Baseball america®
2014 ALMANAC

BASEBALL AMERICA INC. · DURHAM, N.C.

Baseball america
2014 ALMANAC

Editor
Josh Leventhal

Photo Editor
Jim Shonerd

Assistant Editors
Ben Badler, J.J. Cooper, Matt Eddy, Aaron Fitt,
Vincent Lara-Cinisomo, Will Lingo, Clint Longenecker,
John Manuel, Josh Norris, Jim Shonerd

Editorial Assistants
Mat Batts, Ian Fraser,
Michael Lananna

Database and Application Development
Brent Lewis

Design & Production
Sara Hiatt McDaniel,
Linwood Webb

Contributing Writer
John Perrotto

Programming & Technical Development
Brent Lewis

Cover Photo
Justin Upton by Cliff Welch

Distributed by Simon & Schuster ISBN-13: 978-1-932391-48-0

Statistics provided by Major League Baseball Advanced Media and Compiled by Baseball America

Baseball america

PRESIDENT/PUBLISHER Lee Folger
DIRECTOR OF EDITORIAL AND OPERATIONS Will Lingo

EDITORIAL
EDITOR IN CHIEF John Manuel
MANAGING EDITOR J.J. Cooper
NEWS EDITOR Josh Leventhal
ASSOCIATE EDITOR Matt Eddy
WEB EDITOR Vincent Lara-Cinisomo
NATIONAL WRITERS Ben Badler, Aaron Fitt
ASSISTANT EDITORS Clint Longenecker, Josh Norris, Jim Shonerd

PRODUCTION
DESIGN & PRODUCTION DIRECTOR Sara Hiatt McDaniel
MULTIMEDIA MANAGER Linwood Webb
PRODUCTION MANAGER Christina Ponce

ADVERTISING
DIRECT MARKETING MANAGER Ximena Caceres
MARKETPLACE MANAGER Kristopher M. Lull
ADVERTISING ACCOUNT EXECUTIVE Abbey Langdon

BUSINESS
CUSTOMER SERVICE Melissa Hales, Ronnie McCabe
ACCOUNTING/OFFICE MANAGER Hailey Carpenter
TECHNOLOGY MANAGER Brent Lewis
ADMINISTRATIVE ASSISTANT Shannon Tuohey

WHERE TO DIRECT QUESTIONS
ADVERTISING: advertising@baseballamerica.com
BUSINESS BEAT: joshleventhal@baseballamerica.com
COLLEGES: aaronfitt@baseballamerica.com
DESIGN/PRODUCTION: production@baseballamerica.com
DRAFT: johnmanuel@baseballamerica.com
HIGH SCHOOLS: clintlongenecker@baseballamerica.com
INDEPENDENT LEAGUES: jjcooper@baseballamerica.com
MAJOR LEAGUES: matteddy@baseballamerica.com
MINOR LEAGUES: joshleventhal@baseballamerica.com
PHOTOS: photos@baseballamerica.com
PROSPECTS: benbadler@baseballamerica.com
REPRINTS: production@baseballamerica.com
SUBSCRIPTIONS/CUSTOMER SERVICE: customerservice@baseballamerica.com
WEBSITE: customerservice@baseballamerica.com

GrindMedia

GRINDMEDIA MANAGEMENT
SVP, GROUP PUBLISHER Norb Garrett
norb.garrett@grindmedia.com
VP, DIGITAL Greg Morrow
greg.morrow@grindmedia.com
PRODUCTION DIRECTOR Kasey Kelley
kasey.kelley@grindmedia.com
EDITORIAL DIRECTOR–DIGITAL Chris Mauro
chris.mauro@grindmedia.com
FINANCE DIRECTOR Adam Miner
adam.miner@grindmedia.com
VP, MANUFACTURING & ADVERTISING OPERATIONS
Greg Parnell greg.parnell@sorc.com
SENIOR DIRECTOR, AD OPERATIONS
Pauline Atwood pauline.atwood@sorc.com
DIRECTOR, PUBLISHING TECHNOLOGIES
Dale Bryson dale.bryson@sorc.com
DIRECTOR OF EVENTS Scott Desiderio
scott.desiderio@transworld.net

ADVERTISING SALES
SALES STRATEGY MGR/PRINT & EVENTS
Chris Engelsman
chris.engelsman@grindmedia.com
SALES STRATEGY MGR/DIGITAL Elisabeth Murray
elisabeth.murray@grindmedia.com

DIGITAL
DIRECTOR OF ENGINEERING Jeff Kimmel
jeff.kimmel@grindmedia.com
SENIOR PRODUCT MANAGER Rishi Kumar
rishi.kumar@grindmedia.com
SENIOR PRODUCT MANAGER Marc Bartell
marc.bartell@grindmedia.com
CREATIVE DIRECTOR Peter Tracy
peter.tracy@grindmedia.com

MARKETING AND EVENTS
DIRECTOR OF EVENT SALES Sean Nielsen
sean.nielsen@grindmedia.com

FACILITIES
MANAGER Randy Ward randy.ward@grindmedia.com
OFFICE COORDINATOR Ruth Hosea
ruth.hosea@grindmedia.com
ARCHIVIST Thomas Voehringer
thomas.voehringer@sorc.com

SOURCE INTERLINK MEDIA

OFFICERS OF SOURCE INTERLINK COMPANIES, INC.
PRESIDENT AND CHIEF EXECUTIVE OFFICER /
Michael Sullivan
EVP, CHIEF ADMINISTRATIVE OFFICER
Stephanie Justice
EVP, CHIEF PROCUREMENT OFFICER Kevin Mullan

SOURCE INTERLINK MEDIA, LLC
PRESIDENT Chris Argentieri
GENERAL MANAGER David Algire
CHIEF CREATIVE OFFICER Alan Alpanian
SVP, FINANCE Dan Bednar
VP, SINGLE COPY SALES AND MARKETING Chris Butler
EVP, ENTHUSIAST AUTOMOTIVE Doug Evans
CHIEF CONTENT OFFICER Angus MacKenzie
CHIEF ANALYTICS OFFICER John Marriott
SVP, BUSINESS DEVELOPMENT Tyler Schulze
EVP, SALES AND MARKETING Eric Schwab

CONSUMER MARKETING, ENTHUSIAST MEDIA SUBSCRIPTION COMPANY, INC.
VP, CONSUMER MARKETING Tom Slater
VP, RETENTION AND OPERATIONS FULFILLMENT
Donald T. Robinson III

TABLE OF CONTENTS

KEN BABBITT

MAJOR LEAGUES 6

ORGANIZATION STATISTICS 44

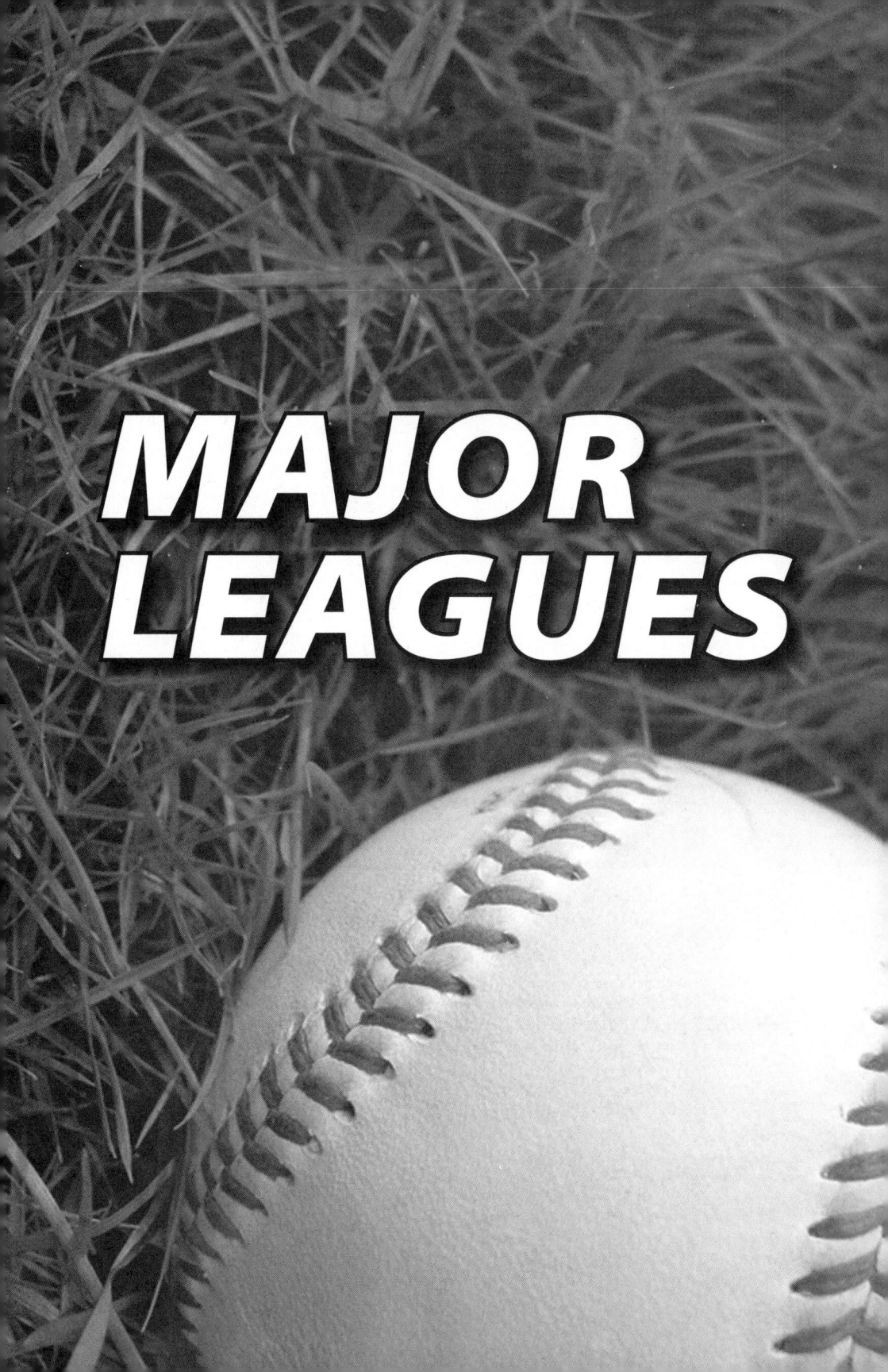

MAJOR LEAGUES

A-Rod, Biogensis flap, mar Red Sox revival

BY JOHN PERROTTO

Alex Rodriguez has made plenty of history during his 20-year career.

The Yankees third baseman has won three American League MVP awards, been selected to play in 14 All-Star Games and won 10 Silver Sluggers. He has also led the AL in home runs five times and his 654 career homers rank fifth in baseball history behind Barry Bonds, Henry Aaron, Babe Ruth and Willie Mays.

Always a lightning rod for controversy, A-Rod still managed to make history in 2013 despite playing in a career-low 44 games after recovering from offseason hip surgery.

It was an infamous bit of history, though, as Rodriguez was suspended for 211 games by Major League Baseball on Aug. 5 for violating its Joint Drug Prevention and Treatment Program. Rodriguez was one of 14 players suspended following MLB's investigation of the now-closed Biogenesis anti-aging clinic in Coral Gables, Fla.

Rodriguez was suspended for the remainder of the season and all of the 2014 season. However, he stayed on the field by appealing the ban, which was to be settled in an offseason hearing.

Once again the specter of performance-enhancing drugs hung over the game despite stricter drug testing and Commissioner Bud Selig's insistence that the game was cleaner than a decade earlier.

That didn't take the sting out of another high-profile player caught up in the Biogenesis scandal. Brewers left fielder Ryan Braun, the 2011 National League MVP, was suspended 65 games—the remainder of the season—on July 23, after admitting to using performance-enhancing drugs.

At the time Rodriguez's suspension was announced, 12 other players received 50-game penalties and none appealed. Among them were three players who took part in the All-Star Game a month earlier—Rangers right fielder Nelson Cruz, Tigers shortstop Jhonny Peralta and Padres shortstop Everth Cabrera.

MLB also announced there would be no further discipline against Athletics righthander Bartolo Colon, Blue Jays outfielder Melky Cabrera and Padres catcher Yasmani Grandal. All were involved in the Biogenesis investigation but had previously served 50-game suspensions after testing positive

Alex Rodriguez returned to a familiar role of villain during the Biogenesis scandal

for elevated levels of testosterone.

"We pursued this matter because it was not only the right thing to do, but the only thing to do," Selig said in a statement. "For weeks, I have noted the many players throughout the game who have strongly voiced their support on this issue, and I thank them for it. I appreciate the unwavering support of our owners and club personnel, who share my ardent desire to address this situation appropriately.

"This case resoundingly illustrates that the strength of our program is not limited only to testing. We continue to attack this issue on every front—from science and research, to education and awareness, to fact-finding and investigative skills."

Cruz said he used PEDs to gain weight after he suffered from a gastrointestinal infection in the 2011-12 offseason that caused him to shed 40 pounds. He returned to the Rangers for their 5-2 loss to the visiting Rays in the AL wild card tiebreaker, receiving a standing ovation from the home crowd before going 0-for-4.

"I should have handled the situation differently and my illness is no excuse," Cruz said.

Peralta's ban ended in time for him to participate in the postseason as the Tigers beat the Athletics in an American League Division Series before losing to the Red Sox in the American League Championship Series. He hit .333 with four doubles and one home run in 10 postseason games.

"I made a mistake and I paid for it with my suspension," Peralta said during the postseason. "I'm embarrassed that it happened and I feel badly that it happened. I am just happy that I've been given a second chance and want to make the most of it."

Rodriguez had been at the heart of an investigation MLB launched after the Miami New Times published a story in late January detailing his ties to Biogenesis, which the report accused of distributing performance-enhancing drugs to players. According to the New Times, citing documents, Rodriguez was paying $12,000 a month and received 19 different drugs and supplements.

Biogenesis founder Tony Bosch agreed to cooperate with MLB investigators after baseball sued him, and his records became a key part of the case against players accused of obtaining PEDs from his clinic.

Rodriguez admitted in 2009 that he had used PEDs while playing with the Rangers from 2001-03. However, he denied having used since, said he believed MLB was on a "witch hunt" in an effort to force him into retirement and vowed not to give in.

MLB said it gave him a longer suspension than the other players because its investigation found that Rodriguez had both bought and tampered with evidence.

"I know people think I'm nuts," Rodriguez said. "I know most people wouldn't want the confrontation. Most people would say, 'Get me out of here. Trade me. Do anything.'

"But I'm the (expletive) crazy man who goes, 'I want to compete. I want to stay in New York. I refuse to quit.' "

Braun received his ban a year after MLB tried to suspend Braun in 2012 for a urine sample with elevated levels of testosterone. However, an arbitrator ruled that a urine sample was mishandled and Braun successfully appealed the suspension then vehemently denied being a PED user.

Braun, though, agreed to a suspension after reportedly being confronted with what was described as "overwhelming evidence" by MLB investigators.

"As I have acknowledged in the past, I am not perfect," Braun said in a statement. "I realize now that I have made some mistakes."

Rob Manfred, MLB's executive vice president for economics and league affairs, said in a statement: "We commend Ryan Braun for taking responsibility for his past actions. We all agree that it is in the best interests of the game to resolve this matter. When Ryan returns, we look forward to him making positive contributions to Major League Baseball, both on and off the field."

High Times In Pittsburgh

One team that certainly never benefited from the Steroids Era was the Pirates. Beginning in 1993, Pittsburgh posted 20 consecutive losing seasons to set the major North American professional sports record for most consecutive seasons with a

---

BIOGENESIS SUSPENSIONS

The names of 17 players affiliated with major league organizations turned up in Biogenesis documents, linking them to the Miami-area, anti-aging clinic that supplied performance-enhancers to athletes. Major League Baseball announced punitive measures for 14 of the players on Aug. 5 after a lengthy investigation.

The big leaguers who received penalties in 2013 included household names such as the Brewers' Ryan Braun, the Rangers' Nelson Cruz, the Tigers' Jhonny Peralta and the Yankees' Alex Rodriguez.

A complete listing of all players tied to Biogenesis:

MAJOR LEAGUERS
On 40-Man Rosters

Player	Pos	Team	Games
Antonio Bastardo	LHP	Phillies	50
Ryan Braun	LF	Brewers	65*
Everth Cabrera	SS	Padres	50
Melky Cabrera	LF	Giants/Blue Jays	50**
Francisco Cervelli	C	Yankees	50
Bartolo Colon	RHP	Athletics	50**
Nelson Cruz	RF	Rangers	50
Yasmani Grandal	C	Padres	50**
Jesus Montero	1B	Mariners	50
Jhonny Peralta	SS	Tigers	50
Cesar Puello	RF	Mets (AA)	50
Alex Rodriguez	3B	Yankees	211***
Jordany Valdespin	2B	Mets (AAA)	50

* Agreed to 65-game penalty on July 22
** Failed a PED test in 2012 but revealed to have ties to Biogenesis
*** Played in 2013 while waiting to appeal penalty in offseason

MINOR LEAGUERS

Player	Pos	Team	Games
Fautino de los Santos	RHP	Padres (AA)	50
Sergio Escalona	LHP	Astros (AA)	50
Fernando Martinez	RF	Yankees (AAA)	50
Jordan Norberto	LHP	Free agent	50

DIAMOND IMAGES

Face of the franchise, and National League MVP, Andrew McCutchen helped the Pirates put to rest 20 years of losing and lifted Pittsburgh to the postseason for the first time since 1992

losing record.

That streak finally ended in 2013, when the Pirates went 94-68 to finish second in the NL Central behind the Cardinals and first in the league's wild-card standings. The Pirates then beat the Reds in the wild-card game before falling to the Cardinals in five games in the NL Division Series.

The Pirates brought an end to their two-decade long skid by notching win No. 82 in a 1-0 victory over the Rangers on Sept. 9 at Arlington.

"We don't really understand what the fans have been through. I know it definitely puts a smile on their face when they see that No. 82 up there," said rookie righthander Gerrit Cole, who threw seven scoreless innings in the win that ended the streak. "We're extremely happy to be able to make them feel like we've got a winning team out there. But we've got a few weeks ahead and those are going to be some real big games."

The Pirates had a much bigger celebration two weeks later when they beat the Cubs 2-1 on Sept. 23 at Wrigley Field to clinch a playoff berth. It was an emotional night for a franchise that has won five World Series titles but had fallen into disrepair.

Star center fielder Andrew McCutchen led the way for the Pirates by hitting .317 with 21 home runs, 84 RBIs and 27 stolen bases in 158 games. Lefthander Francisco Liriano went 16-8.

"Even though I didn't lose for the last 20 years, they make you feel like you (did). You feel like you lost those 20 years," McCutchen said. "That's all you hear. You hear it every single day—'When's it going to change? You think this is the year?'

"You get sick and tired of hearing that. It's awesome that there won't be any questions anymore."

Manager Clint Hurdle best summed up the Pirates' success and the impact it had on the city of Pittsburgh and its fans after the Pirates were eliminated by the Cardinals.

"We were able to take a huge step forward this year in restoring the pride and the passion of the Pittsburgh Pirates' organization, and re-bonding our city with a ball team," he said.

The Tribe's Time

The Pirates weren't the only Rust Belt team to have a surprising season and make the playoffs. The Indians finished the season on a 10-game winning streak, giving them a 92-70 record that left them only one game behind the Tigers in the AL Central and good for first place in the AL wild-card standings.

The Indians were 68-94 in 2012, but first-year manager Terry Francona, who led the Red Sox to

CONTINUED ON PAGE 11

PLAYER OF THE YEAR

Trout tops himself

BY MATT EDDY

Angels center fielder Mike Trout may be the most decorated player in the history of Baseball America—and he only turned 22 in August.

He won Minor League Player of the Year honors while at Double-A Arkansas in 2011, the same year he made his big league debut. An incendiary rookie season for the Angels in 2012—he led the American League with 49 steals and 129 runs despite spending April in Triple-A—earned him the nod as both our Rookie and Major League Player of the Year.

What could he have in store for an encore?

According to the Baseball-Reference advanced metric Wins Above Replacement, Trout was nearly as valuable in 2013 (9.2 WAR) as he had been in 2012 (10.9). He nearly matched his batting and slugging averages, while boosting his on-base percentage by some 30 points in 2013. He again led the AL in runs (109) while also drawing the most walks (110) and batting .323/.432/.557 with 27 homers, 39 doubles, nine triples and 33 steals.

For his all-around blend of excellence, we once again bestow Major League Player of the Year honors on Trout. He edges out worthy challengers such as Dodgers lefthander Clayton Kershaw, the major league ERA champion in each of the past three seasons, and Tigers third baseman Miguel Cabrera, the three-years-running AL batting champ who actually improved on his 2012 Triple Crown

Reigning Rookie and Player of the Year Mike Trout has another historic season

showing this season.

While Trout may be the most talented position player in the majors today, he famously fell to the 25th pick in the 2009 draft because teams struggled to get good looks at the Millville, N.J., prep phenom.

"(His power is) not a surprise, but I am surprised that it has come along to the extent that it has," said Gary Hughes, the Red Sox pro scouting consultant who has been in the business of evaluating players for more than 40 years. It's not like he plays in a small park. But after the last two years of seeing that package of tools, nothing should surprise us.

"Ken Griffey Jr. is probably the highest OFP (overall future potential grade) I've ever had. The game was just so easy for him, and he was just the best kid I've seen at that age. Alex Rodriguez had to be pretty high—he was a man against boys in high school.

"I still think it's unfair to (Trout) to put him on the mountain yet. Mays is the best player I saw. I've been doing this 48 years, and no, he doesn't remind me of Mays. Mays' instincts were better than anybody who ever played.

PREVIOUS POY WINNERS

2003 : Barry Bonds, of, Giants
2004: Barry Bonds, of, Giants
2005: Albert Pujols, 1b, Cardinals
2006: Johan Santana, lhp, Twins
2007: Alex Rodriguez, ss, Yankees
2008: C.C. Sabathia, lhp, Indians/Brewers
2009: Joe Mauer, c, Twins
2010: Roy Halladay, rhp, Phillies
2011: Matt Kemp, of, Dodgers
2012: Mike Trout, Angels

Full list: BaseballAmerica.com/awards

CONTINUED FROM PAGE 9

World Series titles in 2004 and 2007, engineered a quick turnaround following an offseason in which Cleveland signed two big-ticket free agents in first baseman Nick Swisher and center fielder Michael Bourn.

"I'm so crazy about this group of guys," Francona said after the Indians beat the Twins 5-1 at Minnesota on the final day of the regular season to clinch their first playoff berth since 2007. "From ownership to baseball ops to the clubhouse guys. To be able to stand here and say the Indians are going to playoffs, I'm so proud of everybody."

It truly was a team effort for the Indians as no player had more than 22 home runs, 84 RBIs or 14 wins. However, the Indians couldn't carry their late-season momentum into the postseason losing 4-0 at home to the Rays in the AL wild-card game.

"I want our guys to remember how much me and the staff, it was an honor to go through the season with them and how much we care about them," Francona said. "That's what I'll remember more than anything. It was a really special season."

L.A. Story

While the Pirates and Indians made big turn-arounds from the previous season, the Dodgers had an amazing in-season turnaround in 2013.

Any realistic hope the Dodgers had of contending seemed over on the night of June 21, when they lost 5-2 to the Padres at San Diego. The loss dropped the Dodgers to 30-42 and into last place in the NL West, 9½ games out of the lead, and rumors were swirling that manager Don Mattingly

CONTINUED ON PAGE 13

THE BEST YOUNG HITTER EVER?

Mike Trout made his big league debut as a 19-year-old on July 8, 2011, and while he hit just .220 over 40 games as a first-year player, his youth has been the most remarkable aspect of his excellence in 2012 and '13. In fact, baseball has not seen a batter race to such a fast start through his age-21 season since the dawn of the game's Integration Era in 1947. Trout has produced more runs batting than the average player—Rbat being the offensive component of Baseball-Reference's WAR metric— than any member of his peer group in the past 67 seasons, dramatically out-producing even the best Hall of Famers who debuted at early ages, such as Mickey Mantle, Al Kaline and Frank Robinson.

No	Player	Year(s)	Team	Age	AVG	OBP	SLG	Rbat
1	Mike Trout	2011-13	Angels	19-21	.314	.404	.544	121
2	Mickey Mantle	1951-53	Yankees	19-21	.295	.384	.497	76
3	Al Kaline	1953-56	Tigers	18-21	.311	.374	.480	72
4	Frank Robinson	1956-57	Reds	20-21	.307	.378	.543	70
5	Alex Rodriguez	1994-97	Mariners	18-21	.314	.366	.534	67
6	Eddie Mathews	1952-53	Braves	20-21	.274	.366	.541	63
7	Ken Griffey Jr.	1989-91	Mariners	19-21	.299	.367	.479	62
8	Tony Conigliaro	1964-66	Red Sox	19-21	.273	.339	.508	56
9	Cesar Cedeno	1970-72	Astros	19-21	.295	.338	.461	52
10	Albert Pujols	2001	Cardinals	21-21	.329	.403	.610	51

AMERICAN LEAGUE STANDINGS

EAST	W	L	PCT	GB	Manager	General Manager	Attendance	Average	Last Penn.
Boston Red Sox	97	65	.599	—	John Farrell	Ben Cherington	2,833,333	34,979	2013
*Tampa Bay Rays	92	71	.564	5½	Joe Maddon	Andrew Friedman	1,510,300	18,646	2008
Baltimore Orioles	85	77	.525	12	Buck Showalter	Dan Duquette	2,357,551	29,106	1983
New York Yankees	85	77	.525	12	Joe Girardi	Brian Cashman	3,279,589	40,489	2009
Toronto Blue Jays	74	88	.457	23	John Gibbons	Alex Anthopolous	2,536,562	31,316	1993
CENTRAL									
Detroit Tigers	93	69	.574	—	Jim Leyland	Dave Dombrowski	3,083,397	38,067	2012
*Cleveland Indians	92	70	.568	1	Terry Francona	Mark Shapiro	1,572,926	19,662	1997
Kansas City Royals	86	76	.531	7	Ned Yost	Dayton Moore	1,750,754	21,614	1985
Minnesota Twins	66	96	.407	27	Ron Gardenhire	Terry Ryan	2,477,644	30,588	1991
Chicago White Sox	63	99	.389	30	Robin Ventura	Rick Hahn	1,768,413	22,105	2005
WEST									
Oakland Athletics	96	66	.593	—	Bob Melvin	Billy Beane	1,809,302	22,337	1990
Texas Rangers	91	72	.558	5½	Ron Washington	Jon Daniels	3,178,273	38,759	2011
Los Angeles Angels	78	84	.481	18	Mike Scioscia	Jerry Dipoto	3,019,505	37,278	2002
Seattle Mariners	71	91	.438	25	Eric Wedge	Jack Zduriencik	1,761,546	21,747	None
Houston Astros	51	111	.315	45	Bo Porter	Jeff Luhnow	1,651,883	20,394	2005

*Wild card

PLAYOFFS—Wild Card: Rays defeated Indians 4-0 in one-game playoff. **Division Series:** Red Sox defeated Rays 3-1 and Tigers defeated Athletics 3-2 in best-of-five series. **League Championship Series:** Red Sox defeated Tigers 4-2 in best-of-seven series.

ROOKIE OF THE YEAR

A reason to smile in Miami

BY JUAN C. RODRIGUEZ

MIAMI

Their fourth-to-last game of the season, the Miami Marlins found an outlet for Jose Fernandez's inexhaustible verve. They green-lighted his participation for an inning on that evening's television broadcast.

Told of Fernandez's temp job, manager Mike Redmond was thrilled. After Sept. 11, when Fernandez pulled into the neighborhood of his preset innings limit, he wouldn't think twice about using his manager as a sounding board for whatever was on his mind—even in the middle of games.

"He came down and he was talking to me and I told him, 'Hey man, I've got to kind of pay attention here to what's going on in case something comes up,' " said Redmond, recounting an episode from the previous day. "We were just talking about pitching or whatever. I don't even remember exactly. He just wanted to talk. He's great."

That became apparent during an historic 28-start campaign. The combination of a lethal four-pitch repertoire, infectious smile and vibrant personality gave even the most jaded Marlins fan reason to raise an eyebrow throughout a 100-loss season.

Fernandez, who did not turn 21 until July 31, was set to open 2013 in Double-A. He figured half a season of dominating Southern League opposition for Jacksonville would be enough to warrant a promotion.

"It came out a little better than that," said Fernandez, the winning pitcher in 19.4 percent of the Marlins' total victories.

Over his final 18 starts from June 1-Sept. 11, Fernandez was the best pitcher in the majors. He logged a 1.50 ERA (120 innings). Second over that span was Clayton Kershaw (1.96). Fernandez also paced the circuit with a .161 opponents average during that stretch, well ahead of Stephen Strasburg (.194), second among qualifying pitchers.

All but two of Fernandez's last 18 starts

MIKE JANES

Jose Fernandez was the winning pitcher in 19.4 percent of Marlins victories in 2013

were quality. He capped his season with seven innings of five-hit, one-run ball to beat the Braves at Marlins Park. That lowered his ERA to 2.19. In the integration era (since 1947), that's the second-best mark by a qualifying pitcher in his age 20 season, second to Dwight Gooden's 1.53 in 1985.

Fernandez finished the season with a .182 opponents' average. Pedro Martinez (.167) in 2000 was the last qualifying pitcher to stymie major league hitters to that degree.

PREVIOUS ROY WINNERS

2003: Brandon Webb, rhp, Diamondbacks
2004: Khalil Greene, ss, Padres
2005: Huston Street, rhp, Athletics
2006: Justin Verlander, rhp, Tigers
2007: Ryan Braun, 3b, Brewers
2008: Geovany Soto, c, Cubs
2009: Andrew McCutchen, of, Pirates
2010: Jason Heyward, of, Braves
2011: Jeremy Hellickson, rhp, Rays
2012: Mike Trout, Angels

Full list: BaseballAmerica.com/awards

CONTINUED FROM PAGE 11

was on the verge of being fired.

However, the Dodgers beat the Padres 6-1 the next day to begin one of the most torrid 50-game stretches in major league history. The Dodgers went 42-8 in that span, capping their run with a 5-0 win in Philadelphia on Aug. 17.

By then, the Dodgers were 72-50, had an 8 ½-game lead in the NL West and cruised to their first division title since 2009.

"I'm really proud of my club," Mattingly said. "I felt like these guys hung in all year long. People talk all the time about looking forward and turning the page. We did that. Even though you couldn't see it, we knew that light was out there. It was pretty foggy. But we were able to stick to it and keep heading in the right direction. Then the boys took off."

The Dodgers became the fourth team to finish in first place after being in last place July 1, joining the 1914 Boston Braves, 1973 New York Mets and 1995 Seattle Mariners. Of course, the Dodgers also began the season with a $216-million payroll.

"I think the more unusual thing is how we were in last place on July 1," Dodgers team president Stan Kasten said. "The way we played since then is

not the unusual part. What happened to put us in last place on July 1 was the unusual part."

The Dodgers were also involved in a pair of memorable brawls against National League West rivals. Ace Zack Greinke landed on the disabled list with a broken collarbone after just his second start of the season on April 12 at Petco Park. In the bottom of the sixth inning, Greinke plunked

A STRIKING DEBUT

Jose Fernandez needed just one full season in the minors before the Marlins decided he was ready for big league competition. The 2011 first-round pick (14th overall) proved Miami right with a historically dominant season that ended with Baseball America (and National League) Rookie of the Year honors. Fernandez used a four-pitch mix to rack up 9.75 strikeouts per nine innings, which ranks second among all pitchers who threw at least 150 innings in their age-20 season since 1947. The list includes five future Cy Young Award winners, but also several cautionary tales—neither Rick Ankiel nor Ed Correa would pitch another full season in the big leagues. All pitchers on the list were rookies except Bert Blyleven and Dwight Gooden, who made their debuts as 19 year olds.

No.	Player	Team	Year	ERA	W	L	ERA	IP	SO	BB
1	Rick Ankiel	Cardinals	2000	9.98	11	7	3.50	175	194	90
2	Jose Fernandez	Marlins	2013	9.75	12	6	2.19	172	187	58
3	Dwight Gooden	Mets	1985	8.72	24	4	1.53	276	268	69
4	C.C. Sabathia	Indians	2001	8.53	17	5	4.39	180	171	95
5	Fernando Valenzuela	Dodgers	1981	8.42	13	7	2.48	192	180	61
6	Ed Correa	Rangers	1986	8.41	12	14	4.23	202	189	126
7	Felix Hernandez	Mariners	2006	8.29	12	14	4.52	191	176	60
8	Dennis Eckersley	Indians	1975	7.33	13	7	2.60	186	152	90
9	Bert Blyleven	Twins	1971	7.24	16	15	2.81	278	224	59
10	Dave Morehead	Red Sox	1963	7.01	10	13	3.81	174	136	99

NATIONAL LEAGUE STANDINGS

EAST	W	L	PCT	GB	Manager	General Manager	Attendance	Average	Last Penn.
Atlanta Braves	96	66	.593	—	Fredi Gonzalez	John Schuerholz	2,548,679	31,465	1999
Washington Nationals	86	76	.531	10	Davey Johnson	Mike Rizzo	2,652,422	32,746	None
New York Mets	74	88	.457	22	Terry Collins	Sandy Alderson	2,135,657	26,696	2000
Philadelphia Phillies	73	89	.451	23	C. Manuel/R. Sandberg	Ruben Amaro Jr.	3,012,403	37,190	2009
Miami Marlins	62	100	.383	34	Mike Redmond	Dan Jennings	1,586,322	19,584	2003
CENTRAL	W	L	PCT	GB	Manager	General Manager	Attendance	Average	Last Penn.
St. Louis Cardinals	97	65	.599	—	Mike Matheny	John Mozeliak	3,369,769	41,602	2013
*Pittsburgh Pirates	94	68	.580	3	Clint Hurdle	Neal Huntington	2,256,862	28,211	1979
*Cincinnati Reds	90	72	.556	7	Dusty Baker	Walt Jocketty	2,534,369	31,680	1990
Milwaukee Brewers	74	88	.457	23	Ron Roenicke	Doug Melvin	2,531,105	31,248	1982
Chicago Cubs	66	96	.407	31	Dale Sveum	Jed Hoyer	2,642,682	32,626	1945
WEST	W	L	PCT	GB	Manager	General Manager	Attendance	Average	Last Penn.
Los Angeles Dodgers	92	70	.568	—	Don Mattingly	Ned Colletti	3,743,527	46,216	1988
Arizona Diamondbacks	81	81	.500	11	Kirk Gibson	Kevin Towers	2,134,795	26,355	2001
San Diego Padres	76	86	.469	16	Bud Black	Josh Byrnes	2,166,691	26,749	1998
San Francisco Giants	76	86	.469	16	Bruce Bochy	Brian Sabean	3,326,796	41,072	2012
Colorado Rockies	74	88	.457	18	Walt Weiss	Dan O'Dowd	2,793,828	34,492	2007

*Wild card

PLAYOFFS—Wild Card: Pirates defeated Reds in one-game playoff. **Division Series:** Cardinals defeated Pirates 3-2 and Dodgers defeated Braves 3-1 in best-of-five series. **League Championship Series:** Cardinals defeated Dodgers 4-2 in best-of-seven series.

Padres slugger Carlos Quentin, who responded by slowly walking toward the pitcher's mound before charging it. Greinke and Quentin dropped their shoulders and collided, and the 240-pound Quentin tackled his 190-pound adversary and brought him to the grass, leading to a huge scrum.

"I never hit him on purpose," said Greinke, who had previously twice hit Quentin when both played in the American League, and would miss the next month of the season. "I never thought about hitting him on purpose. He always seems to think that I'm hitting him on purpose, but that's not the case. That's all I can really say about it."

Greinke and the Dodgers were involved in another brawl that made national headlines on June 11 against the Diamondbacks at Dodger Stadium. A prolonged scuffle that nearly spilled into the stands resulted in the ejection of Diamondbacks righthander Ian Kennedy, manager Kirk Gibson and assistant hitting coach Turner Ward and Dodgers outfielder Yasiel Puig, righthander Ronald Belisario and hitting coach Mark McGwire. That inning began with Greinke hitting Diamondbacks catcher Miguel Montero in the back. Both teams charged onto the field but no punches were thrown.

Greinke hit Montero in retaliation for Kennedy drilling Puig in the bottom of the sixth, a pitch that hit off Puig's shoulder and grazed his nose. The final straw came in the bottom of the seventh, when Kennedy incited the brawl by hitting Greinke in the upper left shoulder—the ball deflected off his helmet. Kennedy was immediately ejected and calmly walked toward the Diamondbacks dugout before players poured onto the field and relievers ran in from the bullpens.

Puig Power

A big reason for the Dodgers' surge was the play of Puig, who was called up from Double-A Chattanooga on June 3 and inserted into the lineup. The 22-year-old Cuban went on to hit .319/.391/.534 with 19 home runs, 42 RBIs, and 11 stolen bases in 104 games.

Puig quickly earned the nickname "Wild Horse" for his aggressive style of play that helped the Dodgers win some, lose some and generally get under their opponents' skin.

Puig also got under the skin of the Dodgers' manager, as Mattingly twice suspended the high-energy superstar for a lack of hustle and poor judgement in the field.

"We've got to do a better job of helping him to mature and understand what we want done and the way to do it," Mattingly said.

The midseason arrival of Cuban sensation Yasiel Puig keyed Dodgers' playoff surge

BILL NICHOLS

Off To The Races

The other NL division winners were the Braves in the East and Cardinals in the Central. The Braves finished 10 games ahead of the Nationals while the Cardinals overtook the Pirates in September and won by three games over Pittsburgh, then captured their second NL pennant in three years.

The Red Sox completed their major turnaround to win the AL East, going from 69-93 in 2012 to 97-65 in 2013 under first-year manager John Farrell. They finished 5 ½ games in front of the Rays and went on to win their third World Series title in 10 years

The Tigers won their third straight AL Central title by edging out the Indians, while the Athletics repeated as AL West champs, finishing 5 ½ games ahead of the Rangers.

Puig headlined a bumper crop of NL rookies that factored into pennant races, including a trio of Cardinals—righthander Shelby Miller (15-9, 3.06), closer Trevor Rosenthal (2-4, 2.63) and first baseman Matt Adams (.284/.335/.503)—as well as late-season addition Michael Wacha.

Wacha was 4-1, 2.78 in 15 regular season games, including nine starts, then exploded in the postseason as he won his first four starts before taking the loss in Game Six of the World Series, which was the clincher for the Red Sox. All told, Wacha had a 2.64 ERA in October and was named MVP of the NL Championship Series.

ALL-ROOKIE TEAM 2013

Pos	PLAYER, TEAM	AGE	AB	AVG	OBP	SLG	2B	HR	RBI	SB	RUNDOWN
C	Evan Gattis, Braves	27	354	.243	.291	.480	21	21	65	0	Ranked fourth in homers on power-hitting Braves
1B	* Matt Adams, Cardinals	25	296	.284	.335	.503	14	17	51	0	Plugged a hole & then some for injured Allen Craig
2B	Jedd Gyorko, Padres	25	486	.249	.301	.444	26	23	63	1	Just the fifth rookie second sacker with 20 homers
3B	Nolan Arenado, Rockies	22	486	.267	.301	.405	29	10	52	2	Terrific glove makes up for substandard offense
SS	Jose Iglesias, Tigers	23	350	.303	.349	.386	16	3	29	5	Shored-up SS in place of suspended Jhonny Peralta
CF	A.J. Pollock, Diamondbacks	25	443	.269	.322	.409	28	8	38	12	Made most of prolonged injury to Adam Eaton
OF	Wil Myers, Rays	22	332	.295	.353	.482	23	13	53	5	Topped all AL rookies with 23 doubles and 53 RBIs
OF	Yasiel Puig, Dodgers	22	382	.319	.391	.534	21	19	42	11	Sensation belted 27 HR between Double-A and LA
DH	* Kole Calhoun, Angels	25	195	.282	.347	.462	7	8	32	2	RF delivered .809 OPS with strong batting eye

Pos	PITCHER, TEAM	AGE	W	L	SV	ERA	IP	SO	BB	RUNDOWN
SP	Gerrit Cole, Pirates	23	10	7	0	3.22	117	100	28	Ranked second among rookies with 95.5 mph fastball
SP	Jose Fernandez, Marlins	21	12	6	0	2.19	173	187	58	Best season by age-20 pitcher since '85 Dwight Gooden
SP	Shelby Miller, Cardinals	22	15	9	0	3.06	173	169	57	Eye-popping first-half included 2.92 ERA, 1.12 WHIP
SP	* Hyun-Jin Ryu, Dodgers	26	14	8	0	3	192	154	49	Made transition from Korea by topping all rookies in IP
SP	Julio Teheran, Braves	22	14	8	0	3.2	186	170	45	Reversed fortunes of 2012 by adjusting repertoire
RP	Trevor Rosenthal, Cardinals	23	2	4	3	2.63	75	108	20	Used upper-90s heat to strike out 35 pct. of batters faced

*Bats/throws lefthanded

There was no shortage of talented rookies in the National League—12 of the 15 members of BA's All-Rookie Team came from the NL (see above).

The pool of rookies wasn't as deep in the AL but the Rays had two of the best in righthander Chris Archer (9-7, 3.22) and right fielder Wil Myers (.295/.353/.482).

Reds center fielder Billy Hamilton had a debut to remember after being called up in September. He was 13-for-14 in stolen-base attempts over 14 games while hitting .368 (7-for-19) and scoring nine runs.

Long Goodbye

While a number of talented players were saying hello in 2013, all-time saves leader Mariano Rivera, the Yankees' closer, was one of three significant players to retire at the end of the season. Also calling it a career were Yankees lefthander Andy Pettitte and Rockies first baseman Todd Helton.

Rivera's final appearance proved to be one of the most emotional moments in the Yankees' storied history. In the final home game of the season at Yankee Stadium on Sept. 26, manager Joe Girardi called on Rivera to come on in the eighth inning with the Yankees trailing the Rays 4-0.

Rivera got the final two outs of the eighth and the first two outs of the ninth when Pettitte and Yankees shortstop Derek Jeter both popped out of the Yankees' dugout. They strode to the mound and removed Rivera from the bullpen, with Jeter saying, "It's time to go." All three broke into the major leagues with the Yankees in 1995.

Rivera burst into tears and bear-hugged Pettitte for 30 seconds then had a 15-second embrace with Jeter. In all, the ovation lasted four minutes as play-ers from both teams stood on the top step of the dugout and applauded.

It was a scene destined to go down with such other great moments in the Bronx as Lou Gehrig's farewell speech, Babe Ruth's last ballpark appearance, Mickey Mantle Day and the first game after Thurman Munson's death in a plane crash.

"I was bombarded with emotions and feelings that I couldn't describe," Rivera said afterward. "Everything hit at that time. I knew that was the last time. Period. I never felt like that before."

Rivera retreated to the clubhouse between the eighth and ninth innings and said that was when he started to become overwhelmed with a wave of emotion.

"Everything started hitting there," Rivera said. "All the flashbacks, from the minor leagues to the major leagues. They all started hitting at once and I was hoping I could just go back out and pitch without breaking down."

Rivera never lost his cool throughout his 19-year career that included 652 saves and also the all-time record for games finished with 692. Thus, Pettitte was caught off-guard when Rivera started crying.

"I didn't say anything at first when I got out there and I didn't expect him to be so emotional," Pettitte said. "He was really crying, really weeping. I could feel him crying on me."

Two days after Rivera's finale, Pettitte made his final appearance against the Astros in his hometown of Houston.

"It couldn't end any better," Pettitte said.

Pettitte went 256-153 in a 19-year career with a 3.85 ERA. He also finished with 19 career postseason wins, the most in history.

"It all seemed to go by so fast," Pettitte said. "It's

too bad you have to get old and stop playing but the time has come."

The Rockies made sure that Helton could truly ride off into the sunset by giving him a horse as part of a pre-game ceremony before his final home game Sept. 25 against the Red Sox. He followed by going 2-for-3 with a double and a home run in a 15-5 loss.

In his 17 major league seasons, all with the Rockies, Helton had a .316 batting average with 369 home runs and 1,406 RBIs while being selected to five All-Star Games.

"I hoped I would go out and play well," Helton said. "To be able to go out and play well and be productive in my last home game means a lot to me."

And now Helton is going to have to become proficient into something else as he retires with his gift horse to his ranch in suburban Denver.

"I'm going to have to learn to ride a little better," Helton said.

Astros Hit Bottom

The Astros' disastrous season came to an end with a 15-game losing streak, one loss shy of the record for season-ending losing streaks of 16 set by the 1899 Cleveland Spiders.

In their first season after shifting to the AL from the NL, the Astros posted a 51-111 record. No team had lost more games in a season since the Diamondbacks had the identical record in 2004.

Losing has become a familiar scenario in Houston, as the Astros topped the majors in losses for the third consecutive season. In 2014 they will become the first franchise ever to have the No. 1 pick in the June first-year player draft three times in a row. Their 324 losses over three years matched the 1917 Philadelphia Athletics for third-most in major league history, behind the 1962-64 Mets (340) and the 1963-65 Mets (332).

And one other indignity—the Astros set a major league record by striking out 1,535 times.

Relentlessly positive first-year manager Bo Porter was upbeat after the difficult finish.

"I think that we now have enough information that we can actually move forward with the pieces we believe can be a part of that core," Porter said. "We can make additional roster moves that can help put us in a position where we're able to compete in our division for a division championship.

"Then you look at the minor league system with the guys that we have coming—we have some guys that are exciting that can actually come and expedite this whole process because they're impact players."

The Astros outpaced the Marlins in the loss column. Miami finished 62-100 in the team's second season at their publicly funded ballpark. The Marlins' on-field woes followed an offseason in which they purged their roster of veterans by trading shortstop Jose Reyes, lefthander Mark Buehrle, righthander Josh Johnson and catcher John Buck to the Blue Jays. Closer Heath Bell was dealt to the Diamondbacks.

Marlins owner Jeffrey Loria fired president of baseball operations Larry Beinfest late in the season and promoted general manager Michael Hill to take his place. Highly regarded assistant general manager Dan Jennings was moved up to GM.

"There is a lot of room for guys to improve," Marlins manager Mike Redmond said. "We've lost a lot of games, but we've been able to get a lot of guys into games, and get them a lot of at-bats, and a lot of different scenarios."

The Blue Jays opened the season full of optimism and new additions to the roster, including 2012 NL Cy Young Award winner R.A. Dickey and all-star shortstop Jose Reyes from the Mets, but failed to convert it to victories and finished last in the AL East.

Toronto has not reached the playoffs since 1993, the second-longest active drought behind the Royals, who haven't reached the playoffs since winning the World Series in 1985. However, the Royals had a winning season in 2013, their first in 10 years, by going 86-76.

The Nationals failed to live up to manager Davey Johnson's "World Series or bust" proclamation. A year after leading the major leagues with a 98-64 record to win the NL East, the Nationals failed to reach the postseason after going went 86-76. They were under .500 as late as Aug. 22.

No team took a bigger fall, though, than the Giants. One season after winning their second World Series title in three years, the Giants finished 10 games under .500 at 76-86.

General manager Brian Sabean took the blame for the Giants' downfall.

"I think it's pretty simple: We didn't have enough depth," he said. "Last year, we were seemingly able to overcome injuries and lack of performance. We didn't do that this year."

Firing Blanks

Among the few bright spots for the Marlins was righthander Henderson Alvarez throwing a no-hitter against the visiting Tigers on the last day of the season.

It was hardly a typical no-hitter. The game remained scoreless until Marlins right fielder

Giancarlo Stanton scored the winning run on a wild pitch by Luke Putkonen in the bottom of the ninth inning. Alvarez was standing in the on-deck circle and was the first one to greet Stanton and celebrate the no-hitter.

"I was nervous and anxious," Alvarez said. "I started praying, 'Please give us a run.' I was hoping for a wild pitch."

Of the 282 no-hitters in major league history, Alvarez's was the first to end on a wild pitch. It was also the the first walk-off, complete-game, no-hitter since Virgil Trucks threw one for the Tigers on May 15, 1952 against the Washington Senators.

"That's the beauty of baseball," Redmond said. "You never know what you're going to see. On the last day of the season, what a treat."

There were two other no-hitters in 2013, both coming in July, by the Reds' Homer Bailey and the Giants' Tim Lincecum.

Coincidentally, Bailey threw his no-hitter against Lincecum and the Giants on July 2 in a 3-0 win at Cincinnati. It was Bailey's second no-hitter in 10 months as he also had one against the Pirates at Pittsburgh on Sept. 28, 2012.

Bailey became the third Reds pitcher with more than one no-hitter, joining Jim Maloney and Johnny Vander Meer, who is the only major-leaguer to toss two in a row.

"It's something I've already done, so I knew what to expect," Bailey said.

Lincecum had to work for his no-hitter 11 days later in a 9-0 win against the Padres at San Diego as he needed to throw 148 pitches. He struck out 13, walked four and hit a batter.

Lincecum got help to preserve the no-hitter when right fielder Hunter Pence caught Alexi Amarista's sinking liner with a full dive to end the eighth inning. Lincecum pumped his fist as Pence excitedly jumped up with the ball in his glove.

"It's pretty surreal for me just to be part of that," Lincecum said.

Manuel Takes The Fall

The Phillies' Charlie Manuel was the only manager fired during the season but plenty of skippers either got the ax, retired or walked away once the season ended.

The ax fell on Manuel on Aug. 16 with the Phillies languishing at 53-67. He was replaced by bench coach Ryne Sandberg and the Hall of Famer then become the full-time manager at the end of the season after guiding the Phillies to a 20-22 record.

Manuel, 69, managed the Phillies for nine seasons, leading them to two NL pennants and a

AMERICAN LEAGUE BEST TOOLS

A Baseball America survey of American League managers, conducted at midseason 2013, ranked players with the best tools.

BEST HITTER
1. Miguel Cabrera, Tigers
2. Mike Trout, Angels
3. Joe Mauer, Twins

BEST CONTROL
1. Bartolo Colon, Athletics
2. Hisashi Iwakuma, Mariners
3. Felix Hernandez, Mariners

BEST POWER
1. Chris Davis, Orioles
2. Miguel Cabrera, Tigers
3. Edwin Encarnacion, Blue Jays

BEST PICKOFF MOVE
1. Andy Pettitte, Yankees
2. James Shields, Royals
3. Mark Buehrle, Blue Jays

BEST BUNTER
1. Brett Gardner, Yankees
2 (tie). Elvis Andrus, Rangers
2 (tie). Erick Aybar, Angels

BEST RELIEVER
1. Mariano Rivera, Yankees
2. Jesse Crain, White Sox
3. Greg Holland, Royals

BEST STRIKE-ZONE JUDGMENT
1. Miguel Cabrera, Tigers
2. Joe Mauer, Twins
3. David Ortiz, Red Sox

BEST DEFENSIVE CATCHER
1. Salvador Perez, Royals
2. Matt Wieters, Orioles
3. Joe Mauer, Twins

BEST HIT-AND-RUN ARTIST
1. Erick Aybar, Angels
2. Jamey Carroll, Twins
3. Nick Markakis, Orioles

BEST DEFENSIVE 1B
1. Eric Hosmer, Royals
2. James Loney, Rays
3. Justin Smoak, Mariners

BEST BASERUNNER
1. Mike Trout, Angels
2. Jacoby Ellsbury, Red Sox
3. Rajai Davis, Blue Jays

BEST DEFENSIVE 2B
1. Dustin Pedroia, Red Sox
2. Robinson Cano, Yankees
3. Gordon Beckham, White Sox

FASTEST BASERUNNER
1. Mike Trout, Angels
2. Rajai Davis, Blue Jays
3. Jacoby Ellsbury, Red Sox

BEST DEFENSIVE 3B
1. Adrian Beltre, Rangers
2. Manny Machado, Orioles
3. Evan Longoria, Rays

MOST EXCITING PLAYER
1. Mike Trout, Angels
2. Miguel Cabrera, Tigers
3. Chris Davis, Orioles

BEST DEFENSIVE SS
1. J.J. Hardy, Orioles
2. Yunel Escobar, Rays
3. Asdrubal Cabrera, Indians

BEST PITCHER
1. Max Scherzer, Tigers
2. Felix Hernandez, Mariners
3. Matt Moore, Rays

BEST INFIELD ARM
1. Adrian Beltre, Rangers
2. Manny Machado, Orioles
3. Jose Reyes, Blue Jays

BEST FASTBALL
1. Max Scherzer, Tigers
2. Justin Verlander, Tigers
3. Kelvin Herrera, Royals

BEST DEFENSIVE OF
1. Mike Trout, Angels
2. Adam Jones, Orioles
3. Austin Jackson, Tigers

BEST CURVEBALL
1. Clay Buchholz, Red Sox
2. Justin Verlander, Tigers
3. Felix Hernandez, Mariners

BEST OUTFIELD ARM
1. Adam Jones, Orioles
2. Jose Bautista, Blue Jays
3. Josh Reddick, Athletics

BEST SLIDER
1. Chris Sale, White Sox
2. Max Scherzer, Tigers
3. Yu Darvish, Rangers

BEST MANAGER
1. Jim Leyland, Tigers
2 (tie). Bob Melvin, Athletics
2 (tie). Buck Showalter, Orioles

BEST CHANGEUP
1. James Shields, Royals
2. Felix Hernandez, Mariners
3. Fernando Rodney, Rays

World Series victory in 2008, while compiling a 780-636 record.

"I've never quit at nothing in my life and I didn't

CONTINUED ON PAGE 19

Cardinals know the way

BY JOHN MANUEL

Cardinals general manager John Mozeliak was preparing to accept the Organization of the Year award at the 2011 Winter Meetings when it was pointed out to him that Lance Lynn ranked No. 6 on our Top 10, two spots behind righthander Tyrell Jenkins.

Lynn had just finished helping the Cardinals to a World Series championship, making 10 appearances and earning two wins out of St. Louis' bullpen. Jenkins had flashed plenty of promise that summer but was a long way away in the Rookie-level Appalachian League.

"Lance is helping us now!" Mozeliak said with a dose of exasperation. Then he predicted Lynn would be a key member of the Cardinals rotation going forward, adding, "I hope you're right about Tyrell. Because if he's better than Lance, he'll be awfully good."

Of course Mozeliak was right. Lynn has thrown 378 major league innings since then and earned 33 wins. Jenkins has yet to advance out of Class A.

Mozeliak was on point about St. Louis' 2011 talent, and he and his organization have continued to evaluate its own talent well since then, now celebrating its fourth pennant in a decade.

St. Louis turned out a homegrown lineup daily in 2013, with the 2009 draft class contributing more than its fair share of talent. Righthanders Shelby Miller (first round) and Joe Kelly (third) were in the rotation last season, while Trevor Rosenthal (21st) was the closer. The right side of the infield featured second baseman Matt Carpenter (13th) and

Homegrown talent like Carlos Martinez helped St. Louis back to the World Series

KEN BABBITT

first baseman Matt Adams (23rd). Three more pieces came in the 2007 draft in shortstop Pete Kozma (first), utility infielder Daniel Descalso (third) and outfielder Adron Chambers (38th).

Just as important as who the Cardinals drafted and developed is who they correctly let go. The most obvious example is Albert Pujols, whose free agent departure yielded the 19th pick in the 2012 draft from the Angels. St. Louis converted that pick into Michael Wacha.

Lynn was the team's second pick in 2008; the team's first pick, Brett Wallace, was the key piece in the package sent to Oakland in 2008 for Matt Holliday. St. Louis also traded away 2010 first-rounder Zack Cox to the Marlins for reliever Edward Mujica. Adams is a bigger, better version of Wallace, while Cox has flopped and isn't even on the Marlins' 40-man roster.

The Cardinals' entire bullpen aside from Mujica was homegrown, with Rosenthal joined by lefty Kevin Siegrist, a 41st-round pick in 2008. Righthander Carlos Martinez—who originally signed in 2009 with the Red Sox under the name Carlos Matias before the deal was voided—is St. Louis' top international product in the big leagues.

PREVIOUS WINNERS

2003: Florida Marlins
2004: Minnesota Twins
2005: Atlanta Braves
2006: Los Angeles Dodgers
2007: Colorado Rockies
2008: Tampa Bay Rays
2009: Philadelphia Phillies
2010: San Francisco Giants
2011: St. Louis Cardinals
2012: Cincinnati Reds:

Full list: BaseballAmerica.com/awards

quit," Manuel said. "(Management) decided to make a change, I didn't."

Detroit's Jim Leyland resigned after his team lost to the Red Sox in the American League Championship Series. The 68-year-old managed the Tigers for eight seasons, going 700-597, and winning two AL pennants.

"It's been a thrill," Leyland said. "I came here to change talent to team, and I think with the help of this entire organization, I think we've done that. We've won quite a bit. I'm very grateful to have been a small part of that."

Former Tigers catcher Brad Ausmus was hired as Leyland's replacement. Ausmus had most recently been a special assistant to Padres general manager Josh Byrnes, and his lone managerial experience came when he managed Israel in the World Baseball Classic.

The final day of the season marked the end of Davey Johnson's stint as Nationals manager as the 70-year-old announced before the season started that he would retire. After taking the job 83 games into the 2011 season, Johnson compiled a 224-183 record.

"Time to go home," Johnson said after a 3-2 loss to the Diamondbacks at Arizona to end the season. "Put me out to pasture."

The Nationals hired Diamondbacks third-base coach Matt Williams as Johnson's replacement.

Dusty Baker was fired after the Reds lost to the Pirates in the NL wild-card game, despite their third postseason appearance in four years. Baker was replaced by pitching coach Bryan Price. Baker's record was 509-463 in six seasons, the longest tenure by a Reds manager since Sparky Anderson.

Before playing the Pirates, Baker said he thought that management and fans did not give the Reds enough credit for what they had accomplished with the three postseason berths.

"I don't think there are a lot of people that appreciate what we put together, what we've done," Baker said. "We're in a society that there's only one room at the top."

The Cubs fired Dale Sveum after two seasons and a record of 127-197. Cubs president Theo Epstein said they "needed to get it right" with their manager before a wave of talented hitting prospects reaches the major leagues.

Padres bench coach Rick Renteria was brought in as the new skipper.

Sensing he was about to be fired—though general manager Jack Zduriencik denied it—Eric

NATIONAL LEAGUE BEST TOOLS

A Baseball America survey of National League managers, conducted at midseason 2013, ranked players with the best tools.

BEST HITTER
1. Buster Posey, Giants
2. Joey Votto, Reds
3. Yadier Molina, Cardinals

BEST POWER
1. Carlos Gonzalez, Rockies
2. Giancarlo Stanton, Marlins
3. Pedro Alvarez, Pirates

BEST BUNTER
1. Everth Cabrera, Padres
2. Juan Pierre, Marlins
3. Tony Campana, Dbacks

BEST STRIKE-ZONE JUDGMENT
1. Joey Votto, Reds
2. Marco Scutaro, Giants
3. Shin-Soo Choo, Reds

BEST HIT-AND-RUN ARTIST
1. Marco Scutaro, Giants
2. Martin Prado, Diamondbacks
3. Placido Polanco, Marlins

BEST BASERUNNER
1. Everth Cabrera, Padres
2. Andrew McCutchen, Pirates
3. Carlos Gonzalez, Rockies

FASTEST BASERUNNER
1. Everth Cabrera, Padres
2. Carlos Gomez, Brewers
3. Tony Campana, Dbacks

MOST EXCITING PLAYER
1. Andrew McCutchen, Pirates
2. Bryce Harper, Nationals
3. Carlos Gonzalez, Rockies

BEST PITCHER
1. Clayton Kershaw, Dodgers
2. Matt Harvey, Mets
3. Adam Wainwright, Cardinals

BEST FASTBALL
1. Aroldis Chapman, Reds
2. Matt Harvey, Mets
3. Craig Kimbrel, Braves

BEST CURVEBALL
1. Adam Wainwright, Cardinals
2. Clayton Kershaw, Dodgers
3. Jose Fernandez, Marlins

BEST SLIDER
1. Craig Kimbrel, Braves
2. Sergio Romo, Giants
3. Matt Harvey, Mets

BEST CHANGEUP
1. Cole Hamels, Phillies
2. Hyun-Jin Ryu, Dodgers
3. Tyler Clippard, Nationals

BEST CONTROL
1. Adam Wainwright, Cardinals
2. Cliff Lee, Phillies
3. Jordan Zimmermann, Nationals

BEST PICKOFF MOVE
1. Julio Teheran, Braves
2 (tie). Clayton Kershaw, Dodgers
2 (tie). Clayton Richard, Padres

BEST RELIEVER
1. Craig Kimbrel, Braves
2. Jason Grilli, Pirates
3. Aroldis Chapman, Reds

BEST DEFENSIVE CATCHER
1. Yadier Molina, Cardinals
2. Russell Martin, Pirates
3. Buster Posey, Giants

BEST DEFENSIVE 1B
1. Adam LaRoche, Nationals
2. Joey Votto, Reds
3. Paul Goldschmidt, Dbacks

BEST DEFENSIVE 2B
1. Brandon Phillips, Reds
2. Darwin Barney, Cubs
3. Mark Ellis, Dodgers

BEST DEFENSIVE 3B
1. David Wright, Mets
2. Chase Headley, Padres
3. Nolan Arenado, Rockies

BEST DEFENSIVE SS
1. Troy Tulowitzki, Rockies
2. Ian Desmond, Nationals
3. Andrelton Simmons, Braves

BEST INFIELD ARM
1. Ian Desmond, Nationals
2. Andrelton Simmons, Braves
3. Troy Tulowitzki, Rockies

BEST DEFENSIVE OF
1. Carlos Gomez, Brewers
2. Carlos Gonzalez, Rockies
3. Andrew McCutchen, Pirates

BEST OUTFIELD ARM
1. Carlos Gonzalez, Rockies
2. Gerardo Parra, Dbacks
3. Yasiel Puig, Dodgers

BEST MANAGER
1. Bruce Bochy, Giants
2. Clint Hurdle, Pirates
3. Davey Johnson, Nationals

Wedge decided to resign as the Mariners' manager with three days remaining in the season. Wedge said he and Zduriencik had different visions about

CONTINUED ON PAGE 21

Mets ace Matt Harvey posted a 2.27 ERA and struck out 191 hitters in 178 innings

Orioles first baseman Chris Davis led the majors with 53 home runs and 138 RBIs

FIRST TEAM

Pos.	Player, Team	AVG	OBP	SLG	AB	R	H	2B	3B	HR	RBI	BB	SO	SB	CS
C	Yadier Molina, Cardinals	.319	.359	.477	505	68	161	44	0	12	80	30	55	3	2
1B	* Chris Davis, Orioles	.286	.370	.634	584	103	167	42	1	53	138	72	199	4	1
2B	* Matt Carpenter, Cardinals	.318	.392	.481	626	126	199	55	7	11	78	72	98	3	3
3B	Miguel Cabrera, Tigers	.348	.442	.636	555	103	193	26	1	44	137	90	94	3	0
SS	Troy Tulowitzki, Rockies	.312	.391	.540	446	72	139	27	0	25	82	57	85	1	0
CF	Mike Trout, Angels	.323	.432	.557	589	109	190	39	9	27	97	110	136	33	7
OF	Matt Holliday, Cardinals	.300	.389	.490	520	103	156	31	1	22	94	69	86	6	1
OF	Jayson Werth, Nationals	.318	.398	.532	462	84	147	24	0	25	82	60	101	10	1
DH	* David Ortiz, Red Sox	.309	.395	.564	518	84	160	38	2	30	103	76	88	4	0

Pos.	Pitcher, Team	W	L	ERA	G	GS	SV	IP	H	R	ER	HR	BB	SO	WHIP
SP	Yu Darvish, Rangers	13	9	2.83	32	32	0	210	145	68	66	26	80	277	1.07
SP	Felix Hernandez, Mariners	12	10	3.04	31	31	0	204	185	74	69	15	46	216	1.13
SP	* Clayton Kershaw, Dodgers	16	9	1.83	33	33	0	236	164	55	48	11	52	232	0.92
SP	Max Scherzer, Tigers	21	3	2.90	32	32	0	214	152	73	69	18	56	240	0.97
SP	Adam Wainwright, Cardinals	19	9	2.94	34	34	0	242	223	83	79	15	35	219	1.07
RP	Koji Uehara, Red Sox	4	1	1.09	73	0	21	74	33	10	9	5	9	101	0.57

SECOND TEAM

Pos.	Player, Team	AVG	OBP	SLG	AB	R	H	2B	3B	HR	RBI	BB	SO	SB	CS
C	* Joe Mauer, Twins	.324	.404	.476	445	62	144	35	0	11	47	61	89	0	1
1B	Paul Goldschmidt, D-backs	.302	.401	.551	602	103	182	36	3	36	125	99	145	15	7
2B	* Robinson Cano, Yankees	.314	.383	.516	605	81	190	41	0	27	107	65	85	7	1
3B	* Josh Donaldson, Athletics	.301	.384	.499	579	89	174	37	3	24	93	76	110	5	2
SS	Ian Desmond, Nationals	.280	.331	.453	600	77	168	38	3	20	80	43	145	21	6
CF	Andrew McCutchen, Pirates	.317	.404	.508	583	97	185	38	5	21	84	78	101	27	10
OF	* Carlos Gonzalez, Rockies	.302	.367	.591	391	72	118	23	6	26	70	41	118	21	3
OF	Hunter Pence, Giants	.283	.339	.483	629	91	178	35	5	27	99	52	115	22	3
DH	* Joey Votto, Reds	.305	.435	.491	581	101	177	30	3	24	73	135	138	6	3

Pos.	Pitcher, Team	W	L	ERA	G	GS	SV	IP	H	R	ER	HR	BB	SO	WHIP
SP	Jose Fernandez, Marlins	12	6	2.19	28	28	0	173	111	47	42	10	58	187	0.98
SP	Matt Harvey, Mets	9	5	2.27	26	26	0	178	135	46	45	7	31	191	0.93
SP	Hisashi Iwakuma, Mariners	14	6	2.66	33	33	0	220	179	69	65	25	42	185	1.01
SP	Anibal Sanchez, Tigers	14	8	2.57	29	29	0	182	156	56	52	9	54	202	1.15
SP	James Shields, Royals	13	9	3.15	34	34	0	229	215	82	80	20	68	196	1.24
RP	Greg Holland, Royals	2	1	1.21	68	0	47	67	40	11	9	3	18	103	0.87

*Bats/throws lefthanded. #Switch-hitter.

EXECUTIVE OF THE YEAR

Call it Moneyball, or call it whatever you like, but Billy Beane's team-building approach has proven to be nimble. After a five-year retrenching, the A's have finished on top of the AL West—ahead of their deep-pocketed division-mates—the past two seasons, largely thanks to Beane's assertive management.

Billy Beane

Throughout his stewardship, Beane has never shied from trading players at their peak—and peak value—and netted tremendous return. His deals of Trevor Cahill and Gio Gonzalez, for example, have brought rotation mainstays Jarrod Parker and Tommy Milone.

In addition, Beane mined reclamation projects such as 18-game winner Bartolo Colon and Brandon Moss and gotten tremendous return.

PREVIOUS WINNERS

2002: Billy Beane, Athletics
2003: Brian Sabean, Giants
2004: Terry Ryan, Twins
2005: Mark Shapiro, Indians
2006: Dave Dombrowski, Tigers
2007: Jack Zduriencik, Brewers

2008: Theo Epstein, Red Sox
2009: Dan O'Dowd, Rockies
2010: Jon Daniels, Rangers
2011: Doug Melvin, Brewers
2012: Billy Beane, Athletics

Full list: BaseballAmerica.com/awards

MANAGER OF THE YEAR

When Clint Hurdle got to Pittsburgh before the start of the 2011 season, the Pirates had just finished a dispiriting 57-105 campaign, the most losses for a franchise known for losing since 1952.

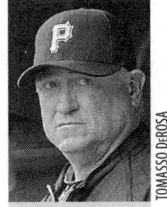

Clint Hurdle

With his mix of enthusiasm and no nonsense, the former major league outfielder coaxed 15 more wins out of the team in 2011, and then nearly ended the Buccos' two-decade-long streak of losing seasons until a late collapse in 2012.

In 2013, emboldened by offseason acquisitions of Francisco Liriano and Russell Martin, Hurdle led the Pirates to a 94-68 season, their first playoff appearance since 1992 and a wild-card playoff win. The season ended in an NL Division Series loss to the Cardinals, but the Pirates appear to be a team on the rise.

PREVIOUS WINNERS

2002: Mike Scioscia, Angels
2003: Jack McKeon, Marlins
2004: Bobby Cox, Braves
2005: Ozzie Guillen, White Sox
2006: Jim Leyland, Tigers
2007: Terry Francona, Red Sox

2008: Ron Gardenhire, Twins
2009: Mike Scioscia, Angels
2010: Bobby Cox, Braves
2011: Joe Maddon, Rays
2012: Buck Showalter, Orioles

Full list: BaseballAmerica.com/awards

CONTINUED FROM PAGE 19

the future of the organization.

Wedge, who missed six weeks after suffering a stroke in late July, compiled a 213-273 record in his three seasons with the Mariners. Tigers hitting coach Lloyd McClendon, who managed the Pirates from 2001-05, was hired to replace Wedge. McClendon becomes Seattle's eighth manager since Lou Piniella's tenure ended after the 2002 season.

In An Instant

Major League Baseball announced that it plans to greatly expand its instant replay system in 2014, making almost every call reviewable with the exception of balls and strikes.

"I couldn't help but sense in the room the acceptance and excitement," Selig said after the plan was unveiled at the quarterly owners' meetings in August in Cooperstown, N.Y. "People understood they were sitting in on something that was historic."

"(This is a chance) for baseball to dramatically reduce the number of incorrect calls that are made in any game that impacts the outcome of that game and hence the outcome of division races," said Braves team president John Schuerholz, a member of the committee that had been studying instant replay. "We believe that not only is it historic, but it will be impactful and very meaningful and useful."

Selig introduced a proposed format that still needs to be approved during the offseason by the Players Association and the World Umpires Association. Under the proposal, reviews will be initiated when a manager informs the umpire that he wants to challenge a play. Managers will be allowed one challenge in the first six innings and two more from the seventh through the end of the game.

If the manager wins his appeal, he retains the challenge. The challenge from the first six innings does not carry over.

If a manager disagrees with a reviewable call, his only recourse would be to use a challenge. Managers would not be able to argue a reviewable call in a bid to get it overturned without the use of replay. A manager could still argue in situations not open to review, such as when defending a player or questioning an improper substitution.

All replays will be reviewed by umpires at MLB Advanced Media's facilities in New York with technicians available to provide the necessary video. However, boundary calls on home runs have been grandfathered and the on-site umpires will retain the right to submit the plays for review or not.

Schuerholz admitted that changes could be made to the system in future seasons.

"It is a phasing plan," he said. "This is but the first phase. At the end of '14, we'll go back and look at what we've done well—what's worked, what hasn't worked—and make adjustments, and then we'll improve it in the next phase, the next rollout, the second iteration.

"And we feel that by no more than a third iteration, we will have diminished to the most minimal level the number of incorrect calls that impact our games."

Instant replay got a trial run during the offseason at the Arizona Fall League. Games featuring many of baseball's brightest prospects were broadcast over a five-day stretch on the MLB Network with a six-camera setup that could be used if the replay system is approved for the 2014 season.

MLB officials and umpires watched in a trailer in the parking lot of the ballpark equipped with TVs and replay feeds from all six cameras. The home-plate umpire donned a headset and communicated with the umps in the truck to review calls.

The MLB officials involved in the instant-replay process included Schuerzholz, MLB executive VP Joe Torre and former Cardinals manager Tony La Russa, currently a special assistant to Selig.

Empty Class In Cooperstown

For the first time since 1965, no living person was inducted into the National Baseball Hall of Fame in Cooperstown, N.Y.

Voters decided against electing such standouts as Barry Bonds and Roger Clemens because of their association with PED use. In fact, nobody received

The Phillies fired manager Charlie Manuel amid their first losing season since 2006

TOMASSO DeROSA

the requisite 75 percent of the vote for induction from 10-year members of the Baseball Writers Association of America.

The three inductees all came from the Veterans Committee ballot and all are deceased: Yankees owner Jacob Ruppert, umpire Hank O'Day and barehanded catcher Deacon White, who last played in 1880.

Just 34 Hall of Famers showed up for the induction ceremony, which was sparsely attended by fans as well.

"It's kind of sad," Hall of Fame third baseman Brooks Robinson said. "It's quiet here.'"

"It's a shame more Hall of Famers aren't here," Hall of Fame pitcher Bert Blyleven said, "because this is really the time they should be here."

However, Robinson and many other Hall of Famers say they hope players with ties to steroids and PEDs never gain entrance into the Hall.

"I'd be very disappointed if any of those guys get in," Robinson said. "I do think though, they will get in. When I'm dead. I get disappointed when I hear guys say, 'I only did it one time.' That upsets me, too. One time, what's the difference? I only robbed a bank once. The way I look at it, those guys cheated. They created an uneven playing field. I don't have any sympathy for them."

CONTINUED ON PAGE 24

All-Star Game all about Mo

BY JOHN PERROTTO

NEW YORK

Officially, it was the 2013 All-Star Game.

Unofficially, it was Mariano Rivera Appreciation Night at Citi Field in New York when the American League blanked the National League 3-0.

The two days of festivities centered on the Yankees closer and baseball's all-time saves leader, who in spring training announced plans to retire at the end of the season. Rivera received a thunderous ovation during pre-game introductions then took the mound to pitch the eighth inning.

AL manager Jim Leyland of the Tigers asked his players to remain in the dugout when Rivera came in from the bullpen, accompanied by his entrance music of Metallica's *Enter Sandman.*

Rivera stood on the field alone as the fans gave him a 90-second ovation and players from both teams applauded.

The 43-year-old Rivera retired the side in order and walked off the mound to another huge ovation.

"It was tough because it was emotional but it was special," Rivera said afterward, holding back tears. "Seeing the fans sharing and both teams standing out of the dugouts and cheering, that was priceless. I will never forget the moment."

Rivera was selected as the game's MVP even though he settled for a hold as Texas' Joe Nathan pitched the ninth for the save.

Leyland was criticized in some circles for not holding Rivera back for potential save opportunity. Leyland feared that the NL might score four runs in the eighth inning to take the lead and might not bat in the bottom of the ninth.

"I just couldn't take the chance," Leyland said. "I'm probably not the most popular manager in baseball for not using him in a save situation but I wouldn't have gotten out of here alive if he didn't get in the game."

Tigers righthander Max Scherzer started and the win went to White Sox lefty Chris Sale.

ALL-STAR GAME

Mariano Rivera earned MVP honors in his 13th and final All-Star Game

JULY 16, 2013

American League 3, National League 0

American	AB	R	H	RBI	National	AB	R	H	BI
Trout, LF-CF	3	0	1	0	Phillips, 2B	2	0	0	0
b-Hunter, To, PH-CF	1	0	0	0	Carpenter, M, 2B	2	0	0	0
Cano, 2B	0	0	0	0	Beltran, RF	2	0	1	0
1-Pedroia, PR-2B	2	0	0	0	2-McCutchen, PR-CF	2	0	0	0
Kipnis, 2B	1	0	1	1	Votto, 1B	2	0	0	0
Cabrera, M, 3B	3	1	1	0	Goldschmidt, 1B	2	0	1	0
Machado, M, 3B	1	0	0	0	Wright, D, 3B	3	0	1	0
Davis, C, 1B	3	0	1	0	Alvarez, P, 3B	1	0	0	0
Fielder, 1B	1	0	1	0	Gonzalez, C, LF	2	0	0	0
Bautista, RF	1	0	0	1	Brown, D, LF	1	0	0	0
Cruz, N, RF	1	0	0	0	Molina, Y, C	2	0	0	0
Ortiz, D, DH	2	0	0	0	Posey, C	1	0	0	0
a-Encarnacion, PH-DH	2	0	0	0	Tulowitzki, SS	2	0	0	0
Jones, Ad, CF	3	1	1	0	Segura, SS	1	0	0	0
Gordon, A, LF	1	0	0	0	Cuddyer, DH	1	0	0	0
Mauer, C	2	0	1	0	c-Craig, PH-DH	1	0	0	0
Perez, S, C	1	1	1	0	Harper, CF-RF	2	0	0	0
Hardy, SS	2	0	0	1	Gomez, C, RF	1	0	0	0
Peralta, Jh, SS	1	0	1	0					
Totals	**31**	**3**	**9**	**3**		**30**	**0**	**3**	**0**
American					000	110	010—3		
National					000	000	000—0		

a-Grounded into a double play for Ortiz, D in the 7th. b-Grounded into a double play for Trout in the 8th. 1-Ran for Cano in the 1st. c-Lined out for Cuddyer in the 8th. 2-Ran for Beltran in the 4th.

LOB—American 4, National 4. **2B**—Trout, M. Cabrera, A. Jones, Kipnis, Goldschmidt. **3B**—Fielder. **SB**—McCutchen.

American	IP	H	R	ER	BB	SO	National	IP	H	R	ER	BB	SO
Scherzer	1	0	0	0	0	1	Harvey	2	1	0	0	0	3
Sale (W)	2	0	0	0	0	2	Kershaw	1	0	0	0	0	0
Hernandez, F	1	1	0	0	0	0	Corbin (L)	1	2	1	1	0	0
Moore, M	1	0	0	0	0	0	Lee, Cl	1	2	1	1	0	0
Balfour	1	0	0	0	1	1	Fernandez, J	1	0	0	0	0	2
Holland, G	1/3	1	0	0	0	0	Chapman	1	0	0	1	1	
Cecil	1/3	0	0	0	0	1	Kimbrel	1	3	1	1	0	1
Delabar	1/3	0	0	0	0	1	Grilli	1	1	0	0	0	0
Rivera	1	0	0	0	0	0							
Nathan (S)	1	1	0	0	0	2							

T—3:06. **A**—45,186.

CONTINUED FROM PAGE 22

Selig Makes It Official

In September, Selig announced he will retire in January, 2015 at age 80.

No replacement has been named for Selig, who will retire as the longest-serving commissioner in the sport's history, but Selig did promote Rob Manfred to chief operating officer in late September. Manfred, who previously served as executive vice president for economics and league affairs, has worked for MLB since 1998 and most recently helped negotiate the Collective Bargaining Agreement with the union after the 2011 season.

Selig took over as interim commissioner in 1992 after owners forced out then-commissioner Fay Vincent, and took the job permanently in 1998. He announced two years ago that the 2014 season would be his last, and owners believed it this time after he had previously hinted at retirement then reconsidered.

Selig presided over an era of unprecedented growth—MLB is now a $9 billion industry—but also multiple labor battles with the players' union, including one that resulted in the cancellation of the 1994 World Series.

Selig's leadership also spanned the period loosely known as baseball's Steroid Era, a tag that began to fade once the league and union collectively bargained for drug testing after the 2002 season. Selig recently has been proud to note that baseball has the toughest drug-testing policy in North America's four major sports.

"It remains my great privilege to serve the game I have loved throughout my life," Selig said in a statement. "Baseball is the greatest game ever invented, and I look forward to continuing its extraordinary growth and addressing several significant issues during the remainder of my term.

Cabrera Keeps On Slugging

Tigers third baseman Miguel Cabrera came up short in his bid to repeat as a Triple Crown winner one year after becoming the first big leaguer to lead a league in batting average, home runs and RBIs since 1967.

However, he did become the first player in more than two decades to win three straight AL batting titles.

Cabrera faded a bit down the stretch while battling abdominal and groin injuries, but still hit a career-high .348 and finished 24 points ahead of the Twins' Joe Mauer.

Cabrera's 44 home runs were second to the 53

ACTIVE LEADERS

Career leaders among players who played in a game in 2013. Batters require 3,000 plate appearances and pitchers 1,000 innings to qualify for percentage titles.

BATTERS			PITCHERS		
AVG	Joe Mauer	.323	ERA	Mariano Rivera	2.21
OBP	Joey Votto	.419	SO/9	Tim Lincecum	9.63
SLG	Albert Pujols	.598	BB/9	Dan Haren	1.87
OPS	Albert Pujols	1.009	HR/9	Mariano Rivera	0.50
R	Alex Rodriguez	1,919	W	Andy Pettitte	256
H	Derek Jeter	3,316	L	Derek Lowe	157
2B	Todd Helton	592	SV	Mariano Rivera	652
3B	Carl Crawford	117	IP	Andy Pettitte	3,316
HR	Alex Rodriguez	654	SO	Jamie Moyer	2,448
RBI	Alex Rodriguez	1,969	BB	Ryan Dempster	1,071
BB	Jason Giambi	1,357	AVG	Mariano Rivera	.211
SO	Jim Thome	2,220	G	Mariano Rivera	1,115
XBH	Alex Rodriguez	1,203	GS	Andy Pettitte	521
SB	Juan Pierre	614	HR	Mark Buehrle	324

by Orioles first baseman Chris Davis. Cabrera also finished second in RBIs, one behind Davis' 138. Cabrera batted .330 in 2012 with 44 homers and 139 RBIs.

"I still had a good season," he said. "I have (almost) the same numbers I had last year."

Davis had a memorable season, too, as he broke the Orioles' single-season home run record of 50 set by Brady Anderson in 1996. Davis had never hit more than 33 homers in his previous five seasons.

A Rockies player won the NL batting title for the eighth time in the franchise's 21-year history when right fielder Michael Cuddyer took home the hardware with a .331 batting average. Cuddyer, who had never hit higher than .284 in his previous 12 major league seasons, finished 10 points ahead of Braves third baseman Chris Johnson at .321.

Playing at Coors Field also helped Andres Galarraga (1994), Larry Walker (1998, '99 and 2001), Todd Helton ('00), Matt Holliday ('07) and Carlos Gonzalez ('10) win batting titles with the Rockies.

"It was nothing that I ever expected, and I really can't wrap my head around it," Cuddyer said. "It just goes to show that no matter what time you're at in your career, something like this can happen if you continue to work hard."

Pirates third baseman Pedro Alvarez and Diamondbacks first baseman Paul Goldschmidt tied for the NL home run lead with 36. Goldschmidt also topped the league in RBIs with 125.

Alvarez became the first Pirate to lead the NL in homers since Willie Stargell had 44 in 1973. Furthermore, it was the lowest total to lead either league since Fred McGriff topped the NL with 35 in 1992 for the Padres.

Mets left fielder Eric Young Jr. followed in the footsteps of his father and led the NL with 46 stolen bases. Eric Young Sr. had a league-best 53 for the Rockies in 1996.

"I'm proud of myself," Young Jr. said. "That's my craft, stolen bases, and you always pride yourself in what your craft is."

Red Sox center fielder Jacoby Ellsbury topped the AL in steals for the third time in his career with 52.

Dodgers lefthander Clayton Kershaw posted a 1.83 ERA to become the first pitcher to lead the major leagues in ERA for three straight seasons since Greg Maddux in 1993-95. Kershaw also led the NL with 232 strikeouts while compiling a 16-9 record.

Tigers righthander Anibal Sanchez's 2.57 ERA led the AL. Rangers righthander Yu Darvish led all major league pitchers with 277 strikeouts, the most since Randy Johnson had 290 for the Diamondbacks in 2004 and the most by an AL pitcher since Pedro Martinez had 284 in 2000.

BILL NICHOLS

Michael Cuddyer was a hit in Colorado, topping the NL with a .331 batting aveage

CABRERA JOINS EXCLUSIVE LIST

Tigers third baseman Miguel Cabrera became the first righthanded batter to win three straight batting titles since Rogers Hornsby claimed six in a row in the National League for the Cardinals from 1920-25. Cabrera, a Triple Crown winner in 2012, became just the fifth player to lead the American League in batting in three consecutive seasons, joining Nap Lajoie (1901-03), Ty Cobb (1907-09, 1911-15 and 1917-19), Rod Carew (1972-75) and Wade Boggs (1985-88). He joins four National League hitters to accomplish the same feat: Tony Gwynn (1987-89 and 1994-97), Stan Musial (1950-52), Rogers Hornsby (1920-25) and Honus Wagner (1906-09).

"He's the best hitter in the game right now," said Tigers manager Jim Leyland, who retired after eight years in Detroit's dugout following Detroit's loss to the Red Sox in the American League Championship Series. "I know I'm biased and see him every day but nobody can do the things Miggy does, day in and day out. He's in a class of his own."

Below is a list of the players in the post-integration era to claim at least three consecutive batting titles.

ANDREW WOOLLEY

Year	Player	League	Team	Average
1997	Tony Gwynn	National	Padres	.372
1996	Tony Gwynn	National	Padres	.353
1995	Tony Gwynn	National	Padres	.368
*1994	Tony Gwynn	National	Padres	.394
1989	Tony Gwynn	National	Padres	.336
1988	Tony Gwynn	National	Padres	.313
1988	Wade Boggs	American	Red Sox	.366
1987	Tony Gwynn	National	Padres	.370
1987	Wade Boggs	American	Red Sox	.363
1986	Wade Boggs	American	Red Sox	.357
1985	Wade Boggs	American	Red Sox	.368
1975	Rod Carew	American	Twins	.359
1974	Rod Carew	American	Twins	.364
1973	Rod Carew	American	Twins	.350
1972	Rod Carew	American	Twins	.318
1952	Stan Musial	National	Cardinals	.336
1951	Stan Musial	National	Cardinals	.355
1950	Stan Musial	National	Cardinals	.346

* Season shortened by players' strike

ARIZONA DIAMONDBACKS

Alfredo Marte	April 2
Charles Brewer	June 10
Zeke Spruill	June 21
Chaz Roe	July 1
Eury De La Rosa	July 14
Tuffy Gosewisch	Aug. 1
Matt Davidson	Aug. 11
David Holmberg	Aug. 27
Chris Owings	Sept. 3

ATLANTA BRAVES

Evan Gattis	April 3
Cory Rasmus	May 22
Alex Wood	May 30
Joey Terdoslavich	July 4
Todd Cunningham	July 30
Philip Gosselin	Aug. 16
David Hale	Sept. 13
Christian Bethancourt	Sept. 29

BALTIMORE ORIOLES

T.J. McFarland	April 6
Zach Clark	May 1
Kevin Gausman	May 23
Henry Urrutia	July 20
Jonathan Schoop	Sept. 25
Mike Belfiore	Sept. 27

BOSTON RED SOX

Jackie Bradley	April 1
Alex Wilson	April 11
Allen Webster	April 21
Steven Wright	April 23
Jose De La Torre	May 12
Jonathan Diaz	June 29
Brandon Workman	July 10
Drake Britton	July 20
Xander Bogaerts	Aug. 20

CHICAGO CUBS

Kyuji Fujikawa	April 1
Hector Rondon	April 3
Junior Lake	July 19
Logan Watkins	Aug. 4
Zach Rosscup	Sept. 3
Chang-Yong Lim	Sept. 7

CHICAGO WHITE SOX

Simon Castro	July 5
Josh Phegley	July 5
Andre Rienzo	July 30
Charlie Leesman	Aug. 9
Jake Petricka	Aug. 22
Erik Johnson	Sept. 4
Marcus Semien	Sept. 4
Daniel Webb	Sept. 4
Miguel Gonzalez	Sept. 10

CINCINNATI REDS

Derrick Robinson	April 5
Justin Freeman	April 17
Donald Lutz	April 29
Neftali Soto	May 18
Curtis Partch	June 9
Nick Christiani	Aug. 23
Billy Hamilton	Sept. 3

CLEVELAND INDIANS

Matt Langwell	June 2
Preston Guilmet	July 10
Danny Salazar	July 11
C.C. Lee	July 14
Jose Ramirez	Sept. 1

COLORADO ROCKIES

Nolan Arenado	April 28
Corey Dickerson	June 22
Chad Bettis	Aug. 1

DETROIT TIGERS

Bruce Rondon	April 25

Evan Reed	May 16
Jose Alvarez	June 9
Nick Castellanos	Sept. 1

HOUSTON ASTROS

Josh Fields	April 2
Paul Clemens	April 9
Brett Oberholtzer	April 21
Jose Cisnero	April 22
Robbie Grossman	April 24
Marc Krauss	June 21
Jarred Cosart	July 12
Jonathan Villar	July 22
Josh Zeid	July 30
Chia-Jen Lo	July 31
Kevin Chapman	Aug. 9
Jorge De Leon	Aug. 9
Max Stassi	Aug. 20
David Martinez	Aug. 21
Cody Clark	Aug. 23

KANSAS CITY ROYALS

Donnie Joseph	July 11
Yordano Ventura	Sept. 17
Chris Dwyer	Sept. 24

LOS ANGELES ANGELS

Luis Jimenez	April 12
Michael Roth	April 13
Ryan Brasier	May 2
Buddy Boshers	Aug. 10
Matt Shoemaker	Sept. 20

LOS ANGELES DODGERS

Hyun-Jin Ryu	April 2
Matt Magill	April 27
Yasiel Puig	June 3
Chris Withrow	June 12
Jose Dominguez	June 30
Onelki Garcia	Sept. 11
Nick Buss	Sept. 14

MIAMI MARLINS

Jose Fernandez	April 7
Kyle Skipworth	April 10
Marcell Ozuna	April 30
Derek Dietrich	May 8
Ed Lucas	May 30
Edgar Olmos	June 3
Jake Marisnick	July 23
Christian Yelich	July 23
Steve Ames	July 30
Arquimedes Caminero	Aug. 16
Brian Flynn	Sept. 4

MILWAUKEE BREWERS

Khris Davis	April 1
Josh Prince	April 6
Hiram Burgos	April 20
Donovan Hand	May 26
Scooter Gennett	June 3
Caleb Gindl	June 15
Sean Halton	June 27
Johnny Hellweg	June 28
Rob Wooten	July 26
Jimmy Nelson	Sept. 6

MINNESOTA TWINS

Aaron Hicks	April 1
Ryan Pressly	April 4
Oswaldo Arcia	April 15
Caleb Thielbar	May 20
Chris Colabello	May 22
Kyle Gibson	June 29
Michael Tonkin	July 11
Andrew Albers	Aug. 6
Josmil Pinto	Sept. 1

NEW YORK METS

Scott Rice	April 1
Juan Lagares	April 23
Zack Wheeler	June 18

Gonzalez Germen	July 12
Wilmer Flores	Aug. 6
Travis d'Arnaud	Aug. 17
Matt den Dekker	Aug. 29
Juan Centeno	Sept. 18
Wilfredo Tovar	Sept. 22

NEW YORK YANKEES

Vidal Nuno	April 29
Preston Claiborne	May 5
Corban Joseph	May 13
David Adams	May 15
Brett Marshall	May 15
Zoilo Almonte	June 19
Cesar Cabral	Sept. 2
JR Murphy	Sept. 2

OAKLAND ATHLETICS

Nate Freiman	April 3
Shane Peterson	April 16
Grant Green	July 8
Sonny Gray	July 10
Michael Choice	Sept. 2

PHILADELPHIA PHILLIES

Jonathan Pettibone	April 22
Cesar Hernandez	May 29
J.C. Ramirez	June 23
Luis Garcia	July 10
Steve Susdorf	July 25
Cody Asche	July 30
Ethan Martin	Aug. 2
Mauricio Robles	Sept. 3
Cameron Rupp	Sept. 10

PITTSBURGH PIRATES

Phil Irwin	April 14
Ryan Reid	June 3
Gerrit Cole	June 11
Brandon Cumpton	June 15
Tony Sanchez	June 23
Duke Welker	June 23
Vic Black	July 25
Andrew Lambo	Aug. 13
Kris Johnson	Aug. 18
Stolmy Pimentel	Sept. 4

SAN DIEGO PADRES

Jedd Gyorko	April 1
Robbie Erlin	April 30
Burch Smith	May 11
Jaff Decker	June 20
Colt Hynes	July 14
Reymond Fuentes	Aug. 26
Chris Robinson	Sept. 4
Tommy Medica	Sept. 11

SAN FRANCISCO GIANTS

Nick Noonan	April 3
Mike Kickham	May 28
Juan Perez	June 9
Jake Dunning	June 16
Kensuke Tanaka	July 9

Roger Kieschnick	July 31
Heath Hembree	Sept. 3
Johnny Monell	Sept. 5
Ehire Adrianza	Sept. 8

SEATTLE MARINERS

Brandon Maurer	April 4
Bobby LaFromboise	April 10
Yoervis Medina	April 16
Jesus Sucre	May 24
Nick Franklin	May 27
Brandon Bantz	June 8
Mike Zunino	June 12
Brad Miller	June 28
Abraham Almonte	Aug. 30
Taijuan Walker	Aug. 30
James Paxton	Sept. 7

ST. LOUIS CARDINALS

Jermaine Curtis	April 27
Seth Maness	May 3
Carlos Martinez	May 3
John Gast	May 14
Tyler Lyons	May 22
Michael Wacha	May 30
Keith Butler	June 1
Kevin Siegrist	June 6
Michael Blazek	June 22
Brock Peterson	July 20
Kolten Wong	Aug. 16
Audry Perez	Sept. 15

TAMPA BAY RAYS

Alex Colome	May 30
Wil Myers	June 18
Tim Beckham	Sept. 19
Enny Romero	Sept. 22
Kevin Kiermaier	Sept. 30

TEXAS RANGERS

Joseph Ortiz	March 31
Leury Garcia	April 6
Nick Tepesch	April 9
Chris McGuiness	June 7
Engel Beltre	June 26
Joey Butler	Aug. 7
Jim Adduci	Sept. 1

TORONTO BLUE JAYS

Sean Nolin	May 24
Kevin Pillar	Aug. 14
Ryan Goins	Aug. 23

WASHINGTON NATIONALS

Anthony Rendon	April 21
Jeff Kobernus	May 25
Nathan Karns	May 28
Erik Davis	June 2
Ian Krol	June 5
Taylor Jordan	June 29
Tanner Roark	Aug. 7
Zach Walters	Sept. 6

Billy Hamilton

GEORGE GOJKOVICH

MAJOR LEAGUES

CLUB BATTING

	AVG	G	AB	R	H	2B	3B	HR	RBI	BB	SO	SB	OBP	SLG
Detroit	.283	162	5735	796	1625	292	23	176	767	531	1073	35	.346	.434
Boston	.277	162	5651	853	1566	363	29	178	819	581	1308	123	.349	.446
Los Angeles	.264	162	5588	733	1476	270	39	164	696	523	1221	82	.329	.414
Texas	.262	163	5585	730	1465	262	23	176	691	462	1067	149	.323	.412
Baltimore	.260	162	5620	745	1460	298	14	212	719	416	1125	79	.313	.431
Kansas City	.260	162	5549	648	1443	254	34	112	620	422	1048	153	.315	.379
Tampa Bay	.257	163	5538	700	1421	296	23	165	670	589	1171	73	.329	.408
Cleveland	.255	162	5465	745	1391	290	23	171	711	562	1283	117	.327	.410
Oakland	.254	162	5521	767	1403	301	25	186	725	573	1178	74	.327	.419
Toronto	.252	162	5537	712	1398	273	24	185	669	510	1123	112	.318	.411
Chicago	.249	162	5563	598	1385	237	19	148	574	411	1207	105	.302	.378
Minnesota	.242	162	5564	614	1346	285	15	151	590	533	1430	52	.312	.380
New York	.242	162	5449	650	1321	247	24	144	614	466	1214	115	.307	.376
Houston	.240	162	5457	610	1307	266	16	148	566	426	1535	110	.299	.375
Seattle	.237	162	5558	624	1318	249	17	188	597	529	1353	49	.306	.390

CLUB PITCHING

	ERA	G	CG	SHO	SV	IP	H	R	ER	HR	BB	SO	AVG
Kansas City	3.45	162	5	12	52	1448.1	1366	601	555	155	469	1208	.250
Oakland	3.56	162	6	13	46	1452	1339	625	574	163	428	1183	.242
Detroit	3.61	162	3	12	39	1462.2	1369	624	587	128	462	1428	.247
Texas	3.62	163	4	10	46	1448.1	1370	636	589	157	498	1309	.248
Tampa Bay	3.74	163	9	17	42	1464	1315	646	608	153	482	1310	.240
Boston	3.79	162	5	8	33	1454	1366	656	613	156	524	1294	.248
Cleveland	3.82	162	3	16	38	1441.1	1359	662	611	147	554	1379	.249
New York	3.94	162	7	10	49	1447.1	1452	671	633	171	437	1233	.261
Chicago	3.98	162	5	5	40	1455	1424	723	643	182	509	1249	.256
Baltimore	4.20	162	2	6	57	1453	1438	709	678	202	473	1169	.259
Los Angeles	4.23	162	4	12	41	1457.2	1475	737	685	167	533	1200	.261
Toronto	4.25	162	4	11	39	1452	1451	756	685	195	500	1208	.259
Seattle	4.31	162	4	14	43	1465	1467	754	702	174	478	1297	.259
Minnesota	4.55	162	1	7	40	1450.1	1591	788	733	168	458	985	.280
Houston	4.79	162	2	5	32	1440	1530	848	766	191	616	1084	.272

CLUB FIELDING

	PCT	PO	A	E	DP		PCT	PO	A	E	DP
Baltimore	.991	4359	1614	54	165	Texas	.986	4390	1549	86	146
Tampa Bay	.990	4392	1593	59	147	Cleveland	.983	4324	1503	98	135
New York	.988	4342	1544	69	139	Oakland	.983	4356	1377	97	112
Boston	.987	4362	1516	80	142	Toronto	.982	4356	1605	111	145
Detroit	.987	4388	1508	76	136	Los Angeles	.981	4373	1500	112	135
Minnesota	.987	4351	1723	81	178	Chicago	.980	4365	1555	121	155
Kansas City	.986	4345	1520	85	136	Houston	.979	4320	1635	125	168
Seattle	.986	4395	1645	88	149						

INDIVIDUAL BATTING LEADERS (MINIMUM 2.7 PA/TEAM GAME)

	AVG	G	AB	R	H	2B	3B	HR	RBI	BB	SO	SB
Cabrera, Miguel, Detroit	.348	148	555	103	193	26	1	44	137	90	94	3
Mauer, Joe, Minnesota	.324	113	445	62	144	35	0	11	47	61	89	0
Trout, Mike, Los Angeles	.323	157	589	109	190	39	9	27	97	110	136	33
Beltre, Adrian, Texas	.315	161	631	88	199	32	0	30	92	50	78	1
Cano, Robinson, New York	.314	160	605	81	190	41	0	27	107	65	85	7
Ortiz, David, Boston	.309	137	518	84	160	38	2	30	103	76	88	4
Hunter, Torii, Detroit	.304	144	606	90	184	37	5	17	84	26	113	3
Nava, Daniel, Boston	.303	134	458	77	139	29	0	12	66	51	93	0
Hosmer, Eric, Kansas City	.302	159	623	86	188	34	3	17	79	51	100	11
Pedroia, Dustin, Boston	.301	160	641	91	193	42	2	9	84	73	75	17

INDIVIDUAL PITCHING LEADERS (MINIMUM 0.8 IP/TEAM GAME)

	W	L	ERA	G	GS	CG	SV	IP	H	R	BB	SO
Sanchez, Anibal, Detroit	14	8	2.57	29	29	1	0	182	156	56	54	202
Colon, Bartolo, Oakland	18	6	2.65	30	30	3	0	190.3	193	60	29	117
Iwakuma, Hisashi, Seattle	14	6	2.66	33	33	0	0	219.7	179	69	42	185
Darvish, Yu, Texas	13	9	2.83	32	32	0	0	209.7	145	68	80	277
Scherzer, Max, Detroit	21	3	2.9	32	32	0	0	214.3	152	73	56	240
Hernandez, Felix, Seattle	12	10	3.04	31	31	0	0	204.3	185	74	46	216
Sale, Chris, Chicago	11	14	3.07	30	30	4	0	214.3	184	81	46	226
Shields, James, Kansas City	13	9	3.15	34	34	2	0	228.7	215	82	68	196
Santana, Ervin, Kansas City	9	10	3.24	32	32	0	0	211	190	85	51	161
Jimenez, Ubaldo, Cleveland	13	9	3.3	32	32	0	0	182.7	163	75	80	194

AWARD WINNERS

Selected by Baseball Writers Association of America

MOST VALUABLE PLAYER

Player	1st	2nd	3rd	Total
Miguel Cabrera, Detroit	23	7	—	385
Mike Trout, Los Angeles	5	19	3	282
Chris Davis, Baltimore	1	4	11	232
Josh Donaldson, Oakland	1	—	14	222
Robinson Cano, New York	—	—	1	150
Evan Longoria, Tampa Bay	—	—	—	103
Dustin Pedroia, Boston	—	—	—	99
Adrian Beltre, Texas	—	—	—	99
Manny Machado, Baltimore	—	—	—	57
David Ortiz, Boston	—	—	—	47
Jason Kipnis, Cleveland	—	—	—	31
Max Scherzer, Detroit	—	—	1	25
Adam Jones, Baltimore	—	—	—	9
Edwin Encarnacion, Toronto	—	—	—	7
Greg Holland, Kansas City	—	—	—	3
Carlos Santana, Cleveland	—	—	—	3
Coco Crisp, Oakland	—	—	—	3
Jacoby Ellsbury, Boston	—	—	—	3
Torii Hunter, Detroit	—	—	—	2
Hisashi Iwakuma, Seattle	—	—	—	2
Koji Uehara, Boston	—	—	—	2
Yu Darvish, Texas	—	—	—	1
Felix Hernandez, Seattle	—	—	—	1
Salvador Perez, Kansas City	—	—	—	1
Shane Victorino, Boston	—	—	—	1

CY YOUNG AWARD

Pitcher	1st	2nd	3rd	Total
Max Scherzer, Detroit	28	1	1	203
Yu Darvish, Texas	—	19	3	93
Hisashi Iwakuma, Seattle	—	6	12	73
Anibal Sanchez, Detroit	1	1	3	46
Chris Sale, Chicago	1	—	5	44
Bartolo Colon, Oakland	—	2	3	25
Koji Uehara, Boston	—	1	2	10
Felix Hernandez, Seattle	—	1	1	6
Matt Moore, Tampa Bay	—	—	—	4
Greg Holland, Kansas City	—	—	—	4
James Shields, Kansas City	—	—	—	2

ROOKIE OF THE YEAR

Player	1st	2nd	3rd	Total
Wil Myers, Tampa Bay	23	5	1	131
Jose Iglesias, Boston/Detroit	5	17	4	80
Chris Archer, Tampa Bay	1	5	15	35
Dan Straily, Oakland	1	2	4	15
J.B. Shuck, Los Angeles	—	1	1	4
Cody Allen, Cleveland	—	—	2	2
Martin Perez, Texas	—	—	2	2
David Lough, Kansas City	—	—	1	1

MANAGER OF THE YEAR

Manager	1st	2nd	3rd	Total
Terry Francona, Indians	16	10	2	112
John Farrell, Red Sox	12	10	6	96
Bob Melvin, Athletics	2	5	11	36
Joe Girardi, Yankees	—	2	5	11
Joe Maddon, Rays	—	2	3	9
Jim Leyland, Tigers	—	1	—	3
Buck Showalter, Orioles	—	—	1	1
Ron Washington, Rangers	—	—	1	1
Ned Yost, Royals	—	—	1	1

GOLD GLOVE WINNERS

Selected by AL managers

C—Salvador Perez, Kansas City. 1B—Eric Hosmer, Kansas City. 2B—Dustin Pedroia, Boston. 3B—Manny Machado, Baltimore. SS—J.J. Hardy, Baltimore. LF—Alex Gordon, Kansas City. CF—Adam Jones, Baltimore. RF—Shane Victorino, Boston. P—R.A. Dickey, Toronto.

SILVER SLUGGER AWARDS

Selected by AL managers, coaches

C—Joe Mauer, Minnesota. 1B—Chris Davis, Baltimore. 2B—Robinson Cano, New York. SS—J.J. Hardy, Baltimore. 3B—Miguel Cabrera, Detroit. OF—Torii Hunter, Detroit. OF—Mike Trout, Los Angeles. OF—Adam Jones, Baltimore. DH—David Ortiz, Boston.

DEPARTMENT LEADERS

BATTING

GAMES
Billy Butler, Kansas City	162
Prince Fielder, Detroit	162
Adrian Beltre, Texas	161
7 players	160

AT-BATS
Manny Machado, Baltimore	667
Adam Jones, Baltimore	653
Dustin Pedroia, Boston	641
Alexei Ramirez, Chicago	637
Nick Markakis, Baltimore	634

PLATE APPEARANCES
Dustin Pedroia, Boston	724
Mike Trout, Los Angeles	716
Prince Fielder, Detroit	712
Manny Machado, Baltimore	710
2 players	700

RUNS
Mike Trout, Los Angeles	109
Miguel Cabrera, Detroit	103
Chris Davis, Baltimore	103
Adam Jones, Baltimore	100
Austin Jackson, Detroit	99

HITS
Adrian Beltre, Texas	199
Miguel Cabrera, Detroit	193
Dustin Pedroia, Boston	193
Robinson Cano, New York	190
Mike Trout, Los Angeles	190

TOTAL BASES
Chris Davis, Baltimore	370
Miguel Cabrera, Detroit	353
Mike Trout, Los Angeles	328
Adam Jones, Baltimore	322
Adrian Beltre, Texas	321

DOUBLES
Manny Machado, Baltimore	51
Jed Lowrie, Oakland	45
Chris Davis, Baltimore	42
Dustin Pedroia, Boston	42
Robinson Cano, New York	41

TRIPLES
Brett Gardner, New York	10
Mike Trout, Los Angeles	9
Stephen Drew, Boston	8
Jacoby Ellsbury, Boston	8
Austin Jackson, Detroit	7

EXTRA-BASE HITS
Chris Davis, Baltimore	96
Mike Trout, Los Angeles	75
Evan Longoria, Tampa Bay	74
Miguel Cabrera, Detroit	71
David Ortiz, Boston	70

HOME RUNS
Chris Davis, Baltimore	53
Miguel Cabrera, Detroit	44
Edwin Encarnacion, Toronto	36
Adam Dunn, Chicago	34
Mark Trumbo, Los Angeles	34

RUNS BATTED IN
Chris Davis, Baltimore	138
Miguel Cabrera, Detroit	137
Adam Jones, Baltimore	108
Robinson Cano, New York	107
Prince Fielder, Detroit	106

SACRIFICES
Elvis Andrus, Texas	16

Munenori Kawasaki, Toronto	10
Leonys Martin, Texas	12
Shane Victorino, Boston	10
2 players	9

SACRIFICE FLIES
Matt Wieters, Baltimore	12
Torii Hunter, Detroit	10
Jason Kipnis, Cleveland	10
Josh Hamilton, Los Angeles	9
9 players	8

HIT BY PITCH
Shane Victorino, Boston	18
Daniel Nava, Boston	15
Josh Willingham, Minnesota	14
Jose Iglesias, Bos/Det	11

Manny Machado

Chris Davis, Baltimore	10

WALKS
Mike Trout, Los Angeles	110
Carlos Santana, Cleveland	93
Miguel Cabrera, Detroit	90
Edwin Encarnacion, Toronto	82
Billy Butler, Kansas City	79

STOLEN BASES
Jacoby Ellsbury, Boston	52
Rajai Davis, Toronto	45
Elvis Andrus, Texas	42
Alex Rios, Chicago/Texas	42
Leonys Martin, Texas	36

CAUGHT STEALING
Jose Altuve, Houston	13

Michael Bourn, Cleveland	12
Brandon Barnes, Houston	11
Ian Kinsler, Texas	11
2 players	9

STOLEN-BASE PERCENTAGE
Alcides Escobar, K.C.	100%
Jacoby Ellsbury, Boston	93%
Craig Gentry, Texas	89%
Rajai Davis, Toronto	88%
Shane Victorino, Boston	88%

STRIKEOUTS
Chris Carter, Houston	212
Chris Davis, Baltimore	199
Adam Dunn, Chicago	189
Mike Napoli, Boston	187
Mark Trumbo, Los Angeles	184

TOUGHEST TO STRIKE OUT
(AT-BATS PER STRIKEOUT)
Victor Martinez, Detroit	9.76
Alberto Callaspo, L.A./Oak	9.64
Alexei Ramirez, Chicago	9.37
Erick Aybar, Los Angeles	9.32
Ian Kinsler, Texas	9.24

GROUNDED INTO DOUBLE PLAYS
Billy Butler, Kansas City	28
Jose Altuve, Houston	24
Victor Martinez, Detroit	23
Dustin Pedroia, Boston	21
2 players	21

MULTI-HIT GAMES
Adrian Beltre, Texas	58
Dustin Pedroia, Boston	58
3 players	56

ON-BASE PERCENTAGE
Miguel Cabrera, Detroit	.442
Mike Trout, Los Angeles	.432
Joe Mauer, Minnesota	.404
David Ortiz, Boston	.395
Daniel Nava, Boston	.385

SLUGGING PERCENTAGE
Miguel Cabrera, Detroit	.636
Chris Davis, Baltimore	.634
David Ortiz, Boston	.564
Mike Trout, Los Angeles	.557
Edwin Encarnacion, Toronto	.534

ON-BASE-PLUS SLUGGING
Miguel Cabrera, Detroit	1.078
Chris Davis, Baltimore	1.004
Mike Trout, Los Angeles	.988
David Ortiz, Boston	.959
Edwin Encarnacion, Toronto	.904

LOWEST AVERAGE
Adam Dunn, Chicago	.219
Mark Reynolds, Cle/N.Y.	.220
Chris Carter, Houston	.223
Mitch Moreland, Texas	.232
Mike Moustakas, K.C.	.233

PITCHING

WINS
Max Scherzer, Detroit	21
Bartolo Colon, Oakland	18
Matt Moore, Tampa Bay	17
C.J. Wilson, Los Angeles	17
Chris Tillman, Baltimore	16

LOSSES
Lucas Harrell, Houston	17
Joe Saunders, Seattle	16

David Price

LARRY GOREN

CLIFF WELCH

4 players	14

GAMES

Joel Peralta, Tampa Bay	80
Cody Allen, Cleveland	77
Matt Lindstrom, Chicago	76
Tanner Scheppers, Texas	76
Dane De La Rosa, Los Angeles	75

GAMES STARTED

R.A. Dickey, Toronto	34
James Shields, Kansas City	34
Justin Verlander, Detroit	34
7 players	33

GAMES FINISHED

Jim Johnson, Baltimore	63
Greg Holland, Kansas City	61
Joe Nathan, Texas	61
Mariano Rivera, New York	60
Addison Reed, Chicago	59

COMPLETE GAMES

David Price, Tampa Bay	4
Chris Sale, Chicago	4
5 players	3

SHUTOUTS

Bartolo Colon, Oakland	3
Justin Masterson, Cleveland	3
6 players	2

SAVES

Jim Johnson, Baltimore	50
Greg Holland, Kansas City	47
Mariano Rivera, New York	44
Joe Nathan, Texas	43
Addison Reed, Chicago	40

INNINGS PITCHED

James Shields, Kansas City	228.7
R.A. Dickey, Toronto	224.7
Hisashi Iwakuma, Seattle	219.7
Justin Verlander, Detroit	218.3
2 players	214.3

HITS ALLOWED

Jeremy Guthrie, Kansas City	236
Joe Saunders, Seattle	232
Doug Fister, Detroit	229
C.C. Sabathia, New York	224
Mark Buehrle, Toronto	223

RUNS ALLOWED

C.C. Sabathia, New York	122
Joe Saunders, Seattle	117

Salvador Perez

ED WOLFSTEIN

R.A. Dickey, Toronto	113
Lucas Harrell, Houston	111
Jeremy Hellickson, Tampa Bay	103

HOME RUNS ALLOWED

A.J. Griffin, Oakland	36
R.A. Dickey, Toronto	35
Chris Tillman, Baltimore	33
Jeremy Guthrie, Kansas City	30
Joe Blanton, Los Angeles	29

WALKS

Lucas Harrell, Houston	88
C.J. Wilson, Los Angeles	85
Yu Darvish, Texas	80
Ubaldo Jimenez, Cleveland	80
Ryan Dempster, Boston	79

WALKS PER NINE INNINGS

David Price, Tampa Bay	1.30
Bartolo Colon, Oakland	1.37

Hisashi Iwakuma, Seattle	1.72
Doug Fister, Detroit	1.90
John Lackey, Boston	1.90

HIT BATTERS

Justin Masterson, Cleveland	17
Doug Fister, Detroit	16
Hector Santiago, Chicago	15
Ivan Nova, New York	14
Chris Sale, Chicago	14

STRIKEOUTS

Yu Darvish, Texas	277
Max Scherzer, Detroit	240
Chris Sale, Chicago	226
Justin Verlander, Detroit	217
Felix Hernandez, Seattle	216

STRIKEOUTS PER NINE INNINGS

Yu Darvish, Texas	11.89
Max Scherzer, Detroit	10.08

Anibal Sanchez, Detroit	9.99
Ubaldo Jimenez, Cleveland	9.56
Felix Hernandez, Seattle	9.51

STRIKEOUTS PER NINE INNINGS (RELIEVERS)

Ernesto Frieri, Los Angeles	12.84
Koji Uehara, Boston	12.23
Cody Allen, Cleveland	11.26
Charlie Furbush, Seattle	11.08
Fernando Rodney, TB	11.07

DOUBLE PLAYS

Kevin Correia, Minnesota	26
Doug Fister, Detroit	26
Joe Saunders, Seattle	26
Felix Hernandez, Seattle	24
Lucas Harrell, Houston	23

PICKOFFS

Mark Buehrle, Toronto	6
Bruce Chen, Kansas City	5
Aaron Loup, Toronto	5
David Price, Tampa Bay	5
Jose Quintana, Chicago	5

WILD PITCHES

Matt Moore, Tampa Bay	17
C.J. Wilson, Los Angeles	14
Felix Hernandez, Seattle	13
Garrett Richards, Los Angeles	11
James Shields, Kansas City	11

WALKS-PLUS-HITS PER INNING

Max Scherzer, Detroit	0.97
Hisashi Iwakuma, Seattle	1.01
Chris Sale, Chicago	1.07
Yu Darvish, Texas	1.07
David Price, Tampa Bay	1.10

OPPONENT AVERAGE

Yu Darvish, Texas	.194
Max Scherzer, Detroit	.198
Hisashi Iwakuma, Seattle	.220
Justin Masterson, Cleveland	.222
A.J. Griffin, Oakland	.226

WORST ERA

Joe Saunders, Seattle	5.26
Jeremy Hellickson, Tampa Bay	5.17
C.C. Sabathia, New York	4.78
Jerome Williams, L.A.	4.57
Ryan Dempster, Boston	4.57

FIELDING

PITCHER

PCT	Doug Fister, Detroit	1.000
PO	Kevin Correia, Minnesota	18
A	R.A. Dickey, Toronto	40
E	Ryan Dempster, Boston	3
	Erik Bedard, Houston	3
	Cody Allen, Cleveland	3
DP	Doug Fister, Detroit	5
	Lucas Harrell, Houston	5

CATCHER

PCT	A.J. Pierzynski, Texas	.998
PO	Matt Wieters, Baltimore	1,021
A	Salvador Perez, Kansas City	71
E	J.P. Arencibia, Toronto	11
DP	A.J. Pierzynski, Texas	8

FIRST BASE

PCT	Chris Davis, Baltimore	.996
PO	Chris Davis, Baltimore	1,339

A	Eric Hosmer, Kansas City	122
E	Eric Hosmer, Kansas City	8
	Nick Swisher, Kansas City	8
	Mark Trumbo, Los Angeles	8
	Adam Dunn, Chicago	8
DP	Chris Davis, Baltimore	153

SECOND BASE

PCT	Ben Zobrist, Tampa Bay	.993
PO	Jose Altuve, Houston	273
A	Brian Dozier, Minnesota	461
E	Ian Kinsler, Texas	13
DP	Jose Altuve, Houston	114

THIRD BASE

PCT	Manny Machado, Baltimore	.973
PO	Josh Donaldson, Oakland	.961
A	Manny Machado, Baltimore	355
E	Matt Dominguez, Houston	16
	Josh Donaldson, Oakland	16

	Mike Moustakas, Kansas City	16
DP	Manny Machado, Baltimore	42

SHORTSTOP

PCT	Yunel Escobar, Tampa Bay	.989
PO	Pedro Florimon, Minnesota	245
A	Alexei Ramirez, Chicago	433
E	Alexei Ramirez, Chicago	22
DP	JJ Hardy, Baltimore	108

OUTFIELD

PCT	Nick Markakis, Baltimore	1.000
PO	Alejandro De Aza, Chicago	368
A	Alex Gordon, Kansas City	17
E	Alejandro De Aza, Chicago	8
	Josh Hamilton, Texas	8
DP	Jose Bautista, Toronto	4
	Brandon Barnes, Houston	4

CLUB BATTING

	AVG	G	AB	R	H	2B	3B	HR	RBI	BB	SO	SB	OBP	SLG
Colorado	.270	162	5599	706	1511	283	36	159	673	427	1204	112	.323	.418
St. Louis	.269	162	5557	783	1494	322	20	125	745	481	1110	45	.332	.401
Los Angeles	.264	162	5491	649	1447	281	17	138	618	476	1146	78	.326	.396
San Francisco	.260	162	5552	629	1446	280	35	107	596	469	1078	67	.320	.381
Arizona	.259	162	5676	685	1468	302	31	130	647	519	1142	62	.323	.391
Milwaukee	.252	162	5474	640	1381	238	43	157	610	407	1183	142	.311	.398
Washington	.251	162	5436	656	1365	259	27	161	621	464	1192	88	.313	.398
Atlanta	.249	162	5441	688	1354	247	21	181	656	542	1384	64	.321	.402
Cincinnati	.249	162	5499	698	1370	274	20	155	664	585	1245	67	.327	.391
Philadelphia	.248	162	5456	610	1355	255	32	140	578	417	1205	73	.306	.384
Pittsburgh	.245	162	5486	634	1346	273	35	161	603	469	1330	94	.313	.396
San Diego	.245	162	5517	618	1349	246	26	146	578	467	1309	118	.308	.378
Chicago	.238	162	5498	602	1307	297	18	172	576	439	1230	63	.300	.392
New York	.237	162	5559	619	1318	263	32	130	593	512	1384	114	.306	.366
Miami	.231	162	5449	513	1257	219	31	95	485	432	1232	78	.293	.335

CLUB PITCHING

	ERA	G	CG	SHO	SV	IP	H	R	ER	HR	BB	SO	AVG
Atlanta	3.18	162	1	12	53	1450.1	1326	548	512	127	409	1232	.244
Los Angeles	3.25	162	7	22	46	1450.1	1321	582	524	127	460	1292	.243
Pittsburgh	3.26	162	3	16	55	1470.2	1299	577	533	101	515	1261	.238
Cincinnati	3.38	162	5	17	43	1473.2	1294	589	554	170	435	1296	.236
St. Louis	3.42	162	7	15	44	1459.2	1366	596	555	112	451	1254	.249
Washington	3.59	162	6	13	47	1445.2	1367	626	576	142	405	1236	.249
Miami	3.71	162	2	13	36	1460	1376	646	602	121	526	1177	.251
New York	3.77	162	4	10	40	1476.2	1442	684	618	152	458	1209	.256
Milwaukee	3.84	162	4	15	40	1442.2	1401	687	615	175	466	1125	.255
Arizona	3.92	162	6	7	38	1495	1460	695	651	176	485	1218	.257
San Diego	3.98	162	3	6	40	1455	1407	700	643	156	525	1171	.255
Chicago	4.00	162	3	6	39	1448	1332	689	643	160	540	1184	.244
San Francisco	4.00	162	2	13	41	1447.1	1380	691	643	145	521	1256	.251
Philadelphia	4.32	162	6	3	32	1436.1	1465	749	689	152	506	1199	.265
Colorado	4.44	162	1	5	35	1436	1545	760	708	136	517	1064	.277

CLUB FIELDING

	PCT	PO	A	E	DP		PCT	PO	A	E	DP
Cincinnati	.988	4421	1643	76	131	Philadelphia	.984	4309	1614	97	141
St. Louis	.988	4379	1718	75	177	Pittsburgh	.984	4412	1924	106	154
Atlanta	.986	4351	1680	85	141	Chicago	.983	4344	1602	100	129
Colorado	.986	4308	1855	90	162	Los Angeles	.982	4351	1723	109	160
Miami	.986	4380	1687	88	144	San Francisco	.982	4342	1537	107	128
San Diego	.986	4365	1698	83	140	Washington	.982	4337	1549	107	146
New York	.985	4430	1642	93	127	Milwaukee	.981	4328	1628	114	153

INDIVIDUAL BATTING LEADERS (MINIMUM 2.7 PA/TEAM GAME)

	AVG	G	AB	R	H	2B	3B	HR	RBI	BB	SO	SB
Cuddyer, Michael, Colorado	.331	130	489	74	162	31	3	20	84	46	100	10
Johnson, Chris, Atlanta	.321	142	514	54	165	34	0	12	68	29	116	0
Freeman, Freddie, Atlanta	.319	147	551	89	176	27	2	23	109	66	121	1
Molina, Yadier, St. Louis	.319	136	505	68	161	44	0	12	80	30	55	3
Werth, Jayson, Washington	.318	129	462	84	147	24	0	25	82	60	101	10
Carpenter, Matt, St. Louis	.318	157	626	126	199	55	7	11	78	72	98	3
McCutchen, Andrew, Pittsburgh	.317	157	583	97	185	38	5	21	84	78	101	27
Craig, Allen, St. Louis	.315	134	508	71	160	29	2	13	97	40	100	2
Tulowitzki, Troy, Colorado	.312	126	446	72	139	27	0	25	82	57	85	1
Votto, Joey, Cincinnati	.305	162	581	101	177	30	3	24	73	135	138	6

INDIVIDUAL PITCHING LEADERS (MINIMUM 0.8 IP/TEAM GAME)

	W	L	ERA	G	GS	CG	SV	IP	H	R	BB	SO
Kershaw, Clayton, Los Angeles	16	9	1.83	33	33	3	0	236	164	55	52	232
Fernandez, Jose, Miami	12	6	2.19	28	28	0	0	172.7	111	47	58	187
Harvey, Matt, New York	9	5	2.27	26	26	1	0	178.3	135	46	31	191
Greinke, Zack, Los Angeles	15	4	2.63	28	28	1	0	177.7	152	54	46	148
Bumgarner, Madison, San Francisco	13	9	2.77	31	31	0	0	201.3	146	68	62	199
Lee, Cliff, Philadelphia	14	8	2.87	31	31	2	0	222.7	193	77	32	222
Wainwright, Adam, St. Louis	19	9	2.94	34	34	5	0	241.7	223	83	35	219
Ryu, Hyun-Jin, Los Angeles	14	8	3	30	30	2	0	192	182	67	49	154
Strasburg, Stephen, Washington	8	9	3	30	30	1	0	183	136	71	56	191
Miller, Shelby, St. Louis	15	9	3.06	31	31	1	0	173.3	152	65	57	169

AWARD WINNERS

Selected by Baseball Writers Association of America

MOST VALUABLE PLAYER

Player	1st	2nd	3rd	Total
Andrew McCutchen, Pittsburgh	28	1	1	409
Paul Goldschmidt, Arizona	—	15	9	242
Yadier Molina, St. Louis	2	8	4	219
Matt Carpenter, St. Louis	—	6	5	194
Freddie Freeman, Atlanta	—	—	—	154
Joey Votto, Cincinnati	—	—	2	149
Clayton Kershaw, Los Angeles	—	8	14	146
Hanley Ramirez, Los Angeles	—	—	1	58
Carlos Gomez, Milwaukee	—	—	—	43
Jay Bruce, Cincinnati	—	—	—	30
Craig Kimbrel, Atlanta	—	—	—	27
Shin Soo Choo, Cincinnati	—	—	—	23
Jayson Werth, Washington	—	—	—	20
Andrelton Simmons, Atlanta	—	—	—	14
Yasiel Puig, Los Angeles	—	—	—	10
Hunter Pence, San Francisco	—	—	—	7
Troy Tulowitzki, Colorado	—	—	—	5
Allen Craig, St. Louis	—	—	—	4
Adrian Gonzalez, Los Angeles	—	—	—	4
Buster Posey, San Francisco	—	—	—	3
Adam Wainwright, St. Louis	—	—	—	3
Michael Cuddyer, Colorado	—	—	—	3
Matt Holliday, St. Louis	—	—	—	2
Russell Martin, Pittsburgh	—	—	—	1

CY YOUNG AWARD

Pitcher	1st	2nd	3rd	Total
Clayton Kershaw, Los Angeles	29	1	—	207
Adam Wainwright, St. Louis	1	15	4	86
Jose Fernandez, Miami	—	9	3	62
Craig Kimbrel, Atlanta	—	4	1	39
Matt Harvey, New York	—	1	8	39
Cliff Lee, Philadelphia	—	—	6	32
Jordan Zimmermann, Washington	—	—	6	21
Zack Greinke, Los Angeles	—	—	2	18
Madison Bumgarner, San Francisco	—	—	—	3
Francisco Liriano, Pittsburgh	—	—	—	3

ROOKIE OF THE YEAR

Player	1st	2nd	3rd	Total
Jose Fernandez, Miami	26	4	—	142
Yasiel Puig, Los Angeles	4	25	—	95
Shelby Miller, St. Louis	—	1	9	12
Hyun-jin Ryu, Los Angeles	—	—	10	10
Julio Teheran, Atlanta	—	—	7	7
Jedd Gyorko, San Diego	—	—	2	2
Nolan Arenado, Colorado	—	—	1	1
Evan Gattis, Atlanta	—	—	1	1

MANAGER OF THE YEAR

Manager	1st	2nd	3rd	Total
Clint Hurdle, Pittsburgh	25	5	—	140
Don Mattingly, Los Angeles	2	17	7	68
Fredi Gonzalez, Atlanta	3	4	16	43
Mike Matheny, St. Louis	—	4	7	19

GOLD GLOVE WINNERS

Selected by NL managers

C—Yadier Molina, St. Louis. 1B—Paul Goldschmidt, Arizona. 2B—Brandon Phillips, Cincinnati. 3B—Nolan Arenado, Colorado. SS—Andrelton Simmons, Atlanta. LF—Carlos Gonzalez, Colorado. CF—Carlos Gomez, Milwaukee. RF—Gerardo Parra, Arizona. P—Adam Wainwright, St. Louis.

SILVER SLUGGER AWARDS

Selected by NL managers, coaches

C—Yadier Molina, St. Louis. 1B—Paul Goldschmidt, Arizona. 2B—Matt Carpenter, St. Louis. SS—Ian Desmond, Washington. 3B—Pedro Alvarez, Pittsburgh. OF—Michael Cuddyer, Colorado. OF—Andrew McCutchen, Pittsburgh. OF—Jay Bruce, Cincinnati. P—Zack Greinke, Los Angeles.

BATTING

GAMES
Hunter Pence, San Francisco	162
Joey Votto, Cincinnati	162
Starlin Castro, Chicago	161
Daniel Murphy, New York	161
4 players	160

AT-BATS
Starlin Castro, Chicago	666
Daniel Murphy, New York	658
Hunter Pence, San Francisco	629
Jay Bruce, Cincinnati	626
Matt Carpenter, St. Louis	626

PLATE APPEARANCES
Joey Votto, Cincinnati	726
Matt Carpenter, St. Louis	717
Shin-Soo Choo, Cincinnati	712
Paul Goldschmidt, Arizona	710
Starlin Castro, Chicago	705

RUNS
Matt Carpenter, St. Louis	126
Shin-Soo Choo, Cincinnati	107
Paul Goldschmidt, Arizona	103
Matt Holliday, St. Louis	103
Joey Votto, Cincinnati	101

HITS
Matt Carpenter, St. Louis	199
Daniel Murphy, New York	188
Andrew McCutchen, Pittsburgh	185
Paul Goldschmidt, Arizona	182
Hunter Pence, San Francisco	178

TOTAL BASES
Paul Goldschmidt, Arizona	332
Hunter Pence, San Francisco	304
Matt Carpenter, St. Louis	301
Jay Bruce, Cincinnati	299
Andrew McCutchen, Pittsburgh	296

DOUBLES
Matt Carpenter, St. Louis	55
Yadier Molina, St. Louis	44
Jay Bruce, Cincinnati	43
Gerardo Parra, Arizona	43
Anthony Rizzo, Chicago	40

TRIPLES
Denard Span, Washington	11
Carlos Gomez, Milwaukee	10
Starling Marte, Pittsburgh	10
Jean Segura, Milwaukee	10
2 players	8

EXTRA-BASE HITS
Paul Goldschmidt, Arizona	75
Jay Bruce, Cincinnati	74
Matt Carpenter, St. Louis	73
Hunter Pence, San Francisco	67
Anthony Rizzo, Chicago	65

HOME RUNS
Pedro Alvarez, Pittsburgh	36
Paul Goldschmidt, Arizona	36
Jay Bruce, Cincinnati	30
4 players	27

RUNS BATTED IN
Paul Goldschmidt, Arizona	125
Jay Bruce, Cincinnati	109
Freddie Freeman, Atlanta	109
Brandon Phillips, Cincinnati	103
2 players	100

SACRIFICES
Bronson Arroyo, Cincinnati	16

Jay Bruce

TOMASSO DeROSA

Zack Cozart, Cincinnati	13
Cole Hamels, Philadelphia	13
Kyle Lohse, Milwaukee	12
3 players	11

SACRIFICE FLIES
Zack Cozart, Cincinnati	10
Adrian Gonzalez, Los Angeles	10
Brandon Phillips, Cincinnati	9
Jonathan Lucroy, Milwaukee	8
5 players	7

HIT BY PITCH
Shin-Soo Choo, Cincinnati	26
Starling Marte, Pittsburgh	24
Neil Walker, Pittsburgh	15
Todd Frazier, Cincinnati	14
Jon Jay, St. Louis	14

WALKS
Joey Votto, Cincinnati	135
Shin-Soo Choo, Cincinnati	112
Paul Goldschmidt, Arizona	99
Andrew McCutchen, Pittsburgh	78
Dan Uggla, Atlanta	77

STOLEN BASES
Eric Young, Col/NYM	46
Jean Segura, Milwaukee	44
Starling Marte, Pittsburgh	41
Carlos Gomez, Milwaukee	40
Everth Cabrera, San Diego	37

CAUGHT STEALING
Starling Marte, Pittsburgh	15
Jean Segura, Milwaukee	13
Norichika Aoki, Milwaukee	12
Everth Cabrera, San Diego	12

Pat Corbin

BILL MITCHELL

2 player	11

STOLEN-BASE PERCENTAGE
Daniel Murphy, New York	88%
Hunter Pence, San Francisco	88%
Carlos Gonzalez, Colorado	88%
Carlos Gomez, Milwaukee	85%
David Wright, New York	85%

STRIKEOUTS
Pedro Alvarez, Pittsburgh	186
Jay Bruce, Cincinnati	185
Dan Uggla, Atlanta	171
Justin Upton, Atlanta	161
B.J. Upton, Atlanta	151

TOUGHEST TO STRIKE OUT
(AT-BATS PER STRIKEOUT)
Norichika Aoki, Milwaukee	14.93
Marco Scutaro, San Francisco	14.35
Martin Prado, Arizona	11.49
Andrelton Simmons, Atlanta	11.02
Yadier Molina, St. Louis	9.18

GROUNDED INTO DOUBLE PLAYS
Matt Holliday, St. Louis	31
Martin Prado, Arizona	29
David Freese, St. Louis	25
Paul Goldschmidt, Arizona	25
Darwin Barney, Chicago	22

MULTI-HIT GAMES
Matt Carpenter, St. Louis	63
Matt Holliday St. Louis, 60	60
Andrew McCutchen, Pittsburgh	60
Hunter Pence, San Francisco	54
Daniel Murphy, New York	53
2 players	52

ON-BASE PERCENTAGE
Joey Votto, Cincinnati	.435
Shin-Soo Choo, Cincinnati	.423
Andrew McCutchen, Pittsburgh	.404
Paul Goldschmidt, Arizona	.401
Jayson Werth, Washington	.398

SLUGGING PERCENTAGE
Paul Goldschmidt, Arizona	.551
Troy Tulowitzki, Colorado	.540
Jayson Werth, Washington	.532
Michael Cuddyer, Colorado	.530
Marlon Byrd, NYM/Pit	.511

ON-BASE-PLUS SLUGGING
Paul Goldschmidt, Arizona	.952
Troy Tulowitzki, Colorado	.931
Jayson Werth, Washington	.931
Joey Votto, Cincinnati	.926
Michael Cuddyer, Colorado	.919

LOWEST AVERAGE
Dan Uggla, Atlanta	.179
Darwin Barney, Chicago	.208
Russell Martin, Pittsburgh	.226
Adeiny Hechavarria, Miami	.227
Anthony Rizzo, Chicago	.233

PITCHING

WINS
Adam Wainwright, St. Louis	19
Jordan Zimmermann, Washington	19
Jorge De La Rosa, Colorado	16
Clayton Kershaw, Los Angeles	16
Francisco Liriano, Pittsburgh	16

LOSSES
Edwin Jackson, Chicago	18
Wily Peralta, Milwaukee	15
Cole Hamels, Philadelphia	14

Dan Haren, Washington 14
Tim Lincecum, San Francisco 14

GAMES
Brad Ziegler, Arizona 78
Ronald Belisario, Los Angeles 77
Paco Rodriguez, Los Angeles 76
6 players 75

GAMES STARTED
Adam Wainwright, St. Louis 34
7 players 33

GAMES FINISHED
Steve Cishek, Miami 62
Craig Kimbrel, Atlanta 60
Rafael Soriano, Washington 58
Aroldis Chapman, Cincinnati 55
Jonathan Papelbon, Philadelphia 54

COMPLETE GAMES
Adam Wainwright, St. Louis 5
Jordan Zimmermann, Washington 4
Clayton Kershaw, Los Angeles 3
Patrick Corbin, Arizona 3
6 players 2

SHUTOUTS
Clayton Kershaw, Los Angeles 2
Adam Wainwright, St. Louis 2
Jordan Zimmermann, Washington 2
17 players 1

SAVES
Craig Kimbrel, Atlanta 50
Rafael Soriano, Washington 43
Aroldis Chapman, Cincinnati 38
Sergio Romo, San Francisco 38
Edward Mujica, St. Louis 37

INNINGS PITCHED
Adam Wainwright, St. Louis 241.7
Clayton Kershaw, L.A. 236
Cliff Lee, Philadelphia 222.7
Cole Hamels, Philadelphia 220
Jeff Samardzija, Chicago 213.7

HITS ALLOWED
Adam Wainwright, St. Louis 223
Eric Stults, San Diego 219
Jeff Samardzija, Chicago 210
Dillon Gee, New York 208
Kyle Kendrick, Philadelphia 207

RUNS ALLOWED
Edinson Volquez, SD/LA 114
Edwin Jackson, Chicago 110

Andrelton Simmons

LARRY GOREN

Jeff Samardzija, Chicago 109
Ian Kennedy, Ari/SD 108
Wily Peralta, Milwaukee 107

HOME RUNS ALLOWED
Bronson Arroyo, Cincinnati 32
Dan Haren, Washington 28
Ian Kennedy, Ari/SD 27
Kyle Lohse, Milwaukee 26
Jeff Samardzija, Chicago 25

WALKS
Jeff Locke, Pittsburgh 84
Jeff Samardzija, Chicago 78
Edinson Volquez, SD/LA 77
3 players tied at 76

WALKS PER NINE INNINGS
Cliff Lee, Philadelphia 1.29
Adam Wainwright, St. Louis 1.30
Bronson Arroyo, Cincinnati 1.51

Matt Harvey, New York 1.56
Kyle Lohse, Milwaukee 1.63

HIT BATTERS
Charlie Morton, Pittsburgh 16
Julio Teheran, Atlanta 13
Ian Kennedy, Ari/SD 12
Stephen Strasburg, Washington 12
Lance Lynn, St. Louis 11

STRIKEOUTS
Clayton Kershaw, L.A. 232
Cliff Lee, Philadelphia 222
Adam Wainwright, St. Louis 219
Jeff Samardzija, Chicago 214
A.J. Burnett, Pittsburgh 209

STRIKEOUTS PER NINE INNINGS
A.J. Burnett, Pittsburgh 9.85
Jose Fernandez, Miami 9.75
Matt Harvey, New York 9.64

Stephen Strasburg, Washington 9.39
Jeff Samardzija, Chicago 9.01

STRIKEOUTS PER NINE INNINGS
(RELIEVERS)
Aroldis Chapman, Cincinnati 15.83
Craig Kimbrel, Atlanta 13.16
Kenley Jansen, L.A. 13.03
Trevor Rosenthal, St. Louis 12.90
Jim Henderson, Milwaukee 11.25

DOUBLE PLAYS
Adam Wainwright, St. Louis 32
Jhoulys Chacin, Colorado 30
Hyun-Jin Ryu, Los Angeles 26
Mike Leake, Cincinnati 23
Wade Miley, Arizona 23

PICKOFFS
Julio Teheran, Atlanta 8
Clayton Kershaw, Los Angeles 7
Madison Bumgarner, S.F. 6
Tony Cingrani, Cincinnati 6
Jeff Locke, Pittsburgh 6

WILD PITCHES
Trevor Cahill, Arizona 17
Edinson Volquez, SD/L.A. 16
Edwin Jackson, Chicago 14
Patrick Corbin, Arizona 13
Wade Miley, Arizona 13

WALKS-PLUS-HITS PER INNING
Clayton Kershaw, L.A. 0.92
Matt Harvey, New York 0.93
Jose Fernandez, Miami 0.98
Cliff Lee, Philadelphia 1.01
Madison Bumgarner, S.F. 1.03

OPPONENT AVERAGE
Jose Fernandez, Miami .182
Clayton Kershaw, L.A. .195
Madison Bumgarner, S.F. .203
Stephen Strasburg, Washington .207
Matt Harvey, New York .209

WORST ERA
Edinson Volquez, SD/LA 5.71
Edwin Jackson, Chicago 4.98
Ian Kennedy, Ari/SD 4.91
Kyle Kendrick, Philadelphia 4.70
Dan Haren, Washington 4.67

PITCHER
PCT Adam Wainwright, St. Louis 1.000
PO Mat Latos, Cincinnati

FIELDING

26
		Mike Leake, Cincinnati	26
A		Kyle Kendrick, Philadelphia	43
E		Jacob Turner, Miami	5
DP		Adam Wainwright, St. Louis	6

CATCHER
PCT	Russell Martin, Pittsburgh	.998
PO	Yadier Molina, St. Louis	976
A	Russell Martin, Pittsburgh	103
E	Welington Castillo, Chicago	10
	Nick Hundley, San Diego	10
DP	Nick Hundley, San Diego	12

FIRST BASE
PCT	Todd Helton, Colorado	.998
PO	Paul Goldschmidt, Arizona	1,494
A	Freddie Freeman, Atlanta	107

E	Adrian Gonzalez, Los Angeles	11
	Adam LaRoche, Washington	11
DP	Adrian Gonzalez, Los Angeles	133

SECOND BASE
PCT	Darwin Barney, Chicago	.993
PO	Brandon Phillips, Cincinnati	278
A	Brandon Phillips, Cincinnati	428
E	Chase Utley, Philadelphia	17
DP	Matt Carpenter, St. Louis	97

THIRD BASE
PCT	Placido Polanco, Miami	.990
PO	Ryan Zimmerman, Washington	98
A	Pedro Alvarez, Pittsburgh	359
E	Pedro Alvarez, Pittsburgh	27
DP	Ryan Zimmerman, Washington	28

SHORTSTOP
PCT	Troy Tulowitzki, Colorado	.986
PO	Andrelton Simmons, Atlanta	240
A	Andrelton Simmons, Atlanta	499
E	Starlin Castro, Chicago	22
DP	Pete Kozma, St. Louis	98

OUTFIELDER
PCT	Denard Span, Washington	1.000
PO	Carlos Gomez, Milwaukee	391
A	Gerardo Parra, Arizona	17
E	Giancarlo Stanton, Miami	8
DP	Andre Ethier, Los Angeles	4
	Marcell Ozuna, Miami	4

KEN BABBITT

David Ortiz lifted the Red Sox to their third World Series championship in 10 years by hitting .688 with two home runs and six RBIs during the six-game victory over the Cardinals

Red Sox reverse course with World Series title

BY JOHN PERROTTO

The Boston Red Sox couldn't quite let go of the 2013 season.

The final out of their Game Six victory over the St. Louis Cardinals in the World Series had been recorded more than three hours earlier and the celebration was still in the process of winding down in their cramped home clubhouse at 101-year-old Fenway Park. On the playing field, some of the players and their children were participating in an impromptu pick-up game, even though it was approaching 3 in the morning.

The Red Sox talked throughout the postseason about how they had developed a unique closeness, beginning on the first day of spring training, and it showed in the aftermath of the franchise's third World Series title in 10 years.

Rarely do postgame celebrations last this long.

The scene was bedlam an hour earlier at Fenway, where the Red Sox hadn't clinched a world championship since 1918 when they had a young lefthanded pitcher named Babe Ruth on their staff. The fans roared when closer Koji Uehara got the final out by striking out Cardinals second baseman Matt Carpenter.

"When the fireworks went off at the presentation of the trophy, when the ballpark was filled with smoke, it was completely surreal," Red Sox manager John Farrell said.

Beating the Cardinals finished a remarkable season in which the Red Sox went from worst to first, rebounding from a 69-93 record under one-and-done manager Bobby Valentine and a last-place finish in the American League East to a world championship.

The Red Sox entered both the 2004 and 2007 seasons with one of the strongest rosters in baseball and it was no surprise—well, some surprise to the Yankees, who led the ALCS 3-0 in 2004— that they wound up as World Series champions. However, few people outside (and perhaps inside) Red Sox Nation expected a World Series winner this time. Some Las Vegas sports books had odds of the Red Sox winning it all at 30-to-1 entering spring training.

"I would say because this is a team that has a lot of players with heart," said DH David Ortiz, the only Red Sox player left from 2004. "We probably don't have the talent that we had in '07 and '04, but we have guys that are capable to stay focused and do the little things. When you win with a ballclub like that, that's special."

Rebuilding The Bond

General manager Ben Cherington set about what he said was "building the next great Red Sox team" following the 2012 debacle. It didn't take him long. The Red Sox won 28 more games following an offseason in which Cherington changed managers by trading with the Toronto Blue Jays for Farrell—the pitching coach on Boston's last championship team in 2007. Cherington also made several key free agent signings, including righthander Ryan Dempster and closer Uehara, catcher David Ross, first baseman Mike Napoli, shortstop Stephen Drew and outfielders Jonny Gomes and Shane Victorino.

"I don't think you'll ever find a team as close as this one was," Ross said. "It started early on in spring training. The bonds formed early. We came together right away. It was something really special. The guys on this team really cared for each other, really had a lot of love for each other.

"You add that to an organization that truly cares about its players and wants to win as much as any organization in baseball, and special things like this happen."

The strong bonds between the Red Sox and New England have been written and talked about for years but they took on an entirely different meaning in 2013.

On April 15, shortly after the Red Sox's traditional Patriots' Day morning game ended against the Rays at Fenway, two bombs exploded near the Boston Marathon finish line in Copley Square. Three people were killed and more than 250 others were injured, many losing limbs.

The city adopted "Boston Strong" as its motto during the recovery from the tragic event, using the "B" logo on the Red Sox cap and the words "strong" as the logo, which was mowed into the center field grass at Fenway Park before every game. The Red Sox also wore the emblem on the left sleeves of their jerseys and affixed a large logo to the Green Monster in left field at Fenway.

"It's hard for me to put sports over a tragedy like that," said Red Sox righthander John Lackey, the Game Six winner. "Hopefully, we helped those who were affected by it forget about it for a few hours every day."

Gomes said the Red Sox rode the wave of emotion to the title.

"I don't think the fans jumped on our back," Gomes said. "It was the other way around. We jumped on the fans' backs. They weren't going to let us fail and here we are. It's very special."

Nobody had a more special Series than the 37-year-old Ortiz, the one constant during a time when Boston not only ended an 84-year title drought in 2004 but smashed the Curse of the Bambino to smithereens, becoming the first team to win three World Series in the new millennium.

The DH, who played first base when the Series shifted to St. Louis, hit .688 as he went 11-for-16 and finished with a .760 on-base percentage by reaching base in 19 of 25 plate appearances to win MVP honors. He had two doubles, two home runs, six RBIs and walked seven times, tying the World Series record set by Boston's Carlton Fisk in 1975.

The rest of the Red Sox hit .234.

"I know I'm one of the forces for this ballclub and I like to take things personal," Ortiz said after Game Six, when St. Louis walked him four times. "That has been that way my whole career, a challenge. I wasn't trying to be the guy but I know I've got to get something done to keep the line moving. Thank God, everything worked out well, and I didn't even have to do anything today, I guess, the rest of the team took over."

Ortiz went hitless in the 6-1 victory in the clincher mainly because the Cardinals wouldn't pitch to him.

"He's as hot as anyone you're going to see this time of year," Cardinals manager Mike Matheny said. "We tried to make tough pitches in tough situations, tried to pitch around him at times."

It didn't work. Ortiz punished the Cardinals' talented pitching staff.

"Let me tell you, I was hitting well, but it wasn't like I was hitting pitches right down the middle of the plate," Ortiz said. "They were trying their best to get me out. I was just putting good swings."

Red Sox lefthander Jon Lester certainly did

enough to earn MVP honors, winnings Games One and Five and holding the Cardinals to only one run in 15 ⅓ innings. However, he became a footnote to Ortiz's exploits.

Lester got the Red Sox off on the right foot by pitching 7 ⅔ scoreless innings in an 8-1 win in the opener at Fenway Park. The game was most notable for the umpires getting together in the first inning to overturn a blown call.

With runners on first and second and one out in the bottom of the first with the game scoreless, Ortiz hit a grounder to Carpenter, whose toss for an attempted force play went off the tip of shortstop Pete Kozma's glove. Second base umpire Dana DeMuth originally ruled an out, indicating Kozma dropped the ball while taking it out of his glove.

Red Sox first baseman Mike Napoli followed with a three-run double to break a scoreless tie.

The Cardinals evened the series with a 4-2 win in Game Two as rookie righthander Michael Wacha allowed two runs in six innings and right fielder Carlos Beltran, a 16-year veteran playing in his first World Series, capped a three-run rally in the seventh inning with an RBI single.

The series shifted to Busch Stadium in St. Louis and Games Three and Four both had bizarre endings.

The Cardinals won 5-4 in Game Three with Allen Craig scoring the winning run on a rare obstruction call in the bottom of the ninth by third-base umpire Jim Joyce. Third baseman Will Middlebrooks dove to his left in an attempt to catch a wild throw from catcher Jarrod Saltalamacchia, unintentionally tripping Craig in the process. That would turn out to be the Cardinals' last win.

The Red Sox evened the series at two games each with a 4-2 victory in Game Four. Gomes hit a tiebreaking three-run home run in the sixth inning and Uehara picked off rookie pinch-runner Kolten Wong at first base to end the game.

Lester shut down the Cardinals in Game Five, giving up one run in 7 ⅔ innings, then Victorino powered the Red Sox to victory in Game Six with four RBIs, including a three-run double off Wacha in the third inning that opened the scoring.

Victorino was also the hero for the Red Sox as they beat the Tigers in the American League Championship Series. His grand slam in the bottom of the seventh off Jose Veras propelled the Red Sox from a one-run deficit to a 5-2 victory in the decisive Game Six.

The Red Sox, however, might not have gotten that far without Ortiz.

Already down 1-0 to Detroit and trailing Game Two 5-1 in the eighth, Ortiz ripped a game-tying grand slam on the first pitch from reliever Joaquin Benoit. Boston won it in the ninth on Saltalamacchia's game-ending single.

Napoli was the difference in Game Three of the ALCS. Against an otherwise-dominant Justin Verlander, he broke a scoreless tie with a homer to straightaway center field for a 1-0 win.

The Tigers pounded Jake Peavy to win Game Four and tie the series again, but it again was a long home run to center field by Napoli—estimated at 460 feet—that rocked Detroit and Anibal Sanchez in Boston's 4-3 win.

That led to the heroics in Game Six from Victorino, who signed a three-year, $39-million contract as a free agent the previous offseason. He quickly became a fan favorite with the Fenway faithful, who sang the chorus to Bob Marley's

AMERICAN LEAGUE CHAMPIONS, 1995–2013

American League postseason results in Wild Card Era, 1995-present, where (*) denotes wild card playoff entrant.

YEAR	CHAMPIONSHIP SERIES	ALCS MVP	DIVISION SERIES 1	DIVISION SERIES 2
2013	Boston 4, Detroit 2	Koji Uehara, rhp, Boston	Boston 3, Tampa Bay* 1	Detrot, 3, Oakland 2
2012	Detroit 4, New York 0	Delmon Young, of, Detroit	New York 3, Baltimore* 2	Detroit 3, Oakland 2
2011	Texas 4, Detroit 2	Nelson Cruz, of, Texas	Detroit 3, New York 2	Texas 3, Tampa Bay* 1
2010	Texas 4, New York 2	Josh Hamilton, of, Texas	Texas 3, Tampa Bay 2	New York* 3, Minnesota 0
2009	New York 4, Los Angeles 2	C.C. Sabathia, lhp, New York	New York 3, Minnesota 0	Los Angeles 3, Boston* 0
2008	Tampa Bay 4, Boston 3	Matt Garza, rhp, Tampa Bay	Boston* 3, Los Angeles 1	Tampa Bay 3, Chicago 1
2007	Boston 4, Cleveland 3	Josh Beckett, rhp, Boston	Boston 3, Los Angeles 0	Cleveland 3, New York* 1
2006	Detroit 4, Oakland 0	Placido Polanco, 2b, Detroit	Detroit* 3, New York 1	Oakland 3, Minnesota 0
2005	Chicago 4, Los Angeles 1	Paul Konerko, 1b, Chicago	Chicago 3, Boston* 0	Los Angeles 3, New York 2
2004	Boston 4, New York 3	David Ortiz, dh, Boston	Boston* 3, Anaheim 0	New York 3, Minnesota 1
2003	New York 4, Boston 3	Mariano Rivera, rhp, New York	New York 3, Minnesota 1	Boston* 3, Oakland 2
2002	Anaheim 4, Minnesota 1	Adam Kennedy, 2b, Anaheim	Anaheim* 3, New York 1	Minnesota 3, Oakland 2
2001	New York 4, Seattle 1	Andy Pettitte, lhp, New York	Seattle 3, Cleveland 2	New York 3, Oakland* 2
2000	New York 4, Seattle 2	David Justice, of, New York	New York 3, Oakland 2	Seattle* 3, Chicago 0
1999	New York 4, Boston 1	Orlando Hernandez, rhp, New York	Boston* 3, Cleveland 2	New York 3, Texas 0
1998	New York 4, Cleveland 2	David Wells, lhp, New York	Cleveland 3, Boston* 1	New York 3, Texas 0
1997	Cleveland 4, Baltimore 2	Marquis Grissom, of, Cleveland	Cleveland 3, New York* 2	Baltimore 3, Seattle 1
1996	New York 4, Baltimore 1	Bernie Williams, of, New York	Baltimore* 3, Cleveland 1	New York 3, Texas 1
1995	Cleveland 4, Seattle 2	Orel Hershiser, rhp, Cleveland	Cleveland 3, Boston 0	Seattle 3, New York* 2

Three Little Birds—Victorino's walkup song—every time he stepped to the plate.

"Don't worry about a thing. 'Cause everything is gonna be all right," Marley sings, and Victorino took care of the rest for the Red Sox.

"The one thing I came here to do is to be part of this city," Victorino said. "With all we went through as a city, there is definitely a bond."

Uehara was named MVP after notching a win and three saves.

Cardinals Come Close

Wacha was the story of the Cardinals' postseason as the 22-year-old went 4-0, 1.00 in four starts until losing the finale at Boston. The Cardinals beat the Dodgers in six games to win the National League Championship Series and Wacha was named MVP when he pitched 13 ⅔ scoreless innings and twice beat Los Angeles ace lefthander Clayton Kershaw.

Pitching dominated the NLCS, as expected. Zack Greinke and Joe Kelly were solid in Game One, won by St. Louis, and then Wacha blanked Kershaw and the Dodgers 1-0 in Game Two.

Righthander Hyun-Jin Ryu got the Dodgers back in the series when it shifted to Los Angeles, stifling the Cardinals and ace Adam Wainwright in Game Three.

The Cards grabbed a 3-1 series lead the next night behind Lance Lynn, and after a rare offensive outburst in Game Five by Los Angeles, Wacha returned in Game Six to blank the Dodgers again and send St. Louis to the World Series.

Wacha was 4-1, 2.78 in 15 regular season games, including nine starts, and foreshadowed his dominant postseason by carrying a no-hitter into ninth inning in his regular season finale before losing it with two outs on an infield single by Nationals third baseman Ryan Zimmerman.

The Cardinals selected Wacha in the first round (19th overall) of the 2012 draft from Texas A&M with the compensation pick they received for the Angels signing Albert Pujols.

"Taking everything into consideration, how this kid was in college 18 months or so ago, and watching the maturity, and watching the progress, too, I think a lot has to be said about that," Cardinals manager Mike Matheny said.

The Cardinals needed all five games to get past the upstart Pirates, who were making their first postseason appearance since 1992, in the National League Division Series while the Dodgers downed the Braves in four games in the other NLDS. The Braves haven't won a postseason series since 2002.

In the American League Division Series, the Red Sox defeated the Rays in four games while the Tigers needed five games to finish off the Athletics.

In the second year of the wild-card round, the Rays beat the Indians in the AL game and the Pirates downed the Reds in the NL in front of a raucous and emotional crowd at PNC Park in Pittsburgh that waited a generation to see postseason baseball.

Reds starter Johnny Cueto became so rattled by the fans chanting "Cueto" that he dropped the ball while in the set position then gave up a two-run home run to Pirates catcher Russell Martin on the next pitch.

"If our city ever thinks they don't make a difference, all they got to do is watch the tape from tonight's game," Pirates manager Clint Hurdle said. "It was special."

NATIONAL LEAGUE CHAMPIONS, 1995–2013

National League postseason results in Wild Card Era, 1995-present, where (*) denotes wild card playoff entrant.

YEAR	CHAMPIONSHIP SERIES	NLCS MVP	DIVISION SERIES	DIVISION SERIES
2013	St. Louis 4, Los Angeles 2	Michael Wacha, rhp, St. Louis	St. Louis 3, Pittsburgh* 2	Los Angeles 3, Atlanta 1
2012	San Francisco 4, St. Louis 3	Marco Scutaro, 2b, San Francisco	St. Louis* 3, Washington 2	San Francisco 3, Cincinnati 2
2011	St. Louis 4, Milwaukee 2	David Freese, 3b, St. Louis	St. Louis* 3, Philadelphia 2	Milwaukee 3, Arizona 2
2010	San Francisco 4, Philadelphia 2	Cody Ross, of, San Francisco	Philadelphia 3, Cincinnati 0	San Francisco 3, Atlanta* 1
2009	Philadelphia 4, Los Angeles 1	Ryan Howard, 1b, Philadelphia	Los Angeles 3, St. Louis 0	Philadelphia 3, Colorado* 1
2008	Philadelphia 4, Los Angeles 1	Cole Hamels, lhp, Philadelphia	Los Angeles 3, Chicago 0	Philadelphia 3, Milwaukee* 1
2007	Colorado 4, Arizona 0	Matt Holliday, of, Colorado	Arizona 3, Chicago 0	Colorado* 3, Philadelphia 0
2006	St. Louis 4, New York 3	Jeff Suppan, rhp, St. Louis	New York 3, Los Angeles* 0	St. Louis 3, San Diego 1
2005	Houston 4, St. Louis 2	Roy Oswalt, rhp, Houston	St. Louis 3, San Diego 0	Houston* 3, Atlanta 1
2004	St. Louis 4, Houston 3	Albert Pujols, 1b, St. Louis	St. Louis 3, Los Angeles 1	Houston* 3, Atlanta 2
2003	Florida 4, Chicago 3	Ivan Rodriguez, c, Florida	Florida* 3, San Francisco 1	Chicago 3, Atlanta 2
2002	San Francisco 4, St. Louis 1	Benito Santiago, c, San Francisco	San Francisco* 3, Atlanta 2	St. Louis 3, Arizona 0
2001	Arizona 4, Atlanta 1	Craig Counsell, ss, Arizona	Atlanta 3, Houston 0	Arizona 3, St. Louis 2
2000	New York 4, St. Louis 1	Mike Hampton, lhp, New York	St. Louis 3, Atlanta 0	New York* 3, San Francisco 1
1999	Atlanta 4, New York 2	Eddie Perez, c, Atlanta	Atlanta 3, Houston 1	New York* 3, Arizona 1
1998	San Diego 4, Atlanta 2	Sterling Hitchcock, lhp, San Diego	Atlanta 3, Chicago* 0	San Diego 3, Houston 1
1997	Florida 4, Atlanta 2	Livan Hernandez, rhp, Florida	Florida* 3, San Francisco 0	Atlanta 3, Houston 0
1996	Atlanta 4, St. Louis 3	Javy Lopez, c, Atlanta	Atlanta 3, Los Angeles* 0	St. Louis 3, San Diego 0
1995	Atlanta 4, Cincinnati 0	Mike Devereaux, of, Atlanta	Atlanta 3, Colorado* 1	Cincinnati 3, Los Angeles 0

Year	Winner	Loser	Result
1903	Boston (AL)	Pittsburgh (NL)	5-3
1904	NO SERIES		
1905	New York (NL)	Philadelphia (AL)	4-1
1906	Chicago (AL)	Chicago (NL)	4-2
1907	Chicago (NL)	Detroit (AL)	4-0
1908	Chicago (NL)	Detroit (AL)	4-1
1909	Pittsburgh (NL)	Detroit (AL)	4-3
1910	Philadelphia (AL)	Chicago (NL)	4-1
1911	Philadelphia (AL)	New York (NL)	4-2
1912	Boston (AL)	New York (NL)	4-3-1
1913	Philadelphia (AL)	New York (NL)	4-1
1914	Boston (NL)	Philadelphia (AL)	4-0
1915	Boston (AL)	Philadelphia (NL)	4-1
1916	Boston (AL)	Brooklyn (NL)	4-1
1917	Chicago (AL)	New York (NL)	4-2
1918	Boston (AL)	Chicago (NL)	4-2
1919	Cincinnati (NL)	Chicago (AL)	5-3
1920	Cleveland (AL)	Brooklyn (NL)	5-2
1921	New York (NL)	New York (AL)	5-3
1922	New York (NL)	New York (AL)	4-0
1923	New York (AL)	New York (NL)	4-2
1924	Washington (AL)	New York (NL)	4-3
1925	Pittsburgh (NL)	Washington (AL)	4-3
1926	St. Louis (NL)	New York (AL)	4-3
1927	New York (AL)	Pittsburgh (NL)	4-0
1928	New York (AL)	St. Louis (NL)	4-0
1929	Philadelphia (AL)	Chicago (NL)	4-1
1930	Philadelphia (AL)	St. Louis (NL)	4-2
1931	St. Louis (NL)	Philadelphia (AL)	4-3
1932	New York (AL)	Chicago (NL)	4-0
1933	New York (NL)	Washington (AL)	4-1
1934	St. Louis (NL)	Detroit (AL)	4-3
1935	Detroit (AL)	Chicago (NL)	4-2
1936	New York (AL)	New York (NL)	4-2
1937	New York (AL)	New York (NL)	4-1
1938	New York (AL)	Chicago (NL)	4-0
1939	New York (AL)	Cincinnati (NL)	4-0
1940	Cincinnati (NL)	Detroit (AL)	4-3
1941	New York (AL)	Brooklyn (NL)	4-1
1942	St. Louis (NL)	New York (AL)	4-1
1943	New York (AL)	St. Louis (NL)	4-1
1944	St. Louis (NL)	St. Louis (AL)	4-2
1945	Detroit (AL)	Chicago (NL)	4-3
1946	St. Louis (NL)	Boston (AL)	4-3
1947	New York (AL)	Brooklyn (NL)	4-3
1948	Cleveland (AL)	Boston (NL)	4-2
1949	New York (AL)	Brooklyn (NL)	4-1
1950	New York (AL)	Philadelphia (NL)	4-0
1951	New York (AL)	New York (NL)	4-2
1952	New York (AL)	Brooklyn (NL)	4-3
1953	New York (AL)	Brooklyn (NL)	4-2
1954	New York (NL)	Cleveland (AL)	4-0
1955	Brooklyn (NL)	New York (AL)	4-3
1956	New York (AL)	Brooklyn (NL)	4-3
1957	Milwaukee (NL)	New York (AL)	4-3
1958	New York (AL)	Milwaukee (NL)	4-3
1959	Los Angeles (NL)	Chicago (AL)	4-2
1960	Pittsburgh (NL)	New York (AL)	4-3
1961	New York (AL)	Cincinnati (NL)	4-1
1962	New York (AL)	San Francisco (NL)	4-3
1963	Los Angeles (NL)	New York (AL)	4-0
1964	St. Louis (NL)	New York (AL)	4-3

KEN BABBITT

Manager John Farrell restored order and guided Boston to its third title in 10 years

Year	Winner	Loser	Result
1965	Los Angeles (NL)	Minnesota (AL)	4-3
1966	Baltimore (AL)	Los Angeles (NL)	4-0
1967	St. Louis (NL)	Boston (AL)	4-3
1968	Detroit (AL)	St. Louis (NL)	4-3
1969	New York (NL)	Baltimore (AL)	4-1
1970	Baltimore (AL)	Cincinnati (NL)	4-1
1971	Pittsburgh (NL)	Baltimore (AL)	4-3
1972	Oakland (AL)	Cincinnati (NL)	4-3
1973	Oakland (AL)	New York (NL)	4-3
1974	Oakland (AL)	Los Angeles (NL)	4-1
1975	Cincinnati (NL)	Boston (AL)	4-3
1976	Cincinnati (NL)	New York (AL)	4-0
1977	New York (AL)	Los Angeles (NL)	4-2
1978	New York (AL)	Los Angeles (NL)	4-2
1979	Pittsburgh (NL)	Baltimore (AL)	4-3
1980	Philadelphia (NL)	Kansas City (AL)	4-2
1981	Los Angeles (NL)	New York (AL)	4-2
1982	St. Louis (NL)	Milwaukee (AL)	4-3
1983	Baltimore (AL)	Philadelphia (NL)	4-1
1984	Detroit (AL)	San Diego (NL)	4-1
1985	Kansas City (AL)	St. Louis (NL)	4-3
1986	New York (NL)	Boston (AL)	4-3
1987	Minnesota (AL)	St. Louis (NL)	4-3
1988	Los Angeles (NL)	Oakland (AL)	4-1
1989	Oakland (AL)	San Francisco (NL)	4-0
1990	Cincinnati (NL)	Oakland (AL)	4-0
1991	Minnesota (AL)	Atlanta (NL)	4-3
1992	Toronto (AL)	Atlanta (NL)	4-2
1993	Toronto (AL)	Philadelphia (NL)	4-2
1994	NO SERIES		
1995	Atlanta (NL)	Cleveland (AL)	4-2
1996	New York (AL)	Atlanta (NL)	4-2
1997	Florida (NL)	Cleveland (AL)	4-3
1998	New York (AL)	San Diego (NL)	4-0
1999	New York (AL)	Atlanta (NL)	4-0
2000	New York (AL)	New York (NL)	4-1
2001	Arizona (NL)	New York (AL)	4-3
2002	Anaheim (AL)	San Francisco (NL)	4-3
2003	Florida (NL)	New York (AL)	4-2
2004	Boston (AL)	St. Louis (NL)	4-0
2005	Chicago (AL)	Houston (NL)	4-0
2006	St. Louis (NL)	Detroit (AL)	4-1
2007	Boston (AL)	Colorado (NL)	4-0
2008	Philadelphia (NL)	Tampa Bay (AL)	4-1
2009	New York (AL)	Philadelphia (NL)	4-2
2010	San Francisco (NL)	Texas (AL)	4-1
2011	St. Louis (NL)	Texas (AL)	4-3
2012	San Francisco (NL)	Detroit (AL)	4-0
2013	Boston (AL)	St. Louis (NL)	4-2

WORLD SERIES BOX SCORES

GAME ONE *October 23, 2013*
BOSTON 8, ST. LOUIS 1

ST. LOUIS	AB	R	H	BI	BB	SO	BOSTON	AB	R	H	BI	BB	SO
Carpenter, M, 2b	4	0	1	0	0	1	Ellsbury, cf	3	1	0	0	1	1
Beltran, rf	1	0	0	0	0	1	Victorino, rf	4	0	0	0	0	0
Jay, cf	2	0	0	0	1	1	Pedroia, 2b	4	2	2	1	0	0
Holliday, lf	4	1	2	1	0	1	Ortiz, D, dh	3	2	2	3	0	0
Craig, dh	4	0	1	0	0	1	Napoli, 1b	4	0	1	3	0	0
Molina, Y, c	4	0	1	0	0	1	Gomes, J, lf	3	0	0	0	0	0
Freese, 3b	4	0	1	0	0	2	a-Nava, ph-lf	1	1	1	0	0	0
Adams, M, 1b	4	0	0	0	0	1	Bogaerts, 3b	3	0	0	1	0	2
Robinson, S, cf-rf	3	0	1	0	0	1	Drew, ss	4	1	1	0	0	2
Kozma, ss	3	0	0	0	0	0	Ross, D, c	4	1	1	0	0	2
TOTAL	**33**	**1**	**7**	**1**	**1**	**10**		**33**	**8**	**8**	**8**	**1**	**7**

St. Louis	000	000	001—1
Boston	320	000	21x—8

a-Doubled for Gomes, J in the 8th.

LOB—Cardinals 6, Red Sox 4. **2B**—Napoli, Nava. **HR**—Holliday, Ortiz. **GIDP**—Freese. **SF**—Ortiz, Bogaerts. **E**—Kozma 2, Freese, Gomes.

ST. LOUIS	IP	H	R	ER	BB	SO	BOSTON	IP	H	R	ER	BB	SO
Wainwright (L)	5	6	5	3	1	4	Lester (W)	7⅔	5	0	0	1	8
Axford	1	0	0	0	0	3	Tazawa	⅓	0	0	0	0	1
Choate	⅓	0	0	0	0	0	Dempster	1	2	1	1	0	1
Maness	⅓	0	1	0	0	0							
Siegrist	⅓	1	1	1	0	0							
Martinez, C	1	1	1	1	0	0							

WP—Martinez, C.
T—3:17. **A**—38,345.

GAME TWO *October 24, 2013*
ST. LOUIS 4, BOSTON 1

ST. LOUIS	AB	R	H	BI	BB	SO	BOSTON	AB	R	H	BI	BB	SO
Carpenter, M, 2b	4	0	0	1	0	1	Ellsbury, cf	4	0	1	0	0	0
Beltran, rf	4	0	2	1	0	0	Victorino, rf	4	0	0	0	0	2
Holliday, lf	4	1	1	0	0	2	Pedroia, 2b	3	1	1	0	1	2
Adams, M, 1b	4	0	1	0	0	0	Ortiz, D, dh	3	1	2	2	1	0
Molina, Y, c	4	0	1	1	0	0	Napoli, 1b	3	0	0	0	1	1
Craig, dh	3	0	1	0	1	1	Gomes, J, lf	4	0	0	0	0	1
Freese, 3b	2	0	0	0	1	1	Saltalamacchia, c	3	0	0	1	2	1
1-Kozma, pr-ss	1	1	0	0	0	0	Drew, ss	3	0	0	0	0	2
Jay, cf	4	1	1	0	0	0	a-Nava, ph	1	0	0	0	0	1
Descalso, ss-3b	3	1	0	0	1	1	Bogaerts, 3b	3	0	0	0	0	2
TOTAL	**33**	**4**	**7**	**3**	**3**	**6**		**31**	**2**	**4**	**2**	**4**	**12**

St. Louis	000	100	300—4
Boston	000	002	000—2

1-Ran for Freese in the 7th. a-Struck out for Drew in the 9th.

LOB—Cardinals 6, Red Sox 6. **2B**—Pedroia. **3B**—Holliday. **HR**—Ortiz (2). **SB**—Kozma, Jay. **SF**—M.Carpenter. **GIDP**—Napoli. **E**—M. Carpenter, Saltalamacchia, Breslow.

ST. LOUIS	IP	H	R	ER	BB	SO	BOSTON	IP	H	R	ER	BB	SO
Wacha (W)	6	3	2	2	4	6	Lackey (L)	6⅓	5	3	3	2	6
Martinez, C	2	1	0	0	0	3	Breslow	⅓	1	1	0	1	0
Rosenthal (S)	1	0	0	0	0	3	Tazawa	⅓	0	0	0	0	0
							Workman	1	1	0	0	0	0
							Uehara	1	0	0	0	0	0

T—3:05. **A**—38,436.

GAME THREE *October 26, 2013*
ST. LOUIS 5, BOSTON 4

BOSTON	AB	R	H	BI	BB	SO	ST. LOUIS	AB	R	H	BI	BB	SO
Ellsbury, cf	5	1	2	0	0	2	Carpenter, M, 2b-3b	5	2	2	0	0	0
Victorino, rf	2	2	0	0	1	0	Beltran, rf	2	1	0	0	1	1
Pedroia, 2b	4	0	0	0	0	0	Holliday, lf	5	1	2	3	0	0
Ortiz, D, 1b	2	0	1	0	2	0	Adams, M, 1b	5	0	2	0	0	3
Nava, lf	4	0	1	2	0	1	Molina, Y, c	4	0	3	1	1	1
Bogaerts, 3b-ss	4	1	2	1	0	0	Freese, 3b	2	0	0	0	2	0
Saltalamacchia, c	3	0	0	0	1	2	1-Descalso, pr	0	0	0	0	0	0
Drew, SS	2	0	0	0	0	2	Rosenthal, p	0	0	0	0	0	0
b-Middlebrooks, ph	2	0	0	0	1	0	e-Craig, ph	1	1	1	0	0	0
Peavy, p	1	0	0	0	0	0	Jay, cf	5	0	1	0	0	0
a-Carp, ph	1	0	0	1	0	0	Kozma, ss	4	0	0	0	0	1
Doubront, p	0	0	0	0	0	0	Kelly, J, p	2	0	0	0	0	1
c-Gomes, J, ph	1	0	0	0	0	0	Choate, p	0	0	0	0	0	0
Breslow, p	0	0	0	0	0	0	Maness, p	0	0	0	0	0	0
Tazawa, p	0	0	0	0	0	0	d-Robinson, S, ph	1	0	0	0	0	0
Workman, p	1	0	0	0	0	1	Siegrist, p	0	0	0	0	0	0
Uehara, p	0	0	0	0	0	0	Martinez, C, p	0	0	0	0	0	0
							Wong, 2b	1	0	1	0	0	1
TOTAL	**32**	**4**	**6**	**4**	**4**	**9**		**37**	**5**	**12**	**4**	**4**	**7**

Boston	000	011	020—4
St. Louis	200	000	201—5

Two out when winning run scored.

a-Grounded into a forceout for Peavy in the 5th. b-Flied out for Drew in the 7th. c-Flied out for Doubront in the 7th. c-Popped out for Maness in the 6th. d-Doubled for Rosenthal in the 9th. 1-Ran for Freese in the 7th.

LOB—Cardinals 12, Red Sox 6. **2B**—Adams, Holliday, Craig. **3B**—Bogaerts. **S**—Beltran. **GIDP**—Bogaerts. **SB**—Wong.

E—Ellsbury (1, fielding), Middlebrooks (1, interference).

BOSTON	IP	H	R	ER	BB	SO	ST. LOUIS	IP	H	R	ER	BB	SO
Peavy	4	6	2	2	1	4	Kelly, J	5⅓	2	2	2	3	6
Doubront	2	1	0	0	1	0	Choate	0	1	0	0	0	0
Breslow	0	1	2	2	0	0	Maness	⅔	1	0	0	0	0
Tazawa	1	1	0	0	1	2	Siegrist	1	0	0	0	0	1
Workman (L)	1.1	2	1	0	1	1	Martinez, C	⅓	1	2	2	1	0
Uehara	0.1	1	0	0	0	0	Rosenthal (W)	1⅔	1	0	0	0	2

IBB—Ortiz, Molina, Beltran. **HBP**—Victorino, Beltran.
T—3:54. **A**—47,432.

Carlos Beltran came up short in the first World Series appearance of his career

KEN BABBITT

GAME FOUR October 27, 2013
BOSTON 4, ST. LOUIS 2

BOSTON	AB	R	H	BI	BB	SO	ST. LOUIS	AB	R	H	BI	BB	SO
Ellsbury, cf	4	0	0	0	0	0	Carpenter, M, 2b	5	1	2	1	0	1
Nava, rf	4	0	0	0	0	0	Beltran, rf	3	0	1	1	1	0
Pedroia, 2b	4	1	1	0	0	2	Holliday, lf	4	0	0	0	0	1
Ortiz, D, 1b	3	2	3	0	1	0	Adams, M, 1b	4	0	0	0	0	1
2-Berry, pr	0	0	0	0	0	0	Molina, Y, c	4	0	0	0	0	0
Lackey, p	0	0	0	0	0	0	Jay, cf	2	0	0	0	2	0
Uehara, p	0	0	0	0	0	0	Freese, 3b	4	0	0	0	0	1
Gomes, J, lf	2	1	1	3	2	0	Descalso, ss	3	0	0	0	1	0
Bogaerts, 3b	3	0	1	0	1	1	Lynn, p	2	0	0	0	0	1
Drew, ss	3	0	0	1	0	0	Maness, p	0	0	0	0	0	0
Ross, D, c	4	0	0	0	0	2	Choate, p	0	0	0	0	0	0
Buchholz, p	1	0	0	0	0	1	a-Robinson, S, ph	1	1	1	0	0	0
c-Carp, ph	1	0	0	0	0	0	Siegrist, p	0	0	0	0	0	0
Doubront, p	1	0	0	0	0	1	Axford, p	0	0	0	0		
Breslow, p	0	0	0	0	0	0	b-Craig, ph	1	0	1		0	0
Tazawa, p	0	0	0	0	0	0	1-Wong, PR	0	0	0	0	0	0
Napoli, 1b	1	0	0	0	0	1							
TOTAL	**31**	**4**	**6**	**4**	**4**	**8**		**33**	**2**	**6**	**2**	**4**	**5**

Boston	000 013 000	—4
St. Louis	001 000 100	—2

a-Doubled for Choate in the 7th. b-Singled for Axford in the 9th. c-Grounded out for Buchholz in the 5th. 1-Ran for Craig in the 9th. 2-Ran for Ortiz, D in the 8th. **LOB**—Red Sox 5, Cardinals 8. **2B**—Molina, Robinson, Ortiz. **HR**—Gomes. **SF**—Drew. **GIDP**—Gomes. **SB**—Berry. **PO**—Wong (by Uehara). **E**—Ellsbury, Bogaerts.

BOSTON	IP	H	R	ER	BB	SO	ST. LOUIS	IP	H	R	ER	BB	SO
Buchholz	4	3	1	0	3	2	Lynn (L)	5⅔	3	3	3	3	5
Doubront (W)	2⅔	1	1	1	0	3	Maness	1	2	1	1	0	1
Breslow	0	1	0	0	1	0	Choate	⅓	0	0	0	0	0
Tazawa	⅓	0	0	0	0	0	Siegrist	⅔	1	0	0	0	0
Lackey	1	0	0	0	0	0	Axford	1⅓	0	0	0	1	2
Uehara (S)	1	1	0	0	0	0							

WP—Buchholz, Lackey. **IBB**—Descalso (by Buchholz). **T**—3:34. **A**—47,469.

A shortstop in Double-A on Opening Day, Xander Bogaerts played third in the Series

KEN BABBITT

GAME FIVE October 28, 2013
BOSTON 3, ST. LOUIS 1

BOSTON	AB	R	H	BI	BB	SO	ST. LOUIS	AB	R	H	BI	BB	SO
Ellsbury, cf	4	0	1	1	0	2	Carpenter, M, 2b	4	0	0	0	0	2
Pedroia, 2b	4	1	1	0	0	0	Robinson, S, cf	3	0	0	0	0	1
Ortiz, D, 1b	4	0	3	1	0	0	b-Jay, ph	1	0	0	0	0	0
Uehara, p	0	0	0	0	0	0	Holliday, lf	4	1	1	1	0	1
Gomes, J, lf	4	0	0	0	0	3	Beltran, rf	3	0	1	0		0
Nava, rf	4	0	0	0	0	2	Molina, Y, c	3	0	0	0	0	1
Bogaerts, 3b	4	1	2	0	0	2	Craig, 1b	3	0	0	0	0	0
Drew, ss	3	1	0	0	1	2	Freese, 3b	3	0	2	0	0	1
Ross, D, c	4	0	2	1	0	2	Kozma, ss	2	0	0	0	0	0
Lester, p	3	0	0	0	0	1	Wainwright, p	2	0	0	0	0	2
Napoli, 1b	0	0	0	0	0	0	Martinez, C, pP	0	0	0	0	0	0
							a-Adams, M, ph	1	0	0	0	0	1
							Rosenthal, p	0	0	0	0	0	0
TOTAL	**34**	**3**	**9**	**3**	**1**	**14**		**29**	**1**	**4**	**1**	**0**	**9**

Boston	100 000 200	—3
St. Louis	000 100 000	—1

a-Struck out for Martinez, C in the 8th. b-Grounded out for Robinson, S in the 9th. LOB—Red Sox 5, Cardinals 2. **2B**—Pedroia, Ortiz, Ross, Freese. **LOB**—Red Sox 5, Cardinals 2. **HR**—Holliday (2). **GIDP**—Nava. **S**—Kozma.

BOSTON	IP	H	R	ER	BB	SO	ST. LOUIS	IP	H	R	ER	BB	SO
Lester (W)	7⅔	4	1	1	0	7	Wainwright (L)	7	8	3	3	1	10
Uehara (S)	1⅓	0	0	0	0	2	Martinez, C	1	1	0	0	0	1
							Rosenthal	1	0	0	0	0	3

T—2:52. **A**—47,436.

GAME SIX October 30, 2013
BOSTON 6, ST. LOUIS 1

ST. LOUIS	AB	R	H	BI	BB	SO	BOSTON	AB	R	H	BI	BB	SO
Carpenter, M, 2B	5	0	3	0	0	1	Ellsbury, CF	4	2	2	0	1	1
Beltran, RF	4	0	1	1	0	0	Pedroia, 2B	5	0	0	0	0	0
Holliday, LF	3	0	0	1	0	0	Ortiz, D, DH	1	0	0	0	4	1
Craig, DH	4	0	2	0	0	0	Napoli, 1B	5	0	1	1	0	4
Molina, Y, C	4	0	1	0	0	0	Gomes, J, LF	3	1	1	1	0	0
Adams, M, 1B	4	0	0	0	0	1	Victorino, RF	3	0	2	4	1	0
Freese, 3B	4	0	0	0	0	2	Bogaerts, 3B	4	0	0	0	0	1
Jay, CF	4	0	1	0	0	1	Drew, SS	4	1	2	1	0	0
Descalso, SS	4	1	1	0	0	1	Ross, D, C	4	0	0	0	0	2
TOTAL	**36**	**1**	**9**	**1**	**1**	**6**		**33**	**6**	**8**	**6**	**7**	**9**

St. Louis	000 000 100	—1
Boston	003 300 000	—6

LOB—Cardinals 9, Red Sox 11. **2B**—Carpenter. Victorino, Ellsbury. **HR**—Drew (1). **E**—Pedroia, Carpenter.

ST. LOUIS	IP	H	R	ER	BB	SO	BOSTON	IP	H	R	ER	BB	SO
Wacha (L)	3⅔	5	6	6	4	5	Lackey (W)	6⅔	9	1	1	1	5
Lynn	0	2	0	0	1	0	Tazawa	⅓	0	0	0	0	0
Maness	⅓	0	0	0	0	1	Workman	1	0	0	0	0	0
Siegrist	1⅓	0	0	0	0	1	Uehara	1	0	0	0	0	1
Martinez, C	1⅔	1	0	0	0	1							
Choate	0	0	0	0	1	0							
Rosenthal	1	0	0	0	1	1							

WP—Lackey 2. **Balk**—Rosenthal. **IBB**—Ortiz 3. **HBP**—Gomes (by Wacha). **T**—3:15. **A**—38,447.

AMERICAN LEAGUE WILD CARD GAME

TAMPA BAY RAYS VS CLEVELAND INDIANS

TAMPA BAY RAYS

PLAYER, POS	AVG	G	AB	R	H	2B	3B	HR	RBI	BB	SO	SB
David DeJesus, lf	.000	1	4	0	0	0	0	0	0	0	1	0
Yunel Escobar, ss	.250	1	4	0	1	0	0	0	1	0	0	0
Sam Fuld, cf	.000	1	1	0	0	0	0	0	0	0	1	0
Desmond Jennings, cf	.667	1	3	0	2	1	0	0	2	0	0	0
James Loney, 1b	.250	1	4	1	1	0	0	0	0	0	1	0
Evan Longoria, 3b	.250	1	4	1	1	0	0	0	0	0	2	0
Jose Molina, c	.000	1	3	0	0	0	0	0	0	1	2	0
Wil Myers, rf	.250	1	4	0	1	0	0	0	0	0	3	0
Delmon Young, dh	.333	1	3	1	1	0	0	1	1	1	1	0
Ben Zobrist, 2b	.250	1	4	1	1	0	0	0	0	0	0	0
Totals	**.235**	**1**	**34**	**4**	**8**	**1**	**0**	**1**	**4**	**2**	**11**	**0**

PITCHER	W	L	ERA	G	GS	SV	IP	H	R	ER	BB	SO
Alex Cobb	1	0	0.00	1	1	0	6.2	8	0	0	1	5
Jake McGee	0	0	0.00	1	0	0	0.1	0	0	0	0	0
Joel Peralta	0	0	0.00	1	0	0	1.0	1	0	0	0	1
Fernando Rodney	0	0	0.00	1	0	0	1.0	0	0	0	0	2
Totals	**1**	**0**	**0.00**	**1**	**1**	**0**	**9.0**	**9**	**0**	**0**	**1**	**9**

CLEVELAND INDIANS

PLAYER, POS	AVG	G	AB	R	H	2B	3B	HR	RBI	BB	SO	SB
Michael Bourn, cf	.000	1	4	0	0	0	0	0	0	0	2	0
Michael Brantley, lf	.250	1	4	0	1	0	0	0	0	0	0	0
Asdrubal Cabrera, ss	.000	1	4	0	0	0	0	0	0	0	1	0
Lonnie Chisenhall, 3b	.750	1	4	0	3	0	0	0	0	0	1	0
Yan Gomes, c	.500	1	4	0	2	1	0	0	0	0	0	0
Jason Kipnis, 2b	.000	1	4	0	0	0	0	0	0	0	0	0
Ryan Raburn, rf	.333	1	3	0	1	1	0	0	0	1	2	0
Carlos Santana, dh	.500	1	4	0	2	1	0	0	0	0	1	0
Nick Swisher, 1b	.000	1	4	0	0	0	0	0	0	0	2	0
Totals	**.257**	**1**	**35**	**0**	**9**	**3**	**0**	**0**	**0**	**1**	**9**	**0**

PITCHER	W	L	ERA	G	GS	SV	IP	H	R	ER	BB	SO
Cody Allen	0	0	0.00	1	0	0	0.1	1	1	0	0	1
Justin Masterson	0	0	0.00	1	1	0	2.0	1	0	0	0	2
Marc Rzepczynski	0	0	0.00	1	0	0	0.1	0	0	0	0	1
Danny Salazar	0	1	6.75	1	1	0	4.0	4	3	3	2	4
Bryan Shaw	0	0	0.00	1	0	0	1.2	1	0	0	0	2
Joe Smith	0	0	0.00	1	0	0	0.2	1	0	0	0	1
Totals	**0**	**1**	**3.00**	**1**	**1**	**0**	**9.0**	**8**	**4**	**3**	**2**	**11**

E—Chisenhall. **LOB**—Tampa Bay 6, Cleveland 9. **DP**—Tampa Bay 1, Cleveland 1. **GIDP**—Loney, Cabrera. HBP: DeJesus (by Masterson). IBB: Young (by Salazar). **CS**—Molina.

SCORE BY INNINGS

Tampa Bay	001 200 001—4
Cleveland	000 000 000—0

AMERICAN LEAGUE DIVISION SERIES

BOSTON RED SOX VS TAMPA BAY RAYS

TAMPA BAY RAYS

PLAYER, POS	AVG	G	AB	R	H	2B	3B	HR	RBI	BB	SO	SB
David DeJesus, lf	.333	4	9	2	3	1	0	0	1	1	5	0
Yunel Escobar, ss	.467	4	15	3	7	2	0	0	1	0	1	0
Sam Fuld, cf	—	1	0	1	0	0	0	0	0	0	0	0
Desmond Jennings, cf	.231	4	13	1	3	0	0	0	0	2	3	1
Kelly Johnson, dh	.333	2	3	0	1	0	0	0	0	0	2	0
Matt Joyce, lf	.000	4	8	0	0	0	0	0	0	0	4	0
Jose Lobaton, c	.286	4	7	1	2	0	0	1	1	0	2	0
James Loney, 1b	.417	4	12	0	5	2	0	0	2	2	2	0
Evan Longoria, 3b	.154	4	13	1	2	0	0	1	3	3	4	0
Jose Molina, c	.000	3	5	0	0	0	0	0	0	0	2	0
Wil Myers, rf	.063	4	16	0	1	0	0	0	0	1	4	0
Sean Rodriguez, lf	.167	4	6	1	1	0	0	1	1	0	0	0
Delmon Young, dh	.250	4	8	0	2	0	0	0	0	2	0	0
Ben Zobrist, 2b	.143	4	14	2	2	0	0	1	2	4	0	
Totals	**.225**	**4**	**129**	**12**	**29**	**5**	**1**	**4**	**12**	**11**	**33**	**1**

PITCHER	W	L	ERA	G	GS	SV	IP	H	R	ER	BB	SO
Chris Archer	0	0	0.00	2	0	0	1.2	1	0	0	0	2
Alex Cobb	0	0	3.60	1	1	0	5.0	5	3	2	2	5
Jeremy Hellickson	0	0	0.00	1	1	0	1.0	1	0	0	2	0
Jake McGee	0	1	6.75	3	0	0	2.2	3	2	2	3	2
Matt Moore	0	1	9.95	2	1	0	6.1	9	8	7	3	7
Joel Peralta	0	0	0.00	2	0	0	2.1	2	0	0	1	3
David Price	0	1	9.00	1	1	0	7.0	9	7	7	2	5
Fernando Rodney	1	0	13.50	2	0	0	1.1	1	2	2	3	2
Alex Torres	0	0	0.00	3	0	0	4.0	2	0	0	0	5
Jamey Wright	0	0	18.00	1	0	0	2.0	4	4	4	3	1
Wesley Wright	0	0	0.00	2	0	0	0.2	1	0	0	1	1
Totals	**1**	**3**	**6.35**	**4**	**4**	**0**	**34.0**	**38**	**26**	**24**	**20**	**33**

BOSTON RED SOX

PLAYER, POS	AVG	G	AB	R	H	2B	3B	HR	RBI	BB	SO	SB
Quintin Berry, dh	—	1	0	0	0	0	0	0	0	0	0	1
Xander Bogaerts, 3b	—	2	0	3	0	0	0	0	0	0	2	0
Mike Carp, ph	.000	1	1	0	0	0	0	0	0	0	1	0
Stephen Drew, ss	.133	4	15	1	2	0	1	0	2	0	2	0
Jacoby Ellsbury, cf	.500	4	18	7	9	2	0	0	2	1	2	4
Jonny Gomes, lf	.222	4	9	3	2	1	0	0	2	2	1	0
Will Middlebrooks, 3b	.231	4	13	1	3	1	0	0	1	3	4	0
Mike Napoli, c	.154	4	13	1	2	1	0	0	1	4	4	0
Daniel Nava, lf	.200	2	5	0	1	0	0	0	0	2	2	0
David Ortiz, dh	.385	4	13	4	5	1	0	2	3	5	2	0
Dustin Pedroia, 2b	.235	4	17	2	4	1	0	0	5	0	3	0
David Ross, c	.200	2	5	1	1	1	0	0	0	0	2	0
Jarrod Saltalamacchia, c	.300	3	10	1	3	1	0	0	3	1	7	0
Shane Victorino, rf	.429	4	14	2	6	0	0	0	3	0	3	1
Totals	**.286**	**4**	**133**	**26**	**38**	**9**	**1**	**2**	**22**	**20**	**33**	**6**

PITCHER	W	L	ERA	G	GS	SV	IP	H	R	ER	BB	SO
Craig Breslow	1	0	0.00	3	0	0	3.2	2	0	0	1	4
Clay Buchholz	0	0	4.50	1	1	0	6.0	7	3	3	3	5
Ryan Dempster	0	0	0.00	1	0	0	1.0	1	0	0	0	2
John Lackey	1	0	6.75	1	1	0	5.1	7	4	4	3	6
Jon Lester	1	0	2.35	1	1	0	7.2	3	2	2	3	7
Franklin Morales	0	0	27.00	1	0	0	0.1	1	1	1	1	0
Jake Peavy	0	0	1.59	1	1	0	5.2	5	1	1	0	3
Junichi Tazawa	0	0	0.00	4	0	0	2.1	1	0	0	0	2
Koji Uehara	0	1	3.00	3	0	2	3.0	1	1	1	0	4
Brandon Workman	0	0	0.00	2	0	0	1.2	1	0	0	1	0
Totals	**3**	**1**	**3.03**	**4**	**4**	**2**	**35.2**	**29**	**12**	**12**	**11**	**33**

E—Molina, Zobrist. **LOB**—Tampa Bay 24, Boston 32. **DP**—Tampa Bay 4, Boston 6. **GIDP**—DeJesus, Escobar, Loney, Longoria, Zobrist, Ellsbury, Gomes, Ortiz. **SAC**—Victorino. **SF**—Young, Pedroia 2. **HBP**—DeJesus (by Lackey), Loney (by Breslow), Victorino 4 (by Cobb, by Moore, by Rodney, by Torres). **IBB**—Gomes 2 (by McGee, by Moore), Middlebrooks (by Wright). **SB**—Jennings, Berry, Ellsbury 4, Victorino. **CS**—Nava. **WP**—Cobb, Moore, Peralta, Rodney, Tazawa. **PB**—Lobaton.

SCORE BY INNINGS

Tampa Bay	020 152 011—12
Boston	302 660 252—26

OAKLAND ATHLETICS VS DETROIT TIGERS

DETROIT TIGERS

PLAYER, POS	AVG	G	AB	R	H	2B	3B	HR	RBI	BB	SO	SB
Alex Avila, c	.133	5	15	1	2	0	0	0	1	4	5	0
Miguel Cabrera, 3b	.250	5	20	1	5	0	0	1	3	1	2	0
Andy Dirks, lf	.000	2	3	2	0	0	0	0	0	1	1	0
Prince Fielder, 1b	.278	5	18	2	5	0	0	0	0	1	2	0
Torii Hunter, rf	.158	5	19	3	3	0	0	0	0	1	6	0
Jose Iglesias, ss	.083	5	12	0	1	0	0	0	0	1	2	0
Omar Infante, 2b	.222	5	18	0	4	1	0	0	3	1	2	0
Austin Jackson, cf	.100	5	20	1	2	1	0	0	1	1	13	0
Don Kelly, lf	.400	3	5	0	2	0	0	0	0	2	1	0
Victor Martinez, dh	.450	5	20	5	9	2	0	1	2	0	2	0
Jhonny Peralta, lf	.417	4	12	1	5	1	0	1	5	0	2	0
Hernan Perez, dh	—	1	0	1	0	0	0	0	0	0	0	0
Totals	**.235**	**5**	**162**	**17**	**38**	**5**	**0**	**3**	**15**	**13**	**38**	**0**

PITCHER	W	L	ERA	G	GS	SV	IP	H	R	ER	BB	SO
Al Alburquerque	0	1	13.50	1	0	0	0.2	2	1	1	1	2
Jose Alvarez	0	0	0.00	1	0	0	3.0	0	0	0	1	3
Joaquin Benoit	0	0	5.40	3	0	2	3.1	3	2	2	1	6
Doug Fister	0	0	4.50	1	1	0	6.0	7	3	3	1	1

	W	L	ERA	G	GS	SV	IP	H	R	ER	BB	SO
Rick Porcello	0	0	—	1	0	0	0.0	1	0	0	0	0
Anibal Sanchez	0	1	10.38	1	1	0	4.1	8	6	5	2	6
Max Scherzer	2	0	3.00	2	1	0	9.0	6	3	3	4	13
Drew Smyly	0	0	0.00	2	0	0	1.0	1	0	0	2	2
Jose Veras	0	0	0.00	1	0	0	1.2	2	0	0	0	3
Justin Verlander	1	0	0.00	2	2	0	15.0	6	0	0	2	21
Totals	3	2	2.86	5	5	2	44.0	36	15	14	14	57

OAKLAND ATHLETICS

PLAYER, POS	AVG	G	AB	R	H	2B	3B	HR	RBI	BB	SO	SB
Daric Barton, 1b	.000	2	3	0	0	0	0	0	0	0	3	0
Alberto Callaspo, 2b	.167	4	6	0	1	1	0	0	0	0	1	0
Yoenis Cespedes, lf	.381	5	21	3	8	1	1	1	4	0	4	0
Coco Crisp, cf	.389	5	18	4	7	2	1	0	2	3	2	1
Josh Donaldson, 3b	.143	5	21	0	3	0	0	0	0	1	8	0
Jed Lowrie, ss	.150	5	20	2	3	1	0	1	3	2	7	0
Brandon Moss, 1b	.111	5	18	2	2	0	0	1	1	3	13	0
Derek Norris, c	.000	1	1	0	0	0	0	0	0	0	1	0
Josh Reddick, rf	.235	5	17	1	4	1	0	1	1	2	5	0
Seth Smith, dh	.313	4	16	1	5	0	0	1	2	1	5	0
Eric Sogard, 2b	.000	4	9	0	0	0	0	0	0	1	1	0
Stephen Vogt, c	.188	5	16	2	3	0	1	0	1	1	7	0
Totals	.217	5	166	15	36	6	3	5	14	14	57	1

PITCHER	W	L	ERA	G	GS	SV	IP	H	R	ER	BB	SO
Brett Anderson	0	0	27.00	1	0	0	0.1	1	1	1	1	1
Grant Balfour	1	0	0.00	3	0	1	3.0	0	0	0	1	3
Bartolo Colon	0	1	4.50	1	1	0	6.0	10	3	3	0	4
Ryan Cook	0	0	27.00	1	0	0	0.2	1	2	2	1	1
Sean Doolittle	0	1	4.15	4	0	0	4.1	3	2	2	2	6
Sonny Gray	0	1	2.08	2	2	0	13.0	10	3	3	6	12
Dan Otero	0	0	0.00	4	0	0	5.2	4	0	0	1	2
Jarrod Parker	1	0	5.40	1	1	0	5.0	5	3	3	1	1
Dan Straily	0	0	4.50	1	1	0	6.0	4	3	3	0	8
Totals	2	3	3.48	5	5	1	44.0	38	17	17	13	38

E—Cabrera, Cespedes. LOB—Detroit 29, Oakland 36. DP—Detroit 1, Oakland 6. GIDP—Fielder, Hunter, Martinez, Peralta, Lowrie. SAC—Iglesias, Sogard. SF—Crisp. HBP—Fielder (by Straily), Hunter (by Colon), Cespedes (by Benoit). IBB—Cabrera (by Gray), Reddick (by Alburquerque), Smith (by Scherzer). SB—Crisp. CS—Fielder, Hunter, Iglesias. WP—Fister, Scherzer, Anderson.

SCORE BY INNINGS

Detroit	300	531	230—17
Oakland	101	250	303—15

AMERICAN LEAGUE CHAMPIONSHIP SERIES

BOSTON RED SOX VS DETROIT TIGERS

DETROIT TIGERS

PLAYER, POS	AVG	G	AB	R	H	2B	3B	HR	RBI	BB	SO	SB
Alex Avila, c	.188	6	16	2	3	0	0	1	3	4	6	0
Miguel Cabrera, 3b	.273	6	22	3	6	0	0	1	4	2	7	1
Andy Dirks, lf	.000	1	2	0	0	0	0	0	0	0	1	0
Prince Fielder, 1b	.182	6	22	1	4	1	0	0	0	2	5	0
Torii Hunter, rf	.231	6	26	2	6	2	0	0	2	1	5	0
Jose Iglesias, ss	.357	6	14	2	5	0	0	0	1	0	3	0
Omar Infante, 2b	.190	6	21	1	4	1	0	0	0	2	4	0
Austin Jackson, cf	.318	6	22	2	7	0	0	0	2	4	5	1
Don Kelly, lf	.000	6	6	0	0	0	0	0	0	1	2	0
Victor Martinez, dh	.364	6	22	4	8	2	0	0	3	1	1	0
Brayan Pena, c	.333	1	3	0	1	0	0	0	1	0	0	0
Jhonny Peralta, lf	.286	6	21	1	6	3	0	0	1	1	3	0
Totals	.254	6	197	18	50	9	0	2	17	18	42	2

PITCHER	W	L	ERA	G	GS	SV	IP	H	R	ER	BB	SO
Al Alburquerque	0	0	2.25	6	0	0	4.0	2	1	1	2	7
Joaquin Benoit	0	0	7.71	3	0	1	2.1	4	2	2	0	4
Phil Coke	0	0	9.00	4	0	0	1.0	1	1	1	0	0
Doug Fister	1	0	1.50	1	1	0	6.0	8	1	1	1	7
Rick Porcello	0	1	—	1	0	0	0.0	2	1	0	0	0
Anibal Sanchez	1	1	2.25	2	2	0	12.0	9	4	3	6	17
Max Scherzer	0	1	2.70	2	2	0	13.1	6	4	4	7	21
Drew Smyly	0	0	4.50	4	0	0	2.0	0	1	1	1	1
Jose Veras	0	0	5.40	5	0	0	3.1	3	2	2	0	6
Justin Verlander	0	1	1.13	1	1	0	8.0	4	1	1	1	10
Totals	2	4	2.77	6	6	1	52.0	39	19	16	18	73

BOSTON RED SOX

PLAYER, POS	AVG	G	AB	R	H	2B	3B	HR	RBI	BB	SO	SB
Quintin Berry, pr	—	1	0	0	0	0	0	0	0	0	0	1
Xander Bogaerts, 3b	.500	4	6	4	3	3	0	0	0	3	1	0
Mike Carp, 1b	.000	3	5	0	0	0	0	0	0	0	2	0
Stephen Drew, ss	.050	6	20	0	1	0	0	0	0	1	10	0
Jacoby Ellsbury, cf	.318	6	22	3	7	1	1	0	3	4	6	2
Jonny Gomes, lf	.188	5	16	3	3	1	0	0	0	0	7	0
Will Middlebrooks, 3b	.100	5	10	1	1	0	0	0	0	0	5	0
Mike Napoli, 1b	.300	6	20	4	6	2	0	2	2	1	11	0
Daniel Nava, lf	.333	2	6	0	2	0	0	0	0	0	3	0
David Ortiz, dh	.091	6	22	1	2	0	0	1	4	3	4	0
Dustin Pedroia, 2b	.273	6	22	1	6	1	0	0	1	4	6	1
David Ross, c	.500	2	4	0	2	1	0	0	1	1	1	0
Jarrod Saltalamacchia, c	.188	5	16	0	3	0	0	0	2	0	8	0
Shane Victorino, rf	.125	6	24	2	3	1	0	1	5	0	9	1
Totals	.202	6	193	19	39	11	1	4	18	18	73	5

PITCHER	W	L	ERA	G	GS	SV	IP	H	R	ER	BB	SO
Craig Breslow	0	0	0.00	4	0	0	3.1	1	0	0	4	2
Clay Buchholz	0	0	5.91	2	2	0	10.7	12	7	7	2	10
Ryan Dempster	0	0	0.00	1	0	0	1.0	1	0	0	0	0
Felix Doubront	0	0	0.00	2	0	0	2.1	1	0	0	2	1
John Lackey	1	0	0.00	1	1	0	6.2	4	0	0	0	8
Jon Lester	1	1	2.31	2	2	0	11.7	13	3	3	4	7
Franklin Morales	0	0	0.00	2	0	0	1.0	2	0	0	1	0
Jake Peavy	0	1	21.00	1	1	0	3.0	5	7	7	3	1
Junichi Tazawa	0	0	3.38	4	0	0	2.2	4	1	1	0	1
Koji Uehara	1	0	0.00	5	0	3	6.0	4	0	0	0	9
Brandon Workman	0	0	0.00	3	0	0	4.2	3	0	0	2	3
Totals	4	2	3.06	6	6	3	53.0	50	18	18	18	42

E—Cabrera, Hunter, Iglesias 2, Drew, Victorino, Workman. LOB—Detroit 44, Boston 39. DP—Detroit 3, Boston 10. GIDP—Cabrera, Hunter 2, Iglesias, Infante 2, Jackson, Pena, Peralta, Ellsbury,Pedroia. SAC—Iglesias 2, Ross. HBP—Avila (by Doubront), Fielder (by Lester), Iglesias (by Lester), Martinez (by Buchholz), Victorino 2 (by Scherzer 2). IBB—Infante (by Breslow), Ellsbury (by Alburquerque). SB—Cabrera, Jackson, Berry, Ellsbury 2, Pedroia, Victorino. CS—Ellsbury. WP—Porcello, Sanchez 3, Scherzer, Verlander, Buchholz. PB—Ross.

SCORE BY INNINGS

Detroit	060	218	100—18
Boston	031	012	642—19

NATIONAL LEAGUE WILD CARD GAME

PITTSBURGH PIRATES VS· CINCINNATI REDS

CINCINNATI REDS

PLAYER, POS	AVG	G	AB	R	H	2B	3B	HR	RBI	BB	SO	SB
Jay Bruce, rf	.250	1	4	0	1	0	0	0	1	0	2	0
Shin-Soo Choo, cf	.333	1	3	2	1	0	0	1	1	0	1	0
Zack Cozart, ss	.000	1	3	0	0	0	0	0	0	1	0	0
Johnny Cueto, p	.000	1	1	0	0	0	0	0	0	0	0	0
Todd Frazier, 3b	.250	1	4	0	1	1	0	0	0	0	1	0
Ryan Hanigan, c	.000	1	3	0	0	0	0	0	0	0	0	0
Chris Heisey, ph	.000	1	1	0	0	0	0	0	0	0	0	0
Ryan Ludwick, lf	.750	1	4	0	3	2	0	0	0	0	0	0
Devin Mesoraco, c	.000	1	1	0	0	0	0	0	0	0	0	0
Brandon Phillips, 2b	.000	1	4	0	0	0	0	0	0	0	0	0
Joey Votto, 1b	.000	1	4	0	0	0	0	0	0	0	2	0
Totals	.188	1	32	2	6	3	0	1	2	1	6	0

PITCHER	W	L	ERA	G	GS	SV	IP	H	R	ER	BB	SO
Johnny Cueto	0	1	10.80	1	1	0	3.1	8	4	4	1	0
J.J. Hoover	0	0	0.00	1	0	0	0.2	0	0	0	0	0
Sam LeCure	0	0	0.00	1	0	0	1.0	1	0	0	0	0
Sean Marshall	0	0	*.**	1	0	0	0.0	1	1	1	2	0
Logan Ondrusek	0	0	9.00	1	0	0	1.0	1	1	1	0	1
Manny Parra	0	0	0.00	1	0	0	0.2	1	0	0	0	1
Alfredo Simon	0	0	0.00	1	0	0	1.1	2	0	0	0	0
Totals	0	1	6.75	1	1	0	8.0	14	6	6	3	2

PITTSBURGH PIRATES

PLAYER, POS	AVG	G	AB	R	H	2B	3B	HR	RBI	BB	SO	SB
Pedro Alvarez, 3b	.000	1	3	0	0	0	0	0	1	0	1	0
Clint Barmes, ss	.250	1	4	0	1	0	0	0	0	0	0	0
Marlon Byrd, rf	.500	1	4	1	2	0	0	1	2	0	0	0
Francisco Liriano, p	.500	1	2	0	1	0	0	0	0	0	0	0
Starling Marte, lf	.400	1	5	1	2	1	0	0	0	0	0	0
Russell Martin, c	.750	1	4	2	3	0	0	2	2	0	0	0
Andrew McCutchen, cf	.667	1	3	1	2	0	0	0	2	0	0	0
Justin Morneau, 1b	.250	1	4	0	1	0	0	0	0	1	0	0
Travis Snider, ph	.000	1	1	0	0	0	0	0	0	0	1	0
Neil Walker, 2b	.400	1	5	1	2	1	0	0	1	0	0	0
Totals	.400	1	35	6	14	2	0	3	6	3	2	0

PITCHER	W	L	ERA	G	GS	SV	IP	H	R	ER	BB	SO
Jason Grilli	0	0	0.00	1	0	0	1.0	0	0	0	0	0
Francisco Liriano	1	0	1.29	1	1	0	7.0	4	1	1	1	5
Tony Watson	0	0	9.00	1	0	0	1.0	2	1	1	0	0
Totals	1	0	2.00	1	1	0	9.0	6	2	2	1	6

Team **LOB**—Cincinnati 5, Pittsburgh 10. **DP**—Cincinnati 1, Pittsburgh 1. **GIDP**—Heisey, Morneau. **SAC**—Liriano. **SF**—Alvarez. HBP: Choo (by Liriano). IBB: McCutchen (by Marshall).

SCORE BY INNINGS

Cincinnati	000	100	010—2
Pittsburgh	021	200	10x—6

NATIONAL LEAGUE DIVISION SERIES

ST· LOUIS CARDINALS VS· PITTSBURGH PIRATES

PITTSBURGH PIRATES

PLAYER, POS	AVG	G	AB	R	H	2B	3B	HR	RBI	BB	SO	SB
Pedro Alvarez, 3b	.353	5	17	4	6	1	0	3	6	2	6	0
Clint Barmes, ss	.286	5	7	0	2	0	0	0	0	0	1	0
A.J. Burnett, p	.000	1	1	0	0	0	0	0	0	0	0	0
Marlon Byrd, rf	.333	5	18	3	6	2	0	0	3	1	6	0
Gerrit Cole, p	.250	2	4	0	1	0	0	0	1	0	2	0
Jeanmar Gomez, p	.000	1	0	0	0	0	0	0	0	0	1	0
Josh Harrison, pr	—	2	0	1	0	0	0	0	0	0	0	0
Garrett Jones, ph	.000	2	2	0	0	0	0	0	0	0	1	0
Francisco Liriano, p	—	1	0	0	0	0	0	0	0	1	0	0
Starling Marte, lf	.053	5	19	1	1	0	0	1	1	1	5	1
Russell Martin, c	.154	5	13	0	2	0	0	0	4	3	5	0
Andrew McCutchen, cf	.278	5	18	2	5	1	0	0	3	3	3	0
Jordy Mercer, ss	.250	5	8	0	2	0	0	0	0	1	2	0
Justin Morneau, 1b	.300	5	20	4	6	1	0	0	0	0	2	0
Charlie Morton, p	.000	1	1	0	0	0	0	0	0	0	0	0
Gaby Sanchez, 1b	.000	2	2	0	0	0	0	0	0	0	0	0

PLAYER, POS	AVG	G	AB	R	H	2B	3B	HR	RBI	BB	SO	SB
Jose Tabata, lf	.000	4	4	0	0	0	0	0	0	0	1	0
Neil Walker, 2b	.000	5	19	0	0	0	0	0	0	2	5	0
Totals	.201	5	154	15	31	5	0	4	15	14	40	1

PITCHER	W	L	ERA	G	GS	SV	IP	H	R	ER	BB	SO
A.J. Burnett	0	1	31.50	1	1	0	2.0	6	7	7	4	0
Gerrit Cole	1	1	2.45	2	2	0	11.0	5	3	3	2	10
Jeanmar Gomez	0	0	0.00	1	0	0	4.0	3	2	0	2	0
Jason Grilli	0	0	0.00	3	0	1	2.1	0	0	0	0	3
Francisco Liriano	0	0	3.00	1	1	0	6.0	3	2	2	2	5
Vin Mazzaro	0	0	0.00	3	0	0	1.2	0	0	0	1	2
Mark Melancon	1	0	9.82	4	0	0	3.2	5	4	4	1	2
Bryan Morris	0	0	0.00	1	0	0	1.0	1	0	0	0	1
Charlie Morton	0	1	3.18	1	1	0	5.2	3	2	2	4	4
Tony Watson	0	0	0.00	3	0	0	3.0	2	0	0	1	1
Justin Wilson	0	0	3.38	2	0	0	2.2	2	1	1	1	3
Totals	2	3	3.98	5	5	1	43.0	33	21	19	17	31

ST. LOUIS CARDINALS

PLAYER, POS	AVG	G	AB	R	H	2B	3B	HR	RBI	BB	SO	SB
Matt Adams, 1b	.316	5	19	3	6	1	0	1	2	1	3	0
Carlos Beltran, rf	.222	5	18	3	4	1	0	2	6	3	1	0
Matt Carpenter, 2b	.053	5	19	1	1	0	0	0	1	6	0	
Adron Chambers, ph	.000	1	0	0	0	0	0	0	0	0	0	0
Daniel Descalso, 3b	.111	5	9	0	1	0	0	0	0	0	2	0
David Freese, 3b	.188	5	16	1	3	0	0	1	4	2	4	0
Matt Holliday, lf	.300	5	20	4	6	1	0	1	2	1	2	0
Jon Jay, cf	.188	5	16	5	3	0	0	0	2	4	4	1
Joe Kelly, p	.000	1	2	0	0	0	0	0	0	0	2	0
Pete Kozma, ss	.400	4	10	1	4	1	0	0	1	1	2	1
Lance Lynn, p	.000	1	1	0	0	0	0	0	0	0	0	0
Yadier Molina, c	.294	5	17	2	5	1	0	1	1	3	3	0
Shane Robinson, ph	.000	1	1	0	0	0	0	0	0	0	0	0
Michael Wacha, p	.000	1	2	0	0	0	0	0	0	0	2	0
Adam Wainwright, p	.000	2	5	1	0	0	0	0	0	1	1	0
Kolten Wong, ph	.000	2	2	0	0	0	0	0	0	0	0	0
Totals	.209	5	158	21	33	5	0	6	18	17	31	2

PITCHER	W	L	ERA	G	GS	SV	IP	H	R	ER	BB	SO
John Axford	0	0	0.00	2	0	0	1.1	0	0	0	2	0
Randy Choate	0	0	0.00	1	0	0	0.2	0	0	0	0	0
Joe Kelly	0	0	3.38	1	1	0	5.1	5	3	2	4	5
Lance Lynn	0	1	10.38	1	1	0	4.1	7	5	5	3	6
Seth Maness	0	0	0.00	2	0	0	1.1	1	0	0	0	0
Carlos Martinez	0	1	9.00	3	0	0	2.0	1	2	2	1	2
Shelby Miller	0	0	9.00	1	0	0	1.0	1	1	1	0	1
Edward Mujica	0	0	0.00	1	0	0	1.0	0	0	0	0	0
Trevor Rosenthal	0	0	0.00	2	0	1	2.0	1	0	0	1	2
Kevin Siegrist	0	0	0.00	2	0	0	1.2	3	1	0	0	0
Michael Wacha	1	0	1.23	1	1	0	7.1	1	1	1	2	9
Adam Wainwright	2	0	1.13	2	2	0	16.0	11	2	2	1	15
Totals	3	2	2.66	5	5	1	44.0	31	15	13	14	40

E—Alvarez, Barmes, Byrd, McCutchen, Freese, Kozma. **LOB**—Pittsburgh 25, St. Louis 29. **DP**—Pittsburgh 2, St. Louis 6. **GIDP**—Morneau, Sanchez, Descalso, Freese. **SAC**—Liriano, Wacha, Wainwright. **SF**—Martin 2. **HBP**— Marte (by Lynn), Adams (by Burnett), Carpenter (by Liriano). **IBB**—Alvarez (by Kelly), Mercer (by Lynn). **SB**—Marte, Jay, Kozma. **CS**—Harrison. **WP**—Liriano.

SCORE BY INNINGS

Pittsburgh	212	031	240—15
St. Louis	027	044	040—21

LOS ANGELES DODGERS VS· ATLANTA BRAVES

LOS ANGELES DODGERS

PLAYER, POS	AVG	G	AB	R	H	2B	3B	HR	RBI	BB	SO	SB
Chris Capuano, p	.000	1	1	0	0	0	0	0	0	0	0	0
Carl Crawford, lf	.353	4	17	6	6	0	0	3	5	2	5	1
A.J. Ellis, c	.333	4	12	2	4	2	0	0	1	2	4	0
Mark Ellis, 2b	.267	4	15	4	4	2	0	0	1	3	5	0
Andre Ethier, ph	.000	4	3	0	0	0	0	0	0	1	1	0
Adrian Gonzalez, 1b	.333	4	18	1	6	0	0	1	4	0	4	0
Dee Gordon, pr	—	1	0	0	0	0	0	0	0	0	0	0
Zack Greinke, p	.000	1	2	0	0	0	0	0	0	0	0	0
Clayton Kershaw, p	.000	2	5	0	0	0	0	0	0	0	3	0
Yasiel Puig, rf	.471	4	17	5	8	1	0	0	2	0	4	0

PLAYER, POS	AVG	G	AB	R	H	2B	3B	HR	RBI	BB	SO	SB
Hanley Ramirez, ss	.500	4	16	4	8	4	1	1	6	2	2	1
Hyun-Jin Ryu, p	—	1	0	0	0	0	0	0	1	0	0	0
Skip Schumaker, cf	.231	4	13	0	3	0	0	0	2	2	2	0
Juan Uribe, 3b	.375	4	16	4	6	1	0	2	4	0	4	0
Michael Young, ph	.333	3	3	0	1	0	0	0	0	0	1	0
Totals	.333	4	138	26	46	10	1	7	26	12	35	2

PITCHER	W	L	ERA	G	GS	SV	IP	H	R	ER	BB	SO
Ronald Belisario	0	0	9.00	3	0	0	1.0	2	1	1	1	1
Chris Capuano	1	0	0.00	1	0	0	3.0	0	0	0	3	3
Zack Greinke	0	1	3.00	1	1	0	6.0	4	2	2	0	3
J.P. Howell	0	0	0.00	3	0	0	2.1	1	0	0	1	3
Kenley Jansen	0	0	0.00	3	0	1	2.1	1	0	0	1	7
Clayton Kershaw	1	0	0.69	2	2	0	13.0	6	3	1	4	18
Paco Rodriguez	0	0	27.00	2	0	0	0.2	4	2	2	1	1
Hyun-Jin Ryu	0	0	12.00	1	1	0	3.0	6	4	4	1	1
Brian Wilson	1	0	0.00	3	0	0	3.0	3	0	0	0	4
Chris Withrow	0	0	27.00	1	0	0	0.2	1	2	2	1	1
Totals	3	1	3.09	4	4	1	35.0	28	14	12	14	42

ATLANTA BRAVES

PLAYER, POS	AVG	G	AB	R	H	2B	3B	HR	RBI	BB	SO	SB
Jose Constanza, ph	1.000	2	1	0	1	0	0	0	1	0	0	0
Freddie Freeman, 1b	.313	4	16	4	5	1	0	0	0	1	4	0
Freddy Garcia, p	.000	1	2	0	0	0	0	0	0	0	0	0
Evan Gattis, lf	.357	4	14	3	5	0	0	0	1	2	3	0
Jason Heyward, cf	.167	4	18	1	3	0	0	1	4	0	7	0
Chris Johnson, 3b	.438	4	16	1	7	0	0	0	5	0	5	0
Elliot Johnson, 2b	.071	4	14	1	1	0	1	0	1	1	4	0
Reed Johnson, ph	.500	3	2	1	1	0	0	0	0	1	0	0
Gerald Laird, c	.000	1	1	0	0	0	0	0	0	0	0	0
Brian McCann, c	.000	4	13	0	0	0	0	0	1	3	6	0
Kris Medlen, p	.000	1	1	0	0	0	0	0	0	0	1	0
Mike Minor, p	.000	1	2	0	0	0	0	0	0	0	0	0
Jordan Schafer, rf	.000	1	1	0	0	0	0	0	0	0	1	0
Andrelton Simmons, ss	.250	4	12	0	3	1	0	0	2	2	3	0
Julio Teheran, p	.000	1	1	0	0	0	0	0	0	0	1	0
B.J. Upton, cf	.000	3	3	1	0	0	0	0	0	0	3	0
Justin Upton, rf	.143	4	14	2	2	1	0	0	0	4	4	0
Alex Wood, p	.000	2	0	0	0	0	0	0	0	0	0	0
Totals	.214	4	131	14	28	3	1	1	14	14	42	0

PITCHER	W	L	ERA	G	GS	SV	IP	H	R	ER	BB	SO
Luis Avilan	0	0	0.00	4	0	0	2.2	3	0	0	1	1
Luis Ayala	0	0	0.00	3	0	0	2.0	1	0	0	2	3
David Carpenter	0	1	13.50	3	0	0	2.2	3	4	4	1	3
Freddy Garcia	0	0	3.00	1	1	0	6.0	8	2	2	2	6
David Hale	0	0	0.00	1	0	0	0.1	0	0	0	0	0
Craig Kimbrel	0	0	0.00	1	0	1	1.1	0	0	0	2	2
Kris Medlen	0	1	11.25	1	1	0	4.0	9	5	5	1	4
Mike Minor	1	0	1.42	1	1	0	6.1	8	1	1	1	5
Julio Teheran	0	1	20.25	1	1	0	2.2	8	6	6	1	5
Jordan Walden	0	0	13.50	2	0	0	2.2	3	4	4	1	3
Alex Wood	0	0	0.00	2	0	0	3.1	3	4	0	0	3
Totals	3	4	5.82	4	4	1	34.0	46	26	22	12	35

E—Gonzalez 2, Johnson, Wood. **LOB**—Los Angeles 28, Atlanta 28. **DP**—Los Angeles 3, Atlanta 5. **GIDP**—Crawford, Ellis, M., Gonzalez, Puig, Schumaker, Johnson, Simmons. **SAC**—Ellis, A., Uribe, Simmons, Wood. **SF**—Ryu, Schumaker. **HBP**—Ellis, A. (by Walden), Puig (by Medlen). **IBB**—Ramirez (by Avilan), Schumaker 2 (by Ayala, by Garcia), Johnson (by Rodriguez). **SB**—Crawford, Ramirez. **CS**—Gordon, Puig. **WP**—Kershaw 2, Teheran, Wood.

SCORE BY INNINGS

LA Dodgers	265 501 070	—26
Atlanta	212 400 302	—14

NATIONAL LEAGUE CHAMPIONSHIP SERIES

ST. LOUIS CARDINALS VS. LOS ANGELES DODGERS

LOS ANGELES DODGERS

PLAYER, POS	AVG	G	AB	R	H	2B	3B	HR	RBI	BB	SO	SB
Carl Crawford, lf	.280	6	25	2	7	1	0	1	1	1	4	0
A.J. Ellis, c	.316	6	19	1	6	2	1	1	2	1	2	0
Mark Ellis, 2b	.240	6	25	1	6	1	1	0	0	0	4	1
Andre Ethier, cf	.150	6	20	1	3	0	0	0	0	2	7	0
Adrian Gonzalez, 1b	.300	6	20	6	6	2	0	2	3	3	3	0
Zack Greinke, p	.200	2	5	0	1	0	0	0	1	0	0	0
Clayton Kershaw, p	.333	2	3	0	1	0	0	0	0	0	0	0
Ricky Nolasco, p	.000	1	1	0	0	0	0	0	0	0	1	0
Yasiel Puig, rf	.227	6	22	1	5	0	1	0	2	1	10	0
Nick Punto, ss	.333	5	6	0	2	1	0	0	0	0	4	0
Hanley Ramirez, ss	.133	5	15	1	2	0	0	0	1	3	5	0
Hyun-Jin Ryu, p	.000	1	2	0	0	0	0	0	0	0	1	0
Skip Schumaker, cf	.000	4	6	0	0	0	0	0	0	0	2	0
Juan Uribe, 3b	.130	6	23	0	3	0	0	0	3	0	7	0
Michael Young, 1b	.000	6	7	0	0	0	0	0	0	0	3	0
Totals	.211	6	199	13	42	7	3	4	13	11	50	1

PITCHER	W	L	ERA	G	GS	SV	IP	H	R	ER	BB	SO
Ronald Belisario	0	0	6.75	4	0	0	2.2	1	2	2	1	1
Zack Greinke	1	0	2.40	2	2	0	15.0	10	4	4	2	14
J.P. Howell	0	0	2.45	4	0	0	3.2	4	1	1	2	3
Kenley Jansen	0	0	9.00	3	0	1	2.0	5	2	2	0	3
Clayton Kershaw	0	2	6.30	2	2	0	10.0	12	8	7	3	10
Carlos Marmol	0	0	0.00	2	0	0	3.2	1	0	0	1	5
Ricky Nolasco	0	1	6.75	1	1	0	4.0	3	3	3	1	4
Hyun-Jin Ryu	1	0	0.00	1	1	0	7.0	3	0	0	1	4
Brian Wilson	0	0	0.00	3	0	0	3.0	1	0	0	2	4
Chris Withrow	0	1	2.08	3	0	0	4.1	2	1	1	5	2
Totals	2	4	3.25	6	6	1	55.1	42	21	20	18	50

ST. LOUIS CARDINALS

PLAYER, POS	AVG	G	AB	R	H	2B	3B	HR	RBI	BB	SO	SB
Matt Adams, 1b	.227	6	22	2	5	1	0	0	2	2	9	0
Carlos Beltran, rf	.286	6	21	2	6	2	1	0	6	5	3	0
Matt Carpenter, 2b	.261	6	23	4	6	2	1	0	2	3	5	1
Adron Chambers, ph	.000	4	4	0	0	0	0	0	0	0	3	0
Daniel Descalso, 3b	.286	5	7	2	2	0	0	0	0	0	3	0
David Freese, 3B	.190	6	21	2	4	1	0	0	0	1	5	0
Matt Holliday, lf	.200	6	25	2	5	2	0	1	3	0	4	0
Jon Jay, cf	.222	6	18	0	4	0	0	0	1	0	3	0
Joe Kelly, p	.250	2	4	1	1	0	0	0	0	0	2	0
Pete Kozma, ss	.067	6	15	1	1	0	0	0	1	3	4	0
Lance Lynn, p	—	2	0	0	0	0	0	0	0	1	0	0
Yadier Molina, c	.227	6	22	2	5	0	0	0	1	3	4	0
Shane Robinson, of	.429	3	7	2	3	0	0	1	3	0	0	0
Michael Wacha, p	.000	2	5	1	0	0	0	0	0	1	3	0
Adam Wainwright, p	.000	1	2	0	0	0	0	0	0	0	1	0
Kolten Wong, 2b	.000	3	3	0	0	0	0	0	0	0	1	0
Totals	.211	6	199	21	42	8	2	2	20	18	50	1

PITCHER	W	L	ERA	G	GS	SV	IP	H	R	ER	BB	SO
John Axford	0	0	4.50	2	0	0	2.0	2	1	1	1	4
Randy Choate	0	0	0.00	4	0	0	2.0	0	0	0	0	1
Joe Kelly	0	1	4.91	2	2	0	11.0	13	6	6	2	8
Lance Lynn	2	0	2.45	2	1	0	7.1	7	2	2	4	6
Seth Maness	0	0	0.00	3	0	0	1.1	2	0	0	0	1
Carlos Martinez	0	0	0.00	4	0	0	4.2	1	0	0	1	4
Edward Mujica	0	0	9.00	1	0	0	1.0	1	1	1	0	0
Trevor Rosenthal	0	0	0.00	4	0	2	5.0	2	0	0	1	7
Kevin Siegrist	0	0	9.00	3	0	0	1.0	1	1	1	0	1
Michael Wacha	2	0	0.00	2	2	0	13.7	7	0	0	2	13
Adam Wainwright	1	1	2.57	1	1	0	7.0	6	2	2	0	5
Totals	4	2	2.09	6	6	2	56.0	42	13	13	11	50

E—Ellis, A., Puig 2, Carpenter. **LOB**—Los Angeles 31, St. Louis 35. **DP**—Los Angeles 7, St. Louis 9. **GIDP**—Ellis, M., Puig, Ramirez, Schumaker, Uribe 3, Young, Freese, Holliday, Molina 2, Robinson. **SAC**—Ellis, M., Lynn. **SF**—Carpenter, Jay. **HBP**—Ramirez (by Kelly), Kozma (by Belisario). **IBB**—Gonzalez (by Wacha), Ramirez 2 (by Lynn, by Rosenthal), Kozma 2 (by Belisario, by Kershaw). **SB**—Ellis, M., Carpenter. **PB**—Ellis, A. **WP**—Howell, Kershaw 2, Withrow, Kelly, Siegrist 2. **BK**—Withrow.

SCORE BY INNINGS

LA Dodgers	023 410 120 000 0	—13
St. Louis	00(11) 060 102 000 0	—21

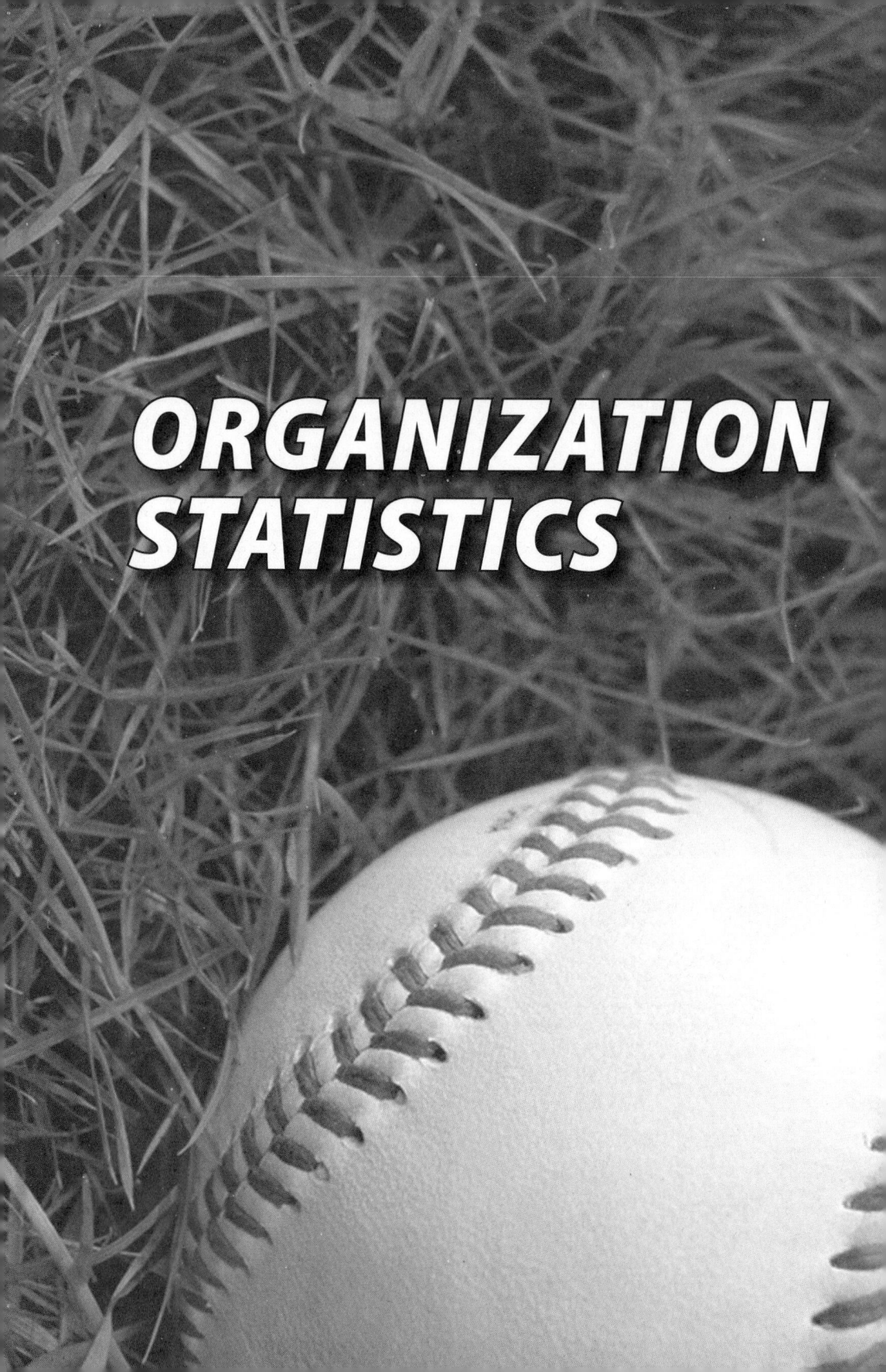

ORGANIZATION STATISTICS

Arizona Diamondbacks

SEASON IN A SENTENCE: Arizona's bid to repeat as National League West champion got off to a good start, and the Diamondbacks led the division through mid-July before their pitching fell short and the resurgent Dodgers zipped past them.

HIGH POINT: Farm-system products Paul Goldschmidt and lefthander Pat Corbin led the Diamondbacks to a 6-1 win July 7 against the Rockies, and at 47-41 the D-Backs had their largest lead of the season, 4½ games. Corbin improved to 10-1 at the time but lost seven of his last 11 decisions. Goldschmidt never really slowed down, though, hitting at least five home runs every month.

LOW POINT: A June 11 loss to the Dodgers in Los Angeles helped awaken the Dodgers as Ian Kennedy started a beanball war by hitting Cuban rookie Yasiel Puig. The loss highlighted bullpen issues, as the Dodgers scored three in the eighth to win, and the demise of Kennedy, who won 36 games the previous two seasons but was traded to the Padres after struggling through his first 21 starts in 2013.

NOTABLE ROOKIES: Outfielder Adam Eaton was injured in the first half, and A.J. Pollock took advantage, posting a solid .730 OPS and ranking second on the team (behind Goldschmidt) with 12 stolen bases. Eaton played most of the second half and underwhelmed offensively while showcasing fine defensive skills. Shortstop Didi Gregorius acquitted himself well after starting the season on the DL. Waiver claim Will Harris, a 28-year-old former Rocky, proved to be a useful bullpen piece.

KEY TRANSACTIONS: GM Kevin Towers made two blockbuster trades in the offseason. In December 2012, he traded 2011 first-round pick Trevor Bauer and two other pitchers to the Indians for Gregorius, lefty Tony Sipp and first baseman Lars Anderson (who was soon lost on waivers). In January, Towers sent Justin Upton and Chris Johnson to the Braves for a group including Martin Prado and righty Randall Delgado.

DOWN ON THE FARM: Low Class A South Bend and Double-A Mobile reached their league finals but lost in the championship series, with the BayBears just falling short of a three-peat. Righty Archie Bradley, the second of two 2011 first-rounders after Bauer, led the system in wins, ERA and strikeouts while spending most of the season at Double-A. Middle infielder Chris Owings led the system in batting at .330.

OPENING DAY PAYROLL: $89.1 million (17th)

PLAYERS OF THE YEAR

MAJOR LEAGUE	MINOR LEAGUE
Paul Goldschmidt **1b**	**Archie Bradley** **rhp**
.302/.401/.551	(High A/Double A)
36 HR, 125 RBIs	Led org with 14 W,
Led NL in HR, RBIs, SLG	1.84 ERA, 162 SO

ORGANIZATION LEADERS

BATTING		*Minimum 250 AB
MAJORS		
* AVG	Goldschmidt, Paul	.302
* OPS	Goldschmidt, Paul	.952
HR	Goldschmidt, Paul	36
RBI	Goldschmidt, Paul	125
MINORS		
* AVG	Owings, Chris, Reno	.330
* OBP	Court, Ryan, Mobile/Visalia/South Bend	.421
* SLG	Flores, Rudy, South Bend	.528
R	Owings, Chris, Reno	104
H	Owings, Chris, Reno	180
TB	Drury, Brandon, South Bend	263
	Owings, Chris, Reno	263
2B	Drury, Brandon, South Bend	51
3B	Brito, Socrates, South Bend	9
	Greene, Justin, Mobile	9
HR	Three tied at	19
RBI	Drury, Brandon, South Bend	85
BB	Court, Ryan, Mobile/Visalia/South Bend	72
SO	Marzilli, Evan, Visalia	143
SB	Inciarte, Ender, Mobile	43

PITCHING		#Minimum 75 IP
MAJORS		
W	Corbin, Patrick	14
# ERA	Corbin, Patrick	3.41
SO	Corbin, Patrick	178
SV	Bell, Heath	15
MINORS		
W	Bradley, Archie, Mobile/Visalia	14
L	Brewer, Charles, Reno	12
# ERA	Bradley, Archie, Visalia/Mobile	1.84
G	Three tied at	55
GS	Chafin, Andrew, Mobile/Visalia	27
	Darrah, Jesse, South Bend	27
SV	Hively, R.J., Visalia, South Bend	33
IP	Chafin, Andrew, Mobile/Visalia	157
	Holmberg, David, Mobile	157
BB	Barbosa, Andrew, Visalia	70
SO	Bradley, Archie, Mobile/Visalia	162
# AVG	Bradley, Archie, Visalia/Mobile	.215

2013 PERFORMANCE

General Manager: Kevin Towers. **Farm Director**: Mike Bell. **Scouting Director**: Ray Montgomery.

Class	Team	League	W	L	PCT	Finish	Manager
Majors	Arizona Diamondbacks	National	81	81	.500	7th (15)	Kirk Gibson
Triple-A	Reno Aces	Pacific Coast	60	84	.417	15th (16)	Brett Butler
Double-A	Mobile BayBears	Southern	79	60	.568	1st (10)	Andy Green
High A	Visalia Rawhide	California	77	63	.550	3rd (10)	Bill Plummer
Low A	South Bend Silver Hawks	Midwest	81	58	.583	4th (16)	Mark Haley
Short season	Hillsboro Hops	Northwest	34	42	.447	6th (8)	Audo Vicente
Rookie	Missoula Osprey	Pioneer	31	42	.425	7th (8)	Robby Hammock
Rookie	Diamondbacks	Arizona	29	27	.518	6th (13)	Luis Urueta
Overall 2013 Minor League Record			391	376	.510	9th (30)	

ORGANIZATION STATISTICS

ARIZONA DIAMONDBACKS
NATIONAL LEAGUE

Batting	B-T	HT	WT	DOB	AVG	vLH	vRH	G	AB	R	H	2B	3B	HR	RBI	BB	HBP	SH	SF	SO	SB	CS	SLG	OBP
Bloomquist, Willie	R-R	5-11	190	11-27-77	.317	.333	.309	48	139	16	44	5	1	0	14	8	2	0	1	11	0	2	.367	.360
Campana, Tony	L-L	5-8	165	5-30-86	.261	.300	.250	29	46	10	12	0	1	0	0	8	0	0	0	14	8	2	.304	.370
Chavez, Eric	L-R	6-1	215	12-7-77	.281	.290	.279	80	228	28	64	14	2	9	44	19	1	0	5	45	1	0	.478	.332
Davidson, Matt	R-R	6-2	225	3-26-91	.237	.231	.240	31	76	8	18	6	0	3	12	10	1	0	0	24	0	1	.434	.333
Eaton, Adam	L-L	5-8	185	12-6-88	.252	.296	.240	66	250	40	63	10	4	3	22	17	6	3	1	44	5	2	.360	.314
Goldschmidt, Paul	R-R	6-3	245	9-10-87	.302	.309	.300	160	602	103	182	36	3	36	125	99	3	0	5	145	15	7	.551	.401
Gosewisch, Tuffy	R-R	5-11	180	8-17-83	.178	.263	.115	14	45	1	8	2	0	0	3	0	0	1	1	8	0	0	.222	.174
Gregorius, Didi	L-R	6-1	185	2-18-90	.252	.200	.275	103	357	47	90	16	3	7	28	37	6	2	1	65	0	2	.373	.332
Hill, Aaron	R-R	5-11	205	3-21-82	.291	.321	.281	87	327	45	95	21	1	11	41	29	5	0	1	48	1	4	.462	.356
Hinske, Eric	L-R	6-2	235	8-5-77	.173	.250	.159	52	52	2	9	3	0	1	6	6	0	0	0	17	0	0	.288	.259
Kubel, Jason	L-R	6-0	220	5-25-82	.220	.162	.230	89	241	21	53	8	1	5	32	24	0	0	2	82	0	1	.324	.288
Marte, Alfredo	R-R	5-11	195	3-31-89	.186	.172	.214	22	43	4	8	3	0	0	4	4	1	0	0	12	0	0	.256	.271
Montero, Miguel	L-R	5-11	210	7-9-83	.230	.190	.244	116	413	44	95	14	0	11	42	51	5	0	6	110	0	2	.344	.318
Nieves, Wil	R-R	5-11	190	9-25-77	.297	.307	.292	71	195	16	58	11	0	1	22	8	0	0	3	32	0	0	.369	.320
Owings, Chris	R-R	5-10	180	8-12-91	.291	.125	.359	20	55	5	16	5	0	0	5	6	0	0	0	10	2	0	.382	.361
Parra, Gerardo	L-L	5-11	200	5-6-87	.268	.198	.297	156	601	79	161	43	4	10	48	48	3	7	4	100	10	10	.403	.323
Pennington, Cliff	B-R	5-10	195	6-15-84	.242	.247	.238	96	269	25	65	13	1	1	18	26	1	2	1	54	2	0	.309	.310
Pollock, A.J.	R-R	6-1	195	12-5-87	.269	.283	.259	137	443	64	119	28	5	8	38	33	2	3	1	82	12	3	.409	.322
Prado, Martin	R-R	6-1	190	10-27-83	.282	.291	.280	155	609	70	172	36	2	14	82	47	2	0	6	53	3	5	.417	.333
Ross, Cody	R-L	5-10	195	12-23-80	.278	.391	.217	94	317	33	88	17	1	8	38	25	3	1	5	50	3	2	.413	.331
Wilson, Josh	R-R	6-0	175	3-26-81	.200	.195	.211	30	60	9	12	1	1	1	4	5	0	0	1	17	0	0	.300	.262

Pitching	B-T	HT	WT	DOB	W	L	ERA	G	GS	CG	SV	IP	H	R	ER	HR	BB	SO	AVG	vLH	vRH	K/9	BB/9
Bell, Heath	R-R	6-3	250	9-29-77	5	2	4.11	69	0	0	15	66	74	30	30	12	16	72	.279	.255	.296	9.87	2.19
Brewer, Charles	R-R	6-3	205	4-7-88	0	0	3.00	4	0	0	0	6	8	2	2	0	2	5	.320	.429	.278	7.50	3.00
Cahill, Trevor	R-R	6-4	220	3-1-88	8	10	3.99	26	25	0	0	147	143	70	65	13	65	102	.261	.275	.246	6.26	3.99
Collmenter, Josh	R-R	6-4	235	2-7-86	5	5	3.13	49	0	0	0	92	79	34	32	8	33	85	.232	.250	.220	8.32	3.23
Corbin, Pat	L-L	6-2	185	7-19-89	14	8	3.41	32	32	3	0	208	189	81	79	19	54	178	.240	.203	.250	7.69	2.33
De La Rosa, Eury	L-L	5-9	165	2-24-90	0	1	7.36	19	0	0	0	15	13	13	12	5	5	16	.232	.115	.333	9.82	3.07
Delgado, Randall	R-R	6-3	200	2-9-90	5	7	4.26	20	19	1	0	116	116	59	55	24	23	79	.264	.260	.268	6.11	1.78
Harris, Will	R-R	6-4	225	8-28-84	4	1	2.91	61	0	0	0	53	50	17	17	3	15	53	.255	.221	.277	9.06	2.56
Hernandez, David	R-R	6-3	230	5-13-85	5	6	4.48	62	0	0	2	62	50	33	31	10	24	66	.215	.234	.198	9.53	3.47
Holmberg, David	R-L	6-3	225	7-19-91	0	0	7.36	1	1	0	0	4	6	3	3	0	3	0	.375	.500	.333	0.00	7.36
Kennedy, Ian	R-R	6-0	190	12-19-84	3	8	5.23	21	21	0	0	124	128	79	72	18	48	108	.268	.285	.251	7.84	3.48
2-team total (10 San Diego)					7	10	4.91	31	31	0	0	181	180	108	99	27	73	163	—	—	—	8.09	3.62
Langwell, Matt	R-R	6-2	220	5-6-86	0	0	5.19	8	0	0	0	9	8	5	5	1	5	6	.242	.200	.261	6.23	5.19
McCarthy, Brandon	R-R	6-7	200	7-7-83	5	11	4.53	22	22	2	0	135	161	71	68	13	21	76	.296	.283	.310	5.07	1.40
Miley, Wade	L-L	6-0	220	11-13-86	10	10	3.55	33	33	0	0	203	201	88	80	21	66	147	.261	.272	.259	6.53	2.93
Paterson, Joe	R-L	6-1	210	5-19-86	0	0	3.86	2	0	0	0	2	2	1	1	0	0	2	.250	.000	.500	7.71	0.00
Putz, J.J.	R-R	6-5	250	2-22-77	3	1	2.36	40	0	0	6	34	26	9	9	4	17	38	.211	.180	.233	9.96	4.46
Reynolds, Matt	L-L	6-5	240	10-2-84	0	2	1.98	30	0	0	2	27	25	7	6	2	5	23	.240	.262	.226	7.57	1.65
Roe, Chaz	R-R	6-5	190	10-9-86	1	0	4.03	21	0	0	0	22	18	10	10	3	13	24	.228	.346	.170	9.67	5.24
Sipp, Tony	L-L	6-0	190	7-12-83	3	2	4.78	56	0	0	0	38	35	22	20	6	22	42	.240	.270	.208	10.04	5.26
Skaggs, Tyler	L-L	6-5	215	7-13-91	2	3	5.12	7	7	0	0	39	38	23	22	7	15	36	.252	.242	.254	8.38	3.49
Spruill, Zeke	B-R	6-5	190	9-11-89	0	2	5.56	6	2	0	0	11	17	11	7	3	5	9	.354	.417	.292	7.15	3.97
Thatcher, Joe	L-L	6-2	230	10-4-81	0	1	6.75	22	0	0	0	9	12	7	7	1	6	7	.343	.368	.313	6.75	5.79
2-team total (50 San Diego)					3	2	3.20	72	0	0	0	39	40	14	14	4	10	36	—	—	—	8.24	2.29
Ziegler, Brad	R-R	6-4	210	10-10-79	8	1	2.22	78	0	0	13	73	61	20	18	3	22	44	.228	.246	.213	5.42	2.71

Fielding

Catcher	PCT	G	PO	A	E	DP	PB
Gosewisch	.989	13	87	2	1	1	0
Montero	.994	112	823	70	5	5	9
Nieves	.994	47	323	14	2	0	1

First Base	PCT	G	PO	A	E	DP
Chavez	1.000	6	20	2	0	3
Goldschmidt	.997	159	1494	99	5	118
Hinske	1.000	6	32	2	0	5

Second Base	PCT	G	PO	A	E	DP
Bloomquist	1.000	15	32	37	0	10
Hill	.995	84	150	232	2	48
Owings	1.000	3	2	10	0	0
Pennington	.980	29	33	64	2	14
Prado	.975	32	53	66	3	12
Wilson	.985	17	22	43	1	11

Third Base	PCT	G	PO	A	E	DP
Chavez	.993	52	30	104	1	6
Davidson	.974	20	10	28	1	3

Pennington	.857	2	0	6	1	0
Prado	.978	113	60	202	6	21
Wilson	1.000	4	0	2	0	0

Shortstop	PCT	G	PO	A	E	DP
Bloomquist	.976	9	12	29	1	7
Gregorius	.971	100	152	279	13	51
Owings	.980	13	18	31	1	4
Pennington	.977	51	58	152	5	30
Prado	—	1	0	0	0	0
Wilson	.667	2	0	2	1	0

Outfield	PCT	G	PO	A	E	DP
Bloomquist	1.000	7	9	0	0	0
Campana	.938	9	14	1	1	0
Eaton	.965	60	103	6	4	1
Kubel	.965	57	76	6	3	0
Marte	1.000	9	11	0	0	0
Parra	.986	155	343	17	5	1
Pollock	.992	118	246	8	2	1
Prado	.973	30	35	1	1	0
Ross	1.000	83	164	5	0	1

RENO ACES — *TRIPLE-A*

PACIFIC COAST LEAGUE

Batting	B-T	HT	WT	DOB	AVG	vLH	vRH	G	AB	R	H	2B	3B	HR	RBI	BB	HBP	SH	SF	SO	SB	CS	SLG	OBP
Belza, Tom	L-R	6-0	190	7-31-89	.500	—	.500	2	4	0	2	1	0	0	0	0	0	0	0	0	0	0	.750	.500
Bloomquist, Willie	R-R	5-11	190	11-27-77	.429	.625	.308	6	21	5	9	0	1	0	9	2	0	0	0	2	0	0	.524	.478
Bortnick, Tyler	R-R	5-11	185	7-3-87	.291	.281	.294	88	251	53	73	11	4	3	33	40	5	1	1	54	19	2	.402	.397
Brenly, Mike	R-R	6-3	250	10-14-86	.118	.333	.071	8	17	1	2	1	0	0	1	1	0	0	0	4	0	0	.176	.167
Campana, Tony	L-L	5-8	165	5-30-86	.293	.339	.284	102	351	65	103	11	6	1	29	34	0	4	2	77	32	8	.368	.354
Chavez, Eric	L-R	6-1	215	12-7-77	.250	.000	.250	3	8	0	2	0	0	0	2	0	0	0	0	1	0	0	.250	.400
Clevlen, Brent	R-R	6-1	205	10-27-83	.200	.200	.200	16	40	6	8	2	0	2	4	5	0	0	1	11	1	0	.400	.283
Davidson, Matt	R-R	6-2	225	3-26-91	.280	.225	.296	115	443	55	124	32	3	17	74	46	5	0	6	134	1	0	.481	.350
Easley, Ed	R-R	6-0	205	12-21-85	.334	.391	.317	87	293	39	98	22	1	6	49	28	3	1	3	50	2	2	.478	.394
Eaton, Adam	L-L	5-8	185	12-6-88	.143	.000	.250	10	35	5	5	2	0	1	5	3	1	0	1	8	0	0	.286	.225
Fox, Jake	R-R	6-0	220	7-20-82	.147	.125	.154	15	34	2	5	2	0	0	2	2	2	0	0	11	0	0	.206	.237
Frey, Evan	L-L	6-0	170	6-7-86	.282	.256	.291	61	149	19	42	5	2	0	8	23	0	3	1	27	9	2	.342	.376
Gosewisch, Tuffy	R-R	5-11	180	8-17-83	.284	.359	.258	72	250	30	71	20	1	7	33	17	1	0	4	40	1	1	.456	.327
Gregorius, Didi	L-R	6-1	185	2-18-90	.387	.500	.333	7	31	7	12	2	0	2	2	2	0	0	1	0	0	0	.645	.424
Harbin, Taylor	R-R	5-9	171	2-13-86	.231	.200	.242	117	364	44	84	16	5	5	36	17	2	1	1	54	6	5	.343	.268
Hill, Aaron	R-R	5-11	205	3-21-82	.375	.667	.333	6	24	8	9	1	1	0	6	1	0	0	1	3	0	0	.500	.385
Hinske, Eric	L-R	6-2	235	8-5-77	.056	.000	.071	5	18	0	1	0	0	0	0	1	0	0	0	5	0	0	.056	.105
Jacobs, Mike	L-R	6-3	215	10-30-80	.304	.256	.322	82	329	53	100	17	0	18	65	31	2	0	2	68	0	0	.520	.365
Ka'aihue, Kila	L-R	6-4	235	3-29-84	.313	.215	.362	53	192	38	60	9	1	16	50	38	2	0	3	41	0	1	.620	.426
Kuhn, Tyler	L-R	5-10	185	9-9-86	.244	.154	.268	50	123	20	30	6	2	1	11	10	0	4	2	22	5	1	.350	.296
Marte, Alfredo	R-R	5-11	195	3-31-89	.280	.259	.287	86	311	37	87	24	1	7	48	22	6	0	4	63	2	1	.431	.335
Owings, Chris	R-R	5-10	180	8-12-91	.330	.306	.338	125	546	104	180	31	8	12	81	22	3	4	0	99	20	7	.482	.359
Rivera, Juan	R-R	6-2	220	7-3-78	.304	.220	.332	96	359	46	109	17	1	10	58	17	6	0	1	30	2	1	.440	.345
Ross, Cody	R-L	5-10	195	12-23-80	.667	.667	—	1	3	1	2	1	0	0	2	1	0	0	0	0	1	0	1.000	.750
Snyder, Brad	L-L	6-3	220	5-25-82	.311	.383	.284	116	411	77	128	29	5	12	60	40	1	1	5	118	7	11	.494	.370
Stovall, Ryan	R-R	5-11	190	12-16-86	.250	.000	.273	10	12	5	3	1	0	0	3	4	0	0	0	2	0	0	.333	.438
Teahen, Mark	L-R	6-3	230	9-6-81	.211	.211	.212	22	71	12	15	3	0	0	5	12	0	0	2	22	0	0	.254	.318
2-team total (10 Round Rock)					.198			32	106	13	21	3	0	0	7	15	0	0	2	33	0	0	.226	.293
Wilson, Josh	R-R	6-0	175	3-26-81	.219	.261	.205	59	192	17	42	8	0	4	20	13	0	1	0	44	1	3	.323	.268

Pitching	B-T	HT	WT	DOB	W	L	ERA	G	GS	CG	SV	IP	H	R	ER	HR	BB	SO	AVG	vLH	vRH	K/9	BB/9
Adcock, Nate	R-R	6-4	230	2-25-88	5	2	6.38	16	10	0	0	66	74	50	47	5	27	41	.287	.353	.230	5.56	3.66
2-team total (10 Omaha)					8	6	6.67	26	19	0	0	113	139	92	84	15	50	69	—	—	—	5.48	3.97
Anderson, Chase	R-R	6-0	185	11-30-87	4	7	5.73	26	13	0	0	88	107	67	56	11	33	80	.301	.274	.323	8.18	3.38
Bolsinger, Mike	R-R	6-2	209	1-29-88	7	7	4.72	17	17	1	0	101	116	60	53	12	39	97	.291	.311	.275	8.64	3.48
Bonine, Eddie	R-R	6-5	220	6-6-81	0	0	6.30	4	1	0	0	10	11	8	7	2	3	6	.275	.308	.214	5.40	2.70
2-team total (7 Tucson)					0	2	8.58	11	5	0	0	28	51	29	27	6	14	10	—	—	—	3.18	4.45
Brewer, Charles	R-R	6-3	205	4-7-88	5	12	4.90	25	22	0	0	140	158	83	76	13	43	107	.289	.264	.310	6.89	2.77
Cahill, Trevor	R-R	6-4	220	3-1-88	0	2	5.94	3	3	0	0	17	16	12	11	3	9	13	.262	.333	.216	7.02	4.86
Camp, Shawn	R-R	6-0	205	11-18-75	0	0	2.42	17	0	0	0	22	22	6	6	2	5	19	.259	.310	.232	7.66	2.01
De La Rosa, Eury	L-L	5-9	165	2-24-90	3	5	5.26	44	0	0	0	50	52	33	29	6	27	49	.272	.202	.333	8.88	4.89
Delgado, Randall	R-R	6-3	200	2-9-90	2	5	5.91	13	13	0	0	64	69	46	42	9	35	57	.272	.285	.258	8.02	4.92
Figueroa, Nelson	R-R	6-1	185	5-18-74	0	3	12.76	4	4	0	0	18	31	27	26	7	8	7	.373	.396	.343	3.44	3.93
Gorgen, Matt	R-R	5-10	210	1-27-87	1	1	7.18	24	0	0	1	31	39	27	25	6	17	23	.305	.361	.254	6.61	4.89
Harris, Will	R-R	6-4	225	8-28-84	0	0	4.63	12	0	0	2	12	12	7	6	1	6	23	.245	.346	.130	17.74	4.63
Henry, Bryan	R-R	6-3	205	2-15-85	0	1	8.27	7	1	0	0	16	26	16	15	1	9	9	.356	.333	.365	4.96	4.96
Hernandez, David	R-R	6-3	230	5-13-85	0	0	0.93	9	0	0	2	10	6	1	1	0	5	12	.176	.250	.111	11.17	4.66
Lorin, Brett	L-R	6-7	245	3-31-87	0	2	3.34	19	0	0	1	30	23	13	11	3	11	21	.217	.229	.211	6.37	3.34
Madrigal, Warner	R-R	6-1	235	3-21-84	1	0	2.75	22	0	0	0	36	21	11	11	2	14	41	.171	.130	.203	10.25	3.50
Marshall, Evan	R-R	6-2	220	4-18-90	3	6	4.34	54	0	0	3	58	75	32	28	2	30	59	.322	.374	.284	9.16	4.66
McCarthy, Brandon	R-R	6-7	200	7-7-83	0	0	6.97	2	2	0	0	10	15	9	8	3	4	3	.333	.412	.286	3.48	2.61
Mock, Garrett	R-R	6-4	230	4-25-83	8	7	6.72	33	11	0	0	75	94	65	56	11	38	54	.310	.322	.302	6.48	4.56
Munson, Kevin	R-R	6-1	215	1-3-89	0	2	5.09	24	0	0	1	23	25	16	13	1	7	27	.269	.297	.250	10.57	2.74
Paredes, Willy	R-R	6-3	180	2-2-89	0	0	10.00	2	2	0	0	9	12	11	10	2	5	6	.324	.357	.304	6.00	5.00
Paterson, Joe	R-L	6-1	210	5-19-86	3	1	1.89	48	1	0	1	52	40	14	11	2	15	53	.221	.151	.295	9.11	2.58
Pauley, David	R-R	6-2	215	6-17-83	0	1	11.12	4	0	0	0	6	10	7	7	2	3	5	.370	.091	.563	7.94	4.76
Putz, J.J.	R-R	6-5	250	2-22-77	0	0	2.25	4	4	0	0	4	2	1	1	0	3	4	.154	.200	.125	9.00	6.75
Roe, Chaz	R-R	6-5	190	10-9-86	0	0	1.23	22	0	0	7	22	15	3	3	0	4	20	.190	.194	.186	8.18	1.64
Rosario, Diogenes	R-R	6-2	179	9-1-88	0	1	4.50	1	1	0	0	6	7	3	3	0	1	6	.318	.313	.333	9.00	1.50
Schultz, Bo	R-R	6-3	215	9-25-85	0	1	5.49	17	0	0	0	20	29	12	12	4	7	23	.345	.321	.357	10.53	3.20

ARIZONA DIAMONDBACKS

Name	B-T	HT	WT	DOB	W	L	ERA	G	GS	CG	SV	IP	H	R	ER	HR	BB	SO	AVG	vLH	vRH	K/9	BB/9
Serrano, Mark	L-R	6-1	185	9-14-85	1	0	1.50	2	2	0	0	12	8	2	2	1	2	4	.182	.174	.190	3.00	1.50
Sipp, Tony	L-L	6-0	190	7-12-83	1	0	0.00	9	0	0	1	10	3	1	0	0	5	12	.088	.125	.056	10.80	4.50
Skaggs, Tyler	L-L	6-5	215	7-13-91	6	10	4.59	19	17	0	0	104	114	62	53	5	39	107	.275	.333	.252	9.26	3.38
Spruill, Zeke	B-R	6-5	190	9-11-89	6	5	4.21	16	16	1	0	92	98	48	43	8	33	48	.277	.281	.274	4.70	3.23
Weller, Blayne	R-R	6-5	220	1-30-90	0	0	0.00	1	0	0	0	1	0	0	0	0	1	1	.000	.000	.000	9.00	9.00
Woodall, Bryan	R-R	6-1	200	10-24-86	1	1	7.08	19	0	0	0	20	34	17	16	3	9	20	.386	.371	.396	8.85	3.98
Wright, Matt	R-R	6-4	270	3-13-82	3	1	6.08	8	4	0	0	27	36	18	18	1	9	25	.321	.372	.290	8.44	3.04

Fielding

Catcher	PCT	G	PO	A	E	DP	PB
Brenly	1.000	5	29	1	0	0	0
Easley	.993	75	496	62	4	3	12
Fox	1.000	3	16	2	0	0	0
Gosewisch	.988	68	516	52	7	2	0

First Base	PCT	G	PO	A	E	DP
Hinske	1.000	1	10	1	0	1
Jacobs	.991	79	726	64	7	62
Ka'aihue	.998	50	413	33	1	38
Rivera	.992	20	105	14	1	21
Teahen	.957	6	42	2	2	3

Second Base	PCT	G	PO	A	E	DP
Bloomquist	1.000	5	6	11	0	1
Bortnick	.979	61	95	141	5	30
Harbin	.990	49	99	100	2	23
Hill	1.000	6	12	18	0	3
Kuhn	1.000	17	19	40	0	9
Owings	.981	11	24	29	1	7

	PCT	G	PO	A	E	DP
Wilson	.964	32	50	84	5	24

Third Base	PCT	G	PO	A	E	DP
Bortnick	1.000	14	5	15	0	2
Chavez	1.000	3	0	4	0	1
Davidson	.936	109	54	195	17	17
Fox	.750	1	0	3	1	0
Harbin	.929	27	16	49	5	4
Kuhn	1.000	2	0	3	0	0
Teahen	.800	2	1	3	1	2
Wilson	1.000	2	0	1	0	0

Shortstop	PCT	G	PO	A	E	DP
Bloomquist	1.000	1	0	4	0	0
Bortnick	.900	4	9	9	2	3
Gregorius	1.000	1	4	5	0	2
Harbin	.952	11	13	27	2	5
Owings	.943	112	128	339	28	71
Wilson	.986	20	22	48	1	11

Outfield	PCT	G	PO	A	E	DP
Belza	—	1	0	0	0	0
Bortnick	—	1	0	0	0	0
Campana	.977	99	166	5	4	0
Clevlen	.900	13	9	0	1	0
Eaton	1.000	2	3	0	0	0
Fox	1.000	7	6	2	0	1
Frey	.988	51	78	1	1	1
Harbin	1.000	26	29	1	0	0
Kuhn	.964	23	26	1	1	0
Marte	.965	85	163	3	6	1
Paterson	—	1	0	0	0	0
Rivera	.982	76	98	9	2	1
Ross	—	1	0	0	0	0
Snyder	.990	103	194	3	2	0
Stovall	1.000	5	7	0	0	0
Teahen	.923	9	11	1	1	0
Wilson	1.000	3	1	0	0	0

MOBILE BAYBEARS — DOUBLE-A

SOUTHERN LEAGUE

Batting	B-T	HT	WT	DOB	AVG	vLH	vRH	G	AB	R	H	2B	3B	HR	RBI	BB	HBP	SH	SF	SO	SB	CS	SLG	OBP
Ahmed, Nick	R-R	6-3	205	3-15-90	.236	.233	.237	136	487	58	115	21	5	4	46	33	5	7	6	72	26	7	.324	.288
Broxton, Keon	R-R	6-3	195	5-7-90	.231	.286	.210	101	334	40	77	13	3	8	41	30	2	4	2	116	5	1	.359	.296
Carroll, Sawyer	L-R	6-4	215	5-9-86	.280	.375	.262	22	50	5	14	3	1	0	10	13	1	1	0	9	1	0	.380	.438
Clevlen, Brent	R-R	6-1	205	10-27-83	.223	.296	.202	38	121	15	27	4	1	4	17	10	1	0	0	32	1	0	.372	.288
Cota, Humberto	R-R	5-11	225	2-7-79	.000	.000	.000	7	16	2	0	0	0	0	0	2	1	0	0	9	0	0	.000	.158
Court, Ryan	R-R	6-2	210	5-28-88	.258	.246	.264	59	178	19	46	14	0	1	19	32	4	0	2	56	2	2	.354	.380
Evans, Nick	R-R	6-2	220	1-30-86	.267	.260	.269	133	454	73	121	24	1	19	81	66	1	0	6	111	2	4	.449	.357
Freeman, Mike	L-R	6-0	192	8-4-87	.247	.230	.253	131	454	61	112	20	0	1	40	65	6	6	5	84	29	10	.297	.345
Gomez, Raywilly	B-R	5-11	192	1-25-90	.272	.270	.273	73	224	19	61	13	0	0	26	30	2	2	3	24	1	1	.330	.359
Greene, Justin	R-R	6-0	185	10-10-85	.308	.374	.276	117	380	75	117	19	9	1	30	42	2	3	3	74	31	12	.413	.377
Griffin, Jon	R-R	6-6	230	4-29-89	.232	.268	.220	61	220	22	51	7	1	3	33	15	3	0	2	70	0	1	.314	.288
Inciarte, Ender	L-L	5-10	160	10-29-90	.281	.260	.289	127	473	68	133	17	3	5	25	27	6	8	2	47	43	8	.362	.327
Martin, Dustin	L-L	6-2	215	4-4-84	.295	.308	.292	73	217	33	64	13	4	8	29	28	2	0	2	50	12	2	.502	.378
Nick, David	R-R	6-2	180	2-3-90	.188	.235	.170	21	64	6	12	4	1	1	7	8	0	0	0	15	2	1	.328	.278
Perez, Rossmel	B-R	5-9	200	8-26-89	.245	.259	.240	74	237	16	58	4	0	2	28	23	3	2	4	16	3	2	.287	.315
Stovall, Ryan	R-R	5-11	190	12-16-86	.229	.189	.247	57	118	8	27	4	1	4	17	4	1	0	1	48	0	2	.381	.258
Weber, Garrett	R-R	5-10	165	3-29-89	.281	.354	.250	104	320	33	90	20	1	4	52	24	7	1	1	62	5	1	.388	.344

Pitching	B-T	HT	WT	DOB	W	L	ERA	G	GS	CG	SV	IP	H	R	ER	HR	BB	SO	AVG	vLH	vRH	K/9	BB/9
Barrett, Jake	R-R	6-3	230	7-22-91	1	1	0.36	24	0	0	14	25	18	4	1	2	3	22	.196	.265	.155	8.03	1.09
Bolsinger, Mike	R-R	6-2	209	1-29-88	4	0	2.51	9	6	1	0	43	35	14	12	0	15	31	.224	.246	.211	6.49	3.14
Bradley, Archie	R-R	6-4	225	8-10-92	12	5	1.97	21	21	2	0	123	93	35	27	5	59	119	.214	.231	.202	8.68	4.31
Chafin, Andrew	R-L	6-2	205	6-17-90	10	7	2.85	21	21	2	0	126	118	46	40	5	41	87	.252	.185	.268	6.20	2.92
Cooper, Blake	R-R	5-11	190	3-30-88	5	2	2.93	39	0	0	0	43	31	20	14	1	22	30	.201	.157	.223	6.28	4.60
Cortes, Dan	R-R	6-6	235	3-4-87	0	1	16.20	10	0	0	0	8	12	15	15	4	14	11	.343	.333	.348	11.88	15.12
Eitel, Derek	R-R	6-4	200	11-21-87	6	2	3.42	42	2	0	1	68	44	31	26	7	27	60	.186	.141	.219	7.90	3.56
Garrison, Steve	B-L	6-1	195	9-12-86	1	1	3.30	47	1	0	0	44	40	16	16	6	14	49	.244	.194	.270	10.10	2.89
Gorgen, Matt	R-R	5-10	210	1-27-87	1	1	2.73	22	0	0	1	26	23	9	8	2	7	29	.232	.243	.226	9.91	2.39
Hagens, Bradin	R-R	6-3	210	5-12-89	11	8	3.47	26	26	0	0	148	147	63	57	10	66	93	.263	.248	.272	5.66	4.01
Holmberg, David	R-L	6-3	225	7-19-91	5	8	2.75	26	26	1	0	157	138	59	48	12	50	116	.239	.240	.238	6.64	2.86
Hudson, Daniel	R-R	6-3	225	3-9-87	0	0	4.50	1	1	0	0	2	2	1	1	0	1	2	.250	.250	.250	4.50	3.50
Lara, Alexis	R-R	6-0	150	3-23-87	1	2	4.23	18	0	0	0	28	35	20	13	4	11	16	.310	.390	.264	5.20	3.58
Lorin, Brett	L-R	6-7	245	3-31-87	5	0	2.45	14	0	0	0	22	22	7	6	2	7	17	.268	.259	.273	6.95	2.86
Meo, Anthony	R-R	6-2	185	2-19-90	4	8	6.37	8	8	0	0	35	31	26	25	6	11	31	.311	.218	.433		6.37
Munson, Kevin	R-R	6-1	215	1-3-89	2	2	3.41	29	0	0	13	32	17	12	12	5	15	39	.157	.171	.151	11.08	4.26
Paredes, Willy	R-R	6-3	180	2-2-89	3	0	1.00	32	0	0	0	36	22	5	4	1	12	33	.173	.143	.192	8.25	3.00
Roe, Chaz	R-R	6-5	190	10-9-86	0	1	0.00	3	0	0	1	2	2	1	0	0	0	3	.200	.000	.286	11.57	0.00
Schultz, Bo	R-R	6-3	215	9-25-85	5	4	2.86	20	16	0	1	85	62	29	27	3	29	52	.205	.174	.230	5.51	3.07
Serrano, Mark	L-R	6-1	185	9-14-85	5	2	3.43	16	4	0	0	45	45	17	17	3	12	40	.265	.328	.226	8.06	2.42
Smith, Eric	R-R	6-3	210	10-15-88	1	3	7.11	33	1	0	3	38	38	30	30	5	21	27	.264	.259	.267	6.39	4.97
Spruill, Zeke	B-R	6-5	190	9-11-89	0	3	1.42	5	5	0	0	32	24	7	5	0	12	20	.224	.295	.175	5.68	3.41
Woodall, Bryan	R-R	6-1	200	10-24-86	1	3	1.94	35	1	0	1	42	27	11	9	5	12	48	.190	.178	.196	10.37	2.59

ARIZONA DIAMONDBACKS *(side tab)*

Fielding

Catcher	PCT	G	PO	A	E	DP	PB
Cota	1.000	7	44	3	0	1	1
Gomez	.992	66	429	39	4	6	5
Perez	.996	74	485	56	2	2	7

First Base	PCT	G	PO	A	E	DP
Carroll	.984	9	55	5	1	5
Court	.971	10	93	6	3	13
Evans	.997	65	536	37	2	39
Griffin	.989	58	512	40	6	61
Stovall	.968	3	25	5	1	4

Second Base	PCT	G	PO	A	E	DP
Ahmed	.833	2	4	6	2	2
Freeman	.986	124	245	334	8	85
Stovall	—	1	0	0	0	0
Weber	.976	22	30	51	2	9

Third Base	PCT	G	PO	A	E	DP
Court	.956	40	27	60	4	7
Evans	.935	49	37	93	9	10
Gomez	—	1	0	0	0	0
Stovall	1.000	1	1	0	0	0
Weber	.949	61	35	115	8	11

Shortstop	PCT	G	PO	A	E	DP
Ahmed	.980	133	196	441	13	88
Freeman	.919	10	8	26	3	4

Outfield	PCT	G	PO	A	E	DP
Broxton	.973	97	172	9	5	1
Carroll	1.000	9	9	0	0	0
Clevlen	.974	32	67	7	2	0
Evans	1.000	6	5	0	0	0
Greene	.987	98	143	7	2	0
Inciarte	.993	121	259	8	2	2
Martin	.990	51	85	10	1	0
Nick	1.000	18	24	0	0	0
Stovall	.974	23	37	1	1	0

VISALIA RAWHIDE

HIGH CLASS A

CALIFORNIA LEAGUE

Batting	B-T	HT	WT	DOB	AVG	vLH	vRH	G	AB	R	H	2B	3B	HR	RBI	BB	HBP	SH	SF	SO	SB	CS	SLG	OBP
Arbelo, Yazy	L-R	6-4	220	4-7-88	.211	.238	.203	26	95	13	20	4	0	3	12	14	3	0	2	31	0	0	.347	.325
Belza, Tom	L-R	6-0	190	7-31-89	.300	.286	.305	128	476	73	143	21	5	10	63	51	2	6	3	93	12	7	.429	.368
Brodin, Joash	B-R	6-3	225	3-24-87	.172	.333	.130	8	29	5	5	0	0	0	2	3	3	0	0	7	0	0	.172	.314
Court, Ryan	R-R	6-2	210	5-28-88	.326	.383	.298	39	141	28	46	10	3	8	29	24	4	0	2	37	2	0	.610	.433
Eaton, Adam	L-L	5-8	185	12-6-88	.321	.280	.357	15	53	12	17	3	0	1	6	10	1	0	0	6	8	1	.434	.438
Ellison, Chris	L-R	6-2	189	12-16-88	.188	.000	.207	17	32	3	6	0	0	0	2	6	0	2	0	11	0	1	.188	.316
Freeman, Ronnie	R-R	6-1	195	1-8-91	.273	.333	.247	31	110	14	30	5	0	0	11	11	1	0	2	22	0	0	.318	.339
Gomez, Raywilly	B-R	5-11	192	1-25-90	.353	.375	.346	21	68	14	24	7	1	0	13	22	1	0	1	12	1	0	.485	.511
Griffin, Jon	R-R	6-6	230	4-29-89	.295	.370	.281	42	166	20	49	9	1	7	29	10	3	0	1	38	0	0	.488	.344
Gutierrez, Yosbel	R-R	5-10	170	1-20-93	.133	.000	.154	4	15	2	2	0	0	1	1	0	0	0	0	7	0	0	.333	.133
Helm, Matt	R-R	6-1	210	9-1-90	.192	.190	.193	66	208	17	40	10	1	4	27	19	1	1	1	88	2	4	.308	.262
Jamieson, Sean	R-R	6-0	193	3-2-89	.287	.247	.297	122	435	80	125	33	5	11	53	48	11	8	3	109	11	5	.462	.370
Jenkins, Kerry	R-R	6-1	210	5-18-89	.228	.216	.233	55	184	12	42	12	1	0	23	11	2	5	0	49	2	2	.304	.279
Lamb, Jake	L-R	6-2	200	10-9-90	.303	.281	.310	64	231	44	70	20	0	13	47	48	2	0	2	70	0	0	.558	.424
Marzilli, Evan	L-L	5-11	175	3-13-91	.250	.232	.255	136	460	67	115	27	4	3	50	59	6	9	2	143	14	6	.346	.342
McMurray, Chris	R-R	6-1	195	10-12-86	.167	.167	.167	15	48	10	8	3	0	1	8	12	0	0	1	17	1	0	.292	.328
Medrano, Kevin	L-R	6-1	155	5-21-90	.297	.167	.322	71	293	48	87	12	1	0	25	36	4	5	2	43	10	4	.345	.379
Montilla, Gerson	R-R	5-10	168	11-13-89	.282	.260	.289	134	542	90	153	28	2	19	72	43	2	14	6	106	8	2	.446	.334
Navarro, Raul	R-R	5-10	170	2-5-92	.247	.282	.233	71	247	36	61	8	1	1	30	22	2	6	1	52	8	2	.300	.313
Nick, David	R-R	6-2	180	2-3-90	.259	.316	.240	71	297	36	77	14	3	10	41	15	0	0	1	58	7	1	.428	.294
Peralta, David	L-L	6-1	160	8-14-87	.346	.258	.362	51	208	29	72	15	0	8	42	9	0	0	2	28	1	0	.534	.370
Perez, Michael	L-R	5-11	180	8-7-92	.173	.162	.176	47	179	21	31	9	0	5	24	11	1	0	2	78	1	1	.307	.223
Rodriguez, Steven	L-R	6-1	200	1-8-90	.197	.214	.195	40	132	17	26	6	0	3	20	24	0	2	1	30	0	0	.311	.318
Ross, Cody	R-L	5-10	195	12-23-80	.125	.250	.083	6	16	2	2	0	0	0	2	1	1	0	1	4	0	0	.125	.211
Stovall, Ryan	R-R	5-11	190	12-16-86	.157	.286	.133	25	89	11	14	5	0	2	7	13	1	0	0	33	1	0	.281	.265

Pitching	B-T	HT	WT	DOB	W	L	ERA	G	GS	CG	SV	IP	H	R	ER	HR	BB	SO	AVG	vLH	vRH	K/9	BB/9
Allen, Brad	L-R	6-4	220	3-26-89	1	1	7.94	3	2	0	0	11	11	10	10	3	5	17	.239	.385	.182	13.50	3.97
Barbosa, Andrew	R-L	6-8	205	11-18-87	11	9	3.81	26	26	1	0	135	115	66	57	11	70	160	.233	.223	.235	10.69	4.68
Barrett, Jake	R-R	6-3	230	7-22-91	2	1	1.98	28	0	0	15	27	21	7	6	2	9	37	.198	.268	.154	12.18	2.96
Bradley, Archie	R-R	6-4	225	8-10-92	2	0	1.26	5	5	0	0	29	22	5	4	1	10	43	.218	.157	.280	13.50	3.14
Chafin, Andrew	R-L	6-2	205	6-17-90	3	1	4.65	6	6	0	0	31	32	16	16	1	14	32	.262	.207	.280	9.29	4.06
Coe, Robert	R-R	6-4	175	1-4-88	2	3	6.58	11	8	0	0	52	58	43	38	10	30	44	.289	.269	.299	7.62	5.19
Cooper, Blake	R-R	5-11	190	3-30-88	0	1	1.59	15	0	0	0	17	14	4	3	0	7	18	.226	.176	.244	9.53	3.71
Fleck, Kaleb	R-R	6-2	190	1-24-89	2	1	2.89	52	0	0	9	56	49	19	18	6	25	60	.236	.266	.222	9.64	4.02
Flynn, Conrad	R-R	6-3	190	11-18-88	7	6	5.24	37	8	0	0	100	114	64	58	20	31	92	.284	.305	.276	8.31	2.80
Green, Tyler	R-R	6-1	185	11-24-91	0	0	5.40	10	0	0	0	10	11	7	6	0	6	7	.268	.400	.226	6.30	5.40
Hessler, Keith	L-L	6-4	215	3-15-89	8	7	5.85	26	26	0	0	137	161	97	89	24	64	126	.303	.288	.308	8.28	4.20
Hively, R.J.	R-R	6-2	205	11-27-88	3	0	2.37	28	0	0	14	30	28	12	8	2	10	38	.255	.241	.259	11.27	2.97
McKiernan, Eddie	R-R	5-11	160	3-21-89	8	3	3.51	12	12	1	0	77	80	35	30	8	20	54	.268	.243	.283	6.31	2.34
Meo, Anthony	R-R	6-2	185	2-19-90	1	1	7.54	21	0	0	0	23	25	22	19	2	22	22	.294	.350	.277	8.74	8.74
Paredes, Willy	R-R	6-3	180	2-2-89	2	1	1.93	15	0	0	0	28	24	7	6	1	10	29	.238	.281	.217	9.32	3.21
Rosario, Diogenes	R-R	6-2	179	9-4-88	5	1	4.60	35	1	0	0	63	57	35	32	8	31	55	.246	.209	.267	7.90	4.45
Sample, Mat	R-R	6-5	200	8-16-88	0	1	5.51	13	0	0	0	16	14	12	10	3	13	17	.241	.364	.167	9.37	7.16
Santana, Frank	R-R	6-2	200	2-21-89	0	0	15.12	6	0	0	0	8	20	14	14	1	6	11	.465	.611	.360	11.88	6.48
Schepel, Kyle	L-R	6-1	230	8-7-90	2	5	8.78	9	7	0	0	40	52	41	39	8	24	32	.317	.355	.284	7.20	5.40
Schuster, Patrick	R-L	6-1	182	10-30-90	0	1	1.83	55	0	0	0	44	30	14	9	3	18	45	.191	.198	.184	9.14	3.65
Simmons, Seth	R-R	5-9	170	6-14-88	6	2	2.44	55	0	0	1	74	48	23	20	8	30	106	.185	.203	.178	12.95	3.67
Sinnery, Brandon	R-R	6-4	170	1-26-90	3	4	5.80	8	8	0	0	50	46	33	32	7	13	47	.236	.261	.222	8.52	2.36
Skaggs, Tyler	L-L	6-5	215	7-13-91	0	0	4.76	1	1	0	0	6	3	3	3	0	8	8	.200	.000	.278	12.71	12.71
Watts, Daniel	L-L	6-3	190	10-26-89	2	4	10.35	9	7	0	0	36	53	43	41	8	26	32	.340	.323	.344	8.07	6.56
Wheeler, Cody	L-L	5-11	160	8-19-89	6	5	5.85	28	13	0	0	80	87	58	52	11	58	99	.274	.360	.247	11.14	6.53
Winkler, Kyle	R-R	5-11	195	6-18-90	1	5	7.63	10	10	0	0	46	67	48	39	10	28	41	.337	.371	.321	8.02	5.48

Fielding

Catcher	PCT	G	PO	A	E	DP	PB
Freeman	.987	31	281	20	4	3	4
Gomez	.981	11	85	16	2	1	3
Gutierrez	.932	4	38	3	3	0	1
McMurray	.992	15	123	9	1	0	2
Perez	.997	42	348	34	1	3	5
Rodriguez	.995	40	364	40	2	2	7

First Base	PCT	G	PO	A	E	DP
Arbelo	.965	17	134	5	5	10
Belza	.991	13	98	10	1	11
Brodin	1.000	7	49	2	0	4
Court	.993	32	270	17	2	32
Griffin	.980	40	270	18	6	29
Helm	.958	32	199	8	9	16
Medrano	1.000	3	21	3	0	1
Stovall	1.000	2	16	1	0	1

Second Base	PCT	G	PO	A	E	DP
Medrano	.991	30	60	50	1	20
Montilla	.988	91	182	213	5	55
Navarro	.981	27	33	72	2	16

Third Base	PCT	G	PO	A	E	DP
Belza	1.000	4	1	4	0	0
Court	.867	6	4	9	2	1
Gomez	.963	9	6	20	1	1
Helm	—	1	0	0	0	0
Lamb	.910	55	30	91	12	12
Medrano	.966	25	14	43	2	2
Montilla	.892	29	18	48	8	6
Navarro	.976	16	9	31	1	1
Stovall	.667	1	0	2	1	0

Shortstop	PCT	G	PO	A	E	DP
Jamieson	.962	112	151	305	18	64
Navarro	.959	32	26	91	5	13

Outfield	PCT	G	PO	A	E	DP
Belza	1.000	107	193	8	0	2
Brodin	1.000	1	3	0	0	0
Eaton	1.000	4	6	0	0	0
Ellison	.929	15	13	0	1	0
Helm	1.000	6	2	0	0	0
Jenkins	.986	43	65	3	1	0
Marzilli	.991	136	328	14	3	8
Montilla	—	1	0	0	0	0
Nick	.969	61	89	5	3	0
Peralta	.987	45	73	4	1	1
Ross	—	2	0	0	0	0
Stovall	.968	19	25	5	1	2

SOUTH BEND SILVER HAWKS LOW CLASS A

MIDWEST LEAGUE

Batting	B-T	HT	WT	DOB	AVG	vLH	vRH	G	AB	R	H	2B	3B	HR	RBI	BB	HBP	SH	SF	SO	SB	CS	SLG	OBP
Aguila, Roidany	R-R	5-10	175	10-22-90	.242	.306	.216	80	289	31	70	18	0	10	30	14	3	0	3	83	1	0	.408	.282
Almadova, Breland	R-R	6-1	195	10-18-90	.237	.250	.231	116	431	66	102	17	5	7	47	50	4	7	1	114	15	8	.348	.321
Bell, Carter	R-R	6-1	195	6-12-90	.233	.274	.211	60	206	21	48	12	2	3	17	15	3	0	3	32	0	1	.354	.291
Brito, Socrates	L-L	6-2	197	9-6-92	.264	.262	.264	129	523	61	138	24	9	2	49	37	2	1	3	124	27	9	.356	.313
Carrasco, Cesar	R-R	6-2	185	10-3-93	.167	.000	.200	6	18	1	3	0	0	0	3	4	0	0	1	8	1	0	.167	.304
Court, Ryan	R-R	6-2	210	5-28-88	.396	.464	.372	29	106	22	42	14	0	2	19	16	2	0	2	26	2	2	.585	.476
Drury, Brandon	R-R	6-2	190	8-21-92	.302	.322	.295	134	526	78	159	51	4	15	85	47	5	0	5	92	1	1	.500	.362
Flores, Rudy	L-R	6-3	205	12-12-90	.274	.237	.289	92	343	43	94	24	3	19	64	31	3	0	3	134	0	2	.528	.337
Freeman, Ronnie	R-R	6-1	195	1-8-91	.238	.227	.241	23	80	6	19	4	0	2	10	7	3	0	0	12	0	0	.363	.322
Glenn, Alex	L-L	5-11	175	6-11-91	.257	.275	.251	106	358	66	92	18	6	11	48	48	7	2	5	85	14	2	.433	.352
Hall, Frazier	L-R	6-4	220	6-3-88	.195	.167	.200	25	82	6	16	3	0	0	8	6	2	0	0	22	0	0	.232	.267
Lang, Michael	R-R	5-11	185	1-13-89	.263	.264	.262	87	293	36	77	13	7	5	22	19	9	4	1	69	7	5	.406	.326
Medrano, Kevin	L-R	6-1	155	5-21-90	.297	.289	.299	45	172	30	51	11	3	0	15	24	5	3	1	32	4	4	.395	.396
Pena, Fidel	R-R	5-10	180	7-19-91	.256	.238	.263	129	540	73	138	33	6	10	75	29	5	3	8	93	18	7	.394	.296
Perez, Michael	L-R	5-11	180	8-7-92	.247	.213	.261	46	162	20	40	12	2	2	14	14	0	0	2	55	0	0	.383	.303
Rodriguez, Steven	L-R	6-1	200	1-8-90	.216	.200	.220	16	51	5	11	2	0	0	3	4	0	0	1	8	0	0	.255	.268
Ruiz, Pedro	B-R	5-11	165	8-30-91	.225	.193	.238	86	276	33	62	9	3	1	26	30	3	2	3	78	2	1	.290	.304
Velazquez, Andrew	B-R	5-8	175	7-14-94	.260	.222	.273	65	235	23	61	10	4	0	16	21	0	0	1	59	7	2	.336	.319
Williams, Justin	L-R	6-2	215	8-20-95	.111	.000	.333	3	9	3	1	0	0	0	0	2	0	0	0	2	0	0	.111	.273

Pitching	B-T	HT	WT	DOB	W	L	ERA	G	GS	CG	SV	IP	H	R	ER	HR	BB	SO	AVG	vLH	vRH	K/9	BB/9
Allen, Brad	L-R	6-4	220	3-26-89	7	6	4.37	20	18	2	0	113	91	57	55	11	31	96	.217	.224	.213	7.62	2.46
Blair, Aaron	R-R	6-5	230	5-26-92	0	2	3.57	3	3	0	0	18	19	10	7	0	4	13	.279	.474	.204	6.62	2.04
Bradley, J.R.	R-R	6-3	185	6-9-92	2	4	7.51	23	2	0	0	38	48	36	32	1	23	30	.300	.351	.272	7.04	5.40
Brendel, Thomas	R-R	6-2	190	5-19-88	6	1	2.98	49	0	0	1	57	44	26	19	2	25	43	.211	.224	.203	6.75	3.92
Burgos, Enrique	R-R	6-4	200	11-23-90	2	2	3.88	49	0	0	17	46	29	23	20	1	49	50	.179	.133	.206	9.71	9.52
Camacho, Yiomar	R-R	6-1	172	2-24-90	0	0	4.61	7	0	0	0	14	12	7	7	0	8	9	.235	.333	.167	5.93	5.27
Capper, Chris	R-R	6-1	203	2-5-91	3	2	2.98	27	0	0	1	42	37	15	14	2	16	27	.240	.241	.240	5.74	3.40
Coe, Robert	R-R	6-1	175	1-4-88	3	1	3.12	12	11	1	0	69	63	27	24	5	18	52	.233	.236	.231	6.75	2.34
Darrah, Jesse	L-R	6-2	190	3-28-90	12	9	3.69	27	27	0	0	151	146	75	62	12	59	101	.250	.274	.231	6.01	3.51
Garcia, Henry	L-L	6-1	170	6-15-90	7	2	2.25	35	0	0	0	60	47	17	15	2	10	63	.214	.253	.193	9.45	1.50
Gibson, Daniel	R-L	6-2	219	10-16-91	0	1	1.08	6	0	0	0	8	6	1	1	0	2	5	.214	.333	.182	5.40	2.16
Green, Tyler	R-R	6-1	185	11-24-91	0	0	5.30	15	0	0	0	19	24	11	11	2	11	18	.308	.414	.245	8.31	5.30
Hively, R.J.	R-R	6-2	205	11-27-88	1	0	1.23	27	0	0	19	29	20	6	4	0	12	30	.187	.122	.227	9.20	3.68
Jeter, Bud	R-R	6-3	205	10-27-91	0	0	9.00	1	0	0	0	1	2	1	1	0	0	0	.400	.000	.500	0.00	0.00
Jose, Jose	L-L	6-2	175	7-21-90	0	1	5.28	16	0	0	5	15	19	10	9	2	7	15	.317	.313	.318	8.80	4.11
Locante, Will	L-L	6-1	190	2-2-90	0	1	5.50	18	0	0	0	18	18	12	11	0	13	21	.265	.346	.214	10.50	6.50
Parra, Geordy	R-R	6-2	165	9-6-93	0	0	0.00	4	0	0	0	4	3	1	0	0	1	4	.200	.000	.273	8.31	2.08
Perry, Blake	R-R	6-5	190	2-3-92	8	7	4.49	26	21	0	1	112	107	71	56	7	67	85	.247	.271	.229	6.81	5.37
Sample, Mat	R-R	6-5	200	8-16-88	0	0	20.25	3	0	0	0	1	2	3	3	0	6	1	.333	1.000	.000	6.75	40.50
Santana, Frank	R-R	6-2	200	2-21-89	4	1	2.20	11	0	0	0	16	14	6	4	1	4	16	.226	.296	.171	8.82	2.20
Schepel, Kyle	L-R	6-1	230	8-7-90	4	3	4.12	18	8	1	0	55	44	26	25	7	30	42	.220	.182	.244	6.91	4.94
Sherfy, Jimmie	R-R	5-10	160	12-27-91	1	1	2.16	9	0	0	2	8	10	2	2	0	3	12	.286	.250	.304	12.96	3.24
Shipley, Braden	R-R	6-3	190	2-22-92	0	1	2.61	4	4	0	0	21	14	6	6	2	8	16	.194	.241	.163	6.97	3.48
Siemens, Taylor	L-L	6-5	200	7-1-89	0	0	9.00	1	1	0	0	1	1	1	1	0	0	0	.250	—	.250	0.00	9.00
Sinnery, Brandon	R-R	6-4	170	1-26-90	7	4	3.04	17	15	2	1	104	95	39	35	9	16	67	.240	.225	.251	5.82	1.39
Watts, Daniel	L-L	6-3	190	10-26-89	10	4	3.18	17	17	0	0	108	94	43	38	7	29	77	.226	.228	.239	6.44	2.42
Wheeler, Cody	L-L	5-11	160	8-19-89	1	0	2.29	4	0	0	0	20	11	5	5	0	11	25	.175	.192	.162	11.44	5.03
Winkler, Kyle	R-R	5-11	195	6-18-90	3	4	3.99	21	9	0	0	70	73	39	31	3	20	69	.264	.265	.263	8.87	2.57

Fielding

Catcher	PCT	G	PO	A	E	DP	PB
Aguila	.984	68	428	57	8	2	10
Freeman	.984	22	167	17	3	1	4
Perez	.997	39	271	28	1	2	6
Rodriguez	.983	16	104	10	2	0	1

First Base	PCT	G	PO	A	E	DP
Aguila	1.000	2	9	0	0	0
Bell	.990	37	280	25	3	22
Carrasco	1.000	2	10	3	0	0
Court	.965	15	128	10	5	8
Flores	.989	71	571	43	7	36
Hall	.989	20	166	13	2	14

Second Base	PCT	G	PO	A	E	DP
Medrano	1.000	19	31	54	0	11
Pena	.982	96	185	254	8	42
Ruiz	1.000	10	18	24	0	3
Velazquez	.964	14	24	29	2	4

Third Base	PCT	G	PO	A	E	DP
Bell	.968	23	16	45	2	3
Carrasco	.900	4	2	7	1	0
Court	.944	6	4	13	1	1
Drury	.959	108	82	224	13	17

Shortstop	PCT	G	PO	A	E	DP
Medrano	.960	16	26	46	3	9
Ruiz	.925	75	109	213	26	30
Velazquez	.934	48	77	107	13	15

Outfield	PCT	G	PO	A	E	DP
Almadova	.983	115	272	11	5	1
Brito	.948	129	260	12	15	2
Glenn	.985	102	196	3	3	0
Lang	.987	71	147	4	2	0
Williams	1.000	2	9	0	0	0

HILLSBORO HOPS · SHORT-SEASON

NORTHWEST LEAGUE

Batting	B-T	HT	WT	DOB	AVG	vLH	vRH	G	AB	R	H	2B	3B	HR	RBI	BB	HBP	SH	SF	SO	SB	CS	SLG	OBP
Bianco, Justin	L-R	5-11	195	8-24-92	.250	.200	.286	3	12	1	3	1	0	0	2	0	0	0	0	6	0	1	.333	.357
Billigen, Brian	R-R	6-0	170	5-11-90	.218	.289	.200	56	188	25	41	10	3	2	21	15	10	2	1	50	4	1	.335	.308
Carrasco, Cesar	R-R	6-2	185	10-3-93	.235	.417	.176	26	98	9	23	3	0	0	6	9	1	0	2	16	0	0	.265	.300
Castillo, William	R-R	5-10	158	7-11-92	.140	.000	.163	21	50	1	7	2	0	0	3	4	0	3	0	16	0	1	.180	.204
Chavez, Denver	B-R	5-8	170	4-20-90	.240	.500	.190	8	25	1	6	3	0	0	7	2	1	1	0	9	2	0	.360	.321
Esquerra, Zach	R-R	6-4	215	12-3-90	.283	.341	.264	46	184	22	52	10	3	8	33	15	3	0	0	62	1	0	.500	.347
Gebhardt, Ryan	R-R	5-10	185	10-5-91	.258	.292	.246	69	252	22	65	13	1	0	19	18	2	4	4	27	5	5	.317	.308
Gutierrez, Yosbel	R-R	5-10	170	1-20-93	.216	.133	.242	34	125	24	27	8	2	1	15	5	5	1	2	34	3	0	.336	.270
Kinsella, Ryan	L-R	6-1	215	3-19-92	.239	.182	.257	30	92	7	22	8	0	1	5	13	1	0	2	29	0	0	.359	.333
Leonard, John	R-R	6-0	159	6-25-92	.168	.114	.200	33	95	7	16	1	1	0	3	9	0	4	1	25	0	2	.200	.238
Linton, Ty	R-R	6-3	195	1-17-91	.213	.095	.259	22	75	7	16	1	0	3	11	5	1	0	1	27	0	0	.347	.268
McCurry, Randy	R-R	6-1	200	1-7-90	.216	.190	.223	55	199	13	43	7	0	0	21	15	1	3	4	37	0	1	.251	.269
Nelson, Grant	R-R	6-1	215	9-8-91	.146	.083	.172	13	41	4	6	0	0	0	3	6	0	0	0	14	0	0	.146	.255
Palka, Daniel	L-L	6-2	220	10-28-91	.340	.333	.341	12	47	10	16	1	2	2	10	7	0	0	1	16	1	0	.574	.418
Parr, Jordan	R-R	6-2	190	11-29-90	.226	.286	.205	46	159	18	36	8	2	2	18	18	2	2	1	32	10	1	.340	.311
Parr, Josh	R-R	5-11	170	9-11-89	.266	.308	.255	19	64	9	17	3	1	2	7	10	1	1	0	14	5	1	.438	.373
Perez-Ramos, Yogey	L-L	6-3	197	10-29-88	.314	.353	.305	67	261	35	82	16	3	0	24	25	5	3	2	39	15	4	.398	.382
Ratliff, Taylor	L-R	6-2	170	6-25-92	.213	.209	.214	59	216	35	46	5	0	0	7	34	3	4	0	56	21	3	.236	.328
Roberts, George	R-R	6-0	210	4-17-90	.251	.327	.227	57	215	34	54	8	1	7	33	17	8	2	2	50	3	0	.395	.326
Soto, Elvin	B-R	5-11	195	2-12-92	.209	.143	.229	45	153	12	32	9	1	1	7	15	2	3	0	41	3	0	.301	.288

Pitching	B-T	HT	WT	DOB	W	L	ERA	G	GS	CG	SV	IP	H	R	ER	HR	BB	SO	AVG	vLH	vRH	K/9	BB/9
Blair, Aaron	R-R	6-5	230	5-26-92	1	1	2.90	8	8	0	0	31	25	10	10	2	13	28	.225	.145	.304	8.13	3.77
Bradley, J.R.	R-R	6-3	185	6-9-92	2	2	2.38	15	0	0	0	23	21	10	6	0	12	24	.244	.233	.256	9.53	4.76
Byo, Alex	R-R	6-2	205	9-2-90	0	1	9.82	5	0	0	0	7	16	9	8	0	6	7	.444	.471	.421	8.59	7.36
Camacho, Yiomar	R-R	6-1	172	2-24-90	3	3	2.36	14	1	0	1	27	20	11	7	1	14	26	.208	.244	.176	8.78	4.73
Carreras, Alexander	L-L	6-1	200	1-9-90	0	1	4.82	6	0	0	0	9	5	5	5	0	7	5	.222	.167	.250	4.82	6.75
Doran, Ryan	R-R	6-1	180	8-5-90	2	0	2.18	3	3	0	0	21	23	5	5	0	3	21	.284	.351	.227	9.15	1.31
Eckels, Ben	R-R	6-0	175	1-27-91	6	6	3.12	15	13	0	0	84	65	35	29	2	40	60	.218	.250	.187	6.45	4.30
Forslund, Blake	R-R	6-4	215	2-16-90	1	2	3.98	11	1	0	0	32	23	16	14	2	23	24	.211	.288	.120	6.82	4.83
Gerdeman, Ross	R-R	6-3	210	11-7-89	3	7	3.56	15	13	1	0	94	88	39	37	4	26	59	.257	.288	.232	5.67	2.50
Gibson, Daniel	R-L	6-2	219	10-16-91	1	0	0.45	14	0	0	3	20	17	5	1	0	8	22	.227	.292	.196	9.90	3.60
Jose, Jose	L-L	6-2	175	7-21-90	0	0	0.00	6	0	0	3	6	1	0	0	0	5	10	.053	.167	.000	14.21	7.11
Locante, Will	L-L	6-1	190	2-2-90	3	1	2.25	21	0	0	1	24	18	13	6	0	18	33	.200	.094	.259	12.38	6.75
Martinez, Jose	R-R	6-1	160	4-14-94	2	3	4.03	10	10	0	0	38	20	20	17	3	25	30	.159	.136	.171	7.11	5.92
Platt, Austin	R-R	6-3	190	3-5-92	4	3	2.62	15	7	1	0	79	71	40	23	5	40	53	.235	.213	.253	6.04	4.56
Pulley, Jonathan	R-R	6-2	215	5-20-93	0	4	3.68	7	5	0	0	29	29	19	12	1	8	17	.259	.260	.258	5.22	2.45
Schepel, Kyle	L-R	6-1	230	8-7-90	1	0	2.84	4	4	1	0	25	19	8	8	0	10	23	.204	.171	.231	8.17	3.55
Sherfy, Jimmie	R-R	5-10	160	12-27-91	0	0	0.00	9	0	0	5	9	3	0	0	1	17	.100	.111	.083	17.00	1.00
Shipley, Braden	R-R	6-3	190	2-21-92	0	2	7.58	8	8	0	0	19	30	18	16	1	6	24	.357	.447	.283	11.37	2.84
Shuttlesworth, Johnny	R-R	6-1	220	9-30-89	3	1	2.01	18	0	0	1	22	16	5	5	1	3	21	.205	.167	.238	8.46	1.21
Smith, Patrick	R-R	6-2	170	1-29-90	1	1	3.34	20	0	0	0	30	36	18	11	1	11	28	.293	.180	.370	8.49	3.34
Stevens, Chase	R-R	5-10	186	8-15-90	0	2	5.51	20	0	0	0	33	36	21	20	2	20	45	.279	.291	.270	12.40	5.51
Triana, Karl	R-R	6-0	180	10-7-92	1	1	4.60	4	3	0	0	16	21	9	8	2	5	11	.344	.259	.412	6.32	2.87
Weller, Blayne	R-R	6-5	220	1-30-90	0	1	2.57	7	0	0	3	7	4	2	2	0	7	8	.160	.000	.211	10.29	9.00

Fielding

Catcher	PCT	G	PO	A	E	DP	PB
Gutierrez	.989	31	227	37	3	3	5
Nelson	.989	10	74	15	1	2	4
Soto	.985	36	273	46	5	3	10

First Base	PCT	G	PO	A	E	DP
Carrasco	1.000	2	16	3	0	3
Kinsella	.986	15	127	10	2	14
Mateo	1.000	9	76	2	0	7
Palka	.980	10	92	6	2	8

Roberts	.987	43	429	42	6	33

Second Base	PCT	G	PO	A	E	DP
Castillo	.935	18	20	52	5	6
Chavez	.970	7	11	21	1	8
Gebhardt	1.000	1	1	1	0	0
Leonard	1.000	28	52	87	0	18
McCurry	.988	17	30	51	1	8
Parr	.935	12	17	26	3	7

Third Base	PCT	G	PO	A	E	DP
Carrasco	.898	20	12	32	5	1
McCurry	.934	37	24	89	8	13
Parr	.750	15	3	15	6	5
Roberts	1.000	5	4	14	0	1

Shortstop	PCT	G	PO	A	E	DP
Gebhardt	.943	68	107	190	18	40
Leonard	.900	4	5	4	1	1
Parr	.867	6	14	11	0	3

Outfield	PCT	G	PO	A	E	DP
Bianco	1.000	3	5	1	0	0
Billigen	.976	54	80	3	2	1
Esquerra	1.000	39	49	2	0	0
Linton	1.000	6	8	0	0	0
McCurry	—	1	0	0	0	0
Parr	.973	25	36	0	1	0
Perez-Ramos	.960	55	90	7	4	0
Ratliff	.991	57	108	6	1	3

AZL DIAMONDBACKS — *ROOKIE*

ARIZONA LEAGUE

Batting	B-T	HT	WT	DOB	AVG	vLH	vRH	G	AB	R	H	2B	3B	HR	RBI	BB	HBP	SH	SF	SO	SB	CS	SLG	OBP
Alcantara, Sergio	B-R	5-10	150	7-10-96	.243	.232	.248	48	169	31	41	5	4	0	16	44	1	2	2	36	3	2	.320	.398
Bloomquist, Willie	R-R	5-11	190	11-27-77	.500	.000	.667	4	12	4	6	1	0	0	1	2	0	0	0	1	0	0	.583	.571
Carrasco, Cesar	R-R	6-2	185	10-3-93	.312	.259	.340	19	77	8	24	4	1	1	6	7	0	0	1	13	0	1	.429	.365
Castillo, Henry	B-R	6-0	180	12-8-94	.313	.400	.273	8	32	3	10	2	0	0	3	1	0	1	0	7	0	0	.375	.333
Chavez, Eric	L-R	6-1	215	12-7-77	.143	.000	.167	3	7	1	1	0	0	1	2	0	0	0	1	0	0	0	.571	.125
Cordero, Jacob	R-R	5-10	174	11-14-94	.259	.273	.250	43	174	20	45	5	3	1	16	12	1	2	3	39	6	8	.339	.305
Eaton, Adam	L-L	5-8	185	12-6-88	.500	.000	.500	1	2	1	1	0	0	0	2	1	1	0	1	1	0	0	.500	.600
Garcia, Raul	R-R	6-0	159	12-14-94	.170	.179	.164	29	94	6	16	1	0	0	5	9	2	0	1	41	0	0	.181	.255
Herum, Marty	R-R	6-3	215	12-16-91	.268	.278	.263	17	56	6	15	2	0	0	8	9	0	0	0	13	1	0	.304	.369
Lamb, Jake	L-R	6-2	200	10-9-90	.294	.125	.444	5	17	4	5	2	0	0	5	2	1	0	1	5	0	0	.412	.381
Llewellyn, Phildrick	B-R	6-1	205	9-25-93	.194	.235	.167	35	129	18	25	5	2	1	8	12	0	3	2	35	3	1	.287	.259
Lopez, B.J.	R-R	5-9	185	9-29-94	.255	.171	.305	31	94	15	24	4	1	0	10	18	1	0	0	29	0	0	.319	.381
McFarland, Dane	R-R	6-4	210	10-24-94	.167	.250	.115	43	156	16	26	5	0	0	12	15	4	0	1	68	4	3	.199	.256
McPhearson, Matt	L-L	5-8	164	4-18-95	.200	.143	.221	42	130	20	26	3	1	0	7	21	0	1	0	45	15	3	.238	.311
Mejias, Ronny	B-R	6-0	170	5-9-94	.198	.250	.180	29	81	18	16	4	3	0	7	9	0	0	2	22	0	0	.321	.272
Montero, Miguel	L-R	5-11	210	7-9-83	.263	.000	.313	6	19	2	5	2	0	0	4	4	0	0	0	4	0	0	.368	.391
Ozuna, Fernery	B-R	5-8	165	11-9-95	.351	.250	.400	10	37	6	13	2	1	0	9	1	1	0	1	7	1	0	.459	.375
Roberts, George	R-R	6-0	210	4-17-90	.300	.000	.375	3	10	2	3	1	1	0	2	2	0	0	0	1	0	0	.600	.417
Rosario, Yeisson	L-L	6-0	185	9-20-92	.238	.235	.239	28	105	12	25	2	3	3	16	14	2	0	0	28	1	1	.400	.339
Smith, Damion	L-R	6-3	170	2-14-94	.159	.143	.170	31	88	9	14	0	1	1	6	11	1	0	1	36	2	0	.216	.257
Thys, Joel	L-R	6-2	210	11-27-90	.208	.111	.267	20	48	2	10	1	0	0	5	3	0	1	0	4	0	0	.229	.255
Vinson, Matt	R-R	6-2	200	10-16-90	.196	.105	.243	18	56	10	11	6	1	1	10	6	2	0	0	20	6	0	.393	.297
Westbrook, Jamie	R-R	5-9	170	6-18-95	.292	.370	.250	40	154	31	45	8	8	1	20	17	4	0	2	21	3	3	.468	.373
Williams, Justin	L-R	6-2	215	8-20-95	.345	.231	.406	37	148	17	51	12	0	1	32	8	5	0	0	35	0	1	.446	.398

Pitching	B-T	HT	WT	DOB	W	L	ERA	G	GS	CG	SV	IP	H	R	ER	HR	BB	SO	AVG	vLH	vRH	K/9	BB/9
Benitez, Anfernee	L-L	6-1	176	7-24-95	3	4	3.74	13	12	0	1	55	56	29	23	3	32	50	.264	.162	.286	8.13	5.20
Byo, Alex	R-R	6-2	205	9-2-90	1	0	2.66	12	0	0	0	24	18	10	7	2	11	27	.212	.194	.222	10.27	4.18
Cahill, Trevor	R-R	6-4	220	3-1-88	0	0	0.00	1	1	0	0	5	1	1	0	0	2	9	.063	.000	.091	16.20	3.60
Doran, Ryan	R-R	6-1	180	8-5-90	3	2	3.36	10	9	0	0	56	54	25	21	4	6	64	.257	.238	.270	10.22	0.96
Forslund, Blake	R-R	6-4	215	2-16-90	0	0	1.50	4	0	0	0	12	10	4	2	0	0	14	.213	.286	.154	10.50	0.00
Furney, Sean	R-R	6-5	220	6-2-91	1	4	2.25	15	5	0	0	52	48	17	13	1	13	64	.241	.259	.234	11.08	2.25
Gonzalez, Jose	R-R	6-2	195	12-17-92	3	2	9.56	8	2	0	1	16	24	19	17	1	18	16	.333	.421	.302	9.00	10.13
Greer, Brody	R-R	6-1	190	5-15-91	1	0	1.64	7	0	0	0	11	6	3	2	0	6	11	.167	.063	.250	9.00	4.91
Hernandez, Luis	R-R	6-2	187	6-22-92	0	1	15.34	14	0	0	0	15	18	29	25	1	39	9	.316	.235	.350	5.52	23.93
Hillier, Bobby	R-R	6-2	205	11-20-89	1	0	3.86	6	0	0	0	12	10	7	5	0	4	14	.222	.273	.174	10.80	3.09
Jameson, Tom	R-R	6-7	245	8-4-91	1	0	0.00	5	0	0	1	9	3	0	0	0	1	13	.103	.143	.067	13.50	1.04
Jeter, Bud	R-R	6-3	205	10-27-91	3	0	0.68	8	0	0	1	13	8	1	1	0	2	16	.186	.105	.250	10.80	1.35
Keller, Brad	R-R	6-5	230	7-27-95	7	3	2.22	13	12	0	0	57	53	22	14	2	26	61	.250	.255	.245	9.69	4.13
Kostuk, Kurtis	L-R	6-2	200	9-8-95	0	3	5.91	12	6	0	0	35	45	30	23	2	18	34	.304	.220	.360	8.74	4.63
Mateo, Wagner	L-L	6-2	190	3-30-93	0	0	10.13	8	0	0	0	8	8	9	9	0	10	8	.267	.333	.250	9.00	11.25
Newton, Dallas	L-R	6-5	215	9-3-94	1	6	5.64	14	8	0	0	53	74	46	33	3	16	39	.322	.294	.344	6.66	2.73
Solis, Jency	R-R	6-1	180	2-22-93	0	2	3.26	13	0	0	0	19	20	10	7	0	1	12	.260	.226	.283	5.59	0.47
Toyfair, Tyler	R-R	6-5	230	4-12-90	0	0	3.00	12	0	0	4	15	10	5	5	0	1	19	.182	.118	.211	11.40	0.60
Van Grouw, Justin	R-R	6-7	225	9-7-90	3	0	3.58	13	1	0	3	28	23	11	11	2	5	38	.217	.179	.239	12.36	1.63

Fielding

Catcher	PCT	G	PO	A	E	DP	PB
Llewellyn	.989	15	154	20	2	1	2
Lopez	.990	31	262	44	3	1	12
Montero	.962	4	24	1	1	0	3
Thys	1.000	13	73	9	0	0	2

First Base	PCT	G	PO	A	E	DP
Carrasco	1.000	13	116	6	0	8
Herum	.990	12	92	4	1	9
Llewellyn	.988	18	148	13	2	8
Mejias	1.000	8	74	2	0	4
Roberts	1.000	3	26	3	0	3
Rosario	.962	4	46	4	2	6
Thys	1.000	1	1	0	0	1

Second Base	PCT	G	PO	A	E	DP
Castillo	.848	7	8	20	5	5
Cordero	.940	14	23	40	4	8
Mejias	1.000	3	3	6	0	1
Ozuna	1.000	5	7	6	0	2
Westbrook	.922	30	49	93	12	16

Third Base	PCT	G	PO	A	E	DP
Carrasco	.786	5	1	10	3	0
Chavez	1.000	1	1	2	0	0
Cordero	.900	18	10	44	6	3
Garcia	.784	16	10	30	11	4
Herum	.875	3	2	5	1	0
Lamb	.778	4	1	6	2	0
Mejias	.900	15	5	13	2	0

Shortstop	PCT	G	PO	A	E	DP
Alcantara	.925	47	66	131	16	28
Bloomquist	1.000	3	4	5	0	2
Cordero	.875	8	8	20	4	3
Mejias	1.000	1	0	1	0	0
Ozuna	1.000	2	2	4	0	1

Outfield	PCT	G	PO	A	E	DP
McFarland	.968	40	59	2	2	0
McPhearson	.933	41	80	3	6	1
Rosario	.943	22	33	0	2	0
Smith	.912	25	29	2	3	0
Vinson	1.000	17	17	4	0	0
Williams	.875	31	34	1	5	0

MISSOULA OSPREY — ROOKIE

PIONEER LEAGUE

Batting	B-T	HT	WT	DOB	AVG	vLH	vRH	G	AB	R	H	2B	3B	HR	RBI	BB	HBP	SH	SF	SO	SB	CS	SLG	OBP
Alvarez, Antonio	B-R	5-10	195	1-16-92	.222	.320	.193	35	108	20	24	1	1	0	9	28	2	2	0	31	8	2	.250	.391
Bianco, Justin	L-R	5-11	195	8-24-92	.232	.321	.206	36	125	12	29	9	0	0	17	11	0	1	0	42	8	4	.304	.294
Bolivar, Anderso	B-R	5-11	165	9-9-92	.228	.286	.211	26	92	12	21	6	0	1	6	5	2	0	0	14	0	0	.326	.283
Bray, Colin	B-L	6-4	205	6-18-93	.276	.286	.273	64	268	43	74	10	2	4	29	26	2	4	3	62	15	9	.373	.341
Chavez, Denver	B-R	5-8	170	4-20-90	.185	.083	.208	20	65	7	12	0	3	0	4	7	3	2	0	12	0	2	.277	.293
Garcia, Yorman	R-R	6-1	175	3-17-94	.228	.152	.250	45	149	18	34	13	0	0	16	17	1	2	1	38	5	2	.315	.310
Kinsella, Ryan	L-R	6-1	215	3-19-92	.293	.111	.344	13	41	9	12	2	2	0	9	10	0	0	0	9	0	0	.439	.431
Linton, Ty	R-R	6-3	195	1-17-91	.171	.091	.200	12	41	8	7	1	0	0	6	2	2	0	0	15	0	0	.195	.244
Mayers, Jacob	R-R	6-2	215	8-8-90	.302	.256	.313	58	215	30	65	16	2	3	41	17	2	0	4	47	1	0	.437	.353
Miller, Jake	R-R	6-2	175	9-26-90	.238	.255	.232	52	185	33	44	7	2	6	31	21	1	4	2	45	4	2	.395	.316
Munoz, Joe	R-R	6-3	195	12-28-93	.263	.257	.264	54	194	32	51	12	3	6	30	20	4	0	1	61	5	0	.448	.342
Nelson, Grant	R-R	6-1	215	9-8-91	.300	.000	.300	7	20	6	6	0	0	1	3	5	0	0	0	4	0	0	.450	.440
Palka, Daniel	L-L	6-2	220	10-28-91	.302	.279	.309	56	205	36	62	20	0	7	38	29	2	0	5	45	2	2	.502	.398
Poma, Danny	R-R	6-1	200	2-23-89	.357	1.000	.308	4	14	2	5	0	0	0	2	0	1	0	0	2	1	0	.357	.400
Queliz, Jose	R-R	6-3	200	8-7-92	.290	.286	.291	49	200	28	58	15	1	4	38	10	0	0	3	38	1	0	.435	.319
Taylor, Chuck	B-L	5-9	185	9-21-93	.291	.294	.290	60	220	38	64	12	3	3	25	28	7	0	2	47	3	5	.414	.385
Trahan, Stryker	L-R	6-1	215	4-25-94	.254	.333	.237	59	236	44	60	15	2	10	33	24	2	0	0	57	1	0	.462	.328
Vinson, Matt	R-R	6-2	200	10-16-90	.000	.000	.000	2	5	0	0	0	0	0	0	2	0	0	0	3	0	0	.000	.286
Westbrook, Jamie	R-R	5-9	170	6-18-95	.254	.444	.224	17	67	12	17	3	0	1	13	6	0	0	0	20	1	0	.343	.315
Williams, Justin	L-R	6-2	215	8-20-95	.412	.250	.426	11	51	12	21	6	0	0	5	1	0	0	0	7	0	0	.529	.423

Pitching	B-T	HT	WT	DOB	W	L	ERA	G	GS	CG	SV	IP	H	R	ER	HR	BB	SO	AVG	vLH	vRH	K/9	BB/9
Blake, Michael	L-L	5-11	190	8-4-90	1	1	3.92	11	0	0	0	21	15	11	9	0	14	27	.200	.200	.200	11.76	6.10
Bracho, Silvino	R-R	5-11	179	7-17-92	0	2	1.71	24	0	0	11	26	23	6	5	2	3	38	.228	.229	.227	12.99	1.03
Buller, Robbie	R-R	6-6	230	10-21-89	0	0	3.97	6	0	0	0	11	9	5	5	2	3	11	.220	.222	.219	8.74	2.38
Furney, Sean	R-R	6-5	220	6-2-91	0	1	9.00	1	0	0	0	3	5	4	3	0	2	0	.385	.571	.167	0.00	6.00
Geyer, Cody	R-R	5-11	215	5-4-92	0	1	5.26	23	0	0	0	26	32	22	15	2	14	15	.317	.289	.333	5.26	4.91
Guzman, Francisco	L-L	6-5	190	7-2-89	0	0	6.23	4	0	0	0	4	2	3	3	0	5	4	.133	.000	.182	8.31	10.38
Hathaway, Steve	L-L	6-1	185	9-13-90	0	1	6.14	3	3	0	0	7	8	8	5	2	1	5	.258	.000	.333	6.14	1.23
Hernandez, Carlos	R-R	5-11	170	4-26-94	4	5	5.06	14	14	0	0	69	66	43	39	4	40	63	.259	.242	.268	8.18	5.19
Hillier, Bobby	R-R	6-2	205	11-20-89	0	3	7.89	10	1	0	0	22	30	24	19	3	12	19	.330	.387	.300	7.89	4.98
Jameson, Tom	R-R	6-7	245	8-4-91	3	0	4.00	9	4	0	1	36	33	21	16	4	12	20	.243	.254	.253	5.00	3.00
Jeter, Bud	R-R	6-3	205	10-27-91	2	3	9.64	6	3	0	0	19	39	22	20	3	9	9	.424	.440	.418	4.34	4.34
Jose, Jose	L-L	6-2	175	7-21-90	0	0	0.00	1	0	0	1	1	1	0	0	0	2	2	.250	—	.250	18.00	0.00
Keller, Brad	R-R	6-5	230	7-27-95	0	0	4.50	2	1	0	0	6	6	3	3	0	4	4	.261	.286	.250	6.00	6.00
Meyerchick, Eric	R-R	6-1	200	2-13-90	1	2	5.45	20	0	0	0	36	49	37	22	3	18	32	.308	.288	.320	7.93	4.46
Miller, Adam	R-R	6-0	185	12-28-89	1	4	4.61	12	9	0	0	53	62	34	27	2	14	35	.291	.406	.236	5.98	2.39
Parra, Geordy	R-R	6-2	165	9-6-93	4	1	0.40	19	0	0	0	23	14	2	1	0	11	35	.167	.280	.119	13.90	4.37
Perez, Felipe	R-R	6-3	190	1-22-94	7	5	4.55	15	14	2	0	89	100	67	45	9	19	50	.283	.345	.255	5.06	1.92
Placido, Anderson	L-L	6-0	190	9-24-93	1	1	5.00	4	4	0	0	18	21	14	10	2	8	17	.300	.381	.265	8.50	4.00
Potter, Andrew	R-R	6-0	208	2-9-94	2	2	6.43	11	8	0	0	49	63	42	35	5	23	41	.315	.274	.339	7.53	4.22
Solis, Jency	R-R	6-1	180	2-22-93	0	1	8.78	9	0	0	1	13	17	15	13	1	4	11	.304	.217	.364	7.43	2.70
Toyfair, Tyler	R-R	6-5	230	4-12-90	1	1	4.26	8	0	0	0	19	19	14	9	1	7	17	.247	.355	.174	8.05	3.32
Triana, Karl	R-R	6-0	180	10-7-92	0	1	5.68	2	1	0	0	6	4	4	1	0	3	2	.240	.500	.190	4.26	0.00
Van Grouw, Justin	R-R	6-7	225	9-7-90	0	2	5.29	5	2	0	0	17	21	13	10	1	5	9	.318	.280	.341	4.76	2.65
Weller, Blayne	R-R	6-5	220	1-30-90	3	5	4.64	10	9	0	0	52	60	34	27	4	17	52	.280	.321	.267	8.94	2.92

Fielding

Catcher	PCT	G	PO	A	E	DP	PB
Nelson	1.000	5	27	10	0	0	2
Queliz	.962	25	177	25	8	1	7
Trahan	.969	44	293	51	11	3	17

First Base	PCT	G	PO	A	E	DP
Kinsella	.989	12	83	8	1	8
Mateo	.971	3	31	3	1	5
Mayers	.974	16	138	10	4	9
Palka	.987	45	431	19	6	36

Second Base	PCT	G	PO	A	E	DP
Alvarez	.958	32	58	102	7	21
Chavez	.964	20	33	47	3	8

	PCT	G	PO	A	E	DP
Miller	.889	5	10	14	3	5
Westbrook	.949	17	22	53	4	9

Third Base	PCT	G	PO	A	E	DP
Alvarez	.900	2	6	3	1	1
Bolivar	.935	12	10	19	2	3
Mayers	.897	36	32	72	12	1
Miller	.886	25	19	51	9	3

Shortstop	PCT	G	PO	A	E	DP
Alvarez	1.000	1	0	2	0	0
Miller	.934	22	20	65	6	13
Munoz	.929	53	98	177	21	36

Outfield	PCT	G	PO	A	E	DP
Bianco	.965	34	50	5	2	2
Bolivar	1.000	6	16	0	0	0
Bray	.974	62	144	6	4	1
Garcia	.938	44	72	4	5	0
Linton	1.000	10	14	0	0	0
Poma	1.000	4	6	0	0	0
Taylor	.975	56	77	2	2	1
Vinson	1.000	2	6	1	0	1
Williams	.818	10	7	2	2	0

DSL DIAMONDBACKS — ROOKIE

DOMINICAN SUMMER LEAGUE

Batting	B-T	HT	WT	DOB	AVG	vLH	vRH	G	AB	R	H	2B	3B	HR	RBI	BB	HBP	SH	SF	SO	SB	CS	SLG	OBP
Alcantara, Frankies	R-R	6-1	190	8-23-95	.215	.111	.233	35	121	11	26	3	1	0	7	4	7	0	0	48	1	3	.256	.280
Castillo, Henry	B-R	6-0	180	12-8-94	.288	.206	.306	51	191	33	55	7	4	1	23	21	3	1	2	39	11	5	.382	.364
De Leon, Jose	R-R	6-2	160	8-9-95	.143	.143	.143	8	28	1	4	0	0	0	1	1	0	0	0	7	2	2	.143	.172
De Oleo, Jesus	R-R	6-0	180	3-27-95	.145	.300	.123	30	83	12	12	1	2	0	3	19	1	0	0	30	7	2	.205	.311
Garcia, Oswaldo	R-R	6-3	210	11-28-95	.227	.152	.245	48	176	34	40	6	2	1	19	28	0	0	0	30	6	4	.301	.333

Name	B-T	HT	WT	DOB	AVG	vLH	vRH	G	AB	R	H	2B	3B	HR	RBI	BB	HBP	SH	SF	SO	SB	CS	OBP	SLG
Graciano, Vicson	R-R	6-1	155	11-23-95	.300	.250	.313	43	140	16	42	6	1	0	21	26	1	1	2	29	3	2	.357	.408
Jimenez, Gerson	R-R	6-1	200	12-2-94	.258	.222	.266	50	151	20	39	6	1	1	16	27	8	0	6	39	5	4	.331	.385
Martinez, Gregory	R-R	6-1	190	12-5-95	.286	.000	.333	11	21	2	6	1	0	0	4	8	0	0	0	8	1	3	.333	.483
Mejias, Ronny	B-R	6-0	170	5-9-94	.267	.500	.231	3	15	2	4	0	2	0	6	0	0	0	0	1	1	0	.533	.267
Ordaz, Jose	L-L	6-1	170	8-11-96	.198	.143	.214	44	126	17	25	4	1	0	8	7	4	0	0	26	13	3	.246	.263
Ozuna, Fernery	B-R	5-8	165	11-9-95	.298	.235	.315	40	161	36	48	9	2	2	15	11	8	0	1	36	12	8	.416	.370
Palacio, Robinson	L-R	5-10	175	5-20-95	.261	.286	.250	21	46	2	12	1	0	0	3	4	1	0	0	8	0	0	.283	.333
Pena, Ismael	L-L	6-3	175	12-15-95	.219	.146	.240	59	219	23	48	13	2	1	23	17	1	1	2	43	7	5	.311	.276
Ramos, Eudy	R-R	6-1	195	2-19-96	.191	.261	.172	35	110	11	21	10	0	2	15	23	2	0	2	36	2	5	.336	.336
Rosario, Yeisson	L-L	6-0	185	9-20-92	.289	.333	.284	30	114	15	33	5	4	1	21	11	0	1	2	13	7	2	.430	.346
Samboy, Raul	R-R	5-11	155	9-25-93	.328	.381	.317	38	125	28	41	12	3	3	18	18	4	0	1	24	8	2	.544	.426
Sanchez, Richi	L-R	5-10	185	5-6-94	.338	.308	.346	58	198	43	67	13	4	3	27	49	5	1	0	29	10	4	.490	.480
Santana, Brandon	R-R	6-2	180	10-13-95	.111	.000	.115	12	27	2	3	1	0	0	0	7	0	0	0	12	0	3	.148	.294
Tineo, Frank	R-R	5-11	165	2-7-96	.167	.143	.170	33	60	9	10	1	0	0	2	2	2	0	1	15	3	6	.183	.215
Veras, Luis	R-R	6-1	180	11-4-93	.295	.303	.292	38	146	16	43	9	2	1	21	5	3	0	2	13	9	3	.404	.327

Pitching	B-T	HT	WT	DOB	W	L	ERA	G	GS	CG	SV	IP	H	R	ER	HR	BB	SO	AVG	vLH	vRH	K/9	BB/9
Basora, Anthony	L-L	6-4	203	2-17-95	5	2	2.50	13	13	0	0	76	69	30	21	0	5	61	.242	.444	.221	7.26	0.59
Castillo, Luis	R-R	6-2	180	3-10-95	4	4	3.58	14	14	1	0	70	74	44	28	1	17	60	.262	.237	.269	7.68	2.18
Cespedes, Christian	R-R	6-2	155	12-22-93	1	3	5.04	16	0	0	0	25	20	16	14	0	26	32	.213	.174	.225	11.52	9.36
Felix, Wellinton	R-R	6-1	185	11-25-94	0	0	3.92	15	1	0	0	21	19	11	9	0	13	23	.235	.321	.189	10.02	5.66
Garcia, Willi	R-R	5-11	180	3-14-95	1	5	4.56	17	0	0	2	26	21	17	13	2	10	25	.223	.227	.222	8.77	3.51
Gonzalez, Jose	R-R	6-2	195	12-17-92	1	2	3.48	7	6	0	0	31	26	13	12	0	7	29	.222	.241	.216	8.42	2.03
Montero, Merkis	R-R	6-2	155	12-1-95	3	2	3.70	10	8	0	0	41	44	26	17	2	11	25	.262	.200	.281	5.44	2.40
Moya, Gabriel	L-L	6-0	175	1-9-95	2	1	1.50	19	0	0	6	30	25	14	5	1	5	33	.221	.357	.202	9.90	1.50
Nunez, Anthony	R-R	6-2	180	4-30-95	1	2	2.97	16	1	0	0	30	27	16	10	0	5	13	.235	.250	.230	3.86	1.48
Placido, Anderson	L-L	6-0	190	9-24-93	4	5	2.59	12	11	0	0	66	45	29	19	1	23	83	.199	.146	.211	11.32	3.14
Pujols, Rafael	R-R	6-6	173	8-21-91	1	0	5.96	15	0	0	0	26	34	20	17	1	11	26	.327	.360	.316	9.12	3.86
Ramirez, Yefrey	R-R	6-2	165	11-28-93	0	6	3.00	13	11	0	0	60	56	31	20	2	16	62	.241	.262	.234	9.30	2.40
Rodriguez, Juan	L-L	6-0	185	8-2-92	3	2	4.19	16	0	0	1	19	24	11	9	0	17	17	.320	.273	.328	7.91	7.91
Solis, Jency	R-R	6-1	180	2-22-93	0	0	3.38	1	1	0	0	3	3	3	1	0	1	3	.250	.125	.500	10.13	3.38
Soto, Alvaro	R-R	6-0	165	7-16-94	0	1	3.93	16	1	0	0	18	17	12	8	1	13	24	.254	.133	.288	11.78	6.38
Vargas, Emilio	R-R	6-3	200	8-12-96	1	2	6.35	16	0	0	0	23	28	19	16	1	8	19	.304	.316	.301	7.54	3.18
Velez, Roger	L-L	6-2	192	12-17-94	1	2	2.84	14	1	0	0	32	32	15	10	0	11	28	.269	.385	.255	7.96	3.13

Fielding

Catcher	PCT	G	PO	A	E	DP	PB
Garcia	.978	27	195	31	5	2	5
Martinez	1.000	8	44	4	0	0	1
Palacio	.983	21	108	10	2	0	5
Sanchez	.991	24	196	27	2	0	10

First Base	PCT	G	PO	A	E	DP
Graciano	.978	10	82	9	2	6
Jimenez	.969	22	186	4	6	17
Pena	1.000	20	124	11	0	4
Ramos	1.000	1	7	2	0	1
Rosario	.975	17	145	9	4	10
Santana	.968	10	56	5	2	5

Second Base	PCT	G	PO	A	E	DP
Castillo	.990	23	39	63	1	11
De Leon	.813	3	8	5	3	0
Graciano	.957	5	12	10	1	3
Mejias	1.000	3	3	1	0	0
Ozuna	.943	26	53	62	7	13
Samboy	.333	1	0	1	2	0
Sanchez	.984	14	36	25	1	4

Third Base	PCT	G	PO	A	E	DP
Castillo	.600	3	1	2	2	1
Graciano	.835	27	17	49	13	0
Mejias	.500	1	1	0	1	0
Ramos	.807	34	23	65	21	5
Samboy	.848	11	6	22	5	0

Shortstop	PCT	G	PO	A	E	DP
Castillo	.880	26	30	80	15	13
De Leon	.929	5	7	19	2	3
De Oleo	.907	30	39	58	10	9
Ozuna	.945	17	27	42	4	9

Outfield	PCT	G	PO	A	E	DP
Alcantara	.949	29	33	4	2	0
Jimenez	.976	27	35	6	1	3
Ordaz	.967	39	57	2	2	0
Pena	.988	45	78	3	1	1
Rosario	1.000	13	21	2	0	1
Samboy	1.000	16	18	2	0	0
Tineo	.969	25	28	3	1	0
Veras	1.000	36	56	2	0	0

Atlanta Braves

SEASON IN A SENTENCE: The Braves won the National League East for the first time since 2005, racking up 96 victories behind a young lineup that led the National League in home runs, a resilient pitching rotation and dominant bullpen, but failed to advance in the playoffs by losing their eighth consecutive postseason series.

HIGH POINT: Atlanta entered August on a win streak and wound up stringing together 14 in a row, with victories No. 11, 12 and 13 of the streak coming in Washington to bury the defending NL East champion Nationals. The clincher, a 6-3 victory, included a two-out, none-on, three-run rally in the eighth inning that effectively ended the division race.

LOW POINT: Aside from the playoffs? Any B.J. Upton or Dan Uggla strikeout would qualify. (And there were plenty to pick from.) The Braves' two highest-paid players combined to make more than $25 million and batted a collective .181 with 322 whiffs. Upton's batting average never topped the .200 mark this season and Uggla, an all-star in 2012, was left off Atlanta's postseason roster. And speaking of the postseason, the Braves' high expectations came crashing down again, as the Dodgers' four-game win in the NL Division Series extended a postseason drought that dates back to the 2001 NL Championship Series.

NOTABLE ROOKIES: Former No. 1 prospect Julio Teheran struggled in Triple-A in 2012 but was the Braves' most consistent righthanded starter in 2013, going 14-8, 3.20. Lefty Alex Wood, a second-round pick in 2012, zoomed to Atlanta and contributed both in the bullpen and rotation. Injuries created playing time at catcher and in left field for Evan Gattis, and the 26-year-old rookie was one of five Braves to hit 20 or more homers, though his defense left plenty to be desired.

KEY TRANSACTIONS: The Braves joined the Upton brothers in the offseason, signing B.J. as a free agent and trading for Justin. The better pickup from the Diamondbacks was actually third baseman Chris Johnson, who finished second in the NL with a .321 batting average.

DOWN ON THE FARM: Only Triple-A Gwinnett failed to have a competitive season among Braves affiliates, but the G-Braves contributed a steady stream of players to Atlanta's roster. The top performer was 2012 first-rounder Lucas Sims, who at just 19 years old led the organization's pitchers in wins and ranked second in strikeouts and ERA.

OPENING DAY PAYROLL: $89.8 million (16th)

PLAYERS OF THE YEAR

MAJOR LEAGUE	MINOR LEAGUE
Freddie Freeman	**Lucas Sims**
1b	**rhp**
.319/.396/.501	(Low A)
23 HR, 109 RBIs	12-4, 2.62
Led team in RBIs, OPS	134 SO, 46 BB

ORGANIZATION LEADERS

BATTING *Minimum 250 AB

MAJORS

* AVG	Johnson, Chris	.321
* OPS	Freeman, Freddie	.897
HR	Upton, Justin	27
RBI	Freeman, Freddie	109

MINORS

* AVG	Rohm, David, Lynchburg	.302
* OBP	Kubitza, Kyle, Lynchburg	.380
* SLG	Mejia, Ernesto, Gwinnett	.497
R	Rohm, David, Lynchburg	77
H	Rohm, David, Lynchburg	150
TB	Mejia, Ernesto, Gwinnett	243
2B	Mejia, Ernesto, Gwinnett	35
3B	Marte, Felix, Rome	9
HR	Mejia, Ernesto, Gwinnett	28
RBI	Elander, Josh, Lynchburg/Rome	93
BB	Marrero, Christian, Mississippi	84
SO	Mejia, Ernesto, Gwinnett	152
SB	Peraza, Jose, Rome	64

PITCHING #Minimum 75 IP

MAJORS

W	Medlen, Kris	15
# ERA	Medlen, Kris	3.11
SO	Minor, Mike	181
SV	Kimbrel, Craig	50

MINORS

W	Sims, Lucas, Rome	12
L	Lafreniere, Frank, Rome	13
# ERA	Schlosser, Gus, Mississippi	2.39
G	Russell, Andrew, Gwinnett/Mississippi	56
GS	Northcraft, Aaron, Mississippi	26
SV	Simmons, Shae, Mississippi/Rome	24
IP	Poveda, Omar, Gwinnett	164
BB	Cabrera, Mauricio, Rome	71
SO	Martin, Cody, Gwinnett/Mississippi	137
# AVG	Sims, Lucas, Rome	.203

General Manager: Frank Wren. **Farm Director:** Ronnie Richardson. **Scouting Director:** Tony DeMacio.

Class	Team	League	W	L	PCT	Finish	Manager
Majors	Atlanta Braves	National	96	66	.593	2nd (15)	Fredi Gonzalez
Triple-A	Gwinnett Braves	International	60	84	.417	14th (14)	Randy Ready
Double-A	Mississippi Braves	Southern	76	63	.547	4th (10)	Aaron Holbert
High A	Lynchburg Hillcats	Carolina	69	70	.496	5th (8)	Luis Salazar
Low A	Rome Braves	South Atlantic	73	66	.525	7th (14)	Randy Ingle
Rookie	Danville Braves	Appalachian	29	36	.446	7th (10)	Jonathan Schuerholz
Rookie	Braves	Gulf Coast	26	34	.433	13th (16)	Rocket Wheeler
Overall 2013 Minor League Record			333	353	.485	22nd (30)	

ORGANIZATION STATISTICS

ATLANTA BRAVES

NATIONAL LEAGUE

Batting	B-T	HT	WT	DOB	AVG	vLH	vRH	G	AB	R	H	2B	3B	HR	RBI	BB	HBP	SH	SF	SO	SB	CS	SLG	OBP
Bethancourt, Christian	R-R	6-2	215	9-2-91	.000	—	.000	1	1	0	0	0	0	0	0	0	0	0	0	1	0	0	.000	.000
Constanza, Jose	L-L	5-9	150	9-1-83	.258	.000	.348	21	31	2	8	0	0	0	3	0	0	0	0	5	0	3	.258	.258
Cunningham, Todd	B-R	6-0	200	3-20-89	.250	.333	.200	8	8	2	2	0	0	0	0	0	0	0	0	3	0	0	.250	.250
DeWitt, Blake	L-R	5-11	195	8-20-85	.333	.000	.500	4	3	0	1	1	0	0	0	0	0	1	0	0	0	0	.667	.333
Francisco, Juan	L-R	6-2	240	6-24-87	.241	.118	.264	35	108	10	26	2	0	5	16	7	0	0	0	43	0	1	.398	.287
2-team total (89 Milwaukee)					.227	—	—	124	348	36	79	12	1	18	48	32	3	0	2	138	0	2	.422	.296
Freeman, Freddie	L-R	6-5	225	9-12-89	.319	.287	.334	147	551	89	176	27	2	23	109	66	7	0	5	121	1	0	.501	.396
Gattis, Evan	R-R	6-4	230	8-18-86	.243	.260	.236	105	354	44	86	21	0	21	65	21	4	0	3	81	0	0	.480	.291
Gosselin, Phil	R-R	6-1	190	10-3-88	.333	.500	.000	4	6	2	2	0	0	0	1	0	0	0	0	2	0	0	.333	.429
Heyward, Jason	L-L	6-5	240	8-9-89	.254	.264	.250	104	382	67	97	22	1	14	38	48	8	1	0	73	2	4	.427	.349
Janish, Paul	R-R	6-2	200	10-12-82	.171	.000	.226	52	41	7	7	2	0	0	2	3	0	0	1	11	0	0	.220	.222
Johnson, Chris	R-R	6-3	220	10-1-84	.321	.383	.299	142	514	54	165	34	0	12	68	29	2	0	2	116	0	4	.457	.358
Johnson, Elliot	B-R	6-1	190	3-9-84	.261	.333	.247	32	92	8	24	5	2	0	10	8	0	1	1	18	8	2	.359	.317
Johnson, Reed	R-R	5-10	180	12-8-76	.244	.291	.206	74	123	13	30	7	1	1	11	6	6	1	0	32	0	0	.341	.311
Laird, Gerald	R-R	6-1	225	11-13-79	.281	.244	.303	47	121	12	34	8	0	1	13	14	3	2	1	23	1	1	.372	.367
McCann, Brian	L-R	6-3	230	2-20-84	.256	.231	.266	102	356	43	91	13	0	20	57	39	5	0	2	66	0	1	.461	.336
Pastornicky, Tyler	R-R	5-11	190	12-13-89	.300	.500	.269	20	30	5	9	1	0	0	0	1	0	2	0	5	0	0	.333	.323
Pena, Ramiro	B-R	5-11	185	7-18-85	.278	.118	.313	50	97	14	27	5	1	3	12	8	0	1	1	18	0	2	.443	.330
Schafer, Jordan	L-L	6-1	190	9-4-86	.247	.129	.265	94	231	32	57	8	3	3	21	29	0	5	0	73	22	6	.346	.331
Simmons, Andrelton	R-R	6-2	170	9-4-89	.248	.216	.257	157	606	76	150	27	6	17	59	40	3	5	4	55	6	5	.396	.296
Terdoslavich, Joey	B-R	6-0	200	9-9-88	.215	.294	.194	55	79	11	17	4	0	0	4	12	0	0	1	24	1	0	.266	.315
Uggla, Dan	R-R	5-11	205	3-11-80	.179	.146	.188	136	448	60	80	10	3	22	55	77	9	0	3	171	2	0	.362	.309
Upton, Justin	R-R	6-2	205	8-25-87	.263	.268	.262	149	558	94	147	27	2	27	70	75	5	1	4	161	8	1	.464	.354
Upton, B.J.	R-R	6-3	185	8-21-84	.184	.157	.194	126	391	30	72	14	0	9	26	44	3	1	6	151	12	5	.289	.268

Pitching	B-T	HT	WT	DOB	W	L	ERA	G	GS	CG	SV	IP	H	R	ER	HR	BB	SO	AVG	vLH	vRH	K/9	BB/9
Avilan, Luis	L-L	6-2	195	7-19-89	5	0	1.52	75	0	0	0	65	40	12	11	1	22	38	.175	.144	.202	5.26	3.05
Ayala, Luis	R-R	6-2	175	1-12-78	1	1	2.90	37	0	0	0	31	34	10	10	1	13	20	.286	.325	.266	5.81	3.77
Beachy, Brandon	R-R	6-3	215	9-3-86	2	1	4.50	5	5	0	0	30	27	17	15	5	4	23	.239	.286	.203	6.90	1.20
Carpenter, David	R-R	6-2	215	7-15-85	4	1	1.78	56	0	0	0	66	45	13	13	5	20	74	.198	.224	.183	10.14	2.74
Downs, Scott	L-L	6-2	220	3-17-76	2	1	3.86	25	0	0	0	14	19	6	6	0	8	15	.339	.367	.308	9.64	5.14
Garcia, Freddy	R-R	6-4	255	10-6-76	1	2	1.65	6	3	0	0	27	23	5	5	2	5	20	.235	.268	.211	6.59	1.65
Gearrin, Cory	R-R	6-3	200	4-14-86	2	1	3.77	37	0	0	1	31	30	13	13	2	16	23	.268	.238	.286	6.68	4.65
Hale, David	R-R	6-2	205	9-27-87	1	0	0.82	2	2	0	0	11	11	1	1	0	1	14	.244	.300	.200	11.45	0.82
Hudson, Tim	R-R	6-1	175	7-14-75	8	7	3.97	21	21	0	0	131	120	60	58	10	36	95	.245	.236	.254	6.51	2.47
Kimbrel, Craig	R-R	5-11	205	5-28-88	4	3	1.21	68	0	0	50	67	39	10	9	4	20	98	.166	.211	.116	13.16	2.69
Loe, Kameron	R-R	6-8	245	9-10-81	1	2	6.17	9	1	0	0	12	17	8	8	2	5	8	.333	.316	.344	6.17	3.86
2-team total (7 Chicago)					1	2	5.85	16	1	0	0	20	29	13	13	5	9	12	—	—	—	5.40	4.05
Maholm, Paul	L-L	6-2	220	6-25-82	10	11	4.41	26	26	0	0	153	169	82	75	17	47	105	.280	.226	.299	6.18	2.76
Martinez, Cristhian	R-R	6-1	185	3-6-82	0	0	7.71	2	0	0	0	2	5	2	2	0	0	0	.417	.571	.200	0.00	0.00
Medlen, Kris	B-R	5-10	190	10-7-85	15	12	3.11	32	31	0	0	197	194	77	68	18	47	157	.258	.256	.259	7.17	2.15
Minor, Mike	R-L	6-4	205	12-26-87	13	9	3.21	32	32	1	0	205	177	79	73	22	46	181	.232	.217	.237	7.96	2.02
O'Flaherty, Eric	L-L	6-2	210	2-5-85	3	0	2.50	19	0	0	0	18	12	5	5	2	5	11	.188	.143	.209	5.50	2.50
Rasmus, Cory	R-R	6-0	200	11-6-87	0	0	8.10	3	0	0	0	7	8	6	6	4	3	6	.286	.417	.188	8.10	4.05
Teheran, Julio	R-R	6-2	175	1-27-91	14	8	3.20	30	30	0	0	186	173	69	66	22	45	170	.246	.289	.204	8.24	2.18
Varvaro, Anthony	R-R	6-0	195	10-31-84	3	1	2.82	62	0	0	1	73	68	25	23	3	25	43	.245	.207	.274	5.28	3.07
Walden, Jordan	R-R	6-5	235	11-16-87	4	3	3.45	50	0	0	1	47	39	19	18	4	14	54	.220	.190	.247	10.34	2.68
Wood, Alex	L-L	6-4	215	1-12-91	3	3	3.13	31	11	0	0	78	76	29	27	3	27	77	.263	.267	.261	8.92	3.13

Fielding

Catcher	PCT	G	PO	A	E	DP	PB
Gattis	.993	42	279	26	2	0	2
Laird	1.000	40	241	16	0	6	1

McCann .995 92 729 34 4 1 3

First Base	PCT	G	PO	A	E	DP
Freeman	.993	147	1228	107	10	114

	PCT	G	PO	A	E	DP
Gattis	.971	4	34	0	1	2
Johnson	1.000	12	103	9	0	12
Terdoslavich	1.000	6	32	1	0	3

Second Base	PCT	G	PO	A	E	DP
Gosselin	1.000	3	2	5	0	1
Janish	1.000	9	11	11	0	2
Johnson	.954	17	22	40	3	5
Pastornicky	1.000	6	4	5	0	2
Pena	1.000	10	12	17	0	4
Uggla	.976	133	247	334	14	81

Third Base	PCT	G	PO	A	E	DP
DeWitt	—	1	0	0	0	0
Francisco	.963	30	18	60	3	6
Janish	1.000	36	3	17	0	2

Johnson	.951	125	62	210	14	14
Johnson	1.000	4	4	9	0	0
Pena	1.000	32	7	25	0	4

Shortstop	PCT	G	PO	A	E	DP
Janish	1.000	6	2	8	0	1
Johnson	1.000	2	1	5	0	1
Pastornicky	1.000	1	2	5	0	1
Pena	1.000	7	5	24	0	3
Simmons	.981	156	240	499	14	94

Outfield	PCT	G	PO	A	E	DP
Constanza	1.000	10	11	0	0	0
Cunningham	—	7	0	0	0	0
Gattis	.943	48	63	3	4	1
Heyward	1.000	102	211	4	0	0
Johnson	1.000	8	8	0	0	0
Johnson	1.000	36	53	0	0	0
Pastornicky	—	1	0	0	0	0
Schafer	.992	68	126	5	1	1
Terdoslavich	1.000	16	21	1	0	0
Upton	.985	147	263	2	4	0
Upton	.983	118	230	3	4	3

GWINNETT BRAVES   TRIPLE-A
INTERNATIONAL LEAGUE

Batting	B-T	HT	WT	DOB	AVG	vLH	vRH	G	AB	R	H	2B	3B	HR	RBI	BB	HBP	SH	SF	SO	SB	CS	SLG	OBP
Boggs, Brandon	B-R	6-0	210	1-9-83	.248	.266	.241	98	335	40	83	17	3	5	28	46	2	2	2	99	4	4	.361	.340
2-team total (21 Rochester)					.236	—	—	119	411	48	97	19	4	7	36	57	3	2	3	124	4	4	.353	.331
Carrithers, Alden	L-R	5-9	170	11-14-84	.299	.211	.315	90	251	34	75	14	1	3	19	32	4	6	0	27	13	4	.398	.387
Constanza, Jose	L-L	5-9	150	9-1-83	.276	.242	.289	83	341	39	94	7	3	0	17	29	0	3	0	49	21	9	.314	.332
Cunningham, Todd	B-R	6-0	200	3-20-89	.265	.298	.252	116	427	60	113	13	5	2	38	41	10	8	1	62	20	7	.333	.342
DeWitt, Blake	L-R	5-11	195	8-20-85	.333	—	.333	2	6	2	2	0	0	0	0	0	0	0	0	1	0	0	.333	.333
Freeman, Freddie	L-R	6-5	225	9-12-89	.500	1.000	.444	3	10	3	5	2	0	0	2	1	1	0	0	3	0	0	.700	.583
Gartrell, Stefan	R-R	6-3	230	1-14-84	.267	.263	.269	75	255	32	68	13	0	9	34	26	4	0	0	88	2	0	.424	.344
Gattis, Evan	R-R	6-4	230	8-18-86	.333	1.000	.300	5	21	1	7	4	0	1	6	1	0	0	0	4	0	0	.667	.364
Golson, Greg	R-R	6-0	190	9-17-85	.462	.444	.500	7	13	2	6	2	0	0	0	1	0	0	0	2	1	1	.615	.500
Gosselin, Phil	R-R	6-1	190	10-9-88	.266	.358	.221	58	207	17	55	4	1	2	15	12	1	7	1	38	1	0	.324	.308
Greene, Tyler	R-R	6-2	190	8-17-83	.333	.250	.385	13	42	8	14	4	0	1	4	3	3	0	0	7	0	0	.500	.417
2-team total (56 Charlotte)					.256	—	—	69	250	34	64	14	2	4	31	18	4	2	0	73	10	3	.376	.316
Heyward, Jason	L-L	6-5	240	8-9-89	.300	.333	.294	6	20	1	6	1	0	0	6	4	1	0	1	7	1	0	.350	.423
Janish, Paul	R-R	6-2	200	10-12-82	.207	.222	.204	41	135	11	28	5	0	0	12	13	2	1	1	32	0	0	.244	.285
Kazmar, Sean	R-R	5-9	180	8-5-84	.228	.239	.222	95	272	26	62	17	1	1	29	18	1	4	1	40	8	4	.309	.277
Kennelly, Matt	R-R	6-1	210	3-21-89	.417	1.000	.364	5	12	2	5	1	0	1	4	0	0	0	1	0	0	0	.750	.385
2-team total (16 Louisville)					.220	—	—	21	59	7	13	2	0	1	6	3	0	0	1	11	0	0	.305	.254
Laird, Gerald	R-R	6-1	225	11-13-79	.000	.000	.000	2	6	0	0	0	0	0	0	0	0	0	0	0	0	0	.000	.000
Leonard, Joe	R-R	6-5	220	8-26-88	.230	.223	.232	119	418	32	96	22	3	0	35	22	3	3	3	91	1	2	.297	.271
McCann, Brian	L-R	6-3	230	2-20-84	.333	1.000	.143	3	9	1	3	0	0	1	2	1	0	0	0	1	0	0	.667	.400
Mejia, Ernesto	R-R	6-5	245	12-2-85	.249	.298	.234	134	489	58	122	35	1	28	83	48	0	6	152	8	2	.497	.323
Nunez, Luis	R-R	5-11	185	11-21-86	.205	.156	.225	40	112	11	23	5	1	2	11	3	2	2	3	12	1	0	.321	.233
Pagnozzi, Matt	R-R	6-2	215	11-10-82	.210	.185	.218	90	290	31	61	10	1	6	31	21	5	4	1	64	0	0	.314	.274
Parraz, Jordan	R-R	6-3	215	10-8-84	.141	.190	.123	29	78	10	11	2	0	4	8	9	0	0	0	25	4	1	.321	.230
Pastornicky, Tyler	R-R	5-11	190	12-13-89	.292	.319	.282	74	288	42	84	13	2	4	28	27	2	1	2	47	9	2	.392	.354
Schafer, Jordan	L-L	6-1	190	9-4-86	.063	.111	.043	8	32	0	2	2	0	0	2	1	0	0	0	4	0	0	.125	.091
Terdoslavich, Joey	B-R	6-0	200	9-9-88	.318	.235	.340	85	321	48	102	24	1	18	58	23	1	0	6	65	3	6	.567	.359
Uggla, Dan	R-R	5-11	205	3-11-80	.286	.250	.333	2	7	1	2	0	0	1	1	0	0	0	0	4	0	0	.714	.286
Upton, B.J.	R-R	6-3	185	8-21-84	.333	.000	.444	3	12	3	4	3	0	0	2	0	0	0	0	4	0	0	.583	.333
Wimberly, Corey	B-R	5-8	170	10-26-83	.234	.267	.226	25	77	9	18	9	0	0	6	4	0	1	1	13	3	0	.351	.268
Yepez, Jose	R-R	6-0	205	6-19-81	.219	.219	.219	56	192	14	42	8	0	0	25	8	3	0	2	22	0	0	.260	.259

Pitching	B-T	HT	WT	DOB	W	L	ERA	G	GS	CG	SV	IP	H	R	ER	HR	BB	SO	AVG	vLH	vRH	K/9	BB/9
Ayala, Luis	R-R	6-2	175	1-12-78	0	1	6.48	8	0	0	0	8	9	6	6	3	4	8	.273	.286	.263	8.64	5.40
Beachy, Brandon	R-R	6-3	215	9-3-86	1	4	3.00	7	7	0	0	30	23	12	10	3	18	26	.211	.200	.222	7.80	5.40
Beimel, Joe	L-L	6-3	205	4-19-77	1	2	4.36	30	0	0	0	33	34	18	16	6	16	24	.264	.290	.239	6.55	4.36
Bisenius, Joe	R-R	6-4	210	9-18-82	3	7	6.00	13	8	0	0	48	72	42	32	4	21	35	.344	.337	.352	6.56	3.94
Buchter, Ryan	L-L	6-3	215	2-13-87	4	0	2.76	51	0	0	5	62	36	23	19	5	51	103	.168	.124	.200	14.95	7.40
Carpenter, David	R-R	6-2	215	7-15-85	1	2	3.52	6	0	0	0	15	17	6	6	1	4	11	.298	.320	.281	6.46	2.35
Cedeno, Juan	L-L	6-1	200	8-19-83	0	3	4.32	37	0	0	0	50	45	26	24	1	25	29	.250	.222	.269	5.22	4.50
2-team total (10 Scranton/W-B)					0	3	3.69	47	0	0	0	61	53	28	25	1	30	38	—	—	—	5.61	4.43
Colon, Roman	R-R	6-5	245	8-13-79	0	1	6.23	6	2	0	0	13	15	11	9	1	3	8	.294	.357	.270	5.54	2.08
2-team total (1 Indianapolis)					0	1	6.75	7	2	0	0	13	16	12	10	2	3	9	—	—	—	6.08	2.03
Corcoran, Tim	R-R	6-2	205	4-15-78	3	4	2.98	10	10	0	0	54	54	20	18	2	31	44	.274	.337	.225	7.29	5.13
Egan, Pat	R-R	6-7	230	10-25-84	1	1	5.60	16	0	0	3	18	22	12	11	3	3	14	.310	.405	.172	7.13	1.53
Flande, Yohan	L-L	6-2	180	1-27-86	9	7	4.18	31	19	1	1	131	142	70	61	9	46	92	.275	.248	.286	6.30	3.15
Garcia, Freddy	R-R	6-4	255	10-6-76	0	1	19.64	1	1	0	0	4	7	8	8	1	5	1	.389	.500	.250	2.45	12.27
2-team total (13 Norfolk)					8	4	3.56	14	14	0	0	86	80	36	34	11	20	62	—	—	—	6.49	2.09
Gilmartin, Sean	L-L	6-2	190	5-8-90	3	8	5.74	17	17	0	0	91	112	61	58	12	33	65	.304	.243	.331	6.43	3.26
Hale, David	R-R	6-2	205	9-27-87	6	9	3.22	22	20	0	0	115	123	50	41	8	36	77	.279	.265	.294	6.04	2.83
Hughes, Dusty	L-L	5-10	190	6-29-82	0	2	6.75	12	0	0	0	12	17	11	9	0	9	14	.327	.278	.353	10.50	6.75
Lamm, Mark	R-R	6-4	215	3-8-88	3	3	3.63	18	0	0	0	22	22	13	9	0	15	22	.250	.343	.189	8.87	6.04
Lee, Mike	R-R	6-7	235	11-18-86	0	0	5.40	1	1	0	0	5	10	3	3	0	3	1	.435	.455	.417	1.80	5.40
Loe, Kameron	R-R	6-8	245	9-10-81	4	4	3.07	27	10	0	2	76	76	32	26	3	17	37	.256	.198	.301	4.36	2.00
Martin, Cody	R-R	6-2	225	9-4-89	3	4	3.49	13	11	1	1	70	59	30	27	6	31	66	.232	.246	.218	8.53	4.00
McCurry, Cole	L-L	6-2	210	9-25-85	1	1	5.73	20	0	0	2	33	44	25	21	5	19	25	.317	.356	.298	6.82	5.18
Obispo, Wirfin	R-R	6-1	160	9-26-84	2	4	3.53	54	0	0	9	64	46	26	25	3	35	70	.204	.188	.212	9.90	4.95

	B-T	HT	WT	DOB	G	GS	CG	SV	IP	H	R	ER	HR	BB	SO	AVG	vLH	vRH	K/9	BB/9
Poveda, Omar	R-R	6-3	235	9-28-87	6	7	3.62	27	25	0	0	164	154	71	66	12	59	133	.249	.286	.207	7.30	3.24
Rasmus, Cory	R-R	6-0	200	11-6-87	3	1	1.72	37	0	0	14	37	20	8	7	2	22	48	.160	.146	.169	11.78	5.40
Rodriguez, Daniel	L-L	6-0	185	12-11-84	3	3	5.77	12	12	0	0	53	49	36	34	3	38	55	.246	.283	.235	9.34	6.45
Russell, Andy	R-R	6-0	200	4-27-84	2	5	3.86	28	0	0	2	33	29	19	14	3	23	27	.242	.278	.212	7.44	6.34
Walden, Jordan	R-R	6-5	235	11-16-87	0	0	0.00	1	0	0	0	1	0	0	0	0	0	1	.000	.000	.000	9.00	0.00
Wood, Alex	L-L	6-4	215	1-12-91	1	0	1.80	1	1	0	0	5	3	1	1	0	2	5	.200	.000	.231	9.00	3.60

Fielding

Catcher	PCT	G	PO	A	E	DP	PB
Gattis	1.000	1	6	1	0	0	0
Kennelly	.895	3	17	0	2	0	0
Laird	.917	2	9	2	1	0	1
McCann	1.000	1	7	0	0	1	0
Pagnozzi	.993	87	611	52	5	4	11
Yepez	.980	55	398	35	9	3	8

First Base	PCT	G	PO	A	E	DP
Freeman	1.000	2	14	1	0	0
Leonard	1.000	13	113	6	0	13
Mejia	.987	125	1021	82	14	110
Terdoslavich	.954	8	56	6	3	1

Second Base	PCT	G	PO	A	E	DP
Carrithers	1.000	17	24	32	0	8
DeWitt	1.000	2	3	8	0	3
Gosselin	.969	47	87	161	8	38
Greene	1.000	5	8	13	0	2
Kazmar	1.000	9	10	23	0	5
Nunez	1.000	4	10	9	0	1

Pastornicky	.957	59	101	144	11	35
Uggla	1.000	2	3	3	0	0
Wimberly	.976	11	17	24	1	7

Third Base	PCT	G	PO	A	E	DP
Carrithers	.932	33	10	45	4	4
Gosselin	—	1	0	0	0	0
Greene	—	1	0	0	0	0
Kazmar	1.000	4	2	6	0	1
Leonard	.965	103	72	201	10	24
Mejia	—	1	0	0	0	0
Nunez	.909	12	9	21	3	5
Pastornicky	1.000	1	1	1	0	0
Wimberly	1.000	1	0	1	0	1

Shortstop	PCT	G	PO	A	E	DP
Gosselin	—	1	0	0	0	0
Greene	1.000	7	14	23	0	5
Janish	.964	41	63	125	7	28
Kazmar	.957	79	96	192	13	39
Nunez	.926	18	29	46	6	9

Pastornicky	.958	8	19	27	2	11

Outfield	PCT	G	PO	A	E	DP
Boggs	.983	74	117	2	2	1
Carrithers	1.000	26	41	2	0	0
Constanza	.988	80	154	4	2	1
Cunningham	.992	112	253	6	2	3
Gartrell	.988	38	77	4	1	1
Gattis	1.000	1	0	1	0	0
Golson	1.000	6	9	0	0	0
Gosselin	1.000	4	9	0	0	0
Heyward	1.000	3	7	0	0	0
Parraz	1.000	13	23	1	0	0
Pastornicky	1.000	3	5	0	0	0
Schafer	1.000	6	13	0	0	0
Terdoslavich	.943	69	106	9	7	2
Upton	1.000	2	5	0	0	0
Wimberly	1.000	10	12	4	0	1

MISSISSIPPI BRAVES · DOUBLE-A

SOUTHERN LEAGUE

Batting	B-T	HT	WT	DOB	AVG	vLH	vRH	G	AB	R	H	2B	3B	HR	RBI	BB	HBP	SH	SF	SO	SB	CS	SLG	OBP
Bethancourt, Christian	R-R	6-2	215	9-2-91	.277	.308	.266	90	358	42	99	21	0	12	45	16	2	5	7	57	11	7	.436	.305
Brewer, Dan	R-R	6-0	195	7-19-87	.265	.309	.248	119	344	51	91	17	4	3	24	42	0	6	2	58	23	8	.363	.343
Carrithers, Alden	L-R	5-9	170	11-14-84	.148	.333	.125	12	27	4	4	0	0	0	0	8	1	1	0	6	3	1	.148	.361
Golson, Greg	R-R	6-0	190	9-17-85	.218	.167	.233	16	55	7	12	3	0	0	3	1	8	1	0	19	6	1	.273	.328
Gosselin, Phil	R-R	6-1	190	10-3-88	.243	.255	.240	59	218	27	53	10	1	1	23	12	4	4	3	31	5	1	.312	.291
Hefflinger, Robby	R-R	6-5	235	1-3-90	.170	.122	.187	53	188	19	32	8	1	6	25	15	0	0	4	64	2	1	.319	.227
Jones, Mycal	R-R	5-10	190	5-30-87	.261	.250	.265	111	345	56	90	18	0	4	36	36	5	7	3	63	29	11	.348	.337
Kleinknecht, Barrett	R-R	6-0	200	7-30-88	.238	.232	.241	93	235	32	56	9	0	8	35	18	3	5	5	43	0	0	.379	.295
La Stella, Tommy	L-R	5-11	185	1-31-89	.343	.338	.344	81	283	32	97	21	2	4	41	37	2	1	0	34	7	1	.473	.422
Landoni, Emerson	B-R	5-11	180	2-19-87	.325	.444	.290	16	40	9	13	2	0	1	7	2	0	1	0	6	0	1	.450	.357
Luna, Omar	R-R	5-11	204	12-13-86	.297	.200	.330	47	138	23	41	7	0	1	9	9	1	2	0	11	2	1	.370	.345
2-team total (29 Chattanooga)					.248	—	—	76	226	26	56	11	0	1	15	12	2	4	0	26	2	2	.310	.292
Marrero, Christian	L-L	6-1	185	7-30-86	.231	.204	.239	130	399	42	92	22	5	8	44	84	2	0	2	72	6	2	.371	.366
Martinez, Jose	R-R	6-7	210	7-25-88	.285	.300	.280	123	431	46	123	19	0	6	39	37	1	4	2	63	6	9	.371	.342
McGill, Shawn	R-R	6-4	225	3-1-84	.387	.250	.407	13	31	6	12	4	0	0	5	3	2	0	0	6	1	0	.516	.472
Nunez, Luis	R-R	5-11	185	11-21-86	.200	.200	.200	37	120	10	24	3	1	1	15	2	1	1	1	12	5	1	.267	.218
Pedroza, Jaime	B-R	5-8	180	9-12-86	.281	.209	.303	117	370	48	104	14	2	4	48	38	2	3	4	66	6	3	.362	.348
Russell, Kyle	L-L	6-4	220	6-27-86	.224	.138	.241	53	170	23	38	6	1	4	17	23	1	0	0	63	3	1	.341	.320
Salcedo, Edward	R-R	6-3	210	7-30-91	.239	.293	.222	132	468	52	112	22	2	12	55	44	1	1	4	111	20	10	.372	.304
Schlehuber, Braeden	R-R	6-2	205	1-7-88	.199	.108	.223	54	176	19	35	4	0	4	17	10	2	3	1	33	2	0	.290	.249
Weglarz, Nick	L-L	6-3	240	12-16-87	.000	.000	.000	2	5	0	0	0	0	0	0	1	0	0	0	3	0	0	.000	.167

Pitching	B-T	HT	WT	DOB	W	L	ERA	G	GS	CG	SV	IP	H	R	ER	HR	BB	SO	AVG	vLH	vRH	K/9	BB/9
Atkins, Mitch	R-R	6-4	225	10-1-85	5	2	3.47	17	16	0	0	96	97	39	37	6	35	76	.266	.255	.272	7.13	3.28
Ayala, Luis	R-R	6-2	175	1-12-78	0	0	0.00	3	0	0	0	3	2	0	0	0	0	2	.182	.250	.000	6.00	0.00
Beachy, Brandon	R-R	6-3	215	9-3-86	1	0	5.40	1	1	0	0	5	6	3	3	1	1	4	.300	.273	.333	7.20	1.80
Bisenius, Joe	R-R	6-4	210	9-18-82	0	1	4.50	1	1	0	0	6	7	4	3	1	1	4	.280	.250	.308	6.00	1.50
Egan, Pat	R-R	6-7	230	10-25-84	7	2	2.10	38	0	0	4	56	48	20	13	1	15	42	.234	.198	.258	6.79	2.43
Flande, Yohan	L-L	6-2	180	1-27-86	0	1	9.64	1	1	0	0	5	9	6	5	0	2	3	.429	.400	.438	5.79	3.86
Graham, J.R.	R-R	5-10	195	1-14-90	1	3	4.04	8	8	0	0	36	39	16	16	0	10	28	.283	.276	.288	7.07	2.52
Hamren, Erik	R-R	6-1	195	8-21-86	0	0	2.55	13	0	0	1	18	18	5	5	0	8	18	.269	.308	.244	9.17	4.08
2-team total (32 Montgomery)					1	2	3.08	45	0	0	3	64	63	25	22	3	31	76	—	—	—	10.63	4.34
Harper, Ryne	R-R	6-3	215	3-27-89	6	3	1.79	41	0	0	11	55	47	17	11	3	18	54	.223	.266	.197	8.78	2.93
Hoyt, James	R-R	6-5	220	9-30-86	0	1	2.48	22	0	0	1	33	17	9	9	1	13	33	.147	.104	.176	9.09	3.58
Jaime, Juan	R-R	6-2	235	8-2-87	2	5	4.07	35	0	0	0	42	30	19	19	1	28	70	.201	.232	.183	15.00	6.00
Jones, Chris	L-L	6-2	205	9-19-88	0	0	13.50	1	0	0	0	1	2	2	2	0	2	1	.333	.000	.400	6.75	13.50
Keeling, Thomas	L-L	6-3	190	3-30-88	1	2	5.68	29	0	0	0	25	25	20	16	5	28	17	.260	.158	.328	6.04	9.95
2-team total (17 Huntsville)					1	3	4.68	46	0	0	1	42	40	29	22	6	38	36	—	—	—	7.65	8.08
Lamm, Mark	R-R	6-4	215	3-8-88	3	3	2.56	35	0	0	10	46	39	14	13	2	21	48	.238	.257	.222	9.46	4.14
Lee, Mike	R-R	6-7	235	11-18-86	9	8	3.71	25	20	1	0	129	160	64	53	10	18	79	.307	.317	.300	5.53	1.26
Martin, Cody	R-R	6-2	225	9-4-89	3	3	2.82	16	11	0	0	67	63	23	21	3	27	71	.250	.270	.234	9.54	3.63
Martinez, Cristhian	R-R	6-1	185	3-6-82	0	0	9.00	2	0	0	0	2	2	2	2	0	2	2	.222	.000	.286	9.00	9.00

	B-T	HT	WT	DOB	W	L	ERA	G	GS	CG	SV	IP	H	R	ER	HR	BB	SO	AVG	vLH	vRH	K/9	BB/9
McCurry, Cole	L-L	6-2	210	9-25-85	0	0	3.38	4	1	0	0	8	7	3	3	1	0	7	.226	.182	.250	7.88	0.00
Moran, Gary	R-R	6-8	265	5-21-85	4	2	3.31	16	6	0	1	49	53	18	18	2	14	25	.279	.241	.306	4.59	2.57
Northcraft, Aaron	R-R	6-4	230	5-28-90	8	8	3.42	26	26	0	0	137	124	66	52	7	51	121	.241	.256	.229	7.95	3.35
Pacheco, Ronan	L-L	6-6	193	7-29-88	1	1	3.60	13	0	0	0	10	7	5	4	0	14	10	.200	.133	.250	9.00	12.60
Russell, Andy	R-R	6-0	200	4-27-84	4	1	2.27	28	0	0	2	44	39	14	11	1	16	34	.242	.338	.167	7.01	3.30
Schlosser, Gus	R-R	6-4	215	10-20-88	7	6	2.39	25	25	0	0	135	118	42	36	5	44	101	.234	.281	.199	6.72	2.93
Shreve, Chase	L-L	6-3	180	7-12-90	3	1	4.43	36	0	0	0	43	43	25	21	1	22	28	.272	.291	.262	5.91	4.64
Simmons, Shae	R-R	5-9	180	9-3-90	0	0	2.45	11	0	0	0	11	5	3	3	0	7	16	.139	.273	.080	13.09	5.73
Thomas, Ian	R-R	6-4	210	4-20-87	7	8	2.76	39	13	0	1	104	72	34	32	7	37	123	.192	.192	.192	10.61	3.19
Wood, Alex	L-L	6-4	215	1-12-91	4	2	1.26	10	10	0	0	57	41	10	8	1	15	57	.195	.185	.199	9.00	2.37
Woolley, Ryan	R-R	6-1	190	2-11-88	0	0	12.27	3	0	0	0	4	7	5	5	0	3	2	.389	.429	.364	4.91	7.36

Fielding

Catcher	PCT	G	PO	A	E	DP	PB
Bethancourt	.983	85	618	65	12	5	13
Kleinknecht	1.000	1	5	0	0	0	0
McGill	1.000	11	75	4	0	0	0
Schlehuber	.988	52	381	36	5	2	4

First Base	PCT	G	PO	A	E	DP
Kleinknecht	.993	41	288	17	2	30
Luna	1.000	6	49	7	0	5
Marrero	.996	108	875	91	4	64
McGill	1.000	1	1	0	0	0
Nunez	.500	1	1	0	1	0

Second Base	PCT	G	PO	A	E	DP
Carrithers	.857	2	1	5	1	0
Gosselin	.969	35	50	107	5	15
Kleinknecht	.977	16	18	24	1	4
La Stella	.980	73	148	203	7	44

	PCT	G	PO	A	E	DP
Landoni	1.000	8	12	22	0	3
Luna	.982	13	19	37	1	6
Nunez	.972	8	13	22	1	7
Pedroza	1.000	1	2	2	0	1

Third Base	PCT	G	PO	A	E	DP
Carrithers	1.000	2	1	2	0	0
Gosselin	1.000	3	1	3	0	0
Kleinknecht	.949	13	7	30	2	3
Landoni	—	1	0	0	0	0
Luna	.962	9	5	20	1	1
Nunez	1.000	3	1	3	0	1
Pedroza	—	1	0	0	0	0
Salcedo	.912	115	72	230	29	15

Shortstop	PCT	G	PO	A	E	DP
Kleinknecht	1.000	16	15	34	0	4
Landoni	1.000	4	2	3	0	0

	PCT	G	PO	A	E	DP
Luna	1.000	9	16	13	0	5
Nunez	.969	24	33	62	3	10
Pedroza	.952	105	124	250	19	57

Outfield	PCT	G	PO	A	E	DP
Brewer	.969	100	153	4	5	0
Carrithers	1.000	6	8	0	0	0
Golson	.962	15	24	1	1	0
Gosselin	1.000	16	17	0	0	0
Hefflinger	1.000	45	64	2	0	1
Jones	.975	103	230	6	6	2
Marrero	1.000	13	19	0	0	0
Martinez	.979	113	175	11	4	3
Russell	.972	45	69	1	2	0
Weglarz	—	2	0	0	0	0

LYNCHBURG HILLCATS

HIGH CLASS A

CAROLINA LEAGUE

Batting	B-T	HT	WT	DOB	AVG	vLH	vRH	G	AB	R	H	2B	3B	HR	RBI	BB	HBP	SH	SF	SO	SB	CS	SLG	OBP
Anselment, Chase	L-R	6-1	208	10-15-90	.080	.000	.083	10	25	3	2	0	0	0	0	6	1	0	0	5	1	0	.080	.281
Beckwith, William	R-L	6-2	220	8-19-90	.229	.283	.211	53	188	26	43	9	0	9	30	27	7	0	4	52	6	3	.420	.341
Brownsten, Cory	R-R	6-0	210	6-3-88	.160	.276	.127	51	131	14	21	2	0	0	10	13	6	3	1	22	0	0	.176	.265
Castro, Daniel	R-R	5-11	170	11-14-92	.284	.450	.235	26	88	10	25	1	1	0	7	7	0	1	0	6	3	1	.318	.337
De La Cruz, Luis	R-R	5-9	165	5-6-89	.202	.227	.194	24	84	7	17	2	0	0	3	6	0	3	0	13	0	0	.226	.256
De Los Santos, Fernando	R-R	6-1	180	1-18-90	.156	.071	.194	16	45	5	7	3	1	0	6	5	1	1	0	13	0	3	.267	.255
Elander, Josh	R-R	6-1	215	3-19-91	.262	.325	.249	61	221	28	58	12	0	4	32	26	3	0	2	48	3	1	.371	.345
Garcia, Eric	L-R	5-11	175	2-18-91	.200	—	.200	3	10	3	2	0	0	0	0	2	0	0	0	1	0	0	.200	.333
Heffley, Ross	R-R	5-7	180	1-21-90	.218	.211	.220	45	165	17	36	10	0	2	14	13	1	6	5	35	2	3	.315	.272
Hefflinger, Robby	R-R	6-5	235	1-3-90	.286	.323	.274	74	280	44	80	17	1	21	52	22	2	0	3	71	1	1	.579	.339
Hyams, Levi	L-R	6-2	205	10-6-89	.191	.286	.178	53	178	17	34	15	1	2	13	25	2	2	1	45	4	5	.320	.296
Kubitza, Kyle	L-R	6-3	190	7-15-90	.260	.253	.261	132	435	75	113	26	6	12	57	80	6	3	3	132	8	16	.434	.380
La Stella, Tommy	L-R	5-11	185	1-31-89	.550	.750	.500	7	20	7	11	1	0	1	4	8	1	0	0	1	1	1	.750	.690
Landoni, Emerson	B-R	5-11	180	2-19-89	.276	.291	.272	65	228	28	63	13	3	2	19	15	3	1	1	25	0	2	.386	.328
Lipka, Matt	R-R	6-1	195	4-15-92	.251	.274	.245	131	525	76	132	29	7	5	40	29	12	4	1	107	37	14	.362	.305
McGill, Shawn	R-R	6-4	225	3-1-84	.269	.400	.238	56	186	20	50	16	2	1	19	16	5	0	1	26	2	0	.392	.341
Moses, Trenton	R-R	6-3	235	2-9-89	.259	.162	.280	64	212	27	55	18	1	3	37	23	8	1	1	46	0	2	.396	.352
Nunez, Anthony	R-R	6-3	205	2-2-90	.133	.182	.118	18	45	3	6	2	0	1	4	3	0	0	0	14	0	0	.244	.188
Reyes, Elmer	R-R	5-11	150	11-26-90	.285	.269	.290	123	438	57	125	30	4	5	60	20	5	5	4	73	7	1	.406	.321
Rohm, David	R-R	6-3	215	1-22-90	.302	.291	.305	130	496	77	150	33	8	2	53	30	2	4	4	92	5	9	.413	.342
Skinner, Will	R-R	6-0	210	6-9-89	.218	.311	.196	71	234	33	51	14	0	16	44	11	0	1	1	89	1	1	.483	.252
Weaver, Matt	R-R	6-0	175	1-27-90	.224	.246	.218	93	281	30	63	11	2	3	35	22	6	7	2	85	7	6	.310	.293
Wren, Kyle	L-L	5-10	174	4-23-91	.000	—	.000	1	1	0	0	0	0	0	0	0	0	0	0	1	0	0	.000	.000

Pitching	B-T	HT	WT	DOB	W	L	ERA	G	GS	CG	SV	IP	H	R	ER	HR	BB	SO	AVG	vLH	vRH	K/9	BB/9
Brewer, Caleb	R-R	6-3	205	2-2-89	0	1	4.01	15	0	0	0	25	29	15	11	2	12	18	.287	.333	.245	6.57	4.38
Bullock, Billy	R-R	6-6	225	2-27-88	0	0	4.00	7	0	0	0	9	6	5	4	0	6	9	.182	.333	.095	9.00	6.00
Chaffee, Matt	L-L	6-0	185	12-19-88	2	2	5.15	24	0	0	1	37	41	24	21	3	18	42	.277	.289	.272	10.31	4.42
Cornely, John	R-R	6-1	195	5-17-89	4	1	3.38	42	0	0	11	51	40	22	19	9	24	70	.211	.239	.184	12.43	4.26
Cunniff, Brandon	R-R	6-0	185	10-7-88	1	0	1.99	20	0	0	0	32	20	8	7	2	21	39	.185	.260	.121	11.08	5.97
Fish, Robert	L-L	6-2	230	1-19-88	2	2	2.25	16	0	0	2	20	17	5	5	0	11	16	.239	.300	.216	7.20	4.95
Hinson, Ryan	L-L	6-3	185	6-3-89	4	4	2.48	10	10	0	0	58	58	17	16	1	19	41	.271	.279	.268	6.36	2.95
Holland, Adam	R-R	6-5	225	12-15-89	5	9	4.80	28	23	0	0	120	130	75	64	7	59	79	.281	.261	.296	5.93	4.43
Hoyt, James	R-R	6-5	220	9-30-86	3	2	4.89	17	3	0	0	50	39	27	27	3	25	72	.213	.155	.250	13.05	4.53
Hyatt, Nathan	R-R	6-0	185	9-26-90	2	4	3.86	43	0	0	12	47	47	21	20	1	30	55	.270	.257	.280	10.61	5.79
Jadofsky, Zach	R-R	6-3	210	6-17-90	0	1	4.91	8	0	0	0	11	14	9	6	0	5	7	.318	.313	.321	5.73	4.09
Lugo, Jose	L-L	6-1	180	4-10-84	0	2	5.40	4	3	0	0	13	17	10	8	0	2	9	.304	.370	.241	6.08	1.35
Miller, Jarrett	R-R	6-1	195	9-28-89	9	8	3.73	30	25	0	0	147	135	69	61	7	63	122	.244	.261	.227	7.47	3.86
Moore, Navery	R-R	6-2	212	8-10-90	7	7	6.16	18	17	0	0	88	111	64	60	8	31	60	.306	.333	.272	6.16	3.18
Pacheco, Ronan	L-L	6-6	193	7-29-88	2	1	2.37	28	0	0	1	38	27	17	10	1	25	36	.193	.070	.247	8.53	5.92

Name	B-T	HT	WT	DOB	W	L	ERA	G	GS	CG	SV	IP	H	R	ER	HR	BB	SO	AVG	vLH	vRH	K/9	BB/9
Perez, Carlos	L-L	6-2	195	11-20-91	0	0	3.95	9	0	0	1	14	6	11	6	1	11	15	.130	.067	.161	9.88	7.24
Perez, Williams	R-R	6-0	185	5-21-91	6	2	2.62	9	9	0	0	55	50	21	16	4	18	47	.239	.259	.226	7.69	2.95
Peterson, Dave	R-R	6-5	205	1-4-90	0	2	2.89	5	4	0	0	19	14	6	6	2	7	17	.212	.229	.194	8.20	3.38
Pope, Mark	R-R	6-2	203	8-29-89	0	2	12.27	5	5	0	0	18	33	29	25	5	15	10	.393	.406	.385	4.91	7.36
Rivera, Wilson	R-R	6-1	195	10-30-89	6	0	2.60	40	0	0	1	62	45	19	18	4	44	86	.208	.200	.216	12.42	6.35
Ross, Greg	R-R	6-3	200	9-6-89	9	6	3.27	23	19	1	0	121	120	58	44	3	36	91	.256	.281	.232	6.77	2.68
Shreve, Chase	L-L	6-3	180	7-12-90	0	1	2.75	14	0	0	2	20	15	7	6	1	8	15	.197	.286	.146	6.86	3.66
Sims, Blaine	L-L	6-0	185	3-10-89	0	6	11.63	6	6	0	0	24	34	33	31	4	26	32	.327	.300	.338	12.00	9.75
Weber, Ryan	R-R	6-0	170	8-12-90	6	5	3.84	22	15	1	0	94	90	50	40	6	15	81	.251	.249	.253	7.78	1.44
Woolley, Ryan	R-R	6-1	190	2-11-88	0	2	6.33	15	0	0	0	21	26	19	15	1	12	17	.289	.214	.354	7.17	5.06

Fielding

Catcher	PCT	G	PO	A	E	DP	PB
Anselment	.917	9	43	12	5	0	3
Brownsten	.984	51	336	41	6	6	7
De La Cruz	.983	24	203	31	4	0	2
McGill	.990	52	368	37	4	3	11
Nunez	.982	18	88	20	2	0	0

First Base	PCT	G	PO	A	E	DP
Beckwith	.983	42	386	22	7	36
Hyams	.970	4	29	3	1	4
Moses	.983	58	493	29	9	51
Weaver	.994	42	338	22	2	29

Second Base	PCT	G	PO	A	E	DP
Castro	.987	17	36	42	1	10
De Los Santos	1.000	2	4	5	0	1
Garcia	1.000	2	7	6	0	4

	PCT	G	PO	A	E	DP
Heffley	.972	42	72	136	6	24
Hyams	.957	36	52	83	6	25
La Stella	1.000	3	3	6	0	0
Landoni	.957	34	58	98	7	24
Weaver	1.000	9	9	20	0	3

Third Base	PCT	G	PO	A	E	DP
Beckwith	—	1	0	0	0	0
De Los Santos	1.000	5	1	5	0	0
Garcia	1.000	1	1	4	0	0
Kubitza	.922	125	78	218	25	26
Landoni	.900	9	5	13	2	0
Weaver	1.000	4	3	6	0	0

Shortstop	PCT	G	PO	A	E	DP
Castro	1.000	6	9	11	0	3
De Los Santos	.926	5	11	14	2	5

	PCT	G	PO	A	E	DP
Landoni	.970	8	11	21	1	4
Reyes	.969	120	170	369	17	77
Weaver	.875	2	5	9	2	3

Outfield	PCT	G	PO	A	E	DP
Elander	.986	51	66	3	1	0
Garcia	—	1	0	0	0	0
Hefflinger	.930	51	51	2	4	0
Lipka	.976	128	236	7	6	1
Rivera	—	1	0	0	0	0
Rohm	.980	106	189	8	4	3
Skinner	.970	53	93	3	3	0
Weaver	.957	38	62	5	3	1
Wren	1.000	1	1	0	0	0

ROME BRAVES

LOW CLASS A

SOUTH ATLANTIC LEAGUE

Batting	B-T	HT	WT	DOB	AVG	vLH	vRH	G	AB	R	H	2B	3B	HR	RBI	BB	HBP	SH	SF	SO	SB	CS	SLG	OBP
Alcantara, Aris	R-R	6-2	170	5-5-90	.123	.125	.123	20	65	6	8	1	0	0	4	10	0	1	1	14	0	1	.138	.237
Anselment, Chase	L-R	6-1	208	10-15-90	.250	.344	.232	55	200	20	50	16	1	5	20	26	0	0	2	59	0	1	.415	.286
Brown, Blake	R-R	6-0	185	6-30-91	.198	.158	.208	62	192	25	38	11	2	1	15	18	2	2	0	81	7	3	.292	.274
Carroll, Dan	R-R	6-1	180	1-6-89	.277	.286	.275	36	119	20	33	9	1	1	17	4	4	2	2	32	10	2	.395	.318
DeSantiago, Nick	L-R	5-11	215	4-17-91	.158	.000	.162	13	38	4	6	3	0	0	2	8	1	1	0	14	0	1	.237	.319
Edmondson, Chris	L-R	6-0	200	4-7-88	.206	.167	.214	10	34	3	7	2	0	1	7	2	0	0	0	10	2	0	.353	.250
Elander, Josh	R-R	6-1	215	3-19-91	.318	.340	.313	74	280	47	89	22	3	11	61	29	0	0	1	61	6	2	.536	.381
Franco, Carlos	R-R	6-2	170	12-20-91	.229	.170	.246	128	454	54	104	20	1	1	48	51	1	1	3	124	15	9	.284	.306
Garcia, Eric	L-R	5-11	175	2-18-91	.255	.273	.252	74	278	36	71	14	2	4	39	34	1	3	1	44	5	9	.363	.338
Heffley, Ross	R-R	5-7	180	1-21-90	.192	.163	.206	47	156	15	30	9	2	0	16	17	2	1	2	35	1	1	.276	.277
Hyams, Levi	R-R	6-0	205	10-6-87	.317	.303	.319	52	199	40	63	9	3	1	26	19	3	0	4	31	12	7	.407	.378
Kalenkosky, Casey	R-R	6-0	204	10-28-89	.247	.260	.243	82	279	35	69	13	2	7	46	34	8	3	7	57	7	5	.384	.338
Luna, Ronald	R-R	6-0	145	8-18-92	.240	.226	.246	64	229	22	55	10	0	0	16	5	5	4	3	27	4	5	.284	.269
Marte, Felix	R-R	6-1	180	11-14-90	.241	.250	.238	104	324	38	78	10	9	3	27	25	1	2	1	106	12	5	.355	.296
McCann, Brian	L-R	6-3	210	2-20-84	.357	.333	.364	4	14	5	5	1	0	3	7	2	0	0	0	2	0	0	1.071	.438
Meneses, Joey	R-R	6-3	190	5-6-92	.257	.235	.263	108	381	36	98	21	4	2	40	28	1	1	3	97	1	5	.349	.308
Moses, Trenton	R-R	6-3	235	2-9-89	.364	.308	.383	33	107	10	39	11	0	2	16	13	3	0	0	26	0	1	.523	.447
Mueller, Tony	R-R	6-0	190	2-22-90	.188	.333	.167	14	48	2	9	1	0	0	4	6	0	1	0	12	2	0	.208	.278
Peraza, Jose	R-R	6-0	165	4-30-94	.288	.268	.293	114	448	72	129	18	8	1	47	34	6	9	7	64	64	15	.371	.341
Sanchez, Edison	R-R	6-4	195	11-1-90	.281	.263	.286	70	242	36	68	18	0	6	36	36	7	0	2	80	4	2	.430	.387
Tewell, Tyler	L-R	5-11	185	7-17-91	.222	.200	.227	86	297	42	66	9	3	9	36	16	5	5	2	71	4	3	.354	.272
Wren, Kyle	L-L	5-10	174	4-23-91	.328	.255	.357	47	195	36	64	11	4	2	20	16	1	3	0	31	32	6	.456	.382

Pitching	B-T	HT	WT	DOB	W	L	ERA	G	GS	CG	SV	IP	H	R	ER	HR	BB	SO	AVG	vLH	vRH	K/9	BB/9
Beachy, Brandon	R-R	6-3	215	9-3-86	1	0	0.00	1	1	0	0	5	3	0	0	0	1	3	.176	.167	.182	5.40	1.80
Briceno, Rafael	R-R	6-2	175	10-29-90	5	9	6.44	24	14	0	0	87	107	74	62	5	47	54	.300	.320	.289	5.61	4.88
Brosius, Tyler	R-R	6-4	230	1-7-92	0	1	1.93	4	0	0	0	5	2	1	1	0	4	9	.125	.200	.091	17.36	7.71
Cabrera, Mauricio	R-R	6-2	180	9-22-93	3	8	4.18	24	24	1	0	131	118	74	61	3	71	107	.243	.236	.247	7.33	4.87
Chaffee, Matt	L-L	6-0	185	12-19-88	2	1	2.92	13	0	0	0	25	11	12	8	0	10	38	.129	.095	.141	13.86	3.65
Fish, Robert	L-L	6-2	230	1-19-88	0	3	6.43	10	0	0	0	14	13	12	10	0	7	21	.255	.214	.270	13.50	4.50
Fitzgerald, Jeremy	R-R	6-0	175	2-4-91	1	0	2.88	17	0	0	2	25	22	8	8	1	12	25	.239	.188	.267	9.00	4.32
Garcia, Bryam	R-R	5-10	190	11-16-88	5	2	5.24	21	0	0	0	34	30	23	20	1	22	37	.238	.333	.190	9.70	5.77
Gilmartin, Sean	L-L	6-2	190	5-8-90	1	0	1.80	1	1	0	0	5	4	1	1	0	0	5	.222	.000	.364	9.00	0.00
Hursh, Jason	R-R	6-3	190	10-2-91	1	1	0.67	9	9	0	0	27	20	9	2	1	10	15	.206	.222	.197	5.00	3.33
Jadofsky, Zach	R-R	6-3	210	6-17-90	6	3	3.79	35	0	0	4	59	59	27	25	6	21	70	.263	.338	.227	10.62	3.19
LaFreniere, Frank	R-R	6-5	185	6-2-90	7	13	5.36	28	22	0	1	136	159	91	81	11	43	97	.299	.316	.290	6.42	2.85
Lugo, Jose	L-L	6-1	180	4-10-84	1	0	4.05	4	0	0	0	7	5	3	3	1	4	5	.217	.000	.263	6.75	5.40
Maholm, Paul	L-L	6-2	220	6-25-82	1	0	1.59	1	1	0	0	6	4	1	1	0	0	6	.190	.125	.231	9.53	0.00
Nelson, Cole	L-L	6-7	235	7-14-89	1	0	6.91	9	0	0	0	14	20	12	11	0	11	15	.339	.059	.452	9.42	6.91
Parsons, Wes	R-R	6-5	190	9-6-92	7	7	2.63	19	19	1	0	110	91	44	32	5	21	101	.224	.254	.209	8.29	1.72
Perez, Carlos	L-L	6-2	195	11-20-91	3	0	2.25	20	0	0	2	32	20	8	8	1	8	37	.179	.207	.169	10.41	2.25
Perez, Williams	R-R	6-0	185	5-21-91	5	4	4.24	14	13	1	0	70	73	34	33	5	18	59	.274	.319	.250	7.59	2.31

Name	B-T	HT	WT	DOB	W	L	ERA	G	GS	CG	SV	IP	H	R	ER	HR	BB	SO	AVG	vLH	vRH	K/9	BB/9
Pfisterer, Eric	L-L	6-2	225	5-18-90	1	0	2.14	21	0	0	2	42	26	12	10	2	9	56	.176	.143	.192	12.00	1.93
Rohde, Brandon	L-L	6-3	215	9-14-89	1	0	9.18	13	0	0	0	17	25	18	17	6	11	17	.329	.286	.339	9.18	5.94
Ross, Greg	R-R	6-3	200	9-6-89	1	0	1.40	7	0	0	0	19	18	4	3	1	1	18	.234	.357	.163	8.38	0.47
Scoggin, Patrick	R-R	6-4	230	2-21-91	7	4	3.34	29	15	0	1	102	91	43	38	11	44	90	.236	.261	.219	7.92	3.87
Silva, Ernesto	R-R	6-4	180	2-5-92	0	0	0.00	1	0	0	0	2	2	0	0	0	0	0	.286	.000	.400	0.00	0.00
Simmons, Shae	R-R	5-9	180	9-3-90	1	1	1.49	39	0	0	24	42	26	12	7	0	15	66	.169	.182	.164	14.03	3.19
Sims, Blaine	L-L	6-0	185	3-10-89	0	1	6.30	4	1	0	0	10	8	7	7	0	8	9	.222	.167	.233	8.10	7.20
Sims, Lucas	R-R	6-2	195	5-10-94	12	4	2.62	28	18	1	0	117	83	44	34	3	46	134	.203	.190	.210	10.34	3.55
Tate, Richie	R-R	6-6	225	4-11-92	0	0	2.70	2	0	0	0	3	2	1	1	0	3	3	.200	.000	.250	8.10	8.10
Ubiera, Andry	R-R	6-0	170	5-22-93	0	0	2.70	1	1	0	0	3	0	1	1	0	4	2	.000	.000	.000	5.40	10.80
Wilson, Alex	R-R	6-5	225	4-3-91	1	3	3.59	33	0	0	8	53	58	26	21	1	11	45	.283	.353	.248	7.69	1.88

Fielding

Catcher	PCT	G	PO	A	E	DP	PB
Anselment	.984	38	276	38	5	2	9
DeSantiago	.956	11	59	6	3	1	0
Kalenkosky	.988	26	214	26	3	1	9
McCann	.905	3	17	2	2	1	0
Tewell	.988	69	550	46	7	6	13

First Base	PCT	G	PO	A	E	DP
Alcantara	.993	14	135	4	1	16
Garcia	1.000	1	9	0	0	1
Kalenkosky	.997	36	301	17	1	27
Luna	1.000	8	59	4	0	3
Moses	.991	26	201	8	2	15
Sanchez	.993	59	518	15	4	50

Second Base	PCT	G	PO	A	E	DP
Garcia	.986	28	58	85	2	21
Heffley	.976	47	76	130	5	32
Hyams	.975	46	82	112	5	26
Luna	.956	22	34	52	4	10

Third Base	PCT	G	PO	A	E	DP
Franco	.897	111	64	188	29	15
Garcia	.933	14	7	21	2	5
Luna	.930	16	7	33	3	5

Shortstop	PCT	G	PO	A	E	DP
Garcia	.943	26	23	60	5	8
Luna	.983	17	19	39	1	11
Peraza	.944	104	150	335	29	64

Outfield	PCT	G	PO	A	E	DP
Brown	.967	60	108	8	4	2
Carroll	.950	33	53	4	3	1
Edmondson	1.000	10	8	0	0	0
Elander	.989	65	83	4	1	1
Marte	.956	91	167	6	8	4
Meneses	.966	101	142	2	5	0
Mueller	1.000	14	29	2	0	2
Sanchez	.833	3	5	0	1	0
Wren	.990	47	101	1	1	0

DANVILLE BRAVES ROOKIE

APPALACHIAN LEAGUE

Batting	B-T	HT	WT	DOB	AVG	vLH	vRH	G	AB	R	H	2B	3B	HR	RBI	BB	HBP	SH	SF	SO	SB	CS	SLG	OBP
Alcantara, Aris	R-R	6-2	170	5-5-90	.158	.000	.188	5	19	2	3	0	0	0	2	0	0	0	3	0	1	.158	.238
Black, Justin	R-R	6-0	195	5-20-93	.144	.146	.143	53	153	13	22	3	1	1	10	13	2	0	1	76	5	3	.222	.219
Brown, Blake	R-R	6-0	185	6-30-91	.212	.091	.254	28	85	13	18	5	0	1	9	14	1	2	0	36	3	2	.306	.330
Camargo, Johan	B-R	6-0	160	12-13-93	.294	.281	.299	57	228	28	67	7	4	0	14	18	5	5	0	31	3	3	.360	.359
Caratini, Victor	R-R	6-0	192	8-17-93	.290	.294	.289	58	200	29	58	23	1	1	25	39	5	0	2	49	0	2	.430	.415
de la Rosa, Bryan	R-R	5-8	193	3-26-94	.261	.250	.267	32	111	9	29	5	0	0	10	11	1	2	2	30	1	2	.306	.328
Dodig, Mike	L-R	6-4	210	7-8-93	.053	.000	.063	14	38	2	2	0	0	0	3	0	1	0	15	0	0	.105	.122
Garcia, Hector	R-R	6-2	170	6-9-92	.213	.200	.219	16	47	6	10	3	0	0	7	4	1	1	0	13	3	0	.277	.288
Laumann, Jackson	R-R	6-3	220	9-21-93	.152	.222	.125	34	99	4	15	1	0	0	5	7	0	3	0	32	0	0	.162	.208
Lien, Connor	R-R	6-3	205	3-15-94	.226	.138	.260	56	212	32	48	11	4	6	27	14	8	1	1	70	10	3	.401	.298
Livesay, Cody	L-L	6-0	160	7-6-93	.267	.250	.269	8	30	6	8	0	0	0	6	6	0	0	0	1	1	3	.267	.389
Luna, Ronald	R-R	6-0	145	8-10-92	.247	.200	.258	23	77	4	19	2	0	0	8	3	0	2	0	11	0	0	.273	.275
Moranda, Seth	R-R	6-2	180	9-26-92	.259	.214	.274	38	112	6	29	6	0	0	9	12	2	3	0	27	2	3	.313	.341
Nunez, Anthony	R-R	6-3	205	2-2-90	.421	.714	.250	8	19	7	8	2	0	0	2	1	3	0	0	1	0	0	.526	.522
Odom, Joseph	R-R	6-2	205	1-9-92	.190	.167	.200	14	42	3	8	1	0	0	3	3	0	0	2	14	0	0	.214	.234
Piloto, Alejandro	R-R	6-0	185	4-8-92	.236	.238	.235	41	144	14	34	6	0	2	22	12	0	1	1	29	2	0	.319	.293
Reyes, Victor	L-R	6-3	170	10-5-94	.321	.211	.355	18	81	12	26	3	0	0	4	3	0	0	0	9	0	0	.358	.345
Reynolds, Mikey	B-R	5-9	170	8-19-90	.309	.361	.292	44	149	21	46	4	3	2	16	15	9	1	1	21	8	3	.416	.402
Sanchez, Carlos	R-R	6-0	178	11-5-93	.250	.345	.215	39	108	4	27	5	0	1	12	8	1	3	2	23	0	0	.324	.303
Schrader, Jake	R-R	6-2	215	3-1-91	.195	.156	.209	36	118	16	23	7	1	5	16	10	3	1	1	36	1	0	.398	.273
Wren, Kyle	L-L	5-10	174	4-23-91	.409	.667	.313	5	22	6	9	3	1	0	4	2	0	1	0	3	3	0	.636	.458

Pitching	B-T	HT	WT	DOB	W	L	ERA	G	GS	CG	SV	IP	H	R	ER	HR	BB	SO	AVG	vLH	vRH	K/9	BB/9
Brosius, Tyler	R-R	6-4	230	1-7-92	2	1	1.76	7	0	0	0	15	7	3	3	0	6	17	.135	.286	.079	9.98	3.52
Buchanan, Chuck	L-L	6-5	220	7-14-90	0	0	3.00	2	0	0	0	3	3	1	1	0	0	3	.250	.000	.300	9.00	0.00
Dettmann, Jared	L-L	6-3	180	5-18-92	2	4	2.09	12	8	0	0	47	37	18	11	4	17	35	.214	.343	.181	6.65	3.23
Dill, Dakota	L-R	6-4	215	5-20-91	2	1	3.67	18	0	0	1	27	27	15	11	0	9	32	.248	.200	.266	10.67	3.00
Flores, Michael	L-L	6-0	180	8-8-92	2	4	4.10	12	11	0	0	53	42	25	24	3	26	66	.210	.276	.199	11.28	4.44
Gil, Yean Carlos	R-R	6-0	160	10-12-90	1	4	3.81	13	11	0	0	50	57	27	21	1	11	36	.294	.174	.331	6.52	1.99
Gunther, Ryan	R-R	6-2	190	11-17-90	0	2	2.54	17	0	0	1	28	27	16	8	4	7	32	.241	.235	.244	10.16	2.22
Holmes, Colby	R-R	5-11	190	10-24-90	0	0	1.84	8	0	0	1	15	14	3	3	0	3	12	.259	.250	.263	7.36	1.84
Janas, Stephen	R-R	6-6	198	4-21-92	0	0	5.79	2	2	0	0	5	9	4	4	3	3	4	.391	.375	.400	5.79	7.71
Kimbrel, Matt	R-R	6-0	190	3-13-90	2	2	12.84	11	0	0	0	20	37	29	29	3	12	10	.398	.385	.403	4.43	5.31
Marksberry, Matt	L-L	6-1	200	8-25-90	1	3	5.08	12	6	0	0	34	32	22	19	1	16	40	.254	.217	.262	10.69	4.28
Merejo, Luis	L-L	6-0	175	10-8-94	1	0	0.00	3	1	0	0	10	8	0	0	0	5	11	.222	.000	.229	9.90	4.50
Montenegro, Jorge	R-R	6-0	170	1-24-91	1	2	5.33	6	6	0	0	25	24	17	15	3	22	19	.267	.317	.224	6.75	7.82
Otero, Andy	L-L	5-9	160	6-3-92	2	0	0.00	15	0	0	0	15	10	1	0	0	1	20	.189	.200	.184	12.27	0.61
Rohde, Brandon	L-L	6-3	215	9-14-89	2	0	12.27	3	0	0	0	4	6	6	5	0	1	3	.353	.200	.417	7.36	2.45
Sechler, Jordan	R-L	6-2	215	11-8-91	2	0	2.73	16	0	0	0	33	27	10	10	1	10	27	.220	.103	.255	7.36	2.73
Silva, Ernesto	R-R	6-4	180	2-5-92	0	1	7.36	3	0	0	0	4	9	3	3	0	1	1	.474	.750	.400	2.45	0.00
Swanner, Michael	R-R	6-4	190	9-23-92	0	3	1.99	16	0	0	6	23	20	7	5	0	6	20	.235	.167	.262	7.94	2.38
Tate, Richie	R-R	6-6	225	4-11-92	2	1	1.80	15	0	0	2	30	27	8	6	0	9	23	.257	.306	.232	6.90	2.70
Ubiera, Andry	R-R	6-0	170	5-22-93	3	2	3.74	11	11	0	0	53	55	30	22	4	21	51	.263	.213	.291	8.66	3.57

Vail, Tyler	R-R	6-0	220	3-3-93	1	0	0.00	2	0	0	0	6	1	0	0	0	2	7	.056	.000	.125	10.50	3.00
Waszak, Andrew	R-R	6-1	205	10-8-90	3	5	2.03	13	9	0	0	53	33	17	12	2	12	47	.175	.228	.136	7.93	2.03
Wright, Clint	R-R	6-6	239	4-29-90	0	0	12.86	5	0	0	0	7	12	10	10	0	6	4	.387	.444	.364	5.14	7.71

Fielding

Catcher	PCT	G	PO	A	E	DP	PB
de la Rosa	.994	21	145	19	1	0	4
Nunez	1.000	7	46	10	0	1	1
Odom	.991	12	107	9	1	0	3
Sanchez	.987	33	210	23	3	3	9

First Base	PCT	G	PO	A	E	DP
Alcantara	1.000	5	30	4	0	3
Laumann	.992	32	245	19	2	16
Luna	1.000	8	57	2	0	7
Schrader	.995	28	207	7	1	18

Second Base	PCT	G	PO	A	E	DP
Luna	.950	10	16	22	2	4
Moranda	.966	34	63	79	5	16
Reynolds	.957	25	39	72	5	17

Third Base	PCT	G	PO	A	E	DP
Camargo	—	1	0	0	0	0
Caratini	.929	47	36	94	10	7
Dodig	.897	12	8	27	4	2
Luna	1.000	3	1	6	0	2
Schrader	1.000	4	1	8	0	0

Shortstop	PCT	G	PO	A	E	DP
Camargo	.960	51	78	137	9	30

Caratini	.750	1	2	1	1	0
Luna	.857	2	2	4	1	2
Reynolds	.950	11	12	26	2	3

Outfield	PCT	G	PO	A	E	DP
Black	.938	46	75	1	5	0
Brown	.972	24	33	2	1	0
Garcia	1.000	15	26	1	0	0
Lien	.977	53	120	5	3	2
Livesay	1.000	8	17	0	0	0
Piloto	.965	31	49	6	2	1
Reyes	1.000	15	17	0	0	0
Wren	1.000	5	13	0	0	0

GCL BRAVES   ROOKIE
GULF COAST LEAGUE

Batting	B-T	HT	WT	DOB	AVG	vLH	vRH	G	AB	R	H	2B	3B	HR	RBI	BB	HBP	SH	SF	SO	SB	CS	SLG	OBP
Arno, Robinson	R-R	6-4	216	3-13-93	.184	.176	.188	36	114	19	21	6	2	2	22	13	5	1	0	43	2	0	.325	.295
Chin, Gerald	L-R	5-10	160	5-29-93	.200	.250	.182	5	15	2	3	0	0	0	1	0	1	0	0	4	0	1	.200	.250
Dodig, Mike	L-R	6-4	210	7-8-93	.300	.353	.261	12	40	6	12	3	0	0	8	2	2	0	0	8	1	0	.375	.364
Garcia, Hector	B-R	6-2	170	6-9-92	.288	.375	.275	19	59	8	17	2	0	0	8	6	0	1	1	13	8	3	.322	.348
Hagenmiller, Ian	R-R	6-1	215	9-3-94	.226	.086	.276	41	133	14	30	5	1	0	12	13	2	0	0	49	1	3	.278	.304
Harper, Reed	R-R	6-2	200	12-21-90	.296	.283	.301	54	189	26	56	13	1	1	16	22	5	1	1	18	4	3	.392	.382
Hass, Nathan	R-R	6-0	195	3-7-94	.125	.000	.143	18	32	4	4	0	0	0	1	2	3	0	0	8	0	0	.125	.243
Livesay, Cody	L-L	6-0	160	7-6-93	.287	.326	.270	41	157	25	45	5	0	0	13	14	1	1	1	25	18	2	.318	.347
Manwaring, Dylan	R-R	6-3	210	9-27-94	.131	.048	.151	37	107	10	14	1	0	0	6	15	0	1	0	37	2	3	.140	.238
McKenzie, Ibrahim	R-R	6-2	185	2-8-94	.212	.136	.232	30	104	12	22	3	1	1	14	4	5	0	0	29	0	2	.288	.274
Mercuri, Mattia	R-R	6-0	190	8-20-94	.107	.231	.081	26	75	5	8	1	0	0	3	3	3	0	0	16	0	0	.120	.173
Monasterio, Luis	R-R	6-0	170	11-11-94	.214	.667	.160	12	28	5	6	2	0	0	5	4	1	1	0	7	1	1	.286	.333
Morel, Jose	B-R	6-1	170	8-2-93	.280	.152	.323	40	132	20	37	6	0	0	21	13	1	0	2	19	13	1	.326	.345
Murphy, Tanner	R-R	6-1	215	2-27-95	.227	.238	.224	32	97	7	22	3	0	0	8	12	1	1	2	34	5	0	.258	.313
Obregon, Omar	B-R	5-10	150	4-18-94	.227	.161	.253	33	110	11	25	0	1	0	11	13	3	4	0	13	5	1	.245	.325
Odom, Joseph	R-R	6-2	205	1-9-92	.250	.400	.182	16	32	6	8	2	0	0	3	7	1	0	0	9	1	0	.313	.400
Oliver, Connor	L-R	6-0	180	10-13-93	.209	.121	.240	37	129	17	27	3	2	0	5	11	0	2	1	27	5	2	.264	.270
Parker, Andrew	R-R	6-0	215	3-26-91	.040	.000	.063	18	25	1	1	0	0	0	1	6	0	2	0	9	0	0	.040	.226
Reyes, Victor	L-R	6-3	170	10-5-94	.357	.529	.282	31	112	22	40	8	1	0	21	12	1	1	3	20	5	1	.446	.414
Sanchez, Fernelys	B-R	6-3	210	3-1-94	.235	.257	.228	46	162	20	38	7	2	2	18	18	1	1	0	73	8	4	.340	.315
Sears, Orrin	R-R	6-3	225	3-20-91	.247	.167	.281	32	81	9	20	5	3	1	16	7	0	0	1	22	2	1	.420	.303

Pitching	B-T	HT	WT	DOB	W	L	ERA	G	GS	CG	SV	IP	H	R	ER	HR	BB	SO	AVG	vLH	vRH	K/9	BB/9
Barczycowski, Chris	R-R	6-8	250	2-11-92	2	0	4.50	15	0	0	0	22	23	16	11	1	10	14	.258	.278	.245	5.73	4.09
Brosius, Tyler	R-R	6-4	230	1-7-92	1	1	4.91	6	0	0	0	7	6	5	4	0	4	9	.214	.300	.167	11.05	4.91
Caicedo, Oriel	L-L	5-11	188	1-14-94	1	1	2.06	11	9	0	0	52	48	21	12	1	16	27	.242	.291	.224	4.64	2.75
Cordero, Daniel	R-R	6-0	180	6-7-93	2	3	3.80	12	8	0	0	45	41	25	19	3	13	40	.238	.290	.204	8.00	2.60
Espinosa, Abraham	R-R	6-1	175	6-3-93	3	4	4.14	14	4	0	2	41	36	21	19	3	12	28	.231	.138	.286	6.10	2.61
Fitzgerald, Jeremy	R-R	6-0	175	2-4-91	0	0	3.00	5	1	0	0	6	4	2	2	1	5	13	.182	.143	.200	19.50	7.50
Gilmartin, Sean	L-L	6-2	190	5-8-90	0	0	0.00	3	2	0	0	9	1	0	0	0	0	11	.034	.100	.000	11.00	0.00
Gonzalez, Francisco	R-R	6-0	170	9-21-94	7	4	6.85	12	10	0	0	47	53	38	36	5	26	30	.285	.250	.314	5.70	4.94
Grosser, Alec	R-R	6-2	186	1-12-95	1	3	2.15	13	5	0	0	29	12	10	7	0	15	23	.125	.167	.100	7.06	4.60
Holmes, Colby	R-R	5-11	190	10-24-90	0	0	1.80	7	0	0	3	10	8	2	2	0	1	3	.216	.222	.211	2.70	0.90
Kimbrel, Matt	R-R	6-0	190	3-13-90	0	0	0.00	5	0	0	0	5	2	0	0	0	4	4	.125	.000	.222	7.20	0.00
Leon, Nelson	L-L	6-0	175	6-29-95	1	1	3.63	5	4	0	0	17	13	12	7	3	5	17	.200	.267	.180	8.83	2.60
Martinez, Cristhian	R-R	6-1	185	3-6-82	0	0	0.00	1	1	0	0	2	1	0	0	0	0	4	.143	.333	.000	18.00	0.00
Merejo, Luis	L-L	6-0	175	10-8-94	0	0	0.00	2	0	0	0	6	4	3	0	0	4	1	.182	.250	.167	1.50	6.00
Moran, Gary	R-R	6-8	265	5-21-85	0	0	0.00	3	2	0	0	7	7	2	0	0	8	8	.250	.125	.300	10.29	0.00
Otero, Andy	L-L	5-9	160	6-3-92	2	1	4.24	9	0	0	1	17	11	8	8	1	5	17	.183	.143	.205	9.00	2.65
Paulino, Richard	R-R	6-2	175	3-28-95	1	1	2.63	7	0	0	1	14	10	6	4	1	6	8	.204	.240	.167	5.27	3.95
Rivero, Adrian	L-L	6-3	185	5-30-91	1	0	3.38	9	0	0	0	13	12	9	5	0	10	8	.235	.176	.265	5.40	6.75
Rodriguez, Rafael	R-R	6-0	170	9-22-90	1	0	2.84	10	0	0	0	13	14	5	4	0	2	13	.280	.222	.313	9.24	1.42
Salazar, Carlos	R-R	6-0	200	11-23-94	0	3	6.92	8	4	0	0	13	18	12	10	0	5	14	.321	.190	.400	9.69	3.46
Santana, Jordany	R-R	6-0	190	7-17-95	1	0	3.18	6	0	0	0	11	6	6	4	2	8	8	.154	.143	.160	6.35	6.35
Schils, Steven	R-R	6-2	220	8-14-90	1	1	7.00	17	0	0	3	18	21	15	14	4	15	19	.304	.435	.239	9.50	7.50
Sims, Blaine	L-L	6-0	185	3-10-89	0	2	5.59	10	1	0	0	19	23	14	12	0	10	15	.284	.250	.298	6.98	4.66
Stiffler, Ian	L-R	6-1	175	2-12-95	0	2	4.91	8	3	0	0	15	21	10	8	3	8	13	.328	.370	.297	7.98	4.91
Vail, Tyler	R-R	6-0	220	3-3-93	1	2	3.20	14	0	0	4	20	18	7	7	1	7	17	.254	.281	.231	7.78	3.20
Volpe, Mike	R-R	6-2	210	1-8-91	0	0	9.00	4	0	0	0	5	6	5	5	2	2	2	.409	.333	.462	3.60	3.60
Weber, Ryan	R-R	6-0	170	8-12-90	0	1	12.00	2	1	0	0	3	5	4	4	1	0	2	.385	.750	.222	6.00	0.00
Zavala, Jorge	R-R	6-4	200	6-10-94	1	3	4.54	11	5	0	0	42	42	28	21	4	13	39	.261	.231	.289	8.42	2.81

ATLANTA BRAVES

Fielding

Catcher	PCT	G	PO	A	E	DP	PB
Hass	.984	18	57	4	1	0	9
Murphy	1.000	30	172	28	0	2	5
Odom	.984	15	56	5	1	1	3
Parker	1.000	14	54	7	0	1	0
Sears	1.000	20	65	4	0	0	5

First Base	PCT	G	PO	A	E	DP
Arno	.984	35	281	28	5	21
McKenzie	.973	28	236	15	7	19

Second Base	PCT	G	PO	A	E	DP
Chin	.933	5	5	9	1	1
Harper	.913	26	41	53	9	11
Mercuri	.957	24	30	58	4	11
Monasterio	.972	12	15	20	1	4
Obregon	1.000	1	2	2	0	0

Third Base	PCT	G	PO	A	E	DP
Dodig	.750	4	2	7	3	0
Hagenmiller	.873	34	23	66	13	7
Manwaring	.889	30	22	42	8	3

Shortstop	PCT	G	PO	A	E	DP
Harper	.991	28	47	68	1	16
Mercuri	.833	2	1	4	1	0
Obregon	.962	32	30	95	5	16

Outfield	PCT	G	PO	A	E	DP
Garcia	1.000	13	24	1	0	0
Livesay	.990	41	93	2	1	2
Morel	1.000	37	65	3	0	1
Oliver	.985	35	60	5	1	1
Reyes	.981	26	47	4	1	0
Sanchez	.886	35	61	1	8	0

DSL BRAVES   ROOKIE

DOMINICAN SUMMER LEAGUE

Batting	B-T	HT	WT	DOB	AVG	vLH	vRH	G	AB	R	H	2B	3B	HR	RBI	BB	HBP	SH	SF	SO	SB	CS	SLG	OBP
Azuaje, Franklin	R-R	6-1	170	3-31-95	.299	.414	.270	43	144	22	43	2	1	0	12	17	8	1	0	21	5	6	.326	.402
Castro, Carlos	R-R	6-1	195	5-24-94	.221	.182	.230	53	181	18	40	8	1	3	31	7	5	0	4	26	1	1	.326	.264
Chin, Gerald	L-R	5-10	160	5-29-93	.280	.240	.288	47	164	31	46	7	4	1	21	28	3	1	1	24	4	4	.390	.393
Cleofa, Nisandro	R-R	5-11	180	10-25-93	.171	.182	.169	48	111	20	19	4	0	1	8	10	7	4	1	44	4	2	.234	.279
Cortes, Jorge	R-R	6-2	175	11-15-95	.208	.211	.208	35	96	10	20	7	0	3	8	8	5	0	1	25	0	0	.375	.300
Didder, Ray-Patrick	R-R	6-0	170	10-1-94	.259	.250	.261	48	135	34	35	2	1	0	12	31	7	6	1	34	8	3	.289	.420
Estevez, Kelvin	R-R	6-1	190	11-17-95	.249	.194	.260	61	205	31	51	8	0	1	21	36	3	4	0	49	6	1	.302	.369
Flores, Alejandro	B-R	6-1	180	12-27-95	.230	.222	.231	47	135	8	31	6	0	1	28	16	1	1	2	29	4	1	.296	.312
Grullon, Yeudi	B-R	6-1	170	7-18-94	.269	.520	.225	51	167	25	45	4	0	0	9	29	3	5	0	21	5	10	.293	.387
Henriquez, Isael	R-R	6-0	180	12-15-93	.200	.571	.146	31	55	9	11	2	1	0	8	9	2	1	2	17	3	2	.273	.324
Lot, Felipe	R-R	6-1	185	1-12-95	.162	.300	.141	27	74	6	12	3	0	0	9	11	5	0	1	23	0	1	.203	.308
Maradaiga, Alvaro	R-R	6-2	190	4-18-94	.150	.400	.067	10	20	1	3	0	0	0	1	1	2	1	0	5	0	0	.150	.261
Martinez, Carlos	R-R	5-11	204	5-2-95	.254	.250	.255	44	122	19	31	5	0	0	13	10	6	2	2	7	2	0	.295	.336
Mendez, Erison	R-R	5-11	170	5-4-92	.212	.385	.187	29	104	11	22	4	0	0	7	6	6	0	2	14	4	6	.250	.288
Puello, Juan	R-R	6-2	214	4-20-92	.167	.053	.208	30	72	9	12	1	0	0	5	16	1	1	0	25	1	1	.181	.326
Robles, Javier	R-R	5-10	175	8-10-94	.364	.600	.167	7	11	7	4	0	0	0	2	2	1	1	0	2	0	1	.364	.500
Tejada, Ledernin	R-R	6-3	168	3-20-96	.220	.097	.248	54	168	21	37	4	3	2	22	19	5	3	3	49	4	3	.315	.313
Tielman, Juruengelo	R-R	6-1	210	5-11-93	.259	.500	.208	19	58	7	15	1	1	0	11	8	0	0	1	11	1	1	.310	.343
Vasquez, Carlos	B-R	6-2	160	2-25-95	.237	.214	.239	47	131	16	31	3	2	0	19	13	1	2	0	29	3	1	.290	.310
Willems, Reangelo	B-R	6-2	165	9-21-94	.100	.500	.056	17	40	6	4	1	0	0	1	5	4	1	1	16	1	4	.125	.260

Pitching	B-T	HT	WT	DOB	W	L	ERA	G	GS	CG	SV	IP	H	R	ER	HR	BB	SO	AVG	vLH	vRH	K/9	BB/9
Falcon, Felix	L-L	6-2	190	8-7-95	9	0	1.90	16	6	1	0	62	54	21	13	1	19	54	.235	.298	.219	7.88	2.77
Gavidia, Angel	R-R	6-2	180	5-16-95	1	1	5.04	16	4	0	0	30	29	23	17	1	20	27	.246	.250	.244	8.01	5.93
Granja, Denis	R-R	6-4	205	5-29-95	0	0	10.80	2	0	0	0	3	7	4	4	0	2	3	.412	.167	.545	8.10	5.40
Henry, Gabriel	R-R	6-3	180	11-16-95	0	0	19.29	5	0	0	0	5	9	11	10	1	8	4	.429	.600	.375	7.71	15.43
Jones, Jesus	R-R	6-2	165	5-31-95	1	0	2.06	19	0	0	1	35	25	12	8	0	16	23	.205	.314	.161	5.91	4.11
Ledezma, Carlos	R-R	6-1	175	8-31-95	0	2	6.00	13	4	0	0	21	24	15	14	0	19	16	.300	.292	.304	6.86	8.14
Leiva, Darrel	R-R	6-1	185	7-31-94	0	4	3.86	7	5	0	0	28	28	19	12	3	8	16	.250	.286	.229	5.14	2.57
Liranzo, Jesus	R-R	6-2	175	3-7-95	0	0	11.57	3	1	0	0	2	3	3	3	0	6	4	.333	.000	.333	15.43	23.14
2-team total (6 Orioles2)					0	1	9.24	9	3	0	0	13	16	21	13	2	12	13	—	—	—	9.24	8.53
Manzanares, Osman	R-R	6-2	192	3-6-95	0	6	7.45	18	3	0	0	29	39	30	24	0	18	13	.325	.313	.333	4.03	5.59
Martinez, Jhon	L-L	6-0	165	2-9-95	1	3	4.75	17	3	0	0	30	29	19	16	0	31	43	.242	.500	.218	12.76	9.20
Matos, David	L-L	6-3	185	5-9-94	4	3	4.21	17	4	0	1	36	38	22	17	1	19	27	.271	.125	.290	6.69	4.71
Miranda, Fernando	R-R	5-11	180	9-5-94	2	2	3.31	19	2	0	5	33	24	18	12	2	12	34	.211	.179	.227	9.37	3.31
Orozco, Evertz	R-R	6-5	192	9-16-94	0	3	6.14	17	0	0	2	22	24	20	15	0	17	18	.270	.267	.271	7.36	6.95
Paulino, Richard	R-R	6-2	175	3-28-95	2	3	5.46	13	6	0	1	30	28	27	18	0	22	33	.252	.194	.275	10.01	6.67
Santana, Jordany	R-R	6-0	190	7-17-95	3	2	4.66	12	6	0	0	46	47	32	24	1	15	29	.261	.258	.263	5.63	2.91
Santiago, Jonathan	R-R	6-1	170	3-1-94	1	6	4.04	15	10	0	1	62	49	35	28	1	26	60	.215	.214	.215	8.66	3.75
Silva, Aldo	R-R	6-1	239	10-19-95	1	2	1.74	18	2	0	2	41	29	14	8	1	16	43	.200	.146	.221	9.36	3.48
Torres, Yeralf	R-R	6-1	175	9-21-95	1	0	4.14	17	7	0	1	37	27	20	17	0	36	48	.200	.300	.169	11.68	8.76
Ventura, Carlos	L-L	6-0	185	9-25-95	0	0	3.52	5	0	0	0	8	9	7	3	0	4	3	.300	.333	.296	3.52	4.70

Fielding

Catcher	PCT	G	PO	A	E	DP	PB
Flores	.967	11	53	5	2	1	4
Lot	.974	22	139	13	4	0	5
Maradaiga	.968	6	28	2	1	0	4
Martinez	.978	44	312	44	8	5	11

First Base	PCT	G	PO	A	E	DP
Castro	.979	45	309	16	7	22
Cortes	.961	14	96	3	4	11
Henriquez	1.000	2	16	2	0	1
Tielman	.962	17	117	8	5	11

Second Base	PCT	G	PO	A	E	DP
Chin	.944	36	86	84	10	21
Didder	.909	2	6	4	1	0
Grullon	.958	30	67	69	6	16
Robles	1.000	2	3	2	0	0
Vasquez	1.000	2	3	2	0	0

Third Base	PCT	G	PO	A	E	DP
Azuaje	.872	40	32	70	15	3
Vasquez	.955	41	35	72	5	6

Shortstop	PCT	G	PO	A	E	DP
Didder	.919	37	55	103	14	17
Grullon	.922	20	22	37	5	3

Mendez	.938	15	18	43	4	8
Robles	1.000	1	3	2	0	1

Outfield	PCT	G	PO	A	E	DP
Cleofa	.961	46	71	2	3	0
Cortes	.913	14	19	2	2	0
Estevez	.920	61	64	5	6	1
Henriquez	.933	23	13	1	1	0
Mendez	.978	15	42	3	1	1
Puello	.950	16	19	0	1	0
Tejada	.979	53	88	7	2	2
Willems	.870	16	20	0	3	0

Baltimore Orioles

SEASON IN A SENTENCE: While the Orioles had a winning season, this workmanlike team fell out of first place in May, never won more than five games in a row and could not keep up with Boston and Tampa Bay in the American League East race.

HIGH POINT: First baseman Chris Davis provided many, starting with a game-winning homer on Opening Day against the Rays, as well as a grand slam in the home opener April 5 in front of 46,653 at Camden Yards. Davis led the AL with 138 RBIs and set an Orioles franchise record with a major league-best 53 home runs.

LOW POINT: Until Sept. 23, any of closer Jim Johnson's nine blown saves might have sufficed. But as the Orioles wrapped a grueling 10-day road trip in September that included an 18-inning loss to the Rays, second-year third baseman Manny Machado got hurt. His left knee bent awkwardly as he hit first base, but his postseason surgery to repair the torn medial patellofemoral ligament should allow him to return by spring training.

NOTABLE ROOKIES: A year after bursting with rookies from Machado to Wei-Yin Chen, the Orioles had only one significant rookie in lefthander T.J. McFarland. The Rule 5 draft pick soaked up 75 innings out of the bullpen—second-most on the team—and was a league-average pitcher. Righthander Kevin Gausman, the team's 2012 first-round pick, came up in August and made five starts but retains his prospect status.

KEY TRANSACTIONS: Baltimore lost some prospect depth due to a series of minor trades intended to fill big league holes. The biggest involved acquiring Bud Norris in exchange for outfielder L.J. Hoes, lefty Josh Hader and a supplemental first-round draft pick in 2014. The O's also acquired Frankie Rodriguez (for Nick Delmonico) from the Brewers and Michael Morse (for Xavier Avery) from the Mariners. Their best offseason pickup turned out to be third baseman Danny Valencia, a journeyman who hit .304/.335/.553 with eight home runs in 161 at-bats.

DOWN ON THE FARM: Orioles top prospect Dylan Bundy came down with a sore arm in spring training and was shut down in April. The right-hander started throwing again in June but required Tommy John surgery after a small tear was discovered in his elbow. Short-season Aberdeen made the playoffs for the first time in the franchise's 12-year history, but didn't score while being swept out of the New York-Penn League playoffs.

OPENING DAY PAYROLL: $90,993,333 (15th)

PLAYERS OF THE YEAR

MAJOR LEAGUE

Chris Davis
1b
.286/.370/.634
53 HR, 1.004 OPS
Led majors in HR

MINOR LEAGUE

Kevin Gausman
rhp
(Double-A/Triple-A)
3-6, 3.51
82/14/82 SO/BB/IP

ORGANIZATION LEADERS

BATTING		*Minimum 250 AB
MAJORS		
* AVG	Davis, Chris	.286
* OPS	Davis, Chris	1.004
HR	Davis, Chris	53
RBI	Davis, Chris	138
MINORS		
* AVG	Ohlman, Michael, Frederick	.313
* OBP	Ohlman, Michael, Frederick	.41
* SLG	Ohlman, Michael, Frederick	.524
R	Joseph, Caleb, Bowie	74
H	Joseph, Caleb, Bowie	155
TB	Joseph, Caleb, Bowie	256
2B	Joseph, Caleb, Bowie	31
3B	Mercedes, Alex, DSL Orioles	10
HR	Waring, Brandon, Norfolk/Bowie	25
RBI	Joseph, Caleb, Bowie	97
BB	Pena, Jerome, Frederick	66
BB	Romero, Niuman, Norfolk/Bowie	66
SO	Lorenzo, Gregory, Delmarva	152
SB	Ruettiger, John, Bowie/Frederick	44

PITCHING		#Minimum 75 IP
MAJORS		
W	Tillman, Chris	16
# ERA	Tillman, Chris	3.71
SO	Tillman, Chris	179
SV	Johnson, Jim	50
MINORS		
W	Berry, Tim, Frederick	11
	Wright, Mike, Norfolk, Bowie	11
L	Clark, Zach, Norfolk/Bowie/Frederick/GCL	15
# ERA	Wright, Mike, Bowie, Norfolk	3.11
G	Delcarmen, Manny, Norfolk	48
GS	Three tied at	27
SV	Asencio, Jairo, Norfolk	28
IP	Berry, Tim, Frederick	152
BB	Clark, Zach, Norfolk/Bowie/Frederick/GCL	75
SO	Bridwell, Parker, Delmarva	144
# AVG	Gamboa, Eddie, Bowie/Norfolk	.232

General Manager: Dan Duquette. **Farm Director:** Brian Graham. **Scouting Director:** Gary Rajsich.

Class	Team	League	W	L	PCT	Finish	Manager
Majors	Baltimore Orioles	American	85	77	.525	8th (15)	Buck Showalter
Triple-A	Norfolk Tides	International	77	67	.535	t-4th (14)	Ron Johnson
Double-A	Bowie Baysox	Eastern	71	71	.500	5th (12)	Gary Kendall
High A	Frederick Keys	Carolina	61	78	.439	7th (8)	Ryan Minor
Low A	Delmarva Shorebirds	South Atlantic	54	82	.397	13th (14)	Luis Pujols
Short-season	Aberdeen Ironbirds	New York-Penn	40	32	.556	4th (14)	Matt Merullo
Rookie	Orioles	Gulf Coast	30	30	.500	6th (16)	Orlando Gomez
Overall 2013 Minor League Record			333	360	.481	25th (30)	

ORGANIZATION STATISTICS

BALTIMORE ORIOLES

AMERICAN LEAGUE

Batting	B-T	HT	WT	DOB	AVG	vLH	vRH	G	AB	R	H	2B	3B	HR	RBI	BB	HBP	SH	SF	SO	SB	CS	SLG	OBP
Betemit, Wilson	B-R	6-2	220	11-2-81	.000	.000	.000	6	10	0	0	0	0	0	0	0	0	0	0	3	0	0	.000	.000
Casilla, Alexi	B-R	5-9	170	7-20-84	.214	.227	.196	62	112	15	24	4	1	1	10	9	0	2	2	20	9	2	.295	.268
Clevenger, Steve	L-R	6-0	195	4-5-86	.267	.333	.250	4	15	1	4	1	0	0	2	0	0	0	0	2	0	0	.333	.267
Davis, Chris	L-R	6-3	230	3-17-86	.286	.235	.316	160	584	103	167	42	1	53	138	72	10	0	7	199	4	1	.634	.370
Dickerson, Chris	L-L	6-4	230	4-10-82	.238	.143	.245	56	105	17	25	5	0	4	13	4	0	0	0	36	5	1	.400	.266
Flaherty, Ryan	L-R	6-3	210	7-27-86	.224	.217	.224	85	246	28	55	11	0	10	27	19	5	1	0	62	2	0	.390	.293
Hardy, J.J.	R-R	6-1	190	8-19-82	.263	.264	.262	159	601	66	158	27	0	25	76	38	0	3	2	73	2	1	.433	.306
Hoes, L.J.	R-R	6-0	190	3-5-90	.000	.000	—	1	3	0	0	0	0	0	0	0	0	0	0	1	0	0	.000	.000
2-team total (46 Houston)					.282	—	—	47	170	24	48	7	2	1	10	12	1	0	1	35	7	1	.365	.332
Ishikawa, Travis	L-L	6-3	220	9-24-83	.118	.000	.125	6	17	0	2	0	0	0	1	1	0	0	0	8	0	0	.118	.167
2-team total (1 New York)					.105	—	—	7	19	0	2	0	0	0	1	1	0	0	0	10	0	0	.105	.150
Johnson, Dan	L-R	6-2	210	8-10-79	.000	—	.000	3	5	0	0	0	0	0	0	0	0	0	0	1	0	0	.000	.000
Jones, Adam	R-R	6-3	225	8-1-85	.285	.251	.300	160	653	100	186	35	1	33	108	25	8	0	3	136	14	3	.493	.318
Machado, Manny	R-R	6-2	180	7-6-92	.283	.292	.279	156	667	88	189	51	3	14	71	29	2	9	3	113	6	7	.432	.314
Markakis, Nick	L-L	6-1	190	11-17-83	.271	.274	.270	160	634	89	172	24	0	10	59	55	3	0	8	76	1	2	.356	.329
McLouth, Nate	L-R	5-11	180	10-28-81	.258	.209	.272	146	531	76	137	31	4	12	36	53	4	4	1	86	30	7	.399	.329
Morse, Michael	R-R	6-5	245	3-22-82	.103	.087	.167	12	29	3	3	0	0	1	0	0	0	0	0	7	0	0	.103	.133
2-team total (76 Seattle)					.215	—	—	88	312	34	67	13	0	13	27	21	3	0	1	87	0	0	.381	.270
Navarro, Yamaico	R-R	5-11	215	10-31-87	.286	.300	.278	8	28	3	8	0	1	0	2	2	0	1	0	8	0	0	.357	.333
Pearce, Steve	R-R	5-11	210	4-13-83	.261	.267	.250	44	119	14	31	7	0	4	13	15	4	0	0	25	1	0	.420	.362
Pridie, Jason	L-R	6-1	205	10-9-83	.200	.200	.200	4	10	0	2	0	0	0	1	0	0	0	0	2	0	0	.200	.200
Reimold, Nolan	R-R	6-4	205	10-12-83	.195	.220	.179	40	128	17	25	3	0	5	12	10	0	0	2	41	0	1	.336	.250
Roberts, Brian	B-R	5-9	175	10-9-77	.249	.284	.227	77	265	33	66	12	1	8	39	26	0	1	4	44	3	1	.392	.312
Schoop, Jonathan	R-R	6-2	210	10-16-91	.286	.500	.250	5	14	5	4	0	0	1	1	1	0	0	0	5	0	0	.500	.333
Snyder, Chris	R-R	6-4	235	2-12-81	.100	.111	.091	9	20	0	2	0	0	0	1	4	0	0	0	7	0	0	.100	.250
Teagarden, Taylor	R-R	6-0	215	12-21-83	.167	.261	.108	23	60	3	10	2	0	2	5	1	0	1	0	18	0	1	.300	.180
Urrutia, Henry	L-R	6-5	200	2-13-87	.276	.143	.294	24	58	5	16	0	1	0	2	0	0	0	0	11	0	0	.310	.276
Valencia, Danny	R-R	6-2	220	9-19-84	.304	.371	.203	52	161	20	49	14	1	8	23	8	0	0	1	33	0	2	.553	.335
Wieters, Matt	B-R	6-5	240	5-21-86	.235	.282	.214	148	523	59	123	29	0	22	79	43	0	1	12	104	2	0	.417	.287

Pitching	B-T	HT	WT	DOB	W	L	ERA	G	GS	CG	SV	IP	H	R	ER	HR	BB	SO	AVG	vLH	vRH	K/9	BB/9
Arrieta, Jake	R-R	6-4	225	3-6-86	1	2	7.23	5	5	0	0	24	25	19	19	2	17	23	.281	.208	.366	8.75	6.46
Asencio, Jairo	R-R	6-2	180	5-30-83	0	0	7.71	4	0	0	0	2	3	2	2	1	2	4	.300	.500	.167	15.43	7.71
Ayala, Luis	R-R	6-2	175	1-12-78	1	0	9.00	2	0	0	0	2	4	2	2	1	0	2	.400	.000	.667	9.00	0.00
Belfiore, Mike	R-L	6-3	220	10-3-88	0	0	13.50	1	0	0	0	1	3	2	2	2	1	0	.500	1.000	.400	0.00	6.75
Britton, Zach	L-L	6-3	195	12-22-87	2	3	4.95	8	7	0	0	40	52	23	22	4	17	18	.321	.327	.319	4.05	3.83
Burnett, Alex	R-R	6-0	220	7-26-87	0	0	20.25	2	0	0	0	1	4	3	3	0	2	2	.500	.000	.800	13.50	13.50
Chen, Wei-Yin	L-L	6-0	195	7-21-85	7	7	4.07	23	23	0	0	137	142	62	62	17	39	104	.272	.223	.286	6.83	2.56
Clark, Zach	R-R	6-0	200	7-11-83	0	0	16.20	1	0	0	0	2	3	3	3	0	2	1	.429	.750	.000	5.40	10.80
Feldman, Scott	L-R	6-7	230	2-7-83	5	6	4.27	15	15	1	0	91	80	45	43	9	31	65	.235	.245	.223	6.45	3.08
Garcia, Freddy	R-R	6-4	255	10-6-76	3	5	5.77	11	10	0	0	53	60	35	34	16	12	26	.287	.292	.281	4.42	2.04
Gausman, Kevin	R-R	6-3	190	1-6-91	3	5	5.66	20	5	0	0	48	51	30	30	8	13	49	.276	.269	.283	9.25	2.45
Gonzalez, Miguel	R-R	6-1	170	5-27-84	11	8	3.78	30	28	0	0	171	157	81	72	24	53	120	.243	.241	.245	6.30	2.78
Hammel, Jason	R-R	6-6	225	9-2-82	7	8	4.97	26	23	0	1	139	155	81	77	22	48	96	.284	.300	.263	6.20	3.10
Hunter, Tommy	R-R	6-3	250	7-3-86	6	5	2.81	68	0	0	4	86	71	28	27	11	14	68	.223	.294	.141	7.09	1.46
Johnson, Jim	R-R	6-6	240	6-27-83	3	8	2.94	74	0	0	50	70	72	26	23	5	18	56	.273	.279	.266	7.17	2.30
Johnson, Steve	R-R	6-1	220	8-31-87	1	1	7.47	9	1	0	0	16	14	13	13	2	13	20	.233	.258	.207	11.49	7.47
Jurrjens, Jair	R-R	6-1	200	1-29-86	0	0	4.91	2	1	0	0	7	9	4	4	1	1	6	.300	.294	.308	7.36	1.23
Matusz, Brian	L-L	6-4	200	2-11-87	2	1	3.53	65	0	0	0	51	43	21	20	3	16	50	.230	.168	.302	8.82	2.82
McFarland, T.J.	L-L	6-3	220	6-8-89	4	1	4.22	38	1	0	0	75	83	37	35	7	28	58	.277	.287	.269	6.99	3.38
Norris, Bud	R-R	6-0	220	3-2-85	4	3	4.80	11	9	0	0	51	61	27	27	6	24	57	.298	.333	.241	10.13	4.26
2-team total (21 Houston)					10	12	4.18	32	30	0	0	177	196	89	82	17	67	147	—	—	—	7.49	3.41
O'Day, Darren	R-R	6-4	220	10-22-82	5	3	2.18	68	0	0	2	62	47	16	15	7	15	59	.210	.309	.154	8.56	2.18
Patton, Troy	B-L	6-1	180	9-3-85	2	0	3.70	56	0	0	0	56	57	25	23	8	16	42	.270	.289	.254	6.75	2.57

	B-T	HT	WT	DOB	W	L	ERA	G	GS	CG	SV	IP	H	R	ER	HR	BB	SO	AVG	vLH	vRH	K/9	BB/9
Rodriguez, Francisco	R-R	6-0	195	1-7-82	2	1	4.50	23	0	0	0	22	25	11	11	5	5	28	.281	.213	.357	11.45	2.05
Stinson, Josh	R-R	6-4	210	3-14-88	0	0	3.18	11	1	0	0	17	10	7	6	4	3	12	.169	.091	.216	6.35	1.59
Strop, Pedro	R-R	6-0	215	6-13-85	0	3	7.25	29	0	0	0	22	23	19	18	4	15	24	.258	.308	.220	9.67	6.04
Tillman, Chris	R-R	6-5	210	4-15-88	16	7	3.71	33	33	1	0	206	184	87	85	33	68	179	.241	.247	.232	7.81	2.97

Fielding

Catcher	PCT	G	PO	A	E	DP	PB
Clevenger	.969	4	30	1	1	0	1
Snyder	1.000	8	39	5	0	2	1
Teagarden	.992	23	108	9	1	0	1
Wieters	.997	140	1021	58	3	6	5

First Base	PCT	G	PO	A	E	DP
Betemit	1.000	1	1	0	0	0
Davis	.996	155	1339	75	6	153
Flaherty	1.000	4	26	0	0	1
Ishikawa	1.000	4	19	1	0	1
Johnson	1.000	1	1	0	0	1
Pearce	1.000	3	23	0	0	2

Second Base	PCT	G	PO	A	E	DP
Casilla	1.000	51	70	99	0	22
Flaherty	.993	65	105	176	2	52
Navarro	.946	8	17	18	2	4
Roberts	.997	60	110	190	1	43
Schoop	.952	4	8	12	1	4

Third Base	PCT	G	PO	A	E	DP
Flaherty	1.000	7	5	7	0	1
Machado	.973	156	116	355	13	42
Valencia	1.000	6	2	2	0	1

Shortstop	PCT	G	PO	A	E	DP
Casilla	1.000	2	0	1	0	0

	PCT	G	PO	A	E	DP
Flaherty	1.000	9	4	8	0	3
Hardy	.981	159	230	403	12	108

Outfield	PCT	G	PO	A	E	DP
Dickerson	1.000	28	41	1	0	0
Hoes	1.000	1	3	0	0	0
Jones	.995	156	352	11	2	0
Markakis	1.000	155	312	7	0	1
McLouth	.996	138	254	4	1	0
Morse	1.000	10	13	0	0	0
Pearce	1.000	18	23	0	0	0
Pridie	.600	4	2	1	2	0
Reimold	1.000	11	24	2	0	1
Urrutia	—	2	0	0	0	0

NORFOLK TIDES   TRIPLE-A
INTERNATIONAL LEAGUE

Batting	B-T	HT	WT	DOB	AVG	vLH	vRH	G	AB	R	H	2B	3B	HR	RBI	BB	HBP	SH	SF	SO	SB	CS	SLG	OBP
Avery, Xavier	L-L	6-0	190	1-1-90	.237	.160	.264	81	295	36	70	12	2	2	23	31	2	3	2	73	17	5	.312	.312
Betemit, Wilson	B-R	6-2	220	11-2-81	.083	.250	.000	4	12	1	1	1	0	0	0	1	0	0	0	5	0	0	.167	.154
Britton, Buck	L-R	5-11	160	5-16-86	.255	.200	.273	62	220	19	56	10	5	2	27	17	3	0	3	32	1	1	.368	.313
Canzler, Russ	R-R	6-2	220	4-11-86	.276	.415	.240	86	323	46	89	15	1	11	49	47	2	0	2	76	1	1	.430	.369
2-team total (39 Indianapolis)					.252	—	—	125	452	55	114	16	2	12	62	62	3	0	5	101	1	1	.376	.343
Clevenger, Steve	L-R	6-0	195	4-5-86	.324	.267	.339	20	71	11	23	2	0	2	11	10	0	0	1	9	0	0	.437	.402
Dickerson, Chris	L-L	6-4	230	4-10-82	.243	.189	.263	37	136	24	33	7	2	2	8	21	2	0	1	35	1	1		.368
.350 Exposito, Luis	R-R	6-3	210	1-20-87	.224	.254	.212	64	205	23	46	13	0	4	23	17	0	0	4	50	0	0	.346	.279
Flaherty, Ryan	L-R	6-3	210	7-27-86	.265	.188	.333	8	34	4	9	1	0	2	5	1	0	0	0	8	0	0	.471	.286
Ford, Lew	R-R	6-0	200	8-12-76	.170	.077	.206	13	47	8	8	3	0	2	4	2	0	0	2	4	0	0	.362	.196
Gil, Jose	R-R	6-0	205	9-4-86	.333	—	.333	2	6	1	2	0	0	0	1	1	0	0	0	3	0	0	.333	.429
2-team total (5 Scranton/W-B)					.304	—	—	7	23	3	7	0	0	0	2	2	0	0	0	3	0	0	.304	.360
Hoes, L.J.	R-R	6-0	190	3-5-90	.304	.284	.310	99	365	62	111	25	1	3	40	58	5	1	1	56	7	7	.403	.406
Ishikawa, Travis	L-L	6-3	220	9-24-83	.316	.263	.331	49	177	29	56	16	0	7	31	29	1	0	1	43	1	0	.525	.413
2-team total (34 Charlotte)					.290	—	—	83	297	46	86	21	2	9	54	44	5	1	1	74	1	0	.465	.389
Jackson, Conor	R-R	6-2	215	5-7-82	.200	.000	.238	9	25	1	5	1	0	0	2	4	1	0	0	4	0	0	.240	.333
Johnson, Dan	R-L	6-2	210	8-10-79	.154	.143	.167	5	13	2	2	0	0	0	1	3	1	0	1	3	0	0	.154	.333
2-team total (133 Scranton/W-B)					.250	—	—	138	472	59	118	26	0	21	70	96	4	0	5	85	1	0	.439	.378
Liddi, Alex	R-R	6-4	225	8-14-88	.222	.292	.197	49	185	20	41	11	3	4	22	11	1	1	0	58	4	1	.378	.269
Martinez, Luis	R-R	6-0	210	4-3-85	.250	.500	.167	2	8	1	2	0	0	0	1	0	0	0	0	2	0	0	.250	.333
Navarro, Yamaico	R-R	5-11	205	10-31-87	.267	.214	.281	107	390	59	104	21	1	12	53	53	3	0	6	73	9	2	.418	.354
Paulino, Ronny	R-R	6-3	250	4-21-81	.174	.200	.167	8	23	2	4	1	0	1	2	4	0	0	0	7	0	0	.348	.296
2-team total (13 Toledo)					.235	—	—	21	68	5	16	3	0	2	8	6	0	0	0	19	0	0	.368	.297
Pridie, Jason	L-R	6-1	205	10-9-83	.269	.256	.274	118	479	69	129	24	5	15	57	43	4	2	3	120	8	2	.434	.333
Roberts, Brian	B-R	5-9	175	10-9-77	.231	.000	.333	4	13	2	3	1	0	0	1	2	0	0	0	3	0	0	.308	.333
Robinson, Chris	R-R	6-0	220	5-12-84	.241	.348	.212	29	108	9	26	4	0	0	5	4	0	1	0	24	0	0	.278	.268
Robinson, Trayvon	B-R	5-10	200	9-1-87	.220	.224	.218	52	177	28	39	5	0	5	15	22	0	2	0	60	9	2	.333	.307
Romero, Niuman	B-R	6-1	190	1-24-85	.167	.200	.158	15	48	7	8	0	1	2	3	10	0	0	0	13	1	2	.333	.310
Schoop, Jonathan	R-R	6-2	210	10-16-91	.256	.211	.271	70	270	30	69	11	0	9	34	13	5	0	1	55	1	2	.396	.301
Snyder, Chris	R-R	6-4	235	2-12-81	.243	.213	.254	52	181	16	44	8	0	6	24	17	0	0	2	47	0	0	.387	.305
Teagarden, Taylor	R-R	6-1	215	12-21-83	.077	.000	.100	5	13	1	1	0	0	1	0	0	0	0	2	0	0	0	.077	.077
Thames, Eric	L-R	6-0	210	11-10-86	.252	.244	.255	36	135	17	34	5	0	3	13	11	2	0	1	33	3	1	.356	.315
Urrutia, Henry	L-L	6-5	200	2-13-87	.316	.273	.333	29	114	16	36	5	1	2	13	8	0	0	1	15	0	0	.430	.358
Valencia, Danny	R-R	6-2	220	9-19-84	.286	.324	.273	65	262	40	75	20	1	14	51	17	0	0	3	48	1	1	.531	.326
Ward, Brian	R-R	5-11	210	10-17-85	—	—	—	1	0	0	0	0	0	0	0	0	0	0	0	0	0	0	—	—
Waring, Brandon	R-R	6-3	215	1-2-86	.222	.182	.240	10	36	3	8	2	0	2	8	5	1	0	0	9	0	0	.444	.333
Wheeler, Zelous	R-R	5-10	220	1-16-87	.268	.325	.249	89	321	38	86	17	1	10	45	30	6	0	2	55	2	1	.421	.340
Wood, Brandon	R-R	6-3	205	3-2-85	.215	.286	.194	48	181	13	39	9	1	2	23	10	0	0	5	37	0	0	.309	.250

Pitching	B-T	HT	WT	DOB	W	L	ERA	G	GS	CG	SV	IP	H	R	ER	HR	BB	SO	AVG	vLH	vRH	K/9	BB/9
Alderson, Tim	R-R	6-6	220	11-3-88	1	2	6.27	15	1	0	0	33	39	23	23	4	10	26	.302	.308	.297	7.09	2.73
2-team total (22 Indianapolis)					4	3	4.32	37	1	0	0	75	79	39	36	9	20	64	—	—	—	7.68	2.40
Arrieta, Jake	R-R	6-4	225	3-6-86	5	3	4.41	9	8	1	0	49	45	26	24	4	14	38	.246	.247	.245	6.98	2.57
Asencio, Jairo	R-R	6-2	180	5-30-83	5	0	2.66	47	0	0	28	51	35	17	15	5	14	56	.191	.208	.179	9.95	2.49
Belfiore, Mike	R-L	6-3	220	10-3-88	2	1	3.18	37	0	0	1	76	81	27	27	6	29	82	.275	.244	.297	9.67	3.42
Britton, Zach	L-L	6-3	195	12-22-87	6	5	4.27	19	19	0	0	103	112	59	49	5	46	75	.279	.208	.303	6.53	4.01
Burnett, Alex	R-R	6-0	220	7-26-87	1	0	1.86	7	0	0	0	10	10	2	2	0	1	8	.256	.313	.217	7.45	0.93
2-team total (2 Buffalo)					1	0	1.50	9	0	0	0	12	11	2	2	0	2	8	—	—	—	6.00	1.50
Clark, Zach	R-R	6-0	200	7-11-83	1	2	4.56	5	5	0	0	26	30	19	13	1	7	20	.288	.281	.298	7.01	2.45
Delaney, Rob	L-R	6-2	250	9-8-84	0	1	10.13	3	0	0	0	5	9	6	6	1	2	2	.409	.444	.385	3.38	3.38
Delcarmen, Manny	R-R	6-2	220	2-16-82	3	3	2.83	48	0	0	0	54	44	18	17	3	22	46	.229	.180	.272	7.67	3.67

Pitching	B-T	HT	WT	DOB	W	L	ERA	G	GS	CG	SV	IP	H	R	ER	HR	BB	SO	AVG	vLH	vRH	K/9	BB/9
Gamboa, Eddie	R-R	6-2	195	12-21-84	2	5	6.23	9	9	1	0	43	41	35	30	2	28	35	.244	.272	.211	7.27	5.82
Garcia, Freddy	R-R	6-4	255	10-6-76	8	3	2.84	13	13	0	0	82	73	28	26	10	15	61	.239	.274	.197	6.67	1.64
2-team total (1 Gwinnett)					8	4	3.56	14	14	0	0	86	80	36	34	11	20	62	—	—	—	6.49	2.09
Gausman, Kevin	R-R	6-3	190	1-6-91	1	2	4.04	8	7	0	0	36	36	16	16	1	9	33	.271	.271	.270	8.33	2.27
Hendrickson, Mark	L-L	6-9	240	6-23-74	5	3	3.06	40	0	0	2	68	55	27	23	8	17	37	.224	.231	.220	4.92	2.26
Johnson, Steve	R-R	6-1	220	8-31-87	2	3	4.11	10	8	0	0	46	40	22	21	4	17	52	.233	.267	.195	10.17	3.33
Jones, Chris	L-L	6-2	205	9-19-88	4	4	2.67	31	2	0	1	71	72	28	21	3	34	47	.268	.196	.311	5.99	4.33
Jurrjens, Jair	R-R	6-1	200	1-29-86	6	6	4.18	16	16	1	0	95	102	48	44	5	24	52	.280	.285	.276	4.94	2.28
2-team total (7 Toledo)					7	10	4.57	23	23	1	0	134	147	72	68	8	38	76	—	—	—	5.10	2.55
Loomis, Andy	L-L	5-10	175	11-25-85	2	3	3.33	14	0	0	0	27	23	11	10	1	10	22	.232	.132	.295	7.33	3.33
McCutchen, Daniel	R-R	6-2	215	9-26-82	2	2	4.74	19	5	0	0	38	41	22	20	5	13	34	.275	.288	.265	8.05	3.08
Petersime, Zach	R-R	6-3	175	1-19-89	0	1	22.50	1	1	0	0	4	11	10	10	1	2	4	.524	.571	.429	9.00	4.50
Pettit, Jake	L-L	6-1	185	10-28-86	3	2	4.56	5	4	0	0	24	24	14	12	2	6	16	.264	.391	.221	6.08	2.28
Proctor, Scott	R-R	6-1	195	1-2-77	0	0	8.59	6	0	0	1	7	10	13	7	1	10	6	.313	.263	.385	7.36	12.27
Rauch, Jon	R-R	6-11	290	9-27-78	1	0	2.89	10	0	0	0	9	9	3	3	2	4	10	.257	.167	.304	9.64	3.86
Russell, Adam	R-R	6-8	250	4-14-83	3	3	2.37	42	3	0	5	61	52	19	16	2	33	59	.231	.241	.225	8.75	4.90
Schlereth, Daniel	L-L	6-0	200	5-9-86	2	0	0.82	12	0	0	0	11	6	2	1	0	8	7	.158	.111	.200	5.73	6.55
Stinson, Josh	R-R	6-4	210	3-14-88	7	6	3.78	23	23	0	0	131	126	60	55	11	54	87	.257	.292	.224	5.98	3.71
Wada, Tsuyoshi	L-L	5-11	180	2-21-81	5	6	4.03	19	19	0	0	103	112	50	46	9	35	80	.281	.275	.284	7.01	3.07
Wright, Mike	R-R	6-6	215	1-3-90	0	0	0.00	1	1	0	0	7	6	0	0	0	0	2	.231	.222	.235	2.70	0.00

Fielding

Catcher	PCT	G	PO	A	E	DP	PB
Clevenger	1.000	11	67	3	0	0	0
Exposito	.979	59	383	35	9	5	8
Gil	1.000	1	7	0	0	0	0
Martinez	1.000	2	15	0	0	0	0
Robinson	.995	27	180	16	1	1	2
Snyder	.995	48	355	30	2	3	12
Teagarden	1.000	2	9	2	0	0	0
Ward	1.000	1	1	0	0	0	0

First Base	PCT	G	PO	A	E	DP
Britton	1.000	17	138	10	0	12
Canzler	.997	35	279	21	1	26
Clevenger	1.000	9	79	7	0	9
Exposito	1.000	1	6	1	0	1
Ishikawa	.991	44	439	24	4	32
Jackson	1.000	2	14	1	0	4
Johnson	1.000	4	31	2	0	4
Liddi	1.000	26	208	14	0	26
Robinson	1.000	1	6	1	0	1
Valencia	.986	6	67	4	1	3
Waring	1.000	1	15	1	0	3

Second Base	PCT	G	PO	A	E	DP
Wood	.972	4	34	1	1	4
Britton	.988	34	63	101	2	27
Canzler	1.000	1	4	3	0	2
Flaherty	.971	8	13	21	1	4
Navarro	.959	15	21	50	3	11
Roberts	1.000	3	1	9	0	0
Romero	1.000	9	17	31	0	7
Schoop	.996	50	87	146	1	36
Wheeler	.971	26	30	70	3	15
Wood	1.000	2	3	5	0	1

Third Base	PCT	G	PO	A	E	DP
Britton	1.000	3	3	7	0	1
Canzler	.818	4	3	6	2	1
Liddi	.926	22	14	36	4	2
Navarro	1.000	2	2	2	0	0
Romero	1.000	2	0	1	0	0
Valencia	.961	50	34	90	5	6
Waring	1.000	8	4	10	0	3
Wheeler	.951	49	29	108	7	10
Wood	.840	9	4	17	4	1

Shortstop	PCT	G	PO	A	E	DP
Liddi	1.000	3	4	15	0	1
Navarro	.962	86	121	262	15	54
Romero	1.000	4	9	9	0	1
Schoop	.930	20	35	72	8	16
Wheeler	.667	2	1	3	2	0
Wood	.975	29	31	87	3	19

Outfield	PCT	G	PO	A	E	DP
Avery	.987	80	150	2	2	0
Britton	1.000	6	9	0	0	0
Canzler	.950	14	18	1	1	0
Dickerson	.984	29	60	3	1	0
Ford	1.000	5	10	0	0	0
Hoes	.973	91	171	6	5	1
Jackson	1.000	5	7	0	0	0
Navarro	1.000	4	4	1	0	0
Pridie	.996	103	259	7	1	4
Robinson	.988	51	78	4	1	1
Thames	1.000	22	38	2	0	1
Urrutia	.967	28	53	5	2	1
Valencia	1.000	5	13	0	0	0

BOWIE BAYSOX   DOUBLE-A
EASTERN LEAGUE

Batting	B-T	HT	WT	DOB	AVG	vLH	vRH	G	AB	R	H	2B	3B	HR	RBI	BB	HBP	SH	SF	SO	SB	CS	SLG	OBP
Adair, Travis	L-R	5-10	180	12-23-87	.250	.250	.250	5	16	1	4	0	0	0	2	1	0	0	0	2	0	0	.250	.294
Alvarez, Dariel	R-R	6-2	180	11-7-88	.194	.333	.160	9	31	2	6	0	0	1	1	1	0	0	0	9	0	0	.290	.219
Avery, Xavier	L-L	6-0	190	1-1-90	.300	.275	.312	39	160	34	48	10	2	1	12	23	1	2	0	44	12	3	.406	.391
Baker, Aaron	L-R	6-2	220	9-10-87	.251	.317	.226	60	215	28	54	13	2	5	21	26	1	0	1	51	1	2	.400	.333
Barber, George	R-R	6-0	180	8-8-89	.333	.667	.167	3	9	2	3	0	0	0	0	0	0	0	0	2	0	0	.333	.333
Betemit, Wilson	B-R	6-2	220	11-2-81	.353	.182	.667	5	17	1	6	0	0	0	3	4	0	0	0	4	0	0	.353	.476
Britton, Buck	L-R	5-11	160	5-16-86	.291	.346	.266	61	247	38	72	12	3	8	52	19	0	2	2	34	5	1	.462	.340
Bumbry, Steve	L-L	5-11	185	4-4-88	.233	.278	.218	25	73	14	17	4	0	5	12	14	2	1	0	26	0	1	.493	.371
Ford, Lew	R-R	6-0	200	8-12-76	.258	.364	.205	17	66	13	17	9	0	3	10	6	3	0	0	9	0	0	.530	.347
Gil, Jose	R-R	6-0	205	9-4-86	.000	.000	.000	1	3	0	0	0	0	0	0	1	0	0	0	1	0	0	.000	.250
2-team total (15 Trenton)					.226	—		16	53	6	12	2	0	0	3	5	1	0	0	13	1	1	.264	.305
Horton, Josh	L-R	6-2	215	2-19-86	.303	.292	.307	74	251	42	76	20	1	2	27	15	1	2	2	48	3	1	.414	.342
Hudson, Kyle	L-L	5-11	175	1-7-87	.292	.290	.293	103	353	66	103	7	1	0	33	55	2	7	4	56	26	8	.317	.386
Iorg, Cale	R-R	6-2	185	9-6-85	.145	.056	.189	18	55	5	8	3	0	1	6	4	0	2	1	22	3	0	.255	.200
Joseph, Caleb	R-R	6-3	180	6-18-86	.299	.416	.252	135	518	74	155	31	2	22	97	39	3	0	10	92	4	2	.494	.346
Kelly, Ty	L-R	6-0	185	7-20-88	.283	.313	.271	72	283	51	80	21	2	1	47	51	2	1	6	49	4	2	.382	.389
Loman, Seth	L-R	6-4	245	12-16-85	.262	.265	.260	56	195	23	51	13	0	6	31	14	6	1	4	57	0	0	.421	.324
Martinez, Luis	R-R	6-0	210	4-3-85	.257	.219	.278	60	206	21	53	16	0	1	20	18	2	0	3	41	0	2	.350	.319
Paulino, Ronny	R-R	6-3	250	4-21-81	.292	.222	.333	8	24	3	7	0	0	0	2	6	0	0	0	7	0	0	.292	.433
Pettit, Chris	R-R	6-0	200	8-15-84	.125	.133	.118	29	64	9	8	3	0	1	5	10	1	2	0	14	0	1	.219	.253
2-team total (18 New Britain)					.127	—		47	126	19	16	7	0	1	10	15	3	3	1	31	1	2	.206	.234
Reimold, Nolan	R-R	6-4	205	10-12-83	.196	.333	.175	12	46	3	9	0	1	1	5	4	0	0	1	13	0	0	.304	.255
Robinson, Trayvon	B-R	5-10	200	9-1-87	.271	.311	.254	55	199	34	54	15	1	6	28	24	0	4	1	55	12	4	.447	.348
Romero, Niuman	B-R	6-1	190	1-24-85	.280	.276	.282	102	371	51	104	21	1	2	47	56	1	9	2	57	7	4	.358	.374
Rosa, Garabez	R-R	6-2	166	10-12-89	.276	.270	.279	125	460	54	127	19	4	6	49	8	2	6	1	77	8	5	.374	.291
Ruettiger, John	L-L	6-1	193	9-21-89	.283	.400	.212	18	53	7	15	2	0	0	3	10	1	1	0	13	1	0	.321	.406
Urrutia, Henry	L-R	6-5	200	2-13-87	.365	.340	.374	52	200	33	73	16	0	7	37	24	0	0	0	36	1	1	.550	.433

	B-T	HT	WT	DOB	AVG	vLH	vRH	G	AB	R	H	2B	3B	HR	RBI	BB	HBP	SH	SF	SO	SB	CS	SLG	OBP
Walker, Christian	R-R	6-0	220	3-28-91	.242	.190	.268	17	62	7	15	5	0	0	1	6	1	0	0	10	0	0	.323	.319
Ward, Brian	R-R	5-11	210	10-17-85	.260	.267	.257	49	154	24	40	9	0	2	23	16	5	4	2	28	1	1	.357	.345
Waring, Brandon	R-R	6-3	215	1-2-86	.213	.254	.192	99	347	46	74	13	0	23	61	48	5	1	3	129	0	0	.450	.315
Wheeler, Zelous	R-R	5-10	220	1-16-87	.299	.154	.361	24	87	11	26	5	0	1	11	15	0	0	0	15	3	0	.391	.402

Pitching	B-T	HT	WT	DOB	W	L	ERA	G	GS	CG	SV	IP	H	R	ER	HR	BB	SO	AVG	vLH	vRH	K/9	BB/9
Bascom, Tim	R-R	6-1	205	1-4-85	2	4	3.72	24	5	0	0	58	51	26	24	2	34	48	.242	.281	.213	7.45	5.28
Beaulac, Eric	R-R	6-5	190	11-13-86	0	0	2.45	5	0	0	0	7	8	2	2	0	7	7	.296	.417	.200	8.59	8.59
Bischoff, Matt	R-R	6-0	190	5-21-87	6	2	4.41	25	1	0	1	51	47	26	25	5	22	50	.242	.272	.221	8.82	3.88
Boleska, Tom	R-R	6-0	190	7-30-86	2	4	5.33	16	0	0	1	25	27	15	15	1	14	28	.276	.182	.352	9.95	4.97
Chen, Wei-Yin	L-L	6-0	195	7-21-85	1	0	3.00	2	2	0	0	12	9	4	4	0	2	8	.214	.250	.206	6.00	1.50
Clark, Zach	R-R	6-0	200	7-11-83	1	4	8.63	6	5	0	0	24	32	26	23	2	20	17	.333	.356	.314	6.38	7.50
Drake, Oliver	R-R	6-4	215	1-13-87	3	0	1.74	19	0	0	8	31	19	8	6	1	13	38	.173	.167	.176	11.03	3.77
Gamboa, Eddie	R-R	6-2	195	12-21-84	4	6	3.64	16	16	2	0	99	82	49	40	6	31	79	.227	.230	.224	7.18	2.82
Gausman, Kevin	R-R	6-3	190	1-6-91	2	4	3.11	8	8	0	0	46	44	21	16	3	5	49	.246	.250	.242	9.52	0.97
Gleason, Sean	L-R	5-11	210	8-21-85	0	0	4.66	5	0	0	0	10	9	7	5	1	3	5	.231	.158	.300	4.66	2.79
Gurka, Jason	L-L	6-0	170	1-10-88	2	2	2.95	20	0	0	4	40	35	13	13	2	18	46	.243	.188	.271	10.44	4.08
Hammel, Jason	R-R	6-6	225	9-2-82	0	0	0.00	1	1	0	0	3	3	0	0	0	3	3	.273	.250	.286	10.13	0.00
Howard, Trent	L-L	6-2	200	10-16-89	0	1	9.00	1	1	0	0	4	4	4	4	0	1	1	.267	.250	.273	2.25	2.25
Jones, Chris	L-L	6-2	205	9-19-88	0	0	2.57	4	0	0	1	7	8	2	2	0	0	6	.286	.222	.316	7.71	0.00
Jones, Devin	R-R	6-2	170	7-4-90	4	7	5.84	24	24	1	0	123	146	95	80	17	48	108	.299	.350	.255	7.88	3.50
Loomis, Andy	L-L	5-10	175	11-25-85	0	3	5.48	12	0	0	1	21	24	15	13	2	12	17	.286	.194	.340	7.17	5.06
McCutchen, Daniel	R-R	6-2	215	9-26-82	2	0	1.21	6	2	0	2	22	15	3	3	2	2	20	.188	.233	.160	8.06	0.81
Petrini, Chris	R-L	6-0	205	2-11-87	5	5	3.11	38	2	0	1	67	59	26	23	3	33	59	.240	.273	.225	7.97	4.46
Pettit, Jake	L-L	6-1	185	10-28-86	7	6	4.42	21	21	1	0	124	122	65	61	12	41	92	.257	.195	.277	6.66	2.97
Prado, Marcel	R-R	6-4	226	11-22-87	1	1	2.45	25	0	0	10	29	25	13	8	1	10	28	.282	.194	.259	8.59	3.07
Rodriguez, Eduardo	L-L	6-2	200	4-7-93	4	3	4.22	11	11	1	0	60	53	28	28	5	24	59	.237	.235	.237	8.90	3.62
Rodriguez, Julio	R-R	6-4	195	8-29-90	0	0	20.25	1	1	0	0	3	2	6	6	1	7	2	.222	.250	.200	6.75	23.63
Schrader, Clay	L-R	5-11	200	4-28-90	5	4	4.34	35	0	0	16	56	50	30	27	6	35	62	.236	.165	.278	9.96	5.63
Walters, David	R-R	6-3	190	8-13-87	1	2	9.00	6	0	0	0	7	16	8	7	1	2	3	.457	.500	.440	3.86	2.57
Wilson, Tyler	R-R	6-2	185	9-25-89	7	5	3.83	16	16	1	0	89	85	40	38	13	22	70	.246	.244	.248	7.05	2.22
Wright, Mike	R-R	6-6	215	1-3-90	11	3	3.26	26	26	0	0	144	152	65	52	9	39	136	.267	.278	.257	8.52	2.44
Zinicola, Zech	R-R	6-1	220	3-2-85	1	5	2.92	46	0	0	13	65	56	23	21	3	22	58	.234	.177	.273	8.07	3.06

Fielding

Catcher	PCT	G	PO	A	E	DP	PB
Gil	1.000	1	8	1	0	0	0
Joseph	.989	64	483	48	6	6	17
Martinez	.982	35	246	28	5	1	4
Paulino	1.000	3	20	3	0	1	0
Ward	.990	46	347	40	4	9	3

First Base	PCT	G	PO	A	E	DP
Baker	.988	49	378	27	5	40
Britton	1.000	6	34	4	0	2
Joseph	.988	12	71	8	1	4
Loman	.991	41	310	17	3	25
Martinez	1.000	1	10	0	0	0
Walker	1.000	14	111	5	0	8
Waring	.984	23	164	21	3	12

Second Base	PCT	G	PO	A	E	DP
Adair	1.000	2	0	2	0	0
Britton	.939	20	26	51	5	9
Horton	.970	58	106	120	7	26

	PCT	G	PO	A	E	DP
Iorg	1.000	8	18	15	0	4
Kelly	.978	18	39	49	2	14
Romero	1.000	1	3	2	0	1
Rosa	.970	26	66	63	4	21
Wheeler	1.000	10	17	20	0	8

Third Base	PCT	G	PO	A	E	DP
Adair	1.000	1	1	2	0	0
Britton	.857	4	2	10	2	2
Kelly	.916	50	37	83	11	8
Rosa	1.000	11	7	19	0	2
Waring	.949	67	49	120	9	11
Wheeler	.923	10	4	20	2	2

Shortstop	PCT	G	PO	A	E	DP
Britton	1.000	1	2	4	0	2
Horton	.952	12	15	25	2	7
Iorg	.897	7	12	14	3	4
Loman	1.000	1	2	0	0	0
Romero	.970	97	125	229	11	41

	PCT	G	PO	A	E	DP
Rosa	.913	23	40	54	9	11
Wheeler	1.000	3	5	5	0	0

Outfield	PCT	G	PO	A	E	DP
Alvarez	.960	9	23	1	1	1
Avery	.957	38	86	2	4	0
Barber	1.000	1	1	0	0	0
Britton	.976	25	41	0	1	0
Bumbry	.945	23	52	0	3	0
Ford	1.000	10	22	2	0	1
Hudson	.990	103	195	6	2	1
Joseph	1.000	16	19	2	0	0
Kelly	1.000	4	5	0	0	0
Pettit	1.000	27	48	1	0	0
Reimold	1.000	7	9	1	0	0
Robinson	.991	53	112	2	1	0
Rosa	.985	64	122	9	2	2
Ruettiger	.971	16	32	1	1	0
Urrutia	1.000	49	82	4	0	1

FREDERICK KEYS HIGH CLASS A

CAROLINA LEAGUE

Batting	B-T	HT	WT	DOB	AVG	vLH	vRH	G	AB	R	H	2B	3B	HR	RBI	BB	HBP	SH	SF	SO	SB	CS	SLG	OBP
Adair, Travis	L-R	5-10	180	12-23-87	.274	.283	.272	73	270	37	74	14	2	3	23	21	1	2	1	30	9	1	.374	.328
Alvarez, Dariel	R-R	6-2	180	11-7-88	.436	—	.436	10	39	5	17	2	0	2	7	2	0	0	0	1	1	2	.641	.463
Baker, Aaron	L-R	6-2	220	9-10-87	.113	.000	.140	14	53	3	6	4	0	1	5	3	0	0	0	16	0	0	.245	.161
Betemit, Wilson	B-R	6-2	220	11-2-81	.294	.000	.294	4	17	1	5	0	0	0	4	0	0	0	0	4	0	0	.294	.294
Bumbry, Steve	L-L	5-11	185	4-4-88	.221	.000	.225	27	95	19	21	3	0	5	17	14	0	0	1	34	2	2	.411	.318
Capellan, Byron	R-R	5-11	150	8-9-93	.000	.000	.000	2	3	0	0	0	0	0	0	0	0	0	0	2	0	0	.000	.000
Caronia, Anthony	L-R	6-0	170	5-22-91	.179	.500	.154	13	28	2	5	0	0	0	1	2	0	1	0	9	2	0	.179	.233
Chavez, Zane	L-R	5-10	200	12-30-86	.295	.186	.314	75	285	40	84	20	0	7	49	46	0	0	2	56	0	0	.439	.390
Cid, Delvi	R-R	6-3	195	7-19-89	.252	.250	.252	41	131	26	33	4	0	5	23	14	3	1	0	31	10	6	.397	.338
Davis, Glynn	R-R	6-3	170	12-7-91	.234	.352	.205	97	364	42	85	17	3	2	32	43	1	2	0	74	19	7	.313	.316
De San Miguel, Allan	R-R	5-9	205	2-14-88	.240	.188	.254	65	221	31	53	10	0	10	33	34	10	1	0	57	3	1	.421	.366
Delmonico, Nick	L-R	6-2	200	7-12-92	.243	.244	.243	61	226	33	55	12	0	13	30	36	1	0	0	59	5	1	.469	.350
Esposito, Jason	R-R	6-2	200	7-19-90	.222	.243	.216	100	365	31	81	12	1	4	41	19	6	3	5	115	8	2	.293	.268
Flaherty, Ryan	L-R	6-3	210	7-27-86	.286	.000	.400	2	7	1	2	0	0	1	2	0	0	0	0	3	0	0	.714	.286
Mosby, Michael	R-R	6-0	195	10-30-89	.278	.111	.309	88	115	16	32	6	0	5	20	16	4	0	1	38	2	1	.461	.382
Mummey, Trent	L-L	5-9	170	1-5-89	.188	.250	.167	10	32	6	6	0	0	1	5	11	0	0	0	4	2	3	.281	.395
Narron, Connor	B-R	6-3	195	11-12-91	.196	.238	.183	27	92	13	18	4	0	1	8	19	1	0	1	26	0	0	.272	.336

Name	B-T	HT	WT	DOB	AVG	vLH	vRH	G	AB	R	H	2B	3B	HR	RBI	BB	HBP	SH	SF	SO	SB	CS	SLG	OBP
Nathans, Tucker	L-R	6-0	200	11-6-88	.277	.296	.273	45	159	17	44	8	1	1	18	16	0	1	1	34	5	2	.358	.341
Ohlman, Michael	R-R	6-4	205	12-14-90	.313	.364	.302	100	361	61	113	29	4	13	53	56	5	0	2	93	5	0	.524	.410
Pearce, Steve	R-R	5-11	210	4-13-83	.167	.000	.200	2	6	0	1	0	0	0	0	1	1	0	0	1	0	0	.167	.375
Pena, Jerome	B-R	5-11	185	11-6-88	.222	.271	.211	120	455	66	101	21	2	11	52	66	3	1	1	123	8	5	.349	.324
Planeta, Mike	R-R	6-4	182	10-17-89	.135	.000	.192	12	37	4	5	1	0	0	1	3	0	0	0	17	0	1	.162	.200
Ruettiger, John	L-L	6-1	193	9-21-89	.246	.203	.254	106	415	52	102	7	2	2	26	45	1	1	4	71	43	7	.287	.320
Starr, Sammie	R-R	5-8	165	5-31-88	.216	.183	.225	115	416	44	90	13	0	6	45	29	13	4	7	62	8	1	.291	.284
Walker, Christian	R-R	6-0	220	3-28-91	.288	.316	.282	55	215	26	62	11	0	8	35	17	3	0	4	41	2	0	.479	.343
Webb, Brenden	L-L	6-1	185	2-24-90	.201	.204	.201	84	293	37	59	14	2	8	31	36	5	1	2	107	7	2	.345	.298

Pitching	B-T	HT	WT	DOB	W	L	ERA	G	GS	CG	SV	IP	H	R	ER	HR	BB	SO	AVG	vLH	vRH	K/9	BB/9
Beal, Jesse	B-R	6-6	210	7-12-90	3	1	4.71	40	0	0	3	73	94	46	38	4	24	67	.306	.342	.286	8.30	2.97
Beaulac, Eric	R-R	6-5	190	11-13-86	2	0	1.64	7	0	0	0	11	6	2	2	0	10	13	.150	.000	.261	10.64	8.18
Berry, Tim	L-L	6-3	180	3-18-91	11	7	3.85	27	27	0	0	152	156	80	65	13	40	119	.265	.217	.285	7.05	2.37
Bischoff, Matt	R-R	6-0	190	5-21-87	1	0	1.20	6	1	0	1	15	12	5	2	0	1	22	.218	.280	.167	13.20	0.60
Chalas, Miguel	R-R	6-0	170	6-27-92	1	3	3.62	22	0	0	2	55	59	23	22	6	10	29	.284	.333	.239	4.77	1.65
Clark, Zach	R-R	6-0	200	7-11-83	1	7	9.74	10	10	0	0	44	51	53	48	3	42	20	.297	.359	.245	4.06	8.53
Davies, Zach	R-R	6-0	150	2-7-93	7	9	3.69	26	26	0	0	149	145	72	61	10	38	132	.256	.254	.257	7.99	2.30
Escat, Gene	R-R	6-2	195	9-3-89	6	7	5.65	41	0	0	6	57	63	38	36	7	25	35	.281	.279	.283	5.49	3.92
Fowler, Zach	L-L	6-4	205	2-27-89	3	4	2.57	37	0	0	2	74	72	25	21	2	28	55	.266	.241	.276	6.72	3.42
Hobgood, Matt	R-R	6-4	245	8-3-90	2	1	5.58	9	0	0	0	31	29	19	19	2	11	25	.254	.204	.292	7.34	3.23
Howard, Trent	L-L	6-2	200	10-16-89	3	2	3.48	28	15	0	1	88	87	45	34	6	25	72	.257	.243	.264	7.36	2.56
Jones, Devin	R-R	6-2	170	7-4-90	1	0	1.50	1	1	0	0	6	3	1	1	0	1	3	.150	.143	.154	4.50	1.50
Petersime, Zach	R-R	6-3	175	1-19-89	2	7	6.44	16	12	0	0	64	89	53	46	0	21	31	.318	.300	.333	4.34	2.94
Prado, Marcel	R-R	6-4	226	11-22-87	2	3	2.30	21	0	0	6	27	26	14	7	1	7	32	.232	.311	.207	10.54	2.30
Price, Matt	R-R	6-2	215	9-8-89	2	2	5.40	25	0	0	2	27	32	21	16	2	13	24	.296	.286	.301	8.10	4.39
Rennie, Luc	R-R	6-2	200	4-26-94	1	2	5.56	3	2	0	0	11	11	9	7	1	6	6	.250	.143	.270	4.76	4.76
Rodriguez, Eduardo	L-L	6-2	200	4-7-93	6	4	2.85	14	14	0	0	85	78	36	27	4	25	66	.245	.306	.222	6.96	2.64
Rodriguez, Julio	R-R	6-4	195	8-29-90	0	3	10.13	4	4	0	0	16	21	21	18	5	10	14	.313	.421	.172	7.88	5.63
Rutledge, Lex	L-L	6-1	195	6-28-91	1	0	7.82	9	0	0	0	13	18	11	11	1	7	15	.327	.250	.359	10.46	4.97
Stinson, Josh	R-R	6-4	210	3-14-88	0	0	4.50	1	0	0	0	2	4	1	1	0	0	1	.400	.000	.500	4.50	0.00
Tolliver, Ashur	L-L	6-0	170	1-24-88	1	0	2.61	12	1	0	0	31	27	9	9	2	9	22	.237	.182	.259	6.39	2.61
Wager, Brady	R-R	6-3	190	11-17-90	3	10	5.23	15	15	1	0	86	93	61	50	5	32	57	.277	.291	.267	5.97	3.35
Walters, David	R-R	6-3	190	8-13-87	0	2	5.08	20	0	0	3	28	37	23	16	5	10	11	.325	.353	.302	3.49	3.18
Wilson, Tyler	R-R	6-2	185	9-25-89	1	1	4.48	11	11	0	0	62	57	34	31	4	25	48	.242	.270	.224	6.93	3.61
Winegardner, Tommy	B-R	5-10	189	3-11-90	1	3	7.29	14	0	0	0	21	29	19	17	4	14	11	.330	.378	.294	4.71	6.00

Fielding

Catcher	PCT	G	PO	A	E	DP	PB
Chavez	.982	45	343	33	7	1	6
De San Miguel	.988	50	307	29	4	3	6
Ohlman	.974	46	311	32	9	1	6

First Base	PCT	G	PO	A	E	DP
Baker	1.000	10	92	10	0	9
Delmonico	.981	6	48	4	1	6
Esposito	.974	19	144	5	4	8
Mosby	.994	32	304	23	2	28
Narron	.988	25	237	12	3	23
Pearce	1.000	1	12	0	0	0
Walker	.994	52	473	16	3	49

Second Base	PCT	G	PO	A	E	DP
Adair	.958	33	51	86	6	24
Caronia	.909	3	4	6	1	1
Esposito	1.000	1	3	2	0	1

	PCT	G	PO	A	E	DP
Flaherty	1.000	2	4	2	0	1
Mosby	1.000	2	0	4	0	0
Nathans	1.000	3	2	12	0	2
Pena	.981	98	198	317	10	73
Starr	1.000	2	1	5	0	0
Winegardner	.500	1	0	1	1	0

Third Base	PCT	G	PO	A	E	DP
Adair	.791	18	11	23	9	4
Caronia	—	1	0	0	0	0
Delmonico	.867	42	16	75	14	6
Esposito	.926	81	62	163	18	10
Mosby	1.000	3	0	2	0	1
Nathans	.800	3	1	3	1	0

Shortstop	PCT	G	PO	A	E	DP
Adair	.929	3	2	11	1	1
Capellan	1.000	1	1	1	0	0

	PCT	G	PO	A	E	DP
Caronia	1.000	6	12	17	0	4
Nathans	1.000	1	1	1	0	0
Pena	.989	19	30	61	1	11
Starr	.955	113	171	354	25	79

Outfield	PCT	G	PO	A	E	DP
Adair	1.000	18	23	1	0	0
Alvarez	.947	10	16	2	1	1
Bumbry	1.000	26	43	4	0	0
Cid	.974	40	69	5	2	1
Davis	.986	95	209	5	3	1
Mummey	1.000	10	11	0	0	0
Nathans	.981	36	52	0	1	0
Planeta	1.000	8	13	0	0	0
Ruettiger	.984	105	180	6	3	1
Webb	.988	81	155	12	2	4

DELMARVA SHOREBIRDS   LOW CLASS A

SOUTH ATLANTIC LEAGUE

Batting	B-T	HT	WT	DOB	AVG	vLH	vRH	G	AB	R	H	2B	3B	HR	RBI	BB	HBP	SH	SF	SO	SB	CS	SLG	OBP
Balog, Nik	L-L	6-3	220	10-14-89	.266	.190	.287	101	380	38	101	29	1	3	32	20	8	0	4	82	1	0	.371	.313
Barber, George	R-R	6-0	180	8-8-89	.234	.214	.240	16	64	10	15	2	1	0	3	6	1	1	0	18	2	1	.297	.310
Bernadina, Roderick	R-R	6-1	162	8-10-92	.238	.208	.245	73	260	34	62	12	2	2	29	17	3	6	1	46	12	1	.323	.292
Boss, Torsten	L-R	6-0	190	12-27-90	.238	.222	.243	106	386	44	92	21	2	7	45	53	3	2	3	106	6	2	.358	.333
Capellan, Byron	R-R	5-11	150	8-9-93	.125	.000	.143	6	16	1	2	0	0	0	0	3	0	0	0	7	0	0	.125	.263
Caronia, Anthony	R-R	6-0	170	5-22-91	.289	.414	.257	45	142	15	41	2	0	0	12	16	1	2	1	35	7	2	.303	.363
Flaherty, Ryan	L-R	6-3	210	7-27-86	.250	.000	.333	2	8	1	2	1	0	0	1	0	0	0	0	3	0	0	.375	.250
Herbst, Lucas	L-L	6-1	185	9-9-90	.276	.225	.293	103	406	43	112	16	4	5	41	20	10	7	2	76	9	10	.372	.324
Hutter, Joel	R-R	6-1	210	2-28-90	.230	.290	.214	120	434	57	100	22	4	5	41	53	5	1	6	76	1	5	.334	.317
Lorenzo, Gregory	R-R	6-0	160	5-31-91	.241	.240	.242	126	489	65	118	18	8	2	41	22	6	7	2	152	40	8	.323	.281
Marin, Adrian	R-R	6-0	165	3-8-94	.265	.213	.279	108	388	30	103	19	2	4	48	23	4	4	3	90	11	4	.356	.311
Mosby, Michael	R-R	6-0	195	10-30-89	.250	.000	.167	4	16	1	2	0	0	0	1	3	0	0	0	5	0	1	.125	.263
Narron, Connor	B-R	6-3	195	11-12-91	.138	.083	.151	21	65	5	9	0	1	0	4	10	1	0	0	17	0	1	.169	.263
Nathans, Tucker	L-R	6-0	200	11-6-88	.271	.333	.255	63	240	33	65	10	5	9	38	21	5	1	4	44	3	3	.467	.337
Perez, Pedro	R-R	5-11	170	5-8-91	.100	.333	.059	6	20	0	2	0	0	0	1	1	0	0	0	2	0	0	.100	.143
Richards, Kris	R-R	6-0	190	12-6-89	.172	.176	.170	36	122	6	21	5	0	0	10	5	0	0	1	44	0	0	.213	.203

	B-T	HT	WT	DOB	AVG	vLH	vRH	G	AB	R	H	2B	3B	HR	RBI	BB	HBP	SH	SF	SO	SB	CS	SLG	OBP
Russell, Steel	L-R	6-0	195	9-5-90	.236	.162	.262	42	140	8	33	5	1	0	14	9	1	2	3	28	0	0	.286	.281
Sawyer, Wynston	R-R	6-3	205	11-14-91	.238	.200	.252	92	315	54	75	18	2	8	38	42	6	0	3	69	1	0	.384	.336
Simpson, Creede	R-R	6-2	185	9-8-89	.248	.220	.257	94	343	48	85	20	0	9	49	42	4	1	3	83	5	1	.385	.334
Vega, Anthony	L-R	6-0	190	12-6-90	.211	.300	.191	34	114	15	24	1	0	0	8	13	2	1	1	41	4	0	.219	.300
Walker, Christian	R-R	6-0	220	3-28-91	.353	.158	.392	31	116	19	41	5	0	3	20	11	3	0	1	16	0	3	.474	.420
Weems, Chase	L-R	6-2	182	1-17-89	.253	.429	.237	22	83	5	21	3	0	0	8	0	0	0	0	27	0	0	.289	.253

Pitching	B-T	HT	WT	DOB	W	L	ERA	G	GS	CG	SV	IP	H	R	ER	HR	BB	SO	AVG	vLH	vRH	K/9	BB/9
Beck, Sander	R-R	6-3	215	10-3-90	1	1	2.61	14	0	0	3	21	14	8	6	1	7	24	.189	.161	.209	10.45	3.05
Blackman, Mark	R-R	6-3	215	4-28-92	4	9	5.53	24	11	0	0	86	110	57	53	1	29	48	.311	.304	.316	5.00	3.02
Bridwell, Parker	R-R	6-4	190	8-2-91	8	9	4.73	26	26	0	0	143	141	86	75	9	59	144	.255	.258	.252	9.08	3.72
Chalas, Miguel	R-R	6-0	170	6-27-92	1	1	3.24	13	0	0	0	33	28	14	12	2	11	29	.231	.245	.221	7.83	2.97
Givens, Mychal	R-R	6-0	207	5-13-90	2	3	4.22	28	0	0	3	43	34	20	20	1	19	36	.219	.222	.217	7.59	4.01
Guzman, Juan	R-R	6-0	160	2-25-91	6	6	4.70	26	19	0	0	111	120	64	58	11	36	88	.278	.290	.266	7.14	2.92
Hader, Josh	L-L	6-3	160	4-7-94	3	6	2.65	17	17	0	0	85	67	41	25	4	42	79	.215	.138	.242	8.36	4.45
Hobgood, Matt	R-R	6-4	245	8-3-90	7	3	3.71	24	1	0	1	63	61	30	26	2	28	47	.256	.273	.242	6.71	4.00
Jacob, Kevin	R-R	6-6	225	3-26-89	0	1	8.59	6	0	0	0	7	9	7	7	0	4	7	.300	.077	.471	8.59	4.91
Kline, Branden	R-R	6-3	195	9-29-91	1	2	5.86	7	7	0	0	35	41	25	23	4	14	32	.289	.293	.287	8.15	3.57
Louico, Williams	R-R	6-2	180	4-10-90	0	2	8.31	10	0	0	0	13	15	16	12	1	20	21	.278	.333	.233	14.54	13.85
Marino, Harry	R-L	6-0	180	7-14-90	1	1	2.57	8	0	0	1	14	12	7	4	1	5	6	.222	.267	.205	3.86	3.21
Nivar, Jose	B-R	6-1	170	2-28-89	1	3	6.65	28	0	0	2	45	50	36	33	5	36	31	.282	.250	.305	6.25	7.25
Parry, Bennett	L-L	6-6	225	8-7-91	2	2	3.49	16	9	0	0	59	55	26	23	6	22	52	.248	.324	.232	7.89	3.34
Price, Matt	R-R	6-2	215	9-8-89	1	1	2.70	16	0	0	8	20	21	6	6	0	8	21	.256	.212	.286	9.45	3.60
Rennie, Luc	R-R	6-2	200	4-26-94	4	5	3.91	10	10	1	0	53	57	30	23	4	13	40	.277	.223	.340	6.79	2.21
Richardson, David	R-R	5-11	170	1-31-91	0	1	8.76	10	0	0	3	12	19	14	12	0	8	12	.358	.464	.240	8.76	5.84
Rutledge, Lex	L-L	6-1	195	6-28-91	4	3	1.45	18	2	0	1	43	28	8	7	1	16	45	.184	.263	.158	9.35	3.32
Taylor, Matt	R-L	6-1	185	4-1-91	4	13	3.77	25	25	0	0	138	134	78	58	5	61	106	.262	.193	.283	6.90	3.97
Tolliver, Ashur	L-L	6-0	170	1-24-88	0	0	3.63	7	0	0	1	17	15	7	7	2	5	20	.231	.167	.255	10.38	2.60
Torres, Dennis	R-R	6-3	200	5-17-90	1	3	3.22	25	0	0	1	45	41	18	16	2	28	37	.246	.329	.186	7.46	5.64
Upperman, Casey	R-R	6-1	185	11-16-90	0	4	8.86	17	0	0	0	21	31	23	21	3	9	26	.333	.324	.339	10.97	3.80
Wager, Brady	R-R	6-3	190	11-17-90	2	3	4.33	9	9	1	0	54	56	27	26	1	14	41	.265	.272	.259	6.83	2.33
Winegardner, Tommy	B-R	5-10	189	3-11-90	1	0	1.42	3	0	0	0	6	3	1	1	0	0	3	.130	.273	.000	4.26	0.00

Fielding

Catcher	PCT	G	PO	A	E	DP	PB
Perez	1.000	6	44	9	0	1	1
Russell	.978	36	250	18	6	2	7
Sawyer	.994	80	572	54	4	4	10
Weems	1.000	17	121	12	0	0	4

First Base	PCT	G	PO	A	E	DP
Balog	.967	22	196	11	7	13
Mosby	.967	2	28	1	1	2
Narron	.992	16	113	11	1	8
Richards	.996	27	219	24	1	24
Sawyer	.963	6	47	5	2	1
Simpson	.982	35	297	27	6	30
Walker	.993	29	254	23	2	17

Second Base	PCT	G	PO	A	E	DP
Boss	.971	96	190	244	13	42
Caronia	.934	20	33	52	6	13
Flaherty	1.000	1	1	4	0	1
Nathans	1.000	12	16	32	0	8
Richards	.963	6	13	13	1	2
Simpson	1.000	2	3	4	0	0

Third Base	PCT	G	PO	A	E	DP
Caronia	.800	3	0	4	1	0
Hutter	.958	118	85	253	15	24
Mosby	1.000	1	2	1	0	0
Nathans	.914	13	5	27	3	1
Richards	1.000	1	1	2	0	0
Simpson	1.000	3	2	6	0	0

Shortstop PCT G PO A E DP

	PCT	G	PO	A	E	DP
Capellan	.864	6	5	14	3	3
Caronia	.914	21	28	46	7	12
Marin	.959	108	163	306	20	51
Nathans	.967	5	15	14	1	3

Outfield	PCT	G	PO	A	E	DP
Balog	.833	2	5	0	1	0
Barber	.963	14	25	1	1	0
Bernadina	.962	72	119	9	5	2
Herbst	.972	99	167	5	5	1
Lorenzo	.949	126	251	11	14	3
Narron	1.000	3	2	0	0	0
Nathans	.964	20	26	1	1	0
Simpson	.977	46	82	3	2	0
Vega	.961	33	48	1	2	0
Weems	—	1	0	0	0	0

ABERDEEN IRONBIRDS

SHORT-SEASON

NEW YORK-PENN LEAGUE

Batting	B-T	HT	WT	DOB	AVG	vLH	vRH	G	AB	R	H	2B	3B	HR	RBI	BB	HBP	SH	SF	SO	SB	CS	SLG	OBP
Barber, George	R-R	6-0	180	8-8-89	.160	.229	.100	27	75	8	12	0	1	1	3	4	2	2	0	16	1	1	.227	.222
Bierfeldt, Conor	R-R	6-2	220	4-2-91	.264	.282	.256	62	231	38	61	15	3	12	36	28	3	0	0	65	4	2	.511	.351
Breen, Jared	R-R	5-11	185	5-11-91	.223	.203	.230	63	238	36	53	6	2	0	13	17	6	0	3	51	14	7	.265	.288
Capellan, Byron	R-R	5-11	150	8-9-93	.200	.200	.200	6	15	2	3	2	0	0	2	1	0	0	0	3	0	0	.333	.250
Castagnini, Federico	R-R	6-0	165	3-15-91	.130	.222	.092	33	92	11	12	1	1	1	3	12	1	1	1	31	2	1	.196	.236
Clevenger, Steve	L-R	6-0	195	4-5-86	.389	.429	.364	5	18	4	7	0	0	0	1	2	0	0	0	0	0	0	.389	.450
Graham, Jack	R-R	5-10	190	10-23-89	.083	.000	.133	15	24	1	2	0	0	0	2	1	0	0	0	12	0	0	.083	.120
Hart, Josh	L-L	6-1	190	10-2-94	.100	.000	.125	3	10	0	1	0	0	0	0	1	0	0	0	4	0	0	.100	.182
Hernandez, Manuel	R-R	6-1	190	8-19-92	.216	.167	.236	55	171	19	37	4	2	2	16	16	3	0	0	56	3	2	.298	.295
Kalush, Scott	R-R	6-1	215	3-22-90	.100	.067	.143	22	50	9	6	0	0	2	8	3	4	0	2	15	0	0	.240	.220
Kemp, Jeff	R-R	6-0	190	3-23-90	.240	.262	.226	48	154	25	37	9	1	3	20	11	6	4	0	50	8	2	.370	.316
Kimmel, Sam	L-R	6-0	185	11-3-89	.277	.207	.294	39	148	19	41	6	3	1	16	9	0	0	1	24	7	3	.378	.316
Ledesma, Ronarsy	R-R	5-11	170	4-19-93	.190	.125	.231	6	21	4	4	1	0	1	4	1	0	0	0	7	0	0	.381	.227
Mancini, Trey	R-R	6-4	215	3-18-92	.328	.405	.297	68	256	43	84	18	2	3	35	20	5	0	4	43	3	1	.449	.382
Murphy, Tanner	L-R	6-1	190	7-4-92	.273	.000	.300	6	11	0	3	0	0	0	2	0	0	0	2	0	1	.273	.385
Perez, Pedro	R-R	5-11	170	5-8-91	.111	.111	.111	5	18	0	2	0	0	0	1	0	0	0	0	3	0	0	.111	.111
Richards, Kris	R-R	6-0	190	12-6-89	.253	.242	.258	25	95	10	24	9	0	0	12	6	1	1	1	26	5	4	.347	.301
Rust, Tanner	B-R	6-2	200	8-3-90	.219	.120	.250	34	105	14	23	2	0	1	6	9	3	2	0	34	3	2	.267	.299
Schoop, Jonathan	R-R	6-2	210	10-16-91	.571	.500	.625	3	14	3	8	1	0	2	9	1	0	0	0	1	0	0	1.071	.600
Segui, Cory	R-R	6-1	200	12-20-91	—	—	—	1	0	0	0	0	0	0	0	0	0	0	0	0	0	0	—	—
Sisco, Chance	L-R	6-2	193	2-24-95	.200	—	.200	2	5	1	1	0	0	0	0	1	0	0	0	2	0	0	.200	.333

Name	B-T	HT	WT	DOB	AVG	vLH	vRH	G	AB	R	H	2B	3B	HR	RBI	BB	HBP	SH	SF	SO	SB	CS	SLG	OBP
Vega, Anthony	L-R	6-0	190	12-6-90	.256	.160	.302	22	78	7	20	2	0	2	5	3	0	0	0	14	4	3	.359	.284
Veloz, Hector	R-R	6-2	192	2-1-94	.213	.233	.204	56	202	17	43	7	1	5	27	17	2	0	3	70	4	2	.332	.277
Viele, Justin	R-R	5-11	185	11-18-90	.300	.000	.333	3	10	2	3	1	0	0	0	2	0	0	0	2	0	0	.400	.417
Wynns, Austin	R-R	6-2	205	12-10-90	.235	.283	.216	54	187	11	44	7	0	0	21	13	1	0	3	33	1	1	.273	.284
Yastrzemski, Mike	L-L	5-11	180	8-23-90	.273	.367	.234	57	205	28	56	13	4	3	25	24	5	0	1	44	8	8	.420	.362

Pitching	B-T	HT	WT	DOB	W	L	ERA	G	GS	CG	SV	IP	H	R	ER	HR	BB	SO	AVG	vLH	vRH	K/9	BB/9
Bill, Augey	L-L	6-9	225	3-22-91	2	0	1.80	8	0	0	0	15	17	4	3	0	3	9	.298	.250	.333	5.40	1.80
Brault, Steven	L-L	6-1	175	4-29-92	1	2	2.09	12	12	0	0	43	35	14	10	1	12	38	.227	.194	.237	7.95	2.51
Cortright, Garrett	R-R	6-5	208	10-2-91	0	0	0.00	2	0	0	0	5	2	0	0	0	2	3	.125	.000	.250	5.40	3.60
Cunningham, Nick	R-R	6-2	205	5-21-91	1	1	5.49	13	0	0	0	20	21	12	12	0	4	18	.284	.324	.250	8.24	1.83
Figuereo, Jose	R-R	6-1	190	3-23-92	1	1	5.55	16	0	0	0	24	26	15	15	2	8	23	.263	.280	.245	8.51	2.96
Green, Eric	L-L	6-1	200	4-18-90	0	0	4.82	6	0	0	0	9	9	5	5	0	6	5	.273	.182	.318	4.82	5.79
Hammel, Jason	R-R	6-6	225	9-2-82	0	0	2.25	1	1	0	0	4	3	1	1	0	1	2	.200	.333	.111	4.50	2.25
Hart, Donnie	L-L	5-11	180	9-6-90	3	1	2.25	19	0	0	5	24	24	10	6	0	7	26	.264	.158	.340	9.75	2.63
Harvey, Hunter	R-R	6-3	175	12-9-94	0	1	2.25	3	3	0	0	12	11	4	3	0	4	15	.239	.350	.154	11.25	3.00
Horacek, Mitch	L-L	6-5	185	12-3-91	5	4	2.78	12	11	0	0	65	54	24	20	1	7	45	.224	.264	.207	6.26	0.97
Johnson, Steve	R-R	6-1	220	8-31-87	0	0	3.00	2	2	0	0	6	5	2	2	1	2	6	.227	.182	.273	9.00	3.00
Joseph, Michael	R-R	6-7	215	9-12-90	1	1	5.40	16	0	0	1	25	33	15	15	0	11	14	.324	.319	.327	5.04	3.96
Keller, Jon	R-R	6-5	206	8-8-92	1	0	3.00	1	0	0	0	3	1	1	1	0	1	2	.100	.200	.000	6.00	3.00
Louico, Williams	R-R	6-1	180	4-10-90	1	1	7.24	11	0	0	0	14	23	15	11	0	8	11	.377	.455	.333	7.24	5.27
Marino, Harry	R-L	6-0	180	7-14-90	2	0	0.82	9	0	0	1	11	10	1	1	0	5	9	.256	.278	.238	7.36	4.09
Rennie, Luc	R-R	6-2	200	4-26-94	0	1	2.79	2	2	0	0	10	9	3	3	0	5	12	.237	.250	.231	11.17	4.66
Rheault, Dylan	R-R	6-9	245	3-21-92	1	2	3.57	13	4	0	0	40	41	17	16	2	16	26	.277	.281	.275	5.80	3.57
Richardson, David	R-R	5-11	170	1-31-91	2	1	6.38	8	2	0	2	18	20	13	13	0	7	16	.263	.233	.283	7.85	3.44
Rivera, Jorge	L-L	6-0	200	10-30-90	2	2	4.41	13	4	0	0	33	29	18	16	1	18	27	.244	.318	.200	7.44	4.96
Santana, Alexander	B-R	5-11	170	8-26-91	1	1	2.14	16	2	0	1	34	23	8	8	1	18	48	.195	.196	.194	12.83	4.81
Severino, Janser	R-R	6-2	140	9-16-91	3	4	3.92	18	9	0	0	62	59	32	27	1	21	57	.246	.205	.285	8.27	3.05
Urban, Austin	R-R	6-1	185	7-8-92	3	5	3.32	13	7	0	1	57	60	30	21	1	29	37	.270	.298	.254	5.84	4.58
Vader, Sebastian	R-R	6-4	175	6-3-92	7	3	2.43	14	13	0	0	85	70	30	23	1	18	64	.222	.208	.234	6.75	1.90
Yacabonis, Jimmy	R-R	6-3	205	3-21-92	3	1	1.52	18	0	0	4	30	15	5	5	0	14	28	.149	.116	.172	8.49	4.25

Fielding

Catcher	PCT	G	PO	A	E	DP	PB
Clevenger	1.000	3	15	6	0	1	0
Graham	1.000	6	15	0	0	0	1
Kalush	.986	21	107	33	2	1	7
Murphy	1.000	4	31	0	0	0	2
Perez	1.000	4	34	5	0	0	0
Sisco	.750	1	3	0	1	0	0
Wynns	.995	45	327	42	2	1	

First Base	PCT	G	PO	A	E	DP
Clevenger	.947	2	16	2	1	1
Mancini	.990	61	524	64	6	51
Richards	.976	5	37	3	1	4
Rust	.967	9	55	3	2	3
Segui	—	1	0	0	0	0
Veloz	1.000	1	1	0	0	0

Second Base	PCT	G	PO	A	E	DP
Capellan	.882	5	7	8	2	2
Castagnini	.945	27	43	60	6	14
Kemp	.975	33	67	89	4	22
Richards	1.000	15	27	26	0	8
Schoop	1.000	2	3	6	0	2
Viele	1.000	2	1	3	0	0

Third Base	PCT	G	PO	A	E	DP
Castagnini	1.000	5	3	10	0	2
Kemp	.714	2	1	4	2	0
Ledesma	.938	6	3	12	1	0
Richards	.789	8	2	13	4	3
Rust	.833	4	1	9	2	0
Veloz	.923	54	41	90	11	5

Shortstop	PCT	G	PO	A	E	DP
Breen	.933	63	102	175	20	40
Capellan	1.000	2	1	2	0	1
Kemp	.939	7	12	19	2	7
Viele	.833	2	2	3	1	0

Outfield	PCT	G	PO	A	E	DP
Barber	.974	25	34	3	1	0
Bierfeldt	.972	45	67	3	2	0
Hart	1.000	3	5	0	0	0
Hernandez	.963	50	75	3	3	1
Kimmel	1.000	22	40	3	0	1
Rust	.941	8	15	1	1	0
Vega	.979	22	47	0	1	1
Yastrzemski	1.000	56	115	7	0	2

GCL ORIOLES
GULF COAST LEAGUE

ROOKIE

Batting	B-T	HT	WT	DOB	AVG	vLH	vRH	G	AB	R	H	2B	3B	HR	RBI	BB	HBP	SH	SF	SO	SB	CS	SLG	OBP
Adair, Travis	L-R	5-10	180	12-23-87	.316	.333	.308	6	19	1	6	1	0	0	1	0	0	0	3	1	0	.368	.381	
Aguilar, Andres	R-R	5-11	175	1-12-94	.233	.214	.242	32	90	13	21	3	1	0	4	3	1	1	1	21	4	1	.289	.263
Alvarez, Dariel	R-R	6-2	180	11-7-88	.444	.500	.400	3	9	2	4	2	1	1	2	1	0	0	0	1	0	0	1.222	.500
Betemit, Wilson	B-R	6-2	220	11-2-81	.375	.667	.308	5	16	1	6	2	0	0	3	2	0	0	0	2	0	0	.500	.444
Capellan, Byron	R-R	5-11	150	8-9-93	.091	.000	.111	5	11	1	1	0	0	0	0	1	0	0	4	0	0	.182	.091	
Chavez, Zane	L-R	5-10	200	12-30-86	.231	.000	.333	5	13	0	3	1	0	0	0	2	1	0	0	3	0	0	.308	.375
Clevenger, Steve	L-R	6-0	195	4-5-86	.231	1.000	.091	4	13	0	3	0	0	0	1	0	0	0	1	3	0	0	.231	.214
Ford, Lew	R-R	6-0	200	8-12-76	.375	.500	.333	3	8	3	3	1	0	0	1	0	0	0	0	3	0	0	.500	.444
Frantini, Brett	R-R	6-1	210	2-7-90	.091	.000	.100	6	11	2	1	0	0	0	0	3	0	1	0	3	0	0	.091	.286
Gassaway, Randolph	R-R	6-4	210	5-23-95	.246	.188	.267	36	122	13	30	8	1	0	8	10	0	0	0	19	3	1	.328	.303
Hart, Josh	L-L	6-1	180	10-7-94	.228	.278	.207	33	123	14	28	5	2	0	9	13	2	1	0	23	11	3	.301	.312
Heim, Jonah	B-R	6-3	190	6-27-95	.185	.125	.211	27	81	8	15	5	0	0	4	10	0	0	0	13	1	1	.247	.275
Hunnicutt, Ray	R-R	5-11	180	12-17-93	.138	.167	.130	16	29	2	4	1	0	0	4	5	0	2	0	8	5	1	.172	.265
Lartiguez, Oswill	R-R	6-1	179	8-11-92	.284	.480	.221	33	102	12	29	0	0	0	12	4	0	0	2	18	4	4	.353	.306
Ledesma, Ronarsy	R-R	5-11	170	4-19-93	.258	.302	.241	53	190	23	49	15	3	2	28	10	8	1	2	35	7	4	.400	.319
Martinez, Jesus	L-R	6-0	175	11-6-90	.230	.267	.219	38	135	11	31	4	2	2	21	6	1	0	0	29	2	0	.333	.268
Mosby, Michael	R-R	6-0	195	10-30-89	.250	.000	.375	4	12	4	3	1	0	0	1	1	0	0	0	6	1	0	.333	.308
Mummey, Trent	L-L	5-9	170	1-5-89	.133	.000	.190	8	30	4	4	1	0	0	2	2	0	0	1	8	0	1	.167	.182
Murphy, Alex	R-R	5-11	210	10-5-94	.231	.389	.192	31	91	11	21	7	1	1	9	12	2	1	1	16	3	1	.363	.330
Pearce, Steve	R-R	5-11	210	4-13-83	.400	.667	.000	2	5	0	2	0	0	0	1	0	0	0	0	0	0	0	.400	.400
Rona, Pita	R-R	6-7	205	7-25-94	.143	.333	.077	19	35	3	5	1	0	1	4	3	0	0	1	12	0	0	.257	.211
Schoop, Jonathan	R-R	6-2	210	10-16-91	.360	.200	.467	8	25	9	9	2	0	3	9	6	0	0	1	6	0	0	.800	.469
Segui, Cory	R-R	6-1	200	12-20-91	.211	.304	.179	33	90	4	19	4	0	0	8	10	4	0	2	25	4	2	.256	.311

Batting	B-T	HT	WT	DOB	AVG	vLH	vRH	G	AB	R	H	2B	3B	HR	RBI	BB	HBP	SH	SF	SO	SB	CS	SLG	OBP
Sisco, Chance	L-R	6-2	193	2-24-95	.371	.333	.384	31	97	15	36	4	1	1	11	17	3	0	1	21	1	1	.464	.475
Thames, Eric	L-R	6-0	210	11-10-86	.375	.667	.308	5	16	4	6	1	0	0	3	4	2	0	0	1	2	0	.438	.545
Vargas, Yariel	R-R	6-0	180	9-25-94	.215	.156	.240	45	149	11	32	4	0	0	14	15	2	0	2	37	0	0	.242	.292
Vasquez, Oscar	B-R	5-11	150	11-22-93	.143	.071	.171	30	49	6	7	1	0	0	4	7	0	2	0	11	2	3	.163	.250
Viele, Justin	R-R	5-11	185	11-18-90	.273	.349	.246	49	161	29	44	7	0	2	14	31	5	6	0	28	9	4	.354	.406
Zorrilla, Andrickson	B-L	6-2	195	3-15-91	.201	.167	.213	49	169	23	34	8	1	3	18	30	1	0	1	60	8	1	.314	.323

Pitching	B-T	HT	WT	DOB	W	L	ERA	G	GS	CG	SV	IP	H	R	ER	HR	BB	SO	AVG	vLH	vRH	K/9	BB/9
Ayers, Danny	L-L	6-3	210	3-24-95	0	2	10.38	4	2	0	0	4	5	7	5	0	9	2	.333	.000	.417	4.15	18.69
Bill, Augey	L-L	6-9	225	3-22-91	3	0	1.08	5	0	0	0	8	5	2	1	1	1	6	.172	.000	.217	6.48	1.08
Bray, Jake	R-R	6-1	185	12-8-92	1	1	2.25	7	1	0	0	12	12	4	3	0	0	13	.267	.273	.261	9.75	0.00
Clark, Zach	R-R	6-0	200	7-11-83	0	2	6.75	4	4	0	0	17	21	15	13	1	6	8	.296	.385	.244	4.15	3.12
Cortright, Garrett	R-R	6-5	208	10-2-91	5	1	1.11	10	4	0	1	41	32	8	5	0	14	29	.219	.195	.250	6.42	3.10
Crichton, Stefan	R-R	6-3	195	2-29-92	3	1	1.96	6	4	0	0	23	13	5	5	1	3	21	.160	.219	.122	8.22	1.17
Delgado, Dariel	R-R	6-0	178	8-26-93	1	3	2.48	17	0	0	7	29	19	9	8	1	9	25	.190	.233	.158	7.76	2.79
Dominguez, Dioni	B-R	6-1	175	10-20-90	2	0	1.26	9	0	0	2	14	5	2	2	0	13	20	.109	.154	.050	12.56	8.16
Green, Eric	L-L	6-1	200	4-18-90	0	0	2.84	9	0	0	1	13	6	5	4	0	10	17	.133	.143	.129	12.08	7.11
Grendell, Kevin	L-L	6-2	210	8-22-93	0	0	0.00	4	0	0	0	6	4	0	0	0	1	8	.174	.500	.143	11.37	1.42
Harvey, Hunter	R-R	6-3	175	12-9-94	0	0	1.35	5	5	0	0	13	10	2	2	0	2	18	.208	.300	.143	12.15	1.35
Hernandez, Ivan	R-R	6-2	249	7-28-91	0	1	5.50	9	6	0	0	18	18	14	11	4	14	14	.261	.167	.333	7.00	2.00
Homick, Max	L-L	6-3	215	6-10-92	1	1	3.80	7	3	0	0	21	20	12	9	0	12	16	.247	.333	.222	6.75	5.06
Isenia, Jonatan	R-R	6-2	180	3-31-93	1	2	3.24	13	0	0	1	25	19	10	9	2	8	24	.207	.227	.188	8.64	2.88
Johnson, Steve	R-R	6-1	220	8-31-87	0	0	0.00	1	1	0	0	2	0	0	0	1	3	.000	.000	.000	13.50	4.50
Keller, Jon	R-R	6-5	206	8-8-92	1	2	4.11	6	5	0	0	15	17	9	7	0	2	18	.274	.333	.255	10.57	1.17
Kellogg, Caleb	R-R	5-11	185	6-3-92	4	1	2.19	15	0	0	0	25	17	8	6	0	10	27	.183	.189	.179	9.85	5.65
Lin, Yi-Hsiang	L-L	6-0	175	12-16-92	0	3	4.40	8	0	0	0	14	10	8	7	1	9	17	.196	.250	.186	10.67	5.65
McAdams, Sean	R-R	6-6	210	11-17-93	2	1	5.40	15	1	0	1	23	20	17	14	0	21	13	.244	.205	.279	5.01	8.10
Nowottnick, Nik	R-R	6-4	195	12-5-91	0	1	2.45	5	0	0	1	7	12	4	2	0	3	5	.375	.385	.368	6.14	3.68
Pinales, Elias	L-L	6-4	155	11-7-92	0	3	3.00	7	5	0	0	27	25	14	9	1	14	25	.248	.231	.253	8.33	4.67
Pintar, Jake	L-R	6-7	200	2-13-94	2	0	2.66	15	0	0	3	20	18	6	6	0	9	16	.240	.281	.209	7.08	3.98
Rodriguez, Julio	R-R	6-4	195	8-29-90	0	0	5.00	2	2	0	0	9	8	5	5	0	1	12	.242	.214	.263	12.00	1.00
Salas, Domingo	R-R	6-2	170	5-11-91	0	2	6.86	6	4	0	0	21	25	17	16	1	7	21	.291	.263	.313	9.00	3.00
Schreurs, Ron	L-L	6-6	205	7-14-92	1	3	2.95	10	2	0	0	37	25	13	12	0	15	28	.194	.238	.172	6.87	3.68
Seabrooke, Travis	R-L	6-5	182	9-16-95	0	0	1.13	3	2	0	0	8	5	2	1	1	5	7	.185	.000	.217	7.88	5.63
Staniewicz, Zachary	R-R	6-3	230	3-11-86	1	1	3.94	12	2	0	0	32	35	17	14	0	16	21	.269	.353	.177	5.91	4.50
Tarpley, Stephen	R-L	6-1	180	2-17-93	0	1	2.14	7	7	0	0	21	20	6	5	0	3	25	.256	.267	.254	10.71	1.29
Wilson, Matt	L-L	6-0	160	1-14-94	0	0	13.50	2	0	0	0	3	7	4	4	0	2	2	.538	.800	.375	6.75	6.75

Fielding

Catcher	PCT	G	PO	A	E	DP	PB
Chavez	1.000	3	9	3	0	0	1
Clevenger	1.000	3	13	2	0	0	0
Frantini	1.000	6	30	3	0	0	0
Heim	1.000	17	123	19	0	2	12
Murphy	.956	21	152	22	8	2	5
Sisco	.987	19	143	10	2	2	2

First Base	PCT	G	PO	A	E	DP
Betemit	1.000	1	3	1	0	1
Gassaway	.981	35	285	25	6	20
Mosby	1.000	2	11	3	0	0
Rona	.974	15	63	12	2	6
Segui	.992	18	122	6	1	7

Second Base	PCT	G	PO	A	E	DP
Adair	1.000	4	8	8	0	3
Capellan	1.000	2	3	4	0	0
Schoop	.947	5	4	14	1	2
Segui	1.000	5	7	10	0	1
Vargas	.957	44	55	99	7	16
Vasquez	.941	11	11	21	2	3

Third Base	PCT	G	PO	A	E	DP
Betemit	1.000	1	0	2	0	0
Ledesma	.911	53	43	80	12	3
Segui	.882	12	5	10	2	1

Shortstop	PCT	G	PO	A	E	DP
Capellan	1.000	3	2	6	0	0

	PCT	G	PO	A	E	DP
Vasquez	.979	14	18	29	1	5
Viele	.965	49	81	111	7	21

Outfield	PCT	G	PO	A	E	DP
Aguilar	1.000	29	30	4	0	0
Alvarez	1.000	3	5	0	0	0
Ford	1.000	3	4	0	0	0
Hart	.988	33	76	3	1	1
Hunnicutt	1.000	11	13	0	0	0
Lartiguez	1.000	33	53	2	0	0
Martinez	.977	28	40	3	1	1
Mummey	1.000	7	9	0	0	0
Pearce	.500	1	1	0	1	0
Thames	1.000	4	10	0	0	0
Zorrilla	.949	47	72	2	4	1

DSL ORIOLES ROOKIE

DOMINICAN SUMMER LEAGUE

Batting	B-T	HT	WT	DOB	AVG	vLH	vRH	G	AB	R	H	2B	3B	HR	RBI	BB	HBP	SH	SF	SO	SB	CS	SLG	OBP
Acosta, Rauel	R-R	6-4	210	12-23-95	.239	.268	.231	56	188	17	45	6	0	3	30	31	5	0	8	42	0	3	.319	.349
Alexander, Rochendrick	R-R	6-3	189	11-10-94	.187	.123	.206	68	246	34	46	4	6	1	25	15	6	2	4	92	3	1	.264	.247
Alvarado, Nicanor	R-R	6-3	205	6-22-94	.061	.000	.074	10	33	2	2	1	0	0	0	4	0	0	0	10	0	0	.091	.162
Betemit, Felipe	B-R	5-11	182	7-6-91	.313	—	—	35	115	13	36	3	1	0	9	13	2	3	2	17	2	4	.357	.386
Cabrera, Jacniel	R-R	5-11	140	6-11-95	.099	.077	.103	33	71	8	7	1	0	0	3	10	3	1	0	26	1	0	.113	.238
Chaves, Luis	R-R	6-2	190	11-16-94	.162	.162	.162	43	142	13	23	6	0	3	18	14	3	0	2	65	3	2	.268	.248
Colla, Richard	R-R	5-9	176	10-27-93	.195	—	—	46	128	15	25	4	1	1	6	13	2	3	2	53	5	3	.266	.276
De Freitas, Nelio	R-R	6-0	210	2-22-93	.171	.300	.129	14	41	1	7	1	0	0	3	2	2	0	0	8	0	0	.195	.244
De La Cruz, Alexander	R-R	6-1	185	8-22-91	.239	—	—	23	71	3	17	3	0	0	11	5	3	0	0	11	0	0	.282	.316
Duran, Brailyn	R-R	6-3	170	11-10-93	.160	.208	.143	35	94	9	15	2	0	1	10	7	2	0	0	36	1	1		.213
.233 Fajardo, Daniel	R-R	6-1	170	11-19-94	.310	.273	.323	43	129	13	40	8	0	0	14	7	0	1	2	11	2	1	.372	.341
Flores, Pedro	B-R	5-10	141	4-18-96	.162	—	—	44	136	11	22	2	0	0	6	15	1	2	0	20	1	2	.176	.250
Franco, Daniel	R-R	6-0	165	10-31-94	.264	.224	.275	57	227	22	60	3	0	0	2	26	3	2	0	58	21	14	.278	.348
Galastica, Gonzalo	B-R	5-11	180	5-15-96	.238	.241	.235	30	80	4	19	1	1	0	5	6	2	0	0	24	1	4	.275	.307
Gil, Geremias	R-R	6-2	190	1-22-96	.171	.235	.151	22	70	4	12	5	0	1	5	9	0	0	1	16	1	3	.286	.263
Guerra, Byron	R-R	5-10	180	10-27-93	.118	.429	.037	10	34	4	4	1	0	0	2	2	1	1	1	3	2	0	.147	.184
Labrador, Alexander	R-R	6-2	190	10-27-94	.047	.077	.033	19	43	1	2	0	0	0	1	3	0	0	0	9	0	0	.047	.109

Name	B-T	HT	WT	DOB	AVG	vLH	vRH	G	AB	R	H	2B	3B	HR	RBI	BB	SO	SB	CS				OBP	SLG
Lamas, Sergio	B-R	6-0	176	11-26-93	.137	.125	.141	39	95	11	13	1	2	0	3	9	5	1	0	41	1	2	.189	.248
Larez, Carlos	R-R	5-11	160	5-11-93	.159	.3	.118	44	44	9	7	0	1	0	2	8	0	1	0	13	4	1	.205	.288
Laureano, Carlos	R-R	6-3	175	6-27-94	.211	.200	.214	61	223	28	47	5	2	3	22	29	8	4	2	70	7	10	.291	.321
Lizardo, Yeridolfo	R-R	6-3	195	6-29-93	.200	.125	.222	11	35	4	7	1	1	1	3	6	2	1	0	11	1	2	.371	.349
Martinez, Rockny	B-R	6-2	175	7-14-92	.297	.239	.315	56	192	22	57	5	2	0	17	12	5	1	1	29	11	8	.344	.352
Medina, Robertico	R-R	6-0	170	1-12-94	.191	.204	.187	61	215	21	41	6	0	3	18	19	4	0	0	88	6	2	.260	.269
Medina, Victor	R-R	6-0	180	11-20-94	.230	.172	.25	69	248	24	57	13	1	1	20	20	5	3	3	60	4	4	.302	.297
Mena, Kelvin	R-R	6-0	200	6-1-93	.200	.167	.212	28	90	9	18	5	0	0	8	13	1	0	0	28	0	1	.256	.308
Mercedes, Alexander	R-R	6-0	160	3-20-92	.336	.308	.346	67	250	47	84	15	10	1	28	31	8	2	5	20	19	6	.488	.418
Mora, Ivan	R-R	6-1	171	7-22-94	.214	.172	.229	39	112	11	24	7	1	1	7	4	3	1	1	19	5	1	.321	.258
Pezzarossi, Paolo	R-R	6-1	200	3-27-93	.067	0	.167	6	15	1	1	1	0	0	1	2	0	0	0	8	0	1	.133	.176
Pichardo, Miguel	L-L	6-1	160	10-21-94	.162	—	—	65	204	22	33	7	3	0	16	21	2	5	1	87	4	6	.225	.246
Rifaela, Ademar	L-L	5-10	180	11-20-94	.244	.212	.254	63	221	38	54	12	5	0	18	41	6	0	1	48	4	8	.344	.375
Rodriguez, Carlos	R-R	6-1	160	3-22-95	.205	.167	.214	53	156	20	32	5	2	0	8	23	7	4	1	48	10	4	.263	.332
Salas, Guillermo	B-R	6-0	175	4-21-94	.252	.258	.25	70	258	40	65	10	4	0	25	22	9	10	3	63	9	4	.322	.329
Soto, Ronald	R-R	6-4	220	10-5-94	.241	—	—	45	145	12	35	5	0	1	18	14	3	0	3	33	2	0	.297	.315
Taveras, Junior	R-R	5-10	187	12-28-92	.245	.261	.24	59	200	14	49	6	0	1	25	21	3	2	3	14	2	5	.290	.322

Pitching	B-T	HT	WT	DOB	W	L	ERA	G	GS	CG	SV	IP	H	R	ER	HR	BB	SO	AVG	vLH	vRH	K/9	BB/9
Almonte, Jefferies	R-R	6-2	190	5-29-92	4	4	1.51	23	0	0	5	36	30	9	6	0	11	36	.231	.184	.250	9.08	2.78
Alvarado, Cristian	R-R	6-2	165	9-20-94	1	7	4.10	13	13	0	0	59	47	34	27	4	12	69	.206	.225	.196	1.47	1.82
Aquino, Wilmer	L-L	5-9	170	12-5-91	6	3	2.89	14	14	1	0	84	78	33	27	2	16	76	.248	.279	.243	8.14	1.71
Bautista, Miguel	R-R	5-11	158	12-11-92	2	2	4.32	15	0	0	0	33	32	17	16	1	18	28	.262	.255	.267	7.56	4.86
Bolivar, Miguel	R-R	6-0	180	1-24-92	3	0	4.03	20	0	0	0	38	36	21	17	1	17	21	.254	.206	.269	4.97	4.03
Cuevas, Yanuel	R-R	5-11	180	10-25-93	2	5	2.94	14	14	0	0	70	69	33	23	2	10	53	.256	.245	.262	6.78	1.28
Diaz, Elvis	R-R	6-3	185	2-6-93	1	2	3.90	14	0	0	0	28	21	15	12	2	6	22	.204	.207	.203	7.16	1.95
Fermin, Yeraldo	R-R	5-11	136	10-2-91	8	0	1.41	19	0	0	4	57	48	14	9	1	7	51	.215	.218	.214	8.01	1.10
Floranus, Wendell	R-R	6-0	158	4-16-95	3	3	1.51	15	15	1	0	78	66	15	13	2	18	43	.232	.227	.234	4.98	2.09
Garcia, Miguel	R-R	6-1	180	3-24-93	1	1	1.29	9	4	0	0	21	12	5	3	0	5	15	.152	.200	.136	6.43	2.14
Gonzalez, Luis	L-L	6-2	170	1-17-92	2	1	1.35	9	0	0	1	13	10	4	2	0	4	23	.192	.250	.182	15.53	2.70
Heredia, Inocencio	R-R	5-11	172	12-11-91	1	3	2.55	27	0	0	12	35	30	17	10	1	8	41	.224	.213	.230	1.44	2.04
Herrera, Alvin	R-R	6-1	165	3-15-93	3	3	2.43	19	0	0	4	41	41	15	11	0	18	33	.265	.320	.238	7.30	3.98
Jimenez, Francisco	R-R	6-1	160	10-4-94	4	4	1.60	14	13	0	0	68	52	24	12	2	19	63	.206	.198	.212	8.38	2.53
LeFranc, Lu Franc-Cito	R-R	6-4	220	3-3-93	0	3	5.85	12	9	0	0	32	25	25	21	0	40	30	.221	.279	.186	8.35	11.13
Leoncio, Tomas	R-R	6-2	180	3-3-95	2	0	3	13	8	0	0	39	32	17	13	0	18	44	.229	.263	.216	1.15	4.15
Liranzo, Jesus	R-R	6-2	175	3-7-95	0	1	8.71	6	2	0	0	10	13	18	10	2	13	9	.283	.364	.257	7.84	5.23
2-team total (3 Braves)					0	1	9.24	9	3	0	0	13	16	21	13	2	12	13	—		—	9.24	8.53
Marrugo, Yeizer	R-R	6-0	170	10-1-94	3	4	1.68	13	13	0	0	59	50	26	11	1	29	29	.227	.273	.197	4.42	4.42
Martinez, Leybi	R-R	6-4	180	1-20-95	0	0	6.52	7	0	0	0	10	8	7	7	0	8	10	.211	.300	.179	9.31	7.45
Medina, Cesar	R-R	6-3	180	6-16-94	5	1	3.09	16	0	0	0	32	24	14	11	1	15	24	.395	.118		6.75	4.22
Mercedes, Daniel	R-R	6-4	180	5-12-92	0	0	4.32	18	0	0	3	33	29	22	16	0	18	31	.234	.152	.282	8.37	4.86
Moreno, Rafael	R-R	6-0	200	2-11-95	7	2	1.23	14	14	1	0	81	74	19	11	4	16	63	.243	.278	.223	7.03	1.79
Ortiz, Elvin	L-L	6-3	180	11-8-91	0	2	6.75	11	1	0	0	15	13	14	11	0	11	23	.220	.333	.191	14.11	6.75
Pacheco, Johalis	L-L	6-0	170	3-29-94	4	4	1.84	14	9	0	1	54	42	15	11	2	19	59	.221	.192	.226	9.89	3.19
Palin, Nelson	R-R	6-3	182	9-22-92	0	0	4.63	9	0	0	0	12	8	7	6	1	11	5	.190	.182	.194	3.86	8.49
Palumbo, Angelo	R-R	6-3	180	11-10-95	0	3	7.61	13	3	0	0	24	27	22	20	0	19	13	.297	.395	.226	4.94	7.23
Rosario, Jose	R-R	6-1	160	2-22-94	1	3	2.49	16	0	0	2	51	48	20	14	2	10	44	.251	.254	.250	7.82	1.78
Salas, Johan	R-R	6-2	195	11-11-94	0	1	4.85	6	0	0	0	13	13	13	7	1	13	5	.250	.222	.265	3.46	9.00
Soler, Fernando	R-R	6-2	180	5-13-94	0	2	8	14	2	0	0	18	25	18	16	2	15	11	.329	.280	.353	5.50	7.50
Sosa, Carlos	R-R	6-6	236	9-6-91	3	4	2.01	18	0	0	2	31	32	10	7	0	11	31	.267	.295	.250	8.90	3.16
Valdez, Juan	R-R	6-2	160	2-6-91	4	2	.82	14	7	0	1	55	31	8	5	1	12	34	.170	.137	.193	5.60	1.98

Fielding

Catcher	PCT	G	PO	A	E	DP	PB
De Freitas	.972	14	96	8	3	2	2
De La Cruz	.987	22	132	18	2	1	2
Fajardo	.985	43	268	51	5	0	3
Labrador	.966	18	72	14	3	1	5
Soto	.978	31	223	43	6	1	11
Taveras	.970	36	235	57	9	2	3

First Base	PCT	G	PO	A	E	DP
Acosta	.974	24	215	8	6	21
Alvarado	.940	7	45	2	3	3
Betemit	1.000	1	14	0	0	0
Gil	.980	7	48	2	1	1
Larez	1.000	1	2	0	0	0
Martinez	.986	32	277	13	4	15
Medina	.982	42	309	20	6	21
Mena	1.000	27	176	12	0	11
Mercedes	1.000	2	2	1	0	1
Mora	1.000	1	9	1	0	2
Soto	.920	3	21	2	2	3
Taveras	.981	12	97	7	2	10

Second Base	PCT	G	PO	A	E	DP
Betemit	1.000	18	35	44	0	10
Cabrera	.959	11	21	26	2	5
Colla	.934	36	53	75	9	8
Flores	.971	35	58	78	4	16
Galastica	.914	15	28	25	5	2
Lamas	.954	17	28	34	3	6
Mercedes	.985	25	63	69	2	15

Third Base	PCT	G	PO	A	E	DP
Betemit	.868	16	5	28	5	6
Colla	.857	3	3	9	2	0
Flores	1.000	2	1	5	0	0
Guerra	.971	10	9	25	1	1
Lamas	.884	22	15	23	5	1
Larez	—	1	0	0	0	0
Lizardo	.935	11	7	22	2	2
Medina	.862	51	31	81	18	4
Pichardo	.942	36	28	85	7	3

Shortstop	PCT	G	PO	A	E	DP
Cabrera	.903	21	23	42	7	5
Flores	.857	4	4	8	2	0
Galastica	.868	16	15	31	7	4
Medina	.814	12	21	27	11	2
Pichardo	.908	34	55	73	13	10
Salas	.916	70	125	191	29	37

Outfield	PCT	G	PO	A	E	DP
Acosta	1.000	4	3	0	0	0
Alexander	.969	66	121	5	4	2
Alvarado	1.000	1	1	0	0	0
Chaves	.970	19	31	1	1	0
Duran	.939	18	28	3	2	2
Franco	1.000	56	132	2	0	0
Gil	.500	1	1	0	1	0
Lamas	—	1	0	0	0	0
Larez	1.000	32	33	4	0	2
Laureano	.967	59	109	8	4	2
Martinez	1.000	6	8	0	0	0
Medina	.969	27	30	1	1	1
Mercedes	1.000	44	87	8	0	2
Mora	.980	23	48	1	1	1
Pezzarossi	1.000	3	0	1	0	0
Rifaela	.990	54	98	2	1	0
Rodriguez	.947	49	66	5	4	2

Boston Red Sox

SEASON IN A SENTENCE: The Red Sox put to rest the memories of a disastrous 2012 campaign and inspired an entire city (not to mention Red Sox Nation) by going from worst in the American League East to first before beating the St. Louis Cardinals in six games to win the World Series, Boston's third title since 2004.

HIGH POINT: How about a few? In the American League Championship Series, already down a game to the Tigers and trailing Game Two 5-1 in the eighth, David Ortiz ripped a game-tying grand slam on the first pitch from reliever Joaquin Benoit. Boston won it in the ninth on Jarrod Saltalamacchia's game-ending single and went on to win the series in six games. Then, with the Cardinals leading the World Series 2-1 and Game Four tied 1-1 in the sixth inning, Jonny Gomes swung the series in the Red Sox's favor with a three-run homer off Seth Maness. As in the ALCS, the Red Sox capitalized on a manager's back-fired decision to lift a starter at a key point in the game.

LOW POINT: The Red Sox led the AL East for 141 days of 164 in the season, so not many low points. But on Aug. 23, a loss to the Dodgers left them tied for the division lead with the Rays. They then won 7 of 8 to increase the lead to 5½ games and didn't look back.

NOTABLE ROOKIES: Xander Bogaerts, Boston's top prospect gave the team a lift when he arrived to the big leagues in late August. But it was his postseason performance that confirmed the Red Sox's belief in him and cemented his place on the 2014 team. In the playoffs, Bogaerts went .296/.412/.481 while moving from shortstop (where he started 95 of 116 games in the minors this season) to third base. He could start at shortstop next season.

KEY TRANSACTIONS: With Clay Buchholz missing most of the second half, the Red Sox went out and acquired righty Jake Peavy from the White Sox. It cost them sure-handed shortstop Jose Iglesias in a three-team deal with the Tigers, but Peavy went 4-1 down the stretch.

DOWN ON THE FARM: The Red Sox seem primed for the likely departure of Jacoby Ellsbury and Jarrod Saltalamacchia to free agency. Jackie Bradley, who made the Opening Day roster but was sent down after struggling, could replace Ellsbury in center field. He had an .842 OPS at Pawtucket. Ryan Lavarnway might step in for Saltalamacchia.

OPENING DAY PAYROLL: $150.6 million (4th)

ORGANIZATIONAL LEADERS

BATTING		*Minimum 250 AB
MAJORS		
* AVG	Ortiz, David	.309
* OPS	Ortiz, David	.959
HR	Ortiz, David	30
RBI	Ortiz, David	103
MINORS		
* AVG	Cecchini, Garin, Portland/Salem	.322
* OBP	Cecchini, Garin, Portland/Salem	.443
* SLG	Betts, Mookie, Salem/Greenville	.506
R	Betts, Mookie, Salem/Greenville	93
H	Cecchini, Garin, Portland/Salem	146
TB	Betts, Mookie, Salem/Greenville	234
2B	Betts, Mookie, Salem/Greenville	36
	De La Cruz, Keury, Salem	36
3B	Thomas, Tony, Pawtucket/Portland	9
HR	Brentz, Bryce, Pawtucket/GCL	19
	Chester, David, Salem/Greenville	19
RBI	De La Cruz, Keury, Salem	89
BB	Cecchini, Garin, Portland/Salem	94
SO	Tavarez, Aneury, Greenville	140
SB	Betts, Mookie, Salem/Greenville	38

PITCHING		#Minimum 75 IP
MAJORS		
W	Lester, Jon	15
# ERA	Lackey, John	3.52
SO	Lester, Jon	177
SV	Uehara, Koji	21
MINORS		
W	Three tied at	11
L	Kukuk, Cody, Greenville	13
# ERA	Owens, Henry, Salem/Portland	2.67
G	Carter, Anthony, Pawtucket	52
GS	Three tied at	26
SV	Carter, Anthony, Pawtucket	24
IP	Doyle, Terry, Pawtucket/Portland	149
BB	Haeger, Charlie, Pawtucket/Portland	83
SO	Owens, Henry, Portland/Salem	169
# AVG	Owens, Henry, Salem/Portland	.177

2013 PERFORMANCE

General Manager: Ben Cherington. **Farm Director:** Ben Crockett. **Scouting Director:** Amiel Sawdaye.

Class	Team	League	W	L	PCT	Finish	Manager
Majors	Boston Red Sox	American	97	65	.599	1st (15)	John Farrell
Triple-A	Pawtucket Red Sox	International	80	63	.559	2nd (14)	Gary DiSarcina
Double-A	Portland Sea Dogs	Eastern	68	73	.472	t-8th (12)	Kevin Boles
High A	Salem Red Sox	Carolina	76	64	.543	3rd (8)	Billy McMillion
Low A	Greenville Drive	South Atlantic	51	87	.370	14th (14)	Carlos Febles
Short-season	Lowell Spinners	New York-Penn	40	33	.548	5th (14)	Bruce Crabbe
Rookie	Red Sox	Gulf Coast	35	25	.583	3rd (16)	Darren Fenster
Overall 2013 Minor League Record			350	345	.504	t-10 (30)	

ORGANIZATION STATISTICS

BOSTON RED SOX

AMERICAN LEAGUE

Batting	B-T	HT	WT	DOB	AVG	vLH	vRH	G	AB	R	H	2B	3B	HR	RBI	BB	HBP	SH	SF	SO	SB	CS	SLG	OBP
Berry, Quintin	L-L	6-0	175	11-21-84	.625	1.000	.571	13	8	5	5	0	0	1	4	1	0	0	0	2	3	0	1.000	.667
Bogaerts, Xander	R-R	6-3	185	10-1-92	.250	.467	.138	18	44	7	11	2	0	1	5	5	0	0	1	13	1	0	.364	.320
Bradley, Jackie	L-R	5-10	195	4-19-90	.189	.080	.229	37	95	18	18	5	0	3	10	10	2	0	0	31	2	0	.337	.280
Carp, Mike	L-R	6-2	210	6-30-86	.296	.269	.300	86	216	34	64	18	2	9	43	22	2	0	3	67	1	0	.523	.362
Ciriaco, Pedro	R-R	6-0	180	9-27-85	.216	.136	.276	28	51	4	11	2	1	1	4	6	0	0	1	12	2	1	.353	.293
2-team total (5 Kansas City)					.210	—	—	33	62	4	13	3	1	1	4	6	0	0	1	13	3	1	.339	.275
Diaz, Jonathan	R-R	5-9	165	4-10-85	.000	.000	.000	5	4	2	0	0	0	0	0	0	0	0	0	0	0	0	.000	.000
Drew, Stephen	L-R	6-0	190	3-16-83	.253	.196	.284	124	442	57	112	29	8	13	67	54	1	0	4	124	6	0	.443	.333
Ellsbury, Jacoby	L-L	6-1	195	9-11-83	.298	.246	.328	134	577	92	172	31	8	9	53	47	5	1	2	92	52	4	.426	.355
Gomes, Jonny	R-R	6-1	230	11-22-80	.247	.236	.258	116	312	49	77	17	0	13	52	43	6	0	5	89	1	0	.426	.344
Holt, Brock	L-R	5-10	180	6-11-88	.203	.111	.220	26	59	9	12	2	0	0	5	1	7	0	3	3	4	1	0	.237	.275
Iglesias, Jose	R-R	5-11	185	1-5-90	.330	.347	.321	63	215	27	71	10	2	1	19	11	6	0	2	30	3	1	.409	.376
2-team total (46 Detroit)					.303	—	—	109	350	39	106	16	2	3	29	15	11	4	2	60	5	2	.386	.349
Lavarnway, Ryan	R-R	6-4	240	8-7-87	.299	.267	.319	25	77	8	23	7	0	1	14	2	2	0	1	17	0	0	.429	.329
McDonald, John	R-R	5-9	180	9-24-74	.250	.000	.400	6	8	1	2	0	0	0	0	1	0	0	0	3	0	0	.250	.333
2-team total (8 Cleveland)					.133	—	—	14	15	3	2	0	0	0	2	0	0	0	4	0	0	.133	.235
Middlebrooks, Will	R-R	6-3	220	9-9-88	.227	.273	.206	94	348	41	79	18	0	17	49	20	2	1	3	98	3	1	.425	.271
Napoli, Mike	R-R	6-0	220	10-31-81	.259	.284	.248	139	498	79	129	38	2	23	92	73	6	0	1	187	1	1	.482	.360
Nava, Daniel	B-L	5-11	200	2-22-83	.303	.252	.322	134	458	77	139	29	0	12	66	51	15	4	8	93	0	2	.445	.385
Ortiz, David	L-L	6-4	250	11-18-75	.309	.260	.339	137	518	84	160	38	2	30	103	76	1	0	5	88	4	0	.564	.395
Pedroia, Dustin	R-R	5-8	165	8-17-83	.301	.354	.278	160	641	91	193	42	2	9	84	73	3	0	7	75	17	5	.415	.372
Ross, David	R-R	6-2	230	3-19-77	.216	.259	.167	36	102	11	22	5	0	4	10	11	1	2	0	42	1	0	.382	.298
Saltalamacchia, Jarrod	B-R	6-4	235	5-2-85	.273	.218	.294	121	425	68	116	40	0	14	65	43	0	0	2	139	4	1	.466	.338
Snyder, Brandon	R-R	6-2	225	11-23-86	.180	.273	.000	27	50	5	9	3	0	2	7	0	2	0	0	16	0	0	.360	.212
Victorino, Shane	B-R	5-9	190	11-30-80	.294	.314	.282	122	477	82	140	26	2	15	61	25	18	10	2	75	21	3	.451	.351

Pitching	B-T	HT	WT	DOB	W	L	ERA	G	GS	CG	SV	IP	H	R	ER	HR	BB	SO	AVG	vLH	vRH	K/9	BB/9
Aceves, Alfredo	R-R	6-2	205	12-8-82	4	1	4.86	11	6	0	0	37	42	21	20	8	22	24	.288	.284	.294	5.84	5.35
Bailey, Andrew	R-R	6-3	240	5-31-84	3	1	3.77	30	0	0	8	29	23	12	12	7	12	39	.223	.185	.265	12.24	3.77
Bard, Daniel	R-R	6-4	215	6-25-85	0	0	9.00	2	0	0	0	1	1	1	1	0	2	1	.250	.500	.000	9.00	18.00
Beato, Pedro	R-R	6-6	230	10-27-86	1	1	3.60	10	0	0	0	10	12	5	4	1	2	5	.279	.158	.375	4.50	1.80
Breslow, Craig	L-L	6-1	190	8-8-80	5	2	1.81	61	0	0	0	60	49	16	12	3	18	33	.228	.253	.208	4.98	2.72
Britton, Drake	L-L	6-2	215	5-22-89	1	1	3.86	18	0	0	0	21	21	9	9	1	7	17	.280	.278	.282	7.29	3.00
Buchholz, Clay	L-R	6-3	190	8-14-84	12	1	1.74	16	16	1	0	108	75	23	21	4	36	96	.199	.187	.216	7.98	2.99
De La Rosa, Rubby	R-R	6-1	205	3-4-89	0	2	5.56	11	0	0	0	11	15	7	7	2	6	13	.313	.250	.344	4.76	1.59
De La Torre, Jose	R-R	5-10	185	10-17-85	0	0	6.35	7	0	0	0	11	10	8	8	2	10	15	.244	.300	.190	11.91	7.94
Dempster, Ryan	R-R	6-2	215	5-3-77	8	9	4.57	32	29	0	0	171	170	97	87	26	79	157	.256	.235	.281	8.25	4.15
Doubront, Felix	L-L	6-2	225	10-23-87	11	6	4.32	29	27	0	0	162	161	84	78	13	71	139	.261	.247	.267	7.71	3.94
Hanrahan, Joel	R-R	6-4	250	10-6-81	0	1	9.82	9	0	0	4	7	10	8	8	4	6	5	.333	.235	.462	6.14	7.36
Lackey, John	R-R	6-6	235	10-23-78	10	13	3.52	29	29	2	0	189	179	80	74	26	40	161	.247	.238	.258	7.65	1.90
Lester, Jon	L-L	6-4	240	1-7-84	15	8	3.75	33	33	1	0	213	209	94	89	19	67	177	.253	.237	.257	7.47	2.83
Miller, Andrew	L-L	6-7	210	5-21-85	1	2	2.64	37	0	0	0	31	25	12	9	3	17	48	.217	.281	.155	14.09	4.99
Morales, Franklin	L-L	6-1	210	1-24-86	2	2	4.62	20	1	0	0	25	24	13	13	2	15	21	.255	.184	.304	7.46	5.33
Mortensen, Clayton	R-R	6-4	185	4-10-85	1	2	5.34	24	0	0	0	30	32	19	18	3	16	21	.267	.317	.211	6.23	4.75
Peavy, Jake	R-R	6-1	195	5-31-81	4	1	4.04	10	10	1	0	65	56	29	29	6	19	45	.230	.212	.246	6.26	2.64
2-team total (13 Chicago)					12	5	4.17	23	23	2	0	145	130	70	67	20	36	121	—	—	—	7.53	2.24
Tazawa, Junichi	R-R	5-11	200	6-6-86	5	4	3.16	71	0	0	0	68	70	25	24	9	12	72	.265	.264	.266	9.48	1.58
Thornton, Matt	L-L	6-6	235	9-15-76	0	1	3.52	20	0	0	0	15	22	6	6	0	5	9	.349	.345	.353	5.28	2.93
2-team total (40 Chicago)					0	4	3.74	60	0	0	0	43	47	20	18	4	15	30	—	—	—	6.23	3.12
Uehara, Koji	R-R	6-2	195	4-3-75	4	1	1.09	73	0	0	21	74	33	10	9	5	9	101	.130	.115	.146	12.23	1.09
Villareal, Brayan	R-R	6-0	170	5-10-87	0	0	—	1	0	0	0	0	0	0	0	0	1	0	—	—	.000	—	—
2-team total (7 Detroit)					0	2	20.77	8	0	0	0	4	8	10	10	1	9	6	—	—	—	12.46	18.69
Webster, Allen	R-R	6-2	190	2-10-90	1	2	8.60	8	7	0	0	30	37	30	29	7	18	23	.308	.391	.214	6.82	5.34
Wilson, Alex	R-R	6-2	215	11-3-86	1	1	4.88	26	0	0	0	28	34	16	15	0	14	22	.306	.200	.431	7.16	4.55

| Workman, Brandon | R-R | 6-4 | 195 | 8-13-88 | 6 | 3 | 4.97 | 20 | 3 | 0 | 0 | 42 | 44 | 23 | 23 | 5 | 15 | 47 | .272 | .253 | .296 | 10.15 | 3.24 |
| Wright, Steven | R-R | 6-1 | 220 | 8-30-84 | 2 | 0 | 5.40 | 4 | 1 | 0 | 0 | 13 | 12 | 8 | 8 | 0 | 9 | 10 | .245 | .297 | .083 | 6.75 | 6.08 |

Fielding

Catcher	PCT	G	PO	A	E	DP	PB
Lavarnway	.993	22	131	8	1	4	6
Ross	.997	36	288	13	1	2	2
Saltalamacchia	.994	119	908	46	6	4	7

First Base	PCT	G	PO	A	E	DP
Carp	.990	29	188	12	2	19
Ciriaco	1.000	1	3	1	0	1
Middlebrooks	1.000	1	10	1	0	0
Napoli	.994	131	976	87	6	96
Nava	.986	19	63	6	1	5
Ortiz	1.000	6	36	1	0	4
Snyder	1.000	6	15	1	0	3

Second Base	PCT	G	PO	A	E	DP
Ciriaco	1.000	3	4	1	0	0

Diaz	—	1	0	0	0	0
Holt	1.000	5	2	2	0	0
Iglesias	1.000	3	2	2	0	0
McDonald	1.000	6	7	6	0	1
Middlebrooks	1.000	2	1	3	0	1
Pedroia	.993	160	254	429	5	102

Third Base	PCT	G	PO	A	E	DP
Bogaerts	1.000	9	9	9	0	1
Ciriaco	.778	10	3	11	4	0
Diaz	1.000	3	2	3	0	0
Holt	.951	20	14	25	2	4
Iglesias	.962	34	19	56	3	4
Middlebrooks	.954	92	53	155	10	12
Snyder	.970	17	8	24	1	4

Shortstop	PCT	G	PO	A	E	DP
Bogaerts	1.000	8	6	20	0	1
Ciriaco	.857	8	9	9	3	4
Drew	.984	124	176	332	8	82
Iglesias	.990	29	34	70	1	17

Outfield	PCT	G	PO	A	E	DP
Berry	1.000	9	4	0	0	0
Bradley	.983	34	57	1	1	0
Carp	1.000	43	43	0	0	0
Ellsbury	.992	134	347	3	3	2
Gomes	.992	101	119	5	1	2
Nava	.984	120	181	5	3	0
Snyder	—	1	0	0	0	0
Victorino	.990	122	296	10	3	3

PAWTUCKET RED SOX   TRIPLE-A
INTERNATIONAL LEAGUE

Batting	B-T	HT	WT	DOB	AVG	vLH	vRH	G	AB	R	H	2B	3B	HR	RBI	BB	HBP	SH	SF	SO	SB	CS	SLG	OBP
Bermudez, Ronald	R-R	6-1	165	6-6-88	.258	.333	.223	46	163	22	42	10	1	0	17	6	2	3	2	30	0	2	.331	.289
Berry, Quintin	L-L	6-0	175	11-21-84	.125	.000	.167	3	8	1	1	0	0	0	1	0	0	0	0	2	2	0	.125	.300
2-team total (49 Toledo)					.166	—	—	52	175	17	29	8	0	1	15	24	4	5	1	47	17	2	.229	.279
Bogaerts, Xander	R-R	6-3	185	10-1-92	.284	.298	.280	60	225	32	64	11	0	9	32	28	2	1	0	44	2	2	.453	.369
Bradley, Jackie	L-R	5-10	195	4-19-90	.275	.267	.279	80	320	57	88	26	3	10	35	41	10	2	1	75	7	7	.469	.374
Brentz, Bryce	R-R	6-0	190	12-30-88	.264	.276	.260	82	326	36	86	16	1	17	56	20	3	0	0	86	1	0	.475	.312
Butler, Dan	R-R	5-10	210	10-17-86	.262	.325	.239	84	282	32	74	19	0	14	45	34	5	0	2	59	1	1	.479	.350
Dent, Ryan	R-R	6-0	190	3-15-89	.167	.100	.192	16	36	3	6	0	0	0	1	2	0	1	0	14	3	1	.167	.211
Diaz, Jonathan	R-R	5-9	165	4-10-85	.253	.272	.246	101	332	45	84	11	2	2	31	47	8	11	1	67	10	3	.316	.358
Hamilton, Mark	L-L	6-4	220	7-29-84	.261	.224	.275	82	283	47	74	21	0	12	57	45	2	0	5	87	1	0	.463	.361
Hassan, Alex	R-R	6-3	220	4-1-88	.321	.323	.320	55	187	26	60	14	0	4	28	36	1	0	1	50	0	1	.460	.431
Hazelbaker, Jeremy	L-R	6-3	200	8-14-87	.257	.182	.287	121	428	62	110	13	2	11	54	36	1	10	5	131	37	7	.374	.313
Hee, Jonathan	B-R	6-0	180	8-11-85	.250	.000	.333	3	4	0	1	0	0	0	0	0	0	0	0	0	0	0	.250	.250
Henry, Justin	L-R	6-2	190	4-30-85	.210	.198	.214	102	357	43	75	17	2	1	36	40	4	4	5	57	9	5	.286	.294
Holt, Brock	L-R	5-10	180	6-11-88	.258	.214	.275	83	291	35	75	6	0	3	24	30	2	2	4	54	8	3	.309	.327
Iglesias, Jose	R-R	5-11	185	1-5-90	.202	.171	.214	33	119	17	24	2	0	4	15	9	1	3	1	18	5	3	.319	.262
Johnson, Matty	B-R	5-8	165	4-10-88	.000	.000	.000	1	4	0	0	0	0	0	0	1	0	0	0	3	0	0	.000	.000
Lavarnway, Ryan	R-R	6-4	240	8-7-87	.250	.263	.246	50	180	23	45	9	0	3	24	25	4	0	5	25	0	0	.350	.346
Linares, Juan Carlos	R-R	5-11	190	9-7-84	.200	.000	.273	14	45	6	9	3	0	0	1	5	1	0	0	12	0	0	.267	.294
Maier, Mitch	L-R	6-3	210	6-30-82	.310	.297	.316	31	113	32	35	7	0	3	22	24	0	0	0	26	3	1	.451	.431
Meneses, Heiker	R-R	5-9	160	7-1-91	.241	.583	.143	18	54	3	13	0	1	0	5	5	1	1	1	12	2	1	.278	.311
Middlebrooks, Will	R-R	6-3	220	9-9-88	.268	.309	.250	45	179	25	48	5	0	10	35	16	0	0	1	38	1	0	.464	.327
Natoli, Nick	R-R	6-1	195	1-17-88	.000	—	.000	1	2	0	0	0	0	0	0	0	0	0	0	0	0	0	.000	.000
Ortiz, David	L-L	6-4	250	11-18-75	.222	.167	.250	6	18	3	4	0	0	1	4	0	0	0	0	6	0	0	.389	.222
Rosario, Alberto	R-R	5-10	190	1-10-87	.233	.267	.217	30	90	13	21	3	0	2	6	7	2	3	0	22	0	0	.333	.303
Ross, David	R-R	6-2	230	3-19-77	.000	.000	.000	4	13	0	0	0	0	0	0	1	0	0	0	5	0	0	.000	.071
Snyder, Brandon	R-R	6-2	225	11-23-86	.261	.246	.266	68	249	37	65	16	1	10	37	20	7	0	1	69	3	1	.454	.332
Sutton, Drew	B-R	6-3	200	6-30-83	.245	.302	.218	102	359	55	88	22	1	2	48	58	1	11	5	78	4	2	.329	.348
Thomas, Tony	R-R	5-10	180	7-10-86	.283	.214	.304	16	60	7	17	4	2	0	3	3	0	0	0	17	2	0	.417	.317
Vazquez, Christian	R-R	5-9	195	8-21-90	.000	.000	.000	3	0	0	0	0	0	0	0	1	0	0	0	0	0	0	.000	.250
Victorino, Shane	B-R	5-9	190	11-30-80	.500	.000	.667	1	4	1	2	0	1	0	0	1	0	0	0	1	0	0	1.250	.500

Pitching	B-T	HT	WT	DOB	W	L	ERA	G	GS	CG	SV	IP	H	R	ER	HR	BB	SO	AVG	vLH	vRH	K/9	BB/9
Aceves, Alfredo	R-R	6-2	205	12-8-82	4	2	4.25	8	8	0	0	49	48	25	23	10	17	39	.254	.241	.265	7.21	3.14
Bailey, Andrew	R-R	6-3	240	5-31-84	0	0	9.00	1	0	0	0	1	2	1	1	1	0	2	.400	—	.400	18.00	0.00
Barnes, Matt	R-R	6-4	205	6-17-90	1	0	0.00	1	1	0	0	5	3	0	0	0	2	7	.167	.111	.222	11.81	3.38
Beato, Pedro	R-R	6-6	230	10-27-86	5	3	2.98	34	0	0	5	51	46	22	17	7	24	45	.245	.267	.225	7.89	4.21
Breslow, Craig	L-L	6-1	190	8-8-80	0	0	2.45	4	0	0	0	4	4	1	1	0	3	4	.308	.167	.429	9.82	7.36
Britton, Drake	L-L	6-2	215	5-22-89	0	1	8.44	1	1	0	0	5	10	5	5	0	1	5	.385	.000	.435	8.44	1.69
Buchholz, Clay	R-R	6-3	190	8-14-84	0	0	2.70	1	1	0	0	3	7	1	1	0	0	2	.438	.333	.500	5.40	0.00
Carpenter, Chris	R-R	6-4	220	12-26-85	0	2	4.96	30	1	0	0	45	50	27	25	3	29	48	.275	.268	.280	9.53	5.76
Carter, Anthony	L-R	6-4	220	4-4-86	2	0	3.47	52	0	0	24	62	56	26	24	6	23	79	.237	.283	.200	11.41	3.32
Contreras, Jose	R-R	6-4	255	12-6-71	0	2	6.52	8	0	0	0	10	9	9	7	2	6	15	.231	.263	.200	13.97	5.59
2-team total (16 Indianapolis)					2	2	2.79	24	0	0	1	29	22	12	9	3	11	39	—	—	—	12.10	3.41
Couch, Keith	L-R	6-2	210	11-5-89	0	0	27.00	1	1	0	0	1	3	4	3	0	2	3	.429	.600	.000	27.00	18.00
De La Rosa, Rubby	R-R	6-1	205	3-4-89	3	3	4.26	24	20	0	0	80	65	40	38	9	48	76	.224	.222	.226	5.55	5.38
De La Torre, Jose	R-R	5-10	185	10-17-85	5	1	2.75	34	0	0	1	52	35	18	16	2	27	59	.187	.200	.176	10.15	4.64
Doyle, Terry	R-R	6-4	250	11-2-85	5	6	5.60	18	11	0	0	80	80	51	50	10	39	64	.258	.252	.264	7.17	4.37
Godfrey, Graham	R-R	6-3	215	8-9-84	4	3	3.83	13	4	0	0	42	44	22	18	5	19	30	.259	.271	.250	6.38	4.04
2-team total (19 Indianapolis)					11	8	3.93	32	15	0	0	119	119	58	52	16	33	75	—	—	—	5.67	2.50
Haeger, Charlie	R-R	6-1	210	9-19-83	4	4	4.38	13	13	0	0	72	77	41	35	11	40	59	.276	.288	.266	7.38	5.00

	B-T	HT	WT	DOB	W	L	ERA	G	GS	CG	SV	IP	H	R	ER	HR	BB	SO	AVG	vLH	vRH	K/9	BB/9
Hanrahan, Joel	R-R	6-4	250	10-6-81	0	0	9.00	2	0	0	0	2	2	2	2	1	1	1	.250	.500	.000	4.50	4.50
Hernandez, Chris	L-L	6-2	195	12-14-88	3	9	5.72	24	16	0	0	102	130	76	65	12	51	61	.308	.287	.316	5.36	4.49
Huntzinger, Brock	R-R	6-3	200	7-2-88	2	2	1.43	24	0	0	0	38	27	10	6	1	16	37	.203	.150	.247	8.84	3.82
Kehrt, Jeremy	R-R	6-2	190	12-21-85	0	2	6.46	5	2	0	1	15	31	12	11	1	4	12	.408	.429	.370	7.04	2.35
Latimer, Will	L-L	6-3	190	12-4-85	0	0	9.39	4	0	0	0	8	11	8	8	1	6	6	.344	.214	.444	7.04	7.04
Lyon, Brandon	R-R	6-1	200	8-10-79	0	0	1.69	4	0	0	2	5	5	2	1	0	1	3	.250	.100	.400	5.06	1.69
Martin, Chris	R-R	6-7	175	6-2-86	3	3	3.18	30	0	0	2	51	51	19	18	3	10	47	.262	.241	.278	8.29	1.76
Morales, Franklin	L-L	6-1	210	1-24-86	0	1	4.76	5	2	0	0	11	5	6	6	3	3	12	.132	.000	.217	9.53	2.38
Mortensen, Clayton	R-R	6-4	185	4-10-85	3	0	2.47	14	6	0	0	44	34	14	12	4	20	39	.222	.294	.165	8.04	4.12
Niesen, Eric	L-L	6-0	185	9-4-85	0	0	6.75	2	0	0	0	1	2	1	1	0	1	1	.333	.000	.400	6.75	6.75
Ranaudo, Anthony	R-R	6-7	230	9-9-89	3	1	2.97	6	5	0	0	30	32	11	10	1	7	21	.271	.231	.303	6.23	2.08
Rowland-Smith, Ryan	L-L	6-3	240	1-26-83	7	0	1.55	37	0	0	1	52	37	12	9	3	15	45	.197	.192	.200	7.74	2.58
Villareal, Brayan	R-R	6-0	170	5-10-87	0	1	1.69	5	0	0	1	5	3	1	1	0	4	6	.188	.250	.125	10.13	6.75
2-team total (28 Toledo)					2	3	2.95	33	0	0	2	40	29	14	13	0	30	47	—	—	—	10.66	6.81
Villarreal, Oscar	L-R	6-0	195	11-22-81	4	2	4.44	14	0	0	0	24	23	13	12	2	9	23	.247	.306	.182	8.51	3.33
Webster, Allen	R-R	6-2	190	2-10-90	8	4	3.60	21	21	0	0	105	71	45	42	9	43	116	.190	.220	.160	9.94	3.69
Wilson, Alex	R-R	6-0	215	11-3-86	3	1	3.71	14	0	0	0	17	17	7	7	2	5	16	.262	.188	.333	8.47	2.65
Workman, Brandon	R-R	6-4	195	8-13-88	3	1	2.80	6	6	0	0	35	39	13	11	6	13	34	.289	.266	.321	8.66	3.31
Wright, Steven	R-R	6-1	220	8-30-84	8	7	3.46	24	24	3	0	135	130	64	52	10	65	99	.254	.266	.246	6.58	4.32

Fielding

Catcher	PCT	G	PO	A	E	DP	PB
Butler	.990	72	541	54	6	4	20
Lavarnway	.994	43	335	24	2	5	13
Rosario	.987	30	211	17	3	1	13
Ross	1.000	4	21	3	0	0	0
Vazquez	1.000	1	7	0	0	0	0

First Base	PCT	G	PO	A	E	DP
Hamilton	.994	19	147	7	1	13
Hassan	.977	10	77	7	2	6
Henry	1.000	1	5	0	0	2
Snyder	.988	41	313	29	4	35
Sutton	.997	77	592	45	2	68

Second Base	PCT	G	PO	A	E	DP
Dent	1.000	1	2	3	0	0
Diaz	.984	43	72	117	3	21
Henry	.991	44	87	129	2	30
Holt	.982	44	66	97	3	21

Meneses	1.000	11	27	32	0	8
Natoli	—	1	0	0	0	0
Thomas	1.000	3	6	3	0	1

Third Base	PCT	G	PO	A	E	DP
Bogaerts	.957	10	10	12	1	3
Dent	1.000	6	3	6	0	1
Diaz	.984	26	15	45	1	5
Hee	—	1	0	0	0	0
Henry	.939	12	7	24	2	1
Holt	.944	7	5	12	1	1
Iglesias	.800	1	2	2	1	0
Middlebrooks	.967	40	38	80	4	3
Snyder	.939	25	31	46	5	7
Sutton	.943	23	19	31	3	2

Shortstop	PCT	G	PO	A	E	DP
Bogaerts	.949	49	74	112	10	32
Diaz	.991	25	37	73	1	14

Hee	.667	2	2	2	2	1
Holt	.985	32	49	82	2	20
Iglesias	.971	32	46	90	4	22
Meneses	.971	7	10	23	1	6

Outfield	PCT	G	PO	A	E	DP
Bermudez	.974	45	109	3	3	1
Berry	1.000	3	4	0	0	0
Bradley	1.000	68	161	4	0	1
Brentz	.935	69	112	3	8	0
Dent	1.000	8	8	1	0	0
Hamilton	1.000	20	27	0	0	0
Hassan	.984	40	60	2	1	0
Hazelbaker	.972	107	200	6	6	1
Henry	1.000	35	63	2	0	1
Linares	1.000	11	14	1	0	0
Maier	1.000	24	50	1	0	0
Thomas	1.000	11	21	1	0	0
Victorino	1.000	1	1	0	0	0

PORTLAND SEA DOGS — DOUBLE-A

EASTERN LEAGUE

Batting	B-T	HT	WT	DOB	AVG	vLH	vRH	G	AB	R	H	2B	3B	HR	RBI	BB	HBP	SH	SF	SO	SB	CS	SLG	OBP
Almanzar, Michael	R-R	6-3	190	12-2-90	.268	.281	.263	131	507	67	136	29	3	16	81	42	6	0	6	100	13	3	.432	.328
Bermudez, Ronald	R-R	6-1	165	6-6-88	.268	.318	.245	21	71	11	19	1	0	1	9	6	0	1	1	15	1	2	.324	.321
Bogaerts, Xander	R-R	6-3	185	10-1-92	.311	.284	.322	56	219	40	68	12	6	6	35	35	2	1	2	51	5	1	.502	.407
Cecchini, Garin	L-R	6-2	200	4-20-91	.296	.333	.277	66	240	36	71	14	3	2	28	51	2	0	2	52	8	2	.404	.420
Dent, Ryan	R-R	6-0	190	3-15-89	.257	.176	.288	56	183	26	47	7	0	3	22	16	1	1	0	39	8	4	.344	.320
Drew, Stephen	L-R	6-0	190	3-16-83	.200	.100	.300	6	20	1	4	2	0	1	4	2	0	0	1	4	0	0	.450	.261
Escobar, Leonel	R-R	5-10	175	9-4-90	.000	.000	.000	1	1	0	0	0	0	0	0	0	1	0	0	1	0	0	.000	.500
Gibson, Derrik	R-R	6-1	170	12-5-89	.250	.342	.210	88	260	40	65	16	1	2	22	37	3	6	2	61	12	5	.342	.348
Heller, Kevin	R-R	5-10	195	9-12-89	.150	.000	.214	7	20	1	3	1	0	0	3	3	0	0	0	6	1	0	.200	.261
Hissey, Pete	L-L	6-1	180	1-17-90	.260	.221	.273	68	262	35	68	15	2	3	24	22	2	5	3	63	17	4	.366	.318
Jacobs, Brandon	R-R	6-1	225	12-8-90	.375	.500	.250	3	8	2	3	1	1	0	0	0	0	0	0	2	0	0	.750	.375
Johnson, Matty	B-R	5-8	165	4-26-89	.280	.172	.328	25	93	12	26	2	1	0	4	9	1	2	0	18	3	7	.323	.350
Linares, Juan Carlos	R-R	5-11	190	9-7-84	.276	.275	.276	81	301	44	83	24	2	8	51	26	10	0	2	72	0	0	.449	.351
Marrero, Deven	R-R	6-1	195	8-25-90	.236	.417	.200	19	72	7	17	0	0	0	5	10	0	1	2	16	6	0	.236	.321
Meneses, Heiker	R-R	5-9	160	7-1-91	.255	.278	.244	92	322	43	82	15	4	3	31	20	7	4	0	84	11	7	.354	.312
Natoli, Nick	R-R	6-1	195	1-17-88	.429	.000	.545	3	14	2	6	1	0	0	2	0	0	0	0	4	1	0	.500	.429
Rosario, Alberto	R-R	5-10	190	1-10-87	.167	.077	.217	11	36	3	6	0	0	0	4	3	1	0	1	4	0	0	.167	.244
Ross, David	R-R	6-2	230	3-19-77	.333	.667	.000	3	6	3	2	2	0	0	2	1	0	0	0	2	0	0	.667	.429
Shaw, Travis	L-R	6-4	225	4-16-90	.221	.230	.217	127	444	57	98	21	4	16	50	78	5	0	2	117	7	3	.394	.342
Spring, Matt	R-R	6-2	215	11-7-84	.222	.200	.230	52	185	21	41	12	0	10	34	10	2	0	1	64	0	0	.449	.268
Thomas, Tony	R-R	5-10	180	7-10-86	.220	.226	.217	107	418	51	92	25	7	11	68	33	8	0	5	113	16	2	.392	.287
Vazquez, Christian	R-R	5-9	195	8-21-90	.289	.333	.272	96	342	48	99	19	1	5	48	47	3	3	4	44	7	5	.395	.376
Vitek, Kolbrin	R-R	6-2	195	4-1-89	.204	.250	.184	58	201	14	41	8	1	0	14	14	2	0	3	52	5	3	.254	.260
Wilkerson, Shannon	R-R	6-0	198	7-20-88	.237	.233	.238	124	465	76	110	23	6	4	37	53	5	9	6	101	23	13	.338	.318

Pitching	B-T	HT	WT	DOB	W	L	ERA	G	GS	CG	SV	IP	H	R	ER	HR	BB	SO	AVG	vLH	vRH	K/9	BB/9
Balcom-Miller, Chris	R-R	6-2	210	3-3-89	0	1	4.12	9	0	0	0	20	20	9	9	3	9	18	.274	.286	.267	8.24	4.12
Bard, Daniel	R-R	6-4	215	6-25-85	0	1	6.39	13	0	0	0	13	13	11	9	1	17	6	.283	.350	.233	4.26	12.08
Barnes, Matt	R-R	6-4	205	6-17-90	5	10	4.33	24	24	0	0	108	112	62	52	11	46	135	.265	.242	.282	11.25	3.83
Breslow, Craig	L-L	6-1	190	8-8-80	0	0	—	1	1	0	0	0	3	3	3	0	1	0	1.000	1.000	1.000	—	—
Britton, Drake	L-L	6-2	215	5-22-89	7	6	3.51	17	16	1	0	97	94	52	38	5	36	80	.254	.187	.281	7.40	3.33

Player	B-T	HT	WT	DOB	W	L	ERA	G	GS	CG	SV	IP	H	R	ER	HR	BB	SO	AVG	vLH	vRH	K/9	BB/9
Celestino, Miguel	R-R	6-6	205	10-10-89	1	9	6.13	39	0	0	1	72	81	52	49	10	36	70	.287	.288	.287	8.75	4.50
Couch, Keith	L-R	6-2	210	11-5-89	11	3	3.47	29	15	2	0	130	132	63	50	11	43	92	.265	.278	.255	6.39	2.98
Doyle, Terry	R-R	6-4	250	11-2-85	1	6	4.06	11	10	2	0	69	73	32	31	6	17	49	.274	.302	.250	6.42	2.23
Haeger, Charlie	R-R	6-1	210	9-19-83	4	4	3.99	12	12	0	0	70	61	36	31	7	43	56	.230	.270	.194	7.20	5.53
Hernandez, Chris	L-L	6-2	195	12-14-88	2	0	1.64	5	5	0	0	33	28	8	6	0	8	19	.235	.261	.219	5.18	2.18
Huntzinger, Brock	R-R	6-3	200	7-2-88	3	0	2.32	25	0	0	13	31	24	12	8	2	12	25	.214	.179	.233	7.26	3.48
Kaminska, Kyle	L-R	6-4	180	10-5-88	0	3	9.00	4	4	0	0	19	34	22	19	1	4	11	.378	.293	.449	5.21	1.89
Kehrt, Jeremy	R-R	6-2	190	12-21-85	2	3	4.33	22	7	0	0	71	78	46	34	6	25	54	.274	.303	.252	6.88	3.18
Kraus, Kyle	R-R	5-11	185	1-19-90	0	0	0.00	1	0	0	0	4	1	0	0	0	1	2	.077	.000	.100	4.50	2.25
Lackey, John	R-R	6-6	235	10-23-78	0	0	0.00	1	1	0	0	4	3	0	0	0	2	5	.231	.250	.222	12.27	4.91
Lanigan, Bobby	R-R	6-4	220	5-5-87	0	2	7.85	8	1	0	2	18	25	18	16	4	4	15	.316	.294	.333	7.36	1.96
2-team total (23 New Britain)					3	3	5.36	31	1	0	3	47	61	35	28	6	15	31	—	—	—	5.94	2.87
Latimer, Will	L-L	6-3	190	12-4-85	2	5	2.18	19	0	0	0	33	38	19	8	0	15	32	.295	.233	.326	8.73	4.09
Maloney, Matt	L-L	6-4	210	1-16-84	1	1	5.14	10	0	0	1	14	18	9	8	1	2	8	.333	.450	.265	5.14	1.29
Martin, Chris	R-R	6-7	175	6-2-86	2	0	0.00	12	0	0	3	21	9	0	0	0	6	27	.132	.238	.085	11.57	2.57
McCarthy, Mike	R-R	6-3	185	11-18-87	1	3	6.03	10	5	0	2	37	45	25	25	4	9	19	.296	.302	.293	4.58	2.17
Morales, Franklin	L-L	6-1	210	1-24-86	1	0	1.13	3	2	0	0	8	10	2	1	0	2	7	.323	.333	.318	7.88	2.25
Niesen, Eric	L-L	6-0	185	9-4-85	1	3	4.34	12	0	0	1	19	18	12	9	1	12	22	.250	.292	.229	10.61	5.79
Ott, Matty	R-R	6-1	190	4-20-90	0	0	0.00	1	0	0	0	4	1	0	0	0	2	1	.077	.000	.111	4.50	2.25
Owens, Henry	L-L	6-6	205	7-21-92	3	1	1.78	6	6	0	0	30	18	8	6	3	15	46	.167	.158	.171	13.65	4.45
Pena, Miguel	L-L	6-2	175	10-24-90	1	1	5.60	3	3	0	0	18	18	11	11	4	5	12	.273	.316	.255	6.11	2.55
Perez, Rafael	L-L	6-3	195	5-15-82	2	2	2.64	25	0	0	6	31	27	9	9	3	5	30	.235	.265	.222	8.80	1.47
Ramirez, Noe	R-R	6-3	180	12-22-89	1	1	2.83	15	0	0	5	29	22	9	9	4	8	31	.218	.268	.183	9.73	2.51
Ranaudo, Anthony	R-R	6-7	230	9-9-89	8	4	2.95	19	19	0	0	110	80	39	36	9	40	106	.204	.212	.199	8.70	3.28
Ruiz, Pete	R-R	6-3	205	8-21-87	3	3	5.23	30	0	0	0	53	50	34	31	4	27	69	.243	.186	.283	11.64	4.56
Striz, Nate	R-R	6-2	220	10-15-88	0	0	6.00	1	0	0	0	3	4	2	2	0	1	3	.364	.000	.400	9.00	3.00
Workman, Brandon	R-R	6-4	195	8-13-88	5	1	3.43	11	10	0	0	66	51	29	25	6	17	74	.216	.226	.210	10.14	2.33

Fielding

Catcher	PCT	G	PO	A	E	DP	PB
Escobar	1.000	1	5	0	0	0	0
Rosario	1.000	8	68	4	0	0	3
Ross	1.000	2	7	1	0	0	0
Spring	.990	39	274	15	3	0	6
Vazquez	.989	93	781	80	10	5	23

First Base	PCT	G	PO	A	E	DP
Almanzar	.990	23	177	18	2	17
Shaw	.992	111	885	77	8	91
Spring	.974	10	68	6	2	8

Second Base	PCT	G	PO	A	E	DP
Dent	1.000	27	56	75	0	23
Gibson	.984	56	105	147	4	35
Meneses	.960	43	68	100	7	22
Natoli	1.000	2	4	5	0	1

	PCT	G	PO	A	E	DP
Thomas	1.000	14	26	36	0	11
Vitek	1.000	1	1	2	0	1

Third Base	PCT	G	PO	A	E	DP
Almanzar	.912	73	45	131	17	19
Cecchini	.956	44	16	93	5	10
Dent	.947	7	5	13	1	2
Gibson	.500	1	0	1	1	0
Natoli	.500	1	1	0	1	0
Shaw	.875	4	1	6	1	1
Vitek	.826	11	5	14	4	1

Shortstop	PCT	G	PO	A	E	DP
Bogaerts	.952	47	57	121	9	26
Dent	1.000	1	1	0	0	0
Drew	1.000	5	6	6	0	0
Gibson	.948	26	35	74	6	10

	PCT	G	PO	A	E	DP
Marrero	.980	19	27	73	2	9
Meneses	.962	48	73	131	8	33

Outfield	PCT	G	PO	A	E	DP
Bermudez	.969	21	31	0	1	0
Dent	.917	20	22	0	2	0
Gibson	1.000	2	1	0	0	0
Heller	1.000	7	6	0	0	0
Hissey	1.000	68	138	5	0	1
Jacobs	1.000	3	4	0	0	0
Johnson	.982	25	55	0	1	0
Linares	.969	70	117	8	4	3
Thomas	.915	70	115	3	11	0
Vitek	.976	27	41	0	1	0
Wilkerson	.990	124	287	7	3	4

SALEM RED SOX

CAROLINA LEAGUE

HIGH CLASS A

Batting	B-T	HT	WT	DOB	AVG	vLH	vRH	G	AB	R	H	2B	3B	HR	RBI	BB	HBP	SH	SF	SO	SB	CS	SLG	OBP
Betts, Mookie	R-R	5-9	156	10-7-92	.341	.250	.362	51	185	30	63	12	3	7	39	23	1	1	1	17	20	2	.551	.414
Blair, Carson	R-R	6-1	190	10-18-89	.250	.179	.271	41	124	21	31	9	2	4	13	23	1	0	0	39	2	1	.452	.372
Cecchini, Garin	L-R	6-2	200	4-20-91	.350	.304	.363	63	214	44	75	19	4	5	33	43	5	0	0	34	15	7	.547	.469
Chester, David	R-R	6-5	270	3-31-89	.273	.357	.239	29	99	12	27	2	0	6	14	11	1	0	1	22	2	0	.475	.348
Coyle, Sean	R-R	5-8	175	1-17-92	.241	.286	.231	48	195	41	47	9	1	14	28	24	1	0	4	65	11	0	.513	.321
De La Cruz, Keury	L-L	5-11	170	11-28-91	.258	.210	.270	133	535	65	138	36	6	9	89	31	2	0	7	130	16	9	.398	.297
Escobar, Leonel	R-R	5-10	175	9-4-90	.167	.500	.100	4	12	0	2	0	0	0	0	0	0	1	0	4	0	0	.167	.167
Frias, Vladimir	B-R	6-2	170	9-6-86	.192	.286	.158	9	26	1	5	0	0	0	2	2	0	2	0	5	1	1	.192	.250
Garcia, Jose	R-R	5-11	165	4-23-91	.176	.095	.195	34	108	2	19	3	1	0	10	5	0	1	2	24	2	3	.222	.209
Gedman, Matt	L-R	6-2	205	9-26-88	.279	.222	.287	65	229	30	64	12	0	7	31	19	1	0	1	33	6	0	.424	.336
Heller, Kevin	R-R	5-10	195	9-12-89	.000	.000	.000	3	9	0	0	0	0	0	0	0	0	0	0	4	0	0	.000	.000
Jacobs, Brandon	R-R	6-1	225	12-8-90	.244	.143	.264	81	291	44	71	24	0	11	44	33	8	0	3	88	10	4	.440	.334
Johns, Bryan	R-R	5-9	180	11-18-88	.186	.000	.229	19	59	6	11	2	0	0	5	5	4	1	0	15	1	0	.220	.294
Johnson, Matty	B-R	5-8	165	4-10-88	.252	.225	.259	56	202	20	51	9	3	0	22	16	1	11	2	31	11	6	.327	.308
Koback, Cody	R-R	6-1	195	4-20-90	.215	.179	.224	54	186	17	40	5	2	0	10	14	6	4	2	29	6	0	.263	.288
Marrero, Deven	R-R	6-1	195	8-25-90	.256	.290	.247	85	332	50	85	20	0	2	21	42	1	1	0	60	21	2	.334	.341
Natoli, Nick	R-R	6-1	195	1-17-88	.185	.125	.200	97	319	43	59	16	1	1	28	51	6	6	2	84	11	2	.251	.307
Ramos, Henry	B-R	6-2	187	4-15-92	.252	.242	.254	129	469	69	118	27	7	12	55	55	3	6	7	100	11	12	.416	.330
Renfroe, David	R-R	6-3	200	11-16-90	.222	.293	.206	62	216	25	48	11	2	3	31	20	3	0	4	50	2	2	.333	.292
Roberson, Tim	R-R	5-10	190	7-19-89	.268	.231	.279	17	56	10	15	2	0	2	8	6	0	0	0	14	0	0	.411	.339
Sanchez, Felix	B-R	6-0	165	6-2-90	.216	.200	.221	32	116	21	25	2	0	1	9	5	2	3	1	43	17	5	.259	.258
Swihart, Blake	B-R	6-1	175	4-3-92	.298	.367	.279	103	376	45	112	29	7	2	42	41	1	1	3	63	7	8	.428	.366
Welch, Stefan	L-R	6-3	190	8-12-88	.292	.226	.308	75	267	48	78	19	0	10	46	45	10	0	3	65	3	2	.476	.409

Pitching	B-T	HT	WT	DOB	W	L	ERA	G	GS	CG	SV	IP	H	R	ER	HR	BB	SO	AVG	vLH	vRH	K/9	BB/9
Augliera, Mike	R-R	6-0	200	6-8-90	9	6	4.23	26	26	1	0	140	146	74	66	10	38	76	.272	.305	.246	4.87	2.44
Balcom-Miller, Chris	R-R	6-2	210	3-3-89	0	0	1.35	4	0	0	0	7	6	2	1	0	2	1	.222	.125	.364	1.35	2.70
Cuevas, William	R-R	6-0	160	10-14-90	8	9	5.05	26	26	1	0	135	139	82	76	13	40	109	.268	.260	.273	7.25	2.66
Diaz, Luis	R-R	6-3	210	4-9-92	2	0	1.38	2	2	0	0	13	11	3	2	0	4	8	.229	.353	.161	5.54	2.77
Johnson, Brian	L-L	6-3	225	12-7-90	1	0	1.64	2	2	0	0	11	9	2	2	0	5	8	.225	.250	.208	6.55	4.09
Kaminska, Kyle	L-R	6-4	180	10-5-88	0	0	4.38	2	2	0	0	12	12	6	6	2	1	7	.261	.296	.211	5.11	0.73
Kraus, Kyle	R-R	5-11	185	1-19-90	4	2	4.04	13	5	0	1	49	52	24	22	5	13	28	.265	.263	.267	5.14	2.39
McCarthy, Mike	R-R	6-3	185	11-18-87	5	2	4.29	21	11	0	1	86	106	50	41	11	18	66	.306	.260	.342	6.91	1.88
Ogando, Nefi	R-R	6-2	185	6-3-89	2	3	4.09	33	0	0	3	55	49	34	25	5	27	44	.238	.225	.246	7.20	4.42
Olivares, Gerardo	R-R	6-0	190	8-14-88	0	0	27.00	2	0	0	0	2	6	7	7	0	4	1	.462	.500	.429	3.86	15.43
Ott, Matty	R-R	6-1	190	4-20-90	4	5	3.82	37	0	0	5	73	67	33	31	4	22	66	.245	.208	.275	8.14	2.71
Owens, Henry	L-L	6-6	205	7-21-92	8	5	2.92	20	20	0	0	105	66	39	34	6	53	123	.180	.221	.166	10.58	4.56
Pena, Miguel	L-L	6-2	175	10-24-90	6	7	4.00	15	15	1	0	81	84	39	36	4	27	54	.274	.365	.239	6.00	3.00
Price, Mathew	R-R	6-3	185	7-8-89	6	0	2.41	35	0	0	6	52	32	15	14	2	22	50	.178	.147	.200	8.60	3.78
Quevedo, Heri	R-R	6-2	211	6-7-90	6	5	4.18	23	11	0	2	97	84	52	45	4	52	91	.229	.218	.238	8.44	4.82
Ramirez, Noe	R-R	6-3	180	12-22-89	2	1	2.11	21	0	0	1	47	41	13	11	0	9	44	.247	.267	.236	8.43	1.72
Rivera, Manny	L-L	6-0	170	9-1-89	0	1	4.58	9	0	0	1	18	22	9	9	1	7	9	.319	.136	.404	4.58	3.57
Scott, Robby	B-L	6-3	220	8-29-89	4	4	2.79	31	0	0	2	68	51	27	21	6	30	44	.214	.239	.204	5.85	3.99
Striz, Nate	R-R	6-2	220	10-15-88	1	4	3.14	38	0	0	8	57	48	21	20	0	26	59	.232	.253	.217	9.26	4.08
Stroup, Kyle	R-R	6-6	235	3-13-90	4	9	5.17	22	20	1	0	87	110	54	50	5	29	58	.310	.281	.327	6.00	3.00
Younginer, Madison	R-R	6-4	195	11-3-90	4	0	3.52	13	0	0	1	23	22	9	9	1	11	25	.253	.258	.250	9.78	4.30

Fielding

Catcher	PCT	G	PO	A	E	DP	PB
Blair	.995	29	180	18	1	2	7
Escobar	1.000	4	28	5	0	1	1
Roberson	.968	10	51	10	2	1	2
Swihart	.988	101	743	88	10	6	6

First Base	PCT	G	PO	A	E	DP
Chester	.995	20	173	11	1	18
Garcia	.989	11	84	10	1	9
Gedman	.988	44	389	25	5	37
Natoli	.957	5	43	2	2	4
Renfroe	.982	44	375	13	7	29
Roberson	1.000	1	8	0	0	1
Welch	1.000	21	183	12	0	16

Second Base	PCT	G	PO	A	E	DP
Betts	.979	50	117	163	6	41
Coyle	.994	36	61	96	1	14
Frias	1.000	1	1	4	0	2
Garcia	.969	14	26	36	2	7
Johns	.982	13	20	35	1	6
Natoli	.969	29	41	83	4	19

Third Base	PCT	G	PO	A	E	DP
Cecchini	.906	59	29	87	12	8
Frias	1.000	4	0	4	0	1
Garcia	.667	1	0	2	1	0
Johns	.667	1	1	1	1	0
Natoli	.960	14	11	37	2	2
Renfroe	.929	19	11	28	3	0
Welch	.992	48	22	95	1	15

Shortstop	PCT	G	PO	A	E	DP
Frias	.842	4	4	12	3	1
Garcia	1.000	1	2	3	0	0
Johns	.967	5	10	19	1	1
Marrero	.990	85	139	264	4	57
Natoli	.954	47	74	135	10	29

Outfield	PCT	G	PO	A	E	DP
De La Cruz	.984	103	175	7	3	2
Heller	1.000	2	3	0	0	0
Jacobs	.976	71	116	4	3	0
Johnson	.989	50	83	5	1	3
Koback	.976	53	121	1	3	0
Natoli	1.000	3	7	0	0	0
Ramos	.984	124	240	9	4	3
Sanchez	.941	20	29	3	2	0

GREENVILLE DRIVE

LOW CLASS A

SOUTH ATLANTIC LEAGUE

Batting	B-T	HT	WT	DOB	AVG	vLH	vRH	G	AB	R	H	2B	3B	HR	RBI	BB	HBP	SH	SF	SO	SB	CS	SLG	OBP
Betts, Mookie	R-R	5-9	156	10-7-92	.296	.230	.320	76	277	63	82	24	1	8	26	58	1	3	1	40	18	2	.477	.418
Briscoe, Keaton	L-R	6-0	190	5-13-91	.206	.195	.209	57	180	26	37	7	3	2	15	20	5	2	0	58	3	2	.311	.302
Chester, David	R-R	6-5	270	3-31-89	.270	.221	.287	94	333	38	90	25	0	13	71	41	6	0	5	89	1	0	.462	.356
Colorado, Jose	L-R	6-1	170	8-26-90	.091	.000	.100	4	11	0	1	1	0	0	0	3	0	0	0	4	0	0	.182	.286
Coyle, Sean	R-R	5-8	175	1-17-92	.320	.250	.333	6	25	4	8	3	0	1	4	3	0	0	0	9	0	1	.560	.393
Escobar, Leonel	R-R	5-10	175	9-4-90	.206	.333	.179	11	34	0	7	1	0	0	2	2	0	1	0	7	0	0	.235	.250
Gragnani, Reed	B-R	5-11	180	9-5-90	.259	.316	.239	38	147	23	38	8	0	1	16	13	6	2	3	22	2	2	.333	.337
Guerrero, Dreily	B-R	5-11	162	10-12-90	.171	.191	.162	56	164	23	28	5	0	1	8	15	1	3	2	56	5	2	.220	.242
Hassan, Alex	R-R	6-3	220	4-1-88	.478	.400	.500	8	23	4	11	2	0	0	7	10	0	0	0	2	0	0	.565	.636
Heller, Kevin	R-R	5-10	195	9-12-89	.248	.212	.262	35	117	12	29	3	2	2	10	10	5	0	0	33	4	0	.359	.333
Hernandez, Jayson	R-R	5-10	200	9-2-88	.267	.333	.243	60	206	13	55	6	0	1	16	9	9	0	1	36	0	2	.311	.324
Johns, Bryan	R-R	5-9	180	11-18-88	.181	.250	.161	21	72	8	13	0	1	2	14	7	1	2	2	21	1	1	.292	.256
Koback, Cody	R-R	6-1	185	4-20-90	.282	.240	.294	61	227	33	64	11	2	0	29	21	6	4	1	45	10	6	.348	.357
Loya, Jesus	L-R	5-11	175	6-15-92	.296	.300	.295	33	125	12	37	6	1	0	9	7	1	1	0	17	3	2	.360	.338
Mager, Kevin	R-R	6-2	185	5-16-89	.245	.417	.189	16	49	8	12	3	0	1	5	8	0	0	0	15	0	0	.367	.351
Martinez, Mario	R-R	6-3	220	11-13-89	.285	.239	.299	76	295	35	84	14	0	9	54	15	5	2	2	81	0	1	.424	.328
Miller, Mike	R-R	5-9	170	9-27-89	.356	.222	.389	15	45	8	16	6	0	0	2	5	2	1	0	5	3	1	.489	.442
Moanaroa, Boss	L-R	6-1	200	7-12-91	.173	.047	.197	84	277	26	48	13	1	4	29	40	2	0	3	107	0	0	.271	.280
Moore, Nick	B-R	6-2	200	12-9-92	.158	.095	.182	24	76	6	12	2	0	2	8	11	0	0	0	47	3	1	.263	.264
Perkins, Kendrick	L-R	6-2	225	9-2-90	.221	.083	.246	45	154	14	34	9	1	2	10	10	2	0	0	57	4	5	.331	.277
Roberson, Tim	R-R	5-10	190	7-19-89	.289	.229	.303	47	187	17	54	9	1	3	29	8	0	0	1	46	0	0	.396	.316
Sanchez, Felix	B-R	6-0	165	6-2-90	.206	.326	.148	43	131	20	27	4	0	0	6	11	8	3	1	49	10	5	.237	.305
Tavarez, Aneury	L-R	5-9	175	4-14-92	.257	.245	.260	125	479	56	123	17	7	7	55	21	6	7	3	140	29	15	.388	.295
Turocy, Drew	L-L	6-3	190	12-26-88	.297	.257	.312	72	279	33	83	25	5	0	20	19	2	0	0	67	6	2	.423	.347
Vinicio, Jose	B-R	5-11	150	7-10-93	.192	.133	.212	107	391	44	75	14	4	1	26	12	5	9	1	108	21	9	.256	.225
Weems, Jordan	L-R	6-3	175	11-7-92	.204	.200	.205	61	201	15	41	8	0	0	13	25	3	0	0	60	2	1	.244	.301

Pitching	B-T	HT	WT	DOB	W	L	ERA	G	GS	CG	SV	IP	H	R	ER	HR	BB	SO	AVG	vLH	vRH	K/9	BB/9
Dahlstrand, Jacob	R-R	6-5	205	3-26-92	4	8	4.65	18	15	1	0	89	95	50	46	9	34	51	.275	.321	.244	5.16	3.44
Diaz, Luis	R-R	6-3	210	4-9-92	7	4	2.05	15	14	1	0	88	74	32	20	5	20	86	.224	.252	.206	8.80	2.05

Garcia, Jason	R-R	6-0	185	11-21-92	2	2	4.21	9	1	0	1	36	33	20	17	3	16	36	.239	.208	.259	8.92	3.96
Gomez, Sergio	R-R	6-3	155	8-24-93	1	3	2.96	5	5	0	0	27	21	10	9	2	10	25	.219	.188	.234	8.23	3.29
Haley, Justin	R-R	6-5	230	6-16-91	7	11	3.68	26	24	0	0	125	97	64	51	10	74	124	.219	.255	.200	8.95	5.34
Johnson, Brian	L-L	6-3	225	12-7-90	1	6	2.87	15	15	0	0	69	50	29	22	4	28	69	.197	.310	.175	9.00	3.65
Kapteyn, Braden	R-R	6-4	225	9-28-89	1	1	4.58	10	0	0	0	18	15	12	9	1	19	15	.246	.222	.256	7.64	9.68
Kraus, Kyle	R-R	5-11	185	1-19-90	2	0	2.29	19	0	0	4	35	32	11	9	1	4	35	.234	.250	.226	8.92	1.02
Kukuk, Cody	L-L	6-4	200	4-10-93	4	13	4.63	26	24	0	1	107	77	69	55	5	81	113	.197	.165	.206	9.50	6.81
Larson, Greg	R-R	6-8	225	9-25-89	0	0	9.45	4	0	0	0	7	12	8	7	0	4	5	.387	.455	.350	6.75	5.40
Light, Pat	R-R	6-5	195	3-29-91	1	4	8.89	10	9	0	0	28	44	33	28	4	14	28	.346	.292	.380	8.89	4.45
Maddox, Austin	R-R	6-2	220	5-13-91	4	6	5.63	33	7	0	1	88	109	67	55	13	22	65	.294	.336	.274	6.65	2.25
Martin, Kyle	R-R	6-7	220	1-18-91	2	1	2.12	9	0	0	1	17	8	5	4	0	7	15	.148	.111	.167	7.94	3.71
McGeary, Jack	L-L	6-3	195	3-19-89	1	1	4.02	9	0	0	0	16	10	7	7	1	13	20	.185	.154	.195	11.49	7.47
Montas, Francellis	R-R	6-2	185	3-21-93	2	9	5.70	19	18	1	0	85	94	62	54	10	32	96	.276	.301	.260	10.13	3.38
2-team total (5 Kannapolis)					5	11	5.43	24	23	1	0	111	114	75	67	11	50	127	—	—	—	10.30	4.05
Morales, Franklin	L-L	6-1	210	1-24-86	0	0	0.00	1	1	0	0	3	1	0	0	2	1	1	.111	.000	.125	3.00	6.00
Olivares, Gerardo	R-R	6-0	190	8-14-88	3	4	5.18	20	0	0	2	40	36	24	23	7	15	26	.247	.170	.290	5.85	3.38
Ortega, Yunior	R-R	5-11	170	8-10-91	2	6	6.55	26	1	0	1	78	96	66	57	14	26	66	.298	.298	.298	7.58	2.99
Rivera, Manny	L-L	6-0	170	9-1-89	0	0	3.38	14	0	0	1	21	22	10	8	1	5	14	.275	.000	.344	5.91	2.11
Smorol, Rob	L-L	6-1	185	2-22-91	0	0	0.00	1	0	0	0	1	0	0	0	1	0	0	.000	—	.000	0.00	9.00
Taveras, Francisco	L-L	6-0	180	5-23-90	3	5	6.69	19	4	0	1	71	80	57	53	15	30	48	.281	.317	.270	6.06	3.79
Vellette, Raynel	R-R	6-2	165	6-10-91	0	3	3.58	15	0	0	0	33	31	14	13	4	16	33	.254	.231	.265	9.09	4.41
Wendelken, J.B.	R-R	6-0	190	3-24-93	2	0	2.77	27	0	0	10	65	59	20	20	4	20	54	.238	.255	.227	7.48	2.77
2-team total (3 Kannapolis)					2	1	3.23	30	0	0	12	70	67	25	25	4	21	62	—	—	—	8.01	2.71
Younginer, Madison	R-R	6-4	195	11-3-90	2	0	5.59	13	0	0	0	19	19	12	12	1	14	30	.247	.250	.245	13.97	6.52

Fielding

Catcher	PCT	G	PO	A	E	DP	PB
Escobar	.976	11	70	11	2	2	2
Hernandez	.986	58	432	53	7	2	7
Roberson	.989	11	85	6	1	1	2
Weems	.994	61	451	35	3	3	5

First Base	PCT	G	PO	A	E	DP
Chester	.991	44	310	20	3	25
Guerrero	1.000	3	2	1	0	0
Mager	.857	1	6	0	1	0
Martinez	.982	12	107	4	2	11
Moanaroa	.994	75	593	35	4	58
Roberson	1.000	8	68	7	0	7

Second Base	PCT	G	PO	A	E	DP
Betts	.964	76	153	169	12	41
Briscoe	.968	7	14	16	1	5
Coyle	1.000	5	7	9	0	1

	PCT	G	PO	A	E	DP
Gragnani	.993	34	60	89	1	23
Guerrero	.967	10	14	15	1	2
Johns	1.000	5	10	3	0	3
Miller	1.000	2	4	6	0	1

Third Base	PCT	G	PO	A	E	DP
Briscoe	.944	46	34	83	7	7
Gragnani	.786	4	2	9	3	0
Guerrero	.842	8	3	13	3	0
Johns	.950	9	5	14	1	0
Mager	.846	4	3	8	2	0
Martinez	.853	36	25	62	15	4
Miller	.895	8	7	10	2	1
Moore	.804	23	11	34	11	1
Roberson	.600	2	1	2	2	0

Shortstop	PCT	G	PO	A	E	DP
Guerrero	.957	26	30	59	4	10

	PCT	G	PO	A	E	DP
Johns	.950	7	5	14	1	1
Miller	.944	4	4	13	1	1
Vinicio	.935	106	160	285	31	67

Outfield	PCT	G	PO	A	E	DP
Briscoe	1.000	2	6	0	0	0
Colorado	.917	4	11	0	1	0
Guerrero	1.000	8	13	1	0	1
Hassan	1.000	4	8	0	0	0
Heller	.948	32	51	4	3	0
Koback	.972	60	130	8	4	1
Loya	1.000	32	64	0	0	0
Mager	1.000	7	15	2	0	1
Perkins	.957	39	64	3	3	1
Sanchez	.991	43	106	3	1	0
Tavarez	.971	121	223	10	7	2
Turocy	.962	70	94	6	4	1

LOWELL SPINNERS   SHORT-SEASON

NEW YORK-PENN LEAGUE

Batting	B-T	HT	WT	DOB	AVG	vLH	vRH	G	AB	R	H	2B	3B	HR	RBI	BB	HBP	SH	SF	SO	SB	CS	SLG	OBP
Allday, Forrestt	R-R	5-11	190	4-24-91	.267	.235	.286	38	135	23	36	5	1	0	11	27	8	0	0	27	8	3	.319	.418
Asuaje, Carlos	R-R	5-9	160	11-2-91	.269	.241	.282	52	171	19	46	12	1	1	20	27	1	2	3	33	4	3	.368	.366
Bethea, Danny	R-R	6-1	210	1-31-90	.261	.368	.205	31	111	21	29	5	0	1	18	11	4	0	2	28	1	0	.333	.344
Blair, Carson	R-R	6-1	190	10-18-89	.250	.000	.250	3	8	1	2	1	0	0	1	4	0	0	1	2	0	0	.375	.462
Colorado, Jose	L-R	6-1	170	8-26-90	.235	.105	.286	21	68	8	16	4	0	1	8	5	0	0	2	23	1	2	.338	.280
Flores, Raymel	B-R	5-9	155	9-22-94	.000	.000	.000	1	0	0	0	0	0	0	0	1	0	0	0	0	1	0	—	1.000
Gragnani, Reed	B-R	5-11	180	9-5-90	.333	.333	.333	14	48	2	16	4	0	0	4	4	3	0	1	4	4	0	.417	.411
Jerez, Williams	L-L	6-4	190	5-16-92	.176	.147	.188	38	119	6	21	5	1	0	8	3	1	2	0	23	4	1	.235	.203
Kapstein, Zach	R-R	5-9	185	5-28-92	.125	.333	.000	2	8	0	1	0	0	1	0	0	0	0	0	3	0	0	.250	.125
King, Aaron	L-L	6-4	205	4-27-89	.238	.122	.287	46	164	13	39	8	1	2	19	17	0	0	2	64	2	1	.335	.306
Lin, Tzu-Wei	L-R	5-9	155	2-15-94	.226	.227	.226	60	230	34	52	9	2	1	20	28	1	1	1	59	12	4	.296	.312
Lopez, Deiner	B-R	6-0	165	5-30-94	.210	.282	.164	28	100	15	21	3	0	0	10	10	2	1	0	23	4	1	.240	.295
Mager, Kevin	R-R	6-2	185	5-16-89	.280	.321	.259	66	236	32	66	13	3	2	36	32	3	5	1	57	3	0	.386	.371
Margot, Manuel	R-R	5-11	170	9-28-94	.270	.222	.290	49	185	29	50	8	2	1	21	22	1	5	3	40	18	8	.351	.346
Meyers, Mike	R-R	6-1	175	12-28-93	.250	.250	.250	2	8	2	2	0	1	0	1	0	0	0	0	3	0	0	.500	.250
Minnich, Nathan	L-R	6-3	245	7-21-90	.226	.190	.238	24	84	8	19	5	0	1	9	7	3	0	2	31	0	0	.321	.302
Moore, Nick	B-R	6-2	200	12-9-92	.183	.203	.173	57	186	21	34	7	1	1	15	20	3	3	3	80	6	1	.247	.269
Perkins, Kendrick	L-R	6-2	225	9-12-91	.227	.250	.217	17	66	9	15	4	0	1	13	6	0	0	0	20	4	0	.333	.292
Rijo, Wendell	R-R	5-11	170	9-4-95	.357	.200	.444	3	14	1	5	1	1	0	1	0	0	0	0	3	0	1	.571	.357
Rodriguez, Miguel	R-R	6-2	170	10-8-90	.150	.133	.160	11	40	1	6	1	0	0	5	1	0	0	0	15	0	1	.175	.171
Romanski, Jake	R-R	5-11	185	12-22-90	.233	.281	.195	20	73	9	17	4	0	2	4	4	2	1	0	11	0	0	.370	.291
Rondon, Cleuluis	R-R	6-0	155	4-13-94	.276	.280	.276	37	123	13	34	4	1	1	10	7	2	6	0	26	6	1	.350	.326
Sopilka, David	R-R	6-0	170	8-30-93	.167	.240	.145	32	108	5	18	2	0	0	3	10	1	0	2	30	0	0	.185	.240
Witte, Jantzen	R-R	6-2	195	1-4-90	.121	.150	.109	20	66	6	8	3	0	0	3	3	4	0	0	15	0	0	.167	.205

Pitching	B-T	HT	WT	DOB	W	L	ERA	G	GS	CG	SV	IP	H	R	ER	HR	BB	SO	AVG	vLH	vRH	K/9	BB/9
Adams, Mike	L-L	6-3	215	10-4-90	0	1	5.27	8	0	0	1	14	18	9	8	1	0	12	.321	.286	.343	7.90	0.00
Alcantara, Mario	R-R	6-2	170	12-27-92	5	5	4.17	14	9	0	0	58	61	42	27	2	29	46	.269	.330	.226	7.10	4.47
Aro, Jonathan	R-R	6-0	172	10-10-90	5	3	2.14	15	1	0	3	55	44	17	13	2	12	49	.222	.265	.180	8.07	1.98
Bard, Daniel	R-R	6-4	215	6-25-85	0	0	0.00	1	0	0	0	1	0	0	0	0	4	2	.000	.000	.000	18.00	36.00
Buchholz, Clay	L-R	6-3	190	8-14-84	0	0	13.50	1	1	0	0	1	1	3	1	0	3	1	.250	.000	1.000	13.50	40.50
Buttrey, Ty	L-R	6-6	230	3-31-93	4	3	2.21	13	13	0	0	61	54	21	15	0	21	35	.242	.287	.188	5.16	3.10
Callahan, Jamie	R-R	6-2	205	8-24-94	5	1	3.92	13	12	0	0	60	48	27	26	4	17	54	.221	.208	.234	8.15	2.56
Carpenter, Chris	R-R	6-4	220	12-26-85	0	0	1.69	4	0	0	0	5	4	2	1	0	1	6	.211	.300	.111	10.13	1.69
Chavez, Dylan	L-L	6-3	190	4-16-91	2	0	5.56	11	0	0	0	23	28	16	14	1	4	24	.295	.250	.322	9.53	1.59
Gomez, Sergio	R-R	6-3	155	8-23-93	3	1	1.60	10	5	0	0	51	40	10	9	2	14	55	.215	.231	.204	9.77	2.49
Grover, Taylor	R-R	6-3	195	4-22-91	0	3	2.63	15	0	0	1	24	20	7	7	1	5	18	.217	.324	.155	6.75	1.88
Gunkel, Joe	R-R	6-5	225	12-30-91	3	0	1.35	14	0	0	5	20	8	4	3	0	3	32	.114	.138	.098	14.40	1.35
Jimenez, Ellis	R-R	6-2	175	6-26-92	0	1	4.50	1	0	0	0	2	1	1	1	0	1	1	.143	.000	.250	4.50	4.50
Larson, Greg	R-R	6-8	225	9-25-89	1	3	2.00	14	0	0	4	18	14	7	4	0	5	16	.206	.250	.167	8.00	2.50
Littrell, Corey	L-L	6-3	185	3-21-92	0	3	1.74	12	10	0	0	31	28	9	6	0	10	30	.237	.324	.198	8.71	2.90
Maloney, Matt	L-L	6-4	210	1-16-84	0	0	0.00	5	0	0	1	6	4	1	0	0	0	4	.182	.100	.250	5.68	0.00
Martin, Kyle	R-R	6-7	220	1-18-91	2	1	0.47	10	0	0	2	19	11	2	1	0	3	15	.159	.139	.182	7.11	1.42
McGeary, Jack	L-L	6-3	195	3-19-89	0	0	7.50	5	0	0	0	6	9	7	5	0	3	10	.321	.375	.250	15.00	4.50
McGrath, Daniel	R-L	6-3	205	7-7-94	3	3	4.86	8	7	0	0	33	29	21	18	2	13	35	.242	.250	.239	9.45	3.51
Mercedes, Simon	R-R	6-4	200	2-17-92	2	2	3.13	13	3	0	1	63	62	24	22	2	17	57	.263	.259	.266	8.10	2.42
Ortega, Yunior	R-R	5-11	170	8-10-91	1	0	4.26	2	0	0	0	6	10	4	3	0	1	4	.357	.333	.375	5.68	1.42
Pinales, Carlos	R-R	6-1	180	4-5-92	2	1	2.67	13	0	0	0	30	24	10	9	2	3	24	.207	.229	.191	7.12	0.89
Quevedo, Heri	R-R	6-2	211	6-7-90	0	0	0.00	1	1	0	0	2	3	0	0	0	1	2	.333	.200	.500	9.00	4.50
Smith, Myles	R-R	6-3	190	9-25-92	0	0	6.75	1	1	0	0	3	4	2	2	0	0	3	.333	.250	.375	10.13	0.00
Spalding, Matt	R-R	5-11	190	10-22-92	0	2	13.50	2	0	0	0	2	1	5	3	0	3	3	.143	.250	.000	13.50	13.50
Stankiewicz, Teddy	R-R	6-4	200	11-25-93	0	0	2.29	9	9	0	0	20	17	6	5	1	2	15	.227	.226	.227	6.86	0.92
Taveras, Francisco	L-L	6-0	180	5-23-90	2	0	1.23	4	1	0	0	15	8	2	2	0	2	16	.151	.188	.135	9.82	1.23
Vellette, Raynel	R-R	6-2	165	6-10-91	0	0	3.38	1	0	0	0	3	2	1	1	0	2	1	.200	.000	.250	3.38	6.75
Villareal, Brayan	R-R	6-0	170	5-10-87	0	0	0.00	2	0	0	0	3	1	0	0	0	0	3	.111	.250	.000	10.13	0.00

Fielding

Catcher	PCT	G	PO	A	E	DP	PB
Bethea	1.000	16	142	9	0	0	2
Blair	1.000	2	14	2	0	0	0
Rodriguez	.984	9	53	7	1	0	1
Romanski	.964	14	95	11	4	0	1
Sopilka	.974	32	266	29	8	2	16

First Base	PCT	G	PO	A	E	DP
Mager	.981	12	100	5	2	6
Minnich	.982	20	150	10	3	11
Moore	.977	39	327	16	8	30
Witte	1.000	3	28	2	0	3

Second Base	PCT	G	PO	A	E	DP
Asuaje	.967	14	25	33	2	3
Gragnani	1.000	7	10	16	0	1
Lopez	.988	19	35	45	1	14
Rijo	.923	3	5	7	1	0
Rondon	.975	30	62	92	4	21

Third Base	PCT	G	PO	A	E	DP
Asuaje	.938	37	21	54	5	5
Gragnani	.667	1	0	2	1	1
Mager	.769	5	0	10	3	0
Moore	.852	17	16	30	8	2
Witte	1.000	15	11	28	0	5

Shortstop	PCT	G	PO	A	E	DP
Lin	.929	58	96	179	21	32
Lopez	.935	9	15	28	3	3
Rondon	1.000	7	13	12	0	3

Outfield	PCT	G	PO	A	E	DP
Allday	.946	33	51	2	3	0
Colorado	.926	18	25	0	2	0
Gragnani	1.000	2	2	0	0	0
Jerez	.968	36	58	2	2	1
Kapstein	—	1	0	0	0	0
King	.971	46	66	2	2	0
Mager	.957	24	43	2	2	0
Margot	.969	47	124	1	4	1
Meyers	1.000	2	1	0	0	0
Perkins	.955	15	21	0	1	0

GCL RED SOX

ROOKIE

GULF COAST LEAGUE

Batting	B-T	HT	WT	DOB	AVG	vLH	vRH	G	AB	R	H	2B	3B	HR	RBI	BB	HBP	SH	SF	SO	SB	CS	SLG	OBP
Austin, Jordon	R-R	5-11	195	3-14-95	.198	.242	.181	40	116	15	23	7	1	0	6	21	1	0	1	55	12	0	.276	.324
Bethea, Danny	R-R	6-1	210	1-31-90	.140	.125	.143	14	43	1	6	2	0	0	6	6	0	0	2	3	0	0	.186	.235
Bishop, Beau	R-R	6-2	200	7-6-93	.000	.000	.000	2	5	0	0	0	0	0	0	0	0	0	0	2	0	0	.000	.000
Brentz, Bryce	R-R	6-0	190	12-30-88	.235	.200	.250	6	17	3	4	2	0	2	8	1	1	0	0	4	0	0	.706	.316
Colorado, Jose	L-R	6-1	170	8-26-90	.188	.091	.216	15	48	4	9	2	0	0	4	3	1	2	1	12	4	1	.229	.245
Conklin, Iseha	R-R	5-11	180	9-11-92	.195	.091	.236	36	77	10	15	2	1	0	5	11	3	2	1	23	3	1	.247	.315
Coste, Carlos	R-R	6-2	186	5-11-93	.194	.000	.241	18	36	2	7	3	0	0	5	1	2	0	0	8	1	1	.278	.256
Coyle, Sean	R-R	5-8	175	1-17-92	.150	.200	.133	6	20	3	3	0	0	1	3	3	1	0	0	6	1	1	.300	.292
Davies, Jake	L-L	6-0	220	9-15-89	.216	.237	.207	43	125	12	27	6	0	1	11	7	0	1	1	30	2	1	.288	.256
Denney, Jonathan	R-R	6-2	205	9-28-94	.203	.192	.208	26	74	9	15	3	0	2	8	3	1	0	1	29	2	0	.243	.379
Dubon, Mauricio	R-R	6-0	160	7-19-94	.245	.300	.212	20	53	8	13	3	0	0	4	1	3	1	0	12	6	2	.302	.298
Flores, Raymel	B-R	5-9	155	9-22-94	.185	.303	.147	49	135	15	25	5	4	0	13	22	4	1	3	41	9	6	.281	.311
Hamilton, Mark	L-L	6-4	220	7-29-84	.304	.500	.200	7	23	2	7	2	0	0	3	4	0	0	0	10	0	0	.391	.400
Hudson, Bryan	R-R	6-1	185	12-00-93	.304	.382	.277	43	135	18	41	6	0	0	15	23	1	2	1	39	6	1	.348	.406
King, Aaron	L-L	6-4	205	4-27-89	.269	.286	.263	7	26	2	7	0	2	0	3	4	0	0	0	7	0	0	.423	.367
Longhi, Nick	R-L	6-2	205	8-16-95	.178	.273	.147	16	45	4	8	5	0	1	4	3	1	0	0	12	1	0	.356	.245
Lopez, Deiner	B-R	6-0	165	5-30-94	.284	.393	.233	25	88	11	25	5	4	0	7	4	4	1	0	20	8	5	.420	.344
Loya, Jesus	L-R	5-11	175	6-15-92	.296	.500	.211	8	27	3	8	3	1	0	4	1	1	1	0	4	2	0	.481	.345
Meyers, Mike	R-R	6-1	175	12-28-93	.256	.214	.276	26	86	10	22	6	0	0	6	8	0	4	1	24	3	3	.326	.316
Minnich, Nathan	L-R	6-3	245	7-21-90	.267	.200	.280	21	60	5	16	10	1	0	7	10	4	0	1	17	0	1	.467	.400
Monge, Joseph	R-R	6-0	170	5-18-95	.225	.212	.231	39	111	18	25	5	0	0	10	9	3	1	0	31	7	6	.270	.301
Oliveras, Rafael	R-R	5-10	180	1-4-95	.000	.000	.000	4	6	0	0	0	0	0	0	2	0	0	0	1	0	0	.000	.250

	B-T	HT	WT	DOB	AVG	vLH	vRH	G	AB	R	H	2B	3B	HR	RBI	BB	HBP	SH	SF	SO	SB	CS	SLG	OBP
Peralta, Aneudis	R-R	5-11	195	8-21-93	.288	.326	.273	44	153	20	44	12	0	0	20	11	2	0	2	22	1	2	.366	.339
Rijo, Wendell	R-R	5-11	170	9-4-95	.271	.271	.270	49	170	28	46	15	0	0	20	22	6	2	3	29	15	5	.359	.368
Suarez, Alixon	R-R	6-1	180	7-25-94	.211	.200	.215	31	109	11	23	6	0	0	13	5	2	0	2	22	1	0	.266	.254
Vitek, Kolbrin	R-R	6-2	195	4-1-89	.286	.500	.200	3	7	0	2	1	0	0	0	0	0	0	0	3	0	0	.429	.286
Witte, Jantzen	R-R	6-2	195	1-4-90	.244	.250	.241	13	41	2	10	2	1	0	7	6	0	0	0	9	1	0	.341	.340

Pitching	B-T	HT	WT	DOB	W	L	ERA	G	GS	CG	SV	IP	H	R	ER	HR	BB	SO	AVG	vLH	vRH	K/9	BB/9
Aceves, Alfredo	R-R	6-2	205	12-8-82	0	0	0.00	2	0	0	0	2	0	0	0	0	1	1	.000	.000	.000	3.86	3.86
Ball, Trey	L-L	6-6	185	6-27-94	0	1	6.43	5	5	0	0	7	10	7	5	1	6	5	.357	.667	.273	6.43	7.71
Bard, Daniel	R-R	6-4	215	6-25-85	0	0	10.80	2	0	0	0	2	1	2	2	0	6	1	.200	.333	.000	5.40	32.40
Drehoff, Jake	L-L	6-4	195	6-5-92	0	2	1.80	5	5	0	0	10	9	2	2	0	6	6	.257	.500	.226	5.40	6.00
Ethington, Willie	R-R	6-3	190	12-8-93	3	4	2.90	9	7	0	0	31	31	18	10	0	8	29	.252	.246	.259	8.42	2.32
Garcia, Edwar	R-R	6-4	175	11-19-93	4	1	3.65	15	3	0	0	44	32	19	18	1	25	41	.204	.293	.152	8.32	5.08
Goetze, Pat	R-R	6-6	200	3-3-94	1	1	3.00	4	1	0	0	6	3	2	2	0	1	4	.158	.200	.143	6.00	1.50
Good, Zach	L-L	6-3	185	6-8-92	0	0	10.50	5	0	0	0	6	7	8	7	0	7	7	.304	.750	.211	10.50	10.50
Gunkel, Joe	R-R	6-5	225	12-30-91	0	0	0.00	1	0	0	0	1	0	0	0	0	0	1	.000	.000	.000	9.00	0.00
Heras, Keivin	R-R	6-1	160	9-21-94	2	0	3.29	11	6	0	0	41	42	18	15	1	8	24	.264	.250	.280	5.27	1.76
Jimenez, Ellis	R-R	6-2	175	6-26-92	2	1	0.40	18	0	0	7	22	19	5	1	1	0	17	.235	.316	.163	6.85	0.00
Johnson, Brian	L-L	6-3	225	12-7-90	0	0	0.00	2	2	0	0	5	1	0	0	0	2	7	.067	.000	.100	12.60	3.60
Light, Pat	R-R	6-5	195	3-29-91	0	0	0.00	3	3	0	0	6	4	0	0	0	2	3	.190	.111	.250	4.50	3.00
Martinez, Enfember	R-R	5-11	140	8-30-95	1	0	3.08	13	1	0	0	26	19	9	9	1	10	15	.207	.188	.227	5.13	3.42
McGrath, Daniel	R-L	6-3	205	7-7-94	0	1	1.35	4	4	0	0	20	8	3	3	2	6	30	.129	.250	.111	13.50	2.70
Ortega, Luis	L-L	5-10	155	4-20-93	3	3	2.45	12	1	0	0	37	38	16	10	2	15	26	.262	.325	.238	6.38	3.68
Perdomo, Christian	L-L	6-6	180	11-9-93	2	1	5.79	7	1	0	0	19	16	12	12	0	11	13	.250	.176	.277	6.27	5.30
Perez, Oscar	R-R	6-1	185	11-9-91	2	2	2.67	16	0	0	8	27	21	15	8	0	9	15	.216	.220	.214	5.00	3.00
Perez, Randy	L-L	5-10	165	4-1-94	3	2	2.39	12	7	0	0	49	32	14	13	1	18	38	.184	.162	.190	6.98	3.31
Pinales, Carlos	R-R	6-1	180	4-5-92	2	0	0.00	3	0	0	0	6	4	0	0	0	1	7	.190	.182	.200	11.12	1.59
Romero, Dioscar	R-R	6-3	230	4-17-95	3	1	3.93	11	4	0	0	34	32	19	15	0	28	22	.256	.190	.323	5.77	7.34
Smith, Myles	R-R	6-1	175	3-23-92	0	0	0.00	4	0	0	0	8	1	0	0	0	0	9	.040	.000	.091	10.13	0.00
Smorol, Rob	L-L	6-1	185	2-22-91	1	0	3.78	13	0	0	2	17	12	7	7	0	7	14	.197	.125	.222	7.56	3.78
Speier, Gabe	R-R	6-0	175	4-12-95	0	0	2.25	3	2	0	0	4	5	1	1	0	1	6	.294	.222	.375	13.50	2.25
Taveras, German	R-R	6-2	180	2-15-93	3	2	2.75	16	0	0	1	36	30	13	11	0	9	30	.227	.295	.169	7.50	2.25
Trader, K.J.	R-R	5-10	160	6-17-94	0	2	10.57	9	1	0	0	8	9	9	9	1	15	4	.281	.333	.250	4.70	17.61
Williams, Jalen	R-R	6-4	210	4-21-95	0	0	1.80	3	3	0	0	5	4	1	1	0	0	4	.211	.000	.364	7.20	0.00
Williams, Stephen	R-R	6-5	210	8-10-92	2	1	3.38	15	0	0	1	19	16	8	7	0	14	16	.229	.212	.243	7.71	6.75
Younginer, Madison	R-R	6-4	195	11-3-90	0	0	3.00	2	0	0	0	3	3	1	1	0	0	2	.273	.333	.000	6.00	0.00

Fielding

Catcher	PCT	G	PO	A	E	DP	PB
Bethea	.944	10	49	2	3	0	0
Bishop	1.000	1	2	0	0	0	1
Coste	.989	18	83	9	1	0	2
Denney	.978	14	78	12	2	0	4
Suarez	.986	29	185	27	3	2	10

First Base	PCT	G	PO	A	E	DP
Davies	.994	42	311	20	2	30
Hamilton	1.000	5	25	4	0	2
Longhi	.970	6	30	2	1	4
Minnich	.992	14	113	7	1	8
Peralta	.918	4	41	4	4	0

Second Base	PCT	G	PO	A	E	DP
Coyle	.923	4	5	7	1	4
Flores	.962	5	12	13	1	7
Lopez	1.000	8	12	23	0	7
Rijo	.975	46	72	126	5	21

Third Base	PCT	G	PO	A	E	DP
Dubon	.938	6	4	11	1	0
Lopez	.947	11	4	14	1	0
Oliveras	1.000	3	1	1	0	0
Peralta	.947	38	26	81	6	11
Witte	1.000	10	5	14	0	0

Shortstop	PCT	G	PO	A	E	DP
Dubon	.906	12	20	28	5	8
Flores	.967	44	62	113	6	22
Lopez	.971	9	10	24	1	4

Outfield	PCT	G	PO	A	E	DP
Austin	.981	33	49	3	1	2
Brentz	1.000	2	5	0	0	0
Colorado	1.000	15	28	0	0	0
Conklin	1.000	33	51	1	0	0
Hudson	1.000	42	78	2	0	0
King	.900	7	18	0	2	0
Longhi	1.000	6	7	0	0	0
Loya	1.000	4	3	1	0	0
Meyers	1.000	20	32	1	0	0
Monge	1.000	36	53	3	0	1
Vitek	1.000	2	4	0	0	0

DSL RED SOX   ROOKIE
DOMINICAN SUMMER LEAGUE

Batting	B-T	HT	WT	DOB	AVG	vLH	vRH	G	AB	R	H	2B	3B	HR	RBI	BB	HBP	SH	SF	SO	SB	CS	SLG	OBP
Acosta, Victor	R-R	5-11	160	6-2-96	.256	.273	.251	63	234	26	60	11	1	8	39	25	3	0	2	23	9	2	.415	.333
Amaya, Anthony	L-L	5-10	160	5-1-94	.192	.000	.294	9	26	2	5	1	0	0	2	3	1	0	0	6	3	0	.231	.300
Andujar, Ricardo	B-R	6-0	160	8-6-92	.202	.043	.242	40	114	14	23	5	0	0	14	19	2	4	1	21	6	4	.246	.324
Bartomolde, Oscar	R-R	6-1	160	11-15-95	.117	.056	.143	25	60	12	7	1	0	0	4	9	0	1	0	18	3	2	.167	.232
Basabe, Luis Alexander	B-R	6-0	160	8-26-96	.225	.286	.210	60	209	49	47	13	2	1	19	49	6	3	1	58	18	5	.321	.385
Basabe, Luis Alejandro	B-R	5-10	160	8-26-96	.192	.077	.215	58	156	25	30	5	4	1	14	33	2	2	5	48	9	2	.295	.332
Benoit, Luis	L-R	5-10	162	11-29-94	.216	.333	.179	15	37	0	8	2	0	0	2	1	0	0	12	0	2	.270	.275
Carrizalez, Gerardo	R-R	6-1	175	7-28-95	.098	.143	.088	14	41	7	4	0	0	0	1	5	1	1	0	9	1	0	.098	.213
Guerra, Javier	L-R	5-11	155	9-29-95	.248	.140	.275	60	210	27	52	9	0	0	23	33	3	6	1	40	7	4	.290	.356
Guzman, Franklin	R-R	5-11	185	2-4-92	.254	.345	.227	64	240	34	61	8	5	2	31	22	4	0	3	44	11	5	.354	.323
Hernandez, Juan	L-R	5-10	155	4-9-96	.247	.364	.233	32	97	8	24	1	0	0	4	9	1	1	0	11	8	2	.258	.318
Lameda, Raiwinson	L-R	5-11	175	10-7-95	.220	.268	.208	56	200	27	44	10	3	0	19	15	3	2	2	35	8	5	.300	.282
Lucena, Isaias	B-R	5-11	160	11-15-94	.216	.133	.233	30	88	12	19	4	1	0	13	18	2	1	1	16	3	1	.284	.358
Nunez, Jhon	B-R	5-9	165	12-5-94	.240	.283	.224	60	200	32	48	6	3	0	16	26	3	2	2	31	6	8	.300	.333
Oliveras, Rafael	R-R	5-10	180	1-4-95	.000	.000	.000	3	5	0	0	0	0	0	0	0	0	0	0	3	0	0	.000	.000
Pena, Darwin	L-L	6-0	180	3-5-93	.236	.173	.254	59	225	22	53	5	4	2	28	21	1	0	1	42	2	1	.320	.302

	B-T	HT	WT	DOB			AVG	G	AB	R	H	2B	3B	HR	RBI	BB	SO	SB	CS				OBP	SLG
Urena, Pablo	R-R	6-0	175	10-17-94	.244	.263	.238	29	82	11	20	5	0	1	8	4	7	1	3	19	2	1	.341	.323
Yovera, Luis	R-R	6-2	170	10-15-95	.103	.214	.040	15	39	1	4	1	0	0	0	4	1	0	0	12	1	2	.128	.205

Pitching	B-T	HT	WT	DOB	W	L	ERA	G	GS	CG	SV	IP	H	R	ER	HR	BB	SO	AVG	vLH	vRH	K/9	BB/9
Almonte, Jose	R-R	6-2	185	9-8-95	3	3	2.50	12	12	0	0	50	38	21	14	1	22	43	.207	.263	.181	7.69	3.93
Caceres, Carlos	R-R	6-3	200	9-30-94	2	0	4.33	12	0	0	1	27	22	14	13	1	11	19	.232	.200	.240	6.33	3.67
El Halaby, Samir	R-R	6-3	175	7-5-95	4	0	0.61	14	1	0	0	29	18	8	2	0	3	17	.171	.125	.185	5.22	0.92
Espitia, Jose	R-R	6-2	180	9-16-93	0	0	0.00	3	0	0	0	4	1	1	0	0	6	4	.071	.167	.000	8.31	12.46
Florian, Wildyn	R-R	6-1	185	10-29-92	0	0	2.70	4	0	0	0	3	2	1	1	0	1	1	.200	.000	.250	2.70	2.70
Garcia, Carlos	L-L	6-0	170	12-15-94	4	3	2.63	14	13	0	0	62	35	21	18	3	23	51	.168	.138	.173	7.44	3.36
Garcia, Edwar	R-R	6-4	175	11-19-93	1	0	5.14	2	0	0	0	7	6	4	4	1	2	7	.222	.200	.235	9.00	2.57
Gonzalez, Daniel	R-R	6-5	180	2-9-96	2	1	0.97	14	2	0	3	46	24	8	5	0	3	42	.147	.188	.137	8.16	0.58
Gonzalez, William	R-R	6-2	180	6-16-93	0	0	7.71	2	0	0	0	2	2	3	2	1	3	3	.222	.000	.333	11.57	11.57
Jimenez, Dedgar	L-L	6-3	240	3-6-96	4	3	1.50	13	13	0	0	60	45	18	10	1	9	55	.204	.222	.200	8.25	1.35
Machuca, Ender	L-R	6-2	200	12-13-93	1	0	6.57	11	0	0	0	12	14	13	9	2	6	7	.275	.222	.286	5.11	4.38
Martinez, Algenis	R-R	6-1	185	9-12-93	7	1	1.28	21	0	0	2	42	24	6	6	1	12	25	.168	.128	.183	5.31	2.55
Martinez, Enfember	R-R	5-11	140	8-30-95	1	0	3.21	6	0	0	0	14	14	5	5	0	3	8	.264	.235	.278	5.14	1.93
Mendoza, Ritzi	R-R	6-2	175	1-10-96	1	2	3.60	12	0	0	0	25	18	14	10	1	17	17	.205	.167	.214	6.12	6.12
Pacheco, Edinxon	R-R	6-4	180	1-6-94	1	1	4.09	8	0	0	1	11	11	7	5	0	4	7	.262	.250	.265	5.73	3.27
Pimentel, Yankory	R-R	6-2	210	9-29-93	5	4	2.62	14	14	0	0	69	59	24	20	2	12	40	.235	.184	.248	5.24	1.57
Ramirez, Victor	R-R	6-1	190	5-12-95	2	2	0.91	22	0	0	15	30	19	3	3	0	6	31	.188	.179	.192	9.40	1.82
Ramos, Luis	L-L	6-1	180	6-5-95	5	3	2.04	12	12	0	0	57	43	18	13	0	4	38	.204	.125	.218	5.97	0.63
Rodriguez, Javier	L-L	6-2	165	5-1-95	2	0	1.72	12	3	0	0	37	29	7	7	1	18	18	.230	.389	.204	4.42	4.42
Torrealba, Jervis	L-L	6-0	165	6-9-95	1	1	1.39	13	0	0	3	32	23	6	5	0	10	28	.190	.273	.172	7.79	2.78

Fielding

Catcher	PCT	G	PO	A	E	DP	PB
Lucena	.989	16	79	12	1	1	7
Nunez	.985	53	327	57	6	2	9
Urena	1.000	11	40	10	0	1	1

First Base	PCT	G	PO	A	E	DP
Amaya	1.000	2	15	1	0	3
Carrizalez	1.000	2	19	0	0	2
Lucena	1.000	2	10	0	0	0
Pena	.993	58	538	31	4	31
Urena	1.000	11	88	7	0	11

Second Base	PCT	G	PO	A	E	DP
Acosta	.963	6	13	13	1	3
Andujar	.968	6	11	19	1	2
Basabe	.962	56	93	136	9	28
Benoit	.950	8	20	18	2	6
Oliveras	1.000	1	0	2	0	0

Third Base	PCT	G	PO	A	E	DP
Acosta	.905	47	51	111	17	13
Andujar	.900	22	13	41	6	2
Benoit	1.000	1	0	2	0	0
Carrizalez	.846	4	3	8	2	0

Shortstop	PCT	G	PO	A	E	DP
Andujar	.886	7	9	22	4	1
Benoit	.852	6	13	10	4	2
Guerra	.954	59	99	190	14	32

Outfield	PCT	G	PO	A	E	DP
Amaya	1.000	7	22	2	0	1
Bartomolde	1.000	23	24	0	0	0
Basabe	.982	53	102	7	2	1
Guzman	.958	48	63	5	3	2
Hernandez	.968	31	53	8	2	3
Lameda	1.000	55	102	4	0	2
Yovera	.947	14	18	0	1	0

Chicago Cubs

SEASON IN A SENTENCE: The franchise remained in rebuilding mode, which prompted trades of established players for prospects. The Cubs were never in contention, particularly because of some regression by young cornerstones such as first baseman Anthony Rizzo (.742 OPS) and shortstop Starlin Castro (.631 OPS). The poor season prompted the firing of manager Dale Sveum at season's end.

HIGH POINT: The Cubs got consistent starting pitching much of the season, particularly in the first half before trading righthanders Scott Feldman and Matt Garza. Lefty Travis Wood earned the team's lone all-star nod.

LOW POINT: There were plenty to choose from, but erstwhile closer Carlos Marmol embodied much of the season by blowing a 3-0 lead against the Mets on June 16, capped by a three-run walk-off homer by the immortal Kirk Nieuwenhuis.

NOTABLE ROOKIES: After trading Soriano, the Cubs shifted infielder Junior Lake to the outfield, and he hit .284/.332/.428 while playing left and center field. More rookies broke through in the bullpen, including former conversion project Blake Parker, a righthander who was effective over 46 innings in his eighth pro season. Lefty Chris Rusin pitched at replacement level in the rotation in the second half, while righty Hector Rondon, stayed healthy and stuck as a Rule 5 draft pick.

KEY TRANSACTIONS: Trading Feldman, Garza and Soriano brought back several key prospects, led by righthander C.J. Edwards (from the Rangers in the Garza deal). Righty Jake Arrieta, acquired for Feldman, showed promise in nine starts. The team's big offseason splash flopped. Righthander Edwin Jackson led the league with 18 losses and struggled to his worst season since his rookie year in the first year of a four-year, $52 million deal.

DOWN ON THE FARM: Javier Baez, the Cubs' 2011 first-round pick, tied for second in the minors with 37 homers—20 of them in 54 games at Double-A Tennessee. No. 2 overall pick Kris Bryant and Edwards helped replace Baez after he was promoted from high Class A Daytona, which won the the Florida State League title. Low Class A Kane County, the team's new affiliate, celebrated bringing in the nearby big league club but struggled on the field, winning 40 percent of its games despite a prospect-heavy team that included outfielder Albert Almora, first baseman Dan Vogelbach and third baseman Jeimer Candelario.

OPENING DAY PAYROLL: $104.3 million (14th)

PLAYERS OF THE YEAR

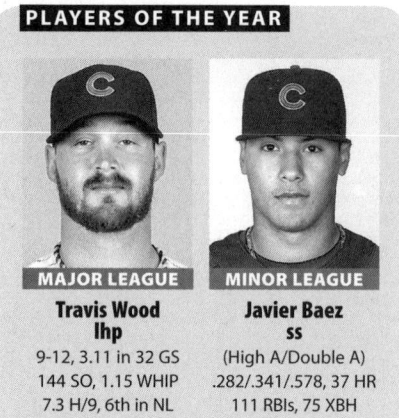

MAJOR LEAGUE	MINOR LEAGUE
Travis Wood	**Javier Baez**
lhp	ss
9-12, 3.11 in 32 GS	(High A/Double A)
144 SO, 1.15 WHIP	.282/.341/.578, 37 HR
7.3 H/9, 6th in NL	111 RBIs, 75 XBH

ORGANIZATION LEADERS

BATTING		*Minimum 250 AB
MAJORS		
* AVG	Schierholtz, Nate	.251
* OPS	Schierholtz, Nate	.77
HR	Rizzo, Anthony	23
RBI	Rizzo, Anthony	80
MINORS		
* AVG	Andreoli, John, Tennessee/Daytona	.305
* OBP	DeVoss, Zeke, Daytona	.393
* SLG	Baez, Javier, Tennessee/Daytona	.578
R	Baez, Javier, Tennessee/Daytona	98
H	Baez, Javier, Tennessee/Daytona	146
TB	Baez, Javier, Tennessee/Daytona	299
2B	Villanueva, Christian, Tennessee	41
3B	Ortiz, Dalfis, DSL Cubs	9
	Silva, Rubi, Tennessee	9
	Zapata, Oliver, Kane County	9
HR	Baez, Javier, Tennessee/Daytona	37
RBI	Baez, Javier, Tennessee/Daytona	111
BB	DeVoss, Zeke, Daytona	80
SO	Baez, Javier, Tennessee/Daytona	147
SB	Andreoli, John, Tennessee/Daytona	40

PITCHING		#Minimum 75 IP
MAJORS		
W	Wood, Travis	9
# ERA	Wood, Travis	3.11
SO	Samardzija, Jeff	214
SV	Gregg, Kevin	33
MINORS		
W	Hendricks, Kyle, Iowa/Tennessee	13
L	Jokisch, Eric, Tennessee	13
# ERA	Hendricks, Kyle, Tennessee/Iowa	2
G	Schlitter, Brian, Iowa/Tennessee	54
GS	Hendricks, Kyle, Iowa/Tennessee	27
SV	Schlitter, Brian, Iowa/Tennessee	22
IP	Hendricks, Kyle, Iowa/Tennessee	166
BB	Struck, Nick, Iowa/Tennessee	72
SO	Jokisch, Eric, Tennessee	137
# AVG	Loosen, Matt, Daytona/Tennessee	.216

General Manager: Jed Hoyer. **Farm Director:** Brandon Hyde. **Scouting Director:** Jaron Madison.

Class	Team	League	W	L	PCT	Finish	Manager
Majors	Chicago Cubs	National	66	96	.407	14th (15)	Dale Sveum
Triple-A	Iowa Cubs	Pacific Coast	66	78	.458	14th (16)	Marty Pevey
Double-A	Tennessee Smokies	Southern	76	62	.571	2nd (10)	Buddy Bailey
High A	Daytona Cubs	Florida State	35	31	.530	1st (12)	Dave Keller
Low A	Kane County Cougars	Midwest	55	80	.407	15th (16)	Mark Johnson
Short-season	Boise Hawks	Northwest	41	35	.539	3rd (8)	Gary Van Tol
Rookie	Cubs	Arizona	27	28	.491	8th (13)	Bobby Mitchell
Overall 2013 Minor League Record			340	334	.504	t-10th (30)	

ORGANIZATION STATISTICS

CHICAGO CUBS

NATIONAL LEAGUE

Batting	B-T	HT	WT	DOB	AVG	vLH	vRH	G	AB	R	H	2B	3B	HR	RBI	BB	HBP	SH	SF	SO	SB	CS	SLG	OBP
Barney, Darwin	R-R	5-10	185	11-8-85	.208	.246	.194	141	501	49	104	25	1	7	41	36	6	4	6	64	4	2	.303	.266
Bogusevic, Brian	L-L	6-3	220	2-18-84	.273	.125	.291	47	143	18	39	7	1	6	16	10	1	0	1	35	2	0	.462	.323
Borbon, Julio	L-L	6-0	195	2-20-86	.202	.206	.200	72	104	10	21	3	1	1	3	12	0	1	0	22	7	1	.279	.284
Boscan, J.C.	R-R	6-2	215	12-26-79	.222	.000	.286	6	9	1	2	1	0	0	0	0	1	0	0	2	0	0	.333	.300
Castillo, Welington	R-R	5-10	210	4-24-87	.274	.247	.282	113	380	41	104	23	0	8	32	34	11	1	2	97	2	0	.397	.349
Castro, Starlin	R-R	5-10	190	3-24-90	.245	.226	.251	161	666	59	163	34	2	10	44	30	7	1	1	129	9	6	.347	.284
Clevenger, Steve	L-R	6-0	195	4-5-86	.125	—	.125	8	8	1	1	0	0	0	0	1	0	0	0	3	0	0	.125	.222
DeJesus, David	L-L	5-11	190	12-20-79	.250	.156	.268	84	284	39	71	19	3	6	27	29	5	0	0	55	3	0	.401	.330
2-team total (3 Washington)					.247			87	287	39	71	19	3	6	27	29	5	1	0	56	3	0	.397	.327
Gillespie, Cole	R-R	6-1	215	6-20-84	.240	.212	.294	25	50	6	12	2	0	0	4	6	1	1	1	13	0	0	.280	.328
2-team total (3 San Francisco)					.203	—	—	28	59	6	12	2	0	0	4	7	1	1	1	13	0	0	.237	.294
Gonzalez, Alberto	R-R	5-10	195	4-18-83	.217	.273	.167	11	23	3	5	1	0	1	2	2	0	0	1	6	0	0	.391	.269
Hairston, Scott	R-R	6-0	205	5-25-80	.172	.179	.143	52	99	13	17	2	0	8	19	7	2	0	4	25	2	0	.434	.232
2-team total (33 Washington)					.191	—	—	85	157	18	30	5	0	10	26	9	2	1	5	44	2	0	.414	.237
Lake, Junior	R-R	6-3	215	3-27-90	.284	.377	.251	64	236	36	67	16	0	6	16	13	4	1	0	68	4	4	.428	.332
Lillibridge, Brent	R-R	5-11	185	9-18-83	.042	.000	.067	9	24	0	1	0	0	0	2	0	0	0	0	9	0	0	.042	.042
McDonald, Darnell	R-R	5-11	205	11-17-78	.302	.429	.160	25	53	4	16	4	0	1	5	4	0	0	0	8	0	0	.434	.351
Murphy, Donnie	R-R	5-10	190	3-10-83	.255	.257	.254	46	149	23	38	8	0	11	23	8	6	0	0	48	2	0	.530	.319
Navarro, Dioner	B-R	5-9	205	2-9-84	.300	.361	.279	89	240	31	72	7	0	13	34	23	2	0	1	36	0	1	.492	.365
Neal, Thomas	R-R	6-2	220	8-17-87	.000	.000	.000	2	4	0	0	0	0	0	0	0	0	0	0	1	0	0	.000	.000
Ransom, Cody	R-R	6-2	200	2-17-76	.203	.234	.156	57	158	21	32	10	1	9	20	22	1	1	0	57	0	0	.449	.304
2-team total (5 San Diego)					.189	—	—	62	169	21	32	10	1	9	20	22	1	1	0	62	0	0	.420	.286
Rizzo, Anthony	L-L	6-3	240	8-8-89	.233	.189	.252	160	606	71	141	40	2	23	80	76	6	0	2	127	6	5	.419	.323
Sappelt, Dave	R-R	5-9	195	1-2-87	.240	.240	.240	31	75	6	18	3	0	0	4	3	0	0	0	14	3	1	.280	.269
Schierholtz, Nate	L-R	6-2	215	2-15-84	.251	.170	.262	137	462	56	116	32	3	21	68	29	6	1	5	94	6	3	.470	.301
Soriano, Alfonso	R-R	6-1	195	1-7-76	.254	.273	.245	93	362	47	92	19	2	17	51	15	3	0	3	89	10	5	.467	.287
Sweeney, Ryan	L-L	6-4	225	2-20-85	.266	.313	.250	70	192	19	51	13	2	6	19	17	0	2	1	31	1	0	.448	.324
Valbuena, Luis	L-R	5-10	170	11-30-85	.218	.226	.217	108	331	34	72	15	1	12	37	53	4	1	2	63	1	4	.378	.331
Watkins, Logan	L-R	5-11	175	8-29-89	.211	.000	.235	27	38	2	8	1	0	0	3	0	1	0	0	14	0	0	.237	.268

Pitching	B-T	HT	WT	DOB	W	L	ERA	G	GS	CG	SV	IP	H	R	ER	HR	BB	SO	AVG	vLH	vRH	K/9	BB/9
Arrieta, Jake	R-R	6-4	225	3-6-86	4	2	3.66	9	9	0	0	52	34	22	21	7	24	37	.185	.176	.194	6.45	4.18
Baker, Scott	R-R	6-4	215	9-19-81	0	0	3.60	3	3	0	0	15	9	6	6	3	4	6	.173	.200	.156	3.60	2.40
Bowden, Michael	R-R	6-3	215	9-9-86	1	3	4.30	34	0	0	0	38	32	18	18	3	15	23	.239	.233	.243	5.50	3.58
Burnett, Alex	R-R	6-0	220	7-26-87	0	0	0.00	1	0	0	0	1	1	0	0	0	0	0	.250	.000	.500	0.00	0.00
Cabrera, Alberto	R-R	6-4	210	10-25-88	0	0	4.50	7	0	0	0	6	7	3	3	0	5	4	.292	.375	.250	6.00	7.50
Camp, Shawn	R-R	6-0	205	11-18-75	1	1	7.04	26	0	0	0	23	34	18	18	7	9	13	.362	.385	.345	5.09	3.52
Dolis, Rafael	R-R	6-4	215	1-10-88	0	0	0.00	5	0	0	0	5	3	2	0	0	2	0	.158	.000	.273	0.00	3.60
Feldman, Scott	L-R	6-7	230	2-7-83	7	6	3.46	15	15	1	0	91	79	42	35	10	25	67	.234	.224	.243	6.63	2.47
Fujikawa, Kyuji	L-R	6-0	190	7-21-80	1	1	5.25	12	0	0	2	12	11	7	7	1	2	14	.239	.217	.261	10.50	1.50
Garza, Matt	R-R	6-4	215	11-26-83	6	1	3.17	11	11	0	0	71	61	26	25	8	20	62	.229	.234	.224	7.86	2.54
Gregg, Kevin	R-R	6-6	245	6-20-78	2	6	3.48	62	0	0	33	62	53	26	24	6	32	56	.230	.163	.286	8.13	4.65
Grimm, Justin	R-R	6-3	200	8-16-88	0	2	2.00	10	0	0	0	9	4	3	2	0	3	8	.133	.000	.182	8.00	3.00
Guerrier, Matt	R-R	6-3	195	8-2-78	2	1	2.13	15	0	0	0	13	11	4	3	0	5	9	.239	.182	.292	6.39	3.55
2-team total (34 Los Angeles)					4	4	4.01	49	0	0	0	43	43	22	19	3	17	30	—	—	—	6.33	3.59
Jackson, Edwin	R-R	6-3	210	9-9-83	8	18	4.98	31	31	0	0	175	197	110	97	16	59	135	.281	.294	.270	6.93	3.03
Lim, Chang-Yong	R-R	5-11	175	6-4-76	0	0	5.40	6	0	0	0	5	5	3	3	0	7	5	.316	.500	.231	9.00	12.60
Loe, Kameron	R-R	6-8	245	9-10-81	0	0	5.40	7	0	0	0	8	12	5	5	3	4	4	.343	.235	.444	4.32	4.32
2-team total (9 Atlanta)					1	2	5.85	16	1	0	0	20	29	13	13	5	9	12	—	—	—	5.40	4.05
Marmol, Carlos	R-R	6-2	215	10-14-82	2	4	5.86	31	0	0	2	28	26	19	18	6	23	32	.252	.119	.344	10.41	6.83
2-team total (21 Los Angeles)					2	4	4.41	52	0	0	2	49	40	26	24	7	40	59	—	—	—	10.84	7.35
Parker, Blake	R-R	6-3	225	6-19-85	1	2	2.72	49	0	0	1	46	39	17	14	4	15	55	.220	.197	.236	10.68	2.91
Putnam, Zach	R-R	6-2	225	7-3-87	0	0	18.90	5	0	0	0	3	9	7	7	1	0	4	.500	.714	.364	10.80	0.00
Raley, Brooks	L-L	6-3	200	6-29-88	0	0	5.14	9	0	0	0	14	11	9	8	2	8	14	.224	.182	.259	9.00	5.14

CHICAGO CUBS

	B-T	HT	WT	DOB			ERA	G				IP	H	R	ER									AVG				
Rodriguez, Henry	R-R	6-1	225	2-25-87	0	0	4.50	5	0	0	0	4	6	4	2	1	4	1	.353	.500	.273	2.25	9.00
2-team total (17 Washington)					0	1	4.09	22	0	0	0	22	20	12	10	2	20	12	—	—	—	4.91	8.18
Rondon, Hector	R-R	6-3	180	2-26-88	2	1	4.77	45	0	0	0	55	52	29	29	6	25	44	.251	.192	.306	7.24	4.12
Rosscup, Zach	R-L	6-2	205	6-9-88	0	0	1.35	10	0	0	0	7	3	1	1	1	7	7	.130	.100	.154	9.45	9.45
Rusin, Chris	L-L	6-2	195	10-22-86	2	6	3.93	13	13	0	0	66	66	30	29	8	24	36	.261	.203	.278	4.88	3.26
Russell, James	L-L	6-4	200	1-8-86	1	6	3.59	74	0	0	0	53	46	21	21	7	18	37	.238	.183	.321	6.32	3.08
Samardzija, Jeff	R-R	6-5	225	1-23-85	8	13	4.34	33	33	2	0	214	210	109	103	25	78	214	.255	.266	.246	9.01	3.29
Sanchez, Eduardo	R-R	5-11	175	2-16-89	0	1	5.68	4	0	0	0	6	5	4	4	1	5	5	.238	.250	.231	7.11	7.11
Strop, Pedro	R-R	6-0	215	6-13-85	2	2	2.83	37	0	0	1	35	22	11	11	1	11	42	.176	.148	.197	10.80	2.83
Takahashi, Hisanori	L-L	5-10	180	4-2-75	0	0	6.00	3	0	0	0	3	3	2	2	1	2	3	.273	.400	.167	9.00	6.00
Villanueva, Carlos	R-R	6-2	215	11-28-83	7	8	4.06	47	15	0	0	129	117	58	58	14	40	103	.248	.260	.240	7.20	2.80
Wood, Travis	R-L	5-11	175	2-6-87	9	12	3.11	32	32	0	0	200	163	73	69	18	66	144	.222	.207	.226	6.48	2.97

Fielding

Catcher	PCT	G	PO	A	E	DP	PB
Boscan	1.000	4	19	2	0	0	0
Castillo	.988	111	730	85	10	3	8
Navarro	.989	55	425	36	5	7	5

First Base	PCT	G	PO	A	E	DP
Ransom	1.000	4	31	0	0	5
Rizzo	.997	159	1287	149	5	114

Second Base	PCT	G	PO	A	E	DP
Barney	.993	141	236	363	4	72
Gonzalez	1.000	10	14	21	0	5
Lillibridge	.958	5	11	12	1	3
Murphy	1.000	2	2	3	0	0
Valbuena	1.000	6	13	13	0	4

Watkins	.929	9	2	11	1	1

Third Base	PCT	G	PO	A	E	DP
Clevenger	1.000	2	1	2	0	0
Gonzalez	1.000	1	1	1	0	1
Lillibridge	1.000	3	6	2	0	0
Murphy	.956	40	27	60	4	10
Ransom	.944	42	21	80	6	8
Valbuena	.967	94	56	150	7	13

Shortstop	PCT	G	PO	A	E	DP
Castro	.967	159	238	416	22	77
Murphy	1.000	3	2	2	0	1
Ransom	1.000	1	1	3	0	0

Outfield	PCT	G	PO	A	E	DP
Bogusevic	1.000	39	86	3	0	0
Borbon	.950	29	37	1	2	0
DeJesus	.995	76	184	2	1	0
Gillespie	1.000	17	22	2	0	1
Hairston	.968	29	28	2	1	0
Lake	.976	56	119	2	3	1
McDonald	1.000	15	33	0	0	0
Neal	1.000	1	3	0	0	0
Sappelt	.968	21	30	0	1	0
Schierholtz	.988	126	242	5	3	1
Soriano	.971	86	160	7	5	0
Sweeney	.993	57	140	1	1	0
Valbuena	—	1	0	0	0	0

IOWA CUBS

TRIPLE-A

PACIFIC COAST LEAGUE

Batting	B-T	HT	WT	DOB	AVG	vLH	vRH	G	AB	R	H	2B	3B	HR	RBI	BB	HBP	SH	SF	SO	SB	CS	SLG	OBP
Barney, Darwin	R-R	5-10	185	11-8-85	.500	—	.500	3	10	4	5	1	0	0	3	0	0	0	0	3	1	0	.600	.615
Bogusevic, Brian	L-L	6-3	220	2-18-84	.317	.265	.341	79	265	50	84	14	3	10	32	41	4	0	0	58	16	2	.506	.416
Borbon, Julio	L-L	6-0	195	2-20-86	.260	.250	.263	24	73	10	19	5	0	0	1	12	0	0	1	15	5	1	.329	.360
Boscan, J.C.	R-R	6-2	215	12-26-79	.232	.205	.245	74	233	17	54	9	0	0	18	21	1	2	1	44	1	1	.270	.297
Brockmeyer, Cael	R-R	6-5	235	10-8-91	.167	.333	.000	2	6	0	1	0	0	0	1	1	0	0	0	3	0	0	.167	.375
Clevenger, Steve	L-R	6-0	195	4-5-86	.327	.391	.276	15	52	14	17	5	0	3	11	9	0	0	0	7	0	0	.596	.426
Flores, Luis	R-R	5-10	195	11-2-86	.204	.191	.208	61	191	17	39	8	0	5	17	23	2	0	1	32	0	0	.325	.295
Giansanti, Anthony	R-R	5-10	195	9-28-88	.345	.600	.292	14	29	3	10	3	0	0	5	1	0	0	0	5	1	0	.448	.367
Gonzalez, Alberto	R-R	5-10	195	4-18-83	.303	.273	.318	10	33	4	10	1	0	0	3	5	0	0	0	4	0	0	.333	.395
Gonzalez, Edgar	R-R	6-0	182	6-14-78	.267	.259	.271	47	165	19	44	9	0	5	20	9	1	0	0	39	8	0	.412	.309
Ha, Jae-Hoon	R-R	6-1	185	10-29-90	.241	.218	.253	62	228	22	55	13	0	5	21	15	0	1	0	42	7	2	.364	.288
Jackson, Brett	L-R	6-2	220	8-2-88	.223	.171	.256	61	215	24	48	7	3	6	23	21	3	2	1	77	7	5	.367	.300
Lake, Junior	R-R	6-3	215	3-27-90	.295	.295	.295	40	156	30	46	10	2	4	18	10	2	0	2	33	14	5	.462	.341
Lillibridge, Brent	R-R	5-11	185	9-18-83	.281	.338	.239	48	160	19	45	8	0	5	13	9	3	1	0	45	6	3	.425	.331
Lockhart, Daniel	L-R	5-11	165	11-4-92	.444	.000	.500	2	9	1	4	1	0	0	0	0	0	0	0	1	1	1	.556	.444
Maysonet, Edwin	R-R	6-1	180	10-17-81	.242	.271	.228	72	219	22	53	15	1	6	33	11	4	2	6	44	1	3	.402	.283
McDonald, Darnell	R-R	5-11	205	11-17-78	.236	.221	.243	92	263	31	62	13	2	4	26	27	1	1	2	50	8	2	.346	.307
Murphy, Donnie	R-R	5-10	190	3-10-83	.265	.297	.251	89	302	32	80	18	1	2	41	27	8	0	3	75	5	3	.457	.338
Nelson, Brad	L-R	6-2	255	12-23-82	.271	.133	.316	126	428	52	116	20	2	20	71	49	3	0	5	90	2	1	.467	.346
Noble, Chad	R-R	6-1	210	11-18-87	.167	.167	.167	6	24	2	4	0	0	0	1	0	0	0	0	4	0	0	.167	.167
Olt, Mike	R-R	6-2	210	8-27-88	.168	.195	.156	39	131	11	22	3	1	3	8	20	0	0	1	37	0	0	.275	.276
2-team total (65 Round Rock)					.197	—	—	104	361	48	71	18	1	14	40	55	1	0	3	126	0	0	.368	.302
Rohan, Greg	R-R	6-0	205	5-11-86	.167	.250	.100	12	36	3	6	0	0	1	2	1	2	0	0	13	0	0	.250	.211
Sappelt, Dave	R-R	5-9	195	1-2-87	.252	.252	.253	90	321	39	81	15	3	5	45	27	0	1	6	38	4	7	.364	.305
Stewart, Ian	L-R	6-3	215	4-5-85	.168	.148	.174	40	113	19	19	6	1	5	20	17	2	0	1	45	0	0	.372	.286
2-team total (27 Albuquerque)					.171	—	—	67	199	32	34	12	1	7	26	34	4	0	1	81	0	0	.347	.303
Sweeney, Ryan	L-L	6-4	225	2-20-85	.337	.320	.345	23	83	12	28	2	2	6	16	8	0	0	0	15	1	0	.627	.396
Torres, Tim	B-R	6-2	180	11-12-83	.207	.182	.219	61	140	12	29	6	1	2	11	9	0	0	2	45	4	1	.307	.252
Vitters, Josh	R-R	6-2	200	8-27-89	.295	.384	.246	28	88	14	26	4	0	5	12	11	1	0	0	19	1	0	.511	.380
Watkins, Logan	L-R	5-11	175	8-29-89	.243	.226	.251	107	412	51	100	18	7	8	26	52	4	3	1	98	10	9	.379	.333
Wright, Ty	R-R	6-0	200	2-26-85	.280	.305	.267	66	232	19	65	14	1	6	36	22	2	0	3	36	3	2	.427	.344

Pitching	B-T	HT	WT	DOB	W	L	ERA	G	GS	CG	SV	IP	H	R	ER	HR	BB	SO	AVG	vLH	vRH	K/9	BB/9
Antigua, Jeffry	R-L	6-1	205	6-23-90	2	2	5.40	16	1	0	0	40	43	26	24	6	14	30	.279	.273	.283	6.75	3.15
Arrieta, Jake	R-R	6-4	225	3-6-86	2	2	3.56	7	7	0	0	30	32	16	12	2	16	39	.271	.313	.216	11.57	4.75
Bowden, Michael	R-R	6-3	215	9-9-86	0	0	2.41	13	0	0	2	19	14	5	5	1	3	28	.197	.226	.175	13.50	1.45
Burnett, Alex	R-R	6-0	220	7-26-87	1	0	8.10	3	0	0	0	3	5	3	3	0	3	1	.357	.500	.250	2.70	8.10
Cabrera, Alberto	R-R	6-4	210	10-25-88	1	3	7.08	15	0	0	0	20	26	16	16	4	12	19	.321	.333	.310	8.41	5.31
Caridad, Esmailin	R-R	5-10	195	10-28-83	3	3	5.02	16	0	0	0	29	27	18	16	2	18	24	.257	.267	.250	7.53	5.65
Carpenter, Drew	R-R	6-3	240	5-18-85	1	4	7.33	6	6	0	0	27	33	23	22	4	15	20	.297	.246	.360	6.67	5.00
2-team total (9 Colorado Springs)					3	7	6.96	15	15	0	0	75	99	59	58	14	30	45	—	—	—	5.40	3.60
Chapman, Jaye	R-R	6-0	195	5-22-87	0	0	17.05	4	0	0	0	6	14	12	12	2	4	4	.438	.429	.455	5.68	5.68

Pitching	B-T	HT	WT	DOB	W	L	ERA	G	GS	CG	SV	IP	H	R	ER	HR	BB	SO	AVG	vLH	vRH	K/9	BB/9
Coleman, Casey	L-R	6-0	185	7-3-87	5	3	3.16	41	4	0	3	88	77	35	31	7	36	66	.241	.265	.220	6.72	3.67
Dolis, Rafael	R-R	6-4	215	1-10-88	1	0	5.40	12	0	0	1	12	11	7	7	1	7	13	.239	.250	.227	10.03	5.40
Fujikawa, Kyuji	L-R	6-0	190	7-21-80	0	0	0.00	1	0	0	0	1	0	0	0	0	1	2	.000	.000	.000	18.00	9.00
Garza, Matt	R-R	6-4	215	11-26-83	1	0	0.96	2	2	0	0	9	6	1	1	0	0	9	.182	.235	.125	8.68	0.00
Grimm, Justin	R-R	6-3	200	8-16-88	2	3	4.68	8	8	0	0	42	46	23	22	1	17	41	.279	.310	.247	8.72	3.61
2-team total (1 Round Rock)					3	3	4.31	9	9	0	0	48	50	24	23	1	19	45	—		—	8.44	3.56
Hatley, Marcus	R-R	6-5	220	3-26-88	3	2	4.22	35	0	0	0	43	40	23	20	2	21	49	.247	.284	.216	10.34	4.43
Hendricks, Kyle	R-R	6-3	190	12-7-89	3	1	2.48	6	6	0	0	40	35	12	11	2	8	27	.235	.313	.176	6.08	1.80
Lewis, Jensen	R-R	6-3	240	5-16-84	0	1	17.18	5	0	0	0	4	10	9	7	4	3	1	.476	.462	.500	2.45	7.36
Lim, Chang-Yong	R-R	5-11	175	6-4-76	0	0	0.79	11	0	0	0	11	5	1	1	0	4	12	.135	.188	.095	9.53	3.18
Loux, Barret	R-R	6-5	230	4-6-89	4	6	4.84	19	16	1	0	80	85	46	43	4	46	76	.274	.310	.232	8.55	5.18
Mateo, Marcos	R-R	6-1	220	4-18-84	0	0	2.76	13	0	0	1	16	15	7	5	0	4	15	.238	.250	.226	8.27	2.20
Moscoso, Guillermo	R-R	6-1	200	11-14-83	7	5	3.93	17	17	0	0	94	75	46	41	14	47	94	.219	.178	.253	9.00	4.50
Negrin, Yoanner	R-R	5-11	190	4-29-84	4	7	4.17	34	14	1	1	108	126	58	50	6	31	118	.295	.333	.262	9.83	2.58
Parker, Blake	R-R	6-3	225	6-19-85	0	1	2.04	16	0	0	7	18	8	4	4	1	10	26	.133	.200	.067	13.25	5.09
Putnam, Zach	R-R	6-2	225	7-3-87	1	1	3.26	17	0	0	4	19	20	7	7	0	6	22	.263	.091	.395	10.24	2.79
Raley, Brooks	L-L	6-3	200	6-29-88	8	10	4.46	27	25	0	1	141	142	73	70	13	45	95	.259	.253	.261	6.05	2.87
Rodriguez, Henry	R-R	6-1	225	2-25-87	0	1	5.40	3	0	0	0	3	5	2	2	0	1	0	.417	.333	.444	0.00	2.70
Rosscup, Zach	R-L	6-2	205	6-9-88	0	1	0.00	9	0	0	0	8	5	5	0	0	6	17	.179	.111	.211	19.96	7.04
Rusin, Chris	L-L	6-2	195	10-22-86	8	7	3.35	19	18	1	0	121	113	49	45	8	27	69	.248	.241	.250	5.13	2.01
Sanchez, Eduardo	R-R	5-11	175	2-16-89	1	1	3.26	24	0	0	2	30	21	12	11	1	19	28	.194	.235	.158	8.31	5.64
2-team total (9 Memphis)					1	1	3.38	33	0	0	3	40	31	16	15	3	23	35	—		—	7.88	5.18
Schlitter, Brian	R-R	6-5	235	12-21-85	1	4	3.24	38	0	0	20	42	38	15	15	4	9	45	.238	.253	.222	9.72	1.94
Struck, Nick	R-R	6-0	205	10-7-89	6	8	6.17	22	20	0	0	109	139	83	75	17	54	56	.317	.307	.327	4.61	4.45
Suarez, Larry	R-R	6-4	245	12-20-89	0	0	0.00	1	0	0	0	1	1	0	0	0	1	1	.250	.333	.000	9.00	9.00
Takahashi, Hisanori	L-L	5-10	180	4-2-75	1	0	1.98	20	0	0	0	27	14	7	6	3	9	25	.152	.207	.127	8.23	2.96
2-team total (18 Colorado Springs)					2	1	4.25	38	0	0	0	53	53	33	25	5	22	61	—		—	10.36	3.74
Wade, Cory	R-R	6-2	185	5-28-83	0	2	7.88	10	0	0	0	16	28	14	14	3	7	16	.389	.432	.343	9.00	3.94
2-team total (2 Las Vegas)					0	3	8.50	12	0	0	1	18	31	17	17	4	7	18	—		—	9.00	3.50

Fielding

Catcher	PCT	G	PO	A	E	DP	PB
Boscan	.993	71	566	31	4	3	4
Brockmeyer	.966	2	27	1	1	0	0
Clevenger	.971	11	59	9	2	2	1
Flores	.991	61	397	38	4	4	2
Maysonet	1.000	1	3	0	0	0	0
Noble	1.000	6	57	3	0	0	1

First Base	PCT	G	PO	A	E	DP
Bogusevic	.977	4	36	7	1	3
Clevenger	1.000	2	14	2	0	2
Gonzalez	.976	4	38	2	1	2
Lillibridge	1.000	18	141	4	0	12
Maysonet	.976	6	38	3	1	5
Nelson	.994	100	769	72	5	64
Rohan	.976	5	37	3	1	6
Stewart	1.000	9	64	6	0	6
Torres	1.000	9	35	4	0	3
Vitters	1.000	4	24	2	0	1
Wright	1.000	2	11	3	0	3

Second Base	PCT	G	PO	A	E	DP
Barney	1.000	3	5	3	0	0
Gonzalez	.977	25	34	52	2	13
Lillibridge	.952	12	22	37	3	10
Lockhart	1.000	2	3	2	0	0
Maysonet	1.000	3	5	8	0	2
Murphy	1.000	7	10	14	0	2
Torres	1.000	9	14	25	0	7
Watkins	.970	90	159	231	12	54

Third Base	PCT	G	PO	A	E	DP
Clevenger	1.000	2	0	3	0	1
Gonzalez	1.000	2	0	1	0	0
Gonzalez	1.000	2	1	1	0	0
Lake	.919	36	26	76	9	8
Lillibridge	.778	4	1	6	2	3
Maysonet	.960	15	7	17	1	0
Murphy	1.000	5	1	8	0	0
Nelson	.800	3	1	3	1	0
Olt	.909	38	29	71	10	0
Rohan	.667	2	0	2	1	0
Stewart	.887	23	10	37	6	1
Torres	.941	10	1	15	1	1
Vitters	.917	18	7	26	3	6

Shortstop	PCT	G	PO	A	E	DP
Gonzalez	1.000	7	6	23	0	3
Lillibridge	.941	4	4	12	1	0
Maysonet	.984	43	62	118	3	30
Murphy	.969	73	101	182	9	38
Torres	.942	11	17	32	3	5
Watkins	.973	13	10	26	1	8

Outfield	PCT	G	PO	A	E	DP
Bogusevic	.994	74	163	6	1	2
Borbon	1.000	20	17	1	0	0
Giansanti	1.000	9	19	0	0	0
Gonzalez	.667	2	2	0	1	0
Ha	.978	61	126	6	3	2
Jackson	.989	52	87	2	1	1
Lake	1.000	6	9	1	0	0
Lillibridge	1.000	10	13	0	0	0
Maysonet	1.000	4	1	0	0	0
McDonald	.980	68	96	3	2	0
Rohan	1.000	2	2	0	0	0
Sappelt	.988	79	152	6	2	2
Sweeney	1.000	20	34	0	0	0
Torres	1.000	12	13	2	0	1
Vitters	.833	2	5	0	1	0
Watkins	1.000	3	3	0	0	0
Wright	.990	51	92	4	1	1

TENNESSEE SMOKIES   DOUBLE-A

SOUTHERN LEAGUE

Batting	B-T	HT	WT	DOB	AVG	vLH	vRH	G	AB	R	H	2B	3B	HR	RBI	BB	HBP	SH	SF	SO	SB	CS	SLG	OBP
Alcantara, Arismendy	B-R	5-10	160	10-29-91	.271	.246	.280	133	494	69	134	36	4	15	69	62	2	9	4	125	31	6	.451	.352
Andreoli, John	R-R	6-1	215	6-9-90	.289	.279	.293	59	201	31	58	12	2	2	19	21	2	0	2	38	17	2	.398	.358
Baez, Javier	R-R	6-0	195	12-1-92	.294	.450	.234	54	218	39	64	15	0	20	54	19	0	0	3	69	8	2	.638	.346
Bour, Justin	L-R	6-4	250	5-28-88	.237	.248	.231	83	317	48	75	17	0	18	64	36	2	0	6	63	0	2	.461	.313
Chen, Pin-Chieh	L-R	6-1	170	7-23-91	.333	.000	.364	8	12	1	4	0	1	0	1	0	0	3	0	2	0	0	.500	.333
Davis, Taylor	R-R	5-11	185	11-28-89	.158	.125	.182	6	19	1	3	2	0	0	1	0	0	0	0	4	0	0	.263	.158
Fernandez, Jair	R-R	6-1	220	10-18-89	.269	.292	.250	18	52	3	14	2	0	1	8	6	0	2	0	11	0	1	.365	.345
Giansanti, Anthony	R-R	5-10	195	9-28-88	.248	.226	.257	40	101	16	25	7	1	0	6	5	2	1	1	22	0	1	.337	.294
Ha, Jae-Hoon	R-R	6-1	185	10-29-90	.284	.400	.231	28	95	21	27	5	0	1	14	13	3	2	1	24	8	1	.368	.384
Jackson, Brett	L-R	6-2	220	8-2-88	.200	.143	.224	30	95	10	19	4	2	0	10	15	2	0	0	37	2	2	.284	.309
Lopez, Rafael	L-R	5-9	190	5-2-88	.247	.197	.263	95	316	44	78	22	0	8	43	49	1	1	0	67	0	1	.392	.350
Mota, Jonathan	R-R	6-0	200	6-1-87	.276	.260	.283	109	301	39	83	15	2	7	40	31	4	2	3	61	2	1	.409	.348
Noble, Chad	R-R	6-1	210	11-18-87	.232	.171	.267	29	95	9	22	6	0	0	8	11	1	1		19	0	0	.295	.288
Rymel, Lance	R-R	6-0	195	5-2-90	.167	.000	.333	2	6	0	1	0	0	0	1	1	0	0	0	1	0	0	.167	.286
Samson, Nate	R-R	6-1	190	8-19-87	.257	.231	.273	30	35	5	9	2	0	0	4	7	0	0	1	7	0	1	.314	.372

Name	B-T	HT	WT	DOB	AVG	vLH	vRH	G	AB	R	H	2B	3B	HR	RBI	BB	HBP	SH	SF	SO	SB	CS	SLG	OBP
Silva, Rubi	L-R	5-11	180	6-25-89	.284	.317	.270	126	468	56	133	30	9	15	52	18	1	0	3	99	13	7	.483	.310
Soto, Elliot	R-R	5-9	160	8-21-89	.190	.179	.195	45	121	12	23	2	0	2	6	13	0	2	0	26	1	2	.256	.269
Szczur, Matt	R-R	6-1	195	7-20-89	.281	.280	.282	128	512	78	144	27	4	3	44	50	6	3	3	75	22	12	.367	.350
Torres, Tim	B-R	6-2	180	11-12-83	.290	.176	.333	22	62	13	18	5	1	2	7	8	1	0	1	18	4	1	.500	.375
Torreyes, Ronald	R-R	5-9	140	9-2-92	.263	.328	.239	65	224	32	59	13	4	2	25	22	6	9	4	15	4	0	.384	.340
Villanueva, Christian	R-R	5-11	160	6-19-91	.261	.239	.270	133	490	60	128	41	2	19	72	34	9	3	6	117	5	7	.469	.317
Wright, Ty	R-R	6-0	200	2-26-85	.253	.277	.243	54	158	14	40	8	0	3	19	12	2	0	1	19	2	0	.361	.312
Zapenas, Brad	R-R	6-3	185	12-8-89	.000	—	.000	1	1	0	0	0	0	0	0	0	0	0	0	0	0	0	.000	.000

Pitching	B-T	HT	WT	DOB	W	L	ERA	G	GS	CG	SV	IP	H	R	ER	HR	BB	SO	AVG	vLH	vRH	K/9	BB/9
Antigua, Jeffry	R-L	6-1	205	6-23-90	2	0	2.03	5	0	0	0	13	7	3	3	0	7	12	.149	.083	.171	8.10	4.73
Batista, Frank	R-R	5-10	170	4-26-89	3	3	2.60	48	0	0	19	62	55	21	18	2	28	52	.246	.292	.215	7.51	4.04
Beeler, Dallas	R-R	6-5	205	6-12-89	4	2	3.13	9	9	0	0	55	43	26	19	3	17	35	.214	.210	.217	5.76	2.80
Cabrera, Alberto	R-R	6-4	210	10-25-88	9	3	3.26	18	18	1	0	113	102	44	40	10	39	107	.250	.315	.200	8.55	3.12
Castillo, Yeiper	R-R	6-3	185	9-6-88	1	2	3.79	21	7	0	1	62	50	32	26	4	31	53	.220	.227	.215	7.74	4.52
Cervenka, Hunter	L-L	6-1	215	1-3-90	5	1	3.05	30	0	0	1	38	29	14	13	1	20	33	.213	.115	.274	7.75	4.70
Diaz, Dayan	R-R	5-10	190	2-10-89	0	0	5.14	5	0	0	0	7	5	4	4	1	3	10	.192	.000	.333	12.86	3.86
Figueroa, Eduardo	R-R	6-1	185	11-30-88	2	2	2.38	6	6	0	0	34	29	9	9	3	8	17	.228	.228	.229	4.50	2.12
Francescon, Patrick	R-R	5-11	185	1-4-89	2	0	4.20	16	0	0	0	30	25	14	14	2	16	21	.238	.306	.203	6.30	4.80
Fujikawa, Kyuji	L-R	6-0	190	7-21-80	0	0	0.00	1	0	0	0	2	1	0	0	0	0	0	.167	.000	.250	0.00	0.00
Garza, Matt	R-R	6-4	215	11-26-83	0	1	1.50	2	2	0	0	6	4	1	1	0	4	2	.182	.125	.214	3.00	6.00
Gutierrez, Carlos	R-R	6-3	230	9-22-86	0	0	0.00	2	0	0	1	4	3	1	0	0	3	2	.200	.143	.250	4.91	7.36
Hatley, Marcus	R-R	6-5	220	3-26-88	1	2	3.00	14	0	0	2	18	13	6	6	1	14	25	.213	.185	.235	12.50	7.00
Hendricks, Kyle	R-R	6-3	190	12-7-89	10	3	1.85	21	21	1	0	126	107	34	26	3	26	101	.227	.257	.204	7.20	1.85
Jokisch, Eric	R-L	6-2	185	7-29-89	11	13	3.42	27	26	2	0	161	144	71	61	14	54	137	.240	.282	.228	7.67	3.02
Kirk, Austin	L-L	6-2	200	5-22-90	2	3	7.02	9	9	0	0	42	52	33	33	3	23	30	.319	.245	.351	6.38	4.89
Lim, Chang-Yong	R-R	5-11	175	6-4-76	0	0	0.00	1	0	0	0	1	1	0	0	0	0	2	.250	1.000	.000	18.00	0.00
Loosen, Matt	R-R	6-2	205	4-10-89	3	3	6.14	16	13	0	0	66	61	49	45	15	48	60	.243	.232	.252	8.18	6.55
Mateo, Marcos	R-R	6-1	220	4-18-84	1	0	1.04	6	0	0	0	9	6	1	1	0	7	7	.188	.182	.190	7.27	7.27
McNutt, Trey	R-R	6-4	220	8-2-89	2	5	4.60	27	0	0	2	31	28	17	16	3	14	23	.250	.317	.211	6.61	4.02
Morris, A.J.	R-R	6-2	185	12-1-86	4	2	4.75	31	10	0	0	72	74	50	38	4	35	53	.266	.266	.266	6.63	4.38
Ramirez, Neil	R-R	6-4	190	5-25-89	0	0	0.00	1	1	0	0	5	1	0	0	0	2	5	.071	.125	.000	9.64	3.86
Rhee, Dae-Eun	L-R	6-2	190	3-23-89	5	1	3.34	11	11	0	0	59	46	24	22	6	20	35	.213	.245	.189	5.31	3.03
Rhoderick, Kevin	R-R	6-1	190	8-19-88	1	5	5.65	33	0	0	3	43	41	29	27	1	42	26	.259	.338	.204	5.44	8.79
Rivero, Armando	R-R	6-4	190	2-1-88	0	1	2.08	6	0	0	0	9	8	2	2	0	3	12	.242	.429	.105	12.46	3.12
Rosscup, Zach	R-L	6-2	205	6-9-88	2	1	2.49	37	0	0	3	43	31	12	12	2	19	66	.197	.164	.219	13.71	3.95
Schlitter, Brian	R-R	6-5	235	12-21-85	0	2	0.83	16	0	0	2	22	24	8	2	0	6	13	.264	.200	.314	5.40	2.49
Struck, Nick	R-R	6-0	205	10-7-89	1	2	3.95	5	5	0	0	27	22	13	12	3	18	12	.218	.208	.226	3.95	5.93
Zych, Tony	R-R	6-3	190	8-7-90	5	5	3.05	47	0	0	3	56	51	30	19	2	21	40	.237	.247	.231	6.43	3.38

Fielding

Catcher	PCT	G	PO	A	E	DP	PB
Davis	.975	6	36	3	1	0	0
Fernandez	.987	17	133	18	2	1	3
Lopez	.984	88	599	58	11	4	9
Noble	.995	28	193	25	1	5	3
Rymel	1.000	2	20	0	0	0	0

First Base	PCT	G	PO	A	E	DP
Bour	.992	74	686	62	6	52
Lopez	1.000	1	7	2	0	1
Mota	.998	52	433	36	1	42
Torres	.990	10	93	8	1	7
Wright	1.000	7	52	5	0	3

Second Base	PCT	G	PO	A	E	DP
Alcantara	.954	64	101	171	13	31
Giansanti	1.000	1	2	3	0	0
Mota	.981	16	19	34	1	5
Samson	.893	7	8	17	3	2
Soto	.966	8	14	14	1	4
Torres	—	1	0	0	0	0
Torreyes	.987	54	84	148	3	32

Third Base	PCT	G	PO	A	E	DP
Mota	.972	16	10	25	1	3
Samson	—	1	0	0	0	0
Soto	1.000	5	2	6	0	1
Torres	1.000	1	1	3	0	0
Villanueva	.930	124	78	240	24	19

Shortstop	PCT	G	PO	A	E	DP
Alcantara	.933	66	93	187	20	38
Baez	.948	50	91	144	13	24
Mota	.929	2	3	10	1	2
Soto	.977	28	44	85	3	13

Outfield	PCT	G	PO	A	E	DP
Andreoli	.981	57	103	3	2	0
Chavez	.944	19	16	1	1	1
Chen	1.000	5	5	0	0	0
Giansanti	.929	27	35	4	3	0
Ha	1.000	25	40	1	0	0
Jackson	1.000	24	38	5	0	1
Mota	1.000	14	13	1	0	0
Silva	.982	122	202	16	4	3
Szczur	.992	126	252	5	2	3
Torres	1.000	5	5	2	0	0
Wright	1.000	30	43	1	0	0

DAYTONA CUBS   HIGH CLASS A

FLORIDA STATE LEAGUE

Batting	B-T	HT	WT	DOB	AVG	vLH	vRH	G	AB	R	H	2B	3B	HR	RBI	BB	HBP	SH	SF	SO	SB	CS	SLG	OBP
Andreoli, John	R-R	6-1	215	6-9-90	.318	.257	.340	68	264	43	84	11	6	0	25	34	1	1	3	57	23	3	.405	.394
Baez, Javier	R-R	6-0	195	12-1-92	.274	.296	.268	76	299	59	82	19	4	17	57	21	11	0	6	78	12	2	.535	.338
Bote, David	R-R	5-11	185	4-7-93	.143	.500	.083	4	14	3	2	1	0	0	3	3	0	0	0	4	0	0	.214	.294
Bruno, Stephen	R-R	5-9	165	11-17-90	.362	.286	.382	19	69	16	25	8	0	0	7	5	4	0	0	16	2	1	.478	.436
Bryant, Kris	R-R	6-5	215	1-4-92	.333	.222	.354	16	57	9	19	5	1	5	14	3	2	0	0	17	1	0	.719	.387
Cabezas, Yaniel	R-R	5-11	185	4-19-89	.237	.130	.270	32	97	9	23	4	0	0	9	3	0	0	0	13	1	0	.278	.302
Carhart, Ben	R-R	5-10	200	1-21-90	.247	.267	.239	112	425	48	105	27	1	3	51	26	6	0	4	54	5	4	.336	.297
Chen, Pin-Chieh	L-R	6-1	170	7-23-91	.281	.313	.268	51	171	21	48	2	2	1	14	22	2	3	0	35	14	5	.351	.369
Darvill, Wes	L-R	6-2	175	9-21-91	.253	.185	.279	79	296	37	75	14	5	3	34	30	3	2	4	67	8	10	.365	.324
Davis, Taylor	R-R	5-11	185	11-28-89	.217	.083	.271	27	83	9	18	2	0	2	8	9	0	0	0	15	0	1	.313	.293
DeVoss, Zeke	B-R	5-10	175	7-17-90	.246	.282	.233	117	415	71	102	17	5	6	51	80	23	6	4	95	39	10	.354	.393

	B-T	HT	WT	DOB	AVG	vLH	vRH	G	AB	R	H	2B	3B	HR	RBI	BB	HBP	SH	SF	SO	SB	CS	SLG	OBP
Easterling, Taiwan	R-R	5-11	195	2-24-89	.216	.230	.211	64	208	23	45	11	2	3	26	17	2	0	0	62	10	2	.332	.282
Geiger, Dustin	R-R	6-2	180	12-2-91	.281	.319	.267	123	456	62	128	28	1	17	86	52	11	0	4	100	6	6	.458	.365
Giansanti, Anthony	R-R	5-10	195	9-28-88	.285	.261	.294	48	165	22	47	6	2	1	19	20	2	1	1	31	3	3	.364	.367
Gibbs, Micah	B-R	5-11	205	7-27-88	.163	.100	.179	16	49	2	8	3	0	1	7	10	1	0	0	16	0	1	.286	.317
Krist, Chadd	R-R	5-11	190	1-28-90	.253	.254	.253	65	225	28	57	14	0	5	34	31	4	0	2	50	4	2	.382	.351
Noble, Chad	R-R	6-1	210	11-18-87	.228	.227	.229	27	92	12	21	3	1	1	6	6	2	0	1	15	1	1	.315	.287
Rademacher, Bijan	L-L	6-0	200	6-15-91	.276	.156	.310	42	145	22	40	7	3	2	20	14	0	0	1	24	3	0	.407	.338
Saunders, Tim	R-R	6-0	180	5-17-90	.226	.179	.242	62	221	42	50	8	2	3	27	23	7	3	2	69	21	3	.321	.316
Soler, Jorge	R-R	6-4	215	2-25-92	.281	.377	.248	55	210	38	59	13	1	8	35	21	1	0	4	38	5	1	.467	.343
Soto, Elliot	R-R	5-9	160	8-21-89	.244	.152	.275	39	135	14	33	8	0	0	18	17	3	2	5	24	2	1	.304	.331
Vogelbach, Dan	L-R	6-0	250	12-17-92	.280	.286	.279	17	50	13	14	2	0	2	5	16	0	0	0	13	1	0	.440	.455
Zapenas, Brad	R-R	6-3	185	12-8-89	.167	.182	.154	9	24	3	4	0	0	0	2	3	0	0	0	5	1	2	.167	.259

Pitching	B-T	HT	WT	DOB	W	L	ERA	G	GS	CG	SV	IP	H	R	ER	HR	BB	SO	AVG	vLH	vRH	K/9	BB/9
Antigua, Jeffry	R-L	6-1	205	6-23-90	1	0	0.00	1	0	0	0	3	1	0	0	0	1	3	.100	—	.100	9.00	3.00
Baker, Scott	R-R	6-4	215	9-19-81	0	1	2.84	2	2	0	0	6	6	3	2	2	2	2	.250	.250	.250	2.84	2.84
Black, Corey	R-R	5-11	175	8-4-91	4	0	2.88	5	5	0	0	25	22	9	8	3	10	28	.237	.143	.277	10.08	3.60
2-team total (19 Tampa)					7	8	3.93	24	24	0	0	108	101	63	47	5	55	116	—	—	—	9.70	4.60
Burke, Kyler	L-L	6-3	205	4-20-88	6	1	3.35	13	8	0	0	51	40	20	19	4	18	40	.214	.222	.211	7.06	3.18
Cales, David	R-R	5-11	205	7-27-87	0	0	2.92	8	0	0	1	12	11	6	4	0	7	16	.239	.286	.219	11.68	5.11
Castillo, Lendy	R-R	6-1	170	4-8-89	2	0	3.60	11	0	0	1	20	21	10	8	2	7	21	.266	.304	.250	9.45	3.15
Castillo, Yeiper	R-R	6-3	185	9-6-88	1	0	2.33	8	3	1	0	27	19	7	7	1	4	27	.200	.172	.212	9.00	1.33
Cates, Zach	R-R	6-3	200	12-17-89	9	9	4.12	28	20	0	3	109	107	56	50	3	48	87	.258	.288	.240	7.16	3.95
Cervenka, Hunter	L-L	6-1	215	1-3-90	1	0	2.91	11	0	0	5	22	13	8	7	0	15	21	.171	.111	.204	8.72	6.23
Del Valle, Frank	L-L	5-11	190	9-16-89	3	3	2.29	31	0	0	9	51	43	15	13	1	30	64	.231	.241	.227	11.29	5.29
Diaz, Dayan	R-R	5-10	190	2-10-89	0	1	2.45	6	0	0	1	11	10	3	3	2	5	14	.227	.200	.241	11.45	4.09
Edwards, C.J.	R-R	6-2	155	9-3-91	0	0	1.96	6	6	0	0	23	14	5	5	1	7	33	.169	.148	.179	12.91	2.74
Figueroa, Eduardo	R-R	6-1	185	11-30-88	1	4	4.10	24	2	0	3	53	64	28	24	1	28	37	.309	.257	.336	6.32	4.78
Francescon, Patrick	R-R	5-11	185	1-4-89	5	4	4.76	14	13	0	0	70	75	40	37	9	21	62	.265	.264	.265	7.97	2.70
Gutierrez, Carlos	R-R	6-3	230	9-22-86	0	0	1.50	3	0	0	1	6	3	2	1	0	2	3	.143	.111	.167	4.50	3.00
Johnson, Pierce	R-R	6-3	170	5-10-91	6	1	2.22	10	8	0	0	49	41	12	12	1	21	50	.240	.239	.240	9.25	3.88
Kirk, Austin	L-L	6-1	200	5-22-90	6	2	4.50	11	10	1	0	54	61	28	27	8	25	42	.293	.200	.323	7.00	4.17
Lim, Chang-Yong	R-R	5-11	175	6-4-76	0	0	1.80	4	0	0	0	5	2	1	1	0	3	6	.125	.000	.154	10.80	5.40
Liria, Luis	B-R	6-2	170	1-15-90	1	4	6.90	20	0	0	2	30	35	24	23	0	20	28	.285	.295	.278	8.40	6.00
Loosen, Matt	R-R	6-2	205	4-10-89	5	2	1.83	9	9	2	0	54	34	11	11	2	17	56	.180	.135	.209	9.33	2.83
Lorick, Jeff	L-L	6-0	205	12-18-87	3	0	3.32	26	0	0	3	43	45	19	16	1	23	35	.269	.246	.282	7.27	4.78
McDonald, Sheldon	L-L	5-11	205	11-5-88	0	1	3.68	18	0	0	0	29	30	15	12	0	14	18	.268	.273	.266	5.52	4.30
Peralta, Starling	R-R	6-4	180	11-11-90	0	1	12.86	5	2	0	0	14	19	20	20	6	7	16	.333	.313	.341	10.29	4.50
Pineyro, Ivan	R-R	6-1	200	9-29-91	3	1	3.40	8	8	0	0	45	44	17	17	2	9	38	.259	.250	.263	7.60	1.80
Reed, Austin	R-R	6-3	200	10-31-91	4	2	4.07	34	0	0	4	66	69	34	30	1	28	40	.266	.293	.251	5.43	3.80
Rivero, Armando	R-R	6-4	190	2-1-88	0	0	2.70	3	0	0	1	3	3	3	1	0	0	5	.200	.143	.250	13.50	0.00
Searle, Ryan	R-R	6-0	190	6-22-89	2	3	5.67	8	2	0	0	27	34	17	17	2	8	28	.306	.265	.325	9.33	2.67
Suarez, Larry	R-R	6-4	245	12-20-89	0	1	3.86	10	0	0	0	14	13	6	6	4	8	11	.260	.267	.257	7.07	5.14
Wang, Yao-Lin	R-R	6-0	180	2-5-91	3	4	3.42	24	8	0	0	71	58	27	27	4	29	64	.222	.234	.216	8.11	3.68
Wells, Ben	R-R	6-2	220	9-10-92	9	6	3.28	23	21	0	0	112	96	50	41	7	40	69	.232	.270	.213	5.53	3.20

Fielding

Catcher	PCT	G	PO	A	E	DP	PB
Cabezas	.996	29	217	13	1	4	3
Davis	.987	9	67	11	1	1	0
Gibbs	1.000	11	100	5	0	0	0
Krist	.982	54	408	35	8	4	3
Noble	1.000	27	186	20	0	2	0

First Base	PCT	G	PO	A	E	DP
Carhart	.987	9	69	8	1	13
Davis	.929	3	11	2	1	0
Geiger	.994	106	917	64	6	90
Giansanti	1.000	5	37	0	0	3
Vogelbach	1.000	7	37	3	0	3

Second Base	PCT	G	PO	A	E	DP
Bote	1.000	1	3	3	0	1
Bruno	.970	15	25	39	2	10
Darvill	.983	55	92	135	4	40
Giansanti	1.000	12	14	27	0	4
Saunders	.984	38	69	111	3	19
Soto	1.000	1	4	0	0	
Zapenas	.971	7	17	16	1	5

Third Base	PCT	G	PO	A	E	DP
Bote	1.000	2	2	4	0	2
Bryant	.975	13	9	30	1	3
Carhart	.963	93	46	186	9	20
Darvill	1.000	8	1	18	0	0
Geiger	.818	5	3	15	4	1
Giansanti	1.000	1	1	1	0	0
Saunders	.950	6	2	17	1	1
Zapenas	1.000	1	0	1	0	0

Shortstop	PCT	G	PO	A	E	DP
Baez	.922	73	141	224	31	51
Bote	1.000	1	2	1	0	0
Darvill	.980	13	22	26	1	2
Giansanti	.500	1	0	1	1	0
Saunders	.967	7	9	20	1	4
Soto	.987	37	44	105	2	27

Outfield	PCT	G	PO	A	E	DP
Andreoli	.976	66	116	4	3	2
Chen	.969	45	91	3	3	1
DeVoss	.974	112	218	7	6	2
Easterling	.971	38	58	9	2	1
Giansanti	1.000	19	29	2	0	1
Gibbs	1.000	1	3	0	0	0
Rademacher	.986	40	66	2	1	1
Saunders	.970	12	30	2	1	0
Soler	.970	55	94	2	3	0

KANE COUNTY COUGARS   LOW CLASS A

MIDWEST LEAGUE

Batting	B-T	HT	WT	DOB	AVG	vLH	vRH	G	AB	R	H	2B	3B	HR	RBI	BB	HBP	SH	SF	SO	SB	CS	SLG	OBP
Almora, Albert	R-R	6-2	180	4-16-94	.329	.417	.308	61	249	39	82	17	4	3	23	17	3	1	2	30	4	4	.466	.376
Amaya, Gioskar	R-R	5-11	175	12-13-92	.252	.265	.247	117	453	65	114	26	6	5	28	42	13	3	5	109	13	6	.369	.329
Bote, David	R-R	5-11	185	4-7-93	.143	.000	.189	17	49	7	7	1	0	1	4	12	0	0	0	8	0	2	.224	.311
Cabezas, Yaniel	R-R	5-11	185	4-19-89	.324	.571	.259	11	34	2	11	1	1	0	6	2	0	2	0	2	0	0	.412	.361
Candelario, Jeimer	B-R	6-1	180	11-24-93	.256	.274	.251	130	500	71	128	35	1	11	57	68	2	0	2	88	1	0	.396	.346
Chen, Pin-Chieh	L-R	6-1	170	7-23-91	.242	.184	.260	44	161	25	39	5	2	0	15	25	1	1	1	23	9	6	.298	.346

Batting	B-T	HT	WT	DOB	AVG	vLH	vRH	G	AB	R	H	2B	3B	HR	RBI	BB	HBP	SH	SF	SO	SB	CS	SLG	OBP
Contreras, Willson	R-R	6-1	175	5-13-92	.248	.329	.222	86	310	46	77	11	5	11	46	26	7	1	1	66	8	3	.423	.320
Darvill, Wes	L-R	6-2	175	9-10-91	.347	.438	.303	15	49	5	17	2	2	0	6	7	0	2	0	9	3	2	.469	.429
Dore, Jose	L-R	6-1	170	2-9-92	.212	.211	.212	26	85	6	18	4	1	1	11	8	0	0	2	18	1	0	.318	.274
Encarnacion, Kevin	B-R	6-0	175	11-23-91	.217	.222	.216	16	60	9	13	2	1	1	3	8	1	0	1	14	1	3	.333	.314
Escobar, Carlos	R-R	6-2	185	12-31-90	.237	.205	.248	49	173	21	41	12	1	4	23	10	5	1	3	43	0	0	.387	.293
Golden, Reggie	R-R	5-10	220	10-10-91	.227	.167	.243	64	233	20	53	7	1	9	29	14	4	0	1	77	1	2	.382	.282
Gretzky, Trevor	L-L	6-4	190	9-14-92	.306	.091	.368	14	49	5	15	0	1	1	2	2	0	0	0	13	0	1	.408	.333
Hernandez, Marco	L-R	6-0	170	9-6-92	.254	.242	.258	111	417	45	106	17	3	4	34	16	4	4	2	72	21	7	.338	.287
Krist, Chadd	R-R	5-11	190	1-28-90	.263	.000	.345	12	38	7	10	2	0	0	2	8	2	0	0	7	0	1	.316	.417
Martin, Trey	R-R	6-2	188	12-11-92	.200	.000	.333	11	35	3	7	2	0	0	5	4	1	0	2	10	2	3	.257	.286
Papaccio, Giuseppe	R-R	6-1	185	6-8-91	.279	.387	.248	37	140	12	39	4	1	2	13	10	1	0	0	24	0	1	.364	.331
Rademacher, Bijan	L-L	6-0	200	6-15-91	.303	.303	.303	55	185	24	56	8	0	2	18	21	2	1	3	25	5	3	.378	.374
Rosario, Neftali	R-R	5-11	193	7-22-93	.222	.500	.143	4	9	0	2	0	0	0	1	0	0	0	0	4	0	0	.222	.300
Shoulders, Rock	L-R	6-2	225	9-26-91	.258	.239	.264	117	431	61	111	27	0	18	74	66	0	0	6	143	0	0	.445	.352
Sweeney, Ryan	L-L	6-4	225	2-20-85	.250	1.000	.000	1	4	0	1	0	0	0	0	0	0	0	0	0	0	0	.250	.250
Valbuena, Luis	L-R	5-10	170	11-30-85	.333	.000	.500	1	3	0	1	0	0	0	0	1	0	0	0	0	0	0	.333	.500
Vogelbach, Dan	L-R	6-0	250	12-17-92	.284	.257	.293	114	433	55	123	21	0	17	71	57	2	0	8	76	4	4	.450	.364
Zapata, Oliver	B-R	5-9	180	9-13-92	.240	.293	.223	114	392	47	94	13	9	7	49	42	3	7	1	89	13	9	.372	.317
Zapenas, Brad	R-R	6-2	185	12-8-89	.255	.333	.244	17	47	7	12	3	0	0	2	13	1	1	1	6	1	0	.319	.419

Pitching	B-T	HT	WT	DOB	W	L	ERA	G	GS	CG	SV	IP	H	R	ER	HR	BB	SO	AVG	vLH	vRH	K/9	BB/9
Amlung, Justin	R-R	6-1	185	5-21-90	5	4	3.75	32	1	0	2	72	71	36	30	6	29	60	.258	.283	.241	7.50	3.63
Antigua, Jeffry	R-L	6-1	205	6-23-90	3	1	2.45	13	0	0	1	26	24	10	7	0	5	30	.242	.242	.242	10.52	1.75
Arias, Jose	R-R	6-6	235	1-17-91	0	0	8.68	4	2	0	0	9	16	13	9	1	11	9	.372	.333	.400	8.68	10.61
Baker, Scott	R-R	6-4	215	9-19-81	1	2	6.17	6	6	0	0	23	29	16	16	4	8	14	.309	.395	.235	5.40	3.09
Camp, Shawn	R-R	6-0	205	11-18-75	0	0	0.00	2	0	0	0	3	2	0	0	0	0	4	.167	.250	.125	12.00	0.00
Castillo, Lendy	R-R	6-1	170	4-8-89	2	5	6.58	19	5	0	0	64	78	52	47	7	32	55	.304	.352	.270	7.69	4.48
Dickson, Ian	R-R	6-5	215	9-16-90	2	2	6.88	11	3	0	1	35	38	28	27	6	15	32	.271	.303	.243	8.15	3.82
Dolis, Rafael	R-R	6-4	215	1-10-88	0	0	—	1	0	0	0	1	0	0	0	0	0	1	1.000	.000	1.000		
Dorris, Nathan	L-L	6-3	185	12-9-90	7	3	2.87	36	2	0	3	69	60	31	22	1	30	55	.234	.098	.277	7.17	3.91
Hamann, Mike	R-R	6-3	165	1-1-91	3	4	2.49	16	0	0	4	22	19	6	6	1	7	17	.247	.269	.235	7.06	2.91
Heesch, Michael	R-L	6-5	245	5-15-90	3	9	3.78	22	20	0	0	119	129	63	50	3	36	60	.278	.165	.308	4.54	2.72
Iannazzo, Matt	L-L	5-9	170	1-8-90	1	1	3.55	10	0	0	0	13	15	6	5	0	10	8	.300	.385	.270	5.68	7.11
Johnson, Pierce	R-R	6-3	170	5-10-91	5	5	3.10	13	13	0	0	70	68	29	24	4	22	74	.255	.250	.250	9.56	2.84
Maples, Dillon	R-R	6-2	195	5-9-92	0	2	8.31	11	7	0	1	35	33	37	32	1	31	34	.248	.194	.303	8.83	8.05
McDonald, Sheldon	L-L	5-11	205	11-5-88	2	0	2.41	17	0	0	0	34	33	12	9	1	8	27	.260	.261	.262	7.22	2.14
McKirahan, Andrew	R-L	6-2	195	2-8-90	2	0	2.75	14	0	0	0	20	14	7	6	0	7	22	.200	.316	.157	10.07	3.20
Orozco, Eddie	R-R	6-2	195	4-11-89	3	3	4.87	17	0	0	2	20	22	13	11	1	13	17	.289	.226	.333	7.52	5.75
Paniagua, Juan Carlos	R-R	6-1	175	4-4-90	0	2	8.22	3	3	0	0	8	10	9	7	0	12	6	.345	.167	.471	7.04	14.09
Pena, Felix	R-R	6-2	186	2-25-90	4	7	3.92	21	17	1	1	103	102	57	45	5	32	77	.257	.206	.293	6.71	2.79
Perakslis, Steve	R-R	6-1	185	1-15-91	1	3	2.93	37	0	0	7	58	51	20	19	2	20	44	.237	.245	.231	6.79	3.09
Peralta, Starling	R-R	6-4	180	11-11-90	2	3	6.06	7	6	0	0	33	34	24	22	3	23	23	.276	.298	.263	6.34	6.34
Pugliese, James	R-R	6-3	195	8-12-92	0	7	7.71	3	3	0	0	14	22	13	12	2	12	12	.373	.500	.317	7.71	7.71
Rivero, Armando	R-R	6-4	190	2-1-88	0	0	5.40	11	0	1	1	18	19	11	11	4	9	28	.264	.333	.229	13.75	4.42
Rosario, Jose	R-R	6-1	170	8-29-90	0	7	7.38	14	11	0	0	65	77	62	53	6	42	33	.296	.328	.268	4.59	5.85
Scott, Tayler	R-R	6-3	165	6-1-92	6	8	4.22	24	24	0	0	130	144	78	61	6	54	67	.282	.292	.274	4.64	3.74
Skulina, Tyler	R-R	6-5	252	9-18-91	0	2	9.31	4	4	0	0	10	14	11	10	1	6	9	.341	.450	.238	8.38	5.59
Smith, Brian	L-L	6-0	170	12-12-92	2	4	4.60	23	7	0	1	61	65	42	31	6	22	46	.273	.217	.292	6.82	3.26
Socorro, Kenny	R-R	5-9	175	6-2-89	0	0	3.00	2	0	0	0	3	6	3	1	0	1	1	.375	.250	.500	3.00	3.00
Torrez, Daury	R-R	6-3	170	6-11-93	0	1	5.40	1	1	0	0	5	5	3	1	1	2	3	.313	.667	.231	3.60	1.80
Yevoli, Al	L-L	6-2	221	1-1-90	0	0	3.15	11	0	0	0	20	23	9	7	0	7	19	.291	.214	.308	8.55	3.15
Zastryzny, Rob	R-L	6-3	205	3-26-92	1	0	0.93	3	0	0	0	10	9	1	1	0	4	6	.257	.091	.333	5.59	3.72

Fielding

Catcher	PCT	G	PO	A	E	DP	PB
Cabezas	1.000	10	74	10	0	0	
Contreras	.968	72	475	70	18	4	19
Escobar	.987	45	279	25	4	2	4
Krist	1.000	12	76	8	0	0	1
Rosario	1.000	1	2	0	0	0	

First Base	PCT	G	PO	A	E	DP
Contreras	1.000	6	48	1	0	6
Escobar	1.000	1	4	0	0	1
Shoulders	.986	45	374	36	6	40
Vogelbach	.986	85	746	54	11	74

Second Base	PCT	G	PO	A	E	DP
Amaya	.959	110	215	299	22	77
Bote	1.000	3	5	10	0	3
Darvill	1.000	5	9	7	0	2
Papaccio	.960	10	19	29	2	7
Zapenas	.978	9	18	26	1	7

Third Base	PCT	G	PO	A	E	DP
Bote	.857	2	0	6	1	1
Candelario	.925	121	88	234	26	24
Darvill	1.000	1	0	4	0	0
Papaccio	.815	9	3	19	5	1
Valbuena	1.000	1	0	1	0	0
Zapenas	1.000	2	2	4	0	0

Shortstop	PCT	G	PO	A	E	DP
Bote	.848	9	11	17	5	3
Darvill	.974	5	12	25	1	5
Hernandez	.939	100	128	318	29	68
Papaccio	.969	17	40	54	3	18
Zapenas	.966	6	12	16	1	2

Outfield	PCT	G	PO	A	E	DP
Almora	.994	59	164	7	1	3
Bote	1.000	2	1	0	0	0
Chen	1.000	44	53	4	0	0
Contreras	—	2	0	0	0	0
Darvill	.800	3	4	0	1	0
Dore	1.000	25	48	3	0	1
Encarnacion	.964	16	26	1	1	0
Golden	.952	63	135	4	7	2
Gretzky	.960	14	24	0	1	0
Martin	.968	11	29	1	1	0
Rademacher	.982	53	101	7	2	2
Shoulders	1.000	16	25	0	0	0
Sweeney	1.000	1	6	0	0	0
Zapata	.965	111	189	6	7	1

NORTHWEST LEAGUE

Batting	B-T	HT	WT	DOB	AVG	vLH	vRH	G	AB	R	H	2B	3B	HR	RBI	BB	HBP	SH	SF	SO	SB	CS	SLG	OBP
Baez, Jeffrey	R-R	6-0	180	10-30-93	.154	.000	.182	4	13	2	2	0	2	0	2	2	1	0	0	6	1	0	.462	.313
Balaguert, Yasiel	R-R	6-2	215	1-2-93	.261	.250	.263	63	238	33	62	15	1	8	48	26	1	0	4	70	1	3	.433	.331
Bote, David	R-R	5-11	185	4-7-93	.250	.274	.241	69	232	39	58	9	0	6	31	23	10	0	5	61	6	4	.366	.337
Brockmeyer, Cael	R-R	6-5	235	10-8-91	.271	.429	.194	33	107	20	29	5	1	0	14	7	0	0	0	22	2	0	.336	.355
Brown, Kevin	L-R	6-0	195	10-30-90	.286	.500	.000	2	7	0	2	0	0	0	1	0	2	0	0	2	0	0	.286	.444
Bryant, Kris	R-R	6-5	215	1-4-92	.354	.476	.295	18	65	13	23	8	1	4	16	8	1	0	3	17	0	0	.692	.416
Dore, Jose	L-R	6-1	170	2-9-92	.200	.133	.213	29	90	6	18	6	1	2	9	11	0	0	1	23	1	0	.356	.284
Dunston Jr., Shawon	L-R	6-2	170	2-5-93	.290	.319	.281	49	193	27	56	8	1	1	19	28	0	1	1	25	12	2	.358	.378
Encarnacion, Kevin	B-R	6-0	175	11-23-91	.355	.237	.391	42	166	34	59	9	1	8	30	21	1	0	0	33	10	5	.566	.431
Gretzky, Trevor	L-L	6-4	190	9-14-92	.256	.435	.190	27	86	11	22	3	0	0	6	3	0	0	0	24	0	0	.291	.281
Hankins, Jordan	L-R	5-10	191	2-18-92	.234	.308	.208	42	145	22	34	5	0	1	8	11	1	0	1	22	2	2	.290	.291
Hannemann, Jacob	L-L	6-1	190	4-29-91	.290	.182	.314	14	62	8	18	4	2	1	5	2	0	0	0	11	3	1	.468	.313
Hodges, Jesse	R-R	6-1	212	3-29-94	.000	.000	.000	3	12	0	0	0	0	0	0	0	0	0	0	5	0	0	.000	.000
Lockhart, Daniel	L-R	5-11	165	11-4-92	.290	.240	.303	67	248	29	72	8	1	0	23	18	4	2	2	39	7	1	.331	.346
Marra, Justin	L-R	5-10	190	1-18-93	.224	.182	.230	25	85	14	19	4	0	6	16	10	1	0	0	30	0	0	.482	.313
Penalver, Carlos	R-R	6-0	170	5-17-94	.261	.333	.240	68	234	43	61	16	2	1	21	25	3	1	1	49	9	3	.359	.338
Rodriguez, Rony	R-R	5-11	210	3-1-90	.270	.309	.247	42	148	24	40	11	0	3	23	10	6	0	0	34	0	0	.405	.341
Rogers, Jacob	L-R	6-5	195	8-23-89	.278	.212	.301	74	259	37	72	11	0	8	47	45	6	0	2	71	2	1	.413	.394
Rosario, Neftali	R-R	5-11	193	7-22-93	.222	1.000	.000	4	9	0	2	0	0	0	0	0	0	0	0	4	0	0	.222	.222
Rymel, Lance	R-R	6-0	195	5-2-90	.253	.318	.229	46	162	22	41	7	0	1	18	15	7	3	3	25	1	0	.315	.337

Pitching	B-T	HT	WT	DOB	W	L	ERA	G	GS	CG	SV	IP	H	R	ER	HR	BB	SO	AVG	vLH	vRH	K/9	BB/9
Arias, Jose	R-R	6-6	235	1-17-91	1	0	0.00	4	0	0	0	11	6	0	0	0	1	9	.158	.188	.136	7.59	0.84
Blackburn, Paul	R-R	6-2	185	12-4-93	2	3	3.33	13	12	0	0	46	41	26	17	3	29	38	.241	.243	.240	7.43	5.67
Bremer, Tyler	R-R	6-2	210	12-7-89	0	3	2.15	23	0	0	7	29	19	9	7	1	11	48	.184	.214	.164	14.73	3.38
Elias, Ethan	R-R	6-3	180	4-27-93	1	0	2.13	6	0	0	0	13	10	3	3	0	5	12	.213	.200	.222	8.53	3.55
Frazier, Scott	R-R	6-7	215	12-3-91	1	2	2.61	14	0	0	1	21	14	6	6	0	10	19	.192	.258	.143	8.27	4.35
Gil, Manuel	R-R	6-6	200	9-29-88	1	2	6.10	5	1	0	0	10	14	8	7	0	2	9	.318	.278	.346	7.84	1.74
Godley, Zack	R-R	6-3	235	4-21-90	2	0	1.75	13	0	0	0	26	20	6	5	0	5	27	.217	.208	.227	9.47	1.75
Hamann, Mike	R-R	6-3	165	1-1-91	0	0	0.00	6	0	0	3	8	4	1	0	0	1	9	.143	.273	.059	10.57	1.17
Hoffner, Corbin	R-R	6-5	235	7-30-93	2	0	1.74	16	0	0	1	47	29	10	9	1	13	42	.180	.194	.172	8.10	2.51
Iannazzo, Matt	L-L	5-9	170	1-8-90	1	1	3.21	14	0	0	4	14	15	6	5	2	2	18	.268	.313	.250	11.57	1.29
Lang, Trey	R-R	6-3	225	5-18-92	0	2	9.82	6	4	0	0	15	17	19	16	2	13	18	.283	.385	.206	11.05	7.98
Maples, Dillon	R-R	6-2	195	5-9-92	5	2	2.14	10	9	0	0	42	37	16	10	0	19	41	.242	.237	.247	8.79	4.07
Martinez-Pumarino, Carlos	R-R	6-4	230	4-2-91	4	2	6.51	18	1	0	0	28	34	24	20	2	14	29	.291	.315	.270	9.43	4.55
Masek, Trey	R-R	6-0	175	1-9-92	1	0	2.16	10	0	0	0	17	11	7	4	0	8	19	.190	.160	.212	10.26	4.32
McKirahan, Andrew	R-L	6-2	195	2-8-90	1	0	2.45	5	0	0	0	7	3	3	2	0	2	11	.120	.250	.059	13.50	2.45
Orozco, Eddie	R-R	6-2	195	4-11-89	0	1	3.77	13	0	0	3	14	14	8	6	0	6	22	.246	.360	.156	13.81	3.77
Padron, Loiger	R-R	6-0	180	1-31-91	2	4	5.87	13	5	0	0	38	39	26	25	2	20	32	.271	.197	.333	7.51	4.70
Paniagua, Juan Carlos	R-R	6-1	175	4-4-90	0	0	11.57	6	2	0	0	14	30	23	18	1	12	18	.423	.375	.462	11.57	7.71
Pugliese, James	R-R	6-3	195	8-12-92	4	3	2.32	12	11	0	0	62	55	21	16	2	12	47	.231	.206	.250	6.82	1.74
Rakkar, Jasvir	R-R	6-2	200	4-27-91	4	1	3.58	20	0	0	1	38	31	16	15	6	10	41	.217	.246	.198	9.80	2.39
Rhee, Dae-Eun	L-R	6-2	190	3-23-89	1	0	0.00	2	2	0	0	4	0	0	0	0	8	1	.143	.188	.083	9.00	0.00
Rosario, Jose	R-R	6-1	170	8-29-90	2	1	5.48	5	5	0	0	23	28	15	14	2	9	20	.295	.324	.276	7.83	3.52
Skulina, Tyler	R-R	6-5	252	9-18-91	0	0	1.20	8	2	0	0	15	9	2	2	0	3	10	.170	.192	.148	6.00	1.80
Underwood, Duane	R-R	6-2	205	7-20-94	3	4	4.97	14	11	0	0	54	62	44	30	4	27	36	.277	.272	.280	5.96	4.47
Wagner, Michael	R-R	6-3	175	10-3-91	0	3	4.38	10	4	0	0	25	31	15	12	2	9	22	.310	.304	.315	8.03	3.28
Wilson, Sam	L-L	6-2	200	7-30-91	3	1	3.33	12	0	0	0	24	26	11	9	0	13	25	.283	.345	.254	9.25	4.81
Zastryzny, Rob	R-L	6-3	205	3-26-92	0	0	3.14	8	7	0	0	14	15	5	5	0	4	16	.268	.176	.308	10.05	2.51

Fielding

Catcher	PCT	G	PO	A	E	DP	PB
Brockmeyer	.994	20	163	11	1	2	0
Marra	1.000	12	93	11	0	0	3
Rosario	1.000	3	7	2	0	0	0
Rymel	.990	44	385	30	4	3	2

First Base	PCT	G	PO	A	E	DP
Bote	1.000	1	5	0	0	0
Brockmeyer	.971	7	64	2	2	4
Rogers	.986	72	573	64	9	56

Second Base	PCT	G	PO	A	E	DP
Bote	.908	25	27	52	8	9
Hankins	.976	9	11	30	1	8
Lockhart	.968	47	87	126	7	27

Third Base	PCT	G	PO	A	E	DP
Bote	.902	20	10	36	5	2
Bryant	.955	16	9	33	2	2
Dore	.700	4	3	4	3	0
Hankins	.938	25	8	37	3	6
Hodges	.857	3	2	4	1	1
Lockhart	.938	13	5	25	2	0

Shortstop	PCT	G	PO	A	E	DP
Bote	.600	2	1	2	2	0
Lockhart	.971	8	13	21	1	6
Penalver	.946	68	102	214	18	38

Outfield	PCT	G	PO	A	E	DP
Baez	.750	3	3	0	1	0
Balaguert	.968	60	87	3	3	1
Bote	1.000	20	35	1	0	0
Brown	1.000	1	2	0	0	0
Dore	1.000	17	28	1	0	0
Dunston Jr.	.971	47	65	3	2	1
Encarnacion	.951	41	74	3	4	0
Gretzky	1.000	22	20	1	0	0
Hannemann	.950	10	19	0	1	0
Rodriguez	1.000	14	24	3	0	0

CHICAGO CUBS

ARIZONA LEAGUE

Batting	B-T	HT	WT	DOB	AVG	vLH	vRH	G	AB	R	H	2B	3B	HR	RBI	BB	HBP	SH	SF	SO	SB	CS	SLG	OBP
Alamo, Tyler	R-R	6-4	200	5-2-95	.111	.111	.111	11	27	1	3	0	0	0	4	2	0	0	1	15	0	0	.111	.167
Baez, Jeffrey	R-R	6-0	180	10-30-93	.287	.261	.297	45	164	31	47	9	2	1	12	16	2	3	0	39	25	3	.384	.357
Balaguert, Yasiel	R-R	6-2	215	1-2-93	.267	.333	.250	4	15	3	4	2	1	0	2	3	0	0	0	4	0	0	.533	.389
Batista, Xavier	R-R	6-3	190	1-18-92	.246	.200	.259	21	69	12	17	7	1	1	8	12	2	0	0	18	0	0	.420	.373
Blair, Zak	L-R	5-10	190	12-19-89	.226	.185	.241	30	106	16	24	4	1	0	17	10	1	0	1	7	3	3	.283	.297
Bogusevic, Brian	L-L	6-3	220	2-18-84	.400	.500	.353	7	25	7	10	4	1	0	5	7	0	0	0	5	3	0	.640	.531
Brown, Kevin	L-R	6-0	195	10-30-90	.230	.219	.235	34	113	17	26	5	2	1	14	22	3	1	0	14	8	2	.336	.370
Bryant, Kris	R-R	6-5	215	1-4-92	.167	1.000	.000	2	6	0	1	1	0	0	2	0	0	0	1	1	0	0	.333	.143
Burks, Charcer	R-R	6-0	170	3-9-95	.269	.231	.280	31	108	13	29	3	0	0	7	10	3	0	1	32	6	1	.296	.344
Castillo, Erick	B-R	5-11	180	2-25-93	.265	.200	.294	16	49	6	13	2	0	1	5	1	0	0	0	6	2	0	.367	.280
Crawford, Rashad	B-R	6-3	185	10-15-93	.210	.158	.230	42	138	20	29	3	3	0	8	16	2	3	1	39	10	1	.275	.299
DeJesus, David	L-L	5-11	190	12-20-79	.333	.667	.222	4	12	4	4	2	0	0	2	0	0	0	0	3	1	0	.500	.429
Freeman, Kelvin	R-R	6-5	245	1-25-91	.262	.313	.245	40	130	18	34	4	0	0	19	18	4	0	5	34	0	2	.292	.357
Hankins, Jordan	L-R	5-10	191	2-18-92	.143	.000	.250	2	7	0	1	0	1	0	2	0	0	0	1	1	0	0	.429	.125
Hannemann, Jacob	L-L	6-1	190	4-29-91	.111	.000	.143	3	9	1	1	1	0	0	2	0	0	1	0	1	1	0	.222	.111
Hodges, Jesse	R-R	6-1	212	3-29-94	.210	.171	.222	47	167	26	35	4	2	2	20	11	4	1	2	44	1	0	.293	.272
Jackson, Brett	L-R	6-2	220	8-2-88	.071	.333	.000	4	14	1	1	0	0	0	1	0	0	0	0	7	0	0	.071	.133
Malave, Mark	B-R	6-3	185	1-5-95	.270	.323	.250	38	115	22	31	6	1	0	15	22	0	1	2	31	0	0	.339	.381
Mineo, Alberto	L-R	5-10	170	7-23-94	.222	.385	.171	16	54	5	12	3	0	0	11	4	2	0	0	17	0	1	.278	.300
Papaccio, Giuseppe	R-R	6-1	185	6-8-91	.313	.000	.400	9	32	3	10	1	1	0	6	3	2	0	1	6	2	0	.406	.395
Penalver, Carlos	R-R	6-0	170	5-17-94	.154	.000	.182	4	13	3	2	0	0	0	2	3	1	0	1	4	0	0	.154	.333
Petit, Wilfredo	B-R	5-11	165	2-9-93	.209	.190	.215	30	86	10	18	2	0	0	14	5	0	2	0	13	0	0	.233	.253
Rohan, Greg	R-R	6-0	205	5-11-86	.286	.000	.353	7	21	4	6	1	0	0	4	5	0	0	1	5	0	0	.333	.407
Rosario, Neftali	R-R	5-11	193	7-22-93	.000	.000	.000	1	4	0	0	0	0	0	0	0	0	0	0	2	0	0	.000	.000
Sanchez, Alex	B-R	6-1	185	9-20-91	.267	.250	.273	6	15	1	4	1	0	0	2	2	0	0	0	0	0	0	.333	.353
Sanchez, Francisco	R-R	6-1	170	12-17-93	.208	.121	.233	41	149	20	31	11	5	1	22	6	1	0	1	53	2	1	.369	.242
Schlecht, Garrett	L-L	6-2	190	2-15-93	.176	.056	.220	29	68	6	12	0	2	0	6	5	2	0	1	23	3	0	.235	.250
Stevens, Trevor	L-R	5-9	170	3-27-89	.257	.211	.275	26	70	8	18	1	2	0	7	13	2	1	0	18	1	0	.329	.388
Sweeney, Ryan	L-L	6-4	225	2-20-85	.286	.333	.250	4	14	4	4	2	0	0	2	3	0	0	0	1	0	0	.429	.412
Valbuena, Luis	L-R	5-10	170	11-30-85	.714	.500	.800	2	7	2	5	2	0	0	3	1	0	0	0	1	1	0	1.000	.750
Vitters, Josh	R-R	6-2	200	8-27-89	.077	.000	.111	5	13	1	1	1	0	0	0	4	0	0	0	5	0	0	.154	.294

Pitching	B-T	HT	WT	DOB	W	L	ERA	G	GS	CG	SV	IP	H	R	ER	HR	BB	SO	AVG	vLH	vRH	K/9	BB/9
Arias, Jose	R-R	6-6	235	1-17-91	0	1	2.53	6	4	0	0	11	6	3	3	0	2	12	.167	.182	.160	10.13	1.69
Beltre, Franyer	R-R	6-1	180	7-24-90	0	1	6.39	12	0	0	0	13	14	11	9	0	17	12	.269	.222	.294	8.53	12.08
Chavez, Johermyn	R-R	6-3	220	1-26-89	1	1	8.53	5	2	0	0	6	6	6	6	1	4	4	.222	.143	.308	5.68	5.68
Clifton, Trevor	R-R	6-4	170	5-11-95	0	0	6.97	8	1	0	0	10	13	8	8	0	8	15	.310	.278	.333	13.06	6.97
Colinas, Augusto	L-L	6-0	190	12-20-92	1	0	5.40	2	0	0	0	2	1	2	1	1	2	0	.200	.000	.250	0.00	10.80
Concepcion, Gerardo	L-L	6-2	180	3-11-92	0	0	0.00	2	2	0	0	4	1	1	0	0	4	2	.083	.000	.091	4.91	9.82
Davis, Josh	R-R	6-3	210	11-3-90	3	1	4.50	12	0	0	0	20	18	11	10	1	7	10	.240	.226	.250	4.50	3.15
Diaz, Dayan	R-R	5-10	190	2-10-89	0	0	0.00	2	1	0	0	3	1	0	0	0	1	5	.100	.000	.200	15.00	3.00
Diaz, Jorge	R-R	6-6	190	1-20-92	1	0	9.53	5	1	0	1	6	6	7	6	1	4	7	.261	.333	.214	11.12	6.35
Dolis, Rafael	R-R	6-4	215	1-10-88	0	0	0.00	3	2	0	0	3	0	0	0	0	1	1	.000	.000	.000	3.00	3.00
Elias, Ethan	R-R	6-3	180	4-27-93	2	1	5.71	9	0	0	0	17	25	16	11	0	5	17	.325	.500	.171	8.83	2.60
Garcia, Victor	L-L	6-2	175	4-1-92	1	0	13.50	2	0	0	0	2	7	4	3	0	2	3	.500	.000	.583	13.50	9.00
Garner, David	R-R	6-1	180	9-21-92	0	2	7.98	9	3	0	0	15	19	15	13	0	9	16	.322	.250	.359	9.82	5.52
Gil, Manuel	R-R	6-6	200	9-29-88	3	1	1.26	10	0	0	0	14	11	3	2	0	4	22	.212	.176	.229	13.81	2.51
Godley, Zack	R-R	6-3	235	4-21-90	0	0	9.00	1	0	0	0	1	2	1	1	0	0	1	.400	.500	.333	9.00	0.00
Graham, Trevor	R-R	6-3	220	11-21-91	0	0	2.01	11	4	0	1	22	18	5	5	2	5	17	.222	.171	.261	6.85	2.01
Guillen, Luis	R-R	6-1	150	12-16-93	0	0	6.91	5	0	0	0	14	19	11	11	3	4	12	.311	.318	.308	7.53	2.51
Gutierrez, Carlos	R-R	6-3	230	9-22-86	0	0	0.00	1	0	0	0	2	0	1	0	0	1	1	.000	.000	.000	4.50	4.50
Hermans, Zak	R-R	6-2	190	6-21-91	1	1	3.12	6	1	0	0	9	10	4	3	0	4	10	.278	.462	.174	10.38	4.15
Ihrig, Tyler	L-L	6-0	190	9-17-91	2	0	0.72	12	0	0	0	25	16	2	2	0	4	30	.184	.211	.176	10.80	1.44
Lang, Trey	R-R	6-3	225	5-18-92	0	1	5.54	11	0	0	0	13	14	8	8	1	9	14	.286	.333	.258	9.69	6.23
Leal, Erick	R-R	6-3	180	3-17-95	3	2	2.77	13	6	0	1	49	50	18	15	2	8	52	.262	.234	.281	9.62	1.48
Lim, Chang-Yong	R-R	5-11	175	6-4-76	0	0	3.60	5	5	0	0	5	5	2	2	0	0	4	.278	.300	.250	7.20	0.00
Masek, Trey	R-R	6-0	175	1-9-92	0	1	15.43	2	0	0	0	2	4	4	4	0	2	2	.400	.200	.600	7.71	7.71
Mateo, Marcos	R-R	6-1	220	4-18-84	1	0	0.00	2	0	0	0	6	3	1	0	0	2	8	.136	.111	.154	12.00	3.00
McKirahan, Andrew	R-L	6-2	195	2-8-90	0	0	4.50	2	0	0	0	2	4	1	1	0	0	4	.500	1.000	.333	18.00	0.00
McNutt, Trey	R-R	6-4	220	8-2-89	0	0	0.00	2	2	0	0	2	3	0	0	0	3	3	.333	.333	.333	13.50	0.00
Mejias, Angel	L-L	6-3	180	10-30-93	0	0	0.00	3	0	0	0	4	3	5	0	0	4	3	.176	.000	.231	6.75	9.00
Paniagua, Juan Carlos	R-R	6-1	175	4-4-90	0	0	0.00	1	0	0	0	3	2	0	0	0	4	.182	.000	.222	12.00	0.00
Peralta, Starling	R-R	6-4	180	11-11-90	0	0	1.35	5	1	0	0	13	11	3	2	0	3	14	.229	.313	.188	9.45	2.03
Prieto, Anthony	L-L	5-11	170	11-16-93	1	2	4.29	4	4	0	0	21	19	15	10	3	12	17	.238	.227	.241	7.29	5.14
Renner, Brad	R-R	6-6	220	5-15-91	0	0	0.00	4	0	0	1	6	2	0	0	0	2	8	.105	.000	.167	12.00	3.00
Rhee, Dae-Eun	L-R	6-2	190	3-23-89	0	0	2.25	2	2	0	0	4	5	3	1	0	1	0	.313	.333	.300	0.00	2.25
Rodriguez, Carlos A.	L-L	5-11	178	7-18-95	1	4	6.97	13	3	0	0	31	44	27	24	0	15	30	.331	.484	.284	8.71	4.35
Santana, Alex	R-R	6-1	170	10-23-93	0	1	4.58	5	2	0	0	18	18	13	9	0	6	16	.257	.179	.310	8.15	3.06
Searle, Ryan	R-R	6-0	190	6-22-89	0	0	4.76	3	3	0	0	6	7	4	3	0	2	6	.259	.286	.250	9.53	3.18
Torrez, Daury	R-R	6-3	170	6-11-93	4	2	3.31	12	2	0	1	49	49	21	18	2	5	49	.255	.171	.303	9.00	0.92
Villalba, Luis	L-L	6-2	182	10-28-92	1	2	2.52	16	0	0	2	25	26	10	7	1	7	32	.265	.179	.300	11.52	2.52

Pitching	B-T	HT	WT	DOB	W	L	ERA	G	GS	CG	SV	IP	H	R	ER	HR	BB	SO	AVG	vLH	vRH	K/9	BB/9
Villegas, David	L-L	6-1	180	9-26-92	0	4	3.68	15	1	0	5	22	21	17	9	0	7	19	.239	.375	.208	7.77	2.86
Wagner, Michael	R-R	6-3	175	10-3-91	1	0	0.00	4	0	0	0	4	4	1	0	0	2	5	.267	.250	.286	11.25	4.50
Wilson, Sam	L-L	6-2	200	7-30-91	0	0	0.00	1	0	0	0	1	1	1	0	0	0	2	.200	.000	.333	18.00	0.00

Fielding

Catcher	PCT	G	PO	A	E	DP	PB
Alamo	.895	3	17	0	2	0	1
Castillo	.977	16	114	14	3	1	2
Malave	1.000	1	2	0	0	0	0
Mineo	.993	16	123	13	1	0	6
Petit	.992	29	218	32	2	5	0
Rosario	1.000	1	7	0	0	0	0

First Base	PCT	G	PO	A	E	DP
Batista	.966	4	25	3	1	4
Brown	1.000	8	67	3	0	5
Freeman	.968	25	196	17	7	14
Malave	.966	18	132	10	5	11
Petit	.875	1	7	0	1	0
Rohan	.951	4	39	0	2	5
Vitters	.857	1	4	2	1	1

Second Base	PCT	G	PO	A	E	DP
Blair	.943	26	50	66	7	14
Malave	.957	11	13	31	2	7
Sanchez	1.000	1	1	5	0	0
Sanchez	.909	6	11	19	3	4
Stevens	.986	16	24	46	1	5

Third Base	PCT	G	PO	A	E	DP
Bryant	.625	2	3	2	3	0
Freeman	1.000	1	1	1	0	0
Hankins	1.000	1	0	3	0	0
Hodges	.859	38	24	61	14	4
Malave	.913	10	4	17	2	1
Papaccio	.750	1	1	2	1	1
Rohan	1.000	1	0	1	0	0
Sanchez	.667	4	0	6	3	0
Valbuena	1.000	1	1	0	0	0
Vitters	.875	3	0	7	1	0

Shortstop	PCT	G	PO	A	E	DP
Batista	—	1	0	0	0	0
Malave	1.000	2	1	8	0	0
Papaccio	.944	8	13	21	2	8
Penalver	.947	4	6	12	1	1
Sanchez	.846	4	2	9	2	1
Sanchez	.902	31	44	85	14	14
Stevens	.923	9	12	12	2	3

Outfield	PCT	G	PO	A	E	DP
Baez	.989	44	76	10	1	0
Balaguert	1.000	3	3	0	0	0
Batista	.917	7	11	0	1	0
Bogusevic	1.000	5	8	0	0	0
Brown	1.000	18	16	1	0	0
Burks	1.000	30	39	0	0	0
Crawford	.988	40	74	5	1	0
DeJesus	1.000	4	6	0	0	0
Hannemann	.667	3	2	0	1	0
Jackson	1.000	4	3	0	0	0
Rohan	1.000	1	1	0	0	0
Schlecht	.923	19	22	2	2	1
Sweeney	1.000	4	4	0	0	0
Vitters	—	1	0	0	0	0

DSL CUBS1

ROOKIE

DOMINICAN SUMMER LEAGUE

Batting	B-T	HT	WT	DOB	AVG	vLH	vRH	G	AB	R	H	2B	3B	HR	RBI	BB	HBP	SH	SF	SO	SB	CS	SLG	OBP
Acosta, Luis	R-R	6-2	195	11-28-94	.122	.222	.105	38	123	13	15	2	0	2	7	21	1	0	0	63	8	2	.187	.255
Alcala, Roney	B-R	6-1	223	2-15-94	.191	.286	.175	12	47	2	9	0	0	0	7	1	0	0	1	7	0	0	.191	.204
Caro, Roberto	B-R	6-0	185	9-25-93	.254	.400	.222	60	197	47	50	8	8	0	18	33	7	4	1	49	18	5	.376	.378
Cuevas, Varonex	B-R	6-0	165	7-24-92	.260	.317	.245	60	204	34	53	11	3	1	20	37	2	1	3	37	13	8	.358	.374
Delarosa, Frandy	R-R	6-1	180	1-24-96	.077	.000	.100	11	39	5	3	0	0	0	3	2	1	1	2	20	2	0	.077	.136
Emeterio, Jenner	R-R	6-1	170	3-19-93	.261	.333	.246	63	203	41	53	2	1	1	23	49	2	2	0	42	37	8	.296	.409
Flete, Bryant	B-R	5-10	146	1-31-93	.136	.000	.167	7	22	4	3	0	0	0	2	6	0	1	1	2	1	0	.136	.310
Garcia, Robert	B-R	5-10	170	12-6-93	.269	.308	.262	25	78	18	21	1	1	0	8	12	3	1	0	20	9	3	.308	.387
Gonzalez, Antonio	B-R	5-10	170	1-27-94	.202	.100	.228	34	99	18	20	2	3	1	11	20	3	1	0	31	6	3	.313	.352
Ortiz, Dalfis	B-R	5-10	160	2-10-92	.343	.237	.373	47	172	39	59	7	9	1	26	25	0	3	5	23	14	7	.506	.416
Paniagua, Jose	R-R	6-2	180	6-7-94	.206	.235	.200	60	209	45	43	13	1	2	24	27	3	0	1	53	5	2	.306	.304
Paula, Adonis	R-R	6-1	185	6-21-94	.281	.279	.281	69	253	44	71	15	5	3	55	36	10	0	3	50	3	3	.415	.387
Pena, Jhonny	R-R	6-0	190	5-24-92	.232	.240	.230	40	125	20	29	6	0	2	11	17	1	0	2	21	1	1	.328	.324
Ramirez, Carlos	R-L	5-9	185	5-27-92	.226	.300	.212	23	62	9	14	0	0	0	6	9	0	0	1	10	1	1	.226	.319
Ubiera, Shamil	R-R	6-0	190	9-28-92	.301	.256	.309	68	256	41	77	18	3	4	56	28	4	0	3	36	13	6	.441	.375
Valerio, Antonio	R-R	6-0	190	3-21-91	.258	.118	.287	56	198	25	51	9	1	1	23	18	0	0	2	22	4	3	.328	.317

Pitching	B-T	HT	WT	DOB	W	L	ERA	G	GS	CG	SV	IP	H	R	ER	HR	BB	SO	AVG	vLH	vRH	K/9	BB/9
Abreu, Gilberto	R-R	6-2	180	8-8-93	2	2	3.49	18	0	0	5	28	20	15	11	2	19	20	.192	.028	.279	6.35	6.04
Araujo, Pedro	R-R	6-3	214	7-2-93	6	0	1.05	8	2	0	0	26	15	3	3	1	3	31	.169	.250	.131	10.87	1.05
Baldayaque, Jesus	R-R	6-2	195	4-17-92	1	3	1.86	12	0	0	2	19	19	6	4	0	7	13	.264	.550	.154	6.05	3.26
De La Cruz, Oscar	R-R	6-4	200	3-4-95	1	0	6.55	4	1	0	0	11	16	8	8	2	5	12	.364	.600	.294	9.82	4.09
Diaz, Andin	L-L	6-0	182	9-2-92	1	0	1.96	5	4	0	0	23	21	9	5	1	3	23	.236	.167	.254	9.00	1.17
Disla, Wagner	R-R	6-4	180	10-21-95	0	0	10.80	4	0	0	0	5	5	6	6	2	6	3	.294	.500	.231	5.40	10.80
Escanio, Luiz	R-R	6-5	190	7-11-94	1	1	2.36	18	0	0	3	27	18	11	7	0	16	32	.186	.161	.197	10.80	5.40
Figueroa, Frailyn	L-L	6-2	203	6-14-95	5	1	1.27	13	5	0	0	50	27	8	7	1	24	53	.161	.143	.164	9.60	4.35
Guillen, Luis	R-R	6-1	150	12-16-93	1	1	1.88	4	2	0	0	14	17	4	3	1	2	13	.315	.333	.306	8.16	1.26
Hernandez, Jeffry	R-R	6-5	215	1-19-95	1	0	4.24	13	5	0	1	34	41	23	16	1	11	17	.297	.286	.302	4.50	2.91
Hernandez, Luis	R-R	6-5	210	3-13-95	2	2	2.50	11	9	0	0	40	34	16	11	1	17	28	.233	.259	.216	6.35	3.86
Llano, Carlos	R-R	6-0	185	2-28-92	6	1	2.95	19	1	0	6	40	39	17	13	2	17	48	.264	.300	.245	10.89	3.86
Mejia, Jefferson	R-R	6-0	175	8-2-94	0	0	3.00	3	3	0	0	9	6	3	3	0	3	6	.222	.250	.217	6.00	3.00
Morel, Jose	R-R	6-6	204	11-13-94	0	0	0.00	2	2	0	0	5	3	0	0	0	5	7	.188	.000	.231	12.60	9.00
Morel, Yomar	R-R	6-1	180	11-18-93	1	1	1.63	10	4	0	1	28	20	5	5	0	4	26	.206	.222	.197	8.46	1.30
Paniagua, Juan Carlos	R-R	6-1	175	4-4-90	0	0	0.00	4	4	0	0	12	4	0	0	0	2	13	.098	.143	.074	9.49	1.46
Paulino, Jose	L-L	6-2	165	4-9-95	5	3	2.33	13	10	0	0	58	47	18	15	1	12	71	.221	.171	.233	11.02	1.86
Pereyra, Jesus	R-R	6-2	175	7-24-93	0	0	12.00	7	0	0	0	6	8	8	8	0	5	5	.333	.455	.231	7.50	7.50
Perez, Hector	R-R	6-1	157	6-25-93	4	3	1.88	13	8	0	1	57	49	16	12	0	13	62	.233	.333	.196	9.73	2.04
Perez, Jesus	L-L	6-1	160	10-20-95	4	2	3.18	10	1	0	0	23	14	9	8	1	19	14	.203	.250	.197	5.56	7.54
Reyes, Amalio	R-R	6-2	175	12-22-91	0	0	4.50	1	1	0	0	2	2	1	1	1	0	3	.286	.500	.200	13.50	0.00
Silverio, Pedro	R-R	6-2	210	6-29-94	1	0	0.00	3	0	0	0	5	2	0	0	0	7	4	.143	.250	.100	7.71	13.50
Vasquez, Dilson	R-R	6-3	200	2-7-92	4	1	3.21	14	0	0	1	28	26	16	10	1	15	18	.252	.343	.206	5.79	4.82
Zapata, Jose	R-R	6-0	170	7-17-93	4	0	1.93	13	9	0	1	56	36	18	12	0	9	49	.181	.273	.146	7.88	1.45

CHICAGO CUBS

Fielding

Catcher	PCT	G	PO	A	E	DP	PB
Alcala	1.000	4	29	5	0	0	2
Pena	.986	11	60	11	1	0	5
Ramirez	.985	19	122	13	2	0	0
Valerio	.993	45	366	54	3	1	3

First Base	PCT	G	PO	A	E	DP
Alcala	.987	9	71	3	1	5
Cuevas	1.000	1	8	2	0	0
Paniagua	.976	31	234	9	6	15
Paula	1.000	1	4	0	0	0
Pena	1.000	27	203	8	0	13
Valerio	.980	11	94	2	2	4

Second Base	PCT	G	PO	A	E	DP
Cuevas	.947	4	10	8	1	2
Emeterio	.951	14	27	31	3	6
Flete	.870	6	14	6	3	0
Gonzalez	.884	10	15	23	5	4
Ortiz	.941	40	73	102	11	15

Third Base	PCT	G	PO	A	E	DP
Cuevas	1.000	2	0	7	0	1
Emeterio	1.000	1	0	1	0	0
Gonzalez	.000	1	0	0	1	0
Paula	.947	67	63	150	12	12
Ubiera	1.000	1	0	1	0	0

Shortstop	PCT	G	PO	A	E	DP
Cuevas	.938	53	65	130	13	13
Delarosa	1.000	10	10	19	0	3
Flete	1.000	1	1	4	0	1
Gonzalez	.975	10	16	23	1	3
Ortiz	1.000	1	3	3	0	2

Outfield	PCT	G	PO	A	E	DP
Acosta	.929	14	11	2	1	1
Caro	.987	50	71	4	1	1
Emeterio	1.000	45	90	6	0	0
Garcia	.977	24	40	2	1	0
Paniagua	.964	30	47	7	2	0
Paula	1.000	1	2	0	0	0
Pena	—	1	0	0	0	0
Ubiera	.943	59	79	3	5	1

VSL CUBS   ROOKIE
VENEZUELAN SUMMER LEAGUE

Batting	B-T	HT	WT	DOB	AVG	vLH	vRH	G	AB	R	H	2B	3B	HR	RBI	BB	HBP	SH	SF	SO	SB	CS	SLG	OBP
Alcala, Roney	B-R	6-1	223	2-15-94	.353	.349	.354	64	241	43	85	15	2	9	49	13	2	0	3	34	5	3	.544	.386
Arcila, Delbis	L-L	6-3	190	4-30-93	.321	.271	.337	64	240	48	77	21	0	10	42	32	0	0	5	62	3	6	.533	.394
Calero, Arnaldo	R-R	6-1	183	11-16-93	.297	.254	.312	61	229	35	68	13	4	5	33	9	10	1	3	53	12	7	.454	.347
Flete, Bryant	B-R	5-10	146	1-31-93	.271	.229	.288	67	247	45	67	11	5	0	23	41	5	2	2	44	17	14	.356	.383
Garcia, Humberto	R-R	5-10	165	5-20-94	.246	.321	.222	62	236	36	58	7	3	1	17	21	2	1	2	48	31	8	.314	.310
Gomez, Victor	R-R	6-2	180	5-25-95	.288	.400	.255	20	66	12	19	2	2	1	7	8	0	1	1	19	4	0	.424	.360
Gonzalez, Jesus	R-R	5-10	145	12-10-95	.130	.000	.170	23	69	8	9	4	1	0	8	10	2	1	0	17	5	1	.217	.259
Gonzalez, Leonardo	R-R	6-1	178	2-17-95	.209	.148	.234	35	91	16	19	8	0	3	11	6	5	2	0	30	0	2	.396	.294
Hodwalker, Martin	R-R	5-11	180	4-1-95	.204	.226	.195	40	108	10	22	3	1	0	9	10	2	1	0	33	3	5	.250	.283
Marcano, Ricardo	L-R	6-2	190	10-18-94	.279	.323	.263	68	251	43	70	19	6	4	45	24	2	0	6	53	13	5	.450	.339
Pereda, Jhonny	R-R	6-1	170	4-18-96	.213	.205	.215	59	188	18	40	9	0	2	21	22	1	1	3	36	0	0	.293	.294
Rico, Miguel	R-R	6-2	204	9-15-93	.231	.348	.195	62	195	39	45	10	0	10	26	23	6	0	4	59	2	1	.436	.325
Vahlis, Roberto	R-R	5-10	190	11-19-93	.241	.130	.281	33	87	10	21	3	0	3	14	9	1	1	0	14	1	0	.379	.320
Vargas, Eufran	R-R	5-11	178	7-14-94	.366	.500	.323	13	41	7	15	4	0	1	13	7	1	0	1	10	0	0	.537	.460

Pitching	B-T	HT	WT	DOB	W	L	ERA	G	GS	CG	SV	IP	H	R	ER	HR	BB	SO	AVG	vLH	vRH	K/9	BB/9
Alzolay, Adbert	R-R	6-0	179	3-1-95	5	3	1.07	15	12	0	0	67	49	16	8	1	10	61	.201	.276	.177	8.19	1.34
Bermudez, Harrinson	R-R	6-4	190	3-6-95	2	1	5.68	12	2	0	0	25	25	20	16	3	18	10	.287	.382	.226	3.55	6.39
Carrillo, Francisco	R-R	6-0	190	3-15-90	8	3	2.09	21	0	0	1	52	48	17	12	1	5	53	.257	.333	.202	9.23	0.87
Castillo, Jesus	R-R	6-2	165	8-27-95	0	2	4.26	5	4	0	0	19	20	13	9	0	3	14	.267	.348	.231	6.63	1.42
Colinas, Augusto	L-L	6-0	190	12-20-92	0	1	2.13	9	0	0	0	13	12	6	3	0	4	3	.250	.667	.222	2.13	2.84
De Los Rios, Enrique	R-R	6-1	175	5-2-95	2	1	2.08	11	9	0	0	43	31	13	10	4	10	26	.204	.266	.159	5.40	2.08
Diaz, Alberto	L-L	5-9	157	6-12-91	3	0	2.18	19	2	0	1	41	33	20	10	2	11	44	.208	.417	.190	9.58	2.40
Eregua, Greyfer	R-R	5-11	160	10-15-93	2	1	1.45	11	6	0	0	43	34	9	7	1	3	42	.217	.213	.218	8.72	0.62
Fuentes, Manuel	L-L	6-1	186	6-6-92	2	0	8.10	17	0	0	0	23	31	24	21	1	13	19	.310	.333	.308	7.33	5.01
Garcia, Victor	L-L	6-2	175	4-1-92	2	4	4.91	13	13	0	0	51	62	38	28	4	7	41	.291	.333	.290	7.19	1.23
Gomez, Yapson	L-L	5-10	158	2-10-93	0	1	4.18	12	2	0	0	24	25	15	11	2	9	15	.263	.133	.288	5.70	3.42
Jerez, Salvador	R-R	6-4	205	3-28-93	0	2	3.29	6	3	0	0	14	9	8	5	0	7	9	.188	.333	.121	5.93	4.61
Mejias, Angel	L-L	6-3	180	10-30-93	3	0	2.45	4	1	0	0	11	7	6	3	1	3	8	.171	.167	.171	6.55	2.45
Pacheco, Yomar	R-R	6-3	200	10-4-89	2	2	2.61	28	0	0	10	41	42	15	12	6	6	37	.266	.135	.330	8.06	1.31
Pieters, Chris	L-L	6-3	183	3-21-94	1	5	12.21	19	4	0	0	24	23	41	33	0	42	19	.261	.143	.272	7.03	15.53
Ramirez, Moises	R-R	6-0	160	12-11-95	1	0	3.38	14	2	0	0	21	20	9	8	1	5	20	.250	.310	.216	8.44	2.11
Rivero, Brohiglyn	R-R	6-3	185	5-3-93	0	1	30.24	11	0	0	0	8	17	28	28	1	18	5	.436	.333	.481	5.40	19.44
Romero, Cesar	R-R	5-11	194	10-2-93	0	1	7.71	7	0	0	0	7	9	6	6	0	7	3	.321	.800	.217	3.86	9.00
Salazar, Victor	R-R	6-3	178	1-21-93	3	2	3.26	18	1	0	2	39	33	15	14	3	9	32	.232	.282	.214	7.45	2.09
Valera, Ramon	R-R	6-2	181	9-9-94	0	1	42.43	8	0	0	0	5	11	22	22	0	11	1	.440	.545	.357	1.93	21.21
Vides, Mauro	R-R	6-2	207	10-19-95	0	1	5.90	15	7	0	0	29	29	24	19	3	19	11	.269	.175	.324	3.41	5.90

Fielding

Catcher	PCT	G	PO	A	E	DP	PB
Alcala	.967	5	28	1	1	0	0
Gonzalez	.991	19	93	17	1	0	4
Pereda	.983	45	297	49	6	2	6
Vahlis	.914	11	45	8	5	0	2
Vargas	1.000	2	10	2	0	0	0

First Base	PCT	G	PO	A	E	DP
Alcala	1.000	5	35	2	0	0
Arcila	.983	34	270	20	5	21
Gonzalez	.982	6	52	2	1	3
Pereda	.969	7	28	3	1	2
Rico	.986	25	207	9	3	13
Vahlis	1.000	1	4	0	0	0
Vargas	1.000	2	9	1	0	1

Second Base	PCT	G	PO	A	E	DP
Alcala	.917	2	5	6	1	2
Flete	.970	16	29	35	2	11
Garcia	.938	37	63	87	10	14
Gonzalez	.926	19	32	31	5	7
Hodwalker	1.000	5	4	7	0	1
Rico	.667	1	1	1	1	0

Third Base	PCT	G	PO	A	E	DP
Alcala	.947	39	29	95	7	9
Garcia	1.000	1	1	3	0	0
Gonzalez	.833	2	3	2	1	0
Hodwalker	.500	2	1	2	3	0
Rico	.880	30	22	66	12	11

Shortstop	PCT	G	PO	A	E	DP
Flete	.891	54	82	154	29	15
Garcia	.943	17	26	40	4	12
Gonzalez	—	2	0	0	0	0

Outfield	PCT	G	PO	A	E	DP
Alcala	1.000	6	6	2	0	0
Arcila	.969	32	54	9	2	1
Calero	.967	56	113	4	4	0
Garcia	.950	9	19	0	1	0
Gomez	.930	20	37	3	3	1
Hodwalker	.977	29	41	1	1	0
Marcano	.973	68	131	13	4	4
Vahlis	—	1	0	0	0	0

Chicago White Sox

SEASON IN A SENTENCE: The White Sox, who contended for most of the 2012 season, collapsed offensively in 2013, ranking last in the American League in runs scored. As a result, the Sox finished with their worst record (63-99) since 1970.

HIGH POINT: Lefthander Chris Sale, the team's 2010 first-round pick, turned in most of them, including a May 15 gem against the Angels, who got only one hit—a one-out single in the seventh to break up a perfect game. The victory started a 10-4 stretch that got the Sox got to the .500 mark.

LOW POINT: Such a season provides many, but a nine-game losing streak in late August and early September summed up the season well. Chicago scored just 25 runs in the nine-game stretch, with lineups that featured veterans such as DH Adam Dunn and first baseman Paul Konerko.

NOTABLE ROOKIES: The White Sox will build the 2014 lineup around outfielder Avisail Garcia, acquired from the Tigers in a three-team deal that sent Jake Peavy to Boston. Garcia lacks selectivity but has profile right-field tools. Catchers Tyler Flowers and Josh Phegley struggled at the plate while replacing A.J. Pierzynski. Conor Gillaspie, acquired in February for minor league righty Jeff Soptic, became the everyday third baseman and had his moments. Righty Andre Reinzo proved homer-prone but made history as the first Brazilian-born pitcher in the majors.

KEY TRANSACTIONS: In his first year as general manager, Rick Hahn recognized his team wasn't a contender and dealt Peavy, outfielder Alex Rios and reliever Jesse Crain. In addition to Garcia, Peavy brought righties Francellis Montas and J.B. Wendelken and shortstop Cleuluis Rondon to Chicago. Rios went to the Rangers for athletic infielder Leurys Garcia.

DOWN ON THE FARM: The news was better on the farm. Phegley had a breakout season that brought him to Chicago and exhausted his rookie eligibility, while fellow Cal Bear alumni Erik Johnson, a righthander, and infielder Marcus Semien blazed through two levels en route to Chicago. Both had started the year with Double-A Birmingham, which was the system's crown jewel, winning the Southern League championship in its first year in a new downtown ballpark. Great Falls had the best record in the Rookie-level Pioneer League regular season but fell in the playoffs. After the season, the Sox kept Great Falls but left Bristol, their Rookie-level Appalachian League affiliate.

OPENING DAY PAYROLL: $119.1 million (8th)

ORGANIZATION LEADERS

BATTING   *Minimum 250 AB

MAJORS

*	AVG	Ramirez, Alexei	.284
*	OPS	Dunn, Adam	.762
	HR	Dunn, Adam	34
	RBI	Dunn, Adam	86

MINORS

*	AVG	Johnson, Micah, Birmingham/W-S/Kannapolis	.312
*	OBP	Black, Dan, Birmingham	.411
*	SLG	Semien, Marcus, Charlotte/Birmingham	.479
	R	Semien, Marcus, Charlotte/Birmingham	110
	H	Johnson, Micah, Birmingham/W-S/Kannapolis	167
	TB	Curley, Chris, Winston-Salem	251
	2B	Coats, Jason, Kannapolis	38
	3B	Johnson, Micah, Birmingham/W-S/Kannapolis	15
	HR	Curley, Chris, Winston-Salem	24
	RBI	Curley, Chris, Winston-Salem	92
	BB	Semien, Marcus, Charlotte/Birmingham	98
	SO	Hawkins, Courtney, Winston-Salem	160
	SB	Johnson, Micah, Birmingham/W-S/Kannapolis	84

PITCHING   #Minimum 75 IP

MAJORS

	W	Sale, Chris	11
#	ERA	Sale, Chris	3.07
	SO	Sale, Chris	226
	SV	Reed, Addison	40

MINORS

	W	Beck, Chris, Birmingham/Winston-Salem	13
		Jaye, Myles, Birmingham/W-S/Kannapolis	13
	L	Stewart, Zach, Charlotte	14
#	ERA	Johnson, Erik, Birmingham/Charlotte	1.96
	G	Thompson, Taylor, Charlotte/Birmingham	44
		Winiarski, Cody, Birmingham/Winston-Salem	44
	GS	Three tied at	28
	SV	Thompson, Taylor, Charlotte/Birmingham	13
		Winiarski, Cody, Birmingham/Winston-Salem	13
	IP	Blough, Bryan, Winston-Salem	172.7
	BB	Cose, Jake, Winston-Salem/Kannapolis	78
	SO	Bassitt, Chris, Birmingham/Winston-Salem	138
#	AVG	Johnson, Erik, Birmingham/Charlotte	.197

2013 PERFORMANCE

General Manager: Rick Hahn. **Farm Director:** Nick Capra. **Scouting Director:** Doug Laumann.

Class	Team	League	W	L	PCT	Finish	Manager
Majors	Chicago White Sox	American	63	99	.389	14th (15)	Robin Ventura
Triple-A	Charlotte Knights	International	65	78	.455	12th (14)	Joel Skinner
Double-A	Birmingham Barons	Southern	77	63	.550	3rd (10)	Julio Vinas
High A	Winston-Salem Dash	Carolina	71	69	.507	4th (8)	Ryan Newman
Low A	Kannapolis Intimidators	South Atlantic	61	76	.445	11th (14)	Tommy Thompson
Rookie	Bristol White Sox	Appalachian	20	45	.308	10th (10)	Mike Gellinger
Rookie	Great Falls Voyagers	Pioneer	48	28	.632	1st (8)	Pete Rose Jr.
Overall 2013 Minor League Record			342	359	.488		

ORGANIZATION STATISTICS

CHICAGO WHITE SOX

AMERICAN LEAGUE

Batting	B-T	HT	WT	DOB	AVG	vLH	vRH	G	AB	R	H	2B	3B	HR	RBI	BB	HBP	SH	SF	SO	SB	CS	SLG	OBP
Anderson, Bryan	L-R	6-1	200	12-16-86	.056	.000	.063	10	18	1	1	1	0	0	2	1	0	0	0	5	0	0	.111	.105
Beckham, Gordon	R-R	6-0	190	9-16-86	.267	.195	.287	103	371	46	99	22	1	5	24	28	4	1	4	56	5	1	.372	.322
Danks, Jordan	L-R	6-4	210	8-7-86	.231	.182	.239	79	160	15	37	7	0	5	12	18	1	0	0	57	7	2	.369	.313
De Aza, Alejandro	L-L	6-0	190	4-11-84	.264	.302	.252	153	607	84	160	27	4	17	62	50	6	6	6	147	20	8	.405	.323
Dunn, Adam	L-R	6-6	285	11-9-79	.219	.197	.226	149	525	60	115	15	0	34	86	76	3	0	3	189	1	1	.442	.320
Flowers, Tyler	R-R	6-4	245	1-24-86	.195	.151	.213	84	256	24	50	11	0	10	24	14	4	0	1	94	0	1	.355	.247
Garcia, Avisail	R-R	6-4	240	6-12-91	.304	.281	.310	42	161	19	49	4	2	5	21	5	1	0	1	38	3	2	.447	.327
2-team total (30 Detroit)					.283	—	—	72	244	31	69	7	3	7	31	9	1	0	2	59	3	3	.422	.309
Garcia, Leury	B-R	5-7	160	3-18-91	.204	.400	.154	20	49	2	10	1	0	0	1	4	0	0	1	18	6	2	.224	.259
2-team total (25 Texas)					.198	—	—	45	101	10	20	1	1	0	2	7	0	2	1	34	7	2	.228	.248
Gillaspie, Conor	L-R	6-1	205	7-18-87	.245	.159	.261	134	408	46	100	14	3	13	40	37	1	0	6	79	0	1	.390	.305
Gimenez, Hector	B-R	5-10	230	9-28-82	.191	.200	.190	26	68	8	13	4	0	2	10	7	2	0	3	22	0	0	.338	.275
Gonzalez, Miguel	R-R	5-11	180	12-3-90	.222	—	.222	5	9	0	2	0	0	0	0	0	0	0	0	3	0	0	.222	.222
Greene, Tyler	R-R	6-2	190	8-17-83	.222	.200	.241	22	54	7	12	2	1	1	3	3	0	0	0	19	0	0	.352	.263
Keppinger, Jeff	R-R	6-0	185	4-21-80	.253	.214	.266	117	423	38	107	13	1	4	40	20	0	2	5	41	0	1	.317	.283
Konerko, Paul	R-R	6-2	220	3-5-76	.244	.313	.226	126	467	41	114	16	0	12	54	45	4	0	4	74	0	0	.355	.313
Morel, Brent	R-R	6-2	225	4-21-87	.200	.231	.167	12	25	3	5	0	0	1	5	0	0	0	0	7	1	1	.200	.333
Phegley, Josh	R-R	5-10	220	2-12-88	.206	.261	.190	65	204	14	42	7	0	4	22	5	0	2	2	41	2	0	.299	.223
Ramirez, Alexei	R-R	6-2	180	9-22-81	.284	.285	.284	158	637	68	181	39	2	6	48	26	3	4	4	68	30	9	.380	.313
Rios, Alex	R-R	6-5	210	2-18-81	.277	.315	.267	109	430	57	119	22	2	12	55	32	1	0	1	78	26	6	.421	.328
2-team total (47 Texas)					.278	—	—	156	616	83	171	33	4	18	81	41	2	0	2	108	42	7	.432	.324
Sanchez, Angel	R-R	6-1	205	9-20-83	.000	.000	.000	1	2	0	0	0	0	0	0	0	0	0	0	0	0	0	.000	.000
Semien, Marcus	R-R	6-1	190	9-17-90	.261	.267	.259	21	69	7	18	4	0	2	7	1	0	0	1	22	2	2	.406	.268
Tekotte, Blake	L-R	5-11	180	5-24-87	.226	.250	.211	20	31	4	7	1	0	1	2	3	1	0	1	9	1	3	.355	.306
Viciedo, Dayan	R-R	5-11	230	3-10-89	.265	.257	.268	124	441	43	117	23	3	14	56	24	3	0	5	98	0	0	.426	.304
Wells, Casper	R-R	6-2	220	11-23-84	.167	.152	.182	37	66	4	11	1	0	0	1	5	0	0	0	22	0	1	.182	.225
2-team total (3 Oakland)					.155	—	—	40	71	4	11	1	0	0	1	5	0	0	0	23	0	1	.169	.211
Wise, Dewayne	L-L	6-0	200	2-24-78	.234	.200	.241	30	64	6	15	3	0	1	3	2	0	0	1	3	2	0	.328	.258

Pitching	B-T	HT	WT	DOB	W	L	ERA	G	GS	CG	SV	IP	H	R	ER	HR	BB	SO	AVG	vLH	vRH	K/9	BB/9
Axelrod, Dylan	R-R	6-0	185	7-30-85	4	11	5.68	30	20	0	0	128	170	89	81	24	43	73	.318	.302	.345	5.12	3.02
Castro, Simon	R-R	6-5	230	4-9-88	0	1	2.70	4	0	0	0	7	5	2	2	1	3	6	.217	.222	.214	8.10	4.05
Crain, Jesse	R-R	6-1	215	7-5-81	2	3	0.74	38	0	0	0	37	31	6	3	0	11	46	.225	.275	.174	11.29	2.70
Danks, John	L-L	6-1	215	4-15-85	4	14	4.75	22	22	0	0	138	151	81	73	28	27	89	.277	.293	.270	5.79	1.76
Floyd, Gavin	R-R	6-6	235	1-27-83	0	4	5.18	5	5	0	0	24	27	15	14	4	12	25	.287	.275	.302	9.25	4.44
Heath, Deunte	R-R	6-4	240	8-8-85	0	0	11.74	5	0	0	0	8	8	10	10	2	12	3	.276	.294	.250	3.52	14.09
Johnson, Erik	R-R	6-3	235	12-30-89	3	2	3.25	5	5	0	0	28	32	16	10	5	11	18	.283	.348	.178	5.86	3.58
Jones, Nate	R-R	6-5	210	1-28-86	4	5	4.15	70	0	0	0	78	69	40	36	5	26	89	.247	.229	.261	10.27	3.00
Leesman, Charlie	L-L	6-4	210	3-10-87	0	0	7.04	8	1	0	0	15	16	14	12	2	16	13	.267	.286	.250	7.63	9.39
Lindstrom, Matt	R-R	6-3	220	2-11-80	2	4	3.12	76	0	0	0	61	64	23	21	2	23	46	.277	.317	.255	6.82	3.41
Omogrosso, Brian	R-R	6-4	240	4-26-84	0	2	9.37	12	0	0	0	16	28	18	17	2	9	16	.378	.429	.313	8.82	4.96
Peavy, Jake	R-R	6-1	195	5-31-81	8	4	4.28	13	13	1	0	80	74	41	38	14	17	76	.244	.265	.218	8.55	1.93
2-team total (10 Boston)					12	5	4.17	23	23	2	0	145	130	70	67	20	36	121	—	—	—	7.53	2.24
Petricka, Jake	R-R	6-5	200	6-5-88	1	1	3.26	16	0	0	0	19	20	7	7	0	10	10	.278	.292	.271	4.66	4.66
Purcey, David	L-L	6-5	235	4-22-82	1	1	2.13	24	0	0	0	25	19	7	6	2	17	23	.209	.205	.213	8.17	6.04
Quintana, Jose	L-L	6-1	215	1-24-89	9	7	3.51	33	33	0	0	200	188	83	78	23	56	164	.247	.260	.242	7.38	2.52
Reed, Addison	R-R	6-4	220	12-27-88	5	4	3.79	68	0	0	40	71	56	31	30	6	23	72	.215	.210	.220	9.08	2.90
Rienzo, Andre	R-R	6-3	190	6-5-88	2	3	4.82	10	10	0	0	56	55	34	30	11	28	38	.253	.248	.264	6.11	4.50
Sale, Chris	L-L	6-6	180	3-30-89	11	14	3.07	30	30	4	0	214	184	81	73	23	46	226	.230	.135	.252	9.49	1.93
Santiago, Hector	R-L	6-0	210	12-16-87	4	9	3.56	34	23	0	0	149	137	69	59	17	72	137	.243	.241	.244	8.28	4.35
Thornton, Matt	L-L	6-6	235	9-15-76	0	3	3.86	40	0	0	0	28	25	14	12	4	10	21	.245	.173	.320	6.75	3.21
2-team total (20 Boston)					0	4	3.74	60	0	0	0	43	47	20	18	4	15	30	—	—	—	6.23	3.12
Troncoso, Ramon	R-R	6-2	215	2-16-83	1	4	4.50	29	0	0	0	30	30	22	15	4	16	18	.256	.360	.179	5.40	4.80
Veal, Donnie	L-L	6-4	235	9-18-84	2	3	4.60	50	0	0	0	29	26	15	15	3	16	29	.236	.257	.200	8.90	4.91
Webb, Daniel	R-R	6-3	210	8-18-89	0	0	3.18	9	0	0	0	11	9	4	4	0	4	10	.220	.261	.167	7.94	3.18

Fielding

Catcher	PCT	G	PO	A	E	DP	PB
Anderson	.981	10	49	2	1	0	0
Flowers	.994	84	640	42	4	4	8
Gimenez	.988	23	146	12	2	3	5
Gonzalez	1.000	4	12	1	0	0	0
Phegley	.989	64	415	29	5	4	8

First Base	PCT	G	PO	A	E	DP
Dunn	.986	71	548	31	8	54
Gillaspie	.981	12	45	6	1	3
Keppinger	.993	20	120	14	1	16
Konerko	.994	76	600	48	4	70
Morel	1.000	3	5	0	0	0

Second Base	PCT	G	PO	A	E	DP
Beckham	.975	103	212	255	12	69
Garcia	.974	9	14	23	1	7
Greene	.966	19	24	33	2	11
Keppinger	.995	45	74	107	1	24
Phegley	—	1	0	0	0	0
Sanchez	1.000	1	0	1	0	0
Semien	1.000	3	1	7	0	0

Third Base	PCT	G	PO	A	E	DP
Garcia	—	2	0	0	0	0
Gillaspie	.943	113	64	200	16	16
Keppinger	.968	41	25	67	3	8
Morel	.952	9	4	16	1	2
Semien	.921	17	5	30	3	2

Shortstop	PCT	G	PO	A	E	DP
Beckham	1.000	2	2	0	0	0
Garcia	1.000	3	3	4	0	1
Ramirez	.968	158	236	433	22	100
Semien	1.000	3	7	13	0	0

Outfield	PCT	G	PO	A	E	DP
Danks	.990	68	100	1	1	1
De Aza	.979	151	368	5	8	2
Dunn	1.000	3	2	0	0	0
Garcia	.976	42	80	1	2	0
Garcia	1.000	6	9	0	0	0
Rios	.987	108	228	8	3	1
Tekotte	1.000	16	21	0	0	0
Viciedo	.970	109	147	12	5	0
Wells	.970	24	31	1	1	1
Wise	.981	26	51	0	1	0

CHARLOTTE KNIGHTS

TRIPLE-A

INTERNATIONAL LEAGUE

Batting	B-T	HT	WT	DOB	AVG	vLH	vRH	G	AB	R	H	2B	3B	HR	RBI	BB	HBP	SH	SF	SO	SB	CS	SLG	OBP
Anderson, Bryan	L-R	6-1	200	12-16-86	.224	.125	.260	64	210	26	47	14	1	7	26	24	0	0	1	60	2	0	.400	.302
Anderson, Lars	L-L	6-4	215	9-25-87	.194	.123	.222	66	227	20	44	7	0	2	14	33	3	1	2	72	1	0	.251	.302
Beckham, Gordon	R-R	6-0	190	9-16-86	.333	.143	.379	8	36	7	12	2	0	0	5	2	0	0	0	6	0	0	.389	.368
Bell, Josh	B-R	6-3	230	11-13-86	.273	.333	.235	15	55	9	15	4	0	0	4	3	0	0	0	18	0	0	.345	.310
2-team total (37 Scranton/W-B)					.226	—	—	52	177	25	40	8	0	5	21	28	0	0	5	45	0	0	.356	.324
Danks, Jordan	L-R	6-4	210	8-7-86	.279	.284	.277	54	208	35	58	9	2	6	28	26	2	1	1	57	3	1	.428	.363
Dowdy, Jeremy	R-R	6-2	215	7-13-90	.000	—	.000	1	3	0	0	0	0	0	0	0	0	0	0	0	0	0	.000	.000
Durango, Luis	B-R	5-9	155	4-23-86	.233	.192	.250	26	90	6	21	2	1	0	4	5	0	1	0	16	5	4	.278	.274
Earley, Michael	R-R	6-0	200	3-15-88	.221	.323	.164	27	86	7	19	3	0	0	8	5	1	1	1	20	0	1	.256	.269
Espino, Damaso	R-R	6-1	210	5-8-83	.000	—	.000	1	4	0	0	0	0	0	0	0	0	0	0	2	0	0	.000	.000
Gallagher, Jimmy	L-L	6-1	195	9-3-85	.245	.213	.256	90	282	39	69	14	1	3	28	31	4	4	1	101	3	0	.333	.327
Garcia, Drew	B-R	6-1	175	4-24-85	.222	.217	.224	24	72	3	16	8	0	0	12	4	2	0	0	19	0	1	.333	.282
Garcia, Avisail	R-R	6-4	240	6-12-91	.370	.429	.308	8	27	6	10	0	1	1	9	4	1	0	0	4	0	0	.556	.469
2-team total (33 Toledo)					.374	—	—	41	174	29	65	7	2	6	32	12	2	0	0	36	4	2	.540	.420
Garcia, Leury	B-R	5-7	160	3-18-91	.267	.250	.269	8	30	3	8	1	0	0	1	1	0	0	0	8	3	0	.300	.313
Gimenez, Hector	B-R	5-10	230	9-28-82	.294	.400	.250	5	17	4	5	1	1	0	2	4	0	1	0	5	0	0	.471	.429
Gonzalez, Miguel	R-R	5-11	180	12-3-90	.280	.250	.308	16	50	5	14	3	0	0	4	6	0	0	2	11	0	0	.340	.345
2-team total (13 Gwinnett)					.256	—	—	69	250	34	64	14	2	4	31	18	4	2	0	73	10	3	.376	.316
Heisler, Adam	L-R	5-10	165	6-7-88	.316	.167	.385	6	19	3	6	0	0	0	2	2	0	1	0	6	1	0	.316	.381
Ishikawa, Travis	L-L	6-3	220	9-24-83	.250	.222	.262	34	120	17	30	5	2	2	23	15	4	1	0	31	0	0	.375	.353
2-team total (49 Norfolk)					.290	—	—	83	297	46	86	21	2	9	54	44	5	1	1	74	1	0	.465	.389
Loman, Seth	L-R	6-4	245	12-16-85	.223	.258	.211	39	121	25	27	6	0	8	19	18	15	0	0	49	0	0	.471	.390
McDade, Mike	B-R	6-1	250	5-8-89	.254	.246	.259	94	354	36	90	18	0	10	46	28	4	0	4	96	1	0	.390	.313
2-team total (21 Columbus)					.250	—	—	115	428	39	107	22	0	10	53	36	5	0	4	120	1	0	.371	.313
Mitchell, Jared	L-L	6-0	205	10-13-88	.132	.071	.154	14	53	7	7	2	0	0	3	10	1	0	1	27	4	1	.170	.277
Morel, Brent	R-R	6-2	225	4-21-87	.266	.327	.241	106	395	55	105	30	3	6	54	48	4	2	3	104	14	3	.403	.349
Phegley, Josh	R-R	5-10	220	2-12-88	.316	.291	.329	61	231	39	73	18	1	15	41	15	7	0	5	38	1	1	.597	.368
Puckett, Cody	R-R	5-9	189	4-3-87	.111	.125	.100	6	18	2	2	0	0	2	2	3	0	0	0	4	0	0	.444	.238
Sanchez, Angel	R-R	6-1	205	9-20-83	.189	.178	.194	43	148	19	28	5	0	1	16	12	3	0	0	25	0	1	.243	.264
Sanchez, Carlos	B-R	5-11	195	6-29-92	.241	.275	.224	112	432	50	104	20	2	0	28	29	4	11	3	76	16	7	.296	.293
Semien, Marcus	R-R	6-1	190	9-17-90	.264	.395	.207	32	125	20	33	11	1	4	17	14	1	0	2	24	4	0	.464	.338
Short, Brandon	R-R	6-0	190	9-9-88	.186	.224	.146	30	97	10	18	4	2	0	6	10	2	4	0	30	1	1	.268	.275
Tekotte, Blake	L-R	5-11	180	5-24-87	.236	.273	.218	76	296	32	70	27	3	4	33	31	6	3	2	74	12	5	.389	.319
Tolleson, Steve	R-R	5-11	185	11-1-83	.288	.299	.283	116	392	47	113	28	1	8	53	59	5	9	8	91	14	5	.426	.381
Viciedo, Dayan	R-R	5-11	230	3-10-89	.200	.250	.182	4	15	2	3	0	0	0	1	0	0	1	0	0	3	0	0	.200	.294
Wilkins, Andy	L-R	6-1	220	9-13-88	.265	.239	.277	58	215	25	57	13	0	7	30	14	2	0	3	52	2	1	.423	.312
Wise, Dewayne	L-L	6-0	200	2-24-78	.170	.200	.167	16	53	4	9	3	1	0	2	3	1	0	0	17	1	1	.264	.228

Pitching	B-T	HT	WT	DOB	W	L	ERA	G	GS	CG	SV	IP	H	R	ER	HR	BB	SO	AVG	vLH	vRH	K/9	BB/9
Arroyo, Spencer	L-L	6-2	166	8-9-88	0	1	5.79	1	1	0	0	5	8	4	3	0	1	4	.364	.400	.353	7.71	1.93
Berken, Jason	R-R	6-0	205	11-27-83	12	12	3.80	27	27	1	0	161	171	74	68	15	46	117	.275	.284	.268	6.54	2.57
Castro, Simon	R-R	6-5	230	4-9-88	3	7	5.83	27	12	0	0	93	98	61	60	14	33	82	.272	.295	.255	7.96	3.21
Danks, John	L-L	6-1	215	4-15-85	1	0	3.45	3	3	0	0	16	13	8	6	1	12	14	.236	.273	.212	8.04	6.89
Gray, Jeff	R-R	6-2	210	11-19-81	2	1	3.27	17	0	0	2	22	16	8	8	2	12	23	.203	.235	.178	9.41	4.91
Heath, Deunte	R-R	6-4	240	8-8-85	2	1	2.20	30	1	0	4	45	36	12	11	1	14	36	.218	.281	.178	7.20	2.80
Johnson, Erik	R-R	6-3	235	12-30-89	4	1	1.57	10	10	0	0	57	43	13	10	1	19	57	.209	.244	.183	8.95	2.98
Leesman, Charlie	L-L	6-4	210	3-10-87	4	3	3.87	16	16	0	0	88	90	50	38	11	41	78	.263	.192	.284	7.95	4.18
Marinez, Jhan	R-R	6-1	200	8-12-88	2	4	6.11	20	0	0	2	28	26	20	19	7	16	26	.243	.238	.246	8.36	5.14
McCray, Stephen	L-R	6-3	230	10-6-87	0	4	8.10	6	2	0	0	13	19	14	12	1	15	11	.333	.429	.241	7.43	5.40
McCully, Nick	R-R	5-11	195	9-5-88	2	3	5.66	9	8	0	0	41	49	31	26	6	18	24	.287	.217	.333	5.23	3.92
Moskos, Daniel	R-L	6-1	200	4-28-86	2	1	4.97	22	0	0	1	29	30	17	16	6	15	28	.273	.324	.247	8.69	4.66

Name	B-T	HT	WT	DOB	W	L	ERA	G	GS	CG	SV	IP	H	R	ER	HR	BB	SO	AVG	vLH	vRH	K/9	BB/9
Nix, Michael	R-R	6-5	235	5-21-83	1	0	5.40	1	1	0	0	5	4	3	3	1	2	5	.222	.231	.200	9.00	3.60
Omogrosso, Brian	R-R	6-4	240	4-26-84	0	1	4.91	10	0	0	2	15	20	8	8	2	4	14	.339	.333	.346	8.59	2.45
Pena Jr., Tony	R-R	6-2	180	3-23-81	5	8	3.87	33	9	0	0	86	97	42	37	4	31	72	.280	.342	.235	7.53	3.24
Petricka, Jake	R-R	6-5	200	6-5-88	2	0	1.17	10	0	0	1	15	9	2	2	0	7	17	.167	.235	.135	9.98	4.11
Purcey, David	L-L	6-5	235	4-22-82	0	2	3.03	26	0	0	3	39	30	14	13	2	12	43	.217	.146	.247	10.01	2.79
Remenowsky, Dan	R-R	6-5	245	4-7-86	0	0	5.40	10	0	0	0	15	17	9	9	2	6	13	.279	.226	.333	7.80	3.60
Rienzo, Andre	R-R	6-3	190	6-5-88	8	6	4.06	20	20	3	0	113	105	62	51	7	46	113	.243	.260	.228	9.00	3.66
Rodriguez, Santos	L-L	6-0	190	1-2-88	1	0	7.30	18	0	0	0	25	21	21	20	3	27	36	.236	.259	.226	13.14	9.85
Septimo, Leyson	L-L	6-1	200	7-7-85	2	1	4.42	28	0	0	0	39	29	21	19	2	33	38	.215	.235	.202	8.84	7.68
Stewart, Zach	R-R	6-2	205	9-28-86	6	14	4.25	28	28	0	0	167	187	89	79	16	37	122	.286	.259	.311	6.56	1.99
Thompson, Taylor	R-R	6-5	225	6-18-87	1	2	7.88	12	0	0	1	16	24	18	14	2	3	16	.324	.483	.222	9.00	1.69
Troncoso, Ramon	R-R	6-2	215	2-16-83	1	1	2.19	21	0	0	8	25	18	9	6	2	7	17	.194	.211	.182	6.20	2.55
Veal, Donnie	L-L	6-4	235	9-18-84	2	2	2.70	17	0	0	2	27	23	8	8	1	14	30	.250	.212	.271	10.13	4.73
Webb, Daniel	R-R	6-3	210	8-18-89	1	1	2.96	21	0	0	4	27	24	15	9	1	17	38	.226	.256	.206	12.51	5.60
Zaleski, Matt	R-R	6-1	205	12-2-81	1	2	5.74	5	5	0	0	27	35	18	17	1	6	20	.321	.294	.345	6.75	2.03

Fielding

Catcher	PCT	G	PO	A	E	DP	PB
Anderson	.996	62	472	27	2	3	5
Dowdy	1.000	1	3	0	0	0	0
Gimenez	.976	5	39	2	1	0	0
Gonzalez	.986	16	136	8	2	2	1
Phegley	.994	60	464	48	3	2	8

First Base	PCT	G	PO	A	E	DP
Anderson	.996	32	252	18	1	12
Bell	.962	3	21	4	1	1
Gallagher	.983	9	56	3	1	5
Ishikawa	1.000	7	59	3	0	9
Loman	1.000	21	170	12	0	12
McDade	.980	34	278	22	6	27
Morel	1.000	4	36	5	0	1
Wilkins	.991	38	297	20	3	34

Second Base	PCT	G	PO	A	E	DP
Beckham	1.000	5	6	15	0	2
Garcia	.982	11	26	28	1	6
Garcia	1.000	5	12	11	0	1
Greene	.966	12	23	34	2	10
Morel	1.000	2	4	3	0	0

	PCT	G	PO	A	E	DP
Puckett	1.000	2	4	2	0	0
Sanchez	.982	13	17	39	1	5
Sanchez	.986	61	126	165	4	38
Tolleson	1.000	37	62	91	0	24

Third Base	PCT	G	PO	A	E	DP
Bell	.667	2	2	4	3	0
Espino	1.000	1	1	1	0	0
Greene	.857	6	2	10	2	1
Morel	.948	87	56	163	12	14
Puckett	1.000	1	0	3	0	1
Sanchez	.943	16	10	23	2	1
Semien	1.000	6	6	16	0	3
Tolleson	.954	23	11	51	3	3
Wilkins	.833	2	4	1	1	0

Shortstop	PCT	G	PO	A	E	DP
Beckham	1.000	2	2	8	0	1
Garcia	.960	12	20	28	2	4
Garcia	.667	2	2	4	3	1
Greene	.789	5	1	14	4	0
Sanchez	.978	14	21	23	1	5
Sanchez	.943	52	65	150	13	29

	PCT	G	PO	A	E	DP
Semien	.917	26	33	55	8	13
Tolleson	.978	33	43	89	3	22

Outfield	PCT	G	PO	A	E	DP
Anderson	1.000	26	38	3	0	1
Danks	1.000	53	98	3	0	0
Durango	1.000	25	50	1	0	0
Earley	.981	27	51	2	1	1
Gallagher	.989	81	166	6	2	2
Garcia	1.000	8	11	1	0	0
Garcia	.500	1	1	0	1	0
Greene	.889	32	35	5	5	0
Heisler	1.000	6	14	0	0	0
Ishikawa	1.000	24	30	0	0	0
Mitchell	.933	14	28	0	2	0
Puckett	1.000	3	2	0	0	0
Short	.978	29	43	1	1	0
Tekotte	.994	75	165	4	1	1
Tolleson	1.000	23	40	3	0	0
Viciedo	.857	3	6	0	1	0
Wise	1.000	15	25	0	0	0

BIRMINGHAM BARONS — DOUBLE-A

SOUTHERN LEAGUE

Batting	B-T	HT	WT	DOB	AVG	vLH	vRH	G	AB	R	H	2B	3B	HR	RBI	BB	HBP	SH	SF	SO	SB	CS	SLG	OBP
Black, Dan	L-R	6-5	240	7-2-87	.290	.320	.280	133	449	70	130	28	1	17	83	91	4	3	4	98	7	2	.470	.411
Blanke, Mike	R-R	6-4	225	10-17-88	.226	.177	.241	94	332	25	75	15	1	7	43	36	1	3	2	75	2	0	.340	.302
De Pinto, Joe	R-R	6-1	190	4-3-89	.375	.400	.333	5	16	2	6	1	0	0	2	4	1	0	0	5	0	1	.438	.524
Dowdy, Jeremy	R-R	6-2	215	7-13-90	.000	.000	.000	1	4	0	0	0	0	0	0	0	0	0	0	1	0	0	.000	.000
Earley, Michael	R-R	6-0	200	3-15-88	.275	.262	.279	66	233	35	64	16	2	4	29	19	4	2	3	37	4	2	.412	.336
Gonzalez, Miguel	R-R	5-11	180	12-3-90	.244	.148	.272	37	119	12	29	5	1	2	16	10	3	0	0	25	3	1	.353	.318
Herbek, David	R-R	6-2	182	4-2-89	.253	.250	.255	29	83	9	21	4	0	0	7	13	1	0	0	17	2	1	.301	.361
Jacobs, Brandon	R-R	6-1	225	12-8-90	.237	.071	.273	43	156	13	37	8	0	2	22	11	3	1	5	50	2	3	.327	.291
Johnson, Micah	B-R	5-11	190	12-18-90	.238	.286	.214	5	21	2	5	0	0	0	1	0	0	0	1	4	1	0	.238	.227
Konerko, Paul	R-R	6-2	220	3-5-76	.400	.500	.375	3	10	1	4	0	0	0	1	1	0	0	0	1	0	0	.400	.455
Manzella, Tommy	R-R	6-2	200	4-16-83	.059	.000	.080	10	34	0	2	0	0	0	0	2	0	0	0	16	1	0	.059	.111
McMurray, Chris	R-R	6-1	195	10-12-86	.200	.167	.208	14	30	4	6	1	0	1	4	0	4	0	6	1	0	.333	.400
Mitchell, Jared	L-L	6-0	205	10-13-88	.174	.156	.180	76	247	23	43	6	2	5	20	41	2	1	0	96	13	5	.275	.297
Puckett, Cody	R-R	5-9	189	4-3-87	.258	.287	.247	102	349	43	90	16	0	15	50	22	1	2	3	47	7	4	.433	.301
Saladino, Tyler	R-R	6-0	200	7-20-89	.229	.178	.246	118	424	49	97	17	2	5	55	51	6	6	6	86	28	8	.314	.316
Semien, Marcus	R-R	6-1	190	9-17-90	.290	.337	.276	105	393	90	114	21	5	15	49	84	4	2	0	66	20	5	.483	.420
Short, Brandon	R-R	6-0	190	9-9-88	.223	.296	.194	29	94	14	21	6	1	1	10	15	2	1	2	14	3	2	.340	.336
2-team total (25 Pensacola)					.225	—	—	54	160	20	36	8	1	2	17	19	3	3	3	26	3	3	.325	.314
Sierra, Luis	L-R	5-11	150	7-23-87	.158	.000	.176	5	19	2	3	1	0	0	2	2	0	0	1	3	0	0	.211	.227
Thompson, Trayce	R-R	6-3	215	3-15-91	.229	.240	.225	135	507	78	116	23	5	15	73	60	13	2	8	139	25	8	.383	.321
Wagner, Daniel	L-R	6-0	185	7-12-88	.274	.196	.288	87	296	33	81	9	0	1	23	19	2	2	0	33	23	7	.314	.322
Walker, Keenyn	B-R	6-3	190	8-12-90	.201	.191	.205	130	462	77	93	16	5	3	32	69	11	8	0	153	38	15	.277	.319
Wilkins, Andy	L-R	6-2	220	9-13-88	.288	.286	.289	67	243	37	70	16	0	10	49	38	2	0	2	58	3	0	.477	.386

Pitching	B-T	HT	WT	DOB	W	L	ERA	G	GS	CG	SV	IP	H	R	ER	HR	BB	SO	AVG	vLH	vRH	K/9	BB/9
Arroyo, Spencer	L-L	6-2	166	8-9-88	9	7	3.42	26	26	1	0	145	134	68	55	9	44	92	.246	.205	.262	5.72	2.74
Ballinger, J.R.	R-R	6-1	190	4-2-88	1	2	6.91	20	0	0	0	27	35	21	21	3	14	33	.307	.417	.256	10.87	4.61
Bassitt, Chris	R-R	6-5	205	2-22-89	4	2	2.27	8	8	0	0	48	35	16	12	2	17	32	.213	.188	.232	6.99	3.21
Beck, Chris	R-R	6-3	210	9-4-90	2	2	2.89	5	5	0	0	28	26	10	9	0	3	22	.250	.244	.254	7.07	0.96
Buch, Ryan	R-R	6-3	205	11-8-87	0	0	4.91	5	0	0	0	7	9	7	4	1	8	5	.265	.267	.263	6.14	9.82
Cales, David	R-R	5-11	205	7-27-87	1	0	1.82	16	0	0	0	25	25	6	5	2	16	22	.258	.242	.266	8.03	5.84

Name	B-T	HT	WT	DOB	W	L	ERA	G	GS	CG	SV	IP	H	R	ER	HR	BB	SO	AVG	vLH	vRH	K/9	BB/9
Carroll, Scott	R-R	6-4	215	9-24-84	0	2	4.32	6	6	0	0	25	25	15	12	2	2	14	.250	.233	.263	5.04	0.72
Casey, Jarrett	R-L	6-0	185	10-27-87	0	1	6.94	7	1	0	0	12	18	12	9	2	2	8	.340	.077	.425	6.17	1.54
Danks, John	L-L	6-1	215	4-15-85	1	0	2.57	1	1	0	0	7	5	2	2	1	1	1	.200	.000	.263	1.29	1.29
Jaye, Myles	B-R	6-3	170	12-28-91	0	1	17.18	1	1	0	0	4	8	7	7	0	0	3	.400	.250	.500	7.36	4.91
Johnson, Erik	R-R	6-3	235	12-30-89	8	2	2.23	14	14	3	0	85	57	22	21	6	21	74	.189	.218	.164	7.87	2.23
Kussmaul, Ryan	R-R	6-4	185	9-19-86	2	1	2.43	23	0	0	5	33	24	11	9	2	7	36	.200	.237	.164	9.72	1.89
Mabee, Henry	R-R	6-4	230	7-10-85	1	0	1.54	7	0	0	0	12	9	2	2	0	2	5	.214	.200	.222	3.86	1.54
McCray, Stephen	L-R	6-3	230	10-6-87	10	7	3.25	22	22	0	0	119	107	53	43	8	48	70	.238	.280	.204	5.29	3.63
McCully, Nick	R-R	5-11	195	9-5-88	7	3	3.08	19	12	0	0	79	52	32	27	8	24	48	.191	.208	.178	5.47	2.73
Molina, Nestor	R-R	6-1	220	1-9-89	1	1	4.71	17	4	0	1	36	44	25	19	2	11	29	.301	.267	.326	7.18	2.72
Nix, Michael	R-R	6-5	235	5-21-83	3	4	5.64	10	9	0	0	53	56	33	33	4	19	39	.273	.247	.295	6.66	3.25
Peavy, Jake	R-R	6-1	195	5-31-81	1	0	1.80	1	1	0	0	5	5	1	1	0	2	4	.250	.333	.182	7.20	3.60
Petricka, Jake	R-R	6-5	200	6-5-88	3	0	2.06	21	1	0	0	39	36	11	9	1	18	41	.255	.277	.245	9.38	4.12
Remenowsky, Dan	R-R	6-5	245	4-7-86	1	2	3.94	19	0	0	1	30	30	14	13	5	6	28	.259	.298	.232	8.49	1.82
Rodriguez, Santos	L-L	6-6	190	1-2-88	1	0	2.35	15	0	0	0	23	13	6	6	1	14	25	.167	.160	.170	9.78	5.48
Romanski, Josh	L-L	6-0	185	10-18-86	1	1	6.26	10	0	0	0	23	30	18	16	3	11	20	.330	.375	.305	7.83	4.30
Sanchez, Salvador	R-R	6-6	195	9-13-85	2	4	2.74	27	0	0	1	43	31	16	13	1	10	46	.197	.203	.194	9.70	2.11
Snodgress, Scott	L-L	6-6	225	9-20-89	11	11	4.70	26	26	2	0	144	146	90	75	9	59	90	.269	.283	.264	5.64	3.70
Thompson, Taylor	R-R	6-5	225	6-18-87	4	2	2.15	32	0	0	12	50	34	15	12	0	13	46	.185	.219	.162	8.23	2.32
Vance, Kevin	R-R	6-0	208	7-8-90	2	6	3.91	40	0	0	7	69	55	31	30	4	36	84	.213	.237	.194	10.96	4.70
Webb, Daniel	R-R	6-3	210	8-18-89	0	0	1.77	13	0	0	4	20	11	4	4	0	5	21	.155	.100	.195	9.30	2.21
Whisler, Wes	L-L	6-5	240	4-7-83	0	2	7.16	8	3	0	0	16	18	15	13	0	10	8	.286	.333	.262	4.41	5.51
Winiarski, Cody	R-R	6-3	190	8-27-89	1	0	0.00	8	0	0	3	11	5	0	0	0	2	18	.135	.125	.143	14.73	1.64

Fielding

Catcher	PCT	G	PO	A	E	DP	PB
Blanke	.990	93	675	51	7	8	8
Dowdy	1.000	1	4	0	0	0	0
Gonzalez	.972	37	218	24	7	4	4
McMurray	.988	14	71	11	1	1	0
Johnson	1.000	5	5	12	0	3	
Puckett	.978	12	16	29	1	6	
Saladino	.986	43	89	127	3	27	
Semien	.956	41	75	99	8	20	
Wagner	.994	34	63	91	1	23	
Saladino	.959	75	112	216	14	52	
Semien	.947	47	60	138	11	29	
Wagner	.500	1	0	1	1	0	

First Base	PCT	G	PO	A	E	DP
Black	.991	92	733	80	7	71
Earley	1.000	5	57	6	0	5
Konerko	1.000	1	10	0	0	0
Puckett	1.000	2	4	0	0	0
Wilkins	.992	43	356	26	3	29

Second Base	PCT	G	PO	A	E	DP
Herbek	.960	10	7	17	1	3

Third Base	PCT	G	PO	A	E	DP
Herbek	1.000	5	0	7	0	0
Puckett	.901	75	46	127	19	8
Semien	.980	17	12	36	1	7
Wagner	.935	48	33	83	8	4

Shortstop	PCT	G	PO	A	E	DP
Herbek	.951	11	13	26	2	3
Manzella	.880	8	5	17	3	2

Outfield	PCT	G	PO	A	E	DP
De Pinto	1.000	4	4	0	0	0
Earley	.986	43	69	3	1	0
Jacobs	1.000	35	65	1	0	0
Mitchell	.975	68	157	1	4	0
Puckett	1.000	3	5	0	0	0
Short	.971	18	33	1	1	0
Thompson	.975	129	261	13	7	2
Walker	.967	124	305	13	11	3

WINSTON-SALEM DASH

HIGH CLASS A

CAROLINA LEAGUE

Batting	B-T	HT	WT	DOB	AVG	vLH	vRH	G	AB	R	H	2B	3B	HR	RBI	BB	HBP	SH	SF	SO	SB	CS	SLG	OBP
Barroso, Yoandy	R-R	6-2	190	11-26-88	.244	.500	.205	15	45	9	11	3	0	0	4	2	3	1	0	14	1	0	.356	.320
Brown, Jake	L-R	5-11	185	2-15-90	.158	.000	.188	6	19	1	3	1	0	0	0	2	0	0	0	6	0	0	.211	.238
Buckner, Grant	R-R	6-2	215	3-21-88	.254	.214	.265	119	422	58	107	24	3	10	62	41	9	0	2	83	3	2	.396	.331
Curley, Chris	R-R	6-0	185	8-25-87	.280	.310	.270	136	533	90	149	24	3	24	92	51	11	1	8	110	14	7	.471	.350
De Pinto, Joe	R-R	6-1	190	4-3-89	.236	.234	.237	58	182	36	43	15	0	3	16	22	5	2	3	26	4	2	.368	.330
DeMichele, Joey	L-R	5-11	185	2-5-91	.246	.301	.228	134	541	87	133	37	2	8	54	62	2	6	4	126	19	7	.366	.323
Farrell, Jeremy	R-R	6-3	200	11-11-86	.253	.213	.264	120	431	70	109	35	1	11	74	44	17	1	0	113	2	2	.415	.346
Haddow, Mark	R-R	6-2	220	12-2-87	.272	.250	.279	87	302	50	82	25	1	3	33	44	8	1	2	75	10	4	.391	.376
Hawkins, Courtney	R-R	6-3	220	11-12-93	.178	.200	.171	103	383	48	68	16	3	19	62	29	9	0	4	160	10	5	.384	.249
Heisler, Adam	L-R	5-10	165	6-7-88	.271	.275	.270	59	218	35	59	8	6	3	30	30	4	3	2	50	11	7	.404	.366
Herbek, David	R-R	6-2	182	4-20-88	.210	.235	.200	38	124	11	26	2	0	1	10	11	2	0	2	27	3	0	.274	.281
Johnson, Micah	B-R	5-11	190	12-18-90	.275	.281	.273	49	211	28	58	7	4	1	15	15	1	5	1	27	22	7	.360	.309
Medina, Martin	R-R	6-0	200	3-24-90	.211	.192	.218	55	185	18	39	7	0	2	14	20	2	1	1	38	1	1	.281	.293
Ravelo, Rangel	R-R	6-2	210	4-24-92	.312	.288	.319	84	301	43	94	27	2	4	53	40	2	1	3	46	4	1	.455	.393
Rice, Bill	L-R	5-11	185	9-7-88	.171	.000	.194	12	41	4	7	3	1	0	1	3	0	0	0	11	4	0	.293	.227
Richmond, Josh	R-R	6-3	205	6-14-89	.254	.207	.272	58	205	30	52	9	3	8	31	19	3	1	3	58	2	1	.444	.322
Smith, Kevan	R-R	6-4	230	6-28-88	.286	.317	.278	101	384	66	110	26	3	12	73	38	15	2	3	66	4	1	.464	.370
Tanner, Brent	L-R	6-2	225	10-1-87	.346	.286	.356	16	52	6	18	6	0	1	7	8	0	0	0	13	0	0	.519	.433
Tracy, Mark	R-R	6-4	220	1-1-88	.223	.154	.244	34	112	13	25	6	1	5	22	10	3	1	2	44	0	0	.429	.299

Pitching	B-T	HT	WT	DOB	W	L	ERA	G	GS	CG	SV	IP	H	R	ER	HR	BB	SO	AVG	vLH	vRH	K/9	BB/9
Ballinger, J.R.	R-R	6-1	190	4-2-88	0	0	2.92	11	0	0	0	12	14	7	4	0	8	14	.292	.448	.053	10.22	5.84
Bassitt, Chris	R-R	6-5	205	2-22-89	7	2	3.46	18	18	0	0	101	90	50	39	9	42	101	.231	.280	.180	8.97	3.73
Beck, Chris	R-R	6-3	210	9-4-90	11	8	3.11	21	21	1	0	119	117	51	41	11	42	57	.262	.286	.239	4.32	3.19
Blough, Bryan	R-R	6-1	190	8-29-89	11	11	3.81	28	28	3	0	173	184	90	73	8	55	98	.275	.298	.255	5.11	2.87
Brackman, Andrew	R-R	6-10	230	12-4-85	0	0	9.00	1	0	0	0	2	2	2	2	1	1	2	.250	.000	.286	9.00	4.50
Brase, Stew	R-R	6-3	195	1-20-90	0	0	5.19	6	0	0	0	9	6	5	5	1	8	5	.194	.222	.182	5.19	8.31
Buch, Ryan	R-R	6-3	205	11-8-87	0	2	5.54	3	3	0	0	13	18	8	8	3	6	11	.316	.273	.343	7.62	4.15
Casey, Jarrett	R-L	6-0	185	10-27-87	2	3	2.91	30	0	0	1	56	36	18	18	4	23	44	.184	.146	.215	7.11	3.72
Collop, Justin	R-R	6-1	185	5-30-88	2	3	5.79	6	0	0	0	28	33	18	18	4	18	21	.295	.208	.359	6.75	5.79
Cose, Jake	B-R	6-5	195	8-28-90	7	5	4.16	17	17	1	0	102	86	48	47	8	57	72	.232	.246	.219	6.37	5.05

Name	B-T	HT	WT	DOB	W	L	ERA	G	GS	CG	SV	IP	H	R	ER	HR	BB	SO	AVG	vLH	vRH	K/9	BB/9
Dvorsky, Joe	R-R	6-2	200	9-19-88	2	4	2.89	21	0	0	2	28	24	16	9	4	8	23	.235	.174	.286	7.39	2.57
Erben, Jeremy	R-R	5-11	195	9-15-87	4	1	5.27	32	0	0	3	56	51	34	33	8	33	52	.242	.250	.235	8.31	5.27
Goldberg, Brad	R-R	6-4	228	2-21-90	0	0	3.18	2	0	0	1	6	5	2	2	1	3	5	.238	.417	.000	7.94	4.76
Hardin, Brandon	R-R	6-0	200	2-17-90	3	3	3.81	34	0	0	6	52	64	24	22	2	15	31	.300	.305	.297	5.37	2.60
Jaye, Myles	B-R	6-3	170	12-28-91	9	6	4.11	20	20	1	0	118	122	60	54	8	44	89	.266	.238	.294	6.77	3.35
Marin, Terance	R-R	6-1	170	8-21-89	5	5	4.76	33	7	0	0	93	101	57	49	5	22	70	.271	.322	.228	6.80	2.14
Ortiz, Braulio	R-R	6-5	205	12-20-91	1	3	6.91	6	6	0	0	27	28	23	21	2	24	29	.252	.250	.254	9.55	7.90
Peterson, Max	L-L	6-2	210	6-27-88	1	5	5.62	35	0	0	4	42	39	35	26	3	36	51	.239	.219	.253	11.02	7.78
Recchia, Mike	R-R	6-1	210	4-2-89	1	0	4.88	5	5	0	0	28	33	15	15	3	12	30	.306	.281	.333	9.76	3.90
Upchurch, Steven	R-R	6-4	180	9-14-89	1	0	5.40	2	0	0	0	3	2	2	2	1	2	4	.182	.125	.333	10.80	5.40
Van Skike, Jason	R-R	6-4	195	4-10-89	3	5	2.80	30	9	0	0	74	76	35	23	4	25	45	.267	.289	.248	5.47	3.04
Webb, Daniel	R-R	6-3	210	8-18-89	1	0	0.00	8	0	0	2	15	10	2	0	0	5	19	.182	.231	.138	11.40	3.00
Wendelken, J.B.	R-R	6-0	190	3-24-93	0	1	4.82	6	0	0	0	9	12	6	5	1	7	16	.308	.250	.348	15.43	6.75
Winiarski, Cody	R-R	6-3	190	8-27-89	0	2	2.91	36	0	0	10	56	49	18	18	3	25	67	.234	.269	.200	10.83	4.04

Fielding

Catcher	PCT	G	PO	A	E	DP	PB
Medina	.989	46	316	41	4	0	3
Smith	.987	92	621	64	9	4	14
Tanner	1.000	4	27	3	0	1	1

First Base	PCT	G	PO	A	E	DP
Buckner	.993	43	386	12	3	26
Farrell	.990	21	203	5	2	14
Medina	1.000	7	60	3	0	7
Ravelo	.991	67	595	41	6	54
Tanner	1.000	7	52	0	0	4
Tracy	.778	1	5	2	2	1

Second Base	PCT	G	PO	A	E	DP
De Pinto	—	1	0	0	0	0
DeMichele	.985	84	139	244	6	48
Herbek	.977	10	9	33	1	6
Johnson	.966	47	68	158	8	24

Third Base	PCT	G	PO	A	E	DP
Buckner	1.000	5	5	15	0	1
Curley	.938	44	42	80	8	7
Farrell	.950	80	56	133	10	14
Herbek	.911	15	9	32	4	4

Shortstop	PCT	G	PO	A	E	DP
Brown	.960	6	9	15	1	3

	PCT	G	PO	A	E	DP
Curley	.940	75	98	201	19	34
DeMichele	.927	47	86	116	16	28
Herbek	.941	13	12	36	3	6

Outfield	PCT	G	PO	A	E	DP
Barroso	1.000	13	28	2	0	0
Buckner	1.000	62	115	3	0	0
De Pinto	.978	52	85	3	2	0
Farrell	1.000	1	1	0	0	0
Haddow	.972	78	136	4	4	0
Hawkins	.955	100	231	4	11	2
Heisler	.981	53	101	2	2	1
Rice	.913	12	21	0	2	0
Richmond	.966	57	84	1	3	0

KANNAPOLIS INTIMIDATORS

LOW CLASS A

SOUTH ATLANTIC LEAGUE

Batting	B-T	HT	WT	DOB	AVG	vLH	vRH	G	AB	R	H	2B	3B	HR	RBI	BB	HBP	SH	SF	SO	SB	CS	SLG	OBP
Almanzar, Jean	B-R	5-7	150	2-7-89	.227	.417	.208	38	132	12	30	6	0	0	9	6	0	3	1	18	1	0	.273	.259
Anderson, Tim	R-R	6-1	180	6-23-93	.277	.234	.291	68	267	45	74	10	5	1	21	23	7	2	2	78	24	4	.363	.348
Barnum, Keon	L-L	6-5	225	1-16-93	.254	.186	.272	56	201	22	51	13	1	5	26	19	0	1	2	65	0	0	.403	.315
Barroso, Yoandy	R-R	6-2	190	11-26-88	.225	.143	.237	36	111	19	25	8	0	1	10	18	3	0	0	34	3	1	.324	.348
Basto, Nick	R-R	6-1	180	4-1-94	.190	.205	.185	54	174	13	33	4	0	1	15	10	1	1	2	44	1	2	.230	.235
Brown, Jake	L-R	5-11	185	2-15-90	.276	.286	.275	21	76	10	21	4	1	0	12	5	0	0	0	18	3	0	.355	.321
Coats, Jason	R-R	6-2	200	2-24-90	.271	.283	.269	133	516	63	140	38	3	12	84	31	8	4	4	85	12	3	.426	.320
Dowdy, Jeremy	R-R	6-2	215	7-13-90	.214	.200	.219	31	98	6	21	3	0	0	5	8	0	0	0	25	0	1	.245	.274
Fisher, Zac	L-R	6-2	195	12-13-91	.268	.000	.292	20	71	8	19	6	1	1	10	7	1	0	2	19	0	2	.423	.333
Grabe, Eric	R-R	5-10	190	8-8-89	.227	.236	.224	70	229	24	52	5	3	1	19	21	2	3	0	46	6	5	.288	.298
Heisler, Adam	L-R	5-10	165	6-7-88	.270	.333	.260	36	122	24	33	7	2	2	15	25	2	1	2	29	11	3	.410	.397
Jirschele, Justin	L-R	5-11	195	4-15-90	.137	.286	.114	15	51	1	7	2	0	0	6	1	0	0	0	5	0	0	.176	.154
Johnson, Micah	B-R	5-11	190	12-18-90	.342	.264	.359	77	304	76	104	17	11	6	42	40	3	3	1	67	61	19	.530	.422
Johnson, Michael	L-R	5-9	170	10-28-88	.286	.271	.289	70	238	32	68	10	2	2	36	35	3	3	2	59	6	4	.370	.381
Kiser, Kale	B-R	5-10	180	3-31-90	.234	.275	.224	120	381	51	89	20	2	4	36	35	11	5	6	65	12	5	.328	.312
Llanos, Alex	R-R	6-1	160	9-21-90	.065	.125	.043	10	31	3	2	1	0	0	2	2	1	0	0	6	1	0	.097	.147
Marjama, Mike	R-R	6-2	205	7-20-89	.277	.268	.280	97	375	48	104	20	1	6	46	20	7	1	4	67	9	5	.384	.323
May, Jacob	B-R	5-10	180	1-23-92	.286	.224	.311	54	206	36	59	6	3	8	28	16	4	2	2	43	19	5	.461	.346
Palmeiro, Patrick	R-R	6-3	210	3-6-90	.190	.148	.200	40	147	17	28	9	0	1	15	7	3	1	1	44	1	0	.272	.241
Ramirez, Juan	R-R	6-4	196	8-28-90	.216	.158	.241	38	125	12	27	3	0	1	10	6	2	1	1	52	3	2	.264	.261
Ravelo, Rangel	R-R	6-2	210	4-24-92	.226	.000	.240	17	53	9	12	4	0	0	9	11	1	0	1	11	1	1	.302	.364
Richmond, Josh	R-R	6-3	205	6-14-89	.375	.583	.318	14	56	9	21	9	2	1	11	1	2	0	0	13	0	1	.661	.407
Robinson, Kyle	R-R	6-3	210	12-2-88	.246	.100	.275	16	61	5	15	1	0	0	7	4	0	0	0	13	3	1	.262	.292
Rondon, Cleulis	R-R	6-0	185	4-13-94	.202	.200	.203	29	94	11	19	0	0	1	6	7	3	0	0	24	1	0	.234	.279
Rosario, Angel	R-R	5-10	175	12-14-91	.091	.000	.111	8	22	2	2	0	0	0	0	2	2	0	0	2	0	0	.091	.231
Sierra Jr., Ruben	L-L	6-2	170	3-10-91	.180	.100	.196	17	61	6	11	3	0	0	4	3	0	0	0	18	1	1	.230	.219
Tanner, Brent	L-R	6-2	225	10-1-87	.235	.200	.242	67	221	24	52	8	0	8	28	27	3	0	1	65	3	2	.380	.325
Williams, Tyler	R-R	6-2	200	1-5-91	.167	.000	.189	27	102	7	17	3	0	2	7	1	0	0	1	52	1	1	.196	.227

Pitching	B-T	HT	WT	DOB	W	L	ERA	G	GS	CG	SV	IP	H	R	ER	HR	BB	SO	AVG	vLH	vRH	K/9	BB/9
Bollinger, Ryan	L-L	6-6	185	2-4-91	0	1	3.17	29	0	0	3	54	57	23	19	5	13	52	.269	.318	.247	8.67	2.17
Bowling, Cal	R-R	6-2	195	10-22-89	0	1	4.26	3	0	0	0	6	3	3	1	1	6	3	.230	.250	.200	8.53	1.42
Brase, Stew	R-R	6-3	195	1-20-89	3	2	2.13	29	0	0	8	42	26	13	10	2	27	54	.181	.279	.139	11.48	5.74
Brennan, Brandon	R-R	6-4	220	7-26-91	4	9	5.53	15	15	0	0	81	99	66	50	7	27	54	.298	.278	.308	5.98	2.99
Bucciferro, Tony	R-R	6-3	205	12-27-89	3	5	2.50	13	12	1	1	72	80	26	20	2	5	71	.275	.272	.277	8.88	0.63
Cales, David	R-R	5-11	205	7-27-87	0	0	0.00	4	0	0	0	4	1	0	0	0	2	10	.316	.333	.308	20.77	4.15
Cose, Jake	B-R	6-5	195	8-28-90	4	3	1.72	10	10	0	0	58	44	19	11	0	21	63	.207	.264	.167	9.83	3.28
Danish, Tyler	R-R	6-2	190	9-12-94	0	0	0.00	2	0	0	0	4	2	0	0	0	0	6	.143	.000	.222	13.50	0.00
Dvorsky, Joe	R-R	6-2	200	9-19-88	0	0	2.52	14	0	0	0	25	27	10	7	3	3	28	.267	.278	.262	10.08	1.08
Evans, Steven	L-L	6-4	210	8-9-89	0	1	40.50	1	0	0	0	1	7	6	6	0	0	3	.636	1.000	.429	20.25	0.00
Goldberg, Brad	R-R	6-4	228	2-21-90	3	0	1.42	12	0	0	2	25	10	6	4	0	6	37	.120	.130	.117	13.14	2.13

	B-T	HT	WT	DOB	W	L	ERA	G	GS	CG	SV	IP	H	R	ER	HR	BB	SO	AVG	vLH	vRH	K/9	BB/9
Gunter, Michael	R-R	6-1	190	7-5-90	0	0	3.68	4	0	0	0	7	5	3	3	0	2	15	.192	.333	.000	18.41	2.45
Hansen, Kyle	R-R	6-8	200	4-20-91	6	9	4.10	21	20	0	1	97	109	57	44	7	27	103	.282	.285	.280	9.59	2.51
Hardin, Brandon	R-R	6-0	200	2-17-90	1	0	0.71	7	0	0	0	13	12	2	1	0	2	8	.245	.263	.233	5.68	1.42
Isler, Zach	R-R	6-5	230	10-31-90	5	4	5.65	27	0	0	4	51	62	39	32	4	20	41	.301	.277	.312	7.24	3.53
Jaye, Myles	B-R	6-3	170	12-28-91	4	1	2.20	7	7	0	0	41	36	17	10	2	17	37	.238	.213	.256	8.12	3.73
Kibby, Todd	L-L	6-4	265	8-31-91	2	0	5.11	15	0	0	0	25	21	17	14	1	15	24	.226	.156	.262	8.76	5.47
Leyer, Euclides	R-R	6-2	172	12-28-92	5	13	5.64	28	20	0	1	113	125	76	71	12	46	81	.276	.258	.285	6.43	3.65
Lopez, Adam	R-R	6-5	195	2-21-90	5	3	2.54	32	7	0	3	99	84	39	28	3	35	129	.223	.227	.222	11.69	3.17
McMillen, Kyle	L-R	6-2	200	3-14-90	0	0	16.20	3	0	0	0	2	1	3	3	0	6	1	.167	.333	.000	5.40	32.40
Montas, Francellis	R-R	6-2	185	3-21-93	3	2	4.56	5	5	0	0	26	20	13	13	1	18	31	.215	.190	.235	10.87	6.31
2-team total (19 Greenville)					5	11	5.43	24	23	1	0	111	114	75	67	11	50	127	—	—	—	10.30	4.05
Olacio, Jefferson	L-L	6-7	270	1-16-94	6	11	4.54	26	25	3	0	137	136	88	69	6	57	89	.256	.183	.273	5.86	3.75
Ortiz, Braulio	R-R	6-5	205	12-20-91	0	4	3.45	22	8	0	3	63	43	30	24	3	39	74	.196	.159	.212	10.63	5.60
Powers, Alex	R-R	6-4	180	2-26-92	0	0	7.56	8	0	0	0	8	9	8	7	2	4	9	.265	.167	.318	9.72	4.32
Putman, David	R-R	6-1	205	2-28-90	0	0	0.00	5	0	0	2	9	3	0	0	0	4	14	.103	.143	.067	13.50	3.86
Recchia, Mike	R-R	6-1	210	4-2-89	5	0	1.45	11	8	0	1	50	36	10	8	1	7	53	.199	.302	.156	9.60	1.27
Throne, Storm	R-R	6-7	215	9-3-90	1	4	6.26	28	0	0	1	42	53	35	29	4	18	40	.303	.333	.291	8.64	3.89
Van Skike, Jason	R-R	6-4	195	4-10-89	0	0	4.50	1	0	0	0	2	2	1	1	0	0	4	.250	.000	1.000	18.00	0.00
Wendelken, J.B.	R-R	6-0	190	3-24-93	0	1	9.64	3	0	0	2	5	8	5	5	0	1	8	.400	.111	.636	15.43	1.93
2-team total (27 Greenville)					2	1	3.23	30	0	0	12	70	67	25	25	4	21	62	—	—	—	8.01	2.71
Wheeler, Andre	L-L	6-1	170	9-27-91	1	0	4.08	9	0	0	3	18	14	9	8	3	5	18	.212	.208	.214	9.17	2.55

Fielding

Catcher	PCT	G	PO	A	E	DP	PB
Dowdy	.996	29	246	32	1	3	7
Fisher	.980	17	137	12	3	0	6
Marjama	.989	71	572	59	7	6	13
Rosario	.983	7	53	4	1	1	2
Tanner	.975	19	134	20	4	3	9

First Base	PCT	G	PO	A	E	DP
Barnum	.978	54	418	28	10	22
Johnson	1.000	8	65	1	0	4
Marjama	.990	9	86	10	1	8
Palmeiro	.974	19	134	13	4	9
Ravelo	1.000	17	145	12	0	12
Robinson	.980	12	95	2	2	5
Rosario	1.000	1	1	0	0	0
Tanner	.981	24	199	13	4	19

Second Base	PCT	G	PO	A	E	DP
Brown	1.000	4	3	6	0	1
Grabe	.970	26	33	65	3	7
Jirschele	1.000	3	4	3	0	1
Johnson	.940	73	121	206	21	35
Johnson	.981	13	22	29	1	5
Rondon	.983	24	44	73	2	13

Third Base	PCT	G	PO	A	E	DP
Basto	.868	54	19	80	15	6
Grabe	.897	34	17	61	9	4
Jirschele	1.000	4	5	12	0	0
Johnson	.927	16	6	32	3	2
Palmeiro	.891	20	10	31	5	1
Williams	.791	14	9	25	9	3

Shortstop	PCT	G	PO	A	E	DP
Almanzar	.930	37	42	105	11	21
Anderson	.934	63	97	174	19	23

	PCT	G	PO	A	E	DP
Brown	.893	12	12	38	6	5
Johnson	.886	21	24	54	10	10
Rondon	1.000	6	6	15	0	2

Outfield	PCT	G	PO	A	E	DP
Barroso	.946	23	34	1	2	0
Coats	.980	118	187	7	4	1
Grabe	1.000	2	2	0	0	0
Heisler	.976	29	40	0	1	0
Jirschele	1.000	7	11	1	0	0
Johnson	.750	6	6	0	2	0
Kiser	.990	111	192	4	2	2
Llanos	.947	9	17	1	1	0
May	.989	50	82	4	1	0
Ramirez	.930	30	65	1	5	0
Richmond	1.000	14	41	1	0	0
Robinson	1.000	3	3	0	0	0
Sierra Jr.	.923	17	23	1	2	1

BRISTOL SOX   ROOKIE

APPALACHIAN LEAGUE

Batting	B-T	HT	WT	DOB	AVG	vLH	vRH	G	AB	R	H	2B	3B	HR	RBI	BB	HBP	SH	SF	SO	SB	CS	SLG	OBP
Ayala, Sammy	L-R	6-2	195	7-12-94	.210	.269	.190	33	105	9	22	3	0	1	7	9	1	1	0	33	0	0	.267	.278
Brown, Jake	L-R	5-11	185	2-15-90	.188	.154	.194	24	80	17	15	3	0	0	7	9	1	4	0	21	9	1	.225	.278
Earley, Nolan	L-L	6-0	205	3-27-91	.310	.342	.303	61	203	23	63	13	2	2	31	32	5	0	4	26	2	8	.424	.410
Glasser, Mitch	R-R	5-10	180	10-15-89	.091	.000	.100	3	11	0	1	1	0	0	0	1	0	0	0	2	0	0	.182	.167
Haddow, Mark	R-R	6-2	220	12-2-87	.391	.400	.389	8	23	4	9	4	0	0	4	3	1	0	1	3	0	0	.565	.464
Hall, Thurman	R-R	6-0	190	2-12-93	.243	.182	.259	58	214	33	52	6	1	0	10	22	10	1	1	60	11	4	.280	.340
Macias, Sam	R-R	6-0	195	12-9-91	.143	.000	.222	16	42	8	6	1	0	0	3	4	0	0	0	23	1	0	.167	.265
Michalczewski, Trey	B-R	6-3	210	2-27-95	.236	.180	.255	56	195	25	46	5	2	3	21	23	3	0	1	56	2	0	.328	.324
Palmeiro, Patrick	R-R	6-3	210	3-6-90	.228	.178	.242	54	202	28	46	14	1	5	27	15	1	0	3	59	0	1	.381	.281
Parent, Nick	R-R	6-3	235	7-30-90	.114	.000	.138	23	70	2	8	0	0	0	5	10	2	0	0	33	0	0	.114	.244
Rodriguez, Antonio	R-R	6-0	180	5-7-95	.120	.000	.136	7	25	1	3	1	0	0	2	1	0	0	0	9	0	0	.160	.154
Rosario, Angel	R-R	5-10	175	12-14-91	.255	.182	.275	17	51	5	13	2	0	1	3	5	1	1	1	16	0	0	.353	.328
Santana, Audry	R-R	5-11	170	2-22-92	.147	.250	.133	11	34	3	5	0	0	0	4	6	0	0	1	7	0	0	.147	.268
Santos, Jeffy	B-R	6-2	150	1-4-93	.152	.059	.171	30	99	8	15	2	2	1	8	5	1	1	0	41	2	2	.242	.200
Stoner, Zach	L-R	6-3	200	12-16-93	.236	.231	.237	33	106	11	25	3	0	2	8	14	2	1	0	39	0	0	.321	.336
Thomas, Toby	R-R	5-11	190	12-2-94	.319	.315	.321	51	210	31	67	10	4	4	30	4	0	0	2	33	2	4	.462	.329
Thomore, Carl	R-R	6-2	212	1-13-93	.207	.194	.211	52	169	13	35	8	1	0	19	29	0	1	2	60	7	2	.266	.320
Velasquez, Victor	B-R	5-11	195	2-5-95	.219	.200	.225	33	105	12	23	4	1	0	7	11	3	5	1	26	3	1	.276	.308
Yount, Cody	L-R	6-1	200	8-19-89	.195	.200	.194	30	82	5	16	1	0	0	6	19	0	1	2	17	0	2	.207	.340

Pitching	B-T	HT	WT	DOB	W	L	ERA	G	GS	CG	SV	IP	H	R	ER	HR	BB	SO	AVG	vLH	vRH	K/9	BB/9
Ball, Matt	R-R	6-5	197	3-25-95	0	1	4.84	14	0	0	0	22	25	18	12	1	8	23	.272	.269	.273	9.27	3.22
Barnette, Tyler	R-R	6-3	190	5-28-92	1	4	5.73	13	6	0	1	33	36	21	21	1	10	19	.286	.231	.310	5.18	2.73
Bengard, Jon	R-R	6-4	185	1-7-91	1	1	4.43	17	0	0	1	22	21	12	11	0	9	22	.250	.292	.233	8.87	3.63
Bowen, Drew	L-R	6-3	215	6-20-89	0	2	6.08	9	6	0	0	24	29	18	16	2	10	15	.302	.205	.368	5.70	3.80
Bowling, Cal	R-R	6-2	195	10-22-89	1	2	6.61	10	0	0	1	16	25	13	12	1	5	21	.342	.333	.347	11.57	2.76
Boydston, Adam	R-L	6-1	190	10-20-88	3	2	4.41	10	0	0	0	16	18	10	8	0	4	14	.295	.333	.286	7.71	2.20
Bucciferro, Tony	R-R	6-3	205	12-27-89	1	1	2.41	3	0	0	0	19	18	8	5	1	1	25	.250	.208	.271	12.05	0.48
Carroll, Scott	R-R	6-4	215	9-24-84	0	0	1.69	5	5	0	0	16	17	4	3	0	4	15	.262	.333	.211	8.44	2.25

Name	B-T	HT	WT	DOB	W	L	ERA	G	GS	CG	SV	IP	H	R	ER	HR	BB	SO	AVG	vLH	vRH	K/9	BB/9
Danish, Tyler	R-R	6-2	190	9-12-94	1	0	1.38	13	1	0	0	26	15	6	4	1	5	22	.165	.143	.179	7.62	1.73
Evans, Steven	L-L	6-4	210	8-9-89	0	0	3.00	2	0	0	0	3	1	1	1	0	1	1	.111	.000	.125	3.00	3.00
Freudenberg, Chris	L-L	6-3	195	6-19-93	1	3	5.40	9	6	0	0	28	35	23	17	3	10	27	.297	.294	.297	8.58	3.18
Gray, Jeff	R-R	6-2	210	11-19-81	0	0	10.80	3	0	0	0	3	6	4	4	0	1	3	.429	1.000	.333	8.10	2.70
Guerrero, Jordan	L-L	6-3	165	5-31-94	0	3	4.26	5	5	0	0	25	31	15	12	4	5	15	.304	.100	.354	5.33	1.78
Leyer, Robin	R-R	6-2	175	3-13-93	2	7	6.35	13	13	0	0	57	74	45	40	5	30	38	.327	.355	.317	6.04	4.76
Lowry, Thaddius	R-R	6-4	215	10-4-94	3	5	5.48	15	7	0	0	44	55	29	27	2	22	30	.313	.263	.336	6.09	4.47
Mabee, Henry	R-R	6-4	230	7-10-85	1	0	4.50	4	0	0	0	6	4	3	3	1	6	4	.211	.375	.091	6.00	9.00
Marinez, Jhan	R-R	6-1	200	8-12-88	0	0	6.75	2	0	0	0	3	2	2	2	0	2	7	.182	.000	.182	23.63	6.75
McGinnis, Cory	L-R	6-0	180	12-24-89	0	0	3.38	3	0	0	0	3	3	1	1	1	1	2	.250	.250	.250	6.75	3.38
McMillen, Kyle	L-R	6-2	200	3-14-90	1	1	7.36	14	0	0	0	15	12	14	12	0	17	10	.222	.235	.216	6.14	10.43
Molina, Nestor	R-R	6-1	220	1-9-89	0	0	0.00	2	1	0	0	3	0	0	0	0	0	2	.000	.000	.000	6.00	0.00
Monroe, Grant	R-R	6-4	220	9-29-88	0	0	0.00	3	0	0	0	4	1	0	0	0	1	4	.077	.000	.100	4.15	2.08
Moore, Devin	R-R	6-3	210	4-1-91	1	1	7.40	18	0	0	1	21	27	18	17	4	10	19	.314	.333	.305	8.27	4.35
Patterson, Jamie	R-R	6-4	165	12-7-93	0	0	7.04	9	0	0	0	8	17	10	6	1	2	7	.486	.636	.417	8.22	2.35
Peralta, Yelmison	R-R	6-0	190	3-3-95	0	3	7.88	10	0	0	0	16	19	17	14	4	13	8	.311	.200	.348	4.50	7.31
Powers, Alex	R-R	6-4	180	2-26-92	1	1	2.79	6	0	0	3	10	8	5	3	0	4	13	.250	.375	.100	12.10	3.72
Sharrer, Charlie	R-R	6-1	205	6-27-91	0	1	4.98	15	1	0	2	22	23	13	12	2	12	23	.264	.241	.276	9.55	4.98
Valerio, Kelvis	R-R	6-1	160	9-26-91	2	6	3.88	12	11	1	0	63	58	32	27	7	18	50	.246	.284	.226	7.18	2.59
Wheeler, Andre	L-L	6-1	170	9-27-91	0	1	2.03	9	0	0	2	13	5	3	3	1	4	20	.111	.143	.105	13.50	2.70

Fielding

Catcher	PCT	G	PO	A	E	DP	PB
Ayala	1.000	26	192	25	0	1	15
Parent	1.000	2	3	0	0	0	0
Rosario	1.000	16	88	7	0	1	5
Stoner	.979	26	179	12	4	3	11

First Base	PCT	G	PO	A	E	DP
Palmeiro	.985	31	247	18	4	22
Parent	1.000	10	58	4	0	5
Yount	.983	28	224	14	4	18

Second Base	PCT	G	PO	A	E	DP
Brown	.971	8	15	18	1	1
Glasser	1.000	2	2	1	0	0

	PCT	G	PO	A	E	DP
Santana	.842	7	8	8	3	1
Santos	.943	13	17	33	3	8
Thomas	.983	10	20	39	1	9
Velasquez	.974	26	48	64	3	18

Third Base	PCT	G	PO	A	E	DP
Glasser	1.000	1	0	1	0	1
Michalczewski	.915	49	27	81	10	7
Palmeiro	.921	13	9	26	3	4
Thomas	1.000	4	1	8	0	2

Shortstop	PCT	G	PO	A	E	DP
Brown	.956	11	14	29	2	5
Santos	.863	17	22	41	10	6

	PCT	G	PO	A	E	DP
Thomas	.942	31	47	98	9	13
Velasquez	.925	7	10	27	3	2

Outfield	PCT	G	PO	A	E	DP
Earley	.977	56	81	3	2	1
Haddow	1.000	6	10	1	0	0
Hall	.963	58	125	4	5	0
Macias	.969	14	28	3	1	0
Palmeiro	.750	5	3	0	1	0
Rodriguez	1.000	7	15	1	0	0
Thomore	.972	50	99	4	3	1

GREAT FALLS VOYAGERS · ROOKIE

PIONEER LEAGUE

Batting	B-T	HT	WT	DOB	AVG	vLH	vRH	G	AB	R	H	2B	3B	HR	RBI	BB	HBP	SH	SF	SO	SB	CS	SLG	OBP
Basto, Nick	R-R	6-1	180	4-1-94	.309	.000	.340	13	55	3	17	0	2	1	11	0	0	0	1	17	0	0	.436	.304
Carballo, Michael	R-R	5-11	188	10-21-91	.127	.222	.109	18	55	5	7	1	0	0	3	1	1	0	0	37	2	0	.145	.158
Engel, Adam	R-R	6-1	215	12-9-91	.301	.352	.286	56	239	44	72	12	3	3	30	21	10	2	2	34	31	8	.414	.379
Fields, Arby	B-R	5-9	195	6-25-91	.167	.000	.200	6	12	5	2	0	0	0	1	6	0	0	0	3	0	0	.167	.444
Fisher, Zac	L-R	6-2	195	12-13-91	.302	.333	.292	42	162	25	49	12	1	6	32	14	3	0	3	24	1	0	.500	.363
Haupt, Dillon	R-R	6-5	225	10-8-91	.284	.118	.324	25	88	12	25	5	0	1	13	7	3	0	0	16	1	0	.375	.357
Hayes, Danny	L-R	6-4	210	9-21-90	.267	.255	.271	58	232	39	62	19	2	5	51	34	0	2	5	51	0	1	.431	.354
Jirschele, Justin	L-R	5-11	195	4-15-90	.304	.255	.317	65	240	33	73	9	1	0	27	18	4	1	2	21	2	1	.350	.360
Kelly, Jairo	B-R	6-0	170	9-20-92	.198	.273	.179	29	106	19	21	7	1	3	18	13	1	0	1	35	2	0	.368	.289
May, Jacob	B-R	5-10	180	1-23-92	.378	.250	.405	12	45	5	17	1	1	0	7	7	2	1	0	6	5	1	.444	.481
Morris, Jacob	R-R	6-3	195	12-19-90	.246	.170	.266	64	224	59	55	12	2	12	33	51	4	1	0	97	7	1	.478	.394
Opel, Dane	L-L	6-2	195	5-22-91	.256	.400	.224	26	82	13	21	6	2	0	11	15	0	1	0	22	1	2	.378	.371
Ruiz, Abe	L-R	6-4	210	3-29-90	.059	.500	.000	4	17	2	1	0	0	0	0	0	0	0	0	9	0	0	.059	.059
Shryock, Tyler	L-R	6-0	170	3-28-91	.286	.296	.284	60	255	42	73	8	4	0	37	25	3	3	2	27	15	4	.349	.354
Stringer, Christian	L-R	5-11	185	6-25-90	.312	.258	.325	47	154	42	48	7	3	1	22	22	7	3	3	12	4	0	.416	.414
Thompson, Corey	R-R	6-3	210	1-30-90	.310	.326	.306	56	226	31	70	13	4	4	40	9	1	0	3	56	0	0	.456	.335
Voight, Zach	R-R	6-0	185	8-26-90	.320	.306	.324	60	225	42	72	21	0	6	41	34	5	1	2	41	2	0	.493	.417
Williams, Alex	L-R	6-6	255	10-1-89	.278	—	.278	4	18	1	5	2	0	0	4	1	0	0	0	1	0	0	.389	.316
Williams, Tyler	R-R	6-2	200	1-5-91	.207	.333	.192	24	82	11	17	4	0	1	7	11	0	0	0	41	0	1	.293	.301
Wimmer, Trey	R-R	6-3	225	5-21-90	.266	.375	.244	37	143	24	38	12	1	6	23	10	2	0	1	25	0	1	.490	.321

Pitching	B-T	HT	WT	DOB	W	L	ERA	G	GS	CG	SV	IP	H	R	ER	HR	BB	SO	AVG	vLH	vRH	K/9	BB/9
Abramson, Matt	R-R	6-2	185	3-22-90	1	1	4.22	18	0	0	2	32	33	19	15	1	13	29	.264	.298	.244	8.16	3.66
Bautista, Jose	L-L	6-1	175	3-31-92	4	2	4.10	16	7	0	0	48	49	31	22	2	23	42	.257	.172	.272	7.82	4.28
Blount, Nick	R-R	6-6	225	9-1-90	4	4	3.18	16	9	0	2	51	55	25	18	1	17	41	.279	.306	.267	7.24	3.00
Brito, Jose	R-R	6-0	175	10-10-92	2	3	5.96	16	8	0	0	48	54	33	32	5	27	31	.289	.250	.309	5.77	5.03
Dykstra, James	R-R	6-4	195	11-22-90	0	0	5.06	6	0	0	0	5	10	4	3	0	5	2	.417	.273	.538	3.38	8.44
Goldberg, Brad	R-R	6-4	228	2-21-90	0	0	0.00	2	0	0	0	4	2	0	0	0	0	7	.133	.000	.167	15.75	0.00
Hagan, Sean	L-L	6-6	215	3-5-91	1	2	6.19	17	0	0	3	32	41	30	22	1	16	20	.318	.296	.324	5.63	4.50
Haselden, David	R-R	6-3	230	10-31-89	6	5	4.14	15	15	0	0	83	91	51	38	2	13	50	.283	.215	.325	5.44	1.42
Hudelson, James	R-R	6-4	215	5-16-90	4	1	4.50	17	2	0	2	46	46	26	23	8	27	45	.254	.308	.233	8.80	5.28
Jaffe, Eric	R-R	6-3	220	6-16-91	1	1	9.89	18	0	0	3	24	32	27	26	1	23	27	.333	.308	.343	10.27	8.75
Kibby, Todd	L-L	6-4	265	8-31-91	7	2	4.39	16	7	0	1	55	55	36	27	2	26	39	.267	.316	.248	6.34	4.23
McKenzie, Jeff	L-L	6-0	170	5-15-91	4	0	1.44	16	0	0	6	25	13	4	4	0	6	23	.160	.000	.203	8.28	2.16
Mitchell, Andrew	R-R	6-3	205	11-9-91	1	3	4.50	14	14	1	0	56	57	34	28	6	30	47	.273	.316	.257	7.55	4.82

					W	L	ERA	G	GS	CG	SV	IP	H	R	ER	HR	BB	SO	AVG	vLH	vRH	K/9	BB/9
Putman, David	R-R	6-1	205	2-28-90	2	1	1.08	13	0	0	3	25	16	6	3	0	17	37	.176	.132	.208	13.32	6.12
Sanchez, Jake	R-R	6-1	205	8-19-89	6	3	2.87	14	14	0	0	82	71	35	26	7	14	76	.230	.239	.224	8.38	1.54
Santiago, Anthony	R-R	5-11	200	9-22-89	3	0	1.59	18	0	0	3	34	19	6	6	1	17	27	.168	.103	.203	7.15	4.50
Wagman, Joey	L-R	6-0	185	7-25-91	1	0	3.57	16	0	0	2	23	23	9	9	0	7	28	.253	.273	.246	11.12	2.78

Fielding

Catcher	PCT	G	PO	A	E	DP	PB
Fisher	.991	27	190	26	2	3	2
Haupt	.994	20	147	14	1	2	3
Wimmer	.989	31	236	34	3	4	3

First Base	PCT	G	PO	A	E	DP
Hayes	.995	52	504	44	3	36
Ruiz	1.000	4	38	3	0	1
Thompson	.980	17	137	9	3	14
Williams	.909	3	29	1	3	0

Second Base	PCT	G	PO	A	E	DP
Jirschele	1.000	22	33	62	0	15
Kelly	1.000	7	6	14	0	1

	PCT	G	PO	A	E	DP
Stringer	.957	47	89	158	11	26
Voight	.909	2	5	5	1	0

Third Base	PCT	G	PO	A	E	DP
Basto	.889	10	6	26	4	1
Jirschele	.889	3	4	4	1	0
Kelly	1.000	7	1	16	0	2
Thompson	1.000	1	0	1	0	0
Voight	.933	54	36	104	10	12
Williams	.750	3	0	9	3	1

Shortstop	PCT	G	PO	A	E	DP
Jirschele	1.000	1	1	5	0	0
Kelly	.884	14	24	37	8	8

	PCT	G	PO	A	E	DP
Shryock	.953	59	73	173	12	25
Voight	.923	2	2	10	1	2

Outfield	PCT	G	PO	A	E	DP
Carballo	.929	15	13	0	1	0
Engel	.986	56	133	9	2	2
Fields	.800	5	4	0	1	0
Jirschele	.964	39	49	5	2	0
May	1.000	12	26	1	0	0
Morris	.956	64	125	6	6	2
Opel	.980	26	46	2	1	0
Thompson	1.000	17	25	1	0	0

DSL WHITE SOX   ROOKIE

DOMINICAN SUMMER LEAGUE

Batting	B-T	HT	WT	DOB	AVG	vLH	vRH	G	AB	R	H	2B	3B	HR	RBI	BB	HBP	SH	SF	SO	SB	CS	SLG	OBP
Ariza, Jose	R-R	6-2	183	12-23-93	.203	.143	.215	27	79	10	16	3	0	2	10	17	1	2	0	14	0	0	.316	.351
Cruz, Johan	R-R	6-2	170	10-8-95	.123	.136	.120	67	244	29	30	7	1	0	7	25	4	4	0	57	18	7	.160	.216
De Jesus, Jhan	R-R	6-2	165	1-30-92	.234	.121	.261	56	167	22	39	6	1	0	19	17	5	0	2	52	0	3	.281	.319
Del Rosario, Robert	R-R	5-11	185	7-25-92	.294	.381	.270	57	194	40	57	10	1	0	25	15	4	1	3	36	14	4	.356	.352
Garcia, Joxelier	R-R	5-10	185	4-30-94	.254	.158	.276	63	201	25	51	13	0	3	25	21	9	9	3	30	1	3	.363	.346
Gonzalez, Carlos	R-R	6-1	175	8-30-93	.190	.125	.200	19	63	3	12	2	0	0	8	5	0	0	1	11	1	2	.222	.246
Gonzalez, Daniel	R-R	6-1	190	12-6-95	.236	.345	.209	46	144	16	34	4	2	0	11	22	5	3	0	15	6	4	.292	.357
Mejia, Carlos	R-R	6-3	90	9-27-95	.190	.158	.196	33	116	4	22	5	0	1	8	4	2	0	0	37	1	1	.259	.230
Otano, Hanleth	R-R	6-3	195	7-16-96	.185	.195	.182	61	222	23	41	9	3	2	26	17	2	0	1	85	2	1	.279	.248
Pizzoli, Franco	R-R	5-9	170	2-1-94	.321	.278	.333	44	159	20	51	7	1	1	23	8	5	1	2	19	0	1	.396	.368
Polanco, Luis	R-R	6-3	190	9-30-91	.217	.250	.208	50	161	26	35	10	2	3	14	10	4	7	2	18	5	1	.360	.277
Ramos, Roger	R-R	6-2	174	10-9-94	.248	.091	.284	39	117	21	29	7	0	2	17	19	6	3	2	46	9	7	.359	.375
Rodriguez, Antonio	R-R	6-0	180	5-7-95	.288	.257	.298	40	156	17	45	8	1	0	18	5	1	2	0	40	4	4	.333	.315
Santana, Vladimir	R-R	6-0	165	1-24-91	.163	.231	.133	12	43	9	7	2	0	1	3	8	1	1	0	9	8	1	.279	.308
Valdez, Robertson	R-R	6-0	204	10-6-92	.238	.296	.221	37	122	19	29	6	0	1	17	10	2	5	3	20	1	2	.311	.299

Pitching	B-T	HT	WT	DOB	W	L	ERA	G	GS	CG	SV	IP	H	R	ER	HR	BB	SO	AVG	vLH	vRH	K/9	BB/9
Arias, Feny	L-L	6-0	175	5-6-91	3	3	4.02	16	10	0	0	63	71	31	28	1	22	55	.289	.375	.268	7.90	3.16
Arteaga, Luis	R-R	6-1	185	10-19-94	1	4	6.75	11	9	0	0	31	34	28	23	1	19	21	.274	.326	.247	6.16	5.58
De La Cruz, Leonardo	L-L	6-4	180	4-29-94	0	1	5.63	11	1	0	0	16	15	14	10	0	10	19	.254	.167	.264	10.69	5.63
Delgado, Johansel	R-R	6-0	175	12-3-90	5	1	0.63	28	0	0	9	43	26	4	3	1	18	64	.170	.060	.223	13.40	3.77
Diaz, Carlos	L-L	6-0	186	1-1-94	1	4	3.54	14	10	0	0	41	32	21	16	1	17	47	.213	.154	.226	10.40	3.76
Diaz, Evandert	R-R	6-3	190	5-20-92	4	4	2.50	20	1	0	2	54	44	21	15	0	23	36	.233	.308	.194	6.00	3.83
Done, Victor	R-R	6-3	195	9-3-95	0	7	6.23	12	12	0	0	30	34	30	21	1	28	26	.279	.386	.218	7.71	8.31
Escorcia, Kevin	L-L	6-1	170	1-5-95	6	0	1.87	16	4	0	0	43	26	11	9	0	18	36	.183	.154	.190	7.48	3.74
Espinosa, Ramon	R-R	6-2	185	11-30-93	0	3	7.22	12	4	0	0	29	36	28	23	1	23	22	.313	.367	.294	6.91	7.22
Garcia, Jose	L-L	5-11	185	4-20-91	0	1	1.42	11	0	0	1	19	13	8	3	0	11	22	.188	.000	.213	10.42	5.21
Ledo, Luis	R-R	6-4	208	5-28-95	1	2	2.82	8	6	0	0	22	17	9	7	0	10	19	.218	.103	.286	7.66	4.03
Percel, Eriberto	R-R	6-5	200	8-2-92	1	0	3.48	13	1	0	0	34	36	23	13	1	15	16	.279	.359	.244	4.28	4.01
Quijada, Jhoan	L-L	6-3	210	12-27-94	2	2	3.99	14	9	0	0	47	38	25	21	4	22	41	.228	.136	.241	7.80	4.18
Rocha, Jaider	R-R	6-1	185	5-23-93	3	2	3.06	19	2	0	0	35	35	24	12	0	24	34	.254	.269	.244	8.66	6.11
Rodriguez, Pedro	R-R	6-0	170	4-12-91	0	0	6.75	3	0	0	0	4	12	7	3	0	0	2	.500	.167	.611	4.50	0.00
Rodriguez, Wilmy	R-R	6-4	225	11-8-90	3	1	2.90	21	0	0	0	50	36	20	16	0	33	38	.208	.315	.160	6.89	5.98
Vargas, Ivan	R-R	6-3	190	8-14-91	0	2	7.79	8	0	0	0	17	29	23	15	0	7	6	.363	.367	.360	3.12	3.63

Fielding

Catcher	PCT	G	PO	A	E	DP	PB
Ariza	.933	4	22	6	2	0	4
Garcia	1.000	15	95	15	0	0	2
Gonzalez	.974	28	197	26	6	1	11
Pizzoli	.966	28	206	49	9	2	5

First Base	PCT	G	PO	A	E	DP
Ariza	.987	21	145	9	2	8
De Jesus	.950	3	18	1	1	1
Del Rosario	.964	6	49	5	2	3
Gonzalez	.976	5	38	2	1	7
Pizzoli	.991	15	104	10	1	7
Polanco	.990	25	201	6	2	12
Ramos	—	1	0	0	0	0
Rocha	1.000	2	3	0	0	0
Valdez	1.000	2	13	1	0	0

Second Base	PCT	G	PO	A	E	DP
De Jesus	.923	20	30	42	6	6
Gonzalez	.935	19	40	46	6	9
Santana	.833	1	2	3	1	0
Valdez	.971	31	62	74	4	10

Third Base	PCT	G	PO	A	E	DP
De Jesus	—	1	0	0	0	0
Garcia	.947	48	53	108	9	7
Pizzoli	.500	2	0	1	1	0
Polanco	.890	22	18	47	8	2
Valdez	.667	1	0	2	1	0

Shortstop	PCT	G	PO	A	E	DP
Cruz	.925	66	134	173	25	25
Polanco	1.000	2	3	3	0	1
Santana	1.000	1	2	4	0	0

Valdez	1.000	3	6	6	0	0

Outfield	PCT	G	PO	A	E	DP
Ariza	—	1	0	0	0	0
De Jesus	.904	30	39	8	5	2
Del Rosario	.901	41	62	2	7	1
Mejia	.882	20	13	2	2	0
Otano	.944	40	49	2	3	0
Polanco	1.000	3	3	0	0	0
Quijada	—	1	0	0	0	0
Ramos	.951	31	39	0	2	0
Rocha	1.000	1	1	0	0	0
Rodriguez	1.000	40	83	3	0	2
Santana	.944	10	16	1	1	0

CHICAGO WHITE SOX

Cincinnati Reds

SEASON IN A SENTENCE: The Reds have gotten accustomed to playing in the playoffs again, but a 90-win season ended with a bitter aftertaste. The Reds were swept by the Pirates in a season-ending series to determine home-field advantage for the wild-card game, then looked sluggish in a 6-2 playoff loss to the Pirates.

HIGH POINT: On Sept. 8, Jay Bruce homered twice and Homer Bailey matched Clayton Kershaw pitch for pitch as the Reds finished off a sweep of a three-game series against the Dodgers. Coming on the heels of beating the Cardinals three games out of four in Cincinnati, the win moved the Reds to within 1.5 games of first place in the Central Division, the first time they'd been that close since late May.

LOW POINT: The Reds would have been better off lobbying for a return to the 154-game schedule. Cincinnati lost its last five regular season games, with back-to-back losses against the hapless Mets preceding a sweep at the hands of the Pirates.

NOTABLE ROOKIES: When Reds ace Johnny Cueto went on the disabled list multiple times with a lat injury, lefthander Tony Cingrani stepped in and provided 105 excellent innings (7-4, 2.92). Righthander J.J. Hoover overcame a rough start to become the club's set-up man (5-5, 2.86, 3 saves). Center fielder Billy Hamilton didn't join the club until Sept. 1, but he stole 13 bases in 13 games to provide an immediate spark.

KEY TRANSACTIONS: An offseason trade brought outfielder Shin-Soo Choo to Cincinnati in a complicated nine-player, three-team deal in which the Reds sent shortstop Didi Gregorius to the Diamondbacks and center fielder Drew Stubbs to the Indians. The Reds' gambled by moving the defensively limited Choo to center field. He responded by hitting .283/.423/.462 as a nearly ideal leadoff hitter.

DOWN ON THE FARM: No Reds domestic minor league affiliate finished with a winning record, and the club finished with the worst overall minor league record among all 30 organizations. After setting the minor league stolen base record in 2012, Hamilton made a successful adjustment to center field in a full season at Triple-A Louisville, but he was limited to 75 steals thanks in large part to his .256/.308/.346 batting line. Righthander Robert Stephenson jumped from low Class A to Double-A during an excellent 7-7, 2.99 season.

OPENING DAY PAYROLL: $107.5 million (13th).

ORGANIZATION LEADERS

BATTING   *Minimum 250 AB

MAJORS

*	AVG	Votto, Joey	.305
*	OPS	Votto, Joey	.926
	HR	Bruce, Jay	30
	RBI	Bruce, Jay	109

MINORS

*	AVG	Mejias-Brean, Seth, Bakersfield/Dayton	.305
*	OBP	Silva, Juan, Bakersfield	.386
*	SLG	Hessman, Mike, Louisville	.495
	R	Arias, Junior, Bakersfield/Dayton	75
		Hamilton, Billy, Louisville	75
	H	Mejias-Brean, Seth, Bakersfield/Dayton	150
	TB	Silverio, Juan, Pensacola/Bakersfield	243
	2B	Mejias-Brean, Seth, Bakersfield/Dayton	36
	3B	Siri, Jose, DSL Reds	9
	HR	Hessman, Mike, Louisville	25
	RBI	Mejias-Brean, Seth, Bakersfield/Dayton	82
	BB	Winker, Jesse, Dayton	63
	SO	Rodriguez, Yorman, Pensacola/Bakersfield	153
	SB	Hamilton, Billy, Louisville	75

PITCHING   #Minimum 75 IP

MAJORS

	W	Three tied at	14
#	ERA	Latos, Mat	3.16
	SO	Bailey, Homer	199
	SV	Chapman, Aroldis	38

MINORS

	W	Reynolds, Greg, Louisville	12
	L	Moscot, Jon, Pensacola/Bakersfield	15
#	ERA	Reynolds, Greg, Louisville	2.42
	G	Hyde, Lee, Louisville/Pensacola	55
	GS	Three tied at	28
	SV	Bell, Trevor, Louisville/Pensacola	17
	IP	Smith, Josh, Pensacola	160
	BB	Guillon, Ismael, Dayton	95
	SO	Moscot, Jon, Pensacola/Bakersfield	140
#	AVG	Stephenson, Robert, Dayton/Bake./Pens.	.217

2013 PERFORMANCE

General Manager: Walt Jocketty. **Farm Director:** Jeff Graupe. **Scouting Director:** Chris Buckley.

Class	Team	League	W	L	PCT	Finish	Manager
Majors	Cincinnati Reds	National	90	72	.556	5th (15)	Dusty Baker
Triple-A	Louisville Bats	International	69	75	.479	9th (14)	Jim Riggleman
Double-A	Pensacola Blue Wahoos	Southern	59	79	.428	t-8th (10)	Delino Deshields
High A	Bakersfield Blaze	California	55	85	.392	10th (10)	Ken Griffey
Low A	Dayton Dragons	Midwest	65	74	.468	11th (16)	Jose Nieves
Rookie	Billings Mustangs	Pioneer	28	46	.378	8th (8)	Pat Kelly
Rookie	AZL Reds	Arizona	18	37	.327	13th (13)	Eli Marrero
Overall 2013 Minor League Record			294	396	.426	30th (30)	

ORGANIZATION STATISTICS

CINCINNATI REDS

NATIONAL LEAGUE

Batting	B-T	HT	WT	DOB	AVG	vLH	vRH	G	AB	R	H	2B	3B	HR	RBI	BB	HBP	SH	SF	SO	SB	CS	SLG	OBP
Bruce, Jay	L-L	6-3	215	4-3-87	.262	.246	.270	160	626	89	164	43	1	30	109	63	2	0	5	185	7	3	.478	.329
Choo, Shin-Soo	L-L	5-11	205	7-13-82	.285	.215	.317	154	569	107	162	34	2	21	54	112	26	3	2	133	20	11	.462	.423
Cozart, Zack	R-R	6-0	195	8-12-85	.254	.245	.257	151	567	74	144	30	3	12	63	26	2	13	10	102	0	0	.381	.284
Frazier, Todd	R-R	6-3	220	2-12-86	.234	.236	.233	150	531	63	124	29	3	19	73	50	14	2	3	125	6	5	.407	.314
Hamilton, Billy	B-R	6-0	160	9-9-90	.368	.000	.389	13	19	9	7	2	0	0	1	2	0	1	0	4	13	1	.474	.429
Hanigan, Ryan	R-R	6-0	210	8-16-80	.198	.222	.190	75	222	17	44	8	0	2	21	29	6	2	1	27	0	1	.261	.306
Hannahan, Jack	L-R	6-2	210	3-4-80	.216	.111	.223	83	139	12	30	5	1	1	14	19	2	0	1	38	0	0	.288	.317
Heisey, Chris	R-R	6-1	210	12-14-84	.237	.259	.223	87	224	29	53	11	1	9	23	9	5	4	2	51	3	0	.415	.279
Izturis, Cesar	B-R	5-9	180	2-10-80	.209	.257	.191	63	129	6	27	8	0	0	11	9	0	3	1	13	0	0	.271	.259
Ludwick, Ryan	R-L	6-2	215	7-13-78	.240	.269	.233	38	129	7	31	5	0	2	12	10	0	0	1	29	0	0	.326	.293
Lutz, Donald	L-R	6-3	250	2-6-89	.241	.267	.233	34	58	5	14	1	0	1	8	1	0	0	0	14	2	0	.310	.254
Mesoraco, Devin	R-R	6-1	230	6-19-88	.238	.321	.212	103	323	31	77	13	0	9	42	24	0	0	5	61	0	2	.362	.287
Miller, Corky	R-R	6-1	250	3-18-76	.257	.267	.250	17	35	2	9	5	0	0	8	5	1	0	0	6	0	0	.400	.366
Paul, Xavier	L-R	5-9	205	2-25-85	.244	.158	.253	97	209	24	51	12	0	7	32	27	3	0	0	53	0	1	.402	.339
Phillips, Brandon	R-R	6-0	200	6-28-81	.261	.254	.263	151	606	80	158	24	2	18	103	39	8	4	9	98	5	3	.396	.310
Robinson, Derrick	B-L	5-11	190	9-28-87	.255	.288	.232	102	192	21	49	7	3	0	8	18	1	5	0	44	4	5	.323	.322
Rodriguez, Henry	B-R	5-8	200	2-9-90	.111	—	.111	9	9	0	1	0	0	0	1	0	0	0	0	4	0	0	.111	.200
Soto, Neftali	R-R	6-1	215	2-28-89	.000	.000	.000	13	12	0	0	0	0	0	0	0	1	0	0	6	0	0	.000	.077
Votto, Joey	L-R	6-2	220	9-10-83	.305	.251	.332	162	581	101	177	30	3	24	73	135	4	0	6	138	6	3	.491	.435

Pitching	B-T	HT	WT	DOB	W	L	ERA	G	GS	CG	SV	IP	H	R	ER	HR	BB	SO	AVG	vLH	vRH	K/9	BB/9
Arroyo, Bronson	R-R	6-4	195	2-24-77	14	12	3.79	32	32	2	0	202	199	88	85	32	34	124	.258	.295	.219	5.52	1.51
Bailey, Homer	R-R	6-4	230	5-3-86	11	12	3.49	32	32	2	0	209	181	85	81	20	54	199	.234	.264	.205	8.57	2.33
Broxton, Jonathan	R-R	6-4	310	6-16-84	2	2	4.11	34	0	0	0	31	27	17	14	4	12	25	.237	.269	.210	7.34	3.52
Chapman, Aroldis	L-L	6-4	205	2-28-88	4	5	2.54	68	0	0	38	64	37	18	18	7	29	112	.164	.137	.172	15.83	4.10
Christiani, Nick	R-R	6-0	190	7-17-87	0	0	2.25	3	0	0	0	4	2	1	1	1	2	1	.167	.333	.111	2.25	4.50
Cingrani, Tony	L-L	6-4	215	7-5-89	7	4	2.92	23	18	0	0	105	72	37	34	14	43	120	.196	.186	.200	10.32	3.70
Cueto, Johnny	R-R	5-11	215	2-15-86	5	2	2.82	11	11	0	0	61	46	20	19	7	18	51	.209	.204	.213	7.57	2.67
Duke, Zach	L-L	6-2	210	4-19-83	0	1	0.84	14	0	0	0	11	8	1	1	1	2	7	.205	.150	.263	5.91	1.69
2-team total (12 Washington)					1	2	6.03	26	1	0	0	31	39	23	21	3	10	18	—	—	—	5.17	2.87
Freeman, Justin	R-R	5-11	175	10-22-86	0	0	18.00	1	0	0	0	1	2	2	2	1	0	0	.400	.333	.500	0.00	0.00
Hoover, J.J.	R-R	6-3	225	8-13-87	5	5	2.86	69	0	0	3	66	47	21	21	6	26	67	.200	.163	.224	9.14	3.55
Latos, Mat	R-R	6-6	245	12-9-87	14	7	3.16	32	32	1	0	211	197	82	74	16	58	187	.247	.247	.246	7.99	2.48
Leake, Mike	R-R	5-10	185	11-12-87	14	7	3.37	31	31	0	0	192	193	78	72	21	48	122	.263	.263	.263	5.71	2.25
LeCure, Sam	R-R	6-0	205	5-4-84	2	1	2.66	63	0	0	1	61	50	18	18	4	24	66	.222	.167	.264	9.74	3.54
Marshall, Sean	L-L	6-7	225	8-30-82	0	1	1.74	16	0	0	0	10	4	3	2	0	2	10	.118	.190	.000	8.71	1.74
Ondrusek, Logan	R-R	6-8	230	2-13-85	4	4	4.09	52	0	0	0	55	53	26	25	8	16	53	.250	.258	.244	8.67	2.62
Parra, Manny	L-L	6-3	205	10-30-82	2	3	3.33	57	0	0	0	46	40	18	17	5	15	56	.238	.167	.310	10.96	2.93
Partch, Curtis	R-R	6-5	240	2-13-87	0	1	6.17	14	0	0	0	23	17	16	16	8	17	16	.210	.161	.240	6.17	6.56
Reynolds, Greg	R-R	6-7	225	7-3-85	1	3	5.52	6	5	0	0	29	38	19	18	5	6	13	.322	.222	.406	3.99	1.84
Simon, Alfredo	R-R	6-6	265	5-8-81	6	4	2.87	63	0	0	1	88	68	31	28	8	26	63	.214	.225	.206	6.47	2.67
Villarreal, Pedro	R-R	6-1	230	12-9-87	0	1	12.71	2	1	0	0	6	13	8	8	4	3	4	.448	.333	.529	6.35	4.76

Fielding

Catcher	PCT	G	PO	A	E	DP	PB
Hanigan	.998	72	538	33	1	1	3
Mesoraco	.993	97	668	55	5	2	4
Miller	.991	16	103	6	1	1	1

First Base	PCT	G	PO	A	E	DP
Hannahan	1.000	10	30	0	0	6
Soto	1.000	5	14	0	0	2
Votto	.990	161	1245	154	14	115

Second Base	PCT	G	PO	A	E	DP
Hannahan	1.000	1	0	6	0	1

	PCT	G	PO	A	E	DP
Izturis	1.000	21	23	37	0	9
Phillips	.987	151	278	428	9	84
Rodriguez	1.000	3	3	3	0	2

Third Base	PCT	G	PO	A	E	DP
Frazier	.970	147	86	241	10	27
Hannahan	.937	37	15	44	4	5
Izturis	.500	1	0	1	1	0

Shortstop	PCT	G	PO	A	E	DP
Cozart	.977	150	222	386	14	83
Izturis	.986	29	23	45	1	10

Outfield	PCT	G	PO	A	E	DP
Bruce	.991	160	330	13	3	3
Choo	.989	153	353	9	4	0
Frazier	—		2	0	0	0
Hamilton	1.000	7	16	0	0	0
Heisey	1.000	75	101	1	0	1
Ludwick	1.000	32	39	0	0	0
Lutz	1.000	18	27	0	0	0
Paul	.973	59	69	3	2	0
Robinson	1.000	73	101	0	0	0

LOUISVILLE BATS

INTERNATIONAL LEAGUE

CINCINNATI REDS

Batting	B-T	HT	WT	DOB	AVG	vLH	vRH	G	AB	R	H	2B	3B	HR	RBI	BB	HBP	SH	SF	SO	SB	CS	SLG	OBP
Ashley, Nevin	R-R	6-1	215	8-14-84	.235	.281	.221	80	238	28	56	13	1	6	28	31	3	4	2	59	4	1	.374	.328
Burriss, Emmanuel	B-R	6-0	190	1-17-85	.241	.269	.230	108	369	32	89	6	0	1	24	22	6	7	1	41	17	8	.266	.294
Chang, Ray	R-R	6-1	195	8-24-83	.222	.208	.238	19	45	5	10	3	0	1	3	4	1	0	0	10	0	0	.356	.300
Costanzo, Mike	L-R	6-2	205	9-9-83	.429	.000	.600	2	7	3	3	2	0	0	4	1	0	0	0	3	0	0	.714	.500
2-team total (66 Syracuse)					.227	—	—	68	225	32	51	10	1	10	33	29	1	1	1	71	2	1	.413	.316
Donald, Jason	R-R	6-1	195	9-4-84	.219	.237	.211	78	251	23	55	15	2	2	17	16	1	2	1	70	2	1	.319	.268
Fellhauer, Josh	L-L	5-11	175	3-24-88	.268	.219	.276	93	246	33	66	10	0	4	26	35	2	2	4	58	3	2	.358	.359
Gonzalez, Yovan	R-R	5-10	186	11-11-89	.200	.000	.333	3	5	0	1	0	0	0	1	0	0	0	0	1	0	0	.200	.200
Hamilton, Billy	B-R	6-0	160	9-9-90	.256	.269	.250	123	504	75	129	18	4	6	41	38	0	4	1	102	75	15	.343	.308
Hanigan, Ryan	R-R	6-0	210	8-16-80	.375	.000	.750	3	8	2	3	0	0	0	2	1	0	0	0	1	0	0	.375	.444
Heisey, Chris	R-R	6-1	210	12-14-84	.200	.000	.211	6	20	1	4	1	0	0	1	1	0	0	1	6	0	0	.250	.227
Hessman, Mike	R-R	6-5	215	3-5-78	.240	.230	.246	121	420	60	101	32	0	25	56	53	4	0	5	134	0	2	.495	.328
Kennelly, Matt	R-R	6-1	210	3-21-89	.170	.143	.182	16	47	5	8	1	0	0	2	3	0	0	0	11	0	0	.191	.220
2-team total (5 Gwinnett)					.220	—	—	21	59	7	13	2	0	1	6	3	0	0	1	11	0	0	.305	.254
LaMarre, Ryan	R-L	6-1	205	11-21-88	.182	.333	.125	3	11	4	2	0	0	0	0	1	2	0	0	1	1	0	.182	.357
Ludwick, Ryan	R-L	6-2	215	7-13-78	.132	.125	.133	10	38	2	5	1	0	1	4	0	1	0	0	9	0	0	.237	.154
Miller, Corky	R-R	6-1	250	3-18-76	.200	.231	.181	44	135	8	27	6	0	4	19	16	3	1	2	23	0	0	.333	.295
Negron, Kris	R-R	6-0	195	2-1-86	.225	.259	.207	116	334	31	75	14	1	5	30	26	9	6	4	93	11	3	.317	.295
Perez, Felix	L-L	6-2	190	11-14-84	.262	.287	.252	126	461	60	121	23	2	10	65	30	8	0	5	91	4	5	.385	.315
Phipps, Denis	R-R	6-2	220	7-22-85	.248	.287	.230	130	423	48	105	27	2	9	49	48	6	2	3	99	14	3	.385	.331
Robinson, Derrick	B-L	5-11	190	9-28-87	.220	.267	.205	15	59	5	13	3	0	0	3	3	0	1	0	20	3	0	.271	.258
Rodriguez, Henry	B-R	5-8	200	2-9-90	.274	.212	.303	126	478	45	131	17	0	4	41	28	5	0	3	69	6	5	.335	.319
Schmidt, Konrad	R-R	5-10	230	8-2-84	.187	.206	.175	28	91	7	17	1	0	1	5	4	0	1	1	32	0	1	.231	.219
Soto, Neftali	R-R	6-1	215	2-28-89	.271	.324	.248	118	461	54	125	21	0	15	61	26	4	0	4	103	3	1	.414	.313

Pitching	B-T	HT	WT	DOB	W	L	ERA	G	GS	CG	SV	IP	H	R	ER	HR	BB	SO	AVG	vLH	vRH	K/9	BB/9
Arredondo, Jose	R-R	6-0	190	3-12-84	2	2	5.87	43	0	0	2	54	43	35	35	3	39	62	.223	.177	.254	10.40	6.54
Bell, Trevor	L-R	6-2	205	10-12-86	1	0	2.45	3	0	0	0	4	5	1	1	0	1	2	.357	.250	.400	4.91	2.45
Broxton, Jonathan	R-R	6-4	310	6-16-84	0	0	0.00	2	2	0	0	2	5	0	0	0	0	3	.455	.500	.429	13.50	0.00
Christiani, Nick	R-R	6-0	190	7-17-87	6	5	3.86	49	0	0	3	56	49	26	24	6	17	49	.236	.306	.187	7.88	2.73
Cingrani, Tony	L-L	6-4	215	7-5-89	3	0	1.15	6	6	0	0	31	14	4	4	1	11	49	.133	.182	.111	14.07	3.16
Corcino, Daniel	R-R	5-11	205	8-26-90	7	14	5.86	28	23	0	0	129	141	95	84	17	73	90	.279	.299	.264	6.28	5.09
Crabbe, Tim	R-R	6-4	195	2-20-88	0	1	0.71	2	2	0	0	13	9	4	1	0	7	8	.196	.214	.188	5.68	4.97
De La Rosa, Wilkin	L-L	5-11	200	2-21-85	0	0	8.10	4	0	0	0	3	4	4	3	0	5	2	.333	.667	.222	5.40	13.50
Dennick, Ryan	L-L	6-0	185	1-10-87	0	1	5.30	8	3	0	0	19	21	11	11	2	9	12	.280	.333	.270	5.79	4.34
Diaz, Jose	R-R	6-4	300	2-27-84	3	4	1.66	44	0	0	13	54	35	11	10	5	21	60	.181	.217	.161	9.94	3.48
Duke, Zach	L-L	6-2	210	4-19-83	2	0	1.30	26	0	0	2	28	19	4	4	2	5	34	.196	.196	.196	11.06	1.63
Freeman, Justin	R-R	5-11	175	10-22-86	0	0	1.29	6	0	0	1	7	5	1	1	2	8	.192	.375	.111	10.29	2.57
Galarraga, Armando	R-R	6-3	230	1-15-82	6	6	2.98	16	16	0	0	85	84	36	28	8	34	60	.260	.234	.212	6.59	3.61
Hensley, Clay	R-R	5-11	190	8-31-79	0	1	4.00	15	0	0	0	18	14	8	8	2	9	20	.226	.167	.281	10.00	4.50
Hyde, Lee	R-L	6-2	205	2-14-85	1	0	0.00	13	0	0	0	7	7	0	0	0	1	6	.259	.333	.111	7.36	1.23
MacDougal, Mike	R-R	6-4	180	3-5-77	0	1	5.49	17	0	0	0	20	21	12	12	2	11	20	.269	.341	.189	9.15	5.03
2-team total (20 Lehigh Valley)					2	2	5.40	37	0	0	0	45	45	27	27	3	28	46	—	—	—	9.20	5.60
Marshall, Sean	L-L	6-7	225	8-30-82	0	0	0.00	2	2	0	0	2	2	0	0	0	0	4	.250	.000	.286	18.00	0.00
Ondrusek, Logan	R-R	6-8	230	2-13-85	0	0	0.00	6	0	0	1	8	4	0	0	0	2	6	.148	.000	.235	6.75	2.25
Partch, Curtis	R-R	6-5	240	2-13-87	1	2	4.13	24	0	0	2	28	27	13	13	2	12	31	.250	.268	.231	9.85	3.81
Pino, Yohan	R-R	6-2	190	12-26-83	5	7	3.26	31	16	1	6	121	114	52	44	7	30	107	.247	.300	.214	7.94	2.23
Prior, Mark	R-R	6-5	230	9-7-80	0	0	4.66	7	0	0	0	10	9	5	5	0	4	9	.243	.182	.269	8.38	3.72
Ravin, Josh	R-R	6-5	225	1-21-88	0	0	6.75	10	0	0	0	11	12	9	8	1	11	9	.286	.308	.276	7.59	9.28
Reineke, Chad	R-R	6-6	230	4-9-82	8	10	4.08	27	21	0	0	130	142	63	59	19	34	83	.275	.270	.279	5.75	2.35
Reynolds, Greg	R-R	6-7	225	7-3-85	12	3	2.42	23	21	3	0	156	139	45	42	6	26	97	.237	.248	.226	5.58	1.50
Rogers, Chad	R-R	5-11	205	8-3-89	5	5	4.22	12	12	0	0	70	66	37	33	9	19	48	.247	.253	.244	6.14	2.43
Texeira, Kanekoa	R-R	6-2	190	2-6-86	0	0	2.42	16	2	0	0	26	25	9	7	1	5	20	.255	.214	.271	6.92	1.73
Van Mil, Loek	R-R	7-1	260	9-15-84	0	1	6.75	3	0	0	0	3	7	2	2	0	2	2	.467	.333	.556	6.75	6.75
Villarreal, Pedro	R-R	6-1	230	12-9-87	4	9	4.43	33	18	0	2	110	115	56	54	17	28	84	.271	.285	.260	6.89	2.30
Whelan, Kevin	R-R	5-11	205	1-8-84	3	3	4.97	47	0	0	6	51	43	31	28	8	33	73	.226	.231	.223	12.97	5.86

Fielding

Catcher	PCT	G	PO	A	E	DP	PB
Ashley	.998	74	503	28	1	8	1
Gonzalez	1.000	3	19	0	0	0	0
Hanigan	.950	3	16	3	1	0	0
Kennelly	1.000	15	80	4	0	1	1
Miller	.989	36	269	9	3	0	5
Schmidt	.991	25	194	19	2	0	3

First Base	PCT	G	PO	A	E	DP
Hessman	.994	103	819	53	5	78
Miller	1.000	4	35	3	0	4
Negron	1.000	1	9	0	0	0
Soto	.994	47	328	27	2	28

Second Base	PCT	G	PO	A	E	DP
Burriss	.985	30	43	85	2	13
Chang	.955	8	12	30	2	5
Donald	.984	49	61	125	3	24
Negron	.958	7	5	18	1	3
Rodriguez	.988	63	105	152	3	39

Third Base	PCT	G	PO	A	E	DP
Chang	1.000	4	2	7	0	1
Christiani	—	1	0	0	0	0
Costanzo	1.000	2	1	3	0	0
Hessman	.917	5	4	7	1	1
Negron	1.000	12	2	17	0	2
Rodriguez	.927	61	40	100	11	16

	PCT	G	PO	A	E	DP
Soto	.920	76	38	135	15	11

Shortstop	PCT	G	PO	A	E	DP
Burriss	.959	67	72	164	10	37
Chang	1.000	2	1	2	0	0
Donald	.941	13	17	31	3	7
Hamilton	1.000	1	0	1	0	0
Negron	.981	73	89	176	5	34

Outfield	PCT	G	PO	A	E	DP
Burriss	1.000	2	1	0	0	0
Donald	1.000	15	22	1	0	1
Fellhauer	1.000	61	90	7	0	1
Hamilton	.980	118	333	8	7	2
Heisey	1.000	4	7	0	0	0

LaMarre	1.000	3	9	0	0	0	Negron	1.000	22	36	2	0	2	Phipps	.975	114	230	6	6	2
Ludwick	1.000	10	11	0	0	0	Perez	.995	99	172	9	1	1	Robinson	1.000	14	28	3	0	1

PENSACOLA BLUE WAHOOS — DOUBLE-A
SOUTHERN LEAGUE

Batting	B-T	HT	WT	DOB	AVG	vLH	vRH	G	AB	R	H	2B	3B	HR	RBI	BB	HBP	SH	SF	SO	SB	CS	SLG	OBP
Barnhart, Tucker	B-R	5-11	195	1-7-91	.260	.172	.280	98	339	31	88	19	1	3	44	45	3	4	4	57	1	0	.348	.348
Berset, Chris	B-R	6-0	192	1-27-88	.182	.125	.205	16	55	5	10	5	0	0	5	6	0	0	1	6	0	0	.273	.258
Bowe, Theo	L-R	5-9	160	8-5-90	.206	.118	.221	99	238	19	49	6	3	4	16	18	0	1	2	54	13	8	.307	.260
Chang, Ray	R-R	6-1	195	8-24-83	.278	.373	.242	67	216	25	60	8	0	2	18	21	0	2	2	35	0	1	.343	.339
Costanzo, Mike	L-R	6-2	205	9-9-83	.261	.306	.248	42	157	19	41	14	1	4	23	27	0	0	1	42	1	0	.439	.368
Durango, Luis	B-R	5-9	165	4-23-84	.245	.222	.253	33	106	8	26	2	0	0	4	21	0	2	0	20	6	3	.264	.370
Fellhauer, Josh	L-L	5-11	175	3-24-88	.250	.000	.261	8	24	2	6	3	0	0	2	1	1	0	0	6	0	0	.375	.308
Gilmartin, Michael	R-R	6-0	180	7-14-87	.169	.143	.172	25	65	7	11	1	0	1	3	14	0	2	0	26	0	1	.231	.316
Greene, Brodie	R-R	6-1	195	9-25-87	.227	.227	.227	92	304	23	69	10	1	3	21	25	1	7	0	39	4	2	.296	.288
Heisey, Chris	R-R	6-1	210	12-14-84	—			1	0	0	0	0	0	0	0	0	0	0	0	0	0	0	—	—
Kennelly, Matt	R-R	6-1	210	3-21-89	.207	.176	.250	9	29	4	6	1	0	0	1	2	1	1	0	4	1	0	.241	.281
LaMarre, Ryan	R-L	6-1	205	11-21-88	.246	.252	.244	126	451	55	111	19	4	10	39	44	11	6	3	93	22	13	.373	.326
Lohman, Devin	R-R	6-1	185	4-14-88	.236	.200	.248	132	484	45	114	22	0	8	53	38	11	11	3	84	16	10	.331	.304
Lutz, Donald	L-R	6-3	250	2-6-89	.245	.190	.265	65	229	35	56	12	4	7	30	19	6	0	1	56	4	1	.424	.318
Mather, Joe	R-R	6-4	215	7-23-82	.174	.182	.172	31	86	6	15	4	0	2	10	14	0	1	1	28	1	1	.291	.287
Mattair, Travis	R-R	6-5	210	12-21-88	.242	.376	.198	132	475	52	115	15	2	13	57	41	10	2	1	106	2	2	.364	.315
Rodriguez, Yorman	R-R	6-3	197	8-15-92	.267	.254	.272	66	262	30	70	15	2	4	31	25	0	0	2	76	4	0	.385	.329
Selsky, Steve	R-R	6-0	203	7-20-89	.181	.250	.137	32	83	7	15	2	0	0	12	10	2	3	1	20	0	0	.205	.281
Short, Brandon	R-R	6-0	190	9-9-88	.227	.200	.239	25	66	6	15	2	0	1	7	4	1	2	1	12	0	1	.303	.278
2-team total (29 Birmingham)					.225	—	—	54	160	20	36	8	1	2	17	19	3	3	3	26	3	3	.325	.314
Silverio, Juan	R-R	6-1	175	4-18-91	.333	—	.333	2	3	1	1	0	0	0	0	0	0	0	0	0	0	0	.667	.333
Smith, Bryson	R-R	6-1	195	12-17-88	.275	.322	.257	60	207	30	57	10	1	5	15	20	9	1	1	33	2	2	.406	.363
Smith, Marquez	R-R	5-10	205	3-20-85	.214	.160	.244	21	70	9	15	5	0	3	11	9	0	0	1	13	0	0	.414	.300
Valor, Humberto	R-R	6-0	208	9-9-92	.000		.000	2	1	0	0	0	0	0	0	0	0	1	0	0	1	0	0	.000	.500
Vicioso, Danny	R-R	6-0	190	10-27-88	.159	.172	.147	21	63	5	10	1	0	1	4	4	1	0	0	16	0	0	.222	.221
Vidal, David	R-R	5-11	185	10-23-89	.206	.184	.215	46	131	9	27	2	0	1	9	15	0	3	1	40	0	0	.244	.286
Wimberly, Corey	B-R	5-8	170	10-26-83	.260	.220	.276	59	177	19	46	3	1	1	10	10	6	3	3	17	6	3	.305	.316

Pitching	B-T	HT	WT	DOB	W	L	ERA	G	GS	CG	SV	IP	H	R	ER	HR	BB	SO	AVG	vLH	vRH	K/9	BB/9
Bell, Trevor	R-R	6-2	205	10-12-86	0	1	1.72	27	0	0	17	31	21	6	6	2	8	37	.193	.200	.188	10.63	2.30
Contreras, Carlos	R-R	5-11	205	1-8-91	3	2	2.76	8	8	0	0	42	36	13	13	2	21	26	.238	.273	.212	5.53	4.46
Crabbe, Tim	R-R	6-4	195	2-20-88	7	8	3.27	25	24	0	0	140	142	59	51	12	36	101	.271	.259	.279	6.48	2.31
De La Rosa, Wilkin	R-R	5-11	200	2-21-85	2	5	5.40	28	0	0	0	35	35	23	21	5	20	28	.269	.304	.250	7.20	5.14
Dennick, Ryan	L-L	6-0	185	1-10-87	5	10	3.55	19	18	1	0	104	101	46	41	8	26	66	.254	.239	.261	5.71	2.25
Doyle, Pat	R-R	6-2	226	5-12-88	0	0	27.00	2	0	0	0	1	4	4	4	0	1	1	.500	.500	.500	6.75	6.75
Ellis, Shaun	R-R	6-4	210	12-2-86	3	2	4.33	26	9	0	0	60	62	34	29	5	25	35	.273	.306	.248	5.22	3.73
Frazier, Parker	R-R	6-5	175	11-11-88	2	3	1.93	13	0	0	0	23	15	5	5	0	10	29	.190	.219	.170	7.71	4.24
Hayes, Drew	R-R	5-11	210	9-3-87	4	3	5.43	51	0	0	2	63	73	42	38	7	33	61	.296	.277	.307	8.71	4.71
Hyde, Lee	R-L	6-2	205	2-14-85	3	4	2.28	42	0	0	2	47	33	13	12	1	17	32	.204	.182	.219	6.08	3.23
Lorenzen, Michael	R-R	6-3	180	1-4-92	0	0	4.50	7	0	0	0	6	3	3	3	1	6	5	.286	.300	.273	7.50	9.00
Lotzkar, Kyle	L-R	6-5	200	10-24-89	0	1	11.88	10	0	0	0	8	16	12	11	0	11	8	.432	.615	.333	8.64	11.88
Manno, Chris	L-L	6-3	170	11-4-88	4	4	3.94	42	0	0	0	62	58	29	27	8	26	59	.248	.242	.250	8.61	3.79
Moscot, Jon	R-R	6-4	205	8-15-91	2	1	3.19	6	6	0	0	31	34	12	11	3	12	28	.281	.286	.278	8.13	3.48
Ondrusek, Logan	R-R	6-8	230	2-13-85	0	0	0.00	3	0	0	0	2	1	0	0	0	0	1	.125	.000	.167	3.86	0.00
Parra, Manny	L-L	6-3	205	10-30-82	0	0	0.00	3	3	0	0	5	3	0	0	0	1	5	.176	.400	.083	9.00	1.80
Partch, Curtis	R-R	6-5	240	2-13-87	0	0	2.16	8	0	0	4	8	6	2	2	0	2	14	.200	.200	.200	15.12	2.16
Pearl, Brian	L-R	6-1	190	5-11-87	3	0	4.58	17	0	0	0	18	23	10	9	2	4	12	.329	.269	.364	6.11	2.04
Pino, Yohan	R-R	6-2	190	12-26-83	0	0	0.00	4	1	0	0	11	3	0	0	0	0	11	.086	.100	.080	9.00	0.00
Ravin, Josh	R-R	6-5	225	1-21-88	1	3	5.58	38	0	0	0	40	44	26	25	4	27	39	.286	.386	.227	8.70	6.02
Renken, Daniel	R-R	6-3	190	7-5-89	6	9	3.99	27	24	0	0	142	129	70	63	18	60	117	.245	.236	.252	7.42	3.80
Rogers, Chad	R-R	5-11	205	8-3-89	3	2	2.20	13	13	0	0	70	47	21	17	5	26	55	.193	.211	.178	7.11	3.36
Smith, Josh	R-R	6-2	220	8-7-87	11	9	3.26	28	28	0	0	160	148	65	58	16	50	139	.245	.285	.220	7.82	2.81
Stephenson, Robert	R-R	6-2	190	2-24-93	0	2	4.86	4	4	0	0	17	17	10	9	2	13	18	.274	.421	.209	9.72	7.02
Van Mil, Loek	R-R	7-1	260	9-15-84	0	9	3.38	48	0	0	0	61	53	24	23	6	28	32	.238	.250	.231	4.70	4.11
Walczak, Jamie	R-R	6-2	195	5-4-87	0	1	3.82	24	0	0	0	33	29	15	14	1	17	43	.244	.250	.240	11.73	4.64

Fielding

Catcher	PCT	G	PO	A	E	DP	PB
Barnhart	.990	96	697	109	8	9	3
Berset	.976	15	113	9	3	1	2
Kennelly	.981	9	47	6	1	2	1
Vicioso	.980	19	130	15	3	1	2

First Base	PCT	G	PO	A	E	DP
Costanzo	.994	34	295	14	2	20
Lutz	.954	8	62	4	3	2
Mather	.956	14	82	5	4	7
Mattair	.995	70	543	44	3	59
Smith	.981	20	150	9	3	12

Second Base	PCT	G	PO	A	E	DP
Chang	.993	32	56	87	1	10
Gilmartin	.950	8	7	12	1	3
Greene	.992	88	168	215	3	51
Wimberly	.970	27	48	48	3	10

Third Base	PCT	G	PO	A	E	DP
Chang	1.000	31	23	41	0	1
Costanzo	1.000	7	5	10	0	2
Gilmartin	1.000	18	4	15	0	1
Mattair	.975	63	47	109	4	10
Silverio	1.000	1	0	1	0	0
Vidal	.955	41	37	48	4	6

Shortstop	PCT	G	PO	A	E	DP
Chang	.947	7	8	10	1	6
Gilmartin	1.000	7	7	14	0	3
Lohman	.946	130	200	310	29	69

Outfield	PCT	G	PO	A	E	DP
Bowe	1.000	61	113	4	0	1
Durango	1.000	30	56	4	0	0
Fellhauer	.857	7	5	1	1	0
Heisey	1.000	1	1	0	0	0

CINCINNATI REDS

LaMarre	.980	121	325	13	7	3				
Lutz	.967	45	83	4	3	0				
Mather	1.000	10	9	0	0	0				
Rodriguez	.953	66	115	8	6	3				
Selsky	.923	22	33	3	3	0				
Short	1.000	17	23	1	0	0				
Smith	.991	55	101	4	1	1				
Wimberly	1.000	11	11	0	0	0				

BAKERSFIELD BLAZE · HIGH CLASS A

CALIFORNIA LEAGUE

Batting	B-T	HT	WT	DOB	AVG	vLH	vRH	G	AB	R	H	2B	3B	HR	RBI	BB	HBP	SH	SF	SO	SB	CS	SLG	OBP
Arias, Junior	R-R	6-1	200	1-9-92	.257	.310	.232	53	222	30	57	12	2	5	20	5	3	0	0	60	20	10	.396	.283
Berset, Chris	B-R	6-0	192	1-27-88	.248	.314	.225	43	137	18	34	8	0	4	12	19	1	2	0	25	0	1	.394	.344
Buckley, Sean	R-R	6-4	220	9-3-89	.053	.000	.083	6	19	1	1	0	0	0	0	2	1	2	0	1	9	0	0	.053	.174
Chavez, Alberti	R-R	5-10	170	7-21-95	.172	.083	.235	9	29	1	5	0	0	0	1	0	0	0	0	8	1	2	.172	.172
D'Anna, Dominic	L-R	6-1	215	12-23-88	.222	.288	.186	44	158	14	35	7	0	3	23	13	2	1	3	36	0	0	.323	.284
Diaz, Sammy	B-R	5-11	170	2-28-91	.200	.182	.222	6	20	4	4	2	0	0	1	3	0	0	1	3	0	0	.300	.292
Duran, Juan	R-R	6-7	205	9-2-91	.251	.308	.229	111	407	55	102	15	3	20	66	45	0	1	3	134	5	6	.450	.323
Gilmartin, Michael	R-R	6-0	180	7-14-87	.200	.250	.185	9	35	5	7	3	0	3	6	4	1	0	0	10	0	0	.543	.300
Gonzalez, Yovan	R-R	5-10	186	11-11-89	.262	.256	.269	74	256	27	67	7	0	2	29	23	3	1	0	34	0	2	.313	.330
Mejias-Brean, Seth	R-R	6-2	216	4-5-91	.308	.333	.250	3	13	3	4	1	0	1	3	0	0	0	0	1	0	0	.615	.308
Morillo, Julio	R-R	5-10	175	12-27-92	.154	.286	.105	18	52	7	8	0	0	0	4	6	1	0	1	5	1	0	.154	.250
O'Shea, Nick	R-R	6-3	215	1-29-91	.300	.333	.286	3	10	2	3	0	0	0	0	0	1	0	0	3	0	1	.500	.364
Perez, Juan	L-R	5-11	182	11-1-91	.251	.268	.244	126	471	63	118	27	5	8	45	34	1	6	5	104	31	11	.380	.299
Peterson, Brent	R-R	5-10	172	10-20-92	.333	.750	.182	5	15	2	5	0	0	0	0	1	0	1	0	1	1	1	.333	.375
Rodriguez, Yorman	R-R	6-3	197	8-15-92	.251	.317	.234	63	251	41	63	20	4	9	35	22	3	1	0	77	6	3	.470	.319
Selsky, Steve	R-R	6-0	203	7-20-89	.297	.372	.272	91	340	54	101	19	5	13	68	37	15	0	2	79	9	4	.497	.388
Silva, Juan	L-L	6-0	190	1-8-91	.271	.250	.280	96	336	51	91	16	4	8	44	61	3	2	2	76	31	13	.414	.386
Silverio, Juan	R-R	6-1	175	4-18-91	.286	.315	.278	126	510	61	146	30	4	19	80	11	4	2	4	109	5	7	.473	.304
Smith, Marquez	R-R	5-10	205	3-20-85	.301	.383	.274	49	183	33	55	11	2	8	26	26	7	0	1	34	2	1	.514	.406
Terry, Joe	L-R	5-10	186	12-18-89	.188	.100	.196	20	69	8	13	1	0	0	4	4	0	0	0	14	3	1	.203	.233
Uxa, Logan	L-R	6-4	220	1-25-91	.000	.000	.000	3	8	1	0	0	0	0	0	1	1	0	0	1	2	0	.000	.100
Vicioso, Danny	R-R	6-0	190	10-27-88	.207	.176	.221	32	111	12	23	4	0	1	4	4	1	1	0	29	1	1	.270	.241
Vidal, David	R-R	5-11	185	10-23-88	.225	.259	.214	60	213	23	48	14	1	3	16	18	3	2	1	61	0	0	.343	.294
Waldrop, Kyle	L-L	6-3	190	11-26-91	.258	.295	.246	129	504	66	130	32	4	21	54	32	2	0	2	121	20	8	.462	.304
Wright, Ryan	R-R	6-1	194	12-3-89	.265	.258	.272	100	411	53	109	23	1	8	52	26	3	1	4	66	5	3	.384	.311

Pitching	B-T	HT	WT	DOB	W	L	ERA	G	GS	CG	SV	IP	H	R	ER	HR	BB	SO	AVG	vLH	vRH	K/9	BB/9
Allen, James	R-R	6-1	197	11-20-89	9	11	4.86	28	28	0	0	144	139	91	78	18	60	85	.254	.294	.234	5.30	3.74
Contreras, Carlos	R-R	5-11	205	1-8-91	5	7	3.80	18	18	0	0	90	70	43	38	9	41	96	.215	.241	.201	9.60	4.10
Dennhardt, Mike	R-R	6-1	205	6-1-90	6	8	4.92	27	13	0	0	82	99	54	45	9	24	70	.298	.327	.283	7.65	2.62
Doyle, Pat	R-R	6-2	226	5-12-88	4	1	2.97	50	0	0	11	73	57	25	24	7	17	69	.216	.177	.232	8.55	2.11
Dyer, Shane	R-R	6-3	185	3-9-88	6	5	3.45	18	18	0	0	107	108	55	41	10	20	84	.259	.273	.249	7.07	1.68
Ellis, Shaun	R-R	6-4	210	12-2-86	0	2	2.65	4	3	0	0	17	18	5	5	1	4	10	.265	.278	.250	5.29	2.12
Gonzalez, Carlos	R-R	6-1	195	6-12-90	3	2	5.33	41	2	0	1	79	88	52	47	6	46	67	.284	.296	.277	7.60	5.22
Housey, Joey	R-R	6-3	190	10-15-89	0	0	0.68	8	0	0	0	13	10	1	1	0	3	8	.213	.278	.172	5.40	2.03
Johnson, Jacob	R-R	6-4	215	9-12-90	7	6	5.10	33	17	0	0	118	140	83	67	14	27	90	.293	.302	.288	7.07	2.05
Klimesh, Ben	R-R	6-4	220	5-14-90	0	1	6.59	21	0	0	1	27	34	23	20	4	12	28	.301	.277	.318	9.22	3.95
Lorenzen, Michael	R-R	6-3	180	1-4-92	0	1	6.35	5	0	0	2	6	6	4	4	1	5	6	.273	.286	.250	9.53	7.94
Lotzkar, Kyle	L-R	6-5	200	10-24-89	1	2	6.98	23	0	0	1	30	31	30	23	1	26	33	.263	.319	.225	10.01	7.89
Lucas, Sean	R-L	6-1	200	4-6-89	0	1	6.92	10	0	0	0	13	12	10	10	0	10	12	.250	.263	.241	8.31	6.92
McMyne, Kyle	R-R	5-11	220	10-18-89	3	4	5.83	40	0	0	2	59	70	41	38	12	30	51	.295	.347	.273	7.82	4.60
Moran, Jimmy	R-R	6-1	180	6-7-90	2	2	4.18	44	0	0	1	60	53	32	28	6	44	61	.239	.319	.200	9.10	6.56
Moscot, Jon	R-R	6-4	205	8-15-91	2	14	4.59	22	22	0	0	116	109	66	59	17	36	112	.247	.265	.238	8.71	2.80
Mugarian, Wes	R-R	6-1	207	9-18-91	1	0	7.11	6	0	0	0	6	5	5	5	0	6	4	.227	.400	.176	5.68	14.21
Muhammad, El'Hajj	R-R	6-2	200	7-7-91	1	0	1.82	22	0	0	5	25	10	5	5	2	19	34	.133	.111	.140	12.41	6.93
Pearl, Brian	L-R	6-1	190	5-17-88	0	0	1.59	10	0	0	3	11	9	2	2	0	5	14	.214	.235	.200	11.12	3.97
Pinckard, Brooks	R-R	6-1	190	8-15-88	2	7	4.57	48	0	0	2	67	55	38	34	5	43	47	.228	.272	.201	6.31	5.78
Quezada, Radhames	R-R	6-2	175	7-6-90	0	1	11.57	2	2	0	0	5	4	7	6	0	14	5	.250	.500	.167	9.64	27.00
Robles, Tanner	L-L	6-4	205	2-24-89	0	4	9.39	6	6	0	0	23	33	27	24	3	19	30	.351	.333	.356	11.74	7.43
Stephenson, Robert	R-R	6-2	190	2-24-93	2	2	3.05	4	4	0	0	21	19	9	7	3	2	22	.235	.267	.216	9.58	0.87
Walczak, Jamie	R-R	6-2	195	5-4-87	0	0	0.00	8	0	0	4	10	3	0	0	0	1	11	.100	.222	.048	10.24	0.93
Williamson, Fabian	R-L	6-2	175	10-20-88	1	4	6.61	7	7	0	0	33	41	25	24	3	19	37	.306	.160	.339	10.19	5.23

Fielding

Catcher	PCT	G	PO	A	E	DP	PB
Berset	.987	43	333	42	5	6	8
Gonzalez	.989	69	549	59	7	4	9
Morillo	.983	16	106	12	2	1	5
O'Shea	1.000	3	29	4	0	0	0
Vicioso	.988	13	76	6	1	0	5

First Base	PCT	G	PO	A	E	DP
D'Anna	.994	37	322	33	2	33
Selsky	.984	68	515	51	9	57
Smith	.983	21	163	10	3	20
Uxa	.926	3	20	5	2	3
Vicioso	.986	17	127	12	2	4

Second Base	PCT	G	PO	A	E	DP
Chavez	1.000	6	14	13	0	5
Diaz	1.000	1	1	3	0	1
Morillo	1.000	2	0	2	0	0
Perez	1.000	12	24	37	0	10
Peterson	.923	3	5	7	1	1
Silverio	.967	25	47	71	4	16
Smith	1.000	10	20	27	0	10
Terry	.923	9	10	14	2	4
Wright	.983	75	147	195	6	54
Gilmartin	.875	4	2	5	1	0
Mejias-Brean	1.000	3	2	5	0	1
Silverio	.916	69	46	151	18	11
Smith	1.000	11	9	29	0	0
Terry	.750	3	1	2	1	0
Vidal	.923	51	38	93	11	14

Third Base	PCT	G	PO	A	E	DP
Chavez	1.000	1	1	1	0	1
Diaz	1.000	2	2	6	0	0

Shortstop	PCT	G	PO	A	E	DP
Diaz	1.000	2	2	6	0	0
Gilmartin	1.000	3	5	11	0	4
Perez	.952	111	155	339	25	71
Peterson	1.000	1	2	2	0	1
Silverio	.913	24	35	59	9	16

CINCINNATI REDS

Outfield	PCT	G	PO	A	E	DP											
Arias	.967	49	117	1	4	1	Duran	.948	97	180	4	10	2	Silva	.988	81	162	5	2	0
Diaz	1.000	1	1	1	0	0	Rodriguez	.952	57	99	1	5	0	Terry	1.000	5	7	0	0	0
							Selsky	1.000	21	42	0	0	0	Waldrop	.974	117	182	6	5	0

DAYTON DRAGONS   LOW CLASS A

MIDWEST LEAGUE

CINCINNATI REDS

Batting	B-T	HT	WT	DOB	AVG	vLH	vRH	G	AB	R	H	2B	3B	HR	RBI	BB	HBP	SH	SF	SO	SB	CS	SLG	OBP
Amaral, Beau	L-L	5-10	177	2-11-91	.258	.369	.224	125	515	67	133	15	5	3	38	34	7	7	2	81	40	12	.324	.312
Arias, Junior	R-R	6-1	200	1-9-92	.284	.309	.278	72	271	45	77	12	4	10	33	13	3	2	1	72	40	10	.469	.323
Dailey, Brandon	R-R	5-10	170	2-10-92	.185	.281	.152	36	124	13	23	5	1	2	19	11	2	1	3	32	0	0	.290	.257
Diaz, Sammy	B-R	5-11	170	2-28-91	.279	.263	.283	72	269	46	75	8	1	3	28	32	5	5	3	32	8	3	.349	.362
Ervin, Phillip	R-R	5-11	190	7-17-92	.349	.143	.389	12	43	7	15	2	0	1	6	8	0	0	0	10	2	1	.465	.451
Gelalich, Jeff	L-R	6-0	207	3-16-91	.245	.222	.252	123	444	61	109	17	2	1	37	57	4	4	9	107	20	6	.300	.331
Gomez, Wagner	B-R	5-11	205	12-2-91	.145	.300	.111	15	55	1	8	1	0	1	4	0	0	1	0	23	0	0	.218	.145
Hudson, Joe	R-R	6-0	205	5-21-91	.247	.236	.250	87	295	36	73	22	0	1	27	32	5	3	3	48	3	1	.332	.328
Ludwick, Ryan	R-L	6-2	215	7-13-78	.167	.000	.167	3	6	2	1	0	0	0	3	0	0	0	0	2	0	0	.167	.444
Matthews, Adam	R-R	6-1	195	4-10-90	.182	.250	.156	13	44	8	8	1	0	1	7	5	0	1	1	15	0	0	.273	.260
Matthews, Jon	R-R	6-1	195	4-6-91	.244	.143	.290	12	45	3	11	1	1	0	5	5	1	1	0	11	5	1	.311	.333
Mejias-Brean, Seth	R-R	6-2	216	4-5-91	.305	.299	.306	127	479	70	146	35	3	10	79	55	6	2	3	83	3	2	.453	.381
O'Shea, Nick	R-R	6-3	215	1-29-89	.138	.176	.122	16	58	6	8	2	0	1	1	1	1	0	1	19	0	0	.328	.177
Peterson, Brent	R-R	5-10	172	10-20-92	.229	.265	.214	53	166	23	38	5	2	0	8	16	1	4	0	49	4	3	.283	.301
Pigott, Daniel	R-R	6-2	205	10-4-89	.280	.275	.282	64	239	33	67	16	3	4	22	18	2	7	1	42	4	4	.423	.335
Rahier, Tanner	R-R	5-11	198	10-12-93	.222	.213	.225	106	410	31	91	15	2	7	61	12	7	0	8	81	0	5	.320	.252
Ramirez, Robert	L-R	6-1	191	7-19-92	.222	.286	.201	48	176	12	39	7	2	2	20	7	1	1	2	48	3	3	.318	.253
Sanchez, Carlos	L-L	5-11	235	4-4-91	.304	.000	.368	8	23	3	7	2	0	0	3	1	0	0	0	3	0	0	.391	.333
Terry, Joe	L-R	5-10	186	12-18-89	.292	.269	.300	27	106	17	31	6	2	1	12	8	2	0	2	18	5	1	.415	.347
Valor, Humberto	R-R	6-0	208	9-9-92	.179	.200	.173	42	123	6	22	3	0	2	12	9	1	3	3	39	2	1	.252	.235
Vincej, Zach	R-R	5-11	177	5-1-91	.263	.280	.258	104	377	51	99	17	5	3	31	36	6	2	4	72	13	7	.358	.333
Winker, Jesse	L-L	6-2	210	8-17-93	.281	.264	.285	112	417	73	117	18	5	16	76	63	4	0	2	75	6	1	.463	.379

Pitching	B-T	HT	WT	DOB	W	L	ERA	G	GS	CG	SV	IP	H	R	ER	HR	BB	SO	AVG	vLH	vRH	K/9	BB/9
Adames, Jesus	R-R	6-6	248	1-25-91	3	3	5.58	38	0	0	1	60	71	39	37	5	27	44	.295	.296	.293	6.64	4.07
Amezcua, Tony	R-R	5-11	184	5-27-91	3	2	5.95	37	0	0	0	79	72	58	52	7	53	67	.240	.230	.247	7.67	6.06
Bender, Joel	L-L	6-3	213	8-3-91	4	2	3.79	36	1	0	2	74	67	35	31	3	23	56	.249	.247	.250	6.84	2.81
Chacin, Alejandro	R-R	5-11	202	6-24-93	4	3	2.91	44	0	0	9	65	42	27	21	4	33	72	.181	.163	.193	9.97	4.57
Cisco, Drew	L-R	5-11	201	7-29-91	5	7	3.86	24	24	0	0	131	148	64	56	11	16	99	.288	.287	.290	6.82	1.10
Cueto, Johnny	R-R	5-11	215	2-15-86	1	0	1.13	2	2	0	0	8	7	1	1	0	0	8	.233	.400	.067	9.00	0.00
De Los Santos, Abel	R-R	6-1	215	5-17-92	1	0	14.46	9	0	0	0	9	12	19	15	2	12	6	.333	.294	.368	5.79	11.57
Diaz, Pedro	R-R	6-0	180	4-29-93	1	6	7.52	11	9	0	0	41	52	38	34	3	22	25	.311	.286	.333	5.53	4.87
Fleece, Nick	R-R	6-2	200	10-24-88	0	0	0.00	3	0	0	0	3	0	0	0	0	0	1	.000	.000	.000	3.38	0.00
Garrett, Amir	L-L	6-5	210	5-3-92	1	3	6.88	8	8	0	0	34	40	26	26	4	16	15	.294	.333	.284	3.97	4.24
Guillon, Ismael	L-L	6-2	218	2-13-92	7	8	4.75	27	26	0	0	121	95	72	64	14	95	134	.220	.196	.228	9.94	7.05
Housey, Joey	R-R	6-3	190	10-15-89	2	1	5.28	11	0	0	1	15	13	10	9	1	11	14	.210	.097	.323	8.22	6.46
Klimesh, Ben	R-R	6-4	220	5-14-90	3	0	2.60	24	0	0	5	35	29	12	10	3	10	45	.230	.273	.207	11.68	2.60
Lively, Ben	R-R	6-4	190	3-5-92	0	1	2.25	1	1	0	0	4	2	2	1	0	1	7	.143	.250	.000	15.75	2.25
Lorenzen, Michael	R-R	6-3	180	1-4-92	1	0	0.00	9	0	0	2	8	7	0	0	0	2	7	.233	.267	.200	7.56	2.16
Lucas, Sean	R-L	6-1	200	4-6-89	3	1	3.34	30	0	0	11	35	29	14	13	3	10	32	.218	.200	.226	8.23	2.57
McMyne, Kyle	R-R	5-11	220	10-18-89	0	0	3.09	10	0	0	3	12	11	5	4	1	5	13	.239	.200	.286	10.03	3.86
Mugarian, Wes	R-R	6-1	207	9-18-91	0	1	5.46	12	0	0	0	30	35	19	18	4	12	26	.304	.300	.307	7.89	3.64
Peralta, Wandy	L-L	6-0	210	7-27-91	2	7	3.80	44	4	0	1	85	91	45	36	9	41	79	.274	.259	.281	8.33	4.32
Romano, Sal	L-R	6-4	250	10-12-93	7	11	4.86	25	25	0	0	120	134	81	65	10	57	89	.291	.322	.267	6.66	4.26
Salter, Austin	R-R	6-4	198	9-5-91	0	1	17.36	4	0	0	0	5	12	10	9	1	4	7	.444	.429	.462	13.50	7.71
Saunders, Mike	R-R	6-2	210	3-7-91	1	1	3.69	6	2	0	1	12	7	5	4	0	5	6	.163	.208	.105	4.63	3.86
Stephens, Jackson	R-R	6-3	205	5-11-94	3	7	4.59	14	6	0	1	65	79	39	33	6	18	55	.312	.379	.272	7.65	2.51
Stephenson, Robert	R-R	6-2	190	2-24-93	5	3	2.57	14	14	0	0	77	56	30	22	5	20	96	.200	.189	.212	11.22	2.34
Taveras, Werleen	R-R	5-11	170	8-19-90	1	2	3.95	11	0	0	0	14	18	8	6	0	7	13	.321	.333	.313	8.56	4.61
Travieso, Nick	R-R	6-2	215	11-3-94	7	4	4.63	17	17	0	0	82	83	47	42	7	27	61	.263	.282	.247	6.72	2.98
Wiley, Mo	R-R	6-4	234	12-11-89	0	0	12.27	4	0	0	0	4	7	6	5	1	4	7	.389	.571	.273	17.18	9.82

Fielding

Catcher	PCT	G	PO	A	E	DP	PB
Dailey	.990	36	252	35	3	3	14
Gomez	.984	15	108	15	2	1	8
Hudson	.989	87	699	87	9	8	15
O'Shea	1.000	2	20	2	0	0	0

First Base	PCT	G	PO	A	E	DP
Diaz	1.000	3	28	3	0	4
Mejias-Brean	.993	79	678	36	5	58
O'Shea	.960	10	69	3	3	6
Pigott	.982	26	207	10	4	20
Ramirez	.993	17	132	12	1	12
Sanchez	1.000	8	57	3	0	5

Valor	.500	1	1	0	1	0

Second Base	PCT	G	PO	A	E	DP
Diaz	.973	60	115	135	7	41
Peterson	.963	33	51	78	5	14
Ramirez	.925	26	34	64	8	11
Terry	.909	12	21	29	5	5
Valor	.974	16	30	45	2	13

Third Base	PCT	G	PO	A	E	DP
Diaz	.667	2	0	2	1	1
Mejias-Brean	.963	48	47	108	6	9
Rahier	.942	89	68	193	16	14
Ramirez	.875	2	0	7	1	0

Shortstop	PCT	G	PO	A	E	DP
Diaz	.917	7	11	11	2	1
Peterson	.960	8	14	10	1	2
Rahier	.846	5	6	5	2	2
Valor	.962	23	26	50	3	12
Vincej	.968	102	142	279	14	57

Outfield	PCT	G	PO	A	E	DP
Amaral	.977	113	243	7	6	3
Arias	.984	49	123	2	2	2
Diaz	1.000	1	1	0	0	0
Ervin	1.000	11	21	0	0	0
Gelalich	.970	101	188	6	6	1

Matthews	1.000	7	16	3	0	1	Peterson	—	1	0	0	0	0	Valor	.667	1	2	0	1	0
Matthews	.958	12	23	0	1	0	Pigott	.978	26	43	2	1	0	Winker	.987	101	144	9	2	1

AZL REDS ROOKIE

ARIZONA LEAGUE

Batting	B-T	HT	WT	DOB	AVG	vLH	vRH	G	AB	R	H	2B	3B	HR	RBI	BB	HBP	SH	SF	SO	SB	CS	SLG	OBP
Aldazoro, Argenis	L-L	6-2	160	9-17-92	.205	.143	.240	10	39	5	8	2	0	0	5	0	1	0	1	9	1	0	.256	.220
Aquino, Aristides	R-R	6-4	190	4-22-94	.278	.292	.274	46	194	37	54	15	6	4	38	10	4	0	1	40	4	3	.479	.325
Bueno, Ronald	B-R	5-10	154	10-4-92	.333	.250	.357	5	18	4	6	2	1	0	0	2	0	0	0	2	1	0	.556	.400
Carter, Dalton	L-L	6-2	200	4-3-95	.205	.129	.229	37	127	19	26	7	0	4	9	19	2	0	1	41	1	1	.354	.315
Chavez, Alberti	R-R	5-10	170	7-21-95	.209	.174	.222	41	163	11	34	6	0	0	9	7	2	2	1	29	8	1	.245	.249
Daal, Carlton	R-R	6-2	160	8-1-93	.143	.000	.214	6	21	3	3	0	0	0	3	1	0	0	0	6	0	0	.143	.182
Duarte, Jose	R-R	6-2	190	4-23-93	.178	.350	.129	29	90	6	16	5	0	0	6	6	1	1	1	22	0	1	.233	.235
Florentino, Oviel	B-R	6-1	160	2-3-94	.161	.160	.162	27	93	11	15	2	0	0	7	10	0	0	1	19	3	1	.183	.240
Franklin, K.J.	R-R	6-1	220	11-24-94	.260	.239	.268	45	173	17	45	15	0	1	25	13	5	3	2	53	1	1	.364	.326
Garcia, Kevin W	R-R	6-1	177	6-19-93	.328	.388	.308	50	195	38	64	13	2	4	23	20	3	5	0	23	6	3	.477	.399
Guzman, Aldi	R-R	6-4	235	2-20-93	.227	.259	.208	23	75	10	17	4	1	3	9	4	3	0	0	41	0	1	.427	.293
Hargreaves, Elliott	L-L	5-10	175	4-1-94	.300	.250	.333	4	10	1	3	0	0	0	1	1	0	0	0	3	0	0	.300	.364
Jocketty, Joe	R-R	5-10	165	10-3-90	.160	.222	.125	9	25	5	4	0	0	0	2	11	0	2	0	5	0	1	.160	.417
Long, Shedric	L-R	5-10	175	8-22-95	.256	.278	.250	24	78	9	20	2	0	1	8	8	1	1	0	17	1	1	.321	.333
Martijn, Jonathan	R-R	6-2	200	2-23-94	.120	.000	.158	7	25	1	3	0	0	0	0	1	0	0	0	9	1	0	.120	.185
Reynolds, J.R.	R-R	6-0	190	7-31-90	.304	.000	.368	9	23	5	7	0	0	1	3	11	1	0	0	5	0	0	.435	.543
Suero, Yonatan	B-R	6-0	170	2-28-93	.235	.370	.167	24	81	10	19	3	0	0	10	5	2	0	1	21	1	0	.272	.292
Thompson, Cory	R-R	5-11	180	9-23-94	.266	.250	.272	48	188	34	50	9	1	1	16	10	12	1	1	30	3	4	.340	.341
Tromp, Chadwick	R-R	5-9	180	3-21-95	.167	.125	.188	9	24	2	4	0	0	0	2	0	1	0	0	4	0	1	.167	.200
Uxa, Logan	L-R	6-4	220	1-25-91	.281	.455	.230	40	146	17	41	10	5	1	28	22	3	0	3	19	2	0	.438	.379

Pitching	B-T	HT	WT	DOB	W	L	ERA	G	GS	CG	SV	IP	H	R	ER	HR	BB	SO	AVG	vLH	vRH	K/9	BB/9
Anselmi, Davide	R-R	6-2	210	1-11-95	0	0	6.75	3	0	0	0	1	1	2	1	0	1	1	.167	.000	.250	6.75	6.75
Arico, Kevin	R-R	6-4	220	8-30-88	1	1	0.00	3	1	0	0	3	0	1	0	0	2	2	.000	.000	.000	6.75	6.75
Armstrong, Mark	R-R	6-2	210	11-26-94	0	0	0.00	2	2	0	0	3	1	0	0	0	0	2	.091	.143	.000	6.00	0.00
Aybar, Manuel	R-R	6-3	185	1-6-93	1	3	3.31	13	10	0	0	52	46	24	19	3	32	36	.249	.237	.257	6.27	5.57
Boyles, Ty	R-L	6-3	270	9-30-95	0	0	1.80	14	0	0	0	30	24	11	6	1	10	31	.216	.185	.226	9.30	3.00
Howell, Blaine	L-L	5-11	210	10-2-88	0	1	4.50	2	2	0	0	2	3	1	1	0	0	1	.429	.000	.600	4.50	0.00
Izold, Jakub	R-L	6-4	205	7-16-93	0	1	8.04	15	0	0	0	16	28	17	14	1	3	16	.389	.533	.351	9.19	1.72
Jones, Chad	L-L	6-2	225	10-5-88	1	1	10.24	13	0	0	0	10	16	17	11	0	11	8	.364	.300	.382	7.45	10.24
Kivel, Jeremy	R-R	6-2	200	10-16-93	0	2	3.91	13	12	0	0	51	50	33	22	4	23	56	.249	.261	.242	9.95	4.09
Lorenzen, Michael	R-R	6-3	180	1-4-92	0	0	0.00	1	1	0	0	1	1	1	0	0	0	1	.200	.333	.000	9.00	0.00
Mahle, Tyler	R-R	6-2	175	9-29-94	1	3	2.36	12	4	0	0	34	32	18	9	0	8	30	.237	.189	.268	7.86	2.10
Marquez, Soid F	R-R	6-3	165	1-3-95	2	1	5.45	16	0	0	0	36	34	24	22	3	16	25	.258	.259	.256	6.19	3.96
Martinez, Juan	L-L	6-2	175	7-15-92	2	3	6.05	16	3	0	0	39	42	29	26	1	17	29	.280	.194	.303	6.75	3.96
Mieres, Oswaldo	R-R	6-3	178	5-14-92	1	2	2.14	14	0	0	3	21	15	8	5	2	6	33	.190	.310	.120	14.14	2.57
Mitchell, Evan	R-R	6-2	175	3-18-92	0	0	3.00	3	0	0	0	3	3	1	1	0	2	5	.250	.200	.286	15.00	6.00
Morillo, Junior	L-L	5-11	167	10-30-91	2	1	1.65	7	6	0	0	33	41	15	6	3	6	27	.297	.255	.319	7.44	0.83
Parra, Jesus	R-R	5-11	175	4-14-91	0	2	8.10	15	0	0	1	13	17	14	12	0	13	10	.321	.350	.303	6.75	8.78
Ramirez, Bernardo	R-R	6-2	180	2-2-93	1	0	4.28	12	4	0	0	34	35	19	16	4	10	27	.276	.200	.325	7.22	2.67
Redan, Ibrahin	R-R	6-3	185	12-11-93	2	4	7.27	19	0	0	0	17	19	17	14	1	13	15	.257	.273	.244	7.79	6.75
Roman, Fabian	R-R	6-0	200	11-22-91	1	1	0.90	8	0	0	1	10	7	2	1	0	0	9	.212	.333	.143	8.10	0.00
Romero, Franderlyn	R-R	6-1	190	2-21-93	3	4	4.89	13	3	0	0	50	51	32	27	5	13	45	.263	.258	.267	8.15	2.36
Routt, Nick	L-L	6-4	215	8-28-90	0	1	3.60	7	7	0	0	15	19	9	6	0	5	16	.297	.313	.292	9.60	3.00
Weiss, Zack	R-R	6-1	200	6-16-92	0	0	0.00	2	0	0	0	2	1	1	0	0	1	2	.143	.250	.000	9.00	4.50

Fielding

Catcher	PCT	G	PO	A	E	DP	PB
Duarte	.974	29	193	32	6	3	5
Long	.993	18	114	20	1	1	12
Reynolds	.971	8	60	8	2	2	3
Tromp	.986	9	63	8	1	7	2

First Base	PCT	G	PO	A	E	DP
Guzman	.953	19	152	12	8	9
Uxa	.982	38	308	27	6	24

Second Base	PCT	G	PO	A	E	DP
Bueno	1.000	5	13	14	0	2

Chavez	.985	14	26	40	1	6
Florentino	.919	20	34	45	7	12
Suero	.933	17	33	37	5	11

Third Base	PCT	G	PO	A	E	DP
Chavez	.929	16	17	35	4	4
Franklin	.811	37	33	53	20	7
Suero	.867	5	2	11	2	1

Shortstop	PCT	G	PO	A	E	DP
Chavez	1.000	1	1	2	0	0
Daal	1.000	5	5	12	0	2

Florentino	.813	5	5	8	3	3
Thompson	.895	47	77	128	24	25

Outfield	PCT	G	PO	A	E	DP
Aquino	.939	44	83	10	6	2
Carter	.937	34	57	2	4	0
Chavez	.833	8	9	1	2	1
Fernandez	.984	33	59	1	1	0
Garcia	.977	45	82	4	2	2
Hargreaves	1.000	4	5	0	0	0
Martijn	1.000	5	5	1	0	1

BILLINGS MUSTANGS ROOKIE

PIONEER LEAGUE

Batting	B-T	HT	WT	DOB	AVG	vLH	vRH	G	AB	R	H	2B	3B	HR	RBI	BB	HBP	SH	SF	SO	SB	CS	SLG	OBP
Aquino, Aristides	R-R	6-4	190	4-22-94	.212	.200	.217	15	66	13	14	1	1	3	10	2	0	0	2	22	1	1	.394	.229
Benedetto, Nick	R-R	6-0	150	2-27-93	.165	.143	.170	37	115	14	19	4	1	1	9	6	0	1	0	39	4	2	.243	.207
Bueno, Ronald	B-R	5-10	154	10-4-92	.274	.343	.254	48	157	28	43	7	3	0	5	14	0	6	3	22	4	1	.357	.328
Daal, Carlton	R-R	6-2	160	8-1-93	.224	.154	.250	15	49	4	11	1	0	0	4	3	0	1	0	13	2	0	.245	.269
Ervin, Phillip	R-R	5-11	190	7-17-92	.326	.238	.343	34	129	27	42	9	1	8	29	17	3	0	0	24	12	0	.597	.416

CINCINNATI REDS

Name	B-T	HT	WT	DOB	AVG	vLH	vRH	G	AB	R	H	2B	3B	HR	RBI	BB	HBP	SH	SF	SO	SB	CS	SLG	OBP
Garcia, Kevin W	R-R	6-1	177	6-19-93	.105	.000	.214	5	19	0	2	1	0	0	1	3	0	0	0	4	2	0	.158	.227
Lopez, Jhimmy	R-R	6-0	215	8-19-92	.189	.136	.205	28	95	3	18	3	0	1	9	10	2	0	0	31	0	1	.253	.280
Matthews, Adam	R-R	6-1	195	4-10-90	.241	.132	.284	35	133	20	32	11	2	2	22	17	1	0	1	40	3	1	.398	.329
Matthews, Jon	R-R	6-1	195	4-6-91	.292	.333	.285	46	154	23	45	5	3	3	8	19	8	0	0	32	22	5	.422	.398
Morillo, Julio	R-R	5-10	175	12-27-92	.120	.000	.125	8	25	2	3	0	0	0	1	0	0	0	0	4	0	0	.120	.120
Ortiz, Jose	R-R	5-11	205	6-11-94	.262	.300	.250	48	164	21	43	14	0	8	32	14	2	0	4	42	1	0	.494	.321
Paula, Daniel	R-R	5-11	180	11-22-92	.262	.167	.281	38	145	20	38	7	1	3	13	4	0	1	0	10	2	0	.386	.282
Rachal, Avain	R-R	6-0	195	2-11-94	.253	.279	.245	53	186	34	47	6	1	4	21	41	4	1	1	39	6	2	.360	.397
Ramirez, Robert	L-R	6-1	191	7-19-92	.185	.118	.196	34	119	16	22	3	2	2	10	6	1	0	1	39	0	2	.303	.228
Reynolds, J.R.	R-R	6-0	190	7-31-90	.235	.143	.259	9	34	1	8	1	1	0	0	2	0	1	0	11	0	0	.324	.278
Reynoso, Jonathan	R-R	6-3	177	1-7-93	.238	.192	.246	38	160	16	38	5	0	2	12	5	0	6	1	29	9	5	.306	.259
Rosa, Gabriel	R-R	6-4	185	7-2-93	.211	.154	.227	51	180	29	38	5	0	6	23	25	6	0	0	46	13	2	.339	.327
Sanchez, Carlos	L-L	5-11	235	4-4-91	.254	.184	.269	55	224	24	57	11	1	6	36	12	1	0	5	42	1	0	.393	.289
Terrasas, Taylor	R-R	5-10	185	7-24-91	.190	.208	.185	38	116	7	22	6	0	1	7	15	6	0	1	28	2	0	.267	.312
Valor, Humberto	R-R	6-0	208	9-9-92	.238	.143	.286	6	21	3	5	1	0	0	3	3	2	0	0	4	0	0	.286	.385
Washington, Ty	R-R	5-9	160	9-1-93	.264	.367	.245	53	193	29	51	12	2	0	22	18	1	5	3	31	10	5	.347	.326

Pitching	B-T	HT	WT	DOB	W	L	ERA	G	GS	CG	SV	IP	H	R	ER	HR	BB	SO	AVG	vLH	vRH	K/9	BB/9
Becker, Nolan	R-L	6-6	225	6-13-91	1	1	6.25	19	0	0	0	32	42	24	22	2	20	28	.326	.500	.258	7.96	5.68
Brattvet, Scott	R-R	6-1	195	7-21-91	2	3	5.35	17	0	0	0	34	27	25	20	4	19	20	.213	.140	.250	5.35	5.08
De Los Santos, Abel	R-R	6-1	215	5-17-92	0	2	3.00	13	0	0	3	15	9	9	5	0	6	20	.176	.217	.143	12.00	3.60
Diaz, Pedro	R-R	6-0	180	4-29-93	2	8	5.28	13	13	0	0	61	78	43	36	6	17	34	.318	.253	.363	4.99	2.49
Fleece, Nick	R-R	6-2	200	10-24-88	0	2	3.50	17	0	0	0	18	18	9	7	1	4	20	.254	.280	.239	10.00	2.00
Garrett, Amir	L-L	6-5	210	5-3-92	1	1	2.66	5	5	0	0	24	22	12	7	0	10	17	.250	.308	.226	6.46	3.80
Guzman, Jose	R-R	6-3	178	9-8-91	3	5	8.49	14	9	0	0	47	61	47	44	10	20	37	.311	.311	.311	7.14	3.86
Housey, Joey	R-R	6-3	190	10-15-89	0	0	2.79	8	0	0	0	10	11	3	3	1	2	15	.282	.143	.360	13.97	1.86
Jones, Chad	L-L	6-2	225	10-5-88	0	0	3.38	3	0	0	0	3	3	3	1	0	4	5	.300	.500	.250	16.88	13.50
Lewis-Walker, Robert	R-R	6-3	195	4-7-93	0	0	4.56	17	0	0	1	26	31	16	13	5	3	15	.292	.243	.319	5.26	1.05
Lively, Ben	R-R	6-4	190	3-5-92	0	3	0.73	12	12	0	0	37	21	7	3	0	12	49	.163	.169	.157	11.92	2.92
Mantoni, Joe	R-R	6-0	220	6-4-91	0	0	0.98	16	0	0	7	18	18	2	2	0	8	30	.250	.167	.292	14.73	3.93
Mieres, Oswaldo	R-R	6-3	178	5-14-92	1	0	3.24	7	0	0	2	8	5	3	3	1	3	8	.167	.200	.160	8.64	3.24
Moran, Luke	R-R	6-2	200	3-6-92	4	6	4.74	15	15	0	0	74	89	44	39	8	16	71	.298	.300	.296	8.64	1.95
Morillo, Junior	L-L	5-11	167	10-30-91	2	3	4.50	7	7	0	0	32	32	17	16	4	7	17	.250	.259	.248	4.78	1.97
Muehring, Austin	R-R	6-3	185	5-18-91	0	1	4.26	21	0	0	6	25	21	13	12	0	16	25	.221	.303	.177	8.88	5.68
Roman, Fabian	R-R	6-0	200	11-22-91	0	1	9.53	13	0	0	0	17	24	18	18	2	10	9	.343	.455	.292	4.76	5.29
Routt, Nick	L-L	6-4	215	8-28-90	0	1	1.29	2	2	0	0	7	7	6	1	0	1	8	.226	.200	.238	10.29	1.29
Salter, Austin	R-R	6-4	198	9-5-91	1	0	2.43	10	0	0	0	33	31	10	9	1	6	28	.248	.250	.246	7.56	1.62
Somsen, Layne	R-R	6-0	190	6-5-89	4	1	1.66	17	0	0	1	43	37	13	8	1	16	40	.236	.241	.232	8.31	3.12
Taveras, Werleen	R-R	5-11	170	8-10-90	2	0	0.63	7	0	0	0	14	5	2	1	1	5	14	.104	.100	.107	8.79	3.14
Weiss, Zack	R-R	6-1	200	6-16-92	2	4	4.39	10	5	0	0	27	30	21	13	7	4	18	.275	.233	.284	6.08	1.35
Wiley, Mo	R-R	6-4	234	12-11-89	0	1	33.75	2	0	0	0	1	4	5	5	0	3	2	.500	.000	.667	13.50	20.25
Wright, Daniel	R-R	6-2	205	4-3-91	3	3	5.91	14	0	0	0	43	57	30	28	4	5	43	.313	.382	.272	9.07	1.05

Fielding

Catcher	PCT	G	PO	A	E	DP	PB
Morillo	1.000	8	62	4	0	2	0
Ortiz	.985	41	301	26	5	1	3
Paula	.988	19	138	29	2	3	1
Reynolds	.970	9	63	1	2	0	0

First Base	PCT	G	PO	A	E	DP
Lopez	.967	19	133	15	5	9
Matthews	1.000	1	2	0	0	0
Ramirez	.800	1	3	1	1	0
Rosa	—	1	0	0	0	0
Sanchez	.996	54	476	25	2	33

Second Base	PCT	G	PO	A	E	DP
Bueno	.929	3	4	9	1	3
Rachal	.948	31	53	74	7	19
Ramirez	—	1	0	0	0	0
Washington	.977	42	62	110	4	16

Third Base	PCT	G	PO	A	E	DP
Rachal	.722	13	6	20	10	1
Ramirez	.926	31	17	46	5	4
Terrasas	.877	36	20	44	9	3
Washington	1.000	1	0	2	0	0

Shortstop	PCT	G	PO	A	E	DP
Bueno	.929	46	70	127	15	27
Daal	.948	15	17	56	4	6
Valor	.882	6	6	24	4	2
Washington	.839	9	6	20	5	4

Outfield	PCT	G	PO	A	E	DP
Aquino	.976	15	41	0	1	0
Benedetto	.988	33	82	3	1	0
Ervin	.946	27	51	2	3	1
Garcia	1.000	5	12	0	0	0
Matthews	1.000	30	54	0	0	0
Matthews	.986	34	66	2	1	2
Reynoso	.959	38	88	6	4	2
Rosa	.952	43	75	5	4	2
Washington	—	1	0	0	0	0

DSL REDS — ROOKIE

DOMINICAN SUMMER LEAGUE

Batting	B-T	HT	WT	DOB	AVG	vLH	vRH	G	AB	R	H	2B	3B	HR	RBI	BB	HBP	SH	SF	SO	SB	CS	SLG	OBP
Azcona, Francis	B-R	5-10	155	11-20-95	.329	.300	.339	46	164	26	54	7	7	0	18	22	2	0	1	31	9	8	.457	.413
Beltre, Michael	B-R	6-3	180	7-3-95	.222	.229	.220	44	126	31	28	5	3	0	11	15	7	1	0	46	6	2	.310	.338
Bernabel, Ery	R-R	6-1	175	7-2-94	.197	.147	.214	43	137	19	27	2	2	0	10	22	1	2	1	41	7	2	.241	.311
Burgos, Deyvi	L-L	6-2	185	7-16-92	.19	.227	.182	44	121	20	23	4	4	0	13	23	3	0	0	35	4	3	.289	.333
Capitillo, Derik	R-R	5-11	205	4-11-95	.188	.18	.191	49	160	24	30	5	2	3	23	25	8	2	0	34	6	3	.3	.326
De Luna, Jose	R-R	6-3	194	3-11-94	.298	.429	.242	13	47	6	14	2	0	0	4	4	1	0	0	11	1	2	.34	.365
Gabo, Erick	R-R	6-3	190	2-22-95	.185	.175	.188	51	168	18	31	3	3	4	16	9	2	0	0	76	4	5	.31	.235
Gonzalez, Luis	R-R	6-0	175	7-28-94	.235	.203	.244	67	264	32	62	10	4	2	28	12	4	2	1	30	18	14	.326	.278
Guerrero, Francis	R-R	6-3	185	11-16-94	.248	.167	.28	31	105	13	26	9	0	0	6	8	1	1	0	32	2	4	.333	.307
Guerrero, Raynay	R-R	6-4	190	2-24-93	.26	.259	.261	54	200	22	52	11	0	4	34	5	7	2	7	35	2	3	.375	.292
Hernandez, Luis	R-R	6-2	180	7-21-94	.131	.077	.149	49	160	8	21	6	1	1	10	9	2	0	2	62	4	1	.2	.185
Jimenez, Daniel	R-R	5-11	175	4-23-96	.266	.27	.265	64	222	25	59	9	5	0	21	11	7	0	1	29	18	7	.351	.32

CINCINNATI REDS

	B-T	HT	WT	DOB	AVG	vLH	vRH	G	AB	R	H	2B	3B	HR	RBI	BB	HBP	SH	SF	SO	SB	CS	OBP	SLG
Jimenez, Olvis	L-L	6-4	175	5-18-94	.253	.147	.286	49	146	20	37	6	2	0	3	19	2	0	0	31	4	4	.322	.347
Lopez, Maikel	B-R	6-2	185	10-31-93	.207	.091	.25	38	121	19	25	8	2	0	11	11	5	0	0	28	5	1	.306	.299
Manzanero, Pabel	R-R	6-3	170	1-30-96	.241	.171	.259	53	170	17	41	6	0	1	21	11	8	0	1	47	2	2	.294	.316
Mateo, Carlos	R-R	6-3	175	5-17-95	.217	.182	.229	38	129	19	28	5	0	0	9	8	1	2	0	36	3	3	.256	.268
Mejia, Cesar	L-R	6-1	165	12-8-94	.204	.095	.236	29	93	6	19	2	0	0	10	15	2	0	0	24	3	2	.226	.327
Mejia, Diohanky	R-R	6-3	190	9-29-95	.278	.128	.333	46	144	20	40	3	1	0	13	22	0	2	1	35	5	11	.313	.371
Mendez, Miguel	L-R	5-10	160	4-16-93	.333	.377	.315	63	234	45	78	20	2	0	28	28	8	3	0	23	32	10	.436	.422
Monegro, Jose	R-R	6-2	165	10-20-95	.222	.3	.203	51	158	14	35	7	0	4	15	15	4	0	1	40	5	2	.342	.303
Noel, Yoel	R-R	6-2	180	2-24-95	.141	—	—	26	85	7	12	3	1	1	4	2	4	0	0	34	0	1	.235	.198
Nunez, Ismael	R-R	6-3	175	8-9-95	.147	.16	.143	44	116	8	17	1	0	0	5	8	3	2	1	39	5	5	.155	.219
Peralta, Henderson	B-R	6-0	195	6-4-91	.232	.282	.216	47	155	21	36	4	4	2	22	12	8	2	0	24	17	9	.348	.32
Raga, Jose	R-R	5-11	190	11-20-93	.138	.103	.149	38	123	6	17	1	0	0	4	5	9	0	0	11	1	1	.146	.226
Rubicondo, Anthony	R-R	6-1	175	4-17-96	.214	.286	.193	57	182	18	39	9	0	0	16	15	5	1	4	58	7	5	.264	.286
Siri, Jose	R-R	6-2	175	7-22-95	.303	.375	.276	63	238	40	72	10	9	5	30	18	5	3	1	57	17	10	.483	.363
Valor, Geraldo	R-R	5-10	155	5-2-94	.259	.188	.281	57	201	41	52	11	1	2	28	23	6	3	0	19	19	8	.353	.352
Vargas, Hector	R-R	6-2	170	1-27-95	.327	.323	.329	61	226	41	74	12	1	0	33	24	8	3	2	18	21	9	.389	.408
Wallace, Raul	R-R	6-2	180	8-19-95	.25	—	—	26	84	9	21	5	2	1	12	5	4	1	0	34	6	2	.393	.323

Pitching

Pitching	B-T	HT	WT	DOB	W	L	ERA	G	GS	CG	SV	IP	H	R	ER	HR	BB	SO	AVG	vLH	vRH	K/9	BB/9
Arias, Junior	R-R	6-3	170	11-10-93	5	3	3.11	13	13	0	0	64	51	27	22	2	18	59	.223	.291	.187	8.34	2.54
Bautista, Wendolyn	R-R	6-0	185	3-27-93	1	10	5.63	14	12	0	0	56	54	47	35	4	33	57	.239	.273	.225	9.16	5.3
Bohorquez, Fabian	R-R	6-2	198	11-28-90	1	0	3.42	20	0	0	1	47	41	26	18	2	22	45	.236	.217	.246	8.56	4.18
Cantalizo, Eury	R-R	6-2	185	9-24-91	2	1	3.23	18	5	0	1	53	55	24	19	0	11	34	.27	.265	.272	5.77	1.87
Castellano, Josue	L-L	6-0	190	1-13-92	1	4	2.03	24	0	0	9	27	25	10	6	0	7	41	.248	.273	.241	13.84	2.36
Constante, Jacob	L-L	6-4	215	3-22-94	0	1	1.86	12	11	0	0	39	28	17	8	0	22	55	.197	.129	.216	12.8	5.12
Cuevas, Israel	R-R	6-1	178	9-19-93	3	3	2.55	11	11	0	0	53	37	16	15	0	29	46	.198	.203	.195	7.81	4.92
Damian, Pedro	R-R	6-1	170	11-29-92	2	3	4.39	13	12	0	0	53	46	35	26	5	30	62	.237	.333	.211	10.46	5.06
De Jesus, Yoel	R-R	6-2	180	10-8-94	1	0	5.7	15	0	0	1	24	26	21	15	1	16	18	.283	.323	.262	6.85	6.08
De Leon, John	R-R	6-4	205	10-13-93	0	4	5.11	18	7	0	0	49	45	34	28	0	30	46	.239	.281	.218	8.39	5.47
De Sousa, Jose	L-L	6-0	180	5-15-92	2	4	2.38	13	13	0	0	57	41	23	15	2	20	51	.203	.24	.198	8.1	3.18
Encarnacion, Carlos	R-R	6-3	180	11-15-93	1	3	2.76	20	0	0	1	33	26	26	10	1	26	29	.213	.214	.213	7.99	7.16
Gonzalez, Luis	L-L	6-1	170	3-25-93	6	2	1.49	18	1	0	0	48	34	11	8	1	3	47	.201	.176	.207	8.75	0.56
Guzman, Hernando	R-R	6-2	170	3-12-96	0	2	3.38	21	0	0	5	27	28	13	10	1	14	22	.277	.289	.27	7.43	4.73
Heredia, Jose	L-L	6-3	200	6-12-92	1	0	21.94	8	0	0	0	5	4	16	13	1	22	3	.235	.5	.2	5.06	37.13
Hernandez, Joyce	R-R	6-2	170	10-28-92	1	2	2.95	18	0	0	1	37	29	15	12	1	12	38	.227	.087	.257	9.33	2.95
Jones, David	R-R	6-4	200	4-26-94	3	1	5.57	12	0	0	0	21	22	15	13	1	08	25	.272	.273	.271	10.71	7.71
Lara, Jean	R-R	6-3	200	4-15-93	3	8	7.28	14	14	1	0	59	79	54	48	0	22	34	.317	.313	.319	5.16	3.34
Martinez, Jairo	L-L	6-1	175	3-21-93	2	1	3.49	14	0	0	2	28	29	12	11	1	21	26	.287	.28	.289	8.26	6.67
Mateo, Alfredo	R-R	6-1	185	10-24-93	0	4	8.89	22	0	0	2	27	38	35	27	1	26	36	.314	.286	.326	11.85	8.56
Moncion, Isaac	R-R	6-5	210	8-11-95	0	1	4.86	8	2	0	0	17	19	13	9	1	12	15	—	—	—	8.1	6.48
Montilla, Franklin	R-R	6-4	203	6-28-94	1	2	4.32	24	0	0	2	42	35	23	20	1	22	42	.238	.212	.253	9.07	4.75
Munoz, Jose	R-R	6-2	180	4-4-92	1	2	4.96	14	0	0	2	16	17	12	9	0	5	13	.283	.385	.255	7.16	2.76
Pena, Warlin	L-L	6-2	170	7-17-95	1	7	5.53	14	11	0	0	42	40	43	26	2	44	30	.247	.276	.241	6.38	9.35
Reinoso, Gregory	L-L	6-1	170	11-17-95	0	1	4.98	22	0	0	1	34	30	30	19	1	36	35	.236	.364	.21	9.17	9.44
Salas, Jose	R-R	6-3	190	2-7-95	3	8	4.1	14	14	0	0	64	61	40	29	3	24	39	.249	.232	.258	5.51	3.39
Santos, Yerry	R-R	6-4	180	11-30-94	2	0	12.38	20	0	0	0	24	32	36	33	4	45	12	.323	.385	.283	4.5	16.88
Taveras, Damian	R-R	6-3	190	1-14-96	3	2	5.71	17	0	0	1	35	36	29	22	1	15	27	.265	.323	.248	7.01	3.89
Telleria, Adolfi	R-R	6-1	170	4-12-94	2	3	3.12	17	1	0	0	35	36	16	12	2	6	35	.261	.32	.227	9.09	1.56
Veras, Jose	R-R	6-4	180	2-10-94	0	2	4.66	14	12	0	0	48	56	32	25	2	25	31	.309	.244	.329	5.77	4.66
Zapata, John	R-R	5-11	190	8-11-92	2	0	5.95	12	0	0	1	20	15	16	13	1	15	19	.221	.3	.188	8.69	6.86

Fielding

Catcher	PCT	G	PO	A	E	DP	PB
Capitillo	.965	32	249	51	11	0	16
Guerrero	.971	24	173	27	6	1	6
Lopez	.964	27	193	23	8	4	8
Manzanero	.976	22	145	17	4	2	9
Peralta	.981	18	133	18	3	0	4
Raga	.986	26	172	33	3	3	9

First Base	PCT	G	PO	A	E	DP
Burgos	.974	31	221	4	6	16
Capitillo	1	7	63	3	0	5
De Luna	1	4	34	1	0	2
Gabo	.981	7	50	1	1	2
Gonzalez	1	1	2	0	0	0
Guerrero	1	4	37	1	0	1
Guerrero	.961	34	277	19	12	21
Manzanero	.976	23	153	10	4	16
Mejia	.969	8	60	3	2	7
Monegro	.972	9	67	3	2	9
Peralta	.993	18	136	3	1	8
Raga	.985	9	65	2	1	5

Second Base	PCT	G	PO	A	E	DP
Azcona	.921	39	56	73	11	9
Bernabel	1	1	2	1	0	0
Gonzalez	1	1	1	3	0	0
Mejia	1	4	8	3	0	1
Mendez	.98	60	132	158	6	21
Rubicondo	.946	34	57	66	7	19
Valor	.97	8	12	20	1	3
Vargas	1	2	1	4	0	1

Third Base	PCT	G	PO	A	E	DP
Bernabel	.878	23	16	27	6	1
Burgos	1	1	0	1	0	0
Jimenez	.5	1	0	1	1	0
Manzanero	.867	6	4	9	2	0
Mejia	.895	15	8	26	4	1
Mendez	1	4	6	6	0	0
Monegro	.8	26	17	39	14	2
Peralta	.813	6	5	8	3	2
Raga	.7	4	3	4	3	0
Rubicondo	.842	24	15	49	12	6
Siri	1	2	4	5	0	0
Valor	.934	33	33	52	6	5
Vargas	.909	3	4	6	1	0
Wallace	.857	6	2	10	2	1

Shortstop	PCT	G	PO	A	E	DP
Azcona	.833	8	11	14	5	5
Gonzalez	.91	65	130	195	32	31
Valor	.897	14	16	36	6	8
Vargas	.948	55	73	147	12	15

Outfield	PCT	G	PO	A	E	DP
Beltre	.927	40	49	2	4	0
Bernabel	.846	7	9	2	2	0
Burgos	.933	9	12	2	1	0
De Luna	.875	7	7	0	1	0
Gabo	.956	37	42	1	2	0
Guerrero	.8	4	4	0	1	0
Hernandez	.986	39	69	3	1	1
Jimenez	.966	56	106	9	4	4
Jimenez	.971	32	31	3	1	1
Mateo	.94	37	71	7	5	2
Mejia	.896	44	41	2	5	0
Monegro	—	1	0	0	0	0
Noel	.971	22	31	2	1	1
Nunez	.9	42	52	2	6	1
Siri	.964	58	99	9	4	3
Wallace	.968	20	29	1	1	0

Cleveland Indians

SEASON IN A SENTENCE: The Indians turned the franchise's fortunes around in one dramatic swoop, improving by 24 wins over 2012 to post their first winning season and playoff appearance since 2007 before a wild-card loss to the Rays.

HIGH POINT: Cleveland entered September four-and-a-half games out of a playoff spot before posting the majors' best record in September at 21-6. The Tribe closed the season on a 10-game winning streak, highlighted by Jason Giambi's memorable walkoff homer with two outs in the ninth against the White Sox on Sept. 24.

LOW POINT: For all the storybook qualities of the Indians' season, it's hard to overlook their struggles with quality opponents. The Indians went just 30-44 against teams with winning records while feasting on the American League's lightweights, including a 23-3 record against the Astros and White Sox.

NOTABLE ROOKIES: A trio of rookies played prominent roles in the Indians' late-season run. Righthander Danny Salazar joined the rotation full-time in August, posted a 3.33 ERA in nine starts down the stretch and got the ball to start the wild-card game against the Rays. Batterymate Yan Gomes, acquired in the offseason from the Blue Jays, earned the lion's share of the catching duties in the second half, displacing Carlos Santana to the DH role, while batting .294/.345/.481 with 11 homers. In the bullpen, righthander Cody Allen, who debuted in 2012, logged the second-most appearances in the AL with 77 and went 6-1, 2.43.

KEY TRANSACTIONS: The hiring of Terry Francona as manager may have been Cleveland's most important move. The culture change continued with the signings of veterans Nick Swisher, Michael Bourn and Giambi. A nine-player, three-team trade that sent Shin-Soo Choo to the Reds brought righthanders Bryan Shaw and Trevor Bauer to Cleveland from Arizona. Shaw made 70 appearances out of the bullpen with a 3.24 ERA.

DOWN ON THE FARM: Bauer, the No. 3 overall pick in 2011, struggled to a 4.15 ERA for Triple-A Columbus and made just four starts for Cleveland. Shortstop Francisco Lindor continued to shine as the farm system's brightest light. Lindor was the top prospect in the high Class A Carolina League and made his Double-A debut as a 19-year-old. The system still isn't particularly deep, and Indians affiliates finished with the second-worst cumulative winning percentage (.445).

OPENING DAY PAYROLL: $77.8 million (21st)

PLAYERS OF THE YEAR

MAJOR LEAGUE	MINOR LEAGUE
Jason Kipnis	**Danny Salazar**
2b	**rhp**
.284/.366/.452	(Double-A/Triple-A)
17 HR, 36 2B, 30 SB	6-5, 2.71, 93 IP
9th in AL in SB	129 SO, 24 BB

ORGANIZATION LEADERS

BATTING		*Minimum 250 AB
MAJORS		
* AVG	Brantley, Michael	.284
* OPS	Santana, Carlos	.832
HR	Swisher, Nick	22
RBI	Kipnis, Jason	84
MINORS		
* AVG	Lindor, Francisco, Akron/Carolina	.303
* OBP	Vick, Logan, Carolina/Lake County	.404
* SLG	Wendle, Joe, Carolina	.513
R	Holt, Tyler, Akron	83
H	Smith, Jordan, Carolina	151
TB	Moncrief, Carlos, Akron	230
2B	Gonzalez, Erik, Carolina/Lake County	32
	Wendle, Joe, Carolina	32
3B	Gonzalez, Erik, Carolina/Lake County	12
HR	Hermida, Jeremy, Columbus	17
HR	Moncrief, Carlos, Akron	17
RBI	Aguilar, Jesus, Akron	105
BB	Vick, Logan, Carolina/Lake County	95
SO	Hermida, Jeremy, Columbus	149
SB	Carrera, Ezequiel, Columbus	43

PITCHING		#Minimum 75 IP
MAJORS		
W	Masterson, Justin	14
# ERA	Jimenez, Ubaldo	3.30
SO	Masterson, Justin	195
SV	Perez, Chris	25
MINORS		
W	Packer, Matt, Akron	12
L	Morimando, Shawn, Carolina	13
# ERA	Anderson, Cody, Carolina/Akron	2.65
G	Flores, Jose, Akron	59
GS	House, T.J., Columbus/Akron	28
	Murata, Toru, Columbus/Akron	28
SV	Guilmet, Preston, Columbus	20
IP	House, T.J., Columbus/Akron	164
BB	Morimando, Shawn, Carolina	76
SO	Espino, Paolo, Columbus/Akron	141
# AVG	Morimando, Shawn, Carolina	.231

2013 PERFORMANCE

General Manager: Chris Antonetti. **Farm Director:** Ross Atkins. **Scouting Director:** Brad Grant.

Class	Team	League	W	L	PCT	Finish	Manager
Majors	Cleveland Indians	American	92	70	.568	4th (15)	Terry Francona
Triple-A	Columbus Clippers	International	71	73	.493	8th (14)	Chris Tremie
Double-A	Akron Aeros	Eastern	68	73	.482	t-8th (12)	Edwin Rodriguez
High A	Carolina Mudcats	Carolina	57	83	.407	8th (8)	David Wallace
Low A	Lake County Captains	Midwest	54	83	.394	16th (16)	Scooter Tucker
Short-season	Mahoning Valley Scrappers	New York-Penn	30	44	.405	13th (14)	Ted Kubiak
Rookie	Indians	Arizona	28	28	.500	7th (13)	Anthony Medrano
Overall 2013 Minor League Record			308	384	.445	29th (30)	

ORGANIZATION STATISTICS

CLEVELAND INDIANS

AMERICAN LEAGUE

Batting	B-T	HT	WT	DOB	AVG	vLH	vRH	G	AB	R	H	2B	3B	HR	RBI	BB	HBP	SH	SF	SO	SB	CS	SLG	OBP
Aviles, Mike	R-R	5-10	205	3-13-81	.252	.232	.269	124	361	54	91	15	0	9	46	15	3	7	8	41	8	5	.368	.282
Bourn, Michael	L-R	5-11	180	12-27-82	.263	.277	.257	130	525	75	138	21	6	6	50	40	2	5	3	132	23	12	.360	.316
Brantley, Michael	L-L	6-2	200	5-15-87	.284	.276	.288	151	556	66	158	26	3	10	73	40	4	3	8	67	17	4	.396	.332
Cabrera, Asdrubal	B-R	6-0	205	11-13-85	.242	.232	.247	136	508	66	123	35	2	14	64	35	8	6	5	114	9	3	.402	.299
Carrera, Ezequiel	L-L	5-10	185	6-11-87	.500	—	.500	2	4	1	2	0	0	0	1	0	0	1	0	1	0	0	.500	.500
Carson, Matt	R-R	6-2	200	7-1-81	.636	1.000	.500	20	11	5	7	0	0	1	3	1	1	0	0	1	3	0	.909	.692
Chisenhall, Lonnie	L-R	6-2	190	10-4-88	.225	.111	.241	94	289	30	65	17	0	11	36	16	2	1	0	56	1	0	.398	.270
Giambi, Jason	L-R	6-3	235	1-8-71	.183	.077	.191	71	186	21	34	8	0	9	31	23	4	0	3	56	0	1	.371	.282
Gomes, Yan	R-R	6-2	215	7-19-87	.294	.327	.275	88	293	45	86	18	2	11	38	18	7	0	4	67	2	0	.481	.345
Kipnis, Jason	L-R	5-11	190	4-3-87	.284	.308	.270	149	564	86	160	36	4	17	84	76	3	5	10	143	30	7	.452	.366
Kubel, Jason	L-R	6-0	220	5-25-82	.167	—	.167	9	18	0	3	1	0	0	5	0	0	0	0	10	0	0	.222	.348
Marson, Lou	R-R	6-1	205	6-26-86	.000	.000	.000	3	3	0	0	0	0	0	0	2	0	0	0	0	0	0	.000	.400
McDonald, John	R-R	5-9	180	9-24-74	.000	.000	.000	8	7	2	0	0	0	0	0	1	0	0	0	1	0	0	.000	.125
2-team total (6 Boston)					.133	—	—	14	15	3	2	0	0	0	0	2	0	0	0	4	0	0	.133	.235
Phelps, Cord	B-R	6-1	210	1-23-87	.000	.000	.000	4	9	0	0	0	0	0	0	0	0	0	0	2	0	0	.000	.000
Raburn, Ryan	R-R	6-0	185	4-17-81	.272	.308	.243	86	243	40	66	18	0	16	55	29	4	0	1	67	0	0	.543	.357
Ramirez, Jose	B-R	5-9	165	9-17-92	.333	.250	.375	15	12	5	4	0	1	0	0	2	0	0	0	2	0	1	.500	.429
Reynolds, Mark	R-R	6-2	220	8-3-83	.215	.215	.215	99	335	40	72	8	0	15	48	43	3	0	3	123	3	0	.373	.307
2-team total (36 New York)					.220	—	—	135	445	55	98	14	0	21	67	51	5	0	3	154	3	1	.393	.306
Santana, Carlos	B-R	5-11	210	4-8-86	.268	.299	.251	154	541	75	145	39	1	20	74	93	4	0	4	110	3	1	.455	.377
Santos, Omir	R-R	6-0	215	4-29-81	.000	—	.000	1	1	0	0	0	0	0	0	0	0	0	0	0	0	0	.000	.000
Shoppach, Kelly	R-R	6-0	220	4-29-80	.000	—	.000	1	2	0	0	0	0	0	0	0	0	0	0	1	0	0	.000	.000
2-team total (35 Seattle)					.193	—	—	36	109	11	21	7	0	3	9	12	3	2	1	46	0	0	.339	.288
Stubbs, Drew	R-R	6-4	205	10-4-84	.233	.266	.216	146	430	59	100	21	2	10	45	44	2	2	3	141	17	2	.360	.305
Swisher, Nick	B-L	6-0	200	11-25-80	.246	.295	.220	145	549	74	135	27	2	22	63	77	4	0	4	138	1	0	.423	.341

Pitching	B-T	HT	WT	DOB	W	L	ERA	G	GS	CG	SV	IP	H	R	ER	HR	BB	SO	AVG	vLH	vRH	K/9	BB/9
Albers, Matt	L-R	6-1	225	1-20-83	3	1	3.14	56	0	0	2	63	57	25	22	2	23	35	.242	.262	.226	5.00	3.29
Allen, Cody	R-R	6-1	210	11-20-88	6	1	2.43	77	0	0	2	70	62	22	19	7	26	88	.233	.230	.236	11.26	3.33
Barnes, Scott	L-L	6-4	200	9-5-87	0	1	7.27	6	0	0	1	9	8	7	7	3	3	10	.242	.200	.278	10.38	3.12
Bauer, Trevor	R-R	6-1	190	1-17-91	1	2	5.29	4	4	0	0	17	15	11	10	3	16	11	.238	.207	.265	5.82	8.47
Carrasco, Carlos	R-R	6-3	210	3-21-87	1	4	6.75	15	7	0	0	47	64	36	35	4	18	30	.330	.351	.309	5.79	3.47
Guilmet, Preston	R-R	6-2	200	7-27-87	0	0	10.13	4	0	0	0	5	8	6	6	0	3	1	.320	.294	.375	1.69	5.06
Hagadone, Nick	L-L	6-5	230	1-1-86	0	1	5.46	36	0	0	0	31	24	21	19	4	21	30	.220	.211	.231	8.62	6.03
Hill, Rich	L-L	6-5	220	3-11-80	1	2	6.28	63	0	0	0	39	38	30	27	3	29	51	.257	.238	.281	11.87	6.75
Huff, David	L-L	6-2	215	8-22-84	0	0	15.00	3	0	0	0	3	7	5	5	0	1	5	.500	.286	.714	15.00	3.00
2-team total (11 New York)					3	1	5.50	14	2	0	0	38	33	23	23	7	9	31	—	—	—	7.41	2.15
Jimenez, Ubaldo	R-R	6-5	210	1-22-84	13	9	3.30	32	32	0	0	183	163	75	67	16	80	194	.239	.223	.258	9.56	3.94
Kazmir, Scott	L-L	6-0	185	1-24-84	10	9	4.04	29	29	0	0	158	162	76	71	19	47	162	.262	.226	.275	9.23	2.68
Kluber, Corey	R-R	6-4	215	4-10-86	11	5	3.85	26	24	0	0	147	153	67	63	15	33	136	.271	.277	.265	8.31	2.02
Langwell, Matt	R-R	6-2	220	5-6-86	1	0	5.06	5	0	0	0	5	5	3	3	1	2	6	.238	.222	.250	10.13	3.38
Lee, C.C.	R-R	5-11	190	10-21-86	0	0	4.15	8	0	0	0	4	4	3	2	0	3	4	.250	.200	.273	8.31	6.23
Martinez, Joe	L-R	6-2	190	2-26-83	1	0	1.80	2	0	0	0	5	4	1	1	0	0	3	.211	.300	.111	5.40	0.00
Masterson, Justin	R-R	6-6	250	3-22-85	14	10	3.45	32	29	3	0	193	156	75	74	13	76	195	.222	.248	.182	9.09	3.54
McAllister, Zach	R-R	6-6	240	12-8-87	9	9	3.75	24	24	0	0	134	134	65	56	13	49	101	.257	.249	.267	6.77	3.28
Myers, Brett	R-R	6-4	240	8-17-80	0	3	8.02	4	3	0	0	21	29	19	19	10	5	12	.319	.300	.333	5.06	2.11
Perez, Chris	R-R	6-4	230	7-1-85	5	3	4.33	54	0	0	25	54	56	27	26	11	21	54	.263	.291	.229	9.00	3.50
Pestano, Vinnie	R-R	6-0	200	2-20-85	1	2	4.08	37	0	0	6	35	37	18	16	6	21	37	.274	.292	.254	9.42	5.35
Rapada, Clay	R-L	6-5	195	3-9-81	0	0	0.00	4	0	0	0	2	1	0	0	0	2	0	.143	.000	.500	0.00	9.00
Rzepczynski, Marc	L-L	6-1	215	8-29-85	0	0	0.89	27	0	0	0	20	11	4	2	1	6	20	.159	.128	.200	8.85	2.66
Salazar, Danny	R-R	6-0	190	1-11-90	2	3	3.12	10	10	0	0	52	44	18	18	7	15	65	.226	.216	.237	11.25	2.60
Shaw, Bryan	B-R	6-1	210	11-8-87	7	3	3.24	70	0	0	1	75	60	31	27	4	28	73	.216	.254	.182	8.76	3.36
Smith, Joe	R-R	6-2	205	3-22-84	6	2	2.29	70	0	0	3	63	56	15	5	23	54	.235	.227	.242	7.71	3.29

Pitching	B-T	HT	WT	DOB	W	L	ERA	G	GS	CG	SV	IP	H	R	ER	HR	BB	SO	AVG	vLH	vRH	K/9	BB/9
Tomlin, Josh	R-R	6-1	190	10-19-84	0	0	0.00	1	0	0	0	2	2	0	0	0	0	0	.250	.000	.333	0.00	0.00
Wood, Blake	R-R	6-5	240	8-8-85	0	0	0.00	2	0	0	0	1	1	0	0	0	3	1	.200	.000	.333	6.75	20.25

Fielding

Catcher	PCT	G	PO	A	E	DP	PB
Gomes	.996	85	663	65	3	1	4
Marson	1.000	3	11	1	0	1	0
Santana	.995	84	694	33	4	2	5
Santos	1.000	1	2	0	0	0	0
Shoppach	.667	1	2	0	1	0	1

First Base	PCT	G	PO	A	E	DP
Gomes	1.000	1	6	0	0	0
Reynolds	.991	41	306	14	3	30
Santana	.995	29	185	9	1	29
Swisher	.991	112	812	88	8	70

Second Base	PCT	G	PO	A	E	DP
Aviles	.978	12	13	31	1	5
Kipnis	.982	147	242	395	12	91
Phelps	.833	3	3	2	1	0
Raburn	1.000	2	7	3	0	1
Ramirez	1.000	5	2	7	0	0

Third Base	PCT	G	PO	A	E	DP
Aviles	.968	56	29	63	3	6
Chisenhall	.955	88	55	134	9	18
McDonald	.875	8	1	6	1	1
Ramirez	.750	2	0	3	1	0
Reynolds	.918	40	18	49	6	8

Shortstop	PCT	G	PO	A	E	DP
Aviles	.976	46	55	106	4	26
Cabrera	.982	129	180	314	9	70
Ramirez	—	2	0	0	0	0

Outfield	PCT	G	PO	A	E	DP
Aviles	1.000	5	13	0	0	0
Bourn	.989	128	272	6	3	2
Brantley	1.000	151	257	11	0	1
Carrera	—	1	0	0	0	0
Carson	1.000	18	10	0	0	0
Kubel	1.000	6	8	1	0	0
Raburn	.979	65	92	3	2	2
Stubbs	.978	142	258	6	6	1
Swisher	.977	27	41	2	1	1

COLUMBUS CLIPPERS   TRIPLE-A
INTERNATIONAL LEAGUE

Batting	B-T	HT	WT	DOB	AVG	vLH	vRH	G	AB	R	H	2B	3B	HR	RBI	BB	HBP	SH	SF	SO	SB	CS	SLG	OBP
Abraham, Adam	R-R	6-0	228	3-27-87	.253	.278	.246	22	79	7	20	3	1	1	7	6	1	0	0	22	0	0	.354	.314
Antonelli, Matt	R-R	6-1	195	4-8-85	.000	.000	.000	3	6	0	0	0	0	0	0	2	0	0	1	0	0		.000	.250
Bourn, Michael	L-R	5-11	180	12-27-82	.143	.250	.000	2	7	0	1	0	0	0	0	1	0	0	0	3	1	0	.143	.250
Carrera, Ezequiel	L-L	5-10	185	6-11-87	.248	.197	.269	105	416	57	103	16	5	5	31	38	2	6	2	87	43	12	.346	.312
Carson, Matt	R-R	6-2	200	7-1-81	.252	.270	.246	121	436	57	110	16	2	14	49	39	7	6	2	119	14	4	.394	.322
Chen, Chun	R-R	5-11	210	11-1-88	.223	.222	.223	94	350	36	78	13	2	9	40	37	4	1	3	105	5	3	.349	.302
Chisenhall, Lonnie	L-R	6-2	190	10-4-88	.390	.310	.421	27	105	21	41	8	2	6	26	12	4	0	4	24	2	0	.676	.456
Cooper, David	L-L	6-0	200	2-12-87	.192	.200	.190	7	26	1	5	0	0	0	1	2	0	0	0	2	0	0	.192	.250
Diaz, Juan	B-R	6-4	200	12-12-88	.242	.212	.252	122	442	45	107	23	0	8	45	46	3	3	1	129	2	1	.348	.317
Fedroff, Tim	L-R	5-10	200	2-4-87	.242	.227	.248	136	513	65	124	13	1	6	48	72	1	4	4	118	22	11	.306	.334
Gomes, Yan	R-R	6-2	215	7-19-87	.300	.300	.333	6	20	2	6	4	0	0	3	4	0	0	0	4	0	0	.500	.417
Hermida, Jeremy	L-R	6-3	220	1-30-84	.247	.219	.258	132	474	62	117	23	3	17	66	88	2	0	3	149	1	3	.416	.365
Hernandez, Luis	B-R	5-10	190	6-26-84	.229	.191	.250	41	131	14	30	4	0	1	8	12	1	6	1	17	3	3	.282	.297
Hunter, Cedric	L-L	6-0	195	3-10-88	.250	.286	.235	32	96	14	24	5	0	2	11	8	0	1	1	14	2	2	.365	.305
LaPorta, Matt	R-R	6-2	215	1-8-85	.238	.262	.230	44	164	21	39	9	0	10	28	17	1	0	2	30	0	0	.476	.310
Lawson, Matt	R-R	6-0	195	11-18-85	.230	.219	.233	45	148	26	34	9	0	1	17	21	3	4	3	44	6	1	.311	.331
Marson, Lou	R-R	6-1	205	6-26-86	.100	.083	.125	8	20	0	2	0	0	0	1	3	0	0	0	8	0	0	.100	.217
McDade, Mike	B-R	6-1	250	5-8-89	.230	.231	.229	21	74	3	17	4	0	0	7	8	1	0	0	24	0	0	.284	.313
2-team total (94 Charlotte)					.250			115	428	39	107	22	0	10	53	36	5	0	4	120	1	0	.371	.313
Medina, Yhoxian	R-R	5-10	165	5-11-90	.286	.000	.333	2	7	1	2	1	0	0	1	0	0	0	0	1	0	0	.429	.286
Perez, Roberto	R-R	5-11	225	12-23-88	.176	.135	.193	67	187	16	33	12	0	0	24	22	3	6	4	59	0	1	.241	.269
Phelps, Cord	B-R	6-1	210	1-23-87	.267	.254	.271	65	255	29	68	16	1	9	46	27	0	2	3	49	4	3	.443	.333
Rohlinger, Ryan	R-R	6-0	195	10-7-83	.266	.269	.266	92	319	44	85	17	0	5	25	36	7	7	1	69	3	2	.367	.353
Santos, Omir	R-R	6-0	215	4-29-81	.248	.256	.246	61	206	14	51	9	2	3	23	10	2	1	3	47	0	0	.354	.285
Shoppach, Kelly	R-R	6-0	220	4-29-80	.333	.333	—	1	3	0	1	0	0	0	0	0	0	0	0	0	1	0	0	.333	.333
3-team total (7 Indianapolis, 10 Syracuse)					.213			18	61	3	13	1	0	0	4	6	2	1	0	18	0	0	.230	.304
Spears, Nate	L-R	5-11	180	5-3-85	.224	.250	.215	68	196	32	44	8	1	4	19	32	2	4	3	50	6	2	.337	.335
Toole, Justin	R-R	6-0	180	9-10-86	.250	.133	.286	20	64	5	16	1	0	0	6	1	0	2	0	7	1	0	.266	.262
Wallace, Chris	R-R	6-0	220	4-27-88	.280	.250	.289	18	50	5	14	5	0	0	9	3	0	0	2	17	0	0	.380	.309

Pitching	B-T	HT	WT	DOB	W	L	ERA	G	GS	CG	SV	IP	H	R	ER	HR	BB	SO	AVG	vLH	vRH	K/9	BB/9
Barnes, Scott	L-L	6-4	200	9-5-87	3	3	7.81	23	0	0	0	28	30	24	24	4	20	35	.286	.263	.299	11.39	6.51
Bauer, Trevor	R-R	6-1	190	1-17-91	6	7	4.15	22	22	1	0	121	119	64	56	14	73	106	.266	.291	.245	7.86	5.41
Bonser, Boof	R-R	6-4	245	10-14-81	0	2	6.00	3	1	0	0	15	20	10	10	1	4	10	.357	.333	.379	6.00	2.40
Brach, Brett	R-R	6-2	190	3-29-88	1	0	2.19	2	2	0	0	12	10	3	3	0	3	11	.222	.160	.300	8.03	2.19
Bryson, Rob	R-R	6-1	200	12-11-87	1	1	6.19	13	0	0	0	16	17	12	11	5	16	16	.274	.222	.295	9.00	9.00
Capps, Matt	R-R	6-2	260	9-3-83	0	0	1.29	6	0	0	0	7	6	1	1	1	1	3	.250	.143	.294	3.86	1.29
Carrasco, Carlos	R-R	6-3	210	3-21-87	3	1	3.14	16	14	0	1	72	59	31	25	6	21	79	.221	.167	.258	9.92	2.64
Cook, Cole	R-R	6-6	220	10-18-88	1	0	12.60	3	0	0	0	5	7	7	7	0	3	2	.350	.333	.357	3.60	5.40
Espino, Paolo	R-R	5-10	190	1-10-87	4	6	3.92	17	8	0	0	62	66	30	27	6	17	68	.269	.255	.281	9.87	2.47
Gil, Jerry	R-R	6-3	215	10-14-82	5	2	4.15	31	1	0	3	48	41	24	22	3	27	41	.233	.246	.225	7.74	5.10
Guilmet, Preston	R-R	6-0	200	7-27-87	5	4	1.68	49	0	0	20	64	43	19	12	4	14	72	.182	.204	.165	10.07	1.96
Hagadone, Nick	L-L	6-5	230	1-1-86	2	3	2.51	27	0	0	7	32	24	9	9	1	17	46	.203	.103	.253	12.80	4.73
Head, Louis	R-R	6-1	180	4-23-90	0	0	0.00	1	0	0	0	2	2	0	0	0	2	2	.333	.000	.400	10.80	10.80
House, T.J.	R-L	6-1	205	9-29-89	7	10	4.32	24	24	2	0	142	163	76	68	11	54	110	.291	.254	.301	6.99	3.43
Huff, David	L-L	6-2	215	8-22-84	3	1	4.07	9	2	0	0	24	28	12	11	2	10	36	.223	.292	.200	10.36	3.33
2-team total (13 Scranton/W-B)					4	7	3.90	22	14	0	1	92	97	44	40	8	22	92	—	—		8.97	2.14
Jakubauskas, Chris	R-R	6-2	215	12-22-78	0	0	3.86	11	0	0	0	14	14	7	6	1	8	13	.259	.200	.294	8.36	5.14
Kazmir, Scott	L-L	6-0	185	1-24-84	1	0	0.00	1	1	0	0	5	5	1	0	0	0	5	.278	.500	.250	9.00	0.00
Kluber, Corey	R-R	6-4	215	4-10-86	1	1	6.57	2	2	0	0	12	14	9	9	2	3	12	.286	.500	.231	8.76	2.19
Landis, Kyle	R-R	6-1	185	5-30-86	1	0	0.00	1	0	0	0	2	1	0	0	0	1		.200	.500	.000	4.50	0.00

	B-T	HT	WT	DOB	W	L	ERA	G	GS	CG	SV	IP	H	R	ER	HR	BB	SO	AVG	vLH	vRH	K/9	BB/9
Langwell, Matt	R-R	6-2	220	5-6-86	3	4	2.24	42	1	0	2	60	54	15	15	1	19	52	.240	.352	.164	7.76	2.83
Lee, C.C.	R-R	5-11	190	10-21-86	1	0	2.37	19	0	0	0	19	14	5	5	1	5	24	.212	.111	.250	11.37	2.37
Martinez, Joe	L-R	6-2	190	2-26-83	3	7	5.26	24	21	0	0	130	163	80	76	19	27	90	.305	.333	.284	6.23	1.87
Matsuzaka, Daisuke	R-R	6-0	185	9-13-80	5	8	3.92	19	19	0	0	103	93	47	45	11	39	95	.245	.238	.250	8.27	3.40
McAllister, Zach	R-R	6-6	240	12-8-87	1	0	0.00	1	1	0	0	6	2	0	0			2	.111	.167	.000	3.00	3.00
Murata, Toru	L-R	6-0	175	5-20-85	0	3	5.67	5	5	0	0	27	37	19	17	7	8	15	.319	.245	.373	5.00	2.67
Nieve, Fernando	R-R	6-0	220	7-15-82	5	3	1.81	22	2	0	0	45	34	12	9	5	12	55	.215	.172	.245	11.08	2.42
Pestano, Vinnie	R-R	6-0	200	2-20-85	0	0	3.29	14	0	0	0	14	13	5	5	0	4	13	.265	.412	.188	8.56	2.63
Price, Bryan	R-R	6-4	210	11-13-86	1	3	2.44	35	1	0	2	59	51	20	16	5	12	75	.229	.217	.236	11.44	1.83
Rapada, Clay	R-L	6-5	195	3-9-81	0	0	1.13	27	0	0	1	24	18	5	3	1	9	20	.220	.188	.265	7.50	3.38
2-team total (10 Scranton/W-B)					1	0	2.14	37	0	0	2	34	31	10	8	2	13	24	—	—	—	6.42	3.48
Romero, J.C.	B-L	5-11	205	6-4-76	0	0	4.50	2	0	0	0	2	1	1	1	0	2	2	.167	.000	.250	9.00	9.00
2-team total (13 Syracuse)					0	1	3.07	15	0	0	0	15	14	6	5	1	6	18	—	—	—	11.05	3.68
Salazar, Danny	R-R	6-0	190	1-11-90	4	2	2.73	14	13	0	1	59	44	21	18	4	14	78	.207	.198	.214	11.83	2.12
Soto, Giovanni	L-L	6-2	190	5-18-91	0	1	5.19	9	1	0	0	9	8	5	5	0	9	8	.267	.000	.320	8.31	9.35
Suarez, Benny	R-R	6-0	190	9-28-91	0	0	1.23	4	0	0	0	7	6	1	1	1	6	9	.214	.200	.222	11.05	7.36
Tomlin, Josh	R-R	6-1	190	10-19-84	2	0	2.40	3	3	0	0	15	12	4	4	0	0	11	.222	.190	.242	6.60	0.00
Valera, Francisco	R-R	6-1	170	10-19-89	1	0	0.00	3	0	0	0	7	2	0	0	0	1	7	.091	.111	.077	9.45	1.35
Wood, Blake	R-R	6-5	240	8-8-85	2	0	2.16	18	0	0	0	17	11	4	4	0	10	23	.186	.227	.162	12.42	5.40

Fielding

Catcher	PCT	G	PO	A	E	DP	PB
Gomes	.962	6	47	3	2	1	0
Marson	1.000	7	46	0	0	0	2
Perez	.989	66	570	43	7	5	4
Santos	.996	61	484	26	2	3	6
Shoppach	1.000	1	10	0	0	0	0
Wallace	.991	18	101	8	1	0	1

First Base	PCT	G	PO	A	E	DP
Abraham	.982	9	51	5	1	4
Chen	.988	71	514	40	7	59
Cooper	1.000	5	50	1	0	2
LaPorta	.995	24	189	2	1	12
McDade	.994	21	159	10	1	21
Phelps	.990	14	98	2	1	6
Spears	1.000	14	84	9	0	7

Second Base	PCT	G	PO	A	E	DP
Antonelli	.900	3	4	5	1	0
Diaz	1.000	12	15	24	0	5
Hernandez	.981	25	46	55	2	15
Lawson	.990	26	33	69	1	10
Medina	1.000	2	2	4	0	0
Phelps	.981	39	63	96	3	28
Rohlinger	.971	9	14	20	1	3
Spears	.970	34	56	75	4	22
Toole	1.000	3	2	5	0	0

Third Base	PCT	G	PO	A	E	DP
Abraham	.966	10	4	24	1	1
Chisenhall	.901	27	19	54	8	2
Diaz	1.000	7	4	14	0	3
Hernandez	.900	8	2	7	1	0
Lawson	.900	3	2	7	1	3
Rohlinger	.936	57	42	105	10	10
Spears	.962	19	15	36	2	5

	PCT	G	PO	A	E	DP
Toole	.946	17	9	26	2	2
Shortstop	PCT	G	PO	A	E	DP
Diaz	.960	102	125	260	16	54
Hernandez	.967	7	8	21	1	5
Lawson	.972	10	12	23	1	4
Rohlinger	1.000	26	36	75	0	22
Outfield	PCT	G	PO	A	E	DP
Abraham	1.000	5	10	0	0	0
Bourn	1.000	2	7	0	0	0
Carrera	.986	94	204	8	3	3
Carson	.988	103	227	19	3	4
Chen	.971	20	32	1	1	0
Fedroff	.991	113	220	9	2	1
Hermida	.958	64	109	4	5	0
Hunter	.964	30	53	1	2	0
Phelps	1.000	13	19	1	0	0
Spears	—	1	0	0	0	0

AKRON AEROS   DOUBLE-A

EASTERN LEAGUE

Batting	B-T	HT	WT	DOB	AVG	vLH	vRH	G	AB	R	H	2B	3B	HR	RBI	BB	HBP	SH	SF	SO	SB	CS	SLG	OBP
Abraham, Adam	R-R	6-0	228	3-27-87	.243	.136	.272	29	103	10	25	4	0	1	9	12	0	0	1	30	0	1	.311	.319
Aguilar, Jesus	R-R	6-3	250	6-30-90	.275	.252	.284	130	499	66	137	28	0	16	105	56	5	0	7	107	0	1	.427	.349
Bellows, Kyle	R-R	6-2	204	8-19-88	.221	.368	.147	33	113	10	25	6	0	1	13	5	0	0	2	25	1	0	.301	.250
Chen, Chun	R-R	5-11	210	11-1-88	.328	.342	.323	38	137	23	45	10	1	6	29	23	2	0	2	41	8	0	.547	.427
Cid, Delvi	R-R	6-3	195	7-19-89	.143	.000	.182	9	28	6	4	0	1	0	0	2	1	0	0	9	1	1	.214	.226
Greenwell, Bo	L-L	6-0	185	10-15-88	.216	.100	.259	10	37	3	8	1	0	1	4	3	0	0	0	9	1	0	.324	.275
Holt, Tyler	R-R	5-10	187	3-10-89	.267	.286	.259	133	521	83	139	24	9	2	42	55	3	7	3	90	28	7	.359	.338
Hunter, Cedric	L-L	6-0	195	3-10-88	.295	.197	.337	61	234	32	69	20	4	12	39	17	2	0	3	35	2	3	.568	.344
Latimore, Quincy	R-R	5-11	175	2-3-89	.231	.244	.225	81	295	34	68	16	1	6	30	26	7	0	2	66	5	3	.353	.306
Lavisky, Alex	R-R	6-1	209	1-13-91	.190	.500	.158	6	21	2	4	1	0	0	2	1	0	0	0	2	0	0	.238	.292
Lawson, Matt	R-R	6-0	195	11-18-85	.246	.281	.229	58	195	30	48	6	1	3	26	26	6	2	2	39	7	3	.333	.349
Lindor, Francisco	B-R	5-11	175	11-14-93	.289	.238	.309	21	76	14	22	3	1	1	7	14	1	0	0	7	5	2	.395	.407
Lowery, Jake	L-R	6-0	195	7-21-90	.275	.204	.297	70	236	22	65	21	1	6	28	33	0	0	1	66	0	0	.449	.363
Lucas, Jeremy	R-R	6-1	205	1-10-91	.200	.333	.000	5	15	2	3	0	0	0	2	5	0	0	0	5	0	0	.200	.400
Marson, Lou	R-R	6-1	205	6-26-86	.333	—	.333	1	3	0	1	0	0	0	0	0	0	0	0	1	0	0	.333	.333
Moncrief, Carlos	L-R	6-0	219	11-3-88	.284	.215	.315	129	489	77	139	26	7	17	75	55	1	6		98	15	7	.470	.354
Monsalve, Alex	R-R	6-2	195	4-22-92	.295	.256	.333	21	78	9	23	4	1	2	6	1	0	1	0	15	0	0	.449	.304
Naquin, Tyler	L-R	6-2	175	4-24-91	.225	.226	.224	18	80	9	18	3	0	1	6	5	0	0	0	22	1	3	.300	.271
Perez, Roberto	R-R	5-11	225	12-23-88	.247	.304	.229	32	93	10	23	6	0	2	10	32	3	0	0	25	1	1	.376	.453
Ramirez, Jose	B-R	5-9	165	9-17-92	.272	.324	.251	113	482	70	131	16	6	3	38	39	1	7	4	41	38	16	.349	.325
Rodriguez, Ronny	R-R	6-0	170	4-17-92	.265	.245	.274	116	468	62	124	25	6	5	52	16	3	6	5	76	12	3	.376	.291
Spears, Nate	L-R	5-11	180	5-3-85	.167	.000	.231	4	18	1	3	1	0	0	3	3	0	0	0	3	0	0	.222	.286
Toole, Justin	R-R	6-0	180	9-10-86	.310	.316	.307	34	113	12	35	6	0	0	7	12	1	2	0	13	1	1	.363	.381
Urshela, Giovanny	R-R	6-0	197	10-11-91	.270	.189	.304	116	445	42	120	23	2	8	43	14	1	4	2	48	1	1	.384	.292
Wallace, Chris	R-R	6-0	220	4-27-88	.299	.280	.313	31	117	17	35	5	0	3	17	10	0	0	2	36	0	0	.419	.349

Pitching	B-T	HT	WT	DOB	W	L	ERA	G	GS	CG	SV	IP	H	R	ER	HR	BB	SO	AVG	vLH	vRH	K/9	BB/9
Adams, Austin	R-R	5-11	190	8-19-86	3	2	2.62	45	0	0	4	55	44	19	16	3	29	76	.215	.286	.158	12.44	4.75
Anderson, Cody	R-R	6-4	220	9-14-90	0	0	5.68	3	3	0	0	13	16	8	8	2	9	10	.320	.115	.542	7.11	6.39
Armstrong, Shawn	R-R	6-2	210	9-11-90	2	3	4.09	30	0	0	0	33	32	18	15	2	21	43	.252	.293	.217	11.73	5.73

Name	B-T	HT	WT	DOB	W	L	ERA	G	GS	CG	SV	IP	H	R	ER	HR	BB	SO	AVG	vLH	vRH	SO/9	BB/9
Berger, Eric	L-L	6-2	205	4-22-86	0	0	4.15	2	0	0	0	4	6	2	2	0	3	2	.333	.500	.286	4.15	6.23
Blair, Kyle	R-R	6-2	236	9-27-88	0	0	0.00	1	0	0	0	2	0	0	0	0	2	1	.000	.000	.000	5.40	10.80
Brach, Brett	R-R	6-2	190	3-29-88	9	9	4.79	27	20	0	0	130	135	77	69	14	34	72	.275	.266	.283	5.00	2.36
Bryson, Rob	R-R	6-1	200	12-11-87	0	1	12.50	16	0	0	1	18	22	25	25	6	18	25	.289	.360	.255	12.50	9.00
Cook, Cole	R-R	6-6	220	10-18-88	2	2	7.17	26	2	0	0	54	66	45	43	9	25	46	.310	.327	.296	7.67	4.17
Cooper, Jordan	R-R	6-2	190	5-10-89	4	4	3.11	18	10	0	0	72	52	25	25	6	32	57	.202	.214	.193	7.09	3.98
Crockett, Kyle	L-L	6-2	170	12-15-91	1	0	0.00	9	0	0	0	10	7	0	0	0	2	9	.200	.273	.167	7.84	1.74
Espino, Paolo	R-R	5-10	190	1-10-87	2	5	5.35	15	13	0	0	79	90	52	47	10	27	73	.283	.279	.287	8.32	3.08
Flores, Jose	R-R	6-3	250	6-4-89	7	3	2.71	59	0	0	16	66	55	26	20	1	27	87	.222	.248	.197	11.80	3.66
Haley, Trey	R-R	6-4	205	6-21-90	1	4	4.70	39	0	0	7	44	37	24	23	0	39	46	.239	.235	.241	9.41	7.98
House, T.J.	R-L	6-1	205	9-29-89	2	1	3.22	4	4	0	0	22	20	8	8	1	3	27	.235	.243	.229	10.88	1.21
Jimenez, Francisco	L-L	5-11	164	10-2-88	0	0	0.00	1	1	0	0	4	3	1	0	0	2	2	.188	.000	.250	4.50	0.00
Johnson, Jeff	R-0	185	2-9-90		0	0	2.49	19	0	0	0	22	12	6	6	1	5	24	.158	.162	.154	9.97	2.08
Landis, Kyle	R-R	6-1	185	5-30-86	1	2	10.54	12	0	0	0	14	23	21	16	3	10	12	.371	.375	.367	7.90	6.59
Lee, C.C.	R-R	5-11	190	10-21-86	0	0	3.38	8	0	0	0	8	3	3	3	0	4	9	.111	.125	.105	10.13	4.50
Martinez, Fabio	R-R	6-3	190	10-29-89	1	0	33.75	3	0	0	0	3	5	10	10	0	5	1	.385	.455	.000	3.38	16.88
McAllister, Zach	R-R	6-6	240	12-8-87	0	0	5.40	1	1	0	0	3	4	2	2	0	1	5	.286	.375	.167	13.50	2.70
Murata, Toru	L-R	6-0	175	5-20-85	6	6	4.19	23	23	0	0	131	143	76	61	18	21	104	.277	.261	.295	7.15	1.44
Myers, Brett	R-R	6-4	240	8-17-80	1	2	3.38	6	3	0	0	11	7	6	4	1	6	6	.175	.045	.333	5.06	5.06
Nixon, Robert	R-R	6-1	225	11-1-88	0	0	2.45	2	0	0	0	4	1	1	1	0	5	6	.083	.167	.000	14.73	12.27
Packer, Matt	L-L	6-0	200	8-28-87	12	9	3.27	28	25	0	0	154	172	71	56	8	44	119	.286	.254	.300	6.95	2.57
Paredes, Edward	L-L	6-0	180	9-30-86	0	1	8.10	6	0	0	0	7	9	6	6	2	3	12	.321	.353	.273	16.20	4.05
Perez, Chris	R-R	6-4	230	7-1-85	0	1	45.00	1	0	0	0	1	5	5	5	3	0	2	.714	1.000	.333	18.00	0.00
Price, Bryan	R-R	6-4	210	11-13-86	1	0	0.56	12	0	0	2	16	6	1	1	0	4	17	.111	.125	.100	9.56	2.25
Rayl, Mike	L-L	6-5	180	11-1-88	0	0	4.50	1	1	0	0	4	5	2	2	1	0	2	.294	.429	.200	4.50	0.00
Reichenbach, J.D.	L-L	6-2	180	8-29-88	0	1	25.20	6	0	0	0	5	15	15	14	0	9	2	.600	.700	.533	16.20	16.20
Roberts, Will	L-R	6-5	195	8-17-90	7	9	4.57	23	21	0	0	134	147	72	68	13	32	90	.285	.322	.251	6.04	2.15
Salazar, Danny	R-R	6-0	190	1-11-90	2	3	2.67	7	7	0	0	34	27	10	10	1	10	51	.220	.262	.172	13.63	2.67
Stowell, Bryce	R-R	6-2	205	9-23-86	4	1	2.58	36	0	0	4	45	33	18	13	2	21	62	.201	.206	.198	12.31	4.17
Tejeda, Enosil	R-R	6-0	175	6-21-89	1	1	0.89	33	0	0	0	41	23	6	4	0	13	36	.169	.290	.068	7.97	2.88
Tomlin, Josh	R-R	6-1	190	10-19-84	0	0	1.50	2	2	0	0	6	3	1	1	0	0	4	.143	.200	.091	6.00	0.00
Whitenack, Robert	R-R	6-5	185	11-20-88	0	2	27.00	3	2	0	0	6	15	18	18	1	11	4	.484	.538	.444	6.00	16.50
Wood, Blake	R-R	6-5	240	8-8-85	0	0	4.50	7	3	0	0	6	8	7	3	0	5	6	.296	.286	.308	9.00	7.50

Fielding

Catcher	PCT	G	PO	A	E	DP	PB
Lavisky	1.000	5	32	2	0	0	0
Lowery	.989	65	439	80	6	4	10
Lucas	1.000	5	40	4	0	1	1
Marson	1.000	1	7	0	0	1	0
Monsalve	.988	20	151	19	2	3	3
Perez	.994	32	318	29	2	5	2
Wallace	.993	16	136	12	1	2	7

First Base	PCT	G	PO	A	E	DP
Abraham	1.000	8	53	9	0	8
Aguilar	.988	128	1053	84	14	112
Chen	.980	5	42	7	1	4
Lawson	1.000	1	2	0	0	0
Lowery	1.000	3	16	1	0	3
Toole	—	1	0	0	0	0
Urshela	1.000	1	2	0	0	1
Wallace	1.000	1	15	2	0	1

Second Base	PCT	G	PO	A	E	DP
Lawson	.985	29	40	92	2	19
Ramirez	.962	53	104	150	10	34
Rodriguez	.962	44	80	120	8	31
Toole	1.000	20	38	45	0	12

Third Base	PCT	G	PO	A	E	DP
Abraham	1.000	4	1	6	0	0
Bellows	.927	13	10	28	3	6
Lawson	.955	10	3	18	1	1
Ramirez	.933	8	8	20	2	2
Spears	1.000	2	3	6	0	0
Urshela	.951	107	55	178	12	21

Shortstop	PCT	G	PO	A	E	DP
Lindor	.953	21	36	46	4	11
Ramirez	.959	50	70	139	9	30
Rodriguez	.948	71	99	190	16	45
Urshela	1.000	3	6	8	0	5

Outfield	PCT	G	PO	A	E	DP
Abraham	1.000	6	7	1	0	0
Bellows	.923	9	12	0	1	0
Cid	.950	7	19	0	1	0
Greenwell	1.000	10	13	1	0	0
Holt	.994	132	302	6	2	1
Hunter	.988	38	81	0	1	0
Latimore	.937	66	100	4	7	2
Lawson	.950	9	18	1	1	0
Moncrief	.973	129	240	16	7	8
Naquin	1.000	18	40	0	0	0
Toole	1.000	6	6	2	0	0

CAROLINA MUDCATS   HIGH CLASS A

CAROLINA LEAGUE

Batting	B-T	HT	WT	DOB	AVG	vLH	vRH	G	AB	R	H	2B	3B	HR	RBI	BB	HBP	SH	SF	SO	SB	CS	SLG	OBP
Battaglia, Ryan	R-R	6-1	202	6-29-92	.226	.143	.256	20	53	2	12	5	0	0	8	7	2	0	0	25	0	0	.321	.339
Gallas, Anthony	R-R	6-2	210	12-14-87	.212	.250	.208	14	52	6	11	3	0	0	2	3	1	0	0	9	0	0	.269	.268
Gonzalez, Erik	R-R	6-1	165	8-31-91	.242	.186	.264	39	153	16	37	9	5	0	27	5	0	1	4	38	1	2	.366	.259
Greenwell, Bo	L-L	6-0	185	10-15-88	.246	.258	.242	65	244	35	60	17	2	4	42	24	3	0	2	35	5	1	.381	.319
Hankins, Todd	R-R	5-9	175	11-18-90	.204	.318	.174	37	108	18	22	6	0	0	6	16	3	2	0	32	14	1	.259	.323
Lavisky, Alex	R-R	6-1	209	1-13-91	.224	.229	.222	39	143	20	32	8	0	3	16	11	3	2	3	34	0	0	.343	.283
Lindor, Francisco	B-R	5-11	175	11-14-93	.306	.237	.327	83	327	51	100	19	6	1	27	35	2	6	3	39	20	5	.410	.373
Lowery, Jake	L-R	6-0	195	7-21-90	.195	.167	.200	12	41	4	8	2	1	1	5	9	0	0	0	12	0	0	.366	.340
MacPhee, Zack	B-R	5-9	175	2-13-90	.219	.243	.212	60	183	15	40	8	1	2	16	30	0	3	2	37	1	1	.306	.326
Matera, Paddy	R-R	5-8	195	10-6-87	.282	.343	.259	73	241	49	68	19	1	4	35	39	18	1	3	54	0	0	.415	.415
Medina, Yhoxian	R-R	5-10	165	5-11-90	.232	.294	.215	23	82	6	19	2	0	0	8	2	2	1	0	18	1	4	.256	.267
Myles, Bryson	R-R	5-11	230	9-18-89	.285	.314	.275	92	337	55	96	20	2	8	52	32	11	1	9	84	15	7	.427	.357
Naquin, Tyler	L-R	6-2	175	4-24-91	.277	.200	.297	108	448	69	124	27	6	9	42	41	6	2	1	112	14	7	.424	.345
Rodriguez, Luigi	B-R	5-11	160	11-13-92	.283	.250	.290	34	113	16	32	11	1	0	11	18	1	1	1	36	3	4	.398	.383
Sabourin, Jerrud	L-L	6-2	210	11-2-89	.260	.258	.261	121	434	43	113	23	1	3	54	56	4	0	8	64	0	2	.339	.345
Sever, Joe	R-R	6-0	205	8-12-90	.316	.182	.338	21	76	11	24	4	0	0	6	5	1	0	0	10	1	0	.368	.366
Siliga, Aaron	L-L	5-8	170	8-24-92	.143	.000	.179	10	35	1	5	2	0	0	3	0	1	0		7	1	0	.200	.211

Batting	B-T	HT	WT	DOB	AVG	vLH	vRH	G	AB	R	H	2B	3B	HR	RBI	BB	HBP	SH	SF	SO	SB	CS	SLG	OBP
Smith, Jordan	L-R	6-4	205	7-5-90	.292	.296	.290	134	518	71	151	29	6	5	54	62	2	2	2	72	18	9	.400	.368
Toole, Justin	R-R	6-0	180	9-10-86	.211	.361	.162	43	147	10	31	4	0	0	19	7	0	5	3	17	3	2	.238	.242
Valerio, Charlie	B-R	6-0	204	11-7-90	.238	.233	.239	53	185	21	44	12	1	2	26	20	0	0	5	48	0	0	.346	.305
Vick, Logan	L-R	5-11	185	10-22-90	.225	.143	.246	20	71	9	16	3	1	2	11	14	1	1	0	19	1	1	.380	.360
Wendle, Joe	L-R	5-11	190	4-26-90	.295	.224	.320	107	413	73	122	32	5	16	64	44	10	1	6	79	10	2	.513	.372
Wolters, Tony	L-R	5-10	177	6-9-92	.277	.279	.276	80	289	36	80	13	0	3	33	41	3	4	3	58	3	6	.353	.369

Pitching	B-T	HT	WT	DOB	W	L	ERA	G	GS	CG	SV	IP	H	R	ER	HR	BB	SO	AVG	vLH	vRH	K/9	BB/9
Anderson, Cody	R-R	6-4	220	9-14-90	9	4	2.34	23	23	0	0	123	105	34	32	6	31	112	.236	.247	.230	8.17	2.26
Araujo, Elvis	L-L	6-6	215	7-15-91	0	0	5.59	2	2	0	0	10	11	8	6	1	4	8	.282	.222	.300	7.45	3.72
Colon, Joseph	R-R	6-0	167	2-18-90	5	3	3.13	15	15	0	0	83	73	36	29	2	25	67	.233	.248	.224	7.24	2.70
Cook, Cole	R-R	6-6	220	10-18-88	2	1	5.63	8	7	0	0	32	35	26	20	7	10	19	.276	.231	.307	5.34	2.81
Cooper, Jordan	R-R	6-2	190	5-10-89	1	2	2.19	4	4	0	0	25	16	7	6	2	7	17	.184	.139	.216	6.20	2.55
Dew, Owen	R-R	6-3	183	9-26-88	3	7	3.86	34	2	0	1	70	74	34	30	8	20	41	.286	.330	.262	5.27	2.57
Goodnight, Michael	R-R	6-4	215	6-10-89	1	0	5.71	21	1	0	0	35	33	23	22	2	29	29	.250	.233	.258	7.53	7.53
Head, Louis	R-R	6-1	180	4-23-90	4	2	3.11	21	0	0	3	38	33	13	13	4	3	41	.244	.204	.267	9.80	0.72
Jimenez, Francisco	L-L	5-11	164	10-2-88	2	1	2.65	31	1	0	0	58	54	24	17	4	23	31	.247	.246	.247	4.84	3.59
Johnson, Jeff	R-R	6-0	185	2-9-90	0	1	2.05	27	0	0	8	26	28	9	6	1	10	26	.267	.314	.243	8.89	3.42
Lee, Jacob	R-R	6-1	190	10-25-89	0	5	6.10	11	11	0	0	52	56	41	35	8	26	39	.272	.299	.259	6.79	4.53
Martin, Josh	R-R	6-5	230	12-30-89	0	2	4.86	16	0	0	0	33	37	18	18	4	11	24	.276	.191	.322	6.48	2.97
Martinez, Fabio	R-R	6-3	190	10-29-89	0	1	8.06	20	0	0	0	26	19	26	23	3	30	26	.200	.194	.203	12.62	10.52
Merritt, Ryan	L-L	6-0	165	2-21-92	0	0	5.00	2	2	0	0	9	7	5	5	1	1	6	.206	.000	.219	6.00	1.00
Morimando, Shawn	L-L	5-11	170	11-20-92	8	13	3.73	27	27	1	0	135	115	68	56	8	76	102	.231	.194	.243	6.80	5.07
Nixon, Robert	R-R	6-1	225	11-1-88	3	6	5.01	43	3	0	5	70	87	45	39	4	29	60	.312	.339	.293	7.71	3.73
Pasquale, Nick	R-R	6-0	190	10-27-90	6	7	3.97	20	20	0	0	102	118	56	45	6	29	51	.291	.310	.281	4.50	2.56
Penny, Cody	R-R	6-3	195	5-15-91	0	0	13.50	1	0	0	0	2	3	3	3	1	1	1	.375	.667	.200	4.50	4.50
Peoples, Scott	R-R	6-5	195	9-5-91	1	4	5.27	8	8	0	0	41	45	30	24	5	13	35	.280	.262	.290	7.68	2.85
Radeke, Mason	R-R	6-1	175	6-13-90	0	2	16.88	2	2	0	0	5	12	11	10	0	4	6	.414	.500	.222	10.13	6.75
Reichenbach, J.D.	L-L	6-2	180	8-29-87	4	5	3.30	41	0	0	1	57	51	25	21	1	24	38	.245	.179	.277	5.97	3.77
Roberts, Will	L-R	6-5	195	8-17-90	1	3	6.10	4	4	0	0	21	26	20	14	4	4	17	.306	.323	.296	7.40	1.74
Sides, Steven	R-R	6-4	215	6-22-89	2	3	6.58	27	0	0	0	40	39	32	29	4	32	44	.264	.241	.278	9.98	7.26
Suarez, Benny	R-R	6-0	190	9-28-91	0	1	2.25	13	0	0	1	16	11	4	4	1	2	8	.193	.150	.216	10.13	4.50
Tejeda, Enosil	R-R	6-0	175	6-21-89	1	2	2.04	14	0	0	2	18	11	7	4	0	9	30	.183	.368	.098	15.28	4.58
Valera, Francisco	R-R	6-1	170	10-19-89	3	5	3.75	24	1	0	0	58	52	26	24	1	23	46	.240	.213	.258	7.18	3.59
Whitenack, Robert	R-R	6-5	185	11-20-88	1	3	4.96	7	7	0	0	33	29	26	18	1	18	16	.228	.229	.228	4.41	4.96

Fielding

Catcher	PCT	G	PO	A	E	DP	PB
Battaglia	1.000	4	22	3	0	0	0
Lavisky	.988	32	231	26	3	3	2
Lowery	1.000	7	41	4	0	0	1
Valerio	.978	41	278	38	7	3	5
Wolters	.993	58	388	45	3	3	6

First Base	PCT	G	PO	A	E	DP
Battaglia	.991	14	93	12	1	11
Lowery	.947	2	18	0	1	1
Matera	.970	3	30	2	1	2
Sabourin	.985	115	926	78	15	88
Sever	.986	7	69	3	1	10
Valerio	1.000	3	27	4	0	2

Second Base	PCT	G	PO	A	E	DP
Hankins	.952	6	12	8	1	6
MacPhee	.973	22	48	59	3	17
Medina	.950	5	9	10	1	2
Sever	1.000	7	11	20	0	6
Toole	1.000	1	1	0	0	0
Wendle	.974	101	208	281	13	57
Wolters	1.000	1	2	2	0	1

Third Base	PCT	G	PO	A	E	DP
Hankins	.911	22	11	30	4	3
MacPhee	.933	24	20	36	4	1
Matera	.936	50	47	85	9	9
Medina	.913	16	10	32	4	3
Sever	.944	6	2	15	1	1
Toole	.937	29	16	43	4	3

Shortstop	PCT	G	PO	A	E	DP
Gonzalez	.949	39	45	122	9	23
Lindor	.952	82	123	234	18	51
Matera	1.000	5	9	12	0	4
Medina	1.000	2	1	3	0	0
Toole	.964	12	15	38	2	7
Wolters	1.000	1	2	4	0	2

Outfield	PCT	G	PO	A	E	DP
Gallas	.909	7	10	0	1	0
Greenwell	.973	42	72	1	2	1
Hankins	1.000	8	19	1	0	0
MacPhee	1.000	6	13	0	0	0
Myles	.993	82	144	7	1	1
Naquin	.985	102	251	11	4	3
Rodriguez	.974	27	34	3	1	0
Siliga	1.000	7	13	0	0	0
Smith	.985	126	252	13	4	3
Vick	.979	20	46	1	1	0

LAKE COUNTY CAPTAINS — LOW CLASS A

MIDWEST LEAGUE

Batting	B-T	HT	WT	DOB	AVG	vLH	vRH	G	AB	R	H	2B	3B	HR	RBI	BB	HBP	SH	SF	SO	SB	CS	SLG	OBP
Bautista, Claudio	R-R	5-11	170	11-29-93	.157	.200	.146	16	51	6	8	2	0	1	5	3	0	1	0	14	0	2	.255	.204
Castillo, Leonardo	R-R	6-2	190	7-9-93	.211	.167	.224	69	228	28	48	11	1	6	24	17	2	3	3	48	5	2	.346	.268
Cervenka, Martin	R-R	6-1	175	8-3-92	.176	.154	.184	15	51	4	9	0	0	0	3	7	0	0	0	17	0	0	.176	.276
Ferrell, Cody	B-R	5-10	195	4-29-90	.246	.235	.250	17	57	3	14	1	0	0	3	3	3	1	0	14	0	0	.263	.317
Garcia, Robel	B-R	6-0	168	3-28-93	.118	.333	.118	16	46	5	8	3	1	0	5	9	1	0	0	11	0	0	.283	.321
Gonzalez, Erik	R-R	6-1	165	8-31-91	.259	.176	.285	93	355	59	92	23	7	9	49	24	1	2	1	71	10	4	.439	.307
Haase, Eric	R-R	5-10	180	12-18-92	.250	.311	.227	104	376	49	94	23	3	14	47	40	1	1	2	117	2	2	.439	.322
Hamilton, Nick	B-R	6-1	200	11-19-89	.241	.226	.250	26	79	6	19	0	0	1	5	8	0	0	0	24	0	1	.278	.310
Hankins, Todd	R-R	5-9	175	11-18-90	.220	.212	.222	37	141	22	31	5	0	4	18	15	2	1	0	36	13	6	.340	.304
Lucas, Jeremy	R-R	6-1	205	1-10-91	.274	.241	.290	75	263	35	72	18	3	6	35	44	3	1	1	50	1	0	.433	.383
MacPhee, Zack	B-R	5-9	175	2-13-90	.209	.233	.198	38	129	12	27	5	0	0	7	19	4	1	1	24	5	3	.248	.327
Martinez, Jorge	B-R	6-1	183	3-29-93	.191	.163	.202	112	393	37	72	20	3	8	45	20	1	3	0	120	3	3	.334	.244
Medina, Yhoxian	R-R	5-10	165	5-11-90	.278	.352	.253	67	216	34	60	11	3	1	14	30	4	4	2	33	7	6	.370	.373
Paulino, Dorssys	R-R	6-0	175	11-21-94	.246	.233	.250	120	476	56	117	28	3	5	46	30	5	11	1	91	12	7	.349	.297
Rodriguez, Luigi	B-R	5-11	160	11-13-92	.263	.333	.241	22	76	14	20	2	0	1	9	10	0	1	1	25	5	3	.329	.345

	B-T	HT	WT	DOB	AVG	vLH	vRH	G	AB	R	H	2B	3B	HR	RBI	BB	HBP	SH	SF	SO	SB	CS	SLG	OBP
Rodriguez, Nelson	R-R	6-2	225	6-12-94	.194	.182	.197	47	160	18	31	7	0	1	13	26	0	1	1	53	0	0	.256	.305
Santander, Anthony	B-R	6-2	187	10-19-94	.242	.208	.251	61	219	27	53	13	0	5	31	13	6	0	0	43	6	3	.370	.303
Sever, Joe	R-R	6-0	205	8-12-90	.272	.260	.276	101	386	48	105	25	2	7	58	32	5	1	3	80	3	3	.402	.333
Siliga, Aaron	L-L	5-8	170	8-24-92	.214	.188	.222	23	70	10	15	3	0	1	11	5	1	2	0	18	4	1	.300	.276
Stock, Richard	R-R	6-2	190	2-8-91	.280	.154	.299	55	193	24	54	8	1	8	31	8	3	0	1	52	1	0	.456	.317
Vick, Logan	L-R	5-11	185	10-22-90	.281	.275	.283	108	349	61	98	23	3	5	45	81	3	2	8	81	25	7	.407	.413
Washington, LeVon	L-R	5-11	170	7-26-91	.321	.205	.356	51	193	33	62	19	4	1	19	32	3	1	0	46	14	4	.477	.425

Pitching	B-T	HT	WT	DOB	W	L	ERA	G	GS	CG	SV	IP	H	R	ER	HR	BB	SO	AVG	vLH	vRH	K/9	BB/9
Aviles, Robbie	L-R	6-4	200	12-17-91	4	5	5.09	16	14	0	0	69	72	42	39	7	26	30	.273	.279	.268	3.91	3.39
Baker, Dylan	R-R	6-2	215	4-6-92	7	6	3.63	27	25	1	0	144	124	68	58	3	62	117	.232	.239	.226	7.33	3.88
Blair, Kyle	R-R	6-2	236	9-27-88	0	0	0.00	1	0	0	0	1	0	0	0	0	0	1	.000	.000	.000	0.00	9.00
Brown, D.J.	R-R	6-6	205	11-28-90	3	4	2.71	27	2	0	1	66	59	26	20	5	20	71	.238	.200	.264	9.63	2.71
Brown, Mitch	R-R	6-1	195	4-13-94	1	1	11.49	5	5	0	0	16	21	21	20	4	11	18	.328	.344	.313	10.34	6.32
Colon, Joseph	R-R	6-0	167	2-18-90	0	1	4.15	2	2	0	0	9	10	5	4	0	2	9	.294	.333	.263	9.35	2.08
Crockett, Kyle	L-L	6-2	170	12-15-91	0	0	1.80	4	0	0	0	5	4	1	1	1	1	7	.211	.429	.083	12.60	1.80
Davenport, Geoff	L-L	6-1	180	3-14-90	0	1	3.38	3	0	0	0	8	7	4	3	1	0	6	.241	.500	.174	6.75	0.00
DeJesus, Luis	R-R	6-3	173	12-16-91	6	11	5.97	27	21	2	0	133	154	100	88	24	46	84	.292	.304	.282	5.70	3.12
Head, Louis	R-R	6-1	180	4-23-90	0	2	1.82	25	0	0	5	30	27	14	6	0	10	23	.245	.196	.281	6.98	3.03
Lee, C.C.	R-R	5-11	190	10-21-86	0	0	0.00	2	0	0	0	2	1	0	0	0	1	4	.167	.500	.000	18.00	4.50
Lugo, Luis	L-L	6-5	200	3-5-94	0	1	3.77	3	3	0	0	14	14	7	6	1	5	14	.250	.222	.255	8.79	3.14
Martin, Josh	R-R	6-5	230	12-30-89	3	3	3.38	23	1	0	2	40	33	18	15	6	7	47	.219	.200	.235	10.58	1.58
Merritt, Ryan	L-L	6-0	165	2-21-92	6	9	3.42	24	23	0	0	126	142	62	48	10	18	91	.287	.325	.270	6.48	1.28
Milbrath, Jordan	R-R	6-6	215	8-1-91	0	1	81.00	1	0	0	0	0	1	4	3	0	2	0	.333	.000	.500	0.00	54.00
Morel, Luis	R-R	6-0	170	11-19-92	5	6	5.36	26	5	0	3	92	99	64	55	4	47	83	.277	.319	.244	8.09	4.58
Pasquale, Nick	R-R	6-0	190	10-27-90	0	0	2.18	9	1	0	1	21	16	9	5	0	5	14	.208	.175	.243	6.10	2.18
Penny, Cody	R-R	6-3	195	5-15-91	1	2	4.42	22	1	0	1	37	42	19	18	3	12	27	.286	.255	.304	6.63	2.95
Peoples, Scott	R-R	6-5	195	9-5-91	1	2	2.64	11	2	0	0	31	35	18	9	0	6	33	.282	.350	.219	9.68	1.76
Perez, Chris	R-R	6-4	230	7-1-85	0	0	0.00	1	0	0	0	1	2	0	0	0	0	1	.667	1.000	.500	9.00	0.00
Pestano, Vinnie	R-R	6-0	200	2-20-85	0	0	0.00	1	0	0	0	1	0	0	0	0	0	1	.000	.000	.000	9.00	0.00
Polanco, Anderson	L-L	6-3	190	9-6-92	1	2	5.02	8	0	0	0	14	9	10	8	3	13	23	.167	.071	.200	14.44	8.16
Radeke, Mason	R-R	6-1	175	6-13-90	1	0	0.00	1	1	0	0	7	5	1	0	0	1	7	.063	.000	.143	12.60	1.80
Santana, Juan	R-R	6-2	170	7-2-93	0	1	11.25	1	1	0	0	4	10	6	5	2	0	3	.455	—	.455	6.75	0.00
Sides, Steven	R-R	6-4	215	6-22-89	2	0	1.38	18	0	0	7	26	15	5	4	0	12	34	.169	.268	.083	11.77	4.15
Sisco, Jake	R-R	6-3	185	12-9-91	4	11	4.86	24	23	1	0	111	118	78	60	13	48	71	.273	.281	.266	5.76	3.89
Sterling, Felix	R-R	6-3	200	3-15-93	3	4	5.13	38	3	0	1	53	68	41	30	5	29	51	.313	.337	.295	8.72	4.96
Stokes, Jim	R-R	6-6	225	10-9-90	0	2	4.50	16	0	0	0	26	31	17	13	2	16	16	.307	.342	.286	5.54	5.54
Suarez, Benny	R-R	6-0	190	9-28-91	2	2	3.38	12	0	0	0	21	20	9	8	0	13	17	.253	.375	.170	7.17	5.48
Tomlin, Josh	R-R	6-1	190	10-19-84	0	0	0.00	3	1	0	0	4	1	0	0	0	0	4	.067	.250	.000	8.31	0.00
Valera, Francisco	R-R	6-1	170	10-19-89	0	1	1.56	13	0	0	1	17	16	9	3	1	6	16	.229	.267	.200	8.31	3.12
Wagoner, Jack	R-R	6-1	205	6-20-89	4	5	5.17	42	0	0	2	56	52	34	32	4	34	58	.250	.244	.254	9.38	5.50
Wood, Blake	R-R	6-5	240	8-8-85	0	0	0.00	3	3	0	0	3	1	0	0	0	3	3	.111	.167	.000	10.13	10.13

Fielding

Catcher	PCT	G	PO	A	E	DP	PB
Cervenka	.973	8	63	10	2	1	2
Haase	.974	73	474	93	15	3	12
Lucas	.987	47	337	52	5	5	7
Stock	.978	12	85	3	2	0	2

First Base	PCT	G	PO	A	E	DP
Castillo	.989	30	241	17	3	23
Gonzalez	1.000	1	2	0	0	0
Hamilton	1.000	1	6	0	0	0
Lucas	1.000	2	6	0	0	0
Martinez	.955	2	19	2	1	0
Rodriguez	.991	40	328	16	3	23
Sever	.991	64	542	35	5	50
Stock	1.000	2	1	0	0	0

Second Base	PCT	G	PO	A	E	DP
Bautista	.968	16	43	48	3	11
Garcia	.946	14	24	29	3	5
Gonzalez	.973	13	19	54	2	8
Hankins	.940	15	26	37	4	7
MacPhee	.971	6	15	18	1	2
Medina	.972	67	139	170	9	41
Sever	1.000	11	18	25	0	4
Siliga	1.000	1	0	3	0	0

Third Base	PCT	G	PO	A	E	DP
Castillo	.869	29	25	48	11	3
Garcia	.750	2	1	2	1	0
Gonzalez	.936	65	62	142	14	23
Hankins	.929	5	3	10	1	0
MacPhee	.952	25	19	40	3	2
Sever	.902	18	10	36	5	4

Shortstop	PCT	G	PO	A	E	DP
Gonzalez	.952	16	19	40	3	3
MacPhee	1.000	8	7	16	0	2
Paulino	.916	116	149	274	39	48

Outfield	PCT	G	PO	A	E	DP
Castillo	1.000	1	4	0	0	0
Ferrell	.976	17	39	1	1	0
Gonzalez	—	1	0	0	0	0
Hamilton	.943	21	31	2	2	0
Hankins	.974	19	34	3	1	1
Martinez	.948	109	171	12	10	2
Rodriguez	.974	21	38	0	1	0
Santander	.959	61	111	6	5	1
Siliga	.960	21	44	4	2	0
Vick	.972	108	227	13	7	5
Washington	.955	50	104	2	5	0

MAHONING VALLEY SCRAPPERS SHORT-SEASON

NEW YORK-PENN LEAGUE

Batting	B-T	HT	WT	DOB	AVG	vLH	vRH	G	AB	R	H	2B	3B	HR	RBI	BB	HBP	SH	SF	SO	SB	CS	SLG	OBP
Battaglia, Ryan	R-R	6-1	202	6-29-92	.200	.200	.200	19	60	8	12	3	0	3	5	6	4	0	0	26	0	1	.400	.314
Bautista, Claudio	R-R	5-11	170	11-29-93	.272	.192	.293	65	250	36	68	16	4	4	24	20	1	2	2	55	3	1	.416	.326
Booth, Tyler	L-L	6-0	155	10-27-92	.154	.000	.176	13	39	3	6	0	0	0	3	1	1	1	0	11	2	0	.154	.233
Boscan, Manuel	R-R	6-0	160	3-10-93	.195	.167	.197	23	77	1	15	1	0	0	9	1	0	0	1	10	0	0	.208	.203
Castillo, Leonardo	R-R	6-2	190	7-9-93	.000	—	.000	1	3	0	0	0	0	0	0	0	0	0	0	2	0	0	.000	.000
Cervenka, Martin	R-R	6-1	175	8-3-92	.188	.273	.172	45	144	9	27	4	0	1	10	17	0	1	2	28	0	0	.236	.270
Ferrell, Cody	R-R	5-10	195	4-29-90	.279	.296	.274	32	111	18	31	2	0	1	3	9	6	2	0	20	0	2	.324	.365
Fink, Grant	R-R	6-3	215	12-14-90	.444	.500	.429	5	18	2	8	2	0	1	3	1	0	0	0	1	0	0	.722	.474
Garcia, Robel	B-R	6-0	168	3-28-93	.216	.262	.201	51	176	17	38	5	4	5	23	20	2	2	3	58	7	5	.375	.299

CLEVELAND INDIANS

Batting	B-T	HT	WT	DOB	AVG	vLH	vRH	G	AB	R	H	2B	3B	HR	RBI	BB	HBP	SH	SF	SO	SB	CS	SLG	OBP
Hamilton, Nick	B-R	6-1	200	11-19-89	.211	.143	.250	7	19	2	4	0	0	0	3	4	3	0	0	6	0	0	.211	.423
Hendrix, Paul	R-R	6-2	187	11-18-91	.258	.279	.252	52	186	9	48	10	2	0	13	20	0	0	0	59	1	1	.333	.330
Herrera, Juan	R-R	5-11	165	6-28-93	.275	.316	.261	39	149	20	41	9	1	1	11	16	6	0	1	30	2	1	.369	.366
2-team total (4 State College)					.256	—	—	43	164	21	42	9	1	1	11	18	6	0	1	31	2	1	.341	.349
Loopstok, Sicnarf	R-R	5-11	195	4-26-93	.205	.294	.179	24	73	4	15	1	1	0	2	4	0	0	0	14	0	1	.247	.247
Mejia, Joel	R-R	5-11	160	4-7-93	.219	.206	.223	40	146	10	32	4	0	0	5	9	4	3	0	42	1	4	.247	.283
Rodriguez, Nelson	R-R	6-2	225	6-12-94	.287	.302	.283	73	261	32	75	16	0	9	37	29	4	0	1	61	0	2	.452	.366
Romero, Juan	R-R	6-1	175	6-16-93	.207	.243	.194	44	145	13	30	5	1	6	14	8	0	0	0	58	8	1	.379	.248
Ruiz, Brian	R-R	6-3	180	9-11-92	.132	.095	.143	32	91	6	12	2	0	0	4	5	0	2	2	33	0	1	.154	.173
Schubert, Josh	R-R	6-4	210	1-25-94	.200	.191	.202	71	240	13	48	9	0	0	11	15	2	3	1	76	7	2	.238	.252
Smith, Garrett	B-R	6-3	180	2-7-90	.167	.000	.200	2	6	1	1	0	0	0	0	0	0	1	0	3	0	0	.167	.167

Pitching	B-T	HT	WT	DOB	W	L	ERA	G	GS	CG	SV	IP	H	R	ER	HR	BB	SO	AVG	vLH	vRH	K/9	BB/9
Blair, Kyle	R-R	6-2	236	9-27-88	1	0	0.00	2	0	0	0	4	4	0	0	0	2	6	.267	.167	.333	13.50	4.50
Carmona, Manuel	R-R	6-0	190	6-21-92	2	2	3.42	21	0	0	3	26	19	15	10	1	19	31	.200	.175	.218	10.59	6.49
Crockett, Kyle	L-L	6-2	170	12-15-91	0	0	0.00	8	0	0	0	9	5	1	0	0	2	16	.152	.100	.174	15.43	1.93
Doane, Kerry	R-R	5-11	175	9-3-90	1	0	4.15	9	0	0	2	17	19	8	8	2	2	19	.264	.219	.300	9.87	1.04
Frank, Trevor	R-R	6-0	195	6-23-91	1	5	2.83	20	0	0	3	35	31	16	11	1	2	39	.233	.302	.171	10.03	0.51
Gomez, Luis	L-L	6-0	195	9-15-92	1	2	3.07	3	3	0	0	15	11	10	5	0	7	16	.200	.111	.243	9.82	4.30
Goodnight, Michael	R-R	6-4	215	6-10-89	0	1	3.79	8	1	0	0	19	20	9	8	0	12	15	.290	.194	.368	7.11	5.68
Guerrero, Harold	L-L	6-4	235	5-21-90	2	1	7.89	20	0	0	1	22	17	23	19	1	24	29	.224	.107	.292	12.05	9.97
Hamrick, Caleb	R-R	6-2	210	9-25-93	3	6	3.20	15	15	0	0	76	73	38	27	9	23	47	.247	.213	.277	5.57	2.72
Heller, Ben	R-R	6-3	205	8-5-91	3	3	3.13	21	1	0	2	37	37	16	13	0	14	39	.252	.292	.220	9.40	3.38
Homblert, Rafael	R-R	6-5	178	9-4-91	0	0	7.43	11	0	0	0	13	19	15	11	2	4	7	.333	.385	.290	4.73	2.70
Kime, Dace	R-R	6-4	200	3-6-92	0	2	2.92	9	9	0	0	25	19	9	8	0	16	26	.224	.214	.233	9.49	5.84
Lugo, Luis	L-L	6-5	200	3-5-94	1	4	1.97	11	11	0	0	50	39	15	11	1	11	30	.222	.250	.208	5.36	1.97
Mathews, Kenny	L-L	6-3	205	8-6-93	0	3	2.52	12	12	0	0	39	35	15	11	0	13	37	.233	.200	.250	8.47	2.97
Melo, Carlos	R-R	6-3	180	2-27-91	1	1	2.25	5	0	0	0	8	6	2	2	0	3	9	.200	.313	.071	10.13	3.38
Myers, Brett	R-R	6-4	240	8-17-80	0	0	0.00	1	0	0	0	1	0	0	0	0	0	1	.000	—	.000	9.00	0.00
Nervis, Joshua	R-R	6-3	230	10-25-88	0	0	7.50	4	0	0	0	6	8	5	5	1	3	6	.320	.300	.333	9.00	4.50
Paredes, Alexis	R-R	6-3	175	1-24-92	2	2	3.35	19	1	0	0	43	32	16	16	2	16	39	.206	.254	.167	8.16	3.35
Perez, Chris	R-R	6-4	230	7-1-85	0	0	0.00	1	0	0	0	1	0	0	0	0	0	1	.000	.000	.000	9.00	0.00
Puerta, Breily	R-R	5-10	180	6-17-92	3	4	2.08	20	0	0	2	35	37	9	8	0	8	38	.274	.281	.268	9.87	2.08
Stokes, Jim	R-R	6-6	225	10-9-90	1	0	0.87	6	0	0	0	10	14	6	1	0	1	8	.318	.375	.286	6.97	0.87
Sulser, Cole	R-R	6-0	190	3-12-90	3	2	1.83	15	9	0	0	54	37	12	11	1	9	60	.191	.220	.165	10.00	1.50
Whitehouse, Matt	L-L	6-1	195	4-13-91	4	2	0.72	14	4	0	0	37	22	9	3	4	4	29	.165	.177	.155	6.99	0.96
Whitenack, Robert	R-R	6-5	185	11-20-88	3	4	3.86	9	8	0	0	44	55	29	19	5	14	28	.307	.358	.265	5.68	2.84
Wood, Blake	R-R	6-5	240	8-8-85	0	0	0.00	1	0	0	0	1	2	0	0	0	0	0	.500	.667	.000	0.00	0.00

Fielding

Catcher	PCT	G	PO	A	E	DP	PB
Battaglia	.973	13	98	10	3	1	3
Boscan	.923	1	12	0	1	0	0
Cervenka	.984	44	339	42	6	4	12
Loopstok	.971	18	118	16	4	2	8

First Base	PCT	G	PO	A	E	DP
Battaglia	1.000	2	11	0	0	2
Boscan	1.000	3	25	1	0	2
Fink	1.000	2	17	0	0	0
Hamilton	1.000	1	9	0	0	0
Rodriguez	.992	67	578	42	5	43

Second Base	PCT	G	PO	A	E	DP
Bautista	.970	39	66	98	5	21
Garcia	1.000	3	3	3	0	1
Hendrix	.960	34	52	92	6	17
Smith	1.000	1	2	3	0	0

Third Base	PCT	G	PO	A	E	DP
Bautista	.918	21	10	35	4	2
Fink	.833	2	1	4	1	0
Garcia	.895	29	21	56	9	8
Herrera	.750	4	1	5	2	0
Roberts	.974	18	11	27	1	2

Shortstop	PCT	G	PO	A	E	DP
Garcia	.848	11	11	17	5	1
Hendrix	.959	11	13	34	2	4
Herrera	.935	31	44	85	9	12
Roberts	.911	21	33	59	9	15

Outfield	PCT	G	PO	A	E	DP
Booth	1.000	13	26	1	0	0
Ferrell	.973	31	70	3	2	1
Hamilton	1.000	3	5	0	0	0
Loopstok	1.000	5	5	1	0	0
Mejia	.963	40	73	4	3	1
Romero	.964	39	74	6	3	2
Ruiz	.974	31	35	2	1	0
Schubert	.922	71	90	5	8	0
Smith	—	1	0	0	0	0

AZL INDIANS — ROOKIE

ARIZONA LEAGUE

Batting	B-T	HT	WT	DOB	AVG	vLH	vRH	G	AB	R	H	2B	3B	HR	RBI	BB	HBP	SH	SF	SO	SB	CS	SLG	OBP
Bautista, Gerald	R-R	6-0	190	7-20-94	.256	.387	.214	41	129	18	33	7	1	0	15	18	3	1	0	36	1	1	.326	.360
Cabral, Victor	R-R	6-2	180	11-5-93	.216	.225	.212	42	153	17	33	6	1	0	13	12	2	2	1	31	8	3	.268	.278
Castillo, Ivan	B-R	5-11	150	5-30-95	.231	.167	.250	42	156	25	36	6	0	0	12	4	2	2	1	23	13	0	.269	.258
Cooper, David	L-L	6-0	200	2-12-87	.440	.286	.500	6	25	4	11	3	0	0	5	2	0	0	0	1	0	0	.560	.481
De Jesus, Victor	R-R	6-2	170	1-13-93	.220	.250	.209	29	91	12	20	2	0	1	8	6	1	1	1	35	5	3	.275	.273
De La Cruz, Juan	B-R	6-1	195	8-5-93	.294	.385	.263	22	51	8	15	6	0	0	10	12	2	0	2	5	1	1	.412	.433
Fink, Grant	R-R	6-3	215	12-14-90	.263	.289	.254	46	160	21	42	14	3	2	23	20	3	0	0	51	2	1	.425	.355
Frazier, Clint	R-R	6-1	190	9-6-94	.297	.318	.289	44	172	32	51	11	5	5	28	17	3	0	4	61	3	2	.506	.362
Giuffre, Mike	R-R	5-11	190	12-14-90	.154	.143	.167	7	13	3	2	1	0	0	1	6	0	0	0	7	1	0	.231	.421
Hankins, Todd	R-R	5-9	175	11-18-90	.333	1.000	.286	4	15	5	5	3	0	0	1	3	1	0	0	5	4	0	.533	.474
Hernandez, Luis	B-R	5-10	190	6-26-84	.158	.000	.176	5	19	1	3	1	0	0	2	3	0	0	1	4	0	0	.211	.261
LaPorta, Matt	R-R	6-2	215	1-8-85	.293	.308	.286	13	41	9	12	4	0	4	12	9	0	0	2	10	0	0	.683	.404
Lora, Felix	R-R	6-3	190	6-18-93	.333	.000	.455	5	15	4	5	0	0	0	2	4	1	0	1	6	0	0	.733	.375
McClure, D'vone	R-R	6-3	190	1-22-94	.218	.080	.263	26	101	16	22	6	1	0	5	5	4	0	0	40	1	0	.297	.282
Mejia, Francisco	B-R	5-10	175	10-27-95	.305	.417	.272	30	105	16	32	9	1	4	24	5	2	1	0	18	3	1	.524	.348

Name	B-T	HT	WT	DOB	AVG	vLH	vRH	G	AB	R	H	2B	3B	HR	RBI	BB	HBP	SH	SF	SO	SB	CS	SLG	OBP
Mejia, Joel	R-R	5-11	160	4-7-93	.299	.313	.294	17	67	20	20	3	4	0	8	7	1	0	1	11	4	0	.463	.368
Mendoza, Yonathan	B-R	5-11	167	2-10-94	.281	.289	.278	43	153	22	43	4	3	0	18	22	0	2	2	26	2	3	.346	.367
Monsalve, Alex	R-R	6-2	225	4-22-92	.231	.500	.111	4	13	1	3	0	0	0	2	1	0	0	0	1	0	0	.231	.286
Rowland, Shane	L-R	6-0	200	11-22-91	.218	.240	.208	27	78	7	17	3	0	1	14	21	1	2	0	20	0	1	.295	.390
Sayles, Silento	R-R	5-9	185	3-28-95	.186	.300	.159	31	102	13	19	4	1	0	4	19	3	3	0	32	5	3	.245	.331
Smith, Garrett	B-R	6-3	180	2-7-90	.059	.000	.081	18	51	7	3	0	0	0	1	7	0	0	0	8	0	0	.059	.172
Tsuchida, Takuya	B-R	5-8	165	5-21-94	.176	.200	.172	19	34	6	6	0	0	0	0	5	0	0	0	20	3	0	.176	.282
Valdez, Ordomar	R-R	5-9	150	4-24-91	.279	.293	.274	41	147	20	41	9	2	1	20	12	0	4	2	24	8	4	.388	.329
Washington, LeVon	L-R	5-11	170	7-26-91	.486	.400	.500	10	37	9	18	1	2	4	13	5	0	0	0	8	2	0	.946	.548

Pitching	B-T	HT	WT	DOB	W	L	ERA	G	GS	CG	SV	IP	H	R	ER	HR	BB	SO	AVG	vLH	vRH	K/9	BB/9
Alcantara, Martin	R-R	5-11	180	9-14-91	4	1	4.03	14	0	0	0	22	19	11	10	0	9	31	.218	.286	.173	12.49	3.63
Armstrong, Shawn	R-R	6-2	210	9-11-90	0	0	4.50	3	0	0	0	4	3	2	2	1	0	5	.200	.000	.273	11.25	0.00
Barnes, Scott	L-L	6-4	200	9-5-87	0	0	27.00	1	1	0	0	1	3	3	3	1	0	0	.500	.500	0.00	0.00	
Beras, Wander	L-L	6-0	160	7-18-88	1	0	4.50	3	0	0	0	4	4	2	2	1	1	6	.250	.200	.273	13.50	2.25
Blair, Kyle	R-R	6-2	236	9-27-88	1	0	3.00	5	0	0	0	6	2	2	2	1	2	7	.125	.000	.250	10.50	3.00
Brady, Sean	L-L	6-0	175	6-9-94	0	1	1.97	10	10	0	0	32	24	11	7	2	6	30	.205	.080	.239	8.44	1.69
Brown, Mitch	R-R	6-1	195	4-13-94	2	4	5.37	12	10	0	0	52	57	32	31	2	29	48	.284	.342	.248	8.31	5.02
Chiang, Shao-Ching	R-R	6-0	175	11-10-93	0	0	0.00	1	0	0	0	1	0	0	0	0	0	0	.000	.000	.000	0.00	0.00
Cleto, Jeffry	R-R	6-3	190	6-14-91	1	1	3.86	5	0	0	0	7	3	3	3	0	6	3	.136	.100	.167	3.86	7.71
Cox, Cortland	R-R	6-1	185	11-3-94	0	0	6.00	2	0	0	0	3	3	2	2	0	2	3	.273	.333	.250	9.00	6.00
Davenport, Geoff	L-L	6-1	180	3-14-90	1	0	0.00	4	1	0	0	6	2	0	0	0	1	4	.105	.000	.133	6.00	1.50
Diaz, Carlos	L-L	6-3	190	2-3-92	1	2	7.62	11	0	0	0	13	12	12	11	0	10	15	.255	.091	.306	10.38	6.92
Gomez, Luis	L-L	6-0	195	9-15-92	1	1	3.60	8	3	0	0	25	19	11	10	0	9	37	.211	.154	.234	13.32	3.24
Hashimoto, Naoki	R-R	5-11	180	6-7-90	0	1	9.50	12	0	0	0	18	22	20	19	0	18	13	.319	.296	.333	6.50	9.00
Kobayashi, Kota	R-R	6-1	175	9-1-91	0	0	1.69	5	0	0	0	5	1	1	1	0	2	1	.053	.000	.091	1.69	3.38
Lovegrove, Kieran	R-R	6-4	185	7-28-94	1	7	5.25	13	12	0	0	58	63	45	34	4	31	51	.272	.250	.283	7.87	4.78
Melo, Carlos	R-R	6-3	180	2-27-91	1	1	2.89	10	0	0	5	9	5	3	3	0	7	10	.156	.091	.190	9.64	6.75
Milbrath, Jordan	R-R	6-6	215	8-1-91	1	1	4.87	13	0	0	0	20	14	12	11	0	15	17	.189	.242	.146	7.52	6.64
Pannone, Thomas	L-L	6-0	180	4-28-94	1	0	9.00	14	0	0	0	16	23	19	16	0	10	20	.338	.316	.347	11.25	5.63
Polanco, Anderson	L-L	6-3	190	9-6-92	2	0	1.78	12	0	0	0	25	15	7	5	0	13	37	.169	.273	.134	13.14	4.62
Rodriguez, Francisco	R-R	6-1	195	2-10-90	0	0	9.00	1	0	0	0	1	1	1	1	0	0	2	.250	.000	.333	9.00	0.00
Rodriguez, Ramon	R-R	5-11	176	3-1-94	2	3	3.48	16	0	0	1	21	20	14	8	1	12	15	.253	.297	.214	6.53	5.23
Santana, Juan	R-R	6-2	170	7-2-93	4	2	4.33	12	11	0	0	52	59	28	25	4	20	37	.278	.286	.274	6.40	3.46
Shane, Casey	R-R	6-4	200	8-23-95	1	1	6.52	11	3	0	1	29	33	23	21	1	16	22	.282	.367	.221	6.83	4.97
Tomlin, Josh	R-R	6-1	190	10-19-84	0	0	0.00	2	2	0	0	2	1	0	0	0	0	2	.143	.000		9.00	0.00
Vizcaya, Anthony	R-R	6-0	180	10-24-93	3	1	6.88	12	3	0	0	35	52	28	27	2	14	33	.340	.377	.320	8.41	3.57
Zapata, Jose	R-R	6-4	200	5-21-93	0	1	3.46	14	0	0	0	26	14	11	10	3	19	30	.169	.250	.118	10.38	6.58

Fielding

Catcher	PCT	G	PO	A	E	DP	PB
De La Cruz	.970	18	84	14	3	0	4
Mejia	.991	25	186	23	2	1	11
Monsalve	1.000	3	23	3	0	0	2
Rowland	.990	24	178	16	2	0	7

First Base	PCT	G	PO	A	E	DP
Bautista	.966	13	108	6	4	7
Cooper	.962	4	23	2	1	0
Fink	.990	38	292	20	3	30
LaPorta	.986	9	66	6	1	4
Smith	1.000	1	6	0	0	0

Second Base	PCT	G	PO	A	E	DP
Giuffre	.857	2	1	5	1	0
Hernandez	1.000	1	3	0	0	0
Mendoza	1.000	2	1	3	0	0
Smith	.909	10	8	22	3	2

	PCT	G	PO	A	E	DP
Tsuchida	.963	15	23	29	2	6
Valdez	.945	38	71	101	10	22

Third Base	PCT	G	PO	A	E	DP
Bautista	.897	15	6	20	3	1
Fink	.925	9	14	23	3	1
Giuffre	.500	4	2	0	2	0
Hankins	.889	3	3	5	1	0
Hernandez	1.000	2	1	7	0	2
Mendoza	.923	28	17	55	6	6
Valdez	.833	1	3	2	1	0

Shortstop	PCT	G	PO	A	E	DP
Castillo	.923	42	55	124	15	19
Hernandez	1.000	1	1	2	0	0
Mendoza	.984	16	21	41	1	11
Smith	.750	1	1	2	1	1

Outfield	PCT	G	PO	A	E	DP
Cabral	.959	42	69	2	3	1
De Jesus	.966	25	25	3	1	0
Frazier	.971	35	64	4	2	0
LaPorta	1.000	1	2	1	0	0
Lora	1.000	3	6	0	0	0
McClure	.923	19	24	0	2	0
Mejia	1.000	1	4	0	0	0
Mejia	1.000	15	24	3	0	1
Sayles	.980	30	48	1	1	1
Smith	1.000	3	1	0	0	0
Tsuchida	—	1	0	0	0	0
Washington	.875	7	6	1	1	0

DSL INDIANS ROOKIE

DOMINICAN SUMMER LEAGUE

Batting	B-T	HT	WT	DOB	AVG	vLH	vRH	G	AB	R	H	2B	3B	HR	RBI	BB	HBP	SH	SF	SO	SB	CS	SLG	OBP
Acosta, Wilkin	L-L	6-0	185	10-8-92	.286	.000	.333	3	7	0	2	0	0	0	0	1	0	0	0	3	0	1	.286	.375
Andujar, Yoan	R-R	6-2	180	5-26-96	.188	.000	.250	11	32	1	6	0	0	0	4	1	0	0	0	10	0	2	.188	.212
Calderon, Kevin	R-R	5-11	180	4-4-94	.160	.184	.149	48	150	19	24	7	0	0	14	15	1	1	1	38	0	2	.207	.240
Caraballo, Joel	R-R	5-11	140	2-8-94	.000	—	.000	2	3	0	0	0	0	0	0	1	0	0	0	2	0	0	.000	.250
Caro, Hector	R-R	6-3	195	10-3-95	.249	.306	.220	52	189	20	47	13	0	0	24	13	2	0	1	27	2	1	.317	.302
Cerda, Erlin	R-R	5-9	170	5-5-94	.253	.243	.258	60	198	29	50	18	2	0	16	35	9	3	1	25	12	7	.364	.387
Cruz, Grofi	R-R	6-2	175	4-3-96	.231	.239	.227	70	260	22	60	11	1	0	22	15	2	4	2	38	2	1	.281	.276
De Los Santos, Alexis	R-R	6-3	0	8-22-94	.237	.240	.235	40	131	13	31	6	0	1	18	16	1	0	1	23	1	2	.305	.322
Depen, Michael	R-R	6-3	186	6-16-92	.231	.174	.262	20	65	8	15	7	2	0	8	1	1	0	1	13	2	0	.400	.250
2-team total (14 Marlins)					.239	—	—	34	109	15	26	7	3	0	12	2	2	0	2	23	4	5	.358	.261
Lunar, Henry	R-R	5-10	170	11-18-93	.200	.000	.250	3	5	0	1	0	0	0	0	0	0	0	0	2	0	0	.200	.200
Marquina, Yoiber	R-R	5-10	190	2-3-96	.133	.077	.156	19	45	1	6	0	0	0	0	9	0	0	0	11	0	1	.133	.278
Martinez, Rubiel	R-R	5-11	175	2-20-93	.158	.375	.000	9	19	6	3	1	0	0	7	1	1	0		2	3	0	.211	.407

Name	B-T	HT	WT	DOB	AVG	vLH	vRH	G	AB	R	H	2B	3B	HR	RBI	BB	HBP	SH	SF	SO	SB	CS	OBP	SLG
Miguel, Francisco	R-R	6-3	206	3-24-95	.205	.209	.203	57	185	21	38	4	1	5	17	24	1	1	1	47	7	5	.319	.299
Moncion, Juan Carlos	L-L	6-2	210	10-24-93	.231	.243	.224	60	195	22	45	13	0	3	28	22	3	1	2	41	1	2	.344	.315
Montero, Luis	L-R	6-1	175	10-11-94	.171	.100	.200	24	35	6	6	0	0	0	1	5	1	1	0	15	3	0	.171	.293
Ramirez, Wagner	R-R	5-11	170	12-11-94	.113	.200	.054	24	62	2	7	1	1	0	4	5	4	1	1	16	0	0	.161	.222
Rodriguez, Jorma	R-R	5-10	150	3-25-96	.201	.188	.207	55	199	28	40	7	2	0	14	27	2	5	0	37	8	4	.256	.303
Sancez, Omar	B-R	6-1	179	2-10-95	.135	.143	.130	29	74	13	10	1	0	0	5	13	2	1	0	28	3	1	.149	.281
Sanchez, Yoel	R-R	6-1	185	1-11-94	.228	.233	.226	33	92	16	21	3	2	1	7	10	0	1	0	29	6	2	.337	.304
Santana, Andri	B-R	6-2	180	7-23-92	.203	.313	.167	20	64	9	13	2	2	1	6	4	2	1	0	23	2	2	.344	.271
Tapia, Emmanuel	L-L	6-3	215	2-26-96	.223	.208	.231	65	224	21	50	11	2	2	13	16	8	0	0	56	6	2	.317	.298

Pitching	B-T	HT	WT	DOB	W	L	ERA	G	GS	CG	SV	IP	H	R	ER	HR	BB	SO	AVG	vLH	vRH	K/9	BB/9
Algarin, Erick	R-R	6-1	195	3-31-95	2	0	2.63	13	5	0	1	41	39	17	12	2	12	34	.244	.283	.220	7.46	2.63
Aquino, Luis	R-R	6-1	170	6-30-93	0	0	0.00	1	0	0	0	1	0	0	0	0	2	2	.000	.000	.000	18.00	18.00
Araujo, Luis	R-R	6-1	155	8-1-96	0	6	4.04	14	14	0	0	49	50	32	22	1	24	36	.266	.250	.274	6.61	4.41
Arias, Jesus	R-R	6-1	185	9-29-93	4	3	3.94	14	1	0	1	32	26	15	14	1	25	26	.226	.286	.207	7.31	7.03
Arosemena, Julio	R-R	6-1	190	7-20-95	2	2	3.82	17	1	0	1	38	34	23	16	0	26	21	.254	.245	.259	5.02	6.21
Beras, Jesus	R-R	6-3	188	1-8-93	0	0	13.50	4	0	0	0	3	3	6	4	0	3	1	.375	.333	.400	3.38	10.13
Espino, Aresante	R-R	6-5	200	12-17-91	1	1	7.53	11	1	0	0	14	16	16	12	0	18	9	.281	.231	.295	5.65	11.30
Estrella, Edward	R-R	6-1	170	1-28-94	3	3	2.86	14	12	1	0	63	50	30	20	3	25	52	.217	.216	.218	7.43	3.57
Fabian, Edward	R-R	6-3	170	8-23-95	0	1	4.73	13	0	0	1	27	23	15	14	0	21	18	.245	.310	.215	6.08	7.09
Gomez, Daniel	R-R	6-1	185	6-2-94	4	4	2.52	18	7	0	0	54	51	30	15	1	19	31	.245	.265	.236	5.20	3.19
Jimenez, Luis	R-R	6-4	170	1-2-95	3	8	5.25	16	10	0	1	48	57	45	28	2	26	28	.289	.273	.300	5.25	4.88
Lopez, Francisco	R-R	5-11	170	2-13-94	0	3	1.83	12	8	0	1	39	32	17	8	2	18	47	.221	.306	.193	10.75	4.12
Manzueta, Cristian	L-L	6-5	205	10-30-94	0	0	5.02	8	0	0	0	14	17	10	8	1	17	9	.293	.167	.308	5.65	10.67
Marte, Daniel	R-R	6-4	175	6-24-94	0	0	13.50	2	0	0	0	2	1	3	3	0	6	2	.167	.000	.250	9.00	27.00
Nivar, Juan	R-R	6-1	170	9-24-92	1	0	9.00	2	0	0	0	2	1	3	2	0	1	1	.167	.000	.333	4.50	4.50
Pineda, Edgar	L-L	5-10	155	9-7-94	0	0	4.29	15	0	0	0	21	6	14	10	0	27	28	.088	.071	.093	12.00	11.57
Puello, Johan	R-R	5-11	165	1-5-94	1	6	4.42	18	6	0	3	39	41	29	19	2	21	29	.272	.255	.275	6.75	4.89
Ramirez, Anderson	R-R	6-2	175	7-28-93	1	0	2.89	8	0	0	0	9	6	4	3	0	5	8	.176	.000	.207	7.71	4.82
Ramirez, Jesus	R-R	6-4	190	3-14-95	1	3	3.00	15	4	0	1	45	46	25	15	1	16	22	.269	.328	.239	4.40	3.20
Rodriguez, Jose	R-R	6-0	185	3-18-95	1	3	2.16	12	2	0	0	25	19	11	6	1	11	19	.200	.171	.217	6.84	3.96
Villasmil, Rodolfo	R-R	6-0	160	1-20-95	0	0	5.11	11	0	0	0	12	12	9	7	0	16	10	.245	.250	.243	7.30	11.68
Vincent, Junior	R-R	6-2	190	2-28-95	0	0	—	1	0	0	0	0	0	1	1	0	4	0	—	.000	.000	—	—

Fielding

Catcher	PCT	G	PO	A	E	DP	PB
Calderon	.976	46	261	59	8	1	12
Lunar	.923	3	11	1	1	0	1
Marquina	.950	18	98	16	6	0	9
Ramirez	.968	13	72	18	3	0	4

First Base	PCT	G	PO	A	E	DP
Cerda	.985	9	63	2	1	5
De Los Santos	.951	5	38	1	2	5
Moncion	.978	56	451	27	11	26
Ramirez	.947	3	17	1	1	4
Tapia	.943	4	29	4	2	0

Second Base	PCT	G	PO	A	E	DP
Andujar	.913	8	19	23	4	5
Caraballo	1.000	1	0	1	0	0
Cerda	.972	45	99	111	6	18
Rodriguez	.968	23	45	46	3	9

Third Base	PCT	G	PO	A	E	DP
Cerda	.871	9	12	15	4	1
Cruz	.853	33	26	61	15	3
De Los Santos	.827	36	40	65	22	4
Sancez	—	1	0	0	0	0

Shortstop	PCT	G	PO	A	E	DP
Caraballo	1.000	1	3	1	0	0
Cruz	.907	33	59	77	14	10
Martinez	.905	8	8	11	2	1
Rodriguez	.913	35	55	91	14	15

Outfield	PCT	G	PO	A	E	DP
Acosta	1.000	2	1	0	0	0
Caro	.977	46	81	3	2	1
Depen	.867	20	25	1	4	0
Miguel	.959	56	87	7	4	1
Montero	.929	19	24	2	2	0
Sancez	.979	26	41	6	1	1
Sanchez	.891	27	39	2	5	1
Santana	1.000	20	31	3	0	0
Tapia	.970	22	31	1	1	0

Colorado Rockies

SEASON IN A SENTENCE: After a strong opening month of the season, the Rockies struggled to both score and prevent runs, finishing in last place for the second consecutive year.

HIGH POINT: The Rockies exited the first month of the year at 16-11 and in first place with the best run differential in the league.

LOW POINT: The Rockies did not have a winning month for the rest of the year. Despite finishing second in the league in runs (706), the Rockies had a below-average offense that was propped up by a strong offensive environment. Troy Tulowitzki (126 games) and Carlos Gonzalez (110), both missed significant time with injuries. Run prevention also hampered the Rockies, as they struck out fewer hitters than any other NL team by both raw totals (1,064) and percent of hitters faced (17 percent). The league average strikeout-walk ratio for NL starting pitchers was 2.6, and the Rockies (1.8) were the only rotation to finish below 2.

NOTABLE ROOKIES: Third baseman Nolan Arenado, 22, held the hot corner for the majority of the year, hitting .267/.301/.405 in 133 games and 514 plate appearances to go with above-average defensive metrics. Arenado was awarded with a Gold Glove. Outfielder Corey Dickerson, 24, had 23 extra-base hits and a .263/.316/.459 line in 213 plate appearances. 2010 second-rounder Chad Bettis, 24, produced lackluster numbers (5.64 ERA, 6.0 strikeouts per nine, 1.5 strikeout-walk ratio) but showed promise with a plus fastball. Charlie Culberson, who was acquired for Marco Scutaro last year, saw time in left field.

KEY TRANSACTIONS: First baseman Todd Helton, who has been entrenched at first since 1998, played his final game, retiring with the only franchise he has ever played for. Helton, 40, finishes his career holding many franchise records including games played (2,247), doubles (592) and home runs (369) to go with a .316/.414/.539 line.

DOWN ON THE FARM: Only one minor league affiliate, high Class A Modesto of the California League, finished with a winning record, but the Nuts lost in the first round of the playoffs. In his nine starts, No. 3 overall pick Jonathan Gray dazzled, striking out 51 in 37 innings. Righthander Eddie Butler, who pitches with premium velocity and made the Futures Game, had one of the best minor league seasons of any pitcher. The 2012 second-rounder posted a 2.02 ERA with nearly a strikeout an inning in 29 starts.

OPENING DAY PAYROLL: $71.9 million (25th)

PLAYERS OF THE YEAR

TONY FARLOW

MAJOR LEAGUE	MINOR LEAGUE
Troy Tulowitzki	**Eddie Butler**
ss	**rhp**
.312/.391/.540	(Lo A/Hi A/Double-A)
25 HR, 27 2B, 82 RBIs	9-5, 1.80 in 28 GS
2nd in NL in SLG, OPS	0.99 WHIP, 8.6 SO/9

ORGANIZATION LEADERS

BATTING		*Minimum 250 PA
MAJORS		
* AVG	Cuddyer, Michael	.331
* OPS	Tulowitzki, Troy	.931
HR	Gonzalez, Carlos	26
RBI	Cuddyer, Michael	84
MINORS		
* AVG	Herrera, Rosell, Asheville	.343
* OBP	Herrera, Rosell, Asheville	.419
* SLG	Murphy, Tom, Tulsa/Asheville	.571
R	Featherston, Taylor, Modesto	87
H	Herrera, Rosell, Asheville	162
TB	Sosa, Francisco, Asheville	244
2B	Sosa, Francisco, Asheville	35
3B	Dickerson, Corey, Colorado Springs	14
HR	Roling, Kiel, Tulsa	24
RBI	Sosa, Francisco, Asheville	89
	Wheeler, Ryan, Colorado Springs	89
BB	Von Tungeln, Kyle, Modesto/Asheville/Tri-City	72
SO	Riggins, Harold, Modesto	192
SB	Ciriaco, Juan, Asheville	50

PITCHING		#Minimum 75 IP
MAJORS		
W	De La Rosa, Jorge	16
# ERA	Chacin, Jhoulys	3.47
SO	Chacin, Jhoulys	126
SV	Brothers, Rex	19
MINORS		
W	Alsup, Ben, Modesto	13
	Winkler, Daniel, Tulsa/Modesto	13
L	Gustafson, Tim, Tulsa	12
# ERA	Butler, Eddie, Asheville/Visalia/Tulsa	1.8
G	Oberg, Scott, Modesto	56
GS	Alsup, Ben, Modesto	29
SV	Oberg, Scott, Modesto	33
IP	Bergman, Christian, Tulsa	171
BB	Matzek, Tyler, Tulsa	76
SO	Winkler, Daniel, Tulsa/Modesto	175
# AVG	Butler, Eddie, Asheville/Visalia/Tulsa	.18

General Manager: Dan O'Dowd. **Farm Director:** Jeff Bridich. **Scouting Director:** Bill Schmidt.

Class	Team	League	W	L	PCT	Finish	Manager
Majors	Colorado Rockies	National	74	88	.457	10th (15)	Walt Weiss
Triple-A	Colorado Springs Sky Sox	Pacific Coast	67	76	.469	13th (16)	Glenallen Hill
Double-A	Tulsa Drillers	Texas	68	70	.493	5th (8)	Kevin Riggs
High A	Modesto Nuts	California	75	65	.536	4th (10)	Lenn Sakata/Fred Nelson
Short-season	Tri-City Dust Devils	Northwest	34	42	.447	7th (8)	Drew Saylor
Rookie	Grand Junction Rockies	Pioneer	35	41	.461	6th (8)	Anthony Sanders
Overall 2013 Minor League Record			342	367	.482	24th (30)	

ORGANIZATION STATISTICS

COLORADO ROCKIES

NATIONAL LEAGUE

Batting	B-T	HT	WT	DOB	AVG	vLH	vRH	G	AB	R	H	2B	3B	HR	RBI	BB	HBP	SH	SF	SO	SB	CS	SLG	OBP
Arenado, Nolan	R-R	6-1	205	4-16-91	.267	.296	.256	133	486	49	130	29	4	10	52	23	1	2	2	72	2	0	.405	.301
Blackmon, Charlie	L-L	6-3	210	7-1-86	.309	.296	.314	82	246	35	76	17	2	6	22	7	3	2	0	49	7	0	.467	.336
Brignac, Reid	L-R	6-3	190	1-16-86	.250	.333	.238	29	48	4	12	3	0	1	6	3	0	2	0	13	0	0	.375	.294
Colvin, Tyler	L-L	6-3	210	9-5-85	.160	.150	.171	27	75	8	12	0	0	3	10	3	0	0	0	27	0	0	.280	.192
Cuddyer, Michael	R-R	6-2	220	3-27-79	.331	.276	.350	130	489	74	162	31	3	20	84	46	2	0	3	100	10	3	.530	.389
Culberson, Charlie	R-R	6-1	200	4-10-89	.293	.283	.302	47	99	12	29	5	0	2	12	4	0	0	1	23	5	1	.404	.317
Dickerson, Corey	L-R	6-1	205	5-22-89	.263	.194	.278	69	194	32	51	13	5	5	17	16	0	1	2	41	2	2	.459	.316
Fowler, Dexter	B-R	6-4	190	3-22-86	.263	.323	.237	119	415	71	109	18	3	12	42	65	6	4	2	105	19	9	.407	.369
Gonzalez, Carlos	L-L	6-1	220	10-17-85	.302	.310	.297	110	391	72	118	23	6	26	70	41	1	0	3	118	21	3	.591	.367
Helton, Todd	L-L	6-2	220	8-20-73	.249	.299	.238	124	397	41	99	22	1	15	61	40	0	0	5	87	0	0	.423	.314
Herrera, Jonathan	B-R	5-9	180	11-3-84	.292	.220	.317	81	195	16	57	7	2	1	16	14	0	4	2	24	3	2	.364	.336
LeMahieu, D.J.	R-R	6-4	205	7-13-88	.280	.276	.281	109	404	39	113	21	3	2	28	19	1	7	3	67	18	7	.361	.311
Nelson, Chris	R-R	5-11	205	9-3-85	.242	.278	.229	21	66	6	16	1	2	0	4	4	0	0	1	19	0	0	.318	.282
Pacheco, Jordan	R-R	6-1	200	1-30-86	.239	.205	.267	95	247	23	59	15	0	1	22	10	3	1	1	38	0	0	.312	.276
Rosario, Wilin	R-R	5-11	220	2-23-89	.292	.323	.279	121	449	63	131	22	1	21	79	15	1	0	1	109	4	1	.486	.315
Rutledge, Josh	R-R	6-1	190	4-21-89	.235	.196	.257	88	285	45	67	6	1	7	19	22	2	4	1	62	12	0	.337	.294
Torrealba, Yorvit	R-R	5-11	200	7-19-78	.240	.293	.225	61	179	16	43	8	0	0	16	13	1	3	0	24	0	0	.285	.295
Tulowitzki, Troy	R-R	6-3	215	10-10-84	.312	.318	.310	126	446	72	139	27	0	25	82	57	4	0	5	85	1	0	.540	.391
Wheeler, Ryan	L-R	6-3	235	7-10-88	.220	.000	.243	28	41	1	9	2	0	0	7	1	0	0	0	10	0	0	.268	.238
Young Jr., Eric	B-R	5-10	180	5-25-85	.242	.281	.222	57	165	22	40	9	3	1	6	11	0	4	0	33	8	4	.352	.290
2-team total (91 New York)					.249			148	539	70	134	27	7	2	32	46	2	10	1	100	46	11	.336	.310

Pitching	B-T	HT	WT	DOB	W	L	ERA	G	GS	CG	SV	IP	H	R	ER	HR	BB	SO	AVG	vLH	vRH	K/9	BB/9
Belisle, Matt	R-R	6-4	225	6-6-80	5	7	4.32	72	0	0	0	73	76	37	35	6	15	62	.269	.283	.259	7.64	1.85
Betancourt, Rafael	R-R	6-2	220	4-29-75	2	5	4.08	32	0	0	16	29	26	15	13	2	11	27	.241	.267	.222	8.48	3.45
Bettis, Chad	R-R	6-1	200	4-26-89	1	3	5.64	16	8	0	0	45	55	34	28	6	20	30	.302	.275	.330	6.04	4.03
Boggs, Mitchell	R-R	6-4	235	2-15-84	0	0	3.12	9	0	0	0	9	7	3	3	2	5	5	.226	.182	.250	5.19	5.19
2-team total (18 St. Louis)					0	3	8.10	27	0	0	2	23	28	23	21	5	20	16	—	—	—	6.17	7.71
Brothers, Rex	L-L	6-0	210	12-18-87	2	1	1.74	72	0	0	19	67	51	16	13	5	36	76	.209	.162	.229	10.16	4.81
Chacin, Jhoulys	R-R	6-3	225	1-7-88	14	10	3.47	31	31	0	0	197	188	82	76	11	61	126	.253	.275	.233	5.75	2.78
Chatwood, Tyler	R-R	6-0	185	12-16-89	8	5	3.15	20	20	1	0	111	118	44	39	5	41	66	.278	.273	.282	5.34	3.31
Corpas, Manny	R-R	6-3	210	12-3-82	1	2	4.54	31	0	0	0	42	40	21	21	5	16	30	.255	.219	.280	6.48	3.46
De La Rosa, Jorge	L-L	6-1	220	4-5-81	16	6	3.49	30	30	0	0	168	170	70	65	11	62	112	.269	.200	.286	6.01	3.33
Escalona, Edgmer	R-R	6-4	235	10-6-86	1	4	5.67	37	0	0	0	46	52	32	29	8	14	34	.280	.312	.257	6.65	2.74
Francis, Jeff	L-L	6-5	205	1-8-81	3	5	6.27	23	12	0	0	70	89	54	49	12	24	63	.306	.208	.341	8.06	3.07
Garland, Jon	R-R	6-6	210	9-27-79	4	6	5.82	12	12	0	0	68	85	45	44	9	23	32	.315	.293	.338	4.24	3.04
Kensing, Logan	R-R	6-1	190	7-3-82	0	0	0.00	1	0	0	0	1	0	0	0	1	1	0	.000	.000	.000	13.50	13.50
Lopez, Wilton	R-R	6-0	205	7-19-83	3	4	4.06	75	0	0	0	75	88	35	34	6	18	48	.293	.278	.305	5.73	2.15
Manship, Jeff	R-R	6-2	210	1-16-85	0	5	7.04	11	4	0	0	31	37	25	24	6	12	18	.298	.304	.294	5.28	3.52
McHugh, Collin	R-R	6-2	195	6-19-87	0	3	9.95	4	4	0	0	19	33	21	21	7	8	8	.384	.424	.358	3.79	0.95
2-team total (3 New York)					0	4	10.04	7	5	0	0	26	45	29	29	6	5	11	—	—	—	3.81	1.73
Nicasio, Juan	R-R	6-3	230	8-31-86	9	9	5.14	31	31	0	0	158	168	97	90	17	64	119	.268	.228	.302	6.79	3.65
Oswalt, Roy	R-R	6-0	190	8-29-77	0	6	8.63	9	6	0	0	32	49	31	31	3	9	34	.358	.375	.342	9.46	2.51
Ottavino, Adam	L-R	6-5	230	11-22-85	1	3	2.64	51	0	0	0	78	73	27	23	5	31	78	.250	.328	.197	8.96	3.56
Outman, Josh	L-L	6-1	205	9-14-84	3	0	4.33	61	0	0	0	54	56	27	26	3	23	53	.268	.198	.347	8.83	3.83
Pomeranz, Drew	R-L	6-5	240	11-22-88	0	4	6.23	8	4	0	0	22	25	15	15	4	19	19	.301	.130	.367	7.89	7.89
Scahill, Rob	R-R	6-2	220	2-15-87	1	0	5.13	23	0	0	0	33	40	19	19	5	9	20	.301	.344	.261	5.40	2.43
Volstad, Chris	R-R	6-8	230	9-23-86	0	0	10.80	6	0	0	0	8	19	10	10	1	1	3	.432	.440	.421	3.24	1.08

Fielding

Catcher	PCT	G	PO	A	E	DP	PB
Pacheco	.979	15	84	8	2	2	2
Rosario	.987	106	646	63	9	2	9
Torrealba	.992	50	336	20	3	4	2

First Base	PCT	G	PO	A	E	DP
Colvin	1.000	1	4	0	0	0
Cuddyer	1.000	15	112	6	0	15
Helton	.998	110	941	92	2	96
LeMahieu	1.000	1	2	0	0	0

Pacheco	.988	43	385	28	5	28
Rosario	.920	4	21	2	2	3
Torrealba	1.000	3	4	0	0	0
Wheeler	1.000	7	39	0	0	4

Second Base	PCT	G	PO	A	E	DP
Brignac	1.000	3	6	8	0	1
Culberson	.857	4	3	3	1	1
Herrera	.968	22	34	56	3	11
LeMahieu	.993	90	168	271	3	57
Rutledge	.982	58	98	171	5	40
Young Jr.	1.000	1	1	0	0	0

Third Base	PCT	G	PO	A	E	DP
Arenado	.973	130	91	309	11	27
Brignac	.875	8	4	10	2	1
Herrera	1.000	5	1	1	0	0

	PCT	G	PO	A	E	DP
LeMahieu	1.000	14	6	24	0	2
Nelson	.938	19	7	38	3	1
Wheeler	.500	1	0	1	1	1

Shortstop	PCT	G	PO	A	E	DP
Brignac	.875	3	4	3	1	0
Herrera	.986	42	50	94	2	27
LeMahieu	—	1	0	0	0	0
Rutledge	.984	14	23	37	1	8
Tulowitzki	.986	121	183	379	8	84

Outfield	PCT	G	PO	A	E	DP
Blackmon	.966	68	112	0	4	0
Brignac	1.000	1	1	0	0	0
Colvin	1.000	23	43	0	0	0
Cuddyer	.990	118	191	6	2	1
Culberson	.976	27	39	2	1	1
Dickerson	1.000	51	94	0	0	0
Fowler	.987	110	231	3	3	2
Gonzalez	.984	106	172	11	3	0
Herrera	—	2	0	0	0	0
Pacheco	1.000	1	0	0	0	0
Wheeler	1.000	1	1	0	0	0
Young Jr.	.967	36	58	0	2	0

COLORADO SPRINGS SKY SOX   TRIPLE-A

PACIFIC COAST LEAGUE

Batting	B-T	HT	WT	DOB	AVG	vLH	vRH	G	AB	R	H	2B	3B	HR	RBI	BB	HBP	SH	SF	SO	SB	CS	SLG	OBP
Arenado, Nolan	R-R	6-1	205	4-16-91	.364	.545	.327	18	66	14	24	11	0	3	21	5	0	1	3	9	0	2	.667	.392
Blackmon, Charlie	L-R	6-3	210	7-1-86	.288	.188	.311	68	257	56	74	15	6	3	40	35	3	1	3	41	7	5	.428	.376
Brignac, Reid	L-R	6-3	190	1-16-86	.230	.146	.265	48	165	25	38	8	0	2	11	20	4	2	2	33	2	1	.315	.325
Colvin, Tyler	L-L	6-3	210	9-5-85	.275	.245	.284	67	229	47	63	8	6	9	32	36	2	1	1	62	6	3	.480	.377
Culberson, Charlie	R-R	6-1	200	4-10-89	.310	.377	.294	97	397	63	123	27	8	14	64	17	1	2	2	74	13	9	.524	.338
Davis, Lars	L-R	6-3	205	11-7-85	.255	.265	.252	82	298	34	76	17	2	3	29	24	2	7	2	85	1	1	.356	.313
Dickerson, Corey	L-R	6-1	205	5-22-89	.371	.349	.377	75	315	61	117	21	14	11	50	26	0	0	4	49	6	10	.632	.414
Fowler, Dexter	B-R	6-4	190	3-22-86	.000	.000	.000	2	6	0	0	0	0	0	0	3	0	0	0	2	1	0	.000	.333
Garcia, Drew	B-R	6-1	175	4-22-86	.236	.333	.192	51	144	21	34	8	1	1	11	9	0	2	0	45	3	0	.326	.281
Golson, Greg	R-R	6-0	190	9-17-85	.244	.205	.258	55	172	22	42	2	5	5	22	10	3	1	0	48	12	2	.401	.297
Gonzalez, Carlos	L-L	6-1	220	10-17-85	.167	—	.167	2	6	0	1	0	0	0	0	1	0	0	0	1	0	0	.167	.286
Gonzalez, Jose	R-R	6-1	165	6-23-87	.185	.276	.143	32	92	7	17	1	1	1	10	12	2	1	1	25	1	1	.250	.290
Iribarren, Hernan	L-R	6-1	195	6-29-84	.312	.253	.337	84	253	33	79	12	3	2	32	23	2	3	5	43	9	3	.407	.367
LeMahieu, D.J.	R-R	6-4	205	7-13-88	.364	.258	.393	33	143	34	52	8	5	1	22	10	2	0	3	19	8	2	.510	.405
Manzella, Tommy	R-R	6-2	200	4-16-83	.190	.261	.171	32	105	9	20	7	1	0	10	7	1	1	1	42	0	1	.276	.246
Matthes, Kent	R-R	6-2	215	1-8-87	.297	.364	.267	47	175	25	52	6	1	11	31	10	0	2	1	40	6	1	.531	.333
McBride, Matt	R-R	6-2	215	5-23-85	.328	.303	.333	48	180	31	59	17	1	15	45	11	0	0	4	21	0	0	.683	.359
Nady, Xavier	R-R	6-2	215	11-14-78	.278	.300	.268	53	187	25	52	14	0	4	22	14	2	0	2	40	3	0	.417	.332
2-team total (71 Omaha)					.296	—	—	124	443	69	131	26	0	15	65	41	6	1	4	91	4	0	.456	.360
Pacheco, Jordan	R-R	6-1	200	1-30-86	.315	.300	.324	18	54	8	17	5	1	1	6	8	0	1	0	3	3	0	.500	.403
Paulsen, Ben	L-R	6-4	205	10-27-87	.292	.222	.316	123	459	64	134	32	10	18	79	37	2	0	4	128	2	2	.523	.345
Rutledge, Josh	R-R	6-1	190	4-21-89	.371	.345	.377	38	143	24	53	17	1	4	24	12	7	0	0	21	1	2	.587	.444
Shepherd, Jaron	L-R	6-1	180	10-30-88	.161	.091	.200	13	31	1	5	0	0	0	1	5	1	2	0	11	1	1	.161	.297
Tarleton, Dallas	L-R	5-11	200	8-5-87	.143	.000	.167	4	14	0	2	1	0	0	1	3	0	0	0	7	0	0	.214	.294
Tulowitzki, Troy	R-R	6-3	215	10-10-84	.800	1.000	.750	2	5	2	4	0	0	0	0	0	1	0	0	0	0	0	.800	.833
Wheeler, Ryan	L-R	6-3	235	7-10-88	.306	.259	.323	116	438	74	134	29	2	12	89	31	3	1	7	91	4	1	.463	.351
Wheeler, Tim	L-R	6-4	205	1-21-88	.262	.250	.267	109	397	59	104	16	3	12	60	33	8	1	1	87	12	7	.355	.330

Pitching	B-T	HT	WT	DOB	W	L	ERA	G	GS	CG	SV	IP	H	R	ER	HR	BB	SO	AVG	vLH	vRH	K/9	BB/9
Berg, Justin	R-R	6-3	225	6-7-84	1	1	5.19	3	3	0	0	17	18	10	10	2	5	4	.277	.242	.313	2.08	2.60
Betancourt, Rafael	R-R	6-2	220	4-29-75	0	0	9.00	1	0	0	0	1	2	1	1	0	0	1	.400	.333	.500	9.00	0.00
Boggs, Mitchell	R-R	6-4	235	2-15-84	1	4	8.27	12	0	0	0	16	33	26	15	1	11	7	.407	.415	.400	3.86	6.06
2-team total (18 Memphis)					1	6	6.75	30	3	0	0	40	63	47	30	3	22	21	—	—	—	4.73	4.95
Carpenter, Drew	R-R	6-3	240	5-18-85	2	3	6.75	9	9	0	0	48	66	36	36	10	15	25	.337	.352	.324	4.69	2.81
2-team total (6 Iowa)					3	7	6.96	15	15	0	0	75	99	59	58	14	30	45	—	—	—	5.40	3.60
Cassevah, Bobby	R-R	6-3	220	9-11-85	1	0	3.29	9	0	0	0	14	21	5	5	2	5	7	.368	.375	.364	4.61	3.29
Chatwood, Tyler	R-R	6-0	185	12-16-89	2	1	2.91	6	6	1	0	34	37	11	11	0	7	33	.278	.244	.295	8.74	1.85
Colon, Roman	R-R	6-5	245	8-13-79	0	1	0.00	2	2	0	0	6	9	7	0	0	1	3	.346	.417	.286	4.76	1.59
Cook, Aaron	R-R	6-3	215	2-8-79	0	5	8.15	8	8	0	0	35	56	38	32	4	11	22	.359	.395	.325	5.60	2.80
Corpas, Manny	R-R	6-3	210	12-3-82	3	3	5.49	21	0	0	1	41	45	26	25	5	15	35	.283	.273	.290	7.68	3.29
Escalona, Edgmer	R-R	6-4	235	10-6-86	0	0	0.00	1	0	0	0	1	1	0	0	0	0	2	.200	.000	.250	13.50	0.00
Fick, C.J.	R-R	6-5	200	11-20-85	0	2	7.36	9	0	0	1	11	14	10	9	1	7	4	.333	.412	.280	3.27	5.73
2-team total (16 Oklahoma City)					1	2	5.97	22	0	0	1	32	41	23	21	2	20	17	—	—	—	4.83	5.68
Francis, Jeff	L-L	6-5	205	1-8-81	2	2	4.34	11	6	0	0	37	42	24	18	1	9	33	.280	.292	.275	7.96	2.17
Frazier, Parker	R-R	6-5	175	11-11-88	0	1	10.67	9	3	0	0	14	34	24	17	1	8	9	.466	.559	.385	5.65	5.02
Friedrich, Christian	R-L	6-4	215	7-8-87	0	1	4.30	4	4	0	0	15	13	12	7	1	8	8	.236	.000	.277	4.91	4.91
Galarraga, Armando	R-R	6-3	230	1-15-82	0	2	5.20	7	7	0	0	36	36	23	21	4	12	21	.259	.243	.277	5.20	2.97
Gallagher, Sean	R-R	6-2	220	12-30-85	2	3	5.77	7	7	0	0	39	46	27	25	4	17	29	.301	.309	.294	6.69	3.92
Hensley, Steven	R-R	6-3	190	12-27-86	0	2	4.69	31	1	0	0	40	49	27	21	7	24	43	.299	.231	.360	9.60	5.36
2-team total (2 Tacoma)					0	2	4.60	33	1	0	0	43	51	28	22	7	26	43	—	—	—	9.00	5.44
Houston, Dan	R-R	6-3	205	10-24-86	0	0	4.91	2	0	0	0	4	4	3	2	0	3	5	.250	.500	.167	12.27	7.36
Jacobson, Brett	R-R	6-6	205	11-9-86	1	1	9.00	10	0	0	0	17	17	17	17	2	26	10	.258	.250	.265	5.29	13.76
Kensing, Logan	R-R	6-1	190	7-3-82	2	5	3.05	44	0	0	15	44	37	22	15	5	22	41	.224	.242	.212	8.32	4.47
Manship, Jeff	R-R	6-1	205	1-16-85	6	8	4.85	24	17	0	0	104	114	66	56	8	32	71	.280	.268	.290	6.14	2.77
McClendon, Mike	R-R	6-5	225	4-3-85	7	8	4.02	45	0	0	3	72	77	38	32	2	35	59	.273	.256	.287	7.41	4.40
McHugh, Collin	R-R	6-2	195	6-19-87	2	2	4.63	9	9	0	0	47	52	25	24	2	14	47	.277	.247	.308	9.06	2.70
2-team total (9 Las Vegas)					5	4	3.69	18	18	0	0	100	109	46	41	5	27	88	—	—	—	7.92	2.43
Nicasio, Juan	R-R	6-3	230	8-31-86	1	0	0.82	2	2	0	0	11	8	1	1	0	1	8	.200	.214	.192	6.55	0.82

COLORADO ROCKIES

Name	B-T	HT	WT	DOB	W	L	ERA	G	GS	CG	SV	IP	H	R	ER	HR	BB	SO	AVG	vLH	vRH	K/9	BB/9
Outman, Josh	L-L	6-1	205	9-14-84	1	0	0.84	5	0	0	0	11	8	2	1	1	4	14	.205	.214	.200	11.81	3.38
Pomeranz, Drew	R-L	6-5	240	11-22-88	8	1	4.20	15	15	0	0	86	83	40	40	6	33	96	.256	.180	.290	10.09	3.47
Riordan, Cory	R-R	6-4	200	5-25-86	4	6	6.75	25	13	0	0	75	114	60	56	12	25	56	.357	.317	.401	6.75	3.01
Scahill, Rob	R-R	6-2	220	2-15-87	5	1	4.50	23	0	0	1	46	53	25	23	6	11	45	.294	.361	.250	8.80	2.15
Schmidt, Nick	L-L	6-5	245	10-10-85	5	3	4.71	37	8	0	1	92	107	52	48	10	38	72	.292	.298	.289	7.07	3.73
Solbach, Mike	R-R	6-3	185	7-31-85	0	0	12.10	20	1	0	0	29	52	43	39	4	23	21	.403	.423	.379	6.52	7.14
Sullivan, Josh	R-R	6-4	205	7-5-84	0	0	13.50	4	0	0	0	3	4	5	5	0	5	2	.308	.400	.250	5.40	13.50
Takahashi, Hisanori	L-L	5-10	180	4-2-75	1	1	6.66	18	0	0	0	26	39	26	19	2	13	36	.345	.308	.365	12.62	4.56
2-team total (20 Iowa)					2	1	4.25	38	0	0	0	53	53	33	25	5	22	61	—	—	—	10.36	3.74
Volstad, Chris	R-R	6-8	230	9-23-86	7	6	4.58	23	22	2	0	128	156	68	65	12	44	57	.308	.342	.278	4.02	3.10
Woods, Coty	R-R	6-2	190	3-14-88	3	3	7.15	33	0	0	4	39	55	33	31	5	23	21	.340	.364	.318	4.85	5.31

Fielding

Catcher	PCT	G	PO	A	E	DP	PB
Davis	.989	76	502	49	6	3	5
Gonzalez	.995	28	187	22	1	2	2
McBride	1.000	28	178	13	0	1	3
Pacheco	.984	9	57	4	1	0	0
Tarleton	1.000	4	32	3	0	0	0

First Base	PCT	G	PO	A	E	DP
Colvin	1.000	4	39	1	0	4
McBride	1.000	3	27	3	0	2
Nady	1.000	3	22	5	0	2
Pacheco	1.000	6	44	1	0	6
Paulsen	.993	116	1043	87	8	116
Wheeler	.993	13	133	3	1	14

Second Base	PCT	G	PO	A	E	DP
Brignac	.933	10	21	21	3	7
Culberson	.979	46	86	146	5	42
Garcia	1.000	23	21	61	0	13
Iribarren	.991	50	86	137	2	26

	PCT	G	PO	A	E	DP
LeMahieu	.900	2	3	6	1	1
Manzella	.966	6	15	13	1	5
Rutledge	.989	16	32	56	1	14

Third Base	PCT	G	PO	A	E	DP
Arenado	.928	17	15	49	5	6
Brignac	.933	19	9	33	3	3
Culberson	1.000	1	0	1	0	0
Garcia	.818	3	2	7	2	1
Iribarren	.750	3	2	7	3	0
LeMahieu	1.000	1	0	2	0	1
Manzella	1.000	9	7	18	0	2
Wheeler	.947	93	44	172	12	13

Shortstop	PCT	G	PO	A	E	DP
Brignac	.941	17	27	37	4	10
Culberson	.958	46	89	159	11	36
Garcia	.963	19	31	48	3	11
LeMahieu	.980	30	36	110	3	20
Manzella	.971	13	25	42	2	16

	PCT	G	PO	A	E	DP
Rutledge	.928	22	30	60	7	15
Tulowitzki	1.000	2	1	4	0	1

Outfield	PCT	G	PO	A	E	DP
Blackmon	.986	65	136	4	2	1
Colvin	.991	59	103	4	1	2
Culberson	1.000	3	7	0	0	0
Dickerson	.983	69	112	6	2	0
Fowler	1.000	2	1	0	0	0
Golson	.953	38	77	4	4	1
Gonzalez	1.000	2	2	0	0	0
Iribarren	1.000	11	11	0	0	0
Matthes	1.000	45	65	4	0	1
McBride	1.000	6	14	0	0	0
Nady	.977	29	42	0	1	0
Shepherd	.962	12	25	0	1	0
Wheeler	1.000	3	3	0	0	0
Wheeler	.952	102	192	8	10	2

TULSA DRILLERS

DOUBLE-A

TEXAS LEAGUE

Batting	B-T	HT	WT	DOB	AVG	vLH	vRH	G	AB	R	H	2B	3B	HR	RBI	BB	HBP	SH	SF	SO	SB	CS	SLG	OBP
Adames, Cristhian	B-R	6-0	160	7-26-91	.267	.299	.257	107	389	45	104	19	2	3	36	34	4	17	2	78	13	7	.350	.331
Cleary, Delta	B-R	6-3	180	8-14-89	.207	.176	.218	116	397	43	82	9	3	2	29	33	5	14	3	93	18	7	.259	.274
Crousset, Juan	L-L	5-11	193	4-30-90	.262	.182	.290	12	42	6	11	2	0	1	5	2	0	0	1	15	0	1	.381	.289
Garneau, Dustin	R-R	6-1	215	8-13-87	.236	.274	.225	96	326	36	77	17	1	13	47	25	13	4	4	57	4	2	.414	.313
Gonzalez, Jose	R-R	6-1	165	6-23-87	.194	.167	.202	38	129	15	25	5	0	3	9	9	3	1	0	42	1	2	.302	.262
Kuhn, Tyler	L-R	5-10	185	9-9-86	.233	.231	.234	61	227	32	53	11	4	1	22	29	3	2	2	34	7	6	.330	.326
Langfels, Jayson	R-R	6-2	205	8-17-88	.218	.256	.207	114	376	48	82	12	0	14	51	33	10	4	4	131	13	8	.362	.296
Matthes, Kent	R-R	6-2	215	1-8-87	.270	.333	.255	68	256	31	69	24	2	9	32	20	5	1	0	66	11	3	.484	.335
Murphy, Tom	R-R	6-1	220	4-3-91	.290	.353	.269	20	69	9	20	5	0	3	9	4	1	0	0	16	0	0	.493	.338
Nina, Angelys	R-R	5-11	165	11-16-88	.280	.231	.293	123	446	45	125	21	6	10	51	30	5	4	2	57	19	9	.422	.331
Ortega, Rafael	L-R	5-11	160	5-15-91	.228	.317	.197	42	158	22	36	4	2	1	10	19	1	0	0	36	6	9	.297	.315
Parker, Kyle	R-R	6-0	200	9-30-89	.288	.305	.283	123	480	70	138	23	3	23	74	40	4	0	4	99	6	6	.492	.345
Roling, Kiel	R-R	6-3	240	1-23-87	.261	.282	.256	112	410	55	107	26	0	24	84	38	3	0	7	107	0	0	.500	.323
Shepherd, Jaron	L-R	6-1	180	10-30-88	.236	.220	.241	64	199	23	47	9	1	0	9	17	3	8	1	44	9	2	.291	.305
Smalling, Tim	R-R	6-3	207	10-14-87	.237	.125	.280	31	114	21	27	7	0	1	10	8	1	2	0	24	0	3	.325	.293
Tanos, Brett	R-R	5-11	175	10-6-88	.100	.500	.000	4	10	0	1	0	0	0	0	1	0	0	0	2	0	0	.100	.182
Tarleton, Dallas	L-R	5-11	200	8-5-87	.210	.077	.245	27	62	5	13	2	0	1	2	7	0	4	0	22	1	0	.290	.290
Wong, Joey	L-R	5-10	175	4-12-88	.240	.154	.260	92	279	26	67	11	1	2	19	18	8	12	1	55	2	4	.330	.304
Wrigley, Henry	R-R	6-2	180	8-9-86	.188	.353	.158	31	112	13	21	6	0	4	10	4	2	0	1	21	1	0	.348	.227

Pitching	B-T	HT	WT	DOB	W	L	ERA	G	GS	CG	SV	IP	H	R	ER	HR	BB	SO	AVG	vLH	vRH	K/9	BB/9
Bergman, Christian	R-R	6-1	180	5-4-88	8	7	3.37	27	27	1	0	171	162	76	64	25	23	111	.253	.289	.225	5.84	1.21
Bettis, Chad	R-R	6-2	200	4-26-89	3	4	3.71	12	12	0	0	63	60	28	26	9	13	68	.255	.231	.275	9.71	1.86
Boggs, Mitchell	R-R	6-4	235	2-15-84	0	0	1.50	4	0	0	1	6	2	1	1	0	3	.095	.000	.143	4.50	0.00
Buch, Ryan	R-R	6-3	205	11-8-87	0	0	31.50	3	0	0	0	2	5	7	7	0	6	2	.500	1.000	.286	9.00	27.00
Butler, Eddie	B-R	6-2	180	3-13-91	1	0	0.65	6	6	0	0	28	13	2	2	0	6	25	.138	.154	.127	8.13	1.95
Frazier, Parker	R-R	6-5	175	11-11-88	1	1	2.57	16	1	0	0	35	31	11	10	3	12	26	.254	.214	.288	6.69	3.09
Froneberger, Isaiah	L-L	5-10	200	6-23-89	1	3	3.89	33	0	0	0	37	35	17	16	3	28	40	.257	.212	.286	9.73	6.81
Gallagher, Sean	R-R	6-2	220	12-30-85	4	5	3.00	12	12	0	0	75	64	26	25	10	28	50	.235	.220	.247	6.00	3.36
Gardner, Joe	R-R	6-4	230	3-18-88	6	4	5.53	35	0	0	2	55	52	38	34	6	18	60	.241	.239	.242	9.79	2.93
Gomez, Leuris	R-R	6-0	170	10-20-86	4	1	1.28	25	0	0	1	42	27	7	6	0	16	56	.178	.190	.170	11.91	3.40
Gonzalez, Juan	R-R	6-2	206	4-5-90	4	3	2.14	39	0	0	4	46	42	15	11	4	8	34	.250	.291	.213	6.60	1.55
Gustafson, Tim	R-R	6-3	210	12-29-84	7	12	5.41	27	27	0	0	146	162	98	88	15	53	105	.290	.312	.272	6.46	3.26
Hensley, Steven	R-R	6-3	190	12-27-86	1	0	2.25	8	0	0	4	8	2	2	2	1	3	.077	.000	.105	9.00	3.38
Houston, Dan	R-R	6-3	205	10-24-86	4	6	3.36	31	13	0	2	102	97	45	38	7	30	67	.249	.256	.244	5.93	2.66
Marbry, Michael	R-R	6-3	185	9-3-84	0	2	3.52	30	0	0	2	38	37	17	15	7	13	22	.261	.262	.259	5.17	3.05
Matzek, Tyler	L-L	6-3	210	10-19-90	8	9	3.79	26	26	0	0	142	147	67	60	13	76	95	.276	.260	.281	6.01	4.81
McHugh, Collin	R-R	6-2	195	6-19-87	1	1	1.38	2	2	0	0	13	9	2	2	1	0	12	.205	.214	.200	8.31	0.00

Name	B-T	HT	WT	DOB	W	L	ERA	G	GS	CG	SV	IP	H	R	ER	HR	BB	SO	AVG	vLH	vRH	K/9	BB/9
Mueller, Josh	R-R	6-4	215	1-18-89	2	1	3.68	23	1	0	0	37	33	17	15	2	14	24	.244	.234	.254	5.89	3.44
Oswalt, Roy	R-R	6-0	190	8-29-77	3	2	2.16	5	5	0	0	33	24	10	8	5	7	25	.211	.196	.224	6.75	1.89
Pomeranz, Drew	R-L	6-5	240	11-22-88	0	1	11.81	1	1	0	0	5	10	7	7	2	1	5	.400	.000	.435	8.44	1.69
Riordan, Cory	R-R	6-4	200	5-25-86	2	0	3.14	7	0	0	0	14	14	5	5	1	1	9	.250	.368	.189	5.65	0.63
Roberts, Kenny	L-L	6-1	200	3-9-88	1	1	7.16	12	0	0	0	16	21	15	13	4	13	6	.333	.316	.341	3.31	7.16
Sexton, Tim	R-R	6-6	185	6-10-87	1	1	4.94	14	0	0	0	24	33	17	13	4	9	10	.337	.325	.345	3.80	3.42
2-team total (15 San Antonio)					2	2	3.24	29	0	0	2	50	53	23	18	5	12	28	—	—	—	5.04	2.16
Solbach, Mike	R-R	6-3	185	7-31-85	3	1	3.28	20	0	0	3	25	19	9	9	1	13	25	.218	.241	.207	9.12	4.74
White, Cole	R-R	6-2	195	1-22-88	2	3	4.38	38	0	0	19	39	37	22	19	2	25	32	.262	.310	.214	7.38	5.77
2-team total (7 NW Arkansas)					2	4	3.97	45	0	0	19	48	44	24	21	2	33	42	—	—	—	7.93	6.23
Winkler, Dan	R-R	6-1	200	2-2-90	1	2	3.04	5	5	0	0	27	23	11	9	3	10	23	.240	.233	.245	7.76	3.38

Fielding

Catcher	PCT	G	PO	A	E	DP	PB
Garneau	.993	77	528	69	4	9	14
Gonzalez	.982	37	242	33	5	5	5
Murphy	.975	14	106	12	3	1	2
Tarleton	.989	11	78	10	1	0	0

First Base	PCT	G	PO	A	E	DP
Garneau	1.000	2	19	0	0	2
Langfels	1.000	4	16	1	0	3
Parker	.975	18	147	12	4	12
Roling	.995	95	873	52	5	108
Smalling	1.000	1	7	0	0	1
Tarleton	.980	6	45	3	1	8
Wrigley	.994	19	160	9	1	10

Second Base	PCT	G	PO	A	E	DP
Adames	.973	7	13	23	1	8
Nina	.980	107	228	319	11	88
Smalling	.920	4	7	16	2	2
Tanos	.938	3	7	8	1	1
Wong	1.000	22	45	74	0	16

Third Base	PCT	G	PO	A	E	DP
Langfels	.959	109	71	230	13	28
Smalling	.950	14	8	30	2	5
Wong	.961	24	13	36	2	10

Shortstop	PCT	G	PO	A	E	DP
Adames	.973	96	167	293	13	65
Nina	.926	5	8	17	2	6
Wong	.971	38	63	136	6	26

Outfield	PCT	G	PO	A	E	DP
Cleary	.996	109	228	8	1	3
Crousset	.923	12	11	1	1	1
Kuhn	.989	55	87	4	1	1
Matthes	.984	61	111	10	2	4
Ortega	.972	39	100	3	3	0
Parker	.972	96	134	7	4	1
Shepherd	.971	54	94	5	3	1
Smalling	1.000	2	3	0	0	0

MODESTO NUTS — HIGH CLASS A
CALIFORNIA LEAGUE

Batting	B-T	HT	WT	DOB	AVG	vLH	vRH	G	AB	R	H	2B	3B	HR	RBI	BB	HBP	SH	SF	SO	SB	CS	SLG	OBP
Beuerlein, Drew	B-R	6-0	205	1-13-88	.200	.077	.243	18	50	4	10	3	0	0	7	7	0	0	2	13	0	0	.260	.288
Casteel, Ryan	R-R	6-1	205	6-6-91	.270	.333	.252	108	411	67	111	30	4	22	76	50	4	0	4	118	1	0	.523	.352
Crousset, Juan	L-L	5-11	193	4-30-90	.238	.353	.193	52	189	15	45	7	2	2	14	11	1	0	3	65	3	2	.328	.279
Espy, Dean	R-R	6-1	210	10-30-89	.000	—	.000	1	2	0	0	0	0	0	0	0	0	0	0	2	0	0	.000	.000
Featherston, Taylor	R-R	6-1	185	10-8-89	.292	.333	.278	116	469	87	137	31	10	13	81	30	9	2	6	110	17	4	.484	.342
Gallego, Niko	R-R	6-0	150	12-29-88	.215	.206	.222	81	228	29	49	11	3	3	17	14	10	2	2	58	14	5	.329	.287
Humphries, Brian	L-R	6-3	195	3-20-90	.300	.261	.310	111	453	62	136	26	5	8	50	14	2	6	1	82	14	6	.433	.323
Kandilas, David	R-R	6-2	185	9-14-90	.265	.286	.258	96	359	47	95	14	3	4	36	44	5	2	5	83	24	5	.354	.349
Massey, Tyler	L-L	6-0	205	7-21-89	.267	.196	.283	116	442	63	118	19	9	11	53	36	9	5	4	95	10	11	.425	.332
Mende, Sam	R-R	6-3	195	1-9-90	.224	.600	.186	16	49	4	11	3	0	0	1	2	3	0	0	18	3	0	.286	.296
Osborne, Zach	R-R	5-8	170	4-00-90	.167	.182	.143	4	18	2	3	0	0	0	0	0	0	0	0	3	0	0	.167	.167
Ribera, Jordan	L-R	6-0	225	12-22-88	.219	.240	.213	59	219	20	48	14	2	3	36	13	0	1	0	62	0	1	.342	.262
Riggins, Harold	R-R	6-2	240	3-6-90	.247	.270	.237	118	413	77	102	25	1	22	65	57	11	0	1	192	4	3	.472	.353
Rivera, Jose	R-R	5-10	170	4-18-90	.183	.174	.185	36	104	16	19	1	0	0	7	5	7	0		19	2	1	.192	.267
Simon, Jared	R-R	6-1	210	3-3-89	.249	.231	.256	78	289	43	72	20	0	10	48	17	11	0	3	76	3	0	.422	.313
Smalling, Tim	R-R	6-3	207	10-14-87	.237	.178	.258	49	177	21	42	8	1	1	18	20	2	1	3	39	2	2	.311	.317
Story, Trevor	R-R	6-1	175	11-15-92	.233	.209	.243	130	497	71	116	34	5	12	65	45	7	4	1	183	23	1	.394	.305
Swanner, Will	R-R	6-2	185	9-10-91	.239	.253	.231	100	355	52	85	25	1	13	51	44	3	0	5	129	7	4	.425	.324
Von Tungeln, Kyle	L-L	5-9	175	9-18-90	.122	.200	.097	14	41	4	5	1	0	0	9	0	0	0		16	3	1	.146	.280
Wessinger, Matt	R-R	6-0	180	9-20-90	.230	.150	.259	19	74	11	17	3	0	0	12	9	0	1	1	9	5	2	.270	.310

Pitching	B-T	HT	WT	DOB	W	L	ERA	G	GS	CG	SV	IP	H	R	ER	HR	BB	SO	AVG	vLH	vRH	K/9	BB/9
Alsup, Ben	R-R	6-3	180	9-9-88	13	8	4.45	29	29	0	0	162	163	93	80	20	59	133	.256	.267	.250	7.40	3.28
Anderson, Tyler	L-L	6-4	215	12-30-89	3	2	3.25	13	13	0	0	75	62	34	27	10	24	63	.224	.263	.208	7.59	2.89
Arrowood, Ryan	R-R	6-3	190	8-24-90	1	0	4.24	10	0	0	0	17	18	8	8	2	6	16	.269	.320	.238	8.47	3.18
Brewer, Russell	R-R	6-0	200	2-25-88	1	0	6.64	19	0	0	0	20	26	15	15	6	10	24	.313	.292	.322	10.62	4.43
Buch, Ryan	R-R	6-3	205	11-8-87	0	1	3.95	11	0	0	0	14	7	6	6	2	7	15	.146	.222	.100	9.88	4.61
Butler, Eddie	B-R	6-2	180	3-13-91	3	4	2.39	13	13	0	0	68	58	29	18	7	21	67	.227	.224	.228	8.91	2.79
Gagnon, Tyler	R-R	6-2	175	3-22-89	12	10	5.50	28	28	0	0	159	183	108	97	17	52	120	.289	.235	.320	6.81	2.95
Gomez, Leuris	R-R	6-0	170	10-20-86	0	0	1.50	11	0	0	0	18	11	3	3	2	5	21	.183	.143	.219	10.50	2.50
Gonzalez, Nelson	R-R	6-1	168	2-15-90	5	6	5.00	55	0	0	0	77	76	46	43	10	16	82	.257	.225	.276	9.54	1.86
Gray, Jonathan	R-R	6-4	255	11-5-91	4	0	0.75	5	5	0	0	24	10	3	2	0	6	36	.128	.139	.119	13.50	2.25
Hernandez, Jefri	R-R	6-1	170	4-27-91	0	0	0.00	3	0	0	0	3	4	0	0	0	2	3	.333	.500	.300	10.13	6.75
Jensen, Chris	R-R	6-4	200	9-30-90	5	8	4.55	28	28	0	0	152	161	86	77	15	39	136	.264	.275	.257	8.04	2.30
Johnson, Patrick	R-R	5-10	170	8-14-88	1	1	4.41	12	0	0	0	16	14	13	8	1	7	23	.230	.211	.238	12.67	3.86
Kern, Bruce	R-R	6-1	175	4-24-88	1	0	2.41	20	0	0	2	19	16	6	5	1	7	17	.229	.242	.216	8.20	3.38
Oakes, T.J.	R-R	6-5	210	7-15-90	0	0	5.40	1	1	0	0	5	4	3	3	0	4	7	.250	.500	.214	12.60	7.20
Oberg, Scott	R-R	6-2	205	3-13-90	1	6	1.86	56	0	0	33	53	34	14	11	4	27	61	.178	.190	.170	10.29	4.56
Parker, Geoff	R-R	6-3	245	3-22-89	4	5	4.59	37	1	0	0	69	73	40	35	4	37	53	.277	.287	.269	6.95	4.85
Rankin, Will	R-R	6-0	192	5-1-89	1	0	5.14	20	0	0	0	21	18	13	12	3	15	15	.228	.179	.255	6.43	6.43
Roberts, Kenny	L-L	6-1	200	3-9-88	0	0	1.30	41	0	0	4	55	52	15	8	0	9	44	.242	.237	.245	7.16	1.46
Schnaitmann, Nick	R-R	6-6	190	11-16-89	2	4	5.75	24	0	0	0	36	31	24	23	4	24	27	.240	.218	.257	6.75	6.00
Sitton, Kraig	L-L	6-5	190	7-13-88	6	5	2.93	52	0	0	2	68	61	26	22	3	27	63	.238	.160	.288	8.38	3.59
Winkler, Dan	R-R	6-1	200	2-2-90	12	5	2.97	22	22	0	0	130	84	48	43	15	37	152	.184	.225	.154	10.50	2.55

Fielding

Catcher	PCT	G	PO	A	E	DP	PB
Beuerlein	1.000	4	13	0	0	0	0
Casteel	.998	57	470	41	1	11	4
Swanner	.986	83	692	59	11	11	18

First Base	PCT	G	PO	A	E	DP
Beuerlein	1.000	4	27	1	0	3
Massey	1.000	3	9	1	0	1
Ribera	.986	41	322	37	5	29
Riggins	.980	96	750	67	17	77

Second Base	PCT	G	PO	A	E	DP
Featherston	.963	109	206	290	19	72
Gallego	.978	21	29	62	2	10

Osborne	1.000	3	3	7	0	0
Rivera	.931	9	8	19	2	6
Smalling	.923	6	10	14	2	4
Wessinger	1.000	1	1	1	0	0

Third Base	PCT	G	PO	A	E	DP
Espy	1.000	1	0	1	0	0
Featherston	.500	2	0	1	1	0
Gallego	.928	46	23	67	7	4
Mende	1.000	16	10	22	0	2
Rivera	.967	27	17	42	2	6
Smalling	.941	44	24	71	6	7
Story	1.000	4	2	6	0	0
Wessinger	.978	19	11	34	1	4

Shortstop	PCT	G	PO	A	E	DP
Featherston	.926	5	9	16	2	5
Gallego	.970	10	11	21	1	7
Smalling	.917	3	3	8	1	2
Story	.957	125	172	336	23	71

Outfield	PCT	G	PO	A	E	DP
Crousset	.949	44	73	2	4	0
Humphries	.975	103	191	2	5	0
Kandilas	.980	90	196	4	4	1
Massey	.981	110	253	5	5	4
Simon	.962	71	118	8	5	3
Von Tungeln	1.000	12	34	0	0	0

ASHEVILLE TOURISTS

LOW CLASS A

SOUTH ATLANTIC LEAGUE

Batting	B-T	HT	WT	DOB	AVG	vLH	vRH	G	AB	R	H	2B	3B	HR	RBI	BB	HBP	SH	SF	SO	SB	CS	SLG	OBP
Argyropoulos, Matt	R-R	6-2	195	8-24-88	.282	.253	.294	85	284	35	80	25	1	2	36	29	3	8	3	72	5	1	.398	.351
Bergin, David	R-R	6-2	235	8-25-89	.367	.125	.455	8	30	5	11	5	0	0	2	3	1	0	0	6	0	1	.533	.441
Beuerlein, Drew	B-R	6-0	205	1-13-88	.342	.333	.344	10	38	7	13	4	0	1	8	4	1	0	0	8	0	0	.526	.419
Briceno, Jose	R-R	6-0	195	9-19-92	.264	.200	.282	26	91	12	24	6	0	1	8	5	0	0	0	10	0	1	.363	.302
Ciriaco, Juan	R-R	5-9	155	7-6-90	.279	.337	.259	100	358	46	100	19	1	2	27	21	1	18	2	62	50	15	.355	.319
Dahl, David	L-R	6-2	185	4-1-94	.275	.250	.281	10	40	9	11	4	1	0	7	2	0	0	0	8	2	0	.425	.310
Espy, Dean	R-R	6-1	210	10-30-89	.333	—	.333	1	3	0	1	0	0	0	0	0	0	0	0	0	0	0	.333	.333
Herrera, Rosell	B-R	6-3	180	10-16-92	.343	.352	.341	126	472	83	162	33	0	16	76	61	3	6	4	96	21	8	.515	.419
Jones, Derek	L-L	6-0	210	6-3-90	.244	.237	.246	114	418	52	102	29	1	19	56	32	11	6	2	124	16	5	.455	.313
Murphy, Tom	R-R	6-1	220	4-3-91	.288	.270	.293	80	288	55	83	26	2	19	74	37	10	3	3	87	4	5	.590	.385
O'Dowd, Chris	B-R	5-11	175	10-4-90	.306	.400	.290	10	36	4	11	3	0	0	3	1	0	1	0	9	3	1	.389	.324
Osborne, Zach	R-R	5-8	170	4-20-90	.256	.357	.207	13	43	5	11	1	0	0	5	1	0	2	0	2	2	1	.279	.273
Ramirez, Michael	R-R	5-10	165	4-27-90	.217	.308	.191	36	115	11	25	8	0	0	7	3	4	10	0	22	0	0	.287	.262
Rivera, Jose	R-R	5-10	170	4-18-90	.272	.309	.314	28	103	22	28	8	2	1	7	14	0	2	0	23	2	1	.417	.359
Sosa, Francisco	R-R	6-4	180	2-27-90	.315	.357	.301	127	461	85	145	35	2	20	89	57	8	1	3	125	30	10	.529	.397
Stolz, Jason	R-R	6-2	200	3-21-90	.233	.197	.246	76	275	36	64	15	1	3	21	16	1	0	0	68	4	3	.327	.277
Thomas, Dillon	L-L	6-1	195	12-10-92	.255	.260	.253	90	330	31	84	14	3	3	36	26	0	2	0	84	10	12	.342	.309
Von Tungeln, Kyle	L-L	5-9	185	9-18-90	.230	.192	.240	55	122	23	28	5	3	1	13	30	2	3	1	24	4	4	.344	.387
Waldrip, Ben	L-L	6-6	245	6-27-90	.196	.200	.195	31	107	10	21	3	0	3	9	5	0	0	0	31	2	0	.308	.232
Wessinger, Matt	R-R	6-0	180	9-20-90	.275	.300	.268	106	404	66	111	28	1	6	42	42	4	12	2	72	22	10	.394	.347
White, Max	L-L	6-0	190	10-10-93	.226	.140	.249	72	243	25	55	16	1	3	21	20	2	2	2	79	11	8	.337	.288
Yan, Julian	R-R	6-2	180	11-27-91	.206	.235	.196	53	189	22	39	12	1	5	20	14	5	2	0	64	12	9	.360	.279

Pitching	B-T	HT	WT	DOB	W	L	ERA	G	GS	CG	SV	IP	H	R	ER	HR	BB	SO	AVG	vLH	vRH	K/9	BB/9
Aquino, Jayson	L-L	6-1	170	11-22-92	0	9	4.78	11	10	0	0	64	66	40	34	4	21	57	.275	.255	.280	8.02	2.95
Arrowood, Ryan	R-R	6-3	190	8-24-90	5	2	3.57	25	6	0	1	68	70	34	27	2	24	83	.263	.300	.244	10.99	3.18
Blank, Trent	R-R	6-2	190	8-31-89	0	1	1.64	17	0	0	0	22	20	6	4	0	6	16	.233	.136	.167	6.55	2.45
Brown, Andrew	R-R	6-2	195	11-11-89	7	1	2.68	21	3	0	0	50	46	19	15	1	10	34	.258	.232	.270	6.08	1.79
Broyles, Shane	R-R	6-1	180	8-19-91	1	9	6.21	21	15	0	0	80	101	64	55	11	32	65	.304	.313	.300	7.34	3.62
Butler, Eddie	B-R	6-2	180	3-13-91	5	1	1.66	9	9	0	0	54	25	16	10	2	25	51	.137	.105	.145	8.45	4.14
Carasiti, Matt	R-R	6-3	205	7-23-91	2	10	7.94	20	20	0	0	93	136	93	82	9	43	60	.341	.335	.345	5.81	4.16
Fernandez, Raul	R-R	6-2	180	6-22-90	2	2	6.29	35	0	0	16	34	40	25	24	6	11	55	.284	.269	.292	14.42	2.88
Flemer, Matt	R-R	6-2	210	11-22-90	4	4	3.64	16	16	1	0	84	91	39	34	7	14	83	.271	.246	.286	8.89	1.50
Gonzalez, Rayan	R-R	6-3	175	10-18-90	2	3	2.68	49	0	0	12	54	51	22	16	0	21	70	.243	.169	.286	11.74	3.52
Hart, Brook	L-L	6-5	220	4-10-89	1	1	4.91	43	0	0	0	55	54	34	30	3	17	52	.256	.058	.321	8.51	2.78
Hughes, Ben	R-R	6-5	215	11-29-89	8	11	5.89	25	25	2	0	136	177	103	89	16	51	71	.316	.330	.306	4.70	3.38
Johnson, Patrick	R-R	5-10	170	8-14-88	3	3	2.83	25	0	0	0	29	20	11	9	1	17	37	.198	.171	.212	11.62	5.34
Mason, Mike	R-L	6-3	190	4-3-90	3	1	3.38	21	0	0	0	29	27	12	11	2	10	28	.239	.233	.259	8.59	3.07
Meaux, Jesse	R-R	6-4	210	8-8-89	0	0	0.90	16	0	0	1	20	17	2	2	1	8	26	.224	.229	.220	11.70	3.60
Mejias, Alving	R-R	6-0	200	12-26-91	5	5	4.73	36	0	0	0	70	84	41	37	9	16	52	.293	.257	.313	6.65	2.05
Newberry, Jacob	R-R	6-2	220	10-10-90	1	0	3.77	11	0	0	0	14	15	6	6	1	6	17	.263	.208	.303	10.67	3.77
Oakes, T.J.	R-R	6-5	210	7-15-90	9	8	4.27	25	25	1	0	139	153	83	66	10	38	86	.279	.317	.256	5.57	2.46
Padilla, Roberto	L-L	6-3	200	6-29-90	1	2	7.43	12	0	0	0	13	18	13	11	3	11	17	.327	.375	.319	11.48	7.43
Slaats, Josh	R-R	6-5	225	12-22-88	1	0	5.65	9	0	0	0	14	16	13	9	3	7	13	.281	.200	.298	8.16	4.40
Vargas, Jonathan	L-L	6-2	150	5-29-89	3	0	5.71	7	7	0	0	35	38	23	22	2	15	16	.279	.167	.304	4.15	3.89

Fielding

Catcher	PCT	G	PO	A	E	DP	PB
Beuerlein	1.000	1	4	1	0	0	0
Briceno	.986	25	190	19	3	1	4
Murphy	.993	69	499	55	4	7	21
O'Dowd	.976	6	31	9	1	0	3
Ramirez	.989	36	249	20	3	3	3

First Base	PCT	G	PO	A	E	DP
Argyropoulos	.993	57	507	27	4	42

Bergin	1.000	7	64	1	0	4
Beuerlein	.989	8	82	6	1	8
Espy	1.000	1	12	2	0	1
Jones	.988	36	302	22	4	28
Stolz	1.000	2	21	1	0	0
Waldrip	.988	29	236	20	3	19

Second Base	PCT	G	PO	A	E	DP
Ciriaco	.954	86	153	245	19	56

Osborne	1.000	5	5	17	0	5
Rivera	.966	12	17	40	2	8
Wessinger	.968	34	60	91	5	23

Third Base	PCT	G	PO	A	E	DP
Argyropoulos	.944	16	8	26	2	0
Rivera	.912	15	8	44	5	4
Stolz	.973	72	55	158	6	17
Wessinger	.896	35	24	79	12	12

Shortstop	PCT	G	PO	A	E	DP
Ciriaco	.857	1	3	3	1	0
Herrera	.930	93	117	257	28	48
Osborne	.964	8	12	15	1	3
Stolz	1.000	2	4	4	0	0
Wessinger	.968	32	56	93	5	17

Outfield	PCT	G	PO	A	E	DP
Ciriaco	—	1	0	0	0	0
Dahl	1.000	8	5	1	0	0
Jones	.984	72	113	7	2	1
Sosa	.952	101	169	11	9	1
Thomas	.952	82	115	5	6	2

	PCT	G	PO	A	E	DP
Von Tungeln	.942	29	49	0	3	0
White	.957	68	153	4	7	0
Yan	.934	53	76	9	6	1

TRI-CITY DUST DEVILS

SHORT-SEASON

NORTHWEST LEAGUE

Batting	B-T	HT	WT	DOB	AVG	vLH	vRH	G	AB	R	H	2B	3B	HR	RBI	BB	HBP	SH	SF	SO	SB	CS	SLG	OBP
Benjamin Jr., Mike	R-R	6-0	190	3-18-92	.233	.333	.204	56	202	24	47	17	1	0	30	18	10	1	3	55	13	6	.327	.322
Derkes, Marcos	B-R	6-0	155	9-12-91	.184	.222	.176	37	103	8	19	3	0	0	8	16	6	3	0	43	7	0	.214	.328
Dwyer, Sean	L-L	6-0	190	12-5-91	.252	.311	.236	58	202	20	51	7	2	1	22	29	4	0	3	60	6	4	.322	.353
Galvez, Cesar	B-R	5-9	145	7-24-91	.161	.029	.204	36	137	11	22	2	0	0	5	10	0	0	0	13	10	6	.175	.218
Graeter, Ashley	R-R	6-1	190	10-3-89	.220	.195	.228	46	164	17	36	7	2	3	22	17	2	1	3	34	5	1	.341	.296
Hutcheson, Pat	L-R	5-10	185	10-9-89	.202	.233	.193	48	178	19	36	7	0	0	8	11	1	4	1	60	12	1	.242	.251
Mehrten, Alec	R-R	6-3	190	7-24-90	.279	.306	.271	60	204	26	57	3	2	1	22	32	15	2	1	27	4	3	.328	.413
Monzon, Jose	R-R	6-0	170	12-30-91	.205	.154	.231	13	39	3	8	1	0	0	1	5	1	0	0	14	0	2	.231	.311
O'Dowd, Chris	B-R	5-11	175	10-4-90	.263	.222	.270	48	175	24	46	5	4	2	18	15	1	4	2	40	13	6	.371	.321
Osborne, Zach	R-R	5-8	170	4-20-90	.250	.000	.333	2	8	1	2	0	0	0	1	1	0	0	0	0	0	0	.250	.333
Popick, Jeff	R-R	6-4	220	6-17-89	.500	.500	—	1	2	1	1	0	0	0	0	0	0	0	0	0	0	0	.500	.500
Rodriguez, Wilfredo	R-R	5-10	200	1-25-94	.270	.250	.277	41	141	15	38	5	0	1	19	18	3	1	4	25	2	4	.326	.355
San Juan, Alex	R-R	5-11	208	4-30-91	.083	.250	.000	4	12	0	1	0	0	0	1	1	0	0	1	6	0	0	.083	.143
Soriano, Wilson	R-R	5-9	140	12-31-91	.175	.167	.178	51	177	11	31	2	0	0	8	10	2	6	2	27	7	6	.186	
.225 Tauchman, Mike	L-L	6-2	200	1-3-91	.297	.327	.287	64	236	38	70	13	3	0	23	33	3	1	1	55	20	7	.377	.388
Valaika, Pat	R-R	5-11	200	9-9-92	.240	.250	.237	42	146	27	35	15	2	1	18	23	2	4	3	33	5	3	.390	.345
Von Tungeln, Kyle	L-L	5-9	175	9-18-90	.199	.133	.217	40	136	27	27	8	3	2	16	33	4	2	0	44	9	5	.346	.370
Waldrip, Ben	L-L	6-6	245	6-27-90	.220	.238	.213	22	82	1	18	3	0	0	6	3	1	1	1	22	2	2	.256	.253
Yan, Julian	R-R	6-2	180	11-27-91	.213	.241	.204	33	127	11	27	3	0	2	16	5	1	0	1	49	6	2	.331	.241

Pitching	B-T	HT	WT	DOB	W	L	ERA	G	GS	CG	SV	IP	H	R	ER	HR	BB	SO	AVG	vLH	vRH	K/9	BB/9
Anderson, Tyler	L-L	6-4	215	12-30-89	1	1	0.60	3	3	0	0	15	9	6	1	0	3	13	.164	.000	.173	7.80	1.80
Aquino, Jayson	L-L	6-1	170	11-22-92	0	1	3.13	4	4	0	0	23	21	8	8	1	5	16	.244	.208	.258	6.26	1.96
Blank, Trent	R-R	6-2	190	8-31-89	0	0	0.00	5	0	0	4	5	0	0	0	0	1	5	.000	.000	.000	9.64	1.93
Brazoban, Huascar	R-R	6-3	155	10-15-89	0	3	7.78	21	0	0	0	20	19	21	17	0	21	24	.238	.269	.222	10.98	9.61
Broyles, Shane	R-R	6-1	180	8-19-91	5	0	0.81	11	0	0	0	22	9	2	2	0	8	38	.118	.043	.151	15.31	3.22
Bryant, Tony	R-R	6-7	220	4-18-91	0	0	1.93	8	0	0	0	9	5	2	2	0	8	13	.156	.250	.063	12.54	7.71
Daniel, Trent	L-L	6-1	190	7-1-90	0	0	1.90	23	0	0	15	24	16	5	5	1	15	23	.193	.200	.190	8.75	5.70
Estevez, Carlos	R-R	6-4	210	12-28-92	1	0	2.45	2	0	0	0	4	3	1	1	1	1	5	.214	.000	.375	12.27	2.45
Jiminian, Johendi	R-R	6-3	170	10-14-92	3	5	3.38	15	14	0	0	83	79	33	31	3	24	57	.256	.291	.225	6.21	2.61
Kern, Bruce	R-R	6-1	175	4-24-88	1	0	0.00	11	0	0	1	11	4	0	0	0	4	12	.118	.100	.143	9.82	3.27
Lezama, Angel	R-R	6-0	164	3-1-94	0	0	7.36	2	0	0	0	4	5	3	3	1	2	4	.313	.667	.231	9.82	4.91
Magliaro, Marc	R-R	5-11	175	2-17-90	2	2	3.90	27	0	0	0	30	36	15	13	1	17	24	.298	.326	.280	7.20	5.10
McCrummen, Jerad	R-R	6-1	190	9-11-90	2	1	1.73	23	0	0	3	26	20	5	5	1	4	24	.211	.289	.158	8.31	1.38
Moll, Sam	L-L	5-10	185	1-3-92	3	1	1.80	10	6	0	0	30	20	9	6	0	10	29	.182	.313	.128	8.70	3.00
Nedeljkovic, Eric	R-R	5-11	175	2-14-90	0	1	7.71	5	0	0	1	5	5	7	4	0	4	2	.263	.000	.333	3.86	7.71
Neiman, Troy	R-R	6-6	195	11-13-90	2	1	3.86	12	0	0	0	23	17	11	10	0	7	22	.200	.184	.213	8.49	2.70
Norris, Logan	R-R	5-10	175	8-27-90	0	4	3.94	6	5	0	0	30	31	17	13	1	13	22	.274	.269	.279	6.67	3.94
Pierpont, Matt	R-R	6-2	215	1-25-91	1	1	3.14	8	0	0	0	14	12	8	5	1	6	16	.231	.267	.182	10.05	3.77
Rodriguez, Alex	L-L	6-4	206	9-14-93	0	0	9.00	6	0	0	0	5	6	5	5	0	7	5	.300	.333	.286	9.00	12.60
Seise, Anthony	R-L	6-1	188	2-23-93	0	0	12.00	5	0	0	0	3	3	8	4	0	6	1	.214	1.000	.154	3.00	18.00
Senzatela, Antonio	R-R	6-1	180	1-21-95	2	4	3.83	8	8	0	0	42	48	23	18	1	13	20	.282	.282	.282	4.25	2.76
Stuart, Shawn	R-R	6-3	210	12-26-88	3	2	5.71	24	0	0	0	35	31	22	22	2	24	19	.238	.280	.213	4.93	6.23
Tago, Peter	R-R	6-2	170	7-5-92	0	2	9.00	2	2	0	0	9	5	11	9	0	10	6	.167	.250	.136	6.00	10.00
Vargas, Jonathan	L-L	6-2	150	5-29-89	2	2	4.21	19	5	0	1	51	51	26	24	1	23	35	.266	.241	.275	6.14	4.03
Wade, Konner	R-R	6-3	190	12-3-91	3	7	3.58	14	14	0	0	65	70	31	26	4	11	37	.270	.298	.248	5.10	1.52
Warner, Ryan	L-R	6-7	195	1-21-94	3	4	3.36	15	15	0	0	88	79	37	33	4	23	46	.239	.233	.242	4.69	2.34

Fielding

Catcher	PCT	G	PO	A	E	DP	PB
Graeter	.982	15	93	14	2	2	8
O'Dowd	.972	42	283	25	9	0	6
Rodriguez	1.000	19	106	8	0	2	2
San Juan	.978	4	37	7	1	0	2

First Base	PCT	G	PO	A	E	DP
Dwyer	.992	41	357	27	3	34
Graeter	1.000	4	45	1	0	8
Hutcheson	.989	11	90	3	1	7
Waldrip	.982	21	204	18	4	25

Second Base	PCT	G	PO	A	E	DP
Galvez	.965	35	78	116	7	27
Hutcheson	.970	24	41	87	4	19
Mehrten	.939	6	16	15	2	5
Valaika	.981	12	17	36	1	6

Third Base	PCT	G	PO	A	E	DP
Benjamin Jr.	.899	46	30	103	15	12
Graeter	.956	16	9	34	2	2
Hutcheson	1.000	8	5	24	0	2
Mehrten	.947	6	4	14	1	0
Osborne	1.000	1	3	0	0	0

Shortstop	PCT	G	PO	A	E	DP
Benjamin Jr.	.927	7	12	26	3	5
Mehrten	.950	38	67	105	9	29
Osborne	1.000	1	2	0	0	0
Soriano	.714	1	2	3	2	1
Valaika	.960	29	40	79	5	19

Outfield	PCT	G	PO	A	E	DP
Derkes	1.000	32	53	2	0	1
Dwyer	1.000	16	15	0	0	0
Monzon	1.000	13	16	1	0	1
Popick	—	1	0	0	0	0
Soriano	.983	50	113	5	2	1
Tauchman	.974	55	113	1	3	0
Von Tungeln	.986	37	66	2	1	1
Yan	.986	28	65	7	1	1

COLORADO ROCKIES

GRAND JUNCTION ROCKIES ROOKIE

PIONEER LEAGUE

Batting	B-T	HT	WT	DOB	AVG	vLH	vRH	G	AB	R	H	2B	3B	HR	RBI	BB	HBP	SH	SF	SO	SB	CS	SLG	OBP
Briceno, Jose	R-R	6-0	195	9-19-92	.333	.270	.353	36	153	32	51	16	0	9	30	5	1	0	1	30	8	2	.614	.356
Dilone, Miguel	L-R	6-2	175	7-8-93	.283	.273	.287	51	173	28	49	9	3	5	23	22	0	3	1	41	3	4	.457	.362
Galvez, Cesar	B-R	5-9	145	7-24-91	.338	.294	.372	21	77	16	26	3	0	0	5	8	0	1	2	7	7	3	.377	.391
Garvey, Ryan	R-R	6-1	190	3-30-93	.232	.200	.243	54	194	21	45	8	3	4	23	16	3	0	0	56	3	8	.366	.300
Jimenez, Emerson	L-R	6-1	160	12-16-94	.309	.239	.333	46	181	32	56	8	1	3	20	9	1	5	1	42	6	3	.414	.344
Jones, Wesley	R-R	6-2	180	8-12-95	.182	.043	.241	23	77	8	14	2	0	0	4	3	2	0	0	20	3	2	.208	.232
McClure, Terry	R-R	6-2	190	9-29-95	.254	.158	.292	41	134	27	34	8	1	0	8	16	4	2	1	59	11	4	.328	.348
McMahon, Ryan	L-R	6-2	185	12-14-94	.321	.311	.325	59	218	42	70	18	3	11	52	28	2	2	1	59	4	6	.583	.402
Norton, Cole	L-L	5-8	180	7-3-91	.258	.250	.260	22	66	13	17	6	1	1	6	12	0	0	1	30	4	1	.424	.367
Nunez, Dom	R-R	6-0	175	1-17-95	.200	.184	.205	55	195	24	39	13	1	3	23	18	1	1	2	34	11	3	.323	.269
Osborne, Zach	R-R	5-8	170	4-20-90	.267	.233	.276	39	135	19	36	9	1	2	12	6	4	6	2	11	3	1	.393	.313
Patterson, Jordan	L-L	6-4	205	2-12-92	.291	.222	.311	60	206	44	60	12	0	10	37	19	16	5	3	37	10	6	.495	.389
Perkins, Robbie	R-R	6-0	175	5-29-94	.162	.143	.167	35	117	16	19	3	0	3	12	8	3	0	0	38	0	0	.265	.234
Popick, Jeff	R-R	6-4	220	6-17-89	.333	.500	.250	2	6	0	2	1	0	0	2	0	0	0	0	0	0	0	.500	.333
Prime, Correlle	R-R	6-5	200	2-18-94	.281	.273	.285	59	224	30	63	12	2	7	39	11	2	0	2	55	11	2	.446	.318
Rosario, Jairo	R-R	5-10	175	1-21-93	.242	.200	.261	44	161	26	39	6	3	4	22	12	2	0	3	33	1	4	.391	.298
Tapia, Raimel	L-L	6-2	160	2-4-94	.357	.368	.353	66	258	53	92	20	6	7	47	15	5	5	3	31	10	9	.562	.399

Pitching	B-T	HT	WT	DOB	W	L	ERA	G	GS	CG	SV	IP	H	R	ER	HR	BB	SO	AVG	vLH	vRH	K/9	BB/9
Balog, Alex	R-R	6-5	210	7-16-92	1	4	9.30	7	7	0	0	30	51	38	31	7	8	17	.383	.362	.395	5.10	2.40
Beck, John	R-R	6-3	195	3-26-92	0	0	0.00	1	0	0	0	1	1	0	0	0	0	1	.250	.000	.500	9.00	0.00
Burke, Devin	R-R	6-1	205	2-20-91	5	2	3.21	13	5	0	0	56	52	21	20	4	12	54	.242	.217	.258	8.68	1.93
Estevez, Carlos	R-R	6-4	210	12-28-92	5	1	3.79	22	0	0	0	36	31	18	15	3	14	31	.240	.289	.214	7.82	3.53
Firth, Scott	R-R	6-0	170	1-2-91	2	2	3.06	25	0	0	3	32	30	19	11	4	12	22	.244	.167	.284	6.12	3.34
Gray, Jonathan	R-R	6-4	255	11-5-91	0	0	4.05	4	4	0	0	13	15	8	6	0	2	15	.278	.250	.289	10.13	1.35
Jemiola, Zach	L-R	6-3	200	4-6-94	2	3	5.21	15	15	1	0	76	78	51	44	6	29	61	.265	.265	.266	7.22	3.43
Lezama, Angel	R-R	6-0	164	3-1-94	2	0	5.03	20	1	0	1	34	46	19	19	3	7	26	.322	.306	.330	6.88	1.85
Mejia, Jordan	R-R	6-2	190	4-6-91	0	0	9.00	9	0	0	1	8	11	8	8	4	4	3	.355	.333	.368	3.38	4.50
Montilla, Manuel	R-R	6-4	205	9-7-91	2	0	7.18	20	1	0	0	36	48	34	29	7	18	21	.318	.283	.337	5.20	4.46
Newberry, Jacob	R-R	6-2	220	10-10-90	0	1	3.95	15	0	0	2	14	12	6	6	0	5	15	.250	.067	.333	9.88	3.29
Norris, Logan	R-R	5-10	175	8-27-90	0	0	12.00	1	1	0	0	3	4	4	4	0	2	0	.333	.167	.500	0.00	6.00
Oswalt, Roy	R-R	6-0	190	8-29-77	1	0	0.00	1	1	0	0	6	3	0	0	0	1	2	.150	.143	.154	3.18	1.59
Palo, Daniel	R-R	6-4	215	11-30-90	1	3	6.06	24	0	0	0	33	45	26	22	2	15	23	.333	.367	.314	6.34	4.13
Payamps, Joel	R-R	6-2	170	4-7-94	4	7	6.06	15	15	0	0	68	87	59	46	6	31	63	.312	.337	.299	8.30	4.08
Rodriguez, Helmis	L-L	5-11	155	6-10-94	2	4	5.10	15	7	0	0	55	60	43	31	5	16	36	.269	.183	.301	5.93	2.63
Shouse, Blake	R-R	6-2	185	3-9-93	0	3	6.89	10	9	0	1	31	32	26	24	5	18	16	.260	.304	.234	4.60	5.17
Stamey, Dylan	R-R	6-2	185	1-7-92	4	1	1.26	24	0	0	7	29	20	6	4	1	5	29	.192	.222	.176	9.10	1.57
Tago, Peter	R-R	6-2	170	7-5-92	3	5	7.14	16	10	0	0	58	77	58	46	4	37	38	.328	.284	.354	5.90	5.74
Waltrip, Billy	L-L	6-2	215	7-1-92	1	1	10.64	20	0	0	0	22	26	30	26	3	23	24	.292	.296	.290	9.82	9.41
Yan, Carlos	R-R	6-5	192	1-28-91	0	4	5.26	26	0	0	2	26	18	19	15	3	18	32	.191	.139	.224	11.22	6.31

Fielding

Catcher	PCT	G	PO	A	E	DP	PB
Briceno	.978	24	202	24	5	3	11
Perkins	.973	23	128	14	4	0	3
Rosario	.967	31	205	27	8	5	12

First Base	PCT	G	PO	A	E	DP
Briceno	.969	4	28	3	1	2
Dilone	.942	9	74	7	5	9
Patterson	.976	10	75	7	2	4
Prime	.982	57	499	37	10	48

Second Base	PCT	G	PO	A	E	DP
Dilone	.896	10	17	26	5	4
Galvez	.980	21	36	63	2	11
Jones	.958	11	18	28	2	9
Nunez	.905	26	48	66	12	17
Osborne	1.000	17	23	52	0	9

Third Base	PCT	G	PO	A	E	DP
Dilone	.829	13	8	26	7	1
Jones	.875	5	5	9	2	0
McMahon	.933	54	49	117	12	12
Nunez	.667	1	1	1	1	0
Osborne	1.000	7	9	10	0	1

Shortstop	PCT	G	PO	A	E	DP
Jimenez	.899	43	65	122	21	21
Jones	1.000	3	3	7	0	1
Nunez	.961	18	26	48	3	7
Osborne	.978	17	44	44	2	11

Outfield	PCT	G	PO	A	E	DP
Dilone	.733	13	10	1	4	0
Garvey	.918	51	69	9	7	1
McClure	.929	40	63	2	5	0
Norton	1.000	21	38	1	0	0
Patterson	.956	50	81	5	4	2
Popick	1.000	2	1	0	0	0
Tapia	.926	63	130	8	11	0

DSL ROCKIES ROOKIE

DOMINICAN SUMMER LEAGUE

Batting	B-T	HT	WT	DOB	AVG	vLH	vRH	G	AB	R	H	2B	3B	HR	RBI	BB	HBP	SH	SF	SO	SB	CS	SLG	OBP
Brito, Antony	R-R	5-11	180	2-15-95	.224	.286	.205	18	58	5	13	1	1	1	7	5	0	0	0	8	1	2	.328	.286
Brito Jr., Luis	L-L	6-0	165	1-28-96	.222	.158	.233	41	135	12	30	6	1	0	18	13	1	1	0	32	3	2	.281	.295
Carrizales, Omar	L-L	6-0	175	1-30-95	.302	.217	.321	66	255	47	77	9	2	0	20	18	4	6	2	27	30	12	.353	.355
Castro, Luis	R-R	6-1	187	9-19-95	.264	.213	.276	70	250	40	66	10	1	2	23	29	9	2	2	43	7	6	.336	.359
Daza, Yonathan	R-R	6-2	190	2-28-94	.291	.375	.262	53	189	26	55	11	1	1	28	9	7	7	1	19	6	3	.376	.345
Diaz, Joel	R-R	6-2	180	9-18-95	.286	.276	.288	44	147	13	42	4	0	0	11	6	6	4	1	17	1	1	.313	.338
Garcia, Henry	R-R	6-2	195	9-21-93	.238	.300	.225	48	172	21	41	18	0	0	31	9	2	0	1	43	1	2	.343	.283
Jean, Luis	R-R	6-1	150	8-17-94	.293	.226	.308	49	164	26	48	8	0	1	17	14	5	9	0	12	19	4	.360	.366
Jimenez, Emerson	L-R	6-1	160	12-16-94	.222	.000	.267	8	36	3	8	1	0	0	1	0	1	0	4	1	2	.250	.243
Jimenez, Wilkyns	R-R	6-2	180	7-18-95	.241	.393	.190	40	112	13	27	4	0	0	7	5	2	1	1	15	3	0	.277	.283

Name	B-T	HT	WT	DOB	AVG	vLH	vRH	G	AB	R	H	2B	3B	HR	RBI	BB	HBP	SH	SF	SO	SB	CS	SLG	OBP
Marte, Hamlet	R-R	5-10	180	2-3-94	.291	.348	.275	59	199	33	58	9	1	7	35	22	9	1	3	31	7	2	.452	.382
Piron, Jonathan	L-R	6-0	175	11-14-94	.224	.273	.210	47	152	14	34	4	4	0	13	8	3	3	0	43	10	2	.303	.276
Reyes, Randy	R-R	6-0	175	9-4-92	.203	.130	.228	54	182	22	37	6	0	1	13	12	3	3	2	32	6	5	.253	.261
Richardson, Denzel	R-R	6-2	174	1-7-94	.256	.138	.292	39	125	18	32	2	1	5	18	9	0	1	2	41	7	7	.408	.301
Rodriguez, Jose	L-R	5-10	135	2-23-96	.167	.148	.172	49	126	14	21	3	0	0	6	12	3	7	2	38	9	5	.190	.252

Pitching	B-T	HT	WT	DOB	W	L	ERA	G	GS	CG	SV	IP	H	R	ER	HR	BB	SO	AVG	vLH	vRH	K/9	BB/9
Brazoban, Gustavo	R-R	6-3	159	8-13-91	2	3	3.64	25	0	0	5	30	29	19	12	0	16	23	.250	.250	.250	6.98	4.85
Fernandez, Julian	R-R	6-2	160	12-5-95	1	1	7.94	10	0	0	0	11	12	14	10	0	12	7	.267	.267	.267	5.56	9.53
Guerrero, Hector	R-R	6-2	195	11-19-92	2	0	4.15	13	0	0	0	22	24	14	10	2	9	8	.270	.273	.269	3.32	3.74
Guillen, Adonis	R-R	6-2	175	11-23-95	0	1	9.00	1	1	0	0	1	2	2	1	0	1	1	.400	.500	.333	9.00	9.00
Guzman, Luis	L-L	6-1	165	2-27-96	0	0	23.14	3	0	0	0	2	5	6	6	0	3	1	.417	.000	.417	3.86	11.57
Harvey, Ronald	R-R	6-0	165	3-15-95	1	1	4.42	14	0	0	2	37	31	19	18	1	12	27	.223	.258	.213	6.63	2.95
Hernandez, Raul	R-R	6-0	175	10-2-92	2	0	0.59	13	0	0	4	15	6	1	1	0	3	15	.115	.267	.054	8.80	1.76
Justo, Salvador	R-R	6-5	210	10-14-94	0	2	4.37	18	0	0	0	23	20	14	11	0	17	18	.235	.250	.230	7.15	6.75
Martinez, David	R-R	6-0	150	2-14-95	2	4	2.95	16	4	0	1	58	53	25	19	2	15	29	.247	.255	.244	4.50	2.33
Matos, Andres	R-R	6-2	160	3-13-96	0	2	3.93	10	4	0	0	18	19	8	8	0	11	8	.271	.364	.229	3.93	5.40
Ozuna, Lorenz	R-R	6-0	175	9-22-94	0	2	4.39	12	4	0	0	27	27	17	13	0	18	19	.267	.233	.282	6.41	6.08
Palacios, Javier	R-R	6-1	165	9-29-93	5	5	3.13	14	14	2	0	72	63	30	25	4	15	54	.237	.219	.243	6.75	1.88
Polanco, Carlos	R-R	6-2	175	2-18-94	4	6	3.14	14	13	0	0	72	57	41	25	2	17	38	.213	.175	.230	4.77	2.13
Quintin, Cristian	R-R	6-3	165	12-27-93	0	1	2.89	7	1	0	1	9	9	6	3	0	1	9	.250	.125	.286	8.68	0.96
Requena, Wilson	R-R	6-0	150	4-16-96	1	0	2.97	16	2	0	0	30	32	15	10	2	16	16	.274	.270	.275	4.75	4.75
Senzatela, Antonio	R-R	6-1	180	1-21-95	6	1	1.76	8	8	1	0	51	32	14	10	1	3	46	.179	.195	.174	8.12	0.53
Suero, Daniel	L-L	6-0	165	9-9-94	0	0	5.06	5	0	0	0	5	5	5	3	0	3	3	.238	.000	.278	5.06	5.06
Torres, Jesus	R-R	6-1	185	5-12-95	2	1	2.92	17	0	0	0	25	22	13	8	1	11	9	.247	.273	.239	3.28	4.01
Valerio, Radhames	L-L	6-2	200	10-17-92	2	2	4.97	13	1	0	1	25	26	21	14	0	13	17	.263	.300	.258	6.04	4.62
Villarroel, Hector	L-L	6-3	150	8-12-95	2	6	3.83	13	13	0	0	52	42	27	22	0	18	34	.220	.167	.228	5.92	3.14
Viloria, Ismael	R-R	6-1	165	3-31-95	0	1	4.82	10	6	0	0	28	32	18	15	1	9	17	.286	.214	.310	5.46	2.89

Fielding

Catcher	PCT	G	PO	A	E	DP	PB
Diaz	.966	23	118	24	5	0	6
Jimenez	.966	34	154	19	6	1	11
Marte	.980	25	125	24	3	0	4

First Base	PCT	G	PO	A	E	DP
Castro	.977	5	40	3	1	2
Diaz	1.000	18	152	10	0	12
Garcia	.998	47	441	21	1	38
Jimenez	1.000	2	2	0	0	0
Marte	1.000	7	61	1	0	2
Reyes	1.000	1	2	0	0	0

Second Base	PCT	G	PO	A	E	DP
Jean	1.000	1	2	3	0	0
Piron	.904	35	69	73	15	17
Rodriguez	.955	42	71	97	8	13

Third Base	PCT	G	PO	A	E	DP
Brito	1.000	1	2	1	0	0
Castro	.890	66	72	196	33	17
Jean	.889	7	5	11	2	2

Shortstop	PCT	G	PO	A	E	DP
Brito	.925	15	19	43	5	4
Jean	.951	39	65	130	10	25
Jimenez	.950	8	8	30	2	2
Piron	.883	13	24	29	7	3

Outfield	PCT	G	PO	A	E	DP
Brito Jr.	1.000	27	36	2	0	1
Carrizales	.977	65	117	8	3	3
Daza	.990	51	92	5	1	3
Diaz	1.000	2	1	0	0	0
Reyes	.984	39	53	7	1	3
Richardson	.976	38	79	4	2	3

Detroit Tigers

SEASON IN A SENTENCE: Miguel Cabrera had a season for the ages that ended with a second straight MVP Award and Max Scherzer led a dominant starting rotation, but after beating the Athletics in the American League Division Series, the Tigers were unable to return to the World Series, falling to the Red Sox in six games in the AL Championship Series.

HIGH POINT: The Tigers ranked second in baseball in runs scored, as Cabrera continued his march toward a Hall of Fame career by hitting .348/.442/.636, leading the majors in those three categories and raising his slash stats from his Triple Crown season in 2012. While Justin Verlander had another stellar season, it was Scherzer who led the rotation, ranking fifth in the AL in ERA (2.90), second in strikeouts (240) and fifth in innings (214 ⅓) while No. 3 starter Anibal Sanchez led the AL with a 2.57 ERA.

LOW POINT: While the Tigers' starters were spectacular, their relievers were a different story, as the Tigers' 4.01 bullpen ERA ranked 24th in baseball and was a liability in the postseason. Cabrera played through injuries in the playoffs while Prince Fielder struggled in October.

NOTABLE ROOKIES: The Tigers didn't lean on their farm system much to help the major league club in 2013. Bruce Rondon, the team's top pitching prospect entering the year, struggled early in the season and spent most of the first half in Triple-A. He helped the Tigers in the second half, flashing triple-digit fastballs that help him overcome occasional command troubles.

KEY TRANSACTIONS: Losing shortstop Jhonny Peralta for 50 games at the end of the season due to his suspension for being involved with Biogenesis hurt the team, though trading for Jose Iglesias helped cushion the blow. The Tigers sent toolsy 22-year-old outfielder Avisail Garcia to the White Sox and righthander Bryan Villareal to the Red Sox, with Boston getting Jake Peavy from Chicago.

DOWN ON THE FARM: Nick Castellanos, the team's top prospect, took a step forward with his hitting approach amidst a challenging assignment to Triple-A Toledo. Castellanos excelled in Triple-A before making his major league debut as a September callup. Devon Travis, a 13th-round pick out of Florida State in 2012, hit .351/.418/.518 in 132 games split between low Class A West Michigan and high Class A Lakeland in his first full season.

OPENING DAY PAYROLL: $148.4 million (5th)

PLAYERS OF THE YEAR

MAJOR LEAGUE	MINOR LEAGUE
Miguel Cabrera	**Nick Castellanos**
3b	of
.348/.442/.636	(Triple-A)
44 HR, 137 RBIs	.276/.343/.450, 18 HR
Led AL in AVG, OBP, SLG	Led IL with 37 2B, 81 R

ORGANIZATION LEADERS

BATTING		*Minimum 250 AB
MAJORS		
* AVG	Cabrera, Miguel	.348
* OPS	Cabrera, Miguel	1.078
HR	Cabrera, Miguel	44
RBI	Cabrera, Miguel	137
MINORS		
* AVG	Travis, Devon, Lakeland/West Michigan	.351
* OBP	Johnson, Jamie, Erie	.420
* SLG	Travis, Devon, Lakeland/West Michigan	.518
R	Travis, Devon, Lakeland/West Michigan	93
H	Travis, Devon, Lakeland/West Michigan	177
TB	Travis, Devon, Lakeland/West Michigan	261
2B	Castellanos, Nick, Toledo	37
3B	Holm, Jeff, West Michigan	8
HR	Dorn, Danny, Toledo	25
RBI	Dorn, Danny, Toledo	82
BB	Johnson, Jamie, Erie	101
SO	Robbins, James, Erie	171
SB	Schotts, Austin, West Michigan/Connecticut	31

PITCHING		#Minimum 75 IP
MAJORS		
W	Scherzer, Max	21
# ERA	Sanchez, Anibal	2.57
SO	Scherzer, Max	240
SV	Benoit, Joaquin	24
MINORS		
W	Lobstein, Kyle, Toledo/Erie	13
L	Hill, Shawn, Toledo	14
# ERA	Alvarez, Jose, Toledo	2.8
G	Nesbitt, Angel, West Michigan	52
GS	Lobstein, Kyle, Toledo/Erie	28
SV	Valdez, Jose, Lakeland/West Michigan	33
IP	Lobstein, Kyle, Toledo/Erie	168
BB	Lobstein, Kyle, Toledo/Erie	52
SO	Lobstein, Kyle, Toledo/Erie	148
# AVG	VerHagen, Drew, Lakeland/Erie	.223

2013 PERFORMANCE

General Manager: Dave Dombrowski. **Farm Director:** Dan Lunetta. **Scouting Director:** Scott Pleis.

Class	Team	League	W	L	PCT	Finish	Manager
Majors	Detroit Tigers	American	93	69	.574	3rd (15)	Jim Leyland
Triple-A	Toledo Mudhens	International	61	83	.424	13th (14)	Phil Nevin
Double-A	Erie SeaWolves	Eastern	76	66	.535	3rd (12)	Chris Cron
High A	Lakeland Flying Tigers	Florida State	64	68	.485	8th (12)	Dave Huppert
Low A	West Michigan Whitecaps	Midwest	69	70	.496	t-7th (16)	Larry Parrish
Short-season	Connecticut Tigers	New York-Penn	33	42	.440	11th (14)	Andrew Graham
Rookie	Tigers	Gulf Coast	32	28	.533	5th (16)	Basilio Cabrera
Overall 2013 Minor League Record			335	357	.484	23rd (30)	

ORGANIZATION STATISTICS

AMERICAN LEAGUE

Batting	B-T	HT	WT	DOB	AVG	vLH	vRH	G	AB	R	H	2B	3B	HR	RBI	BB	HBP	SH	SF	SO	SB	CS	SLG	OBP
Avila, Alex	L-R	5-11	210	1-29-87	.227	.139	.255	102	330	39	75	14	1	11	47	44	1	1	3	112	0	0	.376	.317
Cabrera, Miguel	R-R	6-4	240	4-18-83	.348	.368	.341	148	555	103	193	26	1	44	137	90	5	0	2	94	3	0	.636	.442
Castellanos, Nick	R-R	6-4	210	3-4-92	.278	.273	.286	11	18	1	5	0	0	0	0	0	0	0	0	1	0	0	.278	.278
Dirks, Andy	L-L	6-0	195	1-24-86	.256	.234	.260	131	438	60	112	16	2	9	37	42	2	1	1	84	7	1	.363	.323
Fielder, Prince	L-R	5-11	275	5-9-84	.279	.292	.271	162	624	82	174	36	0	25	106	75	9	0	4	117	1	1	.457	.362
Garcia, Avisail	R-R	6-4	240	6-12-91	.241	.171	.310	30	83	12	20	3	1	2	10	4	0	0	1	21	0	1	.373	.273
2-team total (42 Chicago)					.283	—	—	72	244	31	69	7	3	7	31	9	1	0	2	59	3	3	.422	.309
Holaday, Bryan	R-R	6-0	205	11-19-87	.296	.308	.286	16	27	8	8	1	0	1	2	2	1	3	0	3	0	0	.444	.367
Hunter, Torii	R-R	6-2	225	7-18-75	.304	.300	.305	144	606	90	184	37	5	17	84	26	7	3	10	113	3	2	.465	.334
Iglesias, Jose	R-R	5-11	185	1-5-90	.259	.216	.286	46	135	12	35	6	0	2	10	4	5	4	0	30	2	1	.348	.306
2-team total (63 Boston)					.303	—	—	109	350	39	106	16	2	3	29	15	11	4	2	60	5	2	.386	.349
Infante, Omar	R-R	5-11	195	12-26-81	.318	.301	.326	118	453	54	144	24	3	10	51	20	0	0	3	44	5	2	.450	.345
Jackson, Austin	R-R	6-1	185	2-1-87	.272	.213	.296	129	552	99	150	30	7	12	49	52	4	3	3	129	8	4	.417	.337
Kelly, Don	L-R	6-4	190	2-15-80	.222	.229	.220	112	216	33	48	6	1	6	23	27	2	2	4	28	2	0	.343	.309
Martinez, Victor	B-R	6-2	210	12-23-78	.301	.279	.314	159	605	68	182	36	0	14	83	54	1	0	8	62	0	2	.430	.355
Pena, Brayan	B-R	5-9	230	1-7-82	.297	.264	.325	71	229	19	68	11	0	4	22	6	2	2	4	26	0	2	.397	.315
Peralta, Jhonny	R-R	6-2	215	5-28-82	.303	.352	.282	107	409	50	124	30	0	11	55	35	1	1	2	98	3	3	.457	.358
Perez, Hernan	R-R	6-1	185	3-26-91	.197	.212	.182	34	66	13	13	0	1	0	5	2	0	2	1	15	1	0	.227	.217
Santiago, Ramon	B-R	5-11	175	8-31-79	.224	.196	.234	80	205	27	46	8	1	1	14	21	1	6	1	32	0	1	.288	.298
Tuiasosopo, Matt	R-R	6-2	225	5-10-86	.244	.216	.313	81	164	26	40	7	0	7	30	25	2	0	0	57	0	0	.415	.351
Worth, Danny	R-R	6-1	185	9-30-85	.000	—	.000	3	2	0	0	0	0	0	0	0	0	0	0	1	0	0	.000	.000

Pitching	B-T	HT	WT	DOB	W	L	ERA	G	GS	CG	SV	IP	H	R	ER	HR	BB	SO	AVG	vLH	vRH	K/9	BB/9
Alburquerque, Al	R-R	6-0	195	6-10-86	4	3	4.59	53	0	0	0	49	39	25	25	5	34	70	.213	.228	.202	12.86	6.24
Alvarez, Jose	L-L	5-11	180	5-6-89	1	5	5.82	14	6	0	0	39	42	26	25	7	16	31	.280	.265	.287	7.22	3.72
Benoit, Joaquin	R-R	6-3	220	7-26-77	4	1	2.01	66	0	0	24	67	47	15	15	5	22	73	.197	.194	.202	9.81	2.96
Bonderman, Jeremy	R-R	6-0	220	10-28-82	1	1	6.48	11	0	0	0	17	18	13	12	3	10	16	.281	.400	.176	8.64	5.40
2-team total (7 Seattle)					2	4	5.40	18	7	0	0	55	58	36	33	7	27	32	—	—	—	5.24	4.42
Coke, Phil	L-L	6-1	210	7-19-82	0	5	5.40	49	0	0	1	38	43	24	23	3	21	30	.291	.299	.282	7.04	4.93
Dotel, Octavio	R-R	6-0	230	11-25-73	0	0	13.50	6	0	0	0	5	10	7	7	0	4	4	.417	.273	.538	7.71	7.71
Downs, Darin	R-L	6-3	210	12-26-84	0	2	4.84	29	0	0	0	35	36	20	19	4	11	37	.265	.219	.306	9.42	2.80
Fister, Doug	L-R	6-8	210	2-4-84	14	9	3.67	33	32	1	0	209	229	91	85	14	44	159	.281	.263	.304	6.86	1.90
Ortega, Jose	R-R	5-11	185	10-12-88	0	2	3.86	11	0	0	0	12	10	5	5	2	6	10	.227	.227	.227	7.71	4.63
Porcello, Rick	R-R	6-5	200	12-27-88	13	8	4.32	32	29	1	0	177	185	87	85	18	42	142	.270	.300	.240	7.22	2.14
Putkonen, Luke	R-R	6-6	215	5-10-86	1	3	3.03	30	0	0	0	30	30	11	10	4	9	28	.261	.260	.262	8.49	2.73
Reed, Evan	R-R	6-4	255	12-31-85	0	1	4.24	16	0	0	0	23	28	16	11	2	8	17	.301	.289	.309	6.56	3.09
Rondon, Bruce	R-R	6-3	275	12-9-90	1	2	3.45	30	0	0	1	29	28	11	11	2	11	30	.259	.295	.234	9.42	3.45
Sanchez, Anibal	R-R	6-0	205	2-27-84	14	8	2.57	29	29	1	0	182	156	56	52	9	54	202	.229	.246	.208	9.99	2.67
Scherzer, Max	R-R	6-3	220	7-27-84	21	3	2.90	32	32	0	0	214	152	73	69	18	56	240	.198	.222	.165	10.08	2.35
Smyly, Drew	L-L	6-3	190	6-13-89	6	0	2.37	63	0	0	2	76	62	20	20	4	17	81	.219	.189	.242	9.59	2.01
Valverde, Jose	R-R	6-4	255	3-24-78	0	1	5.59	20	0	0	9	19	18	12	12	6	6	19	.237	.279	.182	8.84	2.79
Veras, Jose	R-R	6-6	240	10-20-80	0	1	3.20	25	0	0	2	20	16	8	7	2	8	16	.213	.244	.176	7.32	3.66
2-team total (42 Houston)					0	5	3.02	67	0	0	21	63	45	23	21	6	22	60	—	—	—	8.62	3.16
Verlander, Justin	R-R	6-5	225	2-20-83	13	12	3.46	34	34	0	0	218	212	94	84	19	75	217	.253	.237	.275	8.95	3.09
Villareal, Brayan	R-R	6-0	170	5-10-87	0	2	20.77	7	0	0	0	4	8	10	10	1	8	6	.444	.714	.273	12.46	16.62
2-team total (1 Boston)					0	2	20.77	8	0	0	0	4	8	10	10	1	9	6	—	—	—	12.46	18.69

Fielding

Catcher	PCT	G	PO	A	E	DP	PB
Avila	.993	98	815	29	6	4	9
Holaday	.974	14	73	3	2	0	0
Martinez	1.000	3	18	4	0	0	0
Pena	.995	64	528	27	3	4	5

First Base	PCT	G	PO	A	E	DP
Fielder	.995	151	1152	96	6	119
Kelly	1.000	4	17	0	0	2
Martinez	1.000	11	85	14	0	3
Pena	1.000	1	1	0	0	0
Tuiasosopo	1.000	13	27	1	0	3

Second Base	PCT	G	PO	A	E	DP
Infante	.980	118	157	342	10	73
Kelly	1.000	3	1	0	0	0
Perez	.975	25	30	48	2	9
Santiago	1.000	33	55	90	0	19

Third Base	PCT	G	PO	A	E	DP
Cabrera	.958	145	87	184	12	24
Iglesias	1.000	3	1	9	0	2
Kelly	1.000	22	8	17	0	2
Perez	1.000	2	0	1	0	0
Santiago	1.000	27	5	19	0	1
Tuiasosopo	1.000	1	0	1	0	0
Worth	.750	2	0	3	1	0

Shortstop	PCT	G	PO	A	E	DP
Iglesias	.988	42	59	103	2	30
Peralta	.991	106	140	294	4	54
Perez	—	2	0	0	0	0
Santiago	.972	27	20	49	2	7

Outfield	PCT	G	PO	A	E	DP
Castellanos	1.000	9	5	0	0	0
Dirks	.992	124	232	7	2	0
Garcia	.980	29	48	0	1	0
Hunter	.987	143	223	9	3	3
Jackson	.993	129	300	5	2	1
Kelly	.977	78	86	0	2	0
Peralta	1.000	3	2	0	0	0
Tuiasosopo	.990	63	97	0	1	0

TOLEDO MUD HENS

TRIPLE-A

INTERNATIONAL LEAGUE

Batting	B-T	HT	WT	DOB	AVG	vLH	vRH	G	AB	R	H	2B	3B	HR	RBI	BB	HBP	SH	SF	SO	SB	CS	SLG	OBP
Avila, Alex	L-R	5-11	210	1-29-87	.250	.000	.268	12	44	5	11	3	0	1	5	7	0	0	0	12	0	0	.386	.353
Berry, Quintin	L-L	6-0	175	11-21-84	.168	.111	.179	49	167	16	28	8	0	1	15	23	3	5	1	45	15	2	.234	.278
2-team total (3 Pawtucket)					.166	—	—	52	175	17	29	8	0	1	15	24	4	5	1	47	17	2	.229	.279
Cabrera, Ramon	B-R	5-8	197	11-5-89	.242	.257	.237	39	149	13	36	9	1	1	15	14	1	1	0	21	0	1	.336	.311
Castellanos, Nick	R-R	6-4	210	3-4-92	.276	.302	.270	134	533	81	147	37	1	18	76	54	3	0	5	100	4	1	.450	.343
Cervenak, Mike	R-R	5-11	195	8-17-76	.291	.329	.281	81	323	35	94	17	0	5	36	19	3	0	7	38	3	1	.390	.330
Davis, Brad	R-R	6-1	190	12-29-82	.202	.294	.187	40	124	20	25	6	1	2	16	8	0	0	3	33	1	0	.315	.244
Diaz, Argenis	R-R	6-0	190	2-12-87	.255	.256	.254	127	471	52	120	30	3	2	48	40	1	6	0	113	4	4	.344	.314
Dorn, Danny	L-L	6-2	205	7-20-84	.258	.262	.257	137	496	67	128	21	2	25	82	58	3	1	7	131	8	2	.460	.335
Douglas, Brandon	R-R	6-0	200	8-27-85	.257	.206	.269	49	179	27	46	9	1	2	16	14	2	1	1	26	3	2	.352	.316
Garcia, Avisail	R-R	6-4	240	6-12-91	.374	.381	.373	33	147	23	55	7	1	5	23	8	1	0	0	32	4	2	.537	.410
2-team total (8 Charlotte)					.374	—	—	41	174	29	65	7	2	6	32	12	2	0	0	36	4	2	.540	.420
Guez, Ben	R-R	5-11	180	1-24-87	.242	.253	.240	128	425	66	103	19	2	18	63	62	8	2	1	136	8	6	.424	.349
Holaday, Bryan	R-R	6-0	205	11-19-87	.260	.286	.254	80	288	28	75	18	1	4	24	18	5	6	3	57	0	1	.372	.312
Infante, Omar	R-R	5-11	195	12-26-81	.211	—	.211	5	19	1	4	0	0	0	1	2	0	0	0	2	0	0	.211	.286
Jackson, Austin	R-R	6-1	185	2-1-87	.231	.250	.222	3	13	1	3	0	0	0	1	1	0	0	0	5	0	0	.231	.286
Jones, Corey	L-R	6-0	202	9-14-87	.190	.250	.176	7	21	0	4	0	0	0	1	2	0	0	0	5	0	0	.190	.261
Lennerton, Jordan	L-L	6-2	217	2-16-86	.278	.255	.284	139	514	68	143	25	1	17	57	84	5	0	4	133	0	3	.430	.382
Lindsey, John	R-R	6-2	255	1-30-77	.200	.125	.219	22	80	8	16	3	1	4	7	4	4	0	0	37	0	1	.413	.273
Murrian, Kody	R-R	6-2	215	6-15-88	.250	.333	.200	3	8	1	2	0	0	1	2	0	0	0	0	1	0	0	.625	.250
Nunez, Gustavo	B-R	5-10	170	2-8-88	.194	.200	.193	61	186	11	36	4	0	0	4	12	0	4	0	45	6	5	.215	.242
Paulino, Ronny	R-R	6-3	250	4-21-81	.267	.571	.211	13	45	3	12	2	0	1	6	2	0	0	0	12	0	0	.378	.298
2-team total (8 Norfolk)					.235	—	—	21	68	5	16	3	0	2	8	6	0	0	0	19	0	0	.368	.297
Perez, Hernan	R-R	6-1	185	3-26-91	.299	.400	.281	16	67	3	20	3	0	0	4	5	1	1	0	7	4	0	.343	.356
Russo, Kevin	R-R	5-11	190	7-8-84	.213	.141	.230	103	376	34	80	27	0	3	41	19	4	7	9	89	9	7	.309	.252
Tuiasosopo, Matt	R-R	6-2	225	5-10-86	.400	.500	.333	2	5	3	2	1	0	0	0	2	1	0	0	2	0	0	.600	.625
Worth, Danny	R-R	6-1	185	9-30-85	.223	.245	.218	82	305	33	68	19	2	1	22	35	1	4	0	91	9	5	.308	.305

Pitching	B-T	HT	WT	DOB	W	L	ERA	G	GS	CG	SV	IP	H	R	ER	HR	BB	SO	AVG	vLH	vRH	K/9	BB/9
Alburquerque, Al	R-R	6-0	195	6-10-86	0	1	3.14	10	0	0	0	14	9	5	5	2	13	27	.176	.238	.133	16.95	8.16
Alvarez, Jose	L-L	5-11	180	5-6-89	8	6	2.80	21	20	1	1	129	114	46	40	11	25	115	.235	.165	.256	8.04	1.75
Below, Duane	L-L	6-3	220	11-15-85	1	2	2.10	4	4	0	0	26	15	6	6	1	4	15	.167	.333	.141	5.26	1.40
Bonderman, Jeremy	R-R	6-0	220	10-28-82	0	0	0.00	7	0	0	0	10	3	0	0	0	0	5	.094	.071	.111	4.66	0.00
Coke, Phil	L-L	6-1	210	7-19-82	0	0	0.00	6	0	0	0	6	5	0	0	0	1	9	.227	.400	.176	13.50	1.50
Crosby, Casey	R-L	6-5	225	9-17-88	2	5	4.84	13	13	0	0	58	55	33	31	3	40	61	.258	.154	.292	9.52	6.24
Dotel, Octavio	R-R	6-0	230	11-25-73	0	0	13.50	3	0	0	0	1	3	2	2	0	2	3	.429	1.000	.333	20.25	13.50
Downs, Darin	R-L	6-3	210	12-26-84	0	1	2.30	12	0	0	0	16	9	5	4	0	6	12	.167	.238	.121	6.89	3.45
Faulk, Kenny	L-L	6-0	235	5-27-87	0	3	3.65	32	0	0	1	44	26	21	18	3	31	52	.170	.064	.217	10.56	6.29
Garcia, Ramon	L-L	6-2	165	10-30-84	3	9	6.39	16	15	0	0	82	105	62	58	9	19	54	.314	.302	.319	5.95	2.09
Hankins, Derek	R-R	6-4	195	7-1-83	4	4	3.03	14	14	0	0	86	84	36	29	9	24	43	.249	.188	.311	4.50	2.51
Hardy, Blaine	L-L	6-2	220	3-14-87	6	1	1.69	14	9	1	0	64	46	12	12	7	19	53	.198	.280	.176	7.45	2.67
Hill, Shawn	R-R	6-2	225	4-28-81	4	14	5.51	26	26	1	0	150	191	105	92	17	47	84	.310	.306	.314	5.03	2.81
Hoffman, Matt	L-L	6-2	225	11-8-88	4	3	2.06	40	0	0	0	35	32	12	8	2	16	35	.246	.224	.264	9.00	4.11
Jurrjens, Jair	R-R	6-1	200	1-29-86	1	4	5.49	7	7	0	0	39	45	24	24	3	14	24	.296	.371	.244	5.49	3.20
2-team total (16 Norfolk)					7	10	4.57	23	23	1	0	134	147	72	68	8	38	76	—	—	—	5.10	2.55
Link, Jon	R-R	6-0	205	3-23-84	0	4	5.56	11	7	0	0	44	51	29	27	6	9	19	.291	.354	.255	3.92	1.85
Lobstein, Kyle	L-L	6-3	200	8-12-89	6	3	3.48	13	13	0	0	72	73	32	28	2	25	65	.267	.314	.246	8.09	3.11
Marte, Luis	R-R	5-11	200	8-26-86	1	2	9.00	3	2	0	0	2	5	5	2	1	2	5	.500	.500	.500	9.00	9.00
Misch, Pat	R-L	6-2	200	8-18-81	3	7	5.07	13	13	0	0	71	95	52	40	11	16	51	.319	.307	.324	6.46	2.03
Morrison, Mike	R-R	6-1	210	12-17-87	0	0	10.80	1	0	0	0	2	2	2	2	0	1	1	.333	.333	.333	5.40	5.40
Ortega, Jose	R-R	5-11	185	10-12-88	3	1	1.86	40	0	0	4	48	28	13	10	2	33	56	.169	.259	.120	10.43	6.14
Putkonen, Luke	R-R	6-6	215	5-10-86	2	0	1.91	20	1	0	1	38	25	10	8	0	13	38	.185	.208	.172	9.08	3.11
Reed, Evan	R-R	6-4	255	12-31-85	1	4	2.54	32	0	0	1	50	38	17	14	1	20	49	.221	.237	.212	8.88	3.62
Rondon, Bruce	R-R	6-3	275	12-9-90	1	1	1.52	30	0	0	14	30	14	6	5	1	13	44	.136	.125	.125	12.13	3.94
Souza, Justin	R-R	6-1	185	10-22-85	0	1	10.29	12	0	0	0	7	16	16	8	3	8	13	.288	.250	.323	8.36	5.14
Todd, Jess	R-R	5-11	210	4-20-86	4	3	2.15	39	0	0	1	63	40	20	15	3	26	65	.175	.091	.229	9.34	3.73
Valverde, Jose	R-R	6-4	255	3-24-78	0	0	4.09	11	0	0	7	11	14	5	5	1	6	10	.333	.389	.292	8.18	4.91
Villareal, Brayan	R-R	6-1	50	5-10-87	2	2	3.15	28	0	0	1	34	26	13	12	0	26	41	.217	.226	.209	10.75	6.82
2-team total (5 Pawtucket)					2	3	2.95	33	0	0	2	40	29	14	13	0	30	47	—	—	—	10.66	6.81
Weinhardt, Robbie	R-R	6-2	205	12-8-85	3	0	2.83	26	2	0	0	60	64	25	19	5	21	38	.277	.313	.250	5.67	3.13

DETROIT TIGERS

Fielding

Catcher	PCT	G	PO	A	E	DP	PB
Avila	1.000	6	37	2	0	0	1
Cabrera	.994	19	168	12	1	1	1
Davis	.981	37	249	11	5	4	1
Holaday	.992	75	568	47	5	2	5
Murrian	1.000	3	11	0	0	0	0
Paulino	1.000	11	63	3	0	0	0

First Base	PCT	G	PO	A	E	DP
Cervenak	1.000	1	7	1	0	1
Dorn	.985	19	129	6	2	13
Lennerton	.996	129	1167	81	5	105

Second Base	PCT	G	PO	A	E	DP
Diaz	1.000	4	4	12	0	3
Douglas	.986	48	81	125	3	27

	PCT	G	PO	A	E	DP
Infante	1.000	4	9	4	0	1
Jones	1.000	5	8	8	0	2
Nunez	.966	36	61	81	5	19
Perez	.988	16	38	44	1	10
Russo	.989	15	35	53	1	10
Worth	.986	29	59	85	2	20

Third Base	PCT	G	PO	A	E	DP
Cervenak	.943	47	27	73	6	7
Diaz	.919	21	7	50	5	0
Jones	.667	1	0	2	1	0
Russo	.946	54	30	111	8	10
Worth	1.000	28	18	51	0	5

Shortstop	PCT	G	PO	A	E	DP
Diaz	.965	103	115	301	15	54
Nunez	.951	21	36	62	5	15
Worth	.943	26	44	72	7	22

Outfield	PCT	G	PO	A	E	DP
Berry	.990	47	98	2	1	1
Castellanos	.987	130	213	8	3	1
Cervenak	1.000	3	4	1	0	0
Dorn	.986	80	135	5	2	0
Garcia	.973	32	71	0	2	0
Guez	.989	119	252	7	3	1
Jackson	1.000	2	2	0	0	0
Nunez	1.000	3	4	1	0	0
Russo	1.000	35	77	1	0	0
Tuiasosopo	1.000	1	1	0	0	0

ERIE SEAWOLVES
DOUBLE-A
EASTERN LEAGUE

Batting	B-T	HT	WT	DOB	AVG	vLH	vRH	G	AB	R	H	2B	3B	HR	RBI	BB	HBP	SH	SF	SO	SB	CS	SLG	OBP
Cabrera, Ramon	B-R	5-8	197	11-5-89	.304	.340	.288	84	312	44	95	22	2	0	54	44	3	0	3	34	4	0	.388	.392
Castillo, Luis	R-R	5-11	160	5-15-89	.242	.257	.234	96	293	42	71	17	2	2	32	35	4	1	3	57	0	1	.334	.328
Collins, Tyler	L-L	5-11	215	6-6-90	.240	.289	.219	129	466	67	112	29	0	21	79	51	8	0	5	122	4	5	.438	.323
Douglas, Brandon	R-R	6-0	200	8-27-85	.303	.258	.327	53	175	19	53	8	2	3	22	13	0	2	1	36	9	1	.423	.349
Fields, Daniel	L-R	6-2	215	1-23-91	.284	.246	.302	118	457	71	130	27	6	10	58	45	8	1	4	130	24	7	.435	.356
Gaynor, Wade	R-R	6-3	225	4-19-88	.226	.219	.229	136	477	66	108	31	2	12	64	37	8	1	5	153	12	3	.375	.290
Hernandez, Michael	R-R	6-1	195	12-18-83	.200	.188	.222	7	25	2	5	1	0	1	3	2	0	0	0	5	0	0	.360	.259
Johnson, Jamie	L-R	5-9	180	4-26-87	.273	.222	.290	123	406	67	111	16	3	2	45	101	7	3	7	74	27	7	.342	.420
Jones, Corey	L-R	6-0	202	9-14-87	.193	.154	.205	20	57	6	11	3	0	0	5	6	2	0	0	11	1	3	.246	.292
Lemon, Marcus	L-R	5-11	173	6-3-88	.241	.169	.267	97	294	43	71	8	7	1	28	25	3	6	1	63	2	4	.327	.307
Maggard, Zach	R-R	5-11	181	8-2-88	.111	.143	.091	15	36	2	4	0	0	0	4	1	3	1	0	15	0	1	.111	.200
McCann, James	B-R	6-2	210	6-13-90	.277	.278	.276	119	441	50	122	30	1	8	54	30	7	1	7	85	3	3	.404	.328
Perez, Hernan	R-R	6-1	185	3-26-91	.301	.298	.302	87	362	45	109	28	2	4	35	12	2	5	3	48	24	7	.423	.325
Robbins, James	L-L	6-0	225	9-26-90	.224	.203	.233	127	468	44	105	26	0	7	43	16	7	3	0	171	3	3	.325	.261
Sanz, Luis	R-R	5-10	165	2-23-91	.333	.500	.000	1	3	0	1	0	0	0	0	0	0	0	0	1	0	0	.333	.333
Suarez, Eugenio	B-R	5-11	180	7-18-91	.253	.265	.248	111	442	53	112	24	4	9	45	46	6	2	0	98	9	11	.387	.332

Pitching	B-T	HT	WT	DOB	W	L	ERA	G	GS	CG	SV	IP	H	R	ER	HR	BB	SO	AVG	vLH	vRH	K/9	BB/9
Clark, Tyler	B-R	6-2	185	1-4-89	1	0	3.58	22	0	0	0	33	37	16	13	1	21	33	.291	.160	.377	9.09	5.79
Clinard, Will	R-R	6-4	225	11-3-89	2	3	5.50	22	0	0	1	34	37	22	21	6	20	26	.280	.233	.303	6.82	5.24
Collier, Tommy	R-R	6-2	205	12-3-89	1	0	5.40	1	1	0	0	5	6	3	3	1	1	2	.300	.250	.375	3.60	1.80
Cooper, Patrick	R-R	6-3	204	8-25-89	2	8	5.84	17	17	0	0	86	115	63	56	11	35	52	.327	.331	.323	5.42	3.65
Crouse, Matt	L-L	6-4	185	7-1-90	9	10	4.47	31	24	0	1	145	149	79	72	21	41	112	.272	.248	.281	6.95	2.54
Garcia, Ramon	L-L	6-2	165	10-30-84	2	4	4.79	9	9	1	0	56	57	32	30	12	9	42	.257	.200	.278	6.71	1.44
Hankins, Derek	R-R	6-4	195	7-1-83	1	1	3.06	3	3	0	0	18	16	9	6	3	2	12	.246	.237	.259	6.11	1.02
Hardy, Blaine	L-L	6-2	220	3-14-87	2	2	1.63	16	0	0	1	28	16	8	5	1	12	26	.170	.154	.178	8.46	3.90
Kopp, David	R-R	6-3	205	10-22-85	3	4	5.44	27	0	0	0	48	52	36	29	6	28	33	.269	.264	.273	6.19	5.25
Larez, Victor	R-R	6-3	160	5-28-87	9	8	4.61	28	24	0	0	137	147	73	70	25	29	90	.270	.249	.287	5.93	1.91
Link, Jon	R-R	6-0	205	3-23-84	3	1	1.13	5	5	2	0	40	30	7	5	1	5	21	.214	.258	.179	4.76	1.13
Lobstein, Kyle	L-L	6-3	205	8-12-89	7	4	3.12	15	15	2	0	92	92	35	33	6	27	83	.262	.269	.259	7.84	2.55
Mercedes, Melvin	R-R	6-3	250	11-2-90	2	1	1.44	26	0	0	12	25	23	10	4	3	9	19	.237	.293	.196	6.84	3.24
Morrison, Mike	R-R	6-1	210	12-17-87	3	3	7.13	30	0	0	0	42	48	37	33	2	31	31	.294	.333	.268	6.70	6.70
Perez, Kelvin	R-R	6-1	140	10-10-85	1	1	6.43	10	0	0	0	42	48	32	30	4	19	30	.279	.354	.215	6.43	4.07
2-team total (9 Trenton)					1	2	5.46	19	8	0	0	58	61	37	35	6	23	45	—	—	—	7.02	3.59
Robowski, Ryan	L-L	6-0	185	2-3-88	4	2	2.88	34	2	0	0	50	39	17	16	5	21	29	.215	.204	.220	5.22	3.78
Saupold, Warwick	R-R	6-1	195	1-16-90	7	6	3.28	22	22	1	0	129	124	54	47	12	51	82	.257	.223	.284	5.72	3.56
Souza, Justin	R-R	6-1	185	10-22-85	5	2	2.63	38	0	0	19	41	33	12	12	4	12	30	.226	.254	.207	6.80	2.63
Startup, Will	L-L	6-0	195	8-4-84	7	1	3.41	33	0	0	4	58	51	25	22	9	16	34	.231	.153	.279	5.28	2.48
Stohr, Tyler	L-R	6-2	210	9-19-86	3	0	5.29	36	0	0	1	48	40	31	28	2	33	32	.231	.197	.255	6.04	6.23
VerHagen, Drew	R-R	6-6	230	10-22-90	2	5	3.00	12	12	1	0	60	53	24	20	3	17	40	.240	.228	.248	6.00	2.55
Weinhardt, Robbie	R-R	6-2	205	12-8-85	0	0	5.19	7	0	0	0	9	13	5	5	3	6	8	.351	.348	.357	8.31	6.23

Fielding

Catcher	PCT	G	PO	A	E	DP	PB
Cabrera	.986	31	198	14	3	2	2
Maggard	.987	14	68	6	1	0	1
McCann	.991	100	614	58	6	5	6
Sanz	1.000	1	10	2	0	0	0

First Base	PCT	G	PO	A	E	DP
Douglas	.979	6	47	0	1	2
Gaynor	1.000	11	85	9	0	0
Robbins	.990	127	1078	80	12	131

Second Base	PCT	G	PO	A	E	DP
Douglas	.987	37	65	87	2	24

	PCT	G	PO	A	E	DP
Jones	.935	10	8	21	2	4
Lemon	.978	44	64	118	4	33
Perez	.983	59	129	158	5	49

Third Base	PCT	G	PO	A	E	DP
Douglas	.800	3	4	4	2	0
Gaynor	.967	125	95	227	11	19
Jones	.933	5	4	10	1	1
Lemon	.892	14	5	28	4	2

Shortstop	PCT	G	PO	A	E	DP
Douglas	.960	4	7	17	1	7

	PCT	G	PO	A	E	DP
Lemon	1.000	1	1	1	0	0
Perez	.928	28	30	73	8	18
Suarez	.951	111	174	329	26	88

Outfield	PCT	G	PO	A	E	DP
Castillo	.989	84	171	7	2	2
Collins	.963	103	200	7	8	1
Fields	.981	111	253	6	5	0
Hernandez	.000	1	0	0	1	0
Johnson	.988	103	235	14	3	3
Lemon	.944	36	68	0	4	0

FLORIDA STATE LEAGUE

DETROIT TIGERS

Batting	B-T	HT	WT	DOB	AVG	vLH	vRH	G	AB	R	H	2B	3B	HR	RBI	BB	HBP	SH	SF	SO	SB	CS	SLG	OBP
Brown, Rashad	L-L	5-11	180	12-17-93	.333	.500	.250	2	6	0	2	0	0	0	0	3	0	0	0	2	0	1	.333	.556
Castro, Harold	L-R	6-0	145	11-30-93	.274	.316	.259	21	73	8	20	2	1	0	11	5	0	1	1	22	3	2	.329	.316
Dean, Jordan	R-R	5-10	170	8-12-90	.250	.250	.250	6	16	2	4	2	0	0	2	2	0	0	1	6	1	1	.375	.316
Garcia, Avisail	R-R	6-4	240	6-12-91	.417	.500	.375	6	24	9	10	0	2	1	4	4	0	0	0	1	2	0	.708	.500
Green, Dean	L-R	6-4	255	6-30-89	.314	.385	.305	29	118	18	37	7	2	2	13	9	2	0	0	22	0	0	.458	.372
Hanover, Tyler	R-R	5-7	170	8-25-89	.230	.250	.220	82	296	35	68	11	0	0	21	33	6	4	4	48	0	1	.267	.316
Hernandez, Michael	R-R	6-1	195	12-18-83	.224	.309	.175	43	152	16	34	9	3	5	23	10	1	0	3	42	0	1	.421	.271
Jones, Corey	L-R	6-0	202	9-14-87	.278	.192	.299	40	133	17	37	9	0	2	21	18	2	1	1	16	0	1	.391	.370
King, Jason	B-R	6-0	216	6-14-89	.135	.100	.148	42	155	13	21	5	0	3	13	16	1	0	1	32	0	0	.226	.220
Kirksey, Zach	L-R	6-1	210	2-17-89	.000	.000	.000	2	8	0	0	0	0	0	0	1	0	0	0	5	0	0	.000	.111
Krizan, Jason	L-R	6-0	185	6-28-89	.288	.208	.315	116	399	48	115	21	5	4	52	62	5	3	3	44	1	1	.396	.388
Leyland, Patrick	R-R	6-2	210	10-11-91	.168	.161	.172	25	95	6	16	2	0	0	2	3	1	2	0	15	0	0	.189	.202
Longley, Andrew	R-R	6-3	215	10-5-88	.000	—	.000	1	2	0	0	0	0	0	0	0	0	0	0	0	0	0	.000	.000
Loy, Brandon	R-R	6-0	190	5-3-90	.202	.273	.173	70	228	22	46	9	0	0	14	35	2	2	1	54	10	2	.241	.312
Machado, Dixon	R-R	6-1	170	2-22-92	.215	.229	.211	37	149	19	32	5	2	1	12	10	0	4	0	19	1	0	.295	.264
Maggard, Zach	R-R	5-11	181	8-2-88	.105	.000	.154	5	19	0	2	0	0	0	0	0	1	0	0	10	0	0	.105	.105
Martinez, Francisco	R-R	6-2	210	9-1-90	.295	.313	.288	74	288	38	85	13	1	3	28	21	3	0	2	55	11	3	.378	.347
McVaney, Jeff	R-R	6-2	210	1-16-90	.252	.289	.238	127	473	62	119	22	6	7	50	39	15	0	2	87	13	8	.368	.327
Moya, Steven	L-R	6-6	230	9-8-91	.255	.219	.269	93	365	52	93	19	5	12	55	18	4	0	1	106	6	0	.433	.296
Murrian, John	R-R	6-2	215	6-15-88	.190	.265	.156	47	158	16	30	8	0	4	17	16	5	0	1	37	0	0	.316	.283
Reaves, Jared	R-R	5-10	185	7-20-90	.276	.444	.200	9	29	6	8	0	0	0	2	2	0	0	0	4	0	0	.276	.364
Reina, Adolfo	R-R	6-0	210	1-22-90	.179	.400	.147	12	39	0	7	2	0	0	7	2	0	0	0	7	0	1	.231	.220
Sanz, Luis	R-R	5-10	165	2-23-91	.249	.286	.235	57	181	21	45	4	0	1	22	24	0	1	3	19	1	0	.287	.332
Suarez, Eugenio	B-R	5-11	180	7-18-91	.311	.381	.293	25	103	17	32	6	2	1	12	14	4	0	1	25	2	3	.437	.410
Travis, Devon	R-R	5-9	183	2-21-91	.350	.321	.361	55	214	38	75	11	2	10	34	18	2	0	3	32	8	1	.561	.401
Westlake, Aaron	L-R	6-4	235	12-27-88	.291	.182	.326	91	358	40	104	29	3	7	62	26	4	0	2	87	0	1	.447	.344
Worth, Danny	R-R	6-1	185	9-30-85	.176	.167	.182	4	17	2	3	1	0	0	3	0	0	0	0	3	0	0	.235	.176
Wright, Chad	L-R	5-10	198	7-27-89	.286	.192	.313	85	329	53	94	12	4	0	30	40	2	7	2	41	10	4	.347	.365

Pitching	B-T	HT	WT	DOB	W	L	ERA	G	GS	CG	SV	IP	H	R	ER	HR	BB	SO	AVG	vLH	vRH	K/9	BB/9
Avila, Nick	R-R	6-2	220	8-29-88	4	2	3.50	23	5	0	0	62	59	24	24	3	28	25	.254	.290	.241	3.65	4.09
Burgos, Alex	L-L	5-11	195	12-1-90	3	5	2.89	30	0	0	2	65	65	25	21	2	32	48	.270	.247	.280	6.61	4.41
Carr, Josh	R-R	6-4	210	11-26-89	1	4	4.35	9	5	0	0	31	38	17	15	1	12	14	.304	.340	.278	4.06	3.48
Clinard, Will	R-R	6-4	225	11-3-89	1	2	1.59	15	0	0	2	28	21	5	5	1	5	23	.210	.200	.214	7.31	1.59
Collier, Tommy	R-R	6-2	205	12-3-89	4	3	4.35	13	13	0	0	62	68	32	30	4	23	52	.281	.274	.285	7.55	3.34
Cooper, Patrick	R-R	6-3	204	8-25-89	2	1	2.86	5	4	0	0	22	17	8	7	0	10	13	.205	.172	.222	5.32	4.09
Davenport, Matt	R-R	6-8	200	10-11-89	1	1	3.81	13	0	0	1	26	22	13	11	0	14	19	.224	.300	.191	6.58	4.85
Dotel, Octavio	R-R	6-0	230	11-25-73	0	1	7.71	5	2	0	0	5	9	4	4	0	0	2	.429	.375	.462	3.86	0.00
Eichhorn, Kevin	R-R	6-0	175	2-6-90	2	6	4.04	12	11	0	0	65	62	32	29	4	20	34	.256	.231	.268	4.73	2.78
Ferrell, Jeff	R-R	6-3	185	11-23-90	6	6	4.00	25	19	0	0	119	121	61	53	15	36	77	.265	.331	.230	5.81	2.72
Gillies, Charlie	R-R	6-2	200	8-30-90	1	0	0.00	1	0	0	0	3	4	0	0	0	1	1	.333	.000	.333	3.00	3.00
Green, Chad	L-R	6-3	210	5-24-91	3	0	3.63	10	2	0	1	17	16	7	7	0	6	10	.242	.280	.220	5.19	3.12
Kubitza, Austin	R-R	6-5	190	11-16-91	0	1	5.82	8	1	0	0	17	16	12	11	0	10	14	.254	.353	.217	7.41	5.29
Mercedes, Melvin	R-R	6-3	250	11-2-90	3	1	0.96	24	0	0	11	28	23	7	3	1	5	17	.221	.206	.229	5.46	1.61
Morrison, Mike	R-R	6-1	210	12-17-87	0	2	3.52	5	0	0	0	8	7	3	3	0	2	9	.241	.286	.227	10.57	2.35
Palacios, Wilsen	R-R	6-3	180	12-15-89	7	8	3.07	24	23	2	0	135	121	56	46	10	44	109	.238	.315	.199	7.28	2.94
Randall, Hudson	R-R	6-4	185	9-22-90	1	8	7.01	11	11	0	0	53	74	48	41	7	12	25	.320	.329	.316	4.27	2.05
Robertson, Montreal	R-R	6-4	220	6-19-90	0	0	4.50	1	0	0	0	4	4	2	2	0	1	0	.250	.286	.222	0.00	2.25
Robowski, Ryan	L-L	6-0	185	2-3-88	1	0	4.96	9	0	0	0	16	13	9	9	1	8	19	.220	.167	.244	10.47	4.41
Rogers, Joe	L-L	6-1	205	2-18-91	1	1	0.00	7	0	0	0	10	11	4	0	0	5	4	.268	.455	.200	3.60	4.50
Ryan, Kyle	L-L	6-5	180	9-25-91	12	7	3.17	24	24	0	0	142	132	58	50	12	37	90	.248	.235	.253	5.70	2.35
Sanchez, Anibal	R-R	6-0	205	2-27-84	0	0	0.00	1	0	0	0	2	2	0	0	0	0	0	.333	1.000	.200	0.00	0.00
Smith, Brennan	R-R	6-3	200	8-4-89	1	1	10.43	11	0	0	0	15	25	18	17	0	7	10	.373	.238	.435	6.14	4.30
Smith, Slade	R-R	6-2	190	9-26-90	3	2	3.56	30	1	0	2	61	64	29	24	2	19	38	.268	.316	.245	5.64	2.82
Todd, Jade	R-L	6-2	190	3-22-90	0	2	6.00	11	0	0	0	21	25	17	14	1	5	20	.291	.320	.279	8.57	2.14
Torrealba, Michael	R-R	5-11	150	11-19-89	1	0	6.09	23	0	0	2	34	42	24	23	2	14	31	.296	.186	.343	8.21	3.71
Valdez, Jose	R-R	6-1	201	3-1-90	1	1	2.74	23	0	0	17	23	16	7	7	1	14	32	.195	.286	.148	12.52	5.48
Valverde, Jose	R-R	6-4	255	3-24-78	0	0	0.00	3	0	0	0	3	1	0	0	0	2	4	.125	.250	.000	12.00	6.00
VerHagen, Drew	R-R	6-6	230	10-22-90	5	3	2.81	12	11	0	0	67	49	27	21	1	27	35	.207	.227	.199	4.68	3.61

Fielding

Catcher	PCT	G	PO	A	E	DP	PB
Leyland	.973	13	70	1	2	0	1
Longley	1.000	1	3	0	0	0	0
Maggard	1.000	5	36	6	0	0	2
Murrian	.978	47	284	28	7	3	3
Reina	.943	12	59	7	4	2	0
Sanz	.992	57	354	30	3	1	5

First Base	PCT	G	PO	A	E	DP
Green	1.000	12	107	6	0	11
Hernandez	1.000	1	6	0	0	1

	PCT	G	PO	A	E	DP
Jones	.990	21	171	19	2	16
Krizan	.994	17	143	13	1	13
Leyland	.980	6	48	1	1	2
Westlake	.991	78	695	63	7	66

Second Base	PCT	G	PO	A	E	DP
Castro	.988	21	34	45	1	11
Dean	1.000	3	8	7	0	1
Hanover	.987	32	63	86	2	21
Jones	1.000	1	1	3	0	0
Loy	.972	23	41	63	3	16

	PCT	G	PO	A	E	DP
Suarez	1.000	1	0	4	0	1
Travis	.979	53	109	125	5	33

Third Base	PCT	G	PO	A	E	DP
Hanover	.906	19	16	42	6	2
Jones	.913	7	3	18	2	0
King	.925	40	21	77	8	3
Martinez	.933	66	57	152	15	22
Westlake	1.000	1	0	1	0	0

Shortstop	PCT	G	PO	A	E	DP
Hanover	1.000	13	21	37	0	6
Loy	.982	47	72	145	4	19
Machado	.957	36	47	107	7	18
Martinez	1.000	7	5	25	0	5
Reaves	.943	8	8	25	2	5

	PCT	G	PO	A	E	DP
Suarez	.931	24	49	86	10	26
Worth	.889	2	3	5	1	1
Outfield	PCT	G	PO	A	E	DP
Garcia	1.000	4	8	0	0	0
Hanover	1.000	4	6	0	0	0
Hernandez	1.000	9	20	2	0	1

	PCT	G	PO	A	E	DP
Kirksey	1.000	2	6	0	0	0
Krizan	.995	97	175	9	1	2
McVaney	.986	121	270	5	4	2
Moya	.987	78	143	7	2	1
Wright	.995	84	188	2	1	3

WEST MICHIGAN WHITECAPS

LOW CLASS A

MIDWEST LEAGUE

Batting	B-T	HT	WT	DOB	AVG	vLH	vRH	G	AB	R	H	2B	3B	HR	RBI	BB	HBP	SH	SF	SO	SB	CS	SLG	OBP
Castro, Harold	L-R	6-0	145	11-30-93	.231	.172	.246	41	147	17	34	7	1	1	11	2	0	3	1	40	5	1	.313	.240
Durham, Lance	L-R	5-11	210	2-20-88	.235	.211	.241	120	421	59	99	30	1	17	68	60	5	0	2	136	4	2	.432	.336
Ficociello, Dominic	B-R	6-4	185	4-10-92	.143	.333	.111	6	21	0	3	1	0	0	3	1	0	0	0	6	1	0	.190	.182
Gonzalez, David	R-R	5-9	140	12-1-93	.247	.250	.246	94	336	44	83	12	2	0	25	35	8	7	1	59	13	5	.295	.332
Green, Austin	R-R	6-1	200	2-22-90	.323	.300	.333	11	31	1	10	4	0	1	4	4	1	0	0	6	0	0	.548	.417
Green, Dean	L-R	6-4	255	6-30-89	.280	.297	.271	28	107	15	30	6	1	5	23	11	3	0	4	19	3	0	.495	.352
Harrell, Connor	R-R	6-3	215	3-24-91	.237	.313	.209	65	241	36	57	14	2	5	29	19	11	0	1	71	4	4	.373	.320
Hernandez, Michael	R-R	6-1	195	12-18-83	.289	.400	.250	11	38	7	11	2	3	0	6	4	2	0	0	8	1	0	.500	.386
Holm, Jeff	L-L	6-3	220	10-17-88	.270	.210	.288	122	459	56	124	15	8	9	74	55	1	1	8	75	16	10	.397	.344
Infante, Omar	R-R	5-11	195	12-26-81	.400	.500	.333	2	5	0	2	0	0	0	0	0	0	1	0	1	0	0	.400	.500
King, Jason	B-R	6-0	216	6-14-89	.263	.284	.256	87	312	38	82	15	2	7	41	43	3	1	6	55	7	1	.391	.352
Kirksey, Zach	L-R	6-1	210	2-17-89	.193	.222	.187	50	161	20	31	9	2	5	21	12	0	0	1	61	10	1	.366	.247
Martinez, Mario	R-R	6-3	220	11-13-89	.234	.200	.243	35	128	13	30	8	0	4	22	5	1	0	2	36	1	0	.391	.265
Perry, Matt	L-R	6-2	182	7-17-87	.071	.000	.083	5	14	2	1	0	0	1	1	2	0	0	0	5	0	0	.286	.188
Pickar, Bennett	R-R	6-1	185	9-14-90	.230	.167	.253	77	270	23	62	15	1	0	15	26	1	0	3	79	1	2	.293	.297
Powell, Curt	R-R	6-0	180	4-30-91	.357	.250	.400	4	14	3	5	0	0	0	1	1	0	0	0	2	2	0	.357	.438
Reaves, Jared	R-R	5-10	185	7-20-90	.271	.299	.260	99	376	49	102	19	1	5	37	28	13	5	2	87	5	4	.367	.341
Reina, Adolfo	R-R	6-0	210	1-22-90	.196	.306	.169	55	184	17	36	9	0	3	22	11	3	0	6	45	1	1	.293	.245
Rhymes, Raph	R-R	6-0	190	10-22-89	.345	.361	.337	32	119	17	41	9	0	0	4	22	4	1	0	13	4	5	.420	.462
Schotts, Austin	R-R	5-11	180	9-16-93	.192	.267	.169	59	193	22	37	6	1	1	17	14	1	3	2	75	9	5	.249	.248
Stewart, Jake	R-R	6-2	195	11-20-90	.214	.286	.189	111	378	50	81	13	3	14	46	35	3	0	2	126	3	4	.394	.285
Travis, Devon	R-R	5-9	183	2-21-91	.352	.387	.342	77	290	55	102	17	2	6	42	35	8	2	4	32	14	3	.486	.430
Vasquez, Danry	L-R	6-3	177	1-8-94	.283	.232	.297	97	375	47	106	16	5	6	40	31	1	8	6	56	9	8	.400	.334
2-team total (32 Quad Cities)					.284	—	—	129	493	59	140	18	6	9	60	37	2	9	8	71	11	8	.400	.331

Pitching	B-T	HT	WT	DOB	W	L	ERA	G	GS	CG	SV	IP	H	R	ER	HR	BB	SO	AVG	vLH	vRH	K/9	BB/9
Briceno, Endrys	R-R	6-5	171	2-7-92	7	9	4.47	25	25	0	0	117	124	72	58	5	51	65	.274	.257	.286	5.01	3.93
De La Rosa, Edgar	R-R	6-6	239	11-20-90	8	6	5.61	25	22	1	0	120	140	83	75	6	41	78	.297	.293	.299	5.83	3.07
Downs, Darin	R-L	6-3	210	12-26-84	0	0	0.00	1	0	0	0	1	0	0	0	0	0	1	.000	.000	.000	9.00	0.00
Drummond, Calvin	R-R	6-3	200	9-22-89	3	2	2.23	23	2	0	1	40	23	17	10	1	16	47	.167	.133	.192	10.49	3.57
Ehlers, Logan	L-L	6-1	190	10-30-91	1	5	4.91	17	1	0	0	29	37	23	16	2	22	20	.306	.292	.315	6.14	6.75
Felix, Julio	R-R	6-1	185	2-23-92	0	3	4.59	22	2	0	0	33	40	27	17	4	14	20	.290	.241	.325	5.40	3.78
Gillies, Charlie	R-R	6-2	200	8-30-90	1	5	4.55	13	13	0	0	61	68	38	31	3	26	41	.282	.299	.271	6.02	3.82
John, Jordan	R-L	6-3	200	7-5-90	9	4	2.92	23	19	0	0	111	107	40	36	2	32	89	.257	.218	.271	7.22	2.59
Knebel, Corey	R-R	6-3	195	11-26-91	2	1	0.87	31	0	0	15	31	14	4	3	0	10	41	.133	.200	.083	11.90	2.90
Knudson, Guido	R-R	6-1	185	8-5-89	1	2	1.79	42	0	0	7	50	41	12	10	3	10	38	.227	.243	.215	6.79	1.79
Lopez, Yorfrank	R-R	6-2	232	12-9-90	8	5	4.89	30	9	0	0	99	108	62	54	8	33	73	.286	.261	.305	6.61	2.99
Maciel, Jon	R-R	6-2	215	11-17-92	0	0	6.00	5	0	0	0	9	10	6	6	2	4	3	.286	.083	.391	3.00	4.00
Nesbitt, Angel	R-R	6-1	237	12-4-90	3	4	3.22	52	0	0	3	67	60	33	24	5	21	54	.235	.219	.248	7.25	2.82
Phillips, Alex	L-L	6-4	205	5-11-90	0	0	18.00	1	0	0	0	2	6	4	4	0	3	1	.500	.250	.625	4.50	13.50
Randall, Hudson	R-R	6-4	185	9-20-88	2	2	1.35	5	5	0	0	27	24	9	4	0	4	10	.240	.293	.203	3.38	1.35
Robertson, Montreal	R-R	6-4	220	6-19-90	3	7	5.91	16	16	0	0	75	87	58	49	4	40	40	.289	.294	.285	4.82	4.82
Smith, Brennan	R-R	6-3	200	8-4-89	2	1	1.23	15	1	0	1	29	20	5	4	1	11	31	.202	.182	.212	9.51	3.38
Smith, Chad	R-R	6-3	215	10-2-89	5	4	2.13	43	2	0	1	72	58	19	17	3	22	73	.223	.226	.221	9.13	2.75
Smith, Slade	R-R	6-2	190	9-26-90	0	0	0.00	3	0	0	0	7	2	0	0	0	4	4	.080	.167	.000	4.91	0.00
Thompson, Jake	R-R	6-4	235	1-31-94	3	3	3.13	17	16	0	0	83	79	38	29	4	32	91	.244	.269	.223	9.83	3.46
Thompson, Jeff	R-R	6-6	245	9-23-91	2	2	3.80	14	6	0	1	45	41	21	19	3	19	42	.240	.254	.230	8.40	3.80
Turley, Josh	L-L	6-0	185	8-26-90	8	4	2.09	51	0	0	2	78	64	25	18	5	17	79	.220	.225	.217	9.15	1.97
Valdez, Jose	R-R	6-1	201	3-1-90	1	1	2.73	27	0	0	16	26	16	9	8	0	20	35	.178	.289	.096	11.96	6.84

Fielding

Catcher	PCT	G	PO	A	E	DP	PB
Green	.989	11	78	10	1	0	1
Pickar	.985	77	554	56	9	4	19
Reina	.985	55	350	32	6	3	4

First Base	PCT	G	PO	A	E	DP
Durham	.974	45	378	28	11	40
Ficociello	1.000	1	9	1	0	1
Green	1.000	22	207	13	0	19
Holm	.994	77	729	38	5	57

Second Base	PCT	G	PO	A	E	DP
Castro	.941	40	63	130	12	23
Ficociello	1.000	1	0	5	0	0
Infante	1.000	1	0	1	0	0
Powell	1.000	2	1	7	0	1
Reaves	.977	30	46	80	3	17
Travis	.982	68	134	239	7	48

Third Base	PCT	G	PO	A	E	DP
Ficociello	.833	3	2	3	1	0
King	.915	80	44	140	17	5
Martinez	.943	35	20	79	6	8
Perry	.750	3	1	5	2	0
Reaves	.953	20	11	30	2	1

Shortstop	PCT	G	PO	A	E	DP
Gonzalez	.937	91	156	259	28	64
Powell	.857	2	1	5	1	1
Reaves	.953	46	61	160	11	31

Outfield	PCT	G	PO	A	E	DP
Harrell	.972	65	133	4	4	2
Hernandez	1.000	1	4	0	0	0
Holm	1.000	36	43	0	0	0
Kirksey	.939	38	61	1	4	0
Rhymes	.936	30	43	1	3	0
Schotts	.962	59	126	2	5	0
Stewart	.974	110	181	8	5	2
Vasquez	.935	96	150	9	11	2

DETROIT TIGERS

CONNECTICUT TIGERS

SHORT-SEASON

NEW YORK-PENN LEAGUE

Batting	B-T	HT	WT	DOB	AVG	vLH	vRH	G	AB	R	H	2B	3B	HR	RBI	BB	HBP	SH	SF	SO	SB	CS	SLG	OBP
Azcona, Javier	R-R	6-0	184	9-28-91	.169	.167	.170	45	136	10	23	10	1	3	14	8	3	2	1	48	2	0	.324	.230
Coffman, Kasey	L-R	6-3	201	9-8-91	.256	.283	.247	63	238	24	61	10	1	2	18	16	12	3	2	55	13	4	.332	.332
Ficociello, Dominic	B-R	6-4	185	4-10-92	.264	.261	.264	59	220	26	58	15	1	3	30	20	2	2	1	56	10	3	.382	.329
Gibson, Tyler	L-R	6-2	190	6-17-93	.203	.194	.206	45	138	20	28	3	3	1	12	22	1	1	2	64	9	3	.290	.313
Green, Austin	R-R	6-1	200	2-22-90	.225	.167	.235	24	80	5	18	2	0	1	6	4	3	0	0	25	0	1	.288	.287
Harrison, Brett	R-R	6-0	185	6-9-92	.216	.250	.207	68	231	27	50	11	3	5	23	14	7	0	5	82	4	5	.355	.276
Johnson, Taylor	L-R	5-8	170	8-21-90	.000	.000	.000	1	4	0	0	0	0	0	0	0	0	0	0	0	0	0	.000	.000
Kirksey, Zach	L-R	6-1	210	2-17-89	.242	.000	.286	10	33	4	8	1	0	0	2	3	1	0	0	13	1	0	.273	.324
Leyland, Patrick	R-R	6-2	210	10-11-91	.206	.160	.219	63	228	18	47	5	0	2	19	10	6	6	1	34	1	2	.254	.257
McAlpine, Duncan	L-R	5-10	215	4-10-91	.201	.290	.178	43	149	14	30	9	1	2	14	10	5	1	2	40	1	2	.315	.271
Negron, Steven	B-R	5-8	175	5-13-93	.167	.263	.122	22	60	5	10	1	0	0	7	14	0	0	2	20	2	0	.183	.316
Powell, Curt	R-R	6-0	180	4-30-91	.249	.231	.255	52	205	28	51	7	2	1	20	11	6	0	2	40	13	2	.317	.304
Remes, Tim	R-R	6-0	205	6-17-92	.143	.000	.167	3	7	1	1	0	0	0	0	4	0	0	0	4	0	1	.143	.455
Rhymes, Raph	R-R	6-0	190	10-22-89	.230	.222	.232	26	87	9	20	4	2	0	8	16	0	0	2	12	3	2	.322	.343
Schotts, Austin	R-R	5-11	180	9-16-93	.229	.269	.217	62	218	25	50	7	3	1	13	20	4	3	1	71	22	3	.303	.305
Smith, Pat	L-L	6-0	170	10-11-91	.000	.000	.000	3	9	1	0	0	0	0	0	2	0	1	0	2	0	0	.000	.182
Taladay, Chris	L-R	6-1	220	5-22-91	.189	.065	.240	32	106	7	20	3	0	1	6	14	0	0	2	19	1	0	.245	.279
Ustariz, Jesus	R-R	6-1	192	4-26-93	.205	.100	.241	11	39	8	8	1	1	1	2	5	2	0	0	6	0	0	.359	.326
Verlander, Ben	R-R	6-3	170	1-31-92	.219	.211	.221	67	256	29	56	12	2	4	29	14	6	2	2	59	6	3	.328	.273

Pitching	B-T	HT	WT	DOB	W	L	ERA	G	GS	CG	SV	IP	H	R	ER	HR	BB	SO	vLH	vRH	K/9	BB/9
Bailey, Tanner	R-R	6-6	240	7-6-90	1	4	3.26	20	0	0	0	39	36	19	14	3	14	35	.250	.228	.222	8.15	3.26
Beck, Ryan	R-L	6-5	230	12-11-90	4	1	2.84	20	0	0	1	44	43	18	14	0	12	34	.247	.200	.283	6.90	2.44
Carmichael, Nick	R-R	6-6	220	4-13-90	1	2	9.58	5	0	0	0	10	19	13	11	2	6	6	.396	.484	.235	5.23	5.23
Crawford, Jonathon	R-R	6-2	205	11-1-91	0	2	1.89	8	8	0	0	19	15	5	4	0	9	21	.205	.205	9.95	4.26
Davenport, Matt	R-R	6-8	200	10-11-89	1	1	2.51	4	0	0	0	14	14	5	4	0	3	13	.246	.273	.229	8.16	1.88
Edwards, Chase	R-R	6-1	180	2-4-94	0	0	2.72	9	9	0	0	40	30	17	12	2	12	25	.205	.203	.208	5.67	2.72
Ehlers, Logan	L-L	6-1	190	10-30-91	2	1	2.35	11	0	0	0	23	18	8	6	1	9	16	.214	.250	.196	6.26	3.52
Farmer, Buck	L-R	6-3	220	2-20-91	0	3	3.09	12	11	0	0	32	32	13	11	1	7	33	.258	.276	.242	9.28	1.97
Felix, Julio	R-R	6-1	185	2-23-92	3	2	3.55	15	2	0	0	46	54	23	18	0	9	32	.297	.288	.304	6.31	1.77
Flattery, Joe	L-L	6-3	190	9-30-90	1	0	2.53	3	2	0	0	11	8	3	3	0	2	8	.205	.250	.174	6.75	1.69
Harrison, Drew	R-R	6-4	260	1-22-91	1	1	3.60	7	0	0	0	10	9	4	4	1	7	8	.231	.333	.167	7.20	6.30
Huber, Brett	R-R	6-3	190	3-23-90	0	2	19.29	3	0	0	0	2	2	6	5	0	6	5	.200	.200	.200	19.29	23.14
Jamison, Preston	L-L	6-6	225	3-2-93	0	2	7.62	4	4	0	0	13	14	12	11	1	13	8	.269	.261	.276	5.54	9.00
Kirkland, Johnnie	R-R	6-1	200	8-25-89	4	2	2.97	21	0	0	2	30	28	10	10	2	10	27	.252	.296	.211	8.01	2.97
LaMarche, Will	R-R	6-2	215	8-7-91	1	0	2.04	15	0	0	2	18	14	5	4	0	7	21	.212	.286	.129	10.70	3.57
Maciel, Jon	R-R	6-2	215	11-17-92	4	1	2.79	17	1	0	0	39	34	12	12	1	9	30	.233	.213	.247	6.98	2.09
Mantiply, Joe	R-L	6-5	200	3-1-91	0	1	2.04	13	12	0	0	35	31	12	8	2	10	30	.235	.200	.247	7.64	2.55
Phillips, Alex	L-L	6-4	205	5-11-90	4	3	3.56	16	14	0	0	81	81	37	32	4	28	55	.264	.212	.291	6.11	3.11
Pritcher, Austin	R-R	6-1	190	2-13-91	3	4	2.72	18	6	0	1	50	55	24	15	3	18	29	.278	.277	.278	5.26	3.26
Reininger, Zac	B-R	6-3	170	1-28-93	1	2	1.00	22	1	0	10	27	17	6	3	0	6	32	.172	.279	.089	10.67	2.00
Scantling, Hunter	R-R	6-8	275	9-12-89	1	2	5.12	13	1	0	0	39	47	28	22	3	12	23	.294	.319	.275	5.35	2.79
Sitz, Scott	R-R	5-10	190	9-10-90	1	4	2.16	21	0	0	3	25	23	14	6	1	4	23	.232	.325	.169	8.28	1.44
Ziomek, Kevin	R-L	6-3	190	3-21-92	0	1	4.50	4	4	0	0	8	5	5	4	0	5	3	.200	.091	.286	3.38	5.63

Fielding

Catcher	PCT	G	PO	A	E	DP	PB
Green	.992	18	107	11	1	0	3
McAlpine	.984	26	180	10	3	2	6
Remes	1.000	3	29	1	0	0	0
Taladay	.987	32	207	16	3	1	4

First Base	PCT	G	PO	A	E	DP
Ficociello	.986	7	61	11	1	3
Leyland	.971	52	436	34	14	37
McAlpine	1.000	1	8	0	0	0
Ustariz	.991	11	102	10	1	11
Verlander	.956	5	42	1	2	2

Second Base	PCT	G	PO	A	E	DP
Azcona	.885	18	40	45	11	10
Ficociello	.974	50	85	144	6	24
Johnson	1.000	1	3	5	0	0
Negron	.906	10	20	38	6	5

Third Base	PCT	G	PO	A	E	DP
Azcona	.938	7	7	8	1	1
Harrison	.918	67	51	129	16	9
McAlpine	.818	4	2	7	2	0
Powell	1.000	1	1	1	0	0

Shortstop	PCT	G	PO	A	E	DP
Azcona	.880	17	29	37	9	5

Negron	.892	11	6	27	4	7
Powell	.962	51	75	150	9	24

Outfield	PCT	G	PO	A	E	DP
Azcona	1.000	1	1	0	0	0
Coffman	.967	49	89	0	3	0
Ficociello	1.000	1	1	0	0	0
Gibson	.985	40	63	4	1	0
Kirksey	1.000	2	6	0	0	0
Rhymes	.962	19	23	2	1	0
Schotts	.974	60	149	1	4	1
Smith	1.000	3	9	0	0	0
Verlander	.980	54	90	6	2	0

GCL TIGERS

ROOKIE

GULF COAST LEAGUE

Batting	B-T	HT	WT	DOB	AVG	vLH	vRH	G	AB	R	H	2B	3B	HR	RBI	BB	HBP	SH	SF	SO	SB	CS	SLG	OBP
Allen, Andrew	R-R	6-1	225	7-10-89	.241	.308	.222	19	58	4	14	1	2	0	10	4	1	0	0	16	1	0	.328	.302
Allen, Jordan	R-R	5-11	200	1-9-92	.311	.444	.278	14	45	6	14	1	2	0	2	1	0	1	0	7	1	0	.422	.326
Betancourt, Javier	R-R	5-10	173	5-8-95	.333	.341	.331	50	177	28	59	9	2	2	22	12	4	7	5	14	5	3	.441	.379
Brown, Rashad	L-L	5-11	180	12-17-93	.313	.306	.315	42	144	16	45	1	2	0	13	12	8	3	1	25	6	2	.347	.394
Castano, Adrian	L-L	6-3	180	8-20-95	.128	.000	.182	19	47	7	6	2	0	0	0	11	1	0	0	24	0	1	.170	.305
Crafort, Samuel	B-R	6-0	147	7-31-93	.339	.375	.333	19	59	14	20	4	0	4	12	9	0	0	1	20	1	1	.610	.420
Dean, Jordan	R-R	5-10	170	8-12-90	.250	—	.250	1	4	0	1	0	0	0	0	1	0	0	0	1	0	0	.250	.400

	B-T	HT	WT	DOB	AVG	vLH	vRH	G	AB	R	H	2B	3B	HR	RBI	BB	HBP	SH	SF	SO	SB	CS	SLG	OBP
Driggers, D.J.	R-R	6-3	195	6-28-92	.250	.000	.286	5	8	1	2	0	0	0	0	1	1	0	0	5	1	0	.250	.400
Fuentes, Steven	B-R	5-11	180	10-21-94	.272	.174	.314	46	151	26	41	10	2	2	24	12	8	1	2	41	5	0	.404	.353
Green, Dean	L-R	6-4	255	6-30-89	.273	.286	.267	8	22	5	6	2	0	1	4	4	1	0	0	4	2	0	.500	.407
Johnson, Taylor	L-R	5-8	170	8-21-90	.154	.000	.200	17	39	6	6	3	0	1	6	3	0	2	0	10	1	1	.308	.239
Kapstein, Jacob	B-R	6-2	215	2-24-94	.247	.333	.207	31	85	13	21	3	1	1	5	9	1	0	0	24	1	1	.341	.326
Kirksey, Zach	L-R	6-1	210	2-17-89	.091	.000	.125	4	11	0	1	0	0	0	0	2	1	0	0	7	0	0	.091	.286
Longley, Andrew	R-R	6-3	215	10-5-88	.192	.250	.175	24	73	6	14	3	0	1	5	5	1	0	1	26	0	0	.274	.250
Machado, Dixon	R-R	6-1	170	2-22-92	.321	.286	.333	7	28	3	9	2	0	0	2	1	0	1	0	5	0	0	.393	.345
Navarro, Franklin	B-R	5-10	181	10-17-94	.258	.263	.256	33	97	13	25	1	2	2	15	6	5	1	2	25	0	1	.371	.327
Negron, Steven	B-R	5-8	175	5-13-93	.265	.304	.244	22	68	15	18	5	2	2	10	13	2	0	1	21	5	1	.485	.393
Paulino, Miguel	R-R	6-1	185	11-3-93	.277	.182	.306	22	47	3	13	5	1	0	7	6	0	0	0	19	2	0	.426	.358
Remes, Tim	R-R	6-0	205	6-17-92	.272	.333	.246	25	81	15	22	4	0	5	19	13	3	0	1	20	0	0	.506	.388
Salgado, Ismael	R-R	6-1	165	1-11-93	.206	.103	.244	41	107	11	22	5	0	0	9	6	0	1	3	25	1	2	.252	.241
Sayers, Aaron	L-R	6-1	175	5-25-94	.159	.000	.204	25	69	9	11	1	1	0	5	11	1	1	0	25	2	0	.203	.284
Taladay, Chris	L-R	6-1	220	5-22-91	.000	—	.000	1	1	0	0	0	0	0	0	0	0	0	0	1	0	0	.000	.000
Tovar, Orvin	R-R	5-11	180	8-6-93	.237	.283	.218	50	156	25	37	8	0	1	16	15	3	2	1	23	2	1	.308	.314
Ustariz, Jesus	R-R	6-1	192	4-26-93	.302	.375	.278	42	129	26	39	11	0	4	21	19	6	1	2	16	5	3	.481	.410
Westlake, Aaron	L-R	6-4	235	12-27-88	.182	.000	.235	6	22	4	4	1	0	1	4	1	1	0	0	10	0	0	.364	.250
Wright, Chad	L-R	5-10	198	7-27-89	.167	.000	.188	7	18	1	3	0	0	0	1	3	1	0	0	2	1	0	.167	.318
Zambrano, Jose	B-R	5-6	151	11-4-93	.227	.349	.180	43	154	21	35	5	1	3	32	14	1	4	6	10	3	6	.331	.286

Pitching

	B-T	HT	WT	DOB	W	L	ERA	G	GS	CG	SV	IP	H	R	ER	HR	BB	SO	AVG	vLH	vRH	K/9	BB/9
Aldridge, Dean	R-R	6-3	190	7-29-94	0	0	5.40	13	0	0	0	20	22	13	12	1	8	20	.272	.231	.291	9.00	3.60
Burgos, Cesar	R-R	6-2	185	3-1-93	3	0	1.98	13	0	0	0	27	27	6	6	0	7	18	.257	.250	.261	5.93	2.30
Carmichael, Nick	R-R	6-6	220	4-13-90	2	2	2.57	8	3	0	0	28	28	9	8	1	5	21	.262	.343	.222	6.75	1.61
Carr, Josh	R-R	6-4	210	11-26-89	0	3	4.15	6	5	0	0	26	26	15	12	2	10	18	.263	.300	.237	6.23	3.46
Chavez, Emanuel	R-R	6-3	175	1-19-95	3	4	6.86	11	10	0	0	42	55	34	32	6	16	40	.316	.245	.347	8.57	3.43
Ciriaco, Ricardo	R-R	6-0	220	8-18-92	0	3	2.78	21	0	0	15	23	18	11	7	0	4	16	.222	.308	.182	6.35	1.59
Cortez, Luis	R-R	6-0	155	1-8-92	0	0	0.00	1	0	0	0	2	1	0	0	0	0	2	.167	.000	.200	9.00	0.00
Dotel, Octavio	R-R	6-0	230	11-25-73	0	0	0.00	2	2	0	0	2	0	0	0	0	0	2	.000	—	.000	9.00	0.00
Drummond, Calvin	R-R	6-3	200	9-22-89	1	0	0.00	2	0	0	0	2	1	0	0	0	0	2	.167	.000	.250	9.00	0.00
Edwards, Chase	R-R	6-1	180	2-4-94	0	0	4.50	2	1	0	0	6	4	3	3	1	2	5	.190	.500	.158	7.50	3.00
Falcon, Juan	R-R	6-3	200	3-7-92	1	0	4.44	13	1	0	0	24	26	21	12	1	17	16	.207	.207	.207	5.92	6.29
Faulk, Kenny	L-L	6-0	235	5-27-87	0	0	0.00	1	0	0	0	1	0	0	0	0	1	2	.000	.000	.000	18.00	9.00
Flattery, Joe	L-L	6-3	190	9-30-90	0	0	0.00	3	0	0	0	4	6	0	0	0	1	7	.353	.667	.286	15.75	2.25
Green, Chad	L-R	6-3	210	5-24-91	1	0	3.00	2	0	0	0	3	3	1	1	0	0	6	.250	.500	.200	18.00	0.00
Harrison, Drew	R-R	6-4	260	1-22-91	1	0	5.40	8	0	0	0	13	15	9	8	2	10	10	.283	.286	.281	6.75	6.75
Huber, Brett	R-R	6-3	190	3-23-90	2	3	2.84	14	0	0	0	25	15	8	8	1	9	36	.169	.182	.161	12.79	3.20
Jamison, Preston	L-L	6-6	225	3-2-93	0	6	5.59	9	9	0	0	39	47	31	24	3	15	26	.307	.304	.308	6.05	3.49
Jimenez, Jon	R-R	6-3	220	1-17-95	3	0	0.50	8	0	0	1	18	9	1	1	0	6	24	.155	.227	.111	12.00	3.00
Kellogg, Micah	R-R	6-4	195	11-29-89	3	2	2.04	12	4	0	0	35	25	12	8	1	12	29	.192	.146	.220	7.39	3.06
Kubitza, Austin	R-R	6-5	190	11-16-91	0	0	2.16	6	0	0	0	8	5	3	2	0	1	5	.185	.444	.056	5.40	1.08
LaMarche, Will	R-R	6-3	220	8-7-91	1	0	0.00	2	0	0	0	2	2	0	0	0	0	3	.250	.000	.333	13.50	0.00
Lara, Confesor	R-R	6-2	170	8-7-90	3	2	3.76	11	11	0	0	53	54	26	22	3	22	46	.265	.397	.199	7.86	3.76
Norris, Daryl	R-R	6-1	220	6-12-91	1	0	3.60	11	0	0	0	20	18	8	8	1	9	22	.231	.161	.277	9.90	4.05
Paulino, David	R-R	6-5	180	2-6-94	2	1	2.70	4	4	0	0	20	16	6	6	1	2	22	.229	.240	.222	9.90	0.90
Perez, Fernando	R-R	6-3	181	12-17-93	5	2	3.23	11	10	0	0	56	47	24	20	3	26	38	.240	.299	.202	6.14	4.20
Rogers, Joe	L-L	6-1	205	2-18-91	0	0	4.50	1	0	0	0	2	3	1	1	0	0	2	.375	.250	.500	9.00	0.00

Fielding

Catcher	PCT	G	PO	A	E	DP	PB
Longley	.993	18	121	13	1	0	5
Navarro	1.000	33	230	33	0	2	10
Remes	.980	14	87	10	2	1	4
Taladay	1.000	1	1	0	0	0	0

First Base	PCT	G	PO	A	E	DP
Allen	.983	16	111	4	2	15
Green	1.000	4	20	0	0	4
Kapstein	.976	7	38	3	1	2
Ustariz	.991	40	311	31	3	23
Westlake	.973	4	36	0	1	2

Second Base	PCT	G	PO	A	E	DP
Betancourt	.938	4	4	11	1	2
Dean	1.000	1	2	1	0	1
Johnson	.885	9	12	11	3	3
Negron	.963	8	5	21	1	2
Sayers	.800	3	5	7	3	4
Zambrano	.966	41	66	103	6	26

Third Base	PCT	G	PO	A	E	DP
Betancourt	.976	17	9	32	1	3
Fuentes	.914	46	26	101	12	12
Negron	—	1	0	0	0	0
Ustariz	1.000	1	0	3	0	0

Shortstop	PCT	G	PO	A	E	DP
Betancourt	.935	31	39	90	9	16
Machado	.962	5	8	17	1	4
Negron	.938	11	10	20	2	5
Sayers	.985	19	26	38	1	7
Zambrano	1.000	2	0	2	0	0

Outfield	PCT	G	PO	A	E	DP
Allen	—	1	0	0	0	0
Allen	1.000	8	8	0	0	0
Brown	.964	41	54	0	2	0
Castano	.929	17	25	1	2	1
Crafort	1.000	16	18	0	0	0
Driggers	1.000	5	4	0	0	0
Kapstein	1.000	12	11	0	0	0
Kirksey	1.000	2	3	0	0	0
Paulino	.969	19	31	0	1	0
Salgado	1.000	40	74	2	0	0
Tovar	1.000	48	71	6	0	1
Wright	1.000	6	7	2	0	0

DSL TIGERS
ROOKIE

DOMINICAN SUMMER LEAGUE

Batting	B-T	HT	WT	DOB	AVG	vLH	vRH	G	AB	R	H	2B	3B	HR	RBI	BB	HBP	SH	SF	SO	SB	CS	SLG	OBP
Acevedo, Sandy	L-L	6-0	170	12-25-92	.215	.208	.217	50	130	29	28	4	6	5	24	18	3	1	0	33	5	1	.454	.325
Adames, Willy	R-R	6-1	180	9-2-95	.245	.229	.248	60	200	48	49	12	5	1	21	56	6	2	3	44	9	12	.370	.419
Contreras, Francisco	R-R	6-1	180	12-3-92	.303	.372	.287	67	238	53	72	15	5	5	48	31	4	1	6	36	9	10	.471	.384
Felipe, Eurys	B-R	5-10	150	3-29-94	.188	.360	.132	36	101	23	19	2	3	0	11	16	2	4	1	23	11	3	.267	.308
Gonzalez, Cesar	R-R	6-2	175	5-31-95	.147	.120	.152	50	150	17	22	5	0	1	8	11	2	3	0	50	3	2	.200	.215

Batting	B-T	HT	WT	DOB	AVG	vLH	vRH	G	AB	R	H	2B	3B	HR	RBI	BB	HBP	SH	SF	SO	SB	CS	SLG	OBP
Hidalgo, Gregoris	R-R	5-10	160	12-18-93	.233	.250	.229	42	129	26	30	5	2	1	19	17	4	2	1	25	9	2	.326	.338
Joseph, Manuel	R-R	5-11	160	5-16-94	.338	.351	.335	61	222	37	75	15	2	3	48	20	10	1	6	32	24	5	.464	.407
Leyba, Domingo	B-R	5-11	160	9-11-95	.348	.360	.347	57	201	51	70	15	8	5	36	34	4	5	3	26	16	8	.577	.446
Ovalles, Victor	R-R	6-4	195	6-23-93	.230	.194	.242	37	122	13	28	9	0	0	16	13	5	1	1	37	1	0	.303	.326
Pena, Yerison	B-R	6-1	180	7-18-91	.282	.222	.296	62	195	43	55	7	2	3	35	56	2	3	3	43	9	3	.385	.441
Rodriguez, Sandy	R-R	6-1	180	10-19-94	.180	.000	.205	36	89	14	16	2	0	1	9	11	5	0		26	2	1	.236	.342
Santana, Felix	R-R	5-10	180	8-19-94	.217	.222	.216	45	161	14	35	7	2	1	27	12	7	0	2	31	3	5	.304	.297
Santana, Felix A.	R-R	5-10	180	8-29-91	.273	.286	.268	39	77	18	21	3	2	0	7	9	5	0	1	19	5	2	.364	.380
Tejeda, Bryan	R-R	6-0	190	1-17-96	.226	.071	.271	29	62	11	14	0	0	0	6	14	1	3	3	15	0	1	.226	.363
Valdez, Ignacio	R-R	6-3	195	7-16-95	.239	.184	.250	65	222	44	53	13	2	2	26	33	4	0	4	59	12	4	.342	.342

Pitching	B-T	HT	WT	DOB	W	L	ERA	G	GS	CG	SV	IP	H	R	ER	HR	BB	SO	AVG	vLH	vRH	K/9	BB/9
Alcantara, Juan	R-R	6-4	195	7-30-94	4	1	2.33	8	8	0	0	39	35	14	10	1	12	38	.233	.185	.260	8.84	2.79
Almonte, Yei	R-R	6-2	210	10-8-95	1	1	6.14	15	0	0	0	22	17	16	15	0	19	14	.224	.231	.220	5.73	7.77
Aybar, Pedro	R-R	6-2	195	11-21-91	0	2	5.29	16	0	0	9	17	15	13	10	2	9	11	.238	.200	.250	5.82	4.76
Baez, Sandy	R-R	6-2	180	11-25-93	8	1	2.05	14	10	1	1	61	41	19	14	0	16	50	.188	.267	.136	7.34	2.35
Cabrera, Rusbell	R-R	6-3	170	9-29-95	4	1	6.00	15	4	0	0	36	48	26	24	2	18	21	.340	.404	.309	5.25	4.50
Guzman, Jesus	L-L	6-3	175	1-2-91	3	3	1.78	24	0	0	10	30	21	6	6	0	10	32	.202	.150	.214	9.49	2.97
Lara, Carlos	R-R	6-3		3-2-94	3	2	1.73	14	10	0	0	57	33	14	11	2	22	61	.165	.143	.175	9.58	3.45
Manzanillo, Rafael	R-R	6-6	190	10-24-91	6	1	3.69	16	4	0	1	46	25	21	19	2	33	47	.167	.163	.168	9.13	6.41
Martinez, Malvin	R-R	6-0	170	4-19-95	3	1	2.35	15	6	0	2	46	39	15	12	1	16	35	.228	.280	.207	6.85	3.13
Martinez, Stanley	R-R	6-3	185	11-29-94	4	2	5.35	14	3	0	1	37	39	31	22	1	33	23	.257	.204	.286	5.59	8.03
Mateo, Jhonny	R-R	6-3	170	8-19-94	2	1	3.70	14	10	0	0	49	39	29	20	1	30	40	.219	.212	.223	7.40	5.55
Montero, Miguel	R-R	6-3	170	12-4-92	0	1	11.81	6	0	0	0	5	9	7	7	0	5	2	.375	.143	.471	3.38	8.44
Moreno, Gerson	R-R	6-0	175	9-10-95	2	1	2.88	15	5	0	1	50	43	21	16	0	21	35	.232	.213	.245	6.30	3.78
Obispo, Janry	R-R	6-3	205	10-10-93	5	0	1.89	22	0	0	0	33	22	7	7	0	12	13	.191	.204	.182	3.51	3.24
Paniagua, Adrian	R-R	6-0	195	5-1-91	0	0	29.25	8	0	0	0	4	6	15	13	0	16	5	.316	.375	.273	11.25	36.00
Rosario, Harold	R-R	5-11	198	10-23-92	3	3	5.21	23	0	0	0	47	47	32	27	2	40	46	.275	.339	.241	8.87	7.71
Soto, Gregory	L-L	6-1	180	2-11-95	1	2	4.82	16	12	0	0	37	29	22	20	1	36	51	.227	.267	.221	12.29	8.68

Fielding

Catcher	PCT	G	PO	A	E	DP	PB
Rodriguez	.977	34	219	33	6	1	4
Santana	.973	32	162	16	5	1	3
Tejeda	.984	27	160	20	3	0	7

First Base	PCT	G	PO	A	E	DP
Acevedo	—	1	0	0	0	0
Contreras	.990	31	266	20	3	26
Ovalles	1.000	1	9	1	0	0
Pena	.997	39	289	30	1	28
Santana	.962	3	21	4	1	0

Second Base	PCT	G	PO	A	E	DP
Felipe	.942	17	29	36	4	8
Hidalgo	.939	30	47	60	7	11
Leyba	.957	36	76	79	7	27

Third Base	PCT	G	PO	A	E	DP
Adams	.929	10	16	2	2	
Contreras	.936	35	23	65	6	8
Joseph	1.000	7	16	18	0	3
Pena	.904	22	18	48	7	3
Santana	1.000	1	0	1	0	0

Shortstop	PCT	G	PO	A	E	DP
Adams	.929	47	85	99	14	30
Hidalgo	1.000	1	0	1	0	0
Joseph	.949	10	14	23	2	2
Leyba	.935	20	26	46	5	7

Outfield	PCT	G	PO	A	E	DP
Acevedo	.986	46	67	1	1	1
Gonzalez	.961	49	69	5	3	0
Joseph	.966	40	54	2	2	1
Santana	—	1	0	0	0	0
Santana	.944	44	50	1	3	0
Valdez	.982	64	102	6	2	3

VSL TIGERS

ROOKIE

VENEZUELAN SUMMER LEAGUE

Batting	B-T	HT	WT	DOB	AVG	vLH	vRH	G	AB	R	H	2B	3B	HR	RBI	BB	HBP	SH	SF	SO	SB	CS	SLG	OBP
Alfaro, Adrian	L-R	5-9	176	9-19-95	.225	.290	.202	67	240	45	54	6	4	0	18	44	2	1	3	47	11	8	.283	.346
Alvarado, Davi	R-R	5-10	156	3-19-95	.191	.200	.188	44	110	13	21	2	0	0	6	14	2	1	1	20	10	2	.209	.291
Azocar, Jose	R-R	5-11	165	5-11-96	.234	.156	.256	62	205	20	48	11	2	0	16	3	2	1	1	43	5	2	.307	.251
Castillo, Eliezer	R-R	6-0	169	1-10-95	.231	.125	.260	53	186	21	43	3	0	0	12	8	6	4	1	43	3	2	.247	.284
Cortez, Victor	L-L	6-1		2-14-96	.155	.091	.164	34	84	3	13	2	0	0	5	6	0	1	3	14	0	1	.179	.204
Flores, Dilinyer	R-R	5-9	187	5-1-96	.162	.182	.158	30	68	3	11	6	0	0	2	1	0	0		26	0	0	.250	.197
Ledezma, Junnell	B-R	5-9	165	11-9-95	.196	.189	.198	52	138	20	27	3	0	1	8	15	7	4	3	32	4	5	.239	.301
Ovalles, Jose	R-R	5-10	205	8-2-93	.294	.343	.283	54	180	20	53	14	1	4	33	21	5	1	2	20	2	2	.450	.380
Padron, Victor	L-R	5-8	160	7-5-94	.341	.353	.337	60	214	38	73	6	0	0	11	24	0	3	0	28	23	8	.369	.408
Perez, Arvicent	R-R	5-10	178	1-14-94	.297	.345	.286	48	148	14	44	5	2	1	26	8	2	1	2	14	3	2	.378	.338
Perez, Carlos	R-R	5-11	174	2-16-94	.271	.200	.296	43	133	27	36	12	0	4	19	11	5	1	0	24	0	0	.451	.349
Sanjur, Mario	R-R	5-7	174	12-23-95	.207	.200	.209	41	116	17	24	4	1	1	12	19	3	1	1	26	0	1	.284	.331
Serrano, Ariel	R-R	5-10	174	6-23-96	.210	.205	.211	53	186	18	39	11	0	4	22	11	3	0	0	35	1	3	.333	.265
Sthormes, Andres	R-R	5-10	171	8-7-96	.232	.444	.191	26	56	6	13	2	0	1	7	4	2	0	0	14	2	1	.321	.306
Tenia, Gabriel	R-R	6-0	203	1-18-93	.296	.250	.311	58	199	29	59	18	4	4	38	40	2	1	4	0	0	53	.548	.375

Pitching	B-T	HT	WT	DOB	W	L	ERA	G	GS	CG	SV	IP	H	R	ER	HR	BB	SO	AVG	vLH	vRH	K/9	BB/9
Belisario, Johan	R-R	5-11	165	8-13-93	5	1	1.15	31	0	0	16	39	24	7	5	0	4	38	.174	.235	.154	8.77	0.92
Camaripano, Junior	L-L	6-2	213	12-21-93	2	2	9.92	23	0	0	0	16	26	19	18	3	10	14	.351	.176	.404	7.71	5.51
Castillo, Oswaldo	R-R	6-0	193	8-18-96	4	3	6.30	12	5	0	0	30	39	25	21	2	15	17	.315	.353	.288	5.10	4.50
Castro, Anthony	R-R	6-0	174	4-13-95	2	2	2.73	13	11	0	0	56	45	24	17	2	17	55	.221	.258	.191	8.84	2.73
Cedeno, Luis	R-R	6-1	185	10-2-93	1	1	3.20	13	4	0	0	39	36	15	14	3	12	36	.248	.258	.241	8.24	2.75
Del Valle, Esmeiro	R-R	6-6	193	10-9-93	1	1	3.86	13	1	0	0	19	17	14	8	0	19	15	.239	.257	.222	7.23	9.16
Fuentes, Jose	R-R	6-0	168	6-6-94	2	6	6.64	13	8	0	0	42	52	37	31	5	14	30	.308	.239	.357	6.43	3.00
Guillen, Victor	R-R	5-11	180	12-22-94	0	1	4.35	13	0	0	0	21	25	13	10	2	5	15	.298	.295	.300	6.53	2.18
Gutierrez, Alfred	R-R	6-0	143	6-12-95	3	1	1.59	18	1	0	3	40	23	14	7	2	10	33	.167	.262	.125	7.49	2.27
Hidrogo, Eudis	L-L	6-1	198	6-6-95	4	4	3.86	13	7	0	0	47	51	21	20	4	12	43	.293	.533	.270	8.29	2.31

Jimenez, Eduardo	R-R	6-0	183	4-4-95	4	2	3.21	14	13	0	0	62	52	26	22	1	25	55	.230	.202	.246	8.03	3.65
Lopez, Jose	R-R	5-9	174	6-21-95	1	0	4.32	5	0	0	0	8	7	4	4	0	2	6	.226	.364	.150	6.48	2.16
Moreno, Willians	R-R	6-0	182	3-30-96	0	1	9.20	11	0	0	0	15	18	18	15	0	12	10	.310	.357	.267	6.14	7.36
Paricaguan, Jesus	R-R	6-0	165	12-3-95	0	1	5.31	14	1	0	0	20	24	12	12	3	10	14	.300	.250	.341	6.20	4.43
Perez, Gerbinson	L-L	5-8	178	5-24-95	1	2	5.89	10	3	0	0	18	22	12	12	1	4	16	.306	.000	.338	7.85	1.96
Robles, Reinaldo	R-R	6-1	191	1-7-95	0	1	4.70	9	0	0	0	8	11	9	4	2	3	9	.344	.385	.316	10.57	3.52
Rodriguez, Jose	R-R	5-11	198	12-30-92	2	2	5.09	13	6	0	0	46	42	27	26	4	15	46	.241	.300	.191	9.00	2.93
Vasquez, Angel	R-R	6-5	190	10-8-93	0	3	6.25	13	8	0	0	40	54	32	28	2	15	21	.314	.350	.295	4.69	3.35
Verastegui, Adenson	R-R	5-11	205	2-19-93	0	2	3.18	26	0	0	1	28	32	11	10	0	8	26	.305	.364	.262	8.26	2.54

Fielding

Catcher	PCT	G	PO	A	E	DP	PB
Ovalles	.986	37	247	41	4	0	5
Perez	.975	22	130	27	4	3	1
Sanjur	.992	21	114	14	1	2	3
Sthormes	1.000	2	7	2	0	0	1
Tenia	1.000	1	3	0	0	0	1

First Base	PCT	G	PO	A	E	DP
Cortez	1.000	2	13	0	0	1
Ovalles	.971	12	92	10	3	11
Perez	.968	5	27	3	1	2
Tenia	.985	53	412	35	7	29

Second Base	PCT	G	PO	A	E	DP
Alfaro	.979	15	18	29	1	5
Alvarado	.939	11	13	18	2	1
Castillo	.968	28	56	65	4	17
Ledezma	.940	21	37	42	5	5

Third Base	PCT	G	PO	A	E	DP
Alvarado	.939	24	25	37	4	0
Castillo	.919	15	9	25	3	1
Flores	.851	18	13	27	7	1
Ledezma	.880	30	23	43	9	4

Shortstop	PCT	G	PO	A	E	DP
Alfaro	.944	55	110	158	16	30
Alvarado	.909	8	18	12	3	3
Castillo	.966	11	20	37	2	3

Outfield	PCT	G	PO	A	E	DP
Azocar	.954	62	118	7	6	1
Cortez	.909	30	28	2	3	0
Flores	.933	11	13	1	1	1
Padron	.985	50	64	2	1	1
Perez	.962	34	51	0	2	0
Serrano	.990	51	91	5	1	1

Houston Astros

SEASON IN A SENTENCE: The favorite to finish last, the Astros lived down to expectations by posting a franchise-record .315 winning percentage while setting a major league record for most strikeouts by a team in a single season.

HIGH POINT: Facing the cross-state and now division-rival Rangers on Opening Day, Houston got solid pitching from Bud Norris and Erik Bedard, a pair of triples from Justin Maxwell and a home run from Rick Ankiel to beat the Rangers 8-2. The Astros would not post a winning record the rest of the season.

LOW POINT: There are plenty of options for this category when a team finishes 60 games under .500, but the Astros saved the worst for last. They won their last game on Sept. 13 then ran off 15 straight losses to end the season.

NOTABLE ROOKIES: Houston shuffled through wave after wave of rookies in search of players who can be part of the club's long-term plans. A couple of righthanders, Jarred Cosart and Brett Oberholtzer, earned spots at the front of the club's 2014 rotation. Cosart went 1-1, 1.95 in 10 starts while Oberholtzer posted 4-5, 2.76 record in 72 innings. There are still questions about shortstop Jonathan Villar's bat after a .243/.321/.319 rookie season, but he showed excellent range in the field.

KEY TRANSACTIONS: Before the season began, Houston sent shortstop Jed Lowrie to the Athletics in exchange for first baseman Chris Carter, righthander Brad Peacock and catcher Max Stassi. All three played in Houston this year. Carter led the club in home runs (29), but he also finished with 212 strikeouts—third most of all-time. The Astros' lacked the veterans to trade in a midseason fire sale, a rite of passage in recent years, but still dealt Norris to the Orioles on July 31 for outfielder L.J. Hoes, lefthander Josh Hader and the Orioles' competitive balance pick in the 2014 draft. Maxwell was traded to the Royals for righthander Kyle Smith.

DOWN ON THE FARM: As bad as the big league club was, the Astros have hope for the future. Houston finished with the best overall record in the minors for a second consecutive year and they did it with prospects. Outfielder George Springer flirted with the minors' first 40-40 season, settling for a still outstanding 37 home runs with 45 steals. Shortstop Carlos Correa, the No. 1 pick in the 2012 draft, hit .320/.405/.467 for low Class A Quad Cities.

OPENING DAY PAYROLL: $22 million (30th).

PLAYERS OF THE YEAR

MAJOR LEAGUE	MINOR LEAGUE
Jason Castro	**George Springer**
c	cf
.276/.350/.485	(Double-A/Triple-A)
18 HR, 35 2B	.303/.411/.600
First-time all-star	37 HR, 45 SB, 108 RBIs

ORGANIZATION LEADERS

BATTING		*Minimum 250 AB
MAJORS		
* AVG	Altuve, Jose	.283
* OPS	Carter, Chris	.770
HR	Carter, Chris	29
RBI	Carter, Chris	82
MINORS		
* AVG	Correa, Carlos, Quad Cities	.32
* OBP	Fontana, Nolan, Lancaster	.415
* SLG	Springer, George, Okla. City/Corpus Christi	.6
R	Springer, George, Okla. City/Corpus Christi	106
H	Tucker, Preston, Corpus Christi/Lancaster	159
TB	Springer, George, Okla. City/Corpus Christi	295
2B	Correa, Carlos, Quad Cities	33
	Laird, Brandon, Oklahoma City	33
	Ruiz, Rio, Quad Cities	33
3B	DeShields, Delino, Lancaster	14
HR	Springer, George, Okla. City/Corpus Christi	37
RBI	Springer, George, Okla. City/Corpus Christi	108
BB	Fontana, Nolan, Lancaster	102
SO	Springer, George, Okla. City/Corpus Christi	161
SB	DeShields, Delino, Lancaster	51

PITCHING		#Minimum 75 IP
MAJORS		
W	Lyles, Jordan	7
# ERA	Keuchel, Dallas	5.15
SO	Bedard, Erik	138
SV	Veras, Jose	19
MINORS		
W	Martinez, David, Okla. City/Corpus Christi	14
L	Tropeano, Nick, Corpus Christi	10
# ERA	Martinez, David, Corpus Christi/Okla. City	2.57
G	Stoffel, Jason, Okla. City/Corpus Christi	51
GS	Buchanan, Jake, Okla. City/Corpus Christi	25
SV	Ballew, Travis, Lancaster	21
IP	Wojciechowski, Asher, Corpus/Okla. City	160
BB	Foltynewicz, Michael, Corpus/Lancaster	66
SO	Cruz, Luis, Corpus Christi/Lancaster	150
# AVG	Wojciechowski, Asher, Corpus/Okla. City	.223

2013 PERFORMANCE

General Manager: Jeff Luhnow. **Farm Director:** Quinton McCracken. **Scouting Director:** Mike Elias.

Class	Team	League	W	L	PCT	Finish	Manager
Majors	Houston Astros	American	51	111	.315	15th (15)	Bo Porter
Triple-A	Oklahoma City Redhawks	Pacific Coast	82	62	.569	1st (16)	Tony DeFrancesco
Double-A	Corpus Christi Hooks	Texas	83	57	.593	1st (8)	Keith Bodie
High A	Lancaster Jethawks	California	82	58	.586	2nd (10)	Rodney Linares
Low A	Quad Cities River Bandits	Midwest	81	57	.587	3rd (16)	Omar Lopez
Short-season	Tri-City Valley Cats	New York-Penn	44	32	.579	2nd (14)	Ed Romero
Rookie	Greeneville Astros	Appalachian	38	30	.559	4th (10)	Josh Bonifay
Rookie	GCL Astros	Gulf Coast	27	33	.450	11th (16)	Ed Alfonzo
Overall 2013 Minor League Record			437	329	.570	1st (30)	

ORGANIZATION STATISTICS

AMERICAN LEAGUE

Batting	B-T	HT	WT	DOB	AVG	vLH	vRH	G	AB	R	H	2B	3B	HR	RBI	BB	HBP	SH	SF	SO	SB	CS	SLG	OBP
Altuve, Jose	R-R	5-5	175	5-6-90	.283	.287	.281	152	626	64	177	31	2	5	52	32	2	4	8	85	35	13	.363	.316
Ankiel, Rick	L-L	6-1	210	7-19-79	.194	.000	.214	25	62	6	12	3	0	5	11	3	0	0	0	35	0	0	.484	.231
Barnes, Brandon	R-R	6-2	205	5-15-86	.240	.296	.212	136	408	46	98	17	1	8	41	21	8	6	2	127	11	11	.346	.289
Carter, Chris	R-R	6-4	245	12-18-86	.223	.232	.220	148	506	64	113	24	2	29	82	70	4	0	5	212	2	0	.451	.320
Castro, Jason	L-R	6-3	215	6-18-87	.276	.242	.286	120	435	63	120	35	1	18	56	50	2	0	4	130	2	1	.485	.350
Cedeno, Ronny	R-R	6-0	195	2-2-83	.220	.298	.167	51	141	12	31	6	1	1	12	6	2	5	1	42	2	1	.298	.260
Clark, Cody	R-R	6-3	200	9-14-81	.105	.100	.111	16	38	1	4	1	0	0	0	1	0	1	0	15	0	0	.132	.128
Corporan, Carlos	B-R	6-2	230	1-7-84	.225	.265	.194	64	191	16	43	5	0	7	20	10	7	1	1	60	0	0	.361	.287
Crowe, Trevor	B-R	5-10	190	11-17-83	.218	.314	.192	60	165	18	36	7	1	1	13	16	0	0	0	39	6	1	.291	.287
Dominguez, Matt	R-R	6-1	215	8-28-89	.241	.235	.244	152	543	56	131	25	0	21	77	30	7	2	7	96	0	1	.403	.286
Elmore, Jake	R-R	5-9	185	6-15-87	.242	.286	.211	52	120	16	29	4	0	2	6	13	0	2	1	20	1	6	.325	.313
Gonzalez, Marwin	B-R	6-1	210	3-14-89	.221	.229	.219	72	204	22	45	8	0	4	14	9	0	8	1	37	6	2	.319	.252
Grossman, Robbie	B-L	6-0	205	9-16-89	.268	.329	.245	63	257	29	69	14	0	4	21	23	2	5	1	70	6	7	.370	.332
Hoes, L.J.	R-R	6-0	190	3-5-90	.287	.273	.295	46	167	24	48	7	2	1	10	12	1	0	1	34	7	1	.371	.337
2-team total (1 Baltimore)					.282	—	—	47	170	24	48	7	2	1	10	12	1	0	1	35	7	1	.365	.332
Krauss, Marc	L-R	6-2	235	10-5-87	.209	.133	.218	52	134	11	28	9	0	4	13	10	1	0	1	45	2	0	.366	.267
Laird, Brandon	R-R	6-1	215	9-11-87	.169	.184	.152	25	71	7	12	3	0	5	11	3	2	0	0	26	0	0	.423	.224
Martinez, Fernando	L-R	6-1	210	10-10-88	.182	.000	.200	11	33	1	6	0	0	1	3	1	1	0	0	12	0	0	.273	.229
Martinez, J.D.	R-R	6-3	220	8-21-87	.250	.229	.260	86	296	24	74	17	0	7	36	10	0	0	3	82	2	0	.378	.272
Maxwell, Justin	R-R	6-5	220	11-6-83	.241	.302	.213	40	137	21	33	10	2	2	8	12	2	0	0	43	4	1	.387	.311
2-team total (35 Kansas City)					.252	—	—	75	234	35	59	16	3	7	25	23	4	0	1	78	6	2	.436	.328
Pagnozzi, Matt	R-R	6-2	215	11-10-82	.143	.400	.063	9	21	1	3	0	0	0	0	1	0	0	0	3	0	0	.143	.182
Paredes, Jimmy	B-R	6-3	200	11-25-88	.192	.105	.230	48	125	8	24	4	0	1	10	6	1	1	2	44	4	4	.248	.231
Pena, Carlos	L-L	6-2	225	5-17-78	.209	.231	.204	85	277	38	58	13	1	8	25	43	4	1	0	89	1	3	.350	.324
2-team total (4 Kansas City)					.207	—	—	89	280	38	58	13	1	8	25	43	4	1	0	92	1	3	.346	.321
Stassi, Max	R-R	5-10	205	3-15-91	.286	.200	.500	3	7	0	2	0	0	0	1	0	0	0	0	2	0	0	.286	.375
Villar, Jonathan	B-R	6-1	195	5-2-91	.243	.250	.240	58	210	26	51	9	2	1	8	24	0	7	0	71	18	8	.319	.321
Wallace, Brett	L-R	6-2	235	8-26-86	.221	.143	.243	79	262	35	58	14	1	13	36	18	5	0	0	104	1	1	.431	.284

Pitching	B-T	HT	WT	DOB	W	L	ERA	G	GS	CG	SV	IP	H	R	ER	HR	BB	SO	AVG	vLH	vRH	K/9	BB/9
Ambriz, Hector	L-R	6-2	235	5-24-84	2	4	5.70	43	0	0	2	36	50	28	23	8	14	27	.325	.373	.295	6.69	3.47
Bedard, Erik	L-L	6-1	200	3-5-79	4	12	4.59	32	26	0	1	151	149	83	77	18	75	138	.260	.309	.244	8.23	4.47
Blackley, Travis	L-L	6-3	205	11-4-82	1	1	4.89	42	0	0	0	35	30	19	19	10	20	29	.234	.200	.265	7.46	5.14
2-team total (4 Texas)					2	2	4.83	46	3	0	0	50	46	27	27	12	22	40	—	—	—	7.15	3.93
Cedeno, Xavier	L-L	6-1	205	8-26-86	0	0	11.37	5	0	0	0	6	10	11	8	0	7	3	.370	.364	.375	4.26	9.95
Chapman, Kevin	L-L	6-3	220	2-19-88	1	1	1.77	25	0	0	1	20	13	6	4	1	13	15	.183	.167	.200	6.64	5.75
Cisnero, Jose	R-R	6-3	230	4-11-89	2	2	4.12	28	0	0	0	44	49	23	20	5	22	41	.283	.293	.275	8.45	4.53
Clemens, Paul	R-R	6-4	195	2-14-88	4	7	5.40	35	5	0	0	73	82	48	44	16	26	49	.283	.275	.291	6.01	3.19
Cosart, Jarred	R-R	6-3	180	5-25-90	1	1	1.95	10	10	0	0	60	46	15	13	3	35	33	.220	.173	.293	4.95	5.25
Cruz, Rhiner	R-R	6-2	215	11-1-86	0	2	3.38	20	0	0	0	21	25	9	8	2	11	10	.305	.225	.381	4.22	4.64
De Leon, Jorge	R-R	6-0	185	8-15-87	0	1	5.40	11	0	0	0	10	12	7	6	1	7	6	.293	.318	.263	5.40	6.30
Fields, Josh	R-R	6-0	180	8-19-85	1	3	4.97	41	0	0	5	38	31	21	21	8	18	40	.220	.246	.200	9.47	4.26
Gonzalez, Edgar	R-R	6-2	210	2-23-83	0	1	7.20	5	0	0	0	10	17	9	8	4	3	8	.370	.261	.478	7.20	2.70
2-team total (3 Toronto)					0	1	7.50	8	0	0	0	18	26	16	15	6	8	11	—	—	—	5.50	4.00
Harrell, Lucas	B-R	6-2	210	6-3-85	6	17	5.86	36	22	0	0	154	174	111	100	20	88	89	.289	.255	.329	5.21	5.15
Humber, Phil	R-R	6-3	210	12-21-82	0	8	7.90	17	7	0	0	55	75	48	48	9	20	36	.322	.433	.189	5.93	3.29
Keuchel, Dallas	L-L	6-3	200	1-1-88	6	10	5.15	31	22	0	0	154	184	96	88	20	52	123	.297	.275	.304	7.20	3.05
LeBlanc, Wade	L-L	6-3	215	8-7-84	0	0	7.11	4	0	0	0	6	9	10	5	1	5	2	.290	.429	.176	2.84	7.11
Lo, Chia-Jen	R-R	5-11	190	8-7-86	0	3	4.19	19	0	0	2	19	14	9	9	3	13	20	.128	.300	.745	7.45	6.05
Lyles, Jordan	R-R	6-4	215	10-19-90	7	9	5.59	27	25	0	1	142	165	98	88	17	49	93	.285	.269	.303	5.91	3.11
Martinez, David	R-R	6-2	180	8-4-87	1	0	7.15	4	0	0	0	11	16	11	9	1	3	6	.381	.417	.367	4.76	2.38
Norris, Bud	R-R	6-0	220	3-2-85	6	9	3.93	21	21	0	0	126	135	62	55	11	43	90	.277	.306	.241	6.43	3.07
2-team total (11 Baltimore)					10	12	4.18	32	30	0	0	177	196	89	82	17	67	147	—	—	—	7.49	3.41
Oberholtzer, Brett	L-L	6-1	235	7-1-89	4	5	2.76	13	10	2	0	72	66	26	22	7	13	45	.237	.280	.219	5.65	1.63
Peacock, Brad	R-R	6-1	175	2-2-88	5	6	5.18	18	14	0	0	83	78	51	48	15	37	77	.241	.286	.184	8.32	4.00

	B-T	HT	WT	DOB	W	L	ERA	G	GS	CG	SV	IP	H	R	ER	HR	BB	SO	AVG	vLH	vRH	K/9	BB/9
Veras, Jose	R-R	6-6	240	10-20-80	0	4	2.93	42	0	0	19	43	29	15	14	4	14	44	.192	.224	.160	9.21	2.93
2-team total (25 Detroit)					0	5	3.02	67	0	0	21	63	45	23	21	6	22	60	—	—	—	8.62	3.16
Wright, Wesley	R-L	5-11	185	1-28-85	0	4	3.92	54	0	0	0	41	45	20	18	5	16	40	.278	.305	.250	8.71	3.48
2-team total (16 Tampa Bay)					0	4	3.69	70	0	0	0	54	54	24	22	7	19	55	—	—	—	9.22	3.19
Zeid, Josh	R-R	6-4	220	3-24-87	0	1	3.90	25	0	0	1	28	26	12	12	3	12	24	.250	.178	.305	7.81	3.90

Fielding

Catcher	PCT	G	PO	A	E	DP	PB
Castro	.993	98	630	44	5	6	10
Clark	.990	16	87	11	1	2	2
Corporan	.984	57	356	17	6	3	2
Elmore	1.000	1	1	0	0	0	0
Pagnozzi	.975	7	37	2	1	0	0
Stassi	1.000	1	1	1	0	0	0

First Base	PCT	G	PO	A	E	DP
Carter	.996	61	472	17	2	45
Cedeno	1.000	1	0	1	0	0
Corporan	—	1	0	0	0	0
Elmore	—	1	0	0	0	0
Krauss	1.000	2	2	0	0	1
Laird	1.000	13	71	2	0	8
Pena	1.000	44	393	30	0	45
Wallace	.992	61	452	40	4	53

Second Base	PCT	G	PO	A	E	DP
Altuve	.987	145	273	393	9	114
Elmore	.982	12	20	36	1	5
Gonzalez	1.000	10	17	38	0	6
Paredes	1.000	3	0	5	0	0

Third Base	PCT	G	PO	A	E	DP
Dominguez	.963	149	92	323	16	28
Elmore	—	1	0	0	0	0
Gonzalez	1.000	4	3	1	0	0
Laird	.900	4	1	8	1	1
Paredes	1.000	1	0	3	0	0
Wallace	1.000	9	4	12	0	3

Shortstop	PCT	G	PO	A	E	DP
Cedeno	.942	41	65	113	11	30
Elmore	.926	20	33	55	7	12
Gonzalez	.956	53	75	143	10	38
Villar	.937	58	95	141	16	38

Outfield	PCT	G	PO	A	E	DP
Ankiel	.957	22	42	3	2	0
Barnes	.991	134	328	9	3	4
Carter	.953	51	61	0	3	0
Crowe	.972	53	103	3	3	1
Elmore	1.000	12	5	0	0	0
Grossman	.976	62	122	2	3	0
Hoes	.956	45	86	0	4	0
Krauss	.953	26	38	3	2	2
Martinez	1.000	10	12	0	0	0
Martinez	.981	70	98	4	2	1
Maxwell	.972	40	100	4	3	2
Paredes	.984	39	61	0	1	0

OKLAHOMA CITY REDHAWKS   TRIPLE-A

PACIFIC COAST LEAGUE

Batting	B-T	HT	WT	DOB	AVG	vLH	vRH	G	AB	R	H	2B	3B	HR	RBI	BB	HBP	SH	SF	SO	SB	CS	SLG	OBP
Amador, Japhet	R-R	6-4	305	1-19-87	.302	.462	.233	10	43	2	13	0	0	0	2	0	0	0	0	8	0	0	.302	.302
Clark, Cody	R-R	6-3	200	9-14-81	.217	.182	.239	44	143	16	31	5	0	1	12	7	1	7	0	32	0	0	.273	.258
Crowe, Trevor	B-R	5-10	190	11-17-83	.304	.212	.339	60	237	40	72	7	2	3	23	22	1	3	1	34	16	7	.388	.364
Elmore, Jake	R-R	5-9	185	6-15-87	.299	.303	.296	70	268	42	80	13	4	5	30	31	7	1	3	37	16	6	.433	.382
Garcia, Rene	R-R	6-0		3-21-90	.246	.091	.278	18	65	8	16	2	0	0	6	3	0	0	0	6	1	1	.277	.279
Gonzalez, Marwin	B-R	6-1	210	3-14-89	.262	.317	.229	44	172	16	45	10	1	1	15	8	0	2	1	23	4	1	.349	.293
Grossman, Robbie	B-L	6-0	205	9-16-89	.281	.298	.268	70	253	42	71	11	2	2	20	48	1	7	1	66	15	8	.364	.396
Jaramillo, Jason	R-R	6-0	215	10-9-82	.130	.217	.087	23	69	4	9	3	1	0	7	11	0	0	0	18	0	0	.203	.250
2-team total (38 Tacoma)					.215	—	—	61	205	17	44	13	1	2	22	20	0	1	1	44	0	0	.317	.283
Krauss, Marc	L-R	6-2	235	10-5-87	.281	.274	.284	78	253	38	71	16	2	10	39	53	2	0	6	52	3	3	.478	.401
Laird, Brandon	R-R	6-1	215	9-11-87	.277	.261	.285	119	470	75	130	33	0	16	79	29	7	0	7	87	1	0	.449	.324
Lin, Che-Hsuan	R-R	6-0	180	9-21-88	.234	.204	.249	121	350	50	82	13	2	3	42	60	9	9	5	56	19	7	.309	.356
Martinez, Fernando	L-R	6-1	210	10-10-88	.219	.175	.246	29	105	12	23	5	1	3	21	11	0	0	1	31	0	0	.371	.291
Martinez, Jose	R-R	5-11	175	1-24-86	.282	.255	.296	81	305	34	86	19	1	6	42	16	2	4	6	24	2	3	.410	.316
Maxwell, Justin	R-R	6-5	220	11-6-83	.179	.182	.176	8	28	5	5	0	0	1	3	3	0	0	1	6	0	0	.286	.250
Paredes, Jimmy	B-R	6-3	200	11-25-88	.287	.298	.282	86	327	50	94	21	6	8	37	28	1	1	1	67	16	7	.462	.345
Perez, Carlos	R-R	6-0	195	10-27-90	.269	.213	.300	75	264	29	71	14	0	2	32	25	0	3	4	39	1	1	.345	.328
Simunic, Andy	R-R	6-0	170	8-7-85	.278	.311	.263	44	144	22	40	3	0	0	15	15	1	1	2	28	9	2	.299	.346
Singleton, Jonathan	L-L	6-2	235	9-18-91	.220	.170	.252	73	245	31	54	13	0	6	31	46	0	0	3	89	1	0	.347	.340
Sosa, Ruben	B-R	5-7	170	9-23-90	.272	.225	.294	46	125	18	34	4	3	1	17	12	1	4	2	35	8	6	.376	.336
Springer, George	R-R	6-3	200	9-19-89	.311	.364	.288	62	219	50	68	7	4	18	53	41	4	0	2	65	22	3	.626	.425
Torrez, Raoul	R-R	5-10	180	3-16-88	.214	.333	.167	16	42	5	9	1	0	0	3	1	1	1	1	15	2	1	.238	.277
Villar, Jonathan	B-R	6-1	195	5-2-91	.277	.221	.315	91	339	47	94	16	8	8	41	32	2	11	2	93	31	7	.442	.341
Wallace, Brett	L-R	6-2	235	8-26-86	.326	.323	.329	60	233	36	76	16	2	11	37	24	4	0	0	69	1	0	.554	.398
Wallace, Chris	R-R	6-0	220	4-27-88	.000	—	.000	1	3	0	0	0	0	0	0	0	0	0	0	2	0	0	.000	.000
Wates, Austin	R-R	6-1	179	9-2-88	.306	.250	.317	15	49	5	15	2	0	0	5	2	1	2	0	3	4	0	.347	.346

Pitching	B-T	HT	WT	DOB	W	L	ERA	G	GS	CG	SV	IP	H	R	ER	HR	BB	SO	AVG	vLH	vRH	K/9	BB/9
Ambriz, Hector	L-R	6-2	235	5-24-84	1	2	5.40	14	0	0	3	17	23	12	10	3	3	12	.315	.242	.375	6.48	1.62
Berger, Eric	L-L	6-2	205	4-22-86	6	3	3.06	44	3	0	1	71	59	28	24	6	32	55	.225	.233	.218	7.00	4.08
Blackley, Travis	L-L	6-3	205	11-4-82	0	0	4.50	1	1	0	0	2	0	1	1	0	0	1	.000	.000	.000	4.50	0.00
2-team total (1 Round Rock)					0	0	1.80	2	2	0	0	5	1	1	1	0	2	3	—	—	—	5.40	3.60
Buchanan, Jake	R-R	6-0	200	9-24-89	5	5	3.89	12	12	0	0	76	85	33	33	6	13	55	.285	.351	.234	6.48	1.53
Chapman, Kevin	L-L	6-3	220	2-19-88	1	2	3.20	45	0	0	2	51	42	23	18	2	36	61	.223	.193	.248	10.84	6.39
Cisnero, Jose	R-R	6-3	230	4-11-89	1	1	8.66	12	1	0	0	18	25	18	17	2	13	24	.333	.366	.294	12.23	6.62
Clemens, Paul	R-R	6-4	195	2-14-88	3	2	4.50	6	6	0	0	30	27	19	15	1	11	16	.235	.208	.254	4.80	3.30
Cosart, Jarred	R-R	6-3	180	5-25-90	7	4	3.29	18	17	1	0	93	74	37	34	5	50	93	.213	.206	.220	9.00	4.84
Cruz, Rhiner	R-R	6-2	215	11-1-86	1	2	4.75	37	0	0	2	42	34	25	22	6	32	38	.227	.310	.174	8.21	6.91
Day, Lance	R-R	6-1	200	10-4-89	0	1	12.00	5	0	0	0	6	15	8	8	0	3	3	.469	.471	.467	4.50	4.50
De Leon, Jorge	R-R	6-0	185	8-15-87	0	0	0.60	12	0	0	6	15	8	1	1	0	2	12	.151	.313	.081	7.20	1.20
Doran, Bobby	R-R	6-6	235	3-21-89	3	0	4.06	8	8	0	0	44	44	21	20	4	15	22	.259	.313	.207	4.47	3.05
Ely, John	R-R	6-2	205	6-28-86	0	0	0.00	1	0	0	1	4	2	0	0	0	2	1	.167	.333	.111	6.75	4.50
Fick, C.J.	R-R	6-5	200	11-20-85	1	0	5.23	16	0	0	0	21	27	13	12	1	13	13	.333	.351	.318	5.66	5.66
2-team total (6 Colorado Springs)					1	2	5.97	22	0	0	1	32	41	23	21	2	20	17	—	—	—	4.83	5.68
Guduan, Reymin	L-L	6-4	185	3-16-92	0	0	3.86	1	0	0	0	2	1	1	1	0	3	4	.143	.000	.167	15.43	11.57

Hallock, Kyle	L-L	6-2	185	8-6-88	1	0	3.72	9	1	0	0	19	17	8	8	2	8	6	.246	.172	.300	2.79	3.72
Humber, Phil	R-R	6-3	210	12-21-82	2	4	4.68	20	7	0	0	50	57	32	26	7	18	38	.285	.296	.275	6.84	3.24
Keuchel, Dallas	L-L	6-3	200	1-1-88	1	0	0.00	1	1	1	0	6	3	0	0	0	0	5	.150	.000	.176	7.50	0.00
LeBlanc, Wade	L-L	6-3	215	8-7-84	3	1	4.71	19	7	0	1	50	55	26	26	5	16	47	.282	.274	.286	8.52	2.90
Lyles, Jordan	R-R	6-4	215	10-19-90	2	2	5.32	6	5	0	0	24	30	15	14	1	6	11	.313	.326	.302	4.18	2.28
Martinez, David	R-R	6-2	180	8-4-87	0	2	9.00	3	3	0	0	11	15	12	11	1	11	10	.326	.300	.346	8.18	9.00
Musick, Wes	L-L	6-0	190	12-30-86	2	0	3.71	9	2	0	0	27	17	11	11	3	10	22	.181	.237	.143	7.43	3.38
Oberholtzer, Brett	L-L	6-1	235	7-1-89	6	6	4.37	16	16	0	0	80	77	48	39	9	25	72	.252	.253	.251	8.07	2.80
Owens, Rudy	L-L	6-3	230	12-18-87	0	3	3.71	4	3	0	0	17	20	8	7	0	9	13	.299	.323	.278	6.88	4.76
Peacock, Brad	R-R	6-1	175	2-2-88	6	2	2.73	14	13	0	0	79	65	29	24	9	22	76	.226	.183	.267	8.66	2.51
Rodgers, Brady	R-R	6-2	187	9-17-90	0	0	1.80	1	1	0	0	5	5	1	1	0	0	4	.263	.143	.333	7.20	0.00
Rollins, David	L-L	6-1	195	12-21-89	1	0	0.00	1	1	0	0	6	3	0	0	0	1	8	.143	.333	.111	12.00	1.50
Seaton, Ross	L-R	6-4	200	9-18-89	3	7	7.34	15	14	0	0	69	97	60	56	13	28	36	.339	.351	.326	4.72	3.67
Sogard, Alex	L-L	6-3	215	7-25-87	2	1	9.39	22	0	0	0	23	30	24	24	1	19	19	.323	.257	.362	7.43	7.43
Stoffel, Jason	R-R	6-2	225	9-15-88	8	1	3.47	44	0	0	0	62	49	24	24	1	30	51	.224	.313	.169	7.36	4.33
Urckfitz, Pat	L-L	6-4	200	7-21-88	0	0	1.64	10	0	0	0	11	14	2	2	0	2	11	.318	.263	.360	9.00	1.64
Valdez, Jose	R-R	6-4	200	1-22-83	3	3	5.72	35	0	0	13	39	42	30	25	4	21	33	.278	.250	.301	7.55	4.81
Walters, Blair	L-L	6-0	200	11-8-89	0	0	4.15	1	1	0	0	4	4	2	2	0	3	4	.267	.333	.250	8.31	6.23
Wojciechowski, Asher	R-R	6-4	235	12-21-88	9	7	3.56	22	21	2	0	134	116	56	53	10	44	104	.229	.218	.239	6.99	2.96
Zeid, Josh	R-R	6-4	220	3-24-87	4	1	3.50	43	0	0	13	44	36	17	17	3	27	53	.231	.242	.223	10.92	5.56

Fielding

Catcher	PCT	G	PO	A	E	DP	PB
Clark	.989	38	254	25	3	1	3
Garcia	1.000	17	114	11	0	1	0
Jaramillo	1.000	19	116	10	0	0	0
Perez	.989	71	551	63	7	7	10

First Base	PCT	G	PO	A	E	DP
Amador	1.000	3	35	1	0	7
Krauss	.987	17	147	9	2	14
Laird	.988	19	145	16	2	16
Singleton	.988	68	547	39	7	45
Wallace	.989	41	345	25	4	40

Second Base	PCT	G	PO	A	E	DP
Elmore	.992	54	98	160	2	34
Gonzalez	1.000	13	26	40	0	10
Martinez	.993	53	118	158	2	32
Paredes	.833	3	2	8	2	2
Simunic	.950	11	14	24	2	8

	PCT	G	PO	A	E	DP
Sosa	.959	8	23	24	2	5
Torrez	1.000	7	13	25	0	8

Third Base	PCT	G	PO	A	E	DP
Elmore	.875	4	1	6	1	1
Gonzalez	1.000	1	0	3	0	0
Laird	.953	85	55	169	11	18
Martinez	.938	18	9	36	3	3
Paredes	.896	20	11	32	5	4
Simunic	.950	9	5	14	1	0
Torrez	.500	1	0	1	1	0
Wallace	.960	10	5	19	1	0

Shortstop	PCT	G	PO	A	E	DP
Elmore	1.000	5	5	15	0	3
Gonzalez	.981	29	36	70	2	12
Paredes	.933	20	30	68	7	13
Torrez	1.000	5	8	13	0	7
Villar	.956	88	132	263	18	63

Outfield	PCT	G	PO	A	E	DP
Crowe	.989	45	82	4	1	1
Elmore	1.000	7	15	0	0	1
Grossman	.983	64	112	5	2	0
Krauss	.984	43	60	1	1	1
Lin	.996	116	249	5	1	1
Martinez	.958	15	23	0	1	0
Maxwell	1.000	8	16	1	0	0
Paredes	.985	35	65	0	1	0
Simunic	1.000	23	50	2	0	0
Sosa	.971	24	30	4	1	0
Springer	1.000	57	121	1	0	1
Torrez	1.000	1	1	0	0	0
Wates	1.000	15	20	0	0	0

CORPUS CHRISTI HOOKS

DOUBLE-A

TEXAS LEAGUE

Batting	B-T	HT	WT	DOB	AVG	vLH	vRH	G	AB	R	H	2B	3B	HR	RBI	BB	HBP	SH	SF	SO	SB	CS	SLG	OBP
Alvarez, Luis	R-R	5-11	230	2-28-90	.250	.250	.250	8	24	2	6	1	0	1	4	1	0	0	1	5	0	1	.417	.269
Burgess, Michael	L-L	5-11	195	10-20-88	.203	.193	.205	98	320	31	65	20	0	12	42	32	2	0	2	93	0	1	.378	.278
Castro, Jason	L-R	6-4	200	11-13-87	.280	.230	.292	117	410	62	115	28	0	18	65	55	2	5	1	105	2	4	.480	.368
Clark, Cody	R-R	6-3	200	9-14-81	.125	—	.125	2	8	0	1	0	0	0	1	0	0	0	1	0	0	0	.125	.111
Duffy, Matt	R-R	6-3	227	2-6-89	.247	.176	.264	24	89	11	22	4	0	5	10	3	3	0	0	22	1	1	.461	.295
Garcia, Rene	R-R	6-0	200	3-21-90	.304	.329	.296	73	303	36	92	18	1	5	36	19	2	4	1	44	1	2	.419	.348
Heras, Leonardo	L-R	5-9	190	5-29-90	.205	.286	.188	10	39	7	8	2	1	1	5	8	1	0	0	11	1	0	.385	.354
Hernandez, Enrique	R-R	5-11	170	8-24-91	.236	.257	.229	116	437	53	103	18	2	13	46	34	5	5	2	70	5	3	.375	.297
Johnson, Zach	R-R	5-11	200	6-16-88	.252	.278	.241	42	123	18	31	6	0	3	7	11	2	1	0	29	1	1	.374	.324
Martinez, Jose	R-R	5-11	175	1-24-88	.455	.571	.423	8	33	7	15	1	0	0	8	3	0	0	0	7	2	1	.485	.500
Martinez, J.D.	R-R	6-3	220	8-21-87	.300	.000	.316	5	20	1	6	2	0	1	6	0	0	0	0	1	0	0	.550	.300
Maxwell, Justin	R-R	6-5	220	11-6-83	.048	.000	.050	6	21	1	1	0	0	0	2	1	0	0	1	8	1	0	.048	.087
McCurdy, Ryan	R-R	5-10	175	12-28-87	.136	.000	.188	10	22	1	3	0	0	0	0	5	4	2	0	3	0	1	.136	.387
Meyer, Jonathan	R-R	6-1	195	11-7-90	.260	.343	.237	129	484	61	126	24	0	15	68	41	3	0	7	109	3	3	.403	.318
Mier, Jio	R-R	6-2	180	8-26-90	.194	.139	.210	104	355	44	69	10	0	5	28	46	4	10	1	97	9	8	.265	.293
Muren, Drew	L-R	6-6	195	11-22-88	.238	.179	.252	93	282	44	67	17	5	1	19	24	8	5	1	67	6	3	.344	.314
Orloff, Ben	R-R	5-11	174	4-26-87	.298	.333	.287	41	131	20	39	5	0	0	11	13	6	9	3	8	5	2	.336	.379
Perez, Carlos	R-R	6-0	195	10-27-90	.283	.267	.289	16	53	6	15	4	0	1	5	4	2	1	0	11	0	0	.415	.356
Santana, Domingo	R-R	6-5	230	8-5-92	.252	.294	.242	112	416	72	105	23	2	25	64	46	13	0	1	139	12	5	.498	.345
Singleton, Jonathan	L-L	6-2	235	9-18-91	.263	.250	.265	11	38	5	10	2	1	2	8	9	0	0	1	16	0	0	.526	.396
Springer, George	R-R	6-3	200	9-19-89	.297	.358	.282	73	273	56	81	20	0	19	55	42	5	2	1	96	23	5	.579	.399
Stassi, Max	R-R	5-10	205	3-15-91	.277	.250	.284	76	289	40	80	20	1	17	60	19	8	2	5	68	1	1	.529	.333
Torreyes, Ronald	R-R	5-9	140	9-2-92	.278	.200	.302	38	151	19	42	6	2	0	12	6	1	4	0	14	1	1	.344	.310
Torrez, Raoul	R-R	5-10	180	11-5-88	.250	.360	.182	28	80	9	20	5	0	3	11	8	2	2	0	32	0	2	.413	.322
Tucker, Preston	L-L	6-0	217	7-6-90	.262	.275	.258	60	237	36	62	14	1	10	29	27	4	0	0	46	0	1	.456	.347
Valenzuela, Rafael	L-R	6-1	175	10-20-87	.000	.000	.000	3	14	1	0	0	0	0	0	1	0	0	0	4	0	0	.000	.067
Wates, Austin	R-R	6-1	179	9-2-88	.310	.333	.304	23	87	14	27	3	3	1	5	14	3	0	0	18	11	1	.448	.423

Pitching	B-T	HT	WT	DOB	W	L	ERA	G	GS	CG	SV	IP	H	R	ER	HR	BB	SO	AVG	vLH	vRH	K/9	BB/9
Alaniz, R.J.	R-R	6-4	175	6-14-91	9	9	4.53	27	19	0	0	113	136	73	57	9	47	65	.298	.322	.278	5.16	3.73
Buchanan, Jake	R-R	6-0	200	9-24-89	7	2	2.09	18	13	0	1	82	67	22	19	4	9	44	.226	.242	.212	4.83	0.99
Cruz, Luis	L-L	5-9	170	9-10-90	2	0	0.53	4	2	1	0	17	5	1	1	0	4	21	.093	.167	.071	11.12	2.12
De Leon, Jorge	R-R	6-0	185	8-15-87	0	3	4.27	29	3	0	6	53	42	26	25	7	15	36	.226	.219	.230	6.15	2.56
Doran, Bobby	R-R	6-6	235	3-21-89	8	2	3.26	23	13	0	2	94	87	40	34	11	23	69	.244	.220	.266	6.61	2.20
Dufek, Jonas	R-R	6-5	215	6-30-88	7	0	0.47	14	0	0	4	19	14	2	1	0	1	20	.212	.333	.143	9.31	0.47
Escalona, Sergio	L-L	6-0	215	8-3-84	1	2	6.60	12	0	0	1	15	25	11	11	3	6	9	.410	.318	.462	5.40	3.60
Fields, Josh	R-R	6-0	180	8-19-85	0	0	3.00	5	0	0	0	6	7	2	2	0	0	4	.292	.250	.333	6.00	0.00
Foltynewicz, Mike	R-R	6-4	200	10-7-91	5	3	2.87	23	16	0	3	103	75	39	33	8	52	95	.207	.181	.227	8.27	4.53
Geith, T.J.	L-L	6-5	175	6-27-89	0	0	7.84	13	0	0	0	21	30	21	18	2	5	13	.345	.310	.362	5.66	2.18
Hallock, Kyle	L-L	6-2	185	8-6-88	0	3	9.40	11	5	0	0	30	31	32	31	7	22	18	.270	.161	.310	5.46	6.67
Heidenreich, Matt	L-R	6-5	185	1-17-91	4	5	8.23	25	7	0	0	55	83	54	50	10	16	34	.356	.351	.361	5.60	2.63
Lamb, Cameron	R-R	6-3	211	5-29-89	0	0	5.68	9	0	0	0	13	15	8	8	3	4	5	.300	.333	.289	3.55	2.84
Lo, Chia-Jen	R-R	5-11	190	4-7-86	0	0	3.52	8	0	0	1	8	9	3	3	1	0	6	.290	.300	.286	7.04	0.00
Long, Kenny	L-L	6-1	155	1-28-89	0	2	9.00	22	0	0	0	21	38	22	21	4	15	13	.400	.380	.422	5.57	6.43
Martinez, David	R-R	6-2	180	8-4-87	14	2	2.02	26	18	2	1	129	109	34	29	10	20	86	.233	.244	.224	5.98	1.39
Quevedo, Carlos	R-R	6-1	222	9-30-89	2	4	3.53	36	5	0	1	82	79	35	32	14	20	59	.251	.292	.216	6.50	2.20
Robinson, Andrew	R-R	6-1	185	2-13-88	5	2	3.28	38	0	0	3	49	47	21	18	6	14	37	.247	.241	.252	6.75	2.55
Rodgers, Brady	R-R	6-2	187	9-17-90	1	0	0.00	1	1	0	0	5	5	0	0	0	0	6	.238	.200	.273	10.80	0.00
Rollins, David	L-L	6-1	195	12-21-89	0	3	4.36	6	6	0	0	33	38	18	16	4	10	33	.295	.290	.296	9.00	2.73
Sanudo, Gonzalo	L-R	6-3	235	1-10-92	0	0	3.86	3	0	0	0	5	6	2	2	1	2	1	.316	.500	.182	1.93	3.86
Seaton, Ross	L-R	6-4	200	9-18-89	3	1	4.77	10	9	0	0	55	56	31	29	7	11	36	.268	.272	.264	5.93	1.81
Sogard, Alex	L-L	6-3	215	7-25-87	0	0	2.88	16	0	0	3	25	26	11	8	3	10	18	.277	.171	.339	6.48	3.60
Stoffel, Jason	R-R	6-2	225	9-15-88	0	0	1.23	7	0	0	5	7	9	3	1	1	0	7	.290	.429	.176	8.59	0.00
Tropeano, Nick	R-R	6-4	205	8-27-90	7	10	4.11	28	20	1	5	134	140	65	61	15	39	130	.275	.318	.241	8.75	2.63
Urckfitz, Pat	L-L	6-4	200	7-21-88	6	3	3.20	40	0	0	7	56	57	21	20	2	20	25	.273	.163	.350	3.99	3.20
Wojciechowski, Asher	R-R	6-4	235	12-21-88	2	1	2.08	6	3	0	1	26	17	6	6	1	7	27	.189	.194	.185	9.35	2.42

Fielding

Catcher	PCT	G	PO	A	E	DP	PB
Alvarez	.980	8	41	7	1	1	2
Clark	1.000	2	18	0	0	0	0
Garcia	.993	60	372	43	3	2	1
McCurdy	.977	10	77	7	2	2	1
Perez	.984	12	107	13	2	3	1
Stassi	.983	50	313	38	6	4	2

First Base	PCT	G	PO	A	E	DP
Burgess	1.000	1	1	0	0	0
Castro	.985	98	906	53	15	94
Duffy	1.000	4	42	5	0	4
Johnson	.992	26	238	9	2	14
Meyer	1.000	1	1	1	0	0
Orloff	.976	5	39	2	1	9
Singleton	.990	10	91	8	1	13
Valenzuela	1.000	2	33	1	0	2

Second Base	PCT	G	PO	A	E	DP
Duffy	—	1	0	0	0	0
Hernandez	.973	104	199	300	14	84
Johnson	1.000	1	0	1	0	0
Martinez	1.000	7	12	23	0	4
Orloff	.977	12	14	29	1	4
Torreyes	1.000	15	34	40	0	9
Torrez	1.000	8	11	30	0	7

Third Base	PCT	G	PO	A	E	DP
Duffy	1.000	7	5	13	0	2
Hernandez	.875	4	2	5	1	0
Johnson	—	1	0	0	0	0
Meyer	.957	123	81	293	17	28
Mier	.667	1	0	2	1	0
Orloff	.952	7	6	14	1	2
Torrez	.875	3	1	6	1	0

Shortstop	PCT	G	PO	A	E	DP
Hernandez	.957	5	8	14	1	3
Mier	.961	101	164	309	19	82
Orloff	.969	14	20	42	2	9
Torreyes	.969	23	32	63	3	7
Torrez	.917	3	3	8	1	4

Outfield	PCT	G	PO	A	E	DP
Burgess	.991	67	98	9	1	2
Heras	1.000	10	20	0	0	0
Hernandez	1.000	5	5	0	0	0
Martinez	1.000	4	2	0	0	0
Maxwell	1.000	5	8	0	0	0
Muren	.996	89	219	12	1	2
Santana	.971	106	187	11	6	2
Springer	.994	70	155	2	1	0
Torrez	1.000	10	15	1	0	0
Tucker	1.000	54	83	7	0	0
Wates	.968	20	29	1	1	0

LANCASTER JETHAWKS   HIGH CLASS A

CALIFORNIA LEAGUE

Batting	B-T	HT	WT	DOB	AVG	vLH	vRH	G	AB	R	H	2B	3B	HR	RBI	BB	HBP	SH	SF	SO	SB	CS	SLG	OBP
Alvarez, Luis	R-R	5-11	230	2-28-90	.261	.500	.133	8	23	7	6	0	1	3	9	2	2	0	0	3	0	0	.739	.370
Aplin, Andrew	L-L	6-0	190	3-21-91	.278	.330	.264	128	500	102	139	32	7	9	107	83	2	3	10	63	24	6	.424	.376
Batista, Jean	B-R	6-2	180	11-15-91	.200	.167	.222	8	30	5	6	1	0	0	1	1	0	0	0	9	0	0	.233	.226
Cokinos, M.P.	R-R	6-2	215	6-18-90	.313	.395	.295	109	425	71	133	28	1	13	94	47	15	1	7	41	1	3	.475	.395
DeShields, Delino	R-R	5-9	205	8-16-92	.317	.272	.327	111	451	100	143	25	14	5	54	57	11	13	2	91	51	18	.468	.405
Duffy, Matt	R-R	6-3	227	2-6-89	.323	.347	.318	100	371	74	120	20	4	19	84	30	18	1	4	80	0	2	.553	.397
Epps, Chris	L-L	6-2	172	12-10-88	.275	.306	.269	115	396	78	109	32	5	16	75	69	3	2	7	116	8	8	.503	.381
Fontana, Nolan	L-R	5-11	190	6-6-91	.259	.267	.257	104	386	88	100	18	6	8	60	102	3	5	3	100	16	5	.399	.415
Gingras, Ricky	L-R	6-2	205	10-18-90	.000	.000	.000	5	15	0	0	0	0	0	1	0	0	0	0	8	0	0	.000	.000
Gulbransen, Dan	L-R	5-11	205	1-5-91	.302	.600	.276	16	63	13	19	3	0	4	16	4	0	0	2	12	1	0	.540	.333
Heineman, Tyler	B-R	5-11	205	6-19-91	.286	.228	.297	104	370	67	106	23	4	13	71	32	15	4	7	47	2	3	.476	.361
Johnson, Zach	R-R	5-11	200	6-16-88	.298	.389	.273	20	84	12	25	10	2	2	20	8	1	1	1	21	0	0	.536	.362
McCurdy, Ryan	R-R	5-10	175	12-28-87	.254	.333	.226	24	71	9	18	2	0	0	8	9	11	0	0	11	0	0	.282	.418
Meredith, Brandon	R-R	6-2	225	12-19-89	.279	.299	.275	105	365	83	102	25	5	16	68	64	12	1	5	88	6	7	.507	.399
Muren, Drew	L-R	6-6	195	11-24-88	.279	.286	.389	12	43	12	16	2	1	2	8	5	1	0	0	12	1	0	.605	.449
Nash, Telvin	R-R	6-1	248	2-20-91	.246	.298	.232	62	228	43	56	10	0	16	48	37	3	0	1	93	1	0	.500	.357
Perdomo, Carlos	R-R	5-10	160	4-25-90	.294	.303	.292	60	187	40	55	9	1	2	29	23	2	0	5	16	8	6	.385	.369
Sclafani, Joe	B-R	5-11	190	4-22-90	.302	.234	.318	92	344	81	104	28	5	7	53	52	4	2	4	60	16	3	.474	.396
Torrez, Raoul	R-R	5-10	180	3-16-88	.215	.200	.218	22	65	15	14	4	0	0	5	2	1	0	1	28	2	0	.277	.278
Tucker, Preston	L-L	6-0	217	7-6-90	.326	.324	.326	75	298	61	97	18	1	15	74	29	2	0	4	45	3	0	.544	.384
Valenzuela, Rafael	L-R	6-1	175	10-20-87	.286	.000	.364	4	14	1	4	2	0	1	3	1	0	0	0	2	0	0	.643	.333
Wierzbicki, Jesse	R-R	6-3	210	11-24-88	.245	.273	.236	25	94	14	23	4	0	2	9	10	6	0	1	11	0	2	.351	.351

Pitching	B-T	HT	WT	DOB	W	L	ERA	G	GS	CG	SV	IP	H	R	ER	HR	BB	SO	AVG	vLH	vRH	K/9	BB/9
Ballew, Travis	R-R	6-0	160	5-1-91	4	5	4.42	50	0	0	21	53	52	33	26	6	22	78	.248	.268	.237	13.25	3.74
Cain, Colton	L-L	6-3	256	2-5-91	3	0	3.24	5	5	0	0	33	36	17	12	2	6	22	.273	.241	.282	5.94	1.62
Cruz, Luis	L-L	5-9	170	9-10-90	8	6	5.16	27	18	0	2	113	111	67	65	10	40	129	.253	.336	.222	10.24	3.18
Devenski, Chris	R-R	6-3	195	11-13-90	4	2	7.88	21	10	0	1	75	106	69	66	13	31	65	.337	.352	.326	7.77	3.70
Dimock, Michael	R-R	6-2	194	10-26-89	4	1	4.10	27	0	0	0	42	41	21	19	5	12	36	.265	.255	.270	7.78	2.59
Dufek, Jonas	R-R	6-5	215	6-30-88	2	2	4.28	36	0	0	0	48	50	29	23	4	19	54	.259	.258	.260	10.06	3.54
Foltynewicz, Mike	R-R	6-4	200	10-7-91	1	0	3.81	7	5	0	0	26	31	16	11	4	14	29	.290	.286	.292	10.04	4.85
Geith, T.J.	L-L	6-5	175	6-27-89	6	0	2.86	31	0	0	1	44	43	15	14	1	15	36	.257	.250	.261	7.36	3.07
Gillingham, Alex	R-R	6-3	200	10-17-89	1	1	11.25	3	1	0	0	8	16	10	10	0	5	6	.432	.571	.348	6.75	5.63
Hallock, Kyle	L-L	6-2	185	8-6-88	4	3	6.41	13	7	0	0	46	55	38	33	9	19	29	.291	.340	.275	5.63	3.69
Hauschild, Mike	R-R	6-3	210	1-22-90	3	3	4.73	8	7	0	0	40	50	26	21	7	14	29	.316	.264	.343	6.53	3.15
Jankowski, Jordan	R-R	6-2	200	5-17-89	0	0	5.40	11	0	0	0	17	15	10	10	3	4	20	.238	.300	.209	10.80	2.16
Lamb, Cameron	R-R	6-3	211	5-29-89	0	0	3.95	19	0	0	1	27	27	17	12	0	10	20	.245	.282	.225	6.59	3.29
Long, Kenny	L-L	6-1	155	1-28-89	2	0	2.83	23	0	0	6	29	25	11	9	2	4	27	.231	.158	.271	8.48	1.26
Perez, Tyson	R-R	6-3	215	12-27-89	4	5	5.85	37	12	0	3	112	142	84	73	16	43	64	.309	.280	.325	5.13	3.45
Quevedo, Carlos	R-R	6-1	222	9-30-89	0	0	0.00	2	0	0	0	3	1	0	0	0	2	1	.091	.000	.143	5.40	0.00
Rodgers, Brady	R-R	6-2	187	9-17-90	10	8	5.38	27	18	0	1	112	135	71	67	14	23	104	.300	.276	.314	8.36	1.85
Rollins, David	L-L	6-1	195	12-21-89	8	5	3.98	23	14	0	3	97	81	50	43	9	32	96	.223	.228	.221	8.88	2.96
Sanchez, Gera	R-R	6-0	188	6-8-89	0	0	1.69	6	0	0	0	11	10	2	2	3	13	.244	.214	.259	10.97	2.53
Shirley, Tommy	R-L	6-5	220	11-11-88	1	4	3.35	27	9	0	1	75	66	31	28	6	24	64	.237	.213	.245	7.65	2.87
Smith, Kyle	R-R	6-0	170	9-10-92	1	1	7.33	5	5	1	0	23	26	19	19	4	9	21	.289	.222	.317	8.10	3.47
Velasquez, Vince	B-R	6-3	203	6-7-92	0	2	6.14	3	3	0	0	15	14	10	10	2	8	19	.259	.231	.286	11.66	4.91
Walters, Blair	L-L	6-0	200	11-8-89	6	2	7.36	34	5	0	0	73	101	71	60	14	40	69	.320	.275	.338	8.47	4.91
West, Aaron	R-R	6-1	195	6-1-90	10	8	5.22	26	21	0	0	109	134	71	63	7	17	112	.300	.324	.283	9.28	1.41

Fielding

Catcher	PCT	G	PO	A	E	DP	PB
Alvarez	.960	7	44	4	2	0	0
Cokinos	.984	14	118	7	2	0	0
Gingras	1.000	4	37	6	0	0	0
Heineman	.991	100	766	90	8	5	8
McCurdy	.980	24	182	19	4	0	0

First Base	PCT	G	PO	A	E	DP
Cokinos	.998	49	384	17	1	36
Duffy	1.000	5	35	1	0	5
Johnson	.993	15	128	11	1	11
Nash	.986	51	406	18	6	25
Perdomo	1.000	1	1	0	0	0
Torrez	.938	3	13	2	1	0
Valenzuela	1.000	4	22	5	0	1
Wierzbicki	.993	18	142	5	1	13

Second Base	PCT	G	PO	A	E	DP
Batista	.667	2	1	1	1	0
DeShields	.952	107	238	238	24	54
Perdomo	.946	21	35	35	4	9
Sclafani	.986	15	34	34	1	8
Torrez	1.000	7	11	11	0	3

Third Base	PCT	G	PO	A	E	DP
Duffy	.949	95	81	215	16	23
Johnson	1.000	1	1	0	0	0
Perdomo	.763	12	3	26	9	0
Sclafani	.934	28	17	54	5	4
Torrez	.960	12	9	15	1	2

Shortstop	PCT	G	PO	A	E	DP
Fontana	.951	95	116	256	19	39
Perdomo	.955	23	25	60	4	9
Sclafani	.929	23	33	59	7	9
Torrez	1.000	1	1	2	0	1

Outfield	PCT	G	PO	A	E	DP
Aplin	.997	125	294	7	1	1
Cokinos	1.000	5	5	0	0	0
Epps	.965	95	131	5	5	0
Gulbransen	.920	14	22	1	2	0
Meredith	.977	95	166	4	4	0
Muren	.969	12	28	3	1	0
Nash	1.000	2	3	1	0	0
Tucker	.991	70	104	7	1	2
Wierzbicki	1.000	8	8	1	0	0

QUAD CITIES RIVER BANDITS

LOW CLASS A

MIDWEST LEAGUE

Batting	B-T	HT	WT	DOB	AVG	vLH	vRH	G	AB	R	H	2B	3B	HR	RBI	BB	HBP	SH	SF	SO	SB	CS	SLG	OBP
Alvarez, Luis	R-R	5-11	230	2-28-90	.294	.313	.286	13	51	5	15	3	0	2	5	1	1	0	0	13	0	0	.471	.321
Blasik, Brian	R-R	5-11	185	3-15-90	.209	.278	.172	67	206	26	43	7	0	3	21	31	4	8	2	33	9	4	.286	.321
Borchering, Bobby	B-R	6-2	205	10-25-90	.203	.196	.207	48	172	17	35	7	1	5	22	21	4	0	0	61	1	0	.343	.305
Correa, Carlos	R-R	6-4	205	9-22-94	.320	.432	.283	117	450	73	144	33	3	9	86	58	8	1	2	83	10	10	.467	.405
Davidson, Chase	L-R	6-5	222	1-14-90	.238	.111	.273	10	42	5	10	3	0	1	5	2	1	0	0	21	1	2	.381	.289
Dineen, Ryan	L-R	6-2	205	3-2-91	.197	.111	.224	27	76	11	15	1	0	0	14	15	2	4	2	20	4	0	.211	.337
Elkins, Austin	B-R	5-11	190	12-21-90	.234	.174	.256	110	354	57	83	15	4	6	26	67	9	9	2	70	19	9	.350	.368
Gulbransen, Dan	L-R	5-11	205	1-5-91	.284	.050	.353	25	88	14	25	7	1	0	7	16	0	2	0	10	1	2	.386	.394
Hamblin, Miles	L-R	6-3	208	10-22-88	.202	.050	.232	35	119	10	24	3	0	1	14	22	0	1	4	39	2	3	.252	.317
Hernandez, Teoscar	R-R	6-2	180	10-15-92	.271	.248	.279	123	499	97	135	25	9	13	55	41	4	17	4	135	24	11	.435	.328
Joyce, Terrell	R-R	6-3	230	5-29-92	.186	.167	.195	72	226	27	42	13	0	3	26	26	5	0	0	80	5	3	.283	.284
Kemp, Tony	L-R	5-6	165	10-31-91	.255	.344	.212	27	98	21	25	1	1	1	9	19	2	1	0	18	4	2	.316	.387
Morales, Jobduan	B-R	5-10	215	6-7-91	.167	.189	.160	66	209	18	35	8	1	2	27	33	0	4	0	67	1	0	.244	.281
Ovando, Ariel	L-L	6-4	226	9-15-93	.172	.059	.200	49	169	12	29	5	0	1	13	18	0	1	1	57	3	0	.219	.250
Pena, Roberto	B-R	6-0	217	6-8-92	.249	.264	.244	86	325	43	81	19	0	5	32	22	1	4	2	52	2	0	.354	.297
Perdomo, Carlos	R-R	5-10	160	4-25-90	.294	.167	.364	5	17	6	5	0	0	0	0	4	0	2	0	3	0	0	.294	.429
Phillips, Brett	L-R	6-0	175	5-30-94	.231	.300	.207	12	39	4	9	2	0	0	3	3	0	2	0	10	1	1	.282	.286
Ruiz, Rio	L-R	6-2	215	5-22-94	.260	.273	.255	114	416	46	108	33	1	12	63	50	0	1	5	92	12	3	.430	.335
Sclafani, Joe	B-R	5-11	190	4-22-90	.241	.286	.227	19	58	13	14	3	0	0	9	17	3	2	1	7	3	2	.293	.430
Scott, Jordan	L-R	6-2	180	9-22-91	.255	.226	.264	125	392	58	100	12	7	0	34	53	0	8	2	78	25	8	.321	.342
Singleton, Jonathan	L-L	6-2	235	9-18-91	.286	1.000	.250	6	21	6	6	2	0	3	5	4	0	0	0	5	0	0	.810	.400
Sosa, Ruben	B-R	5-7	170	9-23-90	.300	.400	.233	16	50	10	15	0	1	0	6	10	0	0	0	14	10	4	.340	.417
Vasquez, Danry	L-R	6-3	177	1-8-94	.288	.361	.256	32	118	12	34	2	1	3	20	6	1	1	2	15	2	0	.398	.323
2-team total (97 West Michigan)					.284	—	—	129	493	59	140	18	6	9	60	37	2	9	8	71	11	8	.400	.331
Wierzbicki, Jesse	R-R	6-3	210	11-24-88	.264	.234	.273	87	330	45	87	21	2	6	54	39	12	0	4	59	9	4	.394	.358

Pitching

Pitching	B-T	HT	WT	DOB	W	L	ERA	G	GS	CG	SV	IP	H	R	ER	HR	BB	SO	AVG	vLH	vRH	K/9	BB/9
Appel, Mark	R-R	6-5	190	7-15-91	3	1	3.82	8	8	0	0	33	30	16	14	2	9	27	.236	.207	.261	7.36	2.45
Bircher, Joe	L-L	6-4	220	3-27-90	3	3	4.15	14	10	0	2	65	71	32	30	5	13	35	.278	.273	.280	4.85	1.80
Cain, Colton	L-L	6-3	256	2-5-91	5	5	4.12	23	14	0	0	87	94	44	40	3	33	66	.277	.187	.310	6.80	3.40
Christensen, Pat	R-R	6-3	205	12-27-90	1	1	1.29	9	0	0	1	14	13	3	2	0	3	22	.245	.235	.250	14.14	1.93
Cotton, Jamaine	R-R	6-1	202	9-27-90	2	5	4.77	26	5	0	2	72	81	51	38	9	27	50	.286	.260	.302	6.28	3.39
Devenski, Chris	R-R	6-3	195	11-13-90	4	3	4.36	8	0	0	0	43	60	22	21	3	9	32	.337	.290	.362	6.65	1.87
Dimock, Michael	R-R	6-2	194	10-26-89	5	0	3.09	10	0	0	0	12	7	4	4	1	2	15	.163	.222	.120	11.57	1.54
Fields, Josh	R-R	6-0	180	8-19-85	0	0	0.00	2	1	0	0	4	2	0	0	0	0	4	.143	.286	.000	9.00	0.00
Hader, Josh	L-L	6-3	160	4-7-94	2	0	3.22	5	5	0	0	22	14	8	8	0	12	16	.182	.158	.190	6.45	4.84
Hallock, Kyle	L-L	6-2	185	8-6-88	0	0	0.00	1	0	0	0	1	0	0	0	0	0	2	.000	.000	.000	18.00	0.00
Hauschild, Mike	R-R	6-3	210	1-22-90	6	1	2.92	20	12	0	0	83	79	32	27	1	16	59	.249	.240	.258	6.37	1.73
Holmes, Brian	L-L	6-4	210	1-30-91	5	3	2.49	15	10	0	0	61	52	21	17	4	19	62	.226	.294	.198	9.10	2.79
Jankowski, Jordan	R-R	6-2	200	5-17-89	3	1	2.61	26	12	0	5	90	79	27	26	9	17	83	.237	.218	.256	8.33	1.71
Lamb, Cameron	R-R	6-3	211	5-29-89	1	2	4.82	12	0	0	3	19	24	12	10	0	9	15	.316	.382	.262	7.23	4.34
Lambson, Mitchell	L-L	6-1	205	7-20-90	8	3	3.03	41	0	0	1	71	61	24	24	3	25	79	.231	.310	.202	9.97	3.15
Lo, Chia-Jen	R-R	5-11	190	4-7-86	0	0	0.00	3	0	0	1	3	1	0	0	1	2	.100	.167	.000	6.00	3.00
McCullers Jr., Lance	L-R	6-2	205	10-2-93	3	5	3.18	25	19	0	0	105	92	49	37	3	49	117	.239	.193	.276	10.06	4.21
Minaya, Juan	R-R	6-4	195	9-18-90	3	6	4.77	24	5	0	8	55	63	34	29	5	23	57	.285	.284	.286	9.38	3.79
Minor, Daniel	R-R	5-11	195	2-9-91	8	3	3.71	31	12	0	1	99	112	48	41	9	29	85	.282	.333	.238	7.70	2.63
Morton, Zach	R-R	6-1	180	7-12-90	0	1	1.45	8	1	0	1	19	18	3	3	0	3	6	.273	.333	.244	2.89	1.45
Neely, John	R-R	6-2	195	7-9-90	2	5	3.82	28	0	0	12	33	41	20	14	0	20	24	.306	.228	.364	6.55	5.45
Osborne, J.D.	R-L	6-5	205	11-13-90	0	0	0.00	1	0	0	0	2	1	0	0	0	0	2	.125	.000	.143	9.00	0.00
Perez, Jorge	R-R	6-0	175	7-30-93	0	0	67.50	1	0	0	0	1	5	5	5	1	1	1	.714	1.000	.667	13.50	13.50
Perez, Juri	R-R	5-11	203	8-8-90	0	2	4.44	11	0	0	0	24	21	12	12	0	15	17	.244	.222	.260	6.29	5.55
Rodriguez, Richard	R-R	6-4	205	3-4-90	0	1	7.33	14	0	0	0	23	29	19	19	4	10	18	.290	.279	.298	6.94	3.86
Sanchez, Gera	R-R	6-0	188	6-8-89	4	2	5.22	30	0	0	0	50	58	39	29	4	14	57	.301	.381	.239	10.26	2.52
Velasquez, Vince	B-R	6-3	203	6-7-92	9	4	3.19	25	16	0	3	110	90	43	39	7	33	123	.221	.230	.212	10.06	2.70
Walter, Andrew	R-R	6-4	200	10-18-90	1	0	0.00	6	0	0	3	13	6	0	0	0	2	10	.140	.154	.133	7.11	1.42

Fielding

Catcher	PCT	G	PO	A	E	DP	PB
Alvarez	.981	6	46	6	1	1	2
Morales	.990	52	379	30	4	0	2
Pena	.993	84	664	74	5	3	6

First Base	PCT	G	PO	A	E	DP
Borchering	.982	40	348	24	7	32
Hamblin	1.000	14	108	10	0	8
Joyce	1.000	1	8	1	0	0
Morales	1.000	10	80	6	0	7
Singleton	1.000	5	44	7	0	5
Wierzbicki	.991	71	582	49	6	49

Second Base	PCT	G	PO	A	E	DP
Blasik	.900	19	28	44	8	7
Elkins	.970	90	146	247	12	48
Kemp	.951	17	25	52	4	15
Pena	.750	1	2	1	1	0

	PCT	G	PO	A	E	DP
Perdomo	.947	3	9	9	1	1
Sclafani	.965	10	20	35	2	7
Sosa	1.000	4	6	10	0	1
Wierzbicki	.800	2	1	3	1	1

Third Base	PCT	G	PO	A	E	DP
Blasik	.750	10	2	16	6	0
Dineen	.854	19	8	27	6	1
Elkins	.778	2	2	5	2	0
Ruiz	.929	111	68	193	20	15

Shortstop	PCT	G	PO	A	E	DP
Blasik	.923	3	1	11	1	1
Correa	.973	115	202	334	15	66
Elkins	.965	13	16	39	2	4
Perdomo	1.000	2	4	11	0	2
Sclafani	.957	10	18	27	2	6

Outfield	PCT	G	PO	A	E	DP
Dineen	—	1	0	0	0	0
Gulbransen	1.000	22	41	1	0	0
Hernandez	.967	123	224	14	8	2
Joyce	.956	52	61	4	3	1
Kemp	.857	3	6	0	1	0
Ovando	.959	46	67	4	3	0
Phillips	1.000	12	27	0	0	0
Scott	.983	123	229	8	4	2
Sosa	1.000	13	25	1	0	1
Vasquez	1.000	32	52	2	0	1
Wierzbicki	1.000	10	15	2	0	1

TRI-CITY VALLEYCATS

SHORT-SEASON

NEW YORK-PENN LEAGUE

Batting	B-T	HT	WT	DOB	AVG	vLH	vRH	G	AB	R	H	2B	3B	HR	RBI	BB	HBP	SH	SF	SO	SB	CS	SLG	OBP
Alvarez, Luis	R-R	5-11	230	2-28-90	.303	.429	.269	12	33	4	10	3	0	1	2	4	1	1	0	3	1	0	.485	.395
Booth, Brett	R-R	5-11	215	10-12-90	.244	.357	.185	26	82	6	20	3	0	0	5	10	3	0	1	16	0	0	.384	.344
Carnahan, Jon	R-R	6-3	225	9-14-89	.000	.000	.000	3	2	0	0	0	0	0	0	0	0	0	0	1	0	0	.000	.000
Dineen, Ryan	L-R	6-2	205	3-2-91	.228	.239	.224	52	162	19	37	4	0	1	15	23	3	3	2	31	3	5	.272	.332
Fernandez, Jose	R-R	6-1	170	5-20-93	.174	.167	.176	7	23	1	4	0	0	0	1	3	0	0	0	6	1	0	.174	.269
Genoves, Ernesto	R-R	5-11	203	6-4-91	.196	.107	.228	37	107	14	21	5	0	2	8	11	4	1	1	25	0	0	.299	.275
Gregor, Conrad	L-R	6-3	220	2-27-92	.289	.282	.292	74	270	36	78	12	1	4	35	37	4	3	3	43	2	2	.385	.379
Gulbransen, Dan	L-R	5-11	205	1-5-91	.397	.444	.375	15	58	15	23	5	0	3	13	3	0	0	0	8	2	0	.638	.426
Kemmer, Jon	L-L	6-2	220	11-17-90	.221	.171	.234	65	199	29	44	7	1	4	16	17	7	1	1	41	1	2	.337	.304
Kemp, Tony	L-R	5-6	165	10-31-91	.282	.295	.276	48	177	25	50	7	2	1	13	21	1	1	4	29	17	9	.362	.355
Lindauer, Thomas	R-R	6-2	175	12-2-91	.073	.063	.080	22	41	6	3	1	0	1	2	1	0	2	0	11	0	0	.171	.095
Marte, Ydarqui	R-R	6-1	188	10-10-92	.200	—	.200	4	5	0	1	0	0	0	1	0	0	0	0	2	0	0	.200	.200
Martinez, Mike	R-R	6-2	215	12-5-89	.225	.250	.216	59	213	22	48	7	0	11	35	16	5	4	3	55	0	0	.413	.291
Mayfield, Jack	R-R	5-11	182	9-30-90	.220	.348	.176	26	91	13	20	3	0	1	7	4	4	1	1	18	1	1	.286	.258
Mejia, Yonathan	B-R	6-2	175	9-19-92	.182	.000	.200	3	11	0	2	1	0	0	0	0	0	0	0	3	0	0	.273	.182
Mitchell, Ronnie	L-L	5-11	200	6-21-90	.256	.256	.256	59	203	22	52	11	2	2	30	18	1	0	2	31	6	4	.360	.317
Moon, Chan	L-R	6-0	160	3-23-91	.263	.184	.292	65	179	21	47	5	4	0	14	16	2	5	2	38	12	1	.335	.327
Nelubowich, Adam	L-R	6-2	195	4-28-91	.185	.067	.212	41	81	7	15	2	0	0	7	5	2	2	2	18	1	0	.210	.244
Ramsay, James	L-L	5-11	180	3-2-92	.258	.281	.250	69	252	40	65	5	4	4	22	29	5	7	0	32	7	5	.357	.346
Rodriguez, Jake	R-R	5-9	185	1-24-92	.209	.189	.224	32	86	6	18	4	0	1	10	10	4	0	0	31	0	1	.291	.320
Toney, D'Andre	R-R	5-8	170	1-24-92	.219	.180	.244	47	128	19	28	7	2	2	12	10	4	3	3	13	13	2	.352	.290
White, Tyler	R-R	5-11	225	10-29-90	.286	.217	.303	28	112	19	32	2	0	3	25	13	1	0	1	9	1	0	.384	.362

Pitching	B-T	HT	WT	DOB	W	L	ERA	G	GS	CG	SV	IP	H	R	ER	HR	BB	SO	AVG	vLH	vRH	K/9	BB/9
Appel, Mark	R-R	6-5	190	7-15-91	0	0	3.60	2	2	0	0	5	6	2	2	0	0	6	.300	.222	.364	10.80	0.00
Basford, Charles	R-R	6-2	210	7-16-90	3	0	2.73	19	0	0	0	26	25	10	8	1	13	26	.255	.353	.203	8.89	4.44
2-team total (1 Staten Island)					3	0	2.86	20	0	0	0	28	29	11	9	2	13	27	—	—	—	8.58	4.13
Brunnemann, Tyler	R-R	6-2	225	8-9-91	0	1	0.90	9	0	0	2	10	4	1	1	1	1	11	.125	.231	.053	9.90	0.90
Bushue, Tanner	R-R	6-4	180	6-20-91	3	4	5.14	13	7	0	0	49	40	29	28	7	13	40	.223	.296	.176	7.35	2.39
Christensen, Pat	R-R	6-3	205	12-27-90	1	1	3.86	14	0	0	2	14	12	6	6	2	0	16	.231	.167	.265	10.29	0.00
Comer, Kevin	R-R	6-3	205	8-1-92	2	5	4.93	15	7	0	1	46	50	28	25	2	18	44	.273	.284	.265	8.67	3.55
Cotton, Chris	R-L	5-10	166	11-21-90	3	3	1.74	8	6	0	0	31	32	11	6	1	2	21	.264	.318	.234	6.10	0.58
Dando, Zach	R-R	6-3	175	1-4-91	1	0	0.00	5	0	0	0	10	9	0	0	0	3	2	.257	.357	.190	1.80	2.70
Fant, Randall	L-L	6-4	180	1-28-91	1	3	3.65	13	6	0	1	44	51	20	18	1	10	31	.287	.298	.282	6.29	2.03
Feliz, Michael	R-R	6-4	210	9-28-93	4	2	1.96	14	10	0	1	69	53	19	15	2	13	78	.209	.226	.194	10.17	1.70
Frias, Edison	R-R	6-1	178	12-18-90	1	0	4.09	3	2	0	0	11	12	5	5	0	2	7	.279	.250	.333	5.73	1.64
Garcia, Christian	R-R	6-2	175	9-24-91	0	0	0.00	2	0	0	0	2	2	0	0	0	2	2	.250	.250	.250	9.00	9.00
Gonzalez, Edgar	R-R	6-2	210	2-23-83	0	0	0.00	1	1	0	0	1	0	0	0	0	0	1	.000	.000	.000	9.00	0.00
Grills, Evan	L-L	6-4	205	6-13-92	7	1	3.34	19	0	0	0	62	66	28	23	4	12	54	.265	.237	.277	7.84	1.74
Hess, Justin	R-R	6-2	205	8-16-90	0	0	13.50	2	0	0	0	1	4	2	2	1	2	1	.500	.000	.500	6.75	13.50
Holley, Krishawn	R-R	6-0	195	2-8-92	1	0	4.00	5	0	0	0	9	8	4	4	2	4	8	.229	.125	.316	8.00	4.00
Houser, Adrian	R-R	6-4	205	2-2-93	0	4	3.42	14	9	0	0	50	57	25	19	1	10	39	.291	.345	.250	7.02	1.80
Lo, Chia-Jen	R-R	5-11	190	4-7-86	0	0	4.50	6	0	0	4	6	5	3	3	1	1	12	.217	.167	.273	18.00	1.50
Minnis, Albert	R-L	6-0	190	11-5-91	2	1	2.57	14	0	0	0	14	12	4	4	1	4	9	.231	.227	.233	5.79	2.57
Morton, Zach	R-R	6-1	180	7-12-90	2	1	1.93	9	4	0	0	33	17	13	7	0	7	16	.152	.244	.099	4.41	1.93
Munnelly, Chris	R-R	6-2	200	2-16-91	0	0	2.08	3	0	0	0	4	5	1	1	0	2	6	.294	.222	.375	12.46	4.15
Osborne, J.D.	R-L	6-5	205	11-13-90	1	0	4.26	12	0	0	2	13	12	6	6	1	11	18	.245	.125	.303	12.79	7.82
Rodriguez, Richard	R-R	6-4	205	3-4-90	4	0	1.29	16	0	0	1	21	17	4	3	2	3	23	.227	.286	.175	9.86	1.29
Sanudo, Gonzalo	L-R	6-3	235	1-10-92	0	0	0.00	9	0	0	8	13	3	0	0	0	1	20	.070	.133	.036	13.85	0.69
Scribner, Troy	R-R	6-3	190	7-2-91	1	2	5.12	6	1	0	0	19	17	12	11	2	7	30	.233	.250	.216	13.97	3.26
Thurman, Andrew	R-R	6-3	200	12-10-91	4	2	3.86	12	5	0	1	40	43	17	17	5	11	43	.277	.225	.321	9.76	2.50
Walter, Andrew	R-R	6-4	200	10-18-90	1	0	2.49	14	0	0	2	25	16	8	7	2	3	26	.184	.207	.172	9.24	1.07
Westwood, Kyle	R-R	6-3	190	4-13-91	2	2	0.81	11	8	0	0	45	28	9	4	3	6	29	.173	.231	.134	5.84	1.21

Fielding

Catcher	PCT	G	PO	A	E	DP	PB
Alvarez	.971	11	57	9	2	0	1
Booth	.989	18	166	17	2	1	1
Carnahan	1.000	3	8	0	0	0	0
Genoves	.987	28	199	21	3	1	0
Rodriguez	.986	30	198	18	3	3	2

First Base	PCT	G	PO	A	E	DP
Gregor	.995	65	508	43	3	40
Martinez	.983	12	115	2	2	8
White	1.000	8	51	2	0	4

Second Base	PCT	G	PO	A	E	DP
Dineen	.968	14	24	36	2	6
Kemp	.985	47	78	124	3	18
Lindauer	1.000	2	2	8	0	0

Mayfield	.972	21	45	59	3	14
Moon	—	1	0	0	0	0

Third Base	PCT	G	PO	A	E	DP
Dineen	.942	38	16	82	6	0
Lindauer	1.000	1	0	1	0	0
Moon	1.000	1	0	4	0	0
Nelubowich	.818	20	8	19	6	1
White	.930	26	15	38	4	4

Shortstop	PCT	G	PO	A	E	DP
Fernandez	.939	7	9	22	2	3
Lindauer	.980	17	15	34	1	6
Mayfield	.893	8	8	17	3	2
Moon	.941	60	72	168	15	27
Nelubowich	—	1	0	0	0	0

Outfield	PCT	G	PO	A	E	DP
Gregor	1.000	11	17	0	0	0
Gulbransen	1.000	11	17	0	0	0
Kemmer	1.000	63	85	5	0	0
Kemp	1.000	3	4	0	0	0
Marte	1.000	2	1	0	0	0
Mitchell	.987	52	70	6	1	0
Nelubowich	1.000	1	1	0	0	0
Ramsay	1.000	68	131	3	0	0
Toney	.938	44	59	2	4	1

GREENEVILLE ASTROS — ROOKIE

APPALACHIAN LEAGUE

Batting	B-T	HT	WT	DOB	AVG	vLH	vRH	G	AB	R	H	2B	3B	HR	RBI	BB	HBP	SH	SF	SO	SB	CS	SLG	OBP
Borchering, Bobby	B-R	6-2	205	10-25-90	.259	.231	.267	17	58	7	15	4	0	2	4	10	0	0	0	15	0	1	.431	.368
Gingras, Ricky	L-R	6-2	205	10-18-90	.275	.250	.279	16	51	10	14	1	0	3	12	9	0	0	0	12	0	0	.471	.383
Gomez, Edwin	B-R	6-3	175	8-26-91	.208	.214	.207	34	120	19	25	5	5	1	11	11	4	3	0	41	0	1	.292	.326
Gonzalez, Alfredo	R-R	6-1	190	7-13-92	.240	.194	.260	33	104	19	25	4	1	2	10	14	2	0	0	24	5	1	.356	.342
Gonzalez, Wallace	R-R	6-5	240	2-11-93	.172	.043	.214	30	93	8	16	7	0	1	7	8	2	0	0	46	0	2	.280	.252
Hipp, Parker	L-R	6-2	200	3-1-91	.159	.231	.140	24	63	3	10	2	0	0	7	11	0	0	1	13	3	1	.190	.280
Holberton, Brian	L-R	5-10	190	6-10-91	.225	.083	.260	37	120	20	27	6	0	5	16	26	4	0	0	21	2	1	.400	.380
Ibanez, Angel	L-R	6-2	220	9-10-90	.239	.148	.267	33	113	14	27	6	0	0	12	10	1	2	2	31	0	0	.292	.302
Lindauer, Thomas	R-R	6-2	175	12-2-91	.247	.208	.260	29	97	16	24	7	0	0	10	7	2	2	2	28	0	2	.320	.306
Mathis, Tanner	L-L	5-11	180	6-27-91	.277	.304	.268	60	188	30	52	3	0	1	14	44	6	7	2	14	7	6	.309	.425
Mayfield, Jack	R-R	5-11	182	9-30-90	.255	.360	.217	29	94	12	24	5	0	3	11	9	3	4	1	19	2	2	.404	.336
McDonald, Chase	R-R	6-4	260	6-2-92	.245	.323	.226	46	155	20	38	6	1	6	33	19	4	0	1	38	0	1	.413	.341
Moronta, Cristian	R-R	5-10	185	12-5-89	.229	.000	.267	11	35	4	8	1	1	0	2	2	1	2	0	9	2	1	.314	.289
Ovando, Ariel	L-L	6-4	200	8-19-93	.216	.189	.224	51	171	25	37	8	0	4	21	23	1	0	2	46	0	1	.333	.310
Phillips, Brett	L-R	6-0	175	5-30-94	.247	.240	.250	29	85	9	21	7	1	0	9	17	1	8	2	21	4	3	.353	.371
Reynoso, Luis	R-R	6-1	170	9-2-94	.250	—	.250	1	4	0	1	0	0	0	0	0	0	0	0	1	0	0	.250	.250
Rivera, Darwin	R-R	5-11	180	10-27-91	.211	.154	.230	40	152	14	32	8	0	2	15	12	2	0	1	34	0	1	.303	.275
Santana, Juan	R-R	6-1	176	8-16-94	.234	.294	.215	60	214	26	50	8	0	3	30	18	1	12	3	37	3	0	.313	.292
Solano, Jose	R-R	6-2	175	3-15-92	.091	.125	.071	7	22	1	2	0	0	0	1	1	1	0	0	7	0	0	.091	.167
White, Tyler	R-R	5-11	225	10-29-90	.344	.364	.340	18	64	10	22	3	0	2	12	7	1	0	1	8	2	0	.484	.411
Wik, Marc	L-R	5-11	195	7-18-92	.266	.182	.292	48	139	22	37	4	2	0	9	40	1	3	0	26	1	4	.324	.433

Pitching	B-T	HT	WT	DOB	W	L	ERA	G	GS	CG	SV	IP	H	R	ER	HR	BB	SO	AVG	vLH	vRH	K/9	BB/9
Abreu, Alan	R-R	6-3	185	6-14-90	0	0	4.50	1	0	0	0	2	2	2	1	1	0	3	.222	.500	.143	13.50	0.00
Brunnemann, Tyler	R-R	6-2	225	8-9-91	2	0	4.66	14	0	0	1	19	18	10	10	0	5	28	.257	.273	.250	13.03	2.33
Chrismon, Austin	R-R	6-2	227	9-16-92	3	1	3.06	11	2	0	1	32	25	13	11	3	8	24	.205	.097	.242	6.68	2.23
Connolly, Ryan	R-R	6-0	180	11-10-90	1	2	5.22	20	0	0	0	29	37	23	17	0	12	20	.303	.289	.310	6.14	3.68
Ferguson, Kevin	L-L	6-0	180	7-4-91	0	1	12.54	6	0	0	0	9	14	13	13	2	6	6	.350	.231	.407	5.79	5.79
Franco, Enderson	R-R	6-2	170	12-29-92	2	5	5.05	12	12	0	0	52	58	35	29	4	18	41	.275	.256	.287	7.14	3.14
Frias, Edison	R-R	6-1	178	12-18-90	3	3	3.09	9	8	0	0	47	49	21	16	2	7	37	.272	.310	.248	7.14	1.35
Garcia, Christian	R-R	6-2	175	9-24-91	2	1	5.85	16	0	0	0	32	32	22	21	2	16	31	.254	.227	.268	8.63	4.45
Gustave, Jandel	R-R	6-2	160	10-12-92	2	3	2.68	10	10	0	0	44	38	23	13	2	23	49	.235	.310	.192	10.10	4.74
Holley, Krishawn	R-R	6-0	195	2-8-92	3	2	2.41	18	0	0	1	34	32	13	9	0	12	33	.244	.275	.231	8.82	3.21
Kessay, Sebastian	L-L	6-2	215	6-19-93	1	0	3.12	13	3	0	0	17	16	7	6	3	9	20	.242	.462	.189	10.38	4.67
Lee, Chris	L-L	6-3	175	8-17-92	2	2	3.10	11	10	0	0	49	37	20	17	3	17	54	.207	.171	.215	9.85	3.10
Mills, Jordan	L-L	6-5	200	5-11-92	5	1	2.08	14	6	0	2	48	36	14	11	2	13	43	.216	.233	.212	8.12	2.45
Montero, Jose	R-R	6-4	190	1-22-93	0	0	2.84	3	1	0	0	6	3	2	2	0	4	10	.143	.250	.118	14.21	5.68
Munnelly, Chris	R-R	6-2	200	2-16-91	2	1	0.53	10	0	0	0	17	4	2	1	1	7	24	.070	.083	.061	12.71	3.71
Ordosgoitti, Luis	R-R	6-4	180	9-22-92	1	0	0.90	2	2	0	0	10	9	3	1	0	4	6	.237	.333	.150	5.40	3.60
Osborne, J.D.	R-L	6-5	205	11-13-90	0	0	0.00	8	0	0	0	14	10	0	0	0	6	22	.196	.500	.156	14.14	3.86
Ramirez, Francis	R-R	6-5	205	1-12-92	0	1	8.22	2	2	0	0	8	11	8	7	1	4	10	.355	.182	.450	11.74	4.70
Ramirez, Gerardo	R-R	6-2	165	1-17-94	1	0	4.26	12	0	0	0	19	22	9	9	1	5	24	.289	.214	.333	11.37	2.37
Rivera, Raul	R-R	6-3	185	2-5-91	4	3	2.14	12	0	0	0	21	18	10	5	2	1	21	.222	.206	.234	9.00	0.43
Sanudo, Gonzalo	L-R	6-3	235	1-10-92	1	2	1.29	18	0	0	11	21	11	3	3	1	1	30	.153	.130	.163	12.86	0.43
Scribner, Troy	R-R	6-3	190	7-2-91	0	0	0.00	2	1	0	0	5	4	0	0	0	4	6	.222	.125	.300	10.80	7.20
Tiburcio, Frederick	R-R	6-3	192	11-1-90	3	2	2.43	12	11	0	0	56	42	18	15	2	19	51	.213	.190	.223	8.25	3.07

Fielding

Catcher	PCT	G	PO	A	E	DP	PB
Gingras	.982	8	50	6	1	0	1
Gonzalez	.989	30	245	21	3	2	6
Holberton	.991	25	199	22	2	2	6
Moronta	.981	10	91	13	2	1	0

First Base	PCT	G	PO	A	E	DP
Borchering	.983	13	111	2	2	6
Gomez	1.000	3	23	0	0	1
Ibanez	.963	14	99	5	4	5
McDonald	.991	38	308	15	3	29
White	1.000	5	45	1	0	3

Second Base	PCT	G	PO	A	E	DP
Hipp	.931	15	19	35	4	6
Mayfield	1.000	4	5	17	0	1
Rivera	.941	6	12	20	2	4
Santana	.977	45	98	119	5	27
Wik	1.000	1	1	3	0	0

Third Base	PCT	G	PO	A	E	DP
Hipp	.917	9	6	16	2	3
Ibanez	.903	15	6	22	3	1
Rivera	.808	32	12	47	14	2
Solano	.889	7	5	11	2	0
White	.935	11	10	19	2	1

Shortstop	PCT	G	PO	A	E	DP
Lindauer	.947	29	44	99	8	16
Mayfield	.968	25	27	64	3	10
Reynoso	1.000	1	0	3	0	0
Santana	.925	16	23	51	6	5

Outfield	PCT	G	PO	A	E	DP
Borchering	.800	3	4	0	1	0
Gomez	1.000	15	20	2	0	1
Gonzalez	.911	27	39	2	4	1
Mathis	.962	56	74	1	3	0
Ovando	.985	45	62	3	1	0
Phillips	1.000	28	61	2	0	0
Wik	1.000	44	54	3	0	2

GCL ASTROS

ROOKIE

GULF COAST LEAGUE

Batting	B-T	HT	WT	DOB	AVG	vLH	vRH	G	AB	R	H	2B	3B	HR	RBI	BB	HBP	SH	SF	SO	SB	CS	SLG	OBP
Batista, Jean	B-R	6-2	180	11-15-91	.280	.273	.282	24	93	17	26	3	6	3	15	1	1	0	0	16	1	0	.538	.295
Booth, Brett	R-R	5-11	215	10-12-90	.308	.316	.303	16	52	6	16	3	1	1	11	8	4	0	1	11	1	0	.462	.431
Clements, Brett	B-R	5-9	185	9-23-90	.222	.333	.167	19	45	5	10	1	0	0	2	5	3	0	0	16	1	0	.244	.340
Coa, Pedro	R-R	6-2	190	12-21-92	.133	.111	.143	26	60	4	8	2	0	0	5	3	1	1	0	12	0	0	.167	.232
Crowe, Trevor	B-R	5-10	190	11-17-83	.250	.000	.333	2	4	0	1	0	0	0	0	0	0	0	0	0	0	1	.250	.250
De La Rosa, Luis	R-R	6-1	162	1-2-92	.134	.167	.125	28	82	8	11	2	1	1	8	3	8	1	0	28	3	2	.220	.237
Estrella, Jean	L-R	5-11	170	4-16-96	.107	.000	.150	8	28	1	3	0	0	0	3	0	0	0	0	9	1	1	.107	.194
Fernandez, Jose	R-R	6-1	170	5-20-93	.258	.400	.216	16	66	10	17	4	2	1	7	5	0	0	0	17	3	2	.424	.310
Gonzalez, Alex	R-R	5-11	165	7-7-91	.233	.200	.245	41	146	22	34	6	0	1	8	10	3	2	0	22	8	6	.295	.296
Laguna, Mesac	R-R	6-2	185	1-12-92	.214	.357	.143	27	84	7	18	7	1	1	14	4	1	0	1	25	1	0	.393	.256
Marte, Ydarqui	R-R	6-1	188	10-10-92	.247	.270	.239	49	146	17	36	9	0	2	15	14	2	5	2	30	3	1	.349	.317
Martin, Jason	L-R	5-10	175	9-5-95	.251	.184	.277	50	179	35	45	8	4	0	17	29	1	4	1	31	11	7	.341	.357
Mejia, Yonathan	R-R	6-2	175	9-19-92	.324	.361	.311	59	222	27	72	19	0	2	32	12	1	1	4	28	6	2	.437	.356
Nottingham, Jacob	R-R	6-3	200	4-3-95	.247	.371	.207	44	146	23	36	10	2	1	20	21	3	0	3	38	4	2	.363	.347
Reynolds, Javaris	L-L	6-1	190	1-24-93	.197	.184	.202	49	152	22	30	0	2	1	15	14	5	7	0	53	9	5	.243	.287
Reynoso, Luis	R-R	6-1	170	9-2-94	.233	.140	.272	43	146	20	34	3	3	1	18	18	3	1	3	35	6	6	.315	.324
Roa, Hector	R-R	6-0	195	3-1-95	.143	.125	.154	6	21	2	3	0	1	0	2	3	0	0	0	8	0	0	.238	.250
Silfa, Yoel	R-R	5-11	160	7-8-93	.212	.143	.244	24	66	6	14	0	0	1	5	2	1	0	1	12	2	1	.258	.243
Solano, Jose	R-R	6-2	175	3-15-92	.300	.250	.320	41	140	27	42	9	1	6	28	11	0	0	1	30	9	3	.507	.349
White, Tyler	R-R	5-11	225	10-29-90	.365	.412	.348	18	63	11	23	9	0	1	15	7	7	0	1	7	0	2	.556	.474
Wikoff, Brandon	L-R	5-8	175	4-5-88	.143	.000	.200	7	7	0	1	0	0	0	0	0	0	0	0	3	0	0	.143	.400

Pitching	B-T	HT	WT	DOB	W	L	ERA	G	GS	CG	SV	IP	H	R	ER	HR	BB	SO	AVG	vLH	vRH	K/9	BB/9
Barrios, Agapito	R-R	6-2	167	11-30-93	3	7	3.44	12	12	0	0	52	55	25	20	2	20	38	.262	.243	.271	6.54	3.44
Bircher, Joe	L-L	6-4	220	3-27-90	1	0	2.08	4	4	0	0	13	15	6	3	0	3	16	.300	.267	.314	11.08	2.08
Corniel, Robert	R-R	6-3	190	6-23-95	0	0	9.00	2	0	0	0	2	1	2	2	0	4	2	.143	.250	.000	9.00	18.00
Culbreth, Brandon	R-R	6-4	200	7-27-92	1	0	2.89	4	1	0	1	9	10	4	3	0	5	18	.250	.300	.235	14.46	3.86
Dando, Zach	R-R	6-3	175	1-4-91	1	1	3.75	15	1	0	0	24	23	12	10	0	15	18	.250	.235	.259	6.75	5.63
De Leon, Ambiorix	L-L	6-3	185	8-7-91	1	0	2.82	5	3	0	0	22	19	9	7	1	8	18	.229	.290	.192	7.25	3.22
De Los Santos, Samil	R-R	6-4	175	1-8-94	3	2	7.86	14	2	0	0	26	34	25	23	1	7	28	.312	.300	.316	9.57	2.39

Name	B-T	HT	WT	DOB	W	L	ERA	G	GS	CG	SV	IP	H	R	ER	HR	BB	SO	AVG	vLH	vRH	K/9	BB/9
Emanuel, Kent	L-L	6-3	190	6-4-92	0	0	0.00	4	4	0	0	9	6	0	0	0	2	8	.188	.091	.238	8.00	2.00
Ferguson, Kevin	L-L	6-0	180	7-4-91	2	0	0.82	9	0	0	0	11	7	1	1	0	2	9	.184	.133	.217	7.36	1.64
German, Devonte	R-R	6-5	240	10-14-94	0	1	14.46	7	0	0	0	9	17	15	15	0	11	9	.405	.391	.421	8.68	10.61
Gonzalez, Erick	R-R	6-1	175	1-10-92	3	5	4.00	20	0	0	4	27	29	23	12	2	13	19	.248	.208	.275	6.33	4.33
Guduan, Reymin	L-L	6-4	185	3-16-92	0	1	4.35	10	2	0	0	21	19	16	10	3	10	28	.235	.192	.255	12.19	4.35
Heidenreich, Matt	L-R	6-5	185	1-17-91	0	0	5.73	6	1	0	0	11	12	9	7	0	2	7	.267	.154	.313	5.73	1.64
Hess, Justin	R-R	6-2	205	8-16-90	1	0	1.04	5	0	0	0	9	6	1	1	0	1	13	.194	.300	.143	13.50	1.04
Holmes, Brian	L-L	6-4	210	1-30-91	0	0	0.00	3	3	0	0	10	3	0	0	0	2	17	.088	.083	.091	14.81	1.74
Juarez, Gerardo	R-R	6-2	175	9-10-92	0	0	1.42	2	1	0	0	6	4	1	1	0	3	8	.174	.000	.222	11.37	4.26
Lozano, Javier	R-R	6-2	190	4-24-93	2	1	5.00	13	1	0	0	18	18	18	10	1	15	15	.254	.258	.250	7.50	7.50
Montero, Jose	R-R	6-4	190	1-22-93	2	2	4.45	11	5	0	0	32	38	18	16	2	15	28	.306	.304	.308	7.79	4.18
Munnelly, Chris	R-R	6-2	200	2-16-91	0	1	2.35	7	0	0	2	8	8	2	2	0	3	7	.258	.091	.350	8.22	3.52
Musgrove, Joe	R-R	6-5	230	12-4-92	1	3	4.41	11	3	0	0	33	43	22	16	1	4	30	.303	.299	.307	8.27	1.10
Nicely, Austin	B-L	6-1	170	12-13-94	0	2	4.91	6	4	0	0	18	17	12	10	1	9	7	.243	.250	.240	3.44	4.42
Ordosgoitti, Luis	R-R	6-4	180	9-22-92	0	0	1.15	4	4	0	0	6	6	3	2	0	6	14	.122	.043	.192	8.04	3.45
Perez, Jorge	R-R	6-0	175	7-30-93	1	1	5.81	17	0	0	0	26	24	19	17	1	18	20	.240	.261	.222	6.84	6.15
Quezada, Euris	R-R	6-6	210	4-6-89	0	0	0.00	1	0	0	0	0	0	0	0	0	0	0	.000	—	.000	0.00	0.00
Ramirez, Francis	R-R	6-5	205	1-12-92	0	1	4.94	9	7	0	0	31	28	19	17	1	17	30	.241	.271	.221	8.71	4.94
Rivera, Raul	R-R	6-3	185	2-5-91	0	0	3.09	9	0	0	0	12	13	7	4	1	4	9	.283	.167	.357	6.94	3.09
Santos, Juan	R-R	6-4	240	8-30-95	2	3	3.96	18	0	0	0	25	16	14	11	2	17	18	.186	.200	.179	6.48	6.12
Scribner, Troy	R-R	6-3	190	7-2-91	3	2	1.26	8	2	0	0	29	16	6	4	1	3	42	.158	.133	.179	13.19	0.94

Fielding

Catcher	PCT	G	PO	A	E	DP	PB
Booth	.988	8	72	9	1	0	1
Clements	.989	15	78	12	1	2	5
Coa	.979	18	76	17	2	1	1
Nottingham	1.000	30	244	14	0	0	12

First Base	PCT	G	PO	A	E	DP
Laguna	.986	11	69	4	1	6
Mejia	.977	53	416	18	10	45
White	1.000	1	7	0	0	1

Second Base	PCT	G	PO	A	E	DP
Estrella	.871	8	11	16	4	4
Fernandez	1.000	1	2	1	0	0
Gonzalez	.964	20	37	43	3	12

	PCT	G	PO	A	E	DP
Reynoso	.895	7	9	25	4	4
Silfa	.895	6	7	10	2	0
Solano	.920	21	42	50	8	14
Wikoff	.714	3	2	3	2	1

Third Base	PCT	G	PO	A	E	DP
Gonzalez	.934	21	9	48	4	5
Mejia	1.000	3	1	3	0	0
Reynoso	.889	2	1	7	1	0
Silfa	.700	4	0	7	3	0
Solano	.907	19	13	36	5	1
White	.909	16	9	31	4	5

Shortstop	PCT	G	PO	A	E	DP
Fernandez	.923	15	20	52	6	15
Gonzalez	—	1	0	0	0	0
Reynoso	.935	34	47	97	10	15
Silfa	.964	14	17	37	2	9

Outfield	PCT	G	PO	A	E	DP
Batista	1.000	7	9	0	0	0
De La Rosa	.946	24	33	2	2	0
Laguna	1.000	17	22	1	0	0
Marte	.980	49	95	3	2	1
Martin	.988	49	79	3	1	1
Reynolds	1.000	49	84	2	0	0
Roa	1.000	3	5	0	0	0

DSL ASTROS   ROOKIE

DOMINICAN SUMMER LEAGUE

Batting	B-T	HT	WT	DOB	AVG	vLH	vRH	G	AB	R	H	2B	3B	HR	RBI	BB	HBP	SH	SF	SO	SB	CS	SLG	OBP
Aquino, Dariel	R-R	6-1	188	1-30-96	.158	.136	.171	22	57	6	9	0	0	0	2	6	2	2	0	23	1	2	.158	.262
Avea, Marlon	R-R	6-1	195	8-31-93	.225	.339	.151	52	142	14	32	8	0	2	14	14	14	9	0	18	1	2	.324	.353
Bermejo, Jesus	R-R	6-1	180	4-8-94	.213	.176	.227	20	61	6	13	1	0	1	9	5	1	1	1	18	0	0	.279	.279
Cesar, Randy	R-R	6-1	180	1-11-95	.235	.205	.250	63	221	29	52	9	1	1	19	29	3	0	1	47	2	4	.299	.331
Cortorreal, Jean Carlos	R-R		170	7-17-94	.204	.143	.229	26	49	4	10	1	0	0	7	10	0	3	1	15	0	1	.224	.333
Estrella, Jean	L-R	5-11	184	4-16-96	.306	.386	.265	50	170	24	52	6	0	0	13	17	4	6	1	22	6	11	.341	.380
Mejia, Brauly	R-R	6-0	185	10-28-94	.240	.200	.264	46	146	14	35	8	1	1	8	10	4	3	1	27	1	0	.329	.304
Melendez, Alexander	R-R	6-1	185	4-21-95	.248	.300	.225	36	129	16	32	8	0	0	12	11	2	3	1	19	5	5	.310	.315
Michelena, Arturo	R-R	5-11	165	10-15-94	.226	.227	.225	67	257	24	58	11	4	0	28	20	2	7	3	37	3	4	.300	.284
Payano, Luis	R-R	6-1	175	5-12-96	.226	.202	.237	69	270	44	61	13	3	3	32	35	4	5	3	64	10	8	.330	.321
Pena, Brian	R-R	6-1	185	6-14-94	.252	.156	.296	31	103	12	26	3	0	1	7	14	2	1	0	18	0	2	.311	.353
Reynoso, Jarico	R-R	5-10	170	1-14-93	.204	.246	.187	65	196	23	40	2	3	1	18	16	6	8	0	47	12	4	.260	.284
Roa, Hector	R-R	6-0	195	3-1-95	.250	.258	.247	56	220	28	55	11	3	7	22	9	3	1	0	54	4	4	.423	.289
Tavarez, Victor	R-R	6-1	193	2-7-95	.195	.115	.232	27	82	6	16	2	0	2	7	8	0	1	0	16	0	1	.293	.267
Toribio, Oliver	R-R	5-10	180	6-7-96	.333	.500	.000	2	3	2	1	0	0	1	0	0	1	0	0	2	0	0	1.000	.500
Trompiz, Kristian	R-R	6-1	170	12-2-95	.202	.169	.215	60	208	18	42	7	4	1	18	25	2	9	2	33	7	9	.288	.291

Pitching	B-T	HT	WT	DOB	W	L	ERA	G	GS	CG	SV	IP	H	R	ER	HR	BB	SO	AVG	vLH	vRH	K/9	BB/9
Acosta, Yhoan	L-L	6-1	172	6-17-95	1	0	3.38	4	0	0	0	5	3	2	2	1	3	4	.158	.500	.118	6.75	5.06
Arauz, Harold	R-R	6-2	185	5-29-95	5	0	1.91	16	12	0	2	66	47	23	14	1	12	43	.195	.179	.204	5.86	1.64
Chevalier, Rayderson	R-R	6-1	165	1-31-95	4	2	2.28	13	5	0	1	43	31	15	11	2	17	33	.203	.200	.204	6.85	3.53
Corniel, Robert	R-R	6-3	190	6-23-95	0	0	3.00	8	0	0	0	6	6	4	2	0	5	7	.273	.400	.235	10.50	7.50
Delis, Juan	R-R	6-1	195	5-29-94	3	3	3.38	13	0	0	0	19	10	11	7	0	18	19	.154	.111	.170	9.16	8.68
Franzua, Geronimo	L-L	6-1	170	9-25-93	1	3	4.42	14	9	0	0	39	30	23	19	0	31	39	.229	.200	.234	9.08	7.22
Garcia, Junior	L-L	6-1	180	10-1-95	2	2	2.67	14	1	0	1	34	24	14	10	1	12	30	.205	.115	.231	8.02	3.21
Hernandez, Elieser	R-R	6-1	170	5-3-95	5	1	1.26	13	12	0	0	57	36	11	8	1	21	46	.184	.156	.197	7.22	3.30
Hernandez, Juan	R-R	6-3	170	1-24-93	1	0	2.37	14	7	0	0	38	26	14	10	0	22	34	.194	.170	.210	8.05	5.21
Juarez, Gerardo	R-R	6-2	175	9-10-92	2	3	1.86	13	5	0	0	53	40	16	11	0	7	50	.212	.162	.240	8.44	1.18
Lozano, Javier	R-R	6-2	190	4-24-93	0	0	0.00	2	1	0	0	6	5	0	0	0	1	8	.208	.250	.167	12.00	1.50
Mesa, Victor	R-R	6-2	170	11-26-93	1	2	4.60	18	0	0	4	31	37	19	16	3	13	27	.303	.300	.305	7.76	3.73
Pinales, Erasmo	R-R	5-11	180	11-25-94	0	0	13.50	1	0	0	0	1	1	1	1	0	2	0	.500	1.000	.000	0.00	27.00
Pinales, Joselo	R-R	6-1	180	11-16-94	2	0	2.14	11	1	0	1	34	18	11	8	0	11	34	.153	.109	.181	9.09	2.94
Rodriguez, Rauldison	R-R	5-11	160	10-21-93	0	0	13.50	2	0	0	0	1	2	2	1	0	2	1	.667	1.000	.500	13.50	27.00

Player	T-B	Ht	Wt	DOB	W	L	ERA	G	GS	CG	SV	IP	H	R	ER	HR	BB	SO	AVG	vLH	vRH		
Sanchez, Starlyng	L-L	5-11	170	8-6-94	0	0	1.13	8	2	0	1	16	12	2	2	0	4	13	.207	.091	.234	7.31	2.25
Santamaria, Cristhopher	L-L	5-11	175	6-19-96	0	1	0.73	15	0	0	1	25	12	2	2	0	6	18	.146	.158	.143	6.57	2.19
Saucedo, Javier	L-L	5-11	160	9-28-93	2	2	3.52	14	1	0	0	23	19	11	9	1	9	26	.241	.278	.230	10.17	3.52
Vasquez, Carlos	R-R	6-2	192	1-23-95	1	1	4.26	8	0	0	0	13	8	7	6	0	15	13	.186	.111	.206	9.24	10.66
Villarroel, Edwin	L-L	6-3	165	5-18-95	5	5	2.51	14	14	0	0	65	60	21	18	4	14	44	.250	.208	.260	6.12	1.95
Yonquelys, Martinez	R-R	6-0	180	4-23-93	1	3	1.74	19	0	0	0	31	18	10	6	1	8	23	.170	.171	.169	6.68	2.32

Fielding

Catcher	PCT	G	PO	A	E	DP	PB
Avea	.985	50	321	68	6	1	10
Bermejo	1.000	1	1	0	0	0	0
Pena	.977	29	226	27	6	0	5

First Base	PCT	G	PO	A	E	DP
Aquino	.917	1	10	1	1	2
Avea	.963	2	23	3	1	3
Cesar	.990	13	99	2	1	4
Cortorreal	1.000	9	57	5	0	5
Pena	.950	2	17	2	1	2
Roa	.990	43	371	29	4	31
Tavarez	.975	9	71	6	2	3
Trompiz	1.000	1	2	0	0	1

Second Base	PCT	G	PO	A	E	DP
Cortorreal	.968	10	11	19	1	4
Estrella	.959	35	59	82	6	18
Michelena	.972	32	56	83	4	17

Third Base	PCT	G	PO	A	E	DP
Cesar	.886	42	33	84	15	6
Cortorreal	—	1	0	0	0	0
Michelena	.903	35	18	66	9	3

Shortstop	PCT	G	PO	A	E	DP
Aquino	.857	8	15	15	5	3
Estrella	.926	8	13	12	2	1
Michelena	1.000	1	0	1	0	0
Trompiz	.954	59	137	173	15	31

Outfield	PCT	G	PO	A	E	DP
Aquino	—	1	0	0	0	0
Mejia	.964	44	50	4	2	0
Melendez	1.000	29	36	3	0	1
Michelena	1.000	1	0	1	0	0
Payano	.968	69	148	4	5	1
Reynoso	.966	64	109	4	4	2
Roa	.895	16	17	0	2	0

Kansas City Royals

SEASON IN A SENTENCE: Kansas City provided thrills and spills in a bi-polar season that included a disastrous 6-22 stretch but also saw the team go 42-27 over the second half of the season on its way to the club's first winning season in 10 years.

HIGH POINT: With playoff hopes seemingly squelched before summer arrived, Kansas City went 17-3 in a late-July/early-August stretch to climb back into the thick of the wild-card race.

LOW POINT: On May 6, James Shields was lifted after eight scoreless innings against the White Sox. Closer Greg Holland blew the save and Jordan Danks homered off of reliever Kelvin Herrera to give Chicago a 2-1 win, snapping a four-game winning streak. That loss started the 6-22 stretch.

NOTABLE ROOKIES: For such a young team, Kansas City relied on few rookies, as most of their core talent arrived in 2011. Outfielder David Lough provided better offense and defense than Jeff Francoeur, the player he eventually replaced in right field. Righthander Yordano Ventura jumped in the middle of the Royals' September chase for a wild-card spot. Ventura left with the lead after pitching 5 ⅔ effective innings in each of his first two starts, but he was chased after giving up four runs in four innings in his final start.

KEY TRANSACTIONS: The Royals' decision to trade outfielder Wil Myers, righthander Jake Odorizzi, lefthander Mike Montgomery and third baseman Patrick Leonard for righthanders James Shields and Wade Davis will be analyzed for years. Shields lived up to expectations, but Davis was a bust as he lost his rotation spot and had to be shuffled back to the bullpen. The Angels were happy to get righthander Ervin Santana off their hands, giving him to Kansas City for pennies on the dollar. Santana responded by giving the Royals a second front-line starter to go with Shields.

DOWN ON THE FARM: Ventura jumped to the majors after dominating the Texas League and holding his own in a promotion to Triple-A Omaha. Omaha made the Pacific Coast League playoffs despite a losing record. Once they got there, the Storm Chasers got hot, won the Pacific Coast League and then beat Durham to claim the Triple-A national championship. After a brutal first two months, 2012 first-rounder Kyle Zimmer showed scouts the plus stuff that make him one of the top pitching prospects in the minors. Shortstop Raul Adalberto Mondesi held his own as a 17-year-old in the South Atlantic League.

OPENING DAY PAYROLL: $81.5 million (19th)

PLAYERS OF THE YEAR

MAJOR LEAGUE	MINOR LEAGUE
James Shields rhp	**Yordano Ventura** rhp
13-9, 3.15 in 34 GS	(Double-A/Triple-A)
229 IP, 1.24 WHIP	8-6, 3.14, 10.4 SO/9
Led AL in GS, IP	September callup

ORGANIZATION LEADERS

BATTING   *Minimum 250 AB

MAJORS

* AVG	Hosmer, Eric	.302
* OPS	Hosmer, Eric	.801
HR	Gordon, Alex	20
RBI	Butler, Billy	79

MINORS

* AVG	Giavotella, Johnny, Omaha	.286
* OBP	Seratelli, Anthony, Omaha	.395
* SLG	Fields, Matt, Northwest Arkansas	.469
R	Adams, Lane, NW Arkansas/Wilmington	86
H	Colon, Christian, Omaha	140
TB	Fields, Matt, Northwest Arkansas	213
2B	Cuthbert, Cheslor, NW Arkansas/Wilmington	37
3B	Eibner, Brett, Northwest Arkansas	9
HR	Fields, Matt, Northwest Arkansas	31
RBI	Fields, Matt, Northwest Arkansas	87
BB	Seratelli, Anthony, Omaha	77
SO	Fields, Matt, Northwest Arkansas	181
SB	Gore, Terrance, Lexington	68

PITCHING   #Minimum 75 IP

MAJORS

W	Guthrie, Jeremy	15
# ERA	Shields, James	3.15
SO	Shields, James	196
SV	Holland, Greg	47

MINORS

W	Selman, Sam, Wilmington	11
L	Lamb, John, Omaha, Wilmington	14
	Marimon, Sugar Ray, Northwest Arkansas	14
# ERA	Binford, Christian, Lexington	2.67
G	Two tied at	47
GS	Dwyer, Chris, Omaha	28
SV	Jackson, Zach, Omaha, Northwest Arkansas	18
	Peterson, Mark, Lexington	18
IP	Brooks, Aaron, NW Arkansas/Wilmington	160
BB	Selman, Sam, Wilmington	85
SO	Ventura, Yordano, Omaha/NW Arkansas	155
# AVG	Selman, Sam, Wilmington	.197

2013 PERFORMANCE

General Manager: Dayton Moore. **Farm Director:** Scott Sharp. **Scouting Director:** Lonnie Goldberg.

Class	Team	League	W	L	PCT	Finish	Manager
Majors	Kansas City Royals	American	86	76	.531	7th (15)	Ned Yost
Triple-A	Omaha Stormchasers	Pacific Coast	70	74	.486	10th (16)	Mike Jirschele
Double-A	Northwest Arkansas Naturals	Texas	59	81	.421	8th (8)	Brian Poldberg
High A	Wilmington Blue Rocks	Carolina	63	77	.450	6th (8)	Vance Wilson
Low A	Lexington Legends	South Atlantic	68	70	.493	8th (14)	Brian Buchanan
Rookie	Idaho Falls Chukars	Pioneer	41	35	.539	3rd (8)	Omar Ramirez
Rookie	Burlington Royals	Appalachian	29	38	.433	8th (10)	Tommy Shields
Rookie	AZL Royals	Arizona	22	33	.400	12th (13)	Daryl Kennedy
Overall 2013 Minor League Record			352	408	.463	27th (30)	

ORGANIZATION STATISTICS

AMERICAN LEAGUE

Batting	B-T	HT	WT	DOB	AVG	vLH	vRH	G	AB	R	H	2B	3B	HR	RBI	BB	HBP	SH	SF	SO	SB	CS	SLG	OBP
Bonifacio, Emilio	B-R	5-11	205	4-23-85	.285	.305	.273	42	158	21	45	6	2	0	11	17	0	3	1	37	16	2	.348	.352
2-team total (94 Toronto)					.243	—	—	136	420	54	102	22	3	3	31	30	2	6	3	103	28	8	.331	.295
Butler, Billy	R-R	6-1	240	4-18-86	.289	.275	.293	162	582	62	168	27	0	15	82	79	3	0	4	102	0	0	.412	.374
Cain, Lorenzo	R-R	6-2	205	4-13-86	.251	.238	.256	115	399	54	100	21	3	4	46	33	4	0	6	90	14	6	.348	.310
Carroll, Jamey	R-R	5-11	175	2-18-74	.111	.130	.077	14	36	5	4	3	0	0	2	4	0	1	2	4	0	1	.194	.190
2-team total (58 Minnesota)					.211	—	—	72	227	26	48	9	0	0	11	17	1	2	2	39	2	1	.251	.267
Ciriaco, Pedro	R-R	6-0	180	9-27-85	.182	.500	.000	5	11	0	2	1	0	0	0	0	0	0	0	1	1	0	.273	.182
2-team total (28 Boston)					.210	—	—	33	62	4	13	3	1	1	4	6	0	0	1	13	3	1	.339	.275
Dyson, Jarrod	L-R	5-9	160	8-15-84	.258	.204	.274	87	213	30	55	9	4	2	17	21	1	3	1	45	34	6	.366	.326
Escobar, Alcides	R-R	6-1	195	12-16-86	.234	.255	.225	158	607	57	142	20	4	4	52	19	3	9	4	84	22	0	.300	.259
Falu, Irving	B-R	5-10	185	6-6-83	.250	.000	1.000	1	4	0	1	0	0	0	0	0	0	0	0	0	0	0	.250	.250
Francoeur, Jeff	R-R	6-4	210	1-8-84	.208	.242	.190	59	183	19	38	8	2	3	13	8	2	0	0	49	2	0	.322	.249
Getz, Chris	L-R	5-11	185	8-30-83	.220	.264	.205	78	209	29	46	6	1	1	18	20	0	8	0	24	16	3	.273	.288
Giavotella, Johnny	R-R	5-8	180	7-10-87	.220	.176	.250	14	41	4	9	3	0	0	4	5	2	0	0	4	0	0	.293	.333
Gordon, Alex	L-R	6-1	220	2-10-84	.265	.307	.244	156	633	90	168	27	6	20	81	52	9	0	6	141	11	3	.422	.327
Hayes, Brett	R-R	6-0	200	2-13-84	.278	.125	.400	5	18	2	5	3	0	1	2	0	0	0	0	3	0	0	.611	.278
Hosmer, Eric	L-L	6-4	220	10-24-89	.302	.323	.291	159	623	86	188	34	3	17	79	51	1	1	4	100	11	4	.448	.353
Johnson, Elliot	B-R	6-1	190	3-9-84	.179	.186	.176	79	162	19	29	2	1	2	9	8	0	3	0	49	14	0	.241	.218
Kottaras, George	L-R	6-0	200	5-10-83	.180	.143	.186	46	100	13	18	4	0	5	12	24	2	0	0	42	1	0	.370	.349
Lough, David	L-L	5-11	180	1-20-86	.286	.292	.284	96	315	35	90	17	4	5	33	10	3	4	3	52	5	2	.413	.311
Maxwell, Justin	R-R	6-5	220	11-6-83	.268	.174	.353	35	97	14	26	6	1	5	17	11	2	0	1	35	2	1	.505	.351
2-team total (40 Houston)					.252	—	—	75	234	35	59	16	3	7	25	23	4	0	1	78	6	2	.436	.328
Moore, Adam	R-R	6-3	215	5-8-84	.300	.200	.400	5	10	1	3	1	0	0	0	1	0	0	0	2	1	0	.400	.364
Moustakas, Mike	L-R	6-0	210	9-11-88	.233	.196	.244	136	472	42	110	26	0	12	42	32	5	1	4	83	2	4	.364	.287
Pena, Carlos	L-L	6-2	225	5-17-78	.000	—	.000	4	3	0	0	0	0	0	0	0	0	0	0	3	0	0	.000	.000
2-team total (85 Houston)					.207	—	—	89	280	38	58	13	1	8	25	43	4	1	0	92	1	3	.346	.321
Perez, Salvador	R-R	6-3	240	5-10-90	.292	.317	.283	138	496	48	145	25	3	13	79	21	4	0	5	63	0	0	.433	.323
Tejada, Miguel	R-R	5-9	220	5-25-74	.288	.253	.329	53	156	15	45	5	0	3	20	6	1	3	1	25	1	0	.378	.317

Pitching	B-T	HT	WT	DOB	W	L	ERA	G	GS	CG	SV	IP	H	R	ER	HR	BB	SO	AVG	vLH	vRH	K/9	BB/9
Bueno, Francisley	L-L	5-10	215	3-5-81	1	0	0.00	7	0	0	0	8	4	0	0	0	2	5	.143	.143	.143	5.40	2.16
Chen, Bruce	L-L	6-2	215	6-19-77	9	4	3.27	34	15	0	0	121	107	46	44	13	36	78	.237	.261	.224	5.80	2.68
Coleman, Louis	R-R	6-4	205	4-4-86	3	0	0.61	27	0	0	0	30	19	2	2	1	6	32	.186	.235	.162	9.71	1.82
Collins, Tim	L-L	5-7	165	8-21-89	3	6	3.54	66	0	0	0	53	49	26	21	3	28	52	.244	.212	.275	8.78	4.73
Crow, Aaron	R-R	6-3	195	11-10-86	7	5	3.38	57	0	0	1	48	49	19	18	6	22	44	.271	.264	.277	8.25	4.13
Davis, Wade	R-R	6-5	225	9-7-85	8	11	5.32	31	24	0	0	135	169	89	80	15	58	114	.307	.326	.286	7.58	3.86
Duffy, Danny	L-L	6-3	200	12-21-88	2	0	1.85	5	5	0	0	24	19	5	5	0	14	22	.213	.296	.177	8.14	5.18
Dwyer, Chris	R-L	6-3	210	4-10-88	0	0	0.00	2	0	0	0	3	2	0	0	0	1	2	.200	.000	.333	6.00	3.00
Guthrie, Jeremy	R-R	6-1	205	4-8-79	15	12	4.04	33	33	3	0	212	236	99	95	30	59	111	.285	.331	.225	4.72	2.51
Gutierrez, J.C.	R-R	6-3	245	7-14-83	0	1	3.38	25	0	0	0	29	30	13	11	2	8	17	.275	.315	.236	5.22	2.45
2-team total (28 Los Angeles)					1	5	4.23	53	0	0	0	55	56	29	26	5	20	45	—	—	—	7.32	3.25
Herrera, Kelvin	R-R	5-10	200	12-31-89	5	7	3.86	59	0	0	2	58	48	27	25	9	21	74	.219	.246	.190	11.42	3.24
Hochevar, Luke	R-R	6-5	215	9-15-83	5	2	1.92	58	0	0	2	70	41	15	15	8	17	82	.169	.198	.138	10.49	2.18
Holland, Greg	R-R	5-10	200	11-20-85	2	1	1.21	68	0	0	47	67	40	11	9	3	18	103	.170	.172	.168	13.84	2.42
Joseph, Donnie	L-L	6-3	190	11-1-87	0	0	0.00	6	0	0	0	6	4	0	0	0	4	7	.200	.000	.308	11.12	6.35
Mendoza, Luis	R-R	6-3	245	10-31-83	2	6	5.36	22	15	0	0	94	106	66	56	10	43	54	.289	.303	.271	5.17	4.12
Santana, Ervin	R-R	6-2	185	12-12-82	9	10	3.24	32	32	0	0	211	190	85	76	26	51	161	.238	.247	.227	6.87	2.18
Shields, James	R-R	6-4	215	12-20-81	13	9	3.15	34	34	2	0	229	215	82	80	20	68	196	.251	.233	.272	7.71	2.68
Smith, Will	R-L	6-5	250	7-10-89	2	1	3.24	19	1	0	0	33	24	16	12	6	7	43	.202	.157	.235	11.61	1.89
Teaford, Everett	L-L	6-0	165	5-15-84	0	0	0.00	1	0	0	0	1	1	0	0	0	0	0	.333	.500	.000	0.00	0.00
Ventura, Yordano	R-R	5-11	180	6-3-91	0	1	3.52	3	3	0	0	15	13	6	6	3	6	11	.224	.211	.250	6.46	3.52

Fielding

Catcher	PCT	G	PO	A	E	DP	PB								
Hayes	1.000	5	45	1	0	0	0	Kottaras	.983	39	212	14	4	0	3
								Moore	.962	5	22	3	1	0	0
								Perez	.993	137	930	71	7	4	3

First Base	PCT	G	PO	A	E	DP
Butler	1.000	7	56	0	0	4
Hosmer	.994	158	1205	122	8	118
Pena	1.000	2	6	0	0	2
Perez	.667	1	2	0	1	0
Tejada	1.000	1	10	0	0	0

Second Base	PCT	G	PO	A	E	DP
Bonifacio	.974	31	40	74	3	15
Carroll	1.000	1	1	1	0	0
Getz	.986	68	106	181	4	39
Giavotella	1.000	13	20	37	0	9
Johnson	.989	57	70	111	2	22
Tejada	1.000	26	28	50	0	10

Third Base	PCT	G	PO	A	E	DP
Bonifacio	1.000	6	3	8	0	2
Carroll	1.000	14	6	11	0	3
Falu	1.000	1	1	0	0	0
Johnson	.909	4	1	9	1	1
Moustakas	.953	134	114	210	16	19
Tejada	.941	22	5	27	2	1

Shortstop	PCT	G	PO	A	E	DP
Ciriaco	1.000	3	8	7	0	3
Escobar	.979	158	222	395	13	89
Johnson	1.000	8	8	10	0	3

Outfield	PCT	G	PO	A	E	DP
Bonifacio	1.000	6	12	0	0	0
Cain	.990	113	296	7	3	0
Dyson	.973	73	176	3	5	2
Francoeur	.990	54	96	3	1	0
Gordon	.997	155	323	17	1	2
Hosmer	—	1	0	0	0	0
Johnson	1.000	3	1	0	0	0
Lough	.989	89	164	8	2	1
Maxwell	.965	31	53	2	2	0

OMAHA STORM CHASERS   TRIPLE-A

PACIFIC COAST LEAGUE

Batting	B-T	HT	WT	DOB	AVG	vLH	vRH	G	AB	R	H	2B	3B	HR	RBI	BB	HBP	SH	SF	SO	SB	CS	SLG	OBP
Berry, Quintin	L-L	6-0	175	11-21-84	.222	.167	.237	48	144	18	32	2	1	2	16	26	1	0	1	34	13	2	.292	.343
Broussard, Ben	L-L	6-2	230	9-24-76	.295	.362	.275	52	200	20	59	14	0	2	24	22	1	0	3	42	0	1	.395	.363
Canham, Mitch	L-R	6-2	205	9-25-84	.333	.143	.500	6	15	0	5	1	0	0	3	4	0	0	1	5	0	0	.400	.450
Ciriaco, Pedro	R-R	6-0	180	9-27-85	.281	.304	.272	43	160	19	45	8	1	1	15	6	1	3	1	22	4	1	.363	.310
Colon, Christian	R-R	5-10	185	5-14-89	.273	.276	.270	131	512	72	140	12	3	12	58	41	7	15	2	57	15	4	.379	.335
Dyson, Jarrod	L-R	5-9	160	8-15-84	.154	.000	.200	15	52	8	8	2	0	0	1	3	2	1	0	12	5	0	.192	.228
Falu, Irving	B-R	5-10	185	6-6-83	.256	.221	.266	135	508	50	130	19	6	2	31	47	1	11	1	51	20	10	.329	.320
Fletcher, Brian	R-R	6-0	190	10-26-88	.250	.240	.253	26	108	14	27	5	0	5	17	5	1	0	1	33	1	0	.435	.287
Getz, Chris	L-R	5-11	185	8-30-83	.310	.263	.323	19	84	7	26	5	1	1	10	1	1	0	2	5	3	1	.429	.318
Giavotella, Johnny	R-R	5-8	180	7-10-87	.286	.190	.316	100	370	48	106	24	0	7	46	51	0	0	5	59	8	4	.408	.369
Hayes, Brett	R-R	6-0	200	2-13-84	.233	.122	.274	78	275	39	64	15	1	17	44	17	2	1	3	64	2	0	.480	.279
Hernandez, Gorkys	R-R	6-0	190	9-7-87	.231	.148	.255	34	121	14	28	6	1	2	10	8	2	2	2	29	3	3	.347	.286
2-team total (90 New Orleans)					.263	—	—	124	430	59	113	17	5	6	32	30	6	6	3	125	25	12	.367	.318
Lambin, Chase	B-R	6-2	195	7-7-79	.246	.316	.211	22	57	10	14	4	1	0	4	4	2	0	0	12	1	0	.351	.317
Lough, David	L-L	5-11	180	1-20-86	.338	.306	.347	37	154	29	52	6	3	3	17	11	3	3	1	21	5	5	.474	.391
Moore, Adam	R-R	6-3	215	5-8-84	.191	.273	.160	41	131	20	25	4	0	8	23	17	0	0	0	52	0	0	.405	.284
Nady, Xavier	R-R	6-2	215	11-14-78	.309	.321	.305	71	256	44	79	12	0	11	43	27	4	1	2	51	1	0	.484	.381
2-team total (53 Colorado Springs)					.296	—	—	124	443	69	131	26	0	15	65	41	6	1	4	91	4	0	.456	.360
Orlando, Paulo	R-R	6-2	210	11-1-85	.276	.328	.266	92	293	41	81	9	3	5	46	22	1	7	3	56	8	3	.379	.326
Pena, Carlos	L-L	6-2	225	5-17-78	.333	.250	.357	5	18	5	6	0	1	2	6	4	0	0	0	3	0	0	.778	.455
Pina, Manny	R-R	6-0	215	6-5-87	.242	.333	.230	28	99	7	24	5	0	2	13	6	1	3	2	10	1	0	.354	.287
Ramirez, Max	R-R	5-11	215	10-11-84	.263	.271	.254	115	411	43	108	19	0	9	55	46	3	0	7	103	0	0	.375	.336
Seratelli, Anthony	B-R	5-10	185	2-27-83	.273	.247	.282	120	400	61	109	17	3	11	41	77	4	6	0	81	24	1	.413	.395
Taveras, Willy	R-R	6-0	180	12-25-81	.239	.216	.243	79	247	36	59	9	5	2	27	18	8	3	3	40	11	2	.340	.308
Tracy, Chad	R-R	6-3	210	7-4-85	.187	.133	.211	45	139	13	26	2	0	4	18	20	3	1	3	37	0	0	.288	.297
Wood, Brandon	R-R	6-3	205	3-2-85	.264	.333	.207	17	53	3	14	1	0	2	7	3	0	0	0	8	0	0	.396	.304

Pitching	B-T	HT	WT	DOB	W	L	ERA	G	GS	CG	SV	IP	H	R	ER	HR	BB	SO	AVG	vLH	vRH	K/9	BB/9
Adcock, Nate	R-R	6-4	230	2-25-88	3	4	7.09	10	9	0	0	47	65	42	37	10	23	28	.332	.316	.347	5.36	4.40
2-team total (16 Reno)					8	6	6.67	26	19	0	0	113	139	92	84	15	50	69	—	—	—	5.48	3.97
Baumann, Buddy	L-L	5-10	175	12-9-87	3	0	2.76	30	0	0	1	49	49	15	15	5	23	66	.257	.226	.268	12.12	4.22
Boyer, Blaine	R-R	6-3	225	7-11-81	0	1	3.00	13	0	0	1	15	15	9	5	3	3	18	.254	.222	.281	10.80	1.80
Bueno, Francisley	L-L	5-10	215	3-5-81	3	3	2.66	36	1	0	1	68	64	27	20	5	24	56	.248	.237	.255	7.45	3.19
Cleto, Maikel	R-R	6-3	250	5-1-89	1	2	3.55	19	1	0	1	38	35	16	15	1	21	36	.248	.258	.240	8.53	4.97
2-team total (16 Memphis)					3	5	5.52	35	10	0	1	91	84	58	56	5	74	89	—	—	—	8.77	7.29
Coleman, Louis	R-R	6-4	205	4-4-86	3	2	1.61	24	0	0	6	45	36	10	8	1	17	52	.218	.141	.277	10.48	3.43
Duffy, Danny	L-L	6-3	200	12-21-88	3	2	4.08	12	10	0	0	53	50	26	24	4	25	59	.249	.212	.262	10.02	4.25
Dwyer, Chris	R-L	6-3	210	4-10-88	10	11	3.55	29	28	0	0	160	140	75	63	15	72	112	.234	.246	.228	6.31	4.06
Garrido, Santiago	R-R	6-1	195	10-4-89	0	0	5.40	1	0	0	0	3	4	2	2	1	2	3	.286	.375	.167	8.10	5.40
Herrera, Kelvin	R-R	5-10	200	12-31-89	0	1	1.13	10	3	0	2	16	6	2	2	1	6	22	.111	.105	.114	12.38	3.38
Jackson, Zach	L-L	6-5	220	5-13-83	0	0	0.00	2	0	0	0	2	1	0	0	0	0	0	.167	1.000	.000	0.00	0.00
Joseph, Donnie	L-L	6-3	190	11-1-87	4	3	3.95	47	0	0	6	55	39	25	24	5	40	84	.199	.160	.226	13.83	6.59
Lamb, John	L-L	6-4	205	7-10-90	1	2	6.75	3	3	0	0	16	15	12	12	1	7	10	.242	.222	.245	5.63	3.94
Mariot, Michael	R-R	5-11	195	10-20-88	4	5	3.56	47	1	0	11	61	59	31	24	4	25	66	.258	.303	.229	9.79	3.71
Marks, Justin	L-L	6-3	195	1-12-88	6	13	4.58	24	20	0	0	130	138	68	66	7	61	117	.273	.187	.309	8.12	4.23
Mortensen, Clayton	R-R	6-4	185	4-10-85	1	0	4.50	1	1	0	0	6	6	3	3	1	3	2	.300	.222	.364	3.00	4.50
Paulino, Felipe	R-R	6-3	270	10-5-83	0	3	8.24	5	5	0	0	20	30	21	18	2	11	18	.353	.447	.277	8.24	5.03
Runion, Sam	R-R	6-4	220	11-9-88	0	0	13.50	1	0	0	0	3	6	4	4	0	1	0	.500	.625	.250	0.00	3.38
Sanches, Brian	R-R	6-1	190	8-8-78	10	3	3.20	27	13	1	0	101	103	43	36	3	21	61	.264	.276	.254	5.42	1.87
Severino, Atahualpa	L-L	5-11	220	11-6-84	0	0	3.00	6	0	0	0	9	6	4	3	2	6	10	.182	.143	.211	10.00	6.00
Sherrill, George	L-L	6-0	215	4-19-77	0	1	6.23	21	0	0	0	22	23	17	15	1	16	13	.277	.233	.302	5.46	5.82
Smith, Will	R-L	6-5	250	7-10-89	6	4	3.03	28	10	0	4	89	81	32	30	7	24	100	.243	.178	.272	10.11	2.43
Teaford, Everett	L-L	6-0	165	5-15-84	4	6	3.49	31	14	0	0	95	92	39	37	7	39	99	.250	.296	.226	9.35	3.68
Ventura, Yordano	R-R	5-11	180	6-3-91	5	4	3.74	15	14	0	0	77	80	35	32	4	33	81	.271	.222	.318	9.47	3.86
Verdugo, Ryan	L-L	6-0	205	4-30-87	2	3	5.16	14	11	0	0	61	69	47	35	10	31	43	.285	.325	.264	6.34	4.57
Wheeler, Dan	R-R	6-3	220	12-10-77	1	3	9.00	11	0	0	0	15	28	17	15	3	5	10	.400	.429	.381	6.00	3.00

KANSAS CITY ROYALS

Fielding

Catcher	PCT	G	PO	A	E	DP	PB
Canham	.973	5	34	2	1	0	1
Hayes	.985	75	558	42	9	5	5
Moore	.986	40	311	42	5	1	2
Pina	.993	28	256	29	2	2	2
Ramirez	1.000	3	22	1	0	1	1

First Base	PCT	G	PO	A	E	DP
Broussard	.991	46	327	21	3	40
Moore	1.000	1	1	0	0	0
Nady	.985	35	248	12	4	22
Pena	1.000	5	44	1	0	10
Ramirez	.979	19	134	5	3	15
Seratelli	1.000	14	98	2	0	6
Tracy	.991	29	220	12	2	21
Wood	1.000	4	23	0	0	3

Second Base	PCT	G	PO	A	E	DP
Ciriaco	1.000	6	10	10	0	4
Colon	.977	75	127	175	7	45

	PCT	G	PO	A	E	DP
Falu	1.000	2	3	3	0	2
Getz	1.000	11	25	23	0	4
Giavotella	.980	46	81	111	4	25
Lambin	.943	9	13	20	2	4
Seratelli	1.000	3	3	5	0	1

Third Base	PCT	G	PO	A	E	DP
Ciriaco	.842	7	2	14	3	2
Falu	.951	74	58	117	9	9
Giavotella	.931	29	26	55	6	2
Hayes	—	1	0	0	0	0
Lambin	.846	6	5	6	2	0
Nady	1.000	3	5	4	0	0
Seratelli	.957	17	10	34	2	5
Wood	.963	13	3	23	1	1

Shortstop	PCT	G	PO	A	E	DP
Ciriaco	.942	30	31	66	6	16
Colon	.952	54	76	124	10	29
Falu	.968	52	69	114	6	38

	PCT	G	PO	A	E	DP
Getz	.909	7	11	19	3	3
Lambin	.778	1	4	3	2	2
Seratelli	.867	3	7	6	2	2
Wood	.833	1	4	1	1	1

Outfield	PCT	G	PO	A	E	DP
Berry	.959	43	69	1	3	0
Canham	—	1	0	0	0	0
Dyson	1.000	14	30	1	0	1
Falu	1.000	11	21	0	0	0
Fletcher	1.000	19	41	0	0	0
Giavotella	.964	20	26	1	1	0
Hernandez	.978	34	84	3	2	2
Lough	.972	37	69	1	2	0
Nady	1.000	22	32	1	0	0
Orlando	.995	89	195	13	1	4
Seratelli	.984	84	175	12	3	3
Taveras	.993	76	127	11	1	2

NORTHWEST ARKANSAS NATURALS

DOUBLE-A

TEXAS LEAGUE

Batting	B-T	HT	WT	DOB	AVG	vLH	vRH	G	AB	R	H	2B	3B	HR	RBI	BB	HBP	SH	SF	SO	SB	CS	SLG	OBP
Adams, Lane	R-R	6-2	198	11-13-89	.244	.214	.250	44	156	30	38	7	1	5	26	18	3	0	0	45	15	0	.397	.333
Bonifacio, Jorge	R-R	6-1	192	6-4-93	.301	.609	.200	25	93	15	28	7	0	2	19	11	0	0	1	23	2	1	.441	.371
Calixte, Orlando	R-R	5-11	160	2-3-92	.250	.324	.230	123	484	59	121	25	4	8	36	42	3	4	3	131	14	11	.368	.312
Canham, Mitch	L-R	6-2	205	9-25-84	.261	.119	.285	91	291	41	76	21	4	2	26	46	0	2	2	54	12	7	.381	.360
Cuthbert, Cheslor	R-R	6-1	190	11-16-92	.215	.163	.227	64	237	25	51	16	0	6	28	20	2	2	3	51	6	2	.359	.279
Eibner, Brett	R-R	6-3	195	12-2-88	.243	.341	.219	114	441	74	107	17	9	19	41	53	6	1	3	149	7	3	.451	.330
Fields, Matt	R-R	6-5	235	7-8-85	.222	.262	.214	131	454	68	101	17	1	31	87	60	9	0	1	181	6	6	.469	.324
Fletcher, Brian	R-R	6-0	190	10-26-88	.314	.325	.311	52	207	37	65	9	1	12	37	13	0	0	1	41	6	2	.541	.353
Franco, Angel	B-R	5-10	155	5-23-90	.294	.321	.288	83	282	27	83	13	3	4	27	19	0	7	1	41	7	7	.404	.338
Graterol, Juan	R-R	6-1	170	2-14-89	.286	.286	.286	56	182	17	52	6	0	3	17	6	2	4	1	22	3	0	.368	.314
Hernandez, Roman	R-R	6-0	195	1-9-88	.262	.254	.265	86	271	20	71	12	2	1	23	23	2	2	1	66	5	6	.332	.323
Llanos, Alex	R-R	6-1	160	9-21-90	.194	.286	.167	9	31	1	6	1	0	0	0	0	1	0	0	14	0	0	.226	.219
McClure, Alex	B-R	6-0	185	6-16-89	.213	.370	.182	50	164	13	35	7	0	0	18	8	1	3	3	33	4	3	.256	.250
Merrifield, Whit	R-R	6-1	175	1-24-89	.270	.362	.245	94	322	31	87	20	5	3	43	22	2	5	2	57	17	7	.391	.319
Navarro, Rey	B-R	5-10	175	12-22-89	.283	.289	.281	119	446	61	126	21	4	12	58	19	2	7	7	54	6	6	.428	.310
Pina, Manny	R-R	6-0	215	6-5-87	.221	.262	.210	58	199	19	44	13	0	5	25	11	2	1	1	30	0	1	.362	.268
Prades, Yem	R-R	6-2	194	3-8-88	.193	.250	.174	84	306	37	59	9	1	6	22	12	1	0	4	71	6	3	.288	.223
Rincon, Edinson	R-R	6-1	215	8-11-90	.154	.000	.186	13	52	3	8	1	0	0	3	1	0	0	0	12	0	0	.173	.170
Testa, Carlo	L-L	6-3	218	12-16-86	.158	.000	.171	13	38	5	6	0	0	1	1	8	0	0	0	14	3	1	.237	.304

Pitching	B-T	HT	WT	DOB	W	L	ERA	G	GS	CG	SV	IP	H	R	ER	HR	BB	SO	AVG	vLH	vRH	K/9	BB/9
Adam, Jason	R-R	6-4	219	8-4-91	8	11	5.19	26	26	0	0	144	153	98	83	12	54	126	.277	.278	.275	7.88	3.38
Alexander, Scott	L-L	6-1	186	7-10-89	2	0	5.18	24	0	0	1	33	38	20	19	0	18	40	.299	.163	.369	10.91	4.91
Arguelles, Noel	L-L	6-3	225	1-12-90	1	8	5.93	25	11	0	0	71	73	60	47	6	53	44	.269	.227	.286	5.55	6.69
Baumann, Buddy	L-L	5-10	175	12-9-87	0	0	0.00	2	0	0	0	4	1	0	0	0	2	6	.091	.143	.000	13.50	4.50
Bergmann, Jason	R-R	6-3	220	9-25-81	0	5	3.67	19	0	0	0	27	26	12	11	2	12	29	.257	.237	.270	9.67	4.00
Brooks, Aaron	R-R	6-4	220	4-27-90	7	7	4.17	16	16	1	0	104	113	51	48	13	11	67	.281	.310	.251	5.82	0.95
Carl, Edwin	R-R	6-0	210	8-31-88	2	1	5.60	25	1	0	4	35	41	22	22	7	15	31	.285	.306	.268	7.90	3.82
Culver, Malcolm	R-R	6-1	205	2-9-90	0	0	0.00	1	0	0	0	2	2	0	0	0	0	1	.250	.000	.500	4.50	0.00
Duffy, Danny	L-L	6-3	200	12-21-88	0	2	3.94	4	4	0	0	16	16	7	7	3	5	28	.267	.154	.298	15.75	2.81
Ferguson, Andy	R-R	6-1	195	9-2-88	3	5	5.16	34	13	0	0	96	95	59	55	11	37	84	.262	.325	.214	7.88	3.47
Garrido, Santiago	R-R	6-1	195	10-4-89	0	5	3.03	39	0	0	2	59	49	28	20	4	37	47	.229	.215	.237	7.13	5.61
Herrera, Kelvin	R-R	5-10	200	12-31-89	0	0	0.00	2	0	0	0	2	1	0	0	0	0	5	.143	.250	.000	22.50	0.00
Jackson, Zach	L-L	6-5	220	5-13-83	2	1	1.38	33	0	0	18	39	32	10	6	3	7	18	.224	.176	.239	4.15	1.62
Keck, Jon	L-L	6-6	215	6-18-88	4	4	3.81	45	0	0	2	52	33	24	22	5	39	50	.185	.193	.182	8.65	6.75
Marimon, Sugar Ray	R-R	6-1	195	9-30-88	6	14	4.31	27	26	2	0	148	159	86	71	26	45	119	.273	.276	.271	7.22	2.73
Marks, Justin	L-L	6-3	195	1-12-88	2	0	1.59	2	2	0	0	11	7	3	2	1	5	12	.167	.286	.143	9.53	3.97
Patton, Spencer	R-R	6-1	185	2-20-88	0	0	1.50	12	0	0	0	18	9	4	3	1	6	27	.155	.077	.219	13.50	3.00
Paulino, Felipe	R-R	6-3	270	10-5-83	0	0	2.25	2	2	0	0	8	5	2	2	1	4	8	.172	.143	.200	9.00	4.50
Pounders, Brooks	R-R	6-4	270	9-26-90	5	7	4.50	27	19	1	1	116	107	63	58	12	42	100	.247	.261	.237	7.76	3.26
Ridings, Matt	R-R	6-0	190	10-17-87	1	1	3.98	15	0	0	1	20	26	9	9	1	10	15	.329	.333	.327	6.64	4.43
Rogers, Nick	R-R	6-2	215	10-2-87	0	0	5.28	12	0	0	1	15	11	10	9	0	12	15	.216	.300	.161	8.80	7.04
Runion, Sam	R-R	6-4	220	11-9-88	4	2	3.72	37	1	0	0	56	53	23	23	4	13	45	.261	.273	.252	7.28	2.10
Sulbaran, Juan Carlos	R-R	6-2	220	11-9-89	3	4	6.99	25	2	0	0	46	47	38	36	9	28	26	.266	.241	.287	5.05	5.44
Triggs, Andrew	R-R	6-4	210	3-16-89	1	0	0.00	4	0	0	0	7	2	0	0	2	0	8	.095	.111	.083	13.50	2.70
Ventura, Yordano	R-R	5-11	180	6-3-91	3	2	2.34	11	11	0	0	58	39	17	15	3	20	74	.189	.187	.191	11.55	3.12
Verdugo, Ryan	L-L	6-0	205	4-10-87	1	0	0.00	3	2	0	0	9	5	0	0	0	0	8	.161	.222	.136	8.00	0.00
White, Cole	R-R	6-2	195	1-22-88	0	1	2.08	7	0	0	0	9	7	2	2	2	6	8	.219	.182	.238	10.38	8.31
2-team total (38 Tulsa)					2	4	3.97	45	0	0	19	48	44	24	21	2	33	42	—	—	—	7.93	6.23
Zimmer, Kyle	R-R	6-3	215	9-13-91	2	1	1.93	4	4	0	0	19	11	4	4	2	5	27	.162	.146	.185	13.02	2.41

Fielding

Catcher	PCT	G	PO	A	E	DP	PB
Canham	.985	46	288	33	5	3	5
Graterol	.990	53	432	52	5	6	4
Pina	.995	48	341	50	2	6	5

First Base	PCT	G	PO	A	E	DP
Canham	.995	27	204	10	1	14
Fields	.986	113	936	46	14	80
Graterol	1.000	1	11	1	0	0
Merrifield	.923	4	24	0	2	3

Second Base	PCT	G	PO	A	E	DP
Calixte	1.000	2	2	3	0	0
Franco	.965	45	91	131	8	34
McClure	.968	23	40	51	3	7
Merrifield	.975	32	63	92	4	20
Navarro	.968	44	74	110	6	24

Third Base	PCT	G	PO	A	E	DP
Calixte	.933	11	11	17	2	3
Canham	—	1	0	0	0	0
Cuthbert	.917	59	40	114	14	10
Franco	.922	26	10	49	5	3
Merrifield	1.000	1	1	1	0	0
Navarro	.900	46	23	76	11	10

Shortstop	PCT	G	PO	A	E	DP
Calixte	.960	101	140	240	16	50
Franco	.889	3	3	5	1	2
McClure	.990	27	36	60	1	11
Navarro	.952	15	15	44	3	8

Outfield	PCT	G	PO	A	E	DP
Adams	.988	39	78	1	1	0
Bonifacio	.946	23	33	2	2	0
Canham	1.000	6	11	0	0	0
Eibner	.987	106	218	10	3	2
Fletcher	.981	32	51	1	1	0
Hernandez	.959	73	108	10	5	3
Llanos	.955	8	21	0	1	0
Merrifield	.993	58	126	7	1	3
Prades	.990	79	186	7	2	1
Rincon	1.000	2	3	0	0	0
Testa	1.000	12	21	1	0	0

WILMINGTON BLUE ROCKS
HIGH CLASS A
CAROLINA LEAGUE

Batting	B-T	HT	WT	DOB	AVG	vLH	vRH	G	AB	R	H	2B	3B	HR	RBI	BB	HBP	SH	SF	SO	SB	CS	SLG	OBP
Adams, Lane	R-R	6-2	198	11-13-89	.276	.296	.271	87	323	56	89	23	2	7	39	43	2	0	2	66	23	6	.424	.362
Bates, Sam	L-R	6-5	230	2-19-89	.245	.182	.263	15	49	6	12	4	0	1	8	6	0	0	2	15	0	0	.388	.316
Beltre, Geulin	B-R	6-0	185	10-27-90	.215	.172	.228	85	288	23	62	11	1	1	19	21	0	8	0	62	6	6	.271	.269
Bonifacio, Jorge	R-R	6-1	192	6-4-93	.296	.324	.290	54	206	32	61	11	3	2	29	23	2	0	3	40	0	2	.408	.368
Chapman, Ethan	L-R	6-0	180	1-5-90	.251	.262	.249	68	219	30	55	6	0	0	16	25	1	10	1	44	14	10	.279	.329
Chism, Tyler	R-R	6-0	205	10-6-88	.213	.120	.235	40	127	16	27	2	1	1	11	11	3	1	1	34	2	1	.268	.289
Cuthbert, Cheslor	R-R	6-1	190	11-16-92	.280	.176	.310	60	225	32	63	21	2	2	31	27	0	0	2	37	1	2	.418	.354
Diekroeger, Kenny	R-R	6-2	190	11-5-90	.207	.188	.210	33	121	8	25	1	1	3	15	3	1	2	0	28	0	3	.306	.232
Elder, Chris	L-R	5-11	205	7-5-88	.176	.143	.185	10	34	3	6	1	1	0	3	2	0	0	0	8	0	1	.265	.222
Espinal, Yowill	R-R	6-0	170	4-1-91	.151	.188	.140	26	73	4	11	1	0	0	2	4	1	3	0	26	0	1	.164	.205
Ferguson, Tim	R-R	6-1	190	10-25-88	.254	.292	.245	39	130	14	33	5	0	2	12	11	1	0	0	35	5	4	.338	.317
Gibbs, Micah	B-R	5-11	205	7-22-87	.208	.333	.179	17	48	3	10	3	0	0	4	9	0	0	0	17	1	0	.271	.333
Hudak, Alex	L-R	5-11	200	4-7-90	.202	.154	.211	26	84	10	17	5	1	2	10	12	0	2	0	32	1	1	.357	.302
Llanos, Alex	R-R	6-1	160	9-21-90	.158	.000	.167	6	19	0	3	0	0	0	0	0	0	0	0	8	0	1	.158	.158
Lopez, Jack	R-R	5-9	165	12-16-92	.230	.263	.224	124	478	62	110	16	4	4	45	36	10	11	1	89	27	11	.301	.297
Mateo, Danny	B-R	6-1	178	8-10-91	.231	.241	.229	119	437	53	101	20	2	9	56	43	5	1	0	83	1	4	.348	.307
McClure, Alex	B-R	6-0	185	6-16-89	.238	.294	.224	24	84	6	20	3	1	0	5	4	1	3	0	23	4	5	.298	.281
Morin, Parker	L-R	5-11	195	7-2-91	.226	.254	.218	88	297	32	67	13	2	1	30	29	3	3	8	68	4	3	.293	.294
Prades, Yem	R-R	6-2	194	3-8-88	.289	.281	.292	39	152	18	44	9	1	1	20	21	5	1	2	30	3	2	.395	.313
Raben, Dennis	L-L	6-3	200	7-31-87	.272	.279	.270	71	254	33	69	12	1	12	41	32	8	0	3	51	2	2	.469	.367
Schlehuber, Jared	R-R	6-3	220	12-24-88	.299	.296	.300	78	284	42	85	24	1	8	59	38	4	0	1	51	1	2	.475	.388
Swab, Kenny	R-R	6-2	215	8-20-88	.212	.136	.227	39	132	18	28	8	2	4	15	10	0	0	2	37	2	1	.394	.264
Trapp, Justin	R-R	5-10	165	10-7-90	.257	.185	.273	128	487	67	125	25	5	10	47	51	12	13	3	118	25	9	.390	.340
Watts, Murray	L-R	6-7	270	10-9-87	.172	.250	.160	16	58	4	10	3	1	0	1	7	0	0	0	22	1	0	.259	.262

Pitching	B-T	HT	WT	DOB	W	L	ERA	G	GS	CG	SV	IP	H	R	ER	HR	BB	SO	AVG	vLH	vRH	K/9	BB/9
Alexander, Scott	L-L	6-1	186	7-10-89	2	0	1.33	12	0	0	1	27	18	5	4	0	8	22	.188	.121	.222	7.33	2.67
Baez, Angel	R-R	6-3	196	2-14-91	3	1	4.38	8	8	0	0	37	34	20	18	3	28	35	.248	.188	.301	8.51	6.81
Brooks, Aaron	R-R	6-4	220	4-27-90	2	3	4.47	10	10	0	0	56	60	28	28	4	11	43	.271	.307	.242	6.87	1.76
Coleman, Louis	R-R	6-4	205	4-4-86	0	0	0.00	2	0	0	0	2	0	0	0	0	0	4	.000	.000	.000	18.00	0.00
Cruz, Antonio	L-L	5-11	200	10-7-91	2	0	2.67	18	0	0	2	30	29	13	9	1	14	29	.248	.218	.274	8.60	4.15
Culver, Malcolm	R-R	6-1	205	2-9-90	5	5	2.79	39	0	0	5	84	55	34	26	3	31	76	.182	.213	.155	8.14	3.32
Davis, Tripp	L-L	6-1	200	2-12-91	0	1	4.50	4	4	0	0	18	22	11	9	2	4	7	.310	.400	.295	3.50	2.00
Davis, Wade	R-R	6-5	225	9-7-85	0	0	0.00	1	0	0	0	2	1	0	0	0	0	5	.143	.000	.167	22.50	0.00
Edwards, Andrew	R-R	6-5	260	10-7-91	0	0	0.00	4	0	0	1	6	2	0	0	0	2	3	.111	.250	.071	4.50	3.00
Fassold, Cody	R-R	6-2	230	10-2-88	5	9	5.11	37	0	0	1	79	85	48	45	4	37	85	.282	.263	.298	9.64	4.20
Hall, Cory	R-R	6-2	232	5-12-88	1	2	5.88	19	0	0	0	26	22	20	17	1	19	15	.229	.256	.208	5.19	6.58
Hernandez, Danny	R-R	6-1	180	4-14-89	0	1	2.17	19	1	0	0	46	44	12	11	3	14	43	.259	.254	.263	8.47	2.76
Lamb, John	L-L	6-4	205	7-10-90	4	12	5.63	19	19	0	0	93	109	61	58	13	19	76	.294	.354	.262	7.38	1.85
Moen, Kellen	B-R	6-2	185	5-30-88	1	4	5.42	35	9	0	0	85	110	63	51	7	25	59	.313	.281	.338	6.27	2.66
Patton, Spencer	R-R	6-1	185	2-20-88	5	2	1.96	25	2	0	2	64	49	19	14	5	20	76	.212	.269	.165	10.63	2.80
Sample, Tyler	L-R	6-7	245	6-27-89	2	4	5.06	18	6	0	0	48	43	33	27	2	49	47	.250	.205	.283	8.81	9.19
Santiago, Leonel	R-R	6-0	180	12-23-89	4	3	3.78	9	1	0	0	50	44	25	21	5	17	25	.238	.218	.255	4.50	3.06
Selman, Sam	R-L	6-3	165	11-14-90	11	9	3.38	27	27	0	0	125	88	63	47	3	85	128	.197	.188	.201	9.19	6.10
Smith, Kyle	R-R	6-0	170	9-10-92	5	4	2.85	19	19	0	0	104	93	38	33	9	29	96	.238	.231	.247	8.28	2.50
Sulbaran, Juan Carlos	R-R	6-2	220	11-9-89	1	3	5.03	8	8	0	0	34	39	23	19	4	14	29	.287	.283	.289	7.68	3.71
Tomchick, Ben	R-R	6-6	205	12-17-89	0	0	0.00	1	0	0	0	1	1	0	0	0	1	1	.250	.000	.333	9.00	0.00
Triggs, Andrew	R-R	6-4	210	3-16-89	5	3	2.54	39	0	0	9	60	58	29	17	1	12	63	.249	.228	.265	9.40	1.79
Williams, Ali	R-R	6-2	185	7-8-89	0	2	5.21	7	0	0	0	19	17	14	11	1	11	15	.230	.231	.229	7.11	5.21
Yambati, Robinson	R-R	6-3	185	1-15-91	0	1	3.82	25	0	0	3	35	33	22	15	2	18	42	.244	.313	.183	10.70	4.58
Zimmer, Kyle	R-R	6-3	215	9-13-91	4	8	4.82	18	18	1	0	90	80	54	48	9	31	113	.237	.235	.238	11.34	3.11

KANSAS CITY ROYALS

Fielding

Catcher	PCT	G	PO	A	E	DP	PB
Gibbs	.992	17	113	15	1	1	1
Morin	.989	88	715	77	9	7	16
Swab	.997	39	294	41	1	2	10

First Base	PCT	G	PO	A	E	DP
Bates	1.000	4	34	1	0	1
Mateo	.988	45	376	27	5	31
Raben	.985	55	436	27	7	49
Schlehuber	.996	27	215	14	1	15
Watts	.969	10	91	3	3	5

Second Base	PCT	G	PO	A	E	DP
Diekroeger	.940	12	18	45	4	9
Espinal	1.000	6	11	11	0	
1 Lopez	.923	6	12	12	2	3

Catcher	PCT	G	PO	A	E	DP
McClure	1.000	7	9	13	0	2
Trapp	.958	111	174	305	21	69

Third Base	PCT	G	PO	A	E	DP
Cuthbert	.917	57	39	83	11	2
Espinal	.889	8	7	9	2	2
Lopez	1.000	1	0	2	0	0
Mateo	.942	60	55	92	9	2
McClure	1.000	2	2	2	0	0
Schlehuber	.944	16	10	24	2	4

Shortstop	PCT	G	PO	A	E	DP
Diekroeger	.941	8	10	22	2	3
Espinal	.923	9	13	23	3	6
Lopez	.950	111	163	293	24	72
McClure	.951	14	22	36	3	7

Outfield	PCT	G	PO	A	E	DP
Adams	.974	85	179	8	5	4
Beltre	.982	79	161	6	3	1
Bonifacio	.968	50	86	5	3	1
Chapman	.980	66	143	4	3	1
Chism	.913	33	40	2	4	0
Elder	1.000	10	19	0	0	0
Ferguson	.978	30	43	2	1	1
Hudak	.944	25	33	1	2	0
Llanos	1.000	6	5	2	0	0
Prades	.965	35	80	3	3	1
Schlehuber	—	1	0	0	0	0
Trapp	1.000	4	4	1	0	0

LEXINGTON LEGENDS
SOUTH ATLANTIC LEAGUE

LOW CLASS A

Batting	B-T	HT	WT	DOB	AVG	vLH	vRH	G	AB	R	H	2B	3B	HR	RBI	BB	HBP	SH	SF	SO	SB	CS	SLG	OBP
Antonio, Mike	R-R	6-2	190	10-26-91	.191	.167	.196	97	341	19	65	15	1	5	35	31	3	1	2	61	3	2	.284	.263
Arteaga, Humberto	R-R	6-1	160	1-23-94	.188	.233	.178	61	240	17	45	5	2	0	13	6	2	3	0	43	0	4	.225	.214
Chapman, Ethan	L-R	6-0	180	1-5-90	.238	.222	.242	62	189	25	45	6	1	0	13	26	1	7	1	36	18	8	.280	.332
Cuckovich, Nicholas	R-R	6-2	200	10-8-91	.171	.091	.187	42	129	12	22	5	0	1	8	8	4	2	0	48	1	2	.233	.241
Diekroeger, Kenny	R-R	6-2	190	11-5-90	.142	.140	.143	66	218	11	31	2	1	1	7	15	1	2	0	101	1	2	.174	.201
Donato, Mark	L-L	6-2	225	11-18-91	.238	.159	.253	75	281	23	67	12	0	7	36	16	2	0	3	48	0	0	.356	.281
Dozier, Hunter	R-R	6-4	220	8-22-91	.327	.625	.277	15	55	6	18	6	0	9	3	1	0	0	5	0	0	.436	.373
Espinal, Yowill	R-R	6-0	170	4-1-91	.165	.211	.146	41	127	17	21	5	1	1	7	14	2	1	0	35	6	4	.244	.259
Ford, Fred	R-R	6-5	200	4-10-92	.193	.141	.206	126	420	47	81	19	4	13	43	52	6	0	4	166	5	2	.350	.288
Gallagher, Cameron	R-R	6-3	210	12-6-92	.212	.193	.218	66	222	19	47	15	0	2	18	24	6	1	3	28	0	0	.306	.302
Gore, Terrance	R-R	5-7	165	6-8-91	.215	.168	.229	128	455	76	98	6	3	0	24	62	19	5	0	120	68	8	.242	.334
Hudak, Alex	L-R	5-11	200	4-7-90	.247	.077	.276	34	89	11	22	5	2	1	7	8	1	1	0	27	3	3	.382	.316
Johnson, Chad	R-R	6-0	190	5-31-94	.429	—	.429	4	14	2	6	3	0	0	1	2	0	0	0	2	0	0	.643	.500
Maggi, Beau	L-R	6-1	208	11-11-90	.000	.000	.000	2	3	0	0	0	0	0	0	1	1	0	0	2	0	0	.000	.400
Marquez, Alex	R-R	5-11	190	12-10-92	.136	.000	.150	16	44	6	6	0	0	0	4	13	0	1	0	12	0	0	.136	.333
Mondesi, Raul Adalberto	B-R	6-1	165	7-27-95	.261	.260	.262	125	482	61	126	13	7	7	47	34	2	15	3	118	24	10	.361	.311
Morales, Adrian	R-R	5-8	180	11-18-88	.098	.273	.060	20	61	8	6	2	0	1	4	11	2	0	0	18	5	0	.180	.257
Shin, Jin-Ho	R-R	6-2	200	10-20-91	.169	.143	.177	67	207	23	35	10	0	2	17	28	6	1	2	65	0	0	.246	.284
Starling, Bubba	R-R	6-4	180	8-3-92	.241	.258	.237	125	435	51	105	21	4	13	63	53	6	0	4	128	22	3	.398	.329
Threlkeld, Mark	R-R	6-1	201	5-2-90	.249	.138	.281	72	257	31	64	25	0	5	36	34	1	1	5	66	2	1	.405	.333
Torres, Ramon	B-R	5-10	155	1-22-93	.218	.286	.197	26	87	8	19	4	0	0	5	7	0	4	1	13	3	3	.264	.274

Pitching	B-T	HT	WT	DOB	W	L	ERA	G	GS	CG	SV	IP	H	R	ER	HR	BB	SO	AVG	vLH	vRH	K/9	BB/9
Alexander, Scott	L-L	6-1	186	7-10-89	1	1	1.20	5	0	0	1	15	7	3	2	0	6	15	.143	.000	.194	9.00	3.60
Allen, Kevin	R-R	6-1	217	3-31-91	3	1	1.82	19	0	0	1	35	25	8	7	2	6	35	.200	.244	.175	9.09	1.56
Almonte, Miguel	R-R	6-2	180	4-4-93	6	9	3.10	25	25	1	0	131	115	53	45	6	36	132	.237	.225	.246	9.09	2.48
Billo, Greg	R-R	6-4	220	7-15-90	3	3	1.35	8	8	0	0	40	32	10	6	2	13	38	.224	.260	.186	8.55	2.93
Binford, Christian	R-R	6-6	217	12-20-92	8	7	2.67	23	23	0	0	135	129	54	40	7	25	130	.253	.304	.218	8.67	1.67
Brickhouse, Bryan	R-R	6-0	195	6-6-92	4	4	2.25	11	11	0	0	60	54	20	15	3	21	49	.238	.190	.266	7.35	3.15
Byrne, Chas	B-R	6-3	185	1-26-89	3	2	4.68	29	0	0	0	50	52	27	26	3	19	41	.268	.232	.288	7.38	3.42
Hall, Cory	R-R	6-2	232	5-12-88	2	1	3.00	19	0	0	0	36	26	12	12	1	19	38	.203	.196	.207	9.50	4.75
Hernandez, Danny	R-R	6-1	180	4-14-89	0	0	0.98	14	0	0	0	28	16	3	3	0	8	31	.160	.071	.224	10.08	2.60
Mills, Alec	R-R	6-4	185	11-30-91	2	3	1.59	18	3	0	6	45	28	11	8	1	9	47	.172	.190	.162	9.33	1.79
Murray, Matt	R-R	6-4	225	12-28-89	1	5	3.21	21	8	1	1	53	39	23	19	2	16	60	.199	.176	.216	10.13	2.70
Nina, Aroni	R-R	6-4	178	4-9-90	8	3	4.19	28	8	0	0	86	75	53	40	2	45	77	.234	.200	.251	8.06	4.71
Peterson, Mark	R-R	6-0	190	9-7-90	0	3	3.06	36	0	0	18	47	40	18	16	2	15	45	.231	.292	.194	8.62	2.87
Rodgers, Colin	L-L	5-10	181	12-2-93	3	3	3.27	9	9	0	0	44	42	24	16	4	21	33	.253	.179	.276	6.75	4.30
Santiago, Leonel	R-R	6-0	180	12-23-89	1	1	3.54	4	4	0	0	20	21	8	8	0	4	15	.269	.286	.260	6.64	1.77
Schulz, Clayton	L-L	6-2	180	6-7-90	3	4	3.03	35	0	0	5	59	48	23	20	1	21	52	.214	.152	.230	7.89	3.19
Simmons, Crawford	R-L	6-2	185	6-10-91	2	3	2.87	14	14	0	0	69	55	29	22	6	29	63	.214	.220	.212	8.22	3.78
Sneed, Zeb	R-R	6-4	195	3-19-91	1	2	5.82	8	0	0	1	22	22	15	14	3	7	19	.262	.115	.328	7.89	2.91
Stumpf, Daniel	L-L	6-2	200	1-4-91	10	10	3.07	25	25	4	0	138	103	58	47	10	50	117	.210	.209	.210	7.65	3.27
Tomchick, Ben	R-R	6-6	205	12-17-89	0	0	9.00	2	0	0	0	4	9	4	4	1	1	6	.450	.286	.538	13.50	2.25
Walter, John	R-R	6-5	225	5-20-91	1	1	1.01	18	0	0	8	27	8	3	3	0	4	31	.090	.118	.073	10.46	1.35
Williams, Ali	R-R	6-2	185	7-8-89	6	4	4.22	28	0	0	0	53	56	28	25	6	25	69	.273	.134	.341	11.64	4.22

Fielding

Catcher	PCT	G	PO	A	E	DP	PB
Gallagher	.991	57	452	73	5	4	6
Johnson	.971	4	32	1	1	0	3
Maggi	1.000	2	13	3	0	0	0
Marquez	.993	16	132	18	1	1	5
Shin	.980	62	483	56	11	4	12
Threlkeld	1.000	1	4	0	0	0	0

First Base	PCT	G	PO	A	E	DP
Cuckovich	.900	4	17	1	2	0
Donato	.994	20	170	6	1	14
Espinal	—	1	0	0	0	0
Ford	.982	47	422	25	8	37
Threlkeld	.989	70	590	38	7	43

Second Base	PCT	G	PO	A	E	DP
Arteaga	.982	34	60	100	3	21
Cuckovich	.900	2	5	4	1	1
Diekroeger	.959	49	82	128	9	29
Espinal	.986	29	55	74	6	15
Morales	1.000	3	5	8	0	1
Torres	.976	23	34	48	2	7

Third Base	PCT	G	PO	A	E	DP
Antonio	.879	81	44	145	26	13
Cuckovich	.907	19	6	33	4	0
Diekroeger	.920	11	9	14	2	0
Dozier	.971	13	9	24	1	4
Espinal	1.000	3	3	3	0	0
Morales	.944	13	8	26	2	0

Shortstop	PCT	G	PO	A	E	DP
Arteaga	.957	24	34	76	5	14
Diekroeger	1.000	1	1	1	0	0
Espinal	.818	3	3	6	2	1
Mondesi	.934	108	125	300	30	50
Torres	.900	3	4	5	1	1

Outfield	PCT	G	PO	A	E	DP
Chapman	.978	60	84	7	2	2
Cuckovich	.967	16	28	1	1	0
Ford	.955	74	122	5	6	0
Gore	.977	126	210	3	5	0
Hudak	.976	29	38	3	1	0
Starling	.988	118	233	6	3	1

BURLINGTON ROYALS

ROOKIE

APPALACHIAN LEAGUE

KANSAS CITY ROYALS

Batting	B-T	HT	WT	DOB	AVG	vLH	vRH	G	AB	R	H	2B	3B	HR	RBI	BB	HBP	SH	SF	SO	SB	CS	SLG	OBP
Allen, Jerrell	R-R	6-2	180	9-6-92	.167	.063	.196	29	72	8	12	1	0	0	5	7	1	1	1	17	5	2	.181	.247
Ayers, Andrew	R-R	5-11	190	4-20-91	.214	.219	.213	44	154	17	33	5	2	1	11	8	1	3	1	27	0	1	.292	.256
Bates, Sam	L-R	6-5	230	2-15-90	.278	.333	.256	51	169	30	47	12	1	10	32	18	3	0	1	25	5	0	.538	.356
Brown, Bobby	L-R	6-3	200	10-14-89	.181	.200	.177	49	149	13	27	3	3	4	18	14	1	0	1	44	1	0	.322	.255
Chism, Tyler	R-R	6-0	205	10-6-88	.333	.323	.337	40	132	28	44	5	2	5	19	24	3	0	0	25	10	3	.515	.447
Cuckovich, Nicholas	R-R	6-2	200	10-8-91	.179	.000	.208	17	56	4	10	4	0	1	3	8	2	0	1	24	0	0	.304	.299
Escalera-Maldonado, Alfredo	R-R	6-1	180	2-17-95	.277	.200	.299	48	184	23	51	14	1	1	13	14	2	3	1	42	3	2	.380	.333
Gonzalez, Pedro	R-R	6-2	162	1-28-92	.279	.281	.278	32	104	7	29	6	0	3	11	4	4	1	2	17	0	1	.423	.325
Henry, Desmond	R-R	6-1	175	7-7-93	.244	.333	.216	48	164	27	40	4	1	2	10	17	1	2	1	45	20	3	.317	.317
Johnson, Chad	R-R	6-0	190	5-31-94	.219	.200	.225	40	137	9	30	1	2	1	14	11	4	0	0	38	0	0	.277	.296
Kuntz, Kevin	B-R	6-1	185	5-29-90	.208	.294	.161	36	96	9	20	2	0	0	6	9	2	3	2	21	1	1	.229	.284
Mercurio, Mike	R-R	6-0	185	1-9-91	.140	.250	.111	25	57	4	8	1	0	1	5	5	3	1	2	14	3	0	.211	.239
Newman, Alex	R-R	6-1	198	12-7-92	.186	.111	.213	51	172	8	32	10	2	1	21	18	0	0	1	75	0	2	.285	.262
Ramos, Mauricio	R-R	6-1	160	2-2-92	.322	.333	.317	42	146	22	47	14	1	0	24	7	2	0	6	17	2	1	.432	.348
Sweeney, Chris	R-R	6-3	185	9-12-91	.203	.125	.213	26	69	10	14	2	3	3	6	8	1	0	0	21	1	0	.449	.295
Torres, Ramon	B-R	5-10	155	1-22-93	.278	.356	.248	42	162	24	45	10	2	3	20	6	1	4	1	12	5	5	.420	.306
Urena, Lewis	R-R	5-8	145	5-6-91	.116	.000	.156	16	43	6	5	0	0	1	6	0	1	0	1	11	0	1	.116	.224
Villegas, Luis	R-R	5-10	170	12-2-92	.222	.211	.229	19	54	4	12	2	0	0	4	0	0	0	1	11	0	0	.259	.276

Pitching	B-T	HT	WT	DOB	W	L	ERA	G	GS	CG	SV	IP	H	R	ER	HR	BB	SO	AVG	vLH	vRH	K/9	BB/9
Deshazier, Torey	R-R	6-0	160	9-16-93	2	1	4.35	11	3	0	0	39	40	22	19	1	23	40	.268	.183	.326	9.15	5.26
Edwards, Andrew	R-R	6-5	260	10-7-91	1	1	1.56	14	0	0	8	17	11	4	3	0	11	14	.186	.149	.227	7.27	5.71
Guevara, Cruz	L-L	6-0	155	5-29-94	3	1	0.47	14	0	0	0	19	20	1	1	0	4	15	.274	.353	.250	7.11	1.89
Jeffreys, Mike	R-R	6-4	190	10-29-91	0	0	0.87	6	0	0	0	10	7	2	1	0	3	14	.184	.235	.143	12.19	2.61
Lewis, Sam	R-R	6-4	195	10-9-91	5	4	3.50	11	6	0	1	44	37	21	17	1	15	37	.231	.205	.256	7.63	3.09
Lovvorn, Zach	R-R	6-0	185	5-26-94	2	3	3.74	11	11	0	0	53	50	24	22	2	21	36	.258	.261	.256	6.11	3.57
Machado, Andres	R-R	6-0	175	4-22-93	0	8	8.34	12	11	0	0	45	75	46	42	7	17	21	.373	.371	.375	4.17	3.38
Mattes, Ryan	R-R	6-7	190	9-7-90	1	2	4.18	15	0	0	1	24	19	12	11	4	2	25	.221	.222	.220	9.51	0.76
McCarthy, Kevin	R-R	6-3	200	2-22-92	4	2	3.40	10	5	0	0	42	49	18	16	2	5	32	.293	.326	.282	6.80	1.06
Newberry, Jake	R-R	6-2	195	11-20-94	1	1	2.68	11	6	0	1	47	39	19	14	3	24	50	.223	.315	.182	9.57	4.60
Ogando, Cesar	R-L	6-3	210	6-6-92	0	5	6.93	11	8	0	1	38	53	41	29	2	24	27	.338	.190	.360	6.45	5.73
Reynoso, Javier	B-L	5-11	182	10-31-92	0	2	2.63	14	0	0	0	24	19	8	7	0	13	27	.216	.154	.227	10.13	4.88
Rodriguez, Jose	R-R	6-2	192	9-18-92	3	2	6.00	16	0	0	2	21	21	19	14	3	15	25	.259	.222	.278	10.71	6.43
Santos, Luis	R-R	6-0	185	2-11-91	4	1	2.25	7	7	1	0	40	33	10	10	0	9	35	.226	.244	.218	7.88	2.03
Stephenson, Niklas	R-R	6-2	195	11-16-93	0	0	8.10	12	0	0	0	23	37	22	21	2	12	15	.378	.533	.309	5.79	4.63
Tenuta, Matt	L-L	6-4	208	12-16-93	2	4	2.81	10	10	0	0	51	42	22	16	4	14	39	.219	.259	.212	6.84	2.45
Tomchick, Ben	R-R	6-6	205	12-17-89	1	1	9.64	11	0	0	0	19	30	21	20	4	10	11	.361	.323	.385	5.30	4.82

Fielding

Catcher	PCT	G	PO	A	E	DP	PB
Gonzalez	.982	14	97	14	2	0	3
Johnson	.997	38	253	40	1	3	6
Villegas	.983	18	101	15	2	0	5

First Base	PCT	G	PO	A	E	DP
Bates	.991	37	312	17	3	22
Brown	.989	31	256	14	3	30
Gonzalez	.947	2	17	1	1	2

Second Base	PCT	G	PO	A	E	DP
Ayers	.983	24	51	65	2	18
Cuckovich	—	1	0	0	0	0

	PCT	G	PO	A	E	DP
Kuntz	.979	35	54	85	3	18
Mercurio	.897	9	9	26	4	7
Urena	1.000	8	12	16	0	1

Third Base	PCT	G	PO	A	E	DP
Ayers	1.000	3	1	3	0	0
Cuckovich	.958	17	10	36	2	0
Gonzalez	1.000	1	0	1	0	0
Henry	—	1	0	0	0	0
Mercurio	.643	13	2	7	5	0
Ramos	.946	39	21	84	6	9
Urena	1.000	2	1	0	0	0

Shortstop	PCT	G	PO	A	E	DP
Ayers	.942	22	39	59	6	15
Mercurio	.500	1	0	1	1	0
Torres	.931	42	58	117	13	26
Urena	.955	6	5	16	1	6

Outfield	PCT	G	PO	A	E	DP
Allen	.897	24	34	1	4	0
Chism	.979	26	40	6	1	0
Escalera-Maldonado	.941	47	93	3	6	3
Henry	.957	46	67	0	3	0
Newman	.962	49	72	3	3	0
Sweeney	.977	20	38	5	1	3

AZL ROYALS

ROOKIE

ARIZONA LEAGUE

Batting	B-T	HT	WT	DOB	AVG	vLH	vRH	G	AB	R	H	2B	3B	HR	RBI	BB	HBP	SH	SF	SO	SB	CS	SLG	OBP
Atkins, Josiah	R-R	6-1	180	12-14-93	.000	.000	.000	4	10	0	0	0	0	0	1	1	0	0	0	8	0	0	.000	.091
Bonifacio, Jorge	R-R	6-1	192	6-4-93	.300	.333	.292	9	30	4	9	3	2	0	6	4	1	0	0	6	1	0	.533	.400
Cano, Cristian	R-R	6-2	170	2-9-94	.258	.357	.213	30	89	12	23	1	0	1	15	11	5	2	3	18	4	3	.303	.361
Dale, Ryan	R-R	6-3	180	3-16-96	.237	.133	.262	27	76	7	18	4	0	0	5	10	0	3	2	33	3	0	.289	.318
Davis, Logan	L-R	6-2	175	8-23-91	.244	.333	.222	25	78	15	19	0	1	0	1	11	1	2	0	8	6	1	.269	.344
Duenez, Samir	L-R	6-1	195	6-11-96	.294	.333	.282	47	187	26	55	12	2	0	19	12	0	0	0	27	6	4	.380	.337

Batting	B-T	HT	WT	DOB	AVG	vLH	vRH	G	AB	R	H	2B	3B	HR	RBI	BB	HBP	SH	SF	SO	SB	CS	SLG	OBP
Dulin, Brandon	L-R	6-3	225	12-29-92	.269	.205	.289	46	186	18	50	11	6	1	22	13	5	0	1	37	5	1	.409	.332
Estades, Ariel	L-R	5-11	150	4-27-94	.250	—	.250	1	4	2	1	0	0	0	0	1	0	0	0	3	0	0	.250	.400
Ferguson, Tim	R-R	6-1	190	10-25-88	.333	.600	.231	6	18	2	6	1	0	0	1	4	0	0	0	2	1	0	.389	.455
Fernandez, Xavier	R-R	5-11	197	7-15-95	.316	.385	.283	21	79	9	25	3	0	0	14	8	0	1	1	11	0	3	.354	.375
Flores, Jecksson	R-R	5-11	145	10-28-93	.246	.194	.264	39	142	25	35	4	0	0	17	23	1	5	2	25	13	3	.275	.351
Franco, Angel	B-R	5-10	155	5-23-90	.346	.400	.313	7	26	5	9	1	0	0	1	5	3	1	0	0	6	1	0	.500	.433
Franco, Wander	R-R	6-2	170	12-13-94	.277	.366	.246	43	159	27	44	11	4	0	23	13	1	2	2	30	2	4	.396	.331
Fukofuka, Amalani	R-R	6-1	180	9-25-95	.244	.190	.263	42	156	28	38	9	2	1	12	27	1	3	0	47	10	2	.346	.359
Gomez, Brawlun	R-R	6-2	185	8-5-92	.277	.270	.279	43	148	26	41	7	0	7	25	20	5	0	1	61	6	3	.466	.379
Gonzalez, Cesar	R-R	6-3	185	11-20-93	.202	.063	.227	33	104	10	21	2	0	0	6	8	2	2	1	25	5	1	.221	.270
Holloway, Marsalis	R-R	5-10	160	9-18-92	.164	.143	.171	27	55	10	9	2	0	0	4	17	5	0	0	21	4	1	.200	.403
King, Riley	R-L	6-4	210	4-23-94	.212	.094	.256	36	118	10	25	3	2	0	17	10	7	4	0	43	3	1	.271	.311
Lara, Luis	R-R	5-11	188	2-3-95	.143	.200	.111	5	14	2	2	1	0	0	1	1	0	0	0	5	0	0	.214	.200
Melo, Eddy	R-R	6-2	180	8-28-93	.105	.222	.069	11	38	2	4	0	0	0	1	3	0	1	1	14	0	0	.105	.167
Patino, Alfredo	R-R	6-0	175	5-18-93	.269	.125	.316	38	130	21	35	6	1	0	15	11	5	2	0	27	4	3	.331	.349
Rincon, Edinson	R-R	6-1	215	8-11-90	.459	.286	.500	11	37	6	17	2	1	0	11	5	0	0	0	2	1	0	.568	.524
Valenzuela, Luis	L-R	5-10	150	8-25-93	.130	.250	.105	5	23	3	3	0	0	0	2	2	0	0	0	1	2	0	.130	.200

Pitching	B-T	HT	WT	DOB	W	L	ERA	G	GS	CG	SV	IP	H	R	ER	BB	SO	AVG	vLH	vRH	K/9	BB/9
Arguelles, Noel	L-L	6-3	225	1-12-90	0	0	0.00	2	2	0	0	3	1	1	0	0	2	5	.111	.000	.125	15.00	6.00
Baez, Angel	R-R	6-3	196	2-14-91	1	0	2.51	6	3	0	0	14	17	6	4	0	3	17	.293	.192	.375	10.67	1.88
Billo, Greg	R-R	6-4	220	7-15-90	0	2	3.00	5	2	0	0	9	5	3	3	1	2	12	.152	.000	.238	12.00	2.00
Black, Alex	R-R	6-3	210	2-27-91	2	2	3.24	15	0	0	3	17	20	6	6	0	7	17	.294	.344	.250	9.18	3.78
Brockett, Andrew	R-R	5-11	185	7-5-92	1	1	0.96	9	0	0	4	9	6	1	1	0	1	11	.182	.200	.174	10.61	0.96
Darhower, Chase	R-R	6-4	215	1-12-93	0	3	6.67	11	2	0	0	30	38	27	22	2	9	24	.306	.282	.318	7.28	2.73
Davis, Tripp	L-L	6-1	200	2-12-91	2	3	3.32	11	1	0	2	22	21	11	8	1	6	15	.253	.182	.279	6.23	2.49
Fairchild, Austin	R-L	6-0	195	3-25-94	0	0	9.20	9	1	0	1	15	17	18	15	0	21	18	.274	.333	.255	11.05	12.89
Feliz, Igol	R-R	6-3	195	5-31-93	4	1	3.47	12	5	0	0	49	50	21	19	3	16	35	.270	.307	.237	6.39	2.92
Fernandez, Pedro	R-R	6-0	175	5-25-94	0	1	1.82	8	7	0	0	35	28	10	7	3	8	38	.215	.214	.216	9.87	2.08
Flecha, Christian	L-L	6-2	150	5-9-95	0	2	5.56	11	0	0	0	11	13	9	7	0	11	12	.283	.231	.303	9.53	8.74
Haynes, Hunter	L-L	6-1	175	2-12-94	0	4	5.20	12	5	0	1	36	36	29	21	3	14	29	.248	.308	.226	7.18	3.47
Herrera, Carlos	L-L	6-3	180	7-4-93	4	1	3.47	7	3	0	0	23	29	10	9	0	4	23	.312	.292	.319	8.87	1.54
Hope, Carter	L-R	6-3	195	2-5-95	0	3	6.08	6	6	0	0	13	21	15	9	1	5	11	.344	.429	.273	7.43	3.38
Melgar, Luis	R-R	6-3	153	2-5-92	0	1	6.75	3	2	0	0	12	15	12	9	1	2	10	.288	.320	.259	7.50	1.50
Melville, Tim	R-R	6-5	210	10-9-89	0	0	0.00	1	1	0	0	1	0	0	0	0	0	1	.000	.000	.000	9.00	0.00
Munoz, Jairo	R-R	6-0	180	8-12-91	1	0	5.29	12	0	0	0	17	23	15	10	1	5	16	.311	.310	.311	8.47	2.65
Ortiz, Jesu	R-R	5-10	170	1-6-91	0	1	9.00	4	0	0	0	6	8	7	6	1	1	3	.286	.222	.316	4.50	1.50
Perez, Kevin	R-R	6-0	205	8-1-93	0	3	3.52	13	0	0	0	15	16	8	6	1	8	15	.271	.048	.395	8.80	4.70
Rico, Luis	L-L	6-1	180	11-29-93	1	0	2.97	11	5	0	0	36	35	19	12	2	13	39	.250	.278	.240	9.66	3.22
Rios, Ronny	R-R	6-2	195	10-18-91	2	2	2.01	13	0	0	0	22	20	8	5	0	6	14	.241	.243	.239	5.64	2.42
Rosario, Harol	R-R	6-3	197	9-15-92	2	0	3.50	12	4	0	0	46	46	25	18	2	19	39	.254	.211	.286	7.58	3.69
Sons, Dylan	L-L	6-3	176	7-15-93	0	5	3.86	11	6	0	0	40	46	33	17	1	19	37	.289	.310	.282	8.39	4.31
Verdugo, Ryan	L-L	6-0	205	4-10-87	2	1	0.00	5	0	0	0	6	4	3	0	0	1	7	.182	.333	.125	11.12	1.59

Fielding

Catcher	PCT	G	PO	A	E	DP	PB
Atkins	1.000	2	1	0	0	0	0
Fernandez	.964	15	122	13	5	0	7
Gonzalez	.978	32	237	24	6	4	22
Lara	1.000	5	30	3	0	0	0
Melo	.986	9	61	12	1	0	1

First Base	PCT	G	PO	A	E	DP
Davis	1.000	1	4	0	0	0
Duenez	.961	23	178	17	8	21
Dulin	.984	33	295	21	5	24

Second Base	PCT	G	PO	A	E	DP
Davis	.961	13	36	38	3	4
Franco	.800	2	2	2	1	1

Franco	.917	4	5	6	1	1
Patino	.960	37	60	85	6	28
Valenzuela	1.000	3	6	7	0	2

Third Base	PCT	G	PO	A	E	DP
Dale	.792	26	13	29	11	2
Franco	1.000	1	0	3	0	0
Franco	.846	36	22	55	14	6

Shortstop	PCT	G	PO	A	E	DP
Davis	.930	15	11	29	3	5
Flores	.925	39	59	114	14	16
Franco	.950	4	5	14	1	2
Franco	.857	5	5	7	2	0
Valenzuela	1.000	2	3	9	0	1

Outfield	PCT	G	PO	A	E	DP
Bonifacio	1.000	8	7	2	0	0
Cano	.957	25	42	3	2	1
Duenez	1.000	6	5	1	0	0
Estades	1.000	1	2	0	0	0
Ferguson	1.000	6	13	1	0	1
Fukofuka	.974	39	73	3	2	0
Gomez	.948	42	83	8	5	3
Holloway	1.000	20	13	1	0	0
King	.952	30	58	1	3	0
Rincon	.833	9	10	0	2	0

IDAHO FALLS CHUKARS

ROOKIE

PIONEER LEAGUE

Batting	B-T	HT	WT	DOB	AVG	vLH	vRH	G	AB	R	H	2B	3B	HR	RBI	BB	HBP	SH	SF	SO	SB	CS	SLG	OBP
Antonio, Mike	R-R	6-2	190	10-26-91	.421	.375	.433	9	38	10	16	8	1	1	8	3	1	0	0	6	0	0	.763	.476
Arteaga, Humberto	R-R	6-1	160	1-23-94	.280	.404	.254	69	300	56	84	15	5	3	58	26	2	10	8	52	11	7	.393	.333
Bringas, Adrian	R-R	5-10	185	7-18-89	.500	.000	.500	8	22	3	11	4	2	0	8	1	1	1	0	2	0	0	.864	.520
Cuckovich, Nicholas	R-R	6-2	200	10-8-91	.226	.333	.205	16	53	13	12	6	0	0	4	8	2	1	0	13	5	2	.340	.349
Davis, Logan	L-R	6-2	175	8-23-91	.234	.167	.244	15	47	8	11	3	0	0	5	4	0	3	0	7	0	0	.298	.294
Dozier, Hunter	R-R	6-4	220	8-22-91	.303	.235	.315	54	218	43	66	24	0	7	43	35	3	0	2	32	3	1	.509	.403
Evans, Zane	R-R	6-2	209	11-29-91	.352	.375	.349	41	162	26	57	18	0	4	31	11	1	0	1	25	1	0	.537	.394
Garcia, Carlos	R-R	6-0	176	3-18-92	.333	.372	.324	64	228	52	76	10	3	2	35	23	4	8	1	34	17	1	.430	.402
Hernandez, Elier	R-R	6-3	200	11-21-94	.301	.286	.304	66	289	44	87	15	8	3	44	18	6	2	4	62	9	2	.439	.350
Maggi, Beau	L-R	6-1	208	11-11-90	.186	.222	.180	21	59	8	11	3	0	1	8	10	1	0	0	13	0	1	.288	.314
Marquez, Alex	R-R	5-11	190	12-10-92	.204	.308	.171	17	54	9	11	2	1	0	4	7	0	1	0	14	0	0	.278	.295

Name	B-T	HT	WT	DOB	AVG	vLH	vRH	G	AB	R	H	2B	3B	HR	RBI	BB	HBP	SH	SF	SO	SB	CS	SLG	OBP
Ramos, Mauricio	R-R	6-1	160	2-2-92	.308	.214	.333	16	65	14	20	5	1	1	4	3	2	0	0	9	0	1	.462	.357
Rivera, Alexis	L-L	6-2	225	6-17-94	.269	.211	.282	57	212	44	57	8	0	4	26	23	3	2	0	37	9	5	.363	.349
Rockett, Daniel	R-R	6-2	200	11-9-90	.310	.517	.279	58	226	42	70	15	1	11	53	13	3	2	3	49	1	2	.531	.351
Schwindel, Frank	R-R	6-1	205	6-29-92	.300	.308	.298	64	260	41	78	14	1	6	42	9	6	1	2	24	0	2	.431	.336
Stubbs, Cody	L-L	6-4	215	1-14-91	.284	.250	.291	64	264	41	75	13	7	6	43	28	4	0	1	61	0	1	.455	.360
Taylor, Dominique	R-R	6-1	190	8-11-92	.322	.313	.324	62	233	50	75	14	2	8	37	15	8	3	2	29	13	5	.502	.380
Urena, Lewis	R-R	5-8	145	5-6-91	.133	.500	.077	8	15	4	2	0	0	0	2	5	1	1	0	4	0	0	.133	.381

Pitching	B-T	HT	WT	DOB	W	L	ERA	G	GS	CG	SV	IP	H	R	ER	HR	BB	SO	AVG	vLH	vRH	K/9	BB/9
Alvarez, Matt	R-R	6-1	186	1-11-91	0	0	6.75	6	0	0	0	5	6	4	4	0	3	2	.300	.273	.333	3.38	5.06
Arguelles, Noel	L-L	6-3	225	1-12-90	0	1	6.75	1	0	0	0	3	3	3	2	1	1	1	.250	.200	.286	3.38	3.38
Bartsch, Kyle	L-L	5-10	210	3-10-91	2	1	2.45	21	0	0	3	29	20	12	8	0	9	37	.190	.171	.200	11.35	2.76
Bonvillain, Brent	L-L	6-2	170	10-10-90	3	2	4.45	17	0	0	0	28	36	21	14	1	14	26	.305	.341	.284	8.26	4.45
Brockett, Andrew	R-R	5-11	185	7-5-92	1	0	4.05	9	0	0	0	13	13	7	6	1	5	10	.250	.227	.267	6.75	3.38
Caramo, Yender	R-R	6-0	175	8-25-91	6	3	3.84	15	8	0	0	61	72	41	26	4	8	37	.295	.336	.254	5.46	1.18
Conroy, Patrick	L-R	6-4	218	1-14-92	6	2	3.30	13	12	0	0	71	65	37	26	3	33	64	.245	.247	.244	8.11	4.18
Dziedzic, Jonathan	R-L	6-0	165	2-4-91	2	0	2.68	12	11	0	0	50	45	16	15	1	14	47	.249	.355	.193	8.40	2.50
Fairchild, Austin	R-L	6-0	195	3-25-94	0	0	21.60	6	0	0	0	3	3	12	8	0	14	4	.231	.333	.200	10.80	37.80
Farrell, Luke	R-R	6-6	210	6-7-91	1	3	6.65	10	10	0	0	43	52	32	32	5	15	45	.311	.349	.288	9.35	3.12
Fitzsimmons, Jon	R-R	6-2	205	11-29-91	0	0	4.00	11	0	0	0	18	15	9	8	1	8	13	.242	.320	.189	6.50	4.00
Goudeau, Ashton	R-R	6-6	205	7-23-92	1	5	10.18	14	5	0	0	41	71	55	46	4	14	23	.382	.474	.318	5.09	3.10
Junis, Jake	R-R	6-3	210	9-16-92	2	6	7.39	13	13	0	0	60	85	59	49	13	17	55	.328	.326	.329	8.30	2.56
Mack, Tyler	R-R	6-4	205	9-3-90	3	4	7.52	13	2	0	0	26	31	28	22	1	22	22	.301	.324	.290	7.52	7.52
Martinez, Josiel	L-L	5-10	160	11-9-91	6	2	5.19	21	0	0	2	43	48	34	25	3	21	33	.270	.291	.260	6.85	4.36
Melville, Tim	R-R	6-5	210	10-9-89	0	1	10.13	3	3	0	0	3	4	6	3	1	4	4	.308	.286	.333	13.50	13.50
Reed, Cody	L-L	6-5	220	4-15-93	0	1	6.07	15	6	0	0	30	31	24	20	0	23	25	.270	.325	.240	7.58	6.98
Rhoney, Corey	R-R	5-9	200	9-2-90	1	0	3.80	20	0	0	5	21	19	10	9	2	7	22	.238	.280	.218	9.28	2.95
Santos, Luis	R-R	6-0	185	2-11-91	3	0	1.40	3	3	0	0	19	9	4	3	0	5	12	.136	.190	.111	5.59	2.33
Sneed, Zeb	R-R	6-4	195	3-19-91	2	1	4.50	8	0	0	0	18	16	9	9	2	4	27	.239	.160	.286	13.50	2.00
Sparkman, Glenn	B-R	6-2	210	5-11-92	1	0	1.72	20	0	0	2	37	25	8	7	1	10	47	.194	.226	.171	11.54	2.45
Tenuta, Matt	L-L	6-4	208	12-16-93	1	1	6.43	3	3	0	0	14	19	12	10	1	4	11	.311	.321	.303	7.07	2.57
Walter, John	R-R	6-5	225	5-20-91	0	0	9.00	1	0	0	0	1	2	2	1	0	0	0	.400	.667	.000	0.00	0.00

Fielding

Catcher	PCT	G	PO	A	E	DP	PB
Evans	.991	27	190	27	2	0	7
Maggi	.989	15	79	7	1	2	2
Marquez	.975	16	106	10	3	1	2
Schwindel	.987	27	190	33	3	1	8

First Base	PCT	G	PO	A	E	DP
Cuckovich	1.000	4	30	0	0	5
Marquez	1.000	1	7	2	0	0
Schwindel	1.000	15	121	11	0	9
Stubbs	.986	57	534	44	8	57

Second Base	PCT	G	PO	A	E	DP
Arteaga	.964	5	15	12	1	4
Bringas	.944	4	4	13	1	5
Davis	1.000	6	6	18	0	0
Garcia	.946	63	129	186	18	44
Ramos	1.000	1	3	4	0	1

Third Base	PCT	G	PO	A	E	DP
Antonio	.889	5	1	7	1	0
Bringas	1.000	3	2	4	0	1
Cuckovich	.813	8	6	20	6	1
Davis	.778	6	3	4	2	1
Dozier	.914	37	24	72	9	6
Ramos	.800	14	4	28	8	2
Urena	.857	6	3	9	2	1

Shortstop	PCT	G	PO	A	E	DP
Arteaga	.946	64	104	196	17	46
Davis	.917	3	5	6	1	2
Dozier	.978	9	12	32	1	8
Urena	1.000	1	0	1	0	0

Outfield	PCT	G	PO	A	E	DP
Cuckovich	—	1	0	0	0	0
Hernandez	.919	63	109	4	10	0
Rivera	.957	51	65	1	3	0
Rockett	.977	57	120	5	3	3
Taylor	.950	58	92	4	5	0

DSL ROYALS   ROOKIE

DOMINICAN SUMMER LEAGUE

Batting	B-T	HT	WT	DOB	AVG	vLH	vRH	G	AB	R	H	2B	3B	HR	RBI	BB	HBP	SH	SF	SO	SB	CS	SLG	OBP
Atencio, Jesus	R-R	5-10	165	8-22-96	.210	.290	.174	33	100	8	21	2	2	0	6	11	2	3	0	10	0	2	.270	.301
Bueno, Misael	R-R	6-1	190	8-10-93	.196	.114	.234	50	138	12	27	9	1	2	10	15	7	0	2	44	4	7	.319	.302
Castellano, Angelo	R-R	6-0	170	1-13-95	.265	.329	.229	67	223	25	59	8	1	0	25	30	3	5	1	25	9	5	.309	.358
Collado, Offerman	R-L	5-10	140	6-10-96	.262	.348	.214	18	65	11	17	1	0	0	6	8	0	1	2	12	3	2	.277	.333
Diaz, Carlos	B-R	5-8	145	11-15-92	.266	.260	.269	65	229	40	61	10	1	0	18	20	8	4	4	23	18	10	.319	.341
Estades, Ariel	L-R	5-11	150	4-27-94	.226	.256	.209	37	106	19	24	3	0	0	7	16	3	3	2	19	8	4	.255	.339
Martinez, Jose	B-R	5-10	150	8-15-96	.263	.244	.274	66	224	26	59	11	5	0	27	19	5	4	3	22	5	4	.357	.331
Melo, Eddy	R-R	6-2	180	8-28-93	.229	.231	.229	29	96	9	22	4	1	0	8	14	1	0	1	15	0	2	.292	.330
Mogollon, Jose	R-R	6-1	170	5-17-96	.125	.238	.078	31	72	8	9	1	0	0	3	13	4	1	0	15	2	2	.139	.292
Saez, Alberto	R-R	6-1	155	7-11-96	.189	.175	.196	43	132	10	25	3	1	0	10	13	1	4	1	36	2	1	.227	.265
Sanchez, Jose	L-L	5-10	155	7-21-94	.219	.122	.274	46	114	9	25	1	1	0	5	12	3	4	0	26	4	3	.246	.310
Solano, Jose	R-R	6-1	170	8-17-93	.171	.455	.067	16	41	5	7	0	1	0	1	2	0	1	0	8	0	3	.220	.209
2-team total (14 Marlins)					.184	—	—	30	87	8	16	2	1	0	2	3	0	1	0	24	1	3	.230	.211
Torres, Jose	R-R	6-0	175	9-16-95	.196	.186	.202	55	168	15	33	5	0	1	16	18	3	3	1	30	5	4	.244	.284
Tovar, Roberto	R-R	6-0	180	11-16-94	.216	.154	.243	54	167	15	36	8	0	0	18	14	3	2	2	24	2	1	.234	.285
Valerio, Cornelio	L-L	5-10	175	3-7-94	.234	.241	.231	36	107	9	25	6	2	1	11	19	5	0	1	18	1	6	.355	.371
Venegas, Ariel	R-R	5-11	155	5-5-95	.237	.235	.238	46	114	16	27	1	0	0	7	19	2	2	0	18	6	4	.246	.356
Vital, Jose	R-R	6-2	180	3-25-96	.211	.250	.192	16	38	3	8	0	1	1	6	4	2	0	1	18	1	2	.342	.311

Pitching

Pitching	B-T	HT	WT	DOB	W	L	ERA	G	GS	CG	SV	IP	H	R	ER	HR	BB	SO	AVG	vLH	vRH	K/9	BB/9
Arias, Yojensy	L-L	6-3	180	7-29-93	1	2	5.71	12	0	0	2	17	17	13	11	1	10	10	.239	.083	.271	5.19	5.19
Arreaza, Cesar	R-R	6-0	175	2-3-94	0	1	5.68	4	0	0	0	6	5	5	4	0	4	2	.208	.000	.313	2.84	5.68
Camacho, Enmanuel	L-L	6-0	160	1-9-95	2	1	2.68	11	10	0	0	40	27	15	12	2	25	32	.193	.364	.161	7.14	5.58
Cepin, Reinaldo	L-L	6-1	160	1-10-94	1	1	2.61	6	0	0	0	10	6	3	3	0	2	9	.171	.000	.200	7.84	1.74
Cordero, Estarlin	L-L	6-0	145	3-3-93	2	2	2.36	16	0	0	3	34	27	11	9	1	16	36	.223	.222	.223	9.44	4.19
Familia, Felix	L-L	6-0	170	11-28-95	6	1	0.76	14	1	0	4	36	20	8	3	0	17	29	.165	.091	.182	7.32	4.29
Fernandez, Pedro	R-R	6-0	175	5-25-94	0	0	0.75	4	2	0	0	12	5	1	1	0	3	15	.128	.235	.045	11.25	2.25
Garabito, Gerson	R-R	6-0	160	8-19-95	1	0	3.04	12	2	0	0	27	23	10	9	0	17	17	.253	.303	.224	5.74	5.74
Garces, Sandy	L-L	6-0	170	10-15-93	3	3	2.70	14	11	1	1	60	53	24	18	4	15	38	.237	.189	.246	5.70	2.25
Gomez, Ofreidy	R-R	6-3	190	7-6-95	3	0	2.35	10	0	0	0	23	15	13	6	0	14	17	.192	.211	.186	6.65	5.48
Herrera, Carlos	L-L	6-3	180	7-4-93	4	1	1.13	7	7	0	0	32	20	7	4	1	10	26	.185	.250	.167	7.31	2.81
Maldonado, Ismael	R-R	6-4	170	9-28-95	0	0	9.00	1	0	0	0	1	1	1	1	0	2	0	.333	.333	—	0.00	18.00
Marte, Yunior	R-R	6-2	165	2-2-95	4	3	1.71	11	8	0	2	47	39	15	9	0	9	36	.229	.317	.182	6.85	1.71
Medrano, Miguel	R-R	6-2	175	6-19-95	2	2	2.91	13	0	0	0	22	20	9	7	0	7	5	.274	.286	.267	2.08	2.91
Melendez, Cesar	R-R	6-1	162	3-20-95	2	0	3.38	14	0	0	6	29	21	12	11	2	8	21	.204	.250	.187	6.44	2.45
Pena, Yimauri	R-R	6-2	160	10-15-93	2	2	2.75	13	5	1	0	39	28	13	12	0	13	33	.193	.229	.175	7.55	2.97
Pinto, Julio	R-R	6-3	185	11-18-95	3	3	2.65	13	13	0	0	54	37	20	16	1	26	43	.197	.274	.159	7.12	4.31
Polanco, Darwin	R-R	6-3	145	5-23-93	0	1	7.50	11	0	0	3	12	12	11	10	0	9	9	.255	.250	.257	6.75	6.75
Reyes, Junior	L-L	6-0	165	3-29-96	2	1	3.48	11	5	0	0	31	28	15	12	2	27	30	.255	.188	.266	8.71	7.84
Tavarez, Yohan	R-R	6-2	185	11-8-94	2	3	0.81	5	4	0	0	22	17	6	2	0	6	15	.218	.357	.188	6.04	2.42
Veras, Jose	R-R	6-1	170	7-15-94	1	2	2.30	13	2	0	5	31	24	12	8	1	10	13	.209	.323	.167	3.73	2.87
Viloria, Alejandro	L-L	6-0	165	6-15-95	0	0	7.04	4	0	0	0	8	7	6	6	1	8	3	.280	.167	.316	3.52	9.39

Fielding

Catcher	PCT	G	PO	A	E	DP	PB
Atencio	.981	23	140	18	3	1	10
Melo	.988	21	140	23	2	0	2
Torres	.984	11	49	14	1	0	1
Tovar	.985	22	114	19	2	1	1

First Base	PCT	G	PO	A	E	DP
Atencio	1.000	1	6	1	0	0
Melo	1.000	6	42	5	0	4
Solano	.952	2	20	0	1	1
Torres	.975	34	260	13	7	25
Tovar	.993	33	274	20	2	26
Venegas	1.000	1	5	0	0	0

Second Base	PCT	G	PO	A	E	DP
Atencio	1.000	1	0	1	0	0
Collado	1.000	10	21	25	0	5
Diaz	.971	53	113	121	7	29
Torres	1.000	5	9	9	0	4
Venegas	.978	17	24	21	1	3

Third Base	PCT	G	PO	A	E	DP
Castellano	.943	66	42	123	10	19
Diaz	.857	5	3	3	1	0
Torres	.929	8	3	10	1	1

Shortstop	PCT	G	PO	A	E	DP
Collado	.800	5	6	10	4	4
Diaz	.917	9	7	15	2	2
Martinez	.945	64	104	173	16	28

Outfield	PCT	G	PO	A	E	DP
Bueno	.980	50	95	4	2	1
Estades	.986	35	62	7	1	4
Mogollon	.938	25	30	0	2	0
Sanchez	.985	42	58	7	1	2
Saez	.950	31	52	5	3	2
Solano	.889	14	16	0	2	0
Valerio	1.000	28	44	5	0	1
Venegas	.917	12	11	0	1	0
Vital	1.000	8	10	0	0	0

Los Angeles Angels

SEASON IN A SENTENCE: Mike Trout is laying the groundwork for a career that could end up among the greatest of all time, but disappointing performances by free agent acquisitions Josh Hamilton and Albert Pujols plus pitching problems led to a second-consecutive third-place finish.

HIGH POINT: In late June and early July, the Angels put together their best stretch of baseball of the season, sweeping the Tigers and taking series against the Cardinals and Red Sox in a 9-2 stretch.

LOW POINT: On June 3, hapless Houston finished off a four-game sweep of the Angels with a 2-1 Astros victory. It was one of only two series all year that the Astros swept. The Angels' lineup, expected to be one of the best in baseball, managed only eight runs in four games against Jordan Lyles, Dallas Keuchel, Erik Bedard and Bud Norris.

NOTABLE ROOKIES: Outfielder J.B. Schuck, who signed as a minor league free agent in late 2012, became the Angels' regular left fielder in 2013 after injuries sidelined outfielder Peter Bourjos. Schuck doesn't have the power teams want in a left fielder, but he held his own by hitting .293/.331/.366. Kole Calhoun also took advantage of the unexpected outfield openings to hit eight home runs in 58 games. Righthander Michael Roth, the club's ninth-round pick in 2012, made it to the majors less than a year after he was picked.

KEY TRANSACTIONS: A year after signing Albert Pujols to a 10-year contract that already looks bad with $212 million left on the deal, the Angels added outfielder Josh Hamilton with a five-year, $123-million agreement. Hamilton responded with the second-worst year of his seven-year career. In need of better starting pitching, the Angels whiffed time after time. First, the club dealt Ervin Santana for Royals minor league lefthander Brandon Sisk. Then Los Angeles traded reliever Jordan Walden for Braves righthander Tommy Hanson, who went 5-3, 5.42 while battling injuries. Free agent acquisition Joe Blanton was worse, going 2-14, 6.02. Ryan Madson, another free agent signing, never got onto the field.

DOWN ON THE FARM: Trading away Jean Segura, Ariel Pena and Johnny Hellweg last year thinned the upper levels of the system. Signing Pujols and Hamilton meant the Angels lacked first-round picks in both the 2012 and 2013 drafts. The Angels did post a winning record overall in the minors, as Triple-A Salt Lake and Double-A Arkansas earned playoff spots.

OPENING DAY PAYROLL: $127.9 million (7th)

PLAYERS OF THE YEAR

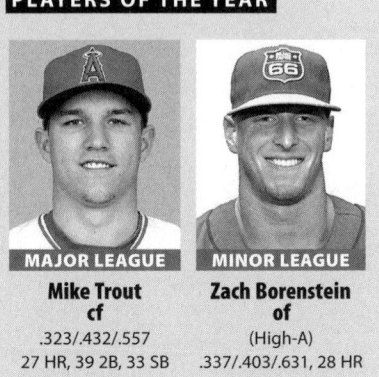

MAJOR LEAGUE	MINOR LEAGUE
Mike Trout	**Zach Borenstein**
cf	of
.323/.432/.557	(High-A)
27 HR, 39 2B, 33 SB	.337/.403/.631, 28 HR
109 R, 110 BB led AL	Cal League MVP

ORGANIZATION LEADERS

BATTING   *Minimum 250 AB

MAJORS

* AVG	Trout, Mike	.323
* OPS	Trout, Mike	.988
HR	Trumbo, Mark	34
RBI	Trumbo, Mark	100

MINORS

* AVG	Borenstein, Zach, Inland Empire	.337
* OBP	Navarro, Efren, Salt Lake	.404
* SLG	Borenstein, Zach, Inland Empire	.631
R	Long, Matt, Salt Lake/Arkansas	96
H	Yarbrough, Alex, Inland Empire	182
TB	Snyder, Michael, Inland Empire	267
	Yarbrough, Alex, Inland Empire	267
2B	Navarro, Efren, Salt Lake	39
3B	Yarbrough, Alex, Inland Empire	10
HR	Borenstein, Zach, Inland Empire	28
RBI	Borenstein, Zach, Inland Empire	95
BB	Johnson, Sherman, Inland Empire/Burlington	69
SO	Snyder, Michael, Inland Empire	149
SB	Perez, Ayendy, DSL Angels	41

PITCHING   #Minimum 75 IP

MAJORS

W	Wilson, C.J.	17
# ERA	Wilson, C.J.	3.39
SO	Wilson, C.J.	188
SV	Frieri, Ernesto	37

MINORS

W	Hynick, Brandon, Arkansas	12
	Sappington, Mark, Arkansas/Inland Empire	12
L	Arenas, Orangel, Salt Lake/Inland Empire	13
	Shoemaker, Matt, Salt Lake	13
# ERA	Hynick, Brandon, Arkansas	2.8
G	Cordero, Chad, Salt Lake/Inland Empire	58
GS	Shoemaker, Matt, Salt Lake	29
SV	Morin, Mike, Arkansas/Inland Empire	23
IP	Shoemaker, Matt, Salt Lake	184
BB	Sappington, Mark, Arkansas/Inland Empire	82
SO	Shoemaker, Matt, Salt Lake	160
# AVG	Hynick, Brandon, Arkansas	.221

General Manager: Jerry Dipoto. **Farm Director:** Bobby Scales. **Scouting Director:** Ric Wilson.

Class	Team	League	W	L	PCT	Finish	Manager
Majors	Los Angeles Angels	American	78	84	.481	10th (15)	Mike Scioscia
Triple-A	Salt Lake Bees	Pacific Coast	78	66	.542	4th (16)	Keith Johnson
Double-A	Arkansas Travelers	Texas	73	66	.525	3rd (8)	Tim Bogar
High A	Inland Empire 66ers	California	69	71	.493	t-5th (10)	Bill Haselman
Low A	Burlington Bees	Midwest	56	78	.418	14th (14)	Jamie Burke
Rookie	Orem Owlz	Pioneer	39	36	.520	4th (8)	Bill Richardson
Rookie	Angels	Arizona	30	26	.536	4th (13)	Denny Hocking
Overall 2013 Minor League Record			345	343	.501	12th (30)	

ORGANIZATION STATISTICS

AMERICAN LEAGUE

Batting	B-T	HT	WT	DOB	AVG	vLH	vRH	G	AB	R	H	2B	3B	HR	RBI	BB	HBP	SH	SF	SO	SB	CS	SLG	OBP
Aybar, Erick	B-R	5-10	180	1-14-84	.271	.288	.264	138	550	68	149	33	5	6	54	23	3	8	5	59	12	7	.382	.301
Bourjos, Peter	R-R	6-1	185	3-31-87	.274	.256	.279	55	175	26	48	3	3	3	12	10	6	4	1	43	6	0	.377	.333
Calhoun, Kole	L-L	5-10	190	10-14-87	.282	.340	.262	58	195	29	55	7	2	8	32	21	1	0	5	41	2	2	.462	.347
Callaspo, Alberto	B-R	5-9	225	4-19-83	.252	.259	.249	86	294	32	74	13	0	5	36	34	0	3	5	22	0	2	.347	.324
2-team total (50 Oakland)					.258	—	—	136	453	52	117	20	0	10	58	53	1	3	6	47	0	2	.369	.333
Conger, Hank	B-R	6-1	220	1-29-88	.249	.250	.249	92	233	23	58	13	1	7	21	17	4	0	1	61	0	1	.403	.310
Cousins, Scott	L-L	6-1	200	1-22-85	.000	—	.000	7	4	1	0	0	0	0	0	0	0	0	0	3	0	0	.000	.200
Cowgill, Collin	R-L	5-9	185	5-22-86	.231	.258	.172	50	91	11	21	3	2	2	8	5	0	3	0	27	1	0	.374	.271
Field, Tommy	R-R	5-10	185	2-22-87	.154	.071	.250	15	26	4	4	0	0	0	0	1	0	0	0	7	0	0	.154	.185
Green, Grant	R-R	6-3	180	9-27-87	.280	.156	.323	40	125	16	35	8	1	1	16	10	1	0	1	38	0	0	.384	.336
2-team total (5 Oakland)					.250	—	—	45	140	16	35	8	1	1	17	10	1	0	2	44	0	0	.343	.301
Hamilton, Josh	L-L	6-4	225	5-21-81	.250	.201	.272	151	576	73	144	32	5	21	79	47	4	0	9	158	4	0	.432	.307
Harris, Brendan	R-R	6-1	200	8-26-80	.206	.028	.296	44	107	14	22	4	0	4	9	6	1	2	1	29	0	1	.355	.252
Hawpe, Brad	L-L	6-2	190	6-22-79	.185	.333	.167	17	27	2	5	0	0	2	5	0	0	0	0	14	0	0	.333	.313
Hester, John	R-R	6-4	230	9-14-83	—	.000	—	1	0	1	0	0	0	0	0	1	0	0	0	0	0	0	—	1.000
Iannetta, Chris	R-R	6-0	230	4-8-83	.225	.266	.198	115	325	40	73	15	0	11	39	68	2	0	4	100	0	1	.372	.358
Jimenez, Luis	R-R	6-1	205	1-18-88	.260	.241	.267	34	104	15	27	6	0	5	2	3	0	1	0	28	0	2	.317	.291
Kendrick, Howard	R-R	5-10	205	7-12-83	.297	.295	.298	122	478	55	142	21	4	13	54	23	6	3	3	89	6	3	.439	.335
Navarro, Efren	L-L	6-0	200	5-14-86	.250	—	.250	4	4	0	1	0	0	0	0	1	2	0	0	1	1	0	.250	.500
Nelson, Chris	R-R	5-11	205	9-3-85	.220	.214	.222	33	109	10	24	1	2	3	18	8	1	0	1	36	2	1	.349	.277
2-team total (10 New York)					.221	—	—	43	145	13	32	3	2	3	20	9	1	0	1	47	2	1	.331	.269
Pujols, Albert	R-R	6-3	230	1-16-80	.258	.213	.272	99	391	49	101	19	0	17	64	40	5	0	7	55	1	1	.437	.330
Romine, Andrew	L-R	6-1	190	12-24-85	.259	.290	.247	47	108	9	28	3	0	0	10	7	1	6	1	24	1	0	.287	.308
Shuck, J.B.	L-L	5-11	195	6-18-87	.293	.310	.288	129	437	60	128	20	3	2	39	27	1	6	7	54	8	4	.366	.331
Trout, Mike	R-R	6-2	230	8-7-91	.323	.309	.327	157	589	109	190	39	9	27	97	110	9	0	8	136	33	7	.557	.432
Trumbo, Mark	R-R	6-4	235	1-16-86	.234	.265	.223	159	620	85	145	30	2	34	100	54	0	0	4	184	5	2	.453	.294

Pitching	B-T	HT	WT	DOB	W	L	ERA	G	GS	CG	SV	IP	H	R	ER	HR	BB	SO	AVG	vLH	vRH	K/9	BB/9
Blanton, Joe	R-R	6-2	220	12-11-80	2	14	6.04	28	20	0	0	133	180	96	89	29	34	108	.317	.300	.339	7.33	2.31
Boshers, Buddy	L-L	6-2	205	5-9-88	0	0	4.70	25	0	0	0	15	13	8	8	0	8	13	.241	.286	.158	7.63	4.70
Brasier, Ryan	R-R	6-0	205	8-26-87	0	0	2.00	7	0	0	0	9	7	2	2	1	4	7	.233	.333	.167	7.00	4.00
Buckner, Billy	R-R	6-2	205	8-27-83	1	0	4.67	7	2	0	0	17	17	9	9	5	7	7	.270	.265	.276	3.63	3.63
Burnett, Sean	L-L	6-1	180	9-17-82	0	0	0.93	13	0	0	0	10	9	1	1	1	4	7	.265	.286	.250	6.52	3.72
Carpenter, David	R-R	6-3	180	9-1-87	0	0	108.00	1	0	0	0	0	2	4	4	1	2	1	.667	1.000	.500	27.00	54.00
Coello, Robert	R-R	6-5	250	11-23-84	2	2	3.71	16	0	0	1	17	14	7	7	1	8	23	.219	.231	.211	12.18	4.24
De La Rosa, Dane	R-R	6-7	245	2-1-83	6	1	2.86	75	0	0	2	72	56	25	23	3	28	65	.219	.191	.248	8.09	3.48
Downs, Scott	L-L	6-2	220	3-17-76	2	3	1.84	43	0	0	0	29	26	7	6	1	11	22	.243	.196	.286	6.75	3.30
Enright, Barry	R-R	6-3	220	3-30-86	0	2	12.96	4	2	0	0	8	12	12	12	2	7	6	.333	.438	.250	6.48	7.56
Frieri, Ernesto	R-R	6-2	205	7-19-85	2	4	3.80	67	0	0	37	69	55	29	29	11	30	98	.216	.155	.292	12.84	3.93
Gutierrez, J.C.	R-R	6-3	245	7-14-83	1	4	5.19	28	0	0	0	26	26	16	15	3	12	28	.255	.245	.265	9.69	4.15
2-team total (25 Kansas City)					1	5	4.23	53	0	0	0	55	56	29	26	5	20	45	—	—	—	7.32	3.25
Hanson, Tommy	R-R	6-6	220	8-28-86	4	3	5.42	15	13	0	0	73	83	47	44	10	30	56	.286	.294	.276	6.90	3.70
Jepsen, Kevin	R-R	6-3	235	7-26-84	1	3	4.50	45	0	0	0	36	41	21	18	3	14	36	.283	.286	.280	9.00	3.50
Kohn, Michael	R-R	6-2	200	6-26-86	1	4	3.74	63	0	0	0	53	42	22	22	7	28	52	.212	.163	.266	8.83	4.75
Lowe, Mark	L-R	6-3	210	6-7-83	1	0	9.26	11	0	0	0	12	11	12	12	1	11	7	.256	.316	.208	5.40	8.49
Maronde, Nick	B-L	6-3	205	9-5-89	0	0	6.75	10	0	0	0	5	4	6	4	1	8	5	.200	.182	.222	8.44	13.50
Rasmus, Cory	R-R	6-0	200	11-6-87	1	1	4.20	16	0	0	0	15	16	9	7	1	9	13	.264	.344	.172	8.40	6.00
Richards, Garrett	R-R	6-3	215	5-27-88	7	8	4.16	47	17	1	1	145	151	73	67	12	44	101	.269	.281	.252	6.27	2.73
Roth, Michael	L-L	6-1	210	2-15-90	1	1	7.20	15	1	0	0	20	24	16	16	0	6	17	.300	.257	.333	7.65	2.70
Shoemaker, Matt	R-R	6-2	225	9-27-86	0	0	0.00	1	1	0	0	5	2	0	0	0	2	5	.118	.182	.000	9.00	3.60
Stange, Daniel	R-R	6-2	210	12-22-85	0	1	16.20	3	0	0	0	2	2	3	3	1	2	1	.286	.400	.000	5.40	10.80
Vargas, Jason	L-L	6-0	215	2-2-83	9	8	4.02	24	24	3	0	150	162	68	67	17	46	109	.276	.327	.256	6.54	2.76
Weaver, Jered	R-R	6-7	210	10-4-82	11	8	3.27	24	24	0	0	154	139	58	56	17	37	117	.237	.227	.254	6.82	2.16
Williams, Jerome	R-R	6-3	240	12-4-81	9	10	4.57	37	25	0	0	169	181	93	86	23	55	107	.272	.283	.259	5.69	2.92
Wilson, C.J.	L-L	6-1	210	11-18-80	17	7	3.39	33	33	0	0	212	200	93	80	15	85	188	.246	.169	.268	7.97	3.60

Fielding

Catcher	PCT	G	PO	A	E	DP	PB
Conger	.986	71	480	30	7	5	1
Hester	1.000	1	1	0	0	0	0
Iannetta	.994	113	725	51	5	6	6

First Base	PCT	G	PO	A	E	DP
Calhoun	.960	6	44	4	2	3
Harris	1.000	6	20	2	0	2
Hawpe	1.000	7	31	3	0	3
Jimenez	1.000	2	2	0	0	0
Navarro	1.000	2	7	2	0	2
Pujols	.990	34	265	29	3	24
Trumbo	.992	123	915	79	8	87

Second Base	PCT	G	PO	A	E	DP
Field	1.000	9	8	1	0	1
Green	.987	40	65	85	2	14

	PCT	G	PO	A	E	DP
Harris	1.000	6	2	8	0	2
Kendrick	.982	118	223	321	10	68
Nelson	1.000	2	0	2	0	0
Romine	1.000	4	5	15	0	4

Third Base	PCT	G	PO	A	E	DP
Callaspo	.948	84	60	141	11	8
Field	1.000	3	1	2	0	0
Harris	.933	7	3	11	1	1
Jimenez	.963	29	34	71	4	13
Nelson	.945	28	13	39	3	2
Romine	.943	24	16	34	3	4
Trumbo	—	1	0	0	0	0

Shortstop	PCT	G	PO	A	E	DP
Aybar	.973	138	217	328	15	78
Field	1.000	5	3	2	0	0

	PCT	G	PO	A	E	DP
Harris	.969	21	22	40	2	9
Jimenez	1.000	1	1	0	0	0
Romine	.979	17	18	29	1	8

Outfield	PCT	G	PO	A	E	DP
Bourjos	.992	53	117	2	1	0
Calhoun	.949	54	108	4	6	3
Cousins	—	4	0	0	0	0
Cowgill	.985	46	63	3	1	0
Hamilton	.968	108	236	4	8	0
Harris	1.000	1	1	0	0	0
Hawpe	.857	6	6	0	1	0
Kendrick	1.000	1	1	0	0	0
Shuck	.988	103	158	7	2	0
Trout	.994	148	359	0	2	0
Trumbo	.981	27	50	1	1	0

SALT LAKE BEES   TRIPLE-A
PACIFIC COAST LEAGUE

Batting	B-T	HT	WT	DOB	AVG	vLH	vRH	G	AB	R	H	2B	3B	HR	RBI	BB	HBP	SH	SF	SO	SB	CS	SLG	OBP
Aybar, Erick	B-R	5-10	180	1-14-84	.400	1.000	.250	1	5	1	2	1	0	1	2	0	0	0	0	0	0	0	1.200	.400
Bourjos, Peter	R-R	6-1	185	3-31-87	.208	.100	.237	12	48	13	10	4	0	2	7	4	2	0	1	19	0	0	.417	.291
Calhoun, Kole	L-L	5-10	190	10-14-87	.354	.439	.328	59	240	48	85	15	6	12	49	32	1	0	1	32	10	2	.617	.431
Carlin, Luke	B-R	5-10	195	12-20-80	.230	.180	.242	77	244	39	56	8	0	4	29	40	1	6	1	53	6	3	.311	.339
Cousins, Scott	L-L	6-1	200	1-22-85	.233	.237	.231	52	193	30	45	3	4	1	19	16	6	4	1	46	7	2	.306	.310
Cowgill, Collin	R-L	5-9	185	5-22-86	.600	.000	.643	4	15	4	9	1	0	2	7	1	1	0	0	3	1	0	1.067	.647
2-team total (33 Las Vegas)					.304			37	138	26	42	7	0	7	19	18	3	3	0	28	5	0	.507	.396
Dalton, Ryan	R-R	6-1	200	7-24-91	.000	.000	.000	2	4	1	0	0	0	0	0	0	0	0	0	0	0	0	.000	.000
Field, Tommy	R-R	5-10	185	2-22-87	.303	.342	.290	81	314	56	95	20	2	11	49	44	5	4	5	68	6	2	.484	.391
Green, Grant	R-R	6-3	180	9-27-87	.333	.000	.421	6	24	2	8	1	0	0	3	3	0	0	1	7	0	1	.375	.393
2-team total (87 Sacramento)					.326			93	402	68	131	28	3	11	53	30	6	3	2	77	4	2		.493
.380Hall, Bill	R-R	6-0	210	12-28-79	.164	.176	.161	21	73	4	12	0	1	1	7	12	0	0	0	25	0	0	.233	.282
Hawpe, Brad	L-L	6-2	190	6-22-79	.305	.295	.310	37	131	21	40	8	0	6	28	21	1	0	0	40	1	1	.504	.405
Heid, Drew	L-R	5-10	175	12-20-87	.331	.250	.364	45	139	24	46	9	5	3	21	21	0	3	3	35	2	4	.532	.411
Hester, John	R-R	6-4	230	9-14-83	.237	.297	.217	74	253	40	60	13	1	8	29	27	0	1	3	75	3	1	.391	.307
Jimenez, Luis	R-R	6-1	205	1-18-88	.284	.222	.303	48	197	28	56	9	2	4	42	12	3	0	6	26	11	3	.411	.326
Long, Matt	L-R	5-11	175	4-30-87	.287	.232	.307	100	369	79	106	21	6	11	52	51	0	5	3	83	17	3	.466	.371
Lopez, Roberto	R-R	6-0	195	10-1-85	.289	.345	.270	127	432	59	125	26	4	10	68	34	4	0	6	74	11	4	.438	.342
Marte, Andy	R-R	6-1	205	10-21-83	.362	.360	.362	26	94	23	34	2	0	6	18	7	0	0	2	16	0	0	.574	.398
Navarro, Efren	L-L	6-0	200	5-14-86	.326	.269	.346	134	513	83	167	39	3	7	81	68	2	0	3	99	8	5	.454	.404
Nelson, Chris	R-R	5-11	205	9-3-85	.328	.300	.337	34	134	20	44	11	0	2	23	4	0	0	2	23	4	0	.545	.361
Oeltjen, Trent	L-L	6-1	205	2-28-83	.255	.329	.232	99	333	60	85	30	2	14	49	37	10	4	3	110	21	7	.483	.345
Rodriguez, Luis	B-R	5-9	190	6-27-80	.267	.255	.270	118	439	58	117	28	4	10	72	41	3	1	7	48	1	4	.417	.329
Romine, Andrew	L-R	6-1	190	12-24-85	.287	.267	.295	89	363	61	104	16	5	4	39	43	4	4	2	68	15	6	.391	.367
Ross, Chance	R-R	6-0	180	2-28-90	.421	.750	.333	6	19	2	8	1	1	0	5	0	0	1	0	4	1	0	.579	.421
Ryal, Rusty	R-R	6-2	200	3-16-83	.400	—	.400	2	5	1	2	1	0	0	1	1	0	0	0	0	0	0	.600	.500
2-team total (106 Albuquerque)					.267	—	—	108	375	51	100	18	3	4	50	20	7	1	4	80	0	0	.363	.313
Snyder, Chris	R-R	6-4	235	2-12-81	.342	.278	.361	21	79	14	27	6	0	7	21	6	0	1	0	22	0	1	.684	.388
Swift, Jimmy	R-R	6-2	190	12-21-87	.303	.250	.321	33	109	11	33	7	0	2	10	4	2	2	1	27	2	0	.422	.336
Widlansky, Robbie	L-R	6-2	210	11-6-84	.367	.313	.394	16	49	10	18	1	0	2	11	8	1	0	1	9	0	0	.510	.458
Young, Matt	L-R	5-8	175	10-3-82	.208	.176	.219	41	130	17	27	4	1	2	13	20	3	1	0	17	11	3	.300	.327

Pitching	B-T	HT	WT	DOB	W	L	ERA	G	GS	CG	SV	IP	H	R	ER	HR	BB	SO	AVG	vLH	vRH	K/9	BB/9
Arenas, Orangel	R-R	6-0	200	3-31-89	1	5	6.57	6	6	0	0	25	34	25	18	4	14	8	.333	.333	.333	2.92	5.11
Berg, Jeremy	R-R	6-0	180	7-17-86	5	0	2.71	52	0	0	1	76	69	24	23	6	17	69	.243	.263	.229	8.14	2.00
Boshers, Buddy	L-L	6-3	205	5-9-88	1	0	3.66	16	0	0	1	20	18	11	8	1	12	26	.247	.176	.308	11.90	5.49
Brasier, Ryan	R-R	6-0	205	8-26-87	5	2	4.13	38	0	0	10	57	59	31	26	6	16	57	.295	.313	.281	9.05	2.54
Buckner, Billy	R-R	6-2	205	8-27-83	7	4	4.87	18	18	0	0	94	101	61	51	7	50	77	.272	.226	.309	7.35	4.77
Cabrera, Fernando	R-R	6-4	225	11-16-81	1	3	3.47	54	3	0	1	73	71	37	28	10	35	71	.252	.284	.229	8.79	4.33
Carpenter, David	R-R	6-3	180	9-1-87	5	1	9.48	24	0	0	2	31	42	35	33	4	27	31	.323	.400	.257	8.90	7.76
Cendejas, Eric	R-R	6-0	175	1-28-88	0	0	4.50	5	2	0	0	12	18	6	6	0	4	5	.333	.276	.455	3.75	3.00
Coello, Robert	R-R	6-5	250	11-23-84	1	0	4.82	15	0	0	4	19	15	10	10	1	11	29	.214	.256	.161	13.98	5.30
Cordero, Chad	R-R	6-0	220	3-18-82	2	3	5.44	52	0	0	2	50	64	31	30	5	11	39	.315	.269	.344	7.07	1.99
De La Rosa, Dane	R-R	6-7	245	2-1-83	1	0	2.70	3	0	0	1	3	1	1	1	0	2	1	.111	.200	.000	2.70	5.40
Delaney, Rob	L-R	6-2	250	9-8-84	1	0	5.14	13	1	0	0	21	24	14	12	1	8	13	.293	.333	.265	5.57	3.43
Ekstrom, Mike	R-R	6-0	190	8-30-83	2	2	5.19	17	0	0	0	26	30	15	15	2	7	22	.294	.300	.290	7.62	2.42
2-team total (21 Sacramento)					3	3	5.14	38	0	0	3	56	69	34	32	5	20	49	—	—	—	7.88	3.21
Enright, Barry	R-R	6-3	220	3-30-86	7	7	7.12	24	22	0	0	116	153	99	92	30	48	78	.317	.329	.307	6.03	3.71
Grube, Jarrett	R-R	6-4	220	11-5-81	7	5	4.47	22	21	0	0	109	113	62	54	12	48	104	.269	.350	.210	8.61	3.98
Hanson, Tommy	R-R	6-6	220	8-28-86	0	2	5.49	4	4	0	0	20	23	14	12	5	6	15	.277	.281	.275	6.86	2.75
Jepsen, Kevin	R-R	6-3	235	7-26-84	0	0	13.50	2	0	0	0	2	3	3	3	2	2	1	.250	.000	.333	4.50	9.00
Johnson, Kevin	L-R	6-4	240	8-19-88	0	1	7.45	16	0	0	3	19	26	16	16	3	12	8	.338	.455	.291	3.72	5.59
Judy, Josh	R-R	6-4	210	2-9-86	0	1	7.02	15	0	0	1	17	30	16	13	3	10	16	.390	.406	.378	5.40	5.40

LOS ANGELES ANGELS

Name	B-T	HT	WT	DOB	W	L	ERA	G	GS	CG	SV	IP	H	R	ER	HR	BB	SO	AVG	vLH	vRH	K/9	BB/9
Kelley, Ty	R-R	6-4	200	8-18-88	0	0	10.80	1	0	0	0	2	6	2	2	0	2	2	.545	.500	.556	10.80	10.80
Kohn, Michael	R-R	6-2	200	6-26-86	0	0	0.00	5	0	0	1	4	2	0	0	0	0	7	.143	.143	.143	14.54	0.00
Ramirez, Elvin	R-R	6-3	210	10-10-87	0	0	12.19	12	0	0	0	10	13	16	14	0	23	7	.325	.444	.227	6.10	20.03
Rasmus, Cory	R-R	6-0	200	11-6-87	1	1	2.79	9	0	0	3	10	6	3	3	0	5	8	.171	.083	.217	7.45	4.66
Richardson, Dustin	L-L	6-6	220	1-9-84	5	2	6.47	20	8	0	0	56	61	42	40	3	32	50	.275	.253	.287	8.08	5.17
Schugel, A.J.	R-R	5-11	185	6-27-89	4	6	7.05	19	19	0	0	89	121	74	70	12	33	76	.324	.259	.370	7.66	3.32
Shoemaker, Matt	R-R	6-2	225	9-27-86	11	13	4.64	29	29	0	0	184	212	99	95	27	29	160	.289	.313	.270	7.81	1.42
Stange, Daniel	R-R	6-2	210	12-22-85	4	1	5.06	26	0	0	5	27	31	16	15	1	13	30	.290	.326	.266	10.13	4.39
2-team total (26 Tucson)					5	1	4.52	52	0	0	5	66	65	37	33	6	37	73	—	—	—	10.01	5.07
Stetter, Mitch	L-L	6-5	215	1-16-81	3	1	4.01	32	0	0	3	25	17	14	11	2	19	26	.195	.200	.188	9.49	6.93
Urquidez, Jason	R-R	6-0	175	9-12-82	1	2	6.92	11	0	0	1	13	15	11	10	3	6	17	.288	.350	.250	11.77	4.15
Vargas, Jason	L-L	6-0	215	2-2-83	0	0	7.71	1	1	0	0	5	4	4	4	3	3	2	.235	.333	.182	3.86	5.79
Wells, Kip	R-R	6-3	205	4-21-77	1	3	10.36	6	6	0	0	24	35	28	28	4	22	9	.343	.368	.328	3.33	8.14
Willis, Dontrelle	L-L	6-4	225	1-12-82	2	1	6.43	5	4	0	0	21	20	16	15	3	14	12	.247	.280	.232	5.14	6.00

Fielding

Catcher	PCT	G	PO	A	E	DP	PB
Carlin	.986	70	532	42	8	3	8
Dalton	.833	1	4	1	1	0	1
Hester	.994	67	471	33	3	2	7
Snyder	.986	9	66	7	1	0	0

First Base	PCT	G	PO	A	E	DP
Hawpe	1.000	5	37	8	0	2
Jimenez	1.000	3	18	2	0	2
Lopez	1.000	4	29	1	0	4
Marte	1.000	1	7	1	0	1
Navarro	.995	130	1061	74	6	110
Rodriguez	1.000	3	19	1	0	3

Second Base	PCT	G	PO	A	E	DP
Field	.978	30	50	83	3	24
Green	1.000	2	6	6	0	2
Hall	.957	10	16	29	2	9
Long	.973	19	33	39	2	8
Nelson	1.000	9	15	17	0	2

	PCT	G	PO	A	E	DP
Rodriguez	.977	59	86	169	6	42
Romine	.965	20	37	45	3	6

Third Base	PCT	G	PO	A	E	DP
Field	.824	6	1	13	3	0
Green	.929	4	2	11	1	2
Hall	.900	9	6	12	2	0
Jimenez	.915	36	27	70	9	12
Lopez	.917	24	18	37	5	2
Marte	1.000	18	16	31	0	5
Nelson	.941	14	6	26	2	4
Rodriguez	.934	27	26	31	4	0
Romine	1.000	11	3	32	0	0
Swift	1.000	11	9	12	0	1

Shortstop	PCT	G	PO	A	E	DP
Aybar	1.000	1	2	3	0	1
Field	.918	46	67	100	15	24
Jimenez	.870	6	6	14	3	2
Nelson	1.000	10	15	28	0	6

	PCT	G	PO	A	E	DP
Rodriguez	1.000	1	1	1	0	1
Romine	.964	59	93	171	10	37
Ross	.947	4	10	8	1	3
Swift	.933	22	28	42	5	10

Outfield	PCT	G	PO	A	E	DP
Bourjos	1.000	7	18	0	0	0
Calhoun	1.000	52	108	0	0	0
Cousins	.985	49	129	0	2	0
Cowgill	1.000	4	8	0	0	0
Hawpe	1.000	9	11	1	0	0
Heid	.985	43	63	3	1	0
Long	.978	81	166	9	4	2
Lopez	.979	86	134	3	3	0
Nelson	1.000	3	4	1	0	0
Oeltjen	.984	90	176	4	3	1
Ryal	—	2	0	0	0	0
Widlansky	1.000	5	7	0	0	0
Young	.985	34	62	2	1	0

ARKANSAS TRAVELERS   DOUBLE-A
TEXAS LEAGUE

Batting	B-T	HT	WT	DOB	AVG	vLH	vRH	G	AB	R	H	2B	3B	HR	RBI	BB	HBP	SH	SF	SO	SB	CS	SLG	OBP
Bandy, Jett	R-R	6-4	210	3-26-90	.241	.305	.220	78	245	26	59	17	2	4	28	14	9	1	3	39	0	1	.376	.303
Bemboom, Anthony	L-R	6-2	190	1-18-90	.154	.000	.222	8	26	1	4	0	0	0	4	1	2	0	0	5	1	0	.154	.241
Cowart, Kaleb	B-R	6-3	195	6-2-92	.221	.279	.202	132	498	48	110	20	1	6	42	38	3	4	3	124	14	5	.301	.279
Cron Jr., C.J.	R-R	6-4	235	1-5-90	.274	.328	.258	134	519	56	142	36	1	14	83	23	15	0	8	83	8	4	.428	.319
Fleury, Mark	L-R	6-0	189	5-4-88	.188	.200	.185	12	32	4	6	1	0	0	4	3	1	1	0	14	1	0	.281	.278
Gomez, Rolando	L-R	5-7	145	6-18-89	.252	.241	.256	97	345	45	87	10	4	4	28	24	0	0	4	88	14	10	.339	.298
Grichuk, Randal	R-R	6-1	195	8-13-91	.256	.286	.246	128	500	85	128	27	8	22	64	28	9	2	3	92	9	5	.474	.306
Hairgrove, Trevor	R-R	6-1	185	9-16-89	.182	.333	.125	4	11	2	2	0	0	0	2	0	0	0	0	3	0	0	.182	.182
Hankerd, Cyle	R-R	6-3	215	1-24-85	.260	.317	.233	35	127	23	33	4	0	6	22	9	10	0	2	35	0	0	.433	.351
Heid, Drew	L-R	5-10	175	12-14-87	.288	.259	.300	63	208	21	60	12	1	3	20	31	0	6	0	49	5	3	.399	.381
Jones, Ryan	L-L	6-0	192	5-19-88	.231	.208	.237	45	117	18	27	5	0	3	16	17	1	4	1	22	5	2	.350	.331
Lindsey, Taylor	L-R	6-0	195	12-2-91	.274	.265	.277	134	508	68	139	22	6	17	56	48	4	3	3	91	4	4	.441	.339
Long, Matt	L-R	5-11	175	4-30-87	.311	.308	.312	32	119	17	37	8	2	3	19	12	0	1	1	29	3	3	.487	.371
Montanez, Lou	R-R	6-1	195	12-15-81	.284	.346	.255	22	81	14	23	5	0	3	14	5	0	0	1	10	3	1	.457	.322
Perales, Danny	L-L	6-0	195	3-18-85	.122	.000	.200	10	41	1	5	0	0	0	1	5	0	0	0	4	0	0	.122	.182
Ramirez, Carlos	R-R	5-11	210	3-19-88	.206	.250	.187	48	155	17	32	12	0	6	22	16	5	4	0	33	1	0	.400	.301
Swift, Jimmy	R-R	6-2	190	12-21-87	.259	.250	.264	83	297	36	77	18	1	4	22	13	2	8	4	73	4	1	.367	.291
Widlansky, Robbie	L-R	6-2	210	11-6-84	.261	.271	.259	88	314	38	82	13	1	8	46	28	6	0	2	58	4	1	.385	.331
Witherspoon, Travis	R-R	6-2	190	4-16-89	.214	.220	.210	129	448	58	96	18	3	11	38	55	1	5	4	118	30	10	.342	.299

Pitching	B-T	HT	WT	DOB	W	L	ERA	G	GS	CG	SV	IP	H	R	ER	HR	BB	SO	AVG	vLH	vRH	K/9	BB/9
Batista, Lay	R-R	6-2	180	8-4-89	5	8	3.38	22	22	0	0	123	105	50	46	8	43	89	.236	.236	.237	6.53	3.15
Berg, Jeremy	R-R	6-0	180	7-17-86	0	0	9.00	3	0	0	0	2	3	2	2	0	1	3	.375	.400	.333	13.50	4.50
Boshers, Buddy	L-L	6-3	205	5-9-88	3	2	3.14	28	0	0	1	29	20	12	10	1	13	35	.196	.234	.164	10.99	4.08
Carpenter, Drew	R-R	6-3	240	5-18-85	3	1	1.44	5	5	0	0	31	20	6	5	3	4	18	.185	.208	.167	5.17	1.15
2-team total (4 Midland)					4	2	2.09	9	9	0	0	52	40	14	12	5	7	30	—	—		5.23	1.22
Carpenter, David	R-R	6-3	180	9-1-87	0	2	3.38	29	0	0	5	29	20	13	11	1	8	21	.194	.209	.183	6.44	2.45
Chaffee, Ryan	R-R	6-2	195	5-18-88	3	2	2.92	47	0	0	6	62	41	28	20	3	35	73	.189	.220	.170	10.65	5.11
Cisco, Mike	R-R	5-11	190	5-23-87	4	4	3.99	46	3	0	1	59	51	26	26	3	24	41	.235	.224	.241	6.29	3.68
Coello, Robert	R-R	6-5	250	11-23-84	0	0	0.00	1	0	0	0	1	0	0	0	0	0	2	.000	.000	.000	18.00	0.00
Correa, Manuarys	R-R	6-3	170	1-5-89	5	12	5.63	26	24	1	1	133	176	93	83	16	23	77	.327	.320	.333	5.22	1.56
Giardina, Carmine	L-L	6-3	225	2-20-88	1	0	3.38	12	0	0	0	11	9	4	4	1	8	7	.237	.267	.217	5.91	6.75
Graham, Caleb	R-R	6-3	220	1-18-87	6	2	3.83	46	0	0	1	45	41	21	19	4	20	38	.243	.319	.213	7.66	4.03
Grube, Jarrett	R-R	6-4	220	11-5-81	4	1	3.12	7	7	0	0	40	32	15	14	4	10	49	.213	.254	.187	10.93	2.23
Hynick, Brandon	R-R	6-3	205	3-7-85	12	5	2.80	24	24	0	0	142	114	50	44	16	34	98	.221	.221	.222	6.23	2.16
Johnson, Kevin	L-R	6-4	240	8-19-88	3	3	2.49	36	0	0	13	43	43	15	12	1	11	24	.267	.292	.247	4.98	2.28

	B-T	HT	WT	DOB	W	L	ERA	G	GS	CG	SV	IP	H	R	ER	HR	BB	SO	AVG	vLH	vRH	K/9	BB/9
Judy, Josh	R-R	6-4	210	2-9-86	1	3	6.50	18	0	0	6	18	20	14	13	6	5	19	.278	.429	.216	9.50	2.50
Kelley, Ty	R-R	6-4	200	8-18-88	0	0	9.00	2	0	0	0	2	3	2	2	0	1	2	.333	.667	.167	9.00	4.50
Maronde, Nick	B-L	6-3	205	9-5-89	2	4	3.51	41	0	0	0	56	41	25	22	4	37	63	.203	.181	.215	10.07	5.91
Morin, Mike	R-R	6-4	218	5-3-91	0	2	2.03	26	0	0	10	31	26	7	7	2	5	33	.230	.333	.145	9.58	1.45
Oye, Matt	R-R	6-5	230	2-25-86	7	8	4.81	23	18	0	0	112	128	65	60	21	34	72	.286	.308	.267	5.77	2.72
Piazza, Mike	R-R	6-4	205	11-24-86	6	2	3.15	21	15	0	0	89	79	33	31	7	37	87	.245	.281	.218	8.83	3.76
Ramirez, Elvin	R-R	6-3	210	10-10-87	1	1	4.09	37	1	0	1	51	47	23	23	1	22	42	.245	.333	.184	7.46	3.91
Roth, Michael	L-L	6-1	210	2-15-90	6	3	4.20	17	15	0	0	79	77	42	37	8	36	51	.262	.219	.274	5.79	4.08
Sappington, Mark	R-R	6-5	209	11-17-90	1	1	3.86	5	5	0	0	26	23	11	11	1	20	26	.240	.268	.218	9.12	7.01
Tillman, Daniel	R-R	6-1	185	3-14-89	0	0	8.64	8	0	0	0	8	3	8	8	0	10	6	.111	.154	.071	6.48	10.80

Fielding

Catcher	PCT	G	PO	A	E	DP	PB
Bandy	.991	76	489	70	5	7	3
Bemboom	1.000	8	52	5	0	2	0
Fleury	.922	12	66	5	6	0	1
Ramirez	.990	48	364	45	4	4	4

First Base	PCT	G	PO	A	E	DP
Cron Jr.	.991	124	1047	82	10	112
Hairgrove	1.000	1	1	0	0	0
Widlansky	1.000	16	112	4	0	12

Second Base	PCT	G	PO	A	E	DP
Gomez	.800	1	1	3	1	1
Lindsey	.972	134	268	361	18	99

	PCT	G	PO	A	E	DP
Long	1.000	2	4	5	0	3
Swift	.917	3	3	8	1	0

Third Base	PCT	G	PO	A	E	DP
Cowart	.923	131	85	213	25	20
Gomez	1.000	1	1	2	0	2
Hairgrove	1.000	1	3	1	0	0
Swift	.923	7	5	19	2	1

Shortstop	PCT	G	PO	A	E	DP
Gomez	.951	73	93	200	15	43
Hairgrove	1.000	2	2	7	0	2
Swift	.975	69	99	215	8	54

Outfield	PCT	G	PO	A	E	DP
Grichuk	.993	118	273	11	2	5
Hankerd	.961	28	49	0	2	0
Heid	.991	55	107	5	1	1
Jones	1.000	34	54	7	0	0
Long	.975	27	38	1	1	1
Montanez	.978	19	44	1	1	1
Perales	1.000	6	10	0	0	0
Swift	1.000	3	9	0	0	0
Widlansky	1.000	9	17	0	0	0
Witherspoon	.980	126	292	8	6	4

INLAND EMPIRE 66ERS

HIGH CLASS A

CALIFORNIA LEAGUE

Batting	B-T	HT	WT	DOB	AVG	vLH	vRH	G	AB	R	H	2B	3B	HR	RBI	BB	HBP	SH	SF	SO	SB	CS	SLG	OBP
Baker, Abel	L-R	6-1	200	10-26-90	.252	.218	.263	87	310	38	78	18	4	5	33	23	1	3	4	91	0	0	.384	.302
Bemboom, Anthony	L-R	6-2	190	1-18-90	.160	.111	.175	23	75	4	12	1	0	1	7	4	2	1	0	19	0	0	.213	.222
Borenstein, Zach	L-R	6-0	205	7-23-90	.337	.321	.342	112	407	76	137	22	7	28	95	43	7	1	7	88	5	5	.631	.403
Bourjos, Peter	R-R	6-1	185	3-31-87	.273	.250	.286	3	11	3	3	0	1	1	2	0	0	0	0	2	0	0	.727	.273
Callaspo, Alberto	B-R	5-9	225	4-19-83	.286	.333	.250	3	7	1	2	0	0	1	3	2	0	0	1	1	0	0	.714	.400
Capote, Joel	R-R	5-11	180	12-8-89	.235	.188	.257	98	319	51	75	11	5	1	33	28	8	3	2	57	11	8	.310	.311
Gowens, Brennan	L-R	6-0	195	3-14-90	.274	.207	.300	77	299	49	82	15	5	0	28	32	4	6	0	65	12	5	.358	.352
Hairgrove, Trevor	R-R	6-1	185	9-16-89	.194	.222	.182	51	144	17	28	6	0	0	7	18	3	5	1	32	1	0	.236	.295
Hernandez, Brian	R-R	6-1	195	11-25-88	.294	.338	.277	140	528	59	155	32	3	6	80	51	4	1	3	89	6	6	.400	.358
Johnson, Sherman	L-R	5-10	178	7-15-90	.308	.333	.294	6	26	3	8	3	1	0	2	3	0	1	1	5	0	0	.500	.367
Jones, Ryan	L-L	6-0	192	5-19-88	.191	.146	.212	40	152	19	29	7	2	5	14	11	0	2	0	37	7	1	.362	.245
Mitchell, Gary	R-R	6-4	235	4-3-89	.246	.250	.245	57	183	23	45	6	3	4	22	23	4	2	0	78	6	2	.377	.343
Ross, Chance	R-R	6-0	180	2-28-90	.259	.235	.270	19	54	5	14	4	0	1	6	4	1	1	0	14	1	0	.389	.322
Scioscia, Matt	R-R	6-2	220	9-20-88	.190	.222	.167	10	21	3	4	0	1	0	2	1	0	0	1	7	0	0	.286	.217
Snyder, Mike	R-R	6-4	230	11-6-85	.280	.275	.282	137	528	70	148	36	2	6	25	92	43	8	0	11	149	0	1	.506	.337
Soto, Wendell	B-R	5-9	170	5-11-92	.125	.222	.000	7	16	1	2	0	0	0	3	2	0	0	1	6	0	0	.125	.211
Stamets, Eric	R-R	6-0	185	9-25-91	.281	.354	.255	126	506	80	142	28	4	4	53	34	8	21	2	66	16	4	.375	.335
Workman, Andy	R-R	6-1	200	11-16-88	.235	.202	.248	125	438	63	103	27	5	9	38	41	8	1	2	119	11	5	.381	.311
Wright, Zach	R-R	6-1	205	1-10-90	.253	.318	.228	68	233	33	59	10	1	4	25	26	7	5	1	58	2	2	.356	.345
Yarbrough, Alex	B-R	5-11	180	8-3-91	.313	.300	.318	136	582	77	182	32	10	11	80	27	1	0	5	106	14	4	.459	.341

Pitching	B-T	HT	WT	DOB	W	L	ERA	G	GS	CG	SV	IP	H	R	ER	HR	BB	SO	AVG	vLH	vRH	K/9	BB/9
Alvarez, R.J.	R-R	6-1	180	6-8-91	4	2	2.96	37	2	0	4	49	34	16	16	2	27	79	.191	.268	.140	14.61	4.99
Arenas, Orangel	R-R	6-0	200	3-31-89	8	8	5.14	19	18	0	0	103	119	65	59	13	26	69	.290	.314	.275	6.01	2.26
Bedrosian, Cam	R-R	6-0	205	10-2-91	0	0	0.00	7	0	0	0	9	4	0	0	0	7	9	.143	.111	.158	9.35	7.27
Boyd, Jake	R-R	6-3	200	1-6-90	0	5	9.00	10	9	0	0	49	72	51	49	11	25	26	.364	.397	.344	4.78	4.59
Burkard, Alex	L-L	6-8	215	1-4-89	0	1	5.40	15	0	0	0	32	33	20	19	3	10	27	.270	.313	.256	7.67	2.84
Burnett, Sean	L-L	6-1	180	9-17-82	0	0	9.00	1	0	0	0	1	1	1	1	0	0	2	.250	—	.250	0.00	0.00
Cendejas, Eric	R-R	6-0	175	1-28-88	6	3	3.69	48	0	0	3	63	58	26	26	4	17	48	.245	.271	.230	6.82	2.42
Cordero, Chad	R-R	6-0	220	3-18-82	0	0	6.35	6	0	0	1	6	9	4	4	0	2	7	.375	.375	.375	11.12	3.18
Diaz, Jairo	R-R	6-0	220	5-27-91	0	2	8.87	13	0	0	0	22	38	27	22	3	14	21	.373	.341	.397	8.46	5.64
Efferson, Brandon	R-R	5-11	175	11-25-88	1	5	6.11	26	8	0	1	71	94	54	48	7	19	53	.324	.349	.310	6.75	2.42
Giardina, Carmine	L-L	6-3	225	2-20-88	1	1	2.82	20	0	0	0	22	17	7	7	3	5	26	.218	.200	.229	10.48	2.01
Graham, Caleb	R-R	6-3	220	1-18-87	0	0	0.00	3	0	0	0	3	2	2	0	0	1	3	.167	.250	.125	9.00	3.00
Hanson, Tommy	R-R	6-6	220	8-28-86	0	1	5.40	1	1	0	0	3	3	2	2	0	1	6	.250	.333	.167	16.20	2.70
Hernandez, Matt	L-L	6-2	190	6-14-91	0	0	12.79	5	0	0	0	6	12	10	9	0	6	6	.414	.583	.294	8.53	8.53
Jepsen, Kevin	R-R	6-3	235	7-26-84	0	0	0.00	1	0	0	0	1	0	0	0	0	0	0	.000	.000	—	0.00	0.00
Jimenez, Eswarlin	L-L	6-1	187	11-27-91	2	5	5.63	21	12	0	0	77	95	54	48	9	21	39	.306	.333	.295	4.58	2.47
Johnson, Michael	L-L	6-2	190	2-5-91	0	2	6.99	26	0	0	1	37	48	33	29	1	17	35	.310	.220	.352	8.44	4.10
Kelley, Ty	R-R	6-4	200	8-18-88	4	2	3.38	38	0	0	4	53	50	24	20	5	24	55	.244	.241	.246	9.28	4.05
Keudell, Alex	R-R	6-3	205	2-25-90	5	1	3.77	11	11	1	0	72	75	35	30	10	17	49	.270	.279	.263	6.15	2.13
Lowe, Mark	L-R	6-3	210	6-11-83	0	0	1.80	3	0	0	1	5	1	1	1	0	0	6	.059	.100	.000	10.80	0.00
Lowery, Pat	R-R	6-5	195	4-2-90	0	0	0.96	3	2	0	0	9	8	1	1	0	5	3	.242	.333	.167	2.89	4.82
Madson, Ryan	L-R	6-6	210	8-28-80	0	0	0.00	1	0	0	1	1	0	0	0	0	0	1	.000	.000	.000	9.00	0.00
Morin, Mike	R-R	6-4	218	5-3-91	3	1	1.85	30	0	0	13	39	30	9	8	2	5	43	.221	.293	.167	9.92	1.15
Pena, Tony	R-R	6-2	240	1-9-82	0	0	9.82	2	0	0	0	4	5	5	4	1	1	5	.294	.250	.308	12.27	2.45

	B-T	HT	WT	DOB	W	L	ERA	G	GS	CG	SV	IP	H	R	ER	HR	BB	SO	AVG	vLH	vRH	K/9	BB/9
Piazza, Mike	R-R	6-4	205	11-24-86	0	1	4.50	2	2	0	0	8	10	4	4	0	4	5	.313	.389	.214	5.63	4.50
Powell, Robbie	R-R	6-0	180	2-7-90	1	0	3.97	25	0	0	1	34	30	15	15	4	12	23	.236	.308	.187	6.09	3.18
Reynolds, Danny	R-R	6-0	170	5-2-91	11	10	5.39	26	26	0	0	145	144	94	87	19	64	114	.262	.267	.259	7.06	3.96
Rucinski, Drew	R-R	6-2	190	12-30-88	2	2	1.86	5	5	0	0	29	29	11	6	0	4	21	.266	.320	.220	6.52	1.24
Santos, Eduard	R-R	6-2	220	10-22-89	2	4	2.87	31	0	0	5	38	36	15	12	4	20	40	.245	.278	.226	9.56	4.78
Sappington, Mark	R-R	6-5	209	11-17-90	11	4	3.38	22	22	0	0	131	103	51	49	10	62	110	.220	.208	.230	7.58	4.27
Sneed, Kramer	L-L	6-3	185	10-7-88	7	4	4.09	16	16	0	0	81	81	41	37	7	23	73	.258	.260	.257	8.08	2.55
Tillman, Daniel	R-R	6-1	185	3-14-89	1	2	6.92	13	0	0	0	13	12	11	10	1	11	13	.240	.273	.214	9.00	7.62
Tobik, Dan	R-R	6-4	195	1-8-91	0	1	45.00	1	1	0	0	1	5	5	5	0	2	0	.556	.000	.833	0.00	18.00
Tromblee, Stephen	L-L	5-11	205	4-3-89	0	1	6.35	4	0	0	0	6	8	5	4	1	3	6	.320	.300	.333	9.53	4.76
Wood, Austin	R-R	6-4	225	7-11-90	0	3	4.15	5	5	0	0	22	25	13	10	1	12	18	.298	.409	.175	7.48	4.98

Fielding

Catcher	PCT	G	PO	A	E	DP	PB
Baker	.986	70	490	54	8	7	5
Bemboom	.994	23	136	20	1	0	3
Wright	.989	51	413	36	5	1	10

First Base	PCT	G	PO	A	E	DP
Baker	1.000	6	1	0	0	
Hairgrove	.984	7	54	8	1	7
Hernandez	1.000	3	32	4	0	4
Mitchell	1.000	2	10	1	0	1
Scioscia	1.000	2	1	1	0	0
Snyder	.988	128	1062	78	14	89

Second Base	PCT	G	PO	A	E	DP
Hairgrove	1.000	11	11	16	0	3
Johnson	1.000	1	4	4	0	2

	PCT	G	PO	A	E	DP
Ross	1.000	3	3	2	0	1
Soto	1.000	2	1	1	0	0
Yarbrough	.982	127	239	314	10	68

Third Base	PCT	G	PO	A	E	DP
Callaspo	1.000	3	0	3	0	1
Hairgrove	.750	5	3	3	2	1
Hernandez	.953	130	92	250	17	22
Johnson	1.000	3	1	10	0	1
Ross	.909	5	3	7	1	1

Shortstop	PCT	G	PO	A	E	DP
Hairgrove	.973	11	16	20	1	5
Ross	.875	4	2	12	2	3
Soto	.909	5	5	15	2	6
Stamets	.972	126	196	400	17	69

Outfield	PCT	G	PO	A	E	DP
Borenstein	.970	81	123	8	4	1
Bourjos	1.000	2	6	0	0	0
Capote	.977	76	123	2	3	2
Gowens	.981	76	148	3	3	2
Hairgrove	1.000	13	19	2	0	0
Johnson	1.000	2	4	0	0	0
Jones	.982	26	54	1	1	0
Mitchell	.974	40	71	5	2	0
Ross	1.000	1	3	0	0	0
Workman	.970	123	305	15	10	2
Wright	—	1	0	0	0	0

BURLINGTON BEES

LOW CLASS A

MIDWEST LEAGUE

Batting	B-T	HT	WT	DOB	AVG	vLH	vRH	G	AB	R	H	2B	3B	HR	RBI	BB	HBP	SH	SF	SO	SB	CS	SLG	OBP
Bemboom, Anthony	L-R	6-2	190	1-18-90	.245	.214	.254	61	229	35	56	11	0	8	25	21	0	3	1	43	0	1	.397	.307
Bolaski, Michael	R-R	6-3	185	2-5-92	.203	.234	.193	77	271	22	55	10	1	6	44	38	0	0	5	74	1	0	.314	.296
Cannizaro, Garrett	R-R	6-0	180	8-10-90	.199	.200	.198	50	176	12	35	8	0	0	14	18	4	3	2	33	1	1	.244	.285
Cayones, Exicardo	L-L	6-0	185	10-9-91	.233	.256	.226	58	202	26	47	6	3	2	15	28	8	2	3	64	11	4	.322	.344
Clarke, Chevy	B-R	6-0	200	1-9-92	.227	.200	.236	124	431	50	98	14	3	7	39	49	5	2	0	138	15	11	.323	.313
Concepcion, Julio	R-R	6-4	194	9-5-89	.219	.370	.159	25	96	10	21	3	1	1	14	3	1	0	1	17	0	0	.302	.248
Good, Riley	L-R	6-0	185	3-7-92	.225	.205	.233	41	142	13	32	1	0	0	6	9	2	2	2	32	0	3	.232	.277
Gowens, Brennan	L-R	6-0	195	3-14-90	.207	.238	.197	25	82	11	17	2	0	0	6	9	0	0	1	13	5	2	.232	.283
Hinkle, Wade	L-L	6-0	225	9-5-89	.270	.259	.274	119	444	57	120	30	2	13	68	54	8	0	1	89	2	2	.435	.359
Johnson, Kyle	R-R	6-0	180	11-9-89	.308	.324	.302	68	247	41	76	16	3	2	30	39	8	5	2	52	30	5	.421	.416
Johnson, Sherman	L-R	5-10	178	7-15-90	.261	.274	.256	105	398	74	104	20	6	4	32	66	6	4	4	87	14	4	.372	.371
Livingston, Zac	R-R	6-2	209	9-30-89	.083	.000	.100	5	12	1	1	0	0	0	0	2	1	0	0	6	0	0	.083	.267
Martinez, Sandy	B-R	5-11	180	7-18-92	.195	.214	.190	44	149	14	29	4	0	2	15	6	2	2	4	15	1	0	.262	.230
Moesquit, Kevin	R-R	5-10	180	6-20-91	.235	.303	.217	49	162	13	38	5	0	0	13	12	7	3	1	29	5	2	.265	.313
Ray, Andrew	R-R	6-1	195	5-1-91	.275	.306	.265	75	287	40	79	27	1	15	52	9	2	0	2	93	0	1	.533	.300
Rosa, Angel	R-R	6-2	185	9-19-92	.270	.371	.239	37	148	19	40	11	2	2	18	8	2	0	1	42	12	3	.412	.314
Ross, Chance	R-R	6-0	180	2-28-90	.250	.268	.243	40	144	24	36	5	1	3	17	9	3	1	0	31	1	2	.361	.308
Scioscia, Matt	R-R	6-2	220	9-20-88	.182	.143	.200	18	66	3	12	0	0	0	4	7	0	1	0	16	0	2	.182	.260
Soto, Wendell	B-R	5-9	170	5-11-92	.197	.149	.212	83	279	30	55	6	6	3	24	29	0	5	1	67	13	6	.294	.272
Toribio, Pedro	R-R	5-10	158	7-21-90	.279	.175	.309	79	283	31	79	10	2	0	26	11	2	5	0	45	32	9	.329	.311
Walsh, Jonathan	B-R	6-2	208	11-14-90	.123	.167	.111	16	57	7	7	1	0	0	7	4	0	0	1	20	0	0	.140	.177
Wright, Zach	R-R	6-1	205	1-10-90	.279	.344	.253	30	111	12	31	8	0	4	17	13	0	3	2	33	4	1	.459	.349

Pitching	B-T	HT	WT	DOB	W	L	ERA	G	GS	CG	SV	IP	H	R	ER	HR	BB	SO	AVG	vLH	vRH	K/9	BB/9
Adams, Austin	R-R	6-2	180	5-5-91	2	1	3.98	27	0	0	1	32	25	17	14	0	17	36	.212	.200	.221	10.23	4.83
Baker, Garrett	L-L	6-5	215	8-1-89	2	1	3.81	21	0	0	2	26	20	14	11	5	6	23	.213	.216	.211	7.96	2.08
Bedrosian, Cam	R-R	6-0	185	10-2-91	1	5	5.30	37	2	0	7	54	55	38	32	4	22	69	.258	.253	.263	11.43	3.64
Blackford, Alex	R-R	5-11	200	11-16-90	0	2	2.54	18	0	0	1	28	21	12	8	5	6	35	.198	.111	.243	11.12	1.91
Boyd, Jake	R-R	6-3	200	1-6-90	3	3	3.35	17	4	1	2	48	42	32	18	3	18	27	.228	.173	.272	5.03	3.35
Crowley, Ryan	L-L	6-3	190	11-15-90	10	7	3.28	26	25	0	0	151	141	63	55	15	35	123	.248	.220	.256	7.33	2.09
Dellatorre, Nic	R-L	5-11	195	8-28-91	0	5	8.90	8	5	0	0	29	43	36	29	9	14	16	.355	.296	.372	4.91	4.30
DeLoach, Tyler	R-L	6-6	240	4-12-91	5	5	3.34	13	13	0	0	70	50	28	26	5	22	79	.201	.190	.204	10.16	2.83
Diaz, Jairo	R-R	6-0	195	5-21-91	3	0	3.97	32	0	0	8	34	27	16	15	3	11	28	.220	.317	.171	7.41	2.91
Efferson, Brandon	R-R	5-11	175	11-25-88	1	2	1.84	10	0	0	0	15	18	7	3	0	4	15	.295	.320	.278	9.20	2.45
Fernandez, Arjenis	R-R	6-4	195	7-29-93	0	1	10.80	2	2	0	0	7	12	9	8	4	5	3	.387	.462	.333	4.05	6.75
Hatcher, Kenny	R-R	6-1	205	5-4-90	0	1	4.50	3	0	0	0	2	3	1	1	0	5	0	.375	.500	.333	0.00	22.50
Hurtado, Daniel	R-R	6-3	180	7-25-92	2	1	3.34	12	2	0	0	32	27	12	12	3	14	24	.223	.197	.255	6.68	3.90
Jimenez, Eswarlin	L-L	6-1	187	11-27-91	1	0	4.00	7	0	0	0	9	11	8	4	1	3	6	.297	.333	.280	6.00	3.00
Keudell, Alex	R-R	6-3	205	2-25-90	4	3	3.11	13	13	0	0	81	73	33	28	4	23	54	.240	.224	.253	6.00	2.56
Krehbiel, Joe	R-R	6-2	185	12-20-92	6	5	2.74	48	1	0	1	66	49	22	20	3	28	70	.204	.265	.159	9.53	3.84
Love, Brandon	L-L	6-3	195	3-6-90	4	7	4.10	20	14	0	1	86	91	42	39	9	30	78	.272	.255	.278	8.19	3.15
Lowery, Pat	R-R	6-5	195	4-2-90	4	10	4.91	21	21	1	0	103	101	64	56	8	57	69	.259	.301	.224	6.05	5.00
Newcomb, Aaron	R-R	6-3	190	3-2-90	1	4	6.24	12	8	0	0	49	62	38	34	6	16	28	.307	.337	.284	5.14	2.94

O'Grady, Chris	L-L	6-4	220	4-17-90	3	1	2.17	21	5	0	0	46	38	13	11	3	9	38	.230	.182	.255	7.49	1.77
Perez, Andres	R-R	6-2	184	2-8-91	0	1	3.95	8	0	0	0	14	14	6	6	1	10	5	.275	.345	.182	3.29	6.59
Powell, Robbie	R-R	6-0	180	2-7-90	3	1	4.57	14	0	0	2	22	21	11	11	2	5	18	.266	.231	.283	7.48	2.08
Santos, Eduard	R-R	6-2	220	10-22-89	1	1	3.38	15	2	0	0	32	27	16	12	2	10	41	.218	.164	.270	11.53	2.81
Scoggins, Reid	R-R	6-3	210	7-18-90	1	4	3.46	21	17	0	0	65	53	30	25	1	35	76	.223	.178	.255	10.52	4.85
Spomer, Kurt	B-R	6-2	215	7-10-89	4	3	2.49	46	0	0	6	65	51	20	18	2	19	45	.217	.247	.197	6.23	2.63

Fielding

Catcher	PCT	G	PO	A	E	DP	PB
Bemboom	.983	58	414	49	8	9	7
Livingston	.949	5	35	2	2	0	2
Martinez	.985	42	305	32	5	4	9
Wright	.989	30	226	32	3	1	3

First Base	PCT	G	PO	A	E	DP
Bolaski	.985	21	180	11	3	13
Cannizaro	.972	4	32	3	1	1
Hinkle	.990	102	900	54	10	94
Ross	1.000	3	26	3	0	1
Scioscia	.979	5	44	3	1	1

Second Base	PCT	G	PO	A	E	DP
Cannizaro	.975	24	41	74	3	14
Johnson	.969	8	12	19	1	6

Martinez	1.000	2	4	4	0	0
Moesquit	.980	20	39	58	2	13
Ross	1.000	20	32	54	0	15
Soto	1.000	9	11	30	0	5
Toribio	.968	56	93	147	8	38

Third Base	PCT	G	PO	A	E	DP
Bolaski	.700	12	6	15	9	1
Cannizaro	.905	16	15	42	6	6
Johnson	.958	90	85	189	12	23
Moesquit	.925	11	12	25	3	4
Rosa	1.000	1	0	1	0	0
Ross	.947	5	6	12	1	1

Shortstop	PCT	G	PO	A	E	DP
Rosa	.901	35	56	90	16	20

Ross	.940	11	24	23	3	6
Soto	.955	73	115	202	15	44
Toribio	.918	18	37	41	7	11

Outfield	PCT	G	PO	A	E	DP
Cayones	1.000	53	90	3	0	0
Clarke	.969	120	213	6	7	2
Concepcion	1.000	17	25	2	0	0
Good	1.000	40	69	4	0	1
Gowens	.974	22	36	2	1	0
Johnson	.992	65	130	2	1	0
Johnson	.875	3	7	0	1	0
Moesquit	1.000	15	27	2	0	0
Ray	.963	57	74	3	3	1
Walsh	1.000	14	12	0	0	0

AZL ANGELS

ROOKIE

ARIZONA LEAGUE

Batting	B-T	HT	WT	DOB	AVG	vLH	vRH	G	AB	R	H	2B	3B	HR	RBI	BB	HBP	SH	SF	SO	SB	CS	SLG	OBP
Allbritton, Alex	R-R	6-2	185	12-9-90	.262	.500	.216	16	61	10	16	1	1	0	4	3	1	0	0	13	5	1	.311	.308
Bayardi, Brandon	R-R	6-2	235	11-27-90	.304	.000	.318	8	23	6	7	4	0	1	6	2	4	0	0	5	3	0	.609	.448
Beltran, Glenn	R-R	6-2	220	12-23-91	.278	.360	.256	35	115	10	32	4	0	0	14	12	4	0	2	32	0	2	.313	.361
Cousins, Scott	L-L	6-2	200	1-22-85	.286	—	.286	2	7	3	2	0	1	0	0	1	0	0	0	3	0	0	.571	.375
Davis, Quinten	R-R	6-1	185	8-1-92	.288	.323	.280	48	156	28	45	9	3	2	23	17	3	1	2	45	13	1	.423	.365
Delgado, Natanael	L-L	6-1	170	10-23-95	.271	.368	.247	51	192	23	52	16	2	3	33	11	2	0	4	43	4	0	.422	.311
Dionicio, Ismael	B-R	5-10	165	7-19-91	.354	.250	.383	47	164	24	58	12	1	0	20	9	1	5	1	29	12	6	.439	.389
Fish, Michael	R-R	6-1	190	1-1-91	.409	.333	.417	20	66	19	27	10	2	2	9	5	0	0	0	14	6	0	.712	.451
Goro, Nate	R-R	6-0	182	11-30-90	.218	.233	.214	48	156	28	34	5	1	1	18	13	3	5	2	43	13	3	.282	.287
Guenther, Brad	L-R	5-10	195	1-13-91	.310	.143	.364	26	58	16	18	2	0	0	5	16	2	1	1	5	10	2	.345	.468
Hermosillo, Michael	R-R	5-9	189	1-17-95	.375	.333	.385	11	16	3	6	0	0	0	1	1	0	0	1	3	1	0	.375	.444
Jimenez, Luis	R-R	6-1	205	1-18-88	.462	—	.462	3	13	3	6	0	0	1	4	0	0	0	0	2	0	0	.692	.462
Johnson, Taylor	R-R	6-2	210	4-17-90	.236	.235	.236	50	182	21	43	11	2	2	22	17	2	1	1	53	3	2	.352	.307
Martinez, Ricky	R-R	6-2	180	11-30-95	.220	.280	.208	40	150	24	33	5	1	2	18	10	0	0	3	57	2	2	.307	.264
McGee, Stephen	R-R	6-3	230	1-7-91	.067	.000	.077	6	15	3	1	0	0	0	0	3	0	0	4	1	1	0	.067	.462
Patterson, Chase	R-R	5-11	185	9-11-93	.165	.067	.184	34	91	11	15	5	0	2	8	12	5	3	0	38	0	2	.286	.296
Pellant, Kirby	L-R	5-10	175	7-13-90	.310	.433	.271	38	126	28	39	8	2	2	15	14	0	5	0	18	15	2	.452	.379
Pizarro, Pedro	R-R	5-10	205	12-19-93	.262	.182	.290	23	42	7	11	2	0	0	4	6	2	0	1	14	3	0	.310	.373
Salcedo, Erick	B-R	5-10	155	6-28-93	.270	.324	.257	48	189	27	51	8	5	0	22	16	0	3	1	32	10	3	.365	.325
Scioscia, Matt	R-R	6-2	220	9-20-88	.213	.182	.222	12	47	2	10	2	0	0	5	2	0	0	0	11	0	1	.255	.245
Shannon, Mark	L-L	6-0	185	4-12-91	.222	.667	.167	8	27	4	6	0	0	1	3	1	0	0	0	7	0	1	.333	.250
Vivas, Enyelber	R-R	6-1	175	8-26-92	—	—	—	1	0	0	0	0	0	0	0	0	0	0	0	0	0	0	—	—
Weiss, Eric	R-R	6-1	195	10-16-90	.254	.222	.260	26	59	8	15	3	0	1	10	4	0	3	1	15	2	0	.356	.297

Pitching	B-T	HT	WT	DOB	W	L	ERA	G	GS	CG	SV	IP	H	R	ER	HR	BB	SO	AVG	vLH	vRH	K/9	BB/9
Blackford, Alex	R-R	5-11	200	11-16-90	0	0	3.00	5	0	0	3	6	4	2	2	0	1	7	.190	.250	.154	10.50	1.50
Carlson, Ben	R-R	6-3	215	11-30-90	4	0	1.73	21	0	0	10	26	22	5	5	0	5	15	.242	.194	.273	5.19	1.73
Clevinger, Mike	R-R	6-4	217	12-21-90	0	0	3.00	2	2	0	0	3	2	1	1	0	2	3	.200	.500	.125	9.00	6.00
Da Silva, Alex	R-R	6-2	195	7-2-93	0	2	10.29	13	0	0	0	14	22	20	16	1	17	12	.338	.345	.333	7.71	10.93
Dellatorre, Nic	R-L	5-11	195	8-28-91	0	3	3.66	5	2	0	0	20	15	12	8	2	4	17	.205	.400	.175	7.78	1.83
Etsell, Ryan	R-R	6-4	180	12-18-91	0	2	1.67	10	5	0	0	27	23	5	5	2	5	20	.221	.184	.242	6.67	1.67
Green, Hunter	L-L	6-4	175	7-12-95	0	1	4.32	8	7	0	0	17	16	14	8	0	16	11	.254	.111	.311	5.94	8.64
Guerra, Angel	R-R	6-1	180	2-2-93	0	3	4.93	10	7	0	0	42	47	28	23	1	18	30	.278	.358	.225	6.43	3.86
Hatcher, Kenny	R-R	6-1	205	5-4-90	1	0	3.90	11	4	0	1	28	28	12	12	0	7	29	.267	.300	.246	9.43	2.28
Hernandez, Matt	L-L	6-2	190	6-14-91	2	0	2.14	11	0	0	0	21	19	6	5	0	8	18	.253	.111	.298	7.71	3.43
Hunter, Kyle	R-L	5-10	180	9-18-91	5	1	4.40	14	1	0	0	31	34	19	15	1	10	29	.276	.333	.258	8.51	2.93
Middleton, Keynan	R-R	6-2	185	9-12-93	0	0	6.35	4	1	0	0	6	3	4	4	0	3	5	.143	.250	.077	7.94	4.76
O'Keefe, Colin	R-L	6-0	175	8-2-92	0	1	18.56	7	0	0	0	5	6	12	11	0	11	2	.300	.000	.353	3.38	18.56
Perez, Andres	R-R	6-2	184	2-8-91	0	0	0.00	1	0	0	0	1	0	1	0	0	1	2	.000	.000	.000	13.50	6.75
Reinoso, Yordany	R-R	6-1	185	10-16-93	0	3	4.15	13	2	0	0	30	38	19	14	4	6	34	.295	.234	.329	10.09	1.78
Rodriguez, Nataniel	L-L	5-10	180	8-27-90	2	1	4.80	13	0	0	1	15	18	14	8	0	16	16	.300	.273	.306	9.60	9.60
Rodriguez, Ramon	R-R	6-0	180	9-20-93	3	0	4.03	9	0	0	0	22	27	12	10	1	5	25	.297	.286	.306	10.07	2.01
Santana, Francisco	L-L	5-10	155	2-1-93	4	1	4.14	16	0	0	0	37	43	20	17	1	10	26	.295	.214	.327	6.32	2.43
Sharp, Clint	R-R	6-2	215	3-20-91	3	4	4.78	15	11	0	0	53	58	36	28	4	15	40	.275	.320	.237	6.84	2.56
Sneed, Kramer	L-L	6-3	185	10-7-88	0	1	2.19	4	4	0	0	12	9	5	3	2	2	12	.209	.357	.138	8.76	1.46
Stetter, Mitch	L-L	6-5	215	1-16-81	0	0	0.00	1	0	0	0	1	1	1	0	0	2	0	.250	.000	.333	18.00	0.00
Terhune, Greg	R-L	6-5	210	8-8-91	2	2	3.49	13	1	0	0	28	40	17	11	0	6	24	.325	.286	.337	7.62	1.91
Tillman, Daniel	R-R	6-1	185	3-14-89	0	0	0.00	3	0	0	0	4	0	0	0	0	0	5	.000	.000	.000	11.25	0.00

	B-T	HT	WT	DOB	W	L	ERA	G	GS	CG	SV	IP	H	R	ER	HR	BB	SO	AVG	vLH	vRH	K/9	BB/9
Tobik, Dan	R-R	6-4	195	1-8-91	4	1	2.89	13	6	0	0	47	37	22	15	2	16	39	.210	.250	.180	7.52	3.09
Wesely, Jonah	L-L	6-2	205	12-8-94	0	0	0.00	1	1	0	0	1	1	0	0	0	1	0	.250	.000	.250	0.00	9.00
Wood, Austin	R-R	6-4	225	7-11-90	0	0	2.08	2	2	0	0	4	4	4	1	0	4	4	.267	.400	.200	8.31	8.31

Fielding

Catcher	PCT	G	PO	A	E	DP	PB
Guenther	1.000	9	26	7	0	0	2
McGee	1.000	4	27	0	0	0	0
Patterson	.975	25	150	9	4	0	10
Pizarro	.921	23	90	15	9	0	5
Vivas	1.000	1	2	0	0	0	0
Weiss	.971	26	122	10	4	1	5

First Base	PCT	G	PO	A	E	DP
Bayardi	1.000	1	9	3	0	1
Goro	1.000	6	50	5	0	5
Guenther	1.000	1	9	0	0	1
Johnson	.986	46	461	36	7	47
Scioscia	.975	5	37	2	1	4

Second Base	PCT	G	PO	A	E	DP
Dionicio	.947	7	12	24	2	4

	PCT	G	PO	A	E	DP
Goro	.978	20	40	51	2	17
Pellant	.978	33	66	111	4	24
Salcedo	1.000	1	3	4	0	2

Third Base	PCT	G	PO	A	E	DP
Allbritton	.980	14	14	35	1	4
Dionicio	.924	37	25	85	9	10
Goro	.800	6	3	9	3	1
Guenther	.000	1	0	0	1	0
Jimenez	1.000	3	1	6	0	2
Johnson	.750	1	1	2	1	0

Shortstop	PCT	G	PO	A	E	DP
Allbritton	1.000	3	4	13	0	2
Goro	.962	6	7	18	1	3
Pellant	1.000	3	2	8	0	0
Salcedo	.945	47	73	167	14	34

Outfield	PCT	G	PO	A	E	DP
Bayardi	1.000	5	7	0	0	0
Beltran	.893	22	23	2	3	0
Cousins	1.000	1	2	0	0	0
Davis	.972	47	67	2	2	1
Delgado	.859	38	54	1	9	0
Fish	1.000	8	9	0	0	0
Goro	.917	10	10	1	1	0
Guenther	1.000	16	16	0	0	0
Hermosillo	.800	7	4	0	1	0
Johnson	1.000	3	6	0	0	0
Martinez	.944	34	33	1	2	0
Patterson	—	1	0	0	0	0
Pellant	—	1	0	0	0	0
Shannon	1.000	7	16	0	0	0

OREM OWLZ
PIONEER LEAGUE

ROOKIE

Batting	B-T	HT	WT	DOB	AVG	vLH	vRH	G	AB	R	H	2B	3B	HR	RBI	BB	HBP	SH	SF	SO	SB	CS	SLG	OBP
Aguilera, Eric	L-L	6-2	218	7-3-90	.306	.250	.316	59	232	27	71	22	1	10	53	14	2	2	7	60	1	1	.539	.341
Alberto, Ranyelmy	R-R	6-2	175	5-27-94	.233	.292	.216	59	210	39	49	13	1	2	23	21	4	1	2	69	6	5	.333	.312
Allbritton, Alex	R-R	6-2	185	12-9-90	.283	.226	.302	37	127	22	36	14	1	0	22	15	3	1	1	36	1	0	.409	.370
Bayardi, Brandon	R-R	6-2	235	11-27-90	.252	.214	.260	37	155	26	39	7	0	5	27	8	6	1	2	32	3	1	.394	.310
Bolden, Ryan	R-L	6-2	195	9-17-91	.130	.125	.133	7	23	1	3	0	0	1	1	4	0	0	0	8	2	0	.261	.259
Cannizaro, Garrett	R-R	6-0	180	8-10-90	.125	.000	.200	4	8	1	1	0	0	0	0	4	0	0	0	2	0	0	.125	.417
Cayones, Exicardo	L-L	6-0	185	10-9-91	.300	.000	.333	3	10	2	3	1	0	0	1	3	1	0	0	2	0	0	.400	.500
Concepcion, Julio	R-R	6-4	194	9-5-89	.444	1.000	.375	2	9	2	4	0	0	1	2	0	0	0	0	1	0	0	.778	.444
Dalton, Ryan	R-R	6-1	200	7-24-91	.236	.194	.248	42	140	18	33	6	0	3	24	16	6	0	4	26	1	1	.343	.331
Davis, Quinten	R-R	6-1	185	8-1-92	.167	.286	.000	4	12	1	2	0	0	0	1	2	0	0	0	4	0	0	.167	.286
Eaves, Kody	L-R	6-0	175	7-8-93	.277	.230	.291	67	264	45	73	14	6	1	24	20	1	4	3	40	22	6	.386	.326
Fish, Michael	R-R	6-1	190	1-3-91	.337	.324	.344	26	98	27	33	8	2	7	33	7	4	0	0	16	1	2	.673	.404
Good, Riley	L-R	6-0	185	3-7-92	.326	.286	.333	9	43	13	14	2	0	0	7	2	0	0	1	7	6	0	.372	.348
Hinshaw, Chad	R-R	6-1	205	9-10-90	.258	.263	.257	26	89	24	23	2	0	0	8	13	11	0	1	21	9	1	.281	.412
Linares, Raul	B-R	5-11	160	10-4-90	.309	.364	.295	52	162	29	50	11	2	3	20	14	0	3	2	31	4	2	.457	.360
Livingston, Zac	R-R	6-2	209	9-30-89	.175	.200	.167	23	63	9	11	4	0	2	5	6	3	1	1	31	1	0	.333	.254
McGee, Stephen	R-R	6-3	230	2-7-91	.300	.231	.333	12	40	2	12	1	0	1	7	6	0	0	1	6	0	0	.400	.383
Moye, Cambric	R-R	6-1	185	4-21-92	.246	.280	.238	35	126	24	31	10	2	6	17	12	4	1	1	41	1	0	.500	.329
Rondon, Jose	R-R	6-1	160	3-3-94	.293	.281	.297	68	276	45	81	22	2	1	50	30	2	1	7	31	13	8	.399	.359
Rosa, Angel	R-R	6-2	185	9-19-92	.278	.182	.302	14	54	6	15	3	0	0	9	1	0	2		20	1	1	.333	.369
Shannon, Mark	L-L	6-0	185	4-12-91	.300	.203	.333	54	230	50	69	16	3	10	33	20	5	0	3	33	9	2	.526	.364
Towey, Cal	L-R	6-1	215	2-6-90	.317	.261	.332	70	230	69	73	16	6	8	53	67	15	0	3	59	13	3	.543	.492

Pitching	B-T	HT	WT	DOB	W	L	ERA	G	GS	CG	SV	IP	H	R	ER	HR	BB	SO	AVG	vLH	vRH	K/9	BB/9
Alcantara, Alfonso	R-R	6-2	190	4-3-93	2	5	7.47	17	12	0	0	59	73	59	49	10	35	48	.304	.270	.325	7.32	5.34
Almonte, Yency	B-R	6-3	185	6-4-94	3	3	6.92	13	11	0	0	53	66	46	41	5	21	35	.304	.319	.297	5.91	3.54
Busenitz, Alan	R-R	6-1	180	8-22-90	5	2	2.33	21	0	0	1	39	37	13	10	3	4	27	.253	.231	.266	6.28	0.93
Bush, Garrett	R-R	6-4	190	10-11-90	2	2	5.45	20	0	0	2	33	34	24	20	4	17	30	.270	.279	.265	8.18	4.64
Carlson, Ben	R-R	6-3	215	11-30-90	0	1	10.80	3	0	0	0	3	4	4	4	0	1	1	.308	.333	.300	2.70	2.70
Clevinger, Mike	R-R	6-4	217	12-21-90	0	1	16.88	1	1	0	0	3	6	6	5	0	2	2	.429	.000	.545	6.75	6.75
Cooney, Harrison	R-R	6-2	175	3-25-92	1	2	5.10	14	0	0	2	30	28	20	17	1	11	18	.241	.241	.241	5.40	3.30
Etsell, Ryan	R-R	6-4	180	12-18-91	0	0	10.80	3	0	0	0	5	6	6	6	1	2	2	.300	.273	.333	3.60	3.60
Fernandez, Arjenis	R-R	6-4	195	7-29-93	4	3	4.89	15	15	0	0	77	97	50	42	10	16	39	.308	.337	.294	4.54	1.86
Foss, Trevor	R-R	6-3	175	11-15-89	3	0	4.31	14	6	0	0	31	44	16	15	3	12	28	.352	.386	.333	8.04	3.45
Gordon, Grant	R-R	6-0	175	9-10-90	3	0	2.57	9	0	0	0	14	12	4	4	0	4	14	.226	.200	.242	9.00	2.57
Hunter, Kyle	R-L	5-10	180	9-14-90	0	0	4.91	4	0	0	1	7	5	2		0	1	8	.389	.250	.500	19.64	2.45
Hurtado, Daniel	R-R	6-3	180	7-25-92	1	0	3.75	5	0	0	0	12	12	5	5	1	6	8	.255	.333	.207	6.00	4.50
Loconsole, Brian	R-R	6-2	215	8-10-90	0	0	9.11	17	0	0	0	27	47	36	27	4	15	20	.392	.349	.416	6.75	5.06
McGowin, Kyle	R-R	6-3	180	11-27-91	1	1	6.28	9	1	0	0	14	12	11	10	2	5	12	.218	.231	.214	7.53	3.14
Middleton, Keynan	R-R	6-2	185	9-12-93	1	3	8.10	6	6	0	0	23	29	24	21	4	15	13	.319	.286	.333	5.79	5.79
Morris, Elliot	R-R	6-4	210	4-26-92	2	2	3.95	11	2	0	0	27	29	12	12	1	11	25	.279	.189	.328	8.23	3.62
Nuss, Garrett	R-R	6-1	180	4-15-93	4	3	5.15	13	9	0	0	51	66	36	29	2	13	44	.319	.263	.354	7.82	2.31
O'Grady, Chris	L-L	6-4	220	4-17-90	0	0	2.25	3	0	0	0	8	8	4	2	1	2	8	.267	.333	.222	9.00	2.25
Rodriguez, Nataniel	L-L	5-10	185	8-27-90	0	0	9.00	2	0	0	0	2	5	2	2	0	1	2	.500	1.000	.444	9.00	4.50
Smith, Michael	R-R	6-0	195	1-31-90	4	2	1.95	21	0	0	0	28	29	9	6	1	6	18	.269	.400	.205	5.86	1.95
Smith, Nate	L-L	6-3	200	8-28-91	2	2	3.86	15	9	0	0	35	34	19	15	4	7	31	.264	.159	.318	7.97	1.80
Swanson, Cole	L-L	6-5	200	4-5-92	2	2	4.31	16	2	0	0	31	36	19	15	3	12	40	.288	.310	.277	12.06	3.45
Tobik, Dan	R-R	6-4	195	1-8-91	0	0	0.00	2	1	0	0	5	5	2	0	0	3	4	.278	.444	.111	7.71	5.79
Trygg, Spencer	R-R	6-2	210	6-2-90	0	1	5.67	20	0	0	0	27	34	24	17	0	15	28	.293	.212	.359	9.33	5.00
Van Eaton, Jonathan	R-R	6-2	205	5-16-91	0	0	3.79	17	0	0	10	19	17	8	8	3	4	23	.233	.185	.261	10.89	1.89

Fielding

Catcher	PCT	G	PO	A	E	DP	PB
Dalton	.992	20	108	18	1	1	8
Livingston	.936	21	122	24	10	1	7
McGee	.991	12	97	11	1	1	4
Moye	.982	28	183	37	4	1	14

First Base	PCT	G	PO	A	E	DP
Aguilera	.977	43	397	30	10	37
Allbritton	.988	10	76	3	1	11
Bayardi	1.000	1	4	0	0	0
Dalton	.979	17	137	6	3	16
Linares	.984	7	58	2	1	3
Livingston	1.000	1	9	0	0	1
Towey	1.000	1	9	0	0	0

Second Base	PCT	G	PO	A	E	DP
Allbritton	1.000	7	15	24	0	7
Cannizaro	1.000	1	2	5	0	0

Eaves	.960	65	141	193	14	51
Linares	1.000	1	3	2	0	0
Rosa	1.000	3	6	14	0	3

Third Base	PCT	G	PO	A	E	DP
Allbritton	.907	12	11	28	4	3
Cannizaro	.833	3	2	8	2	1
Linares	.750	7	2	7	3	1
Livingston	1.000	1	0	1	0	0
Rosa	.933	5	3	11	1	0
Towey	.899	53	33	119	17	11

Shortstop	PCT	G	PO	A	E	DP
Allbritton	.912	7	8	23	3	5
Linares	.500	1	0	1	1	0
Rondon	.955	66	109	213	15	49
Rosa	.941	4	12	4	1	0

Outfield	PCT	G	PO	A	E	DP
Aguilera	1.000	1	1	0	0	0
Alberto	.949	56	106	6	6	1
Bayardi	.977	24	41	2	1	0
Bolden	.875	7	6	1	1	0
Cayones	1.000	3	4	0	0	0
Concepcion	1.000	1	1	0	0	0
Davis	1.000	4	11	0	0	0
Fish	1.000	24	40	3	0	0
Good	1.000	9	13	0	0	0
Hinshaw	.953	24	37	4	2	1
Linares	1.000	31	43	4	0	0
Shannon	.943	49	94	5	6	1
Towey	—	3	0	0	0	0

DSL ANGELS
DOMINICAN SUMMER LEAGUE

ROOKIE

Batting	B-T	HT	WT	DOB	AVG	vLH	vRH	G	AB	R	H	2B	3B	HR	RBI	BB	HBP	SH	SF	SO	SB	CS	SLG	OBP
Almao, Angel	R-R	5-10	145	11-5-94	.202	.261	.187	37	114	16	23	1	0	0	3	17	1	4	0	17	5	3	.211	.311
Arias, Jonathan	R-R	6-2	170	1-31-96	.148	.138	.150	39	142	13	21	4	0	0	7	10	2	2	1	29	3	1	.176	.213
Espinoza, Luis	R-R	6-3	180	1-13-94	.252	.233	.256	45	155	12	39	11	0	1	17	22	3	0	2	32	3	6	.342	.352
Fernandez, Jesus	R-R	6-1	185	3-6-94	.056	.143	.034	15	36	0	2	0	0	0	1	3	2	1	0	20	0	0	.056	.171
Genao, Angel	R-R	6-2	175	3-22-93	.171	.182	.169	27	82	8	14	2	1	0	9	12	2	0	1	22	0	0	.220	.289
Herrera, Jose	B-R	6-0	155	1-14-93	.244	.242	.244	62	197	24	48	6	0	0	27	34	8	1	3	33	2	2	.274	.372
Jolly, Luis	R-R	6-2	180	3-21-93	.154	.107	.167	45	136	18	21	4	2	1	7	25	1	5	0	61	12	5	.235	.290
Martinez, Mario	R-R	5-10	185	7-31-96	.247	.194	.260	53	162	24	40	9	2	1	28	21	15	1	7	34	4	5	.346	.371
Mateo, Steven	R-R	6-2	188	8-19-92	.279	.302	.273	66	219	44	61	20	1	2	39	55	4	0	2	62	14	6	.406	.429
Montilla, Angel	R-R	6-1	170	4-18-93	.234	.043	.270	40	145	26	34	2	0	0	11	12	8	1	3	27	16	5	.248	.321
Moreno, Juan	R-R	6-1	160	11-17-94	.273	.250	.277	38	132	21	36	4	1	0	13	20	4	3	0	19	12	5	.318	.385
Mota, Darlyn	R-R	6-1	165	8-2-96	.195	.333	.157	46	154	21	30	4	0	0	12	25	4	1	0	49	3	1	.221	.322
Perez, Ayendy	L-R	5-9	160	9-10-93	.317	.250	.333	58	208	46	66	7	4	0	25	38	4	8	1	25	41	10	.389	.430
Richiez, Danny	R-R	6-2	175	8-13-96	.146	.097	.157	44	158	18	23	6	0	1	9	16	2	0	0	67	10	3	.203	.233
Santana, Gabriel	R-R	6-2	180	8-18-95	.206	.231	.202	30	97	8	20	1	0	0	9	10	3	1	0	14	1	3	.216	.300
Soto, Yeffri	B-R	5-9	145	3-12-93	.196	.278	.177	32	97	8	19	2	2	0	9	10	1	2	1	26	4	0	.258	.275

Pitching	B-T	HT	WT	DOB	W	L	ERA	G	GS	CG	SV	IP	H	R	ER	HR	BB	SO	AVG	vLH	vRH	K/9	BB/9
Barria, Jaime	R-R	6-1	180	7-18-96	0	1	10.80	4	0	0	0	5	13	8	6	0	1	4	.481	.222	.611	7.20	1.80
Cruz, Marcelis	R-R	6-0	180	1-29-94	1	2	2.78	20	1	0	5	36	35	14	11	1	9	17	.255	.250	.257	4.29	2.27
De La Cruz, Miguel	R-R	6-1	175	8-5-92	1	0	3.00	12	0	0	0	21	17	11	7	0	11	9	.227	.273	.208	3.86	4.71
Gonzalez, Raymundo	R-R	6-3	190	9-8-95	0	0	2.57	6	0	0	0	7	5	2	2	0	3	8	.250	.143	.286	10.29	3.86
Heredia, Andres	R-R	6-3	175	8-15-96	1	6	7.50	15	10	0	0	42	46	44	35	0	41	34	.284	.302	.277	7.29	8.79
Lopez, Eduar	R-R	6-0	180	2-21-95	6	3	1.88	14	13	0	0	62	27	19	13	0	42	83	.132	.023	.160	11.98	6.06
Mendoza, Jose	R-R	6-2	165	7-29-94	5	4	2.52	14	14	0	0	79	65	32	22	1	11	33	.220	.197	.228	3.78	1.26
Mieses, Crusito	R-R	6-5	187	9-5-97	0	1	2.13	4	3	0	0	13	13	4	3	0	6	10	.271	.200	.303	7.11	4.26
Paredes, Eduardo	R-R	6-1	170	3-6-95	2	1	2.82	17	0	0	8	22	27	10	7	1	4	14	.297	.200	.333	5.64	1.61
Pimentel, Yunior	L-L	6-4	180	9-9-94	4	5	3.41	14	13	0	0	61	57	32	23	1	33	46	.254	.310	.246	6.82	4.90
Reyes, Carlos	R-R	6-3	170	6-7-94	2	2	2.66	14	0	0	0	20	14	8	6	0	5	14	.194	.286	.172	6.20	2.21
Reyes, Jose	R-R	6-2	160	2-3-93	4	0	2.19	17	0	0	1	37	27	10	9	0	15	29	.211	.207	.212	7.05	3.65
Rodriguez, Jose	R-R	6-2	155	8-29-95	3	3	1.64	22	2	0	1	44	33	10	8	1	12	38	.213	.256	.198	7.77	2.45
Rodriguez, Ramon	R-R	6-0	180	9-20-93	0	1	3.52	11	0	0	1	15	15	8	6	0	8	11	.268	.368	.216	9.49	4.70
Rondon, Manuel	L-L	6-1	165	3-7-95	2	1	2.83	20	2	0	1	41	31	23	13	2	21	30	.203	.235	.199	6.53	4.57
Rosales, Engerberg	L-L	6-1	160	4-16-96	0	0	3.65	10	0	0	0	12	9	7	5	0	13	10	.205	.000	.243	7.30	9.49
Rosario, Edisson	L-L	6-0	180	8-13-94	2	4	3.41	14	13	0	0	63	51	30	24	1	29	52	.224	.194	.228	7.39	4.12
Sanchez, Luis	R-R	6-1	170	1-30-94	0	0	10.80	5	0	0	0	5	4	6	6	0	7	2	.250	.667	.154	3.60	12.60
Valdez, Alexander	R-R	6-0	175	1-28-94	3	1	3.41	21	0	0	1	29	37	19	11	0	7	27	.316	.306	.321	8.38	2.17

Fielding

Catcher	PCT	G	PO	A	E	DP	PB
Fernandez	.941	11	42	6	3	0	2
Genao	.939	22	119	19	9	0	2
Herrera	1.000	1	1	0	0	0	0
Martinez	.961	44	295	50	14	3	15
Santana	1.000	2	11	1	0	0	1

First Base	PCT	G	PO	A	E	DP
Herrera	.882	2	15	0	2	1
Mateo	.977	51	435	32	11	42
Santana	.973	21	173	9	5	15

Second Base	PCT	G	PO	A	E	DP
Almao	.968	15	33	27	2	8

Arias	.800	1	1	3	1	1
Herrera	.986	15	40	33	1	11
Moreno	.983	30	94	77	3	25
Mota	.950	4	6	13	1	1
Soto	1.000	8	17	22	0	3

Third Base	PCT	G	PO	A	E	DP
Arias	1.000	2	1	4	0	2
Herrera	.910	36	30	111	14	14
Moreno	.950	3	4	15	1	1
Mota	1.000	1	0	1	0	0
Richiez	.846	31	21	67	16	5
Soto	—	1	0	0	0	0

Shortstop	PCT	G	PO	A	E	DP
Arias	.877	32	51	70	17	7
Moreno	.958	6	7	16	1	3
Mota	.930	34	52	108	12	21

Outfield	PCT	G	PO	A	E	DP
Almao	1.000	19	32	4	0	2
Espinoza	.946	44	50	3	3	0
Herrera	1.000	2	3	1	0	0
Jolly	.959	40	68	2	3	0
Montilla	.987	39	74	1	1	0
Perez	.983	57	110	4	2	1
Soto	1.000	19	34	0	0	0

Los Angeles Dodgers

SEASON IN A SENTENCE: After a series of block-buster trades and splashy signings, the Dodgers were off to a disappointing start, but a second-half surge helped the Dodgers win the National League West and advance to the NL Championship Series, where they lost in six games to the Cardinals.

HIGH POINT: Clayton Kershaw cemented his status as baseball's best pitcher, leading the major leagues in ERA (1.83) for the third straight season. His 232 strikeouts also led the NL, while his 236 innings ranked second. The Dodgers went 45-23 in the second half fueled by the return of shortstop Hanley Ramirez from a jammed thumb, as he hit .345/.402/.638 in 86 games. Cuban right fielder Yasiel Puig started in Double-A but quickly forced his way to L.A., making his major league debut on June 3 and hitting .319/.391/.534 in 104 games.

LOW POINT: Manager Don Mattingly nearly lost his job after the Dodgers started 30-42 to drop to 9 ½ games back in the NL West.

NOTABLE ROOKIES: Puig signed a seven-year, $42 million deal in June 2012 that had other teams scratching their heads because few were able to scout him before he signed. He quickly became a fan favorite for his five-tool ability and athleti-cism from a hulking 6-foot-3, 245-pound frame. Lefthander Hyun-Jin Ryu, who signed a six-year, $36 million contract before the season after the Dodgers won the posting free with a $25.7 million bid to the Hanwha Eagles of the Korean Baseball Organization, also made an immediate impact with a 3.00 ERA in 192 innings.

KEY TRANSACTIONS: The Dodgers added to a stacked starting rotation of Kershaw, Ryu and Zack Greinke by acquiring righthander Ricky Nolasco and an international bonus slot from the Marlins in July for three minor league righthanders: Angel Sanchez, Josh Wall and Steve Ames. Nolasco deliv-ered a 3.56 ERA in 16 games with the Dodgers.

DOWN ON THE FARM: Joc Pederson had a strong season in Double-A Chattanooga and should make an already crowded outfield even more compli-cated. Corey Seager, a shortstop who likely will end up at third base, showed a polished hitting approach as a 19-year-old who reached high Class A in his first full season. Righthander Zach Lee pitched well in Double-A and could contribute in 2014. Mexican lefthander Julio Urias is further away, but he posted a 2.48 remarkable things for a 16-year-old in the low Class A Midwest League, where he had a 2.48 ERA in 54 innings.

OPENING DAY PAYROLL: $216.6 million (2nd)

PLAYERS OF THE YEAR

MAJOR LEAGUE	MINOR LEAGUE
Clayton Kershaw	**Joc Pederson**
lhp	**cf**
16-9, 1.83 in 33 GS	(Double-A)
232 SO, 0.92 WHIP	.278/.381/.497
Led NL in ERA, SO, WHIP	22 HR, 31 SB, 70 BB

ORGANIZATION LEADERS

BATTING		*Minimum 250 AB
MAJORS		
* AVG	Gonzalez, Adrian	.293
* OPS	Gonzalez, Adrian	.803
HR	Gonzalez, Adrian	22
RBI	Gonzalez, Adrian	22
MINORS		
* AVG	Buss, Nick, Albuquerque	.303
* OBP	Ogle, Tyler, Great Lakes	.401
* SLG	Schebler, Scott, Rancho Cucamonga	.581
R	Schebler, Scott, Rancho Cucamonga	95
H	Sweeney, Darnell, Rancho Cucamonga	152
TB	Schebler, Scott, Rancho Cucamonga	277
2B	Sweeney, Darnell, Rancho Cucamonga	34
3B	Sweeney, Darnell, Rancho Cucamonga	16
HR	Schebler, Scott, Rancho Cucamonga	27
RBI	Buss, Nick, Albuquerque	100
BB	Ogle, Tyler, Great Lakes	96
SO	Baldwin, James, Great Lakes	154
SB	Gordon, Dee, Albuquerque	49

PITCHING		#Minimum 75 IP
MAJORS		
W	Kershaw, Clayton	16
# ERA	Kershaw, Clayton	1.83
SO	Kershaw, Clayton	232
SV	Jansen, Kenley	28
MINORS		
W	Brown, Geoff, Great Lakes	12
L	Gould, Garrett, Chattanooga/R. Cucamonga	12
	Santiago, Andres, Chattanooga	12
# ERA	Stripling, Ross, R. Cucamonga/Chattanooga	2.82
G	Coulombe, Daniel, Rancho Cucamonga	54
GS	Lee, Zach, Chattanooga	25
	Reed, Chris, Chattanooga	25
	Santiago, Andres, Chattanooga	25
SV	Garcia, Yimi, Chattanooga	19
IP	Caughel, Lindsey, R. Cucamonga/Great Lakes	144
BB	Santiago, Andres, Chattanooga	74
SO	Caughel, Lindsey, R. Cucamonga/Great Lakes	138
# AVG	Santiago, Andres, Chattanooga	.238

General Manager: Ned Colletti. **Farm Director:** De Jon Watson. **Scouting Director:** Logan White.

Class	Team	League	W	L	PCT	Finish	Manager
Majors	Los Angeles Dodgers	National	92	70	.568	4th (15)	Don Mattingly
Triple-A	Albuquerque Isotopes	Pacific Coast	76	68	.528	t-6th (16)	Lorenzo Bundy
Double-A	Chattanooga Lookouts	Southern	59	80	.424	10th (10)	Jody Reed
High A	Rancho Cucamonga Quakes	California	65	75	.464	7th (10)	Carlos Subero
Low A	Great Lakes Loons	Midwest	67	72	.482	10th (16)	Razor Shines
Rookie	Ogden Raptors	Pioneer	36	40	.474	5th (8)	Damon Berryhill
Rookie	Dodgers	Arizona	34	22	.607	2nd (13)	P.J. Forbes
Overall 2013 Minor League Record			337	357	.486	21st (30)	

ORGANIZATION STATISTICS

NATIONAL LEAGUE

Batting	B-T	HT	WT	DOB	AVG	vLH	vRH	G	AB	R	H	2B	3B	HR	RBI	BB	HBP	SH	SF	SO	SB	CS	SLG	OBP
Buss, Nick	L-R	6-2	195	12-15-86	.105	.000	.125	8	19	0	2	0	0	0	0	1	0	0	0	1	0	0	.105	.150
Butera, Drew	R-R	6-1	200	8-9-83	.143	.000	.333	4	7	0	1	0	0	0	0	0	0	0	0	4	0	0	.143	.143
Castellanos, Alex	R-R	6-0	200	8-4-86	.167	.250	.100	8	18	2	3	1	0	1	1	0	0	0	0	5	0	0	.389	.167
Crawford, Carl	L-L	6-2	215	8-5-81	.283	.206	.308	116	435	62	123	30	3	6	31	28	3	0	2	66	15	4	.407	.329
Cruz, Luis	R-R	6-1	210	2-10-84	.127	.158	.113	45	118	12	15	2	0	1	6	5	2	2	1	20	0	0	.169	.175
Ellis, A.J.	R-R	6-3	220	4-9-81	.238	.200	.249	115	390	43	93	17	1	10	52	45	3	4	6	78	0	2	.364	.318
Ellis, Mark	R-R	5-10	190	6-6-77	.270	.282	.265	126	433	46	117	13	2	6	48	26	10	6	5	74	4	1	.351	.323
Ethier, Andre	L-L	6-2	205	4-10-82	.272	.221	.294	142	482	54	131	33	2	12	52	61	7	0	3	95	4	3	.423	.360
Federowicz, Tim	R-R	5-10	215	8-5-87	.231	.213	.239	56	160	12	37	8	0	4	16	10	0	2	1	56	0	0	.356	.275
Gonzalez, Adrian	L-L	6-2	225	5-8-82	.293	.273	.303	157	583	69	171	32	0	22	100	47	1	0	10	98	1	0	.461	.342
Gordon, Dee	L-R	5-11	160	4-22-88	.234	.273	.222	38	94	9	22	1	1	1	6	10	1	1	0	21	10	2	.298	.314
Hairston Jr., Jerry	R-R	5-10	195	5-29-76	.211	.179	.230	96	204	17	43	7	0	2	22	14	2	3	3	22	0	0	.275	.265
Hernandez, Ramon	R-R	6-0	220	5-20-76	.208	.231	.200	17	48	4	10	2	0	3	6	6	0	0	1	7	1	0	.438	.291
Herrera, Elian	B-R	5-10	190	2-1-85	.250	.333	.200	4	8	0	2	0	0	0	0	0	0	0	0	2	0	0	.250	.250
Kemp, Matt	R-R	6-4	215	9-23-84	.270	.320	.250	73	263	35	71	15	0	6	33	22	2	0	3	76	9	0	.395	.328
Puig, Yasiel	R-R	6-3	245	12-7-90	.319	.340	.312	104	382	66	122	21	2	19	42	36	11	0	3	97	11	8	.534	.391
Punto, Nick	B-R	5-9	195	11-8-77	.255	.309	.228	116	294	34	75	15	0	2	21	33	0	6	2	67	3	3	.327	.328
Ramirez, Hanley	R-R	6-2	225	12-23-83	.345	.349	.344	86	304	62	105	25	2	20	57	27	3	0	2	52	10	2	.638	.402
Schumaker, Skip	L-R	5-10	195	2-3-80	.263	.255	.265	125	319	31	84	16	0	2	30	28	5	3	0	54	2	2	.332	.332
Sellers, Justin	R-R	5-10	160	2-1-86	.188	.238	.167	27	69	6	13	1	0	1	2	5	2	1	0	20	0	0	.246	.263
Uribe, Juan	R-R	6-0	235	3-22-79	.278	.242	.290	132	388	47	108	22	2	12	50	30	2	3	3	81	5	0	.438	.331
Van Slyke, Scott	R-R	6-5	250	7-24-86	.240	.234	.246	53	129	13	31	8	0	7	19	20	1	0	2	37	1	1	.465	.342
Young, Michael	R-R	6-1	200	10-19-76	.314	.368	.281	21	51	3	16	2	1	0	4	1	0	0	1	5	0	0	.392	.321
2-team total (126 Philadelphia)					.279	—	—	147	519	52	145	26	5	8	46	43	1	0	2	83	1	0	.395	.335

Pitching	B-T	HT	WT	DOB	W	L	ERA	G	GS	CG	SV	IP	H	R	ER	HR	BB	SO	AVG	vLH	vRH	K/9	BB/9
Beckett, Josh	R-R	6-5	225	5-15-80	0	5	5.19	8	8	1	0	43	50	30	25	8	15	41	.289	.318	.261	8.52	3.12
Belisario, Ronald	R-R	6-3	240	12-31-82	5	7	3.97	77	0	0	1	68	72	34	30	3	28	49	.274	.305	.260	6.49	3.71
Billingsley, Chad	R-R	6-1	240	7-29-84	1	0	3.00	2	2	0	0	12	12	4	4	1	5	6	.286	.261	.316	4.50	3.75
Capuano, Chris	L-L	6-3	215	8-19-78	4	7	4.26	24	20	0	0	106	125	57	50	11	24	81	.295	.248	.312	6.90	2.04
Dominguez, Jose	R-R	6-0	160	8-7-90	0	0	2.16	9	0	0	0	8	11	3	2	0	3	4	.314	.333	.300	4.32	3.24
Fife, Stephen	R-R	6-3	220	10-4-86	4	4	3.70	12	10	0	0	58	69	28	24	7	20	45	.304	.336	.263	6.94	3.09
Garcia, Onelki	L-L	6-3	220	8-2-89	0	0	13.50	3	0	0	0	1	1	2	2	1	4	1	.200	.333	.000	6.75	27.00
Greinke, Zack	R-R	6-2	195	10-21-83	15	4	2.63	28	28	1	0	178	152	54	52	13	46	148	.234	.254	.216	7.50	2.33
Guerra, Javy	R-R	6-1	190	10-31-85	0	0	6.75	9	0	0	0	11	15	9	8	1	6	12	.319	.333	.308	10.13	5.06
Guerrier, Matt	R-R	6-3	195	8-2-78	2	3	4.80	34	0	0	0	30	32	18	16	3	12	21	.283	.211	.320	6.30	3.60
2-team total (15 Chicago)					4	4	4.01	49	0	0	0	43	43	22	19	3	17	30	—	—	—	6.33	3.59
Howell, J.P.	L-L	6-0	185	4-25-83	4	1	2.18	67	0	0	0	62	42	15	15	2	23	54	.193	.164	.222	7.84	3.34
Jansen, Kenley	B-R	6-5	260	9-30-87	4	3	1.88	75	0	0	28	77	48	16	16	6	18	111	.177	.204	.158	13.03	2.11
Kershaw, Clayton	L-L	6-3	220	3-19-88	16	9	1.83	33	33	3	0	236	164	55	48	11	52	232	.195	.165	.202	8.85	1.98
League, Brandon	R-R	6-2	215	3-16-83	6	4	5.30	58	0	0	14	54	69	37	32	8	15	28	.305	.312	.301	4.64	2.48
Lilly, Ted	L-L	6-0	195	1-4-76	0	2	5.09	5	5	0	0	23	27	16	13	4	10	18	.276	.400	.244	7.04	3.91
Magill, Matt	R-R	6-3	210	11-10-89	0	2	6.51	6	6	0	0	28	27	25	20	6	28	26	.257	.279	.242	8.46	9.11
Marmol, Carlos	R-R	6-2	215	10-14-82	0	0	2.53	21	0	0	0	21	14	7	6	1	19	27	.187	.207	.174	11.39	8.02
2-team total (31 Chicago)					2	4	4.41	52	0	0	2	49	40	26	24	7	40	59	—	—	—	10.84	7.35
Moylan, Peter	R-R	6-2	225	12-2-78	1	0	6.46	14	0	0	0	15	23	11	11	3	7	6	.365	.440	.316	3.52	4.11
Nolasco, Ricky	R-R	6-2	235	12-13-82	8	3	3.52	16	15	0	0	87	83	40	34	6	21	75	.247	.243	.251	7.76	2.17
2-team total (18 Miami)					13	11	3.70	34	33	0	0	199	195	90	82	17	46	165	—	—	—	7.45	2.08
Rodriguez, Paco	L-L	6-3	220	4-16-91	3	4	2.32	76	0	0	2	54	30	15	14	5	19	63	.164	.131	.202	10.44	3.15
Ryu, Hyun-Jin	L-L	6-2	255	3-25-87	14	8	3.00	30	30	2	0	192	182	67	64	15	49	154	.252	.270	.245	7.22	2.30
Tolleson, Shawn	R-R	6-2	210	1-19-88	0	0	—	1	0	0	0	0	0	0	0	0	2	0	—	.000	.000	—	—
Volquez, Edinson	R-R	6-0	225	7-3-83	0	2	4.18	6	5	0	0	28	25	14	13	5	8	26	.234	.231	.236	8.36	2.57
2-team total (27 San Diego)					9	12	5.71	33	32	0	0	170	193	114	108	19	77	142	—	—	—	7.50	4.07
Wall, Josh	R-R	6-6	215	1-21-87	0	1	18.00	6	0	0	0	7	17	14	14	2	6	7	.486	.333	.565	9.00	7.71

	B-T	HT	WT	DOB	W	L	ERA	G				IP	H	R	ER	BB		SO	AVG	vLH	vRH	K/9	BB/9
Wilson, Brian	R-R	6-2	205	3-16-82	2	1	0.66	18	0	0	0	14	8	1	1	0	4	13	.178	.091	.206	8.56	2.63
Withrow, Chris	R-R	6-4	215	4-1-89	3	0	2.60	26	0	0	1	35	20	10	10	5	13	43	.165	.217	.133	11.16	3.38

Fielding

Catcher	PCT	G	PO	A	E	DP	PB
Butera	1.000	2	3	0	0	0	0
Ellis	.997	113	855	73	3	8	6
Federowicz	.986	45	323	40	5	0	2
Hernandez	.990	11	89	8	1	0	2

First Base	PCT	G	PO	A	E	DP
Butera	1.000	2	15	0	0	1
Cruz	1.000	1	5	0	0	1
Federowicz	—	2	0	0	0	0
Gonzalez	.992	151	1294	84	11	133
Hairston Jr.	1.000	13	57	4	0	2
Hernandez	1.000	2	3	0	0	0
Uribe	.950	4	18	1	1	1
Van Slyke	1.000	4	24	0	0	4
Young	1.000	8	28	2	0	4

Second Base	PCT	G	PO	A	E	DP
Ellis	.989	119	225	302	6	78
Gordon	1.000	3	0	4	0	1
Hairston Jr.	—	1	0	0	0	0
Punto	.989	33	41	47	1	15
Schumaker	.970	44	85	79	5	25
Young	1.000	2	0	4	0	0

Third Base	PCT	G	PO	A	E	DP
Cruz	.972	28	21	49	2	6
Ellis	—	1	0	0	0	0
Hairston Jr.	.887	28	12	35	6	5
Punto	.932	35	15	40	4	3
Sellers	—	1	0	0	0	0
Uribe	.983	123	62	230	5	22
Young	.900	8	0	9	1	1

Shortstop	PCT	G	PO	A	E	DP
Cruz	.983	15	12	46	1	9

	PCT	G	PO	A	E	DP
Gordon	.936	27	29	73	7	11
Punto	.981	49	47	109	3	30
Ramirez	.960	76	105	210	13	43
Sellers	.959	22	22	48	3	11
Young	1.000	1	0	2	0	0

Outfield	PCT	G	PO	A	E	DP
Buss	1.000	6	7	0	0	0
Castellanos	1.000	8	2	0	0	0
Crawford	.977	107	165	3	4	0
Cruz	—	1	0	0	0	0
Ethier	.992	133	247	8	2	4
Hairston Jr.	1.000	27	33	1	0	0
Herrera	.000	2	0	0	1	0
Kemp	.964	70	133	2	5	0
Puig	.971	100	162	8	5	1
Schumaker	.976	74	80	1	2	1
Van Slyke	.968	41	59	1	2	0

ALBUQUERQUE ISOTOPES   TRIPLE-A
PACIFIC COAST LEAGUE

Batting	B-T	HT	WT	DOB	AVG	vLH	vRH	G	AB	R	H	2B	3B	HR	RBI	BB	HBP	SH	SF	SO	SB	CS	SLG	OBP
Alfonzo, Eliezer	R-R	5-11	220	2-7-79	.284	.455	.250	19	67	5	19	5	0	3	14	0	1	0	0	14	1	0	.493	.294
Amezaga, Alfredo	B-R	5-11	165	1-16-78	.339	.442	.284	37	124	19	42	10	1	2	25	14	1	0	2	20	1	1	.484	.404
Angle, Matt	L-R	5-10	180	9-10-85	.283	.298	.275	120	400	70	113	20	8	8	62	51	9	5	3	104	22	5	.433	.374
Baker, John	L-R	6-1	215	1-20-81	.203	.189	.208	40	133	14	27	1	0	4	17	18	0	0	2	33	0	1	.301	.294
2-team total (4 Tucson)					.205	—	—	44	146	16	30	1	0	4	18	20	1	0	2	38	0	1	.295	.302
Barden, Brian	R-R	5-11	190	4-2-81	.277	.295	.268	123	415	49	115	22	3	5	56	41	7	5	3	66	1	1	.381	.350
Buss, Nick	L-R	6-2	195	12-15-86	.303	.282	.311	131	459	84	139	29	11	17	100	41	7	3	8	90	21	2	.525	.363
Butera, Drew	R-R	6-1	200	8-9-83	.135	.154	.128	16	52	3	7	3	1	0	3	4	0	1	0	14	0	0	.231	.196
Castellanos, Alex	R-R	6-0	200	8-4-86	.257	.202	.282	105	385	75	99	14	5	19	61	41	12	1	0	112	19	5	.468	.347
Cilladi, Steve	R-R	5-9	182	3-15-87	.000	.000	.000	1	7	0	0	0	0	0	0	0	0	0	0	3	0	0	.000	.000
Espino, Damaso	R-R	6-1	210	5-8-83	.333	.292	.359	19	63	7	21	5	0	0	6	8	0	0	1	6	0	0	.413	.403
Federowicz, Tim	R-R	5-10	215	8-5-87	.418	.476	.397	21	79	20	33	8	1	8	25	14	1	2	2	26	0	0	.848	.500
Flores, Jesus	R-R	6-1	210	10-26-84	.164	.103	.205	22	73	5	12	5	0	0	7	4	1	2	0	18	0	0	.233	.218
Gonzalez, Elevys	B-R	5-11	175	10-23-89	.229	.267	.200	14	35	6	8	1	1	2	5	6	2	3	0	12	4	0	.486	.372
Gordon, Dee	L-R	5-11	160	4-22-88	.297	.270	.310	92	374	65	111	17	9	0	33	51	3	4	1	70	49	11	.390	.385
Gwynn Jr., Tony	L-R	5-11	195	10-4-82	.300	.292	.304	104	333	53	100	12	5	2	27	49	3	4	2	52	12	9	.384	.393
Herrera, Elian	B-R	5-10	190	2-1-85	.282	.255	.297	108	408	69	115	13	1	7	43	48	8	10	2	76	16	3	.370	.367
Kemp, Matt	R-R	6-4	215	9-23-84	.182	.000	.200	3	11	3	2	2	0	0	0	1	0	0	0	6	1	0	.364	.250
Martinez, Ozzie	R-R	5-10	200	5-7-88	.233	.294	.192	13	43	6	10	4	1	0	4	7	0	0	0	6	1	0	.372	.340
Moore, Jeremy	L-R	6-1	195	6-29-87	.220	.200	.226	45	141	13	31	8	1	3	17	14	1	0	0	42	4	2	.355	.295
Ricardo, Dashenko	R-R	6-0	205	3-1-90	.000	.000	.000	2	7	0	0	0	0	0	0	1	0	0	0	4	0	0	.000	.125
Rodriguez, Leo	R-R	5-11	160	12-11-91	1.000	—	1.000	1	1	0	1	0	0	0	0	0	0	0	0	0	0	0	1.000	1.000
Ryal, Rusty	R-R	6-2	200	3-16-83	.265	.257	.269	106	370	50	98	17	3	4	49	19	7	1	4	80	0	0	.359	.310
2-team total (2 Salt Lake)					.267	—	—	108	375	51	100	18	3	4	50	20	7	1	4	80	0	0	.363	.313
Sellers, Justin	R-R	5-10	160	2-1-86	.270	.329	.252	89	326	39	88	26	4	6	65	25	5	4	6	54	4	0	.429	.326
Stewart, Ian	L-R	6-3	215	4-5-85	.174	.160	.180	27	86	13	15	6	0	2	6	17	2	0	0	36	0	0	.314	.324
2-team total (40 Iowa)					.171	—	—	67	199	32	34	12	1	7	26	34	4	0	1	81	0	0	.347	.303
Towles, J.R.	R-R	6-2	200	2-11-84	.200	.375	.000	4	15	2	3	0	0	1	2	0	0	2	0	3	1	0	.400	.200
2-team total (19 Memphis)					.230	—	—	23	74	17	17	3	1	6	16	8	4	2	0	13	1	0	.541	.337
Van Slyke, Scott	R-R	6-5	250	7-24-86	.348	.403	.321	60	204	55	71	17	2	12	48	50	5	0	4	61	8	2	.627	.479
Wallach, Matt	L-R	6-1	210	2-17-86	.245	.211	.253	30	98	13	24	2	0	4	13	16	0	0	1	25	0	0	.388	.348

Pitching	B-T	HT	WT	DOB	W	L	ERA	G	GS	CG	SV	IP	H	R	ER	HR	BB	SO	AVG	vLH	vRH	K/9	BB/9
Aguasviva, Geison	L-L	6-2	166	8-3-87	4	4	5.12	33	0	0	1	46	57	29	26	5	25	22	.326	.279	.351	4.34	4.93
Ames, Steve	R-R	6-1	205	3-15-88	2	2	3.67	30	0	0	8	34	45	20	14	4	13	29	.317	.302	.329	7.60	3.41
2-team total (9 New Orleans)					3	2	3.69	39	0	0	8	46	59	25	19	6	17	34	—	—	—	6.60	3.30
Capuano, Chris	L-L	6-3	215	8-19-78	0	0	1.93	2	2	0	0	9	8	2	2	0	3	9	.229	.250	.217	8.68	2.89
Castro, Angel	R-R	5-11	200	11-14-82	8	5	3.48	25	19	0	0	116	123	50	45	7	37	91	.272	.279	.265	7.04	2.86
Cofield, Kyle	R-R	6-5	220	1-23-87	0	0	36.00	1	0	0	0	1	3	4	4	2	1	0	.500	.750	.000	0.00	9.00
De La Cruz, Kelvin	L-L	6-5	190	8-1-88	3	1	2.89	47	0	0	7	62	62	23	20	3	35	78	.254	.217	.273	11.26	5.63
Dominguez, Jose	R-R	6-0	160	8-7-90	1	0	0.00	8	0	0	0	8	1	0	0	0	5	12	.040	.111	.000	13.50	5.63
Fife, Stephen	R-R	6-3	220	10-4-86	2	4	6.03	10	8	0	0	37	46	31	25	3	21	33	.307	.277	.343	7.96	5.06
Garcia, Onelki	L-L	6-3	220	8-2-89	1	0	3.72	10	0	0	0	10	6	4	4	0	11	10	.176	.161	.188	13.03	2.79
Guerra, Javy	R-R	6-1	190	10-31-85	0	4	3.66	27	0	0	12	39	46	18	16	6	14	36	.301	.316	.284	8.24	3.20
Infante, Greg	R-R	6-2	215	7-10-87	0	0	13.50	1	0	0	0	2	2	3	3	0	3	2	.286	.000	.500	9.00	13.50
Johnson, Blake	R-R	6-5	200	6-14-85	6	6	4.77	22	16	1	0	94	102	56	50	8	29	82	.275	.299	.254	7.82	2.77
Laffey, Aaron	L-L	6-0	200	4-15-85	4	3	5.61	12	11	0	0	61	72	40	38	12	22	29	.299	.316	.291	4.28	3.25
2-team total (11 Nashville)					6	8	6.34	23	22	0	0	111	140	85	78	17	41	55	—	—	—	4.47	3.33

Batting	B-T	HT	WT	DOB	W	L	ERA	G	GS	CG	SV	IP	H	R	ER	HR	BB	SO	AVG	SLG	OBP

	B-T	HT	WT	DOB			ERA												AVG	SLG	OBP
Lilly, Ted	L-L	6-0	195	1-4-76	0	1	7.50	1	1	0	0	6	8	6	5	1	1	5	.308	.667	.261	7.50	1.50
Magill, Matt	R-R	6-3	210	11-10-89	6	2	3.47	18	16	0	0	86	72	34	33	7	50	101	.238	.234	.243	10.61	5.25
Moylan, Peter	R-R	6-2	225	12-2-78	4	1	2.74	38	0	0	4	46	38	14	14	1	20	45	.236	.255	.226	8.80	3.91
Ortega, Anthony	R-R	6-0	185	8-24-85	4	4	4.79	39	1	0	0	62	62	34	33	9	29	49	.259	.270	.250	7.11	4.21
Palmer, Matt	R-R	6-2	235	3-21-79	6	8	3.84	25	22	0	0	134	127	65	57	15	56	131	.253	.231	.271	8.82	3.77
Patterson, Red	R-R	6-3	210	5-11-87	7	4	3.03	39	12	0	1	107	99	45	36	14	49	109	.249	.222	.276	9.17	4.12
Rasmussen, Rob	R-L	5-9	160	4-2-89	0	7	6.46	12	10	0	0	54	64	42	39	10	32	37	.296	.241	.315	6.13	5.30
Sanchez, Jonathan	L-L	6-0	195	11-19-82	7	3	5.13	14	14	1	0	67	72	40	38	12	42	79	.281	.215	.311	10.67	5.67
Smith, Steve	R-R	6-2	215	5-15-86	1	0	3.72	14	1	0	0	29	36	16	12	3	17	21	.298	.339	.262	6.52	5.28
Tolleson, Shawn	R-R	6-2	210	1-19-88	0	0	0.00	3	0	0	2	6	2	0	0	0	2	6	.125	.200	.091	9.53	3.18
Vasquez, Luis	R-R	6-4	175	4-3-86	0	0	1.69	7	0	0	0	11	12	2	2	0	5	12	.316	.375	.273	10.13	4.22
Wall, Josh	R-R	6-6	215	1-21-87	1	2	5.60	25	0	0	3	27	27	19	17	3	16	25	.270	.205	.321	8.23	5.27
2-team total (20 New Orleans)					2	3	4.56	45	0	0	4	49	50	28	25	3	24	46	—	—	—	8.39	4.38
White, Sean	R-R	6-4	210	4-25-81	6	6	3.51	34	7	0	0	74	72	31	29	5	43	43	.270	.289	.255	5.21	5.21
Wilson, Brian	R-R	6-2	205	3-16-82	0	0	0.00	3	0	0	0	3	1	0	0	0	0	2	.091	.125	.000	5.40	0.00
Withrow, Chris	R-R	6-4	215	4-1-89	4	0	1.71	25	0	0	0	26	25	10	5	0	13	33	.248	.239	.255	11.28	4.44

Fielding

Catcher	PCT	G	PO	A	E	DP	PB
Alfonzo	1.000	1	2	0	0	0	0
Baker	.997	37	296	25	1	2	1
Butera	1.000	16	132	17	0	1	3
Cilladi	1.000	1	14	0	0	0	0
Espino	.993	18	132	15	1	2	1
Federowicz	1.000	19	170	15	0	3	0
Flores	.994	21	150	20	1	1	5
Ricardo	1.000	2	4	0	0	0	0
Towles	1.000	4	34	5	0	0	0
Wallach	.986	27	194	22	3	3	1

First Base	PCT	G	PO	A	E	DP
Alfonzo	.972	9	66	3	2	13
Barden	.995	29	206	11	1	16
Espino	1.000	1	2	0	0	1
Ryal	.989	67	487	33	6	60
Stewart	1.000	1	4	0	0	1
Van Slyke	.989	51	402	40	5	53
Wallach	1.000	2	4	0	0	1

Second Base	PCT	G	PO	A	E	DP
Amezaga	.931	24	34	61	7	18
Barden	.929	8	7	6	1	3
Castellanos	1.000	1	1	1	0	1
Gonzalez	.952	13	31	28	3	7
Gordon	.990	20	48	50	1	13
Herrera	.974	76	142	198	9	55
Martinez	.909	3	5	5	1	2
Rodriguez	—	1	0	0	0	0
Ryal	1.000	3	2	7	0	0
Sellers	.977	19	46	39	2	10

Third Base	PCT	G	PO	A	E	DP
Amezaga	.842	6	5	11	3	1
Barden	.974	90	46	145	5	18
Herrera	.933	20	12	30	3	1
Martinez	.000	2	0	0	1	0
Ryal	.889	10	7	9	2	4
Sellers	1.000	11	4	13	0	1
Stewart	.984	26	19	44	1	3

Shortstop	PCT	G	PO	A	E	DP
Amezaga	1.000	6	10	14	0	2
Gonzalez	1.000	1	2	2	0	1
Gordon	.951	73	119	228	18	62
Herrera	1.000	1	0	1	0	1
Martinez	.951	9	11	28	2	6
Sellers	.970	60	93	169	8	45

Outfield	PCT	G	PO	A	E	DP
Angle	.986	107	202	9	3	2
Buss	.986	116	196	9	3	2
Castellanos	.986	91	134	11	2	2
Gwynn Jr.	.993	84	139	7	1	0
Herrera	1.000	18	23	1	0	0
Kemp	1.000	2	4	0	0	0
Moore	1.000	36	50	3	0	0
Ryal	.889	7	7	1	1	0
Van Slyke	1.000	10	14	0	0	0

CHATTANOOGA LOOKOUTS

DOUBLE-A

SOUTHERN LEAGUE

Batting	B-T	HT	WT	DOB	AVG	vLH	vRH	G	AB	R	H	2B	3B	HR	RBI	BB	HBP	SH	SF	SO	SB	CS	SLG	OBP
Burroughs, Sean	L-R	6-1	195	9-12-80	.220	.103	.245	57	168	14	37	10	1	0	18	25	1	1	0	24	2	1	.292	.325
Cavazos-Galvez, Brian	R-R	6-0	215	5-17-87	.263	.238	.275	115	377	38	99	16	1	7	40	15	8	0	2	52	15	6	.366	.303
Coyle, Bobby	L-L	6-1	215	3-6-89	.171	.133	.177	42	111	8	19	2	1	0	8	10	1	1	1	33	0	0	.207	.244
Ellis, Mark	R-R	5-10	190	6-6-77	.000	—	.000	2	4	1	0	0	0	0	0	1	0	0	0	2	0	0	.000	.200
Erickson, Gorman	B-R	6-4	220	3-11-88	.199	.254	.169	59	181	20	36	10	1	9	18	31	3	1	1	52	0	3	.414	.324
Garcia, Jon	R-R	5-11	175	11-11-91	.168	.132	.182	56	185	15	31	7	2	1	9	12	0	0	1	60	1	1	.243	.217
Gonzalez, Elevys	B-R	5-11	175	10-23-89	.000	.000	.000	10	22	0	0	0	0	0	1	1	0	2	0	5	0	0	.000	.043
Grider, Casio	R-R	6-1	165	8-17-87	.000	.000	.000	3	7	0	0	0	0	0	0	1	0	1	0	4	0	1	.000	.125
Guerrero, Pedro	R-R	6-3	185	12-3-88	—	—	—	1	0	0	0	0	0	0	0	0	0	0	0	0	0	0	—	—
Jacobs, Chris	R-R	6-5	257	11-25-88	.188	.053	.227	29	85	9	16	3	0	3	12	10	0	0	1	33	0	0	.329	.271
Luna, Omar	R-R	5-11	204	12-13-86	.170	.259	.131	29	88	3	15	4	0	0	6	3	1	2	0	15	0	1	.216	.207
2-team total (47 Mississippi)					.248	—	—	76	226	26	56	11	0	1	15	12	2	4	0	26	2	2	.310	.292
Martinez, Ozzie	R-R	5-10	200	5-7-88	.249	.266	.241	76	253	20	63	11	0	4	19	19	2	3	0	35	5	4	.340	.307
Moore, Jeremy	L-R	6-1	195	6-20-87	.192	.115	.219	32	99	10	19	2	1	4	13	9	3	1	2	41	1	2	.354	.274
Pederson, Joc	L-L	6-1	185	4-21-92	.278	.200	.316	123	439	81	122	24	3	22	58	70	5	2	3	114	31	8	.497	.381
Puig, Yasiel	R-R	6-3	245	12-7-90	.313	.244	.340	40	147	26	46	12	3	8	37	15	3	0	2	29	13	5	.599	.383
Retherford, C.J.	R-R	5-10	195	8-14-85	.219	.191	.232	47	146	18	32	11	2	4	26	9	3	4	3	28	0	0	.404	.273
Ricardo, Dashenko	R-R	6-0	205	3-31-84	.250	1.000	.143	9	16	3	4	1	0	1	3	1	0	0	0	2	0	0	.500	.294
Rojas, Miguel	R-R	6-0	150	2-24-89	.233	.225	.237	130	420	45	98	12	2	5	32	40	3	13	2	49	10	4	.307	.303
Smith, Blake	L-R	6-2	225	12-9-87	.233	.214	.241	74	240	30	56	14	1	6	28	27	1	0	2	62	3	1	.375	.311
Songco, Angelo	L-R	6-0	190	9-9-88	.214	.188	.219	74	210	21	45	12	2	6	27	18	2	2	1	43	1	0	.376	.281
Vazquez, Jan	B-R	5-10	165	4-29-91	.190	.097	.221	44	126	14	24	1	0	6	12	14	3	1	1	42	3	1	.341	.285
Wallach, Matt	L-R	6-1	210	2-17-86	.215	.229	.210	45	135	8	29	4	0	6	16	4	3	0	0	39	0	1	.244	.316
Wise, J.T.	R-R	6-0	210	6-2-86	.245	.269	.229	106	278	30	68	20	0	8	35	39	2	1	1	88	0	2	.403	.341
Ynoa, Rafael	R-R	6-0	180	8-7-87	.267	.274	.264	128	484	56	129	30	1	4	36	29	1	6	33	51	7	0	.370	.338

Pitching	B-T	HT	WT	DOB	W	L	ERA	G	GS	CG	SV	IP	H	R	ER	HR	BB	SO	AVG	vLH	vRH	K/9	BB/9
Acosta, Ryan	R-R	6-1	184	11-4-88	0	1	13.11	9	0	0	0	12	21	18	17	0	9	8	.389	.500	.313	6.17	6.94
Aguasviva, Geison	L-L	6-2	166	8-3-87	0	0	3.60	2	0	0	0	5	5	2	2	1	1	3	.278	.000	.385	5.40	1.80
Baez, Pedro	R-R	6-2	195	3-11-88	1	1	4.24	16	0	0	0	23	26	13	11	3	8	23	.283	.370	.246	8.87	3.09
Cofield, Kyle	R-R	6-5	220	1-23-87	1	2	2.78	18	1	0	0	32	23	10	10	2	17	29	.200	.217	.188	8.07	4.73
Cotton, Jharel	R-R	5-11	195	1-19-92	0	2	8.10	8	0	0	0	10	15	12	9	0	3	11	.341	.500	.267	9.90	2.70
De La Cruz, Kelvin	L-L	6-5	190	8-1-88	0	0	0.00	3	0	0	0	5	4	1	0	0	6	.211	.222	.200	10.80	0.00	

LOS ANGELES DODGERS

Name		HT	WT	DOB	W	L	ERA	G	GS	CG	SV	IP	H	R	ER	HR	BB	SO	AVG	vLH	vRH	K/9	BB/9
Dominguez, Jose	R-R	6-0	160	8-7-90	1	0	2.60	14	0	0	5	17	8	5	5	0	8	28	.138	.111	.161	14.54	4.15
Eadington, Eric	R-L	6-2	220	2-9-88	2	0	11.42	10	0	0	0	9	13	12	11	1	9	10	.351	.250	.400	10.38	9.35
Elbert, Scott	L-L	6-2	220	8-13-85	1	0	4.15	5	1	0	1	4	3	2	2	1	0	3	.200	.000	.250	6.23	0.00
Frias, Carlos	R-R	6-4	194	11-13-89	1	1	3.94	8	2	0	0	16	15	7	7	2	7	8	.254	.296	.219	4.50	3.94
Garcia, Onelki	L-L	6-3	220	8-2-89	2	3	2.75	25	6	0	1	52	41	19	16	3	32	53	.215	.143	.244	9.11	5.50
Garcia, Yimi	R-R	6-1	175	8-18-90	4	6	2.54	49	0	0	19	60	35	17	17	9	14	85	.164	.210	.136	12.68	2.09
Gould, Garrett	R-R	6-4	190	7-19-91	3	5	5.88	11	6	0	0	41	42	32	27	5	15	45	.264	.231	.287	9.80	3.27
Infante, Greg	R-R	6-2	215	7-10-87	1	1	3.35	27	0	0	0	38	33	14	14	2	25	36	.250	.364	.193	8.60	5.97
Lee, Zach	R-R	6-3	190	9-13-91	10	10	3.22	28	25	1	0	143	132	57	51	13	35	131	.247	.255	.242	8.26	2.21
Lima, Joel	R-R	6-0	165	8-7-89	1	0	3.00	1	0	0	0	3	3	1	1	0	0	1	.250	.500	.125	3.00	0.00
Marmol, Carlos	R-R	6-2	215	10-14-82	0	0	0.00	2	0	0	0	2	0	0	0	0	1	2	.000	.000	.000	9.00	4.50
Martin, Jarret	L-L	6-4	227	8-14-89	0	0	1.69	11	0	0	0	11	11	2	2	0	12	11	.289	.294	.286	9.28	10.13
Miller, Aaron	L-L	6-3	200	9-18-87	0	2	6.00	11	1	0	0	24	30	16	16	1	12	26	.316	.276	.333	9.75	4.50
Nelo, Hector	R-R	6-1	200	11-5-86	5	2	2.67	45	0	0	3	61	51	23	18	2	29	50	.231	.253	.218	7.42	4.30
Rasmussen, Rob	R-L	5-9	160	4-2-89	3	4	2.55	16	14	0	0	81	60	26	23	5	28	76	.203	.217	.199	8.41	3.10
Reed, Chris	L-L	6-4	195	5-20-90	4	11	3.86	29	25	1	0	138	128	64	59	9	63	106	.250	.171	.276	6.93	4.12
Santiago, Andres	R-R	6-1	218	10-26-89	5	12	4.97	30	25	1	0	134	116	78	74	9	74	109	.238	.263	.221	7.32	4.97
Smith, Steve	R-R	6-2	215	5-15-86	1	4	5.15	18	4	0	0	44	42	26	25	3	13	40	.266	.351	.218	8.24	2.68
Stripling, Ross	R-R	6-3	190	11-23-89	6	4	2.78	21	16	0	1	94	91	33	29	4	19	83	.251	.259	.247	7.95	1.82
Thomas, Mike	L-L	6-2	185	1-6-89	1	1	3.23	34	1	0	2	47	45	17	17	2	21	51	.260	.263	.259	9.70	3.99
Vasquez, Luis	R-R	6-4	175	4-3-86	3	3	2.88	18	0	0	0	25	15	9	8	1	23	34	.176	.115	.203	12.24	8.28
von Schamann, Duke	R-R	6-5	220	6-3-91	3	5	5.00	16	12	0	0	67	82	39	37	7	20	50	.309	.269	.335	6.75	2.70

Fielding

Catcher	PCT	G	PO	A	E	DP	PB
Erickson	.991	57	481	49	5	5	0
Ricardo	.963	4	22	4	1	0	1
Vazquez	.987	39	277	32	4	1	4
Wallach	.981	44	313	39	7	2	1

First Base	PCT	G	PO	A	E	DP
Burroughs	1.000	4	28	1	0	4
Jacobs	.982	27	216	6	4	26
Luna	1.000	1	4	0	0	1
Songco	.995	59	521	31	3	47
Wise	.994	72	506	33	3	51

Second Base	PCT	G	PO	A	E	DP
Ellis	1.000	2	6	4	0	3
Gonzalez	1.000	3	2	5	0	2

	PCT	G	PO	A	E	DP
Grider	1.000	2	1	6	0	2
Luna	.942	15	17	32	3	8
Martinez	.960	7	9	15	1	4
Rojas	1.000	3	1	6	0	1
Ynoa	.987	122	203	325	7	72

Third Base	PCT	G	PO	A	E	DP
Burroughs	.956	48	21	88	5	11
Gonzalez	1.000	7	0	7	0	0
Luna	.941	8	5	11	1	2
Martinez	.957	47	15	74	4	2
Retherford	.968	46	18	72	3	6
Ynoa	1.000	5	2	7	0	1

Shortstop	PCT	G	PO	A	E	DP
Martinez	.898	15	8	36	5	8

	PCT	G	PO	A	E	DP
Rojas	.973	129	172	403	16	89
Ynoa	1.000	6	6	11	0	6

Outfield	PCT	G	PO	A	E	DP
Cavazos-Galvez	.983	90	110	9	2	1
Coyle	1.000	27	34	1	0	0
Garcia	.948	54	89	3	5	1
Luna	1.000	1	1	0	0	0
Martinez	.846	11	9	2	2	0
Moore	1.000	28	49	0	0	0
Pederson	.980	117	234	10	5	2
Puig	1.000	38	65	3	0	1
Smith	.981	66	95	6	2	1
Songco	.000	1	0	0	1	0
Wise	—	1	0	0	0	0

RANCHO CUCAMONGA QUAKES   HIGH CLASS A

CALIFORNIA LEAGUE

Batting	B-T	HT	WT	DOB	AVG	vLH	vRH	G	AB	R	H	2B	3B	HR	RBI	BB	HBP	SH	SF	SO	SB	CS	SLG	OBP
Cannon, John	R-R	6-0	180	5-11-90	.286	.286	.286	7	21	2	6	1	0	0	0	0	0	0	0	4	0	0	.333	.286
Coyle, Bobby	L-L	6-1	215	3-6-89	.267	.128	.307	56	210	29	56	6	2	15	26	12	2	0	4	47	1	2	.529	.307
Crawford, Carl	L-L	6-2	215	8-5-81	.385	—	.385	4	13	2	5	1	0	0	1	0	0	0	0	2	1	0	.462	.429
Cuevas, Noel	R-R	6-2	187	10-2-91	.284	.256	.294	123	476	80	135	25	10	12	66	37	7	11	5	107	38	15	.454	.341
Dickson, O'Koyea	R-R	5-11	215	2-9-90	.280	.254	.289	122	468	68	131	32	3	15	88	29	17	0	9	68	4	2	.457	.338
Ellis, A.J.	R-R	6-2	220	4-9-81	.000	—	.000	2	7	0	0	0	0	0	0	0	0	0	0	3	0	0	.000	.000
Franco, Bladimir	R-R	6-1	172	2-4-91	.198	.125	.215	24	81	4	16	3	2	0	8	7	0	1	0	29	2	1	.284	.261
Garcia, Jon	R-R	5-11	175	11-11-91	.287	.316	.275	68	258	51	74	13	5	17	44	16	4	1	1	82	9	3	.574	.337
Garvey, Robbie	L-L	5-8	165	4-26-89	.255	.000	.317	19	51	9	13	2	0	0	6	12	2	4	0	11	9	7	.294	.415
Gonzalez, Elevys	B-R	5-11	175	10-23-89	.167	.190	.148	18	48	5	8	1	1	1	2	10	0	1	0	15	5	1	.292	.310
Grider, Casio	R-R	6-1	165	8-17-87	.258	.269	.254	94	298	48	77	11	7	1	28	29	10	9	2	80	29	13	.352	.342
Guerrero, Pedro	R-R	6-3	185	12-3-88	.199	.171	.210	49	146	20	29	4	0	2	16	10	0	2	1	47	2	1	.267	.248
Hairston Jr., Jerry	R-R	5-10	195	5-21-76	.000	.000	.000	5	0	0	0	0	0	0	0	0	0	0	0	0	0	0	.000	.000
Jacobs, Chris	R-R	6-5	257	11-25-88	.286	.267	.293	73	248	42	71	13	1	14	40	34	7	0	5	96	3	0	.516	.381
Kemp, Matt	R-R	6-4	215	9-23-84	.000	.000	.000	5	18	0	0	0	0	0	0	1	0	0	0	7	0	1	.000	.053
Maynard, Pratt	L-R	6-0	215	11-19-89	.246	.310	.232	69	236	33	58	14	0	6	27	41	1	1	0	41	3	2	.381	.360
McDonald, James	B-R	5-10	170	12-16-91	.172	.125	.180	19	58	8	10	2	1	0	3	6	1	4	0	15	1	1	.241	.262
Mount, Ryan	L-R	6-0	190	8-17-86	.333	.400	.315	43	165	22	55	13	2	7	37	15	1	0	1	26	0	2	.564	.390
O'Brien, Chris	B-R	6-0	219	7-24-89	.195	.183	.200	64	210	28	41	12	1	3	21	18	0	3	2	51	0	0	.305	.257
Ramirez, Hanley	R-R	6-2	225	12-23-83	.333	—	.333	5	15	1	5	2	0	0	6	1	0	0	1	3	0	0	.467	.353
Rivas, Webster	R-R	6-2	200	8-8-90	.213	.154	.238	26	89	13	19	4	0	1	7	3	0	2	1	18	1	1	.292	.265
Schebler, Scott	L-R	6-1	208	10-6-90	.296	.301	.294	125	477	95	141	29	13	27	91	35	15	4	3	140	16	5	.581	.360
Seager, Corey	L-R	6-4	215	4-27-94	.160	.219	.132	27	100	10	16	2	1	4	15	12	0	0	2	31	1	0	.320	.246
Shines, Devin	R-L	5-10	185	5-15-89	.133	.118	.143	15	45	6	6	2	0	0	5	0	0	0	0	13	2	1	.178	.220
Songco, Angelo	L-R	6-0	190	9-9-88	.310	.294	.317	43	171	24	53	8	4	5	38	9	1	0	4	39	1	1	.491	.341
Sweeney, Darnell	B-R	6-1	150	2-1-91	.275	.282	.273	134	552	79	152	34	16	11	77	43	5	6	7	151	48	20	.455	.329
Van Slyke, Scott	R-R	6-5	250	7-24-86	.429	.000	.429	2	7	2	3	0	0	0	2	0	0	0	0	1	0	0	.429	.556
Wingo, Scott	L-R	5-11	175	3-25-89	.227	.222	.229	101	286	47	65	11	4	4	24	50	16	11	1	81	9	2	.336	.371

Pitching

Pitching	B-T	HT	WT	DOB	W	L	ERA	G	GS	CG	SV	IP	H	R	ER	HR	BB	SO	AVG	vLH	vRH	K/9	BB/9
Acosta, Ryan	R-R	6-1	184	11-4-88	0	0	13.50	5	0	0	0	7	13	10	10	4	1	8	.394	.500	.316	10.80	1.35
Aguasviva, Geison	L-L	6-2	166	8-3-87	0	3	10.05	4	4	0	0	14	22	18	16	1	9	9	.349	.467	.313	5.65	5.65
Baez, Pedro	R-R	6-2	195	3-11-88	2	2	3.63	32	0	0	2	35	41	17	14	3	15	32	.295	.375	.253	8.31	3.89
Billingsley, Chad	R-R	6-1	240	7-29-84	0	0	6.75	1	1	0	0	4	7	4	3	0	3	2	.389	.556	.222	4.50	6.75
Cabrera, Freddie	R-R	6-5	210	1-25-90	3	5	6.01	33	6	0	0	67	94	52	45	7	28	51	.328	.371	.298	6.82	3.74
Campbell, James	R-R	6-1	195	9-20-91	1	4	6.61	17	5	0	0	33	32	32	24	2	20	17	.246	.231	.256	4.68	5.51
Carl, Edwin	R-R	6-0	210	8-31-88	1	1	1.17	11	0	0	0	15	10	3	2	0	7	24	.182	.143	.206	14.09	4.11
Caughel, Lindsey	R-R	6-3	205	8-13-90	4	7	4.01	20	19	0	0	117	131	63	52	12	21	112	.279	.273	.283	8.64	1.62
Cotton, Jharel	R-R	5-11	195	1-19-92	0	0	1.59	2	2	0	0	6	4	1	1	0	3	3	.190	.200	.188	4.76	4.76
Coulombe, Danny	L-L	5-10	185	10-26-89	4	2	4.05	54	0	0	1	67	46	37	30	7	48	85	.189	.195	.185	11.48	6.48
Eadington, Eric	R-L	6-2	220	2-9-88	5	5	5.55	39	0	0	6	49	52	34	30	9	22	65	.267	.286	.258	12.02	4.07
Elbert, Scott	L-L	6-2	220	8-13-85	1	0	0.00	3	0	0	0	3	1	0	0	0	1	4	.100	.000	.200	12.00	3.00
Fife, Stephen	R-R	6-3	220	10-4-86	0	1	6.75	1	1	0	0	4	6	4	3	1	1	3	.333	.400	.250	6.75	2.25
Frias, Carlos	R-R	6-4	194	11-13-89	2	3	4.11	8	8	0	0	46	52	22	21	4	11	48	.280	.301	.265	9.39	2.15
Gomez, Gustavo	R-R	6-1	150	5-24-91	5	6	5.50	22	22	0	0	108	117	74	66	11	50	102	.279	.275	.283	8.50	4.17
Gould, Garrett	R-R	6-4	190	7-19-91	2	7	7.04	16	15	0	0	77	89	64	60	10	31	59	.290	.295	.286	6.93	3.64
Greinke, Zack	R-R	6-2	195	10-21-83	0	0	6.23	1	1	0	0	4	6	3	3	1	0	4	.286	.333	.222	8.31	0.00
Jones, Owen	R-R	6-1	190	6-12-89	0	1	7.84	8	0	0	2	10	15	10	9	1	5	13	.333	.600	.200	11.32	4.35
Lilly, Ted	L-L	6-0	195	1-4-76	1	4	8.14	5	5	0	0	24	35	23	22	5	7	24	.340	.357	.333	8.88	2.59
Lima, Joel	R-R	6-0	165	8-7-89	2	0	5.47	31	1	0	1	49	56	38	30	8	21	33	.273	.274	.273	6.02	3.83
Marmol, Carlos	R-R	6-2	215	10-14-82	0	0	6.00	3	0	0	1	3	4	2	2	1	4	.308	.125	.600	12.00	3.00
Martin, Jarret	L-L	6-4	227	8-14-89	6	7	4.62	29	14	0	2	86	85	58	44	8	50	95	.255	.268	.252	9.98	5.25
Noriega, Juan	R-R	5-7	145	9-3-90	1	2	1.45	14	0	0	0	19	16	3	3	1	7	20	.239	.200	.262	9.64	3.38
Ozoria, Arismendy	R-R	6-1	195	8-7-90	0	0	13.50	2	0	0	0	3	1	4	4	1	4	1	.111	.250	.000	3.38	13.50
Redding, JonMichael	R-R	6-1	195	11-16-87	4	5	3.87	32	13	0	0	100	113	63	43	7	36	81	.285	.341	.255	7.29	3.24
Sanchez, Angel	R-R	6-3	177	11-28-89	0	0	3.00	2	1	0	0	9	8	4	3	0	2	12	.235	.200	.263	12.00	2.00
Sanchez, Raydel	R-R	6-3	177	3-11-90	2	3	3.89	43	1	0	1	74	74	43	32	6	26	48	.258	.302	.236	5.84	3.16
Shelton, Matt	R-R	6-4	205	11-30-88	5	2	2.45	32	2	0	3	48	40	16	13	2	18	47	.226	.265	.202	8.87	3.40
Stem, Craig	R-R	6-5	215	1-5-90	2	1	6.15	21	0	0	3	26	24	19	18	3	12	24	.245	.143	.302	8.20	4.10
Stripling, Ross	R-R	6-3	190	11-23-89	2	0	2.94	6	6	0	0	34	24	11	11	1	11	34	.198	.121	.227	9.09	2.94
Thomas, Mike	L-L	6-2	185	1-6-89	0	0	1.46	11	0	0	9	12	8	2	2	1	3	17	.178	.143	.208	12.41	2.19
Tolleson, Shawn	R-R	6-2	210	1-19-88	1	0	9.00	1	0	0	0	1	1	1	1	1	0	1	.250	.000	.500	9.00	0.00
Villa, Francisco	R-R	6-0	194	4-1-92	0	1	11.25	1	1	0	0	4	7	5	5	2	3	1	.412	.429	.400	2.25	6.75
von Schamann, Duke	R-R	6-5	220	6-3-91	8	2	4.34	11	11	0	0	64	64	32	31	8	18	50	.267	.306	.245	6.99	2.52
Wilson, Brian	R-R	6-2	205	3-16-82	0	0	0.00	1	1	0	0	1	0	0	0	0	0	1	.000	.000	.000	9.00	0.00

Fielding

Catcher	PCT	G	PO	A	E	DP	PB
Cannon	.981	6	45	8	1	0	0
Maynard	.988	63	494	63	7	6	4
O'Brien	.980	60	457	42	10	5	3
Rivas	.994	19	134	20	1	2	3

First Base	PCT	G	PO	A	E	DP
Coyle	—	1	0	0	0	0
Dickson	.985	59	492	26	8	27
Gonzalez	1.000	2	3	0	0	0
Guerrero	.897	7	22	4	3	1
Jacobs	.990	50	374	31	4	36
Rivas	.976	5	38	3	1	2
Songco	.984	26	237	6	4	18

Second Base	PCT	G	PO	A	E	DP
Gonzalez	1.000	6	5	12	0	0
Grider	.989	26	31	58	1	12
Guerrero	.957	6	12	10	1	3
McDonald	.984	17	28	35	1	6
Sweeney	.986	29	64	82	2	11
Wingo	.979	68	119	166	6	38

Third Base	PCT	G	PO	A	E	DP
Dickson	.750	5	5	10	5	0
Franco	.882	21	7	38	6	4
Gonzalez	.900	8	10	17	3	3
Grider	.884	16	11	27	5	2
Guerrero	.883	36	19	72	12	4
Hairston Jr.	1.000	1	0	1	0	0
Mount	.826	40	22	73	20	4
Seager	1.000	1	1	0	0	0
Wingo	.913	26	16	47	6	3

Shortstop	PCT	G	PO	A	E	DP
Gonzalez	.875	2	1	6	1	0
Grider	1.000	4	5	10	0	2
Guerrero	1.000	1	0	1	0	0
Ramirez	1.000	4	5	10	0	4
Seager	.914	25	33	52	8	11
Sweeney	.929	108	169	278	34	52
Wingo	.800	1	0	4	1	0

Outfield	PCT	G	PO	A	E	DP
Coyle	.985	38	63	1	1	0
Crawford	1.000	2	8	0	0	0
Cuevas	.967	122	227	7	8	0
Dickson	1.000	1	1	0	0	0
Franco	—	1	0	0	0	0
Garcia	.977	68	113	12	3	2
Garvey	.977	17	43	1	1	0
Grider	.985	54	130	1	2	1
Hairston Jr.	—	1	0	0	0	0
Kemp	1.000	1	3	1	0	0
McDonald	1.000	2	1	0	0	0
Mount	—	1	0	0	0	0
Schebler	.971	121	197	5	6	0
Shines	.952	14	16	4	1	0
Van Slyke	1.000	1	1	0	0	0
Wingo	1.000	4	4	0	0	0

GREAT LAKES LOONS
LOW CLASS A

MIDWEST LEAGUE

Batting	B-T	HT	WT	DOB	AVG	vLH	vRH	G	AB	R	H	2B	3B	HR	RBI	BB	HBP	SH	SF	SO	SB	CS	SLG	OBP
Aguilar, Alexis	R-R	5-10	150	6-17-91	.250	.300	.235	13	44	5	11	3	0	0	5	1	0	0	0	7	2	0	.318	.267
Baldwin III, James	L-R	6-3	205	10-10-91	.238	.200	.249	118	369	49	88	22	6	7	49	41	7	9	4	154	42	11	.388	.323
Capellan, Jose	R-R	6-0	210	10-10-90	.249	.267	.242	68	209	22	52	11	1	1	28	16	0	4	2	44	3	2	.325	.300
Cowen, Austin	R-R	5-11	195	9-15-89	.077	.000	.083	5	13	0	1	0	0	0	0	0	0	1	0	5	0	0	.077	.143
Dixon, Brandon	R-R	6-2	215	1-29-92	.185	.104	.209	59	211	28	39	11	1	1	17	11	1	3	2	65	6	2	.261	.227
Franco, Bladimir	R-R	6-1	172	2-4-91	.000	.000	.000	3	7	2	0	0	0	0	0	1	0	0	1	0	0	0	.000	.125
Garvey, Robbie	L-L	5-8	165	4-26-89	.270	.295	.262	86	330	47	89	9	4	1	24	33	2	4	1	74	25	12	.330	.339
Gonzalez, Elevys	B-R	5-11	175	10-23-89	.206	.071	.300	11	34	1	7	1	1	0	4	6	0	0	1	11	1	0	.294	.317
Grider, Casio	R-R	6-1	165	8-17-87	.143	.000	.200	2	7	1	1	0	0	0	1	3	0	0	0	1	1	0	.143	.400
Hoenecke, Paul	L-R	6-2	205	7-8-90	.230	.200	.243	43	152	19	35	10	0	2	11	15	0	1	1	25	2	0	.336	.298
Holland, Malcolm	R-R	5-11	165	6-18-92	.207	.234	.195	84	251	37	52	4	1	0	23	45	0	11	0	67	27	16	.231	.328

LOS ANGELES DODGERS

Batting	B-T	HT	WT	DOB	AVG	vLH	vRH	G	AB	R	H	2B	3B	HR	RBI	BB	HBP	SH	SF	SO	SB	CS	SLG	OBP
Linares, Jonathan	R-R	6-0	160	4-29-93	.250	—	.250	2	4	0	1	0	0	0	1	0	0	0	0	3	0	0	.250	.250
Ogle, Tyler	R-R	5-10	210	8-9-90	.252	.269	.246	130	437	60	110	24	0	12	57	96	13	2	0	76	6	7	.389	.401
Rathjen, Jeremy	R-R	6-5	195	1-28-90	.232	.256	.223	131	444	65	103	29	1	7	61	56	15	11	1	99	33	6	.349	.337
Ricardo, Dashenko	R-R	6-0	205	3-1-90	.202	.269	.172	26	84	8	17	4	0	0	7	3	2	0	1	24	0	1	.250	.244
Rivas, Webster	R-R	6-2	200	8-8-90	.262	.333	.250	20	61	7	16	2	0	0	5	4	1	2	1	6	0	1	.295	.313
Rodriguez, Leo	R-R	5-11	160	12-11-91	.256	.284	.247	89	308	33	79	9	0	0	20	31	5	5	1	52	5	2	.286	.333
Seager, Corey	L-R	6-4	215	4-27-94	.309	.262	.322	74	272	45	84	18	3	12	57	34	3	1	2	58	9	4	.529	.389
Shines, Devin	R-L	5-10	185	5-15-89	.211	.267	.182	37	133	10	28	8	0	2	16	12	1	1	1	35	2	1	.316	.279
Smith, Eric	L-R	6-1	190	10-10-90	.221	.222	.220	45	145	15	32	11	0	1	15	24	2	3	2	22	2	1	.317	.335
Stover, Pat	R-R	6-4	220	9-12-90	.173	.194	.162	35	110	12	19	6	0	2	10	4	3	1	1	43	0	1	.282	.220
Taylor, Kevin	L-R	6-0	200	7-13-91	.247	.229	.251	77	259	42	64	7	1	5	29	32	4	4	0	43	4	4	.340	.339
Trinkwon, Brandon	L-R	6-1	165	3-30-92	.168	.160	.171	26	95	9	16	3	1	2	12	3	1	0	2	8	5	0	.284	.198
Valdez, Jesus	R-R	6-3	195	3-27-92	.188	.056	.226	28	80	9	15	2	0	0	10	3	3	0	1	22	1	0	.213	.241
Valentin, Jesmuel	B-R	5-9	180	5-12-94	.212	.263	.180	33	99	12	21	6	1	0	5	16	1	5	1	28	4	3	.293	.325
Winker, Joey	L-L	6-1	190	8-28-89	.240	.444	.195	15	50	8	12	4	0	2	2	6	0	1	0	13	0	1	.440	.321

Pitching	B-T	HT	WT	DOB	W	L	ERA	G	GS	CG	SV	IP	H	R	ER	HR	BB	SO	AVG	vLH	vRH	K/9	BB/9
Anderson, Chris	R-R	6-4	215	7-29-92	3	0	1.96	12	12	0	0	46	32	15	10	0	24	50	.201	.277	.149	9.78	4.70
Bare, Crayton	L-L	5-11	185	9-18-90	1	1	5.18	29	0	0	2	33	35	21	19	3	4	36	.265	.130	.337	9.82	1.09
Bird, Zach	R-R	6-4	205	7-14-94	2	5	5.10	19	11	0	0	60	56	38	34	5	45	50	.249	.308	.195	7.50	6.75
Brown, Geoff	L-L	5-11	188	1-20-89	12	1	2.08	28	1	0	0	78	59	20	18	4	20	56	.208	.167	.225	6.46	2.31
Campbell, James	R-R	6-1	195	9-20-91	0	3	12.46	4	0	0	0	4	12	11	6	0	3	2	.444	.636	.313	4.15	6.23
Carela, Danny	R-R	6-3	230	9-18-87	0	1	54.00	2	0	0	0	1	5	6	6	0	2	0	.625	1.000	.500	0.00	18.00
Cash, Ralston	R-R	6-3	215	8-20-91	4	3	3.19	16	8	0	0	54	40	30	19	4	33	56	.206	.244	.179	9.39	5.53
Caughel, Lindsey	R-R	6-3	205	8-13-90	0	3	2.00	5	5	0	0	27	22	12	6	2	2	26	.214	.200	.221	8.67	0.67
Cotton, Jharel	R-R	5-11	195	1-19-92	2	5	3.55	11	9	1	0	58	42	23	23	4	17	58	.200	.156	.237	8.95	2.62
Downing, Gregg	L-L	5-10	175	11-8-90	0	1	9.00	4	0	0	1	5	6	8	5	0	7	2	.273	.333	.231	3.60	12.60
Frias, Carlos	R-R	6-4	194	11-13-89	5	3	2.63	12	12	0	0	68	66	26	20	3	23	49	.258	.271	.244	6.45	3.03
Garcia, Alan	R-R	6-4	253	12-25-90	1	1	5.63	12	0	0	1	16	17	11	10	2	10	21	.266	.323	.212	11.81	5.63
Gonzalez, Sawil	R-R	6-1	169	3-24-90	2	3	6.30	16	0	0	0	20	27	16	14	0	11	27	.355	.306	.400	12.15	4.95
Griggs, Scott	R-R	6-4	215	5-13-91	2	7	2.56	34	0	0	4	46	28	18	13	1	33	74	.169	.188	.155	14.58	6.50
Hermsen, Jake	R-L	6-0	205	11-16-89	0	0	10.80	5	0	0	0	7	5	11	8	1	9	5	.208	.167	.222	6.75	12.15
Hershiser, Jordan	R-R	6-8	245	9-15-88	0	1	0.00	1	0	0	0	2	2	1	0	0	1	4	.286	.500	.000	18.00	4.50
Jones, Owen	R-R	6-1	190	6-12-89	3	4	2.13	42	0	0	7	51	43	13	12	2	13	68	.229	.205	.248	12.08	2.31
Lima, Joel	R-R	6-0	165	8-7-89	0	0	5.87	6	0	0	0	8	10	5	5	2	1	4	.303	.231	.350	4.70	1.17
Martinez, Brandon	R-R	6-4	150	11-25-90	2	4	4.73	15	12	0	0	72	87	43	38	4	27	43	.298	.259	.336	5.35	3.36
Martinez, Jonathan	R-R	6-1	194	6-27-94	3	4	3.51	15	7	0	0	67	65	30	26	3	16	42	.263	.235	.283	5.67	2.16
Mesa, Luis	R-R	6-4	200	7-31-91	4	1	3.96	51	0	0	4	73	77	37	32	8	32	41	.272	.304	.247	5.06	3.96
Ozoria, Arismendy	R-R	6-1	195	8-7-90	2	7	5.98	32	2	0	0	59	56	45	39	10	33	66	.248	.232	.260	10.13	5.06
Rogers, Rob	R-R	5-11	205	10-25-90	2	0	3.86	11	0	0	0	23	26	11	10	1	5	19	.277	.270	.281	7.33	1.93
Sanchez, Angel	R-R	6-3	177	11-28-89	2	7	4.88	14	14	0	0	72	80	50	39	6	28	70	.273	.244	.297	8.75	3.50
Shelton, Matt	R-R	6-4	205	11-30-88	1	0	0.00	1	0	0	0	2	1	0	0	0	2	1	.000	.000	.000	9.00	18.00
Stem, Craig	R-R	6-5	215	1-5-90	1	0	1.38	32	0	0	14	39	25	7	6	0	15	24	.187	.226	.153	5.54	3.46
Sulbaran, Miguel	L-L	5-10	185	3-19-94	6	4	3.01	23	16	0	1	93	89	40	31	3	27	85	.250	.281	.238	8.26	2.62
2-team total (4 Cedar Rapids)					9	4	2.96	27	20	0	1	113	110	49	37	3	32	101	—	—		8.07	2.56
Taylor, Thomas	R-R	6-4	220	2-26-90	2	2	6.00	10	0	0	0	12	16	11	8	0	8	14	.291	.273	.303	10.50	6.00
Urias, Julio	L-L	5-11	160	8-12-96	2	0	2.48	18	18	0	0	54	44	15	15	5	16	67	.227	.214	.232	11.10	2.65
Windle, Tom	L-L	6-4	215	3-10-92	5	1	2.68	13	12	0	0	54	50	19	16	2	20	51	.242	.292	.218	8.55	3.35

Fielding

Catcher	PCT	G	PO	A	E	DP	PB
Capellan	.993	67	512	67	4	7	3
Cowen	.971	5	32	2	1	0	1
Linares	.938	2	12	3	1	1	1
Ogle	1.000	14	87	10	0	1	0
Ricardo	.994	22	141	24	1	0	5
Rivas	.983	15	97	17	2	0	1
Smith	.991	28	214	17	2	0	6

First Base	PCT	G	PO	A	E	DP
Hoenecke	1.000	6	60	7	0	8
Miller	.957	5	38	7	2	2
Ogle	.993	102	787	66	6	53
Rivas	1.000	2	13	1	0	1
Shines	1.000	2	15	1	0	1
Valdez	.995	26	181	17	1	12
Winker	1.000	3	13	3	0	2

Second Base	PCT	G	PO	A	E	DP
Aguilar	.927	12	19	19	3	4
Grider	1.000	2	3	1	0	0
Holland	.984	36	51	76	2	8
Rodriguez	.964	37	60	73	5	12
Taylor	.966	48	71	126	7	18
Valentin	.971	16	29	39	2	9

Third Base	PCT	G	PO	A	E	DP
Dixon	.836	58	31	91	24	5
Franco	.600	3	2	1	2	0
Gonzalez	.864	10	7	12	3	0
Hoenecke	.864	30	18	58	12	5
Rodriguez	.930	25	17	36	4	1
Smith	1.000	3	1	2	0	0
Taylor	.914	16	12	20	3	1

Shortstop	PCT	G	PO	A	E	DP
Aguilar	1.000	2	2	3	0	0
Rodriguez	.955	30	32	53	4	8
Seager	.961	74	101	172	11	31
Trinkwon	.953	26	37	64	5	15
Valentin	.873	17	26	29	8	8

Outfield	PCT	G	PO	A	E	DP
Baldwin III	.969	115	240	10	8	1
Garvey	.989	84	173	10	2	2
Holland	.966	46	54	2	2	0
Miller	1.000	2	2	0	0	0
Ogle	—	1	0	0	0	0
Rathjen	.979	125	217	11	5	1
Shines	.984	32	57	3	1	0
Stover	.889	30	40	0	5	0
Taylor	1.000	1	3	0	0	0
Winker	1.000	8	8	1	0	0

AZL DODGERS

ROOKIE

ARIZONA LEAGUE

Batting	B-T	HT	WT	DOB	AVG	vLH	vRH	G	AB	R	H	2B	3B	HR	RBI	BB	HBP	SH	SF	SO	SB	CS	SLG	OBP
Ahmed, Mike	R-R	6-2	195	1-20-92	.276	.233	.286	43	156	22	43	11	0	0	13	19	1	0	0	34	4	3	.346	.358
Alexander, Theo	L-R	6-1	195	8-25-94	.253	.238	.258	27	83	16	21	5	1	5	20	16	3	0	0	35	5	2	.518	.392
Bellinger, Cody	L-L	6-4	180	7-13-95	.210	.195	.215	47	162	25	34	9	6	1	30	31	1	1	0	46	3	3	.358	.340

Batting

Player	B-T	HT	WT	DOB	AVG	vLH	vRH	G	AB	R	H	2B	3B	HR	RBI	BB	HBP	SH	SF	SO	SB	CS	OBP	SLG
Chigbogu, Justin	L-L	6-1	240	7-8-94	.326	.133	.419	11	46	12	15	3	1	5	19	3	0	0	1	18	0	0	.761	.360
Compton, David	R-R	6-1	195	9-29-89	.091	.000	.200	4	11	2	1	0	0	0	0	0	0	0	0	6	0	0	.091	.091
Cordero, Josmar	R-R	5-10	175	9-10-91	.272	.296	.264	36	114	17	31	9	0	5	28	8	3	1	2	29	4	0	.482	.331
de la Fuente, Dimitri	R-R	6-0	195	6-25-90	.000	—	.000	1	4	0	0	0	0	0	0	0	1	0	0	1	0	0	.000	.200
Erickson, Gorman	B-R	6-4	220	3-11-88	.286	.400	.250	8	21	7	6	0	0	1	3	9	0	0	0	8	0	1	.429	.500
Gomez, Cristian	R-R	5-11	185	1-11-96	.173	.200	.165	42	156	18	27	4	1	4	14	6	2	0	3	48	1	1	.288	.210
Gwynn Jr., Tony	L-R	5-11	195	10-4-82	.182	.500	.000	3	11	2	2	1	0	0	2	0	0	1	1	2	0	0	.273	.167
Harris, Jaylen	B-R	5-9	175	9-25-93	.243	.250	.241	32	103	25	25	3	1	0	8	14	1	7	0	26	3	4	.291	.339
Henderson, Josh	L-L	6-0	184	11-16-93	.299	.211	.328	22	77	11	23	9	0	1	10	4	2	1	3	12	3	0	.455	.337
Henderson, Stefen	R-R	6-1	197	1-11-92	.250	.000	.294	8	20	3	5	0	1	1	3	4	0	0	0	9	1	1	.500	.375
Hennessey, Blake	R-R	6-0	172	9-28-94	.195	.200	.193	24	77	14	15	0	1	1	8	12	3	2	1	30	2	1	.260	.323
Hoenecke, Paul	L-R	6-2	205	7-8-90	.176	.182	.174	9	34	4	6	2	0	2	3	3	0	0	0	6	1	0	.412	.243
Law, Adam	R-R	6-0	193	2-5-90	.357	.250	.392	33	129	29	46	6	1	0	15	13	5	5	2	23	21	3	.419	.430
Leon, Julian	R-R	5-11	215	1-24-96	.247	.286	.233	26	81	12	20	3	1	3	19	7	3	0	3	21	0	1	.420	.319
Linares, Jonathan	R-R	6-0	160	4-29-93	.000	—	.000	1	1	0	0	0	0	0	0	0	0	0	0	1	0	0	.000	.000
McDonald, James	R-R	5-10	170	12-16-91	.294	.292	.295	24	85	19	25	2	1	3	14	15	0	1	1	26	2	2	.447	.396
Moore, Jeremy	L-R	6-1	195	6-29-87	.273	.000	.429	3	11	4	3	2	0	0	1	1	0	0	0	3	0	0	.455	.333
O'Brien, Chris	B-R	6-0	219	7-24-89	.226	.286	.208	9	31	4	7	0	0	2	5	4	0	0	1	7	0	0	.419	.306
Oguisten, Faustino	R-R	6-2	165	1-17-91	.296	.385	.274	30	81	23	24	4	1	1	7	16	3	1	1	18	15	3	.407	.426
Pederson, Tyger	R-R	5-11	175	10-22-89	.317	.188	.364	18	60	10	19	2	0	0	7	13	0	0	0	15	1	1	.350	.438
Reid-Foley, David	L-R	6-3	190	1-2-91	.208	.182	.216	16	48	5	10	1	0	1	4	8	1	1	0	13	0	0	.292	.333
Rojas, Jeffry	B-R	6-0	170	8-18-92	.190	.333	.133	6	21	0	4	1	0	0	2	3	1	0	0	7	0	0	.238	.320
Santana, Melvin	R-R	5-10	160	10-4-94	.149	.200	.139	30	94	11	14	5	2	0	8	7	1	0	2	21	4	3	.245	.213
Scott, Ryan	R-R	6-1	180	2-7-95	.143	.143	.143	16	49	4	7	0	0	1	5	7	1	2	1	20	0	0	.204	.259
Smith, Eric	L-R	6-1	190	10-10-90	.333	—	.333	1	3	0	1	0	0	0	0	2	0	0	0	1	0	0	.333	.600
Torres, Reymundo	R-R	5-11	170	1-25-94	.178	.333	.147	31	90	13	16	3	4	1	12	9	2	1	0	31	3	0	.333	.267
Wingo, Scott	L-R	5-11	175	3-25-89	.333	.375	.316	7	27	5	9	2	2	1	0	1	5	2	0	0	8	0	0	.481	.471

Pitching	B-T	HT	WT	DOB	W	L	ERA	G	GS	CG	SV	IP	H	R	ER	HR	BB	SO	AVG	vLH	vRH	K/9	BB/9
Arano, Victor	R-R	6-2	196	2-7-95	3	2	4.20	13	8	0	0	49	52	34	23	4	13	49	.255	.276	.236	8.94	2.37
Bermudez, Jhosue	L-L	6-0	195	4-21-93	3	1	4.03	15	0	0	1	22	23	15	10	2	8	16	.264	.318	.246	6.45	3.22
Bock, Edinson	R-R	6-2	190	4-15-94	5	1	2.35	15	1	0	1	23	18	11	6	0	22	15	.217	.321	.164	5.87	8.61
Campbell, James	R-R	6-1	195	9-20-91	0	1	12.00	3	2	0	0	3	7	9	4	0	5	1	.412	.429	.400	3.00	15.00
Cash, Ralston	R-R	6-3	215	8-20-91	0	0	0.00	1	0	0	0	2	1	0	0	0	0	5	.125	.000	.200	22.50	0.00
De Leon, Jose	R-R	6-2	185	8-7-92	2	3	4.01	9	8	0	0	34	32	18	15	1	18	35	.256	.324	.231	9.36	4.81
Flamion, Billy	L-L	6-1	200	1-19-93	0	0	1.38	9	0	0	0	13	6	2	2	0	8	19	.143	.154	.138	13.15	5.54
Gonzalez, Pablo	R-R	6-4	195	3-1-91	0	1	3.60	11	1	0	0	25	21	11	10	2	16	22	.223	.167	.259	7.92	5.76
Gonzalez, Victor	L-L	6-0	200	11-16-95	3	2	3.79	11	10	0	0	38	31	24	16	1	12	45	.223	.167	.247	10.66	2.84
Guerra, Javy	R-R	6-1	190	10-31-85	0	0	0.00	1	1	0	0	3	1	0	0	0	0	2	.100	.250	.000	6.00	0.00
Harris, Greg	R-R	6-2	170	8-17-94	2	3	5.29	10	7	0	0	34	33	22	20	4	9	22	.256	.320	.215	5.82	2.38
Johnson, Blake	R-R	6-5	200	6-14-85	1	0	0.00	2	2	0	0	8	4	0	0	0	1	12	.143	.111	.158	13.50	1.13
Johnson, Michael	L-L	6-1	185	1-3-91	1	0	4.50	4	0	0	1	4	6	3	2	0	2	6	.333	1.000	.294	13.50	4.50
Keener, Nick	R-R	5-11	180	1-17-91	2	0	6.17	10	0	0	0	12	10	8	2	6	7	.243	.438	.111	5.40	4.63
Magill, Matt	R-R	6-3	210	11-10-89	0	0	0.00	1	1	0	0	3	1	0	0	0	3	.100	.167	.000	9.00	0.00
Mateo, Jackson	R-R	6-0	193	8-22-92	0	0	1.42	9	0	0	2	13	10	3	2	0	2	9	.204	.267	.176	6.39	1.42
Munoz, Bryan	R-R	6-2	180	7-26-95	0	1	3.28	13	0	0	2	25	29	10	9	3	6	16	.282	.310	.262	5.84	2.19
Osuna, Lenix	R-R	6-1	220	11-11-95	2	1	1.82	17	0	0	1	25	18	13	5	2	15	23	.202	.263	.157	8.39	5.47
Perez, Franklin	R-R	6-1	180	5-11-94	0	0	0.00	2	0	0	0	2	3	0	0	0	1	3	.375	.667	.200	13.50	4.50
Reyes, Bernardo	R-R	6-0	175	7-22-95	0	0	2.59	11	5	0	0	24	22	8	7	0	9	21	.242	.222	.255	7.77	3.33
Rogers, Rob	R-R	5-11	205	10-25-90	0	0	1.29	5	0	0	3	7	6	1	1	0	1	7	.222	.333	.133	9.00	1.29
Sandoval, Nelson	R-R	6-0	190	2-26-94	1	2	6.97	10	3	0	0	21	34	23	16	1	4	14	.354	.270	.407	6.10	1.74
Serrano, Wellington	L-L	6-0	170	9-5-94	0	0	4.50	2	0	0	0	2	3	2	1	0	0	1	.375	.000	.429	4.50	0.00
Soto, William	R-R	6-4	185	2-13-96	0	0	3.86	6	0	0	0	9	10	8	4	0	4	10	.244	.263	.227	9.64	3.86
Teodo, Wascar	R-R	6-4	185	6-25-94	5	1	2.55	16	0	0	3	35	21	11	10	0	14	35	.175	.208	.149	8.92	3.57
Tolleson, Shawn	R-R	6-2	210	1-19-88	0	0	0.00	1	0	0	0	1	0	0	0	0	1	0	.000	.000	.000	9.00	
Underwood, J.D.	L-R	6-2	215	9-2-92	0	0	2.57	2	1	0	0	7	4	2	2	0	1	12	.160	.300	.067	15.43	1.29
Velasquez, Abdiel	R-R	6-3	184	3-4-93	3	2	4.72	14	6	0	1	48	40	31	25	4	20	44	.229	.200	.245	8.31	3.78

Fielding

Catcher	PCT	G	PO	A	E	DP	PB
Cordero	.988	11	76	5	1	2	5
de la Fuente	1.000	1	6	0	0	0	3
Erickson	1.000	5	43	4	0	0	0
Leon	.956	16	74	13	4	0	7
O'Brien	.955	6	37	5	2	1	1
Reid-Foley	.963	13	91	12	4	1	0
Scott	.985	15	121	12	2	2	7

First Base	PCT	G	PO	A	E	DP
Bellinger	.986	43	383	32	6	30
Chigbogu	.966	6	51	5	2	7
Cordero	.965	11	74	8	3	7

Second Base	PCT	G	PO	A	E	DP
Hennessey	.938	11	16	29	3	6
Law	1.000	1	0	2	0	0
McDonald	.942	10	23	26	3	6
Oguisten	1.000	3	6	16	0	3
Pederson	.984	12	29	34	1	7
Santana	.966	20	33	51	3	13
Wingo	1.000	1	0	2	0	0

Third Base	PCT	G	PO	A	E	DP
Ahmed	.961	38	33	89	5	8
Gomez	1.000	1	1	2	0	0
Hoenecke	.824	5	4	10	3	2
Law	1.000	2	3	1	0	0
Oguisten	1.000	1	2	2	0	0
Rojas	.750	5	1	8	3	2
Santana	.769	4	3	7	3	0

Shortstop	PCT	G	PO	A	E	DP
Ahmed	1.000	1	0	2	0	0
Gomez	.877	41	60	111	24	18
Hennessey	.917	3	5	6	1	2
Law	1.000	1	3	0	2	
Oguisten	1.000	10	12	25	0	3
Wingo	1.000	2	4	5	0	0

LOS ANGELES DODGERS

Outfield	PCT	G	PO	A	E	DP
Alexander	.960	20	23	1	1	0
Compton	1.000	4	3	0	0	0
Gwynn Jr.	1.000	2	4	0	0	0
Harris	1.000	1	2	1	0	0

	PCT	G	PO	A	E	DP
Harris	.886	27	57	5	8	0
Henderson	.933	22	27	1	2	0
Henderson	1.000	5	8	1	0	1
Hennessey	1.000	10	15	1	0	1
Law	.920	29	43	3	4	3

	PCT	G	PO	A	E	DP
McDonald	.952	14	20	0	1	0
Moore	1.000	3	1	0	0	0
Oguisten	.964	14	26	1	1	1
Torres	.952	29	38	2	2	0
Wingo	1.000	4	5	0	0	0

OGDEN RAPTORS · ROOKIE

PIONEER LEAGUE

Batting	B-T	HT	WT	DOB	AVG	vLH	vRH	G	AB	R	H	2B	3B	HR	RBI	BB	HBP	SH	SF	SO	SB	CS	SLG	OBP
Babitt, Zach	L-R	5-7	165	9-1-89	.215	.250	.208	27	93	13	20	3	1	0	10	19	0	3	0	11	2	1	.269	.348
Chaplin, Jake	L-L	6-0	180	1-27-90	.172	.200	.167	12	29	6	5	0	0	0	3	6	0	0	0	7	2	1	.172	.314
Chigbogu, Justin	L-L	6-1	240	7-8-94	.254	.323	.241	49	189	34	48	9	1	9	31	22	0	0	1	72	2	1	.455	.330
Cowen, Austin	R-R	5-11	195	9-15-89	.274	.174	.298	29	117	15	32	8	0	2	18	6	1	0	1	17	0	0	.393	.312
Curletta, Joey	R-R	6-4	225	3-8-94	.326	.237	.344	62	230	41	75	16	0	5	42	27	3	0	1	42	2	4	.461	.402
de la Fuente, Dimitri	R-R	6-0	195	6-25-90	.125	.000	.138	9	32	0	4	2	1	0	2	0	0	0	2	7	0	0	.250	.118
Farmer, Kyle	R-R	6-0	195	8-17-90	.347	.250	.370	41	167	37	58	19	0	4	36	7	6	0	4	21	1	1	.533	.386
Law, Adam	R-R	6-0	193	2-5-90	.327	.450	.299	25	107	21	35	7	1	0	15	7	1	3	0	13	19	1	.411	.374
Moyer, Dillon	R-R	6-1	185	7-18-91	.167	.263	.151	41	138	14	23	7	1	1	14	14	1	0	4	45	2	2	.254	.242
Navin, Spencer	R-R	6-1	185	8-11-92	.190	.000	.211	7	21	2	4	2	0	0	2	4	0	0	6	0	1	.286	.320
Nunez, Gerson	R-R	5-11	178	12-21-90	.296	.185	.327	34	125	25	37	2	2	5	23	18	2	2	0	28	2	3	.464	.393
Oguisten, Faustino	R-R	6-2	165	1-17-91	.300	.333	.286	4	10	2	3	1	0	0	1	1	1	0	0	3	1	1	.400	.417
Santana, Alex	R-R	6-4	200	8-21-93	.327	.300	.333	55	205	39	67	10	4	2	27	20	3	0	2	39	7	3	.444	.391
Scavuzzo, Jacob	R-R	6-4	195	1-15-94	.307	.211	.325	63	244	49	75	18	3	14	42	17	1	0	4	47	3	5	.578	.350
Stover, Pat	R-R	6-4	220	9-12-90	.312	.300	.315	50	189	35	59	16	3	4	33	25	5	0	0	51	9	2	.492	.406
Trinkwon, Brandon	L-R	6-1	165	3-30-92	.362	.296	.378	33	138	26	50	13	3	4	27	10	2	1	1	18	3	3	.587	.411
Valdez, Jesus	R-R	6-3	195	3-27-92	.272	.275	.272	53	202	32	55	9	2	9	37	18	2	1	2	55	1	0	.470	.335
Valentin, Jesmuel	B-R	5-9	180	5-12-94	.284	.205	.301	62	250	53	71	10	3	4	24	33	6	3	1	34	11	7	.396	.379
Yates, Hank	R-R	6-2	190	10-19-90	.307	.214	.328	39	153	26	47	7	3	3	23	17	1	1	1	41	6	4	.451	.378

Pitching	B-T	HT	WT	DOB	W	L	ERA	G	GS	CG	SV	IP	H	R	ER	HR	BB	SO	AVG	vLH	vRH	K/9	BB/9
Araujo, Victor	R-R	5-11	171	11-9-92	5	3	6.48	15	15	0	0	76	90	58	55	7	20	75	.292	.300	.288	8.84	2.36
Barlow, Scott	R-R	6-3	170	12-18-92	4	3	6.20	15	15	0	0	70	82	54	48	13	32	51	.295	.314	.283	6.59	4.13
Baune, Jamie	R-R	6-3	190	9-27-91	1	1	3.07	20	0	0	0	29	33	14	10	0	5	25	.280	.204	.333	7.67	1.53
Bird, Zach	R-R	6-4	205	7-14-94	2	4	5.77	9	9	0	0	44	43	30	28	3	19	44	.247	.283	.228	9.07	3.92
De Leon, Jose	R-R	6-2	185	8-7-92	1	2	12.10	5	5	0	0	19	35	30	26	5	3	18	.380	.359	.396	8.38	1.40
De Paula, Luis	L-L	6-1	170	4-26-92	3	5	4.25	15	8	0	0	55	60	36	26	2	29	43	.271	.226	.286	7.04	4.75
Diaz, Jose Agusto	R-R	5-11	185	1-15-91	1	0	6.20	18	0	0	1	25	24	18	17	4	10	32	.258	.314	.224	11.68	3.65
Fisher, Jake	L-L	5-11	178	9-16-90	2	3	5.97	16	2	0	0	38	46	27	25	4	9	29	.305	.265	.324	6.93	2.15
Flamion, Billy	L-L	6-1	200	1-19-93	0	0	5.40	4	0	0	0	5	4	3	3	0	6	7	.211	.429	.083	12.60	10.80
Gonzalez, Sawil	R-R	6-1	169	3-24-90	1	1	4.21	22	0	0	6	26	26	16	12	3	10	38	.257	.278	.246	13.32	3.51
Hershiser, Jordan	R-R	6-8	245	9-15-88	2	2	4.86	17	0	0	1	37	41	22	20	4	10	40	.289	.356	.258	9.73	2.43
Hooper, Kyle	R-R	6-4	195	5-28-91	3	0	4.82	18	0	0	0	28	30	16	15	4	8	36	.278	.382	.230	11.57	2.57
Johnson, Michael	L-L	6-1	185	1-3-91	2	2	3.18	16	0	0	0	23	17	15	8	2	12	31	.205	.258	.173	12.31	4.76
Martinez, Jonathan	R-R	6-1	194	6-27-94	3	1	4.96	6	6	0	0	33	39	22	18	2	4	11	.298	.327	.278	3.03	1.10
Mateo, Jackson	R-R	6-0	193	8-22-92	0	0	6.75	7	0	0	0	11	20	12	8	1	4	8	.392	.176	.500	6.75	3.38
Perez, Franklin	R-R	6-1	180	5-11-94	0	1	18.00	1	0	0	0	1	2	2	2	1	1	0	.500	.000	.333	0.00	9.00
Perez, Ricardo	R-R	5-11	185	5-24-90	1	1	4.55	20	0	0	0	30	34	20	15	1	14	24	.296	.302	.292	7.28	4.25
Rhame, Jacob	R-R	6-1	190	3-16-93	1	2	4.58	20	0	0	8	20	19	13	10	2	9	21	.257	.364	.171	9.61	4.12
Rogers, Rob	R-R	5-11	205	10-25-90	1	1	3.18	5	0	0	0	6	7	3	2	0	5	5	.318	.429	.267	7.94	7.94
Serrano, Wellington	L-L	6-0	170	9-5-94	0	0	9.00	1	0	0	0	1	3	1	1	0	0	1	.500	.000	.600	9.00	0.00
Taylor, Thomas	R-R	6-4	220	2-26-90	1	0	5.23	8	0	0	0	10	9	8	6	2	4	10	.214	.250	.192	8.71	3.48
Teodo, Wascar	R-R	6-4	185	6-25-94	0	0	27.00	1	0	0	0	1	2	3	3	0	1	1	.400	.333	.500	9.00	9.00
Underwood, J.D.	L-R	6-2	215	9-2-92	0	2	12.60	7	4	0	0	15	26	22	21	2	6	13	.366	.318	.388	7.80	3.60
Villa, Francisco	R-R	6-0	194	4-1-92	3	5	4.35	12	12	0	0	62	71	38	30	8	26	48	.287	.245	.317	6.97	3.77

Fielding

Catcher	PCT	G	PO	A	E	DP	PB
Cowen	.973	28	184	29	6	0	8
de la Fuente	.965	8	69	14	3	2	1
Farmer	.987	35	282	32	4	4	13
Navin	.948	6	48	7	3	0	0

First Base	PCT	G	PO	A	E	DP
Chaplin	1.000	9	62	6	0	5
Chigbogu	.977	34	283	12	7	31
Valdez	.991	36	300	19	3	26

Second Base	PCT	G	PO	A	E	DP
Babitt	.975	27	46	70	3	17
Law	1.000	1	0	1	0	0
Valentin	.969	48	113	139	8	39

Third Base	PCT	G	PO	A	E	DP
Law	.950	24	14	43	3	7
Moyer	.900	13	11	25	4	1
Santana	.817	39	19	66	19	10

Shortstop	PCT	G	PO	A	E	DP
Moyer	.942	28	36	78	7	17
Oguisten	.857	3	3	15	3	0
Trinkwon	.974	32	45	106	4	21
Valentin	.949	13	18	38	3	7

Outfield	PCT	G	PO	A	E	DP
Curletta	.954	62	122	3	6	1
Nunez	.983	33	56	2	1	2
Scavuzzo	.949	61	108	3	6	1
Stover	.982	33	56	0	1	0
Valdez	1.000	2	1	0	0	0
Yates	.976	39	79	4	2	0

DOMINICAN SUMMER LEAGUE

Batting	B-T	HT	WT	DOB	AVG	vLH	vRH	G	AB	R	H	2B	3B	HR	RBI	BB	HBP	SH	SF	SO	SB	CS	SLG	OBP
Alcantara, Luis	R-R	6-1	185	10-23-92	.221	.219	.222	60	149	19	33	7	0	0	11	13	8	2	2	25	5	4	.268	.314
Almarante, Bernys	R-R	6-0	185	9-12-93	.136	.200	.118	11	22	2	3	2	0	0	4	9	0	3	3	6	0	1	.227	.353
Aquino, Carlos	B-R	6-0	165	10-20-95	.182	.167	.188	7	22	3	4	0	0	0	0	1	0	0	0	3	0	2	.182	.217
Castillo, Deivy	L-L	6-3	170	7-21-95	.190	.162	.202	37	121	11	23	0	3	0	9	15	6	1	1	32	5	7	.240	.308
Gomez, Rafael	R-R	6-0	170	1-5-95	.256	.182	.269	41	78	15	20	2	2	0	9	16	1	4	0	21	4	6	.333	.389
Hernandez, Ravel	B-R	6-0	145	10-20-95	.167	—	.167	3	6	0	1	0	1	0	1	0	0	0	0	3	0	0	.500	.167
Isabel, Ibandel	R-R	6-4	185	6-20-95	.327	.320	.329	57	196	25	64	15	5	3	31	20	4	2	1	50	1	3	.500	.398
Javier, Jose Luis	R-R	5-10	160	10-31-92	.305	.200	.339	64	223	36	68	4	6	1	20	25	2	3	1	52	23	7	.390	.378
Medina, Michael	R-R	6-2	190	8-24-96	.198	.224	.189	56	192	32	38	7	2	10	31	21	4	0	1	94	4	3	.411	.289
Ortiz, Samuel	B-R	5-11	170	8-4-96	.182	.231	.167	20	55	9	10	1	0	0	4	9	2	0	1	9	5	0	.200	.313
Palmer, Nelson	R-R	6-2	170	4-27-92	.239	.222	.243	61	197	28	47	10	1	1	17	16	1	3	0	48	2	2	.315	.299
Paz, Luis	L-R	6-1	190	5-7-96	.161	.037	.198	41	118	14	19	2	0	1	12	16	3	1	3	27	2	1	.203	.271
Perez, Jimy	R-R	6-2	185	2-12-94	.209	.286	.180	44	153	14	32	3	3	2	21	15	4	1	2	47	7	5	.307	.293
Rodriguez, Luis	R-R	5-11	180	2-12-95	.196	.182	.203	40	112	15	22	8	1	1	10	14	2	1	2	28	3	2	.313	.292
Romano, Albert	R-R	6-1	171	7-14-95	.143	.333	.000	3	7	0	1	0	0	0	1	0	0	0	0	2	0	1	.143	.143
Sandoval, Ariel	R-R	6-2	180	11-6-95	.255	.322	.234	63	243	26	62	7	2	0	16	15	1	4	2	39	19	12	.300	.299
Santana, Dennis	R-R	6-2	160	4-12-96	.198	.205	.195	56	172	18	34	4	0	2	25	25	5	5	3	53	4	7	.256	.312
Subero, Luis	R-R	5-11	185	3-21-95	.188	.059	.231	35	69	9	13	1	0	0	1	16	1	0	0	12	2	2	.203	.349

Pitching	B-T	HT	WT	DOB	W	L	ERA	G	GS	CG	SV	IP	H	R	ER	HR	BB	SO	AVG	vLH	vRH	K/9	BB/9
Alcantara, Geuris	R-R	6-2	185	5-29-92	0	0	0.00	2	0	0	0	3	3	0	0	0	2	1	.231	1.000	.091	2.70	5.40
Bautista, Angel	R-R	6-3	190	4-25-95	0	0	6.30	8	0	0	1	10	14	10	7	1	7	2	.333	.300	.344	1.80	6.30
Bock, Edinson	R-R	6-2	190	4-15-94	0	1	10.80	1	1	0	0	3	6	4	4	0	3	1	.429	.500	.417	2.70	8.10
Canelo, Willie	L-L	6-2	180	5-27-92	0	0	2.45	2	0	0	0	4	2	1	1	0	3	4	.154	.000	.182	9.82	7.36
Chica, Dennys	L-L	6-3	175	8-31-95	1	0	3.63	8	2	0	0	17	14	9	7	2	6	11	.215	.286	.196	5.71	3.12
Cruz, Oscar	R-R	6-1	170	8-25-94	0	2	3.15	11	7	0	0	34	19	13	12	3	16	21	.160	.118	.176	5.50	4.19
Escudero, Jose	R-R	5-11	170	5-24-95	2	1	2.81	19	1	0	1	32	23	14	10	1	8	23	.189	.205	.179	6.47	2.25
Fernandez, Roberth	L-L	6-1	165	3-21-95	3	2	3.81	17	0	0	0	26	23	11	11	2	13	16	.228	.063	.259	5.54	4.50
German, Angel	R-R	6-4	185	5-25-96	0	5	6.10	10	6	0	0	21	21	22	14	1	17	10	.256	.200	.288	4.35	7.40
Guzman, Kevin	R-R	6-3	165	11-6-94	3	5	2.34	13	8	0	1	42	40	14	11	1	7	32	.247	.191	.270	6.80	1.49
Jean, Elou	R-R	5-11	205	4-29-92	0	3	6.75	20	0	0	4	21	25	21	16	0	13	10	.281	.385	.238	4.22	5.48
Jimenez, Luis	R-R	6-1	178	5-29-95	3	4	4.59	25	0	0	1	33	31	19	17	3	8	20	.246	.162	.281	5.40	2.16
Londono, Miguel	L-L	6-1	160	4-30-96	0	0	4.15	5	0	0	0	4	4	3	2	0	5	1	.250	.333	.231	2.08	10.38
Longa, Roniel	R-R	6-2	180	7-12-94	0	1	5.40	4	0	0	0	3	4	6	2	1	6	3	.267	.000	.444	8.10	16.20
Martinez, Francisco	R-R	6-0	190	12-3-91	5	2	1.99	12	9	1	0	54	39	21	12	3	4	35	.198	.138	.211	5.80	0.66
Pacheco, Jairo	L-L	6-0	165	7-6-96	1	1	1.24	17	6	0	0	44	26	9	6	1	13	45	.169	.075	.202	9.27	2.68
Pena, Angel	R-R	6-1	180	7-19-94	0	0	3.86	14	0	0	1	23	16	14	10	0	14	11	.193	.250	.149	4.24	5.40
Perez, Franklin	R-R	6-1	180	5-11-94	1	0	1.84	18	0	0	3	29	25	10	6	1	11	24	.231	.262	.212	7.36	3.38
Querales, Mario	R-R	6-1	175	11-15-94	0	0	3.45	19	0	0	1	31	25	17	12	2	9	15	.216	.227	.208	4.31	2.59
Ramirez, Osiris	R-R	6-3	185	9-14-95	1	1	6.06	7	5	0	0	16	23	18	11	0	6	13	.315	.350	.302	7.16	3.31
Rodriguez, Hector	R-R	6-3	190	10-17-94	0	4	7.18	14	7	0	0	31	31	30	25	1	20	21	.254	.205	.282	6.03	5.74
Rosario, Diomailin	L-L	6-2	180	11-14-93	1	2	6.43	22	0	0	0	28	42	26	20	2	13	19	.359	.316	.367	6.11	4.18
Sandoval, Nelson	R-R	6-0	190	2-26-94	0	0	0.00	1	1	0	0	4	1	0	0	0	2	7	.071	.167	.000	15.75	4.50
Serrano, Wellington	L-L	6-0	170	9-5-94	6	3	1.99	12	10	0	0	50	41	23	11	0	14	32	.227	.421	.175	5.80	2.54
Soto, Algenis	R-R	6-4	185	5-24-96	0	0	0.00	1	0	0	0	1	0	1	0	0	3	0	.000	.000	.000	0.00	40.50
Urena, Miguel	R-R	6-8	210	2-27-95	0	6	7.76	12	7	0	0	27	33	29	23	1	16	21	.300	.357	.280	7.09	5.40

Fielding

Catcher	PCT	G	PO	A	E	DP	PB
Alcantara	.990	27	87	9	1	0	1
Paz	.950	17	65	11	4	0	9
Rodriguez	.974	28	165	24	5	1	6
Subero	.983	30	98	16	2	0	11

First Base	PCT	G	PO	A	E	DP
Alcantara	.979	23	173	10	4	15
Gomez	1.000	1	5	0	0	1
Palmer	.981	50	387	16	8	36
Perez	.955	9	59	5	3	2
Rodriguez	1.000	1	3	0	0	0

Second Base	PCT	G	PO	A	E	DP
Almarante	1.000	4	7	7	0	1
Aquino	.903	5	13	15	3	4

	PCT	G	PO	A	E	DP
Gomez	.931	26	38	43	6	10
Hernandez	.875	2	1	6	1	0
Javier	.975	35	71	82	4	19
Ortiz	.860	12	15	22	6	3
Romano	1.000	2	4	6	0	2

Third Base	PCT	G	PO	A	E	DP
Alcantara	.879	14	6	23	4	1
Almarante	1.000	1	2	3	0	0
Gomez	.800	3	3	9	3	1
Javier	.943	28	23	76	6	7
Perez	.871	37	32	76	16	10

Shortstop	PCT	G	PO	A	E	DP
Almarante	.833	4	5	10	3	0
Aquino	.875	2	2	5	1	2

	PCT	G	PO	A	E	DP
Javier	.895	9	16	18	4	5
Ortiz	.875	8	8	13	3	1
Romano	—	1	0	0	0	0
Santana	.905	53	76	152	24	28

Outfield	PCT	G	PO	A	E	DP
Castillo	.985	35	64	2	1	1
Gomez	1.000	2	3	0	0	0
Isabel	.922	41	69	2	6	1
Javier	.833	2	5	0	1	0
Medina	.953	49	77	4	4	0
Mieses	.882	16	30	0	4	0
Palmer	.920	15	22	1	2	0
Sandoval	.968	60	118	4	4	0

Miami Marlins

SEASON IN A SENTENCE: Doomed from the start, the Marlins' jettisoned of nearly every big-name or big-money player but ended with one of the strangest no-hitters in baseball history.

HIGH POINT: The no-hitter referenced above, which was thrown by righty Henderson Alvarez. He was acquired in the deal that sent Jose Reyes, Mark Buehrle, Josh Johnson and others to Toronto for a package of six youngsters and Jeff Mathis. Alvarez held the Tigers hitless through nine innings, but the Marlins couldn't plate him a run of support until the bottom of the ninth, when Luke Putkonen's wild pitch brought home Giancarlo Stanton home from third with the winner. The kicker? Alvarez was in the on-deck circle when the game ended.

LOW POINT: Miami had two months that featured 20 or more losses, but May takes the cake. The season's second month found the Marlins losers 22 times, including a stretch of nine in a row from May 21-30. During that stretch they scored just 22 runs and allowed 46.

NOTABLE ROOKIES: Jose Fernandez earned NL rookie of the year honors and would have had a shot at the Cy Young Award if not for Clayton Kershaw's campaign. The Cuban righty, who had never thrown a pitch above high Class A, fanned 187 over 173 innings and surrendered just 111 hits. Miami also received contributions from outfielders Jake Marisnick, Christian Yelich and Marcell Ozuna, as well as infielder Derek Dietrich.

KEY TRANSACTIONS: In addition to the late-2012 blockbuster, Miami sent Heath Bell to the desert in October in a three-team rendezvous with Arizona and Oakland, flipped Yunel Escobar to the Rays in December, and traded Ricky Nolasco to the Dodgers at midseason. For all of those pieces, the Marlins received salary relief, Dietrich, Yordy Cabrera and three farmhands from Los Angeles.

DOWN ON THE FARM: The jewel of the Marlins system is lefty Andrew Heaney, who ate up the competition at high Class A and Double-A en route to 89 strikeouts against 26 walks in 96 innings across both levels. He's complemented by Colin Moran, the sixth overall pick in the 2013 draft out of North Carolina. He hit .299/.354/.442 with four home runs at low Class A Greensboro before finishing his season in the Arizona Fall League. Lefty Justin Nicolino, also acquired in the swap with the Jays, whiffed 95 hitters between Jupiter and Jacksonville.

OPENING DAY PAYROLL: $36.3 million (29th)

PLAYERS OF THE YEAR

MAJOR LEAGUE

Jose Fernandez
rhp
12-6, 2.19 in 28 GS
187 SO, 0.98 WHIP
BA Rookie of the Year

MINOR LEAGUE

Andrew Heaney
lhp
(High-A/Double-A)
9-3, 1.60 in 19 G
1.07 WHIP, 8.4 SO/9

ORGANIZATION LEADERS

BATTING		*Minimum 250 AB
MAJORS		
* AVG	Stanton, Giancarlo	.249
* OPS	Stanton, Giancarlo	.845
HR	Stanton, Giancarlo	24
RBI	Stanton, Giancarlo	62
MINORS		
* AVG	Keys, Brent, Jacksonville/Jupiter	.341
* OBP	Keys, Brent, Jacksonville/Jupiter	.415
* SLG	Jensen, Kyle, New Orleans/Jacksonville	.492
R	Jensen, Kyle, New Orleans/Jacksonville	74
H	Keys, Brent, Jacksonville/Jupiter	141
TB	Jensen, Kyle, New Orleans/Jacksonville	220
2B	Petersen, Bryan, New Orleans	33
3B	Dean, Austin, Greensboro/Batavia	7
	Mattison, Kevin, New Orleans	7
	Yelich, Christian, Jax/Jupiter/GCL	7
HR	Jensen, Kyle, New Orleans/Jacksonville	28
RBI	Jensen, Kyle, New Orleans/Jacksonville	78
BB	Rosa, Viosergy, Greensboro	74
SO	Jensen, Kyle, New Orleans/Jacksonville	144
SB	Solorzano, Jesus, Greensboro	33

PITCHING		#Minimum 75 IP
MAJORS		
W	Fernandez, Jose	12
# ERA	Fernandez, Jose	2.19
SO	Fernandez, Jose	187
SV	Cishek, Steve	34
MINORS		
W	Conley, Adam, Jacksonville	11
L	Flynn, Brian, New Orleans/Jacksonville	12
# ERA	Flynn, Brian, Jacksonville/New Orleans	2.63
G	Hatcher, Chris, New Orleans	60
GS	Flynn, Brian, New Orleans/Jacksonville	27
	Nicolino, Justin, Jacksonville/Jupiter	27
SV	Hatcher, Chris, New Orleans	33
IP	Flynn, Brian, New Orleans/Jacksonville	161
BB	Brice, Austin, Greensboro	82
SO	Flynn, Brian, New Orleans/Jacksonville	147
# AVG	Conley, Adam, Jacksonville	.236

General Manager: Dan Jennings. **Farm Director:** Brian Chattin. **Scouting Director:** Stan Meek.

Class	Team	League	W	L	PCT	Finish	Manager
Majors	Miami Marlins	National	62	100	.383	15th (15)	Mike Redmond
Triple-A	New Orleans Zephyrs	Pacific Coast	72	72	.500	9th (16)	Ron Hassey
Double-A	Jacksonville Suns	Southern	73	63	.537	5th (10)	Andy Barkett
High A	Jupiter Hammerheads	Florida State	68	69	.496	5th (12)	Andy Haines
Low A	Greensboro Grasshoppers	South Atlantic	65	72	.474	9th (14)	Jorge Hernandez
Short-season	Batavia Muckdogs	New York-Penn	39	36	.520	6th (14)	Angel Espada
Rookie	GCL Marlins	Gulf Coast	25	34	.424	14th (16)	Julio Garcia
2013 Overall Minor League Record			342	346	.497	t-13th (30)	

ORGANIZATION STATISTICS

NATIONAL LEAGUE

Batting	B-T	HT	WT	DOB	AVG	vLH	vRH	G	AB	R	H	2B	3B	HR	RBI	BB	HBP	SH	SF	SO	SB	CS	SLG	OBP
Brantly, Rob	L-R	6-1	195	7-14-89	.211	.056	.241	67	223	11	47	9	0	1	18	15	2	0	3	53	0	0	.265	.263
Brown, Jordan	L-L	6-0	220	12-18-83	.200	.000	.231	14	15	0	3	1	0	0	5	1	0	0	1	1	0	0	.267	.235
Coghlan, Chris	L-R	6-0	195	6-18-85	.256	.333	.244	70	195	10	50	10	3	1	10	17	1	0	1	43	2	0	.354	.318
Diaz, Matt	R-R	6-0	215	3-3-78	.167	.167	.167	10	18	1	3	1	0	0	1	1	0	0	0	3	0	0	.222	.211
Dietrich, Derek	L-R	6-0	200	7-18-89	.214	.259	.199	57	215	32	46	10	2	9	23	11	7	0	0	56	1	0	.405	.275
Dobbs, Greg	L-R	6-1	210	7-2-78	.228	.143	.250	114	237	21	54	11	0	2	22	22	5	0	3	40	1	1	.300	.303
Green, Nick	R-R	5-11	190	9-10-78	.236	.000	.342	18	55	4	13	2	0	1	6	3	3	2	2	14	0	0	.327	.302
Hechavarria, Adeiny	R-R	6-0	185	4-15-89	.227	.234	.224	148	543	30	123	14	8	3	42	30	0	4	1	96	11	10	.298	.267
Hill, Koyie	B-R	6-1	210	3-9-79	.155	.350	.053	18	58	3	9	2	0	0	2	0	1	0	18	0	0	.190	.183
Kearns, Austin	R-R	6-3	240	5-20-80	.185	.200	.167	19	27	3	5	0	0	0	4	0	0	0	8	0	0	.185	.290
Kotchman, Casey	L-L	6-3	220	2-22-83	.000	.000	.000	6	20	0	0	0	0	0	1	1	0	0	1	0	0	.000	.048
Lucas, Ed	R-R	6-3	210	5-21-82	.256	.330	.224	94	351	43	90	14	1	4	28	26	2	4	1	78	1	1	.336	.311
Mahoney, Joe	L-L	6-6	245	2-1-87	.276	.000	.320	9	29	2	8	1	0	1	4	0	0	0	4	0	0	.414	.276
Marisnick, Jake	R-R	6-3	225	3-30-91	.183	.188	.182	40	109	6	20	2	1	1	5	6	1	1	27	3	1	.248	.231
Mathis, Jeff	R-R	6-0	205	3-31-83	.181	.214	.167	73	232	14	42	7	1	5	29	21	1	1	76	0	0	.284	.251
Morrison, Logan	L-L	6-3	245	8-25-87	.242	.183	.261	85	293	32	71	13	4	6	36	38	2	0	56	0	0	.375	.333
Olivo, Miguel	R-R	6-0	230	7-15-78	.203	.250	.167	33	74	5	15	2	0	4	9	5	0	0	23	0	0	.392	.250
Ozuna, Marcell	R-R	6-1	220	11-12-90	.265	.318	.249	70	275	31	73	17	4	3	32	13	2	1	57	5	1	.389	.303
Pierre, Juan	L-L	5-10	180	8-14-77	.247	.175	.265	113	308	36	76	11	2	1	8	13	3	6	27	23	6	.305	.284
Polanco, Placido	R-R	5-9	190	10-10-75	.260	.317	.232	118	377	33	98	13	0	1	23	23	9	3	31	2	0	.302	.315
Ruggiano, Justin	R-R	6-1	210	4-12-82	.222	.248	.210	128	424	49	94	18	1	18	50	41	5	1	114	15	8	.396	.298
Skipworth, Kyle	L-R	6-4	225	3-1-90	.000	—	.000	4	3	0	0	0	0	0	1	0	0	1	0	0	.000	.250
Solano, Donovan	R-R	5-9	195	12-17-87	.249	.216	.263	102	361	33	90	13	1	3	34	23	7	2	57	3	1	.316	.305
Stanton, Giancarlo	R-R	6-6	240	11-8-89	.249	.278	.240	116	425	62	106	26	0	24	62	74	4	0	140	1	0	.480	.365
Valaika, Chris	R-R	5-11	210	8-14-85	.219	.280	.179	22	64	4	14	5	0	1	9	3	1	1	16	0	0	.344	.261
Velazquez, Gil	R-R	6-2	185	10-17-79	.000	.000	—	1	1	0	0	0	0	0	0	0	0	0	0	0	.000	.000
Yelich, Christian	L-R	6-4	195	12-5-91	.288	.165	.362	62	240	34	69	12	1	4	16	31	1	0	66	10	0	.396	.370

Pitching	B-T	HT	WT	DOB	W	L	ERA	G	GS	CG	SV	IP	H	R	ER	HR	BB	SO	AVG	vLH	vRH	K/9	BB/9
Alvarez, Henderson	R-R	6-0	210	4-18-90	5	6	3.59	17	17	1	0	103	90	42	41	2	27	57	.237	.269	.206	5.00	2.37
Ames, Steve	R-R	6-1	205	3-15-88	0	1	4.50	4	0	0	0	4	6	2	2	0	2	4	.375	.429	.333	9.00	4.50
Below, Duane	L-L	6-3	220	11-15-85	0	1	10.13	2	0	0	0	3	6	3	3	0	2	2	.500	.500	.500	6.75	6.75
Caminero, Arquimedes	R-R	6-4	255	6-16-87	0	0	2.77	13	0	0	0	13	10	4	4	2	3	12	.208	.300	.143	8.31	2.08
Cishek, Steve	R-R	6-6	215	6-18-86	4	6	2.33	69	0	0	34	70	53	19	18	3	22	74	.211	.235	.185	9.56	2.84
Dunn, Mike	L-L	6-0	205	5-23-85	3	4	2.66	75	0	0	2	68	53	21	20	5	28	72	.212	.192	.231	9.58	3.72
Dyson, Sam	R-R	6-1	210	5-7-88	0	2	9.00	5	1	0	0	11	16	12	11	2	5	5	.348	.368	.333	4.09	4.09
Eovaldi, Nate	R-R	6-2	210	2-13-90	4	6	3.39	18	18	0	0	106	100	44	40	7	40	78	.249	.246	.251	6.60	3.39
Fernandez, Jose	R-R	6-2	240	7-31-92	12	6	2.19	28	28	0	0	173	111	47	42	10	58	187	.182	.188	.175	9.75	3.02
Flynn, Brian	L-L	6-7	240	4-19-90	0	2	8.50	4	4	0	0	18	27	17	17	4	13	15	.370	.400	.362	7.50	6.50
Hand, Brad	L-L	6-3	215	3-20-90	1	1	3.05	7	2	0	0	21	13	7	7	2	8	15	.176	.192	.167	6.53	3.48
Hatcher, Chris	R-R	6-1	205	1-12-85	0	1	12.46	7	0	0	0	9	13	13	12	1	4	7	.325	.308	.333	7.27	4.15
Jennings, Dan	L-L	6-3	210	4-17-87	2	1	3.76	47	0	0	0	41	39	17	17	1	16	38	.255	.282	.221	8.41	3.54
Koehler, Tom	R-R	6-3	235	6-29-86	5	10	4.41	29	23	0	0	143	140	72	70	14	54	92	.261	.235	.283	5.79	3.40
LeBlanc, Wade	L-L	6-3	215	8-7-84	1	5	5.18	13	7	0	0	49	63	30	28	6	15	31	.312	.328	.304	5.73	2.77
Maine, John	R-R	6-4	220	5-8-81	0	0	12.27	4	0	0	0	7	15	10	10	2	5	7	.441	.364	.478	8.59	6.14
Nolasco, Ricky	R-R	6-2	235	12-13-82	5	8	3.85	18	18	0	0	112	112	50	48	11	25	90	.261	.268	.253	7.21	2.00
2-team total (16 Los Angeles)					13	11	3.70	34	33	0	0	199	195	90	82	17	46	165	—	—	—	7.45	2.08
Olmos, Edgar	L-L	6-4	215	4-12-90	0	1	7.20	5	0	0	0	5	7	9	4	2	3	2	.350	.222	.455	3.60	5.40
Phillips, Zach	L-L	6-0	190	9-21-86	0	1	5.40	3	0	0	0	2	3	1	1	0	3	1	.429	.667	.250	5.40	16.20
Qualls, Chad	R-R	6-4	240	8-17-78	5	2	2.61	66	0	0	0	62	57	18	18	4	19	49	.251	.239	.259	7.11	2.76
Ramos, A.J.	R-R	5-10	210	9-20-86	3	4	3.15	68	0	0	0	80	58	32	28	4	43	86	.201	.220	.185	9.68	4.84
Rauch, Jon	R-R	6-11	290	9-27-78	1	2	7.56	15	0	0	0	17	23	14	14	1	7	15	.329	.310	.341	8.10	3.78
Sanabia, Alex	R-R	6-2	210	9-8-88	3	7	4.88	10	10	0	0	55	69	33	30	10	25	31	.317	.369	.262	5.04	4.07
Slowey, Kevin	R-R	6-2	200	5-4-84	3	6	4.11	20	14	0	0	92	106	44	42	12	18	76	.291	.307	.276	7.43	1.76
Turner, Jacob	R-R	6-5	215	5-21-91	3	8	3.74	20	20	1	0	118	116	55	49	11	54	77	.262	.254	.269	5.87	4.12
Webb, Ryan	R-R	6-6	245	2-5-86	2	6	2.91	66	0	0	0	80	70	30	26	5	27	54	.244	.244	.244	6.05	3.02

MIAMI MARLINS

Fielding

Catcher	PCT	G	PO	A	E	DP	PB
Brantly	.990	65	440	42	5	5	9
Hill	.991	18	107	6	1	0	1
Mathis	.998	73	520	30	1	2	5
Olivo	.977	21	114	12	3	1	1
Skipworth	1.000	1	2	0	0	0	0

First Base	PCT	G	PO	A	E	DP
Dobbs	.998	51	363	50	1	33
Green	1.000	6	47	3	0	4
Kotchman	.976	6	39	2	1	4
Lucas	1.000	25	180	14	0	17
Mahoney	.979	7	44	3	1	6
Morrison	.996	79	678	68	3	65
Olivo	1.000	1	4	0	0	0
Valaika	.909	3	8	2	1	2

Second Base	PCT	G	PO	A	E	DP
Coghlan	1.000	1	0	1	0	0
Dietrich	.992	57	98	158	2	31
Green	1.000	2	5	1	0	1
Lucas	1.000	20	17	30	0	5
Solano	.983	93	172	284	8	69
Valaika	1.000	6	8	11	0	3

Third Base	PCT	G	PO	A	E	DP
Coghlan	.870	8	4	16	3	3
Green	1.000	2	1	2	0	0
Lucas	.961	61	37	111	6	14
Polanco	.990	109	52	153	2	13
Solano	—	2	0	0	0	0
Valaika	.750	5	0	3	1	0
Velazquez	—	1	0	0	0	0

Shortstop	PCT	G	PO	A	E	DP
Green	1.000	8	15	23	0	6
Hechavarria	.976	148	197	401	15	89
Lucas	.962	6	7	18	1	4
Valaika	.947	6	5	13	1	3

Outfield	PCT	G	PO	A	E	DP
Coghlan	1.000	39	99	4	0	0
Diaz	1.000	4	4	2	0	1
Dobbs	1.000	1	1	0	0	0
Kearns	1.000	4	13	0	0	0
Lucas	1.000	1	5	0	0	0
Marisnick	1.000	32	75	5	0	2
Ozuna	.988	69	157	8	2	4
Pierre	1.000	64	146	0	0	0
Ruggiano	.984	110	242	3	4	0
Stanton	.968	116	233	7	8	0
Yelich	1.000	62	114	0	0	0

NEW ORLEANS ZEPHYRS

TRIPLE-A

PACIFIC COAST LEAGUE

Batting	B-T	HT	WT	DOB	AVG	vLH	vRH	G	AB	R	H	2B	3B	HR	RBI	BB	HBP	SH	SF	SO	SB	CS	SLG	OBP
Brantly, Rob	L-R	6-1	195	7-14-89	.186	.167	.192	20	70	9	13	3	0	1	3	3	0	1	0	8	0	0	.271	.219
Brown, Jordan	L-L	6-0	220	12-18-83	.289	.274	.294	97	291	31	84	22	0	2	28	24	3	3	3	34	0	2	.385	.346
Burg, Alex	R-R	6-0	190	8-9-87	.300	.600	.257	12	40	3	12	1	0	2	8	4	1	0	1	15	1	0	.475	.370
Ciriaco, Audy	R-R	6-3	195	6-16-87	.154	.167	.143	4	13	2	2	0	0	1	3	1	0	0	0	2	0	0	.385	.214
Coghlan, Chris	L-R	6-0	195	6-18-85	.500	.500	.500	3	12	1	6	1	0	1	3	2	0	0	0	0	1	1	.833	.571
Cox, Zack	L-R	5-11	225	5-9-89	.000	—	.000	2	5	0	0	0	0	0	1	0	0	0	0	0	0	0	.000	.167
Diaz, Matt	R-R	6-0	215	3-3-78	.341	.467	.273	24	85	8	29	4	0	2	10	6	0	0	0	7	6	0	.459	.385
Downs, Matt	R-R	6-1	190	3-19-84	.215	.112	.265	82	270	27	58	11	2	8	35	24	3	0	4	54	0	1	.359	.282
Goetz, Ryan	L-R	5-10	185	5-16-88	.222	.000	.235	9	18	0	4	1	0	0	1	2	0	0	0	3	0	0	.278	.300
Gran, Paul	R-R	5-11	182	4-7-86	.195	.179	.208	28	87	9	17	7	2	0	3	6	2	1	0	27	0	0	.322	.263
Green, Nick	R-R	5-11	190	9-10-78	.214	.186	.224	90	318	39	68	11	1	12	34	18	4	2	1	82	1	2	.368	.264
Gutierrez, Chris	R-R	5-9	185	3-12-84	.447	.417	.462	17	38	5	17	4	0	0	3	5	1	3	0	10	0	1	.553	.523
Hernandez, Gorkys	R-R	6-0	190	9-7-87	.275	.333	.244	90	309	45	85	11	4	4	22	22	4	4	1	96	22	9	.375	.330
2-team total (34 Omaha)					.263	—	—	124	430	59	113	17	5	6	32	30	6	3	1	125	25	12	.367	.318
Hill, Koyie	B-R	6-1	210	3-9-79	.237	.229	.243	60	190	18	45	14	0	1	14	15	0	1	0	30	0	0	.326	.291
Jefferies, Jake	L-R	6-1	210	10-30-87	.200	.222	.190	9	30	1	6	2	0	0	3	0	1	0	3	0	0	.267	.273
Jensen, Kyle	R-L	6-3	247	5-20-88	.233	.224	.235	60	202	31	47	15	0	12	36	17	2	1	4	71	1	0	.485	.293
Kouzmanoff, Kevin	R-R	6-1	210	7-25-81	.294	.290	.295	60	218	20	64	14	0	6	42	14	5	0	4	27	2	0	.440	.344
Krick, Taylor	R-R	6-1	215	3-31-88	.000	—	.000	1	3	0	0	0	0	0	0	1	0	0	0	0	0	0	.000	.250
Lasater, Ben	R-R	6-3	225	5-25-84	.217	.217	.217	49	175	13	38	4	1	4	19	18	2	1	0	53	0	0	.320	.297
Lucas, Ed	R-R	6-3	205	5-21-82	.304	.377	.267	46	181	26	55	12	0	5	14	12	2	1	0	37	2	1	.453	.354
Mahoney, Joe	L-L	6-6	245	2-1-87	.190	.213	.182	55	195	9	37	8	0	2	16	3	0	0	2	66	1	0	.262	.200
Mathis, Jeff	R-R	6-0	205	3-31-83	.222	.250	.200	2	9	1	2	1	0	1	2	1	0	0	0	5	0	0	.667	.300
Mattison, Kevin	L-L	6-1	195	9-20-85	.216	.235	.209	106	334	55	72	16	7	7	31	36	2	5	3	138	18	9	.368	.293
Petersen, Bryan	L-R	6-0	195	4-9-86	.275	.203	.303	136	506	61	139	33	5	8	49	65	6	2	117	12	4	.407	.363
Skipworth, Kyle	L-R	6-4	225	3-1-90	.188	.146	.197	73	239	22	45	13	2	11	30	12	5	0	1	82	0	0	.397	.241
Smolinski, Jake	R-R	5-11	185	2-9-89	.258	.264	.256	95	314	36	81	14	2	9	31	37	5	0	1	61	8	1	.401	.345
Solano, Donovan	R-R	5-9	195	12-17-87	.379	.467	.353	17	66	8	25	3	1	2	9	4	1	0	2	11	0	0	.545	.411
Valaika, Chris	R-R	5-11	210	8-14-85	.246	.194	.263	37	130	17	32	6	0	3	11	10	2	0	1	25	1	1	.362	.308
Valdez, Wilson	R-R	5-11	170	5-20-81	.232	.231	.233	35	112	7	26	3	0	0	8	7	0	2	1	17	4	1	.259	.275
Velazquez, Gil	R-R	6-2	185	10-17-79	.277	.300	.266	74	256	30	71	8	0	2	24	43	0	4	4	53	3	5	.309	.376

Pitching	B-T	HT	WT	DOB	W	L	ERA	G	GS	CG	SV	IP	H	R	ER	HR	BB	SO	AVG	vLH	vRH	K/9	BB/9
Aardsma, David	R-R	6-3	205	12-27-81	1	0	2.57	10	0	0	0	14	9	5	4	2	8	12	.180	.211	.161	7.71	5.14
2-team total (8 Las Vegas)					1	0	2.05	18	0	0	3	22	14	6	5	3	15	23	—	—	—	9.41	6.14
Albaladejo, Jonathan	R-R	6-5	270	10-30-82	4	5	3.80	57	0	0	4	73	83	34	31	5	23	72	.282	.311	.266	8.84	2.82
Ames, Steve	R-R	6-1	205	3-15-88	1	0	3.75	9	0	0	0	12	14	5	5	2	4	5	.304	.250	.324	3.75	3.00
2-team total (30 Albuquerque)					3	2	3.69	39	0	0	8	46	59	25	19	6	17	34	—	—	—	6.60	3.30
Battisto, A.J.	R-R	6-0	193	9-30-83	1	1	7.65	17	6	0	0	38	49	35	32	7	24	24	.327	.217	.400	5.73	5.73
Below, Duane	L-L	6-3	220	11-15-85	5	5	2.55	13	13	0	0	74	77	31	21	3	21	53	.270	.305	.256	6.45	2.55
Caminero, Arquimedes	R-R	6-4	255	6-16-87	1	0	0.00	1	0	0	0	2	0	0	0	0	1	0	.000	.000	.000	4.50	0.00
Conley, Jordan	R-R	6-1	180	7-19-86	1	0	3.00	2	0	0	0	3	2	1	1	1	0	2	.182	.333	.125	6.00	0.00
Dyson, Sam	R-R	6-1	210	5-7-88	1	3	2.61	5	5	0	0	31	23	10	9	1	12	16	.213	.133	.244	4.65	3.48
Flynn, Brian	L-L	6-7	240	4-19-90	6	11	2.80	23	23	0	0	138	127	52	43	7	40	122	.246	.258	.242	7.96	2.61
Hand, Brad	L-L	6-3	215	3-20-90	3	5	3.42	15	15	0	0	82	69	33	31	7	45	81	.232	.274	.215	8.93	4.96
Hatcher, Chris	R-R	6-1	205	1-12-85	4	3	3.61	60	0	0	33	67	69	27	27	8	28	65	.262	.237	.282	8.69	3.74
Jackson, Jay	R-R	6-1	195	10-27-87	1	2	4.68	7	4	0	0	25	29	16	13	3	11	20	.299	.325	.281	7.20	3.96
Jennings, Dan	L-L	6-3	210	4-17-87	4	2	1.80	18	0	0	1	25	19	8	5	1	11	25	.209	.184	.226	9.00	3.96
Koehler, Tom	R-R	6-3	235	6-29-86	0	2	2.74	4	4	0	0	23	16	8	7	2	12	18	.200	.257	.156	7.04	4.70
Leverton, James	R-L	6-2	185	5-13-86	3	2	2.66	30	0	0	2	51	29	15	15	5	21	48	.167	.150	.175	8.53	3.73
Maine, Scott	L-L	6-3	225	2-2-85	0	0	9.35	11	0	0	0	9	11	11	9	0	16	11	.297	.158	.444	11.42	16.62

Name	B-T	HT	WT	DOB	W	L	ERA	G	GS	CG	SV	IP	H	R	ER	HR	BB	SO	AVG	vLH	vRH	K/9	BB/9
Mathis, Doug	R-R	6-3	230	6-7-83	5	8	3.85	24	21	1	0	115	107	57	49	10	53	85	.249	.258	.240	6.67	4.16
McGough, Scott	R-R	6-0	170	10-31-89	0	1	5.06	2	1	0	0	5	8	3	3	1	2	3	.364	.333	.385	5.06	3.38
Morey, Robert	R-R	6-1	185	11-27-88	1	0	3.60	3	1	0	0	10	9	4	4	3	8	4	.243	.200	.273	3.60	7.20
Nappo, Greg	L-L	6-0	190	8-25-88	0	0	0.00	2	0	0	0	2	1	0	0	0	0	0	.143	.000	.333	0.00	0.00
Neil, Matthew	R-R	6-6	225	9-5-86	3	3	4.47	10	8	0	0	50	57	29	25	6	16	48	.286	.315	.262	8.58	2.86
Nygren, James	R-R	6-0	195	3-8-89	0	0	8.31	2	0	0	0	4	9	4	4	1	2	4	.450	.455	.444	8.31	4.15
Phillips, Zach	L-L	6-0	190	9-21-86	4	2	2.44	50	0	0	1	59	49	19	16	3	24	74	.224	.176	.258	11.29	3.66
Reifer, Adam	R-R	6-2	195	6-3-86	2	1	1.32	28	0	0	1	41	19	11	6	2	25	37	.143	.132	.150	8.12	5.49
Rogers, Jared	R-R	6-7	202	5-9-88	7	4	4.25	17	16	0	0	85	91	46	40	11	22	62	.266	.284	.251	6.59	2.34
Smith, Jordan	R-R	6-3	220	2-4-86	3	1	5.28	29	0	0	0	44	59	26	26	6	15	25	.330	.288	.358	5.08	3.05
Talbot, Mitch	R-R	6-1	180	10-17-83	1	0	0.00	1	1	0	0	5	2	0	0	0	2	3	.111	.167	.000	5.40	3.60
2-team total (1 Las Vegas)					1	0	4.15	2	2	0	0	9	9	7	4	0	5	3	—	—	—	3.12	5.19
Turner, Jacob	R-R	6-5	215	5-21-91	3	4	4.47	10	10	0	0	56	59	25	28	7	14	35	.268	.243	.295	5.59	2.24
Varner, Rett	R-R	6-4	185	2-3-88	3	4	2.80	30	7	0	1	61	54	20	19	6	24	55	.242	.217	.257	8.11	3.54
Villanueva, Elih	R-R	6-2	230	7-27-86	2	3	3.50	8	8	0	0	46	41	18	18	5	11	31	.238	.278	.210	6.02	2.14
Waite, Rob	R-R	6-3	210	1-9-87	1	0	5.06	7	1	0	0	11	13	6	6	1	2	12	.302	.389	.240	10.13	1.69
Wall, Josh	R-R	6-6	215	1-21-87	1	1	3.27	20	0	0	1	22	23	9	8	0	8	21	.264	.212	.296	8.59	3.27
2-team total (25 Albuquerque)					2	3	4.56	45	0	0	4	49	50	28	25	3	24	46	—	—	—	8.39	4.38

Fielding

Catcher	PCT	G	PO	A	E	DP	PB
Brantly	.992	19	121	10	1	0	0
Hill	.995	57	378	33	2	5	3
Jefferies	1.000	9	72	8	0	0	0
Krick	.917	1	11	0	1	0	0
Mathis	1.000	2	29	0	0	0	0
Skipworth	.983	68	484	45	9	7	8

First Base	PCT	G	PO	A	E	DP
Brown	.986	52	394	26	6	43
Diaz	1.000	3	16	1	0	0
Downs	1.000	8	64	5	0	5
Kouzmanoff	.984	9	55	6	1	9
Lasater	.986	30	266	19	4	22
Mahoney	.998	48	381	29	1	38

Second Base	PCT	G	PO	A	E	DP
Downs	.968	30	44	76	4	18
Goetz	1.000	5	4	9	0	1
Green	.983	25	56	59	2	20
Gutierrez	.933	3	10	4	1	0
Lucas	.989	22	31	60	1	12

	PCT	G	PO	A	E	DP
Solano	1.000	9	18	28	0	10
Valaika	.972	23	36	67	3	17
Valdez	.981	13	21	32	1	4
Velazquez	1.000	22	45	60	0	15

Third Base	PCT	G	PO	A	E	DP
Burg	.955	7	0	21	1	1
Ciriaco	1.000	4	4	11	0	2
Coghlan	1.000	3	2	4	0	0
Cox	1.000	2	1	5	0	0
Downs	.891	22	10	39	6	5
Gran	.944	25	13	38	3	4
Green	.897	14	9	26	4	2
Gutierrez	1.000	12	6	12	0	3
Kouzmanoff	.948	38	29	62	5	9
Lasater	1.000	6	7	18	0	0
Lucas	1.000	4	4	10	0	0
Solano	.889	4	1	7	1	1
Valaika	.909	5	3	7	1	0
Valdez	1.000	4	3	5	0	0

Shortstop	PCT	G	PO	A	E	DP
Downs	.959	17	20	50	3	11
Green	.979	43	63	123	4	22
Gutierrez	—	1	0	0	0	0
Lucas	.961	17	26	48	3	9
Solano	1.000	3	4	8	0	1
Valaika	1.000	6	7	14	0	0
Valdez	.959	14	26	45	3	13
Velazquez	.972	50	69	136	6	32

Outfield	PCT	G	PO	A	E	DP
Brown	.967	20	28	1	1	0
Burg	1.000	2	2	0	0	0
Diaz	1.000	13	19	2	0	1
Goetz	—	1	0	0	0	0
Green	1.000	1	1	0	0	0
Hernandez	.994	75	154	4	1	0
Jensen	.990	47	92	6	1	2
Mattison	.992	86	229	12	2	1
Petersen	.985	123	249	13	4	4
Smolinski	.977	84	166	5	4	0

JACKSONVILLE SUNS

DOUBLE-A

SOUTHERN LEAGUE

Batting	B-T	HT	WT	DOB	AVG	vLH	vRH	G	AB	R	H	2B	3B	HR	RBI	BB	HBP	SH	SF	SO	SB	CS	SLG	OBP
Barnes, Austin	R-R	5-10	190	12-28-89	.339	.286	.354	19	62	10	21	2	2	1	7	12	0	0	0	10	0	0	.484	.446
Black, Danny	L-R	6-3	180	8-19-88	.200	.197	.201	98	315	45	63	5	4	2	21	35	2	0	0	74	8	3	.260	.284
Burg, Alex	R-R	6-0	190	8-9-87	.132	.000	.161	11	38	3	5	1	0	0	2	1	0	0	0	9	0	0	.158	.154
Canha, Mark	R-R	6-2	195	2-15-89	.273	.313	.259	128	425	63	116	32	2	13	58	54	15	5	5	102	6	1	.449	.371
Ciriaco, Audy	R-R	6-3	195	6-16-87	.231	.182	.253	84	247	33	57	7	2	5	26	21	3	0	3	43	7	2	.336	.296
Cox, Zack	L-R	5-11	225	5-9-89	.269	.189	.297	86	283	32	76	15	2	3	29	38	2	0	2	68	2	0	.367	.357
Dietrich, Derek	L-R	6-0	200	7-18-89	.271	.246	.280	63	218	35	59	13	3	11	38	29	10	0	0	60	3	0	.509	.381
Dudley, Aaron	L-R	6-3	193	2-17-88	.148	.286	.128	30	54	5	8	1	0	2	6	10	0	0	0	8	1	0	.278	.281
Fisher, Ryan	L-R	6-3	195	4-24-88	.221	.100	.252	50	145	22	32	9	0	5	24	16	5	2	0	45	2	1	.386	.319
Galloway, Isaac	R-R	6-2	190	10-10-89	.173	.171	.173	37	139	10	24	5	1	2	14	7	0	3	0	48	5	3	.266	.212
Gutierrez, Chris	R-R	5-9	185	3-12-84	.212	.239	.200	85	236	19	50	9	2	3	18	28	3	3	1	41	2	2	.305	.302
Jensen, Kyle	R-L	6-3	247	5-20-88	.237	.297	.215	70	245	43	58	16	0	16	42	33	12	0	1	73	5	3	.498	.354
Keys, Brent	L-R	6-1	210	7-14-90	.281	.000	.346	8	32	3	9	0	0	0	0	5	0	1	0	3	1	0	.281	.378
Krick, Taylor	R-R	6-1	215	3-31-88	.265	.152	.319	43	102	14	27	6	0	1	16	14	4	0	0	27	1	0	.353	.375
Main, Michael	R-R	6-1	170	12-14-88	.223	.208	.228	67	206	17	46	5	1	0	11	16	3	1	0	38	3	5	.257	.288
Marisnick, Jake	R-R	6-3	225	3-30-91	.294	.313	.286	67	265	43	78	13	3	12	46	17	11	2	3	68	11	6	.502	.358
Mathis, Jeff	R-R	6-0	205	3-31-83	.273	.000	.300	3	11	1	3	1	0	1	6	1	0	1	0	6	0	0	.636	.333
McClure, Alex	B-R	6-0	185	6-16-89	.000	.000	.000	7	11	0	0	0	0	0	0	1	0	0	0	6	0	0	.000	.083
Morrison, Logan	L-L	6-3	245	8-25-87	.182	.250	.143	10	33	5	6	0	0	2	7	2	0	0	0	4	0	0	.364	.129
Othman, Sharif	B-R	6-0	195	3-23-89	.250	—	.250	2	4	1	1	0	0	0	1	1	0	0	0	2	0	0	.250	.400
Ozuna, Marcell	R-R	6-1	220	11-12-90	.333	.286	.357	10	42	6	14	3	1	5	15	3	1	0	1	9	1	0	.810	.383
Perio, Noah	L-R	6-0	170	11-14-91	.232	.128	.269	57	177	20	41	7	0	1	14	16	1	1	1	27	2	0	.288	.297
Pertusati, Danny	R-R	6-1	185	4-27-90	.210	.208	.211	92	252	27	53	10	3	6	38	17	3	1	3	45	2	3	.345	.265
Realmuto, J.T.	R-R	6-1	205	3-18-91	.239	.217	.248	106	368	41	88	21	3	5	39	36	5	0	7	68	9	1	.353	.310
Smolinski, Jake	R-R	5-11	185	2-9-89	.196	.273	.178	24	56	8	11	1	0	0	4	13	1	0	0	10	1	0	.214	.357
Yelich, Christian	L-R	6-1	195	12-5-91	.280	.194	.321	49	193	33	54	13	6	7	29	32	5	2	5	55	2	5	.518	.365

Pitching	B-T	HT	WT	DOB	W	L	ERA	G	GS	CG	SV	IP	H	R	ER	HR	BB	SO	AVG	vLH	vRH	K/9	BB/9
Alvarez, Henderson	R-R	6-0	210	4-18-90	1	0	0.00	2	2	0	0	14	9	0	0	0	0	13	.106	.125	.087	8.16	0.00
Andrelczyk, Pete	R-R	6-1	185	11-10-85	0	1	3.10	16	0	0	2	20	19	8	7	1	6	15	.244	.364	.156	6.64	2.66

Brady, Mike	R-R	6-0	215	3-21-87	2	2	1.53	49	0	0	23	53	42	12	9	2	9	55	.216	.263	.184	9.34	1.53
Caminero, Arquimedes	R-R	6-4	255	6-16-87	5	2	3.61	42	0	0	5	52	34	23	21	4	21	68	.183	.244	.135	11.69	3.61
Cargill, Collin	R-R	6-2	190	10-6-87	4	1	1.61	38	0	0	0	56	29	13	10	2	15	27	.158	.172	.150	4.34	2.41
Conley, Adam	L-L	6-3	185	5-24-90	11	7	3.25	26	25	3	0	139	125	61	50	7	37	129	.236	.226	.239	8.37	2.40
Conley, Jordan	R-R	6-1	180	7-19-86	1	1	5.51	12	0	0	0	16	16	13	10	5	8	15	.242	.250	.238	8.27	4.41
Dayton, Grant	L-L	6-2	205	11-25-87	4	4	2.37	30	0	0	1	38	33	10	10	4	12	56	.226	.140	.262	13.26	2.84
DeSclafani, Anthony	R-R	6-2	195	4-18-90	5	4	3.36	13	13	0	0	75	74	31	28	7	14	62	.263	.252	.273	7.44	1.68
Dyson, Sam	R-R	6-1	210	5-7-88	3	7	2.63	16	15	0	0	75	72	36	22	0	23	41	.254	.261	.248	4.90	2.75
Eovaldi, Nate	R-R	6-2	210	2-13-90	1	0	5.40	3	3	0	0	12	13	7	7	0	4	9	.289	.286	.292	6.94	3.09
Evans, Bryan	R-R	6-3	205	2-25-87	7	5	3.32	21	11	1	1	79	75	33	29	9	7	81	.245	.235	.253	9.27	0.80
Flynn, Brian	L-L	6-7	240	4-19-90	1	1	1.57	4	4	0	0	23	18	4	4	2	3	25	.222	.185	.241	9.78	1.17
Heaney, Andrew	L-L	6-2	190	6-5-91	4	1	2.94	6	6	1	0	34	31	11	11	2	9	23	.242	.300	.224	6.15	2.41
Jackson, Jay	R-R	6-1	195	10-27-87	3	6	3.16	14	14	0	0	80	59	32	28	6	22	73	.203	.216	.196	8.25	2.49
Lazo, Raudel	L-L	5-9	165	4-12-89	1	0	0.00	5	0	0	1	7	3	0	0	0	1	9	.130	.111	.143	11.57	1.29
Leverton, James	R-L	6-2	185	5-13-86	1	1	5.85	11	1	0	0	20	22	14	13	2	2	19	.289	.211	.316	8.55	0.90
McGough, Scott	R-R	6-0	170	10-31-89	4	3	2.63	36	0	0	1	62	48	21	18	4	18	56	.209	.272	.174	8.17	2.63
Morey, Robert	R-R	6-1	185	11-27-88	4	8	5.31	20	20	2	0	103	119	65	61	10	41	69	.292	.280	.303	6.01	3.57
Neil, Matthew	R-R	6-6	225	9-5-86	2	2	3.05	15	10	0	0	59	57	24	20	3	15	49	.253	.299	.212	7.47	2.29
Nicolino, Justin	L-L	6-3	190	11-22-91	3	2	4.96	9	9	1	0	45	63	29	25	2	12	31	.341	.425	.317	6.15	2.38
Ojala, Mike	R-R	6-3	195	8-24-87	1	1	6.12	16	1	0	0	25	36	17	17	3	12	15	.346	.432	.283	5.40	4.32
Olmos, Edgar	L-L	6-4	215	4-12-90	4	2	2.50	38	0	0	1	50	47	20	14	1	27	41	.244	.260	.238	7.33	4.83
Ravago, Robert	R-R	6-1	180	9-4-90	0	0	9.00	1	0	0	0	1	2	1	1	0	2	1	.400	.000	.400	9.00	18.00
Varner, Rett	R-R	6-4	185	2-3-88	1	1	5.25	10	0	0	0	12	17	8	7	3	3	10	.333	.313	.343	7.50	2.25
Waite, Rob	R-R	6-3	210	1-9-87	0	1	4.63	6	2	0	0	12	14	6	6	0	6	7	.298	.235	.333	5.40	4.63
Wittgren, Nick	R-R	6-3	210	5-29-91	0	0	0.00	4	0	0	1	4	0	0	0	0	0	4	.000	.000	.000	9.00	0.00

Fielding

Catcher	PCT	G	PO	A	E	DP	PB
Barnes	1.000	11	75	8	0	1	0
Krick	.988	26	159	12	2	3	4
Mathis	1.000	3	26	1	0	0	1
Othman	1.000	1	5	1	0	0	0
Realmuto	.990	100	769	52	8	7	12

First Base	PCT	G	PO	A	E	DP
Canha	.992	111	899	71	8	71
Ciriaco	1.000	2	7	1	0	0
Cox	1.000	3	19	4	0	0
Dudley	1.000	10	72	4	0	6
Fisher	1.000	6	45	4	0	2
Krick	1.000	4	22	1	0	2
Morrison	1.000	7	53	6	0	3
Perio	1.000	1	8	0	0	0
Pertusati	1.000	1	7	0	0	0

Second Base	PCT	G	PO	A	E	DP
Barnes	1.000	4	12	12	0	2
Black	.964	13	19	34	2	8
Dietrich	.976	51	90	114	5	21
Gutierrez	.955	29	49	58	5	14
Perio	.964	53	90	127	8	21

Third Base	PCT	G	PO	A	E	DP
Burg	1.000	3	2	4	0	1
Ciriaco	1.000	32	16	49	0	7
Cox	.919	67	25	89	10	6
Dietrich	.955	8	7	14	1	2
Fisher	.924	33	10	63	6	6
Gutierrez	1.000	7	5	11	0	0
Krick	.000	2	0	0	1	0

Shortstop	PCT	G	PO	A	E	DP
Black	.939	66	78	185	17	27
Ciriaco	.959	39	40	102	6	17

	PCT	G	PO	A	E	DP
Gutierrez	.930	38	37	96	10	13
McClure	.917	3	3	8	1	4

Outfield	PCT	G	PO	A	E	DP
Black	1.000	13	22	2	0	0
Burg	1.000	6	14	3	0	0
Canha	.962	12	24	1	1	0
Ciriaco	1.000	3	1	0	0	0
Fisher	.889	8	8	0	1	0
Galloway	1.000	36	77	1	0	0
Gutierrez	1.000	2	5	1	0	0
Jensen	.973	65	101	6	3	1
Keys	.895	8	17	0	2	0
Main	.975	63	110	5	3	1
Marisnick	.969	67	152	6	5	0
Ozuna	1.000	10	17	0	0	0
Pertusati	.984	71	116	4	2	0
Smolinski	1.000	17	25	0	0	0
Yelich	.989	48	87	3	1	0

JUPITER HAMMERHEADS   HIGH CLASS A

FLORIDA STATE LEAGUE

Batting	B-T	HT	WT	DOB	AVG	vLH	vRH	G	AB	R	H	2B	3B	HR	RBI	BB	HBP	SH	SF	SO	SB	CS	SLG	OBP
Adams, Josh	R-R	5-11	185	3-7-89	.218	.165	.252	79	248	20	54	8	0	5	31	20	1	1	1	56	3	1	.310	.278
Barnes, Austin	R-R	5-10	190	12-28-89	.260	.241	.269	98	350	42	91	15	1	4	38	52	10	0	5	59	5	2	.343	.367
Brown, Brandon	R-R	6-3	200	6-5-91	.125	.000	.167	4	8	0	1	0	0	0	0	0	0	0	0	0	0	0	.125	.125
Burg, Alex	R-R	6-0	190	8-9-87	.266	.276	.260	58	203	29	54	10	1	4	32	22	2	1	1	58	0	1	.384	.342
Cabrera, Yordy	R-R	6-1	205	9-3-90	.237	.175	.270	30	114	12	27	5	0	1	17	7	1	0	0	29	0	0	.307	.287
Coghlan, Chris	L-R	6-0	195	6-18-85	.185	.154	.214	9	27	1	5	0	1	0	2	1	0	0	0	6	0	0	.259	.214
Cordova, Rehiner	B-R	6-0	150	1-11-94	.200	.333	.143	3	10	0	2	0	0	0	0	0	0	0	0	2	0	0	.200	.200
Dayleg, Terrence	R-R	6-0	170	9-19-87	.250	—	.250	3	4	0	1	1	0	0	0	1	0	0	0	1	0	0	.500	.400
Fisher, Ryan	L-R	6-3	195	4-24-88	.294	.250	.316	69	255	43	75	21	2	4	28	25	9	0	4	71	2	2	.439	.372
Flynn, Cameron	L-R	6-0	195	2-24-90	.250	.000	.333	1	4	0	1	0	0	0	0	0	0	0	0	1	0	0	.500	.250
Galloway, Isaac	R-R	6-2	190	10-10-89	.271	.252	.280	89	347	39	94	24	4	5	40	12	3	5	5	73	26	11	.406	.297
Gimenez, Wilfredo	R-R	5-11	235	12-18-90	.237	.202	.257	80	278	23	66	16	1	0	33	10	3	3	3	52	1	0	.302	.269
Goetz, Ryan	L-R	5-10	185	5-16-88	.218	.190	.229	92	294	29	64	7	4	0	22	28	0	4	3	66	6	2	.269	.283
Hechavarria, Adeiny	R-R	6-0	185	4-15-89	.429	.000	.500	2	7	0	3	1	0	0	1	2	0	0	0	1	1	0	.571	.556
Keys, Brent	L-R	6-1	210	11-9-90	.346	.319	.362	95	381	57	132	14	0	2	33	46	2	3	2	26	13	9	.399	.418
Kotchman, Casey	L-L	6-3	220	2-22-83	.295	.320	.278	18	61	7	18	4	0	0	8	7	1	0	0	7	0	0	.361	.377
Lopez, Alfredo	R-R	5-10	160	10-7-89	.297	.254	.317	59	209	29	62	8	1	1	17	25	4	0	3	31	5	3	.359	.378
Mahoney, Joe	L-L	6-6	245	2-1-87	.303	.357	.263	9	33	4	10	1	0	2	2	1	0	0	0	9	0	0	.515	.324
Main, Michael	R-R	6-1	170	12-14-88	.250	.250	.417	3	13	4	5	0	0	0	2	0	0	0	0	3	1	0	.385	.385
Marisnick, Jake	R-R	6-3	225	3-30-91	.200	.000	.214	3	15	2	3	1	0	0	0	0	0	0	0	1	0	0	.267	.200
Mathis, Jeff	R-R	6-0	205	3-31-83	.286	.500	.125	4	14	1	4	2	0	0	4	1	1	0	0	4	0	0	.429	.375
McIntyre, Ryan	L-R	6-2	195	5-26-90	.269	.290	.250	23	67	6	18	3	1	0	8	8	1	0	1	15	3	2	.343	.342
Morrison, Logan	L-L	6-3	245	8-25-87	.174	.250	.091	6	23	0	4	0	0	0	3	4	0	0	0	0	0	1	.174	.296
Nola, Austin	R-R	6-0	180	12-28-89	.232	.287	.199	124	413	39	96	22	3	1	40	54	8	12	2	92	6	3	.308	.331

Player	B-T	HT	WT	DOB	AVG	vLH	vRH	G	AB	R	H	2B	3B	HR	RBI	BB	HBP	SH	SF	SO	SB	CS	OBP	SLG
Othman, Sharif	B-R	6-0	195	3-23-89	.250	.200	.294	8	32	5	8	3	0	2	8	2	0	1	0	3	1	0	.531	.294
Ozuna, Marcell	R-R	6-1	220	11-12-90	.267	.400	.200	4	15	1	4	1	0	0	1	0	0	0	0	4	1	0	.333	.267
Perez, Yefri	R-R	5-11	162	2-24-91	.111	.000	.250	4	9	1	1	0	0	0	1	0	0	0	0	2	0	0	.111	.111
Perio, Noah	L-R	6-0	170	11-14-91	.241	.207	.260	43	162	17	39	4	0	0	16	10	0	4	2	12	6	2	.265	.282
Pertusati, Danny	R-R	6-1	185	4-27-90	.132	.222	.086	15	53	6	7	0	0	1	5	5	0	0	1	9	1	0	.189	.203
Rieger, Ryan	L-L	6-2	205	8-10-90	.257	.215	.276	119	421	52	108	13	4	7	38	48	3	4	3	78	7	3	.356	.335
Senne, Aaron	L-L	6-2	180	11-5-87	.080	.000	.133	8	25	1	2	0	0	0	0	1	0	1	0	8	0	0	.080	.115
Smith, Matt	R-R	6-3	230	12-13-87	.216	.250	.185	14	51	5	11	1	0	0	1	2	0	0	0	20	0	0	.235	.245
Solano, Donovan	R-R	5-9	195	12-17-87	.429	.571	.286	4	14	0	6	1	0	0	1	0	0	0	0	2	0	0	.500	.429
Stanton, Giancarlo	R-R	6-6	240	11-8-89	.000	.000	.000	5	15	0	0	0	0	0	0	2	0	0	0	5	1	0	.000	.118
Valaika, Chris	R-R	5-11	210	8-14-85	.200	.111	.226	11	40	3	8	1	0	1	4	2	1	0	0	6	0	1	.300	.256
Vaughn, Michael	R-R	6-2	190	12-19-90	.143	.143	.143	5	14	0	2	1	0	0	3	0	0	0	0	5	0	0	.214	.143
Vigil, Rodrigo	R-R	6-0	164	1-3-93	.000	—	.000	2	4	0	0	0	0	0	0	0	0	0	0	0	0	0	.000	.000
Wilson, Ross	R-R	5-11	185	11-9-88	.222	.248	.205	97	311	34	69	7	3	1	16	29	8	6	3	68	5	4	.273	.302
Yelich, Christian	L-R	6-4	195	12-5-91	.231	.214	.250	7	26	3	6	0	0	2	4	4	0	0	0	8	0	0	.462	.333

Pitching	B-T	HT	WT	DOB	W	L	ERA	G	GS	CG	SV	IP	H	R	ER	HR	BB	SO	AVG	vLH	vRH	K/9	BB/9
Alvarez, Henderson	R-R	6-0	210	4-18-90	1	0	2.70	2	2	0	0	10	9	3	3	1	1	2	.250	.313	.200	1.80	0.90
Alvis, Sam	R-R	6-0	195	6-11-90	0	1	9.00	2	0	0	0	3	1	3	3	0	3	1	.125	.000	.143	3.00	9.00
Andrelczyk, Pete	R-R	6-1	185	11-10-85	1	2	2.55	11	0	0	2	18	14	6	5	3	5	21	.209	.182	.222	10.70	2.55
Barnes, Blake	R-R	6-1	180	7-9-90	3	1	5.76	17	0	0	1	25	29	16	16	4	10	18	.290	.243	.317	6.48	3.60
Cargill, Collin	R-R	6-2	190	10-6-87	0	0	0.00	5	0	0	0	7	4	2	0	0	1	6	.154	.286	.105	7.36	1.23
Ceda, Jose	R-R	6-5	280	1-28-87	0	1	22.50	3	0	0	0	2	6	7	5	0	2	3	.500	.500	.500	13.50	9.00
Conley, Jordan	R-R	6-1	180	7-19-86	1	0	0.63	13	0	0	4	14	9	1	1	1	5	17	.180	.231	.162	10.67	3.14
Cravey, Kevin	R-R	6-1	180	8-15-87	3	4	4.66	40	1	0	0	58	61	36	30	2	28	52	.279	.319	.259	8.07	4.34
Del Pozo, Miguel	L-L	6-1	180	10-14-92	0	0	0.00	2	0	0	0	2	1	2	0	0	2	0	.125	.500	.000	0.00	9.00
DeSclafani, Anthony	R-R	6-2	195	4-18-90	4	2	1.67	12	12	0	0	54	48	18	10	3	9	53	.236	.198	.265	8.83	1.50
Donatello, Sean	R-R	6-2	205	8-24-90	0	3	11.12	9	0	0	0	11	26	16	14	1	3	8	.464	.500	.444	6.35	2.38
Easley, Josh	R-R	6-3	190	12-9-90	0	0	0.00	1	0	0	0	2	1	0	0	1	3	0	.000	.000	.000	13.50	4.50
Effertz, Joel	R-R	6-2	235	9-27-90	0	1	6.75	2	0	0	0	4	4	4	3	0	2	6	.267	.111	.500	6.75	4.50
Eovaldi, Nate	R-R	6-2	210	2-13-90	0	1	3.00	2	2	0	0	9	9	3	3	1	2	6	.265	.000	.310	6.00	2.00
Esch, Jacob	R-R	6-4	190	3-27-90	2	10	4.69	23	19	0	0	94	99	57	49	5	38	57	.270	.267	.272	5.46	3.64
Fermin, Miguel	R-R	5-11	175	2-11-85	1	1	1.59	18	0	0	0	28	24	5	5	2	5	20	.235	.282	.206	6.35	1.59
Heaney, Andrew	L-L	6-2	190	6-5-91	5	2	0.88	13	12	0	0	62	45	11	6	2	17	66	.193	.229	.184	9.63	2.48
Higgins, Tyler	R-R	6-3	215	4-22-91	2	7	4.01	45	0	0	0	58	63	35	26	5	26	64	.268	.345	.223	9.87	4.01
Hodges, Josh	R-R	6-7	235	6-21-91	4	6	3.60	27	22	0	0	132	130	64	53	9	31	84	.260	.303	.236	5.71	2.11
Jackson, Justin	R-R	6-4	201	12-14-88	0	0	45.00	1	0	0	0	1	6	5	5	1	0	1	.667	1.000	.400	9.00	0.00
Lyman, Scott	R-R	6-4	215	3-21-90	3	2	3.62	6	6	0	0	32	30	14	13	0	16	15	.246	.304	.211	4.18	4.45
McCarthy, Casey	R-R	6-4	215	4-13-90	0	0	18.00	1	0	0	0	2	6	4	4	0	0	0	.600	1.000	.556	0.00	0.00
Merkling, Patrick	L-L	6-1	165	3-21-91	1	0	5.06	7	0	0	0	11	10	6	6	0	5	9	.238	.125	.308	7.59	4.22
Nappo, Greg	L-L	6-0	190	8-25-88	5	1	1.15	36	0	0	1	55	42	8	7	0	9	56	.210	.208	.211	9.16	1.47
Nicolino, Justin	L-L	6-3	190	11-22-91	5	2	2.23	18	18	1	0	97	89	27	24	4	18	64	.247	.237	.249	5.96	1.68
Nygren, James	R-R	6-0	195		7	4	3.26	38	1	0	0	58	64	24	21	2	11	27	.281	.296	.272	4.19	1.71
O'Gara, Joey	R-R	6-7	205	4-20-88	0	1	6.30	7	0	0	0	10	16	9	7	2	4	5	.381	.412	.360	4.50	3.60
Ojala, Mike	R-R	6-3	195	8-24-87	0	0	0.00	2	0	0	0	2	0	0	0	0	0	4	.000	.000	.000	18.00	0.00
Ravago, Robert	R-R	6-1	180	9-4-90	0	1	6.75	9	0	0	0	11	16	8	8	1	6	10	.364	.333	.379	8.44	5.06
Reed, Frankie	L-L	6-1	185	2-2-88	1	0	0.75	10	0	0	0	12	13	1	1	0	5	9	.289	.071	.387	6.75	3.75
Rogers, Jared	R-R	6-7	202	5-9-88	1	2	2.68	9	6	0	0	40	40	14	12	1	6	20	.258	.313	.234	4.46	1.34
Sanchez, Angel	R-R	6-3	177	11-28-89	4	3	3.22	10	10	1	0	50	45	19	18	5	21	42	.233	.217	.242	7.51	3.75
Suggs, Colby	R-R	5-11	230	10-25-91	1	3	3.93	14	0	0	0	18	9	8	8	0	14	26	.141	.167	.125	12.76	6.87
Urena, Jose	R-R	6-3	172	9-12-91	10	7	3.73	27	26	0	0	150	148	69	62	8	29	107	.257	.274	.247	6.43	1.74
Waite, Rob	R-R	6-3	210	1-9-87	1	0	2.70	2	0	0	0	3	2	1	1	0	1	3	.200	.200	.200	8.10	2.70
Wittgren, Nick	R-R	6-3	210	5-29-91	2	1	0.83	48	0	0	25	54	42	7	5	1	10	59	.211	.250	.191	9.77	1.66

Fielding

Catcher	PCT	G	PO	A	E	DP	PB
Adams	—	1	0	0	0	0	0
Barnes	.987	64	412	34	6	3	5
Brown	1.000	4	21	1	0	0	0
Burg	1.000	1	2	0	0	0	0
Gimenez	.988	61	435	41	6	2	7
Mathis	1.000	3	14	1	0	0	0
Othman	1.000	7	52	3	0	0	1
Vaughn	1.000	4	14	2	0	1	0
Vigil	1.000	1	2	0	0	0	0

First Base	PCT	G	PO	A	E	DP
Adams	.992	12	113	6	1	11
Burg	1.000	4	20	1	0	5
Fisher	.976	6	39	2	1	4
Gimenez	1.000	5	26	5	0	3
Kotchman	.986	10	64	5	1	7
Mahoney	1.000	8	73	7	0	5
Morrison	.969	3	27	4	1	2
Rieger	.991	90	735	42	7	57
Smith	.974	12	111	2	3	9

	PCT	G	PO	A	E	DP
Valaika	1.000	2	13	1	0	1

Second Base	PCT	G	PO	A	E	DP
Dayleg	1.000	3	2	6	0	0
Goetz	.917	13	13	31	4	9
Lopez	.979	21	39	55	2	13
Perez	1.000	1	3	1	0	0
Perio	.974	41	86	103	5	22
Solano	1.000	1	3	0	0	0
Valaika	1.000	1	1	1	0	0
Wilson	.983	64	114	168	5	37

Third Base	PCT	G	PO	A	E	DP
Adams	.875	56	22	104	18	7
Burg	.500	1	0	1	1	0
Cabrera	.963	10	8	18	1	0
Coghlan	.833	6	3	2	1	0
Fisher	.933	54	35	117	11	14
Goetz	.950	12	3	16	1	1
Lopez	.909	4	1	9	1	0
Solano	1.000	2	0	4	0	0
Valaika	.875	3	0	7	1	0

	PCT	G	PO	A	E	DP
Wilson	—	1	0	0	0	0

Shortstop	PCT	G	PO	A	E	DP
Cordova	1.000	2	5	3	0	2
Goetz	1.000	8	17	24	0	6
Hechavarria	1.000	2	2	2	0	1
Lopez	1.000	6	5	6	0	1
Nola	.974	122	165	390	15	68
Solano	1.000	1	2	2	0	0
Valaika	1.000	3	5	8	0	2

Outfield	PCT	G	PO	A	E	DP
Burg	.963	40	72	5	3	3
Cabrera	.938	14	29	1	2	0
Flynn	1.000	1	2	0	0	0
Galloway	.973	87	176	7	5	2
Goetz	.969	55	122	2	4	0
Keys	.971	95	187	12	6	2
Lopez	.980	23	49	1	1	0
Main	1.000	3	5	0	0	0
Marisnick	1.000	3	7	0	0	0
McIntyre	1.000	19	43	1	0	1

Ozuna	1.000	4	6	0	0	0
Perez	1.000	2	6	0	0	0
Pertusati	1.000	15	27	1	0	0
Rieger	.969	22	30	1	1	0
Senne	1.000	7	6	0	0	0
Stanton	1.000	4	8	0	0	0
Wilson	.962	27	50	1	2	0
Yelich	1.000	6	7	0	0	0

GREENSBORO GRASSHOPPERS

LOW CLASS A

SOUTH ATLANTIC LEAGUE

Batting	B-T	HT	WT	DOB	AVG	vLH	vRH	G	AB	R	H	2B	3B	HR	RBI	BB	HBP	SH	SF	SO	SB	CS	SLG	OBP
Barber, Blake	R-R	5-10	180	4-4-90	.286	.397	.233	53	192	29	55	14	1	8	30	10	2	2	2	47	1	1	.495	.325
Behar, Jose	R-R	6-1	200	4-30-89	.202	.222	.193	36	119	12	24	6	0	2	13	7	4	3	2	28	0	1	.303	.265
Bohn, Justin	R-R	6-0	180	11-2-92	.250	.200	.286	12	48	5	12	1	0	0	2	4	0	2	0	12	4	0	.271	.308
Cabrera, Yordy	R-R	6-1	205	9-3-90	.237	.210	.246	91	337	55	80	13	1	13	45	28	11	0	2	78	5	2	.398	.315
Caldwell, Tony	R-R	5-10	195	12-2-88	.182	.178	.183	54	165	21	30	8	2	3	23	18	6	5	3	49	1	1	.309	.281
Cordova, Rehiner	B-R	6-0	150	1-11-94	.220	.143	.250	20	50	5	11	1	1	0	3	4	0	1	0	17	0	0	.280	.278
Dean, Austin	R-R	6-1	190	10-14-93	.200	.167	.214	7	20	4	4	1	0	1	3	4	1	0	1	5	0	0	.400	.346
Flynn, Cameron	L-R	6-0	195	2-24-90	.308	.204	.347	97	357	49	110	17	5	7	44	32	3	3	1	62	2	2	.443	.369
Gomez, Anthony	R-R	6-0	190	11-26-90	.271	.290	.265	117	447	61	121	14	1	5	55	23	4	15	6	45	12	5	.340	.308
Hernandez, Yeison	B-R	5-10	150	6-29-92	.253	.259	.252	54	182	23	46	7	0	0	18	13	1	2	2	18	3	2	.291	.303
Juengel, Matt	R-R	6-2	185	1-13-90	.270	.345	.244	123	444	61	120	22	1	14	63	40	11	0	4	56	6	4	.419	.343
Keefer, Cody	L-R	6-1	185	11-6-90	.240	.174	.258	97	325	32	78	16	2	4	39	35	4	2	3	74	1	1	.338	.319
Lopez, Alfredo	R-R	5-10	160	10-7-89	.216	.147	.250	30	102	11	22	6	0	0	7	8	0	2	1	14	2	2	.275	.270
Main, Michael	R-R	6-1	170	12-14-88	.228	.389	.189	23	92	10	21	3	0	1	7	6	1	3	0	24	4	2	.293	.283
Martinez, Juancito	R-R	6-1	170	6-10-89	.223	.235	.217	60	229	33	51	7	3	2	19	14	3	2	0	54	26	9	.306	.276
McClure, Alex	B-R	6-0	185	6-16-89	.185	.222	.167	8	27	3	5	1	0	0	2	2	0	1	0	9	0	0	.222	.241
Moran, Colin	L-R	6-4	190	10-1-92	.299	.267	.319	42	154	19	46	8	1	4	23	15	1	0	5	25	1	0	.442	
.354 Othman, Sharif	B-R	6-0	195	3-23-89	.167	.286	.146	17	48	5	8	2	0	2	4	5	1	2	0	13	0	0	.333	.259
Perez, Yefri	R-R	5-11	162	2-24-91	.196	.222	.190	13	51	7	10	2	1	0	7	4	0	0	0	4	8	1	.275	.255
Romero, Avery	R-R	5-11	195	5-11-93	.147	.100	.167	9	34	5	5	1	0	0	5	4	0	2	0	5	0	0	.265	.237
Rosa, Viosergy	L-L	6-3	185	6-16-90	.252	.223	.261	133	465	68	117	22	1	23	69	74	8	0	2	119	3	1	.452	.362
Solorzano, Jesus	R-R	6-0	190	8-8-90	.285	.296	.281	129	484	72	138	29	3	15	66	24	7	3	5	111	33	4	.450	.325
Vaughn, Michael	R-R	6-2	190	12-19-90	.211	.267	.190	34	109	12	23	5	1	3	10	9	0	2	0	30	0	0	.358	.271
Wilson, Ross	R-R	5-11	185	11-9-88	.364	.250	.429	4	11	4	4	1	0	0	2	2	1	0	0	2	0	0	.455	.500

Pitching	B-T	HT	WT	DOB	W	L	ERA	G	GS	CG	SV	IP	H	R	ER	HR	BB	SO	AVG	vLH	vRH	K/9	BB/9
Barnes, Blake	R-R	6-1	180	7-9-90	1	1	0.90	14	0	0	7	20	8	2	2	1	4	22	.125	.143	.111	9.90	1.80
Beltre, Andy	R-R	6-4	195	7-6-93	0	1	7.20	2	0	0	0	5	5	4	4	1	2	8	.263	.273	.250	14.40	3.60
Brice, Austin	R-R	6-4	205	6-19-92	8	11	5.73	26	23	0	0	113	118	84	72	11	82	111	.268	.288	.247	8.84	6.53
Del Orbe, Ramon	R-R	5-11	190	2-17-92	5	8	4.75	23	23	0	0	116	139	75	61	13	41	77	.296	.338	.262	5.99	3.19
Donatello, Sean	R-R	6-2	205	8-24-90	2	1	1.11	14	0	0	0	24	12	4	3	1	9	20	.148	.091	.188	7.40	3.33
Ellington, Brian	R-R	6-4	200	8-4-90	3	2	4.64	16	2	0	0	43	40	26	22	3	23	27	.250	.250	.250	5.70	4.85
Fermin, Miguel	R-R	5-11	175	2-11-85	0	2	3.30	22	0	0	1	30	35	13	11	2	4	33	.285	.271	.297	9.90	1.20
Hope, Mason	R-R	6-3	190	6-27-92	6	6	4.94	26	17	0	1	98	100	73	54	12	53	73	.263	.278	.250	6.68	4.85
Jackson, Justin	R-R	6-4	201	12-14-88	1	0	0.00	1	0	0	0	5	4	0	0	0	3	2	.222	.286	.000	3.60	5.40
James, Chad	L-L	6-4	180	1-23-91	2	6	5.74	13	13	0	0	53	57	37	34	6	28	57	.278	.360	.252	9.62	4.73
Logan, Blake	R-R	6-1	245	1-12-92	2	6	5.01	41	0	0	11	59	57	37	33	9	20	67	.253	.295	.223	10.16	3.03
Lyman, Scott	R-R	6-4	215	3-21-90	4	6	4.11	20	20	0	0	105	101	53	48	11	37	102	.251	.274	.234	8.74	3.17
Manzueta, Jheyson	R-R	6-2	162	12-5-89	4	5	3.08	39	0	0	2	79	62	38	27	7	22	66	.213	.230	.201	7.52	2.51
Milroy, Matt	L-R	6-2	185	10-5-90	2	0	5.49	17	9	0	0	57	63	41	35	5	33	59	.276	.297	.255	9.26	5.18
Oliver, Dejai	R-R	6-2	200	8-28-90	6	4	4.77	20	18	0	0	100	103	56	53	16	38	78	.260	.242	.277	7.02	3.42
Ravago, Robert	R-R	6-1	180	9-4-90	0	0	0.00	3	0	0	0	7	2	0	0	0	2	4	.095	.091	.100	5.40	2.70
Reed, Frankie	L-L	6-1	185	2-12-88	5	0	0.60	36	0	0	12	45	26	6	3	1	17	40	.167	.143	.180	8.06	3.43
Reyes, Helpi	R-R	6-1	200	7-27-92	0	2	3.86	14	1	0	0	28	28	12	12	3	14	16	.269	.321	.216	5.14	4.50
Smith, Chipper	L-L	6-2	195	1-22-90	8	3	2.74	34	6	0	2	89	70	34	27	7	33	98	.223	.196	.234	9.95	3.35
Steckenrider, Drew	R-R	6-5	215	1-10-91	1	1	4.58	5	4	0	0	20	15	14	10	2	10	28	.205	.172	.227	12.81	4.58
Stone, Dane	R-R	6-7	225	6-14-91	5	5	4.92	32	0	0	2	53	57	39	29	10	16	61	.264	.272	.259	10.36	2.72
Williams, Trevor	R-R	6-3	228	4-25-92	0	0	0.00	1	0	0	0	3	2	0	0	0	0	3	.182	.222	.000	9.00	0.00
Wright, Beau	L-L	6-2	255	1-2-91	2	0	2.36	14	0	0	0	27	19	8	7	1	10	18	.207	.250	.183	6.08	3.38

Fielding

Catcher	PCT	G	PO	A	E	DP	PB
Behar	.991	36	292	41	3	2	5
Caldwell	.988	54	437	45	6	2	3
Othman	.983	17	105	12	2	0	0
Vaughn	.978	34	211	16	5	2	7

First Base	PCT	G	PO	A	E	DP
Juengel	.992	30	220	19	2	22
Rosa	.986	109	918	61	14	67

Second Base	PCT	G	PO	A	E	DP
Barber	.963	40	83	97	7	22
Cordova	.947	12	15	21	2	5
Gomez	.977	21	39	47	2	9
Hernandez	.982	30	70	95	3	26

	PCT	G	PO	A	E	DP	PB
Lopez	.965	27	42	69	4	9	
McClure	1.000	4	4	9	0	3	
Romero	.943	9	13	20	2	5	
Wilson	.750	1	2	1	1	0	

Third Base	PCT	G	PO	A	E	DP
Cabrera	.888	72	42	109	19	6
Cordova	—	1	0	0	0	0
Juengel	.904	31	19	56	8	1
Lopez	—	1	0	0	0	0
Moran	.927	34	22	54	6	3
Wilson	1.000	1	1	2	0	0

Shortstop	PCT	G	PO	A	E	DP
Bohn	1.000	12	19	28	0	5

	PCT	G	PO	A	E	DP
Cordova	.917	7	8	14	2	3
Gomez	.966	94	117	277	14	50
Hernandez	.952	23	23	56	4	7
McClure	1.000	4	5	11	0	3

Outfield	PCT	G	PO	A	E	DP
Barber	1.000	10	7	1	0	0
Dean	1.000	7	10	0	0	0
Flynn	.977	95	165	8	4	1
Keefer	.973	92	139	4	4	0
Main	1.000	22	59	1	0	1
Martinez	.970	60	124	5	4	1
Perez	.960	13	22	2	1	0
Solorzano	.966	122	245	9	9	2

NEW YORK-PENN LEAGUE

Batting	B-T	HT	WT	DOB	AVG	vLH	vRH	G	AB	R	H	2B	3B	HR	RBI	BB	HBP	SH	SF	SO	SB	CS	SLG	OBP
Aper, Ryan	R-R	6-3	175	6-6-93	.122	.063	.152	17	49	3	6	1	1	1	6	6	3	1	0	23	1	1	.245	.259
Avila, Juan	R-R	6-1	180	10-18-91	.190	.222	.182	12	42	6	8	2	0	0	3	1	2	0	1	7	0	0	.238	.239
Barber, Blake	R-R	5-10	180	4-4-90	.750	1.000	.000	1	4	2	3	0	0	1	2	0	0	0	0	0	0	0	1.500	.750
Behar, Jose	R-R	6-1	200	4-30-89	.000	.000	.000	2	6	1	0	0	0	0	0	1	0	0	0	2	0	0	.000	.143
Blanton, Aaron	R-R	6-2	175	9-1-93	.286	.000	.400	2	7	1	2	1	0	0	0	0	0	0	0	3	0	0	.429	.286
Bohn, Justin	R-R	6-0	180	11-2-92	.177	.121	.194	40	141	12	25	4	0	0	8	15	5	1	1	32	4	2	.206	.278
Burke, Connor	R-R	6-1	195	8-20-92	.149	.095	.174	25	67	5	10	2	1	0	8	7	1	1	1	21	1	0	.209	.237
Carcaise, Scott	L-L	6-5	230	5-13-92	.229	.250	.222	35	118	14	27	7	1	3	19	19	4	0	1	46	0	0	.381	.352
Castillo, Felix	R-R	5-1	170	7-16-91	.160	.238	.130	22	75	3	12	3	0	1	6	5	1	0	0	13	0	0	.240	.222
Castro, Victor	R-R	6-1	198	1-10-92	.133	.000	.167	4	15	0	2	0	0	0	0	0	0	0	0	2	0	0	.133	.133
Ceballos, Jose	R-R	6-0	190	12-27-88	.323	.462	.222	10	31	3	10	2	0	0	4	0	2	0	1	6	0	0	.387	.353
Cordova, Rehiner	B-R	6-0	150	1-11-94	.237	.231	.240	12	38	5	9	3	0	0	0	10	5	0	2	2	12	2	0	.316	.311
Dean, Austin	R-R	6-1	190	10-14-93	.268	.203	.295	56	213	28	57	12	7	2	19	17	1	0	0	47	0	2	.418	.325
Johnson, Coco	R-R	5-11	205	5-3-91	.172	.171	.172	46	134	14	23	1	0	0	8	17	4	1	2	26	1	2	.179	.280
Lopez, Carlos	L-R	6-2	210	7-16-89	.318	.347	.310	61	223	28	71	10	6	0	24	26	0	1	3	32	1	3	.417	.385
Lopez, Javier	R-R	6-3	180	9-13-94	.174	.132	.188	45	155	14	27	4	3	1	13	13	2	0	3	47	1	2	.258	.243
Munoz, Felix	L-L	6-1	193	4-7-92	.301	.261	.316	69	246	33	74	19	0	4	40	28	0	0	4	28	0	2	.427	.367
Ortiz, Luis	B-R	5-10	161	3-14-92	.242	.250	.239	28	91	13	22	3	0	1	12	5	1	0	2	17	9	3	.308	.283
Othman, Sharif	B-R	6-0	195	3-23-89	.200	.500	.125	3	10	1	2	0	0	0	1	2	0	0	0	2	0	0	.200	.333
Perez, Yefri	R-R	5-11	162	2-24-91	.250	.303	.232	31	128	18	32	6	1	3	10	5	1	2	0	18	12	1	.383	.284
Pujols, Wildert	L-L	6-1	175	6-7-94	.275	.250	.286	15	51	6	14	0	0	1	1	1	0	0	0	21	0	0	.275	.288
Riddle, J.T.	L-R	6-3	175	10-12-91	.243	.254	.239	59	222	38	54	10	0	2	18	10	5	4	3	28	6	1	.315	.288
Romero, Avery	R-R	5-11	195	5-11-93	.297	.241	.318	56	209	27	62	18	0	2	30	15	7	0	4	34	3	4	.411	.357
Vaughn, Michael	R-R	6-2	190	12-19-90	.231	.000	.273	9	26	2	6	1	0	0	2	2	0	0	0	8	1	0	.269	.286
Wallach, Chad	R-R	6-3	210	11-4-91	.226	.190	.240	43	146	19	33	6	0	0	13	11	4	0	2	27	0	0	.267	.294

Pitching	B-T	HT	WT	DOB	W	L	ERA	G	GS	CG	SV	IP	H	R	ER	HR	BB	SO	AVG	vLH	vRH	K/9	BB/9
Adames, Jose	R-R	6-2	165	1-17-93	0	0	0.00	2	0	0	0	2	3	0	0	0	1	5	.300	.333	.286	22.50	4.50
Crabaugh, Cody	L-R	6-6	210	12-25-90	1	0	0.00	1	1	0	0	6	2	0	0	0	3	5	.111	.000	.125	7.50	4.50
Del Pozo, Miguel	L-L	6-1	180	10-14-92	2	1	4.81	17	0	0	0	24	24	15	13	1	17	36	.242	.238	.246	13.32	6.29
Donatello, Sean	R-R	6-2	205	8-24-90	0	0	1.29	2	0	0	0	7	4	2	1	1	1	5	.160	.000	.286	6.43	1.29
Easley, Josh	R-R	6-3	190	12-9-90	4	0	0.40	14	0	0	3	23	9	3	1	0	4	30	.118	.069	.149	11.91	1.59
Effertz, Joel	R-R	6-3	235	9-27-90	2	0	2.08	3	2	0	1	13	12	3	3	1	0	14	.235	.267	.222	9.69	0.00
Ellington, Brian	R-R	6-4	200	8-4-90	1	2	3.72	6	1	0	0	19	16	14	8	0	9	21	.222	.212	.231	9.78	4.19
Garcia, Jarlin	L-L	6-2	170	1-18-93	2	3	3.10	15	15	0	0	70	58	31	24	7	18	74	.221	.225	.220	9.56	2.33
Garner, Max	R-R	6-3	200	6-11-90	0	2	1.62	14	14	0	0	44	40	13	8	2	16	30	.244	.266	.224	6.09	3.25
German, Domingo	R-R	6-2	175	8-4-92	2	3	1.76	8	8	0	0	41	33	14	8	0	5	34	.213	.242	.191	7.46	1.10
Jackson, Justin	R-R	6-4	201	12-14-88	7	1	3.83	13	2	0	0	56	55	24	24	2	14	45	.259	.266	.254	7.19	2.24
Kane, Tyler	R-R	6-1	190	8-23-92	0	0	1.93	3	0	0	0	5	5	1	1	1	1	4	.294	.500	.182	7.71	1.93
Kinley, Tyler	R-R	6-4	205	1-31-91	0	0	22.50	1	0	0	0	2	6	5	5	0	1	1	.545	1.000	.444	4.50	4.50
McCarthy, Casey	R-R	6-4	215	4-13-90	2	5	4.11	23	0	0	6	35	41	19	16	1	10	24	.299	.345	.268	6.17	2.57
Merkling, Patrick	L-L	6-1	165	3-21-91	0	0	9.14	16	0	0	1	22	25	26	22	2	12	22	.284	.303	.273	9.14	4.98
Newell, Ryan	R-R	6-2	215	6-18-91	5	4	2.09	14	14	0	0	82	60	30	19	1	21	75	.203	.228	.179	8.23	2.30
Ravago, Robert	R-R	6-1	180	9-4-90	2	1	5.40	12	0	0	1	20	30	14	12	0	10	20	.366	.394	.347	9.00	4.50
Redman, Reid	R-R	6-0	180	11-22-88	2	2	1.91	19	0	0	1	28	24	9	6	1	9	25	.233	.255	.212	7.94	2.86
Reyes, Helpi	R-R	6-1	200	7-27-92	1	5	8.31	7	7	0	0	26	36	25	24	2	16	12	.330	.367	.286	4.15	5.54
Rincon, Junior	R-R	6-2	185	12-7-91	0	0	6.43	5	0	0	0	7	8	7	5	0	2	7	.276	.083	.412	9.00	2.57
Robinson, C.J.	R-R	6-0	215	5-11-93	1	1	1.61	15	0	0	0	22	17	6	4	1	6	24	.207	.188	.220	9.67	2.42
Stone, Dane	R-R	6-7	225	6-14-91	1	1	3.38	10	1	0	2	16	16	6	6	2	2	18	.267	.226	.310	10.13	1.13
Suggs, Colby	R-R	5-11	230	10-25-91	1	0	1.13	7	0	0	3	8	5	2	1	0	2	11	.200	.250	.154	12.38	2.25
Townsley, Sean	L-L	6-7	240	9-19-90	0	1	2.08	7	0	0	1	13	7	3	3	0	0	20	.152	.150	.154	13.85	0.00
Williams, Trevor	R-R	6-3	228	4-25-92	0	2	2.48	10	10	0	0	29	26	13	8	0	8	20	.228	.259	.196	6.21	2.48
Wooster, James	L-L	6-1	200	6-19-89	1	2	11.50	14	0	0	0	18	27	26	23	1	16	18	.338	.387	.306	9.00	8.00
Wright, Beau	L-L	6-2	255	1-2-91	2	0	2.08	3	0	0	0	9	5	2	2	0	6	6	.185	.000	.263	6.23	6.23

Fielding

Catcher	PCT	G	PO	A	E	DP	PB
Behar	1.000	1	5	2	0	0	0
Castillo	.990	22	178	15	2	1	3
Othman	1.000	3	26	2	0	0	0
Vaughn	.984	8	52	8	1	1	2
Wallach	.984	43	330	47	6	2	12

First Base	PCT	G	PO	A	E	DP
Carcaise	.975	10	77	2	2	8
Ceballos	1.000	1	4	0	0	0
Lopez	1.000	3	22	1	0	2
Munoz	.990	65	566	55	6	47

Second Base	PCT	G	PO	A	E	DP
Burke	1.000	1	0	2	0	0
Cordova	.943	12	21	29	3	3
Ortiz	.976	8	16	25	1	6
Riddle	1.000	4	11	9	0	3
Romero	.961	53	70	179	10	35

Third Base	PCT	G	PO	A	E	DP
Avila	.846	11	9	24	6	4
Barber	1.000	1	2	1	0	0
Bohn	.917	8	4	18	2	2
Ortiz	.759	10	8	14	7	3
Riddle	.929	47	22	82	8	9

Shortstop	PCT	G	PO	A	E	DP
Blanton	1.000	2	4	4	0	1
Bohn	.947	28	41	83	7	17
Lopez	.899	38	71	89	18	24
Riddle	.967	8	11	18	1	4

Outfield	PCT	G	PO	A	E	DP
Aper	.926	17	25	0	2	0
Burke	.931	24	25	2	2	0
Carcaise	1.000	7	6	0	0	0
Castro	.625	3	5	0	3	0
Dean	.968	56	88	3	3	1
Johnson	.947	46	67	4	4	0
Lopez	.966	36	51	5	2	3
Perez	.980	30	48	2	1	1
Pujols	.938	15	29	1	2	0

MIAMI MARLINS

GULF COAST LEAGUE

Batting	B-T	HT	WT	DOB	AVG	vLH	vRH	G	AB	R	H	2B	3B	HR	RBI	BB	HBP	SH	SF	SO	SB	CS	SLG	OBP
Aper, Ryan	R-R	6-3	175	6-6-93	.150	.125	.157	31	113	10	17	2	1	1	6	12	3	0	0	35	4	1	.212	.250
Avila, Juan	R-R	6-1	180	10-18-91	.189	.262	.158	42	143	12	27	4	1	1	11	9	5	0	0	23	1	1	.252	.261
Blanton, Aaron	R-R	6-2	175	9-1-93	.250	.281	.240	47	136	13	34	5	0	0	6	27	2	0	2	35	2	2	.287	.377
Brown, Brandon	R-R	6-3	200	6-5-91	.194	.375	.143	12	36	1	7	1	0	0	4	3	0	0	1	1	0	0	.222	.250
Caldwell, Tony	R-R	5-10	195	12-2-88	.471	.500	.462	6	17	4	8	3	0	0	2	2	1	0	0	3	0	0	.647	.550
Castro, Victor	R-R	6-1	198	1-10-92	.286	.129	.341	35	119	12	34	11	0	4	20	9	3	0	1	27	0	1	.479	.348
Cordova, Rehiner	B-R	6-0	150	1-11-94	.091	.000	.105	6	22	1	2	0	0	0	1	2	0	0	0	5	0	1	.091	.167
Cruz, David	R-R	6-0	201	1-23-92	.270	.333	.250	13	37	6	10	0	0	3	8	4	2	0	1	10	0	0	.514	.364
Duran, Carlos	L-R	6-1	192	5-24-92	.257	.261	.256	45	171	13	44	12	1	2	20	8	2	0	0	13	0	0	.374	.298
Hernandez, Yeison	B-R	5-10	150	6-29-92	.216	.200	.220	16	51	4	11	3	1	0	6	3	0	1	0	10	1	0	.314	.259
Jimenez, Joel	R-R	5-11	189	4-30-92	.237	.250	.231	14	38	2	9	3	0	0	3	3	1	0	0	3	0	1	.316	.310
Lasater, Ben	R-R	6-3	225	5-25-84	.250	.200	.267	6	20	3	5	0	0	1	5	2	1	0	0	3	0	0	.400	.348
Martinez, Juancito	R-R	6-1	170	6-10-89	.175	.111	.194	12	40	6	7	1	0	0	4	4	1	0	0	16	1	2	.200	.267
Miller, Ron	R-R	5-11	205	1-7-94	.182	.267	.161	44	154	12	28	6	1	2	8	11	5	0	0	52	1	0	.273	.259
Olivencia, Iramis	R-R	5-9	175	11-6-94	.142	.171	.133	44	148	13	21	3	4	2	14	8	2	1	1	47	0	0	.257	.195
Othman, Sharif	B-R	6-0	195	3-23-89	.313	.500	.200	5	16	2	5	1	0	0	1	1	0	0	0	3	0	0	.375	.353
Pujols, Wildert	L-L	6-1	175	6-7-94	.238	.111	.274	25	80	8	19	3	1	0	7	9	1	0	0	17	1	1	.300	.322
Rivera, Christian	R-R	5-10	165	2-10-94	.148	.091	.169	29	81	11	12	2	0	1	8	17	1	0	0	26	1	0	.210	.303
Sappelt, Eddie	B-R	5-11	175	7-16-94	.438	.500	.429	10	16	6	7	1	0	0	3	10	1	0	0	1	1	1	.500	.667
Smolinski, Jake	R-R	5-11	185	2-9-89	.500	.500	.500	2	6	1	3	0	0	0	1	0	0	0	0	0	0	0	.500	.571
Vigil, Rodrigo	R-R	6-0	164	1-3-93	.282	.385	.262	24	78	12	22	2	1	1	2	4	4	0	0	8	0	0	.372	.349
Williams, Miles	R-R	5-10	185	7-18-92	.157	.107	.170	42	134	13	21	7	0	1	12	11	0	0	0	51	0	2	.231	.280
Woods, K.J.	L-R	6-3	230	7-9-95	.201	.152	.216	43	144	15	29	4	0	1	6	17	6	0	1	53	3	1	.250	.310
Yelich, Christian	L-R	6-4	195	12-5-91	.294	.333	.286	5	17	2	5	0	1	0	0	1	0	0	0	5	0	0	.412	.333

Pitching	B-T	HT	WT	DOB	W	L	ERA	G	GS	CG	SV	IP	H	R	ER	HR	BB	SO	AVG	vLH	vRH	K/9	BB/9
Adames, Jose	R-R	6-2	165	1-17-93	1	3	2.51	14	3	0	1	32	26	16	9	0	13	33	.211	.239	.195	9.19	3.62
Alvis, Sam	R-L	6-0	195	6-11-92	1	0	3.24	12	0	0	0	17	15	8	6	0	9	14	.238	.294	.217	7.56	4.86
Aquino, Francisco	L-L	6-3	185	9-15-92	1	0	1.80	3	0	0	0	5	5	1	1	0	2	4	.278	.333	.267	7.20	3.60
Castellanos, Gabriel	L-L	6-1	165	12-28-93	3	4	3.45	12	12	0	0	47	40	24	18	0	19	56	.227	.132	.268	10.72	3.64
Cavanerio, Jorgan	R-R	6-1	155	8-18-94	4	1	2.74	9	8	0	0	43	43	16	13	1	10	29	.267	.341	.190	6.12	2.11
Ceda, Jose	R-R	6-5	280	1-28-87	0	0	0.00	2	1	0	0	2	0	0	0	0	0	3	.000	.000	.000	13.50	0.00
Crabaugh, Cody	L-R	6-6	210	12-25-90	2	1	3.53	13	3	0	1	36	33	16	14	1	3	29	.241	.216	.256	7.32	0.76
Cruz, Edward	R-R	6-2	175	8-22-90	1	3	7.59	14	0	0	0	21	28	19	18	0	18	21	.315	.211	.392	8.86	7.59
De La Rosa, Esmerling	R-R	6-2	199	5-15-91	0	1	3.63	14	0	0	0	17	18	11	7	0	9	21	.281	.267	.294	10.90	4.67
Dyson, Sam	R-R	6-1	210	5-7-88	0	1	3.60	1	1	0	0	5	6	3	2	0	1	5	.316	.286	.333	9.00	1.80
Easley, Josh	R-R	6-3	190	12-9-90	1	0	1.50	3	0	0	1	6	5	2	1	0	0	10	.208	.250	.188	15.00	0.00
Effertz, Joel	R-R	6-3	235	9-27-90	0	4	6.86	8	3	0	0	21	28	17	16	3	3	18	.326	.324	.327	7.71	1.29
Ellington, Brian	R-R	6-4	200	8-4-90	0	0	0.00	2	0	0	0	3	0	0	0	0	3	4	.000	.000	.000	12.00	9.00
German, Domingo	R-R	6-2	175	8-4-92	3	0	1.38	5	5	0	0	26	15	4	4	1	5	27	.167	.079	.231	9.35	1.73
Hand, Brad	L-L	6-3	215	3-20-90	0	1	1.13	2	2	0	0	8	5	2	1	0	2	11	.179	.100	.222	12.38	2.25
Harris, Cody	R-R	6-3	195	4-4-92	2	2	4.45	13	2	0	1	28	23	14	14	1	12	12	.223	.205	.234	3.81	3.81
Kane, Tyler	R-R	6-1	190	8-23-92	2	1	1.54	8	0	0	1	12	8	3	2	0	3	3	.190	.053	.304	2.31	2.31
Kinley, Tyler	R-R	6-4	205	1-31-91	0	1	4.50	6	2	0	0	12	15	8	6	0	7	5	.306	.417	.200	3.75	5.25
Maine, Scott	L-L	6-3	225	2-2-85	0	0	0.00	9	0	0	3	11	6	2	0	0	3	15	.146	.100	.161	12.66	2.53
Rincon, Junior	R-R	6-2	185	12-24-92	0	0	3.65	10	0	0	1	12	13	8	5	0	6	11	.255	.278	.242	8.03	4.38
Santamaria, Rigoberto	R-R	6-2	195	4-27-94	0	0	9.00	1	0	0	0	1	2	1	1	0	0	1	.400	.333	.500	9.00	0.00
Suggs, Colby	R-R	5-11	230	10-25-91	0	0	9.00	1	0	0	0	1	1	1	1	0	2	1	.250	.333	.000	9.00	18.00
Talbot, Mitch	R-R	6-1	180	10-17-83	1	1	2.25	2	1	0	0	8	6	4	2	0	1	8	.194	.214	.176	9.00	1.13
Townsley, Sean	L-L	6-7	240	9-19-90	0	1	0.98	13	0	0	3	18	17	7	2	0	4	21	.236	.252	.232	10.31	1.96
Villanueva, Elih	R-R	6-2	230	7-27-86	2	0	1.00	4	4	0	0	18	20	2	2	0	3	19	.278	.314	.243	9.50	1.50
Wertenberger, Ryan	R-R	6-2	215	1-22-90	0	2	5.09	15	0	0	2	18	34	15	10	0	6	17	.415	.333	.462	8.66	3.06
Westmoreland, Adam	L-L	6-4	280	1-10-90	0	6	6.40	11	8	0	0	32	40	32	23	4	7	33	.288	.289	.287	9.19	1.95
White, Will	L-L	6-3	190	7-18-93	0	1	2.08	5	2	0	0	13	7	6	3	0	6	12	.149	.000	.194	8.31	4.15
Williams, Trevor	R-R	6-3	228	4-25-92	0	0	4.50	1	1	0	0	2	3	2	1	0	0	1	.300	.750	.000	4.50	0.00
Zulueta, Nelson	R-R	6-3	175	8-10-94	1	0	2.19	4	1	0	0	12	8	3	3	0	4	4	.186	.200	.174	2.92	2.92

Fielding

Catcher	PCT	G	PO	A	E	DP	PB
Brown	.981	7	46	7	1	0	1
Caldwell	1.000	5	33	2	0	0	0
Cruz	.972	10	66	4	2	0	3
Jimenez	1.000	14	90	6	0	2	3
Othman	.975	5	37	2	1	0	2
Vigil	.985	24	169	22	3	1	13

First Base	PCT	G	PO	A	E	DP
Brown	1.000	1	13	0	0	0
Duran	.991	25	204	11	2	16
Lasater	.970	3	30	2	1	6
Miller	.990	31	273	15	3	27
Rivera	1.000	1	2	0	0	1

Second Base	PCT	G	PO	A	E	DP
Cordova	1.000	1	2	0	0	0
Hernandez	1.000	11	17	25	0	4
Olivencia	.932	39	58	93	11	20
Rivera	.957	9	15	29	2	12

Third Base	PCT	G	PO	A	E	DP
Avila	.914	42	32	85	11	10
Cordova	.857	2	1	5	1	1
Lasater	.857	3	0	6	1	0
Rivera	.903	14	6	22	3	2

Shortstop	PCT	G	PO	A	E	DP
Blanton	.913	47	69	140	20	31
Cordova	1.000	3	3	9	0	1
Hernandez	.833	5	3	12	3	1
Rivera	.926	6	5	20	2	3

Outfield	PCT	G	PO	A	E	DP
Aper	.985	30	61	3	1	2
Brown	1.000	2	2	0	0	0
Castro	.882	33	44	1	6	1
Martinez	1.000	12	13	1	0	1
Olivencia	1.000	5	9	0	0	0
Pujols	.964	21	26	1	1	0
Sappelt	1.000	9	12	0	0	0
Smolinski	1.000	2	4	0	0	0
Williams	1.000	32	32	1	0	0
Woods	.875	36	53	3	8	0
Yelich	1.000	4	6	1	0	1

DOMINICAN SUMMER LEAGUE

Batting	B-T	HT	WT	DOB	AVG	vLH	vRH	G	AB	R	H	2B	3B	HR	RBI	BB	HBP	SH	SF	SO	SB	CS	SLG	OBP
Almonte, Erwin	L-L	6-0	170	2-22-95	.208	.136	.228	53	202	11	42	10	0	0	14	16	4	0	1	27	1	0	.257	.278
Avello, Roger	R-R	6-2	189	12-5-94	.235	.182	.250	38	98	12	23	4	0	0	6	16	2	1	0	25	12	4	.276	.353
Cabrera, Rony	R-R	5-11	175	1-29-96	.253	.171	.273	45	178	27	45	11	4	1	18	14	4	1	3	39	6	3	.376	.317
Corcino, Sonner	R-R	6-2	190	12-26-92	.195	.167	.200	12	41	0	8	1	0	0	3	1	0	0	0	6	0	0	.220	.214
De La Cruz, Dionicio	R-R	6-2	175	1-31-94	.210	.200	.213	16	62	9	13	2	0	0	2	6	1	0	0	8	3	1	.242	.290
Depen, Michael	R-R	6-3	186	6-16-92	.250	.286	.243	14	44	7	11	0	1	0	4	1	1	0	1	10	1	3	.295	.277
2-team total (20 Indians)					.239	—	—	34	109	15	26	7	3	0	12	2	2	0	2	23	4	5	.358	.261
Heredia, Jorge	L-L	6-1	180	10-15-94	.145	.150	.143	26	83	4	12	3	0	0	8	6	2	0	2	29	0	0	.181	.215
Heredia, Juan	R-R	5-11	145	7-4-92	.269	1.000	.240	10	26	3	7	0	0	0	2	6	0	1	1	4	3	0	.269	.394
2-team total (13 Phillies)					.226	—	—	23	62	5	14	1	0	0	3	12	0	2	2	9	5	1	.242	.342
Javier, Sony	R-R	6-0	195	6-15-91	.238	.000	.238	7	21	2	5	2	1	0	1	2	0	0	0	1	0	1	.429	.304
Made, Pedro	B-R	6-2	160	9-29-94	.155	.000	.203	41	97	13	15	2	1	0	5	20	2	2	0	29	9	2	.196	.311
Molina, Leudy	L-R	6-0	160	11-20-94	.199	.171	.207	45	151	11	30	7	1	0	8	22	3	0	4	48	1	0	.258	.313
Moscat, Galvi	R-R	6-0	180	6-29-94	.259	.133	.288	23	81	10	21	4	0	0	6	8	1	0	0	16	3	2	.309	.333
Peguero, Alinson	R-R	6-2	175	4-13-94	.216	.194	.221	50	176	16	38	7	0	3	21	12	5	0	3	65	0	1	.307	.281
Pinto, Yobanis	R-R	5-11	190	2-15-96	.192	.071	.220	23	73	6	14	3	0	0	6	8	5	0	2	5	1	0	.233	.307
Reyes, Angel	R-R	6-0	175	5-6-95	.224	.111	.256	56	201	18	45	13	1	1	21	22	2	1	3	53	2	3	.313	.303
Richards, Jonathan	B-R	6-0	180	6-16-95	.255	.244	.258	56	196	19	50	6	1	0	11	23	1	3	1	21	10	12	.296	.335
Sanchez, Alberto	R-R	6-2	205	2-14-96	.168	.261	.141	28	101	6	17	2	1	0	6	6	1	0	1	16	1	0	.208	.220
Santana, Geuris	L-R	6-3	195	6-30-95	.176	.278	.161	44	136	4	24	4	0	0	2	22	3	1	0	27	5	6	.206	.304
Silva, Geral	R-R	6-1	155	10-29-94	.246	.278	.237	51	167	19	41	2	0	0	12	18	4	0	2	31	10	5	.257	.330
Solano, Jose	R-R	6-1	170	8-17-93	.196	.375	.158	14	46	3	9	2	0	0	1	1	0	0	0	16	1	0	.239	.213
2-team total (16 Royals)					.184	—	—	30	87	8	16	2	1	0	2	3	0	1	0	24	1	3	.230	.211
Ynoa, Christopher	R-R	6-1	175	1-28-93	.167	—	.167	3	6	1	1	0	0	0	2	1	0	0	1	1	1	0	.167	.250

Pitching	B-T	HT	WT	DOB	W	L	ERA	G	GS	CG	SV	IP	H	R	ER	HR	BB	SO	AVG	vLH	vRH	K/9	BB/9
Adames, Ayron	B-R	6-0	190	3-1-94	1	3	2.45	13	7	0	0	55	39	20	15	0	24	37	.197	.225	.190	6.05	3.93
Aquino, Francisco	L-L	6-3	185	9-15-92	1	3	2.01	10	6	0	2	40	39	19	9	0	16	40	.248	.211	.254	8.93	3.57
Arias, Juan	R-R	6-2	170	12-30-94	0	0	3.86	3	0	0	1	5	5	9	2	0	5	6	.238	.429	.143	11.57	9.64
Bautista, Felix	R-R	6-5	190	6-20-95	0	3	2.73	11	3	0	1	26	21	14	8	0	14	17	.214	.258	.194	5.81	4.78
Cuello, Pedro	R-R	6-3	175	6-29-94	0	2	6.35	5	0	0	1	6	6	5	4	0	1	3	.286	.500	.200	4.76	1.59
De La Rosa, Gregory	R-R	6-4	200	3-15-93	0	1	8.38	7	1	0	0	10	8	11	9	0	14	4	.216	.455	.115	3.72	13.03
De La Rosa, Leurys	R-R	6-2	160	11-5-94	4	3	2.55	11	6	0	1	49	43	18	14	0	6	42	.230	.193	.246	7.66	1.09
De Leon, Anderson	R-R	6-2	170	5-18-95	0	2	36.00	4	1	0	0	2	3	11	8	0	10	0	.375	.400	.333	0.00	45.00
Del Rosario, Yeison	R-R	6-1	165	2-15-94	2	3	2.88	10	5	0	1	41	28	17	13	0	14	53	.188	.150	.202	11.73	3.10
Diaz, Jose	R-R	6-2	180	5-7-93	4	2	1.95	13	6	0	1	55	49	19	12	0	17	31	.240	.128	.267	5.04	2.77
Jaramillo, Jose	R-R	6-1	180	12-2-95	0	2	3.63	8	1	0	0	22	22	10	9	0	10	12	.272	.304	.259	4.84	4.03
Jean, Victor	R-R	6-2	185	4-25-94	2	1	2.28	12	6	1	1	51	41	19	13	0	10	42	.214	.241	.201	7.36	1.75
Lara, Erick	R-R	6-2	150	3-24-94	1	1	2.08	10	3	0	0	26	21	11	6	0	14	22	.219	.364	.176	7.62	4.85
Martes, Francis	R-R	6-0	170	11-24-95	3	3	3.04	12	6	0	0	50	51	21	17	1	14	33	.267	.288	.259	5.90	2.50
Mendoza, Yeims	R-R	6-2	155	2-27-93	4	5	3.00	15	10	0	0	78	71	34	26	1	15	83	.239	.306	.212	9.58	1.73
Ogando, Cristofer	R-R	6-3	195	10-23-93	0	0	8.53	5	0	0	0	6	9	9	6	0	6	5	.321	.400	.278	7.11	8.53
Perez, Yonqueli	R-R	6-4	175	6-6-93	1	5	3.93	12	6	0	1	34	34	25	15	0	21	44	.243	.190	.252	11.53	5.50
Ramos, Felix	B-L	6-0	175	12-2-93	3	1	1.95	16	0	0	4	32	24	9	7	0	7	27	.205	.176	.210	7.52	1.95
Romero, Derlin	R-R	6-2	175	10-8-94	0	0	32.40	4	0	0	0	2	2	7	6	0	9	1	.333	.000	.400	5.40	48.60
Ruiz, Leonel	L-L	5-9	170	3-15-93	0	5	2.70	12	4	0	0	37	22	22	11	0	33	30	.183	.286	.177	7.36	8.10

Fielding

Catcher	PCT	G	PO	A	E	DP	PB
Molina	.971	10	51	15	2	0	3
Pinto	1.000	18	141	19	0	0	4
Reyes	.971	45	322	83	12	0	8

First Base	PCT	G	PO	A	E	DP
Almonte	.980	37	279	16	6	14
Corcino	.979	11	91	1	2	3
Molina	1.000	2	3	0	0	0
Pinto	1.000	3	26	2	0	1
Reyes	.875	2	6	1	1	0
Sanchez	.980	7	50	0	1	4
Santana	.984	22	173	15	3	8
Silva	1.000	1	5	0	0	0
Ynoa	1.000	2	11	0	0	0

Second Base	PCT	G	PO	A	E	DP
Cabrera	.962	13	24	27	2	4
Heredia	1.000	1	3	2	0	0
Heredia	.944	7	18	16	2	0

	PCT	G	PO	A	E	DP	
Richards	.929	22	45	60	8	8	
Silva	.959	13	28	19	2	2	
Solano	.961	20	34	40	3	5	

Third Base	PCT	G	PO	A	E	DP
Cabrera	.909	15	11	39	5	0
Heredia	1.000	1	3	1	0	0
Heredia	1.000	2	1	7	0	0
Molina	.333	2	0	1	2	0
Sanchez	.848	19	11	28	7	3
Santana	.880	22	19	47	9	5
Silva	.914	16	8	24	3	0
Solano	.600	4	2	1	2	0
Ynoa	.750	1	0	3	1	0

Shortstop	PCT	G	PO	A	E	DP
Cabrera	.929	13	21	44	5	5
Richards	.914	27	43	85	12	7
Silva	.879	24	31	71	14	5
Solano	.926	9	10	15	2	2

Outfield	PCT	G	PO	A	E	DP
Almonte	.946	25	32	3	2	0
Avello	.952	38	58	2	3	2
De La Cruz	1.000	16	32	2	0	0
Depen	.917	14	22	0	2	0
Heredia	.895	16	14	3	2	0
Javier	1.000	5	12	0	0	0
Made	.959	38	69	2	3	2
Molina	.000	1	0	0	2	0
Moscat	.917	23	33	0	3	0
Peguero	.973	43	67	4	2	0
Richards	1.000	4	11	0	0	0
Romero	1.000	1	1	0	0	0
Silva	—	1	0	0	0	0
Solano	—	1	0	0	0	0
Solano	.966	14	28	0	1	0

Milwaukee Brewers

SEASON IN A SENTENCE: Two years after reaching the National League Championship Series, the losses of Ryan Braun, Corey Hart and Aramis Ramirez—for various reasons—left the depleted Brewers in fourth place in the NL Central, 23 games behind St. Louis.

HIGH POINT: Well, as you might imagine, it came early. After beating the Pirates 12-8 on April 30, Milwaukee was in second place, just a half-game out. It didn't last. Meanwhile, shortstop Jean Segura, acquired from the Angels in the Zack Greinke deal was an all-star in his first full season.

LOW POINT: Losing 22 of 28 in May left the Brew Crew 15 games out of first and buried. But the real downer, of course, came when Braun was suspended on July 22 for the remainder of the season—65 games—for his use of PEDs supplied by Biogenesis. Braun, who in 2012 had a positive PED test overturned for alleged chain of command issues, a month later apologized to his teammates and fans for using a cream and a lozenge in 2011 to speed his recovery from a calf injury. In his apology, Braun acknowledged he "deserved to be" suspended. His suspension ended on Oct. 31.

NOTABLE ROOKIES: Khris Davis, a 25-year-old outfielder drafted in 2009, finally got his shot after Braun was suspended. Davis slugged .596 with 11 homers and the Brewers are planning a big role for him in 2014. Second baseman Scooter Gennett might supplant Rickie Weeks despite Weeks' massive contract. Gennett hit .324 and had an .834 OPS in 69 games.

KEY TRANSACTIONS: While the Brewers traded former closer John Axford to the Cardinals, the biggest move was extending the contract of—and not trading—blossoming center fielder Carlos Gomez. Now signed through 2016, Gomez improved upon a solid 2012 with 61 extra-base hits and continued to play an excellent outfield.

DOWN ON THE FARM: Tyler Thornberg, the Brewers' No. 2 prospect entering last season, went 3-1 in a late-season, big league audition. Clint Coulter, their 2012 top pick, struggled at two higher levels before getting hot in the Arizona League. The Brewers plan to keep him at catcher. Meanwhile, 2011 first-round pick Tyler Jungmann posted a 10-10, 4.33 record in 153 innings at Double-A Huntsville, and first baseman Hunter Morris, who was the system's 2012 player of the year after hitting 28 home runs with Huntsville, belted another 24 in 2013 with Triple-A Nashville.

OPENING DAY PAYROLL: $84 million (18th)

PLAYERS OF THE YEAR

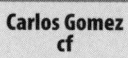

MAJOR LEAGUE	MINOR LEAGUE
Carlos Gomez cf	**Jimmy Nelson** rhp
.284/.338/.506	(Double-A/Triple-A)
24 HR, 40 SB, 61 XBH	10-10, 3.25, 9.6 SO/9
Won first Gold Glove	September callup

ORGANIZATION LEADERS

BATTING		*Minimum 250 AB	
MAJORS			
*	AVG	Segura, Jean	.294
*	OPS	Gomez, Carlos	.843
	HR	Gomez, Carlos	24
	RBI	Lucroy, Jonathan	82
MINORS			
*	AVG	Reed, Michael, Wisconsin	.286
*	OBP	Reed, Michael, Wisconsin	.385
*	SLG	Rogers, Jason, Huntsville	.468
	R	Davis, Kentrail, Nashville/Huntsville	78
	H	Davis, Kentrail, Nashville/Huntsville	134
	TB	Morris, Hunter, Nashville	227
	2B	Haniger, Mitch, Brevard County/Wisconsin	36
	3B	Reed, Michael, Wisconsin	13
	HR	Kjeldgaard, Brock, Huntsville	24
		Morris, Hunter, Nashville	24
	RBI	Rogers, Jason, Huntsville	87
	BB	Reed, Michael, Wisconsin	71
	SO	Ramirez, Nick, Brevard County	171
	SB	Garcia, Omar, Helena	28

PITCHING		#Minimum 75 IP	
MAJORS			
	W	Gallardo, Yovani	12
#	ERA	Lohse, Kyle	3.35
	SO	Gallardo, Yovani	144
	SV	Henderson, Jim	28
MINORS			
	W	Hellweg, Johnny, Nashville/Wisconsin	13
	L	Kroenke, Zach, Nashville	16
#	ERA	Hellweg, Johnny, Wisconsin/Nashville	3.14
	G	Webb, Travis, Nashville	56
	GS	Nelson, Jimmy, Nashville/Huntsville	27
		Pena, Ariel, Huntsville	27
	SV	Toledo, Tommy, Brevard County	20
		Wooten, Rob, Nashville	20
	IP	Nelson, Jimmy, Nashville/Huntsville	152
	BB	Hellweg, Johnny, Nashville/Wisconsin	83
	SO	Nelson, Jimmy, Nashville/Huntsville	163
#	AVG	Goforth, David, Brevard County/Huntsville	.217

General Manager: Doug Melvin. **Farm Director:** Reid Nichols. **Scouting Director:** Bruce Seid.

Class	Team	League	W	L	PCT	Finish	Manager
Majors	Milwaukee Brewers	National	74	88	.457	11th (15)	Ron Roenicke
Triple-A	Nashville Sounds	Pacific Coast	57	87	.396	16th (16)	Mike Guerrero
Double-A	Huntsville Stars	Southern	59	79	.428	t-8th (10)	Darnell Coles
High A	Brevard County Manatees	Florida State	66	68	.493	7th (12)	Joe Ayrault
Low A	Wisconsin Timber Rattlers	Midwest	59	76	.437	13th (16)	Matt Erickson
Rookie	Helena Brewers	Pioneer	43	33	.566	2nd (8)	Tony Diggs
Rookie	Brewers	Arizona	23	33	.411	10th (13)	Nestor Corredor
2013 Overall Minor League Record			307	376	.449	28th (30)	

ORGANIZATION STATISTICS

NATIONAL LEAGUE

Batting	B-T	HT	WT	DOB	AVG	vLH	vRH	G	AB	R	H	2B	3B	HR	RBI	BB	HBP	SH	SF	SO	SB	CS	SLG	OBP
Aoki, Norichika	L-R	5-9	175	1-5-82	.286	.339	.264	155	597	80	171	20	3	8	37	55	11	8	3	40	20	12	.370	.356
Betancourt, Yuniesky	R-R	5-10	205	1-31-82	.212	.198	.219	137	391	35	83	15	1	13	46	14	1	0	3	71	0	0	.355	.240
Bianchi, Jeff	R-R	5-11	180	10-5-86	.237	.258	.229	100	236	22	56	8	1	1	25	11	1	2	2	46	4	4	.292	.272
Braun, Ryan	R-R	6-2	205	11-17-83	.298	.368	.262	61	225	30	67	14	2	9	38	27	0	0	1	56	4	5	.498	.372
Davis, Khris	R-R	5-11	200	12-21-87	.279	.244	.297	56	136	27	38	10	0	11	27	11	5	0	1	34	3	0	.596	.353
Francisco, Juan	L-R	6-2	240	6-24-87	.221	.200	.222	89	240	26	53	10	1	13	32	25	3	0	2	95	0	1	.433	.300
2-team total (35 Atlanta)					.227	—		124	348	36	79	12	1	18	48	32	3	0	2	138	0	2	.422	.296
Gennett, Scooter	L-R	5-10	180	5-1-90	.324	.154	.362	69	213	29	69	11	2	6	21	10	1	5	1	42	2	1	.479	.356
Gindl, Caleb	L-L	5-7	205	8-31-88	.242	.333	.233	57	132	17	32	7	2	5	14	20	0	2	1	25	2	1	.439	.340
Gomez, Carlos	R-R	6-3	215	12-4-85	.284	.315	.274	147	536	80	152	27	10	24	73	37	10	1	6	146	40	7	.506	.338
Gonzalez, Alex	R-R	6-1	210	2-15-77	.177	.135	.197	41	113	14	20	3	0	1	8	3	1	0	1	26	0	0	.230	.203
Halton, Sean	R-R	6-4	260	6-7-87	.238	.212	.250	42	101	9	24	4	0	4	17	5	3	1	1	31	0	0	.396	.291
Lalli, Blake	L-R	6-1	210	5-12-83	.125	.000	.143	16	24	1	3	0	0	0	2	0	0	0	0	7	0	0	.125	.125
Lucroy, Jonathan	R-R	6-0	195	6-13-86	.280	.312	.270	147	521	59	146	25	6	18	82	46	5	0	8	69	9	1	.455	.340
Maldonado, Martin	R-R	6-0	235	8-16-86	.169	.159	.173	67	183	13	31	7	1	4	22	13	3	3	0	53	0	0	.284	.236
Prince, Josh	R-R	6-0	180	1-26-88	.125	.000	.200	8	8	3	1	1	0	0	0	1	0	0	0	1	0	0	.250	.222
Ramirez, Aramis	R-R	6-1	210	6-25-78	.283	.299	.278	92	304	43	86	18	0	12	49	36	8	0	3	55	0	1	.461	.370
Schafer, Logan	L-L	6-1	180	9-8-86	.211	.175	.220	134	298	29	63	15	3	4	33	25	3	11	0	60	7	1	.322	.279
Segura, Jean	R-R	5-10	200	3-17-90	.294	.317	.287	146	588	74	173	20	10	12	49	25	6	2	2	84	44	13	.423	.329
Weeks, Rickie	R-R	5-10	215	9-13-82	.209	.226	.201	104	350	40	73	20	1	10	24	40	9	0	0	105	7	3	.357	.306

Pitching	B-T	HT	WT	DOB	W	L	ERA	G	GS	CG	SV	IP	H	R	ER	HR	BB	SO	AVG	vLH	vRH	K/9	BB/9
Axford, John	R-R	6-5	220	4-1-83	6	7	4.45	62	0	0	0	55	62	29	27	10	23	54	.286	.280	.291	8.89	3.79
2-team total (13 St. Louis)					7	7	4.02	75	0	0	0	65	73	32	29	10	26	65	—	—	—	9.00	3.60
Badenhop, Burke	R-R	6-5	220	2-8-83	2	3	3.47	63	0	0	1	62	62	32	24	6	12	42	.266	.338	.229	6.06	1.73
Blazek, Michael	R-R	6-0	200	3-16-89	0	1	3.86	7	0	0	0	7	6	4	3	1	3	4	.222	.273	.188	5.14	3.86
2-team total (11 St. Louis)					0	1	5.71	18	0	0	0	17	16	12	11	3	13	14	—	—	—	7.22	6.75
Burgos, Hiram	R-R	5-11	210	8-4-87	1	2	6.44	6	6	0	0	29	38	23	21	5	11	18	.309	.339	.284	5.52	3.38
Estrada, Marco	R-R	5-11	200	7-5-83	7	4	3.87	21	21	0	0	128	109	56	55	19	29	118	.229	.214	.242	8.30	2.04
Fiers, Mike	R-R	6-2	195	6-15-85	1	4	7.25	11	3	0	0	22	28	20	18	8	6	15	.298	.304	.289	6.04	2.42
Figaro, Alfredo	R-R	6-0	175	7-7-84	3	3	4.14	33	5	0	1	74	77	41	34	15	15	54	.265	.246	.282	6.57	1.82
Gallardo, Yovani	R-R	6-2	215	2-27-86	12	10	4.18	31	31	0	0	181	180	92	84	18	66	144	.261	.249	.272	7.17	3.29
Gonzalez, Mike	R-L	6-2	200	5-23-78	0	3	4.68	75	0	0	0	50	58	28	26	10	25	60	.283	.274	.293	10.80	4.50
Gorzelanny, Tom	L-L	6-2	210	7-12-82	3	6	3.90	43	10	0	0	85	77	41	37	11	31	83	.241	.184	.266	8.75	3.27
Hand, Donovan	R-R	6-3	210	4-20-86	1	5	3.69	31	7	0	0	68	71	29	28	10	21	37	.280	.286	.273	4.87	2.77
Hellweg, Johnny	R-R	6-9	205	10-29-88	1	4	6.75	8	7	0	0	31	40	30	23	3	26	9	.325	.381	.267	2.64	7.63
Henderson, Jim	L-R	6-5	220	10-21-82	5	5	2.70	61	0	0	28	60	44	18	18	8	24	75	.200	.238	.165	11.25	3.60
Kintzler, Brandon	R-R	5-10	185	8-1-84	3	3	2.69	71	0	0	0	77	66	25	23	2	16	58	.234	.220	.244	6.78	1.87
Lohse, Kyle	R-R	6-2	210	10-4-78	11	10	3.35	32	32	2	0	199	196	78	74	26	36	125	.259	.256	.262	5.66	1.63
Narveson, Chris	L-L	6-3	205	12-20-81	0	0	0.00	2	0	0	0	2	1	0	0	0	1	0	.143	.000	.200	0.00	4.50
Nelson, Jimmy	R-R	6-5	245	6-5-89	0	0	0.90	4	1	0	0	10	7	1	1	0	5	8	.065	.125	.000	7.20	4.50
Peralta, Wily	R-R	6-1	245	5-8-89	11	15	4.37	32	32	2	0	183	187	107	89	19	73	129	.264	.259	.269	6.33	3.58
Rodriguez, Francisco	R-R	6-0	195	1-7-82	1	1	1.09	25	0	0	10	25	17	3	3	2	9	26	.198	.102	.324	9.49	3.28
Thornburg, Tyler	R-R	5-11	190	9-29-88	3	1	2.03	18	7	0	0	67	53	17	15	1	26	48	.225	.192	.261	6.48	3.51
Wooten, Rob	R-R	6-1	210	7-21-85	3	1	3.90	27	0	0	0	28	27	12	12	1	8	18	.257	.245	.268	5.86	2.60

Fielding

Catcher	PCT	G	PO	A	E	DP	PB
Lalli	1.000	1	2	0	0	0	0
Lucroy	.991	126	857	56	8	5	7
Maldonado	.997	47	281	35	1	3	3

First Base	PCT	G	PO	A	E	DP
Betancourt	.993	68	389	25	3	38
Francisco	.983	67	538	25	10	57
Gonzalez	.994	22	145	9	1	13
Halton	1.000	25	168	8	0	18

	PCT	G	PO	A	E	DP
Lalli	.957	5	45	0	2	1
Lucroy	.972	14	66	4	2	5
Maldonado	.956	10	62	3	3	4

Second Base	PCT	G	PO	A	E	DP
Betancourt	1.000	5	5	7	0	0
Bianchi	.970	19	25	40	2	10
Gennett	.981	59	113	146	5	39
Weeks	.975	95	143	254	10	56

Third Base	PCT	G	PO	A	E	DP
Betancourt	.934	59	29	84	8	3
Bianchi	.965	42	27	84	4	9
Francisco	.600	4	1	5	4	2
Gonzalez	.864	11	5	14	3	1
Halton	—	1	0	0	0	0
Prince	—	1	0	0	0	0
Ramirez	.955	80	45	103	7	7

Shortstop	PCT	G	PO	A	E	DP
Betancourt	1.000	3	3	1	0	0
Bianchi	.957	20	35	55	4	16
Gonzalez	.933	3	2	12	1	0
Segura	.978	144	199	459	15	96

Outfield	PCT	G	PO	A	E	DP
Aoki	.990	149	290	9	3	0
Betancourt	—	2	0	0	0	0
Bianchi	1.000	3	0	1	0	0
Braun	.984	59	116	5	2	1
Davis	.980	34	47	1	1	0
Gindl	.962	34	49	2	2	0
Gomez	.988	145	391	12	5	2
Halton	1.000	6	6	1	0	0
Prince	1.000	3	2	0	0	0
Schafer	1.000	91	174	4	0	2

NASHVILLE SOUNDS — TRIPLE-A

PACIFIC COAST LEAGUE

MILWAUKEE BREWERS

Batting	B-T	HT	WT	DOB	AVG	vLH	vRH	G	AB	R	H	2B	3B	HR	RBI	BB	HBP	SH	SF	SO	SB	CS	SLG	OBP
Bianchi, Jeff	R-R	5-11	180	10-5-86	.244	.207	.333	10	41	6	10	1	1	1	6	2	0	0	0	8	0	0	.390	.279
Buller, Dayton	R-R	5-10	203	6-22-81	.245	.368	.176	21	53	7	13	0	0	1	4	9	0	0	0	15	0	0	.302	.355
Chavez, Ozzie	B-R	6-1	175	7-13-83	.202	.200	.204	43	109	6	22	2	0	0	7	5	0	2	1	28	1	1	.220	.235
Davis, Blake	L-R	5-11	170	12-22-83	.256	.257	.256	102	332	33	85	16	5	2	31	19	1	3	2	71	5	5	.352	.297
Davis, Kentrail	L-R	5-9	200	6-29-88	.270	.210	.299	49	196	27	53	7	3	2	14	22	3	2	0	51	8	6	.367	.353
Davis, Khris	R-R	5-11	200	12-21-87	.255	.260	.253	69	243	35	62	12	1	13	37	31	5	0	2	59	6	4	.473	.349
De La Rosa, Anderson	R-R	5-11	188	8-1-84	.270	.239	.293	69	211	17	57	15	0	2	20	12	2	0	2	45	3	0	.370	.313
Diaz, Robinzon	R-R	5-11	215	9-19-83	.328	.305	.339	50	177	27	58	9	1	4	20	14	0	1	1	16	0	2	.458	.375
Garner, Cole	R-R	6-2	215	12-15-84	.192	.202	.183	71	214	18	41	9	1	8	29	17	3	0	0	89	2	0	.355	.261
Gennett, Scooter	L-R	5-10	180	5-1-90	.280	.257	.298	79	321	44	90	10	5	3	22	21	2	3	2	59	10	5	.371	.327
Gindl, Caleb	L-L	5-7	205	8-31-88	.295	.268	.300	83	312	33	92	21	3	11	51	30	2	1	2	72	1	2	.487	.358
Halton, Sean	R-R	6-4	260	6-7-87	.273	.273	.272	96	352	51	96	29	2	11	51	35	8	0	4	92	6	2	.460	.348
Lalli, Blake	L-R	6-2	210	5-12-83	.282	.253	.293	82	284	36	80	14	0	11	35	22	1	3	1	68	0	0	.447	.334
Morris, Hunter	L-R	6-2	226	10-7-88	.247	.211	.269	134	497	61	123	26	3	24	73	43	3	0	3	122	3	1	.457	.310
Paciorek, Joey	R-R	6-2	225	9-20-88	.071	.000	.143	8	14	3	1	0	0	0	1	0	1	0	0	3	0	0	.071	.133
Parker, Steve	L-R	6-2	205	9-3-87	.218	.185	.234	125	399	44	87	20	1	8	43	47	5	3	2	106	3	1	.333	.307
Prince, Josh	R-R	6-0	180	1-26-88	.237	.246	.232	115	418	68	99	18	2	11	53	60	5	5	2	105	25	8	.368	.338
Statia, Hainley	B-R	5-11	184	1-19-86	.241	.217	.251	114	291	40	70	10	0	5	23	50	0	2	0	46	6	5	.326	.352
Velez, Eugenio	B-R	6-1	170	5-16-82	.377	.306	.412	38	151	23	57	10	3	2	21	19	0	1	4	25	9	3	.523	.437

Pitching	B-T	HT	WT	DOB	W	L	ERA	G	GS	CG	SV	IP	H	R	ER	HR	BB	SO	AVG	vLH	vRH	K/9	BB/9
Burgos, Hiram	R-R	5-11	210	8-4-87	1	4	3.82	7	7	0	0	31	25	14	13	6	12	24	.238	.256	.226	7.04	3.52
De La Cruz, Frankie	R-R	5-11	214	3-12-84	1	7	7.93	12	10	0	0	48	57	43	42	6	37	30	.303	.302	.305	5.66	6.99
Dillard, Tim	R-R	6-4	220	7-19-83	4	2	4.40	38	0	0	0	47	43	27	23	2	25	29	.238	.355	.176	5.55	4.79
Estrada, Marco	R-R	5-11	200	7-5-83	0	0	6.75	1	1	0	0	3	3	2	2	0	2	2	.273	.333	.200	6.75	6.75
Fiers, Mike	R-R	6-2	195	6-15-85	1	2	2.20	5	5	1	0	29	24	8	7	3	12	30	.224	.173	.273	9.42	3.77
Figaro, Alfredo	R-R	6-0	175	7-7-84	1	0	2.77	3	3	0	0	13	14	6	4	0	9	8	.286	.250	.320	5.54	6.23
Hand, Donovan	R-R	6-3	210	4-20-86	3	1	3.28	20	0	0	0	36	34	15	13	4	11	38	.243	.274	.218	9.59	2.78
Heckathorn, Kyle	R-R	6-6	225	6-17-88	8	3	3.60	48	1	0	1	65	50	31	26	5	31	46	.207	.196	.215	6.37	4.29
Hellweg, Johnny	R-R	6-9	205	10-29-88	12	5	3.15	23	23	0	0	126	103	55	44	6	81	89	.228	.308	.160	6.37	5.80
Hensley, Clay	R-R	5-11	190	8-3-79	0	0	3.38	4	0	0	0	3	4	1	1	0	3	2	.333	.333	.333	6.75	10.13
Hoey, Jim	R-R	6-6	205	12-30-82	0	1	29.70	3	0	0	0	3	12	11	11	3	2	3	.600	.400	.667	8.10	5.40
Holle, Greg	R-R	6-8	240	11-16-88	0	0	0.00	2	0	0	0	2	2	0	0	0	1	1	.286	.333	.250	4.50	4.50
Jakubauskas, Chris	R-R	6-2	215	12-22-78	1	0	3.29	8	0	0	0	14	14	5	5	0	4	12	.269	.318	.233	7.90	2.63
Kroenke, Zach	R-L	6-2	215	4-21-84	5	16	4.51	32	19	1	0	130	134	73	65	10	49	89	.270	.279	.265	6.18	3.40
Laffey, Aaron	L-L	6-0	200	4-15-85	2	5	7.25	11	11	0	0	50	68	45	40	5	19	26	.325	.400	.308	4.71	3.44
2-team total (12 Albuquerque)					6	8	6.34	23	22	0	0	111	140	85	78	17	41	55	—	—	—	4.47	3.33
Leach, Brent	L-L	6-5	215	11-18-82	0	3	5.19	17	0	0	0	17	15	10	10	2	10	21	.227	.219	.235	10.90	5.19
Lowe, Johnnie	R-R	6-5	220	3-21-85	0	1	3.53	37	5	0	0	79	94	39	31	7	21	62	.298	.301	.296	7.06	2.39
Molleken, Dustin	L-R	6-4	230	8-21-84	0	0	3.14	10	0	0	1	14	9	5	5	0	4	13	.176	.100	.226	8.16	2.51
Narveson, Chris	L-L	6-3	205	12-20-81	4	7	5.14	15	15	0	0	77	85	54	44	9	24	59	.276	.294	.271	6.90	2.81
Nelson, Jimmy	R-R	6-5	245	6-5-89	5	6	3.67	15	15	1	0	83	74	39	34	2	50	91	.240	.250	.231	9.83	5.40
Olmsted, Michael	R-R	6-6	245	5-2-87	1	1	6.71	49	0	0	0	52	54	41	39	6	40	52	.263	.238	.281	8.94	6.88
Rodriguez, Francisco	R-R	6-0	195	1-7-82	0	0	0.00	2	0	0	0	2	1	0	0	0	2	3	.143	.000	.250	13.50	9.00
Sanchez, Jesus	R-R	5-11	200	9-8-87	4	3	2.83	48	0	0	7	70	69	29	22	5	18	50	.257	.281	.239	6.43	2.31
Seidel, R.J.	R-R	6-5	225	9-3-87	2	4	4.64	18	14	0	0	76	75	42	39	12	31	80	.259	.248	.267	9.52	3.69
Thornburg, Tyler	R-R	5-11	190	9-29-88	0	3	5.79	15	15	1	0	75	90	54	48	11	29	87	.297	.315	.279	10.49	3.50
Webb, Travis	L-L	6-4	205	8-2-84	2	6	7.04	56	0	0	1	55	64	51	43	8	43	67	.287	.295	.281	10.96	7.04
Wooten, Rob	R-R	6-1	210	7-21-85	0	1	2.94	40	0	0	20	52	40	17	17	4	12	45	.209	.228	.189	7.79	2.08

Fielding

Catcher	PCT	G	PO	A	E	DP	PB
Buller	.985	16	125	9	2	0	8
De La Rosa	.987	57	398	49	6	8	10
Diaz	.970	23	147	12	5	3	2
Lalli	.983	56	392	21	7	1	10

First Base	PCT	G	PO	A	E	DP
Diaz	1.000	1	2	0	0	0
Halton	1.000	15	105	8	0	9
Lalli	1.000	14	83	11	0	4
Morris	.992	123	1010	53	9	98
Parker	1.000	4	7	2	0	2

Second Base	PCT	G	PO	A	E	DP
Bianchi	1.000	2	7	6	0	2
Chavez	.923	4	3	9	1	1
Gennett	.990	77	162	228	4	48
Prince	1.000	4	4	7	0	1
Statia	.980	27	39	58	2	13
Velez	.971	35	73	93	5	27

Third Base	PCT	G	PO	A	E	DP
Bianchi	.800	3	1	3	1	0
Chavez	1.000	4	3	4	0	0
Davis	1.000	5	1	1	0	0
Diaz	.838	15	6	25	6	1

	PCT	G	PO	A	E	DP
Parker	.943	118	73	192	16	20
Prince	.929	4	4	9	1	1
Statia	.889	14	2	14	2	1
Velez	—	2	0	0	0	0

Shortstop	PCT	G	PO	A	E	DP
Bianchi	.889	3	3	5	1	2
Chavez	.980	29	34	65	2	8
Davis	.960	89	138	265	17	52
Prince	.936	31	33	98	9	27
Statia	.913	7	7	14	2	2

Outfield	PCT	G	PO	A	E	DP
Bianchi	—	1	0	0	0	0
Davis	1.000	4	6	0	0	0
Davis	.973	49	106	1	3	0
Davis	.959	65	116	2	5	0

De La Rosa	—	1	0	0	0	0
Garner	.967	63	112	4	4	1
Gindl	.993	80	142	8	1	3
Halton	.986	72	135	5	2	1
Paciorek	—	1	0	0	0	0

Prince	.963	83	152	3	6	2
Statia	.982	31	52	2	1	0
Velez	.875	3	7	0	1	0

HUNTSVILLE STARS

DOUBLE-A

SOUTHERN LEAGUE

Batting	B-T	HT	WT	DOB	AVG	vLH	vRH	G	AB	R	H	2B	3B	HR	RBI	BB	HBP	SH	SF	SO	SB	CS	SLG	OBP
Bianchi, Jeff	R-R	5-11	180	10-5-86	.267	.333	.250	5	15	0	4	0	0	0	1	1	0	0	0	2	0	1	.267	.313
Chavez, Ozzie	B-R	6-1	175	7-13-83	.226	.235	.222	17	62	6	14	2	0	0	7	4	0	2	1	16	0	1	.258	.269
Davis, Kentrail	L-R	5-9	200	6-29-88	.266	.209	.289	88	304	51	81	19	4	5	33	45	7	1	2	74	18	5	.405	.372
De La Rosa, Anderson	R-R	5-11	188	8-1-84	.290	.500	.217	8	31	4	9	4	0	0	2	1	0	0	0	8	0	0	.419	.313
Diaz, Robinzon	R-R	5-11	215	9-19-83	.276	.292	.266	58	174	12	48	12	1	3	22	4	0	1	0	14	1	1	.408	.292
Gomez, Hector	R-R	6-2	185	3-5-88	.196	.275	.162	113	368	23	72	12	2	2	25	18	3	16	1	77	6	9	.255	.238
Kjeldgaard, Brock	R-R	6-5	235	1-22-86	.222	.233	.218	134	446	61	99	11	2	24	70	66	10	0	4	151	0	0	.417	.333
Mittelstaedt, T.J.	L-R	5-10	185	2-13-88	.137	.000	.200	20	51	3	7	2	0	1	2	7	0	0	0	23	1	1	.235	.241
Owings, Micah	R-R	6-5	220	9-28-82	.195	.250	.143	21	41	3	8	0	0	1	3	3	0	1	0	17	0	0	.268	.250
Paciorek, Joey	R-R	6-2	225	9-20-88	.252	.233	.267	41	103	11	26	5	0	2	9	17	1	0	1	25	0	0	.359	.361
Patterson, Eric	L-R	6-0	170	4-8-83	.204	.063	.232	38	98	8	20	3	0	0	6	12	0	1	0	20	2	3	.235	.291
Rogers, Jason	R-R	6-2	260	3-13-88	.270	.338	.243	133	481	69	130	25	2	22	87	59	1	0	8	86	7	2	.468	.346
Shaw, Nick	R-R	5-11	160	8-25-88	.253	.245	.256	124	450	50	114	10	2	2	27	63	2	9	6	71	8	4	.298	.344
Stang, Chad	R-R	6-2	190	3-26-89	.229	.276	.213	58	218	27	50	7	1	1	9	19	3	2	2	75	6	2	.284	.298
Tosoni, Rene	L-R	6-0	195	7-2-86	.238	.225	.242	131	446	48	106	17	2	11	46	39	5	4	3	83	5	6	.359	.304
Vucinich, Shea	R-R	6-1	185	12-1-88	.199	.205	.195	98	221	25	44	11	0	2	13	40	3	2	2	67	4	1	.276	.327
Walker, Mike	L-R	6-2	240	6-12-88	.223	.226	.222	119	368	42	82	15	1	12	41	49	3	0	2	108	2	2	.367	.318
Weisenburger, Adam	R-R	5-10	185	12-13-88	.251	.382	.192	63	175	21	44	8	1	5	24	24	9	3	2	48	0	2	.394	.367
Zarraga, Shawn	R-R	6-0	248	1-21-89	.292	.190	.325	74	168	15	49	9	0	1	15	14	3	4	1	30	0	1	.363	.355

Pitching	B-T	HT	WT	DOB	W	L	ERA	G	GS	CG	SV	IP	H	R	ER	HR	BB	SO	AVG	vLH	vRH	K/9	BB/9
De La Cruz, Frankie	R-R	5-11	214	3-12-84	2	4	4.87	24	1	0	1	41	41	23	22	5	21	35	.263	.246	.276	7.75	4.65
Gagnon, Drew	R-R	6-4	195	6-26-90	4	9	5.57	16	16	1	0	84	94	54	52	12	42	58	.288	.226	.333	6.21	4.50
Garman, Brian	L-L	5-10	180	7-19-88	1	0	4.25	20	0	0	0	30	32	15	14	3	10	22	.278	.250	.293	6.67	3.03
Goforth, David	R-R	6-0	188	10-11-88	4	3	3.28	20	4	1	5	47	32	19	17	1	18	36	.192	.148	.217	6.94	3.47
Hall, Brooks	R-R	6-5	200	6-26-90	2	4	4.01	17	13	0	1	61	65	31	27	8	23	39	.283	.269	.289	5.79	3.41
Holle, Greg	R-R	6-8	240	11-16-88	4	3	3.96	51	0	0	10	64	63	32	28	2	24	51	.265	.316	.231	7.21	3.39
Jungmann, Taylor	R-R	6-6	210	12-18-89	10	10	4.33	26	26	0	0	139	117	75	67	11	73	82	.232	.232	.232	5.30	4.72
Keeling, Thomas	L-L	6-3	190	3-30-88	0	1	3.18	17	0	0	1	17	15	9	6	1	10	19	.242	.273	.225	10.06	5.29
2-team total (29 Mississippi)					1	3	4.68	46	0	0	1	42	40	29	22	6	38	36	—	—	—	7.65	8.08
Leach, Brent	L-L	6-5	215	11-18-82	0	0	0.00	4	0	0	1	5	6	0	0	0	1	5	.333	.375	.300	8.44	1.69
Leon, Arcenio	R-R	6-1	220	9-22-86	2	7	5.68	35	10	0	0	71	60	49	45	8	58	41	.235	.268	.215	5.17	7.32
Manzanillo, Santo	R-R	6-2	225	12-20-88	1	3	7.45	26	0	0	0	29	39	28	24	3	21	19	.333	.356	.319	5.90	6.52
Marzec, Eric	R-R	5-11	210	1-13-88	5	0	1.99	43	0	0	0	54	49	17	12	2	20	51	.238	.317	.185	8.45	3.31
Meadows, Dan	L-L	6-6	220	11-3-87	0	2	4.60	13	0	0	0	16	11	8	8	2	16	6	.200	.211	.194	3.45	9.19
Medlen, Casey	R-R	6-0	155	8-4-89	3	4	3.77	48	0	0	8	60	53	32	25	5	34	47	.237	.250	.228	7.09	5.13
Moye, Andy	R-R	6-5	180	9-11-87	6	15	4.25	26	25	2	0	127	114	73	60	18	41	88	.238	.266	.215	6.24	2.91
Nelson, Jimmy	R-R	6-5	245	6-5-89	5	4	2.74	12	12	1	0	69	63	34	21	5	15	72	.241	.277	.215	9.39	1.96
Olmsted, Michael	R-R	6-6	245	5-2-87	0	0	0.00	6	0	0	0	7	2	0	0	0	3	8	.080	.000	.125	9.82	3.68
Pena, Ariel	R-R	6-3	240	5-20-89	8	9	3.73	27	27	0	0	142	115	63	59	17	79	131	.224	.200	.241	8.28	5.00
Rogers, Mark	R-R	6-3	240	1-30-86	0	0	11.12	5	0	0	0	6	8	7	7	2	8	1	.348	.400	.308	1.59	12.71
Seidel, R.J.	R-R	6-5	225	9-3-87	1	0	4.85	8	0	0	0	13	15	7	7	2	4	14	.278	.348	.226	9.69	2.77
Shackelford, Kevin	R-R	6-5	215	4-7-89	1	1	0.92	20	0	0	6	29	23	6	3	1	7	25	.217	.237	.206	7.67	2.15
Williams, Alan	L-L	6-3	195	3-5-90	0	2	3.00	13	3	0	1	30	26	13	10	2	11	32	.243	.265	.233	9.60	3.30
Williams, Mark	R-R	6-3	240	8-12-89	0	0	5.40	15	1	0	0	30	29	18	18	7	22	28	.264	.388	.164	8.40	6.60

Fielding

Catcher	PCT	G	PO	A	E	DP	PB
De La Rosa	1.000	8	54	9	0	2	3
Diaz	.980	29	183	15	4	2	8
Paciorek	.947	11	65	7	4	1	4
Weisenburger	.990	60	355	35	4	3	4
Zarraga	.994	44	274	33	2	3	9

First Base	PCT	G	PO	A	E	DP
Kjeldgaard	1.000	3	23	2	0	1
Rogers	.993	130	1108	84	9	109
Walker	.971	11	62	4	2	5

Second Base	PCT	G	PO	A	E	DP
Bianchi	1.000	2	4	5	0	1
Chavez	1.000	5	9	12	0	2
Gomez	1.000	1	3	2	0	0

	PCT	G	PO	A	E	DP	PB
Mittelstaedt	.929	6	9	17	2	3	
Paciorek	.857	2	2	4	1	0	
Patterson	1.000	10	18	27	0	3	
Shaw	.985	102	146	249	6	53	
Vucinich	.990	26	45	57	1	14	

Third Base	PCT	G	PO	A	E	DP
Bianchi	1.000	1	1	0	0	0
Mittelstaedt	1.000	5	1	5	0	1
Vucinich	.974	14	13	24	1	1
Walker	.953	99	62	161	11	17

Shortstop	PCT	G	PO	A	E	DP
Bianchi	1.000	2	3	4	0	0
Chavez	.882	11	17	28	6	9

	PCT	G	PO	A	E	DP
Gomez	.965	110	195	330	19	70
Shaw	.933	26	35	77	8	11

Outfield	PCT	G	PO	A	E	DP
Davis	.968	88	171	9	6	1
Diaz	1.000	1	1	0	0	0
Kjeldgaard	.977	119	195	13	5	3
Mittelstaedt	1.000	6	7	1	0	0
Owings	.923	7	12	0	1	0
Paciorek	1.000	3	3	0	0	0
Patterson	1.000	17	26	1	0	0
Rogers	1.000	2	2	1	0	0
Stang	.990	55	100	4	1	4
Tosoni	.978	124	218	9	5	1
Vucinich	1.000	9	17	0	0	0

FLORIDA STATE LEAGUE

MILWAUKEE BREWERS

Batting	B-T	HT	WT	DOB	AVG	vLH	vRH	G	AB	R	H	2B	3B	HR	RBI	BB	HBP	SH	SF	SO	SB	CS	SLG	OBP
Dean, Brent	R-R	6-1	210	7-26-86	.000	.000	—	1	4	0	0	0	0	0	0	0	0	0	0	0	0	0	.000	.000
Delmonico, Nick	L-R	6-2	200	7-12-92	.194	.357	.155	21	72	8	14	4	1	0	9	12	3	0	0	21	2	1	.278	.333
Dishon, Johnny	R-R	5-11	193	3-21-89	.208	.056	.259	23	72	7	15	1	1	1	3	6	0	2	1	19	2	3	.292	.266
Garfield, Cameron	R-R	6-1	195	5-23-91	.250	.269	.241	109	420	40	105	20	5	8	48	14	4	0	2	99	1	2	.379	.280
Haniger, Mitch	R-R	6-2	180	12-23-90	.250	.232	.258	88	328	52	82	24	3	6	43	32	4	0	1	68	2	2	.396	.323
Hawn, Cody	L-R	6-1	195	8-11-88	.248	.200	.261	89	326	32	81	14	0	9	35	24	1	0	2	82	1	1	.374	.300
Hinojosa, Dionis	R-R	6-0	192	8-14-90	.178	.071	.226	14	45	7	8	1	1	0	4	6	0	0	0	13	4	0	.244	.275
Hopkins, Greg	R-R	6-1	200	11-22-88	.237	.236	.238	129	497	55	118	25	0	6	63	25	3	6	1	99	9	4	.324	.278
Macias, Brandon	R-R	5-10	185	10-10-88	.208	.237	.195	107	360	34	75	21	3	3	27	18	12	6	2	56	7	4	.308	.268
McMahan, Ben	R-R	6-0	201	10-14-89	.246	.305	.212	72	228	28	56	11	2	5	30	15	1	0	2	56	10	4	.377	.293
Mittelstaedt, T.J.	L-R	5-10	185	2-13-88	.211	.151	.227	76	251	42	53	13	0	11	33	53	2	1	2	91	4	6	.394	.351
Neda, Rafael	R-R	6-1	215	10-12-88	.203	.087	.258	44	143	4	29	5	0	0	11	7	2	1	0	24	1	0	.238	.250
Ramirez, Nick	L-L	6-3	225	8-1-89	.258	.208	.280	134	500	70	129	27	3	19	81	54	0	0	7	171	5	0	.438	.326
Richardson, D'Vontrey	R-R	6-1	200	7-30-88	.325	.368	.309	52	209	25	68	12	2	1	13	14	2	2	1	43	13	6	.416	.372
Rivera, Yadiel	R-R	6-2	175	5-2-92	.241	.219	.249	129	478	51	115	16	2	5	37	32	9	4	1	80	13	8	.314	.300
Roenicke, Lance	R-R	6-1	190	6-8-88	.223	.191	.237	68	224	19	50	11	0	4	19	7	4	2	2	65	3	6	.326	.257
Stang, Chad	R-R	6-2	190	3-26-89	.254	.246	.258	68	228	32	58	6	3	3	16	23	2	5	1	71	11	6	.346	.327
Williams, Adrian	R-R	6-0	175	1-3-91	.143	.143	.143	7	14	3	2	0	0	0	1	1	0	0	0	5	1	0	.143	.200

Pitching	B-T	HT	WT	DOB	W	L	ERA	G	GS	CG	SV	IP	H	R	ER	HR	BB	SO	AVG	vLH	vRH	K/9	BB/9
Arnett, Eric	R-R	6-5	230	1-25-88	0	1	0.87	6	0	0	0	10	11	3	1	1	2	8	.306	.200	.381	6.97	1.74
Barnes, Jacob	R-R	6-2	230	4-14-90	9	6	3.08	21	14	1	0	105	98	43	36	6	36	66	.250	.255	.247	5.64	3.08
Bradley, Jed	L-L	6-4	225	6-12-90	4	4	4.14	16	16	1	0	78	81	42	36	6	39	58	.270	.239	.279	6.66	4.48
Burgos, Hiram	R-R	5-11	210	8-4-87	0	0	4.50	1	1	0	0	4	5	2	2	0	0	4	.313	.333	.300	9.00	0.00
Cravy, Tyler	R-R	6-3	194	7-13-89	4	2	2.04	25	9	0	0	79	61	22	18	1	24	59	.210	.195	.219	6.69	2.72
Fiers, Mike	R-R	6-2	195	6-15-85	0	0	6.00	1	1	0	0	6	6	4	4	1	0	8	.250	.222	.267	12.00	0.00
Gagnon, Drew	R-R	6-4	195	6-26-90	3	4	5.16	10	10	0	0	45	46	27	26	2	15	50	.263	.254	.269	9.93	2.98
Goforth, David	R-R	6-0	188	10-11-88	7	5	3.10	14	14	0	0	78	67	33	27	4	28	58	.231	.228	.233	6.66	3.22
Hall, Brooks	R-R	6-5	200	6-26-90	2	3	2.78	11	10	0	0	58	47	24	18	1	18	40	.217	.224	.212	6.17	2.78
Harvey, Seth	L-R	6-2	205	1-20-88	1	0	4.02	16	0	0	10	16	19	8	7	1	10	11	.302	.296	.306	6.32	5.74
Lamontagne, Andre	B-R	6-4	230	3-24-86	1	0	3.00	19	0	0	0	21	20	8	7	1	12	19	.244	.130	.288	8.14	5.14
Leach, Brent	L-L	6-5	215	11-18-82	1	0	0.00	3	0	0	1	5	1	0	0	0	1	7	.067	.167	.000	12.60	1.80
Magnifico, Damien	R-R	6-1	185	5-24-91	0	2	6.08	10	10	0	0	27	32	21	18	2	17	17	.311	.286	.328	5.74	5.74
Mangum, Taylor	R-R	6-1	190	3-4-89	1	3	5.09	7	1	0	0	23	26	14	13	2	8	16	.283	.302	.265	6.26	3.13
Manzanillo, Santo	R-R	6-2	225	12-20-88	0	5	4.25	20	0	0	2	30	32	16	14	3	18	16	.278	.326	.250	4.85	5.46
Marzec, Eric	R-R	5-11	210	1-13-88	1	0	1.59	3	0	0	0	6	3	1	1	0	5	1	.176	.000	.231	7.94	0.00
Meadows, Dan	L-L	6-6	220	11-3-87	1	0	5.81	23	0	0	0	26	22	18	17	1	31	20	.234	.233	.234	6.84	10.59
Miller, Matt	R-R	6-6	220	1-30-89	4	3	5.08	34	0	0	0	57	53	38	32	3	42	40	.255	.224	.276	6.35	6.67
Moore, Alex	R-R	6-2	210	1-16-91	0	2	4.85	13	0	0	0	26	27	16	14	1	17	13	.278	.326	.241	4.50	5.88
Peterson, Stephen	L-L	6-3	210	11-6-87	5	1	3.23	41	0	0	1	64	61	23	23	5	12	58	.249	.250	.249	8.16	1.69
Pierce, Chad	R-R	6-1	215	11-20-87	6	6	3.40	30	11	0	0	109	93	44	41	6	52	106	.237	.207	.253	8.78	4.31
Rodriguez, Francisco	R-R	6-0	195	1-7-82	0	0	0.00	2	0	0	0	2	0	0	0	0	1	4	.000	.000	.000	18.00	4.50
Rogers, Mark	R-R	6-3	240	1-30-86	0	2	3.60	6	6	0	0	15	17	11	6	0	7	12	.279	.200	.355	7.20	4.20
Scarpetta, Cody	R-R	6-3	250	8-25-88	0	5	7.15	12	11	0	0	34	37	33	27	2	36	25	.282	.243	.298	6.62	9.53
Shackelford, Kevin	R-R	6-5	215	4-7-89	1	3	5.06	24	0	0	2	32	39	18	18	3	4	23	.300	.255	.329	6.47	1.13
Suter, Brent	R-L	6-5	195	8-29-89	7	9	3.63	21	20	1	0	124	125	57	50	11	36	97	.263	.254	.266	7.04	2.61
Toledo, Tommy	R-R	6-3	198	12-13-88	4	2	2.11	43	0	0	20	55	43	16	13	3	18	44	.214	.333	.147	7.16	2.93
Williams, Mark	R-R	6-3	240	8-12-89	4	0	1.61	13	0	0	1	28	17	5	5	0	12	22	.183	.286	.121	7.07	3.86

Fielding

Catcher	PCT	G	PO	A	E	DP	PB
Dean	1.000	1	7	2	0	0	0
Garfield	.985	93	645	59	11	4	11
Neda	.984	43	271	29	5	2	3

First Base	PCT	G	PO	A	E	DP
Hawn	.996	26	217	10	1	15
Hopkins	1.000	1	2	0	0	0
Ramirez	.989	108	918	64	11	115

Second Base	PCT	G	PO	A	E	DP
Hopkins	.984	124	245	326	9	84

Mittelstaedt	.968	7	13	17	1	4
Williams	1.000	5	7	9	0	3

Third Base	PCT	G	PO	A	E	DP
Delmonico	.900	15	14	22	4	5
Hopkins	1.000	2	1	5	0	0
Macias	.931	101	63	180	18	13
Mittelstaedt	.952	20	10	50	3	1

Shortstop	PCT	G	PO	A	E	DP
Macias	1.000	5	9	9	0	1
Rivera	.963	129	200	429	24	103

Outfield	PCT	G	PO	A	E	DP
Dishon	.980	23	44	4	1	0
Haniger	.972	87	202	8	6	0
Hinojosa	.946	14	34	1	2	0
McMahan	.961	61	95	4	4	1
Mittelstaedt	.988	46	74	5	1	1
Richardson	.979	51	135	4	3	2
Roenicke	.990	57	98	4	1	1
Stang	.963	66	128	3	5	1

MIDWEST LEAGUE

Batting	B-T	HT	WT	DOB	AVG	vLH	vRH	G	AB	R	H	2B	3B	HR	RBI	BB	HBP	SH	SF	SO	SB	CS	SLG	OBP
Arcia, Orlando	R-R	6-0	165	8-4-94	.251	.195	.271	120	442	67	111	14	5	4	39	35	6	2	1	40	20	9	.333	.314
Berberet, Parker	R-R	6-3	205	10-20-89	.257	.252	.259	95	339	35	87	17	2	7	35	31	6	1	3	58	0	2	.381	.327
Cooper, Garrett	R-R	6-6	230	12-25-90	.287	.273	.292	32	122	15	35	6	2	2	20	10	1	0	0	22	1	0	.434	.346
Coulter, Clint	R-R	6-3	210	7-30-93	.207	.241	.195	33	116	18	24	5	1	3	13	11	5	1	2	31	1	0	.345	.299
Dean, Brent	R-R	6-1	210	7-26-86	.167	.222	.154	13	48	3	8	3	0	0	4	2	1	1	0	20	1	0	.229	.216

	B-T	HT	WT	DOB	AVG	vLH	vRH	G	AB	R	H	2B	3B	HR	RBI	BB	HBP	SH	SF	SO	SB	CS	SLG	OBP
Garza, Mike	R-R	6-1	195	3-11-90	.282	.327	.264	106	412	43	116	15	9	4	41	18	1	6	2	79	4	5	.391	.312
Giacalone, Adam	L-R	6-2	218	12-22-91	.249	.250	.249	64	229	27	57	13	0	0	25	28	2	1	4	61	0	1	.306	.331
Haniger, Mitch	R-R	6-2	180	12-23-90	.297	.357	.272	41	145	24	43	12	2	5	25	25	3	0	5	24	7	0	.510	.399
Houle, Dustin	R-R	6-1	205	11-9-93	.261	.500	.077	7	23	5	6	4	0	0	1	3	1	0	0	2	0	0	.435	.370
McFarland, Chris	R-R	6-0	190	11-24-92	.238	.247	.233	87	307	35	73	12	8	3	42	22	5	3	2	90	7	3	.358	.298
Reed, Michael	R-R	6-0	190	11-18-92	.286	.349	.261	118	455	68	130	23	13	1	40	71	4	7	2	108	26	10	.400	.385
Roache, Victor	R-R	6-1	225	9-17-91	.248	.306	.228	119	459	62	114	14	4	22	74	46	6	0	5	137	6	2	.440	.322
Roberts, Tyler	R-R	6-0	226	10-25-90	.259	.250	.261	33	112	13	29	9	0	1	13	14	3	1	1	43	0	1	.366	.354
Rodriguez, Alfredo	R-R	6-0	175	5-26-90	.270	.241	.274	109	392	52	106	15	0	2	35	50	9	10	4	52	10	11	.324	.363
Roenicke, Lance	R-R	6-1	190	6-8-88	.250	.500	.167	10	32	4	8	0	0	1	3	2	2	0	0	7	0	0	.344	.333
Sermo, Jose	B-R	6-0	190	3-22-91	.179	.200	.172	35	117	10	21	4	2	2	18	8	1	1	2	38	5	3	.299	.234
Taylor, Tyrone	R-R	6-0	185	1-22-94	.274	.292	.267	122	485	69	133	33	2	8	57	35	14	11	4	63	19	8	.400	.338
Walla, Max	L-L	5-11	205	4-12-91	.254	.200	.265	71	256	15	65	19	2	0	27	19	3	1	1	71	6	2	.344	.312
Williams, Adrian	R-R	6-0	175	1-3-91	.140	.240	.098	38	86	9	12	2	0	0	3	12	0	4	0	22	2	1	.163	.245

Pitching	B-T	HT	WT	DOB	W	L	ERA	G	GS	CG	SV	IP	H	R	ER	HR	BB	SO	AVG	vLH	vRH	K/9	BB/9
Armold, Jonathan	R-R	6-2	200	1-15-89	4	3	3.89	26	0	0	3	39	36	21	17	5	21	41	.252	.262	.244	9.38	4.81
Blaski, Austin	R-R	6-3	200	8-2-90	3	2	2.01	12	8	0	0	54	40	20	12	1	20	30	.207	.248	.163	5.03	3.35
Burgos, Hiram	R-R	5-11	210	8-4-87	0	1	4.50	1	1	0	0	2	2	1	1	0	1	3	.250	.000	.400	13.50	4.50
Estrada, Marco	R-R	5-11	200	7-5-83	0	1	20.25	1	1	0	0	3	8	6	6	1	1	5	.500	.625	.375	16.88	3.38
Fasano, Ryan	R-R	6-1	195	11-10-89	0	0	1.93	3	0	0	0	5	5	1	1	1	0	3	.263	.111	.400	5.79	0.00
Fernandez, Rodolfo	R-R	6-2	220	3-21-90	4	4	2.35	25	2	0	4	61	53	26	16	5	11	50	.229	.248	.213	7.34	1.61
Gainey, Preston	R-R	6-3	205	2-13-91	4	7	5.11	25	13	0	0	99	114	62	56	10	51	70	.295	.297	.292	6.39	4.65
Gibbard, Ryan	R-R	6-3	220	11-28-89	4	7	5.69	25	10	0	2	100	124	69	63	9	45	63	.313	.291	.337	5.69	4.06
Hellweg, Johnny	R-R	6-9	205	10-29-88	1	0	3.00	1	1	0	0	6	5	2	2	0	2	4	.217	.400	.077	6.00	3.00
Henderson, Jim	L-R	6-2	220	10-21-82	0	0	0.00	1	0	0	0	1	1	0	0	0	0	3	.250	.500	.000	27.00	0.00
Johnson, Hobbs	R-L	5-11	205	4-29-91	0	0	0.69	7	0	0	1	13	13	2	1	0	4	23	.255	.267	.250	15.92	2.77
Lopez, Jorge	R-R	6-4	165	2-10-93	7	8	5.23	25	22	0	2	117	120	78	68	13	48	92	.264	.227	.302	7.08	3.69
Lorenzo, Leonard	R-R	6-0	190	7-16-91	2	5	6.13	17	8	0	2	62	72	53	42	6	32	42	.300	.390	.230	6.13	4.67
Magnifico, Damien	R-R	6-1	185	5-24-91	5	1	3.83	11	8	0	0	54	51	25	23	4	24	46	.250	.211	.284	7.67	4.00
Mangum, Taylor	R-R	6-1	190	3-4-89	2	6	3.35	20	0	0	5	48	48	20	18	4	17	47	.265	.255	.276	8.75	3.17
Martin, Harvey	L-R	6-1	200	7-12-89	2	5	4.63	12	0	0	3	35	43	24	18	5	10	23	.297	.353	.247	5.91	2.57
Razo, Chris	R-R	5-11	210	6-22-90	1	1	6.43	4	0	0	0	7	9	5	5	0	3	3	.310	.316	.300	3.86	3.86
Ross, Austin	R-R	6-2	200	8-12-88	2	0	2.38	10	10	0	0	45	37	15	12	1	12	41	.224	.171	.277	8.14	2.38
Semmelhack, Eric	R-R	6-5	230	1-7-91	2	6	4.99	22	15	0	1	106	128	72	59	18	42	52	.299	.276	.321	4.40	3.55
Strong, Mike	L-L	6-0	194	11-17-88	3	4	3.31	25	8	0	1	87	79	46	32	4	45	98	.236	.264	.223	10.14	4.66
Suter, Brent	R-L	6-5	195	8-29-89	0	1	1.80	3	3	0	0	15	14	4	3	0	5	16	.241	.294	.220	9.60	3.00
Viramontes, Martin	R-R	6-5	225	7-12-89	1	1	5.16	15	0	0	1	30	25	19	17	3	25	41	.223	.235	.213	12.44	7.58
Wagner, Tyler	R-R	6-3	195	1-24-91	10	8	3.21	27	25	1	0	149	129	59	53	10	56	116	.236	.248	.226	7.02	3.39
Wall, Taylor	L-L	6-2	190	1-8-90	2	3	2.15	33	0	0	7	50	40	15	12	2	18	35	.229	.208	.238	6.26	3.22
Williams, Alan	L-L	6-3	195	3-5-90	0	2	7.11	3	0	0	0	6	10	6	5	0	3	6	.400	.714	.278	8.53	4.26

Fielding

Catcher	PCT	G	PO	A	E	DP	PB
Berberet	.992	59	428	60	4	3	8
Coulter	.962	28	173	29	8	1	17
Dean	.971	12	90	11	3	2	2
Houle	1.000	7	57	10	0	1	0
Roberts	.982	33	202	19	4	1	5

First Base	PCT	G	PO	A	E	DP
Berberet	.990	32	273	29	3	32
Cooper	.985	26	244	17	4	20
Garza	.973	23	139	7	4	13
Giacalone	.992	63	543	51	5	44
Walla	.867	2	12	1	2	1

Second Base	PCT	G	PO	A	E	DP
McFarland	.947	74	105	198	17	30
Rodriguez	.968	46	72	143	7	25
Williams	.971	19	24	43	2	4

Third Base	PCT	G	PO	A	E	DP
Garza	.933	83	53	142	14	8
Rodriguez	.893	35	26	49	9	6
Sermo	.933	25	17	53	5	5
Williams	—	1	0	0	0	0

Shortstop	PCT	G	PO	A	E	DP
Arcia	.963	120	253	353	23	79
Rodriguez	1.000	9	22	21	0	7

	PCT	G	PO	A	E	DP
Williams	1.000	9	21	34	0	7

Outfield	PCT	G	PO	A	E	DP
Haniger	.958	35	62	7	3	2
Reed	.983	107	166	9	3	1
Roache	.932	86	146	5	11	2
Roenicke	.923	8	12	0	1	0
Sermo	—	1	0	0	0	0
Taylor	.986	112	270	13	4	3
Walla	.977	56	80	5	2	1
Williams	1.000	3	8	1	0	0

AZL BREWERS   ROOKIE
ARIZONA LEAGUE

Batting	B-T	HT	WT	DOB	AVG	vLH	vRH	G	AB	R	H	2B	3B	HR	RBI	BB	HBP	SH	SF	SO	SB	CS	SLG	OBP
Andrade, Joe	L-R	5-10	195	4-21-90	.175	.091	.207	16	40	4	7	2	0	0	2	5	0	0	0	9	0	0	.225	.267
Aviles, Luis	R-R	6-1	170	3-16-95	.207	.185	.213	42	121	14	25	2	2	0	14	10	1	2	2	40	6	1	.256	.269
Castillo, Francisco	B-R	5-11	170	6-4-93	.282	.294	.279	45	170	23	48	5	3	0	14	14	3	5	0	32	15	6	.347	.348
Cleary, Jack	R-R	6-2	212	6-20-90	.233	.263	.222	25	73	8	17	5	0	0	7	4	1	0	1	13	0	0	.301	.278
Coulter, Clint	R-R	6-3	210	7-30-93	.350	.333	.354	17	60	12	21	5	1	3	15	5	1	0	0	15	1	1	.617	.409
Davis, Johnny	B-R	5-9	172	4-26-90	.294	.400	.268	30	102	11	30	5	1	0	9	8	1	1	0	21	17	5	.363	.351
Denson, David	L-R	6-4	245	11-17-95	.244	.250	.242	40	127	22	31	6	1	6	17	29	2	0	3	45	2	2	.449	.385
Diaz, Brandon	R-R	5-11	175	4-14-95	.286	.364	.266	45	161	37	46	9	5	3	26	28	1	2	0	39	21	9	.460	.395
Eshleman, Paul	R-R	6-3	220	9-3-90	.286	.364	.273	26	77	12	22	3	0	1	8	5	1	0	1	18	0	0	.364	.333
Halcomb, Steven	L-R	5-10	180	8-7-92	.317	.556	.250	27	82	12	26	3	0	0	7	11	2	1	1	10	5	4	.354	.406
Hernandez, Yonki	B-R	5-10	160	10-5-90	.255	.143	.303	25	47	13	12	2	3	1	6	6	0	0	0	17	7	0	.489	.340
Neuhaus, Tucker	L-R	6-3	190	6-18-95	.231	.182	.245	51	195	29	45	12	1	0	24	23	0	0	1	56	6	3	.303	.311
Norton, Tanner	L-R	6-0	190	7-9-95	.191	.190	.191	30	110	4	21	2	0	0	13	6	2	0	1	29	0	1	.209	.244
Owings, Micah	R-R	6-5	220	9-28-82	.222	.000	.250	4	9	1	2	2	0	0	0	1	0	0	0	4	0	0	.444	.300

Name	B-T	HT	WT	DOB	AVG	vLH	vRH	G	AB	R	H	2B	3B	HR	RBI	BB	HBP	SH	SF	SO	SB	CS	SLG	OBP
Richardson, D'Vontrey	R-R	6-1	200	7-30-88	.292	.286	.294	5	24	3	7	0	0	0	3	1	0	1	0	6	0	0	.292	.320
Rivera, Edgardo	L-R	6-0	155	4-12-94	.180	.105	.200	29	89	14	16	1	2	0	3	10	0	3	2	21	8	4	.236	.257
Rubio, Elvis	R-R	6-3	215	7-2-94	.314	.107	.367	42	137	18	43	11	0	4	26	10	6	1	0	30	4	3	.482	.386
Sermo, Jose	B-R	6-0	190	3-22-91	.372	.444	.353	13	43	5	16	3	1	1	8	4	0	0	0	9	4	4	.558	.426
Sharkey, Alan	L-L	6-1	185	11-8-93	.209	.059	.246	29	86	12	18	4	1	0	8	10	2	2	2	11	1	0	.279	.300
Williams, Eric	R-R	5-10	190	4-25-95	.260	.261	.260	37	127	16	33	3	1	0	13	14	1	3	2	21	6	2	.299	.333

Pitching	B-T	HT	WT	DOB	W	L	ERA	G	GS	CG	SV	IP	H	R	ER	HR	BB	SO	AVG	vLH	vRH	K/9	BB/9
Arnett, Eric	R-R	6-5	230	1-25-88	0	0	7.20	4	0	0	0	5	8	4	4	0	1	3	.348	.167	.412	5.40	1.80
Brock, Dylan	R-R	6-2	225	4-6-93	0	0	2.84	9	0	0	0	13	15	4	4	1	2	3	.283	.077	.350	2.13	1.42
Bucci, Nick	R-R	6-2	195	7-16-90	0	0	0.00	1	1	0	0	1	1	3	0	0	0	1	.333	.500	.000	13.50	27.00
Deeter, Ryan	R-R	6-0	180	7-27-91	1	0	0.00	7	0	0	1	11	5	0	0	0	4	9	.135	.167	.120	7.36	3.27
Dicent, Joel	R-R	6-3	176	8-4-91	0	1	5.00	3	0	0	0	9	7	5	5	2	7	8	.212	.286	.158	8.00	7.00
Estrada, Marco	R-R	5-11	200	7-5-83	0	0	3.38	1	1	0	0	3	3	1	1	0	0	4	.273	.000	.333	13.50	0.00
Figaro, Alfredo	R-R	6-0	175	7-7-84	0	0	0.00	1	1	0	0	2	1	0	0	0	0	4	.125	.000	.143	15.43	0.00
Garman, Brian	L-L	5-10	180	7-19-88	0	0	0.00	3	2	0	0	2	3	0	0	0	1	2	.300	.500	.200	7.71	3.86
Ghelfi, Drew	R-R	6-3	190	9-10-90	2	5	7.49	14	6	0	0	34	41	32	28	3	17	31	.295	.250	.325	8.29	4.54
Gomez, Milton	R-R	6-1	172	4-22-94	1	1	5.95	9	2	0	0	20	24	16	13	0	7	22	.304	.243	.357	10.07	3.20
Harkin, Scott	R-R	6-2	200	8-6-91	2	0	1.08	13	0	0	4	17	11	2	2	0	8	18	.190	.111	.225	9.72	4.32
Lavandero, Alex	L-R	6-3	180	11-21-93	1	1	3.71	14	2	0	1	34	30	24	14	3	22	32	.248	.302	.218	8.47	5.82
Lieser, Scott	R-R	6-3	195	4-23-90	0	2	3.38	11	0	0	0	19	21	11	7	1	3	19	.273	.226	.304	9.16	1.45
Matulis, Chris	L-L	6-6	217	4-9-90	1	1	7.06	11	0	0	0	22	27	18	17	0	11	15	.314	.381	.292	6.23	4.57
Moore, Alex	R-R	6-2	210	1-16-91	0	1	10.80	3	0	0	1	3	8	5	4	0	0	2	.421	.714	.250	5.40	0.00
Ortega, Jorge	R-R	6-1	165	6-20-93	2	5	4.15	14	5	0	0	56	61	38	26	5	10	41	.266	.233	.287	6.55	1.60
Poppe, Tanner	R-R	6-6	225	7-19-90	1	0	0.00	2	0	0	0	6	5	2	0	0	0	8	.238	.125	.308	12.00	0.00
Rizzo, Gian	R-R	6-1	160	9-5-93	1	2	4.28	14	7	0	1	48	58	29	23	1	6	53	.286	.333	.254	9.87	1.12
Rogers, Mark	R-R	6-3	240	1-30-86	0	0	0.00	1	1	0	0	2	1	0	0	0	0	4	.143	.000		18.00	0.00
Ross, Austin	R-R	6-2	200	8-12-88	0	2	14.29	6	6	0	0	11	20	19	18	1	4	10	.385	.412	.371	7.94	3.18
Spurlin, Tyler	R-R	6-3	195	6-17-91	3	0	0.90	12	0	0	1	20	16	9	2	0	2	23	.208	.241	.188	10.35	0.90
Terry, Clint	L-L	6-4	195	6-9-92	3	1	1.54	14	4	0	0	47	36	11	8	2	10	56	.211	.200	.213	10.80	1.93
Uhen, Josh	R-R	6-4	185	4-7-92	2	6	4.54	14	6	0	0	38	35	31	19	2	23	31	.248	.231	.258	7.41	5.50
Viramontes, Martin	R-R	6-5	225	7-12-89	0	1	1.23	4	4	0	0	7	6	4	1	0	5	11	.207	.267	.143	13.50	6.14
Wardour, Sean	B-R	6-5	230	8-7-91	1	0	5.95	11	0	0	1	20	29	14	13	1	6	19	.345	.429	.304	8.69	2.75
West, Will	L-L	6-4	170	7-23-92	0	0	5.06	3	2	0	0	5	3	4	3	1	3	4	.150	.250	.125	6.75	5.06
Williams, Alan	L-L	6-3	195	3-5-90	0	0	7.71	2	0	0	0	2	4	2	2	0	1	2	.400	.600	.200	7.71	3.86
Williams, Devin	R-R	6-3	165	9-21-94	1	3	3.38	13	6	0	1	35	28	17	13	0	22	39	.215	.158	.239	10.13	5.71

Fielding

Catcher	PCT	G	PO	A	E	DP	PB
Andrade	1.000	7	27	1	0	0	2
Cleary	.979	22	170	20	4	1	3
Coulter	.955	7	40	2	2	0	0
Eshleman	.983	16	107	8	2	1	1
Norton	.967	17	141	4	5	1	6

First Base	PCT	G	PO	A	E	DP
Denson	.987	35	288	13	4	24
Eshleman	1.000	2	9	1	0	0
Sharkey	.978	24	211	12	5	11

Second Base	PCT	G	PO	A	E	DP
Castillo	.935	44	63	111	12	15

	PCT	G	PO	A	E	DP
Diaz	.667	1	2	2	2	0
Halcomb	.974	9	10	28	1	4
Sermo	.913	4	7	14	2	3

Third Base	PCT	G	PO	A	E	DP
Andrade	1.000	3	2	3	0	0
Aviles	.860	18	12	31	7	2
Halcomb	1.000	6	4	11	0	1
Neuhaus	.934	27	18	53	5	4
Sermo	.917	9	3	8	1	2
Williams	.333	2	1	0	2	0

Shortstop	PCT	G	PO	A	E	DP
Aviles	.947	23	35	55	5	11

	PCT	G	PO	A	E	DP
Halcomb	.953	12	11	50	3	4
Neuhaus	.922	24	28	67	8	11

Outfield	PCT	G	PO	A	E	DP
Davis	.930	25	39	1	3	0
Diaz	.955	43	60	4	3	1
Hernandez	1.000	17	15	0	0	0
Owings	1.000	1	2	0	0	0
Richardson	1.000	5	11	1	0	0
Rivera	.964	27	48	5	2	0
Rubio	.920	33	42	4	4	0
Williams	.948	35	53	2	3	2

HELENA BREWERS   ROOKIE

PIONEER LEAGUE

Batting	B-T	HT	WT	DOB	AVG	vLH	vRH	G	AB	R	H	2B	3B	HR	RBI	BB	HBP	SH	SF	SO	SB	CS	SLG	OBP
Brennan, Taylor	R-R	6-0	210	1-31-92	.247	.176	.262	58	198	44	49	10	2	12	45	39	2	1	2	67	4	4	.500	.373
Cleary, Jack	R-R	6-2	212	6-20-90	.308	.000	.364	3	13	2	4	0	0	0	1	0	0	0	0	1	0	0	.308	.308
Cooper, Garrett	R-R	6-6	230	12-25-90	.274	.154	.306	16	62	11	17	4	0	4	10	7	1	0	0	18	0	0	.532	.357
Coulter, Clint	R-R	6-3	210	7-30-93	.216	.000	.267	20	74	8	16	4	0	1	8	4	1	1	5	14	1	0	.311	.263
Garcia, Omar	R-R	5-11	170	8-1-93	.305	.421	.279	54	203	39	62	4	1	0	27	34	9	5	1	39	28	6	.335	.425
Giacalone, Adam	L-R	6-2	218	12-22-91	.337	.286	.348	43	166	31	56	4	0	5	34	25	3	0	3	31	2	1	.452	.426
Harris, Jalen	R-R	6-2	210	7-7-92	.287	.333	.275	52	181	24	52	11	1	1	32	18	2	0	1	47	1		.376	.356
Hinojosa, Dionis	R-R	6-0	192	8-14-90	.273	.200	.283	33	128	29	35	6	1	1	8	11	0	1	0	23	5	7	.359	.331
Houle, Dustin	R-R	6-1	205	11-9-93	.250	.226	.255	46	180	23	45	8	0	1	19	7	4	1	2	35	1	2	.311	.290
Jenkins, Renaldo	R-R	6-0	180	3-1-93	.289	.391	.272	45	159	27	46	5	3	2	25	7	2	5	0	22	9	7	.396	.327
Markson, Charlie	R-R	6-2	180	2-6-91	.288	.333	.279	46	177	35	51	12	1	0	21	22	5	2	3	35	8	4	.367	.377
Orf, Nathan	R-R	5-9	180	2-1-90	.312	.370	.297	43	138	35	43	10	2	0	24	25	10	1	1	21	3	3	.413	.448
Ortega, Angel	R-R	6-2	170	9-11-93	.222	.143	.239	63	243	38	54	5	2	2	22	15	3	7	2	52	5	3	.284	.274
Pena, Jose	R-R	6-2	192	3-3-93	.272	.088	.307	57	213	29	58	19	0	10	35	21	4	0	3	46	5	3	.502	.344
Ratterree, Michael	R-R	6-1	190	2-9-91	.314	.326	.311	65	258	63	81	22	6	12	58	26	9	0	4	72	7	3	.585	.391
Sanchez, Ruben	L-L	6-2	198	8-20-91	.286	.364	.273	22	77	12	22	1	1	0	9	6	0	0	0	9	4	1	.325	.337
Turay, Michael	R-R	5-10	175	1-8-90	.256	.375	.226	23	78	12	20	6	0	3	16	9	2	1	0	16	2	0	.449	.348
Weiss, Jesse	R-R	6-0	200	9-27-90	.273	.200	.289	15	55	10	15	2	1	0	3	4	2	0	1	17	0	0	.345	.339

Pitching	B-T	HT	WT	DOB	W	L	ERA	G	GS	CG	SV	IP	H	R	ER	HR	BB	SO	AVG	vLH	vRH	K/9	BB/9
Albury, Sean	R-R	5-11	180	3-24-89	2	0	2.00	14	0	0	3	18	16	7	4	0	5	17	.229	.074	.326	8.50	2.50
Alexander, Tyler	L-L	6-1	180	9-22-91	2	0	1.72	13	0	0	1	16	7	3	3	1	3	27	.125	.067	.146	15.51	1.72
Archer, Tristan	R-R	6-2	200	10-18-90	2	1	3.08	15	3	0	1	38	37	20	13	4	5	25	.243	.235	.248	5.92	1.18
Astin, Barrett	R-R	6-1	190	10-22-91	1	1	4.30	12	8	0	0	38	41	25	18	6	11	31	.266	.309	.233	7.41	2.63
Banda, Anthony	L-L	6-3	175	8-10-93	3	4	4.45	14	14	0	0	61	64	40	30	7	25	45	.274	.318	.256	6.68	3.71
Encarnacion, Estevenson	R-R	6-4	186	6-4-90	1	1	3.38	15	0	0	1	24	20	15	9	1	15	16	.222	.323	.169	6.00	5.63
Fasano, Ryan	R-R	6-1	195	11-10-89	2	2	4.09	13	0	0	1	22	25	15	10	3	5	13	.275	.091	.379	5.32	2.05
Hillis, Andy	R-R	6-6	218	11-6-90	3	1	0.44	17	0	0	5	21	14	2	1	0	12	23	.192	.258	.143	10.02	5.23
Johnson, Hobbs	R-L	5-11	205	4-29-91	0	0	1.13	4	0	0	1	8	7	2	1	0	0	9	.219	.125	.250	10.13	0.00
Keller, Daniel	R-R	6-5	190	6-30-92	1	3	7.15	12	5	0	0	34	35	29	27	2	25	18	.269	.146	.326	4.76	6.62
Linehan, Tyler	L-L	6-0	240	8-30-91	2	2	2.45	14	4	0	3	40	31	19	11	1	26	35	.214	.214	.214	7.81	5.80
Martin, Harvey	L-R	6-1	200	7-12-89	0	0	2.08	2	0	0	0	4	7	1	1	0	1	6	.389	.400	.375	12.46	2.08
Moore, Brandon	R-R	6-3	230	2-27-92	1	3	6.68	13	8	0	0	32	41	29	24	3	11	22	.308	.280	.325	6.12	3.06
Otterman, David	R-L	6-3	210	5-15-91	1	4	4.84	14	7	0	0	45	45	34	24	3	38	26	.254	.214	.267	5.24	7.66
Poppe, Tanner	R-R	6-6	225	7-19-90	1	0	2.75	13	0	0	2	20	16	6	6	2	6	16	.222	.194	.244	7.32	2.75
Quintana, Zachary	R-R	5-11	180	4-15-94	4	4	6.95	14	14	0	0	66	95	60	51	5	32	42	.347	.362	.328	5.73	4.36
Razo, Chris	R-R	5-11	210	6-22-90	6	0	2.61	11	0	0	0	21	16	8	6	0	6	11	.208	.200	.214	4.79	2.61
Reyes, Eduard	R-R	6-0	174	8-23-90	4	5	7.38	15	5	0	1	57	66	51	47	9	29	53	.287	.313	.276	8.32	4.55
Santiago, Juan	L-L	5-11	176	12-23-90	4	0	4.83	17	0	0	3	32	29	18	17	2	27	25	.246	.222	.260	7.11	7.67
Seidenberger, Trevor	L-L	6-2	196	6-9-92	0	1	6.75	10	2	0	0	27	32	23	20	3	12	19	.302	.333	.286	6.41	4.05
Williams, Taylor	B-R	5-11	165	7-21-91	3	1	4.25	12	6	0	0	42	42	22	20	5	17	42	.258	.296	.228	8.93	3.61

Fielding

Catcher	PCT	G	PO	A	E	DP	PB
Cleary	.950	3	15	4	1	0	1
Coulter	.980	14	89	11	2	2	3
Houle	.975	43	276	38	8	1	7
Turay	.974	19	134	17	4	0	3

First Base	PCT	G	PO	A	E	DP
Cooper	.978	15	128	8	3	9
Giacalone	.990	39	370	22	4	31
Harris	.991	24	205	13	2	14
Weiss	1.000	2	18	1	0	1

Second Base	PCT	G	PO	A	E	DP
Harris	.977	8	22	20	1	4
Jenkins	.968	32	57	94	5	14
Orf	.941	40	72	121	12	29

Third Base	PCT	G	PO	A	E	DP
Brennan	.897	57	36	121	18	8
Harris	.855	19	14	33	8	3
Turay	1.000	2	0	5	0	0

Shortstop	PCT	G	PO	A	E	DP
Jenkins	.968	15	24	36	2	7
Ortega	.955	63	120	223	16	36

Outfield	PCT	G	PO	A	E	DP
Garcia	.958	54	114	1	5	0
Hinojosa	.935	24	41	2	3	0
Markson	.946	34	52	1	3	0
Pena	.955	45	60	3	3	0
Ratterree	.968	57	85	6	3	0
Sanchez	.931	18	25	2	2	0

DSL BREWERS — ROOKIE

DOMINICAN SUMMER LEAGUE

Batting	B-T	HT	WT	DOB	AVG	vLH	vRH	G	AB	R	H	2B	3B	HR	RBI	BB	HBP	SH	SF	SO	SB	CS	SLG	OBP
Belonis, Carlos	R-R	6-3	175	8-19-94	.167	—	.167	2	6	1	1	0	0	0	0	0	0	0	0	3	0	0	.167	.167
Chal, Roosevert	L-R	5-9	152	4-9-94	.200	.200	.200	15	35	4	7	0	1	0	5	3	0	1	0	7	1	2	.257	.263
Colatosti, Raphachel	R-R	6-1	173	7-3-93	.227	.143	.242	44	141	19	32	1	2	0	11	12	2	4	0	20	2	4	.262	.297
De Leon, Juan	R-R	6-4	217	2-27-92	.197	.147	.212	50	147	15	29	3	0	0	5	19	9	1	0	64	0	0	.218	.326
De Los Santos, Juan	R-R	5-11	170	1-11-94	.281	.389	.257	62	203	29	57	13	2	2	31	25	11	1	3	46	9	1	.394	.384
Leonardo, Daniel	B-R	5-9	157	8-28-95	.233	.119	.260	60	219	32	51	7	2	1	22	33	4	1	3	46	8	7	.297	.340
Martinez, Kevin	B-R	5-10	180	1-11-95	.215	.111	.245	40	121	16	26	6	1	0	17	8	3	0	1	18	1	2	.281	.278
Martinez, Yerald	R-R	6-2	180	12-3-95	.198	.194	.199	57	187	32	37	14	1	0	19	26	1	3	1	60	8	4	.283	.298
Matos, Sthervin	R-R	6-1	185	2-31-94	.232	.227	.233	35	125	13	29	9	1	4	16	10	4	0	0	28	8	2	.416	.309
Mejia, Natanael	R-R	6-0	175	7-10-92	.253	.400	.224	35	91	14	23	5	0	3	13	9	3	1	3	19	0	0	.407	.330
Munoz, Gregory	L-R	5-9	160	2-6-94	.292	.323	.286	54	185	31	54	1	6	0	18	22	3	2	0	36	13	3	.362	.376
Ortiz, Juan	L-R	6-1	175	9-20-94	.200	.190	.202	61	235	29	47	10	1	4	24	12	8	0	2	67	4	4	.302	.261
Otano, Leudi	R-R	5-11	180	2-21-91	.281	.265	.284	57	203	30	57	14	1	3	25	30	0	0	1	57	5	4	.404	.372
Quiterio, Jorge	R-R	6-0	171	12-10-94	.278	.300	.273	60	216	35	60	12	2	5	37	25	6	0	3	37	8	5	.421	.364
Santana, Yunior	R-R	6-3	210	9-10-93	.232	.091	.257	62	224	31	52	9	3	2	30	22	4	0	2	78	16	9	.326	.310

Pitching	B-T	HT	WT	DOB	W	L	ERA	G	GS	CG	SV	IP	H	R	ER	HR	BB	SO	AVG	vLH	vRH	K/9	BB/9
Arguila, Nelson	R-R	6-0	180		1	0	11.05	6	0	0	0	7	4	9	9	1	16	4	.200	.000	.235	4.91	19.64
Arias, Doni	R-R	6-3	187	7-26-92	1	0	3.94	16	0	0	6	16	9	7	7	0	10	16	.167	.100	.206	9.00	5.63
Benoit, Rodrigo	R-R	6-2	170	2-23-94	0	2	6.75	6	2	0	0	13	22	10	10	1	2	9	.373	.500	.333	6.08	1.35
Cordero, Axel	R-R	6-4	175	7-13-91	2	1	4.59	17	0	0	2	33	37	25	17	2	11	19	.278	.390	.228	5.13	2.97
De La Cruz, Joan	L-L	6-3	175	9-30-94	0	6	5.11	14	12	0	0	49	52	37	28	2	27	56	.274	.250	.278	10.22	4.93
Diaz, Miguel	R-R	6-1	175	11-28-94	3	2	2.40	11	9	0	0	49	36	17	13	0	21	34	.211	.204	.214	6.29	3.88
Diaz, Victor	R-R	6-1	170	10-6-93	5	8	3.34	14	11	0	0	70	65	37	26	5	26	56	.243	.321	.211	7.20	3.34
Dicent, Joel	R-R	6-3	176	8-4-91	0	1	9.00	3	0	0	0	5	4	6	5	0	8	7	.222	.000	.286	12.60	14.40
Diplan, Nattino	R-R	6-3	180	12-30-93	1	3	7.49	14	4	0	0	40	39	35	33	3	30	32	.258	.196	.286	7.26	6.81
Flores, Junior	R-R	6-1	175	10-13-94	1	2	12.54	15	1	0	0	19	25	29	26	3	31	18	.316	.364	.298	8.68	14.95
Leal, Yosmer	R-R	6-4	170	2-26-96	2	3	8.05	13	10	0	0	35	32	36	31	2	38	28	.248	.256	.244	7.27	9.87
Nova, Boanerges	L-L	6-2	170	2-6-93	0	0	3.75	15	0	0	0	12	10	5	5	0	12	20	.204	.167	.210	7.50	4.50
Padilla, Marcos	L-L	6-2	175	1-1-94	0	1	10.80	11	1	0	0	13	13	17	16	1	19	11	.277	.375	.256	7.43	12.83
Paulino, Felix	R-R	5-11	165	5-21-91	0	0	1.07	8	0	0	2	25	12	3	3	0	6	16	.135	.129	.138	5.68	2.13
Peguero, Pedro	R-R	6-6	215	8-10-93	0	7	10.67	14	8	0	0	29	28	41	34	1	38	26	.257	.265	.253	8.16	11.93
Rizzo, Gian	R-R	6-1	160	9-5-93	0	1	3.75	3	3	0	0	12	11	5	5	2	4	5	.234	.267	.219	3.75	3.00
Tejada, Melvin	R-R	6-3	175	1-24-95	1	1	4.71	7	0	0	0	21	23	13	11	0	7	7	.284	.367	.235	3.00	3.00
Torres, Joshua	R-R	6-0	160	4-26-94	2	4	3.70	15	4	0	0	49	43	22	20	2	14	38	.247	.171	.271	7.03	2.59
Torrez, Orlando	R-R	6-3	195	4-14-92	2	1	4.89	13	2	0	0	39	45	34	21	1	20	22	.283	.297	.279	5.12	4.66
Ventura, Angel	R-R	6-2	185	4-7-93	5	2	2.70	12	4	1	0	60	47	29	18	1	22	65	.211	.247	.192	9.75	3.30

Fielding

Catcher	PCT	G	PO	A	E	DP	PB
Martinez	.973	38	222	32	7	2	7
Mejia	.986	31	188	25	3	1	6
Otano	.981	17	81	23	2	0	7

First Base	PCT	G	PO	A	E	DP
Colatosti	1.000	3	17	4	0	0
De Leon	.991	39	313	22	3	12
De Los Santos	.995	28	179	15	1	13
Ortiz	.966	10	79	6	3	5

Second Base	PCT	G	PO	A	E	DP
Chal	.913	10	10	11	2	3
Colatosti	.971	17	33	33	2	6
Leonardo	.962	6	15	10	1	1
Munoz	.937	19	27	32	4	7
Otano	.857	1	2	4	1	0
Quiterio	.941	24	46	65	7	7
Santana	1.000	1	0	1	0	0

Third Base	PCT	G	PO	A	E	DP
Chal	1.000	1	0	1	0	0
Colatosti	.873	19	11	37	7	0
De Los Santos	.857	4	1	5	1	1
Matos	.855	34	34	72	18	3
Quiterio	.857	22	24	30	9	2

Shortstop	PCT	G	PO	A	E	DP
Leonardo	.930	44	97	115	16	20
Munoz	.947	29	43	65	6	8

Outfield	PCT	G	PO	A	E	DP
Belonis	1.000	2	3	0	0	0
Colatosti	1.000	2	2	0	0	0
De Leon	—	1	0	0	0	0
De Los Santos	.920	19	23	0	2	0
Martinez	.955	55	105	2	5	1
Ortiz	.951	50	70	7	4	0
Otano	.909	31	47	3	5	1
Quiterio	1.000	1	1	0	0	0
Santana	.944	61	112	7	7	1

Minnesota Twins

SEASON IN A SENTENCE: The Twins met pre-season expectations as one of baseball's worst teams by finishing 66-96, fourth in the American League Central and tied with the Cubs for the fourth-worst record in the big leagues.

HIGH POINT: Joe Mauer was one of the lone bright spots for the Twins' offense. The 30-year-old catcher posted an on-base percentage north of .400 for the sixth time in his career, batting .324/.404/.476 in 113 games, including 75 games behind the plate. His on-base percentage ranked fourth in the AL and he finished second in the batting race, with a lifetime .323 average that ranks first among active players. Second baseman Brian Dozier, 26, emerged as a pleasant surprise with a team-high 18 home runs, while Glen Perkins was an effective closer.

LOW POINT: Perkins gave the Twins more value than any of their starting pitchers, and their pitching staff as a whole was a disaster. The 788 runs the Twins allowed were the second-most in the majors, while they ranked last in baseball in strikeouts. The Twins didn't fare much better on offense, as their 614 runs scored ranked 25th in baseball.

NOTABLE ROOKIES: Trading Ben Revere to the Phillies before the season cleared a surprisingly quick path to the majors for 2008 first-rounder Aaron Hicks, who broke camp as Minnesota's Opening Day center fielder. Hicks, who had never played above Double-A entering the year, hit just .192/.259/.338 in 81 big league games. Corner outfielder Oswaldo Arcia moved back and forth between Triple-A Rochester and Minnesota and batted .251/.304/.430 in 97 games.

KEY TRANSACTIONS: With Justin Morneau's contract ending after the season, the Twins dealt their former star first baseman to the Pirates for outfielder Alex Presley and righthander Duke Welker, both of whom could be role players.

DOWN ON THE FARM: Byron Buxton, the No. 2 overall pick in the 2012 draft, firmly established himself as the best prospect in baseball. Buxton has the potential for five legitimately above-average tools, and between low Class A Cedar Rapids and high Class A Fort Myers, he hit .334/.424/.520 with 55 stolen bases en route to winning BA's Minor League Player of the Year award. Miguel Sano will rack up more strikeouts than Buxton, but the third baseman's power grades out at the top of the charts. Between high Class A and Double-A, Sano batted .280/.382/.610 with 35 homers.

OPENING DAY PAYROLL: $75.8 million (22nd)

PLAYERS OF THE YEAR

MAJOR LEAGUE	MINOR LEAGUE
Joe Mauer	**Byron Buxton**
c	cf
.324/.404/.476	(Low-A/High-A)
11 HR, 35 2B, 61 BB	.334/.424/.520, 55 SB
2nd in AL batting race	BA Minor League POY

ORGANIZATION LEADERS

BATTING   *Minimum 250 AB

MAJORS

*	AVG	Mauer, Joe	.324
*	OPS	Mauer, Joe	.88
	HR	Dozier, Brian	18
	RBI	Morneau, Justin	74

MINORS

*	AVG	Colabello, Chris, Rochester	.352
*	OBP	Colabello, Chris, Rochester	.427
*	SLG	Colabello, Chris, Rochester	.639
	R	Buxton, Byron, Fort Myers/Cedar Rapids	109
	H	Buxton, Byron, Fort Myers/Cedar Rapids	163
	TB	Sano, Miguel, New Britain/Fort Myers	268
	2B	Hicks, Dalton, Fort Myers/Cedar Rapids	39
	3B	Buxton, Byron, Fort Myers/Cedar Rapids	18
	HR	Sano, Miguel, New Britain/Fort Myers	35
	RBI	Hicks, Dalton, Fort Myers/Cedar Rapids	110
	BB	Buxton, Byron, Fort Myers/Cedar Rapids	76
	SO	Sano, Miguel, New Britain/Fort Myers	142
	SB	Buxton, Byron, Fort Myers/Cedar Rapids	55

PITCHING   #Minimum 75 IP

MAJORS

	W	Correia, Kevin	9
#	ERA	Correia, Kevin	4.18
	SO	Correia, Kevin	101
		Pelfrey, Mike	101
	SV	Perkins, Glen	36

MINORS

	W	Baxendale, D.J., New Britain/Fort Myers	12
	L	Dean, Pat, Rochester/New Britain	13
#	ERA	Albers, Andrew, Rochester	2.86
	G	Tonkin, Michael, Rochester/New Britain	52
	GS	Dean, Pat, Rochester/New Britain	28
	SV	Tonkin, Michael, Rochester/New Britain	21
	IP	Dean, Pat, Rochester/New Britain	165
	BB	May, Trevor, New Britain	67
	SO	May, Trevor, New Britain	159
#	AVG	Summers, Matthew, Fort Myers/New Britain	.232

2013 PERFORMANCE

General Manager: Terry Ryan. **Farm Director:** Brad Steil. **Scouting Director:** Deron Johnson.

Class	Team	League	W	L	PCT	Finish	Manager
Majors	Minnesota Twins	American	66	96	.407	13th (15)	Ron Gardenhire
Triple-A	Rochester Red Wings	International	77	67	.535	t-4th (14)	Gene Glynn
Double-A	New Britain Rock Cats	Eastern	66	76	.465	10th (12)	Jeff Smith
High A	Fort Myers Miracle	Florida State	79	56	.585	2nd (12)	Doug Mientkiewicz
Low A	Cedar Rapids Kernels	Midwest	88	50	.638	1st (16)	Jake Mauer
Rookie	Elizabethton Twins	Appalachian	37	31	.544	5th (10)	Ray Smith
Rookie	GCL Twins	Gulf Coast	28	32	.467	9th (16)	Ramon Borrego
2013 Overall Minor League Record			375	312	.546	t-4th (30)	

ORGANIZATION STATISTICS

AMERICAN LEAGUE

Batting	B-T	HT	WT	DOB	AVG	vLH	vRH	G	AB	R	H	2B	3B	HR	RBI	BB	HBP	SH	SF	SO	SB	CS	SLG	OBP
Arcia, Oswaldo	L-R	6-0	220	5-9-91	.251	.254	.249	97	351	34	88	17	2	14	43	23	4	0	0	117	1	2	.430	.304
Bernier, Doug	R-R	6-1	185	6-24-80	.226	.278	.200	33	53	9	12	3	0	0	5	8	1	2	0	15	2	1	.283	.339
Butera, Drew	R-R	6-1	200	8-9-83	.000	.000	.000	2	3	0	0	0	0	0	0	0	0	0	0	1	0	0	.000	.000
Carroll, Jamey	R-R	5-11	175	2-18-74	.230	.326	.203	58	191	21	44	6	0	0	9	13	1	1	0	35	2	0	.262	.283
2-team total (14 Kansas City)					.211	—	—	72	227	26	48	9	0	0	11	17	1	2	2	39	2	1	.251	.267
Colabello, Chris	R-R	6-4	220	10-24-83	.194	.191	.195	55	160	14	31	3	0	7	17	20	1	0	0	58	0	1	.344	.287
Doumit, Ryan	B-R	6-1	220	4-3-81	.247	.290	.229	135	485	49	120	28	1	14	55	48	1	0	4	99	1	0	.396	.314
Dozier, Brian	R-R	5-11	190	5-15-87	.244	.328	.219	147	558	72	136	33	4	18	66	51	6	3	4	120	14	7	.414	.312
Escobar, Eduardo	B-R	5-10	175	1-5-89	.236	.233	.238	66	165	23	39	5	2	3	10	11	0	2	1	34	0	2	.345	.282
Florimon, Pedro	B-R	6-2	180	12-10-86	.221	.180	.234	134	403	44	89	17	0	9	44	33	2	5	3	115	15	6	.330	.281
Fryer, Eric	R-R	6-2	215	8-26-85	.385	.667	.143	6	13	2	5	1	0	1	4	3	0	0	0	3	0	0	.692	.500
Herrmann, Chris	L-R	6-0	200	11-24-87	.204	.172	.211	57	157	16	32	7	0	4	18	18	0	3	0	49	0	1	.325	.286
Hicks, Aaron	B-R	6-2	190	10-2-89	.192	.203	.189	81	281	37	54	11	3	8	27	24	2	4	2	84	9	3	.338	.259
Mastroianni, Darin	R-R	5-11	190	8-26-85	.185	.227	.163	30	65	5	12	2	0	0	5	3	1	3	1	23	2	1	.215	.229
Mauer, Joe	L-R	6-5	230	4-19-83	.324	.322	.324	113	445	62	144	35	0	11	47	61	0	0	2	89	0	1	.476	.404
Morneau, Justin	L-R	6-4	215	5-15-81	.259	.209	.281	127	495	56	128	32	0	17	74	37	6	0	5	98	0	0	.426	.315
Parmelee, Chris	L-L	6-1	220	2-24-88	.228	.172	.242	101	294	21	67	13	0	8	24	33	3	0	3	81	1	1	.354	.309
Pinto, Josmil	R-R	5-11	210	3-31-89	.342	.294	.356	21	76	10	26	5	0	4	12	6	1	0	0	22	0	0	.566	.398
Plouffe, Trevor	R-R	6-2	205	6-15-86	.254	.300	.240	129	477	44	121	22	1	14	52	34	6	1	4	112	2	1	.392	.309
Presley, Alex	L-L	5-10	190	7-25-85	.283	.300	.274	28	113	9	32	4	1	1	11	8	1	0	0	21	1	3	.363	.336
Ramirez, Wilkin	R-R	6-2	230	10-25-85	.272	.333	.235	35	81	5	22	6	1	0	6	3	1	0	1	23	0	0	.370	.302
Thomas, Clete	L-R	5-11	195	11-14-83	.214	.175	.229	92	290	39	62	15	0	4	13	30	1	1	0	92	1	3	.307	.290
Willingham, Josh	R-R	6-2	230	2-17-79	.208	.219	.205	111	389	42	81	20	0	14	48	66	14	0	2	128	1	0	.368	.342

Pitching	B-T	HT	WT	DOB	W	L	ERA	G	GS	CG	SV	IP	H	R	ER	HR	BB	SO	AVG	vLH	vRH	K/9	BB/9
Albers, Andrew	R-L	6-1	195	10-6-85	2	5	4.05	10	10	1	0	60	64	34	27	6	7	25	.271	.290	.264	3.75	1.05
Burton, Jared	R-R	6-5	225	6-2-81	2	9	3.82	71	0	0	2	66	61	29	28	6	22	61	.242	.256	.229	8.32	3.00
Correia, Kevin	R-R	6-3	200	8-24-80	9	13	4.18	31	31	0	0	185	218	89	86	24	45	101	.297	.295	.299	4.90	2.19
Deduno, Samuel	R-R	6-3	190	7-2-83	8	8	3.83	18	18	0	0	108	105	48	46	7	41	67	.259	.204	.331	5.58	3.42
DeVries, Cole	R-R	6-1	180	2-12-85	0	2	10.80	4	2	0	0	15	22	18	18	6	9	12	.333	.292	.444	7.20	5.40
Diamond, Scott	L-L	6-3	220	7-30-86	6	13	5.43	24	24	0	0	131	163	88	79	21	36	52	.306	.310	.304	3.57	2.47
Duensing, Brian	L-L	6-0	200	2-22-83	6	2	3.98	73	0	0	1	61	68	28	27	4	22	56	.283	.303	.263	8.26	3.25
Fien, Casey	R-R	6-2	205	10-21-83	5	2	3.92	73	0	0	0	62	51	28	27	9	12	73	.225	.242	.213	10.60	1.74
Gibson, Kyle	R-R	6-6	210	10-23-87	2	4	6.53	10	10	0	0	51	69	38	37	7	20	29	.327	.341	.307	5.12	3.53
Hendriks, Liam	R-R	6-1	205	2-10-89	1	3	6.85	10	8	0	0	47	67	39	36	10	14	34	.327	.327	.326	6.46	2.66
Hernandez, Pedro	L-L	5-10	210	4-12-89	3	3	6.83	14	12	0	0	57	80	43	43	10	23	29	.338	.290	.354	4.61	3.65
Martis, Shairon	R-R	6-1	225	3-30-87	0	1	5.59	6	0	0	0	10	6	6	6	3	4	7	.171	.211	.125	6.52	3.72
Pelfrey, Mike	R-R	6-7	250	1-14-84	5	13	5.19	29	29	0	0	153	184	92	88	13	53	101	.300	.270	.337	5.95	3.12
Perkins, Glen	L-L	6-0	205	3-2-83	2	0	2.30	61	0	0	36	63	43	16	16	5	15	77	.196	.236	.183	11.06	2.15
Pressly, Ryan	R-R	6-3	205	12-15-88	3	3	3.87	49	0	0	0	77	71	37	33	5	27	49	.251	.289	.216	5.75	3.17
Robertson, Tyler	L-L	6-5	255	12-23-87	0	0	9.00	2	0	0	0	1	1	1	1	0	2	2	.250	.500	.000	18.00	18.00
Roenicke, Josh	R-R	6-3	200	8-4-82	3	1	4.35	63	0	0	1	62	63	31	30	6	36	45	.263	.295	.241	6.53	5.23
Swarzak, Anthony	R-R	6-4	210	9-10-85	3	2	2.91	48	0	0	0	96	89	33	31	7	22	69	.249	.268	.233	6.47	2.06
Thielbar, Caleb	L-L	6-0	195	1-31-87	3	2	1.76	49	0	0	0	46	24	11	9	4	14	39	.154	.143	.165	7.63	2.74
Tonkin, Mike	R-R	6-7	220	11-19-89	0	0	0.79	9	0	0	0	11	9	6	1	0	3	10	.205	.160	.263	7.94	2.38
Walters, P.J.	R-R	6-4	215	3-12-85	2	5	5.95	8	8	0	0	39	51	30	26	5	18	22	.311	.288	.333	5.03	4.12
Worley, Vance	R-R	6-2	230	9-25-87	1	5	7.21	10	10	0	0	49	82	43	39	9	15	25	.381	.368	.396	4.62	2.77

Fielding

Catcher	PCT	G	PO	A	E	DP	PB
Butera	1.000	2	3	0	0	0	0
Doumit	.992	43	229	20	2	2	3
Fryer	1.000	5	28	2	0	0	0
Herrmann	.987	27	136	13	2	0	0
Mauer	.996	75	495	30	2	7	3
Pinto	.983	20	112	4	2	1	0

First Base	PCT	G	PO	A	E	DP
Colabello	.991	26	206	16	2	19
Mauer	.988	8	78	3	1	9
Morneau	.997	112	999	86	3	117
Parmelee	1.000	23	152	12	0	15
Plouffe	1.000	2	2	0	0	0

Second Base	PCT	G	PO	A	E	DP
Bernier	1.000	4	1	2	0	0
Carroll	1.000	17	24	32	0	10
Dozier	.992	146	267	461	6	110
Escobar	1.000	7	8	17	0	4
Mastroianni	—	1	0	0	0	0

Third Base	PCT	G	PO	A	E	DP
Bernier	1.000	7	0	2	0	0
Carroll	.976	33	23	59	2	10
Escobar	.917	23	4	18	2	3
Plouffe	.956	120	91	194	13	25
Shortstop	PCT	G	PO	A	E	DP
Bernier	1.000	20	17	46	0	9
Carroll	1.000	3	2	9	0	2

	PCT	G	PO	A	E	DP
Escobar	.952	38	31	69	5	9
Florimon	.973	133	245	401	18	101
Outfield	PCT	G	PO	A	E	DP
Arcia	.989	83	167	5	2	2
Colabello	.938	11	14	1	1	0
Doumit	.984	33	55	5	1	2
Escobar	—	1	0	0	0	0
Herrmann	1.000	24	29	3	0	2

	PCT	G	PO	A	E	DP
Hicks	1.000	81	215	9	0	2
Mastroianni	1.000	28	40	1	0	0
Parmelee	.982	68	105	6	2	0
Presley	1.000	28	80	2	0	1
Ramirez	1.000	25	49	1	0	0
Thomas	.986	86	212	6	3	1
Willingham	.992	72	125	5	1	1

ROCHESTER RED WINGS

TRIPLE-A

INTERNATIONAL LEAGUE

Batting	B-T	HT	WT	DOB	AVG	vLH	vRH	G	AB	R	H	2B	3B	HR	RBI	BB	HBP	SH	SF	SO	SB	CS	SLG	OBP
Arcia, Oswaldo	L-R	6-0	220	5-9-91	.313	.224	.367	38	128	25	40	6	0	10	30	22	4	0	1	37	2	1	.594	.426
Benson, Joe	R-R	6-1	215	3-5-88	.192	.146	.214	42	151	20	29	7	2	1	9	10	3	0	0	50	4	2	.285	.256
Beresford, James	L-R	6-1	170	1-19-89	.298	.143	.324	58	198	34	59	7	1	0	21	16	2	5	1	29	5	2	.343	.355
Bernier, Doug	R-R	6-1	185	6-24-80	.295	.307	.290	92	302	47	89	15	5	3	41	31	7	10	3	74	4	2	.407	.370
Bigley, Evan	R-R	6-1	200	3-9-87	.303	.333	.296	19	66	10	20	4	0	2	3	9	1	0	0	14	1	0	.455	.395
Boggs, Brandon	B-R	6-0	210	1-9-83	.184	.200	.180	21	76	8	14	2	1	2	8	11	1	0	1	25	0	0	.316	.292
2-team total (98 Gwinnett)					.236	—	—	119	411	48	97	19	4	7	36	57	3	2	3	124	4	4	.353	.331
Butera, Drew	R-R	6-1	200	8-9-83	.218	.217	.219	27	87	8	19	2	0	2	10	2	2	1	2	15	0	0	.310	.247
Clement, Jeff	L-R	6-1	220	8-21-83	.220	.237	.213	123	446	45	98	25	1	16	70	45	1	0	3	106	1	1	.388	.291
Colabello, Chris	R-R	6-4	220	10-24-83	.352	.341	.355	89	338	58	119	25	0	24	76	43	5	0	5	89	2	1	.639	.427
Dinkelman, Brian	L-R	5-11	195	11-10-83	.215	.118	.232	89	237	35	51	10	2	6	23	32	3	3	4	40	6	0	.350	.312
Escobar, Eduardo	B-R	5-10	175	1-5-89	.307	.302	.309	43	166	22	51	16	2	4	27	17	3	1	1	37	6	2	.500	.380
Farris, Eric	R-R	5-9	180	3-3-86	.248	.226	.258	117	404	44	100	13	2	3	31	31	2	7	5	53	23	5	.312	.301
Fryer, Eric	R-R	6-2	215	8-26-85	.215	.233	.207	65	200	32	43	11	2	5	31	35	4	1	3	47	8	0	.365	.339
Hanson, Nate	R-R	6-0	195	2-8-87	.172	.286	.116	20	64	5	11	2	0	2	9	4	2	0	1	13	0	0	.297	.239
Herrmann, Chris	L-R	6-0	200	11-24-87	.227	.263	.216	69	247	31	56	9	3	2	22	24	1	2	1	61	3	2	.312	.297
Hicks, Aaron	B-R	6-2	190	10-2-89	.222	.385	.186	22	72	7	16	4	2	0	5	10	0	0	0	21	1	0	.333	.317
Lehmann, Danny	R-R	5-11	190	9-5-85	.250	.333	.214	9	20	2	5	0	0	0	2	1	0	1	0	6	0	0	.250	.286
Mastroianni, Darin	R-R	5-11	190	8-26-85	.240	.286	.233	15	50	9	12	1	0	0	5	10	3	0	0	11	4	0	.260	.397
Mitchell, Jermaine	L-L	6-0	215	11-2-84	.286	.424	.240	43	133	19	38	3	2	2	11	9	0	0	0	42	7	4	.383	.331
2-team total (63 Lehigh Valley)					.268	—	—	106	340	62	91	16	7	7	29	37	1	5	0	105	20	8	.418	.341
Olmedo, Ray	B-R	5-11	165	5-31-81	.234	.224	.238	105	312	42	73	12	1	2	38	36	3	7	3	47	10	2	.298	.316
Parmelee, Chris	L-L	6-1	220	2-24-88	.231	.200	.241	45	173	23	40	13	1	3	22	22	1	0	2	32	1	0	.370	.318
Pinto, Josmil	R-R	5-11	210	3-31-89	.314	.389	.288	19	70	6	22	9	0	1	6	2	1	0	2	12	0	0	.486	.333
Plouffe, Trevor	R-R	6-2	205	6-15-86	.333	.375	.286	4	15	3	5	0	0	1	3	2	0	0	0	3	0	0	.533	.412
Richardson, Antoan	B-R	5-8	165	10-8-83	.265	.193	.292	82	302	57	80	14	7	0	29	52	5	9	1	70	25	2	.358	.381
Rodriguez, Jairo	R-R	5-11	180	8-24-88	.000	.000	—	1	1	0	0	0	0	0	0	0	0	0	0	1	0	0	.000	.000
Rohlfing, Dan	R-R	6-0	200	2-12-89	.314	.421	.229	26	86	16	27	2	1	2	12	14	0	1	2	20	0	1	.430	.402
Romero, Deibinson	R-R	6-1	215	9-25-86	.266	.230	.281	86	304	40	81	15	1	10	50	47	4	0	3	75	4	0	.421	.369
Sobolewski, Mark	R-R	6-1	215	12-24-86	.182	.143	.200	12	44	3	8	1	0	1	4	4	0	0	0	15	0	0	.273	.250
Thomas, Clete	L-R	5-11	195	11-14-83	.296	.275	.306	36	125	17	37	8	0	9	25	18	0	0	0	35	6	4	.576	.385
Willingham, Josh	R-R	6-2	230	2-17-79	.111	.000	.125	3	9	1	1	0	0	1	1	2	0	0	0	2	0	0	.444	.273

Pitching	B-T	HT	WT	DOB	W	L	ERA	G	GS	CG	SV	IP	H	R	ER	HR	BB	SO	AVG	vLH	vRH	K/9	BB/9
Achter, A.J.	R-R	6-5	205	8-27-88	1	2	3.04	16	0	0	1	24	17	9	8	4	14	20	.198	.263	.146	7.61	5.32
Albers, Andrew	R-L	6-1	195	10-6-85	11	5	2.86	22	22	3	0	132	124	46	42	14	32	116	.251	.237	.255	7.89	2.18
Blackburn, Nick	R-R	6-4	240	2-24-82	0	1	10.80	1	1	0	0	5	10	6	6	2	0	0	.455	.500	.375	0.00	0.00
Darnell, Logan	L-L	6-2	210	2-2-89	4	4	4.26	12	11	0	0	57	63	33	27	5	22	43	.292	.194	.336	6.79	3.47
Dean, Pat	L-L	6-1	180	5-25-89	3	2	2.03	6	6	0	0	40	38	14	9	0	5	22	.253	.163	.297	4.95	1.13
Deduno, Samuel	R-R	6-3	190	7-2-83	0	0	2.70	3	3	0	0	17	14	6	5	1	10	17	.237	.273	.192	9.18	5.40
DeVries, Cole	R-R	6-1	205	8-12-85	3	4	7.02	10	10	0	0	50	77	40	39	6	13	24	.358	.364	.352	4.32	2.34
Diamond, Scott	L-L	6-3	220	7-30-86	4	0	2.41	6	6	1	0	41	33	13	11	4	9	19	.217	.218	.216	4.17	1.98
Eppley, Cody	R-R	6-5	205	10-8-85	2	0	4.88	22	0	0	0	24	23	13	13	0	13	20	.253	.313	.220	7.50	4.88
2-team total (19 Scranton/W-B)					4	2	6.49	41	0	0	3	43	53	31	31	1	28	39	—	—	—	8.16	5.86
Gibson, Kyle	R-R	6-6	210	10-23-87	7	5	2.92	17	17	2	0	102	85	36	33	5	33	87	.227	.225	.228	7.70	2.92
Hendriks, Liam	R-R	6-1	205	2-10-89	4	8	4.67	16	16	1	0	98	115	56	51	9	15	62	.294	.289	.299	5.67	1.37
Hernandez, Pedro	L-L	5-10	210	4-12-89	2	1	4.50	8	7	1	0	46	53	24	23	8	12	33	.290	.192	.328	6.46	2.35
Ibarra, Edgar	L-L	6-0	189	5-31-89	1	0	1.96	16	0	0	0	18	9	4	4	1	9	14	.150	.250	.100	6.87	4.42
Lanigan, Bobby	R-R	6-4	220	5-5-87	0	0	0.00	1	0	0	1	1	0	0	0	0	0	1	.000	.000	.000	13.50	0.00
Martin, Blake	L-L	6-2	182	6-19-86	0	0	4.02	12	0	0	0	16	12	7	7	6	12	15	.218	.200	.225	8.62	6.89
Martis, Shairon	R-R	6-1	225	3-30-87	2	4	4.26	42	3	0	11	80	68	39	38	8	31	65	.227	.163	.273	7.28	3.47
O'Connor, Mike	L-L	6-3	185	8-17-80	0	1	4.86	13	0	0	0	17	18	10	9	0	6	17	.343	.286	.385	9.18	3.24
Perdomo, Luis	R-R	6-0	180	4-27-84	5	4	5.95	45	0	0	6	65	67	48	43	9	43	59	.263	.213	.299	8.17	5.95
Perez, Rafael	L-L	6-3	195	5-15-82	1	0	2.25	4	0	0	0	4	2	1	1	1	3	2	.154	.333	.100	4.50	6.75
Pugh, Bruce	R-R	6-3	180	7-18-88	0	0	19.80	5	0	0	0	5	14	11	11	1	3	1	.538	.750	.200	1.80	5.40
Robertson, Tyler	L-L	6-5	255	12-23-87	2	0	3.05	21	0	0	1	21	22	7	7	0	16	20	.289	.176	.381	8.71	6.97
2-team total (26 Syracuse)					4		23.04	47	1	0	2	47	55	19	16	2	24	44	—	—	—	8.37	4.56
Slama, Anthony	R-R	6-3	195	1-6-84	0	4	13.50	14	0	0	2	13	16	21	20	2	14	9	.302	.320	.286	6.08	9.45
Thielbar, Caleb	L-L	6-0	195	1-31-87	1	1	3.76	17	0	0	1	24	26	17	13	1	8	34	.260	.159	.333	11.62	2.73
Thompson, Aaron	L-L	6-3	200	2-28-87	3	2	3.48	31	1	0	6	44	49	20	17	3	13	42	.285	.304	.276	8.59	2.66
Tonkin, Mike	R-R	6-7	220	11-19-89	1	2	4.41	30	0	0	14	33	33	18	16	3	8	36	.256	.250	.259	9.92	2.20
Turpen, Dan	R-R	6-4	245	8-17-86	2	0	6.93	21	0	0	1	25	34	24	19	6	13	19	.337	.316	.349	6.93	4.74

	B-T	HT	WT	DOB	W	L	ERA	G	GS	CG	SV	IP	H	R	ER	HR	BB	SO	AVG	vLH	vRH	K/9	BB/9
Vasquez, Virgil	R-R	6-3	205	6-7-82	4	7	4.41	23	13	0	1	88	100	47	43	12	19	60	.288	.279	.297	6.16	1.95
Walters, P.J.	R-R	6-4	215	3-12-85	7	5	4.18	19	19	1	0	103	110	54	48	5	46	82	.278	.298	.257	7.14	4.01
Wood, Tim	R-R	6-0	180	11-16-82	1	1	6.75	7	0	0	1	8	9	6	6	1	5	9	.273	.375	.176	10.13	5.63
Worley, Vance	R-R	6-2	230	9-25-87	6	3	3.88	9	9	3	0	58	65	31	25	3	17	34	.281	.265	.295	5.28	2.64

Fielding

Catcher	PCT	G	PO	A	E	DP	PB
Butera	.987	22	139	8	2	0	6
Fryer	.994	61	436	25	3	3	10
Herrmann	.993	40	264	27	2	0	1
Lehmann	1.000	8	45	2	0	0	1
Pinto	.979	14	91	4	2	0	2
Rohlfing	1.000	8	43	1	0	1	0

First Base	PCT	G	PO	A	E	DP
Clement	.987	53	432	31	6	49
Colabello	.990	67	540	40	6	60
Dinkelman	1.000	5	10	0	0	0
Parmelee	.996	28	225	20	1	18
Rohlfing	1.000	1	7	1	0	2

Second Base	PCT	G	PO	A	E	DP
Beresford	.985	56	108	158	4	41
Dinkelman	.938	4	8	7	1	2
Escobar	1.000	6	11	21	0	3

	PCT	G	PO	A	E	DP
Farris	.987	58	108	123	3	31
Olmedo	.992	31	53	66	1	16

Third Base	PCT	G	PO	A	E	DP
Dinkelman	1.000	15	10	28	0	4
Escobar	.941	6	2	14	1	2
Hanson	.889	8	3	13	2	1
Olmedo	.958	46	15	53	3	6
Plouffe	.900	3	4	5	1	0
Romero	.938	78	47	165	14	18
Sobolewski	.920	12	6	17	2	1

Shortstop	PCT	G	PO	A	E	DP
Bernier	.985	91	141	250	6	53
Escobar	.959	29	35	82	5	14
Olmedo	.954	31	59	85	7	21

Outfield	PCT	G	PO	A	E	DP
Arcia	1.000	19	30	3	0	0

	PCT	G	PO	A	E	DP
Benson	.974	40	73	3	2	0
Bigley	.968	18	29	1	1	0
Boggs	1.000	21	37	1	0	0
Colabello	.962	15	25	0	1	0
Dinkelman	.985	55	65	1	1	0
Farris	1.000	55	109	5	0	0
Hanson	1.000	5	7	0	0	0
Herrmann	.969	20	28	3	1	0
Hicks	1.000	19	45	0	0	0
Mastroianni	.906	14	27	2	3	0
Mitchell	1.000	43	74	3	0	0
Parmelee	1.000	18	31	1	0	1
Richardson	1.000	79	195	4	0	1
Rohlfing	1.000	17	23	1	0	0
Thomas	.988	33	76	4	1	0
Willingham	1.000	1	2	0	0	0

NEW BRITAIN ROCK CATS

DOUBLE-A

EASTERN LEAGUE

Batting	B-T	HT	WT	DOB	AVG	vLH	vRH	G	AB	R	H	2B	3B	HR	RBI	BB	HBP	SH	SF	SO	SB	CS	SLG	OBP
Beresford, James	L-R	6-1	170	1-19-89	.316	.214	.353	45	158	21	50	5	0	0	19	14	2	4	3	22	5	0	.348	.373
Bigley, Evan	R-R	6-1	200	3-9-87	.216	.239	.208	50	190	22	41	9	1	2	25	11	2	0	3	58	0	2	.305	.262
Boyer, Brad	L-R	6-0	185	10-4-83	.244	.000	.303	11	41	5	10	2	0	0	5	6	0	1	0	7	2	1	.293	.340
Christian, Jason	L-R	6-3	185	6-16-87	.189	.125	.200	23	53	6	10	2	2	0	4	6	0	1	0	18	2	2	.302	.271
Farris, Eric	R-R	5-9	180	3-3-86	.500	—	.500	1	2	1	1	0	0	0	0	1	0	0	0	1	0	1	.500	.667
Garcia, Harold	B-R	5-11	200	10-25-86	.217	.400	.167	7	23	3	5	0	0	2	5	0	3	0	0	5	0	0	.478	.308
Goncalves, Jonathan	R-R	5-11	205	5-13-89	.196	.120	.222	31	97	12	19	5	1	2	9	9	2	2	1	27	1	0	.330	.275
Hanson, Nate	R-R	6-0	195	2-8-87	.253	.281	.244	101	367	47	93	22	3	7	47	38	6	3	5	60	1	0	.387	.329
Knudson, Kyle	R-R	6-3	212	9-12-87	.295	.190	.328	28	88	8	26	5	0	0	12	10	3	0	1	13	0	0	.352	.382
Lehmann, Danny	R-R	5-11	190	9-5-85	.273	.250	.286	9	22	4	6	0	0	1	3	3	1	0	1	7	0	0	.409	.370
Morales, Angel	R-R	6-1	180	11-24-89	.169	.208	.153	57	166	20	28	6	1	5	16	12	2	1	3	63	3	1	.307	.230
Ortiz, Danny	L-L	5-11	175	1-5-90	.258	.236	.265	133	484	63	125	27	4	12	60	27	4	2	4	88	1	4	.405	.301
Parraz, Jordan	R-R	6-3	215	10-8-84	.261	.351	.222	74	241	36	63	11	0	11	33	25	7	1	1	53	5	1	.444	.347
Pettersen, Adam	R-R	5-9	170	11-19-88	.150	.257	.106	49	120	13	18	4	0	0	5	17	3	0	1	17	3	2	.183	.292
Pettit, Chris	R-R	6-0	200	8-15-84	.129	.150	.119	18	62	10	8	4	0	0	5	2	1	0	1	17	1	1	.194	.214
2-team total (29 Bowie)					.127	—		47	126	19	16	7	0	1	10	15	3	3	1	31	1	2	.206	.234
Pinto, Josmil	R-R	5-11	210	3-31-89	.308	.290	.315	107	386	59	119	23	1	14	68	64	3	0	0	71	0	2	.482	.411
Ramirez, Wilkin	R-R	6-2	230	10-25-85	.172	.273	.111	7	29	3	5	1	0	0	2	0	0	0	0	6	1	0	.207	.226
Richardson, Antoan	B-R	5-8	165	10-8-83	.336	.304	.344	33	119	26	40	6	1	0	14	22	5	7	1	25	14	5	.403	.456
Rodriguez, Reynaldo	R-R	6-0	195	2-7-86	.231	.196	.243	121	415	70	96	33	4	21	57	44	3	0	7	108	5	4	.482	.305
Rohlfing, Dan	R-R	6-0	200	2-12-89	.253	.274	.244	86	289	31	73	13	1	1	30	34	3	2	1	76	0	0	.315	.336
Romero, Deibinson	R-R	6-1	215	9-24-86	.355	.333	.364	8	31	6	11	2	0	3	6	4	0	0	0	7	0	0	.710	.429
Rosario, Eddie	L-R	6-0	170	9-28-91	.284	.287	.282	70	289	40	82	19	3	4	38	21	0	1	2	67	7	4	.412	.330
Sano, Miguel	R-R	6-3	195	5-11-93	.236	.299	.211	67	233	35	55	15	3	19	55	36	4	0	3	81	2	1	.571	.344
Santana, Danny	B-R	5-11	173	11-7-90	.297	.323	.286	131	539	66	160	22	10	2	45	24	8	11	5	94	30	13	.386	.333
Smith, Curt	R-R	5-10	210	9-9-86	.231	.222	.235	45	147	17	34	8	0	4	19	12	4	2	3	45	0	0	.367	.301
Sobolewski, Mark	R-R	6-1	215	12-24-86	.165	.200	.154	33	121	12	20	4	0	2	15	9	2	0	2	37	0	0	.248	.231
Turner, Stuart	R-R	6-2	220	12-27-91	.500	.667	.000	1	4	1	2	0	0	0	0	0	0	0	0	1	0	0	.500	.500

Pitching	B-T	HT	WT	DOB	W	L	ERA	G	GS	CG	SV	IP	H	R	ER	HR	BB	SO	AVG	vLH	vRH	K/9	BB/9
Achter, A.J.	R-R	6-5	205	8-27-88	2	0	2.21	25	0	0	3	37	28	10	9	3	19	36	.209	.146	.244	8.84	4.66
Baxendale, D.J.	R-R	6-2	190	12-8-90	5	7	5.63	16	16	1	0	93	110	65	58	13	22	64	.293	.275	.306	6.22	2.14
Blackburn, Nick	R-R	6-4	240	2-24-82	0	1	5.06	2	2	0	0	11	10	6	6	0	3	4	.270	.450	.059	3.38	2.53
Darnell, Logan	L-L	6-2	210	2-2-89	6	6	2.61	15	15	1	0	97	96	34	28	4	23	77	.263	.236	.274	7.17	2.14
Davies, Kyle	R-R	6-1	210	9-9-83	3	0	3.49	6	6	0	0	28	29	12	11	2	2	24	.264	.182	.318	7.62	0.64
Dean, Pat	L-L	6-1	180	5-25-89	6	11	4.68	22	22	2	0	125	151	72	65	12	17	61	.295	.255	.310	4.39	1.22
DeVries, Cole	R-R	6-1	180	2-12-85	0	2	1.69	3	3	0	0	16	12	7	3	3	2	11	.203	.207	.200	6.19	1.13
Fuentes, Nelvin	L-L	6-0	206	4-7-89	0	0	10.13	4	0	0	0	5	9	6	6	2	5	4	.391	.400	.389	3.38	3.38
Gonzalez, Jose	L-L	5-9	166	2-3-90	2	0	6.13	31	0	0	0	40	49	35	27	4	21	35	.299	.250	.327	7.94	4.76
Hauser, Matt	R-R	6-2	195	3-30-88	3	5	6.00	26	1	0	3	39	42	28	26	6	12	35	.276	.206	.326	8.08	2.77
Hermsen, B.J.	R-R	6-5	240	12-1-89	1	10	4.81	30	14	0	0	86	117	58	46	6	28	35	.328	.290	.362	3.66	2.93
Hernandez, Pedro	L-L	5-10	210	4-12-89	1	0	0.82	2	1	0	0	11	9	1	1	0	3	6	.209	.067	.286	4.91	2.45
Ibarra, Edgar	L-L	6-0	189	5-31-89	2	2	1.91	31	0	0	2	42	32	11	9	2	20	40	.212	.157	.240	8.50	4.25
Johnson, Cole	R-R	6-3	200	10-6-88	1	3	4.38	28	0	0	3	39	35	21	19	6	15	48	.235	.250	.224	11.08	3.46
Lanigan, Bobby	R-R	6-4	220	5-5-87	3	1	3.77	23	0	0	1	29	36	17	12	2	11	16	.300	.346	.265	5.02	3.45
2-team total (8 Portland)					3	3	5.36	31	1	0	3	47	61	35	28	6	15	31	—			5.94	2.87

MINNESOTA TWINS

Name	B-T	HT	WT	DOB	W	L	ERA	G	GS	CG	SV	IP	H	R	ER	HR	BB	SO	AVG	vLH	vRH	K/9	BB/9
Martin, Blake	L-L	6-2	182	6-19-86	2	2	6.10	25	3	0	0	41	46	32	28	5	33	37	.288	.225	.308	8.06	7.19
May, Trevor	R-R	6-5	215	9-23-89	9	9	4.51	27	27	2	0	152	149	79	76	14	67	159	.256	.257	.255	9.44	3.98
Meyer, Alex	R-R	6-9	220	1-3-90	4	3	3.21	13	13	0	0	70	60	29	25	3	29	84	.226	.207	.243	10.80	3.73
O'Rourke, Ryan	R-L	6-3	217	4-30-88	0	2	4.67	17	0	0	2	17	15	10	9	0	7	19	.238	.200	.286	9.87	3.63
Popham, Marty	R-R	6-6	235	8-4-87	2	1	10.80	6	0	0	0	8	11	10	10	1	8	10	.306	.250	.321	10.80	8.64
Pugh, Bruce	R-R	6-3	180	7-18-88	1	1	7.82	18	0	0	0	25	27	23	22	4	20	19	.273	.357	.211	6.75	7.11
Sattler, Dan	R-R	6-3	190	11-11-83	0	0	11.37	8	0	0	1	6	8	8	8	0	9	6	.296	.308	.286	8.53	12.79
Stuifbergen, Tom	R-R	6-3	270	9-26-88	3	1	6.16	8	6	0	0	31	34	21	21	5	9	20	.270	.274	.266	5.87	2.64
Summers, Matt	R-R	6-1	205	8-17-89	1	2	6.45	6	5	0	0	22	25	17	16	1	12	13	.284	.262	.304	5.24	4.84
Thompson, Aaron	L-L	6-3	200	2-28-87	0	1	0.61	11	0	0	3	15	11	1	1	0	3	11	.204	.158	.229	6.75	1.84
Tonkin, Mike	R-R	6-7	220	11-19-89	1	2	2.22	22	0	0	7	24	21	10	6	0	8	30	.216	.065	.288	11.10	2.96
Turpen, Dan	R-R	6-4	245	8-17-86	1	1	3.79	26	0	0	3	40	35	22	17	3	27	30	.236	.167	.293	6.69	6.02
Vasquez, Virgil	R-R	6-3	205	6-7-82	3	3	3.14	7	7	2	0	49	42	23	17	4	8	34	.227	.284	.189	6.29	1.48
Watts, Dakota	R-R	6-5	201	11-16-87	3	0	0.74	28	0	0	8	36	31	5	3	0	10	31	.230	.190	.264	7.68	2.48
Williams, Corey	L-L	5-10	204	7-4-90	1	0	0.00	1	0	0	0	2	2	0	0	0	2	3	.250	.500	.167	13.50	9.00

Fielding

Catcher	PCT	G	PO	A	E	DP	PB
Knudson	.995	28	194	16	1	2	4
Lehmann	.985	9	59	6	1	1	0
Pinto	.989	60	407	26	5	2	6
Rohlfing	.987	51	350	24	5	0	3

First Base	PCT	G	PO	A	E	DP
Hanson	.992	31	228	21	2	16
Rodriguez	.992	93	761	61	7	79
Rohlfing	1.000	6	48	1	0	5
Smith	.987	16	140	14	2	11

Second Base	PCT	G	PO	A	E	DP
Beresford	.982	38	63	102	3	22
Boyer	1.000	2	2	5	0	0
Christian	.939	13	15	16	2	4
Farris	1.000	1	4	7	0	3
Garcia	1.000	5	9	13	0	5
Hanson	1.000	4	4	9	0	2
Pettersen	.986	19	29	43	1	10

	PCT	G	PO	A	E	DP
Rosario	.965	65	122	157	10	37
Santana	1.000	3	6	7	0	2

Third Base	PCT	G	PO	A	E	DP
Beresford	1.000	2	2	1	0	1
Boyer	.889	3	4	4	1	0
Christian	.867	6	2	11	2	0
Hanson	.924	32	14	47	5	5
Pettersen	1.000	8	1	9	0	1
Romero	1.000	5	3	7	0	0
Sano	.935	64	44	128	12	9
Sobolewski	.845	31	22	49	13	2

Shortstop	PCT	G	PO	A	E	DP
Beresford	.957	4	10	12	1	1
Boyer	1.000	2	7	8	0	0
Christian	1.000	1	0	1	0	0
Pettersen	.958	14	16	30	2	5
Santana	.946	125	204	357	32	78

Outfield	PCT	G	PO	A	E	DP
Bigley	1.000	48	86	4	0	2
Boyer	1.000	2	5	2	0	0
Christian	1.000	1	2	0	0	0
Garcia	—	1	0	0	0	0
Goncalves	.963	31	50	2	2	0
Hanson	1.000	18	17	0	0	0
Morales	.985	57	131	4	2	0
Ortiz	.963	129	219	17	9	1
Parraz	.994	73	166	5	1	0
Pettersen	1.000	4	8	0	0	0
Pettit	1.000	17	43	0	0	0
Ramirez	1.000	3	8	0	0	0
Richardson	.986	33	70	1	1	0
Rodriguez	.900	9	8	1	1	0
Rohlfing	.976	24	40	0	1	0
Smith	1.000	4	6	0	0	0

FORT MYERS MIRACLE   HIGH CLASS A
FLORIDA STATE LEAGUE

Batting	B-T	HT	WT	DOB	AVG	vLH	vRH	G	AB	R	H	2B	3B	HR	RBI	BB	HBP	SH	SF	SO	SB	CS	SLG	OBP
Bigley, Evan	R-R	6-1	200	3-9-87	.353	.167	.455	4	17	3	6	2	0	1	1	1	2	0	0	4	0	0	.647	.450
Bryant, Adam	R-R	5-11	170	5-21-89	—	—	—	1	0	0	0	0	0	0	0	0	0	0	0	0	0	0	—	—
Buxton, Byron	R-R	6-2	189	12-18-93	.326	.339	.321	57	218	41	71	4	8	4	22	32	2	0	1	49	23	8	.472	.415
Goncalves, Jonathan	R-R	5-11	205	5-13-89	.266	.313	.244	84	301	43	80	20	3	2	25	31	6	1	4	72	16	5	.372	.342
Gonzales, Mike	L-R	6-6	264	6-16-88	.238	.188	.255	18	63	16	15	1	1	4	15	10	1	0	3	17	0	0	.476	.338
Haar, Bryan	R-R	6-3	215	12-9-89	.500	—	.500	1	2	1	1	0	0	1	1	0	0	0	1	0	0	1.000	.667
Hicks, D.J.	L-R	6-5	228	4-2-90	.270	.257	.274	42	148	18	40	8	0	4	28	22	2	0	4	38	0	1	.405	.364
Knudson, Kyle	R-R	6-3	212	9-12-87	.280	.161	.339	29	93	6	26	3	0	2	9	9	3	0	0	19	0	1	.376	.362
Koch, Matt	R-R	6-0	219	11-21-88	.278	.286	.275	98	352	38	98	20	1	7	40	35	3	0	3	75	1	1	.401	.346
Kvasnicka, Mike	R-R	6-2	200	12-7-88	.282	.338	.259	69	248	35	70	13	2	9	40	23	0	0	2	59	4	1	.460	.341
Leachman, Drew	R-R	6-3	200	4-21-89	.193	.188	.195	18	57	4	11	0	0	0	4	6	1	1	1	7	2	1	.193	.277
Leer, Andy	R-R	6-2	200	1-3-88	.195	.182	.201	66	205	29	40	10	1	4	19	17	1	8	2	66	4	1	.312	.258
Licon, Joel	R-R	5-10	180	12-21-90	.400	1.000	.333	2	10	1	4	1	0	0	2	0	0	0	0	1	0	0	.500	.400
Mastroianni, Darin	R-R	5-11	190	8-26-85	.400	—	.400	3	10	4	4	2	0	0	0	2	0	0	0	1	2	0	.600	.500
Mejia, Aderlin	B-R	5-11	170	5-12-92	.308	.289	.318	75	292	41	90	10	1	0	28	26	0	5	5	30	14	10	.349	.359
Michael, Levi	B-R	5-10	180	2-9-91	.229	.240	.223	94	315	40	72	15	4	4	28	49	2	3	6	67	21	2	.340	.331
Morales, Angel	R-R	6-1	180	11-21-89	.297	.391	.254	55	202	35	60	17	4	7	36	20	3	6	3	64	5	6	.525	.364
Murphy, Jonathan	R-R	6-1	189	6-23-90	.248	.244	.250	38	129	14	32	6	0	1	9	5	2	1	0	27	5	3	.318	.287
Pettersen, Adam	R-R	5-9	170	11-19-88	.248	.239	.253	37	129	20	32	4	0	1	10	9	8	4	3	10	4	1	.302	.329
Pimentel, Candido	R-R	5-11	160	7-19-90	.278	.240	.310	19	54	7	15	4	0	0	9	1	1	2	0	10	2	1	.352	.304
Ramirez, Wilkin	R-R	6-2	230	10-25-85	.111	.000	.125	3	9	3	1	0	0	0	2	0	0	0	0	2	0	0	.111	.273
Ray, Lance	L-R	6-1	194	9-2-89	.200	.143	.228	23	85	10	17	4	0	1	8	10	0	0	1	20	1	1	.282	.281
Roberts, Nate	L-L	6-1	200	2-25-89	.250	.000	.250	1	4	0	1	0	0	0	1	0	1	0	0	0	0	0	.500	.400
Rodriguez, Jairo	R-R	5-11	190	8-7-89	.246	.162	.280	37	130	8	32	3	0	0	14	3	2	2	2	10	0	0	.269	.270
Rosario, Eddie	L-R	6-0	170	9-28-91	.329	.300	.343	52	207	40	68	13	5	6	35	17	2	0	5	29	3	6	.527	.377
Sano, Miguel	R-R	6-3	195	5-11-93	.330	.301	.346	56	206	51	68	15	2	16	48	29	6	0	2	61	9	2	.655	.424
Vargas, Kennys	R-R	6-5	215	8-1-90	.267	.282	.260	125	457	68	122	33	1	19	93	50	7	0	6	105	0	0	.468	.344
Wickens, Stephen	R-R	5-10	170	3-5-89	.260	.244	.267	112	389	60	101	22	3	3	44	45	12	0	6	55	20	3	.355	.350
Williams, J.D.	B-R	5-11	183	11-20-90	.236	.176	.255	42	140	17	33	5	0	1	16	19	2	0	1	38	11	6	.293	.333

Pitching	B-T	HT	WT	DOB	W	L	ERA	G	GS	CG	SV	IP	H	R	ER	HR	BB	SO	AVG	vLH	vRH	K/9	BB/9
Bard, Luke	R-R	6-3	195	11-13-90	0	0	0.00	1	0	0	0	1	0	0	0	0	0	2	.000	—	.000	18.00	0.00
Baxendale, D.J.	R-R	6-2	190	12-8-90	7	0	1.10	9	9	0	0	57	34	9	7	2	11	48	.171	.165	.175	7.53	1.73
Boer, Madison	R-R	6-4	215	11-9-89	1	0	11.81	3	2	0	0	11	20	14	14	2	7	5	.417	.500	.367	4.22	5.91

Name	B-T	HT	WT	DOB	W	L	ERA	G	GS	CG	SV	IP	H	R	ER	HR	BB	SO	AVG	vLH	vRH	K/9	BB/9
Davies, Kyle	R-R	6-1	210	9-9-83	1	3	4.01	5	5	0	0	25	28	13	11	3	13	16	.277	.333	.237	5.84	4.74
DeVries, Cole	R-R	6-1	180	2-12-85	1	0	1.00	2	2	0	0	9	8	2	1	0	0	6	.229	.176	.278	6.00	0.00
Diamond, Scott	L-L	6-3	220	7-30-86	0	0	7.20	1	1	0	0	5	6	4	4	1	0	3	.286	.300	.273	5.40	0.00
Duffey, Tyler	R-R	6-3	225	12-27-90	4	5	4.45	15	9	0	0	63	67	37	31	3	17	44	.272	.275	.271	6.32	2.44
Fuentes, Nelvin	L-L	6-0	206	4-7-89	2	1	3.33	29	0	0	0	46	38	19	17	4	15	56	.221	.205	.227	10.96	2.93
Gonzalez, Jose	L-L	5-9	166	2-3-90	0	1	2.51	10	0	0	0	14	11	4	4	3	3	19	.208	.250	.200	11.93	1.88
Gruver, Steven	L-L	6-2	205	6-30-89	0	0	3.98	9	0	0	0	20	20	9	9	1	13	14	.263	.261	.264	6.20	5.75
Hauser, Matt	R-R	6-2	195	3-30-88	1	0	0.00	4	0	0	0	7	3	0	0	0	2	7	.125	.143	.118	9.00	2.57
Hurlbut, David	L-L	6-3	221	11-24-89	1	1	3.54	4	4	0	0	20	25	9	8	0	5	18	.309	.333	.303	7.97	2.21
Johnson, Cole	R-R	6-3	200	10-6-88	2	0	0.82	13	0	0	2	22	13	2	2	0	5	20	.171	.241	.128	8.18	2.05
Jones, Tyler	R-R	6-4	247	9-5-89	1	3	4.20	12	0	0	4	15	18	7	7	0	4	22	.305	.462	.261	13.20	2.40
Jones, Zack	R-R	6-1	185	12-4-90	4	3	1.85	39	0	0	14	49	28	11	10	2	28	70	.172	.185	.165	12.95	5.18
Munoz, Miguel	R-R	6-2	182	8-4-88	0	0	3.97	6	0	0	0	11	13	5	5	1	0	5	.277	.176	.333	3.97	0.00
O'Rourke, Ryan	R-L	6-3	217	4-30-88	5	1	2.22	17	0	0	3	28	19	7	7	3	8	21	.190	.118	.205	6.67	2.54
Rodgers, Chad	L-L	6-3	225	11-23-87	8	2	4.13	31	0	0	0	52	56	34	24	4	19	38	.272	.267	.274	6.54	3.27
Rogers, Taylor	L-L	6-3	175	12-17-90	11	6	2.55	22	21	3	0	131	119	46	37	5	32	83	.248	.200	.264	5.72	2.20
Salcedo, Adrian	R-R	6-4	175	2-5-91	6	3	3.70	34	0	0	2	58	53	25	24	6	15	54	.239	.253	.231	8.33	2.31
Soliman, Manuel	R-R	6-2	185	8-11-89	1	8	5.47	14	11	1	0	51	73	35	31	10	32	35	.333	.348	.327	6.18	5.65
Stuifbergen, Tom	R-R	6-3	270	9-26-88	2	3	3.65	11	10	0	0	57	56	31	23	5	2	28	.250	.225	.264	4.45	0.32
Summers, Matt	R-R	6-1	205	8-17-89	6	5	2.47	21	21	1	0	120	100	38	33	2	34	87	.222	.228	.218	6.51	2.54
Tomshaw, Matthew	L-L	6-2	202	12-17-88	4	4	3.94	17	14	0	1	96	104	44	42	7	21	58	.281	.313	.272	5.44	1.97
Watts, Dakota	R-R	6-5	201	11-16-87	1	1	9.90	7	0	0	0	10	17	12	11	0	6	7	.378	.294	.429	6.30	5.40
Wheeler, Jason	L-L	6-8	265	10-27-90	9	4	3.70	26	26	0	0	143	156	72	59	16	58	91	.284	.257	.291	5.71	3.64
Williams, Corey	L-L	5-10	204	7-4-90	0	2	5.16	35	0	0	10	45	44	28	26	7	23	43	.257	.245	.262	8.54	4.57
Wood, Tim	R-R	6-0	180	11-16-82	1	0	20.25	2	0	0	0	1	5	3	3	0	1	0	.625	1.000	.400	0.00	6.75

Fielding

Catcher	PCT	G	PO	A	E	DP	PB
Knudson	1.000	26	132	20	0	2	6
Koch	.987	81	559	63	8	6	5
Kvasnicka	1.000	1	1	0	0	0	0
Rodriguez	.995	31	192	15	1	2	6

First Base	PCT	G	PO	A	E	DP
Gonzales	.978	8	87	3	2	6
Haar	1.000	1	4	1	0	0
Hicks	.994	34	291	15	2	34
Koch	1.000	3	14	1	0	4
Leachman	1.000	3	32	1	0	2
Leer	1.000	7	48	7	0	6
Vargas	.985	81	708	39	11	68

Second Base	PCT	G	PO	A	E	DP
Leer	.967	18	36	52	3	13
Mejia	1.000	13	17	22	0	7
Michael	.979	39	83	100	4	23

Third Base	PCT	G	PO	A	E	DP
Pimentel	.941	10	23	25	3	7
Rosario	.985	50	109	162	4	44
Wickens	.917	7	11	11	2	5

Third Base	PCT	G	PO	A	E	DP
Goncalves	.864	8	6	13	3	1
Leer	.778	8	3	11	4	1
Mejia	1.000	1	1	3	0	1
Sano	.928	56	34	108	11	8
Wickens	.970	68	54	141	6	13

Shortstop	PCT	G	PO	A	E	DP
Mejia	.973	50	62	154	6	30
Michael	.941	49	59	147	13	32
Pettersen	.992	30	39	87	1	28
Wickens	.971	7	7	27	1	2

Outfield	PCT	G	PO	A	E	DP
Bigley	1.000	2	3	0	0	0
Bryant	—	1	0	0	0	0
Buxton	.993	55	140	6	1	4
Goncalves	.986	72	130	10	2	0
Koch	1.000	2	3	0	0	0
Kvasnicka	.987	62	151	3	2	0
Leachman	.950	7	18	1	1	0
Leer	1.000	25	51	1	0	1
Mastroianni	1.000	3	3	0	0	0
Mejia	1.000	9	9	2	0	0
Morales	.977	53	127	1	3	0
Murphy	.971	35	65	2	2	0
Pettersen	1.000	6	11	0	0	0
Pimentel	1.000	3	5	0	0	0
Ramirez	1.000	2	1	0	0	0
Ray	.970	17	32	0	1	0
Roberts	1.000	1	3	0	0	0
Wickens	.975	20	38	1	1	0
Williams	.982	40	51	5	1	0

CEDAR RAPIDS KERNELS   LOW CLASS A

MIDWEST LEAGUE

Batting	B-T	HT	WT	DOB	AVG	vLH	vRH	G	AB	R	H	2B	3B	HR	RBI	BB	HBP	SH	SF	SO	SB	CS	SLG	OBP
Altobelli, Bo	R-R	6-1	199	2-6-91	.310	.294	.315	19	71	4	22	2	0	0	9	3	1	0	1	10	0	0	.338	.342
Arias, Jhonatan	R-R	5-10	180	2-18-89	.236	.267	.228	22	72	4	17	4	0	0	5	3	0	0	0	14	0	0	.292	.267
Buxton, Byron	R-R	6-2	189	12-18-93	.341	.357	.338	68	270	68	92	15	10	8	55	44	1	3	3	56	32	11	.559	.431
Gonzales, Mike	L-R	6-6	264	6-16-88	.252	.194	.284	29	103	17	26	7	0	5	18	7	6	0	4	22	1	0	.466	.325
Goodrum, Niko	B-R	6-3	170	2-28-92	.260	.253	.262	103	385	62	100	22	4	4	45	60	4	4	2	105	20	4	.369	.364
Grimes, Tyler	R-R	5-10	187	7-3-90	.256	.253	.257	89	293	54	75	11	4	6	30	45	13	3	2	87	3	1	.382	.377
Harrison, Travis	R-R	6-1	215	10-17-92	.253	.206	.266	129	450	66	114	28	0	15	59	68	14	2	3	125	2	4	.416	.366
Hicks, D.J.	L-R	6-5	228	4-2-90	.297	.220	.320	89	354	50	105	31	0	13	82	34	2	3	7	85	0	1	.494	.355
Jimenez, Romy	R-R	6-2	170	5-14-91	.095	.000	.111	21	74	5	7	2	0	0	6	4	1	0	1	22	0	0	.122	.150
Kepler, Max	L-L	6-4	180	2-10-93	.237	.117	.278	61	236	35	56	11	3	9	40	24	2	0	1	43	2	0	.424	.312
Leachman, Drew	R-R	6-3	200	4-21-89	.346	.500	.318	6	26	4	9	1	1	0	4	0	0	0	1	4	1	0	.462	.333
Licon, Joel	R-R	5-10	180	12-21-90	.241	.234	.244	53	187	22	45	13	0	2	29	16	1	1	1	38	1	1	.342	.302
Murphy, Jonathan	R-R	6-1	189	6-23-90	.272	.175	.305	56	224	31	61	7	4	2	22	24	3	2	0	55	7	4	.366	.351
Pimentel, Candido	B-R	5-11	160	7-19-90	.269	.192	.283	47	171	32	46	2	2	0	11	18	0	0	1	39	11	3	.304	.337
Pineda, Jeremias	R-R	5-11	180	11-16-90	.239	.355	.196	68	230	35	55	6	1	2	21	20	7	1	1	64	16	4	.300	.318
Polanco, Jorge	B-R	5-11	165	7-5-93	.308	.309	.307	115	465	76	143	32	10	5	78	42	3	3	10	59	4	4	.452	.362
Quesada, Michael	R-R	6-1	184	2-1-90	.202	.217	.198	62	208	28	42	13	1	2	21	34	1	0	1	57	0	0	.303	.316
Rodriguez, Jairo	R-R	5-11	180	8-24-88	.140	.000	.152	16	50	8	7	2	0	0	4	6	0	1	1	7	0	0	.180	.228
Walker, Adam Brett	R-R	6-4	225	10-18-91	.278	.254	.285	129	508	83	141	31	7	27	109	31	4	1	9	115	10	0	.526	.319
Walker, Ryan	L-R	6-1	170	3-26-92	.250	.400	.200	6	20	3	5	1	0	0	2	0	1	1	0	4	0	0	.300	.286
Williams, J.D.	B-R	5-11	183	11-20-90	.281	.259	.287	80	267	65	75	12	6	8	42	47	4	2	4	67	15	7	.461	.391

Pitching	B-T	HT	WT	DOB	W	L	ERA	G	GS	CG	SV	IP	H	R	ER	HR	BB	SO	AVG	vLH	vRH	K/9	BB/9
Atherton, Tim	R-R	6-2	209	11-7-89	8	5	2.54	31	11	0	1	96	76	41	27	4	33	102	.217	.224	.212	9.60	3.10
Berrios, Jose	R-R	6-0	187	5-27-94	7	7	3.99	19	19	0	0	104	105	58	46	6	40	100	.262	.252	.272	8.68	3.47

Name	B-T	HT	WT	DOB	W	L	ERA	G	GS	CG	SV	IP	H	R	ER	HR	BB	SO	AVG	vLH	vRH	K/9	BB/9
Bixler, Brandon	R-L	5-11	170	12-31-91	1	0	4.66	9	0	0	0	10	13	5	5	0	8	12	.317	.357	.296	11.17	7.45
Boer, Madison	R-R	6-4	215	11-9-89	1	1	3.04	18	0	0	7	27	26	9	9	0	8	23	.263	.200	.305	7.76	2.70
Boyd, Hudson	R-R	6-2	225	10-18-92	4	5	4.98	29	16	0	0	103	101	62	57	10	56	72	.260	.269	.249	6.29	4.89
Brewer, Caleb	R-R	6-3	205	2-2-89	1	1	6.53	12	0	0	1	21	28	17	15	3	10	18	.333	.313	.346	7.84	4.35
Burris, Josh	B-R	5-10	183	11-28-91	0	0	10.80	8	0	0	0	10	11	12	12	2	9	8	.306	.357	.273	7.20	8.10
Duffey, Tyler	R-R	6-3	225	12-27-90	3	2	2.78	9	9	0	0	58	49	19	18	5	6	47	.221	.234	.204	7.25	0.93
Gallant, Dallas	R-R	6-3	195	1-25-89	1	0	5.51	14	0	0	1	16	13	11	10	3	13	28	.213	.071	.333	15.43	7.16
Gilbert, Brian	R-R	6-1	215	8-9-92	1	1	1.06	13	0	0	5	17	12	2	2	0	0	7	.190	.167	.212	3.71	0.00
Gruver, Steven	L-L	6-2	205	6-30-89	5	2	2.45	24	2	0	3	59	50	22	16	6	16	62	.226	.222	.228	9.51	2.45
Hurlbut, David	L-L	6-3	221	11-24-89	3	1	2.52	24	3	0	6	50	40	20	14	3	8	46	.207	.304	.177	8.28	1.44
Jones, Tyler	R-R	6-4	247	9-5-89	4	3	1.93	24	0	0	9	37	19	14	8	0	16	44	.146	.240	.088	10.61	3.86
Lee, Brett	L-L	6-4	206	9-20-90	8	4	2.95	23	19	2	0	116	117	49	38	7	26	89	.259	.164	.290	6.91	2.02
Mazza, Chris	R-R	6-4	180	10-17-89	0	0	6.23	7	0	0	2	9	12	6	6	0	3	10	.333	.444	.222	10.38	3.12
Melotakis, Mason	R-L	6-2	206	6-28-91	11	4	3.16	24	18	0	1	111	106	50	39	6	39	84	.249	.258	.245	6.81	3.16
Merck, Kaleb	R-R	6-0	215	2-17-91	1	1	7.50	6	0	0	1	12	16	10	10	1	3	9	.320	.350	.300	6.75	2.25
Montanez, Josue	L-L	6-1	222	1-15-92	7	5	3.97	26	12	0	1	91	88	51	40	13	30	55	.258	.143	.296	5.46	2.98
Muren, Alex	R-R	6-3	195	11-6-91	6	1	2.85	33	0	0	2	60	50	24	19	3	18	36	.223	.218	.228	5.40	2.70
Pelfrey, Mike	R-R	6-7	250	1-14-84	1	0	3.00	1	1	0	0	6	2	2	2	1	0	6	.100	.111	.091	9.00	0.00
Powell, Christian	L-R	6-5	210	7-3-91	3	5	5.81	14	10	0	0	62	83	43	40	5	34	50	.325	.283	.367	7.26	4.94
Robb, Hein	L-L	6-0	185	5-12-92	0	0	7.59	3	3	0	0	11	11	10	9	0	9	10	.250	.375	.222	8.44	7.59
Rogers, Taylor	L-L	6-3	175	12-17-90	0	1	7.20	3	3	0	0	10	14	12	8	1	4	10	.304	.313	.300	9.00	3.60
Shibuya, Tim	R-R	6-1	190	9-14-89	4	0	0.96	10	4	1	1	38	23	5	4	0	4	25	.173	.159	.186	5.97	0.96
Soliman, Manuel	R-R	6-2	185	8-11-89	3	1	5.28	17	0	0	1	29	29	21	17	1	18	28	.264	.193	.340	8.69	5.59
Sulbaran, Miguel	L-L	5-10	185	3-19-94	3	0	2.70	4	4	0	0	20	21	9	6	0	5	16	.269	.333	.246	7.20	2.25
2-team total (23 Great Lakes)					9	4	2.96	27	20	0	1	113	110	49	37	3	32	101	—	—	—	8.07	2.56
Tomshaw, Matthew	L-L	6-2	200	12-17-88	2	0	5.10	9	4	0	0	30	36	17	17	4	8	24	.290	.200	.333	7.20	2.40

Fielding

Catcher	PCT	G	PO	A	E	DP	PB
Altobelli	.988	12	74	10	1	2	1
Arias	.987	21	146	8	2	0	0
Grimes	.984	43	264	38	5	2	2
Quesada	.991	51	396	35	4	3	3
Rodriguez	.985	15	122	13	2	2	1

First Base	PCT	G	PO	A	E	DP
Altobelli	1.000	3	30	1	0	3
Gonzales	.994	16	144	10	1	8
Goodrum	1.000	5	36	3	0	1
Hicks	.990	85	796	57	9	65
Kepler	.987	24	218	17	3	24
Leachman	1.000	1	6	1	0	1
Quesada	1.000	5	44	2	0	2

Second Base	PCT	G	PO	A	E	DP
Goodrum	.941	6	10	22	2	6
Grimes	.973	13	25	46	2	4
Licon	.953	31	53	70	6	17
Pimentel	.935	35	70	103	12	18
Polanco	.966	57	90	167	9	39

Third Base	PCT	G	PO	A	E	DP
Goodrum	.944	6	3	14	1	1
Harrison	.915	12	59	221	26	16
Licon	.984	21	16	47	1	3
Pimentel	1.000	1	1	3	0	0

Shortstop	PCT	G	PO	A	E	DP
Goodrum	.941	81	100	280	24	49
Grimes	—	1	0	0	0	0

	PCT	G	PO	A	E	DP
Pimentel	.917	2	3	8	1	0
Polanco	.956	49	67	128	9	24
Walker	.875	6	6	22	4	4

Outfield	PCT	G	PO	A	E	DP
Buxton	.994	66	155	3	1	1
Harrison	—	1	0	0	0	0
Jimenez	.944	14	17	0	1	0
Kepler	.942	30	65	0	4	0
Licon	—	1	0	0	0	0
Murphy	.971	55	127	8	4	3
Pineda	.927	56	82	7	7	1
Walker	.981	122	204	6	4	1
Williams	.985	73	127	6	2	0

ELIZABETHTON TWINS   ROOKIE

APPALACHIAN LEAGUE

Batting	B-T	HT	WT	DOB	AVG	vLH	vRH	G	AB	R	H	2B	3B	HR	RBI	BB	HBP	SH	SF	SO	SB	CS	SLG	OBP
Altobelli, Bo	R-R	6-1	199	2-6-91	.300	.500	.214	7	20	2	6	1	0	0	0	2	0	0	0	3	0	0	.350	.364
Avila, Carlos	R-R	5-10	180	3-28-90	.206	.077	.236	24	68	6	14	1	0	0	4	10	1	2	1	18	1	2	.221	.313
Garver, Mitch	R-R	6-1	210	1-15-91	.243	.241	.243	56	202	16	49	15	2	2	30	17	2	1	1	31	0	0	.366	.313
Granite, Zach	L-L	6-1	175	9-17-92	.285	.500	.243	61	242	39	69	4	5	0	24	29	2	2	3	25	14	7	.343	.362
Haar, Bryan	R-R	6-3	215	12-9-89	.293	.316	.289	60	232	33	68	14	5	6	30	18	0	1	2	59	7	4	.474	.341
Jimenez, Romy	R-R	6-2	170	5-14-91	.254	.290	.246	50	173	23	44	8	1	1	13	10	0	0	1	32	4	4	.329	.293
Larson, Zach	R-R	6-2	185	10-8-93	.301	.182	.323	20	73	14	22	5	1	1	11	9	4	0	0	16	3	2	.438	.407
Ortiz, Kelvin	R-R	5-11	178	10-19-91	.195	.182	.198	37	133	16	26	4	1	1	14	13	7	0	3	56	12	4	.263	.295
Pimentel, Javier	R-R	6-2	175	3-13-94	.216	.171	.229	45	153	17	33	11	2	0	14	12	1	0	1	61	0	1	.314	.275
Proctor, Jake	R-R	6-2	215	12-15-90	.194	.250	.179	10	36	5	7	2	1	0	3	2	0	0	0	12	0	0	.306	.237
Rhodes, Rory	R-R	6-9	220	7-28-91	.242	.156	.259	52	194	28	47	14	0	4	30	22	0	0	3	69	5	2	.376	.315
Rodriguez, Dereck	R-R	6-1	180	6-5-92	.222	.250	.215	41	153	23	34	11	0	3	19	8	2	1	1	46	7	1	.353	.268
Santy, Bryan	R-R	6-1	201	6-28-90	.256	.111	.297	23	82	4	21	3	0	0	12	1	1	0	1	14	1	2	.293	.279
Turner, Stuart	R-R	6-2	220	12-27-91	.264	.292	.258	34	121	15	32	5	0	3	19	12	4	1	4	22	0	1	.380	.340
Vavra, Tanner	R-R	5-11	180	7-6-89	.246	.219	.255	42	134	20	33	3	1	0	8	21	3	4	1	36	1	2	.284	.358
Vielma, Engelb	B-R	5-11	151	6-22-94	.217	.000	.238	6	23	7	5	0	0	0	1	1	2	0	0	7	1	0	.217	.308
Wade, Logan	B-R	6-1	190	11-13-91	.303	.467	.274	32	99	10	30	3	3	2	12	5	0	1	1	33	2	2	.455	.333
Walker, Ryan	L-R	6-1	170	3-26-92	.267	.161	.298	42	135	18	36	4	0	1	14	17	0	0	3	27	4	1	.319	.342

Pitching	B-T	HT	WT	DOB	W	L	ERA	G	GS	CG	SV	IP	H	R	ER	HR	BB	SO	AVG	vLH	vRH	K/9	BB/9
Bard, Luke	R-R	6-3	195	11-13-90	1	0	1.08	7	0	0	0	8	2	1	1	0	6	6	.091	.000	.125	6.48	6.48
Bixler, Brandon	R-L	5-11	170	12-31-91	1	1	0.73	6	0	0	0	12	6	2	1	0	4	18	.143	.091	.161	13.14	2.92
Burris, Josh	B-R	5-10	183	11-28-91	4	2	3.70	12	8	0	0	41	32	21	17	2	32	48	.219	.245	.206	10.45	6.97
Eades, Ryan	R-R	6-2	178	12-15-91	0	0	4.60	10	0	0	0	16	13	9	8	0	12	13	.236	.143	.294	7.47	6.89
Ferreira, Andrew	R-L	6-2	200	10-22-90	1	0	2.57	13	0	0	0	21	11	6	6	1	14	30	.162	.083	.179	12.86	6.00
Gallant, Dallas	R-R	6-3	195	1-25-89	2	1	5.40	8	0	0	0	10	8	6	6	0	4	8	.229	.118	.333	7.20	3.60
Gilbert, Brian	R-R	6-1	215	8-9-92	1	0	0.00	5	0	0	1	6	1	0	0	0	1	7	.050	.200	.000	10.50	1.50

					W	L	ERA	G	GS	CG	SV	IP	H	R	ER	HR	BB	SO	AVG	vLH	vRH	K/9	BB/9
Goldsmith, Carson	R-R	6-3	200	7-25-90	1	2	5.50	14	0	0	1	18	19	11	11	1	10	29	.271	.227	.292	14.50	5.00
Gonsalves, Stephen	L-L	6-5	190	7-8-94	1	1	1.29	3	3	0	0	14	10	2	2	0	4	21	.200	.273	.179	13.50	2.57
Irby, C.K.	R-R	6-1	200	5-6-92	0	1	3.29	10	0	0	1	14	10	6	5	1	7	10	.204	.167	.226	6.59	4.61
Jorge, Felix	R-R	6-2	170	1-2-94	2	2	2.95	12	12	0	0	61	56	26	20	2	18	72	.245	.327	.183	10.62	2.66
Landa, Yorman	R-R	6-0	175	6-11-94	3	4	2.78	12	12	0	0	55	46	25	17	1	29	46	.227	.324	.171	7.53	4.75
Lo, Kuo Hua	R-R	5-10	195	10-28-92	2	1	2.37	15	4	0	2	38	29	10	10	3	14	34	.209	.128	.250	8.05	3.32
Malinowski, Austin	R-L	6-4	210	11-30-92	4	3	2.01	20	0	0	1	40	27	11	9	0	17	43	.190	.171	.196	9.60	3.79
Martinez, Andre	L-L	6-0	185	6-22-93	0	1	8.18	19	1	0	0	22	24	29	20	4	25	29	.264	.188	.280	11.86	10.23
Mendonca, Tanner	R-R	6-4	215	6-18-92	2	1	8.49	12	7	0	0	23	24	26	22	2	37	23	.279	.244	.311	8.87	14.27
Mildren, Ethan	R-R	6-4	215	6-4-91	1	1	1.65	12	0	0	0	16	15	4	3	0	7	13	.254	.333	.172	7.16	3.86
Nunez, Luis	L-L	5-11	160	9-26-91	0	0	0.00	4	0	0	3	5	4	0	0	0	3	8	.211	.250	.200	14.40	5.40
Peterson, Brandon	R-R	6-1	190	9-23-91	0	2	2.96	19	0	0	5	27	22	9	9	3	9	40	.224	.310	.161	13.17	2.96
Robb, Hein	L-L	6-0	185	5-12-92	4	4	2.71	11	11	1	0	63	63	20	19	2	13	52	.263	.220	.271	7.43	1.86
Rosario, Randy	L-L	6-0	160	5-18-94	4	3	2.82	9	9	0	0	45	42	16	14	0	18	37	.251	.237	.256	7.46	3.63
Shibuya, Tim	R-R	6-1	190	9-14-89	3	1	2.33	6	0	0	0	19	17	6	5	0	4	13	.230	.211	.250	6.05	1.86
Slegers, Aaron	R-R	6-10	250	9-4-92	0	0	0.47	9	0	0	3	19	16	2	1	0	2	18	.246	.391	.167	8.53	0.95
Stewart, Kohl	R-R	6-3	195	10-7-94	0	0	0.00	1	1	0	0	4	1	0	0	0	1	8	.077	.111	.000	18.00	2.25

Fielding

Catcher	PCT	G	PO	A	E	DP	PB
Altobelli	.969	7	58	4	2	0	0
Garver	1.000	23	210	23	0	3	5
Santy	.980	13	85	15	2	1	1
Turner	.987	28	267	26	4	1	1

First Base	PCT	G	PO	A	E	DP
Garver	1.000	1	2	0	0	0
Haar	.986	24	189	19	3	20
Rhodes	.995	44	366	30	2	41

Second Base	PCT	G	PO	A	E	DP
Vavra	.968	42	82	101	6	33
Wade	.976	29	51	70	3	14

Third Base	PCT	G	PO	A	E	DP
Haar	.925	24	16	33	4	4
Pimentel	.899	45	18	62	9	7
Wade	1.000	1	0	1	0	1
Walker	—	1	0	0	0	0

Shortstop	PCT	G	PO	A	E	DP
Avila	.924	24	26	59	7	12

	PCT	G	PO	A	E	DP
Vielma	.968	6	8	22	1	7
Wade	1.000	1	6	9	0	2
Walker	.970	40	56	105	5	23

Outfield	PCT	G	PO	A	E	DP
Granite	.976	61	118	3	3	1
Jimenez	.947	46	65	6	4	3
Larson	.913	19	21	0	2	0
Ortiz	.938	35	43	2	3	0
Proctor	1.000	9	12	1	0	0
Rodriguez	.969	39	58	4	2	2

GCL TWINS

ROOKIE

GULF COAST LEAGUE

Batting	B-T	HT	WT	DOB	AVG	vLH	vRH	G	AB	R	H	2B	3B	HR	RBI	BB	HBP	SH	SF	SO	SB	CS	SLG	OBP
Bigley, Evan	R-R	6-1	200	3-9-87	.240	.200	.250	5	2	6	4	1	0	4	4	0	0	0	4	0	0	.480	.345
Christensen, Chad	R-R	6-3	190	10-6-90	.235	.224	.240	47	162	23	38	7	3	3	21	13	4	2	4	21	4	2	.370	.301
Fernandez, Jorge	B-R	6-3	188	3-30-94	.236	.244	.231	36	123	14	29	7	2	3	19	6	2	0	3	19	2	1	.398	.276
Gonzales, Mike	L-R	6-6	264	6-16-88	.313	.111	.571	5	16	2	5	0	0	1	2	3	0	0	0	6	0	0	.500	.421
Hurt, Will	R-R	5-11	175	12-22-93	.243	.217	.255	26	74	11	18	1	1	0	6	16	2	0	1	17	7	1	.284	.387
Kanzler, Jason	R-R	6-0	190	8-20-90	.220	.167	.243	44	159	19	35	6	6	3	15	13	2	1	1	50	13	1	.390	.286
Larson, Zach	R-R	6-2	185	10-8-93	.317	.279	.338	35	120	25	38	6	0	4	19	10	4	1	2	23	9	0	.467	.382
Mastroianni, Darin	R-R	5-11	190	8-26-85	.143	.000	.250	3	7	1	1	0	0	0	2	2	1	0	1	2	0		.143	.364
Minier, Amaurys	B-R	6-2	190	1-30-96	.214	.135	.253	31	112	10	24	5	2	6	17	6	0	0	1	29	1	1	.455	.252
Molina, Nelson	L-R	6-3	175	4-30-95	.110	.107	.111	36	109	13	12	1	0	0	3	6	3	2	0	15	2	3	.119	.178
Navarreto, Brian	R-R	6-4	220	12-29-94	.226	.213	.233	42	137	15	31	10	0	3	16	15	4	1	1	35	3	1	.365	.318
Pacheco, Adonis	L-L	5-11	175	7-14-91	.225	.146	.257	46	142	16	32	6	4	1	12	14	0	0	2	19	5	2	.345	.291
Polanco, Joel	R-R	5-11	175	8-15-92	.203	.231	.189	25	79	5	16	6	1	0	12	8	4	0	2	24	0	1	.304	.301
Ramirez, Wilkin	R-R	6-2	230	10-25-85	.273	.000	.333	4	11	2	3	1	0	1	1	1	0	0	0	2	0	0	.636	.333
Ray, Lance	L-R	6-1	194	9-2-89	.231	.300	.188	7	26	4	6	1	0	0	2	4	1	0	0	6	1	0	.269	.355
Schwarz, Rick	R-R	6-2	195	8-10-94	.148	.083	.175	26	81	5	12	2	0	0	6	6	3	1	2	23	1	0	.173	.228
Swim, Alex	B-R	5-11	180	3-26-91	.287	.289	.286	37	122	16	35	7	0	0	12	14	1	2	3	14	0	0	.344	.357
Thomas, Ivory	R-R	5-9	175	8-24-91	.255	.143	.297	16	51	6	13	3	0	0	3	8	2	1	0	13	5	1	.314	.377
Tufts, Ryan	R-R	6-4	240	2-1-89	.193	.171	.208	28	88	5	17	5	0	0	4	6	3	0	0	25	0	1	.250	.268
Vielma, Engelb	B-R	5-11	151	6-22-94	.237	.171	.267	42	131	20	31	3	0	0	11	15	2	2	2	23	7	3	.260	.320
Ynojoso, Jonatan	B-R	5-11	150	10-23-92	.236	.318	.198	48	140	24	33	4	5	0	15	14	1	3	0	28	10	2	.336	.310

Pitching	B-T	HT	WT	DOB	W	L	ERA	G	GS	CG	SV	IP	H	R	ER	HR	BB	SO	AVG	vLH	vRH	K/9	BB/9
Abreu, Jose	R-R	5-11	170	7-13-92	2	3	1.61	18	0	0	5	28	18	7	5	1	5	30	.184	.222	.161	9.64	1.61
Bard, Luke	R-R	6-3	195	11-13-90	0	0	12.00	4	0	0	0	3	5	5	4	0	3	1	.333	.167	.444	3.00	9.00
Blackburn, Nick	R-R	6-4	240	2-24-82	1	0	2.77	3	3	0	0	13	15	4	4	0	0	10	.300	.267	.350	6.92	0.00
Boer, Madison	R-R	6-4	215	11-9-89	0	0	0.00	2	0	0	1	3	5	2	0	0	0	5	.357	.400	.333	15.00	0.00
Booser, Cameron	L-L	6-3	225	5-4-92	0	0	2.45	3	0	0	0	4	3	2	1	0	0	3	.200	.000	.250	7.36	0.00
Davies, Kyle	R-R	6-1	210	9-9-83	0	0	0.00	1	1	0	0	5	3	0	0	0	1	7	.167	.154	.200	12.60	1.80
Defrank, Damian	R-R	6-3	200	2-1-95	2	0	2.33	8	2	0	0	19	20	5	5	1	5	12	.274	.343	.211	5.59	2.33
DeVries, Cole	R-R	6-1	180	2-12-85	0	0	0.00	1	0	0	0	3	0	0	0	0	0	4	.000	.000	.000	12.00	0.00
Easton, Brandon	L-L	6-5	190	9-21-92	1	3	7.45	10	3	0	0	19	25	21	16	0	13	11	.313	.417	.294	5.12	6.05
Gibbons, Sam	L-R	6-4	190	12-12-93	3	3	1.91	13	8	0	0	42	40	16	9	0	10	30	.250	.290	.224	6.38	2.13
Gonsalves, Stephen	L-L	6-5	190	7-8-94	1	0	0.63	5	2	0	0	14	8	1	1	0	7	18	.163	.357	.086	11.30	4.40
Gonzalez, Miguel	R-R	6-1	180	10-12-94	0	0	1.05	20	0	0	3	26	20	6	3	0	9	33	.215	.235	.203	11.57	3.16
Guerra, Deolis	R-R	6-5	245	4-17-89	0	1	4.50	3	0	0	0	4	3	2	2	0	1	3	.214	.222	.200	6.75	2.25
Guyer, Josh	R-R	6-2	185	5-27-94	1	2	5.30	15	0	0	1	19	18	15	11	2	13	22	.254	.250	.256	10.61	6.27
Hayden, Jason	R-R	6-2	215	10-29-91	1	0	0.00	10	0	0	0	9	7	0	0	0	5	6	.206	.111	.240	6.00	5.00
Hernandez, Pedro	L-L	5-10	210	4-12-89	0	1	2.57	2	1	0	0	7	8	2	2	0	0	6	.308	.333	.304	7.71	0.00
Hu, Chih-Wei	R-R	6-1	209	11-4-93	2	0	2.45	12	5	0	0	37	28	11	10	0	8	39	.207	.197	.216	9.57	1.96

	B-T	HT	WT	DOB	W	L	ERA	G	GS	CG	SV	IP	H	R	ER	HR	BB	SO	AVG	vLH	vRH	K/9	BB/9
Meyer, Alex	R-R	6-9	220	1-3-90	0	0	1.08	3	3	0	0	8	7	1	1	1	3	16	.233	.200	.267	17.28	3.24
Oliveros, Lester	R-R	6-0	235	5-28-88	0	0	0.00	6	0	0	2	6	4	0	0	0	3	8	.200	.286	.000	11.37	4.26
Penilla, Derrick	L-L	6-2	180	12-31-91	1	2	5.40	14	1	0	3	13	19	11	8	0	7	13	.339	.467	.293	8.78	4.73
Pugh, Bruce	R-R	6-3	180	7-18-88	0	0	5.40	3	0	0	0	3	3	3	2	0	3	4	.214	.143	.286	10.80	8.10
Romero, Fernando	R-R	6-0	215	12-24-94	2	0	1.60	12	6	0	0	45	32	12	8	0	13	47	.196	.227	.170	9.40	2.60
Sattler, Dan	R-R	6-3	190	11-11-83	1	3	5.40	10	0	0	0	10	11	9	6	1	2	8	.268	.261	.278	7.20	1.80
Solbach, Markus	R-R	6-5	195	8-26-91	1	1	0.96	5	0	0	0	9	8	4	1	0	1	5	.222	.333	.143	4.82	0.96
Stewart, Kohl	R-R	6-3	195	10-7-94	0	0	1.69	6	3	0	0	16	12	7	3	0	3	16	.188	.258	.121	9.00	1.69
Stirewalt, Tyler	R-R	6-3	210	12-6-90	1	1	0.57	12	0	0	1	16	8	1	1	0	5	20	.148	.273	.063	11.49	2.87
Thorpe, Lewis	R-L	6-1	160	11-23-95	4	1	2.05	12	8	0	0	44	32	13	10	2	6	64	.203	.071	.250	13.09	1.23
Wagner, Seth	L-L	6-7	220	12-27-94	0	0	2.53	6	0	0	0	11	5	4	3	0	7	8	.139	.143	.138	6.75	5.91
Wilson, Jared	R-R	6-4	210	4-26-90	3	2	5.23	10	3	0	0	29	19	13	12	0	10	22	.244	.257	.233	9.58	4.35
Wimmers, Alex	L-R	6-2	195	11-1-88	0	1	7.20	6	6	0	0	15	25	15	12	1	5	18	.357	.242	.459	10.80	3.00
Zazueta, Leonel	R-R	6-0	170	9-27-94	0	5	4.67	14	4	0	0	27	35	18	14	1	11	19	.310	.333	.299	6.33	3.67
Zoquiel, Reyson	L-L	5-11	175	11-5-93	1	3	9.64	15	0	0	0	14	17	18	15	0	17	12	.293	.385	.267	7.71	10.93

Fielding

Catcher

	PCT	G	PO	A	E	DP	PB
Fernandez	.987	15	139	10	2	3	5
Navarreto	.989	19	165	21	2	1	5
Polanco	.972	13	94	12	3	2	8
Swim	.979	17	129	14	3	3	5

First Base

	PCT	G	PO	A	E	DP
Christensen	.973	11	98	12	3	11
Fernandez	1.000	11	75	4	0	5
Gonzales	1.000	1	5	0	0	0
Minier	1.000	1	5	1	0	1
Molina	1.000	1	5	1	0	0
Navarreto	1.000	19	130	10	0	10
Pacheco	.956	9	37	6	2	4
Polanco	1.000	6	39	4	0	1
Swim	.975	10	76	2	2	9

Second Base

	PCT	G	PO	A	E	DP
Hurt	.925	17	21	41	5	7
Molina	.967	12	22	37	2	7
Ynojoso	.955	35	47	80	6	19

Third Base

	PCT	G	PO	A	E	DP
Christensen	.878	27	26	39	9	3
Minier	.889	23	15	33	6	2
Molina	1.000	3	3	4	0	1
Navarreto	.875	4	1	6	1	0
Vielma	.875	6	4	10	2	0
Ynojoso	.500	4	1	2	3	1

Shortstop

	PCT	G	PO	A	E	DP
Hurt	1.000	5	2	14	0	3
Molina	.914	18	18	46	6	10
Vielma	.924	36	48	86	11	19
Ynojoso	.821	8	9	14	5	5

Outfield

	PCT	G	PO	A	E	DP
Bigley	1.000	6	7	1	0	0
Christensen	.941	10	16	0	1	0
Kanzler	.969	43	84	9	3	3
Larson	1.000	32	57	2	0	1
Mastroianni	.750	2	3	0	1	0
Pacheco	.965	36	52	3	2	0
Ramirez	1.000	3	4	0	0	0
Ray	1.000	5	8	0	0	0
Schwarz	1.000	20	24	1	0	0
Thomas	.933	12	13	1	1	0
Tufts	.972	24	34	1	1	0

DSL TWINS   ROOKIE

DOMINICAN SUMMER LEAGUE

Batting	B-T	HT	WT	DOB	AVG	vLH	vRH	G	AB	R	H	2B	3B	HR	RBI	BB	HBP	SH	SF	SO	SB	CS	SLG	OBP
Alvarez, Jhonathan	R-R	6-0	190	2-18-96	.138	.259	.083	34	87	10	12	3	0	1	6	13	4	0	0	31	1	2	.207	.279
Amarante, Junior	L-L	5-11	185	3-21-95	.195	.118	.217	29	77	10	15	1	0	0	3	12	0	0	0	21	7	3	.208	.303
Andrade, Jorge	B-R	5-10	170	12-7-94	.179	.000	.227	11	28	10	5	1	1	0	4	9	0	1	0	8	3	4	.286	.378
Baez, Dubal	R-R	6-0	175	6-14-93	.335	.295	.350	57	164	43	55	8	1	0	14	29	5	2	1	37	27	11	.396	.447
Concepcion, Eddy	B-R	5-11	185	1-25-93	.215	.281	.194	38	130	12	28	5	2	2	20	16	2	0	3	29	2	2	.331	.305
Encarnacion, Frank	R-L	6-1	195	11-1-95	.273	.231	.283	39	139	15	38	13	2	2	25	13	4	0	2	32	6	3	.439	.348
Gonzalez, Luis	B-R	5-11	180	10-10-94	.077	.000	.083	7	26	1	2	0	0	0	0	2	1	0	0	8	1	0	.077	.172
Guzman, Manuel	B-R	5-9	160	2-10-95	.291	.262	.303	44	151	29	44	4	3	1	16	24	3	5	2	19	14	11	.377	.394
Hernandez, Jet	L-R	6-2	185	11-23-94	.174	.231	.150	30	86	18	15	4	1	0	9	21	1	2	0	35	11	4	.244	.343
Martinez, Carlos	R-R	5-11	170	4-6-94	.219	.111	.255	49	146	18	32	9	2	0	9	18	2	1	2	31	11	6	.308	.310
Mateo, Francis	L-L	5-11	185	4-24-93	.269	.275	.267	47	167	18	45	10	2	2	28	5	4	0	2	42	3	2	.389	.303
Montesino, Ariel	B-R	5-10	170	9-21-95	.270	.308	.250	23	74	10	20	2	3	1	11	12	3	1	0	19	8	2	.419	.393
Parra, Jorge	R-R	6-0	176	6-14-95	.195	.195	.195	45	159	19	31	5	1	0	15	15	2	1	2	44	7	4	.239	.270
Ramirez, Joel	B-R	6-0	170	9-4-93	.252	.200	.269	53	143	36	36	7	1	0	20	29	6	5	2	33	20	8	.315	.394
Silva, Rainis	R-R	6-1	183	3-20-96	.223	.222	.223	45	148	15	33	4	0	0	15	13	2	1	3	33	1	1	.250	.289
Tovar, Antonio	R-R	6-0	196	6-1-96	.191	.227	.172	44	131	15	25	2	0	0	7	24	2	1	0	29	12	1	.206	.325
Valera, Rafael P	R-R	5-11	180	8-15-94	.257	.295	.244	55	171	31	44	5	2	0	28	42	7	2	3	28	19	10	.310	.417
Ynfante, Gabriel A.	B-R	5-11	158	11-15-94	.235	.276	.222	43	119	19	28	4	1	1	16	23	2	2	1	30	8	2	.311	.366

Pitching	B-T	HT	WT	DOB	W	L	ERA	G	GS	CG	SV	IP	H	R	ER	HR	BB	SO	AVG	vLH	vRH	K/9	BB/9
Aponte, Carlos	R-R	5-11	185	9-13-95	6	3	4.41	19	3	0	0	35	40	27	17	0	11	24	.292	.289	.293	6.23	2.86
Cabrera, Robener	R-R	6-3	205	1-25-94	1	2	4.66	20	2	0	2	37	34	23	19	0	12	26	.239	.316	.212	6.38	2.95
Del Rosario, Eduardo	R-R	6-0	145	5-9-95	2	3	2.03	15	9	0	1	44	22	19	10	1	25	30	.154	.171	.147	6.09	5.08
Hernandez, Onesimo	R-R	5-11	200	2-16-92	2	3	4.08	14	8	0	0	46	48	32	21	1	17	32	.274	.313	.260	6.22	3.30
Herrera, Ramses	R-R	6-3	190	9-14-93	1	2	4.54	13	7	0	0	38	30	21	19	3	21	31	.222	.320	.200	7.41	5.02
Jimenez, Jadison	L-L	6-0	180	3-19-94	2	2	3.90	13	3	0	1	30	28	15	13	1	12	21	.255	.286	.250	6.30	3.60
Liranzo, Wilfredy	R-R	5-11	185	10-26-94	3	4	3.07	16	6	0	0	41	21	17	14	0	27	62	.151	.140	.157	13.61	5.93
Perez, Randolph	R-R	6-0	170	4-23-94	0	0	6.23	9	0	0	1	9	10	8	6	0	5	9	.278	.200	.290	9.35	5.19
Perez, Sebastian	R-R	6-1	175	5-17-95	2	2	4.64	20	0	0	3	33	33	28	17	1	16	18	.258	.167	.279	4.91	4.36
Quezada, Johan	R-R	6-6	200	8-15-94	0	1	10.29	11	5	0	0	14	21	16	16	0	28	12	.264	.200	.289	7.71	18.00
Ramirez, Jose	R-R	6-0	170	8-19-92	1	2	3.51	13	9	0	0	41	37	21	16	1	20	34	.240	.220	.250	7.46	4.39
Ramirez, Williams	R-R	6-1	200	8-8-92	3	1	2.45	17	2	0	0	33	13	11	9	0	25	35	.123	.188	.095	9.55	6.82
Reyes, Reudis	R-R	6-4	175	3-18-93	0	1	13.50	1	0	0	0	1	1	1	1	0	2	0	.000	—	.000	0.00	27.00
Rosario, Gabriel	R-R	6-1	185	9-8-94	2	0	7.36	14	0	0	0	18	28	16	15	1	9	12	.350	.421	.328	5.89	4.42
Silva, Argenis	R-R	6-0	190	7-24-95	0	0	19.29	4	0	0	0	2	2	6	5	1	7	0	.222	.333	.167	0.00	27.00
Tapia, Alexis	R-R	6-2	195	8-10-95	2	1	2.13	11	7	0	0	42	32	13	10	2	5	31	.203	.206	.202	6.59	1.06
Vargas, Javier	R-R	6-1	185	1-26-93	4	1	2.70	12	4	0	0	33	38	14	10	1	9	26	.292	.355	.273	7.02	2.43
Villasana, Elias	R-R	6-1	190	3-22-93	1	1	2.79	18	4	0	1	39	39	22	12	2	9	26	.252	.333	.234	6.05	2.09
Zarzuela, Ezequiel	R-R	6-1	170	11-18-90	1	1	2.50	11	0	0	1	18	15	6	5	0	5	13	.234	.192	.263	6.50	2.50

Fielding

Catcher	PCT	G	PO	A	E	DP	PB
Alvarez	.976	28	146	18	4	1	14
Concepcion	1.000	4	27	4	0	0	2
Gonzalez	1.000	2	20	1	0	0	0
Silva	.972	43	271	45	9	3	11

First Base	PCT	G	PO	A	E	DP
Concepcion	.996	25	212	11	1	14
Gonzalez	1.000	3	27	1	0	1
Martinez	.991	14	108	6	1	7
Mateo	1.000	1	2	0	0	0
Parra	.989	21	168	10	2	11
Valera	.986	7	66	4	1	7
Ynfante	.980	8	47	3	1	4

Second Base	PCT	G	PO	A	E	DP
Andrade	.897	6	13	13	3	3
Guzman	.992	25	47	78	1	12
Montesino	1.000	8	16	30	0	4
Ramirez	.952	9	21	19	2	4
Valera	1.000	3	5	8	0	1
Ynfante	.981	26	46	57	2	10

Third Base	PCT	G	PO	A	E	DP
Martinez	.882	34	28	69	13	10
Ramirez	.926	8	11	14	2	2
Valera	.902	29	23	60	9	2
Ynfante	1.000	6	2	4	0	0

Shortstop	PCT	G	PO	A	E	DP
Andrade	1.000	2	1	4	0	0
Guzman	.899	22	19	61	9	6
Montesino	.955	13	30	34	3	4
Ramirez	.886	36	52	95	19	14
Valera	1.000	1	2	2	0	0
Ynfante	1.000	2	2	3	0	0

Outfield	PCT	G	PO	A	E	DP
Amarante	.920	22	22	1	2	0
Baez	.959	54	89	5	4	2
Encarnacion	.959	38	43	4	2	0
Martinez	—	1	0	0	0	0
Mateo	.887	35	48	7	7	3
Parra	.971	24	32	1	1	0
Tovar	.983	37	54	3	1	0
Valera	1.000	18	31	2	0	1

New York Mets

SEASON IN A SENTENCE: The Mets finished with the same 74-88 record as the 2012 club, and have turned in five straight losing efforts since falling short of the playoffs on the final day of the 2008 season.

HIGH POINT: With the All-Star Game festivities taking place at Citi Field, the local fans were treated to a heavy dose of Mets power pitching. Righthanders Noah Syndergaard (U.S.) and Rafael Montero (World) started the Future Game on Sunday, each delivering a scoreless inning, while Matt Harvey got the nod for the NL in Tuesday's main attraction. The 24-year-old ace worked two scoreless innings.

LOW POINT: After losing to the Phillies on April 26, the Mets never again sniffed .500, but the worst came on Aug. 24. That's when Harvey left a start against the Tigers having allowed a career high 13 hits. Days later the baseball world learned that the righthander had a torn UCL in his elbow, and would require Tommy John surgery.

NOTABLE ROOKIES: The Mets received expected contributions from righthander and top prospect Zack Wheeler, who went 7-5, 3.42 in 17 starts while averaging 94 mph on his fastball. Less expected were the callups of center fielder Juan Lagares, who didn't hit much (.242/.281/.352) but showed off plus range and a strong arm, and first baseman Josh Satin, who filled in capably (.279/.376/.405) while Ike Davis endured a season-long slump.

KEY TRANSACTIONS: Under Sandy Alderson, the Mets have been among the most adept clubs at importing talented prospects in trades. They turned Marlon Byrd and John Buck into low Class A second baseman Dilson Herrera and big league-ready reliever Vic Black in an August trade with the Pirates. The previous December, he acquired top prospects Syndergaard and Travis d'Arnaud from the Blue Jays in exchange for reigning Cy Young Award winner R.A. Dickey.

DOWN ON THE FARM: Just two minor league clubs won more games than Double-A Binghamton (86-55), but the real pride of the system was the low Class A Savannah pitching staff. Led by Gabriel Ynoa and fellow prospects such as lefty Steve Matz and righty Matt Koch, the Sand Gnats easily paced the full-season minors with a 4.3 K-BB ratio. Savannah cruised through the Sally League playoffs to win the franchise's first title in 17 years.

OPENING DAY PAYROLL: $73.4 million (23rd).

PLAYERS OF THE YEAR

MAJOR LEAGUE

Matt Harvey
rhp
9-5, 2.27
191 SO, 0.93 WHIP
Started All-Star Game

MINOR LEAGUE

Rafael Montero
rhp
(Double-A/Triple-A)
12-7, 2.78
150 SO, 155 IP

ORGANIZATION LEADERS

BATTING		*Minimum 250 AB
MAJORS		
* AVG	Murphy, Daniel	.286
* OPS	Murphy, Daniel	.733
HR	Byrd, Marlon	21
RBI	Murphy, Daniel	78
MINORS		
* AVG	Boyd, Jayce, St. Lucie/Savannah	.33
* OBP	Dykstra, Allan, Binghamton	.436
* SLG	Taijeron, Travis, Binghamton/St. Lucie	.531
R	Muno, Daniel, Binghamton	86
H	Boyd, Jayce, St. Lucie/Savannah	151
TB	Lawley, Dustin, Las Vegas/St. Lucie	251
2B	Plawecki, Kevin, St. Lucie/Savannah	38
	Taijeron, Travis, Binghamton/St. Lucie	38
3B	Pina, Eudy, Savannah	8
HR	Lawley, Dustin, Las Vegas/St. Lucie	26
RBI	Lawley, Dustin, Las Vegas/St. Lucie	96
BB	Dykstra, Allan, Binghamton	102
SO	Nimmo, Brandon, Savannah	131
	Taijeron, Travis, Binghamton/St. Lucie	131
SB	Ceciliani, Darrell, Binghamton	31

PITCHING		#Minimum 75 IP
MAJORS		
W	Gee, Dillon	12
# ERA	Harvey, Matt	2.27
SO	Harvey, Matt	191
SV	Parnell, Bobby	22
MINORS		
W	Ynoa, Gabriel, Savannah	15
L	Three tied at	9
# ERA	Ynoa, Gabriel, Savannah	2.72
G	Hampson, Justin, Las Vegas	64
GS	Schwinden, Chris, Las Vegas	28
SV	Walters, Jeff, Binghamton	38
IP	Montero, Rafael, Las Vegas/Binghamton	155
BB	Tapia, Domingo, St. Lucie	63
SO	Montero, Rafael, Las Vegas/Binghamton	150
# AVG	Montero, Rafael, Binghamton/Las Vegas	.232

2013 PERFORMANCE

General Manager: Sandy Alderson. **Farm Director:** Paul DePodesta. **Scouting Director:** Tom Tanous.

Class	Team	League	W	L	PCT	Finish	Manager
Majors	New York Mets	National	74	88	.457	12th (15)	Terry Collins
Triple-A	Las Vegas 51s	Pacific Coast	81	63	.563	2nd (16)	Wally Backman
Double-A	Binghamton Mets	Eastern	86	55	.610	1st (12)	Pedro Lopez
High A	St. Lucie Mets	Florida State	71	60	.542	3rd (12)	Ryan Ellis
Low A	Savannah Sand Gnats	South Atlantic	77	61	.558	4th (14)	Luis Rojas
Short-season	Brooklyn Cyclones	New York-Penn	38	37	.507	7th (14)	Rich Donnelly
Rookie	Kingsport Mets	Appalachian	40	27	.597	3rd (10)	Jose Leger
Rookie	GCL Mets	Gulf Coast	20	40	.333	16th (16)	Jose Carreno
2013 Overall Minor League Record			413	343	.546	t-4th (30)	

ORGANIZATION STATISTICS

NATIONAL LEAGUE

Batting	B-T	HT	WT	DOB	AVG	vLH	vRH	G	AB	R	H	2B	3B	HR	RBI	BB	HBP	SH	SF	SO	SB	CS	SLG	OBP
Ankiel, Rick	L-L	6-1	210	7-19-79	.182	.250	.177	20	66	7	12	4	1	2	7	5	0	0	0	25	0	1	.364	.239
Baxter, Mike	L-R	6-0	195	12-7-84	.189	.333	.175	74	132	14	25	6	1	0	4	17	5	0	1	28	5	2	.250	.303
Brown, Andrew	R-R	6-0	185	9-10-84	.227	.234	.219	68	150	16	34	5	0	7	24	13	0	2	0	44	1	0	.400	.288
Buck, John	R-R	6-3	245	7-7-80	.215	.175	.229	101	368	38	79	11	0	15	60	29	8	0	2	99	2	1	.367	.285
2-team total (9 Pittsburgh)					.222	—	—	110	392	39	87	11	0	15	62	29	8	0	2	104	2	1	.365	.288
Byrd, Marlon	R-R	6-0	245	8-30-77	.285	.345	.255	117	425	61	121	26	5	21	71	25	7	1	6	124	2	4	.518	.330
2-team total (30 Pittsburgh)					.291	—	—	147	532	75	155	35	5	24	88	31	8	1	7	144	2	4	.511	.336
Centeno, Juan	L-R	5-10	170	11-16-89	.300	—	.300	4	10	0	3	0	0	0	1	0	0	0	0	1	0	0	.300	.300
Cowgill, Collin	R-L	5-9	185	5-22-86	.180	.222	.120	23	61	7	11	2	0	2	8	2	0	0	0	15	0	0	.311	.206
d'Arnaud, Travis	R-R	6-2	195	2-10-89	.202	.083	.240	31	99	4	20	3	0	1	5	12	0	0	1	21	0	0	.263	.286
Davis, Ike	L-L	6-4	230	3-22-87	.205	.145	.222	103	317	37	65	14	0	9	33	57	1	0	2	101	4	0	.334	.326
den Dekker, Matt	L-L	6-1	205	8-10-87	.207	.000	.222	27	58	7	12	1	0	1	6	4	1	0	0	23	4	1	.276	.270
Duda, Lucas	L-R	6-4	255	2-3-86	.223	.183	.240	100	318	42	71	16	0	15	33	55	9	0	2	102	0	3	.415	.352
Flores, Wilmer	R-R	6-3	190	8-6-91	.211	.188	.222	27	95	8	20	5	0	1	13	5	0	0	1	23	0	0	.295	.248
Lagares, Juan	R-R	6-1	175	3-17-89	.242	.241	.243	121	392	35	95	21	5	4	34	20	2	5	2	96	6	3	.352	.281
Lutz, Zach	R-R	6-1	220	6-3-86	.300	.429	.231	15	20	2	6	2	0	0	2	6	0	0	0	6	0	0	.400	.462
Murphy, Daniel	L-R	6-2	205	4-1-85	.286	.273	.292	161	658	92	188	38	4	13	78	32	2	0	5	95	23	3	.415	.319
Nieuwenhuis, Kirk	L-R	6-3	215	8-7-87	.189	.000	.207	47	95	10	18	3	1	3	14	12	0	0	1	32	2	0	.337	.278
Quintanilla, Omar	L-R	5-9	185	10-24-81	.222	.203	.229	95	315	28	70	9	2	2	21	38	1	3	2	70	2	0	.283	.306
Recker, Anthony	R-R	6-2	240	8-29-83	.215	.208	.218	50	135	17	29	7	0	6	19	13	0	1	2	49	0	1	.400	.280
Satin, Josh	R-R	6-2	200	12-23-84	.279	.317	.250	75	190	23	53	15	0	3	17	30	0	0	1	56	1	1	.405	.376
Tejada, Ruben	R-R	5-11	185	10-27-89	.202	.274	.171	57	208	20	42	12	0	0	10	15	1	3	0	24	2	1	.260	.259
Tovar, Wilfredo	R-R	5-10	160	8-11-91	.200	.200	.200	7	15	1	3	0	0	0	2	1	1	2	0	3	1	0	.200	.294
Turner, Justin	R-R	6-0	210	11-23-84	.280	.272	.287	86	200	12	56	13	1	2	16	11	1	1	1	34	0	1	.385	.319
Valdespin, Jordany	L-R	6-0	190	12-23-87	.188	.105	.202	66	153	15	25	3	1	4	16	8	3	0	0	28	4	3	.316	.250
Wright, David	R-R	6-0	210	12-20-82	.307	.336	.296	112	430	63	132	23	6	18	58	55	5	0	2	79	17	3	.514	.390
Young Jr., Eric	B-R	5-10	180	5-25-85	.251	.248	.253	91	374	48	94	18	4	1	26	35	2	6	1	67	38	7	.329	.318
2-team total (57 Colorado)					.249	—	—	148	539	70	134	27	7	2	32	46	2	10	1	100	46	11	.336	.310

Pitching	B-T	HT	WT	DOB	W	L	ERA	G	GS	CG	SV	IP	H	R	ER	HR	BB	SO	AVG	vLH	vRH	K/9	BB/9
Aardsma, David	R-R	6-3	205	12-27-81	2	2	4.31	43	0	0	0	40	39	20	19	7	19	36	.257	.218	.278	8.17	4.31
Atchison, Scott	R-R	6-2	200	3-29-76	3	3	4.37	50	0	0	0	45	45	27	22	4	12	28	.254	.254	.254	5.56	2.38
Black, Vic	R-R	6-4	215	5-23-88	3	0	3.46	15	0	0	1	13	11	5	5	1	4	12	.224	.238	.214	8.31	2.77
2-team total (3 Pittsburgh)					3	0	3.71	18	0	0	1	17	17	7	7	1	6	15	—	—	—	7.94	3.18
Burke, Greg	R-R	6-4	215	9-21-82	0	3	5.68	32	0	0	0	32	43	27	20	3	15	28	.312	.319	.308	7.96	4.26
Byrdak, Tim	L-L	5-11	190	10-31-73	0	0	7.71	8	0	0	0	5	5	4	4	2	2	3	.263	.273	.250	5.79	3.86
Carson, Robert	L-L	6-4	240	1-23-89	0	0	8.24	14	0	0	0	20	21	19	18	9	7	8	.269	.265	.273	3.66	3.20
Edgin, Josh	L-L	6-1	225	12-17-86	1	1	3.77	34	0	0	1	29	26	12	12	2	12	20	.243	.250	.236	6.28	3.77
Familia, Jeurys	R-R	6-4	230	10-10-89	0	0	4.22	9	0	0	1	11	12	5	5	2	9	8	.293	.313	.280	6.75	7.59
Feliciano, Pedro	L-L	5-10	195	8-25-76	0	2	3.97	25	0	0	0	11	11	5	5	1	6	9	.262	.176	.625	7.15	4.76
Francisco, Frank	R-R	6-2	250	9-11-79	1	0	4.26	8	0	0	1	6	4	3	3	0	3	6	.182	.222	.154	8.53	4.26
Gee, Dillon	R-R	6-1	205	4-28-86	12	11	3.62	32	32	2	0	199	208	84	80	24	47	142	.268	.288	.252	6.42	2.13
Germen, Gonzalez	R-R	6-2	200	9-23-87	1	2	3.93	29	0	0	1	34	32	15	15	1	16	33	.241	.226	.250	8.65	4.19
Harang, Aaron	R-R	6-7	260	5-9-78	0	1	3.52	4	4	0	0	23	20	10	9	5	12	26	.230	.256	.208	10.17	4.70
Harvey, Matt	R-R	6-4	225	3-27-89	9	5	2.27	26	26	1	0	178	135	46	45	7	31	191	.209	.178	.240	9.64	1.56
Hawkins, LaTroy	R-R	6-5	220	12-21-72	3	2	2.93	72	0	0	13	71	71	27	23	6	10	55	.264	.248	.275	7.00	1.27
Hefner, Jeremy	R-R	6-4	215	3-11-86	4	8	4.34	24	23	0	0	131	132	75	63	20	37	99	.260	.286	.240	6.82	2.55
Henn, Sean	R-L	6-3	235	4-23-81	0	1	3.38	4	0	0	0	3	3	1	1	1	3	1	.300	.500	.167	3.38	10.13
Laffey, Aaron	L-L	6-0	200	4-15-85	0	0	7.20	4	2	0	0	10	16	8	8	1	5	9	.390	.357	.407	8.10	4.50
Lyon, Brandon	R-R	6-1	200	8-10-79	2	2	4.98	37	0	0	0	34	43	20	19	3	13	23	.323	.271	.353	6.03	3.41
Marcum, Shaun	R-R	6-0	195	12-14-81	1	10	5.29	14	12	0	0	78	85	48	46	7	21	60	.284	.302	.272	6.89	2.41
Matsuzaka, Daisuke	R-R	6-0	185	9-13-80	3	3	4.42	7	7	0	0	39	32	21	19	4	16	33	.227	.250	.200	7.68	3.72
McHugh, Collin	R-R	6-2	195	6-19-87	0	1	10.29	3	1	0	0	7	12	8	8	2	3	3	.400	.467	.333	3.86	3.86
2-team total (4 Colorado)					0	4	10.04	7	5	0	0	26	45	29	29	6	5	11	—	—	—	3.81	1.73
Mejia, Jenrry	R-R	6-0	205	10-11-89	1	2	2.30	5	5	0	0	27	28	9	7	2	4	27	.269	.261	.276	8.89	1.32

	B-T	HT	WT	DOB	W	L	ERA	G	GS	CG	SV	IP	H	R	ER	HR	BB	SO	AVG	vLH	vRH	K/9	BB/9
Niese, Jon	L-L	6-4	215	10-27-86	8	8	3.71	24	24	1	0	143	158	68	59	10	48	105	.281	.239	.294	6.61	3.02
Parnell, Bobby	R-R	6-4	200	9-8-84	5	5	2.16	49	0	0	22	50	38	17	12	1	12	44	.211	.211	.211	7.92	2.16
Rice, Scott	L-L	6-6	225	9-21-81	4	5	3.71	73	0	0	0	51	42	22	21	1	27	41	.235	.174	.362	7.24	4.76
Torres, Carlos	R-R	6-1	185	10-22-82	4	6	3.44	33	9	0	0	86	79	34	33	15	17	75	.242	.268	.226	7.82	1.77
Wheeler, Zack	R-R	6-4	185	5-30-90	7	5	3.42	17	17	0	0	100	90	42	38	10	46	84	.243	.259	.230	7.56	4.14

Fielding

Catcher	PCT	G	PO	A	E	DP	PB
Buck	.995	97	704	40	4	1	6
Centeno	1.000	4	28	2	0	0	0
d'Arnaud	1.000	14	214	10	0	0	3
Recker	.990	38	289	17	3	2	2

First Base	PCT	G	PO	A	E	DP
Brown	1.000	1	1	0	0	0
Davis	.989	96	805	38	9	62
Duda	1.000	34	237	18	0	19
Lutz	1.000	1	1	0	0	0
Murphy	.974	7	70	5	2	3
Satin	.993	33	257	16	2	27
Turner	.989	15	87	6	1	9

Second Base	PCT	G	PO	A	E	DP
Flores	1.000	2	3	2	0	1

Murphy	.976	150	263	391	16	86
Turner	1.000	12	5	7	0	1
Valdespin	.974	12	14	24	1	4
Young Jr.	1.000	3	1	4	0	1

Third Base	PCT	G	PO	A	E	DP
Flores	.971	26	13	55	2	4
Lutz	1.000	3	0	5	0	1
Quintanilla	—	1	0	0	0	0
Satin	.912	17	10	21	3	0
Turner	.968	23	9	21	1	1
Wright	.973	111	86	235	9	18

Shortstop	PCT	G	PO	A	E	DP
Quintanilla	.978	92	107	248	8	45
Tejada	.969	55	72	177	8	37
Tovar	1.000	7	5	15	0	4

Turner	1.000	18	19	32	0	8
Valdespin	—	1	0	0	0	0

Outfield	PCT	G	PO	A	E	DP
Ankiel	1.000	18	35	1	0	0
Baxter	.988	46	84	1	1	0
Brown	.966	38	52	4	2	0
Byrd	.986	112	201	7	3	2
Cowgill	1.000	20	20	0	0	0
den Dekker	1.000	24	34	0	0	0
Duda	.978	58	90	1	2	1
Lagares	.983	116	281	15	5	0
Nieuwenhuis	1.000	33	46	2	0	0
Turner	—	1	0	0	0	0
Valdespin	.972	25	34	1	1	0
Young Jr.	.989	90	181	7	2	0

LAS VEGAS 51S
TRIPLE-A

PACIFIC COAST LEAGUE

Batting	B-T	HT	WT	DOB	AVG	vLH	vRH	G	AB	R	H	2B	3B	HR	RBI	BB	HBP	SH	SF	SO	SB	CS	SLG	OBP
Baxter, Mike	L-R	6-0	195	12-7-84	.289	.200	.302	53	187	38	54	12	5	7	22	24	4	0	1	27	4	5	.519	.380
Bixler, Brian	R-R	6-1	195	10-22-82	.259	.214	.280	101	309	40	80	16	2	5	27	26	4	4	2	89	7	4	.372	.323
Brown, Andrew	R-R	6-0	185	9-10-84	.346	.320	.359	41	153	39	53	15	6	7	41	23	4	0	5	34	0	0	.660	.432
Campbell, Eric	R-R	6-3	220	4-9-87	.314	.339	.302	120	341	61	107	25	3	8	66	66	10	4	4	60	12	4	.475	.435
Centeno, Juan	L-R	5-10	170	11-16-89	.305	.310	.304	67	213	25	65	10	2	0	28	12	3	6	3	24	1	1	.371	.346
Cowgill, Collin	R-L	5-9	185	5-22-86	.268	.200	.301	33	123	22	33	6	0	5	12	17	2	3	0	25	4	0	.439	.366
2-team total (4 Salt Lake)					.304	—	—	37	138	26	42	7	0	7	19	18	3	3	0	28	5	0	.507	.396
d'Arnaud, Travis	R-R	6-2	195	2-10-89	.304	.375	.275	19	56	19	17	8	0	2	12	21	0	0	1	12	0	0	.554	.487
Davis, Ike	L-L	6-4	230	3-22-87	.293	.292	.294	21	75	21	22	7	0	7	13	17	0	0	0	18	0	0	.667	.424
den Dekker, Matt	L-L	6-1	205	8-10-87	.296	.135	.338	53	179	34	53	8	4	6	38	20	1	0	2	46	8	1	.486	.366
Duda, Lucas	L-R	6-4	255	2-3-86	.306	.333	.298	18	62	13	19	3	0	0	8	14	0	0	2	15	1	0	.355	.423
Flores, Wilmer	R-R	6-3	190	8-6-91	.321	.348	.311	107	424	69	136	36	4	15	86	25	3	3	8	63	1	3	.531	.357
Gronauer, Kai	R-R	6-1	215	11-28-86	.250	.389	.111	18	36	3	9	3	0	1	4	2	0	1	0	10	0	1	.417	.289
Havens, Reese	L-R	6-1	195	10-20-86	.237	.200	.239	38	97	9	23	4	1	1	8	10	1	0	1	27	1	0	.330	.312
Hicks, Brandon	R-R	6-2	200	9-14-85	.283	.278	.285	95	318	57	90	12	4	11	49	29	3	3	1	111	9	2	.450	.348
Hoffmann, Jamie	R-R	6-3	235	8-20-84	.277	.315	.264	116	365	48	101	29	1	9	56	22	6	0	2	59	8	1	.436	.327
Lagares, Juan	R-R	6-1	175	3-17-89	.346	.292	.370	17	78	13	27	3	2	3	9	4	0	0	0	14	2	3	.551	.378
Lawley, Dustin	R-R	6-1	195	4-11-89	.300	.143	.385	6	20	3	6	2	0	1	6	2	0	1	0	2	0	0	.550	.333
Lutz, Zach	R-R	6-1	220	6-3-86	.293	.221	.316	111	399	62	117	27	4	13	80	54	4	2	7	102	0	2	.479	.377
Nieuwenhuis, Kirk	L-R	6-3	215	8-7-87	.248	.210	.264	74	282	60	70	15	2	14	37	40	2	5	1	78	6	2	.465	.345
Pena, Francisco	R-R	6-2	230	10-12-89	.257	.300	.244	68	218	22	56	15	1	9	39	10	3	1	4	40	1	0	.459	.294
Powell, Landon	R-R	6-3	265	3-19-82	.159	.250	.095	28	69	7	11	3	0	2	3	12	0	1	0	21	0	1	.290	.284
Quintanilla, Omar	L-R	5-9	185	10-24-81	.333	.240	.356	48	126	26	42	9	2	2	18	20	0	0	2	25	1	1	.484	.419
Recker, Anthony	R-R	6-2	240	8-29-83	.400	.400	.400	5	10	3	4	0	1	1	4	2	0	0	0	2	0	0	.900	.500
Sandoval, Rylan	R-R	5-10	185	8-10-87	.327	.458	.291	38	110	20	36	8	0	4	12	9	0	0	0	26	4	2	.509	.378
Satin, Josh	R-R	6-2	200	12-23-84	.305	.354	.280	60	220	46	67	14	0	9	32	43	1	0	4	45	0	2	.491	.420
Tejada, Ruben	R-R	5-11	185	10-27-89	.288	.319	.280	60	240	38	69	14	1	2	24	14	6	5	4	30	1	1	.379	.337
Valdespin, Jordany	L-R	6-0	190	12-23-87	.466	.375	.480	16	58	14	27	4	2	3	24	8	1	0	0	7	2	3	.759	.537

Pitching	B-T	HT	WT	DOB	W	L	ERA	G	GS	CG	SV	IP	H	R	ER	HR	BB	SO	AVG	vLH	vRH	K/9	BB/9
Aardsma, David	R-R	6-3	205	12-27-81	0	0	1.13	8	0	0	3	8	5	1	1	1	7	11	.185	.091	.250	12.38	7.88
2-team total (10 New Orleans)					1	0	2.05	18	0	0	3	22	14	6	5	3	15	23	—	—	—	9.41	6.14
Alvarado, Giancarlo	R-R	6-4	210	1-24-78	5	4	3.49	12	12	0	0	59	67	25	23	2	30	41	.289	.333	.256	6.22	4.55
Burke, Greg	R-R	6-4	215	9-21-82	2	2	4.55	31	0	0	5	32	33	16	16	3	10	34	.275	.368	.232	9.66	2.84
Byrdak, Tim	L-L	5-11	190	10-31-73	2	0	0.00	11	0	0	0	6	0	0	0	0	5	10	.000	.250	.176	11.25	5.63
Carson, Robert	L-L	6-4	240	1-23-89	3	3	4.06	43	0	0	11	44	48	25	20	3	19	36	.274	.320	.240	7.31	3.86
Church, John	R-R	6-2	235	11-4-86	3	0	3.21	23	0	0	3	28	27	10	10	2	13	27	.267	.171	.333	8.68	4.18
deGrom, Jake	L-R	6-4	185	6-19-88	4	2	4.52	14	14	0	0	76	87	41	38	6	24	63	.288	.257	.315	7.49	2.85
Edgin, Josh	L-L	6-1	225	12-17-86	2	0	5.91	11	0	0	1	14	14	7	7	1	2	12	.318	.294	.333	10.13	1.69
Familia, Jeurys	R-R	6-4	230	10-10-89	0	0	0.00	4	0	0	1	5	5	0	0	0	1	4	.278	.143	.364	7.20	1.80
Feliciano, Pedro	L-L	5-10	195	8-25-76	0	0	0.00	3	0	0	1	2	0	0	0	0	1	.000	.000	.000	4.50	0.00
Fox, Matt	R-R	6-3	190	12-4-82	8	4	4.59	20	20	0	0	112	133	62	57	11	27	76	.302	.267	.332	6.13	2.18
Germen, Gonzalez	R-R	6-2	200	9-23-87	3	3	5.52	35	0	0	4	44	47	29	27	7	11	51	.270	.304	.242	10.43	2.25
Gorski, Darin	L-L	6-4	210	10-6-87	1	1	6.59	4	3	0	0	14	17	11	10	1	9	7	.315	.381	.273	4.61	5.93
Hampson, Justin	L-L	6-1	205	5-24-80	6	4	3.63	64	0	0	2	67	78	32	27	4	27	56	.293	.263	.326	7.52	3.63
Harang, Aaron	R-R	6-7	260	5-9-78	0	0	4.50	1	0	0	0	4	7	2	2	1	1	5	.389	.286	.455	11.25	2.25
Henn, Sean	R-L	6-3	235	4-23-81	3	5	2.81	52	0	0	2	58	60	25	18	0	32	49	.275	.295	.257	7.65	4.99

Kolarek, Adam	L-L	6-3	215	1-14-89	0	0	11.25	2	0	0	0	4	5	5	5	0	3	1	.294	.111	.500	2.25	6.75
Leathersich, Jack	R-L	5-11	205	7-14-90	2	0	7.76	28	0	0	0	29	32	33	25	2	29	47	.278	.304	.261	14.59	9.00
McHugh, Collin	R-R	6-2	195	6-19-87	3	2	2.87	9	9	0	0	53	57	21	17	3	13	41	.277	.294	.258	6.92	2.19
2-team total (9 Colorado Springs)					5	4	3.69	18	18	0	0	100	109	46	41	5	27	88	—	—	—	7.92	2.43
Mitchell, D.J.	R-R	6-0	160	5-13-87	6	6	7.71	34	13	0	0	82	116	77	70	12	47	64	.349	.344	.354	7.05	5.18
2-team total (1 Tacoma)					6	6	7.67	35	14	0	0	86	119	80	73	12	54	66	—	—	—	6.93	5.67
Montero, Rafael	R-R	6-0	170	10-17-90	5	4	3.05	16	16	0	0	89	85	35	30	4	25	78	.254	.272	.239	7.92	2.54
Owen, Dylan	R-R	5-11	185	7-12-86	0	3	7.50	15	0	0	0	18	23	15	15	3	11	12	.311	.243	.378	6.00	5.50
Peavey, Greg	R-R	6-2	185	7-11-88	4	3	5.74	39	1	0	0	63	67	42	40	7	28	41	.273	.289	.264	5.89	4.02
Rodriguez, Armando	R-R	6-3	250	1-28-88	1	2	4.30	39	0	0	0	44	55	22	21	8	26	40	.311	.358	.271	8.18	5.32
Schwinden, Chris	R-R	6-3	215	9-22-86	6	9	5.78	29	28	0	0	146	188	102	94	23	45	89	.313	.315	.311	5.47	2.77
Talbot, Mitch	R-R	6-1	180	10-17-83	0	0	9.82	1	1	0	0	4	7	7	4	0	3	0	.412	.462	.250	0.00	7.36
2-team total (1 New Orleans)					1	0	4.15	2	2	0	0	9	9	7	4	0	5	3	—	—	—	3.12	5.19
Thompson, Daryl	R-R	6-0	205	11-2-85	2	0	3.97	4	2	0	0	11	12	5	5	2	3	10	.267	.304	.227	7.94	2.38
Torres, Carlos	R-R	6-1	185	10-22-82	6	3	3.89	12	12	2	0	72	71	36	31	7	19	67	.253	.241	.265	8.41	2.39
Wade, Cory	R-R	6-2	185	5-28-83	0	1	13.50	2	0	0	1	2	3	3	3	1	0	2	.429	.000	.750	9.00	0.00
2-team total (10 Iowa)					0	3	8.50	12	0	0	1	18	31	17	17	4	7	18	—	—	—	9.00	3.50
Wheeler, Zack	R-R	6-4	185	5-30-90	4	2	3.93	13	13	0	0	69	61	35	30	9	27	73	.236	.220	.252	9.57	3.54

Fielding

Catcher	PCT	G	PO	A	E	DP	PB
Centeno	.993	62	388	46	3	1	5
d'Arnaud	.986	18	130	11	2	1	5
Gronauer	1.000	6	24	2	0	0	1
Pena	.990	57	368	47	4	3	2
Powell	1.000	18	119	8	0	2	2
Recker	.944	3	17	0	1	0	0

First Base	PCT	G	PO	A	E	DP
Brown	1.000	4	20	1	0	3
Campbell	.986	27	192	15	3	20
Davis	1.000	19	137	16	0	19
Duda	1.000	12	88	5	0	19
Flores	.988	11	73	6	1	5
Hicks	.952	3	19	1	1	2
Lutz	.995	28	197	16	1	21
Sandoval	1.000	5	40	4	0	5
Satin	.998	47	395	35	1	42

Second Base	PCT	G	PO	A	E	DP
Bixler	1.000	13	22	22	0	5

Flores	.975	79	132	213	9	54
Havens	.952	9	17	23	2	6
Hicks	.986	26	63	79	2	26
Quintanilla	—	1	0	0	0	0
Sandoval	.953	12	15	26	2	1
Tejada	—	1	0	0	0	0
Valdespin	.951	14	20	38	3	8

Third Base	PCT	G	PO	A	E	DP
Bixler	.917	18	9	13	2	0
Campbell	.927	28	16	33	4	5
Flores	.857	4	1	5	1	1
Havens	.929	15	6	20	2	3
Hicks	.923	25	23	25	4	1
Lawley	1.000	2	4	5	0	1
Lutz	.962	69	36	92	5	14
Sandoval	.824	7	5	9	3	0

Shortstop	PCT	G	PO	A	E	DP
Bixler	.943	17	19	31	3	8
Hicks	.953	41	67	96	8	32

Quintanilla	.947	43	62	99	9	30
Sandoval	1.000	3	4	5	0	1
Tejada	.969	58	98	150	8	37

Outfield	PCT	G	PO	A	E	DP
Baxter	.984	45	59	4	1	1
Bixler	.989	48	87	0	1	0
Brown	.958	33	63	6	3	1
Campbell	1.000	55	101	3	0	0
Cowgill	.974	32	74	2	2	0
den Dekker	.992	51	115	2	1	1
Duda	1.000	3	6	1	0	0
Hoffmann	.972	99	133	7	4	0
Lagares	.963	17	48	4	2	0
Lawley	1.000	3	1	0	0	0
Lutz	1.000	9	11	0	0	0
Mitchell	1.000	1	3	0	0	0
Nieuwenhuis	.994	71	150	4	1	1
Satin	1.000	1	1	0	0	0
Valdespin	.750	2	3	0	1	0

BINGHAMTON METS   DOUBLE-A

EASTERN LEAGUE

Batting	B-T	HT	WT	DOB	AVG	vLH	vRH	G	AB	R	H	2B	3B	HR	RBI	BB	HBP	SH	SF	SO	SB	CS	SLG	OBP
Bonfe, Joe	R-R	6-4	220	12-28-87	.245	.297	.219	43	110	11	27	4	0	1	12	6	4	0	3	31	2	1	.309	.301
Carrillo, Xorge	R-R	6-1	220	4-12-89	.296	.154	.341	34	108	12	32	6	0	0	13	8	2	1	2	21	0	0	.352	.350
Ceciliani, Darrell	L-L	6-1	220	6-22-90	.268	.243	.276	113	418	61	112	17	6	6	44	29	6	4	4	105	31	7	.380	.322
Centeno, Juan	L-R	5-10	170	11-16-89	.261	.250	.263	6	23	4	6	1	0	0	3	0	0	1	0	5	0	0	.391	.261
d'Arnaud, Travis	R-R	6-2	195	2-10-89	.222	.200	.227	7	27	2	6	2	1	1	3	3	0	0	0	9	0	0	.481	.300
Dykstra, Allan	L-R	6-5	215	5-21-87	.274	.265	.277	122	372	56	102	22	0	21	82	102	9	6	123	0	0	0	.503	.436
Forsythe, Blake	R-R	6-2	220	7-31-89	.192	.200	.190	88	307	36	59	18	2	10	33	32	2	0	2	101	3	0	.362	.271
Harris, Alonzo	R-R	5-11	165	1-16-91	.218	.293	.191	101	354	43	77	17	1	4	24	34	1	2	4	89	25	9	.305	.285
Hughes, Rhyne	L-L	6-2	215	9-9-83	.278	.189	.304	53	162	20	45	11	2	5	30	20	3	0	2	61	1	1	.463	.364
Lucas, Richard	R-R	6-1	205	11-2-88	.206	.204	.206	99	345	42	71	12	1	8	32	21	4	2	3	103	5	3	.316	.257
Muno, Danny	B-R	5-11	175	2-9-89	.249	.234	.254	127	449	86	112	27	2	9	67	92	9	6	5	97	15	11	.379	.384
Pena, Francisco	R-R	6-2	230	10-12-89	.246	.217	.261	21	69	4	17	6	0	4	7	1	1	1	4	0	1	.333	.321
Puello, Cesar	R-R	6-2	195	4-1-91	.326	.421	.298	91	331	63	108	21	2	16	73	28	16	0	2	82	24	7	.547	.403
Reynolds, Matt	R-R	6-1	198	12-3-90	.000	—	.000	1	3	0	0	0	0	0	0	0	0	0	0	0	0	0	.000	.000
Rodriguez, Josh	R-R	6-0	185	12-18-84	.272	.272	.272	127	441	77	120	30	2	6	52	70	3	2	6	94	5	3	.390	.371
Taijeron, Travis	R-R	6-2	200	1-20-89	.246	.217	.256	65	232	33	57	18	0	14	42	24	3	0	2	77	0	0	.504	.322
Tovar, Wilfredo	R-R	5-10	160	8-11-91	.263	.292	.255	133	441	70	116	14	4	4	36	33	7	3	2	49	12	7	.340	.323
Turner, Justin	R-R	6-0	210	11-23-84	.400	.333	.417	4	15	5	6	2	0	0	1	1	0	0	2	0	0	.533	.471
Vaughn, Cory	R-R	6-3	225	5-1-89	.267	.344	.242	71	262	40	70	9	1	10	50	24	8	0	1	78	9	1	.424	.346

Pitching	B-T	HT	WT	DOB	W	L	ERA	G	GS	CG	SV	IP	H	R	ER	HR	BB	SO	AVG	vLH	vRH	K/9	BB/9
Atchison, Scott	R-R	6-2	200	3-29-76	1	0	0.00	4	0	0	0	4	2	0	0	0	0	4	.154	.143	.167	9.00	0.00
Bennett, Hamilton	R-L	6-1	180	6-26-88	1	0	1.46	8	0	0	0	12	7	2	2	1	2	12	.156	.000	.219	8.76	1.46
Bradford, Chase	R-R	6-1	185	8-5-89	3	1	0.71	20	0	0	1	25	19	6	2	1	8	18	.211	.250	.185	6.39	2.84
Church, John	R-R	6-2	235	11-4-86	2	4	3.44	32	0	0	0	37	30	15	14	2	13	41	.221	.310	.181	10.06	3.19
Cohoon, Mark	L-L	6-2	195	9-15-87	9	5	3.99	25	21	2	0	120	146	65	53	9	28	89	.311	.277	.325	6.69	2.11
Cuan, Angel	L-L	5-11	150	5-29-89	0	1	4.50	1	1	0	0	6	7	3	3	0	1	5	.333	.333	.333	7.50	1.50
deGrom, Jake	L-R	6-4	185	6-19-88	2	5	4.80	10	10	0	0	60	69	38	32	4	20	44	.295	.318	.282	6.60	3.00
Edgin, Josh	L-L	6-1	225	12-17-86	0	0	7.88	5	0	0	0	8	10	7	7	2	5	10	.313	.176	.467	11.25	5.63
Feliciano, Pedro	L-L	5-10	195	8-25-76	0	0	1.26	14	0	0	0	14	9	2	2	0	2	14	.180	.167	.192	8.79	1.26

	B-T	HT	WT	DOB	W	L	ERA	G	GS	CG	SV	IP	H	R	ER	HR	BB	SO	AVG	vLH	vRH	K/9	BB/9
Francisco, Frank	R-R	6-2	250	9-11-79	0	0	0.00	2	0	0	0	2	2	0	0	0	1	1	.286	.333	.250	4.50	4.50
Fraser, Ryan	R-R	6-3	190	8-27-88	1	2	5.63	27	0	0	0	38	51	30	24	4	26	25	.323	.349	.305	5.87	6.10
Fuller, Jim	L-L	5-10	180	6-1-87	3	2	7.50	9	0	0	0	18	18	16	15	1	9	27	.250	.227	.260	13.50	4.50
Goeddel, Erik	R-R	6-3	185	12-20-88	9	7	4.37	25	25	0	0	134	135	72	65	14	58	125	.265	.287	.243	8.40	3.90
Gorski, Darin	L-L	6-4	210	10-6-87	6	1	1.83	14	13	1	0	79	46	17	16	1	22	67	.172	.279	.140	7.67	2.52
Huchingson, Chase	L-L	6-5	200	4-14-89	3	2	1.61	45	0	0	1	67	55	20	12	4	29	68	.225	.125	.267	9.13	3.90
Kolarek, Adam	L-L	6-3	215	1-14-89	3	3	1.71	44	0	0	1	63	47	15	12	3	22	63	.204	.227	.194	9.00	3.14
Leathersich, Jack	R-L	5-11	205	7-14-90	2	0	1.53	24	0	0	3	29	19	5	5	1	16	55	.181	.367	.107	16.88	4.91
Mateo, Luis	R-R	6-3	185	3-22-90	0	1	12.00	1	1	0	0	3	6	4	4	1	3	2	.400	1.000	.250	6.00	9.00
Mazzoni, Cory	R-R	6-1	190	10-19-89	5	3	4.36	13	12	0	0	66	70	43	-32	4	19	74	.275	.258	.290	10.09	2.59
Mejia, Jenrry	R-R	6-0	205	10-11-89	2	0	0.82	2	2	0	0	16	6	1	1	1	4	9	.167	.222	.148	7.36	3.27
Montero, Rafael	R-R	6-0	170	10-17-90	7	3	2.43	11	11	0	0	67	51	21	18	2	10	72	.204	.223	.188	9.72	1.35
Niese, Jon	L-L	6-4	215	10-27-86	1	0	3.60	1	1	0	0	5	4	2	2	0	3	6	.235	.200	.250	10.80	5.40
Owen, Dylan	R-R	5-11	185	7-12-86	0	0	9.00	2	0	0	0	2	4	3	2	0	2	0	.400	.333	.429	0.00	9.00
Peavey, Greg	R-R	6-2	185	7-11-88	2	2	3.00	6	5	0	0	33	27	13	11	1	10	22	.229	.273	.190	6.55	2.73
Pill, Tyler	R-R	6-1	185	5-29-90	1	1	7.58	4	4	0	0	19	29	17	16	1	8	17	.349	.333	.358	8.05	3.79
Rodriguez, Armando	R-R	6-3	250	1-28-88	1	2	5.95	11	0	0	0	20	17	14	13	2	7	21	.239	.278	.200	9.61	3.20
Rosario, Adrian	R-R	6-4	180	9-30-89	0	0	10.13	6	0	0	0	8	7	11	9	1	12	9	.233	.286	.217	10.13	13.50
Syndergaard, Noah	L-R	6-6	240	8-29-92	6	1	3.00	11	11	0	0	54	46	23	18	8	12	69	.228	.295	.168	11.50	2.00
Teufel, Shawn	L-L	6-3	215	7-16-86	0	0	4.26	15	0	0	0	19	14	10	9	2	20	21	.209	.136	.244	9.95	9.47
Verrett, Logan	R-R	6-2	180	6-19-90	12	6	4.25	24	24	0	0	146	136	72	69	21	31	132	.249	.256	.243	8.14	1.91
Walters, Jeff	R-R	6-3	170	11-6-87	4	3	2.09	53	0	0	38	56	46	13	13	2	16	60	.224	.218	.228	9.64	2.57

Fielding

Catcher	PCT	G	PO	A	E	DP	PB
Carrillo	.993	33	289	16	2	1	3
Centeno	.982	6	51	4	1	0	0
d'Arnaud	.968	7	49	12	2	1	0
Forsythe	.999	80	657	43	1	7	4
Pena	.988	18	161	8	2	0	1

First Base	PCT	G	PO	A	E	DP
Bonfe	.984	10	59	3	1	8
Dykstra	.987	59	426	38	6	40
Hughes	.996	36	263	16	1	17
Lucas	.985	45	310	13	5	32

Second Base	PCT	G	PO	A	E	DP
Harris	1.000	1	4	3	0	1
Muno	.980	115	197	282	10	59
Rodriguez	.962	26	35	65	4	18
Tovar	.867	4	4	9	2	2
Turner	1.000	2	4	8	0	0

Third Base	PCT	G	PO	A	E	DP
Bonfe	.857	2	3	3	1	0
Lucas	.906	51	28	78	11	6
Rodriguez	.939	100	54	146	13	14

Shortstop	PCT	G	PO	A	E	DP
Muno	.904	17	19	28	5	6

	PCT	G	PO	A	E	DP
Reynolds	.800	1	1	3	1	1
Tovar	.981	128	161	304	9	65
Turner	.875	2	3	4	1	0

Outfield	PCT	G	PO	A	E	DP
Bonfe	.971	23	32	2	1	1
Ceciliani	.969	105	210	6	7	0
Forsythe	1.000	1	1	0	0	0
Harris	.982	97	215	9	4	2
Hughes	1.000	3	5	0	0	0
Puello	.980	89	184	8	4	3
Taijeron	.980	63	93	3	2	0
Vaughn	.981	60	101	4	2	0

ST. LUCIE METS

HIGH CLASS A

FLORIDA STATE LEAGUE

Batting	B-T	HT	WT	DOB	AVG	vLH	vRH	G	AB	R	H	2B	3B	HR	RBI	BB	HBP	SH	SF	SO	SB	CS	SLG	OBP
Bonfe, Joe	R-R	6-4	220	12-28-87	.250	—	.250	3	8	0	2	1	0	0	0	0	0	0	1	0	1	0	.375	.250
Boyd, Jayce	R-R	6-3	185	12-30-90	.292	.247	.316	58	209	28	61	13	1	4	37	26	2	2	2	29	2	0	.421	.372
Carrillo, Xorge	R-R	6-1	220	4-12-89	.000	.000	.000	2	7	0	0	0	0	0	0	0	0	0	0	2	0	0	.000	.000
Clark, Jonathan	L-R	6-1	180	9-28-90	.190	.250	.176	20	42	5	8	2	0	0	1	5	0	2	0	13	4	3	.238	.277
Cordero, Albert	R-R	5-11	175	1-14-90	.220	.250	.200	24	82	9	18	4	0	0	6	7	2	0	0	6	1	2	.268	.297
De La Cruz, Yucarybert	R-R	6-0	160	10-23-90	.189	.077	.225	17	53	3	10	4	0	0	8	4	0	0	0	15	1	1	.264	.246
den Dekker, Matt	L-L	6-1	205	8-10-87	.276	.286	.267	14	58	8	16	2	0	0	4	3	0	0	1	6	1	0	.310	.306
Duda, Lucas	L-R	6-4	255	2-3-86	.250	.375	.200	7	28	4	7	2	0	1	5	2	0	0	0	7	0	0	.429	.300
Gomez, Gilbert	R-R	6-3	190	3-8-92	.216	.231	.210	115	366	40	79	14	0	1	27	46	4	7	1	110	4	7	.262	.309
Harrison, Brian	R-R	6-2	180	12-15-88	.219	.385	.105	9	32	5	7	1	0	1	5	4	3	0	1	4	0	1	.344	.350
Hicks, Brandon	R-R	6-2	200	9-14-85	.250	—	.250	2	8	1	2	1	0	0	2	0	0	0	0	2	0	0	.375	.250
Johnson, Kyle	R-R	6-0	180	11-9-89	.278	.383	.228	48	187	42	52	8	1	3	14	17	4	2	4	35	12	5	.380	.344
Lawley, Dustin	R-R	6-1	195	4-11-89	.260	.312	.239	122	469	69	122	33	5	25	92	36	3	0	6	111	6	3	.512	.313
Maron, Cam	L-R	6-1	175	1-20-91	.235	.165	.265	84	285	25	67	13	2	0	29	38	1	1	0	49	1	0	.295	.327
Plawecki, Kevin	R-R	6-2	205	2-26-91	.294	.296	.293	60	204	25	60	14	0	2	37	19	14	1	1	21	0	0	.392	.391
Ponce, Dimas	R-R	5-11	140	1-22-91	.038	.091	.000	10	26	1	1	0	0	0	2	2	0	0	1	10	0	0	.038	.103
Reynolds, Matt	R-R	6-1	198	12-3-90	.226	.230	.225	117	433	59	98	21	6	5	49	36	13	1	5	80	9	2	.337	.302
Rivera, T.J.	R-R	6-1	190	4-13-88	.289	.316	.277	125	502	76	145	23	1	2	51	34	13	7	3	73	6	2	.351	.348
Rodriguez, Aderlin	R-R	6-3	210	11-18-91	.260	.286	.253	62	246	27	64	14	0	9	41	11	3	0	4	43	1	1	.427	.295
Rohan, Eddie	R-R	6-0	205	8-15-88	.250	.000	.333	4	4	0	1	0	0	0	0	0	0	0	0	0	0	0	.250	.250
Sandoval, Rylan	R-R	5-10	185	8-10-87	.243	.173	.279	63	222	28	54	8	3	1	22	16	6	1	2	49	3	2	.320	.309
Shields, Robbie	R-R	6-1	195	12-2-87	.231	.248	.223	93	337	31	78	19	1	2	19	25	1	1	0	71	5	5	.312	.287
Taijeron, Travis	R-R	6-2	200	1-20-89	.303	.255	.321	55	188	33	57	20	1	9	27	23	8	3	0	54	1	1	.564	.396
Thurber, Charley	L-L	6-4	220	12-28-89	.227	.195	.242	79	277	38	63	15	1	5	39	25	4	3	0	64	3	3	.343	.301
Turner, Justin	R-R	6-0	210	11-23-84	.000	—	.000	1	1	0	0	0	0	0	0	0	0	0	0	0	0	0	.000	.000
Vaughn, Cory	R-R	6-3	225	5-1-89	.205	.167	.212	12	39	5	8	1	1	0	3	8	1	0	0	9	5	0	.282	.354
Zapata, Nelfi	R-R	6-0	203	12-13-90	.133	.000	.167	10	30	3	4	2	0	0	3	5	0	0	0	10	0	0	.200	.257

Pitching	B-T	HT	WT	DOB	W	L	ERA	G	GS	CG	SV	IP	H	R	ER	HR	BB	SO	AVG	vLH	vRH	K/9	BB/9
Acosta, Octavio	R-R	6-0	165	8-3-90	1	1	5.79	2	2	0	0	9	8	6	6	1	6	10	.242	.316	.143	9.64	5.79
Atchison, Scott	R-R	6-2	200	3-29-76	0	0	0.00	1	0	0	1	1	0	0	0	0	0	1	.000	.000	.000	9.00	0.00
Bennett, Hamilton	R-L	6-1	180	6-26-88	3	0	1.96	38	0	0	9	46	39	10	10	0	12	48	.227	.138	.272	9.39	2.35
Bowman, Matt	R-R	6-0	165	5-31-91	6	4	3.18	16	16	0	0	96	83	36	34	8	31	90	.232	.231	.232	8.41	2.90

Name	B-T	HT	WT	DOB	W	L	ERA	G	GS	CG	SV	IP	H	R	ER	HR	BB	SO	AVG	vLH	vRH	SO/9	BB/9
Bradford, Chase	R-R	6-1	185	8-5-89	6	2	3.71	30	0	0	3	44	45	18	18	3	9	43	.257	.355	.204	8.86	1.85
Byrdak, Tim	L-L	5-11	190	10-31-73	1	1	2.19	14	0	0	3	12	6	3	3	0	7	13	.146	.083	.172	9.49	5.11
Camarena, Marcos	R-R	6-3	202	9-8-90	0	1	8.83	6	3	0	0	17	28	17	17	4	12	9	.368	.438	.318	4.67	6.23
Chism, T.J.	L-L	5-10	190	8-9-88	1	4	2.21	47	0	0	20	61	52	16	15	2	15	56	.229	.188	.245	8.26	2.21
Cuan, Angel	L-L	5-11	150	5-29-89	8	3	3.57	27	12	0	1	103	101	46	41	14	22	82	.256	.196	.275	7.14	1.92
deGrom, Jake	L-R	6-4	185	6-19-88	1	0	3.00	2	2	0	0	12	12	4	4	1	2	13	.261	.389	.179	9.75	1.50
Familia, Jeurys	R-R	6-4	230	10-10-89	0	1	3.00	3	1	0	0	3	2	1	1	0	2	3	.182	.200	.167	9.00	6.00
Feliciano, Pedro	L-L	5-10	195	8-25-76	0	0	1.93	5	0	0	0	5	5	3	1	0	2	4	.313	.143	.444	7.71	3.86
Fontanez, Randy	R-R	6-1	205	5-18-89	9	7	3.41	45	0	0	1	61	55	27	23	2	17	83	.231	.292	.195	12.31	2.52
Francisco, Frank	R-R	6-2	250	9-11-79	0	0	0.00	5	0	0	0	5	1	0	0	0	2	6	.067	.000	.067	10.80	3.60
Fraser, Ryan	R-R	6-3	190	8-27-88	0	0	4.15	5	0	0	0	4	5	2	2	0	2	0	.294	.375	.222	0.00	4.15
Frias, Darwin	R-R	6-0	192	2-18-92	0	0	27.00	1	0	0	0	4	1	1	0	0	0	.800	.750	1.000	0.00	0.00
Fuller, Jim	L-L	5-10	180	6-1-87	1	0	0.84	16	0	0	0	32	15	4	3	1	16	31	.142	.116	.159	8.72	4.50
Fulmer, Michael	R-R	6-3	200	3-15-93	2	2	3.44	7	7	0	0	34	24	13	13	1	18	29	.198	.208	.191	7.68	4.76
Gsellman, Robert	R-R	6-4	200	7-18-93	1	0	3.00	2	2	0	0	9	5	3	3	1	5	5	.152	.125	.176	5.00	5.00
Lara, Rainy	R-R	6-4	180	3-14-91	4	5	3.76	14	13	0	0	79	78	40	33	5	20	54	.258	.271	.249	6.15	2.28
Mateo, Luis	R-R	6-3	185	3-22-90	1	1	4.15	3	1	0	0	9	10	4	4	1	3	11	.303	.357	.263	11.42	3.12
Mejia, Jenrry	R-R	6-0	205	10-11-89	0	0	4.50	2	2	0	0	8	10	4	4	0	4	14	.303	.250	.353	15.75	4.50
Mesa, Wanel	R-R	6-3	190	1-15-87	0	1	10.13	12	0	0	0	13	16	15	15	3	13	10	.302	.263	.324	6.75	8.78
Mitchell, Bret	R-R	6-2	190	12-10-88	1	0	1.76	21	0	0	0	31	19	8	6	2	22	34	.178	.095	.231	9.98	6.46
Morel, Estarlin	R-R	6-0	185	10-2-89	4	3	4.33	21	0	0	0	35	40	19	17	4	10	19	.288	.304	.277	4.84	2.55
Niese, Jon	L-L	6-4	215	10-27-86	0	0	0.00	1	1	0	0	4	2	0	0	0	1	4	.167	.500	.000	9.00	2.25
Panteliodis, Alex	L-L	6-2	235	7-7-90	6	6	4.75	19	19	0	0	102	129	67	54	11	29	56	.309	.282	.318	4.93	2.55
Robles, Hansel	R-R	5-11	185	8-13-90	5	4	3.72	16	15	0	0	85	83	38	35	8	29	66	.259	.250	.264	7.02	3.08
Satterwhite, Cody	R-R	6-4	205	1-27-87	2	2	2.78	16	0	0	0	23	24	12	7	1	13	23	.273	.364	.218	9.13	5.16
Syndergaard, Noah	L-R	6-6	240	8-29-92	3	3	3.11	12	12	0	0	64	61	25	22	3	16	64	.255	.297	.219	9.05	2.26
Tapia, Domingo	R-R	6-4	186	12-16-91	3	9	4.62	23	22	0	0	101	87	60	52	3	63	89	.231	.243	.224	7.90	5.60
Teufel, Shawn	L-L	6-3	215	7-16-86	1	0	6.00	7	0	0	0	9	11	7	6	0	8	7	.324	.167	.357	7.00	8.00
Vazquez, Carlos	L-L	5-11	180	9-3-91	1	0	2.29	10	1	0	0	20	15	5	5	1	3	13	.221	.267	.208	5.95	1.37
Williams, Ty	R-R	6-2	195	2-21-94	0	0	18.00	2	0	0	0	2	6	4	4	0	2	3	.500	.600	.429	13.50	9.00

Fielding

Catcher	PCT	G	PO	A	E	DP	PB
Carrillo	1.000	2	20	2	0	0	0
Cordero	.987	17	143	12	2	1	6
Maron	.986	74	515	53	8	10	4
Plawecki	.994	42	292	20	2	1	3
Rohan	1.000	1	11	1	0	1	0
Zapata	1.000	1	4	1	0	0	0

First Base	PCT	G	PO	A	E	DP
Bonfe	1.000	3	12	1	0	2
Boyd	.980	9	93	6	2	5
Harrison	1.000	9	88	7	0	8
Plawecki	.993	17	136	15	1	10
Rodriguez	.994	17	150	16	1	7
Sandoval	.987	45	364	19	5	29
Shields	.991	28	209	17	2	16
Zapata	1.000	10	69	4	0	6

Second Base	PCT	G	PO	A	E	DP
De La Cruz	1.000	2	2	6	0	2
Ponce	.833	3	1	4	1	0
Rivera	.982	111	198	288	9	69
Sandoval	1.000	1	3	1	0	0
Shields	1.000	20	33	49	0	12
Turner	1.000	1	0	1	0	0

Third Base	PCT	G	PO	A	E	DP
De La Cruz	.964	13	5	22	1	1
Hicks	1.000	1	0	3	0	0
Lawley	.933	15	11	31	3	4
Ponce	.800	6	3	1	2	0
Rodriguez	.921	43	20	85	9	7
Sandoval	.865	12	11	21	5	0
Shields	.943	44	32	118	9	12

Shortstop	PCT	G	PO	A	E	DP
De La Cruz	.900	3	4	5	1	3
Hicks	1.000	1	1	2	0	0
Reynolds	.957	114	145	304	20	57
Rivera	.977	15	17	26	1	5
Sandoval	1.000	4	3	5	0	2

Outfield	PCT	G	PO	A	E	DP
Clark	1.000	9	12	0	0	0
den Dekker	.967	14	28	1	1	0
Duda	1.000	5	9	0	0	0
Gomez	.951	107	207	5	11	3
Johnson	.991	48	109	3	1	0
Lawley	.994	99	147	14	1	2
Taijeron	.981	48	99	2	2	1
Thurber	.982	56	107	5	2	1
Vaughn	1.000	12	28	1	0	0

SAVANNAH SAND GNATS   LOW CLASS A

SOUTH ATLANTIC LEAGUE

Batting	B-T	HT	WT	DOB	AVG	vLH	vRH	G	AB	R	H	2B	3B	HR	RBI	BB	HBP	SH	SF	SO	SB	CS	SLG	OBP
Boyd, Jayce	R-R	6-3	185	12-30-90	.361	.486	.340	65	249	40	90	16	1	5	46	35	2	0	2	32	0	4	.494	.441
Cordero, Albert	R-R	5-11	175	1-14-90	.233	.222	.237	40	129	10	30	5	0	0	10	9	2	1	0	28	2	0	.271	.293
de la Cruz, Maikis	R-R	5-11	174	9-6-90	.261	.287	.252	96	349	50	91	20	5	3	41	39	6	0	4	81	17	3	.372	.342
De La Cruz, Yucarybert	R-R	6-0	160	10-23-90	.212	.205	.214	48	170	23	36	13	0	0	5	11	1	6	1	35	3	2	.288	.262
Evans, Phillip	R-R	5-10	185	9-10-92	.203	.203	.203	106	350	35	71	13	1	2	25	30	3	1	5	60	4	2	.263	.268
Frenzel, Cole	L-R	6-2	215	3-13-90	.235	.212	.241	119	422	51	99	24	1	7	60	51	13	0	3	85	2	0	.346	.333
Glenn, Jeff	R-R	6-3	185	9-22-91	.196	.093	.220	70	225	21	44	9	0	3	30	34	2	2	3	75	1	0	.276	.303
Harrison, Brian	R-R	6-2	180	12-15-88	.133	.154	.122	23	75	6	10	3	0	0	6	6	3	0	1	28	0	1	.173	.224
Herrera, Dilson	R-R	5-10	150	3-3-94	.316	.000	.375	7	19	6	6	0	0	0	4	3	1	0	1	6	3	0	.316	.417
2-team total (109 West Virginia)					.267	—	—	116	442	75	118	27	3	11	60	40	8	6	7	116	14	6	.416	.334
Johnson, Kyle	R-R	6-0	180	11-9-89	.185	.143	.200	8	27	1	5	1	0	0	3	5	3	0	0	2	2	1	.222	.371
Nimmo, Brandon	L-R	6-3	185	3-27-93	.273	.240	.284	110	395	62	108	16	6	2	40	71	11	1	2	131	10	7	.359	.397
Pina, Eudy	R-R	6-3	188	4-12-91	.233	.208	.241	126	450	72	105	27	8	10	49	57	12	2	2	123	21	7	.396	.334
Plawecki, Kevin	R-R	6-2	205	2-26-91	.314	.460	.277	65	245	35	77	24	1	6	43	23	10	0	4	32	1	0	.494	.390
Ponce, Dimas	R-R	5-11	140	1-22-91	.198	.171	.212	34	101	12	20	7	0	0	2	6	1	3	0	20	1	0	.267	.250
Pron, Greg	R-R	6-6	195	1-3-89	.188	.238	.172	56	176	16	33	9	0	1	21	25	3	2	1	47	8	3	.256	.298
Reynolds, Jeff	R-R	5-10	175	7-28-88	.242	.263	.236	96	330	31	80	14	0	2	33	26	8	1	1	75	0	5	.303	.312
Rivero, Jorge	B-R	6-0	183	1-6-89	.279	.306	.269	33	129	18	36	5	1	0	10	11	1	1	0	19	3	2	.333	.340
Sabol, Stefan	R-R	6-0	200	2-2-92	.203	.143	.219	105	365	42	74	18	5	8	42	47	3	1	1	116	13	7	.345	.298
Zapata, Nelfi	R-R	6-0	203	12-13-90	.216	.250	.207	23	74	9	16	0	0	1	10	8	1	0	1	24	0	0	.257	.298
Zurcher, Chad	R-R	6-1	170	8-25-88	.276	.250	.283	50	174	25	48	7	0	0	12	37	3	3	1	30	4	3	.316	.409

Pitching	B-T	HT	WT	DOB	W	L	ERA	G	GS	CG	SV	IP	H	R	ER	HR	BB	SO	AVG	vLH	vRH	K/9	BB/9
Bowman, Matt	R-R	6-0	165	5-31-91	4	0	2.64	5	5	0	0	31	28	9	9	0	4	26	.237	.239	.236	7.63	1.17
Camarena, Marcos	R-R	6-3	202	9-8-90	5	4	3.27	17	10	1	0	77	81	34	28	2	15	39	.274	.270	.276	4.56	1.75
Carnevale, Hunter	R-R	5-11	200	8-27-88	0	3	3.57	44	0	0	2	58	49	23	23	5	18	66	.220	.151	.263	10.24	2.79
Cessa, Luis	R-R	6-3	190	4-25-92	8	4	3.12	21	21	1	0	130	136	53	45	11	19	124	.268	.256	.275	8.58	1.32
Gsellman, Robert	R-R	6-4	200	7-18-93	2	3	3.72	5	5	0	0	29	35	17	12	2	6	14	.310	.343	.295	4.34	1.86
Hilario, Julian	R-R	6-1	190	8-17-90	7	7	3.77	35	5	0	1	86	84	36	36	5	27	76	.256	.248	.261	7.95	2.83
Koch, Matt	L-R	6-3	185	11-2-90	6	4	4.70	18	15	1	0	82	100	52	43	7	4	68	.295	.314	.284	7.43	0.44
Kuebler, Jake	R-R	6-5	200	9-3-89	3	6	2.76	21	11	0	1	82	75	31	25	3	17	57	.244	.292	.214	6.28	1.87
Lara, Rainy	R-R	6-4	180	3-14-91	4	2	1.42	8	8	0	0	51	39	12	8	1	6	51	.204	.324	.138	9.06	1.07
Lugo, Jacob	R-R	6-4	185	11-17-89	2	2	2.53	5	5	0	0	32	22	9	9	2	6	39	.196	.119	.283	10.97	1.69
Matz, Steve	R-L	6-2	192	5-29-91	5	6	2.62	21	21	1	0	106	86	36	31	4	38	121	.225	.261	.214	10.24	
3.22 Mesa, Wanel	R-R	6-3	190	1-15-87	2	2	5.46	15	0	0	1	31	30	21	19	1	19	37	.259	.231	.273	10.63	5.46
Mitchell, Bret	R-R	6-2	190	12-10-88	3	2	2.35	22	0	0	10	31	23	9	8	2	7	41	.205	.289	.162	12.03	2.05
Morel, Estarlin	R-R	6-0	185	10-2-89	1	1	1.89	10	0	0	0	19	17	4	4	0	2	15	.246	.222	.262	7.11	0.95
Peterson, Tim	R-R	6-1	190	2-22-91	1	0	5.13	18	3	0	0	26	29	16	15	3	6	30	.279	.245	.314	10.25	2.05
Sewald, Paul	R-R	6-2	190	5-26-90	3	2	1.77	35	0	0	8	56	48	11	11	0	7	67	.229	.203	.243	10.77	1.13
Taylor, Logan	R-R	6-5	205	12-13-91	1	1	2.67	7	7	0	0	30	28	10	9	0	9	35	.246	.326	.197	10.38	2.67
Teufel, Shawn	L-L	6-3	215	7-16-86	0	0	2.79	9	0	0	1	10	7	3	3	0	4	11	.194	.000	.259	10.24	3.72
Vanderheiden, Tyler	R-R	6-2	174	6-27-90	4	2	5.97	30	0	0	0	38	49	26	25	3	21	34	.318	.306	.324	8.12	5.02
Wheeler, Beck	R-R	6-3	215	12-13-88	1	6	2.32	43	0	0	19	50	34	14	13	5	16	74	.190	.157	.211	13.23	2.86
Ynoa, Gabriel	R-R	6-2	158	5-26-93	15	4	2.72	22	22	1	0	136	123	45	41	9	16	106	.238	.213	.254	7.03	1.06

Fielding

Catcher	PCT	G	PO	A	E	DP	PB
Cordero	.992	40	327	33	3	5	0
Glenn	.988	54	363	35	5	2	6
Plawecki	.992	46	451	33	4	2	2
Zapata	1.000	1	5	0	0	0	0

First Base	PCT	G	PO	A	E	DP
Boyd	.993	51	410	38	3	31
Frenzel	.992	59	459	29	4	34
Harrison	.993	17	134	9	1	7
Zapata	.992	17	114	6	1	9

Second Base	PCT	G	PO	A	E	DP
De La Cruz	.986	37	56	87	2	13
Herrera	1.000	6	7	16	0	4

Ponce	1.000	2	3	2	0	0
Reynolds	.970	29	43	55	3	9
Rivero	.962	30	48	79	5	13
Zurcher	.989	44	69	119	2	22

Third Base	PCT	G	PO	A	E	DP
De La Cruz	.923	8	3	9	1	0
Frenzel	.903	62	26	104	14	6
Harrison	—	1	0	0	0	0
Ponce	.933	6	3	11	1	1
Reynolds	.933	70	39	115	11	8
Rivero	1.000	1	0	2	0	0

Shortstop	PCT	G	PO	A	E	DP
De La Cruz	.889	4	2	6	1	1

Evans	.942	106	146	279	26	47
Ponce	.979	26	30	65	2	14
Rivero	1.000	1	0	2	0	0
Zurcher	.966	6	10	18	1	2

Outfield	PCT	G	PO	A	E	DP
de la Cruz	.978	74	125	8	3	1
Johnson	1.000	7	9	0	0	0
Nimmo	.971	106	226	6	7	1
Pina	.980	100	188	7	4	1
Pron	.979	37	45	2	1	0
Reynolds	1.000	2	2	0	0	0
Rivero	—	2	0	0	0	0
Sabol	.993	93	145	3	1	1

BROOKLYN CYCLONES   SHORT-SEASON

NEW YORK-PENN LEAGUE

Batting	B-T	HT	WT	DOB	AVG	vLH	vRH	G	AB	R	H	2B	3B	HR	RBI	BB	HBP	SH	SF	SO	SB	CS	SLG	OBP
Biondi, Patrick	L-R	5-9	160	1-9-91	.249	.246	.250	50	193	29	48	6	2	0	14	28	2	2	1	40	17	4	.301	.348
Cecchini, Gavin	R-R	6-1	180	12-22-93	.273	.267	.275	51	194	18	53	8	0	0	14	14	0	2	2	30	2	3	.314	.319
Chavez, Anthony	R-R	6-2	185	11-8-92	.201	.246	.180	56	179	17	36	10	1	2	12	18	2	0	1	62	0	0	.302	.280
Clark, Jonathan	L-R	6-1	180	9-20-89	.176	.200	.170	32	119	17	21	1	1	1	5	11	1	0	0	43	9	3	.227	.252
Concepcion, Julio	R-R	6-4	194	9-5-89	.238	.333	.200	6	21	2	5	1	0	0	3	0	0	0	0	7	0	0	.286	.238
Gamboa, Juan Carlos	L-R	5-7	152	4-18-91	.195	.444	.174	32	118	11	23	3	0	2	9	12	0	4	0	24	2	0	.271	.269
King, Jared	B-L	5-11	208	10-12-91	.266	.328	.244	63	222	32	59	15	0	1	21	35	2	1	4	49	5	0	.347	.365
Mazzilli, L.J.	R-R	6-0	185	9-6-90	.278	.254	.287	70	273	24	76	12	2	4	34	22	1	0	5	53	3	0	.381	.329
Nido, Tomas	R-R	6-0	200	4-12-94	.185	.240	.170	33	119	3	22	6	0	1	11	4	1	1	0	21	0	1	.261	.218
Oberste, Matt	R-R	6-2	209	8-9-91	.208	.306	.176	68	255	21	53	7	2	3	24	10	4	0	4	56	0	0	.286	.245
Peguero, Eris	L-R	6-1	175	11-29-89	.184	.333	.174	18	49	2	9	1	0	0	1	2	0	1	0	8	0	0	.204	.216
Plaia, Colton	R-R	6-2	225	9-25-90	.170	.211	.160	27	94	8	16	3	0	0	8	8	1	1	0	26	0	0	.202	.243
Rivero, Jorge	B-R	6-0	183	1-6-89	.339	.389	.318	15	62	6	21	4	0	0	4	3	0	1	1	12	0	0	.403	.364
Roche, James	R-R	6-3	210	7-26-91	.243	.258	.237	67	235	26	57	14	2	5	28	24	5	0	1	68	8	2	.383	.325
Rohan, Eddie	R-R	6-0	205	8-15-88	.269	.524	.152	20	67	6	18	7	0	2	7	4	4	0	0	15	0	1	.463	.347
Sanchez, Alex	R-R	6-3	200	11-28-90	.239	.267	.230	62	234	20	56	10	1	4	22	12	0	0	2	39	0	0	.342	.274
Tijerina, Ismael	R-R	6-0	165	8-19-89	.214	.207	.218	28	84	14	18	3	0	0	6	11	2	2	1	18	2	0	.250	.316
Turner, Justin	R-R	6-0	210	11-23-84	.300	.400	.200	3	10	2	3	1	0	0	3	0	0	0	0	0	0	0	.400	.417

Pitching	B-T	HT	WT	DOB	W	L	ERA	G	GS	CG	SV	IP	H	R	ER	HR	BB	SO	AVG	vLH	vRH	K/9	BB/9
Alvarez, Dario	L-L	6-1	170	1-17-89	2	4	3.10	12	12	0	0	58	48	27	20	1	26	57	.221	.184	.229	8.84	4.03
Bay, Shane	L-L	6-2	225	2-29-92	0	1	1.80	3	0	0	0	5	7	1	1	0	3	5	.368	.500	.333	9.00	5.40
Chivilli, Cristian	R-R	6-2	200	2-19-91	3	2	3.30	19	0	0	0	30	17	13	11	1	21	21	.173	.140	.200	6.30	6.30
Diaz, Miller	R-R	6-1	209	6-22-92	7	3	2.03	13	12	0	0	67	44	22	15	1	33	87	.183	.183	.184	11.75	4.46
Familia, Jeurys	R-R	6-4	230	10-10-89	0	0	0.00	1	1	0	0	1	1	1	0	0	0	2	.250	.000	.500	0.00	0.00
Frias, Darwin	R-R	6-0	192	2-18-92	1	1	4.44	12	4	0	1	47	44	25	23	4	13	56	.250	.325	.192	10.80	2.51
Gant, John	R-R	6-3	175	8-6-92	6	4	2.89	13	13	1	0	72	53	30	23	3	18	81	.206	.174	.235	10.17	3.52
Griffin, Cameron	R-R	6-3	195	6-25-91	1	0	2.00	5	0	0	0	9	5	3	2	0	6	7	.172	.133	.214	7.00	6.00
Gsellman, Robert	R-R	6-4	200	7-18-93	3	3	2.06	12	12	0	0	70	59	23	16	2	12	64	.220	.245	.203	8.23	1.54
Knapp, Ricky	R-R	6-0	185	5-20-92	0	2	3.76	13	1	0	3	26	29	13	11	1	9	19	.282	.358	.200	6.49	3.08
Lugo, Jacob	R-R	6-4	185	11-17-89	2	4	4.19	7	7	0	0	34	34	16	16	3	13	27	.260	.317	.233	7.08	3.41
Magliozzi, Johnny	R-R	5-10	195	7-21-91	0	0	1.17	14	0	0	9	15	6	2	2	0	5	12	.120	.040	.200	7.04	2.93

Name	B-T	HT	WT	DOB	W	L	ERA	G	GS	CG	SV	IP	H	R	ER	HR	BB	SO	AVG	vLH	vRH	K/9	BB/9
McGowan, Kevin	R-R	6-6	215	10-18-91	0	2	5.28	14	1	0	3	31	33	20	18	2	8	27	.275	.298	.260	7.92	2.35
Mincone, John	L-L	6-1	215	7-23-89	2	1	1.47	14	0	0	6	18	8	3	3	0	1	15	.136	.150	.128	7.36	0.49
Morris, Akeel	R-R	6-1	170	11-14-92	4	1	1.00	14	3	0	1	45	29	7	5	1	23	60	.184	.220	.162	12.00	4.60
Paez, Paul	L-L	5-9	185	4-29-92	2	2	3.74	16	0	0	0	22	19	11	9	0	9	15	.238	.226	.245	6.23	3.74
Peterson, Tim	R-R	6-1	190	2-22-91	0	0	0.00	9	0	0	1	18	7	0	0	0	4	20	.119	.080	.147	10.19	2.04
Teufel, Shawn	L-L	6-3	215	7-16-86	0	1	1.23	6	0	0	3	7	5	2	1	1	1	9	.200	.125	.235	11.05	1.23
Urbina, Juan	L-L	6-2	170	5-31-93	2	1	4.67	13	0	0	0	17	11	11	9	0	13	15	.167	.278	.125	7.79	6.75
Valdez, Carlos	L-L	6-0	170	9-30-90	2	2	2.58	9	9	0	0	45	41	17	13	1	17	33	.237	.174	.260	6.55	3.38
Vanderheiden, Tyler	R-R	6-2	174	6-27-90	0	0	5.68	4	0	0	0	6	4	4	4	1	1	2	.200	.222	.182	2.84	1.42
Wynn, David	B-L	5-10	168	10-16-89	1	2	2.28	21	0	0	1	28	20	12	7	1	16	28	.200	.250	.176	9.11	5.20

Fielding

Catcher	PCT	G	PO	A	E	DP	PB
Nido	.987	28	264	31	4	1	3
Plaia	.977	27	227	26	6	0	3
Rohan	.994	20	152	22	1	0	2

First Base	PCT	G	PO	A	E	DP
Oberste	.990	53	454	22	5	28
Sanchez	.992	24	230	8	2	22

Second Base	PCT	G	PO	A	E	DP
Gamboa	1.000	1	1	4	0	1
Mazzilli	.977	68	126	210	8	36

	PCT	G	PO	A	E	DP
Tijerina	.913	6	3	18	2	3
Turner	1.000	1	3	2	0	0

Third Base	PCT	G	PO	A	E	DP
Chavez	.892	53	32	100	16	7
Gamboa	.923	20	11	37	4	4
Tijerina	1.000	5	2	5	0	1

Shortstop	PCT	G	PO	A	E	DP
Cecchini	.964	50	71	144	8	24
Gamboa	.974	11	13	25	1	2
Tijerina	.967	16	15	43	2	6

	PCT	G	PO	A	E	DP
Turner	1.000	2	3	7	0	0

Outfield	PCT	G	PO	A	E	DP
Biondi	1.000	49	84	3	0	1
Clark	.954	28	61	1	3	0
Concepcion	1.000	1	2	0	0	0
King	.991	63	104	6	1	1
Peguero	.889	12	16	0	2	0
Rivero	1.000	13	19	0	0	0
Roche	.980	66	94	6	2	0

KINGSPORT METS

APPALACHIAN LEAGUE

ROOKIE

Batting	B-T	HT	WT	DOB	AVG	vLH	vRH	G	AB	R	H	2B	3B	HR	RBI	BB	HBP	SH	SF	SO	SB	CS	SLG	OBP
Abreu, Adrian	R-R	6-0	185	6-14-91	.182	.103	.220	31	88	12	16	4	1	1	7	20	1	3	0	19	6	3	.284	.339
Bernal, Michael	R-R	6-1	195	12-27-91	.237	.286	.222	26	93	9	22	5	0	5	15	7	2	2	0	42	4	1	.452	.304
Cruzado, Victor	B-R	5-11	178	6-3-92	.328	.273	.346	40	137	21	45	8	1	3	22	21	3	0	3	26	1	2	.467	.421
De Leon, Jeyckol	R-R	6-2	185	7-25-90	.298	.378	.274	43	161	24	48	9	0	4	33	15	4	0	2	30	1	0	.429	.368
Diehl, Jeff	R-R	6-4	195	9-30-93	.266	.265	.266	53	207	32	55	13	1	5	19	15	2	0	1	68	2	1	.411	.320
Leroux, Jon	R-R	6-1	205	9-19-90	.286	.333	.266	41	133	20	38	15	1	6	32	17	2	0	2	42	0	2	.549	.370
Marquez, Brad	R-R	6-1	185	12-14-92	.250	.294	.239	27	84	17	21	5	0	1	9	4	1	1	2	21	3	1	.345	.286
Mathieu, Zach	R-R	6-7	265	11-25-91	.138	.217	.105	30	80	5	11	4	0	0	2	14	0	0	0	21	1	0	.188	.266
McNeil, Jeff	L-R	6-1	165	4-8-92	.329	.259	.343	47	164	26	54	9	2	0	18	17	10	3	5	14	11	2	.409	.413
Peguero, Eris	L-R	6-1	175	11-29-89	.333	.500	.313	5	18	3	6	3	1	0	3	2	0	0	0	3	0	1	.611	.400
Perez, Pedro	B-R	6-1	190	8-31-94	.264	.327	.236	45	159	21	42	5	1	3	24	11	2	0	3	52	4	2	.365	.314
Rodriguez, Richie	R-R	5-9	170	2-15-90	.191	.105	.224	41	136	17	26	6	0	3	18	9	1	2	1	21	4	0	.301	.245
Rosario, Amed	R-R	6-2	170	11-20-95	.241	.188	.256	58	212	22	51	8	4	3	23	11	1	0	2	43	2	6	.358	.279
Ruiz, Yeixon	B-R	6-0	155	3-19-91	.304	.292	.308	52	194	34	59	9	0	0	12	15	1	3	0	38	12	1	.351	.357
Smith, Dominic	L-L	6-0	185	6-15-95	.667	.000	.667	3	2	4	4	0	0	4	2	0	0	0	0	0	1	0	1.333	.750
Stuart, Champ	R-R	6-0	175	10-11-92	.240	.261	.231	43	150	26	36	8	3	1	14	34	3	0	1	58	11	2	.353	.388
Tuschak, Joe	L-R	6-0	185	10-17-92	.271	.233	.281	56	210	23	57	7	3	3	24	10	4	1	3	50	4	0	.376	.313

Pitching	B-T	HT	WT	DOB	W	L	ERA	G	GS	CG	SV	IP	H	R	ER	HR	BB	SO	AVG	vLH	vRH	K/9	BB/9
Almonte, Gaby	R-R	6-0	185	8-15-92	1	0	1.50	1	1	0	0	6	3	1	1	3	3		.158	.250	.133	4.50	4.50
Arias, Martires	R-R	6-7	207	11-10-90	1	7	5.81	12	11	0	0	53	51	40	34	3	28	36	.254	.270	.246	6.15	4.78
Baldonado, Alberto	L-L	6-2	160	2-1-93	2	0	3.94	14	0	0	0	30	25	17	13	2	14	41	.221	.174	.233	12.44	4.25
Bashlor, Ty	R-R	6-0	220	4-16-93	0	1	5.74	13	0	0	0	16	14	12	10	1	12	18	.226	.231	.222	10.34	6.89
Coles, Robby	R-R	6-2	160	8-20-91	4	1	1.83	15	0	0	6	20	14	5	4	1	8	20	.200	.263	.176	9.15	3.66
Dotson, Zach	L-L	6-1	180	10-30-90	0	0	6.00	3	0	0	0	3	4	2	2	1	2	4	.308	—	.308	12.00	6.00
Flexen, Chris	R-R	6-3	215	7-1-94	8	1	2.09	11	11	2	0	69	53	18	16	6	12	62	.209	.174	.230	8.09	1.57
Gomez, Carlos	R-R	6-1	160	3-30-92	2	0	0.00	5	3	0	1	23	14	2	0	1	4	12	.177	.115	.208	4.70	1.57
Gonzalez, Yoan	L-L	6-0	178	1-29-91	4	4	4.24	11	9	0	0	47	58	30	22	2	20	46	.309	.400	.294	8.87	3.86
Jacquez, Ricky	R-R	5-9	160	5-6-93	2	0	1.74	16	0	0	6	21	11	6	4	0	9	33	.162	.174	.156	14.37	3.92
Massie, Andrew	R-R	6-1	170	1-27-94	2	2	5.92	10	6	0	0	38	34	30	25	2	19	24	.238	.220	.250	5.68	4.50
Ortega, Flabio	R-R	6-1	170	8-19-90	1	0	5.06	5	0	0	0	5	7	3	3	0	2	6	.333	.167	.400	10.13	3.38
Oswalt, Corey	R-R	6-4	200	9-3-93	0	1	3.46	3	2	0	0	13	14	6	5	0	1	11	.280	.300	.267	7.62	0.69
Perez, Andres	R-R	6-2	184	2-8-91	0	1	5.52	7	1	0	0	15	15	10	9	2	5	11	.259	.238	.270	6.75	3.07
Rengel, Luis	R-R	6-2	165	3-19-90	3	1	1.60	15	0	0	0	34	26	11	6	2	12	38	.208	.171	.226	10.16	3.21
Reyes, Persio	R-R	6-2	151	3-17-93	4	5	4.40	10	9	1	0	57	52	33	28	2	15	52	.237	.247	.231	8.16	2.35
Reyes, Ruben	R-R	6-4	178	9-22-90	0	0	4.32	14	0	0	1	17	12	9	8	0	18	18	.188	.294	.149	9.72	9.72
Villasmil, Edioglis	R-R	6-2	164	4-10-92	1	1	7.89	13	0	0	1	30	31	29	26	5	15	31	.267	.304	.243	9.40	4.55
Welch, Brandon	R-R	6-1	185	8-24-91	2	0	2.38	2	2	0	0	11	9	4	3	0	2	10	.214	.235	.200	7.94	1.59
Whalen, Rob	R-R	5-2	200	1-31-94	3	2	1.87	12	12	0	0	72	50	26	15	1	17	76	.187	.226	.157	9.46	2.12

Fielding

Catcher	PCT	G	PO	A	E	DP	PB
Abreu	.970	31	265	28	9	1	6
De Leon	.993	35	258	25	2	3	10
Leroux	.933	3	11	3	1	0	3

First Base	PCT	G	PO	A	E	DP
De Leon	.970	4	30	2	1	4

	PCT	G	PO	A	E	DP
Diehl	.981	28	239	16	5	18
Leroux	.917	5	18	4	2	1
Mathieu	.977	25	201	9	5	7
Perez	.976	10	78	4	2	10
Rodriguez	1.000	1	2	0	0	0
Smith	1.000	1	16	0	0	1

Second Base	PCT	G	PO	A	E	DP
McNeil	.977	45	89	128	5	25
Rodriguez	1.000	17	31	39	0	4
Ruiz	.929	11	9	30	3	3

Third Base	PCT	G	PO	A	E	DP
Perez	.891	31	21	61	10	1

Rodriguez	.893	22	11	39	6	6
Ruiz	.914	20	11	42	5	3

Shortstop	PCT	G	PO	A	E	DP
Rosario	.941	58	70	154	14	23
Ruiz	.926	12	12	38	4	6

Outfield	PCT	G	PO	A	E	DP
Bernal	.909	21	28	2	3	0
Cruzado	.957	32	43	1	2	0
Diehl	.967	21	29	0	1	0
Marquez	.980	26	48	2	1	0

McNeil	—	1	0	0	0	0
Peguero	.923	5	11	1	1	0
Ruiz	.944	10	16	1	1	0
Stuart	.989	43	85	2	1	1
Tuschak	.986	51	68	1	1	0

GCL METS   ROOKIE

GULF COAST LEAGUE

Batting	B-T	HT	WT	DOB	AVG	vLH	vRH	G	AB	R	H	2B	3B	HR	RBI	BB	HBP	SH	SF	SO	SB	CS	SLG	OBP
Arrizurieta, Luis	R-R	5-10	160	8-10-91	.250	.000	.393	18	44	5	11	3	0	0	4	2	1	0	0	5	3	0	.318	.298
Becerra, Wuilmer	R-R	6-4	190	10-1-94	.243	.204	.261	52	173	21	42	6	0	1	25	20	10	1	2	60	5	6	.295	.351
Brosher, Brandon	R-R	6-3	225	2-17-95	.180	.250	.156	22	61	10	11	1	0	3	6	12	1	0	0	23	1	2	.344	.324
Canelon, Leon	R-R	5-11	150	9-10-91	.278	.220	.300	47	151	25	42	6	2	1	21	11	2	2	4	32	7	1	.364	.327
Caraballo, Oswald	R-R	6-2	180	1-5-93	.195	.111	.219	44	123	13	24	9	3	0	12	9	3	0	4	19	1	2	.317	.259
d'Arnaud, Travis	R-R	6-2	195	2-10-89	.318	.167	.500	6	22	4	7	3	0	0	5	1	0	0	0	2	0	0	.455	.348
Duda, Lucas	L-R	6-4	255	2-3-86	.000	.000	.000	4	13	1	0	0	0	0	3	0	0	0	0	8	0	0	.000	.188
Garcia, Jose	B-R	6-0	200	11-3-94	.229	.188	.244	39	118	11	27	1	0	0	12	12	2	1	0	23	1	0	.237	.311
Guillorme, Luis	L-R	5-10	170	9-27-94	.258	.114	.313	41	159	22	41	4	0	0	11	17	2	4	0	17	6	4	.283	.337
Harrison, Brian	R-R	6-0	180	12-15-88	.179	.182	.176	7	28	1	5	1	0	0	4	1	0	1	1	9	1	0	.214	.200
Hilario, Manuel	R-R	5-10	172	2-10-92	.100	.500	.000	5	10	1	1	0	0	0	1	0	0	0	0	5	0	0	.100	.100
Kaupe, Branden	B-R	5-7	175	4-10-94	.214	.262	.191	41	131	20	28	0	0	0	3	29	0	1	1	33	8	1	.214	.354
Lupo, Vicente	R-R	6-0	180	11-26-94	.220	.241	.213	37	109	13	24	4	1	4	15	13	2	0	2	50	4	3	.385	.310
Machillanada, Alex	R-R	5-11	180	10-1-91	.357	.125	.450	8	28	2	10	3	0	0	2	0	0	0	0	8	0	1	.464	.357
Rodriguez, Jean	B-R	6-0	160	9-3-92	.206	.224	.198	46	155	19	32	6	1	0	17	13	0	4	2	36	4	2	.258	.265
Sanchez, Elvis	R-R	6-2	190	2-8-94	.109	.111	.109	20	55	5	6	1	0	2	4	12	2	0	0	22	0	0	.236	.290
Smith, Dominic	L-L	6-0	185	6-15-95	.287	.276	.294	48	167	23	48	9	1	3	22	24	4	0	3	37	2	4	.407	.384
Tejada, Ruben	R-R	5-11	185	10-27-89	.333	.000	.429	3	9	1	3	1	0	0	2	0	1	0	0	5	0	0	.444	.400
Turner, Justin	R-R	6-0	210	11-23-84	.000	.000	.000	1	4	0	0	0	0	0	0	1	0	0	0	2	0	0	.000	.200
Urena, Jhoan	B-R	6-1	200	9-1-94	.299	.200	.346	47	157	19	47	6	3	0	20	13	0	0	1	34	4	1	.376	.351
Vaughn, Cory	R-R	6-3	225	5-1-89	.172	.182	.167	9	29	4	5	1	2	0	1	9	0	1	1	9	2	0	.345	.359
Wilson, Ivan	R-R	6-3	220	5-26-95	.219	.188	.232	47	160	16	35	4	3	1	15	22	2	0	0	65	13	2	.300	.321

Pitching	B-T	HT	WT	DOB	W	L	ERA	G	GS	CG	SV	IP	H	R	ER	HR	BB	SO	AVG	vLH	vRH	K/9	BB/9
Acosta, Octavio	R-R	6-0	165	8-3-90	1	2	2.28	9	6	0	0	43	31	12	11	2	8	40	.201	.184	.210	8.31	1.66
Almonte, Gaby	R-R	6-0	185	8-15-92	3	2	2.31	10	7	0	0	47	43	15	12	3	19	34	.249	.290	.225	6.56	3.66
Atchison, Scott	R-R	6-2	200	3-29-76	0	1	4.50	2	2	0	0	4	3	2	2	1	1	0	.333	.250	.400	13.50	0.00
Bumgardner, Gaither	R-R	6-6	210	1-29-91	2	2	4.68	18	0	0	3	25	28	14	13	0	10	23	.275	.366	.213	8.28	3.60
Byrdak, Tim	L-L	5-11	190	10-31-73	0	0	0.00	1	1	0	0	1	0	0	0	0	1	1	.000	.000	.000	9.00	9.00
Celas, Jose	R-R	6-1	180	1-12-91	0	2	4.26	4	3	0	0	19	15	10	9	0	9	10	.231	.333	.191	4.74	4.26
Chapman, Ryan	R-R	6-3	215	12-27-90	1	0	4.70	7	0	0	0	8	4	4	4	0	10	6	.154	.125	.167	7.04	11.74
Church, Andrew	R-R	6-2	190	10-7-94	3	3	5.91	9	6	0	0	35	49	26	23	2	8	19	.336	.377	.306	4.89	2.06
Encarnacion, Jose	R-R	6-4	190	10-7-94	0	0	10.24	11	0	0	1	10	13	11	11	0	16	10	.333	.182	.393	9.31	14.90
Estevez, Ramon	R-R	6-0	165	10-27-90	1	0	6.65	15	0	0	0	22	24	17	16	1	16	12	.289	.412	.204	4.98	6.65
Francisco, Frank	R-R	6-2	250	9-11-79	0	2	1.80	5	4	0	0	5	5	2	1	1	0	7	.250	.000	.385	12.60	0.00
Fulmer, Michael	R-R	6-3	200	3-15-93	1	1	3.00	2	2	0	0	12	9	4	4	0	1	13	.205	.176	.222	9.75	0.75
Griffin, Cameron	R-R	6-3	195	6-25-91	0	0	3.77	13	0	0	5	14	15	6	6	1	7	14	.268	.368	.216	8.79	4.40
Herrmann, Dan	R-R	6-4	205	9-2-94	0	4	9.60	9	1	0	0	15	18	21	16	1	19	8	.286	.400	.233	4.80	11.40
McMinn, Brent	R-R	6-2	195	12-2-90	0	0	0.00	1	0	0	0	1	1	1	0	0	1	1	.250	.500	.000	9.00	9.00
Meisner, Casey	R-R	6-7	190	5-22-95	1	3	3.06	10	4	0	0	35	31	17	12	0	10	28	.238	.370	.167	7.13	2.55
Mejia, Jenrry	R-R	6-0	205	10-11-89	0	0	3.18	2	2	0	0	8	8	4	2	0	2	3	.320	.250	.385	4.74	3.18
Missigman, Craig	R-R	6-4	175	8-5-93	0	4	3.95	9	3	0	0	27	26	13	12	3	7	22	.257	.222	.277	7.24	2.30
Molina, Marcos	R-R	6-3	188	3-8-95	4	3	4.39	11	6	1	0	53	56	31	26	3	14	43	.271	.274	.268	7.26	2.36
Montgomery, Christian	R-R	6-1	230	11-20-92	0	0	10.50	3	0	0	0	6	8	9	7	0	5	7	.320	.286	.333	10.50	7.50
Niese, Jon	L-L	6-4	215	10-27-86	0	0	4.50	1	1	0	0	2	3	4	1	0	0	1	.300	.250	.333	4.50	0.00
Nuez, Yoryi	R-R	6-1	153	2-13-93	2	2	3.89	11	7	0	1	39	38	21	17	0	22	32	.257	.220	.276	7.32	5.03
Robles, Hansel	R-R	5-11	185	8-10-90	0	1	4.22	2	2	0	0	11	12	6	5	0	2	5	.300	.318	.278	4.22	1.69
Rodriguez, Waldo	L-L	5-11	176	10-20-90	1	2	2.49	16	0	0	0	25	25	13	7	1	10	13	.258	.214	.275	4.62	3.55
Rosario, Lenny	L-L	6-1	162	5-15-91	1	2	6.52	6	2	0	0	19	18	14	14	0	14	20	.261	.150	.306	9.31	6.52
Welch, Brandon	R-R	6-1	185	8-24-91	0	0	0.82	4	1	0	0	11	6	3	1	0	2	6	.154	.091	.179	4.91	1.64
Williams, Ty	R-R	6-2	195	2-21-94	0	3	6.89	11	0	0	0	16	19	15	12	2	8	11	.284	.259	.300	6.32	4.60

Fielding

Catcher	PCT	G	PO	A	E	DP	PB
Arrizurieta	.972	18	94	12	3	0	4
Canelon	1.000	1	1	0	0	0	0
d'Arnaud	.971	5	28	5	1	1	2
Garcia	.979	39	240	40	6	2	0
Hilario	1.000	1	2	1	0	0	1
Machillanada	1.000	7	41	6	0	1	0

First Base	PCT	G	PO	A	E	DP
Harrison	1.000	3	9	0	0	0
Sanchez	.978	16	124	10	3	13
Smith	.984	43	341	27	6	29

Second Base	PCT	G	PO	A	E	DP
Canelon	.970	21	36	60	3	9
Kaupe	.946	37	66	108	10	20
Rodriguez	1.000	5	9	7	0	6

Third Base	PCT	G	PO	A	E	DP
Canelon	1.000	7	5	8	0	1
Harrison	1.000	2	1	4	0	0
Rodriguez	.821	18	14	18	7	5
Urena	.833	42	23	62	17	6

Shortstop	PCT	G	PO	A	E	DP
Canelon	1.000	7	7	22	0	3
Guillorme	.956	37	71	104	8	23
Rodriguez	.904	17	25	50	8	6
Tejada	1.000	3	2	6	0	1

Outfield	PCT	G	PO	A	E	DP
Becerra	.980	51	91	8	2	1
Brosher	1.000	5	4	0	0	0
Canelon	1.000	5	6	0	0	0
Caraballo	.973	42	69	3	2	1
Duda	1.000	3	4	1	0	0
Lupo	.978	33	43	2	1	1
Vaughn	1.000	7	16	1	0	0
Wilson	.947	46	106	2	6	0

DOMINICAN SUMMER LEAGUE

Batting	B-T	HT	WT	DOB	AVG	vLH	vRH	G	AB	R	H	2B	3B	HR	RBI	BB	HBP	SH	SF	SO	SB	CS	SLG	OBP
Carrion, Junior	R-R	6-0	198	12-16-93	.187	—	—	48	139	17	26	10	1	2	25	11	9	3	3	44	3	4	.317	.284
Correa, Franklin	R-R	5-9	176	1-1-96	.205	.129	.221	61	185	21	38	9	2	0	15	18	7	2	1	63	6	5	.276	.299
Crisostomo, Luis	L-R	6-1	180	12-9-93	.235	.231	.236	43	149	19	35	1	1	0	11	14	3	2	1	19	9	12	.255	.311
Diaz, Alejandro	B-R	6-0	150	3-2-96	.182	—	—	37	110	7	20	3	1	0	15	11	3	3	2	15	4	4	.227	.270
Diaz, Edwin	L-R	6-2	180	11-30-95	.193	.156	.200	56	192	20	37	5	1	1	18	25	1	0	1	70	1	5	.245	.288
Guzman, Rafael	R-R	6-1	175	10-5-95	.145	—	—	53	131	12	19	5	0	0	7	14	7	1	0	52	3	3	.183	.263
Infante, Santos	R-R	6-3	195	4-15-95	.163	—	—	61	208	15	34	5	1	4	18	9	1	3	1	98	2	3	.255	.201
Leal, Miguel	R-R	6-0	184	7-4-91	.241	—	—	59	199	23	48	5	1	0	18	29	1	1	0	28	6	3	.276	.341
Maria, Jose	R-R	5-9	194	11-30-94	.250	—	—	55	172	18	43	11	0	2	25	17	1	0	3	40	2	2	.349	.316
Martinez, Jose	R-R	6-1	159	1-18-94	.166	.176	.164	64	199	23	33	12	2	0	14	32	6	1	0	51	2	5	.246	.300
Montero, Luis	R-R	6-2	190	1-16-96	.182	.125	.196	37	121	16	22	3	2	0	12	14	6	0	0	24	1	0	.240	.298
Mora, John	L-L	5-10	165	5-31-93	.310	—	—	68	242	36	75	15	5	0	46	31	6	3	3	34	16	14	.413	.397
Ortega, Luis	R-R	5-10	187	4-5-93	.257	—	—	67	230	19	59	15	1	2	32	28	8	1	7	35	10	8	.357	.348
Patino, Miguel	R-R	5-11	155	12-17-95	.172	—	—	13	29	5	5	0	0	0	2	4	0	1	0	2	2	1	.172	.273
Pierre, Ysidro	B-R	6-1	171	11-30-93	.196	.132	.210	63	219	41	43	5	0	0	8	32	11	2	0	73	25	13	.219	.328
Rasquin, Walter	R-R	5-9	160	3-21-96	.167	.250	.125	4	12	1	2	0	0	0	3	0	0	0	4	1	0	.167	.333
Rodriguez, Dionis	R-R	6-0	183	2-15-95	.189	—	—	30	90	19	17	8	0	0	15	18	7	0	0	27	3	0	.278	.365
Sanchez, Carlos	R-R	5-11	170	6-6-96	.178	—	—	53	169	10	30	3	0	0	13	14	4	0	1	42	3	3	.195	.255
Sierra, Johanny	R-R	6-4	180	1-3-92	.185	—	—	54	146	19	27	6	1	0	12	32	3	1	0	63	7	2	.240	.343
Valencia, Gregory	R-R	6-3	185	3-19-93	.225	—	—	69	253	28	57	5	1	0	16	30	2	0	2	84	13	5	.253	.310
Figuera, Jose	R-R	6-2	180	6-10-93	.243	.326	.225	67	247	53	60	16	1	0	17	33	10	4	0	59	16	5	.316	.355
Maracaro, Alvin	R-R	5-9	178	2-10-93	.258	.200	.269	66	221	29	57	14	3	0	25	30	6	1	2	54	8	8	.348	.359
Marte, Santo	R-R	5-9	168	9-30-93	.246	.200	.256	59	199	36	49	7	1	0	13	31	2	4	1	29	13	6	.291	.352
Moscote, Victor	R-R	6-1	155	5-10-94	.250	.344	.232	53	196	20	49	12	0	1	30	15	3	0	2	51	4	4	.327	.310
Ramos, Natanael	R-R	5-10	170	6-19-93	.333	1.000	.000	1	3	1	1	0	0	0	0	0	0	0	0	1	0	0	.333	.333
Reyes, Alfredo	R-R	6-2	160	10-4-93	.316	.342	.310	59	212	37	67	15	1	2	22	27	2	5	4	40	16	5	.425	.392
Rojas, Hengelbert	R-R	6-1	188	10-27-93	.314	.500	.289	16	51	10	16	6	0	0	11	7	3	0	2	10	0	0	.431	.413
Zabala, Enmanuel	R-R	6-0	185	9-29-94	.263	.200	.277	55	194	29	51	11	3	1	24	29	7	2	4	32	12	4	.366	.372

Pitching	B-T	HT	WT	DOB	W	L	ERA	G	GS	CG	SV	IP	H	R	ER	HR	BB	SO	AVG	vLH	vRH	K/9	BB/9
Almeida, Adrian	L-L	6-0	150	2-25-95	3	3	3.89	12	12	0	0	42	31	19	18	0	27	43	—	—	—	9.29	5.83
Alvarez, Jean	R-R	6-1	160	5-1-95	1	2	5.40	16	0	0	0	27	29	22	16	0	30	10	—	—	—	3.38	1.13
Arias, Eucebio	R-R	6-1	173	9-20-94	0	1	2.86	6	6	0	0	28	22	14	9	2	8	28	.210	.261	.195	8.89	2.54
Berihuete, Enmanuel	R-R	6-0	174	11-5-93	0	1	9.15	14	0	0	0	20	22	23	20	0	18	17	.306	.231	.348	7.78	8.24
Blanco, Rolgenis	R-R	6-0	160	2-7-93	0	1	4.09	12	2	0	0	22	19	11	10	0	22	12	.247	.185	.280	4.91	8.18
Caminero, Franly	L-L	5-11	175	12-3-92	0	0	5.84	12	0	0	1	12	17	11	8	0	6	16	—	—	—	11.68	4.38
Canelon, Kevin	L-L	6-1	175	1-16-94	6	2	2.86	14	14	1	0	63	51	23	20	1	16	50	.223	.222	.223	7.14	2.29
Carreno, Luis	R-R	6-0	169	8-12-95	1	3	9.98	16	5	0	2	31	34	38	34	2	21	31	.276	.371	.239	9.10	6.16
Castillo, Yrelvis	R-R	6-4	197	7-13-91	0	1	4.73	17	0	0	1	27	35	17	14	0	15	13	—	—	—	4.39	5.06
Celis, Jorge	L-L	5-10	160	9-11-94	0	1	4.82	16	0	0	1	19	19	14	10	0	13	20	.271	.125	.315	9.64	6.27
Cespedes, Jorge	R-R	6-5	174	12-4-94	2	2	3.71	25	0	0	1	27	27	15	11	1	3	22	.252	.310	.231	7.43	1.01
Crismatt, Nabil	R-R	6-1	197	12-25-94	4	2	1.33	24	0	0	8	41	23	8	6	0	13	46	.174	.077	.215	1.18	2.88
Debora, Nicolas	R-R	6-5	170	12-6-93	1	3	2.81	8	5	0	0	26	28	10	8	1	3	20	—	—	—	7.01	1.05
Estevez, Gregorix	R-R	6-5	200	4-12-94	3	1	3.24	15	0	0	1	25	22	13	9	0	12	20	.234	.345	.185	7.20	4.32
Feliz, Gabriel	L-L	5-11	160	11-12-92	3	1	3.12	14	2	0	2	49	43	20	17	1	13	31	.236	.211	.239	5.69	2.39
German, Audry	R-R	5-11	163	8-16-92	1	4	3.38	17	2	0	6	37	37	23	14	1	14	32	—	—	—	7.71	3.38
Gonzalez, Marcos	R-R	6-0	175	10-22-92	5	2	3.65	20	0	0	5	25	18	11	10	0	5	17	.217	.207	.222	6.20	1.82
Gonzalez, Merandy	R-R	6-1	175	10-9-95	4	1	2.82	14	2	0	1	45	39	18	14	0	16	29	.234	.275	.216	5.84	3.22
Guedez, Ronald	R-R	6-1	160	1-26-96	2	4	5.18	14	10	0	0	42	48	31	24	1	24	38	.296	.293	.298	8.21	5.18
Gutierrez, Miguel	L-L	6-0	180	12-3-94	0	4	3.55	15	5	0	0	38	42	25	15	2	19	30	—	—	—	7.11	4.50
Lugo, Jesus	R-R	6-1	165	3-31-94	1	1	6.35	4	0	0	1	6	3	4	4	1	3	6	.150	.333	.118	9.53	4.76
Marte, Juan	R-R	6-3	208	8-29-90	2	2	2.01	15	5	0	2	54	35	13	12	2	17	33	—	—	—	5.53	2.83
Martinez, Wimbert	R-R	6-2	175	12-18-93	4	1	3.25	21	2	0	7	36	30	15	13	0	14	33	.231	.152	.274	8.25	3.50
Medina, Jose	L-L	6-2	180	8-25-96	2	0	.35	12	12	0	0	52	35	5	2	0	6	41	.190	.200	.189	7.10	1.04
Mendez, Jose	R-R	6-2	230	12-29-94	2	9	5.03	16	15	0	1	59	70	48	33	3	27	38	.290	.277	.297	5.80	4.12
Merilan, Claudio	R-R	6-1	184	5-3-94	2	1	8.69	14	0	0	0	29	39	34	28	3	18	22	.322	.268	.350	6.83	5.59
Montero, Randi	R-R	6-2	165	11-8-92	2	2	5.03	15	6	0	0	34	25	19	19	1	19	19	.207	.088	.253	5.03	5.03
Olivo, Aneury	L-L	6-2	159	10-24-94	0	1	2.28	13	0	0	1	24	20	11	6	0	12	23	—	—	—	8.75	4.56
Popa, Luis	R-R	5-11	185	10-27-94	1	1	2.89	8	0	0	0	9	7	3	3	0	4	6	.233	.167	.278	5.79	3.86
Ramos, Darwin	R-R	6-2	195	11-23-95	3	2	3.43	11	11	0	0	42	37	17	16	2	5	40	.239	.196	.257	8.57	1.07
Reina, Richard	R-R	6-2	183	2-7-95	0	1	6.23	9	0	0	0	9	10	7	6	0	13	7	—	—	—	7.27	13.50
Reyes, Scarlyn	R-R	6-3	190	11-7-91	5	3	1.41	12	11	1	0	64	51	19	10	0	18	56	—	—	—	7.88	2.53
Rodriguez, Edgar	R-R	6-2	155	8-31-94	0	1	1.24	10	0	0	0	10	15	16	11	0	15	4	—	—	—	3.72	13.97
Rodriguez, Euner	R-R	6-0	170	2-10-94	0	0	6.75	11	1	0	0	13	11	10	10	0	18	15	.234	.154	.265	1.13	12.15
Rodriguez, Jhonaiker	R-R	6-1	178	6-26-94	1	2	4.43	14	0	0	0	22	20	14	11	1	13	9	.233	.200	.250	3.63	5.24
Rodriguez, Ramon	R-R	5-11	169	12-27-91	2	4	3.57	13	10	0	0	53	46	25	21	3	21	35	.238	.180	.259	5.94	3.57
Suazo, Randinson	R-R	6-0	190	4-19-95	1	4	9.39	16	0	0	0	23	33	29	24	0	20	10	—	—	—	3.91	7.83
Uceta, Adonis	R-R	6-1	195	5-10-94	2	2	5.59	14	4	0	0	47	43	32	29	1	26	43	—	—	—	8.29	5.01

NEW YORK METS

Fielding

Catcher	PCT	G	PO	A	E	DP	PB
Guzman	.947	24	129	15	8	1	8
Leal	1.000	25	178	22	0	2	4
Maria	.983	41	267	26	5	6	7
Moscote	1.000	8	60	3	0	0	3
Ortega	.983	19	100	16	2	1	3
Ramos	1.000	1	5	2	0	0	0
Rasquin	1.000	1	6	1	0	0	0
Rodriguez	.976	19	104	17	3	0	7
Sanchez	.977	33	151	22	4	0	6

First Base	PCT	G	PO	A	E	DP
Crisostomo	.975	7	35	4	1	2
Figuera	.977	6	42	1	1	6
Guzman	.949	12	86	7	5	7
Leal	.996	31	248	12	1	23
Maria	.947	9	52	2	3	6
Marte	1.000	1	11	0	0	0
Moscote	.990	21	197	7	2	16
Ortega	.991	14	103	8	1	14
Patino	1.000	3	14	1	0	1
Rasquin	.962	3	24	1	1	2
Sanchez	.968	18	112	10	4	7
Valencia	.994	40	322	19	2	26

Second Base	PCT	G	PO	A	E	DP
Correa	.969	57	96	120	7	31
Crisostomo	.906	11	14	15	3	2
Diaz	.967	15	25	33	2	9
German	.333	1	1	0	2	0
Maracaro	.970	30	64	65	4	18
Marte	.979	35	54	83	3	18
Ortega	.900	2	5	4	1	1
Patino	1.000	4	2	3	0	0
Rasquin	1.000	1	1	1	0	0
Sanchez	1.000	1	3	2	0	1

Third Base	PCT	G	PO	A	E	DP
Correa	1.000	2	2	1	0	0
Crisostomo	.833	2	1	4	1	0
Diaz	.846	5	4	7	2	1
Leal	.667	3	1	5	3	0
Maracaro	.919	34	29	84	10	6
Marte	1.000	5	0	5	0	0
Martinez	.750	8	0	12	4	3
Montero	.859	34	25	60	14	5
Ortega	.931	37	24	84	8	9
Sanchez	1.000	1	1	1	0	0
Valencia	.918	30	29	60	8	5

Shortstop	PCT	G	PO	A	E	DP
Crisostomo	.846	9	11	22	6	3
Diaz	.981	15	24	28	1	8
Marte	.935	13	13	30	3	2
Martinez	.921	55	110	135	21	27
Reyes	.948	59	93	161	14	30

Outfield	PCT	G	PO	A	E	DP
Carrion	.903	36	62	3	7	0
Crisostomo	1.000	6	7	0	0	0
Diaz	.903	47	46	10	6	2
Figuera	.973	65	102	7	3	2
Guzman	.857	10	6	0	1	0
Infante	.940	48	75	3	5	0
Marte	.778	6	6	1	2	0
Mora	.991	68	104	4	1	1
Ortega	1.000	5	3	0	0	0
Pierre	.969	61	145	11	5	3
Rojas	1.000	13	13	1	0	0
Sierra	1.000	39	55	5	0	1
Valencia	1.000	5	5	0	0	0
Zabala	.984	55	117	4	2	1

NEW YORK METS

New York Yankees

SEASON IN A SENTENCE: From Curtis Granderson's first spring at-bat until the final month, the Yankees' season was hopelessly bogged down by a spate of injuries to nearly all of their high-value, high-dollar players.

HIGH POINT: All the tension and vitriol from a lost season was momentarily eased during Mariano Rivera's final home game, when hoodie-clad Derek Jeter and Andy Pettitte came to retrieve Rivera in the ninth inning. The closer broke down in Pettitte's arms, creating yet another piece of indelible pinstriped imagery.

LOW POINT: The Yankees' bottoming out came when Alex Rodriguez returned, and the year became a circus of awkward questions, venom-filled columns from scribes both local and national. Ensnared in the Biogenesis scandal, Rodriguez was still better than the rest of the third basemen the Bombers threw out there all year, but at the cost of whatever sanity remained in the clubhouse.

NOTABLE ROOKIES: After two seasons toiling in the Scranton/Wilkes-Barre rotation, righthander Adam Warren emerged as the Yankees' most reliable long man and spot starter. He made 34 appearances (two starts) and worked to a 3-2, 3.39 record with 64 strikeouts in 77 innings. Righty Preston Claiborne fizzled down the stretch but otherwise contributed 50 innings of near league-average relief.

KEY TRANSACTIONS: Still in the playoff hunt at midseason, New York shipped reliever Corey Black to the Cubs for left fielder Alfonso Soriano, who swatted 17 longballs in 58 games back where he started his career. He also drove in 50 runs and put together a .256/.325/.525 line.

DOWN ON THE FARM: The Trenton Thunder swept their way through the Double-A Eastern League playoffs en route to their third title. It was an otherwise disappointing year for Yankees affiliates. Manny Banuelos missed the season with Tommy John surgery. Center fielder Mason Williams underwhelmed all year long. Tyler Austin missed a chunk of the second half with a wrist injury. Slade Heathcott's year ended with knee tendinitis just after he'd reached a career high in games played. Michael Pineda never recovered enough from labrum surgery to make it to the big leagues. About the only high points were Gary Sanchez continuing to hit and first baseman Greg Bird's coming-out party at low Class A Charleston (.288/.428/.511 with 20 longballs and 107 walks).

OPENING DAY PAYROLL: $228.2 million (1st)

PLAYERS OF THE YEAR

MAJOR LEAGUE	MINOR LEAGUE
Robinson Cano	**Greg Bird**
2b	**1b**
.314/.383/.516	(Low-A)
27 2B, 41 2B, 107 RBIs	.288/.428/.511
5th Silver Slugger	20 HR, 36 2B, 107 BB

ORGANIZATION LEADERS

BATTING		*Minimum 250 AB
MAJORS		
* AVG	Cano, Robinson	.314
* OPS	Cano, Robinson	.899
HR	Cano, Robinson	27
RBI	Cano, Robinson	107
MINORS		
* AVG	Refsnyder, Robert, Tampa/Charleston	.293
* OBP	Bird, Greg, Charleston	.428
* SLG	O'Brien, Peter, Tampa/Charleston	.544
R	Bird, Greg, Charleston	84
H	Flores, Ramon, Trenton	139
TB	O'Brien, Peter, Tampa/Charleston	243
2B	O'Brien, Peter, Tampa/Charleston	39
3B	Heathcott, Slade, Trenton	7
	Valera, Junior, DSL Yankees	7
HR	O'Brien, Peter, Tampa/Charleston	22
RBI	O'Brien, Peter, Tampa/Charleston	96
BB	Bird, Greg, Charleston	107
SO	Roller, Kyle, Trenton	143
SB	Mateo, Jorge, DSL Yankees	49

PITCHING		#Minimum 75 IP
MAJORS		
W	Sabathia, C.C.	14
# ERA	Kuroda, Hiroki	3.31
SO	Sabathia, C.C.	175
SV	Rivera, Mariano	44
MINORS		
W	Greene, Shane, Trenton/Tampa	12
L	Mitchell, Bryan, Trenton/Tampa	11
	Nuding, Zach, Scranton/Trenton	11
# ERA	Allen, Scottie, Tampa/Trenton	3.21
G	Burawa, Danny, Trenton	46
	Kahnle, Tommy, Trenton	46
GS	Turley, Nik, Scranton/Trenton	27
SV	Kahnle, Tommy, Trenton	15
IP	Greene, Shane, Trenton/Tampa	154
BB	Turley, Nik, Scranton/Trenton	76
SO	De Paula, Rafael, Tampa/Charleston	146
# AVG	Turley, Nik, Trenton/Scranton	.226

2013 PERFORMANCE

General Manager: Brian Cashman. **Farm Director:** Mark Newman. **Scouting Director:** Damon Oppenheimer.

Class	Team	League	W	L	PCT	Finish	Manager
Majors	New York Yankees	American	85	77	.525	9th (15)	Joe Girardi
Triple-A	Scranton/Wilkes-Barre RailRiders	International	68	76	.472	10th (14)	Dave Miley
Double-A	Trenton Thunder	Eastern	74	67	.525	4th (12)	Tony Franklin
High A	Tampa Yankees	Florida State	58	78	.426	11th (12)	Luis Sojo
Low A	Charleston RiverDogs	South Atlantic	75	63	.543	6th (14)	Al Pedrique
Short-season	Staten Island Yankees	New York-Penn	34	41	.453	10th (14)	Justin Pope
Rookie	GCL Yankees 1	Gulf Coast	28	32	.467	10th (16)	Tom Nieto
Rookie	GCL Yankees 2	Gulf Coast	36	24	.600	2nd (16)	Mario Garza
2013 Overall Minor League Record			373	381	.495	17th (30)	

ORGANIZATION STATISTICS

AMERICAN LEAGUE

Batting	B-T	HT	WT	DOB	AVG	vLH	vRH	G	AB	R	H	2B	3B	HR	RBI	BB	HBP	SH	SF	SO	SB	CS	SLG	OBP
Adams, David	R-R	6-1	205	5-15-87	.193	.197	.190	43	140	10	27	5	1	2	13	9	2	1	0	43	0	0	.286	.252
Almonte, Zoilo	B-R	6-0	205	6-10-89	.236	.200	.250	34	106	9	25	4	0	1	9	6	0	0	1	19	3	1	.302	.274
Boesch, Brennan	L-L	6-4	235	4-12-85	.275	.250	.282	23	51	6	14	2	1	3	8	2	0	0	0	9	0	0	.529	.302
Brignac, Reid	L-R	6-3	190	1-16-86	.114	.143	.108	17	44	1	5	1	0	0	1	0	0	0	1	17	0	0	.136	.133
Cano, Robinson	L-R	6-0	210	10-22-82	.314	.291	.329	160	605	81	190	41	0	27	107	65	6	0	5	85	7	1	.516	.383
Cervelli, Francisco	R-R	6-1	205	3-6-86	.269	.227	.300	17	52	12	14	3	0	3	8	8	1	0	0	9	0	0	.500	.377
Cruz, Luis	R-R	6-1	210	2-10-84	.182	.000	.208	16	55	6	10	1	0	0	5	1	2	1	0	13	1	0	.200	.224
Francisco, Ben	R-R	6-1	195	10-23-81	.114	.088	.200	21	44	4	5	0	0	1	5	1	5	1	0	11	0	0	.182	.220
Gardner, Brett	L-L	5-10	185	8-24-83	.273	.247	.285	145	539	81	147	33	10	8	52	52	8	7	3	127	24	8	.416	.344
Gonzalez, Alberto	R-R	5-10	195	4-18-83	.176	.000	.222	13	34	3	6	1	0	0	4	0	0	0	0	6	0	0	.206	.176
Granderson, Curtis	L-R	6-1	195	3-16-81	.229	.242	.224	61	214	31	49	13	2	7	15	27	1	2	1	69	8	2	.407	.317
Hafner, Travis	L-R	6-3	240	6-3-77	.202	.173	.210	82	262	31	53	8	1	12	37	32	5	0	0	79	2	0	.378	.301
Ishikawa, Travis	L-L	6-3	220	9-24-83	.000	—	.000	1	2	0	0	0	0	0	0	0	0	0	0	2	0	0	.000	.000
2-team total (6 Baltimore)					.105	—		7	19	0	2	0	0	1	1	0	0	0	0	10	0	0	.105	.150
Jeter, Derek	R-R	6-3	195	6-26-74	.190	.350	.116	17	63	8	12	1	0	1	7	8	1	0	1	10	0	0	.254	.288
Joseph, Corban	L-R	6-0	180	10-28-88	.167	—	.167	2	6	1	1	1	0	0	0	1	0	0	0	1	0	0	.333	.286
Lillibridge, Brent	R-R	5-11	185	9-18-83	.171	.154	.182	11	35	2	6	1	0	0	3	1	0	1	0	8	1	0	.200	.194
Mesa, Melky	R-R	6-1	190	1-31-87	.385	.600	.250	5	13	2	5	2	0	0	1	1	0	0	0	2	0	1	.538	.429
Murphy, J.R.	R-R	5-11	195	5-13-91	.154	.250	.071	16	26	3	4	1	0	0	1	1	0	0	0	9	0	0	.192	.185
Neal, Thomas	R-R	6-2	220	8-17-87	.182	.286	.000	4	11	1	2	0	0	0	0	1	1	0	0	4	0	0	.182	.308
Nelson, Chris	R-R	5-11	205	9-3-85	.222	.429	.172	10	36	3	8	2	0	0	2	1	0	0	0	11	0	0	.278	.243
2-team total (33 Los Angeles)					.221	—		43	145	13	32	3	2	3	20	9	1	0	1	47	2	1	.331	.269
Nix, Jayson	R-R	5-11	195	8-26-82	.236	.266	.220	87	267	32	63	9	1	3	24	24	5	4	3	80	13	1	.311	.308
Nunez, Eduardo	R-R	6-0	185	6-15-87	.260	.225	.277	90	304	38	79	17	4	3	28	20	3	4	5	51	10	3	.372	.307
Overbay, Lyle	L-L	6-2	235	1-28-77	.240	.190	.258	142	445	43	107	24	1	14	59	36	0	0	4	111	2	0	.393	.295
Reynolds, Mark	R-R	6-2	220	8-3-83	.236	.245	.228	36	110	15	26	6	0	6	19	8	2	0	0	31	0	1	.455	.300
2-team total (99 Cleveland)					.220	—	—	135	445	55	98	14	0	21	67	51	5	0	3	154	3	1	.393	.306
Rodriguez, Alex	R-R	6-3	225	7-27-75	.244	.200	.264	44	156	21	38	7	0	7	19	23	2	0	0	43	4	2	.423	.348
Romine, Austin	R-R	6-0	215	11-22-88	.207	.233	.196	60	135	15	28	9	0	1	10	8	1	3	1	37	1	0	.296	.255
Ryan, Brendan	R-R	6-2	195	3-26-82	.220	.238	.211	17	59	7	13	2	0	1	1	2	1	0	0	13	0	0	.305	.258
2-team total (87 Seattle)					.197	—	—	104	319	30	63	12	0	4	22	23	2	4	1	73	4	2	.273	.255
Soriano, Alfonso	R-R	6-1	195	1-7-76	.256	.329	.221	58	219	37	56	8	0	17	50	21	2	0	1	67	8	4	.525	.325
Stewart, Chris	R-R	6-4	210	2-19-82	.211	.188	.220	109	294	28	62	6	0	4	25	30	6	6	4	49	4	0	.272	.293
Suzuki, Ichiro	L-R	5-11	170	10-22-73	.262	.321	.235	150	520	57	136	15	3	7	35	26	1	6	2	63	20	4	.342	.297
Teixeira, Mark	B-R	6-3	215	4-11-80	.151	.248	.086	15	53	5	8	1	0	3	12	8	1	0	1	19	0	0	.340	.270
Wells, Vernon	R-R	6-1	230	12-8-78	.233	.269	.207	130	424	45	99	16	0	11	50	30	0	0	4	73	7	3	.349	.282
Youkilis, Kevin	R-R	6-1	220	3-15-79	.219	.086	.286	28	105	12	23	7	0	2	8	8	5	0	0	31	0	0	.343	.305

Pitching	B-T	HT	WT	DOB	W	L	ERA	G	GS	CG	SV	IP	H	R	ER	HR	BB	SO	AVG	vLH	vRH	K/9	BB/9
Betances, Dellin	R-R	6-8	260	3-23-88	0	0	10.80	6	0	0	0	5	9	6	6	1	2	10	.375	.571	.294	18.00	3.60
Bootcheck, Chris	R-R	6-5	210	10-24-78	0	0	9.00	1	0	0	0	2	1	2	2	1	2	1	.400	.000	.500	9.00	18.00
Cabral, Cesar	L-L	6-3	250	2-11-89	0	0	2.45	8	0	0	0	4	3	1	1	0	1	6	.231	.125	.400	14.73	2.45
Chamberlain, Joba	R-R	6-2	250	9-23-85	2	1	4.93	45	0	0	1	42	47	23	23	8	26	38	.278	.257	.295	8.14	5.57
Claiborne, Preston	R-R	6-2	225	1-21-88	0	2	4.11	44	0	0	0	50	51	23	23	7	14	42	.260	.323	.204	7.51	2.50
Daley, Matt	R-R	6-2	180	6-23-82	1	0	0.00	7	0	0	0	6	2	0	0	0	8	1	.100	.125	.083	12.00	0.00
Eppley, Cody	R-R	6-5	205	10-8-85	0	0	21.60	2	0	0	0	2	4	4	4	0	0	1	.500	1.000	.200	5.40	0.00
Huff, David	L-L	6-2	215	8-22-84	3	1	4.67	11	2	0	0	35	26	18	18	7	8	26	.208	.268	.179	6.75	2.08
2-team total (3 Cleveland)					3	1	5.50	14	2	0	0	38	31	23	23	7	9	31	—	—	—	7.41	2.15
Hughes, Phil	R-R	6-5	240	6-24-86	4	14	5.19	30	29	0	0	146	170	91	84	24	42	121	.293	.298	.286	7.48	2.59
Kelley, Shawn	R-R	6-2	220	4-26-84	4	2	4.39	57	0	0	0	53	47	28	26	8	23	71	.233	.244	.225	11.98	3.88
Kuroda, Hiroki	R-R	6-1	205	2-10-75	11	13	3.31	32	32	1	0	201	191	79	74	20	43	150	.249	.265	.232	6.71	1.92
Logan, Boone	R-L	6-5	215	8-13-84	5	2	3.23	61	0	0	0	39	33	15	14	7	13	50	.236	.221	.254	11.54	3.00
Marshall, Brett	R-R	6-1	195	3-22-90	0	0	4.50	3	0	0	0	12	13	6	6	3	7	7	.283	.261	.304	5.25	5.25
Miller, Jim	R-R	6-1	200	4-28-82	0	0	20.25	1	0	0	0	1	3	3	3	1	1	0	.500	.000	.500	0.00	6.75
Nova, Ivan	R-R	6-4	225	1-12-87	9	6	3.10	23	20	3	0	139	135	49	48	9	44	116	.258	.264	.251	7.49	2.84

	B-T	HT	WT	DOB	W	L	ERA	G	GS	CG	SV	IP	H	R	ER	HR	BB	SO	AVG	vLH	vRH	SLG	OBP
Nuno, Vidal	L-L	5-11	195	7-26-87	1	2	2.25	5	3	0	0	20	16	5	5	2	6	9	.213	.188	.220	4.05	2.70
Pettitte, Andy	L-L	6-5	225	6-15-72	11	11	3.74	30	30	1	0	185	198	85	77	17	48	128	.275	.195	.299	6.22	2.33
Phelps, David	R-R	6-2	200	10-9-86	6	5	4.98	22	12	0	0	87	88	50	48	8	35	79	.265	.255	.280	8.20	3.63
Rivera, Mariano	R-R	6-2	195	11-29-69	6	2	2.11	64	0	0	44	64	58	16	15	6	9	54	.236	.244	.225	7.59	1.27
Robertson, David	R-R	5-11	195	4-9-85	5	1	2.04	70	0	0	3	66	51	15	15	5	18	77	.213	.175	.257	10.45	2.44
Sabathia, C.C.	L-L	6-7	290	7-21-80	14	13	4.78	32	32	2	0	211	224	122	112	28	65	175	.272	.242	.281	7.46	2.77
Warren, Adam	R-R	6-1	200	8-25-87	3	2	3.39	34	2	0	1	77	80	29	29	10	30	64	.268	.301	.231	7.48	3.51
Zagurski, Mike	L-L	6-0	240	1-27-83	0	0	54.00	1	0	0	0	0	1	2	2	0	0	0	.500	.000	1.000	0.00	0.00

Fielding

Catcher	PCT	G	PO	A	E	DP	PB
Cervelli	.969	17	121	6	4	1	0
Murphy	1.000	15	65	7	0	0	0
Romine	.991	59	315	24	3	1	4
Stewart	.997	108	741	55	2	6	12

First Base	PCT	G	PO	A	E	DP
Adams	1.000	4	26	4	0	2
Ishikawa	1.000	1	7	0	0	0
Joseph	1.000	1	7	2	0	1
Lillibridge	1.000	1	7	0	0	1
Overbay	.996	130	933	67	4	93
Reynolds	.995	24	199	3	1	14
Stewart	1.000	2	4	0	0	2
Teixeira	1.000	14	100	8	0	9
Wells	1.000	1	6	0	0	0
Youkilis	1.000	6	45	1	0	1

Second Base	PCT	G	PO	A	E	DP
Adams	1.000	9	16	19	0	4
Cano	.991	153	247	404	6	88
Cervelli	—	1	0	0	0	0
Joseph	1.000	1	1	4	0	0
Nix	1.000	4	3	6	0	3
Nunez	1.000	2	6	3	0	2
Reynolds	1.000	2	4	3	0	1
Wells	—	1	0	0	0	0

Third Base	PCT	G	PO	A	E	DP
Adams	.985	31	14	53	1	6
Cruz	.974	13	9	29	1	0
Gonzalez	.857	6	2	4	1	0
Lillibridge	.947	9	4	14	1	0
Nelson	1.000	10	5	12	0	0
Nix	.968	41	24	66	3	8
Nunez	.933	14	5	23	2	1
Reynolds	.963	14	7	19	1	7
Rodriguez	.987	27	22	52	1	9
Wells	1.000	1	0	1	0	0
Youkilis	.925	22	12	25	3	1

Shortstop	PCT	G	PO	A	E	DP
Brignac	1.000	17	17	27	0	7
Cano	—	1	0	0	0	0
Cruz	.917	5	9	13	2	1
Gonzalez	1.000	5	13	14	0	2
Jeter	.962	13	23	27	2	6
Nix	.979	48	58	133	4	26
Nunez	.953	75	88	156	12	34
Ryan	.987	17	15	61	1	12

Outfield	PCT	G	PO	A	E	DP
Almonte	1.000	28	56	0	0	0
Boesch	.967	15	28	1	1	1
Francisco	1.000	8	8	0	0	0
Gardner	.991	138	327	5	3	1
Gonzalez	—	2	0	0	0	0
Granderson	1.000	46	107	1	0	0
Lillibridge	1.000	1	1	0	0	0
Mesa	1.000	4	11	0	0	0
Neal	1.000	3	6	0	0	0
Overbay	1.000	4	5	0	0	0
Soriano	.991	48	106	5	1	2
Suzuki	.989	138	254	5	3	0
Wells	1.000	96	177	8	0	1

SCRANTON/WILKES-BARRE RAILRIDERS   TRIPLE-A

INTERNATIONAL LEAGUE

Batting	B-T	HT	WT	DOB	AVG	vLH	vRH	G	AB	R	H	2B	3B	HR	RBI	BB	HBP	SH	SF	SO	SB	CS	SLG	OBP
Adams, David	R-R	6-1	205	5-15-87	.268	.263	.270	59	220	28	59	11	2	5	21	29	5	1	0	43	0	0	.405	.366
Almonte, Zoilo	B-R	6-0	205	6-10-89	.297	.281	.303	68	259	30	77	12	1	6	36	30	1	0	3	47	4	1	.421	.369
Bell, Josh	B-R	6-3	230	11-13-86	.205	.206	.205	37	122	16	25	4	0	5	17	25	0	0	5	27	0	0	.361	.329
2-team total (15 Charlotte)					.226	—	—	52	177	25	40	8	0	5	21	28	0	0	5	45	0	0	.356	.324
Boesch, Brennan	L-L	6-4	235	4-12-85	.200	.300	.150	8	30	6	6	2	0	0	2	7	0	0	0	8	0	0	.267	.351
Corona, Reegie	B-R	5-11	185	11-7-86	.118	.200	.083	5	17	2	2	0	0	0	0	1	0	0	0	6	0	0	.118	.167
Crespo, Hector	R-R	5-10	175	8-30-91	.111	.000	.200	4	9	0	1	0	0	0	0	0	0	0	0	2	0	0	.111	.111
Farnham, Jeff	R-R	6-1	190	8-30-87	.205	.400	.138	14	39	4	8	1	0	0	3	8	1	0	0	9	0	0	.231	.354
Fiorito, Dan	R-R	6-4	215	8-20-90	.240	.167	.308	6	25	2	6	1	0	0	0	0	1	0	2	2	2	0	.280	.240
Garcia, Adonis	R-R	5-9	190	4-12-85	.256	.231	.265	50	199	17	51	9	1	3	10	11	5	1	0	21	4	4	.357	.312
Gil, Jose	R-R	6-0	205	9-4-86	.294	.167	.600	5	17	2	5	0	0	0	1	1	0	0	0	0	0	0	.294	.333
2-team total (2 Norfolk)					.304	—	—	7	23	3	7	0	0	0	2	2	0	0	0	3	0	0	.304	.360
Gonzalez, Alberto	R-R	5-10	195	4-18-83	.183	.250	.161	55	191	10	35	4	0	1	12	14	1	3	2	33	0	2	.220	.240
Granderson, Curtis	L-R	6-1	195	3-16-81	.400	.571	.308	5	20	2	8	0	0	1	3	1	0	0	0	4	0	0	.550	.429
Grice, Cody	R-R	6-0	220	1-19-90	.238	.269	.222	23	80	10	19	1	2	2	9	6	0	2	1	29	3	0	.375	.287
Harris, Brendan	R-R	6-1	200	8-26-80	.233	.286	.220	22	73	9	17	3	0	1	4	13	1	0	0	12	0	0	.315	.356
Ibarra, Walter	B-R	5-11	180	11-1-87	.254	.172	.280	38	122	14	31	5	0	2	9	8	0	0	4	21	1	1	.344	.300
Jeter, Derek	R-R	6-3	195	6-26-74	.222	.167	.250	7	18	4	4	1	0	0	1	5	0	0	0	3	0	0	.278	.391
Johnson, Dan	L-R	6-2	210	8-10-79	.253	.229	.262	133	459	57	116	26	0	21	69	93	3	0	4	82	1	0	.447	.379
2-team total (5 Norfolk)					.250	—	—	138	472	59	118	26	0	21	70	96	4	0	5	85	1	0	.439	.378
Johnson, Cody	L-R	6-2	240	8-18-88	.167	.125	.174	18	54	6	9	2	0	1	4	10	0	0	0	32	0	0	.259	.297
Joseph, Corban	L-R	6-0	180	10-28-88	.239	.149	.270	47	188	30	45	9	0	6	19	21	4	0	0	39	2	0	.383	.329
Lillibridge, Brent	R-R	5-11	185	9-18-83	.273	.333	.252	41	150	24	41	8	1	7	18	13	3	0	2	36	12	2	.480	.339
Mahoney, Kevin	L-R	6-1	200	5-11-87	.273	.333	.250	5	11	3	3	1	0	0	2	3	0	1	0	2	0	0	.364	.429
Martinez, Fernando	L-R	6-1	210	10-10-88	.325	.313	.328	22	83	9	27	7	0	4	18	6	4	0	1	12	1	0	.554	.394
Maruszak, Addison	R-R	6-1	190	12-21-86	.254	.271	.246	94	299	42	76	21	1	4	32	32	3	1	3	58	0	1	.371	.329
Medchill, Neil	L-R	6-4	220	6-25-87	.219	.111	.261	11	32	3	7	1	0	1	6	8	1	0	0	10	0	0	.344	.390
Mesa, Melky	R-R	6-1	190	1-31-87	.261	.211	.277	84	314	40	82	15	3	13	39	11	5	0	2	112	13	2	.452	.295
Murphy, J.R.	R-R	5-11	195	5-13-91	.270	.339	.244	59	230	26	62	19	0	6	21	23	0	1	1	41	0	1	.430	.342
Murton, Luke	R-R	6-4	225	5-21-86	.188	.294	.109	23	80	5	15	2	0	6	6	6	0	0	1	26	0	0	.213	.241
Mustelier, Ronnier	R-R	5-10	210	8-8-84	.272	.305	.259	84	334	35	91	21	0	7	39	23	0	0	4	44	4	2	.398	.319
Neal, Thomas	R-R	6-2	220	8-17-87	.325	.333	.321	72	265	36	86	17	0	2	29	23	7	0	2	53	2	1	.411	.391
Patterson, Corey	L-R	5-10	180	8-13-79	.206	.167	.217	53	209	22	43	9	0	6	14	7	1	2	1	42	4	2	.335	.234
Pirela, Jose	B-R	5-11	210	11-21-89	.304	.143	.375	5	23	3	7	0	0	0	1	1	0	0	2	1	0	0	.304	.333
Rodriguez, Alex	R-R	6-3	225	7-27-75	.250	—	.250	3	12	1	3	0	0	1	2	0	0	0	5	0	0	.500	.250
Romine, Austin	R-R	6-0	215	11-22-88	.333	.182	.387	14	42	5	14	0	0	1	4	4	0	0	0	12	0	0	.405	.391
Ruiz, Randy	R-R	6-3	250	10-19-77	.274	.303	.265	71	277	38	76	15	0	17	42	14	3	0	0	75	0	0	.513	.316
Stevenson, Casey	L-R	6-3	200	8-18-88	.417	.500	.375	4	12	3	5	1	0	3	5	1	0	1	0	2	3	1	1.250	.471
Velazquez, Gil	R-R	6-2	185	10-17-79	.173	.188	.167	27	75	4	13	0	0	1	5	3	0	0	2	0	1	0	.173	.253
Wilson, Bobby	R-R	6-0	220	4-8-83	.208	.176	.223	66	216	28	45	12	0	7	38	32	1	2	2	38	0	0	.361	.311

NEW YORK YANKEES

Pitching

Pitching	B-T	HT	WT	DOB	W	L	ERA	G	GS	CG	SV	IP	H	R	ER	HR	BB	SO	AVG	vLH	vRH	K/9	BB/9
Baker, Ryan	R-R	5-9	205	11-9-84	0	0	6.23	2	0	0	0	4	7	3	3	1	2	0	.368	.364	.375	0.00	4.15
Betances, Dellin	R-R	6-8	260	3-23-88	6	4	2.68	38	6	0	5	84	52	25	25	2	42	108	.178	.203	.153	11.57	4.50
Bootcheck, Chris	R-R	6-5	210	10-24-78	10	7	3.69	24	23	2	0	137	135	61	56	15	41	97	.258	.228	.288	6.39	2.70
Cabral, Cesar	L-L	6-3	250	2-11-89	0	1	7.20	10	0	0	0	10	12	8	8	0	5	16	.293	.200	.438	14.40	4.50
Cedeno, Juan	L-L	6-1	200	8-19-83	0	0	0.82	10	0	0	0	11	8	2	1	0	5	9	.211	.278	.150	7.36	4.09
2-team total (37 Gwinnett)					0	3	3.69	47	0	0	0	61	53	28	25	1	30	38	—	—	—	5.61	4.43
Chamberlain, Joba	R-R	6-2	250	9-23-85	0	0	0.00	1	1	0	0	1	2	0	0	0	0	0	.400	.333	.500	0.00	0.00
Claiborne, Preston	R-R	6-2	225	1-21-88	0	0	3.48	8	0	0	3	10	14	5	4	0	1	10	.333	.158	.478	8.71	0.87
Cotham, Caleb	R-R	6-3	215	11-6-87	6	6	5.48	21	17	0	0	95	115	64	58	11	34	60	.304	.322	.290	5.66	3.21
Daley, Matt	R-R	6-2	180	6-23-82	2	3	2.54	30	0	0	1	39	28	12	11	3	6	53	.197	.295	.123	12.23	1.38
Demel, Sam	R-R	6-0	205	10-23-85	1	1	1.72	35	0	0	3	52	38	11	10	3	23	65	.201	.217	.186	11.18	3.96
Eppley, Cody	R-R	6-5	205	10-8-85	2	2	8.53	19	0	0	3	19	30	18	18	1	15	19	.375	.500	.292	9.00	7.11
2-team total (22 Rochester)					4	2	6.49	41	0	0	3	43	53	31	31	1	28	39	—	—	—	8.16	5.86
Garrison, Taylor	R-R	5-11	165	5-24-90	0	0	0.00	1	0	0	0	2	1	1	0	0	0	0	.400	.500	.000	0.00	0.00
Heredia, Jairo	R-R	6-1	190	10-8-89	0	0	4.50	1	0	0	1	4	5	2	2	0	1	3	.278	.273	.286	6.75	2.25
Herndon, David	R-R	6-5	200	9-4-85	1	0	1.74	6	0	0	0	10	11	3	2	0	3	8	.275	.316	.238	6.97	2.61
Huff, David	L-L	6-2	215	8-22-84	1	6	3.84	13	12	0	1	68	76	31	29	4	13	64	.279	.253	.289	8.47	1.72
2-team total (9 Columbus)					4	7	3.90	22	14	0	1	92	97	44	40	8	22	92	—	—	—	8.97	2.14
Lewis, Freddy	L-L	6-2	210	12-16-86	0	0	0.00	1	0	0	0	1	0	0	0	0	1	2	.000	.000	.000	13.50	6.75
Marshall, Brett	R-R	6-1	195	3-22-90	7	10	5.13	25	25	0	0	139	144	88	79	17	68	120	.271	.276	.267	7.79	4.41
Miller, Jim	R-R	6-1	200	4-28-82	3	5	3.55	43	1	0	6	63	55	27	25	8	25	92	.229	.176	.273	13.07	3.55
Montgomery, Mark	R-R	5-11	205	8-30-90	2	3	3.38	25	0	0	0	40	36	17	15	4	25	49	.250	.238	.259	11.03	5.63
Nova, Ivan	R-R	6-4	225	1-12-87	2	0	2.04	3	3	0	0	18	15	6	4	1	4	17	.234	.250	.214	8.66	2.04
Nuding, Zach	R-R	6-4	260	3-29-90	0	0	4.76	1	1	0	0	6	7	3	3	1	3	5	.304	.333	.294	7.94	4.76
Nuno, Vidal	L-L	5-11	195	7-26-87	2	0	1.44	5	5	0	0	25	14	4	4	2	2	30	.157	.103	.183	10.80	0.72
Perez, Kelvin	R-R	6-1	140	10-10-85	0	4	9.00	8	4	0	0	18	32	18	18	2	9	13	.400	.471	.348	6.50	4.50
Pineda, Michael	R-R	6-7	260	1-18-89	1	1	3.86	6	6	0	0	23	18	10	10	2	6	26	.205	.244	.170	10.03	2.31
Pope, Ryan	R-R	6-3	205	5-21-86	1	0	2.92	5	1	0	0	12	14	4	4	1	1	7	.298	.360	.227	5.11	0.73
Ramirez, Jose	R-R	6-3	190	1-21-90	1	3	4.88	8	8	0	0	31	29	20	17	3	21	28	.259	.283	.237	8.04	6.03
Rapada, Clay	R-L	6-5	195	3-9-81	1	0	4.66	10	0	0	1	10	13	5	5	1	4	4	.351	.250	.429	3.72	3.72
2-team total (27 Columbus)					1	0	2.14	37	0	0	2	34	31	10	8	2	13	24	—	—	—	6.42	3.48
Romanski, Josh	R-R	6-0	185	10-18-86	0	1	45.00	1	0	0	0	1	4	5	5	1	2	2	.571	.667	.500	18.00	18.00
Rondon, Francisco	L-L	6-0	190	4-19-88	0	0	3.12	3	1	0	0	9	6	3	3	1	4	6	.194	.167	.211	6.23	4.15
Spence, Josh	L-L	6-1	190	1-22-88	1	1	3.98	33	0	0	1	43	50	19	19	0	17	41	.296	.257	.323	8.58	3.56
Stoneburner, Graham	R-R	6-0	205	9-29-87	4	6	4.57	16	14	0	0	67	70	38	34	8	21	32	.267	.260	.274	4.30	2.82
Tateyama, Yoshinori	R-R	5-10	165	12-26-75	2	2	1.70	21	1	0	1	42	37	9	8	2	4	42	.230	.192	.265	8.93	0.85
Turley, Nik	L-L	6-4	195	9-11-89	0	0	1.50	1	1	0	0	6	2	1	1	0	3	4	.105	.500	.059	6.00	4.50
Wang, Chien-Ming	R-R	6-4	225	3-31-80	4	4	2.33	9	9	1	0	58	57	17	15	2	10	25	.256	.231	.277	3.88	1.55
2-team total (9 Buffalo)					8	7	2.87	18	17	2	0	110	103	39	35	5	22	55	—	—	—	4.51	1.81
Whitley, Chase	R-R	6-3	215	6-14-89	3	2	3.06	29	5	0	3	68	61	24	23	3	21	62	.247	.193	.297	8.25	2.79
Zagurski, Mike	L-L	6-0	240	1-27-83	5	3	3.08	20	0	0	1	26	22	11	9	2	12	38	.237	.150	.302	12.99	4.10
2-team total (19 Indianapolis)					6	3	2.66	39	0	0	2	47	37	16	14	4	21	75	—	—	—	14.26	3.99

Fielding

Catcher	PCT	G	PO	A	E	DP	PB
Farnham	.971	14	88	14	3	2	1
Gil	1.000	3	18	1	0	0	0
Murphy	.991	56	487	42	5	4	6
Romine	1.000	14	95	5	0	0	1
Wilson	.992	60	468	37	4	2	4

First Base	PCT	G	PO	A	E	DP
Adams	1.000	2	16	2	0	2
Bell	1.000	5	43	4	0	2
Gil	1.000	1	8	0	0	1
Johnson	.992	114	876	70	8	92
Joseph	1.000	3	25	3	0	6
Lillibridge	1.000	3	20	2	0	0
Maruszak	1.000	2	10	2	0	0
Murton	.957	5	39	5	2	5
Ruiz	1.000	11	75	3	0	4
Wilson	1.000	2	11	3	0	0

Second Base	PCT	G	PO	A	E	DP
Adams	.975	28	48	71	3	27
Corona	1.000	3	5	2	0	1
Garcia	1.000	1	2	1	0	1
Gonzalez	1.000	11	20	39	0	6
Harris	1.000	7	7	15	0	4
Ibarra	.977	13	16	27	1	7
Joseph	.967	44	83	122	7	26
Lillibridge	.971	17	29	39	2	8
Mahoney	1.000	3	5	4	0	1
Maruszak	.980	13	18	32	1	4
Pirela	1.000	5	15	11	0	4
Stevenson	1.000	3	3	6	0	1
Velazquez	1.000	2	2	6	0	3

Third Base	PCT	G	PO	A	E	DP
Adams	.955	30	20	44	3	4
Bell	.983	21	21	38	1	4
Fiorito	.667	3	2	2	2	0
Gonzalez	.893	6	6	19	3	1
Harris	1.000	5	2	8	0	0
Johnson	.769	5	3	7	3	1
Lillibridge	1.000	18	13	20	0	3
Mahoney	1.000	2	1	3	0	0
Maruszak	.947	19	11	25	2	0
Mustelier	.936	41	13	75	6	11
Rodriguez	—	1	0	0	0	0
Stevenson	.857	2	2	4	1	0

Shortstop	PCT	G	PO	A	E	DP
Corona	1.000	2	2	4	0	0

Outfield	PCT	G	PO	A	E	DP
Crespo	.846	4	1	10	2	0
Fiorito	1.000	3	6	6	0	2
Gonzalez	.976	39	69	97	4	17
Harris	.977	10	20	22	1	8
Ibarra	.988	24	28	52	1	8
Jeter	.824	6	4	10	3	0
Lillibridge	.818	4	4	5	2	0
Maruszak	.986	41	54	91	2	25
Velazquez	.983	26	38	77	2	18
Almonte	.972	67	105	1	3	0
Boesch	1.000	7	11	0	0	0
Garcia	.989	47	90	3	1	2
Granderson	1.000	4	5	0	0	0
Grice	.984	23	61	2	1	0
Ibarra	—	1	0	0	0	0
Johnson	1.000	5	4	1	0	0
Martinez	1.000	21	39	0	0	0
Maruszak	1.000	24	26	2	0	0
Medchill	1.000	11	23	0	0	0
Mesa	.995	84	182	4	1	1
Mustelier	.974	45	70	4	2	0
Neal	.977	62	125	4	3	1
Patterson	1.000	50	91	2	0	0

NEW YORK YANKEES

Batting	B-T	HT	WT	DOB	AVG	vLH	vRH	G	AB	R	H	2B	3B	HR	RBI	BB	HBP	SH	SF	SO	SB	CS	SLG	OBP
Angelini, Carmen	R-R	6-2	185	9-22-88	.220	.192	.233	66	236	24	52	13	1	4	28	21	2	2	1	52	7	3	.335	.288
Arcia, Francisco	B-R	5-11	195	9-14-89	.176	.158	.184	19	68	4	12	1	0	2	9	4	0	0	0	18	0	0	.279	.222
Austin, Tyler	R-R	6-1	220	9-6-91	.257	.292	.243	83	319	43	82	17	1	6	40	41	3	0	3	79	4	0	.373	.344
Blaser, Tyson	R-R	6-2	225	12-8-87	.214	.400	.111	4	14	1	3	1	0	0	2	1	0	0	0	1	0	0	.286	.267
Brown, Shane	R-R	5-11	197	1-11-88	.174	.192	.163	23	69	6	12	2	0	0	5	8	4	1	1	16	0	0	.203	.293
Butler, Saxon	L-L	6-3	225	5-11-90	.125	.125	.125	8	24	2	3	1	0	0	6	4	2	0	0	8	0	0	.167	.300
Castillo, Ali	R-R	5-10	165	6-19-89	.218	.176	.230	46	156	15	34	4	3	0	22	12	4	3	1	29	4	4	.282	.289
Clark, Andrew	L-L	6-2	220	8-12-87	.277	.157	.344	39	141	19	39	12	0	3	20	12	0	0	0	31	0	0	.426	.333
Corona, Reegie	B-R	5-11	185	11-7-86	.245	.258	.240	88	318	41	78	16	0	5	37	28	2	1	4	66	6	0	.343	.307
Farnham, Jeff	R-R	6-1	190	8-30-87	.174	.185	.167	22	69	4	12	0	0	0	4	6	0	1	0	18	0	0	.174	.240
Fiorito, Dan	R-R	6-4	215	8-20-90	.000	.000	.000	3	7	0	0	0	0	0	0	1	0	0	0	4	0	0	.000	.125
Flores, Ramon	L-L	5-10	150	3-26-92	.260	.245	.267	136	534	79	139	25	6	6	55	77	2	3	4	98	7	6	.363	.353
Gamel, Ben	L-L	5-11	185	5-17-92	.239	.238	.239	16	67	5	16	4	0	0	1	5	4	0	1	0	18	1	0	.343	.282
Gil, Jose	R-R	6-0	205	9-4-86	.240	.500	.158	15	50	6	12	2	0	0	3	4	1	0	0	12	1	1	.280	.309
2-team total (1 Bowie)					.226	—		16	53	6	12	2	0	0	3	5	1	0	0	13	1	1	.264	.305
Granderson, Curtis	L-R	6-1	195	3-16-81	.333	.000	.333	2	6	1	2	0	1	0	0	3	0	0	0	1	0	0	.667	.556
Grice, Cody	R-R	6-0	220	1-19-90	.190	.179	.196	27	84	13	16	0	1	1	8	9	4	3	0	32	5	3	.250	.299
Heathcott, Slade	L-L	6-0	195	9-28-90	.261	.298	.246	103	399	59	104	22	7	8	49	36	4	3	2	107	15	8	.411	.327
Higashioka, Kyle	R-R	6-0	200	4-20-90	.320	.357	.273	7	25	1	8	3	0	1	5	0	0	1	0	5	0	0	.560	.320
Ibarra, Walter	B-R	5-11	180	11-1-87	.312	.333	.305	20	77	12	24	2	1	1	6	2	0	1	2	21	2	1	.403	.321
Mahoney, Kevin	L-R	6-1	205	5-11-87	.203	.163	.224	39	128	14	26	4	0	1	8	14	1	1	1	48	2	0	.258	.285
McCoy, Nick	R-R	5-10	180	3-2-87	.160	.200	.150	9	25	2	4	3	0	0	2	2	1	0	0	6	0	0	.280	.250
Medchill, Neil	L-R	6-4	220	6-25-87	.247	.200	.264	53	190	20	47	9	0	4	23	17	1	0	2	70	3	0	.358	.310
Murphy, J.R.	R-R	5-11	195	5-13-91	.268	.212	.280	49	183	34	49	10	0	6	25	24	1	1	2	32	1	0	.421	.352
Nunez, Eduardo	R-R	6-0	185	6-15-87	.375	.400	.333	2	8	1	3	0	0	0	1	0	0	0	0	2	0	0	.375	.444
Oliberto, Mikeson	R-R	5-10	164	8-23-90	.500	—	.500	1	2	2	2	0	0	0	0	0	0	0	0	0	0	0	.500	.500
Pirela, Jose	B-R	5-11	210	11-21-89	.272	.303	.260	124	459	73	125	27	5	10	62	56	9	1	5	61	18	3	.418	.359
Rodriguez, Alex	R-R	6-3	225	7-27-75	.333	.375	.000	4	9	3	3	0	0	2	5	5	0	0	1	2	0	0	1.000	.533
Roller, Kyle	L-R	6-1	250	3-27-88	.253	.293	.238	124	443	59	112	24	1	17	69	53	12	0	2	143	0	2	.427	.347
Rosario, Francisco	B-R	6-1	170	7-12-90	.182	.333	.125	3	11	0	2	0	0	0	2	0	0	0	0	2	0	0	.182	.182
Sanchez, Gary	R-R	6-2	220	12-2-92	.250	.241	.254	23	92	12	23	6	0	2	10	13	4	0	1	16	0	0	.380	.364
Sanchez, Yeral	R-R	6-0	210	7-18-85	.182	.182	.182	31	110	11	20	4	0	2	9	7	3	0	0	37	0	0	.273	.250
Segedin, Rob	R-R	6-2	220	11-10-88	.338	.211	.385	18	71	16	24	10	0	3	17	6	2	0	3	18	0	1	.606	.390
Stevenson, Casey	L-R	6-3	200	5-18-88	.228	.211	.234	67	202	19	46	10	0	2	16	20	5	2	2	43	1	1	.307	.310
Teixeira, Mark	B-B	6-3	215	4-11-80	.200	—	.200	2	5	0	1	0	0	0	0	1	0	0	0	1	0	0	.200	.333
Williams, Mason	L-R	6-1	180	8-21-91	.153	.190	.137	17	72	7	11	3	1	1	4	1	0	3	0	18	0	0	.264	.164
Youkilis, Kevin	R-R	6-1	220	3-15-79	.200	—	.200	2	5	1	1	0	0	0	1	1	0	0	0	0	0	0	.200	.333

Pitching	B-T	HT	WT	DOB	W	L	ERA	G	GS	CG	SV	IP	H	R	ER	HR	BB	SO	AVG	vLH	vRH	K/9	BB/9
Allen, Scottie	R-R	6-1	170	7-3-91	2	0	1.59	4	4	0	0	23	18	5	4	0	14	9	.217	.226	.212	3.57	5.56
Arrebato, Rigoberto	L-L	5-11	190	2-4-86	2	1	3.50	10	0	0	1	18	17	7	7	2	10	24	.246	.211	.260	12.00	5.00
Barreda, Manuel	R-R	5-11	195	10-8-88	0	1	4.35	5	0	0	0	10	7	5	5	0	8	12	.200	.231	.182	10.45	6.97
Black, Sean	R-R	6-3	185	4-23-88	2	3	4.22	6	6	0	0	32	35	16	15	4	11	15	.280	.250	.299	4.22	3.09
Bleich, Jeremy	L-L	6-2	200	6-18-87	2	1	2.76	27	4	0	2	65	57	27	20	1	39	57	.242	.288	.224	7.85	5.37
Burawa, Daniel	R-R	6-2	210	12-30-88	6	3	2.59	46	0	0	4	66	47	25	19	1	42	66	.202	.257	.176	9.00	5.73
Cabral, Cesar	L-L	6-3	250	2-11-89	1	0	5.49	15	0	0	0	20	22	12	12	2	9	22	.286	.296	.280	10.07	4.12
Cotham, Caleb	R-R	6-3	215	11-6-87	2	1	3.72	7	6	0	0	29	27	13	12	1	13	26	.245	.182	.309	8.07	4.03
Daley, Matt	R-R	6-2	180	6-23-82	3	0	1.00	10	0	0	0	9	5	1	1	0	4	11	.161	.154	.167	11.00	4.00
Dott, Aaron	R-L	6-4	215	5-17-88	1	2	4.66	36	1	0	1	46	54	27	24	3	16	55	.287	.268	.295	10.68	3.11
Greene, Shane	R-R	6-3	200	11-17-88	8	4	3.18	14	13	1	0	79	92	35	28	6	20	68	.289	.344	.254	7.71	2.27
Hall, Shaeffer	R-L	6-1	205	10-2-87	3	0	3.32	10	0	0	0	19	19	9	7	0	6	12	.264	.250	.271	5.68	2.84
Herndon, David	R-R	6-5	200	9-4-85	1	0	0.00	5	0	0	1	10	6	0	0	0	4	14	.171	.200	.150	13.03	3.72
Kahnle, Tommy	R-R	6-1	230	8-7-89	1	3	2.85	46	0	0	15	60	38	20	19	4	45	74	.182	.159	.197	11.10	6.75
Lewis, Freddy	L-L	6-2	210	12-16-86	0	4	2.28	20	5	0	0	43	46	14	11	3	20	39	.279	.306	.267	8.10	4.15
Mitchell, Bryan	L-R	6-3	205	4-19-91	0	0	1.93	3	3	0	0	19	14	5	4	0	5	16	.206	.130	.244	7.71	2.41
Moreno, Diego	R-R	6-1	177	7-21-87	1	0	0.96	6	0	0	0	9	4	1	1	0	2	12	.129	.167	.105	11.57	1.93
Nuding, Zach	R-R	6-4	260	3-29-90	5	11	4.21	31	21	1	1	128	141	75	60	9	57	101	.279	.243	.305	7.08	4.00
O'Brien, Mikey	R-R	5-11	190	3-3-90	7	8	4.12	21	19	0	0	107	107	54	49	10	44	90	.261	.282	.246	7.57	3.70
Perez, Kelvin	R-R	6-1	140	10-10-85	0	1	2.87	9	0	0	0	16	13	5	5	2	4	15	.228	.250	.212	8.62	2.30
2-team total (10 Erie)					1	2	5.46	19	8	0	0	58	61	37	35	6	23	45	—	—	—	7.02	3.59
Phelps, David	R-R	6-2	200	10-9-86	0	0	3.52	2	2	0	0	8	5	3	3	2	5	12	.185	.231	.143	14.09	5.87
Pinder, Branden	R-R	6-3	210	1-26-89	1	1	6.29	19	0	0	5	24	28	19	17	2	16	22	.295	.324	.276	8.14	5.92
Pineda, Michael	R-R	6-7	260	1-18-89	1	0	4.00	2	2	0	0	9	6	4	4	0	2	8	.182	.063	.294	8.00	6.00
Ramirez, Jose	R-R	6-3	190	1-21-90	1	3	2.76	9	8	0	0	42	28	15	13	7	15	50	.192	.171	.211	10.63	3.19
Romanski, Josh	L-L	6-0	185	10-18-86	2	0	2.00	6	0	0	0	9	10	3	2	0	2	11	.270	.143	.348	11.00	2.00
Rondon, Francisco	L-L	6-0	190	4-19-88	4	3	4.01	30	6	0	3	74	56	44	33	6	50	79	.203	.195	.206	9.61	6.08
Short, Charlie	R-R	6-2	220	8-13-88	2	2	3.86	3	0	0	0	5	4	3	2	0	4	5	.267	1.000	.154	9.64	7.71
Smith, Caleb	R-L	6-2	175	7-28-91	0	0	2.45	1	1	0	0	4	3	1	1	0	1	5	.214	.500	.167	12.27	2.45
Stoneburner, Graham	R-R	6-0	205	9-29-87	0	1	3.52	14	1	0	1	23	25	10	9	0	6	10	.287	.387	.232	3.91	2.35
Tracy, Matt	L-L	6-3	215	11-26-88	4	5	5.51	14	13	0	0	64	67	42	39	6	37	60	.279	.266	.284	8.48	5.23
Turley, Nik	L-L	6-4	195	9-11-89	11	8	3.88	27	26	0	0	139	119	69	60	11	73	137	.230	.171	.248	8.87	4.73
Venditte, Pat	R-B	6-1	180	6-30-85	1	2	3.97	8	0	0	0	11	13	5	5	1	3	13	.283	.154	.333	10.32	2.38

Fielding

Catcher	PCT	G	PO	A	E	DP	PB
Arcia	1.000	19	153	15	0	1	2
Blaser	.919	4	32	2	3	0	0
Farnham	.969	22	135	22	5	3	4
Gil	1.000	14	117	8	0	2	1
Higashioka	1.000	7	43	10	0	1	0
McCoy	.987	9	67	8	1	1	0
Murphy	.989	49	408	47	5	4	7
Sanchez	.982	20	204	15	4	2	2

First Base	PCT	G	PO	A	E	DP
Butler	1.000	7	58	2	0	1
Clark	.982	24	203	14	4	26
Gil	1.000	1	7	0	0	0
Mahoney	1.000	5	46	1	0	2
Roller	.990	94	629	71	7	56
Stevenson	.981	15	97	7	2	11
Teixeira	1.000	2	9	1	0	0

Second Base	PCT	G	PO	A	E	DP
Castillo	1.000	1	3	3	0	0
Corona	.972	22	47	56	3	13
Ibarra	1.000	5	7	17	0	3
Mahoney	1.000	2	4	2	0	0
Pirela	.966	111	209	247	16	61
Stevenson	.750	1	1	2	1	0

Third Base	PCT	G	PO	A	E	DP
Corona	.957	55	34	100	6	6
Fiorito	1.000	2	1	3	0	0
Mahoney	.984	31	18	43	1	4
Pirela	—	1	0	0	0	0
Rodriguez	1.000	4	1	11	0	2
Rosario	1.000	1	2	3	0	0
Segedin	.827	16	12	31	9	1
Stevenson	.915	39	27	70	9	5
Youkilis	1.000	2	1	0	0	0

Shortstop	PCT	G	PO	A	E	DP
Angelini	.981	66	101	161	5	39
Castillo	.980	44	79	118	4	19
Corona	.933	13	18	24	3	3
Fiorito	1.000	1	1	1	0	0
Ibarra	.958	15	31	38	3	4
Nunez	1.000	1	2	4	0	2
Rosario	1.000	2	2	6	0	3
Stevenson	1.000	3	2	6	0	0

Outfield	PCT	G	PO	A	E	DP
Austin	.991	69	109	7	1	2
Brown	.864	15	19	0	3	0
Flores	.976	125	193	13	5	1
Gamel	.976	14	37	3	1	0
Granderson	—	1	0	0	0	0
Grice	.958	27	66	2	3	0
Heathcott	.966	90	191	8	7	4
Mahoney	1.000	1	2	0	0	0
Medchill	.980	29	46	3	1	1
Oliberto	1.000	1	2	0	0	0
Pirela	1.000	5	11	0	0	0
Sanchez	.982	27	54	2	1	1
Stevenson	.882	11	14	1	2	0
Williams	1.000	15	35	0	0	0

TAMPA YANKEES
HIGH CLASS A
FLORIDA STATE LEAGUE

Batting	B-T	HT	WT	DOB	AVG	vLH	vRH	G	AB	R	H	2B	3B	HR	RBI	BB	HBP	SH	SF	SO	SB	CS	SLG	OBP
Angelini, Carmen	B-R	6-2	185	9-22-88	.312	.231	.349	32	125	14	39	4	1	5	22	5	1	0	1	20	6	2	.480	.344
Arcia, Francisco	B-R	5-11	195	9-14-89	.233	.270	.217	36	129	16	30	3	1	2	12	12	4	2	0	24	1	0	.318	.317
Blaser, Tyson	R-R	6-2	225	12-8-87	.221	.256	.203	34	113	11	25	3	2	0	8	13	2	0	0	32	3	1	.283	.313
Butler, Saxon	L-L	6-3	225	5-11-90	.257	.258	.256	67	226	23	58	13	1	4	25	20	4	0	2	49	1	2	.376	.325
Castillo, Ali	R-R	5-10	165	6-19-89	.234	.282	.211	73	244	24	57	4	1	3	24	21	2	4	2	44	7	6	.295	.297
Culver, Cito	R-R	6-0	190	8-26-92	.355	.333	.360	16	62	13	22	5	0	1	5	4	0	0	0	14	0	1	.484	.394
Dugas, Taylor	L-L	5-8	170	12-15-89	.321	.273	.341	55	193	34	62	7	0	1	16	32	4	4	1	15	7	7	.373	.426
Farnham, Jeff	R-R	6-1	190	8-30-87	.268	.429	.214	17	56	3	15	0	0	0	3	10	2	0	1	10	1	0	.268	.391
Feliz, Anderson	B-R	6-0	175	5-11-92	.265	.195	.295	36	136	18	36	4	2	1	17	16	0	1	1	37	4	4	.346	.340
Fiorito, Dan	R-R	6-4	215	8-20-90	.272	.323	.255	73	250	32	68	10	1	1	18	28	5	1	1	52	6	2	.332	.356
Gamel, Ben	L-L	5-11	185	5-17-92	.272	.211	.303	96	364	50	99	28	4	3	49	48	1	3	7	77	21	5	.396	.352
Granderson, Curtis	L-L	6-1	195	3-16-81	.154	.125	.200	4	13	2	2	0	0	0	1	1	0	0	0	4	0	0	.154	.214
Grice, Cody	R-R	6-0	220	1-19-90	.204	.265	.176	36	108	12	22	5	1	0	10	9	1	0	1	33	8	1	.269	.269
Gumbs, Angelo	R-R	6-0	175	10-13-92	.214	.286	.175	39	159	16	34	10	2	0	11	8	3	0	0	31	6	1	.302	.265
Kuo, Fu-Lin	R-R	6-0	185	1-7-91	.181	.320	.106	23	72	9	13	1	0	1	8	8	1	0	3	27	0	1	.236	.262
Mustelier, Ronnier	R-R	5-10	210	8-8-84	—			1	0	0	0	0	0	0	0	0	0	0	0	0	0	0	—	—
Nix, Jayson	R-R	5-11	195	8-26-82	.100	.167	.000	3	10	1	1	1	0	0	1	1	0	0	0	1	0	0	.200	.182
Nunez, Eduardo	R-R	6-0	185	6-15-87	.333	—	.333	3	3	2	1	0	0	0	0	2	0	0	0	2	0	0	.333	.600
Nunez, Reymond	R-R	6-4	210	9-25-90	.176	.000	.188	5	17	1	3	3	0	0	4	1	0	0	0	4	0	0	.353	.222
O'Brien, Peter	R-R	6-3	215	7-15-90	.265	.215	.287	66	253	31	67	17	3	11	55	19	2	0	6	76	0	1	.486	.314
Oliberto, Mikeson	R-R	5-10	164	8-23-90	.208	.182	.218	23	77	13	16	4	1	1	6	4	0	0	0	22	5	3	.325	.247
Rabago, Hector	R-R	5-10	185	8-24-88	.333	.333	—	1	3	0	1	0	0	0	0	0	0	0	0	0	0	0	.333	.333
Refsnyder, Robert	R-R	6-1	205	3-26-91	.283	.299	.276	117	413	66	117	28	2	6	51	78	11	2	3	70	16	6	.404	.408
Rodriguez, Alex	R-R	6-3	225	7-27-75	.176	.500	.133	6	17	2	3	1	0	0	3	1	2	0	0	5	0	0	.235	.300
Sanchez, Gary	R-R	6-2	220	12-2-92	.254	.270	.247	94	362	38	92	21	0	13	61	28	5	0	4	71	3	1	.420	.313
Sanchez, Yeral	R-R	6-0	210	7-18-85	.226	.162	.256	32	115	9	26	9	1	2	16	5	1	0	2	31	0	0	.374	.260
Snyder, Matt	L-R	6-5	200	6-17-90	.159	.214	.122	20	69	8	11	3	0	3	8	12	2	0	0	12	0	0	.333	.301
Sosa, Eduardo	L-L	6-0	180	3-14-91	.204	.156	.218	43	142	12	29	4	0	0	12	13	2	2	1	36	5	3	.232	.278
Stevenson, Casey	L-R	6-3	200	6-17-90	.200	.111	.250	17	50	4	10	0	0	0	7	7	0	0	2	7	2	1	.260	.311
Toussen, Jose	R-R	6-1	155	11-13-89	.231	.277	.211	89	268	26	62	11	0	1	23	28	1	5	2	50	5	5	.284	.304
Valera, Jackson	R-R	6-1	175	4-8-92	.273	.273	.273	7	22	0	6	0	0	0	1	1	0	0	1	2	0	0	.273	.292
Williams, Mason	L-R	6-1	180	8-21-91	.261	.227	.281	100	406	56	106	21	3	3	24	39	2	11	3	61	15	9	.350	.327
Wilson, Zach	R-R	6-1	205	8-6-90	.308	.340	.305	8	13	3	4	2	0	0	4	0	0	0	0	2	0	0	.462	.471

Pitching	B-T	HT	WT	DOB	W	L	ERA	G	GS	CG	SV	IP	H	R	ER	HR	BB	SO	AVG	vLH	vRH	K/9	BB/9
Allen, Scottie	R-R	6-1	170	7-3-91	9	5	3.54	21	21	1	0	112	108	50	44	9	32	75	.259	.292	.246	6.03	2.57
Arneson, Zach	R-R	6-2	190	11-17-88	1	2	9.97	16	0	0	1	22	34	30	24	1	17	21	.362	.500	.303	8.72	7.06
Arrebato, Rigoberto	L-L	5-11	190	2-4-86	2	2	1.88	21	0	0	0	38	35	10	8	1	13	40	.240	.227	.245	9.39	3.05
Barreda, Manuel	R-R	5-11	195	10-8-88	2	2	3.96	33	0	0	3	52	46	28	23	6	19	58	.227	.236	.221	9.97	3.27
Bautista, Rony	L-L	6-7	200	9-17-91	1	0	0.00	1	1	0	0	5	3	0	0	0	1	3	.278	.250	.286	5.40	1.80
Black, Corey	R-R	5-11	175	8-4-91	3	8	4.25	19	19	0	0	83	79	54	39	2	45	88	.243	.169	.285	9.58	4.90
2-team total (5 Daytona)					7	8	3.93	24	24	0	0	108	101	63	47	5	55	116	—	—	—	9.70	4.60
Black, Sean	R-R	6-3	185	4-23-88	2	0	1.66	12	7	0	0	43	31	8	8	2	12	31	.204	.226	.189	6.44	2.49
Brebbia, John	R-R	6-1	185	5-30-90	0	3	3.98	16	0	0	0	32	33	16	14	2	12	20	.258	.224	.278	5.68	3.41
Cabral, Cesar	L-L	6-3	250	2-11-89	0	0	2.57	5	0	0	0	7	6	2	2	0	8	5	.250	.286	.235	6.43	10.29
Canela, Erick	R-R	5-11	155	10-2-90	0	0	27.00	1	0	0	0	2	11	6	6	0	0	0	.688	.700	.667	0.00	0.00
Claiborne, Preston	R-R	6-2	225	1-21-88	0	0	0.00	1	1	0	0	1	0	0	0	0	1	1	.000	.000	.000	9.00	9.00
Daley, Matt	R-R	6-2	180	6-23-82	0	0	0.00	4	0	0	0	5	5	0	0	0	0	10	.238	.400	.188	16.88	0.00

Player	B-T	HT	WT	DOB																			
De La Cruz, Joel	B-R	6-1	190	6-9-89	6	3	3.28	33	6	0	1	85	70	35	31	2	27	73	.225	.287	.189	7.73	2.86
De Paula, Rafael	R-R	6-2	212	3-24-91	1	3	6.06	11	10	0	0	49	54	35	33	5	30	50	.283	.293	.273	9.18	5.51
Enns, Dietrich	L-L	6-1	195	5-16-91	0	5	5.63	9	7	0	0	38	36	34	24	4	21	43	.248	.154	.269	10.10	4.93
Garrison, Taylor	R-R	5-11	165	5-24-90	5	3	1.87	30	0	0	8	43	25	13	9	1	11	35	.166	.161	.168	7.27	2.28
Goody, Nick	B-R	5-11	195	7-6-91	1	0	3.00	2	0	0	0	3	2	1	1	1	2	3	.182	.167	.200	9.00	6.00
Greene, Shane	R-R	6-3	200	11-17-88	4	6	3.60	13	13	0	0	75	83	36	30	4	10	69	.279	.278	.280	8.28	1.20
Heredia, Jairo	R-R	6-1	190	10-8-89	3	1	3.22	7	7	0	0	36	33	17	13	5	14	34	.236	.270	.208	8.42	3.47
Herndon, David	R-R	6-5	200	9-4-85	1	2	5.73	7	1	0	0	11	19	7	7	0	3	10	.388	.350	.414	8.18	2.45
Lail, Brady	R-R	6-2	175	8-9-93	1	0	7.04	2	1	0	0	8	14	7	6	1	3	5	.389	.250	.500	5.87	3.52
Lewis, Freddy	L-L	6-2	210	12-16-86	0	0	3.86	8	0	0	0	14	14	7	6	0	4	19	.237	.357	.200	12.21	2.57
Long, Jaron	R-R	6-0	185	8-28-91	0	1	9.00	2	0	0	0	4	6	5	4	0	2	2	.353	.429	.300	4.50	4.50
Maher, Joey	R-R	6-5	200	8-5-92	0	1	54.00	1	1	0	0	1	6	8	8	0	4	1	.600	.600	.600	6.75	27.00
Mahoney, Dan	R-R	6-3	195	2-17-88	0	2	6.86	15	0	0	0	20	19	18	15	1	20	12	.253	.269	.245	5.49	9.15
Martinez, Dallas	R-R	6-0	174	10-28-94	0	1	15.00	1	1	0	0	3	6	8	5	1	3	3	.400	.333	.500	9.00	9.00
Mascheri, Rich	L-L	5-10	190	8-7-89	0	0	0.00	1	0	0	0	2	0	0	0	0	0	2	.000	.000	.000	9.00	9.00
Mejia, Edison	R-R	6-1	185	7-2-90	0	0	9.64	3	0	0	0	5	9	8	5	3	1	0	.429	.429	.429	0.00	1.93
Mitchell, Bryan	L-R	6-3	205	4-19-91	4	11	5.12	24	23	1	0	127	144	83	72	5	53	104	.289	.280	.293	7.39	3.77
Moreno, Diego	R-R	6-1	177	7-21-87	2	4	4.88	18	0	0	0	28	26	16	15	2	10	25	.241	.182	.267	8.13	3.25
O'Brien, Mikey	R-R	5-11	190	3-3-90	1	2	4.39	6	6	0	0	27	33	17	13	0	8	34	.300	.333	.288	11.48	2.70
Paullus, Robert	R-R	6-1	190	8-31-89	0	0	5.56	6	0	0	0	11	15	7	7	0	2	6	.300	.190	.379	4.76	1.59
Pinder, Branden	R-R	6-3	210	1-26-89	1	2	3.49	21	5	0	1	49	39	20	19	4	11	50	.225	.250	.210	9.18	2.02
Pineda, Michael	R-R	6-7	260	1-18-89	0	0	1.08	2	2	0	0	8	7	3	1	0	2	7	.206	.143	.250	7.56	2.16
Rincon, Angel	R-R	6-1	180	9-26-92	0	1	7.20	1	1	0	0	5	6	4	4	1	2	4	.286	.308	.250	7.20	3.60
Ruth, Eric	R-R	6-0	195	9-26-90	0	0	0.00	2	0	0	0	5	1	0	0	0	2	4	.059	.000	.167	6.75	3.38
Short, Charlie	R-R	6-0	220	8-13-88	4	1	2.20	25	0	0	2	45	29	14	11	2	12	59	.176	.193	.167	11.80	2.40
Smith, Alex	R-R	6-3	200	9-29-89	2	2	4.55	18	0	0	1	32	38	21	16	2	9	24	.295	.333	.274	6.82	2.56
Varce, Zach	R-R	6-0	195	12-14-88	0	0	0.00	3	0	0	1	6	5	0	0	0	5	10	.208	.364	.077	15.00	7.50
Vargas, Cesar	R-R	6-1	160	12-30-91	0	3	11.68	3	3	0	0	12	23	19	16	1	8	9	.434	.474	.412	6.57	5.84
Venditte, Pat	R-B	6-1	180	6-30-85	0	1	1.80	4	0	0	0	5	2	1	1	0	4	4	.133	.143	.125	7.20	7.20
Woods, Zach	R-R	6-0	190	11-15-87	0	1	3.60	5	0	0	0	10	6	4	4	1	6	9	.176	.294	.059	8.10	5.40
Wooten, Eric	L-L	6-3	180	3-18-90	1	0	2.45	3	0	0	0	7	6	2	2	0	2	12	.214	.308	.133	14.73	2.45

Fielding

Catcher	PCT	G	PO	A	E	DP	PB
Arcia	1.000	15	105	8	0	0	2
Blaser	.991	15	94	13	1	1	4
Farnham	.984	17	107	13	2	0	0
O'Brien	.991	12	99	10	1	1	1
Rabago	1.000	1	8	0	0	0	1
Sanchez	.990	76	630	75	7	5	11
Valera	1.000	3	25	2	0	1	1

First Base	PCT	G	PO	A	E	DP
Arcia	.978	10	82	6	2	5
Blaser	.989	11	82	6	1	4
Butler	.980	64	466	23	10	42
Fiorito	.980	6	46	2	1	4
Kuo	.968	10	89	1	3	3
Nunez	1.000	5	43	4	0	2
Sanchez	1.000	1	1	0	0	0
Snyder	.976	19	154	6	4	12
Stevenson	.980	7	47	3	1	4
Toussen	.984	9	58	4	1	4
Valera	.968	4	26	4	1	2
Wilson	1.000	1	7	0	0	1

Second Base	PCT	G	PO	A	E	DP
Angelini	1.000	3	3	9	0	0
Castillo	1.000	7	7	19	0	4
Feliz	.800	4	3	9	3	2
Gumbs	.973	24	48	59	3	14
Refsnyder	.949	95	160	212	20	47
Stevenson	1.000	1	0	1	0	0
Toussen	1.000	4	4	4	0	2

Third Base	PCT	G	PO	A	E	DP
Angelini	1.000	2	4	4	0	0
Castillo	.750	1	3	0	1	0
Feliz	.792	24	14	43	15	3
Fiorito	.900	29	18	36	6	2
Kuo	.826	10	6	13	4	3
Mustelier	1.000	1	0	1	0	0
Nix	.667	3	1	1	1	0
O'Brien	.802	38	21	52	18	4
Rodriguez	1.000	3	1	4	0	0
Stevenson	.962	10	5	20	1	4
Toussen	.959	22	16	31	2	1
Wilson	.875	3	2	5	1	1

Shortstop	PCT	G	PO	A	E	DP
Angelini	.941	25	31	80	7	17
Castillo	.970	57	76	154	7	23
Culver	.972	16	27	42	2	7
Feliz	1.000	3	2	10	0	0
Fiorito	.962	31	29	73	4	11
Nunez	1.000	3	0	4	0	0
Toussen	.821	5	9	14	5	4

Outfield	PCT	G	PO	A	E	DP
Castillo	1.000	7	19	1	0	0
Dugas	.992	54	116	5	1	3
Feliz	.800	3	3	1	1	0
Gamel	.988	93	167	2	2	0
Granderson	1.000	3	3	1	0	0
Grice	.946	34	49	4	3	1
Kuo	1.000	1	4	0	0	0
Oliberto	.952	23	38	2	2	0
Sanchez	.983	31	55	3	1	2
Sosa	.948	43	86	6	5	0
Stevenson	1.000	1	5	0	0	0
Toussen	1.000	30	41	1	0	1
Williams	.984	98	243	8	4	5

CHARLESTON (SC) RIVERDOGS   LOW CLASS A
SOUTH ATLANTIC LEAGUE

Batting	B-T	HT	WT	DOB	AVG	vLH	vRH	G	AB	R	H	2B	3B	HR	RBI	BB	HBP	SH	SF	SO	SB	CS	SLG	OBP
Afenir, Ty	R-R	6-1	185	8-26-91	.197	.188	.200	27	76	11	15	2	1	0	0	6	2	3	0	19	1	1	.250	.274
Aldrich, Daniel	L-R	6-2	210	10-5-90	.225	.158	.241	30	102	7	23	2	1	2	13	5	6	0	1	46	3	1	.324	.298
Bichette Jr., Dante	R-R	6-1	215	9-26-92	.214	.253	.204	114	435	47	93	16	1	11	61	43	6	0	2	119	1	0	.331	.292
Bird, Greg	L-R	6-3	215	11-9-92	.288	.264	.295	130	458	84	132	36	3	20	84	107	6	0	2	132	1	1	.511	.428
Butler, Saxon	L-L	6-3	225	5-11-90	.286	.500	.258	9	35	4	10	6	0	1	6	4	1	0	0	8	0	0	.543	.375
Calderon, Yeicok	L-L	6-2	185	12-23-91	.189	.227	.182	43	159	21	30	8	0	5	23	14	1	0	1	57	2	1	.333	.257
Culver, Cito	R-R	6-0	180	8-26-92	.232	.248	.227	104	410	57	95	18	2	8	29	48	0	7	1	124	13	5	.344	.312
Custodio, Claudio	R-R	5-10	155	10-30-90	.240	.333	.217	43	150	24	36	8	2	3	19	18	1	3	0	34	18	2	.380	.325
De Leon, Kelvin	R-R	6-2	180	10-29-90	.221	.182	.232	68	258	28	57	13	0	5	32	15	3	0	1	67	3	3	.329	.271
Dugas, Taylor	L-L	5-8	170	12-15-89	.250	.275	.244	58	196	32	49	8	0	1	18	32	12	1	2	24	10	4	.306	.384
Gates, Aaron	L-L	6-1	200	4-12-90	.313	.250	.333	17	64	5	20	1	1	0	5	1	1	0	0	15	0	1	.359	.333
Gumbs, Angelo	R-R	6-0	175	10-13-92	.213	.237	.203	52	202	20	43	10	3	4	26	13	1	0	2	55	10	5	.351	.261
Herrera, Roybell	R-R	5-11	177	12-30-90	.200	.000	.250	1	5	0	1	0	0	0	1	0	0	0	2	0	0	.200	.333
Kuo, Fu-Lin	R-R	6-0	185	1-7-91	.209	.227	.203	30	91	8	19	5	0	0	4	8	2	0	1	36	1	2	.264	.284

Batting	B-T	HT	WT	DOB	AVG	vLH	vRH	G	AB	R	H	2B	3B	HR	RBI	BB	HBP	SH	SF	SO	SB	CS	SLG	OBP
Leonora, Ericson	R-R	5-11	174	8-25-92	.302	.419	.269	38	139	15	42	13	1	4	16	7	2	2	2	35	2	1	.496	.340
McCoy, Nick	R-R	5-10	180	3-2-87	.118	.000	.167	22	68	5	8	2	0	0	3	8	2	1	0	18	0	0	.147	.231
Nunez, Eduardo	R-R	6-0	185	6-15-87	.400	—	.400	2	5	1	2	0	0	0	0	1	0	0	0	0	1	0	.400	.500
Nunez, Reymond	R-R	6-4	210	9-25-90	.260	.261	.259	100	366	37	95	18	2	15	62	22	10	0	4	93	1	0	.443	.316
O'Brien, Peter	R-R	6-3	215	7-15-90	.325	.273	.335	53	194	47	63	22	1	11	41	22	4	0	6	58	0	0	.619	.394
Oh, Danny	L-L	6-0	190	12-28-89	.266	.212	.285	82	259	32	69	13	0	0	12	31	13	1	0	58	10	2	.317	.373
Refsnyder, Robert	R-R	6-1	205	3-26-91	.370	.375	.370	13	54	9	20	4	1	0	6	6	2	0	0	12	7	0	.481	.452
Rodriguez, Alex	R-R	6-3	225	7-27-75	.000	—	.000	2	4	0	0	0	0	0	0	0	0	0	0	1	0	0	.000	.000
Rosario, Francisco	B-R	6-1	170	7-12-90	.106	.067	.118	25	66	5	7	0	0	0	2	13	0	0	1	26	1	2	.106	.250
Rosario, Jose	R-R	5-11	160	11-29-91	.184	.182	.185	37	114	13	21	5	0	3	10	11	4	9	1	23	5	1	.307	.277
Valera, Jackson	R-R	6-1	175	4-8-92	.300	.273	.308	29	100	9	30	3	0	2	11	9	1	0	1	11	0	1	.390	.360
Wilson, Wes	R-R	6-0	210	8-18-89	.190	.182	.192	36	121	8	23	7	0	0	8	5	2	0	0	35	0	0	.248	.234

Pitching	B-T	HT	WT	DOB	W	L	ERA	G	GS	CG	SV	IP	H	R	ER	HR	BB	SO	AVG	vLH	vRH	K/9	BB/9
Arneson, Zach	R-R	6-2	190	11-17-88	0	0	5.63	4	0	0	0	8	7	5	5	0	11	10	.259	.429	.200	11.25	12.38
Beriguete, Victor	R-R	6-1	185	11-6-88	0	1	108.00	1	0	0	0	0	3	5	4	0	2	0	.750	1.000	.500	0.00	54.00
Brebbia, John	R-R	6-1	185	5-30-90	0	2	4.14	18	0	0	1	37	40	19	17	2	4	29	.272	.229	.293	7.05	0.97
Camarena, Daniel	L-L	6-0	200	11-9-92	4	6	4.42	25	21	0	0	112	109	67	55	11	19	83	.251	.350	.228	6.67	1.53
Campos, Jose	R-R	6-4	195	7-27-92	4	2	3.41	26	19	0	2	87	82	37	33	5	16	77	.249	.262	.241	7.97	1.66
Castro, Kelvin	R-R	6-3	164	12-14-87	1	0	2.70	5	0	0	0	10	13	5	3	0	4	11	.317	.158	.455	9.90	3.60
Davis, Rookie	R-R	6-3	235	4-29-93	0	0	0.00	2	2	0	0	10	9	0	0	0	0	8	.237	.238	.235	7.20	0.00
De Paula, Rafael	R-R	6-2	212	3-24-91	6	2	2.94	13	13	0	0	64	43	21	21	3	23	96	.189	.191	.187	13.43	3.22
Encinas, Gabe	R-R	6-3	195	12-21-91	3	0	0.77	7	7	0	0	35	22	5	3	0	16	31	.177	.233	.148	7.97	4.11
Enns, Dietrich	L-L	6-1	195	5-16-91	4	1	0.61	19	1	0	1	44	23	5	3	0	14	69	.151	.152	.151	14.01	2.84
Garrison, Taylor	R-R	5-11	165	5-24-90	0	0	0.69	8	0	0	3	13	5	2	1	0	3	16	.109	.188	.067	11.08	2.08
Gerritse, Brett	R-R	6-4	220	3-4-91	8	7	3.56	30	9	0	0	101	93	47	40	2	31	108	.242	.242	.243	9.62	2.76
Niebla, Luis	R-R	6-2	180	1-4-91	5	6	4.61	18	12	0	1	80	99	51	41	9	20	60	.308	.200	.373	6.75	2.25
Paullus, Robert	R-R	6-1	190	8-31-89	6	3	2.54	32	0	0	9	60	46	20	17	2	26	60	.208	.190	.218	9.85	3.88
Pazos, James	R-L	6-3	230	5-5-91	3	1	4.05	24	0	0	1	33	27	15	15	3	8	32	.220	.192	.227	8.64	2.16
Rutckyj, Evan	R-L	6-5	213	1-31-92	10	9	5.03	25	19	0	0	118	128	76	66	10	60	102	.276	.259	.280	7.78	4.58
Severino, Luis	R-R	6-0	195	2-20-94	1	1	4.08	4	4	0	0	18	21	9	8	1	4	21	.292	.280	.298	10.70	2.04
Short, Charlie	R-R	6-0	220	8-13-88	0	1	0.71	8	0	0	1	13	8	1	1	0	3	21	.178	.000	.276	14.92	2.13
Smith, Adam	R-R	6-3	200	12-15-89	5	2	4.02	27	0	0	0	47	41	26	21	4	21	39	.240	.167	.274	7.47	4.02
Smith, Alex	R-R	6-3	200	9-29-89	3	3	1.01	20	0	0	4	36	26	6	4	0	4	38	.198	.188	.205	9.59	1.01
Vargas, Cesar	R-R	6-1	160	12-30-91	4	5	3.24	22	22	1	0	108	86	48	39	6	35	83	.216	.200	.225	6.90	2.91
Varnadore, Derek	R-R	6-3	215	7-10-90	2	7	3.77	32	3	0	2	60	59	32	25	4	19	45	.257	.295	.232	6.79	2.87
Webb, Tyler	R-L	6-6	225	7-20-90	3	1	3.86	16	0	0	2	30	24	14	13	4	6	40	.216	.207	.220	11.87	1.78
Wetherell, Phil	R-R	6-5	225	10-9-89	1	0	3.06	23	0	0	2	47	45	20	16	3	14	46	.247	.210	.267	8.81	2.68
Wooten, Eric	L-L	6-3	180	3-18-90	2	3	1.88	9	6	0	1	43	41	14	9	0	4	39	.253	.167	.283	8.16	0.84

Fielding

Catcher	PCT	G	PO	A	E	DP	PB
Herrera	.882	1	15	0	2	0	0
McCoy	.994	22	157	12	1	0	2
O'Brien	.989	53	503	46	6	6	16
Valera	.988	29	233	19	3	0	7
Wilson	.993	36	250	36	2	0	0

First Base	PCT	G	PO	A	E	DP
Bird	.987	90	768	40	11	59
Butler	.980	4	45	3	1	2
Kuo	1.000	1	0	1	0	0
Nunez	.992	45	370	25	3	21
Rosario	1.000	1	6	1	0	0

Second Base	PCT	G	PO	A	E	DP
Afenir	1.000	7	7	20	0	2
Custodio	.947	29	36	54	5	8
Gumbs	.968	51	81	129	7	26
Kuo	.906	17	28	30	6	7

	PCT	G	PO	A	E	DP	PB
Refsnyder	.898	13	19	25	5	6	
Rosario	.932	14	17	24	3	3	
Rosario	.985	16	30	35	1	12	

Third Base	PCT	G	PO	A	E	DP
Afenir	.879	14	11	18	4	1
Bichette Jr.	.941	112	64	225	18	14
Custodio	.833	2	2	3	1	0
Kuo	.875	3	2	5	1	1
Rodriguez	1.000	2	0	1	0	1
Rosario	.964	11	4	23	1	3
Rosario	1.000	1	0	1	0	0

Shortstop	PCT	G	PO	A	E	DP
Afenir	.958	7	8	15	1	1
Culver	.960	103	146	308	19	45
Custodio	.941	12	9	39	3	7
Nunez	.900	2	6	3	1	1
Rosario	1.000	1	0	1	0	0

	PCT	G	PO	A	E	DP
Rosario	.935	20	36	50	6	11

Outfield	PCT	G	PO	A	E	DP
Aldrich	.848	23	27	1	5	0
Calderon	.938	41	74	2	5	0
Cave	.992	114	241	5	2	1
Custodio	—	1	0	0	0	0
De Leon	.964	46	52	2	2	0
Dugas	.990	55	93	2	1	1
Gates	1.000	16	18	2	0	2
Gumbs	—	1	0	0	0	0
Kuo	1.000	8	6	1	0	0
Leonora	.957	38	63	4	3	1
Oh	.989	80	176	3	2	0
Rosario	—	1	0	0	0	0
Wilson	—	1	0	0	0	0

STATEN ISLAND YANKEES

SHORT-SEASON

NEW YORK-PENN LEAGUE

Batting	B-T	HT	WT	DOB	AVG	vLH	vRH	G	AB	R	H	2B	3B	HR	RBI	BB	HBP	SH	SF	SO	SB	CS	SLG	OBP
Aldrich, Daniel	L-R	6-2	210	10-5-90	.080	.000	.100	7	25	1	2	0	0	0	0	2	0	0	0	9	0	0	.080	.148
Avelino, Abiatal	R-R	5-11	186	2-14-95	.243	.158	.275	17	70	10	17	2	0	0	6	4	2	0	0	6	2	0	.271	.303
Calderon, Yeicok	L-L	6-2	185	12-23-91	.268	.324	.247	66	254	34	68	18	1	10	43	22	0	0	2	68	0	1	.465	.324
Crespo, Hector	R-R	5-10	175	8-30-91	.220	.250	.210	24	82	11	18	1	0	0	5	7	2	0	0	22	2	0	.232	.297
Ford, Mike	L-R	6-0	225	7-4-92	.235	.148	.261	33	115	19	27	7	0	3	17	20	0	0	1	23	0	0	.374	.346
Garrison, Trent	L-R	6-0	185	5-24-90	.262	.143	.293	29	103	9	27	6	0	3	13	1	3	0	1	14	0	0	.408	.287
Haddad, Radley	L-R	6-1	190	5-11-90	.267	.500	.231	5	15	2	4	0	0	0	4	4	1	0	0	3	0	0	.267	.450
Jagielo, Eric	L-R	6-2	195	5-17-92	.266	.405	.231	51	184	19	49	14	1	6	27	26	7	0	1	54	0	0	.451	.376
Jones, Bubba	L-R	6-1	205	8-20-92	.284	.291	.282	60	211	26	60	17	0	2	26	15	6	1	1	66	0	1	.393	.348
Lopez, Daniel	R-R	6-2	175	1-17-92	.209	.261	.195	36	110	19	23	4	1	1	12	21	1	1	0	33	5	1	.291	.341
Lopez, Jerison	R-R	5-11	177	8-24-91	.600	1.000	.500	2	5	1	3	0	0	0	1	0	0	0	0	1	0	0	.600	.600

	B-T	HT	WT	DOB	AVG	vLH	vRH	G	AB	R	H	2B	3B	HR	RBI	BB	HBP	SH	SF	SO	SB	CS	SLG	OBP
Murphy, John	L-R	5-11	185	4-2-91	.173	.194	.167	37	127	9	22	3	0	1	12	6	3	0	1	20	2	2	.220	.226
O'Neill, Michael	R-R	6-1	195	6-12-92	.219	.247	.208	64	256	26	56	17	1	0	14	14	9	1	1	93	9	7	.293	.282
Oliberto, Mikeson	R-R	5-10	164	8-23-90	.174	.154	.182	12	46	3	8	0	0	0	2	0	0	0	0	10	2	0	.174	.174
Orozco, Jamiel	R-R	5-11	160	1-29-93	.333	.500	.000	1	3	0	1	0	0	0	0	0	0	0	0	2	0	0	.333	.333
Rosario, Francisco	B-R	6-1	170	7-12-90	.125	.000	.167	3	8	0	1	1	0	0	2	1	0	0	0	5	0	0	.250	.222
Rosario, Jose	R-R	5-11	160	11-29-91	.268	.286	.262	30	112	15	30	6	0	0	10	6	1	2	2	24	6	1	.321	.306
Sumner, Kale	R-R	5-11	205	6-16-91	.253	.182	.279	46	166	22	42	5	0	3	16	24	5	0	2	42	0	0	.337	.360
Tejeda, Isaias	R-R	6-0	195	10-28-91	.200	.190	.204	43	145	19	29	5	0	3	13	13	5	0	1	27	0	0	.297	.287
Thomas, Brandon	B-R	6-3	180	2-7-91	.214	.180	.223	66	243	27	52	8	2	6	31	30	7	0	0	90	9	6	.337	.318
Toadvine, Derek	R-R	5-10	175	3-20-92	.237	.164	.266	57	215	23	51	7	1	0	7	23	7	0	1	53	7	6	.279	.329
Wade, Tyler	L-R	6-1	180	11-23-94	.077	.000	.083	4	13	0	1	0	0	0	1	2	0	0	0	4	0	0	.077	.200

Pitching	B-T	HT	WT	DOB	W	L	ERA	G	GS	CG	SV	IP	H	R	ER	HR	BB	SO	AVG	vLH	vRH	K/9	BB/9
Acevedo, Andury	R-R	6-4	200	8-23-90	1	0	4.50	17	0	0	0	20	18	14	10	0	18	21	.237	.259	.224	9.45	8.10
Agnew-Wieland, Sam	R-R	6-2	205	5-31-92	2	1	3.72	17	1	0	1	39	33	24	16	5	17	42	.220	.186	.242	9.78	3.96
Basford, Charles	R-R	6-2	210	7-16-90	0	0	4.50	1	0	0	0	2	4	1	1	1	0	1	.444	1.000	.286	4.50	0.00
2-team total (19 Tri-City)					3	0	2.86	20	0	0	0	28	29	11	9	2	13	27	—	—	—	8.58	4.13
Benak, Andrew	R-R	6-5	225	1-31-90	3	3	5.48	17	2	0	1	43	48	29	26	8	7	44	.281	.273	.286	9.28	1.48
Beresford, Andy	R-R	6-7	200	2-26-90	3	2	1.80	19	0	0	0	30	32	12	6	1	5	19	.274	.295	.260	5.70	1.50
Castro, Kelvin	R-R	6-3	164	12-14-87	1	2	3.42	15	0	0	2	24	24	9	9	6	7	33	.253	.333	.203	12.55	2.66
Coshow, Cale	R-R	6-5	260	7-16-92	0	2	3.76	15	4	0	0	41	36	27	17	2	22	36	.232	.245	.225	7.97	4.87
Davis, Rookie	R-R	6-3	235	4-29-93	2	4	2.36	11	11	0	0	42	46	19	11	1	13	39	.267	.306	.240	8.36	2.79
Gallegos, Giovanny	R-R	6-2	175	8-14-91	2	8	4.27	16	16	0	0	65	71	32	31	9	14	43	.278	.289	.272	5.92	1.93
Giel, Tim	R-R	6-2	220	9-29-90	1	0	0.00	1	0	0	0	2	2	0	0	0	1	1	.250	.333	.200	3.86	3.86
Haslup, Charlie	R-R	6-3	180	8-23-91	2	0	1.80	19	0	0	2	30	28	14	6	1	12	24	.255	.311	.215	7.20	3.60
Hebert, Chaz	L-L	6-2	180	9-4-92	0	0	3.00	1	1	0	0	6	5	2	2	0	0	4	.238	.444	.083	6.00	0.00
Heredia, Jairo	R-R	6-1	190	10-8-89	1	1	3.45	6	6	0	0	29	29	11	11	2	4	31	.266	.300	.246	9.73	1.26
Kendrick, Conner	L-L	6-1	185	8-18-92	1	3	4.15	13	8	0	0	43	39	22	20	3	18	27	.245	.224	.255	5.61	3.74
Lopez, Stefan	R-R	6-2	190	6-4-91	1	1	1.09	19	0	0	3	33	24	7	4	0	7	40	.198	.143	.246	10.91	1.91
McNamara, Dillon	R-R	6-5	220	10-6-91	4	3	2.19	20	1	0	0	37	23	10	9	2	17	31	.181	.209	.167	7.54	4.14
Palladino, David	R-R	6-8	235	3-15-93	3	3	4.67	15	12	0	0	54	57	32	28	4	26	49	.270	.233	.290	8.17	4.33
Pazos, James	R-L	6-3	230	5-5-91	0	0	0.00	1	0	0	0	1	1	0	0	0	1	1	.250	.000	.333	9.00	9.00
Rumbelow, Nick	R-R	6-0	190	6-12-91	2	2	2.35	19	0	0	7	23	12	13	6	1	5	20	.148	.148	.148	7.83	1.96
Smith, Caleb	R-L	6-2	175	7-28-91	1	2	1.89	13	9	0	0	48	33	15	10	0	15	52	.195	.296	.148	9.82	2.83
Taylor, Chad	R-R	6-1	180	8-29-90	1	0	0.00	1	0	0	0	3	2	0	0	0	1	3	.182	.250	.143	9.00	3.00
Walby, Philip	L-R	6-2	190	7-24-92	3	1	2.75	14	4	0	0	36	24	12	11	1	30	37	.186	.229	.160	9.25	7.50
Webb, Tyler	R-L	6-6	225	7-20-90	0	0	0.00	4	0	0	1	5	0	0	0	0	2	8	.000	.000	.000	14.40	3.60

Fielding

Catcher	PCT	G	PO	A	E	DP	PB
Garrison	.988	29	226	28	3	3	5
Haddad	1.000	5	43	8	0	1	1
Tejeda	.979	43	325	41	8	1	11

First Base	PCT	G	PO	A	E	DP
Ford	.983	18	165	7	3	10
Jones	.980	52	416	30	9	30
Sumner	1.000	7	59	5	0	3

Second Base	PCT	G	PO	A	E	DP
Crespo	.925	19	29	45	6	9
Lopez	.500	1	0	1	1	1
Murphy	.947	3	4	14	1	2
Rosario	.929	3	8	5	1	1

Toadvine	.965	54	105	142	9	25

Third Base	PCT	G	PO	A	E	DP
Calderon	1.000	1	0	2	0	0
Crespo	1.000	7	2	13	0	2
Ford	.833	4	3	7	2	0
Jagielo	.969	42	25	70	3	4
Lopez	.750	1	3	0	1	0
Rosario	1.000	3	4	4	0	0
Rosario	1.000	2	1	2	0	0
Sumner	.894	19	10	32	5	1

Shortstop	PCT	G	PO	A	E	DP
Avelino	.914	17	21	43	6	10
Murphy	.959	34	44	74	5	15

	PCT	G	PO	A	E	DP
Orozco	1.000	1	2	3	0	1
Rosario	.908	21	24	65	9	8
Toadvine	.778	2	3	4	2	0
Wade	1.000	4	4	7	0	2

Outfield	PCT	G	PO	A	E	DP
Aldrich	1.000	3	4	0	0	0
Calderon	.967	56	87	1	3	0
Lopez	.885	33	45	1	6	1
O'Neill	.970	60	122	6	4	1
Oliberto	.885	11	22	1	3	0
Sumner	1.000	4	4	0	1	0
Thomas	.992	64	125	3	1	0

GCL YANKEES1

GULF COAST LEAGUE

ROOKIE

Batting	B-T	HT	WT	DOB	AVG	vLH	vRH	G	AB	R	H	2B	3B	HR	RBI	BB	HBP	SH	SF	SO	SB	CS	SLG	OBP
Afenir, Ty	R-R	6-1	185	8-26-91	.136	.333	.063	11	22	1	3	0	0	0	3	3	1	0	5	3	0	.136	.321
Aparicio, Jesus	R-R	5-11	186	8-18-94	.200	.286	.167	10	25	3	5	0	1	0	1	5	1	0	0	7	0	0	.280	.355
Aune, Austin	L-R	6-2	190	9-6-93	.192	.186	.195	41	156	13	30	9	1	0	12	8	0	0	1	72	0	2	.263	.230
Avelino, Abiatal	R-R	5-11	186	2-14-95	.259	.176	.293	17	58	14	15	2	1	0	4	7	1	1	0	7	9	3	.328	.348
2-team total (17 Yankees2)					.336	—	—	38	125	35	43	7	5	0	17	16	3	1	0	11	26	4	.469	.422
Barnes, Jordan	R-R	5-11	180	6-19-94	.200	.244	.183	48	150	13	30	2	0	0	9	14	3	2	0	30	7	5	.213	.281
Breen, Chris	R-R	6-3	215	3-26-94	.214	.189	.223	53	201	31	43	10	3	5	34	19	4	0	2	56	3	0	.368	.292
Brito, Sandy	R-R	6-3	170	6-9-93	.133	.038	.184	22	75	7	10	5	0	1	3	7	0	2	0	30	2	0	.240	.207
2-team total (18 Yankees2)					.161	—	—	40	124	17	20	6	1	2	6	17	0	2	0	54	4	0	.274	.262
Cornelius, Kevin	R-R	6-1	178	8-28-92	.274	.261	.279	24	84	9	23	8	0	0	6	7	0	1	1	17	1	0	.369	.326
2-team total (3 Yankees2)					.269	—	—	27	93	12	25	10	0	0	6	9	0	1	1	19	1	0	.376	.330
Cuevas, Bryan	R-R	5-10	179	10-14-93	.240	.136	.269	26	100	16	24	4	1	2	13	9	0	1	2	20	4	0	.360	.297
2-team total (21 Yankees2)					.269	—	—	47	186	33	50	7	3	3	17	15	1	1	2	42	6	3	.387	.324
Custodio, Claudio	R-R	5-10	155	10-30-90	.000	—	.000	1	3	1	0	0	0	0	0	0	0	0	0	1	0	0	.000	.000
2-team total (1 Yankees2)					.000	—	—	2	6	2	0	0	0	0	0	0	0	1	0	1	0	0	.000	.143
de Oleo, Eduardo	R-R	5-10	180	1-25-93	.283	.184	.320	37	138	15	39	10	1	3	26	10	4	0	0	25	1	1	.435	.349
Duran, Matt	R-R	6-1	205	5-1-93	.200	.111	.273	6	20	0	4	0	0	0	4	2	0	0	1	6	0	0	.200	.261

BaseballAmerica.com

Name	B-T	HT	WT	DOB	AVG	vLH	vRH	G	AB	R	H	2B	3B	HR	RBI	BB	HBP	SH	SF	SO	SB	CS	OBP	SLG
Falla, Jimmy	R-R	6-2	230	9-19-90	.215	.194	.222	35	121	16	26	7	0	0	17	10	3	0	1	32	0	1	.273	.289
Fowler, Dustin	L-L	6-0	185	12-29-94	.241	.250	.239	30	112	8	27	8	4	0	9	4	1	0	0	23	3	1	.384	.274
Garcia, Adonis	R-R	5-9	190	4-12-85	.111	.167	.000	3	9	1	1	0	0	1	1	0	0	0	0	3	0	0	.444	.111
2-team total (3 Yankees2)					.278	—	—	6	18	1	5	0	0	1	2	0	0	1		3	0	0	.444	.263
Haddad, Radley	L-R	6-1	190	5-11-90	.118	.000	.143	13	34	3	4	0	0	0	1	6	0	0	0	13	0	0	.118	.250
Jagielo, Eric	L-R	6-2	195	5-17-92	.000	.000	.000	1	2	1	0	0	0	0	0	0	1	0	0	0	0	0	.000	.333
2-team total (3 Yankees2)					.222	—	—	4	9	3	2	0	0	0	1	1	0	0		2	0	0	.444	.364
Katoh, Gosuke	L-R	6-2	180	10-8-94	.310	.315	.308	50	184	28	57	11	5	6	25	27	2	1	1	44	4	2	.522	.402
Leonora, Ericson	R-R	5-11	174	8-25-92	.235	.500	.091	6	17	2	4	1	0	0	3	2	0	0	0	8	1	0	.294	.316
Lopez, Jerison	R-R	5-11	177	8-24-91	.154	.000	.250	4	13	2	2	1	0	0	1	0	0	0	0	1	2	0	.231	.154
2-team total (3 Yankees2)					.182	—	—	7	22	3	4	2	0	0	1	0	0	0	0	2	3	0	.273	.182
Lopez, Jose	R-R	5-10	178	8-13-91	.114	.000	.161	19	44	0	5	0	0	0	4	4	0	0	1	5	0	0	.114	.184
Martini, Renzo	R-R	6-1	190	8-25-92	.224	.238	.221	28	98	11	22	5	0	2	13	9	2	0	1	17	0	0	.337	.300
2-team total (25 Yankees2)					.267	—	—	53	191	24	51	14	0	3	24	17	3	0	3	32	1	1	.387	.332
Moronta, Eladio	R-R	5-11	175	12-16-88	.207	.133	.233	24	58	5	12	3	0	0	6	6	1	0	1	22	1	2	.259	.288
Mustelier, Ronnier	R-R	5-10	210	8-8-84	.308	.000	.400	4	13	3	4	1	0	0	2	1	0	0	0	2	1	0	.385	.357
2-team total (1 Yankees2)					.313	—	—	5	16	4	5	1	0	0	2	1	0	0	0	3	1	0	.375	.353
Nix, Jayson	R-R	5-11	195	8-26-82	.000	.000	.000	1	2	0	0	0	0	0	0	0	0	1	0	0	1	0	0	.000	.333
Snyder, Matt	L-R	6-5	200	6-17-90	.500	.250	.750	2	8	0	4	0	0	0	2	0	0	0	0	0	0	0	.500	.500
2-team total (5 Yankees2)					.250	—	—	7	24	0	6	0	0	0	3	2	0	0	0	1	0	0	.250	.308
Tamarez, Christopher	R-R	6-2	170	10-25-93	.235	.217	.241	33	102	12	24	7	0	0	11	6	2	3	1	24	0	1	.304	.288
Wade, Tyler	L-R	6-1	180	11-23-94	.309	.282	.317	46	162	37	50	10	0	0	12	32	2	2	0	42	11	1	.370	.429

Pitching	B-T	HT	WT	DOB	W	L	ERA	G	GS	CG	SV	IP	H	R	ER	HR	BB	SO	AVG	vLH	vRH	K/9	BB/9
Aquino, Daury	R-R	6-1	179	4-4-91	3	4	5.55	18	1	0	0	36	49	28	22	2	14	25	.333	.353	.323	6.31	3.53
Bautista, Rony	L-L	6-7	200	9-17-91	0	0	4.05	4	4	0	0	13	12	6	6	1	10	18	.235	.133	.278	12.15	6.75
2-team total (6 Yankees2)					1	1	2.52	10	6	0	0	36	24	12	10	1	22	48	—	—		12.11	5.55
Bello, Hector	L-L	6-1	175	5-19-91	1	0	3.62	14	0	0	0	27	24	18	11	0	12	27	.240	.040	.307	8.89	3.95
Beriguete, Victor	R-R	6-1	185	11-6-88	1	1	1.95	21	0	0	11	28	20	8	6	1	9	32	.198	.257	.167	10.41	2.93
Canela, Erick	R-R	6-1	155	10-2-90	4	1	3.23	11	9	0	0	47	45	19	17	1	13	35	.253	.229	.274	6.65	2.47
Checo, Mariel	R-R	6-3	190	10-16-89	0	1	3.86	17	0	0	0	28	26	16	12	1	14	40	.234	.302	.191	12.86	4.50
Clarkin, Ian	L-L	6-2	186	2-14-95	0	2	10.80	3	3	0	0	5	5	6	6	2	4	4	.263	.429	.167	7.20	7.20
Cortes, Nestor	R-L	5-11	190	12-10-94	0	1	4.42	10	3	0	1	18	22	9	9	0	5	20	.293	.350	.273	9.82	2.45
Diaz, Jose	R-L	6-1	178	9-1-94	0	2	9.82	9	0	0	0	11	11	13	12	1	14	12	.262	.200	.281	9.82	11.45
2-team total (1 Yankees2)					0	2	9.00	10	1	0	0	12	12	13	12	1	14	14	—	—		10.50	10.50
Flight, Tim	L-L	6-4	195	12-27-90	2	2	3.22	13	0	0	0	22	16	12	8	1	14	33	.195	.143	.213	13.30	5.64
Garcia, Samuel	R-R	6-0	180	3-4-93	1	2	3.66	11	0	0	0	20	16	8	8	1	8	25	.216	.303	.146	11.44	3.66
2-team total (4 Yankees2)					1	3	3.12	15	0	0	0	26	20	11	9	1	9	37	—	—		12.81	3.12
Hebert, Chaz	L-L	6-2	180	9-4-92	4	5	5.60	18	0	0	0	45	62	33	28	1	18	47	.343	.321	.352	9.40	3.60
Joseph, Francis	R-R	5-10	165	10-4-93	1	5	4.18	16	0	0	0	28	34	17	13	2	4	29	.306	.395	.260	9.32	1.29
Lail, Brady	R-R	6-2	175	8-9-93	4	1	2.33	12	11	0	0	54	39	15	14	0	5	51	.200	.198	.202	8.50	0.83
Luis, Omar	L-L	6-2	210	10-13-92	0	1	27.00	1	1	0	0	2	3	5	5	0	2	1	.375	.500	.333	5.40	10.80
2-team total (10 Yankees2)					0	2	5.68	11	11	0	0	32	30	25	20	0	29	43	—	—		12.22	8.24
Martinez, Dallas	R-R	6-0	174	10-28-94	0	1	7.04	4	4	0	0	15	24	12	12	1	3	11	.369	.321	.405	6.46	1.76
2-team total (6 Yankees2)					1	1	4.03	10	6	0	0	29	33	14	13	1	5	22	—	—		6.83	1.55
Mejia, Edison	R-R	6-1	185	7-2-90	1	1	4.50	2	0	0	0	2	1	1	1	0	1	1	.500	.600	.333	4.50	0.00
2-team total (6 Yankees2)					3	1	0.75	8	0	0	0	12	10	1	1	0	1	10	—	—		7.50	0.75
Montgomery, Mark	R-R	5-11	205	8-30-90	0	0	5.40	2	2	0	0	3	4	2	2	0	0	8	.286	.333	.250	21.60	0.00
2-team total (2 Yankees2)					0	0	3.38	4	4	0	0	5	5	2	2	0	0	10	—	—		16.88	0.00
Morton, Taylor	R-R	6-3	194	12-18-91	0	0	4.50	3	0	0	0	4	4	2	2	0	2	1	.250	.000	.308	2.25	4.50
Rodriguez, Wilton	R-R	6-3	195	11-6-90	0	0	16.20	2	1	0	0	2	3	3	3	0	1	1	.375	.000	.600	5.40	5.40
2-team total (3 Yankees2)					0	1	16.20	5	4	0	0	3	4	6	6	0	5	2	—	—		5.40	13.50
Ruth, Eric	R-R	6-0	195	9-26-90	1	0	0.75	16	0	0	5	24	19	4	2	0	4	40	.213	.300	.169	15.00	1.50
Severino, Luis	R-R	6-0	195	2-20-94	3	1	1.37	6	4	0	0	26	16	5	4	0	6	32	.172	.208	.159	10.94	2.05
Sharp, Hayden	R-R	6-6	195	10-30-92	1	0	4.18	6	4	0	0	28	27	14	13	3	9	18	.250	.318	.203	5.79	2.89
Taylor, Chad	R-R	6-1	180	8-29-90	1	0	1.77	13	1	0	0	20	14	5	4	0	8	17	.194	.120	.234	7.52	3.54
2-team total (4 Yankees2)					2	2	1.32	17	1	0	0	27	21	7	4	0	8	23	—	—		7.57	2.63
Venditte, Pat	R-B	6-1	180	6-30-85	0	1	4.50	5	4	0	0	6	9	5	3	0	1	5	.346	.444	.294	7.50	1.50
2-team total (4 Yankees2)					0	1	3.65	9	6	0	0	12	12	7	5	0	1	13	—	—		9.49	0.73
Woods, Zach	R-R	6-0	190	11-15-87	0	0	0.00	6	0	0	0	10	8	0	0	0	1	17	.211	.182	.222	14.81	0.87

Fielding

Catcher	PCT	G	PO	A	E	DP	PB
Aparicio	.971	10	61	5	2	0	1
de Oleo	.987	32	256	37	4	2	7
Haddad	.988	11	76	4	1	1	1
Lopez	.994	19	139	14	1	0	2

First Base	PCT	G	PO	A	E	DP
Breen	.976	32	265	20	7	21
Falla	.962	14	96	5	4	11
Martini	1.000	17	141	15	0	8
Snyder	1.000	1	3	0	0	0

Second Base	PCT	G	PO	A	E	DP
Afenir	.967	7	12	17	1	6
Cornelius	.833	1	2	3	1	3
Cuevas	.969	13	28	34	2	7
Katoh	.977	42	82	90	4	19

Third Base	PCT	G	PO	A	E	DP
Cornelius	.915	23	15	50	6	5
Duran	.917	4	1	10	1	2
Falla	1.000	1	0	3	0	0
Jagielo	1.000	1	1	1	0	0
Martini	.750	6	2	4	2	0
Nix	—	1	0	0	0	0
Tamarez	.968	32	16	44	2	3

Shortstop	PCT	G	PO	A	E	DP
Afenir	1.000	5	4	9	0	0
Avelino	.861	12	8	23	5	5
Cornelius	.500	1	0	1	1	0
Cuevas	.842	7	6	10	3	3
Custodio	1.000	1	1	3	0	2
Lopez	.765	4	8	5	4	1
Martini	—	1	0	0	0	0
Wade	.953	39	40	102	7	17

Outfield	PCT	G	PO	A	E	DP
Aune	.903	39	53	3	6	0
Barnes	.960	48	92	4	4	2

Breen	1.000	13	13	0	0	0	Fowler	.969	27	29	2 1 0	Moronta	.968	24	30	0 1 0
Brito	.931	21	27	0	2	0	Garcia	1.000	2	1	1 0 0	Mustelier	.750	4	4	2 2 0
Falla	.944	16	34	0	2	0	Leonora	1.000	5	4	0 0 0				

GCL YANKEES2   ROOKIE
GULF COAST LEAGUE

Batting	B-T	HT	WT	DOB	AVG	vLH	vRH	G	AB	R	H	2B	3B	HR	RBI	BB	HBP	SH	SF	SO	SB	CS	SLG	OBP
Agramonte, Wilson	L-L	6-3	180	11-10-94	.132	.083	.154	16	38	7	5	1	0	0	3	9	0	0	0	11	1	1	.158	.298
Alcantara, Jorge	R-R	6-1	195	8-9-91	.215	.189	.224	47	135	20	29	14	0	2	28	22	2	1	2	38	15	5	.363	.329
Aldrich, Daniel	L-R	6-2	210	10-5-90	.250	.000	.500	2	8	0	2	1	0	0	0	0	1	0	0	2	0	0	.375	.333
Anderson, Jake	L-R	6-0	170	12-3-91	.236	.222	.243	20	55	10	13	4	0	0	9	6	0	1	2	21	3	3	.309	.302
Andujar, Miguel	R-R	6-0	175	3-2-95	.323	.333	.319	34	133	18	43	11	0	4	25	7	3	0	1	21	4	1	.496	.368
Austin, Tyler	R-R	6-1	220	9-6-91	.667		.667	2	6	1	4	0	0	0	0	1	0	0	0	0	0	0	.667	.714
Avelino, Abiatal	R-R	5-11	186	2-14-95	.400	.560	.311	17	70	21	28	5	4	0	13	9	2	0	0	4	17	1	.586	.481
2-team total (17 Yankees1)					.336	—		34	128	35	43	7	5	0	17	16	3	1	0	11	26	4	.469	.422
Bridges, Drew	L-R	6-4	230	2-3-95	.153	.087	.184	22	72	9	11	1	1	1	9	11	1	0	1	24	1	0	.236	.271
Brito, Sandy	R-R	6-3	170	6-9-93	.204	.308	.167	18	49	10	10	1	1	1	3	10	0	0	0	24	2	0	.327	.339
2-team total (22 Yankees1)					.161	—		40	124	17	20	6	1	2	6	17	0	2	0	54	4	0	.274	.262
Coleman, Kendall	L-L	6-4	190	5-22-95	.143	.000	.182	10	28	1	4	1	0	0	2	0	0	0	0	11	0	0	.179	.200
Cornelius, Kevin	R-R	6-1	178	8-28-92	.222	—	.222	3	9	3	2	2	0	0	2	0	0	0	0	2	0	0	.444	.364
2-team total (24 Yankees1)					.269	—		27	93	12	25	10	0	0	6	9	0	1	1	19	1	0	.376	.330
Cuevas, Bryan	R-R	5-10	179	10-14-93	.302	.227	.328	21	86	17	26	3	2	1	4	6	1	0	0	22	2	3	.419	.355
2-team total (26 Yankees1)					.269	—		47	186	33	50	7	3	3	17	15	1	1	2	42	6	3	.387	.324
Custodio, Claudio	R-R	5-10	155	10-30-90	.000	—	.000	1	3	1	0	0	0	0	0	0	1	0	0	0	0	0	.000	.250
2-team total (1 Yankees1)					.000	—		2	6	2	0	0	0	0	0	0	1	0	0	1	0	0	.000	.143
Estrada, Thairo	R-R	5-10	154	2-22-96	.278	.400	.237	50	176	28	49	11	5	2	17	12	8	2	1	30	7	5	.432	.350
Figueroa, Jose	L-R	5-10	170	12-9-92	.252	.286	.233	51	159	25	40	5	2	1	17	23	1	2	3	31	13	3	.327	.344
Garcia, Adonis	R-R	5-9	190	4-12-85	.444	.333	.500	3	9	0	4	0	0	0	1	0	0	0	1	0	0	0	.444	.400
2-team total (3 Yankees1)					.278	—		6	18	1	5	0	0	1	2	0	0	0	1	3	0	0	.444	.263
Herrera, Roybell	R-R	5-11	177	12-30-90	.189	.273	.154	24	37	4	7	4	0	1	5	3	1	0	1	11	0	0	.378	.262
Jagielo, Eric	L-R	6-2	195	5-17-92	.286	.250	.333	3	7	2	2	2	0	0	0	1	0	0	0	2	0	0	.571	.375
2-team total (1 Yankees1)					.222	—		4	9	3	2	2	0	0	0	1	1	0	0	2	0	0	.444	.364
Javier, Jose	R-R	5-10	160	9-16-92	.247	.250	.246	45	158	22	39	10	3	2	21	10	0	3	4	29	11	1	.386	.285
Lopez, Jerison	R-R	5-11	177	8-24-91	.222	.000	.333	3	9	1	2	1	0	0	0	0	0	0	0	1	1	0	.333	.222
2-team total (4 Yankees1)					.182	—		7	22	3	4	2	0	0	1	0	0	0	0	2	3	0	.273	.182
Martini, Renzo	R-R	6-1	190	8-25-92	.312	.440	.265	29	93	13	29	9	0	1	18	8	1	0	2	15	1	1	.441	.365
2-team total (28 Yankees1)					.267	—		53	191	24	51	14	0	3	24	17	3	0	3	32	1	1	.387	.332
Mikolas, Nathan	L-L	6-0	200	12-30-93	.256	.275	.250	56	195	27	50	12	1	5	35	25	7	0	4	50	6	2	.405	.355
Mustelier, Ronnier	R-R	5-10	210	8-8-84	.333	.000	.333	1	3	1	1	0	0	0	0	0	0	0	0	1	0	0	.333	.333
2-team total (4 Yankees1)					.313	—		5	16	4	5	1	0	0	2	1	0	0	0	3	1	0	.375	.353
Noriega, Alvaro	R-R	6-0	198	11-9-94	.295	.381	.270	33	95	8	28	6	0	1	16	4	3	0	2	13	1	0	.389	.337
Smith, Dalton	R-R	6-3	205	6-29-94	.169	.182	.164	26	83	12	14	3	0	1	5	4	1	0	1	23	0	1	.241	.213
Snyder, Matt	L-R	6-5	200	6-17-90	.125	.125	.125	5	16	0	2	0	0	0	1	2	0	0	0	1	0	0	.125	.222
2-team total (2 Yankees1)					.250	—		7	24	0	6	0	0	0	3	2	0	0	0	1	0	0	.250	.308
Steiger, Brady	L-R	6-1	195	12-28-90	.233	.100	.260	18	60	8	14	4	0	0	5	14	4	0	0	9	1	2	.300	.410
Torrens, Luis	R-R	6-0	171	5-2-96	.241	.222	.250	48	174	17	42	7	0	1	14	27	2	0	1	40	2	0	.299	.348

Pitching	B-T	HT	WT	DOB	W	L	ERA	G	GS	CG	SV	IP	H	R	ER	HR	BB	SO	AVG	vLH	vRH	K/9	BB/9
Acuna, Joaquin	R-R	6-2	185	3-7-91	3	0	3.25	14	1	0	0	28	29	13	10	0	12	13	.266	.318	.231	4.23	3.90
Agramonte, Kenedy	R-R	5-10	150	12-4-90	6	0	0.71	16	0	0	0	25	9	3	2	0	12	31	.114	.192	.075	11.01	4.26
Bautista, Rony	L-L	6-7	200	9-17-91	1	1	1.61	6	2	0	0	22	12	6	4	0	12	30	.145	.227	.115	12.09	4.84
2-team total (4 Yankees1)					1	1	2.52	10	6	0	0	36	24	12	10	1	22	48	—	—	—	12.11	5.55
Bello, Yoely	L-L	6-2	150	12-16-90	0	2	6.29	16	0	0	1	24	24	20	17	0	16	29	.245	.091	.323	10.73	5.92
Carnes, Ethan	L-L	6-3	205	12-30-91	1	0	3.86	9	0	0	0	16	18	7	7	0	7	16	.273	.125	.320	8.82	3.86
Cote, Jordan	R-R	6-5	215	11-13-92	0	1	0.96	9	5	0	0	28	18	7	3	1	5	20	.182	.289	.115	6.43	1.61
Dawe, Dayton	R-R	6-2	175	4-13-94	0	1	11.81	13	0	0	0	16	17	26	21	2	22	19	.274	.333	.237	10.69	12.38
Diaz, Jose	R-L	6-1	178	9-1-94	0	0	0.00	1	1	0	0	1	1	0	0	0	2	.333	.000	1.000	10.50	10.50
2-team total (9 Yankees1)					0	2	9.00	10	1	0	0	12	12	13	12	1	14	14	—	—	—	10.50	10.50
Garcia, Samuel	R-R	6-0	180	3-4-93	0	1	1.42	4	0	0	0	6	4	3	1	0	1	12	.160	.111	.188	17.05	1.42
2-team total (11 Yankees1)					1	3	3.12	15	0	0	0	26	20	11	9	3	9	37	—	—	—	12.81	3.12
Giel, Tim	R-R	6-2	220	9-29-90	0	2	2.18	15	0	0	2	21	25	14	5	1	4	20	.284	.231	.327	8.71	1.74
Gonzalez, Felipe	R-R	6-2	165	8-15-91	4	1	2.23	11	5	0	1	48	40	17	12	1	17	45	.225	.194	.243	8.38	3.17
Herndon, David	R-R	6-5	200	9-4-85	0	0	3.86	3	2	0	0	5	6	2	2	0	4	.316	.500	.182	7.71	0.00
Long, Jaron	R-R	6-0	185	8-28-91	1	0	0.00	4	0	0	0	7	4	1	0	0	1	7	.182	.375	.071	9.45	1.35
Luis, Omar	L-L	6-0	210	10-13-92	0	1	4.50	10	10	0	0	30	27	20	15	0	27	42	.227	.143	.245	12.60	8.10
2-team total (1 Yankees1)					0	2	5.68	11	11	0	0	32	30	25	20	0	29	43	—	—	—	12.22	8.24
Maher, Joey	R-R	6-5	200	8-5-92	5	3	1.91	12	10	0	0	57	37	16	12	1	17	28	.188	.221	.162	4.45	2.70
Martinez, Dallas	R-R	6-0	174	10-28-94	1	0	0.66	6	2	0	0	14	9	2	1	0	2	11	.184	.353	.094	7.24	1.32
2-team total (4 Yankees1)					1	1	4.03	10	6	0	0	29	33	14	13	1	5	22	—	—	—	6.83	1.55
Mascheri, Rich	L-L	5-10	190	8-7-89	3	1	1.27	11	0	0	1	21	8	4	3	0	9	32	.116	.400	.037	13.50	3.80
Matos, Juan	R-R	6-2	190	10-6-93	1	4	4.50	4	1	0	0	10	15	6	5	0	2	6	.375	.278	.455	5.40	1.80
Mejia, Edison	R-R	6-1	185	7-2-90	2	0	0.00	6	0	0	0	10	6	0	0	0	1	9	.176	.231	.143	8.10	0.90
2-team total (2 Yankees1)					3	1	0.75	8	0	0	0	12	11	1	1	0	1	10	—	—	—	7.50	0.75
Montgomery, Mark	R-R	5-11	205	8-30-90	0	0	0.00	2	2	0	0	2	1	0	0	0	0	2	.143	.000	.200	9.00	0.00

2-team total (2 Yankees1)				0	0	3.38	4	4	0	0	5	5	2	2	0	0	10	—	—	—	16.88	0.00
Pena, Jose	R-R	6-0	190	3-22-91	1	1	4.01	21	0	0	10	25	22	11	11	0	9	36	.244	.289	.212	13.14	3.28
Perez, Elvin	R-R	6-4	193	8-3-90	4	2	3.91	12	7	0	0	51	53	29	22	4	5	42	.260	.245	.273	7.46	0.89
Polanco, Alex	R-R	6-4	230	5-8-94	1	0	0.00	4	0	0	0	3	1	2	0	0	4	3	.077	.000	.111	8.10	10.80
Rincon, Angel	R-R	6-1	180	9-26-92	1	3	2.77	10	7	0	0	39	33	15	12	0	11	24	.224	.284	.175	5.54	2.54
Rodriguez, Wilton	R-R	6-3	195	11-6-90	1	1	16.20	3	3	0	0	2	1	3	3	0	4	1	.167	.200	.000	5.40	21.60
2-team total (2 Yankees1)				0	1	16.20	5	4	0	0	3	4	6	6	0	5	2	—	—	—	5.40	13.50
Taylor, Chad	R-R	6-1	180	8-29-90	1	2	0.00	4	0	0	0	7	7	2	0	0	0	6	.259	.400	.176	7.71	0.00
2-team total (13 Yankees1)				2	2	1.32	17	1	0	0	27	21	7	4	0	8	23	—	—	—	7.57	2.63
Venditte, Pat	R-B	6-1	180	6-30-85	0	0	2.84	4	2	0	0	6	3	2	2	0	0	8	.136	.167	.125	11.37	0.00
2-team total (5 Yankees1)				0	1	3.65	9	6	0	0	12	12	7	5	0	1	13	—	—	—	9.49	0.73

Fielding

Catcher	PCT	G	PO	A	E	DP	PB
Herrera	1.000	21	69	10	0	1	2
Noriega	.981	29	184	19	4	1	3
Torrens	.993	32	236	41	2	2	13

First Base	PCT	G	PO	A	E	DP
Alcantara	1.000	4	32	0	0	6
Bridges	1.000	7	63	2	0	5
Herrera	.955	3	21	0	1	2
Javier	1.000	1	10	1	0	1
Martini	.980	10	96	2	2	3
Smith	.982	22	157	3	3	11
Snyder	.969	4	30	1	1	2
Steiger	.992	15	114	4	1	10

Second Base	PCT	G	PO	A	E	DP
Anderson	.930	10	12	28	3	2
Cornelius	1.000	2	1	5	0	2
Cuevas	.946	13	25	28	3	8

	PCT	G	PO	A	E	DP
Estrada	.975	9	19	20	1	5
Javier	.935	29	43	57	7	11
Lopez	.889	2	4	4	1	2
Steiger	1.000	1	1	5	0	1

Third Base	PCT	G	PO	A	E	DP
Anderson	.750	6	0	6	2	0
Andujar	.869	26	16	57	11	2
Bridges	.882	10	4	11	2	2
Cornelius	.800	1	1	3	1	0
Jagielo	1.000	3	1	3	0	0
Javier	.714	6	1	7	8	0
Martini	.907	16	7	32	4	1
Mustelier	—	1	0	0	0	0
Smith	1.000	2	0	5	0	0

Shortstop	PCT	G	PO	A	E	DP
Avelino	.947	15	26	45	4	8
Cornelius	1.000	1	1	0	0	0

	PCT	G	PO	A	E	DP
Cuevas	.923	3	5	7	1	1
Custodio	1.000	1	0	2	0	0
Estrada	.942	40	59	103	10	21
Javier	.778	4	4	3	2	1
Lopez	1.000	1	1	1	0	0

Outfield	PCT	G	PO	A	E	DP
Agramonte	.955	15	21	0	1	0
Alcantara	.952	43	57	2	3	1
Aldrich	1.000	2	4	0	0	0
Austin	1.000	2	3	1	0	0
Brito	.970	18	32	0	1	0
Coleman	.923	10	11	1	1	1
Figueroa	.989	51	88	1	1	0
Garcia	1.000	3	3	0	0	0
Mikolas	.964	52	78	2	3	0

DSL YANKEES
ROOKIE

DOMINICAN SUMMER LEAGUE

Batting	B-T	HT	WT	DOB	AVG	vLH	vRH	G	AB	R	H	2B	3B	HR	RBI	BB	HBP	SH	SF	SO	SB	CS	SLG	OBP
Aguilar, Angel	R-R	6-0	170	6-13-95	.262	.229	.268	62	229	35	60	18	3	3	37	17	7	2	5	44	2	1	.406	.326
Aparicio, Jesus	R-R	5-11	186	8-18-94	.208	.083	.244	17	53	10	11	3	0	2	7	9	4	1	0	18	0	0	.377	.364
Aquino, Melvin	R-R	5-11	160	7-14-92	.313	.281	.321	48	163	24	51	15	4	2	28	13	6	0	3	41	18	3	.491	.378
Asencio, Hector	R-R	6-0	170	2-22-94	.234	.217	.241	34	77	16	18	2	1	1	10	7	0	1	1	30	4	0	.325	.294
Barrios, Daniel	R-R	5-11	183	4-18-95	.234	.231	.235	49	145	18	34	2	0	3	13	23	1	0	5	42	2	0	.310	.333
Cedeno, Oliver	R-R	5-10	165	5-24-96	.164	.2	.154	42	116	17	19	2	0	0	7	22	2	1	1	27	1	0	.181	.305
Chevalier, Ignacio	R-R	6-1	190	1-10-94	.091	.167	.063	9	22	5	2	0	0	0	3	3	0	0	0	7	0	0	.091	.286
Coa, Rainiero	R-R	5-10	170	1-3-93	.203	0	.255	30	69	11	14	2	0	1	12	11	1	2	2	11	1	2	.275	.313
Corredera, Yeison	R-R	5-11	175	1-30-94	.188	.25	.175	21	48	11	9	3	1	0	5	10	2	1	0	10	3	0	.292	.35
Davis, Eduardo	R-R	6-0	190	11-10-93	.213	.214	.212	18	47	4	10	3	0	0	4	3	2	0	0	11	0	2	.277	.288
De la Rosa, Jenso	R-R	6-1	170	5-22-95	.097	.133	.085	27	62	6	6	1	0	0	3	9	2	1	0	26	0	2	.113	.233
Encarnacion, Greidy	L-L	5-11	156	4-1-94	.187	.125	.198	41	107	10	20	6	1	0	8	15	0	0	1	31	1	5	.262	.285
Frias, Frank	R-R	6-2	185	3-29-94	.305	.29	.308	55	203	44	62	8	3	4	26	38	8	0	0	57	26	10	.433	.434
Gil, Miguel	R-R	6-2	170	3-9-96	.071	0	.111	8	14	0	1	0	0	0	1	3	0	0	1	7	0	0	.071	.222
Gomez, Jhoan	R-R	6-0	175	2-14-93	.215	.211	.216	34	93	14	20	3	0	0	9	12	1	1	1	22	5	2	.247	.308
Guzman, Tirson	B-R	6-2	165	6-3-94	.231	.207	.238	43	134	17	31	7	3	1	12	20	2	1	0	35	7	6	.351	.34
Lorenzo, Juan	R-R	6-0	180	6-7-93	.277	.333	.264	52	173	26	48	6	2	2	22	13	7	0	0	30	10	6	.37	.352
Martinez, Miguel	R-R	6-2	190	9-14-94	.166	.182	.161	48	145	19	24	5	0	1	11	17	13	1	0	54	13	3	.221	.309
Mateo, Jorge	R-R	6-0	188	6-23-95	.287	.163	.312	64	258	50	74	9	6	7	26	34	5	0	2	52	49	10	.45	.378
Mojica, Miguel	R-R	6-2	180	8-23-92	.333	.429	.313	35	117	21	39	8	4	1	23	17	3	0	2	14	3	2	.496	.424
Munoz, Barfil	R-R	6-1	207	5-21-94	.188	.125	.195	44	144	14	27	8	1	3	21	22	1	0	3	58	2	3	.319	.294
Munoz, Miguel	R-R	6-2	170	12-27-92	.201	.167	.207	47	169	16	34	7	1	6	19	10	2	0	3	51	1	1	.361	.25
Palma, Alexander	R-R	6-0	201	10-18-95	.287	.167	.304	37	143	15	41	6	0	2	16	7	1	0	0	15	4	1	.371	.325
Perez, Bolivar	R-R	5-9	190	3-21-93	.326	—	—	16	43	5	14	3	0	0	5	5	0	0	0	5	1	1	.395	.396
Ramirez, Alan	R-R	6-1	185	2-15-94	.167	.192	.161	47	144	15	24	3	1	2	12	11	4	0	0	42	2	1	.243	.245
Rey, Victor	R-R	6-2	178	6-29-95	.194	.25	.183	62	222	16	43	3	1	1	23	13	2	2	5	55	0	0	.23	.24
Reyes, Allison	R-R	6-2	165	9-16-92	.24	.162	.26	50	183	32	44	8	3	2	17	20	6	3	1	34	10	12	.35	.333
Reyes, Brian	R-R	6-0	190	6-28-95	.246	—	—	54	175	28	43	9	0	5	27	25	6	1	1	50	1	2	.383	.357
Rodriguez, Wascar	R-R	6-2	198	10-14-94	.165	.091	.182	39	121	9	20	5	0	2	7	11	1	1	2	51	0	2	.256	.237
Romero, Wilmer	R-R	6-1	185	12-19-93	.227	.167	.238	43	154	28	35	7	0	6	28	23	5	0	0	31	2	2	.39	.346
Silva, Adam	R-R	6-2	202	3-27-94	.357	.2	.444	5	14	3	5	1	0	0	1	0	1	0	0	2	1	0	.429	.4
Taveras, Oscar	R-R	5-11	180	9-13-92	.294	.5	.231	28	68	13	20	1	1	2	10	12	3	0	0	24	6	3	.426	.422
Urena, Pedro	R-R	6-3	195	10-16-93	.237	.286	.225	61	215	33	51	6	0	6	39	33	3	0	4	63	0	1	.349	.341
Valera, Junior	R-R	6-0	180	9-27-92	.318	.25	.333	48	179	35	57	10	7	0	15	25	3	1	0	25	24	5	.453	.411
Valerio, Allen	R-R	6-1	173	1-11-93	.279	.226	.287	68	226	49	63	14	3	8	46	48	5	2	7	46	9	5	.473	.406
Ventura, Darwin	R-R	6-0	195	12-21-92	.19	.125	.2	41	121	8	23	7	0	0	9	9	5	1	0	22	0	1	.248	.274

Pitching

Pitching	B-T	HT	WT	DOB	W	L	ERA	G	GS	CG	SV	IP	H	R	ER	HR	BB	SO	AVG	vLH	vRH	K/9	BB/9
Acevedo, Domingo	R-R	6-7	242	6-3-94	1	2	2.63	11	10	0	0	41	42	20	12	0	11	43	.259	.286	.245	9.44	2.41
Alcantara, Brayan	R-R	6-1	175	8-6-92	0	1	2.77	17	0	0	1	26	27	17	8	1	16	31	.27	.333	.239	1.73	5.54
Arias, Freddery	R-R	6-1	196	10-24-94	0	3	3.71	21	0	0	2	44	38	21	18	2	25	33	.233	.176	.259	6.8	5.15
Batista, Jean	R-R	6-4	175	10-27-91	0	4	4.26	11	11	1	0	44	42	31	21	1	19	36	.249	.288	.231	7.31	3.86
Burgos, Havid	L-L	6-1	188	8-6-94	3	1	1.29	12	0	0	1	21	20	13	3	1	11	15	.235	.25	.232	6.43	4.71
Cabrera, Cristofer	R-R	6-0	180	12-25-92	3	2	3.72	14	11	0	1	56	50	31	23	0	30	52	.233	.265	.218	8.41	4.85
Casanova, Jeris	R-R	6-0	155	5-11-94	1	2	7.36	5	0	0	0	7	15	6	6	0	4	6	.455	.545	.409	7.36	4.91
Cedeno, Luis	R-R	5-11	154	7-14-94	5	0	.53	5	0	0	0	17	11	4	1	0	3	13	.183	.083	.208	6.88	1.59
Cedeno, Moises	R-R	6-0	188	8-29-95	4	2	3.45	12	11	0	0	47	43	29	18	1	22	50	.246	.232	.255	9.57	4.21
De La Rosa, Maikel	L-L	6-2	190	11-25-90	0	4	3.91	19	0	0	5	25	24	19	11	0	11	28	.247	.158	.269	9.95	3.91
De la Rosa, Pablo	R-R	6-1	180	4-7-94	0	3	1.95	12	0	0	0	12	13	18	15	0	13	4	.265	.158	.333	2.92	9.49
De la Rosa, Simon	R-R	6-3	185	5-11-93	1	1	3.77	14	14	0	0	45	33	24	19	1	33	60	.204	.232	.189	11.91	6.55
Diaz, Carlos	L-L	6-2	170	5-24-95	2	2	3.34	7	6	0	0	32	37	14	12	1	6	26	.287	.333	.278	7.24	1.67
Espinal, Raynel	R-R	6-5	165	10-6-93	5	1	3.55	17	0	0	2	33	29	18	13	1	21	38	.234	.25	.226	1.36	5.73
Garcia, Leonardo	R-R	6-0	180	12-31-93	1	2	9	22	0	0	1	31	38	36	31	1	21	15	.306	.189	.356	4.35	6.1
Garcia, Luis	L-L	6-3	180	9-30-95	1	6	7.68	13	11	0	0	36	44	41	31	2	22	29	.293	.407	.268	7.18	5.45
Gomez, Anyelo	R-R	6-1	171	3-1-93	1	5	4.75	14	3	0	1	30	21	18	16	0	22	24	.204	.172	.216	7.12	6.53
Guzman, Raudy	R-R	6-1	211	9-27-94	2	4	4.25	9	9	0	0	36	40	23	17	2	15	26	.284	.233	.306	6.5	3.75
Hurtado, Erick	L-L	6-4	190	11-21-94	0	0	0	1	0	0	0	1	0	0	0	0	1	0	0	0	0	0	6.75
Jose, Fernando	R-R	6-2	190	11-27-92	0	1	4.7	2	2	0	0	8	4	8	4	0	9	6	.143	.111	.158	7.04	1.57
Juliana, Hershelon	R-R	6-1	171	2-6-93	4	2	4.34	15	0	0	0	19	16	13	9	2	6	17	.225	.136	.265	8.2	2.89
Magallanes, Kelvin	R-R	6-1	175	7-15-94	0	2	8.49	18	4	0	0	30	23	33	28	0	32	23	.213	.281	.184	6.98	9.71
McCoy, Corby	L-L	6-3	180	10-5-95	1	0	4.35	19	0	0	1	31	21	20	15	0	23	25	.188	.143	.194	7.26	6.68
Mora, Abel	L-L	6-5	175	12-3-91	0	2	4.73	8	0	0	1	13	14	10	7	0	6	14	—	—	—	9.45	4.05
Morban, Jhon	R-R	6-4	190	6-3-92	1	5	2.59	16	0	0	2	31	22	15	9	1	12	31	.19	.263	.154	8.9	3.45
Morla, Melvin	R-R	6-4	185	5-26-93	0	3	7.85	11	5	0	0	29	41	33	25	0	22	19	.331	.405	.299	5.97	6.91
Ordaz, Rafael	R-R	6-4	201	2-17-95	0	3	6.66	16	0	0	0	26	26	21	19	4	17	20	.271	.216	.305	7.01	5.96
Ovalles, Jordan	R-R	6-1	160	1-17-94	3	3	2.39	19	0	0	1	38	35	14	10	0	13	23	.269	.31	.257	5.5	3.11
Perez, Braudy	R-R	6-0	170	6-26-93	0	1	1.22	12	0	0	0	12	20	22	14	0	20	8	.364	.588	.263	5.84	14.59
Pichardo, Jose	R-R	5-11	164	7-21-93	0	0	3	16	0	0	1	21	22	7	7	1	10	13	—	—	—	5.57	4.29
Polanco, Reynaldo	R-R	6-2	178	5-20-93	5	4	3.54	13	12	0	0	61	59	32	24	1	20	54	.255	.301	.23	7.97	2.95
Pujols, Jose	R-R	6-6	183	11-19-92	0	2	4.61	19	0	0	0	41	48	33	21	2	26	20	.306	.275	.321	4.39	5.71
Ramirez, Jean	R-R	6-4	180	3-1-93	0	0	0	1	0	0	0	2	0	0	0	0	1	0	0	0	0	4.5	0
Reyes, Aderlis	R-R	6-2	182	10-23-91	2	1	3.82	16	0	0	0	31	20	14	13	3	26	27	.192	.189	.194	7.92	7.63
Reyes, Manolo	R-R	6-1	190	11-14-89	0	1	3.32	5	5	0	0	22	17	12	8	0	20	25	.221	.143	.265	1.38	8.31
Rivera, Eduardo	R-R	6-5	190	9-24-92	1	5	3.5	13	13	0	0	46	40	30	18	0	32	48	.226	.146	.256	9.32	6.22
Rodriguez, David	R-R	5-11	156	1-15-93	4	2	2.57	17	5	0	1	49	43	18	14	2	19	44	.235	.274	.215	8.08	3.49
Santiago, Felix	R-R	6-0	170	12-7-93	2	0	3.12	17	0	0	1	26	27	10	9	0	12	23	.276	.333	.246	7.96	4.15
Vargas, Daris	R-R	6-3	195	8-12-92	2	4	4.31	14	9	0	0	48	34	30	23	1	31	33	.205	.151	.23	6.19	5.81

Fielding

Catcher	PCT	G	PO	A	E	DP	PB
Aparicio	.981	13	101	5	2	1	3
Aquino	1.000	1	5	0	0	0	0
Cedeno	.972	42	257	53	9	1	16
Chevalier	1.000	9	62	5	0	1	5
Coa	.969	21	108	17	4	1	6
Davis	.833	4	9	1	2	0	1
Perez	.949	15	56	18	4	1	7
Reyes	.984	52	375	60	7	1	15
Ventura	.957	12	51	15	3	1	1

First Base	PCT	G	PO	A	E	DP
Aquino	1.000	6	58	1	0	5
Barrios	.978	37	291	24	7	28
Coa	.960	9	67	5	3	7
Davis	1.000	4	29	2	0	2
Gomez	.985	28	183	9	3	14
Lorenzo	.889	3	16	0	2	3
Mojica	.977	14	123	4	3	9
Urena	1.000	7	46	3	0	4
Valerio	.960	30	252	14	11	20
Ventura	.981	21	148	9	3	9

Second Base	PCT	G	PO	A	E	DP
Aquino	1.000	1	0	1	0	0

Barrios	1.000	5	11	10	0	3
Corredera	1.000	6	5	3	0	1
Guzman	.975	25	31	47	2	
6 Lorenzo	.979	25	49	45	2	7
Reyes	.920	45	86	86	15	18
Taveras	1.000	7	11	17	0	5
Valera	.971	45	108	95	6	21
Ventura	1.000	1	2	1	0	1

Third Base	PCT	G	PO	A	E	DP
Aquino	.867	29	27	51	12	4
Barrios	.800	4	2	10	3	0
Corredera	1.000	4	2	6	0	1
Gil	.762	8	5	11	5	0
Gomez	.864	7	5	14	3	1
Guzman	1.000	4	0	6	0	1
Lorenzo	.667	2	0	2	1	0
Rey	.899	61	48	147	22	15
Taveras	.892	15	13	20	4	1
Valerio	.753	23	19	45	21	1
Ventura	1.000	1	1	0	0	0

Shortstop	PCT	G	PO	A	E	DP
Aguilar	.913	60	110	172	27	29
Aparicio	1.000	1	1	2	0	0

Aquino	.864	6	9	10	3	3
Corredera	.903	8	10	18	3	0
Guzman	.714	3	2	3	2	1
Lorenzo	.682	5	10	5	7	3
Mateo	.927	56	97	146	19	28
Valerio	.933	8	9	19	2	3

Outfield	PCT	G	PO	A	E	DP
Asencio	.964	26	26	1	1	1
De la Rosa	.950	20	18	1	1	0
Encarnacion	.985	35	56	8	1	3
Frias	.969	50	89	5	3	3
Gomez	1.000	2	1	0	0	0
Lorenzo	—	1	0	0	0	0
Martinez	.945	45	83	3	5	0
Mojica	.964	18	24	3	1	1
Munoz	.951	36	36	3	2	0
Munoz	.968	43	58	2	2	0
Palma	.975	33	68	10	2	2
Ramirez	.984	43	56	5	1	1
Rodriguez	.913	28	39	3	4	1
Romero	.913	34	34	8	4	0
Silva	1.000	4	7	0	0	0
Urena	.984	47	57	4	1	1

Oakland Athletics

SEASON IN A SENTENCE: The Athletics won their second straight American League West title, but suffered an all-too-familiar Division Series Game Five loss to Justin Verlander and the Tigers.

HIGH POINT: The A's once again outpaced their big-spending AL West rivals in Los Angeles and Texas, capturing the division by five games and winning 96, their highest total since 2003. The A's put the division away with a three-game sweep of the Rangers in Arlington on Sept. 13-15, highlighted by all-star Bartolo Colon outpitching Yu Davish in a 1-0 win. Third baseman Josh Donaldson homered twice in the series as well, part of a breakout season in which the 27-year-old led the A's in batting average (.301) and RBIs (93).

LOW POINT: While the 2012 A's could be excused for a happy-to-be-here feeling after their unlikely run to a playoff berth, the same couldn't be said for the 2013 team. The A's had a 2-games-to-1 lead in the ALDS and opened up a 3-0 lead in Game Four before the wheels fell off in an 8-6 loss. Verlander then stonewalled the A's in a Game Five for the second straight year, carrying a no-hitter into the seventh en route to a 3-0 Detroit win.

NOTABLE ROOKIES: Sonny Gray, who took the loss in Game Five, shined in throwing eight shut-out inning against the Tigers in Game Two of that series and had a 2.67 ERA after being called up in the second-half. Righthander Dan Straily, a revelation in 2012, spent the year in the A's rotation and went 10-8, 3.96. Nate Freiman, an Astros Rule 5 draft pick who the A's subsequently picked up off waivers, saw plenty of action as a first-base platoon option. Another waiver pickup, righty Dan Otero, posted a 1.38 ERA over 39 innings of relief.

KEY TRANSACTIONS: The A's didn't make any drastic changes to the core of their 2012 team but got strong returns by adding Jed Lowrie at short-stop, and veteran John Jaso and rookie Stephen Vogt as part of the catching rotation.

DOWN ON THE FARM: Only low Class A Beloit, reached the postseason, but there were still several individual success stories. First-round picks Gray (2011) and Michael Choice (2010) made their big league debuts, and 2012 first-rounder Addison Russell cemented his place as one of the sport's elite prospects by hitting .305 in the second half as a 19-year-old in high Class A. First baseman Max Muncy also had a breakout year, hitting 25 homers between high Class A and Double-A in his first full season.

OPENING DAY PAYROLL: $60.7 million (27th)

PLAYERS OF THE YEAR

MAJOR LEAGUE	MINOR LEAGUE
Bartolo Colon rhp	**Michael Choice** of
18-6, 2.65, 190 IP	(Triple-A)
117 SO, 29 BB	.302/.390/.445
2nd in AL in ERA, W	14 HR, 89 RBIs

ORGANIZATION LEADERS

BATTING		*Minimum 250 AB
MAJORS		
* AVG	Donaldson, Josh	.301
* OPS	Donaldson, Josh	.883
HR	Moss, Brandon	30
RBI	Donaldson, Josh	93
MINORS		
* AVG	Green, Grant, Sacramento	.325
* OBP	Barton, Daric, Sacramento	.423
* SLG	Green, Grant, Sacramento	.5
R	Weeks, Jemile, Sacramento	96
H	Aliotti, Anthony, Sacramento/Midland	160
TB	Muncy, Max, Midland/Stockton	249
2B	Coleman, Dusty, Sacramento/Midland	35
	Richard, Myrio, Stockton	35
3B	Oberacker, Chad, Midland	12
HR	Muncy, Max, Midland/Stockton	25
RBI	Muncy, Max, Midland/Stockton	100
BB	Muncy, Max, Midland/Stockton	88
SO	Vollmuth, B.A., Stockton	161
SB	Penalo, Rodolfo, DSL Athletics	29

PITCHING		#Minimum 75 IP
MAJORS		
W	Colon, Bartolo	18
# ERA	Colon, Bartolo	2.65
SO	Griffin, A.J.	171
SV	Balfour, Grant	38
MINORS		
W	Billings, Bruce, Sacramento	13
L	Werner, Andrew, Sacramento	14
# ERA	Hernandez, Carlos, Midland/Sacramento	2.66
G	Gordon, Brian, Sacramento	51
GS	Three tied at	28
SV	Gordon, Brian, Sacramento	23
IP	Neal, Zach, Midland	166
	Peters, Tanner, Stockton	166
BB	Granier, Drew, Midland/Stockton	82
SO	Peters, Tanner, Stockton	159
# AVG	Hernandez, Carlos, Midland/Sacramento	.245

2013 PERFORMANCE

General Manager: Billy Beane. **Farm Director:** Keith Lieppman. **Scouting Director:** Eric Kubota.

Class	Team	League	W	L	PCT	Finish	Manager
Majors	Oakland Athletics	American	96	66	.593	2nd (15)	Bob Melvin
Triple-A	Sacramento	Pacific Coast	79	65	.549	3rd (16)	Steve Scarsone
Double-A	Midland Rockhounds	Texas	62	78	.443	7th (8)	Aaron Nieckula
High A	Stockton Ports	California	69	71	.493	t-5th (10)	Webster Garrison
Low A	Beloit Snappers	Midwest	77	62	.554	5th (16)	Ryan Christenson
Short-season	Vermont Lake Monsters	New York-Penn	33	43	.434	12th (14)	Rick Magnante
Rookie	AZL Athletics	Arizona	25	30	.455	9th (13)	Marcus Jensen
Overall 2013 Minor League Record			345	349	.497	t-13th (30)	

ORGANIZATION STATISTICS

AMERICAN LEAGUE

Batting	B-T	HT	WT	DOB	AVG	vLH	vRH	G	AB	R	H	2B	3B	HR	RBI	BB	HBP	SH	SF	SO	SB	CS	SLG	OBP
Barton, Daric	L-R	6-0	205	8-16-85	.269	.269	.269	37	104	15	28	2	0	3	16	13	1	0	2	18	0	0	.375	.350
Callaspo, Alberto	B-R	5-9	225	4-19-83	.281	.263	.250	50	159	20	43	7	0	5	22	19	1	0	1	25	0	0	.409	.350
2-team total (86 Los Angeles)					.258	—	—	136	453	52	117	20	0	10	58	53	1	3	6	47	0	2	.369	.333
Cespedes, Yoenis	R-R	5-10	210	10-18-85	.240	.280	.223	135	529	74	127	21	4	26	80	37	5	0	3	137	7	7	.442	.294
Choice, Michael	R-R	6-0	215	11-10-89	.278	.250	.300	9	18	2	5	1	0	0	1	0	0	0	0	6	0	0	.333	.316
Crisp, Coco	B-R	5-10	185	11-1-79	.261	.218	.286	131	513	93	134	22	3	22	66	61	0	2	8	65	21	5	.444	.335
Donaldson, Josh	R-R	6-0	220	12-8-85	.301	.335	.285	158	579	89	174	37	3	24	93	76	6	1	6	110	5	2	.499	.384
Freiman, Nate	R-R	6-8	250	12-31-86	.274	.304	.167	80	190	10	52	8	1	4	24	14	2	0	2	31	0	0	.389	.327
Green, Grant	R-R	6-3	180	9-27-87	.000	.000	—	5	15	0	0	0	0	0	1	0	0	0	1	6	0	0	.000	.000
2-team total (40 Los Angeles)					.250			45	140	16	35	8	1	1	17	10	1	0	2	44	0	0	.343	.301
Jaso, John	L-R	6-2	205	9-19-83	.271	.192	.282	70	207	31	56	12	0	3	21	38	2	1	1	45	2	1	.372	.387
Lowrie, Jed	B-R	6-0	190	4-17-84	.290	.305	.282	154	603	80	175	45	2	15	75	50	2	3	4	91	1	0	.446	.344
Montz, Luke	R-R	6-1	230	7-7-83	.179	.200	.000	13	28	2	5	3	0	1	5	2	1	0	0	8	0	0	.393	.200
Moss, Brandon	L-R	6-0	210	9-16-83	.256	.200	.268	145	446	73	114	23	3	30	87	50	6	0	3	140	4	2	.522	.337
Norris, Derek	R-R	6-0	210	2-14-89	.246	.320	.149	98	264	41	65	16	0	9	30	37	4	1	2	71	5	0	.409	.345
Parrino, Andy	B-R	6-0	190	10-31-85	.118	.167	.063	14	34	2	4	2	0	0	1	2	0	0	0	12	0	0	.176	.167
Peterson, Shane	L-L	6-0	210	2-11-88	.143	.333	.000	2	7	1	1	0	0	0	1	1	0	0	0	3	0	0	.143	.250
Reddick, Josh	L-R	6-2	180	2-19-87	.226	.200	.238	114	385	54	87	19	2	12	56	46	2	1	7	86	9	2	.379	.307
Rosales, Adam	R-R	6-1	195	5-20-83	.191	.244	.121	51	136	11	26	5	0	4	8	10	4	4	0	31	0	0	.316	.267
2-team total (17 Texas)					.190	—	—	68	147	15	28	5	0	5	12	10	4	4	1	34	0	2	.327	.259
Sizemore, Scott	R-R	6-0	185	1-4-85	.167	.200	.000	2	6	0	1	1	0	0	0	0	0	0	0	2	0	0	.333	.167
Smith, Seth	L-L	6-3	210	9-30-82	.253	.235	.258	117	368	49	93	27	0	8	40	39	3	0	0	94	0	0	.391	.329
Sogard, Eric	L-R	5-10	190	5-22-86	.266	.230	.274	130	368	45	98	24	3	2	35	27	5	6	4	51	10	5	.364	.322
Suzuki, Kurt	R-R	5-11	205	10-4-83	.303	.313	.294	15	33	6	10	2	0	2	7	2	0	0	0	3	0	0	.545	.343
Taylor, Michael	R-R	6-5	255	12-19-85	.043	.091	.000	9	23	0	1	0	0	0	0	2	0	0	0	5	0	0	.043	.120
Vogt, Stephen	L-R	6-0	215	11-1-84	.252	.222	.256	47	135	18	34	6	1	4	16	9	0	2	2	28	0	1	.400	.295
Weeks, Jemile	B-R	5-9	160	1-26-87	.111	.000	.125	8	9	3	1	0	0	0	0	0	0	0	0	5	0	0	.111	.111
Wells, Casper	R-R	6-2	220	11-23-84	.000	.000	.000	3	5	0	0	0	0	0	0	0	0	0	0	1	0	0	.000	.000
2-team total (37 Chicago)					.155	—	—	40	71	4	11	1	0	1	5	0	0	0	0	23	0	1	.169	.211
Young, Chris	R-R	6-2	190	9-5-83	.200	.209	.193	107	335	46	67	18	3	12	40	36	2	0	2	93	10	3	.379	.280

Pitching	B-T	HT	WT	DOB	W	L	ERA	G	GS	CG	SV	IP	H	R	ER	HR	BB	SO	AVG	vLH	vRH	K/9	BB/9
Anderson, Brett	L-L	6-4	235	2-1-88	1	4	6.04	16	5	0	3	45	51	32	30	5	21	46	.287	.283	.288	9.27	4.23
Balfour, Grant	R-R	6-2	200	12-30-77	1	3	2.59	65	0	0	38	63	48	20	18	7	27	72	.206	.192	.222	10.34	3.88
Blevins, Jerry	L-L	6-6	175	9-6-83	5	0	3.15	67	0	0	0	60	47	23	21	7	17	52	.218	.253	.190	7.80	2.55
Chavez, Jesse	R-R	6-2	160	8-21-83	2	4	3.92	35	0	0	1	57	50	27	25	3	20	55	.230	.246	.212	8.63	3.14
Colon, Bartolo	R-R	5-11	265	5-24-73	18	6	2.65	30	30	3	0	190	193	60	56	14	29	117	.264	.261	.268	5.53	1.37
Cook, Ryan	R-R	6-2	215	6-30-87	6	4	2.54	71	0	0	2	67	62	22	19	2	25	67	.238	.279	.207	8.96	3.34
Doolittle, Sean	L-L	6-3	210	9-26-86	5	5	3.13	70	0	0	2	69	53	24	24	4	13	60	.214	.188	.227	7.83	1.70
Figueroa, Pedro	L-L	6-0	215	11-23-85	0	0	12.00	5	0	0	0	3	6	4	4	2	3	3	.400	.429	.375	9.00	9.00
Gray, Sonny	R-R	5-11	200	11-7-89	5	3	2.67	12	10	0	0	64	51	22	19	4	20	67	.214	.226	.198	9.42	2.81
Griffin, A.J.	R-R	6-5	230	1-28-88	14	10	3.83	32	32	1	0	200	171	91	85	36	54	171	.226	.226	.226	7.70	2.43
Milone, Tommy	L-L	6-0	205	2-16-87	12	9	4.14	28	26	1	0	156	160	83	72	25	39	126	.258	.298	.247	7.25	2.25
Neshek, Pat	B-R	6-3	210	9-4-80	2	1	3.35	45	0	0	0	40	40	17	15	6	15	29	.252	.315	.219	6.47	3.35
Okajima, Hideki	L-L	6-1	195	12-25-75	0	0	2.25	5	0	0	0	4	7	1	1	1	2	1	.368	.444	.300	2.25	4.50
Otero, Dan	R-R	6-3	215	2-19-85	2	0	1.38	33	0	0	0	39	42	7	6	0	6	27	.276	.269	.284	6.23	1.38
Parker, Jarrod	R-R	6-1	195	11-24-88	12	8	3.97	32	32	1	0	197	178	92	87	25	63	134	.242	.257	.221	6.12	2.88
Resop, Chris	R-R	6-3	225	11-4-82	1	1	6.00	18	0	0	0	18	22	13	12	3	10	13	.293	.324	.268	6.50	5.00
Scribner, Evan	R-R	6-3	190	7-19-85	0	0	4.39	18	0	0	0	27	26	13	13	3	7	19	.243	.220	.263	6.41	2.36
Straily, Dan	R-R	6-2	215	12-1-88	10	8	3.96	27	27	0	0	152	132	74	67	16	57	124	.233	.244	.221	7.33	3.37

Fielding

Catcher	PCT	G	PO	A	E	DP	PB
Jaso	.989	48	269	12	3	1	0
Norris	.995	91	562	30	3	4	6
Suzuki	.986	15	65	5	1	0	3
Vogt	.997	44	299	14	1	2	6

First Base	PCT	G	PO	A	E	DP
Barton	.996	36	232	23	1	25
Donaldson	—	1	0	0	0	0
Freiman	.997	59	292	17	1	23
Jaso	1.000	1	1	0	0	0
Montz	—	1	0	0	0	0
Moss	.990	111	663	47	7	52
Norris	1.000	1	4	0	0	0
Peterson	1.000	2	8	2	0	1

Second Base	PCT	G	PO	A	E	DP
Callaspo	.970	32	39	57	3	9

Green	.895	5	10	7	2	3
Lowrie	.972	24	33	36	2	10
Parrino	.952	5	12	8	1	2
Rosales	1.000	13	8	16	0	1
Sizemore	1.000	2	4	2	0	2
Sogard	.985	113	207	258	7	68
Weeks	1.000	4	5	6	0	1

Third Base	PCT	G	PO	A	E	DP
Callaspo	.895	9	6	11	2	0
Donaldson	.961	155	143	255	16	22
Moss	—	2	0	0	0	0
Parrino	1.000	2	1	2	0	0
Rosales	1.000	2	1	2	0	0

Shortstop	PCT	G	PO	A	E	DP
Donaldson	1.000	1	0	1	0	0
Lowrie	.962	119	139	266	16	56

Parrino	1.000	7	1	12	0	1
Rosales	.954	36	46	99	7	13
Sogard	.965	15	27	28	2	2

Outfield	PCT	G	PO	A	E	DP
Cespedes	.983	108	224	10	4	1
Choice	1.000	7	10	0	0	0
Crisp	1.000	110	307	2	0	1
Moss	.983	34	56	1	1	0
Reddick	.981	113	244	9	5	3
Rosales	1.000	1	2	0	0	0
Smith	1.000	58	114	1	0	0
Taylor	1.000	8	12	0	0	0
Weeks	1.000	2	2	0	0	0
Wells	1.000	2	1	0	0	0
Young	.992	96	240	2	2	0

SACRAMENTO RIVER CATS

TRIPLE-A

PACIFIC COAST LEAGUE

Batting	B-T	HT	WT	DOB	AVG	vLH	vRH	G	AB	R	H	2B	3B	HR	RBI	BB	HBP	SH	SF	SO	SB	CS	SLG	OBP
Aliotti, Anthony	L-L	6-0	204	7-16-87	.266	.171	.294	42	154	17	41	4	1	2	20	15	0	1	1	44	0	0	.344	.329
Barfield, Jeremy	R-L	6-5	220	7-12-88	.188	.267	.161	35	117	14	22	3	0	4	15	14	0	0	3	31	0	0	.316	.269
Barton, Daric	L-R	6-0	205	8-16-85	.297	.250	.314	110	391	77	116	29	1	7	69	87	3	1	6	57	1	2	.430	.423
Cespedes, Yoenis	R-R	5-10	210	10-18-85	.333	—	.333	3	9	5	3	0	0	1	4	2	0	0	0	3	1	0	.667	.455
Choice, Michael	R-R	6-0	215	11-10-89	.302	.308	.300	132	510	90	154	29	1	14	89	69	11	0	10	115	1	2	.445	.390
Coleman, Dusty	R-R	6-2	185	4-20-87	.143	.000	.158	6	21	4	3	1	0	0	1	0	1	0	0	5	1	0	.190	.182
Crumbliss, Conner	L-R	5-8	175	4-19-87	.136	.143	.133	20	59	11	8	2	1	3	11	12	2	1	1	19	1	0	.356	.297
Freitas, David	R-R	6-3	225	3-18-89	.268	.400	.234	29	97	13	26	8	0	1	9	11	2	0	0	14	0	0	.381	.355
Goebbert, Jake	L-L	6-0	205	9-24-87	.229	.238	.224	21	70	13	16	3	0	4	6	15	0	0	0	16	0	0	.443	.365
Green, Grant	R-R	6-3	180	9-27-87	.325	.385	.310	87	378	66	123	27	3	11	50	27	6	3	1	70	4	1	.500	.379
2-team total (6 Salt Lake)					.326	—	—	93	402	68	131	28	3	11	53	30	6	3	2	77	4	2	.493	.380
Horton, Josh	L-R	6-2	215	2-19-86	.224	.333	.192	17	67	5	15	2	1	2	8	2	0	0	0	12	0	1	.373	.246
Ladendorf, Tyler	R-R	6-0	210	3-7-88	.107	.125	.100	8	28	0	3	1	0	0	2	4	0	0	0	3	0	0	.143	.219
Montz, Luke	R-R	6-1	230	7-7-83	.246	.267	.239	33	122	17	30	9	0	9	29	19	2	0	2	45	0	1	.541	.352
Moore, Scott	L-R	6-2	195	11-17-83	.276	.226	.290	81	293	51	81	26	0	11	56	36	5	1	4	76	0	1	.478	.361
2-team total (39 Tucson)					.271	—	—	120	424	66	115	33	0	14	66	50	6	1	4	107	0	2	.448	.353
Nakajima, Hiroyuki	R-R	5-11	200	7-31-82	.283	.282	.284	90	346	40	98	17	0	4	34	23	6	0	9	83	3	1	.367	.331
Norris, Derek	R-R	6-0	210	2-14-89	.429	.333	.455	3	14	3	6	0	0	2	4	0	0	0	0	3	0	0	.857	.429
Ortiz, Ryan	R-R	6-3	200	9-29-87	.270	.111	.318	36	115	18	31	7	1	3	9	11	1	1	1	24	0	0	.426	.336
Parrino, Andy	B-R	6-0	190	10-31-85	.210	.240	.202	108	367	43	77	16	3	4	36	43	5	3	2	102	3	1	.302	.300
Peterson, Shane	L-L	6-0	210	2-11-88	.251	.284	.240	126	463	70	116	25	1	12	79	77	4	3	6	127	17	2	.387	.358
Reddick, Josh	L-R	6-2	180	2-19-87	.182	1.000	.100	3	11	5	2	0	0	0	3	0	0	0	0	1	2	0	.182	.357
Rosales, Adam	R-R	6-1	195	5-20-83	.211	.286	.194	9	38	4	8	2	0	0	6	3	0	0	1	7	1	1	.263	.262
Russell, Addison	R-R	6-0	195	1-23-94	.077	.000	.091	3	13	1	1	0	0	0	0	0	0	0	0	9	0	0	.077	.077
Taylor, Michael	R-R	6-5	255	12-19-85	.281	.178	.309	112	420	54	118	25	1	18	85	50	5	0	6	88	5	2	.474	.360
Vogt, Stephen	L-R	6-0	215	11-1-84	.324	.277	.338	75	296	55	96	21	3	13	58	38	0	1	3	45	0	1	.547	.398
Weeks, Jemile	R-R	5-9	160	1-26-87	.271	.226	.284	130	520	96	141	19	10	4	40	80	8	5	1	99	17	2	.369	.376
Young, Chris	R-R	6-2	190	9-5-83	1.000	1.000	—	1	1	1	1	0	0	0	0	0	0	2	0	0	0	1	0	1.000	1.000

Pitching	B-T	HT	WT	DOB	W	L	ERA	G	GS	CG	SV	IP	H	R	ER	HR	BB	SO	AVG	vLH	vRH	K/9	BB/9
Anderson, Brett	L-L	6-4	235	2-1-88	0	0	7.71	1	1	0	0	2	3	2	2	0	3	2	.333	.500	.200	7.71	11.57
Banwart, Travis	R-R	6-3	220	2-14-86	10	5	4.60	29	23	0	0	131	145	74	67	20	54	125	.280	.309	.252	8.59	3.71
Billings, Bruce	R-R	6-0	210	11-18-85	13	8	4.31	28	26	0	0	148	140	78	71	17	51	135	.248	.246	.251	8.19	3.09
Byrd, Darren	R-R	6-3	200	10-24-86	1	1	5.71	23	2	0	0	35	37	25	22	3	22	35	.268	.286	.253	9.09	5.71
Chavez, Jesse	R-R	6-2	160	8-21-83	2	2	2.70	5	5	0	0	30	35	16	9	1	5	26	.285	.354	.240	7.80	1.50
Ekstrom, Mike	R-R	6-0	190	8-30-83	1	1	5.10	21	0	0	3	30	39	19	17	3	13	27	.317	.389	.261	8.10	3.90
2-team total (17 Salt Lake)					3	3	5.14	38	0	0	3	56	69	34	32	5	20	49	—	—	—	7.88	3.21
Figueroa, Pedro	L-L	6-0	215	11-23-85	3	4	4.10	46	1	0	2	59	57	29	27	9	33	49	.252	.216	.282	7.43	5.01
Gordon, Brian	L-R	6-0	190	8-16-78	4	0	3.57	51	0	0	23	63	61	27	25	4	9	66	.249	.257	.243	9.43	1.29
Gray, Sonny	R-R	5-11	200	11-7-89	10	7	3.42	20	20	1	0	118	117	51	45	5	39	118	.259	.244	.274	8.97	2.97
Hall, Shaeffer	R-L	6-1	205	10-2-87	1	0	0.00	1	0	0	0	3	2	0	0	0	0	3	.182	.167	.200	9.00	0.00
Hernandez, Carlos	L-L	5-11	155	3-4-87	1	3	5.85	4	4	0	0	20	33	17	13	1	3	10	.363	.395	.340	4.50	1.35
Leon, Arnold	R-R	6-1	205	9-6-88	5	3	4.42	12	11	0	0	71	81	36	35	4	13	49	.287	.338	.240	6.18	1.64
Milone, Tommy	L-L	6-0	205	2-16-87	0	0	1.74	2	2	0	0	10	16	5	2	0	1	15	.348	.000	.390	13.06	0.87
Neshek, Pat	B-R	6-3	210	9-4-80	0	0	0.00	2	0	0	0	2	2	0	1	0	2	2	.250	.200	.333	9.00	9.00
Newby, Kyler	R-R	6-4	225	7-4-85	2	1	3.58	24	0	0	1	28	29	11	11	2	12	28	.276	.273	.299	9.11	3.90
Nieve, Fernando	R-R	6-0	220	7-15-82	1	0	2.19	7	1	0	0	12	9	3	3	1	2	9	.184	.130	.231	6.57	1.46
Norberto, Jordan	L-L	6-0	195	12-8-86	0	1	40.50	3	0	0	0	1	5	6	6	0	7	4	.556	.750	.400	27.00	47.25
Okajima, Hideki	L-L	6-1	195	12-25-75	1	3	4.22	37	0	0	1	43	40	21	20	5	9	45	.244	.182	.299	9.49	1.90
Otero, Dan	R-R	6-3	215	2-19-85	1	0	0.99	23	0	0	15	27	14	4	3	0	1	22	.147	.152	.143	7.24	0.33
Resop, Chris	R-R	6-3	225	11-4-82	1	2	6.81	26	1	0	0	36	48	27	27	5	13	29	.322	.339	.310	7.32	3.28
Scribner, Evan	R-R	6-3	190	7-19-85	3	1	2.22	31	0	0	1	45	32	12	11	2	9	58	.192	.164	.213	11.69	1.81

Name	B-T	HT	WT	DOB	W	L	ERA	G	GS	CG	SV	IP	H	R	ER	HR	BB	SO	AVG	vLH	vRH	K/9	BB/9
Simmons, James	R-R	6-3	220	9-29-86	0	2	7.16	12	0	0	0	16	27	17	13	1	8	13	.365	.357	.370	7.16	4.41
Smyth, Paul	R-R	5-11	210	4-1-87	0	0	2.45	32	0	0	1	37	36	11	10	2	16	31	.265	.350	.197	7.61	3.93
Straily, Dan	R-R	6-2	215	12-1-88	3	1	1.14	5	5	0	0	32	24	11	4	1	9	33	.202	.174	.219	9.38	2.56
Thomas, Justin	L-L	6-3	220	1-18-84	3	6	4.48	16	16	0	0	84	92	47	42	8	34	68	.273	.240	.292	7.26	3.63
Vidal, Pedro	R-R	6-1	215	7-31-87	0	0	12.27	3	0	0	0	4	3	5	5	1	3	4	.214	.125	.333	9.82	7.36
Viola, Pedro	L-L	6-1	185	6-29-83	1	0	4.05	7	0	0	0	7	14	5	3	0	4	6	.438	.500	.375	8.10	5.40
Werner, Andrew	L-L	6-2	215	2-25-87	12	14	5.78	27	26	1	0	165	202	110	106	20	38	111	.305	.279	.319	6.05	2.07
Zagurski, Mike	L-L	6-0	240	1-27-83	0	0	6.00	6	0	0	0	6	7	6	4	0	3	8	.280	.333	.231	12.00	4.50

Fielding

Catcher	PCT	G	PO	A	E	DP	PB
Freitas	.990	27	183	9	2	0	1
Montz	.980	21	176	19	4	1	2
Norris	.941	2	16	0	1	0	0
Ortiz	.979	33	215	20	5	2	3
Vogt	.997	65	528	51	2	4	6

First Base	PCT	G	PO	A	E	DP
Aliotti	.994	42	323	31	2	36
Barton	.991	80	617	68	6	46
Green	.857	1	6	0	1	3
Montz	1.000	2	11	1	0	2
Moore	.989	11	84	6	1	7
Peterson	.990	13	92	7	1	10

Second Base	PCT	G	PO	A	E	DP
Barton	—	1	0	0	0	0
Coleman	1.000	2	5	6	0	2
Green	.968	73	112	156	9	44

	PCT	G	PO	A	E	DP
Nakajima	.987	19	33	41	1	10
Parrino	1.000	5	10	17	0	2
Rosales	1.000	1	1	5	0	0
Weeks	.974	45	87	103	5	22

Third Base	PCT	G	PO	A	E	DP
Barton	.892	29	13	45	7	2
Coleman	.714	4	1	4	2	0
Horton	.875	14	8	20	4	0
Moore	.935	45	28	59	6	5
Nakajima	.952	37	23	57	4	6
Ortiz	1.000	1	0	1	0	0
Parrino	.917	18	17	27	4	3

Shortstop	PCT	G	PO	A	E	DP
Horton	1.000	2	0	7	0	2
Ladendorf	1.000	1	1	4	0	2
Nakajima	.966	28	44	69	4	20
Parrino	.961	85	132	237	15	46

	PCT	G	PO	A	E	DP
Rosales	.968	7	12	18	1	5
Russell	.667	2	0	2	1	1
Weeks	.946	23	32	56	5	10

Outfield	PCT	G	PO	A	E	DP
Barfield	1.000	34	64	3	0	0
Cespedes	.667	1	2	0	1	0
Choice	.983	116	225	4	4	0
Crumbliss	.972	20	34	1	1	0
Goebbert	1.000	15	32	1	0	0
Ladendorf	1.000	7	17	0	0	0
Moore	.958	16	22	1	1	0
Peterson	.987	106	220	9	3	3
Reddick	1.000	1	2	0	0	0
Taylor	.987	103	212	9	3	3
Weeks	.968	25	60	1	2	0
Young	1.000	1	2	0	0	0

MIDLAND ROCKHOUNDS   DOUBLE-A

TEXAS LEAGUE

Batting	B-T	HT	WT	DOB	AVG	vLH	vRH	G	AB	R	H	2B	3B	HR	RBI	BB	HBP	SH	SF	SO	SB	CS	SLG	OBP
Aliotti, Anthony	L-L	6-0	204	7-16-87	.350	.230	.391	91	340	49	119	29	0	12	51	66	0	0	3	83	3	2	.541	.452
Barfield, Jeremy	R-L	6-5	220	7-12-88	.242	.056	.284	26	99	19	24	3	0	8	18	14	0	0	1	17	1	1	.515	.333
Catricala, Vinnie	R-R	6-3	220	10-31-88	.221	.098	.247	61	231	21	51	9	0	4	26	14	4	1	4	56	3	1	.312	.273
Coleman, Dusty	R-R	6-2	185	4-20-87	.260	.292	.253	130	484	65	126	34	10	3	61	57	6	5	2	155	17	10	.390	.344
Crumbliss, Conner	L-R	5-8	175	4-19-87	.280	.311	.266	92	347	66	97	19	2	10	34	69	6	5	3	57	12	4	.432	.405
Fabiaschi, Michael	R-R	5-11	185	8-17-88	.240	.200	.250	9	25	0	6	2	0	0	2	3	0	0	0	9	0	0	.320	.321
Freitas, David	R-R	6-3	225	3-18-89	.214	.111	.234	61	224	34	48	6	0	9	21	20	2	0	0	39	0	0	.362	.285
Goebbert, Jake	L-L	6-0	205	9-24-87	.268	.205	.286	105	396	57	106	20	5	18	75	47	8	1	7	83	6	3	.480	.352
Head, Miles	R-R	6-0	215	5-2-91	.196	.150	.203	40	148	13	29	4	0	2	8	12	2	0	1	42	0	1	.264	.264
Ladendorf, Tyler	R-R	6-0	180	3-7-88	.263	.320	.241	83	266	34	70	16	1	6	40	27	5	2	2	45	2	0	.398	.340
Lipkin, Ryan	R-R	6-0	205	10-8-87	.119	.059	.143	18	59	4	7	2	0	1	6	5	1	0	0	10	0	0	.203	.200
Lopez, Diomendes	R-R	6-2	195	1-30-89	.111	1.000	.000	3	9	1	1	0	0	0	0	0	1	1	0	3	0	0	.111	.200
Marte, Jefry	R-R	6-1	190	6-21-91	.278	.344	.254	66	245	33	68	17	1	2	28	25	4	0	4	49	8	1	.380	.349
Muncy, Max	L-R	6-0	190	8-25-90	.250	.244	.252	47	172	22	43	12	2	4	24	24	0	0	1	34	0	1	.413	.340
Myers, D'Arby	R-R	6-3	175	12-9-88	.285	.400	.249	118	485	75	138	29	3	5	51	16	10	9	2	70	20	10	.388	.320
Oberacker, Chad	L-L	5-11	195	1-14-89	.237	.131	.261	120	448	55	106	26	12	6	54	41	6	5	6	101	17	1	.388	.305
Perez, Darwin	B-R	5-10	160	7-27-89	.237	.207	.245	115	393	55	93	19	5	3	34	50	4	1	4	103	19	4	.333	.326
Rickles, Nick	R-R	6-3	220	2-2-90	.500	—	.500	1	4	1	2	0	0	0	1	0	0	0	0	1	0	0	.500	.500
Taylor, Beau	L-R	6-0	205	2-13-90	.191	.135	.205	76	267	21	51	11	0	3	32	33	2	1	3	71	1	0	.266	.282
Whitaker, Josh	R-R	5-11	225	2-8-89	.240	.243	.239	32	125	22	30	12	1	3	16	11	1	0	1	35	2	0	.424	.304

Pitching	B-T	HT	WT	DOB	W	L	ERA	G	GS	CG	SV	IP	H	R	ER	HR	BB	SO	AVG	vLH	vRH	K/9	BB/9
Anderson, Brett	L-L	6-4	235	2-1-88	0	1	14.73	1	1	0	0	4	6	6	6	0	4	3	.353	.000	.429	7.36	9.82
Arnesen, Erik	R-R	6-3	260	3-19-84	0	1	10.03	3	2	0	0	12	16	14	13	3	6	7	.348	.474	.259	5.40	4.63
Bowman, Josh	R-R	6-2	195	9-9-88	2	1	4.54	8	8	0	0	40	41	26	20	5	21	18	.275	.333	.239	4.08	4.76
Brown, Jake	R-L	6-2	230	12-28-86	0	0	10.80	3	0	0	0	3	10	4	4	0	1	3	.556	.429	.636	8.10	2.70
Byrd, Darren	R-R	6-3	200	10-24-86	0	0	1.35	3	0	0	1	7	2	1	1	0	2	4	.091	.200	.059	5.40	2.70
Carpenter, Drew	R-R	6-3	240	5-18-85	1	1	3.10	4	4	0	0	20	20	8	7	2	3	12	.238	.216	.255	5.31	1.33
2-team total (5 Arkansas)					4	2	2.09	9	9	0	0	52	40	14	12	5	7	30	—	—		5.23	1.22
Castillo, Jesus	R-R	6-0	205	5-31-84	0	0	0.00	6	0	0	1	10	7	0	0	0	2	5	.200	.133	.250	4.50	1.80
Daley, Gary	R-R	6-3	200	11-1-85	0	1	12.46	8	0	0	0	9	14	14	12	1	7	6	.359	.250	.435	6.23	7.27
DeMark, Mike	R-R	6-0	210	5-20-83	3	3	5.59	31	0	0	4	39	42	25	24	4	20	33	.280	.364	.245	7.68	4.66
Dull, Ryan	R-R	5-11	175	10-2-89	0	1	4.63	10	0	0	1	12	15	9	6	2	3	13	.319	.353	.265	9.23	2.31
Fisher, Carlos	R-R	6-4	220	2-22-83	1	2	3.88	37	0	0	0	49	38	24	21	4	33	71	.207	.239	.188	13.13	6.10
Gailey, Frank	L-L	5-9	190	11-18-85	2	3	2.61	39	0	0	3	62	58	20	18	3	11	54	.245	.243	.246	7.84	1.60
Granier, Drew	R-R	6-0	180	11-24-88	3	6	5.23	14	14	0	0	72	82	48	42	9	42	56	.286	.300	.275	6.97	5.23
Hassebrock, Blake	R-R	6-4	212	7-15-89	0	2	6.61	12	0	0	0	16	18	13	12	1	7	5	.295	.200	.387	2.76	3.86
Hernandez, Carlos	L-L	5-11	155	3-4-87	7	7	2.18	25	20	0	0	132	109	43	32	5	38	96	.223	.224	.223	6.55	2.59
Hunter, Brett	R-R	6-4	215	6-27-87	2	1	3.38	23	0	0	2	32	16	12	12	1	19	42	.145	.154	.141	11.81	5.34
Leon, Arnold	R-R	6-1	205	9-6-88	4	5	3.84	13	13	0	0	73	87	40	31	6	16	48	.295	.359	.253	5.94	1.98
Long, Nathan	R-R	6-2	210	2-9-86	2	2	3.86	32	1	0	0	63	67	36	27	2	20	57	.269	.236	.288	8.14	2.86
Murphy, Sean	B-R	6-6	215	8-23-88	8	8	4.08	25	24	0	0	137	137	65	62	9	50	121	.263	.256	.268	7.97	3.29

	B-T	HT	WT	DOB	W	L	ERA	G	GS	CG	SV	IP	H	R	ER	HR	BB	SO	AVG	vLH	vRH	K/9	BB/9
Neal, Zach	R-R	6-3	220	11-9-88	8	12	4.35	28	28	1	0	166	172	95	80	18	36	96	.266	.259	.272	5.22	1.96
Newby, Kyler	R-R	6-4	225	2-22-85	4	4	1.95	23	0	0	6	32	28	10	7	1	7	31	.237	.318	.189	8.63	1.95
Perez, Sergio	R-R	6-3	230	12-5-84	0	0	27.00	1	0	0	0	2	1	1	0	0	0		.667	.500	1.000	0.00	0.00
Smith, Murphy	R-R	6-3	210	8-25-87	9	8	3.48	26	25	0	0	150	157	69	58	14	46	98	.274	.297	.257	5.88	2.76
Smyth, Paul	R-R	5-11	210	4-1-87	2	2	2.74	13	0	0	1	23	14	8	7	2	4	24	.179	.211	.150	9.39	1.57
Urlaub, Jeff	L-L	6-2	160	4-24-87	2	2	3.86	40	0	0	1	47	49	20	20	2	13	40	.274	.273	.275	7.71	2.51
Vidal, Pedro	R-R	6-1	215	7-31-87	0	4	5.21	8	0	0	0	19	15	12	11	4	2	20	.214	.286	.167	9.47	0.95
Viola, Pedro	L-L	6-1	185	6-29-83	2	1	5.60	12	0	0	0	18	15	11	11	1	5	25	.224	.192	.244	12.74	2.55

Fielding

Catcher	PCT	G	PO	A	E	DP	PB
Freitas	.982	54	402	32	8	4	2
Lipkin	.983	17	104	12	2	0	2
Lopez	1.000	3	20	2	0	0	0
Rickles	1.000	1	5	0	0	0	0
Taylor	.990	68	461	39	5	1	7

First Base	PCT	G	PO	A	E	DP
Aliotti	.997	75	644	44	2	53
Catricala	.984	8	54	9	1	2
Freitas	1.000	1	3	0	0	0
Goebbert	.991	10	96	11	1	5
Head	1.000	3	26	2	0	3
Marte	1.000	2	19	0	0	2
Muncy	.986	43	399	34	6	25

Second Base	PCT	G	PO	A	E	DP
Coleman	.975	52	100	137	6	28
Crumbliss	1.000	16	23	50	0	8
Fabiaschi	1.000	1	3	4	0	0
Ladendorf	.987	31	69	80	2	17
Perez	.960	45	64	129	8	22

Third Base	PCT	G	PO	A	E	DP
Catricala	.939	38	17	60	5	3
Coleman	1.000	6	4	17	0	1
Fabiaschi	.923	7	1	11	1	0
Head	.818	19	8	19	6	3
Ladendorf	.931	32	16	38	4	3
Marte	.875	47	17	74	13	12
Perez	1.000	1	1	2	0	0

Shortstop	PCT	G	PO	A	E	DP
Coleman	.957	66	116	221	15	35
Ladendorf	.907	7	16	23	4	3
Perez	.956	67	86	198	13	37

Outfield	PCT	G	PO	A	E	DP
Barfield	.982	23	54	2	1	1
Crumbliss	.948	74	122	6	7	1
Goebbert	.966	62	135	6	5	1
Ladendorf	1.000	14	23	2	0	0
Myers	.992	117	242	6	2	0
Oberacker	.980	110	228	13	5	4
Perez	1.000	1	3	0	0	0
Whitaker	.986	28	67	1	1	0

STOCKTON PORTS
HIGH CLASS A
CALIFORNIA LEAGUE

Batting	B-T	HT	WT	DOB	AVG	vLH	vRH	G	AB	R	H	2B	3B	HR	RBI	BB	HBP	SH	SF	SO	SB	CS	SLG	OBP
Crocker, Bobby	R-R	6-3	220	5-1-90	.276	.260	.281	113	449	73	124	31	8	11	53	32	14	1	1	159	22	9	.454	.343
Delgado, Ryan	R-R	5-11	215	1-11-88	.231	.176	.243	25	91	15	21	3	1	4	12	7	2	0	0	21	0	0	.418	.300
Dixon, Rashun	R-R	6-2	210	8-27-90	.207	.171	.219	86	285	46	59	17	1	12	38	48	11	0	4	116	8	1	.400	.339
Fabiaschi, Michael	R-R	5-11	185	8-17-88	.222	.000	.250	6	18	6	4	1	0	2	4	3	1	1		5	1	0	.611	.375
Kirkland, Wade	R-R	5-10	197	4-4-89	.220	.140	.243	67	223	25	49	18	0	6	27	10	5	0	1	65	1	2	.381	.268
Lamas, Antonio	B-R	5-9	165	12-30-89	.255	.254	.256	125	517	64	132	23	3	12	72	29	8	2	2	93	1	2	.381	.304
Maxwell, Bruce	L-R	6-2	235	12-20-90	.263	.107	.293	47	175	19	46	8	0	5	21	19	1	0	2	34	0	0	.394	.335
Muncy, Max	L-R	6-0	190	8-25-90	.285	.238	.300	93	351	67	100	13	1	21	76	64	7	0	6	68	1	1	.507	.400
Ortiz, Ryan	R-R	6-3	200	9-29-87	.202	.105	.229	26	89	12	18	4	1	3	7	13	4	0	0	31	0	1	.371	.330
Pohl, Phil	R-R	5-11	195	7-22-90	.227	.200	.236	54	194	32	44	8	0	9	20	12	7	0	4	68	1	0	.407	.290
Reddick, Josh	L-R	6-2	180	2-19-87	.333	—	.333	1	3	0	1	0	0	0	0	0	0	0	0	0	0	0	.333	.333
Richard, Myrio	R-R	6-1	190	8-27-88	.256	.304	.240	111	465	64	119	35	0	11	40	33	7	0	2	90	13	7	.402	.314
Robinson, Dusty	R-R	6-0	205	9-9-89	.210	.192	.214	123	458	67	96	16	3	21	64	41	4	0	2	146	18	4	.395	.279
Rosales, Adam	R-R	6-1	195	5-20-83	.500	.571	.400	5	12	3	6	2	0	1	1	0	0	0	0	0	0	0	.917	.500
Russell, Addison	R-R	6-0	195	1-23-94	.275	.252	.282	107	429	85	118	29	10	17	60	61	11	0	3	116	21	3	.508	.377
Thompson, Tony	R-R	6-4	220	12-19-88	.250	.247	.251	116	460	58	115	26	1	18	92	48	3	0	4	96	3	0	.428	.322
Vollmuth, B.A.	R-R	6-3	215	12-23-89	.212	.211	.213	125	471	66	100	25	2	21	70	56	7	2	7	161	0	0	.408	.301
Whitaker, Josh	R-R	6-3	225	2-8-89	.270	.283	.266	53	204	29	55	13	0	9	41	22	6	0	2	49	6	3	.466	.355

Pitching	B-T	HT	WT	DOB	W	L	ERA	G	GS	CG	SV	IP	H	R	ER	HR	BB	SO	AVG	vLH	vRH	K/9	BB/9
Alcantara, Raul	R-R	6-3	180	12-4-92	5	5	3.76	14	14	0	0	79	73	45	33	8	17	66	.243	.252	.238	7.52	1.94
Anderson, Brett	L-L	6-4	235	2-1-88	0	1	13.50	1	1	0	0	3	5	5	5	2	2	6	.333	.333	.333	16.20	5.40
Avila, Andres	R-R	6-0	185	6-20-90	0	3	9.30	5	5	0	0	20	26	22	21	3	7	19	.302	.279	.326	8.41	3.10
Barham, Trey	L-L	6-0	215	11-7-85	0	0	3.86	9	0	0	0	12	16	8	5	1	7	16	.320	.316	.323	12.34	5.40
Bowman, Josh	R-R	6-2	195	9-9-88	7	6	5.56	17	15	1	0	100	117	67	62	13	23	74	.293	.309	.283	6.64	2.06
Brown, Jake	R-L	6-2	230	12-28-86	2	3	4.21	27	3	0	1	58	59	27	27	8	11	43	.262	.264	.261	6.71	1.72
Byrd, Darren	R-R	6-3	200	10-24-86	0	0	4.91	3	0	0	0	4	6	2	2	1	3	1	.353	.429	.300	2.45	7.36
Doolittle, Ryan	R-R	6-2	205	3-25-88	0	2	4.76	2	2	0	0	6	5	3	3	1	4	12	.227	.333	.100	6.35	1.59
Dull, Ryan	R-R	5-11	175	10-2-89	1	3	1.59	15	0	0	6	23	13	4	4	0	3	31	.165	.250	.118	12.31	1.19
Duran, Omar	L-L	6-3	209	2-26-90	3	1	4.58	33	0	0	0	53	38	30	27	4	41	83	.200	.149	.228	14.09	6.96
Frankoff, Seth	R-R	6-5	200	8-27-88	2	0	2.78	48	0	0	4	74	57	32	23	6	23	93	.208	.250	.177	11.26	2.78
Granier, Drew	R-R	6-0	180	11-24-88	6	3	3.25	14	14	0	0	83	71	32	30	5	40	97	.228	.209	.243	10.52	4.34
Hall, Shaeffer	R-L	6-1	205	10-2-87	4	4	6.58	16	12	0	1	64	81	52	47	14	12	37	.309	.238	.332	5.18	1.68
Hassebrock, Blake	R-R	6-4	212	7-15-89	2	4	4.28	26	5	0	1	65	57	34	29	4	29	68	.251	.274	.238	10.03	4.28
Healy, Tucker	L-R	6-1	195	6-15-90	1	1	1.86	15	0	0	3	19	13	4	4	2	5	31	.186	.240	.156	14.43	2.33
Hunter, Brett	R-R	6-4	215	6-27-87	0	0	2.25	3	0	0	0	4	3	1	1	0	1	7	.200	.000	.300	15.75	2.25
Jimenez, Deyvi	R-R	6-3	220	12-30-89	0	3	6.56	9	9	0	0	36	45	28	26	4	15	33	.296	.298	.295	8.33	3.79
Joseph, Jonathan	R-R	6-1	180	5-17-88	5	5	3.50	47	0	0	6	64	46	33	25	6	28	76	.203	.180	.220	10.63	3.92
Macias, Jose	R-R	6-2	180	7-18-89	1	2	2.76	22	0	0	5	33	24	12	10	1	7	28	.207	.167	.235	7.71	1.93
Mota, David	R-R	6-4	180	2-18-87	0	1	6.49	22	0	0	0	26	28	21	19	2	13	17	.275	.356	.211	5.81	4.44
Murphy, Sean	R-R	6-6	215	9-8-88	2	1	2.89	3	3	0	0	19	19	8	6	4	4	19	.268	.296	.250	9.16	1.93
Perez, Sergio	R-R	6-3	230	12-5-84	0	1	13.50	3	3	0	0	8	13	12	12	4	6	11	.342	.333	.350	12.38	6.75
Perlman, Max	R-L	6-7	235	2-2-88	0	1	5.06	4	0	0	0	5	4	3	3	0	6	3	.222	.333	.111	5.06	10.13
Peters, Tanner	R-R	6-0	155	8-6-90	12	8	4.07	28	28	0	0	166	167	86	75	24	27	159	.261	.265	.257	8.64	1.47
Simmons, James	R-R	6-2	220	9-29-86	8	8	5.48	20	20	0	0	113	131	76	69	24	25	86	.291	.283	.296	6.83	1.99
Vidal, Pedro	R-R	6-1	215	7-31-87	0	1	3.57	26	0	0	2	40	37	17	16	3	11	41	.240	.306	.196	9.15	2.45

OAKLAND ATHLETICS

OAKLAND ATHLETICS *(sidebar)*

	B-T	HT	WT	DOB	W	L	ERA	G	GS	CG	SV	IP	H	R	ER	HR	BB	SO	AVG	vLH	vRH	K/9	BB/9
Viola, Pedro	L-L	6-1	185	6-29-83	2	0	1.50	4	0	0	1	6	3	1	1	0	1	12	.143	.286	.071	18.00	1.50
Walz, T.J.	R-R	6-0	175	11-21-88	4	2	6.13	42	0	0	0	62	79	52	42	7	32	73	.312	.289	.327	10.65	4.67
Ynoa, Michael	R-R	6-7	210	9-24-91	1	2	7.71	7	6	0	1	21	23	20	18	2	17	20	.274	.321	.250	8.57	7.29

Fielding

Catcher	PCT	G	PO	A	E	DP	PB
Delgado	.987	24	208	15	3	0	1
Maxwell	.993	45	420	30	3	2	9
Ortiz	.992	26	239	11	2	1	4
Pohl	.986	48	397	23	6	1	6

First Base	PCT	G	PO	A	E	DP
Muncy	.996	85	678	47	3	66
Thompson	.986	47	385	28	6	24
Vollmuth	.983	8	54	5	1	8

Second Base	PCT	G	PO	A	E	DP
Fabiaschi	.941	4	6	10	1	0

	PCT	G	PO	A	E	DP
Kirkland	.969	26	49	75	4	16
Lamas	.966	110	201	282	17	60
Rosales	—	1	0	0	0	0

Third Base	PCT	G	PO	A	E	DP
Kirkland	1.000	1	1	0	0	0
Thompson	.876	28	26	52	11	7
Vollmuth	.900	111	68	203	30	14

Shortstop	PCT	G	PO	A	E	DP
Fabiaschi	1.000	2	4	2	0	0
Kirkland	.950	35	41	92	7	18
Rosales	1.000	1	0	2	0	1

	PCT	G	PO	A	E	DP
Russell	.968	105	149	274	14	53

Outfield	PCT	G	PO	A	E	DP
Crocker	.991	108	223	5	2	0
Dixon	.993	76	132	6	1	1
Kirkland	1.000	3	3	0	0	0
Reddick	—	1	0	0	0	0
Richard	.988	85	164	7	2	2
Robinson	.952	111	193	5	10	2
Whitaker	.989	44	84	3	1	1

BELOIT SNAPPERS

LOW CLASS A

MIDWEST LEAGUE

Batting

	B-T	HT	WT	DOB	AVG	vLH	vRH	G	AB	R	H	2B	3B	HR	RBI	BB	HBP	SH	SF	SO	SB	CS	SLG	OBP
Alexander, Dayton	R-R	6-1	195	2-4-91	.236	.220	.247	53	148	20	35	7	1	2	8	17	0	1	1	53	7	2	.338	.313
Bostick, Chris	R-R	5-11	185	3-24-93	.282	.275	.285	129	489	75	138	25	8	14	89	51	6	4	5	122	25	8	.452	.354
Delgado, Ryan	R-R	5-11	215	1-11-88	.215	.239	.204	43	144	18	31	6	0	2	14	17	3	0	2	35	3	0	.299	.307
Dixon, Rashun	R-R	6-2	210	8-27-90	.278	.222	.296	11	36	11	10	0	0	4	7	9	0	0	0	8	3	0	.611	.422
Lewis, Chad	R-R	6-3	200	12-10-91	.200	.158	.217	18	65	6	13	4	0	1	8	1	1	0	0	20	0	0	.308	.224
Mathews, Ryan	R-R	6-4	195	8-1-89	.260	.219	.275	122	419	64	109	32	2	14	55	45	4	3	1	98	7	4	.446	.337
Maxwell, Bruce	L-R	6-2	235	12-20-90	.286	.327	.271	57	199	25	57	14	0	2	28	24	0	3	2	29	0	0	.387	.360
Nunez, Renato	R-R	6-1	185	4-4-94	.258	.258	.258	128	508	69	131	27	0	19	85	28	5	1	3	136	2	2	.423	.301
Olson, Matt	L-R	6-4	236	3-29-94	.225	.180	.241	134	481	69	108	32	0	23	93	72	2	0	3	148	4	3	.435	.326
Pohl, Phil	R-R	5-11	195	7-22-90	.250	.333	.222	3	12	1	3	0	0	0	0	0	0	0	0	3	0	0	.250	.250
Rickles, Nick	R-R	6-3	220	2-2-90	.258	.289	.246	81	283	27	73	10	3	7	33	11	2	2	2	52	0	1	.389	.289
Roberts, Sam	L-R	6-1	190	2-23-89	.204	.268	.188	65	206	24	42	9	3	2	15	29	0	1	0	61	2	7	.306	.302
Robertson, Daniel	R-R	6-0	190	3-22-94	.277	.297	.269	101	401	59	111	21	1	9	46	41	7	0	2	79	1	7	.401	.353
Shipman, Aaron	L-L	6-0	175	1-27-92	.279	.293	.272	68	244	44	68	7	2	0	16	47	1	0	0	50	17	8	.324	.397
Solano, Wilfredo	R-R	6-2	205	1-15-93	.143	.000	.200	2	7	1	1	0	0	0	0	0	0	0	0	3	0	0	.143	.143
Tanis, Jacob	R-R	6-1	190	6-30-89	.182	.188	.179	12	44	4	8	4	0	1	5	2	0	0	0	11	0	0	.341	.217
Vertigan, Brett	L-L	5-9	175	8-21-90	.243	.255	.240	123	436	65	106	24	5	0	27	55	6	10	4	64	21	6	.321	.333
Wooten, John	R-R	6-3	190	1-19-91	.257	.284	.247	133	495	76	127	22	2	20	69	53	5	0	2	113	5	3	.430	.333

Pitching

	B-T	HT	WT	DOB	W	L	ERA	G	GS	CG	SV	IP	H	R	ER	HR	BB	SO	AVG	vLH	vRH	K/9	BB/9
Alcantara, Raul	R-R	6-3	180	12-4-92	7	1	2.44	13	13	1	0	77	84	29	21	3	7	58	.272	.261	.281	6.75	0.81
Avila, Andres	R-R	6-0	185	6-20-90	7	4	5.01	23	11	0	2	88	106	61	49	9	44	55	.300	.305	.296	5.63	4.50
Bacus, Dakota	R-R	6-2	200	4-2-91	9	5	3.56	26	16	0	0	121	124	55	48	6	38	90	.263	.293	.238	6.68	2.82
Bayless, Trevor	R-R	6-3	210	10-6-91	1	2	9.00	6	0	0	0	8	14	8	8	2	4	8	.412	.700	.292	9.00	4.50
Bragg, Sam	R-R	6-2	190	3-23-93	0	0	0.00	2	0	0	0	2	0	0	0	0	0	3	.000	.000	.000	13.50	0.00
Covey, Dylan	R-R	6-2	195	8-14-91	1	1	4.75	10	10	0	0	47	64	28	25	4	17	31	.327	.361	.306	5.89	3.23
De Young, Derek	R-R	6-0	165	12-17-91	8	5	4.22	27	16	0	2	113	118	58	53	7	41	83	.271	.215	.318	6.61	3.27
Dull, Ryan	R-R	5-11	175	10-2-89	1	1	2.10	20	0	0	12	26	16	6	6	1	3	35	.176	.174	.178	12.27	1.05
Finnegan, Kyle	R-R	6-2	170	9-4-91	1	1	9.82	2	2	0	0	7	12	8	8	1	6	5	.375	.538	.263	6.14	7.36
Hall, Kris	R-R	6-3	215	6-8-91	4	2	4.92	30	2	0	1	53	52	33	29	6	35	56	.260	.286	.241	9.51	5.94
Healy, Tucker	L-R	6-1	195	6-15-90	0	1	0.94	18	0	0	2	29	20	7	3	5	43	.190	.214	.175	13.50	1.57
House, Austin	R-R	6-4	200	1-24-91	3	4	3.97	36	9	1	9	100	93	48	44	9	43	72	.249	.286	.222	6.50	3.88
Jimenez, Deyvi	R-R	6-3	220	12-30-89	2	6	6.02	12	9	0	0	58	80	41	39	6	18	40	.325	.355	.302	6.17	2.78
Lamb, Chris	B-L	6-1	185	6-29-90	2	5	4.53	32	0	0	2	50	56	30	25	4	22	39	.289	.326	.277	7.07	3.99
Mota, David	R-R	6-4	265	2-18-87	1	0	1.86	6	0	0	0	10	7	2	2	1	7	10	.206	.235	.176	9.31	6.52
Powers, Brent	L-L	6-1	185	5-25-89	3	2	6.00	8	2	0	0	18	19	16	12	1	11	16	.284	.429	.245	8.00	5.50
Pudenz, Stuart	R-R	6-5	215	9-15-90	3	1	2.40	25	0	0	3	41	35	14	11	0	15	35	.240	.236	.242	7.62	3.27
Sanburn, Nolan	R-R	6-0	175	7-21-91	1	3	1.38	14	1	0	0	26	17	4	4	1	9	20	.191	.212	.179	6.92	3.12
Streich, Seth	L-R	6-3	215	2-19-91	10	6	3.82	21	21	1	0	111	114	56	47	2	41	82	.268	.229	.308	6.67	3.33
Tyson, Drew	R-R	6-4	215	8-11-89	1	1	8.10	3	0	0	0	7	9	6	6	0	2	6	.310	.294	.333	8.10	2.70
Vail, Tyler	R-R	6-1	208	11-3-91	5	5	4.15	39	0	0	7	56	61	29	26	2	20	38	.276	.255	.293	6.07	3.20
Voiro, Vince	R-R	6-3	195	2-23-90	5	5	3.67	30	12	0	3	101	110	53	41	3	44	69	.283	.310	.255	6.17	3.93
Ynoa, Michael	R-R	6-7	210	9-24-91	2	1	2.14	15	15	0	0	55	45	19	13	3	18	48	.221	.214	.228	7.90	2.96

Fielding

Catcher	PCT	G	PO	A	E	DP	PB
Delgado	.987	30	202	28	3	3	7
Maxwell	.993	38	272	26	2	3	8
Pohl	1.000	3	25	1	0	0	6
Rickles	.987	74	467	80	7	11	3

First Base	PCT	G	PO	A	E	DP
Delgado	1.000	1	10	0	0	3
Lewis	.938	4	25	5	2	1

	PCT	G	PO	A	E	DP
Olson	.993	127	1109	102	9	97
Tanis	1.000	2	15	1	0	1
Wooten	.983	6	55	3	1	6

Second Base	PCT	G	PO	A	E	DP
Bostick	.963	125	234	340	22	78
Roberts	.967	14	25	33	2	5
Wooten	—	1	0	0	0	0

Third Base	PCT	G	PO	A	E	DP
Lewis	.722	9	4	9	5	0
Nunez	.884	114	79	218	39	23
Rickles	.800	2	2	2	1	1
Tanis	.875	5	8	6	2	0
Wooten	.971	10	10	24	1	0

Shortstop	PCT	G	PO	A	E	DP
Roberts	.961	40	46	103	6	19
Robertson	.971	99	163	271	13	64
Solano	1.000	2	3	7	0	1

Outfield	PCT	G	PO	A	E	DP
Alexander	.979	46	91	4	2	1
Dixon	1.000	6	13	0	0	0
Mathews	.986	88	137	3	2	1

Roberts	.667	2	2	0	1	0
Shipman	.983	61	112	6	2	1
Vertigan	.985	120	251	7	4	3
Wooten	.961	105	170	3	7	2

VERMONT LAKE MONSTERS

SHORT-SEASON

NEW YORK-PENN LEAGUE

Batting	B-T	HT	WT	DOB	AVG	vLH	vRH	G	AB	R	H	2B	3B	HR	RBI	BB	HBP	SH	SF	SO	SB	CS	SLG	OBP
Baez, Luis	R-R	6-3	200	5-24-91	.184	.188	.183	54	174	11	32	5	0	1	12	8	1	3	1	39	4	0	.230	.223
Booker, Austin	L-R	5-10	170	4-11-88	.158	.000	.200	6	19	2	3	1	0	0	2	0	0	0	0	4	0	0	.211	.158
Boyd, B.J.	L-R	5-10	220	7-16-93	.285	.290	.283	71	260	39	74	13	2	8	32	35	3	1	1	66	8	6	.442	.375
Brugman, Jaycob	L-L	6-0	190	1-18-92	.261	.275	.256	49	165	13	43	9	4	1	23	7	3	0	1	48	7	0	.382	.301
Gorton, Ryan	R-R	6-2	220	2-27-90	.212	.115	.244	35	104	7	22	2	0	1	4	19	1	3	0	20	1	1	.260	.339
Healy, Ryon	R-R	6-5	205	1-10-92	.233	.226	.235	36	146	12	34	10	0	4	21	2	2	0	1	24	2	1	.384	.312
Huck, Ryan	R-R	6-5	255	2-24-91	.238	.303	.220	46	160	15	38	12	0	3	15	25	0	0	0	53	1	0	.369	.341
Lopez, Diomedes	R-R	6-2	195	1-30-89	.125	—	.125	5	16	2	2	0	0	0	2	2	1	1	0	9	0	0	.125	.263
Macklin, Xavier	R-R	6-1	190	9-5-90	.155	.238	.108	19	58	4	9	4	0	1	3	3	1	0	0	26	0	0	.276	.210
Marincov, Tyler	R-R	6-2	200	10-20-91	.215	.200	.220	62	214	20	46	8	2	3	20	25	3	1	3	56	5	4	.313	.302
Mateo, Reynaldo	R-R	5-9	235	7-16-89	.056	.250	.000	7	18	0	1	1	0	0	1	0	0	1	0	9	0	0	.111	.056
McKinney, Billy	L-L	6-1	195	8-23-94	.353	.222	.400	9	34	5	12	2	1	1	6	3	0	0	0	4	1	1	.559	.405
Mercedes, Melvin	B-R	5-8	170	1-13-92	.228	.152	.250	49	145	15	33	3	0	0	9	21	2	3	1	30	5	6	.248	.331
Miller, Josh	R-R	5-9	205	5-11-91	.176	.136	.183	40	131	17	23	5	0	0	6	9	2	1	0	23	4	2	.214	.239
Pinder, Chad	R-R	6-2	195	3-29-92	.200	.214	.196	42	140	14	28	4	0	3	8	12	6	0	3	41	1	0	.293	.286
Powell, Boog	L-L	5-10	175	1-14-93	.283	.196	.307	59	212	30	60	7	3	0	14	26	1	6	0	34	14	6	.344	.364
Rojas, Kelvin	R-R	6-2	188	8-7-89	.226	.250	.222	10	31	3	7	1	0	1	6	2	0	0	1	9	1	1	.355	.265
Solano, Wilfredo	R-R	6-2	205	1-15-93	.161	.129	.173	31	112	9	18	6	0	0	7	10	1	1	1	15	1	2	.214	.234
Soto, Michael	R-R	6-3	215	11-17-91	.206	.320	.167	55	194	17	40	14	1	3	15	12	2	0	1	54	2	3	.335	.258
Wolfe, Chris	B-R	5-11	160	2-2-90	.219	.167	.236	25	73	9	16	3	0	1	5	2	1	0	0	19	1	0	.274	.263

Pitching	B-T	HT	WT	DOB	W	L	ERA	G	GS	CG	SV	IP	H	R	ER	HR	BB	SO	AVG	vLH	vRH	K/9	BB/9
Adkins, Hunter	R-R	6-4	190	9-20-90	0	3	2.81	5	4	0	0	26	23	10	8	3	6	16	.230	.192	.271	5.61	2.10
Bahramzadeh, Kayvon	R-R	6-2	190	1-22-90	1	1	1.80	11	0	0	1	20	12	4	4	0	4	14	.179	.194	.161	6.30	1.80
Bayless, Trevor	R-R	6-3	210	10-6-91	1	0	1.10	14	0	0	7	16	14	2	2	1	5	21	.219	.154	.263	11.57	2.76
Bragg, Sam	R-R	6-2	190	3-23-93	0	2	1.83	13	0	0	5	20	16	6	4	1	9	20	.222	.214	.227	9.15	4.12
Covey, Dylan	R-R	6-2	195	8-14-91	0	0	0.00	4	4	0	0	12	9	1	0	0	1	15	.205	.130	.286	11.25	0.75
Cruzado, Fernand	R-R	6-2	210	10-25-89	1	3	4.99	21	0	0	1	31	35	21	17	2	17	24	.289	.268	.308	7.04	4.99
Duran, Omar	L-L	6-3	209	2-26-90	0	0	0.00	4	0	0	3	5	1	0	0	0	2	8	.063	.143	.000	13.50	3.38
Finnegan, Kyle	R-R	6-2	170	9-4-91	3	3	2.70	11	11	0	0	50	43	18	15	0	12	35	.231	.178	.294	6.30	2.16
Grundy, Jerad	L-L	5-11	200	9-11-90	2	2	7.14	12	3	0	0	29	37	29	23	1	13	14	.306	.250	.323	4.34	4.03
Hansen, Derek	R-R	6-1	195	8-21-90	2	2	2.60	11	0	0	0	17	9	10	5	1	11	15	.153	.143	.158	7.79	5.71
Herrera, Ronald	R-R	5-10	168	5-3-95	1	0	5.87	2	1	0	0	8	10	6	5	0	2	8	.303	.261	.400	9.39	2.35
Jimenez, Deyvi	R-R	6-3	220	12-30-89	2	1	2.41	4	3	0	0	19	10	5	5	2	8	17	.152	.172	.135	8.20	3.86
Johnson, Tyler	R-R	6-1	205	7-18-90	1	1	1.71	20	1	0	3	42	32	11	8	2	17	24	.212	.194	.226	5.14	3.64
Massey, Taylor	L-L	6-0	190	1-14-89	0	1	13.50	4	0	0	0	3	3	7	5	0	6	2	.333	.167	.286	5.40	16.20
Mendez, Junior	R-R	6-1	210	9-20-92	0	0	0.93	9	0	0	0	19	13	4	2	0	9	19	.181	.270	.086	8.84	4.19
Michaud, Joe	R-R	6-4	200	4-4-91	0	1	3.86	2	0	0	0	5	4	4	2	0	1	6	.190	.154	.250	11.57	1.93
Mota, David	R-R	6-4	265	2-18-87	0	0	0.00	2	0	0	0	3	3	0	0	0	2	2	.273	.167	.400	6.00	6.00
Paulino, Gregory	R-R	6-3	200	2-4-93	2	3	2.79	7	5	0	0	29	28	11	9	2	8	22	.257	.268	.245	6.83	2.48
Perez, Cristhian	R-R	6-2	180	9-13-91	1	1	5.29	5	2	0	0	17	22	12	10	3	4	7	.314	.306	.324	3.71	2.12
Powers, Brent	L-L	6-1	185	5-25-89	6	3	2.43	14	14	1	0	78	69	23	21	3	18	69	.234	.259	.224	8.00	2.09
Sosa, Lee	R-R	6-2	215	9-3-91	1	4	4.09	14	5	0	0	44	33	24	20	3	33	30	.213	.273	.169	6.14	6.75
Stalcup, Matt	L-L	6-2	195	7-6-90	2	4	2.83	11	4	0	0	29	22	12	9	0	15	19	.222	.205	.236	5.97	4.71
Torres, Jose	L-L	6-2	175	9-24-93	3	2	2.64	9	5	0	0	31	28	15	9	2	12	21	.228	.281	.209	6.16	3.52
Trivino, Lou	R-R	6-5	225	10-1-91	3	4	3.12	14	10	0	0	61	53	31	21	2	20	47	.231	.235	.228	6.97	2.97
Vattuone, Dominique	R-R	6-4	170	2-12-91	1	1	4.61	9	0	0	0	14	12	8	7	2	8	17	.222	.259	.185	11.20	5.27
Wahl, Bobby	R-R	6-2	210	3-21-92	0	0	3.92	9	4	0	2	21	20	10	9	3	6	27	.241	.281	.216	11.76	2.61

Fielding

Catcher	PCT	G	PO	A	E	DP	PB
Gorton	.992	34	221	24	2	4	9
Lopez	.957	4	18	4	1	0	0
Mateo	1.000	5	28	4	0	2	1
Miller	.986	36	260	26	4	1	2

First Base	PCT	G	PO	A	E	DP
Baez	1.000	2	6	0	0	1
Healy	.949	7	51	5	3	5
Huck	.985	41	307	24	5	25
Soto	.974	31	247	19	7	25

Second Base	PCT	G	PO	A	E	DP
Baez	.973	7	14	22	1	4
Booker	.875	5	8	13	3	5
Mercedes	.966	44	77	124	7	32
Solano	1.000	6	8	18	0	3
Wolfe	.949	20	40	35	4	5

Third Base	PCT	G	PO	A	E	DP
Baez	.899	34	25	64	10	5
Healy	.810	26	18	33	12	5
Pinder	.857	2	2	4	1	2
Solano	—	1	0	0	0	0
Soto	.921	20	9	26	3	3

Shortstop	PCT	G	PO	A	E	DP
Baez	.934	15	21	36	4	10
Mercedes	.810	7	8	9	4	3
Pinder	.944	33	59	77	8	16
Solano	.948	25	30	79	6	11

Outfield	PCT	G	PO	A	E	DP
Boyd	.992	66	121	0	1	0
Brugman	.971	36	61	6	2	1
Macklin	1.000	7	12	0	0	0
Marincov	.973	54	106	2	3	0
McKinney	1.000	9	22	1	0	0
Powell	.992	54	112	9	1	3
Rojas	.882	8	14	1	2	0

ARIZONA LEAGUE

OAKLAND ATHLETICS

Batting	B-T	HT	WT	DOB	AVG	vLH	vRH	G	AB	R	H	2B	3B	HR	RBI	BB	HBP	SH	SF	SO	SB	CS	SLG	OBP
Akau, Iolana	R-R	5-11	180	8-31-95	.133	.143	.130	11	30	2	4	1	0	0	1	2	0	0	1	10	0	0	.167	.182
Bennie, Joe	R-R	6-0	200	5-7-91	.246	.250	.245	20	65	10	16	3	1	1	7	14	0	0	0	22	1	1	.369	.380
Contreras, Franklin	R-R	6-2	165	6-10-90	.000	.000	.000	3	8	0	0	0	0	0	0	1	0	0	0	3	0	0	.000	.111
De La Cruz, Vicmal	L-L	6-0	185	11-20-93	.213	.265	.193	33	122	10	26	2	0	2	11	7	2	0	0	28	0	0	.279	.267
Diaz, Edwin	R-R	6-2	195	8-25-95	.239	.308	.212	27	92	7	22	6	1	1	6	5	0	0	1	25	1	1	.359	.276
Duinkerk, Shawn	L-R	6-5	195	8-18-94	.246	.333	.219	35	138	22	34	7	3	0	20	8	0	0	0	32	4	3	.341	.288
Healy, Ryon	R-R	6-5	205	1-10-92	.214	.273	.176	11	28	4	6	0	1	2	8	3	0	0	2	4	0	0	.500	.273
Higley, Justin	L-R	6-4	200	12-25-92	.275	.242	.283	42	153	31	42	7	4	6	29	21	2	0	3	57	4	3	.490	.363
Huck, Ryan	R-R	6-5	255	2-24-91	.475	.667	.393	10	40	9	19	7	1	2	11	3	2	0	0	6	0	0	.850	.533
Kim, Seongmin	R-R	6-1	200	5-12-93	.148	.000	.182	10	27	6	4	0	0	1	3	0	0	0	7	0	0	.148	.233
Kitamura, Pi'ikea	R-R	6-0	190	6-20-91	.233	.194	.247	34	116	9	27	5	0	0	12	11	0	0	1	22	0	0	.276	.297
Kubala, A.J.	R-R	6-0	205	6-7-94	.147	.167	.140	26	68	12	10	2	0	4	11	8	3	1	0	41	0	0	.353	.266
Lopez, Diomendes	R-R	6-2	195	1-30-89	.200	.200	.200	10	25	3	5	2	0	1	2	6	2	0	0	10	0	0	.400	.394
Marte, Jefry	R-R	6-1	190	6-21-91	.167	.000	.222	5	12	0	2	0	0	0	3	0	0	0	5	0	0	.167	.333
Masik, Scott	R-R	6-2	180	1-10-91	.250	.471	.170	22	64	12	16	2	1	0	4	16	2	1	0	16	2	0	.313	.415
McKinney, Billy	L-L	6-1	195	8-23-94	.320	.415	.281	46	181	31	58	7	2	2	20	17	4	0	4	29	7	0	.414	.383
McQuown, Ben	R-R	5-10	175	2-6-90	.277	.208	.299	33	101	22	28	7	1	0	7	22	3	1	1	30	10	2	.366	.417
Munoz, Yairo	R-R	6-1	165	1-23-95	.194	.250	.176	25	67	8	13	3	0	1	5	7	2	0	1	11	1	0	.284	.286
Paz, Andy	R-R	6-0	170	1-5-93	.228	.364	.186	33	92	7	21	4	0	2	11	10	0	0	0	18	0	1	.337	.304
Raga, Argenis	R-R	6-1	176	7-22-94	.189	.231	.180	24	74	11	14	2	0	1	3	5	1	2	0	22	0	0	.257	.250
Santana, Gabriel	R-R	6-0	165	8-23-92	.267	.219	.279	45	161	19	43	7	1	1	12	4	6	1	3	19	0	1	.342	.305
Shipman, Aaron	L-L	6-0	175	1-27-92	.421	.667	.375	6	19	7	8	1	1	0	3	4	1	0	0	2	0	0	.579	.542
Solano, Wilfredo	R-R	6-2	205	1-15-93	.154	.286	.105	7	26	2	4	1	0	0	4	5	0	0	0	9	0	0	.192	.290
Wheeler, Kyle	R-R	5-11	195	10-16-90	.269	.071	.342	17	52	8	14	5	0	1	12	3	2	0	1	16	0	0	.423	.328
Whitaker, Josh	R-R	6-3	225	2-8-89	.000	.000	.000	1	3	0	0	0	0	0	0	0	0	0	0	2	0	0	.000	.000
Zarraga, Jonesy	R-R	6-1	170	6-3-92	.275	.276	.275	34	109	15	30	3	3	3	18	7	4	0	1	31	4	0	.440	.339

Pitching	B-T	HT	WT	DOB	W	L	ERA	G	GS	CG	SV	IP	H	R	ER	HR	BB	SO	AVG	vLH	vRH	K/9	BB/9
Acevedo, Rony	R-R	6-2	165	9-18-88	2	1	4.91	16	0	0	1	22	22	14	12	1	4	23	.259	.194	.296	9.41	1.64
Adkins, Hunter	R-R	6-4	190	9-20-90	0	1	3.94	8	3	0	0	16	14	10	7	0	6	17	.230	.231	.229	9.56	3.38
Azor, Jose	R-R	6-1	185	10-12-88	1	0	16.88	3	0	0	0	3	5	6	5	1	7	1	.455	1.000	.333	3.38	23.63
Barham, Trey	L-L	6-0	215	11-7-85	0	0	3.72	7	7	0	0	10	9	4	4	0	3	14	.243	.111	.286	13.03	2.79
Bragg, Sam	R-R	6-2	190	3-23-93	1	0	0.00	4	0	0	1	7	2	0	0	0	2	14	.080	.167	.053	17.18	2.45
Burke, A.J.	R-R	6-3	225	7-12-90	1	3	7.84	15	0	0	0	21	29	19	18	1	6	18	.326	.270	.365	7.84	2.61
Doolittle, Ryan	R-R	6-2	205	3-25-88	1	0	0.79	4	3	0	0	11	6	1	1	0	1	6	.158	.056	.250	4.76	0.79
Driver, Dustin	R-R	6-2	210	10-11-94	0	2	7.15	7	4	0	0	11	18	12	9	0	11	4	.367	.333	.387	3.18	8.74
Herrera, Ronald	R-R	5-10	168	5-3-95	4	4	3.82	14	9	0	0	71	76	36	30	3	11	58	.272	.238	.292	7.39	1.40
Kohler, Chris	L-L	6-3	190	5-4-95	1	2	2.78	13	4	0	1	23	19	10	7	0	9	32	.224	.063	.261	12.71	3.57
Massad, Jon	R-R	6-1	200	4-19-91	1	4	3.90	17	2	0	0	30	34	15	13	3	5	24	.281	.170	.351	7.20	1.50
McMullen, Blake	R-R	6-1	205	2-15-91	0	2	5.11	15	1	0	0	25	31	22	14	1	14	20	.313	.214	.386	7.30	5.11
Mendez, Junior	R-R	6-1	210	9-20-92	0	1	4.50	10	1	0	0	20	19	10	10	2	6	21	.244	.320	.208	9.45	2.70
Michaud, Joe	R-R	6-4	200	4-4-91	1	0	3.77	10	2	0	0	14	17	8	6	1	9	24	.288	.250	.308	15.07	5.65
Navas, Carlos	R-R	6-1	170	8-13-92	1	2	4.83	12	7	0	0	50	55	31	27	4	12	23	.281	.250	.295	4.11	2.15
Nolasco, Alex	L-L	6-4	190	9-11-90	2	3	5.66	14	5	0	0	41	38	28	26	3	33	22	.253	.212	.265	4.79	7.19
Peralta, Jensi	R-R	6-2	180	7-2-91	2	1	5.50	15	0	0	0	18	15	14	11	0	13	19	.227	.267	.194	9.50	6.50
Perez, Cristhian	R-R	6-2	180	9-13-91	3	3	3.92	10	5	0	0	44	43	24	19	5	5	36	.251	.213	.281	7.42	1.03
Pitcher, Travis	R-R	6-4	225	1-30-91	1	0	1.69	14	0	0	3	21	19	10	4	1	13	27	.238	.231	.241	11.39	5.48
Sanburn, Nolan	R-R	6-0	175	7-21-91	0	0	2.25	2	1	0	0	4	3	1	1	0	1	6	.200	.200	.200	13.50	2.25
Vattuone, Dominique	R-R	6-4	175	2-12-91	1	1	3.31	9	0	0	2	16	13	7	6	1	4	21	.220	.273	.189	11.57	2.20
Wahl, Bobby	R-R	6-2	210	3-21-92	0	0	9.00	1	1	0	0	1	0	1	1	0	2	1	.000	.000	.000	9.00	18.00

Fielding

Catcher	PCT	G	PO	A	E	DP	PB
Akau	.987	9	61	14	1	1	3
Kim	.962	9	40	10	2	2	4
Lopez	.983	10	57	2	1	0	1
Paz	1.000	29	183	20	0	2	3
Wheeler	.980	13	87	12	2	1	4

First Base	PCT	G	PO	A	E	DP
Duinkerk	.979	19	171	14	4	18
Healy	1.000	8	59	2	0	2
Huck	1.000	10	83	3	0	8
Kubala	.968	5	28	2	1	3
Santana	.993	23	146	6	1	11

Second Base	PCT	G	PO	A	E	DP
Bennie	.964	19	28	52	3	8
Contreras	1.000	3	5	10	0	3
Kitamura	.974	18	31	44	2	11
Munoz	1.000	7	5	8	0	2
Raga	.900	3	4	5	1	1
Santana	1.000	10	21	22	0	5
Solano	1.000	3	6	4	0	2

Third Base	PCT	G	PO	A	E	DP
Bennie	1.000	1	0	2	0	0
Kitamura	1.000	8	1	11	0	0
Kubala	.821	20	5	27	7	2
Marte	1.000	5	1	10	0	2
Raga	.860	18	4	39	7	8
Santana	.905	21	13	25	4	2
Munoz	.944	20	19	49	4	5
Santana	.500	1	1	1	2	1
Solano	.857	5	6	12	3	2

Outfield	PCT	G	PO	A	E	DP
De La Cruz	.958	25	45	1	2	0
Duinkerk	.955	14	21	0	1	0
Higley	.980	32	50	0	1	0
Masik	1.000	18	22	3	0	1
McKinney	.964	29	53	1	2	0
McQuown	.972	30	66	4	2	0
Shipman	1.000	6	6	0	0	0
Whitaker	1.000	1	4	0	0	0
Zarraga	.968	22	29	1	1	0

Shortstop	PCT	G	PO	A	E	DP
Diaz	.950	27	40	56	5	14
Kitamura	.938	10	14	31	3	5

DOMINICAN SUMMER LEAGUE

Batting	B-T	HT	WT	DOB	AVG	vLH	vRH	G	AB	R	H	2B	3B	HR	RBI	BB	HBP	SH	SF	SO	SB	CS	SLG	OBP
Barrera, Luis	L-L	6-0	180	11-15-95	.190	.250	.167	39	126	15	24	5	4	4	20	18	3	0	2	22	3	3	.389	.302
Chavez, Jose	R-R	5-11	175	5-8-95	.223	.091	.256	30	112	7	25	4	0	0	9	2	1	2	0	4	2	2	.259	.243
Godard, Javier	R-R	6-0	170	12-13-95	.156	.097	.176	40	122	15	19	4	1	1	10	10	5	2	0	16	4	3	.230	.248
Guzman, Miguel	R-R	6-2	210	3-10-95	.167	.200	.156	23	60	4	10	2	0	0	4	5	3	1	0	16	0	1	.200	.265
Hernandez, Luis	R-R	5-11	203	9-3-94	.211	.080	.275	27	76	5	16	2	0	0	3	12	0	2	0	9	2	1	.237	.318
Marinez, Eric	B-R	6-1	160	9-12-95	.246	.070	.305	51	171	18	42	12	3	0	17	12	1	1	4	53	1	4	.351	.293
Martes, Mitchell	R-R	6-5	170	11-3-94	.157	.156	.158	55	178	14	28	6	1	2	14	11	2	3	1	61	3	6	.236	.214
Martinez, Robert	R-R	6-1	180	2-8-94	.235	.250	.230	36	119	12	28	8	2	1	16	15	2	1	0	32	3	3	.361	.331
Mercedes, Miguel	R-R	6-4	200	9-12-95	.169	.137	.179	68	213	29	36	9	2	0	10	29	6	0	1	72	5	5	.230	.285
Mullen, Robert	R-R	6-0	170	5-23-96	.267	.294	.260	30	90	12	24	6	0	1	12	6	4	1	0	15	1	2	.367	.340
Penalo, Rodolfo	B-R	5-7	130	8-27-92	.311	.250	.340	51	151	38	47	6	4	0	9	25	4	4	0	21	29	10	.404	.422
Pimentel, Sandber	R-R	6-3	216	9-12-94	.255	.267	.250	32	102	15	26	5	3	2	14	15	1	0	1	22	1	5	.422	.353
Rivas, Jesus	R-R	6-0	180	3-22-94	.333	.333	.333	2	6	1	2	0	0	0	2	0	0	0	1	0	0	0	.333	.286
Rivas, Raymond	L-R	6-1	180	9-23-95	.275	.233	.288	51	182	16	50	5	0	0	15	8	2	2	0	27	4	5	.302	.313
Rodriguez, Jean Carlo	R-R	5-10	170	1-12-96	.302	.373	.271	64	222	33	67	12	1	1	20	19	7	5	1	20	12	5	.378	.373
Rodriguez, Jhonny	L-L	6-3	170	7-20-96	.247	.191	.268	67	251	20	62	15	7	0	32	11	2	2	1	46	2	8	.363	.283
Silva, Andys	R-R	5-11	160	9-12-95	.194	.241	.176	36	103	10	20	3	1	0	1	17	1	5	0	27	2	5	.243	.314

Pitching	B-T	HT	WT	DOB	W	L	ERA	G	GS	CG	SV	IP	H	R	ER	HR	BB	SO	AVG	vLH	vRH	K/9	BB/9
Andueza, Ivan	L-L	5-11	180	2-7-95	2	7	3.09	14	14	0	0	67	68	28	23	1	22	49	.269	.235	.274	6.58	2.96
Benzant, Leonel	R-R	6-6	213	12-20-91	3	1	2.94	17	0	0	1	34	33	16	11	1	16	22	.266	.342	.233	5.88	4.28
Blanco, Argenis	R-R	6-1	165	5-23-96	1	3	4.99	18	1	0	0	31	29	22	17	1	17	27	.254	.257	.253	7.92	4.99
Castillo, Jose	R-R	6-2	185	2-22-91	2	3	2.78	17	1	0	0	32	15	14	10	1	22	42	.139	.111	.153	11.69	6.12
Duno, Angel	R-R	6-0	180	1-10-94	3	4	3.19	15	12	0	0	73	76	36	26	2	15	52	.272	.231	.293	6.38	1.84
Ferreras, Kevin	L-L	6-0	170	7-5-93	1	1	0.99	17	0	0	5	27	12	4	3	0	12	36	.130	.111	.133	11.85	3.95
Hoyos, Renaldo	L-L	6-0	167	5-23-94	0	2	4.97	16	0	0	0	25	27	17	14	1	11	20	.267	.125	.312	9.59	3.91
Magallanes, Wilfredo	R-R	6-2	185	11-15-95	1	1	4.24	15	0	0	0	23	18	13	11	1	17	14	.209	.240	.197	5.40	6.56
Mata, Anderson	L-L	5-11	165	11-17-93	2	3	3.65	15	0	0	0	25	25	16	10	0	14	22	.263	.227	.274	8.03	5.11
Mendoza, Juan	R-R	6-2	170	4-15-96	6	2	1.88	15	14	0	0	72	69	25	15	2	21	42	.257	.296	.239	5.27	2.64
Ortiz, Phillip	R-R	6-0	190	3-6-95	0	2	1.69	9	0	0	1	11	7	4	2	0	9	7	.200	.167	.207	5.91	7.59
Ramos, Julio	L-L	6-1	190	2-13-88	0	0	0.00	2	2	0	0	2	1	0	0	0	1	4	.143	1.000	.000	18.00	4.50
Trejo, Jose	R-R	6-3	175	3-31-96	0	0	6.35	16	0	0	3	23	28	19	16	2	11	16	.301	.238	.319	6.35	4.37
Vargas, Alejandro	R-R	6-1	160	1-29-95	2	1	2.03	18	0	0	0	27	12	11	6	2	19	22	.138	.086	.173	7.43	6.41
Veliz, Victor	L-L	5-11	170	10-6-93	5	3	1.39	14	14	0	0	71	53	17	11	1	18	46	.211	.263	.202	5.83	2.28
Zambrano, Jesus	R-R	5-11	170	8-23-96	2	6	4.40	14	14	1	0	61	62	34	30	4	12	48	.262	.227	.278	7.04	1.76

Fielding

Catcher	PCT	G	PO	A	E	DP	PB
Chavez	.989	22	148	36	2	0	2
Guzman	.978	17	76	12	2	1	0
Hernandez	.974	27	161	25	5	1	5
Mullen	.962	15	85	17	4	3	2
Pimentel	1.000	1	10	0	0	0	0

First Base	PCT	G	PO	A	E	DP
Chavez	1.000	1	9	0	0	0
Martes	.982	48	413	33	8	40
Mercedes	.975	17	149	6	4	13
Pimentel	.979	12	87	8	2	8

Second Base	PCT	G	PO	A	E	DP
Chavez	.957	6	10	12	1	5

	PCT	G	PO	A	E	DP
Godard	.981	32	75	84	3	22
Penalo	1.000	8	12	14	0	2
Rodriguez	.938	22	41	65	7	10
Rodriguez	1.000	1	1	1	0	0
Silva	.935	9	22	21	3	6

Third Base	PCT	G	PO	A	E	DP
Godard	1.000	2	3	7	0	0
Martes	1.000	3	6	6	0	0
Mercedes	.870	43	30	84	17	11
Rodriguez	.914	20	16	48	6	5
Silva	.963	8	7	19	1	4

Shortstop	PCT	G	PO	A	E	DP
Marinez	.893	50	80	137	26	23

	PCT	G	PO	A	E	DP
Rodriguez	.918	9	18	27	4	4
Silva	.958	14	19	27	2	5

Outfield	PCT	G	PO	A	E	DP
Barrera	.960	29	45	3	2	0
Martes	1.000	1	1	0	0	0
Martinez	.962	35	49	1	2	0
Penalo	.986	36	64	5	1	0
Pimentel	.950	11	18	1	1	0
Rivas	1.000	2	3	0	0	0
Rivas	.975	46	74	5	2	2
Rodriguez	1.000	7	7	0	0	0
Rodriguez	.978	63	79	8	2	2

OAKLAND ATHLETICS

Philadelphia Phillies

SEASON IN A SENTENCE: Already reeling from a poor 2012, the Phillies banked once more on their erstwhile core of Jimmy Rollins, Ryan Howard, Chase Utley, Roy Halladay, Cliff Lee and Cole Hamels and wound up falling even further into the doldrums.

HIGH POINT: For one day, July 19, everything was good for the Phillies. Against the division foe Mets, The Mets got home runs from the old guard (Utley), new guard (a pair from Domonic Brown), and an offseason import (Michael Young). At the end of the day, the win was their third in a row, and it put them over .500 for the first time all season and just 6 ½ games out of the division lead. Alas, the hope was both fleeting and false, and the Phillies lost 14 of their next 16.

LOW POINT: The firing of Charlie Manuel ended a six-year era of good feelings in Philly. Provided with an aging core bolstered only by Youngs Delmon and Michael, as well as an abominable bullpen, Manuel took the fall on Aug. 16, and was replaced, first on an interim basis and then permanently, by Ryne Sandberg.

NOTABLE ROOKIES: Jonathan Pettibone came up in late April when Halladay's shoulder gave out and promptly won his first three starts. He didn't allow more than three earned runs in any start until May 30, his eighth start, against the Red Sox. Corn-fed masher Darin Ruf also swatted 14 longballs, good for third-most on the team behind only Utley and Brown, and put together an OPS+ of 121.

KEY TRANSACTIONS: For the most part, the Phillies stood pat, with their only move being the shipment of Michael Young to the Dodgers down the stretch. Otherwise, their most significant movement involved the comings and goings of Ryan Howard, Roy Halladay and Erik Kratz to and from the disabled list. They also lost catcher Carlos Ruiz to the suspended list for the first 25 games after he was deemed to have used amphetamines.

DOWN ON THE FARM: Cody Asche is just getting his feet wet, but he may already be hearing footsteps. Maikel Franco slugged 31 homers between high Class A and Double-A and is the organization's top prospect. Jesse Biddle battled control issues, whooping cough and plantar fasciitis to accumulate the third-most strikeouts in the Eastern League, and first-rounder J.P. Crawford wowed scouts in the Gulf Coast League with his polish and overall skills.

OPENING DAY PAYROLL: $165.3 million (3rd)

ORGANIZATION LEADERS

BATTING		*Minimum 250 AB
MAJORS		
* AVG	Utley, Chase	.284
* OPS	Utley, Chase	.823
HR	Brown, Domonic	27
RBI	Brown, Domonic	83
MINORS		
* AVG	Franco, Maikel, Reading/Clearwater	.32
* OBP	Hernandez, Cesar, Lehigh Valley/Reading	.378
* SLG	Franco, Maikel, Reading/Clearwater	.569
R	Franco, Maikel, Reading/Clearwater	89
H	Franco, Maikel, Reading/Clearwater	173
TB	Franco, Maikel, Reading/Clearwater	308
2B	Altherr, Aaron, Clearwater	36
	Franco, Maikel, Reading/Clearwater	36
3B	Collier, Zach, Reading	9
	Hernandez, Cesar, Lehigh Valley/Reading	9
HR	Franco, Maikel, Reading/Clearwater	31
RBI	Franco, Maikel, Reading/Clearwater	103
BB	Alonso, Carlos, Clearwater	59
	Murphy, Jim, Reading	59
SO	Greene, Larry, Lakewood	163
SB	Hernandez, Cesar, Lehigh Valley/Reading	33

PITCHING		#Minimum 75 IP
MAJORS		
W	Lee, Cliff	14
# ERA	Lee, Cliff	2.87
SO	Lee, Cliff	222
SV	Papelbon, Jonathan	29
MINORS		
W	Milner, Hoby, Clearwater	12
L	Biddle, Jesse, Reading	14
# ERA	Hollands, Mario, Clearwater/Reading	2.86
G	Johnson, Jay, Lehigh Valley/Reading	55
GS	Buchanan, David, Lehigh Valley/Reading	28
SV	Four tied at	11
IP	Buchanan, David, Lehigh Valley/Reading	170
BB	Biddle, Jesse, Reading	82
SO	Biddle, Jesse, Reading	154
# AVG	Biddle, Jesse, Reading	.21

PHILADELPHIA PHILLIES

2013 PERFORMANCE

General Manager: Ruben Amaro Jr. **Farm Director:** Joe Jordan. **Scouting Director:** Marti Wolever.

Class	Team	League	W	L	PCT	Finish	Manager(s)
Majors	Philadelphia Phillies	National	73	89	.451	13th (15)	C. Manuel/Ryne Sandberg
Triple-A	Lehigh Valley IronPigs	International	72	72	.500	7th (14)	Dave Brundage
Double-A	Reading Fightin' Phils	Eastern	62	80	.437	12th (12)	Dusty Wathan
High A	Clearwater Threshers	Florida State	67	68	.496	6th (12)	Chris Truby
Low A	Lakewood BlueClaws	South Atlantic	56	80	.412	12th (14)	Mickey Morandini
Short-season	Williamsport Crosscutters	New York-Penn	37	38	.493	9th (14)	Nelson Prada
Rookie	GCL Phillies	Gulf Coast	30	30	.500	7th (16)	Roly DeArmas
Overall 2013 Minor League Record			324	368	.468	26th (30)	

ORGANIZATION STATISTICS

NATIONAL LEAGUE

Batting	B-T	HT	WT	DOB	AVG	vLH	vRH	G	AB	R	H	2B	3B	HR	RBI	BB	HBP	SH	SF	SO	SB	CS	SLG	OBP
Asche, Cody	L-R	6-1	180	6-30-90	.235	.219	.238	50	162	18	38	8	1	5	22	15	1	0	1	43	1	0	.389	.302
Bernadina, Roger	L-L	6-2	200	6-12-84	.187	.154	.194	27	75	8	14	4	1	2	5	4	3	1	0	21	1	0	.347	.256
2-team total (85 Washington)					.181	—	—	112	227	26	41	10	2	4	11	16	5	2	0	65	4	0	.295	.250
Brown, Domonic	L-L	6-5	205	9-3-87	.272	.252	.281	139	496	65	135	21	4	27	83	39	1	0	4	97	8	3	.494	.324
Carrera, Ezequiel	L-L	5-10	185	6-11-87	.077	.000	.091	13	13	2	1	0	0	0	0	1	2	0	0	4	0	0	.077	.250
Frandsen, Kevin	R-R	6-0	185	5-24-82	.234	.311	.202	119	252	27	59	10	1	5	26	12	11	1	2	29	1	0	.341	.296
Galvis, Freddy	B-R	5-10	170	11-14-89	.234	.245	.230	70	205	13	48	5	4	6	19	13	1	3	0	45	1	0	.385	.283
Hernandez, Cesar	B-R	5-10	175	5-23-90	.289	.262	.304	34	121	17	35	5	0	0	10	9	1	0	0	26	0	3	.331	.344
Howard, Ryan	L-L	6-4	240	11-19-79	.266	.173	.302	80	286	34	76	20	2	11	43	23	2	0	6	95	0	0	.465	.319
Kratz, Erik	R-R	6-4	255	6-15-80	.213	.079	.245	68	197	21	42	7	0	9	26	18	1	0	2	45	0	0	.386	.280
Lerud, Steve	L-R	6-1	215	10-13-84	.000	.000	.000	6	5	0	0	0	0	0	0	0	0	0	0	4	0	0	.000	.000
Martinez, Michael	B-R	5-9	175	9-16-82	.175	.167	.176	29	40	5	7	0	0	0	3	0	0	0	0	12	1	0	.175	.175
Mayberry Jr., John	R-R	6-6	225	12-21-83	.227	.240	.221	134	353	47	80	23	1	11	39	27	3	0	1	90	5	3	.391	.286
McDonald, John	R-R	5-9	180	9-24-74	.174	.000	.267	21	23	5	4	0	0	1	3	1	0	1	0	4	0	0	.304	.208
2-team total (16 Pittsburgh)					.111	—	—	37	54	5	6	1	0	1	4	4	1	1	0	12	0	0	.185	.186
Nix, Laynce	L-L	6-1	220	10-30-80	.180	.111	.185	81	128	11	23	4	0	2	7	8	0	0	0	44	1	0	.258	.228
Orr, Pete	L-R	6-1	195	6-8-79	.200	.333	.176	15	20	1	4	0	0	0	0	2	0	0	0	8	0	0	.200	.273
Quintero, Humberto	R-R	5-9	215	8-2-79	.250	.545	.189	24	64	3	16	4	0	2	9	3	1	0	0	15	0	0	.406	.294
Revere, Ben	L-R	5-9	170	5-3-88	.305	.370	.285	88	315	37	96	9	3	0	17	16	0	5	0	36	22	8	.352	.338
Rollins, Jimmy	B-R	5-8	180	11-27-78	.252	.252	.252	160	600	65	151	36	2	6	39	59	1	3	3	93	22	6	.348	.318
Ruf, Darin	R-R	6-3	220	7-28-86	.247	.188	.269	73	251	36	62	11	0	14	30	33	7	0	2	91	0	0	.458	.348
Ruiz, Carlos	R-R	5-10	205	1-22-79	.268	.300	.257	92	310	30	83	16	0	5	37	18	7	4	2	39	1	0	.368	.320
Rupp, Cameron	R-R	6-1	240	9-28-88	.308	.250	.333	4	13	1	4	1	0	0	2	1	0	0	0	4	0	0	.385	.357
Susdorf, Steve	L-L	6-1	195	3-28-86	.143	.000	.200	3	7	1	1	0	0	0	0	0	0	0	0	1	0	0	.143	.143
Utley, Chase	L-R	6-1	200	12-17-78	.284	.245	.302	131	476	73	135	25	6	18	69	45	5	0	5	79	8	3	.475	.348
Wells, Casper	R-R	6-2	220	11-23-84	.042	.200	.000	12	24	2	1	1	0	0	0	2	0	0	0	8	0	0	.083	.115
Young, Delmon	R-R	6-3	240	9-14-85	.261	.286	.254	80	272	32	71	13	0	8	31	14	3	0	2	69	0	0	.397	.302
Young, Michael	R-R	6-1	200	10-19-76	.276	.235	.289	126	468	49	129	24	4	8	42	42	1	0	1	78	1	0	.395	.336
2-team total (21 Los Angeles)					.279	—	—	147	519	52	145	26	5	8	46	43	1	0	2	83	1	0	.395	.335

Pitching	B-T	HT	WT	DOB	W	L	ERA	G	GS	CG	SV	IP	H	R	ER	HR	BB	SO	AVG	vLH	vRH	K/9	BB/9
Adams, Mike	R-R	6-5	195	7-29-78	1	4	3.96	28	0	0	0	25	23	11	11	5	11	23	.242	.257	.233	8.28	3.96
Aumont, Phillippe	L-R	6-7	260	1-7-89	1	3	4.19	22	0	0	0	19	24	11	9	0	13	19	.308	.433	.229	8.84	6.05
Bastardo, Antonio	L-L	5-11	200	9-21-85	3	2	2.32	48	0	0	2	43	33	12	11	2	21	47	.217	.194	.233	9.91	4.43
Cloyd, Tyler	R-R	6-3	210	5-16-87	2	7	6.56	13	11	0	0	60	83	45	44	7	25	41	.328	.308	.346	6.12	3.73
De Fratus, Justin	R-R	6-4	220	10-28-87	3	3	3.86	58	0	0	0	47	45	21	20	3	25	42	.259	.170	.291	8.10	4.82
Diekman, Jake	L-L	6-4	200	1-21-87	1	4	2.58	45	0	0	0	38	34	15	11	1	16	41	.234	.148	.298	9.63	3.76
Durbin, Chad	R-R	6-2	225	12-3-77	1	0	9.00	16	0	0	0	16	25	17	16	4	9	16	.357	.357	.357	9.00	5.06
Garcia, Luis	R-R	6-2	225	1-30-87	1	1	3.73	24	0	0	0	31	27	15	13	3	23	23	.237	.214	.250	6.61	6.61
Halladay, Roy	R-R	6-6	225	5-14-77	4	5	6.82	13	13	1	0	62	55	48	47	12	36	51	.238	.248	.230	7.40	5.23
Hamels, Cole	L-L	6-3	195	12-27-83	8	14	3.60	33	33	1	0	220	205	94	88	21	50	202	.246	.257	.243	8.26	2.05
Horst, Jeremy	L-L	6-3	215	10-1-85	0	2	6.23	28	0	0	0	26	35	19	18	4	12	21	.330	.286	.359	7.27	4.15
Jimenez, Cesar	L-L	5-11	220	11-12-84	1	1	3.71	19	0	0	0	17	14	7	7	1	10	11	.226	.143	.294	5.82	5.29
Kendrick, Kyle	R-R	6-3	210	8-26-84	10	13	4.70	30	30	2	0	182	207	96	95	18	47	110	.285	.246	.318	5.44	2.32
Lannan, John	L-L	6-4	235	9-27-84	3	6	5.33	14	14	0	0	74	86	48	44	6	27	38	.296	.323	.288	4.60	3.27
Lee, Cliff	L-L	6-3	205	8-30-78	14	8	2.87	31	31	2	0	223	193	77	71	22	32	222	.232	.210	.239	8.97	1.29
Martin, Ethan	R-R	6-2	195	6-6-89	2	5	6.08	15	8	0	0	40	42	27	27	9	26	41	.284	.241	10.58	5.85	
Miner, Zach	R-R	6-4	225	3-12-82	0	2	4.40	16	3	0	0	29	33	14	14	4	17	20	.297	.281	.304	6.28	5.34
Papelbon, Jonathan	R-R	6-4	225	11-23-80	5	1	2.92	61	0	0	29	62	59	23	20	6	11	57	.247	.241	.252	8.32	1.61
Pettibone, Jonathan	L-R	6-6	225	7-19-90	5	4	4.04	18	18	0	0	100	109	50	45	9	38	66	.284	.306	.261	5.92	3.41
Ramirez, J.C.	R-R	6-4	250	8-16-88	0	1	7.50	18	0	0	0	24	30	22	20	6	15	16	.313	.378	.271	6.00	5.63
Robles, Mauricio	L-L	5-10	215	3-5-89	0	0	1.93	3	0	0	0	5	7	3	1	0	3	6	.318	.375	.286	11.57	5.79
Rosenberg, B.J.	R-R	6-3	220	9-17-85	2	0	4.58	22	0	0	1	20	20	10	10	0	9	19	.263	.333	.231	8.69	4.12
Savery, Joe	L-L	6-3	235	11-4-85	2	0	3.15	18	0	0	0	20	15	11	7	1	11	14	.205	.409	.118	6.30	4.95
Stutes, Mike	R-R	6-1	185	9-4-86	3	1	4.58	16	0	0	0	18	14	11	9	1	8	9	.212	.346	.125	4.58	4.08
Valdes, Raul	L-L	5-11	190	11-27-77	1	1	7.46	17	1	0	0	35	42	29	29	7	8	37	.300	.229	.337	9.51	2.06

Fielding

Catcher	PCT	G	PO	A	E	DP	PB
Kratz	.998	60	414	26	1	5	1
Lerud	1.000	5	7	0	0	0	0
Quintero	.972	21	123	14	4	1	0
Ruiz	.996	86	657	44	3	9	4
Rupp	1.000	3	25	1	0	0	0

First Base	PCT	G	PO	A	E	DP
Frandsen	.996	40	256	16	1	18
Howard	.998	76	618	42	1	55
Mayberry Jr.	.975	7	36	3	1	7
Nix	1.000	4	24	0	0	2
Ruf	.993	36	248	21	2	29
Young	1.000	26	176	8	0	17

Second Base	PCT	G	PO	A	E	DP
Frandsen	.976	20	38	43	2	13
Galvis	.980	23	40	56	2	13

	PCT	G	PO	A	E	DP
Hernandez	.939	10	12	19	2	4
McDonald	1.000	1	1	0	0	0
Utley	.971	125	247	317	17	65
Third Base	**PCT**	**G**	**PO**	**A**	**E**	**DP**
Asche	.959	44	29	87	5	3
Frandsen	.857	4	2	4	1	0
Galvis	.976	16	7	33	1	2
Martinez	1.000	2	1	0	0	0
McDonald	1.000	8	3	7	0	4
Orr	.667	2	0	2	1	0
Young	.961	99	58	166	9	12
Shortstop	**PCT**	**G**	**PO**	**A**	**E**	**DP**
Galvis	1.000	11	11	26	0	7
Martinez	1.000	3	5	3	0	1
McDonald	.947	6	5	13	1	3
Rollins	.982	153	190	424	11	89

Outfield	PCT	G	PO	A	E	DP
Bernadina	1.000	23	46	2	0	0
Brown	.975	133	190	9	5	0
Carrera	1.000	7	11	0	0	0
Galvis	1.000	10	20	0	0	0
Hernandez	.918	22	45	0	4	0
Martinez	1.000	16	18	1	0	1
Mayberry Jr.	.995	118	203	3	1	0
McDonald	1.000	1	1	0	0	0
Nix	.979	27	47	0	1	0
Orr	1.000	2	4	0	0	0
Revere	.991	87	220	6	2	3
Ruf	1.000	47	74	4	0	0
Susdorf	.750	2	3	0	1	0
Wells	1.000	5	14	1	0	1
Young	.960	64	115	4	5	2

LEHIGH VALLEY IRONPIGS   TRIPLE-A
INTERNATIONAL LEAGUE

Batting	B-T	HT	WT	DOB	AVG	vLH	vRH	G	AB	R	H	2B	3B	HR	RBI	BB	HBP	SH	SF	SO	SB	CS	SLG	OBP
Abreu, Miguel	R-R	5-10	190	11-14-84	.125	.200	.091	9	16	4	2	0	0	0	0	0	0	0	0	4	0	0	.125	.125
Asche, Cody	L-R	6-1	180	6-30-90	.295	.261	.308	104	404	52	119	24	4	15	68	35	3	0	4	95	11	3	.485	.352
Castro, Leandro	R-R	5-11	175	6-15-89	.256	.328	.228	117	438	48	112	23	1	8	55	15	0	4	1	77	20	7	.368	.280
Fields, Josh	R-R	6-2	225	12-14-82	.289	.348	.264	109	377	43	109	26	3	4	45	28	1	2	3	110	10	3	.406	.337
Galvis, Freddy	B-R	5-10	170	11-14-89	.245	.316	.223	62	241	26	59	14	2	3	25	11	1	7	6	51	3	1	.357	.274
Gillies, Tyson	L-R	6-2	205	10-31-88	.220	.170	.234	63	214	31	47	7	2	3	8	19	1	3	0	55	13	2	.313	.286
Hanzawa, Troy	R-R	5-9	155	9-12-85	.283	.300	.267	19	60	6	17	5	0	0	5	3	1	2	0	8	0	1	.367	.328
Henson, Tyler	R-R	6-1	205	12-15-87	.316	.353	.308	31	95	12	30	8	0	4	14	9	2	2	3	30	3	1	.526	.376
Hernandez, Cesar	B-R	5-10	175	5-23-90	.309	.321	.305	104	391	59	121	12	9	2	34	41	1	5	2	81	32	8	.402	.375
Joseph, Tommy	R-R	6-1	215	7-16-91	.209	.167	.218	21	67	6	14	1	0	3	14	4	1	0	0	15	0	1	.358	.264
Kratz, Erik	R-R	6-4	255	6-15-80	.167	.333	.111	3	12	0	2	1	0	0	1	0	0	0	0	1	0	0	.250	.167
Lerud, Steve	L-R	6-1	215	10-13-84	.217	.212	.218	61	180	20	39	8	0	3	21	35	3	1	0	50	1	0	.311	.353
Martinez, Michael	B-R	5-9	175	9-16-82	.300	.343	.283	71	243	35	73	11	3	3	28	18	2	2	1	35	6	5	.407	.352
Mitchell, Derrick	R-R	6-3	210	1-5-87	.248	.300	.228	33	109	15	27	7	0	4	15	11	0	0	2	36	5	1	.422	.311
Mitchell, Jermaine	L-L	6-0	215	11-2-84	.256	.267	.253	63	207	43	53	13	5	5	18	28	1	5	0	63	13	4	.440	.347
2-team total (43 Rochester)					.268	—	—	106	340	62	91	16	7	7	29	37	1	5	0	105	20	8	.418	.341
Orr, Pete	L-R	6-1	195	6-8-79	.258	.188	.277	95	325	40	84	17	6	4	31	17	3	5	2	61	9	7	.385	.300
Overbeck, Cody	R-R	6-1	200	6-5-86	.255	.308	.235	122	440	52	112	29	0	19	65	28	8	0	6	140	2	4	.450	.307
Quintero, Humberto	R-R	5-9	215	8-2-79	.292	.250	.333	8	24	7	7	1	0	2	4	4	2	1	1	5	0	0	.583	.419
Ruf, Darin	R-R	6-3	220	7-28-86	.266	.288	.259	83	305	44	81	22	0	7	46	36	3	0	6	88	1	2	.407	.343
Ruiz, Carlos	R-R	5-10	205	1-22-79	.200	.000	.333	2	5	1	1	0	0	0	0	0	0	0	0	0	0	0	.200	.200
Rupp, Cameron	R-R	6-1	240	9-28-88	.269	.404	.215	53	182	18	49	10	0	6	24	10	1	0	1	55	1	1	.423	.309
Suomi, John	L-R	5-11	200	10-5-80	.269	.455	.133	10	26	3	7	1	0	1	3	3	0	0	0	6	0	0	.423	.345
Susdorf, Steve	L-L	6-1	195	3-28-86	.313	.279	.321	101	310	43	97	20	1	2	36	37	6	0	6	52	11	7	.403	.390
Tolbert, Matt	B-R	6-0	185	5-4-82	.000	.000	.000	4	13	0	0	0	0	0	0	1	0	0	0	2	0	0	.000	.071
Young, Delmon	R-R	6-3	240	9-14-85	.294	.500	.267	4	17	2	5	1	0	0	1	0	0	0	0	4	0	0	.353	.294

Pitching	B-T	HT	WT	DOB	W	L	ERA	G	GS	CG	SV	IP	H	R	ER	HR	BB	SO	AVG	vLH	vRH	K/9	BB/9
Aumont, Phillippe	L-R	6-7	260	1-7-89	0	2	4.04	32	0	0	2	36	29	16	16	0	38	42	.230	.231	.230	10.60	9.59
Bramhall, Zach	L-L	5-11	190	7-13-85	0	0	6.39	6	0	0	0	13	17	10	9	3	4	4	.321	.350	.303	2.84	2.84
2-team total (2 Syracuse)					0	0	6.75	9	0	0	0	16	20	13	12	5	6	6	—			3.38	3.38
Buchanan, David	R-R	6-3	190	5-11-89	4	2	3.00	6	6	0	0	39	36	14	13	2	12	22	.250	.091	.348	5.08	2.77
Cloyd, Tyler	R-R	6-3	210	5-16-87	9	4	4.71	19	19	2	0	113	125	70	59	21	26	93	.276	.288	.288	7.43	2.08
Cochran, Tom	L-L	6-2	195	10-16-82	3	8	5.44	19	19	0	0	91	108	61	55	8	47	65	.296	.242	.314	6.43	4.65
De Fratus, Justin	B-R	6-4	220	10-21-87	3	0	1.89	13	0	0	0	19	18	5	4	0	6	17	.269	.296	.250	8.05	2.84
Diekman, Jake	L-L	6-4	200	1-21-87	1	0	5.70	30	0	0	11	30	31	22	19	1	24	37	.270	.316	.310	11.10	7.20
Friend, Justin	R-R	6-1	210	6-21-86	5	4	3.79	46	0	0	3	71	61	35	30	8	43	57	.231	.321	.168	7.19	5.43
Garcia, Luis	R-R	6-2	215	1-30-87	0	0	0.82	8	0	0	3	11	5	1	1	0	4	8	.132	.231	.080	6.55	3.27
Garner, Perci	R-R	6-3	225	12-13-88	1	0	3.18	1	1	0	0	6	6	2	2	0	2	7	.273	.500	.222	11.12	3.18
Horst, Jeremy	L-L	6-1	215	10-11-85	0	0	4.50	2	0	0	0	2	1	1	1	0	0	3	.167	.333	.000	13.50	0.00
Jimenez, Cesar	L-L	5-11	200	11-12-84	1	2	3.12	36	3	0	3	66	61	24	23	3	26	64	.247	.276	.234	8.68	3.53
Johnson, Jay	R-L	6-2	210	12-21-89	0	2	4.08	17	0	0	0	18	9	8	8	1	19	22	.158	.130	.176	11.21	9.68
MacDougal, Mike	B-R	6-4	180	3-5-77	2	1	5.33	20	0	0	0	25	24	15	15	1	17	26	.258	.313	.230	9.24	6.04
2-team total (17 Louisville)					2	2	5.40	37	0	0	0	45	45	27	27	3	28	46	—			9.20	5.60
Martin, Ethan	R-R	6-2	195	6-6-89	11	5	4.12	21	21	1	0	116	94	56	53	11	67	107	.229	.249	.211	8.33	5.21
Miner, Zach	R-R	6-4	225	3-12-82	5	6	3.90	27	12	0	2	85	90	43	37	5	28	54	.276	.268	.284	5.70	2.95
Morgan, Adam	L-L	6-1	195	2-27-90	2	7	4.04	16	16	0	0	71	84	41	32	10	26	49	.296	.284	.300	6.18	3.28
Nesseth, Mike	R-R	6-5	215	4-19-88	0	0	0.00	3	1	0	0	7	2	1	0	1	2	2	.091	.143	.067	2.57	1.29
Pettibone, Jonathan	L-R	6-6	225	7-19-90	0	2	6.75	4	4	0	0	17	26	15	13	1	5	10	.371	.355	.385	5.19	2.60
Ramirez, J.C.	R-R	6-4	250	8-16-88	4	2	4.71	30	0	0	3	42	42	24	22	2	23	36	.253	.288	.234	7.71	4.93
Robles, Mauricio	L-L	5-10	215	3-5-89	2	2	1.42	34	0	0	7	38	16	7	6	0	31	26	.137	.195	.105	6.16	7.34

PHILADELPHIA PHILLIES

Rosenberg, B.J.	R-R	6-3	220	9-17-85	3	6	4.52	28	10	0	2	76	80	41	38	5	34	59	.270	.276	.266	7.02	4.04
Savery, Joe	L-L	6-3	235	11-4-85	3	1	3.80	20	0	0	2	24	18	11	10	2	9	29	.209	.194	.218	11.03	3.42
Smith, Greg	L-L	6-1	190	12-22-83	8	4	3.31	23	14	0	0	98	107	38	36	6	19	50	.282	.236	.299	4.59	1.74
Stutes, Mike	R-R	6-1	185	9-4-86	1	2	3.33	20	0	0	2	27	21	11	10	1	11	25	.208	.194	.214	8.33	3.67
Valdes, Raul	L-L	5-11	190	11-27-77	4	5	2.86	14	14	0	0	79	67	26	25	5	22	66	.228	.269	.213	7.55	2.52
Zambrano, Carlos	B-R	6-4	275	6-1-81	1	0	3.32	4	4	0	0	19	19	10	7	0	10	18	.257	.316	.194	8.53	4.74

Fielding

Catcher	PCT	G	PO	A	E	DP	PB
Joseph	.993	21	140	8	1	0	9
Kratz	1.000	2	16	0	0	0	0
Lerud	.982	60	401	31	8	4	10
Quintero	1.000	8	69	7	0	2	1
Ruiz	1.000	2	7	0	0	0	4
Rupp	.995	52	344	32	2	2	4
Suomi	.983	9	55	4	1	0	3

First Base	PCT	G	PO	A	E	DP
Fields	.987	31	204	22	3	22
Henson	.963	3	24	2	1	1
Overbeck	.994	97	727	55	5	78
Ruf	1.000	19	144	12	0	15
Suomi	1.000	1	2	0	0	0
Susdorf	.909	1	10	0	1	0

Second Base	PCT	G	PO	A	E	DP
Abreu	1.000	4	12	10	0	2

Galvis	1.000	3	4	6	0	1
Hernandez	.976	79	157	203	9	62
Martinez	.968	12	28	32	2	7
Orr	.987	46	114	121	3	23
Tolbert	.933	3	6	8	1	2

Third Base	PCT	G	PO	A	E	DP
Abreu	1.000	1	1	5	0	0
Asche	.959	103	54	202	11	18
Fields	.964	12	5	22	1	4
Galvis	1.000	2	3	4	0	0
Henson	.953	24	15	46	3	5
Martinez	.800	2	0	4	1	0
Orr	1.000	2	1	4	0	0
Tolbert	.667	1	1	1	1	0

Shortstop	PCT	G	PO	A	E	DP
Galvis	.988	57	100	144	3	32
Hanzawa	1.000	19	27	45	0	11

Hernandez	—	1	0	0	0	0
Martinez	.954	46	64	122	9	26
Orr	.976	28	49	72	3	20

Outfield	PCT	G	PO	A	E	DP
Castro	.968	115	235	8	8	0
Fields	1.000	10	17	0	0	0
Gillies	.963	63	121	9	5	1
Hernandez	.941	21	48	0	3	0
Martinez	1.000	10	27	3	0	1
Mitchell	1.000	33	73	2	0	0
Mitchell	.992	57	123	1	1	0
Orr	1.000	14	26	2	0	0
Ruf	.978	60	90	1	2	0
Susdorf	.970	64	94	3	3	0
Young	1.000	4	7	0	0	0

READING FIGHTIN' PHILS

DOUBLE-A

EASTERN LEAGUE

Batting	B-T	HT	WT	DOB	AVG	vLH	vRH	G	AB	R	H	2B	3B	HR	RBI	BB	HBP	SH	SF	SO	SB	CS	SLG	OBP
Abreu, Miguel	R-R	5-10	190	11-14-84	.242	.250	.239	36	99	14	24	4	1	3	11	3	1	1	0	13	4	2	.394	.272
Cartwright, Albert	R-R	5-10	180	10-31-87	.254	.254	.253	128	489	76	124	16	5	7	42	30	16	4	7	111	26	9	.350	.314
Collier, Zach	L-L	6-2	185	9-8-90	.222	.236	.218	123	446	57	99	14	9	8	36	47	11	7	2	129	17	6	.348	.310
Dalles, Justin	R-R	6-2	205	12-30-88	.219	.500	.091	12	32	3	7	2	0	1	2	0	0	1	0	8	0	0	.375	.219
Dugan, Kelly	B-R	6-3	195	9-18-90	.264	.296	.253	56	212	25	56	12	1	10	23	5	6	2	1	54	0	1	.472	.299
Duran, Edgar	R-R	5-11	155	2-10-91	.225	.222	.225	117	405	35	91	19	2	4	33	22	9	9	5	91	12	6	.311	.277
Franco, Maikel	R-R	6-1	180	8-26-92	.339	.314	.348	69	277	47	94	13	2	15	51	10	2	0	3	31	1	2	.563	.363
Gillies, Tyson	L-R	6-2	205	10-31-88	.267	.240	.272	51	176	24	47	8	4	7	21	12	0	2	1	39	4	3	.477	.312
Gonzalez, Andy	R-R	6-3	215	12-15-81	.143	.000	.185	12	35	3	5	1	0	0	1	7	0	0	0	5	0	0	.171	.286
Hanzawa, Troy	R-R	5-9	155	9-12-85	.295	.294	.296	60	193	22	57	12	2	1	17	5	4	5	1	28	2	2	.394	.325
Henson, Tyler	R-R	6-1	205	12-15-87	.264	.190	.278	80	258	31	68	17	4	4	23	26	5	3	2	86	10	3	.407	.340
Hernandez, Cesar	B-R	5-10	175	5-23-90	.500	.400	.600	3	10	2	5	1	0	0	3	1	0	1	1	1	1	0	.600	.500
Hewitt, Anthony	R-R	6-1	190	4-27-89	.244	.389	.199	116	386	50	94	16	4	16	51	26	3	1	1	134	21	9	.430	.294
Joseph, Tommy	R-R	6-1	215	7-16-91	.273	.000	.333	3	11	0	3	1	0	0	1	1	0	0	0	1	0	0	.364	.333
Kratz, Erik	R-R	6-4	255	6-15-80	.000	—	.000	1	4	0	0	0	0	0	0	0	0	0	0	1	0	0	.000	.000
Mendonca, Tommy	L-R	6-1	200	4-12-88	.257	.231	.260	40	136	13	35	8	2	1	20	7	1	0	0	34	0	0	.368	.299
Mitchell, Derrick	R-R	6-3	210	1-5-87	.241	.255	.236	72	220	36	53	15	1	9	25	25	1	1	1	50	8	4	.441	.320
Murphy, Jim	R-R	6-4	240	9-16-85	.273	.300	.267	139	505	62	138	24	2	23	83	59	7	0	8	119	1	1	.465	.352
Ruiz, Carlos	R-R	5-10	205	1-22-79	.167	.500	.000	2	6	0	1	1	0	0	1	0	0	0	0	0	0	0	.333	.286
Rupp, Cameron	R-R	6-1	240	9-28-88	.245	.105	.266	41	143	18	35	6	0	8	21	14	4	0	0	36	0	0	.455	.329
Suomi, John	L-R	5-11	200	10-5-80	.235	.077	.265	35	81	12	19	0	0	2	10	11	0	0	0	6	0	0	.309	.326
Tolbert, Matt	B-R	6-0	185	5-4-82	.308	.300	.310	25	78	10	24	1	1	0	5	4	0	1	1	7	1	2	.346	.337
Utley, Chase	L-R	6-1	200	12-17-78	.000	.000	.000	2	9	0	0	0	0	0	0	0	0	0	0	1	0	0	.000	.000
Valle, Sebastian	R-R	6-1	205	7-24-90	.203	.198	.205	98	354	38	72	15	2	12	41	19	1	3	2	88	1	1	.359	.245
Welty, Ronnie	R-R	6-3	204	1-19-88	.162	.143	.167	15	37	3	6	0	0	1	3	3	0	0	1	15	2	0	.243	.220

Pitching	B-T	HT	WT	DOB	W	L	ERA	G	GS	CG	SV	IP	H	R	ER	HR	BB	SO	AVG	vLH	vRH	K/9	BB/9
Biddle, Jesse	L-L	6-4	225	10-22-91	5	14	3.64	27	27	2	0	138	104	59	56	10	82	154	.210	.195	.215	10.02	5.33
Bramhall, Bobby	L-L	5-11	190	7-13-85	1	3	3.67	23	7	0	0	56	55	31	23	6	25	43	.246	.294	.224	6.87	3.99
Buchanan, David	R-R	6-3	190	5-11-89	6	11	4.82	22	22	0	0	131	142	78	70	15	41	86	.281	.245	.314	5.92	2.82
Cochran, Tom	L-L	6-2	195	10-16-82	0	3	5.73	3	2	0	0	11	12	7	7	3	7	6	.279	.375	.222	4.91	5.73
Colvin, Brody	R-R	6-3	195	8-14-90	3	2	6.40	21	13	0	0	77	79	56	55	9	54	36	.272	.288	.261	4.19	6.28
Demmin, Ryan	L-L	6-1	210	4-5-88	1	2	4.58	3	3	0	0	20	22	11	10	3	4	8	.301	.217	.340	3.66	1.83
Erbe, Brandon	R-R	6-4	190	12-25-87	0	0	9.82	3	0	0	0	4	3	4	4	0	8	6	.231	.333	.143	14.73	19.64
Friend, Justin	R-R	6-1	210	6-21-86	0	1	22.50	2	0	0	0	2	5	5	5	0	4	2	.500	.833	.000	9.00	18.00
Garcia, Luis	R-R	6-2	215	1-30-87	2	1	2.45	11	0	0	1	11	10	3	3	1	3	13	.250	.353	.174	10.64	2.45
Garner, Perci	R-R	6-3	225	12-13-88	0	0	6.52	2	2	0	0	10	11	9	7	1	10	7	.256	.269	.235	6.52	9.31
Gonzalez, Severino	R-R	6-1	153	9-28-92	1	0	2.70	1	1	0	0	7	8	2	2	0	0	6	.308	.333	.286	8.10	0.00
Hollands, Mario	L-L	6-5	205	8-26-88	3	2	4.31	13	10	0	0	63	70	32	30	6	20	53	.279	.299	.270	7.61	2.87
Johnson, Jay	R-L	6-2	210	12-21-89	2	2	2.65	38	0	0	3	37	32	15	11	1	25	46	.222	.213	.229	11.09	6.03
Knigge, Tyler	R-R	6-4	215	10-27-88	4	3	4.25	48	0	0	3	66	60	33	31	8	30	55	.237	.235	.238	7.54	4.11
Lannan, John	L-L	6-4	235	9-27-84	0	1	2.57	1	1	0	0	7	7	2	2	0	1	1	.280	.273	.286	1.29	1.29
Neris, Hector	R-R	6-2	175	6-14-89	6	4	4.55	46	8	0	0	97	89	51	49	14	39	93	.241	.268	.222	8.63	3.62
Nesseth, Mike	R-R	6-5	210	4-19-88	1	4	1.64	35	0	0	9	44	39	14	8	2	14	24	.247	.281	.223	4.91	2.86

Name	B-T	HT	WT	DOB	W	L	ERA	G	GS	CG	SV	IP	H	R	ER	HR	BB	SO	AVG	vLH	vRH	K/9	BB/9
Pettibone, Jonathan	L-R	6-6	225	7-19-90	0	0	5.40	1	1	0	0	5	5	3	3	0	1	4	.294	.000	.500	7.20	1.80
Ramirez, J.C.	R-R	6-4	250	8-16-88	1	0	0.00	4	0	0	0	7	2	0	0	0	2	8	.083	.111	.067	10.29	2.57
Robles, Mauricio	L-L	5-10	215	3-5-89	3	1	2.77	17	0	0	2	26	19	8	8	1	13	37	.204	.238	.194	12.81	4.50
Rosin, Seth	R-R	6-6	250	11-2-88	9	6	4.33	26	23	1	0	127	120	69	61	13	35	96	.248	.261	.237	6.82	2.49
Shreve, Colby	R-R	6-5	210	1-5-88	1	2	5.52	19	0	0	1	29	29	19	18	2	15	21	.266	.234	.290	6.44	4.60
Simon, Kyle	R-R	6-6	220	8-18-90	2	6	4.45	45	0	0	11	57	58	30	28	4	22	33	.262	.301	.234	5.24	3.49
Smith, Greg	L-L	6-1	190	12-22-83	1	2	3.50	3	3	0	0	18	17	11	7	2	4	7	.239	.231	.241	3.50	2.00
Sosa, Juan	R-R	6-2	165	10-11-89	3	5	5.58	35	2	0	2	71	78	54	44	7	41	56	.284	.271	.291	7.10	5.20
Wright, Austin	L-L	6-4	235	9-26-89	6	5	5.92	27	16	0	0	94	91	66	62	13	59	77	.253	.240	.258	7.35	5.63
Zambrano, Carlos	B-R	6-4	275	6-1-81	1	0	1.50	1	1	0	0	6	3	1	1	1	3	7	.176	.000	.333	10.50	4.50

Fielding

Catcher	PCT	G	PO	A	E	DP	PB
Dalles	.976	6	38	2	1	0	0
Joseph	1.000	3	21	3	0	0	0
Kratz	1.000	1	5	0	0	0	0
Ruiz	1.000	2	13	0	0	0	0
Rupp	.985	32	230	29	4	1	2
Suomi	1.000	12	76	5	0	0	4
Valle	.999	90	622	54	1	7	10

First Base	PCT	G	PO	A	E	DP
Abreu	—	1	0	0	0	0
Franco	.986	8	65	4	1	3
Gonzalez	1.000	2	8	0	0	1
Henson	1.000	9	56	1	0	5
Murphy	.992	125	992	61	8	89
Suomi	1.000	3	16	2	0	0

Second Base	PCT	G	PO	A	E	DP
Abreu	.870	5	8	12	3	1

Second Base (cont.)	PCT	G	PO	A	E	DP
Cartwright	.976	105	201	255	11	49
Duran	.983	12	28	31	1	10
Gonzalez	1.000	3	3	9	0	1
Hanzawa	.963	11	29	23	2	7
Tolbert	1.000	13	18	32	0	6
Utley	1.000	2	6	3	0	3

Third Base	PCT	G	PO	A	E	DP
Abreu	.875	17	10	25	5	4
Franco	.947	59	53	109	9	9
Gonzalez	.917	5	3	8	1	1
Hanzawa	.824	5	4	10	3	0
Henson	.921	33	19	63	7	3
Mendonca	.900	23	12	51	7	3
Tolbert	1.000	6	2	15	0	0

Shortstop	PCT	G	PO	A	E	DP
Abreu	.944	4	10	7	1	2
Duran	.947	101	144	247	22	52

Shortstop (cont.)	PCT	G	PO	A	E	DP
Gonzalez	.909	2	3	7	1	1
Hanzawa	.972	41	43	96	4	16
Tolbert	—	1	0	0	0	0

Outfield	PCT	G	PO	A	E	DP
Abreu	1.000	2	4	0	0	0
Cartwright	.979	20	45	1	1	1
Collier	.996	118	261	9	1	2
Dugan	.983	50	109	4	2	1
Gillies	.990	48	101	3	1	0
Henson	1.000	30	51	2	0	2
Hernandez	.929	3	13	0	1	0
Hewitt	.967	98	166	9	6	1
Mitchell	1.000	62	102	10	0	4
Murphy	1.000	3	4	0	0	0
Tolbert	1.000	2	7	1	0	0
Valle	1.000	1	1	0	0	0
Welty	1.000	9	14	0	0	0

CLEARWATER THRESHERS

HIGH CLASS A

FLORIDA STATE LEAGUE

Batting	B-T	HT	WT	DOB	AVG	vLH	vRH	G	AB	R	H	2B	3B	HR	RBI	BB	HBP	SH	SF	SO	SB	CS	SLG	OBP
Abreu, Miguel	R-R	5-10	190	11-14-84	.143	.105	.162	16	56	5	8	0	1	0	5	2	2	0	0	4	2	1	.179	.200
Alonso, Carlos	R-R	5-11	205	2-15-88	.260	.216	.280	120	453	70	118	24	2	4	43	59	14	6	4	71	2	2	.349	.360
Altherr, Aaron	R-R	6-5	190	1-14-91	.275	.254	.283	123	466	57	128	36	6	12	69	45	3	5	8	140	23	5	.455	.337
Alvarez, Miguel	R-R	6-1	172	9-27-89	.250	—	.250	1	4	1	1	0	0	0	0	0	0	0	0	1	0	0	.500	.250
Dugan, Kelly	B-R	6-3	195	9-18-90	.318	.379	.291	56	217	37	69	12	3	10	36	24	6	0	0	60	1	3	.539	.401
Franco, Maikel	R-R	6-1	180	8-26-92	.299	.284	.305	65	264	42	79	23	1	16	52	20	2	0	3	39	0	0	.576	.349
Gonzalez, Gustavo	R-R	6-2	190	1-23-91	.000	—	.000	1	3	0	0	0	0	0	0	0	0	0	0	2	0	1	.000	.000
Hudson, Kyrell	R-R	6-1	180	12-6-90	.202	.255	.179	50	168	24	34	5	0	1	6	9	3	1	2	61	8	4	.250	.253
James, Jiwan	B-R	6-4	180	4-11-89	.260	.180	.302	36	146	19	38	5	2	0	10	7	2	4	1	27	8	1	.322	.301
Joseph, Tommy	R-R	6-1	215	7-16-91	.095	.000	.133	11	42	4	4	2	0	0	1	0	0	0	0	13	0	0	.143	.095
Lavin, Peter	L-L	5-11	180	12-27-87	.224	.217	.227	58	214	18	48	14	5	0	14	28	1	0	2	39	5	7	.336	.314
Ludy, Josh	R-R	5-10	210	4-18-90	.250	.200	.286	4	12	1	3	0	0	1	2	2	0	0	0	2	0	0	.500	.357
Martinez, Gustavo	R-R	5-11	155	9-22-93	.250	.500	.000	3	8	0	2	0	0	0	1	0	1	0	0	2	0	0	.250	.333
Martinez, Harold	R-R	6-3	210	5-3-90	.272	.247	.282	91	323	34	88	21	1	2	29	21	1	0	2	81	6	1	.362	.317
Mojica, Jose	R-R	6-0	145	12-26-88	.233	.279	.212	87	275	34	64	10	1	0	25	17	4	2	1	49	1	1	.276	.286
Moore, Logan	L-R	6-3	190	8-22-90	.185	.187	.185	91	302	25	56	12	1	4	28	28	2	3	3	72	1	1	.272	.257
Morelos, Jair	L-R	5-10	150	2-2-94	—	.000	—	1	1	0	0	0	0	0	0	0	0	0	0	0	0	0	—	—
Perkins, Cameron	R-R	6-5	195	9-27-90	.295	.317	.284	103	387	54	114	30	5	6	53	25	7	2	3	57	4	5	.444	.346
Roof, Jonathan	R-R	6-1	175	1-23-89	.246	.221	.256	68	248	36	61	11	3	4	29	24	0	1	2	34	4	4	.363	.310
Ruiz, Carlos	R-R	5-10	205	1-22-79	.125	.000	.250	2	8	1	1	0	0	1	3	2	0	0	0	0	0	0	.500	.300
Serritella, Chris	L-R	6-3	205	2-21-90	.244	.159	.276	126	484	53	118	22	2	12	53	32	2	0	4	125	0	0	.372	.291
Stassi, Brock	L-L	6-2	190	8-7-89	.295	.316	.288	88	288	32	85	11	5	3	32	23	1	2	2	43	8	1	.399	.347
Stumpo, Bob	B-R	6-4	220	7-17-87	.210	.156	.233	37	105	12	22	2	0	2	11	14	1	1	1	21	0	0	.286	.306
Tolbert, Matt	B-R	6-0	185	5-4-82	.404	.538	.353	13	47	5	19	1	0	0	5	0	1	0	0	4	3	1	.426	.462
Young, Delmon	R-R	6-3	240	9-14-85	.462	.667	.400	3	13	1	6	1	0	0	1	0	0	0	1	3	0	0	.538	.429

Pitching	B-T	HT	WT	DOB	W	L	ERA	G	GS	CG	SV	IP	H	R	ER	HR	BB	SO	AVG	vLH	vRH	K/9	BB/9
Arias, Gabirel	R-R	6-2	185	12-6-89	6	2	2.47	12	7	1	0	55	50	19	15	2	14	39	.248	.224	.257	6.42	2.30
Arteaga, Alejandro	R-R	6-2	176	4-30-94	0	1	4.70	2	2	0	0	8	8	4	4	0	2	5	.276	.750	.200	5.87	2.35
Broussard, Geoff	R-R	6-0	185	9-21-90	0	0	6.43	3	0	0	0	7	8	5	5	1	3	7	.286	.300	.278	9.00	3.86
Carela, Danny	R-R	6-3	230	9-18-87	1	0	2.45	6	0	0	0	11	7	5	3	0	8	13	.189	.188	.190	10.64	6.55
Child, Dan	R-R	6-5	230	7-24-92	0	0	1.38	11	0	0	2	13	9	2	2	0	5	4	.209	.235	.192	2.77	3.46
Cochran, Tom	L-L	6-2	195	10-16-82	0	0	2.08	1	1	0	0	4	3	1	1	0	1	5	.188	.250	.167	2.08	10.38
Erbe, Brandon	R-R	6-4	190	12-25-87	0	1	2.84	4	0	0	0	6	7	4	2	0	1	7	.250	.167	.273	9.95	1.42
Forsythe, Cody	L-L	6-0	170	9-17-90	0	0	0.00	1	0	0	0	1	0	0	0	0	1	1	.250	.000	.500	9.00	9.00
Garcia, Luis	R-R	6-2	215	1-30-87	0	1	1.37	14	0	0	7	20	15	3	3	2	5	20	.208	.333	.119	9.15	2.29
Garner, Perci	R-R	6-2	225	12-13-88	6	6	4.30	22	22	0	0	121	130	75	58	6	62	95	.278	.267	.286	7.05	4.60
Giles, Kenny	R-R	6-2	190	9-20-90	2	2	6.31	24	0	0	6	26	23	19	18	4	19	34	.237	.282	.207	11.92	6.66
Gonzalez, Severino	R-R	6-1	153	9-28-92	3	5	2.02	20	9	0	0	76	66	23	17	4	19	82	.239	.309	.203	9.75	2.26
Grimmett, Zach	R-R	6-3	210	2-5-90	0	0	37.80	3	0	0	0	2	8	7	7	3	7	0	.615	.667	.571	0.00	37.80

Name	B-T	HT	WT	DOB	W	L	ERA	G	GS	CG	SV	IP	H	R	ER	HR	BB	SO	AVG	vLH	vRH	K/9	BB/9
Guth, Jordan	R-R	6-5	200	4-7-91	3	3	6.28	26	0	0	0	43	50	35	30	3	31	26	.303	.327	.291	5.44	6.49
Hanson, Nic	R-R	6-7	210	4-15-92	0	2	6.23	5	5	0	0	26	35	20	18	3	4	8	.321	.326	.318	2.77	1.38
Hernandez, Nick	L-L	6-4	216	7-30-88	3	5	5.28	18	18	0	0	89	102	58	52	8	36	86	.291	.188	.316	8.73	3.65
Hollands, Mario	L-L	6-5	205	8-26-88	4	1	1.56	14	10	1	0	69	60	15	12	2	12	61	.234	.271	.223	7.92	1.56
Horst, Jeremy	L-L	6-3	215	10-1-85	0	0	0.00	1	1	0	0	1	0	0	0	0	0	0	.250	.000	.333	0.00	0.00
Inch, Steven	R-R	6-4	190	2-1-91	4	1	2.50	16	0	0	1	40	30	13	11	2	21	19	.213	.286	.182	4.31	4.76
Kleven, Colin	R-R	6-5	200	4-15-91	0	3	14.29	3	3	0	0	11	21	18	18	3	5	19	.389	.467	.359	15.09	3.97
Lannan, John	L-L	6-4	235	9-27-84	0	1	2.25	1	1	0	0	4	6	2	1	0	1	5	.333	.167	.417	11.25	2.25
Leiter Jr., Mark	R-R	6-0	195	3-13-91	1	0	3.00	2	1	0	0	6	6	3	2	1	1	4	.261	.300	.231	6.00	1.50
Martinez, Manaure	R-R	6-1	155	12-31-91	0	0	0.00	1	0	0	0	1	0	0	0	0	3	1	.000	.000	.000	9.00	27.00
Milner, Hoby	L-L	6-2	165	1-13-91	12	7	3.83	26	25	0	0	143	147	62	61	11	39	108	.270	.189	.294	6.78	2.45
Murray, Colton	R-R	6-0	195	4-22-90	5	7	5.02	47	0	0	11	66	66	38	37	6	27	75	.256	.218	.275	10.18	3.66
Nesseth, Mike	R-R	6-5	210	4-19-88	0	1	5.71	10	0	0	0	17	25	11	11	1	5	8	.347	.476	.294	4.15	2.60
Nichols, Chris	R-R	6-2	180	8-21-90	0	1	8.53	5	0	0	0	6	12	8	6	2	1	5	.414	.333	.450	7.11	1.42
O'Hare, Chris	L-L	6-2	195	9-23-90	0	0	0.00	1	0	0	0	1	0	0	0	0	0	1	.000	—	.000	0.00	9.00
O'Sullivan, Ryan	R-R	6-2	190	9-5-90	4	5	2.52	53	0	0	6	75	71	33	21	5	35	45	.256	.237	.267	5.40	4.20
Paulino, Luis	R-R	6-1	215	6-16-89	7	6	4.56	31	7	0	2	73	82	42	37	6	35	65	.287	.318	.268	8.01	4.32
Ridenhour, Lee	R-R	6-4	230	8-7-89	0	0	18.00	3	0	0	0	3	7	6	6	2	1	0	.438	.500	.400	0.00	3.00
Savery, Joe	L-L	6-3	235	11-4-85	0	0	0.00	1	0	0	0	1	0	0	0	0	0	1	.000	.000	.000	9.00	0.00
Shreve, Colby	R-R	6-5	210	1-5-88	2	1	3.32	22	0	0	0	38	38	14	14	2	19	27	.266	.265	.266	6.39	4.50
Sosa, Juan	R-R	6-2	165	10-11-89	2	0	0.00	7	0	0	1	12	5	0	0	0	4	13	.132	.100	.143	9.75	3.00
Stewart, Ethan	L-L	6-5	210	1-19-91	1	6	6.00	21	21	2	0	96	111	72	64	8	80	64	.298	.341	.284	6.00	7.50
Zambrano, Carlos	B-R	6-4	275	6-1-81	1	0	0.00	2	2	0	0	10	7	0	0	0	4	5	.184	.118	.238	4.35	3.48

Fielding

Catcher	PCT	G	PO	A	E	DP	PB
Joseph	1.000	8	61	12	0	0	2
Ludy	.967	4	26	3	1	0	0
Moore	.989	91	641	80	8	6	8
Ruiz	1.000	2	19	1	0	0	0
Stumpo	.983	37	210	27	4	2	3

First Base	PCT	G	PO	A	E	DP
Martinez	.989	11	90	3	1	11
Serritella	.993	68	549	41	4	58
Stassi	.994	60	455	41	3	51

Second Base	PCT	G	PO	A	E	DP
Alonso	.996	117	240	297	2	75
Roof	.967	18	16	43	2	8
Tolbert	1.000	3	6	5	0	1

Third Base	PCT	G	PO	A	E	DP
Abreu	1.000	2	0	4	0	1
Alonso	1.000	3	0	6	0	0
Franco	.967	64	41	106	5	10
Martinez	.939	59	35	103	9	12
Tolbert	.962	9	6	19	1	1

Shortstop	PCT	G	PO	A	E	DP
Abreu	.915	12	15	28	4	7
Gonzalez	1.000	1	2	4	0	1
Mojica	.954	83	122	227	17	52
Roof	.960	45	73	121	8	26
Tolbert	1.000	1	0	1	0	0

Outfield	PCT	G	PO	A	E	DP
Abreu	1.000	2	3	0	0	0
Alonso	1.000	2	1	0	0	0
Altherr	.993	114	249	17	2	0
Alvarez	1.000	1	7	0	0	0
Dugan	1.000	50	119	5	0	2
Hudson	.976	46	120	3	3	1
James	1.000	34	92	3	0	2
Lavin	.942	50	91	6	6	0
Martinez	1.000	3	5	0	0	0
Perkins	.961	89	163	9	7	3
Roof	.923	7	10	2	1	0
Stassi	1.000	12	9	2	0	1
Young	.833	3	5	0	1	0

LAKEWOOD BLUECLAWS
LOW CLASS A

SOUTH ATLANTIC LEAGUE

Batting	B-T	HT	WT	DOB	AVG	vLH	vRH	G	AB	R	H	2B	3B	HR	RBI	BB	HBP	SH	SF	SO	SB	CS	SLG	OBP
Abreu, Miguel	R-R	5-10	190	11-14-84	.100	.000	.111	2	10	1	1	0	0	0	1	0	0	0	0	3	0	0	.100	.100
Brown, Domonic	L-L	6-5	205	9-3-87	.600	.000	.750	1	5	2	3	0	0	1	2	0	0	0	0	0	0	1	.600	.600
Carman, Chad	R-R	5-10	189	5-9-89	.311	.000	.358	18	61	8	19	3	0	0	3	1	3	0	0	9	0	0	.361	.354
Carmona, William	B-R	5-11	185	3-9-91	.303	.279	.310	121	462	60	140	34	4	6	54	39	0	2	2	93	1	0	.433	.356
Charles, Art	L-L	6-6	220	11-10-90	.251	.167	.276	123	442	64	111	34	2	11	72	58	5	0	8	125	1	6	.412	.339
Crawford, J.P.	L-R	6-2	180	1-11-95	.208	.182	.214	14	53	10	11	1	0	0	2	7	0	0	0	10	2	1	.226	.300
Dalles, Justin	R-R	6-2	205	12-30-88	.317	.407	.250	19	63	8	20	7	0	4	20	5	2	0	3	8	0	0	.619	.370
Gonzalez, Gustavo	R-R	6-2	190	1-23-91	.194	.111	.227	13	31	1	6	0	0	1	3	4	0	2	1	14	0	2	.290	.278
Greene, Larry	L-R	6-0	235	2-10-93	.213	.148	.239	111	400	45	85	22	1	4	28	55	0	2	3	163	8	8	.303	.306
Greene, Tyler	R-R	6-2	175	12-1-92	.100	—	.100	4	10	0	1	0	0	0	0	1	0	0	4	0	0	.100	.250
Lino, Gabriel	R-R	6-3	200	5-17-93	.242	.286	.231	10	33	4	8	3	1	0	9	1	2	0	1	13	0	1	.394	.297
Ludy, Josh	R-R	5-10	245	9-8-88	.245	.298	.200	33	102	6	25	5	0	1	6	7	1	0	0	38	0	0	.343	.300
Mora, Angelo	B-R	5-11	151	2-25-93	.214	.227	.210	110	407	45	87	16	3	3	34	30	1	7	1	87	17	9	.290	.283
Numata, Chace	B-R	6-0	175	8-14-92	.231	.284	.214	94	308	27	71	14	0	3	37	30	6	3	4	45	4	1	.305	.307
Olmo, Yan	R-R	6-3	200	12-15-90	.222	.500	.200	8	27	2	6	1	0	0	2	0	1	0	1	9	0	0	.259	.241
Pointer, Brian	L-L	6-0	190	1-28-92	.216	.190	.223	119	416	54	90	25	3	6	44	58	19	1	2	125	22	7	.334	.337
Quaranto, Kevin	L-R	6-3	215	5-13-88	.000	—	.000	1	3	0	0	0	0	0	0	1	0	0	0	3	0	0	.000	.250
Quinn, Roman	B-R	5-10	170	5-14-93	.238	.266	.230	67	260	37	62	7	3	5	21	27	6	4	1	64	32	9	.346	.323
Roof, Jonathan	R-R	6-1	175	1-23-89	.289	.288	.313	16	59	11	17	4	0	2	13	5	3	0	2	8	1	2	.458	.362
Taylor, Zach	L-R	6-3	215	5-3-91	.240	.222	.245	60	179	22	43	14	4	2	14	10	0	0	6	66	1	2	.397	.295
Tocci, Carlos	R-R	6-2	160	8-23-95	.209	.223	.203	118	421	40	88	17	0	0	26	22	9	3	4	77	6	7	.249	.261
Tromp, Jiandido	R-R	5-11	175	9-27-93	.150	.125	.156	13	40	2	6	1	2	0	3	2	2	0	0	16	0	1	.275	.227
Villalobos, Alejandro	R-R	5-11	170	8-20-91	.272	.333	.244	75	257	22	70	8	0	0	25	19	5	2	2	30	3	3	.335	.323
Walding, Mitch	L-R	6-3	190	9-10-92	.224	.210	.228	115	402	50	90	18	2	1	42	57	3	0	2	121	6	7	.286	.323

Pitching	B-T	HT	WT	DOB	W	L	ERA	G	GS	CG	SV	IP	H	R	ER	HR	BB	SO	AVG	vLH	vRH	K/9	BB/9
Aizenstadt, Andrew	R-R	6-5	185	8-4-89	0	0	8.38	7	0	0	0	10	9	9	9	1	11	7	.281	.333	.250	6.52	10.24
Brady, Kevin	L-R	6-3	200	9-7-90	1	2	5.47	6	6	0	0	26	23	17	16	1	16	28	.245	.256	.236	9.57	5.47
Broussard, Geoff	R-R	6-0	185	9-21-90	4	3	3.29	32	0	0	1	66	76	33	24	4	9	54	.285	.304	.273	7.40	1.23
Burgess, Chris	R-R	6-2	210	8-24-90	2	4	3.19	20	0	0	5	31	32	12	11	1	14	24	.274	.277	.271	6.97	4.06

Name	B-T	HT	WT	DOB	W	L	ERA	G	GS	CG	SV	IP	H	R	ER	HR	BB	SO	AVG	vLH	vRH	K/9	BB/9
Carela, Danny	R-R	6-3	230	9-18-87	0	0	4.70	10	0	0	0	15	14	10	8	3	11	18	.250	.263	.243	10.57	6.46
Cooper, Zach	R-R	5-10	185	1-6-90	1	3	3.97	33	0	0	2	48	56	22	21	2	24	39	.293	.338	.268	7.36	4.53
Demmin, Ryan	L-L	6-1	210	4-5-88	0	2	3.46	2	2	0	0	13	12	7	5	1	1	14	.245	.167	.256	9.69	0.69
Francisco, Delvy	R-R	6-1	190	8-24-92	4	5	3.18	46	0	0	9	62	55	36	22	2	46	75	.231	.253	.216	10.83	6.64
Gonzalez, Severino	R-R	6-1	153	9-28-92	3	0	1.69	4	4	0	0	21	10	4	4	1	3	31	.137	.194	.095	13.08	1.27
Guth, Jordan	R-R	6-5	200	4-7-91	1	4	3.22	14	5	0	1	45	38	26	16	4	19	36	.226	.234	.221	7.25	3.83
Halladay, Roy	R-R	6-6	225	5-14-77	0	0	1.50	1	1	0	0	6	7	2	1	0	3	4	.333	.500	.267	6.00	4.50
Hanson, Nic	R-R	6-7	210	4-15-92	2	2	2.49	16	10	0	1	76	77	31	21	1	12	60	.260	.261	.259	7.11	1.42
Inch, Steven	R-R	6-4	190	2-1-91	1	4	4.68	29	2	0	10	42	44	26	22	0	24	27	.273	.258	.283	5.74	5.10
Leiter Jr., Mark	R-R	6-0	195	3-13-91	2	0	0.00	3	3	0	0	16	11	0	0	0	5	20	.193	.320	.094	11.25	2.81
Martinez, Lino	L-L	6-0	165	9-17-92	1	3	5.19	17	2	0	0	26	31	20	15	3	18	25	.290	.270	.300	8.65	6.23
Mecias, Yoel	L-L	6-2	160	10-11-93	4	3	3.79	13	11	0	1	57	53	27	24	3	25	70	.244	.207	.258	11.05	3.95
Musser, Jonathan	R-R	6-5	205	12-19-91	1	8	6.16	16	14	0	0	73	89	61	50	11	38	43	.308	.302	.311	5.30	4.68
Nichols, Chris	R-R	6-2	180	8-21-90	0	2	5.59	9	0	0	0	19	25	17	12	0	6	13	.301	.323	.288	6.05	2.79
Nunez, Miguel	R-R	6-6	215	10-27-92	10	8	4.22	26	22	0	0	130	136	74	61	5	38	80	.270	.315	.239	5.54	2.63
O'Hare, Chris	L-L	6-2	195	9-23-90	0	1	6.00	3	0	0	0	3	4	2	2	0	1	6	.308	.286	.333	18.00	3.00
Oviedo, Ramon	R-R	6-6	175	7-24-90	1	4	5.45	11	6	0	0	36	45	23	22	0	14	30	.310	.349	.280	7.43	3.47
Paulino, Luis	R-R	6-1	215	6-16-89	3	0	3.00	7	0	0	0	12	10	4	4	1	3	15	.217	.313	.167	11.25	2.25
Prosinski, Jon	R-R	6-3	180	2-17-91	2	2	3.13	8	8	0	0	37	48	16	13	3	8	24	.316	.343	.294	5.79	1.93
Ridenhour, Lee	R-R	6-4	230	8-7-89	1	0	1.46	7	0	0	1	12	10	3	2	0	1	10	.233	.313	.185	7.30	0.73
Santos, Felix	R-R	5-11	170	9-10-90	1	2	5.67	17	0	0	0	33	36	24	21	1	15	31	.275	.264	.282	8.37	4.05
Stefan, Jeb	R-R	6-4	225	4-21-90	6	7	3.55	35	13	0	0	112	101	61	44	11	37	93	.234	.267	.212	7.50	2.98
Walter, Kevin	R-R	6-5	215	5-1-92	0	2	5.92	23	5	0	0	52	53	37	34	3	28	36	.265	.241	.282	6.27	4.88
Warner, Josh	R-R	6-3	185	10-10-92	1	3	7.50	6	6	0	0	24	29	21	20	1	15	20	.299	.367	.269	7.50	5.63
Watson, Shane	R-R	6-4	200	8-13-93	4	6	4.75	16	16	0	0	72	63	44	38	12	28	53	.230	.183	.261	6.63	3.50

Fielding

Catcher	PCT	G	PO	A	E	DP	PB
Carman	.992	17	104	14	1	0	3
Dalles	.977	17	114	13	3	2	1
Lino	.987	10	71	6	1	2	4
Ludy	.975	9	33	6	1	0	0
Numata	.979	90	662	89	16	5	28

First Base	PCT	G	PO	A	E	DP
Carmona	.993	32	270	20	2	19
Charles	.985	106	861	46	14	91

Second Base	PCT	G	PO	A	E	DP
Abreu	1.000	1	3	1	0	1
Gonzalez	1.000	6	8	12	0	2

	PCT	G	PO	A	E	DP
Greene	.909	2	2	8	1	0
Mora	.963	57	135	153	11	37
Roof	1.000	8	11	21	0	5
Villalobos	.977	63	118	175	7	43

Third Base	PCT	G	PO	A	E	DP
Carmona	.921	24	15	43	5	3
Villalobos	1.000	2	1	0	0	0
Walding	.923	112	82	219	25	25

Shortstop	PCT	G	PO	A	E	DP
Crawford	.984	14	23	38	1	11
Gonzalez	.909	7	11	9	2	2
Mora	.938	54	67	159	15	30

	PCT	G	PO	A	E	DP
Quinn	.878	66	83	141	31	26
Roof	.800	2	4	4	2	1

Outfield	PCT	G	PO	A	E	DP
Abreu	1.000	1	4	0	0	0
Brown	1.000	1	3	0	0	0
Greene	.927	111	162	4	13	0
Olmo	.917	8	11	0	1	0
Pointer	.972	114	201	10	6	4
Roof	1.000	5	10	1	0	0
Taylor	.933	45	80	3	6	0
Tocci	.987	117	297	10	4	3
Tromp	1.000	12	20	1	0	0

WILLIAMSPORT CROSSCUTTERS   SHORT-SEASON

NEW YORK-PENN LEAGUE

Batting	B-T	HT	WT	DOB	AVG	vLH	vRH	G	AB	R	H	2B	3B	HR	RBI	BB	HBP	SH	SF	SO	SB	CS	SLG	OBP
Bass, Corey	R-R	5-9	200	4-27-91	.155	.133	.163	21	58	3	9	2	0	0	5	5	5	0	2	19	1	0	.190	.271
Canelo, Malquin	R-R	5-10	156	9-5-94	.220	.250	.206	57	182	22	40	9	1	1	13	17	3	2	4	47	10	2	.297	.291
Cardozo, Jairo	B-R	5-11	160	1-27-94	.196	.156	.217	32	92	8	18	1	1	0	3	9	0	1	0	15	2	1	.228	.267
Carman, Chad	R-R	5-10	189	5-9-89	.200	.286	.154	7	20	3	4	0	0	0	2	3	1	0	0	1	0	0	.200	.333
Cozens, Dylan	L-L	6-6	235	5-31-94	.265	.247	.273	68	245	50	65	19	2	9	35	28	2	0	2	64	11	6	.469	.343
Dove, Sam	R-R	6-2	190	11-27-90	.179	.308	.121	25	84	5	15	1	0	1	6	3	0	0	0	14	0	0	.226	.207
Green, Zach	R-R	6-3	210	3-7-94	.252	.218	.266	74	270	52	68	20	1	13	41	31	8	0	2	91	8	5	.478	.344
Hiciano, Samuel	R-R	6-1	203	1-25-94	.243	.326	.204	42	136	27	33	5	1	7	20	18	4	0	0	39	1	5	.449	.348
Knapp, Andrew	B-R	6-1	190	11-9-91	.253	.214	.267	62	217	30	55	20	0	4	23	22	7	0	1	57	7	5	.401	.340
Lino, Gabriel	R-R	6-3	200	5-17-93	.256	.191	.284	46	156	14	40	6	0	4	23	10	1	0	0	47	2	1	.372	.305
Martinez, Gustavo	R-R	5-11	155	9-22-93	.257	.259	.257	55	210	24	54	6	1	0	11	11	1	2	0	45	16	8	.295	.297
Mora, Angelo	B-R	5-11	175	2-25-93	.286	.375	.250	7	28	5	8	2	0	2	7	2	1	0	0	5	4	1	.571	.355
Parr, Justin	L-R	6-2	190	11-29-90	.247	.275	.237	56	190	21	47	10	5	0	19	21	3	2	0	42	8	4	.353	.332
Pierce, Logan	L-R	6-0	215	2-1-90	.266	.170	.293	68	237	28	63	15	0	5	29	27	8	0	3	41	1	1	.392	.356
Pullin, Andrew	L-R	6-0	190	9-25-93	.261	.311	.240	51	211	20	55	13	5	3	23	7	0	0	1	37	1	3	.412	.283
Rodriguez, Herlis	L-L	6-0	157	6-10-94	.204	.000	.238	13	49	5	10	2	0	0	4	5	1	1	0	5	3	0	.245	.291
Tromp, Jiandido	R-R	5-11	175	9-27-93	.299	.214	.329	33	107	9	32	9	1	1	8	8	1	1	0	25	6	2	.430	.353

Pitching	B-T	HT	WT	DOB	W	L	ERA	G	GS	CG	SV	IP	H	R	ER	HR	BB	SO	AVG	vLH	vRH	K/9	BB/9
Anderson, Drew	R-R	6-3	185	3-22-94	6	3	2.00	15	15	0	0	76	58	21	17	5	20	54	.214	.207	.220	6.37	2.36
Buckley, Tyler	R-R	6-5	230	11-9-90	0	2	2.22	21	0	0	4	28	20	10	7	2	13	27	.202	.231	.183	8.58	4.13
Burgess, Chris	R-R	6-2	210	8-24-90	0	1	7.20	4	0	0	0	5	4	4	4	0	3	4	.211	.167	.231	7.20	5.40
Gueller, Mitch	R-R	6-3	210	11-10-93	3	8	5.86	14	14	1	0	58	83	47	38	4	26	35	.337	.379	.311	5.40	4.01
Marcello, Rob	L-L	6-3	230	10-16-90	2	0	5.55	18	0	0	1	24	33	16	15	1	11	16	.320	.172	.378	5.92	4.07
Martin, Shane	R-R	6-4	210	4-27-91	5	3	4.31	15	15	0	0	71	63	33	26	7	16	44	.232	.286	.203	5.60	2.04
Martinez, Lino	L-L	6-0	165	9-17-92	1	1	4.66	7	0	0	2	10	9	5	5	1	5	12	.231	.286	.200	11.17	4.66
Martinez, Manaure	R-R	6-1	155	12-31-91	0	1	3.00	19	0	0	0	24	23	15	8	3	13	27	.245	.351	.175	10.13	4.88
Meadors, Mark	R-R	6-4	200	2-10-92	2	2	3.26	18	0	0	2	30	20	13	11	0	11	23	.192	.156	.220	6.82	3.26
Musser, Jonathan	R-R	6-5	205	12-19-91	1	1	6.17	5	0	0	0	12	14	10	8	1	8	6	.292	.368	.241	4.63	6.17
Nichols, Chris	R-R	6-2	180	8-21-90	2	1	1.72	9	1	0	0	16	10	3	3	0	2	9	.189	.158	.206	5.17	1.15

	B-T	HT	WT	DOB	W	L	ERA	G	GS	CG	SV	IP	H	R	ER	HR	BB	SO	AVG	vLH	vRH	K/9	BB/9
Oviedo, Ramon	R-R	6-6	175	7-24-90	1	0	3.60	5	0	0	0	10	9	5	4	0	1	3	.237	.375	.136	2.70	0.90
Prosinski, Jon	R-R	6-3	180	2-17-91	1	1	3.86	5	5	0	0	16	26	8	7	1	3	14	.347	.350	.343	7.71	1.65
Reyes, Julio	R-R	6-3	190	4-19-91	3	2	3.14	16	12	0	0	63	34	26	22	3	30	58	.160	.217	.116	8.29	4.29
Ridenhour, Lee	R-R	6-4	230	8-7-89	0	0	2.18	11	0	0	2	21	16	7	5	1	3	18	.211	.226	.200	7.84	1.31
Rios, Yacksel	R-R	6-3	185	6-27-93	5	3	3.59	15	10	0	0	53	52	24	21	1	19	39	.265	.272	.261	6.66	3.25
Rojas, Keivi	R-R	6-0	170	2-26-93	1	2	3.00	22	0	0	2	36	27	17	12	3	13	44	.200	.158	.231	11.00	3.25
Santos, Felix	R-R	5-11	170	9-10-90	2	1	2.09	21	0	0	3	43	40	12	10	0	10	37	.252	.288	.230	7.74	2.09
Soren, Matt	R-R	6-5	225	5-27-91	0	1	6.91	8	0	0	0	14	17	13	11	1	9	10	.309	.333	.286	6.28	5.65
Warner, Josh	R-R	6-3	185	10-10-92	2	4	4.11	20	3	0	1	46	59	24	21	3	12	32	.319	.347	.301	6.26	2.35

Fielding

Catcher	PCT	G	PO	A	E	DP	PB
Bass	.935	15	79	8	6	1	7
Carman	.976	6	35	5	1	0	0
Knapp	.974	21	140	10	4	2	10
Lino	.994	39	262	53	2	2	6

First Base	PCT	G	PO	A	E	DP
Dove	.984	7	58	3	1	5
Lino	.943	5	29	4	2	2
Pierce	.987	65	588	25	8	49

Second Base	PCT	G	PO	A	E	DP
Canelo	1.000	1	1	1	0	0
Cardozo	.963	13	24	28	2	7
Dove	.959	17	35	58	4	12
Pullin	.976	49	87	116	5	25

Third Base	PCT	G	PO	A	E	DP
Cardozo	1.000	5	1	1	0	0
Green	.921	72	39	158	17	17

Shortstop	PCT	G	PO	A	E	DP
Canelo	.945	56	96	163	15	28

	PCT	G	PO	A	E	DP
Cardozo	.948	13	20	35	3	7
Mora	1.000	7	11	18	0	2

Outfield	PCT	G	PO	A	E	DP
Cozens	.982	60	106	4	2	1
Hiciano	.958	37	66	2	3	0
Martinez	.981	51	95	7	2	2
Parr	.976	44	76	6	2	1
Rodriguez	.966	12	25	3	1	0
Tromp	.970	30	63	1	2	0

GCL PHILLIES
GULF COAST LEAGUE
ROOKIE

Batting	B-T	HT	WT	DOB	AVG	vLH	vRH	G	AB	R	H	2B	3B	HR	RBI	BB	HBP	SH	SF	SO	SB	CS	SLG	OBP
Abreu, Miguel	R-R	5-10	190	11-14-84	.000	—	.000	1	3	0	0	0	0	0	0	0	0	0	0	0	0	0	.000	.000
Biter, Venn	L-R	6-1	181	10-27-94	.288	.182	.351	18	59	9	17	3	2	0	2	4	0	1	1	19	0	1	.407	.328
Canelo, Malquin	R-R	5-10	156	9-5-94	.235	.000	.267	4	17	1	4	1	0	0	2	0	0	0	0	1	0	1	.294	.235
Carman, Chad	R-R	5-10	189	5-9-89	.167	.000	.200	7	12	1	2	0	0	0	2	1	1	0	0	3	0	0	.167	.286
Crawford, J.P.	L-R	6-2	180	1-11-95	.345	.283	.382	39	142	24	49	8	3	1	19	25	0	1	0	25	12	5	.465	.443
Dove, Sam	R-R	6-2	190	11-27-90	.143	.000	.214	9	21	3	3	1	0	1	3	0	1	0	0	3	0	1	.333	.182
Ferdinand, Nick	R-R	6-1	210	12-31-89	.261	.261	.260	39	142	14	37	9	1	5	22	10	3	1	0	26	2	1	.444	.323
Golden, Steven	R-R	6-3	180	9-12-94	.185	.190	.182	23	65	6	12	4	0	0	1	4	0	2	0	16	1	3	.246	.232
Gonzalez, Gustavo	R-R	6-2	190	1-23-91	.167	.000	.250	4	12	1	2	0	0	0	1	0	1	0	0	4	0	0	.167	.231
Grullon, Deivi	R-R	6-1	180	2-17-96	.273	.462	.183	41	121	13	33	8	0	1	14	10	1	0	0	18	0	0	.364	.333
Hernandez, Jan	R-R	6-1	195	1-3-95	.210	.303	.176	39	124	16	26	6	1	3	14	12	3	0	2	50	7	2	.347	.291
James, Jiwan	B-R	6-4	180	4-11-89	.321	.167	.364	8	28	5	9	1	1	1	5	2	0	1	0	9	0	1	.536	.367
Joseph, Tommy	R-R	6-1	215	7-16-91	.333	.000	.500	1	3	0	1	0	0	0	0	2	0	0	0	1	0	0	.333	.600
Knight, Johnny	R-R	6-3	175	6-3-93	.109	.059	.132	28	55	3	6	1	0	1	2	8	0	0	0	21	2	1	.182	.222
Mayorga, Jose	R-R	5-10	175	8-20-92	.196	.167	.205	30	51	3	10	2	0	0	2	9	2	0	0	5	0	0	.235	.339
Morelos, Jair	L-R	5-10	150	2-3-94	.291	.263	.303	39	127	15	37	5	0	0	8	7	0	3	0	11	1	3	.331	.328
Oberto, Wilmer	L-L	5-11	188	11-2-92	.316	.288	.328	51	187	31	59	10	4	6	45	16	7	0	2	37	0	0	.508	.387
Perkins, Cameron	R-R	6-5	195	9-27-90	.571	.500	.600	2	7	1	4	1	0	1	1	1	0	0	0	0	0	0	1.143	.625
Pujols, Jose	R-R	6-3	175	9-29-95	.188	.256	.165	45	160	27	30	7	2	6	18	19	1	1	0	56	1	3	.369	.278
Rodriguez, Herlis	L-L	6-0	157	6-10-94	.389	.440	.369	28	90	17	35	7	0	2	15	10	0	1	3	15	4	5	.533	.437
Sandberg, Cord	L-L	6-3	215	1-2-95	.207	.218	.202	48	169	23	35	3	1	2	14	24	2	1	0	36	4	3	.272	.313
Sweaney, Jake	R-R	6-3	180	11-17-94	.164	.100	.189	31	73	7	12	2	0	0	3	5	4	1	0	31	2	0	.192	.256
Tolbert, Matt	R-R	6-0	185	5-4-82	.500	.500	.500	4	12	1	6	1	0	2	3	2	0	0	0	1	0	0	1.667	.571
Torres, Robinson	R-R	5-10	160	2-12-92	.283	.283	.283	46	159	26	45	9	1	2	20	13	5	1	0	19	10	1	.390	.356
Williams, Trey	R-R	6-1	210	3-9-94	.208	.294	.176	39	125	20	26	3	0	3	9	13	5	0	1	27	0	0	.304	.306

Pitching	B-T	HT	WT	DOB	W	L	ERA	G	GS	CG	SV	IP	H	R	ER	HR	BB	SO	AVG	vLH	vRH	K/9	BB/9
Alezones, Lewis	R-R	6-3	170	11-29-95	1	1	1.82	14	0	0	0	25	16	6	5	0	16	15	.180	.226	.155	5.47	5.84
Angulo, Rivar	L-L	6-3	185	7-1-91	0	1	40.50	1	0	0	0	1	3	3	0	3	1	.333	.000	.500	13.50	40.50
Arteaga, Alejandro	R-R	6-2	176	4-30-94	4	2	3.27	11	10	0	0	52	55	25	19	4	9	35	.271	.295	.252	6.02	1.55
Bielski, Ricky	R-R	6-3	190	10-25-94	3	1	1.17	18	0	0	4	23	19	5	3	0	4	15	.226	.242	.216	5.87	1.57
Casimiro, Ranfi	R-R	6-8	200	7-16-92	2	6	5.21	11	11	0	0	48	66	35	28	0	15	30	.324	.387	.287	5.59	2.79
Child, Dan	R-R	6-5	230	7-24-92	0	0	1.59	4	0	0	0	6	1	1	1	0	3	8	.190	.125	.231	12.71	4.76
Dygestile-Therrien, Jesen	R-R	6-2	200	3-18-93	2	3	5.45	11	6	0	0	38	42	32	23	4	15	26	.276	.345	.237	6.16	3.55
Elliott, Jordan	R-R	6-1	195	12-9-89	2	0	1.80	4	0	0	0	10	5	2	2	0	1	6	.147	.000	.278	5.40	0.90
Forsythe, Cody	L-L	6-0	170	9-17-90	3	0	2.38	18	0	0	2	23	21	7	6	0	3	18	.259	.318	.237	7.15	1.19
Garcia, Elniery	L-L	6-0	155	12-24-94	1	3	5.15	9	9	0	0	37	43	29	21	1	14	31	.291	.258	.299	7.61	3.44
Halladay, Roy	R-R	6-6	225	5-14-77	0	0	4.50	1	1	0	0	6	6	3	3	1	3	4	.261	.231	.300	6.00	4.50
Hanson, Nic	R-R	6-7	210	4-15-92	0	0	0.00	1	1	0	0	4	1	0	0	0	1	1	.083	.333	.000	2.25	2.25
Keys, Denton	L-L	6-3	190	9-30-94	2	2	5.68	9	2	0	0	19	23	15	12	0	5	15	.311	.313	.310	5.21	2.37
Leiter Jr., Mark	R-R	6-0	195	3-13-91	1	0	1.57	11	0	0	0	23	17	4	4	0	7	26	.207	.111	.255	10.17	2.74
Meadors, Mark	R-R	6-4	200	2-10-92	0	0	0.00	2	0	0	0	4	1	0	0	0	1	5	.071	.000	.100	11.25	2.25
Mendez, Ronald	R-R	6-5	211	2-24-93	1	1	3.15	15	0	0	3	20	21	11	7	2	2	12	.263	.259	.264	5.40	0.90
Morgan, Adam	L-L	6-1	195	2-27-90	0	1	2.57	2	2	0	0	7	6	2	2	0	0	8	.231	.222	.235	10.29	0.00
Morris, Will	L-R	6-4	180	5-2-93	1	3	4.15	17	0	0	3	30	33	20	14	1	6	24	.266	.386	.200	7.12	1.78
Motta, Chris	R-R	6-1	195	3-22-90	0	1	4.91	4	0	0	0	7	11	4	4	0	4	6	.355	.400	.333	7.36	4.91
O'Hare, Chris	L-L	6-2	195	9-23-90	0	0	0.00	1	0	0	0	1	1	0	0	0	0	3	.333	—	.333	0.00	0.00
Sanchez, Feliberto	R-R	6-1	175	9-30-93	3	3	4.12	12	10	0	0	55	58	27	25	1	22	33	.279	.333	.250	5.43	3.62

	B-T	HT	WT	DOB	W	L	ERA	G	GS	CG	SV	IP	H	R	ER	HR	BB	SO	HBP			AVG	vLH	vRH	K/9	BB/9
Savery, Joe	L-L	6-3	235	11-4-85	0	0	0.00	1	1	0	0	1	0	0	0	0	0	1				.000	.000	.000	9.00	0.00
Shull, Braden	L-L	6-6	215	5-8-93	0	1	12.00	4	0	0	0	3	4	5	4	0	8	0				.400	.667	.286	0.00	24.00
Soren, Matt	R-R	6-5	225	5-27-91	1	0	3.12	6	0	0	0	9	6	3	3	0	1	10				.176	.273	.130	10.38	1.04
Southard, Matt	R-R	6-9	220	4-18-92	0	1	7.80	9	1	0	0	15	17	13	13	1	11	11				.279	.227	.308	6.60	6.60
Vargas, Franklyn	L-L	6-4	205	8-21-94	2	0	4.34	13	0	0	0	19	9	12	9	0	20	13				.148	.235	.114	6.27	9.64
Viza, Tyler	R-R	6-3	170	10-21-94	1	0	1.41	12	6	0	0	32	21	5	5	1	10	20				.193	.234	.161	5.63	2.81

Fielding

Catcher	PCT	G	PO	A	E	DP	PB
Carman	1.000	7	23	2	0	0	0
Grullon	.974	38	173	18	5	0	9
Joseph	1.000	1	7	2	0	0	0
Mayorga	1.000	21	65	13	0	0	2
Sweaney	.982	26	96	14	2	3	4

First Base	PCT	G	PO	A	E	DP
Mayorga	1.000	7	37	10	0	6
Oberto	.992	40	352	25	3	33
Williams	.978	15	122	11	3	7

Second Base	PCT	G	PO	A	E	DP
Abreu	1.000	1	1	1	0	1
Dove	.750	4	2	1	1	0

Morelos	1.000	14	33	28	0	8
Tolbert	1.000	2	3	1	0	1
Torres	.959	44	80	105	8	26

Third Base	PCT	G	PO	A	E	DP
Dove	.929	5	5	8	1	0
Hernandez	.893	36	21	71	11	8
Tolbert	.667	1	1	1	1	0
Torres	.333	2	0	1	2	0
Williams	.877	23	16	48	9	4

Shortstop	PCT	G	PO	A	E	DP
Canelo	1.000	4	9	13	0	0
Crawford	.950	31	60	91	8	16
Gonzalez	1.000	4	6	7	0	0

Hernandez	—	1	0	0	0	0
Morelos	.927	24	32	69	8	13
Tolbert	1.000	1	0	2	0	0

Outfield	PCT	G	PO	A	E	DP
Biter	1.000	18	36	3	0	1
Ferdinand	1.000	25	43	2	0	0
Golden	.960	20	23	1	1	0
James	1.000	7	12	0	0	0
Knight	1.000	24	27	3	0	0
Perkins	1.000	2	4	0	0	0
Pujols	.964	42	81	0	3	0
Rodriguez	.975	18	37	2	1	1
Sandberg	1.000	44	103	5	0	0

DSL PHILLIES   ROOKIE

DOMINICAN SUMMER LEAGUE

Batting	B-T	HT	WT	DOB	AVG	vLH	vRH	G	AB	R	H	2B	3B	HR	RBI	BB	HBP	SH	SF	SO	SB	CS	SLG	OBP
Arrocha, Hugo	R-R	5-11	150	10-2-95	.263	.241	.268	49	167	29	44	8	2	0	19	20	1	3	6	29	14	10	.335	.335
Garcia, Enmanuel	R-R	6-0	180	7-23-94	.250	.250	.250	66	244	33	61	11	5	1	30	14	6	2	3	48	13	5	.348	.303
Heredia, Juan	R-R	5-11	145	7-4-92	.194	.333	.167	13	36	2	7	1	0	0	1	6	0	1	1	5	2	1	.222	.302
2-team total (10 Marlins)					.226	—	—	23	62	5	14	1	0	0	3	12	0	2	2	9	5	1	.242	.342
Marrero, Ronaldo	R-R	6-0	160	2-7-96	.178	.167	.179	16	45	4	8	1	0	0	2	2	3	0	1	9	1	1	.200	.255
Marte, Olvy	B-R	5-9	154	8-8-94	.338	.317	.343	63	213	41	72	12	6	1	29	25	4	5	1	33	21	18	.465	.416
Miranda, Pedro	R-R	6-0	180	7-6-92	.290	.238	.300	65	255	33	74	8	1	0	22	19	6	2	0	25	18	6	.329	.354
Morillo, Leomar	B-R	5-10	165	1-6-94	.221	.143	.239	39	113	12	25	2	1	1	9	5	2	2	1	17	3	1	.283	.264
Olivera, Deiber	R-R	5-11	155	8-25-92	.304	.263	.310	41	148	20	45	6	0	1	16	8	3	3	1	11	5	1	.365	.350
Posso, Jesus	R-R	5-11	201	2-10-95	.212	.400	.170	52	165	17	35	9	0	2	17	20	7	2	1	31	2	4	.303	.321
Reyes, Yunior	R-R	6-3	190	3-11-95	.250	.000	1.000	1	4	0	1	0	0	0	0	0	0	0	0	3	0	0	.250	.250
Rios, Fernando	R-R	6-0	175	8-22-92	.198	.222	.191	35	86	5	17	1	0	0	2	11	5	3	0	16	0	1	.209	.324
Rosario, Francisco	R-R	6-1	175	1-26-91	.276	.333	.269	10	29	4	8	2	0	0	6	4	0	0	1	3	0	1	.345	.353
Salas, Emmanuel	R-R	6-2	172	12-18-94	.181	.167	.184	67	215	19	39	7	1	2	21	16	4	5	0	37	6	8	.251	.251
Santana, Henry	R-R	6-3	180	12-19-94	.222	.333	.214	13	45	4	10	0	1	0	2	1	0	0	1	9	2	3	.267	.234
Serra, Enmanuel	B-R	5-10	166	12-17-92	.265	.195	.282	61	211	29	56	5	0	0	14	21	3	11	1	20	18	11	.289	.339
Soto, Raymer	R-R	6-1	207	12-18-92	.188	.222	.178	43	117	12	22	10	0	0	8	3	2	0	26	1	1	.274	.258
Torres, Wilber	R-R	5-11	206	5-9-94	.219	.174	.225	60	183	32	40	7	0	3	20	16	3	3	1	30	11	3	.306	.291
Valdez, Hector	B-R	5-11	171	3-8-93	.213	.278	.186	22	61	7	13	1	0	1	8	5	1	1	2	10	5	2	.279	.275

Pitching	B-T	HT	WT	DOB	W	L	ERA	G	GS	CG	SV	IP	H	R	ER	HR	BB	SO	AVG	vLH	vRH	K/9	BB/9
Alejo, Francibel	L-L	6-3	170	1-21-93	3	4	3.07	15	4	0	1	44	46	23	15	0	14	21	.272	.259	.275	4.30	2.86
Cabrera, Joel	R-R	6-1	175	6-9-94	0	0	2.57	6	0	0	0	7	11	4	2	1	1	0	.324	.375	.308	0.00	1.29
Campusano, Edgar	R-R	6-4	177	11-20-93	4	4	3.44	18	11	0	0	65	68	35	25	2	26	47	.273	.338	.250	6.47	3.58
Cedeno, Erick	R-L	6-3	220	2-25-93	0	1	5.09	10	0	0	2	18	12	10	10	0	8	11	.207	.200	.208	5.60	4.08
Contreras, Roberto	L-R	6-3	170	7-12-94	0	0	3.38	10	0	0	0	11	12	5	4	0	8	6	.267	.235	.286	5.06	6.75
De La Cruz, Yan	R-R	6-4	180	4-28-95	1	1	7.52	14	0	0	0	20	29	19	17	1	8	11	.322	.353	.315	4.87	3.54
Dominguez, Seranthony	R-R	6-1	183	11-25-94	4	6	2.96	14	14	2	0	76	60	34	25	1	30	58	.217	.300	.194	6.87	3.55
Dottin, Henry	R-R	6-3	170	10-10-92	0	0	24.75	5	0	0	0	4	6	11	11	0	11	4	.375	.167	.500	9.00	24.75
Emelenciano, Pedro	R-R	6-4	175	7-23-93	3	3	5.75	16	0	0	1	20	22	17	13	0	11	11	.265	.222	.277	4.87	4.87
Figueroa, Juan	L-L	6-0	185	8-31-92	0	0	4.13	18	0	0	0	24	27	15	11	0	12	17	.284	.267	.288	6.38	4.50
Gonzalez, Yonathan	R-R	6-3	165	10-31-95	0	0	7.04	8	1	0	0	15	14	14	12	1	16	4	.255	.167	.297	2.35	9.39
Mejia, Angel	R-R	6-0	160	2-10-95	2	3	2.01	21	0	0	7	40	28	11	9	2	18	26	.209	.167	.221	5.80	4.02
Santos, Gregorio	R-R	6-3	190	3-1-93	9	1	1.47	14	14	1	0	86	58	18	14	3	15	57	.190	.170	.194	5.97	1.57
Serrano, Jorge	R-R	6-2	180	9-21-93	5	5	3.35	14	13	0	0	78	77	31	29	2	33	52	.259	.259	.259	6.00	3.81
Solano, San Lazaro	R-R	5-11	170	12-17-90	1	0	2.21	12	0	0	3	20	11	5	5	1	5	17	.159	.231	.116	7.52	2.21
Torres, Raymer	R-R	6-4	197	9-11-92	0	3	2.04	19	0	0	0	40	39	17	9	0	19	26	.244	.283	.213	5.90	4.31
Valera, Masilis	R-R	6-3	182	2-5-93	1	0	2.70	3	0	0	0	3	2	1	1	0	4	3	.200	.000	.250	8.10	10.80
Vasquez, Gerard	R-R	6-2	190	6-3-94	4	3	3.57	14	14	0	0	63	57	32	25	1	34	46	.246	.226	.257	6.57	4.86

Fielding

Catcher	PCT	G	PO	A	E	DP	PB
Posso	.983	10	51	6	1	0	2
Rosario	1.000	5	32	4	0	0	0
Soto	1.000	15	57	9	0	0	5
Torres	.977	54	287	56	8	4	9

First Base	PCT	G	PO	A	E	DP
Garcia	1.000	13	101	8	0	9
Marte	1.000	1	2	0	0	0
Morillo	1.000	1	4	0	0	1
Olivera	.959	7	45	2	2	3

Posso	.983	13	106	7	2	7
Rios	.994	23	167	10	1	11
Rosario	1.000	5	38	1	0	2
Soto	.978	23	170	10	4	9
Torres	1.000	2	12	0	0	1

Second Base	PCT	G	PO	A	E	DP
Arrocha	1.000	7	11	10	0	2
Heredia	.957	6	9	13	1	1
Marte	.971	38	88	79	5	9
Morillo	1.000	2	2	3	0	1
Olivera	1.000	9	12	18	0	5
Serra	.981	12	24	28	1	5
Valdez	.981	14	27	24	1	6

Third Base	PCT	G	PO	A	E	DP
Arrocha	.750	1	0	3	1	0

	PCT	G	PO	A	E	DP
Olivera	.800	10	8	20	7	1
Posso	.904	31	19	84	11	5
Serra	.926	32	37	88	10	8
Valdez	1.000	6	0	7	0	0

Shortstop	PCT	G	PO	A	E	DP
Arrocha	.932	42	78	100	13	12
Heredia	.912	7	17	14	3	4
Marrero	.941	9	7	25	2	3
Marte	1.000	3	5	1	0	0
Serra	.978	18	29	61	2	9

Outfield	PCT	G	PO	A	E	DP
Garcia	1.000	43	89	8	0	3
Marte	1.000	26	56	4	0	1
Miranda	.979	62	93	2	2	1
Morillo	.939	27	25	6	2	0
Salas	.977	60	123	4	3	0
Santana	.963	13	26	0	1	0
Soto	—	1	0	0	0	0
Valdez	1.000	4	7	0	0	0

VSL PHILLIES

ROOKIE

VENEZUELAN SUMMER LEAGUE

Batting	B-T	HT	WT	DOB	AVG	vLH	vRH	G	AB	R	H	2B	3B	HR	RBI	BB	HBP	SH	SF	SO	SB	CS	SLG	OBP
Acosta, Adrian	R-R	5-11	165	3-15-96	.253	.250	.253	41	99	11	25	7	0	1	7	4	0	0	1	22	2	0	.354	.279
Cuicas, William	B-R	5-11	160	2-1-95	.257	.190	.282	47	152	21	39	5	0	1	13	14	2	3	1	35	8	5	.309	.325
Cumana, Grenny	B-R	5-5	143	11-10-95	.293	.340	.274	62	188	36	55	13	4	0	22	17	10	4	0	21	7	4	.404	.381
Duran, Carlos	R-R	6-2	170	11-22-94	.305	.283	.312	58	203	32	62	14	2	3	19	29	4	1	0	33	20	6	.438	.403
Fernandez, Rafael	R-R	5-10	168	5-13-92	.258	.243	.264	43	124	17	32	10	0	4	18	11	2	1	0	14	1	1	.435	.328
Garcia, Wilson	B-R	5-11	160	1-11-94	.304	.245	.326	57	191	19	58	14	2	1	31	13	2	1	3	16	3	0	.414	.349
Gonzalez, Damaso	B-R	6-1	152	4-11-96	.218	.259	.203	38	101	6	22	1	0	0	7	4	0	0	0	29	0	3	.228	.248
Herrera, Francisco	R-R	5-11	185	9-15-93	.277	.378	.240	40	137	16	38	6	0	3	19	11	3	0	1	19	3	1	.387	.342
Isava, Willerker	B-R	5-11	174	1-21-96	.237	.000	.310	16	38	0	9	1	0	0	3	1	0	1	0	8	0	1	.263	.256
Jimenez, Enger	R-R	6-1	165	7-4-95	.194	.200	.193	52	144	19	28	12	0	3	18	10	2	3	4	40	7	3	.340	.250
Miranda, Joseph	B-R	6-2	186	4-30-95	.236	.185	.255	58	203	27	48	16	2	2	27	21	2	0	2	51	2	1	.365	.311
Perdomo, Alexander	B-R	5-9	155	5-24-93	.250	.300	.235	51	132	16	33	8	4	0	10	17	7	5	1	25	8	5	.371	.363
Rivero, Gregori	R-R	5-11	194	5-27-96	.266	.267	.265	40	128	16	34	8	1	0	8	3	8	2	1	37	1	1	.344	.321
Rodriguez, Anthony	R-R	5-9	148	12-3-94	.227	.500	.071	18	22	4	5	1	0	1	3	4	2	0	0	5	0	0	.409	.393
Rojo, Lucas	R-R	5-6	153	4-5-94	.260	.250	.262	57	181	29	47	10	2	7	22	11	12	4	2	26	2	1	.453	.340
Zorrilla, Freddy	R-R	6-4	195	10-19-94	.299	.375	.275	58	197	29	59	11	1	4	26	15	5	2	0	61	2	5	.426	.364

Pitching	B-T	HT	WT	DOB	W	L	ERA	G	GS	CG	SV	IP	H	R	ER	HR	BB	SO	AVG	vLH	vRH	K/9	BB/9
Bermudez, Gabriel	R-R	6-3	184	6-24-93	1	0	2.57	5	0	0	1	7	5	2	2	1	2	9	.208	.200	.211	11.57	2.57
Chavez, Jesus	L-L	6-3	175	11-22-93	9	0	2.18	14	14	0	0	74	67	21	18	1	9	72	.248	.206	.262	8.72	1.09
Delgado, Victor	R-R	6-2	182	2-3-95	2	4	4.60	14	13	0	0	59	73	38	30	5	8	40	.297	.291	.299	6.14	1.23
Diaz, Oberdan	R-L	6-1	175	1-27-95	2	1	5.11	15	0	0	1	25	25	14	14	2	14	24	.269	.300	.265	8.76	5.11
Dun, Christian	R-R	6-6	232	9-15-93	0	2	8.10	14	0	0	0	17	25	19	15	1	8	6	.329	.263	.351	3.24	4.32
Fernandez, Yeisson	L-L	6-4	170	5-17-94	0	0	3.25	15	0	0	0	28	31	18	10	1	10	21	.277	.222	.287	6.83	3.25
Gonzalez, Manuel	R-R	6-2	188	8-15-91	2	0	2.62	18	0	0	4	34	29	11	10	3	3	27	.225	.241	.213	7.08	0.79
Gonzalez, Reiwal	R-R	6-2	196	11-11-94	1	1	5.12	12	0	0	0	19	23	13	11	1	13	17	.291	.304	.286	7.91	6.05
Indriago, Carlos	R-R	6-2	197	6-29-94	2	3	6.43	9	1	0	0	21	30	19	15	2	6	14	.319	.412	.267	6.00	2.57
Perez, Alfredo	L-L	6-1	176	10-23-94	1	1	3.45	13	1	0	0	16	9	7	6	0	15	14	.170	.143	.174	8.04	8.62
Pinto, Ricardo	R-R	6-0	165	1-20-94	3	5	2.86	14	14	0	0	63	55	29	20	4	12	51	.228	.226	.230	7.29	1.71
Ramos, Edubray	R-R	6-0	165	12-19-92	2	3	5.08	14	5	0	1	34	36	21	19	0	13	36	.269	.356	.200	9.62	3.48
Rivas, Frank	R-R	5-11	180	7-17-92	3	3	2.01	24	0	0	10	31	16	8	7	2	7	33	.150	.088	.178	9.48	2.01
Rivero, Alexis	R-R	6-0	192	10-18-94	5	2	2.03	14	13	0	0	71	57	22	16	1	15	43	.218	.266	.163	5.45	1.90
Suarez, Ranger	L-L	6-0	177	8-26-95	0	0	3.18	8	1	0	1	17	18	8	6	2	0	13	.257	.364	.237	6.88	0.00
Velis, Sergio	L-L	5-11	182	1-16-95	2	7	4.35	15	6	0	0	52	50	33	25	2	24	34	.259	.360	.244	5.92	4.18

Fielding

Catcher	PCT	G	PO	A	E	DP	PB
Acosta	.979	35	155	31	4	1	11
Fernandez	.975	20	99	20	3	2	3
Garcia	.954	27	130	15	7	0	3
Herrera	1.000	1	3	2	0	0	0
Rivero	.945	14	52	17	4	0	2
Rodriguez	1.000	2	9	1	0	0	0

First Base	PCT	G	PO	A	E	DP
Acosta	1.000	2	12	1	0	0
Fernandez	.987	12	74	1	1	6
Garcia	.985	30	243	19	4	13
Herrera	.996	29	234	20	1	13
Miranda	.986	9	67	4	1	5
Rivero	.944	3	15	2	1	0
Rodriguez	.600	2	3	0	2	0

Second Base	PCT	G	PO	A	E	DP
Cuicas	.974	8	16	21	1	2
Gonzalez	1.000	1	0	1	0	0
Isava	.920	7	11	12	2	1
Perdomo	.978	45	74	105	4	16
Rojo	.991	24	46	60	1	11

Third Base	PCT	G	PO	A	E	DP
Cuicas	.914	31	15	70	8	5
Cumana	.869	17	15	38	8	1
Gonzalez	.857	6	3	9	2	0
Herrera	.500	1	0	1	1	0
Rojo	.930	29	20	46	5	5

Shortstop	PCT	G	PO	A	E	DP
Cuicas	.923	8	7	17	2	2
Cumana	.939	42	46	93	9	10
Gonzalez	.846	27	35	53	16	9
Isava	.727	8	4	4	3	1

Outfield	PCT	G	PO	A	E	DP
Cumana	.857	5	6	0	1	0
Duran	.957	58	108	2	5	0
Jimenez	.956	51	62	3	3	3
Miranda	.984	52	59	1	1	0
Rodriguez	—	1	0	0	0	0
Zorrilla	.940	56	106	4	7	0

Pittsburgh Pirates

SEASON IN A SENTENCE: After teasing fans in 2012 and spending more than two decades with flashbacks of Sid Bream singed onto their fans' frontal cortexes, the Pirates finally made their return trip to October baseball.

HIGH POINT: Andrew McCutchen's throw to Russell Martin on Sept. 23 at Wrigley Field nailed Nate Schierholtz at the dish, ended the game, and clinched Pittsburgh's spot in the playoffs.

LOW POINT: Fans survived an agonizing four-game losing skid between their 81st and 82nd wins, a 96-hour waiting period before the Bucs faithful could finally say their team was a winner.

NOTABLE ROOKIES: Gerrit Cole was the king of this crop. After getting two months of seasoning at Triple-A Indianapolis, the Pirates summoned their ace-in-waiting. In the season's final month, the 2011 No. 1 overall pick went 4-0, 1.69. He allowed just 24 hits in 32 innings and fanned 39 against just 10 walks and zero longballs. He started twice in the postseason, including the season-ending loss to Adam Wainwright and the Cardinals in Game Five of the Division Series.

KEY TRANSACTIONS: Plucking Francisco Liriano off the scrap heap for a mere one year and $6 million was the inarguable masterstroke of general manager Neal Huntington's offseason. The lefthander went 16-8, 3.02 and surrendered just 134 hits in 161 innings and fanned 100 more than he walked. The addition of Martin, who, considering the alternatives, was bizarrely allowed to walk from the Bronx without so much as a parting offer, was also smart. The pickups of Marlon Byrd and Justin Morneau from the Mets and Twins also proved worthwhile during the stretch run.

DOWN ON THE FARM: As rosy as the major league picture looks, it gets even better in the minors, where several blue chips remain if they choose to continue the youth movement or strike for Marlins superstar Giancarlo Stanton in the offseason. On the hill, they have righty Jameson Taillon, who used a fastball-hook-change melange to ring up 143 hitters in as many innings between Double-A Altoona and Triple-A Indianapolis. Closely behind Taillon is outfielder Gregory Polanco, who zoomed from high Class A Bradenton to the Futures Game in Queens to Indianapolis for the International League playoffs. Righty Tyler Glasnow lit up the Sally League with an eye-popping 54 hits allowed and 164 whiffs in 111 innings with West Virginia.

OPENING DAY PAYROLL: $ 79.6 million(20th)

PLAYERS OF THE YEAR

MAJOR LEAGUE

Andrew McCutchen
cf

.317/.404/.553
21 HR, 27 SB, 78 BB
Ranked 3rd in NL OBP

MINOR LEAGUE

Gregory Polanco
cf

(Hi A/AA/AAA)
.285/.356/.434
12 HR, 38 SB, 52 BB

ORGANIZATION LEADERS

BATTING   *Minimum 250 AB

MAJORS

* AVG	McCutchen, Andrew	.317
* OPS	McCutchen, Andrew	.911
HR	Alvarez, Pedro	36
RBI	Alvarez, Pedro	100

MINORS

* AVG	Gourley, Walker, West Virginia	.304
* OBP	Hague, Matt, Indianapolis	.378
* SLG	Lambo, Andrew, Indianapolis/Altoona	.574
R	Bell, Josh, West Virginia	75
	Gourley, Walker, West Virginia	75
	Moroff, Max, West Virginia	75
H	Hague, Matt, Indianapolis	153
TB	Lambo, Andrew, Indianapolis/Altoona	255
2B	Bell, Josh, West Virginia	37
	Hague, Matt, Indianapolis	37
3B	Hanson, Alen, Altoona/Bradenton	13
HR	Lambo, Andrew, Indianapolis/Altoona	32
RBI	Lambo, Andrew, Indianapolis/Altoona	99
BB	Allie, Stetson, Bradenton/West Virginia	77
SO	Allie, Stetson, Bradenton/West Virginia	161
SB	Pie, Felix, Indianapolis	38
	Polanco, Gregory, Indy/Altoona/Bradenton	38

PITCHING   #Minimum 75 IP

MAJORS

W	Liriano, Francisco	16
# ERA	Burnett, A.J.	3.30
SO	Burnett, A.J.	209
SV	Grilli, Jason	33

MINORS

W	Sadler, Casey, Indianapolis/Altoona	11
L	Navarro, Eliecer, Altoona/Bradenton	17
# ERA	Johnson, Kris, Indianapolis	2.39
G	Welker, Duke, Indianapolis	48
GS	Pimentel, Stolmy, Indianapolis/Altoona	27
SV	Black, Vic, Indianapolis	17
IP	Pimentel, Stolmy, Indianapolis/Altoona	169
BB	Oliver, Andy, Indianapolis	112
SO	Glasnow, Tyler, West Virginia	164
# AVG	Oliver, Andy, Indianapolis	.220

General Manager: Neal Huntington. **Farm Director:** Larry Broadway. **Scouting Director:** Joe Delli Carri

Class	Team	League	W	L	PCT	Finish	Manager
Majors	Pittsburgh Pirates	National	94	68	.580	3rd (15)	Clint Hurdle
Triple-A	Indianapolis Indians	International	80	64	.556	3rd (14)	Dean Treanor
Double-A	Altoona Curve	Eastern	63	79	.444	11th (12)	Carlos Garcia
High A	Bradenton Marauders	Florida State	57	77	.425	12th (12)	Frank Kremblas
Low A	West Virginia Power	South Atlantic	82	58	.586	2nd (14)	Michael Ryan
Short-season	Jamestown Jammers	New York-Penn	43	32	.573	3rd (14)	Dave Turgeon
Rookie	GCL Pirates	Gulf Coast	33	27	.550	4th (16)	Milver Reyes
Overall 2013 Minor League Record			358	337	.515	8th (30)	

ORGANIZATION STATISTICS

NATIONAL LEAGUE

Batting	B-T	HT	WT	DOB	AVG	vLH	vRH	G	AB	R	H	2B	3B	HR	RBI	BB	HBP	SH	SF	SO	SB	CS	SLG	OBP
Alvarez, Pedro	L-R	6-3	235	2-6-87	.233	.180	.249	152	558	70	130	22	2	36	100	48	4	0	4	186	2	0	.473	.296
Barmes, Clint	R-R	6-1	200	3-6-79	.211	.185	.216	108	304	22	64	15	0	5	23	14	2	9	1	70	0	0	.309	.249
Buck, John	R-R	6-3	245	7-7-80	.333	.000	.348	9	24	1	8	0	0	0	2	0	0	0	0	5	0	0	.333	.333
2-team total (101 New York)					.222	—	—	110	392	39	87	11	0	15	62	29	8	0	2	104	2	1	.365	.288
Byrd, Marlon	R-R	6-0	245	8-30-77	.318	.333	.313	30	107	14	34	9	0	3	17	6	1	0	1	20	0	0	.486	.357
2-team total (117 New York)					.291	—	—	147	532	75	155	35	5	24	88	31	8	1	7	144	2	4	.511	.336
Harrison, Josh	R-R	5-8	200	7-8-87	.250	.350	.167	60	88	10	22	1	2	3	14	2	3	2	0	10	2	0	.409	.290
Inge, Brandon	R-R	5-11	190	5-19-77	.181	.171	.186	50	105	5	19	3	0	1	7	2	1	2	0	32	0	0	.238	.204
Jones, Garrett	L-L	6-4	230	6-21-81	.233	.095	.241	144	403	41	94	26	2	15	51	31	2	0	4	101	2	0	.419	.289
Lambo, Andrew	L-L	6-3	220	8-11-88	.233	1.000	.207	18	30	4	7	2	0	1	2	3	0	0	0	11	0	1	.400	.303
Marte, Starling	R-R	6-1	185	10-9-88	.280	.402	.254	135	510	83	143	26	10	12	35	25	24	6	1	138	41	15	.441	.343
Martin, Russell	R-R	5-10	215	2-15-83	.226	.194	.235	127	438	51	99	21	0	15	55	58	8	1	1	108	9	5	.377	.327
McCutchen, Andrew	R-R	5-10	190	10-10-86	.317	.388	.302	157	583	97	185	38	5	21	84	78	9	0	4	101	27	10	.508	.404
McDonald, John	R-R	5-9	180	9-24-74	.065	.000	.087	16	31	0	2	1	0	0	1	3	1	0	0	8	0	0	.097	.171
2-team total (21 Philadelphia)					.111	—	—	37	54	5	6	1	0	1	4	4	1	1	0	12	0	0	.185	.186
McKenry, Mike	R-R	5-10	210	3-4-85	.217	.207	.221	41	115	9	25	6	0	3	14	5	2	0	0	24	0	0	.348	.262
Mercer, Jordy	R-R	6-3	205	8-27-86	.285	.410	.247	103	333	33	95	22	2	8	27	22	4	5	1	62	3	2	.435	.336
Morneau, Justin	L-R	6-4	215	5-15-81	.260	.188	.279	25	77	6	20	4	0	0	3	13	1	0	1	12	0	0	.312	.370
Pie, Felix	L-L	6-2	190	2-8-85	.138	.000	.167	27	29	5	4	1	0	0	2	2	0	0	0	13	1	2	.172	.194
Presley, Alex	L-L	5-10	190	7-25-85	.264	.300	.258	29	72	8	19	1	1	2	4	1	0	0	0	18	0	1	.389	.274
Sanchez, Gaby	R-R	6-1	235	9-2-83	.254	.333	.204	136	264	29	67	18	0	7	36	44	4	0	7	51	1	0	.402	.361
Sanchez, Tony	R-R	5-11	230	5-20-88	.233	.235	.233	22	60	9	14	4	0	2	5	3	2	0	1	14	0	0	.400	.288
Snider, Travis	L-L	6-0	235	2-2-88	.215	.091	.226	111	261	28	56	12	2	5	25	24	0	0	0	75	2	3	.333	.281
Tabata, Jose	R-R	5-11	210	8-12-88	.282	.250	.292	106	308	35	87	17	5	6	33	23	5	5	0	45	3	1	.429	.342
Walker, Neil	B-R	6-3	210	9-10-85	.251	.225	.256	133	478	62	120	24	4	16	53	50	15	5	3	85	1	2	.418	.339

Pitching	B-T	HT	WT	DOB	W	L	ERA	G	GS	CG	SV	IP	H	R	ER	HR	BB	SO	AVG	vLH	vRH	K/9	BB/9
Black, Vic	R-R	6-4	215	5-23-88	0	0	4.50	3	0	0	0	4	6	2	2	0	2	3	.333	.000	.500	6.75	4.50
2-team total (15 New York)					3	0	3.71	18	0	0	1	17	17	7	7	1	6	15	—	—	—	7.94	3.18
Burnett, A.J.	R-R	6-4	225	1-3-77	10	11	3.30	30	30	1	0	191	165	79	70	11	67	209	.231	.263	.203	9.85	3.16
Cole, Gerrit	R-R	6-4	235	9-8-90	10	7	3.22	19	19	0	0	117	109	43	42	7	28	100	.253	.250	.255	7.67	2.15
Contreras, Jose	R-R	6-4	255	12-6-71	0	0	9.00	7	0	0	0	5	7	5	5	1	6	5	.318	.273	.364	9.00	10.80
Cumpton, Brandon	R-R	6-2	210	11-16-88	2	1	2.05	6	5	0	0	31	26	8	7	1	5	22	.226	.259	.197	6.46	1.47
Farnsworth, Kyle	R-R	6-4	230	4-14-76	1	1	1.04	9	0	0	2	9	6	1	1	1	3	9	.200	.214	.188	9.35	3.12
Gomez, Jeanmar	R-R	6-3	220	2-10-88	3	0	3.35	34	8	0	0	81	65	35	30	6	28	53	.223	.222	.225	5.91	3.12
Grilli, Jason	R-R	6-4	235	11-11-76	0	2	2.70	54	0	0	33	50	40	15	15	4	13	74	.214	.244	.188	13.32	2.34
Hughes, Jared	R-R	6-7	240	7-4-85	2	3	4.78	29	0	0	0	32	37	17	17	2	16	23	.291	.392	.224	6.47	4.50
Irwin, Phil	R-R	6-3	210	2-25-87	0	0	7.71	1	1	0	0	5	6	5	4	0	4	4	.316	.286	.333	7.71	7.71
Johnson, Kris	L-L	6-4	195	10-14-84	0	2	6.10	4	1	0	0	10	12	7	7	0	4	9	.300	.267	.320	7.84	3.48
Leroux, Chris	R-R	6-6	225	4-14-84	0	0	6.75	2	0	0	0	4	4	3	3	1	6	3	.267	.286	.250	6.75	13.50
Liriano, Francisco	L-L	6-2	220	10-26-83	16	8	3.02	26	26	2	0	161	134	54	54	9	63	163	.224	.131	.249	9.11	3.52
Locke, Jeff	L-L	6-0	190	11-20-87	10	7	3.52	30	30	0	0	166	146	69	65	11	84	125	.242	.286	.229	6.76	4.55
Mazzaro, Vin	R-R	6-2	220	9-27-86	8	2	2.81	57	0	0	1	74	68	23	23	3	21	46	.246	.211	.272	5.62	2.57
McDonald, James	L-R	6-4	205	10-19-84	2	2	5.76	6	6	0	0	30	29	24	19	1	20	25	.252	.232	.271	7.58	6.07
Melancon, Mark	R-R	6-2	215	3-28-85	3	2	1.39	72	0	0	16	71	60	15	11	1	8	70	.223	.148	.286	8.87	1.01
Morris, Bryan	R-R	6-3	225	3-28-87	5	7	3.46	55	0	0	0	65	57	25	25	8	28	37	.243	.265	.226	5.12	3.88
Morton, Charlie	R-R	6-5	245	11-12-83	7	4	3.26	20	20	0	0	116	113	51	42	6	36	85	.261	.314	.222	6.59	2.79
Pimentel, Stolmy	R-R	6-3	235	2-1-90	0	0	1.93	5	0	0	0	9	6	4	2	0	2	9	.171	.071	.238	8.68	1.93
Reid, Ryan	R-R	5-11	210	4-24-85	0	0	1.64	7	0	0	1	11	9	2	2	1	3	7	.231	.333	.167	5.73	2.45
Rodriguez, Wandy	R-L	5-10	195	1-18-79	6	4	3.59	12	12	0	0	63	58	26	25	10	12	46	.240	.250	.236	6.61	1.72
Sanchez, Jonathan	L-L	6-0	195	11-19-82	0	3	11.85	5	4	0	0	14	25	18	18	7	8	15	.397	.375	.404	9.88	5.27
Watson, Tony	L-L	6-4	225	5-30-85	3	1	2.39	67	0	0	2	72	51	19	19	5	12	54	.198	.206	.192	6.78	1.51
Welker, Duke	R-R	6-7	240	2-10-86	0	0	0.00	2	0	0	0	1	0	0	0	0	1	0	.000	.000	.000	0.75	6.00
Wilson, Justin	L-L	6-2	205	8-18-87	6	1	2.08	58	0	0	0	74	50	17	17	4	28	59	.192	.200	.189	7.21	3.42
Zagurski, Mike	L-L	6-0	240	1-27-83	0	0	15.00	6	0	0	0	6	10	10	10	1	8	5	.385	.545	.267	7.50	12.00

Fielding

Catcher	PCT	G	PO	A	E	DP	PB
Buck	1.000	7	42	1	0	0	0
Martin	.998	120	885	103	2	6	4
McKenry	.991	31	210	16	2	0	1
Sanchez	1.000	16	98	7	0	0	1

First Base	PCT	G	PO	A	E	DP
Inge	1.000	4	6	1	0	1
Jones	.992	83	671	52	6	73
Mercer	1.000	1	1	0	0	0
Morneau	.996	25	223	14	1	16
Sanchez	.996	113	696	58	3	55

Second Base	PCT	G	PO	A	E	DP
Harrison	1.000	11	18	24	0	5
Inge	1.000	13	18	26	0	6
McDonald	1.000	4	6	6	0	1

	PCT	G	PO	A	E	DP	
Mercer	.972	26	31	72	3	13	
Walker	.989	132	256	397	7	88	
Third Base	PCT	G	PO	A	E	DP
Alvarez	.941	150	72	359	27	27
Harrison	.923	7	1	11	1	0
Inge	1.000	10	4	25	0	2
Martin	1.000	3	3	3	0	0
Mercer	1.000	1	0	3	0	0
Sanchez	—	1	0	0	0	0

Shortstop	PCT	G	PO	A	E	DP
Barnes	.968	106	107	282	13	53
Harrison	1.000	4	1	1	0	0
Inge	1.000	1	0	1	0	1
McDonald	.933	13	9	19	2	6
Mercer	.962	78	89	214	12	49

Outfield	PCT	G	PO	A	E	DP
Byrd	.955	29	39	3	2	1
Harrison	1.000	15	7	2	0	1
Inge	1.000	6	6	1	0	0
Jones	.974	32	37	1	1	0
Lambo	1.000	8	6	0	0	0
Marte	.966	130	193	6	7	0
Martin	1.000	1	1	0	0	0
McCutchen	.982	155	321	11	6	3
Pie	1.000	19	10	0	0	0
Presley	.968	21	30	0	1	0
Snider	.992	81	117	5	1	0
Tabata	1.000	89	106	0	0	0

INDIANAPOLIS INDIANS   TRIPLE-A
INTERNATIONAL LEAGUE

Batting	B-T	HT	WT	DOB	AVG	vLH	vRH	G	AB	R	H	2B	3B	HR	RBI	BB	HBP	SH	SF	SO	SB	CS	SLG	OBP
Andino, Robert	R-R	6-0	195	4-25-84	.302	.250	.319	25	96	7	29	8	0	0	9	5	0	2	2	20	0	1	.385	.330
Bocock, Brian	R-R	5-11	185	3-9-85	.172	.286	.153	31	99	9	17	4	0	3	7	7	1	2	0	22	1	0	.303	.234
2-team total (22 Syracuse)					.175	—		53	143	10	25	5	0	3	9	11	1	2	1	30	3	1	.287	.237
Canzler, Russ	R-R	6-2	220	4-11-86	.194	.190	.195	39	129	9	25	1	1	1	13	15	1	0	3	25	0	0	.240	.277
2-team total (86 Norfolk)					.252	—		125	452	55	114	16	2	12	62	62	3	0	5	101	1	1	.376	.343
Carroll, Brett	R-R	5-11	210	10-3-82	.222	.247	.213	89	275	42	61	9	1	13	38	39	5	1	1	74	7	2	.404	.328
d'Arnaud, Chase	R-R	6-1	205	1-21-87	.233	.208	.240	61	240	33	56	8	4	4	20	18	1	2	1	43	17	5	.350	.288
De Jesus Jr., Ivan	R-R	5-11	200	5-1-87	.319	.305	.324	103	304	36	97	27	3	3	32	29	4	3	5	65	5	2	.457	.380
Ford, Darren	R-R	5-9	190	10-1-85	.230	.205	.244	83	239	36	55	7	2	2	19	27	1	4	3	56	29	11	.301	.307
Goedert, Jared	R-R	6-1	210	5-25-85	.241	.239	.242	130	464	57	112	32	2	11	62	51	1	0	3	110	4	0	.390	.316
Hague, Matt	R-R	6-3	225	8-20-85	.285	.320	.275	142	536	67	153	37	2	8	69	71	11	1	3	96	4	3	.407	.378
Harrison, Josh	R-R	5-8	200	7-8-87	.317	.361	.301	64	268	50	85	29	5	4	34	20	4	4	0	39	19	7	.507	.373
Inge, Brandon	R-R	5-11	190	5-19-77	.150	.143	.152	18	60	4	9	2	0	2	6	12	3	0	0	17	1	0	.283	.320
Jeroloman, Brian	L-R	5-11	190	5-10-85	.222	.429	.091	11	18	6	4	1	0	0	2	9	0	2	0	4	0	1	.278	.481
2-team total (30 Syracuse)					.221	—		41	113	15	25	5	0	0	9	22	1	4	1	32	0	1	.265	.350
Lambo, Andrew	L-L	6-3	220	8-11-88	.272	.250	.280	62	224	32	61	15	1	18	53	24	2	1	3	67	1	0	.589	.344
Larish, Jeff	L-R	6-2	200	10-11-82	.167	.111	.179	20	48	2	8	1	0	2	5	10	0	0	0	17	0	0	.313	.310
May, Lucas	R-R	6-0	200	10-24-84	.226	.167	.243	57	186	18	42	3	1	3	21	12	2	1	2	43	1	0	.301	.277
McDonald, John	R-R	5-9	180	9-24-74	.265	.167	.286	10	34	5	9	1	0	0	1	2	1	0	0	3	1	0	.294	.324
Mercer, Jordy	R-R	6-3	205	8-27-86	.333	.350	.329	26	96	11	32	6	1	1	19	12	0	1	0	17	3	1	.448	.404
Paulino, Carlos	R-R	6-0	175	9-24-89	.273	—	.273	3	11	1	3	0	0	0	2	1	0	0	0	1	0	0	.273	.333
Pie, Felix	L-L	6-2	190	2-8-85	.251	.053	.290	105	354	53	89	17	4	8	40	37	2	2	1	83	38	9	.390	.325
Polanco, Gregory	L-L	6-4	170	9-14-91	.222	—	.222	2	9	1	2	0	0	0	0	0	0	0	0	2	0	0	.222	.222
Presley, Alex	L-L	5-10	190	7-25-85	.298	.250	.315	89	342	57	102	17	6	5	27	40	4	3	2	56	17	6	.427	.376
Sanchez, Tony	R-R	5-11	230	5-20-88	.288	.324	.276	76	260	35	75	26	0	10	42	28	6	0	2	60	0	0	.504	.368
Sands, Jerry	R-R	6-4	225	9-28-87	.207	.218	.204	106	343	37	71	17	2	7	34	50	2	1	1	105	0	1	.329	.311
Shoppach, Kelly	R-R	6-0	220	4-29-80	.192	.250	.167	7	26	0	5	1	0	0	2	1	0	0	0	8	0	0	.231	.222
3-team total (1 Columbus, 10 Syracuse)					.213	—		18	61	3	13	1	0	0	4	6	2	1	0	18	0	0	.230	.304
Snider, Travis	L-L	6-0	235	2-2-88	.344	.267	.412	8	32	4	11	1	0	0	5	5	0	0	1	8	1	1	.375	.421
Solis, Ali	R-R	5-11	175	9-29-87	.217	.286	.188	9	23	2	5	0	0	0	2	2	0	0	1	4	0	0	.217	.269
Tabata, Jose	R-R	5-11	210	8-12-88	.179	.500	.091	9	28	1	5	1	0	0	3	1	0	0	1	7	1	0	.214	.281
Tejeda, Oscar	R-R	6-1	170	12-26-89	.085	.182	.056	21	47	3	4	3	0	0	3	7	0	0	0	14	2	0	.149	.204
Walker, Neil	B-R	6-3	210	9-10-85	.222	.000	.286	3	9	2	2	1	0	0	2	0	0	0	1	0	0	0	.333	.364

Pitching	B-T	HT	WT	DOB	W	L	ERA	G	GS	CG	SV	IP	H	R	ER	HR	BB	SO	AVG	vLH	vRH	K/9	BB/9
Alderson, Tim	R-R	6-6	220	11-3-88	3	1	2.79	22	0	0	0	42	40	16	13	5	10	38	.247	.221	.266	8.14	2.14
2-team total (15 Norfolk)					4	3	4.32	37	1	0	0	75	79	39	36	9	20	64	—	—	—	7.68	2.40
Black, Vic	R-R	6-4	215	5-23-88	5	3	2.51	38	0	0	17	47	28	15	13	2	21	63	.169	.179	.159	12.15	4.05
Bromberg, David	L-R	6-5	245	9-14-87	1	1	3.38	2	2	0	0	11	12	4	4	1	3	8	.293	.333	.276	6.75	2.53
Brown, Brooks	R-R	6-3	205	6-20-85	6	5	4.75	37	8	0	0	91	95	53	48	11	24	69	.272	.323	.232	6.82	2.37
Cole, Gerrit	R-R	6-4	235	9-8-90	5	3	2.91	12	12	0	0	68	44	23	22	4	28	47	.190	.227	.144	6.22	3.71
Colon, Roman	R-R	6-5	245	8-13-79	0	1	27.00	1	0	0	0	1	1	1	1	0	2	0	.500	.500	—	27.00	0.00
2-team total (6 Gwinnett)					0	2	6.75	7	2	0	0	13	16	12	10	2	3	9	—	—	—	6.08	2.03
Contreras, Jose	R-R	6-4	255	12-6-71	2	0	0.93	16	0	0	1	19	13	3	2	1	5	24	.203	.214	.194	11.17	2.33
2-team total (8 Pawtucket)					2	2	2.79	24	0	0	1	29	22	12	9	3	11	39	—	—	—	12.10	3.41
Cordier, Erik	R-R	6-4	250	2-25-86	4	2	4.58	44	0	0	4	53	51	29	27	3	28	65	.256	.319	.200	11.04	4.75
Cumpton, Brandon	R-R	6-2	210	11-16-88	6	7	3.32	21	19	1	0	122	115	52	45	6	44	90	.253	.302	.210	6.64	3.25
Farnsworth, Kyle	R-R	6-4	230	4-14-76	1	1	4.05	6	0	0	0	7	7	3	3	0	4	3	.292	.182	.385	4.05	5.40
Godfrey, Graham	R-R	6-3	215	8-9-84	7	5	3.99	19	11	0	0	77	75	36	34	11	14	45	.254	.286	.226	5.28	1.64
2-team total (13 Pawtucket)					11	8	3.93	32	15	0	0	119	119	58	52	16	33	75	—	—	—	5.67	2.50
Gomez, Jeanmar	R-R	6-3	220	2-10-88	1	0	1.13	2	2	0	0	8	3	2	1	0	4	7	.111	.200	.059	7.88	4.50
Hollingsworth, Ethan	R-R	6-2	200	5-4-87	0	1	4.50	2	2	0	0	10	15	9	5	1	1	6	.319	.350	.296	5.40	0.90
Hughes, Jared	R-R	6-7	240	7-4-85	1	0	0.43	18	1	0	2	21	17	1	1	0	7	18	.227	.243	.211	7.71	3.00

Player	B-T	HT	WT	DOB	W	L	ERA	G	GS	CG	SV	IP	H	R	ER	HR	BB	SO	AVG	vLH	vRH	H/9	BB/9
Irwin, Phil	R-R	6-3	210	2-25-87	1	0	0.90	2	2	0	0	10	5	1	1	0	3	8	.147	.071	.200	7.20	2.70
Johnson, Kris	L-L	6-4	195	10-14-84	10	4	2.39	26	21	1	2	136	116	37	36	6	43	94	.234	.219	.240	6.24	2.85
Liriano, Francisco	L-L	6-2	220	10-26-83	2	0	3.38	3	3	0	0	16	15	6	6	1	1	23	.238	.375	.218	12.94	0.56
Mathis, Doug	R-R	6-3	230	6-7-83	0	1	7.50	2	1	0	0	6	11	6	5	2	0	4	.407	.444	.389	6.00	0.00
Mazzaro, Vin	R-R	6-2	220	9-27-86	1	0	0.00	3	0	0	0	7	3	0	0	0	1	9	.130	.143	.111	11.57	1.29
McDonald, James	L-R	6-4	205	10-19-84	1	3	6.53	4	4	0	0	21	26	16	15	2	9	12	.321	.343	.304	5.23	3.92
McPherson, Kyle	B-R	6-4	215	11-11-87	0	1	19.29	2	2	0	0	5	11	10	10	0	4	2	.440	.400	.500	3.86	7.71
Morris, Bryan	L-R	6-3	225	3-28-87	0	0	1.42	5	0	0	5	6	5	1	1	0	1	4	.217	.300	.154	5.68	1.42
Morton, Charlie	R-R	6-5	245	11-12-83	0	1	3.79	4	4	0	0	19	16	10	8	1	10	12	.229	.242	.216	5.68	4.74
Oliver, Andy	L-L	6-3	215	12-3-87	5	4	4.05	29	24	0	0	124	99	63	56	6	112	138	.220	.271	.206	9.99	8.11
Pimentel, Stolmy	R-R	6-3	235	2-1-90	2	6	3.13	14	14	1	0	92	76	38	32	6	21	62	.224	.245	.210	6.07	2.05
Reid, Ryan	L-R	5-11	210	4-24-85	7	2	2.73	36	0	0	2	59	49	22	18	4	22	56	.223	.194	.244	8.49	3.34
Rodriguez, Wandy	R-L	5-10	195	1-18-79	0	0	2.25	1	1	0	0	4	4	1	1	0	1	5	.235	.167	.273	11.25	2.25
Sadler, Casey	R-R	6-4	200	7-13-90	0	0	4.50	1	1	0	0	6	7	3	3	1	1	5	.280	.333	.263	7.50	1.50
Severino, Atahualpa	L-L	5-11	220	11-6-84	0	3	3.72	33	2	0	1	46	48	21	19	5	13	48	.270	.179	.311	9.39	2.54
Taillon, Jameson	R-R	6-6	235	11-18-91	1	3	3.89	6	6	0	0	37	31	16	16	1	16	37	.223	.233	.219	9.00	3.89
Thornton, Zach	R-R	6-3	213	5-19-88	3	1	3.91	13	0	0	0	25	22	14	11	3	4	31	.224	.318	.148	11.01	1.42
Waldrop, Kyle	R-R	6-5	220	10-27-85	1	0	2.37	5	2	0	0	19	13	5	5	0	3	15	.194	.258	.139	7.11	1.42
Welker, Duke	L-R	6-7	240	2-10-86	3	4	3.57	48	0	0	9	63	53	28	25	3	31	65	.231	.231	.232	9.29	4.43
Zagurski, Mike	L-L	6-0	240	1-27-83	1	0	2.14	19	0	0	1	21	15	5	5	2	9	37	.188	.259	.151	15.86	3.86
2-team total (20 Scranton/W-B)					6	3	2.66	39	0	0	2	47	37	16	14	4	21	75	—	—	—	14.26	3.99

Fielding

Catcher	PCT	G	PO	A	E	DP	PB
Jeroloman	.974	10	69	5	2	0	2
May	.991	54	401	25	4	4	7
Paulino	1.000	3	31	2	0	0	0
Sanchez	.976	72	533	44	14	4	7
Shoppach	.981	7	49	3	1	0	0
Solis	1.000	8	61	5	0	0	1

First Base	PCT	G	PO	A	E	DP
Canzler	1.000	9	62	5	0	10
Goedert	1.000	1	2	0	0	0
Hague	.991	132	1213	56	12	127
Inge	1.000	1	10	2	0	2
Lambo	.857	1	6	0	1	2
Sands	.986	7	69	3	1	4

Second Base	PCT	G	PO	A	E	DP
Andino	1.000	1	5	2	0	0
Bocock	1.000	9	20	16	0	5
d'Arnaud	.971	16	29	38	2	10
De Jesus Jr.	.970	68	119	203	10	59
Goedert	.966	7	10	18	1	2

Catcher (cont.)	PCT	G	PO	A	E	DP
Harrison	.987	33	50	103	2	24
Inge	1.000	6	11	20	0	3
McDonald	1.000	4	3	8	0	0
Mercer	1.000	2	3	11	0	4
Tejeda	1.000	9	20	33	0	9
Walker	1.000	3	7	4	0	2

Third Base	PCT	G	PO	A	E	DP
Canzler	.903	10	4	24	3	2
De Jesus Jr.	.929	11	8	18	2	2
Goedert	.924	12	59	221	23	25
Hague	.926	13	4	21	2	2
Inge	.833	4	0	5	1	0
Mercer	1.000	1	1	6	0	0
Tejeda	1.000	2	3	2	0	0

Shortstop	PCT	G	PO	A	E	DP
Andino	.965	24	31	80	4	11
Bocock	.957	20	16	74	4	15
d'Arnaud	.954	39	47	118	8	28
De Jesus Jr.	.846	6	6	16	4	4
Harrison	.978	30	34	101	3	22

(Third Base cont.)	PCT	G	PO	A	E	DP
Inge	1.000	1	0	2	0	0
McDonald	1.000	6	9	15	0	4
Mercer	.983	23	34	79	2	19
Tejeda	1.000	4	5	10	0	4

Outfield	PCT	G	PO	A	E	DP
Canzler	1.000	5	6	0	0	0
Carroll	.957	68	102	8	5	3
d'Arnaud	1.000	5	10	0	0	0
Ford	1.000	55	92	1	0	0
Harrison	1.000	1	1	0	0	0
Inge	1.000	3	2	0	0	0
Lambo	.990	53	98	3	1	0
Larish	1.000	1	1	0	0	0
Pie	.950	89	151	1	8	0
Polanco	1.000	2	4	0	0	0
Presley	.994	82	162	1	1	0
Sands	.994	87	150	12	1	5
Snider	.818	5	8	1	2	0
Tabata	1.000	8	12	0	0	0

ALTOONA CURVE

DOUBLE-A

EASTERN LEAGUE

Batting	B-T	HT	WT	DOB	AVG	vLH	vRH	G	AB	R	H	2B	3B	HR	RBI	BB	HBP	SH	SF	SO	SB	CS	SLG	OBP
Brown, Kelson	R-R	6-3	175	11-7-87	.192	.133	.237	53	104	13	20	3	0	0	5	12	2	2	1	16	4	1	.221	.286
Cunningham, Jarek	R-R	6-1	195	12-25-89	.216	.182	.231	131	468	53	101	18	4	19	49	30	9	5	3	127	12	6	.393	.275
Curry, Matt	L-R	6-1	225	7-27-88	.248	.115	.291	26	105	11	26	4	0	4	16	5	1	0	1	35	2	0	.400	.286
Cutler, Charlie	L-R	6-0	200	7-29-86	.298	.269	.305	86	255	32	76	16	3	3	26	39	4	1	2	37	3	0	.420	.397
d'Arnaud, Chase	R-R	6-1	205	1-21-87	.143	.000	.182	4	14	1	2	0	0	0	1	0	0	0	0	1	1	0	.143	.200
Dickerson, Alex	L-L	6-3	235	5-26-90	.288	.298	.284	126	451	61	130	36	3	17	68	27	8	2	3	89	10	7	.494	.337
Hanson, Alen	B-R	5-11	152	10-22-92	.255	.250	.259	35	137	13	35	4	5	1	10	8	1	3	1	26	6	2	.380	.299
Howard, Justin	L-R	6-0	205	8-28-87	.314	.242	.335	98	283	40	89	15	1	8	38	38	5	2	0	62	7	6	.459	.405
Lambo, Andrew	L-L	6-3	220	8-11-88	.291	.243	.313	58	220	35	64	9	4	14	46	20	2	2	3	60	6	1	.559	.351
Maggi, Drew	R-R	6-0	185	5-16-89	.254	.316	.207	95	264	38	67	14	2	1	25	27	9	4	5	49	18	6	.333	.338
Ngoepe, Gift	B-R	5-10	165	1-18-90	.177	.174	.179	72	220	29	39	10	2	3	16	28	4	4	3	82	10	3	.282	.278
Paulino, Carlos	R-R	6-0	175	9-24-84	.220	.278	.191	99	323	23	71	9	4	0	38	28	5	2	3	48	5	1	.272	.290
Perez, Miguel	R-R	6-3	235	9-25-83	.143	.000	.167	4	7	1	1	0	0	0	0	0	0	0	0	1	0	0	.143	.143
Polanco, Gregory	L-L	6-4	170	9-14-91	.263	.281	.253	68	243	36	64	13	2	6	41	36	1	1	5	36	13	7	.407	.354
Rojas Jr., Mel	R-B	6-3	215	5-24-90	.274	.291	.266	120	446	57	122	29	8	5	41	38	3	5	4	100	14	8	.410	.332
Sanchez, Tony	R-R	5-11	230	5-20-88	.176	.400	.083	4	17	2	3	1	0	0	0	0	0	0	0	3	0	0	.235	.176
Santos, Adalberto	R-R	5-11	185	9-28-87	.281	.289	.278	118	409	62	115	23	1	6	47	59	5	5	4	70	21	8	.386	.375
Snider, Travis	L-L	6-0	235	2-2-88	.333	.333	.333	2	6	1	2	0	0	0	0	0	0	0	0	0	0	0	.333	.333
Solis, Ali	R-R	5-11	175	9-29-87	.164	.400	.118	20	61	7	10	3	0	0	1	3	1	1	0	17	2	0	.213	.215
Tejeda, Oscar	R-R	6-1	170	12-26-89	.262	.263	.261	29	84	10	22	2	0	2	12	5	0	2	0	18	0	0	.357	.303
Vasquez, Andy	L-R	6-2	175	10-8-87	.248	.294	.237	94	262	32	65	5	4	4	27	15	2	2	1	71	12	9	.344	.293
Walker, Neil	B-R	6-3	210	9-10-85	.417	.333	.500	4	12	0	5	1	0	0	1	1	0	0	0	2	0	0	.500	.462
Welch, Stefan	L-R	6-3	190	8-12-88	.149	.231	.131	29	74	6	11	2	0	1	6	10	0	0	0	16	0	0	.216	.250

Pitching

Pitching	B-T	HT	WT	DOB	W	L	ERA	G	GS	CG	SV	IP	H	R	ER	HR	BB	SO	AVG	vLH	vRH	K/9	BB/9
Alderson, Tim	R-R	6-6	220	11-3-88	1	0	1.32	7	0	0	2	14	4	3	2	0	2	17	.091	.045	.136	11.20	1.32
Baker, Nate	L-L	6-3	190	12-27-87	4	4	6.05	38	7	0	3	80	92	63	54	8	45	68	.295	.291	.296	7.62	5.04
Beckman, Ryan	R-R	6-4	185	1-2-90	0	1	2.37	15	0	0	1	19	19	7	5	0	7	15	.257	.276	.244	7.11	3.32
Bromberg, David	L-R	6-5	245	9-14-87	6	12	3.51	26	20	0	0	136	120	64	53	10	52	127	.240	.222	.256	8.40	3.44
Cevette, Dan	L-L	6-4	235	10-19-83	0	0	0.00	2	0	0	0	2	3	1	0	0	1	2	.273	.000	.375	7.71	3.86
Contreras, Jose	R-R	6-4	255	12-6-71	0	0	0.00	2	0	0	0	2	0	0	0	0	0	1	.000	.000	.000	4.50	0.00
Cumpton, Brandon	R-R	6-2	210	11-16-88	0	1	7.45	2	2	0	0	10	11	9	8	0	5	7	.282	.278	.286	6.52	4.66
Dodson, Zack	L-L	6-2	190	7-23-90	0	1	13.50	1	1	0	0	4	8	6	6	0	4	2	.500	.667	.462	4.50	9.00
Grilli, Jason	R-R	6-4	235	11-11-76	0	0	0.00	2	2	0	0	2	2	0	0	0	4	4	.222	.500	.000	18.00	0.00
Hollingsworth, Ethan	R-R	6-2	200	5-4-87	6	5	3.55	24	9	0	0	84	70	38	33	11	20	47	.226	.217	.233	5.06	2.15
Hughes, Jared	R-R	6-7	240	7-4-85	0	0	0.00	1	1	0	0	2	1	0	0	0	0	4	.143	.333	.000	18.00	0.00
Inman, Jeff	R-R	6-3	180	11-24-87	1	1	2.65	10	0	0	2	17	15	5	5	1	6	14	.242	.292	.211	7.41	3.18
Karstens, Jeff	R-R	6-3	185	9-24-82	0	0	0.00	1	1	0	0	4	2	0	0	0	2	4	.133	.100	.200	9.00	4.50
Kasparek, Kenn	R-R	6-10	245	9-23-85	4	2	3.26	38	1	0	2	61	62	27	22	3	16	44	.263	.323	.221	6.53	2.37
Kingham, Nick	R-R	6-5	220	11-8-91	3	3	2.70	14	12	0	0	73	70	24	22	1	30	69	.253	.266	.242	8.47	3.68
Liriano, Francisco	L-L	6-2	220	10-26-83	0	1	13.50	1	1	0	0	3	4	4	4	1	3	4	.333	.000	.400	13.50	10.13
McDonald, James	L-R	6-4	205	10-19-84	0	1	5.79	2	2	0	0	5	4	3	3	1	5	2	.250	.500	.214	3.86	9.64
Miller, Quinton	R-R	6-1	185	11-28-89	1	5	3.75	31	2	0	1	58	49	25	24	3	36	45	.236	.198	.260	7.02	5.62
Morton, Charlie	R-R	6-5	245	11-12-83	1	1	2.41	4	4	0	0	19	10	5	5	2	6	11	.154	.220	.042	5.30	2.89
Navarro, Eliecer	L-L	5-9	177	10-26-87	4	8	4.52	15	14	0	0	76	76	44	38	8	35	55	.254	.268	.250	6.54	4.16
Pimentel, Stolmy	R-R	6-3	235	2-1-90	4	3	3.61	13	13	1	0	77	74	36	31	8	35	61	.252	.282	.227	7.10	4.07
Ramos, Jhonatan	L-L	6-0	199	8-7-89	3	2	4.72	36	0	0	1	48	53	25	25	4	11	42	.277	.275	.279	7.93	2.08
Sadler, Casey	R-R	6-4	200	7-13-90	11	7	3.31	23	23	1	0	130	116	54	48	11	42	67	.242	.246	.239	4.63	2.90
Sanz, Luis	R-R	6-1	173	11-19-87	3	5	4.94	47	3	0	16	62	61	38	34	8	35	61	.256	.280	.241	8.85	5.08
Taillon, Jameson	R-R	6-6	235	11-18-91	4	7	3.67	20	19	0	0	110	112	54	45	8	36	106	.257	.261	.254	8.65	2.94
Thornton, Zach	R-R	6-3	213	5-19-88	2	1	2.00	19	1	0	2	36	24	9	8	1	7	45	.182	.191	.176	11.25	1.75
Townsend, Jason	R-R	6-3	190	9-17-88	5	5	6.71	36	1	0	3	54	71	50	40	7	27	38	.311	.350	.280	6.37	4.53
Waldron, Tyler	R-R	6-2	185	5-1-89	0	3	4.81	8	3	0	0	24	31	18	13	1	10	13	.313	.326	.304	4.81	3.70

Fielding

Catcher	PCT	G	PO	A	E	DP	PB
Cutler	1.000	30	226	18	0	1	0
Paulino	.990	94	598	69	7	9	7
Perez	1.000	2	7	2	0	0	0
Sanchez	1.000	2	14	3	0	0	1
Solis	.986	18	128	13	2	1	0

First Base	PCT	G	PO	A	E	DP
Brown	1.000	14	91	14	0	7
Curry	.988	19	154	17	2	13
Cutler	.935	6	25	4	2	3
Howard	.995	77	575	56	3	43
Lambo	.972	18	125	14	4	12
Maggi	1.000	14	83	5	0	10
Perez	1.000	1	2	0	0	0
Tejeda	.923	2	12	0	1	2
Welch	1.000	19	112	14	0	12

Second Base	PCT	G	PO	A	E	DP
Brown	1.000	10	17	20	0	7
Cunningham	.984	126	220	333	9	68
Maggi	1.000	10	13	26	0	4
Tejeda	1.000	1	3	3	0	1
Vasquez	1.000	2	1	0	0	0
Walker	.909	4	3	7	1	2

Third Base	PCT	G	PO	A	E	DP
Brown	1.000	6	4	8	0	0
Cunningham	1.000	4	0	10	0	0
Maggi	1.000	4	1	0	0	0
Santos	.895	108	64	209	32	26
Tejeda	.824	7	6	8	3	0
Vasquez	.973	17	10	26	1	2
Welch	1.000	8	5	10	0	2

Shortstop	PCT	G	PO	A	E	DP
Brown	.938	8	4	11	1	3
d'Arnaud	.929	4	5	8	1	1

Hanson	.950	35	41	92	7	17
Maggi	.948	26	37	73	6	10
Ngoepe	.962	72	78	176	10	32
Vasquez	.825	9	14	19	7	5

Outfield	PCT	G	PO	A	E	DP
Brown	—		1	0	0	0
Curry	1.000	5	8	0	0	0
Dickerson	.995	119	197	6	1	1
Howard	1.000	5	4	0	0	0
Lambo	1.000	46	93	3	0	0
Maggi	1.000	27	49	1	0	0
Polanco	.989	68	172	6	2	2
Rojas Jr.	.980	119	240	5	5	0
Santos	1.000	4	6	1	0	0
Snider	1.000	3	2	0	0	0
Tejeda	.917	6	10	1	1	0
Vasquez	.975	52	72	5	2	0

BRADENTON MARAUDERS   HIGH CLASS A

FLORIDA STATE LEAGUE

Batting	B-T	HT	WT	DOB	AVG	vLH	vRH	G	AB	R	H	2B	3B	HR	RBI	BB	HBP	SH	SF	SO	SB	CS	SLG	OBP
Allie, Stetson	R-R	6-2	238	3-13-91	.229	.242	.221	66	236	28	54	18	0	4	25	41	2	0	5	82	2	3	.356	.342
Avila, Eric	R-R	6-1	165	6-9-90	.234	.286	.203	33	111	6	26	7	2	3	17	4	0	2	1	25	3	2	.414	.259
Crumlich, D.J.	R-R	6-0	190	4-23-90	.145	.184	.111	27	83	9	12	2	0	0	9	13	1	1	3	15	1	2	.169	.260
d'Arnaud, Chase	R-R	6-1	205	1-21-87	.333	.000	.400	2	6	2	2	0	1	0	0	0	0	0	1	1	.667	.429
Diaz, Elias	R-R	6-1	175	11-17-90	.279	.263	.290	57	183	30	51	12	2	6	35	31	1	3	2	33	4	4	.399	.382
Gamache, Daniel	L-R	5-11	190	11-20-90	.258	.268	.252	133	480	58	124	34	3	5	54	58	5	6	4	139	8	9	.373	.342
Garcia, Willy	R-R	6-3	180	9-4-92	.256	.273	.245	118	449	51	115	21	6	16	60	23	2	3	154	13	6	.437	.294
Gonzalez, Benji	R-R	5-11	160	1-16-90	.232	.224	.237	105	384	55	89	15	3	1	25	43	4	9	2	66	27	13	.294	.314
Grovatt, Dan	L-L	6-1	195	10-29-88	.226	.143	.281	18	53	4	12	1	0	2	5	1	2	5	8	1	1	.358	.281
Hanson, Alen	B-R	5-11	152	10-22-92	.281	.214	.322	92	367	51	103	23	8	7	48	33	2	2	5	70	24	14	.444	.339
Ivany, Devin	R-R	6-2	185	7-27-82	.429	.500	.000	2	7	0	3	0	0	0	1	0	1	0	0	0	0	.429	.500
Lashmet, Chris	R-R	6-4	230	4-25-89	.198	.231	.179	34	106	13	21	5	0	1	8	11	4	2	1	25	4	1	.274	.295
Lewis, Taylor	L-L	6-0	200	12-18-89	.207	.192	.217	95	323	42	67	11	12	2	39	22	5	6	5	103	17	3	.334	.265
Mesa, Carlos	R-R	6-2	215	2-10-88	.225	.256	.201	81	275	25	62	21	0	9	40	11	2	3	1	99	2	2	.400	.260
Ngoepe, Gift	B-R	5-10	165	1-18-90	.292	.310	.278	28	96	17	28	7	3	0	6	21	1	5	0	35	7	1	.427	.424
Osuna, Jose	R-R	6-2	213	12-12-92	.244	.281	.221	123	454	47	111	25	1	8	48	35	2	4	5	76	18	6	.357	.298
Polanco, Gregory	L-L	6-4	190	9-14-91	.312	.241	.359	57	218	29	68	17	0	6	30	16	3	2	2	37	24	4	.472	.364
Ponce, Ashley	R-R	5-11	140	1-22-91	.235	.194	.260	26	81	9	19	2	0	0	6	3	1	4	1	16	1	0	.259	.267
Sosa, Junior	L-L	5-10	139	10-3-90	.247	.226	.256	53	178	17	44	8	1	0	16	0	6	4	33	4	4	.303	.303
Stallings, Jacob	R-R	6-5	215	12-22-89	.219	.290	.177	78	251	36	55	16	2	6	23	45	7	2	1	62	1	1	.371	.352

Pitching	B-T	HT	WT	DOB	W	L	ERA	G	GS	CG	SV	IP	H	R	ER	HR	BB	SO	AVG	vLH	vRH	K/9	BB/9
Beckman, Ryan	R-R	6-4	185	1-2-90	2	0	4.00	13	0	0	1	18	20	9	8	2	5	11	.282	.167	.321	5.50	2.50
Benedict, Matt	R-R	6-5	220	2-3-89	3	9	4.17	28	9	0	5	86	109	51	40	4	24	48	.310	.336	.297	5.00	2.50
Castro, Orlando	L-L	5-11	190	3-17-92	2	3	4.32	13	4	0	1	33	39	18	16	3	11	21	.295	.227	.309	5.67	2.97
Cevette, Dan	L-L	6-4	235	10-19-83	0	0	0.00	2	0	0	0	3	1	0	0	0	1	3	.100	.500	.000	9.00	3.00
Contreras, Jose	R-R	6-4	255	12-6-71	0	1	9.00	1	0	0	0	2	2	2	2	0	1	2	.286	.333	.250	9.00	4.50
De Leon, Emmanuel	B-R	6-1	175	12-25-90	3	2	3.49	30	2	0	4	59	58	29	23	5	20	58	.262	.250	.269	8.80	3.03
Dodson, Zack	L-L	6-2	190	7-23-90	6	8	4.40	21	20	0	0	110	111	64	54	11	37	53	.255	.206	.270	4.32	3.02
Espinoza, Roberto	R-R	6-1	189	5-7-92	0	0	0.00	1	0	0	0	1	0	0	0	0	0	2	.000	.000	.000	13.50	0.00
Fuesser, Zac	L-L	6-2	190	7-19-90	2	4	3.18	37	0	0	3	68	73	27	24	4	15	52	.281	.197	.312	6.88	1.99
Harlan, Tom	L-L	6-6	215	3-7-90	1	0	0.00	3	0	0	0	6	9	1	0	0	2	9	.321	.200	.389	13.50	3.00
Karstens, Jeff	R-R	6-3	185	9-24-82	0	0	3.00	1	1	0	0	3	4	1	1	0	0	4	.308	.200	.375	12.00	0.00
Kilcrease, Robert	L-L	5-11	175	3-14-89	5	2	1.36	40	0	0	11	66	48	11	10	1	26	43	.208	.115	.235	5.86	3.55
Kingham, Nick	R-R	6-5	220	11-8-91	6	3	3.09	13	13	0	0	70	55	25	24	6	14	75	.212	.220	.209	9.64	1.80
Liriano, Francisco	L-L	6-2	220	10-26-83	0	0	0.00	1	1	0	0	3	0	0	0	0	0	6	.000	.000	.000	18.00	0.00
Lopez, Cesar	R-R	6-3	210	12-3-90	0	0	18.00	2	0	0	0	3	7	6	6	0	3	2	.467	.600	.400	6.00	9.00
Ludwig, Pat	R-R	6-1	185	10-11-89	2	2	3.90	13	9	0	0	55	57	26	24	1	14	41	.273	.305	.252	6.67	2.28
McDonald, James	L-R	6-4	205	10-19-84	0	0	9.00	1	0	0	0	2	4	2	2	1	0	1	.400	.600	.200	4.50	0.00
Medina, Jhondaniel	R-R	5-11	158	2-8-93	0	0	2.53	9	0	0	0	11	3	3	3	0	11	13	.091	.083	.091	9.78	9.28
Miller, Quinton	R-R	6-1	185	11-28-89	1	3	3.77	10	0	0	0	14	17	11	6	1	5	18	.288	.217	.333	11.30	3.14
Montero, Joan	R-R	6-0	186	10-26-88	4	6	3.03	40	3	0	2	68	67	31	23	5	34	49	.253	.290	.230	6.45	4.48
Morton, Charlie	R-R	6-5	245	11-12-83	0	0	6.00	1	1	0	0	3	2	2	2	1	0	2	.250	.200	.286	6.00	0.00
Navarro, Eliecer	L-L	5-9	177	10-26-87	1	9	2.86	13	11	0	0	69	62	25	22	4	13	62	.235	.194	.249	8.05	1.69
Ramos, Jhonatan	L-L	6-0	199	8-7-89	0	0	0.63	5	0	0	0	14	7	2	1	0	3	6	.143	.167	.135	3.77	1.88
Rocha, Oderman	R-R	6-3	165	11-7-92	0	0	4.50	2	0	0	2	6	4	3	3	0	2	4	.190	.222	.167	6.00	3.00
Rodriguez, Joely	L-L	6-1	175	11-14-91	4	3	2.67	12	12	0	0	67	63	24	20	4	19	44	.251	.169	.280	5.88	2.54
Rowland, Robby	R-R	6-4	215	12-15-91	4	11	4.82	27	24	0	0	127	132	89	68	10	48	67	.268	.352	.214	4.75	3.40
Sampson, Adrian	R-R	6-3	200	10-7-91	5	8	5.14	25	24	1	0	140	177	87	80	18	22	85	.310	.337	.295	5.46	1.41
Singer, Kirk	R-R	6-2	170	12-1-89	1	0	6.00	5	0	0	0	6	4	4	4	1	6	3	.200	.500	.071	4.50	9.00
Thornton, Zach	R-R	6-3	213	5-19-88	2	1	1.93	10	0	0	3	14	12	5	3	0	1	14	.222	.308	.195	9.00	0.64
Von Rosenberg, Zack	R-R	6-5	205	9-24-90	2	1	3.91	14	0	0	0	23	27	14	10	2	12	9	.287	.355	.254	3.52	4.70
Waldron, Tyler	R-R	6-2	185	5-1-89	1	0	7.88	5	0	0	2	8	11	9	7	1	4	11	.297	.000	.355	12.38	4.50
Yacko, Kurt	R-R	5-11	180	8-22-87	0	0	18.56	3	0	0	0	5	11	11	11	0	7	2	.423	.556	.353	3.38	11.81

Fielding

Catcher	PCT	G	PO	A	E	DP	PB
Diaz	.987	55	332	39	5	2	10
Ivany	1.000	1	3	1	0	0	0
Stallings	.991	78	478	57	5	2	3
Ponce	1.000	2	2	2	0	2	
Ponce	1.000	6	5	19	0	2	
Singer	1.000	1	0	1	0	0	

First Base	PCT	G	PO	A	E	DP
Allie	.992	49	473	26	4	45
Avila	.950	2	18	1	1	5
Lashmet	1.000	7	60	7	0	4
Osuna	.991	77	721	52	7	60

Second Base	PCT	G	PO	A	E	DP
Crumlich	1.000	1	0	1	0	0
Gamache	.969	120	232	331	18	64
Gonzalez	1.000	13	33	44	0	12

Third Base	PCT	G	PO	A	E	DP
Avila	.896	27	20	49	8	9
Crumlich	.916	26	16	71	8	7
Gonzalez	.966	51	26	115	5	6
Lashmet	.824	17	9	47	12	2
Ponce	.914	19	9	44	5	3

Shortstop	PCT	G	PO	A	E	DP
Avila	.857	1	1	5	1	2
d'Arnaud	1.000	2	2	6	0	0
Gonzalez	.956	9	12	31	2	4
Hanson	.942	92	118	286	25	49
Ngoepe	.978	28	34	100	3	17

Outfield	PCT	G	PO	A	E	DP
Garcia	.970	116	243	20	8	7
Gonzalez	.976	38	78	5	2	0
Grovatt	1.000	14	20	0	0	0
Lashmet	—	1	0	0	0	0
Lewis	.989	94	173	4	2	1
Mesa	.986	45	68	1	1	0
Osuna	1.000	1	1	0	0	0
Polanco	.952	56	137	3	7	0
Sosa	.991	51	104	2	1	1

WEST VIRGINIA POWER

SOUTH ATLANTIC LEAGUE

LOW CLASS A

Batting	B-T	HT	WT	DOB	AVG	vLH	vRH	G	AB	R	H	2B	3B	HR	RBI	BB	HBP	SH	SF	SO	SB	CS	SLG	OBP
Allie, Stetson	R-R	6-2	238	3-13-91	.324	.267	.337	66	244	42	79	16	1	17	61	36	3	0	2	79	6	1	.607	.414
Aponte, Francisco	B-R	5-11	135	2-9-91	.000	.000	.000	2	5	1	0	0	0	0	1	1	0	1	1	2	0	0	.000	.143
Barnes, Barrett	R-R	6-1	195	7-29-91	.268	.207	.279	46	183	26	49	9	0	5	24	17	3	2	1	48	10	3	.399	.338
Bell, Josh	B-R	6-3	213	8-14-92	.279	.302	.272	119	459	75	128	37	2	13	76	52	3	0	5	90	1	2	.453	.353
Crumlich, D.J.	R-R	6-0	190	4-23-90	.253	.269	.250	51	174	23	44	9	0	0	20	35	3	1	2	28	2	1	.305	.383
Diaz, Chris	R-R	6-0	180	11-9-90	.239	.148	.268	33	109	16	26	2	1	1	15	10	3	3	2	9	0	2	.303	.315
Diaz, Francisco	B-R	5-11	183	3-21-90	.255	.270	.251	66	212	29	54	12	1	1	17	28	3	1	3	35	0	0	.335	.348
Emsley-Pai, Kawika	B-R	5-11	195	9-3-88	.189	.172	.194	43	122	19	23	4	0	0	14	36	2	0	1	37	3	0	.221	.379
Fortunato, Raul	R-R	6-2	190	9-5-90	.248	.238	.251	123	440	47	109	21	5	5	52	31	2	1	1	95	12	8	.352	.300
Gourley, Walker	R-R	6-0	185	6-28-91	.304	.261	.315	119	444	75	135	19	2	6	43	26	6	3	1	86	36	10	.396	.350
Herrera, Dilson	R-R	5-10	150	3-3-94	.265	.310	.253	109	423	69	112	27	3	11	56	37	7	6	6	110	11	6	.421	.330
2-team total (7 Savannah)					.267	—	—	116	442	75	118	27	3	11	60	40	8	6	7	116	14	6	.416	.334
Mathisen, Wyatt	R-R	6-1	210	12-30-93	.185	.154	.194	32	119	13	22	3	0	0	9	9	3	5	2	22	1	0	.210	.256
Moroff, Max	R-R	6-0	175	5-13-93	.233	.220	.237	115	429	75	100	18	3	8	48	65	2	7	3	102	8	8	.345	.335
Ponce, Ashley	R-R	5-11	140	1-22-91	.244	.333	.226	36	127	22	31	8	0	0	16	13	2	4	1	15	4	1	.354	.322
Rider, Jimmy	R-R	5-8	175	5-9-90	.302	.273	.313	14	43	8	13	4	0	2	11	4	1	0	1	6	0	0	.535	.367
Schwind, Jonathan	R-R	6-0	185	10-20-90	.216	.200	.220	75	232	27	50	9	0	2	25	25	2	5	0	56	11	1	.280	.297
Sosa, Junior	L-L	5-10	139	10-3-90	.242	.240	.242	38	124	13	30	9	0	0	15	12	2	1	4	22	6	2	.315	.310
Steranka, Jordan	L-R	6-1	205	11-14-89	.247	.219	.256	67	263	29	65	11	2	3	25	9	1	1	3	90	2	3	.338	.272
Urena, Luis	R-R	6-4	198	8-21-92	.194	.091	.225	28	93	11	18	6	1	2	5	5	1	0	0	50	2	2	.344	.242
Wood, Eric	R-R	6-2	195	11-22-92	.255	.228	.263	97	364	40	93	20	0	6	51	29	3	4	2	88	2	3	.360	.314

PITTSBURGH PIRATES

Pitching	B-T	HT	WT	DOB	W	L	ERA	G	GS	CG	SV	IP	H	R	ER	HR	BB	SO	AVG	vLH	vRH	K/9	BB/9
Breedlove, Lance	R-R	6-1	180	9-1-90	3	2	5.97	26	0	0	0	35	46	28	23	3	10	36	.311	.359	.274	9.35	2.60
Burnette, Jake	R-R	6-4	180	8-10-92	0	3	16.88	5	4	0	0	11	19	20	20	2	13	14	.365	.333	.400	11.81	10.97
Castro, Orlando	L-L	5-11	190	3-17-92	7	4	1.93	13	13	0	0	75	65	19	16	5	6	63	.236	.190	.249	7.59	0.72
Creasy, Jason	R-R	6-4	197	5-13-92	6	4	2.74	32	13	0	3	108	106	43	33	7	24	96	.250	.268	.235	7.98	1.99
Glasnow, Tyler	L-R	6-7	195	8-23-93	9	3	2.18	24	24	0	0	111	54	35	27	9	61	164	.142	.137	.147	13.26	4.93
Hafner, Ryan	R-R	6-6	205	11-22-91	7	0	3.00	40	1	0	3	87	69	34	29	6	40	102	.216	.285	.159	10.55	4.14
Harlan, Tom	L-L	6-6	215	3-7-90	6	3	2.27	31	1	0	1	71	55	29	18	6	14	74	.208	.241	.193	9.34	1.77
Haynes, Kyle	R-R	6-2	190	2-11-91	1	5	2.38	41	8	0	7	83	64	29	22	1	36	85	.214	.284	.158	9.18	3.89
Heredia, Luis	R-R	6-6	205	8-10-94	7	3	3.05	14	13	0	0	65	52	22	22	5	37	55	.224	.207	.243	7.62	5.12
Holmes, Clay	R-R	6-5	230	3-27-93	5	6	4.08	26	25	0	0	119	106	59	54	7	69	90	.240	.259	.224	6.81	5.22
Jagoditsh, David	B-R	6-7	230	9-4-90	0	3	18.47	6	0	0	0	6	8	14	13	0	16	6	.308	.333	.294	8.53	24.16
Kuchno, John	R-R	6-5	210	5-21-91	9	5	4.01	24	22	0	0	123	124	61	55	7	45	89	.266	.263	.268	6.49	3.28
Lopez, Cesar	R-R	6-3	210	12-3-90	3	2	3.86	15	0	0	2	23	19	11	10	2	3	30	.218	.205	.233	11.57	1.16
Ludwig, Pat	R-R	6-1	185	10-11-89	6	0	3.12	24	1	0	1	49	38	21	17	4	16	44	.213	.195	.228	8.08	2.94
Medina, Jhondaniel	R-R	5-11	158	2-8-93	2	2	1.78	28	0	0	13	35	21	11	7	1	21	55	.164	.205	.109	14.01	5.35
Perez, Clario	R-R	6-1	185	8-30-92	0	2	4.19	21	1	0	1	34	29	18	16	0	22	29	.227	.211	.239	7.60	5.77
Rodriguez, Joely	L-L	6-1	175	11-14-91	5	5	2.72	14	14	0	0	73	79	36	22	4	20	57	.280	.247	.294	7.06	2.48
Smith, Josh	L-L	6-3	200	10-11-89	1	1	6.75	13	0	0	1	24	30	19	18	1	10	17	.297	.333	.284	6.38	3.75
Trepagnier, Bryton	R-R	6-5	180	9-18-91	5	5	4.95	43	0	0	3	73	71	46	40	5	39	69	.254	.234	.271	8.55	4.83

Fielding

Catcher	PCT	G	PO	A	E	DP	PB
Diaz	.980	65	528	49	12	10	6
Emsley-Pai	.982	43	353	36	7	2	9
Mathisen	.990	32	280	24	3	0	11
Schwind	1.000	1	7	0	0	0	1

First Base	PCT	G	PO	A	E	DP
Allie	.992	41	339	27	3	26
Crumlich	1.000	5	48	6	0	8
Gourley	.991	49	387	34	4	35
Rider	1.000	2	12	0	0	1
Schwind	1.000	2	6	0	0	0
Steranka	.991	46	407	19	4	33

Second Base	PCT	G	PO	A	E	DP
Aponte	1.000	1	2	4	0	1
Diaz	1.000	12	19	31	0	8
Gourley	.875	2	2	5	1	1
Herrera	.970	104	195	296	15	55
Ponce	.976	18	38	44	2	15
Rider	1.000	4	4	14	0	4

Third Base	PCT	G	PO	A	E	DP
Aponte	1.000	1	1	2	0	0
Crumlich	.946	40	25	81	6	5
Diaz	.957	8	8	14	1	1
Gourley	.923	5	2	10	1	2
Ponce	1.000	1	0	2	0	0
Rider	1.000	9	5	15	0	0
Wood	.873	77	47	146	28	15

Shortstop	PCT	G	PO	A	E	DP
Diaz	.950	13	17	40	3	7
Moroff	.933	110	158	302	33	52
Ponce	1.000	18	18	53	0	10

Outfield	PCT	G	PO	A	E	DP
Barnes	.977	45	85	0	2	0
Bell	.978	84	129	5	3	1
Crumlich	1.000	1	2	0	0	0
Fortunato	.969	118	180	9	6	2
Gourley	.988	53	71	8	1	2
Schwind	.990	64	89	8	1	1
Sosa	.982	38	54	0	1	0
Urena	.949	27	36	1	2	0

JAMESTOWN JAMMERS   SHORT-SEASON

NEW YORK-PENN LEAGUE

Batting	B-T	HT	WT	DOB	AVG	vLH	vRH	G	AB	R	H	2B	3B	HR	RBI	BB	HBP	SH	SF	SO	SB	CS	SLG	OBP
Aponte, Francisco	B-R	5-11	135	2-9-91	.181	.227	.160	27	72	7	13	1	1	1	4	7	0	4	0	15	4	0	.264	.253
Barrios, Yhonathan	B-R	5-11	180	12-1-91	.143	.429	.048	11	28	3	4	0	0	1	6	2	0	1	1	9	1	1	.250	.194
Carvajal, Jodaneli	R-R	5-9	160	4-20-92	.290	.000	.333	8	31	6	9	2	3	0	5	2	0	1	1	2	1	2	.548	.324
Collins, Danny	R-R	6-2	205	2-11-91	.259	.269	.256	64	228	39	59	15	2	7	25	17	4	2	2	46	5	4	.434	.319
Dennis, Andrew	R-R	6-2	180	3-30-93	.214	.333	.167	16	42	4	9	2	0	0	6	4	0	1	0	15	0	0	.262	.283
Escobar, Elvis	L-L	5-10	180	9-6-94	.268	.258	.270	56	183	25	49	8	2	1	23	9	0	1	6	47	9	4	.350	.293
Espinal, Edwin	R-R	6-3	210	1-23-94	.288	.280	.289	67	240	22	69	9	0	2	41	9	3	4	4	38	1	1	.350	.316
Fransoso, Mike	L-R	6-0	180	7-27-90	.253	.235	.259	67	225	37	57	9	0	2	25	34	3	14	0	55	14	6	.320	.359
Frazier, Adam	L-R	5-11	170	12-14-91	.321	.322	.321	58	224	34	72	7	1	0	27	25	6	0	3	31	5	8	.362	.399
Jhang, Jin-De	L-R	5-11	220	5-17-93	.277	.262	.282	53	184	22	51	8	1	5	34	17	2	4	4	24	0	1	.413	.338
Jones, JaCoby	R-R	6-3	200	5-10-92	.311	.412	.273	55	61	9	19	2	2	1	10	3	2	0	1	14	3	2	.459	.358
Landecker, Adam	R-R	6-0	200	2-1-91	.224	.111	.250	17	49	6	11	1	0	0	9	1	0	0	0	9	3	1	.245	.240
Maffei, Justin	R-R	6-1	180	8-27-91	.206	.111	.240	14	34	4	7	0	0	0	2	3	2	0	1	14	2	0	.206	.300
Mathisen, Wyatt	R-R	6-1	210	12-30-93	.269	.600	.190	8	26	4	7	0	0	0	3	5	1	0	1	7	1	0	.269	.394
McGuire, Reese	L-R	6-0	180	3-2-95	.250	.000	.267	4	16	3	4	0	0	0	1	0	0	0	1	1	0	.250	.294
Meadows, Austin	L-L	6-3	200	5-3-95	.529	.500	.533	5	17	8	9	0	0	2	2	5	0	0	0	4	0	0	.882	.636
Myles, Candon	L-R	5-10	185	10-24-92	.255	.200	.262	16	47	8	12	0	2	0	4	12	0	1	0	9	7	2	.340	.407
Ramirez, Harold	R-R	5-11	175	9-6-94	.285	.224	.301	71	274	42	78	11	4	5	40	23	8	2	3	52	23	11	.409	.354
Rider, Jimmy	R-R	5-8	175	5-9-90	.246	.250	.244	23	61	4	15	3	0	0	11	2	2	3	1	11	3	1	.295	.288
Rossiter, Max	R-R	5-11	195	10-5-90	.333	.000	.500	1	3	1	1	0	0	0	2	1	0	0	0	1	0	0	.333	.500
Roy, Jeff	L-L	5-9	168	1-24-92	.292	.327	.278	53	185	28	54	4	1	0	19	25	1	3	2	52	23	4	.324	.376
Valesente, Dave	R-R	6-2	220	7-15-88	.250	.360	.171	20	60	3	15	3	0	0	4	4	3	0	14	2	1	.300	.297
Vasquez, Jesus	R-R	6-2	198	12-10-91	.250	.143	.294	9	24	4	6	0	0	0	2	1	0	0	10	1	0	.250	.333
Wallace, Beau	R-R	6-1	205	7-28-92	.100	.143	.087	10	30	6	3	1	0	0	2	3	1	0	0	8	0	1	.133	.206
Weiss, Erich	L-R	6-3	180	9-11-91	.273	.200	.287	41	121	21	33	7	2	0	10	13	2	3	2	40	4	2	.364	.348

Pitching	B-T	HT	WT	DOB	W	L	ERA	G	GS	CG	SV	IP	H	R	ER	HR	BB	SO	AVG	vLH	vRH	K/9	BB/9
Borden, Buddy	R-R	6-3	210	4-29-92	0	0	1.08	6	3	0	0	17	10	2	2	0	5	23	.169	.250	.114	12.42	2.70
Breedlove, Lance	R-R	6-1	180	9-1-90	1	0	0.00	3	0	0	0	7	4	0	0	0	3	12	.167	.000	.308	15.43	3.86
Brewer, Colten	R-R	6-4	200	10-29-92	2	0	3.29	3	3	0	0	14	16	6	5	1	5	6	.296	.261	.323	3.95	3.29
Carle, Shane	R-R	6-4	185	8-30-91	1	0	2.15	14	4	0	1	50	47	18	12	3	6	43	.247	.253	.247	7.69	1.07
Diaz, Axel	R-R	6-2	170	3-14-91	4	3	3.60	19	0	0	0	30	28	16	12	1	19	36	.250	.182	.294	10.80	5.70
Dickson, Cody	L-L	6-3	180	4-27-92	2	0	2.37	14	14	0	0	57	42	18	15	3	24	59	.209	.286	.174	9.32	3.79

Player	B-T	HT	WT	DOB	W	L	ERA	G	GS	CG	SV	IP	H	R	ER	HR	BB	SO	AVG	vLH	vRH	K/9	BB/9
Espinoza, Roberto	R-R	6-1	189	5-7-92	3	2	2.55	18	0	0	5	25	15	9	7	0	15	26	.181	.290	.115	9.49	5.47
Hirsch, Henry	R-R	6-3	185	9-29-92	2	0	1.50	15	0	0	2	24	13	4	4	1	5	26	.159	.118	.188	9.75	1.88
Jagoditsh, David	B-R	6-7	230	9-4-90	0	1	33.75	3	0	0	0	1	0	5	5	0	2	2	.000	.000	.000	13.50	13.50
Kendall, Will	B-L	6-3	180	9-7-91	0	2	3.09	12	0	0	0	23	26	9	8	4	4	22	.286	.357	.254	8.49	1.54
Kleis, Kevin	R-R	6-8	225	8-31-91	1	1	3.77	11	0	0	2	14	13	7	6	1	3	8	.241	.263	.229	5.02	1.88
Kuhl, Chad	R-R	6-3	215	9-10-92	3	4	2.11	13	13	0	0	55	53	22	13	0	6	33	.255	.250	.258	5.37	0.98
Lodge, Jackson	L-L	6-2	158	10-12-93	4	5	5.18	15	10	0	0	57	67	37	33	9	7	30	.291	.263	.301	4.71	1.10
Lopez, Cesar	R-R	6-3	210	12-3-90	2	1	2.81	8	0	0	1	16	10	5	5	0	4	15	.179	.238	.143	8.44	2.25
Lopez, Jovany	L-L	5-10	155	3-11-91	1	1	4.63	6	0	0	0	12	7	7	6	1	14	4	.179	.250	.161	3.09	10.80
McKinney, Brett	R-R	6-2	225	11-19-90	1	0	3.45	23	0	0	10	29	27	12	11	5	9	27	.248	.250	.246	8.48	2.83
Mulderig, Jerry	R-R	6-4	205	6-17-92	0	0	0.00	1	0	0	0	2	1	3	0	0	1	1	.143	.500	.000	5.40	5.40
Neverauskas, Dovydas	R-R	6-3	175	1-14-93	4	4	4.01	15	15	0	0	61	55	33	27	8	22	39	.243	.250	.236	5.79	3.26
Otamendi, Andy	L-L	5-11	170	5-15-92	2	2	5.89	11	0	0	0	18	15	12	12	4	9	19	.221	.250	.208	9.33	4.42
Rocha, Oderman	R-R	6-3	165	11-7-92	0	0	6.14	5	0	0	0	7	4	6	5	1	7	10	.167	.200	.143	12.27	8.59
Sanchez, Isaac	R-R	6-0	170	10-14-92	1	1	3.45	14	13	0	0	57	52	28	22	4	26	47	.242	.165	.287	7.38	4.08
Topa, Justin	R-R	6-4	200	3-7-91	5	2	2.19	19	0	0	0	37	33	11	9	1	10	33	.237	.172	.284	8.03	2.43
Yacko, Kurt	R-R	5-11	180	8-22-87	2	1	3.18	12	0	0	0	17	17	10	6	1	3	14	.258	.344	.176	7.41	1.59

Fielding

Catcher	PCT	G	PO	A	E	DP	PB
Dennis	.976	14	78	5	2	0	1
Jhang	.992	45	333	57	3	5	11
Mathisen	1.000	5	43	4	0	1	0
McGuire	1.000	3	17	3	0	1	1
Rossiter	1.000	1	10	1	0	1	1
Valesente	1.000	13	62	10	0	0	4

First Base	PCT	G	PO	A	E	DP
Collins	.985	29	240	15	4	20
Espinal	.992	49	448	29	4	44
Rider	1.000	2	3	0	0	0

Second Base	PCT	G	PO	A	E	DP
Aponte	1.000	10	18	23	0	3
Barrios	1.000	5	9	11	0	3
Carvajal	.955	8	13	29	2	7

	PCT	G	PO	A	E	DP
Fransoso	.969	37	60	95	5	27
Frazier	.975	15	31	48	2	14
Landecker	1.000	2	2	7	0	3
Rider	1.000	3	4	5	0	1

Third Base	PCT	G	PO	A	E	DP
Aponte	.939	12	5	26	2	5
Barrios	.667	1	1	1	1	0
Espinal	.857	1	0	6	1	0
Landecker	1.000	14	8	26	0	5
Rider	.978	17	10	35	1	0
Wallace	.824	5	3	11	3	2
Weiss	.875	35	28	63	13	7

Shortstop	PCT	G	PO	A	E	DP
Fransoso	.967	27	32	86	4	13
Frazier	.959	43	47	116	7	23

	PCT	G	PO	A	E	DP
Jones	.926	5	9	16	2	6

Outfield	PCT	G	PO	A	E	DP
Aponte	.900	4	9	0	1	0
Barrios	1.000	5	9	1	0	0
Collins	1.000	8	17	0	0	0
Escobar	.902	49	71	3	8	1
Jones	1.000	10	17	0	0	0
Maffei	.967	10	29	0	1	0
Meadows	1.000	5	14	0	0	0
Myles	.957	15	21	1	1	0
Ramirez	.955	70	125	3	6	0
Roy	.970	53	92	5	3	3
Vasquez	.917	6	9	2	1	1

GCL PIRATES   ROOKIE

GULF COAST LEAGUE

Batting	B-T	HT	WT	DOB	AVG	vLH	vRH	G	AB	R	H	2B	3B	HR	RBI	BB	HBP	SH	SF	SO	SB	CS	SLG	OBP
Arbet, Trae	R-R	6-0	185	7-1-94	.174	.111	.188	42	144	16	25	7	3	0	10	4	7	3	0	43	4	2	.264	.232
Arribas, Danny	R-R	6-0	185	9-30-92	.307	.257	.321	50	166	32	51	8	2	0	19	23	3	7	1	36	5	3	.380	.399
Buckner, Nick	L-L	6-1	205	8-9-95	.245	.161	.267	40	147	11	36	8	2	1	31	8	3	2	4	41	4	3	.347	.290
Chambers, Evan	R-R	5-11	210	3-24-89	.077	.167	.000	4	13	1	1	0	0	0	0	0	0	0	0	3	0	0	.154	.077
Curry, Matt	L-R	6-1	225	7-27-88	.111	—	.111	3	9	0	1	0	0	0	0	1	0	0	0	2	0	0	.111	.111
Diaz, Chris	R-R	6-0	180	11-9-90	.240	.250	.238	9	25	5	6	2	1	0	5	2	1	2	0	3	1	0	.400	.321
Gonzalez, Samuel	R-R	6-0	180	2-24-89	.071	.000	.100	5	14	0	1	0	0	0	0	1	0	0	0	3	0	0	.071	.133
Landecker, Adam	R-R	6-0	200	2-1-91	.220	.269	.206	36	123	19	27	8	2	0	17	15	4	1	1	19	1	3	.317	.322
Maffei, Justin	R-R	6-1	180	8-27-91	.237	.364	.215	22	76	6	18	4	2	0	7	4	3	1	1	13	0	0	.342	.298
Mathisen, Wyatt	R-R	6-1	210	12-30-93	.409	.500	.357	8	22	5	9	1	0	0	3	7	0	0	0	2	0	0	.455	.552
McGuire, Reese	L-R	6-0	181	3-2-95	.330	.310	.336	46	176	30	58	11	0	0	21	15	3	2	2	18	5	1	.392	.388
Meadows, Austin	L-L	6-3	200	5-3-95	.294	.250	.310	43	160	29	47	11	5	5	20	24	4	1	0	42	3	2	.519	.399
Montilla, Ulises	R-R	5-11	170	5-12-92	.290	.324	.281	43	155	18	45	16	2	1	33	16	3	5	2	25	0	0	.439	.364
Morales, Tomas	R-R	6-0	190	7-30-91	.303	.600	.250	15	33	4	10	3	0	0	4	0	1	0	0	3	1	0	.394	.324
Myles, Candon	L-R	5-10	185	10-24-92	.291	.314	.283	37	141	22	41	2	0	0	10	15	2	3	0	29	8	4	.305	.367
Ozuna, Carlos	B-R	5-11	162	7-19-93	.204	.138	.221	39	142	16	29	4	2	0	20	10	1	7	2	36	2	3	.261	.258
Rivera, Maximo	R-R	5-11	182	12-22-92	.244	.353	.217	31	86	14	21	2	3	0	7	9	3	2	2	21	6	2	.337	.330
Rosario, Henrry	L-L	5-9	180	4-5-93	.178	.111	.194	14	45	6	8	0	0	0	1	5	0	4	0	10	2	1	.178	.260
Ross, Kevin	R-R	6-0	205	9-17-93	.000	.000	.000	5	14	0	0	0	0	0	0	1	2	1	0	4	0	0	.000	.176
Sands, Jerry	R-R	6-4	225	9-28-87	.364	.333	.375	4	11	4	4	4	0	0	2	3	2	0	0	4	0	0	.909	.462
Urena, Luis	R-R	6-4	198	8-25-91	.290	.333	.278	19	69	6	20	4	1	1	6	4	1	1	0	23	1	1	.420	.338
Vallejo, Enyel	R-R	6-1	175	10-15-90	.306	.667	.250	29	111	19	34	5	2	3	20	2	2	1	2	14	4	1	.468	.325
Wallace, Beau	R-R	6-1	205	7-28-92	.149	.133	.153	27	87	11	13	1	0	0	3	12	4	1	0	24	3	1	.161	.282

Pitching	B-T	HT	WT	DOB	W	L	ERA	G	GS	CG	SV	IP	H	R	ER	HR	BB	SO	AVG	vLH	vRH	K/9	BB/9
Campos, Luis	R-R	6-0	188	8-28-90	1	1	6.65	19	0	0	1	23	28	19	17	4	16	21	.301	.300	.302	8.22	6.26
Cevette, Dan	L-L	6-4	235	10-19-83	1	0	0.00	2	0	0	0	4	0	0	0	0	0	4	.000	.000	.000	12.00	0.00
Del Rosario, Mervin	L-L	6-3	190	3-15-92	2	3	5.87	15	2	0	1	38	38	27	25	4	6	32	.259	.216	.273	7.51	1.41
Espinoza, Roberto	R-R	6-1	189	5-7-92	0	0	0.00	2	0	0	2	1	1	0	0	0	0	3	.200	—	.200	20.25	0.00
Gibbs, Jeff	R-R	6-4	185	4-23-91	2	0	14.46	10	0	0	0	9	6	15	15	0	17	5	.214	.300	.167	4.82	16.39
Griffin, Cameron	L-L	6-1	210	11-7-91	0	0	1.90	18	0	0	0	24	17	6	5	0	14	29	.200	.148	.224	11.03	5.32
Grullon, Adrian	R-R	6-0	180	9-17-92	0	3	5.09	7	5	0	0	18	20	10	10	1	6	20	.282	.320	.261	10.19	3.06
Hernandez, Jimy	R-R	6-2	210	5-22-92	2	0	5.14	15	0	0	0	21	20	12	12	1	14	12	.256	.250	.261	5.14	6.00
Herrand, Jhonatan	R-R	6-5	230	9-11-91	0	0	0.00	2	0	0	0	2	1	0	0	0	4	1	.167	.000	.250	5.40	21.60
Hirsch, Henry	R-R	6-3	185	9-29-92	1	0	0.00	2	0	0	0	3	1	0	0	0	1	1	.125	.000	.143	3.00	3.00

Hurst, Hayden	R-R	6-5	235	8-24-93	0	0	27.00	1	0	0	0	0	0	1	1	0	5	0	—	.000	.000	0.00 135.00
Kendall, Will	B-L	6-3	180	9-7-91	0	0	0.00	1	0	0	0	1	1	0	0	0	2	.250	.000	.333	18.00	0.00
Kozikowski, Neil	R-R	6-4	180	5-26-95	1	1	2.63	7	6	0	0	24	24	11	7	2	3	13	.253	.179	.304	4.88 1.13
Lopez, Jovany	L-L	5-10	155	3-11-91	2	0	2.35	12	0	0	5	15	15	4	4	1	5	12	.250	.333	.222	7.04 2.93
McDonald, James	L-R	6-4	205	10-19-84	0	0	6.35	3	3	0	0	6	5	4	4	0	1	5	.238	.429	.143	7.94 1.59
Mulderig, Jerry	L-R	6-4	205	6-17-92	0	1	2.25	10	0	0	2	12	11	4	3	0	3	8	.244	.231	.250	6.00 2.25
Otamendi, Andy	L-L	5-11	170	5-15-92	3	0	1.62	9	0	0	3	17	13	3	3	0	2	23	.213	.200	.217	12.42 1.08
Pimentel, Cesilio	L-L	6-2	185	1-5-93	2	3	3.97	14	6	0	0	34	27	19	15	2	13	30	.211	.250	.198	7.94 3.44
Rocha, Oderman	R-R	6-3	165	11-7-92	1	0	2.18	10	0	0	0	21	16	7	5	1	7	16	.213	.185	.229	6.97 3.05
Rosario, Miguel	R-R	6-0	182	1-30-93	1	1	3.61	15	5	0	0	42	45	29	17	5	13	33	.257	.318	.220	7.02 2.76
Roth, Billy	R-R	6-3	184	6-5-95	0	1	3.26	6	6	0	0	19	15	7	7	1	9	10	.231	.172	.278	4.66 4.19
Sanchez, Angel	L-L	6-7	190	3-2-93	3	2	3.25	15	0	0	0	36	30	15	13	4	9	26	.219	.235	.214	6.50 2.25
Sandfort, Jon	B-R	6-6	215	8-27-94	2	2	4.95	10	9	0	0	36	39	22	20	3	14	35	.281	.333	.247	8.67 3.47
Santiago, Cristian	R-R	6-4	232	6-14-90	3	2	4.62	16	0	0	1	25	30	19	13	2	13	14	.306	.300	.310	4.97 4.62
Singer, Kirk	R-R	6-2	170	12-1-89	0	1	5.68	6	0	0	0	6	5	4	4	0	2	3	.208	.333	.133	4.26 2.84
Smith, Josh	L-L	6-3	200	10-11-89	1	0	0.00	1	0	0	0	1	1	0	0	0	1	1	.333	.000	.500	9.00 9.00
Taylor, Blake	L-L	6-3	220	8-17-95	0	2	2.57	8	7	0	0	21	7	8	6	0	9	13	.104	.143	.087	5.57 3.86
Wang, Wei-Chung	L-L	6-1	160	4-25-92	1	3	3.23	12	11	0	0	47	37	18	17	2	4	42	.209	.278	.179	7.99 0.76

Fielding

Catcher	PCT	G	PO	A	E	DP	PB
Arribas	.990	21	176	13	2	2	6
Gonzalez	1.000	3	17	4	0	0	0
Mathisen	1.000	6	32	3	0	0	0
McGuire	.977	25	138	31	4	3	1
Morales	.986	15	62	7	1	0	1

First Base	PCT	G	PO	A	E	DP
Arribas	.997	28	289	19	1	21
Curry	1.000	1	4	0	0	0
Gonzalez	1.000	1	7	1	0	1
Rivera	.996	30	224	23	1	20
Ross	1.000	5	30	1	0	3
Sands	1.000	1	9	1	0	1

Second Base	PCT	G	PO	A	E	DP
Diaz	1.000	1	6	5	0	1
Landecker	1.000	3	6	9	0	2
Montilla	.968	40	70	112	6	27
Ozuna	.967	17	40	48	3	13

Third Base	PCT	G	PO	A	E	DP
Landecker	.928	31	22	55	6	7
Rivera	1.000	1	0	1	0	1
Vallejo	.643	5	0	9	5	2
Wallace	.929	24	17	75	7	7

Shortstop	PCT	G	PO	A	E	DP
Arbet	.876	38	43	105	21	16
Diaz	.971	8	13	20	1	3
Ozuna	.893	19	21	54	9	9

Outfield	PCT	G	PO	A	E	DP
Buckner	.981	33	49	2	1	0
Chambers	1.000	2	4	0	0	0
Maffei	.970	21	32	0	1	0
Meadows	.987	36	74	3	1	1
Myles	.962	37	49	2	2	0
Rosario	.952	14	19	1	1	0
Sands	1.000	3	1	1	0	0
Urena	1.000	17	21	2	0	1
Vallejo	.930	22	38	2	3	0

DSL PIRATES   ROOKIE

DOMINICAN SUMMER LEAGUE

Batting	B-T	HT	WT	DOB	AVG	vLH	vRH	G	AB	R	H	2B	3B	HR	RBI	BB	HBP	SH	SF	SO	SB	CS	SLG	OBP
Adames, Yunerky	L-L	6-1	200	8-26-90	.262	.231	.269	19	65	15	17	4	0	5	14	8	4	0	2	15	8	4	.554	.367
Aquiles, Yunior	R-R	6-3	185	11-11-93	.158	.1	.17	37	57	5	9	1	1	0	2	6	0	1	0	20	1	3	.211	.238
Barrios, Gustavo	R-R	5-10	157	12-15-93	.250	.267	.248	44	124	29	31	2	5	0	13	26	4	4	0	28	7	3	.347	.396
Bastardo, Alexis	R-R	5-11	190	2-26-94	.276	.226	.286	56	185	38	51	12	3	2	34	32	15	1	3	39	11	3	.405	.417
Benitez, Luis	B-R	5-9	153	12-8-93	.223	.319	.198	65	224	42	50	6	4	0	17	31	5	0	0	47	33	10	.286	.331
Cerda, Reggie	R-R	6-0	185	9-10-94	.230	.176	.241	10	100	9	23	4	0	0	10	5	2	2	1	13	0	1	.270	.275
Chourio, Bealyn	B-R	6-0	150	3-31-94	.177	.233	.167	59	186	26	33	4	0	0	17	41	1	4	2	52	8	4	.242	.326
De Jesus, Johan	B-R	6-0	165	8-1-96	.190	.3	.156	54	168	16	32	2	0	0	17	14	1	5	2	46	6	4	.202	.254
De La Cruz, Julio	B-R	6-1	190	10-5-95	.199	.095	.225	61	211	22	42	12	1	4	37	21	17	0	3	48	4	1	.322	.317
De La Cruz, Michael	L-L	6-1	165	7-10-96	.292	.237	.303	62	226	51	66	11	3	0	20	58	3	2	4	50	14	11	.367	.436
De La Mota, Steven	L-L	6-0	190	10-21-93	.274	.429	.243	53	168	34	46	3	2	1	22	25	5	7	0	39	10	3	.333	.384
Esqueda, Carlos	R-R	5-8	135	12-6-91	.170	.188	.167	34	100	17	17	4	0	0	11	19	5	1	1	28	7	5	.210	.328
Figueroa, Edgar	L-L	5-10	156	2-12-94	.270	.143	.297	61	237	38	64	7	8	2	42	28	0	10	4	40	7	3	.392	.342
Garcia, Deybi	R-R	5-11	185	2-11-92	.207	.208	.206	39	121	11	25	6	0	0	12	7	3	1	1	29	0	0	.256	.265
Gonzalez, Yoel	R-R	6-1	180	8-1-96	.188	.105	.2	44	149	20	28	7	1	1	14	11	3	3	2	24	0	0	.268	.255
Guzman, Rudy	B-R	6-0	175	7-28-91	.275	.379	.238	29	109	20	30	1	4	0	11	13	0	3	1	27	19	3	.358	.350
Herrera, Jhoan	L-R	6-1	185	6-14-95	.238	.163	.255	64	235	36	56	9	2	2	36	25	7	3	2	48	1	2	.319	.327
Hurtarte, Dennis	B-R	6-2	221	6-10-93	.247	.25	.246	44	150	19	37	12	0	0	16	17	3	2	0	37	2	0	.327	.335
Marquez, Carlos	L-R	6-2	180	4-29-93	.212	.125	.24	17	33	6	7	0	0	0	3	9	0	0	0	11	0	0	.212	.381
Morales, Tomas	R-R	6-0	190	7-30-94	.125	.2	.105	9	24	5	3	0	0	0	2	1	0	0	3	1	0	.125	.222
Munoz, Carlos	L-L	5-11	225	6-29-94	.319	.286	.324	67	207	40	66	16	2	3	36	54	3	2	6	27	0	1	.459	.456
Munoz, Edgard	B-R8-May	150	10-31-91	.400	—	.4	4	10	5	4	0	0	0	2	2	0	0	0	1	0	0	.400	.500
Padilla, Fredys	B-R	5-11	168	1-12-94	.260	.4	.234	45	127	13	33	9	1	0	17	22	1	3	4	23	2	5	.346	.364
Pena, Ramses	B-R	5-10	152	10-9-92	.243	.267	.236	51	140	26	34	7	1	0	7	24	2	3	1	32	21	5	.307	.359
Perez, Ramy	R-R	6-0	170	9-29-94	.239	.231	.24	26	88	13	21	3	1	1	15	11	0	2	3	17	2	0	.330	.314
Polanco, Yomifer	R-R	6-1	187	2-15-93	.304	—	—	39	125	16	38	9	0	0	21	15	1	1	2	30	5	3	.376	.378
Polo, Tito	R-R	5-11	180	8-23-94	.275	.171	.304	45	160	29	44	3	3	2	16	15	4	5	0	41	22	5	.369	.352
Polonia, Rodney	L-R	5-10	160	9-19-92	.235	.353	.2	45	149	21	35	2	3	0	14	12	2	5	2	33	1	4	.289	.297
Rangel, Eduardo	R-R	6-2	188	1-19-93	.071	0	.086	26	42	9	3	0	0	0	2	9	4	2	0	20	0	0	.071	.291
Reyes, Pablo	R-R	5-10	150	9-5-93	.304	.324	.3	52	184	27	56	8	3	3	28	23	0	4	3	21	15	4	.429	.376
Reyes, Patrick	R-R	6-0	190	9-11-92	.179	.091	.214	22	39	2	7	0	0	0	3	4	1	0	0	16	0	1	.179	.273
Ronco, Jesus	R-R	5-10	171	3-31-94	.194	—	—	33	67	8	13	6	0	0	8	12	7	5	0	17	2	0	.284	.372
Rosario, Henrry	L-L9-May	180	4-5-93	.200	.357	.164	28	75	12	15	1	4	1	9	14	1	5	0	20	3	1	.360	.333
Salazar, Jose	R-R	6-2	174	7-11-94	.227	.2	.234	44	132	16	30	6	0	0	20	15	11	5	2	25	1	2	.273	.350
Santos, Sandy	R-R	6-3	185	4-20-94	.205	.189	.209	54	171	20	35	2	2	2	18	11	1	4	4	47	6	3	.275	.251

Pitching	B-T	HT	WT	DOB	W	L	ERA	G	GS	CG	SV	IP	H	R	ER	HR	BB	SO	AVG	vLH	vRH	K/9	BB/9
Agrazal, Dario	R-R	6-3	190	12-28-94	6	0	2.40	13	12	0	0	60	57	21	16	2	17	32	.249	.25	.248	4.80	2.55
Almonte, Brayan	R-R	6-7	188	10-9-91	1	3	8.00	16	0	0	0	18	17	19	16	0	22	14	.246	.333	.222	7.00	11.00
Basulto, Omar	L-L	6-3	190	8-24-93	5	3	2.09	15	14	0	0	69	60	24	16	3	14	62	.233	.13	.243	8.09	1.83
Batista, Jose	L-L	6-2	175	2-1-96	3	0	2.24	16	10	0	0	56	46	19	14	1	27	36	.237	.226	.239	5.75	4.31
Beltrez, Marcus	L-L	6-0	204	10-20-92	4	1	1.08	19	0	0	2	42	27	8	5	1	12	34	.184	.074	.208	7.34	2.59
Brun, Luis	R-R	6-0	170	12-28-94	2	0	6.50	12	0	0	1	18	18	15	13	0	21	9	.257	.19	.286	4.50	10.50
Calderin, Oscar	L-L	6-4	175	2-22-91	0	0	4.76	4	0	0	1	6	7	4	3	0	1	1	.304	.333	.3	1.59	1.59
Ceballo, Addelin	R-R	6-0	190	6-29-91	3	2	2.93	13	0	0	0	28	33	11	9	0	9	12	.308	.29	.316	3.90	2.93
De Aza, Remy	R-R	6-3	207	9-8-94	0	2	7.20	7	1	0	1	10	10	11	8	0	12	5	.286	.125	.333	4.50	10.80
De Leon, Christopher	R-R	6-0	158	8-2-92	2	3	3.62	17	0	0	4	27	16	16	11	1	15	32	—	—	—	10.54	4.94
Esqueda, Jherson	L-R	6-1	175	6-9-95	1	1	2.31	10	1	0	0	23	20	10	6	1	5	13	.227	.217	.231	5.01	1.93
Ferreras, Miguel	R-R	6-5	221	9-19-91	1	5	4.14	14	13	0	0	54	49	32	25	0	33	46	.249	.28	.238	7.62	5.47
Garcia, Hector	L-L	6-0	170	10-4-95	3	2	2.40	17	1	0	1	41	30	15	11	1	22	41	.2	.136	.211	8.93	4.79
Gutierrez, Alexander	R-R	6-2	213	3-25-93	1	1	7.62	12	0	0	0	13	11	13	11	0	21	12	.224	.333	.217	8.31	14.54
Henriquez, Cristian	L-L	6-0	175	6-20-92	4	1	1.72	17	9	0	1	63	55	14	12	0	14	38	.246	.208	.25	5.46	2.01
Hiciano, Delvin	R-R	6-2	175	12-24-91	1	0	1.08	5	0	0	0	8	7	3	1	0	7	3	.241	.167	.261	3.24	7.56
Lorenzo, Arquimedes	R-R	6-2	190	5-29-91	4	1	3.40	16	0	0	2	40	39	21	15	2	13	19	.258	.267	.256	4.31	2.95
Martinez, Edgar	R-R	6-0	145	9-1-90	0	0	3.97	6	0	0	2	11	10	6	5	0	6	11	.238	.333	.2	8.74	4.76
Mendoza, Andres	R-R	6-2	220	6-3-92	2	0	3.03	18	1	0	5	33	27	13	11	0	7	27	—	—	—	7.44	1.93
Minier, Jonathan	R-R	6-1	180	3-8-90	1	0	1.35	12	0	0	4	20	15	5	3	0	8	14	.211	.3	.176	6.30	3.60
Miranda, Luylli	L-L	5-11	180	1-29-92	2	1	3.57	14	0	0	5	23	23	9	9	1	6	22	.267	.5	.25	8.74	2.38
Mitchell, Richard	R-R	6-2	185	7-29-95	4	4	4.74	18	0	0	0	38	28	23	20	1	25	21	.209	.222	.204	4.97	5.92
Navarro, Gerardo	L-R	6-2	194	8-23-93	4	0	3.43	19	0	0	2	42	31	25	16	3	31	21	.214	.267	.2	4.50	6.64
Paredes, Jesus	L-L	6-2	162	1-18-93	6	3	2.34	18	1	0	0	35	32	13	9	2	21	34	.246	.286	.241	8.83	5.45
Perez, Jesus	R-R	6-2	228	1-1-94	0	1	11.57	5	0	0	0	7	9	9	9	0	11	3	.31	.091	.444	3.86	14.14
Ramos, Horelbin	L-L	6-1	180	1-14-94	3	1	2.30	19	0	0	2	43	36	13	11	1	15	33	.225	.077	.238	6.91	3.14
Regalado, Jose	R-R	6-3	180	11-19-91	6	4	2.60	14	14	0	0	69	58	26	20	2	4	52	.227	.321	.2	6.75	0.52
Rodriguez, Francis	R-R	6-2	170	11-28-92	2	4	3.48	15	7	0	2	52	47	28	20	2	15	29	.239	.302	.221	5.05	2.61
Rodriguez, Ramon	R-R	6-4	196	3-23-93	1	5	2.86	14	14	0	0	63	58	28	20	2	20	36	.243	.203	.256	5.14	2.86
Ruiz, Carlos	R-R	6-2	169	4-13-91	2	1	1.20	18	0	0	5	30	21	10	4	1	8	34	.189	.212	.179	10.20	2.40
Urbina, Dan	R-R	6-3	158	11-27-93	3	0	2.19	5	5	0	0	16	17	8	6	1	5	10	.185	.276	.143	3.65	1.82
Vasquez, Jandy	R-R	6-4	195	7-11-94	3	6	5.53	14	14	0	0	55	59	43	34	1	24	28	.28	.308	.273	4.55	3.90
Vera, Eduardo	R-R	6-3	177	7-3-94	1	0	1.95	14	13	0	0	60	53	22	13	1	14	44	.233	.208	.247	6.60	2.10
Vivas, Julio	R-R	6-2	227	10-1-93	5	2	2.30	14	13	0	0	63	55	24	16	1	16	52	.238	.314	.205	7.47	2.30

Fielding

Catcher	PCT	G	PO	A	E	DP	PB
Cerda	.943	28	157	7	10	0	8
Garcia	.977	37	185	29	5	6	1
Gonzalez	.994	44	260	54	2	0	14
Marquez	1.000	6	18	2	0	0	0
Morales	1.000	5	11	3	0	0	0
Perez	.946	19	118	23	8	1	9
Rangel	1.000	20	70	11	0	0	0
Reyes	.987	18	66	8	1	1	3

First Base	PCT	G	PO	A	E	DP
Adames	1.000	13	113	6	0	9
De La Mota	1.000	7	37	0	0	1
Hurtarte	.983	44	387	20	7	42
Munoz	.990	57	483	16	5	35
Pena	.988	18	152	8	2	17
Reyes	1.000	1	1	1	0	0
Salazar	1.000	17	127	7	0	13

Second Base	PCT	G	PO	A	E	DP
Barrios	.964	38	85	105	7	15
Esqueda	.968	14	31	30	2	8

	PCT	G	PO	A	E	DP
Padilla	.978	39	99	80	4	20
Pena	1.000	17	39	44	0	10
Polonia	.951	22	43	55	5	9
Reyes	.962	27	74	77	6	25
Ronco	1.000	1	2	0	0	0
Salazar	1.000	3	1	2	0	0

Third Base	PCT	G	PO	A	E	DP
De Jesus	1.000	1	0	1	0	1
De La Cruz	.879	32	15	72	12	7
Esqueda	.914	16	15	38	5	4
Herrera	.859	52	36	92	21	5
Munoz	1.000	2	0	2	0	0
Pena	.692	7	1	8	4	1
Polonia	.931	16	18	49	5	7
Reyes	—	1	0	0	0	0
Ronco	.909	14	10	20	3	4
Salazar	.962	20	17	34	2	4

Shortstop	PCT	G	PO	A	E	DP
Chourio	.953	59	88	155	12	18
De Jesus	.888	49	53	137	24	22

	PCT	G	PO	A	E	DP
Esqueda	.933	5	3	11	1	1
Pena	1.000	1	1	2	0	0
Reyes	.946	23	36	70	6	10
Ronco	.867	18	13	26	6	3
Salazar	.952	5	9	11	1	2

Outfield	PCT	G	PO	A	E	DP
Adames	1.000	1	4	0	0	0
Aquiles	1.000	23	21	1	0	1
Bastardo	1.000	45	60	7	0	3
Benitez	.972	63	130	8	4	0
De La Cruz	.985	57	122	6	2	1
De La Mota	1.000	34	45	3	0	0
Figueroa	.956	59	105	3	5	0
Guzman	.980	27	47	2	1	1
Padilla	1.000	8	4	1	0	0
Pena	1.000	4	2	0	0	0
Polanco	.976	27	41	3	1	1
Polo	.990	44	93	2	1	1
Rosario	.907	23	38	1	4	0
Santos	.981	48	101	4	2	3

St. Louis Cardinals

SEASON IN A SENTENCE: Any team that doesn't win it all ends up disappointed, but it was an amazing run as St. Louis made it to the World Series despite losing two starting pitchers, its closer and its top prospect to injury.

HIGH POINT: The Cardinals shut out the Dodgers on two hits in the deciding Game Six of the National League Championship Series with a trio of hard-throwing rookie righthanders—Michael Wacha, Carlos Martinez and Trevor Rosenthal. St. Louis' pitching staff had a sparkling 2.09 ERA during the NLCS after similarly shutting down the Pirates in their Division Series.

LOW POINT: On July 31, St. Louis added to its season-worst seven game losing streak with a 5-4 loss to the Pirates that dropped St. Louis 2 ½ games behind the Pirates in the National League Central race. The loss was a fourth straight at the hands of the Pirates.

NOTABLE ROOKIES: St. Louis promoted wave after wave of strong-armed rookie pitchers, led by bullpen stalwarts like playoff closer Trevor Rosenthal (2-4, 2.63), lefthander Kevin Siegrist (3-1, 0.45) and righthander Seth Maness (5-2, 2.32). Righthander Shelby Miller was a rotation fixture, going 15-9, 3.06. Wacha joined the rotation late in the season. His 4-1, 2.78 record doesn't include his outstanding run through the playoffs, where he went 4-1, 2.64 and was named NLCS MVP. Righthander Carlos Martinez, like Wacha, played a minor role in the club's regular season run to the playoffs, but was a key member of the bullpen when October arrived. First baseman Matt Adams hit 17 home runs in a part-time role.

KEY TRANSACTIONS: Because of the depth of the farm system, all of the significant moves were promotions from the minor leagues. The Cardinals used 10 different starting pitchers to overcome injuries to Chris Carpenter and Jaime Garcia. Righthanded reliever John Axford, acquired from the Brewers at the end of August, did make six appearances in the playoffs.

DOWN ON THE FARM: Six of the club's top seven prospects heading into the season ended up contributing to the club's run to the World Series, so the farm system is understandably a little thinner than it was a year ago. St. Louis likely would have gone seven for seven on big league contributions if outfielder Oscar Taveras, the club's No. 1 prospect, had not missed much of the season with a nagging high ankle sprain that required surgery.

OPENING DAY PAYROLL: $115.2 million (11th)

PLAYERS OF THE YEAR

MAJOR LEAGUE

Adam Wainwright
rhp

19-9, 2.94 in 242 IP
8.2 SO/9, 1.07 WHIP
Led NL in W, IP

MINOR LEAGUE

Michael Wacha
rhp

(Triple-A)
5-3, 2.65, 0.99 WHIP
NLCS MVP (13²/₃, 0 R)

ORGANIZATION LEADERS

BATTING	*Minimum 250 AB	
MAJORS		
* AVG	Molina, Yadier	.319
* OPS	Holliday, Matt	.879
HR	Beltran, Carlos	24
RBI	Craig, Allen	97
MINORS		
* AVG	O'Neill, Mike, Memphis/Springfield	.314
* OBP	O'Neill, Mike, Memphis/Springfield	.424
* SLG	Peterson, Brock, Memphis	.531
R	O'Neill, Mike, Memphis/Springfield	82
H	Valera, Breyvic, Peoria	159
TB	Peterson, Brock, Memphis	242
2B	Rodriguez, Jonathan, Palm Beach	34
3B	Wong, Kolten, Memphis	8
HR	Scruggs, Xavier, Springfield	29
RBI	Gotay, Ruben, Springfield	89
BB	O'Neill, Mike, Memphis/Springfield	91
SO	Scruggs, Xavier, Springfield	177
SB	Ramos, Steven, Peoria/State College	22

PITCHING	#Minimum 75 IP	
MAJORS		
W	Wainwright, Adam	19
# ERA	Wainwright, Adam	2.94
SO	Wainwright, Adam	219
SV	Mujica, Edward	37
MINORS		
W	Cooney, Tim, Springfield/Palm Beach	10
	McGregor, Scott, Memphis/Springfield	10
L	Cooney, Tim, Springfield/Palm Beach	13
# ERA	Petrick, Zach, Peoria/Palm Beach/Springfield	1.99
G	Stoppelman, Lee, Memphis/Springfield/P.B.	55
GS	Whiting, Boone, Memphis/Springfield	27
SV	Shaban, Ronnie, Palm Beach	18
IP	Cooney, Tim, Springfield/Palm Beach	154
BB	Ferrara, Anthony, Springfield	54
SO	Cooney, Tim, Springfield/Palm Beach	148
# AVG	Petrick, Zach, Peoria/Palm Beach/Springfield	.213

General Manager: John Mozeliak. **Farm Director:** Gary LaRocque. **Scouting Director:** Dan Kantrovitz.

Class	Team	League	W	L	PCT	Finish	Manager
Majors	St. Louis Cardinals	National	97	65	.599	1st (15)	Mike Matheny
Triple-A	Memphis Redbirds	Pacific Coast	69	75	.486	11th (16)	Ron Warner
Double-A	Springfield Cardinals	Texas	64	74	.464	6th (8)	Mike Shildt
High A	Palm Beach Cardinals	Florida State	64	71	.474	10th (12)	Johnny Rodriguez
Low A	Peoria Chiefs	Midwest	68	69	.496	t-7th (16)	Dann Bilardello
Short-season	State College Spikes	New York-Penn	48	27	.640	1st (14)	Oliver Marmol
Rookie	Johnson City Cardinals	Appalachian	36	31	.480	6th (10)	Joe Kruzel
Rookie	GCL Cardinals	Gulf Coast	24	35	.407	15th (16)	Steve Turco
Overall 2013 Minor League Record			373	382	.494	18th (30)	

ORGANIZATION STATISTICS

ST. LOUIS CARDINALS

NATIONAL LEAGUE

Batting	B-T	HT	WT	DOB	AVG	vLH	vRH	G	AB	R	H	2B	3B	HR	RBI	BB	HBP	SH	SF	SO	SB	CS	SLG	OBP
Adams, Matt	L-R	6-3	260	8-31-88	.284	.231	.295	108	296	46	84	14	0	17	51	23	0	0	0	80	0	1	.503	.335
Beltran, Carlos	B-R	6-1	210	4-24-77	.296	.252	.315	145	554	79	164	30	3	24	84	38	1	1	6	90	2	1	.491	.339
Carpenter, Matt	L-R	6-3	215	11-26-85	.318	.294	.329	157	626	126	199	55	7	11	78	72	9	3	7	98	3	3	.481	.392
Chambers, Adron	L-L	5-10	200	10-8-86	.154	.000	.190	25	26	5	4	1	0	0	1	3	0	0	0	11	0	1	.192	.241
Craig, Allen	R-R	6-2	215	7-18-84	.315	.278	.327	134	508	71	160	29	2	13	97	40	10	0	5	100	2	0	.457	.373
Cruz, Tony	R-R	5-11	215	8-18-86	.203	.088	.247	51	123	13	25	6	1	1	13	4	2	0	0	25	0	0	.293	.240
Curtis, Jermaine	R-R	5-11	190	7-10-87	.000	.000	.000	5	3	0	0	0	0	0	0	1	1	0	0	1	0	0	.000	.400
Descalso, Daniel	L-R	5-10	190	10-19-86	.238	.183	.250	123	328	43	78	25	1	5	43	22	3	3	2	56	6	3	.366	.290
Freese, David	R-R	6-2	225	4-28-83	.262	.275	.257	138	462	53	121	26	1	9	60	47	9	0	3	106	1	2	.381	.340
Holliday, Matt	R-R	6-4	250	1-15-80	.300	.298	.301	141	520	103	156	31	1	22	94	69	9	0	4	86	6	1	.490	.389
Jackson, Ryan	R-R	6-3	180	5-10-88	.000	.000	.000	7	7	0	0	0	0	0	0	0	0	0	0	2	0	0	.000	.000
Jay, Jon	L-L	5-11	195	3-15-85	.276	.220	.291	157	548	75	151	27	2	7	67	52	14	9	5	103	10	5	.370	.351
Johnson, Rob	R-R	6-1	220	7-22-82	.171	.000	.231	20	35	2	6	1	1	0	2	3	0	0	0	6	0	0	.257	.237
Kozma, Pete	R-R	6-0	190	4-11-88	.217	.184	.232	143	410	44	89	20	0	1	35	34	0	1	3	91	3	1	.273	.275
Molina, Yadier	R-R	5-11	220	7-13-82	.319	.333	.315	136	505	68	161	44	0	12	80	30	3	0	3	55	3	2	.477	.359
Perez, Audry	R-R	5-9	230	12-23-88	.000	—	.000	2	1	0	0	0	0	0	0	0	0	0	0	0	0	0	.000	.000
Peterson, Brock	R-R	6-3	215	11-20-83	.077	.056	.125	23	26	0	2	0	0	0	2	2	0	0	0	11	0	0	.077	.143
Robinson, Shane	R-R	5-9	165	10-30-84	.250	.228	.277	99	144	22	36	2	1	2	16	23	0	0	4	17	5	1	.319	.345
Wigginton, Ty	R-R	6-0	225	10-11-77	.158	.115	.194	47	57	9	9	2	0	0	3	5	1	0	0	19	0	1	.193	.238
Wong, Kolten	L-R	5-9	185	10-10-90	.153	.000	.173	32	59	6	9	1	0	0	3	0	0	0	0	12	3	0	.169	.194

Pitching	B-T	HT	WT	DOB	W	L	ERA	G	GS	CG	SV	IP	H	R	ER	HR	BB	SO	AVG	vLH	vRH	K/9	BB/9
Axford, John	R-R	6-5	220	4-1-83	1	0	1.74	13	0	0	0	10	11	3	2	0	3	11	.282	.357	.240	9.58	2.61
2-team total (62 Milwaukee)					7	7	4.02	75	0	0	0	65	73	32	29	10	26	65	—	—	—	9.00	3.60
Blazek, Michael	R-R	6-0	200	3-16-89	0	0	6.97	11	0	0	0	10	10	8	8	2	10	10	.244	.133	.308	8.71	8.71
2-team total (7 Milwaukee)					0	1	5.71	18	0	0	0	17	16	12	11	3	13	14	—	—	—	7.27	6.75
Boggs, Mitchell	R-R	6-4	235	2-15-84	0	3	11.05	18	0	0	2	15	21	20	18	3	15	11	.339	.290	.387	6.75	9.20
2-team total (9 Colorado)					0	3	8.10	27	0	0	2	23	28	23	21	5	20	16	—	—	—	6.17	7.71
Butler, Keith	R-R	6-0	170	1-30-89	0	0	4.05	16	0	0	0	20	13	9	9	0	11	16	.181	.212	.154	7.20	4.95
Choate, Randy	L-L	6-1	210	9-5-75	2	1	2.29	64	0	0	0	35	26	9	9	0	11	28	.208	.176	.275	7.13	2.80
Cleto, Maikel	R-R	6-3	250	5-1-89	0	0	19.29	1	0	0	0	2	5	5	5	1	1	5	.417	.500	.375	19.29	3.86
Freeman, Sam	R-L	5-11	165	6-24-87	1	0	2.19	13	0	0	0	12	8	3	3	0	5	8	.182	.200	.167	5.84	3.65
Garcia, Jaime	L-L	6-2	215	7-8-86	5	2	3.58	9	9	0	0	55	57	26	22	6	15	43	.263	.333	.239	6.99	2.44
Gast, John	L-L	6-1	195	2-16-89	2	0	5.11	3	3	0	0	12	11	7	7	1	5	8	.234	.385	.176	5.84	3.65
Kelly, Joe	R-R	6-1	175	6-9-88	10	5	2.69	37	15	0	0	124	124	42	37	10	44	79	.259	.245	.270	5.73	3.19
Lynn, Lance	R-R	6-5	240	5-12-87	15	10	3.97	33	33	0	0	202	189	92	89	14	76	198	.252	.259	.247	8.84	3.39
Lyons, Tyler	B-L	6-4	200	2-21-88	2	4	4.75	12	8	0	0	53	49	29	28	5	16	43	.241	.228	.247	7.30	2.72
Maness, Seth	R-R	6-0	190	10-14-88	5	2	2.32	66	0	0	1	62	65	17	16	4	13	35	.281	.274	.285	5.08	1.89
Marte, Victor	R-R	6-2	260	11-8-80	0	1	6.00	4	0	0	0	3	4	2	2	0	3	2	.308	.250	.333	6.00	9.00
Martinez, Carlos	R-R	6-0	185	9-21-91	2	1	5.08	21	1	0	1	28	31	16	16	1	9	24	.282	.326	.250	7.62	2.86
Miller, Shelby	R-R	6-3	215	10-10-90	15	9	3.06	31	31	1	0	173	152	65	59	20	57	169	.234	.266	.205	8.78	2.96
Mujica, Edward	R-R	6-3	225	5-10-84	2	1	2.78	65	0	0	37	65	60	20	20	9	5	46	.245	.232	.256	6.40	0.70
Rosenthal, Trevor	R-R	6-2	220	5-29-90	2	4	2.63	74	0	0	3	75	63	25	22	4	20	108	.223	.236	.213	12.90	2.39
Rzepczynski, Marc	L-L	6-1	215	8-29-85	0	0	7.84	11	0	0	0	10	16	9	9	1	4	9	.364	.294	.407	7.84	3.48
Salas, Fernando	R-R	6-2	210	5-30-85	0	3	4.50	27	0	0	0	28	27	15	14	3	6	22	.255	.293	.231	7.07	1.93
Siegrist, Kevin	L-L	6-5	215	7-20-89	3	1	0.45	45	0	0	0	40	17	2	2	1	18	50	.128	.118	.138	11.34	4.08
Wacha, Michael	R-R	6-6	210	7-1-91	4	1	2.78	15	9	0	0	65	52	20	20	5	19	65	.219	.197	.242	9.05	2.64
Wainwright, Adam	R-R	6-7	235	8-30-81	19	9	2.94	34	34	5	0	242	223	83	79	15	35	219	.248	.242	.254	8.16	1.30
Westbrook, Jake	R-R	6-3	210	9-29-77	7	8	4.63	21	19	1	0	117	132	69	60	7	50	44	.293	.337	.255	3.39	3.86

Fielding

Catcher	PCT	G	PO	A	E	DP	PB		First Base	PCT	G	PO	A	E	DP				
Cruz	.996	44	234	14	1	1	2		Adams	.997	74	598	50	2	70		Peterson	1.000	4	17	2	0	1
Johnson	1.000	15	52	3	0	0	1		Carpenter	1.000	2	10	0	0	0		Wigginton	1.000	7	36	3	0	6
Molina	.996	131	976	63	4	11	3		Craig	.999	95	780	57	1	85								
Perez	1.000	1	1	0	0	0			Molina	1.000	5	17	1	0	1								

Second Base	PCT	G	PO	A	E	DP
Carpenter	.985	132	211	370	9	97
Descalso	.974	39	55	92	4	22
Jackson	1.000	2	1	2	0	0
Wong	1.000	18	22	43	0	8

Third Base	PCT	G	PO	A	E	DP
Carpenter	.958	42	11	58	3	9
Cruz	1.000	3	0	1	0	0
Descalso	.921	38	6	29	3	4
Freese	.957	132	55	190	11	21

	PCT	G	PO	A	E	DP
Jackson	—	3	0	0	0	0
Wigginton	.900	5	0	9	1	0

Shortstop	PCT	G	PO	A	E	DP
Descalso	.964	55	51	135	7	28
Jackson	1.000	1	0	1	0	0
Kozma	.984	139	155	397	9	98

Outfield	PCT	G	PO	A	E	DP
Beltran	.980	137	242	4	5	1
Carpenter	1.000	2	1	1	0	0
Chambers	.875	14	7	0	1	0
Craig	1.000	46	67	1	0	1
Curtis	—	1	0	0	0	0
Holliday	.995	136	212	2	1	1
Jay	.997	152	335	4	1	3
Kozma	1.000	1	2	0	0	0
Peterson	1.000	5	2	0	0	0
Robinson	.973	77	108	0	3	0
Wigginton	1.000	6	1	0	0	0

MEMPHIS REDBIRDS   TRIPLE-A
PACIFIC COAST LEAGUE

Batting	B-T	HT	WT	DOB	AVG	vLH	vRH	G	AB	R	H	2B	3B	HR	RBI	BB	HBP	SH	SF	SO	SB	CS	SLG	OBP
Albitz, Vance	R-R	5-7	170	1-31-88	.268	.194	.314	28	82	12	22	3	0	1	9	2	2	1	1	9	3	0	.341	.299
Chambers, Adron	L-L	5-10	200	10-8-86	.252	.143	.289	101	333	51	84	13	4	8	43	39	7	8	6	75	16	2	.387	.338
Christian, Justin	R-R	6-1	195	4-3-80	.270	.231	.291	107	374	41	101	16	3	3	29	31	4	1	1	44	14	4	.353	.332
Curtis, Jermaine	R-R	5-11	190	7-10-87	.257	.217	.278	115	370	45	95	17	1	5	49	52	7	2	5	53	10	2	.349	.355
Freese, David	R-R	6-2	225	4-28-83	.333	.500	.250	3	12	2	4	2	0	0	4	1	0	0	0	2	0	0	.500	.385
Garcia, Greg	L-R	6-0	190	8-8-89	.271	.265	.274	116	354	50	96	23	4	3	35	49	11	10	0	70	14	2	.384	.377
Huffman, Chad	R-R	6-1	215	4-29-85	.282	.248	.298	108	309	49	87	18	1	13	55	47	4	1	4	70	2	0	.472	.379
Jackson, Ryan	R-R	6-3	180	5-10-88	.278	.331	.246	121	442	49	123	19	1	3	34	52	2	7	7	91	9	0	.346	.352
Johnson, Rob	R-R	6-1	220	7-22-82	.236	.284	.211	59	195	27	46	8	1	7	32	24	0	0	2	42	0	2	.395	.317
Mateo, Luis	R-R	6-0	175	5-23-90	.286	.429	.143	5	14	3	4	0	0	1	2	0	0	0	3	0	0	.286	.375
O'Neill, Mike	L-L	5-9	170	2-12-88	.295	.281	.300	32	112	16	33	3	0	0	3	20	0	1	0	11	1	0	.321	.402
Perez, Audry	R-R	5-9	230	12-23-88	.211	.147	.250	25	90	7	19	3	0	0	7	2	0	1	0	10	0	0	.244	.228
Peterson, Brock	R-R	6-3	215	11-20-83	.296	.341	.271	122	456	69	135	30	1	25	86	44	6	0	2	114	1	1	.531	.364
Pham, Tommy	R-R	6-1	175	3-8-88	.264	.300	.242	30	106	6	28	6	1	1	13	7	0	0	0	25	2	1	.368	.310
Ramsey, James	L-R	6-0	190	12-19-89	.000	.000	.000	1	3	0	0	0	0	0	0	0	0	0	0	1	0	0	.000	.000
Romak, Jamie	R-R	6-3	226	9-30-85	.242	.267	.229	134	458	69	111	32	1	22	74	49	6	2	3	115	6	1	.461	.322
Swauger, Chris	L-L	6-0	195	8-11-86	.212	.219	.208	48	104	10	22	6	0	2	12	7	0	1	1	34	1	1	.327	.259
Tartamella, Travis	R-R	5-11	200	12-17-87	.244	.220	.254	53	176	11	43	4	0	3	18	14	1	1	1	54	0	1	.318	.302
Taveras, Oscar	L-L	6-2	200	6-19-92	.306	.222	.366	46	173	25	53	12	0	5	32	9	1	1	2	22	5	1	.462	.341
Towles, J.R.	R-R	6-2	200	2-11-84	.237	.118	.286	19	59	15	14	3	1	5	14	8	4	0	0	10	0	0	.576	.366
2-team total (4 Albuquerque)					.230	—	—	23	74	17	17	3	1	6	16	8	4	2	0	13	1	0	.541	.337
Wong, Kolten	L-R	5-9	185	10-10-90	.303	.289	.310	107	412	68	125	21	8	10	45	41	4	2	4	60	20	1	.466	.369

Pitching	B-T	HT	WT	DOB	W	L	ERA	G	GS	CG	SV	IP	H	R	ER	HR	BB	SO	AVG	vLH	vRH	K/9	BB/9
Additon, Nick	L-L	6-5	215	12-16-87	9	7	4.10	24	21	1	0	132	117	63	60	15	38	117	.237	.223	.244	8.00	2.60
Almarante, Jose	R-R	6-1	172	12-19-88	0	0	0.00	1	0	0	0	1	3	0	0	0	1	3	.429	1.000	.333	6.75	0.00
Blazek, Michael	R-R	6-0	200	3-16-89	1	2	2.77	19	0	0	2	26	17	8	8	1	16	27	.185	.130	.239	9.35	5.54
Boggs, Mitchell	R-R	6-4	235	2-15-84	0	2	5.70	18	3	0	0	24	30	21	15	2	11	14	.297	.367	.231	5.32	4.18
2-team total (12 Colorado Springs)					1	6	6.75	30	3	0	0	40	63	47	30	3	22	21	—	—	—	4.73	4.95
Browning, Barret	L-L	6-2	230	12-28-84	1	2	4.58	13	0	0	0	20	24	10	10	2	6	17	.312	.250	.340	7.78	2.75
Butler, Keith	R-R	6-0	170	1-30-89	3	2	3.62	20	1	0	2	27	21	12	11	3	9	28	.210	.175	.233	9.22	2.96
Carpenter, Chris	R-R	6-6	230	4-27-75	0	1	10.80	1	1	0	0	3	9	4	4	0	2	2	.529	.700	.286	5.40	5.40
Castillo, Richard	R-R	5-11	165	10-11-89	1	2	1.93	5	5	0	0	28	22	6	6	1	14	17	.216	.235	.196	5.46	4.50
Cleto, Maikel	R-R	6-3	250	5-1-89	2	3	6.92	16	9	0	0	53	49	42	41	4	53	53	.246	.286	.208	8.94	8.94
2-team total (19 Omaha)					3	5	5.52	35	10	0	1	91	84	58	56	5	74	89	—	—	—	8.77	7.29
Delgado, Ramon	R-R	6-3	195	9-3-86	0	0	4.05	4	0	0	0	7	6	3	3	2	1	6	.261	.300	.231	8.10	1.35
Fornataro, Eric	R-R	6-1	225	1-2-88	1	4	6.02	37	4	0	1	55	65	42	37	5	23	39	.300	.340	.263	6.34	3.74
Freeman, Sam	R-L	5-11	165	6-24-87	7	2	2.97	49	0	0	2	70	57	25	23	4	27	66	.218	.237	.207	8.53	3.49
Gast, John	L-L	6-1	195	2-16-89	3	1	1.16	7	7	0	0	39	28	6	5	3	10	35	.214	.216	.213	8.15	3.03
Greenwood, Nick	R-L	6-1	180	9-28-87	2	8	5.63	22	7	0	0	54	65	39	34	9	19	24	.305	.303	.306	3.98	3.15
Hooker, Deryk	R-R	6-4	215	6-21-89	0	0	5.23	15	0	0	0	21	20	12	12	2	8	14	.253	.313	.213	6.10	3.48
Lyons, Tyler	B-L	6-4	200	2-21-88	7	2	3.32	17	16	0	0	100	85	40	37	6	19	86	.230	.220	.234	7.71	1.70
Maness, Seth	R-R	6-0	190	10-14-88	2	2	4.32	4	4	0	0	25	34	12	12	3	3	18	.333	.316	.356	6.48	1.08
Marte, Victor	R-R	6-2	260	11-8-80	2	3	4.94	45	0	0	11	55	62	31	30	2	27	55	.283	.298	.267	9.05	4.45
Martinez, Carlos	R-R	6-0	185	9-21-91	5	3	2.51	13	13	0	0	68	54	22	19	3	27	63	.213	.250	.168	8.34	3.57
McGregor, Scott	R-R	6-2	193	12-19-86	6	10	4.83	18	17	0	0	101	111	61	54	10	29	67	.283	.307	.254	5.99	2.59
Rondon, Jorge	R-R	6-1	215	2-16-88	3	5	3.06	51	0	0	1	68	72	31	23	6	17	45	.274	.236	.307	5.59	4.92
Rzepczynski, Marc	L-L	6-1	215	8-29-85	1	2	3.07	32	0	0	0	44	44	23	15	1	18	31	.263	.185	.314	6.34	3.68
Salas, Fernando	R-R	6-2	210	5-30-85	1	2	1.90	22	0	0	12	24	15	8	5	1	5	21	.181	.083	.255	7.99	1.90
Sanchez, Eduardo	R-R	5-11	175	2-16-89	0	0	3.72	9	0	0	1	10	10	4	4	2	4	7	.270	.286	.261	6.52	3.72
2-team total (24 Iowa)					1	1	3.38	33	0	0	3	40	31	16	15	3	23	35	—	—	—	7.88	5.18
Siegrist, Kevin	L-L	6-5	215	7-20-89	1	0	1.17	5	0	0	0	8	3	2	1	0	3	9	.111	.125	.105	10.57	3.52
Stoppelman, Lee	L-L	6-2	210	5-24-90	1	0	4.50	3	0	0	0	2	4	1	1	0	2	2	.400	.400	.400	9.00	9.00
Thomas, Kevin	R-R	6-3	215	7-8-86	0	1	10.80	4	0	0	0	3	5	4	4	1	5	4	.313	.143	.444	13.50	2.70
Wacha, Michael	R-R	6-6	210	7-1-91	5	3	2.65	15	15	0	0	85	65	26	25	9	19	73	.210	.242	.178	7.73	2.01
Whiting, Boone	R-R	6-1	175	8-20-89	5	5	4.09	21	21	1	0	106	107	51	48	11	40	99	.261	.274	.249	8.43	3.41

Fielding

Catcher	PCT	G	PO	A	E	DP	PB
Johnson	.995	57	398	38	2	2	6
Perez	.990	25	175	17	2	0	0
Tartamella	.997	52	357	33	1	3	3
Towles	1.000	15	112	11	0	1	1

First Base	PCT	G	PO	A	E	DP
Peterson	.992	118	923	74	8	72
Romak	.993	38	246	25	2	18
Swauger	1.000	1	7	0	0	0

Second Base	PCT	G	PO	A	E	DP
Albitz	1.000	17	24	50	0	10
Curtis	1.000	2	6	7	0	2
Garcia	.988	21	40	39	1	8
Jackson	1.000	10	19	22	0	3
Mateo	1.000	1	2	7	0	3
Wong	.974	102	195	296	13	49

Third Base	PCT	G	PO	A	E	DP
Albitz	1.000	2	1	4	0	0
Curtis	.948	104	65	154	12	7
Freese	1.000	2	3	1	0	0
Garcia	1.000	13	5	17	0	0
Jackson	.984	32	20	42	1	3
Mateo	1.000	1	0	1	0	0
Romak	.947	13	5	13	1	0

Shortstop	PCT	G	PO	A	E	DP
Albitz	.955	6	9	12	1	2
Garcia	.962	73	113	168	11	33
Jackson	.973	72	102	183	8	30
Mateo	.947	3	4	14	1	2

Outfield	PCT	G	PO	A	E	DP
Albitz	—	1	0	0	0	0
Chambers	.984	98	230	10	4	2
Christian	.989	102	185	3	2	0
Huffman	.985	51	66	1	1	0
Jackson	1.000	7	10	0	0	0
O'Neill	1.000	31	44	3	0	1
Pham	.975	29	78	1	2	0
Ramsey	1.000	1	1	0	0	0
Romak	.979	89	133	7	3	0
Swauger	1.000	28	34	0	0	0
Tartamella	1.000	1	1	0	0	0
Taveras	.988	39	82	2	1	0

SPRINGFIELD CARDINALS

DOUBLE-A

TEXAS LEAGUE

Batting	B-T	HT	WT	DOB	AVG	vLH	vRH	G	AB	R	H	2B	3B	HR	RBI	BB	HBP	SH	SF	SO	SB	CS	SLG	OBP
Adams, Matt	L-R	6-3	260	8-31-88	.250	.000	.273	3	12	1	3	1	0	0	2	0	0	0	0	4	0	0	.333	.250
Albitz, Vance	R-R	5-7	170	1-31-88	.250	.313	.232	50	144	14	36	4	0	2	16	5	3	7	3	19	3	1	.319	.284
Castillo, Juan	R-R	5-11	190	12-13-89	.182	—	.182	4	11	0	2	1	0	0	0	0	0	0	0	5	0	0	.273	.182
Gotay, Ruben	R-R	5-11	175	12-25-82	.279	.263	.283	133	498	75	139	31	0	16	89	72	0	0	6	95	16	7	.438	.366
Lemmerman, Jake	R-R	6-1	192	5-4-89	.231	.262	.223	98	308	46	71	16	1	8	36	55	4	3	1	89	11	1	.367	.353
Longmire, Nick	R-R	6-3	180	1-5-89	.125	.333	.000	2	8	1	1	0	0	0	0	2	0	0	0	5	0	0	.125	.300
Mateo, Luis	R-R	6-0	175	5-23-90	.237	.316	.213	99	346	48	82	13	0	5	30	16	3	6	1	54	14	7	.318	.276
Melker, Adam	L-L	5-11	180	1-31-88	.258	.222	.267	107	318	42	82	17	2	8	32	28	4	4	3	75	7	7	.399	.323
O'Neill, Mike	L-L	5-9	170	2-12-88	.320	.348	.314	98	359	66	115	13	2	2	35	71	0	2	2	26	18	4	.384	.431
Perez, Audry	R-R	5-9	230	12-23-88	.209	.333	.182	57	215	16	45	12	0	6	26	3	4	0	0	39	0	1	.349	.234
Pham, Tommy	R-R	6-1	175	3-8-88	.301	.370	.287	45	163	27	49	6	6	6	28	20	4	0	1	42	6	3	.521	.388
Piscotty, Stephen	R-R	6-3	210	1-14-91	.299	.415	.266	49	184	17	55	9	0	6	24	19	1	1	2	19	7	3	.446	.364
Pritchard, Neal	R-R	6-0	195	2-21-89	.172	.000	.200	14	29	1	5	1	0	0	0	2	1	2	0	8	0	1	.207	.250
Rahmatulla, Tyler	R-R	5-10	190	2-26-90	.098	.200	.083	24	41	4	4	1	0	0	1	10	2	0	0	11	1	0	.122	.302
Ramsey, James	R-L	6-0	190	12-19-89	.251	.214	.262	93	347	61	87	11	2	15	44	53	6	6	4	108	8	4	.424	.356
Rasmus, Casey	L-R	5-10	175	3-29-90	.292	.222	.308	15	48	7	14	1	0	0	4	2	0	2	0	7	7	0	.313	.320
Robinson, Shane	R-R	5-9	165	10-30-84	.200	.000	.400	3	10	0	2	0	0	0	0	2	0	0	0	1	0	0	.200	.333
Rodriguez, Starlin	B-R	5-10	175	12-13-89	.254	.283	.248	77	248	25	63	12	2	6	36	14	7	3	3	62	8	2	.391	.309
Scruggs, Xavier	R-R	6-1	210	9-23-87	.248	.300	.235	133	448	67	111	18	1	29	81	82	12	1	3	177	11	7	.487	.376
Stanley, Cody	L-R	5-10	190	12-21-88	.250	.294	.240	75	272	31	68	10	0	5	34	16	2	2	2	54	4	0	.342	.295
Swauger, Chris	L-L	6-0	195	8-11-86	.266	.182	.291	77	286	34	76	10	2	8	39	17	3	0	3	70	6	4	.399	.311
Tartamella, Travis	R-R	5-11	200	12-17-87	.087	.200	.000	8	23	2	2	1	0	0	1	1	0	0	1	6	0	0	.130	.120
Walsh, Colin	B-R	6-0	190	9-26-89	.220	.087	.253	32	118	15	26	5	0	2	6	16	0	0	0	24	3	0	.314	.313
Williams, Matt	R-R	6-0	170	8-29-89	.107	.000	.143	9	28	1	3	0	0	0	1	1	0	1	1	3	1	0	.107	.133

Pitching	B-T	HT	WT	DOB	W	L	ERA	G	GS	CG	SV	IP	H	R	ER	HR	BB	SO	AVG	vLH	vRH	K/9	BB/9
Almarante, Jose	R-R	6-1	172	12-19-88	2	2	2.75	27	0	0	3	39	29	19	12	1	11	31	.206	.213	.202	7.09	2.52
Baker, Corey	R-R	6-1	170	11-23-89	0	1	6.41	8	1	0	0	20	24	17	14	6	7	7	.312	.350	.298	3.20	3.20
Blair, Seth	R-R	6-2	185	3-3-89	3	9	5.07	24	22	0	0	130	149	83	73	18	48	117	.298	.332	.271	8.12	3.33
Blazek, Michael	R-R	6-0	200	3-16-89	0	0	0.92	17	0	0	7	20	11	4	2	0	10	25	.157	.080	.200	11.44	4.58
Butler, Keith	R-R	6-0	170	1-30-89	0	0	0.66	13	0	0	7	14	8	1	1	1	2	21	.163	.182	.148	13.83	1.32
Carpenter, Chris	R-R	6-6	230	4-27-75	0	1	6.75	1	1	0	0	3	6	3	2	1	2	5	.400	.800	.200	16.88	6.75
Castillo, Richard	R-R	5-11	165	10-11-89	7	9	4.59	21	21	0	0	120	123	69	61	17	39	70	.267	.256	.275	5.26	2.93
Cooney, Tim	L-L	6-3	195	12-19-90	7	10	3.80	20	20	0	0	118	132	58	50	8	18	125	.284	.324	.271	9.51	1.37
Cornelius, Jonathan	L-L	6-1	190	5-31-88	6	6	4.46	18	14	0	0	79	84	46	39	9	29	66	.277	.253	.285	7.55	3.32
Delgado, Ramon	R-R	6-3	195	9-3-86	1	0	2.92	16	0	0	0	25	22	8	8	0	4	21	.239	.355	.180	7.66	1.46
Ferrara, Anthony	R-L	6-1	175	9-2-89	7	6	5.84	23	20	0	0	99	94	66	64	16	54	85	.249	.207	.261	7.75	4.93
Gorgen, Scott	R-R	5-10	190	1-27-87	0	1	12.27	1	0	0	0	4	4	5	5	2	0	2	.308	.250	.400	4.91	0.00
Greenwood, Nick	R-L	6-1	180	9-28-87	3	4	3.98	11	7	1	0	41	50	25	18	3	11	22	.301	.243	.318	4.87	2.43
Hooker, Deryk	R-R	6-4	215	6-21-89	1	4	3.64	39	0	0	8	47	38	19	19	4	10	61	.217	.200	.227	11.68	1.91
Kiekhefer, Dean	L-L	6-0	175	6-7-89	0	2	3.86	11	0	0	0	16	20	9	7	1	1	10	.294	.136	.370	5.51	0.55
Martinez, Carlos	R-R	6-0	185	9-21-91	1	0	2.31	3	3	0	0	12	11	3	3	1	1	9	.239	.304	.174	6.94	0.77
McGregor, Scott	R-R	6-2	193	12-19-86	4	1	2.44	8	8	0	0	48	42	14	13	5	11	48	.233	.232	.234	9.00	2.06
Miller, Travis	R-R	6-0	195	3-15-90	0	0	0.00	1	0	0	0	2	1	0	0	1	0	2	.111	.000	.125	7.71	3.86
Miranda, Danny	L-L	6-0	225	8-25-90	1	1	6.25	16	0	0	0	22	28	16	15	2	6	6	.301	.357	.277	6.65	2.49
Petrick, Zach	R-R	6-3	195	7-29-89	3	3	3.99	9	9	0	0	47	44	22	21	3	15	44	.247	.175	.287	8.37	2.85
Russell, Zach	R-R	6-2	185	7-27-89	0	2	8.16	10	0	0	0	14	16	18	13	2	8	15	.271	.227	.297	9.42	5.02
Sherriff, Ryan	L-L	6-1	185	5-25-90	2	1	3.33	5	5	0	0	27	34	10	10	0	9	18	.318	.321	.316	6.00	3.00
Siegrist, Kevin	L-L	6-5	215	7-20-89	1	1	2.25	13	0	0	1	20	8	5	5	2	7	35	.121	.095	.133	15.75	3.15
Stoppelman, Lee	L-L	6-2	210	5-24-90	3	1	1.35	37	0	0	6	40	20	6	6	3	14	50	.150	.217	.115	11.25	3.15
Thomas, Kevin	R-R	6-3	215	7-8-86	6	4	2.56	46	0	0	1	60	49	18	17	4	17	75	.224	.167	.248	11.31	2.56
Westbrook, Jake	R-R	6-3	210	9-29-77	0	0	2.45	1	1	0	0	4	6	1	1	0	0	5	.375	.429	.333	12.27	0.00

	B-T	HT	WT	DOB	W	L	ERA	G	GS	CG	SV	IP	H	R	ER	HR	BB	SO	AVG	vLH	vRH	K/9	BB/9
Whiting, Boone	R-R	6-1	175	8-20-89	3	2	2.93	6	6	0	0	31	28	14	10	2	7	34	.237	.200	.260	9.98	2.05
Wright, Justin	L-L	5-9	175	8-18-89	1	1	5.34	50	0	0	0	59	71	39	35	6	25	64	.290	.229	.314	9.76	3.81
Wyatt, Heath	R-R	6-2	185	8-27-88	3	1	3.26	36	0	0	0	47	46	18	17	5	10	38	.254	.295	.241	7.28	1.91

Fielding

Catcher	PCT	G	PO	A	E	DP	PB
Castillo	1.000	3	23	1	0	0	1
Perez	.989	56	499	44	6	3	3
Rasmus	.983	15	108	10	2	2	0
Stanley	1.000	59	414	73	0	4	2
Tartamella	.973	8	64	7	2	1	0

First Base	PCT	G	PO	A	E	DP
Adams	1.000	3	27	3	0	2
Gotay	1.000	1	1	0	0	0
Scruggs	.988	129	1131	62	14	86
Swauger	1.000	11	73	7	0	7

Second Base	PCT	G	PO	A	E	DP
Albitz	1.000	25	40	52	0	13
Mateo	.989	43	69	114	2	26
Pritchard	1.000	4	6	6	0	2
Rahmatulla	1.000	2	0	6	0	0

	PCT	G	PO	A	E	DP
Rodriguez	.971	42	99	100	6	23
Walsh	.926	30	51	75	10	18
Williams	1.000	6	9	12	0	2

Third Base	PCT	G	PO	A	E	DP
Albitz	.940	17	10	37	3	2
Gotay	.944	102	51	201	15	14
Lemmerman	.667	2	0	4	2	0
Mateo	1.000	6	7	12	0	2
Pritchard	1.000	8	6	7	0	2
Rahmatulla	.958	13	4	19	1	0

Shortstop	PCT	G	PO	A	E	DP
Albitz	1.000	6	7	16	0	3
Lemmerman	.934	85	92	236	23	44
Mateo	.980	49	60	141	4	21
Rodriguez	—	1	0	0	0	0

Outfield	PCT	G	PO	A	E	DP
Longmire	1.000	2	4	0	0	0
Melker	.992	90	120	6	1	3
O'Neill	.985	87	119	10	2	0
Pham	1.000	37	86	1	0	0
Piscotty	.989	48	88	3	1	1
Ramsey	.978	88	169	6	4	2
Robinson	1.000	2	5	0	0	0
Rodriguez	.911	26	51	0	5	0
Scruggs	—	1	0	0	0	0
Stanley	—	1	0	0	0	0
Swauger	.987	49	73	5	1	0
Williams	—	1	0	0	0	0

PALM BEACH CARDINALS HIGH CLASS A

FLORIDA STATE LEAGUE

Batting	B-T	HT	WT	DOB	AVG	vLH	vRH	G	AB	R	H	2B	3B	HR	RBI	BB	HBP	SH	SF	SO	SB	CS	SLG	OBP
Castillo, Juan	R-R	5-11	190	12-13-89	.244	.250	.242	39	131	11	32	4	0	0	11	11	0	3	0	26	0	1	.275	.303
Castillo, Ronard	R-R	6-5	200	6-16-92	.273	.333	.250	3	11	3	3	0	0	1	2	0	0	0	0	2	0	0	.545	.273
Ehrlich, Adam	L-R	6-1	205	12-13-92	.150	.000	.176	7	20	1	3	0	0	0	3	4	0	0	0	4	0	0	.150	.292
Garcia, Anthony	R-R	6-0	180	1-4-92	.217	.179	.232	98	345	37	75	16	1	13	45	26	9	2	4	95	6	2	.383	.286
Gil, Ronny	B-R	5-10	150	3-15-89	.230	.222	.233	90	261	29	60	13	3	1	22	25	1	4	0	57	11	4	.314	.300
Keener, Jonathan	R-R	6-0	195	12-10-89	.333	—	.333	1	3	0	1	0	0	0	0	0	0	0	0	0	0	0	.333	.333
Klein, Geoff	B-R	6-3	200	3-27-88	.000	.000	.000	1	1	2	0	0	0	0	0	1	2	0	0	0	0	0	.000	.750
Lewis, Adam	L-R	6-0	200	4-12-89	.220	.000	.275	17	50	7	11	5	0	0	2	5	0	1	0	8	0	0	.320	.291
Longmire, Nick	R-R	6-3	180	1-5-89	.229	.299	.194	113	428	40	98	21	4	9	46	20	1	4	0	88	3	8	.360	.265
Mejia, Alex	R-R	6-1	200	1-18-91	.207	.211	.205	81	295	26	61	14	0	0	24	13	4	10	4	39	6	3	.254	.247
Montero, Jesus	R-R	5-10	220	6-21-91	.208	.224	.200	47	154	10	32	7	0	3	21	8	1	3	1	43	1	2	.312	.250
Parque, Jimmy	L-L	5-9	170	10-3-88	.176	.333	.143	5	17	1	3	0	0	1	0	2	0	0		4	0	0	.176	.263
Piscotty, Stephen	R-R	6-3	210	1-14-91	.292	.259	.310	63	243	30	71	14	2	9	35	18	3	0	0	27	4	5	.477	.348
Popkins, David	L-R	6-3	215	11-16-89	.317	.356	.297	93	350	49	111	21	6	6	45	27	8	9	2	78	9	7	.463	.377
Rahmatulla, Tyler	R-R	5-10	190	2-26-90	.205	.188	.211	23	73	8	15	2	0	0	2	6	0	0	0	11	2	0	.233	.266
Ramsey, James	L-R	6-0	190	12-19-89	.361	.182	.400	16	61	17	22	5	2	1	7	12	3	0	1	12	1	0	.557	.481
Rasmus, Casey	L-R	5-10	175	3-29-90	.310	.200	.370	12	42	1	13	1	1	0	10	1	0	1	0	12	3	1	.381	.326
Rodriguez, Jonathan	R-R	6-2	205	8-21-89	.284	.264	.293	126	455	71	129	34	1	18	72	60	6	0	2	101	21	4	.481	.373
Rodriguez, Starlin	B-R	5-10	175	12-13-89	.293	.375	.247	35	133	19	39	9	0	1	14	13	2	0	2	21	3	1	.383	.360
Stanley, Cody	L-R	5-10	190	12-21-88	.226	.048	.286	23	84	7	19	1	2	1	11	2	2	0	1	21	1	0	.321	.256
Stienstra, Danny	R-R	6-2	200	3-1-89	.276	.325	.257	117	417	28	115	14	1	4	38	28	2	3	1	47	1	3	.343	.324
Tilson, Charlie	L-L	5-11	175	12-2-92	.294	.167	.364	9	34	1	10	1	1	0		5	0	0	0	6	0	0	.382	.385
Valera, Cesar	R-R	6-1	180	3-8-92	.174	.300	.077	8	23	2	4	1	0	0	1	1	0	0	1	2	0	0	.217	.240
Walsh, Colin	B-R	6-0	190	9-26-89	.262	.288	.249	94	351	59	92	20	6	4	34	58	2	1	0	68	11	1	.387	.370
Williams, Matt	R-R	6-0	170	8-29-89	.262	.265	.260	76	237	39	62	10	0	3	12	26	2	1	0	33	11	4	.342	.340
Wilson, Jacob	R-R	5-11	180	7-29-90	.179	.162	.188	32	117	12	21	4	0	3	10	17	2	1	0	20	0	1	.291	.294
Wisdom, Patrick	R-R	6-2	210	8-27-91	.250	.270	.236	25	92	8	23	4	0	2	11	9	0	1	0	31	0	0	.359	.317

Pitching	B-T	HT	WT	DOB	W	L	ERA	G	GS	CG	SV	IP	H	R	ER	HR	BB	SO	AVG	vLH	vRH	K/9	BB/9
Adamek, Brady	R-R	6-5	230	4-13-90	0	0	0.00	1	0	0	0	1	0	0	0	0	0	1	.000	.000	.000	6.75	0.00
Almarante, Jose	R-R	6-1	172	12-19-88	0	2	5.54	16	1	0	0	26	31	18	16	2	10	26	.295	.244	.328	9.00	3.46
Baker, Corey	R-R	6-1	170	11-23-89	2	2	3.90	14	2	0	1	32	32	14	14	1	12	23	.267	.286	.256	6.40	3.34
Bautista, Juan	R-R	5-11	195	6-16-93	0	0	3.21	3	3	0	0	14	11	5	5	0	4	6	.234	.091	.360	3.86	2.57
Billbrough, Logan	R-R	6-5	225	8-4-89	0	0	2.12	12	0	0	0	17	14	4	4	0	5	21	.222	.222	.222	11.12	2.65
Booden, Jacob	R-R	6-7	235	8-14-90	1	0	5.40	3	0	0	0	3	6	3	2	0	3	1	.375	.167	.500	2.70	8.10
Cooney, Tim	L-L	6-3	195	12-19-90	3	3	2.75	6	6	1	0	36	38	14	11	4		23	.273	.231	.290	5.75	1.00
Cornelius, Jonathan	L-L	6-1	190	5-31-88	2	1	2.66	11	5	0	1	44	39	18	13	0	7	31	.239	.212	.252	6.34	1.43
Corrigan, Chris	R-R	6-2	155	12-24-87	0	1	5.14	2	1	0	0	7	6	5	4	0	4	4	.250	.000	.353	5.14	5.14
Creath, Brandon	R-R	6-3	200	2-16-89	0	2	4.26	12	0	0	0	19	19	10	9	3	12	19	.260	.143	.308	9.00	5.68
Cuda, Joey	R-R	5-9	195	9-13-89	4	0	1.40	7	7	0	0	39	33	8	6	0	9	29	.226	.161	.267	6.75	1.40
Gaviglio, Sam	R-R	6-1	200	5-22-90	4	1	2.72	7	7	0	0	40	29	13	12	2	12	30	.207	.239	.191	6.81	2.72
Gonzales, Marco	L-L	6-0	185	2-16-92	0	0	1.62	4	4	0	0	17	10	3	3	1	5	13	.179	.313	.125	7.02	2.70
Gorgen, Scott	R-R	5-10	190	1-27-87	3	2	4.55	6	5	0	0	30	30	17	15	4	10	21	.261	.288	.222	6.98	3.03
Hald, Kyle	L-L	6-0	190	5-27-89	5	8	4.42	24	24	0	0	136	153	80	67	5	31	74	.288	.324	.275	4.89	2.05
Hernandez, Hector	B-L	6-1	189	2-20-91	3	3	3.77	9	8	0	0	45	49	23	19	5	20	28	.288	.268	.295	5.56	3.97
Heyer, Kurt	L-R	6-2	185	1-23-91	6	5	3.42	15	14	0	0	84	75	35	32	7	22	61	.246	.272	.230	6.51	2.35
Jenkins, Tyrell	R-R	6-4	204	7-20-92	0	0	4.50	3	3	0	0	10	13	6	5	0	1	6	.310	.308	.310	5.40	0.90
Kiekhefer, Dean	L-L	6-0	175	6-7-89	4	3	3.27	25	0	0	7	44	48	18	16	1	8	28	.277	.275	.278	5.73	1.64

Name	B-T	HT	WT	DOB	W	L	ERA	G	GS	CG	SV	IP	H	R	ER	HR	BB	SO	AVG	vLH	vRH	K/9	BB/9
Lee, Thomas	R-R	6-1	190	10-20-89	0	1	0.00	2	0	0	1	4	4	1	0	0	1	1	.286	.200	.333	2.45	2.45
Lucas, Aiden	R-R	6-2	225	4-21-88	0	1	4.70	6	0	0	1	8	11	6	4	0	4	6	.344	.400	.138	7.04	4.70
Melling, Tyler	R-L	6-2	170	9-4-88	3	4	4.93	17	13	0	0	73	80	46	40	6	21	43	.276	.279	.275	5.30	2.59
Miller, Travis	R-R	6-0	195	3-15-90	2	10	5.23	26	9	0	0	65	79	44	38	2	35	43	.307	.298	.313	5.92	4.82
Miranda, Danny	L-L	6-0	225	8-25-90	3	1	1.58	24	0	0	3	40	33	10	7	2	6	29	.220	.209	.224	6.53	1.35
Nazario, Iden	L-L	6-0	190	3-28-89	1	4	4.42	38	0	0	3	55	49	30	27	6	24	64	.238	.231	.240	10.47	3.93
Petrick, Zach	R-R	6-3	195	7-29-89	3	0	0.27	9	4	0	1	33	21	4	1	0	4	32	.176	.093	.224	8.64	1.08
Shaban, Ronnie	L-R	6-1	195	3-8-90	2	5	1.73	45	0	0	18	52	39	14	10	2	20	41	.211	.183	.224	7.10	3.46
Sherriff, Ryan	L-L	6-1	185	5-25-90	4	4	2.31	13	13	1	0	78	67	25	20	3	13	41	.231	.214	.235	4.73	1.50
Stock, Robert	L-R	6-1	200	11-21-89	2	0	4.37	18	0	0	0	23	20	14	11	2	16	27	.238	.174	.262	10.72	6.35
Stoppelman, Lee	L-L	6-2	210	5-24-90	2	1	1.50	15	0	0	0	24	16	8	4	0	10	26	.184	.160	.194	9.75	3.75
Swagerty, Jordan	B-R	6-2	175	7-14-89	0	1	13.50	6	0	0	0	7	11	10	10	0	8	4	.407	.375	.421	5.40	10.80
Voss, Jay	L-L	6-4	195	4-22-87	1	4	13.50	8	5	0	0	21	34	33	32	5	18	10	.370	.222	.405	4.22	7.59
Watson, Brad	R-R	6-0	185	8-8-89	1	0	2.00	2	1	0	0	9	9	5	2	0	1	5	.243	.214	.261	5.00	1.00
Wyatt, Heath	R-R	6-2	185	8-27-88	2	2	2.16	16	0	0	3	25	24	7	6	1	7	18	.270	.323	.241	6.48	2.52

Fielding

Catcher	PCT	G	PO	A	E	DP	PB
Castillo	.980	39	216	27	5	1	7
Ehrlich	.980	7	46	2	1	1	2
Keener	1.000	1	3	0	0	0	0
Klein	1.000	1	9	0	0	0	0
Lewis	1.000	17	94	9	0	1	0
Montero	.991	46	290	34	3	5	6
Rasmus	1.000	11	69	4	0	1	0
Stanley	.992	18	117	12	1	3	1

First Base	PCT	G	PO	A	E	DP
Rodriguez	.994	109	864	66	6	88
Stienstra	.989	28	255	11	3	27

Second Base	PCT	G	PO	A	E	DP
Gil	.938	13	31	45	5	13
Rahmatulla	1.000	6	11	12	0	5

	PCT	G	PO	A	E	DP
Walsh	.980	79	151	189	7	51
Williams	1.000	9	11	13	0	3
Wilson	.976	31	66	95	4	19

Third Base	PCT	G	PO	A	E	DP
Gil	—	1	0	0	0	0
Rahmatulla	.850	9	6	11	3	1
Rodriguez	1.000	1	0	1	0	0
Stienstra	.935	68	47	98	10	13
Williams	.930	44	21	72	7	8
Wisdom	.947	24	18	36	3	5

Shortstop	PCT	G	PO	A	E	DP
Gil	.919	38	49	110	14	26
Mejia	.957	80	108	224	15	43
Valera	1.000	8	22	25	0	5
Williams	.956	11	15	28	2	5

Outfield	PCT	G	PO	A	E	DP
Castillo	1.000	2	8	0	0	0
Garcia	.961	82	165	7	7	0
Gil	.944	23	66	2	4	0
Longmire	.992	100	240	7	2	2
Parque	.857	2	5	1	1	0
Piscotty	.992	60	118	5	1	2
Popkins	.969	68	122	1	4	1
Ramsey	1.000	18	45	0	0	0
Rodriguez	1.000	13	28	1	0	1
Rodriguez	.986	32	72	1	1	0
Tilson	1.000	9	20	1	0	1
Williams	.857	2	6	0	1	0

PEORIA CHIEFS — LOW CLASS A

MIDWEST LEAGUE

Batting	B-T	HT	WT	DOB	AVG	vLH	vRH	G	AB	R	H	2B	3B	HR	RBI	BB	HBP	SH	SF	SO	SB	CS	SLG	OBP
Caldwell, Bruce	L-R	5-11	175	11-27-91	.179	.182	.177	24	84	6	15	2	0	1	5	8	0	1	1	23	0	0	.238	.247
Ehrlich, Adam	L-R	6-1	205	12-13-92	.348	1.000	.318	7	23	5	8	2	0	0	6	1	0	1	0	6	0	0	.435	.375
Herrera, Juan	R-R	5-11	165	6-28-93	.271	.231	.288	23	85	5	23	4	0	0	3	7	1	1	0	22	2	0	.318	.333
Keener, Jonathan	R-R	6-0	195	12-10-89	.208	.182	.216	16	48	3	10	1	0	0	1	1	1	2	1	9	0	0	.229	.235
Kelly, Carson	R-R	6-2	200	7-14-94	.219	.200	.224	43	146	18	32	6	0	2	13	13	2	5	2	25	0	0	.301	.288
Klein, Geoff	B-R	6-3	200	3-27-88	.179	.125	.200	10	28	2	5	0	0	1	8	4	2	1	0	11	0	1	.286	.324
Martin, Trevor	R-R	6-0	190	8-3-91	.373	.366	.377	29	110	11	41	6	2	2	22	2	2	1	0	23	0	1	.518	.395
Martini, Nick	L-L	5-11	205	6-27-90	.252	.205	.267	106	365	36	92	18	2	2	36	40	9	0	2	40	9	8	.329	.339
Mateo, Leandro	R-R	5-11	170	3-17-90	.091	.000	.125	4	11	0	1	0	0	0	0	0	0	0	0	3	0	0	.091	.091
McElroy Jr., C.J.	R-R	5-10	180	5-29-93	.240	.261	.231	58	242	24	58	9	3	0	23	17	0	6	1	40	8	8	.302	.288
Mejia, Alex	R-R	6-1	200	1-18-91	.281	.304	.271	40	153	26	43	9	2	1	13	9	2	4	1	29	2	1	.386	.327
Montero, Jesus	R-R	5-10	220	6-21-91	.220	.235	.214	19	59	9	13	3	0	2	4	6	5	1	0	20	0	0	.373	.343
Parque, Jimmy	L-L	5-9	170	10-3-88	.163	.100	.182	17	43	5	7	0	0	1	3	4	4	0	0	12	0	0	.233	.294
Perez, Luis	R-R	5-10	165	7-24-91	1.000	1.000	—	1	1	1	1	0	0	1	3	0	0	0	0	0	0	0	4.000	1.000
Popkins, David	L-R	6-3	215	11-16-89	.000	.000	.000	4	8	1	0	0	0	0	0	1	0	0		3	0	0	.000	.111
Ramos, Steve	R-R	6-0	160	7-4-90	.071	—	.071	4	14	0	1	0	0	0	0	1	1	0	0	1	6	0	0	.071	.125
Rasmus, Casey	L-R	5-10	175	3-29-90	.296	.200	.333	25	71	13	21	2	1	0	6	6	1	3	0	10	4	2	.352	.359
Schaffer, Jeremy	R-R	6-1	205	1-16-90	.214	.188	.224	75	281	25	60	14	1	11	33	22	3	0	5	61	2	2	.388	.273
Swinson, Mike	L-R	6-2	185	9-24-89	.207	.211	.206	40	135	17	28	4	3	0	13	17	1	3	1	39	8	0	.281	.299
Tilson, Charlie	L-L	5-11	175	12-2-92	.303	.265	.317	100	376	49	114	8	6	4	30	25	2	7	1	58	15	6	.388	.349
Valera, Breyvic	B-R	5-11	160	8-1-92	.309	.313	.307	128	515	71	159	18	6	0	48	40	1	4	2	30	13	7	.367	.358
Vargas, Ildemaro	R-R	6-0	170	7-16-91	.248	.239	.252	115	419	54	104	15	3	1	39	31	3	13	1	49	8	4	.305	.304
Velazco, Gerwuins	R-R	6-0	190	10-7-91	.206	.131	.231	77	247	25	51	4	1	1	13	30	0	6	2	45	5	0	.243	.290
Walton, Jordan	L-L	5-11	185	3-13-90	.278	.255	.285	109	403	47	112	24	3	3	49	31	5	2	5	77	5	5	.375	.333
Washington, David	L-L	6-5	200	11-20-90	.333	.000	.429	3	9	1	3	2	0	0	1	6	0	0	0	2	0	0	.556	.600
Wiley, Brett	L-R	5-10	175	11-24-91	.167	.000	.250	2	6	2	1	0	1	0	1	2	0	0	0	1	0	0	.500	.375
Wilson, Jacob	R-R	5-11	180	4-28-90	.264	.288	.257	97	348	63	92	19	1	5	72	40	10	3	8	54	6	5	.468	.350
Wisdom, Patrick	R-R	6-2	210	8-27-91	.231	.247	.226	104	372	54	86	20	4	13	62	42	3	3	3	114	4	1	.411	.312
Young, Matt	R-R	6-3	230	8-17-90	.214	1.000	.154	4	14	0	3	1	0	0	1	0	0	0	0	5	0	0	.286	.267

Pitching	B-T	HT	WT	DOB	W	L	ERA	G	GS	CG	SV	IP	H	R	ER	HR	BB	SO	AVG	vLH	vRH	K/9	BB/9
Adamek, Brady	R-R	6-5	230	4-13-90	1	1	2.05	17	0	0	1	26	22	6	6	0	15	27	.227	.146	.286	9.23	5.13
Aldrete, Mike	R-R	5-10	165	9-30-89	2	2	5.31	27	0	0	1	42	45	28	25	2	20	45	.269	.227	.297	9.57	4.25
Baker, Corey	R-R	6-1	170	11-23-89	1	1	1.85	14	0	0	1	24	21	5	5	0	2	29	.236	.278	.208	10.73	0.74
Cuda, Joey	R-R	5-9	195	9-13-89	5	4	4.28	15	15	0	0	76	92	43	36	5	18	77	.303	.323	.287	9.16	2.14
Donofrio, Joey	R-R	6-3	185	5-10-89	6	2	2.63	40	0	0	5	68	56	25	20	3	17	85	.220	.266	.194	11.20	2.24
Garcia, Silfredo	R-R	6-2	170	7-19-91	4	5	3.82	18	18	1	0	99	100	51	42	6	30	64	.256	.282	.235	5.82	2.73

	B-T	HT	WT	DOB	W	L	ERA	G	GS	CG	SV	IP	H	R	ER	HR	BB	SO	AVG	vLH	vRH	K/9	BB/9
Helisek, Kyle	L-L	6-0	170	4-23-90	7	7	3.13	23	23	0	0	129	128	56	45	5	42	101	.258	.265	.255	7.03	2.92
Hernandez, Hector	B-L	6-1	189	2-20-91	5	3	3.42	13	13	0	0	76	65	29	29	8	28	60	.226	.185	.239	7.07	3.30
Heyer, Kurt	L-R	6-2	185	1-23-91	3	2	3.40	8	8	0	0	40	44	16	15	2	12	35	.280	.224	.333	7.94	2.72
Jenkins, Tyrell	R-R	6-4	204	7-20-92	4	4	4.74	10	10	2	0	49	51	28	26	4	24	34	.267	.236	.294	6.20	4.38
Jones, Cory	R-R	6-5	225	9-20-91	8	2	2.04	11	11	0	0	66	52	17	15	4	16	52	.215	.196	.231	7.06	2.17
Lee, Thomas	R-R	6-1	190	10-20-89	5	1	2.44	24	1	0	0	48	41	14	13	5	5	46	.229	.256	.208	8.63	0.94
Llorens, Dixon	R-R	5-10	170	11-18-92	3	3	2.85	37	0	0	11	47	34	15	15	2	23	71	.199	.292	.131	13.50	4.37
Lucas, Josh	R-R	6-6	185	11-5-90	0	4	6.53	4	4	0	0	21	37	22	15	2	5	8	.394	.304	.479	3.48	2.18
Mayers, Mike	R-R	6-4	185	12-6-91	0	3	3.70	5	5	0	0	24	29	10	10	2	5	14	.302	.277	.327	5.18	1.85
O'Shea, Ben	L-L	6-5	255	9-9-91	1	4	5.70	6	6	0	0	30	42	20	19	2	9	17	.328	.324	.330	5.10	2.70
Perry, Chris	L-R	6-2	215	7-15-90	2	4	3.91	9	9	0	0	48	50	27	21	3	15	40	.266	.333	.218	7.45	2.79
Petrick, Zach	R-R	6-3	195	7-29-89	1	0	0.83	16	0	0	7	33	24	5	3	1	8	46	.200	.200	.200	12.67	2.20
Polanco, Jhonny	R-R	6-3	195	4-28-92	2	1	5.09	8	0	0	0	18	19	11	10	2	9	22	.271	.250	.289	11.21	4.58
Russell, Zach	R-R	6-2	185	7-27-89	0	0	0.82	11	0	0	5	11	5	1	1	1	2	17	.132	.133	.130	13.91	1.64
Sabatino, Steve	L-L	6-2	190	3-8-90	0	1	1.54	7	0	0	1	12	9	3	2	0	5	15	.209	.091	.250	11.57	3.86
Scanio, Joe	R-R	6-4	230	1-30-90	3	4	3.95	40	0	0	0	73	76	34	32	3	24	58	.278	.308	.256	7.15	2.96
Stock, Robert	L-R	6-1	200	11-21-89	0	1	2.30	14	0	0	4	16	11	4	4	0	10	15	.208	.077	.250	8.62	5.74
Thomas, Chris	R-R	6-2	200	3-16-88	1	0	2.35	4	0	0	0	8	5	2	2	0	2	11	.192	.091	.267	12.91	2.35
Tuivailala, Sam	R-R	6-3	195	10-19-92	0	3	5.35	28	0	0	1	35	31	22	21	0	20	50	.233	.233	.233	12.74	5.09
Villanueva, Dail	L-L	6-3	190	1-23-90	0	2	11.74	3	3	0	0	8	12	12	10	0	8	2	.364	.000	.414	2.35	9.39
Voss, Jay	L-L	6-4	195	4-22-87	0	0	1.50	6	0	0	0	12	9	2	2	1	5	11	.209	.273	.188	8.25	3.75
Watson, Brad	R-R	6-4	185	8-8-89	3	5	4.27	11	11	0	0	65	74	35	31	8	17	55	.284	.321	.255	7.58	2.34
Westbrook, Jake	R-R	6-3	210	9-29-77	1	0	1.29	1	1	0	0	7	4	1	1	0	0	5	.167	.167	.167	6.43	0.00

Fielding

Catcher	PCT	G	PO	A	E	DP	PB
Ehrlich	.944	6	46	5	3	0	1
Keener	.980	15	134	15	3	2	2
Klein	.920	3	23	0	2	0	1
Montero	.987	18	139	8	2	2	1
Rasmus	.995	21	167	22	1	2	1
Velazco	.996	77	603	65	3	6	11

First Base	PCT	G	PO	A	E	DP
Klein	1.000	1	12	0	0	3
Schaffer	.989	61	527	31	6	50
Walton	.981	50	391	33	8	41
Washington	1.000	3	34	0	0	0
Wisdom	.992	28	249	15	2	21

Second Base	PCT	G	PO	A	E	DP
Caldwell	.962	21	46	56	4	15
Mateo	.857	3	5	7	2	0

		G	PO	A	E	DP
Valera	.964	46	80	136	8	36
Vargas	.963	5	7	19	1	3
Wiley	1.000	2	7	3	0	3
Wilson	.981	65	115	187	6	37

Third Base	PCT	G	PO	A	E	DP
Kelly	.905	31	19	38	6	5
Martin	.795	12	5	26	8	2
Valera	.941	16	8	24	2	2
Vargas	.985	21	14	52	1	3
Wisdom	.913	63	49	119	16	13

Shortstop	PCT	G	PO	A	E	DP
Herrera	.950	20	21	74	5	12
Mejia	.960	38	58	110	7	21
Valera	.935	9	16	27	3	8
Vargas	.966	76	90	223	11	39

Outfield	PCT	G	PO	A	E	DP
Martini	.989	105	170	9	2	2
McElroy Jr.	1.000	58	134	2	0	0
Parque	.955	16	19	2	1	0
Perez	1.000	1	1	0	0	0
Popkins	1.000	4	1	0	0	0
Ramos	1.000	4	5	2	0	0
Swinson	.961	38	46	3	2	1
Tilson	.966	99	193	8	7	1
Valera	.947	48	66	5	4	0
Vargas	1.000	7	15	0	0	0
Walton	.955	44	62	2	3	0
Wilson	—	1	0	0	0	0
Young	1.000	4	3	0	0	0

STATE COLLEGE SPIKES — SHORT-SEASON

NEW YORK-PENN LEAGUE

Batting	B-T	HT	WT	DOB	AVG	vLH	vRH	G	AB	R	H	2B	3B	HR	RBI	BB	HBP	SH	SF	SO	SB	CS	SLG	OBP
Bosco, Jimmy	L-R	5-10	170	5-21-91	.300	.226	.321	65	240	34	72	18	6	3	27	21	2	2	1	54	3	6	.463	.360
Bryan, Vaugn	B-R	6-0	185	6-5-93	.125	.200	.000	2	8	1	1	0	0	0	0	0	0	0	0	2	0	0	.250	.125
Caldwell, Bruce	L-R	5-11	175	11-27-91	.321	.250	.343	36	131	30	42	9	0	1	15	22	1	1	2	29	6	1	.412	.417
Castillo, Ronard	R-R	6-5	200	6-16-92	.341	.341	.340	37	138	18	47	6	2	2	28	7	0	0	1	23	4	1	.457	.370
DeLeon, Alex	R-R	6-1	215	2-9-91	.197	.125	.246	38	117	9	23	4	1	4	13	11	4	0	2	36	1	1	.350	.284
Herrera, Juan	R-R	5-11	165	6-28-93	.067	.167	.000	4	15	1	1	0	0	0	0	2	0	0	0	1	0	0	.067	.176
2-team total (39 Mahoning Valley)					.256	—	—	43	164	21	42	9	1	1	11	18	6	0	1	31	2	1	.341	.349
Katz, Mason	L-R	5-10	188	8-23-90	.249	.279	.235	56	197	27	49	13	1	2	23	21	9	0	2	49	2	1	.355	.345
Kelly, Carson	R-R	6-2	200	7-14-94	.277	.278	.276	70	271	35	75	16	1	4	32	20	6	2	0	31	1	0	.387	.340
Lewis, Adam	L-R	6-0	200	4-12-89	.300	.000	.375	3	10	1	3	1	0	0	2	1	0	0	1	2	0	0	.400	.333
Martin, Trevor	R-R	6-0	190	8-3-91	.244	.238	.250	12	41	4	10	1	0	1	6	2	0	0	0	10	1	0	.341	.279
Perez, Luis	R-R	5-10	165	7-24-91	.214	.211	.216	24	70	8	15	3	0	0	7	6	2	1	3	9	3	1	.257	.284
Ramos, Steve	R-R	6-0	160	7-4-90	.341	.337	.343	67	252	40	86	12	3	2	24	15	2	4	2	47	22	4	.437	.380
Rosenberg, Dante	R-R	5-11	180	7-5-90	.139	.300	.077	16	36	2	5	1	0	0	1	1	2	1	0	4	0	0	.167	.205
Schulze, Michael	L-R	6-1	175	5-13-91	.275	.167	.306	35	109	16	30	5	1	0	12	5	2	0	2	10	2	2	.339	.314
Valera, Cesar	R-R	6-1	180	3-8-92	.265	.250	.272	67	268	43	71	13	4	2	27	19	11	2	1	45	13	3	.366	.338
Vigo-Suarez, Brian	R-R	6-1	175	12-12-91	.188	.167	.200	8	16	2	3	2	0	0	1	1	0	0	4	0	0	.313	.278
Voit, Luke	R-R	6-3	225	2-13-91	.242	.303	.224	46	149	14	36	7	0	2	16	21	6	0	1	29	1	0	.329	.356
Washington, David	L-L	6-5	200	11-20-90	.261	.239	.268	72	261	34	68	17	0	10	50	40	5	0	4	76	4	2	.441	.365
Wiley, Brett	L-R	5-10	175	11-24-91	.337	.389	.324	25	89	17	30	2	4	2	18	9	1	1	3	13	7	0	.517	.392
Young, Matt	R-R	6-3	230	8-17-90	.252	.341	.212	45	143	18	36	10	0	2	13	16	0	1	1	30	17	2	.364	.301

Pitching	B-T	HT	WT	DOB	W	L	ERA	G	GS	CG	SV	IP	H	R	ER	HR	BB	SO	AVG	vLH	vRH	K/9	BB/9
Adamek, Brady	R-R	6-5	230	4-13-90	1	0	0.96	6	0	0	3	9	3	1	1	0	1	8	.188	.182	.190	7.71	0.96
Aldrete, Mike	R-R	5-10	165	9-30-89	1	0	6.97	13	0	0	1	21	29	18	16	2	13	18	.315	.194	.393	7.84	5.66
Bautista, Juan	R-R	5-11	195	6-16-93	1	5	4.87	12	12	0	0	61	76	46	33	5	27	31	.318	.361	.275	4.57	3.98
Booden, Jacob	R-R	6-7	235	8-14-90	5	0	1.19	16	0	0	4	30	21	4	4	1	11	39	.184	.140	.219	11.57	3.26
Brookshire, Chase	R-L	6-0	190	3-7-91	1	0	1.59	9	2	0	2	23	20	9	4	0	3	19	.233	.222	.240	7.54	1.19

Name	B-T	HT	WT	DOB	W	L	ERA	G	GS	CG	SV	IP	H	R	ER	HR	BB	SO	AVG	vLH	vRH	K/9	BB/9
De Leon, Victor	R-R	6-2	190	4-19-92	5	2	2.87	17	1	0	0	38	31	14	12	2	17	37	.230	.255	.213	8.84	4.06
Harris, Mitch	R-R	6-4	215	11-7-85	4	1	0.81	20	0	0	1	33	22	4	3	0	15	29	.193	.245	.148	7.83	4.05
Herget, Kevin	R-R	5-10	185	4-3-91	7	0	2.89	14	8	0	0	53	63	20	17	2	8	36	.306	.286	.324	6.11	1.36
Lucas, Josh	R-R	6-6	185	11-5-90	0	0	7.36	1	1	0	0	4	6	4	3	0	1	4	.333	.375	.300	9.82	2.45
O'Shea, Ben	L-L	6-5	255	9-9-91	3	2	5.79	6	6	0	0	28	24	18	18	4	9	22	.229	.364	.193	7.07	2.89
Paulino, Willy	R-R	6-3	172	6-21-90	2	3	3.09	15	9	1	0	58	44	24	20	2	34	52	.210	.226	.198	8.02	5.25
Perry, Chris	L-R	6-2	215	7-15-90	2	0	1.61	4	4	0	0	22	17	6	4	0	5	15	.207	.143	.255	6.04	2.01
Petree, Nick	R-R	6-1	195	7-16-90	3	1	1.62	12	9	0	0	56	46	11	10	2	16	46	.230	.215	.243	7.44	2.59
Pierce, Andrew	R-R	6-3	170	1-26-91	2	2	2.11	12	7	0	2	43	43	11	10	0	7	36	.262	.256	.267	7.59	1.48
Polanco, Jhonny	R-R	6-3	195	4-28-92	4	3	2.63	22	0	0	1	38	34	14	11	2	14	44	.234	.159	.303	10.51	3.35
Rauh, Jeff	R-R	6-2	200	1-24-90	3	2	4.05	23	0	0	5	27	23	13	12	3	17	28	.245	.238	.250	9.45	5.74
Reed, Jimmy	L-L	5-11	165	12-18-90	3	2	2.05	12	9	0	2	53	52	19	12	2	12	40	.255	.290	.239	6.84	2.05
Reyes, Artie	R-R	5-11	185	4-6-92	1	2	2.08	10	7	0	0	43	37	13	10	3	15	25	.234	.310	.149	5.19	3.12
Webb, Kyle	R-R	6-0	185	3-8-91	1	2	3.12	17	0	0	2	26	27	12	9	0	4	20	.270	.349	.211	6.92	1.38

Fielding

Catcher	PCT	G	PO	A	E	DP	PB
DeLeon	.994	22	144	11	1	0	3
Lewis	1.000	3	14	1	0	1	0
Rosenberg	.988	16	75	10	1	0	3
Voit	.992	45	309	42	3	3	13

First Base	PCT	G	PO	A	E	DP
DeLeon	.971	12	96	4	3	12
Martin	1.000	4	32	7	0	2
Washington	.982	62	557	41	11	62

Second Base	PCT	G	PO	A	E	DP
Caldwell	.990	23	35	64	1	15
Katz	.963	38	82	129	8	28
Martin	1.000	2	4	7	0	3

	PCT	G	PO	A	E	DP
Schulze	1.000	2	5	9	0	3
Wiley	.966	12	25	31	2	10

Third Base	PCT	G	PO	A	E	DP
Caldwell	.833	3	2	3	1	0
Kelly	.942	65	47	100	9	8
Schulze	.842	8	3	13	3	1
Wiley	1.000	1	0	1	0	0

Shortstop	PCT	G	PO	A	E	DP
Caldwell	1.000	1	1	3	0	1
Herrera	1.000	2	3	16	0	2
Schulze	1.000	10	13	20	0	7
Valera	.952	64	127	207	17	49

Outfield	PCT	G	PO	A	E	DP
Bosco	.961	62	94	5	4	1
Bryan	.875	2	7	0	1	0
Castillo	.940	35	47	0	3	0
Perez	.885	21	20	3	3	0
Ramos	.978	64	129	5	3	1
Vigo-Suarez	1.000	6	5	1	0	0
Washington	1.000	8	11	0	0	0
Young	.947	42	67	4	4	0

JOHNSON CITY CARDINALS — ROOKIE

APPALACHIAN LEAGUE

Batting	B-T	HT	WT	DOB	AVG	vLH	vRH	G	AB	R	H	2B	3B	HR	RBI	BB	HBP	SH	SF	SO	SB	CS	SLG	OBP
Acevedo, Johan	R-R	6-1	173	3-28-93	.293	.304	.289	27	99	13	29	4	0	1	14	8	0	2	1	18	6	1	.364	.343
Altobelli, J.J.	R-R	6-1	190	12-9-90	.284	.241	.304	48	169	18	48	12	2	2	18	16	2	1	0	30	4	2	.414	.353
Bean, Steve	L-R	6-2	190	9-15-93	.229	.152	.259	32	118	15	27	4	0	2	14	11	2	2	1	44	0	0	.314	.303
Bryan, Vaugn	B-R	6-0	185	6-5-93	.280	.231	.298	57	236	45	66	8	5	3	24	22	1	0	2	54	13	3	.394	.341
Garcia, Ronnierd	R-R	6-2	175	3-8-94	.286	.368	.259	59	231	41	66	17	2	5	39	24	1	1	1	53	2	0	.442	.362
Gonzalez, Yoenny	R-R	5-9	170	1-31-92	.192	.280	.165	32	104	8	20	4	2	0	10	4	0	5	1	22	0	3	.269	.220
Grieshaber, Kyle	R-R	6-0	200	6-24-91	.190	.200	.186	31	105	12	20	2	1	1	12	7	2	0	2	27	5	1	.257	.250
Jeffries, Lance	R-R	5-9	185	3-28-93	.235	.273	.228	20	68	10	16	2	0	0	4	6	1	0	0	32	7	2	.265	.307
Keener, Jonathan	R-R	6-0	195	12-10-89	.148	.100	.176	7	27	4	4	0	0	0	5	0	0	1	0	7	0	0	.148	.143
Lacy, Devante	R-R	5-9	180	4-20-94	.190	.222	.178	20	63	6	12	1	1	0	5	3	1	0	1	23	0	0	.238	.235
Mateo, Leandro	B-R	5-11	170	3-17-90	.161	.133	.171	18	56	11	9	0	0	1	3	5	1	0	1	11	4	1	.214	.238
Pedroza, Richy	B-R	5-6	150	7-21-91	.270	.304	.263	36	122	24	33	7	2	0	16	27	2	0	1	15	2	4	.361	.408
Peoples, Kenny	R-R	6-1	180	8-16-93	.300	.230	.324	59	237	41	71	11	4	7	35	15	4	1	0	73	9	3	.468	.352
Perez, Luis	R-R	5-10	165	7-24-91	.292	.389	.255	16	65	9	19	3	0	2	6	3	2	0	0	16	2	2	.431	.343
Reyes, Robelys	B-R	5-9	170	7-25-90	.167	.200	.154	5	18	1	3	1	0	0	0	1	0	2	0	2	1	1	.222	.211
Ringo, Justin	L-R	6-0	195	12-24-90	.300	.267	.310	53	200	34	60	9	1	6	34	26	3	1	1	22	2	2	.445	.387
Rodriguez, Frankie	R-R	5-9	175	7-27-95	.121	.000	.211	14	33	2	4	1	0	0	2	2	0	1	0	12	0	0	.152	.171
Vigo-Suarez, Brian	R-R	6-1	175	12-12-91	.119	.200	.074	17	42	4	5	0	0	0	0	2	0	1	0	15	3	1	.119	.159
Wick, Rowan	L-R	6-3	220	11-9-92	.256	.231	.265	56	207	28	53	11	1	10	35	30	2	1	1	71	2	1	.464	.334
Wiley, Brett	L-R	5-10	175	11-24-91	.294	.182	.333	33	126	16	37	6	2	2	24	18	4	0	0	29	3	3	.421	.399

Pitching	B-T	HT	WT	DOB	W	L	ERA	G	GS	CG	SV	IP	H	R	ER	HR	BB	SO	AVG	vLH	vRH	K/9	BB/9
Anderson, Will	R-R	6-3	205	8-26-92	2	3	4.71	11	9	0	0	42	48	26	22	4	6	28	.291	.382	.245	6.00	1.29
Baez, Fernando	R-R	6-1	190	1-2-92	1	0	0.82	26	0	0	6	33	15	3	3	0	23	47	.140	.125	.147	12.82	6.27
Booden, Jacob	R-R	6-7	235	8-14-90	0	0	1.13	2	1	0	0	8	8	1	1	0	3	7	.276	.385	.188	7.88	3.38
Brito, Ismael	L-L	5-11	170	3-23-93	0	1	4.76	5	0	0	0	6	8	3	3	0	3	9	.320	.667	.211	14.29	4.76
De Los Santos, Hansel	R-R	6-3	160	8-7-91	1	3	5.93	6	6	0	0	27	32	19	18	4	9	22	.291	.244	.319	7.24	2.96
Gerdel, Anderson	R-R	6-4	204	3-22-93	3	1	3.78	21	0	0	0	33	39	22	14	4	7	30	.291	.356	.258	8.10	1.89
Grana, Kyle	R-R	6-4	245	4-26-91	1	0	2.45	7	0	0	0	7	4	2	2	0	1	9	.160	.286	.111	11.05	1.23
Holback, Michael	R-R	6-1	195	9-15-92	2	0	2.18	16	4	0	1	33	24	11	8	1	17	44	.203	.133	.227	12.00	4.64
Lee, Brandon	R-R	6-0	200	11-18-90	1	1	2.91	12	0	0	0	22	27	11	7	1	6	16	.293	.321	.281	6.65	2.49
Lomascolo, Nick	R-L	6-1	190	11-9-89	2	3	2.90	13	3	0	1	31	21	15	10	2	22	43	.196	.273	.176	12.48	6.39
Lopez, Stalyn	L-L	5-9	160	12-28-91	1	0	3.86	15	0	0	0	21	15	10	9	0	25	29	.214	.357	.179	12.43	10.71
Loraine, Zach	R-R	6-3	205	8-8-90	3	1	2.04	24	0	0	3	40	29	10	9	1	11	47	.200	.263	.178	10.66	2.50
Martinez, Dailyn	R-R	6-2	170	4-19-93	4	3	2.70	12	12	0	0	63	61	31	19	3	23	31	.254	.173	.291	4.41	3.27
McKnight, Blake	R-R	6-1	182	2-13-91	3	1	2.69	11	10	0	0	60	58	19	18	1	8	46	.249	.288	.236	6.86	1.19
Mills, Tyler	R-R	6-3	205	1-10-90	0	0	11.81	7	0	0	0	5	7	8	7	1	10	4	.350	.111	.545	6.75	16.88
Paredes, Norge	R-R	6-3	170	2-12-91	2	2	3.58	19	0	0	1	38	34	19	15	5	21	40	.243	.333	.204	9.56	5.02
Perdomo, Luis	R-R	6-0	170	5-9-93	1	5	5.40	12	10	0	0	42	59	44	25	4	14	29	.316	.385	.279	6.26	3.02
Reyes, Alex	R-R	6-3	185	8-29-94	6	4	3.39	12	12	0	0	58	54	26	22	1	28	68	.249	.328	.216	10.49	4.32
Sabatino, Steve	L-L	6-2	190	3-8-91	3	2	4.84	11	0	0	0	22	21	12	12	0	12	33	.241	.385	.216	13.30	4.84

Fielding

Catcher	PCT	G	PO	A	E	DP	PB
Bean	.990	31	261	31	3	4	5
Keener	1.000	7	61	7	0	0	2
Rodriguez	1.000	8	43	5	0	1	2
Wick	1.000	25	207	22	0	2	8

First Base	PCT	G	PO	A	E	DP
Garcia	.985	20	182	14	3	16
Ringo	.983	49	404	10	7	38

Second Base	PCT	G	PO	A	E	DP
Gonzalez	—	1	0	0	0	0
Mateo	.952	10	16	24	2	5
Pedroza	.952	28	51	69	6	13

	PCT	G	PO	A	E	DP
Reyes	.889	4	3	13	2	4
Wiley	.963	26	49	81	5	20

Third Base	PCT	G	PO	A	E	DP
Altobelli	.989	29	23	65	1	9
Garcia	.870	32	23	64	13	6
Gonzalez	—	1	0	0	0	0
Grieshaber	.800	9	5	11	4	1
Wiley	—	1	0	0	0	0

Shortstop	PCT	G	PO	A	E	DP
Altobelli	.958	16	25	43	3	9
Mateo	.857	5	8	10	3	1
Peoples	.916	47	76	142	20	27

Outfield	PCT	G	PO	A	E	DP
Acevedo	.966	26	53	3	2	0
Bryan	.991	57	111	3	1	1
Gonzalez	.973	31	32	4	1	0
Grieshaber	1.000	8	4	0	0	0
Jeffries	.903	17	25	3	3	0
Lacy	1.000	20	34	3	0	1
Mateo	—	1	0	0	0	0
Pedroza	1.000	1	1	0	0	0
Perez	1.000	14	15	4	0	0
Reyes	1.000	1	1	0	0	0
Vigo-Suarez	.889	15	15	1	2	0
Wick	.897	23	32	3	4	0

GCL CARDINALS   ROOKIE
GULF COAST LEAGUE

Batting	B-T	HT	WT	DOB	AVG	vLH	vRH	G	AB	R	H	2B	3B	HR	RBI	BB	HBP	SH	SF	SO	SB	CS	SLG	OBP
Acevedo, Johan	R-R	6-1	173	3-28-93	.250	.320	.227	28	100	16	25	5	0	1	6	12	1	0	1	15	3	4	.330	.333
Almaraz, Joe	L-R	6-3	185	5-6-92	.136	.118	.141	29	81	4	11	3	0	0	8	1	1	0	0	37	0	0	.173	.157
Alvarez, Eliezer	B-R	5-11	165	10-15-94	.209	.143	.226	20	67	12	14	2	3	1	7	4	1	1	0	14	6	2	.373	.264
Asbury, De'Andre	R-R	6-3	170	8-5-95	.179	.273	.143	43	117	4	21	5	1	0	7	9	6	3	0	36	3	2	.239	.273
Bautista, Ricardo	L-R	6-0	185	12-27-95	.255	.100	.293	34	102	14	26	7	0	0	13	15	2	1	4	28	0	2	.324	.350
Collymore, Malik	R-R	5-11	190	4-29-95	.228	.286	.209	19	57	2	13	3	0	1	3	3	0	0	0	23	0	1	.333	.267
Cruz, Luis	R-R	6-2	180	5-26-93	.321	.357	.310	17	56	10	18	3	0	3	5	5	2	0	1	10	0	2	.536	.391
Deol, Dutch	R-R	6-3	200	10-20-92	.188	.250	.167	5	16	0	3	0	0	0	0	2	0	0	0	8	0	1	.188	.278
Garcia, Anthony	R-R	6-0	180	1-4-92	.000	.000	.000	1	4	0	0	0	0	0	0	0	0	0	0	1	0	0	.000	.000
Godoy, Jose	L-R	5-11	180	10-13-94	.263	.318	.250	36	114	15	30	5	0	0	13	14	5	0	0	18	0	0	.307	.368
Gomez, Jose	R-R	5-11	183	1-30-92	.320	.267	.343	19	50	4	16	1	1	0	4	3	1	0	2	11	0	0	.380	.357
McElroy Jr., C.J.	R-R	5-10	180	5-29-93	.300	.250	.333	3	10	0	3	1	0	0	0	0	1	0	0	2	1	1	.400	.364
Medina, Rafael	R-R	6-2	170	10-24-91	.282	.297	.279	51	177	29	50	10	1	2	24	19	1	0	4	20	2	2	.384	.348
Mercado, Oscar	R-R	6-2	175	12-16-94	.209	.132	.232	42	163	18	34	5	4	1	14	17	3	0	3	39	12	4	.307	.290
Pina, Leobaldo	R-R	6-2	160	6-29-94	.273	.239	.285	48	176	29	48	3	5	0	13	12	2	0	0	30	8	2	.347	.326
Ray, Anthony	L-R	6-1	165	3-3-95	.233	.091	.262	43	129	16	30	3	2	0	5	7	2	1	1	30	6	3	.287	.281
Rivera, Chris	R-R	5-11	150	3-10-95	.195	.115	.215	39	133	18	26	6	0	5	19	9	2	0	1	33	1	1	.353	.255
Rodriguez, Elier	B-R	6-2	210	2-15-95	.280	.333	.265	37	107	14	30	6	0	0	11	10	2	1	2	27	0	1	.336	.347
Stone, Jake	L-R	6-0	220	10-22-90	.298	.118	.361	41	131	15	39	11	2	1	20	14	3	0	2	22	0	1	.435	.373
Taveras, Oscar	L-L	6-2	200	6-19-92	1.000	—	1.000	1	1	0	1	0	0	0	0	0	0	0	0	0	0	0	2.000	1.000
Torres, Carlos	R-R	6-3	160	10-1-92	.224	.156	.243	45	147	14	33	3	1	4	22	10	1	1	3	35	6	3	.340	.273

Pitching	B-T	HT	WT	DOB	W	L	ERA	G	GS	CG	SV	IP	H	R	ER	HR	BB	SO	AVG	vLH	vRH	K/9	BB/9
Barraclough, Kyle	R-R	6-3	225	5-23-90	0	1	13.50	3	0	0	0	3	7	5	5	0	2	5	.438	.375	.500	13.50	5.40
Billbrough, Logan	R-R	6-5	225	8-4-89	0	1	3.00	7	5	0	0	9	9	3	3	0	0	11	.265	.400	.158	11.00	0.00
Brito, Ismael	L-L	5-11	170	3-23-93	3	1	1.73	11	0	0	0	26	21	5	5	3	5	27	.228	.190	.239	9.35	1.73
Caballero, Juan	R-R	6-4	175	8-20-92	2	1	5.33	18	0	0	2	25	26	16	15	3	6	21	.257	.300	.230	7.46	2.13
Corrigan, Chris	R-R	6-2	155	12-24-87	0	0	11.57	2	0	0	0	2	4	4	3	0	1	4	.364	.500	.286	15.43	3.86
Escudero, Jhonatan	R-R	6-1	165	7-7-93	1	1	2.81	20	0	0	0	32	28	14	10	1	14	41	.239	.200	.269	11.53	3.94
Farinaro, Steven	R-R	6-0	170	8-18-95	1	3	6.29	10	6	0	0	24	36	18	17	2	6	21	.340	.413	.283	7.77	2.22
Flores, Fidencio	R-R	6-0	160	9-10-91	5	2	4.69	13	2	0	0	40	44	24	21	2	16	25	.267	.361	.212	5.58	3.57
Fornataro, Eric	R-R	6-1	225	1-2-88	0	0	3.00	3	0	0	0	3	3	2	1	0	1	3	.250	.000	.429	9.00	3.00
Gaviglio, Sam	R-R	6-1	200	5-22-90	0	0	0.00	2	1	0	0	8	4	0	0	0	1	9	.143	.000	.167	10.13	1.13
Gonzales, Marco	L-L	6-0	185	2-16-92	0	0	5.40	4	2	0	0	7	8	5	4	0	3	10	.276	.500	.190	13.50	4.05
Grana, Kyle	R-R	6-4	245	4-26-91	1	0	1.69	15	0	0	4	21	18	9	4	0	7	24	.240	.333	.167	10.13	2.95
Hawkins, Dylan	L-L	6-2	215	6-26-93	3	2	2.61	16	2	0	0	31	22	11	9	2	9	34	.198	.262	.159	9.87	2.61
Kaminsky, Rob	R-L	5-11	191	9-2-94	0	3	3.68	8	5	0	0	22	23	14	9	1	9	28	.261	.190	.284	11.45	3.68
Lee, Brandon	R-R	6-0	200	11-18-90	0	0	2.08	3	0	0	0	4	4	2	1	0	1	5	.222	.200	.231	10.38	2.08
Lopez, Stalyn	L-L	5-9	160	12-28-91	0	0	43.20	2	0	0	0	2	3	8	8	0	7	0	.500	1.000	.400	0.00	37.80
Lucas, Josh	R-R	6-6	185	11-5-90	0	1	13.50	1	0	0	0	3	6	6	5	0	0	3	.333	.250	.400	8.10	0.00
Machuca, Javier	L-L	6-3	200	11-21-92	0	0	0.00	3	0	0	0	3	0	0	0	0	2	0	.000	.000	.000	5.40	0.00
Mayers, Mike	R-R	6-4	185	12-6-91	1	0	1.50	5	3	0	0	12	6	4	2	1	6	13	.146	.118	.167	9.75	4.50
McKinney, Ian	L-L	5-11	185	11-18-94	1	0	0.89	10	5	0	0	30	23	7	3	0	12	24	.217	.043	.265	7.12	3.56
Nazario, Iden	L-L	6-0	190	3-28-89	0	0	0.00	1	0	0	0	2	0	0	0	0	1	2	.000	.000	.000	9.00	4.50
Perez, Dewen	L-L	6-0	175	9-29-94	2	4	3.23	11	7	0	0	39	29	19	14	0	23	34	.216	.222	.214	7.85	5.31
Perez, Juan	R-R	6-2	195	7-22-95	1	3	4.69	11	10	0	0	40	36	30	21	0	37	40	.242	.354	.155	8.93	8.26
Russell, Zach	R-R	6-2	185	7-27-89	0	0	0.00	2	0	0	0	2	2	0	0	0	0	2	.286	1.000	.167	9.00	0.00
Salazar, Hector	R-R	6-2	165	6-29-94	0	5	6.44	16	5	0	0	41	41	30	25	3	18	30	.256	.232	.269	6.53	3.92
Silva, Isaac	L-L	6-2	190	9-12-92	1	4	5.51	11	4	0	0	33	33	25	20	2	21	37	.266	.294	.256	10.19	5.79
Swagerty, Jordan	B-R	6-2	175	7-14-89	0	0	0.00	3	2	0	0	4	2	0	0	0	0	5	.154	.143	.167	11.25	0.00
Villegas, Kender	R-R	6-2	170	6-8-93	1	1	1.23	22	0	0	2	29	20	5	4	0	7	32	.196	.216	.185	9.82	2.15
Voss, Jay	L-L	6-4	195	4-22-87	1	1	0.00	4	0	0	0	4	4	2	0	0	1	6	.235	.000	.286	13.50	2.25

Fielding

Catcher	PCT	G	PO	A	E	DP	PB
Cruz	.971	8	60	6	2	0	4
Godoy	.988	24	215	29	3	3	4
Gomez	.990	16	88	9	1	0	0
Rodriguez	.993	19	132	13	1	2	16

First Base	PCT	G	PO	A	E	DP
Almaraz	.975	22	108	7	3	9
Cruz	1.000	4	19	1	0	1
Medina	1.000	5	40	2	0	4
Rodriguez	1.000	1	0	1	0	0
Stone	.993	39	267	18	2	21

Second Base	PCT	G	PO	A	E	DP
Alvarez	.951	8	17	22	2	7
Collymore	.826	14	18	20	8	3
Pina	1.000	5	3	18	0	2
Rivera	.947	34	51	73	7	19
Rodriguez	1.000	1	0	1	0	0

Third Base	PCT	G	PO	A	E	DP
Acevedo	—	1	0	0	0	0
Almaraz	1.000	3	0	3	0	0
Alvarez	.905	7	6	13	2	1
Medina	.938	44	45	60	7	7
Pina	.952	8	5	15	1	2

Shortstop	PCT	G	PO	A	E	DP
Mercado	.905	33	70	73	15	17
Pina	.948	26	42	68	6	10

Outfield	PCT	G	PO	A	E	DP
Acevedo	.984	26	60	3	1	2
Alvarez	—	1	0	0	0	0
Asbury	.971	42	63	3	2	1
Bautista	.956	29	41	2	2	0
Deol	1.000	4	4	0	0	0
McElroy Jr.	1.000	3	1	0	0	0
Pina	—	2	0	0	0	0
Ray	.952	40	60	0	3	0
Taveras	—	1	0	0	0	0
Torres	.937	43	85	4	6	1

DSL CARDINALS   ROOKIE
DOMINICAN SUMMER LEAGUE

Batting	B-T	HT	WT	DOB	AVG	vLH	vRH	G	AB	R	H	2B	3B	HR	RBI	BB	HBP	SH	SF	SO	SB	CS	SLG	OBP
Alvarado, Henry	R-R	6-3	195	1-30-96	.150	.200	.138	57	187	17	28	7	0	3	18	17	4	0	2	78	0	2	.235	.233
Baez, Jorge	R-R	5-11	180	3-17-94	.233	.000	.273	34	103	9	24	3	2	2	16	10	1	1	0	38	0	1	.359	.307
Bandes, Luis	R-R	6-1	200	5-15-96	.185	.217	.176	61	222	20	41	11	2	2	18	17	6	0	3	50	3	1	.279	.258
Cerdas, Jeffry	B-R	6-0	160	1-12-95	.230	.235	.228	28	74	11	17	1	0	1	2	10	1	1	0	13	1	0	.284	.329
Cordoba, Allen	R-R	6-1	175	12-6-95	.272	.227	.282	41	125	20	34	5	1	0	7	19	5	3	0	24	5	3	.328	.389
De La Cruz, Joaquin	R-R	6-2	195	10-13-95	.215	.161	.231	42	135	10	29	6	0	1	14	20	6	0	3	35	1	1	.281	.335
Encarnacion, Ruben	B-R	6-0	170	6-8-94	.225	.231	.224	43	160	29	36	3	2	0	9	21	3	1	1	24	15	5	.269	.324
Franco, Bladimil	R-R	6-0	170	10-29-93	.355	.467	.324	38	138	23	49	8	3	3	29	12	1	0	3	16	5	3	.522	.403
Lopez, Joshua	R-R	5-10	188	3-4-96	.173	.239	.148	55	168	20	29	10	0	2	21	29	3	0	2	54	7	1	.268	.302
Luna, Ramon	R-R	6-1	175	8-16-94	.164	.176	.161	49	152	20	25	6	0	1	10	18	0	2	0	44	10	3	.224	.253
Paulino, Diory	R-R	6-0	170	7-13-94	.200	.200	.200	18	55	5	11	1	0	1	7	5	4	0	1	16	2	2	.273	.308
Pena, Dionenrys	R-R	6-1	185	4-20-95	.226	.250	.222	23	62	9	14	3	1	0	5	3	2	1	0	13	0	0	.306	.284
Reyes, Robelys	B-R	5-9	150	7-25-90	.317	.333	.312	30	104	21	33	4	3	0	13	13	2	0	3	14	7	2	.413	.393
Ripoll, Sergio	R-R	6-0	180	4-16-94	.200	.214	.196	41	135	13	27	6	0	1	13	18	11	0	0	27	1	1	.267	.341
Sanchez, Yunior	R-R	5-11	160	6-12-95	.152	.000	.172	27	66	13	10	1	1	0	6	9	0	2	1	21	2	1	.197	.250
Sierra, Magneuris	L-L	5-11	160	4-7-96	.269	.279	.266	63	212	44	57	6	3	1	21	29	4	3	4	33	15	7	.340	.361
Sosa, Edmundo	R-R	5-11	170	3-6-96	.314	.436	.277	47	169	33	53	8	3	3	27	22	3	1	3	15	7	5	.450	.396

Pitching	B-T	HT	WT	DOB	W	L	ERA	G	GS	CG	SV	IP	H	R	ER	HR	BB	SO	AVG	vLH	vRH	K/9	BB/9
Arias, Estarlin	R-R	6-1	175	5-22-94	1	0	1.38	3	3	0	0	13	7	2	2	0	2	11	.163	.167	.160	7.62	1.38
Changarotty, Will	R-R	6-0	165	10-19-95	5	3	2.36	12	6	0	0	53	41	16	14	1	14	46	.211	.159	.237	7.76	2.36
De La Cruz, Andy	L-L	6-1	185	8-29-94	3	3	2.01	14	1	0	0	31	24	12	7	0	15	23	.209	.308	.180	6.61	4.31
Encarnacion, Virgilio	R-R	6-2	190	2-8-92	2	1	2.01	11	0	0	4	22	14	5	5	0	10	20	.194	.200	.193	8.06	4.03
Gavin, Frendy	L-L	6-0	170	9-14-94	1	1	6.32	10	0	0	0	16	12	14	11	0	15	10	.218	.385	.167	5.74	8.62
Gonzalez, Derian	R-R	6-3	190	1-31-95	1	2	4.83	12	6	0	2	41	40	26	22	0	28	40	.256	.256	.257	8.78	6.15
Lara, Jose	R-R	6-2	175	3-26-94	2	0	3.82	14	0	0	2	31	37	16	13	0	7	24	.298	.385	.259	7.04	2.05
Mateo, Julio	R-R	6-3	180	9-29-95	1	4	2.50	11	9	1	0	50	40	27	14	0	16	56	.207	.270	.177	10.01	2.86
Medina, Yeison	R-R	6-2	206	10-2-92	1	1	1.26	17	0	0	6	29	21	8	4	0	12	35	.202	.200	.203	10.99	3.77
Medrano, Ronald	R-R	6-0	170	9-17-95	2	2	2.80	8	8	0	0	35	37	12	11	1	11	28	.262	.273	.258	7.13	2.80
Negrette, Alirio	L-L	5-11	176	3-29-95	1	1	3.22	11	0	0	2	22	24	16	8	0	10	15	.270	.200	.284	6.04	4.03
Oca, David	L-L	5-10	165	7-4-95	2	3	3.63	11	6	0	0	45	41	28	18	3	19	51	.240	.098	.285	10.28	3.83
Parra, Frederis	R-R	6-3	162	10-22-94	4	1	2.08	9	9	0	0	43	31	15	10	2	15	28	.199	.240	.179	5.82	3.12
Rodriguez, Jorge L.	R-R	6-2	175	3-18-94	2	5	2.72	13	8	0	2	50	42	19	15	2	19	57	.226	.286	.200	10.33	3.44
Sanchez, Ronald	R-R	6-5	180	9-20-93	2	1	5.56	11	0	0	0	11	11	10	7	1	12	9	.234	.150	.296	7.15	9.53
Santos, Ramon	R-R	6-0	170	9-20-94	3	4	2.48	12	12	0	0	58	52	26	16	1	16	55	.240	.270	.223	8.53	2.48
Urena, Rigobert	L-L	6-4	170	2-8-95	0	2	4.56	9	3	0	0	24	21	14	12	2	16	17	.244	.222	.247	6.46	6.08
Vallejo, Esteban	R-R	6-4	190	12-9-93	1	2	2.89	12	0	0	1	28	25	17	9	0	18	18	.229	.194	.244	5.79	5.79

Fielding

Catcher	PCT	G	PO	A	E	DP	PB
Baez	1.000	2	12	1	0	0	0
Lopez	.963	52	339	56	15	0	11
Pena	.919	17	87	4	8	0	3
Ripoll	.981	14	90	15	2	1	2

First Base	PCT	G	PO	A	E	DP
Alvarado	.989	22	173	9	2	11
Baez	.994	21	162	13	1	18
De La Cruz	.978	10	85	3	2	8
Ripoll	.983	27	207	19	4	12

Second Base	PCT	G	PO	A	E	DP
Cerdas	.943	21	39	43	5	9
Cordoba	.963	11	26	26	2	4

	PCT	G	PO	A	E	DP
Encarnacion	.930	25	42	51	7	9
Reyes	.958	3	10	13	1	6
Sanchez	.964	18	35	46	3	10

Third Base	PCT	G	PO	A	E	DP
Baez	.882	12	7	23	4	2
Cerdas	.778	4	3	4	2	0
Cordoba	.857	1	1	5	1	1
De La Cruz	.856	30	18	59	13	7
Paulino	.871	10	9	18	4	2
Reyes	.935	22	18	40	4	5

Shortstop	PCT	G	PO	A	E	DP
Cerdas	1.000	1	1	1	0	0
Cordoba	.928	26	40	63	8	7

	PCT	G	PO	A	E	DP
Paulino	.826	5	6	13	4	1
Reyes	1.000	3	4	8	0	1
Sosa	.935	41	59	143	14	16

Outfield	PCT	G	PO	A	E	DP
Alvarado	.870	19	18	2	3	0
Bandes	.986	45	68	4	1	0
Encarnacion	.950	19	19	0	1	0
Franco	.952	34	36	4	2	0
Luna	.947	46	68	3	4	0
Sanchez	—	1	0	0	0	0
Sierra	.966	62	108	7	4	0

San Diego Padres

SEASON IN A SENTENCE: A middle-of-the-road offense and pitch-to-contact staff combined for a second straight 76-86 season, the Padres' fifth losing year out of the last six.

HIGH POINT: The Padres went 45-36 at home and 30-26 overall in May and June, though their opponents outscored them across both samples. The top individual moment came on Sept. 16, when 27-year-old righthander Andrew Cashner one-hit the Pirates while striking out seven, walking none and facing the minimum 27 batters. He carried a perfect game into the seventh inning that day, and in the bigger picture he turned in his best (and healthiest) big league season, going 10-9, 3.09 in 31 appearances (26 starts) while notching 6.6 strikeouts per nine innings and a 1.13 WHIP.

LOW POINT: Injuries once again dominated the headlines in San Diego. Starters Casey Kelly, Cory Luebke and Joe Wieland did not pitch at all as they rehabbed from Tommy John surgery. Meanwhile, catcher Yasmani Grandal sat out the first 50 games while serving a suspension for performance-enhancer use, then in game No. 28 of his comeback tore the ACL in his knee during a home-plate collision.

NOTABLE ROOKIES: Second baseman Jedd Gyorko took to his new position, batting .249/.301/.444 and leading the club—not to mention all rookies—with 23 home runs. He became the fifth rookie second baseman in history to belt 20 or more homers. Lefty Robbie Erlin (3-3, 4.12 in 11 games) and righty Burch Smith (1-3, 6.44 in 10 games) had varying degrees of success in the rotation. Righty relievers Brad Boxberger and Nick Vincent missed plenty of bats out of the bullpen.

KEY TRANSACTIONS: Though they weren't contenders in the National League in the second half, general manager Josh Byrnes jumped on the chance to acquire veteran talent when the Diamondbacks made Ian Kennedy available. The command-oriented 28-year-old went 4-2, 4.24 in 10 starts wearing a Padres uniform. San Diego surrendered bullpen lefty Joe Thatcher, Double-A closer Matt Stites and a supplemental second-round pick in 2014 to get a deal done.

DOWN ON THE FARM: Padres domestic affiliates finished with a .496 winning percentage, ranking No. 16, but Double-A San Antonio rode a dominant pitching staff to the Texas League title. Missions pitchers led the TL with a 3.20 ERA and 3.1 K-BB ratio.

OPENING DAY PAYROLL: $67.1 million (26th).

PLAYERS OF THE YEAR

MAJOR LEAGUE	MINOR LEAGUE
Will Venable rf	**Matt Wisler** rhp
.268/.312/.484	(High-A/Double-A)
22 HR, 22 SB	10-6, 2.78
Career-high 52 XBH	131 SO, 33 BB

ORGANIZATION LEADERS

BATTING *Minimum 250 AB

MAJORS

* AVG	Denorfia, Chris	.279
* OPS	Venable, Will	.796
HR	Gyorko, Jedd	23
RBI	Gyorko, Jedd	63

MINORS

* AVG	Anna, Dean, Tucson	.331
* OBP	Fuentes, Reymond, Tucson/San Antonio	.413
* SLG	Decker, Cody, Tucson/San Antonio	.515
R	Robertson, Dan, Tucson	91
H	Anna, Dean, Tucson	165
TB	Anna, Dean, Tucson	240
2B	Anna, Dean, Tucson	38
3B	Peterson, Jace, Lake Elsinore	13
HR	Medica, Tommy, San Antonio/AZL	20
RBI	Baltz, Jeremy, Lake Elsinore/Fort Wayne	87
BB	Kral, Robert, San Antonio/Lake Elsinore	78
SO	Adams, Brian, Fort Wayne	134
SB	Jankowski, Travis, Lake Elsinore	71

PITCHING #Minimum 75 IP

MAJORS

W	Stults, Eric	11
# ERA	Cashner, Andrew	3.09
SO	Stults, Eric	131
SV	Street, Huston	33

MINORS

W	Sampson, Keyvius, Tucson/San Antonio	12
L	Roach, Donn, San Antonio	12
# ERA	Eflin, Zach, Fort Wayne	2.73
G	McBryde, Jeremy, San Antonio	61
GS	Roach, Donn, San Antonio	28
SV	Mikolas, Miles, Tucson	26
IP	Roach, Donn, San Antonio	143
BB	Sampson, Keyvius, Tucson/San Antonio	62
SO	Sampson, Keyvius, Tucson/San Antonio	135
# AVG	Wisler, Matt, Lake Elsinore/San Antonio	.217

General Manager: Josh Byrnes. **Farm Director:** Randy Smith. **Scouting Director:** Billy Gasparino.

Class	Team	League	W	L	PCT	Finish	Manager
Majors	San Diego Padres	National	76	86	.469	8th (15)	Bud Black
Triple-A	Tucson Padres	Pacific Coast	77	67	.535	5th (16)	Pat Murphy
Double-A	San Antonio Missions	Texas League	78	61	.561	2nd (8)	Rich Dauer
High A	Lake Elsinore Storm	California	61	79	.436	9th (10)	Shawn Wooten
Low A	Fort Wayne Tincaps	Midwest	72	69	.511	6th (16)	Jose Valentin
Short-season	Eugene Emeralds	Northwest	27	49	.365	8th (8)	Jim Gabella
Rookie	Padres	Arizona	28	26	.519	5th (13)	Michael Collins
Overall 2013 Minor League Record			343	349	.436	16th (30)	

ORGANIZATION STATISTICS

NATIONAL LEAGUE

Batting	B-T	HT	WT	DOB	AVG	vLH	vRH	G	AB	R	H	2B	3B	HR	RBI	BB	HBP	SH	SF	SO	SB	CS	SLG	OBP
Alonso, Yonder	L-R	6-2	250	4-8-87	.281	.242	.296	97	334	34	94	11	0	6	45	32	2	0	7	47	6	0	.368	.341
Amarista, Alexi	L-R	5-8	150	4-6-89	.236	.220	.239	146	368	35	87	14	4	5	32	22	2	3	1	57	4	2	.337	.282
Baker, John	L-R	6-1	215	1-20-81	.150	.167	.147	16	40	0	6	0	0	0	2	6	0	0	0	12	0	0	.150	.261
Blanks, Kyle	R-R	6-6	265	9-11-86	.243	.282	.220	88	280	31	68	14	0	8	35	21	5	0	2	85	1	1	.379	.305
Cabrera, Everth	B-R	5-10	190	11-17-86	.283	.365	.248	95	381	54	108	15	5	4	31	41	2	10	1	69	37	12	.381	.355
Cedeno, Ronny	R-R	6-0	195	2-2-83	.268	.324	.247	38	123	12	33	2	2	2	9	8	1	1	0	31	3	3	.366	.318
Ciriaco, Pedro	R-R	6-0	180	9-27-85	.238	.241	.235	23	63	5	15	1	1	1	4	3	1	1	0	10	6	0	.333	.284
Decker, Jaff	L-L	5-10	190	2-23-90	.154	.000	.167	13	26	3	4	0	0	1	2	3	0	1	1	4	0	1	.269	.233
Denorfia, Chris	R-R	6-0	195	7-15-80	.279	.284	.276	144	473	67	132	21	2	10	47	42	1	0	4	84	11	0	.395	.337
Forsythe, Logan	R-R	6-1	195	1-14-87	.214	.211	.215	75	220	22	47	6	1	6	19	19	2	1	1	54	6	1	.332	.281
Fuentes, Reymond	L-L	6-0	160	2-12-91	.152	.167	.148	23	33	4	5	0	0	0	1	3	0	0	0	16	3	0	.152	.222
Grandal, Yasmani	B-R	6-2	215	11-8-88	.216	.233	.200	28	88	13	19	8	0	1	9	18	1	0	1	18	0	0	.341	.352
Guzman, Jesus	R-R	6-1	200	6-14-84	.226	.245	.208	126	288	33	65	17	0	9	35	27	2	1	0	79	3	0	.378	.297
Gyorko, Jedd	R-R	5-10	210	9-23-88	.249	.264	.244	125	486	62	121	26	0	23	63	32	4	0	2	123	1	1	.444	.301
Headley, Chase	B-R	6-2	220	5-9-84	.250	.248	.251	141	520	59	130	35	2	13	50	67	11	0	2	142	8	4	.400	.347
Hundley, Nick	R-R	6-1	195	9-8-83	.233	.183	.250	114	373	35	87	19	0	13	44	26	5	1	3	98	1	0	.389	.290
Kotsay, Mark	L-L	6-0	220	12-2-75	.194	.118	.203	104	155	8	30	2	0	1	12	13	0	1	2	25	0	2	.226	.253
Maybin, Cameron	R-R	6-3	205	4-4-87	.157	.133	.167	14	51	7	8	1	0	1	5	4	1	1	0	9	4	1	.235	.232
Medica, Tommy	R-R	6-1	190	4-9-88	.290	.154	.321	19	69	9	20	2	0	3	10	10	0	0	0	23	0	0	.449	.380
Quentin, Carlos	R-R	6-2	240	8-28-82	.275	.284	.272	82	276	42	76	21	0	13	44	31	9	0	4	55	0	0	.493	.363
Ransom, Cody	R-R	6-2	200	2-17-76	.000	.000	.000	5	11	0	0	0	0	0	0	0	0	0	0	5	0	0	.000	.000
2-team total (57 Chicago)					.189	—	—	62	169	21	32	10	1	9	20	22	1	1	0	62	0	0	.420	.286
Rivera, Rene	R-R	5-10	230	7-31-83	.254	.235	.260	23	67	4	17	3	1	0	7	2	0	0	2	16	0	0	.328	.268
Robinson, Chris	R-R	6-0	205	5-12-84	.167	.167	.167	8	12	1	2	0	0	0	0	3	0	0	0	3	0	0	.417	.167
Venable, Will	L-L	6-2	210	10-29-82	.268	.276	.266	151	481	64	129	22	8	22	53	29	2	2	1	118	22	6	.484	.312

Pitching	B-T	HT	WT	DOB	W	L	ERA	G	GS	CG	SV	IP	H	R	ER	HR	BB	SO	AVG	vLH	vRH	K/9	BB/9
Bass, Anthony	R-R	6-2	195	11-1-87	0	0	5.36	24	0	0	0	42	51	26	25	4	20	31	.297	.299	.295	6.64	4.29
Boxberger, Brad	R-R	6-2	220	5-27-88	0	1	2.86	18	0	0	1	22	19	9	7	3	13	24	.250	.182	.302	9.82	5.32
Brach, Brad	R-R	6-6	215	4-12-86	1	0	3.19	33	0	0	0	31	36	15	11	3	19	31	.303	.232	.365	9.00	5.52
Cashner, Andrew	R-R	6-6	220	9-11-86	10	9	3.09	31	26	1	0	175	151	68	60	12	47	128	.233	.251	.217	6.58	2.42
Erlin, Robbie	L-L	5-11	190	10-8-90	3	3	4.12	11	9	0	0	55	53	26	25	6	15	40	.255	.318	.225	6.59	2.47
Gregerson, Luke	L-R	6-3	200	5-14-84	6	8	2.71	73	0	0	4	66	49	24	20	3	18	64	.203	.216	.192	8.68	2.44
Hynes, Colt	L-L	5-11	200	6-28-85	0	0	9.00	22	0	0	0	17	25	17	17	3	9	13	.338	.156	.476	6.88	4.76
Kennedy, Ian	R-R	6-0	190	12-19-84	4	2	4.24	10	10	0	0	57	52	29	27	9	25	55	.239	.219	.257	8.63	3.92
2-team total (21 Arizona)					7	10	4.91	31	31	0	0	181	180	108	99	27	73	163	—	—	—	8.09	3.62
Layne, Tommy	L-L	6-0	190	11-2-84	0	2	2.08	14	0	0	0	9	10	4	2	1	5	6	.323	.333	.300	6.23	5.19
Marquis, Jason	R-R	6-1	220	8-21-78	9	5	4.05	20	20	0	0	118	111	61	53	18	68	72	.257	.267	.249	5.51	5.20
Mikolas, Miles	R-R	6-5	215	8-23-88	0	0	0.00	2	0	0	0	2	0	0	0	0	1	1	.000	.000	.000	5.40	5.40
O'Sullivan, Sean	R-R	6-1	240	9-1-87	0	2	3.96	7	3	0	0	25	31	12	11	0	14	12	.310	.348	.278	4.32	5.04
Richard, Clayton	L-L	6-5	245	9-12-83	2	5	7.01	12	11	0	0	53	65	44	41	13	21	24	.308	.226	.335	4.10	3.59
Ross, Tyson	R-R	6-6	230	4-22-87	3	8	3.17	35	16	0	0	125	100	51	44	8	44	119	.225	.252	.198	8.57	3.17
Smith, Burch	R-R	6-4	215	4-12-90	1	3	6.44	10	7	0	0	36	39	26	26	9	21	46	.269	.275	.263	11.39	5.20
Stauffer, Tim	R-R	6-1	215	6-2-82	3	1	3.75	43	0	0	0	70	59	29	29	7	20	64	.231	.190	.269	8.27	2.58
Street, Huston	R-R	6-0	195	8-2-83	2	5	2.70	58	0	0	33	57	44	17	17	12	14	46	.213	.208	.217	7.31	2.22
Stults, Eric	L-L	6-0	230	12-9-79	11	13	3.93	33	33	2	0	204	219	97	89	18	40	131	.274	.185	.301	5.79	1.77
Thatcher, Joe	L-L	6-2	230	10-4-81	3	1	2.10	50	0	0	0	30	28	7	7	3	4	29	.243	.215	.280	8.70	1.20
2-team total (22 Arizona)					3	2	3.20	72	0	0	0	39	40	14	14	4	10	36	—	—	—	8.24	2.29
Thayer, Dale	R-R	6-0	215	12-17-80	3	5	3.32	69	0	0	1	65	59	25	24	8	22	64	.244	.261	.229	8.86	3.05
Vincent, Nick	R-R	6-0	185	7-12-86	6	3	2.14	45	0	0	1	46	33	11	11	1	11	49	.202	.301	.122	9.52	2.14
Volquez, Edinson	R-R	6-0	225	7-3-83	0	2	6.01	27	27	0	0	142	168	100	95	14	69	116	.291	.305	.276	7.33	4.36
2-team total (6 Los Angeles)					9	12	5.71	33	32	0	0	170	193	114	108	19	77	142	—	—	—	7.50	4.07
Weber, Thad	R-R	6-2	205	9-28-84	0	0	2.00	3	0	0	0	9	5	2	2	1	5	6	.172	.125	.190	6.00	5.00

SAN DIEGO PADRES

Fielding

Catcher

Catcher	PCT	G	PO	A	E	DP	PB
Baker	1.000	14	81	9	0	2	0
Grandal	.990	26	195	11	2	1	1
Hundley	.988	112	729	63	10	12	4
Rivera	1.000	21	185	13	0	1	2
Robinson	1.000	2	8	0	0	0	0

First Base

First Base	PCT	G	PO	A	E	DP
Alonso	.996	92	761	58	3	72
Blanks	.991	34	199	14	2	19
Grandal	1.000	1	4	0	0	1
Guzman	.990	38	280	15	3	24
Kotsay	1.000	5	26	2	0	2
Medica	1.000	19	153	13	0	6

Second Base

Second Base	PCT	G	PO	A	E	DP
Alonso	—	1	0	0	0	0
Amarista	.989	23	40	48	1	10

	PCT	G	PO	A	E	DP
Ciriaco	1.000	2	3	6	0	1
Forsythe	.988	34	59	99	2	21
Guzman	1.000	1	1	0	0	0
Gyorko	.992	117	196	302	4	54

Third Base

Third Base	PCT	G	PO	A	E	DP
Alonso	—	1	0	0	0	0
Amarista	1.000	9	3	5	0	1
Cedeno	—	1	0	0	0	0
Forsythe	.950	11	5	14	1	0
Guzman	.714	3	3	2	2	0
Gyorko	.933	13	1	27	2	0
Headley	.968	140	83	252	11	18
Ransom	.900	4	1	8	1	0

Shortstop

Shortstop	PCT	G	PO	A	E	DP
Amarista	.974	13	11	26	1	5
Cabrera	.987	95	143	298	6	59

	PCT	G	PO	A	E	DP
Cedeno	.985	35	46	84	2	14
Ciriaco	.957	18	25	42	3	12
Forsythe	.961	11	15	34	2	4

Outfield

Outfield	PCT	G	PO	A	E	DP
Alonso	—	1	0	0	0	0
Amarista	.982	95	160	5	3	1
Blanks	.980	61	94	2	2	2
Decker	1.000	8	15	2	0	0
Denorfia	.981	139	247	13	5	3
Forsythe	1.000	13	11	0	0	0
Fuentes	.958	17	23	0	1	0
Guzman	.980	40	50	0	1	0
Kotsay	1.000	25	17	1	0	0
Maybin	1.000	14	33	0	0	0
Quentin	.991	69	105	1	1	0
Venable	.989	143	271	3	3	1

TUCSON PADRES   TRIPLE-A
PACIFIC COAST LEAGUE

Batting	B-T	HT	WT	DOB	AVG	vLH	vRH	G	AB	R	H	2B	3B	HR	RBI	BB	HBP	SH	SF	SO	SB	CS	SLG	OBP
Allen, Brandon	L-R	6-2	235	2-12-86	.267	.195	.282	119	423	64	113	24	7	17	76	55	0	0	6	87	6	0	.478	.347
Alonso, Yonder	L-R	6-2	250	4-8-87	.571	.167	.875	4	14	1	8	0	0	0	2	0	0	0	0	0	0	1	.571	.571
Anna, Dean	L-R	5-11	180	11-24-86	.331	.288	.340	132	498	90	165	38	5	9	73	61	11	4	8	65	3	7	.482	.410
Baker, John	L-R	6-1	215	1-20-81	.231	.400	.125	4	13	2	3	0	0	0	0	2	1	0	0	5	0	0	.231	.375
2-team total (40 Albuquerque)					.205	—	—	44	146	16	30	1	0	4	18	20	1	0	2	38	0	1	.295	.302
Blanks, Kyle	R-R	6-6	265	9-11-86	.237	.333	.219	12	38	8	9	3	0	1	4	6	2	0	0	10	0	0	.395	.370
Buck, Travis	L-R	6-2	230	11-18-83	.256	.185	.276	35	125	19	32	11	0	5	26	7	1	0	2	20	0	0	.464	.296
Burke, Chris	R-R	6-1	205	4-25-90	.333	.000	.333	4	3	0	1	0	0	0	0	0	0	0	0	1	0	0	.333	.333
Carroll, Sawyer	L-R	6-4	215	5-9-86	.167	—	.167	5	12	1	2	0	0	0	2	0	0	0	0	4	0	1	.167	.286
Contreras, Anthony	L-R	5-11	185	9-26-83	.154	.000	.167	7	13	2	2	1	0	0	2	1	0	0	0	2	0	0	.231	.214
Darnell, James	R-R	6-2	215	1-19-87	.246	.250	.245	15	61	5	15	5	1	0	10	3	0	0	0	12	0	2	.361	.281
Decker, Cody	R-R	5-11	220	1-17-87	.272	.229	.283	113	324	45	88	24	5	17	60	24	5	3	1	98	0	0	.534	.349
Decker, Jaff	L-L	5-10	190	2-23-90	.286	.260	.291	105	350	63	100	23	1	10	40	55	1	6	3	94	4	6	.443	.381
Forsythe, Logan	R-R	6-1	195	1-14-87	.360	.250	.412	8	25	6	9	2	2	2	5	8	0	0	0	7	0	0	.840	.515
Francisco, Ben	R-R	6-1	195	10-23-81	.241	.268	.233	60	187	20	45	8	1	1	16	18	1	2	1	38	6	1	.310	.309
Fuentes, Reymond	L-L	6-0	160	2-12-91	.418	.308	.452	14	55	7	23	4	0	0	8	10	1	1	0	10	6	1	.491	.515
Gale, Rocky	R-R	6-0	180	2-22-88	.200	.500	.167	8	20	1	4	1	0	0	2	0	0	0	0	2	0	0	.250	.200
Galvez, Jonathan	R-R	6-2	200	1-18-91	.278	.244	.288	112	410	66	114	24	1	6	51	34	7	2	2	104	22	7	.385	.342
Grandal, Yasmani	B-R	6-2	215	11-8-88	.306	.263	.385	9	36	3	11	3	0	0	2	2	0	0	0	8	0	0	.389	.342
Hagerty, Jason	B-R	6-3	230	9-13-87	.160	.000	.182	12	25	2	4	0	0	0	3	5	1	0	0	3	0	0	.160	.323
Maybin, Cameron	R-R	6-3	205	4-4-87	.261	.308	.242	15	46	7	12	1	0	4	5	10	0	0	0	9	1	1	.543	.393
Merchan, Jesus	R-R	5-11	180	3-26-81	.254	.294	.238	70	181	18	46	9	1	0	18	9	3	2	1	22	1	2	.315	.299
Miller, Justin	R-R	5-9	190	12-14-88	.360	.364	.357	9	25	7	9	1	0	2	1	0	0	0	0	5	1	0	.400	.385
Moore, Scott	L-R	6-2	195	11-17-83	.260	.261	.259	39	131	15	34	7	0	3	10	14	1	0	0	31	0	1	.382	.336
2-team total (81 Sacramento)					.271	—	—	120	424	66	115	33	0	14	66	50	6	1	4	107	0	2	.448	.353
Moreno, Edwin	L-L	6-1	190	10-27-93	.500	—	.500	2	2	0	1	0	0	0	1	0	0	0	0	0	0	0	.500	.500
Petit, Gregorio	R-R	5-10	195	12-10-84	.292	.276	.295	134	503	55	147	26	3	4	61	40	2	6	4	75	5	3	.380	.344
Rivera, Rene	R-R	5-10	230	7-31-83	.343	.373	.333	74	251	36	86	18	0	5	38	17	2	1	5	42	0	2	.474	.382
Robertson, Dan	R-R	5-8	175	9-30-85	.285	.276	.289	136	484	91	138	24	9	2	53	60	10	5	6	63	23	6	.384	.371
Robinson, Chris	R-R	6-0	220	5-12-84	.316	.303	.320	39	133	20	42	5	0	0	17	3	2	3	1	18	2	2	.353	.338
Rodriguez, Eddy	R-R	6-0	220	12-1-85	.210	.000	.239	27	81	8	17	9	0	2	10	4	0	0	0	26	0	0	.395	.247
Sams, Kalian	R-R	6-2	248	8-25-86	.160	.444	.098	24	50	5	8	2	0	1	3	7	0	0	0	21	0	0	.260	.263
Wilson, Mike	R-R	6-2	245	6-29-83	.291	.323	.280	76	220	32	64	13	1	7	42	20	3	0	3	63	1	8	.455	.354

Pitching	B-T	HT	WT	DOB	W	L	ERA	G	GS	CG	SV	IP	H	R	ER	HR	BB	SO	AVG	vLH	vRH	K/9	BB/9
Andriese, Matt	R-R	6-3	210	8-28-89	3	5	4.45	12	10	0	0	59	64	32	29	2	12	42	.287	.312	.255	6.44	1.84
Bass, Anthony	R-R	6-2	195	11-1-87	4	6	5.45	15	15	0	0	79	108	51	48	11	17	60	.331	.379	.293	6.81	1.93
Bonine, Eddie	R-R	6-5	220	6-6-81	0	2	9.82	7	4	0	0	18	40	21	20	4	11	4	.460	.538	.396	1.96	5.40
2-team total (4 Reno)					0	2	8.58	11	5	0	0	28	51	29	27	6	14	10	—	—	—	3.18	4.45
Boscan, Wilfredo	R-R	6-2	160	10-26-89	1	3	6.70	14	6	0	1	43	61	35	32	9	10	22	.330	.333	.327	4.60	2.09
Boxberger, Brad	R-R	6-2	220	5-27-88	2	4	3.61	42	0	0	5	57	50	24	23	3	19	89	.235	.182	.272	13.97	2.98
Brach, Brad	R-R	6-6	215	4-12-86	4	3	2.84	33	0	0	3	44	43	15	14	5	14	44	.254	.329	.198	8.93	2.84
Branham, Matt	R-R	6-2	205	9-28-87	0	1	15.00	1	1	0	0	3	7	5	5	1	3	2	.438	.444	.429	6.00	9.00
Cortes, Dan	R-R	6-6	235	3-4-87	0	0	0.00	3	0	0	0	4	2	0	0	0	0	1	.143	.000	.222	2.25	0.00
De Los Santos, Fautino	R-R	6-2	225	2-15-86	0	1	3.86	2	0	0	0	2	4	1	1	0	2	1	.400	.500	.333	15.43	0.00
Erlin, Robbie	L-L	5-11	190	10-8-90	8	3	5.07	20	20	0	0	99	125	65	56	11	34	84	.307	.306	.307	7.61	3.08
Geer, Josh	R-R	6-3	195	6-2-83	0	1	6.75	1	1	0	0	4	5	3	3	0	2	1	.333	.400	.200	2.25	4.50
Gonzalez, Greg	R-R	5-11	190	9-19-88	0	0	3.38	4	0	0	0	5	6	3	2	1	3	3	.273	.250	.286	5.06	5.06
Hynes, Colt	L-L	5-11	200	6-28-85	1	3	1.80	31	0	0	4	35	33	10	7	1	2	42	.248	.169	.311	10.80	0.51
Ibarra, Jeff	L-L	6-0	180	8-18-87	0	0	30.86	2	0	0	0	2	8	8	8	1	5	2	.533	.667	.500	7.71	11.57
Jackson, Matt	R-R	6-4	195	12-18-87	0	0	8.10	1	1	0	0	3	7	3	3	0	2	4	.412	.000		10.80	5.40
Kelly, Ryan	R-R	6-2	180	10-30-87	1	1	3.60	14	1	0	1	20	22	8	8	1	9	18	.293	.367	.244	8.10	4.05

					W	L	ERA	G	GS	CG	SV	IP	H	R	ER	HR	BB	SO	AVG	vLH	vRH	H/9	BB/9
Kloess, Brandon	R-R	6-2	195	12-9-84	3	6	4.99	41	14	0	0	101	120	63	56	10	39	97	.294	.339	.259	8.64	3.48
Lane, Jason	R-L	6-2	225	12-22-76	2	2	5.24	11	6	0	0	46	55	31	27	7	6	33	.293	.271	.302	6.41	1.17
Layne, Tommy	L-L	6-2	190	11-2-84	2	4	4.50	49	0	0	0	46	49	29	23	1	27	41	.275	.227	.311	8.02	5.28
Lollis, Matt	R-R	6-9	250	9-11-90	0	1	6.23	3	0	0	0	4	7	5	3	0	4	5	.350	.400	.333	10.38	8.31
Lopez, Arturo	L-L	5-9	165	2-22-83	1	0	4.61	6	2	0	0	14	14	7	7	3	2	8	.259	.385	.220	5.27	1.32
Mikolas, Miles	R-R	6-5	215	8-23-88	4	2	3.25	54	0	0	26	61	62	25	22	6	17	40	.265	.266	.264	5.90	2.51
O'Sullivan, Sean	R-R	6-1	240	9-1-87	8	5	3.83	20	20	0	0	115	130	55	49	7	31	99	.283	.246	.310	7.75	2.43
Quackenbush, Kevin	R-R	6-3	220	11-28-88	8	2	2.91	28	0	0	4	34	33	14	11	0	19	38	.256	.204	.293	10.06	5.03
Ray, Jason	R-R	5-11	210	7-14-84	0	0	9.95	5	0	0	0	6	8	8	7	2	2	4	.320	.364	.286	5.68	2.84
Reyes, Jorge	B-R	6-3	195	12-7-87	6	3	5.28	42	4	0	0	75	83	45	44	5	38	72	.287	.285	.289	8.64	4.56
Richard, Clayton	L-L	6-5	245	9-12-83	0	1	2.25	2	2	0	0	12	10	3	3	0	0	12	.227	.125	.250	9.00	0.00
Ross, Tyson	R-R	6-6	230	4-22-87	1	1	4.63	4	2	0	0	12	12	6	6	0	6	9	.273	.238	.304	6.94	4.63
Sampson, Keyvius	R-R	6-0	185	1-6-91	2	3	7.11	9	9	0	0	38	44	32	30	5	29	25	.306	.367	.262	5.92	6.87
Smith, Burch	R-R	6-4	215	4-12-90	5	1	3.39	12	12	0	0	61	56	24	23	4	17	65	.246	.263	.233	9.59	2.51
Stange, Daniel	R-R	6-2	210	12-22-85	1	0	4.15	26	0	0	0	39	34	21	18	5	24	43	.233	.234	.232	9.92	5.54
2-team total (26 Salt Lake)					5	1	4.52	52	0	0	5	66	65	37	33	6	37	73	—	—		10.01	5.07
Stauffer, Tim	R-R	6-1	215	6-2-82	2	2	3.16	8	8	0	0	43	50	16	15	1	15	38	.299	.264	.338	8.02	3.16
Vincent, Nick	R-R	6-0	185	7-12-86	4	3	3.55	24	0	0	0	25	26	11	10	4	12	24	.257	.289	.238	8.53	4.26
Weber, Thad	R-R	6-2	205	9-28-84	4	1	3.93	6	6	0	0	34	38	16	15	0	4	26	.277	.329	.219	6.82	1.05

Fielding

Catcher	PCT	G	PO	A	E	DP	PB
Baker	1.000	3	18	1	0	1	1
Decker	1.000	10	26	1	0	0	2
Gale	1.000	7	28	6	0	0	1
Grandal	1.000	5	36	6	0	0	0
Hagerty	.978	8	43	1	1	0	1
Rivera	.993	68	513	56	4	10	9
Robinson	.994	39	292	27	2	4	3
Rodriguez	.988	24	154	13	2	2	1

First Base	PCT	G	PO	A	E	DP
Allen	.997	82	580	46	2	44
Alonso	1.000	4	28	1	0	2
Blanks	.980	7	44	5	1	6
Darnell	1.000	1	11	1	0	3
Decker	.998	69	472	43	1	40
Hagerty	1.000	1	1	0	0	0
Rivera	1.000	3	35	3	0	5

Second Base	PCT	G	PO	A	E	DP
Anna	.982	72	105	216	6	40
Contreras	1.000	2	5	4	0	1

	PCT	G	PO	A	E	DP
Forsythe	.900	3	4	5	1	0
Galvez	.959	74	116	185	13	28
Merchan	1.000	2	2	4	0	2
Robertson	1.000	1	0	4	0	1

Third Base	PCT	G	PO	A	E	DP
Anna	1.000	7	8	6	0	1
Contreras	.667	3	0	2	1	0
Darnell	1.000	3	1	4	0	0
Decker	.800	1	0	4	1	0
Galvez	.818	13	4	14	4	2
Merchan	.946	58	29	76	6	3
Miller	1.000	1	0	1	0	0
Moore	.964	36	26	54	3	7
Petit	.975	48	41	77	3	5
Robertson	—	1	0	0	0	0

Shortstop	PCT	G	PO	A	E	DP
Anna	.979	60	63	172	5	32
Forsythe	.895	4	8	9	2	3
Merchan	1.000	1	0	3	0	0
Petit	.963	91	131	230	14	46

Outfield	PCT	G	PO	A	E	DP
Allen	.941	41	46	2	3	2
Anna	—	1	0	0	0	0
Blanks	1.000	5	9	0	0	0
Buck	1.000	30	49	2	0	0
Carroll	.750	3	3	0	1	0
Darnell	1.000	9	11	1	0	0
Decker	.976	104	192	13	5	6
Francisco	.981	45	47	5	1	1
Fuentes	1.000	14	46	0	0	0
Galvez	1.000	22	36	2	0	0
Lane	1.000	1	1	0	0	0
Maybin	1.000	13	26	0	0	0
Miller	1.000	5	7	0	0	0
Robertson	.976	129	277	12	7	2
Sams	.929	13	13	0	1	0
Wilson	.990	56	90	6	1	1

SAN ANTONIO MISSIONS
DOUBLE-A

TEXAS LEAGUE

Batting	B-T	HT	WT	DOB	AVG	vLH	vRH	G	AB	R	H	2B	3B	HR	RBI	BB	HBP	SH	SF	SO	SB	CS	SLG	OBP
Asencio, Yeison	R-R	6-1	225	11-14-89	.261	.230	.270	74	291	25	76	15	3	2	32	13	3	0	2	29	3	2	.354	.298
Bisson, Chris	L-R	5-11	185	8-14-89	.191	.200	.190	32	89	8	17	5	1	0	11	10	1	0	0	28	2	2	.270	.280
Blackwood, Jake	R-R	6-0	195	9-14-85	.259	.300	.251	126	478	53	124	24	1	7	61	22	3	0	2	78	2	2	.358	.295
Burke, Chris	R-R	6-1	205	4-25-90	.200	.000	.200	4	5	1	1	1	0	0	4	1	1	1	0	2	0	0	.400	.429
Buschini, Adam	R-R	6-2	205	5-6-87	.239	.267	.231	91	285	40	68	9	3	8	32	19	2	4	2	52	13	6	.375	.289
Cabrera, Felix	R-R	6-0	170	7-14-89	.000	.000	.000	2	3	0	0	0	0	0	0	1	0	0	0	1	0	0	.000	.250
Contreras, Anthony	L-R	5-11	185	9-26-83	.167	.200	.163	16	54	4	9	1	1	0	2	7	0	0	0	8	1	0	.222	.262
Decker, Cody	R-R	5-11	220	1-17-87	.171	.000	.194	10	35	6	6	0	0	2	6	5	0	0	0	14	0	0	.343	.275
Del Castillo, Miguel	R-R	5-10	170	10-14-91	.000	—	.000	1	1	0	0	0	0	0	0	0	0	0	0	1	0	0	.000	.000
Fuentes, Reymond	L-L	6-0	160	2-12-91	.316	.292	.320	93	345	56	109	21	2	6	35	41	6	9	2	71	29	10	.441	.399
Gale, Rocky	R-R	6-0	180	2-22-88	.246	.278	.240	62	207	15	51	5	0	1	22	10	2	3	2	19	0	4	.285	.285
Gyorko, Jedd	R-R	5-10	210	9-23-88	1.000	—	1.000	1	1	0	1	0	0	0	0	0	0	0	0	0	0	0	1.000	1.000
Hedges, Austin	R-R	6-1	190	8-18-92	.224	.167	.236	20	67	4	15	3	0	0	8	6	1	1	0	9	3	1	.269	.297
Kirby-Jones, A.J.	R-R	6-0	215	10-2-88	.238	.250	.235	58	168	18	40	10	0	5	22	15	2	0	1	55	1	2	.387	.306
Kral, Robert	L-R	5-10	195	3-28-89	.154	.125	.158	21	65	6	10	1	0	3	8	15	0	1	0	14	0	0	.308	.313
Limonta, Johan	L-L	6-0	205	8-4-83	.255	.163	.275	72	247	30	63	12	0	4	19	37	1	0	1	55	0	1	.352	.353
Medica, Tommy	R-R	6-1	190	4-9-88	.296	.264	.304	76	280	48	83	20	3	18	57	28	8	0	4	67	4	2	.582	.372
Miller, Justin	R-R	5-9	190	12-14-88	.195	.333	.171	19	41	8	8	0	0	0	2	6	3	0	1	16	4	2	.195	.333
Noel, Rico	R-R	5-9	175	1-11-89	.266	.272	.265	131	496	74	132	23	5	0	41	52	13	10	5	119	59	19	.333	.348
Orr, Lee	R-R	6-3	215	10-23-88	.226	.200	.231	19	62	9	14	4	0	1	6	4	4	0	1	24	1	2	.339	.310
Rodriguez, Eddy	R-R	6-0	220	12-1-85	.240	.240	.240	56	200	20	48	11	1	4	26	12	0	0	2	58	0	1	.365	.280
Rodriguez, Jeremy	B-R	5-8	185	8-30-89	.250	.000	.300	5	12	0	3	1	0	0	0	0	0	0	0	1	0	0	.333	.250
Sams, Kalian	R-R	6-2	248	8-25-86	.250	.273	.246	26	80	16	20	7	0	10	27	20	2	0	0	24	4	0	.713	.412
2-team total (20 Frisco)					.268		—	46	157	27	42	8	0	14	37	28	2	0	1	44	10	0	.586	.383
Spangenberg, Cory	R-L	6-0	195	3-16-91	.289	.234	.305	76	287	35	83	10	3	2	20	17	2	11	2	61	19	11	.366	.331
Valdez, Jeudy	R-R	5-10	190	5-5-89	.251	.284	.245	125	443	46	111	29	5	10	49	27	5	1	2	106	16	12	.406	.300
Williams, Everett	L-R	5-10	200	10-1-90	.257	.180	.270	89	331	37	85	11	1	2	31	28	0	1	3	81	10	4	.314	.312

Pitching

Pitching	B-T	HT	WT	DOB	W	L	ERA	G	GS	CG	SV	IP	H	R	ER	HR	BB	SO	AVG	vLH	vRH	K/9	BB/9
Andriese, Matt	R-R	6-3	210	8-28-89	8	2	2.37	15	15	0	0	76	71	26	20	3	17	63	.242	.238	.246	7.46	2.01
Bonine, Eddie	R-R	6-5	220	6-6-81	4	3	3.76	11	11	1	0	69	66	32	29	5	16	15	.260	.265	.255	1.95	2.08
Boscan, Wilfredo	R-R	6-2	160	10-26-89	0	1	4.26	5	4	0	0	19	21	11	9	3	7	11	.266	.184	.341	5.21	3.32
Branham, Matt	R-R	6-5	220	9-28-87	4	2	2.61	22	0	0	0	31	20	11	9	2	14	36	.183	.211	.169	10.45	4.06
Campos, Leonel	R-R	6-3	185	7-17-87	1	0	0.88	26	0	0	2	31	14	5	3	0	16	43	.137	.175	.113	12.62	4.70
DePaula, Jose	L-L	6-1	170	3-4-90	4	6	3.86	14	14	0	0	75	84	42	32	3	11	57	.284	.290	.282	6.87	1.33
Geer, Josh	R-R	6-3	195	6-2-83	8	5	3.41	34	11	0	2	100	114	47	38	11	24	79	.288	.270	.300	7.09	2.15
Hynes, Colt	L-L	5-11	200	6-28-85	1	0	0.73	10	0	0	0	12	10	1	1	0	0	16	.233	.063	.333	11.68	0.00
Ibarra, Jeff	L-L	6-6	180	8-18-87	3	1	5.88	57	0	0	0	52	59	35	34	5	11	52	.278	.250	.298	9.00	1.90
Jackson, Matt	R-R	6-4	195	12-18-87	0	1	12.00	2	0	0	0	3	5	4	4	0	3	1	.385	.400	.375	3.00	9.00
Kelly, Ryan	R-R	6-2	180	10-30-87	1	2	5.13	37	0	0	1	47	49	27	27	8	20	37	.266	.257	.272	7.04	3.86
Lara, Robert	R-R	6-2	225	11-25-86	0	0	8.68	8	0	0	0	9	11	9	9	2	4	9	.289	.176	.381	8.68	3.86
Lollis, Matt	R-R	6-9	250	9-11-90	1	3	6.28	32	0	0	0	39	51	29	27	6	24	27	.311	.318	.306	6.28	5.59
McBryde, Jeremy	R-R	6-2	225	5-1-87	4	4	2.35	61	0	0	15	61	41	18	16	6	15	73	.186	.244	.154	10.71	2.20
Mejia, Ruben	R-R	6-1	175	2-23-92	1	0	0.00	1	0	0	0	2	2	0	0	1	4	.250	.250	.250	18.00	4.50
Oramas, Juan	L-L	5-10	215	5-11-90	3	2	3.07	12	12	0	0	56	52	22	19	4	16	64	.249	.280	.239	10.35	2.59
Quackenbush, Kevin	R-R	6-3	220	11-28-88	2	0	0.29	29	0	0	13	31	16	4	1	1	10	46	.151	.196	.117	13.35	2.90
Rearick, Chris	L-L	6-3	190	12-5-87	3	0	1.89	35	0	0	0	38	31	11	8	1	10	42	.223	.233	.219	9.95	2.37
Roach, Donn	R-R	6-1	200	12-14-89	8	12	3.53	28	28	0	0	143	138	73	56	7	40	77	.252	.265	.242	4.86	2.52
Sampson, Keyvius	R-R	6-0	185	1-6-91	10	4	2.26	19	18	0	0	103	74	31	26	9	33	110	.199	.212	.191	9.58	2.87
Sexton, Tim	R-R	6-6	185	6-10-87	1	1	1.71	15	0	0	2	26	20	6	5	1	3	18	.215	.132	.273	6.15	1.03
2-team total (14 Tulsa)					2	2	3.24	29	0	0	2	50	53	23	18	5	12	28	—	—	—	5.04	2.16
Smith, Burch	R-R	6-4	215	4-12-90	1	2	1.15	6	6	0	0	31	17	8	4	1	6	37	.155	.154	.155	10.63	1.72
Stites, Matt	R-R	5-11	170	5-28-90	2	2	2.08	46	0	0	14	52	37	16	12	6	8	51	.194	.237	.165	8.83	1.38
Wisler, Matt	R-R	6-3	195	9-12-92	8	5	3.00	20	20	0	0	105	85	36	35	7	27	103	.223	.261	.188	8.83	2.31
Zavada, Clay	L-L	6-1	185	6-28-84	0	2	3.80	21	0	0	1	21	19	17	9	2	12	17	.244	.212	.267	7.17	5.06

Fielding

Catcher	PCT	G	PO	A	E	DP	PB
Del Castillo	1.000	1	1	0	0	0	0
Gale	.993	59	406	51	3	4	2
Hedges	.982	18	152	10	3	1	0
Kral	1.000	7	52	2	0	0	1
Rodriguez	.982	55	446	58	9	4	8
Rodriguez	.963	4	21	5	1	1	0

First Base	PCT	G	PO	A	E	DP
Burke	—	1	0	0	0	0
Buschini	1.000	2	6	0	0	0
Decker	.974	5	34	3	1	1
Kirby-Jones	.989	23	171	7	2	11
Kral	.971	5	32	1	1	1
Limonta	.992	57	484	38	4	31
Medica	.996	51	438	50	2	35
Orr	.971	4	33	1	1	3

Second Base	PCT	G	PO	A	E	DP
Bisson	.947	14	14	40	3	3
Blackwood	1.000	3	3	5	0	2
Buschini	.971	33	46	89	4	13
Cabrera	1.000	2	1	1	0	0
Contreras	.909	3	4	6	1	2
Gyorko	1.000	1	2	1	0	0
Spangenberg	.988	75	109	225	4	46
Valdez	.931	16	30	37	5	6

Third Base	PCT	G	PO	A	E	DP
Blackwood	.928	124	69	251	25	17
Burke	.800	3	2	2	1	0
Buschini	.927	18	9	29	3	4
Contreras	—	1	0	0	0	0
Miller	—	1	0	0	0	0

Shortstop	PCT	G	PO	A	E	DP
Bisson	.931	14	24	30	4	6
Buschini	.900	7	6	12	2	0
Contreras	.959	13	20	27	2	4
Valdez	.935	111	152	249	28	48

Outfield	PCT	G	PO	A	E	DP
Asencio	.970	73	153	11	5	1
Buschini	.972	25	35	0	1	0
Fuentes	.959	90	158	6	7	0
Limonta	—	5	0	0	0	0
Medica	1.000	1	1	0	0	0
Miller	1.000	8	14	0	0	0
Noel	.975	130	330	15	9	5
Orr	1.000	9	22	0	0	0
Sams	1.000	15	29	2	0	1
Spangenberg	—	1	0	0	0	0
Williams	.983	70	112	4	2	1

LAKE ELSINORE STORM — HIGH CLASS A

CALIFORNIA LEAGUE

Batting	B-T	HT	WT	DOB	AVG	vLH	vRH	G	AB	R	H	2B	3B	HR	RBI	BB	HBP	SH	SF	SO	SB	CS	SLG	OBP
Adamson, Corey	L-R	6-2	205	2-23-92	.300	.333	.295	18	70	10	21	4	3	0	7	7	1	0	0	16	8	1	.443	.372
Asencio, Yeison	R-R	6-1	225	11-14-89	.296	.306	.293	57	243	34	72	20	2	5	44	10	0	0	4	29	1	1	.457	.319
Baltz, Jeremy	R-R	6-3	195	9-17-90	.309	.359	.300	67	262	42	81	19	2	10	54	22	5	0	3	58	2	1	.511	.370
Bernard, Wynton	R-R	6-2	200	9-24-90	.214	.200	.222	4	14	4	3	0	1	0	0	1	0	0	0	2	0	1	.357	.267
Brugueira, Reynaldo	B-R	5-10	170	11-5-91	.167	.000	.176	8	18	2	3	1	1	0	4	1	1	0	0	6	0	0	.333	.250
Burke, Chris	R-R	6-1	205	4-25-90	.276	.263	.279	24	87	14	24	7	0	0	15	7	3	0	0	26	1	1	.356	.351
Cedeno, Ronny	R-R	6-0	195	2-2-83	.125	.000	.143	2	8	1	1	1	0	0	0	2	0	0	0	1	0	0	.250	.300
Contreras, Anthony	L-R	5-11	185	9-26-83	.222	.000	.240	7	27	2	6	1	0	0	1	1	0	0	0	2	0	0	.259	.250
Del Castillo, Miguel	R-R	5-10	170	10-14-91	.125	.333	.000	5	16	0	2	0	0	0	0	1	0	0	0	3	0	1	.125	.176
Domoromo, Luis	L-L	6-1	215	2-4-92	.198	.157	.213	50	192	19	38	7	1	5	21	12	6	1	0	54	2	1	.323	.267
Gaedele, Kyle	R-R	6-3	220	11-1-89	.256	.212	.268	127	450	77	115	26	9	13	57	43	9	2	4	128	27	7	.440	.330
Guinn, Brian	B-R	6-1	180	4-4-89	.252	.194	.268	96	321	44	81	13	8	4	45	32	4	10	4	79	7	8	.380	.324
Gyorko, Jedd	R-R	5-10	210	9-23-88	.571	—	.571	2	7	2	4	1	0	0	1	0	0	0	0	1	0	0	.714	.571
Headley, Chase	B-R	6-2	220	5-9-84	.250	.333	.167	4	12	0	3	1	0	0	0	0	0	0	0	2	0	0	.333	.250
Hedges, Austin	R-R	6-1	190	8-18-92	.270	.300	.262	66	233	34	63	22	1	4	30	22	6	1	4	45	5	4	.425	.343
Hunt, Bridger	R-R	5-11	165	7-24-85	.337	.250	.373	20	83	10	28	4	0	2	13	8	0	1	0	5	2	2	.458	.396
Jankowski, Travis	L-R	6-2	190	6-15-91	.286	.239	.301	122	493	89	141	19	6	1	38	54	2	3	4	96	71	14	.355	.356
Jones, Duanel	R-R	6-3	220	5-11-93	.225	.211	.228	123	449	49	101	21	2	7	54	31	5	0	2	124	1	3	.327	.281
Kirby-Jones, A.J.	R-R	5-10	215	10-2-88	.262	.091	.287	46	172	20	45	16	1	7	32	22	3	0	2	54	0	1	.477	.352
Kral, Robert	L-R	5-10	195	3-28-89	.286	.191	.318	80	269	57	77	16	5	13	45	63	5	0	3	51	2	0	.528	.426
Miller, Justin	R-R	5-9	190	12-14-88	.213	.154	.226	21	75	6	16	0	1	1	9	8	1	2	0	14	4	3	.280	.298
Orr, Lee	R-R	6-3	215	10-23-88	.276	.232	.288	70	268	40	74	17	4	10	36	17	4	0	0	92	8	4	.481	
Peterson, Jace	L-R	6-0	205	5-9-90	.303	.337	.293	113	423	78	128	17	13	7	66	54	5	7	7	58	42	10	.454	.382

	B-T	HT	WT	DOB	AVG	vLH	vRH	G	AB	R	H	2B	3B	HR	RBI	BB	HBP	SH	SF	SO	SB	CS	SLG	OBP
Phillips, Dane	L-R	6-1	195	12-18-90	.173	.000	.200	14	52	7	9	3	2	0	6	2	0	0	1	8	0	0	.308	.200
Richardson, Ronnie	B-R	5-6	175	5-5-90	.211	.188	.220	16	57	9	12	2	2	1	4	6	1	0	0	12	0	1	.368	.297
Rodriguez, Jeremy	B-R	5-8	185	8-30-89	.295	.529	.250	36	105	12	31	7	1	0	13	27	2	0	0	17	1	0	.381	.448
Ruiz, Jose	R-R	6-1	190	10-21-94	.200	—	.200	1	5	1	1	0	0	0	1	0	0	0	0	3	0	0	.200	.200
Spangenberg, Cory	B-R	5-10	195	3-16-91	.296	.333	.278	54	226	33	67	13	6	4	31	23	1	3	0	51	17	3	.460	.364
Whitmore, Travis	L-R	6-1	195	7-5-88	.213	.189	.219	54	183	22	39	4	1	1	18	11	1	1	2	45	0	0	.262	.259

Pitching	B-T	HT	WT	DOB	W	L	ERA	G	GS	CG	SV	IP	H	R	ER	HR	BB	SO	AVG	vLH	vRH	K/9	BB/9
Alger, Brandon	L-L	6-3	190	7-4-91	4	9	5.68	37	9	0	0	90	128	71	57	7	18	67	.331	.342	.326	6.68	1.79
Barbato, Johnny	R-R	6-2	185	7-11-92	3	6	5.01	49	7	0	14	88	90	54	49	8	33	89	.269	.261	.276	9.10	3.38
Branham, Matt	R-R	6-5	220	9-28-87	1	2	5.92	22	0	0	0	38	47	27	25	6	9	29	.305	.409	.227	6.87	2.13
Cabrera, Erik	R-R	6-2	190	8-15-90	0	0	3.00	2	0	0	0	3	3	1	1	0	2	4	.273	.000	.273	12.00	6.00
Chabot, Matt	R-R	6-2	190	9-11-91	0	0	3.86	1	0	0	0	2	1	2	1	1	0	3	.111	.000	.333	11.57	0.00
Church, Joe	R-R	6-2	190	9-29-89	0	0	13.50	2	0	0	0	3	5	5	4	0	3	2	.385	.222	.750	6.75	10.13
Cortes, Dan	R-R	6-6	235	3-4-87	2	0	5.86	20	0	0	1	28	29	24	18	6	20	23	.259	.184	.297	7.48	6.51
De La Cruz, Luis	R-R	6-6	225	6-15-89	5	5	5.40	55	0	0	1	67	61	46	40	6	49	69	.237	.238	.237	9.32	6.62
Garces, Frank	L-L	5-11	175	1-17-90	7	9	5.67	26	26	0	0	121	131	86	76	15	57	126	.275	.197	.301	9.40	4.25
Gonzalez, Greg	R-R	5-11	190	9-19-88	0	0	1.80	4	0	0	0	5	5	1	1	0	3	5	.263	.000	.357	9.00	5.40
Hancock, Justin	R-R	6-4	185	10-28-90	3	7	5.14	14	14	0	0	63	81	52	36	5	36	39	.307	.306	.307	5.57	5.14
Hebner, Cody	R-R	6-0	175	11-21-90	2	2	3.62	58	0	0	4	75	57	31	30	3	41	78	.207	.280	.153	9.40	4.94
Holder, Trevor	R-R	6-2	185	1-8-87	4	7	6.39	25	16	0	0	100	138	76	71	13	35	55	.326	.305	.336	4.95	3.15
Hussey, John	R-R	6-3	190	11-22-86	2	3	6.49	35	2	0	0	60	80	54	43	10	24	32	.325	.276	.352	4.83	3.62
Jackson, Matt	R-R	6-4	195	12-18-87	6	4	5.83	17	16	1	0	88	115	63	57	11	18	58	.313	.310	.315	5.93	1.84
Lara, Robert	R-R	6-2	225	11-25-86	0	1	5.63	13	0	0	1	16	17	11	10	1	10	17	.279	.250	.310	9.56	5.63
Lloyd, Kyle	R-R	6-4	210	10-16-90	0	0	6.00	2	0	0	0	3	2	2	2	0	2	4	.182	.250	.143	12.00	6.00
Lollis, Matt	R-R	6-9	250	9-11-90	2	4	2.32	23	0	0	0	31	28	11	8	2	11	31	.239	.283	.203	9.00	3.19
Morrow, Bryce	R-R	6-2	200	1-2-88	4	2	4.81	7	7	0	0	39	45	28	21	4	10	23	.281	.333	.245	5.26	2.29
Needy, James	R-R	6-3	200	3-30-91	10	5	3.76	27	27	0	0	134	144	70	56	11	51	98	.274	.291	.264	6.58	3.43
O'Grady, Dennis	R-R	5-10	200	5-17-89	3	7	3.86	54	0	0	10	70	70	35	30	4	29	69	.258	.254	.261	8.87	3.73
Quigley, Ryan	R-R	6-2	205	4-11-85	1	0	5.13	19	0	0	0	26	23	16	15	2	15	31	.232	.340	.135	10.59	5.13
Rea, Colin	R-R	6-5	220	7-1-90	0	5	6.07	15	9	0	0	43	43	34	29	3	39	45	.272	.300	.244	9.42	8.16
Street, Huston	R-R	6-0	195	8-2-83	0	0	0.00	1	1	0	0	1	0	0	0	0	0	0	.000	.000	.000	0.00	0.00
Wisler, Matt	R-R	6-3	195	9-12-92	2	1	2.03	6	6	0	0	31	22	7	7	1	6	28	.196	.229	.172	8.13	1.74

Fielding

Catcher	PCT	G	PO	A	E	DP	PB
Del Castillo	1.000	5	36	1	0	1	0
Hedges	.979	61	449	56	11	5	7
Kral	.993	36	266	19	2	2	5
Phillips	.976	13	72	10	2	0	3
Rodriguez	1.000	32	212	17	0	1	5
Ruiz	1.000	1	6	1	0	0	0

First Base	PCT	G	PO	A	E	DP
Burke	.985	8	61	3	1	6
Kirby-Jones	.994	38	314	20	2	22
Kral	.996	32	257	15	1	22
Miller	.973	5	36	0	1	1
Orr	.982	48	359	27	7	33
Whitmore	1.000	15	101	8	0	9

Second Base	PCT	G	PO	A	E	DP
Brugeura	1.000	4	4	2	0	1
Burke	.974	9	19	18	1	0
Contreras	.875	3	4	3	1	1

	PCT	G	PO	A	E	DP
Guinn	.959	68	123	159	12	35
Gyorko	1.000	2	2	5	0	1
Hunt	1.000	2	0	6	0	0
Spangenberg	.966	53	78	119	7	23
Whitmore	.941	12	19	29	3	5

Third Base	PCT	G	PO	A	E	DP
Brugeura	—	1	0	0	0	
Burke	.857	3	3	3	1	0
Contreras	1.000	2	2	4	0	0
Guinn	.875	7	1	13	2	1
Headley	1.000	3	1	4	0	0
Hunt	1.000	1	2	0	0	0
Jones	.891	115	65	180	30	12
Miller	1.000	1	0	1	0	0
Orr	.800	1	2	2	1	0
Whitmore	.825	16	7	26	7	3

Shortstop	PCT	G	PO	A	E	DP
Cedeno	.941	2	9	7	1	2
Contreras	.933	3	5	9	1	2
Guinn	.888	19	29	42	9	10
Hunt	.953	16	27	34	3	8
Peterson	.956	107	183	277	21	53

Outfield	PCT	G	PO	A	E	DP
Adamson	.933	16	28	0	2	0
Asencio	1.000	49	69	5	0	0
Baltz	.965	58	108	1	4	0
Bernard	1.000	2	5	0	0	0
Domoromo	.941	32	60	4	4	0
Gaedele	.982	116	213	10	4	3
Hunt	1.000	2	3	0	0	0
Jankowski	.994	118	333	6	2	0
Miller	1.000	7	15	1	0	1
Orr	.957	12	21	1	1	0
Richardson	1.000	15	31	1	0	0

FORT WAYNE TINCAPS — LOW CLASS A

MIDWEST LEAGUE

Batting	B-T	HT	WT	DOB	AVG	vLH	vRH	G	AB	R	H	2B	3B	HR	RBI	BB	HBP	SH	SF	SO	SB	CS	SLG	OBP
Adams, Brian	R-R	6-4	215	2-28-91	.211	.184	.218	100	351	43	74	17	3	6	45	19	0	6	2	134	17	8	.328	.250
Adamson, Corey	L-R	6-2	205	2-23-92	.269	.288	.264	99	342	58	92	13	5	3	36	48	5	6	4	76	24	9	.363	.363
Baltz, Jeremy	R-R	6-3	195	9-17-90	.268	.167	.290	43	168	18	45	11	1	5	33	7	5	0	2	37	4	0	.435	.313
Bernard, Wynton	R-R	6-2	200	9-24-90	.200	.400	.100	5	15	1	3	0	1	0	3	1	0	0	0	5	1	1	.333	.250
Brugeura, Reynaldo	B-R	5-10	170	11-5-91	.326	.318	.328	23	86	9	28	3	1	1	11	6	0	1	0	17	1	3	.419	.370
Burke, Chris	R-R	6-1	205	4-25-90	.307	.341	.295	44	166	22	51	7	1	4	22	6	9	3	1	35	1	1	.434	.363
Cabrera, Everth	B-R	5-10	190	11-17-86	.000	.000	.000	2	7	1	0	0	0	0	0	1	0	0	0	5	0	0	.000	.125
Cabrera, Felix	R-R	6-0	170	7-14-89	.161	.143	.167	10	31	6	5	1	0	0	1	3	0	0	0	8	0	0	.194	.235
Carmon, Stephen	L-R	5-7	155	2-19-90	.253	.240	.256	50	154	19	39	8	3	1	14	19	3	3	3	22	1	2	.364	.341
Charles, Eric	R-R	5-10	180	12-18-88	.133	—	.133	6	15	1	2	0	0	0	2	0	0	0	0	6	0	0	.133	.133
Daal, Rodney	R-R	5-11	190	3-23-94	.271	.203	.295	79	269	30	73	13	2	8	39	14	5	9	2	58	6	4	.424	.317
Del Castillo, Miguel	R-R	5-10	170	10-14-91	.129	.000	.190	9	31	1	4	0	0	0	3	0	0	0	0	6	0	0	.129	.206
Domoromo, Luis	L-L	6-1	215	2-4-92	.233	.200	.241	59	215	26	50	9	5	4	30	14	2	2	4	44	3	1	.377	.281
Goris, Diego	R-R	6-2	165	12-8-90	.266	.277	.262	96	361	43	96	19	1	6	52	16	1	3	7	47	1	0	.334	.294
Martinez, Alberth	R-R	6-1	170	1-23-91	.277	.244	.287	97	358	63	99	24	9	10	58	39	8	9	1	68	10	4	.478	.360
Miller, Ryan	R-R	6-3	215	11-17-92	.167	.000	.200	3	6	1	1	0	0	0	1	0	0	0	0	1	0	0	.167	.167

Name	B-T	HT	WT	DOB	AVG	vLH	vRH	G	AB	R	H	2B	3B	HR	RBI	BB	HBP	SH	SF	SO	SB	CS	SLG	OBP
Phillips, Dane	L-R	6-1	195	12-18-90	.281	.133	.304	58	224	34	63	15	2	5	23	19	3	0	2	53	1	0	.433	.343
Quintana, Gabriel	R-R	6-2	190	9-7-92	.305	.293	.309	88	347	50	106	20	1	9	44	11	5	0	2	91	6	2	.447	.334
Renfroe, Hunter	R-R	6-1	200	1-28-92	.212	.143	.244	18	66	6	14	5	0	2	7	4	1	1	0	23	0	0	.379	.268
Smith, Mallex	L-R	5-9	155	5-6-93	.262	.341	.240	110	424	81	111	17	2	4	29	59	12	11	1	84	64	16	.340	.367
Stubblefield, Tyler	R-R	5-10	185	11-19-87	.267	.302	.256	64	225	26	60	16	3	4	19	16	1	6	1	31	4	0	.418	.317
Tejada, Luis	R-R	6-3	175	10-12-92	.227	.235	.225	112	423	44	96	19	4	2	37	19	5	3	4	92	18	5	.305	.266
Tissenbaum, Maxx	B-R	5-10	185	7-25-91	.277	.280	.276	111	415	48	115	28	0	2	49	43	19	5	8	36	4	2	.359	.365

Pitching	B-T	HT	WT	DOB	W	L	ERA	G	GS	CG	SV	IP	H	R	ER	HR	BB	SO	AVG	vLH	vRH	K/9	BB/9
Cabrera, Erik	R-R	6-1	180	8-15-90	0	3	10.35	9	3	0	0	20	30	27	23	2	15	14	.361	.395	.333	6.30	6.75
Campos, Leonel	R-R	6-3	185	7-17-87	2	1	2.23	28	0	0	5	36	19	9	9	2	22	63	.150	.192	.120	15.61	5.45
Chabot, Matt	R-R	6-2	190	9-11-91	6	1	5.31	29	0	0	0	61	65	43	36	6	21	57	.266	.243	.285	8.41	3.10
Church, Joe	R-R	6-2	190	9-29-89	3	3	5.63	22	0	0	1	40	53	32	25	2	19	34	.321	.338	.309	7.65	4.28
Eflin, Zach	R-R	6-4	200	4-8-94	7	6	2.73	22	22	0	0	119	110	53	36	7	31	86	.239	.216	.258	6.52	2.35
Fried, Max	L-L	6-4	185	1-18-94	6	7	3.49	23	23	0	0	119	107	54	46	7	56	100	.249	.174	.275	7.58	4.25
Gott, Trevor	R-R	6-0	190	8-26-92	2	2	2.56	27	0	0	4	32	23	11	9	1	12	33	.205	.095	.271	9.38	3.41
Guerrero, Tayron	R-R	6-7	189	1-9-91	0	1	7.36	4	0	0	0	4	8	8	3	0	8	4	.471	.429	.500	9.82	19.64
Guzman, Jorge	R-R	6-1	170	7-15-89	1	1	2.86	20	0	0	0	28	23	12	9	1	14	21	.213	.125	.283	6.67	4.45
Hancock, Justin	R-R	6-4	185	10-28-90	5	1	1.73	12	12	0	0	68	54	20	13	0	20	44	.222	.234	.208	5.85	2.66
Hussey, John	R-R	6-3	190	11-22-86	2	0	1.59	6	0	0	0	17	12	5	3	0	2	9	.185	.242	.125	4.76	1.06
Kelly, Mike	R-R	6-4	185	9-6-92	2	1	5.00	15	0	0	0	18	17	10	10	1	12	16	.262	.294	.226	8.00	6.00
Madrid, Roman	R-R	6-0	185	2-26-91	6	4	2.72	51	0	0	22	56	45	24	17	0	29	56	.216	.236	.202	8.95	4.63
Mejia, Ruben	R-R	6-1	175	2-23-92	3	5	3.18	25	5	0	0	62	63	31	22	2	21	58	.263	.292	.239	8.37	3.03
Nunn, Chris	L-L	6-5	200	10-5-90	8	2	2.77	55	0	0	9	65	62	23	20	3	30	66	.259	.267	.255	9.14	4.15
Portillo, Adys	R-R	6-2	235	12-20-91	0	1	4.82	3	3	0	0	9	14	8	5	0	4	10	.350	.292	.438	9.64	3.86
Rea, Colin	R-R	6-5	220	7-1-90	2	1	2.09	16	3	0	0	43	34	11	10	1	22	38	.218	.288	.175	7.95	4.60
Reyes, Genison	R-R	6-5	190	9-19-91	3	1	7.07	13	0	0	0	14	16	15	11	0	15	5	.271	.346	.212	3.21	9.64
Richardson, Josh	R-R	6-0	175	8-1-91	0	0	0.00	2	0	0	0	3	2	0	0	2	4		.182	.000	.250	12.00	6.00
Rodriguez, Bryan	R-R	6-5	180	7-6-91	2	8	3.19	19	14	0	0	85	88	48	30	5	32	52	.269	.229	.299	5.53	3.40
Ross, Joe	R-R	6-3	185	5-21-93	5	8	3.75	23	23	0	0	122	124	55	51	7	40	79	.267	.276	.258	5.81	2.94
Shepherd, Matt	R-R	6-3	185	5-2-90	4	4	4.04	36	8	0	1	94	85	48	42	8	44	79	.240	.218	.259	7.59	4.23
Weickel, Walker	R-R	6-6	195	11-14-93	3	6	5.04	24	23	0	0	111	125	72	62	8	43	82	.283	.295	.274	6.67	3.50

Fielding

Catcher	PCT	G	PO	A	E	DP	PB
Daal	.971	79	516	78	18	5	13
Del Castillo	.988	9	75	7	1	1	2
Miller	1.000	3	20	2	0	0	0
Phillips	.991	51	392	35	4	1	7

First Base	PCT	G	PO	A	E	DP
Goris	.992	31	242	19	2	17
Tejada	.986	111	972	74	15	97

Second Base	PCT	G	PO	A	E	DP
Brugeura	.924	14	27	46	6	10
Cabrera	.974	9	14	24	1	7
Charles	1.000	3	2	2	0	0
Goris	.979	30	55	88	3	22
Quintana	—	1	0	0	0	0
Stubblefield	1.000	1	0	2	0	0

	PCT	G	PO	A	E	DP
Tissenbaum	.967	92	153	228	13	52

Third Base	PCT	G	PO	A	E	DP
Burke	.882	35	36	61	13	6
Charles	1.000	2	1	3	0	0
Daal	—	1	0	0	0	0
Goris	.870	21	14	33	7	2
Quintana	.876	84	47	144	27	13
Stubblefield	1.000	1	2	3	0	0

Shortstop	PCT	G	PO	A	E	DP
Brugeura	.870	6	8	12	3	1
Cabrera	1.000	2	1	6	0	0
Cabrera	1.000	1	0	2	0	1
Carmon	.934	50	66	131	14	28
Charles	.000	1	0	0	1	0
Goris	.857	5	5	13	3	4

	PCT	G	PO	A	E	DP
Stubblefield	.967	61	106	156	9	35
Tissenbaum	.930	22	24	56	6	14

Outfield	PCT	G	PO	A	E	DP
Adams	.977	86	165	8	4	2
Adamson	.982	86	150	17	3	3
Baltz	1.000	16	20	1	0	0
Bernard	1.000	4	7	0	0	0
Brugeura	—	1	0	0	0	0
Domoromo	.991	52	100	8	1	1
Martinez	.973	93	203	11	6	1
Renfroe	.923	16	24	0	2	0
Smith	.976	67	162	4	4	3
Tejada	.000	1	0	0	1	0

EUGENE EMERALDS   SHORT-SEASON

NORTHWEST LEAGUE

Batting	B-T	HT	WT	DOB	AVG	vLH	vRH	G	AB	R	H	2B	3B	HR	RBI	BB	HBP	SH	SF	SO	SB	CS	SLG	OBP
Bass, Michael	R-R	5-9	155	9-10-91	.234	.111	.267	51	171	21	40	8	0	0	16	16	1	2	2	34	7	1	.281	.300
Bernard, Wynton	R-R	6-2	200	9-24-90	.250	.214	.266	39	136	19	34	5	1	1	10	18	1	2	4	33	7	4	.324	.333
Blanco, Felipe	R-R	6-1	175	12-9-93	.209	.128	.248	52	148	11	31	10	2	2	11	12	2	4	1	48	5	3	.345	.276
Brito, Malquiel	L-R	6-1	187	8-24-93	.239	.238	.239	32	113	13	27	6	0	4	12	4	1	1	1	34	1	1	.398	.269
Brugeura, Reynaldo	B-R	5-10	170	11-5-91	.154	—	.154	5	13	1	2	0	0	0	0	2	2	0	0	5	1	0	.154	.353
Charles, Eric	R-R	5-10	180	12-18-88	.000	.000	.000	2	4	0	0	0	0	0	0	0	2	0	0	1	0	0	.000	.333
Charles, Henry	L-L	6-1	174	1-3-94	.239	.239	.239	60	205	26	49	10	1	4	21	9	8	2	1	47	3	2	.356	.296
Davis, Marcus	L-L	6-3	200	4-26-92	.176	.241	.151	35	102	5	18	3	0	0	8	9	2	0	2	24	2	1	.206	.252
Del Castillo, Miguel	R-R	5-10	170	10-14-91	.238	.167	.250	16	42	3	10	1	0	1	4	3	0	1	0	8	0	1	.333	.289
Filpo, Fabel	B-R	6-1	180	9-28-92	.107	.000	.115	10	28	0	3	1	0	0	1	3	2	0	0	5	0	0	.143	.242
Goree, Jalen	R-R	5-10	195	6-15-93	.067	.000	.071	6	15	0	1	0	0	0	0	0	0	0	0	4	0	0	.067	.067
Jensen, Chase	R-R	6-3	175	1-29-91	.162	.219	.141	38	117	8	19	2	0	1	6	10	4	1	0	36	0	0	.205	.252
Kreuter, Cade	R-R	6-5	205	4-27-91	.000	—	.000	2	6	0	0	0	0	0	0	0	0	0	0	4	0	0	.000	.000
Lopez, Yair	R-R	6-3	150	9-9-91	.077	.000	.105	12	26	1	2	0	0	0	1	0	0	0	0	5	0	1	.077	.077
Masiello, Danny	R-R	5-6	180	12-19-91	.167	.200	.000	2	6	0	1	0	0	0	0	0	0	0	0	0	0	0	.167	.167
Miller, Michael	R-R	6-2	200	5-27-92	.194	.211	.186	38	124	9	24	5	0	1	7	10	4	0	0	16	0	0	.258	.275
Miller, Ryan	R-R	6-3	215	11-17-92	.245	.225	.253	43	139	12	34	6	1	0	9	13	2	0	1	31	3	1	.302	.316
Moreno, Edwin	L-L	6-1	190	10-27-93	.182	.074	.210	39	132	10	24	9	0	0	9	4	0	1	2	39	1	1	.250	.203
Perez, Fernando	L-R	6-2	190	9-13-93	.213	.161	.232	59	211	15	45	9	1	3	27	15	2	0	2	68	0	1	.308	.270
Renfroe, Hunter	R-R	6-1	200	1-28-92	.308	.250	.333	25	104	20	32	9	0	4	18	5	0	0	2	26	2	0	.510	.333

	B-T	HT	WT	DOB	AVG	vLH	vRH	G	AB	R	H	2B	3B	HR	RBI	BB	HBP	SH	SF	SO	SB	CS	SLG	OBP
Reyes, Franmil	R-R	6-4	200	7-5-95	.205	.273	.182	12	44	4	9	1	0	1	4	1	0	0	0	10	0	0	.295	.222
Richardson, Ronnie	B-R	5-6	175	5-5-90	.298	.250	.323	48	151	24	45	14	1	2	13	38	14	3	1	37	7	8	.444	.475
Santos, Trae	L-L	6-1	235	10-11-92	.248	.273	.239	56	210	18	52	15	0	3	20	12	5	1	0	58	1	0	.362	.304
Tate, Donavan	R-R	6-3	200	9-27-90	.213	.231	.210	23	75	6	16	4	2	0	6	11	2	0	0	29	3	1	.320	.330
Torres, Anthony	B-R	6-0	156	10-3-92	.196	.289	.169	53	168	19	33	4	1	0	8	13	5	1	1	46	0	2	.232	.273

Pitching	B-T	HT	WT	DOB	W	L	ERA	G	GS	CG	SV	IP	H	R	ER	HR	BB	SO	AVG	vLH	vRH	K/9	BB/9
Beatty, Max	R-R	6-2	210	3-27-91	0	1	13.50	5	0	0	0	6	12	9	9	0	3	4	.400	.455	.368	6.00	4.50
Brasoban, Yimmi	R-R	6-1	185	6-22-94	2	3	4.17	13	13	0	0	58	44	33	27	10	23	39	.212	.221	.202	6.02	3.55
Cabrera, Erik	R-R	6-1	180	8-15-90	1	7	4.32	21	10	0	0	58	59	41	28	2	40	55	.254	.239	.264	8.49	6.17
Cimber, Adam	R-R	6-4	180	8-15-90	3	1	2.56	28	0	0	10	32	25	10	9	2	7	27	.216	.145	.296	7.67	1.99
Cowgill, Coby	R-R	6-1	200	3-23-91	3	2	2.78	17	7	0	0	55	46	21	17	3	20	62	.221	.194	.243	10.15	3.27
De La Cruz, Vladimir	R-R	6-3	174	9-23-90	0	3	5.89	8	5	0	0	18	27	16	12	4	20	20	.360	.308	.388	9.82	9.82
Enloe, Jeffrey	L-L	6-5	215	8-13-89	2	3	6.75	18	6	0	0	41	49	36	31	4	18	44	.290	.280	.294	9.58	3.92
Fry, Brandon	L-L	6-3	195	3-28-93	0	2	4.15	11	0	0	0	13	14	6	6	0	9	11	.286	.400	.235	7.62	6.23
Gott, Trevor	R-R	6-0	190	8-26-92	0	0	2.08	4	0	0	0	4	4	2	1	0	3	8	.250	.250	.250	16.62	6.23
Guerrero, Tayron	R-R	6-7	189	1-9-91	1	4	4.50	15	3	0	0	32	24	21	16	1	25	35	.209	.128	.265	9.84	7.03
Guzman, Jorge	R-R	6-1	170	7-15-89	2	0	0.00	4	0	0	2	5	2	0	0	0	7	4	.118	.100	.143	12.60	0.00
Hale, Tyler	R-R	5-10	170	7-12-90	3	3	5.32	12	2	0	0	22	24	13	13	4	12	17	.286	.342	.239	6.95	4.91
Kelly, Mike	R-R	6-4	185	9-6-92	1	1	6.10	18	0	0	0	38	36	37	26	2	35	33	.257	.319	.226	7.75	8.22
Livengood, Justin	R-R	6-3	210	3-2-90	0	1	5.87	5	0	0	0	8	8	5	5	0	5	13	.250	.214	.278	15.26	5.87
Lloyd, Kyle	R-R	6-4	210	10-16-90	4	1	2.30	19	0	0	0	47	42	18	12	5	15	51	.237	.257	.224	9.77	2.87
Miller, Christian	L-L	6-3	170	5-21-93	0	0	1.80	2	1	0	0	5	5	1	1	1	2	3	.278	.143	.364	5.40	3.60
Mutz, Nick	R-R	6-1	190	6-15-90	0	0	3.86	3	0	0	0	7	7	4	3	2	2	9	.241	.083	.353	11.57	2.57
Reyes, Genison	R-R	6-5	190	9-19-91	1	2	3.53	25	0	0	0	36	34	18	14	1	13	37	.241	.340	.191	9.34	3.28
Richardson, Josh	R-R	6-0	175	8-1-91	1	2	2.43	24	0	0	2	33	29	10	9	1	12	30	.236	.263	.212	8.10	3.24
Rizzotti, Tony	R-R	6-4	205	4-21-92	1	2	3.86	11	1	0	0	21	23	9	9	2	6	22	.274	.243	.298	9.43	2.57
Schoenrock, Erik	R-L	6-2	200	8-12-91	2	3	2.51	14	14	0	0	57	48	19	16	1	15	52	.227	.245	.222	8.16	2.35
Verbitsky, Bryan	R-R	5-11	205	6-11-92	0	6	4.01	14	14	0	0	49	42	25	22	2	38	47	.239	.233	.244	8.57	6.93

Fielding

Catcher	PCT	G	PO	A	E	DP	PB
Del Castillo	.987	16	136	19	2	0	8
Masiello	1.000	2	11	1	0	0	0
Miller	.979	22	177	13	4	1	8
Miller	1.000	41	317	65	0	5	8

First Base	PCT	G	PO	A	E	DP
Davis	.984	14	119	7	2	14
Jensen	1.000	4	28	1	0	2
Kreuter	1.000	2	19	0	0	1
Miller	.946	4	31	4	2	2
Santos	.985	56	430	20	7	57

Second Base	PCT	G	PO	A	E	DP
Bass	.949	43	86	118	11	32
Blanco	.941	2	7	9	1	1
Brugeura	1.000	1	0	1	0	0

	PCT	G	PO	A	E	DP
Charles	1.000	1	5	3	0	2
Goree	.947	4	7	11	1	3
Perez	1.000	3	7	7	0	3
Torres	.950	30	49	64	6	16

Third Base	PCT	G	PO	A	E	DP
Bass	.900	7	6	12	2	2
Brugeura	1.000	4	1	5	0	0
Jensen	.948	22	20	53	4	5
Perez	.849	49	27	63	16	7

Shortstop	PCT	G	PO	A	E	DP
Bass	1.000	1	1	0	0	0
Blanco	.937	49	73	121	13	35
Jensen	.980	11	17	31	1	9
Torres	.935	25	43	58	7	16

Outfield	PCT	G	PO	A	E	DP
Bass	1.000	2	6	0	0	0
Bernard	.966	34	55	2	2	1
Brito	.941	14	16	0	1	0
Charles	.960	42	70	2	3	1
Davis	1.000	13	23	0	0	0
Filpo	1.000	5	5	0	0	0
Lopez	.917	10	11	0	1	0
Moreno	.955	17	20	1	1	1
Renfroe	.978	25	41	4	1	1
Reyes	.882	11	14	1	2	1
Richardson	.951	47	74	3	4	0
Tate	1.000	22	30	3	0	3

AZL PADRES ROOKIE

ARIZONA LEAGUE

Batting	B-T	HT	WT	DOB	AVG	vLH	vRH	G	AB	R	H	2B	3B	HR	RBI	BB	HBP	SH	SF	SO	SB	CS	SLG	OBP
Bauers, Jake	L-L	6-1	195	10-6-95	.282	.167	.322	47	163	22	46	8	2	1	25	14	3	3	5	31	2	0	.374	.341
Belen, Carlos	R-R	6-1	213	2-28-96	.211	.000	.267	5	19	3	4	0	0	1	1	1	0	0	7	1	0	.368	.286
Bernard, Wynton	R-R	6-2	200	9-24-90	.400	.250	.500	3	10	1	4	0	0	0	3	0	0	0	3	2	1	.400	.400
Boykin, Rod	R-R	6-1	175	4-17-95	.279	.273	.281	41	154	22	43	3	1	0	10	12	7	0	0	40	11	1	.312	.358
Brito, Malquiel	L-R	6-1	187	8-24-95	.333	.333	.667	3	12	3	7	0	1	0	3	0	0	0	2	0	0	.750	.583
Brugeura, Reynaldo	B-R	5-10	170	11-5-91	.087	.000	.125	7	23	2	2	0	0	1	3	3	0	0	7	0	1	.217	.192
Charles, Eric	R-R	5-10	180	12-18-88	.286	.333	.250	2	7	3	2	2	0	0	0	1	0	0	1	0	0	.571	.375
Contreras, Anthony	L-R	5-11	185	9-26-83	.083	.000	.111	4	12	2	1	0	0	0	0	1	0	0	4	0	0	.083	.154
Cordero, Franchy	L-R	6-3	175	9-2-94	.333	.314	.340	35	141	23	47	4	6	3	17	10	2	2	2	33	11	0	.511	.381
Dial, Tyler	L-R	5-10	185	11-19-91	.271	.261	.277	23	70	18	19	5	0	0	13	6	1	0	0	14	2	0	.343	.338
Ford, Adam	R-R	5-11	170	2-4-94	.212	.429	.169	31	85	11	18	2	2	0	3	9	1	0	0	23	5	1	.282	.295
Galvez, Jonathan	R-R	6-2	200	1-18-91	.000	—	.000	1	3	0	0	0	0	0	0	0	0	0	1	0	0	.000	.000
Goree, Jalen	R-R	5-10	195	6-15-93	.309	.357	.293	16	55	9	17	3	1	0	8	4	2	1	2	12	2	0	.400	.365
Jimenez, Miguel	L-L	6-2	185	10-17-93	.121	.000	.160	11	33	4	4	1	0	0	1	5	0	0	1	15	0	0	.152	.231
Martinez, Cristhofer	B-R	6-1	175	11-23-92	.270	.278	.267	24	63	9	17	4	1	1	10	3	0	1	0	15	2	0	.413	.308
Masiello, Danny	R-R	5-6	180	12-19-91	.100	.000	.167	11	10	0	1	0	0	0	0	1	0	0	2	0	0	.100	.250
Medica, Tommy	R-R	6-1	190	4-9-88	.294	.500	.182	5	17	5	5	2	0	2	8	1	0	0	0	7	0	0	.765	.333
Minaya, Euri	R-R	6-4	205	10-11-95	.000	.000	.000	2	5	1	0	0	0	0	0	0	0	0	3	0	0	.000	.000
Perez, Fernando	L-R	6-2	190	9-13-93	.417	.500	.375	4	12	3	5	1	0	1	4	1	0	0	2	0	0	.750	.462
Peterson, Dustin	R-R	6-2	190	9-10-94	.293	.265	.306	38	157	20	46	8	0	0	18	9	3	0	3	33	3	0	.344	.337
Quintana, Gabriel	R-R	6-2	190	9-7-92	.333	.200	.375	6	21	4	7	2	0	0	3	1	2	0	0	4	0	0	.429	.417
Reyes, Franmil	R-R	6-4	200	7-5-95	.315	.308	.317	45	165	24	52	12	2	3	30	20	0	0	1	39	5	5	.467	.387
Ruiz, Jose	R-R	6-1	190	10-21-94	.224	.158	.239	33	107	10	24	6	2	0	16	2	3	0	1	25	0	0	.318	.257

	B-T	HT	WT	DOB	AVG	vLH	vRH	G	AB	R	H	2B	3B	HR	RBI	BB	HBP	SH	SF	SO	SB	CS	SLG	OBP
Smith, Mason	R-R	6-2	195	3-16-95	.209	.267	.179	37	129	13	27	11	2	0	11	14	2	0	0	45	3	1	.326	.297
Urena, Jose	R-R	6-3	180	1-14-95	.257	.161	.296	49	191	32	49	11	5	9	34	22	3	0	1	54	1	2	.508	.341
Valenzuela, Ricardo	R-R	6-0	190	8-4-90	.221	.217	.222	19	68	8	15	3	0	0	6	5	0	0	0	13	0	0	.265	.274
VanMeter, Josh	L-R	5-11	165	3-10-95	.278	.259	.288	44	158	33	44	7	2	0	16	24	2	1	1	25	10	4	.348	.378

Pitching	B-T	HT	WT	DOB	W	L	ERA	G	GS	CG	SV	IP	H	R	ER	HR	BB	SO	AVG	vLH	vRH	K/9	BB/9
Baskette, Payton	L-L	6-1	175	10-1-93	2	2	1.37	16	6	0	2	46	36	14	7	0	11	43	.207	.250	.196	8.41	2.15
Beatty, Max	R-R	6-2	210	3-27-91	1	1	3.09	16	0	0	1	23	25	12	8	0	5	23	.275	.341	.220	8.87	1.93
Bonine, Eddie	R-R	6-5	220	6-6-81	0	0	4.50	1	0	0	0	2	1	2	1	0	2	1	.143	.500	.000	4.50	9.00
Bostjancic, Cory	R-R	6-0	180	7-14-92	1	2	10.13	11	0	0	1	13	13	18	15	0	18	17	.277	.357	.242	11.48	12.15
Constanza, Alexander	L-L	6-3	190	7-27-94	0	1	2.45	3	1	0	0	7	6	5	2	0	3	6	.222	.286	.200	7.36	3.68
De Horta, Adrian	R-R	6-3	185	3-13-95	0	2	4.06	12	11	0	0	31	28	15	14	1	13	40	.241	.179	.273	11.61	3.77
De La Cruz, Vladimir	R-R	6-3	174	9-23-90	0	0	6.97	11	0	0	0	21	23	19	16	0	7	25	.277	.357	.236	10.89	3.05
Diaz, Malcom	R-R	6-2	185	3-2-94	2	0	13.98	16	0	0	0	19	15	30	29	1	35	16	.224	.179	.256	7.71	16.88
Gonzalez, Greg	R-R	5-11	190	9-19-88	0	0	1.59	5	0	0	0	6	7	1	1	0	3	10	.292	.500	.143	15.88	4.76
Guerrero, Tayron	R-R	6-7	189	1-9-91	1	0	5.79	3	1	0	0	5	5	4	3	0	0	5	.263	.333	.250	9.64	0.00
Hale, Tyler	R-R	5-10	170	7-12-90	0	0	4.50	4	0	0	0	6	8	4	3	1	0	6	.333	.273	.385	9.00	0.00
Holland, Sam	R-R	6-4	200	2-20-94	2	2	2.25	27	0	0	8	32	35	10	8	0	6	34	.267	.296	.247	9.56	1.69
Kelich, Pete	R-R	6-2	185	2-16-91	7	1	1.40	13	10	1	1	58	43	14	9	1	1	69	.200	.237	.172	10.71	0.16
Liriano, Elvin	L-L	6-3	190	10-17-92	0	0	17.18	3	0	0	0	4	5	9	7	0	5	3	.313	1.000	.267	7.36	12.27
Lockett, Walker	R-R	6-5	225	5-19-94	0	0	11.57	3	0	0	0	2	5	3	3	0	2	2	.455	.429	.500	7.71	7.71
Long, Chris	R-R	6-2	190	3-24-93	0	0	0.00	1	0	0	0	1	0	0	0	0	1	1	.000	—	.000	9.00	9.00
Marcano, Ivan	R-R	6-3	220	6-1-91	2	3	12.75	18	0	0	0	24	35	36	34	2	31	13	.354	.349	.357	4.88	11.63
Miller, Christian	L-L	6-3	170	5-21-93	3	1	9.87	7	0	0	0	17	24	22	19	0	6	10	.312	.188	.344	5.19	3.12
Oramas, Juan	L-L	5-10	215	5-11-90	0	0	1.29	2	2	0	0	7	6	1	1	0	2	15	.214	.500	.100	19.29	2.57
Rizzotti, Tony	R-R	6-4	205	4-21-92	0	0	19.29	2	0	0	0	2	5	5	5	0	3	0	.500	.333	.571	0.00	11.57
Russell, Griffin	L-L	6-0	190	3-5-94	0	1	6.30	9	3	0	0	20	22	16	14	1	13	24	.286	.250	.298	10.80	5.85
Santos, Wilson	R-R	6-2	200	10-20-91	0	0	4.80	23	0	0	0	30	32	26	16	0	21	27	.248	.234	.256	8.10	6.30
Severino, Miguel	R-R	6-3	180	5-30-93	1	4	8.85	9	6	0	0	20	25	21	20	3	26	17	.325	.323	.326	7.52	11.51
Stewart, Cam	L-R	6-8	220	9-9-94	4	5	4.15	13	13	0	0	52	51	35	24	2	23	40	.259	.319	.227	6.92	3.98
Yardley, Eric	R-R	6-0	165	8-18-90	2	0	1.89	12	0	0	2	19	15	5	4	0	2	18	.205	.261	.180	8.53	0.95

Fielding

Catcher	PCT	G	PO	A	E	DP	PB
Dial	.974	16	99	12	3	0	9
Masiello	1.000	11	19	0	0	0	3
Ruiz	.965	33	264	35	11	0	11
Valenzuela	.988	11	76	7	1	0	6

First Base	PCT	G	PO	A	E	DP
Bauers	.987	43	353	31	5	24
Jimenez	1.000	8	60	6	0	6
Martinez	—	1	0	0	0	0
Medica	.941	2	15	1	1	0
Valenzuela	.977	5	40	3	1	4

Second Base	PCT	G	PO	A	E	DP
Brugeura	.952	3	5	15	1	2
Charles	.923	2	5	7	1	0

	PCT	G	PO	A	E	DP
Contreras	.800	1	1	3	1	1
Ford	.949	21	30	45	4	6
Galvez	1.000	1	2	2	0	0
Goree	.984	13	23	38	1	8
Martinez	.900	3	5	4	1	1
Perez	1.000	1	0	3	0	0
VanMeter	.962	15	30	45	3	5

Third Base	PCT	G	PO	A	E	DP
Belen	.917	5	0	11	1	0
Brugeura	1.000	3	2	6	0	0
Contreras	—	1	0	0	0	0
Martinez	.933	15	6	22	2	0
Perez	1.000	1	1	0	0	0
Peterson	.827	31	21	46	14	5
Quintana	.778	3	1	6	2	0

Shortstop	PCT	G	PO	A	E	DP
Brugeura	—	1	0	0	0	0
Cordero	.899	30	29	69	11	10
VanMeter	.941	25	38	89	8	17

Outfield	PCT	G	PO	A	E	DP
Bernard	1.000	2	1	0	0	0
Boykin	.963	40	75	3	3	0
Brito	.875	3	7	0	1	0
Jimenez	—	2	0	0	0	0
Minaya	—	1	0	0	0	0
Reyes	.917	38	62	4	6	1
Smith	.986	36	66	3	1	0
Urena	.974	44	67	8	2	0

DSL PADRES

ROOKIE

DOMINICAN SUMMER LEAGUE

Batting	B-T	HT	WT	DOB	AVG	vLH	vRH	G	AB	R	H	2B	3B	HR	RBI	BB	HBP	SH	SF	SO	SB	CS	SLG	OBP
Barahona, Luis	B-R	5-11	170	11-27-93	.300	.298	.301	56	213	30	64	9	3	0	21	26	4	4	2	41	16	6	.371	.384
Belen, Carlos	R-R	6-1	213	2-28-96	.247	.267	.242	64	231	34	57	9	4	7	27	26	6	0	2	60	5	6	.411	.336
Beltre, Moises	R-R	5-11	190	11-15-90	.000	.000	.000	2	7	0	0	0	0	0	0	0	0	0	0	3	0	0	.000	.000
Bravo, Daniel	R-R	6-0	160	2-16-95	.220	.250	.212	60	200	30	44	7	2	1	11	18	7	4	0	48	6	7	.290	.307
Brito, Malquiel	L-R	6-1	187	8-24-93	.233	.273	.211	14	60	7	14	2	1	0	8	4	1	0	0	9	1	1	.300	.292
Castillo, Fabian	R-R	6-1	175	9-26-93	.259	.207	.277	34	112	8	29	4	0	0	10	6	3	2	0	12	0	1	.295	.314
Contreras, Ronaldo	R-R	6-3	195	7-15-96	.242	.225	.246	59	211	26	51	16	0	6	29	25	6	0	1	78	4	4	.403	.337
De La Cruz, Wilfri	R-R	5-11	180	12-29-93	.298	.308	.296	28	94	13	28	10	2	0	11	9	2	0	0	19	1	1	.447	.371
Diaz, Yorky	R-R	6-2	185	6-18-93	.227	.200	.233	31	88	8	20	2	0	0	10	9	0	0	2	36	0	3	.250	.293
Lantigua, Jonas	L-R	6-5	205	12-15-94	.273	.240	.282	64	238	22	65	15	2	1	38	24	4	0	1	55	0	2	.366	.348
Lendor, Moises	B-R	6-1	170	6-25-93	.290	.333	.278	28	69	11	20	2	0	0	2	7	1	1	0	24	2	3	.319	.364
Minaya, Euri	R-R	6-4	205	10-11-95	.182	.100	.202	42	154	22	28	5	1	5	16	16	7	0	1	74	0	1	.325	.287
Munoz, Christian	L-R	5-10	185	7-12-94	.190	.182	.191	25	79	11	15	4	1	0	8	14	1	0	0	27	0	1	.266	.319
Pena, Jhonatan	R-R	6-2	180	4-18-94	.297	.280	.300	41	155	23	46	11	2	0	13	15	2	1	0	32	9	4	.394	.366
Pomare, Derwin	R-R	5-11	160	5-11-95	.270	.258	.273	49	152	30	41	5	4	0	13	21	0	3	0	25	3	2	.355	.358
Ugueto, Luis	R-R	6-1	180	8-5-96	.188	.176	.143	39	112	11	18	1	1	0	12	15	1	2	2	37	1	4	.172	.243
Vizcaino, Manuel	R-R	6-0	165	1-8-96	.204	.100	.216	29	98	12	20	2	0	0	5	10	4	0	0	35	0	2	.224	.304

Pitching	B-T	HT	WT	DOB	W	L	ERA	G	GS	CG	SV	IP	H	R	ER	HR	BB	SO	AVG	vLH	vRH	K/9	BB/9
Carrillo, Jhonathan	L-L	6-1	170	2-2-94	2	2	3.07	22	3	0	1	41	29	25	14	2	24	30	.195	.227	.189	6.59	5.27
Constanza, Alexander	L-L	6-3	190	7-27-94	1	3	3.44	10	10	0	0	37	36	22	14	1	21	34	.259	.313	.252	8.35	5.15
Davis, Jose	R-R	6-4	225	5-19-93	1	0	2.25	8	0	0	0	8	6	4	2	0	8	8	.207	.143	.227	9.00	9.00

Diaz, Adonis	R-R	6-1	185	12-8-94	4	2	2.33	18	0	0	2	27	21	9	7	0	6	21	.219	.200	.230	7.00	2.00
Gonzalez, Cesar	R-R	6-0	185	12-18-91	2	2	5.12	20	0	0	5	19	16	21	11	0	19	21	.216	.318	.173	9.78	8.84
Gonzalez, Manuel	R-R	6-4	195	10-21-94	1	4	4.53	13	13	0	0	60	63	37	30	1	14	57	.257	.250	.261	8.60	2.11
Linares, Joel	R-R	6-1	175	12-8-94	0	2	4.22	13	13	0	0	49	31	27	23	3	40	36	.178	.205	.169	6.61	7.35
Liriano, Elvin	L-L	6-3	190	10-17-92	0	4	4.35	13	8	0	0	39	34	24	19	2	26	33	.236	.500	.212	7.55	5.95
Lora, Carlos	R-R	6-3	190	8-24-91	2	1	2.51	13	0	0	2	14	9	6	4	1	5	9	.173	.125	.194	5.65	3.14
Martinez, Deninson	L-L	6-0	180	2-1-94	1	2	2.55	10	0	0	1	18	21	13	5	0	4	15	.292	.286	.292	7.64	2.04
Montas, Ernesto	R-R	6-3	180	7-18-91	3	4	3.76	13	13	0	0	55	63	33	23	0	15	27	.286	.284	.288	4.42	2.45
Pena, Arturo	R-R	6-4	200	5-13-94	3	2	3.29	29	0	0	1	41	40	18	15	0	24	35	.268	.260	.268	7.68	5.27
Ramirez, Emmanuel	R-R	6-2	190	7-15-94	1	3	8.92	24	0	0	0	36	36	51	36	1	49	41	.255	.250	.257	10.16	12.14
Ramos, Emmanuel	R-R	6-2	185	7-23-94	2	4	4.12	21	0	0	0	39	37	25	18	2	24	30	.262	.217	.284	6.86	5.49
Reyes, Manuel	R-R	6-4	195	6-8-93	0	0	27.00	6	0	0	0	4	2	13	12	0	16	4	.154	.000	.222	9.00	36.00
Reyes, Ramon	L-L	6-3	170	11-23-95	1	5	6.00	24	0	0	0	27	18	29	18	2	36	28	.189	.154	.195	9.33	12.00
Sanchez, Alejandro	R-R	6-2	170	9-7-92	2	1	3.98	23	0	0	0	32	27	25	14	1	30	29	.237	.282	.213	8.24	8.53
Ynfante, Starling	R-R	6-2	200	2-23-94	0	2	2.33	14	9	0	0	39	20	16	10	3	33	45	.152	.156	.149	10.47	7.68

Fielding

Catcher	PCT	G	PO	A	E	DP	PB
Beltre	.947	2	16	2	1	0	0
Castillo	.982	33	228	43	5	4	10
De La Cruz	.963	21	135	23	6	1	2
Munoz	.977	18	106	23	3	1	8

First Base	PCT	G	PO	A	E	DP
De La Cruz	1.000	6	55	3	0	2
Diaz	.976	4	39	2	1	1
Lantigua	.978	50	425	17	10	36
Lendor	1.000	1	7	0	0	0
Pomare	.990	15	96	7	1	7

Second Base	PCT	G	PO	A	E	DP
Lendor	.882	7	9	6	2	3
Pomare	.962	12	19	31	2	6
Ugueto	.922	34	61	69	11	12
Vizcaino	.851	21	30	44	13	11

Third Base	PCT	G	PO	A	E	DP
Belen	.879	64	47	149	27	11
Lendor	.667	1	1	1	1	0
Pomare	.900	3	4	5	1	0
Vizcaino	.889	3	4	4	1	0

Shortstop	PCT	G	PO	A	E	DP
Bravo	.907	58	90	165	26	30
Lendor	.846	8	3	8	2	1
Pomare	.839	7	10	16	5	3
Ugueto	.900	5	9	9	2	5

Outfield	PCT	G	PO	A	E	DP
Barahona	.952	48	74	5	4	1
Bravo	1.000	1	1	0	0	0
Brito	.968	12	28	2	1	1
Contreras	.934	56	79	6	6	2
Diaz	1.000	22	37	2	0	1
Lendor	1.000	4	2	0	0	0
Minaya	.927	30	46	5	4	0
Pena	.986	39	66	6	1	4
Pomare	.875	6	7	0	1	0

SAN DIEGO PADRES

San Francisco Giants

SEASON IN A SENTENCE: Brimming with great expectations after slaying the Tigers in the World Series, the Giants' season fell shorter than Tim Lincecum's new hairdo.

HIGH POINT: Lincecum's no-hitter, which put yet another jewel in the career of the two-time Cy Young Award winner. Lincecum performed his masterwork, which featured 10 punchouts, four walks and 148 pitches, against the Padres at Petco Park. Yusmiero Petit flirted with perfection late in the season, but his bid fell short after pinch-hitter Eric Chavez's single with two outs in the ninth

LOW POINT: A three-game sweep at the hands of the Dodgers in June, during which the Giants scored just eight runs. That whitewashing was sandwiched in the middle of a six-game skid, and a stretch where they dropped 14 out of 16.

NOTABLE ROOKIES: Reliever Jean Machi, 31, contributed 53 innings and a 2.38 ERA. Righty Jake Dunning pitched in a dozen games in relief, and highly touted prospects Mike Kickham and Heath Hembree made their debuts. Infielders Nick Noonan and Ehire Adrianza also got their first tastes of the highest level. Francisco Peguero also got a cup of coffee for the second straight season.

KEY TRANSACTIONS: The biggest (and only) trade they made was to send Conor Gillaspie to the White Sox for pitcher Jeff Soptic. With that in mind, the biggest deal would have to be the two-year, $35 million extension the Giants handed Lincecum after the season was over. Because it came on the heels of two seasons in which he produced negative WAR, this deal is almost certainly tied more to his past performance, rather than what the Giants expect him to do in the future. It also seems to have a bit to do with his status, along with Buster Posey, as one of the faces of the franchise.

DOWN ON THE FARM: Kyle Crick, the team's top prospect, missed two months with a strained oblique, but otherwise pitched well. He produced a 1.57 ERA and 95 strikeouts in just 69 innings over 14 starts in high Class A San Jose. Lefty Edwin Escobar pitched to a 2.80 ERA across the high Class A California and Double-A Eastern leagues, fanning 146 hitters along the way. Chris Stratton, who spent most of his time at low Class A Augusta, went 9-3, 3.27 in 22 starts. Outfielder Mac Williamson hit .292/.375/.502 with 25 longballs at San Jose, and Peguero hit .316/.354/.408 at Triple-A Fresno.

OPENING DAY PAYROLL: $140.3 million (6th)

PLAYERS OF THE YEAR

BILL MITCHELL

MAJOR LEAGUE	MINOR LEAGUE
Buster Posey	**Mac Williamson**
c	of
.294/.371/.450	(High A)
15 HR, 34 2B, 60 BB	.292/.375/.504
2nd straight A-S Game	25 HR, 31 2B, 89 RBIs

ORGANIZATION LEADERS

BATTING		*Minimum 250 AB
MAJORS		
* AVG	Scutaro, Marco	.297
* OPS	Belt, Brandon	.841
HR	Pence, Hunter	27
RBI	Pence, Hunter	99
MINORS		
* AVG	Tanaka, Kensuke, Fresno	.329
* OBP	Tanaka, Kensuke, Fresno	.400
* SLG	Williamson, Mac, San Jose	.504
R	Williamson, Mac, San Jose	94
H	Williamson, Mac, San Jose	152
TB	Williamson, Mac, San Jose	262
2B	Harris, Devin, San Jose	40
3B	Lofton, Chris, San Jose	11
HR	Williamson, Mac, San Jose	25
RBI	Williamson, Mac, San Jose	89
BB	Minicozzi, Mark, Richmond	62
SO	Parker, Jarrett, Richmond	161
SB	Galindo, Jesus, Augusta	48

PITCHING		#Minimum 75 IP
MAJORS		
W	Bumgarner, Madison	13
# ERA	Bumgarner, Madison	2.77
SO	Bumgarner, Madison	199
SV	Romo, Sergio	38
MINORS		
W	Blach, Ty, San Jose	12
	Snodgrass, Jack, Richmond	12
L	Westcott, Craig, Richmond	12
# ERA	Flores, Kendry, Augusta	2.73
G	McCormick, Phil, Richmond	58
GS	Westcott, Craig, Richmond	27
SV	Hembree, Heath, Fresno	31
IP	Gloor, Chris, Richmond	156
BB	Rogers, Taylor, Richmond	56
	Westcott, Craig, Richmond	56
SO	Escobar, Edwin, Richmond/San Jose	146
# AVG	Flores, Kendry, Augusta	.216

2013 PERFORMANCE

General Manager: Brian Sabean. **Farm Director:** Fred Stanley. **Scouting Director:** John Barr.

Class	Team	League	W	L	PCT	Finish	Manager(s)
Majors	San Francisco Giants	National	76	86	.469	9th (15)	Bruce Bochy
Triple-A	Fresno Giants	Pacific Coast	68	75	.476	12th (16)	Bob Mariano
Double-A	Richmond Flying Squirrels	Eastern	70	72	.493	6th (12)	Dave Machemer
High A	San Jose Giants	California	83	57	.593	1st (10)	Andy Skeels
Low A	Augusta Greenjackets	South Atlantic	82	55	.599	1st (14)	Mike Goff
Short-season	Salem-Keizer Volcanoes	Northwest	47	29	.618	1st (8)	Gary Davenport
Rookie	Giants	Arizona	41	15	.745	1st (13)	Derin McMains/Nestor Rojas
Overall 2013 Minor League Record			391	302	.564	2nd (30)	

ORGANIZATION STATISTICS

NATIONAL LEAGUE

Batting	B-T	HT	WT	DOB	AVG	vLH	vRH	G	AB	R	H	2B	3B	HR	RBI	BB	HBP	SH	SF	SO	SB	CS	SLG	OBP
Abreu, Tony	B-R	5-9	200	11-13-84	.268	.309	.241	53	138	21	37	12	3	2	14	6	1	1	1	33	0	2	.442	.301
Adrianza, Ehire	B-R	6-1	165	8-21-89	.222	.167	.333	9	18	3	4	1	0	1	3	1	0	1	0	5	0	0	.444	.263
Arias, Joaquin	R-R	6-1	160	9-21-84	.271	.270	.272	102	225	17	61	9	2	1	19	4	1	4	2	33	1	0	.342	.284
Belt, Brandon	L-L	6-5	220	4-20-88	.289	.261	.297	150	509	76	147	39	4	17	67	52	6	1	3	125	5	2	.481	.360
Blanco, Gregor	L-L	5-11	185	12-24-83	.265	.246	.269	141	452	50	120	17	6	3	41	52	1	3	3	95	14	9	.350	.341
Crawford, Brandon	L-R	6-2	215	1-21-87	.248	.199	.269	149	499	52	124	24	3	9	43	42	5	1	3	96	1	2	.363	.311
Francoeur, Jeff	R-R	6-4	210	1-8-84	.194	.188	.200	22	62	1	12	2	0	0	4	1	0	0	0	12	1	0	.226	.206
Gillespie, Cole	R-R	6-1	215	6-20-84	.000	.000	.000	3	9	0	0	0	0	0	1	0	0	0	0	0	0	.000	.100
2-team total (25 Chicago)					.203	—	—	28	59	6	12	2	0	0	4	7	1	1	1	13	0	0	.237	.294
Kieschnick, Roger	L-R	6-3	220	1-21-87	.202	.083	.222	38	84	6	17	0	1	0	5	11	0	0	0	29	0	0	.226	.295
Monell, Johnny	L-R	6-0	210	3-27-86	.125	—	.125	8	8	2	1	0	0	0	1	0	1	0	0	3	0	0	.125	.222
Noonan, Nick	L-R	6-1	170	5-4-89	.219	.300	.211	62	105	12	23	2	0	0	5	6	0	0	0	24	0	0	.238	.261
Pagan, Angel	B-R	6-2	200	7-2-81	.282	.305	.273	71	280	44	79	16	3	5	30	23	0	0	2	36	9	4	.414	.334
Peguero, Francisco	R-R	6-0	190	6-1-88	.207	.214	.200	18	29	4	6	1	0	1	1	0	0	0	1	2	2	0	.345	.233
Pence, Hunter	R-R	6-4	220	4-13-83	.283	.309	.274	162	629	91	178	35	5	27	99	52	3	0	3	115	22	3	.483	.339
Perez, Juan	R-R	5-11	185	11-13-86	.258	.208	.333	34	89	8	23	5	0	1	8	6	0	1	1	21	2	0	.348	.302
Pill, Brett	R-R	6-4	225	9-9-84	.224	.193	.286	48	85	11	19	4	0	3	12	5	1	0	1	17	0	0	.376	.272
Posey, Buster	R-R	6-1	220	3-27-87	.294	.320	.283	148	520	61	153	34	1	15	72	60	8	0	7	70	2	1	.450	.371
Quiroz, Guillermo	R-R	6-1	210	11-29-81	.186	.121	.226	43	86	5	16	7	0	1	6	5	1	2	1	21	0	0	.302	.237
Sanchez, Hector	B-R	6-0	235	11-17-89	.248	.341	.205	63	129	8	32	4	0	3	19	7	3	0	1	29	0	0	.349	.300
Sandoval, Pablo	B-R	5-11	240	8-11-86	.278	.270	.281	141	525	52	146	27	2	14	79	47	6	0	6	79	0	0	.417	.341
Scutaro, Marco	R-R	5-10	185	10-30-75	.297	.309	.292	127	488	57	145	23	3	2	31	45	2	9	3	34	2	0	.369	.357
Tanaka, Kensuke	L-R	5-9	170	5-20-81	.267	.000	.286	15	30	4	8	0	0	0	2	4	0	0	0	3	2	0	.267	.353
Torres, Andres	B-R	5-10	195	1-26-78	.250	.291	.206	103	272	33	68	17	1	2	21	22	0	2	4	61	4	3	.342	.302

Pitching	B-T	HT	WT	DOB	W	L	ERA	G	GS	CG	SV	IP	H	R	ER	HR	BB	SO	AVG	vLH	vRH	K/9	BB/9
Affeldt, Jeremy	L-L	6-4	225	6-6-79	1	5	3.74	39	0	0	0	34	27	14	14	2	17	21	.225	.196	.250	5.61	4.54
Bumgarner, Madison	R-L	6-5	235	8-1-89	13	9	2.77	31	31	0	0	201	146	68	62	15	62	199	.203	.161	.215	8.90	2.77
Cain, Matt	R-R	6-3	230	10-1-84	8	10	4.00	30	30	0	0	184	158	85	82	23	55	158	.228	.215	.239	7.71	2.69
Casilla, Santiago	R-R	6-0	210	7-25-80	7	2	2.16	57	0	0	2	50	39	14	12	2	25	38	.222	.217	.224	6.84	4.50
Dunning, Jake	R-R	6-4	190	8-12-88	0	2	2.84	29	0	0	0	25	20	8	8	2	11	16	.225	.171	.259	5.68	3.91
Gaudin, Chad	R-R	5-10	185	3-24-83	5	2	3.06	30	12	0	0	97	81	34	33	6	40	88	.227	.271	.193	8.16	3.71
Hembree, Heath	R-R	6-4	210	1-13-89	0	0	0.00	9	0	0	0	8	4	0	0	0	2	12	.148	.125	.158	14.09	2.35
Kickham, Mike	L-L	6-4	220	12-12-88	0	3	10.16	12	3	0	0	28	46	34	32	8	10	29	.351	.362	.345	9.21	3.18
Kontos, George	R-R	6-3	215	6-12-85	2	2	4.39	52	0	0	0	55	60	30	27	7	18	47	.282	.339	.258	7.64	2.93
Lincecum, Tim	L-R	5-11	170	6-15-84	10	14	4.37	32	32	1	0	198	184	102	96	21	76	193	.248	.235	.260	8.79	3.46
Lopez, Javier	L-L	6-5	220	7-11-77	4	2	1.83	69	0	0	1	39	30	10	8	1	12	37	.208	.156	.296	8.47	2.75
Machi, Jean	R-R	6-0	260	2-1-82	3	1	2.38	51	0	0	0	53	46	15	14	2	12	51	.234	.247	.226	8.66	2.04
Mijares, Jose	L-L	5-11	265	10-29-84	0	3	4.22	60	0	0	0	49	67	24	23	3	20	54	.321	.276	.360	9.92	3.67
Moscoso, Guillermo	R-R	6-1	200	11-14-83	2	2	5.10	13	2	0	0	30	20	17	17	5	21	31	.192	.139	.221	9.30	6.30
Petit, Yusmeiro	R-R	6-1	255	11-22-84	4	1	3.56	8	7	1	0	48	46	19	19	4	11	47	.251	.209	.276	8.81	2.06
Ramirez, Ramon	R-R	5-11	200	8-31-81	0	0	11.12	6	0	0	0	6	9	8	7	2	5	0	.429	.455	.400	0.00	7.94
Romo, Sergio	R-R	5-10	185	3-4-83	5	8	2.54	65	0	0	38	60	53	20	17	5	12	58	.226	.279	.183	8.65	1.79
Rosario, Sandy	R-R	6-1	210	8-22-85	3	2	3.02	43	0	0	0	42	38	15	14	1	20	24	.245	.196	.269	5.18	4.32
Surkamp, Eric	L-L	6-5	215	7-16-87	0	1	23.63	1	1	0	0	3	9	7	7	2	0	0	.563	.500	.600	0.00	0.00
Vogelsong, Ryan	R-R	6-4	215	7-22-77	4	6	5.73	19	19	0	0	104	124	73	66	15	38	67	.299	.266	.327	5.82	3.30
Zito, Barry	L-L	6-2	205	5-13-78	5	11	5.74	30	25	0	0	133	173	94	85	19	54	86	.318	.330	.315	5.81	3.65

Fielding

Catcher	PCT	G	PO	A	E	DP	PB
Monell	1.000	1	4	0	0	0	0
Posey	.993	121	907	53	7	5	3
Quiroz	1.000	35	144	13	0	0	0
Sanchez	.996	33	210	15	1	0	5

First Base	PCT	G	PO	A	E	DP
Arias	1.000	6	41	1	0	4
Belt	.993	143	1066	88	8	100
Pill	1.000	13	73	6	0	6
Posey	.986	21	137	6	2	11

Second Base	PCT	G	PO	A	E	DP
Abreu	.981	30	45	57	2	15
Arias	.980	13	28	21	1	9
Noonan	.981	22	22	30	1	11
Scutaro	.976	121	221	299	13	69

Third Base	PCT	G	PO	A	E	DP
Abreu	1.000	3	0	2	0	0
Arias	.959	55	15	55	3	4
Noonan	1.000	15	7	16	0	2
Sandoval	.940	137	77	206	18	14

Shortstop	PCT	G	PO	A	E	DP
Abreu	.900	3	2	7	1	0
Adrianza	.941	6	4	12	1	4

	PCT	G	PO	A	E	DP
Arias	.984	24	21	42	1	12
Crawford	.974	147	185	388	15	75
Noonan	—	1	0	0	0	0

Outfield	PCT	G	PO	A	E	DP
Blanco	1.000	136	232	6	0	1
Francoeur	.962	18	23	2	1	0
Gillespie	1.000	3	4	0	0	0
Kieschnick	1.000	25	38	1	0	0

	PCT	G	PO	A	E	DP
Pagan	.975	71	149	5	4	1
Peguero	1.000	13	15	0	0	0
Pence	.982	162	374	2	7	1
Perez	.987	32	67	8	1	1
Pill	1.000	8	8	0	0	0
Tanaka	1.000	9	6	0	0	0
Torres	.968	85	152	1	5	0

FRESNO GRIZZLIES — TRIPLE-A
PACIFIC COAST LEAGUE

Batting	B-T	HT	WT	DOB	AVG	vLH	vRH	G	AB	R	H	2B	3B	HR	RBI	BB	HBP	SH	SF	SO	SB	CS	SLG	OBP
Abreu, Tony	B-R	5-9	200	11-13-84	.338	.417	.321	22	65	9	22	9	0	1	9	1	3	0	2	15	1	1	.523	.366
Adrianza, Ehire	B-R	6-1	165	8-21-89	.310	.300	.314	45	145	23	45	7	6	0	12	23	2	6	1	31	6	2	.441	.409
Arias, Joaquin	R-R	6-1	160	9-21-84	.250	—	.250	2	8	0	2	0	0	0	0	0	0	0	0	3	0	0	.250	.250
Brown, Gary	R-R	6-1	190	9-28-88	.231	.272	.221	137	558	79	129	29	6	13	50	33	10	6	1	135	17	11	.375	.286
Ciriaco, Juan	R-R	6-0	160	8-15-83	.239	.314	.189	36	88	7	21	5	0	0	5	8	0	1	0	16	3	0	.295	.302
Dominguez, Chris	R-R	6-5	235	11-22-86	.294	.258	.304	132	466	60	137	24	5	15	65	23	6	0	2	112	4	5	.464	.334
Francoeur, Jeff	R-R	6-4	210	1-8-84	.222	.000	.222	4	18	0	4	0	0	0	2	0	0	0	0	3	0	0	.222	.222
Gillespie, Cole	R-R	6-1	215	6-20-84	.277	.303	.266	74	235	35	65	11	2	9	31	32	0	0	2	52	7	0	.455	.361
Jurica, Carter	R-R	5-11	185	9-23-88	.249	.169	.269	107	357	38	89	15	2	2	32	38	5	2	1	83	3	3	.319	.329
Kieschnick, Roger	L-R	6-3	220	1-21-87	.273	.289	.268	101	374	50	102	27	9	13	56	40	1	0	7	102	4	1	.497	.339
LaTorre, Tyler	L-R	6-0	235	4-22-83	.111	.000	.143	6	9	0	1	0	0	0	0	3	0	0	0	6	0	0	.111	.333
Linden, Todd	B-R	6-2	225	6-30-80	.204	.212	.202	47	137	12	28	8	1	1	15	11	3	0	1	48	0	0	.299	.276
Monell, Johnny	L-R	6-0	210	3-27-86	.275	.250	.281	121	415	71	114	27	2	20	64	59	2	0	5	105	6	3	.494	.364
Noonan, Nick	L-R	6-1	170	5-4-89	.255	.129	.284	48	165	20	42	13	1	0	20	17	1	2	3	44	1	2	.345	.323
Pagan, Angel	B-R	6-2	200	7-2-81	.278	.000	.294	5	18	1	5	0	0	0	3	2	1	0	1	2	0	0	.278	.364
Peguero, Francisco	R-R	6-0	190	6-1-88	.316	.308	.319	70	272	38	86	12	2	3	30	13	3	0	0	51	3	0	.408	.354
Perez, Juan	R-R	5-11	185	11-13-86	.291	.269	.296	101	382	52	111	27	5	10	50	15	5	4	3	75	18	6	.466	.323
Pill, Brett	R-R	6-4	225	9-9-84	.344	.344	.344	68	276	48	95	21	2	18	79	15	3	0	4	40	1	0	.630	.379
Quiroz, Guillermo	R-R	6-1	210	11-29-81	.294	.182	.348	14	34	2	10	2	0	0	8	6	1	0	1	7	0	0	.353	.405
Sanchez, Hector	B-R	6-0	235	11-17-89	.271	.263	.273	32	85	10	23	4	0	3	11	12	1	0	1	15	0	0	.424	.364
Tanaka, Kensuke	L-R	5-9	170	5-20-81	.329	.262	.345	107	343	54	113	14	3	1	32	42	3	5	7	36	22	10	.397	.400
Villegas, Ydwin	B-R	5-10	178	9-1-90	.274	.269	.275	39	106	10	29	4	2	0	13	9	1	0	0	28	0	0	.349	.336
Wagner, Mark	R-R	6-1	205	6-11-84	.000	.000	.000	3	3	0	0	0	0	0	0	0	0	0	0	1	0	0	.000	.000
Williams, Jackson	R-R	5-11	200	5-14-86	.230	.154	.249	85	261	30	60	14	2	5	30	21	2	2	3	48	0	0	.356	.289

Pitching	B-T	HT	WT	DOB	W	L	ERA	G	GS	CG	SV	IP	H	R	ER	HR	BB	SO	AVG	vLH	vRH	K/9	BB/9
Bochy, Brett	R-R	6-2	190	8-27-87	1	1	3.99	45	0	0	2	56	51	27	25	2	16	57	.238	.275	.205	9.11	2.56
Bonser, Boof	R-R	6-4	245	10-14-81	2	6	5.87	15	15	0	0	80	95	57	52	9	40	46	.301	.248	.339	5.20	4.52
Bowlin, Drew	R-R	6-1	190	12-28-86	0	0	20.25	1	0	0	0	1	2	3	3	1	3	1	.400	.500	.333	6.75	20.25
Castillo, Fabio	R-R	6-1	235	2-19-89	4	5	6.47	23	5	0	0	57	75	44	41	6	26	51	.321	.345	.298	8.05	4.11
Dunning, Jake	R-R	6-4	190	8-12-88	2	2	1.49	34	0	0	1	48	47	14	8	3	14	44	.263	.216	.295	8.19	2.61
Dunnington, Jacob	L-R	6-2	160	2-2-91	0	1	18.00	1	0	0	0	1	3	2	2	1	2	0	.500	.750	.000	18.00	18.00
Edlefsen, Steve	B-R	6-2	195	6-27-85	2	2	6.28	47	0	0	0	53	56	45	37	3	45	42	.271	.278	.265	7.13	7.64
Fitzgerald, Justin	R-R	6-5	230	3-3-86	2	8	5.61	14	14	0	0	77	87	52	48	12	33	65	.284	.305	.265	7.60	3.86
Fleet, Austin	R-R	6-2	200	4-17-87	1	5	3.52	13	9	0	0	61	59	24	24	11	17	47	.251	.308	.191	6.90	2.49
Hembree, Heath	R-R	6-4	210	1-13-89	1	4	4.07	54	0	0	31	55	54	26	25	7	16	63	.248	.269	.232	10.25	2.60
Heston, Chris	R-R	6-4	185	4-10-88	7	6	5.80	19	19	1	0	109	129	75	70	14	46	97	.301	.352	.258	8.03	3.81
Kickham, Mike	L-L	6-4	220	12-12-88	7	7	4.31	20	20	0	0	111	105	60	53	9	49	90	.250	.228	.258	7.32	3.98
Kontos, George	R-R	6-3	215	6-12-85	3	2	4.18	18	0	0	4	24	19	11	11	3	3	26	.209	.351	.111	9.89	1.14
Kown, Andrew	L-R	6-7	210	10-7-82	0	1	12.15	2	2	0	0	7	14	12	9	3	4	3	.400	.214	.524	4.05	5.40
Lively, Mitch	R-R	6-5	240	9-7-85	7	5	4.72	30	20	0	0	124	111	73	65	15	55	99	.235	.214	.254	7.19	3.99
Loux, Shane	R-R	6-2	225	8-31-79	5	2	4.09	9	9	1	0	51	42	26	23	6	18	17	.223	.240	.202	3.02	3.20
Machi, Jean	R-R	6-0	260	2-1-82	3	1	0.98	16	0	0	2	18	13	4	2	0	3	19	.206	.231	.189	9.33	1.47
Maday, Daryl	R-R	6-2	225	8-12-85	0	1	5.55	14	3	0	0	24	29	16	15	2	11	19	.302	.300	.304	7.03	4.07
Mejia, Adalberto	L-L	6-3	195	6-20-93	0	0	3.60	1	1	0	0	5	5	2	2	2	2	2	.250	.364	.111	3.60	3.60
Petit, Yusmeiro	R-R	6-1	255	11-22-84	5	6	4.52	15	15	1	0	88	92	45	44	16	13	91	.268	.313	.236	9.34	1.33
Ramirez, Ramon	R-R	5-11	200	8-31-81	2	1	3.46	20	0	0	0	26	18	11	10	2	13	31	.189	.171	.204	10.73	4.50
Rosario, Sandy	R-R	6-1	210	8-22-85	1	1	2.78	21	0	0	4	32	30	11	10	1	10	35	.244	.200	.279	9.74	2.78
Runzler, Dan	L-L	6-4	235	3-30-85	3	7	5.68	51	0	0	1	52	58	39	33	5	37	50	.284	.260	.299	8.60	6.36
Surkamp, Eric	L-L	6-5	215	7-16-87	7	1	2.78	11	11	0	0	71	56	23	22	4	20	54	.221	.203	.228	6.81	2.52
Teller, Carlos	L-L	5-11	180	10-3-86	0	1	1.69	2	0	0	0	5	6	1	1	1	3	2	.316	.500	.111	3.38	5.06
Tobin, Mason	R-R	6-3	210	7-8-87	3	0	5.24	31	0	0	0	34	36	22	20	3	17	23	.269	.278	.263	6.03	4.46
Vessella, Tom	R-L	6-6	205	10-12-85	0	0	0.00	1	0	0	0	1	0	0	0	0	2	2	.000	.000	.000	13.50	13.50

Fielding

Catcher	PCT	G	PO	A	E	DP	PB
Monell	.967	48	350	29	13	2	6
Quiroz	.987	10	73	2	1	0	2
Sanchez	.986	18	124	12	2	1	3
Williams	.995	77	538	47	3	2	10

First Base	PCT	G	PO	A	E	DP
Dominguez	.990	23	180	23	2	17

	PCT	G	PO	A	E	DP
Linden	.983	17	108	6	2	14
Monell	.995	47	372	24	2	37
Pill	.985	65	474	49	8	37

Second Base	PCT	G	PO	A	E	DP
Abreu	1.000	16	20	33	0	7
Ciriaco	.875	1	5	2	1	1
Gillespie	.981	12	29	24	1	4

	PCT	G	PO	A	E	DP
Jurica	.967	28	42	47	3	11
Noonan	.993	36	52	94	1	24
Tanaka	.937	55	91	133	15	28
Villegas	.985	16	30	34	1	8

SAN FRANCISCO GIANTS

Third Base	PCT	G	PO	A	E	DP
Abreu	.500	1	1	0	1	0
Ciriaco	1.000	2	2	3	0	0
Dominguez	.937	96	53	156	14	14
Jurica	.970	14	8	24	1	3
Monell	—	1	0	0	0	0
Noonan	1.000	9	5	8	0	2
Perez	.942	34	15	50	4	5
Pill	1.000	3	1	6	0	1

Shortstop	PCT	G	PO	A	E	DP
Adrianza	.943	44	62	121	11	25
Arias	.800	1	1	3	1	0
Ciriaco	.926	22	34	53	7	13
Jurica	.960	57	83	157	10	31
Noonan	.941	3	4	12	1	2
Perez	.784	11	9	20	8	1
Villegas	.987	18	29	45	1	10

Outfield	PCT	G	PO	A	E	DP
Brown	.974	136	324	17	9	3
Ciriaco	—	1	0	0	0	0
Dominguez	1.000	3	5	1	0	0
Francoeur	1.000	4	3	1	0	0
Gillespie	.989	47	83	3	1	0
Kieschnick	.969	93	183	6	6	0
Linden	.938	11	15	0	1	0
Pagan	.889	5	8	0	1	0
Peguero	.992	65	122	4	1	0
Perez	.981	59	149	3	3	0
Tanaka	.982	30	52	4	1	0
Williams	1.000	1	1	0	0	0

RICHMOND FLYING SQUIRRELS

DOUBLE-A

EASTERN LEAGUE

Batting	B-T	HT	WT	DOB	AVG	vLH	vRH	G	AB	R	H	2B	3B	HR	RBI	BB	HBP	SH	SF	SO	SB	CS	SLG	OBP
Adrianza, Ehire	B-R	6-1	165	8-21-89	.240	.218	.250	73	250	31	60	12	0	2	23	31	4	4	2	45	11	6	.312	.331
Ciriaco, Juan	R-R	6-0	160	8-15-83	.250	.063	.325	25	56	5	14	0	0	2	5	2	0	1	0	7	0	0	.357	.276
Duvall, Adam	R-R	6-1	205	9-4-88	.252	.265	.247	105	385	61	97	23	4	17	58	35	5	2	3	72	2	1	.465	.320
Herrera, Javier	R-R	5-11	225	4-9-85	.296	.301	.294	131	480	70	142	37	3	16	74	57	7	4	4	117	23	8	.485	.376
Krill, Brett	R-R	6-4	220	1-24-89	.258	.222	.281	85	225	27	58	10	0	2	28	11	8	2	2	55	3	1	.329	.313
LaTorre, Tyler	L-R	6-0	235	4-22-83	.138	.000	.159	26	80	6	11	2	0	1	9	10	0	1	0	26	0	0	.200	.233
Lollis, Ryan	L-L	6-2	185	12-16-86	.267	.267	.266	136	469	60	125	24	2	8	57	50	8	4	8	61	6	3	.377	.345
Minicozzi, Mark	R-R	6-1	210	2-11-83	.309	.313	.308	128	443	74	137	30	0	10	66	62	8	0	5	123	3	1	.445	.400
Moss, Brad	R-R	5-8	160	10-10-89	.200	.333	.000	5	5	1	1	0	0	0	0	0	0	0	0	2	0	0	.400	.200
Navarro, Jesus	R-R	6-0	180	1-3-88	.200	.222	.192	17	35	3	7	4	0	0	3	1	1	0	16	0	0	.314	.282
Oropesa, Ricky	L-R	6-3	225	12-15-89	.207	.188	.217	66	241	19	50	6	0	6	23	15	1	0	2	74	0	0	.307	.255
Panik, Joe	L-R	6-1	190	10-30-90	.257	.248	.260	137	522	64	134	27	4	4	57	58	5	8	6	68	10	5	.347	.333
Parker, Jarrett	L-L	6-4	210	1-1-89	.245	.248	.245	131	444	72	109	18	5	18	57	60	15	5	0	161	13	11	.430	.355
Relaford, Travious	R-R	5-11	160	5-13-92	.188	.250	.156	32	69	10	13	1	0	0	5	12	2	2	0	22	0	3	.203	.325
Stromsmoe, Skyler	B-R	5-10	175	3-30-84	.263	.360	.237	48	118	19	31	7	1	1	5	10	2	3	1	15	1	3	.364	.328
Susac, Andrew	R-R	6-2	210	3-22-90	.256	.345	.213	84	262	32	67	17	0	12	46	42	3	1	2	68	1	0	.458	.362
Tomlinson, Kelby	R-R	6-2	180	6-6-90	.198	.105	.221	33	96	13	19	5	0	0	4	16	0	4	0	27	3	1	.250	.313
Villalona, Angel	R-R	6-3	257	8-13-90	.235	.333	.208	52	196	23	46	11	0	8	28	8	3	0	2	60	0	0	.413	.273
Wagner, Mark	R-R	6-1	205	6-11-84	.172	.233	.152	47	122	7	21	5	0	1	13	16	2	0	1	33	1	0	.238	.277
Zambrano, Eliezer	B-R	5-11	195	9-16-86	.273	.000	.333	5	11	0	3	0	0	0	0	1	0	0	0	1	0	0	.273	.333

Pitching	B-T	HT	WT	DOB	W	L	ERA	G	GS	CG	SV	IP	H	R	ER	HR	BB	SO	vLH	vRH	K/9	BB/9
Bowlin, Drew	R-R	6-1	190	12-28-86	4	3	4.87	32	0	0	0	44	36	25	24	4	24	33	.221	.250	.207	6.70	4.87
Bradley, Ryan	B-L	6-1	180	7-15-88	0	6	6.37	23	11	0	1	65	100	59	46	7	34	37	.361	.387	.353	5.12	4.71
Castillo, Fabio	R-R	6-1	235	2-19-89	2	2	3.34	14	2	0	0	32	25	15	12	1	17	44	.205	.308	.088	12.25	4.73
Escobar, Edwin	L-L	6-2	200	9-4-88	5	4	2.67	10	10	0	0	54	44	18	16	2	13	54	.219	.233	.215	9.00	2.17
Fitzgerald, Justin	R-R	6-5	230	3-3-86	3	0	1.09	6	0	0	0	33	30	6	4	2	8	41	.233	.208	.263	11.18	2.18
Gloor, Chris	L-L	6-6	255	3-7-87	9	7	4.03	26	26	0	0	156	163	77	70	16	41	121	.271	.240	.283	6.97	2.36
Hall, Cody	R-R	6-4	220	1-6-88	2	2	2.39	20	0	0	8	26	17	8	7	4	8	27	.181	.167	.188	9.23	2.73
Javier, Omar	R-R	6-3	165	10-4-87	4	0	5.58	27	2	0	0	50	55	32	31	7	28	45	.282	.276	.289	8.10	5.04
Maday, Daryl	R-R	6-2	225	8-12-85	1	1	2.84	26	0	0	13	25	21	8	8	0	9	20	.223	.256	.196	7.11	3.20
McCormick, Phil	L-L	6-1	184	9-7-88	4	5	3.97	58	0	0	3	57	49	32	25	3	34	57	.234	.187	.271	9.05	5.40
Osich, Josh	L-L	6-2	230	9-3-88	2	3	4.85	22	0	0	3	30	26	16	16	2	12	28	.241	.226	.247	8.49	3.64
Quirarte, Edwin	R-R	6-2	185	12-20-86	3	5	2.61	56	0	0	10	72	66	22	21	2	28	44	.253	.270	.242	5.47	3.48
Rogers, Taylor	R-R	6-4	200	6-5-87	5	9	5.43	26	18	0	1	104	108	73	63	5	56	70	.266	.296	.233	6.04	4.83
Shuman, Scott	R-R	6-3	205	3-28-88	0	0	9.51	28	0	0	0	24	15	28	25	0	42	39	.179	.243	.128	14.83	15.97
Snodgrass, Jack	L-L	6-6	210	12-10-87	12	4	3.70	25	25	1	0	141	126	64	58	10	39	81	.241	.225	.246	5.17	2.49
Teller, Carlos	L-L	5-11	180	10-3-86	1	4	5.64	11	11	0	0	45	42	30	28	7	36	33	.259	.161	.282	6.65	7.25
Valdez, Jose	R-R	6-7	250	8-1-88	3	2	5.46	38	1	0	0	56	64	37	34	2	48	53	.295	.300	.291	8.52	7.71
Vessella, Tom	R-L	6-6	205	10-18-87	3	3	5.55	33	1	0	2	47	63	31	29	4	23	28	.342	.397	.314	5.36	4.40
Vogelsong, Ryan	R-R	6-4	215	7-22-77	2	0	0.82	2	2	0	0	11	10	1	1	1	2	8	.256	.308	.231	6.55	1.64
Westcott, Craig	L-R	6-4	215	3-1-86	5	12	4.19	27	27	0	0	144	158	77	67	12	56	92	.282	.312	.258	5.75	3.50

Fielding

Catcher	PCT	G	PO	A	E	DP	PB
LaTorre	.982	26	160	8	3	2	7
Moss	1.000	5	13	1	0	0	1
Navarro	.988	15	78	4	1	0	2
Susac	.992	71	477	38	4	4	9
Wagner	.996	42	217	25	1	3	9
Zambrano	1.000	5	28	0	0	0	0

First Base	PCT	G	PO	A	E	DP
Duvall	1.000	7	59	3	0	7
Minicozzi	.992	30	225	18	2	20
Oropesa	.989	59	500	36	6	52
Stromsmoe	.889	4	6	2	1	0
Susac	.986	9	66	3	1	2
Villalona	.985	44	359	31	6	20

Second Base	PCT	G	PO	A	E	DP
Ciriaco	1.000	1	3	4	0	3
Minicozzi	.973	10	16	20	1	7
Panik	.987	117	234	304	7	73
Relaford	.957	11	20	25	2	6
Stromsmoe	.981	10	24	27	1	7

Third Base	PCT	G	PO	A	E	DP
Ciriaco	.917	8	4	7	1	2
Duvall	.931	90	47	195	18	11
Minicozzi	.916	45	21	77	9	11
Relaford	1.000	3	4	4	0	1
Stromsmoe	1.000	9	9	12	0	0

Shortstop	PCT	G	PO	A	E	DP
Adrianza	.982	72	106	221	6	47
Ciriaco	1.000	8	1	20	0	3
Panik	.980	20	37	59	2	11
Relaford	.952	7	8	12	1	2
Stromsmoe	.934	16	19	38	4	10
Tomlinson	.977	32	44	82	3	19

Outfield	PCT	G	PO	A	E	DP
Herrera	.995	122	176	11	1	4
Krill	.976	56	75	6	2	1
Lollis	.983	129	284	5	5	1
Minicozzi	.957	13	20	2	1	0
Parker	.981	124	251	13	5	3
Stromsmoe	1.000	2	4	0	0	0

SAN FRANCISCO GIANTS

SAN JOSE GIANTS
CALIFORNIA LEAGUE

HIGH CLASS A

Batting	B-T	HT	WT	DOB	AVG	vLH	vRH	G	AB	R	H	2B	3B	HR	RBI	BB	HBP	SH	SF	SO	SB	CS	SLG	OBP
Arnold, Jeff	R-R	6-2	205	1-13-88	.251	.242	.254	97	350	53	88	26	4	13	61	38	6	0	2	116	4	0	.460	.333
Blair, Elliott	R-R	6-1	181	2-3-88	.229	.310	.200	69	223	34	51	14	1	3	26	29	11	2	2	60	4	6	.341	.343
Bond, Brock	B-R	5-10	185	9-11-85	.240	.260	.234	92	367	54	88	16	3	3	39	49	8	1	4	63	6	4	.324	.339
Brown, Trevor	R-R	6-2	195	11-15-91	.172	.417	.109	14	58	5	10	4	0	0	4	4	0	0	0	10	0	0	.241	.226
Cavan, Ryan	B-R	5-11	180	6-28-87	.283	.217	.303	75	300	41	85	16	0	3	38	21	2	1	3	42	1	4	.367	.331
Duffy, Matt	R-R	6-2	170	1-15-91	.292	.391	.265	26	106	17	31	6	1	5	14	7	1	1	0	16	3	1	.509	.342
Haney, Bobby	L-R	6-1	165	8-16-88	.257	.150	.280	102	346	40	89	14	1	4	38	34	3	10	4	75	3	1	.338	.326
Harris, Devin	R-R	6-3	225	4-23-88	.258	.284	.252	129	508	75	131	40	5	23	84	41	7	0	7	123	1	1	.492	.318
Lofton, Chris	L-R	6-1	175	5-20-90	.258	.221	.266	120	446	72	115	18	11	4	41	45	6	14	5	105	23	13	.374	.331
Oropesa, Ricky	L-R	6-3	225	12-15-89	.295	.241	.313	57	220	30	65	16	0	8	38	24	4	0	5	55	0	0	.477	.368
Pagan, Angel	B-R	6-2	200	7-2-81	.000	—	.000	1	2	0	0	0	0	0	0	0	1	0	0	0	0	0	.000	.333
Payne, Shawn	R-R	6-1	190	7-13-89	.229	.345	.200	73	275	43	63	14	2	1	29	34	5	6	5	62	21	10	.305	.320
Polonius, John	R-R	6-1	160	1-13-91	.221	.231	.220	26	95	10	21	4	1	1	7	7	2	3	1	26	2	0	.316	.286
Relaford, Travious	R-R	5-11	160	5-13-92	.156	.111	.167	12	45	7	7	3	0	0	3	2	1	0	0	14	0	0	.222	.208
Sanchez, Hector	B-R	6-0	235	11-17-89	.250	.000	.300	4	12	1	3	1	0	0	3	1	0	0	1	4	0	0	.333	.286
Sandoval, Pablo	B-R	5-11	240	8-11-86	.667	.333	1.000	2	6	2	4	0	0	2	2	0	0	0	0	0	0	0	1.667	.667
Schroder, Myles	R-R	5-11	180	8-1-87	.296	.329	.284	86	291	42	86	20	6	6	33	25	5	3	2	73	12	4	.467	.359
Sim, Eric	R-R	6-2	215	1-3-89	.276	.143	.294	17	58	3	16	3	0	0	10	5	0	1	1	13	0	0	.328	.328
Stromsmoe, Skyler	B-R	5-10	175	3-30-84	.262	.400	.243	16	42	9	11	2	0	0	2	8	2	1	0	9	2	1	.310	.404
Tomlinson, Kelby	R-R	6-2	180	6-16-90	.276	.355	.252	32	134	13	37	7	0	0	16	12	1	0	1	32	5	1	.328	.338
Villalona, Angel	R-R	6-3	257	8-13-90	.229	.241	.226	73	284	37	65	16	0	14	42	15	6	0	4	76	0	0	.433	.278
Villegas, Ydwin	B-R	5-10	178	9-1-90	.189	.333	.146	16	53	3	10	2	0	0	3	1	0	0	0	23	1	0	.226	.204
Williamson, Mac	R-R	6-5	240	7-15-90	.292	.259	.301	136	520	94	152	31	2	25	89	51	21	0	5	132	10	1	.504	.375
Zambrano, Eliezer	R-R	5-11	195	9-16-86	.242	.240	.243	28	95	5	23	7	0	1	11	6	3	2	4	13	0	1	.347	.296

Pitching	B-T	HT	WT	DOB	W	L	ERA	G	GS	CG	SV	IP	H	R	ER	HR	BB	SO	AVG	vLH	vRH	K/9	BB/9
Bandilla, Bryce	L-L	6-4	235	1-17-90	1	4	3.65	38	0	0	5	44	26	20	18	5	25	72	.167	.178	.162	14.62	5.08
Blach, Ty	R-L	6-1	200	10-20-90	12	4	2.90	22	20	0	0	130	124	46	42	8	18	117	.248	.246	.248	8.08	1.24
Blackburn, Clayton	L-R	6-3	220	1-6-93	7	5	3.65	23	23	0	0	133	111	67	54	12	35	138	.224	.238	.215	9.34	2.37
Bowlin, Drew	R-R	6-1	190	12-28-86	0	0	5.40	3	0	0	0	5	3	3	3	0	4	7	.300	.286	.308	12.60	7.20
Bucardo, Jorge	R-R	6-4	190	10-18-89	2	0	4.82	5	0	0	0	9	8	5	5	0	3	7	.242	.214	.263	6.75	2.89
Casilla, Jose	R-R	6-1	210	5-21-89	3	7	3.22	43	2	0	5	67	74	28	24	3	13	48	.276	.318	.256	6.45	1.75
Casilla, Santiago	R-R	6-0	210	7-25-80	0	0	5.40	5	2	0	0	5	7	3	3	0	5	2	.350	.000	.500	3.60	9.00
Concepcion, Edward	R-R	6-2	215	10-3-88	0	1	27.00	3	0	0	0	2	6	7	7	2	3	3	.462	.000	.667	11.57	11.57
Crick, Kyle	L-R	6-4	220	11-30-92	3	1	1.57	14	14	0	0	69	48	20	12	1	39	95	.201	.264	.150	12.45	5.11
Dunnington, Jacob	L-R	6-2	160	2-2-91	0	0	1.69	4	0	0	0	5	4	1	1	1	2	9	.211	.500	.077	15.19	3.38
Escobar, Edwin	L-L	6-2	200	4-22-92	3	8	2.89	16	14	0	0	75	68	33	24	3	17	92	.234	.262	.227	11.09	2.05
Fleet, Austin	R-R	6-2	200	4-17-87	6	2	3.92	15	8	0	0	57	53	27	25	3	16	54	.244	.222	.260	8.48	2.51
Forjet, Jason	R-R	6-2	185	1-4-90	4	3	4.52	19	10	0	0	64	69	34	32	8	25	55	.280	.311	.267	7.77	3.53
Hall, Cody	R-R	6-4	220	1-6-88	2	0	1.34	26	0	0	2	34	15	8	5	2	7	48	.130	.206	.099	12.83	1.87
Harrold, Stephen	R-R	6-1	200	3-12-89	5	2	4.09	39	0	0	3	55	58	29	25	6	22	46	.265	.264	.265	7.53	3.60
Law, Derek	R-R	6-3	218	9-14-90	4	0	2.10	22	0	0	11	26	20	7	6	1	1	45	.208	.182	.222	15.78	0.35
Marlowe, Chris	R-R	6-0	175	10-26-89	3	2	3.97	26	7	0	0	70	71	34	31	4	35	55	.273	.278	.269	7.04	4.48
Marte, Kelvin	R-R	5-9	170	11-24-87	6	4	3.67	25	15	0	0	105	102	46	43	14	19	80	.258	.237	.264	6.84	1.62
Mejia, Adalberto	L-L	6-3	195	6-20-93	7	4	3.31	16	16	0	0	87	75	34	32	11	23	89	.228	.191	.242	9.21	2.38
Osich, Josh	L-L	6-2	230	9-3-88	3	1	2.45	34	0	0	12	40	32	13	11	1	10	48	.213	.213	.214	10.71	2.23
Rojas, Luis	R-R	5-10	185	7-29-89	7	6	4.86	49	1	0	0	70	74	40	38	3	42	56	.269	.206	.303	7.17	5.37
Sandbrink, Danny	R-R	6-2	190	6-23-89	1	2	9.12	14	1	0	1	25	45	29	25	7	6	19	.398	.514	.342	6.93	2.19
Soptic, Jeff	R-R	6-6	220	4-8-91	3	2	6.26	32	0	0	0	42	40	34	29	2	36	46	.255	.246	.260	9.94	7.78
Strickland, Hunter	R-R	6-4	220	9-24-88	1	0	0.86	20	0	0	9	21	10	2	2	1	5	23	.145	.217	.109	9.86	2.14
Surkamp, Eric	L-L	6-5	215	7-16-87	0	0	2.93	5	5	0	0	15	8	6	5	2	3	17	.157	.333	.119	9.98	1.76
Teller, Carlos	L-L	5-11	180	10-3-86	0	1	21.00	3	0	0	0	3	4	8	7	0	8	5	.308	.000	.364	15.00	24.00
Vander Tuig, Nick	R-R	6-3	190	12-9-91	0	0	11.57	1	1	0	0	2	4	3	3	1	2	3	.444	.400	.500	11.57	7.71
Vogelsong, Ryan	R-R	6-4	215	7-22-77	0	1	6.75	1	1	0	0	3	1	2	2	1	1	3	.111	1.000	.000	10.13	3.38

Fielding

Catcher	PCT	G	PO	A	E	DP	PB
Arnold	.991	95	884	64	9	3	6
Brown	1.000	1	9	1	0	0	0
Sanchez	1.000	3	30	2	0	0	1
Schroder	1.000	2	5	0	0	0	0
Sim	.993	16	118	15	1	1	3
Zambrano	1.000	28	236	10	0	0	5

First Base	PCT	G	PO	A	E	DP
Blair	1.000	10	62	3	0	10
Oropesa	.990	55	458	29	5	46
Schroder	1.000	11	78	3	0	4
Villalona	.989	70	530	22	6	46

Second Base	PCT	G	PO	A	E	DP
Bond	.974	39	57	91	4	15
Brown	.982	12	17	37	1	6
Cavan	.947	25	65	61	7	22
Haney	.991	28	44	67	1	19
Polonius	.981	13	29	24	1	6
Relaford	.969	8	12	19	1	7
Schroder	.840	6	6	15	4	3
Stromsmoe	1.000	2	4	5	0	0
Villegas	.956	14	16	27	2	6

Third Base	PCT	G	PO	A	E	DP
Blair	.000	1	0	0	1	0
Bond	.957	17	13	32	2	3
Cavan	.950	49	35	99	7	10

Haney	1.000	2	0	1	0	0
Polonius	.917	3	5	6	1	0
Relaford	.778	2	1	6	2	0
Sandoval	.750	2	1	2	1	0
Schroder	.942	65	36	144	11	17
Stromsmoe	.864	8	4	15	3	1

Shortstop	PCT	G	PO	A	E	DP
Duffy	.969	25	24	70	3	
12 Haney	.967	74	88	178	9	31
Polonius	.926	11	8	17	2	3
Relaford	1.000	2	2	4	0	3
Schroder	1.000	2	3	4	0	1
Tomlinson	.954	30	42	82	6	19
Villegas	.917	3	2	9	1	3

Outfield	PCT	G	PO	A	E	DP
Blair	1.000	60	112	3	0	3
Harris	.946	97	154	5	9	1

Lofton	.989	119	271	4	3	0
Pagan	1.000	1	3	0	0	0
Payne	.951	37	56	2	3	0

Stromsmoe	1.000	6	13	0	0	0
Williamson	.971	115	216	15	7	5

AUGUSTA GREENJACKETS

LOW CLASS A

SOUTH ATLANTIC LEAGUE

Batting	B-T	HT	WT	DOB	AVG	vLH	vRH	G	AB	R	H	2B	3B	HR	RBI	BB	HBP	SH	SF	SO	SB	CS	SLG	OBP
Branca, Stephen	R-R	6-1	170	4-10-89	.234	.231	.234	46	137	16	32	6	1	1	12	12	1	5	0	33	2	2	.314	.300
Brown, Trevor	R-R	6-2	195	11-15-91	.250	.257	.248	97	384	48	96	18	1	3	40	27	5	2	5	52	10	9	.326	.304
Cain, Andrew	R-R	6-6	220	3-24-90	.240	.222	.245	110	358	54	86	15	8	9	44	32	5	3	3	94	20	3	.402	.309
Delfino, Mitch	R-R	6-2	210	1-15-91	.270	.320	.257	122	477	63	129	25	2	13	76	35	5	0	5	76	4	4	.413	.324
Duffy, Matt	R-R	6-2	170	1-15-91	.307	.308	.306	78	287	48	88	14	3	4	43	45	3	3	1	41	22	6	.418	.405
Galindo, Jesus	B-R	5-11	175	8-23-90	.273	.327	.262	89	326	66	89	9	2	1	25	31	5	4	4	80	48	6	.322	.342
Hollick, Tyler	L-R	6-1	185	9-16-92	.178	.222	.167	15	45	2	8	0	2	0	2	4	0	2	0	15	4	0	.267	.245
Houck, Shayne	R-R	6-1	210	5-29-90	.235	.179	.252	96	336	42	79	18	1	5	43	36	15	0	5	80	1	2	.339	.332
Jones, Chuckie	R-R	6-3	235	7-28-92	.236	.233	.237	128	407	58	96	21	2	10	51	47	7	5	6	140	12	8	.371	.321
Moreno, Rando	R-R	5-11	164	6-6-92	.353	.417	.318	13	34	4	12	1	2	0	4	1	0	2	0	6	2	2	.500	.371
Moss, Brad	R-R	5-8	160	10-10-89	.147	.125	.154	14	34	4	5	1	0	0	2	5	0	0	0	7	0	0	.176	.256
Pare, Matt	L-R	6-0	205	11-17-90	.111	.000	.125	3	9	0	1	0	0	0	1	0	1	2	0	3	1	0	.111	.200
Payne, Shawn	R-R	6-1	190	7-13-89	.259	.294	.248	36	135	29	35	10	1	4	21	21	2	1	3	29	6	2	.437	.360
Rapp, Joey	R-R	6-2	225	11-27-89	.267	.244	.274	91	344	42	92	19	0	6	54	19	14	2	4	98	2	2	.375	.328
Relaford, Travious	R-R	5-11	160	5-13-92	.221	.114	.252	48	154	19	34	3	1	2	18	17	3	1	0	35	10	3	.292	.310
Robles, Alberto	R-R	6-1	155	9-14-90	.304	.279	.311	62	194	33	59	9	2	1	21	13	5	3	2	22	13	7	.387	.360
Rodriguez, Rafael	R-R	6-5	198	7-13-92	.208	.237	.203	73	250	30	52	10	1	4	25	15	4	0	2	52	4	4	.304	.262
Sim, Eric	R-R	6-2	215	1-3-89	.193	.212	.190	63	207	20	40	7	0	2	20	16	14	0	3	59	2	1	.256	.292
Turner, Ben	R-R	6-5	225	4-27-90	.249	.208	.259	100	378	40	94	19	0	2	38	20	2	6	6	24	4	1	.315	.286
Zambrano, Eliezer	B-R	5-11	195	9-16-86	.230	.000	.259	20	61	7	14	0	0	0	6	6	0	2	1	10	2	1	.230	.294

Pitching	B-T	HT	WT	DOB	W	L	ERA	G	GS	CG	SV	IP	H	R	ER	HR	BB	SO	AVG	vLH	vRH	K/9	BB/9
Agosta, Martin	R-R	6-1	180	4-7-91	9	3	2.06	18	18	0	0	92	57	24	21	4	43	109	.180	.216	.164	10.70	4.22
Biagini, Joe	R-R	6-4	215	5-29-90	7	6	5.03	20	20	0	0	97	102	63	54	5	42	79	.267	.241	.282	7.36	3.91
Bucardo, Jorge	R-R	6-4	190	10-18-89	2	1	1.84	27	0	0	6	44	31	9	9	1	11	40	.197	.220	.184	8.18	2.25
Concepcion, Edward	R-R	6-2	215	10-3-88	1	0	6.75	3	2	0	0	7	7	5	5	0	6	3	.292	.000	.389	4.05	8.10
Dunnington, Jacob	L-R	6-2	160	2-2-91	1	0	3.29	9	0	0	1	14	10	5	5	0	8	18	.208	.176	.226	11.85	5.27
Farley, Brandon	R-R	6-2	215	8-1-90	4	4	3.65	28	0	0	1	57	61	27	23	1	23	39	.282	.323	.265	6.19	3.65
Flores, Kendry	R-R	6-2	175	11-24-91	10	6	2.73	22	22	1	0	142	113	47	43	11	17	137	.216	.194	.233	8.70	1.08
Gardeck, Ian	R-R	6-2	215	11-21-90	4	3	3.21	44	0	0	1	56	45	24	20	2	40	66	.226	.203	.240	10.61	6.43
Gregorio, Joan	R-R	6-7	180	1-12-92	6	3	4.00	14	13	0	0	70	65	34	31	3	17	84	.243	.140	.305	10.85	2.20
Johnson, Stephen	R-R	6-4	205	2-21-91	5	1	3.61	45	0	0	8	52	41	24	21	2	30	71	.215	.284	.177	12.21	5.16
Kurrasch, Joe	L-L	6-0	205	6-19-91	5	0	1.78	7	4	0	0	25	19	7	5	1	8	32	.207	.219	.200	11.37	2.84
Law, Derek	R-R	6-3	218	9-14-90	3	0	2.31	19	0	0	3	35	27	12	9	1	10	48	.206	.270	.181	12.34	2.57
Lujan, Matt	L-L	6-1	210	8-23-88	7	0	3.33	15	12	0	0	78	77	32	29	5	28	64	.264	.244	.272	7.35	3.22
McVay, Mason	L-L	6-7	230	8-15-90	3	5	4.12	51	1	0	1	68	71	39	31	5	18	75	.271	.226	.296	9.98	2.39
Mizenko, Tyler	R-R	6-1	200	4-9-90	1	4	2.75	48	0	0	25	52	45	19	16	3	24	50	.227	.212	.235	8.60	4.13
Okert, Steven	L-L	6-3	210	7-9-91	2	2	2.97	44	0	0	2	61	55	27	20	3	24	59	.244	.189	.272	8.75	3.56
Reyes, Jose	R-R	6-1	184	1-3-91	1	3	9.53	6	6	0	0	17	17	19	18	2	15	11	.258	.063	.320	5.82	7.94
Sandbrink, Danny	R-R	6-2	190	6-23-89	0	0	1.59	7	0	0	0	11	8	3	2	0	1	6	.195	.308	.143	4.76	0.79
Schumer, Justin	R-R	6-0	180	8-2-88	5	8	4.59	22	17	0	0	96	95	51	49	8	33	59	.260	.238	.272	5.53	3.09
Stratton, Chris	R-R	6-3	186	8-22-90	9	3	3.27	22	22	1	0	132	128	48	48	5	47	123	.258	.285	.238	8.39	3.20

Fielding

Catcher	PCT	G	PO	A	E	DP	PB
Brown	1.000	13	100	8	0	1	0
Moss	1.000	12	91	11	0	1	1
Pare	1.000	2	19	2	0	1	0
Sim	.995	60	485	62	3	7	8
Turner	1.000	45	340	34	0	2	1
Zambrano	.986	14	135	9	2	1	3

First Base	PCT	G	PO	A	E	DP
Branca	1.000	2	23	2	0	2
Houck	.978	14	84	3	2	8
Rapp	.991	88	738	48	7	61
Turner	.994	37	324	19	2	26

Second Base	PCT	G	PO	A	E	DP
Branca	.968	17	24	36	2	5

	PCT	G	PO	A	E	DP
Brown	.970	76	133	188	10	40
Houck	1.000	1	0	1	0	0
Moreno	1.000	10	16	24	0	3
Relaford	.981	12	16	35	1	5
Robles	.966	29	33	80	4	17

Third Base	PCT	G	PO	A	E	DP
Branca	.960	10	5	19	1	2
Delfino	.947	101	56	175	13	13
Houck	.928	27	17	47	5	2
Moreno	—	2	0	0	0	0
Relaford	1.000	4	4	7	0	1
Robles	—	1	0	0	0	0

Shortstop	PCT	G	PO	A	E	DP
Branca	.862	7	9	16	4	4

	PCT	G	PO	A	E	DP
Duffy	.966	74	86	230	11	37
Moreno	1.000	1	1	1	0	1
Relaford	.956	34	49	82	6	15
Robles	.938	32	41	79	8	17

Outfield	PCT	G	PO	A	E	DP
Branca	1.000	1	2	0	0	0
Cain	.968	109	175	6	6	1
Galindo	.988	86	162	4	2	1
Hollick	1.000	13	21	2	0	1
Houck	1.000	9	6	1	0	0
Jones	.987	127	224	6	3	2
Payne	.982	31	54	2	1	1
Rapp	—	1	0	0	0	0
Rodriguez	.990	66	95	1	1	0

NORTHWEST LEAGUE

Batting	B-T	HT	WT	DOB	AVG	vLH	vRH	G	AB	R	H	2B	3B	HR	RBI	BB	HBP	SH	SF	SO	SB	CS	SLG	OBP
Bednar, Brandon	R-R	6-4	185	3-21-92	.272	.271	.273	50	202	36	55	9	0	6	34	14	5	3	2	28	11	3	.406	.332
Blair, Elliott	R-R	6-1	181	2-3-88	.237	.286	.226	11	38	7	9	2	0	0	0	8	2	0	0	8	2	0	.289	.396
Cornier, Gabriel	B-R	6-0	190	6-10-92	.197	.333	.167	25	66	10	13	2	1	1	8	11	1	1	1	17	0	0	.303	.316
Eberle, Sam	R-R	6-0	215	2-1-90	.235	.255	.229	60	204	32	48	14	3	5	30	35	6	0	2	36	2	0	.407	.360
Escalante, Geno	R-R	5-10	185	6-25-91	.300	.320	.295	39	130	19	39	8	1	1	19	11	7	0	3	34	0	1	.400	.377
Hill, Kentrell	R-R	6-0	180	10-27-90	.200	.167	.222	16	45	5	9	3	0	0	4	1	3	0	1	14	1	1	.267	.280
Hollick, Tyler	L-R	6-0	185	9-16-92	.262	.186	.278	63	237	47	62	7	1	3	27	37	6	0	1	53	20	5	.338	.374
Honeycutt, Ryan	L-R	6-0	195	9-6-88	.269	.000	.292	7	26	3	7	2	0	1	6	2	0	0	0	4	1	0	.462	.321
Horan, Tyler	L-R	6-2	230	12-2-90	.295	.324	.288	44	176	25	52	11	3	4	25	20	2	0	1	34	4	0	.460	.372
Jones, Jonathan	R-R	6-0	205	2-15-92	.230	.357	.191	17	61	8	14	2	1	1	10	10	0	0	0	21	0	0	.344	.338
Jones, Ryan	R-R	5-10	175	9-8-90	.336	.241	.360	42	143	24	48	12	0	0	23	22	3	3	2	25	9	0	.420	.429
McCall, Shilo	R-R	6-1	210	6-2-94	.235	.200	.248	55	196	31	46	14	3	4	30	21	7	3	0	67	3	2	.398	.330
Miller, Blake	R-R	6-3	195	4-25-90	.309	.389	.291	25	97	18	30	8	0	3	12	9	2	0	2	19	3	1	.485	.373
Ortiz, Randy	R-R	5-11	170	6-15-93	.253	.205	.270	48	150	27	38	4	3	0	7	14	6	3	0	36	16	3	.320	.341
Otero, Cristian	R-R	6-0	170	3-30-93	.237	.500	.115	16	38	4	9	1	1	0	7	3	2	0	0	12	0	1	.316	.326
Polonius, John	R-R	6-1	160	1-13-91	.270	.375	.241	39	148	15	40	4	4	1	25	9	5	0	0	24	5	3	.372	.333
Ragira, Brian	R-R	6-2	185	1-22-92	.263	.237	.270	47	179	29	47	12	1	3	36	26	6	0	2	54	1	1	.391	.371
Rojas, Leo	R-R	5-11	182	6-11-90	.306	.368	.279	17	62	8	19	7	0	1	9	2	4	0	0	12	0	0	.468	.368
Ross, Ty	R-R	6-1	203	1-17-92	.243	.208	.253	31	103	17	25	11	0	0	8	10	1	2	1	21	1	0	.350	.313
Sy, Jeremy	R-R	5-8	180	10-14-89	.294	.256	.307	46	170	37	50	12	1	8	41	26	3	0	3	44	13	2	.518	.391
Tuntland, Ryan	R-R	6-1	190	4-30-91	.254	.333	.235	36	122	16	31	6	1	3	19	26	2	1	0	30	2	3	.393	.393

Pitching	B-T	HT	WT	DOB	W	L	ERA	G	GS	CG	SV	IP	H	R	ER	HR	BB	SO	AVG	vLH	vRH	K/9	BB/9
Connolly, Mike	R-R	6-1	180	10-31-91	0	2	10.61	6	0	0	0	9	18	11	11	1	6	9	.419	.476	.364	8.68	5.79
Encinosa, E.J.	R-R	6-5	215	8-5-91	0	0	3.12	14	0	0	1	17	8	6	6	1	10	21	.143	.154	.133	10.90	5.19
Fern, Chris	L-L	6-4	215	8-22-91	0	0	15.95	8	0	0	0	7	25	16	13	2	2	7	.556	.357	.645	8.59	2.45
Johnson, Chase	R-R	6-3	185	1-9-92	3	2	4.17	10	10	0	0	41	36	24	19	3	12	37	.240	.286	.192	8.12	2.63
Johnson, Chris	R-R	6-4	205	8-24-91	6	3	2.49	15	15	0	0	83	65	27	23	1	8	78	.207	.238	.180	8.46	0.87
Jones, Christian	L-L	6-3	210	1-27-91	2	0	3.29	11	0	0	0	14	14	8	5	1	2	14	.250	.231	.267	9.22	1.32
Kurrasch, Joe	L-L	6-0	205	6-19-91	2	4	5.03	9	8	0	0	34	45	23	19	0	12	25	.308	.278	.318	6.62	3.18
Leenhouts, Drew	L-L	6-3	200	3-28-90	9	2	2.39	15	15	0	0	72	68	23	19	5	14	53	.255	.247	.258	6.66	1.76
Maltos-Garcia, Arturo	R-R	6-1	190	8-2-91	0	0	6.89	10	0	0	0	16	19	13	12	1	10	11	.302	.321	.286	6.32	5.74
Marlowe, Chris	R-R	6-0	175	10-26-89	0	0	1.08	7	0	0	0	8	5	2	1	0	1	6	.156	.125	.167	6.48	1.08
McVey, Cameron	R-R	6-5	205	10-18-88	3	2	3.19	22	0	0	1	42	34	15	15	1	14	48	.218	.222	.214	10.20	2.98
Mendoza, Lorenzo	R-R	5-10	190	8-6-91	3	1	4.68	9	2	0	1	25	28	19	13	4	5	17	.275	.212	.340	6.12	1.80
Montero, Raymundo	R-R	6-2	185	9-20-89	2	2	1.82	25	0	0	14	30	20	8	6	2	7	43	.183	.211	.169	13.04	2.12
Moronta, Reyes	R-R	6-0	175	1-6-93	2	2	4.98	6	6	0	0	22	24	15	12	2	8	22	.279	.256	.302	9.14	3.32
Neff, Steven	L-L	6-2	195	2-24-89	1	0	2.49	14	0	0	0	22	25	6	6	0	5	23	.291	.323	.273	9.55	2.08
Nova, Juan	R-R	6-3	190	10-7-91	1	1	6.92	10	0	0	0	13	12	12	10	3	10	8	.250	.364	.154	5.54	6.92
Paniagua, Armando	R-R	5-11	155	1-11-90	0	1	2.48	25	1	0	2	36	34	14	10	2	20	22	.252	.388	.118	5.45	4.95
Reyes, Jose	R-R	6-1	184	1-3-91	2	1	2.00	4	4	0	0	18	13	4	4	0	9	9	.203	.167	.250	4.50	4.50
Rogers, Tyler	R-R	6-5	187	12-17-90	1	1	3.10	14	0	0	0	20	16	7	7	0	9	16	.219	.268	.156	7.08	3.98
Shadle, Jake	R-R	6-2	175	4-25-90	4	1	3.03	21	0	0	0	39	32	17	13	2	12	40	.221	.270	.183	9.31	2.79
Slania, Dan	R-R	6-5	275	5-24-92	1	1	3.95	12	0	0	3	14	13	7	6	1	3	14	.245	.188	.333	9.22	1.98
Smith, Jake	R-R	6-4	190	6-2-90	2	2	3.61	19	4	0	0	42	37	19	17	2	21	54	.230	.276	.176	11.48	4.46
Soptic, Jeff	R-R	6-6	220	4-8-91	0	0	2.25	4	0	0	0	4	2	1	1	1	6	.154	.333	.100	13.50	2.25
Vander Tuig, Nick	R-R	6-3	190	12-9-91	0	0	13.50	3	3	0	0	7	15	10	10	1	2	5	.441	.400	.474	6.75	2.70
Young, Pat	R-R	6-5	200	3-24-92	3	1	0.92	8	8	0	0	39	26	7	4	2	9	27	.186	.172	.197	6.18	2.06

Fielding

Catcher	PCT	G	PO	A	E	DP	PB
Cornier	.972	22	151	21	5	1	4
Escalante	.983	30	213	22	4	1	4
Rojas	1.000	2	10	1	0	0	2
Ross	.977	31	238	20	6	0	6

First Base	PCT	G	PO	A	E	DP
Blair	1.000	3	26	1	0	1
Eberle	.996	27	260	12	1	31
Jones	.994	17	145	15	1	18
Miller	.969	14	150	7	5	12
Ragira	.987	18	149	4	2	9

Second Base	PCT	G	PO	A	E	DP
Bednar	.955	20	31	75	5	16
Jones	.980	42	60	135	4	20
Otero	.941	11	20	28	3	11
Polonius	1.000	7	13	24	0	3

Third Base	PCT	G	PO	A	E	DP
Bednar	.933	9	6	22	2	1
Eberle	.891	18	12	37	6	3
Miller	1.000	11	4	14	0	3
Otero	1.000	1	1	1	0	0
Polonius	1.000	7	3	12	0	0
Tuntland	.874	34	19	57	11	7

Shortstop	PCT	G	PO	A	E	DP
Bednar	.910	17	25	46	7	8
Miller	1.000	1	1	0	0	0
Otero	1.000	4	1	2	0	0
Polonius	.979	24	44	97	3	20
Sy	.919	34	49	98	13	22

Outfield	PCT	G	PO	A	E	DP
Blair	1.000	6	17	0	0	0
Hill	.944	14	16	1	1	0
Hollick	1.000	62	102	3	0	1
Horan	.982	38	53	2	1	0
McCall	.924	49	69	4	6	0
Ortiz	.952	43	57	2	3	1
Ragira	.972	26	35	0	1	0

AZL GIANTS ROOKIE

ARIZONA LEAGUE

Batting	B-T	HT	WT	DOB	AVG	vLH	vRH	G	AB	R	H	2B	3B	HR	RBI	BB	HBP	SH	SF	SO	SB	CS	SLG	OBP
Arenado, Jonah	R-R	6-4	195	2-3-95	.211	.400	.143	12	38	6	8	0	1	0	8	4	0	0	0	8	0	0	.263	.286
Arroyo, Christian	R-R	6-1	180	5-30-95	.326	.308	.333	45	184	47	60	18	5	2	39	19	2	0	4	32	3	2	.511	.388
Bednar, Brandon	R-R	6-4	185	3-21-92	.000	.000	.000	1	2	0	0	0	0	0	0	1	1	0	0	1	0	0	.000	.500
Callaway, Will	R-R	6-0	205	12-14-89	.271	.233	.288	31	96	13	26	8	2	1	16	10	2	2	2	19	0	0	.427	.345
Cavan, Ryan	B-R	5-11	180	6-28-87	.526	.500	.536	11	38	8	20	4	1	0	11	4	1	0	1	3	0	0	.684	.568
Delgado, Jean	R-R	5-11	150	2-5-93	.167	.375	.000	8	18	2	3	0	0	0	1	3	0	0	0	4	0	0	.167	.286
Fargas, Johneshwy	R-R	6-1	165	12-15-94	.299	.263	.310	30	77	21	23	4	0	0	2	9	3	1	0	11	8	3	.351	.393
Fuentes, Leonardo	R-R	6-4	215	11-29-92	.261	.211	.280	21	69	12	18	5	2	3	12	6	2	0	0	30	0	1	.522	.338
Horan, Tyler	L-R	6-2	230	12-2-90	.245	.200	.265	13	49	14	12	5	1	0	5	6	0	0	1	12	1	0	.388	.321
Jones, Jonathan	R-R	6-0	205	2-15-92	.225	.379	.176	32	120	18	27	10	0	5	25	16	4	0	1	34	0	0	.433	.333
Jones, Ryder	L-R	6-2	200	6-7-94	.317	.361	.303	37	145	29	46	9	0	1	18	14	5	0	1	38	0	0	.400	.394
Kay, Brett	R-R	5-11	165	4-11-91	.255	.250	.257	29	94	18	24	2	1	1	12	16	2	1	2	26	3	0	.351	.368
Leslie, Ben	L-L	6-1	185	6-28-94	.348	.455	.250	15	23	7	8	2	0	0	2	9	0	0	0	9	1	1	.435	.531
Massoni, Craig	R-R	6-2	215	10-29-91	.272	.300	.259	37	125	27	34	8	0	2	22	19	8	0	0	29	2	1	.384	.401
Melendez, Rene	R-R	6-1	190	1-20-95	.154	.000	.167	4	13	0	2	1	0	0	2	0	0	0	0	6	0	0	.231	.154
Mercedes, Hector	R-R	6-3	185	10-5-91	.215	.150	.233	32	93	15	20	4	2	2	17	4	1	0	0	39	1	0	.366	.255
Miller, Blake	R-R	6-3	195	4-25-90	.211	.250	.192	16	38	9	8	1	0	0	3	10	3	0	0	12	0	0	.237	.412
Moreno, Rando	R-R	5-11	164	6-6-92	.342	.366	.329	28	117	18	40	7	3	0	18	12	0	1	0	18	10	4	.453	.403
Otero, Cristian	R-R	6-0	170	3-30-93	.000	—	.000	2	1	0	0	0	0	0	0	0	0	0	0	1	0	0	.000	.000
Pagan, Angel	B-R	6-2	200	7-2-81	.182	.000	.250	4	11	3	2	1	0	0	2	0	0	0	0	0	0	0	.364	.308
Pare, Matt	L-R	6-0	205	11-17-90	.200	.250	.188	9	20	3	4	0	0	1	5	4	0	0	1	6	0	0	.350	.320
Paulino, Cristian	R-R	5-10	168	9-4-91	.307	.469	.232	34	101	22	31	9	1	2	16	5	3	1	0	17	13	2	.475	.358
Peguero, Francisco	R-R	6-0	190	6-1-88	.308	.333	.300	6	26	5	8	0	1	1	7	0	0	0	0	2	0	0	.500	.308
Pena, Julio	R-R	6-0	185	12-13-92	.238	.214	.248	48	185	27	44	17	3	2	24	8	4	1	1	56	1	0	.395	.283
Pujadas, Fernando	R-R	6-1	179	1-2-92	.306	.344	.288	34	98	12	30	4	2	1	22	12	2	3	1	17	0	0	.418	.389
Ragira, Brian	R-R	6-2	185	1-22-92	.357	.444	.316	7	28	4	10	1	1	0	6	1	0	0	0	6	0	0	.464	.379
Riley, John	R-R	6-0	210	2-14-94	.200	.217	.190	21	65	6	13	2	2	0	8	12	0	0	1	25	0	0	.292	.321
Ross, Ty	R-R	6-1	203	1-17-92	.182	.333	.125	3	11	2	2	1	0	0	2	2	0	0	0	1	0	0	.273	.308
Sanchez, Hector	B-R	6-0	235	11-17-89	.333	—	.333	1	3	0	1	1	0	0	2	0	0	0	0	1	0	0	.667	.333
Stiner, Drew	R-R	6-1	200	9-5-92	.297	.286	.304	14	37	5	11	2	0	1	10	2	0	0	3	10	0	0	.432	.310
Tomlinson, Kelby	R-R	6-2	180	6-16-90	.286	.111	.368	7	28	9	8	1	1	1	2	3	0	0	0	7	1	1	.500	.355
Tuntland, Ryan	R-R	6-1	190	4-30-91	.360	.429	.333	7	25	6	9	3	0	0	3	4	1	0	0	2	0	0	.480	.467

Pitching	B-T	HT	WT	DOB	W	L	ERA	G	GS	CG	SV	IP	H	R	ER	HR	BB	SO	AVG	vLH	vRH	K/9	BB/9
Alvarado, Carlos	R-R	6-4	175	10-22-89	2	0	2.20	15	2	0	5	29	23	10	7	2	6	37	.215	.277	.167	11.62	1.88
Barrios, Marvin	R-R	6-3	145	9-23-92	0	0	9.82	9	0	0	0	7	12	8	8	0	4	8	.375	.375	.375	9.82	4.91
Brooks, Dylan	R-R	6-7	230	8-20-95	0	0	6.14	8	0	0	0	7	6	7	5	0	11	8	.240	.308	.167	9.82	13.50
Connolly, Mike	R-R	6-1	180	10-31-91	2	0	1.32	8	0	0	0	14	8	3	2	0	7	7	.174	.222	.143	4.61	4.61
De Jesus, Enmanuel	L-L	6-0	175	1-6-94	0	0	7.71	3	0	0	0	2	4	2	2	0	1	4	.364	1.000	.125	15.43	3.86
Diaz, Carlos	L-L	6-2	176	11-18-93	2	3	4.99	12	11	0	0	40	43	26	22	1	21	51	.283	.400	.241	11.57	4.76
Feliz, Keurin	R-L	6-0	180	8-17-90	2	0	1.00	9	0	0	2	9	4	1	1	0	5	8	.121	.333	.074	8.00	5.00
Fitzgerald, Justin	R-R	6-5	230	3-3-86	0	0	2.25	1	1	0	0	4	4	1	1	1	2	6	.267	.286	.250	13.50	4.50
Flores, Alejandro	R-R	6-3	180	9-25-93	1	1	7.16	11	4	0	0	16	25	15	13	0	9	11	.338	.385	.313	6.06	4.96
Freite, Renzo	R-R	6-1	170	1-3-93	3	3	5.59	17	0	0	0	19	18	13	12	0	11	17	.257	.270	.242	7.91	5.12
Gonzalez, Nick	L-L	6-4	220	6-26-92	2	1	1.04	7	0	0	1	17	6	8	2	0	3	17	.100	.143	.087	8.83	1.56
Hernandez, Ariel	R-R	6-3	180	3-2-92	0	0	10.57	10	0	0	1	8	4	10	9	0	12	10	.154	.100	.188	11.74	14.09
Hernandez, Rayan	R-R	6-4	230	9-24-95	0	1	8.31	9	0	0	0	9	14	8	8	0	6	8	.378	.412	.350	8.31	6.23
Hughes, Garrett	L-L	6-9	230	8-27-91	2	0	4.70	9	0	0	0	8	8	4	4	1	8	7	.276	.182	.333	8.22	9.39
Johnson, Chase	R-R	6-3	185	1-9-92	1	0	1.69	3	0	0	0	5	5	1	1	0	1	7	.263	.250	.273	11.81	1.69
Jones, Christian	L-L	6-3	210	1-27-91	0	0	1.69	4	0	0	0	5	3	1	1	0	2	4	.167	.250	.143	6.75	3.38
Jones, Nick	L-L	6-6	215	9-15-91	0	0	1.93	17	0	0	2	19	9	4	4	0	9	18	.155	.111	.175	8.68	4.34
Knight, Dusten	R-R	6-0	185	9-7-90	5	1	1.13	18	0	0	2	32	24	8	4	1	11	43	.209	.261	.174	12.09	3.09
Law, Derek	R-R	6-3	218	9-14-90	1	0	3.18	5	0	0	0	6	4	2	2	0	1	9	.200	.222	.182	14.29	1.59
McCasland, Jake	R-R	6-2	215	9-13-91	0	0	4.73	15	0	0	0	13	17	8	7	0	10	13	.321	.348	.300	8.78	6.75
Mella, Keury	R-R	6-2	200	8-2-93	3	2	2.25	10	9	0	0	36	34	12	9	0	11	41	.252	.246	.257	10.25	2.75
Miller, Ethan	R-R	6-5	220	11-19-90	1	0	3.27	8	0	0	0	11	10	5	4	0	5	16	.233	.368	.125	13.09	4.09
Neff, Steven	L-L	6-2	195	2-24-89	0	0	0.96	8	0	0	0	9	6	1	1	0	3	16	.176	.167	.182	15.43	2.89
Nova, Juan	R-R	6-3	190	10-7-91	0	0	13.50	2	0	0	0	2	5	4	3	1	2	3	.417	.500	.333	13.50	9.00
Petit, Yusmeiro	R-R	6-1	255	11-22-84	1	0	1.80	1	1	0	0	5	3	1	1	0	0	8	.150	.250	.083	14.40	0.00
Pino, Luis	R-R	6-0	175	11-4-94	0	1	3.94	14	6	0	0	30	30	17	13	0	18	26	.259	.273	.246	7.89	5.46
Reyes, Jose	R-R	6-1	184	1-3-91	2	0	2.84	6	0	0	0	6	4	2	2	1	1	7	.182	.364	.000	9.95	1.42
Rogers, Tyler	R-R	6-5	187	12-17-90	0	0	0.00	6	0	0	0	7	6	0	0	0	3	15	.214	.100	.278	19.29	3.86
Sanchez, Eury	R-R	5-10	170	11-8-92	1	0	1.13	14	0	0	7	16	12	2	2	0	4	26	.211	.273	.171	14.63	2.25
Simpson, William	R-R	6-3	210	9-15-91	1	0	2.35	8	0	0	0	8	5	3	2	0	5	9	.179	.250	.083	10.57	5.87
Snelten, D.J.	L-L	6-6	215	5-29-92	3	1	1.57	14	6	0	0	34	27	11	6	0	13	39	.208	.209	.207	10.22	3.41
Vander Tuig, Nick	R-R	6-3	190	12-9-91	0	0	0.00	1	1	0	0	1	0	0	0	0	0	2	.000	.000	.000	18.00	0.00
Vogelsong, Ryan	R-R	6-4	215	7-22-77	0	0	0.00	1	1	0	0	2	2	0	0	0	0	2	.286	.000	.333	9.00	0.00
Young, Pat	R-R	6-5	200	3-24-92	1	0	3.60	2	1	0	0	5	4	2	2	0	1	5	.222	.143	.273	9.00	1.80
Ysla, Luis	L-L	6-1	185	4-27-92	4	0	2.65	12	12	0	0	51	38	18	15	1	13	52	.204	.200	.206	9.18	2.29

SAN FRANCISCO GIANTS

Fielding

Catcher	PCT	G	PO	A	E	DP	PB
Melendez	.967	4	26	3	1	0	1
Pare	1.000	9	70	4	0	1	9
Pujadas	.978	31	241	21	6	0	8
Riley	.981	14	97	6	2	0	7
Ross	.957	2	22	0	1	0	0
Sanchez	1.000	1	8	2	0	0	0
Stiner	.980	12	94	5	2	1	5

First Base	PCT	G	PO	A	E	DP
Jones	.997	32	271	34	1	22
Massoni	.973	15	101	7	3	7
Miller	1.000	6	41	2	0	1
Ragira	.980	7	47	1	1	5

Second Base	PCT	G	PO	A	E	DP
Callaway	.970	18	27	37	2	8
Cavan	1.000	5	8	13	0	3
Delgado	.846	4	5	6	2	1
Kay	.979	13	19	27	1	2
Moreno	.961	23	38	61	4	14

Third Base	PCT	G	PO	A	E	DP
Arenado	.952	9	5	15	1	1
Callaway	1.000	7	1	9	0	0
Cavan	.750	4	0	3	1	0
Delgado	.909	4	4	6	1	0
Jones	.909	31	7	53	6	2
Miller	.938	9	1	14	1	1
Paulino	1.000	1	1	0	0	0
Tuntland	.333	3	0	1	2	1

Shortstop	PCT	G	PO	A	E	DP
Arroyo	.958	40	56	128	8	25
Kay	.935	12	8	21	2	3
Moreno	.913	7	4	17	2	1
Otero	1.000	2	1	0	0	0
Tomlinson	.933	7	12	16	2	1

Outfield	PCT	G	PO	A	E	DP
Fargas	1.000	24	27	0	0	0
Fuentes	1.000	16	15	1	0	0
Horan	.941	12	14	2	1	0
Leslie	1.000	14	8	1	0	0
Massoni	.957	18	22	0	1	0
Mercedes	1.000	30	29	4	0	0
Pagan	1.000	4	8	0	0	0
Paulino	.941	31	45	3	3	0
Peguero	1.000	6	4	1	0	0
Pena	.984	48	58	3	1	0

DSL GIANTS   ROOKIE
DOMINICAN SUMMER LEAGUE

Batting	B-T	HT	WT	DOB	AVG	vLH	vRH	G	AB	R	H	2B	3B	HR	RBI	BB	HBP	SH	SF	SO	SB	CS	SLG	OBP
Angomas, Jean	L-R	6-0	170	6-5-95	.286	.250	.296	51	175	32	50	7	5	0	15	25	3	1	0	17	9	9	.383	.384
Antunez, Robert	R-R	5-10	160	3-22-96	.233	.333	.208	28	30	13	7	1	0	0	4	9	0	2	0	11	6	1	.267	.410
Astacio, Royel	B-R	6-2	197	9-27-93	.184	.214	.177	47	141	19	26	9	1	1	14	34	2	0	0	44	3	4	.284	.350
Barias, Raiby	R-R	6-2	185	9-29-95	.071	.143	.048	13	28	3	2	0	0	0	0	2	0	0	0	15	0	0	.071	.133
Cabrera, Gustavo	R-R	6-2	190	1-23-96	.247	.250	.246	54	186	38	46	7	4	2	22	30	10	2	1	54	21	7	.360	.379
Cartagena, Carlos	R-R	6-2	190	12-22-93	.200	.250	.186	41	110	23	22	1	1	4	18	25	5	0	1	35	7	1	.336	.369
Gomez, Anthony	R-R	6-3	200	11-19-94	.154	.143	.156	16	39	3	6	2	0	0	1	9	1	0	0	10	0	0	.205	.327
Gomez, Miguel	B-R	5-10	185	12-17-92	.315	.391	.295	35	111	16	35	12	1	2	23	10	1	0	1	27	1	0	.495	.374
Guzman, Marco	R-R	6-0	170	8-7-94	.254	.167	.280	46	130	19	33	9	1	1	10	23	1	1	1	26	4	4	.362	.368
Hernandez, Emmanuel	R-R	6-1	185	11-2-93	.245	.174	.267	32	98	8	24	6	1	0	14	13	0	0	0	25	1	0	.327	.333
Javier, Nathanael	R-R	6-3	185	10-10-95	.229	.190	.243	59	236	23	54	13	2	2	28	12	5	1	4	43	4	4	.326	.276
Medina, Hengerber	R-R	5-11	158	10-12-94	.162	.175	.157	53	148	22	24	3	1	0	9	17	7	3	0	37	7	3	.196	.279
Medrano, Robinson	R-R	6-3	180	4-20-96	.225	.176	.240	40	138	17	31	3	1	1	11	7	1	0	0	35	7	2	.283	.267
Mora, Jose	R-R	5-11	175	1-16-93	.310	.222	.327	23	58	8	18	4	2	0	11	5	0	1	0	6	1	0	.448	.365
Morles, Jose	L-R	5-10	180	8-18-94	.231	.333	.200	20	52	5	12	2	0	0	3	10	1	0	0	12	0	1	.269	.365
Parra, Nicoll	L-L	5-9	160	7-28-94	.244	.269	.237	40	119	23	29	3	1	0	18	36	6	0	0	21	20	5	.286	.441
Rivas, Kleiber	L-R	5-11	200	6-22-95	.250	.200	.272	42	116	8	29	8	0	2	20	19	1	0	1	15	2	2	.371	.358
Rodriguez, Richard	R-R	6-1	170	10-3-92	.227	.143	.253	43	119	20	27	0	1	0	9	20	1	2	0	18	7	4	.244	.340
Valdez, Carlos	R-R	5-11	180	6-22-94	.273	.278	.271	37	132	22	36	2	3	5	13	20	2	0	0	22	4	3	.447	.377

Pitching	B-T	HT	WT	DOB	W	L	ERA	G	GS	CG	SV	IP	H	R	ER	HR	BB	SO	AVG	vLH	vRH	K/9	BB/9
Castillo, Luis	R-R	6-2	170	12-12-92	0	1	0.64	27	0	0	20	28	15	5	2	0	3	34	.150	.167	.145	10.80	0.95
De La Cruz, Jose	L-L	6-2	175	6-19-93	0	2	6.14	10	0	0	0	15	14	12	10	1	16	15	.255	.083	.302	9.20	9.82
Encarnacion, Eusebio	R-R	5-11	170	8-6-94	5	1	1.72	14	10	0	1	68	56	19	13	2	12	49	.225	.194	.235	6.49	1.59
Gomez, Shawn	R-R	6-4	180	8-24-94	7	0	2.76	18	0	0	0	42	41	14	13	3	15	27	.268	.372	.227	5.74	3.19
Guzman, Eber	R-R	6-3	195	4-8-93	4	4	3.34	14	13	0	0	70	60	33	26	2	24	59	.236	.280	.218	7.59	3.09
Loaisiga, Jonathan	R-R	5-11	165	11-2-94	8	1	2.75	13	13	0	0	69	60	29	21	4	16	40	.240	.397	.193	5.24	2.10
Morel, Jose	R-R	6-2	190	9-6-93	6	0	1.22	22	1	0	6	59	48	13	8	1	6	55	.223	.316	.203	8.39	0.92
Parra, Olbis	R-R	6-2	180	10-1-94	5	3	4.13	13	13	0	0	57	57	33	26	1	17	37	.260	.250	.265	5.88	2.70
Revolledo, Dainer	L-L	6-3	200	12-1-93	1	1	4.24	7	0	0	1	17	12	10	8	0	13	6	.207	.143	.216	3.18	6.88
Richardson, Clarence	R-R	6-3	190	5-11-94	0	1	5.16	14	0	0	2	23	17	17	13	1	14	33	.202	.190	.206	13.10	5.56
Rodriguez, Reymi	R-R	6-2	195	8-30-94	7	1	1.36	17	2	0	1	46	24	10	7	0	23	49	.155	.228	.112	9.52	4.47
Santos, Michael	R-R	6-4	170	5-29-95	1	2	2.75	4	4	0	0	20	18	7	6	0	6	18	.240	.172	.283	8.24	2.75
Vizcaino, Raffi	R-R	6-1	195	12-2-95	0	3	3.80	11	11	0	0	47	46	26	20	2	17	41	.254	.178	.279	7.80	3.23
Yanez, Cesar	R-R	6-5	175	9-30-94	2	2	2.23	13	0	0	0	32	26	16	8	0	15	32	.218	.100	.258	8.91	4.18

Fielding

Catcher	PCT	G	PO	A	E	DP	PB
Gomez	.981	19	130	23	3	0	3
Mora	.993	23	117	19	1	0	2
Morles	.993	20	113	22	1	1	8
Rivas	.976	20	110	12	3	0	2
Rodriguez	.750	1	3	0	1	0	0

First Base	PCT	G	PO	A	E	DP
Astacio	.994	34	305	14	2	25
Gomez	.985	8	63	2	1	1
Gomez	1.000	4	41	1	0	6
Hernandez	.996	25	236	10	1	13
Rodriguez	1.000	1	3	0	0	0
Rodriguez	1.000	8	12	0	0	1

Second Base	PCT	G	PO	A	E	DP
Antunez	.946	17	19	34	3	3
Guzman	.964	36	60	75	5	14
Rivas	—	1	0	0	0	0
Rodriguez	.973	30	45	64	3	13

Third Base	PCT	G	PO	A	E	DP
Astacio	1.000	6	7	16	0	0
Gomez	.833	4	0	5	1	0
Javier	.911	59	47	127	17	15
Rodriguez	—	1	0	0	0	0

Shortstop	PCT	G	PO	A	E	DP
Gomez	.667	1	1	1	1	1
Guzman	1.000	16	18	36	0	5

Medina	.962	52	83	145	9	22
Rodriguez	1.000	1	3	1	0	0
Rodriguez	.892	8	13	20	4	2

Outfield	PCT	G	PO	A	E	DP
Angomas	.970	44	61	3	2	1
Barias	1.000	5	1	0	0	0
Cabrera	.966	53	110	5	4	1
Cartagena	1.000	34	52	3	0	0
Medrano	.922	39	42	5	4	0
Parra	1.000	20	33	1	0	1
Valdez	.861	31	29	2	5	0

Seattle Mariners

SEASON IN A SENTENCE: Any thoughts that the rebuilding Mariners could be a factor in the ultra-competitive AL West fell to the wayside quickly, and the team stumbled its way to a fourth consecutive losing season at 71-91.

HIGH POINT: The Mariners had only one winning month (15-10 in July), so high points were few and far between. July did include Seattle's longest winning streak at eight games, highlighted by Felix Hernandez throwing eight shutout innings against the Angels on July 13. Hernandez and rotation-mate Hisashi Iwakuma were the Mariners' only all-stars and both finished among the AL's top 10 in ERA.

LOW POINT: Any good feelings from the Mariners' July winning streak were tempered on July 22 when manager Eric Wedge suffered a stroke. The Mariners lurched to the finish line by going 9-18 in September, punctuating the season with a dispiriting 9-0 loss to the division-winning Athletics at Safeco Field.

NOTABLE ROOKIES: The Mariners imported plenty of youth with 11 players making their major league debuts. Among the most notable, Mike Zunino became the first position player from the 2012 draft to reach the majors and took over the everyday catching duties. Second baseman Nick Franklin and shortstop Brad Miller formed a homegrown double-play tandem in the second half while showing flashes of their offensive potential.

KEY TRANSACTIONS: The Mariners looked to give their lineup some veteran punch, trading for Michael Morse and Kendrys Morales and signing Raul Ibanez in free agency, but the results were mixed at best. Despite the changes, the Mariners produced an offense that finished last in the AL in average (.237) and 12th in runs. Ibanez and Morales, who led the team with a .277 average and 80 RBIs, did their parts, but Morse struggled to a .226/.283/.410 line before being traded away.

DOWN ON THE FARM: For all the young talent making its way to Seattle, one glaring absence was lefthander Danny Hultzen, the second overall pick in 2011. Hultzen was shut down and needed shoulder surgery. There was brighter news elsewhere, however. Top pitching prospect Taijuan Walker lived up to his considerable billing, posting a 2.93 ERA between Double-A and Triple-A. Rookie-level Pulaski captured the Appalachian League title, led by league pitcher of the year Edwin Diaz and player of the year Tyler Smith.

OPENING DAY PAYROLL: $72 million (24th)

PLAYERS OF THE YEAR

MAJOR LEAGUE

Hisashi Iwakuma
rhp

14-6, 2.66 in 33 GS
1.01 WHIP, 7.6 SO/9
3rd in AL ERA race

MINOR LEAGUE

Taijuan Walker
rhp

(Double-A/Triple-A)
9-10, 2.93 in 25 GS
1.20 WHIP, 10.2 SO/9

ORGANIZATION LEADERS

BATTING   *Minimum 250 AB

MAJORS

* AVG	Morales, Kendrys	.277
* OPS	Morales, Kendrys	.785
HR	Ibanez, Raul	29
RBI	Morales, Kendrys	80

MINORS

* AVG	Taylor, Chris, Jackson/High Desert	.314
* OBP	Taylor, Chris, Jackson/High Desert	.409
* SLG	Choi, Ji-Man, Tacoma/Jackson/High Desert	.535
R	Taylor, Chris, Jackson/High Desert	108
H	Taylor, Chris, Jackson/High Desert	165
TB	Rivers, Kevin, High Desert	250
2B	Pizzano, Dario, Clinton	40
3B	Taylor, Chris, Jackson/High Desert	11
HR	Blash, Jabari, Jackson/High Desert	25
RBI	Rivers, Kevin, High Desert	97
BB	Taylor, Chris, Jackson/High Desert	84
SO	Peguero, Carlos, Tacoma	156
SB	Austin, Jamal, High Desert	40

PITCHING   #Minimum 75 IP

MAJORS

W	Iwakuma, Hisashi	14
# ERA	Iwakuma, Hisashi	2.66
SO	Hernandez, Felix	216
SV	Wilhelmsen, Tom	24

MINORS

W	DeCecco, Scott, High Desert/Clinton	10
L	Three tied at	11
# ERA	Sanchez, Victor, Clinton	2.78
G	Bawcom, Logan, Tacoma	51
	Wood, Grady, High Desert/Clinton	51
GS	DeCecco, Scott, High Desert/Clinton	27
SV	Bawcom, Logan, Tacoma	21
IP	DeCecco, Scott, High Desert/Clinton	150
BB	Paxton, James, Tacoma	58
SO	Walker, Taijuan, Tacoma/Jackson	160
# AVG	Walker, Taijuan, Jackson/Tacoma	.217

General Manager: Jack Zduriencik. **Farm Director:** Chris Gwynn. **Scouting Director:** Tom McNamara.

Class	Team	League	W	L	PCT	Finish	Manager(s)
Majors	Seattle Mariners	American	71	91	.438	12th (15)	Eric Wedge
Triple-A	Tacoma Rainiers	Pacific Coast	73	68	.518	t-6th (16)	Daren Brown/John Stearns
Double-A	Jackson Generals	Southern	62	73	.459	7th (10)	Jim Pankovits
High A	High Desert Mavericks	California	64	76	.457	8th (10)	Jim Horner
Low A	Clinton Lumber Kings	Midwest	67	72	.482	9th (16)	Eddie Menchaca
Short-season	Everett Aquasox	Northwest	44	32	.579	2nd (8)	Rob Mummau
Rookie	Pulaski Mariners	Appalachian	41	27	.603	1st (10)	Chris Prieto
Rookie	AZL Mariners	Arizona	22	32	.407	11th (13)	Darrin Garner
Overall 2013 Minor League Record			376	380	.497	t-13th (30)	

ORGANIZATION STATISTICS

AMERICAN LEAGUE

Batting	B-T	HT	WT	DOB	AVG	vLH	vRH	G	AB	R	H	2B	3B	HR	RBI	BB	HBP	SH	SF	SO	SB	CS	SLG	OBP
Ackley, Dustin	L-R	6-1	195	2-26-88	.253	.259	.250	113	384	40	97	18	2	4	31	37	1	4	1	72	2	3	.341	.319
Almonte, Abe	B-R	5-9	205	6-27-89	.264	.207	.302	25	72	10	19	4	0	2	9	6	0	2	2	21	1	0	.403	.313
Andino, Robert	R-R	6-0	195	4-25-84	.184	.290	.111	29	76	5	14	4	0	0	4	7	0	2	0	27	0	0	.237	.253
Bantz, Brandon	R-R	6-1	205	1-7-87	.000	.000	—	1	2	0	0	0	0	0	0	0	0	0	0	1	0	0	.000	.000
Bay, Jason	R-R	6-2	210	9-20-78	.204	.226	.180	68	206	30	42	6	0	11	20	26	2	1	1	62	3	1	.393	.298
Blanco, Henry	R-R	5-11	220	8-29-71	.125	.138	.119	35	96	8	12	2	0	3	14	10	1	0	0	26	0	0	.240	.215
2-team total (15 Toronto)					.142			50	134	11	19	5	0	3	14	14	1	1	0	36	0	0	.246	.228
Chavez, Endy	L-L	5-11	170	2-7-78	.267	.254	.271	97	266	22	71	10	0	2	14	9	0	3	1	31	1	3	.327	.290
Franklin, Nick	B-R	6-1	195	3-2-91	.225	.210	.232	102	369	38	83	20	1	12	45	42	0	0	1	113	6	1	.382	.303
Gutierrez, Franklin	R-R	6-2	195	2-21-83	.248	.218	.267	41	145	18	36	7	0	10	24	5	0	1	0	43	3	1	.503	.273
Ibanez, Raul	L-R	6-2	225	6-2-72	.242	.244	.242	124	454	54	110	20	2	29	65	42	0	0	1	128	0	0	.487	.306
Liddi, Alex	R-R	6-4	225	8-14-88	.059	.000	.071	8	17	0	1	1	0	0	0	1	0	0	0	7	0	0	.118	.111
Miller, Brad	L-R	6-2	185	10-18-89	.265	.270	.262	76	306	41	81	11	6	8	36	24	1	2	2	52	5	3	.418	.318
Montero, Jesus	R-R	6-3	230	11-28-89	.208	.167	.225	29	101	6	21	1	1	3	9	8	0	0	1	21	0	1	.327	.264
Morales, Kendrys	B-R	6-1	225	6-20-83	.277	.282	.275	156	602	64	167	34	0	23	80	49	5	0	1	114	0	0	.449	.336
Morse, Michael	R-R	6-5	245	3-22-82	.226	.245	.216	76	283	31	64	13	0	13	27	20	3	0	1	80	0	0	.410	.283
2-team total (12 Baltimore)					.215			88	312	34	67	13	0	13	27	21	3	0	1	87	0	0	.381	.270
Peguero, Carlos	L-L	6-5	260	2-22-87	.333	—	.333	2	6	1	2	0	0	1	1	1	0	0	0	2	1	0	.833	.429
Quintero, Humberto	R-R	5-9	215	8-2-79	.224	.194	.250	22	67	5	15	1	0	2	4	3	0	2	0	15	0	0	.328	.257
Ryan, Brendan	R-R	6-2	195	3-26-82	.192	.179	.199	87	260	23	50	10	0	3	21	21	1	4	1	60	4	2	.265	.254
2-team total (17 New York)					.197			104	319	30	63	12	0	4	22	23	2	4	1	73	4	2	.273	.255
Saunders, Michael	L-R	6-4	225	11-19-86	.236	.211	.249	132	406	59	96	23	3	12	46	54	1	1	6	118	13	5	.397	.323
Seager, Kyle	L-R	6-0	215	11-3-87	.260	.235	.276	160	615	79	160	32	2	22	69	68	7	0	5	122	9	3	.426	.338
Shoppach, Kelly	R-R	6-0	220	4-29-80	.196	.167	.208	35	107	11	21	7	0	3	9	12	3	2	1	45	0	0	.346	.293
2-team total (1 Cleveland)					.193			36	109	11	21	7	0	3	9	12	3	2	1	46	0	0	.339	.288
Smoak, Justin	B-L	6-4	220	12-5-86	.238	.192	.260	131	454	53	108	19	0	20	50	64	2	0	1	119	0	0	.412	.334
Sucre, Jesus	R-R	6-0	225	4-30-88	.192	.250	.167	8	26	1	5	0	0	0	3	2	0	0	1	0	0	0	.192	.241
Triunfel, Carlos	R-R	5-11	205	2-27-90	.136	.143	.130	17	44	1	6	1	0	0	2	0	1	1	1	11	0	0	.159	.152
Zunino, Mike	R-R	6-2	220	3-25-91	.214	.217	.213	52	173	22	37	5	0	5	14	16	3	0	1	49	1	0	.329	.290

Pitching	B-T	HT	WT	DOB	W	L	ERA	G	GS	CG	SV	IP	H	R	ER	HR	BB	SO	AVG	vLH	vRH	K/9	BB/9
Beavan, Blake	R-R	6-7	255	1-17-89	0	2	6.13	12	2	0	0	40	46	27	27	8	8	27	.284	.279	.287	6.13	1.82
Bonderman, Jeremy	R-R	6-0	220	10-28-82	1	3	4.93	7	7	0	0	38	40	23	21	4	17	16	.267	.308	.203	3.76	3.99
2-Team total (11 Detroit)					2	4	5.40	18	7	0	0	55	58	36	33	7	27	32	—	—	—	5.24	4.42
Capps, Carter	R-R	6-5	220	8-7-90	3	3	5.49	53	0	0	0	59	73	37	36	12	23	66	.302	.323	.288	10.07	3.51
Farquhar, Danny	R-R	5-9	180	2-17-87	0	3	4.20	46	0	0	16	56	44	29	26	2	22	79	.217	.171	.265	12.77	3.56
Furbush, Charlie	L-L	6-5	215	4-11-86	2	6	3.74	71	0	0	0	65	48	33	27	5	29	80	.199	.173	.221	11.08	4.02
Harang, Aaron	R-R	6-7	260	5-9-78	5	11	5.76	22	22	2	0	120	133	81	77	21	28	87	.274	.291	.651	2.09	
Hernandez, Felix	R-R	6-3	230	4-8-86	12	10	3.04	31	31	0	0	204	185	74	69	15	46	216	.242	.251	.232	9.51	2.03
Iwakuma, Hisashi	R-R	6-3	210	4-12-81	14	6	2.66	33	33	0	0	220	179	69	65	25	42	185	.220	.216	.225	7.58	1.72
LaFromboise, Bobby	L-L	6-4	215	6-25-86	0	1	5.91	10	0	0	0	11	12	8	7	0	4	11	.286	.286	.286	9.28	3.38
Loe, Kameron	R-R	6-8	245	9-10-81	1	1	10.80	4	0	0	0	7	11	8	8	6	1	3	.367	.400	.350	4.05	1.35
Luetge, Lucas	L-L	6-4	205	3-24-87	1	3	4.86	35	0	0	0	37	42	22	20	2	16	27	.296	.259	.318	6.57	3.89
Maurer, Brandon	R-R	6-5	215	7-3-90	5	8	6.30	22	14	0	0	90	114	66	63	16	27	70	.311	.321	.299	7.00	2.70
Medina, Yoervis	R-R	6-3	245	7-27-88	4	6	2.91	63	0	0	1	68	49	22	22	5	40	71	.201	.191	.209	9.40	5.29
Noesi, Hector	R-R	6-3	205	1-26-87	0	1	6.59	12	1	0	0	27	42	21	20	3	12	21	.353	.373	.333	6.91	3.95
Paxton, James	L-L	6-4	220	11-6-88	3	0	1.50	4	4	0	0	24	15	5	4	2	7	21	.172	.313	.141	7.88	2.63
Perez, Oliver	L-L	6-3	220	8-15-81	3	3	3.74	61	0	0	2	53	50	23	22	6	26	74	.249	.291	.256	12.57	4.42
Pryor, Stephen	R-R	6-4	250	7-23-89	0	0	0.00	7	0	0	0	7	3	0	0	0	1	7	.120	.000	.158	8.59	1.23
Ramirez, Erasmo	R-R	5-11	200	5-2-90	5	3	4.98	14	13	0	0	72	79	44	40	12	26	57	.273	.286	.254	7.09	3.24
Ruffin, Chance	R-R	6-0	195	9-8-88	0	2	8.38	9	0	0	0	10	14	10	9	3	5	15	.333	.333	.333	13.97	4.66
Saunders, Joe	L-L	6-3	215	6-16-81	11	16	5.26	32	32	2	0	183	232	117	107	25	61	107	.311	.214	.337	5.26	3.00
Walker, Taijuan	R-R	6-4	210	8-13-92	1	0	3.60	3	3	0	0	15	11	7	6	0	4	12	.204	.194	.222	7.20	2.40
Wilhelmsen, Tom	R-R	6-6	220	12-16-83	0	3	4.12	59	0	0	24	59	45	28	27	2	33	45	.213	.287	.145	6.86	5.03

Fielding

Catcher	PCT	G	PO	A	E	DP	PB
Bantz	1.000	1	5	0	0	0	0
Blanco	.989	34	246	13	3	4	2
Montero	.995	26	207	11	1	0	3
Quintero	.994	21	158	12	1	3	2
Shoppach	.996	35	263	14	1	0	2
Sucre	1.000	8	60	6	0	1	0
Zunino	.995	50	363	22	2	1	2

First Base	PCT	G	PO	A	E	DP
Ackley	1.000	6	11	1	0	0
Liddi	1.000	6	34	0	0	4
Morales	.997	31	293	13	1	26
Morse	1.000	7	59	3	0	9
Smoak	.995	125	1035	60	5	101

Second Base	PCT	G	PO	A	E	DP
Ackley	1.000	53	81	150	0	30
Andino	1.000	8	15	27	0	9
Franklin	.975	96	139	326	12	64
Miller	.979	13	22	25	1	5
Triunfel	1.000	4	5	6	0	2

Third Base	PCT	G	PO	A	E	DP
Andino	1.000	4	1	5	0	0
Miller	1.000	3	0	1	0	0
Seager	.964	160	94	308	15	38
Triunfel	1.000	1	1	0	0	0

Shortstop	PCT	G	PO	A	E	DP
Andino	.953	18	12	29	2	8
Franklin	1.000	3	4	10	0	3

Miller	.972	68	87	155	7	30
Ryan	.968	84	96	240	11	52
Triunfel	.944	10	11	23	2	6

Outfield	PCT	G	PO	A	E	DP
Ackley	.993	59	134	1	1	1
Almonte	.895	23	33	1	4	0
Bay	1.000	61	103	2	0	0
Chavez	.975	82	149	4	4	2
Gutierrez	.987	38	78	0	1	0
Ibanez	.977	100	165	6	4	1
Morse	.991	62	108	1	1	0
Peguero	1.000	2	3	0	0	0
Saunders	.996	126	255	7	1	2

TACOMA RAINIERS
PACIFIC COAST LEAGUE

TRIPLE-A

Batting	B-T	HT	WT	DOB	AVG	vLH	vRH	G	AB	R	H	2B	3B	HR	RBI	BB	HBP	SH	SF	SO	SB	CS	SLG	OBP
Ackley, Dustin	L-R	6-1	195	2-26-88	.365	.296	.390	25	104	21	38	8	0	2	14	19	2	1	0	14	0	0	.500	.472
Almonte, Abe	L-R	5-9	205	6-27-89	.314	.254	.330	94	338	63	106	17	5	11	50	49	2	6	1	66	20	7	.491	.403
Almonte, Denny	B-R	6-2	190	9-24-88	.163	.200	.153	28	92	13	15	3	1	3	9	6	0	2	1	50	4	1	.315	.212
Andino, Robert	R-R	6-0	195	4-25-84	.229	.391	.200	44	153	17	35	5	1	3	12	12	0	0	2	38	2	1	.333	.281
Avery, Xavier	L-L	6-0	190	1-1-90	.500	1.000	.455	3	12	5	6	1	0	1	3	1	0	1	0	1	1	0	.833	.538
Bantz, Brandon	R-R	6-1	205	1-7-87	.252	.333	.238	37	123	8	31	2	2	2	11	11	2	1	0	27	0	3	.350	.324
Bonilla, Leury	R-R	6-2	195	2-8-85	.254	.182	.269	42	130	18	33	4	0	2	7	11	0	8	0	26	2	5	.331	.312
Chavez, Endy	L-L	5-11	170	2-7-78	.429	.000	.462	6	28	8	12	1	0	0	1	3	0	0	0	3	0	2	.464	.484
Choi, Ji-Man	L-R	6-1	195	5-19-91	.244	.500	.189	13	45	9	11	2	0	2	6	4	2	1	0	7	0	0	.422	.333
Dunigan, Joe	L-L	6-1	240	3-29-86	.193	.167	.200	25	88	13	17	2	1	4	11	10	1	0	1	44	3	0	.375	.280
Franklin, Nick	B-R	6-1	195	3-2-91	.324	.333	.321	39	142	28	46	9	0	4	20	30	1	2	2	20	7	0	.472	.440
Gutierrez, Franklin	R-R	6-2	195	2-21-83	.211	.294	.182	47	194	27	41	16	0	3	25	15	2	0	2	60	4	2	.340	.272
Jaramillo, Jason	B-R	6-0	215	10-9-82	.257	.375	.221	38	136	13	35	10	0	2	15	9	0	1	1	26	0	0	.375	.301
2-team total (23 Oklahoma City)					.215	—	—	61	205	17	44	13	1	2	22	20	2	1	1	44	0	0	.317	.283
Jones, James	L-L	6-4	193	9-24-88	.333	.200	.400	4	15	2	5	2	0	0	1	2	0	0	0	2	0	0	.467	.412
Kelly, Ty	L-R	6-0	185	7-20-88	.320	.406	.278	54	197	34	63	6	1	3	17	51	0	2	2	41	3	7	.406	.456
Liddi, Alex	R-R	6-4	225	8-14-88	.263	.333	.247	59	240	46	63	9	2	11	43	20	1	1	0	86	7	1	.454	.322
Miller, Brad	L-R	6-2	185	10-18-89	.356	.399	.347	26	104	26	37	5	1	6	28	15	0	0	3	18	2	1	.596	.426
Montero, Jesus	R-R	6-3	230	11-28-89	.247	.474	.167	19	73	12	18	6	2	1	9	8	0	0	1	24	0	0	.425	.317
Morse, Michael	R-R	6-5	245	3-22-82	.250	.200	.263	6	24	3	6	1	0	1	2	2	0	0	0	6	0	0	.417	.308
Patterson, Corey	L-R	5-10	180	8-13-79	.175	.250	.164	19	63	6	11	1	1	1	8	3	1	1	0	16	2	0	.270	.224
Peguero, Carlos	L-L	6-5	260	2-22-87	.260	.219	.274	118	454	60	118	28	3	19	83	42	2	0	7	156	11	8	.460	.321
Poythress, Rich	R-R	6-4	235	8-11-87	.252	.200	.267	100	365	47	92	24	1	13	57	46	2	0	3	77	3	1	.430	.337
Romero, Stefen	R-R	6-2	220	10-17-88	.277	.213	.295	93	375	51	104	23	4	11	74	28	4	0	4	87	8	4	.448	.331
Saunders, Michael	L-R	6-4	225	11-19-86	.182	.500	.111	3	11	2	2	1	1	0	2	3	1	0	1	0	0	0	.455	.375
Savastano, Scott	R-R	6-4	190	6-12-86	.235	.225	.238	58	183	16	43	4	2	3	20	15	2	0	5	41	4	2	.328	.293
Smoak, Justin	B-L	6-4	220	12-5-86	.238	.375	.154	5	21	2	5	2	0	0	1	0	1	0	0	5	0	0	.333	.273
Sucre, Jesus	R-R	6-0	225	4-30-88	.299	.222	.319	23	87	10	26	3	0	0	8	7	0	1	0	11	1	1	.333	.351
Tenbrink, Nate	L-R	6-2	202	12-21-86	.267	.202	.283	124	430	77	115	24	4	15	60	62	5	3	5	135	12	7	.447	.363
Thames, Eric	L-R	6-0	210	11-10-86	.295	.300	.294	57	217	32	64	15	2	7	33	29	2	0	1	62	3	1	.479	.382
Torres, Dan	R-R	6-0	175	5-29-92	.000	.000	—	1	1	0	0	0	0	0	0	0	0	0	0	0	0	0	.000	.000
Triunfel, Carlos	R-R	5-11	205	2-27-90	.282	.304	.276	100	383	55	108	22	3	5	31	17	10	2	1	76	6	4	.394	.328
Zunino, Mike	R-R	6-2	220	3-25-91	.227	.231	.226	52	203	38	46	12	3	11	43	17	5	0	4	66	0	0	.478	.297

Pitching	B-T	HT	WT	DOB	W	L	ERA	G	GS	CG	SV	IP	H	R	ER	HR	BB	SO	AVG	vLH	vRH	K/9	BB/9
Arias, Jonathan	R-R	6-3	210	2-8-88	4	2	5.58	32	2	0	2	60	63	40	37	10	26	64	.274	.312	.248	9.65	3.92
Bawcom, Logan	R-R	6-2	220	11-2-88	1	4	2.91	51	0	0	21	65	56	24	21	4	24	64	.235	.234	.236	8.86	3.32
Beavan, Blake	R-R	6-7	255	1-19-89	6	6	5.55	16	16	0	0	94	120	61	58	15	23	47	.317	.298	.333	4.50	2.20
Bonderman, Jeremy	R-R	6-0	220	10-28-82	2	4	4.52	11	11	0	0	64	77	34	32	7	18	33	.302	.369	.250	4.66	2.54
Burgoon, Tyler	R-R	5-10	160	4-25-89	1	0	10.80	2	0	0	0	3	3	4	4	0	2	3	.250	.333	.222	8.10	5.40
Capps, Carter	R-R	6-5	220	8-7-90	0	0	1.64	7	0	0	0	11	6	3	2	0	4	9	.167	.222	.148	7.36	3.27
Carraway, Andrew	R-R	6-2	205	9-24-86	6	8	5.61	22	22	0	0	119	139	86	74	18	55	84	.290	.299	.282	6.37	4.17
Farquhar, Danny	R-R	5-9	180	2-17-87	0	1	2.25	15	0	0	6	20	17	6	5	1	4	30	.221	.321	.163	13.50	1.80
Gillheeney, Jimmy	L-L	6-1	200	11-8-87	2	2	4.50	6	5	0	0	32	30	17	16	5	9	25	.254	.220	.273	7.03	2.53
Hensley, Steven	R-R	6-3	190	12-27-86	0	0	3.38	2	0	0	0	3	2	1	1	0	2	0	.200	.000	.400	0.00	6.75
2-team total (31 Colorado Springs)					0	2	4.60	33	1	0	0	43	51	28	22	7	26	43	—	—	—	9.00	5.44
Hill, Nick	L-L	6-0	190	1-30-85	1	0	3.00	2	0	0	0	3	2	1	1	0	0	2	.200	.333	.143	6.00	0.00
Hultzen, Danny	L-L	6-3	200	11-28-89	4	1	2.05	6	6	0	0	31	19	9	7	1	7	34	.168	.097	.195	9.98	2.05
Kinney, Josh	R-R	6-0	220	3-31-79	2	2	4.36	30	0	0	1	33	20	16	16	1	10	32	.168	.240	.116	8.73	2.73
Kittredge, Andrew	R-R	6-1	200	3-17-90	0	0	7.27	10	1	0	0	17	24	14	14	3	9	8	.329	.414	.273	4.15	4.67
LaFromboise, Bobby	L-L	6-4	215	6-25-86	6	0	3.39	45	0	0	5	61	66	29	23	5	18	63	.277	.280	.275	9.30	2.66
Luetge, Lucas	L-L	6-4	205	3-24-87	0	0	4.35	22	0	0	1	31	28	16	15	4	16	45	.243	.250	.239	13.06	4.65
Maurer, Brandon	R-R	6-5	215	7-3-90	3	4	5.21	10	10	0	0	47	48	29	27	2	26	47	.262	.244	.276	9.06	5.01

Name	B-T	HT	WT	DOB	W	L	ERA	G	GS	CG	SV	IP	H	R	ER	HR	BB	SO	AVG	vLH	vRH	K/9	BB/9
Medina, Yoervis	R-R	6-3	245	7-27-88	0	1	1.50	4	0	0	0	6	2	1	1	0	3	7	.111	.000	.200	10.50	4.50
Mitchell, D.J.	R-R	6-0	160	5-13-87	0	0	6.75	1	1	0	0	4	3	3	3	0	7	2	.200	.222	.167	4.50	15.75
2-team total (34 Las Vegas)					6	6	7.67	35	14	0	0	86	119	80	73	12	54	66	—	—		6.93	5.67
Moran, Brian	L-L	6-3	210	9-30-88	2	5	3.45	48	0	0	4	63	70	28	24	4	20	85	.290	.235	.341	12.21	2.87
Noesi, Hector	R-R	6-3	205	1-26-87	3	3	5.83	15	11	0	0	66	80	45	43	12	14	49	.291	.292	.290	6.65	1.90
Nunez, Jhonny	R-R	6-3	215	11-26-85	3	2	7.67	20	0	0	0	29	43	27	25	8	14	13	.331	.426	.277	3.99	4.30
Paxton, James	L-L	6-4	220	11-6-88	8	11	4.45	28	26	2	0	146	158	84	72	10	58	131	.277	.222	.294	8.09	3.58
Pryor, Stephen	R-R	6-4	250	7-23-89	0	0	15.00	4	0	0	0	3	5	5	5	0	2	1	.333	.286	.375	3.00	6.00
Ramirez, Erasmo	R-R	5-11	200	5-2-90	3	3	3.09	7	7	0	0	44	43	17	15	4	14	42	.256	.234	.269	8.66	2.89
Ruffin, Chance	R-R	6-0	195	9-8-88	1	2	3.94	15	2	0	0	30	28	13	13	3	6	25	.248	.310	.211	7.58	1.82
Snow, Forrest	R-R	6-6	220	12-30-88	4	0	2.93	19	1	0	0	40	34	13	13	5	17	43	.228	.203	.247	9.68	3.83
Sweeney, Brian	R-R	6-2	200	6-13-74	8	3	3.96	36	10	0	0	98	104	46	43	10	21	77	.272	.238	.299	7.10	1.94
Walker, Taijuan	R-R	6-4	210	8-13-92	5	3	3.61	11	11	0	0	57	54	25	23	5	27	64	.249	.161	.315	10.05	4.24
Wilhelmsen, Tom	R-R	6-6	220	12-16-83	0	1	10.50	8	2	0	0	12	19	14	14	3	5	15	.380	.400	.371	11.25	3.75

Fielding

Catcher	PCT	G	PO	A	E	DP	PB
Bantz	.985	37	301	33	5	1	1
Jaramillo	.997	38	286	16	1	2	3
Montero	1.000	1	3	1	0	0	0
Sucre	.991	23	193	17	2	1	1
Torres	1.000	1	2	0	0	0	0
Zunino	.993	50	378	31	3	2	4

First Base	PCT	G	PO	A	E	DP
Choi	.988	10	70	9	1	6
Liddi	.981	7	47	4	1	7
Montero	.984	16	117	7	2	14
Poythress	.999	85	674	56	1	59
Romero	1.000	2	4	0	0	0
Savastano	.987	20	144	10	2	13
Smoak	.923	3	12	0	1	2
Tenbrink	1.000	13	70	6	0	12

Second Base	PCT	G	PO	A	E	DP
Ackley	.984	12	26	34	1	13
Andino	1.000	19	25	42	0	8
Bonilla	.921	8	10	25	3	3
Franklin	.981	23	43	60	2	16
Kelly	.975	45	89	103	5	27

	PCT	G	PO	A	E	DP
Miller	1.000	3	5	6	0	4
Romero	1.000	2	5	3	0	0
Savastano	1.000	4	5	9	0	1
Tenbrink	.958	21	22	46	3	8
Triunfel	.984	13	19	41	1	9

Third Base	PCT	G	PO	A	E	DP
Andino	.867	7	5	8	2	0
Bonilla	.900	19	13	32	5	4
Kelly	.952	9	7	13	1	1
Liddi	.943	51	25	91	7	5
Poythress	—	1	0	0	0	0
Savastano	.976	17	14	27	1	2
Tenbrink	.937	51	45	88	9	13
Triunfel	.889	2	2	6	1	0

Shortstop	PCT	G	PO	A	E	DP
Andino	.969	18	23	40	2	14
Bonilla	.750	2	1	2	1	0
Franklin	.957	15	26	41	3	7
Miller	.935	22	21	66	6	13
Tenbrink	.941	6	7	9	1	2
Triunfel	.943	84	117	214	20	48

Outfield	PCT	G	PO	A	E	DP
Ackley	1.000	12	22	0	0	0
Almonte	.983	91	220	8	4	2
Almonte	.963	28	74	3	3	2
Avery	1.000	3	6	0	0	0
Bonilla	1.000	11	17	0	0	0
Chavez	1.000	6	14	0	0	0
Dunigan	.938	13	30	0	2	0
Gutierrez	.981	27	51	1	1	0
Jones	1.000	4	7	0	0	0
Kelly	1.000	2	1	1	0	0
Morse	1.000	3	6	0	0	0
Patterson	1.000	17	41	2	0	1
Peguero	.966	89	162	9	6	3
Romero	1.000	75	143	2	0	0
Saunders	1.000	1	1	0	0	0
Savastano	1.000	3	3	0	0	0
Tenbrink	.987	41	70	5	1	2
Thames	.983	38	55	3	1	0

JACKSON GENERALS DOUBLE-A

SOUTHERN LEAGUE

Batting	B-T	HT	WT	DOB	AVG	vLH	vRH	G	AB	R	H	2B	3B	HR	RBI	BB	HBP	SH	SF	SO	SB	CS	SLG	OBP
Almonte, Abe	B-R	5-9	205	6-27-89	.255	.143	.297	29	102	18	26	6	1	4	18	18	0	0	0	28	6	1	.451	.367
Almonte, Denny	B-R	6-2	190	9-24-88	.179	.151	.187	70	240	26	43	12	1	6	26	22	2	3	3	89	9	7	.313	.251
Bantz, Brandon	R-R	6-1	205	1-7-87	.159	.105	.180	22	69	5	11	2	0	1	4	4	0	1	0	21	1	0	.232	.205
Blash, Jabari	R-R	6-5	224	7-4-89	.309	.407	.271	29	97	13	30	3	0	9	21	20	3	0	0	28	1	1	.619	.442
Bonilla, Leury	R-R	6-2	195	2-8-85	.235	.333	.185	33	98	9	23	2	0	0	11	16	0	1	0	24	3	1	.255	.342
Brady, Patrick	R-R	5-10	176	2-5-88	.344	.400	.294	12	32	4	11	3	0	1	3	4	0	0	0	10	1	0	.531	.417
Catricala, Vinnie	R-R	6-3	220	10-31-88	.253	.347	.216	48	174	23	44	8	0	3	21	15	3	0	3	39	2	1	.351	.318
Choi, Ji-Man	L-R	6-1	195	5-19-91	.268	.239	.276	61	198	21	53	10	3	9	39	32	4	0	2	28	2	2	.485	.377
Cohoes, Cavan	R-R	6-2	185	5-3-93	.000	—	.000	1	1	0	0	0	0	0	0	0	0	0	0	0	0	0	.000	.000
Dowd, Mike	R-R	5-9	205	4-10-90	.196	.067	.216	36	112	9	22	4	0	1	3	4	4	0	0	20	0	1	.259	.250
Dunigan, Joe	L-L	6-1	240	3-29-86	.273	—	.273	3	11	3	3	0	0	1	2	1	0	0	0	4	0	0	.545	.333
Hicks, John	R-R	6-2	210	8-31-89	.236	.229	.239	80	296	40	70	14	1	4	29	22	6	1	2	62	13	4	.331	.301
Jones, James	L-L	6-4	193	9-24-88	.275	.262	.281	101	363	44	100	14	10	6	45	40	0	2	0	72	28	9	.419	.347
Landry, Leon	L-R	5-11	185	9-20-89	.216	.222	.214	114	422	43	91	15	2	6	37	26	1	9	2	71	22	7	.303	.262
Mack, Chantz	L-L	5-11	205	5-4-91	.227	.250	.214	5	22	2	5	0	0	0	1	0	0	0	0	5	1	0	.227	.227
Marder, Jack	R-R	5-11	185	2-21-90	.218	.280	.195	90	275	32	60	10	2	4	22	24	8	6	2	59	8	4	.313	.298
Martinez, Francisco	R-R	6-2	210	9-1-90	.206	.212	.204	34	126	8	26	6	0	0	5	6	0	4	0	43	7	0	.254	.242
Miller, Brad	L-R	6-2	185	10-18-89	.294	.200	.333	42	153	27	45	7	1	6	25	20	1	1	0	30	4	3	.471	.379
Morban, Julio	L-L	6-1	205	2-13-92	.295	.241	.315	86	295	46	87	20	5	7	44	28	3	0	0	95	7	2	.468	.362
Moria, Ramon	R-R	6-1	203	11-20-89	.244	.321	.221	65	246	24	60	12	5	8	41	18	3	0	1	87	5	2	.431	.302
Noriega, Gabriel	R-R	6-2	170	9-10-90	.256	.295	.239	104	371	35	95	15	4	2	30	14	1	13	3	72	7	2	.334	.283
Paolini, Dan	R-R	6-0	190	10-11-89	.165	.107	.187	31	103	6	17	5	1	0	4	18	0	1	0	24	1	2	.233	.289
Poythress, Rich	R-R	6-4	235	8-11-87	.286	.000	.400	4	14	4	4	1	0	2	4	4	0	0	0	1	0	0	.786	.444
Proscia, Steve	R-R	6-2	210	6-26-90	.201	.209	.197	90	314	37	63	9	1	10	28	20	1	2	2	92	11	4	.331	.249
Tanabe, Carlton	R-R	6-0	190	10-28-91	.111	.000	.143	3	9	1	1	0	0	0	0	0	1	0	0	3	0	0	.111	.200
Taylor, Chris	R-R	6-0	170	8-29-90	.293	.304	.290	67	256	46	75	12	4	1	16	40	2	1	1	55	18	3	.383	.391

Pitching	B-T	HT	WT	DOB	W	L	ERA	G	GS	CG	SV	IP	H	R	ER	HR	BB	SO	AVG	vLH	vRH	K/9	BB/9
Arias, Jonathan	R-R	6-3	210	2-8-88	0	1	4.43	12	0	0	0	20	16	10	10	3	10	28	.216	.250	.200	12.39	4.43
Burgoon, Tyler	R-R	5-10	160	4-25-89	4	3	3.58	36	0	0	4	50	45	22	20	6	23	65	.246	.317	.211	11.62	4.11
Elias, Roenis	L-L	6-2	178	8-1-88	6	11	3.18	22	22	0	0	130	112	57	46	9	50	121	.232	.160	.253	8.38	3.46

Name	T	HT	WT	DOB	W	L	ERA	G	GS	CG	SV	IP	H	R	ER	HR	BB	SO	AVG	vLH	vRH	K/9	BB/9
Fernandez, Anthony	L-L	6-4	210	6-8-90	9	8	4.43	22	22	1	0	120	117	69	59	13	40	74	.258	.284	.249	5.55	3.00
Gillheeney, Jimmy	L-L	6-1	200	11-8-87	7	7	4.08	20	20	0	0	104	98	51	47	13	39	62	.259	.292	.248	5.38	3.39
Hernandez, Moises	R-R	6-1	168	3-18-84	1	2	4.98	23	2	0	0	47	45	26	26	5	17	20	.262	.279	.250	3.83	3.26
Hill, Nick	L-L	6-0	190	1-30-85	2	3	2.17	42	0	0	0	50	44	12	12	0	24	46	.237	.171	.276	8.34	4.35
Hobson, Cameron	L-L	6-0	190	4-10-89	1	2	3.00	3	3	1	0	18	18	6	6	3	7	10	.265	.118	.314	5.00	3.50
Hunter, Kyle	L-L	6-2	207	6-18-89	3	0	1.40	34	4	0	1	58	47	11	9	2	16	43	.222	.189	.233	6.71	2.50
Kittredge, Andrew	R-R	6-1	200	3-17-90	1	3	6.23	17	0	0	0	22	39	16	15	0	12	27	.382	.333	.409	11.22	4.98
Kohlscheen, Stephen	R-R	6-6	223	9-20-88	7	3	2.30	41	0	0	2	67	47	18	17	6	25	85	.203	.235	.184	11.48	3.38
Leone, Dominic	R-R	5-11	185	10-26-91	1	2	2.50	16	0	0	4	18	12	6	5	2	5	17	.182	.125	.214	8.50	2.50
McCoy, Kevin	L-R	6-4	220	7-12-91	0	0	0.00	1	0	0	0	1	1	0	0	0	2	1	.250	.000	.500	9.00	18.00
Miller, Trevor	R-R	6-3	190	6-13-91	3	2	4.82	8	8	0	0	47	45	27	25	5	22	28	.265	.224	.306	5.40	4.24
Noesi, Hector	R-R	6-0	205	1-26-87	1	0	0.00	2	2	0	0	11	5	0	0	3	12	.135	.118	.150	9.82	2.45
Ramirez, Erasmo	R-R	5-11	200	5-2-90	0	0	1.80	1	1	0	0	5	3	2	1	0	2	3	.158	.333	.000	5.40	3.60
Ruffin, Chance	R-R	6-0	195	9-8-88	4	4	3.90	16	16	1	0	83	82	40	36	11	23	57	.256	.259	.254	6.18	2.49
Shackleford, Stephen	R-R	6-1	185	5-5-89	1	2	2.89	23	0	0	1	28	26	11	9	1	15	23	.250	.310	.210	7.39	4.82
Shankin, Brett	R-R	6-0	200	10-30-89	3	1	4.04	8	8	0	0	42	49	28	19	4	20	22	.293	.446	.196	4.68	4.25
Smith, Carson	R-R	6-6	215	10-19-89	1	3	1.98	44	0	0	15	50	33	12	11	1	17	71	.183	.233	.158	12.78	3.06
Snow, Forrest	R-R	6-6	220	12-30-88	1	5	3.00	23	1	0	0	42	27	14	14	2	11	41	.186	.157	.202	8.79	2.36
Vasquez, Anthony	L-L	6-0	190	9-19-86	2	4	4.26	12	12	1	0	70	66	37	33	13	19	31	.255	.235	.260	4.00	2.45
Walker, Taijuan	R-R	6-4	210	8-13-92	4	7	2.46	14	14	0	0	84	58	31	23	6	30	96	.195	.211	.182	10.29	3.21

Fielding

Catcher	PCT	G	PO	A	E	DP	PB
Bantz	1.000	22	160	22	0	0	3
Dowd	.985	35	228	27	4	2	6
Hicks	.994	79	574	62	4	5	17
Marder	—	1	0	0	0	0	0
Tanabe	1.000	2	19	1	0	0	2

First Base	PCT	G	PO	A	E	DP
Bonilla	1.000	7	51	3	0	0
Catricala	.946	4	34	1	2	4
Choi	.997	43	327	17	1	39
Morla	1.000	2	4	0	0	1
Paolini	1.000	12	102	6	0	6
Poythress	1.000	4	38	3	0	3
Proscia	.993	66	539	34	4	54

Second Base	PCT	G	PO	A	E	DP
Bonilla	1.000	5	6	10	0	2
Brady	1.000	12	25	23	0	6
Marder	.984	58	111	128	4	34
Miller	1.000	6	13	18	0	6
Noriega	.969	32	79	77	5	23
Taylor	.962	25	66	61	5	20

Third Base	PCT	G	PO	A	E	DP
Bonilla	.960	21	21	51	3	5
Catricala	.909	38	22	78	10	7
Marder	1.000	6	2	8	0	0
Miller	.857	3	3	3	1	1
Morla	.940	60	55	133	12	23
Noriega	1.000	4	4	11	0	3
Proscia	.727	7	5	11	6	0

Shortstop	PCT	G	PO	A	E	DP
Miller	.934	29	41	72	8	11
Noriega	.976	68	80	169	6	29
Taylor	.928	39	52	115	13	25

Outfield	PCT	G	PO	A	E	DP
Almonte	.977	20	40	2	1	0
Almonte	.994	66	179	1	1	0
Blash	.983	25	56	1	1	0
Catricala	—	1	0	0	0	0
Cohoes	—	1	0	0	0	0
Dunigan	1.000	2	3	0	0	0
Jones	.966	81	137	7	5	1
Landry	.984	106	177	10	3	1
Mack	1.000	5	9	0	0	0
Marder	.974	24	36	2	1	0
Martinez	.969	28	63	0	2	0
Morban	.975	52	75	3	2	0
Paolini	1.000	9	12	1	0	0

HIGH DESERT MAVERICKS   HIGH CLASS A

CALIFORNIA LEAGUE

Batting	B-T	HT	WT	DOB	AVG	vLH	vRH	G	AB	R	H	2B	3B	HR	RBI	BB	HBP	SH	SF	SO	SB	CS	SLG	OBP
Austin, Jamal	R-R	5-9	170	8-26-90	.288	.301	.285	126	520	107	150	15	10	0	58	44	4	13	5	69	40	13	.356	.346
Baron, Steve	R-R	6-0	205	12-7-90	.208	.242	.201	86	331	31	69	18	5	5	47	18	0	1	3	93	7	0	.338	.247
Blash, Jabari	R-R	6-5	224	7-4-89	.258	.281	.251	80	283	42	73	16	3	16	53	40	6	0	3	85	14	8	.505	.358
Brady, Patrick	R-R	5-10	176	2-5-88	.279	.333	.264	57	222	36	62	13	2	11	37	22	1	3	1	39	6	4	.505	.346
Choi, Ji-Man	L-R	6-1	195	5-19-91	.337	.200	.376	48	181	34	61	24	3	7	40	27	2	0	1	33	0	1	.619	.427
Dowd, Mike	R-R	5-9	205	4-10-90	.281	.241	.293	32	128	21	36	7	0	3	14	2	5	0	2	17	0	1	.406	.314
Hazlett, Dillon	R-R	6-1	190	1-22-89	.211	.179	.220	76	270	38	57	15	2	7	31	21	1	3	2	63	7	2	.359	.269
Hebert, Brock	R-R	5-10	180	5-11-91	.281	.417	.250	17	64	13	18	6	1	1	11	8	2	1	1	16	0	1	.453	.373
Henry, Jabari	R-R	6-1	200	11-11-90	.238	.364	.205	29	105	19	25	5	2	4	17	16	0	1	1	24	0	1	.438	.336
Kivlehan, Patrick	R-R	6-2	210	12-22-89	.320	.314	.321	68	266	48	85	13	2	13	59	26	5	0	5	65	10	3	.530	.384
Lara, Jordy	R-R	6-3	180	5-21-91	.311	.222	.327	15	61	11	19	2	0	3	9	1	1	0	0	13	0	0	.492	.333
Marte, Ketel	B-R	6-1	180	10-12-93	.256	.357	.236	19	86	18	22	0	2	1	8	4	0	2	0	11	4	3	.337	.289
McGee, Mike	R-R	6-0	185	3-7-89	.149	.100	.172	29	94	10	14	1	0	2	6	15	0	1	1	35	2	1	.223	.264
Melendres, Nathan	R-R	5-10	187	4-4-90	.260	.309	.246	69	258	39	67	18	3	6	38	12	3	2	5	39	6	2	.422	.295
Morales, Alfredo	R-R	6-2	210	11-6-92	.196	.182	.200	15	51	7	10	2	0	0	7	7	0	0	0	19	0	0	.235	.293
Morla, Ramon	R-R	6-1	203	11-20-89	.303	.275	.311	45	175	32	53	17	1	10	33	12	1	0	0	48	7	1	.583	.351
Paolini, Dan	R-R	6-0	190	10-11-89	.284	.280	.286	92	334	62	95	21	2	18	69	57	8	1	7	56	2	2	.521	.394
Phillips, Anthony	R-R	5-9	160	4-11-90	.259	.216	.272	124	413	70	107	23	4	9	43	49	12	6	5	92	5	7	.400	.351
Pimentel, Guillermo	L-L	6-1	206	10-5-92	.333	.444	.315	15	63	10	21	3	1	4	14	2	1	0	1	18	0	0	.603	.358
Proscia, Steve	R-R	6-2	210	6-26-90	.306	.421	.273	21	85	15	26	8	1	4	18	4	6	0	2	15	5	1	.565	.371
Rivers, Kevin	L-R	6-2	210	10-8-89	.297	.255	.307	128	485	92	144	36	5	20	97	66	2	0	4	127	8	3	.515	.381
Romero, Stefan	R-R	6-2	220	10-17-88	.278	.286	.273	5	18	1	5	1	0	0	2	2	1	0	0	1	0	0	.333	.381
Taylor, Chris	R-R	6-0	170	8-29-90	.335	.286	.352	67	269	62	90	16	7	7	44	44	2	0	4	62	20	2	.524	.426
Villasuso, David	R-R	5-10	195	12-31-89	.227	.269	.210	24	88	9	20	5	0	3	8	4	1	1	2	16	2	1	.386	.263

Pitching	B-T	HT	WT	DOB	W	L	ERA	G	GS	CG	SV	IP	H	R	ER	HR	BB	SO	AVG	vLH	vRH	K/9	BB/9
Anderson, Matt	R-R	6-1	210	11-18-91	2	4	5.90	10	10	0	0	50	47	38	33	8	28	43	.245	.226	.263	7.69	5.01
Blandford, Tyler	R-R	6-3	165	1-25-88	0	0	15.30	7	0	0	0	10	13	17	17	2	12	4	.317	.071	.444	3.60	10.80
Brazis, Matt	R-R	6-3	205	9-6-89	2	5	4.60	42	0	0	1	59	61	41	30	3	27	57	.268	.323	.225	8.74	4.14
Colvin, David	R-R	6-3	215	1-7-89	5	0	2.34	32	1	0	1	58	57	19	15	2	13	62	.257	.289	.232	9.68	2.03
DeCecco, Scott	R-L	6-0	175	5-8-91	1	1	2.55	3	3	0	0	18	17	7	5	3	4	15	.250	.188	.269	7.64	2.04

	B-T	HT	WT	DOB	W	L	ERA	G	GS	CG	SV	IP	H	R	ER	HR	BB	SO	AVG	vLH	vRH	K/9	BB/9
Dobbs, Jeremy	L-L	6-3	185	10-12-89	5	2	5.62	35	0	0	1	50	56	34	31	4	18	49	.284	.221	.318	8.88	3.26
Guaipe, Mayckol	R-R	6-3	175	8-11-90	3	4	5.64	35	3	0	5	59	59	39	37	5	29	57	.267	.290	.248	8.69	4.42
Hauser, Blake	R-R	6-2	180	4-14-91	0	0	6.75	9	0	0	0	15	15	11	11	4	3	14	.263	.286	.241	8.59	1.84
Hobson, Cameron	L-L	6-0	190	4-10-89	5	9	5.24	23	23	0	0	115	137	73	67	9	41	88	.298	.254	.319	6.89	3.21
Hunter, Kyle	L-L	6-2	207	6-18-89	1	1	3.65	8	0	0	0	12	12	7	5	2	4	12	.240	.241	.238	8.76	2.92
Kaalekahi, Charles	B-R	6-2	175	5-13-92	0	0	11.25	1	1	0	0	4	5	5	5	1	6	3	.294	.000	.385	6.75	13.50
Kim, Seon Gi	R-R	6-2	185	9-1-91	5	5	7.00	46	1	0	1	73	74	61	57	12	39	71	.263	.278	.253	8.71	4.79
Kittredge, Andrew	R-R	6-1	200	3-17-90	0	2	5.87	14	0	0	1	23	28	17	15	6	3	23	.295	.300	.291	9.00	1.17
Landazuri, Steve	R-R	6-0	175	1-6-92	6	7	4.63	23	23	0	0	117	125	74	60	16	32	115	.274	.250	.292	8.87	2.47
Leone, Dominic	R-R	5-11	185	10-26-91	0	1	2.50	29	0	0	12	40	31	11	11	2	9	37	.220	.237	.207	8.39	2.04
Mieses, George	R-R	6-2	180	5-3-91	3	4	7.96	33	0	0	1	46	55	43	41	10	22	44	.296	.291	.299	8.55	4.27
Miller, Trevor	R-R	6-3	190	6-13-91	4	7	4.82	18	18	0	0	93	110	63	50	11	33	78	.295	.259	.324	7.52	3.18
Pries, Jordan	B-R	6-1	195	1-27-90	8	6	5.13	24	23	0	0	125	129	77	71	14	40	104	.264	.237	.281	7.51	2.89
Shackleford, Stephen	R-R	6-1	185	5-5-89	2	2	2.52	24	0	0	7	25	16	8	7	1	17	23	.180	.189	.173	8.28	6.12
Shankin, Brett	R-R	6-0	200	10-30-89	2	5	5.69	12	12	0	0	55	69	44	35	5	17	39	.317	.349	.284	6.34	2.77
Shellhorn, Rusty	L-L	5-10	170	2-25-90	0	0	5.40	2	0	0	0	2	4	3	1	0	1	1	.400	.250	.500	5.40	5.40
Shipers, Jordan	R-L	5-10	168	6-27-91	4	3	6.50	11	11	0	0	54	56	43	39	6	24	33	.276	.323	.255	5.50	4.00
Shore, Bobby	R-R	6-1	170	1-27-89	6	5	5.42	34	11	0	0	81	93	57	49	15	31	63	.287	.248	.317	6.97	3.43
Wood, Grady	R-R	6-2	195	5-18-90	0	3	5.01	23	0	0	0	41	40	23	23	4	21	37	.263	.250	.272	8.06	4.57

Fielding

Catcher	PCT	G	PO	A	E	DP	PB
Baron	.991	86	676	70	7	8	8
Dowd	.992	32	224	29	2	3	5
Villasuso	.990	24	179	24	2	3	5

First Base	PCT	G	PO	A	E	DP
Brady	1.000	4	37	2	0	1
Choi	.984	41	343	28	6	26
Dowd	1.000	1	1	0	0	1
Lara	.992	15	121	9	1	12
Morla	.972	15	129	10	4	11
Paolini	.997	40	329	25	1	26
Proscia	1.000	21	167	10	0	17
Rivers	.980	11	91	8	2	8

Second Base	PCT	G	PO	A	E	DP
Brady	.977	21	35	51	2	14
Hazlett	.968	34	61	89	5	25

Hebert	.981	13	21	30	1	6
Marte	1.000	2	1	8	0	1
Melendres	.970	15	30	34	2	3
Phillips	.964	59	97	173	10	30
Taylor	1.000	2	2	8	0	0

Third Base	PCT	G	PO	A	E	DP
Brady	.909	3	2	8	1	0
Choi	1.000	4	3	3	0	0
Hazlett	.870	28	13	47	9	10
Kivlehan	.943	66	65	134	12	14
Melendres	.952	9	2	18	1	3
Morla	.878	29	13	59	10	4
Phillips	.923	4	1	11	1	0
Romero	1.000	4	7	7	0	1

Shortstop	PCT	G	PO	A	E	DP
Hazlett	.889	1	5	3	1	1

Hebert	.900	2	3	6	1	2
Marte	.922	15	18	41	5	7
Phillips	.976	61	90	196	7	36
Taylor	.948	61	86	188	15	33

Outfield	PCT	G	PO	A	E	DP
Austin	.984	118	238	12	4	4
Blash	.946	58	85	3	5	1
Brady	.956	18	40	3	2	2
Hebert	1.000	1	2	0	0	0
Henry	.962	27	46	4	2	1
McGee	1.000	20	35	1	0	1
Melendres	.989	45	85	2	1	2
Morales	.900	10	9	0	1	0
Paolini	1.000	26	44	1	0	0
Pimentel	.923	9	11	1	1	0
Rivers	.959	97	150	13	7	1

CLINTON LUMBERKINGS
MIDWEST LEAGUE

LOW CLASS A

Batting	B-T	HT	WT	DOB	AVG	vLH	vRH	G	AB	R	H	2B	3B	HR	RBI	BB	HBP	SH	SF	SO	SB	CS	SLG	OBP
Ard, Taylor	R-R	6-2	230	1-31-90	.240	.261	.235	118	420	47	101	23	1	8	53	45	6	0	4	63	2	1	.357	.320
Caballero, Luis	R-R	6-1	157	7-8-92	.280	.250	.286	8	25	1	7	2	0	0	2	2	1	0	0	6	0	1	.360	.357
Guerrero, Gabriel	R-R	6-3	190	12-11-93	.271	.225	.285	125	469	60	127	23	3	4	50	21	3	0	6	113	12	3	.358	.303
Hebert, Brock	R-R	5-10	180	5-11-91	.277	.275	.279	59	191	41	53	9	0	1	16	22	5	3	1	42	15	6	.340	.365
Henry, Jabari	R-R	6-1	200	11-11-90	.268	.259	.271	71	257	41	69	18	2	7	40	47	3	0	3	49	9	6	.436	.384
Kivlehan, Patrick	R-R	6-2	210	12-22-89	.283	.327	.269	60	223	26	63	12	1	3	31	17	5	0	2	42	5	3	.386	.344
Lara, Jordy	R-R	6-3	180	5-21-91	.260	.214	.275	98	339	39	88	25	3	10	63	29	2	0	5	68	3	0	.440	.317
Littleway, Marcus	B-R	6-3	194	3-18-92	.230	.250	.221	60	213	26	49	18	1	3	18	40	0	2	1	58	1	0	.366	.350
Lopes, Timmy	R-R	5-11	180	6-24-94	.272	.263	.275	92	334	40	91	15	3	1	36	20	2	6	3	46	10	7	.344	.315
Marlette, Tyler	R-R	5-11	195	1-23-93	.304	.200	.322	75	270	36	82	17	2	6	37	24	3	0	0	53	10	4	.448	.367
Marte, Ketel	B-R	6-1	180	10-12-93	.304	.250	.317	98	378	61	115	15	5	0	29	15	1	9	3	39	16	8	.370	.330
McGruder, Jamodrick	L-R	5-8	155	8-4-91	.145	.214	.130	30	83	10	12	0	0	0	3	13	1	3	1	17	3	0	.145	.265
Morales, Alfredo	R-R	6-2	210	11-6-92	.257	.176	.271	31	113	12	29	7	0	1	7	19	0	0	0	32	1	0	.345	.364
Peguero, Martin	R-R	6-1	185	11-3-93	.232	.244	.229	53	181	17	42	8	0	0	24	4	0	4	2	22	2	2	.276	.246
Peterson, D.J.	R-R	6-1	190	12-31-91	.293	.333	.282	26	99	16	29	5	1	7	20	7	1	0	0	24	1	0	.576	.346
Pimentel, Guillermo	L-L	6-1	206	10-5-92	.257	.289	.248	55	202	24	52	10	2	6	30	20	2	0	0	68	4	3	.416	.330
Pizzano, Dario	L-R	5-11	200	4-25-91	.311	.287	.317	126	463	75	144	40	5	8	70	61	3	0	4	48	8	4	.471	.392
Shank, Zach	R-R	6-1	180	1-6-91	.286	.000	.353	8	21	4	6	0	0	1	4	1	2	0	1	3	1	0	.429	.360
Tanabe, Carlton	R-R	6-0	190	10-28-91	.105	.125	.091	6	19	0	2	1	0	0	1	0	0	0	0	3	0	0	.158	.105
Torres, Dan	R-R	6-0	175	5-29-92	.333	.500	.000	2	6	0	2	0	0	0	0	1	0	0	0	1	0	0	.333	.429
Villasuso, David	R-R	5-10	195	12-31-89	.250	.500	.125	4	12	2	3	1	0	0	1	0	0	0	0	4	0	0	.333	.250
Werman, Keith	L-R	5-7	150	10-1-89	.077	.000	.087	10	26	1	2	0	0	0	0	1	3	0	6	0	1	0	.115	.111
Zorrilla, Janelfry	R-R	6-3	205	9-2-90	.257	.281	.250	84	296	43	76	11	1	6	34	21	4	6	3	68	3	5	.361	.312

Pitching	B-T	HT	WT	DOB	W	L	ERA	G	GS	CG	SV	IP	H	R	ER	HR	BB	SO	AVG	vLH	vRH	K/9	BB/9
Anderson, Matt	R-R	6-1	210	11-18-91	4	6	3.86	16	16	0	0	86	79	41	37	8	26	54	.237	.241	.234	5.63	2.71
Bordonaro, Mark	R-R	6-0	170	8-17-90	3	4	4.65	21	0	0	3	31	22	20	16	0	21	35	.198	.171	.214	10.16	6.10
Copping, Cameron	R-R	6-6	220	4-24-90	0	0	9.90	6	0	0	0	10	17	14	11	2	3	5	.354	.333	.375	4.50	2.70
DeCecco, Scott	R-L	6-0	175	5-8-91	9	8	4.49	24	24	1	0	132	136	72	66	12	42	77	.266	.284	.258	5.24	2.86
Dobbs, Jeremy	L-L	6-3	185	10-12-89	1	0	6.14	4	0	0	0	7	5	6	5	0	12	8	.200	.231	.167	9.82	14.73
Ewing, Steve	L-L	6-1	220	8-8-91	1	2	8.62	3	3	0	0	16	19	16	15	3	9	10	.306	.438	.261	5.74	5.17
Garcia, Oliver	R-R	6-2	205	12-7-90	7	5	3.82	41	1	0	2	68	60	36	29	5	39	59	.232	.216	.246	7.77	5.14

	B-T	HT	WT	DOB	W	L	ERA	G	GS	CG	SV	IP	H	R	ER	HR	BB	SO	AVG	vLH	vRH	K/9	BB/9
Garcia, Rigoberto	R-R	6-5	202	9-23-93	2	5	5.23	10	8	0	0	52	55	37	30	6	20	41	.267	.232	.299	7.14	3.48
Hauser, Blake	R-R	6-2	180	4-14-91	0	3	6.10	9	0	0	2	10	12	8	7	1	6	7	.308	.250	.348	6.10	5.23
Holman, David	R-R	6-6	220	5-31-90	4	8	3.25	38	7	1	3	111	104	52	40	6	20	53	.249	.200	.293	4.31	1.63
Holovach, Blake	L-L	6-5	195	3-27-91	1	2	5.02	30	3	0	1	57	68	37	32	3	28	51	.302	.348	.283	8.01	4.40
Kaalekahi, Charles	B-R	6-2	175	5-13-92	5	5	4.50	15	14	0	0	74	74	42	37	11	44	50	.259	.197	.315	6.08	5.35
Landazuri, Steve	R-R	6-0	175	1-6-92	1	0	1.50	3	3	0	0	12	8	4	2	0	8	14	.186	.214	.133	10.50	6.00
Leone, Dominic	R-R	5-11	185	10-26-91	0	0	0.00	3	0	0	0	6	6	1	0	0	4	10	.250	.214	.300	14.21	5.68
Mieses, George	R-R	6-2	180	5-3-91	0	1	1.88	12	0	0	2	24	21	8	5	0	10	19	.244	.324	.192	7.13	3.75
Ogando, Jochi	R-R	6-5	210	5-27-93	1	3	3.32	33	0	0	3	60	53	29	22	1	32	56	.243	.255	.233	8.45	4.83
Pike, Tyler	L-L	6-0	180	1-26-94	7	4	2.37	22	22	0	0	110	73	41	29	5	57	90	.194	.204	.190	7.34	4.65
Sanchez, Victor	R-R	6-0	255	1-30-95	6	6	2.78	20	20	1	0	113	106	42	35	4	18	79	.241	.262	.223	6.27	1.43
Shellhorn, Rusty	L-L	5-10	170	2-25-90	0	1	5.49	9	4	0	0	20	24	16	12	2	13	14	.316	.391	.283	6.41	5.95
Unsworth, Dylan	R-R	6-1	175	9-23-92	4	1	2.32	11	11	1	0	66	58	18	17	2	2	46	.237	.260	.220	6.27	0.27
Vargas, Richard	R-R	6-3	185	4-19-91	1	1	4.38	19	0	0	3	25	27	13	12	2	13	24	.270	.205	.321	8.76	4.74
Vasquez, Anthony	L-L	6-0	190	9-19-86	0	2	3.31	3	3	0	0	16	15	12	6	1	4	10	.234	.136	.286	5.51	2.20
Vedo, Matt	L-R	6-3	205	1-12-90	5	2	7.20	22	0	0	2	35	35	30	28	4	25	34	.263	.273	.254	8.74	6.43
White, Richard	R-R	5-11	170	2-1-93	1	1	10.32	8	0	0	0	11	17	13	13	2	9	5	.362	.615	.265	3.97	7.15
Wood, Grady	R-R	6-2	195	5-18-90	4	2	2.50	28	0	0	7	40	29	17	11	1	14	32	.199	.227	.175	7.26	3.18

Fielding

Catcher	PCT	G	PO	A	E	DP	PB
Littlewood	.989	57	323	37	4	4	8
Marlette	.995	73	483	66	3	3	10
Tanabe	.979	6	35	11	1	0	0
Torres	1.000	2	10	0	0	0	0
Villasuso	1.000	4	25	4	0	0	2

First Base	PCT	G	PO	A	E	DP
Ard	.987	111	960	74	14	93
Caballero	1.000	2	6	1	0	0
Lara	.981	30	250	15	5	15

Second Base	PCT	G	PO	A	E	DP
Caballero	1.000	3	5	7	0	2
Hebert	.958	17	26	43	3	6
Lopes	.963	77	139	224	14	42

	PCT	G	PO	A	E	DP
Marte	.991	24	50	62	1	15
McGruder	.946	10	16	19	2	3
Peguero	1.000	2	2	4	0	0
Shank	.960	5	8	16	1	6
Werman	1.000	10	19	33	0	12

Third Base	PCT	G	PO	A	E	DP
Caballero	1.000	3	0	3	0	1
Hebert	.500	2	1	2	3	1
Kivlehan	.911	49	38	75	11	6
Lara	.941	46	38	89	8	7
McGruder	.500	1	1	0	1	0
Peguero	.884	20	13	25	5	3
Peterson	.902	21	16	30	5	6
Shank	.909	3	3	7	1	1

Shortstop	PCT	G	PO	A	E	DP
Caballero	1.000	1	0	1	0	0
Hebert	.948	37	55	110	9	24
Lopes	.800	7	1	11	3	3
Marte	.946	70	111	206	18	40
Peguero	.950	32	55	96	8	20

Outfield	PCT	G	PO	A	E	DP
Guerrero	.970	121	244	12	8	2
Hebert	.500	2	0	1	1	0
Henry	.983	61	111	3	2	0
McGruder	1.000	10	16	0	0	0
Morales	.960	29	45	3	2	0
Pimentel	.931	39	64	3	5	1
Pizzano	.987	84	148	4	2	1
Zorrilla	.971	81	195	3	6	1

EVERETT AQUASOX   SHORT-SEASON
NORTHWEST LEAGUE

Batting	B-T	HT	WT	DOB	AVG	vLH	vRH	G	AB	R	H	2B	3B	HR	RBI	BB	HBP	SH	SF	SO	SB	CS	SLG	OBP
Brito, Bryan	R-R	6-2	170	2-16-92	.265	.282	.261	59	196	26	52	5	2	0	13	11	2	2	2	62	12	5	.311	.308
Carmichael, Christian	R-R	5-11	190	4-25-92	.252	.300	.239	40	143	16	36	7	2	3	13	14	1	3	0	33	1	2	.392	.323
Castillo, Phillips	R-R	6-2	190	2-2-94	.183	.089	.207	61	219	22	40	12	0	6	26	16	6	0	1	70	1	3	.320	.256
Faulkner, Mike	L-L	5-9	150	6-28-91	.237	.162	.257	51	173	32	41	7	1	0	9	29	1	3	0	37	13	3	.289	.350
Hebert, Brock	R-R	5-10	180	5-11-91	.217	—	.217	6	23	3	5	2	1	0	1	3	2	0	0	4	2	0	.391	.357
Kauppila, Lonnie	R-R	6-1	170	1-17-92	.182	.200	.176	37	110	12	20	4	0	1	12	9	1	1	3	19	1	1	.245	.244
Lawson, Reggie	R-R	6-4	245	8-14-91	.232	.205	.241	52	177	16	41	7	2	1	21	15	3	1	2	60	1	3	.311	.299
Mack, Chantz	L-L	5-11	205	5-4-91	.280	.360	.258	35	118	12	33	9	0	2	14	13	2	3	1	34	5	1	.407	.358
McGruder, Jamodrick	L-R	5-8	155	8-4-91	.328	.318	.333	21	61	15	20	2	3	1	7	14	6	3	0	13	7	4	.508	.494
Miller, Ian	L-R	6-0	170	2-21-92	.333	.714	.257	12	42	7	14	0	0	0	1	4	0	2	0	6	3	1	.333	.391
Morales, Alfredo	R-R	6-2	210	11-6-92	.226	.000	.280	9	31	7	7	2	0	1	3	8	0	0	1	6	0	1	.387	.375
Peguero, Martin	R-R	6-1	185	11-3-93	.389	.200	.462	5	18	4	7	0	0	0	3	4	1	0	1	2	1	0	.389	.500
Peterson, D.J.	R-R	6-1	190	12-31-91	.312	.259	.329	29	109	20	34	6	0	6	27	13	0	0	1	18	0	1	.532	.382
Petty, Kyle	R-R	6-5	215	3-1-91	.264	.250	.267	27	91	10	24	4	0	2	12	7	2	0	1	23	5	1	.374	.327
Reinheimer, Jack	R-R	6-0	165	7-19-92	.269	.262	.271	66	249	39	67	6	1	2	30	32	4	4	2	51	18	5	.325	.359
Seager, Justin	R-R	6-1	195	5-5-92	.267	.364	.245	61	240	29	64	13	0	3	30	14	7	0	2	62	1	1	.358	.323
Tanabe, Carlton	R-R	6-0	190	10-28-91	.233	.156	.257	38	133	11	31	6	1	2	17	8	1	1	0	26	4	1	.338	.282
Torres, Dan	R-R	6-0	175	5-29-92	.000	—	.000	2	7	1	0	0	0	0	0	1	0	0	0	3	0	0	.000	.125
Wilson, Austin	R-R	6-4	210	2-7-92	.241	.250	.239	56	203	22	49	11	3	6	27	17	6	0	0	4	2	4	.414	.319
Zamarripa, James	L-L	5-10	190	9-17-93	.249	.295	.234	53	185	20	46	5	0	0	11	27	0	1	1	53	11	4	.276	.343

Pitching	B-T	HT	WT	DOB	W	L	ERA	G	GS	CG	SV	IP	H	R	ER	HR	BB	SO	AVG	vLH	vRH	K/9	BB/9
Brooks, Aaron	R-R	6-6	210	5-15-92	1	2	4.50	21	0	0	0	28	24	17	14	2	13	31	.222	.347	.119	9.96	4.18
Burns, Tommy	R-R	6-1	180	9-27-93	2	2	6.34	11	6	0	1	38	45	33	27	3	24	25	.302	.351	.253	5.87	5.63
Carraway, Andrew	R-R	6-2	205	9-4-86	0	0	3.00	3	3	0	0	15	13	7	5	1	1	14	.241	.214	.269	8.40	0.60
Chen, Min-Sih	R-R	6-3	205	12-6-89	2	2	2.78	21	0	0	2	32	41	15	10	4	10	34	.318	.345	.296	9.46	2.78
Copping, Cameron	R-R	6-6	220	4-24-90	0	2	4.02	10	0	0	0	16	18	7	7	0	5	11	.310	.214	.400	6.32	2.87
Ewing, Steve	L-L	6-1	220	8-8-91	1	3	4.11	12	10	0	1	57	49	32	26	2	18	56	.236	.153	.279	8.84	2.84
Garcia, Rigoberto	R-R	6-5	202	9-23-93	4	0	2.22	5	5	0	0	28	23	7	7	0	10	21	.223	.208	.236	6.67	3.18
Horstman, Ryan	L-L	6-1	185	7-20-92	0	0	4.50	1	1	0	0	2	3	2	1	0	0	3	.375	.667	.200	13.50	0.00
Huijer, Lars	R-R	6-4	183	9-22-93	8	2	3.03	14	13	0	0	71	57	25	24	2	23	61	.218	.212	.224	7.70	2.90
Koneski, Nate	R-L	6-0	175	3-11-90	2	1	4.20	11	4	0	0	30	28	14	14	3	13	32	.252	.220	.271	9.60	3.90
Medina, Jefferson	R-R	6-2	184	5-31-94	1	0	1.69	1	1	0	0	5	3	1	1	0	4	2	.188	.222	.143	3.38	6.75
Olson, Tyler	R-L	6-3	190	10-2-89	2	4	4.33	18	8	1	1	54	61	33	26	1	20	48	.282	.307	.270	8.00	3.33
Pagan, Emilio	L-R	6-3	205	5-7-91	0	1	4.50	5	0	0	0	6	8	4	3	1	1	8	.320	.250	.385	12.00	1.50

SEATTLE MARINERS

Pitching	B-T	HT	WT	DOB	W	L	ERA	G	GS	CG	SV	IP	H	R	ER	HR	BB	SO	AVG	vLH	vRH	K/9	BB/9
Pereira, Ricardo	R-B	6-3	150	4-18-91	1	2	6.94	20	1	0	1	35	42	28	27	3	20	17	.313	.286	.333	4.37	5.14
Pryor, Stephen	R-R	6-4	250	7-23-89	0	0	27.00	1	1	0	0	1	3	3	2	1	0	1	.600	.500	.667	13.50	0.00
Ramirez, Erasmo	R-R	5-11	200	5-2-90	0	0	1.69	1	1	0	0	5	6	2	1	0	1	10	.286	.231	.375	16.88	1.69
Taylor, Luke	R-R	6-6	200	7-14-92	0	0	0.00	2	0	0	0	3	4	3	0	0	0	1	.286	.500	.000	3.00	0.00
Valdivia, Jose	R-R	6-4	235	3-19-92	3	0	2.23	20	0	0	3	32	16	9	8	1	14	36	.148	.186	.123	10.02	3.90
Valenza, Nick	R-L	5-10	180	3-31-93	3	1	6.52	22	0	0	4	29	32	22	21	1	15	28	.271	.286	.263	8.69	4.66
Vargas, Richard	R-R	6-3	185	4-19-91	0	0	0.00	4	0	0	3	6	3	0	0	0	0	12	.136	.200	.083	17.05	0.00
Vieira, Thyago	R-R	6-2	210	1-7-93	4	5	3.84	14	13	0	0	68	60	30	29	2	34	51	.244	.243	.245	6.75	4.50
White, Richard	R-R	5-11	170	2-1-93	3	2	5.63	22	0	0	1	24	21	22	15	4	23	27	.241	.186	.295	10.13	8.63
Wright, Tyler	L-L	6-2	180	3-12-91	2	0	1.99	19	0	0	1	32	23	9	7	2	18	39	.202	.206	.200	11.08	5.12
Zokan, Jake	R-L	6-1	195	4-27-91	5	3	4.18	10	9	0	0	52	46	24	24	7	13	54	.250	.235	.256	9.41	2.26

Fielding

Catcher	PCT	G	PO	A	E	DP	PB
Carmichael	.986	40	322	30	5	0	7
Tanabe	.991	38	279	47	3	4	8
Torres	1.000	2	7	3	0	0	0

First Base	PCT	G	PO	A	E	DP
Lawson	.977	23	199	13	5	18
Peterson	1.000	1	6	0	0	0
Petty	.995	24	188	9	1	15
Seager	.987	33	284	21	4	27

Second Base	PCT	G	PO	A	E	DP
Brito	.926	26	58	80	11	19
Hebert	1.000	4	9	11	0	2
Kauppila	.992	22	45	73	1	16

	PCT	G	PO	A	E	DP
McGruder	.952	18	34	46	4	6
Peguero	1.000	2	3	8	0	2
Reinheimer	.968	7	11	19	1	2

Third Base	PCT	G	PO	A	E	DP
Brito	.901	25	17	47	7	3
Kauppila	.833	4	2	3	1	0
Peguero	1.000	1	0	2	0	0
Peterson	.913	24	9	33	4	5
Seager	.915	27	17	37	5	3

Shortstop	PCT	G	PO	A	E	DP
Brito	.947	6	8	10	1	0
Hebert	1.000	2	2	6	0	3
Kauppila	1.000	11	14	30	0	8

	PCT	G	PO	A	E	DP
Peguero	1.000	2	1	3	0	0
Reinheimer	.982	57	88	179	5	36

Outfield	PCT	G	PO	A	E	DP
Brito	—	1	0	0	0	0
Castillo	.976	56	81	2	2	0
Faulkner	1.000	41	80	4	0	0
Lawson	1.000	6	6	0	0	0
Mack	1.000	16	17	0	0	0
Miller	.938	9	15	0	1	0
Morales	1.000	9	20	1	0	0
Wilson	.974	50	72	3	2	3
Zamarripa	.989	50	85	9	1	1

PULASKI MARINERS   ROOKIE
APPALACHIAN LEAGUE

Batting	B-T	HT	WT	DOB	AVG	vLH	vRH	G	AB	R	H	2B	3B	HR	RBI	BB	HBP	SH	SF	SO	SB	CS	SLG	OBP
Barbosa, Aaron	L-R	5-10	157	4-14-92	.356	.391	.346	30	101	23	36	4	1	0	6	19	0	2	1	14	19	3	.416	.455
Brito, Kristian	R-R	6-5	240	12-20-94	.249	.328	.219	56	209	27	52	14	0	10	38	13	1	0	2	71	3	2	.459	.293
Calderon, Yordi	R-R	6-2	185	2-15-94	.000	—	.000	1	3	0	0	0	0	0	0	1	0	0	0	3	0	0	.000	.250
Cowan, Jordan	L-R	6-0	160	4-13-95	.125	.000	.143	2	8	1	1	0	0	0	0	1	0	0	0	1	0	0	.125	.222
DeCarlo, Joe	R-R	5-10	205	9-13-93	.250	.261	.247	27	96	18	24	4	0	4	15	17	1	0	0	42	0	1	.417	.368
DeMello, Toby	R-R	6-2	220	1-3-90	.273	.182	.303	27	88	7	24	8	0	3	14	8	0	0	0	33	3	0	.466	.333
Diaz, Franklin	B-R	6-1	170	7-20-90	.267	.167	.310	19	60	9	16	4	1	0	6	3	0	0	1	16	0	1	.367	.297
Franca, Gabriel	R-R	5-11	160	9-11-93	.213	.229	.205	54	160	28	34	2	1	0	9	37	2	0	0	29	14	6	.238	.367
Guarnaccia, Luke	R-R	5-11	210	7-11-92	.314	.233	.336	38	137	15	43	11	1	2	16	5	1	0	0	31	5	3	.453	.343
Kemp, Dan	R-R	6-3	195	8-7-91	.235	.250	.231	15	51	9	12	2	0	0	6	8	1	0	0	14	2	1	.275	.350
Martinez, Wilton	R-R	6-4	195	12-11-93	.209	.322	.162	53	201	29	42	9	1	12	33	12	3	0	2	65	3	2	.443	.261
Michel, Raysheron	B-R	6-2	175	11-30-92	.282	.286	.281	12	39	4	11	3	1	1	5	1	0	0	0	12	1	1	.487	.300
Miller, Ian	L-R	6-0	170	2-21-92	.297	.400	.277	40	155	30	46	5	0	1	13	16	3	2	0	29	14	6	.348	.374
Shank, Zach	R-R	6-1	180	1-6-91	.230	.222	.232	52	183	30	42	11	5	1	19	21	5	4	2	22	9	0	.361	.322
Smith, Tyler	R-R	6-0	195	7-1-91	.320	.271	.336	52	200	33	64	16	3	2	34	18	9	2	4	32	12	5	.460	.394
Torres, Dan	R-R	6-0	175	5-29-92	.148	.167	.143	9	27	4	4	0	0	1	2	2	0	0		8	0	0	.148	.258
Ugueto, Jesus	R-R	6-0	170	5-30-91	.261	.294	.248	49	184	27	48	10	5	8	39	9	2	3	2	47	5	2	.500	.299
Werman, Keith	L-R	5-7	150	10-1-89	.118	.143	.100	5	17	2	2	0	0	0	0	3	0	0	0	1	0	1	.118	.250
Yates, Isaiah	R-L	5-9	185	8-31-94	.269	.236	.283	50	193	28	52	12	3	4	30	22	3	1	0	62	10	4	.425	.353
Zimmerman, Jeff	L-L	6-3	220	7-5-92	.305	.214	.322	47	174	27	53	10	4	5	39	11	5	0	1	40	0	1	.494	.361

Pitching	B-T	HT	WT	DOB	W	L	ERA	G	GS	CG	SV	IP	H	R	ER	HR	BB	SO	AVG	vLH	vRH	K/9	BB/9
Campbell, Ed	L-L	6-0	190	1-17-92	3	3	3.72	11	9	0	0	48	36	22	20	2	22	66	.212	.273	.203	12.29	4.10
Cleto, Ramire	R-R	6-0	190	4-4-93	4	3	3.49	12	11	0	0	57	66	32	22	5	21	35	.297	.315	.285	5.56	3.34
Copping, Cameron	R-R	6-6	220	4-24-90	0	0	0.00	2	0	0	0	4	1	0	0	0	0	5	.077	.000	.125	11.25	0.00
De La Cruz, Noel	R-R	6-3	180	12-17-91	3	3	4.63	13	12	0	0	58	57	36	30	10	17	37	.259	.214	.280	5.71	2.62
De Meyer, Dylan	R-R	6-4	165	9-16-92	1	1	6.59	17	2	0	1	29	41	24	21	2	6	30	.345	.432	.293	9.42	1.88
Diaz, Edwin	R-R	6-2	165	3-22-94	5	2	1.43	13	13	0	0	69	45	14	11	5	18	79	.191	.173	.201	10.30	2.35
Flores, Jose	R-R	6-2	190	12-31-92	6	1	3.00	12	12	0	0	72	42	19	19	6	22	58	.208	.200	.211	9.16	3.47
Gohara, Luiz	L-L	6-3	210	7-31-96	1	2	4.15	6	6	0	0	22	22	14	10	1	9	27	.256	.231	.260	11.22	3.74
Gonzalez, Isliexel	R-R	6-3	185	5-10-91	0	0	3.60	8	0	0	0	15	10	7	6	1	11	24	.182	.176	.184	14.40	6.60
Marte, Wander	L-L	6-2	180	6-30-92	1	1	2.25	17	0	0	0	16	5	4	4	1	13	17	.100	.100	.100	9.56	7.31
Mathis, Will	L-L	6-3	180	8-18-90	0	1	5.40	1	0	0	0	2	2	1	1	0	0	1	.400	.000	.500	5.40	0.00
Misell, Carlos	R-R	6-1	165	4-25-92	2	0	0.00	3	0	0	0	5	2	0	0	1	0	10	.125	.286	.000	19.29	1.93
Munoz, Leoncio	L-L	6-4	170	8-18-90	7	1	1.69	17	0	0	1	37	25	11	7	0	10	43	.188	.200	.185	10.37	2.41
Pagan, Emilio	L-R	6-2	205	5-7-91	1	0	0.00	15	0	0	12	20	9	0	0	0	5		.127	.211	.096	11.95	2.21
Pina, Luis	L-L	6-2	178	12-6-93	2	1	3.71	18	0	0	1	34	35	17	14	2	22	22	.267	.310	.255	5.82	3.18
Pineda, Rafael	R-R	6-5	200	2-3-91	2	3	4.25	20	0	0	3	30	26	14	14	1	7	40	.226	.162	.256	12.13	2.12
Ronnenbergh, Scott	L-L	6-2	170	1-11-92	1	2	4.61	15	0	0	0	27	31	16	14	4	17	28	.277	.333	.259	9.22	5.60
Saquilon, Gabe	R-R	6-0	180	6-7-93	1	2	3.72	15	3	0	1	39	27	17	16	1	20	25	.206	.333	.140	5.82	4.66
Thieben, Daniel	R-R	6-4	195	9-18-93	1	0	6.95	18	0	0	0	22	24	18	17	3	25	19	.304	.296	.308	7.77	10.23
Zokan, Jake	R-L	6-1	195	4-27-91	0	0	2.08	3	0	0	0	4	6	1	1	0	0	5	.286	.750	.176	10.38	1.09

Fielding

Catcher	PCT	G	PO	A	E	DP	PB
DeMello	.992	25	225	30	2	2	5
Diaz	.986	18	128	13	2	0	4
Guarnaccia	.990	21	175	20	2	2	6
Torres	.973	9	64	7	2	3	2

First Base	PCT	G	PO	A	E	DP
Brito	.997	43	340	20	1	32
DeMello	1.000	2	7	0	0	1
Zimmerman	.996	29	243	14	1	26

Second Base	PCT	G	PO	A	E	DP
Cowan	1.000	2	7	5	0	1
Franca	.969	21	41	54	3	15

	PCT	G	PO	A	E	DP
Shank	.995	43	84	129	1	36
Werman	1.000	3	4	7	0	2

Third Base	PCT	G	PO	A	E	DP
Brito	.750	3	0	3	1	1
Calderon	1.000	1	1	1	0	1
DeCarlo	.957	27	15	51	3	4
Franca	.942	21	8	41	3	3
Kemp	.923	15	10	26	3	1
Shank	.818	3	0	9	2	1
Werman	—	1	0	0	0	0

Shortstop	PCT	G	PO	A	E	DP
Franca	.941	11	15	33	3	8

	PCT	G	PO	A	E	DP
Shank	.946	6	12	23	2	5
Smith	.963	51	71	161	9	31
Werman	1.000	1	1	3	0	0

Outfield	PCT	G	PO	A	E	DP
Barbosa	.951	27	39	0	2	0
Martinez	.957	41	66	1	3	1
Michel	.917	10	10	1	1	0
Miller	.967	40	55	3	2	0
Pineda	—	1	0	0	0	0
Ugueto	.959	44	66	5	3	1
Yates	.963	46	77	2	3	0

AZL MARINERS ROOKIE

ARIZONA LEAGUE

Batting	B-T	HT	WT	DOB	AVG	vLH	vRH	G	AB	R	H	2B	3B	HR	RBI	BB	HBP	SH	SF	SO	SB	CS	SLG	OBP
Ammirati, Nick	B-R	5-10	195	7-31-91	.100	.000	.111	7	20	2	2	0	0	0	1	2	0	1	0	4	0	1	.100	.182
Berro, Noe	L-R	6-3	180	8-21-93	.239	.185	.256	33	117	18	28	3	3	0	12	15	4	1	2	36	5	3	.316	.341
Brito, Miguel	R-R	6-3	228	9-11-92	.270	.185	.298	30	111	11	30	5	0	0	8	5	0	0	1	31	1	0	.315	.299
Caballero, Luis	R-R	6-1	157	7-8-92	.280	.250	.289	43	150	29	42	5	1	0	13	21	5	2	2	41	5	4	.327	.382
Calderon, Yordi	R-R	6-2	185	2-14-94	.143	.000	.172	12	35	3	5	1	1	0	1	6	1	0	0	10	0	0	.229	.286
Cohoes, Cavan	R-R	6-2	185	5-3-93	.151	.063	.171	31	86	7	13	1	0	0	4	14	0	2	0	36	6	2	.163	.270
Cowan, Jordan	L-R	6-0	160	4-13-95	.262	.100	.321	42	149	26	39	7	2	0	13	15	1	1	1	26	3	5	.336	.331
Dunigan, Joe	L-L	6-1	240	3-29-86	.333	.333	.333	10	30	6	10	1	1	4	9	0	0	0	0	11	0	0	.833	.333
Fontaine, Lachlan	L-R	6-2	190	8-27-95	.200	.286	.176	18	65	6	13	2	0	0	2	8	0	0	0	13	0	0	.231	.288
Franco, Joshua	R-R	5-11	193	9-10-93	.000	—	.000	1	3	0	0	0	0	0	0	0	0	0	0	1	0	0	.000	.000
Howell, Dan	R-R	6-4	235	11-26-89	.176	.000	.231	6	17	1	3	0	0	1	2	4	0	0	0	5	0	0	.353	.333
Kauppila, Lonnie	R-R	6-1	170	1-17-92	.385	.250	.409	8	26	7	10	1	0	0	6	5	0	0	2	6	1	0	.423	.455
Mack, Chantz	L-L	5-11	205	5-4-91	.304	.500	.250	13	46	8	14	5	1	0	11	11	1	0	2	16	0	3	.457	.433
Mejia, Erick	B-R	5-11	155	11-9-94	.360	.250	.412	7	25	4	9	2	0	0	2	2	0	2	0	5	2	0	.440	.407
Michel, Raysheron	B-R	6-2	175	11-30-92	.125	.333	.077	15	32	5	4	0	3	0	2	3	0	2	0	15	2	0	.313	.200
Montero, Jesus	R-R	6-3	230	11-28-89	.261	.000	.316	8	23	3	6	1	0	0	2	3	1	0	1	5	0	0	.304	.357
Morales, Estarlyn	R-R	6-3	180	10-28-92	.258	.235	.264	47	182	19	47	6	2	2	19	18	1	1	1	40	2	3	.346	.327
O'Neill, Tyler	R-R	5-11	205	6-22-95	.310	.217	.338	28	100	12	31	5	3	1	15	12	4	0	0	27	2	4	.450	.405
Palma, Alexy	R-R	6-3	195	12-24-92	.261	.290	.250	38	119	12	31	9	1	3	21	19	4	0	0	42	0	1	.429	.380
Perez, Georvic	B-R	6-0	198	4-15-95	.177	.267	.149	22	62	3	11	1	0	0	7	5	1	0	1	12	0	0	.194	.246
Petty, Kyle	R-R	6-5	215	3-1-91	.349	.250	.381	22	83	15	29	8	1	0	13	3	2	1	0	23	6	0	.470	.386
Pimentel, Guillermo	L-L	6-1	206	10-5-92	.300	.333	.294	6	20	1	6	2	0	0	2	0	0	0	0	6	0	0	.400	.300
Sanchez, Miguel	R-R	6-2	180	9-7-91	.266	.278	.263	24	94	7	25	6	1	0	15	4	0	1	0	22	1	0	.351	.293
Scammell, Cory	L-R	6-5	205	7-28-93	.284	.278	.286	42	148	23	42	7	4	0	14	14	3	0	0	46	5	2	.385	.358
Simpson, Corey	R-R	6-2	210	12-8-93	.244	.200	.257	14	45	7	11	2	0	3	7	6	0	0	0	13	0	0	.489	.333
Sucre, Jesus	R-R	6-0	225	4-30-88	.316	.600	.214	6	19	1	6	1	0	0	3	1	0	0	0	2	0	0	.368	.350
Thomas, Brett	L-R	6-1	190	2-21-94	.269	.400	.238	8	26	3	7	3	0	0	2	1	1	0	0	4	0	0	.385	.321
Torres, Dan	R-R	6-0	175	5-29-92	.240	.286	.222	17	50	7	12	2	0	0	1	4	0	2	0	11	1	1	.280	.296

Pitching	B-T	HT	WT	DOB	W	L	ERA	G	GS	CG	SV	IP	H	R	ER	HR	BB	SO	AVG	vLH	vRH	K/9	BB/9
Burns, Tommy	R-R	6-1	180	9-27-93	1	0	0.00	3	1	0	0	8	9	0	0	0	2	11	.281	.308	.263	11.88	2.16
Claudio, Ricky	R-R	6-3	190	12-20-90	0	2	1.86	15	0	0	6	19	14	4	4	0	10	23	.212	.231	.208	10.71	4.66
Fry, Paul	L-L	6-0	190	7-26-92	2	3	4.50	14	4	0	1	34	41	22	17	3	8	34	.306	.179	.340	9.00	2.12
Gonzalez, Isliexel	R-R	6-3	185	5-10-91	1	1	2.92	7	0	0	0	12	11	8	4	0	7	19	.239	.333	.194	13.86	5.11
Guzman, Michaelangelo	L-L	6-0	215	2-27-91	1	0	2.73	15	0	0	1	26	15	9	8	0	25	38	.174	.136	.188	12.99	8.54
Hauser, Blake	R-R	6-2	180	4-14-91	0	0	0.00	2	1	0	0	3	2	0	0	0	2	3	.182	.000	.333	9.00	6.00
Hultzen, Danny	L-L	6-3	200	11-28-89	1	0	1.80	1	1	0	0	5	3	1	1	0	0	8	.167	.000	.188	14.40	0.00
Koneski, Nate	R-L	6-0	175	3-11-90	0	0	4.50	4	1	0	0	10	11	5	5	1	4	6	.268	.357	.222	5.40	3.60
Littell, Zack	R-R	6-3	190	10-5-95	0	6	5.94	10	7	0	1	33	39	27	22	2	13	28	.291	.300	.286	7.56	3.51
Mathis, Will	L-L	6-3	180	8-18-90	1	0	3.81	16	0	0	1	38	32	16	12	2	13	29	.281	.200	.310	9.21	4.13
McCoy, Kevin	L-R	6-4	220	7-12-91	2	1	2.59	15	0	0	4	24	17	9	7	0	10	36	.193	.152	.218	13.32	3.70
Medina, Jefferson	R-R	6-2	184	5-31-94	4	3	2.58	11	8	0	1	52	44	18	15	1	14	34	.228	.257	.210	5.85	2.41
Misell, Carlos	R-R	6-1	165	4-25-92	0	0	0.00	2	0	0	0	3	2	0	0	0	3	2	.200	.667	.000	9.00	9.00
Missaki, Daniel	R-R	6-0	170	4-9-96	0	1	6.23	7	3	0	0	13	17	9	9	1	5	15	.400	.282	.400	10.38	3.46
Osorio, Neritzon	R-R	6-1	180	12-29-93	2	3	6.47	14	4	0	0	40	51	36	29	5	15	27	.319	.277	.347	6.02	3.35
Pereira, Cruz	L-L	5-10	175	12-18-90	1	3	2.66	12	0	0	0	24	23	11	7	1	11	14	.245	.238	.247	5.32	4.18
Roy, Alex	L-L	6-2	165	7-28-95	0	0	8.00	9	0	0	0	9	7	9	8	0	15	5	.219	.250	.208	5.00	15.00
Scott, Troy	R-R	6-3	200	11-17-93	0	0	4.76	9	0	0	0	17	21	16	9	1	6	24	.296	.318	.286	12.71	3.18
Seifrit, Logan	B-R	5-11	165	8-25-94	2	4	7.94	11	9	0	0	34	41	32	30	2	16	26	.291	.310	.277	6.88	4.24
Shipers, Jordan	R-R	6-3	168	6-21-91	1	0	3.86	4	4	0	0	14	11	6	6	1	5	12	.220	.250	.211	7.71	3.21
Sparger, Tyler	R-R	6-5	220	2-20-92	0	0	0.00	1	0	0	0	1	2	0	0	0	1	0	.500	.333	1.000	0.00	9.00
Torres, Jose	R-R	6-4	165	9-1-93	0	0	1.50	6	0	0	0	6	4	2	1	0	5	3	.190	.091	.300	4.50	7.50
Unsworth, Dylan	R-R	6-1	175	9-23-92	0	0	4.50	3	3	0	0	6	4	3	3	1	0	10	.190	.167	.222	15.00	0.00
Urbina, Ugueth	R-R	6-1	185	10-28-94	3	2	5.76	11	4	0	0	45	61	37	29	1	17	30	.332	.358	.311	5.96	3.38
Urquides, Melchor	B-L	6-0	180	7-26-95	0	2	5.74	9	4	0	0	16	20	18	10	1	13	16	.282	.167	.340	9.19	7.47

Fielding

Catcher	PCT	G	PO	A	E	DP	PB
Ammirati	.979	6	45	2	1	1	0
Perez	.977	17	107	21	3	2	5
Sanchez	.969	22	168	22	6	4	13
Sucre	.966	4	27	1	1	0	0
Torres	1.000	16	108	15	0	1	1

First Base	PCT	G	PO	A	E	DP
Brito	.967	11	85	4	3	5
Franco	.900	1	9	0	1	0
Howell	.921	4	32	3	3	2
Montero	1.000	6	28	0	0	1
Petty	.989	18	161	11	2	11
Scammell	.956	19	167	7	8	19

Second Base	PCT	G	PO	A	E	DP
Berro	.881	27	52	66	16	10

Caballero	1.000	2	2	3	0	0
Cowan	.969	24	48	75	4	19
Kauppila	1.000	2	5	1	0	2
Mejia	1.000	2	3	5	0	0

Third Base	PCT	G	PO	A	E	DP
Berro	.818	5	0	9	2	1
Brito	.929	15	7	32	3	3
Caballero	.870	8	3	17	3	1
Calderon	.875	11	7	14	3	2
Fontaine	.882	18	12	33	6	6

Shortstop	PCT	G	PO	A	E	DP
Caballero	.977	30	41	87	3	20
Cowan	.974	18	27	47	2	4
Kauppila	.966	5	11	17	1	4
Mejia	1.000	5	6	19	0	2

Outfield	PCT	G	PO	A	E	DP
Caballero	1.000	2	1	0	0	0
Cohoes	.957	29	45	0	2	0
Dunigan	1.000	7	5	0	0	0
Mack	.957	13	22	0	1	0
Michel	1.000	12	15	2	0	1
Morales	.988	40	75	6	1	2
O'Neill	1.000	17	22	4	0	0
Palma	.975	32	36	3	1	0
Pimentel	.857	4	6	0	1	0
Scammell	1.000	16	21	1	0	0
Simpson	.941	11	16	0	1	0
Thomas	1.000	7	7	0	0	0

DSL MARINERS   ROOKIE

DOMINICAN SUMMER LEAGUE

Batting	B-T	HT	WT	DOB	AVG	vLH	vRH	G	AB	R	H	2B	3B	HR	RBI	BB	HBP	SH	SF	SO	SB	CS	SLG	OBP
Alcantara, Ismael	R-R	6-0	185	12-15-93	.275	.243	.289	66	233	32	64	8	4	2	37	33	7	0	3	31	7	13	.369	.377
Almonte, Adalfi	R-R	6-1	170	4-19-96	.235	.348	.177	61	196	40	46	16	2	4	22	43	5	3	2	56	12	3	.398	.382
Almonte, Miguel	R-R	6-0	180	1-5-94	.151	.138	.158	38	86	13	13	4	1	0	6	8	4	1	0	35	4	1	.221	.255
Baez, Cesar	L-R	6-0	160	7-6-95	.129	.179	.095	27	70	7	9	0	0	0	3	6	3	0	0	23	3	3	.129	.228
De la Cruz, Adonis	R-R	6-2	170	12-20-94	.155	.130	.169	41	129	14	20	5	0	1	8	17	5	3	1	39	3	1	.217	.276
Dominguez, Anthony	R-R	6-0	170	6-6-96	.179	.158	.189	61	179	27	32	5	1	0	20	34	2	4	6	30	5	7	.218	.308
Franco, Joshua	R-R	5-11	193	9-10-93	.201	.164	.223	50	164	6	33	10	0	0	12	12	5	1	0	47	0	2	.262	.276
Gonzalez, Ivan	R-R	6-0	175	10-28-95	.209	.077	.267	12	43	7	9	0	1	0	7	4	2	0	2	3	5	4	.256	.294
Jimenez, Angel	R-R	6-1	180	9-8-94	.251	.111	.308	59	187	30	47	8	1	5	31	31	6	4	2	36	11	4	.385	.372
Liberato, Luis	L-L	6-1	175	12-18-95	.255	.203	.276	57	204	39	52	8	3	2	17	23	3	2	1	50	14	8	.353	.338
Martinez, Hersin	R-R	6-5	220	2-27-95	.198	.244	.167	28	101	12	20	5	0	0	10	11	2	0	1	33	0	3	.248	.287
Mejia, Erick	B-R	5-11	155	11-9-94	.261	.297	.235	24	88	16	23	3	1	0	3	14	1	1	1	10	11	7	.318	.365
Nieto, Arturo	R-R	6-2	195	12-9-92	.299	.265	.316	52	147	18	44	3	0	1	17	24	9	3	0	27	8	3	.340	.428
Ramirez, Gregory	R-R	6-4	190	7-24-95	.236	.218	.247	50	144	14	34	5	1	1	16	17	6	3	1	42	7	5	.306	.339
Rosa, Jose	R-R	6-0	175	3-7-94	.212	.333	.129	36	104	12	22	4	0	1	8	9	1	0	0	24	3	2	.279	.281
Vargas, Leurys	L-R	6-3	225	8-30-96	.185	.182	.186	47	168	11	31	5	1	5	24	9	3	0	0	38	3	3	.315	.239

Pitching	B-T	HT	WT	DOB	W	L	ERA	G	GS	CG	SV	IP	H	R	ER	HR	BB	SO	AVG	vLH	vRH	K/9	BB/9
Arias, Jefferson	R-R	6-4	185	4-8-93	1	2	7.36	12	1	0	0	15	13	14	12	2	16	20	.224	.286	.205	12.27	9.82
Asencio, Oliver	L-L	6-2	199	1-18-93	4	2	2.17	13	11	1	0	62	49	19	15	1	27	42	.215	.225	.213	6.06	3.90
Brito, Frankely	R-R	6-0	170	11-1-92	0	5	8.18	10	10	0	0	22	29	26	20	0	25	16	.333	.240	.371	6.55	10.23
Cortoreal, Leonel	L-L	6-5	175	9-6-92	1	1	3.86	12	1	0	0	21	22	11	9	1	15	12	.268	.158	.302	5.14	6.43
Dominguez, Ronald	R-R	6-2	180	1-13-94	1	0	3.89	15	0	0	2	39	41	22	17	5	6	31	.277	.270	.279	7.09	1.37
Feliz, Jose	R-R	6-0	170	12-23-94	3	4	1.81	13	2	0	1	45	46	20	9	0	8	33	.277	.316	.257	6.65	1.61
Franco, Arismendy	R-R	6-1	165	4-15-94	0	0	4.11	8	0	0	1	15	10	9	7	1	14	7	.182	.158	.194	4.11	8.22
Garcia, Andres	R-R	6-4	170	3-11-92	2	1	4.15	14	0	0	1	26	29	14	12	1	6	21	.296	.223	.308	7.27	2.08
Gonzalez, Yeuri	R-R	6-2	170	12-22-92	8	3	1.63	14	14	1	0	83	75	33	15	1	14	55	.235	.299	.203	5.96	1.52
Manzueta, Romulo	L-L	6-2	160	10-9-95	3	1	5.08	10	3	0	0	28	24	17	16	1	17	28	.231	.056	.267	8.89	5.40
Millord, Yohailys	R-R	6-2	180	12-4-93	1	1	4.74	11	0	0	1	19	18	13	10	1	14	19	.261	.286	.255	9.00	6.63
Paulino, Darel	R-R	6-6	225	11-24-92	3	2	1.88	13	0	0	0	24	17	5	5	0	13	13	.207	.222	.203	4.88	4.88
Paulino, Roberto	R-R	6-2	187	11-16-93	0	0	15.75	3	0	0	0	4	7	7	7	0	2	4	.412	.800	.250	9.00	4.50
Pedie, Raul	R-R	6-0	175	8-14-92	4	0	0.61	17	0	0	8	30	16	3	2	1	5	32	.151	.107	.167	9.71	1.52
Peralta, Freddy	R-R	5-11	175	6-4-96	3	3	1.46	13	10	1	0	55	38	14	9	0	15	49	.198	.219	.189	7.97	2.44
Reyes, Pedro	L-L	6-0	155	5-28-93	2	1	1.36	17	0	0	3	40	24	7	6	0	16	38	.175	.125	.186	8.62	3.63
Santiago, Jose	R-R	6-1	190	3-1-94	0	3	4.30	14	14	0	0	52	50	33	25	0	34	44	.258	.295	.247	7.57	5.85
Tamarez, Albert	R-R	6-1	185	11-30-93	0	3	5.33	13	2	0	0	25	23	21	15	0	17	14	.242	.175	.291	4.97	6.04
Urquides, Melchor	B-L	6-0	180	7-26-95	1	1	6.52	3	2	0	0	10	10	7	7	1	4	14	.256	.000	.333	13.03	3.72

Fielding

Catcher	PCT	G	PO	A	E	DP	PB
Almonte	.987	14	69	8	1	2	9
Nieto	.981	51	313	51	7	1	6
Rosa	.962	21	108	19	5	1	4

First Base	PCT	G	PO	A	E	DP
Alcantara	.989	9	78	9	1	5
Almonte	.968	4	28	2	1	2
Franco	.975	15	113	4	3	9
Nieto	1.000	1	13	1	0	2
Ramirez	1.000	1	1	0	0	0
Rosa	.983	13	108	5	2	2
Vargas	.991	36	313	17	3	17

Second Base	PCT	G	PO	A	E	DP
Alcantara	.940	30	49	76	8	8
Baez	.925	19	22	40	5	7
Dominguez	.951	18	41	37	4	7
Gonzalez	.926	5	7	18	2	1
Jimenez	.875	4	8	6	2	1
Mejia	1.000	2	3	5	0	0

Third Base	PCT	G	PO	A	E	DP
Alcantara	.970	9	11	21	1	0
Dominguez	1.000	1	0	3	0	0
Franco	.863	17	15	29	7	2
Gonzalez	.800	1	2	2	1	1
Jimenez	.860	49	43	92	22	2
Rosa	1.000	1	0	1	0	0

Shortstop	PCT	G	PO	A	E	DP
Baez	.857	5	5	7	2	1
Dominguez	.927	42	55	109	13	13
Gonzalez	.939	7	15	16	2	0
Jimenez	.917	4	6	5	1	0
Mejia	.939	22	47	77	8	11

Outfield	PCT	G	PO	A	E	DP
Alcantara	.824	14	13	1	3	1
Almonte	.970	61	85	11	3	2
De la Cruz	.912	33	26	5	3	0
Liberato	.986	55	134	6	2	2
Martinez	.930	22	37	3	3	0
Ramirez	1.000	42	47	4	0	0

VENEZUELAN SUMMER LEAGUE

Batting	B-T	HT	WT	DOB	AVG	vLH	vRH	G	AB	R	H	2B	3B	HR	RBI	BB	HBP	SH	SF	SO	SB	CS	SLG	OBP
Ascanio, Rayder	B-R	5-11	155	3-17-96	.266	.235	.275	50	143	28	38	9	3	3	18	23	3	1	1	33	3	3	.434	.376
Calderon, Yordi	R-R	6-2	185	2-15-94	.343	.368	.335	68	239	68	82	20	3	11	42	39	8	0	2	48	16	10	.590	.448
Capriata, Alexander	R-R	5-11	190	8-3-92	.288	.261	.300	26	73	12	21	4	1	2	16	10	2	1	0	4	4	2	.452	.388
Fernandez, Rafael	B-R	5-10	180	4-21-94	.284	.250	.296	58	211	40	60	6	3	2	18	21	2	6	2	24	17	5	.370	.352
Gonzalez, Ricardo	R-R	6-0	206	3-25-92	.215	.308	.192	21	65	12	14	4	0	3	12	11	1	0	0	26	5	1	.415	.338
Guedez, Jose	R-R	6-2	175	9-6-94	.145	.167	.140	35	69	9	10	4	0	1	8	4	1	0	1	22	1	2	.246	.200
Herrera, Albert	R-R	5-11	160	3-7-96	.220	.100	.258	21	41	9	9	0	1	0	1	6	3	1	0	15	2	0	.268	.360
Laya, Alexdray	R-R	6-1	185	10-6-95	.037	.000	.045	13	27	2	1	0	0	0	1	7	0	0	0	6	0	1	.037	.235
Leal, Bryan	L-R	6-0	164	8-20-96	.191	.143	.200	18	47	2	9	0	1	0	7	1	1	0	0	14	0	1	.234	.224
Leal, Jose	R-R	6-3	215	2-16-95	.243	.277	.232	57	189	39	46	10	3	6	37	19	7	1	7	52	6	3	.423	.324
Mina, Diego	R-R	5-11	181	10-13-92	.297	.167	.339	33	74	12	22	3	0	2	17	3	3	2	0	22	4	4	.419	.350
Morales, Jhonbaker	R-R	6-0	170	7-17-94	.314	.265	.326	51	172	30	54	10	0	1	24	11	6	5	2	20	1	4	.390	.372
Quevedo, Johan	B-R	6-1	212	11-6-93	.295	.364	.271	59	210	48	62	14	1	3	48	20	3	0	3	16	10	2	.414	.360
Sojo, Danilo	R-R	6-4	211	4-29-95	.074	.091	.065	30	68	4	5	2	0	1	7	3	2	0	1	33	1	0	.147	.135
Talos, Felipe	L-R	5-11	170	2-3-95	.266	.227	.275	44	124	12	33	10	3	0	18	16	3	0	0	22	5	3	.395	.364
Tenias, Raymon	B-R	5-8	185	4-15-94	.119	.200	.111	22	59	8	7	2	2	0	8	4	0	0	1	21	1	0	.220	.172
Velasquez, Alberto	L-L	6-5	240	3-7-94	.339	.458	.310	46	124	15	42	7	1	1	23	16	2	0	2	8	1	1	.435	.417
Villa, Hilario	R-R	6-3	167	7-1-92	.203	.200	.204	32	69	7	14	4	2	0	7	7	0	1	1	18	1	0	.319	.273
Wawoe, Gianfranco	R-R	5-11	170	7-25-94	.328	.404	.307	68	244	63	80	19	4	6	30	33	4	2	1	25	21	7	.512	.415

Pitching	B-T	HT	WT	DOB	W	L	ERA	G	GS	CG	SV	IP	H	R	ER	HR	BB	SO	AVG	vLH	vRH	K/9	BB/9
Breto, Liarvis	L-L	5-11	175	4-10-93	5	3	3.57	13	11	0	0	58	48	28	23	3	26	50	.223	.233	.222	7.76	4.03
Carrera, Rafael	R-R	6-0	190	10-29-92	0	1	3.86	3	3	0	0	12	8	6	5	1	5	10	.211	.200	.217	7.71	3.86
Carrillo, Rohimard	R-L	5-11	175	8-19-94	2	2	6.59	8	0	0	0	14	13	10	10	2	6	11	.250	.500	.190	7.24	3.95
Gadea, Kevin	R-R	6-5	188	12-6-94	9	1	2.65	14	14	0	0	71	71	28	21	3	23	48	.264	.205	.293	6.06	2.90
Hernandez, Anjul	R-R	6-2	192	1-2-96	5	1	4.31	13	9	0	1	54	62	35	26	1	19	31	.300	.382	.252	5.13	3.15
Hidalgo, Hector	R-R	6-1	182	9-21-92	2	0	1.43	14	0	0	7	38	27	7	6	2	10	24	.197	.159	.215	5.73	2.39
Jimenez, Jonathan	R-R	6-1	196	2-14-92	0	2	2.13	13	0	0	5	25	25	7	6	0	2	15	.260	.219	.281	5.33	0.71
Lopez, Pablo	R-R	6-3	196	3-7-96	7	1	2.57	12	12	0	0	67	51	25	19	2	11	38	.209	.148	.239	5.13	1.49
Marruffo, Wladimir	R-R	6-0	173	5-29-93	4	1	2.23	12	0	0	1	36	36	14	9	1	12	24	.263	.349	.223	5.94	2.97
Mata, Daniel	R-R	6-2	180	7-3-93	2	1	2.93	14	0	0	4	31	31	13	10	2	9	23	.258	.308	.235	6.75	2.64
Miliani, Eduardo	R-R	5-11	178	7-8-93	2	2	5.18	14	1	0	3	43	43	29	19	3	9	24	.316	.289	.330	6.55	2.45
Morales, Osmel	R-R	6-3	196	10-30-92	5	1	1.86	15	3	0	5	53	29	12	11	2	14	66	.162	.161	.162	11.14	2.36
Pena, Andres	R-R	6-3	200	1-16-95	1	2	4.64	11	11	0	0	33	27	21	17	0	28	22	.229	.171	.260	6.00	7.64
Quintanilla, Kevin	R-R	6-0	174	5-21-92	2	1	3.14	14	0	0	2	29	28	12	10	1	14	18	.252	.289	.233	5.65	4.40
Rodriguez, Carlos	R-R	6-0	190	5-23-95	2	1	0.75	6	1	0	0	12	10	1	1	1	1	7	.227	.200	.250	5.25	0.75
Suarez, Michael	L-L	6-2	180	3-21-95	0	0	5.02	15	3	0	0	29	36	17	16	0	10	23	.310	.400	.302	7.22	3.14

Fielding

Catcher	PCT	G	PO	A	E	DP	PB
Capriata	.993	23	118	23	1	1	3
Gonzalez	.984	9	56	4	1	1	2
Quevedo	.995	31	176	33	1	5	0
Tenias	.953	17	74	7	4	0	2

First Base	PCT	G	PO	A	E	DP
Calderon	.990	25	187	3	2	15
Capriata	1.000	1	8	0	0	0
Gonzalez	1.000	2	2	1	0	0
Laya	1.000	1	9	0	0	1
Mina	1.000	12	74	0	0	12
Quevedo	.992	11	115	4	1	6
Sojo	1.000	2	7	0	0	1
Velasquez	.992	36	247	13	2	24

Second Base	PCT	G	PO	A	E	DP
Ascanio	.967	7	16	13	1	3
Fernandez	.987	14	36	40	1	16
Herrera	.915	18	25	29	5	8
Laya	1.000	1	2	1	0	1
Mina	1.000	5	10	7	0	3
Morales	.842	4	8	8	3	3
Wawoe	.959	38	71	92	7	22

Third Base	PCT	G	PO	A	E	DP
Ascanio	.966	9	5	23	1	4
Calderon	.871	19	13	41	8	7
Fernandez	.964	10	3	24	1	2
Laya	.857	9	5	7	2	4
Morales	.941	34	28	84	7	8

Shortstop	PCT	G	PO	A	E	DP
Ascanio	.933	33	42	98	10	13
Fernandez	.944	20	22	63	5	13
Herrera	1.000	3	2	3	0	1
Laya	1.000	1	0	1	0	0
Morales	.982	14	18	38	1	6
Wawoe	.927	10	17	21	3	4

Outfield	PCT	G	PO	A	E	DP
Calderon	.950	32	38	0	2	0
Fernandez	1.000	18	41	3	0	1
Guedez	.936	34	44	0	3	0
Leal	.842	16	16	0	3	0
Leal	.941	54	89	7	6	1
Sojo	.941	19	15	1	1	0
Talos	.967	34	54	5	2	2
Villa	.955	32	40	2	2	1
Wawoe	1.000	19	29	3	0	1

SEATTLE MARINERS

Tampa Bay Rays

SEASON IN A SENTENCE: The Rays remained a shining example of how to compete on a budget, making the postseason for the fourth time in six years, but they were unable to overcome the Red Sox juggernaut.

HIGH POINT: The Rays were neck-and-neck with the Red Sox in the AL East race for most of the year on their way to 92 wins, peaking with a majors-best 21-5 record in July. In the end, Tampa had to survive a tight wild-card race, winning game 163 on the road in Texas and then the AL wild-card game in Cleveland on the strength of back-to-back strong pitching performances from David Price and Alex Cobb.

LOW POINT: The Rays needed a late charge to get into the playoffs as a wild-card team after an August and early September swoon doomed their division title hopes. Tampa went just 4-12 from Aug. 25-Sept. 11, dropping from a first-place tie with Boston to a 9 ½ game deficit.

NOTABLE ROOKIES: The Rays plugged top prospect Wil Myers into right field in June and the 22-year-old quickly became a catalyst in the middle of their lineup, batting .293/.354/.478 with 13 homers and leading AL rookies in doubles (23) and RBIs (53). Righthander Chris Archer was a key part of the Rays' hot July, going 4-0, 0.73 in five July outings, and went 9-7, 3.22 for the year.

KEY TRANSACTIONS: The Rays made one of the offseason's bigger trades when they landed four players, led by Myers and righthander Jake Odorizzi, from the Royals for a trio of big leaguers in James Shields, Wade Davis and Elliot Johnson. That deal came a few days after the Rays found their new shortstop in Yunel Escobar in a trade from the Marlins. General manager Andrew Friedman also scored a coup in free agency with first baseman James Loney, who revitalized his career by hitting .299 with 13 homers while costing the Rays just a $2 million salary.

DOWN ON THE FARM: Despite losing Myers and Archer to promotions, Triple-A Durham posted the best record in the International League and won the IL title. The Bulls were one of three Rays full-season affiliates to qualify for postseason play, and the organization's .524 cumulative winning percentage was the seventh-best in baseball. Durham's J.D. Martin was named the International League's most valuable pitcher, while low Class A Bowling Green outfielder Andrew Toles won the Midwest League batting title.

OPENING DAY PAYROLL: $57.9 million (28th)

PLAYERS OF THE YEAR

MAJOR LEAGUE	MINOR LEAGUE
Evan Longoria	**Enny Romero**
3b	**lhp**
.269/.343/.498,	(Double-A/Triple-A)
32 HR, 39 2B, 88 RBIs	11-7, 2.61, 148 IP
7th in AL in HR	114 H, 112 SO, 75 BB

ORGANIZATION LEADERS

BATTING — *Minimum 250 AB

MAJORS

*	AVG	Loney, James	.299
*	OPS	Longoria, Evan	.842
	HR	Longoria, Evan	32
	RBI	Longoria, Evan	88

MINORS

*	AVG	Toles, Andrew, Bowling Green	.326
*	OBP	Belnome, Vince, Durham	.408
*	SLG	Kang, Kyeong, Montgomery/Charlotte	.479
	R	Kiermaier, Kevin, Durham/Montgomery	89
	H	Toles, Andrew, Bowling Green	169
	TB	Toles, Andrew, Bowling Green	242
	2B	Belnome, Vince, Durham	35
		Toles, Andrew, Bowling Green	35
	3B	Toles, Andrew, Bowling Green	16
	HR	Kang, Kyeong, Montgomery/Charlotte	16
	RBI	Anderson, Leslie, Durham	74
	BB	Coyle, Thomas, Bowling Green	91
	SO	Kang, Kyeong, Montgomery/Charlotte	121
	SB	Toles, Andrew, Bowling Green	62

PITCHING — #Minimum 75 IP

MAJORS

	W	Moore, Matt	17
#	ERA	Price, David	3.33
	SO	Price, David	151
	SV	Rodney, Fernando	37

MINORS

	W	Martin, J.D., Durham	16
	L	Kelly, Merrill, Durham/Montgomery	10
		Thompson, Jacob, Montgomery	10
#	ERA	Floro, Dylan, Bowling Green/Charlotte	1.77
	G	Sandoval, Juan, Durham/Montgomery	58
	GS	Buschmann, Matt, Durham/Montgomery	28
		Romero, Enny, Durham/Montgomery	28
	SV	Yates, Kirby, Durham	20
	IP	Buschmann, Matt, Durham/Montgomery	161
	BB	Romero, Enny, Durham/Montgomery	75
	SO	Buschmann, Matt, Durham/Montgomery	167
#	AVG	Ames, Jeff, Bowling Green	.21

2013 PERFORMANCE

General Manager: Andrew Friedman. **Farm Director:** Mitch Lukevics. **Scouting Director:** R.J. Harrison

Class	Team	League	W	L	PCT	Finish	Manager
Majors	Tampa Bay Rays	American	92	71	.564	5th (15)	Joe Maddon
Triple-A	Durham Bulls	International	87	57	.604	1st (14)	Charlie Montoyo
Double-A	Montgomery Biscuits	Southern	71	69	.507	6th (10)	Billy Gardner Jr.
High A	Charlotte Stone Crabs	Florida State	67	65	.508	4th (12)	Brady Williams
Low A	Bowling Green Hot Rods	Midwest	82	56	.594	2nd (14)	Jared Sandberg
Short-season	Hudson Valley Renegades	New York-Penn	38	37	.507	8th (14)	Michael Johns
Rookie	Princeton Rays	Appalachian	25	43	.368	9th (10)	Danny Sheaffer
Rookie	GCL Rays	Gulf Coast	27	33	.450	12th (16)	Jim Morrison
Overall 2013 Minor League Record			358	337	.524	7th (30)	

ORGANIZATION STATISTICS

TAMPA BAY RAYS

AMERICAN LEAGUE

Batting	B-T	HT	WT	DOB	AVG	vLH	vRH	G	AB	R	H	2B	3B	HR	RBI	BB	HBP	SH	SF	SO	SB	CS	SLG	OBP
Beckham, Tim	R-R	6-0	190	1-27-90	.429	.500	.333	5	7	1	3	0	0	0	1	0	0	0	1	0	0	0	.429	.375
Bourgeois, Jason	R-R	5-9	190	1-4-82	.188	.167	.250	9	16	2	3	0	0	1	2	2	0	0	0	4	0	0	.375	.278
DeJesus, David	L-L	5-11	190	12-20-79	.260	.182	.269	35	104	13	27	10	0	2	11	10	1	1	1	23	2	3	.413	.328
Duncan, Shelley	R-R	6-5	215	9-29-79	.182	.080	.267	20	55	6	10	1	0	2	6	9	0	0	0	14	0	0	.309	.297
Escobar, Yunel	R-R	6-2	210	11-2-82	.256	.279	.245	153	508	61	130	27	1	9	56	57	3	6	4	73	4	4	.366	.332
Fuld, Sam	L-L	5-10	175	11-20-81	.199	.273	.155	118	176	25	35	0	3	2	17	17	1	4	2	28	8	2	.267	.270
Gimenez, Chris	R-R	6-2	220	12-27-82	.333	.000	.333	4	3	0	1	1	0	0	0	1	0	0	0	1	0	0	.667	.500
Guzman, Freddy	B-R	5-10	165	1-20-81	—		.000	1	0	1	0	0	0	0	0	0	0	0	0	1	0		—	—
Jennings, Desmond	R-R	6-2	200	10-30-86	.252	.299	.231	139	527	82	133	31	6	14	54	64	3	5	115	20	8	.414	.334
Johnson, Kelly	L-R	6-1	200	2-22-82	.235	.291	.218	118	366	41	86	12	2	16	52	35	3	0	3	99	7	4	.410	.305
Joyce, Matt	L-R	6-2	205	8-3-84	.235	.164	.246	140	413	61	97	22	0	18	47	59	2	0	7	87	7	3	.419	.328
Kiermaier, Kevin	L-R	6-1	200	4-22-90	—			1	0	0	0	0	0	0	0	0	0	0	0	0	0		—	—
Lobaton, Jose	B-R	6-0	210	10-21-84	.249	.242	.253	100	277	38	69	15	2	7	32	30	0	2	2	65	0	1	.394	.320
Loney, James	L-L	6-3	220	5-7-84	.299	.299	.299	158	549	54	164	33	0	13	75	44	0	1	4	77	3	1	.430	.348
Longoria, Evan	R-R	6-2	210	10-7-85	.269	.301	.256	160	614	91	165	39	3	32	88	70	3	6	162	1	0	.498	.343
Molina, Jose	R-R	6-2	250	6-3-75	.233	.242	.229	99	283	26	66	14	0	2	18	22	2	3	3	63	2	1	.304	.290
Myers, Wil	R-R	6-3	205	12-10-90	.293	.293	.292	88	335	50	98	23	0	13	53	33	1	0	4	91	5	2	.478	.354
Roberts, Ryan	R-R	5-11	185	9-19-80	.247	.305	.188	60	162	15	40	6	0	5	17	11	0	0	0	39	0	2	.377	.295
Rodriguez, Sean	R-R	6-0	200	4-26-85	.246	.252	.225	96	195	21	48	10	1	5	23	17	5	3	2	59	1	3	.385	.320
Scott, Luke	L-R	6-0	220	6-25-78	.241	.269	.229	91	253	27	61	13	2	9	40	30	4	0	4	63	1	1	.415	.326
Young, Delmon	R-R	6-3	240	9-14-85	.258	.200	.297	23	62	8	16	3	0	3	7	6	1	0	1	9	0	0	.452	.329
Zobrist, Ben	B-R	6-3	210	5-26-81	.275	.250	.287	157	612	77	168	36	3	12	71	72	7	1	6	91	11	3	.402	.354

Pitching	B-T	HT	WT	DOB	W	L	ERA	G	GS	CG	SV	IP	H	R	ER	HR	BB	SO	AVG	vLH	vRH	K/9	BB/9
Archer, Chris	R-R	6-3	200	9-26-88	9	7	3.22	23	23	2	0	129	107	49	46	15	38	101	.226	.261	.176	7.06	2.66
Beliveau, Jeff	L-L	6-1	195	1-17-87	0	0	0.00	1	0	0	0	1	1	0	0	0	1	0	.333	.500	.000	0.00	13.50
Cobb, Alex	R-R	6-3	190	10-7-87	11	3	2.76	22	22	1	0	143	120	46	44	13	45	134	.228	.235	.217	8.41	2.83
Colome, Alex	R-R	6-2	185	12-31-88	1	1	2.25	3	3	0	0	16	14	8	4	2	9	12	.230	.258	.200	6.75	5.06
Farnsworth, Kyle	R-R	6-4	230	4-14-76	2	0	5.76	39	0	0	0	30	37	19	19	4	7	19	.306	.273	.325	5.76	2.12
Gomes, Brandon	R-R	5-11	185	7-15-84	3	1	6.52	26	0	0	0	19	18	15	14	4	7	29	.247	.357	.178	13.50	3.26
Hellickson, Jeremy	R-R	6-1	190	4-8-87	12	10	5.17	32	31	0	0	174	185	103	100	24	50	135	.274	.274	.274	6.98	2.59
Hernandez, Roberto	R-R	6-4	230	8-30-80	6	13	4.89	32	24	1	1	151	164	87	82	24	38	113	.281	.305	.253	6.74	2.26
Lueke, Josh	R-R	6-5	220	12-5-84	0	2	5.06	19	0	0	0	21	23	12	12	3	12	25	.277	.250	.298	10.55	5.06
McGee, Jake	L-L	6-3	230	8-6-86	5	3	4.02	71	0	0	1	63	52	28	28	8	22	75	.223	.235	.217	10.77	3.16
Moore, Matt	L-L	6-3	210	6-18-89	17	4	3.29	27	27	1	0	150	119	58	55	14	76	143	.216	.221	.214	8.56	4.55
Odorizzi, Jake	R-R	6-2	185	3-27-90	0	1	3.94	7	4	0	1	30	28	13	13	3	8	22	.252	.293	.208	6.67	2.43
Peralta, Joel	R-R	5-11	205	3-23-76	3	8	3.41	80	0	0	1	71	47	31	27	7	34	74	.184	.163	.213	9.34	4.29
Price, David	L-L	6-6	220	8-26-85	10	8	3.33	27	27	4	0	187	178	78	69	16	27	151	.252	.189	.271	7.28	1.30
Ramos, Cesar	L-L	6-2	205	6-22-84	2	2	4.14	48	0	0	1	67	66	31	31	6	22	53	.256	.272	.245	7.08	2.94
Rodney, Fernando	R-R	5-11	220	3-18-77	5	4	3.38	68	0	0	37	67	53	27	25	3	36	82	.211	.248	.169	11.07	4.86
Romero, Enny	L-L	6-3	165	1-24-91	0	0	0.00	1	1	0	0	5	1	0	0	0	4	0	.071	.000	.083	0.00	7.71
Torres, Alex	L-L	5-10	175	12-8-87	4	2	1.71	39	0	0	0	58	32	12	11	1	20	62	.159	.175	.149	9.62	3.10
Wright, Wesley	R-L	5-11	185	1-28-85	0	0	2.92	16	0	0	0	12	9	4	4	2	3	15	.200	.154	.263	10.95	2.19
2-team total (54 Houston)					0	4	3.69	70	0	0	0	54	54	24	22	7	19	55	—	—	—	9.22	3.19
Wright, Jamey	R-R	6-6	235	12-24-74	2	2	3.09	66	1	0	0	70	65	25	24	4	23	65	.240	.230	.255	8.36	2.96

Fielding

Catcher	PCT	G	PO	A	E	DP	PB
Gimenez	1.000	1	1	0	0	0	0
Lobaton	.996	96	643	40	3	6	2
Molina	.994	96	674	34	4	5	8

First Base	PCT	G	PO	A	E	DP
Duncan	1.000	4	14	1	0	2

Gimenez	1.000	1	3	0	0	0
Johnson	1.000	3	21	0	0	2
Loney	.995	154	1203	98	7	115
Roberts	1.000	3	2	1	0	0
Rodriguez	1.000	23	124	3	0	11
Scott	1.000	5	12	0	0	0

Second Base	PCT	G	PO	A	E	DP
Beckham	1.000	3	0	5	0	0
Johnson	1.000	22	21	37	0	8
Roberts	.970	48	46	84	4	17
Rodriguez	1.000	5	1	5	0	1
Zobrist	.993	125	218	332	4	73

Third Base	PCT	G	PO	A	E	DP
Gimenez	1.000	1	0	1	0	0
Johnson	.978	16	13	31	1	3
Longoria	.972	147	96	279	11	27
Roberts	.972	9	3	14	0	3
Shortstop	**PCT**	**G**	**PO**	**A**	**E**	**DP**
Beckham	—	1	0	0	0	0
Escobar	.989	153	208	395	7	88

	PCT	G	PO	A	E	DP
Rodriguez	.917	7	3	8	1	1
Zobrist	.980	21	11	37	1	5
Outfield	**PCT**	**G**	**PO**	**A**	**E**	**DP**
Bourgeois	1.000	7	8	0	0	0
DeJesus	1.000	33	46	0	0	0
Fuld	.992	105	126	2	1	1
Jennings	.991	136	320	2	3	2
Johnson	.965	53	77	6	3	1

	PCT	G	PO	A	E	DP
Joyce	.994	110	168	2	1	1
Kiermaier	—	1	0	0	0	0
Myers	1.000	77	140	2	0	1
Rodriguez	1.000	54	56	1	0	0
Scott	.833	6	5	0	1	0
Young	—	1	0	0	0	0
Zobrist	1.000	42	49	4	0	1

DURHAM BULLS · TRIPLE-A

INTERNATIONAL LEAGUE

Batting	B-T	HT	WT	DOB	AVG	vLH	vRH	G	AB	R	H	2B	3B	HR	RBI	BB	HBP	SH	SF	SO	SB	CS	SLG	OBP
Albernaz, Craig	R-R	5-8	185	10-30-82	.225	.333	.174	33	102	11	23	5	0	1	11	7	1	4	1	22	3	0	.304	.279
Anderson, Leslie	L-L	6-1	205	3-30-82	.292	.173	.330	119	431	52	126	28	1	14	74	50	8	0	5	58	2	3	.459	.372
Apodaca, Juan	R-R	5-11	180	7-15-86	.238	.300	.219	29	84	11	20	5	1	1	8	9	3	1	0	25	0	1	.357	.333
Beckham, Tim	R-R	6-0	190	1-27-90	.276	.282	.282	122	460	71	127	25	7	4	51	44	5	8	5	108	17	7	.387	.342
Belnome, Vince	L-R	5-11	205	3-11-88	.300	.289	.305	127	444	77	133	35	3	8	67	84	0	1	4	109	0	2	.446	.408
Bourgeois, Jason	R-R	5-9	190	1-4-82	.290	.292	.290	90	348	52	101	15	3	2	61	31	0	6	6	38	22	6	.368	.343
Duncan, Shelley	R-R	6-5	215	9-29-79	.215	.207	.217	90	335	36	72	21	1	11	54	33	3	0	5	82	0	0	.382	.287
Figueroa, Cole	L-R	5-10	185	6-30-87	.286	.281	.288	129	461	65	132	20	4	3	62	54	4	6	8	30	10	2	.367	.361
Flores, Jesus	R-R	6-1	210	10-26-84	.178	.169	.182	52	180	8	32	6	0	2	18	7	1	0	1	42	0	0	.244	.212
Fontenot, Mike	L-R	5-8	170	6-9-80	.264	.257	.266	120	417	53	110	32	2	4	42	37	9	4	3	87	6	1	.379	.335
Frey, Evan	L-L	6-0	170	6-7-86	.230	.075	.302	47	126	18	29	4	0	0	10	19	0	2	1	27	9	2	.262	.329
Gimenez, Chris	R-R	6-2	220	12-27-82	.224	.198	.235	95	308	43	69	16	0	3	22	57	4	4	2	63	1	1	.305	.350
Guyer, Brandon	R-R	6-2	210	1-28-86	.301	.319	.294	98	356	73	107	23	6	7	41	29	14	4	2	62	22	3	.458	.374
Kiermaier, Kevin	L-R	6-2	200	4-22-90	.263	.275	.256	39	137	24	36	7	6	1	13	14	2	0	1	26	7	1	.423	.338
Lee, Hak-Ju	L-R	6-2	170	11-4-90	.422	.333	.455	15	45	13	19	3	1	1	7	1	0	1	0	9	6	2	.600	.536
Myers, Wil	R-R	6-3	205	12-10-90	.286	.328	.273	64	252	44	72	13	2	14	57	29	2	0	6	71	7	1	.520	.356
Roberts, Ryan	R-R	5-11	185	9-19-80	.210	.214	.207	37	124	12	26	5	0	1	13	21	0	1	2	30	3	1	.274	
.320 Scott, Luke	L-R	6-0	220	6-25-78	.333	.667	.222	3	12	2	4	0	0	0	2	0	0	0	1	0	0	.333	.429
Thompson, Rich	L-R	6-2	190	4-23-79	.249	.190	.265	50	189	33	47	6	3	0	20	16	6	5	1	38	22	3	.312	.325

Pitching	B-T	HT	WT	DOB	W	L	ERA	G	GS	CG	SV	IP	H	R	ER	HR	BB	SO	AVG	vLH	vRH	K/9	BB/9
Archer, Chris	R-R	6-3	200	9-26-88	5	3	3.96	10	10	0	0	50	50	26	22	6	23	52	.251	.247	.255	9.36	4.14
Beliveau, Jeff	L-L	6-1	195	1-17-87	2	3	2.62	38	0	0	1	45	41	15	13	1	22	76	.237	.183	.265	15.31	4.43
Buschmann, Matt	R-R	6-3	195	2-13-84	8	2	2.97	18	17	0	1	97	80	37	32	4	44	104	.226	.263	.191	9.65	4.08
Colome, Alex	R-R	6-2	185	12-31-88	4	6	3.07	14	14	0	0	70	63	30	24	5	29	72	.236	.248	.226	9.21	3.71
De Los Santos, Frank	L-L	6-0	165	11-17-87	1	2	5.34	26	0	0	1	32	37	22	19	3	14	21	.287	.158	.341	5.91	3.94
Geltz, Steve	R-R	5-9	185	11-1-87	5	3	2.82	41	0	0	3	67	35	21	21	8	24	80	.156	.116	.180	10.75	3.22
Gomes, Brandon	R-R	5-11	185	7-15-84	0	0	0.00	9	0	0	0	7	3	3	1	1	6	14	.189	.182	.200	12.19	0.87
Hubbard, Austin	R-R	6-2	206	6-14-88	0	0	67.50	1	0	0	0	1	4	5	5	0	3	1	.800	.667	1.000	13.50	40.50
Inman, Will	R-R	5-11	220	2-6-87	0	2	6.47	21	0	0	0	32	26	23	23	4	27	25	.224	.190	.243	7.03	7.59
Kelly, Merrill	R-R	6-1	170	10-14-88	8	4	3.19	15	14	0	0	85	74	37	30	4	34	70	.233	.250	.219	7.44	3.61
Lara, Braulio	L-L	6-1	190	12-20-88	0	0	0.00	1	0	0	0	3	0	0	0	0	1	3	.000	.000	.000	9.00	3.00
Liberatore, Adam	L-L	6-3	225	5-12-87	5	3	3.58	43	0	0	0	60	50	27	24	1	25	69	.228	.164	.260	10.29	3.73
Lueke, Josh	R-R	6-5	220	12-5-84	3	1	0.63	40	0	0	17	57	41	6	4	1	15	81	.196	.236	.167	12.72	2.35
Martin, J.D.	R-R	6-4	220	1-2-83	16	4	2.75	27	27	1	0	160	168	58	49	15	26	116	.267	.257	.275	6.51	1.46
Montgomery, Mike	L-L	6-4	200	7-1-89	7	8	4.72	20	19	1	0	109	111	65	57	9	48	77	.268	.230	.278	6.38	3.98
Moore, Matt	L-L	6-3	210	6-18-89	0	0	9.00	1	1	0	0	4	8	4	4	0	2	2	.444	1.000	.333	4.50	4.50
Odorizzi, Jake	R-R	6-2	185	3-27-90	9	6	3.33	22	22	0	0	124	101	49	46	12	40	124	.225	.216	.235	8.98	2.90
Paduch, Jim	R-R	6-2	190	11-2-82	2	3	7.54	12	3	0	0	37	51	34	31	10	17	23	.331	.311	.350	5.59	4.14
Ramirez, Ramon	R-R	5-11	200	8-31-81	0	0	2.84	6	0	0	0	6	5	2	2	0	1	7	.208	.200	.211	9.95	1.42
Riefenhauser, C.J.	L-L	6-0	180	1-30-90	2	1	3.05	17	0	0	0	21	14	9	7	2	8	22	.189	.118	.250	9.58	3.48
Romero, Enny	L-L	6-3	165	1-24-91	0	0	0.00	1	1	0	0	4	0	0	0	2	1	2	.154	.125	.200	2.25	2.25
Sandoval, Juan	R-R	6-2	170	1-12-81	1	1	3.13	12	2	0	0	23	18	10	8	2	5	16	.214	.176	.240	6.26	1.96
Torres, Alex	L-L	5-10	175	12-8-87	2	2	3.52	9	9	0	0	46	34	23	18	2	21	61	.200	.182	.206	11.93	4.11
Wade, Cory	R-R	6-2	185	5-28-83	4	1	2.17	30	5	0	1	50	41	13	12	3	14	33	.230	.232	.229	5.98	2.54
Yates, Kirby	R-R	5-10	170	3-25-87	3	2	1.90	51	0	0	20	62	38	14	13	2	23	93	.175	.143	.193	13.57	3.36

Fielding

Catcher	PCT	G	PO	A	E	DP	PB
Albernaz	.991	29	205	18	2	1	3
Apodaca	.991	25	215	10	2	1	2
Flores	.991	45	400	24	4	3	3
Gimenez	.998	56	449	22	1	0	3
First Base	**PCT**	**G**	**PO**	**A**	**E**	**DP**	
Anderson	.988	44	305	26	4	22	
Apodaca	1.000	1	2	0	0	0	
Belnome	.992	63	445	26	4	53	
Duncan	.989	35	243	16	3	27	
Gimenez	.976	7	38	2	1	2	
Second Base	**PCT**	**G**	**PO**	**A**	**E**	**DP**	
Beckham	.953	15	27	34	3	9	

	PCT	G	PO	A	E	DP	PB
Belnome	1.000	13	23	14	0	0	
Figueroa	.982	20	19	37	1	9	
Fontenot	.982	82	138	189	6	49	
Roberts	.953	19	33	48	4	8	
Third Base	**PCT**	**G**	**PO**	**A**	**E**	**DP**	
Belnome	.971	32	20	47	2	3	
Figueroa	.951	94	58	118	9	17	
Fontenot	.943	13	10	23	2	2	
Gimenez	.500	1	0	1	1	0	
Roberts	.929	9	3	10	1	2	
Shortstop	**PCT**	**G**	**PO**	**A**	**E**	**DP**	
Beckham	.954	106	162	273	21	65	
Figueroa	1.000	12	14	32	0	3	

	PCT	G	PO	A	E	DP
Fontenot	.920	15	17	29	4	5
Lee	.927	15	23	28	4	7
Outfield	**PCT**	**G**	**PO**	**A**	**E**	**DP**
Anderson	1.000	49	65	2	0	0
Bourgeois	.970	78	153	8	5	1
Duncan	1.000	11	11	0	0	0
Figueroa	1.000	6	4	0	0	0
Frey	1.000	44	78	4	0	0
Gimenez	.966	31	55	1	2	0
Guyer	.989	96	177	4	2	1
Kiermaier	1.000	38	107	2	0	1
Myers	.984	56	120	0	2	0
Thompson	.990	46	99	3	1	0

MONTGOMERY BISCUITS — DOUBLE-A

SOUTHERN LEAGUE

Batting	B-T	HT	WT	DOB	AVG	vLH	vRH	G	AB	R	H	2B	3B	HR	RBI	BB	HBP	SH	SF	SO	SB	CS	SLG	OBP
Acosta, Mayobanex	R-R	6-1	205	11-20-87	.197	.226	.186	71	234	18	46	8	0	7	30	21	0	3	4	61	0	0	.321	.259
Brett, Ryan	R-R	5-9	180	10-9-91	.238	.233	.242	25	105	19	25	6	1	3	16	8	0	0	1	14	4	0	.400	.289
Casali, Curt	R-R	6-2	220	11-9-88	.383	.421	.366	35	120	25	46	11	0	5	31	21	3	0	1	18	0	0	.600	.483
Castillo, Keith	B-R	6-4	215	7-10-87	.190	.097	.224	34	116	10	22	8	0	1	11	16	0	0	0	34	0	0	.284	.288
Estrada, Robi	B-R	5-10	170	10-8-88	.247	.185	.273	77	215	21	53	12	1	3	24	22	0	4	1	29	2	1	.353	.315
Frey, Evan	L-L	6-0	170	6-7-86	.167	.000	.176	4	18	0	3	0	0	0	1	0	0	0	0	3	0	1	.167	.167
Glaesmann, Todd	R-R	6-4	220	10-24-90	.240	.271	.227	132	487	53	117	28	3	11	54	26	10	0	6	110	6	2	.378	.289
Guevara, Hector	R-R	6-0	192	10-7-91	.230	.176	.253	34	113	11	26	4	0	0	10	12	1	1	0	17	2	1	.265	.310
Kang, K.D.	L-L	6-2	200	2-6-88	.251	.250	.252	107	346	52	87	17	7	15	45	53	3	0	1	102	3	0	.471	.355
Kiermaier, Kevin	L-R	6-1	200	4-22-90	.307	.309	.307	97	371	65	114	14	9	5	28	31	8	4	3	61	14	11	.434	.370
Mahtook, Mikie	R-R	6-1	200	11-30-89	.254	.245	.258	132	511	71	130	30	8	7	68	43	10	0	4	102	25	8	.386	.322
Morrison, Ty	L-R	6-2	170	7-22-90	.211	.158	.231	17	71	11	15	0	2	0	6	6	1	0	2	19	1	2	.268	.275
O'Malley, Shawn	R-R	5-11	160	12-28-87	.262	.260	.262	91	321	53	84	12	6	3	32	32	6	11	3	60	24	3	.364	.337
Price, Robby	L-R	5-10	188	4-20-88	.226	.222	.227	121	420	39	95	10	0	5	31	48	10	10	3	43	2	3	.286	.318
Seitzer, Cameron	L-R	6-5	220	1-11-90	.268	.245	.273	139	489	58	131	25	1	6	61	81	8	0	1	98	1	1	.360	.380
Sexton, Greg	R-R	6-2	205	2-8-85	.212	.250	.176	12	33	4	7	2	0	1	2	7	0	0	0	7	1	0	.364	.350
Thomas, Mark	R-R	6-1	180	5-5-88	.151	.157	.148	53	186	18	28	7	2	4	23	8	3	2	3	57	1	1	.274	.195
Tinoco, Steve	R-R	6-0	191	4-11-88	.151	.135	.163	33	86	8	13	4	1	0	2	7	1	0	0	15	0	0	.221	.223
Torrez, Riccio	R-R	6-0	205	10-14-89	.247	.273	.239	89	299	37	74	16	2	5	44	16	19	0	4	56	2	1	.365	.322
Young, Delmon	R-R	6-3	240	9-14-85	.233	.286	.188	7	30	4	7	0	0	1	3	1	0	0	0	7	0	0	.333	.258

Pitching	B-T	HT	WT	DOB	W	L	ERA	G	GS	CG	SV	IP	H	R	ER	HR	BB	SO	AVG	vLH	vRH	K/9	BB/9
Beliveau, Jeff	L-L	6-1	195	1-17-87	0	0	0.00	2	0	0	0	2	0	0	0	0	1	5	.000	.000	.000	22.50	4.50
Bellatti, Andrew	R-R	6-1	190	8-5-91	1	1	7.09	14	0	0	1	27	32	24	21	6	11	18	.296	.324	.284	6.08	3.71
Buschmann, Matt	R-R	6-3	195	2-13-84	6	3	2.69	11	11	0	0	64	59	24	19	6	23	63	.247	.319	.200	8.91	3.25
Colla, Mike	R-R	6-2	220	12-23-86	6	2	3.70	14	14	0	0	75	74	35	31	10	19	49	.258	.252	.262	5.85	2.27
Fisher, Carlos	R-R	6-4	220	2-22-83	0	0	4.50	5	0	0	0	8	10	6	4	1	7	7	.303	.200	.348	7.88	7.88
Fleming, Marquis	R-R	6-1	180	9-11-86	4	7	5.18	41	8	0	0	92	104	57	53	10	34	89	.289	.258	.307	8.71	3.33
Floethe, Jake	R-R	6-3	192	5-29-89	1	6	5.86	10	10	0	0	51	65	40	33	4	27	32	.311	.222	.367	5.68	4.80
Hamren, Erik	R-R	6-1	195	8-21-86	1	2	3.28	32	0	0	2	47	45	20	17	3	23	58	.241	.262	.230	11.19	4.44
2-team total (13 Mississippi)					1	2	3.08	45	0	0	3	64	63	25	22	3	31	76	—	—	—	10.63	4.34
Hubbard, Austin	R-R	6-2	206	6-14-88	1	0	7.67	28	0	0	0	32	34	28	27	8	22	19	.268	.265	.269	5.40	6.25
Kelly, Merrill	R-R	6-1	170	10-14-88	5	6	4.15	13	12	0	0	74	54	34	34	3	31	41	.208	.202	.211	5.01	3.79
Lara, Braulio	L-L	6-1	190	12-20-88	4	2	4.38	45	0	0	0	72	68	42	35	6	43	53	.253	.192	.277	6.63	5.38
Liberatore, Adam	L-L	6-3	225	5-12-87	0	0	0.00	1	0	0	1	2	1	0	0	0	3	3	.143	.000	.167	13.50	0.00
Mateo, Victor	R-R	6-5	180	7-27-89	7	9	3.93	27	26	2	0	153	120	76	67	17	55	94	.215	.209	.220	5.52	3.23
Nevarez, Matt	R-R	6-4	220	2-26-87	2	1	2.31	9	0	0	1	12	9	3	3	0	5	13	.243	.333	.200	10.03	3.86
Patterson, Jimmy	R-L	6-0	190	2-9-89	1	4	4.17	17	1	0	0	41	40	20	19	4	9	27	.252	.224	.264	5.93	1.98
Quate, Jacob	R-R	6-1	200	9-12-87	0	0	18.90	8	0	0	0	7	16	15	14	2	6	6	.471	.444	.480	8.10	8.10
Riefenhauser, C.J.	L-L	6-0	180	1-30-90	4	0	0.51	34	0	0	11	53	28	10	3	3	11	48	.153	.125	.163	8.15	1.87
Romero, Enny	L-L	6-3	165	1-24-91	11	7	2.76	27	27	0	0	140	110	51	43	9	73	110	.215	.289	.194	7.05	4.68
Sandoval, Juan	R-R	6-2	170	1-12-81	5	3	3.24	46	0	0	19	58	73	26	21	2	20	47	.303	.333	.289	7.25	3.09
Schenk, Neil	L-L	6-3	220	6-17-86	1	2	7.03	32	0	0	0	40	53	35	31	4	21	27	.325	.375	.304	6.13	4.76
Suarez, Albert	R-R	6-3	235	10-8-89	0	0	1.42	2	2	0	0	6	10	2	1	0	2	6	.345	.455	.278	8.53	2.84
Thompson, Jake	R-R	6-2	225	8-8-89	11	10	4.18	27	26	0	0	149	149	80	69	13	59	101	.264	.258	.267	6.11	3.57
Van Meter, Joe	R-R	6-2	195	10-18-88	0	4	6.50	5	3	0	0	18	21	13	13	3	7	16	.300	.391	.255	8.00	3.50

Fielding

Catcher	PCT	G	PO	A	E	DP	PB
Acosta	1.000	62	425	62	0	3	1
Casali	.995	25	169	26	1	1	4
Thomas	.974	53	347	31	10	2	7

First Base	PCT	G	PO	A	E	DP
Acosta	1.000	2	15	1	0	0
Seitzer	.991	136	1137	68	11	94
Tinoco	1.000	5	32	0	0	1

Second Base	PCT	G	PO	A	E	DP
Brett	.967	25	46	72	4	15
Estrada	.989	23	38	54	1	17
Guevara	1.000	2	2	8	0	0

	PCT	G	PO	A	E	DP	PB
O'Malley	1.000	1	2	3	0	0	
Price	.986	94	196	242	6	47	

Third Base	PCT	G	PO	A	E	DP
Estrada	.909	5	4	6	1	2
Guevara	.944	20	8	26	2	1
Price	.971	26	17	49	2	6
Sexton	.941	6	6	10	1	1
Tinoco	.786	4	6	5	3	0
Torrez	.932	86	50	171	16	17

Shortstop	PCT	G	PO	A	E	DP
Estrada	.936	42	61	114	12	14
Guevara	.906	12	16	32	5	5

	PCT	G	PO	A	E	DP
O'Malley	.959	89	116	231	15	43

Outfield	PCT	G	PO	A	E	DP
Estrada	—	2	0	0	0	0
Frey	.889	4	8	0	1	0
Glaesmann	.979	125	227	10	5	0
Kang	.956	61	106	2	5	0
Kiermaier	.989	89	254	6	3	1
Mahtook	.973	127	276	8	8	1
Morrison	1.000	13	27	2	0	0
Tinoco	.952	12	19	1	1	0

CHARLOTTE STONE CRABS — HIGH CLASS A

FLORIDA STATE LEAGUE

Batting	B-T	HT	WT	DOB	AVG	vLH	vRH	G	AB	R	H	2B	3B	HR	RBI	BB	HBP	SH	SF	SO	SB	CS	SLG	OBP
Argo, Willie	R-R	6-1	220	10-15-89	.308	.326	.300	95	305	58	94	18	2	4	30	43	7	3	1	76	37	5	.420	.404
Bailey, Luke	R-R	6-0	198	3-11-91	.180	.192	.172	43	139	8	25	4	0	1	18	6	2	0	2	44	1	0	.230	.221
Brett, Ryan	R-R	5-9	180	10-9-91	.340	.323	.347	51	206	38	70	11	4	4	22	15	4	0	0	27	22	7	.490	.396
Carter, Kes	L-L	6-2	205	3-3-90	.235	.178	.258	118	409	52	96	18	9	7	34	32	5	6	2	100	10	7	.374	.297
Casali, Curt	R-R	6-2	220	11-9-88	.267	.316	.241	46	165	15	44	6	1	5	22	18	1	0	0	31	1	0	.406	.342

Name	B-T	HT	WT	DOB	AVG	vLH	vRH	G	AB	R	H	2B	3B	HR	RBI	BB	HBP	SH	SF	SO	SB	CS	OBP	SLG
DePew, Jake	R-R	6-1	220	3-1-92	.223	.190	.236	61	211	16	47	5	0	1	19	15	0	4	0	39	0	3	.261	.274
Guevara, Hector	R-R	6-0	192	10-7-91	.260	.303	.241	82	288	37	75	16	2	7	39	8	5	2	2	22	10	2	.403	.290
Hager, Jake	R-R	6-1	170	3-4-93	.258	.257	.259	113	449	56	116	15	3	0	33	38	3	4	4	81	12	8	.305	.318
Jennings, Desmond	R-R	6-2	200	10-30-86	.333	.333	—	1	3	1	1	0	0	0	0	0	0	0	0	0	1	1	0	.333	.333
Kang, K.D.	L-L	6-2	200	2-6-88	.339	.214	.378	17	59	13	20	6	1	1	4	9	0	0	0	19	1	1	.525	.426
Kline, Ben	R-R	6-3	200	12-2-88	.192	.188	.194	19	52	6	10	1	0	0	3	3	1	0	0	12	0	0	.212	.250
Malm, Jeff	L-L	6-3	225	10-31-90	.239	.240	.239	119	422	51	101	22	0	14	57	36	7	0	2	96	4	3	.391	.308
McChesney, Ryan	L-R	6-0	200	2-3-90	.222	.250	.200	4	9	1	2	0	0	0	0	1	0	0	0	1	0	0	.222	.300
Motter, Taylor	R-R	6-1	190	9-18-89	.290	.348	.262	66	210	26	61	14	2	3	21	22	1	5	1	29	20	8	.419	.359
Nommensen, Brett	L-L	5-11	190	10-6-86	.467	.444	.500	5	15	0	7	1	0	0	0	2	0	0	0	2	2	0	.533	.529
Paulino, Enmanuel	R-R	6-1	175	11-28-93	.261	.222	.286	8	23	2	6	1	0	0	2	0	1	0	0	9	0	0	.304	.292
Quinonez, Jonathan	R-R	6-1	187	11-27-90	.302	.333	.278	21	63	8	19	9	0	0	7	0	2	0	0	8	0	0	.444	.323
Scott, Luke	L-R	6-0	220	6-25-78	.222	.400	.154	5	18	2	4	1	0	0	2	0	1	0	0	5	0	0	.278	.263
Segovia, Alejandro	R-R	6-0	185	4-27-90	.281	.281	.280	109	374	48	105	22	1	14	51	44	15	0	3	66	0	1	.457	.376
Shaffer, Richie	R-R	6-3	218	3-15-91	.254	.273	.245	122	469	55	119	33	1	11	73	35	6	0	9	106	6	0	.399	.308
Tinoco, Steve	R-R	6-0	191	4-11-88	.245	.278	.226	13	49	2	12	0	0	0	5	2	1	1	0	13	1	0	.245	.288
Vettleson, Drew	L-R	6-1	185	7-19-91	.274	.228	.295	121	467	50	128	29	6	4	62	40	2	2	5	78	5	7	.388	.331

Pitching

Name	B-T	HT	WT	DOB	W	L	ERA	G	GS	CG	SV	IP	H	R	ER	HR	BB	SO	AVG	vLH	vRH	K/9	BB/9
Bellatti, Andrew	R-R	6-1	190	8-5-91	6	3	2.95	22	0	0	2	55	39	19	18	2	17	52	.195	.219	.181	8.51	2.78
Bierman, Sean	L-L	6-0	195	10-20-88	1	1	2.11	5	1	0	0	21	16	5	5	0	0	16	.198	.208	.193	6.75	0.00
Brandt, Kevin	R-L	6-1	195	11-24-89	1	0	4.15	6	0	0	0	13	14	6	6	0	6	6	.280	.261	.296	4.15	4.15
Cabrera, Luis	R-R	6-2	185	8-14-90	0	1	7.71	2	0	0	0	5	8	4	4	0	7	6	.381	.500	.353	11.57	13.50
Carpenter, Ryan	L-L	6-5	208	8-22-90	7	6	4.67	24	22	0	0	118	131	69	61	14	37	97	.280	.321	.268	7.42	2.83
Cobb, Alex	R-R	6-3	190	10-7-87	0	1	4.32	3	3	0	0	8	8	4	4	0	4	8	.258	.286	.235	8.64	4.32
Crawford, Shay	L-L	6-2	190	12-12-87	4	3	1.34	31	0	0	2	54	34	9	8	1	29	43	.181	.058	.228	7.21	4.86
De Los Santos, Frank	L-L	6-0	165	11-17-87	1	0	0.00	2	0	0	0	3	1	0	0	0	0	1	.111	.000	.143	3.00	0.00
Fernandez, Mario	R-R	6-0	206	9-7-93	0	1	17.18	2	0	0	0	4	6	8	7	0	5	1	.400	.286	.500	2.45	12.27
Floethe, Jake	R-R	6-3	192	5-29-89	4	3	3.56	10	1	0	0	43	44	20	17	3	18	27	.268	.273	.266	5.65	3.77
Floro, Dylan	L-R	6-2	175	12-27-90	2	0	1.61	4	4	2	0	28	20	5	5	0	2	14	.206	.250	.170	4.50	0.64
Garcia, Nate	R-R	6-1	184	5-9-88	3	4	3.48	41	0	0	13	54	46	24	21	3	24	49	.230	.286	.204	8.12	3.98
Garvin, Grayson	L-L	6-6	225	10-27-89	0	1	1.08	5	5	0	0	17	8	7	2	0	4	12	.138	.143	.136	6.48	2.16
Gomes, Brandon	R-R	5-11	185	7-15-84	0	0	7.50	5	4	0	0	6	9	5	5	3	0	5	.346	.385	.308	7.50	0.00
Gomez, Roberto	R-R	6-5	178	8-3-89	5	8	4.69	21	19	1	0	111	115	66	58	7	39	65	.274	.273	.274	5.25	3.15
Hahn, Jesse	R-R	6-5	182	7-30-89	2	1	2.15	19	19	0	0	67	55	20	16	1	18	63	.218	.227	.213	8.46	2.42
Harrison, Jordan	R-L	6-1	180	4-9-91	0	1	10.13	2	0	0	0	3	1	3	3	0	3	4	.111	.000	.143	13.50	10.13
Hubbard, Austin	R-R	6-2	206	6-14-88	1	0	3.00	12	0	0	4	18	12	8	6	0	9	25	.176	.105	.204	12.50	4.50
Kirsch, Chris	L-L	6-2	185	11-15-91	2	0	3.60	5	0	0	0	10	12	4	4	1	5	3	.300	.000	.353	2.70	4.50
Linsky, Lenny	R-R	6-2	220	3-4-90	7	5	3.22	39	2	0	5	73	73	32	26	3	27	52	.268	.218	.296	6.44	3.34
Markel, Parker	R-R	6-4	220	9-15-90	4	7	6.37	18	16	0	0	82	99	64	58	7	35	71	.298	.362	.269	7.79	3.84
Montgomery, Mike	L-L	6-4	200	7-1-89	0	1	6.23	2	2	0	0	9	9	7	6	0	3	10	.273	.000	.300	10.38	3.12
Mortensen, Jared	L-R	5-11	205	6-1-88	2	0	1.04	4	1	1	0	17	8	3	2	1	5	18	.133	.125	.136	9.35	2.60
Partridge, Jacob	L-L	6-3	200	12-21-90	2	5	3.75	33	8	0	2	94	65	41	39	4	55	80	.198	.105	.231	7.69	5.28
Patterson, Jimmy	R-L	6-0	190	2-9-89	0	0	4.50	2	0	0	0	6	6	3	3	1	0	8	.261	.000	.316	12.00	0.00
Price, David	L-L	6-6	220	8-26-85	1	0	1.23	2	2	0	0	7	4	2	1	0	3	12	.148	.000	.167	14.73	3.68
Ramirez, Ramon	R-R	5-11	200	8-31-81	1	0	3.00	1	0	0	0	3	2	1	1	1	1	4	.182	.000	.182	12.00	3.00
Ramsey, Matt	R-R	5-11	205	9-24-89	1	1	3.28	12	0	0	0	25	27	10	9	0	15	22	.290	.306	.281	8.03	5.47
Rivero, Felipe	L-L	6-0	150	7-5-91	9	7	3.40	25	23	2	0	127	122	63	48	7	52	91	.257	.235	.263	6.45	3.69
Suero, Bruedlin	L-L	6-4	170	2-28-90	0	1	5.49	11	0	0	0	20	29	12	12	1	3	16	.333	.385	.311	7.32	1.37
Suero, Eliazer	R-R	6-4	170	6-7-89	1	4	6.36	22	1	0	1	47	56	38	33	9	22	39	.296	.338	.274	7.52	4.24

Fielding

Catcher	PCT	G	PO	A	E	DP	PB
Bailey	.989	39	241	23	3	0	6
Casali	.987	37	274	27	4	3	4
DePew	.991	58	387	48	4	4	8
McChesney	.947	4	16	2	1	0	1

First Base	PCT	G	PO	A	E	DP
Kline	—	1	0	0	0	0
Malm	.989	94	783	52	9	73
Segovia	.983	41	313	24	6	25
Tinoco	1.000	3	20	0	0	1

Second Base	PCT	G	PO	A	E	DP
Brett	.968	48	97	115	7	31
Guevara	.980	60	102	137	5	37
Kline	.958	7	9	14	1	5
Motter	.969	13	23	39	2	9
Paulino	1.000	1	1	1	0	0
Quinonez	1.000	8	20	25	0	5

Third Base	PCT	G	PO	A	E	DP
Guevara	1.000	6	3	11	0	2
Kline	.864	9	5	14	3	1
Motter	.933	5	8	6	1	1
Paulino	—	1	0	0	0	0
Quinonez	1.000	6	3	11	0	1
Segovia	1.000	1	0	3	0	1
Shaffer	.934	108	54	201	18	16

Shortstop	PCT	G	PO	A	E	DP
Guevara	.978	9	12	32	1	5
Hager	.952	110	143	313	23	63
Motter	.971	9	13	20	1	4
Paulino	.923	6	8	16	2	5
Quinonez	1.000	2	1	7	0	1

Outfield	PCT	G	PO	A	E	DP
Argo	.989	86	177	3	2	0
Carter	.981	115	308	8	6	1
Jennings	1.000	1	1	0	0	0
Kang	.900	16	26	1	3	1
Malm	1.000	14	25	1	0	0
Motter	.970	39	62	3	2	0
Nommensen	1.000	5	5	0	0	0
Quinonez	1.000	5	9	0	0	0
Tinoco	1.000	7	7	0	0	0
Vettleson	.945	120	227	13	14	4

BOWLING GREEN HOT RODS

LOW CLASS A

MIDWEST LEAGUE

Batting	B-T	HT	WT	DOB	AVG	vLH	vRH	G	AB	R	H	2B	3B	HR	RBI	BB	HBP	SH	SF	SO	SB	CS	SLG	OBP
Araiza, Jesus	R-R	5-11	185	6-19-93	.500	.000	1.000	1	2	0	1	0	0	0	0	0	0	0	0	0	0	0	.500	.500
Coyle, Tommy	L-R	5-7	170	10-24-90	.278	.258	.283	126	454	79	126	24	8	6	58	91	3	1	3	78	40	8	.405	.399
Dunn, Ryan	R-R	5-10	180	10-28-88	.209	.148	.227	83	277	40	58	11	1	4	25	37	3	4	1	63	6	0	.300	.308
Gantt, Marty	R-L	5-11	179	2-11-90	.267	.211	.282	123	435	67	116	23	5	7	65	46	5	3	7	110	19	3	.391	.339
Goeddel, Tyler	R-R	6-4	186	10-20-92	.249	.159	.269	112	450	63	112	18	12	7	65	40	3	1	3	98	30	5	.389	.313
Goetzman, Granden	R-R	6-4	200	11-14-92	.153	.176	.145	21	72	5	11	1	1	1	9	4	2	0	0	15	4	1	.236	.218
Hernandez, Oscar	R-R	6-0	196	7-9-93	.222	.000	.250	3	9	1	2	0	0	1	2	0	0	0	1	0	0	.222	.364
Kline, Ben	R-R	6-3	200	12-2-88	.281	.143	.320	10	32	5	9	3	0	0	8	2	2	0	2	5	0	2	.375	.342
Leonard, Patrick	R-R	6-4	225	10-20-92	.225	.198	.233	123	440	52	99	26	0	9	57	42	8	1	2	118	4	1	.345	.303
Maile, Luke	R-R	6-3	220	2-6-91	.283	.228	.298	95	361	45	102	25	3	4	49	41	0	0	5	54	8	2	.402	.351
Martin, Brandon	R-R	5-11	185	10-26-91	.206	.200	.208	73	262	29	54	10	3	7	39	19	5	1	5	65	10	5	.347	.268
O'Conner, Justin	R-R	6-0	190	3-31-92	.233	.220	.237	102	399	49	93	17	0	14	56	31	3	1	5	111	5	0	.381	.290
Reginatto, Leonardo	R-R	6-2	179	4-10-90	.325	.319	.327	112	412	68	134	17	4	1	49	43	3	2	6	58	11	7	.393	.388
Rickard, Joey	R-L	6-1	183	5-21-91	.270	.280	.267	127	452	79	122	29	5	8	63	78	16	5	8	98	30	10	.409	.390
Rowan, Geoff	R-R	5-9	190	10-30-89	.169	.000	.220	22	65	5	11	1	0	0	2	3	1	3	0	15	1	0	.185	.217
Toles, Andrew	L-R	5-10	185	5-24-92	.326	.305	.331	121	519	79	169	35	16	2	57	22	7	1	3	105	62	17	.466	.359

Pitching	B-T	HT	WT	DOB	W	L	ERA	G	GS	CG	SV	IP	H	R	ER	HR	BB	SO	AVG	vLH	vRH	K/9	BB/9
Ames, Jeff	R-R	6-4	225	1-31-91	9	4	2.98	23	23	0	0	115	87	39	38	10	38	83	.210	.210	.210	6.51	2.98
Bierman, Sean	L-L	6-0	195	10-20-88	5	4	2.69	13	13	0	0	67	57	25	20	7	14	52	.226	.238	.220	6.99	1.88
Brandt, Kevin	R-L	6-1	195	11-24-89	3	0	2.13	4	4	0	0	25	23	6	6	2	3	20	.247	.313	.234	7.11	1.07
Crawford, Shay	L-L	6-2	190	12-12-87	1	0	0.00	3	0	0	0	5	2	0	0	0	2	8	.125	.000	.154	15.43	3.86
Floro, Dylan	L-R	6-2	175	12-27-90	9	2	1.81	19	19	0	0	109	103	34	22	4	19	85	.251	.274	.229	7.00	1.56
Garton, Ryan	R-R	5-11	170	12-5-89	4	3	2.44	40	0	0	8	70	54	19	19	3	34	62	.212	.207	.215	7.97	4.37
Guerrieri, Taylor	R-R	6-3	195	12-1-92	6	2	2.01	14	14	0	0	67	54	17	15	5	12	51	.225	.219	.230	6.85	1.61
Hanse, Andrew	R-R	6-7	210	5-13-91	1	0	0.49	10	0	0	3	18	13	2	1	0	2	21	.206	.286	.143	10.31	0.98
Harrison, Jordan	R-L	6-1	180	4-9-91	5	2	2.69	15	9	0	0	60	52	20	18	4	22	53	.231	.224	.234	7.91	3.28
Henderson, Brandon	L-L	6-3	175	4-19-92	2	1	3.16	13	1	0	0	37	34	16	13	2	8	30	.234	.211	.243	7.30	1.95
Lopez, Reinaldo	R-R	6-3	221	4-27-91	7	5	2.95	26	18	0	1	116	109	46	38	7	33	86	.247	.248	.246	6.67	2.56
Molina, Jose	L-L	5-11	160	6-26-91	4	4	4.07	42	0	0	4	84	73	41	38	6	27	81	.237	.224	.244	8.68	2.89
Proctor, Marcus	R-R	6-3	170	8-21-91	6	4	2.99	45	0	0	6	78	69	28	26	6	13	70	.235	.229	.241	8.04	1.49
Pruitt, Austin	R-R	5-11	165	8-31-89	0	2	1.71	9	2	0	1	26	17	6	5	3	3	24	.181	.191	.170	8.20	1.03
Quinonez, Eduar	R-R	6-3	190	8-9-89	6	5	6.47	17	6	0	0	57	54	46	41	7	28	43	.249	.253	.246	6.79	4.42
Ramsey, Matt	R-R	5-11	205	9-24-89	0	1	2.42	20	0	0	6	26	24	8	7	1	10	36	.245	.182	.326	12.46	3.46
Sawyer, Nick	R-R	5-11	175	9-23-91	2	5	4.22	36	0	0	5	60	33	31	28	3	59	80	.165	.172	.159	12.07	8.90
Snell, Blake	L-L	6-4	180	12-4-92	4	9	4.27	23	23	0	0	99	90	55	47	8	73	106	.245	.200	.262	9.64	6.64
Spann, Matt	L-L	6-7	185	2-17-91	4	3	2.87	19	4	0	2	60	67	29	19	5	21	35	.284	.282	.285	5.28	3.17
Speer, Stone	L-L	5-11	180	6-10-91	3	0	3.48	13	1	0	2	31	25	13	12	3	18	21	.221	.219	.222	6.10	5.23
Suero, Bruedlin	L-L	6-4	170	2-28-90	1	0	2.16	3	1	0	0	8	9	2	2	1	1	10	.273	.200	.304	10.80	1.08

Fielding

Catcher	PCT	G	PO	A	E	DP	PB
Hernandez	1.000	2	14	0	0	0	0
Maile	.991	64	480	66	5	3	2
O'Conner	.984	62	466	74	9	3	2
Rowan	.981	12	91	11	2	1	2

First Base	PCT	G	PO	A	E	DP
Dunn	.976	38	341	28	9	29
Kline	.943	3	31	2	2	2
Leonard	.985	99	918	45	15	77
Maile	1.000	1	4	0	0	0

Second Base	PCT	G	PO	A	E	DP
Coyle	.978	121	188	341	12	68
Dunn	1.000	4	7	8	0	1
Reginatto	1.000	13	18	30	0	5

Third Base	PCT	G	PO	A	E	DP
Dunn	.818	5	2	7	2	0
Goeddel	.894	94	74	204	33	11
Kline	.917	4	1	10	1	1
Leonard	.871	12	6	21	4	1
Reginatto	.915	24	11	43	5	4

Shortstop	PCT	G	PO	A	E	DP
Goeddel	.929	8	7	19	2	3
Martin	.963	68	116	221	13	46
Reginatto	.974	62	95	168	7	34

Outfield	PCT	G	PO	A	E	DP
Dunn	1.000	36	54	3	0	2
Gantt	.995	121	180	9	1	2
Goetzman	.960	15	23	1	1	0
Reginatto	1.000	6	8	1	0	0
Rickard	.987	124	221	9	3	0
Toles	.971	116	232	6	7	3

TAMPA BAY RAYS

HUDSON VALLEY RENEGADES

SHORT-SEASON

NEW YORK-PENN LEAGUE

Batting	B-T	HT	WT	DOB	AVG	vLH	vRH	G	AB	R	H	2B	3B	HR	RBI	BB	HBP	SH	SF	SO	SB	CS	SLG	OBP
Alexander, John	L-L	6-5	200	4-25-93	.215	.200	.219	66	233	20	50	13	1	1	29	9	1	4	1	48	3	2	.292	.246
Antunez, Ismel	L-R	5-7	166	6-17-91	.222	.000	.286	3	9	1	2	0	0	0	1	3	0	0	0	4	2	0	.222	.417
Blair, Pat	R-R	5-10	180	10-1-91	.168	.217	.155	32	107	19	18	5	0	1	5	17	6	3	0	28	7	1	.243	.315
Field, Johnny	R-R	5-10	190	2-20-92	.252	.236	.257	60	238	22	60	20	1	2	24	12	6	1	5	38	14	6	.370	.299
George, Darryl	R-R	6-1	213	3-14-93	.286	.269	.294	61	227	21	65	8	2	0	18	23	5	2	1	40	9	0	.339	.363
Goetzman, Granden	R-R	6-4	200	11-14-92	.220	.241	.213	55	209	25	46	8	6	2	22	7	1	0	5	50	19	7	.344	.243
Harris, James	R-R	6-1	180	8-7-93	.258	.233	.268	67	217	31	56	10	3	1	21	17	0	1	2	68	16	7	.346	.309
Hernandez, Oscar	R-R	6-0	196	7-9-93	.228	.195	.238	43	167	22	38	6	0	6	33	11	2	0	1	24	9	1	.371	.282
Kline, Ben	R-R	6-3	200	12-2-88	.294	.273	.304	11	34	3	10	1	0	0	4	3	1	0	0	6	0	0	.324	.368
McChesney, Ryan	L-R	6-0	200	2-3-90	.250	.063	.304	23	72	6	18	4	0	1	9	16	3	0	0	20	1	1	.347	.407
Milone, Thomas	L-L	5-11	190	6-7-93	.667	1.000	.600	2	6	3	4	0	0	1	2	0	1	0	0	1	0	1	1.167	.714
Morillo, Julian	L-L	5-11	167	12-10-91	.220	.235	.213	32	109	9	24	2	0	1	9	5	2	1	0	15	2	1	.266	.267
Narvaez, Omar	B-R	5-10	172	2-10-92	.267	.233	.275	39	150	13	40	6	2	0	13	8	2	1	1	21	0	2	.333	.311

	B-T	HT	WT	DOB	AVG	vLH	vRH	G	AB	R	H	2B	3B	HR	RBI	BB	HBP	SH	SF	SO	SB	CS	SLG	OBP
Quinonez, Jonathan	R-R	6-1	187	11-27-90	.337	.414	.306	25	101	14	34	13	0	1	8	7	5	0	0	14	2	2	.495	.407
Ridings, Julian	L-R	6-2	175	3-1-92	.255	.333	.232	53	216	25	55	14	2	0	13	9	2	3	2	43	10	5	.338	.288
Soriano, Ariel	R-R	5-11	160	11-24-90	.267	.329	.246	68	273	36	73	12	5	6	31	12	5	2	0	50	18	6	.414	.310
Young, Ty	L-R	5-10	173	7-17-92	.217	.250	.210	58	221	26	48	13	2	2	22	24	6	0	1	57	8	5	.321	.310

Pitching

	B-T	HT	WT	DOB	W	L	ERA	G	GS	CG	SV	IP	H	R	ER	HR	BB	SO	AVG	vLH	vRH	K/9	BB/9
Brandt, Kevin	R-L	6-1	195	11-24-89	4	3	2.00	10	5	0	0	45	31	13	10	3	11	45	.197	.200	.196	9.00	2.20
Choate, Justin	R-R	6-0	170	12-31-90	1	3	2.88	16	0	0	6	41	45	25	13	2	9	35	.271	.274	.269	7.75	1.99
Echarry, Eli	R-R	6-1	150	7-1-92	5	3	2.70	18	2	0	2	53	47	20	16	5	21	44	.242	.222	.254	7.43	3.54
Farrell, John	R-R	6-2	210	2-18-91	0	0	8.44	3	3	0	0	5	8	6	5	0	2	4	.348	.429	.313	6.75	3.38
Gabay, Willie	R-R	6-0	180	7-3-91	0	0	0.00	2	0	0	0	3	1	0	0	0	2	2	.100	.000	.200	6.00	6.00
Gauthier, Tyler	L-R	6-5	245	6-3-92	0	1	5.40	8	0	0	0	10	16	7	6	0	3	6	.356	.353	.357	5.40	2.70
Gil, Isaac	R-R	6-5	230	10-8-91	0	0	0.00	1	0	0	1	3	3	0	0	0	0	2	.300	.500	.167	6.00	0.00
Griffin, Aaron	R-R	6-4	200	6-17-91	3	3	2.02	17	12	0	1	76	67	28	17	4	8	54	.233	.222	.242	6.42	0.95
Griset, Ben	L-L	6-1	175	3-12-92	3	3	3.41	14	14	0	0	66	79	31	25	3	10	55	.289	.388	.257	7.50	1.36
Hanse, Andrew	R-R	6-7	210	5-13-91	2	2	4.71	12	0	0	2	21	21	11	11	2	7	14	.273	.357	.224	6.00	3.00
Harrison, Jordan	R-L	6-1	180	4-9-91	4	1	2.73	5	4	0	0	26	17	8	8	3	8	26	.177	.192	.171	8.89	2.73
Jordan, Cory	R-R	6-5	220	1-17-91	1	3	4.00	18	0	0	2	27	28	13	12	0	11	26	.267	.306	.232	8.67	3.67
Kirsch, Chris	L-L	6-2	185	11-15-91	4	3	2.94	16	16	0	0	83	83	40	27	2	28	46	.269	.300	.261	5.01	3.05
Loera, Derek	L-L	5-11	180	2-9-91	3	1	2.45	14	4	0	3	44	38	14	12	3	4	36	.229	.207	.241	7.36	0.82
MacDonald, Corey	R-R	6-6	205	5-19-91	0	0	3.72	7	0	0	2	10	11	6	4	0	3	9	.289	.250	.308	8.38	2.79
Pruitt, Austin	R-R	5-11	165	8-31-89	0	1	1.14	5	5	0	0	24	19	6	3	0	2	15	.226	.256	.195	5.70	0.76
Reavis, Colton	R-R	6-0	195	12-16-89	3	1	2.10	13	0	0	0	34	23	11	8	1	14	28	.183	.204	.167	7.34	3.67
Schreiber, Brad	R-R	6-3	225	2-13-91	0	0	1.50	4	0	0	0	6	3	1	1	0	4	7	.150	.333	.000	10.50	6.00
Schultz, Jaime	R-R	5-10	190	6-20-91	1	2	3.05	17	10	0	0	44	32	17	15	3	29	55	.206	.161	.232	11.17	5.89
Sidhu, Harmen	R-R	6-1	185	8-11-90	0	2	9.00	6	0	0	1	8	9	10	8	1	5	7	.300	.364	.263	7.88	5.63
Teasley, Rick	L-L	6-2	210	4-22-91	3	4	2.77	16	0	0	2	39	40	18	12	3	9	34	.270	.259	.277	7.85	2.08
Tzamtzis, Anthony	R-R	6-0	185	11-4-90	1	1	4.34	12	0	0	1	19	16	13	9	2	13	22	.229	.133	.300	10.61	6.27

Fielding

Catcher	PCT	G	PO	A	E	DP	PB
Hernandez	.994	38	279	41	2	3	6
McChesney	.977	10	79	7	2	0	2
Narvaez	.992	30	212	25	2	2	4

First Base	PCT	G	PO	A	E	DP
Alexander	.986	66	590	34	9	66
George	.976	9	77	6	2	9
Kline	.920	3	21	2	2	0

Second Base	PCT	G	PO	A	E	DP
Morillo	.918	20	32	57	8	13
Quinonez	1.000	2	6	7	0	2

Soriano	.972	56 117 157 8 44

Third Base	PCT	G	PO	A	E	DP
George	.921	8	11	24	3	4
Morillo	.862	8	6	19	4	1
Quinonez	.846	4	2	9	2	2
Young	.910	56	35	97	13	10

Shortstop	PCT	G	PO	A	E	DP
Blair	.911	32	52	92	14	24
George	.949	34	53	114	9	25
Morillo	.867	5	5	8	2	2
Quinonez	.957	8	10	35	2	6

Outfield	PCT	G	PO	A	E	DP
Antunez	.833	3	5	0	1	0
Field	.990	54	92	6	1	3
George	1.000	7	14	0	0	0
Goetzman	.969	42	93	2	3	1
Harris	.947	61	122	4	7	2
Kline	.714	5	5	0	2	0
Milone	1.000	2	7	0	0	0
Quinonez	1.000	7	10	0	0	0
Ridings	.990	50	97	4	1	1

PRINCETON RAYS ROOKIE

APPALACHIAN LEAGUE

Batting	B-T	HT	WT	DOB	AVG	vLH	vRH	G	AB	R	H	2B	3B	HR	RBI	BB	HBP	SH	SF	SO	SB	CS	SLG	OBP
Araiza, Jesus	R-R	5-11	185	6-19-93	.277	.292	.271	49	177	20	49	6	1	0	10	20	4	1	1	31	1	2	.322	.361
Araujo, Yoel	R-R	6-0	190	12-3-93	.223	.161	.250	57	206	27	46	6	0	7	26	20	3	1	1	66	6	3	.354	.300
Blanchard, Coty	R-R	6-0	180	12-16-91	.213	.244	.202	52	164	17	35	10	1	0	8	26	2	2	2	32	3	1	.287	.325
Correa, Leopoldo	L-R	6-0	186	12-3-91	.223	.182	.232	38	121	7	27	4	2	1	13	8	3	2	0	20	0	0	.314	.288
Dominguez, Wilmer	R-R	5-10	182	6-19-90	.164	.000	.214	18	55	3	9	0	0	0	7	4	0	1	0	16	0	0	.164	.220
Duran, Douglas	B-R	5-10	150	11-17-92	.191	.231	.176	18	47	5	9	1	0	0	7	0	0	0	0	14	1	0	.213	.296
Edwards, Spencer	R-R	6-0	170	4-7-93	.232	.240	.229	51	194	29	45	9	2	2	16	15	1	3	0	50	13	3	.330	.290
Eierman, Johnny	R-R	6-1	195	8-23-92	.228	.250	.217	34	101	13	23	6	2	4	10	7	0	3	0	29	0	0	.446	.278
Flores, Travis	R-R	6-1	215	7-12-92	.179	.130	.197	50	168	19	30	5	0	7	24	21	4	0	1	46	2	3	.333	.284
Garcia, David	R-R	5-7	175	3-30-91	.236	.227	.240	51	165	23	39	9	0	4	25	16	5	1	1	46	2	3	.364	.321
Jackson, Bralin	R-L	6-2	183	12-2-93	.216	.177	.231	60	231	20	50	4	3	3	16	19	2	4	1	56	11	5	.299	.281
Lockwood, Hunter	R-R	5-10	180	9-16-92	.243	.224	.252	64	235	26	57	10	6	9	34	16	3	0	4	76	0	1	.451	.295
Nacapoy, Chad	R-R	5-7	220	7-28-89	.158	.111	.172	13	38	2	6	0	0	0	1	2	0	1	0	14	1	0	.158	.200
Paulino, Enmanuel	R-R	6-1	175	11-28-93	.242	.250	.239	27	95	15	23	4	1	1	6	8	1	0	0	26	3	0	.337	.308
Rosa, Adderly	B-R	6-0	167	7-4-91	.083	.000	.105	10	24	3	2	0	0	0	2	2	0	2	1	5	0	0	.083	.148
Torres, Elias	R-R	6-1	176	2-22-92	.256	.335	.225	41	133	19	34	11	0	2	18	9	5	2	1	28	4	3	.383	.324

Pitching	B-T	HT	WT	DOB	W	L	ERA	G	GS	CG	SV	IP	H	R	ER	HR	BB	SO	AVG	vLH	vRH	K/9	BB/9
Armenta, Oscar	R-L	5-11	170	10-15-93	2	3	5.80	19	0	0	2	36	44	29	23	6	8	27	.299	.371	.277	6.81	2.02
Cabrera, Luis	R-R	6-2	185	8-14-90	0	5	3.71	15	1	0	2	34	37	20	14	1	12	32	.262	.231	.281	8.47	3.18
Crum, Clayton	R-R	6-1	190	1-26-92	4	1	3.07	12	0	0	0	29	27	12	10	5	8	25	.243	.200	.263	7.67	2.45
De La Cruz, Geisel	L-L	6-0	139	4-11-93	0	0	14.40	3	1	0	0	5	9	9	8	0	5	4	.409	.667	.368	7.20	9.00
Faria, Jacob	R-R	6-3	175	7-30-93	3	3	2.02	12	12	0	0	62	53	21	14	2	9	71	.227	.207	.238	10.25	1.30
Fernandez, Mario	R-R	6-0	206	9-7-93	1	0	0.00	3	0	0	0	9	3	2	0	0	3	7	.107	.182	.059	7.00	3.00
Fischer, Darren	L-L	6-2	185	8-8-92	0	3	5.30	12	0	0	0	19	12	11	11	4	7	17	.182	.118	.204	8.20	3.38
Gannon, Nolan	R-R	6-5	195	11-3-93	1	5	7.43	11	10	0	0	40	45	40	33	3	11	34	.274	.240	.289	7.65	2.48
Gil, Isaac	R-R	6-5	230	10-8-91	3	2	1.55	18	0	0	4	29	21	6	5	1	12	17	.208	.171	.227	5.28	3.72
Gomez, Edgar	R-R	5-11	190	1-5-93	0	1	7.20	11	0	0	0	15	21	19	12	1	5	10	.313	.333	.302	6.00	3.00
Havlicek, Stepan	R-L	6-1	160	2-25-93	0	0	5.86	13	0	0	1	28	33	24	18	7	9	14	.297	.276	.305	4.55	2.93

	B-T	HT	WT	DOB			ERA	G				IP	H	R	ER						SO				SLG	OBP
Kimborowicz, Josh	R-R	6-3	215	3-17-92	2	4	4.54	18	2	0	1	38	37	24	19	4	19	32	.261	.229	.277	7.65	4.54
Marquez, German	R-R	6-1	184	2-22-95	2	5	4.05	12	12	0	0	53	46	27	24	2	20	38	.232	.244	.224	6.41	3.38
Rodriguez, Jorge	R-R	5-11	187	12-15-91	0	5	3.90	13	12	0	1	60	72	28	26	2	9	51	.303	.329	.291	7.65	1.35
Slaton, D.J.	R-R	6-2	195	10-10-92	4	3	2.66	12	12	0	0	61	61	25	18	5	14	42	.261	.244	.270	6.20	2.07
Speer, Stone	L-L	5-11	180	6-10-91	0	0	3.52	4	0	0	0	8	6	3	3	1	3	8	.200	.000	.261	9.39	3.52
Teasley, Rick	L-L	6-2	210	4-22-91	0	0	0.00	1	0	0	0	2	0	0	0	0	0	2	.000	.000	.000	7.71	0.00
Wood, Hunter	R-R	6-1	171	8-12-93	3	3	3.80	16	6	0	2	45	38	20	19	5	11	59	.224	.222	.224	11.80	2.20

Fielding

Catcher	PCT	G	PO	A	E	DP	PB
Araiza	.992	47	344	46	3	4	5
Dominguez	.970	17	118	10	4	0	2
Nacapoy	.971	5	29	4	1	0	1

First Base	PCT	G	PO	A	E	DP
Correa	.979	23	181	10	4	12
Flores	.993	49	400	16	3	30

Second Base	PCT	G	PO	A	E	DP
Blanchard	.953	50	80	124	10	23
Duran	.975	12	20	19	1	4

	PCT	G	PO	A	E	DP
Garcia	1.000	1	2	1	0	1
Paulino	.933	5	3	11	1	2
Rosa	.957	4	10	12	1	1

Third Base	PCT	G	PO	A	E	DP
Correa	.936	15	13	31	3	1
Garcia	.914	44	25	71	9	3
Paulino	.897	13	2	24	3	1
Rosa	1.000	1	1	1	0	1

Shortstop	PCT	G	PO	A	E	DP
Correa	1.000	1	1	4	0	1

	PCT	G	PO	A	E	DP
Duran	.889	7	6	18	3	2
Edwards	.923	50	51	130	15	21
Paulino	.824	9	13	15	6	4
Rosa	.944	5	9	8	1	2

Outfield	PCT	G	PO	A	E	DP
Araujo	.905	52	90	5	10	1
Eierman	1.000	30	59	5	0	1
Jackson	.965	60	133	4	5	1
Lockwood	.971	25	32	2	1	1
Torres	.957	38	64	2	3	0

GCL RAYS   ROOKIE
GULF COAST LEAGUE

Batting	B-T	HT	WT	DOB	AVG	vLH	vRH	G	AB	R	H	2B	3B	HR	RBI	BB	HBP	SH	SF	SO	SB	CS	SLG	OBP
Brett, Ryan	R-R	5-9	180	10-9-91	.000	—	.000	1	4	0	0	0	0	0	0	0	0	0	0	2	0	0	.000	.000
Ciuffo, Nick	L-R	6-1	205	3-7-95	.258	.306	.236	43	159	11	41	6	1	0	25	9	0	0	1	40	0	0	.308	.296
Hadley, Jeremy	R-R	6-0	205	11-21-94	.205	.138	.229	33	112	9	23	2	2	0	8	4	0	0	0	32	2	1	.259	.233
Hager, Jake	R-R	6-1	170	3-4-93	.500	—	.500	1	4	1	2	1	0	0	1	0	0	0	0	0	0	0	.750	.500
Hawkins, Taylor	R-R	5-11	188	9-17-93	.171	.114	.193	38	123	13	21	7	0	1	12	11	4	0	1	37	4	1	.252	.259
Henley, Ryan	R-R	5-9	180	7-9-91	.217	.263	.203	28	83	9	18	3	1	1	11	4	1	0	2	12	1	3	.313	.256
Henning, Clayton	L-L	6-3	180	11-9-93	.260	.286	.250	33	96	6	25	4	1	0	8	12	0	3	1	36	10	2	.323	.339
Milone, Thomas	L-L	5-11	190	1-26-95	.190	.205	.184	40	142	18	27	2	4	0	4	7	3	1	0	38	5	1	.261	.243
Montes, Hector	R-R	6-0	235	2-21-92	.228	.227	.228	25	79	7	18	3	0	1	9	8	2	0	0	14	0	1	.304	.315
Motter, Taylor	R-R	6-1	190	9-18-89	.364	.000	.444	4	11	1	4	2	0	0	2	0	0	0	1	0	0	0	.545	.462
Natera, Jiminson	R-R	6-0	180	4-10-92	.214	.000	.231	6	14	1	3	1	0	0	1	3	1	0	0	6	0	0	.286	.389
Paez, Jose	B-R	6-0	165	8-11-93	.236	.238	.235	45	182	20	43	6	6	1	14	9	3	1	0	48	9	6	.352	.284
Paulino, Enmanuel	R-R	6-1	175	11-28-93	.143	.000	.167	2	7	4	1	0	0	0	2	1	0	0	0	3	0	0	.143	.400
Pendleton, Adam	R-R	6-0	210	7-17-90	.140	.000	.176	14	43	2	6	1	0	0	2	5	0	0	0	8	1	0	.163	.229
Rosa, Adderly	B-R	6-0	167	7-4-91	.310	.333	.304	12	29	5	9	2	0	0	3	12	2	0	1	9	6	2	.379	.523
Simon, Alexander	B-R	6-2	182	9-28-92	.293	.258	.310	58	208	25	61	6	5	0	22	19	1	0	1	50	12	8	.370	.354
Smedley, Sean	R-R	6-1	195	9-30-90	.000	.000	.000	2	5	0	0	0	0	0	0	1	0	0	1	0	0	0	.000	.167
Toribio, Cristian	R-R	5-11	170	9-13-94	.266	.366	.224	44	139	21	37	4	3	0	4	18	1	2	0	39	10	2	.338	.354
Unroe, Riley	B-R	5-10	180	8-3-95	.246	.196	.264	46	167	34	41	7	3	1	15	33	2	0	0	43	7	2	.341	.376
Vasquez, Erick	R-R	6-1	186	9-27-93	.179	.125	.198	35	123	6	22	5	0	0	14	7	4	0	2	41	5	1	.220	.243
Wong, Kean	L-R	5-11	190	4-17-95	.328	.294	.341	62	247	27	81	7	2	1	30	17	3	1	3	30	22	7	.390	.377

Pitching	B-T	HT	WT	DOB	W	L	ERA	G	GS	CG	SV	IP	H	R	ER	HR	BB	SO	AVG	vLH	vRH	K/9	BB/9
Almonte, Yomelbin	R-R	6-0	202	2-22-93	0	2	5.93	12	2	0	1	27	19	20	18	1	19	23	.196	.205	.190	7.57	6.26
Alonzo, Jose	R-R	6-4	191	2-24-93	7	2	2.22	12	7	0	0	57	47	17	14	3	14	35	.221	.213	.227	5.56	2.22
Alvarez, Freddy	R-R	5-10	203	9-10-93	2	5	3.60	12	4	0	0	40	30	21	16	1	26	41	.211	.250	.183	9.23	5.85
Carroll, Damion	R-R	6-3	198	1-31-94	0	0	3.86	2	2	0	0	2	1	1	1	0	2	3	.000	.000	.000	11.57	7.71
Castillo, Jose	L-L	6-4	200	1-10-96	2	2	5.87	12	3	0	0	31	34	21	20	1	8	25	.288	.174	.316	7.34	2.35
Crisostomo, Christopher	L-L	6-2	177	3-8-94	1	5	4.85	10	4	0	0	39	46	27	21	4	21	25	.305	.375	.286	5.77	4.85
De La Cruz, Geisel	L-L	6-0	139	4-11-93	2	1	2.04	7	0	0	0	18	19	5	4	0	7	14	.288	.214	.308	7.13	3.57
De Los Santos, Frank	L-L	6-0	165	11-17-87	0	0	4.91	2	2	0	0	4	2	2	2	0	0	4	.154	.500	.091	9.82	0.00
Fernandez, Mario	R-R	6-0	206	9-7-93	2	1	3.18	8	6	0	0	34	38	15	12	3	10	27	.284	.206	.352	7.15	2.65
Formo, Hyrum	R-R	6-1	185	4-13-92	0	0	2.16	6	0	0	0	8	11	4	2	0	0	6	.333	.400	.304	6.48	0.00
Fredrick, Eric	L-L	6-3	208	8-5-89	0	2	1.93	14	0	0	3	28	23	6	6	0	13	22	.221	.286	.205	7.07	4.18
Gabay, Willie	R-R	6-0	180	7-3-91	0	1	4.50	3	1	0	0	4	4	2	2	0	0	4	.250	.250	.250	9.00	0.00
Garvin, Grayson	L-L	6-6	225	10-27-89	0	1	2.31	6	6	0	0	12	11	3	3	1	4	12	.244	.444	.194	9.26	3.09
Gomes, Brandon	R-R	5-11	185	7-15-84	0	0	0.00	1	1	0	0	1	0	0	0	0	0	1	.000	.000	.000	9.00	0.00
Gomez, Edgar	R-R	5-11	190	1-5-93	1	0	0.00	3	0	0	1	5	2	0	0	0	1	4	.125	.000	.222	7.20	1.80
Gonzalez, Andres	R-R	6-3	205	2-20-94	3	0	2.06	11	1	0	2	39	36	10	9	1	2	30	.252	.279	.232	6.86	0.46
Hahn, Jesse	R-R	6-5	182	7-30-89	0	0	0.00	1	1	0	0	2	4	1	0	0	4	4	.364	.500	.286	18.00	0.00
Hurtado, Jhefferson	R-R	6-0	181	12-19-91	0	2	5.66	11	0	0	0	21	24	20	13	0	18	10	.304	.207	.360	4.35	7.84
Mujica, Jose	R-R	6-2	200	6-29-96	3	2	3.09	12	5	0	1	32	32	14	11	0	3	20	.244	.196	.275	5.63	0.84
Paredes, Ruben	R-R	6-1	180	9-21-93	1	1	1.38	14	0	0	8	26	15	5	4	1	8	23	.174	.242	.132	7.96	2.77
Ramirez, Roel	R-R	6-1	205	5-26-95	3	4	5.86	12	1	0	0	28	35	22	18	0	6	16	.307	.259	.357	5.20	1.95
Regalado, Yael	R-R	6-2	200	2-23-93	0	2	5.48	12	0	0	2	21	26	15	13	3	6	18	.289	.278	.296	7.59	2.53
Rodriguez, Wilking	R-R	6-1	180	3-2-90	0	0	0.00	8	6	0	0	9	6	0	0	0	3	9	.207	.333	.150	9.00	3.00
Shull, Trevor	R-R	6-4	180	8-7-90	0	0	2.25	4	4	0	0	8	5	2	2	1	2	9	.185	.250	.158	10.13	2.25
Suero, Bruedlin	L-L	6-0	175	2-25-95	0	0	0.00	2	0	0	0	3	1	0	0	0	1	1	.111	.000	.125	6.00	3.00
Swilley, Matt	R-R	6-2	175	12-19-90	0	0	8.10	3	2	0	0	3	4	3	3	0	4	3	.308	.429	.167	8.10	10.80
Tzamtzis, Anthony	R-R	6-0	185	11-4-90	0	0	9.00	1	0	0	0	1	2	1	1	0	1	1	.500	1.000	.333	9.00	9.00

Fielding

Catcher	PCT	G	PO	A	E	DP	PB
Ciuffo	.983	25	147	23	3	1	11
Hawkins	.950	31	197	32	12	3	9
Pendleton	.972	5	32	3	1	1	1
Smedley	1.000	1	7	0	0	0	0

First Base	PCT	G	PO	A	E	DP
Montes	1.000	1	1	0	0	0
Pendleton	1.000	6	59	2	0	6
Simon	.994	54	475	34	3	36
Smedley	1.000	1	4	0	0	0

Second Base	PCT	G	PO	A	E	DP
Brett	1.000	1	2	2	0	0
Henley	.970	11	13	19	1	0

Rosa	1.000	5	9	16	0	3
Toribio	.955	5	9	12	1	2
Wong	.979	39	79	108	4	29

Third Base	PCT	G	PO	A	E	DP
Henley	.882	15	5	25	4	2
Montes	.911	22	18	33	5	6
Motter	1.000	2	0	5	0	0
Paulino	1.000	1	0	2	0	0
Rosa	.960	7	6	18	1	4
Toribio	.953	18	15	46	3	2

Shortstop	PCT	G	PO	A	E	DP
Hager	1.000	1	0	6	0	0
Paulino	1.000	1	0	1	0	0

Toribio	.917	19	28	38	6	7
Unroe	.953	39	60	103	8	19

Outfield	PCT	G	PO	A	E	DP
Hadley	.979	32	45	1	1	0
Henley	1.000	1	3	0	0	0
Henning	.948	33	55	0	3	0
Milone	.988	39	84	1	1	0
Motter	1.000	2	1	0	0	0
Natera	1.000	2	3	0	0	0
Paez	.949	43	68	6	4	0
Vasquez	.960	32	47	1	2	0

DSL RAYS · ROOKIE

DOMINICAN SUMMER LEAGUE

Batting	B-T	HT	WT	DOB	AVG	vLH	vRH	G	AB	R	H	2B	3B	HR	RBI	BB	HBP	SH	SF	SO	SB	CS	SLG	OBP
Astacio, Joseph	L-R	6-0	155	6-5-94	.173	.091	.208	22	75	12	13	1	0	0	4	6	2	0	1	13	5	3	.187	.250
Hernandez, Miguel	R-R	6-2	175	12-28-95	.211	.205	.213	65	247	22	52	11	1	2	27	17	6	0	0	73	8	8	.287	.278
Herrera, Julio	R-R	5-9	184	10-9-92	.312	.278	.326	38	125	11	39	7	0	2	12	11	5	0	2	24	0	3	.416	.385
Jumes, Joel	L-R	6-1	192	1-24-93	.179	.242	.156	39	123	14	22	4	0	0	5	18	1	1	0	34	0	2	.211	.289
Maria, Eric	R-R	6-0	180	6-30-94	.211	.188	.223	41	142	17	30	5	0	0	18	11	2	2	2	21	1	2	.246	.274
Mella, Raybell	L-R	5-11	170	1-3-94	.152	.154	.150	16	33	2	5	0	1	0	3	6	1	2	0	13	4	1	.212	.300
Moreno, Angel	R-R	6-2	180	7-31-96	.305	.231	.348	38	141	26	43	9	3	4	22	10	1	1	1	24	5	4	.496	.353
Paulino, Enmanuel	R-R	6-1	175	11-28-93	.368	.500	.321	11	38	8	14	3	1	1	7	3	0	1	0	9	3	2	.579	.415
Perez, Angel	R-R	6-2	185	1-10-95	.400	.000	.500	2	5	1	2	1	1	0	1	0	0	0	0	0	0	0	1.000	.400
Pina, Julio	R-R	5-9	190	6-18-91	.222	.500	.188	8	18	3	4	1	0	1	5	2	0	0	2	7	0	0	.444	.273
Pujols, Bill	R-R	5-11	160	7-19-94	.301	.355	.276	64	239	54	72	14	2	3	27	33	5	6	1	26	14	8	.414	.396
Ramirez, Daulin	L-R	6-1	185	5-1-95	.085	.030	.107	39	117	10	10	2	0	1	5	12	0	2	0	39	0	0	.128	.171
Rodriguez, Darinel	R-R	5-10	175	1-8-95	.249	.212	.268	67	249	39	62	9	2	2	22	27	4	3	1	36	7	4	.325	.331
Rojas, Jose	R-R	6-0	175	3-11-93	.280	.247	.298	69	250	51	70	21	1	8	51	39	8	1	5	31	5	3	.468	.387
Rosario, Jilber	B-R	5-11	175	9-20-94	.271	.400	.212	13	48	8	13	1	0	0	2	8	3	1	0	9	8	2	.292	.407
Sanchez, Manuel	R-R	6-2	220	10-6-95	.247	.195	.270	69	251	47	62	14	1	13	52	36	0	0	6	47	8	1	.466	.334
Trinidad, Jesus	R-R	5-11	166	1-11-95	.172	.214	.153	28	87	5	15	4	1	0	7	7	1	2	1	23	0	0	.241	.240

Pitching	B-T	HT	WT	DOB	W	L	ERA	G	GS	CG	SV	IP	H	R	ER	HR	BB	SO	AVG	vLH	vRH	K/9	BB/9
Adames, Mario	R-R	6-2	210	5-29-92	5	2	1.55	19	1	0	3	46	33	14	8	1	6	45	.192	.148	.212	8.74	1.17
Cano, Joselito	L-L	6-5	190	9-16-92	2	2	2.25	18	0	0	3	24	21	8	6	1	16	34	.239	.182	.247	12.75	6.00
Castillo, Eddy	L-L	6-1	165	1-2-94	2	2	7.36	11	0	0	0	15	24	14	12	0	12	9	.353	.333	.358	5.52	7.36
Castillo, Erodis	R-R	6-1	173	11-29-93	0	5	3.83	14	13	0	1	56	55	35	24	4	22	35	.256	.212	.275	5.59	3.51
Cordova, Rafael	R-R	6-2	175	11-16-94	5	1	0.81	15	0	0	0	44	27	7	4	0	3	30	.173	.302	.124	6.09	0.61
Crisostomo, Christopher	L-L	6-2	177	3-8-94	1	0	1.56	4	4	0	0	17	13	6	3	1	9	14	.213	.105	.262	7.27	4.67
Disla, Jose	R-R	6-2	165	3-11-96	1	1	4.97	6	0	0	0	13	12	7	7	1	4	14	.255	.313	.226	9.95	2.84
Feliz, Junior	R-R	6-0	160	1-17-94	5	3	1.95	14	14	0	0	65	40	23	14	1	23	41	.178	.191	.169	5.71	3.20
Garcia, Carlos	R-R	6-2	218	12-1-90	4	1	3.03	18	0	0	1	36	28	18	12	0	17	24	.212	.235	.198	6.06	4.29
Germoso, Herminio	R-R	6-2	178	10-21-94	0	0	3.86	7	0	0	0	5	1	6	2	0	15	3	.071	.167	.000	5.79	28.93
Gracia, Ariel	L-L	5-11	173	9-17-94	3	1	1.49	14	14	0	0	67	60	20	11	2	12	59	.243	.227	.246	7.97	1.62
Hernandez, Wilmer	R-R	6-3	175	8-29-91	1	5	5.12	19	0	0	5	32	38	24	18	2	1	33	.311	.341	.296	9.38	0.28
Inoa, Odelis	R-R	6-1	180	9-2-94	0	1	3.86	13	9	0	0	28	27	15	12	0	9	18	.255	.256	.254	5.79	2.89
Martinez, Ramon	R-R	6-0	190	11-24-93	3	0	2.81	18	0	0	0	32	24	16	10	3	18	29	.198	.176	.207	8.16	5.06
Mendez, Deivy	R-R	6-2	160	10-27-95	0	4	6.55	14	14	0	0	33	49	27	24	1	17	22	.348	.417	.324	6.00	4.64
Mercedes, Luis	L-L	5-11	170	3-30-92	1	3	3.00	21	0	0	7	27	31	15	9	0	11	26	.290	.333	.277	8.67	3.67
Ortiz, Roquely	R-R	5-11	179	1-21-94	0	1	5.40	9	0	0	0	12	7	12	7	1	15	5	.194	.182	.200	3.86	11.57
Ortiz, Willy	R-R	6-1	174	7-20-95	1	1	3.12	12	2	0	1	35	40	21	12	0	12	23	.290	.222	.323	5.97	3.12
Rodriguez, Estarlin	R-R	5-10	165	8-20-94	1	1	5.01	15	0	0	1	23	12	18	13	0	28	22	.154	.045	.196	8.49	10.80
Soto, Gustavo	L-L	5-10	170	5-19-91	1	1	1.86	15	0	0	0	19	12	10	4	1	21	21	.171	.071	.196	9.78	9.78

Fielding

Catcher	PCT	G	PO	A	E	DP	PB
Herrera	.978	15	105	27	3	0	9
Maria	.940	39	244	36	18	0	18
Pina	1.000	2	2	1	0	0	0
Trinidad	.971	19	134	31	5	0	4

First Base	PCT	G	PO	A	E	DP
Herrera	.983	12	108	7	2	4
Jumes	.982	20	159	9	3	10
Maria	—	1	0	0	0	0
Paulino	1.000	3	36	5	0	3
Rojas	.982	40	311	23	6	25
Trinidad	1.000	3	18	0	0	0

Second Base	PCT	G	PO	A	E	DP
Astacio	.935	4	13	16	2	2
Mella	.953	10	27	14	2	7
Paulino	1.000	2	5	4	0	2
Pujols	.965	17	34	48	3	7
Rodriguez	.967	35	66	82	5	7
Rojas	1.000	2	2	2	0	2
Rosario	.865	10	14	18	5	2
Trinidad	—	1	0	0	0	0

Third Base	PCT	G	PO	A	E	DP
Paulino	.889	5	1	7	1	0
Pujols	.939	20	18	44	4	6

Ramirez	.792	22	12	30	11	0
Rodriguez	.864	6	5	14	3	2
Rojas	.885	28	23	62	11	3

Shortstop	PCT	G	PO	A	E	DP
Astacio	.918	17	33	45	7	5
Mella	1.000	3	6	9	0	1
Paulino	1.000	1	2	3	0	0
Pujols	.908	29	48	71	12	7
Rodriguez	.925	24	49	62	9	17
Rosario	.938	2	4	11	1	0

Outfield	PCT	G	PO	A	E	DP
Cano	1.000	2	5	0	0	0
Hernandez	.955	63	101	6	5	0
Herrera	—	1	0	0	0	0

	PCT	G	PO	A	E	DP
Jumes	.952	17	20	0	1	0
Mella	—	1	0	0	0	0
Moreno	.973	37	70	3	2	0
Perez	1.000	1	2	0	0	0

	PCT	G	PO	A	E	DP
Rodriguez	.000	1	0	0	1	0
Sanchez	.955	61	97	8	5	1
Vasquez	.940	47	77	2	5	0

VSL RAYS

ROOKIE

VENEZUELAN SUMMER LEAGUE

Batting	B-T	HT	WT	DOB	AVG	vLH	vRH	G	AB	R	H	2B	3B	HR	RBI	BB	HBP	SH	SF	SO	SB	CS	SLG	OBP
Apaez, Cesar	R-R	6-1	182	5-19-95	.176	.143	.185	53	193	19	34	5	0	2	11	10	3	0	0	65	5	4	.233	.228
Aray, Edduin	R-R	6-0	175	4-13-94	.200	.125	.220	28	75	8	15	2	1	1	11	8	4	0	0	22	4	2	.293	.310
Auciello, Kreiber	R-R	5-10	176	2-23-95	.375	.167	.417	25	72	14	27	7	2	2	11	8	0	0	0	5	0	1	.611	.438
Barrios, Kevin	R-R	6-1	190	2-28-95	.272	.273	.272	64	257	30	70	17	0	10	38	11	3	0	1	44	1	0	.455	.309
Castillo, Manuel	R-R	6-0	190	12-11-94	.204	.280	.178	33	98	16	20	3	1	4	14	14	4	0	0	30	1	0	.378	.328
Colina, David	R-R	6-1	173	3-20-94	.274	.342	.255	46	175	19	48	8	2	2	20	8	6	0	1	32	1	3	.377	.326
Hernandez, Jose	R-R	6-0	191	11-9-92	.264	.262	.265	42	144	17	38	11	2	1	10	7	3	0	0	30	1	3	.389	.312
Lugo, Henry	R-R	5-11	160	11-30-95	.134	.036	.162	40	127	9	17	4	0	0	6	10	2	0	0	31	3	0	.165	.209
Maestre, Roni	R-R	6-3	170	4-22-95	.261	.313	.248	41	153	23	40	5	0	2	18	3	2	1	1	21	4	0	.333	.283
Rivero, Nohisglin	R-R	6-0	180	1-26-90	.203	.160	.212	37	138	13	28	5	3	1	4	2	1	0	0	27	4	1	.304	.220
Rodriguez, David	R-R	5-11	200	2-25-96	.329	.442	.297	64	237	44	78	14	0	12	29	24	8	0	0	62	5	2	.540	.409
Rojas, Oscar	R-R	5-11	165	7-5-96	.275	.392	.240	54	218	21	60	17	5	6	28	11	3	2	1	41	5	10	.482	.318
Suarez, Norly	R-R	5-11	156	9-17-93	.083	.125	.063	15	24	0	2	0	0	1	2	0	0	0	9	1	1	.083	.154
Teran, Jhonnathan	R-R	6-1	161	12-13-94	.248	.267	.244	47	153	18	38	8	1	1	13	7	6	0	1	22	4	1	.333	.305
Torres, Enneider	R-R	5-10	150	5-29-96	.200	.286	.176	52	190	25	38	3	0	2	14	13	3	2	1	26	6	3	.247	.261

Pitching	B-T	HT	WT	DOB	W	L	ERA	G	GS	CG	SV	IP	H	R	ER	HR	BB	SO	AVG	vLH	vRH	K/9	BB/9
Alvarado, Jose	L-L	6-0	180	5-21-95	1	8	1.97	13	13	0	0	46	41	23	10	2	21	54	.238	.280	.231	10.64	4.14
Bastardo, Armando	R-R	6-0	172	7-11-94	2	4	4.74	16	0	0	1	44	54	25	23	6	18	27	.312	.260	.350	5.56	3.71
Casanas, Alberto	R-R	6-2	158	11-27-93	3	1	4.14	16	0	0	1	41	42	23	19	4	23	34	.269	.333	.226	7.40	5.01
Centeno, Henry	R-R	6-2	174	8-24-94	2	2	2.62	10	10	0	0	34	27	11	10	0	7	24	.213	.207	.217	6.29	1.83
Chirinos, Yonny	R-R	6-2	170	12-26-93	3	3	3.27	13	12	0	0	55	59	21	20	4	11	42	.277	.253	.294	6.87	1.80
Duarte, Jorman	R-R	6-2	190	11-16-94	2	5	4.37	14	14	0	0	60	74	39	29	4	10	38	.303	.267	.336	5.73	1.51
Guarecuco, Roimar	R-R	6-1	170	1-25-95	0	3	6.21	11	0	0	0	29	31	20	20	5	15	18	.282	.229	.323	5.59	4.66
Guzman, Pablo	R-R	6-3	185	6-21-95	0	0	11.74	8	0	0	0	15	18	24	20	2	17	4	.290	.250	.324	2.35	9.98
Hernandez, E, Edgardo	R-R	6-3	201	11-9-94	0	4	4.62	14	0	0	2	49	54	28	25	9	8	38	.277	.276	.278	7.03	1.48
Leon, Carlos	R-R	6-2	195	4-10-92	0	2	6.30	7	0	0	1	10	15	8	7	2	2	8	.341	.353	.320	1.80	1.80
Marval, Johan	R-R	6-1	195	11-24-93	2	4	3.79	18	0	0	2	40	42	23	17	7	4	40	.261	.325	.202	8.93	0.89
Molina, Benjamin	L-L	6-0	144	11-18-94	0	4	3.40	12	11	0	0	53	51	26	20	8	12	47	.254	.385	.222	7.98	2.04
Navas, Adrian	R-R	6-2	200	4-13-96	0	1	1.86	3	3	0	0	10	12	2	2	0	3	10	.316	.267	.348	9.31	2.79
Nieves, Wilce	R-R	6-0	175	5-12-92	0	1	5.68	8	0	0	0	19	26	15	12	2	6	13	.329	.375	.298	6.16	2.84
Pilar, Daniel	R-R	6-4	185	6-6-95	0	2	10.73	15	0	0	0	26	37	37	31	4	20	20	.322	.350	.307	6.92	6.92
Prado, Enderson	R-R	6-1	165	1-3-95	2	4	6.35	13	1	0	0	28	27	21	20	4	23	14	.248	.294	.207	4.45	7.31
Rivas, Frehumar	L-L	6-1	175	5-20-95	0	0	12.79	7	2	0	0	6	7	9	9	0	14	1	.318	.000	.350	1.42	19.89
Rodriguez, Jesus	L-L	6-2	145	8-19-95	0	1	24.08	9	0	0	0	12	29	39	33	5	20	10	.439	.417	.444	7.30	14.59
Veliz, Oliver	R-R	6-0	175	2-22-96	0	1	6.43	5	0	0	0	7	10	6	5	0	2	4	.303	.294	.313	5.14	2.57
Yepez, Angel	R-R	6-1	215	4-27-95	1	0	5.06	5	2	0	0	11	13	9	6	2	5	7	.317	.267	.346	5.91	4.22

Fielding

Catcher	PCT	G	PO	A	E	DP	PB
Auciello	1.000	20	89	22	0	0	4
Rivero	.899	10	59	12	8	0	5
Rodriguez	.988	43	290	38	4	1	6

First Base	PCT	G	PO	A	E	DP
Barrios	.991	60	505	38	5	38
Colina	1.000	1	2	2	0	0
Januario	.962	4	23	2	1	2
Rivero	1.000	6	46	7	0	3

Second Base	PCT	G	PO	A	E	DP
Colina	1.000	1	1	0	0	0
Hernandez	1.000	22	29	55	0	4
Lugo	.976	10	19	22	1	7
Suarez	1.000	10	13	12	0	4
Teran	.986	16	29	43	1	8
Torres	.967	19	53	36	3	9

Third Base	PCT	G	PO	A	E	DP
Colina	.891	33	24	82	13	8
Hernandez	.929	18	23	29	4	4
Suarez	.667	1	1	3	2	0
Teran	.973	25	20	51	2	4

Shortstop	PCT	G	PO	A	E	DP
Lugo	.918	30	44	79	11	10
Teran	.967	6	10	19	1	0
Torres	.844	34	57	73	24	13

Outfield	PCT	G	PO	A	E	DP
Apaez	.951	52	93	5	5	2
Aray	.935	25	43	0	3	0
Castillo	.875	32	46	3	7	0
Maestre	.980	40	90	9	2	1
Rivero	.957	17	42	3	2	0
Rojas	.980	53	95	4	2	0
Suarez	—	2	0	0	0	0

Texas Rangers

SEASON IN A SENTENCE: For the fourth straight season, the Rangers finished with at least 90 wins, but it wasn't good enough to make the playoffs, as Texas finished in a three-way tie for the American League wild card and lost 5-2 to the Rays in the Game 163 tiebreaker.

HIGH POINT: Team ace Yu Darvish led the majors with 277 strikeouts in 210 innings and ranked fifth in the AL with a 2.83 ERA. Third baseman Adrian Beltre hit 30 home runs (his third consecutive season with at least 30 homers) with a .315/.371/.509 batting line.

LOW POINT: The Rangers entered September in first place in the AL West, but went just 12-16 in September. The loss of Nelson Cruz to a 50-game suspension for his involvement with Biogenesis left the team with an offensive hole, as they struggled to find production from their outfield corners, first base and DH. After the season, CEO Nolan Ryan announced he was leaving the team.

NOTABLE ROOKIES: The future is still bright for 20-year-old shortstop Jurickson Profar, but he struggled at the plate in 85 games as the Rangers essentially used him as a utility player to squeeze him into a lineup with Elvis Andrus, Ian Kinsler and Beltre already in the infield. The talent in the farm system—particularly from the international ranks—has started to bubble up to the big leagues, with the Rangers getting solid contributions in 2013 from Venezuelan lefthander Martin Perez and Cuban center fielder Leonys Martin.

KEY TRANSACTIONS: The Rangers traded for Alex Rios from the White Sox to make up for Cruz's absence, parting with speedy 22-year-old utility man Leury Garcia. Their midseason acquisition of Matt Garza, who became a free agent after the season, could prove more costly, as that deal included prized righthander C.J. Edwards.

DOWN ON THE FARM: The middle infield picture will only get more crowded in the near future with Profar and 19-year-old second baseman Rougned Odor, who reached Double-A by the end of the season and dominated the circuit in his brief time there, showing a sweet lefty swing and a mature hitting approach. Low Class A Hickory had plenty of physical power hitters with big strikeout rates, none more fascinating than 18-year-old third baseman Joey Gallo. The 6-foot-5 lefthanded hitter hit 38 home runs and 165 strikeouts games with Hickory. plus another two homers in the Rookie-level Arizona League.

OPENING DAY PAYROLL: $114.1 million (12th)

PLAYERS OF THE YEAR

MAJOR LEAGUE	MINOR LEAGUE
Yu Darvish	**Rougned Odor**
rhp	**2b**
13-9, 2.83 in 32 GS	(High A/Double-A)
Led AL with 277 SO,	.305/.365/.474
11.9 SO/9, 6.2 H/9	11 HR, 41 2B, 32 SB

ORGANIZATION LEADERS

BATTING		*Minimum 250 AB
MAJORS		
* AVG	Beltre, Adrian	.315
* OPS	Beltre, Adrian	.88
HR	Beltre, Adrian	30
RBI	Beltre, Adrian	92
MINORS		
* AVG	Odor, Rougned, Frisco/Myrtle Beach	.305
* OBP	Butler, Joey, Round Rock	.395
* SLG	Gallo, Joey, Hickory	.61
R	Rua, Ryan, Frisco/Hickory	89
H	Odor, Rougned, Frisco/Myrtle Beach	156
TB	Gallo, Joey, Hickory/AZL	256
2B	Odor, Rougned, Frisco/Myrtle Beach	41
3B	Williams, Nick, Hickory	12
HR	Gallo, Joey, Hickory/AZL	40
RBI	Nicholas, Brett, Frisco	91
	Rua, Ryan, Frisco/Hickory	91
BB	Robinson, Drew, Myrtle Beach	72
SO	Brinson, Lewis, Hickory	191
SB	Three tied at	32

PITCHING		#Minimum 75 IP
MAJORS		
W	Darvish, Yu	13
# ERA	Darvish, Yu	2.83
SO	Darvish, Yu	277
SV	Nathan, Joe	43
MINORS		
W	Martinez, Nick, Frisco/Myrtle Beach	12
W	Sadzeck, Connor, Hickory	12
L	McBride, Nick, Round Rock/Frisco, M.B.	12
# ERA	Jackson, Luke, Myrtle Beach/Frisco	2.04
G	Rowen, Ben, Round Rock/Frisco	51
GS	Eickhoff, Jerad, Frisco/Myrtle Beach	27
SV	Burns, Cory, Round Rock	20
IP	Martinez, Nick, Frisco/Myrtle Beach	151
BB	Pucetas, Kevin, Frisco/Myrtle Beach	65
SO	Asher, Alec, Myrtle Beach	139
# AVG	Jackson, Luke, Myrtle Beach/Frisco	.202

General Manager: Jon Daniels. **Farm Director:** Tim Purpura. **Scouting Director:** A.J. Preller.

Class	Team	League	W	L	PCT	Finish	Manager
Majors	Texas Rangers	American	91	72	.558	6th (15)	Ron Washington
Triple-A	Round Rock Express	Pacific Coast	73	71	.507	8th (16)	Bobby Jones
Double-A	Frisco RoughRiders	Texas	70	70	.500	4th (8)	Steve Buechele
High A	Myrtle Beach Pelicans	Carolina	77	62	.554	2nd (8)	Jason Wood
Low A	Hickory Crawdads	South Atlantic	76	63	.547	5th (14)	Corey Ragsdale
Short-season	Spokane Indians	Northwest	38	38	.500	5th (8)	Tim Hulett
Rookie	AZL Rangers	Arizona	32	23	.582	3rd (13)	Kenny Holmberg
Overall 2013 Minor League Record			366	327	.528	6th (30)	

ORGANIZATION STATISTICS

AMERICAN LEAGUE

Batting	B-T	HT	WT	DOB	AVG	vLH	vRH	G	AB	R	H	2B	3B	HR	RBI	BB	HBP	SH	SF	SO	SB	CS	SLG	OBP
Adduci, Jim	L-L	6-2	210	5-15-85	.258	.333	.240	17	31	2	8	1	0	0	3	0	0	0	9	2	0	.290	.324
Andrus, Elvis	R-R	6-0	200	8-26-88	.271	.273	.270	156	620	91	168	17	4	4	67	52	4	16	6	97	42	8	.331	.328
Baker, Jeff	R-R	6-2	210	6-21-81	.279	.314	.204	74	154	21	43	8	0	11	21	18	2	0	1	48	1	0	.545	.360
Beltre, Adrian	R-R	5-11	220	4-7-79	.315	.325	.312	161	631	88	199	32	0	30	92	50	7	0	2	78	1	0	.509	.371
Beltre, Engel	L-L	6-2	180	11-1-89	.250	.167	.265	22	40	7	10	1	0	0	2	0	1	1	0	5	1	2	.275	.268
Berkman, Lance	B-L	6-1	220	2-10-76	.242	.254	.238	73	256	27	62	10	1	6	34	38	0	0	0	52	0	0	.359	.340
Borbon, Julio	L-L	6-0	195	2-20-86	.000	—	.000	1	1	1	0	0	0	0	0	0	0	0	0	0	0	0	.000	.000
Butler, Joey	R-R	6-2	220	3-12-86	.333	.400	.000	8	12	3	4	2	0	0	1	3	0	0	0	6	0	0	.500	.467
Chirinos, Robinson	R-R	6-1	205	6-5-84	.179	.154	.200	13	28	3	5	3	0	0	0	2	0	0	0	6	0	0	.286	.233
Cruz, Nelson	R-R	6-2	230	7-1-80	.266	.279	.262	109	413	49	110	18	0	27	76	35	4	0	4	109	5	1	.506	.327
Garcia, Leury	R-R	5-7	160	3-18-91	.192	.188	.194	25	52	8	10	0	1	0	1	3	0	2	0	16	1	0	.231	.236
2-team total (20 Chicago)					.198	—	—	45	101	10	20	1	1	0	2	7	0	2	1	34	7	2	.228	.248
Gentry, Craig	R-R	6-2	190	11-29-83	.280	.280	.281	106	246	39	69	12	4	2	22	29	8	3	1	46	24	3	.386	.373
Kinsler, Ian	R-R	6-0	200	6-22-82	.277	.306	.265	136	545	85	151	31	2	13	72	51	8	3	7	59	15	11	.413	.344
Martin, Leonys	L-L	6-2	190	3-6-88	.260	.226	.275	147	457	66	119	21	6	8	49	28	8	12	3	104	36	9	.385	.313
McGuiness, Chris	L-L	6-1	210	4-11-88	.176	.111	.200	10	34	0	6	1	0	0	1	0	0	0	0	13	0	0	.206	.176
Moreland, Mitch	L-L	6-2	240	9-6-85	.232	.241	.227	147	462	60	107	24	1	23	60	45	3	0	8	117	0	0	.437	.299
Murphy, David	L-L	6-4	210	10-18-81	.220	.223	.219	142	436	51	96	26	1	13	45	37	1	0	1	59	1	4	.374	.282
Pierzynski, A.J.	L-R	6-3	235	12-30-76	.272	.279	.269	134	503	48	137	24	1	17	70	11	9	0	6	76	1	1	.425	.297
Profar, Jurickson	B-R	6-0	165	2-20-93	.234	.188	.258	85	286	30	67	11	0	6	26	26	5	6	1	63	2	4	.336	.308
Rios, Alex	R-R	6-5	210	2-18-81	.280	.310	.266	47	186	26	52	11	2	6	26	9	1	0	1	30	16	1	.457	.315
2-team total (109 Chicago)					.278	—	—	156	616	83	171	33	4	18	81	41	2	0	2	108	42	7	.432	.324
Rosales, Adam	R-R	6-1	195	5-20-83	.182	.167	.200	17	11	4	2	0	0	1	4	0	0	0	1	3	0	0	.455	.167
2-team total (51 Oakland)					.190	—	—	68	147	15	28	5	0	5	12	10	4	4	1	34	0	0	.327	.259
Soto, Geovany	R-R	6-1	235	1-20-83	.245	.200	.272	54	163	20	40	9	0	9	22	20	0	1	0	60	1	2	.466	.328

Pitching	B-T	HT	WT	DOB	W	L	ERA	G	GS	CG	SV	IP	H	R	ER	HR	BB	SO	AVG	vLH	vRH	K/9	BB/9
Blackley, Travis	L-L	6-3	205	11-4-82	1	1	4.70	4	3	0	0	15	16	8	8	2	2	11	.281	.467	.214	6.46	1.17
2-team total (42 Houston)					2	2	4.83	46	3	0	0	50	46	27	27	12	22	40	—	—	—	7.15	3.93
Burns, Cory	R-R	6-0	205	10-9-87	1	0	3.18	10	0	0	0	11	12	4	4	1	7	5	.261	.286	.240	3.97	5.56
Cotts, Neal	L-L	6-1	200	3-25-80	8	3	1.11	58	0	0	1	57	36	8	7	2	18	65	.180	.204	.157	10.26	2.84
Darvish, Yu	R-R	6-5	225	8-16-86	13	9	2.83	32	32	0	0	210	145	68	66	26	80	277	.194	.212	.165	11.89	3.43
Feliz, Neftali	R-R	6-3	225	5-2-88	0	0	0.00	6	0	0	0	5	5	0	0	0	2	4	.278	.200	.308	7.71	3.86
Font, Wilmer	R-R	6-4	230	5-24-90	0	0	0.00	2	0	0	0	1	1	0	0	0	2	0	.200	.250	.000	0.00	13.50
Frasor, Jason	R-R	5-9	180	8-9-77	4	3	2.57	60	0	0	0	49	36	15	14	4	20	48	.203	.152	.234	8.82	3.67
Garza, Matt	R-R	6-4	215	11-26-83	4	5	4.38	13	13	1	0	84	89	47	41	12	22	74	.271	.301	.237	7.90	2.35
Grimm, Justin	R-R	6-3	200	8-16-88	7	7	6.37	17	17	0	0	89	116	67	63	15	31	68	.314	.309	.319	6.88	3.13
Harrison, Matt	L-L	6-4	250	9-16-85	0	2	8.44	2	2	0	0	11	14	11	10	2	7	12	.326	.182	.375	10.13	5.91
Holland, Derek	B-L	6-2	210	10-9-86	10	9	3.42	33	33	2	0	213	210	90	81	20	64	189	.259	.265	.258	7.99	2.70
Kirkman, Michael	L-L	6-4	220	9-18-86	0	2	8.18	25	0	0	1	22	36	20	20	2	15	25	.364	.341	.379	10.23	6.14
Lindblom, Josh	R-R	6-4	240	6-15-87	1	3	5.46	8	3	0	0	31	35	19	19	4	11	21	.278	.286	.262	6.03	3.16
Lowe, Derek	R-R	6-6	230	6-1-73	1	0	9.00	9	0	0	0	13	16	13	13	3	3	8	.308	.368	.273	5.54	2.08
McClellan, Kyle	R-R	6-2	215	6-12-84	0	1	7.71	7	0	0	0	9	7	8	8	2	5	3	.212	.125	.294	2.89	4.82
Nathan, Joe	R-R	6-4	230	11-22-74	6	2	1.39	67	0	0	43	65	36	10	10	2	22	73	.162	.171	.152	10.16	3.06
Ogando, Alexi	R-R	6-4	200	10-5-83	7	4	3.11	23	18	0	0	104	87	38	36	11	41	72	.231	.210	.258	6.21	3.54
Ortiz, Joe	L-L	5-7	175	8-13-90	2	2	4.23	32	0	0	0	45	46	26	21	5	10	27	.269	.257	.277	5.44	2.01
Perez, Martin	L-L	6-0	190	4-4-91	10	6	3.62	20	20	1	0	124	129	55	50	15	37	84	.267	.282	.262	6.08	2.68
Ross, Robbie	L-L	5-11	215	6-24-89	4	2	3.03	65	0	0	0	62	63	21	21	4	19	58	.259	.341	.211	8.37	2.74
Scheppers, Tanner	R-R	6-4	200	1-17-87	6	2	1.88	76	0	0	1	77	58	21	16	6	24	59	.214	.218	.210	6.93	2.82
Soria, Joakim	R-R	6-3	200	5-18-84	1	0	3.80	26	0	0	0	24	18	10	10	2	14	28	.212	.068	.366	10.65	5.32
Tepesch, Nick	R-R	6-4	225	10-12-88	4	6	4.84	19	17	0	0	93	100	53	50	12	27	76	.272	.297	.239	7.35	2.61
Wolf, Ross	R-R	6-0	180	10-18-82	1	3	4.15	22	3	0	0	48	58	24	22	5	15	21	.307	.356	.247	3.97	2.83

Fielding

Catcher	PCT	G	PO	A	E	DP	PB								First Base	PCT	G	PO	A	E	DP
Chirinos	1.000	3	22	0	0	0	0	Pierzynski	.998	119	892	65	2	8	6						
								Soto	.995	53	395	27	2	3	1	Adduci	.923	4	12	0	1	3

	PCT	G	PO	A	E	DP
Baker	1.000	21	109	3	0	7
Berkman	.978	4	38	6	1	3
Chirinos	.964	4	23	4	1	2
McGuiness	1.000	10	77	6	0	5
Moreland	.996	146	1045	96	5	108
Rosales	1.000	4	4	1	0	1

Second Base	PCT	G	PO	A	E	DP
Baker	1.000	1	1	0		1
Garcia	.980	12	16	33	1	7
Kinsler	.978	124	211	371	13	89
Profar	.970	32	54	75	4	16
Rosales	1.000	2	0	1	0	0

Third Base	PCT	G	PO	A	E	DP
Baker	.950	10	5	14	1	1
Beltre	.959	146	93	232	14	25
Chirinos	1.000	3	0	1	0	0
Garcia	1.000	4	0	2	0	0
Profar	.923	10	8	16	2	1
Rosales	—	2	0	0	0	0
Soto	—	1	0	0	0	0

Shortstop	PCT	G	PO	A	E	DP
Andrus	.976	146	212	362	14	97
Garcia	1.000	4	1	9	0	0
Profar	.970	18	22	43	2	9
Rosales	1.000	3	0	2	0	1

Outfield	PCT	G	PO	A	E	DP
Adduci	1.000	8	10	0	0	0
Baker	1.000	22	20	0	0	0
Beltre	1.000	16	26	0	0	0
Butler	1.000	5	3	0	0	0
Cruz	.985	102	195	1	3	0
Gentry	.990	102	183	7	2	1
Martin	.985	142	317	14	5	1
Moreland	—	1	0	0	0	0
Murphy	.990	129	195	10	2	1
Profar	1.000	4	8	0	0	0
Rios	1.000	47	99	1	0	0

ROUND ROCK EXPRESS   TRIPLE-A

PACIFIC COAST LEAGUE

Batting	B-T	HT	WT	DOB	AVG	vLH	vRH	G	AB	R	H	2B	3B	HR	RBI	BB	HBP	SH	SF	SO	SB	CS	SLG	OBP
Adduci, Jim	L-L	6-2	210	5-15-85	.298	.258	.318	127	473	75	141	24	3	16	65	65	2	5	6	107	32	9	.463	.381
Beltre, Engel	L-L	6-2	180	11-1-89	.292	.206	.332	94	394	58	115	19	1	7	34	28	3	9	5	84	15	12	.398	.340
Berkman, Lance	B-L	6-1	220	2-10-76	.429	—	.429	2	7	1	3	0	0	1	2	0	0	0	0	1	0	0	.857	.429
Bianucci, Mike	R-R	6-1	215	6-26-86	.281	.354	.228	56	196	31	55	14	0	12	46	21	2	0	2	43	0	1	.536	.353
Buchholz, Alex	R-R	6-0	185	9-30-87	.262	.154	.295	45	168	24	44	13	0	4	22	16	1	2	1	30	2	0	.411	.328
Butler, Joey	R-R	6-2	220	3-12-86	.291	.288	.293	119	426	71	124	26	0	12	51	69	6	1	3	119	1	2	.437	.395
Chirinos, Robinson	R-R	6-1	205	6-5-84	.257	.279	.249	74	265	35	68	10	2	8	40	38	4	2	2	55	2	0	.400	.356
Cunningham, Aaron	R-R	5-11	195	4-24-86	.247	.273	.237	115	421	63	104	31	2	10	50	50	9	1	4	84	12	3	.401	.337
Felix, Jose	R-R	5-10	200	6-28-88	.270	.357	.217	32	111	9	30	2	1	0	13	4	0	0	2	17	0	0	.306	.291
Garcia, Leury	B-R	5-7	160	3-18-91	.264	.270	.262	47	193	31	51	8	4	4	19	14	0	1	0	53	12	4	.409	.314
Harris, Brendan	R-R	6-1	200	8-26-80	.244	.182	.267	12	41	7	10	0	0	2	5	7	1	0	0	7	0	0	.390	.367
Hoying, Jared	L-R	6-3	190	5-18-89	.266	.207	.292	53	188	31	50	5	5	8	24	6	1	0	1	60	4	2	.473	.291
McGuiness, Chris	L-L	6-1	210	4-11-88	.246	.287	.231	104	362	52	89	29	1	11	63	68	4	0	2	86	1	0	.423	.369
Miclat, Greg	B-R	5-8	180	7-23-87	.238	.267	.223	79	265	25	63	11	0	0	26	35	1	8	0	47	10	5	.279	.329
Olt, Mike	R-R	6-2	210	8-27-88	.213	.286	.171	65	230	37	49	15	0	11	32	35	1	0	2	89	0	0	.422	.317
2-team total (39 Iowa)					.197	—	—	104	361	48	71	18	1	14	40	55	1	0	3	126	0	0	.368	.302
Onaka, Hirotoshi	B-R	5-10	175	7-11-88	.000	—	.000	1	2	0	0	0	0	0	0	0	0	0	0	0	0	0	.000	.000
Profar, Jurickson	B-R	6-0	165	2-20-93	.278	.263	.283	37	144	27	40	7	2	4	19	21	0	1	0	24	6	1	.438	.370
Ramirez, Manny	R-R	6-0	225	5-30-72	.259	.333	.227	30	108	7	28	3	0	3	13	10	1	0	0	14	0	0	.370	.328
Rodriguez, Guilder	B-R	6-1	160	7-24-83	.319	.364	.306	12	47	10	15	1	0	0	3	6	0	1	0	8	2	0	.340	.396
Solarte, Yangervis	B-R	5-11	195	7-7-87	.276	.321	.255	133	526	66	145	31	0	12	75	39	2	2	8	69	3	0	.403	.323
Teahen, Mark	L-R	6-3	230	9-6-81	.171	.273	.125	10	35	1	6	0	0	0	2	3	0	0	0	11	0	0	.171	.237
2-team total (22 Reno)					.198	—	—	32	106	13	21	3	0	0	7	15	0	0	2	33	0	0	.226	.293
Whiteside, Eli	R-R	6-2	220	10-22-79	.187	.186	.187	67	225	21	42	6	0	5	25	16	1	0	2	61	0	0	.280	.242
Zaneski, Zach	R-R	6-2	215	6-27-86	.217	.200	.222	7	23	4	5	2	0	1	6	3	0	1	0	7	0	0	.435	.308

Pitching	B-T	HT	WT	DOB	W	L	ERA	G	GS	CG	SV	IP	H	R	ER	HR	BB	SO	AVG	vLH	vRH	K/9	BB/9
Balester, Collin	R-R	6-5	200	6-6-86	1	4	7.33	6	5	0	0	27	34	23	22	4	9	22	.309	.365	.234	7.33	3.00
Beliveau, Jeff	L-L	6-1	195	1-17-87	0	0	0.00	1	0	0	0	2	1	0	0	0	0	0	.143	.000	.167	0.00	0.00
Blackley, Travis	L-L	6-3	205	11-4-82	0	0	0.00	1	1	0	0	3	1	0	0	0	2	2	.125	.000	.167	6.00	6.00
2-team total (1 Oklahoma City)					0	0	1.80	2	2	0	0	5	1	1	0	2	3		—	—	—	5.40	3.60
Bleier, Richard	L-L	6-3	215	4-16-87	1	1	3.79	8	2	0	0	19	23	9	8	1	7	8	.315	.321	.311	3.79	3.32
Bonilla, Lisalverto	R-R	6-0	175	6-18-90	5	5	7.95	26	2	0	0	43	52	42	38	8	24	56	.299	.291	.305	11.72	5.02
Brigham, Jake	R-R	6-3	210	2-10-88	5	5	4.51	26	18	0	2	114	125	65	57	7	46	78	.287	.285	.288	6.18	3.64
Burns, Cory	R-R	6-0	205	10-9-87	0	2	2.15	38	0	0	20	38	39	11	9	0	15	48	.264	.229	.295	11.47	3.58
Cotts, Neal	L-L	6-1	200	3-25-80	3	1	0.78	15	0	0	2	23	13	3	2	1	5	42	.171	.000	.271	16.43	1.96
Feierabend, Ryan	L-L	6-3	225	8-22-85	6	5	3.66	24	16	1	0	120	128	54	49	10	33	79	.280	.248	.296	5.91	2.47
Feliz, Neftali	R-R	6-3	225	5-2-88	0	0	0.00	9	0	0	0	9	4	0	0	2	9		.133	.063	.214	9.35	2.08
Font, Wilmer	R-R	6-4	230	5-24-90	1	0	0.45	16	0	0	4	20	8	3	1	0	10	26	.119	.107	.128	11.70	4.50
Grimm, Justin	R-R	6-3	200	8-16-88	1	0	1.59	1	1	0	0	6	4	1	1	0	2	4	.200	.200	.200	6.35	3.18
2-team total (8 Iowa)					3	3	4.31	9	9	0	0	48	50	24	23	1	19	45	—	—	—	8.44	3.56
Harrison, Matt	L-L	6-4	250	9-16-85	0	1	9.00	1	1	0	0	3	3	4	3	1	2	0	.231	.200	.250	0.00	6.00
Kirkman, Michael	L-L	6-4	220	9-18-86	2	3	6.98	6	5	0	0	30	31	23	23	3	19	23	.282	.231	.298	6.98	5.76
Lewis, Colby	R-R	6-4	240	8-2-79	0	1	9.00	2	2	0	0	6	10	6	6	1	4	4	.385	.273	.467	6.00	6.00
Lindblom, Josh	R-R	6-4	240	6-15-87	8	4	3.08	20	18	0	0	108	86	39	37	12	31	79	.214	.207	.220	6.58	2.58
Mavare, Jose	R-R	6-0	175	2-19-90	1	1	4.15	2	0	0	0	4	3	2	2	0	2	4	.188	.111	.286	8.31	4.15
McBride, Nick	R-R	6-4	180	5-13-91	0	0	12.00	1	0	0	0	3	6	4	4	1	2	2	.462	.400	.500	6.00	6.00
McClellan, Kyle	R-R	6-2	215	6-12-84	1	0	2.57	9	0	0	2	7	8	3	2	1	2	9	.276	.000	.421	11.57	2.57
Meek, Evan	R-R	6-2	215	5-12-83	6	9	4.50	33	15	0	4	108	115	62	54	9	46	80	.273	.250	.295	6.67	3.83
Miller, Justin	R-R	6-3	215	6-13-87	0	1	9.82	11	0	0	1	11	14	16	12	4	9	12	.292	.348	.240	9.82	7.36
Mills, Brad	L-L	6-0	185	3-5-85	7	5	3.87	18	17	0	0	98	92	48	42	9	29	73	.248	.239	.252	6.73	2.67
Ogando, Alexi	R-R	6-4	200	10-5-83	1	0	6.23	3	3	0	0	13	12	9	9	0	4	9	.240	.222	.250	2.77	2.77
Ortiz, Joe	L-L	5-7	195	8-13-90	2	1	3.08	19	0	0	2	26	24	9	9	3	8	29	.245	.263	.167	9.91	2.73
Perez, Martin	L-L	6-0	190	4-4-91	5	1	1.75	6	6	0	0	36	29	8	7	1	8	28	.225	.206	.242	7.00	2.00
Pimentel, Carlos	R-R	6-3	180	12-1-89	0	0	1.59	6	0	0	0	11	8	3	2	1	7	11	.200	.100	.300	8.74	5.56
Richmond, Scott	R-R	6-5	220	8-30-79	6	7	5.91	20	20	0	0	113	123	77	74	17	45	56	.279	.313	.246	4.47	3.59
Robertson, Nate	R-L	6-2	225	9-3-77	4	4	3.04	45	0	0	0	50	45	21	17	0	23	40	.243	.213	.267	7.15	4.11
Rodebaugh, Ryan	L-R	6-0	165	3-30-89	1	0	3.34	22	0	0	1	30	20	12	11	3	15	23	.192	.227	.167	6.98	4.55

					W	L	ERA	G	GS	CG	SV	IP	H	R	ER	HR	BB	SO	AVG	vLH	vRH	K/9	BB/9
Rowen, Ben	R-R	6-4	190	11-15-88	3	1	0.84	20	0	0	3	32	18	5	3	0	6	30	.157	.148	.164	8.44	1.69
Soria, Joakim	R-R	6-3	200	5-18-84	0	0	0.00	2	0	0	0	2	1	0	0	0	0	3	.143	.000	.250	13.50	0.00
Tateyama, Yoshinori	R-R	5-10	165	12-26-75	0	1	4.24	23	0	0	1	34	37	16	16	5	10	44	.270	.258	.280	11.65	2.65
Tepesch, Nick	R-R	6-4	225	10-12-88	1	0	0.00	1	1	0	0	5	5	1	0	0	0	5	.250	.200	.267	9.00	0.00
Wells, Randy	R-R	6-5	230	8-28-82	0	4	6.08	5	5	0	0	24	32	19	16	4	12	20	.317	.347	.288	7.61	4.56
Wolf, Ross	R-R	6-0	180	10-18-82	1	1	1.77	7	6	0	0	36	27	8	7	1	10	26	.214	.226	.203	6.56	2.52
Yan, Johan	R-R	6-4	185	9-27-88	2	2	4.68	44	0	0	3	58	63	33	30	4	21	53	.284	.378	.210	8.27	3.28

Fielding

Catcher	PCT	G	PO	A	E	DP	PB
Chirinos	.987	51	342	33	5	3	6
Felix	.995	25	180	11	1	1	3
Whiteside	.992	65	470	36	4	2	7
Zaneski	1.000	7	47	5	0	0	0

First Base	PCT	G	PO	A	E	DP
Adduci	.997	33	288	34	1	28
Bianucci	.995	19	174	12	1	18
Chirinos	1.000	3	27	2	0	4
McGuiness	.998	90	778	73	2	82

Second Base	PCT	G	PO	A	E	DP
Buchholz	.921	7	14	21	3	5
Miclat	.987	45	86	144	3	39
Profar	.970	7	18	14	1	1

	Solarte	.980	88	151	234	8	60

Third Base	PCT	G	PO	A	E	DP
Bianucci	.833	8	7	13	4	1
Buchholz	.921	34	25	57	7	4
Chirinos	.895	10	3	14	2	0
Miclat	1.000	3	1	6	0	1
Olt	.923	63	30	125	13	9
Solarte	.956	20	9	34	2	4
Teahen	.929	10	12	14	2	1

Shortstop	PCT	G	PO	A	E	DP
Garcia	.962	42	62	139	8	35
Harris	.947	12	18	36	3	11
Miclat	.929	31	52	66	9	14
Profar	.959	30	51	88	6	28

	Rodriguez	.948	12	20	35	3	9
	Solarte	.977	20	35	50	2	12

Outfield	PCT	G	PO	A	E	DP
Adduci	.994	95	169	0	1	0
Beltre	.995	94	212	4	1	2
Bianucci	1.000	3	2	0	0	0
Butler	.972	101	170	4	5	2
Cunningham	.993	85	138	1	1	0
Garcia	1.000	5	7	0	0	0
Hoying	.970	45	94	4	3	1
McGuiness	.917	5	11	0	1	0
Onaka	1.000	1	1	0	0	0
Solarte	1.000	6	3	0	0	0

FRISCO ROUGHRIDERS   DOUBLE-A
TEXAS LEAGUE

Batting	B-T	HT	WT	DOB	AVG	vLH	vRH	G	AB	R	H	2B	3B	HR	RBI	BB	HBP	SH	SF	SO	SB	CS	SLG	OBP
Alberto, Hanser	R-R	5-11	175	10-17-92	.213	.155	.228	100	356	37	76	6	4	4	40	16	5	1	6	41	13	5	.287	.253
Baker, Jeff	R-R	6-2	210	6-21-81	.182	—	.182	3	11	0	2	0	0	0	0	0	0	0	0	2	0	0	.182	.182
Benson, Joe	R-R	6-1	215	3-5-88	.205	.233	.196	37	132	18	27	4	3	5	16	15	2	0	1	44	3	1	.394	.293
Berkman, Lance	B-L	6-1	220	2-10-76	.250	—	.250	2	4	2	1	0	0	0	1	3	0	0	0	1	0	0	.250	.571
Buchholz, Alex	R-R	6-0	185	9-30-87	.279	.305	.273	79	301	37	84	17	1	13	40	17	10	1	1	31	1	1	.472	.337
Chiang, Chih-Hsien	L-R	6-2	195	2-21-88	.263	.273	.260	125	476	61	125	36	2	11	52	23	2	3	3	88	0	1	.416	.298
Gentry, Craig	R-R	6-2	190	11-29-83	.231	—	.231	4	13	2	3	1	0	0	1	1	0	0	1	3	0	0	.308	.267
Herrera, Odubel	L-R	5-11	165	12-29-91	.257	.238	.262	101	389	37	100	12	7	2	30	17	1	3	2	67	15	5	.339	.289
Hoying, Jared	L-R	6-3	190	5-18-89	.242	.273	.233	40	153	17	37	9	3	5	24	13	1	0	1	45	3	1	.438	.304
Kinsler, Ian	R-R	6-0	200	6-22-82	.000	—	.000	2	8	0	0	0	0	0	0	0	0	0	0	3	0	0	.000	.111
Martinez, Teodoro	R-R	5-11	155	3-16-92	.248	.305	.235	117	443	51	110	11	1	15	47	18	4	4	1	68	21	9	.379	.283
Miclat, Greg	B-R	5-8	180	7-23-87	.200	.600	.100	5	25	5	5	0	0	0	1	0	0	0	0	9	0	0	.200	.231
Moreland, Mitch	L-L	6-2	240	9-6-85	.500	.400	.571	3	12	3	6	3	0	0	3	0	0	0	0	1	0	0	.500	.500
Nicholas, Brett	L-R	6-2	210	7-18-88	.289	.239	.303	136	506	71	146	25	3	21	91	46	13	0	10	123	2	1	.474	.357
Odor, Rougned	L-R	5-11	170	2-3-94	.306	.345	.295	30	134	20	41	8	2	6	19	9	1	0	0	24	5	2	.530	.354
Olt, Mike	R-R	6-2	210	8-27-88	.333	—	.333	3	12	1	4	2	0	1	2	0	0	0	0	6	0	0	.750	.333
Pierzynski, A.J.	L-R	6-3	235	12-30-76	.167	.000	.333	2	6	0	1	0	0	0	0	0	0	0	0	1	0	0	.167	.167
Rodriguez, Guilder	B-R	6-1	160	7-24-83	.236	.283	.224	85	301	44	71	8	0	1	13	37	2	6	2	34	15	7	.272	.322
Rua, Ryan	R-R	6-2	180	3-11-90	.233	.350	.197	23	86	19	20	2	1	3	9	7	2	0	0	24	1	0	.384	.305
Sams, Kalian	R-R	6-2	248	8-25-86	.286	.214	.302	20	77	11	22	1	0	4	10	8	0	0	1	20	6	0	.455	.349
2-team total (26 San Antonio)					.268	—	—	46	157	27	42	8	0	14	37	28	2	0	1	44	10	0	.586	.383
Sardinas, Luis	B-R	6-1	150	5-16-93	.259	.387	.221	29	135	12	35	4	0	1	15	4	1	1	0	21	5	2	.311	.286
Selen, Alejandro	R-R	5-10	175	3-20-89	.222	.239	.217	61	189	23	42	8	1	3	13	3	4	2	0	55	1	1	.323	.250
Serrato, Barrett	L-R	6-2	185	9-1-90	.250	—	.250	1	4	0	1	0	0	0	0	0	0	0	0	1	0	0	.250	.250
Strausborger, Ryan	R-R	6-0	180	3-4-88	.217	.256	.208	133	461	50	100	20	5	10	51	38	7	11	1	102	28	9	.347	.286
Telis, Tomas	B-R	5-8	175	6-18-91	.264	.250	.267	91	348	32	92	19	0	4	43	10	4	3	4	46	8	2	.353	.290
Teschner, Brett	R-R	6-3	225	8-23-91	.250	.000	.333	2	4	1	1	0	0	0	0	0	1	0	0	0	1	0	.250	.400
Zaneski, Zach	R-R	6-2	215	6-27-86	.190	.216	.179	47	163	15	31	5	0	5	19	15	1	0	0	45	0	1	.313	.263

Pitching	B-T	HT	WT	DOB	W	L	ERA	G	GS	CG	SV	IP	H	R	ER	HR	BB	SO	AVG	vLH	vRH	K/9	BB/9
Bleier, Richard	L-L	6-3	215	4-16-87	5	5	3.18	34	2	0	4	62	61	27	22	5	13	41	.254	.131	.321	5.92	1.88
Bonilla, Lisalverto	R-R	6-0	175	6-18-90	2	0	0.30	21	0	0	6	30	16	1	1	0	9	50	.152	.167	.143	14.84	2.67
Brigham, Jake	R-R	6-3	210	2-20-88	0	0	0.00	7	0	0	2	14	5	0	0	0	7	17	.116	.200	.043	11.20	4.61
Buckel, Cody	R-R	6-1	185	6-18-92	0	5	20.25	6	5	0	0	9	10	27	21	2	28	9	.303	.364	.273	8.68	27.00
Claudio, Alexander	L-L	6-3	160	1-31-92	1	5	2.84	21	0	0	0	32	28	16	10	2	11	29	.243	.116	.319	8.24	3.13
Edwards, Jon	R-R	6-5	230	1-8-88	0	1	5.28	9	0	0	0	15	15	10	9	3	8	16	.259	.353	.220	9.39	4.70
Eickhoff, Jerad	R-R	6-4	200	7-2-90	1	1	7.45	6	6	0	0	29	34	24	24	6	14	13	.304	.292	.313	4.03	4.34
Feierabend, Ryan	L-L	6-3	225	8-22-85	1	2	3.86	5	5	0	0	28	31	14	12	4	5	22	.292	.235	.303	7.07	1.61
Font, Wilmer	R-R	6-4	230	5-24-90	1	2	1.41	26	0	0	10	32	14	8	5	2	24	45	.132	.119	.141	12.66	6.75
Harrison, Matt	L-L	6-4	250	9-16-85	0	1	1.80	2	2	0	0	5	5	1	1	0	2	5	.263	.143	.333	9.00	3.60
Henry, Randy	R-R	6-3	190	5-10-90	2	0	1.07	31	0	0	1	51	32	9	6	1	7	40	.178	.133	.210	7.11	1.24
Jackson, Luke	R-R	6-2	185	8-24-91	2	0	0.67	6	4	0	0	27	13	2	2	0	12	30	.144	.119	.167	10.00	4.00
Klein, Phil	R-R	6-7	240	4-30-89	5	1	2.52	29	2	0	0	54	45	23	15	3	44	74	.230	.256	.209	12.41	7.38
Lewis, Colby	R-R	6-4	240	8-2-79	0	1	7.00	5	5	0	0	18	23	14	14	4	6	15	.295	.385	.211	7.50	2.00
Martinez, Nick	L-R	6-1	175	8-5-90	2	0	1.13	5	4	0	0	32	11	6	4	1	7	23	.107	.111	.103	6.47	1.97
Mavare, Jose	R-R	6-0	175	2-19-90	3	3	5.29	27	6	0	0	68	66	42	40	12	30	66	.257	.213	.289	8.74	3.97
McBride, Nick	R-R	6-4	180	5-13-91	2	7	6.19	13	13	0	0	57	82	43	39	2	23	31	.349	.372	.333	4.92	3.65

Name	B-T	HT	WT	DOB	W	L	ERA	G	GS	CG	SV	IP	H	R	ER	HR	BB	SO	AVG	vLH	vRH	K/9	BB/9
McClellan, Kyle	R-R	6-2	215	6-12-84	2	0	3.33	19	0	0	0	27	29	11	10	2	6	27	.282	.333	.257	9.00	2.00
Mendez, Roman	R-R	6-3	190	7-25-90	2	0	1.82	16	0	0	2	25	12	6	5	1	11	24	.146	.148	.145	8.76	4.01
Mendoza, Francisco	R-R	6-0	175	12-7-87	0	1	1.50	9	0	0	0	12	8	3	2	2	8	10	.195	.238	.150	7.50	6.00
Miller, Justin	R-R	6-3	215	6-13-87	1	0	6.19	16	0	0	2	16	16	12	11	1	7	21	.254	.417	.154	11.81	3.94
Ogando, Alexi	R-R	6-4	200	10-5-83	1	0	0.00	1	0	0	0	6	4	2	0	1	0	4	.190	.222	.167	6.00	0.00
Perez, Martin	L-L	6-0	190	4-4-91	0	1	11.05	2	2	0	0	7	14	9	9	1	2	2	.400	.364	.417	2.45	2.45
Pimentel, Carlos	R-R	6-3	180	12-1-89	8	7	4.09	22	21	0	0	117	102	59	53	16	37	122	.233	.267	.211	9.41	2.85
Pucetas, Kevin	R-R	6-4	225	11-27-84	10	8	4.67	22	19	1	0	118	128	69	61	11	36	64	.286	.353	.239	4.90	2.75
Ramirez, Neil	R-R	6-4	190	5-25-89	9	3	3.84	21	21	0	0	103	77	46	44	8	42	127	.213	.200	.222	11.10	3.67
Reyes, Jimmy	L-L	5-10	195	3-7-89	2	4	2.69	44	0	0	0	67	56	25	20	5	20	57	.221	.176	.244	7.66	2.69
Rodebaugh, Ryan	L-R	6-0	165	3-30-89	1	1	3.18	20	1	0	2	34	21	13	12	3	13	41	.176	.289	.108	10.85	3.44
Rowen, Ben	R-R	6-4	190	11-15-88	3	0	0.53	31	0	0	10	34	23	3	2	1	11	28	.198	.208	.191	7.49	2.94
Soria, Joakim	R-R	6-3	200	5-18-84	0	0	0.00	4	0	0	0	4	0	0	0	0	0	4	.000	.000	.000	9.00	0.00
Tepesch, Nick	R-R	6-4	225	10-12-88	0	0	1.50	2	2	0	0	6	7	1	1	0	2	3	.280	.300	.267	4.50	3.00
Tufts, Tyler	R-R	6-3	200	12-5-86	3	5	3.34	27	19	0	0	100	106	42	37	11	21	40	.277	.251	.296	3.61	1.90
Van Meter, Joe	R-R	6-0		10-18-88	0	4	7.56	6	0	0	0	8	13	7	7	1	2	7	.361	.400	.333	7.56	2.16
Wolf, Ross	R-R	6-0	180	10-18-82	0	1	5.40	1	0	0	0	2	3	1	1	0	0	1	.429	.333	.500	5.40	0.00

Fielding

Catcher	PCT	G	PO	A	E	DP	PB
Nicholas	.992	14	108	11	1	2	1
Pierzynski	1.000	1	5	2	0	2	0
Telis	.991	82	608	68	6	2	12
Teschner	.857	1	6	0	1	0	0
Zaneski	.998	44	363	38	1	1	4

First Base	PCT	G	PO	A	E	DP
Baker	1.000	1	9	0	0	1
Buchholz	1.000	1	13	0	0	0
Moreland	1.000	2	13	1	0	0
Nicholas	.994	117	991	79	7	98
Rodriguez	.990	20	181	8	2	10
Serrato	1.000	1	9	0	0	2

Second Base	PCT	G	PO	A	E	DP
Herrera	.975	93	171	261	11	58

	PCT	G	PO	A	E	DP
Kinsler	1.000	1	3	2	0	1
Miclat	1.000	1	2	3	0	1
Odor	.955	30	78	93	8	20
Rodriguez	1.000	14	19	44	0	7
Selen	1.000	1	2	0	0	0
Strausborger	.800	1	1	3	1	2

Third Base	PCT	G	PO	A	E	DP
Buchholz	.952	71	40	137	9	11
Miclat	1.000	2	3	3	0	0
Olt	1.000	3	1	5	0	0
Rodriguez	.979	36	24	71	2	8
Rua	.855	23	11	36	8	3
Selen	.833	6	5	10	3	1

Shortstop	PCT	G	PO	A	E	DP
Alberto	.964	98	175	283	17	59

	PCT	G	PO	A	E	DP
Herrera	1.000	1	1	1	0	0
Miclat	1.000	2	7	8	0	5
Rodriguez	.979	13	17	30	1	3
Sardinas	.956	29	44	85	6	18

Outfield	PCT	G	PO	A	E	DP
Baker	1.000	1	1	0	0	0
Benson	.986	37	66	5	1	2
Chiang	.976	93	150	13	4	3
Gentry	1.000	3	4	0	0	0
Hoying	.987	37	69	6	1	2
Martinez	.973	102	170	8	5	1
Sams	1.000	14	22	1	0	0
Selen	1.000	15	14	0	0	0
Strausborger	.997	128	287	8	1	2

MYRTLE BEACH PELICANS — HIGH CLASS A

CAROLINA LEAGUE

Batting	B-T	HT	WT	DOB	AVG	vLH	vRH	G	AB	R	H	2B	3B	HR	RBI	BB	HBP	SH	SF	SO	SB	CS	SLG	OBP
Adams, Trever	R-R	6-0	200	9-30-88	.257	.224	.267	135	506	69	130	28	2	11	82	53	9	1	8	118	10	6	.385	.333
Alberto, Hanser	R-R	5-11	175	10-17-92	.258	.238	.263	29	97	6	25	5	0	0	7	4	2	1	0	8	3	1	.309	.301
Alfaro, Jorge	R-R	6-2	185	6-11-93	.182	.000	.182	3	11	4	2	0	0	0	2	0	0	0		5	0	0	.182	.308
Beck, Preston	L-R	6-2	190	10-26-90	.245	.300	.227	98	322	38	79	14	4	3	39	47	3		4	62	10	4	.342	.345
Bolinger, Royce	R-R	6-2	200	8-12-90	.261	.224	.273	72	272	33	71	17	3	4	25	17	3	3		68	5	4	.390	.308
Cantwell, Pat	R-R	6-2	190	4-10-90	.249	.208	.265	70	257	35	64	13	0	1	24	17	8	5	2	44	5	2	.311	.313
Cone, Zach	R-R	6-2	205	12-14-89	.308	.600	.238	7	26	3	8	2	0	0	0	1	0	0		9	1	0	.385	.333
Deglan, Kellin	L-R	6-2	195	5-3-92	.231	.278	.220	89	308	37	71	10	2	12	49	33	14	2	2	94	0	0	.393	.331
Garcia, Edwin	B-R	6-1	170	3-1-91	.263	.304	.249	86	308	30	81	16	0	2	34	22	0	2	6	48	3	2	.334	.307
Grayson, Chris	L-L	6-0	190	9-15-89	.199	.155	.215	112	372	52	74	18	3	4	28	51	4	5	6	71	19	9	.296	.298
Herrera, Odubel	L-R	5-11	165	12-29-91	.295	.333	.288	29	95	13	28	2	1	1	5	16	1	2	1	19	2	2	.368	.398
Maloney, Joe	R-R	6-2	190	7-27-90	.200	.167	.211	74	285	28	57	17	1	6	46	10	8	1	4	85	0	1	.330	.244
Odor, Rougned	L-R	5-11	170	2-3-94	.305	.258	.319	100	377	65	115	33	4	5	59	26	15	2	5	67	27	8	.454	.369
Onaka, Hirotoshi	B-R	5-10	175	7-11-88	.200	—	.200	1	5	0	1	0	0	0	0	0	0	0	0	1	0	1	.200	.200
Robinson, Drew	L-R	6-1	185	4-20-92	.257	.239	.262	122	436	62	112	26	7	8	70	72	7	5	3	124	10	2	.404	.369
Sardinas, Luis	B-R	6-1	150	5-16-93	.269	.289	.307	97	383	69	114	15	3	1	31	32	7	5	5	54	27	8	.360	.358
Skole, Jake	L-R	6-1	200	1-17-92	.211	.118	.232	117	361	59	76	22	1	3	40	69	2	2	3	94	8	4	.302	.338
Torres, Kevin	L-R	6-3	195	2-24-90	.205	.107	.232	38	127	18	26	5	0	3	12	12	4	1	2	30	2	0	.315	.290

Pitching	B-T	HT	WT	DOB	W	L	ERA	G	GS	CG	SV	IP	H	R	ER	HR	BB	SO	AVG	vLH	vRH	K/9	BB/9
Asher, Alec	R-R	6-4	218	10-4-91	9	7	2.90	26	25	0	0	133	120	60	43	10	40	139	.235	.241	.232	9.38	2.70
Dennis, Taylor	R-R	6-1	175	3-31-89	1	3	5.55	19	1	0	0	36	30	24	22	3	18	22	.240	.200	.263	5.55	4.54
Edwards, Jon	R-R	6-5	230	1-8-88	3	1	3.57	26	0	0	4	40	28	19	16	0	31	51	.196	.255	.159	11.38	6.92
Ege, Cody	L-L	6-1	185	5-8-91	1	0	0.00	2	0	0	0	2	1	0	0	0	0	3	.200	.200	.000	16.20	0.00
Eickhoff, Jerad	R-R	6-4	200	7-2-90	7	3	3.41	21	21	0	0	116	110	52	44	9	26	80	.252	.216	.292	6.21	2.02
Gonzalez, Alex	R-R	6-2	195	1-15-92	0	0	2.84	5	5	0	0	19	15	8	6	1	9	15	.221	.250	.194	7.11	4.26
Harvey, Ryan	L-R	6-2	210	1-31-91	7	2	3.41	42	1	0	8	58	48	26	22	3	36	54	.233	.242	.224	8.38	5.59
Jackson, Luke	R-R	6-2	185	8-24-91	9	4	2.41	19	19	0	0	101	79	30	27	6	47	104	.216	.218	.215	9.27	4.19
Kendall, Cody	R-R	6-2	210	12-12-89	1	1	3.63	9	0	0	0	17	13	11	7	1	9	6	.206	.231	.189	3.12	4.67
Klein, Phil	R-R	6-7	240	4-30-89	1	0	1.98	7	0	0	0	14	6	4	3	0	3	12	.128	.222	.069	7.90	1.98
Lamb, Will	L-L	6-6	180	9-9-90	5	3	5.17	39	1	0	1	70	60	42	40	8	39	62	.234	.195	.251	8.01	5.04
Martinez, Nick	L-R	6-1	175	8-5-90	10	7	2.87	22	21	1	0	119	106	47	38	5	38	105	.236	.211	.254	7.92	2.87
Mavare, Jose	R-R	6-0	175	2-19-90	0	1	2.38	7	0	0	2	11	7	5	3	1	3	12	.188	.160		9.53	2.38
McBride, Nick	R-R	6-4	180	5-13-91	0	5	3.88	19	5	1	2	53	58	26	23	2	19	31	.280	.304	.261	5.23	3.21
McElwee, Josh	R-R	6-4	227	6-12-89	3	2	1.04	17	0	0	0	35	10	4	2		11	34	.212	.208	.215	8.83	2.86
Mendoza, Francisco	R-R	6-0	175	12-7-87	3	2	3.55	27	0	0	7	38	39	22	15	1	21	46	.277	.322	.244	10.89	4.97

Name	B-T	HT	WT	DOB	W	L	ERA	G	GS	CG	SV	IP	H	R	ER	HR	BB	SO	AVG	vLH	vRH	K/9	BB/9
Monegro, Jose	R-R	6-3	200	9-19-89	0	0	5.06	8	0	0	1	11	9	7	6	3	4	9	.231	.214	.240	7.59	3.38
Parra, Luis	L-L	6-2	160	11-21-91	0	2	3.71	5	5	0	0	27	29	12	11	2	10	18	.276	.292	.272	6.08	3.38
Payano, Victor	L-L	6-5	185	10-17-92	5	7	6.29	22	21	0	0	87	85	64	61	11	57	96	.256	.225	.264	9.89	5.87
Pucetas, Kevin	R-R	6-4	225	11-27-84	1	3	4.78	6	6	0	0	32	32	20	17	3	29	22	.281	.205	.320	6.19	8.16
Rojas, Randol	R-R	6-0	160	9-28-90	4	3	4.96	39	0	0	3	69	66	53	38	5	30	64	.245	.243	.247	8.35	3.91
Schwendel, Paul	R-R	6-5	220	8-9-89	2	2	4.89	19	3	0	1	46	49	26	25	3	20	34	.280	.224	.323	6.65	3.91
Smith, Tyler	R-R	6-3	195	2-3-92	0	0	1.08	4	0	0	1	8	3	1	1	1	1	9	.107	.222	.053	9.72	1.08
Van Meter, Joe	R-R	6-2	195	10-18-88	3	4	3.62	24	6	0	4	55	53	26	22	5	26	64	.255	.224	.287	10.54	4.28
Zouzalik, Michael	L-R	6-3	195	7-13-90	2	0	3.95	9	0	0	1	14	15	8	6	0	8	13	.294	.308	.280	8.56	5.27

Fielding

Catcher	PCT	G	PO	A	E	DP	PB
Cantwell	.993	66	524	60	4	13	16
Deglan	.985	71	545	57	9	5	10
Maloney	1.000	3	19	3	0	0	1
Torres	1.000	4	29	3	0	1	0

First Base	PCT	G	PO	A	E	DP
Adams	.993	49	424	23	3	47
Alfaro	.875	1	6	1	1	2
Garcia	1.000	3	21	3	0	4
Maloney	.981	54	390	23	8	48
Torres	.981	34	297	10	6	27

Second Base	PCT	G	PO	A	E	DP
Garcia	.974	35	58	90	4	25
Herrera	.929	23	39	65	8	18
Odor	.957	84	153	229	17	58
Sardinas	.667	1	2	0	1	0

Third Base	PCT	G	PO	A	E	DP
Garcia	.918	25	15	52	6	3
Robinson	.929	115	92	197	22	25

Shortstop	PCT	G	PO	A	E	DP
Alberto	.953	29	54	88	7	26

	PCT	G	PO	A	E	DP
Garcia	.969	22	28	65	3	18
Sardinas	.936	92	128	236	25	54

Outfield	PCT	G	PO	A	E	DP
Adams	1.000	33	51	1	0	0
Beck	.961	34	134	13	6	6
Bolinger	.980	70	138	8	3	2
Cone	1.000	7	18	0	0	0
Grayson	.965	108	186	8	7	1
Onaka	1.000	1	2	1	0	0
Skole	.996	111	235	10	1	3

HICKORY CRAWDADS
SOUTH ATLANTIC LEAGUE
LOW CLASS A

Batting	B-T	HT	WT	DOB	AVG	vLH	vRH	G	AB	R	H	2B	3B	HR	RBI	BB	HBP	SH	SF	SO	SB	CS	SLG	OBP
Akins, Jordan	R-R	6-3	192	4-19-92	.221	.240	.216	95	358	36	79	19	1	7	35	7	2	0	1	129	9	6	.338	.239
Alfaro, Jorge	R-R	6-2	185	6-11-93	.258	.257	.258	104	372	63	96	22	1	16	53	28	18	0	2	111	16	3	.452	.338
Beck, Preston	L-R	6-2	190	10-26-90	.333	.000	.364	8	24	6	8	2	0	1	5	1	0	0	0	4	0	0	.417	.467
Brinson, Lewis	R-R	6-3	170	5-8-94	.237	.253	.233	122	447	64	106	18	2	21	52	48	8	0	0	191	24	7	.427	.322
Gallo, Joey	L-R	6-5	205	11-19-93	.245	.309	.228	106	392	82	96	19	5	38	78	48	5	0	1	165	14	1	.610	.334
Garia, Chris	B-R	6-0	165	12-16-92	.156	.200	.143	26	109	10	17	0	0	2	6	3	3	1	1	23	6	4	.193	.198
Guzman, Ronald	L-L	6-5	205	10-20-94	.272	.195	.295	49	173	17	47	8	0	4	26	11	4	0	3	27	0	0	.387	.325
Lyon, David	B-R	5-11	190	1-19-90	.239	.214	.246	77	255	31	61	14	2	9	31	28	3	0	1	85	1	0	.416	.321
Maloney, Joe	R-R	6-2	190	7-27-90	.230	.250	.224	43	148	16	34	10	0	8	22	14	2	0	0	57	1	1	.459	.305
Marte, Luis	R-R	6-1	170	12-15-93	.217	.205	.221	125	423	46	92	16	0	3	27	13	3	14	1	99	16	4	.277	.245
Mazara, Nomar	L-L	6-4	195	4-26-95	.236	.165	.254	126	453	48	107	23	2	13	62	44	6	0	3	131	1	2	.382	.310
Mendez, Luis	B-R	5-9	155	1-1-93	.204	.125	.220	16	49	7	10	2	0	0	4	3	1	1	1	11	2	1	.245	.259
Onaka, Hirotoshi	B-R	5-10	175	7-11-88	.170	.143	.175	16	47	2	8	1	0	2	7	2	0	2	1	10	0	0	.319	.200
Rua, Ryan	R-R	6-2	180	3-11-90	.251	.288	.240	104	367	70	92	24	1	29	82	49	12	0	2	91	13	2	.559	.356
Selen, Alejandro	R-R	5-10	175	3-20-89	.400	.500	.333	7	20	4	8	3	0	2	8	3	2	0	1	3	0	0	.850	.500
Teschner, Brett	R-R	6-3	225	8-23-91	.158	.000	.250	5	19	1	3	2	0	0	0	0	0	0	0	9	0	0	.263	.158
Torres, Kevin	L-R	6-3	195	2-6-90	.235	.000	.289	28	102	7	24	6	0	1	8	2	4	1	0	20	0	0	.324	.279
Urbanus, Nick	B-R	6-1	175	3-29-92	.150	.184	.139	55	160	15	24	5	0	0	6	15	2	5	1	50	3	1	.181	.230
Vickerson, Nick	R-R	5-11	205	7-8-89	.217	.215	.218	72	244	45	53	11	0	7	24	52	6	3	1	69	14	4	.348	.366
Williams, Nick	L-L	6-3	195	9-8-93	.293	.265	.300	95	376	70	110	19	12	17	60	15	11	0	2	110	8	5	.543	.337
Wrenn, Taylor	L-R	5-11	175	12-22-89	.182	.000	.190	6	22	3	4	1	0	1	2	2	1	1	0	8	0	0	.364	.280

Pitching	B-T	HT	WT	DOB	W	L	ERA	G	GS	CG	SV	IP	H	R	ER	HR	BB	SO	AVG	vLH	vRH	K/9	BB/9
Bores, Ryan	R-R	6-3	190	10-10-90	3	2	4.61	24	6	0	1	68	78	36	35	6	20	34	.286	.298	.278	4.48	2.63
Brooks, Eric	R-R	6-2	198	8-29-90	0	0	9.00	3	3	0	0	11	19	13	11	0	6	9	.396	.321	.500	7.36	4.91
Burns, Joe	L-L	6-0	200	8-3-89	4	5	4.89	31	0	0	2	50	51	32	27	4	18	35	.266	.283	.259	6.34	3.26
Claudio, Alexander	L-L	6-3	160	1-31-92	3	1	1.15	24	0	0	11	47	22	7	6	2	7	62	.139	.149	.135	11.87	1.34
Cowgill, Coby	R-R	6-1	200	3-23-91	0	0	2.87	10	0	0	0	16	11	7	5	3	12	12	.190	.185	.194	6.89	6.89
Edwards, C.J.	R-R	6-2	155	9-3-91	8	2	1.83	18	18	1	0	93	62	28	19	0	34	122	.186	.180	.190	11.76	3.28
Ege, Cody	L-L	6-1	185	5-8-91	3	0	0.42	10	0	0	1	22	12	5	1	0	5	29	.160	.056	.193	12.05	2.08
Faulkner, Andrew	R-L	6-3	180	9-12-92	6	5	3.48	21	19	0	0	111	123	54	43	8	37	84	.280	.310	.267	6.79	2.99
Kela, Keone	R-R	6-1	190	4-16-93	2	2	2.41	12	0	0	1	19	18	6	5	0	6	20	.250	.219	.275	9.64	2.89
Kendall, Cody	R-R	6-2	210	12-12-89	2	2	3.43	25	0	0	7	42	47	21	16	1	6	25	.278	.311	.259	5.36	1.29
Kukuruda, John	R-R	6-4	180	9-12-90	2	1	3.81	9	1	0	0	26	28	15	11	1	13	28	.272	.146	.355	9.69	4.50
Leclerc, Anyelo	R-R	6-0	165	12-19-93	3	4	3.36	39	0	0	5	59	53	26	22	2	21	77	.240	.325	.191	11.75	3.20
Lopez, Frank	L-L	6-1	175	2-18-94	3	7	4.79	16	16	0	0	73	74	46	39	2	35	79	.261	.263	.260	9.70	4.30
McElwee, Josh	R-R	6-4	227	6-12-89	2	1	10.13	11	0	0	2	13	23	18	15	5	10	22	.371	.346	.389	14.85	6.75
Monegro, Jose	R-R	6-3	200	9-19-89	1	2	4.78	15	5	0	2	49	49	28	26	10	12	34	.259	.219	.284	6.24	2.20
Niggli, John	R-R	6-4	185	5-2-90	1	1	2.92	2	2	0	0	12	13	6	4	0	1	8	.260	.308	.243	5.84	0.73
Parra, Luis	L-L	6-2	160	11-21-91	5	4	2.34	15	15	0	0	81	74	30	21	2	32	65	.239	.213	.249	7.25	3.57
Perez, Santo	R-R	6-5	200	11-22-88	0	3	3.00	6	0	0	0	12	13	4	4	1	4	3	.295	.263	.320	3.00	2.25
Sadzeck, Connor	R-R	6-5	195	10-1-91	12	4	2.25	24	24	0	0	132	102	43	33	4	51	78	.216	.241	.198	5.32	3.48
Schwendel, Paul	R-R	6-5	220	8-9-89	1	2	4.18	5	5	0	0	28	27	16	13	1	8	21	.255	.211	.279	6.75	2.57
Slack, Ryne	L-L	6-2	221	12-22-92	0	1	9.00	9	0	0	0	14	16	15	14	3	13	18	.291	.267	.300	11.57	8.36
Smith, Tyler	R-R	6-3	195	2-3-92	4	5	5.49	26	11	0	0	79	78	54	48	7	40	67	.262	.303	.235	7.67	4.58
Stafford, Sam	L-L	6-4	200	4-27-90	3	6	5.37	28	7	0	1	57	64	38	34	2	37	63	.290	.273	.297	9.95	5.84
Valdespina, Jose	R-R	6-6	220	3-22-92	4	1	5.70	30	0	0	2	43	51	33	27	2	20	46	.287	.296	.280	9.70	4.22
Vasquez, Kelvin	R-R	6-4	191	4-6-93	2	2	6.49	8	7	0	0	26	31	23	19	4	18	19	.292	.259	.302	6.49	6.15
Wolff, Sam	R-R	6-1	190	4-14-91	1	0	0.00	11	0	0	5	14	8	1	0	0	3	23	.160	.105	.194	15.15	1.98

Fielding

Catcher	PCT	G	PO	A	E	DP	PB
Alfaro	.986	82	618	80	10	7	26
Lyon	.996	59	427	58	2	6	7
Vickerson	.893	5	22	3	3	0	1

First Base	PCT	G	PO	A	E	DP
Alfaro	1.000	17	123	7	0	9
Beck	1.000	5	46	2	0	5
Guzman	.977	45	361	19	9	38
Maloney	.975	37	324	34	9	34
Mendez	1.000	1	12	1	0	0
Teschner	1.000	1	11	1	0	0
Torres	.981	28	245	13	5	23
Vickerson	.974	9	71	4	2	8

Second Base	PCT	G	PO	A	E	DP
Mendez	1.000	6	10	16	0	3
Onaka	1.000	2	2	4	0	0
Rua	.968	88	169	256	14	58
Selen	1.000	7	9	23	0	8
Urbanus	.971	25	46	55	3	12
Vickerson	.957	13	18	26	2	6
Wrenn	1.000	6	12	16	0	2

Third Base	PCT	G	PO	A	E	DP
Gallo	.924	101	57	186	20	13
Rua	.905	8	7	12	2	1
Urbanus	.897	17	7	28	4	1
Vickerson	.891	16	10	31	5	2

Shortstop	PCT	G	PO	A	E	DP
Marte	.940	125	197	383	37	84

	PCT	G	PO	A	E	DP
Mendez	.867	4	7	6	2	3
Urbanus	.917	13	16	39	5	8

Outfield	PCT	G	PO	A	E	DP
Akins	.963	73	123	7	5	2
Beck	1.000	1	2	0	0	0
Brinson	.966	120	247	9	9	1
Garia	.917	13	21	1	2	0
Mazara	.950	115	178	13	10	2
Mendez	—	1	0	0	0	0
Onaka	1.000	9	10	0	0	0
Rua	—	1	0	0	0	0
Urbanus	1.000	1	1	0	0	0
Vickerson	.944	17	17	0	1	0
Williams	.942	81	91	6	6	3

SPOKANE INDIANS

SHORT-SEASON

NORTHWEST LEAGUE

Batting	B-T	HT	WT	DOB	AVG	vLH	vRH	G	AB	R	H	2B	3B	HR	RBI	BB	HBP	SH	SF	SO	SB	CS	SLG	OBP
Akins, Jordan	R-R	6-3	192	4-19-92	.209	.118	.230	22	91	13	19	6	0	4	11	3	2	0	0	24	1	2	.407	.250
Castro, JanLuis	B-R	5-9	165	1-4-94	.254	.216	.264	69	248	28	63	11	1	4	37	16	3	0	1	46	0	1	.355	.306
Cordell, Ryan	R-R	6-4	205	3-31-92	.241	.309	.220	64	232	34	56	12	0	5	23	23	5	1	1	53	19	4	.358	.322
Duran, Robbie	R-R	5-11	190	7-4-90	.097	.200	.048	12	31	1	3	0	0	0	3	2	0	0	0	11	0	0	.097	.152
Garcia, Brandon	L-R	6-1	195	6-26-90	.179	.250	.169	26	67	9	12	5	0	2	5	11	0	0	0	25	0	0	.343	.295
Garia, Chris	B-R	6-0	165	12-16-92	.256	.225	.264	42	180	29	46	4	5	4	19	7	4	5	0	36	18	5	.400	.298
Greene, Marcus	R-R	5-11	195	8-19-94	.227	.261	.217	58	203	27	46	11	1	3	15	41	4	0	0	49	3	2	.335	.367
Jackson, Joe	L-R	6-1	180	5-5-92	.215	.152	.232	45	158	15	34	5	1	2	16	20	1	0	0	36	1	0	.297	.307
Jarmon, Jamie	R-R	6-1	190	6-21-94	.150	.269	.117	37	120	14	18	3	0	1	14	10	1	0	0	42	0	1	.200	.221
Johnson, Saquan	R-R	6-2	175	2-26-93	.113	.095	.120	24	71	6	8	0	2	0	3	7	1	1	0	39	1	2	.169	.203
Moorman, Chuck	R-R	5-11	200	1-9-94	.222	.000	.222	3	9	0	2	0	0	0	2	0	1	0	3	0	0	.222	.364
Onaka, Hirotoshi	B-R	5-10	175	7-11-88	.182	.000	.182	6	11	2	2	1	0	0	4	4	0	1	1	2	1	.273	.375
Pinto, Eduard	L-L	5-11	150	10-23-94	.250	.214	.258	22	80	3	20	1	0	0	2	5	1	2	0	7	0	1	.263	.302
Roa, Gabriel	R-R	5-8	165	3-26-92	.240	.239	.240	66	200	23	48	5	1	0	23	25	8	2	2	32	4	1	.275	.345
Schiller, Cam	B-R	6-0	195	11-30-89	.222	.203	.227	69	257	25	57	11	2	1	19	22	2	1	0	51	2	0	.292	.288
Serrato, Barrett	L-R	6-2	185	9-1-90	.220	.242	.215	50	168	15	37	6	0	2	19	25	1	1	5	50	1	0	.292	.317
Torres, Kevin	L-R	6-3	195	2-24-90	.291	.324	.281	39	148	16	43	9	1	3	18	11	0	0	3	25	0	0	.426	.333
Triunfel, Alberto	R-R	5-11	160	2-1-94	.217	.273	.204	32	115	14	25	7	1	2	18	12	2	3	1	23	2	6	.348	.300
Van Hoosier, Evan	R-R	5-11	185	12-24-93	.249	.282	.238	46	169	21	42	9	2	2	9	16	5	1	0	31	3	1	.361	.332

Pitching	B-T	HT	WT	DOB	W	L	ERA	G	GS	CG	SV	IP	H	R	ER	HR	BB	SO	AVG	vLH	vRH	K/9	BB/9
Alvarez, Richard	R-R	6-2	200	8-14-92	2	2	3.58	16	0	0	0	33	33	16	13	1	16	33	.270	.310	.234	9.09	4.41
Anderson, Brett	R-R	6-3	185	9-3-90	1	0	7.00	7	0	0	0	9	9	8	7	1	4	8	.250	.091	.320	8.00	4.00
Brooks, Eric	R-R	6-2	198	8-29-90	2	3	2.79	16	6	0	0	58	48	21	18	3	16	61	.219	.206	.230	9.47	2.48
Castro, Kyle	R-R	6-5	194	8-18-93	1	3	8.31	10	5	0	0	30	39	30	28	2	22	35	.310	.256	.337	10.38	6.53
de la Cruz, Alex	R-R	5-11	200	10-2-91	2	0	0.46	10	0	0	1	20	15	2	1	0	4	20	.205	.214	.200	9.15	1.83
De Los Santos, Abel	R-R	6-2	180	11-21-92	4	1	3.48	20	0	0	0	41	33	16	16	4	13	48	.219	.230	.211	10.45	2.83
Dean, Travis	R-R	6-5	217	5-3-91	2	1	2.64	16	0	0	0	31	30	13	9	0	19	31	.254	.256	.253	9.10	5.58
Ege, Cody	L-L	6-1	185	5-8-91	0	0	2.70	5	0	0	1	7	6	3	2	0	0	7	.231	.125	.278	9.45	0.00
Gonzalez, Alex	R-R	6-2	195	1-15-92	0	4	4.56	9	9	0	0	24	30	16	12	1	7	20	.313	.214	.389	7.61	2.66
Kela, Keone	R-R	6-1	190	4-16-93	1	2	3.78	12	0	0	2	17	17	8	7	1	6	26	.250	.278	.219	14.04	3.24
Ledbetter, David	L-R	5-11	188	2-13-92	3	3	2.93	13	13	0	0	58	53	20	19	3	19	51	.243	.206	.273	7.87	2.93
McElwee, Josh	R-R	6-4	227	6-12-89	1	0	1.93	6	0	0	1	9	6	3	2	1	3	22	.176	.176	.176	21.21	2.89
Mendez, Yohander	L-L	6-4	178	1-17-95	1	2	3.78	8	8	0	0	33	31	18	14	4	17	23	.240	.238	.241	6.21	4.59
Niggli, John	R-R	6-4	185	5-2-90	1	1	1.59	3	3	0	0	17	11	3	3	0	3	8	.193	.108	.350	4.24	1.59
Pollorena, Luis	L-L	5-8	170	1-14-91	1	2	2.76	8	0	0	1	16	16	6	5	0	5	14	.267	.316	.244	7.71	2.76
Rodriguez, Ricardo	R-R	6-2	220	8-31-92	0	2	6.30	7	0	0	1	10	13	9	7	2	2	11	.325	.222	.409	9.90	1.80
Slack, Ryne	L-L	6-2	221	7-22-92	2	0	2.63	17	5	0	0	48	45	16	14	2	18	58	.250	.217	.317	10.88	3.38
Sprenger, Justin	R-R	6-4	199	6-11-91	3	2	4.23	19	0	0	4	28	22	13	13	1	13	31	.216	.224	.208	10.08	4.23
Straka, John	L-R	6-2	213	1-19-90	2	2	4.88	19	0	0	1	31	38	17	17	3	6	27	.299	.328	.275	7.76	1.72
Vasquez, Kelvin	R-R	6-4	191	4-6-93	2	2	2.13	14	13	0	0	63	46	18	15	3	34	72	.199	.284	.113	10.23	4.83
Wiles, Collin	R-R	6-4	212	5-30-94	2	7	3.09	14	14	0	0	67	71	32	23	4	21	40	.283	.327	.248	5.37	2.82
Wolff, Sam	R-R	6-1	190	4-14-91	3	0	1.10	10	0	0	0	16	12	2	2	0	6	21	.203	.208	.200	11.57	3.31
Zouzalik, Michael	L-R	6-3	195	7-13-90	2	0	1.35	14	0	0	4	20	13	3	3	1	6	14	.186	.222	.163	6.30	2.70

Fielding

Catcher	PCT	G	PO	A	E	DP	PB
Garcia	1.000	2	8	0	0	0	0
Greene	.982	27	250	20	5	5	1
Jackson	.987	28	213	14	3	3	7
Moorman	1.000	3	23	5	0	0	0
Torres	.995	22	186	19	1	1	2

First Base	PCT	G	PO	A	E	DP
Cordell	1.000	1	2	0	0	0

Duran	1.000	3	13	0	0	0
Garcia	.900	3	8	1	1	1
Jackson	1.000	1	9	0	0	1
Schiller	.992	28	227	15	2	20
Serrato	.993	32	270	23	2	29
Torres	1.000	17	164	6	0	13

Second Base	PCT	G	PO	A	E	DP
Castro	.976	27	36	85	3	20

Roa	1.000	14	21	32	0	8
Schiller	.864	6	3	16	3	3
Triunfel	1.000	1	2	1	0	0
Van Hoosier	.958	36	45	92	6	15

Third Base	PCT	G	PO	A	E	DP
Castro	.886	38	12	50	8	2
Duran	1.000	7	3	7	0	1
Roa	.929	6	2	11	1	2

Schiller	.933	32	21	63	6	6
Serrato	1.000	2	0	2	0	0

Shortstop	PCT	G	PO	A	E	DP
Roa	.948	46	65	118	10	26
Schiller	1.000	4	4	8	0	2
Triunfel	.945	31	54	84	8	18

Outfield	PCT	G	PO	A	E	DP
Akins	1.000	21	39	0	0	0
Cordell	.974	63	110	4	3	2
Garcia	.917	10	10	1	1	0
Garia	.986	38	69	3	1	1
Greene	.958	12	23	0	1	0
Jackson	—	1	0	0	0	0

	PCT	G	PO	A	E	DP
Jarmon	.935	35	43	0	3	0
Johnson	.786	22	10	1	3	0
Onaka	1.000	3	2	0	0	0
Pinto	.957	20	42	2	2	1
Serrato	.955	12	18	3	1	0
Van Hoosier	1.000	6	4	1	0	0

AZL RANGERS   ROOKIE

ARIZONA LEAGUE

Batting	B-T	HT	WT	DOB	AVG	vLH	vRH	G	AB	R	H	2B	3B	HR	RBI	BB	HBP	SH	SF	SO	SB	CS	SLG	OBP
Alfaro, Jorge	R-R	6-2	185	6-11-93	.429	.333	.467	6	21	5	9	2	0	2	8	2	2	0	1	6	2	0	.810	.500
Benson, Joe	R-R	6-1	215	3-5-88	.417	.000	.500	7	24	10	10	3	0	1	5	4	1	0	1	5	2	0	.667	.500
Beras, Jairo	R-R	6-5	178	12-25-95	.250	.316	.222	17	64	11	16	2	2	2	15	5	1	0	0	19	1	0	.438	.314
Bolinger, Royce	R-R	6-2	200	8-12-90	.292	.333	.286	6	24	4	7	3	0	0	2	1	2	0	0	7	1	1	.417	.370
Caraballo, Oliver	R-R	6-1	180	8-25-94	.192	.227	.176	26	73	9	14	3	0	1	11	6	1	0	1	19	3	0	.274	.259
Cedeno, Diego	L-L	5-11	160	5-19-92	.213	.276	.194	40	122	12	26	5	1	0	13	19	3	0	1	20	4	3	.270	.331
Demeritte, Travis	R-R	6-0	178	9-30-94	.285	.184	.321	39	144	31	41	5	3	4	20	29	2	0	0	49	5	1	.444	.411
Duran, Robbie	R-R	5-11	190	7-4-90	.000	—	.000	1	4	0	0	0	0	0	0	0	0	0	0	2	0	0	.000	.000
Gallo, Joey	L-R	6-5	205	11-19-93	.368	.250	.400	5	19	4	7	4	0	2	10	2	0	0	0	7	1	0	.895	.429
Garay, Carlos	R-R	6-0	178	10-5-94	.214	.261	.200	32	98	11	21	4	0	0	16	13	1	2	1	16	0	0	.255	.310
Gonzalez, Jose	R-R	6-1	175	3-16-94	.280	.293	.275	50	189	27	53	9	2	1	12	17	1	0	2	32	7	3	.365	.340
Johnson, Saquan	R-R	6-2	175	2-26-93	.259	.267	.256	18	58	8	15	5	2	0	5	9	1	0	1	18	1	1	.414	.362
Kiner-Falefa, Isiah	R-R	5-10	165	3-23-95	.322	.128	.391	41	149	36	48	5	0	0	11	15	1	4	0	24	12	3	.356	.388
Lantigua, Smerling	R-R	6-2	180	2-3-94	.211	.270	.194	45	166	23	35	11	2	5	23	7	2	1	1	52	1	2	.392	.250
McDonald, Todd	L-R	6-3	180	10-23-95	.241	.188	.263	42	162	14	39	4	4	0	15	16	1	0	0	45	4	3	.315	.309
Mendez, Luis	B-R	5-9	155	1-1-93	.281	.259	.289	53	196	29	55	6	5	1	19	20	3	4	0	33	9	5	.378	.356
Miclat, Greg	B-R	5-8	180	7-23-87	.462	.000	.600	4	13	3	6	1	0	0	2	2	0	0	0	2	0	0	.538	.533
Moorman, Chuck	R-R	5-11	200	1-9-94	.210	.235	.200	34	119	16	25	5	0	3	14	6	3	1	1	39	0	0	.328	.264
Onaka, Hirotoshi	B-R	5-10	175	7-11-88	.341	.167	.414	13	41	6	14	1	0	0	4	12	1	0	0	8	2	0	.366	.500
Pinto, Eduard	L-L	5-11	150	10-23-94	.315	.333	.311	14	54	5	17	3	0	0	4	0	0	0	0	6	0	0	.370	.315
Serrato, Barrett	L-R	6-2	185	9-1-90	.267	.333	.250	5	15	1	4	1	0	1	5	4	1	0	0	4	1	0	.533	.450
Teschner, Brett	R-R	6-3	225	8-23-91	.200	.500	.125	3	10	1	2	0	0	0	1	3	0	0	0	2	0	0	.200	.385
Vivili, Fernando	R-R	6-3	210	1-9-94	.180	.136	.192	28	100	10	18	5	0	6	18	6	3	0	1	35	1	0	.410	.245
Wrenn, Taylor	L-R	5-11	175	12-22-89	.317	.143	.407	11	41	6	13	2	1	0	3	4	1	1	1	5	0	1	.415	.383

Pitching	B-T	HT	WT	DOB	W	L	ERA	G	GS	CG	SV	IP	H	R	ER	HR	BB	SO	AVG	vLH	vRH	K/9	BB/9
Anderson, Brett	R-R	6-3	185	9-3-90	1	1	3.29	8	0	0	0	14	13	7	5	0	6	11	.250	.227	.267	7.24	3.95
Bostick, Akeem	R-R	6-4	180	5-4-95	4	1	2.83	14	6	0	1	41	42	16	13	0	12	33	.264	.317	.232	7.19	2.61
Brill, Zach	L-L	6-6	215	2-10-94	0	0	4.50	4	0	0	0	4	2	2	2	0	6	2	.143	.333	.000	4.50	13.50
Buckel, Cody	R-R	6-1	185	6-18-92	0	1	27.00	2	2	0	0	1	0	4	4	0	7	4	.000	.000	.000	27.00	47.25
Dula, Chris	R-R	6-2	200	8-6-92	0	0	4.00	4	0	0	0	6	5	4	4	1	3	5	.227	.286	.200	7.50	4.50
Feliz, Neftali	R-R	6-3	225	5-2-88	0	0	0.00	2	1	0	0	2	1	0	0	0	2	4	.167	.250	.000	18.00	9.00
Gardewine, Nick	R-R	6-1	160	8-15-93	3	3	3.21	14	6	0	1	48	34	21	17	2	20	37	.193	.217	.178	6.99	3.78
Gates, David	R-R	6-2	185	9-15-92	0	0	5.40	11	0	0	0	13	17	11	8	1	6	8	.321	.333	.313	5.40	4.05
Kela, Keone	R-R	6-1	190	4-16-93	2	0	7.36	3	0	0	0	4	8	3	3	0	3	6	.421	.500	.364	14.73	7.36
Kennelly, Tim	R-R	6-0	180	12-5-86	0	0	18.00	2	0	0	0	1	2	2	2	0	4	2	.000	.000	.000	18.00	36.00
Kukuruda, John	R-R	6-4	180	6-9-92	2	2	7.71	12	0	0	0	12	18	14	10	1	9	10	.360	.529	.273	7.71	6.94
Lanphere, Luke	R-R	6-2	175	9-30-95	1	1	3.50	8	2	0	0	18	14	7	7	1	6	14	.203	.036	.317	7.00	3.00
Leclerc, Angelo	R-R	6-0	170	10-9-91	2	0	2.66	9	1	0	0	20	18	6	6	0	3	27	.247	.250	.244	11.95	1.33
Ledbetter, Ryan	R-R	6-1	190	2-13-92	3	0	4.26	15	0	0	0	19	11	9	9	3	11	18	.169	.143	.182	8.53	5.21
Napiontek, Easton	R-R	6-8	250	4-18-93	2	0	1.25	15	0	0	0	22	17	4	3	1	5	18	.227	.231	.224	7.48	2.08
Niggli, John	R-R	6-4	185	5-2-90	2	1	4.35	11	1	0	1	21	23	12	10	1	7	15	.277	.222	.319	6.53	3.05
Palumbo, Joe	L-L	6-1	150	10-26-94	1	1	5.03	13	0	0	0	20	19	11	11	0	14	22	.250	.269	.240	10.07	6.41
Perez, David	R-R	6-5	200	12-20-92	0	1	6.75	3	2	0	0	3	3	2	2	0	2	3	.429	.000	.600	10.13	6.75
Perez, Santo	R-R	6-5	200	11-22-88	2	1	0.96	14	0	0	2	19	11	2	2	0	6	15	.160	.160	.175	7.23	2.89
Pollorena, Luis	L-L	5-8	170	1-14-91	0	0	1.04	7	0	0	0	9	6	1	1	0	2	7	.214	.167	.227	7.27	2.08
Rodriguez, Ricardo	R-R	6-2	220	8-31-92	0	1	1.59	13	0	0	7	17	14	3	3	0	2	28	.219	.200	.227	14.82	1.06
Samayoa, Jose	R-R	6-1	200	3-9-90	0	2	3.70	14	12	0	0	56	58	26	23	3	15	75	.261	.351	.214	12.05	2.41
Smith, Jarred	R-R	6-0	190	3-19-93	0	0	4.91	3	0	0	1	4	4	2	2	1	5	5	.267	.250	.273	12.27	2.45
Soria, Joakim	R-R	6-3	200	5-18-84	0	0	0.00	1	1	0	0	1	0	0	0	0	0	1	.000	.000	.000	9.00	0.00
Sosa, Kevin	R-R	6-1	192	1-6-95	2	3	3.58	12	9	0	0	50	48	24	20	0	15	32	.245	.224	.261	5.72	2.68
Thompson, Derek	L-L	6-4	180	8-8-92	2	2	2.41	13	9	0	0	41	35	13	11	0	14	47	.229	.302	.200	10.32	3.07
West, Matt	R-R	6-1	200	11-21-88	0	1	—	1	1	0	0	2	2	2	2	0	2	0	1.000	1.000	1.000	—	—
Wiper, Cole	R-R	6-4	185	6-3-92	3	1	2.13	10	2	0	0	25	21	10	6	0	8	26	.228	.250	.208	9.24	2.84

Fielding

Catcher	PCT	G	PO	A	E	DP	PB
Alfaro	.971	4	33	0	1	0	2
Caraballo	1.000	1	2	1	0	0	3
Garay	.989	23	156	20	2	1	1
Moorman	.986	23	192	23	3	1	3
Teschner	1.000	2	11	3	0	0	0
Vivili	.987	11	62	13	1	1	5

First Base	PCT	G	PO	A	E	DP
Caraballo	1.000	10	74	2	0	6
Cedeno	.979	8	86	7	2	9
Lantigua	.970	22	184	9	6	19
Moorman	1.000	8	67	3	0	5
Serrato	1.000	3	16	2	0	1
Vivili	.989	10	87	6	1	11

Second Base	PCT	G	PO	A	E	DP
Kiner-Falefa	.953	24	39	82	6	20
Mendez	.990	23	36	66	1	16
Onaka	.750	2	2	1	1	1
Wrenn	.976	10	12	29	1	3

Third Base	PCT	G	PO	A	E	DP
Caraballo	.000	2	0	0	3	0

	PCT	G	PO	A	E	DP
Demeritte	.897	14	8	18	3	1
Duran	.500	1	0	1	1	0
Gallo	.909	4	3	7	1	0
Lantigua	.849	22	16	29	8	5
Mendez	.889	20	14	26	5	1
Moorman	.500	1	0	1	1	0
Onaka	1.000	2	1	2	0	0
Shortstop	**PCT**	**G**	**PO**	**A**	**E**	**DP**
Demeritte	.946	24	45	94	8	26

	PCT	G	PO	A	E	DP
Kiner-Falefa	.956	19	36	50	4	10
Mendez	.950	11	9	29	2	5
Miclat	.857	4	2	10	2	0
Wrenn	.875	1	1	6	1	1
Outfield	**PCT**	**G**	**PO**	**A**	**E**	**DP**
Benson	1.000	5	5	2	0	1
Beras	.933	15	27	1	2	0
Bolinger	.800	4	4	0	1	0
Caraballo	1.000	15	21	0	0	0

	PCT	G	PO	A	E	DP
Cedeno	.970	32	31	1	1	0
Gonzalez	.974	45	69	7	2	0
Johnson	1.000	16	22	2	0	0
McDonald	.980	33	49	1	1	0
Onaka	1.000	11	11	0	0	0
Pinto	1.000	11	13	1	0	0
Serrato	1.000	2	1	0	0	0

DSL RANGERS ROOKIE

DOMINICAN SUMMER LEAGUE

Batting	B-T	HT	WT	DOB	AVG	vLH	vRH	G	AB	R	H	2B	3B	HR	RBI	BB	HBP	SH	SF	SO	SB	CS	SLG	OBP
Adames, Crisford	B-R	6-1	160	1-26-95	.234	.333	.204	57	184	31	43	3	2	1	23	34	5	2	2	38	0	2	.288	.364
Arroyo, Carlos	L-R	5-11	150	6-28-93	.288	.377	.265	69	264	57	76	9	7	2	36	26	4	9	2	27	11	3	.398	.358
Ayarza, Rodrigo	B-R	5-8	145	2-20-95	.309	.231	.333	32	55	17	17	2	4	1	9	7	0	6	0	7	0	1	.545	.387
Carvajal, Ronny	R-R	6-3	180	10-9-95	.287	.500	.250	38	94	17	27	11	0	0	15	9	5	1	0	21	2	0	.404	.380
Castillo, Elio	R-R	6-1	160	3-1-94	.291	.362	.273	65	230	30	67	6	3	0	38	34	4	3	5	32	10	3	.343	.385
Castro, Rubell	R-R	6-3	180	8-13-96	.121	.000	.133	13	33	3	4	2	0	1	3	5	2	0	0	19	0	0	.273	.275
Cedeno, Diego	L-L	5-11	160	5-19-92	.161	.000	.238	11	31	9	5	2	0	0	5	14	0	2	0	2	0	0	.226	.422
Fajardo, Kelvin	R-R	5-11	160	3-8-96	.218	.154	.231	36	78	9	17	0	0	0	10	9	1	0	1	8	1	1	.218	.303
Gonzalez, Jesus	R-R	6-1	180	9-12-94	.284	.316	.275	37	88	21	25	5	0	1	11	12	2	1	2	15	2	0	.375	.375
Gonzalez, Jose	R-R	6-1	175	3-16-94	.289	.385	.250	13	45	7	13	3	0	0	7	7	1	4	0	7	1	0	.356	.396
Lacrus, Sherman	R-R	5-11	180	12-23-93	.330	.410	.307	54	179	36	59	4	1	3	21	21	16	2	2	18	8	4	.413	.440
Martinez, Jesus	L-L	5-10	165	5-7-95	.293	.261	.302	61	208	38	61	7	4	1	27	37	4	2	2	23	6	7	.380	.406
Matos, Josue	L-R	5-10	200	1-26-95	.176	.167	.179	24	51	11	9	2	0	0	7	9	2	0	1	4	0	0	.216	.317
McDonald, Todd	L-R	6-3	180	10-23-95	.143	.667	.000	4	14	1	2	0	0	0	1	4	4	0	0	1	5	1	0	.143	.316
Mendoza, Kevin	B-R	5-10	155	8-16-95	.305	.308	.330	46	118	21	36	9	0	0	27	20	3	2	0	13	0	1	.381	.418
Perez, Brallan	R-R	5-10	165	1-27-96	.325	.279	.337	61	206	43	67	10	1	0	31	32	6	2	3	14	9	6	.383	.425
Profar, Juremi	R-R	6-1	185	1-30-96	.281	.196	.304	63	217	38	61	13	1	0	44	22	7	2	3	13	1	4	.350	.361
Terrero, Luis	R-R	6-0	185	11-11-95	.258	.178	.279	62	217	39	56	8	4	0	35	24	10	2	2	27	9	2	.332	.356
Valencia, Ricardo	R-R	6-0	185	1-13-93	.228	.231	.227	28	79	14	18	6	0	2	12	10	0	0	2	21	0	0	.380	.308

Pitching	B-T	HT	WT	DOB	W	L	ERA	G	GS	CG	SV	IP	H	R	ER	HR	BB	SO	AVG	vLH	vRH	K/9	BB/9
Beaton, Raul	R-R	6-1	185	8-31-93	0	0	20.25	2	0	0	0	1	3	4	3	0	1	0	.429	.000	.500	0.00	6.75
Beltre, Dario	R-R	6-3	170	11-19-92	6	1	1.34	24	0	0	1	40	25	10	6	0	12	53	.176	.276	.150	11.83	2.68
Carvallo, Felix	L-L	6-1	175	10-5-93	1	1	0.90	25	0	0	8	30	22	3	3	0	2	41	.206	.100	.216	12.30	0.60
Cedeno, Rafael	R-R	6-5	210	10-5-94	1	0	2.89	12	0	0	0	19	14	7	6	0	11	16	.209	.222	.207	7.71	5.30
Decena, Albert	R-R	6-3	185	5-12-91	4	2	1.36	22	0	0	1	40	30	12	6	0	14	47	.213	.188	.220	10.66	3.18
Fandino, Jesus	R-R	6-2	165	1-27-94	0	0	15.00	3	0	0	0	3	6	7	5	0	2	1	.429	1.000	.333	3.00	6.00
Fracchiolla, Gionny	L-L	5-7	156	9-10-91	2	0	2.25	13	0	0	0	20	14	5	5	0	4	24	.189	.200	.186	10.80	1.80
Garcia, Christopher	R-R	6-4	220	8-26-95	2	1	1.76	12	0	0	0	15	7	3	3	0	10	7	.152	.111	.162	4.11	5.87
Hernandez, Jonathan	R-R	6-2	150	7-6-96	3	1	1.21	13	8	0	0	45	28	14	6	2	22	38	.176	.222	.167	7.66	4.43
Juan, Johan	R-R	6-1	180	4-14-94	2	0	0.33	7	4	0	0	28	20	5	1	0	7	20	.204	.171	.222	6.51	2.28
Jurado, Ariel	R-R	6-1	180	1-30-96	6	0	2.39	9	9	0	0	49	48	21	13	1	3	47	.254	.286	.245	8.63	0.55
Leal, Werner	R-R	6-1	160	7-8-95	3	1	2.11	17	4	0	0	38	44	13	9	0	7	42	.284	.316	.274	9.86	1.64
Lopez, Omarlin	R-R	6-3	175	10-8-93	3	1	3.15	13	13	0	0	60	62	26	21	1	10	47	.274	.273	.275	7.05	1.50
Marte, Juan	R-R	6-4	160	5-8-90	1	1	3.48	13	0	0	0	21	22	12	8	0	8	16	.293	.273	.297	6.97	3.48
Martinez, Emerson	R-R	6-1	185	1-11-95	1	1	1.20	5	2	0	0	15	12	2	2	0	4	16	.222	.308	.195	9.60	2.40
Nunez, Nerfy	L-L	6-3	210	8-12-92	0	0	7.54	11	4	0	0	23	27	21	19	2	12	12	.303	.500	.267	4.76	4.76
Payano, Pedro	R-R	6-2	170	9-27-94	5	5	3.34	14	12	0	0	67	66	29	25	6	11	56	.265	.190	.290	7.49	1.47
Pena, Richelson	R-R	6-1	170	9-29-93	9	1	2.29	11	11	0	0	75	57	21	19	1	11	76	.215	.270	.198	9.16	1.33
Rodriguez, Argenis	R-R	6-3	190	3-7-96	3	1	7.20	11	1	0	0	20	28	17	16	1	8	10	.350	.300	.367	4.50	3.60
Rodriguez, Ricardo	R-R	6-2	220	8-31-92	0	1	1.80	6	0	0	4	5	4	1	1	0	2	3	.211	.000	.286	5.40	3.60
Sosa, Kevin	R-R	6-1	192	1-6-95	2	0	1.80	3	3	0	0	15	8	5	3	0	4	14	.157	.214	.135	8.40	2.40

Fielding

Catcher	PCT	G	PO	A	E	DP	PB
Adames	1.000	1	8	3	0	0	0
Gonzalez	.987	23	124	26	2	1	1
Lacrus	.976	7	34	7	1	0	4
Matos	1.000	6	12	1	0	0	0
Mendoza	.982	40	236	40	5	0	6
Profar	1.000	1	9	2	0	0	0
Valencia	.994	22	144	12	1	0	2

First Base	PCT	G	PO	A	E	DP
Adames	.992	41	345	15	3	34
Castillo	.992	31	235	10	2	16
Gonzalez	1.000	2	4	0	0	0
Matos	.960	8	22	2	1	2
Profar	1.000	1	6	1	0	0
Valencia	1.000	1	2	0	0	0

Second Base	PCT	G	PO	A	E	DP
Ayarza	.959	21	39	32	3	10
Fajardo	1.000	5	5	7	0	2
Perez	.989	61	120	142	3	28
Profar	—	1	0	0	0	0

Third Base	PCT	G	PO	A	E	DP
Adames	1.000	4	3	5	0	2
Castillo	.930	27	15	65	6	6
Fajardo	.870	13	3	17	3	0
Profar	.980	23	12	38	1	2
Terrero	.870	15	8	32	6	2

Shortstop	PCT	G	PO	A	E	DP
Adames	.857	4	9	3	2	3
Castillo	.909	3	4	6	1	2
Fajardo	—	1	0	0	0	0
Profar	.944	36	53	99	9	21

	PCT	G	PO	A	E	DP
Terrero	.912	38	50	84	13	15
Valencia	1.000	2	3	4	0	0
Outfield	**PCT**	**G**	**PO**	**A**	**E**	**DP**
Arroyo	.970	67	125	5	4	0
Ayarza	—	1	0	0	0	0
Carvajal	.935	24	28	1	2	0
Castro	.889	9	7	1	1	1
Cedeno	.947	11	17	1	1	0
Fajardo	1.000	10	10	1	0	1
Gonzalez	—	1	0	0	0	0
Gonzalez	1.000	13	31	2	0	0
Lacrus	1.000	44	47	2	0	0
Martinez	.981	61	94	7	2	0
McDonald	.857	2	6	0	1	0
Terrero	1.000	2	1	0	0	0

Toronto Blue Jays

SEASON IN A SENTENCE: After aggressive off-season moves swapped highly-regarded prospects for established major league veterans, the Blue Jays sputtered to a slow start to the season, were outscored by 44 runs on the year and finished in last place with 74 wins—one more than in 2012.

HIGH POINT: After accumulating a winning percentage of .438 over the first two plus months of the season amid key injuries and slow starts by key players, the Blue Jays won 11 straight games to put the club two games above .500 and five games out of first place on June 23.

LOW POINT: That was the high water mark for the season, as the Blue Jays then entered July at the .500 mark, which they never sniffed again. June was the only month the Jays had a winning record. Excluding that winning month of June, the Jays were outscored by 86 runs on the season. The pitching staff in particular struggled, posting the fourth-highest ERA in the league (4.26) with below-average strikeout and walk rates, while allowing the second most home runs in the league (195).

NOTABLE ROOKIES: Despite his age (32), shortstop Munenori Kawasaki retained rookie eligibility after coming over from Japan in 2012. He filled in after Jose Reyes was injured, and struggled offensively with a .229/.326/.308 line and 12 extra-base hits in 289 plate appearances. Righthander Todd Redmond, 28, struck out nearly a man an inning with a 3.3 strikeout-walk ratio in 14 starts and 17 games. Lefthander Aaron Loup, 25, was a reliable bullpen arm who posted a 2.47 ERA with above-average command and a 4.1 strikeout-walk ratio.

KEY TRANSACTIONS: Although these were off-season moves, the Jays made two large trades that pushed the organization in a different direction with a greater emphasis on current production. The Jays brought in reigning NL Cy Young winner R.A. Dickey from the Mets and a legion of talent (Josh Johnson, Jose Reyes, Mark Buehrle and others) from the Marlins. The Jays dug into their deep, talented farm system. Once the season began, the Jays made only one trade.

DOWN ON THE FARM: While one full-season club (Buffalo) finished above .500, the Vancouver Canadians won their third straight Northwest League title and the Bluefield Blue Jays made the Appalachian League playoffs. The bulk of the organization's talent was concentrated at the lower levels.

OPENING DAY PAYROLL: $117.5 million (9th)

PLAYERS OF THE YEAR

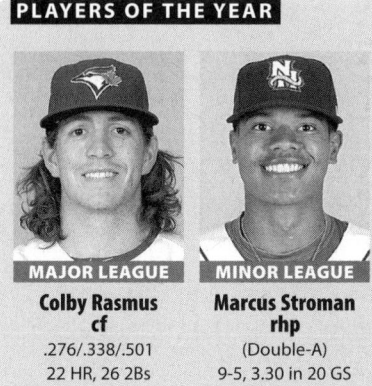

MAJOR LEAGUE	MINOR LEAGUE
Colby Rasmus	**Marcus Stroman**
cf	**rhp**
.276/.338/.501	(Double-A)
22 HR, 26 2Bs	9-5, 3.30 in 20 GS
2nd in ISO among CFs	10.4 SO/9, 4.8 SO:BB

ORGANIZATION LEADERS

BATTING		*Minimum 250 AB
MAJORS		
* AVG	Lind, Adam	.288
* OPS	Encarnacion, Edwin	.904
HR	Encarnacion, Edwin	36
RBI	Encarnacion, Edwin	104
MINORS		
* AVG	Pillar, Kevin, Buffalo/New Hampshire	.307
* OBP	Smith, Dwight Jr., Lansing	.365
* SLG	Gomez, Mauro, Buffalo	.521
R	Berti, Jon, Dunedin	85
	Burns, Andy, New Hampshire/Dunedin	85
H	Pillar, Kevin, Buffalo/New Hampshire	155
TB	Burns, Andy, New Hampshire/Dunedin	241
2B	Pillar, Kevin, Buffalo/New Hampshire	39
3B	Pompey, Dalton, Lansing	9
HR	Gomez, Mauro, Buffalo	29
RBI	Burns, Andy, New Hampshire/Dunedin	85
BB	Schimpf, Ryan, New Hampshire	79
SO	Patterson, Kevin, Dunedin/Lansing	140
SB	Berti, Jon, Dunedin	56

PITCHING		#Minimum 75 IP
MAJORS		
W	Dickey, R.A.	14
# ERA	Buehrle, Mark	4.15
SO	Dickey, R.A.	177
SV	Janssen, Casey	34
MINORS		
W	Bibens-Dirkx, Austin, Dunedin/N.H.	12
L	Walden, Marcus, New Hampshire	14
# ERA	Bibens-Dirkx, Austin, Dunedin/N.H.	2.48
G	Carreno, Joel, Buffalo/New Hampshire	50
	Sikula, Arik, Lansing	50
GS	Cole, Taylor, Dunedin/Lansing	27
SV	Sikula, Arik, Lansing	19
IP	Bibens-Dirkx, Austin, Dunedin/N.H.	167
BB	Romero, Ricky, Buffalo/Dunedin	63
SO	Bibens-Dirkx, Austin, Dunedin/N.H.	155
# AVG	Bibens-Dirkx, Austin, Dunedin/N.H.	.211

2013 PERFORMANCE

General Manager: Alex Anthopoulos. **Farm Director:** Charlie Wilson. **Scouting Director:** Brian Parker.

Class	Team	League	W	L	PCT	Finish	Manager
Majors	Toronto Blue Jays	American	74	88	.457	11th (15)	John Gibbons
Triple-A	Buffalo Bisons	International	74	70	.514	6th (14)	Marty Brown
Double-A	New Hampshire Fisher Cats	Eastern	68	72	.486	7th (10)	Gary Allenson
High A	Dunedin Blue Jays	Florida State	63	68	.481	9th (12)	Bobby Meacham
Low A	Lansing Lugnuts	Midwest	61	78	.439	12th (16)	John Tamargo
Short-season	Vancouver Canadians	Northwest	39	37	.513	4th (8)	Clayton McCullough
Rookie	Bluefield Blue Jays	Appalachian	40	27	.597	2nd (10)	Dennis Holmberg
Rookie	GCL Blue Jays	Gulf Coast	28	32	.467	8th (16)	John Schneider
Overall 2013 Minor League Record			373	384	.493	19th (30)	

ORGANIZATION STATISTICS

AMERICAN LEAGUE

Batting	B-T	HT	WT	DOB	AVG	vLH	vRH	G	AB	R	H	2B	3B	HR	RBI	BB	HBP	SH	SF	SO	SB	CS	SLG	OBP
Arencibia, J.P.	R-R	6-0	200	1-5-86	.194	.204	.190	138	474	45	92	18	0	21	55	18	3	0	2	148	0	2	.365	.227
Bautista, Jose	R-R	6-0	190	10-19-80	.259	.250	.261	118	452	82	117	24	0	28	73	69	3	0	4	84	7	2	.498	.358
Blanco, Henry	R-R	5-11	220	8-29-71	.184	.167	.200	15	38	3	7	3	0	0	4	0	1	0	0	10	0	0	.263	.262
2-team total (35 Seattle)					.142	—	—	50	134	11	19	5	0	3	14	14	1	1	0	36	0	0	.246	.228
Bonifacio, Emilio	B-R	5-11	205	4-23-85	.218	.161	.235	94	262	33	57	16	1	3	20	13	2	3	2	66	12	6	.321	.258
2-team total (42 Kansas City)					.243	—	—	136	420	54	102	22	3	3	31	30	2	6	3	103	28	8	.331	.295
Cabrera, Melky	B-L	6-0	200	8-11-84	.279	.253	.290	88	344	39	96	15	2	3	30	23	0	2	3	47	2	2	.360	.322
Davis, Rajai	R-R	5-9	195	10-19-80	.260	.319	.228	108	331	49	86	16	2	6	24	21	5	1	2	67	45	6	.375	.312
DeRosa, Mark	R-R	6-1	215	2-26-75	.235	.267	.178	88	204	23	48	12	1	7	36	28	1	0	3	49	0	0	.407	.326
Encarnacion, Edwin	R-R	6-2	230	1-7-83	.272	.270	.272	142	530	90	144	29	1	36	104	82	4	0	5	62	7	1	.534	.370
Goins, Ryan	L-R	5-10	170	2-13-88	.252	.233	.263	34	119	11	30	5	0	2	8	2	0	0	0	28	0	0	.345	.264
Gose, Anthony	L-L	6-1	195	8-10-90	.259	.179	.287	52	147	15	38	6	5	2	12	5	0	1	0	37	4	3	.408	.283
Izturis, Maicer	B-R	5-8	170	9-12-80	.236	.259	.225	107	365	33	86	12	0	5	32	27	1	3	3	38	1	5	.310	.288
Kawasaki, Munenori	L-R	5-10	165	6-3-81	.229	.152	.247	96	240	27	55	6	5	1	24	32	4	10	3	41	7	1	.308	.326
Langerhans, Ryan	L-L	6-3	220	2-20-80	.273	.400	.167	4	11	3	3	0	0	0	0	2	0	0	0	2	1	0	.273	.385
LaRoche, Andy	R-R	6-0	205	9-13-83	.000	—	.000	1	4	0	0	0	0	0	0	0	0	0	0	1	0	0	.000	.000
Lawrie, Brett	R-R	6-0	225	1-18-90	.254	.219	.266	107	401	41	102	18	3	11	46	30	7	1	3	68	9	5	.397	.315
Lind, Adam	L-L	6-2	220	7-17-83	.288	.208	.309	143	465	67	134	26	1	23	67	51	1	0	4	103	1	0	.497	.357
Nickeas, Mike	R-R	6-0	215	2-13-83	—	—	—	1	0	0	0	0	0	0	0	0	0	0	0	0	0	0	—	—
Pillar, Kevin	R-R	6-0	200	1-4-89	.206	.235	.191	36	102	11	21	4	0	3	13	4	2	2	0	29	0	1	.333	.250
Rasmus, Colby	L-L	6-2	190	8-11-86	.276	.256	.284	118	417	57	115	26	1	22	66	37	3	0	1	135	0	1	.501	.338
Reyes, Jose	B-R	6-1	195	6-11-83	.296	.247	.311	93	382	58	113	20	0	10	37	34	1	0	2	47	15	6	.427	.353
Sierra, Moises	R-R	6-0	230	9-24-88	.290	.235	.315	35	107	11	31	13	1	1	13	14	0	0	1	29	1	0	.458	.369
Thole, Josh	L-R	6-0	215	10-28-86	.175	.182	.173	45	120	11	21	3	1	1	8	12	1	2	0	25	0	0	.242	.256

Pitching	B-T	HT	WT	DOB	W	L	ERA	G	GS	CG	SV	IP	H	R	ER	HR	BB	SO	AVG	vLH	vRH	K/9	BB/9
Buehrle, Mark	L-L	6-2	245	3-23-79	12	10	4.15	33	33	1	0	204	223	100	94	24	51	139	.276	.256	.283	6.14	2.25
Bush, Dave	R-R	6-2	205	11-9-79	0	0	15.00	1	0	0	0	3	5	5	5	4	1	1	.357	.286	.429	3.00	3.00
Cecil, Brett	R-L	6-1	215	7-2-86	5	1	2.82	60	0	0	1	61	44	20	19	4	23	70	.201	.191	.212	10.38	3.41
Delabar, Steve	R-R	6-4	230	7-17-83	5	5	3.22	55	0	0	1	59	50	25	21	4	29	82	.231	.216	.244	12.58	4.45
Dickey, R.A.	R-R	6-2	215	10-29-74	14	13	4.21	34	34	3	0	225	207	113	105	35	71	177	.242	.255	.228	7.09	2.84
Drabek, Kyle	R-R	6-1	230	12-8-87	0	0	7.71	3	0	0	0	2	4	2	2	1	2	3	.364	.200	.500	11.57	7.71
Germano, Justin	R-R	6-2	210	8-6-82	0	0	9.00	1	0	0	0	2	6	2	2	1	0	1	.500	.800	.286	4.50	0.00
Gonzalez, Edgar	R-R	6-2	210	2-23-83	0	0	7.88	3	0	0	0	8	9	7	7	2	5	3	.281	.263	.308	3.38	5.63
2-team total (5 Houston)					0	1	7.50	8	0	0	0	18	26	16	15	6	8	11	—	—	—	5.50	4.00
Happ, J.A.	L-L	6-6	195	10-19-82	5	7	4.56	18	18	0	0	93	91	53	47	10	45	77	.250	.304	.229	7.48	4.37
Janssen, Casey	R-R	6-3	225	9-17-81	4	1	2.56	56	0	0	34	53	39	17	15	3	13	50	.202	.244	.135	8.54	2.22
Jeffress, Jeremy	R-R	6-0	195	9-21-87	1	0	0.87	10	0	0	0	10	8	1	1	1	5	12	.211	.118	.286	10.45	4.35
Jenkins, Chad	R-R	6-3	225	12-22-87	1	0	2.70	10	3	0	0	33	31	13	10	3	6	15	.250	.235	.268	4.05	1.62
Johnson, Josh	L-R	6-7	250	1-31-84	2	8	6.20	16	16	0	0	81	105	64	56	15	30	83	.305	.275	.350	9.18	3.32
Laffey, Aaron	L-L	6-0	205	4-15-85	0	0	6.75	1	1	0	0	3	2	2	2	0	5	0	.286	.250	.333	0.00	16.88
Lincoln, Brad	L-R	6-0	225	5-25-85	1	2	3.98	22	0	0	0	32	28	17	14	4	22	25	.233	.224	.242	7.11	6.25
Loup, Aaron	L-L	6-0	210	12-19-87	4	6	2.47	64	0	0	2	69	66	23	19	5	13	53	.258	.200	.295	6.88	1.69
McGowan, Dustin	R-R	6-3	230	3-24-82	0	0	2.45	25	0	0	0	26	19	11	7	2	12	26	.190	.188	.192	9.12	4.21
Morrow, Brandon	R-R	6-3	200	7-26-84	2	3	5.63	10	10	0	0	54	63	39	34	12	18	42	.286	.301	.268	6.96	2.98
Nolin, Sean	L-L	6-5	235	12-26-89	0	1	40.50	1	1	0	0	1	7	6	6	1	1	0	.700	1.000	.500	0.00	6.75
Oliver, Darren	R-L	6-3	250	10-6-70	3	4	3.86	50	0	0	0	49	47	24	21	6	15	40	.257	.324	.211	7.35	2.76
Ortiz, Ramon	R-R	6-0	175	5-23-73	1	2	6.04	7	4	0	0	25	34	17	17	7	11	8	.337	.327	.348	2.84	3.91
Perez, Juan	R-L	6-0	170	9-3-78	1	2	3.69	19	0	0	0	32	23	17	13	3	15	33	.200	.200	.200	9.38	4.26
Perez, Luis	L-L	6-0	210	12-26-84	0	1	5.40	6	0	0	0	5	4	3	3	0	2	6	.211	.300	.111	10.80	3.60
Redmond, Todd	R-R	6-3	235	5-17-85	4	3	4.32	17	14	0	0	77	70	38	37	13	23	76	.239	.208	.273	8.88	2.69
Rogers, Esmil	R-R	6-1	190	8-14-85	5	9	4.77	44	20	0	0	138	152	76	73	21	44	96	.279	.297	.258	6.28	2.88
Romero, Ricky	R-L	6-0	225	11-6-84	0	2	11.05	4	2	0	0	7	11	9	9	2	8	5	.355	.667	.158	6.14	9.82
Santos, Sergio	R-R	6-3	240	7-4-83	1	1	1.75	29	0	0	0	26	11	5	5	1	4	28	.131	.118	.140	9.82	1.40

	B-T	HT	WT	DOB	W	L	ERA	G	GS	CG	SV	IP	H	R	ER	BB	SO	SB	AVG	vLH	vRH	K/9	BB/9
Storey, Mickey	R-R	6-1	185	3-16-86	0	0	6.75	3	0	0	0	4	6	3	3	0	1	6	.353	.333	.375	13.50	2.25
Wagner, Neil	R-R	6-0	215	1-1-84	2	4	3.79	36	0	0	0	38	39	17	16	5	13	33	.271	.270	.272	7.82	3.08
Wang, Chien-Ming	R-R	6-4	225	3-31-80	1	2	7.67	6	6	0	0	27	40	24	23	5	9	14	.351	.429	.276	4.67	3.00
Weber, Thad	R-R	6-2	205	9-28-84	0	1	3.00	5	0	0	0	6	7	3	2	1	3	4	.318	.500	.167	6.00	4.50

Fielding

Catcher	PCT	G	PO	A	E	DP	PB
Arencibia	.988	131	891	49	11	6	13
Blanco	1.000	13	85	4	0	0	8
Nickeas	—	1	0	0	0	0	0
Thole	.993	39	253	13	2	2	9

	PCT	G	PO	A	E	DP	PB
DeRosa	1.000	29	28	47	0	8	
Goins	.993	32	53	94	1	27	
Izturis	.975	59	73	123	5	28	
Kawasaki	.986	18	26	45	1	6	
Lawrie	.913	6	12	9	2	2	

	PCT	G	PO	A	E	DP
Goins	1.000	2	1	3	0	0
Izturis	.961	28	22	51	3	8
Kawasaki	.977	60	79	136	5	39
Reyes	.974	92	95	240	9	51

First Base	PCT	G	PO	A	E	DP
Bautista	1.000	1	2	0	0	0
DeRosa	1.000	17	82	9	0	7
Encarnacion	.992	79	689	44	6	66
Langerhans	1.000	4	28	0	0	4
Lind	.989	76	579	51	7	56
Thole	.900	2	9	0	1	0

Third Base	PCT	G	PO	A	E	DP
Bautista	1.000	3	1	1	0	0
DeRosa	.915	25	13	30	4	2
Encarnacion	.950	10	12	26	2	2
Izturis	.968	36	18	42	2	3
LaRoche	1.000	1	1	3	0	1
Lawrie	.963	103	68	189	10	19

Outfield	PCT	G	PO	A	E	DP
Bautista	.976	109	192	8	5	4
Bonifacio	1.000	32	56	0	0	0
Cabrera	.992	77	126	3	1	0
Davis	.989	97	173	4	2	1
DeRosa	—	1	0	0	0	0
Gose	.955	49	81	4	4	0
Pillar	1.000	34	57	1	0	0
Rasmus	.987	114	308	1	4	1
Sierra	.966	31	57	0	2	0

Second Base	PCT	G	PO	A	E	DP
Bonifacio	.973	59	101	156	7	43

Shortstop	PCT	G	PO	A	E	DP
Bonifacio	1.000	1	1	1	0	0

BUFFALO BISONS
INTERNATIONAL LEAGUE

TRIPLE-A

Batting	B-T	HT	WT	DOB	AVG	vLH	vRH	G	AB	R	H	2B	3B	HR	RBI	BB	HBP	SH	SF	SO	SB	CS	SLG	OBP
Cabrera, Melky	B-L	6-0	200	8-11-84	.600	1.000	.333	2	5	1	3	0	0	0	1	0	0	0	1	0	0	0	.600	.500
Gailen, Blake	L-L	5-9	180	3-27-85	.286	.250	.313	8	28	2	8	2	0	1	3	0	0	1	1	4	2	0	.464	.276
Glenn, Brad	R-R	6-2	220	4-2-87	.246	.318	.205	18	61	8	15	1	0	5	10	7	1	0	1	13	0	0	.508	.329
Goins, Ryan	L-R	5-10	170	2-13-88	.257	.206	.276	111	377	42	97	22	1	6	46	29	1	9	2	85	3	5	.369	.311
Gomez, Mauro	R-R	6-2	230	9-7-84	.249	.269	.242	110	405	58	101	21	1	29	73	43	2	0	3	131	2	2	.521	.322
Gose, Anthony	L-L	6-1	195	8-10-90	.239	.250	.235	106	393	64	94	17	6	3	27	38	7	3	2	121	22	13	.336	.316
Hernandez, Ramon	R-R	6-0	220	5-20-76	.105	.167	.077	5	19	0	2	0	0	0	2	0	0	0	0	3	0	0	.105	.105
Jimenez, A.J.	R-R	6-0	210	5-1-90	.233	.182	.263	8	30	0	7	1	0	0	1	0	0	0		2	0	1	.267	.258
Jimenez, Luis	L-L	6-3	280	5-7-82	.285	.280	.287	99	354	57	101	16	2	18	73	39	1	0	8	65	3	1	.494	.351
Kawasaki, Munenori	L-R	5-10	165	6-3-81	.250	.300	.240	25	60	9	15	0	0	0	3	14	1	6	0	12	3	0	.250	.400
Langerhans, Ryan	L-L	6-3	220	2-20-80	.221	.320	.190	64	208	27	46	7	2	9	26	38	1	1	0	69	1	2	.404	.344
LaRoche, Andy	R-R	6-0	205	9-13-83	.271	.298	.263	104	365	45	99	21	1	12	51	37	4	0	7	55	4	4	.433	.339
Lawrie, Brett	R-R	6-0	215	1-18-90	.167	.400	.000	3	12	2	2	0	0	1	3	1	0	0	0	7	1	0	.417	.231
Loewen, Adam	L-L	6-4	235	4-9-84	.000	.000	.000	1	3	0	0	0	0	0	2	0	0	0	0	0	0	0	.000	.400
McCoy, Mike	R-R	5-9	180	4-2-81	.245	.295	.222	108	355	50	87	15	1	4	22	59	3	13	0	68	29	7	.327	.357
Murphy, Jack	B-R	6-4	235	4-6-88	.250	.400	.000	3	8	2	2	1	0	0	1	0	0	0	0	2	0	0	.375	.250
Nanita, Ricardo	L-L	6-1	195	6-12-81	.261	.267	.258	38	134	16	35	11	0	2	14	8	0	1	1	22	1	0	.388	.301
Negrych, Jim	L-R	5-9	185	3-2-85	.285	.276	.288	108	382	60	109	27	1	3	44	44	2	7	2	63	5	4	.385	.360
Nickeas, Mike	R-R	6-0	215	2-13-83	.166	.182	.158	58	175	16	29	12	0	1	11	17	4	4	0	40	0	0	.251	.255
Ochinko, Sean	R-R	5-11	205	10-21-87	.220	.222	.219	50	150	9	33	5	0	3	17	17	0	1	3	35	0	2	.313	.294
Pillar, Kevin	R-R	6-0	200	1-4-89	.299	.387	.259	52	201	30	60	19	4	4	27	12	2	1	2	39	8	5	.493	.341
Reyes, Jose	B-R	6-1	195	6-11-83	.412	.600	.333	4	17	3	7	1	0	0	1	0	0	0	0	1	0		.471	.412
Robinson, Clint	L-L	6-5	230	2-16-85	.213	.063	.276	35	108	13	23	9	0	2	12	19	0	0	3	33	0	0	.352	.323
Sierra, Moises	R-R	6-0	230	9-24-88	.261	.219	.276	100	379	57	99	18	5	11	51	16	12	1	4	106	12	4	.422	.309
Thole, Josh	L-R	6-0	215	10-28-86	.322	.357	.314	41	149	18	48	5	1	7	31	14	2	0	2	25	0	1	.510	.383
Velez, Eugenio	B-R	6-1	170	5-16-82	.270	.296	.258	69	222	31	60	10	3	7	24	35	1	1	0	38	21	5	.437	.372
Zawadzki, Lance	B-R	5-11	185	5-26-85	.222	.000	.286	7	18	1	4	1	0	0	2	2	0	1	0	5	2	0	.278	.300

Pitching	B-T	HT	WT	DOB	W	L	ERA	G	GS	CG	SV	IP	H	R	ER	HR	BB	SO	AVG	vLH	vRH	K/9	BB/9
Batista, Miguel	R-R	6-1	210	2-19-71	1	2	8.36	8	7	0	0	28	41	29	26	4	16	17	.345	.268	.413	5.46	5.14
Beck, Chad	R-R	6-4	250	1-17-85	1	1	7.11	8	0	0	0	13	19	10	10	3	8	3	.365	.409	.333	2.13	5.68
Brummett, Tyson	R-R	6-0	185	8-15-84	0	1	108.00	1	1	0	0	0	3	5	4	0	3	1	.600	1.000	.000	27.00	81.00
Burnett, Alex	R-R	6-0	220	7-26-87	0	0	0.00	2	0	0	0	2	1	0	0	0	1	0	.125	.200	.000	0.00	3.86
2-team total (7 Norfolk)					1	0	1.50	9	0	0	0	12	11	2	2	0	2	8	—	—	—	6.00	1.50
Bush, Dave	R-R	6-2	205	11-9-79	8	7	4.20	19	15	1	0	90	95	47	42	16	17	69	.264	.290	.244	6.90	1.70
Carlyle, Buddy	L-R	6-3	210	12-21-77	4	2	3.86	36	2	0	0	56	47	28	24	10	20	76	.226	.238	.218	12.21	3.21
Carreno, Joel	R-R	6-2	220	3-7-87	4	2	2.97	28	0	0	1	39	27	18	13	5	16	46	.191	.275	.111	10.53	3.66
Drabek, Kyle	R-R	6-1	230	12-8-87	1	2	3.77	4	3	0	0	14	14	6	6	1	2	12	.250	.200	.333	7.53	1.26
Everts, Clint	B-R	6-2	195	8-10-84	0	2	9.39	6	0	0	0	8	7	11	8	1	10	1	.250	.308	.200	1.17	11.74
Germano, Justin	R-R	6-2	210	8-6-82	8	9	4.47	25	24	2	0	151	184	84	75	12	27	103	.302	.319	.286	6.14	1.61
Gonzalez, Edgar	R-R	6-2	210	2-23-83	1	0	5.49	4	4	0	0	20	26	12	12	2	2	15	.331	.268	.375	6.86	0.92
Gracey, Scott	R-R	6-2	190	10-15-86	1	0	5.00	8	0	0	0	9	9	5	5	0	4	9	.250	.176	.316	9.00	4.00
Happ, J.A.	L-L	6-6	195	10-19-82	0	2	6.75	3	3	0	0	13	17	10	10	2	8	13	.321	.316	.324	8.78	5.40
Hinshaw, Alex	L-L	6-2	175	10-31-82	1	0	3.27	12	0	0	0	11	9	4	4	0	17	16	.220	.167	.241	13.09	13.91
Hottovy, Tommy	L-L	6-1	205	7-9-81	0	0	3.44	24	0	0	0	18	20	9	7	3	9	19	.270	.158	.389	9.33	4.42
Hutchison, Drew	L-R	6-2	195	8-22-90	0	3	6.63	5	5	0	0	19	28	16	14	2	6	20	.341	.405	.275	9.47	2.84
Jeffress, Jeremy	R-R	6-0	195	9-21-87	1	0	1.65	25	0	0	7	27	22	6	5	0	13	28	.229	.263	.207	9.22	4.28
Jenkins, Chad	R-R	6-3	225	12-22-87	0	3	7.48	5	5	0	0	22	33	20	18	6	4	8	.344	.289	.392	3.32	1.66
Johnson, Josh	R-R	6-7	250	1-31-84	0	1	6.23	2	2	0	0	9	9	6	6	0	4	6	.273	.273	.273	6.23	4.15

	B-T	HT	WT	DOB	W	L	ERA	G	GS	CG	SV	IP	H	R	ER	HR	BB	SO	AVG	vLH	vRH	K/9	BB/9
Korecky, Bobby	R-R	5-11	185	9-16-79	3	0	4.45	26	2	0	0	57	69	33	28	9	15	39	.297	.299	.296	6.19	2.38
Lawrence, Casey	R-R	6-2	170	10-28-87	0	1	11.25	1	1	0	0	4	10	6	5	0	2	3	.455	.300	.583	6.75	4.50
Lincoln, Brad	L-R	6-0	225	5-25-85	3	2	2.05	23	0	0	5	26	22	7	6	2	8	29	.244	.200	.273	9.91	2.73
McGowan, Dustin	R-R	6-3	230	3-24-82	0	0	7.00	8	0	0	0	9	10	7	7	1	6	12	.278	.313	.250	12.00	6.00
Nolin, Sean	L-L	6-5	235	12-26-89	1	1	1.53	3	3	0	0	18	13	3	3	1	10	13	.232	.143	.262	6.62	5.09
Ortiz, Ramon	R-R	6-0	175	5-23-73	2	0	2.18	4	3	0	0	21	15	5	5	4	7	13	.203	.190	.219	5.66	3.05
Perez, Juan	R-L	6-0	170	9-3-78	2	1	0.86	17	0	0	3	21	12	2	2	0	11	25	.162	.000	.218	10.71	4.71
Perez, Luis	L-L	6-0	210	1-20-85	0	0	2.45	2	0	0	0	4	3	1	1	0	2	1	.231	.200	.250	2.45	4.91
Redmond, Todd	R-R	6-3	235	5-17-85	3	1	5.06	6	5	0	0	27	29	15	15	2	5	29	.284	.320	.250	9.79	1.69
Romero, Ricky	R-L	6-0	225	11-6-84	5	8	5.78	22	22	1	0	114	136	81	73	11	63	81	.303	.330	.294	6.41	4.99
Santos, Sergio	R-R	6-3	240	7-4-83	0	0	7.50	6	0	0	0	6	8	7	5	0	2	5	.308	.375	.278	7.50	3.00
Schwimer, Michael	R-R	6-8	240	2-19-86	0	0	0.00	6	0	0	0	6	1	0	0	0	7	6	.056	.200	.000	9.00	10.50
Stilson, John	R-R	6-3	200	7-28-90	6	2	2.09	33	0	0	4	47	36	13	11	3	15	47	.211	.164	.245	8.94	2.85
Storey, Mickey	R-R	6-1	185	3-16-86	0	2	2.56	36	0	0	2	60	43	21	17	5	16	70	.198	.247	.161	10.56	2.41
Vargas, Claudio	R-R	6-4	235	6-19-78	5	7	5.86	20	14	0	0	83	97	57	54	10	36	55	.295	.258	.326	5.96	3.90
Wagner, Neil	R-R	6-0	215	1-1-84	1	0	0.76	23	0	0	16	24	13	2	2	0	9	38	.167	.267	.104	14.45	3.42
Wang, Chien-Ming	R-R	6-4	225	3-31-80	4	3	3.48	9	8	1	0	52	46	22	20	3	12	30	.237	.231	.241	5.23	2.09
2-team total (9 Scranton/W-B)					8	7	2.87	18	17	2	0	110	103	39	35	5	22	55	—	—	—	4.51	1.81
Weber, Thad	R-R	6-2	205	9-28-84	8	5	2.61	18	15	1	0	100	91	35	29	5	21	88	.243	.245	.242	7.92	1.89

Fielding

Catcher	PCT	G	PO	A	E	DP	PB
Hernandez	.957	3	22	0	1	0	1
Jimenez	1.000	7	49	10	0	1	1
Murphy	1.000	3	19	0	0	0	0
Nickeas	.998	57	433	29	1	3	5
Ochinko	1.000	43	299	17	0	1	3
Thole	.993	37	259	19	2	3	3

First Base	PCT	G	PO	A	E	DP
Gomez	.989	60	493	30	6	51
Hernandez	1.000	1	5	1	0	0
Jimenez	.988	39	311	21	4	34
LaRoche	1.000	6	47	3	0	4
Loewen	1.000	1	5	2	0	1
Ochinko	1.000	7	47	3	0	4
Robinson	.989	32	255	16	3	21
Thole	1.000	1	8	1	0	2

Second Base	PCT	G	PO	A	E	DP
Goins	1.000	9	21	21	0	7

	PCT	G	PO	A	E	DP	PB
Kawasaki	.982	11	25	30	1	7
LaRoche	.964	7	9	18	1	5
Lawrie	1.000	3	3	7	0	1
McCoy	.976	34	45	78	3	14
Negrych	.984	70	127	188	5	51
Velez	.923	13	17	31	4	8
Zawadzki	.923	2	3	9	1	0

Third Base	PCT	G	PO	A	E	DP
Goins	1.000	1	1	3	0	0
Gomez	.889	10	4	20	3	2
LaRoche	.961	89	61	161	9	28
McCoy	.953	16	15	26	2	2
Negrych	.919	25	11	46	5	6
Velez	.800	3	3	5	2	1
Zawadzki	1.000	3	0	6	0	2

Shortstop	PCT	G	PO	A	E	DP
Goins	.980	101	132	299	9	59
Kawasaki	.962	12	13	37	2	6

	PCT	G	PO	A	E	DP
McCoy	.971	31	43	91	4	15
Reyes	1.000	3	3	4	0	2
Zawadzki	.500	1	0	1	1	0

Outfield	PCT	G	PO	A	E	DP
Cabrera	1.000	2	3	0	0	0
Gailen	.917	8	10	1	1	0
Glenn	1.000	18	25	2	0	1
Gose	.975	106	218	15	6	4
Langerhans	.990	61	100	4	1	1
McCoy	.970	29	62	2	2	0
Nanita	.943	24	32	1	2	1
Negrych	1.000	2	3	0	0	0
Pillar	.991	52	109	5	1	0
Robinson	.750	2	3	0	1	0
Sierra	.963	98	198	9	8	4
Velez	.985	39	64	2	1	0

NEW HAMPSHIRE FISHER CATS

DOUBLE-A

EASTERN LEAGUE

Batting	B-T	HT	WT	DOB	AVG	vLH	vRH	G	AB	R	H	2B	3B	HR	RBI	BB	HBP	SH	SF	SO	SB	CS	SLG	OBP
Ahrens, Kevin	B-R	6-1	195	4-26-89	.218	.200	.236	73	238	20	52	15	1	4	29	23	0	2	2	55	0	0	.340	.285
Burns, Andy	R-R	6-2	190	8-7-90	.253	.308	.224	64	265	40	67	19	2	7	32	23	0	0	3	55	12	5	.419	.309
Cabrera, Melky	B-L	6-0	200	8-11-84	.364	—	.364	3	11	1	4	0	0	1	2	0	0	0	0	1	1	0	.636	.364
Glenn, Brad	R-R	6-2	220	4-2-87	.264	.223	.281	111	425	61	112	28	2	17	69	44	3	1	4	104	2	2	.459	.334
Jacobo, Gabe	R-R	6-3	200	4-14-87	.366	.421	.341	32	123	21	45	8	0	7	19	10	2	0	0	20	1	0	.602	.422
Jimenez, A.J.	R-R	6-0	210	5-1-90	.276	.259	.283	50	203	28	56	15	0	3	29	16	1	0	3	37	1	2	.394	.327
Jones, Jonathan	R-R	5-11	185	8-2-89	.154	.167	.143	4	13	2	2	0	0	0	1	2	1	0	0	0	1	0	.154	.313
Lawrie, Brett	R-R	6-0	225	1-18-90	.333	.000	.429	3	9	3	3	0	0	0	0	4	0	0	0	2	0	0	.333	.538
Loewen, Adam	L-L	6-5	235	4-9-84	.269	.244	.280	115	431	60	116	22	3	15	60	57	3	0	0	125	10	5	.439	.358
Manzella, Tommy	R-R	6-2	190	4-16-83	.265	.308	.238	21	68	10	18	5	0	0	6	10	6	0	1	21	1	0	.338	.320
Murphy, Jack	B-R	6-4	235	4-6-88	.218	.208	.224	56	197	19	43	11	1	3	22	14	0	2	1	37	0	0	.330	.269
Nanita, Ricardo	L-L	6-1	195	6-24-81	.255	.200	.283	36	137	25	35	3	0	4	11	13	1	0	1	18	2	1	.365	.322
Nolan, Kevin	R-R	6-2	200	12-13-87	.262	.265	.260	120	451	59	118	24	3	9	60	44	3	2	4	65	5	4	.388	.329
Ochinko, Sean	R-R	5-11	205	10-21-87	.243	.298	.216	41	144	14	35	13	0	2	20	17	2	0	1	27	1	1	.375	.329
Pillar, Kevin	R-R	6-0	200	1-4-89	.313	.387	.273	71	304	44	95	20	2	5	30	19	4	0	0	31	15	8	.441	.361
Rankin, Pierce	R-R	6-1	190	4-26-89	.200	.000	.300	4	15	1	3	0	0	1	2	1	0	0	0	6	0	0	.400	.250
Robinson, Clint	L-L	6-5	230	2-16-85	.270	.220	.293	76	289	41	78	14	2	11	43	40	3	0	0	50	1	2	.446	.364
Schaeffer, Chris	R-R	5-10	195	11-19-87	.000	.000	.000	2	5	1	0	0	0	0	0	1	0	0	0	3	0	0	.000	.167
Schimpf, Ryan	L-R	5-9	180	4-11-88	.210	.215	.208	126	442	67	93	21	3	23	65	79	7	0	1	138	3	3	.428	.338
Talley, Jon	L-R	6-3	200	2-18-89	.163	.125	.167	29	80	5	13	5	0	2	10	2	3	0	0	25	0	0	.300	.212
Tolisano, John	B-R	5-11	190	10-7-88	.243	.224	.258	64	222	26	54	16	1	5	31	21	2	1	2	56	3	3	.392	.312
Van Kirk, Brian	R-R	6-1	200	8-10-85	.278	.314	.257	70	234	39	65	10	1	2	29	53	1	0	1	40	3	2	.355	.412
Wilson, Kenny	B-R	5-10	185	1-30-90	.259	.264	.256	55	216	31	56	14	1	3	11	19	5	2	0	56	16	6	.375	.333
Zawadzki, Lance	B-R	5-11	185	5-26-85	.220	.111	.273	25	82	9	18	1	0	1	4	7	1	1	1	21	3	1	.268	.286
Zazueta, Amadeo	R-R	5-10	160	1-31-86	.213	.138	.267	48	155	13	33	8	0	1	10	2	1	2	0	17	0	0	.284	.228

Pitching	B-T	HT	WT	DOB	W	L	ERA	G	GS	CG	SV	IP	H	R	ER	HR	BB	SO	AVG	vLH	vRH	K/9	BB/9
Antolin, Dustin	R-R	6-2	195	8-9-89	0	2	11.41	26	0	0	2	32	44	42	41	4	28	31	.324	.327	.321	8.63	7.79
Beck, Chad	R-R	6-2	250	1-17-85	1	0	2.70	13	0	0	6	17	15	8	5	1	9	26	.246	.174	.289	14.04	4.86
Bibens-Dirkx, Austin	R-R	6-1	210	4-29-85	3	4	1.92	12	10	0	0	66	47	19	14	3	17	57	.195	.202	.190	7.81	2.33
Boone, Randy	R-R	6-0	200	8-6-84	3	3	3.47	33	0	0	1	62	67	35	24	5	16	49	.275	.299	.261	7.07	2.31

Name	B-T	HT	WT	DOB	W	L	ERA	G	GS	CG	SV	IP	H	R	ER	HR	BB	SO	AVG	vLH	vRH		
Brummett, Tyson	R-R	6-0	185	8-15-84	1	7	5.36	33	9	1	2	87	90	57	52	8	31	76	.263	.291	.244	7.83	3.19
Carreno, Joel	R-R	6-2	220	3-7-87	2	1	1.65	22	0	0	7	27	12	8	5	0	8	44	.128	.189	.088	14.49	2.63
Crawford, Evan	R-L	6-2	190	9-2-86	2	2	5.68	32	0	0	1	38	48	28	24	1	19	33	.314	.244	.343	7.82	4.50
Drabek, Kyle	R-R	6-1	230	12-8-87	0	1	3.38	2	2	0	0	8	4	3	3	2	1	3	.138	.063	.231	3.38	1.13
Everts, Clint	B-R	6-2	195	8-10-84	0	0	6.75	5	1	0	0	8	8	9	6	2	6	7	.250	.222	.261	7.88	6.75
Farina, Alan	R-R	5-11	190	8-9-86	1	1	2.88	21	0	0	7	25	23	9	8	3	8	32	.228	.333	.153	11.52	2.88
Gracey, Scott	R-R	6-2	190	10-15-86	4	1	2.00	19	0	0	2	27	23	7	6	0	11	31	.225	.176	.250	10.33	3.67
Griffith, Shawn	R-R	5-10	180	5-24-87	0	0	7.20	2	0	0	0	5	10	4	4	1	1	4	.417	.385	.455	7.20	1.80
Hernandez, Fernando	R-R	5-11	216	7-31-84	0	0	1.17	5	0	0	1	8	6	1	1	0	5	5	.222	.250	.211	5.87	5.87
Hottovy, Tommy	L-L	6-1	205	7-9-81	0	1	4.74	18	0	0	1	25	26	16	13	3	8	23	.274	.172	.318	8.39	2.92
Hutchison, Drew	L-R	6-2	195	8-22-90	0	1	4.70	2	2	0	0	8	6	5	4	0	2	10	.207	.375	.000	11.74	2.35
Jenkins, Chad	R-R	6-3	225	12-22-87	0	0	1.20	4	3	0	0	15	11	4	2	0	2	9	.190	.192	.188	5.40	1.20
Lawrence, Casey	R-R	6-2	170	10-28-87	0	0	2.70	2	2	0	0	10	9	4	3	2	3	6	.250	.125	.286	5.40	2.70
Magnuson, Trystan	L-R	6-7	220	6-6-85	1	1	9.00	10	0	0	0	12	19	14	12	0	6	12	.339	.316	.351	9.00	4.50
Marze, Dayton	R-R	6-2	185	1-1-89	1	0	12.00	7	0	0	0	6	11	9	8	0	6	6	.393	.571	.333	9.00	9.00
McGuire, Deck	R-R	6-6	235	6-23-89	9	10	4.86	27	26	1	0	157	148	90	85	12	59	143	.247	.215	.266	8.18	3.38
Nolin, Sean	L-L	6-5	235	12-26-89	8	3	3.01	17	17	1	0	93	89	33	31	6	25	103	.251	.256	.249	10.00	2.43
Spoone, Chorye	R-R	6-1	215	9-16-85	4	3	3.99	28	0	0	0	50	46	24	22	2	31	58	.250	.306	.214	10.51	5.62
Stilson, John	R-R	6-3	200	7-28-90	0	0	3.86	2	0	0	1	2	3	1	1	0	0	6	.333	.667	.167	23.14	0.00
Stroman, Marcus	R-R	5-9	185	5-1-91	9	5	3.30	20	20	0	0	112	99	48	41	13	27	129	.234	.171	.284	10.40	2.18
Tepera, Ryan	R-R	6-1	190	11-3-87	10	8	4.50	33	20	0	1	116	109	65	58	11	56	105	.248	.229	.259	8.15	4.34
Walden, Marcus	R-R	6-0	195	9-13-88	6	14	3.71	26	26	1	0	162	184	76	67	9	50	88	.289	.312	.276	4.88	2.77
Wright, Matt	L-L	5-10	170	5-7-87	3	4	6.57	29	2	0	0	63	77	50	46	14	27	54	.297	.333	.284	7.71	3.86

Fielding

Catcher	PCT	G	PO	A	E	DP	PB
Jimenez	1.000	40	314	25	0	2	3
Murphy	.990	56	475	34	5	5	5
Ochinko	.994	40	326	28	2	3	3
Rankin	1.000	4	19	2	0	0	4
Schaeffer	1.000	2	21	0	0	0	0
Talley	1.000	3	7	0	0	0	0

First Base	PCT	G	PO	A	E	DP
Ahrens	.997	37	283	19	1	7
Jacobo	.995	21	187	10	1	16
Loewen	.988	11	76	3	1	5
Robinson	.989	70	613	30	7	51
Talley	.984	9	60	3	1	7

Second Base	PCT	G	PO	A	E	DP
Burns	1.000	1	1	0	0	0

	PCT	G	PO	A	E	DP
Manzella	.941	10	9	23	2	5
Schimpf	.994	38	60	102	1	20
Tolisano	.941	53	85	138	14	29
Zawadzki	.971	17	19	47	2	10
Zazueta	.965	25	43	67	4	16

Third Base	PCT	G	PO	A	E	DP
Ahrens	.913	26	13	60	7	5
Burns	.903	58	25	115	15	9
Lawrie	1.000	2	0	6	0	0
Manzella	.957	8	5	17	1	2
Schimpf	.933	49	30	81	8	12

Shortstop	PCT	G	PO	A	E	DP
Burns	.941	4	1	15	1	2
Manzella	.857	2	2	4	1	0
Nolan	.948	116	152	325	26	60

	PCT	G	PO	A	E	DP
Zazueta	.957	22	20	46	3	5

Outfield	PCT	G	PO	A	E	DP
Cabrera	1.000	3	4	0	0	0
Glenn	.986	107	202	6	3	3
Jones	1.000	4	7	1	0	0
Loewen	.973	87	178	3	5	0
Manzella	1.000	1	1	0	0	0
Nanita	1.000	9	19	0	0	0
Pillar	.976	71	149	12	4	3
Robinson	1.000	2	0	1	0	0
Schimpf	.979	25	46	0	1	0
Tolisano	.667	1	2	0	1	0
Van Kirk	.983	62	111	3	2	0
Wilson	.951	55	96	1	5	0

DUNEDIN BLUE JAYS

HIGH CLASS A

FLORIDA STATE LEAGUE

Batting	B-T	HT	WT	DOB	AVG	vLH	vRH	G	AB	R	H	2B	3B	HR	RBI	BB	HBP	SH	SF	SO	SB	CS	SLG	OBP
Baligod, Nick	L-R	5-11	190	9-28-87	.283	.242	.296	83	272	33	77	19	1	2	19	27	2	1	1	23	5	2	.382	.351
Berti, Jon	R-R	5-10	175	1-22-90	.250	.275	.237	128	505	85	126	18	5	3	44	57	11	2	1	90	56	19	.323	.338
Burns, Andy	R-R	6-2	190	8-7-90	.327	.419	.287	64	248	45	81	15	5	8	53	25	2	0	7	38	21	9	.524	.383
Cabrera, Melky	B-L	6-0	200	8-11-84	.167	.333	.000	2	6	0	1	0	0	0	0	0	0	0	0	2	0	0	.167	.167
Chung, Derrick	R-R	5-11	180	2-23-88	.287	.299	.281	71	244	24	70	12	0	0	21	20	1	3	2	30	3	1	.336	.341
Compton, Brian	R-R	6-2	195	9-29-89	.250	—	.250	1	4	0	1	0	0	0	0	0	0	0	0	3	0	0	.500	.250
Crouse, Michael	R-R	6-4	215	11-22-90	.250	.289	.232	85	300	34	75	18	2	8	41	39	5	0	3	92	21	9	.403	.343
Davis, Rajai	R-R	5-9	195	10-19-80	.300	.400	.200	3	10	2	3	1	0	0	0	0	0	0	0	1	0	0	.500	.300
Dominguez, Oliver	B-R	5-9	156	4-23-89	.218	.191	.233	42	133	13	29	5	1	3	11	12	0	0	1	34	0	2	.338	.281
Flores, Jorge	R-R	5-5	160	11-25-91	.193	.208	.182	19	57	7	11	5	1	0	4	6	2	0	0	6	1	2	.316	.292
Guerrero, Emilio	R-R	6-4	189	8-17-92	.143	—	.143	2	7	1	1	1	0	0	0	0	0	0	0	2	0	0	.286	.143
Hobson, K.C.	L-L	6-2	205	8-22-90	.215	.202	.220	108	396	37	85	22	0	19	72	26	0	0	9	69	2	0	.414	.258
Jacobo, Gabe	R-R	6-3	200	4-14-87	.278	.259	.288	46	169	30	47	13	1	4	36	17	2	0	3	37	1	0	.438	.346
Jimenez, A.J.	R-R	6-0	210	5-1-90	.429	.364	.471	9	28	5	12	3	0	1	9	1	0	0	0	3	0	0	.643	.448
Jones, Jonathan	R-R	5-11	185	8-2-89	.227	.282	.190	28	97	11	22	5	1	0	7	10	0	0	0	15	8	0	.299	.299
Knecht, Marcus	R-R	6-1	200	6-21-90	.239	.271	.222	116	419	42	100	21	3	11	46	27	9	0	3	106	10	4	.382	.297
Lawrie, Brett	R-R	6-0	225	1-18-90	.500	.667	.444	4	12	1	6	1	1	0	2	1	0	0	0	0	0	0	.750	.538
Leblebijian, Jason	R-R	5-8	190	5-13-91	.278	.250	.300	7	18	2	5	1	0	1	4	2	0	0	0	4	0	0	.500	.350
Mooney, Peter	L-R	5-6	155	8-19-90	.244	.269	.236	80	262	35	64	8	3	2	22	47	4	1	2	38	6	2	.321	.365
Munoz, Aaron	R-R	5-9	190	12-24-88	.257	.167	.304	10	35	3	9	1	0	0	3	2	0	1	0	7	0	0	.286	.297
Newman, Matt	L-L	5-10	170	9-20-88	.290	.238	.306	102	348	42	101	25	3	6	37	29	3	1	4	66	5	7	.431	.346
Opitz, Shane	L-R	6-1	180	1-10-92	.309	.236	.338	60	188	27	58	10	1	0	20	17	0	2	2	25	10	5	.399	.362
Patterson, Kevin	L-R	6-4	220	9-28-88	.169	.214	.159	22	83	8	14	4	0	0	9	4	0	0	2	33	0	0	.217	.202
Pierre, Gustavo	R-R	6-2	202	12-28-91	.210	.182	.225	54	195	19	41	10	1	3	15	2	1	1	3	66	3	0	.318	.219
Rankin, Pierce	R-R	6-1	190	4-26-89	.154	.122	.170	48	149	11	23	6	0	1	7	18	0	0	0	40	1	1	.215	.246
Reyes, Jose	B-R	6-1	195	6-11-83	.417	.000	.455	3	12	3	5	0	0	0	1	0	0	0	0	2	1	0	.417	.417
Schaeffer, Chris	R-R	5-10	195	11-19-87	.161	.091	.200	21	62	2	10	1	0	0	5	7	0	0	1	14	0	0	.177	.243
Talley, Jon	L-R	6-3	220	2-18-89	.208	.222	.200	14	53	7	11	7	0	1	3	3	0	0	1	21	0	0	.396	.246
Wilson, Kenny	B-R	5-10	185	1-30-90	.625	—	.625	2	8	4	5	2	0	0	1	2	0	0	0	1	1	0	.875	.700

Pitching	B-T	HT	WT	DOB	W	L	ERA	G	GS	CG	SV	IP	H	R	ER	HR	BB	SO	AVG	vLH	vRH	K/9	BB/9
Anderson, John	L-L	6-2	200	11-9-88	5	3	3.56	24	5	0	2	48	43	28	19	1	25	48	.238	.250	.232	9.00	4.69
Antolin, Dustin	R-R	6-2	195	8-9-89	2	1	2.35	20	0	0	2	23	16	7	6	0	7	28	.190	.171	.204	10.96	2.74
Barnes, Dan	L-R	6-1	195	10-21-89	1	1	22.50	3	0	0	0	2	5	5	5	0	1	2	.500	.000	.625	9.00	4.50
Bibens-Dirkx, Austin	R-R	6-1	210	4-29-85	9	5	2.85	17	13	0	0	101	84	43	32	6	26	98	.220	.259	.197	8.73	2.32
Boyd, Matt	L-L	6-3	215	2-2-91	0	2	5.40	3	2	0	0	10	7	6	6	2	3	11	.206	.364	.130	9.90	2.70
Brown, Eric	L-R	6-1	185	2-23-89	0	0	0.00	1	0	0	0	3	2	0	0	0	1	0	.200	.000	.222	0.00	3.38
Browning, Wil	R-R	6-3	190	9-8-88	2	0	1.02	10	0	0	0	18	13	2	2	0	0	15	.206	.238	.190	7.64	0.00
Champlin, Kramer	R-R	6-6	200	3-8-90	0	1	11.37	3	0	0	0	6	12	14	8	4	2	5	.400	.364	.421	7.11	2.84
Cole, Taylor	R-R	6-1	190	8-20-89	0	1	1.80	1	1	0	0	5	6	2	1	0	2	2	.300	.455	.111	3.60	3.60
Copeland, Scott	R-R	6-3	210	12-15-87	9	8	3.74	26	23	2	0	147	158	75	61	9	52	99	.277	.317	.251	6.08	3.19
Crawford, Evan	R-L	6-2	190	9-2-86	0	0	5.14	5	0	0	0	7	6	4	4	1	4	11	.231	.100	.313	14.14	5.14
Davis, Tony	B-L	5-11	185	1-16-88	4	1	3.71	43	0	0	0	51	45	22	21	1	19	71	.239	.155	.291	12.53	3.35
Delabar, Steve	R-R	6-4	230	7-17-83	0	0	0.00	1	0	0	0	1	0	0	0	0	0	0	.000	.000	.000	0.00	0.00
Drabek, Kyle	R-R	6-1	230	12-8-87	0	1	2.61	8	6	0	0	21	14	6	6	2	3	20	.192	.185	.196	8.71	1.31
Farina, Alan	R-R	5-11	190	8-9-86	0	0	1.50	6	0	0	1	6	5	1	1	1	0	6	.227	.500	.071	9.00	0.00
Ghysels, Chuck	R-R	5-11	225	11-28-89	0	0	0.00	1	0	0	0	1	1	0	0	0	0	1	.250	1.000	.000	6.75	0.00
Gracey, Scott	R-R	6-2	190	10-15-86	3	0	2.61	14	0	0	0	21	15	6	6	1	2	19	.200	.118	.268	8.27	0.87
Grifantini, Marco	R-R	6-3	185	9-17-85	3	2	5.21	21	6	0	1	48	59	29	28	4	23	27	.306	.318	.299	5.03	4.28
Griffith, Shawn	R-R	5-10	180	5-24-87	1	3	5.87	13	1	0	0	23	22	15	15	1	18	23	.250	.258	.246	9.00	7.04
Happ, J.A.	L-L	6-6	195	10-19-82	0	0	0.00	1	1	0	0	5	3	0	0	0	0	7	.176	.000	.200	12.60	0.00
Hernandez, Jesse	R-R	6-1	200	8-23-88	7	12	3.49	26	20	0	0	134	134	64	52	9	38	89	.258	.273	.248	5.98	2.55
Hutchison, Drew	L-R	6-2	195	8-22-90	0	0	1.04	3	2	0	0	9	2	1	1	0	6	12	.080	.000	.125	12.46	6.23
Jackson, Justin	R-R	6-2	190	12-11-88	0	0	5.28	10	0	0	0	15	19	9	9	3	5	8	.302	.240	.342	4.70	2.93
Jeffress, Jeremy	R-R	6-0	195	9-21-87	0	0	0.00	3	0	0	0	5	1	0	0	0	0	2	.059	.250	.000	3.60	0.00
Johnson, Josh	L-R	6-7	250	1-31-84	0	0	3.00	1	1	0	0	3	3	1	1	0	0	6	.250	.000	.300	15.00	0.00
Lawrence, Casey	R-R	6-2	170	10-28-87	4	6	4.43	16	15	0	0	89	107	48	44	7	15	54	.302	.299	.304	5.44	1.51
Marze, Dayton	R-R	6-2	185	1-1-89	1	1	3.41	22	0	0	0	34	26	13	13	3	11	20	.211	.205	.215	5.24	2.88
McFarland, Blake	R-R	6-5	230	2-2-88	0	8	3.72	48	0	0	18	46	46	23	19	4	19	49	.263	.269	.259	9.59	3.72
McGowan, Dustin	R-R	6-3	230	3-24-82	0	0	0.00	3	0	0	0	3	1	0	0	0	1	5	.100	.000	.167	15.00	3.00
Meyer, Ajay	L-R	6-6	185	7-19-87	3	2	2.77	48	0	0	8	68	65	23	21	7	8	76	.247	.286	.227	10.01	1.05
Morrow, Brandon	R-R	6-3	200	7-26-84	0	0	13.50	1	1	0	0	2	5	3	3	1	1	0	.556	.750	.400	0.00	4.50
Nieves, Efrain	L-L	6-0	169	11-15-89	2	2	5.49	7	4	0	0	20	23	15	12	1	7	13	.291	.300	.288	5.95	3.20
Norris, Daniel	L-L	6-2	180	4-25-93	1	0	0.00	1	1	0	0	5	1	0	0	0	2	1	.063	.000	.083	1.80	3.60
Oliver, Darren	R-L	6-3	250	10-6-70	0	0	0.00	2	2	0	0	2	0	0	0	0	0	4	.000	.000	.000	18.00	0.00
Perez, Luis	L-L	6-0	210	1-20-85	0	0	1.50	4	2	0	0	6	1	1	1	0	2	5	.200	.000	.250	7.50	3.00
Romero, Ricky	R-L	6-0	225	11-6-84	0	0	1.29	1	1	0	0	7	6	1	1	0	6		.240	.333	.227	5.14	0.00
Sanchez, Aaron	R-R	6-4	190	7-1-92	4	5	3.34	22	20	0	0	86	63	40	32	4	40	75	.202	.207	.199	7.82	4.17
Santos, Sergio	R-R	6-3	240	7-4-83	0	0	5.79	5	4	0	0	5	4	3	3	0	2	2	.250	.500	.167	3.86	3.86
Ybarra, Tyler	L-L	6-2	170	12-11-89	2	3	1.95	39	0	0	2	55	30	16	12	0	33	65	.156	.131	.168	10.57	5.37

Fielding

Catcher	PCT	G	PO	A	E	DP	PB
Chung	.998	64	443	64	1	5	7
Compton	1.000	1	8	0	0	0	0
Jimenez	.981	7	49	2	1	0	0
Munoz	1.000	10	89	8	0	0	1
Rankin	.974	36	243	24	7	2	7
Schaeffer	1.000	20	131	11	0	2	4

First Base	PCT	G	PO	A	E	DP
Dominguez	1.000	1	6	0	0	2
Hobson	.992	93	811	65	7	67
Jacobo	.995	22	185	14	1	14
Opitz	1.000	5	40	7	0	1
Patterson	1.000	7	73	6	0	9
Rankin	1.000	1	5	2	0	0
Talley	.989	8	79	7	1	8

Second Base	PCT	G	PO	A	E	DP
Berti	.978	116	181	341	12	69

	PCT	G	PO	A	E	DP
Dominguez	1.000	8	13	19	0	4
Flores	1.000	2	1	1	0	1
Lawrie	1.000	2	8	6	0	4
Leblebijian	1.000	1	5	5	0	1
Opitz	1.000	5	10	17	0	6

Third Base	PCT	G	PO	A	E	DP
Burns	.928	59	29	125	12	7
Chung	1.000	2	2	1	0	0
Dominguez	1.000	6	4	12	0	0
Guerrero	1.000	1	0	2	0	1
Lawrie	1.000	2	1	0	0	0
Opitz	.944	11	8	26	2	3
Pierre	.897	51	42	89	15	7
Rankin	.833	4	2	8	2	1

Shortstop	PCT	G	PO	A	E	DP
Burns	1.000	6	5	18	0	3
Dominguez	.938	2	8	7	1	3

	PCT	G	PO	A	E	DP
Flores	.986	18	24	46	1	11
Guerrero	.889	2	3	5	1	2
Leblebijian	.933	4	6	8	1	1
Mooney	.969	77	89	224	10	43
Opitz	.943	30	41	74	7	16
Reyes	1.000	2	0	3	0	0

Outfield	PCT	G	PO	A	E	DP
Baligod	.967	77	116	3	4	1
Cabrera	—	1	0	0	0	0
Crouse	.988	80	154	4	2	4
Davis	1.000	2	2	0	0	0
Jacobo	1.000	9	22	0	0	0
Jones	1.000	26	44	1	0	1
Knecht	.972	109	164	8	5	1
Newman	.995	95	192	11	1	3
Rankin	1.000	2	0	1	0	0
Wilson	1.000	2	7	1	0	1

LANSING LUGNUTS

LOW CLASS A

MIDWEST LEAGUE

Batting	B-T	HT	WT	DOB	AVG	vLH	vRH	G	AB	R	H	2B	3B	HR	RBI	BB	HBP	SH	SF	SO	SB	CS	SLG	OBP
Conner, Seth	R-R	6-2	205	1-29-92	.159	.143	.161	34	107	11	17	2	0	0	8	10	1	1	1	26	0	0	.178	.235
Flores, Jorge	R-R	5-5	160	11-25-91	.247	.200	.269	58	194	24	48	17	1	1	18	23	7	2	0	30	8	7	.361	.348
Fuenmayor, Balbino	R-R	6-3	230	11-26-89	.208	.133	.222	26	96	13	20	4	1	4	17	8	3	0	1	32	0	0	.396	.287
Guerrero, Emilio	R-R	6-4	189	8-21-92	.277	.267	.281	98	343	48	95	15	2	8	52	39	4	2	3	58	17	6	.402	.355
Hawkins, Chris	L-R	6-2	195	8-17-91	.226	.278	.214	108	380	44	86	12	6	3	28	32	1	6	2	65	9	5	.313	.287
Klein, Dan	R-R	5-10	185	8-29-90	.250	.158	.289	19	64	11	16	7	0	3	11	3	1	1	2	13	0	0	.500	.286
Lawrie, Brett	R-R	6-2	225	1-18-90	.000	.000	.000	1	6	1	0	0	0	0	0	2	0	0	0	1	0	0	.000	.250
Leblebijian, Jason	R-R	6-1	190	5-13-91	.231	.275	.211	50	160	23	37	6	1	0	12	17	5	0	2	33	3	2	.281	.321
Leyland, Jordan	R-R	6-4	205	9-6-89	.231	.071	.275	37	130	16	30	2	1	2	19	17	1	0	2	33	2	1	.308	.320
Lopes, Christian	R-R	6-0	185	10-1-92	.245	.281	.234	129	497	52	122	24	3	5	66	40	8	0	7	78	2	1	.336	.308

	B-T	HT	WT	DOB	AVG	vLH	vRH	G	AB	R	H	2B	3B	HR	RBI	BB	HBP	SH	SF	SO	SB	CS	SLG	OBP
Melendez, Ronnie	R-R	5-10	170	9-29-89	.061	.000	.077	10	33	2	2	0	0	0	2	2	1	1	0	10	3	1	.061	.139
Munoz, Aaron	R-R	5-9	190	12-24-88	.224	.172	.241	40	116	12	26	4	1	0	7	13	3	2	2	20	1	0	.276	.313
Nessy, Santiago	R-R	6-2	230	12-8-92	.241	.322	.212	61	224	23	54	15	0	5	23	13	4	0	1	59	0	0	.375	.293
Opitz, Shane	L-R	6-1	180	1-10-92	.370	.300	.386	15	54	9	20	5	1	0	3	5	0	0	0	13	0	1	.500	.424
Patterson, Kevin	L-R	6-4	220	9-28-88	.212	.238	.204	94	344	48	73	15	2	18	62	44	2	0	5	107	0	0	.424	.301
Pierre, Gustavo	R-R	6-2	202	12-28-91	.292	.289	.293	61	233	33	68	15	2	5	33	2	1	0	1	62	15	6	.438	.300
Pompey, Dalton	B-R	6-1	170	12-11-92	.261	.273	.256	115	437	68	114	22	9	6	40	63	5	3	3	106	38	10	.394	.358
Ramirez, Carlos	R-R	6-3	172	4-24-91	.228	.257	.217	114	395	53	90	27	5	7	41	33	6	1	0	102	14	5	.375	.297
Smith Jr., Dwight	L-R	5-11	180	10-25-92	.284	.196	.310	109	423	57	120	17	3	7	46	52	3	0	1	82	25	5	.388	.365
Sweeney, Kellen	L-R	6-0	180	9-14-91	.185	.191	.183	109	352	33	65	10	5	5	32	40	1	4	1	94	1	1	.284	.269

Pitching	B-T	HT	WT	DOB	W	L	ERA	G	GS	CG	SV	IP	H	R	ER	HR	BB	SO	AVG	vLH	vRH	K/9	BB/9
Avendano, Javier	R-R	6-3	220	9-6-90	8	6	3.76	26	22	0	0	115	114	69	48	8	62	99	.254	.257	.252	7.75	4.85
Boyd, Matt	L-L	6-3	215	2-2-91	0	1	0.64	5	3	0	0	14	7	1	1	0	1	12	.140	.200	.114	7.71	0.64
Brown, Eric	L-R	6-1	185	2-23-89	2	3	3.81	7	5	0	0	28	33	16	12	2	8	15	.297	.278	.316	4.76	2.54
Browning, Wil	R-R	6-3	190	9-8-88	2	3	2.44	32	0	0	4	44	29	19	12	0	24	66	.178	.276	.125	13.40	4.87
Champlin, Kramer	R-R	6-6	200	3-8-90	6	4	3.67	26	2	1	0	81	65	35	33	6	16	73	.215	.179	.240	8.11	1.78
Cole, Taylor	R-R	6-1	190	8-20-89	7	11	4.02	26	26	0	0	132	141	75	59	5	59	101	.273	.277	.270	6.89	4.02
Donahue, Tucker	R-R	6-2	200	8-27-90	3	3	6.09	41	0	0	0	55	65	41	37	4	28	45	.298	.315	.287	7.41	4.61
Ghysels, Chuck	R-R	5-11	225	11-28-89	2	1	5.09	14	0	0	3	18	18	13	10	0	14	19	.277	.280	.275	9.68	7.13
Girodo, Chad	L-L	6-1	195	2-6-91	1	1	4.18	14	0	0	0	24	21	11	11	0	5	24	.236	.179	.262	9.13	1.90
Gonzalez, Alonzo	L-L	6-5	200	1-15-92	2	9	5.56	18	16	0	0	79	100	79	49	9	42	48	.333	.367	.321	5.45	4.76
Graveman, Kendall	R-R	6-2	185	12-21-90	1	3	4.31	10	10	0	0	40	41	23	19	3	13	25	.266	.280	.253	5.67	2.95
Jackson, Justin	R-R	6-2	190	12-11-88	0	2	2.36	23	0	0	0	34	38	15	9	1	24	26	.275	.254	.299	6.82	6.29
Johnson, Matt	R-R	6-3	210	5-26-89	0	0	6.00	9	0	0	0	9	15	11	6	1	4	3	.341	.412	.296	3.00	4.00
Kadish, Ian	L-R	6-0	200	8-29-88	5	4	3.36	49	0	0	0	67	63	30	25	6	15	79	.247	.306	.204	10.61	2.01
Murphy, Griffin	R-L	6-3	200	1-16-91	1	3	4.18	36	0	0	1	71	80	43	33	6	31	60	.287	.337	.262	7.61	3.93
Nieves, Efrain	L-L	6-0	169	11-15-89	2	2	4.09	28	0	0	0	55	48	33	25	0	25	54	.229	.148	.262	8.84	4.09
Norris, Daniel	L-L	6-2	180	4-25-93	1	7	4.20	23	22	0	0	86	84	46	40	6	44	99	.255	.308	.234	10.40	4.62
Osuna, Roberto	R-R	6-2	230	2-7-95	3	5	5.53	10	10	0	0	42	39	28	26	6	11	51	.242	.339	.182	10.84	2.34
Sikula, Arik	R-R	6-1	195	12-21-88	6	1	1.93	50	0	0	19	61	41	14	13	2	18	60	.191	.230	.164	8.90	2.67
Turner, Colton	L-L	6-3	185	1-17-91	1	0	2.61	4	0	0	0	10	8	3	3	0	6	9	.229	.286	.190	7.84	5.23
White, Ben	R-R	6-2	185	5-10-89	8	9	4.33	28	23	1	0	137	152	85	66	11	46	98	.277	.255	.294	6.42	3.01

Fielding

Catcher	PCT	G	PO	A	E	DP	PB
Conner	.976	32	224	22	6	3	17
Klein	.986	19	124	19	2	0	4
Munoz	.989	40	307	42	4	3	9
Nessy	.984	54	398	46	7	4	18

First Base	PCT	G	PO	A	E	DP
Fuenmayor	.995	25	212	9	1	16
Leblebijian	1.000	16	118	8	0	16
Leyland	.993	34	281	19	2	18
Opitz	.972	5	31	4	1	1
Patterson	.976	36	293	32	8	23
Sweeney	.988	28	222	17	3	21

Second Base	PCT	G	PO	A	E	DP
Flores	.981	10	24	28	1	8
Leblebijian	1.000	2	1	4	0	1
Lopes	.974	114	193	339	14	74
Sweeney	.938	15	20	41	4	4

Third Base	PCT	G	PO	A	E	DP
Guerrero	1.000	2	2	2	0	0
Lawrie	.875	2	0	7	1	3
Leblebijian	.899	21	18	44	7	5
Opitz	1.000	1	3	0	0	0
Pierre	.873	58	33	98	19	7
Sweeney	.882	59	34	86	16	3

Shortstop	PCT	G	PO	A	E	DP
Flores	.932	35	66	85	11	27
Guerrero	.917	89	138	226	33	45
Leblebijian	1.000	7	8	17	0	3
Lopes	1.000	3	6	8	0	2
Opitz	.909	7	6	14	2	1

Outfield	PCT	G	PO	A	E	DP
Hawkins	.969	89	153	4	5	1
Leyland	.857	5	6	0	1	0
Melendez	1.000	10	16	1	0	0
Pompey	1.000	114	223	8	0	0
Ramirez	.956	102	163	11	8	1
Smith Jr.	.967	104	202	6	7	1

TORONTO BLUE JAYS

VANCOUVER CANADIANS   SHORT-SEASON
NORTHWEST LEAGUE

Batting	B-T	HT	WT	DOB	AVG	vLH	vRH	G	AB	R	H	2B	3B	HR	RBI	BB	HBP	SH	SF	SO	SB	CS	SLG	OBP
Arcila, Daniel	L-R	6-1	170	7-4-90	.212	.125	.227	24	52	7	11	1	1	1	4	9	1	1	0	18	2	3	.327	.339
Atkinson, Justin	R-R	6-1	205	7-24-93	.230	.378	.196	64	239	27	55	9	1	1	24	31	2	1	1	74	2	1	.289	.322
Conner, Seth	R-R	6-2	205	1-29-92	.208	.375	.175	14	48	3	10	2	0	0	1	6	1	0	0	16	0	0	.250	.283
Dantzler, L.B.	L-R	5-11	200	5-22-91	.302	.278	.309	59	232	32	70	20	0	9	35	30	2	0	1	47	0	1	.504	.385
Fermin, Andy	L-R	6-0	180	7-27-89	.274	.297	.269	57	212	29	58	11	2	1	29	25	1	1	2	25	1	2	.358	.350
Frank, Chaz	L-L	5-10	170	10-17-90	.282	.286	.281	49	181	35	51	9	3	0	16	36	4	1	0	36	8	5	.365	.412
Garcia, Melvin	R-R	6-0	175	9-17-91	.231	.316	.208	33	91	6	21	5	1	0	11	11	4	1	3	36	1	0	.308	.330
Harris, David	R-R	6-1	190	8-10-91	.263	.265	.263	45	152	21	40	9	0	2	19	4	4	0	2	37	6	2	.362	.296
Hitt, Matt	R-R	5-11	190	8-16-89	.033	.000	.042	14	30	7	1	0	0	0	4	3	0	0	0	13	0	0	.033	.091
Kalfus, Brenden	B-R	6-0	190	8-22-91	.268	.234	.276	63	228	30	61	11	2	1	19	25	5	2	3	53	9	3	.346	.349
Klein, Dan	R-R	5-10	185	8-29-90	.183	.059	.233	19	60	7	11	1	1	2	11	5	2	0	2	22	1	0	.333	.261
Leblebijian, Jason	R-R	6-1	190	5-13-91	.333	.667	.278	5	21	3	7	1	1	1	5	2	0	0	0	5	1	0	.619	.391
Leyland, Jordan	R-R	6-4	205	9-6-89	.341	.433	.314	36	135	21	46	11	0	2	22	24	0	0	2	34	1	1	.467	.435
Lugo, Dawel	R-R	6-0	188	12-13-94	.246	.429	.200	16	69	6	17	4	0	1	8	1	0	0	0	13	0	0	.348	.257
Melendez, Ronnie	R-R	5-10	170	9-29-89	.171	.333	.138	13	35	6	6	1	1	0	4	4	0	1	1	8	5	1	.257	.250
Parmley, Ian	L-L	5-11	175	12-19-89	.257	.306	.245	66	257	31	66	7	0	0	15	23	3	2	2	61	23	2	.284	.323
Reeves, Mike	L-R	6-2	195	9-16-90	.275	.343	.259	55	193	26	53	6	0	1	25	28	4	0	2	36	2	1	.321	.374
Taylor, Nico	R-R	6-4	215	2-9-90	.234	.750	.186	16	47	6	11	3	1	0	4	7	1	0	0	12	3	1	.340	.345
Thon, Dickie Joe	R-R	6-2	185	11-16-91	.280	.314	.271	45	164	31	46	7	3	1	21	18	7	1	3	54	5	4	.378	.370
Valeriote, Shaun	L-L	5-11	175	12-19-89	.040	.000	.056	12	25	3	1	0	0	0	3	8	0	1	0	10	0	0	.040	.273
Vazquez, Christian	B-R	5-10	170	9-11-89	.203	.105	.220	34	128	9	26	2	0	0	9	8	2	2	1	18	2	0	.219	.259
Vega-Rosado, Jorge	R-R	5-8	175	12-5-91	.114	.000	.128	15	44	4	5	0	0	0	2	4	3	0	0	12	5	0	.114	.235

Pitching

Pitching	B-T	HT	WT	DOB	W	L	ERA	G	GS	CG	SV	IP	H	R	ER	HR	BB	SO	AVG	vLH	vRH	K/9	BB/9
Anderson, Kyle	R-L	6-2	205	5-24-90	5	3	2.71	15	15	0	0	83	74	31	25	2	12	58	.233	.270	.219	6.29	1.30
Brechbuehler, Tim	R-R	6-8	205	10-21-89	0	1	10.80	13	0	0	0	12	20	15	14	0	12	12	.370	.353	.378	9.26	9.26
Brisker, Markus	R-R	6-3	210	8-21-90	1	1	7.71	6	0	0	0	5	5	4	4	0	10	4	.278	.200	.308	7.71	19.29
Brosnahan, Bobby	L-L	6-0	155	6-2-89	1	1	7.45	7	3	0	0	19	31	17	16	0	8	13	.383	.444	.352	6.05	3.72
Brown, Eric	R-L	6-1	185	2-23-89	5	1	1.37	9	9	0	0	53	43	9	8	1	8	46	.226	.278	.180	7.86	1.37
D'Alessandro, Justin	R-R	6-4	190	9-27-89	1	1	7.36	3	0	0	0	4	2	3	3	0	4	3	.182	.500	.000	7.36	9.82
Dawson, Shane	R-L	6-1	180	9-9-93	1	1	2.89	4	4	0	0	19	17	6	6	0	4	26	.246	.200	.265	12.54	1.93
Dermody, Matt	R-L	6-5	190	7-4-90	5	1	1.77	15	2	0	0	41	45	12	8	0	4	50	.280	.193	.327	11.07	0.89
Dorsett, Brandon	R-R	6-3	200	11-1-89	1	0	7.58	18	0	0	0	19	20	17	16	1	16	8	.267	.217	.288	3.79	7.58
Gabryszwski, Jeremy	R-R	6-4	195	3-16-93	5	2	2.82	14	14	0	0	77	71	35	24	0	10	40	.241	.261	.225	4.70	1.17
Ghysels, Chuck	R-R	5-11	225	11-28-89	0	3	2.15	28	0	0	11	29	19	14	7	1	13	51	.178	.214	.154	15.65	3.99
Gonzalez, Alonzo	L-L	6-5	200	1-15-92	0	2	2.68	11	4	0	0	37	30	12	11	1	12	30	.231	.306	.202	7.30	2.92
James, Justin	R-R	6-1	195	3-17-90	1	7	3.86	20	2	0	0	44	45	27	19	0	15	29	.256	.230	.270	5.89	3.05
Jimenez, Alvido	R-R	6-1	160	11-22-91	0	0	0.93	8	0	0	0	10	3	2	1	0	3	9	.100	.100	.100	8.38	2.79
Johnson, Matt	R-R	6-3	210	5-26-88	0	1	2.30	26	0	0	1	31	28	11	8	2	6	12	.235	.133	.297	3.45	1.72
Kountis, Jonathan	R-R	6-3	220	3-15-88	0	0	5.79	10	0	0	3	9	16	8	6	0	5	10	.364	.400	.345	9.64	4.82
Permison, Drew	R-R	5-10	170	2-24-89	1	0	7.20	5	0	0	0	5	8	4	4	0	1	5	.364	.286	.400	9.00	1.80
Pickens, Garrett	R-R	6-1	185	4-17-90	1	4	3.29	20	0	0	1	27	21	10	10	1	15	15	.226	.316	.164	4.94	4.94
Robson, Tom	R-R	6-4	200	6-27-93	3	0	0.94	7	7	0	0	38	28	5	4	0	11	29	.212	.214	.211	6.81	2.58
Silverstein, Scott	L-L	6-5	250	5-27-90	2	2	4.58	14	4	0	1	37	41	22	19	2	13	31	.279	.360	.237	7.47	3.13
Spano, Joe	L-L	5-10	175	10-27-89	2	1	4.84	19	0	0	0	22	22	13	12	0	21	30	.253	.242	.259	12.09	8.46
Turner, Colton	L-L	6-3	185	1-17-91	4	5	2.96	13	12	1	0	67	56	29	22	4	17	39	.224	.246	.216	5.24	2.28

Fielding

Catcher	PCT	G	PO	A	E	DP	PB
Conner	.990	10	100	4	1	0	1
Hitt	.972	10	34	1	1	0	1
Klein	1.000	15	81	17	0	0	1
Reeves	.984	51	322	43	6	2	5

First Base	PCT	G	PO	A	E	DP
Arcila	.984	9	60	2	1	8
Atkinson	.986	23	193	12	3	13
Conner	1.000	1	10	1	0	6
Dantzler	.993	40	382	30	3	32
Leyland	1.000	10	118	8	0	12

Second Base	PCT	G	PO	A	E	DP
Fermin	.981	19	34	71	2	18

	PCT	G	PO	A	E	DP
Harris	.944	32	56	97	9	18
Vazquez	.951	15	29	48	4	7
Vega-Rosado	.968	14	22	39	2	9

Third Base	PCT	G	PO	A	E	DP
Atkinson	.941	38	18	78	6	7
Dantzler	1.000	1	2	0	0	
Fermin	.961	30	15	58	3	7
Harris	.938	6	1	14	1	1
Leblebijian	.875	3	3	4	1	0
Valeriote	.944	8	4	13	1	2

Shortstop	PCT	G	PO	A	E	DP
Atkinson	—	1	0	0	0	
Harris	1.000	2	3	7	0	0

Outfield	PCT	G	PO	A	E	DP
Leblebijian	1.000	2	3	8	0	2
Lugo	.935	16	27	73	7	11
Thon	.911	40	59	105	16	21
Vazquez	.946	20	26	62	5	14
Frank	1.000	47	93	3	0	2
Garcia	.951	31	38	1	2	0
Kalfus	.961	61	90	8	4	1
Leyland	.955	12	21	0	1	0
Melendez	1.000	11	21	1	0	0
Parmley	.974	66	141	7	4	2
Taylor	1.000	15	20	0	0	0
Thon	1.000	1	1	0	0	0

BLUEFIELD BLUE JAYS   ROOKIE
APPALACHIAN LEAGUE

Batting	B-T	HT	WT	DOB	AVG	vLH	vRH	G	AB	R	H	2B	3B	HR	RBI	BB	HBP	SH	SF	SO	SB	CS	SLG	OBP
Arce, Eric	L-R	5-9	205	11-29-91	.219	.250	.208	13	32	4	7	1	1	3	8	7	0	0	0	14	0	0	.594	.359
Barreto, Franklin	R-R	5-9	174	2-27-96	.204	.222	.200	15	54	4	11	5	1	0	7	2	2	0	0	14	0	2	.333	.259
Custons, Garrett	R-R	5-11	200	9-14-90	.222	.176	.243	17	54	6	12	5	0	0	7	4	2	0	1	14	3	2	.315	.295
Davis, D.J.	L-R	6-1	180	7-25-94	.240	.271	.229	58	225	35	54	8	7	6	25	8	3	1	3	76	13	8	.418	.323
Davis, Jonathan	R-R	5-8	188	5-12-92	.238	.231	.242	43	130	21	31	11	3	2	14	14	8	2	1	26	4	2	.415	.346
Dean, Matt	R-R	6-3	190	12-22-92	.338	.379	.322	63	210	37	71	14	3	6	35	14	5	2	2	57	8	5	.519	.390
Garcia, Melvin	R-R	6-0	175	9-17-91	.250	.000	.333	8	20	2	5	1	0	0	1	0	0	0	1	4	0	0	.300	.238
Gonzalez, Jesus	R-R	6-0	180	1-11-95	.183	.194	.179	45	120	8	22	4	1	1	18	6	4	0	3	53	0	2	.258	.241
Jones, Dennis	R-R	6-3	185	9-4-92	.267	.333	.222	32	30	15	8	0	0	1	3	4	3	0	0	14	2	0	.367	.405
Locastro, Tim	R-R	6-1	175	7-14-92	.283	.256	.293	43	138	28	39	5	3	1	13	13	6	4	1	12	12	2	.384	.367
Loveless, Derrick	L-R	6-1	200	3-7-93	.226	.257	.218	59	177	22	40	6	6	2	22	10	8	0	3	47	3	1	.362	.329
Lugo, Dawel	R-R	6-0	188	12-13-94	.297	.104	.361	51	192	28	57	11	2	6	36	5	2	0	3	28	1	0	.469	.317
Maldonado, Alex	R-R	5-9	175	6-12-91	.260	.316	.247	34	100	16	26	0	1	0	11	13	1	2	0	20	1	1	.280	.351
Moseby, Lydell	R-R	6-6	230	3-15-92	.182	.375	.120	16	33	3	6	1	0	0	2	0	0	2	0	7	0	0	.212	.270
Nay, Mitch	R-R	6-3	195	9-20-93	.300	.246	.318	64	230	41	69	11	0	6	42	25	0	0	3	35	0	1	.426	.364
Rojas, Angel	R-R	5-11	160	4-7-93	.125	.077	.136	30	72	4	9	2	0	1	4	2	2	2	1	19	0	0	.194	.167
Saez, Jorge	R-R	5-10	185	8-28-90	.247	.233	.252	51	158	21	39	10	0	2	22	14	2	0	3	39	2	0	.348	.311
Silviano, John	L-R	5-11	190	7-11-94	.141	.600	.110	34	78	5	11	2	0	3	10	10	0	0	0	34	0	0	.282	.239
Sotillo, Andres	R-R	5-11	180	12-28-93	.200	.400	.150	12	25	2	5	2	0	0	3	1	1	0	3	0	0	.280	.310
Taylor, Nico	R-R	6-4	215	2-9-90	.262	.320	.225	24	65	14	17	6	0	2	13	13	0	0	0	13	1	0	.446	.385

Pitching	B-T	HT	WT	DOB	W	L	ERA	G	GS	CG	SV	IP	H	R	ER	HR	BB	SO	AVG	vLH	vRH	K/9	BB/9
Barber, Brett	R-R	6-1	180	11-7-90	2	2	3.80	19	0	0	7	21	17	16	9	2	5	23	.200	.200	.207	9.70	2.11
Biggs, Mark	R-R	6-3	205	5-10-93	1	0	4.91	11	3	0	0	29	39	20	16	2	13	17	.315	.289	.326	5.22	3.99
Cardona, Adonys	R-R	6-1	170	1-16-94	0	2	6.75	8	5	0	1	25	35	20	19	1	13	27	.327	.292	.337	9.59	4.62
Castro, Miguel	R-R	6-5	190	12-24-94	0	0	0.00	1	0	0	0	2	1	2	0	0	0	3	.111	.500	.000	13.50	0.00
Cordero, Jimmy	R-R	6-3	195	10-19-91	0	0	0.00	1	0	0	0	1	0	0	0	0	1	0	.000	—	.000	9.00	9.00
D'Alessandro, Justin	R-R	6-4	190	9-27-89	1	1	7.94	8	0	0	0	11	19	12	10	3	8	11	.373	.391	.357	8.74	6.35
Dawson, Shane	R-L	6-1	180	9-9-93	1	3	3.29	7	3	0	0	27	17	10	10	1	6	35	.179	.250	.172	11.52	1.98
DeJong, Chase	L-R	6-4	185	12-29-93	2	3	3.05	13	10	1	0	56	58	21	19	0	10	66	.261	.274	.255	10.61	1.61
Del Rosario, Yeyfry	R-R	6-2	182	4-27-94	4	2	2.54	16	0	0	2	28	24	11	8	3	15	33	.224	.303	.189	10.48	4.76

Dragmire, Brady	R-R	6-1	180	2-5-93	3	2	2.16	14	8	0	2	50	39	17	12	5	8	40	.209	.313	.154	7.20	1.44
Gracesqui, Francisco	L-L	6-0	175	11-26-91	4	0	2.82	17	0	0	0	22	22	8	7	1	12	16	.253	.368	.221	6.45	4.84
Hollon, Clint	R-R	6-1	195	12-24-94	0	1	10.13	2	1	0	0	5	6	7	6	1	3	5	.261	.300	.231	8.44	5.06
Jimenez, Alvido	R-R	6-1	160	11-22-91	3	0	1.29	12	0	0	4	21	11	3	3	0	7	27	.149	.111	.161	11.57	3.00
Kelly, Adaric	R-R	5-10	180	12-1-92	2	1	2.70	15	0	0	0	23	22	10	7	1	14	22	.242	.286	.222	8.49	5.40
Kish, Phil	R-R	6-0	175	8-30-89	0	2	1.96	11	0	0	2	18	14	6	4	1	6	16	.219	.389	.152	7.85	2.95
Labourt, Jairo	L-L	6-4	204	3-7-94	2	2	1.92	12	8	0	0	52	39	16	11	3	14	45	.204	.190	.208	7.84	2.44
Lovecchio, Joey	R-R	6-2	190	9-6-90	4	2	6.08	13	1	0	0	24	30	19	16	3	9	20	.313	.310	.313	7.61	3.42
Mayza, Tim	L-L	6-3	205	1-15-92	1	2	6.95	10	3	0	0	22	30	20	17	2	10	17	.323	.417	.309	6.95	4.09
Robson, Tom	R-R	6-4	200	6-27-93	3	0	1.38	6	5	0	0	26	15	4	4	1	5	18	.172	.129	.196	6.23	1.73
Silverstein, Scott	L-L	6-5	250	5-27-90	0	0	1.50	1	1	0	0	6	4	1	1	0	0	4	.200	.333	.143	6.00	0.00
Tirado, Alberto	R-R	6-1	177	12-10-94	3	0	1.68	12	8	0	0	48	41	13	9	1	20	44	.236	.290	.200	8.19	3.72
Wasilewski, Zak	L-L	6-1	190	6-16-93	4	2	3.16	13	11	0	0	51	46	21	18	1	30	47	.247	.273	.244	8.24	5.26

Fielding

Catcher	PCT	G	PO	A	E	DP	PB
Custons	.993	17	130	14	1	1	1
Saez	.995	47	337	40	2	4	14
Sotillo	.986	12	67	2	1	0	3

First Base	PCT	G	PO	A	E	DP
Dean	.996	57	464	30	2	50
Moseby	.982	9	53	3	1	4
Rojas	.971	10	63	3	2	10

Second Base	PCT	G	PO	A	E	DP
Locastro	.955	31	58	69	6	19

Maldonado	.944	31	54	80	8	16
Rojas	1.000	15	18	40	0	9
Third Base	**PCT**	**G**	**PO**	**A**	**E**	**DP**
Dean	1.000	4	1	6	0	0
Moseby	—	1	0	0	0	0
Nay	.901	63	35	120	17	12
Rojas	1.000	3	1	2	0	1
Shortstop	**PCT**	**G**	**PO**	**A**	**E**	**DP**
Barreto	.852	15	20	32	9	11
Locastro	.966	5	6	22	1	5

Lugo	.946	48	57	134	11	28
Rojas	1.000	3	3	5	0	0
Outfield	**PCT**	**G**	**PO**	**A**	**E**	**DP**
Arce	1.000	6	2	0	0	0
Davis	.946	57	86	1	5	1
Davis	.962	31	50	0	2	0
Garcia	.933	7	13	1	1	2
Gonzalez	1.000	43	65	2	0	2
Jones	1.000	12	14	0	0	0
Loveless	.959	57	69	2	3	0
Taylor	1.000	14	15	0	0	0

GCL BLUE JAYS   ROOKIE

GULF COAST LEAGUE

Batting	B-T	HT	WT	DOB	AVG	vLH	vRH	G	AB	R	H	2B	3B	HR	RBI	BB	HBP	SH	SF	SO	SB	CS	SLG	OBP
Alford, Anthony	R-R	6-1	193	7-20-94	.227	.400	.176	6	22	4	5	2	1	0	2	6	1	1	0	6	2	0	.409	.414
Almonte, Josh	R-R	6-3	193	1-28-94	.167	.186	.158	48	144	16	24	6	0	1	10	8	4	2	1	58	5	3	.229	.229
Arcila, Daniel	L-R	6-1	170	7-4-90	.333	1.000	.200	1	6	1	2	1	0	0	2	1	0	0	0	2	1	1	.500	.429
Barreto, Franklin	R-R	5-9	174	2-27-96	.299	.267	.316	44	174	30	52	16	6	4	19	13	6	1	0	42	10	4	.529	.368
Cenas, Gabriel	R-R	6-1	155	10-16-93	.259	.133	.319	44	139	16	36	9	2	3	32	17	4	0	4	32	0	2	.417	.348
Collins, Boomer	R-R	6-0	200	6-13-89	.305	.295	.310	52	187	36	57	13	3	2	25	23	4	0	1	29	6	0	.439	.391
Dantzler, L.B.	L-R	5-11	200	5-22-91	.333	1.000	.000	1	3	0	1	0	0	0	1	0	1	0	0	0	0	0	.333	.500
De Aza, Andres	R-R	6-4	200	11-17-94	.235	.222	.241	39	119	11	28	6	0	2	17	9	1	0	1	39	1	1	.336	.292
De La Cruz, Michael	R-R	5-10	175	5-15-93	.133	.250	.091	13	30	3	4	0	1	0	3	4	0	0	0	8	0	0	.200	.235
DeSouza, Nathan	L-R	6-0	185	7-13-94	.192	.000	.246	29	73	6	14	2	2	2	12	6	0	0	2	14	0	0	.356	.247
Devonshire, Daniel	L-R	6-1	220	3-30-92	.154	.000	.167	21	39	2	6	1	0	0	4	6	1	1	0	10	0	0	.179	.283
Dupont, Will	R-R	6-0	170	12-1-94	.262	.150	.317	26	61	13	16	3	0	0	10	6	1	0	0	13	3	2	.311	.338
Florides, Andrew	R-R	6-1	170	1-22-95	.152	.222	.125	17	33	4	5	0	0	0	3	1	0	1	0	12	0	0	.152	.243
Fuentes, Edwin	R-R	6-0	170	8-14-94	.206	.148	.240	51	165	24	34	5	0	0	9	16	4	2	1	29	7	1	.236	.290
Hurley, Sean	R-R	6-4	235	5-5-92	.216	.214	.216	49	139	21	30	7	2	2	12	23	2	1	0	42	1	0	.338	.335
Jansen, Danny	R-R	6-2	215	4-15-95	.246	.308	.213	36	114	19	28	4	0	0	18	21	2	0	3	10	0	0	.281	.364
Kraemer, Koby	R-R	5-9	185	10-14-89	.190	.222	.179	29	105	9	20	4	0	0	9	10	2	0	0	17	1	0	.229	.274
Moseby, Lydell	R-R	6-6	230	3-15-91	.294	.167	.364	8	17	2	5	1	0	0	3	2	0	0	0	6	0	0	.353	.368
Pascazi, Trey	R-R	6-1	175	8-7-93	.083	.000	.103	19	36	2	3	0	0	0	1	1	0	0	0	24	0	1	.083	.108
Segovia, Rolando	B-R	5-11	165	10-26-94	.219	.143	.256	22	64	12	14	1	1	1	8	8	1	0	0	16	1	2	.313	.315
Sierra, Moises	R-R	6-0	230	9-24-88	.333	.250	.500	3	6	2	2	1	0	0	3	1	2	0	1	1	1	0	.500	.500
Sotillo, Andres	R-R	5-11	180	12-28-93	.302	.278	.311	18	63	8	19	1	1	0	3	4	0	1	0	15	0	0	.349	.366
Tellez, Rowdy	L-L	6-4	220	3-16-95	.234	.256	.224	34	124	10	29	5	3	2	20	15	1	0	1	26	1	0	.371	.319
Tolisano, John	B-R	5-11	190	10-7-88	.300	.333	.286	6	20	6	6	1	0	1	2	5	0	0	0	4	0	0	.500	.440
Urena, Richard	L-R	6-1	170	2-26-96	.333	.143	.400	7	27	3	9	2	0	0	3	3	0	1	0	6	0	0	.407	.400
Vazquez, Christian	B-R	5-11	170	3-26-93	.333	.400	.286	4	12	3	4	1	0	0	1	2	1	1	0	3	0	0	.417	.467
Wilson, Kenny	B-R	5-10	185	1-30-90	.222	.333	.167	3	9	2	2	0	0	0	1	2	0	0	0	2	0	1	.222	.364
Zawadzki, Lance	B-R	5-11	185	5-26-85	.000	.000	.000	2	6	0	0	0	0	0	0	0	0	0	0	0	0	0	.000	.000

Pitching	B-T	HT	WT	DOB	W	L	ERA	G	GS	CG	SV	IP	H	R	ER	HR	BB	SO	AVG	vLH	vRH	K/9	BB/9
Adams, Zak	L-L	6-2	190	3-19-92	0	1	13.50	2	0	0	0	2	4	3	3	0	1	3	.444	.333	.500	13.50	4.50
Barnes, Dan	L-R	6-1	195	10-21-89	0	0	0.00	1	0	0	0	1	0	0	0	0	3	0	.000	.000	27.00	0.00
Beck, Chad	R-R	6-4	250	1-17-85	1	0	2.16	9	1	0	1	8	8	4	2	0	4	6	.250	.100	.318	6.48	4.32
Brentz, Jake	L-L	6-2	175	9-14-94	0	0	10.57	9	0	0	0	8	5	9	9	1	12	8	.192	.143	.211	9.39	14.09
Cabrera, Oscar	L-L	6-2	215	5-22-94	0	3	6.93	13	4	0	0	25	35	19	19	0	15	26	.347	.233	.394	9.49	5.47
Castro, Miguel	R-R	6-5	190	12-24-94	1	0	2.40	3	2	0	1	15	11	4	4	0	2	14	.212	.208	.214	8.40	1.20
Cordero, Jimmy	R-R	6-3	195	10-19-91	4	2	5.68	15	2	0	0	25	30	20	16	0	17	30	.280	.262	.292	10.66	6.04
Delabar, Steve	R-R	6-4	230	7-17-83	0	0	0.00	1	0	0	0	1	0	0	0	0	0	0	.000	.000	.000	0.00	0.00
Dermody, Matt	L-L	6-5	190	7-24-90	0	0	0.00	1	1	0	0	3	1	0	0	0	1	1	.100	.000	.125	3.38	0.00
Diaz, Francisco	R-R	6-5	200	2-27-93	3	3	4.41	15	3	0	0	33	28	22	16	1	20	27	.228	.317	.183	7.44	5.51
Duvall, Myles	R-R	6-5	220	4-23-89	1	0	0.00	3	0	0	0	3	2	1	0	0	1	3	.182	.000	.222	9.00	3.00
Fernandez, Jose	L-L	6-3	170	2-13-93	1	0	2.70	16	0	0	2	20	19	8	6	0	3	13	.250	.192	.280	5.85	1.35
Gonzales, Tyler	R-R	6-2	175	1-22-93	1	1	10.45	9	0	0	0	10	12	13	12	0	12	9	.300	.333	.263	7.84	10.45

Name	B-T	HT	WT	DOB	W	L	ERA	G	GS	CG	SV	IP	H	R	ER	HR	BB	SO	AVG	vLH	vRH	K/9	BB/9
Gorman, Corey	R-L	6-0	185	8-18-90	2	0	1.91	13	5	0	0	38	34	10	8	0	13	24	.258	.289	.241	5.73	3.11
Greene, Conner	R-R	6-5	165	4-4-95	1	1	5.28	11	4	0	0	31	37	19	18	1	15	20	.308	.408	.239	5.87	4.40
Happ, J.A.	L-L	6-6	195	10-19-82	0	0	0.00	1	1	0	0	3	4	2	0	0	0	0	.286	.000	.333	0.00	0.00
Hollon, Clint	R-R	6-1	195	12-24-94	1	0	0.00	4	2	0	0	12	2	0	0	0	3	10	.056	.000	.105	7.50	2.25
Jenkins, Chad	R-R	6-3	225	12-22-87	0	0	0.00	2	2	0	0	3	0	0	0	0	0	2	.000	.000	.000	6.00	0.00
Kish, Phil	R-R	6-0	175	8-30-89	2	1	0.64	9	0	0	2	14	9	1	1	0	3	19	.184	.118	.219	12.21	1.93
Lietz, Daniel	L-L	6-2	200	6-1-94	2	3	4.75	12	6	0	0	36	47	33	19	4	11	35	.297	.239	.321	8.75	2.75
Lovecchio, Joey	R-R	6-2	190	9-6-90	0	0	0.00	1	0	0	0	2	2	0	0	0	1	2	.250	.000	.333	9.00	4.50
Mayza, Tim	L-L	6-3	205	1-15-92	0	2	10.29	3	2	0	0	7	11	8	8	0	2	10	.355	.571	.292	12.86	2.57
Permison, Drew	R-R	5-10	170	2-24-89	0	0	0.00	5	0	0	0	5	1	0	0	0	1	3	.067	.000	.100	5.40	1.80
Pickens, Garrett	R-R	6-1	185	4-17-90	1	0	0.00	3	0	0	1	4	4	1	0	0	3	2	.235	.500	.154	4.15	6.23
Ratcliffe, Sean	L-R	6-4	200	4-11-95	1	1	5.63	8	0	0	1	8	8	6	5	0	4	8	.235	.143	.300	9.00	4.50
Rowley, Chris	R-R	6-2	195	8-14-90	4	0	1.10	9	5	0	0	33	19	5	4	1	3	39	.162	.140	.183	10.74	0.83
Santos, Sergio	R-R	6-3	240	7-4-83	0	0	0.00	1	1	0	0	1	1	0	0	0	0	2	.200	.500	.000	18.00	0.00
Smith, Evan	R-L	6-5	190	8-17-95	0	1	7.50	8	0	0	1	12	15	12	10	0	9	10	.294	.385	.263	7.50	6.75
Smoral, Matt	L-L	6-8	220	3-18-94	0	2	7.01	15	5	0	0	26	22	23	20	1	26	27	.237	.250	.231	9.47	9.12
Solarte, Alejandro	L-L	6-4	180	9-22-94	1	1	2.96	9	3	0	0	24	28	11	8	0	5	15	.286	.269	.292	5.55	1.85
Tinoco, Jesus	R-R	6-4	190	4-30-95	0	5	5.09	12	9	0	1	46	49	28	26	0	21	45	.271	.338	.218	8.80	4.11
Usui, Kamakami	R-R	6-1	180	2-27-90	1	3	3.86	18	0	0	2	21	23	10	9	2	3	15	.288	.370	.245	6.43	1.29
Wine, Cale	R-R	6-2	225	8-6-90	0	2	5.00	13	2	0	0	27	40	18	15	2	2	15	.357	.333	.373	5.00	0.67

Fielding

Catcher	PCT	G	PO	A	E	DP	PB
Cenas	1.000	2	8	1	0	0	0
De La Cruz	.986	13	66	6	1	1	1
Jansen	.996	35	249	23	1	1	6
Sotillo	.993	17	118	19	1	0	3

First Base	PCT	G	PO	A	E	DP
Cenas	.971	19	152	18	5	17
Dantzler	1.000	1	9	0	0	0
Devonshire	.955	5	20	1	1	1
Fuentes	1.000	7	53	4	0	3
Moseby	.956	8	41	2	2	1
Tellez	.984	27	237	13	4	19

Second Base	PCT	G	PO	A	E	DP
Dupont	.970	20	30	34	2	8
Florides	—	1	0	0	0	0
Fuentes	—	1	0	0	0	0
Kraemer	.979	11	23	24	1	7
Pascazi	.974	9	15	23	1	7
Segovia	.983	20	21	37	1	7
Tolisano	.938	5	8	7	1	1
Vazquez	.923	2	7	5	1	1
Zawadzki	1.000	2	4	7	0	1

Third Base	PCT	G	PO	A	E	DP
Cenas	.800	1	1	3	1	0
Florides	1.000	2	1	0	0	1
Fuentes	.968	40	31	89	4	9
Kraemer	.943	20	17	33	3	2

Shortstop	PCT	G	PO	A	E	DP
Barreto	.899	42	52	118	19	13
Florides	.906	12	15	14	3	6
Fuentes	.500	2	2	1	3	1
Pascazi	.778	4	2	5	2	0
Urena	.914	7	7	25	3	5
Vazquez	1.000	2	4	7	0	1

Outfield	PCT	G	PO	A	E	DP
Alford	.933	6	14	0	1	0
Almonte	.968	46	85	7	3	1
Collins	1.000	51	59	5	0	1
De Aza	.951	32	35	4	2	1
DeSouza	.962	17	25	0	1	0
Hurley	.944	46	64	3	4	1
Sierra	1.000	2	5	1	0	0
Wilson	1.000	3	2	0	0	0

DSL BLUE JAYS   ROOKIE

DOMINICAN SUMMER LEAGUE

Batting	B-T	HT	WT	DOB	AVG	vLH	vRH	G	AB	R	H	2B	3B	HR	RBI	BB	HBP	SH	SF	SO	SB	CS	SLG	OBP
Alcantara, Eddy	R-R	6-3	182	7-22-94	.268	.200	.283	18	56	13	15	1	0	0	7	10	1	1	2	19	2	0	.286	.377
Almanzar, Jean	R-R	6-0	150	2-12-95	.059	.100	.042	16	34	7	2	0	0	0	1	9	1	0	0	11	2	1	.059	.273
Barreto, Deiferson	R-R	5-10	165	5-19-95	.300	.371	.288	64	243	56	73	14	3	0	26	31	12	3	1	23	19	5	.383	.404
Bell, Dean	R-R	5-9	175	10-14-92	.245	.429	.214	44	147	23	36	3	3	0	13	10	0	2	0	35	4	1	.306	.293
De Aza, Andres	R-R	6-4	200	11-17-94	.188	.250	.167	5	16	0	3	0	1	0	5	4	1	0	3	7	0	0	.313	.333
De La Cruz, Michael	R-R	5-10	175	5-15-93	.288	.299	.295	45	156	22	45	9	5	1	29	38	2	1	2	33	16	5	.429	.429
Demorizi, Ronniel	B-R	6-0	170	7-19-95	.212	.200	.215	58	193	31	41	6	1	5	28	33	1	3	1	50	6	2	.332	.329
Dominguez, Luis	R-R	6-2	190	12-26-95	.150	.160	.147	34	100	15	15	4	0	0	10	18	1	1	1	41	0	2	.190	.283
Fuente, Juan	R-R	6-0	155	11-8-93	.284	.333	.273	62	194	42	55	6	4	0	22	31	11	3	1	67	30	8	.356	.409
Garcia, Leudy	R-R	6-4	195	4-18-95	.200	.241	.192	58	175	16	35	14	0	1	18	33	3	1	1	46	5	2	.297	.335
Hernandez, Javier	R-R	6-1	180	7-21-96	.223	.160	.235	48	157	20	35	5	0	0	6	9	8	1	2	28	4	2	.255	.295
Kelly, Juan	L-R	5-10	155	7-16-94	.254	.389	.226	65	213	36	54	8	1	2	27	52	2	2	1	30	14	2	.329	.403
Orozco, Rodrigo	B-R	5-11	155	4-2-95	.269	.429	.239	40	130	21	35	10	2	2	22	19	3	3	1	21	5	4	.423	.373
Tejada, Juan	R-R	6-3	180	2-13-94	.196	.242	.188	66	219	30	43	7	2	2	36	29	7	1	3	57	20	6	.274	.306
Urena, Richard	L-R	6-1	170	2-26-96	.296	.235	.306	64	243	45	72	19	2	1	35	30	4	2	1	43	9	5	.403	.381

Pitching	B-T	HT	WT	DOB	W	L	ERA	G	GS	CG	SV	IP	H	R	ER	HR	BB	SO	AVG	vLH	vRH	K/9	BB/9
Aleton, Wilfri	L-L	6-5	165	11-18-95	0	0	4.82	9	3	0	0	19	16	11	10	1	18	13	.246	.286	.241	6.27	8.68
Brito, Jose	R-R	6-2	185	12-19-94	0	1	5.68	4	0	0	0	13	12	12	8	0	6	12	.235	.125	.286	8.53	4.26
Burgos, Miguel	L-L	5-9	155	6-16-95	3	3	3.12	15	2	0	1	49	40	22	17	0	16	34	.223	.350	.208	6.24	2.94
Castillo, Rauly	R-R	6-2	195	6-8-93	3	1	4.50	17	0	0	1	30	21	16	15	0	11	23	.202	.222	.195	6.90	3.30
Castro, Miguel	R-R	6-5	190	12-24-94	5	2	1.36	11	10	0	0	53	40	14	8	0	12	71	.208	.183	.220	12.06	2.04
Conde, Greylor	R-R	6-4	195	6-25-94	0	2	7.94	7	0	0	0	11	19	11	10	3	4	10	.388	.444	.375	7.94	3.18
Cordova, Manuel	R-R	6-3	190	1-17-95	2	1	6.48	13	0	0	1	25	30	25	18	3	16	21	.283	.414	.234	7.56	5.76
Diaz, Denis	R-R	6-1	180	11-20-94	1	0	9.00	12	0	0	0	15	24	17	15	0	15	12	.393	.313	.422	7.20	9.00
Diaz, Francisco	R-R	6-5	200	2-27-93	0	1	6.00	2	2	0	0	6	7	5	4	0	4	8	.304	.750	.211	12.00	6.00
Diaz, Pedro	R-R	6-1	187	12-10-94	4	1	1.98	10	1	0	0	14	8	5	3	1	4	8	.170	.211	.143	5.27	2.63
Eduardo, Francis	R-R	6-2	190	5-24-94	3	3	2.88	16	7	0	3	50	41	22	16	3	19	40	.227	.353	.177	7.20	3.42
Gutierrez, Osman	R-R	6-4	185	12-15-94	0	1	3.86	8	2	0	0	12	17	7	5	1	4	8	.340	.444	.281	5.40	4.63
Guzman, Alberto	R-R	6-1	180	12-7-92	5	1	2.65	15	12	0	0	54	43	23	16	2	28	49	.222	.250	.210	8.12	4.64
Herdenez, Yonardo	R-R	6-1	170	9-20-95	1	0	6.08	13	0	0	2	24	27	19	16	1	8	11	.284	.233	.308	4.18	3.04
Hernandez, Jhonny	R-R	6-1	170	2-12-93	0	1	6.35	8	5	0	1	17	18	14	12	1	6	10	.281	.250	.292	5.29	3.18

Higuera, Juliandry	L-L	6-1	180	9-6-94	4	1	2.54	13	4	1	0	46	40	19	13	2	10	40	.235	.190	.242	7.83	1.96
Perdomo, Angel	L-L	6-6	200	5-7-94	0	1	3.04	12	2	0	2	27	16	12	9	1	18	43	.172	.083	.185	14.51	6.08
Rios, Francisco	R-R	6-1	180	5-6-95	4	6	4.47	15	9	0	1	52	51	36	26	1	19	48	.258	.239	.267	8.25	3.27
Rodriguez, Dalton	R-R	6-1	180	8-20-96	3	1	1.80	13	6	0	2	50	40	20	10	1	14	32	.214	.309	.160	5.76	2.52
Rosario, Jairo	R-R	6-4	190	10-21-93	1	2	3.18	20	2	0	10	23	16	11	8	1	16	23	.195	.192	.196	9.13	6.35
Suero, Hamly	R-R	6-3	195	10-17-94	1	0	6.14	5	0	0	0	7	4	5	5	1	7	6	.167	.167	.167	7.36	8.59
Torres, Jonathan	L-L	6-4	190	12-31-94	1	0	2.84	7	0	0	0	13	6	5	4	0	12	17	.140	.200	.132	12.08	8.53

Fielding

Catcher	PCT	G	PO	A	E	DP	PB
De La Cruz	.973	16	127	15	4	0	7
Dominguez	1.000	7	23	2	0	0	1
Hernandez	.980	39	303	37	7	2	15
Kelly	.992	18	104	19	1	0	6

First Base	PCT	G	PO	A	E	DP
De La Cruz	.995	22	176	18	1	12
Demorizi	1.000	1	5	0	0	0
Dominguez	.956	14	83	3	4	12
Hernandez	1.000	1	1	0	0	0
Kelly	.982	38	245	28	5	23
Tejada	1.000	2	12	0	0	2

Second Base	PCT	G	PO	A	E	DP
Almanzar	.929	6	13	13	2	1

	PCT	G	PO	A	E	DP
Barreto	.942	56	105	124	14	22
Bell	.870	6	12	8	3	4
Demorizi	.957	7	12	10	1	3
Orozco	1.000	1	5	3	0	1

Third Base	PCT	G	PO	A	E	DP
Barreto	.921	10	13	22	3	1
Bell	.868	20	15	31	7	1
De La Cruz	.800	4	4	8	3	1
Demorizi	.835	41	37	49	17	1
Kelly	1.000	5	10	12	0	3

Shortstop	PCT	G	PO	A	E	DP
Almanzar	.857	3	2	4	1	2
Barreto	1.000	1	1	0	0	0
Demorizi	.947	5	7	11	1	2

	PCT	G	PO	A	E	DP
Fuente	1.000	6	7	5	0	4
Urena	.936	61	115	150	18	31

Outfield	PCT	G	PO	A	E	DP
Alcantara	.952	14	17	3	1	1
De Aza	1.000	5	10	0	0	0
De La Cruz	1.000	7	5	0	0	0
Demorizi	.875	9	13	1	2	0
Fuente	.990	57	97	3	1	0
Garcia	.967	39	56	3	2	0
Herdenez	—	1	0	0	0	0
Orozco	.909	37	48	2	5	1
Tejada	.953	65	98	3	5	1

Washington Nationals

SEASON IN A SENTENCE: The Nationals entered the season as a World Series favorite but scuffled through the first four months, and a strong finish couldn't salvage a postseason berth.

HIGH POINT: Washington rallied in the final two months, going 32-16 after Aug. 8, highlighted by a seven-game winning streak in mid-September. Jordan Zimmermann threw a two-hit shutout against the Marlins on Sept. 20 to help the Nats draw within four games of a wild-card spot.

LOW POINT: The Nats played .500 ball for the first three months of the season, then went 11-16 in July to fall out of contention in the NL East. After the Braves closed out a three-game sweep in Washington on Aug. 7, the Nationals fell to a season-worst six games below .500, and 15½ games behind first-place Atlanta.

NOTABLE ROOKIES: Top prospect Anthony Rendon made his big league debut in April, was sent back to the minors in May, then returned to Washington for good in early June. A third baseman by trade, Rendon took over the second base job after Danny Espinosa broke his wrist. The Nationals also got boosts on the mound from Taylor Jordan, Tanner Roark and Ian Krol, each of whom showed power stuff.

KEY TRANSACTIONS: Washington's key offseason move was shipping power-armed prospect Alex Meyer to the Twins for center fielder Denard Span. Span struggled offensively before stringing together a late-season 29-game hittng streak and providing strong defense in center field. Washington's top free agent acquisition, righthander Dan Haren, went just 4-10, 5.61 in the first half of the season but proved to be a durable back-of-the-rotation innings eater. And the Nationals reacquired righthander A.J. Cole—one of the key pieces of their deal for Gio Gonzalez the previous offseason—in a three-team trade for expendable slugger Michael Morse in spring training.

DOWN ON THE FARM: The Rookie-level Gulf Coast League Nationals posted the best record in organized baseball, going an 49-9, thanks in part to strong U.S. debuts from several products of Washington's rejuvenated Latin American program. At the higher levels, pitchers like Cole, Robbie Ray, Sammy Solis and Nate Karns turned in strong seasons, but top hitting prospect Brian Goodwin ran into some adversity in Double-A, and top power prospect Matt Skole missed almost the entire season with wrist and elbow injuries.

OPENING DAY PAYROLL: $116 million (10th).

PLAYERS OF THE YEAR

MAJOR LEAGUE	MINOR LEAGUE
Jordan Zimmermann rhp	**Robbie Ray** lhp
19-9, 3.25	(Double-A/High-A)
161 SO, 213 IP	11-5, 3.36
Led NL in W	Led org with 160 SO

ORGANIZATION LEADERS

BATTING *Minimum 250 AB

MAJORS

*	AVG	Werth, Jayson	.318
*	OPS	Werth, Jayson	.931
	HR	Zimmerman, Ryan	26
	RBI	Werth, Jayson	82

MINORS

*	AVG	Kobernus, Jeff, Syracuse	.318
*	OBP	Burns, Billy, Harrisburg/Potomac	.425
*	SLG	Walters, Zach, Syracuse	.517
	R	Renda, Tony, Hagerstown	99
	H	Renda, Tony, Hagerstown	153
	TB	Walters, Zach, Syracuse	252
	2B	Renda, Tony, Hagerstown	43
	3B	Goodwin, Brian, Harrisburg	11
	HR	Walters, Zach, Syracuse	29
	RBI	Miller, Brandon, Potomac/Hagerstown	88
	BB	Dykstra, Cutter, Potomac	77
	SO	Miller, Brandon, Potomac/Hagerstown	164
	SB	Burns, Billy, Harrisburg/Potomac	74

PITCHING #Minimum 75 IP

MAJORS

	W	Zimmermann, Jordan	19
#	ERA	Strasburg, Stephen	3
	SO	Gonzalez, Gio	192
	SV	Soriano, Rafael	43

MINORS

	W	Schwartz, Blake, Potomac/Hagerstown	13
	L	Rosenbaum, Danny, Syracuse	11
#	ERA	Schwartz, Blake, Hagerstown/Potomac	2.51
	G	Barrett, Aaron, Harrisburg	51
		Crotta, Michael, Syracuse	51
	GS	Rosenbaum, Danny, Syracuse	28
	SV	Benincasa, Robert, Potomac/Hagerstown	27
	IP	Hill, Taylor, Syracuse, Harrisburg/Potomac	165
	BB	Tatusko, Ryan, Syracuse/Harrisburg	81
	SO	Ray, Robbie, Harrisburg/Potomac	160
#	AVG	Ray, Robbie, Potomac/Harrisburg	.224

General Manager: Mike Rizzo. **Farm Director:** Bob Boone. **Scouting Director:** Kris Kline.

Class	Team	League	W	L	PCT	Finish	Manager
Majors	Washington Nationals	National	86	76	.531	6th (15)	Davey Johnson
Triple-A	Syracuse Chiefs	International	66	78	.458	11th (14)	Tony Beasley
Double-A	Harrisburg Senators	Eastern	77	65	.542	2nd (12)	Matt LeCroy
High A	Potomac Nationals	Carolina	84	55	.604	1st (8)	Brian Daubach
Low A	Hagerstown Suns	South Atlantic	80	57	.584	3rd (14)	Tripp Keister
Short-season	Auburn Doubledays	New York-Penn	26	49	.347	14th (14)	Gary Cathcart
Rookie	GCL Nationals	Gulf Coast	49	9	.845	1st (16)	Patrick Anderson
Overall 2013 Minor League Record			382	313	.550	3rd (30)	

ORGANIZATION STATISTICS

NATIONAL LEAGUE

Batting	B-T	HT	WT	DOB	AVG	vLH	vRH	G	AB	R	H	2B	3B	HR	RBI	BB	HBP	SH	SF	SO	SB	CS	SLG	OBP
Bernadina, Roger	L-L	6-2	200	6-12-84	.178	.111	.187	85	152	18	27	6	1	2	6	12	2	1	0	44	3	0	.270	.247
2-team total (27 Philadelphia)					.181	—	—	112	227	26	41	10	2	4	11	16	5	2	0	65	4	0	.295	.250
Brown, Corey	L-L	6-1	210	11-26-85	.167	—	.167	14	12	2	2	1	0	1	1	3	0	0	0	4	1	0	.500	.333
DeJesus, David	L-L	5-11	190	12-20-79	.000	—	.000	3	3	0	0	0	0	0	0	0	0	0	0	1	0	0	.000	.000
2-team total (84 Chicago)					.247	—	—	87	287	39	71	19	3	6	27	29	5	1	0	56	3	0	.397	.327
Desmond, Ian	R-R	6-3	210	9-20-85	.280	.281	.280	158	600	77	168	38	3	20	80	43	5	2	5	145	21	6	.453	.331
Espinosa, Danny	B-R	6-0	205	4-25-87	.158	.125	.167	44	158	11	25	9	0	3	12	4	3	1	1	47	1	0	.272	.193
Hairston, Scott	R-R	6-0	205	5-25-80	.224	.271	.000	33	58	5	13	3	0	2	7	2	0	1	1	19	0	0	.379	.246
2-team total (52 Chicago)					.191	—	—	85	157	18	30	5	0	10	26	9	2	1	5	44	2	0	.414	.237
Harper, Bryce	L-R	6-2	230	10-16-92	.274	.214	.300	118	424	71	116	24	3	20	58	61	5	3	4	94	11	4	.486	.368
Kobernus, Jeff	R-R	6-2	210	6-30-88	.167	.208	.000	24	30	8	5	0	0	1	5	1	0	0	6	3	2	.267	.306
LaRoche, Adam	L-L	6-2	200	11-6-79	.237	.198	.250	152	511	70	121	19	3	20	62	72	3	0	4	131	4	1	.403	.332
Leon, Sandy	B-R	5-11	215	3-13-89	.000	—	.000	2	1	0	0	0	0	0	0	0	0	0	0	1	0	0	.000	.000
Lombardozzi Jr., Steve	B-R	6-0	200	9-20-88	.259	.273	.254	118	290	25	75	15	1	2	22	8	1	5	3	34	4	3	.338	.278
Marrero, Chris	R-R	6-3	230	7-2-88	.125	.167	.000	8	16	0	2	0	0	0	1	0	0	0	0	4	0	0	.125	.125
Moore, Tyler	R-R	6-2	220	1-30-87	.222	.189	.247	63	167	16	37	9	0	4	21	8	1	1	1	58	0	0	.347	.260
Perez, Eury	R-R	6-0	180	5-30-90	.125	.167	.000	9	8	1	1	0	0	0	0	0	0	0	0	3	1	0	.125	.125
Ramos, Wilson	R-R	6-0	220	8-10-87	.272	.282	.269	78	287	29	78	9	0	16	59	15	0	0	1	42	0	1	.470	.307
Rendon, Anthony	R-R	6-0	195	6-6-90	.265	.294	.253	98	351	40	93	23	1	7	35	31	5	2	5	69	1	1	.396	.329
Solano, Jhonatan	R-R	5-9	205	8-12-85	.146	.150	.143	24	48	2	7	2	0	0	2	2	0	0	0	7	0	1	.188	.180
Span, Denard	L-L	6-0	210	2-27-84	.279	.223	.298	153	610	75	170	28	11	4	47	42	2	7	1	77	20	6	.380	.327
Suzuki, Kurt	R-R	5-11	205	10-4-83	.222	.222	.222	79	252	19	56	11	1	3	25	20	3	2	4	32	2	0	.310	.283
Tracy, Chad	L-R	6-1	205	5-22-80	.202	.333	.192	92	129	6	26	4	0	4	11	7	0	0	0	25	0	2	.326	.243
Walters, Zach	B-R	6-2	220	9-5-89	.375	.333	.400	8	8	2	3	0	1	0	1	1	0	0	0	0	0	.625	.444
Werth, Jayson	R-R	6-5	225	5-20-79	.318	.350	.309	129	462	84	147	24	0	25	82	60	5	0	5	101	10	1	.532	.398
Zimmerman, Ryan	R-R	6-3	230	9-28-84	.275	.259	.280	147	568	84	156	26	2	26	79	60	2	0	3	133	6	0	.465	.344

Pitching	B-T	HT	WT	DOB	W	L	ERA	G	GS	CG	SV	IP	H	R	ER	HR	BB	SO	AVG	vLH	vRH	K/9	BB/9
Abad, Fernando	L-L	6-1	220	12-17-85	0	3	3.35	39	0	0	0	38	42	14	14	3	10	32	.271	.306	.247	7.65	2.39
Cedeno, Xavier	L-L	6-1	205	8-26-86	0	0	1.50	11	0	0	0	6	5	1	1	0	1	6	.227	.133	.429	9.00	1.50
Clippard, Tyler	R-R	6-3	200	2-14-85	6	3	2.41	72	0	0	0	71	37	19	19	9	24	73	.152	.152	.151	9.25	3.04
Davis, Erik	R-R	6-2	190	10-8-86	1	0	3.12	10	0	0	0	9	10	3	3	0	1	12	.278	.286	.273	12.46	1.04
Detwiler, Ross	R-L	6-5	200	3-6-86	2	7	4.04	13	13	0	0	71	92	37	32	5	14	39	.315	.312	.316	4.92	1.77
Duke, Zach	L-L	6-2	210	4-19-83	1	1	8.71	12	1	0	0	21	31	22	20	2	8	11	.352	.448	.305	4.79	3.48
2-team total (14 Cincinnati)					1	2	6.03	26	1	0	0	31	39	23	21	3	10	18	—	—	—	5.17	2.87
Gonzalez, Gio	R-L	6-0	200	9-19-85	11	8	3.36	32	32	1	0	196	169	79	73	17	76	192	.231	.204	.239	8.83	3.50
Haren, Dan	R-R	6-5	215	9-17-80	10	14	4.67	31	30	0	1	170	179	92	88	28	31	151	.268	.253	.281	8.01	1.64
Jordan, Taylor	R-R	6-3	190	1-17-89	1	3	3.66	9	9	0	0	52	59	27	21	3	11	29	.291	.308	.277	5.05	1.92
Karns, Nate	R-R	6-3	230	11-25-87	0	1	7.50	3	3	0	0	12	17	11	10	5	6	11	.321	.370	.269	8.25	4.50
Krol, Ian	L-L	6-1	210	5-9-91	2	1	3.95	32	0	0	0	27	28	12	12	5	8	22	.264	.220	.304	7.24	2.63
Mattheus, Ryan	R-R	6-3	215	11-10-83	0	2	6.37	37	0	0	0	35	52	26	25	1	15	22	.351	.438	.286	5.60	3.82
Maya, Yunesky	R-R	5-11	205	8-28-81	0	1	54.00	1	0	0	0	0	2	2	2	1	0	0	.667	.500	1.000	0.00	0.00
Ohlendorf, Ross	R-R	6-4	240	8-8-82	4	1	3.28	16	7	0	0	60	56	22	22	8	14	45	.245	.268	.227	6.71	2.09
Roark, Tanner	R-R	6-2	220	10-5-86	7	1	1.51	14	5	0	0	54	38	11	9	1	11	40	.202	.263	.157	6.71	1.84
Rodriguez, Henry	R-R	6-1	225	2-25-87	0	1	4.00	17	0	0	0	18	14	8	8	1	16	11	.203	.211	.194	5.50	8.00
2-team total (5 Chicago)					0	1	4.09	22	0	0	0	22	20	12	10	2	20	12	—	—	—	4.91	8.18
Soriano, Rafael	R-R	6-1	210	12-19-79	3	3	3.11	68	0	0	43	67	65	24	23	7	17	51	.251	.274	.235	6.89	2.30
Stammen, Craig	R-R	6-3	215	3-9-84	7	6	2.76	55	0	0	0	82	78	30	25	4	27	79	.262	.282	.249	8.71	2.98
Storen, Drew	B-R	6-1	225	8-11-87	4	2	4.52	68	0	0	3	62	65	34	31	7	19	58	.267	.267	.268	8.46	2.77
Strasburg, Stephen	R-R	6-4	200	7-20-88	8	9	3.00	30	30	1	0	183	136	71	61	16	56	191	.207	.218	.197	9.39	2.75
Zimmermann, Jordan	R-R	6-2	220	5-23-86	19	9	3.25	32	32	4	0	213	192	81	77	19	40	161	.239	.262	.212	6.79	1.69

Fielding

Catcher	PCT	G	PO	A	E	DP	PB								
Leon	1.000	1	2	0	0	0	0	Solano	.990	19	96	6	1	0	0
Ramos	.987	77	593	35	8	1	5	Suzuki	.992	78	556	30	5	5	0

First Base	PCT	G	PO	A	E	DP
LaRoche	.991	149	1164	76	11	117
Marrero	1.000	3	12	2	0	1

WASHINGTON NATIONALS

	PCT	G	PO	A	E	DP
Moore	1.000	14	97	4	0	12
Tracy	.983	10	55	4	1	5
Second Base	**PCT**	**G**	**PO**	**A**	**E**	**DP**
Espinosa	.991	43	96	119	2	32
Lombardozzi Jr.	.987	48	92	129	3	28
Rendon	.976	82	147	213	9	50
Third Base	**PCT**	**G**	**PO**	**A**	**E**	**DP**
Lombardozzi Jr.	1.000	4	1	4	0	0
Rendon	.868	15	7	26	5	4
Tracy	.947	14	5	13	1	3

	PCT	G	PO	A	E	DP
Walters	1.000	2	0	1	0	0
Zimmerman	.945	141	98	260	21	28
Shortstop	**PCT**	**G**	**PO**	**A**	**E**	**DP**
Desmond	.971	158	234	446	20	96
Espinosa	1.000	1	1	0	0	0
Rendon	.846	4	9	2	2	1
Walters	1.000	2	0	6	0	1
Outfield	**PCT**	**G**	**PO**	**A**	**E**	**DP**
Bernadina	1.000	63	70	4	0	1
Brown	1.000	9	7	0	0	0

	PCT	G	PO	A	E	DP
DeJesus	—	3	0	0	0	0
Hairston	1.000	17	16	0	0	0
Harper	.973	115	202	13	6	1
Kobernus	1.000	10	13	0	0	0
Lombardozzi Jr.	1.000	23	32	1	0	0
Moore	.971	35	34	0	1	0
Perez	1.000	7	11	0	0	0
Span	1.000	153	379	5	0	1
Werth	.992	126	235	7	2	1

SYRACUSE CHIEFS   TRIPLE-A

INTERNATIONAL LEAGUE

Batting	B-T	HT	WT	DOB	AVG	vLH	vRH	G	AB	R	H	2B	3B	HR	RBI	BB	HBP	SH	SF	SO	SB	CS	SLG	OBP
Bocock, Brian	R-R	5-11	185	3-9-85	.182	.182	.182	22	44	1	8	3	0	0	2	4	0	0	1	8	2	1	.250	.245
2-team total (31 Indianapolis)					.175	—	—	53	143	10	25	7	0	3	9	11	1	2	1	30	3	1	.287	.237
Brown, Corey	L-L	6-1	210	11-26-85	.254	.210	.270	107	389	57	99	26	1	19	56	40	3	3	3	132	12	4	.473	.326
Costanzo, Mike	L-R	6-2	205	9-9-83	.220	.140	.240	66	218	29	48	8	1	10	29	28	1	1	1	68	2	1	.404	.310
2-team total (2 Louisville)					.227	—	—	68	225	32	51	10	1	10	33	29	1	1	1	71	2	1	.413	.316
Espinosa, Danny	B-R	6-0	205	4-25-87	.216	.195	.223	75	283	32	61	12	1	2	22	19	7	2	1	101	6	1	.286	.280
Head, Jerad	R-R	6-0	210	11-15-82	.231	.000	.250	6	13	2	3	1	0	0	1	2	0	1	0	4	0	0	.308	.333
Howell, Jeff	R-R	6-0	205	4-1-83	.217	.400	.167	13	46	6	10	3	0	1	3	1	0	0	0	15	0	0	.348	.234
Jeroloman, Brian	L-R	5-11	190	5-10-85	.221	.167	.246	30	95	9	21	4	0	0	7	13	1	2	1	28	0	0	.263	.318
2-team total (11 Indianapolis)					.221	—	—	41	113	15	25	5	0	0	9	22	1	4	1	32	0	1	.265	.350
Johnson, Josh R.	B-R	5-11	170	1-11-86	.341	.400	.310	35	88	14	30	6	1	1	14	18	1	4	0	12	6	0	.466	.458
Kobernus, Jeff	R-R	6-2	210	6-30-88	.318	.391	.296	95	371	59	118	19	2	1	36	28	2	8	3	59	42	9	.388	.366
Komatsu, Erik	L-L	5-10	175	10-1-87	.160	.167	.158	9	25	3	4	0	0	0	3	0	0	0	0	7	0	0	.160	.250
Maldonado, Carlos	R-R	6-2	260	1-3-79	.098	.154	.071	14	41	2	4	0	0	0	1	3	0	2	0	18	0	0	.098	.159
Marrero, Chris	R-R	6-3	230	7-2-88	.270	.293	.260	111	408	48	110	17	2	11	59	36	3	0	3	67	0	1	.402	.331
Moore, Tyler	R-R	6-2	220	1-30-87	.318	.366	.303	45	173	26	55	14	1	10	46	23	1	0	3	39	1	0	.584	.395
Owings, Micah	R-R	6-5	220	9-28-82	.265	.295	.252	57	200	28	53	13	3	8	31	10	2	0	1	71	2	0	.480	.305
Palace, Sam	R-R	6-1	210	6-3-86	.000	—	.000	1	4	0	0	0	0	0	0	0	0	0	0	2	0	0	.000	.000
Perez, Eury	R-R	6-0	180	5-30-90	.300	.366	.275	96	403	55	121	18	5	7	28	13	9	8	0	64	23	8	.402	.336
Rahl, Chris	R-R	5-10	185	12-5-83	.293	.327	.280	111	399	53	117	21	5	8	42	10	1	3	6	97	14	6	.431	.308
Rendon, Anthony	R-R	6-0	195	6-6-90	.182	—	.182	3	11	2	2	1	0	0	2	1	0	0	3	0	0	.273	.357
Rhymes, Will	L-R	5-9	190	4-1-83	.274	.230	.284	133	453	53	124	15	5	3	51	65	0	5	7	29	7	5	.349	.360
Rivero, Carlos	R-R	6-3	200	5-20-88	.233	.214	.243	63	210	15	49	7	0	1	16	22	2	1	4	40	2	2	.281	.307
Shoppach, Kelly	R-R	6-0	220	4-29-80	.219	.417	.100	10	32	3	7	0	0	2	5	1	0	8	0	0	.219	.359
3-team total (1 Columbus, 7 Indianapolis)					.213	—	—	18	61	3	13	1	0	4	6	2	1	0	18	0	0	.230	.304
Solano, Jhonatan	R-R	5-9	205	4-24-85	.214	.389	.154	40	140	9	30	7	1	0	10	5	1	1	1	17	0	0	.279	.245
Soriano, Francisco	B-R	5-11	169	6-16-87	.267	.500	.231	7	15	2	4	1	0	0	3	1	0	1	0	4	0	0	.333	.313
VanOstrand, Jimmy	R-R	6-4	210	8-7-84	.296	.316	.288	21	71	8	21	5	0	0	5	1	0	1	0	14	0	1	.366	.311
Walters, Zach	B-R	6-2	220	9-9-89	.253	.244	.256	134	487	69	123	32	5	29	77	20	5	3	6	134	4	3	.517	.286
Watts, Kris	L-R	6-1	210	7-15-84	.211	.152	.232	43	128	12	27	6	0	3	14	21	5	1	1	25	0	0	.328	.342

Pitching	B-T	HT	WT	DOB	W	L	ERA	G	GS	CG	SV	IP	H	R	ER	HR	BB	SO	AVG	vLH	vRH	K/9	BB/9
Abad, Fernando	L-L	6-1	220	12-17-85	1	0	1.06	17	0	0	0	17	17	2	2	0	2	12	.254	.310	.211	6.35	1.06
Accardo, Jeremy	R-R	6-0	195	12-8-81	2	1	5.56	17	0	0	0	23	24	14	14	3	12	18	.273	.313	.250	7.15	4.76
Bramhall, Bobby	L-L	5-11	190	7-13-85	0	0	8.10	2	0	0	0	3	3	3	3	2	2	2	.250	.300	.000	5.40	5.40
2-team total (6 Lehigh Valley)					0	0	6.75	8	0	0	0	16	20	13	12	5	6	6	—	—	—	3.38	3.38
Broadway, Mike	R-R	6-5	215	3-30-87	1	1	2.28	18	0	0	6	24	16	6	6	2	7	26	.188	.186	.190	9.89	2.66
Cedeno, Xavier	L-L	6-1	205	8-26-86	2	0	1.31	39	0	0	4	34	23	11	5	2	16	45	.189	.164	.209	11.80	4.19
Clay, Caleb	R-R	6-2	180	2-15-88	5	2	2.49	14	13	0	0	83	68	26	23	5	14	51	.223	.184	.261	5.53	1.52
Crotta, Mike	R-R	6-6	235	9-25-84	6	7	3.57	51	0	0	4	58	59	26	23	0	25	44	.265	.302	.236	6.83	3.88
Davis, Erik	R-R	6-2	190	10-8-86	3	7	3.10	45	0	0	15	52	55	25	18	4	20	54	.267	.267	.267	9.29	3.44
Demny, Paul	R-R	6-2	200	8-3-89	0	1	10.80	1	1	0	0	5	9	7	6	1	1	6	.391	.556	.316	10.80	1.80
Dupra, Brian	R-R	6-3	200	12-15-88	0	0	27.00	1	0	0	0	1	6	4	4	1	1	2	.545	.571	.500	6.75	6.75
Garcia, Christian	R-R	6-5	230	8-24-85	1	0	3.24	7	2	0	0	8	5	4	3	0	6	10	.172	.105	.300	10.80	6.48
Hill, Taylor	R-R	6-3	233	3-12-89	1	0	4.22	2	2	0	0	11	18	6	5	0	2	9	.383	.333	.414	7.59	1.69
Kimball, Cole	R-R	6-3	240	8-1-85	0	0	8.06	23	0	0	1	26	31	23	23	4	14	25	.304	.381	.250	8.77	4.91
Krol, Ian	L-L	6-1	210	5-9-91	1	1	4.91	5	0	0	0	4	2	2	2	0	1	7	.154	.143	.167	17.18	2.45
Lowe, Mark	L-R	6-3	210	6-7-83	3	1	3.14	24	0	0	1	29	31	11	10	3	10	37	.272	.326	.235	11.62	3.14
Mandel, Jeff	B-R	6-3	190	4-30-85	3	9	4.61	36	10	0	0	107	128	59	55	11	27	80	.299	.345	.261	6.71	2.26
Mattheus, Ryan	R-R	6-3	215	11-10-83	0	0	1.23	6	0	0	0	7	6	1	1	1	1	4	.214	.231	.200	4.91	1.23
Maya, Yunesky	R-R	5-11	205	8-28-81	8	8	3.87	24	24	2	0	146	157	73	63	10	31	99	.275	.245	.298	6.09	1.91
McCoy, Patrick	L-L	6-3	220	8-3-88	0	0	9.95	7	0	0	0	6	12	12	7	2	2	3	.414	.333	.471	4.26	2.84
Ohlendorf, Ross	R-R	6-4	240	8-8-82	4	6	4.22	14	13	2	0	75	65	36	35	5	30	71	.230	.230	.229	8.56	3.62
Perry, Ryan	R-R	6-5	215	2-13-87	1	4	7.93	12	8	0	0	42	54	40	37	9	23	27	.309	.356	.275	5.79	4.93
Roark, Tanner	R-R	6-2	220	10-5-86	9	3	3.15	33	11	0	2	106	85	43	37	6	20	84	.217	.198	.235	7.15	1.70
Robertson, Tyler	L-L	6-5	255	12-23-87	2	2	3.60	14	1	0	1	27	33	12	9	2	8	24	.303	.319	.290	8.10	2.70
2-team total (21 Rochester)					4	2	3.04	47	1	0	2	47	55	19	16	2	24	44	—	—	—	8.37	4.56
Romero, J.C.	B-L	5-11	205	6-4-76	0	1	2.84	13	0	0	0	13	13	5	4	1	4	16	.255	.174	.321	11.37	2.84
2-team total (2 Columbus)					0	1	3.07	15	0	0	0	15	14	6	5	1	6	18	—	—	—	11.05	3.68

	B-T	HT	WT	DOB	W	L	ERA	G	GS	CG	SV	IP	H	R	ER	HR	BB	SO	AVG	vLH	vRH	K/9	BB/9
Rosenbaum, Danny	R-L	6-1	210	10-10-87	7	11	3.87	28	28	0	0	158	167	84	68	10	67	102	.276	.263	.281	5.80	3.81
Storen, Drew	B-R	6-1	225	8-11-87	0	0	5.68	6	1	0	0	6	7	5	4	1	0	11	.269	.429	.083	15.63	0.00
Tatusko, Ryan	R-R	6-5	200	3-27-85	5	8	4.33	28	18	0	0	121	114	66	58	7	77	100	.255	.270	.240	7.46	5.74
Torra, Matt	R-R	6-3	225	6-29-84	0	3	5.53	5	5	0	0	28	39	19	17	3	7	15	.333	.352	.317	4.88	2.28
Young, Chris	R-R	6-10	260	5-25-79	1	2	7.88	7	7	0	0	32	50	31	28	9	14	16	.352	.413	.304	4.50	3.94

Fielding

Catcher	PCT	G	PO	A	E	DP	PB
Howell	.981	13	94	8	2	1	5
Jeroloman	.987	30	218	12	3	0	2
Maldonado	.989	14	84	3	1	0	2
Palace	1.000	1	8	1	0	0	0
Shoppach	1.000	10	67	7	0	0	2
Solano	.997	38	262	31	1	3	2
Watts	.997	40	271	26	1	1	1

First Base	PCT	G	PO	A	E	DP
Bocock	1.000	2	15	1	0	3
Costanzo	.987	18	146	9	2	18
Marrero	.990	97	860	57	9	82
Moore	.990	19	182	11	2	13
Rivero	.977	10	78	6	2	7
VanOstrand	1.000	5	47	1	0	6

Second Base	PCT	G	PO	A	E	DP
Bocock	.947	5	9	9	1	3
Espinosa	.968	41	71	112	6	33

Johnson	.968	9	10	20	1	1
Kobernus	.988	15	26	56	1	11
Rendon	.875	3	4	10	2	2
Rhymes	.983	82	147	248	7	61
Soriano	—	1	0	0	0	0

Third Base	PCT	G	PO	A	E	DP
Bocock	1.000	8	3	6	0	1
Costanzo	.951	22	10	29	2	1
Johnson	.972	16	6	29	1	6
Kobernus	.972	11	12	23	1	1
Rhymes	.894	24	6	53	7	7
Rivero	.930	42	21	98	9	7
Soriano	.889	2	3	5	1	2
VanOstrand	.857	6	1	5	1	0
Walters	.910	27	16	55	7	7

Shortstop	PCT	G	PO	A	E	DP
Bocock	1.000	1	1	2	0	1
Espinosa	.961	35	44	104	6	22

Rivero	.952	6	3	17	1	2
Walters	.935	104	133	313	31	64

Outfield	PCT	G	PO	A	E	DP
Brown	.973	99	205	10	6	2
Costanzo	.909	6	10	0	1	0
Head	1.000	6	5	0	0	0
Johnson	1.000	9	13	0	0	0
Kobernus	1.000	69	111	6	0	0
Komatsu	.944	9	16	1	1	0
Moore	.975	21	34	5	1	0
Owings	.923	31	46	2	4	0
Perez	.979	92	186	4	4	0
Rahl	.984	95	183	5	3	1
Rhymes	1.000	1	2	0	0	0
Rivero	1.000	6	5	1	0	0
Soriano	1.000	4	2	0	0	0
Watts	—	1	0	0	0	0

HARRISBURG SENATORS

DOUBLE-A

EASTERN LEAGUE

Batting	B-T	HT	WT	DOB	AVG	vLH	vRH	G	AB	R	H	2B	3B	HR	RBI	BB	HBP	SH	SF	SO	SB	CS	SLG	OBP
Bloxom, Justin	R-B	6-1	205	4-29-88	.250	.248	.251	131	460	56	115	22	1	8	67	73	3	1	7	113	5	1	.354	.352
Burns, Billy	B-R	5-9	180	8-30-89	.325	.378	.290	30	114	26	37	4	0	0	8	20	2	2	0	17	20	2	.360	.434
Goodwin, Brian	L-L	6-1	195	11-2-90	.252	.204	.272	122	457	82	115	19	11	10	40	66	8	1	1	121	19	11	.407	.355
Hague, Rick	R-R	6-2	190	9-18-88	.245	.287	.227	128	437	57	107	19	4	8	55	33	3	4	2	101	3	3	.362	.301
Harper, Bryce	L-R	6-2	230	10-16-92	.286	.000	.400	2	7	3	2	0	1	0	2	2	0	0	0	3	0	0	.571	.444
Head, Jerad	R-R	6-0	210	11-15-82	.253	.263	.248	111	392	46	99	21	0	13	46	23	11	0	0	79	2	1	.406	.312
Hood, Destin	R-R	6-1	225	4-3-90	.224	.284	.199	112	392	44	88	18	5	4	40	27	4	1	5	116	5	7	.327	.278
Howell, Jeff	R-R	6-0	205	4-1-83	.280	.433	.206	30	93	11	26	4	1	5	11	4	0	2	1	19	0	1	.505	.306
Jeroloman, Brian	L-R	5-11	190	5-10-85	.239	.185	.275	21	67	5	16	2	1	0	6	6	0	1	0	21	0	0	.299	.301
Johnson, Josh R.	B-R	5-11	170	1-11-86	.267	.352	.224	53	161	32	43	7	1	7	28	21	0	5	1	29	4	2	.453	.350
Komatsu, Erik	L-L	5-10	175	10-1-87	.172	.000	.333	7	29	4	5	1	0	0	1	3	0	1	0	6	0	0	.207	.250
Leon, Sandy	B-R	5-11	215	3-13-89	.177	.250	.145	95	310	35	55	12	1	3	26	47	3	0	1	57	0	0	.252	.291
Lozada, Jose	B-R	6-0	180	12-29-85	.204	.250	.194	81	201	11	41	5	1	1	19	17	4	5	3	53	3	2	.254	.276
Manuel, Craig	L-R	6-1	205	5-22-90	.000	—	.000	1	1	0	0	0	0	0	0	0	0	0	0	0	0	0	.000	.000
Martinson, Jason	R-R	6-1	190	10-15-88	.185	.207	.174	54	173	19	32	3	3	4	19	20	1	1	1	56	2	0	.306	.272
Nicol, Sean	R-R	5-10	175	9-25-86	.254	.214	.277	97	276	31	70	12	2	2	33	37	1	7	3	41	5	4	.333	.341
Oduber, Randolph	R-L	6-3	190	3-18-89	.111	.143	.091	5	18	1	2	0	0	1	3	1	0	0	0	9	0	0	.278	.158
Ramos, Wilson	R-R	6-0	220	8-10-87	.500	.667	.000	2	4	1	2	1	0	0	1	0	0	0	0	0	0	0	.750	.600
Rendon, Anthony	R-R	6-0	195	6-6-90	.319	.200	.382	33	116	17	37	11	2	6	24	30	3	0	3	25	1	0	.603	.461
Rivero, Carlos	R-R	6-3	200	5-20-88	.253	.208	.271	51	186	18	47	12	0	4	22	9	1	1	2	54	0	1	.382	.288
Skole, Matt	L-R	6-4	220	7-30-89	.200	.500	.000	2	5	1	1	1	0	0	1	2	0	0	0	2	0	0	.400	.429
Soriano, Francisco	B-R	5-11	169	6-16-87	.208	.286	.176	10	24	2	5	0	0	0	0	4	0	1	0	9	0	0	.208	.321
Souza, Steven	R-R	6-3	220	4-24-89	.300	.305	.298	77	273	54	82	23	1	15	44	41	5	0	4	76	20	6	.557	.396
VanOstrand, Jimmy	R-R	6-4	210	8-7-84	.252	.184	.281	76	254	35	64	19	0	10	37	25	4	0	0	28	0	1	.445	.329
Watts, Kris	L-R	6-1	210	7-15-84	.333	.000	.375	5	18	1	6	2	0	0	4	3	0	0	0	4	0	0	.444	.368

Pitching	B-T	HT	WT	DOB	W	L	ERA	G	GS	CG	SV	IP	H	R	ER	HR	BB	SO	AVG	vLH	vRH	K/9	BB/9
Barrett, Aaron	R-R	6-4	215	1-2-88	1	1	2.15	51	0	0	26	50	40	14	12	2	15	69	.215	.210	.219	12.34	2.68
Bray, Bill	L-L	6-3	215	6-5-83	0	0	0.00	4	0	0	0	4	2	0	0	0	1	6	.143	.333	.091	12.46	2.08
Broadway, Mike	R-R	6-5	215	3-30-87	1	0	2.70	12	0	0	0	17	18	6	5	1	5	14	.281	.231	.316	7.56	2.70
Broderick, Brian	R-R	6-6	205	9-1-86	1	3	5.21	7	7	0	0	38	48	23	22	7	8	30	.312	.342	.282	7.11	1.89
Clay, Caleb	R-R	6-2	180	2-15-88	6	3	3.46	13	13	2	0	75	64	33	29	6	17	59	.228	.185	.261	7.05	2.03
Cole, A.J.	R-R	6-4	180	1-5-92	4	2	2.18	7	7	0	0	45	31	13	11	3	10	49	.188	.228	.151	9.73	1.99
Demny, Paul	R-R	6-2	200	8-3-89	5	6	4.95	18	15	0	0	84	81	53	46	10	35	86	.253	.282	.226	9.25	3.76
Frias, Marcos	R-R	6-2	190	12-19-88	0	2	6.16	14	0	0	2	19	26	16	13	1	9	19	.313	.293	.333	9.00	2.37
Garcia, Christian	R-R	6-5	230	8-24-85	0	1	2.25	3	2	0	0	4	5	2	1	0	2	4	.294	.250	.400	9.00	4.50
Gilliam, Rob	R-R	6-1	195	11-29-87	3	6	4.40	19	18	0	0	90	83	46	44	9	38	77	.242	.235	.249	7.70	3.80
Grace, Matt	L-L	6-3	190	12-14-88	6	3	3.79	28	0	0	1	38	42	17	16	2	7	31	.284	.263	.297	7.34	1.66
Herron, Tyler	R-R	6-3	190	8-5-86	6	2	3.11	33	1	0	5	46	45	17	16	2	21	58	.247	.221	.271	11.27	4.08
Hill, Taylor	R-R	6-3	233	3-12-89	2	7	2.71	11	11	0	0	70	67	25	21	7	16	41	.256	.355	.184	5.30	2.07
Holder, Trevor	R-R	6-2	185	1-8-87	0	1	2.89	7	1	0	1	19	16	9	6	0	4	13	.246	.300	.194	6.27	1.93
Holland, Neil	R-R	6-0	190	8-14-88	1	4	2.84	41	0	0	1	51	48	16	16	3	11	63	.250	.254	.248	11.19	1.95
Jordan, Taylor	R-R	6-3	190	1-17-89	7	0	0.83	9	8	2	0	54	37	6	5	0	9	43	.194	.188	.200	7.17	1.50
Karns, Nate	R-R	6-3	230	11-25-87	10	6	3.26	23	23	3	0	133	109	54	48	14	48	155	.224	.212	.237	10.52	3.26

Name	B-T	HT	WT	DOB	W	L	ERA	G	GS	CG	SV	IP	H	R	ER	HR	BB	SO	AVG	vLH	vRH	K/9	BB/9
Krol, Ian	L-L	6-1	210	5-9-91	0	0	0.69	21	0	0	1	26	14	4	2	1	7	29	.157	.122	.188	10.04	2.42
Lehman, Pat	R-R	6-3	210	10-18-86	1	3	5.49	13	0	0	1	20	23	12	12	2	7	23	.291	.324	.262	10.53	3.20
Mattheus, Ryan	R-R	6-3	215	11-10-83	0	0	2.25	3	0	0	0	4	5	1	1	0	2	0	.357	.667	.125	0.00	4.50
McCoy, Patrick	L-L	6-3	220	8-3-88	2	1	4.32	39	0	0	0	42	48	24	20	5	12	36	.279	.313	.257	7.78	2.59
Mirowski, Richie	R-R	6-2	190	4-30-89	2	0	2.61	13	0	0	1	21	15	6	6	0	4	29	.197	.222	.175	12.63	1.74
Perry, Ryan	R-R	6-5	215	2-13-87	2	5	4.43	18	0	0	2	22	14	11	11	3	13	22	.189	.171	.205	8.87	5.24
Rauh, Brian	R-R	6-2	200	7-23-91	0	0	2.25	1	0	0	1	4	1	1	1	0	1	2	.077	.143	.000	4.50	2.25
Ray, Robbie	L-L	6-2	170	10-1-91	5	2	3.72	11	11	1	0	58	56	28	24	4	21	60	.247	.215	.259	9.31	3.26
Swynenberg, Matt	R-R	6-5	215	2-16-89	4	0	3.16	36	4	1	0	74	66	32	26	6	30	58	.238	.319	.180	7.05	3.65
Tatusko, Ryan	R-R	6-5	200	3-27-85	1	0	0.00	1	1	0	0	7	4	1	0	0	4	5	.174	.154	.200	5.14	5.14
Treinen, Blake	R-R	6-4	215	6-30-88	6	7	3.64	21	20	0	0	119	125	54	48	9	33	86	.269	.295	.245	6.52	2.50
Wort, Rob	R-R	6-2	170	2-7-89	1	0	13.50	4	0	0	0	3	4	5	5	2	4	2	.286	.286	.286	5.40	10.80

Fielding

Catcher	PCT	G	PO	A	E	DP	PB
Howell	1.000	28	189	18	0	2	1
Jeroloman	1.000	19	162	11	0	1	0
Leon	.993	93	764	61	6	1	9
Ramos	1.000	2	6	3	0	0	0
Watts	1.000	5	37	3	0	0	2

First Base	PCT	G	PO	A	E	DP
Bloxom	.991	105	820	44	8	75
Head	.981	14	95	7	2	9
Lozada	1.000	4	21	1	0	3
Nicol	1.000	1	1	1	0	0
Skole	1.000	2	15	0	0	0
VanOstrand	.990	23	183	12	2	16

Second Base	PCT	G	PO	A	E	DP
Hague	.970	117	204	289	15	55
Johnson	.947	3	8	10	1	4
Lozada	.935	10	17	12	2	3
Nicol	1.000	13	18	17	0	5
Rendon	.947	5	10	8	1	1
Soriano	1.000	4	7	12	0	5

Third Base	PCT	G	PO	A	E	DP
Bloxom	.805	18	12	21	8	0
Lozada	.915	17	10	33	4	2
Nicol	.950	42	43	72	6	8
Rendon	.958	24	13	55	3	6
Rivero	.961	49	35	88	5	8

Shortstop	PCT	G	PO	A	E	DP
Hague	.950	7	5	14	1	1
Johnson	.931	42	49	112	12	22
Lozada	.978	29	40	91	3	19
Martinson	.944	53	71	130	12	26
Nicol	.937	17	21	38	4	7
Rendon	1.000	1	2	2	0	1
Soriano	1.000	3	5	5	0	3

Outfield	PCT	G	PO	A	E	DP
Bloxom	.000	3	0	0	1	0
Burns	.986	30	67	2	1	1
Goodwin	.982	116	261	5	5	0
Harper	1.000	2	4	0	0	0
Head	.981	62	100	4	2	1
Hood	.979	104	174	10	4	0
Komatsu	1.000	7	9	0	0	0
Lozada	.800	10	8	0	2	0
Nicol	1.000	17	22	2	0	0
Oduber	1.000	5	9	0	0	0
Soriano	1.000	2	2	0	0	0
Souza	.979	76	130	8	3	1
VanOstrand	1.000	6	9	0	0	0

POTOMAC NATIONALS HIGH CLASS A

CAROLINA LEAGUE

Batting	B-T	HT	WT	DOB	AVG	vLH	vRH	G	AB	R	H	2B	3B	HR	RBI	BB	HBP	SH	SF	SO	SB	CS	SLG	OBP
Burns, Billy	B-R	5-9	180	8-30-89	.312	.313	.312	91	330	70	103	8	9	0	29	52	12	6	2	37	54	5	.391	.422
Difo, Wilmer	R-R	6-0	175	4-2-92	.222	1.000	.176	6	18	2	4	1	0	0	1	2	0	0	0	3	0	1	.278	.300
Dykstra, Cutter	R-R	5-11	180	6-29-89	.283	.306	.275	107	361	42	102	26	0	4	43	77	5	0	3	72	16	4	.388	.413
Gilmartin, Michael	R-R	6-0	180	7-14-87	.241	.276	.235	59	191	26	46	9	0	3	21	29	6	1	2	37	5	2	.335	.355
Harper, Bryce	L-R	6-2	230	10-16-92	.500	—	.500	2	4	2	2	1	0	1	1	1	0	0	0	1	0	0	1.500	.600
Higley, J.R.	R-R	6-3	210	6-21-88	.000	.000	.000	4	10	0	0	0	0	0	1	1	0	1	0	2	0	0	.000	.091
Kelso, Blake	R-R	5-10	180	3-28-89	.375	.667	.308	5	16	2	6	3	0	0	2	0	0	0	0	1	0	0	.563	.375
Keyes, Kevin	R-R	6-3	225	3-15-89	.233	.182	.246	117	437	54	102	24	0	13	79	34	5	1	5	132	9	4	.378	.293
Leonida, Cole	R-R	6-2	220	12-25-88	.225	.214	.228	58	178	24	40	6	0	10	25	21	5	3	3	58	1	2	.427	.319
Manuel, Craig	L-R	6-1	205	5-22-90	.400	.333	.444	4	15	2	6	0	0	0	1	0	0	0	0	1	0	0	.400	.438
Martinson, Jason	R-R	6-1	190	10-15-88	.268	.321	.254	73	254	44	68	11	4	12	53	38	8	0	5	89	15	2	.484	.374
Miller, Brandon	R-R	6-2	215	10-8-89	.300	.217	.322	30	110	11	33	6	3	2	16	7	2	0	1	29	3	1	.464	.350
Miller, Justin	R-R	6-0	180	11-28-88	.253	.232	.262	74	237	33	60	16	2	5	29	17	3	3	2	47	12	3	.401	.309
Nieto, Adrian	B-R	6-0	200	11-12-89	.285	.208	.304	110	390	68	111	29	1	11	53	53	4	1	4	82	4	2	.449	.373
Norfork, Khayyan	R-R	5-10	190	1-19-89	.200	.231	.182	11	35	5	7	0	0	1	2	3	0	2	0	8	2	1	.286	.263
Oduber, Randolph	R-L	6-3	190	3-18-89	.238	.239	.238	103	323	45	77	18	3	3	39	17	11	2	2	101	15	7	.341	.297
Piwnica-Worms, Will	R-R	6-3	215	4-1-90	.273	.200	.333	4	11	1	3	0	0	0	1	0	0	0	0	1	0	1	.273	.273
Ramos, Wilson	R-R	6-0	220	8-10-87	.000	—	.000	3	10	0	0	0	0	0	0	1	1	0	0	1	0	0	.000	.167
Ramsey, Caleb	L-R	6-2	215	10-7-88	.290	.266	.296	127	483	81	140	20	4	6	59	32	5	2	6	69	13	8	.385	.337
Sanchez, Adrian	B-R	6-0	160	8-10-90	.241	.238	.242	120	428	43	103	14	4	1	42	17	6	10	2	61	8	4	.299	.278
Soriano, Francisco	B-R	5-11	169	6-16-87	.209	.140	.227	72	206	40	43	8	6	1	20	46	2	4	0	52	8	6	.320	.358
Taylor, Michael	R-R	6-4	205	3-26-91	.263	.275	.260	133	509	79	134	41	6	10	87	55	8	2	7	131	51	7	.426	.340
Valdez, Jean Carlos	R-R	6-2	190	3-14-93	.000	—	.000	1	1	0	0	0	0	0	0	0	0	0	0	0	0	0	.000	.000
Werth, Jayson	R-R	6-5	225	5-20-79	.556	.500	.625	6	18	4	10	1	0	2	8	2	0	0	0	0	0	0	.944	.600
Zimmerman, Ryan	R-R	6-3	230	9-28-84	.000	—	.000	1	3	0	0	0	0	0	0	0	0	0	0	0	0	0	.000	.000

Pitching	B-T	HT	WT	DOB	W	L	ERA	G	GS	CG	SV	IP	H	R	ER	HR	BB	SO	AVG	vLH	vRH	K/9	BB/9
Bates, Colin	R-R	6-1	175	3-10-88	5	4	2.61	36	0	0	1	62	58	30	18	4	8	48	.244	.260	.232	6.97	1.16
Benincasa, Robert	R-R	6-2	180	9-5-90	0	4	3.30	25	0	0	17	30	28	14	11	2	9	34	.243	.240	.246	10.20	2.70
Cole, A.J.	R-R	6-4	180	1-5-92	6	3	4.25	18	18	0	0	97	96	50	46	12	23	102	.257	.263	.252	9.43	2.13
Demny, Paul	R-R	6-2	200	8-3-89	2	2	3.69	8	8	1	0	32	34	19	13	1	15	34	.272	.213	.328	9.66	4.26
Detwiler, Ross	R-L	6-5	200	3-6-86	0	0	2.45	1	1	0	0	4	7	1	1	0	0	4	.389	.167	.500	9.82	0.00
Dupra, Brian	R-R	6-3	200	12-15-88	1	7	4.96	29	3	0	0	62	64	36	34	7	28	46	.263	.270	.258	6.42	4.09
Fischer, David	R-R	6-5	175	4-10-90	4	0	4.30	21	0	0	1	44	29	26	21	2	44	53	.190	.197	.184	10.84	9.00
Frias, Marcos	R-R	6-2	190	12-19-88	2	1	7.59	6	2	0	0	11	21	9	9	2	4	7	.420	.409	.429	5.91	3.38
Gilliam, Rob	R-R	6-1	195	11-29-87	0	1	7.04	2	2	0	0	8	10	6	6	2	5	7	.313	.429	.280	8.22	5.87
Grace, Matt	L-L	6-3	190	12-14-88	3	0	3.18	14	0	0	0	28	26	11	10	0	7	24	.245	.300	.224	7.62	2.22
Hawkins, Ben	L-L	6-2	175	11-4-89	0	0	5.63	7	0	0	0	8	14	9	5	1	6	9	.389	.467	.333	10.13	6.75
Henke, Travis	R-R	6-6	241	7-9-88	0	0	2.25	7	0	0	1	12	10	3	3	1	2	11	.222	.250	.200	8.25	1.50

	B-T	HT	WT	DOB	W	L	ERA	G	GS	CG	SV	IP	H	R	ER	HR	BB	SO	AVG	vLH	vRH	K/9	BB/9
Herron, Tyler	R-R	6-3	190	8-5-86	1	1	1.77	10	0	0	1	20	16	5	4	0	11	32	.222	.133	.286	14.16	4.87
Hill, Taylor	R-R	6-3	233	3-12-89	6	2	2.99	15	14	2	0	84	73	31	28	6	11	54	.233	.235	.231	5.76	1.17
Holt, Greg	R-R	6-2	205	6-19-89	9	0	3.71	42	0	0	1	70	67	32	29	8	33	55	.255	.275	.240	7.04	4.22
Jordan, Taylor	R-R	6-3	190	1-17-89	2	1	1.24	6	6	0	0	36	31	9	5	1	6	29	.228	.233	.222	7.18	1.49
Martin, Rafael	R-R	6-3	215	5-16-84	0	0	1.04	17	0	0	2	26	12	5	3	1	14	33	.135	.212	.089	11.42	4.85
Meza, Christian	L-L	6-0	185	8-3-90	0	0	6.62	10	0	0	1	18	26	17	13	1	12	24	.333	.320	.340	12.23	6.11
Mirowski, Richie	R-R	6-2	190	4-30-89	8	3	1.50	32	0	0	6	48	32	17	8	6	11	59	.180	.229	.137	11.06	2.06
Mooneyham, Brett	L-L	6-5	235	1-24-90	0	3	13.50	3	3	0	0	11	17	19	17	2	13	6	.354	.333	.361	4.76	10.32
Ohlendorf, Ross	R-R	6-4	240	8-8-82	0	0	6.75	1	1	0	0	4	8	3	3	0	1	2	.444	.300	.625	4.50	2.25
Pineyro, Ivan	R-R	6-1	200	9-29-91	1	0	3.68	3	3	0	0	15	14	6	6	1	5	8	.255	.297	.167	4.91	3.07
Purke, Matt	L-L	6-4	205	7-17-90	5	3	4.43	12	12	0	0	61	67	36	30	3	18	41	.284	.333	.259	6.05	2.66
Rauh, Brian	R-R	6-2	200	7-23-91	4	2	4.22	16	12	0	0	64	69	32	30	8	18	35	.278	.293	.264	4.92	2.53
Ray, Robbie	L-L	6-2	170	10-1-91	6	3	3.11	16	16	3	0	84	60	30	29	9	41	100	.205	.194	.211	10.71	4.39
Schwartz, Blake	R-R	6-3	200	10-9-89	11	4	2.65	23	23	1	0	133	117	47	39	8	26	80	.236	.218	.250	5.43	1.76
Self, Derek	R-R	6-3	205	1-14-90	4	2	6.29	23	0	0	4	24	30	18	17	3	10	20	.309	.357	.273	7.40	3.70
Selik, Cameron	R-R	6-2	235	8-25-87	1	3	5.73	10	0	0	1	11	9	7	7	1	5	10	.237	.200	.261	8.18	4.09
Silvestre, Hector	L-L	6-3	180	12-14-92	0	1	2.45	1	1	0	0	4	2	5	1	1	4	1	.154	.143	.167	2.45	9.82
Solis, Sammy	R-L	6-5	230	8-10-88	2	1	3.43	13	12	0	0	58	58	23	22	3	19	40	.270	.291	.257	6.24	2.97
Thomas, Justin	L-L	6-2	195	10-21-90	0	0	0.00	1	0	0	0	1	1	0	0	0	2	0	.250	.000	.250	0.00	18.00
Turnbull, Kylin	R-L	6-5	205	9-12-89	0	3	14.81	3	3	0	0	10	20	18	17	1	8	3	.426	.455	.417	2.61	6.97
Wort, Rob	R-R	6-2	170	2-7-89	1	1	3.71	31	0	0	6	34	25	16	14	1	29	48	.210	.222	.200	12.71	7.68

Fielding

Catcher	PCT	G	PO	A	E	DP	PB
Leonida	.993	52	369	37	3	5	3
Manuel	1.000	4	23	4	0	0	0
Nieto	.991	86	656	74	7	6	14
Ramos	1.000	2	10	4	0	1	0

First Base	PCT	G	PO	A	E	DP
Keyes	.987	100	778	32	11	77
Miller	.981	30	197	12	4	9
Ramsey	.990	13	91	8	1	4
Soriano	1.000	2	17	3	0	1

Second Base	PCT	G	PO	A	E	DP
Difo	1.000	1	4	3	0	1
Dykstra	.976	33	49	73	3	10
Gilmartin	.980	35	62	84	3	16
Kelso	1.000	1	1	0	0	0
Norfork	1.000	9	24	35	0	8

	PCT	G	PO	A	E	DP
Sanchez	.972	56	103	136	7	30
Soriano	.964	12	22	31	2	10

Third Base	PCT	G	PO	A	E	DP
Dykstra	.923	62	47	73	10	9
Gilmartin	.805	18	13	20	8	3
Kelso	1.000	4	4	6	0	1
Miller	.920	35	25	44	6	3
Sanchez	.875	9	5	9	2	1
Soriano	.960	24	16	32	2	1
Valdez	—	1	0	0	0	0
Zimmerman	1.000	1	2	1	0	0

Shortstop	PCT	G	PO	A	E	DP
Difo	.867	4	2	11	2	1
Dykstra	.964	8	10	17	1	3
Martinson	.968	55	70	140	7	23
Sanchez	.961	56	83	139	9	30

	PCT	G	PO	A	E	DP
Soriano	.967	23	26	63	3	10

Outfield	PCT	G	PO	A	E	DP
Burns	.994	89	162	5	1	2
Gilmartin	—	1	0	0	0	0
Harper	1.000	1	0	0	0	0
Higley	1.000	4	7	0	0	0
Miller	.967	26	53	5	2	1
Miller	1.000	14	23	2	0	0
Norfork	1.000	1	1	0	0	0
Oduber	.979	68	134	3	3	1
Piwnica-Worms	1.000	4	4	0	0	0
Ramsey	.976	102	159	6	4	2
Soriano	1.000	6	8	0	0	0
Taylor	.986	121	325	21	5	4
Werth	1.000	6	12	1	0	1

HAGERSTOWN SUNS

LOW CLASS A

SOUTH ATLANTIC LEAGUE

Batting	B-T	HT	WT	DOB	AVG	vLH	vRH	G	AB	R	H	2B	3B	HR	RBI	BB	HBP	SH	SF	SO	SB	CS	SLG	OBP
Bailey, Hunter	R-R	6-0	180	5-17-89	.182	.333	.143	16	44	5	8	1	0	0	3	4	1	0	0	11	2	0	.205	.265
Ballou, Isaac	L-R	6-2	205	3-17-90	.111	.000	.120	6	27	2	3	0	0	0	2	2	0	0	0	6	1	0	.111	.172
Difo, Wilmer	R-R	6-0	175	4-2-92	.220	.143	.233	16	50	7	11	2	0	2	11	5	0	0	1	13	4	1	.380	.286
Fernandez, Erick	R-R	5-11	190	11-30-88	.192	.500	.100	10	26	1	5	1	0	0	3	1	0	0	1	6	0	0	.231	.214
Foat, Matt	R-R	6-0	185	3-20-90	.247	.176	.268	22	73	11	18	3	0	0	9	6	3	1	0	18	1	0	.288	.329
Higley, J.R.	R-R	6-3	210	6-21-88	.235	.400	.217	15	51	7	12	2	1	0	5	4	3	0	0	12	1	1	.314	.328
Lippincott, Bryan	L-R	6-3	210	9-26-89	.219	.000	.269	10	32	5	7	1	0	0	2	6	0	0	0	10	0	0	.281	.342
Lopez, Carlos	R-R	6-2	220	1-18-90	.296	.000	.333	9	27	4	8	3	0	0	1	7	0	0	0	7	0	0	.407	.441
Manuel, Craig	L-R	6-1	205	5-22-90	.273	.350	.261	48	154	25	42	6	1	1	25	23	0	2	4	19	2	0	.344	.359
Martinez, Estarlin	L-R	6-1	185	3-8-92	.253	.282	.246	98	364	57	92	22	1	4	48	36	4	2	4	74	20	4	.352	.324
McQuillan, Mike	L-R	5-11	175	10-2-89	.277	.227	.286	73	264	32	73	10	4	2	29	40	2	5	3	66	15	6	.367	.372
Mesa, Narciso	R-R	5-11	175	11-16-91	.298	.300	.297	53	205	35	61	6	2	1	19	17	4	6	0	29	13	8	.361	.363
Miller, Brandon	R-R	6-2	215	10-8-89	.243	.263	.238	103	395	62	96	26	2	18	72	34	6	0	7	135	3	1	.456	.308
Norfork, Khayyan	R-R	6-0	185	11-25-88	.250	.262	.247	88	316	50	79	15	5	4	42	32	6	3	3	71	14	6	.367	.328
Palace, Sam	R-R	6-1	210	6-3-86	.308	.200	.375	3	13	2	4	0	0	1	6	0	0	0	0	3	0	0	.538	.308
Perez, Stephen	B-R	5-11	175	12-16-90	.236	.212	.242	128	432	59	102	23	2	4	54	40	3	8	3	107	7	9	.326	.303
Perrott, Geoff	R-R	6-2	205	12-13-90	.333	.000	.364	3	12	2	4	0	0	0	2	0	0	0	0	3	0	0	.333	.333
Piwnica-Worms, Will	R-R	6-3	215	4-1-90	.257	.276	.253	93	303	53	78	15	2	3	44	55	9	3	2	64	11	4	.350	.385
Pleffner, Shawn	L-R	6-5	225	8-17-89	.288	.290	.288	101	361	55	104	24	2	4	52	59	2	0	6	76	11	2	.399	.386
Ramirez, Andruth	R-R	5-11	180	3-10-89	.250	.000	.500	1	4	0	1	1	0	0	0	0	0	0	0	1	0	0	.500	.250
Ramos, Wander	R-R	6-2	180	4-26-91	.264	.291	.257	76	265	43	70	17	3	7	49	33	2	1	2	81	4	1	.430	.348
Renda, Tony	R-R	5-10	170	1-24-91	.294	.296	.293	135	521	99	153	43	3	3	51	68	8	4	5	65	30	6	.405	.380
Schill, Wes	R-R	5-9	170	11-22-89	.215	.189	.222	90	247	48	53	9	2	1	34	45	1	5	4	57	13	2	.279	.333
Severino, Pedro	R-R	6-1	180	7-20-93	.241	.322	.220	84	282	28	68	19	2	1	45	13	1	3	3	54	1	0	.333	.274

Pitching	B-T	HT	WT	DOB	W	L	ERA	G	GS	CG	SV	IP	H	R	ER	HR	BB	SO	AVG	vLH	vRH	K/9	BB/9
Anderson, Dixon	R-R	6-5	225		5	5	3.20	15	15	0	0	79	62	35	28	3	30	72	.215	.196	.233	8.24	3.43
Bacus, Dakota	R-R	6-2	200	4-2-91	1	0	0.00	2	1	0	0	8	2	0	0	0	4	5	.074	.045	.200	5.40	4.32
Bafidis, Cory	L-L	6-0	190	8-22-90	0	0	9.00	2	0	0	0	3	4	3	3	0	5	2	.308	.000	.500	6.00	15.00
Benincasa, Robert	R-R	6-2	180	9-5-90	0	1	2.57	20	0	0	10	21	17	6	6	2	5	30	.213	.231	.204	12.86	2.14

	B-T	HT	WT	DOB	W	L	ERA	G	GS	CG	SV	IP	H	R	ER	HR	BB	SO	AVG	vLH	vRH	K/9	BB/9
Davis, Cody	R-R	5-9	170	7-21-90	2	3	2.76	35	0	0	1	42	40	14	13	1	14	46	.237	.313	.190	9.78	2.98
Dickson, Ian	R-R	6-5	215	9-16-90	5	3	4.39	16	10	0	2	66	65	33	32	8	17	71	.265	.250	.279	9.73	2.33
Dupra, Brian	R-R	6-3	200	12-15-88	1	2	3.72	5	1	0	0	19	22	9	8	2	6	12	.293	.382	.220	5.59	2.79
Encarnacion, Pedro	R-R	6-4	175	6-26-91	10	9	3.58	25	24	1	0	128	116	68	51	10	37	113	.235	.283	.186	7.92	2.59
Fischer, David	R-R	6-5	175	4-10-90	1	0	3.65	9	0	0	3	25	20	10	10	2	8	28	.217	.188	.233	10.22	2.92
Harper, Bryan	L-L	6-5	205	12-29-89	5	1	3.97	34	0	0	1	45	32	22	20	2	32	43	.194	.189	.196	8.54	6.35
Henke, Travis	R-R	6-6	241	7-9-88	3	1	2.72	30	0	0	2	60	49	21	18	3	17	41	.230	.233	.228	6.18	2.56
Hollins, L.J.	R-R	6-3	185	7-31-91	0	0	4.50	1	0	0	0	2	3	2	1	0	2	1	.300	.000	.375	4.50	9.00
Hudgins, Will	R-R	6-4	200	2-12-90	2	1	4.79	16	0	0	1	21	19	13	11	3	14	18	.232	.250	.220	7.84	6.10
Johansen, Jake	R-R	6-6	235	1-23-91	0	2	5.79	2	2	0	0	9	13	9	6	1	5	7	.317	.429	.259	6.75	4.82
Lee, Nick	L-L	5-11	185	1-13-91	6	4	3.96	19	17	0	0	91	83	48	40	7	43	102	.249	.218	.260	10.09	4.25
Lopez, Reynaldo	R-R	6-0	185	1-4-94	0	0	6.75	1	1	0	0	4	8	3	3	1	1	4	.444	.333	.667	9.00	2.25
Mattheus, Ryan	R-R	6-3	215	11-10-83	0	0	9.00	1	1	0	0	1	1	1	1	0	0	0	.200	.333	.000	0.00	0.00
McKenzie, Chris	R-R	6-3	185	12-6-89	0	1	5.25	8	0	0	0	12	11	8	7	1	10	7	.256	.286	.241	5.25	7.50
Mendez, Gilberto	R-R	6-0	165	11-17-92	3	2	0.91	24	0	0	7	30	18	3	3	1	10	33	.173	.122	.218	10.01	3.03
Meza, Christian	L-L	6-0	185	8-3-90	3	1	4.06	19	0	0	1	31	27	14	14	2	14	36	.241	.256	.232	10.45	4.06
Mooneyham, Brett	L-L	6-5	235	1-24-90	10	3	1.94	17	17	0	0	93	50	21	20	5	41	79	.161	.151	.166	7.65	3.97
Pena, Ronald	R-R	6-4	195	9-19-91	4	3	3.48	28	10	0	1	88	89	40	34	4	34	55	.263	.266	.262	5.63	3.48
Pineyro, Ivan	R-R	6-1	200	9-29-91	5	3	3.14	13	13	0	0	66	57	26	23	4	17	65	.237	.227	.244	8.86	2.32
Purke, Matt	L-L	6-4	205	7-17-90	1	1	2.48	6	6	0	0	29	25	9	8	3	7	41	.229	.318	.207	12.72	2.17
Rauh, Brian	R-R	6-2	200	7-23-91	3	2	5.21	14	0	0	2	38	37	22	22	3	15	31	.261	.344	.192	7.34	3.55
Schwartz, Blake	R-R	6-3	200	10-9-89	2	0	1.26	4	1	0	1	14	5	4	2	1	2	21	.102	.074	.136	13.19	1.26
Self, Derek	R-R	6-3	205	1-14-90	0	3	3.41	24	0	0	4	32	34	12	12	2	6	29	.281	.289	.276	8.24	1.71
Smith, Jason	R-R	6-3	180	8-7-90	0	1	9.39	3	0	0	0	8	11	8	8	1	4	8	.344	.273	.381	9.39	4.70
Thomas, Justin	L-L	6-2	195	10-21-90	1	0	4.60	10	0	0	0	16	17	11	8	2	1	21	.254	.143	.333	12.06	0.57
Turnbull, Kylin	R-L	6-5	205	9-12-89	6	5	3.58	16	16	0	0	83	97	47	33	10	16	67	.287	.286	.288	7.27	1.73
Voth, Austin	R-R	6-1	190	6-26-92	1	0	3.38	2	2	0	0	11	8	4	4	0	2	9	.195	.231	.133	7.59	1.69
Walsh, Jake	L-L	6-3	195	1-1-91	0	0	0.00	1	0	0	0	1	1	0	0	0	0	1	.250	.000	.500	9.00	0.00

Fielding

Catcher	PCT	G	PO	A	E	DP	PB
Fernandez	.963	10	47	5	2	0	0
Manuel	.992	46	351	44	3	2	5
Palace	1.000	3	26	2	0	0	0
Plutko	1.000	2	21	1	0	0	0
Severino	.980	82	590	108	14	4	16

First Base	PCT	G	PO	A	E	DP
Foat	1.000	2	14	2	0	1
Lippincott	1.000	5	49	1	0	5
Lopez	1.000	9	73	4	0	4
Martinez	.993	34	273	13	2	23
Pleffner	.986	94	813	53	12	65

Second Base	PCT	G	PO	A	E	DP
Bailey	.950	5	11	8	1	2

Norfork	1.000	17	31	43	0	6
Renda	.973	119	191	340	15	73

Third Base	PCT	G	PO	A	E	DP
Bailey	1.000	6	4	14	0	1
Difo	.889	11	5	19	3	2
McQuillan	.885	52	27	96	16	4
Norfork	.937	49	29	90	8	8
Schill	.893	21	8	42	6	1

Shortstop	PCT	G	PO	A	E	DP
Bailey	.667	4	0	2	1	0
Difo	.867	2	7	6	2	1
Norfork	1.000	1	1	2	0	1
Perez	.969	125	167	371	17	69
Schill	.971	8	16	17	1	3

Outfield	PCT	G	PO	A	E	DP
Ballou	1.000	6	17	0	0	0
Foat	1.000	3	1	0	0	0
Higley	1.000	15	32	0	0	0
Lippincott	1.000	3	4	0	0	0
Martinez	.947	54	70	1	4	0
McQuillan	1.000	2	1	0	0	0
Mesa	.957	51	109	3	5	1
Miller	.989	102	167	14	2	2
Norfork	1.000	1	3	0	0	0
Piwnica-Worms	.994	91	170	5	1	0
Ramirez	—	1	0	0	0	0
Ramos	.945	46	64	5	4	1
Schill	.944	58	66	2	4	1

AUBURN DOUBLEDAYS
SHORT-SEASON

NEW YORK-PENN LEAGUE

Batting	B-T	HT	WT	DOB	AVG	vLH	vRH	G	AB	R	H	2B	3B	HR	RBI	BB	HBP	SH	SF	SO	SB	CS	SLG	OBP
Allen, Brenton	L-L	6-1	200	11-2-91	.197	.158	.204	41	117	13	23	7	0	1	10	15	8	0	0	33	3	1	.282	.329
Attl, Kyle	R-R	6-0	180	8-16-91	.171	.071	.238	11	35	2	6	1	0	1	7	1	0	2	0	9	0	1	.286	.194
Ballou, Isaac	L-R	6-2	205	3-17-90	.294	.289	.295	59	211	33	62	14	1	2	20	30	10	1	1	31	8	3	.398	.405
Chubb, Austin	R-R	6-1	200	4-17-89	.200	.222	.192	32	105	7	21	4	0	0	6	2	4	1	1	12	0	1	.238	.241
Dent, Cody	L-R	5-11	190	4-17-88	.217	.188	.220	50	157	16	34	3	0	0	8	19	1	2	1	47	5	2	.236	.303
Difo, Wilmer	R-R	6-0	175	4-2-92	.217	.281	.193	33	120	15	26	3	4	1	6	10	3	2	1	17	3	2	.333	.291
Fernandez, Erick	R-R	5-11	190	11-30-88	.120	.250	.059	9	25	5	3	1	0	0	1	7	1	0	0	3	0	0	.160	.333
Foat, Matt	R-R	6-0	185	3-20-90	.200	.233	.187	42	150	12	30	4	1	2	16	16	1	0	2	24	1	0	.280	.278
Gunter, Cody	L-R	6-3	195	4-18-94	.224	.174	.237	62	223	21	50	5	2	3	19	20	0	1	1	64	0	2	.305	.287
Leon, Sandy	B-R	5-11	215	3-13-89	.077	.000	.100	3	13	0	1	0	0	0	0	0	0	0	0	3	0	0	.077	.077
Lippincott, Bryan	L-R	6-3	210	9-26-89	.283	.268	.288	44	166	30	47	9	0	7	29	19	1	0	1	29	3	0	.464	.358
Masters, David	R-R	6-1	185	4-23-93	.183	.222	.162	45	153	11	28	7	1	0	8	10	5	1	1	33	0	0	.242	.254
Mesa, Narciso	R-R	5-11	175	11-16-91	.083	.000	.167	3	12	1	1	0	0	0	2	3	0	0	0	1	0	0	.083	.267
Poole, Jordan	R-R	6-3	210	9-11-91	.220	.154	.239	18	59	6	13	4	0	3	13	5	0	1	1	35	0	0	.441	.277
Ramirez, Andruth	R-R	5-11	180	3-10-89	.158	.083	.178	21	57	2	9	1	0	0	2	2	0	1	1	10	1	0	.175	.183
Reistetter, Matt	L-R	5-10	180	5-5-92	.253	.133	.281	24	79	9	20	1	2	1	5	10	0	0	0	9	0	1	.354	.337
Rodriguez, Wilman	R-R	6-1	190	6-7-91	.239	.274	.224	57	205	18	49	6	0	1	15	13	7	0	1	46	8	3	.283	.305
Valdez, Jean Carlos	R-R	6-2	190	3-14-93	.251	.345	.210	48	179	24	45	9	2	3	19	9	1	2	0	35	0	1	.374	.291
Yezzo, Jimmy	L-R	6-0	200	2-27-92	.258	.255	.259	66	252	19	65	8	2	2	26	6	1	1	3	40	0	1	.329	.275
Zebrack, Greg	L-R	6-0	200	8-28-90	.233	.326	.181	44	129	14	30	5	1	1	14	12	6	0	0	38	7	4	.310	.327

Pitching	B-T	HT	WT	DOB	W	L	ERA	G	GS	CG	SV	IP	H	R	ER	HR	BB	SO	AVG	vLH	vRH	K/9	BB/9
Bafidis, Cory	L-L	6-0	190	8-22-90	2	1	2.18	10	0	0	0	21	15	6	5	0	8	15	.211	.238	.200	6.53	3.48
Barrientos, Joel	L-L	6-2	145	8-16-93	1	5	7.08	11	8	0	0	41	54	34	32	6	27	24	.331	.346	.324	5.31	5.98
Cooper, Andrew	R-R	6-1	200	6-27-92	2	1	4.18	13	0	0	0	24	25	13	11	1	7	15	.275	.405	.185	5.70	2.66
Derosier, Matt	R-R	6-2	200	7-13-94	0	0	0.00	1	0	0	0	3	1	0	0	0	1	1	.111	.333	.000	3.38	0.00

Name	B-T	HT	WT	DOB	W	L	ERA	G	GS	CG	SV	IP	H	R	ER	HR	BB	SO	AVG	vLH	vRH	K/9	BB/9
Dicharry, Austin	R-R	6-4	200	11-27-89	0	2	14.54	3	0	0	0	4	8	7	7	0	2	4	.421	.333	.462	8.31	4.15
Garcia, Christian	R-R	6-5	230	8-24-85	0	0	0.00	1	0	0	0	1	0	0	0	0	0	2	.000	—	.000	18.00	0.00
Giolito, Lucas	R-R	6-6	225	7-14-94	1	0	0.64	3	3	0	0	14	9	1	1	1	4	14	.191	.182	.200	9.00	2.57
Grisz, Ben	R-R	6-1	230	1-26-90	1	0	0.00	5	0	0	0	8	4	0	0	0	1	7	.143	.182	.118	7.88	1.13
Hollins, L.J.	R-R	6-3	185	7-31-91	1	4	2.84	23	0	0	6	44	45	23	14	0	14	35	.268	.321	.241	7.11	2.84
Hudgins, Will	R-R	6-4	200	2-12-90	1	1	3.75	4	0	0	0	12	6	6	5	1	7	10	.140	.125	.148	7.50	5.25
Johansen, Jake	R-R	6-6	235	1-23-91	1	1	1.06	10	10	0	0	42	22	8	5	1	18	44	.147	.197	.112	9.35	3.83
Joyce, Jake	R-R	6-0	185	8-19-91	1	3	5.04	20	0	0	2	30	37	23	17	0	12	27	.301	.435	.221	8.01	3.56
Lopez, Reynaldo	R-R	6-0	185	1-4-94	0	1	47.25	1	1	0	0	1	7	7	7	0	0	0	.700	.571	1.000	0.00	0.00
Medina, Silvio	R-R	6-1	190	6-3-90	1	3	4.08	19	0	0	0	35	33	19	16	2	25	48	.241	.250	.236	12.23	6.37
Mudron, Mike	R-L	6-0	185	2-4-90	1	3	6.82	19	0	0	0	30	43	27	23	0	15	32	.328	.313	.343	9.49	4.45
Napoli, David	R-L	5-10	180	10-3-90	1	0	1.14	14	0	0	3	24	16	4	3	0	10	28	.176	.212	.155	10.65	3.80
Orlan, R.C.	R-L	6-0	185	9-28-90	1	5	3.65	13	11	0	0	57	54	27	23	2	22	47	.256	.294	.238	7.46	3.49
Pivetta, Nic	R-R	6-5	220	2-14-93	0	1	3.38	5	5	0	0	21	19	8	8	1	11	17	.238	.286	.212	7.17	4.64
Selsor, Casey	L-L	6-2	185	2-23-90	0	6	4.29	14	7	0	0	42	56	27	20	1	14	30	.322	.273	.345	6.43	3.00
Simko, Todd	L-L	6-5	220	12-5-88	3	0	6.00	4	0	0	0	6	8	4	4	1	3	10	.333	.200	.368	15.00	4.50
Simms, John	R-R	6-3	205	1-17-92	0	3	5.79	11	2	0	1	28	41	19	18	0	7	31	.336	.373	.310	9.96	2.25
Spezial, Niko	R-L	6-3	205	11-1-90	0	0	5.40	3	0	0	0	3	5	2	2	0	3	4	.333	.333	.333	10.80	8.10
Sylvestri, Mike	R-R	5-10	180	6-14-90	2	1	11.42	7	0	0	0	9	12	12	11	0	8	7	.333	.429	.273	7.27	8.31
Thomas, Justin	L-L	6-2	195	10-21-90	0	0	0.00	2	0	0	1	3	1	0	0	0	0	3	.100	.333	.000	8.10	0.00
Treinen, Blake	R-R	6-4	215	6-30-88	0	0	0.00	2	2	0	0	6	1	0	0	0	0	7	.056	.091	.000	10.50	0.00
Turnbull, Kylin	R-L	6-5	205	9-12-89	2	0	1.96	4	4	0	0	18	16	9	4	1	3	15	.229	.375	.185	7.36	1.47
Ullmann, Ryan	R-R	6-6	230	8-12-91	2	2	5.30	8	6	0	0	37	52	27	22	4	10	23	.333	.384	.289	5.54	2.41
Voth, Austin	R-R	6-1	190	6-26-92	2	0	1.47	7	0	0	0	31	21	6	5	0	4	42	.193	.209	.182	12.33	1.17
Waterman, Elliott	L-L	6-5	230	11-24-90	0	0	6.75	4	0	0	0	7	13	5	5	2	3	4	.406	.286	.440	5.40	4.05
Williams, Deion	R-R	6-3	190	11-11-92	0	6	9.42	8	8	0	0	29	40	32	30	1	17	23	.339	.346	.333	7.22	5.34
Young, Chris	R-R	6-10	260	5-25-79	0	0	0.00	1	1	0	0	3	1	0	0	0	1	3	.100	—	.100	9.00	3.00

Fielding

Catcher	PCT	G	PO	A	E	DP	PB
Chubb	.996	29	215	26	1	1	5
Fernandez	.969	7	57	5	2	1	2
Leon	1.000	3	23	4	0	1	0
Ramirez	.986	21	126	12	2	0	12
Reistetter	.988	22	139	20	2	1	2

First Base	PCT	G	PO	A	E	DP
Foat	1.000	1	5	3	0	0
Lippincott	.977	8	42	0	1	3
Valdez	.989	9	86	3	1	4
Yezzo	.993	60	504	31	4	48

Second Base	PCT	G	PO	A	E	DP
Attl	1.000	8	16	21	0	6
Dent	.975	29	53	65	3	11
Difo	.948	13	18	37	3	7
Foat	.951	21	40	57	5	14
Masters	1.000	7	17	19	0	4

Third Base	PCT	G	PO	A	E	DP
Attl	1.000	1	0	1	0	0
Dent	—	2	0	0	0	0
Gunter	.885	59	36	118	20	9
Valdez	.956	15	15	28	2	0

Shortstop	PCT	G	PO	A	E	DP
Attl	.800	2	0	4	1	0
Dent	.945	21	25	61	5	12
Difo	.971	18	27	40	2	
Masters	.936	38	53	108	11	17

Outfield	PCT	G	PO	A	E	DP
Allen	.940	33	47	0	3	0
Ballou	.982	54	102	8	2	1
Foat	1.000	4	3	1	0	0
Lippincott	.979	29	45	2	1	2
Mesa	1.000	3	6	0	0	0
Poole	.963	14	26	0	1	0
Rodriguez	.992	57	116	10	1	3
Zebrack	1.000	38	48	1	0	1

GCL NATIONALS

ROOKIE

GULF COAST LEAGUE

Batting	B-T	HT	WT	DOB	AVG	vLH	vRH	G	AB	R	H	2B	3B	HR	RBI	BB	HBP	SH	SF	SO	SB	CS	SLG	OBP
Abreu, Osvaldo	R-R	6-0	170	6-13-94	.286	.216	.309	44	147	24	42	12	1	0	24	19	1	3	1	24	16	6	.381	.369
Allen, Brenton	L-L	6-1	200	11-2-91	.000	.000	.000	2	5	0	0	0	0	0	0	0	0	0	0	2	0	0	.000	.000
Alvarez, Carlos	B-R	5-11	175	11-25-85	.333	—	.333	4	6	3	2	0	0	2	3	1	0	0	0	2	0	0	1.333	.429
Attl, Kyle	R-R	6-0	180	8-16-91	.286	.000	.333	16	28	5	8	0	0	0	3	2	1	1	1	4	3	1	.286	.344
Bautista, Rafael	R-R	6-2	165	3-8-93	.322	.375	.297	52	202	44	65	7	2	1	27	18	9	5	1	34	26	7	.391	.400
Difo, Wilmer	R-R	6-0	175	4-2-92	.211	.125	.273	6	19	6	4	1	0	1	3	4	0	0	0	3	2	0	.421	.348
Eusebio, Diomedes	R-R	6-0	185	9-8-92	.330	.296	.342	36	100	17	33	6	0	2	16	7	2	3	1	18	2	2	.450	.382
Flynn, Kevin	R-R	5-10	200	11-3-87	.158	.000	.188	17	19	5	3	1	0	0	3	2	0	0	0	3	1	1	.211	.333
Gordon, Garrett	R-R	6-0	210	2-26-93	.257	.296	.243	37	101	16	26	4	1	0	13	12	4	1	1	27	6	2	.317	.356
Guzman, Luis	L-L	5-11	183	9-10-95	.222	.179	.236	36	117	15	26	3	1	0	10	5	4	0	0	32	3	1	.265	.278
Jennings, Hayden	L-L	6-0	170	10-16-92	.248	.219	.257	44	137	22	34	7	3	0	17	11	2	4	0	48	12	3	.343	.313
Kelso, Blake	R-R	5-10	170	3-28-89	.250	—	.250	2	4	1	1	0	0	0	0	0	0	0	0	1	0	0	.250	.250
Kieboom, Spencer	R-R	6-0	199	3-16-91	.333	.250	.500	4	6	0	2	0	0	0	1	2	0	0	0	1	0	0	.333	.500
Marmolejos-Diaz, Jose	R-L	6-1	185	1-2-93	.312	.323	.309	43	141	27	44	11	0	2	21	14	1	0	2	27	1	1	.433	.373
McQuillan, Mike	L-R	5-11	175	10-24-82	.417	.250	.500	5	12	8	5	3	0	0	2	8	0	0	0	3	1	0	.667	.650
Medina, Willie	R-R	5-10	160	1-25-91	.228	.333	.179	39	114	21	26	1	0	0	12	9	6	0	1	24	10	4	.237	.315
Mejia, Bryan	B-R	6-1	170	3-2-94	.262	.273	.258	44	168	30	44	6	7	0	20	3	5	2	1	25	10	2	.381	.294
Novas, Randy	R-R	6-3	180	7-31-94	.349	.303	.358	34	109	22	38	8	1	3	12	16	1	0	0	25	5	3	.523	.437
Perrott, Geoff	R-R	6-2	205	12-13-90	.000	.000	—	1	1	0	0	0	0	0	0	0	0	0	0	0	0	0	.000	.000
Pleffner, Shawn	L-R	6-5	225	8-17-89	.500	1.000	.300	5	14	3	7	2	0	0	9	1	0	0	1	0	0	0	.643	.500
Poole, Jordan	R-R	6-3	210	9-11-91	.231	.000	.300	4	13	1	3	0	0	0	2	1	0	0	0	3	0	0	.231	.286
Ramos, Wander	R-R	6-3	192	4-26-90	.250	.000	.250	2	4	0	1	1	0	0	2	1	0	0	0	1	0	0	.500	.400
Ramos, Wilson	R-R	6-0	220	8-10-87	.000	—	.000	2	3	0	0	0	0	0	0	1	0	0	0	1	0	0	.000	.400
Read, Raudy	R-R	6-0	170	10-29-93	.252	.267	.245	40	147	9	37	5	0	2	17	6	2	1	2	17	2	6	.327	.287
Ruiz, Adderling	R-R	6-1	175	5-3-91	.302	.381	.237	26	86	13	26	6	0	1	15	12	4	1	0	17	4	3	.407	.412
Souza, Steven	R-R	6-3	220	4-24-89	.300	.500	.000	4	10	3	2	1	0	0	2	3	1	0	1	4	0	0	.300	.400
Ward, Drew	L-R	6-4	210	11-25-94	.292	.364	.229	49	168	24	49	13	0	1	28	25	6	0	0	44	2	4	.387	.402

Pitching

Pitching	B-T	HT	WT	DOB	W	L	ERA	G	GS	CG	SV	IP	H	R	ER	HR	BB	SO	AVG	vLH	vRH	K/9	BB/9
Bafidis, Cory	L-L	6-0	190	8-22-90	0	0	1.93	3	0	0	1	5	3	1	1	0	1	6	.188	.667	.077	11.57	1.93
Boyden, Mike	R-R	6-0	180	6-18-90	0	0	4.61	13	0	0	1	14	17	12	7	1	14	15	.309	.286	.324	9.88	9.22
Broderick, Brian	R-R	6-6	205	9-1-86	1	0	9.00	1	0	0	0	3	4	3	3	1	1	3	.333	.250	.375	9.00	3.00
Cooper, Andrew	R-R	6-1	200	6-27-92	0	0	0.00	1	0	0	0	2	4	0	0	0	0	1	.444	.500	.400	4.50	0.00
Derosier, Matt	R-R	6-2	200	7-13-94	2	1	2.67	11	1	0	2	27	24	8	8	2	5	20	.238	.324	.188	6.71	1.67
Giolito, Lucas	R-R	6-6	225	7-14-94	1	1	2.78	8	8	0	0	23	19	8	7	0	10	25	.232	.300	.192	9.93	3.97
Kimball, Cole	R-R	6-3	240	8-1-85	0	0	0.00	2	1	0	0	3	3	0	0	0	1	3	.273	.200	.333	10.13	3.38
Lehman, Pat	R-R	6-3	210	10-18-86	1	0	0.90	8	0	0	0	10	4	1	1	0	1	7	.121	.083	.143	6.30	0.90
Martin, Rafael	R-R	6-3	215	5-16-84	0	0	0.00	4	0	0	0	5	3	0	0	0	0	6	.176	.167	.182	10.80	0.00
Mattheus, Ryan	R-R	6-3	215	11-10-83	0	0	0.00	1	1	0	0	1	1	0	0	0	0	3	.250	.500	.000	27.00	0.00
Meyers, Brad	R-R	6-6	205	9-13-85	0	0	0.00	2	2	0	0	5	3	0	0	0	1	2	.176	.222	.125	3.60	1.80
Ott, Travis	L-L	6-4	170	6-29-95	3	0	4.03	10	7	0	0	29	24	15	13	2	12	32	.240	.280	.207	9.93	3.72
Pivetta, Nic	R-R	6-5	220	2-14-93	1	0	2.13	4	3	0	0	13	11	4	3	0	2	8	.234	.222	.241	5.68	1.42
Ramos, David	R-R	6-0	175	9-13-91	5	3	6.95	14	0	0	1	22	23	17	17	2	10	16	.267	.212	.302	6.55	4.09
Reyes, Luis	R-R	6-2	175	9-26-94	0	1	6.75	1	1	0	0	4	4	3	3	1	2	1	.267	.182	.500	2.25	4.50
Rodriguez, Jefry	R-R	6-5	185	7-26-93	3	2	2.45	12	12	0	0	48	40	15	13	1	20	43	.229	.246	.218	8.12	3.78
Rodriguez, Kelvin	R-R	6-0	190	11-6-91	5	0	3.07	13	1	0	0	29	31	13	10	2	6	15	.277	.271	.281	4.60	1.84
Selik, Cameron	R-R	6-2	235	8-25-87	0	0	0.00	3	0	0	1	3	1	0	0	0	0	3	.100	.200	.000	8.10	0.00
Silvestre, Hector	L-L	6-3	180	12-14-92	7	0	1.82	13	8	0	0	49	33	13	10	1	8	40	.190	.143	.201	7.30	1.46
Simms, John	R-R	6-3	205	1-17-92	0	1	4.50	1	0	0	0	2	2	1	1	0	0	3	.250	.333	.200	13.50	0.00
Solis, Sammy	R-L	6-5	230	8-10-88	0	0	0.00	1	0	0	0	2	1	0	0	0	0	3	.167	.000	.250	13.50	0.00
Spezial, Niko	R-L	6-3	220	11-1-90	1	0	2.87	12	0	0	1	16	11	6	5	1	5	17	.196	.308	.163	9.77	2.87
Suero, Wander	R-R	6-3	175	9-15-91	8	1	1.65	13	3	0	0	49	27	10	9	2	13	46	.156	.131	.170	8.45	2.39
Sylvestri, Mike	R-R	5-10	180	6-14-90	1	0	0.00	6	0	0	1	10	9	0	0	0	1	7	.231	.167	.259	6.52	0.93
Thomas, Justin	L-L	6-2	195	10-21-90	0	0	0.00	3	0	0	2	3	3	0	0	0	0	4	.250	.500	.200	12.00	0.00
Ullmann, Ryan	R-R	6-6	230	8-12-91	1	0	3.00	4	1	0	0	12	12	4	4	0	3	15	.261	.174	.348	11.25	2.25
Valdez, Phillip	R-R	6-2	160	11-16-91	3	0	1.95	14	3	0	2	32	16	8	7	0	12	27	.148	.075	.191	7.52	3.34
Voth, Austin	R-R	6-1	190	6-26-92	0	0	0.00	2	2	0	0	5	4	0	0	0	0	4	.235	.200	.250	7.20	0.00
Walsh, Jake	L-L	6-3	195	1-1-91	0	0	1.40	16	0	0	8	19	10	3	3	0	5	17	.156	.125	.167	7.91	2.33
Waterman, Elliott	L-L	6-5	230	11-24-90	2	0	1.53	10	0	0	0	18	17	4	3	1	9	9	.268	.188	.269	4.58	4.58
Webb, Joey	L-L	6-5	230	9-27-90	2	0	1.89	12	0	0	2	19	13	5	4	0	6	25	.183	.143	.193	11.84	2.84
Williams, Deion	R-R	6-3	190	11-11-92	2	1	2.08	3	2	0	0	13	13	6	3	0	9	7	.283	.143	.344	4.85	6.23
Young, Chris	R-R	6-10	260	5-25-79	0	0	0.00	1	1	0	0	2	1	0	0	0	1	2	.143	.333	.000	9.00	4.50

Fielding

Catcher	PCT	G	PO	A	E	DP	PB
Flynn	1.000	13	46	3	0	1	0
Plutko	1.000	1	4	1	0	0	0
Ramos	.875	2	7	0	1	0	0
Read	.996	31	222	20	1	3	5
Ruiz	.989	24	154	18	2	0	4

First Base	PCT	G	PO	A	E	DP
Eusebio	1.000	26	166	7	0	14
Marmolejos-Diaz	.993	37	261	19	2	21
Mejia	1.000	1	9	0	0	0
Pleffner	1.000	5	22	2	0	4
Poole	1.000	4	25	1	0	3

Second Base	PCT	G	PO	A	E	DP
Abreu	1.000	5	8	7	0	2
Alvarez	1.000	1	0	1	0	0

	PCT	G	PO	A	E	DP
Difo	1.000	2	5	6	0	2
Eusebio	1.000	1	1	3	0	0
Flynn	—	1	0	0	0	0
Medina	.974	18	25	49	2	7
Mejia	.952	35	73	87	8	25

Third Base	PCT	G	PO	A	E	DP
Alvarez	.667	2	1	3	2	0
Attl	.941	8	4	12	1	1
Difo	1.000	2	1	3	0	0
Eusebio	.920	9	7	16	2	1
Kelso	1.000	1	3	0	0	0
McQuillan	1.000	3	4	2	0	0
Medina	—	1	0	0	0	0
Mejia	1.000	7	5	14	0	1
Ward	.950	35	19	57	4	9

Shortstop	PCT	G	PO	A	E	DP
Abreu	.940	38	58	98	10	15
Attl	1.000	4	5	7	0	2
Difo	1.000	1	1	2	0	0
Kelso	1.000	1	0	1	0	0
Medina	.958	19	34	57	4	8
Mejia	1.000	2	1	6	0	1

Outfield	PCT	G	PO	A	E	DP
Allen	1.000	2	2	0	0	0
Bautista	.990	52	96	2	1	0
Gordon	.979	27	43	4	1	1
Guzman	1.000	33	52	2	0	0
Jennings	1.000	44	58	4	0	1
Novas	.947	21	35	1	2	0
Ramos	1.000	2	3	0	0	0
Souza	1.000	4	9	0	0	0

DSL NATIONALS ROOKIE

DOMINICAN SUMMER LEAGUE

Batting	B-T	HT	WT	DOB	AVG	vLH	vRH	G	AB	R	H	2B	3B	HR	RBI	BB	HBP	SH	SF	SO	SB	CS	SLG	OBP
Aguero, Younaifred	R-R	6-2	170	4-10-93	.253	.290	.245	57	170	20	43	6	1	0	16	14	3	6	2	27	13	3	.300	.317
Alvarez, Thomas	R-R	6-1	165	2-15-95	.203	.256	.190	64	207	20	42	5	1	0	12	38	3	4	1	47	11	9	.237	.333
Atencio, Miguel	R-R	6-0	165	5-3-95	.183	.250	.167	23	60	5	11	0	0	0	4	3	2	3	0	11	0	1	.183	.246
Cerda, Kevin	R-R	6-2	170	6-11-93	.125	.000	.150	9	24	1	3	0	0	0	1	3	1	0	0	6	1	2	.125	.250
Corredor, Aldrem	L-L	6-0	202	10-27-95	.265	.182	.282	57	196	32	52	8	3	0	18	27	1	1	3	23	4	4	.337	.352
Florentino, Darryl	L-R	6-2	175	1-1-96	.226	.179	.235	58	190	24	43	7	5	0	21	28	1	2	1	49	6	10	.316	.327
Gutierrez, Kelvin	R-R	6-3	185	8-28-94	.255	.162	.275	60	208	35	53	13	2	0	23	23	2	1	1	36	9	2	.337	.333
Lora, Edwin	R-R	6-1	150	9-14-95	.205	.152	.217	55	185	29	38	8	0	2	13	18	3	2	0	44	6	4	.281	.286
Mendoza, Pedro	R-R	5-11	175	11-16-94	.186	.143	.200	23	59	2	11	2	0	0	1	3	1	2	0	21	1	0	.220	.238
Mercedes, Yermin	R-R	5-11	175	2-14-93	.255	.304	.241	41	106	12	27	2	1	2	21	14	5	0	3	17	3	4	.349	.359
Mota, Israel	R-R	6-2	175	1-3-96	.215	.167	.228	52	144	21	31	9	1	1	12	27	6	0	3	38	4	2	.313	.356
Ortiz, Oliver	L-L	6-0	170	5-6-96	.307	.125	.325	26	88	14	27	5	1	0	8	13	1	0	0	19	2	2	.386	.402
Peguero, Francys	R-R	6-2	170	10-4-95	.000	.000	.000	6	12	0	0	0	0	0	0	0	0	0	0	3	0	1	.000	.000
Pilier, Neivy	R-R	6-1	185	8-1-96	.163	.200	.154	17	49	6	8	1	1	1	3	5	6	0	0	15	1	2	.286	.317
Ramirez, Joshual	R-R	6-3	185	5-20-96	.000	—	.000	2	1	0	0	0	0	0	0	0	0	0	0	3	0	0	.000	.000
Rosario, Dionicio	R-R	6-3	180	2-14-98	.221	.143	.235	56	190	29	42	7	0	4	26	21	4	0	1	39	1	3	.321	.310
Serrata, Brayan	R-R	6-3	175	6-17-94	.242	.130	.262	49	149	16	36	4	3	0	19	11	2	1	1	41	2	0	.309	.301

	B-T	HT	WT	DOB	AVG	vLH	vRH	G	AB	R	H	2B	3B	HR	RBI	BB	SO	SB	CS	OBP	SLG
Suarez, Wester	L-L	6-2	195	11-10-94	.192	.182	.194	25	73	13	14	3	0	1	4	8	1	0	0	22	1	0	.274	.280
Tillero, Jorge	R-R	5-11	160	12-21-93	.262	.167	.288	30	84	8	22	5	0	1	7	6	0	1	1	13	2	2	.357	.308
Vilorio, Luis	R-R	6-1	180	8-28-93	.000	—	.000	2	3	0	0	0	0	0	0	0	1	0	0	2	0	1	.000	.250

Pitching	B-T	HT	WT	DOB	W	L	ERA	G	GS	CG	SV	IP	H	R	ER	HR	BB	SO	AVG	vLH	vRH	K/9	BB/9
Aquino, Jonathan	R-R	6-1	185	3-28-95	4	1	4.58	14	0	0	0	20	21	16	10	2	10	16	.280	.429	.246	7.32	4.58
Charlis, Fiyeral	R-R	6-2	180	9-17-94	1	0	1.53	12	0	0	0	18	14	8	3	0	13	17	.219	.409	.119	8.66	6.62
Feliz, John	R-R	6-2	180	10-28-93	4	2	2.54	20	0	0	1	39	33	15	11	1	5	33	.224	.179	.241	7.62	1.15
Green, Adrian	R-R	6-2	185	5-1-91	0	2	5.40	12	0	0	2	10	12	9	6	1	8	8	.300	.333	.280	7.20	7.20
Morales, Jose	R-R	6-3	180	2-12-95	4	3	1.13	16	8	0	0	56	35	14	7	3	5	37	.180	.213	.165	5.98	0.81
Pena, Yefri	R-R	6-2	175	2-8-95	2	1	3.62	17	2	0	2	37	37	20	15	2	15	29	.252	.191	.280	6.99	3.62
Ramirez, Jean	R-R	6-4	180	10-24-94	1	1	3.71	14	4	0	0	34	32	19	14	2	16	27	.252	.263	.247	7.15	4.24
Reyes, Luis	R-R	6-2	175	9-26-94	5	3	2.82	12	12	0	0	54	38	19	17	1	20	65	.199	.273	.177	10.77	3.31
Reynoso, Yorlin	L-L	6-2	200	11-20-95	1	1	2.70	19	1	0	0	37	27	20	11	1	13	31	.203	.095	.223	7.61	3.19
Rosario, Ramses	R-R	6-3	180	10-18-95	1	3	3.54	7	2	0	0	20	22	13	8	0	6	15	.282	.350	.211	6.64	2.66
Salazar, Melvi	R-R	6-1	175	12-17-94	4	0	0.98	22	0	0	13	28	21	4	3	1	10	21	.214	.233	.206	6.83	3.25
Sanchez, Mario	R-R	6-1	166	10-31-94	2	3	2.33	18	5	0	0	58	46	17	15	2	14	54	.216	.243	.201	8.38	2.17
Torres, Luis	R-R	6-3	190	6-4-94	1	3	3.91	13	9	0	0	53	54	33	23	1	17	51	.261	.221	.285	8.66	2.89
Valerio, Maximo	R-R	6-2	175	7-22-95	3	4	2.86	14	13	0	0	63	55	27	20	5	17	56	.234	.179	.265	8.00	2.43
Yrizarri, Deibi	R-R	6-1	170	10-3-94	5	3	1.99	14	13	0	0	68	59	19	15	0	16	50	.230	.205	.243	6.62	2.12

Fielding

Catcher	PCT	G	PO	A	E	DP	PB
Mendoza	1.000	8	28	3	0	1	2
Mercedes	1.000	3	19	1	0	0	1
Serrata	.980	47	291	50	7	2	8
Tillero	.986	28	182	27	3	1	7
Vilorio	1.000	1	1	0	0	0	0

First Base	PCT	G	PO	A	E	DP
Aguero	1.000	1	4	0	0	0
Cerda	1.000	5	27	1	0	2
Corredor	1.000	12	58	3	0	2
Gutierrez	1.000	3	11	0	0	1
Mendoza	1.000	2	11	1	0	0
Mercedes	.988	16	79	4	1	6
Ortiz	.985	23	185	8	3	15
Pilier	1.000	1	8	0	0	2

	PCT	G	PO	A	E	DP
Rosario	.941	3	16	0	1	3
Suarez	.970	21	157	6	5	18
Second Base	PCT	G	PO	A	E	DP
Alvarez	.968	28	54	68	4	14
Lora	.940	43	93	80	11	20
Ramirez	1.000	1	0	2	0	0
Third Base	PCT	G	PO	A	E	DP
Aguero	.893	48	36	97	16	6
Cerda	1.000	1	1	3	0	0
Corredor	1.000	1	0	1	0	0
Gutierrez	.909	13	12	28	4	6
Lora	—	1	0	0	0	0
Peguero	1.000	2	2	1	0	0
Pilier	.809	16	20	18	9	0
Ramirez	.714	1	1	4	2	0

Shortstop	PCT	G	PO	A	E	DP
Aguero	.947	3	5	13	1	1
Alvarez	.976	20	37	46	2	8
Gutierrez	.921	42	68	95	14	15
Lora	.911	9	13	28	4	6
Peguero	1.000	3	4	3	0	1
Outfield	PCT	G	PO	A	E	DP
Aguero	1.000	3	2	0	0	0
Alvarez	1.000	11	23	2	0	0
Atencio	.970	23	31	1	1	0
Corredor	.958	44	66	3	3	0
Florentino	.966	56	110	4	4	0
Mota	.945	50	60	9	4	0
Ortiz	1.000	3	5	0	0	0
Rosario	.956	38	60	5	3	2

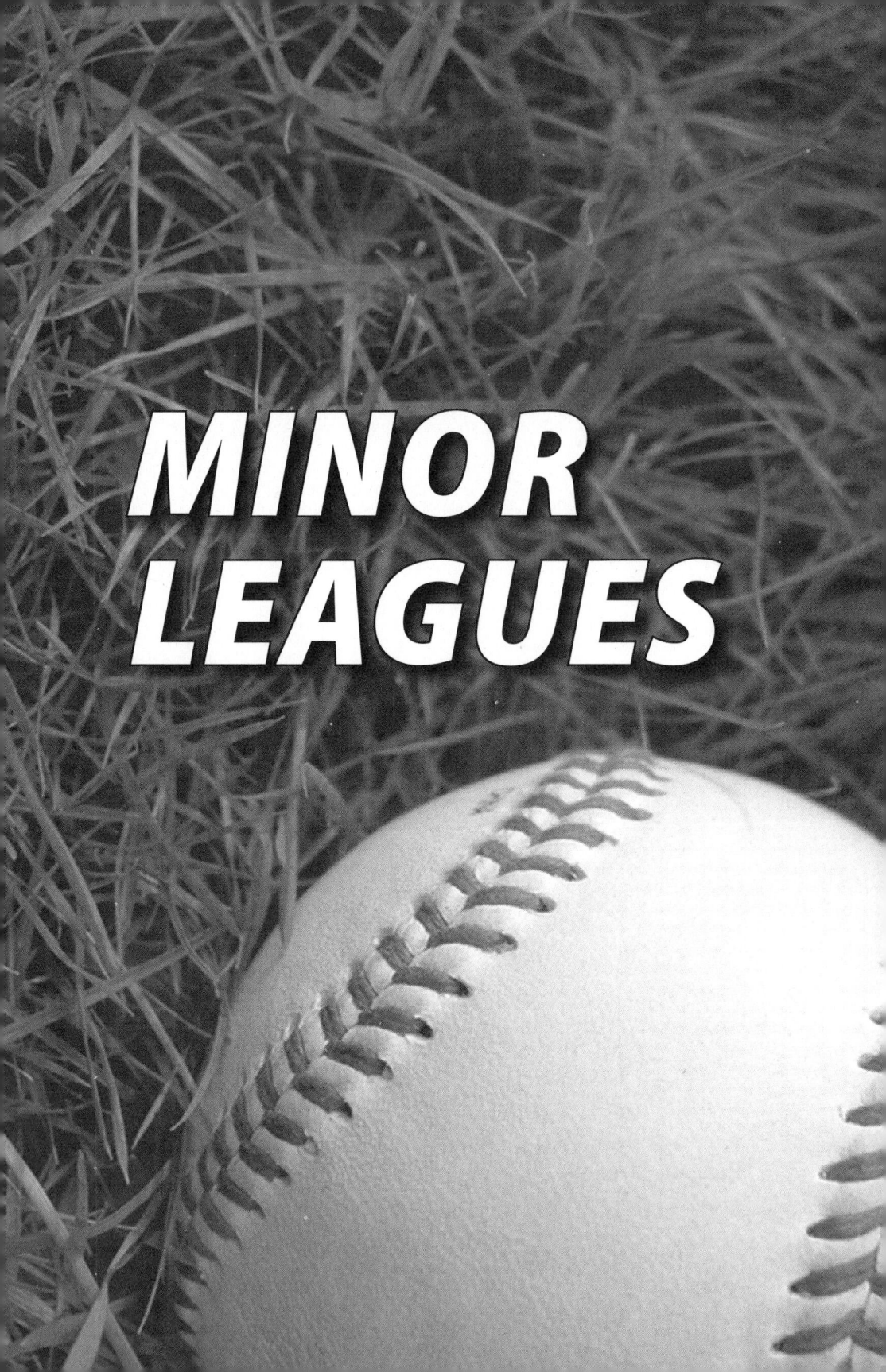

MINOR
LEAGUES

Midwest League ballparks like Wisconsin's Fox Cities Stadium were often iced over in April

Minors deliver through rain, sleet and snow

BY JOSH LEVENTHAL

A sour economy spoiled minor league baseball's streak of attendance records five years ago and limited the industry to being satisfied with holding steady at the gate in the years that followed.

The sport, however, met a different foil in 2013. Rotten weather was to blame for much of minor league baseball's challenges, as a Midwestern freeze and Southern thunderstorms combined to force the most cancellations the industry had endured in 13 years.

"It seems like every day and every time you turn on the news there is a pocket of weather (affecting a team)," Minor League Baseball president Pat O'Conner said.

The result left attendance in essentially the same spot as the previous two seasons, ticking up to 41,553,781 fans—roughly 250,000 more than the 2012 total, which was up just a fraction from the 2011 season. That growth is a far cry from the high times of 2004-08, when attendance spiked 3.3 million while setting annual records.

Yet a ray of hope could still be found amid the storms of 2013, as average attendance increased nearly 2 percent to 4,040—the biggest growth since those record-breaking days.

"We've taken it on the chin pretty good," said Daytona Cubs general manager Brady Ballard, whose team rolled to a Florida State League title but played just 126 of 140 scheduled regular season games. "But when we get playable weather, we get great support and great crowds."

The D-Cubs weren't alone, as 86 of minor league baseball's 140 teams saw an increase at the gate compared to 58 in 2012. The biggest improvement came at the Triple-A level, where 17 of 30 teams grew their average attendance after just seven did the year before.

"If you have a flat average in this weather you are doing well," O'Conner said. "It shows that you're still drawing fans in horrible weather."

In the Midwest League, where teams got off to a frigid and wet start to the season, Clinton LumberKings general manager Ted Tornow couldn't believe his eyes as he stared out at Ashford University Field after yet another gulley-washer dumped six inches of rain in early April.

Where the team's center fielder would normally roam, he saw a family of ducks, paddling away as if the field "was another tributary of the Mississippi River," Tornow said.

Playing fields throughout the Midwest League were better suited for mallards than minor leaguers during the first month of the season. A run of rain, snow and freezing temperatures forced the postponement or cancellation of 24 games by April 15—the same number of openings the 16-team league lost in all of the 2012 season. That number eventually topped the 59 openings lost in 2011, which Midwest League president George Spelius said was the most during his 27-year tenure.

"It's (impacting) player development and umpire development," Spelius said. "They can't develop when the outfield is up to your ankles in some spots—and those are at our nicer facilities."

The Midwest League's 65 openings lost was only third-worst in the minors behind the Florida State (82) and South Atlantic (74) leagues. The Lakeland Flying Tigers lost 17 of their 70 home dates, the most in the minors, followed by Daytona at 12 and Colorado Springs (Pacific Coast) and Charlotte (International) with nine each.

But there were also success stories. The Columbus Clippers (International), one of the oldest franchises in the minors, returned to the top of the attendance ladder for the first time since 1987. In its fifth season at downtown Huntington Park, Columbus topped the minors with an average crowd of 9,212. And if not for two rainouts, the Clippers likely would have surpassed fellow IL franchise Indianapolis for the top overall attendance in the minors. Columbus drew 635,613 in 69 openings, second to the Indians' 637,579 in 71 openings.

"The weather was a little iffy in April, May and June. Then things got nice and we kind of got on a roll," said Columbus general manager Ken Schnacke, whose team drew at least 9,000 fans in each of its final 11 home games of the season. "You never know year to year what the weather is going to be like, but you got a sense that the economy was improving this year. Our group (sales) business was up quite a bit and companies are back to doing things (at the ballpark)."

New Ballparks Bring Crowds

The addition of new ballparks and the replacement of struggling markets has driven minor league baseball's growth over the past 25 years from a mom-and-pop business to a multimillion dollar industry. The pace of ballpark construction slowed during the recent economic downturn—49 ballparks opened from 2000-09, but just eight in the last four seasons—but the addition of three new ones in 2013 may signal another uptick.

CANCELATIONS BY LEAGUE

LEAGUE	OPENINGS LOST	LEAGUE	OPENINGS LOST
Florida State	82	Carolina	31
South Atlantic	74	Appalachian	31
Midwest	65	Ny Penn	27
International League	45	Texas	19
Eastern	41	Pioneer	9
Southern	39	Northwest	5
Pacific Coast League	32	California	3
		TOTAL	**503**

The Scranton/Wilkes-Barre (International) franchise changed its name from Yankees to RailRiders and welcomed a new front office headed by GM Rob Crain as part of its move into a much-needed new home. The inclusion of a promotional schedule that featured giveaways at every game at $53.3 million PNC Park helped the team increase average attendance 40 percent from 2011 (the team spent all of 2012 on the road) and overall from 298,098 to 435,839.

The Birmingham Barons had similar results, as the Southern League franchise left its longtime home in suburban Hoover for Regions Field, a new $64 million downtown stadium. Concerns that fans wouldn't come into the city for games were alleviated for at least one season, as the team topped the Southern League at 398,820 while increasing average attendance 89 percent to 5,669.

In its first season after leaving Yakima, Wash., the Northwest League's Hillsboro Hops—a name celebrating the suburban Portland community's passion for growing the key ingredient in beer—were a hit in their new ballpark, more than doubling the franchise's 1,629 average in Yakima in 2012.

What's In A Name?

Going off the beaten path has become the mainstream approach to naming and branding minor league baseball teams. The wackier the name the better and more likely to appeal to their young fans—which remain teams' target audience.

Scranton/Wilkes-Barre changed its name from Yankees to RailRiders, while Reading transformed from Phillies to Fightin' Phils, with their logo featuring a fighting ostrich, designed after the team's popular Crazy Hot Dog Vendor mascot.

Remarkably, that was just a warmup to the name and logo changes of two teams following the season.

The new El Paso franchise, which will debut in the Pacific Coast League in 2014 after spending the previous three seasons in Tucson, was going with an off-the-board selection no matter which of the five nominations it selected for its name and logo. In the end, they may have strayed as far from center as possible by picking Chihuahuas.

The team, led by president Alan Ledford and general manager Brad Taylor, settled on Chihuahuas for many reasons, but none bigger than the appeal they believe it will have for the youngsters.

When people look at the new logo "through the eyes of a kid and think about it that way . . . they all smile," Ledford said before the unveiling. "That is our aim. That is our goal in this process."

The name created quite a stir, with many of the team's new fans taking to social media in protest. Ledford predicted opposition will quickly turn to support once their new downtown ballpark opens.

Akron followed a similar formula when the Eastern League franchise decided to replace the Aeros moniker that has been part of the team since its debut in 1997 with RubberDucks.

The new name provides both a local connection—nicknamed Rubber City, Akron once housed all four major rubber companies and is still home to Goodyear and the Bridgestone/Firestone Technology Center—and a kid-friendly element.

A tire-treaded, grimacing duck surrounded by burned-out flames highlight the team's primary logo, with the name RubberDucks written in a tread-style font.

"During this rebranding process, we listened to our fans," second-year owner Ken Babby said. "It was evident that our fans wanted to honor the history of Akron and the rubber industry while creating a new identity that was fun, exciting and family-friendly, just like our baseball team."

Buxton Vs. Springer

No performance on the field was more impressive than the superlative factory that is Twins center fielder Byron Buxton, who took home Minor League Player of the Year honors. But Astros outfielder George Springer finished a close second.

In just about any other year, the former University of Connecticut star, who bid for a rare 40-homer, 40-steal season in the minor leagues, would have walked away with the hardware.

His 37 home runs, a career high for the 23-year-old, tied him for second in the minors with Cubs prospect Javier Baez and placed him just three behind Rangers slugger Joey Gallo for the top spot.

As is often the case with big-time power guys, Springer's game also features a ton of swing-and-miss. He fanned 161 times this season, putting him among the top 15 in the minors.

However, he salved evaluators' concerns about his high strikeout proclivity by adding 83 walks

ORGANIZATION STANDINGS

Cumulative domestic farm club records for major league organizations, with winning percentages going back five years. Most organizations have six affiliates.

	2013 W	L	PCT	2012	2011	2010	2009
1. Houston	437	329	.570	.546	.408	.436	.426
2. San Francisco	391	302	.564	.506	.539	.524	.603
3. Washington	382	313	.550	.506	.511	.501	.501
4. N.Y. Mets	413	343	.546	.509	.498	.511	.466
4. Minnesota	375	312	.546	.525	.490	.434	.535
6. Texas	366	327	.528	.517	.565	.522	.495
7. Tampa Bay	397	360	.524	.515	.497	.534	.502
8. Pittsburgh	358	337	.515	.505	.512	.511	.499
9. Arizona	391	376	.510	.499	.488	.489	.476
10. Chi. Cubs	340	334	.504	.470	.507	.542	.487
10. Boston	350	345	.504	.504	.490	.491	.505
12. L.A. Angels	345	343	.501	.449	.507	.507	.514
13. Oakland	345	349	.497	.496	.514	.527	.494
13. Seattle	376	380	.497	.528	.483	.530	.528
13. Miami	342	346	.497	.524	.495	.490	.502
16. San Diego	343	349	.496	.455	.515	.485	.501
17. N.Y. Yankees	373	381	.495	.529	.494	.538	.554
18. St. Louis	373	382	.494	.505	.518	.569	.498
19. Toronto	373	384	.493	.524	.515	.506	.467
20. Chi. White Sox	342	359	.488	.504	.500	.489	.551
21. L.A. Dodgers	337	357	.486	.528	.543	.508	.498
22. Atlanta	333	353	.485	.461	.471	.457	.503
23. Detroit	335	357	.484	.482	.467	.485	.492
24. Colorado	342	367	.482	.540	.495	.480	.513
25. Baltimore	333	360	.481	.456	.487	.463	.475
26. Philadelphia	324	368	.468	.498	.522	.508	.507
27. Kansas City	352	408	.463	.492	.494	.492	.482
28. Milwaukee	307	376	.449	.459	.466	.493	.488
29. Cleveland	308	384	.445	.506	.515	.504	.501
30. Cincinnati	294	396	.426	.449	.503	.466	.453

POSTSEASON RESULTS

LEAGUE	CHAMPION	RUNNER-UP
International	Durham	Pawtucket
Pacific Coast	Omaha	Salt Lake
Eastern	Trenton	Harrisburg
Southern	Birmingham	Mobile
Texas	San Antonio	Frisco
California	Lancaster	Arkansas
Carolina	Salem	Potomac
Florida State	Daytona	Charlotte
Midwest	Quad Cities	South Bend
South Atlantic	Savannah	Hagerstown
New York-Penn	Tri-City	State College
Northwest	Vancouver	Boise
Appalachian	Pulaski	Greeneville
Pioneer	Idaho Falls	Helena
Arizona	Giants	Dodgers
Gulf Coast	Nationals	Red Sox

and an on-base percentage of .411, by far the best among those with 161 or more punchouts.

One American League scouting director said that, at the major league level, Springer's whiffs would be much easier to swallow if they were supplemented with a healthy dose of patience.

"The strikeouts are a concern for sure, but he's also maintained a quality walk rate, which

Rangers slugger Joey Gallo and the Hickory Crawdads produced plenty of hits—and misses

mitigates the strikeout red flag to a certain extent," the scouting director said. "I'm a personal believer that tolerance for strikeouts is directly correlated to walk rate."

Hard-Hitting Hickory

The Daytona Cubs secured Minor League Team of the Year honors for their overall dominance, but if an award went to the most entertaining squad, the Hickory Crawdads (South Atlantic) would be coming home with the hardware.

In any inning, on any pitch, something amazing might happen. And most every night, you were likely to see a home run or three.

Joey Gallo—the ultimate high-risk, high-reward Crawdad—hit a minor league-best 40 home runs. Center fielder Lewis Brinson became the first Crawdad in team history to go 20-20, with 21 home runs and 24 steals. Before he was promoted to Double-A, second baseman Ryan Rua matched Gallo home run for home run and finished the season tied for fifth in the minors with 32.

With 178 home runs, Hickory led all other South Atlantic League clubs by a chasm of 70 homers. Just two other teams—Greensboro and Asheville—even reached triple-digits in homers and the Crawdads' more than tripled Lakewood's 49-homer output. Just two other clubs in all of baseball, the Stockton Ports (California) and Baltimore Orioles, hit more home runs.

The good, of course, came with the bad. Hickory struck out at a rate that would make Mark Reynolds cringe. The Crawdads' 1,403 strikeouts led all of Organized Baseball.

"I would say (Hickory) has as many prospects as any team I've seen since I've been involved with (baseball)," said one scout with a National League club who has spent several decades in the game.

UP AND DOWN YEAR

Despite overall attendance in the minor leagues remaining flat for a third straight season, average attendance across the minors grew by nearly 2 percent as 86 of the minors' 140 teams saw an increase at the gate.

Below is a list of teams that saw the biggest gains in average attendance in 2013:

TEAM (LEAGUE)	DIFFERENCE
Hillsboro (Northwest)	118.35%
Birmingham (Southern)	88.72%
Scranton/WB (International)	62.50%
South Bend (Midwest)	30.98%
Bakersfield (California)	26.37%
Potomac (Carolina)	19.67%
Bradenton (Florida State)	16.96%
Cedar Rapids (Midwest)	16.25%
Connecticut (New York-Penn)	15.06%
Lakeland (Florida State)	14.61%
Peoria (Midwest)	13.61%
Buffalo (International)	12.25%
Akron (Eastern)	11.90%
Mobile (Southern)	10.75%
Mahoning Valley (New York-Penn)	10.38%
Inland Empire (California)	10.35%
Kane County (Midwest)	10.15%

Tucson Loses Team, Again

Mike Feder toed the rubber before the start of the San Diego Padres' home finale, and while his name and face may not be familiar to most baseball fans, he is certainly a popular figure in San Diego's clubhouse and front office.

Feder spent the past three seasons as GM of the Padres Triple-A Tucson affiliate—a not-so-glamorous post considering the team was never supposed to be there in the first place.

Feder, who was named Pacific Coast League executive of the year after ensuring Padres pros-

CONTINUED ON PAGE 350

Buxton puts tools to work

BY MATT EDDY

More than 250 players in the full-season minors out-homered Byron Buxton this season. Yet that didn't prevent the 19-year-old center fielder from ranking as the No. 1 prospect in baseball at midseason or from winning the Midwest League MVP award or from ranking as the top prospect in two Class A leagues.

The Twins even ticketed their uber-prospect—in the words of one scout, "The best minor leaguer I've ever seen"—for the Arizona Fall League in October.

Now, Buxton can add one more feather to his cap: Baseball America Minor League Player of the Year, a distinction he sewed up with an all-around game seldom seen from a teenager in his first full season.

In stops at low Class A Cedar Rapids and—following a late-June promotion—high Class A Fort Myers, Buxton hit a cumulative .334/.424/.520 with 49 extra-base hits, 55 stolen bases and a sparkling 76-to-105 walk-to-strikeout ratio in 125 games. He led the minors with 18 triples, finished second with 109 runs scored and 12th in stolen bases.

More impressively, Buxton ranked sixth in the minor league batting race, 10th in hits (163) and seventh in on-base percentage, despite being a full year younger than any other member of those top-10 lists.

Adding another layer to his accomplishments is the fact that just 15 months ago, scouts voiced concern about Buxton's ability to adjust to quality pitching as he left the high school ranks for pro ball. The rapidity at which Buxton, the second pick in the 2012 draft from Appling County High in Baxley, Ga., has put those concerns to rest truly belies his youth.

"You think, 'How can he get better?' Well he's going to get better," a pro scout for an American League club said. "He's just going to get better with repetitions and with a little tweaking here and there."

So while Buxton's 12 home runs this season, eight of them in low Class A, don't overwhelm when compared with the output from top young sluggers such as the Rangers' Joey Gallo

Byron Buxton

(40), the Cubs' Javier Baez (37), the Astros' George Springer (37) or the Twins' own Miguel Sano (35), he's on virtually the same trajectory as another five-tool stud for whom power developed later—and suddenly.

Angels center fielder Mike Trout took the baseball world by storm as a rookie in 2012, mashing 30 homers and leading the majors with 49 stolen bases and 129 runs scored. Yet just two years prior to that, a teen-aged Trout hit 10 home runs in 131 games during his full-season debut at two Class A levels, one of them the notoriously hitter-friendly California League.

Trout in 2010 excelled at many of the same things that Buxton did this season. He hit for average, drew walks, stole bases and showed budding extra-base power. He even played for the same Cedar Rapids club, back when it was an Angels affiliate.

"The books are full of guys who didn't show the power numbers in the low minors," the AL scout said, "and (Buxton) is already showing it."

While scouts don't necessarily see Buxton developing into the 30-homer beast that Trout has become, they feel confident that he'll go deep 20-25 times a year once he matures.

"Trout has more power, but Buxton probably does more (things). He has a better arm. He is a better defender than Trout, with better range and jumps," said high Class A Palm Beach manager Johnny Rodriguez, who managed against Trout in the Midwest League in 2010.

PREVIOUS WINNERS

2003: Joe Mauer, c, Fort Myers/New Britain (Twins)
2004: Jeff Francis, lhp, Tulsa/Colorado Springs (Rockies)
2005: Delmon Young, of, Montgomery/Durham (Devil Rays)
2006: Alex Gordon, 3b, Wichita (Royals)
2007: Jay Bruce, of, Sarasota/Chattanooga/Louisville (Reds)
2008: Matt Wieters, c, Frederick/Bowie (Orioles)
2009: Jason Heyward, Myrtle Beach/Mississippi (Braves)
2010: Jeremy Hellickson, Montgomery/Durham (Rays)
2011: Mike Trout, Arkansas (Angels)
2012: Wil Myers, Northwest Arkansas/Omaha (Royals)

Full list: BaseballAmerica.com/awards

MINOR LEAGUES

Omaha for everyone

Martie Cordaro knew there would be no do-overs when, in 2011, it came time for Omaha's Pacific Coast League franchise to move from a historic stadium on a hill to one being in built in a cornfield south of the city.

Get it right, and the Storm Chasers had a chance to start a wonderful new chapter in Omaha's baseball history. Mess it up, and Cordaro knew it would take years for the franchise to dig out of the hole. That Cordaro is BA's Minor League Executive of the Year is testament to how well he did.

"What Martie did was masterful," said Rob Crain, now the general manager of the Scranton Wilkes-Barre Yankees (International) but then Cordaro's top lieutenant in Omaha. "He did it by making sure we had a vision, that we knew what change was going to look like.

"He gave us a story, and then told us to go out in the community and tell us. He did a tremendous job of rallying the troops and making sure we were all on the proverbial same page."

Omaha's new ballpark in suburban Sarpy

County has been a hit and a way to bring the region together. In its debut season, Werner Park drew more than 410,000 fans. The franchise attracted almost 416,000 fans in 2012 and 390,000 during a weather-challenged 2013 season.

CONTINUED FROM PAGE 348

pects had a quality place to play before moving on to a new ballpark in El Paso next year, and his wife Pattie were the Padres' guests in San Diego, and as part of the team's appreciation for him, Feder threw out the ceremonial first pitch before San Diego's game against the Diamondbacks.

Feder had been out of baseball for a decade when Pacific Coast League president Branch Rickey III called him in early 2011 with a not-so-appealing offer. Rickey needed Feder to bail out a PCL franchise that was being squeezed out of Portland, Ore., with no permanent destination in its future. Rickey wanted the team to play in Tucson for one season until it could settle on a home, and he thought Feder was the man for the job.

The Tucson Padres debuted at Kino Stadium a few months later with then-owner Jeff Moorad, who doubled as chief operating officer of the Padres, planning to move the team to a ballpark in the San Diego suburb of Escondido. That ballpark never got built, Moorad's bid to buy the Padres failed and he ultimately sold his minor league team. Meanwhile, one year in Tucson turned into three for Feder's ballclub.

The team only came to Tucson after former Portland Beavers owner Merritt Paulson converted his team's ballpark into a soccer-only facility on the assumption the city would pay for a new home for the baseball team—which it did not.

The Padres finished at the bottom of the PCL in attendance each season in Tucson and drew 200,007 fans in 2013—128,000 fewer than any other team in the league.

Now Feder's run has come to an end yet again. And while he laments the team never catching on as he had hoped—"People just weren't going to put their hearts into the team because they knew it was going to leave," he said—he is walking away on top. Being named PCL executive of the year by his peers means a lot, Feder said.

"This is not just a parting gift," Minor League Baseball president Pat O'Conner said. "He did a hell of a job under trying circumstances."

Suspensions Continue

The Biogenesis scandal that ensnared numerous big leaguers also led to the suspensions of seven minor leaguers.

The list included Double-A San Antonio right-hander Fautino de los Santos (Padres), Double-A Corpus Christi lefthander Sergio Escalona (Astros), Triple-A Scranton/Wilkes-Barre out-

Building Boston's foundation

After two years in the Angels front office, Gary DiSarcina had a mission in 2013 in his return to the Red Sox as manager of the organization's Triple-A affiliate.

"We're here to get you out of here," DiSarcina said of his approach to working with players on the doorstep of the big leagues. "Use us."

It was an approach that had made DiSarcina a valued member of the Red Sox player development staff from 2007-10 as a manager for short-season Lowell (2007-09) and as a roving infield instructor in 2010 before he was hired by the Angels. And in his return to the Sox, the 45-year-old had the opportunity to help a number of familiar prospects whom he had seen previously at much earlier stages of their player development.

But this time, the conversations were different. Where DiSarcina had largely been trying to help players such as Will Middlebrooks and Xander Bogaerts develop a foundation near the start of their careers, this time he proved a critical contributor in the latter stages of their apprenticeships.

At a level of the minors where it can prove challenging to maintain a positive clubhouse attitude among players who feel like they belong in the majors, DiSarcina managed to keep them focused on their development and productivity.

MANAGER OF THE YEAR

PREVIOUS 10 WINNERS

2003: Dave Brundage, San Antonio (Mariners)
2004: Marty Brown, Buffalo (Indians)
2005: Ken Oberkfell, Norfolk (Mets)
2006: Todd Claus, Portland (Red Sox)
2007: Matt Wallbeck, Erie (Tigers)
2008: Rocket Wheeler, Myrtle Beach (Braves)
2009: Charlie Montoyo, Durham Bulls (Rays)
2010: Mike Sarbaugh, Columbus Clippers (Indians)
2011: Ryne Sandberg, Lehigh Valley IronPigs (Phillies)
2012: Dave Miley, Scranton/Wilkes-Barre (Yankees)

Full list: BaseballAmerica.com/awards

---

fielder Fernando Martinez (Yankees), Triple-A Tacoma catcher Jesus Montero (Mariners), free agent lefthander Jordan Norberto, Double-A Binghamton outfielder Cesar Puello (Mets) and Triple-A Las Vegas second baseman Jordany Valdespin (Mets).

Montero, Puello and Valdespin were on 40-man rosters at the time of the suspensions, though every player on the list, save for Puello, has recent major league experience.

In all, 45 minor leaguers were suspended in 2013 through early November, a significant decrease from the 108 in 2012, with the majority coming in the Rookie-level Dominican Summer and Venezuelan Summer leagues.

There were several notable players in domestic leagues nabbed, including Rays righthander Taylor Guerrieri, the 24th overall pick in the 2011 draft, who was suspended 50 games after a second positive test for a drug of abuse.

The 20-year-old is rehabbing from Tommy John surgery he had in late July and because of how the rules work, he will be able to serve his suspension during his injury rehabilitation in 2014 and likely will miss no actual games because of the suspension.

Guerreri's suspension gives the Rays a streak that no team would want to have. Tampa Bay's first-round picks in 2008 (Tim Beckham), 2010 (Josh Sale) and 2011 (Guerreri) all have all been suspended after testing positive for drugs of abuse. Ryan Brett, the Rays' 2010 third-round pick, also earned a drug suspension.

Astros On Top

The Astros didn't have many reasons to celebrate at the big league level. Houston finished with the worst mark in the majors for a third straight season and in 2014 will become the first franchise in draft history to select No. 1 overall three years in a row.

However, Astros general manager Jeff Luhnow's willingness to trade veterans for prospects was starting to bear fruit at the minor league level. Houston finished at the top of the organization standings for a second straight season, boosting their domestic minor league winning percentage from .546 in 2012 to .570 this season (see chart on page 348).

Houston took things a step further this season by placing its top six affiliates in the playoffs, which according to Minor League Baseball had not been accomplished since the Pirates in 2003.

The Astros' three most junior affiliates to qualify for the postseason wound up advancing to their

TRIPLE-A

Pos	Player, Team (Org)	League	AVG	OBP	SLG	AB	R	H	2B	3B	HR	RBI	BB	SO	SB	CS
C	Josh Phegley, Charlotte (White Sox)	IL	.316	.368	.597	231	39	73	18	1	15	41	15	38	1	1
1B	Chris Colabello, Rochester (Twins)	IL	.352	.427	.639	338	58	119	25	0	24	76	43	89	2	1
2B	Wilmer Flores, Las Vegas (Mets)	PCL	.321	.357	.531	424	69	136	36	4	15	86	25	63	1	3
3B	Cody Asche, Lehigh Valley (Phillies)	IL	.295	.352	.485	404	52	119	24	4	15	68	35	95	11	3
SS	Chris Owings, Reno (Diamondbacks)	PCL	.330	.359	.482	546	104	180	31	8	12	81	22	99	20	7
CF	Billy Hamilton, Louisville (Reds)	IL	.256	.308	.343	504	75	129	18	4	6	41	38	102	75	15
OF	Nick Castellanos, Toledo (Tigers)	IL	.276	.343	.450	533	81	147	37	1	18	76	54	100	4	1
OF	Michael Choice, Sacramento (Athletics)	PCL	.302	.390	.445	510	90	154	29	1	14	89	69	115	1	2
DH	Corey Dickerson, Colorado Springs (Rockies)	PCL	.371	.414	.632	315	61	117	21	14	11	50	26	49	6	10

Pos	Pitcher, Team (Org)	League	W	L	ERA	G	GS	SV	IP	H	HR	BB	SO	G/F	WHIP	AVG
SP	Brian Flynn, New Orleans (Marlins)	PCL	6	11	2.80	23	23	0	138	127	7	40	122	1.41	.246	1.21
SP	Sonny Gray, Sacramento (Athletics)	PCL	10	7	3.42	20	20	0	118	117	5	39	118	1.44	.259	1.32
SP	Rafael Montero, Las Vegas (Mets)	PCL	5	4	3.05	16	16	0	89	85	4	25	78	0.72	.254	1.24
SP	Tyler Skaggs, Reno (Diamondbacks)	PCL	6	10	4.59	19	17	0	104	114	5	39	107	1.08	.275	1.47
RP	Heath Hembree, Fresno (Giants)	PCL	1	4	4.07	54	0	31	55	54	7	16	63	0.57	.248	1.27

Player of the Year: Chris Colabello, Rochester (Twins). **Pitcher of the Year:** Sonny Gray, Sacramento (Athletics). **Manager of the Year:** Charlie Montoyo, Durham (Rays).

DOUBLE-A

Pos	Player, Team (Org)	League	AVG	OBP	SLG	AB	R	H	2B	3B	HR	RBI	BB	SO	SB	CS
C	Josmil Pinto, New Britain (Twins)	EL	.308	.411	.482	386	59	119	23	1	14	68	64	71	0	2
1B	Anthony Aliotti, Midland (Athletics)	TL	.350	.452	.541	340	49	119	29	0	12	51	66	83	3	2
2B	Arismendy Alcantara, Tennessee (Cubs)	SL	.271	.352	.451	494	69	134	36	4	15	69	62	125	31	6
3B	Maikel Franco, Reading (Phillies)	EL	.339	.363	.563	277	47	94	13	2	15	51	10	31	1	2
SS	Marcus Semien, Birmingham (White Sox)	SL	.290	.420	.483	393	90	114	21	5	15	49	84	66	20	5
CF	George Springer, Corpus Christi (Astros)	TL	.297	.399	.579	273	56	81	20	0	19	55	42	96	33	5
OF	Joc Pederson, Chattanooga (Dodgers)	SL	.278	.381	.497	439	81	122	24	3	22	58	70	114	31	8
OF	Domingo Santana, Corpus Christi (Astros)	TL	.252	.345	.498	416	72	105	23	2	25	64	46	139	12	5
DH	Kyle Parker, Tulsa (Rockies)	TL	.285	.343	.490	480	70	137	23	3	23	74	40	99	7	6

Pos	Pitcher, Team (Org)	League	W	L	ERA	G	GS	SV	IP	H	HR	BB	SO	G/F	WHIP	AVG
SP	Archie Bradley, Mobile (Diamondbacks)	SL	12	5	2.04	21	21	0	123	93	5	59	119	1.03	1.23	.214
SP	Kyle Hendricks, Tennessee (Cubs)	SL	10	3	1.85	21	21	0	126	107	3	26	101	1.80	1.05	.227
SP	Erik Johnson, Birmingham (White Sox)	SL	8	2	2.23	14	14	0	85	57	6	21	74	1.14	0.92	.189
SP	Taijuan Walker, Jackson (Mariners)	SL	4	7	2.46	14	14	0	84	58	6	30	96	1.16	1.05	.195
RP	C.J. Riefenhauser, Montgomery (Rays)	SL	4	0	0.51	34	0	11	53	28	3	11	48	1.14	0.74	.153

Player of the Year: George Springer, Corpus Christi (Astros). **Pitcher of the Year:** Archie Bradley, Mobile (Diamondbacks). **Manager of the Year:** Pedro Lopez, Binghamton (Mets).

HIGH CLASS A

Pos	Player, Team (Org)	League	AVG	OBP	SLG	AB	R	H	2B	3B	HR	RBI	BB	SO	SB	CS
C	Michael Ohlman, Frederick (Orioles)	CAR	.313	.410	.524	361	61	113	29	4	13	53	56	93	5	0
1B	Jonathan Rodriguez, Palm Beach (Cardinals)	FSL	.284	.373	.481	455	71	129	34	1	18	72	60	101	21	4
2B	Delino Deshields Jr., Lancaster (Astros)	CAL	.317	.405	.468	451	100	143	25	14	5	54	57	91	51	18
3B	Miguel Sano, Fort Myers (Twins)	FSL	.330	.424	.655	206	51	68	15	2	16	48	29	61	9	2
SS	Addison Russell, Stockton (Athletics)	CAL	.275	.377	.508	429	85	118	29	10	17	60	61	116	21	3
CF	Byron Buxton, Fort Myers (Twins)	FSL	.326	.415	.472	218	41	71	4	8	4	22	32	49	23	8
OF	Zach Borenstein, Inland Empire (Angels)	CAL	.337	.403	.631	407	76	137	22	7	28	95	43	88	5	5
OF	Mac Williamson, San Jose (Giants)	CAL	.292	.375	.504	520	94	152	31	2	25	89	51	132	10	1
DH	Garin Cecchini, Salem (Red Sox)	CAR	.350	.469	.547	214	44	75	19	4	5	33	43	34	14	7

Pos	Pitcher, Team (Org)	League	W	L	ERA	G	GS	SV	IP	H	HR	BB	SO	G/F	WHIP	AVG
SP	Clayton Blackburn, San Jose (Giants)	CAL	7	5	3.65	23	23	0	133	111	12	35	138	1.34	1.10	.224
SP	Henry Owens, Salem (Red Sox)	CAR	8	5	2.92	20	20	0	105	66	6	53	123	1.06	1.14	.180
SP	Dan Winkler, Modesto (Rockies)	CAL	12	5	2.97	22	22	0	130	84	15	37	152	0.80	0.93	.184
SP	Kyle Zimmer, Wilmington (Royals)	CAR	4	8	4.82	18	18	0	90	80	9	31	113	1.58	1.24	.237
RP	Nick Wittgren, Jupiter (Marlins)	FSL	2	1	0.83	48	0	25	54	42	1	10	59	1.20	0.96	.211

Player of the Year: Miguel Sano, Fort Myers (Twins). **Pitcher of the Year:** Henry Owens, Salem (Red Sox). **Manager of the Year:** Rodney Linares, Lancaster (Astros).

league finals, with low Class A Quad Cities winning the Midwest League, short-season Tri-City claiming the New York-Penn League championship and Rookie-level Greeneville finishing runner-up in the Appalachian League.

And winning in the minor league postseason mattered to the Astros, perhaps more than racking up a few more big league victories in September.

LOW CLASS A

Pos	Player, Team (Org)	League	AVG	OBP	SLG	AB	R	H	2B	3B	HR	RBI	BB	SO	SB	CS
C	Tom Murphy, Asheville (Rockies)	SAL	.288	.385	.590	288	55	83	26	2	19	74	37	87	4	5
1B	Greg Bird, Charleston (Yankees)	SAL	.288	.428	.511	458	84	132	36	3	20	84	107	132	1	1
2B	Micah Johnson, Kannapolis (White Sox)	SAL	.342	.422	.530	304	76	104	17	11	6	42	40	67	61	19
3B	Joey Gallo, Hickory (Rangers)	SAL	.245	.334	.610	392	82	96	19	5	38	78	48	165	14	1
SS	Carlos Correa, Quad Cities (Astros)	MWL	.320	.405	.467	450	73	144	33	3	9	86	58	83	10	10
CF	Byron Buxton, Cedar Rapids (Twins)	MWL	.341	.431	.559	270	68	92	15	10	8	55	44	56	32	11
OF	Adam Walker, Cedar Rapids (Twins)	MWL	.276	.317	.524	508	83	140	31	7	27	109	31	115	10	0
OF	Nick Williams, Hickory (Rangers)	SAL	.293	.337	.543	376	70	110	19	12	17	60	15	110	8	5
DH	Rosell Herrera, Asheville (Rockies)	SAL	.343	.419	.515	472	83	162	33	0	16	76	61	96	21	8

Pos	Pitcher, Team (Org)	League	W	L	ERA	G	GS	SV	IP	H	HR	BB	SO	G/F	WHIP	AVG
SP	C.J. Edwards, Hickory (Rangers)	SAL	8	2	1.83	18	18	0	93	62	0	34	122	1.60	1.03	.186
SP	Dylan Floro, Bowling Green (Rays)	MWL	9	2	1.81	19	19	0	109	103	4	19	85	2.83	1.12	.251
SP	Tyler Glasnow, West Virginia (Pirates)	SAL	9	3	2.18	24	24	0	111	54	9	61	164	1.16	1.03	.142
SP	Vincent Velasquez, Quad Cities (Astros)	MWL	9	4	3.19	25	16	3	110	90	7	33	123	1.58	1.12	.221
RP	Shae Simmons, Rome (Braves)	SAL	1	1	1.49	39	0	24	42	26	0	15	66	2.05	0.97	.169

Player of the Year: Byron Buxton, Cedar Rapids (Twins). **Pitcher of the Year:** C.J. Edwards, Hickory (Rangers). **Manager of the Year:** Mark Haley, South Bend (Diamondbacks).

SHORT-SEASON

Pos	Player, Team (Org)	League	AVG	OBP	SLG	AB	R	H	2B	3B	HR	RBI	BB	SO	SB	CS
C	Wilfredo Rodriguez, Tri-City (Rockies)	NWL	.270	.355	.326	141	15	38	5	0	1	19	18	25	2	4
1B	L.B. Dantzler, Vancouver (Blue Jays)	NWL	.302	.385	.504	232	32	70	20	0	9	35	30	47	0	1
2B	Avery Romero, Batavia (Marlins)	NYP	.297	.357	.411	209	27	62	18	0	2	30	15	34	3	4
3B	Zach Green, Williamsport (Phillies)	NYP	.252	.344	.478	270	52	68	20	1	13	41	31	91	8	5
SS	Adam Frazier, Jamestown (Pirates)	NYP	.321	.399	.362	224	34	72	7	1	0	27	25	31	5	8
CF	Harold Ramirez, Jamestown (Pirates)	NYP	.285	.354	.409	274	42	78	11	4	5	40	23	52	23	11
OF	B.J. Boyd, Vermont (Athletics)	NYP	.285	.375	.442	260	39	74	13	2	8	32	35	66	8	6
OF	Hunter Renfroe, Eugene (Padres)	NWL	.308	.333	.510	104	20	32	9	0	4	18	5	26	2	0
DH	Kris Bryant, Boise (Cubs)	NWL	.354	.416	.692	65	13	23	8	1	4	16	8	17	0	0

Pos	Pitcher, Team (Org)	League	W	L	ERA	G	GS	SV	IP	H	HR	BB	SO	G/F	WHIP	AVG
SP	Miller Diaz, Brooklyn (Mets)	NYP	7	3	2.03	13	12	0	67	44	1	33	87	1.68	1.16	.183
SP	Michael Feliz, Tri-City (Astros)	NYP	4	2	1.96	14	10	1	69	53	2	13	78	1.42	0.96	.209
SP	Robert Gsellman, Brooklyn (Mets)	NYP	3	3	2.06	12	12	0	70	59	2	12	64	1.67	1.01	.220
SP	Chris Johnson, Salem-Keizer (Giants)	NWL	6	3	2.49	15	15	0	83	65	1	8	78	2.46	0.88	.207
RP	Zac Reininger, Connecticut (Tigers)	NYP	1	2	1.00	22	1	10	27	17	0	6	32	1.43	0.85	.172

Player of the Year: Zach Green, Williamsport (Phillies). **Pitcher of the Year:** Michael Feliz, Tri-City (Astros). **Manager of the Year:** Clayton McCullough, Vancouver (Blue Jays).

ROOKIE

Pos	Player, Team (Org)	League	AVG	OBP	SLG	AB	R	H	2B	3B	HR	RBI	BB	SO	SB	CS
C	Jose Briceno, Grand Junction (Rockies)	PIO	.333	.356	.614	153	32	51	16	0	9	30	5	30	8	2
1B	Matt Dean, Bluefield (Blue Jays)	APP	.338	.390	.519	210	37	71	14	3	6	35	14	57	8	5
2B	Gosuke Katoh, GCL Yankees-1	GCL	.310	.402	.522	184	28	57	11	5	6	25	27	44	4	2
3B	Hunter Dozier, Idaho Falls (Royals)	PIO	.303	.403	.509	218	43	66	23	0	7	43	35	32	3	1
SS	Christian Arroyo, AZL Giants	AZL	.326	.388	.511	184	47	60	18	5	2	39	19	32	3	2
CF	Raimel Tapia, Grand Junction (Rockies)	PIO	.357	.399	.562	258	53	92	20	6	7	47	15	31	10	9
OF	Phillip Ervin, Billings (Reds)	PIO	.326	.416	.597	129	27	42	9	1	8	29	17	24	12	0
OF	Austin Meadows, GCL Pirates	GCL	.294	.399	.519	160	29	47	11	5	5	20	24	42	3	2
DH	Clint Frazier, AZL Indians	AZL	.297	.362	.506	172	32	51	11	5	5	28	17	61	3	2

Pos	Pitcher, Team (Org)	League	W	L	ERA	G	GS	SV	IP	H	HR	BB	SO	G/F	WHIP	AVG
SP	Edwin Diaz, Pulaski (Mariners)	APP	5	2	1.43	13	13	0	69	45	5	18	79	1.19	0.91	.191
SP	Chris Flexen, Kingsport (Mets)	APP	8	1	2.09	11	11	0	69	53	6	12	62	1.56	0.94	.209
SP	Ben Lively, Billings (Reds)	PIO	0	3	0.73	12	12	0	37	21	0	12	49	1.03	0.89	.163
SP	Keury Mella, AZL Giants	AZL	3	2	2.25	10	9	0	36	34	0	11	41	2.39	1.25	.252
RP	Geordy Parra, Missoula (D-backs)	PIO	4	1	0.40	19	0	0	23	14	0	11	35	1.33	1.10	.167

Player of the Year: Christian Arroyo, AZL Giants. **Pitcher of the Year:** Edwin Diaz, Pulaski (Mariners). **Manager of the Year:** Patrick Anderson, GCL Nationals.

MINOR LEAGUES

The Astros opted to keep Springer at Triple-A Oklahoma City when major league rosters expanded on Aug. 31.

"It's important some of these guys stay here to try and win a championship," Luhnow told The Oklahoman on the eve of the Pacific Coast League playoffs. "Guys like Jon Singleton and George Springer have a chance to do something special."

Dodgers outfielder Joc Pederson hit 22 home runs at Double-A Chattanooga

Arizona ace Archie Bradley fanned 162 batters in 152 innings at two levels

PHOTOS BY TONY FARLOW

FIRST TEAM

Pos	Player, Level (Organization)	Age	AVG	OBP	SLG	G	AB	R	H	2B	3B	HR	RBI	BB	SO	SB
C	Josmil Pinto, AA/AAA (Twins)	24	.309	.400	.482	126	456	65	141	32	1	15	74	66	83	0
1B	Chris Colabello, AAA (Twins)	29	.352	.427	.639	89	338	58	119	25	0	24	76	43	89	2
2B	Marcus Semien, AA/AAA (White Sox)	22	.284	.401	.479	137	518	110	147	32	6	19	66	98	90	24
3B	Miguel Sano, AA/Hi A (Twins)	20	.280	.382	.610	123	439	86	123	30	5	35	103	65	142	11
SS	Xander Bogaerts, AA/AAA (Red Sox)	20	.297	.388	.477	116	444	72	132	23	6	15	67	63	95	7
CF	Byron Buxton, Lo A/Hi A (Twins)	19	.334	.424	.520	125	488	109	163	19	18	12	77	76	105	55
OF	Joc Pederson, AA (Dodgers)	21	.278	.381	.497	123	439	81	122	24	3	22	58	70	114	31
OF	George Springer, AA/AAA (Astros)	23	.303	.411	.600	135	492	106	149	27	4	37	108	83	161	45
DH	Javier Baez, Hi A/AA (Cubs)	20	.282	.341	.578	130	517	98	146	34	4	37	111	40	147	20

Pos	Pitcher, Level (Organization)	Age	W	L	ERA	G	GS	SV	IP	H	HR	BB	SO	G/F	AVG	WHIP
SP	Archie Bradley, AA/Hi A (D-backs)	21	14	5	1.84	26	26	0	152	115	6	69	162	0.99	.215	1.21
SP	Eddie Butler, Hi A/Lo A/AAA (Rockies)	22	9	5	1.80	28	28	0	150	96	9	52	143	2.14	.180	0.99
SP	C.J. Edwards, Lo A/Hi A (Rangers/Cubs)	21	8	2	1.86	24	24	0	116	76	1	41	155	1.41	.182	1.01
SP	Erik Johnson, AA/AAA (White Sox)	23	12	3	1.96	24	24	0	142	100	7	40	131	1.13	.197	0.99
SP	Rafael Montero, AAA/AA (Mets)	22	12	7	2.78	27	27	0	155	136	6	35	150	0.74	.232	1.10
RP	C.J. Riefenhauser, AA/AAA (Rays)	23	6	1	1.22	51	0	11	74	42	5	19	70	0.96	.163	0.83

SECOND TEAM

Pos	Player, Level (Organization)	Age	AVG	OBP	SLG	G	AB	R	H	2B	3B	HR	RBI	BB	SO	SB
C	Tom Murphy, Lo A/AA (Rockies)	22	.289	.376	.571	100	357	64	103	31	2	22	83	41	103	4
1B	Greg Bird, Lo A (Yankees)	20	.288	.428	.511	130	458	84	132	36	3	20	84	107	132	1
2B	Mookie Betts, Lo A/Hi A (Red Sox)	20	.314	.417	.506	127	462	93	145	36	4	15	65	81	57	38
3B	Maikel Franco, AA/Hi A (Phillies)	21	.320	.356	.569	134	541	89	173	36	3	31	103	30	70	1
SS	Rosell Herrera, Lo A (Rockies)	20	.343	.419	.515	126	472	83	162	33	0	16	76	61	96	21
CF	Billy Burns, Hi A/AA (Nationals)	24	.315	.425	.383	121	444	96	140	12	9	0	37	72	54	74
OF	Zach Borenstein, Hi A (Angels)	23	.337	.403	.631	112	407	76	137	22	7	28	95	43	88	5
OF	Corey Dickerson, AAA (Rockies)	24	.371	.414	.632	75	315	61	117	21	14	11	50	26	49	6
DH	Joey Gallo, Lo A/AZL (Rangers)	19	.251	.338	.623	111	411	86	103	23	5	40	88	50	172	15

Pos	Pitcher, Level (Organization)	Age	W	L	ERA	G	GS	SV	IP	H	HR	BB	SO	G/F	AVG	WHIP
SP	Tyler Glasnow, Lo A (Pirates)	20	9	3	2.18	24	24	0	111	54	9	61	164	1.16	.142	1.03
SP	Kyle Hendricks, AA/AAA (Cubs)	23	13	4	2.00	27	27	0	166	142	5	34	128	1.86	.229	1.06
SP	Henry Owens, Hi A/AA (Red Sox)	21	11	6	2.67	26	26	0	135	84	9	68	169	0.89	.177	1.13
SP	Yordano Ventura, AAA/AA (Royals)	22	8	6	3.14	26	25	0	135	119	7	53	155	0.92	.238	1.28
SP	Taijuan Walker, AA/AAA (Mariners)	21	9	10	2.93	25	25	0	141	112	11	57	160	1.12	.217	1.20
RP	Matt Stites, AA (Padres)	23	2	2	2.08	46	0	14	52	37	6	8	51	1.06	.194	0.87

MINOR LEAGUES

Daytona's dream season

BY SEAN KERNAN

Manager Dave Keller saw some things that he hadn't witnessed in 31 years of pro ball. First baseman Dustin Geiger saw some things he may never see again if he plays for 20 more years.

That was the kind of season 2013 was for the high Class A Daytona Cubs, a team that had two no-hitters, a four-homer game from shortstop Javier Baez, the most prospects in the franchise's 21-year history and—oh, by the way—a 5-1 playoff run that won the Florida State League title.

"Being there from day one, the first night we turned on the lights at Jackie Robinson Ballpark, to coming back on the bus from Port Charlotte as Florida State League champion, it was definitely an eventful run," said Geiger, who was among the FSL leaders in RBIs (86), OPS (.824) and slugging (.458).

A two-game sweep of the Dunedin Blue Jays put Daytona in the championship series against the Charlotte Stone Crabs. The Cubs took the best-of-five title series in four games, closing it out on the second combined shutout of the postseason for C.J. Edwards and Ryan Searle. The two combined for 17 strikeouts, allowing just three hits and four walks in victories over the Blue Jays and Stone Crabs.

Edwards, acquired from the Rangers in the Matt Garza deal, was nearly unhittable in the playoffs, after going a combined 8-2, 1.86 with 155 strikeouts in 116 innings.

The Cubs also put out the welcome wagon for Corey Black, obtained from the Yankees for Alfonso Soriano, and Ivan Pineyro, acquired from the Nationals for Scott Hairston. Along with Johnson, who was promoted from low Class A Kane County near the end of June, that gave Daytona's rotation an extreme makeover.

Not only were three of the five starters at the end of the season not with Daytona in the first half, but three—Edwards, Black and Pineryo—weren't even in the organization.

"Coming together as a team, it was a very good season from that aspect," Geiger said. "They meshed very well with everybody in

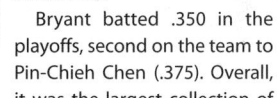

OF THE YEAR

the locker room, and we welcomed them with open arms."

Baez began his monumental season in Daytona. He led the minors in extra-base hits (75) and RBIs (111), and was tied for second with 37 homers—17 of which came as a D-Cub.

Though Baez was long gone from Daytona, promoted to Double-A Tennessee, and Soler was sidelined in June with a broken bone in his leg, the Cubs' parade of prospects continued when 2013 first-rounder Kris Bryant and 2011 second-rounder Dan Vogelbach added some pop to the lineup for the stretch run.

Bryant batted .350 in the playoffs, second on the team to Pin-Chieh Chen (.375). Overall, it was the largest collection of prospects the franchise had seen in its 20 years as a Cubs affiliate.

Matt Loosen spun Daytona's first nine-inning no-hitter in 19 seasons, and Ben Wells, Kyler Burke and Zach Cates combined on a most unusual seven-inning no-no at home on Aug. 27 in the completion of a suspended game that was started six days earlier in Dunedin. So, the Cubs actually threw a no-hitter at the Jack as the visiting team.

But in the end, the 2013 Cubs will be remembered for storming through the playoffs behind incredible starting pitching.

"It was amazing, funny, difficult, energizing. It was all that," Edwards said of the finish.

Javier Baez

MIKE JANES

PREVIOUS 10 WINNERS

2003: Sacramento/Pacific Coast (Athletics)
2004: Lancaster/California (Diamondbacks)
2005: Jacksonville/Southern (Dodgers)
2006: Tucson/Pacific Coast (Diamondbacks)
2007: San Antonio/Texas (Padres)
2008: Frisco/Texas (Rangers)
2009: Akron/Eastern (Indians)
2010: Northwest Arkansas/Texas (Royals)
2011: Mobile BayBears/Southern (Diamondbacks)
2012: Springfield Cardinals/Texas (Cardinals)

Full list: BaseballAmerica.com/awards

MINOR LEAGUES

MINOR LEAGUES

BY J.J. COOPER

NEW YORK

Sorry, Hall of Fame, you can't have Matt Davidson's bat.

The Futures Game MVP is honored to be asked to add his bat to the Hall of Fame's collection of baseball's history. "Those are like little kid dreams to get something into the Hall of Fame," is how the Diamondbacks prospect described it.

But even if he got to dress in a big league clubhouse and play on a big league field for a day, Davidson is a minor leaguer, and as such good bats are precious. And this is a very good bat. It's the one he used to hit a two-run home run off of Michael Ynoa that turned a one-run World lead into a one-run U.S. lead in the Futures Game at Citi Field. The U.S. never trailed again as an insurance run in the eighth led to the final 4-2 score.

"I told the Hall of Fame I'm on an unbelievable pace of breaking bats," Davidson said. "I've broken like 40 of them this year. It's unreal. I've got to get through the season. I have to have this bat. I hit a home run with it so I better keep it."

Davidson offered his batting gloves and batting helmet as a suitable substitute. His Futures Game jersey is going to his family as a memento of a game he'll always remember.

Davidson was the MVP of a game dominated by pitchers throwing excellent one-inning stints, so no one player really made this game his own. If there was an overriding theme of the day, it was Arizona's day to shine.

In addition to Davidson winning the MVP award for his home run, Diamondbacks shortstop Chris Owings was the defensive star of the game, making an over-the-shoulder catch while running away from home plate out to the left field line. He then teamed with second baseman Kolten Wong to turn double plays to end the fifth, sixth and seventh innings.

Diamondbacks righthander Archie Bradley pitched a perfect inning, showcasing a 94-98 mph fastball and a good breaking ball.

Red Sox righthander Anthony Ranaudo got tagged by the World team just days after he had a rough outing in the Eastern League all-star game. Ranaudo gave up two runs and walked two in two-thirds of an inning; the rest of the U.S. staff allowed only one hit. Cubs second baseman Arismendy Alcantara homered to

lead off the fourth inning against him. Xander Bogaerts singled to follow up and came around to score on a Jordan Lennerton sacrifice fly to give the World a 2-1 lead.

The U.S. rallied in the top of the fifth when C.J. Cron turned around a Ynoa fastball for a single and Davidson followed with a home run that put the U.S. ahead for good.

The World threatened in the ninth when Giants righthander Kyle Crick walked two batters before Nationals righthander A.J. Cole struck out Ji-Man Choi and then watched Jesus Galindo ground out to Kolten Wong to end the game. It was the first save of Cole's pro career and the ninth win for the U.S. in 15 Futures Games.

FUTURES GAME BOX SCORE

JULY 14

UNITED STATES 17, WORLD 5

WORLD	AB	R	H	BI	U.S.	AB	R	H	BI
Fuentes, lf	3	0	0	0	Hamilton, B cf-pr	2	1	0	0
Ascencio, lf	1	0	0	0	Buxton, cf	2	0	0	0
Alcantara, 2b	3	1	1	1	DeShields, 2b	2	0	0	0
Herrera, D, 2b	1	0	0	0	Wong, 2b	2	0	1	0
Bogaerts, ss	3	1	2	0	Springer, rf	3	0	1	0
Sano, 3b	2	0	0	0	Cron, 1b	4	1	2	0
Urrutia, rf	3	0	0	0	Davidson, 3b	2	1	1	2
Lennerton, 1b	0	0	0	1	Cecchini, 3b	2	0	1	1
Choi J, 1b	2	0	0	0	Pederson, lf	1	1	1	0
Polanco, cf	1	0	0	0	Yelich, dh	2	0	2	1
Gallindo, cf	1	0	0	0	Walker, ph-dh	2	0	0	0
Franco, dh	2	0	0	0	Russell, A,ss	2	0	0	0
Lindor, ph-dh	2	0	0	0	Owings, ss	2	0	0	0
Correa, ss	0	0	0	0	Hedges, c	2	0	0	0
Jimenez, c	1	0	0	0	McCann, c	1	0	0	0
Bethancourt, c	1	0	0	0					
Totals	**25**	**2**	**3**	**2**	**Totals**	**33**	**4**	**9**	**4**

WORLD	000	200	000—2
U.S.	010	200	08X—4

LOB: World 5, U.S. 7. **2B:** Yelich, Cecchini. **HR:** Davidson. **GIDP:** Alcantara, Urrutia, Lindor. **SB:** Wong. **CS:** Bogaerts.

WORLD	IP	H	R	ER	BB	SO	U.S.	IP	H	R	ER	BB	SO
Montero	1	0	0	0	0	0	Syndergaard	1	1	0	0	0	1
Romero	1	2	1	1	0	2	Walker, T	1	0	0	0	1	0
Rienzo	1	0	0	0	0	1	Bradley, A	1	0	0	0	0	0
Ynoa (L)	1	3	2	2	1	1	Ranaudo	⅔	2	2	2	2	0
De Paula	1	1	0	0	0	1	Biddle (W)	1⅓	0	0	0	1	1
Rodriguez, E	1	1	0	0	0	1	Butler	1	0	0	0	0	1
Almonte	1	0	0	0	0	1	Nelson	1	0	0	0	1	0
Contreras	⅔	3	1	1	0	1	Riefenhauser	1	0	0	0	0	0
Ventura	⅓	0	0	0	0	0	Wheeler	⅓	0	0	0	2	0
							Cole (S)	⅔	0	0	0	0	1
Totals	**8**	**9**	**4**	**4**	**1**	**8**	**Totals**	**9**	**3**	**2**	**2**	**7**	**4**

Umpires: HP—Pat Hoberg. 1B—Gabe Morales. 2B—Ryan Goodman. 3B—Nick Lentz.

TRIPLE-A: After six runs crossed the plate in the first two innings, 15 pitchers combined to allow only one the rest of the way as the International League took a 4-3 win against the Pacific Coast League before an Aces Ballpark -record 10,135 fans in Reno.

Indianapolis catcher Tony Sanchez put the IL on top for good with a three-run home run in the second inning, and the IL bullpen limited the PCL to four hits the rest of the way.

Durham righthander J.D. Martin and Indianapolis lefty Kris Johnson each threw a scoreless inning before Scranton righty Chris Bootcheck tossed two scoreless frames. Pawtucket's Anthony Carter and Durham's Kirby Yates each followed in tow, and Indianapolis' Vic Black and Columbus' Preston Guilmet split the ninth as the IL improved to 9-7 in the series.

EASTERN LEAGUE: The West division blanked the East, 5-0, in New Britian. Richmond outfielder Javier Herrera hit a three-run homer off Eastern starter Anthony Ranaudo (Portland) in the first inning, which proved to be more than enough for the West pitching staff. Nine West pitchers combined for a five-hit shutout, which included eight strikeouts and no walks. Bowie righthander Mike Wright (Orioles) picked up the win for the West, tossing one hitless inning with one strikeout.

George Springer

SOUTHERN LEAGUE: The Southern Division seized control early and let its pitching go to work, dominating the North in a 6-0 win in Jacksonville. Mobile outfielder Justin Greene hit an RBI triple in the first inning to open the scoring, which was enough for him to earn MVP honors, but the South's pitching was the story. The South used 11 pitchers to combine on a one-hit shutout, led by a pair of Mobile lefthanders in David Holmberg and Andrew Chafin.

TEXAS LEAGUE: Corpus Christi outfielder George Springer smacked a pair of homers to earn MVP honors and lead the Southern Division to a 6-0 rout of the Northern Division at Northwest Arkansas' Arvest Field. Springer, a 2011 Astros first-rounder, added two runs and a walk to an impressive all-star showing.

CALIFORNIA-CAROLINA LEAGUE: Consecutive five-run innings capped the offensive assault unleashed by the Carolina League all-stars, pacing them to a 12-2 win against their West Coast counterparts at San Jose's Municipal Stadium. The Carolina League busted out in the fourth, scoring four runs with two outs, capped off by a two-RBI double from Carolina shortstop Francisco Lindor. The team did the same in the following frame, receiving a pair of two-out, two-RBI singles from Lynchburg right fielder David Rohm and Myrtle Beach shortstop Luis Sardinas.

FLORIDA STATE LEAGUE: A three-run homer by Bradenton shortstop Alen Hanson capped a five-run fifth inning, helping the South to an 8-1 win in Dunedin. The North's pitching staff kept the South scoreless through four frames. A solo homer by Palm Beach right fielder Stephen Piscotty tied the game in the fifth, and a sacrifice fly from Charlotte third baseman Richie Shaffer put the game out of reach.

MIDWEST LEAGUE: The Western Division nearly stole the all-star game with a three-run ninth-inning rally that tied the game in Dayton. But with two on and two outs in the bottom of the ninth, East center fielder Dalton Pompey took a Ryan Dull payoff pitch up the middle to seal a 6-5 East win.

The game featured 26 pitchers and plenty of prospects, particularly on the West roster. The West had the 2012 No. 1 overall pick, Carlos Correa, playing shortstop and the No. 2 pick, Byron Buxton, manning center field.

SOUTH ATLANTIC LEAGUE: Rain delayed the game by nearly three hours, but there was certainly no delay from Northern Division speedster Micah Johnson (Kannapolis) after he singled in the third. Johnson broke for second on the first pitch, allowing the runner on third, Dilson Herrera (Pirates), to break for home and tie the score at 1-1. On the next pitch, Johnson swiped third base, then scored on a Lewis Brinson (Rangers) groundout. That 2-1 lead would hold up as the North won the game and Johnson took MVP honors.

*Full-season teams only

TEAM

WINS

Cedar Rapids (Midwest)	88
Durham (International)	87
Binghamton (Eastern)	86
Potomac (Carolina)	84
Corpus Christi (Texas)	83
San Jose (California)	83

LONGEST WINNING STREAK*

Fort Myers (Florida State)	12
Oklahoma City (Pacific Coast)	12
Birmingham (Southern)	11
Cedar Rapids (Midwest)	11
Jacksonville (Southern)	11

LOSSES

Greenville (South Atlantic)	87
Nashville (Pacific Coast)	87
Bakersfield (California)	85
Gwinnett (International)	84
Reno (Pacific Coast)	84

LONGEST LOSING STREAK*

Gwinnett (International)	14
Louisville (International)	12
Charlotte (Florida State)	11
Chattanooga (Southern)	11
3 teams tied at	10

BATTING AVERAGE*

Lancaster (California)	.289
Las Vegas (Pacific Coast)	.287
Salt Lake (Pacific Coast)	.287
Colorado Springs (Pacific Coast)	.284
Tucson (Pacific Coast)	.283

RUNS

Lancaster (California)	976
Las Vegas (Pacific Coast)	828
High Desert (California)	827
Salt Lake (Pacific Coast)	809
Sacramento (Pacific Coast)	773

HOME RUNS

Stockton (California)	183
Hickory (South Atlantic)	178
Corpus Christi (Texas)	158
High Desert (California)	154
Lancaster (California)	153

STOLEN BASES

Bowling Green (Midwest)	230
Potomac (Carolina)	216
Asheville (South Atlantic)	211
Lake Elsinore (California)	201
Rome (South Atlantic)	188

EARNED RUN AVERAGE*

Lexington (South Atlantic)	2.99
Mobile (Southern)	3.03
Bowling Green (Midwest)	3.06
Mississippi (Southern)	3.07
Savannah (South Atlantic)	3.15

STRIKEOUTS

San Jose (California)	1282
Visalia (California)	1272
Stockton (California)	1258
Durham (International)	1246
Columbus (International)	1239

INDIVIDUAL BATTING

BATTING AVERAGE

Chris Colabello (Rochester)	.352
Devon Travis (West Michigan/Lakeland)	.351
Rosell Herrera (Asheville)	.343
Brent Keys (Jupiter/Jacksonville)	.341
Zach Borenstein (Inland Empire)	.337

RUNS

Marcus Semien (Birmingham/Charlotte)	110
Byron Buxton (Cedar Rapids/Fort Myers)	109
Chris Taylor (High Desert/Jackson)	108
Jamal Austin (High Desert)	107
Micah Johnson (Kannapolis/W-S/Birm.)	106

George Springer (Corpus Christi/Okla. City)	106

HITS

Alex Yarbrough (Inland Empire)	182
Chris Owings (Reno)	180
Devon Travis (West Michigan/Lakeland)	177
Maikel Franco (Clearwater/Reading)	173
Andrew Toles (Bowling Green)	169

TOP HITTING STREAKS

D'Arby Myers (Midland)	33
Raimel Tapia (Grand Junction)	29
Billy Burns (Potomac)	25
Patrick Kivlehan (High Desert)	25
Corey Thompson (Great Falls)	25

MOST HITS (ONE GAME)

Abraham Almonte (Tacoma)	6
Willy Garcia (Bradenton)	6
Emilio Guerrero (Lansing)	6
Nathan Melendres (High Desert)	6
Carlos Peguero (Tacoma)	6
Moises Sierra (Buffalo)	6
Aaron Westlake (Lakeland)	6

TOTAL BASES

Maikel Franco (Clearwater/Reading)	308
Javier Baez (Daytona/Tennessee)	299
George Springer (Corpus Christi/Okla. City)	295
Scott Schebler (Rancho Cucamonga)	277
Preston Tucker (Corpus Christi/Lancaster)	270

EXTRA-BASE HITS

Javier Baez (Daytona/Tennessee)	75
Brandon Drury (South Bend)	70
Maikel Franco (Clearwater/Reading)	70
Miguel Sano (Fort Myers/New Britain)	70
Scott Schebler (Rancho Cucamonga)	69

DOUBLES

Brandon Drury (South Bend)	51
Tony Renda (Hagerstown)	43
Rougned Odor (Myrtle Beach/Frisco)	41
Michael Taylor (Potomac)	41
Christian Villanueva (Tennessee)	41

TRIPLES

Byron Buxton (Cedar Rapids/Fort Myers)	18
Darnell Sweeney (Rancho Cucamonga)	16
Andrew Toles (Bowling Green)	16
Micah Johnson (Kannapolis/W-Salem/ Birmingham)	15
Kevin Kiermaier (Montgomery/Durham)	15

HOME RUNS

Joey Gallo (AZL Rangers/Hickory)	40
Javier Baez (Daytona/Tennessee)	37
George Springer (Corpus Christi/Okla. City)	37
Miguel Sano (Fort Myers/New Britain)	35
Andrew Lambo (Altoona/Indianapolis)	32
Ryan Rua (Hickory/Frisco)	32

RUNS BATTED IN

Javier Baez (Daytona/Tennessee)	111
Dalton Hicks (Cedar Rapids/Fort Myers)	110
Adam Walker (Cedar Rapids)	109
George Springer (Corpus Christi/Okla. City)	108
Andrew Aplin (Lancaster)	107

MOST RBIS (ONE GAME)

Jake Marisnick (Jacksonville)	9
Tony Thompson (Stockton)	9
10 players tied at	8

WALKS

Greg Bird (Charleston)	107
Allan Dykstra (Binghamton)	102
Nolan Fontana (Lancaster)	102
Ty Kelly (Bowie/Tacoma)	102
Jamie Johnson (Erie)	101

INTENTIONAL WALKS

Max Muncy (Stockton/Midland)	10
David Washington (Peoria/State College)	9
Dan Black (Birmingham)	8
Justin Bour (Tennessee)	8
Anthony Seratelli (Omaha)	8

STRIKEOUTS

Harold Riggins (Modesto)	192

Lewis Brinson (Hickory)	191
Trevor Story (Modesto)	183
Matt Fields (NW Arkansas)	181
Xavier Scruggs (Springfield)	177

STOLEN BASES

Micah Johnson (Kannapolis/W-Salem/ Birmingham)	84
Billy Hamilton (Louisville)	75
Billy Burns (Potomac/Harrisburg)	74
Travis Jankowski (Lake Elsinore)	71
Terrance Gore (Lexington)	68

CAUGHT STEALING

Micah Johnson (Kannapolis/W-Salem/ Birmingham)	26
Junior Arias (Dayton/Bakersfield)	20
Darnell Sweeney (Rancho Cucamonga)	20
4 players tied at	19

ON-BASE PERCENTAGE*

Garin Cecchini (Salem/Portland)	.443
Allan Dykstra (Binghamton)	.436
Eric Campbell (Las Vegas)	.435
Greg Bird (Charleston)	.428
Chris Colabello (Rochester)	.427

SLUGGING PERCENTAGE*

Chris Colabello (Rochester)	.639
Zach Borenstein (Inland Empire)	.631
Miguel Sano (Fort Myers/New Britain)	.610
Joey Gallo (Hickory)	.610
George Springer (Corpus Christi/Okla. City)	.600

ON-BASE PLUS SLUGGING (OPS)*

Chris Colabello (Rochester)	1.066
Zach Borenstein (Inland Empire)	1.034
George Springer (Corpus Christi/Okla. City)	1.010
Miguel Sano (Fort Myers/New Britain)	.992
Tom Murphy (Asheville/Tulsa)	.948

HIT BY PITCH

Kevin Plawecki (Savannah/St. Lucie)	24
Zeke DeVoss (Daytona)	23
Matt Duffy (Lancaster/Corpus Christi)	21
Seth Loman (Charlotte/Bowie)	21
Mac Williamson (San Jose)	21

SACRIFICE BUNTS

Eric Stamets (Inland Empire)	21
Juan Ciriaco (Asheville)	18
Cristhian Adames (Tulsa)	17
Ethan Chapman (Lexington/Wilmington)	17
Teoscar Hernandez (Quad Cities)	17

SACRIFICE FLIES

Peter O'Brien (Charleston/Tampa)	12
Dalton Hicks (Cedar Rapids/Fort Myers)	11
Michael Snyder (Inland Empire)	11
6 players tied at	10

GROUNDED INTO DOUBLE PLAY

Chris Dominguez (Fresno)	23
Yangervis Solarte (Round Rock)	22
Joseph Sever (Carolina/Lake County)	21
7 players tied at	20

BATTING AVERAGE*

CATCHERS

Michael Ohlman (Frederick)	.313
M.P. Cokinos (Lancaster)	.313
Josmil Pinto (New Britain/Rochester)	.309
Kevin Plawecki (St. Lucie/St. Lucie)	.305
Caleb Joseph (Bowie)	.299

FIRST BASEMEN

Chris Colabello (Rochester)	.352
Jayce Boyd (Savannah/St. Lucie)	.330
Efren Navarro (Salt Lake)	.326
Anthony Aliotti (Midland/Sacramento)	.324
Seth Mejias-Brean (Bakersfield/Bakersfield)	.305

SECOND BASEMEN

Devon Travis (West Michigan/Lakeland)	.351
Dean Anna (Tucson)	.331
Kensuke Tanaka (Fresno)	.329
Grant Green (Sacramento/Salt Lake)	.326
Wilmer Flores (Las Vegas)	.321

THIRD BASEMEN

Garin Cecchini (Salem/Portland)	.322
Maikel Franco (Clearwater/Reading)	.320
Ryan Court (South Bend/Visalia/Mobile)	.315
Mark Minicozzi (Richmond)	.309
Matt Duffy (Lancaster/Corpus Christi)	.309

SHORTSTOPS

Rosell Herrera (Asheville)	.343
Chris Owings (Reno)	.330
Leonardo Reginatto (Bowling Green)	.325
Carlos Correa (Quad Cities)	.320
Chris Taylor (Jackson/Jackson)	.314

OUTFIELDERS

Brent Keys (Jupiter/Jacksonville)	.341
Zach Borenstein (Inland Empire)	.337
Byron Buxton (Cedar Rapids/Fort Myers)	.334
Reymond Fuentes (San Antonio/Tucson)	.330
Andrew Toles (Bowling Green)	.326

DESIGNATED HITTERS

Willie Carmona (Lakewood)	.303
Alejandro Segovia (Charlotte)	.281
David Chester (Greenville/Salem)	.271
Nik Balog (Delmarva)	.266
Rock Shoulders (Kane County)	.258

INDIVIDUAL PITCHING

EARNED RUN AVERAGE*

Dylan Floro (Bowling Green/Charlotte)	1.77
Eddie Butler (Asheville/Modesto/Tulsa)	1.80
Archie Bradley (Visalia/Mobile)	1.84
C.J. Edwards (Hickory/Daytona)	1.86
Erik Johnson (Birmingham/Charlotte)	1.96

WORST ERA*

Barry Enright (Salt Lake)	7.12
Nate Adcock (Omaha/Reno)	6.67
Garrett Gould (R. Cucamonga/Chattanooga)	6.64
Chris Devenski (Lancaster/Quad Cities)	6.60
Ross Seaton (Corpus Christi/Okla. City)	6.20

WINS

J.D. Martin (Durham)	16
Gabriel Ynoa (Savannah)	15
Archie Bradley (Visalia/Mobile)	14
Matt Buschmann (Montgomery/Durham)	14
David Martinez (Corpus Christi/Okla. City)	14

LOSSES

Eliecer Navarro (Bradenton/Altoona)	17
Zach Kroenke (Nashville)	16
Zach Clark (Norfolk/Bowie/GCL/Frederick)	15
Jon Moscot (Bakersfield/Pensacola)	15
Andy Moye (Huntsville)	15

GAMES

Justin Hampson (Las Vegas)	64
Jeremy McBryde (San Antonio)	61
Chris Hatcher (New Orleans)	60
Jose Flores (Akron)	59
Jeff Ibarra (Tucson/San Antonio)	59

GAMES STARTED

Ben Alsup (Modesto)	29
Matt Shoemaker (Salt Lake)	29
24 players tied at	28

COMPLETE GAMES

Robbie Ray (Potomac/Harrisburg)	4
Daniel Stumpf (Lexington)	4
12 players tied	3

SHUTOUTS

Steven Wright (Pawtucket)	3
12 players tied	2

GAMES FINISHED

Chris Hatcher (New Orleans)	55
Jose Flores (Akron)	53
RJ Hively (South Bend/Visalia)	52
Jeff Walters (Binghamton)	52
Miles Mikolas (Tucson)	50

HOLDS

Cody Hebner (Lake Elsinore)	23
Patrick Schuster (Visalia)	20
Leonel Campos (Fort Wayne/San Antonio)	18
Jeff Ibarra (Tucson/San Antonio)	18
Manny Delcarmen (Norfolk)	17

Henry Owens

RODGER WOOD

SAVES

Jeff Walters (Binghamton)	38
Chris Hatcher (New Orleans)	33
R.J. Hively (South Bend/Visalia)	33
Scott Oberg (Modesto)	33
Jose Valdez (West Michigan/Lakeland)	33

INNINGS PITCHED

Matt Shoemaker (Salt Lake)	184.1
Bryan Blough (Winston-Salem)	172.2
Christian Bergman (Tulsa)	171.0
David Buchanan (Reading/Lehigh Valley)	169.2
Stolmy Pimentel (Altoona/Indianapolis)	169.1

WALKS

Andy Oliver (Indianapolis)	112
Ismael Guillon (Dayton)	95
Sam Selman (Wilmington)	85
Charlie Haeger (Portland/Pawtucket)	83
Johnny Hellweg (Wisconsin/Nashville)	83

STRIKEOUTS

Daniel Winkler (Modesto/Tulsa)	175
Henry Owens (Salem/Portland)	169
Matt Buschmann (Montgomery/Durham)	167
Tyler Glasnow (West Virginia)	164
Jimmy Nelson (Huntsville/Nashville)	163

HITS ALLOWED

Matt Shoemaker (Salt Lake)	212
Andrew Werner (Sacramento)	202
Shawn Hill (Toledo)	191
Pat Dean (New Britain/Rochester)	189
Chris Schwinden (Las Vegas)	188

HOME RUNS ALLOWED

Barry Enright (Salt Lake)	30
Matt Shoemaker (Salt Lake)	27
Sugar Ray Marimon (NW Arkansas)	26
Christian Bergman (Tulsa)	25
Victor Larez (Erie)	25
Toru Murata (Columbus/Akron)	25

STRIKEOUTS PER NINE INNINGS (STARTERS)*

C.J. Edwards (Hickory/Daytona)	11.99
Matt Barnes (Portland/Pawtucket)	11.28
Henry Owens (Salem/Portland)	11.27
Robert Stephenson (Dayton/Bake./Pens.)	10.71
Andrew Barbosa (Visalia)	10.69

STRIKEOUTS PER NINE INNINGS (RELIEVERS)*

Jack Leathersich (Binghamton/Las Vegas)	15.74
Ryan Buchter (Gwinnett)	14.95
Leonel Campos (Fort Wayne/San Antonio)	14.24
Brad Boxberger (Tucson)	13.97
Derek Law (Augusta/San Jose)	13.80

OPPONENT BATTING AVERAGE (STARTERS)*

Henry Owens (Salem/Portland)	.177
Eddie Butler (Asheville/Modesto/Tulsa)	.180
C.J. Edwards (Hickory/Daytona)	.182
Daniel Winkler (Modesto/Tulsa)	.193
Sam Selman (Wilmington)	.197

OPPONENT BATTING AVERAGE (RELIEVERS)*

Leonel Campos (Fort Wayne/San Antonio)	.144
Cody Hall (San Jose/Richmond)	.153
Steve Geltz (Durham)	.156
Collin Cargill (Jupiter/Jacksonville)	.157
Taylor Garrison (Charleston/Tampa/Scranton)	.158

MOST STRIKEOUTS/ONE GAME

Jesse Biddle (Reading)	16
Kendry Flores (Augusta)	15
5 players tied at	14

WILD PITCHES

Malcom Diaz (AZL Padres)	28
Bryan Mitchell (Tampa/Trenton)	27
Ismael Guillon (Dayton)	26
Andres Heredia (DSL Angels)	23
Connor Sadzeck (Hickory)	23

BALKS

Matt Carasiti (Asheville)	9
Edgar De La Rosa (West Michigan)	8
Carlos Teller (San Jose/Fresno/Richmond)	8
Aroni Nina (Lexington)	7
3 players tied at	6

HIT BATTERS

Brett Shankin (Jackson/High Desert)	24
Matt Miller (Brevard County)	19
Blake Perry (South Bend)	19
5 players tied at	17

GROUND BALL DOUBLE PLAYS

Danny Rosenbaum (Syracuse)	31
Chris Reed (Chattanooga)	27
Taylor Rogers (Cedar Rapids/Fort Myers)	26
Matt Packer (Akron)	25
Logan Darnell (New Britain/Rochester)	24
Kyle Lobstein (Erie/Toledo)	24

INDIVIDUAL FIELDING

ERRORS

Javier Baez (Daytona/Tennessee)	44
Renato Nunez (Beloit)	39
Dorssys Paulino (Lake County)	39
Zach Walters (Syracuse/Syracuse)	38
Luis Marte (Hickory)	37

MINOR LEAGUES

MINOR LEAGUES

	INTERNATIONAL LEAGUE	PACIFIC COAST LEAGUE	EASTERN LEAGUE	SOUTHERN LEAGUE	TEXAS LEAGUE	CALIFORNIA LEAGUE	CAROLINA LEAGUE	FLORIDA STATE LEAGUE	MIDWEST LEAGUE	SOUTH ATLANTIC LEAGUE
Best Batting Prospect	Nick Castellanos, Indianapolis	Chris Owings, Reno	Xander Bogaerts, Portland	Christian Yelich, Jacksonville	George Springer, Corpus Christi	Addison Russell, Stockton	Garin Cecchini, Salem	Miguel Sano, Fort Myers	Byron Buxton, Cedar Rapids	Rosell Herrera, Asheville
Best Power Prospect	Wil Myers, Durham	Matt Davidson, Reno	Miguel Sano, New Britain	Kyle Jensen, Jacksonville	George Springer, Corpus Christi	Mac Williamson, San Jose	Courtney Hawkins, Winston-Salem	Miguel Sano, Fort Myers	Adam Brett Walker, Cedar Rapids	Joey Gallo, Hickory
Best Strike-Zone Judgment	Cole Figueroa, Durham	Kolten Wong, Memphis	Josmil Pino, New Britain	Marcus Semien, Birmingham	Anthony Aliotti, Midland	Nolan Fontana, Lancaster	Garin Cecchini, Salem	Brent Keys, Jupiter	Tommy Coyle, Bowling Green	Mookie Betts, Greenville
Best Baserunner	Billy Hamilton, Louisville	Tony Campana, Reno	Jose Ramirez, Akron	Ender Inciarte, Mobile	Rico Noel, San Antonio	Travis Jankowski, Lake Elsinore	Billy Burns, Potomac	Jon Berti, Dunedin	Mallex Smith, Fort Wayne	Micah Johnson, Kannapolis
Fastest Baserunner	Billy Hamilton, Louisville	Gary Brown, Fresno	Jose Ramirez, Akron	Keenyn Walker, Birmingham	Rico Noel, San Antonio	Travis Jankowski, Lake Elsinore	Billy Burns, Potomac	Byron Buxton, Fort Myers	Andrew Toles, Bowling Green	Terrence Gore, Lexington
Best Pitching Prospect	Gerrit Cole, Indianapolis	Zack Wheeler, Las Vegas	Noah Syndergaard, Binghamton	Archie Bradley, Mobile	Mike Foltynewicz, Corpus Christi	Kyle Crick, San Jose	Kyle Zimmer, Wilmington	Noah Syndergaard, St. Lucie	Robert Stephenson, Dayton	Tyler Glasnow, West Virginia
Best Fastball	Bruce Rondon, Toledo	Zack Wheeler, Las Vegas	Noah Syndergaard, Binghamton	Archie Bradley, Mobile	Mike Foltynewicz, Corpus Christi	Kyle Crick, San Jose	Kyle Zimmer, Wilmington	Noah Syndergaard, St. Lucie	Robert Stephenson, Dayton	Tyler Glasnow, West Virginia
Best Breaking Pitch	Trevor Bauer, Columbus	Sonny Gray, Sacramento	Jesse Biddle, Reading	Taijuan Walker, Jackson	Mike Foltynewicz, Corpus Christi	Clayton Blackburn, San Jose	Kyle Zimmer, Wilmington	Aaron Sanchez, Dunedin	Lance McCullers Jr., Quad Cities	Lucas Sims, Rome
Best Changeup	Jose Alvarez, Toledo	Michael Wacha, Memphis	Kevin Gausman, Bowie	Marquis Fleming, Montgomery	Neil Ramirez, Frisco	Tanner Peters, Stockton	Henry Owens, Salem	Justin Nicolino, Jupiter	Ismael Guillon, Dayton	Alexander Claudio, Hickory
Best Control	Jose Alvarez, Toledo	Sonny Gray, Sacramento	Kevin Gausman, Bowie	Kyle Hendricks, Tennessee	David Martinez, Corpus Christi	Ty Blach, San Jose	Taylor Hill, Potomac	Justin Nicolino, Jupiter	Dylan Unsworth, Clinton	Gabriel Ynoa, Savannah
Best Reliever	Vic Black, Indianapolis	Chris Hatcher, New Orleans	Aaron Barrett, Harrisburg	C.J. Riefenhauser, Montgomery	Matt Stites, San Antonio	Jake Barrett, Visalia	Cody Winiarski, Winston-Salem	Nick Wittgren, Jupiter	Scott Griggs, Great Lakes	Tyler Mizenko, Augusta
Best Defensive Catcher	Josh Phegley, Charlotte	Tuffy Gosewisch, Reno	Christian Vazquez, Portland	J.T. Realmuto, Jacksonville	Rene Garcia, Tulsa	Austin Hedges, Lake Elsinore	Blake Swihart, Salem	Elias Diaz, Bradenton	Luke Maile, Bowling Green	Tom Murphy, Asheville
Best Defensive First Baseman	Jordan Lennerton, Toledo	Efren Navarro, Salt Lake	Travis Shaw, Portland	Christian Marrero, Mississippi	Anthony Aliotti, Midland	Max Muncy, Stockton	Jerrud Sabourin, Carolina	Jonathan Rodriguez, Palm Beach	Matt Olson, Beloit	Jayce Boyd, Savannah
Best Defensive Second Baseman	Cesar Hernandez, Lehigh Valley	Kolten Wong, Memphis	Hernan Perez, Erie	Marcus Semien, Birmingham	Taylor Lindsey, Arkansas	Alex Yarbrough, Inland Empire	Rougned Odor, Myrtle Beach	Carlos Alonso, Clearwater	Jorge Polanco, Cedar Rapids	Dilson Herrera, West Virginia
Best Defensive Third Baseman	Cody Asche, Lehigh Valley	Mike Olt, Iowa	Giovanny Urshela, Akron	Christian Villanueva, Tennessee	Jonathan Meyer, Corpus Christi	Juan Silverio, Bakersfield	Kyle Kubitza, Lynchburg	Andy Burns, Dunedin	Brandon Drury, South Bend	Joey Gallo, Hickory
Best Defensive Shortstop	Jose Iglesias, Pawtucket	Jonathan Villar, Oklahoma City	Danny Santana, New Britain	Nick Ahmed, Mississippi	Orlando Calixte, Northwest Arkansas	Trevor Story, Modesto	Franisco Lindor, Carolina	Jadiel Rivera, Brevard County	Carlos Correa, Quad Cities	Raul A. Mondesi, Lexington
Best Infield Arm	Tim Beckham, Durham	Jonathan Villar, Oklahoma City	Miguel Sano, New Britain	Arismendy Alcantara, Tennessee	Jonathan Meyer, Corpus Christi	Trevor Story, Modesto	Deven Marrero, Salem	Javier Baez, Daytona	Carlos Correa, Quad Cities	Joey Gallo, Hickory
Best Defensive Outfielder	Jackie Bradley, Pawtucket	Gary Brown, Fresno	Brian Goodwin, Harrisburg	Joc Pederson, Chattanooga	George Springer, Corpus Christi	Travis Jankowski, Lake Elsinore	Michael Taylor, Potomac	Byront Buxton, Fort Myers	Byron Buxton, Cedar Rpids	Lewis Brinson, Hickory
Best Outfield Arm	Moises Sierra, Buffalo	Che-Hsuan Lin, Oklahoma City	Carlos Moncrief, Akron	Rubi Silva, Tennessee	Kent Matthes, Tulsa	Jon Garcia, Rancho Cucamonga	Tyler Naquin, Carolina	Wily Garcia, Bradenton	Gabriel Guerrero, Clinton	Jesus Solarzano, Greensboro
Most Exciting Player	Billy Hamilton, Louisville	George Springer, Oklahoma City	Cesar Puello, Binghamton	Joc Pederson, Chattanooga	George Springer, Corpus Christi	Addison Russell, Stockton	Francisco Lindor, Carolina	Miguel Sano, Fort Myers	Byron Buxton, Cedar Rapids	Rosell Herrera, Asheville
Best Manager Prospect	Gary DiSarcina, Pawtucket	Keith Johnson, Salt Lake	Pedro Lopez, Binghamton	Julio Vinas, Birmingham	Tim Bogar, Arkansas	Webster Garrison, Stockton	Jason Wood, Myrtle Beach	Andy Haines, Jupiter	Jake Mauer, Cedar Rapids	Mike Goff, Augusta

Awards honor sustained success

TRIPLE-A
Indianapolis Indians (International)

The Indianapolis Indians have bucked a significant trend around minor league baseball over the past five seasons. As most teams, and the industry as a whole, saw a decrease in attendance during the economic downturn, Indianapolis' turnstiles were spinning at a record pace that climaxed in 2013 with the Indians drawing a minor league-best 637,579 fans.

From 2009-2013, Indianapolis' average attendance increased 9.5 percent—from 8,202 to 8,980—the biggest gain among International League teams during that span. Overall attendance grew by 88,027 fans, the biggest increase among all Triple-A teams.

Adding a degree of difficulty is the competition the team faces for sports fans. Indianapolis is a major league city, with the NBA's Indiana Pacers and NFL's Indianapolis Colts each playing just up the road from the Indians' Victory Field.

DOUBLE-A
Tulsa Drillers (Texas)

You can't make something out of nothing. Yet the Tulsa Drillers (Texas) have seemingly done just that, by turning their new stadium into a catalyst for the community.

ONEOK Field opened in downtown Tulsa in 2010, surrounded by plenty of empty space. Since then, each of the bustling districts in the distance have expanded to the ballpark, creating a revitalized environment.

The organization has offered a great experience for many years, which is something that general manager Mike Melega credits to its ownership. Longtime owner Went Hubbard died in September 2012, leaving a legacy that has been embraced by the new owners, his two sons.

"The best thing about working for the Drillers is working for Dale and Jeff Hubbard, to be completely honest with you," Melega said.

CLASS A
Clearwater Threshers (Florida State)

The lights never go out at Bright House Field.

Whether the Clearwater Threshers are playing or not, the front office has made a point of making the ballpark a place for members of the community to attend and host events. It's exactly that philosophy that has people coming back for more.

Bright House Field plays host to a variety of events, from fundraisers to a weekly Wednesday night happy hour to a Halloween extravaganza, with hayrides on the warning track and 35 candy stations for trick-or-treaters.

It's also a hit during the season. The Phillies-owned franchise led the FSL in overall (172,151) and average (2,608) attendance in 2013, extending a streak that began when Bright House Field opened in 2004.

SHORT-SEASON
State College Spikes (New York-Penn)

The State College Spikes may not seem like a natural match for a town that reveres its college football team like no other. But just because the Spikes sit in the shadow of Penn State football doesn't mean that the team is obscured by it.

"We provide the things that minor league baseball as an industry brings—that connection to a community, affordability and a fun atmosphere," Spikes general manager Jason Dambach said.

The team made history before it ever took the field. Its 5,500-seat ballpark debuted on June 20, 2006, as the first stadium in the world to earn a Leadership in Energy and Environmental Design (LEED) certification, an honor handed out by the U.S. Green Building Council for the construction and operation of a high-performance green building.

MINOR LEAGUES

PREVIOUS WINNERS

TRIPLE-A	DOUBLE-A	CLASS A	SHORT-SEASON
2003: Pawtucket (International)	**2003:** New Britain (Eastern)	**2003:** Modesto (California)	**2003:** Spokane (Northwest)
2004: Sacramento (Pacific Coast)	**2004:** Round Rock (Texas)	**2004:** Dayton (Midwest)	**2004:** Burlington (Appalachian)
2005: Toledo (International)	**2005:** Tulsa (Texas)	**2005:** Lakewood (South Atlantic)	**2005:** Brooklyn (New York-Penn)
2006: Durham (International)	**2006:** Altoona (Eastern)	**2006:** Daytona (Florida State)	**2006:** Aberdeen (New York-Penn)
2007: Albuquerque (Pacific Coast)	**2007:** Frisco (Texas)	**2007:** Lake Elsinore (California)	**2007:** Missoula (Pioneer)
2008: Columbus (International)	**2008:** Birmingham (Southern)	**2008:** Greensboro (South Atlantic)	**2008:** Greeneville (Appalachian)
2009: Iowa (Pacific Coast)	**2009:** New Hamshire (Eastern)	**2009:** San Jose (California)	**2009:** Tri-City (New York-Penn)
2010: Louisville (International)	**2010:** Corpus Christi (Texas)	**2010:** Lynchburg (Carolina)	**2010:** Idaho Falls (Pioneer)
2011: Colo. Springs (Pacific Coast)	**2011:** Harrisburg (Eastern)	**2011:** Fort Wayne (Midwest)	**2011:** Vancouver (Northwest)
2012: Lehigh Valley (International)	**2012:** N-West Arkansas (Texas)	**2012:** Greenville (South Atlantic)	**2012:** Billings (Pioneer)

BY JOHN MANUEL

The Durham Bulls started the year with two of the top prospects in the minors on their Triple-A roster.

Wil Myers was in his first year in the Rays organization, after arriving from the Royals in the off-season trade for James Shields. Chris Archer was in his second year as a Ray. Both are North Carolina natives playing in their home state on what they hoped would be their last minor league stop.

With Archer and Myers, the Bulls could be expected to get off to a strong start. And when they earned promotions to the majors (and helped the Rays reach the playoffs), it would have been reasonable for Durham to fall back to the IL pack.

But that never happened. Behind a fortified pitching staff and a stellar postseason effort from righthander Jake Odorizzi, Durham won its fourth Governor's Cup title since joining the International League in 1998, defeating Pawtucket in the league finals.

Durham led the league with 698 runs scored (despite a league-low 77 home runs) and in ERA at 3.33.

It was the second IL title for manager Charlie Montoyo, who has led the Bulls to the playoffs five times in his seven-year tenure. This year's team, which also withstood an April knee injury to shortstop Hak-Ju Lee, was built around 2008 No. 1 overall pick Tim Beckham and a slew of trade acquisitions such as Odorizzi, who came over with Myers in the Shields trade, and first baseman Vince Belnome, who was acquired from the Padres.

The Bulls gave up only three runs in the series with the PawSox, with the key win being a 2-1 14-inning victory in Game Two that turned the series after the PawSox had won the opener.

TOP 20 PROSPECTS

1. Xander Bogaerts, ss, Pawtucket (Red Sox)
2. Wil Myers, of, Durham (Rays)
3. Gerrit Cole, rhp, Indianapolis (Pirates)
4. Chris Archer, rhp, Durham (Rays)
5. Nick Castellanos, of, Toledo (Tigers)
6. Danny Salazar, rhp, Columbus (Indians)
7. Avisail Garcia, of, Toledo (Tigers)/Charlotte (White Sox)
8. Jackie Bradley, of, Pawtucket (Red Sox)
9. Cody Asche, 3b, Lehigh Valley (Phillies)
10. Billy Hamilton, of, Louisville (Reds)
11. Erik Johnson, rhp, Charlotte (White Sox)
12. Oswaldo Arcia, of, Rochester (Twins)
13. Allen Webster, rhp, Pawtucket (Red Sox)
14. Jonathan Schoop, 2b/ss, Norfolk (Orioles)
15. Jake Odorizzi, rhp, Durham (Rays)
16. Trevor Bauer, rhp, Columbus (Indians)
17. Darin Ruf, of/1b, Lehigh Valley (Phillies)
18. Carlos Sanchez, 2b/ss, Charlotte (White Sox)
19. Kevin Pillar, of, Buffalo (Blue Jays)
20. Joey Terdoslavich, of, Gwinnett (Braves)

The league's MVP was also one of its best stories. The Twins signed Chris Colabello after he spent six years in independent ball, and after playing for Italy in the World Baseball Classic. He finished sixth in the league in home runs despite playing just 89 games, won the batting title at .352 and earned his first big league tour.

Another minor league veteran, righthander J.D. Martin (a 2001 first-round pick), led the league with a Bulls-record 16 wins. But it was Odorizzi who shined in the playoffs, striking out 16 and allowing just five hits and four walks in 14 scoreless innings.

Charlotte spent its final season in its South Carolina ballpark and will move into a new downtown Charlotte ballpark in 2014. The Knights, who will host the Triple-A National Championship in 2014, had the league's only no-hitter—a seven-inning job, pitched by Brazilian righty Andre Rienzo.

OVERALL STANDINGS

Team (Organization)	W	L	PCT	GB	Manager(s)	Attendance	Average	Last Pennant
Durham Bulls (Rays)	87	57	.604	—	Charlie Montoyo	498,735	7,125	2013
Pawtucket Red Sox (Red Sox)	80	63	.559	6½	Gary DiSarcina	540,034	7,827	2012
Indianapolis Indians (Pirates)	80	64	.556	7	Dean Treanor	637,579	8,980	2000
Norfolk Tides (Orioles)	77	67	.535	10	Ron Johnson	382,195	5,704	1985
Rochester Red Wings (Twins)	77	67	.535	10	Gene Glynn	420,751	6,098	1997
Buffalo Bisons (Blue Jays)	74	70	.514	13	Marty Brown	537,747	8,273	2004
Lehigh Valley IronPigs (Phillies)	72	72	.500	15	Dave Brundage	613,075	9,016	1995
Columbus Clippers (Indians)	71	73	.493	16	Mike Sarbaugh	635,613	9,212	2010
Louisville Bats (Reds)	69	75	.479	18	Jim Riggleman	581,114	8,185	2001
Scranton/Wilkes-Barre RailRiders (Yankees)	68	76	.472	19	Dave Miley	435,839	6,409	2008
Syracuse Chiefs (Nationals)	66	78	.458	21	Tony Beasley	345,047	5,150	1976
Charlotte Knights (White Sox)	65	78	.455	21½	Joel Skinner	254,834	3,803	1999
Toledo Mudhens (Tigers)	61	83	.424	26	Phil Nevin	560,080	7,779	2006
Gwinnett Braves (Braves)	60	84	.417	27	Randy Ready	323,799	4,762	2007

Semifinals: Durham defeated Indianapolis 3-0 and Pawtucket defeated Rochester 3-2 in best-of-five series. **Finals:** Durham defeated Pawtucket 3-1 in a best-of-five series

CLUB BATTING

	AVG	G	AB	R	H	2B	3B	HR	RBI	BB	SO	SB	OBP	SLG
Durham	.267	144	4811	698	1285	269	40	77	631	554	928	137	.347	.388
Lehigh Valley	.267	144	4771	612	1274	263	36	98	568	395	1147	141	.326	.399
Syracuse	.260	144	4824	600	1256	241	33	114	558	395	1094	123	.320	.395
Norfolk	.258	144	4873	638	1259	250	20	127	594	503	1072	66	.330	.396
Rochester	.258	144	4826	669	1244	236	36	114	624	561	1082	123	.339	.392
Buffalo	.257	144	4618	621	1186	242	28	128	575	492	1043	120	.331	.405
Pawtucket	.256	143	4734	663	1211	235	16	120	618	540	1090	101	.337	.388
Indianapolis	.255	144	4880	622	1243	278	35	105	572	548	1096	153	.334	.391
Scranton/W-B	.254	144	4806	576	1220	240	11	133	539	499	1023	55	.329	.391
Gwinnett	.253	144	4741	541	1198	237	23	89	503	395	993	101	.315	.369
Toledo	.252	144	4985	599	1258	268	17	111	565	493	1173	78	.323	.380
Charlotte	.248	143	4689	589	1163	268	25	89	547	475	1212	98	.325	.373
Columbus	.244	144	4794	577	1172	219	20	101	541	547	1200	115	.325	.362
Louisville	.244	144	4739	523	1156	215	12	94	486	390	1065	144	.307	.354

CLUB PITCHING

	ERA	G	CG	SHO	SV	IP	H	R	ER	HR	BB	SO	AVG
Durham	3.33	144	2	9	44	1262	1102	533	467	95	469	1246	.234
Indianapolis	3.45	144	3	10	44	1298	1144	555	497	90	500	1153	.237
Toledo	3.68	144	3	10	32	1299	1234	611	531	103	483	1080	.250
Columbus	3.70	144	3	9	37	1287	1230	589	529	118	471	1239	.253
Louisville	3.75	144	4	13	38	1259	1185	578	525	120	452	1061	.248
Scranton/W-B	3.80	144	3	12	30	1254	1224	576	529	102	454	1157	.257
Norfolk	3.81	144	3	8	38	1271	1245	606	538	99	464	999	.259
Pawtucket	3.90	143	3	13	37	1255	1201	615	544	126	556	1122	.252
Lehigh Valley	3.95	144	3	12	38	1238	1197	608	544	96	554	998	.256
Gwinnett	4.03	144	2	9	39	1248	1241	640	559	94	571	1041	.261
Syracuse	4.08	144	4	9	34	1251	1297	656	567	104	444	999	.267
Buffalo	4.16	144	6	4	38	1227	1267	646	567	122	435	1046	.267
Charlotte	4.16	143	4	9	30	1238	1242	651	572	111	487	1094	.261
Rochester	4.21	144	12	10	46	1265	1316	664	592	120	447	983	.270

CLUB FIELDING

	PCT	PO	A	E	DP		PCT	PO	A	E	DP
Louisville	.982	3778	1380	97	123	Columbus	.980	3861	1342	108	127
Pawtucket	.982	3765	1375	93	134	Norfolk	.979	3812	1558	113	133
Lehigh Valley	.981	3715	1413	99	127	Charlotte	.978	3714	1398	117	113
Rochester	.981	3795	1435	102	135	Durham	.978	3786	1211	113	113
Scranton/W-B	.981	3761	1357	97	126	Gwinnett	.975	3743	1500	136	137
Toledo	.981	3897	1484	103	133	Indianapolis	.975	3895	1586	143	155
Buffalo	.980	3682	1432	102	137	Syracuse	.974	3755	1579	143	136

INDIVIDUAL BATTING LEADERS *(Minimum 2.7 PA/Team Game)*

	AVG	G	AB	R	H	HR	RBI
Kobernus, Jeff, Syracuse	.318	95	371	59	118	1	36
# Hernandez, Cesar, Lehigh Valley	.309	104	391	59	121	2	34
Hoes, L.J., Norfolk	.304	99	365	62	111	3	40
Guyer, Brandon, Durham	.301	98	356	73	107	7	41
Perez, Eury, Syracuse	.300	96	403	55	121	7	28
* Belnome, Vince, Durham	.300	127	444	77	133	8	67
* Asche, Cody, Lehigh Valley	.295	104	404	52	119	15	68
Rahl, Chris, Syracuse	.293	111	399	53	117	8	42
* Anderson, Leslie, Durham	.292	119	431	52	126	14	74
Fields, Josh, Lehigh Valley	.289	109	377	43	109	4	45

INDIVIDUAL PITCHING LEADERS *(Minimum 0.8 IP/team game)*

Pitcher, Club	W	L	ERA	IP	H	BB	SO
* Johnson, Kris, Indianapolis	10	4	2.39	136	116	43	94
Reynolds, Greg, Louisville	12	3	2.42	156	139	26	97
Martin, J.D., Durham	16	4	2.75	160	168	26	116
* Alvarez, Jose, Toledo	8	6	2.80	129	114	25	115
* Albers, Andrew, Rochester	11	5	2.86	132	124	32	116
Pino, Yohan, Louisville	5	7	3.26	121	114	30	107
Cumpton, Brandon, Indianapolis	6	7	3.32	122	115	44	90
Odorizzi, Jake, Durham	9	6	3.33	124	101	40	124
Wright, Steven, Pawtucket	8	7	3.46	135	129	65	99
Poveda, Omar, Gwinnett	6	7	3.62	164	154	59	124

ALL-STAR TEAM

C: Tony Sanchez, Indianapolis. **1B:** Chris Colabello, Rochester. **2B:** Cesar Hernandez, Lehigh Valley. **3B:** Cody Asche, Lehigh Valley. **SS:** Zach Walters, Syracuse. **OF:** Nick Castellanos, Toledo; Billy Hamilton, Louisville; Joey Terdoslavich, Gwinnett. **DH:** Mauro Gomez, Buffalo. **UT:** Vince Belnome, Durham. **SP:** J.D. Martin, Durham. **RP:** Jairo Ascencio, Norfolk.
Most Valuable Player: Chris Colabello, Rochester. **Most Valuable Pitcher:** J.D. Martin, Durham.
Rookie of the Year: Chris Colabello, Rochester. **Manager of the Year:** Charlie Montoyo, Durham.

DEPARTMENT LEADERS

BATTING

OBP	Colabello, Chris, Rochester	.427
SLG	Colabello, Chris, Rochester	.639
OPS	Colabello, Chris, Rochester	1.066
R	Castellanos, Nick, Toledo	81
H	Hague, Matt, Indianapolis	153
TB	Walters, Zach, Syracuse	252
XBH	Walters, Zach, Syracuse	66
2B	Castellanos, Nick, Toledo	37
	Hague, Matt, Indianapolis	37
3B	Hernandez, Cesar, Lehigh Valley	9
HR	Gomez, Mauro, Buffalo	29
	Walters, Zach, Syracuse	29
RBI	Mejia, Ernesto, Gwinnett	83
SAC	McCoy, Mike, Buffalo	13
BB	Johnson, Dan, Scranton/Norfolk	96
HBP	Loman, Seth, Charlotte	15
SO	Mejia, Ernesto, Gwinnett	152
SB	Hamilton, Billy, Louisville	75
CS	Hamilton, Billy, Louisville	15
AB/SO	Rhymes, Will, Syracuse	15.62

PITCHING

G	Obispo, Wirfin, Gwinnett	54
GS	Rosenbaum, Danny, Syracuse	28
	Stewart, Zach, Charlotte	28
GF	Asencio, Jairo, Norfolk	40
	Carter, Anthony, Pawtucket	40
SV	Asencio, Jairo, Norfolk	28
W	Martin, J.D., Durham	16
L	Three tied at	14
IP	Stewart, Zach, Charlotte	167.1
H	Hill, Shawn, Toledo	191
R	Hill, Shawn, Toledo	105
ER	Hill, Shawn, Toledo	92
HB	Webster, Allen, Pawtucket	16
BB	Oliver, Andy, Indianapolis	112
SO	Oliver, Andy, Indianapolis	138
SO/9	Oliver, Andy, Indianapolis	9.99
SO/9(RP)	Buchter, Ryan, Gwinnett	15
BB/9	Martin, J.D., Durham	1.46
WP	Montgomery, Mike, Durham	15
BK	Three tied at	4
HR	Cloyd, Tyler, Lehigh Valley	21
AVG	Oliver, Andy, Indianapolis	.220

FIELDING

C	PCT	Ashley, Nevin, Louisville	.998
	PO	Pagnozzi, Matt, Gwinnett	611
	A	Butler, Dan, Pawtucket	54
	DP	Ashley, Nevin, Louisville	8
	E	Sanchez, Tony, Indianapolis	14
	PB	Butler, Dan, Pawtucket	20
1B	PCT	Lennerton, Jordan, Toledo	.996
	PO	Hague, Matt, Indianapolis	1213
	A	Mejia, Ernesto, Gwinnett	82
	DP	Hague, Matt, Indianapolis	127
	E	Mejia, Ernesto, Gwinnett	14
2B	PO	Hernandez, Cesar, Lehigh Valley	157
	A	Rhymes, Will, Syracuse	248
	DP	Hernandez, Cesar, Lehigh Valley	62
	E	Pastornicky, Tyler, Gwinnett	11
3B	PCT	Leonard, Joe, Gwinnett	.965
	PO	Leonard, Joe, Gwinnett	72
	A	Goedert, Jared, Indianapolis	221
	DP	LaRoche, Andy, Buffalo	28
	E	Goedert, Jared, Indianapolis	23
SS	PCT	Goins, Ryan, Buffalo	.980
	PO	Beckham, Tim, Durham	162
	A	Walters, Zach, Syracuse	313
	DP	Beckham, Tim, Durham	65
	E	Walters, Zach, Syracuse	31
OF	PCT	Pridie, Jason, Norfolk	.996
	PO	Hamilton, Billy, Louisville	333
	A	Carson, Matt, Columbus	19
	DP	Sands, Jerry, Indianapolis	5
	E	Four tied at	8

MINOR LEAGUES

BY JOHN MANUEL

Baseball has boomed in Omaha, which tore down iconic Johnny Rosenblatt Stadium but built two new ballparks in the last four years. Downtown TD Ameritrade Park houses the College World Series, but suburban Sarpy County has proved a fine home for the Storm Chasers.

Omaha won the Northern Division of the PCL's American Conference with a losing record, rallying past Memphis by a game, then streaked through the PCL playoffs to win the league championship. It's the second championship in three years for the Storm Chasers, who went on to win the Triple-A National Championship.

Omaha's strength all season was pitching, as its 3.91 ERA ranked third in the league. The Chasers swept Oklahoma City in the first round and beat Salt Lake in four games in the best-of-five finals.

Omaha blended young, prospect arms such as hard-throwing Yordano Ventura and lefty Chris Dwyer with veterans like Brian Sanches, a 1999 Royals second-round pick who rejoined the organization this year for the first time since being traded in 2003. Sanches, 35, went 10-3, 3.20 in the regular season, then won a pair of playoff starts, including the clincher against the Bees. Another contributing vet was 36-year-old first baseman Ben Broussard, who hadn't played in the domestic minors since 2009 prior to 2013.

Prospects also played a key role in the PCL in 2013. The two top hitters in the minors opened the season in the PCL, with Rangers shortstop Jurickson Profar in Round Rock and Cardinals outfielder Oscar Taveras in Memphis.

Neither player's season went as hoped. Profar reached the majors in late May but never caught

fire, either in the minors or with Texas. Taveras had a tougher go, injuring his right ankle in May, returning to the lineup in June, before being shut down in July and having surgery in August.

Oklahoma City was the scene for more prospect happenings, as Astros outfielder George Springer joined the RedHawks from Double-A in late June and continued his quest for a 40-homer, 40-stolen base season. The 2011 first-round pick out of Connecticut reached 40 steals but didn't homer in his final eight games, finishing with 37.

Oklahoma City won despite graduating many players to its 110-loss big league team in Houston, such as righthanders Jarred Cosart, Paul Clemens and Brad Peacock. But the team's pitching remained strong thanks to promotions of pitchers such as Jake Buchanan and Asher Wojciechowski, who tossed the league's only one-hitter on July 8.

TOP 20 PROSPECTS

1. Oscar Taveras, of, Memphis (Cardinals)
2. Jurickson Profar, ss, Round Rock (Rangers)
3. George Springer, of, Oklahoma City (Astros)
4. Zack Wheeler, rhp, Las Vegas (Mets)
5. Michael Wacha, rhp, Memphis (Cardinals)
6. Taijuan Walker, rhp, Tacoma (Mariners)
7. Carlos Martinez, rhp, Memphis (Cardinals)
8. Chris Owings, ss, Reno (Diamondbacks)
9. Nick Franklin, 2b/ss, Tacoma (Mariners)
10. Yordano Ventura, rhp, Omaha (Royals)
11. Jarred Cosart, rhp, Oklahoma City (Astros)
12. Sonny Gray, rhp, Sacramento (Athletics)
13. Jonathan Singleton, 1b, Oklahoma City (Astros)
14. Matt Davidson, 3b, Reno (Diamondbacks)
15. Wilmer Flores, 2b/1b, Las Vegas (Mets)
16. Kolten Wong, 2b, Memphis (Cardinals)
17. Tyler Skaggs, lhp, Reno (Diamondbacks)
18. Rafael Montero, rhp, Las Vegas (Mets)
19. Jonathan Villar, ss, Oklahoma City (Astros)
20. Michael Choice, of, Sacramento (Athletics)

OVERALL STANDINGS

Team (Organization)	W	L	PCT	GB	Manager(s)	Attendance	Average	Last Pennant
Oklahoma City RedHawks(Astros)	82	62	.569	—	Tony DeFrancesco	400,025	5,797	1965
Las Vegas 51s (Mets)	81	63	.563	1	Wally Backman	328,266	4,690	1998
Sacramento River Cats (Athletics)	79	65	.549	3	Steve Scarsone	607,329	8,435	2008
Salt Lake Bees (Angels)	78	66	.542	4	Keith Johnson	531,221	7,482	1979
Tucson Padres (Padres)	77	67	.535	5	Pat Murphy	200,077	2,818	2006
Albuquerque Isotopes (Dodgers)	76	68	.528	6	Lorenzo Bundy	567,568	7,994	1994
Tacoma Rainiers (Mariners)	76	68	.528	6	Daren Brown/John Stearns	320,080	4,446	2010
Round Rock Express (Rangers)	73	71	.507	9	Bobby Jones	589,042	8,181	Never
New Orleans Zephyrs (Marlins)	72	72	.500	10	Ron Hassey	344,998	4,929	2001
Omaha Storm Chasers (Royals)	70	74	.486	12	Mike Jirschele	390,957	5,666	2013
Memphis Redbirds (Cardinals)	69	75	.479	13	Ron Warner	498,362	7,223	2009
Fresno Grizzlies (Giants)	68	75	.476	13 1/2	Bob Mariano	487,536	6,771	Never
Colorado Springs Sky Sox (Rockies)	67	76	.469	14 1/2	Glenallen Hill	326,374	5,181	1995
Iowa Cubs (Cubs)	66	78	.458	16	Marty Pevey	467,481	6,977	Never
Reno Aces (Diamondbacks)	60	84	.417	22	Brett Butler	349,364	4,921	2012
Nashville Sounds (Brewers)	57	87	.396	25	Mike Guerrero	355,003	5,071	2005

Semifinals: Omaha defeated Oklahoma City 3-0 and Salt Lake City defeated Las Vegas 3-1 in best-of-five series. **Finals:** Omaha defeated Salt Lake City 3-1 in a best-of-five series.

CLUB BATTING

	AVG	G	AB	R	H	2B	3B	HR	RBI	BB	SO	SB	OBP	SLG
Las Vegas	.287	144	4934	828	1418	311	47	148	764	548	1061	73	.362	.459
Salt Lake	.287	144	4949	809	1421	285	47	136	756	562	1030	138	.362	.446
Colorado Springs	.284	143	4925	747	1400	283	71	125	703	416	1106	101	.343	.447
Reno	.283	144	5062	757	1432	277	42	124	700	439	1071	109	.342	.429
Tucson	.283	144	4914	723	1391	292	38	97	669	494	1003	81	.352	.417
Fresno	.273	143	4978	656	1358	278	50	114	627	431	1115	96	.334	.417
Sacramento	.272	144	4920	773	1336	276	27	129	720	643	1098	58	.359	.417
Albuquerque	.271	144	4898	746	1325	250	57	110	695	552	1125	165	.351	.412
Oklahoma City	.271	144	4751	677	1289	234	39	105	612	530	985	172	.347	.403
Tacoma	.269	144	5031	762	1352	268	40	146	704	547	1291	105	.343	.425
Memphis	.265	144	4790	634	1267	244	27	116	600	508	971	104	.340	.399
Omaha	.264	144	4807	621	1267	201	30	110	575	486	887	125	.335	.387
Round Rock	.263	144	4850	686	1277	257	21	131	635	554	1076	102	.341	.406
Nashville	.255	144	4777	589	1216	237	31	119	550	465	1150	88	.324	.392
Iowa	.250	144	4786	565	1197	234	31	126	534	468	1079	106	.320	.391
New Orleans	.248	144	4866	546	1205	245	27	105	499	427	1206	83	.313	.374

CLUB PITCHING

	ERA	G	CG	SHO	SV	IP	H	R	ER	HR	BB	SO	AVG
New Orleans	3.54	144	1	12	44	1283	1227	578	505	116	504	1074	.253
Memphis	3.91	144	2	15	32	1257	1204	611	546	104	474	1038	.252
Omaha	3.91	144	1	8	33	1254	1240	622	545	103	537	1183	.258
Albuquerque	4.05	144	2	5	38	1260	1291	638	567	130	586	1135	.269
Round Rock	4.06	144	1	9	45	1270	1244	639	573	114	470	1032	.258
Oklahoma City	4.21	144	4	7	42	1254	1219	645	586	105	530	1036	.256
Iowa	4.25	144	3	11	42	1259	1259	658	595	112	504	1088	.261
Sacramento	4.29	144	2	4	47	1266	1350	683	603	115	414	1131	.272
Tacoma	4.50	144	2	11	40	1264	1363	711	646	140	461	1145	.271
Nashville	4.51	144	4	7	30	1250	1257	717	626	116	582	1059	.261
Tucson	4.56	144	0	4	44	1256	1429	703	636	112	439	1103	.288
Fresno	4.62	143	3	4	45	1274	1292	725	654	141	516	1079	.263
Las Vegas	4.65	144	2	5	33	1257	1420	728	649	124	498	1049	.287
Reno	5.05	144	2	7	19	1264	1402	793	709	129	507	1083	.283
Colorado Springs	5.29	143	3	6	26	1240	1507	836	729	120	507	949	.302
Salt Lake	5.37	144	0	5	39	1260	1447	832	752	160	541	1070	.288

CLUB FIELDING

	PCT	PO	A	E	DP		PCT	PO	A	E	DP
New Orleans	.981	3850	1454	105	135	Las Vegas	.977	3770	1383	120	148
Oklahoma City	.981	3762	1501	102	140	Reno	.977	3793	1543	128	133
Tucson	.981	3767	1466	100	119	Salt Lake	.977	3779	1346	121	130
Memphis	.980	3771	1435	104	96	Tacoma	.977	3873	1366	121	125
Albuquerque	.979	3779	1501	115	161	Omaha	.976	3762	1295	126	129
Colorado Springs	.978	3721	1545	119	153	Sacramento	.976	3797	1328	127	115
Iowa	.978	3778	1442	120	122	Nashville	.974	3749	1448	139	126
Round Rock	.978	3810	1506	118	143	Fresno	.972	3822	1397	152	113

INDIVIDUAL BATTING LEADERS (Minimum 2.7 PA/Team Game)

Batter, Club	AVG	G	AB	R	H	HR	RBI
* Anna, Dean, Tucson	.331	132	498	90	165	9	73
Owings, Chris, Reno	.330	125	546	104	180	12	81
* Tanaka, Kensuke, Fresno	.329	107	343	54	113	1	32
* Navarro, Efren, Salt Lake	.324	134	513	83	166	7	81
Green, Grant, Sacramento	.323	93	402	68	130	11	53
Flores, Wilmer, Las Vegas	.321	107	424	69	136	15	86
Campbell, Eric, Las Vegas	.314	120	341	61	107	8	66
Almonte, Abe, Tacoma	.314	94	338	63	106	11	50
* Snyder, Brad, Reno	.311	116	411	77	128	12	60
Culberson, Charlie, Colorado Springs	.310	97	397	63	123	14	64

INDIVIDUAL PITCHING LEADERS (Minimum 0.8 IP/team game)

Pitcher, Club	W	L	ERA	IP	H	BB	SO
* Flynn, Brian, New Orleans	6	11	2.80	138	127	40	122
Hellweg, Johnny, Nashville	12	5	3.22	126	103	81	89
* Rusin, Chris, Iowa	8	7	3.35	121	113	27	69
Gray, Sonny, Sacramento	10	7	3.42	118	117	39	118
Castro, Angel, Albuquerque	8	5	3.48	116	123	37	91
* Dwyer, Chris, Omaha	10	11	3.55	160	140	72	112
Wojciechowski, Asher, Oklahoma City	9	7	3.56	134	116	44	104
* Feierabend, Ryan, Round Rock	6	5	3.66	120	128	33	79
Palmer, Matt, Albuquerque	6	8	3.84	134	127	56	131
* Additon, Nick, Memphis	9	7	4.10	132	117	38	117

ALL-STAR TEAM

C: Stephen Vogt, Sacramento. **1B:** Efren Navarro, Salt Lake. **2B:** Dean Anna, Tucson. **3B:** Ryan Wheeler, Colorado Springs. **SS:** Chris Owings, Reno. **OF:** Nick Buss, Albuquerque; Michael Choice, Sacramento; Corey Dickerson, Colorado Springs. **DH:** Brock Peterson, Memphis. **RHP:** Johnny Hellweg, Nashville. **LHP:** Brian Flynn, New Orleans. **RP:** Chris Hatcher, New Orleans.
Most Valuable Player: Chris Owings, Reno. **Pitcher of the Year:** Johnny Hellweg, Nashville.
Rookie of the Year: Chris Owings, Reno. **Manager of the Year:** Keith Johnson, Salt Lake

DEPARTMENT LEADERS

BATTING

OBP	Campbell, Eric, Las Vegas	.435
SLG	Dickerson, Corey, Col. Springs	.632
OPS	Campbell, Eric, Las Vegas	.910
R	Owings, Chris, Reno	104
H	Owings, Chris, Reno	180
TB	Owings, Chris, Reno	263
XBH	Paulsen, Ben, Colorado Springs	60
2B	Navarro, Efren, Salt Lake	39
3B	Dickerson, Corey, Colorado Springs	14
HR	Peterson, Brock, Memphis	25
RBI	Buss, Nick, Albuquerque	100
SAC	Colon, Christian, Omaha	15
BB	Barton, Daric, Sacramento	87
HBP	Castellanos, Alex, Albuquerque	12
SO	Peguero, Carlos, Tacoma	156
SB	Gordon, Dee, Albuquerque	49
CS	Beltre, Engel, Round Rock	12
	Hernandez, Gorkys, N. Orleans, Omaha	12
AB/SO	Falu, Irving, Omaha	9.96

PITCHING

G	Hampson, Justin, Las Vegas	64
GS	Shoemaker, Matt, Salt Lake	29
GF	Hatcher, Chris, New Orleans	55
SV	Hatcher, Chris, New Orleans	33
W	Billings, Bruce, Sacramento	13
L	Kroenke, Zach, Nashville	16
IP	Shoemaker, Matt, Salt Lake	184.1
H	Shoemaker, Matt, Salt Lake	212
R	Werner, Andrew, Sacramento	110
ER	Werner, Andrew, Sacramento	106
HB	Hellweg, Johnny, Nashville	14
BB	Hellweg, Johnny, Nashville	81
SO	Shoemaker, Matt, Salt Lake	160
SO/9	Gray, Sonny, Sacramento	8.97
SO/9(RP)	Moran, Brian, Tacoma	12.2
BB/9	Shoemaker, Matt, Salt Lake	1.42
WP	Adcock, Nate, Omaha, Reno	19
BK	16 tied at	2
HR	Enright, Barry, Salt Lake	30
AVG	Hellweg, Johnny, Nashville	.228

FIELDING

C	PCT	Williams, Jackson, Fresno	.995
	PO	Boscan, J.C., Iowa	566
	A	Perez, Carlos, Oklahoma City	63
	DP	Rivera, Rene, Tucson	10
	E	Monell, Johnny, Fresno	13
	PB	Easley, Ed, Reno	12
1B	PCT	Navarro, Efren, Salt Lake	.995
	PO	Navarro, Efren, Salt Lake	1061
	A	Paulsen, Ben, Colorado Springs	87
	DP	Paulsen, Ben, Colorado Springs	116
	E	Morris, Hunter, Nashville	9
2B	PCT	Wong, Kolten, Memphis	.974
	PO	Wong, Kolten, Memphis	195
	A	Wong, Kolten, Memphis	296
	DP	Solarte, Yangervis, Round Rock	60
	E	Tanaka, Kensuke, Fresno	15
3B	PCT	Curtis, Jermaine, Memphis	.948
	PO	Parker, Stephen, Nashville	73
	A	Olt, Mike, Round Rock, Iowa	196
	DP	Parker, Stephen, Nashville	20
	E	Olt, Mike, Round Rock, Iowa	23
SS	PCT	Owings, Chris, Reno	.943
	PO	Davis, Blake, Nashville	138
	A	Owings, Chris, Reno	339
	DP	Owings, Chris, Reno	71
	E	Owings, Chris, Reno	28
OF	PCT	Lin, Che-Hsuan, Oklahoma City	.996
	PO	Brown, Gary, Fresno	324
	A	Brown, Gary, Fresno	17
	DP	Decker, Jaff, Tucson	6
	E	Wheeler, Tim, Colorado Springs	10

MINOR LEAGUES

BY JOSH NORRIS

After falling just shy against Akron a year prior, the Trenton Thunder sealed their third Eastern League championship with authority in 2013.

Trenton, infused by a late-season boost of prospects that included catcher Gary Sanchez, center fielder Mason Williams and righty Bryan Mitchell, as well as the return from the disabled list of right fielder Tyler Austin, swept first through league wins leader Binghamton and then through Western Division champ Harrisburg.

The title was the third in seven seasons for manager Tony Franklin, the longest-tenured skipper in franchise history. Franklin has taken the team to the postseason in five of those years.

"It never gets old," Franklin told the Trentonian after the Thunder's decisive 11-4 win over the Senators. "I can't believe we (swept the series)."

The title came despite underwhelming seasons from outfielders Austin, Slade Heathcott and Ramon Flores, who combined for just 20 home runs in 1,430 plate appearances.

Mets outfielder Allan Dykstra, 26, put together a .274/.436/.503 average with 21 homers and 82 RBIs, good enough to earn league MVP honors.

Back from a litany of injuries, Portland righty Anthony Ranaudo took home the pitcher of the year award after posting an 8-4, 2.95 record with 106 strikeouts and 40 walks in 110 innings.

Altoona outfielder and Pirates outfield prospect Alex Dickerson won the rookie of the year with a .288/.337/.494 line with 17 homers and 68 RBIs.

Ranaudo, who pitched for Pawtucket in the International League finals, was the lone member of the trio to crack the league's Top 20. Ranaudo's teammate Xander Bogaerts, even at just 20 years old, stood out in his brief time with the Sea Dogs as the league's top talent. Evaluators raved about his package of hitting, defense and burgeoning

TOP 20 PROSPECTS

1. Xander Bogaerts, ss, Portland (Red Sox)
2. Miguel Sano, 3b, New Britain (Twins)
3. Noah Syndergaard, rhp, Binghamton (Mets)
4. Maikel Franco, 3b, Reading (Phillies)
5. Alex Meyer, rhp, New Britain (Twins)
6. Jameson Taillon, rhp, Altoona (Pirates)
7. Gregory Polanco, of, Altoona (Pirates)
8. Anthony Rendon, 3b, Harrisburg (Nationals)
9. Eduardo Rodriguez, lhp, Bowie (Orioles)
10. Marcus Stroman, rhp, New Hampshire (Blue Jays)
11. Jesse Biddle, lhp, Reading (Phillies)
12. Taylor Jordan, rhp, Harrisburg (Nationals)
13. Rafael Montero, rhp, Binghamton (Mets)
14. Garin Cecchini, 3b, Portland (Red Sox)
15. Nick Kingham, rhp, Altoona (Pirates)
16. Anthony Ranaudo, rhp, Portland (Red Sox)
17. Jose Ramirez, 2b/ss, Akron (Indians)
18. J.R. Murphy, c, Trenton (Yankees)
19. Brandon Workman, rhp, Portland (Red Sox)
20. Josmil Pinto, c, New Britain (Twins)

power, and the Red Sox showed their faith in the kid by adding him to their playoff roster as they secured their third World Series title since 2004.

New Britain third baseman Miguel Sano and his 19 homers in a half-season with the Rock Cats wasn't far behind. The same goes for Reading third sacker Maikel Franco, who socked 17 bombs with the Fightin Phils.

Binghamton righty Noah Syndergaard paced the hurlers and started Game One of the playoffs for the B-Mets, which won a franchise-best 86 games before bowing to Trenton in three games in the Division Series.

Akron made headlines after the season when the Indians affiliate announced that it is dropping its longtime Aeros moniker and will now be called the RubberDucks. The team made the change following its first season under owner Ken Babby, a former Washington Post business executive who ramped up the team's promotions and customer service to see average attendance increase 11.9 percent to 4,221.

OVERALL STANDINGS

Team (Organization)	W	L	PCT	GB	Manager(s)	Attendance	Average	Last Pennant
Binghamton Mets (Mets)	86	55	.610	—	Pedro Lopez	185,093	2,804	1994
Harrisburg Senators (Nationals)	77	65	.542	9 ½	Matt LeCroy	284,361	4,121	1999
Erie Seawolves (Tigers)	76	66	.535	10 ½	Chris Cron	206,780	3,086	Never
Trenton Thunder (Yankees)	74	67	.525	12	Tony Franklin	360,010	5,373	2013
Bowie Baysox (Orioles)	71	71	.500	15 ½	Gary Kendall	252,593	3,715	Never
Richmond Flying Squirrels (Giants)	70	72	.493	16 ½	Dave Machemer	434,769	6,689	2002
New Hampshire Fisher Cats (Blue Jays)	68	72	.486	17 ½	Gary Allenson	353,639	5,125	2011
Akron Aeros (Indians)	68	73	.482	18	Edwin Rodriguez	295,459	4,221	2012
Portland Sea Dogs (Red Sox)	68	73	.482	18	Kevin Boles	341,420	5,096	2006
New Britain Rock Cats (Twins)	66	76	.465	20 ½	Jeff Smith	307,097	4,653	2001
Altoona Curve (Pirates)	63	79	.444	23 ½	Carlos Garcia	286,227	4,209	2010
Reading Fightin Phils (Phillies)	62	80	.437	24 ½	Dusty Wathan	436,134	6,321	2001

Semifinals: Trenton defeated Binghamton 3-0 and Harrisburg defeated Erie 3-1 in best-of-five series. **Finals:** Trenton defeated Harrisburg 3-0 in a best-of-five series.

CLUB BATTING

	AVG	G	AB	R	H	2B	3B	HR	RBI	BB	SO	SB	OBP	SLG
Bowie	.274	142	4765	697	1305	267	20	105	646	518	1001	91	.347	.404
Akron	.268	141	4896	654	1314	255	41	96	593	466	909	127	.334	.396
Erie	.259	142	4714	621	1220	270	31	80	571	463	1103	122	.332	.380
New Hampshire	.255	140	4759	640	1214	272	22	126	599	517	1010	81	.332	.401
New Britain	.254	142	4716	637	1200	248	35	112	595	456	1074	83	.327	.393
Binghamton	.253	141	4545	668	1152	239	25	115	604	542	1161	132	.340	.393
Portland	.253	141	4690	640	1187	250	42	91	578	519	1088	149	.333	.383
Altoona	.252	142	4591	569	1157	218	44	94	520	437	1026	146	.323	.380
Richmond	.252	142	4628	611	1164	243	19	109	577	510	1115	77	.333	.383
Reading	.249	142	4692	585	1170	211	42	132	524	344	1118	111	.308	.397
Trenton	.245	141	4681	609	1147	235	28	88	558	494	1117	77	.324	.364
Harrisburg	.242	142	4585	602	1110	221	35	101	542	521	1090	89	.324	.372

CLUB PITCHING

	ERA	G	CG	SHO	SV	IP	H	R	ER	HR	BB	SO	AVG
Harrisburg	3.43	142	9	15	42	1237	1139	533	471	101	391	1168	.243
Binghamton	3.53	141	3	13	44	1225	1136	560	481	93	419	1185	.247
Trenton	3.63	141	2	9	35	1226	1137	577	494	85	597	1151	.247
Portland	3.90	141	5	8	34	1235	1193	634	535	106	471	1126	.254
Altoona	3.92	142	2	10	33	1213	1164	614	528	97	480	975	.252
Bowie	3.96	142	6	9	42	1227	1183	620	540	98	467	1099	.253
Erie	4.08	142	7	5	39	1228	1226	630	557	141	445	868	.262
New Britain	4.25	142	8	12	36	1237	1282	673	584	105	452	1000	.266
New Hampshire	4.25	140	4	9	32	1241	1234	669	586	102	462	1150	.257
Akron	4.31	141	0	6	34	1260	1251	687	603	108	480	1150	.260
Richmond	4.32	142	1	15	41	1219	1221	661	585	91	559	955	.263
Reading	4.46	142	3	4	32	1222	1174	675	605	122	564	985	.253

CLUB FIELDING

	PCT	PO	A	E	DP		PCT	PO	A	E	DP
Binghamton	.978	3676	1272	109	111	Bowie	.976	3682	1284	122	111
Akron	.977	3779	1449	124	150	Erie	.976	3683	1408	123	152
Altoona	.977	3638	1440	121	115	Harrisburg	.976	3711	1337	123	113
Portland	.977	3704	1386	122	126	New Hampshire	.975	3722	1396	132	113
Reading	.977	3666	1339	120	113	New Britain	.974	3710	1358	135	119
Richmond	.977	3657	1484	122	131	Trenton	.973	3677	1359	138	115

INDIVIDUAL BATTING LEADERS (Minimum 2.7 PA/Team Game)

Batter, Club	AVG	G	AB	R	H	HR	RBI
Minicozzi, Mark, Richmond	.309	128	443	75	137	10	66
Pinto, Josmil, New Britain	.308	107	386	59	119	14	68
Joseph, Caleb, Bowie	.297	135	518	74	154	22	97
# Santana, Danny, New Britain	.295	131	539	66	159	2	45
Herrera, Javier, Richmond	.293	131	481	70	141	16	74
* Hudson, Kyle, Bowie	.292	103	353	66	103	0	33
Vazquez, Christian, Portland	.289	96	342	48	99	5	48
* Dickerson, Alex, Altoona	.288	126	451	61	130	17	68
* Moncrief, Carlos, Akron	.284	129	489	77	139	17	75
* Fields, Daniel, Erie	.282	118	457	71	129	10	58

INDIVIDUAL PITCHING LEADERS (Minimum 0.8 IP/team game)

Pitcher, Club	W	L	ERA	IP	H	BB	SO
Karns, Nate, Harrisburg	10	6	3.26	133	108	48	155
Wright, Mike, Bowie	11	3	3.26	144	152	39	136
Sadler, Casey, Altoona	11	7	3.31	130	116	42	67
* Packer, Matt, Akron	12	9	3.33	154	172	44	119
Saupold, Warwick, Erie	7	6	3.42	129	125	51	82
Couch, Keith, Portland	11	3	3.47	130	132	43	92
Bromberg, David, Altoona	6	12	3.51	136	120	52	127
Treinen, Blake, Harrisburg	6	7	3.64	119	125	33	86
* Biddle, Jesse, Reading	5	14	3.64	138	104	82	154
* Snodgrass, Jack, Richmond	12	4	3.70	141	125	39	81

ALL-STAR TEAM

C: Josmil Pinto, New Britain. **1B:** Allan Dykstra, Binghamton. **2B:** Hernan Perez, Erie. **3B:** Mark Minicozzi, Richmond. **SS:** Danny Santana, New Britain. **OF:** Alex Dickerson, Altoona; Javier Herrera, Richmond; Carlos Moncrief, Akron. **DH:** Jesus Aguilar, Akron. **UT:** Caleb Joseph, Bowie. **RHP:** Anthony Ranaudo, Portland. **LHP:** Jack Snodgrass, Richmond. **RP:** Jeff Walters, Binghamton.
Most Valuable Player: Allan Dykstra, Binghamton. **Pitcher of the Year:** Anthony Ranaudo, Portland. **Rookie of the Year:** Alex Dickerson, Altoona. **Manager of the Year:** Pedro Lopez, Binghamton.

DEPARTMENT LEADERS

BATTING

OBP	Dykstra, Allan, Binghamton	.436
SLG	Puello, Cesar, Binghamton	.547
OPS	Dykstra, Allan, Binghamton	.938
R	Muno, Daniel, Binghamton	86
H	Santana, Danny, New Britain	160
TB	Joseph, Caleb, Bowie	256
XBH	Rodriguez, Reynaldo, New Britain	58
2B	Herrera, Javier, Richmond	37
3B	Goodwin, Brian, Harrisburg	11
HR	Three tied at	23
RBI	Aguilar, Jesus, Akron	105
SAC	Santana, Danny, New Britain	11
BB	Dykstra, Allan, Binghamton	102
HBP	Cartwright, Albert, Reading	16
	Puello, Cesar, Binghamton	16
SO	Robbins, James, Erie	171
SB	Ramirez, Jose, Akron	38
CS	Ramirez, Jose, Akron	16
AB/SO	Ramirez, Jose, Akron	11.76

PITCHING

G	Flores, Jose, Akron	59
GS	Three tied at	27
GF	Flores, Jose, Akron	53
SV	Walters, Jeff, Binghamton	38
W	Three tied at	12
L	Biddle, Jesse, Reading	14
	Walden, Marcus, New Hampshire	14
IP	Walden, Marcus, New Hampshire	162.1
H	Walden, Marcus, New Hampshire	184
R	Jones, Devin, Bowie	95
ER	McGuire, Deck, New Hampshire	85
HB	Turley, Nik, Trenton	16
BB	Biddle, Jesse, Reading	82
SO	May, Trevor, New Britain	159
SO/9	Karns, Nathan, Harrisburg	10.52
SO/9(RP)	Flores, Jose, Akron	11.8
BB/9	Dean, Pat, New Britain	1.22
WP	Gamboa, Eddie, Bowie	15
BK	Turley, Nik, Trenton	6
HR	Larez, Victor, Erie	25
AVG	Biddle, Jesse, Reading	.210

FIELDING

C	PCT	Forsythe, Blake, Binghamton	.999
	PO	Vazquez, Christian, Portland	781
	A	Lowery, Jake, Akron	80
		Vazquez, Christian, Portland	80
	DP	Paulino, Carlos, Altoona	9
		Ward, Brian, Bowie	9
	E	Vazquez, Christian, Portland	10
	PB	Vazquez, Christian, Portland	23
1B	PCT	Murphy, Jim, Reading	.992
	PO	Robbins, James, Erie	1078
	A	Aguilar, Jesus, Akron	84
	DP	Robbins, James, Erie	131
	E	Aguilar, Jesus, Akron	14
2B	PCT	Panik, Joe, Richmond	.987
	PO	Panik, Joe, Richmond	234
	A	Cunningham, Jarek, Altoona	333
	DP	Panik, Joe, Richmond	73
	E	Pirela, Jose, Trenton	16
3B	PCT	Gaynor, Wade, Erie	.967
	PO	Gaynor, Wade, Erie	95
	A	Gaynor, Wade, Erie	227
	DP	Santos, Adalberto, Altoona	26
	E	Santos, Adalberto, Altoona	32
SS	PCT	Tovar, Wilfredo, Binghamton	.981
	PO	Santana, Danny, New Britain	204
	A	Santana, Danny, New Britain	357
	DP	Suarez, Eugenio, Erie	88
	E	Santana, Danny, New Britain	32
OF	PCT	Collier, Zach, Reading	.996
	PO	Holt, Tyler, Akron	302
	A	Ortiz, Daniel, New Britain	17
	DP	Moncrief, Carlos, Akron	8
	E	Thomas, Tony, Portland	11

MINOR LEAGUES

MINOR LEAGUES

BY MATT EDDY

Fans of the Double-A Southern League saw more big leaguers in 2013 than any circuit this side of the majors.

Not only did Chattanooga right fielder Yasiel Puig (Dodgers) and Mississippi lefthander Alex Wood (Braves) matriculate from the SL to the heat of the National League pennant race over Memorial Day weekend, but the Marlins promoted six players directly from Jacksonville to Miami.

That Marlins list includes not only big-time outfield prospects Jake Marisnick, Marcell Ozuna and Christian Yelich, but also second baseman Derek Dietrich and relievers Arquimedes Caminero and Edgar Olmos.

The White Sox raided the Birmingham roster to shuttle righthanders Erik Johnson and Daniel Webb and middle infielder Marcus Semien to Triple-A Charlotte during the summer and then to Chicago in September. Semien, a sixth-round pick from California in 2011, led the SL in on-base percentage (.420), ranked second in slugging (.483) and walks (84) and third in the batting race (.290). He led the minors with 110 runs scored and won the SL's MVP award.

The Mariners didn't wait until September to accelerate their rebuild, calling up shortstop Brad Miller in late June and righthander Taijuan Walker at the end of August after both players made stopovers at Triple-A Tacoma.

The Barons won the league title despite losing Johnson, Semien, et al., to in-season promotions, vanquishing two-time defending champion Mobile. The Baybears scored two runs in the top of the first inning of the deciding fifth game of the league finals, yet the Diamondbacks affiliate failed to score again and thus failed—narrowly—to three-peat as SL champions.

Birmingham took home the SL crown, its first since 2002, with a 4-2 win in Game Five. Second baseman Micah Johnson, who led the minors with 84 steals this season, went 2-for-4 in the deciding game with a leadoff home run and an RBI single in

the second inning. He went 14-for-38 (.368) with 12 runs scored, seven walks and seven steals in 10 games to sew up MVP honors for the playoffs.

The Barons, who went 33-37 in the second half, required the full five games to advance in both rounds of playoffs, despite jumping out to two-games-to-none leads both times. They dispatched Tennessee (Cubs) in round one, where in the other bracket Mobile trounced Mississippi (Braves), winning Game Four by a score of 15-0.

TOP 20 PROSPECTS

1. Yasiel Puig, of, Chattanooga (Dodgers)
2. Archie Bradley, rhp, Mobile (Diamondbacks)
3. Javier Baez, ss, Tennessee (Cubs)
4. Taijuan Walker, rhp, Jackson (Mariners)
5. Chistian Yelich, of, Jacksonville (Marlins)
6. Alex Wood, lhp, Mississippi (Braves)
7. Joc Pederson, of, Chattanooga (Dodgers)
8. Christian Bethencourt, c, Mississippi (Braves)
9. Arismendy Alcantara, ss/2b, Tennessee (Cubs)
10. Jake Marisnick, of, Jacksonville (Marlins)
11. Erik Johnson, rhp, Birmingham (White Sox)
12. Enny Romero, lhp, Montgomery (Rays)
13. Brad Miller, ss, Jackson (Mariners)
14. Marcus Semien, ss/2b, Birmingham (White Sox)
15. Zach Lee, rhp, Chattanooga (Dodgers)
16. Tommy La Stella, 2b, Mississippi (Braves)
17. Julio Morban, of, Jackson (Mariners)
18. Jimmy Nelson, rhp, Huntsville (Brewers)
19. Edward Salcedo, 3b, Mississippi (Braves)
20. Yorman Rodriguez, Pensacola (Reds)

STANDINGS: SPLIT SEASON

FIRST HALF

NORTH	W	L	PCT	GB
Birm.	44	26	.629	—
Chatt.	35	35	.500	9
Tennessee	34	35	.493	9.5
Jackson	29	37	.439	13
Huntsville	29	39	.426	14

SOUTH	W	L	PCT	GB
Mobile	39	30	.565	—
Mississippi	38	32	.543	1.5
Mont.	37	33	.529	2.5
Jacksonville	34	33	.507	4
Pensacola	25	44	.362	14

SECOND HALF

NORTH	W	L	PCT	GB
Tennessee	42	27	.609	—
Jackson	33	36	.478	9
Birm.	33	37	.471	9.5
Huntsville	30	40	.429	12.5
Chatt.	24	45	.348	18

SOUTH	W	L	PCT	GB
Mobile	40	30	.571	—
Jacksonville	39	30	.565	0.5
Mississippi	38	31	.551	1.5
Pensacola	34	35	.493	5.5
Mont.	34	36	.486	6

Playoffs—Semifinals: Birmingham defeated Tennessee 3-2, Mobile defeated Mississippi 3-1 in best-of-five series. **Finals:** Birmingham defeated Mobile 3-2 in best-of-five series.

OVERALL STANDINGS

Team (Organization)	W	L	PCT	GB	Manager	Attendance	Average	Last Pennant
Mobile BayBears (Diamondbacks)	79	60	.568	—	Andy Green	149,675	2,339	2012
Tennessee Smokies (Cubs)	76	62	.551	2½	Buddy Bailey	244,984	3,828	2004
Birmingham Barons (White Sox)	77	63	.550	2½	Julio Vinas	396,820	5,669	2013
Mississippi Braves (Braves)	76	63	.547	3	Aaron Holbert	200,268	2,861	2008
Jacksonville Suns (Marlins)	73	63	.537	4½	Andy Barkett	295,258	4,407	2010
Montgomery Biscuits (Rays)	71	69	.507	8½	Billy Gardner	258,532	3,917	2007
Jackson Generals (Mariners)	62	73	.459	15	Jim Pankovits	119,202	1,954	2000
Huntsville Stars (Brewers)	59	79	.428	19½	Darnell Coles	123,904	1,877	2001
Pensacola Blue Wahoos (Reds)	59	79	.428	19½	Delino DeShields	307,094	4,653	Never
Chattanooga Lookouts (Dodgers)	59	80	.424	20	Jody Reed	220,854	3,398	1998

CLUB BATTING

	AVG	G	AB	R	H	2B	3B	HR	RBI	BB	SO	SB	OBP	SLG
Tennessee	.258	138	4611	618	1190	279	32	118	573	451	1010	120	.328	.409
Mobile	.254	139	4528	563	1150	203	31	65	509	466	966	163	.327	.356
Mississippi	.251	139	4574	556	1150	217	19	79	502	455	901	137	.321	.359
Montgomery	.246	140	4571	577	1123	214	43	82	522	459	913	88	.323	.365
Birmingham	.245	140	4521	619	1107	209	25	103	571	598	1030	183	.338	.370
Jackson	.242	135	4399	525	1065	190	41	91	481	417	1064	157	.312	.366
Jacksonville	.235	136	4333	552	1019	197	35	104	515	471	1035	77	.320	.369
Pensacola	.234	138	4508	461	1055	188	22	73	431	444	970	83	.310	.334
Huntsville	.233	138	4372	484	1017	176	18	94	446	491	1068	60	.315	.346
Chattanooga	.230	139	4413	479	1015	210	21	101	446	447	995	100	.306	.356

CLUB PITCHING

	ERA	G	CG	SHO	SV	IP	H	R	ER	HR	BB	SO	AVG
Mobile	3.03	139	6	9	35	1210	1026	478	407	88	475	960	.232
Mississippi	3.07	139	1	14	31	1229	1128	489	420	60	454	1080	.244
Jacksonville	3.29	136	8	13	36	1166	1073	499	427	79	329	1003	.244
Jackson	3.41	135	4	9	27	1166	1035	506	442	105	432	983	.240
Tennessee	3.46	138	4	12	37	1217	1065	545	468	83	528	992	.236
Birmingham	3.55	140	6	15	34	1218	1083	563	480	76	427	970	.238
Pensacola	3.61	138	1	12	33	1223	1139	544	491	103	481	993	.251
Chattanooga	3.81	139	3	14	32	1198	1090	555	507	85	498	1118	.245
Huntsville	4.06	138	5	12	35	1179	1077	614	532	117	565	921	.246
Montgomery	4.11	140	2	14	35	1222	1175	641	558	114	510	932	.253

CLUB FIELDING

	PCT	PO	A	E	DP		PCT	PO	A	E	DP
Mobile	.982	3631	1480	95	134	Mississippi	.976	3688	1466	125	111
Chattanooga	.981	3594	1478	100	140	Tennessee	.976	3652	1536	130	121
Pensacola	.978	3668	1334	110	120	Jacksonville	.975	3499	1344	124	96
Jackson	.977	3497	1324	113	117	Montgomery	.975	3667	1395	132	104
Huntsville	.976	3536	1438	122	131	Birmingham	.973	3654	1393	139	119

INDIVIDUAL BATTING LEADERS *(Minimum 2.7 PA/Team Game)*

Batter, Club	AVG	G	AB	R	H	HR	RBI
* Kiermaier, Kevin, Montgomery	.310	97	371	65	115	5	28
Greene, Justin, Mobile	.308	117	380	75	117	1	30
Semien, Marcus, Birmingham	.290	105	393	90	114	15	49
* Black, Dan, Birmingham	.290	133	449	70	130	17	83
Martinez, Jose, Mississippi	.285	123	431	46	123	6	39
* Silva, Rubi, Tennessee	.284	126	468	56	133	15	52
# Pedroza, Jaime, Mississippi	.281	117	370	48	104	4	44
Szczur, Matt, Tennessee	.279	128	512	78	143	3	44
* Inciarte, Ender, Mobile	.279	128	473	69	132	5	25
* Pederson, Joc, Chattanooga	.278	123	439	81	122	22	58

INDIVIDUAL PITCHING LEADERS *(Minimum 0.8 IP/team game)*

Pitcher, Club	W	L	ERA	IP	H	BB	SO
Hendricks, Kyle, Tennessee	10	3	1.85	126	107	26	101
Bradley, Archie, Mobile	12	5	1.97	123	93	59	119
Schlosser, Gus, Mississippi	7	6	2.39	135	118	44	101
* Holmberg, David, Mobile	5	8	2.75	157	137	50	116
* Romero, Enny, Montgomery	11	7	2.76	140	110	73	110
* Chafin, Andrew, Mobile	10	7	2.99	126	118	41	87
* Elias, Roenis, Jackson	6	11	3.18	130	111	50	121
Cabrera, Alberto, Tennessee	9	3	3.20	113	102	39	107
Lee, Zach, Chattanooga	10	10	3.22	143	132	35	131
* Conley, Adam, Jacksonville	11	7	3.25	139	125	37	129

ALL-STAR TEAM

C: Christian Bethancourt, Mississippi. 1B: Jason Rogers Huntsville. 2B: Arismendy Alcantara, Tennessee. 3B: Christian Villanueva, Tennessee. SS: Javier Baez, Tennessee. OF: Justin Greene, Mobile; Kevin Kiermaier, Montgomery; Joc Pederson, Chattanooga; Matt Szczur, Tennessee. DH: Dan Black, Birmingham. UT: Marcus Semien, Birmingham. RHP: Kyle Hendricks, Tennessee. LHP: Enny Romero, Montgomery. RP: Michael Brady, Jacksonville.
Most Valuable Player: Marcus Semien, Birmingham. Most Outstanding Pitcher: Archie Bradley, Mobile. Manager of the Year: Andy Green, Mobile.

DEPARTMENT LEADERS

BATTING

OBP	Semien, Marcus, Birmingham	.420
SLG	Pederson, Joc, Chattanooga	.497
OPS	Semien, Marcus, Birmingham	.903
R	Semien, Marcus, Birmingham	90
H	Szczur, Matt, Tennessee	144
TB	Villanueva, Christian, Tennessee	230
XBH	Villanueva, Christian, Tennessee	62
2B	Villanueva, Christian, Tennessee	41
3B	Jones, James, Jackson	10
HR	Kjeldgaard, Brock, Huntsville	24
RBI	Rogers, Jason, Huntsville	87
SAC	Gomez, Hector, Huntsville	16
BB	Black, Dan, Birmingham	91
HBP	Torrez, Riccio, Montgomery	19
SO	Walker, Keenyn, Birmingham	153
SB	Inciarte, Ender, Mobile	43
CS	Walker, Keenyn, Birmingham	15
AB/SO	Inciarte, Ender, Mobile	10.06

PITCHING

G	Hayes, Drew, Pensacola	51
	Holle, Greg, Huntsville	51
GS	Smith, Josh, Pensacola	28
GF	Brady, Michael, Jacksonville	44
	Garcia, Yimi, Chattanooga	44
SV	Brady, Michael, Jacksonville	23
W	Bradley, Archie, Mobile	12
L	Moye, Andy, Huntsville	15
IP	Jokisch, Eric, Tennessee	160.2
H	Lee, Michael, Mississippi	160
R	Snodgrass, Scott, Birmingham	90
ER	Snodgrass, Scott, Birmingham	75
HB	Northcraft, Aaron, Mississippi	14
BB	Pena, Ariel, Huntsville	79
SO	Smith, Josh, Pensacola	139
SO/9	Bradley, Archie, Mobile	8.68
SO/9(RP)	Garcia, Yimi, Chattanooga	12.7
BB/9	Lee, Michael, Mississippi	1.26
WP	Three tied at	12
BK	Garcia, Onelki, Chattanooga	4
HR	Moye, Andy, Huntsville	18
AVG	Bradley, Archie, Mobile	.214

FIELDING

C	PCT	Perez, Rossmel, Mobile	.996
	PO	Realmuto, J.T., Jacksonville	769
	A	Barnhart, Tucker, Pensacola	109
	DP	Barnhart, Tucker, Pensacola	9
	E	Bethancourt, Christian, Miss.	12
	PB	Hicks, John, Jackson	17
1B	PCT	Marrero, Christian, Mississippi	.996
	PO	Seitzer, Cameron, Montgomery	1137
	A	Marrero, Christian, Mississippi	91
	DP	Rogers, Jason, Huntsville	109
	E	Seitzer, Cameron, Montgomery	11
2B	PCT	Ynoa, Rafael, Chattanooga	.987
	PO	Freeman, Mike, Mobile	245
	A	Freeman, Mike, Mobile	334
	DP	Freeman, Mike, Mobile	85
	E	Alcantara, Arismendy, Tennessee	13
3B	PCT	Walker, Mike, Huntsville	.953
	PO	Villanueva, Christian, Tennessee	78
	A	Villanueva, Christian, Tennessee	240
	DP	Morla, Ramon, Jackson	23
	E	Salcedo, Edward, Mississippi	29
SS	PCT	Ahmed, Nick, Mobile	.980
	PO	Lohman, Devin, Pensacola	200
	A	Ahmed, Nick, Mobile	441
	DP	Rojas, Miguel, Chattanooga	89
	E	Lohman, Devin, Pensacola	29
OF	PCT	Inciarte, Ender, Mobile	.993
	PO	LaMarre, Ryan, Pensacola	325
	A	Silva, Rubi, Tennessee	16
	DP	Stang, Chadwin, Huntsville	4
	E	Walker, Keenyn, Birmingham	11

BY VINCENT LARA-CINISOMO

It wasn't quite 2012, when Wil Myers, Jurickson Profar and Oscar Taveras dotted rosters, but the Texas League was again dominated by premium prospects.

Near the top of the list were Astros farmhands George Springer (who belted 19 home runs in half a season) and Mike Foltynewicz (who posted a 2.87 ERA over a full season as a 21-year-old), but it's hard to overlook the story of one 30-year-old pitcher.

While Corpus Christi won the South Division in part due to Springer and Foltynewicz, San Antonio won the league championship thanks to Josh Geer, who pitched five strong innings as the Missions, a Padres affiliate, beat the Arkansas Travelers in Game Five of the title series.

Geer, selected by the Padres in the third round of the 2005 draft, missed all of the 2011 season as he battled stage 3 melanoma. He rebounded to full health in 2013 and went 8-5, 3.41 in 100 innings.

As for what we're all here for, the prospects: Corpus Christi had Springer and Foltynewicz; San Antonio won behind three righthanded pitchers—Matt Wisler, Keyvius Sampson and Matt Andriese; and Northwest Arkansas had power righthander Yordano Ventura, third baseman Cheslor Cuthbert and shortstop Orlando Calixte making the grade.

Springer graduated to Triple-A, but was in the Texas League long enough to finish in the top 10 in home runs while topping the cirucit with a .579 slugging percentage.

Wisler held batters to a .223 average; Sampson struck out 110 in 103 innings pitched and Andriese went 8-3, 2.37.

Ventura dominated Texas League hitters, holding them to a .180 batting average as he climbed all the way to Kansas City by season's end.

San Antonio's Reymond Fuentes—acquired from the Red Sox in the Adrian Gonzalez deal—also jumped to Triple-A and then San Diego after finally flashing some bat skills. Between the Texas and Pacific Coast leagues, Fuentes hit .330/.413/.448 with 35 stolen bases.

Arkansas Travelers first baseman C.J. Cron saw

his homers fall off during the regular season, from 27 in 2012 to 14 in 2013, but he hit four in the Texas League playoffs after belting five in August.

In other developments following the season, the Travelers revealed a new logo. Arkansas began building anticipation for its makeover late last season, when it held a retirement celebration for Shelly, the team's horse mascot of 17 years.

General manager Paul Allen said the new logo, which features a stallion with a capital A blended into its bridle, will help rekindle excitement in the team that has faded a bit since the opening of the new ballpark.

TOP 20 PROSPECTS

1. George Springer, of, Corpus Christi (Astros)
2. Mike Foltynewicz, rhp, Corpus Christi (Astros)
3. Yordano Ventura, rhp, Northwest Arkansas (Royals)
4. Rougned Odor, 2b, Frisco (Rangers)
5. Matt Wisler, rhp, San Antonio (Padres)
6. Domingo Santana, of, Corpus Christi (Astros)
7. Keyvius Sampson, rhp, San Antonio (Padres)
8. Jason Adam, rhp, Northwest Arkansas (Royals)
9. Stephen Piscotty, of, Springfield (Cardinals)
10. Taylor Lindsey, 2b, Arkansas (Angels)
11. Luis Sardinas, ss, Frisco (Rangers)
12. Tim Cooney, lhp, Springfield (Cardinals)
13. Kyle Parker, of/1b, Tulsa (Rockies)
14. Chad Bettis, rhp, Tulsa (Rockies)
15. Matt Andriese, rhp, San Antonio (Padres)
16. Max Stassi, c, Corpus Christi (Astros)
17. Randal Grichuk, of, Arkansas (Angels)
18. Orlando Calixte, ss/3b, Northwest Arkansas (Royals)
19. Reymond Fuentes, of, San Antonio (Padres)
20. Cheslor Cuthbert, 3b, Northwest Arkansas (Royals)

STANDINGS: SPLIT SEASON

FIRST HALF					SECOND HALF				
NORTH	W	L	PCT	GB	NORTH	W	L	PCT	GB
Tulsa	34	34	.500	—	Arkansas	40	30	.571	—
Springfield	33	35	.485	1	NW Ark.	34	36	.486	6
Arkansas	33	36	.478	1½	Tulsa	34	36	.486	6
NW Ark.	25	45	.357	10	Springfield	31	39	.443	9
SOUTH	W	L	PCT	GB	SOUTH	W	L	PCT	GB
C. Christi	42	28	.600	—	C. Christi	41	29	.586	—
Frisco	39	31	.557	3	San Antonio	40	30	.571	1
San Antonio	38	31	.551	3½	Frisco	31	39	.443	10
Midland	33	37	.471	9	Midland	29	41	.414	12

PLAYOFFS—Semifinals: Arkansas defeated Tulsa 3-0 and San Antonio defeated Corpus Christi 3-2 in best-of-five series; **Finals:** San Antonio defeated Arkansas 3-2 in best-of-five.

OVERALL STANDINGS

Team (Organization)	W	L	PCT	GB	Manager	Attendance	Average	Last Pennant
Corpus Christi Hooks (Astros)	83	57	.593	—	Keith Bodie	379,395	5,498	2006
San Antonio Missions (Padres)	78	61	.561	4½	Rich Dauer	294,346	4,329	2013
Arkansas Travelers (Angels)	73	66	.525	9½	Tim Bogar	293,749	4,519	2008
Frisco Roughriders (Rangers)	70	70	.500	13	Steve Buechele	479,873	7,057	2004
Tulsa Drillers (Rockies)	68	70	.493	14	Kevin Riggs	393,600	5,704	1998
Springfield Cardinals (Cardinals)	64	74	.464	18	Mike Shildt	338,345	5,205	2012
Midland Rockhounds (Athletics)	62	78	.443	21	Aaron Nieckula	317,233	4,598	2009
Northwest Arkansas Naturals (Royals)	59	81	.421	24	Brian Poldberg	318,592	4,685	2010

TEXAS LEAGUE STATISTICS

CLUB BATTING

	AVG	G	AB	R	H	2B	3B	HR	RBI	BB	SO	SB	OBP	SLG
San Antonio	.256	139	4623	562	1183	223	29	85	520	396	1017	171	.321	.372
Corpus Christi	.255	140	4739	657	1210	253	19	158	606	472	1123	85	.331	.417
Midland	.255	140	4767	647	1215	270	42	99	586	534	1063	111	.335	.391
Springfield	.254	138	4532	607	1152	194	18	124	567	512	1034	131	.335	.387
Arkansas	.250	139	4591	578	1149	228	31	114	530	366	970	106	.313	.388
Northwest Arkansas	.250	140	4656	583	1164	220	57	131		392	1089	118	.311	.390
Frisco	.249	140	4750	569	1183	201	33	115	539	303	906	127	.300	.378
Tulsa	.245	138	4559	549	1116	222	25	115	513	376	1019	115	.310	.380

CLUB PITCHING

	ERA	G	CG	SHO	SV	IP	H	R	ER	HR	BB	SO	AVG
San Antonio	3.19	139	1	14	50	1235	1113	527	438	93	352	1088	.239
Frisco	3.58	140	1	8	39	1253	1115	578	499	112	470	1111	.240
Tulsa	3.67	138	1	11	38	1230	1161	572	502	129	426	943	.254
Arkansas	3.76	139	1	13	39	1222	1124	566	511	112	441	976	.247
Corpus Christi	3.84	140	4	14	44	1255	1253	603	536	133	372	917	.263
Midland	3.94	140	1	6	20	1245	1237	634	545	102	413	987	.259
Springfield	4.02	138	1	10	33	1210	1202	619	540	123	380	1125	.259
Northwest Arkansas	4.19	140	4	9	31	1234	1167	653	575	126	497	1074	.252

CLUB FIELDING

	PCT	PO	A	E	DP		PCT	PO	A	E	DP
Tulsa	.980	3691	1571	107	162	Springfield	.976	3631	1443	126	110
Frisco	.979	3759	1477	110	125	Midland	.974	3734	1437	140	107
Arkansas	.978	3666	1413	115	144	NW Arkansas	.973	3701	1374	141	119
Corpus Christi	.978	3765	1612	121	156	San Antonio	.972	3705	1427	149	97

INDIVIDUAL BATTING LEADERS (Minimum 2.7 PA/Team Game)

Batter, Club	AVG	G	AB	R	H	HR	RBI
* Aliotti, Anthony, Midland	.350	91	340	49	119	12	51
* O'Neill, Mike, Springfield	.320	98	359	66	115	2	35
* Fuentes, Reymond, San Antonio	.316	93	345	56	109	6	35
* Nicholas, Brett, Frisco	.289	136	506	71	146	21	91
Parker, Kyle, Tulsa	.288	123	480	70	138	23	74
Myers, D'Arby, Midland	.285	118	485	75	138	5	51
# Navarro, Rey, NW Arkansas	.284	119	447	61	127	12	58
Castro, Erik, Corpus Christi	.280	117	410	62	115	18	65
Nina, Angelys, Tulsa	.280	123	446	45	125	10	51
* Crumbliss, Conner, Midland	.280	92	347	66	97	10	34

INDIVIDUAL PITCHING LEADERS (Minimum 0.8 IP/team game)

Pitcher, Club	W	L	ERA	IP	H	BB	SO
Martinez, David, Corpus Christi	14	2	2.02	129	109	20	86
* Hernandez, Carlos, Midland	7	7	2.18	132	109	38	96
Hynick, Brandon, Arkansas	12	5	2.80	142	114	34	98
Bergman, Christian, Tulsa	8	7	3.37	171	162	23	111
Batista, Lay, Arkansas	5	8	3.38	123	105	43	89
Roach, Donn, San Antonio	8	12	3.41	143	137	40	77
Smith, Murphy, Midland	9	8	3.48	150	156	46	98
* Matzek, Tyler, Tulsa	8	9	3.79	142	147	76	95
* Cooney, Tim, Springfield	7	10	3.80	118	132	18	125
Murphy, Sean, Midland	8	8	4.08	137	137	50	121

ALL-STAR TEAM

C: Max Stassi, Corpus Christi. 1B: Anthony Aliotti, Midland. 2B: Taylor Lindsey, Arkansas. 3B: Ruben Gotay, Springfield. SS: Cristhian Adames, Tulsa. UT: Angelys Nina, Tulsa. OF: Reymond Fuentes, San Antonio; Mike O'Neill, Springfield; Kyle Parker, Tulsa; George Springer, Corpus Christi. DH: Brett Nicholas, Frisco. P: Christian Bergman, Tulsa; Mike Foltynewicz, Corpus Christi; Carlos Hernandez, Midland; Brandon Hynick, Arkansas; Jeremy McBryde, San Antonio; David Martinez, Corpus Christi; Kevin Quackenbush, San Antonio; Neil Ramirez, Frisco; Keyvius Sampson, San Antonio.
Player of the Year: George Springer, Corpus Christi. **Pitcher of the Year:** David Martinez, Corpus Christi. **Manager of the Year:** Rich Dauer, San Antonio.

DEPARTMENT LEADERS

BATTING

OBP	Aliotti, Anthony, Midland	.452
SLG	Aliotti, Anthony, Midland	.541
OPS	Aliotti, Anthony, Midland	.993
R	Grichuk, Randal, Arkansas	85
H	Nicholas, Brett, Frisco	146
TB	Nicholas, Brett, Frisco	240
XBH	Grichuk, Randal, Arkansas	57
2B	Chiang, Chih-Hsien, Frisco	36
	Cron, C.J., Arkansas	36
3B	Oberacker, Chad, Midland	12
HR	Fields, Matt, NW Arkansas	31
RBI	Nicholas, Brett, Frisco	91
SAC	Adames, Cristhian, Tulsa	17
BB	Scruggs, Xavier, Springfield	82
HBP	Cron, C.J., Arkansas	15
SO	Fields, Matt, NW Arkansas	181
SB	Noel, Rico, San Antonio	59
CS	Noel, Rico, San Antonio	19
AB/SO	O'Neill, Mike, Springfield	13.81

PITCHING

G	McBryde, Jeremy, San Antonio	61
GS	Neal, Zach, Midland	28
	Roach, Donn, San Antonio	28
GF	Jackson, Zach, NW Arkansas	31
SV	White, Cole, NW Arkansas, Tulsa	19
W	Martinez, David, Corpus Christi	14
L	Marimon, Sugar Ray, NW Arkansas	14
IP	Bergman, Christian, Tulsa	171
H	Correa, Henry, Arkansas	176
R	Adam, Jason, NW Arkansas	98
	Gustafson, Tim, Tulsa	98
ER	Gustafson, Tim, Tulsa	88
HB	Adam, Jason, NW Arkansas	15
BB	Matzek, Tyler, Tulsa	76
SO	Tropeano, Nick, Corpus Christi	130
SO/9	Cooney, Tim, Springfield	9.51
SO/9(RP)	Thomas, Kevin, Springfield	11.3
BB/9	Bergman, Christian, Tulsa	1.21
WP	Fisher, Carlos, Midland	15
BK	Marimon, Sugar Ray, NW Arkansas	4
HR	Marimon, Sugar Ray, NW Arkansas	26
AVG	Hynick, Brandon, Arkansas	.221

FIELDING

C	PCT	Garneau, Dustin, Tulsa	.993
	PO	Telis, Tomas, Frisco	608
	A	Stanley, Cody, Springfield	73
	DP	Garneau, Dustin, Tulsa	9
	E	Rodriguez, Eddy, San Antonio	9
	PB	Garneau, Dustin, Tulsa	14
1B	PCT	Roling, Kiel, Tulsa	.995
	PO	Scruggs, Xavier, Springfield	1131
	A	Cron, C.J., Arkansas	82
	DP	Cron, C.J., Arkansas	112
	E	Castro, Erik, Corpus Christi	15
2B	PCT	Nina, Angelys, Tulsa	.980
	PO	Lindsey, Taylor, Arkansas	268
	A	Lindsey, Taylor, Arkansas	361
	DP	Lindsey, Taylor, Arkansas	99
	E	Lindsey, Taylor, Arkansas	18
3B	PCT	Langfels, Jayson, Tulsa	.959
	PO	Cowart, Kaleb, Arkansas	85
	A	Meyer, Jonathan, Corpus Christi	293
	DP	Langfels, Jayson, Tulsa	28
		Meyer, Jonathan, Corpus Christi	28
	E	Blackwood, Jake, San Antonio	25
		Cowart, Kaleb, Arkansas	25
SS	PCT	Adames, Cristhian, Tulsa	.973
	PO	Alberto, Hanser, Frisco	175
	A	Mier, Jiovanni, Corpus Christi	309
	DP	Mier, Jiovanni, Corpus Christi	82
	E	Valdez, Jeudy, San Antonio	28
OF	PCT	Strausborger, Ryan, Frisco	.997
	PO	Noel, Rico, San Antonio	330
	A	Noel, Rico, San Antonio	15
	DP	Grichuk, Randal, Arkansas	5
		Noel, Rico, San Antonio	5
	E	Noel, Rico, San Antonio	9

MINOR LEAGUES

BY JIM SHONERD

nland Empire went just 69-71 in the regular season, but they played their best when the stakes were the highest. The 66ers took down the teams that posted the league's two best records, Lancaster and San Jose, on their way to the title.

To get to the finals, the 66ers had to survive a 15-inning marathon in the decisive fifth game of their division final against Lancaster, finally scoring the decisive run on Abel Baker's two-out RBI double in the top of the 15th.

San Jose, Inland Empire's final opponent, boasted the league's best pitching staff, leading the league in ERA at 3.66. But the 66ers outscored the Giants 16-2 in a three-game sweep, getting successive strong starts from Orangel Arenas, Dan Reynolds and Drew Rucinski.

The 66ers lost their best pitching prospect, righthander Mark Sappington, to a second-half promotion. Their offense, which placed three players on the league's end-of-season all-star team, remained intact and was spearheaded by league MVP Zach Borenstein and second baseman Alex Yarbrough. Borenstein nearly won the California League triple crown, leading the way in average (.337) and homers (28) and finishing third in RBIs (95). First baseman Mike Snyder led the charge in the playoffs, batting .342 with two homers in 10 postseason games.

San Jose rode its pitching staff to the league's best regular season record at 83-57, and all five members of its rotation were legitimate prospects. In the usually hitter-friendly circuit where the average ERA was 4.64, all five Giants starters— Kyle Crick, Edwin Escobar, Adalberto Mejia, Ty Blach and Clayton Blackburn—posted marks of 3.65 or better.

Crick was one of a handful of true blue-chip prospects to spend significant time in the league, and the general sense was that its talent level was down in 2013. There was a clear separation from the top three prospects of Stockton's Addison Russell, Modesto's Eddie Butler and Crick to the rest of the crop. A few other big names made brief stops in the Cal League, most notably Diamondbacks righthander Archie Bradley, who opened the season with Visalia and made five starts before a promotion, and the Rockies' Jonathan Gray, the No. 3 overall pick in this year's draft who joined Modesto in August.

TOP 20 PROSPECTS

1. Addison Russell, ss, Stockton (Athletics)
2. Eddie Butler, rhp, Modesto (Rockies)
3. Kyle Crick, rhp, San Jose (Giants)
4. Delino DeShields Jr., 2b, Lancaster (Astros)
5. Austin Hedges, c, Lake Elsinore (Padres)
6. Edwin Escobar, lhp, San Jose (Giants)
7. Patrick Kivlehan, 3b, High Desert (Mariners)
8. Jace Peterson, ss, Lake Elsinore (Padres)
9. Alex Yarbrough, 2b, Inland Empire (Angels)
10. Adalberto Mejia, lhp, San Jose (Giants)
11. Chris Taylor, ss, High Desert (Mariners).
12. Travis Jankowski, of, Lake Elsinore (Padres).
13. Yorman Rodriguez, of, Bakersfield (Reds).
14. Max Muncy, 1b, Stockton (Athletics).
15. Ty Blach, lhp, San Jose (Giants).
16. Mark Sappington, rhp, Inland Empire (Angels).
17. R.J. Alvarez, rhp, Inland Empire (Angels).
18. Mac Williamson, of, San Jose (Giants).
19. Trevor Story, ss, Modesto (Rockies).
20. Clayton Blackburn, rhp, San Jose (Giants).

STANDINGS: SPLIT SEASON

FIRST HALF

NORTH	W	L	PCT	GB
San Jose	43	27	.614	—
Visalia	39	31	.557	4
Stockton	38	32	.543	5
Modesto	32	38	.457	11
Bakersfield	29	41	.414	14

SOUTH	W	L	PCT	GB
Lancaster	39	31	.557	—
I. Empire	37	33	.529	2
High Desert	34	36	.486	5
Rancho Cuca.	31	39	.443	8
Lake Elsinore	28	42	.400	11

SECOND HALF

NORTH	W	L	PCT	GB
Modesto	43	27	.614	—
San Jose	40	30	.571	3
Visalia	38	32	.543	5
Stockton	31	39	.443	12
Bakersfield	26	44	.371	17

SOUTH	W	L	PCT	GB
Lancaster	43	27	.614	—
Rancho Cuca.	34	36	.486	9
Lake Elsinore	33	37	.471	10
I. Empire	32	38	.457	11
High Desert	30	40	.429	13

PLAYOFFS—Division Series: Visalia defeated Modesto 2-0 and Inland Empire defeated Rancho Cucamonga 2-1 in best-of-three series. **Semifinals:** San Jose defeated Visalia 3-2 and Inland Empire defeated Lancaster 3-2 in best-of-five series. **Finals:** Inland Empire defeated San Jose 3-0 in a best-of-five series.

OVERALL STANDINGS

Team (Organization)	W	L	PCT	GB	Manager	Attendance	Average	Last Pennant
San Jose Giants (Giants)	83	57	.593	—	Andy Skeels	201,011	2,872	2010
Lancaster Jethawks (Astros)	82	58	.586	1	Rodney Linares	158,266	2,294	2012
Visalia Rawhide (Diamondbacks)	77	63	.550	6	Bill Plummer	115,321	1,647	1978
Modesto Nuts (Rockies)	75	65	.536	8	Lenn Sakata/Fred Nelson	177,700	2,539	2004
Inland Empire 66ers (Angels)	69	71	.493	14	Bill Haselman	192,549	2,751	2013
Stockton Ports (Athletics)	69	71	.493	14	Webster Garrison	199,742	2,853	2008
Rancho Cucamonga Quakes (Dodgers)	65	75	.464	18	Carlos Subero	172,306	2,462	1994
High Desert Mavericks (Mariners)	64	76	.457	19	Jim Horner	92,379	1,359	1997
Lake Elsinore Storm (Padres)	61	79	.436	22	Shawn Wooten	217,869	3,158	2011
Bakersfield Blaze (Reds)	55	85	.393	28	Ken Griffey	56,345	805	1989

CLUB BATTING

	AVG	G	AB	R	H	2B	3B	HR	RBI	BB	SO	SB	OBP	SLG
Lancaster	.289	140	4823	976	1395	296	57	153	897	669	957	140	.384	.469
High Desert	.274	140	4850	827	1329	285	56	154	763	503	1066	144	.346	.451
Inland Empire	.270	140	4839	675	1308	254	58	106	625	416	1089	92	.334	.412
Lake Elsinore	.267	140	4820	718	1286	257	72	96	658	487	1082	201	.340	.410
Visalia	.266	140	4754	704	1265	261	28	110	639	522	1172	89	.343	.402
Rancho Cucamonga	.262	140	4759	728	1245	245	73	145	674	441	1208	185	.333	.435
San Jose	.259	140	4836	690	1251	280	37	116	633	460	1142	98	.331	.404
Bakersfield	.257	140	4780	635	1229	254	35	136	596	396	1104	142	.319	.410
Modesto	.252	140	4839	695	1221	275	46	124	630	429	1372	135	.321	.405
Stockton	.247	140	4894	731	1207	272	31	183	698	497	1319	96	.326	.427

CLUB PITCHING

	ERA	G	CG	SHO	SV	IP	H	R	ER	HR	BB	SO	AVG
San Jose	3.66	140	0	8	48	1266	1165	590	515	103	425	1282	.243
Modesto	3.88	140	0	7	41	1260	1166	633	544	126	441	1178	.243
Stockton	4.55	140	1	5	32	1268	1263	738	641	143	419	1258	.258
Bakersfield	4.61	140	0	6	33	1237	1224	736	633	131	540	1089	.259
Inland Empire	4.64	140	1	3	35	1245	1291	713	642	122	467	1039	.269
Visalia	4.83	140	2	9	39	1225	1244	739	657	158	588	1272	.264
Rancho Cucamonga	4.90	140	0	5	31	1245	1324	804	677	132	519	1147	.270
Lake Elsinore	5.04	140	1	4	31	1232	1376	818	690	122	529	1028	.281
Lancaster	5.09	140	1	3	40	1234	1372	792	698	140	414	1144	.280
High Desert	5.24	140	0	2	30	1227	1311	816	715	146	478	1074	.274

CLUB FIELDING

	PCT	PO	A	E	DP		PCT	PO	A	E	DP
Inland Empire	.977	3734	1470	122	112	Lancaster	.973	3702	1352	142	100
San Jose	.976	3798	1312	128	115	High Desert	.972	3682	1504	149	121
Visalia	.976	3675	1330	124	122	Bakersfield	.970	3710	1445	162	132
Modesto	.974	3781	1382	136	130	Lake Elsinore	.968	3695	1313	164	106
Stockton	.974	3803	1287	137	110	Rancho Cuca.	.963	3734	1381	198	101

INDIVIDUAL BATTING LEADERS (Minimum 2.7 PA/Team Game)

Batter, Club	AVG	G	AB	R	H	HR	RBI
* Borenstein, Zach, Inland Empire	.339	111	404	76	137	28	95
Duffy, Matt, Lancaster	.323	100	371	74	120	19	84
DeShields, Delino, Lancaster	.317	111	451	100	143	5	54
Cokinos, M.P., Lancaster	.314	108	421	70	132	13	92
# Yarbrough, Alex, Inland Empire	.313	135	579	76	181	11	80
* Humphries, Brian, Modesto	.302	110	450	62	136	8	49
# Sclafani, Joe, Lancaster	.302	91	341	79	103	7	53
* Peterson, Jace, Lake Elsinore	.300	112	420	78	126	7	66
Selsky, Steve, Bakersfield	.299	90	338	53	101	13	68
* Rivers, Kevin, High Desert	.299	127	482	91	144	20	97

INDIVIDUAL PITCHING LEADERS (Minimum 0.8 IP/team game)

Pitcher, Club	W	L	ERA	IP	H	BB	SO
* Blach, Ty, San Jose	12	4	2.90	130	124	18	117
Winkler, Dan, Modesto	12	5	2.97	130	84	37	152
Sappington, Mark, Inland Empire	11	4	3.38	131	103	62	110
Blackburn, Clayton, San Jose	7	5	3.65	133	111	35	138
Needy, James, Lake Elsinore	10	5	3.76	134	143	51	98
* Barbosa, Andrew, Visalia	11	9	3.81	135	115	70	160
Caughel, Lindsey, R. Cucamonga	4	7	4.01	117	131	21	112
Peters, Tanner, Stockton	12	8	4.07	166	167	27	159
Alsup, Ben, Modesto	13	8	4.45	162	163	59	133
Jensen, Chris, Modesto	5	8	4.55	152	161	39	136

ALL-STAR TEAM

C: Ryan Casteel, Modesto. **1B:** Mike Snyder, Inland Empire. **2B:** Alex Yarbrough, Inland Empire. **3B:** Matt Duffy, Lancaster. **SS:** Addison Russell, Stockton. **OF:** Scott Schebler, Rancho Cucamonga; Andrew Aplin, Lancaster; Travis Jankowski, Lake Elsinore. **DH:** Zach Borenstein, Inland Empire. **UT:** M.P. Cokinos, Lancaster. **P:** Andrew Barbosa, Visalia; Ty Blach, San Jose; Mark Sappington, Inland Empire; Dan Winkler, Modesto.
Most Valuable Player: Zach Borenstein, Inland Empire. **Pitcher of the Year:** Dan Winkler, Modesto. **Rookie of the Year:** Addison Russell, Stockton. **Manager of the Year:** Rodney Linares, Lancaster.

DEPARTMENT LEADERS

BATTING

OBP	Fontana, Nolan, Lancaster	.415
SLG	Borenstein, Zach, Inland Empire	.631
OPS	Borenstein, Zach, Inland Empire	1.034
R	Austin, Jamal, High Desert	107
H	Yarbrough, Alex, Inland Empire	182
TB	Schebler, Scott, R. Cucamonga	277
XBH	Schebler, Scott, R. Cucamonga	69
2B	Harris, Devin, San Jose	40
3B	Sweeney, Darnell, R. Cucamonga	16
HR	Borenstein, Zach, Inland Empire	28
RBI	Aplin, Andrew, Lancaster	107
SAC	Stamets, Eric, Inland Empire	21
BB	Fontana, Nolan, Lancaster	102
HBP	Williamson, Mac, San Jose	21
SO	Riggins, Harold, Modesto	192
SB	Jankowski, Travis, Lake Elsinore	71
CS	Sweeney, Darnell, R. Cucamonga	20
AB/SO	Cokinos, MP, Lancaster	10.37

PITCHING

G	Cody Hebner, Lake Elsinore	58
GS	Alsup, Ben, Modesto	29
GF	Oberg, Scott, Modesto	49
SV	Oberg, Scott, Modesto	33
W	Alsup, Ben, Modesto	13
L	Moscot, Jon, Bakersfield	14
IP	Peters, Tanner, Stockton	165.2
H	Gagnon, Tyler, Modesto	183
R	Gagnon, Tyler, Modesto	108
ER	Gagnon, Tyler, Modesto	97
HB	Two tied at	16
BB	Barbosa, Andrew, Visalia	70
SO	Barbosa, Andrew, Visalia	160
SO/9	Barbosa, Andrew, Visalia	10.69
SO/9(RP)	Simmons, Seth, Visalia	13
BB/9	Blach, Ty, San Jose	1.24
WP	Coulombe, Daniel, R. Cucamonga	17
BK	Reynolds, Dan, Inland Empire	6
HR	Hessler, Keith, Visalia	24
	Peters, Tanner, Stockton	24
AVG	Winkler, Daniel, Modesto	.184

FIELDING

C	PCT	Heineman, Tyler, Lancaster	.991
	PO	Arnold, Jeff, San Jose	884
	A	Heineman, Tyler, Lancaster	90
	DP	Two tied at	11
	E	Hedges, Austin, Lake Elsinore	11
		Swanner, Will, Modesto	11
	PB	Swanner, Will, Modesto	18
1B	PCT	Snyder, Michael, Inland Empire	.988
	PO	Snyder, Michael, Inland Empire	1062
	A	Snyder, Michael, Inland Empire	78
	DP	Snyder, Michael, Inland Empire	89
	E	Riggins, Harold, Modesto	17
2B	PCT	Yarbrough, Alex, Inland Empire	.982
	PO	Yarbrough, Alex, Inland Empire	239
	A	Yarbrough, Alex, Inland Empire	314
	DP	Featherston, Taylor, Modesto	72
	E	DeShields, Delino, Lancaster	24
3B	PCT	Hernandez, Brian, Inland Empire	.953
	PO	Hernandez, Brian, Inland Empire	92
	A	Hernandez, Brian, Inland Empire	250
	DP	Duffy, Matt, Lancaster	23
	E	Jones, Duanel, Lake Elsinore	30
		Vollmuth, B.A., Stockton	30
SS	PCT	Stamets, Eric, Inland Empire	.972
	PO	Stamets, Eric, Inland Empire	196
	A	Stamets, Eric, Inland Empire	400
	DP	Two tied at	71
	E	Sweeney, Darnell, R. Cucamonga	34
OF	PCT	Belza, Tom, Visalia	1.000
	PO	Jankowski, Travis, Lake Elsinore	333
	A	Williamson, Mac, San Jose	15
		Workman, Andy, Inland Empire	15
	DP	Marzilli, Evan, Visalia	8
	E	Three tied at	10

MINOR LEAGUES

BY JOSH LEVENTHAL

The eight-team Carolina League usually runs thin on talent beyond a handful of elite prospects. The league was unusually deep this year, however, thanks in part to the strength of the Nationals, Rangers and Red Sox farm systems. They produced eight of the top 10 prospects and 13 players overall.

Boston's recent investment in its farm system paid off with a championship. Salem, whose roster at various points included seven players drafted over the past four years who signed for nearly a combined $10 million, swept through the postseason to claim the franchise's first Carolina League title since 2001. The Red Sox took home the Mills Trophy in three games over Potomac, even after bidding farewell to two of the league's top players at midseason.

Salem third baseman Garin Cecchini hit .350/.469/.547 in just 214 at-bats before moving on to Double-A Portland after the all-star break. (His combined .443 on-base percentage topped the minors.) Lefthander Henry Owens topped the CL in strikeouts (123) at the time of his promotion, and saved his best for last, tossing 11 hitless innings over two starts against Frederick and Potomac in late July before moving up to Double-A.

The Red Sox had plenty in the tank without those two—including catcher Blake Swihart (who threw out a league-high 42 percent of basestealers), shortstop Deven Marrero (who challenged top prospect Francisco Lindor as the circuit's top defender), second baseman Sean Coyle (who returned from injury to hit .417 in the finals), and late callup Mookie Betts (the second baseman who swiped 20 bases and hit .341 in 185 at-bats).

The league was particularly deep in position players. Myrtle Beach featured one of the best double-play combinations in shortstop Luis Sardinas and second baseman Rougned Odor, while the Nationals paired speedy outfielders Billy Burns and Michael Taylor, who combined for 105 steals.

One year after playing as the youngest position player in the Midwest League, Indians shortstop Lindor spent the first half of this season as the second-youngest regular in the CL at age 19. Once again, he looked more like a wily veteran than an overmatched teenager, drawing as much praise for his leadership skills and high baseball IQ as his physical tools.

Winston-Salem outfielder Courtney Hawkins, the 13th overall pick in the 2012 draft who signed for $2.475 million, ranked among the league's Top 20 prospects despite a disastrous first full pro season. The circuit's youngest player topped the league with 160 strikeouts yet showed off plenty of raw power, as 38 of his 68 hits went for extra bases.

TOP 20 PROSPECTS

1. Francisco Lindor, ss, Carolina (Indians)
2. Kyle Zimmer, rhp, Wilmington (Royals)
3. Rougned Odor, 2b, Myrtle Beach (Rangers)
4. Henry Owens, lhp, Salem (Red Sox)
5. Blake Swihart, c, Salem (Red Sox)
6. Garin Cecchini, 3b, Salem (Red Sox)
7. Mookie Betts, 2b, Salem (Red Sox)
8. Eduardo Rodriguez, lhp, Frederick (Orioles)
9. Luke Jackson, rhp, Myrtle Beach (Rangers)
10. A.J. Cole, rhp, Potomac (Nationals)
11. Jorge Bonifacio, of, Wilmington (Royals)
12. Michael Taylor, of, Potomac (Nationals)
13. Deven Marrero, ss, Salem (Red Sox)
14. Luis Sardinas, ss, Myrtle Beach (Rangers)
15. Courtney Hawkins, of, Winston-Salem (White Sox)
16. Robbie Ray, lhp, Potomac (Nationals)
17. Robby Hefflinger, of, Lynchburg (Braves)
18. Michael Ohlman, c, Frederick (Orioles)
19. Billy Burns, of, Potomac (Nationals)
20. Cody Anderson, rhp, Carolina (Indians)

STANDINGS: SPLIT SEASON

FIRST HALF

NORTH	W	L	PCT	GB
Potomac	42	27	.609	—
Lynchburg	36	33	.522	6
Frederick	34	35	.493	8
Wilmington	33	37	.471	9½

SOUTH	W	L	PCT	GB
Myrtle B.	40	29	.580	—
W-S	38	32	.543	2½
Salem	33	37	.471	7½
Carolina	22	48	.314	18½

SECOND HALF

NORTH	W	L	PCT	GB
Potomac	42	28	.600	—
Lynchburg	33	37	.471	9
Wilmington	30	40	.429	12
Frederick	27	43	.386	15

SOUTH	W	L	PCT	GB
Salem	43	27	.614	—
Myrtle B.	37	33	.529	6
Carolina	35	35	.500	8
W-S	33	37	.471	10

PLAYOFFS—Semifinals: Potomac defeated Lynchburg 2-0 and Salem defeated Myrtle Beach 2-0 in best-of-three series. **Finals:** Salem defeated Potomac 3-0 in a best-of-five series.

OVERALL STANDINGS

Team (Organization)	W	L	PCT	GB	Manager	Attendance	Average	Last Pennant
Potomac Nationals (Nationals)	84	55	.604	—	Brian Daubach	236,772	3,534	2010
Myrtle Beach Pelicans (Rangers)	77	62	.554	7	Jason Wood	222,406	3,370	2000
Salem Red Sox (Red Sox)	76	64	.543	8½	Billy McMillon	172,293	2,735	2013
Winston-Salem Dash (White Sox)	71	69	.507	13½	Ryan Newman	301,366	4,498	2003
Lynchburg Hillcats (Braves)	69	70	.496	15	Luis Salazar	160,537	2,396	2012
Wilmington Blue Rocks (Royals)	63	77	.450	21½	Vance Wilson	292,319	4,429	1999
Frederick Keys (Orioles)	61	78	.439	23	Ryan Minor	324,311	4,914	2011
Carolina Mudcats (Indians)	57	83	.407	27½	David Wallace	224,736	3,354	2006

CLUB BATTING

	AVG	G	AB	R	H	2B	3B	HR	RBI	BB	SO	SB	OBP	SLG
Carolina	.266	140	4693	637	1247	278	39	63	569	523	939	111	.345	.382
Potomac	.262	140	4580	680	1200	242	42	85	611	506	1017	216	.343	.389
Salem	.256	140	4625	644	1184	268	39	96	578	514	1019	175	.335	.393
Winston-Salem	.254	140	4691	703	1193	281	34	116	653	486	1093	114	.334	.403
Lynchburg	.253	139	4517	607	1144	266	37	89	540	410	1001	88	.323	.388
Myrtle Beach	.249	140	4548	621	1134	243	31	64	551	484	1001	132	.330	.359
Wilmington	.246	140	4609	572	1133	222	36	69	519	452	1024	123	.319	.355
Frederick	.245	139	4702	612	1154	218	17	109	561	549	1110	141	.330	.369

CLUB PITCHING

	ERA	G	CG	SHO	SV	IP	H	R	ER	HR	BB	SO	AVG
Potomac	3.69	140	7	11	42	1214	1151	590	498	98	448	1057	.251
Myrtle Beach	3.71	140	2	8	35	1211	1091	605	499	87	535	1105	.241
Wilmington	3.89	140	2	7	24	1222	1136	635	528	82	498	1137	.246
Salem	3.90	140	4	10	31	1221	1165	596	529	79	442	971	.253
Winston-Salem	3.94	140	6	13	29	1221	1202	630	534	94	521	956	.257
Carolina	4.09	140	1	9	23	1216	1180	657	553	89	500	960	.256
Lynchburg	4.12	139	2	8	31	1194	1165	642	547	75	546	1088	.255
Frederick	4.43	139	1	2	26	1228	1299	721	604	87	434	930	.272

CLUB FIELDING

	PCT	PO	A	E	DP		PCT	PO	A	E	DP
Salem	.978	3664	1508	114	129	Frederick	.971	3685	1515	158	134
Potomac	.975	3641	1302	128	107	Lynchburg	.970	3581	1483	159	132
Carolina	.973	3648	1438	139	114	Myrtle Beach	.970	3635	1389	153	146
Winston-Salem	.973	3663	1407	141	114	Wilmington	.969	3667	1369	160	117

INDIVIDUAL BATTING LEADERS (Minimum 2.7 PA/Team Game)

Batter, Club	AVG	G	AB	R	H	HR	RBI
Ohlman, Michael, Frederick	.313	100	361	61	113	13	53
# Burns, Billy, Potomac	.310	90	326	69	101	0	29
* Odor, Rougned, Myrtle Beach	.302	99	374	65	113	5	59
Rohm, David, Lynchburg	.301	129	492	76	148	2	53
# Sardinas, Luis, Myrtle Beach	.298	96	379	69	113	1	29
# Swihart, Blake, Salem	.298	103	376	45	112	2	42
* Smith, Jordan, Carolina	.293	134	518	71	152	5	55
* Wendle, Joe, Carolina	.293	107	413	73	121	16	64
* Ramsey, Caleb, Potomac	.291	126	478	80	139	6	58
Myles, Bryson, Carolina	.285	92	337	55	96	8	52

INDIVIDUAL PITCHING LEADERS (Minimum 0.8 IP/team game)

Pitcher, Club	W	L	ERA	IP	H	BB	SO
Anderson, Cody, Carolina	9	4	2.34	123	105	31	112
Schwartz, Blake, Potomac	11	4	2.58	133	116	26	80
Martinez, Nick, Myrtle Beach	10	7	2.87	119	106	38	105
Asher, Alec, Myrtle Beach	9	7	2.90	133	120	40	139
Beck, Chris, Winston-Salem	11	8	3.19	119	117	42	57
Ross, Greg, Lynchburg	9	6	3.27	121	120	36	91
Eickhoff, Jerad, Myrtle Beach	7	3	3.41	116	110	26	80
* Selman, Sam, Wilmington	11	9	3.45	125	88	85	128
Davies, Zach, Frederick	7	8	3.69	149	145	38	132
* Morimando, Shawn, Carolina	8	13	3.73	135	115	76	102

ALL-STAR TEAM

C: Michael Ohlman, Frederick. 1B: Trever Adams, Myrtle Beach. 2B: Rougned Odor, Myrtle Beach. 3B: Chris Curley, Winston-Salem. SS: Francisco Lindor, Carolina. UT-IF: Joe Wendle, Carolina. OF: Billy Burns, Potomac; Keury de la Cruz, Salem; Michael Taylor, Potomac. UT-OF: David Rohm, Lynchburg. DH: Robby Hefflinger, Lynchburg. SP: Cody Anderson, Carolina. RP: Robert Benincasa, Potomac. Most Valuable Player: Chris Curley, Winston-Salem. Pitcher of the Year: Cody Anderson, Carolina. Manager of the Year: Jason Wood, Myrtle Beach.

DEPARTMENT LEADERS

BATTING

OBP	Burns, Billy, Potomac	.422
SLG	Ohlman, Michael, Frederick	.524
OPS	Ohlman, Michael, Frederick	.934
R	Curley, Chris, Winston-Salem	90
H	Smith, Jordan, Carolina	151
TB	Curley, Chris, Winston-Salem	251
XBH	Taylor, Michael, Potomac	57
2B	Taylor, Michael, Potomac	41
3B	Burns, Billy, Potomac	9
HR	Curley, Chris, Winston-Salem	24
RBI	Curley, Chris, Winston-Salem	92
SAC	Trapp, Justin, Winston-Salem	13
BB	Kubitza, Kyle, Lynchburg	80
HBP	Matera, Paddy, Carolina	18
SO	Hawkins, Courtney, W-S	160
SB	Burns, Billy, Potomac	54
CS	Kubitza, Kyle, Lynchburg	16
AB/SO	Burns, Billy, Potomac	8.92

PITCHING

G	Nate Hyatt, Lynchburg	43
	Rob Nixon, Carolina	43
GS	Blough, Bryan, Winston-Salem	28
GF	Triggs, Andrew, Wilmington	37
SV	Benincasa, Robert, Potomac	17
W	Five tied at	11
L	Morimando, Shawn, Carolina	13
IP	Blough, Bryan, Winston-Salem	172.2
H	Blough, Bryan, Winston-Salem	184
R	Blough, Bryan, Winston-Salem	90
ER	Cuevas, William, Salem	76
HB	Holland, A.J., Lynchburg	17
BB	Selman, Sam, Wilmington	85
SO	Asher, Alec, Myrtle Beach	139
SO/9	Asher, Alec, Myrtle Beach	9.38
SO/9(RP)	Rivera, Wilson, Lynchburg	12.4
BB/9	Schwartz, Blake, Potomac	1.76
WP	Miller, Jarrett, Lynchburg	16
BK	Martinez, Nick, Myrtle Beach	3
	Morimando, Shawn, Carolina	3
HR	Berry, Tim, Frederick	13
	Cuevas, William, Salem	13
	Lamb, John, Wilmington	13
AVG	Selman, Sam, Wilmington	.197

FIELDING

C	PCT	Nieto, Adrian, Potomac	.991
	PO	Swihart, Blake, Salem	743
	A	Swihart, Blake, Salem	88
	DP	Cantwell, Pat, Myrtle Beach	13
	E	Swihart, Blake, Salem	10
	PB	Cantwell, Pat, Myrtle Beach	16
		Morin, Parker, Wilmington	16
1B	PCT	Keyes, Kevin, Potomac	.987
	PO	Sabourin, Jerrud, Carolina	926
	A	Sabourin, Jerrud, Carolina	78
	DP	Sabourin, Jerrud, Carolina	88
	E	Sabourin, Jerrud, Carolina	15
2B	PCT	Pena, Jerome, Frederick	.981
	PO	Wendle, Joe, Carolina	208
	A	Pena, Jerome, Frederick	317
	DP	Pena, Jerome, Frederick	73
	E	Trapp, Justin, Wilmington	21
3B	PCT	Robinson, Drew, Myrtle Beach	.929
	PO	Robinson, Drew, Myrtle Beach	92
	A	Kubitza, Kyle, Lynchburg	218
	DP	Kubitza, Kyle, Lynchburg	26
	E	Kubitza, Kyle, Lynchburg	25
SS	PCT	Reyes, Elmer, Lynchburg	.969
	PO	Starr, Sammie, Frederick	171
	A	Reyes, Elmer, Lynchburg	369
	DP	Starr, Sammie, Frederick	79
	E	Sardinas, Luis, Myrtle Beach	25
		Starr, Sammie, Frederick	25
OF	PCT	Skole, Jake, Myrtle Beach	.996
	PO	Taylor, Michael, Potomac	325
	A	Taylor, Michael, Potomac	21
	DP	Beck, Preston, Myrtle Beach	6
	E	Hawkins, Courtney, W-S	11

MINOR LEAGUES

BY JOHN MANUEL

The easiest way to describe the Florida State League in 2013 is fun.

League managers and scouts who covered the league agreed the top-end talent and depth was as good as it had been in years, and the league had several of the minors' top storylines.

Fort Myers proved interesting all year long, starting with 2000 Olympic hero and longtime big leaguer Doug Mientkiewicz managing for the first time and piloting a team with two of the minors' best prospects. First it was Miguel Sano, trailed by a documentary film crew and capable of launching—and admiring—tape-measure home runs at any time.

Then, after Sano left, the game's best prospect showed up, and outfielder Byron Buxton lived up to the hype. In fact, he exceeded it, building his case for the Minor League Player of the Year award.

Meanwhile, precocious hitters zoomed through the league, which started the year with one of the best pitching prospects in Noah Syndergaard.

Daytona won the league title behind righthander C.J. Edwards and third baseman Kris Bryant, the 2013 No. 2 overall pick. Edwards pitched 10 scoreless innings in the postseason, giving up only one hit while striking out 11. Bryant hit five homers in 16 games before batting .364 in the playoffs.

Daytona gave up just four runs in six playoff outings, posting four shutouts behind Edwards and fellow pitchers Pierce Johnson, Ivan Pineyro and Corey Black. The Cubs also claimed the league's lone no-hitter, a nine-inning job by righthander Matt Loosen on July 8 against Dunedin.

The Cubs won the league title after losing shortstop Javier Baez to a promotion to Double-A (Baez hit 37 homers on the season, second in the minors) and outfielder Jorge Soler to a broken leg. Baez signaled he was ready with a five-hit, three-double game on June 1 in which he also homered and drove in six runs, then one-upped himself with a four-homer, seven-RBI effort June 10.

Soler also was involved in one of the league's more newsworthy incidents when he was suspended five games for his part in an April fracas, when he charged the Clearwater dugout while wielding a bat. He was stopped before doing any harm.

TOP 20 PROSPECTS

1. Byron Buxton, of, Fort Myers (Twins)
2. Miguel Sano, 3b, Fort Myers (Twins)
3. Javier Baez, ss, Daytona (Cubs)
4. Gregory Polanco, of, Bradenton (Pirates)
5. Maikel Franco, 3b, Clearwater (Phillies)
6. Noah Syndergaard, rhp, St. Lucie (Mets)
7. Gary Sanchez, c, Tampa (Yankees)
8. Jorge Soler, of, Daytona (Cubs)
9. Andrew Heaney, lhp, Jupiter (Marlins)
10. Aaron Sanchez, rhp, Dunedin (Blue Jays)
11. Nick Kingham, rhp, Bradenton (Pirates)
12. Eddie Rosario, 2b, Fort Myers (Twins)
13. Alen Hanson, ss, Bradenton (Pirates)
14. Stephen Piscotty, of, Palm Beach (Cardinals)
15. Pierce Johnson, rhp, Daytona (Cubs)
16. Justin Nicolino, lhp, Jupiter (Marlins)
17. Devon Travis, 2b, Lakeland (Tigers)
18. Anthony DeSclafani, rhp, Jupiter (Marlins)
19. Mason Williams, of, Tampa (Yankees)
20. Aaron Altherr, of, Clearwater (Phillies)

STANDINGS: SPLIT SEASON

FIRST HALF

NORTH	W	L	PCT	GB
Dunedin	37	29	.561	—
Brevard Co	37	30	.552	½
Daytona	35	31	.530	2
Clearwater	35	33	.515	3
Lakeland	30	38	.441	8
Tampa	28	40	.412	10

SOUTH	W	L	PCT	GB
Fort Myers	45	22	.672	—
St. Lucie	37	30	.552	8
Jupiter	36	32	.529	9½
Charlotte	29	38	.433	16
Palm Beach	29	39	.426	16½
Bradenton	26	42	.382	19½

SECOND HALF

NORTH	W	L	PCT	GB
Daytona	40	20	.667	—
Lakeland	34	30	.531	8
Clearwater	32	35	.478	11½
Tampa	30	38	.441	14
Brevard Co	29	38	.433	14½
Dunedin	26	39	.400	16.5

SOUTH	W	L	PCT	GB
Charlotte	38	27	.585	—
St. Lucie	34	30	.531	3½
Palm Beach	35	32	.522	4
Fort Myers	34	34	.500	5½
Bradenton	31	35	.470	7½
Jupiter	32	37	.464	8

PLAYOFFS—Semifinals: Charlotte defeated Fort Myers 2-0 and Daytona defeated Dunedin 2-0 in best-of-three series.
Finals: Daytona defeated Charlotte 3-1 in a best-of-five series.

OVERALL STANDINGS

Team (Organization)	W	L	PCT	GB	Manager	Attendance	Average	Last Pennant
Daytona Cubs (Cubs)	75	51	.595	—	Dave Keller	146,049	2,518	2011
Fort Myers Miracle (Twins)	79	56	.585	½	Doug Mientkiewicz	121,832	1,904	1985
St. Lucie Mets (Mets)	71	60	.542	½	Ryan Ellis	98,664	1,542	2006
Charlotte Stone Crabs (Rays)	67	65	.508	11	Brady Williams	107,995	1,770	1990
Jupiter Hammerheads (Marlins)	68	69	.496	12½	Andy Haines	64,813	997	1991
Clearwater Threshers (Phillies)	67	68	.496	12½	Chris Truby	172,151	2,608	2007
Brevard County Manatees (Brewers)	66	68	.493	13	Joe Ayrault	97,238	1,451	2001
Lakeland Flying Tigers (Tigers)	64	68	.485	14	Dave Huppert	60,011	1,177	2012
Dunedin Blue Jays (Blue Jays)	63	68	.481	14½	Bobby Meacham	50,695	768	Never
Palm Beach Cardinals (Cardinals)	64	71	.474	15½	Johnny Rodriguez	64,121	972	2005
Tampa Yankees (Yankees)	58	78	.426	22	Luis Sojo	118,770	1,827	2010
Bradenton Marauders (Pirates)	57	77	.425	22	Frank Kremblas	109,845	1,772	1963

CLUB BATTING

	AVG	G	AB	R	H	2B	3B	HR	RBI	BB	SO	SB	OBP	SLG
Fort Myers	.271	135	4472	653	1210	237	36	96	585	474	937	147	.345	.404
Charlotte	.264	133	4405	545	1162	232	32	76	504	369	865	133	.328	.383
Daytona	.261	127	4171	606	1089	213	36	81	558	472	899	162	.345	.388
Clearwater	.257	135	4533	562	1166	243	38	78	507	388	950	76	.320	.379
Lakeland	.257	132	4427	558	1139	209	38	63	508	431	839	69	.329	.364
Jupiter	.254	137	4570	517	1161	196	26	43	459	430	893	94	.324	.337
Palm Beach	.254	135	4428	518	1125	221	30	79	479	396	883	101	.321	.371
Dunedin	.253	131	4322	533	1093	235	29	75	498	401	870	155	.319	.373
Tampa	.253	136	4490	549	1137	222	26	63	501	478	920	125	.330	.356
St. Lucie	.250	131	4344	565	1084	235	23	70	523	392	875	65	.321	.363
Bradenton	.246	134	4344	529	1068	245	44	72	481	433	1079	162	.317	.372
Brevard County	.241	134	4399	509	1058	211	26	81	473	343	1063	90	.301	.356

CLUB PITCHING

	ERA	G	CG	SHO	SV	IP	H	R	ER	HR	BB	SO	AVG
Jupiter	3.24	137	2	10	33	1202	1161	514	433	64	346	941	.253
Fort Myers	3.46	135	5	13	36	1169	1134	520	450	87	374	900	.255
Dunedin	3.51	131	2	9	35	1141	1056	526	445	72	378	982	.245
Palm Beach	3.59	135	2	13	39	1161	1133	551	463	61	364	837	.258
St. Lucie	3.61	131	0	15	38	1140	1081	518	457	80	416	993	.250
Daytona	3.64	127	4	16	38	1108	1037	497	448	67	457	964	.248
Brevard County	3.66	134	3	6	37	1164	1089	547	474	67	496	906	.250
Lakeland	3.76	132	2	9	38	1143	1127	543	477	68	399	775	.258
Charlotte	3.82	133	6	14	29	1151	1084	563	489	70	449	923	.249
Bradenton	3.83	134	1	2	34	1167	1200	593	497	85	360	820	.266
Clearwater	4.08	135	4	13	36	1184	1217	617	536	87	517	955	.269
Tampa	4.17	136	2	5	18	1181	1173	655	547	69	451	1077	.257

CLUB FIELDING

	PCT	PO	A	E	DP		PCT	PO	A	E	DP
Clearwater	.980	3551	1367	100	131	Brevard County	.975	3492	1374	124	137
Dunedin	.978	3424	1434	110	116	Jupiter	.975	3606	1400	127	123
Fort Myers	.977	3507	1397	113	131	Palm Beach	.975	3484	1323	125	127
Lakeland	.977	3429	1420	115	121	Bradenton	.972	3502	1518	143	121
Daytona	.976	3323	1297	116	126	Charlotte	.972	3454	1310	137	114
St. Lucie	.976	3419	1337	118	103	Tampa	.968	3543	1424	159	101

INDIVIDUAL BATTING LEADERS (Minimum 2.7 PA/Team Game)

Batter, Club	AVG	G	AB	R	H	HR	RBI
* Keys, Brent, Jupiter	.346	95	382	57	132	2	33
* Popkins, David, Palm Beach	.320	92	347	49	111	6	45
Perkins, Cameron, Clearwater	.295	103	387	54	114	6	53
* Westlake, Aaron, Lakeland	.291	91	358	40	104	7	62
* Newman, Matt, Dunedin	.290	102	348	42	101	6	37
Rivera, T.J., St. Lucie	.289	125	502	76	145	2	51
* Krizan, Jason, Lakeland	.288	116	399	48	115	4	52
* Wright, Chad, Lakeland	.286	85	329	53	94	0	30
Rodriguez, Jonathan, Palm Beach	.285	125	453	71	129	18	72
Refsnyder, Robert, Tampa	.283	117	413	66	117	6	51

INDIVIDUAL PITCHING LEADERS (Minimum 0.8 IP/team game)

Pitcher, Club	W	L	ERA	IP	H	BB	SO
Summers, Matt, Fort Myers	6	5	2.47	120	100	34	87
* Rogers, Taylor, Fort Myers	11	6	2.53	132	120	32	85
Palacios, Wilsen, Lakeland	7	8	3.07	135	121	44	109
* Ryan, Kyle, Lakeland	12	7	3.17	142	132	37	90
Wells, Ben, Daytona	9	6	3.28	112	96	40	69
Pierce, Chad, Brevard County	6	6	3.40	109	93	52	106
Hernandez, Jesse, Dunedin	7	12	3.49	134	134	38	89
Allen, Scottie, Tampa	9	5	3.54	112	108	32	75
Hodges, Josh, Jupiter	4	6	3.60	132	130	31	84
* Rivero, Felipe, Charlotte	9	7	3.61	127	123	52	91

ALL-STAR TEAM

C: Gary Sanchez, Tampa; Matt Koch, Fort Myers. **1B:** Jonathan Rodriguez, Palm Beach. **2B:** Jon Berti, Dunedin. **3B:** Richie Shaffer, Charlotte. **SS:** Javier Baez, Daytona. **UT-IF:** T.J. Rivera, St. Lucie. **LF:** Dustin Lawley, St. Lucie. **CF:** Brent Keys, Jupiter. **RF:** David Popkins, Palm Beach. **UT-OF:** Aaron Altherr, Clearwater. **DH:** Kennys Vargas, Fort Myers. **P:** Matt Bowman, St. Lucie; Justin Nicolino, Jupiter; Taylor Rogers, Fort Myers; Kyle Ryan, Lakeland. **RP:** Ronnie Shaban, Palm Beach; Nick Wittgren, Clearwater.
Player of the Year: Dustin Lawley, St. Lucie. **Pitcher of the Year:** Justin Nicolino, Jupiter.
Manager of the Year: Doug Mientkiewicz, Fort Myers.

DEPARTMENT LEADERS

BATTING

OBP	Keys, Brent, Jupiter	.418
SLG	Lawley, Dustin, St. Lucie	.512
OPS	Rodriguez, Jonathan, Palm Beach	.854
R	Berti, Jon, Dunedin	85
H	Rivera, T.J., St. Lucie	145
TB	Lawley, Dustin, St. Lucie	240
XBH	Lawley, Dustin, St. Lucie	63
2B	Altherr, Aaron, Clearwater	36
3B	Lewis, Taylor, Bradenton	12
HR	Lawley, Dustin, St. Lucie	25
RBI	Vargas, Kennys, Fort Myers	93
SAC	Nola, Austin, Jupiter	12
BB	DeVoss, Zeke, Daytona	80
HBP	DeVoss, Zeke, Daytona	23
SO	Ramirez, Nick, Brevard County	171
SB	Berti, Jon, Dunedin	56
CS	Berti, Jon, Dunedin	19
AB/SO	Keys, Brent, Jupiter	14.65

PITCHING

G	O'Sullivan, Ryan, Clearwater	53
GS	Urena, Jose, Jupiter	26
	Wheeler, Jason, Fort Myers	26
GF	Shaban, Ronnie, Palm Beach	41
SV	Wittgren, Nick, Jupiter	25
W	Milner, Hoby, Clearwater	12
	Ryan, Kyle, Lakeland	12
L	Hernandez, Jesse, Dunedin	12
IP	Urena, Jose, Jupiter	149.2
H	Sampson, Adrian, Bradenton	177
R	Rowland, Robby, Bradenton	89
ER	Sampson, Adrian, Bradenton	80
HB	Miller, Matt, Brevard County	19
BB	Stewart, Ethan, Clearwater	80
SO	Black, Corey, Tampa, Daytona	116
SO/9	Carpenter, Ryan, Charlotte	7.42
SO/9(RP)	Fontanez, Randy, St. Lucie	12.3
BB/9	Sampson, Adrian, Bradenton	1.41
WP	Mitchell, Bryan, Tampa	23
BK	Hald, Kyle, Palm Beach	4
HR	Sampson, Adrian, Bradenton	18
AVG	Summers, Matthew, Fort Myers	.222

FIELDING

C	PCT	Stallings, Jacob, Bradenton	.991
	PO	Garfield, Cameron, Brevard Co.	645
	A	Moore, Logan, Clearwater	80
	DP	Maron, Cam, St. Lucie	10
	E	Garfield, Cameron, Brevard Co.	11
	PB	Garfield, Cameron, Brevard Co.	11
		Sanchez, Gary, Tampa	11
1B	PCT	Geiger, Dustin, Daytona	.994
	PO	Ramirez, Nick, Brevard County	918
	A	Rodriguez, Jonathan, Palm Beach	66
	DP	Ramirez, Nick, Brevard County	115
	E	Ramirez, Nick, Brevard County	11
		Vargas, Kennys, Fort Myers	11
2B	PCT	Alonso, Carlos, Clearwater	.996
	PO	Hopkins, Gregory, Brevard Co.	245
	A	Berti, Jon, Dunedin	341
	DP	Hopkins, Gregory, Brevard Co.	84
	E	Refsnyder, Robert, Tampa	20
3B	PCT	Shaffer, Richie, Charlotte	.934
	PO	Macias, Brandon, Brevard Co.	63
	A	Shaffer, Richie, Charlotte	201
	DP	Martinez, Francisco, Lakeland	22
	E	Four tied at	18
SS	PCT	Nola, Austin, Jupiter	.974
	PO	Rivera, Yadiel, Brevard County	200
	A	Rivera, Yadiel, Brevard County	429
	DP	Rivera, Yadiel, Brevard County	103
	E	Baez, Javier, Daytona	31
OF	PCT	Newman, Matt, Dunedin	.995
	PO	Carter, Kes, Charlotte	308
	A	Garcia, Willy, Bradenton	20
	DP	Garcia, Willy, Bradenton	7
	E	Vettleson, Drew, Charlotte	14

MINOR LEAGUES

MINOR LEAGUES

BY J.J. COOPER

They may not have been the best team in the regular season, but the Quad Cities River Bandits don't have to worry about being tagged as a fluke.

The River Bandits finished the regular season 81-57, the second-best record in the Western Division and third best overall in the Midwest League. The club's overall consistency wasn't enough to win either the first- or second-half division titles, but it did easily earn them a wild-card spot. And once they got into the playoffs, they had little trouble trouncing all competition. Quad Cities swept Cedar Rapids in the best-of-three quarterfinal series, won a deciding Game Three of their semifinal series against Beloit and then swept South Bend in the championship series to win the club's sixth Midwest League title.

In going 7-1 through the playoffs, Quad Cities had a 2.15 ERA that was more than a run better than anyone else in the league. What was impressive is the River Bandits dominated the playoffs with pitching even though the pitching staff that had gotten them to the playoffs had disappeared. Vince Velasquez, Lance McCullers Jr. and Mark Appel had each been shut down.

No problem, Josh Hader, acquired from the Orioles in a midseason trade, went 2-0, 0.64 in two starts. Joe Bircher went 2-0, 0.90.

Quad Cities won the title, but the 2013 season will likely be most fondly remembered in Cedar Rapids. Just four seasons after Mike Trout roamed center field for the Kernels, Cedar Rapids once again had a future star in center. Byron Buxton established his credentials as the best prospect in the game with an outstanding .341/.431/.559 first-half that earned him a promotion.

TOP 20 PROSPECTS

1. Byron Buxton, of, Cedar Rapids (Twins)
2. Carlos Correa, ss, Quad Cities (Astros)
3. Robert Stephenson, rhp, Dayton (Reds)
4. Corey Seager, ss, Great Lakes (Dodgers)
5. Lance McCullers Jr, rhp, Quad Cities (Astros)
6. Albert Almora, of, Kane County (Cubs)
7. Julio Urias, lhp, Great Lakes (Dodgers)
8. Max Fried, lhp, Fort Wayne (Padres)
9. Jesse Winker, of, Dayton (Reds)
10. Pierce Johnson, rhp, Kane County (Cubs)
11. Zach Eflin, rhp, Fort Wayne (Padres)
12. Vince Velasquez, rhp, Quad Cities (Astros)
13. Jose Berrios, rhp, Cedar Rapids (Twins)
14. Joe Ross, rhp, Fort Wayne (Padres)
15. Adam Brett Walker, of, Cedar Rapids (Twins)
16. Brandon Drury, 3b, South Bend (Diamondbacks)
17. Dan Vogelbach, 1b, Kane County (Cubs)
18. Taylor Guerrieri, rhp, Bowling Green (Rays)
19. Andrew Toles, of, Bowling Green (Rays)
20. Jorge Polanco, 2b/ss, Cedar Rapids (Twins)

STANDINGS: SPLIT SEASON

FIRST HALF					SECOND HALF				
NORTH	W	L	PCT	GB	NORTH	W	L	PCT	GB
South Bend	44	25	.638	—	Bowling G.	44	26	.629	—
Fort Wayne	43	26	.623	1	Great Lakes	40	29	.580	3½
Bowling G.	38	30	.559	5½	Dayton	37	33	.529	7
W. Michigan	33	37	.471	11½	South Bend	37	33	.529	7
Lansing	32	37	.464	12	W. Michigan	36	33	.522	7½
Dayton	28	41	.406	16	Lake Co.	31	39	.443	13
Great Lakes	27	43	.386	17½	Fort Wayne	29	41	.414	15
Lake Co.	23	44	.343	20	Lansing	29	41	.414	15
SOUTH	W	L	PCT	GB	SOUTH	W	L	PCT	GB
Beloit	43	27	.614	—	Cedar Rapids	48	22	.686	—
Cedar Rapids	40	28	.588	2	Quad Cities	43	26	.623	4½
Peoria	38	29	.567	3½	Beloit	34	35	.493	13½
Quad Cities	38	31	.551	4½	Clinton	34	36	.486	14
Clinton	33	36	.478	9½	Burlington	30	39	.435	17½
Kane Co.	36	36	.455	11	Peoria	30	40	.429	18
Wisconsin	29	36	.446	11½	Wisconsin	30	40	.429	18
Burlington	26	39	.400	14½	Kane Co.	25	44	.362	22½

PLAYOFFS—Division Series: South Bend defeated Great Lakes 2-0, Fort Wayne defeated Bowling Green 2-0, Beloit defeated Clinton 2-0 and Quad Cities defeated Cedar Rapids 2-0 in best-of-three series. **Semifinals:** South Bend defeated Fort Wayne 2-1 and Quad Cities defeated Beloit 2-1 in best-of-three series. **Finals:** Quad Cities defeated South Bend 3-0 in a best-of-five series.

OVERALL STANDINGS

Team (Organization)	W	L	PCT	GB	Manager	Attendance	Average	Last Pennant
Cedar Rapids Kernels (Twins)	88	50	.638	—	Jake Mauer	180,688	2,697	1994
Bowling Green Hot Rods (Rays)	82	56	.594	6	Jared Sandberg	216,301	3,228	Never
Quad Cities River Bandits (Astros)	81	57	.587	7	Omar Lopez	226,112	3,533	2013
South Bend Silver Hawks (Diamondbacks)	81	58	.583	7½	Mark Haley	237,448	3,598	2005
Beloit Snappers (Athletics)	77	62	.554	11½	Ryan Christenson	61,045	939	1995
Fort Wayne Tincaps (Padres)	72	67	.518	16½	Jose Valentin	403,596	5,766	2009
West Michigan Whitecaps (Tigers)	69	70	.496	19½	Larry Parrish	377,948	5,558	2007
Peoria Chiefs (Cardinals)	68	69	.496	19½	Dann Bilardello	208,616	3,114	2002
Clinton Lumberkings (Mariners)	67	72	.482	21½	Eddie Menchaca	113,880	1,779	1991
Great Lakes Loons (Dodgers)	67	72	.482	21½	Razor Shines	231,639	3,564	2000
Dayton Dragons (Reds)	65	74	.468	23½	Jose Nieves	579,946	8,405	Never
Lansing Lugnuts (Blue Jays)	61	78	.439	27½	John Tamargo	334,806	5,231	2003
Wisconsin Timber Rattlers (Brewers)	59	76	.437	27½	Matt Erickson	241,938	3,780	2012
Burlington Bees (Angels)	56	78	.418	30	Jamie Burke	62,932	1,015	2008
Kane County Cougars (Cubs)	55	80	.407	31½	Mark Johnson	406,152	6,154	2001
Lake County Captains (Indians)	54	83	.394	33½	Scooter Tucker	235,002	3,561	2010

CLUB BATTING

	AVG	G	AB	R	H	2B	3B	HR	RBI	BB	SO	SB	OBP	SLG
Clinton	.268	139	4640	629	1244	261	30	72	569	429	875	106	.333	.384
Cedar Rapids	.267	138	4664	752	1243	253	53	108	692	530	1078	125	.346	.413
Bowling Green	.263	138	4641	666	1219	240	58	70	603	501	994	230	.339	.385
Fort Wayne	.261	139	4700	632	1228	245	44	76	558	367	979	166	.323	.381
South Bend	.260	139	4700	624	1224	275	54	89	551	418	1128	99	.325	.399
Kane County	.259	135	4539	582	1177	220	39	97	521	480	956	87	.334	.389
Wisconsin	.257	135	4577	594	1178	220	53	65	515	442	979	114	.330	.371
Dayton	.256	139	4685	614	1198	210	38	71	539	428	962	158	.323	.362
Peoria	.256	138	4616	573	1184	196	39	61	506	406	817	91	.322	.356
Beloit	.254	138	4618	658	1171	244	27	120	598	502	1086	97	.331	.396
West Michigan	.253	139	4620	591	1169	227	35	90	551	456	1093	113	.326	.376
Lake County	.247	138	4490	591	1109	250	34	84	521	481	1068	116	.325	.374
Quad Cities	.247	138	4525	636	1119	225	32	76	556	578	1039	151	.338	.362
Burlington	.242	134	4416	545	1068	198	31	72	486	444	1039	147	.317	.350
Lansing	.240	139	4588	581	1103	219	43	79	520	458	1024	138	.315	.359
Great Lakes	.238	139	4497	590	1069	217	23	66	516	522	1055	181	.324	.340

CLUB PITCHING

	ERA	G	CG	SHO	SV	IP	H	R	ER	HR	BB	SO	AVG
Bowling Green	3.06	138	0	15	38	1219	1049	483	415	87	440	1057	.232
Peoria	3.54	138	3	9	37	1215	1191	546	478	71	398	1112	.256
Fort Wayne	3.59	139	0	10	42	1227	1181	621	489	63	516	1011	.253
Quad Cities	3.62	138	0	7	43	1214	1204	559	488	73	394	1086	.259
West Michigan	3.62	139	1	10	40	1214	1169	605	489	61	448	976	.254
Great Lakes	3.66	139	1	13	34	1203	1124	595	490	76	492	1113	.246
South Bend	3.68	139	6	13	47	1221	1095	577	499	76	484	987	.237
Cedar Rapids	3.69	138	3	6	42	1212	1152	604	497	84	428	1021	.249
Burlington	3.82	134	2	6	31	1165	1075	588	494	98	424	1006	.244
Beloit	3.88	139	3	7	43	1206	1261	612	520	73	452	943	.270
Clinton	3.90	139	4	6	29	1194	1123	625	517	81	480	883	.248
Lansing	3.98	139	2	7	27	1202	1211	681	532	76	496	1066	.260
Wisconsin	4.09	135	1	4	32	1194	1206	651	542	102	496	953	.264
Lake County	4.24	138	4	8	24	1185	1205	691	559	99	457	983	.264
Kane County	4.49	135	1	6	24	1174	1238	708	586	72	506	891	.272
Dayton	4.50	139	0	6	37	1225	1219	712	612	104	531	1084	.261

CLUB FIELDING

	PCT	PO	A	E	DP		PCT	PO	A	E	DP
Dayton	.974	3675	1377	137	122	Wisconsin	.969	3581	1494	163	123
Peoria	.974	3646	1498	140	129	Great Lakes	.968	3610	1326	163	91
Bowling Green	.973	3657	1507	143	120	Clinton	.967	3583	1452	172	119
Quad Cities	.973	3643	1475	142	114	West Michigan	.967	3643	1545	176	125
Beloit	.972	3619	1462	149	130	Kane County	.966	3523	1490	174	131
South Bend	.971	3662	1385	149	86	Fort Wayne	.965	3682	1435	187	128
Cedar Rapids	.970	3635	1525	159	116	Lansing	.964	3607	1433	186	110
Burlington	.969	3494	1410	155	130	Lake County	.962	3556	1407	196	107

INDIVIDUAL BATTING LEADERS (Minimum 2.7 PA/Team Game)

Batter, Club	AVG	G	AB	R	H	HR	RBI
Reginato, Leonardo, Bowling Green	.328	112	412	68	135	1	49
* Toles, Andrew, Bowling Green	.326	121	519	79	169	2	57
Correa, Carlos, Quad Cities	.320	117	450	73	144	9	86
* Pizzano, Dario, Clinton	.311	126	463	75	144	8	70
# Valera, Breyvic, Peoria	.309	128	515	71	159	0	48
# Polanco, Jorge, Cedar Rapids	.308	115	465	76	143	5	78
Mejias-Brean, Seth, Dayton	.305	127	479	70	146	10	80
# Marte, Ketel, Clinton	.304	98	378	61	115	0	29
* Tilson, Charlie, Peoria	.303	100	376	49	114	4	30
Drury, Brandon, South Bend	.302	134	526	78	159	15	85

INDIVIDUAL PITCHING LEADERS (Minimum 0.8 IP/team game)

Pitcher, Club	W	L	ERA	IP	H	BB	SO
Eflin, Zach, Fort Wayne	7	6	2.73	119	110	31	86
Sanchez, Victor, Clinton	6	6	2.78	113	106	18	79
Lopez, Reinaldo, Bowling Green	7	5	2.95	116	109	33	86
* Lee, Brett, Cedar Rapids	8	4	2.95	116	116	26	89
Ames, Jeff, Bowling Green	9	4	2.98	115	87	38	83
* Helisek, Kyle, Peoria	7	7	3.13	129	128	42	101
* Melotakis, Mason, Cedar Rapids	11	4	3.16	111	106	39	84
Wagner, Tyler, Wisconsin	10	8	3.21	149	129	56	116
* Crowley, Ryan, Burlington	10	7	3.28	151	141	35	123
* Merritt, Ryan, Lake County	6	9	3.42	126	142	18	91

ALL-STAR TEAM

C: Luke Maile, Bowling Green. **1B:** Dalton Hicks, Cedar Rapids. **2B:** Devon Travis, West Michigan. **3B:** Brandon Drury, South Bend. **SS:** Carlos Correa, Quad Cities. **OF:** Byron Buxton, Cedar Rapids; Andrew Toles, Bowling Green; Adam Brett Walker, Cedar Rapids. **DH:** Rock Shoulders, Kane County. **RHSP:** Dylan Floro, Bowling Green. **LHSP:** Tyler Pike, Clinton. **RHRP:** R.J. Hively, South Bend. **LHRP:** Geoff Brown, Great Lakes. **Most Valuable Player:** Byron Buxton, Cedar Rapids. **Prospect of the Year:** Byron Buxton, Cedar Rapids. **Manager of the Year:** Mark Haley, South Bend.

DEPARTMENT LEADERS

BATTING

OBP	Vick, Logan, Lake County	.413
SLG	Flores, Rudy, Great Lakes	.528
OPS	Correa, Carlos, Quad Cities	.872
R	Hernandez, Teoscar, Quad Cities	97
H	Toles, Andrew, Bowling Green	169
TB	Walker II, Adam Brett, C. Rapids	267
XBH	Drury, Brandon, South Bend	70
2B	Drury, Brandon, South Bend	51
3B	Toles, Andrew, Bowling Green	16
HR	Walker II, Adam Brett, C. Rapids	27
RBI	Walker II, Adam Brett, C. Rapids	109
SAC	Hernandez, Teoscar, Quad Cities	17
BB	Ogle, Tyler, Great Lakes	96
HBP	Tissenbaum, Maxx, Fort Wayne	19
SO	Baldwin, James, Great Lakes	154
SB	Smith, Mallex, Fort Wayne	64
CS	Toles, Andrew, Bowling Green	17
AB/SO	Valera, Breyvic, Peoria	17.17

PITCHING

G	Nunn, Chris, Fort Wayne	55
GS	Darrah, Jesse, South Bend	27
GF	Sikula, Arik, Lansing	42
SV	Madrid, Roman, Fort Wayne	22
W	Brown, Geoff, Great Lakes	12
	Darrah, Jesse, South Bend	12
L	Four tied at	11
IP	Darrah, Jesse, South Bend	151.1
H	DeJesus, Luis, Lake County	154
R	DeJesus, Luis, Lake County	100
ER	DeJesus, Luis, Lake County	88
HB	Perry, Blake, South Bend	19
BB	Guillon, Ismael, Dayton	95
SO	Guillon, Ismael, Dayton	134
SO/9	Guillon, Ismael, Dayton	9.94
SO/9(RP)	Sawyer, Nick, Bowling Green	12.1
BB/9	Cisco, Drew, Dayton	1.1
WP	Guillon, Ismael, Dayton	26
BK	De La Rosa, Edgar, West Michigan	8
HR	DeJesus, Luis, Lake County	24
AVG	Ames, Jeff, Bowling Green	.210

FIELDING

C	PCT	Velazco, Gerwuins, Peoria	.996
	PO	Hudson, Joe, Dayton	699
	A	Haase, Eric, Lake County	93
	DP	Rickles, Nick, Beloit	11
	E	Contreras, Willson, Kane County	18
		Daal, Rodney, Fort Wayne	18
	PB	O'Conner, Justin, Bowling Green	22
1B	PCT	Ogle, Tyler, Great Lakes	.993
	PO	Olson, Matt, Beloit	1109
	A	Olson, Matt, Beloit	102
	DP	Olson, Matt, Beloit	97
		Tejada, Luis, Fort Wayne	97
	E	Leonard, Patrick, Bowling Green	15
		Tejada, Luis, Fort Wayne	15
2B	PCT	Pena, Fidel, South Bend	.982
	PO	Bostick, Chris, Beloit	234
	A	Coyle, Thomas, Bowling Green	341
	DP	Bostick, Chris, Beloit	78
	E	Amaya, Gioskar, Kane County	22
		Bostick, Chris, Beloit	22
3B	PCT	Drury, Brandon, South Bend	.959
	PO	Candelario, Jeimer, Kane County	88
	A	Candelario, Jeimer, Kane County	234
	DP	Candelario, Jeimer, Kane County	24
	E	Nunez, Renato, Beloit	39
SS	PCT	Correa, Carlos, Quad Cities	.973
	PO	Arcia, Orlando, Wisconsin	253
	A	Arcia, Orlando, Wisconsin	353
	DP	Arcia, Orlando, Wisconsin	79
	E	Paulino, Dorssys, Lake County	39
OF	PCT	Pompey, Dalton, Lansing	1.000
	PO	Almadova, Breland, South Bend	272
	A	Adamson, Corey, Fort Wayne	17
	DP	Vick, Logan, Lake County	5
	E	Brito, Socrates, South Bend	15

BY J.J. COOPER

All season clubs facing Savannah knew that runs would be hard to come by.

The Sand Gnats finished second in the league during the regular season in ERA (3.15) behind a pitching staff with excellent control—Savannah walked more than 100 fewer batters than anyone else in the league.

So facing Savannah, the game plan for any club had to be to take advantage of any opportunity, because you weren't going to get many big innings.

Those big innings were few and far between in the playoffs. Savannah rolled to the South Atlantic League title by sweeping its semifinal series and going 3-1 against Hagerstown in the championship series. Over those six games, Savannah allowed more than two runs only once. They had three shutouts, including back-to-back ones against Hagerstown to clinch the title.

Steven Matz was on the mound for the clincher as he worked his second of two scoreless playoff starts. Matz struck out 17 while allowing only seven baserunners over 12 ⅔ innings.

Matz may have gotten the win in the deciding game but Gabriel Ynoa was nearly as effective, going 2-0, 1.23 in two starts.

While Savannah may have won the league title, Hickory was easily the league's most fascinating team. The Rangers' low Class A affiliate was a prospect watcher's dream. Some scouts said they could turn in a full lineup of nine players (counting the pitcher) who projected as future big leaguers.

"It's the only group of kids I've seen—not only in my scouting career, but in my life playing-wise—where there's eight guys who are going to be one of the best players in the game," a scout said.

Joey Gallo, the Crawdads' third baseman, led the minors with 40 home runs. Righthander C.J. Edwards, who was traded to the Cubs during the season, went 8-2, 1.83 with Hickory. Asheville also fielded a fascinating club with righthander Eddie Butler (5-1, 1.66) and shortstop Rosell Herrera (.343/.419/.515).

TOP 20 PROSPECTS

1. Eddie Butler, rhp, Asheville (Rockies)
2. Tyler Glasnow, rhp, West Virginia (Pirates)
3. C.J. Edwards, rhp, Hickory (Rangers/Cubs)
4. Raul Adalberto Mondesi, ss, Lexington (Royals)
5. Rosell Herrera, ss, Asheville (Rockies)
6. Miguel Almonte, rhp, Lexington (Royals)
7. Colin Moran, 3b, Greensboro (Marlins)
8. Mookie Betts, 2b, Greenville (Red Sox)
9. Lucas Sims, rhp, Rome (Braves)
10. Mauricio Cabrera, rhp, Rome (Braves)
11. Lewis Brinson, of, Hickory (Rangers)
12. Joey Gallo, 3b, Hickory (Rangers)
13. Nick Williams, of, Hickory (Rangers)
14. Jorge Alfaro, c, Hickory (Rangers)
15. Nomar Mazara, of, Hickory (Rangers)
16. Jose Peraza, ss, Rome (Braves)
17. Rafael De Paula, rhp, Charleston (Yankees)
18. Carlos Tocci, of, Lakewood (Phillies)
19. Bubba Starling, of, Lexington (Royals)
20. Steve Matz, lhp, Savannah (Mets)

STANDINGS: SPLIT SEASON

FIRST HALF					SECOND HALF				
NORTH	**W**	**L**	**PCT**	**GB**	**NORTH**	**W**	**L**	**PCT**	**GB**
Hagerstown	38	29	.567	—	W. Virginia	45	25	.643	—
Hickory	39	31	.557	½	Hagerstown	42	28	.600	3
W. Virginia	37	33	.529	2½	Hickory	37	32	.536	7½
Greensboro	33	36	.478	6	Kannapolis	34	35	.493	10½
Delmarva	30	37	.448	8	Greensboro	32	36	.471	12
Kannapolis	27	41	.397	11½	Lakewood	30	39	.435	14½
Lakewood	26	41	.388	12	Delmarva	24	45	.348	20½
SOUTH	**W**	**L**	**PCT**	**GB**	**SOUTH**	**W**	**L**	**PCT**	**GB**
Savannah	43	26	.623	—	Augusta	44	24	.647	—
Charleston	39	29	.574	3½	Rome	37	33	.529	8
Asheville	38	30	.559	4½	Charleston	36	34	.514	9
Augusta	38	31	.551	5	Lexington	35	35	.500	10
Rome	36	33	.522	7	Savannah	34	35	.493	10½
Lexington	33	35	.485	9½	Greenville	29	40	.420	15½
Greenville	22	47	.319	21	Asheville	25	43	.368	19

PLAYOFFS—Semifinals: Savannah defeated Augusta 2-0 and Hagerstown defeated West Virginia 2-1 in best-of-three series. **Finals:** Savannah defeated Hagerstown 3-1 in a best-of-five series.

OVERALL STANDINGS

Team (Organization)	W	L	PCT	GB	Manager	Attendance	Average	Last Pennant
Augusta Greenjackets (Giants)	82	55	.599	—	Mike Goff	176,762	2,851	2008
West Virginia Power (Pirates)	82	58	.586	1½	Michael Ryan	149,198	2,331	1990
Hagerstown Suns (Nationals)	80	57	.584	2	Tripp Keister	65,606	1,058	Never
Savannah Sand Gnats (Mets)	77	61	.558	5½	Luis Rojas	131,763	2,027	2013
Hickory Crawdads (Rangers)	76	63	.547	7	Corey Ragsdale	143,157	2,169	2004
Charleston RiverDogs (Yankees)	75	63	.543	7½	Al Pedrique	283,274	4,292	Never
Rome Braves (Braves)	73	66	.525	10	Randy Ingle	168,026	2,625	2003
Lexington Legends (Royals)	68	70	.493	14½	Brian Buchanan	274,805	4,102	2001
Greensboro Grasshoppers (Marlins)	65	72	.474	17	Jorge Hernandez	362,274	5,489	2011
Asheville Tourists (Rockies)	63	73	.463	18½	Fred Ocasio	163,664	2,518	2012
Kannapolis Intimidators (White Sox)	61	76	.445	21	Tommy Thompson	125,811	1,906	2005
Lakewood BlueClaws (Phillies)	56	80	.412	25½	Mickey Morandini	400,299	5,975	2010
Delmarva Shorebirds (Orioles)	54	82	.397	27½	Luis Pujols	206,772	3,335	2001
Greenville Drive (Red Sox)	51	87	.370	31½	Carlos Febles	300,402	4,768	1998

MINOR LEAGUES

CLUB BATTING

	AVG	G	AB	R	H	2B	3B	HR	RBI	BB	SO	SB	OBP	SLG
Asheville	.272	136	4450	644	1209	299	20	105	567	423	1086	211	.341	.419
Hagerstown	.258	137	4468	692	1152	248	33	56	608	530	988	153	.341	.366
Rome	.257	139	4580	603	1179	236	45	60	550	418	1069	188	.324	.368
West Virginia	.256	140	4609	660	1181	244	24	82	584	480	1070	117	.331	.373
Greensboro	.254	137	4492	606	1141	207	24	108	559	385	901	112	.320	.383
Kannapolis	.251	137	4525	595	1136	220	37	62	514	397	1067	183	.319	.357
Augusta	.250	137	4557	625	1141	205	29	67	546	402	956	169	.320	.352
Delmarva	.248	136	4547	532	1126	209	33	57	484	390	1067	102	.313	.346
Charleston	.247	138	4595	599	1134	257	25	97	522	491	1218	108	.329	.377
Greenville	.246	138	4505	541	1109	237	29	60	484	404	1221	125	.317	.352
Savannah	.242	138	4454	565	1079	231	29	50	492	534	1049	95	.333	.341
Lakewood	.238	136	4451	521	1060	237	30	49	465	448	1131	104	.315	.338
Hickory	.237	139	4560	643	1079	225	28	178	593	392	1403	128	.309	.415
Lexington	.213	138	4358	469	929	179	26	59	397	448	1148	159	.294	.307

CLUB PITCHING

	ERA	G	CG	SHO	SV	IP	H	R	ER	HR	BB	SO	AVG
Lexington	2.99	138	6	15	47	1197	1002	486	398	62	400	1143	.226
Savannah	3.15	138	5	13	43	1192	1124	471	417	65	267	1131	.248
Charleston	3.40	138	1	14	30	1216	1100	550	460	69	368	1165	.240
Augusta	3.42	137	2	12	48	1207	1076	519	458	62	445	1175	.239
West Virginia	3.42	140	0	11	35	1206	1055	555	458	75	503	1175	.234
Hagerstown	3.44	137	1	16	36	1175	1043	526	449	84	419	1098	.237
Hickory	3.73	139	1	11	40	1197	1147	605	496	70	468	1084	.251
Rome	3.77	139	4	9	44	1202	1100	602	503	64	462	1144	.244
Kannapolis	3.80	137	4	12	35	1180	1143	625	498	69	428	1163	.251
Lakewood	4.14	136	0	10	31	1178	1199	670	542	75	476	987	.263
Greensboro	4.16	137	0	5	38	1178	1123	656	545	122	501	1070	.250
Delmarva	4.27	136	2	6	24	1169	1162	649	554	66	494	995	.259
Greenville	4.44	138	3	6	23	1168	1116	682	577	114	508	1055	.250
Asheville	4.59	136	4	7	30	1158	1265	699	591	93	403	989	.277

CLUB FIELDING

	PCT	PO	A	E	DP		PCT	PO	A	E	DP
Augusta	.979	3620	1394	107	107	Greenville	.969	3505	1276	153	109
Savannah	.977	3575	1337	118	91	Lexington	.969	3590	1400	161	106
Charleston	.973	3648	1397	141	95	Asheville	.968	3475	1469	162	120
Hagerstown	.973	3525	1438	137	107	West Virginia	.968	3619	1443	165	115
Greensboro	.971	3535	1352	148	97	Hickory	.965	3591	1491	186	131
Rome	.971	3607	1375	150	130	Lakewood	.964	3533	1349	184	125
Delmarva	.970	3507	1438	155	107	Kannapolis	.961	3539	1365	201	95

INDIVIDUAL BATTING LEADERS (Minimum 2.7 PA/Team Game)

Batter, Club	AVG	G	AB	R	H	HR	RBI
# Herrera, Rosell, Asheville	.343	126	472	83	162	16	76
Sosa, Francisco, Asheville	.315	127	461	85	145	20	89
* Flynn, Cameron, Greensboro	.308	97	357	49	110	7	44
Gourley, Walker, West Virginia	.304	119	444	75	135	6	43
# Carmona, William, Lakewood	.303	121	462	60	140	6	54
Renda, Tony, Hagerstown	.292	135	521	99	152	3	51
* Williams, Nick, Hickory	.290	95	376	70	109	17	60
* Pleffner, Shawn, Hagerstown	.288	101	361	55	104	4	52
Peraza, Jose, Rome	.288	114	448	72	129	1	47
* Bird, Greg, Charleston	.288	130	459	84	132	20	84

INDIVIDUAL PITCHING LEADERS (Minimum 0.8 IP/team game)

Pitcher, Club	W	L	ERA	IP	H	BB	SO
Sadzeck, Connor, Hickory	12	4	2.25	132	102	51	78
Sims, Lucas, Rome	12	4	2.62	117	83	46	134
Binford, Christian, Lexington	8	6	2.67	135	129	25	130
Ynoa, Gabriel, Savannah	15	4	2.72	136	123	16	106
Flores, Kendry, Augusta	10	6	2.73	142	113	17	137
Almonte, Miguel, Lexington	6	9	2.89	131	114	36	132
* Stumpf, Daniel, Lexington	10	10	3.07	138	103	50	117
Cessa, Luis, Savannah	8	4	3.12	130	136	19	124
Stratton, Chris, Augusta	9	3	3.27	132	128	47	123
* Faulkner, Andrew, Hickory	6	5	3.48	111	123	37	84

ALL-STAR TEAM

C: Tom Murphy, Asheville. **1B:** Greg Bird, Charleson. **2B:** Micah Johnson, Kannapolis. **3B:** Joey Gallo, Hickory. **SS:** Rosell Herrera, Asheville. **UT-IF:** Tony Renda, Hagerstown. **OF:** Josh Bell, West Virginia; Francisco Sosa, Asheville; Nick Williams, Hickory. **UT-OF:** Cameron Flynn, Greensboro. **DH:** Ryan Rua, Hickory. **RHP:** Tyler Glasnow, West Virginia. **LHP:** Daniel Stumpf, Lexington. **RP:** Shae Simmons, Rome.
Most Valuable Player: Rosell Herrera, Asheville. **Most Outstanding Pitcher:** Gabriel Ynoa, Savannah. **Most Outstanding MLB Prospect:** Rossell Herrera, Asheville. **Manager of the Year:** Tripp Keister, Hagerstown.

DEPARTMENT LEADERS

BATTING

OBP	Bird, Greg, Charleston	.428
SLG	Gallo, Joey, Hickory	.610
OPS	Gallo, Joey, Hickory	.944
R	Renda, Tony, Hagerstown	99
H	Herrera, Rosell, Asheville	162
TB	Sosa, Francisco, Asheville	244
XBH	Gallo, Joey, Hickory	62
2B	Renda, Tony, Hagerstown	43
3B	Williams, Nick, Hickory	12
HR	Gallo, Joey, Hickory	38
RBI	Sosa, Francisco, Asheville	89
SAC	Ciriaco, Juan, Asheville	18
BB	Bird, Greg, Charleston	107
HBP	Gore, Terrance, Lexington	19
	Pointer, Brian, Lakewood	19
SO	Brinson, Lewis, Hickory	191
SB	Gore, Terrance, Lexington	68
CS	Johnson, Micah, Kannapolis	19
AB/SO	Turner, Ben, Augusta	15.75

PITCHING

G	McVay, Mason, Augusta	51
GS	Bridwell, Parker, Delmarva	26
GF	Mizenko, Tyler, Augusta	44
SV	Mizenko, Tyler, Augusta	25
W	Ynoa, Gabriel, Savannah	15
L	Four tied at	13
IP	Bridwell, Parker, Delmarva	142.2
H	Hughes, Ben, Asheville	177
R	Hughes, Ben, Asheville	103
ER	Hughes, Ben, Asheville	89
HB	Oakes, T.J., Asheville	16
BB	Brice, Austin, Greensboro	82
SO	Glasnow, Tyler, West Virginia	164
SO/9	Sims, Lucas, Rome	10.34
SO/9(RP)	Lopez, Adam, Kannapolis	13.7
BB/9	Ynoa, Gabriel, Savannah	1.06
WP	Sadzeck, Connor, Hickory	23
BK	Carasiti, Matt, Asheville	9
HR	Hughes, Ben, Asheville	16
	Oliver, Daniel, Greensboro	16
AVG	Sims, Lucas, Rome	.203

FIELDING

C	PCT	Sawyer, Wynston, Delmarva	.994
	PO	Numata, Chace, Lakewood	662
	A	Severino, Pedro, Hagerstown	108
	DP	Diaz, Francisco, West Virginia	10
	E	Numata, Chace, Lakewood	16
	PB	Numata, Chace, Lakewood	28
1B	PCT	Pleffner, Shawn, Hagerstown	.986
	PO	Rosa, Viosergy, Greensboro	918
	A	Rosa, Viosergy, Greensboro	61
	DP	Charles, Art, Lakewood	91
	E	Charles, Art, Lakewood	14
		Rosa, Viosergy, Greensboro	14
2B	PCT	Renda, Tony, Hagerstown	.973
	PO	Herrera, Dilson, W. Va., Savannah	202
	A	Renda, Tony, Hagerstown	340
	DP	Renda, Tony, Hagerstown	73
	E	Johnson, Micah, Kannapolis	21
3B	PCT	Hutter, Joel, Delmarva	.958
	PO	Hutter, Joel, Delmarva	85
	A	Hutter, Joel, Delmarva	253
	DP	Walding, Mitch, Lakewood	25
	E	Franco, Carlos, Rome	29
SS	PCT	Perez, Stephen, Hagerstown	.969
	PO	Marte, Luis, Hickory	197
	A	Marte, Luis, Hickory	383
	DP	Marte, Luis, Hickory	84
	E	Marte, Luis, Hickory	37
OF	PCT	Cave, Jake, Charleston	.992
	PO	Tocci, Carlos, Lakewood	297
	A	Pointer, Brian, Lakewood	14
	DP	Marte, Felix, Rome	4
		Pointer, Brian, Lakewood	4
	E	Lorenzo, Gregory, Delmarva	14

BY AARON FITT

The Tri-City ValleyCats reached the New York-Penn League finals for the third time in four years and took home their second title in that span, sweeping the State College Spikes in the best-of-three championship series.

State College, in its first year as a Cardinals affiliate, won a 2-1 pitchers' duel in the opener, but Tri-City jumped out to a 5-0 lead in the second game and held on for a 5-4 win. In the winner-takes-all Game Three, the ValleyCats erased a 1-0 deficit with four runs in the sixth en route to a 4-3 victory. The opportunistic ValleyCats managed to score four runs without hitting a ball out of the infield in the sloppy sixth.

Righthander Kyle Westwood allowed just a run on six hits while striking out four over six innings to pick up his second series-clinching win of the playoffs.

"We've been up and down the whole year," Tri-City manager Ed Romero said afterward. "These guys—just watching these guys toughen up and play the game the way they've played it the last month—it's unbelievable.

"I cannot describe how proud I am of these guys. They showed a lot of character."

Tri-City lost to Hudson Valley in the NY-P finals in 2012. Their only previous title came in 2010, when they swept Brooklyn in the championship series. State College reached the finals for the first time.

The ValleyCats and Spikes were two of the oldest teams in the league, and each placed only one player on the league's Top 20 prospects list (not counting Juan Herrera, who played just four games for State College after a late-July trade). Williamsport landed three players in the top seven, while Lowell and Brooklyn also placed three play-

TOP 20 PROSPECTS

1. Harold Ramirez, of, Jamestown (Pirates)
2. Oscar Hernandez, c, Hudson Valley (Rays)
3. Michael Feliz, rhp, Tri-City (Astros)
4. Zach Green, 3b, Williamsport (Phillies)
5. Carson Kelly, 3b, State College (Cardinals)
6. Eric Jagielo, 3b, Staten Island (Yankees)
7. Manuel Margot, of, Lowell (Red Sox)
8. Avery Romero, 2b, Batavia (Marlins)
9. Dylan Cozens, of, Williamsport (Phillies)
10. Simon Mercedes, rhp, Lowell (Red Sox)
11. Gavin Cecchini, ss, Brooklyn (Mets)
12. B.J. Boyd, of, Vermont (Athletics)
13. Jake Johansen, rhp, Auburn (Nationals)
14. Trevor Williams, rhp, Batavia (Marlins)
15. Jamie Callahan, rhp, Lowell (Red Sox)
16. Steven Brault, lhp, Aberdeen (Orioles)
17. Zac Reininger, rhp, Connecticut (Tigers)
18. Robert Gsellman, rhp, Brooklyn (Mets)
19. Juan Herrera, ss, M. Valley (Indians)/S. College (Cardinals)
20. Miller Diaz, rhp, Brooklyn (Mets)

ers apiece in the Top 20.

Several of the biggest arms to pass through the NY-P in 2013 failed to qualify for that list—most notably first-rounders Mark Appel (Astros), Jonathon Crawford (Tigers), Lucas Giolito (Nationals) and Hunter Harvey (Orioles)—each of whom likely would have ranked in the top five if they had met the minimum innings requirement.

Fellow first-rounders Austin Meadows (Pirates) and Billy McKinney (Athletics) also made very positive impressions in short NY-P stints but fell short of the plate appearances minimum. As a result, Yankees third baseman Eric Jagielo was the only 2013 first-rounder to make the list, which includes just five college products—considerably fewer than usual.

Most of the league's top prospects were young international signees or premium 2012 high school draftees who performed well against older competition.

OVERALL STANDINGS

Team (Organization)	W	L	PCT	GB	Manager(s)	Attendance	Average	Last Pennant
State College Spikes (Cardinals)	48	27	.640	—	Oliver Marmol	133,637	3,517	1994
Tri-City Valleycats (Astros)	44	32	.579	4 ½	Ed Romero	156,712	4,235	2013
Jamestown Jammers (Pirates)	43	32	.573	5	Dave Turgeon	38,728	1,076	1991
Aberdeen Ironbirds (Orioles)	40	32	.556	6 ½	Matt Merullo	189,879	5,274	1983
Lowell Spinners (Red Sox)	40	33	.548	7	Bruce Crabbe	156,358	4,343	Never
Batavia MuckDogs (Marlins)	39	36	.520	9	Angel Espada	33,909	969	2008
Brooklyn Cyclones (Mets)	38	37	.507	10	Rich Donnelly	232,224	6,276	2001
Hudson Valley Renegades (Rays)	38	37	.507	10	Michael Johns	164,230	4,322	2012
Williamsport Crosscutters (Phillies)	37	38	.493	11	Nelson Prada	64,188	1,783	2003
Staten Island Yankees (Yankees)	34	41	.453	14	Justin Pope	128,441	3,471	2011
Connecticut Tigers (Tigers)	33	42	.440	15	Andrew Graham	68,757	1,910	1998
Vermont Lake Monsters (Athletics)	33	43	.434	15 ½	Rick Magnante	81,683	2,334	1996
Mahoning Valley Scrappers (Indians)	30	44	.405	17 ½	Ted Kubiak	114,598	3,371	2004
Auburn Doubledays (Nationals)	26	49	.347	22	Gary Cathcart	39,381	1,158	2007

PLAYOFFS—Semifinals: Tri-City defeated Aberdeen 2-0 and State College defeated Jamestown 2-1 in best-of-three series. **Finals:** Tri-City defeated State College 2-1 in a best-of-three series.

CLUB BATTING

	AVG	G	AB	R	H	2B	3B	HR	RBI	BB	SO	SB	OBP	SLG
State College	.275	75	2561	354	703	141	23	37	314	234	505	77	.345	.391
Jamestown	.270	75	2465	355	666	93	21	27	314	229	528	113	.338	.358
Hudson Valley	.248	75	2589	296	641	135	24	25	264	183	527	121	.307	.347
Williamsport	.247	75	2492	324	616	140	18	50	272	227	594	81	.320	.378
Tri-City	.246	76	2515	324	618	94	16	41	273	248	482	68	.322	.345
Batavia	.242	75	2447	296	591	115	20	21	257	211	502	42	.309	.331
Aberdeen	.241	72	2433	312	587	104	20	39	265	204	608	67	.309	.349
Staten Island	.236	75	2508	295	591	121	7	38	262	241	669	44	.316	.335
Brooklyn	.235	75	2528	258	594	112	11	25	223	220	574	48	.300	.318
Lowell	.235	73	2351	279	553	109	15	15	241	249	620	78	.316	.313
Mahoning Valley	.233	74	2373	219	553	93	13	32	198	199	621	33	.302	.324
Auburn	.230	75	2447	258	563	92	16	28	226	209	518	40	.302	.315
Vermont	.225	76	2406	244	541	110	13	30	211	233	583	60	.299	.319
Connecticut	.221	75	2444	261	539	101	20	27	223	207	650	88	.294	.311

CLUB PITCHING

	ERA	G	CG	SHO	SV	IP	H	R	ER	HR	BB	SO	AVG
State College	2.80	75	1	5	23	665	621	261	207	30	229	549	.249
Brooklyn	2.81	75	1	8	28	673	526	264	210	22	262	662	.214
Hudson Valley	2.92	75	0	7	23	688	640	299	223	37	204	573	.246
Lowell	2.95	73	0	8	18	635	557	262	208	20	180	574	.234
Mahoning Valley	2.96	74	0	5	13	629	561	278	207	27	209	576	.237
Tri-City	2.98	76	0	5	25	673	606	267	223	42	161	619	.238
Vermont	3.06	76	1	7	22	649	565	285	221	33	250	520	.231
Staten Island	3.19	75	0	6	17	655	591	305	232	47	242	606	.239
Connecticut	3.20	75	0	3	19	654	629	299	233	27	218	577	.250
Jamestown	3.26	75	0	10	21	654	579	292	237	50	218	551	.238
Aberdeen	3.29	72	0	6	15	648	600	279	237	12	227	541	.246
Batavia	3.42	75	0	6	19	647	594	313	246	26	210	606	.242
Williamsport	3.50	75	1	5	17	656	617	313	255	37	228	512	.249
Auburn	4.19	75	0	5	13	638	670	358	297	25	256	575	.270

CLUB FIELDING

	PCT	PO	A	E	DP		PCT	PO	A	E	DP
Tri-City	.975	2020	824	73	55	Vermont	.964	1948	756	102	66
Brooklyn	.974	2020	786	74	53	Hudson Valley	.963	2065	852	113	85
Jamestown	.971	1963	817	83	73	Lowell	.963	1904	710	100	57
State College	.970	1995	822	87	82	Mahoning Valley	.963	1887	762	102	53
Aberdeen	.969	1945	816	88	68	Staten Island	.963	1965	776	104	51
Auburn	.968	1913	754	88	63	Batavia	.961	1942	805	111	67
Williamsport	.966	1969	796	98	62	Connecticut	.961	1963	794	113	54

INDIVIDUAL BATTING LEADERS (Minimum 2.7 PA/Team Game)

Batter, Club	AVG	G	AB	R	H	HR	RBI
Ramos, Steve, State College	.341	67	252	40	86	2	24
Mancini, Trey, Aberdeen	.328	68	256	43	84	3	36
* Frazier, Adam, Jamestown	.321	58	224	34	72	0	27
* Lopez, Carlos, Batavia	.318	61	223	28	71	0	24
Munoz, Felix, Batavia	.301	69	246	33	74	4	40
* Bosco, Jimmy, State College	.300	65	240	34	72	3	27
Romero, Avery, Batavia	.297	56	209	27	62	2	30
* Ballou, Isaac, Auburn	.294	59	211	33	62	2	20
* Roy, Jeff, Jamestown	.290	53	186	28	54	0	19
* Gregor, Conrad, Tri-City	.289	74	270	36	78	4	35

INDIVIDUAL PITCHING LEADERS (Minimum 0.8 IP/team game)

Pitcher, Club	W	L	ERA	IP	H	BB	SO
Feliz, Michael, Tri-City	4	2	1.96	69	53	13	78
Anderson, Drew, Williamsport	6	3	2.00	76	58	20	54
Griffin, Aaron, Hudson Valley	3	3	2.02	76	66	8	54
Diaz, Miller, Brooklyn	7	3	2.03	67	44	33	87
Gsellman, Robert, Brooklyn	3	3	2.06	70	59	12	64
Newell, Ryan, Batavia	5	4	2.09	82	60	21	75
Buttrey, Ty, Lowell	4	3	2.21	61	54	21	35
Vader, Sebastian, Aberdeen	7	3	2.43	85	70	18	64
* Powers, Brent, Vermont	6	3	2.43	78	69	18	69
* Horacek, Mitch, Aberdeen	5	4	2.78	65	54	7	45

DEPARTMENT LEADERS

BATTING

OBP	Ballou, Isaac, Auburn	.405
SLG	Bierfeldt, Conor, Aberdeen	.511
OPS	Bierfeldt, Conor, Aberdeen	.862
R	Green, Zach, Williamsport	52
H	Ramos, Steven, State College	86
TB	Green, Zach, Williamsport	129
XBH	Green, Zach, Williamsport	34
2B	Three tied at	20
3B	Dean, Austin, Batavia	7
HR	Green, Zach, Williamsport	13
RBI	Washington, David, State College	50
SAC	Fransoso, Michael, Jamestown	14
BB	Washington, David, State College	40
HBP	Coffman, Kasey, Connecticut	12
SO	O'Neill, Michael, Staten Island	93
SB	Ramirez, Harold, Jamestown	23
	Roy, Jeff, Jamestown	23
CS	Ramirez, Harold, Jamestown	11
AB/SO	Munoz, Felix, Batavia	8.79

PITCHING

G	Four tied at	23
GS	Gallegos, Giovanny, Staten Island	16
	Kirsch, Chris, Hudson Valley	16
GF	McCarthy, Casey, Batavia	19
SV	McKinney, Brett, Jamestown	10
	Reininger, Zac, Connecticut	10
W	Five tied at	7
L	Gallegos, Giovanny, Staten Island	8
	Gueller, Mitch, Williamsport	8
IP	Vader, Sebastian, Aberdeen	85.1
H	Gueller, Mitch, Williamsport	83
	Kirsch, Chris, Hudson Valley	83
R	Gueller, Mitch, Williamsport	47
ER	Gueller, Mitch, Williamsport	38
HB	Neverauskas, Dovydas, Jamestown	10
BB	Paulino, Willy, State College	34
SO	Diaz, Miller, Brooklyn	87
SO/9	Diaz, Miller, Brooklyn	11.75
SO/9 RP)	Morris, Akeel, Brooklyn	12.7
BB/9	Griffin, Aaron, Hudson Valley	0.95
WP	Newell, Ryan, Batavia	13
BK	Lugo, Luis, Mahoning Valley	4
HR	Three tied at	9
AVG	Reyes, Julio, Williamsport	.160

FIELDING

C	PCT	Wynns, Austin, Aberdeen	.995
	PO	Cervenka, Martin, Mahon. Valley	339
	A	Jhang, Jin-De, Jamestown	57
	DP	Jhang, Jin-De, Jamestown	5
	E	Sopilka, David, Lowell	8
		Tejeda, Isaias, Staten Island	8
	PB	Sopilka, David, Lowell	16
1B	PCT	Gregor, Conrad, Tri-City	.995
	PO	Alexander, John, Hudson Valley	590
	A	Mancini, Trey, Aberdeen	64
	DP	Alexander, John, Hudson Valley	66
	E	Leyland, Pat, Connecticut	14
2B	PCT	Mazzilli, L.J., Brooklyn	.977
	PO	Mazzilli, L.J., Brooklyn	126
	A	Mazzilli, L.J., Brooklyn	210
	DP	Soriano, Ariel, Hudson Valley	44
	E	Azcona, Javier, Connecticut	11
3B	PCT	Kelly, Carson, State College	.942
	PO	Harrison, Brett, Connecticut	51
	A	Green, Zach, Williamsport	158
	DP	Green, Zach, Williamsport	17
	E	Gunter, Cody, Auburn	20
SS	PCT	Powell, Curt, Connecticut	.962
	PO	Valera, Cesar, State College	127
	A	Valera, Cesar, State College	207
	DP	Valera, Cesar, State College	49
	E	Lin, Tzu-Wei, Lowell	21
OF	PCT	Three tied at	1.000
	PO	Schotts, Austin, Connecticut	149
	A	Rodriguez, Wilman, Auburn	10
	DP	Five tied at	3
	E	Escobar, Elvis, Jamestown	8
		McAdams, Josh, Mahoning Valley	8

MINOR LEAGUES

BY VINCENT LARA-CINISOMO

L ed by British Columbia native Tom Robson, the Vancouver Canadians (Blue Jays) won their third straight Northwest League title.

Robson, who grew up 30 minutes south of the Canadians' stadium, pitched into the seventh inning of a 5-0 shutout of the Boise Hawks (Cubs) in the third and deciding game of the championship series.

Vancouver was led by first baseman L.B. Dantzler, who led the ciruit in homers with nine and doubles (20). His two-run double broke a tie in the deciding game of the title series.

But any talk of the Northwest League has to include Cubs power-hitting third baseman Kris Bryant. The second overall pick in June, Bryant started hitting in the spring and continued straight through the Northwest League season and on to the Florida State League and the Arizona Fall League.

What's relevant here is his great 77-plate appearance stretch in the Northwest League. The 21-year-old batted .354/.416/.692, rapping eight doubles, a triple and four home runs in just 65 at-bats.

"He killed us. You can see why the Cubs took him (second overall)," Vancouver manager Clayton McCullough said. "He's just a monster—the best looking hitter we saw all year. With (Eugene third baseman D.J.) Peterson and (Everett outfielder Hunter) Renfroe, you could make good pitches and have a chance.

"But Bryant hit everything."

Bryant wasn't alone among the Northwest League mashers. Giants' second-rounder Ryan Jones hit .336/.429/.420 in 143 at-bats for Salem-Keizer. Renfroe, the 13th overall pick of the Padres out of Mississippi State, hit .308/.333/.510 with an .843 OPS. Peterson, the 12th overall pick by the Mariners out of New Mexico, hit six homers in just 109 at-bats.

Meanwhile, after spending three years in the Dominican Summer League because of visa issues, Boise outfielder Kevin Encarnacion crushed Northwest League pitching, leading the league in

batting (.355) and slugging (.566).

Among the pitchers, Diamondbacks second-rounder Aaron Blair (Hillsboro) held opponents to a .225 average in eight starts, Spokane righthander Kelvin Vasquez (Rangers) struck out 72 in 63 innings, and Boise righthander Dillon Maples, a 2011 pick by the Cubs who missed the 2012 season, posted a 2.14 ERA.

As for Robson, the 20-year-old's championship win topped off a great 2013. He was 3-0, 1.38 in the Appalachian League before going 3-0, 0.94 in 38 innings with Vancouver.

TOP 20 PROSPECTS

1. Kris Bryant, 3b, Boise (Cubs)
2. Hunter Renfroe, of, Eugene (Padres)
3. D.J. Peterson, 3b, Everett (Mariners)
4. Aaron Blair, rhp, Hillsboro (Diamondbacks)
5. Austin Wilson, of, Everett (Mariners)
6. Kelvin Vasquez, rhp, Spokane (Rangers)
7. Paul Blackburn, rhp, Boise (Cubs)
8. Chase Johnson, rhp, Salem-Keizer (Giants)
9. Yasiel Balaguert, of, Boise (Cubs)
10. Dillon Maples, rhp, Boise (Cubs)
11. David Ledbetter, rhp, Spokane (Rangers)
12. Shawon Dunston Jr., of, Boise (Cubs)
13. Tom Robson, rhp, Vancouver (Blue Jays)
14. Jack Reinheimer, ss, Everett (Mariners)
15. Daniel Gibson, lhp, Hillsboro (Diamondbacks)
16. Ryan Warner, rhp, Tri-City (Rockies)
17. Kevin Encarnacion, of, Boise (Cubs)
18. Lars Huijer, rhp, Everett (Mariners)
19. L.B. Dantzler, 1b, Vancouver (Blue Jays)
20. Jose Martinez, rhp, Hillsboro (Diamondbacks)

STANDINGS: SPLIT SEASON

FIRST HALF

NORTH	W	L	PCT	GB
Everett	23	15	.605	—
Vancouver	22	16	.579	1
Spokane	20	18	.526	3
Tri-City	19	19	.500	4

SOUTH	W	L	PCT	GB
S.-Keizer	23	15	.605	—
Boise	21	17	.553	2
Eugene	13	25	.342	10
Hillsboro	11	27	.289	12

SECOND HALF

NORTH	W	L	PCT	GB
Everett	21	17	.553	—
Spokane	18	20	.474	3
Vancouver	17	21	.447	4
Tri-City	15	23	.395	6

SOUTH	W	L	PCT	GB
S.-Keizer	24	14	.632	—
Hillsboro	23	15	.605	1
Boise	20	18	.526	4
Eugene	14	24	.368	10

PLAYOFFS—Semifinals: Vancouver defeated Everett 2-0 and Boise defeated Salem-Keizer 2-0 in best-of-three series.
Finals: Vancouver defeated Boise 2-1 in a best-of-three series.

OVERALL STANDINGS

Team (Organization)	W	L	PCT	GB	Manager	Attendance	Average	Last Pennant
Salem-Keizer Volcanoes (Giants)	47	29	.618	—	Gary Davenport	98,024	2,580	2009
Everett Aquasox (Mariners)	44	32	.579	3	Rob Mummau	92,489	2,569	2010
Boise Hawks (Cubs)	41	35	.539	6	Gary Van Tol	91,324	2,468	2004
Vancouver Canadians (Blue Jays)	39	37	.513	8	Clayton McCullough	184,042	4,843	2013
Spokane Indians (Rangers)	38	38	.500	9	Tim Hulett	187,371	5,064	2008
Hillsboro Hops (Diamondbacks)	34	42	.447	13	Audo Vicente	135,167	3,557	Never
Tri-City Dust Devils (Rockies)	34	42	.447	13	Drew Saylor	83,987	2,270	Never
Eugene Emeralds (Padres)	27	49	.355	20	Jim Gabella	112,028	2,948	1980

MINOR LEAGUES

CLUB BATTING

	AVG	G	AB	R	H	2B	3B	HR	RBI	BB	SO	SB	OBP	SLG
Boise	.269	76	2561	384	690	129	13	50	337	265	573	57	.347	.389
Salem-Keizer	.266	76	2593	418	691	151	24	45	376	320	593	94	.360	.395
Vancouver	.255	76	2643	350	673	120	17	23	291	311	640	77	.341	.339
Everett	.250	76	2528	324	631	108	16	36	277	259	624	88	.328	.348
Hillsboro	.238	76	2583	298	615	119	20	29	256	245	613	73	.313	.333
Tri-City	.231	76	2471	284	572	101	22	13	243	279	607	119	.320	.306
Spokane	.227	76	2558	295	581	106	17	35	258	262	585	57	.307	.323
Eugene	.221	76	2490	245	551	122	10	27	211	208	649	43	.295	.311

CLUB PITCHING

	ERA	G	CG	SHO	SV	IP	H	R	ER	HR	BB	SO	AVG
Vancouver	3.23	76	1	8	17	688	645	306	247	15	220	550	.247
Spokane	3.28	76	0	3	17	687	637	293	250	37	260	681	.246
Hillsboro	3.29	76	3	7	17	684	610	319	250	27	305	596	.240
Salem-Keizer	3.49	76	0	5	22	674	634	314	261	38	212	615	.246
Tri-City	3.53	76	0	3	25	676	604	316	265	23	270	518	.238
Boise	3.58	76	0	7	20	662	618	330	263	30	260	646	.245
Everett	4.01	76	1	7	21	670	629	349	299	40	280	622	.252
Eugene	4.02	76	0	8	14	671	627	371	300	48	342	656	.247

CLUB FIELDING

	PCT	PO	A	E	DP		PCT	PO	A	E	DP
Everett	.971	2011	823	85	65	Tri-City	.969	2027	854	91	79
Spokane	.971	2060	794	84	73	Boise	.967	1986	798	96	65
Vancouver	.971	2065	909	89	74	Salem-Keizer	.966	2022	863	100	71
Hillsboro	.969	2052	877	95	74	Eugene	.961	2014	775	112	84

INDIVIDUAL BATTING LEADERS (Minimum 2.7 PA/Team Game)

Batter, Club	AVG	G	AB	R	H	HR	RBI
* Perez-Ramos, Yogey, Hillsboro	.314	67	261	35	82	0	24
* Dantzler, L.B., Vancouver	.302	59	232	32	70	9	35
* Tauchman, Mike, Tri-City	.297	64	236	38	70	0	24
* Dunston, Shawon, Boise	.290	49	193	27	56	1	19
* Lockhart, Daniel, Boise	.289	67	249	29	72	0	23
* Frank, Chaz, Vancouver	.282	49	181	35	51	0	16
Mehrten, Alec, Tri-City	.279	60	204	26	57	1	22
* Rogers, Jacob, Boise	.278	74	259	37	72	8	47
* Reeves, Mike, Vancouver	.275	55	193	26	53	1	25
* Fermin, Andy, Vancouver	.274	57	212	29	58	1	29

INDIVIDUAL PITCHING LEADERS (Minimum 0.8 IP/team game)

Pitcher, Club	W	L	ERA	IP	H	BB	SO
* Leenhouts, Drew, Salem-Keizer	9	2	2.26	72	66	14	53
Vasquez, Kelvin, Spokane	2	2	2.27	63	47	34	72
Pugliese, James, Boise	4	3	2.32	62	55	12	47
Johnson, Chris, Salem-Keizer	6	3	2.49	83	65	8	78
Platt, Austin, Hillsboro	4	3	2.62	79	71	40	53
* Anderson, Kyle, Vancouver	5	3	2.71	83	74	12	58
Gabryszwski, Jeremy, Vancouver	5	2	2.82	77	71	10	40
* Turner, Colton, Vancouver	4	5	2.96	67	56	17	39
Huijer, Lars, Everett	8	2	3.03	71	57	23	61
Wiles, Collin, Spokane	2	7	3.09	67	71	21	40

DEPARTMENT LEADERS

BATTING

OBP	Richardson, Ronnie, Eugene	.475
SLG	Encarnacion, Kevin, Boise	.566
OPS	Richardson, Ronnie, Eugene	.919
R	Hollick, Tyler, Salem-Keizer	47
H	Perez-Ramos, Yogey, Hillsboro	82
TB	Dantzler, L.B., Vancouver	117
XBH	Dantzler, L.B., Vancouver	29
2B	Dantzler, L.B., Vancouver	20
3B	Garia, Chris, Spokane	5
HR	Dantzler, L.B., Vancouver	9
RBI	Balaguert, Yasiel, Boise	48
SAC	Soriano, Wilson, Tri-City	6
BB	Rogers, Jacob, Boise	45
HBP	Mehrten, Alec, Tri-City	15
SO	Atkinson, Justin, Vancouver	74
SB	Parmley, Ian, Vancouver	23
CS	Richardson, Ronnie, Eugene	8
AB/SO	Gebhardt, Ryan, Hillsboro	9.33

PITCHING

G	Cimber, Adam, Eugene	28
	Ghysels, Chuck, Vancouver	28
GS	Four tied at	15
GF	Montero, Raymundo, Salem-Keizer	24
SV	Daniel, Trent, Tri-City	15
W	Leenhouts, Andrew, Salem-Keizer	9
L	Five tied at	7
IP	Gerderman, Ross, Hillsboro	93.2
H	Gerderman, Ross, Hillsboro	88
R	Underwood, Duane, Boise	44
ER	Gerderman, Ross, Hillsboro	37
HB	Vieira, Thyago, Everett	16
BB	Three tied at	40
SO	Johnson, Chris, Salem-Keizer	78
SO/9	Vasquez, Kelvin, Spokane	10.23
SO/9(RP)	Stevens, Chase, Hillsboro	12.4
BB/9	Johnson, Chris, Salem-Keizer	0.87
WP	Brazoban, Huascar, Tri-City	16
BK	Brasoban, Jimmy, Eugene	4
HR	Brasoban, Jimmy, Eugene	10
AVG	Vasquez, Kelvin, Spokane	.199

FIELDING

C	PCT	Miller, Ryan, Eugene	1.000
	PO	Rymel, Lance, Boise	385
	A	Miller, Ryan, Eugene	65
	DP	Greene, Marcus, Spokane	5
		Miller, Ryan, Eugene	5
	E	O'Dowd, Chris, Tri-City	9
	PB	Soto, Elvin, Hillsboro	10
1B	PCT	Rogers, Jacob, Boise	.986
	PO	Rogers, Jacob, Boise	573
	A	Rogers, Jacob, Boise	64
	DP	Santos, Trae, Eugene	57
	E	Rogers, Jacob, Boise	9
2B	PO	Lockhart, Danny, Boise	87
	A	Jones, Ryan, Salem-Keizer	135
	DP	Bass, Michael, Eugene	32
	E	Bass, Michael, Eugene	11
		Brito, Bryan, Everett	11
3B	PO	Benjamin, Michael, Tri-City	30
	A	Benjamin, Michael, Tri-City	103
	DP	McCurry, Randy, Hillsboro	13
	E	Perez, Fernando, Eugene	16
SS	PCT	Reinheimer, Jack, Everett	.982
	PO	Gebhardt, Ryan, Hillsboro	107
	A	Penalver, Carlos, Boise	214
	DP	Gebhardt, Ryan, Hillsboro	40
	E	Gebhardt, Ryan, Hillsboro	18
		Penalver, Carlos, Boise	18
OF	PCT	Hollick, Tyler, Salem-Keizer	1.000
	PO	Parmley, Ian, Vancouver	141
	A	Zamarripa, James, Everett	9
	DP	Three tied at	3
	E	McCall, Shilo, Salem-Keizer	6

MINOR LEAGUES

BY CLINT LONGENECKER

The Pulaski Mariners posted the league's best regular season record at 41-27 and went undefeated through the playoffs to win their first league championship since 1991.

Pulaski second baseman Gabrial Franca hit a bases-loaded walkoff single to give the Mariners a 6-5 victory against the Greenville Astros in the championship game, which made this the second consecutive season the Appalachian League title game ended on a walkoff.

The Mariners, in their first year in Pulaski, were the second-youngest team in the league and had the circuit's highest-scoring offense. Pulaski led the league in all three triple-slash categories (.265/.339/.412), home runs (53) and steals (101).

Pulaski had both the Appalachian League player of the year and pitcher of the year. Shortstop Tyler Smith, a 22-year-old eighth-round pick out of Oregon State in 2013, won league MVP honors, finishing in the top 10 in all three triple-slash categories (.320/.394/.460) while providing dependable defense. Righthander Edwin Diaz, a 2012 third-round pick out of Puerto Rico, led the league with a 1.43 ERA in 69 innings, to go with 10.4 strikeouts per nine.

Righthander Emilio Pagan, a 10th-round pick in 2013, was named the league's top reliever, after not allowing an earned run in 20 innings. Right fielder Wilton Martinez, a 19-year-old with big raw power out of the Dominican Republic, led the league with 12 home runs.

The Astros, who finished second in the Western division and were led by leaguer manager of the year Josh Bonifay, defeated Western division champ Kingsport in the semifinals.

Despite losing to the Mariners in the semifinals, the Blue Jays had the league's most prospect-laden club. Seven Blue Jays made the Top 20 Prospects list, including five in the top 10. Outfielder D.J. Davis (second), third baseman Mitch Nay (fourth)

TOP 20 PROSPECTS

1. Amed Rosario, ss, Kingsport (Mets)
2. D.J. Davis, of, Bluefield (Blue Jays)
3. Victor Caratini, 3b, Danville (Braves)
4. Mitch Nay, 3b, Bluefield (Blue Jays)
5. Dawel Lugo, ss, Bluefield (Blue Jays)
6. Chase DeJong, rhp, Bluefield (Blue Jays)
7. Alex Reyes, rhp, Johnson City (Cardinals)
8. Alberto Tirado, rhp, Bluefield (Blue Jays)
9. Edwin Diaz, rhp, Pulaski (Mariners)
10. Tyler Danish, rhp, Bristol (White Sox)
11. Johan Camargo, ss, Danville (Braves)
12. Jairo Labourt, lhp, Bluefield (Blue Jays)
13. Wilton Martinez, of, Pulaski (Mariners)
14. Felix Jorge, rhp, Elizabethton (Twins)
15. Rob Whalen, rhp, Kinsport (Mets)
16. Adonys Cardona, rhp, Bluefield (Blue Jays)
17. Kenny Peoples, ss, Johnson City (Cardinals)
18. Stuart Turner, c, Elizabethton (Twins)
19. Chris Flexen, rhp, Kingsport (Mets)
20. Steve Bean, c, Johnson City (Cardinals)

and shortstop Dawel Lugo (fifth) formed a strong core of position players. Corner infielder Matt Dean led the league in batting average at .338 in his second tour of the circuit.

The Jays placed four power arms on the list, three of whom (righthander Alberto Tirado, lefthander Jairo Labourt and righthander Adonys Cardona) are products of Toronto's increased international spending before the current collective bargaining agreement was formed.

From a prospect perspective, the Appalachian League was down this year from a banner 2012 season. This year's crop was hamstrung by a lack of impact players. Last year's crop benefited greatly from the earlier signing deadline, which enabled three 2012 first-round picks to garner enough playing time to become eligible. While the 2012 group boasted Byron Buxton, Courtney Hawkins and Lucas Sims, this year lacked a single 2013 first-round pick who qualified. The highest drafted 2013 player was righthander Tyler Danish, a second-round pick who posted a 1.38 ERA and 4.4 strikeout-walk ratio in 26 innings.

OVERALL STANDINGS

Team (Organization)	W	L	PCT	GB	Manager(s)	Attendance	Average	Last Pennant
Pulaski (Mariners)	41	27	.603	—	Chris Prieto	25,842	783	2013
Bluefield (Blue Jays)	40	27	.597	½	Dennis Holmberg	28,232	856	2001
Kingsport (Mets)	40	27	.597	½	Jose Leger	23,476	757	1995
Greeneville (Astros)	38	30	.559	3	Josh Bonifay	45,261	1,372	2004
Elizabethton (Twins)	37	31	.544	4	Ray Smith	24,725	798	2012
Johnson City (Cardinals)	36	31	.537	4 ½	Joe Kruzel	25,612	826	2011
Danville (Braves)	29	36	.446	10 ½	Jonathan Schuerholz	25,152	898	2009
Burlington (Royals)	29	38	.433	11 ½	Tommy Shields	32,200	1,238	1993
Princeton (Rays)	25	43	.368	16	Danny Sheaffer	24,610	746	1994
Bristol (White Sox)	20	45	.308	19 ½	Mike Gellinger	20,309	700	2002

Semifinals: Pulaski defeated Bluefield 2-0 and Greeneville defeated Kingsport 2-1 in best-of-three series. **Finals:** Pulaski defeated Greeneville 2-0 in a best-of-three series.

CLUB BATTING

	AVG	G	AB	R	H	2B	3B	HR	RBI	BB	SO	SB	OBP	SLG
Kingsport	.265	67	2232	314	591	122	18	38	279	224	548	66	.338	.387
Pulaski	.265	68	2286	352	606	125	26	53	323	227	572	101	.339	.412
Johnson City	.259	67	2326	338	602	103	23	42	300	230	576	65	.332	.377
Elizabethton	.253	68	2273	296	576	108	22	24	258	212	567	62	.322	.352
Bluefield	.252	67	2143	316	539	105	28	42	281	205	529	50	.326	.385
Danville	.243	65	2094	237	509	99	17	19	203	200	530	42	.319	.334
Burlington	.239	67	2120	253	506	96	20	36	219	188	486	56	.307	.354
Greeneville	.237	68	2142	289	507	95	7	35	246	304	491	31	.339	.337
Bristol	.232	65	2026	238	470	81	14	19	202	222	564	39	.316	.314
Princeton	.225	68	2154	248	484	85	18	40	216	200	555	47	.299	.337

CLUB PITCHING

	ERA	G	CG	SHO	SV	IP	H	R	ER	HR	BB	SO	AVG
Elizabethton	3.10	68	1	8	17	599	498	248	206	22	291	626	.228
Bluefield	3.21	67	1	9	20	571	529	257	204	34	209	537	.243
Greeneville	3.30	68	0	4	22	591	528	271	217	32	201	593	.237
Johnson City	3.40	67	0	4	12	593	567	294	224	32	249	583	.251
Pulaski	3.43	68	0	3	19	596	515	268	227	44	236	598	.235
Danville	3.53	65	0	4	11	559	524	272	219	26	206	519	.247
Kingsport	3.64	67	3	9	15	578	497	294	234	32	218	552	.229
Princeton	4.01	68	0	4	13	573	565	320	255	49	165	490	.256
Burlington	4.25	67	1	5	14	557	582	312	263	35	222	463	.271
Bristol	4.88	65	1	1	11	541	585	345	293	42	215	457	.277

CLUB FIELDING

	PCT	PO	A	E	DP		PCT	PO	A	E	DP
Pulaski	.977	1789	739	60	67	Burlington	.966	1671	708	84	62
Danville	.972	1677	662	68	49	Bristol	.965	1622	664	82	50
Elizabethton	.972	1796	699	72	68	Johnson City	.964	1779	700	92	59
Greeneville	.968	1774	700	82	52	Kingsport	.962	1735	697	97	47
Bluefield	.966	1714	680	85	70	Princeton	.962	1718	638	93	47

INDIVIDUAL BATTING LEADERS (Minimum 2.7 PA/Team Game)

Batter, Club	AVG	G	AB	R	H	HR	RBI
Dean, Matt, Bluefield	.338	63	210	37	71	6	35
* McNeil, Jeff, Kingsport	.327	47	165	26	54	0	18
Smith, Tyler, Pulaski	.320	52	200	33	64	2	34
Thomas, Toby, Bristol	.319	51	210	31	67	4	30
* Earley, Nolan, Bristol	.310	61	203	23	63	2	31
* Zimmerman, Jeff, Pulaski	.305	47	174	27	53	5	39
# Ruiz, Yeixon, Kingsport	.304	52	194	34	59	0	12
Nay, Mitch, Bluefield	.300	64	230	41	69	6	42
* Ringo, Justin, Johnson City	.300	53	200	34	60	6	34
Lugo, Dawel, Bluefield	.297	51	192	28	57	6	36

INDIVIDUAL PITCHING LEADERS (Minimum 0.8 IP/team game)

Pitcher, Club	W	L	ERA	IP	H	BB	SO
Diaz, Edwin, Pulaski	5	2	1.43	69	45	18	79
Whalen, Robert, Kingsport	3	2	1.87	72	50	17	76
Faria, Jacob, Princeton	3	3	2.02	62	53	9	71
Waszak, Andrew, Danville	3	5	2.03	53	33	12	47
Flexen, Chris, Kingsport	8	1	2.09	69	53	12	62
Tiburcio, Frederick, Greeneville	3	2	2.43	56	42	19	51
Slaton, D.J., Princeton	4	3	2.66	61	61	14	42
McKnight, Blake, Johnson City	3	1	2.69	60	58	8	46
Martinez, Dailyn, Johnson City	4	3	2.70	63	61	23	31
* Robb, Hein, Elizabethton	4	4	2.71	63	62	13	52

ALL-STAR TEAM

C: Rowan Wick, Johnson City. **1B:** Sam Bates, Burlington. **2B:** Yeixon Ruiz, Kingsport. **3B:** Mitch Nay, Bluefield. **SS:** Tyler Smith, Pulaski. **UT-IF:** Kenny Peoples, Johnson City. **OF:** Vaughn Bryan, Johnson City; Nolan Earley, Bristol; Zack Granite, Elizabethton. **UT-OF:** Ian Miller, Pulaski. **DH:** Matt Dean, Bluefield. **RHP:** Edwin Diaz, Pulaski. **LHP:** Jairo LaBourt, Bluefield. **RP:** Emilio Pagan, Pulaski. **Player of the Year:** Tyler Smith, Pulaski. **Pitcher of the Year:** Edwin Diaz, Pulaski. **Manager of the Year:** Josh Bonifay, Greeneville.

DEPARTMENT LEADERS

BATTING

OBP	Wik, Marc, Greeneville	.433
SLG	Bates, Sam, Burlington	.538
OPS	Dean, Matt, Bluefield	.909
R	Bryan, Vaughn, Johnson City	45
H	Dean, Matt, Bluefield	71
	Peoples-Walls, Kenneth, Jo. City	71
TB	Peoples-Walls, Kenneth, Jo. City	111
XBH	Three tied at	25
2B	Caratini, Victor, Danville	23
3B	Davis, D.J., Bluefield	7
HR	Martinez, Wilton, Pulaski	12
RBI	Nay, Mitch, Bluefield	42
SAC	Santana, Juan, Greeneville	12
BB	Mathis, Tanner, Greeneville	44
HBP	Hall, Thurman, Bristol	10
	McNeil, Jeff, Kingsport	10
SO	Three tied at	76
SB	Henry, Desmond, Burlington	20
CS	Davis, D.J., Bluefield	8
	Earley, Nolan, Bristol	8
AB/SO	Mathis, Tanner, Greeneville	13.43

PITCHING

G	Baez, Fernando, Johnson City	26
GS	Diaz, Edwin, Pulaski	13
	Leyer, Robinson, Bristol	13
GF	Three tied at	16
SV	Pagan, Emilio, Pulaski	12
W	Flexen, Chris, Kingsport	8
L	Machado, Andres, Burlington	8
IP	Whalen, Robert, Kingsport	72.1
H	Machado, Andres, Burlington	75
R	Machado, Andres, Burlington	46
ER	Machado, Andres, Burlington	42
HB	De La Cruz, Noel, Pulaski	9
BB	Mendonca, Tanner, Elizabethton	37
SO	Diaz, Edwin, Pulaski	79
SO/9	Jorge, Felix, Elizabethton	10.62
SO/9(RP)	Peterson, Brandon, Elizabethton	13.2
BB/9	McKnight, Blake, Johnson City	1.19
WP	Flores, Michael, Danville	10
WP	Paredes, Norge, Johnson City	10
BK	Five tied at	2
HR	De La Cruz, Noel, Pulaski	10
AVG	Whalen, Robert, Kingsport	.187

FIELDING

C	PCT	Johnson, Chad, Burlington	.997
	PO	Araiza, Armando, Princeton	344
	A	Araiza, Armando, Princeton	46
	DP	Three tied at	4
	E	Abreu, Adrian, Kingsport	9
	PB	Ayala, Sammy, Bristol	15
1B	PCT	Dean, Matt, Bluefield	.996
	PO	Dean, Matt, Bluefield	464
	A	Dean, Matt, Bluefield	30
		Rhodes, Rory, Elizabethton	30
	DP	Dean, Matt, Bluefield	50
	E	Ringo, Justin, Johnson City	7
2B	PCT	Blanchard, Coty, Princeton	.953
	PO	Santana, Juan, Greeneville	98
	A	Shank, Zach, Pulaski	129
	DP	Shank, Zach, Pulaski	36
	E	Blanchard, Coty, Princeton	10
3B	PCT	Caratini, Victor, Danville	.929
	PO	Caratini, Victor, Danville	36
	A	Nay, Mitch, Bluefield	120
	DP	Nay, Mitch, Bluefield	12
	E	Nay, Mitch, Bluefield	17
SS	PCT	Smith, Tyler, Pulaski	.963
	PO	Camargo, Johan, Danville	78
	A	Smith, Tyler, Pulaski	161
	DP	Smith, Tyler, Pulaski	31
	E	Peoples-Walls, Kenneth, Jo. City	20
OF	PCT	Bryan, Vaughn, Johnson City	.991
	PO	Jackson, Bralin, Princeton	133
	A	Three tied at	6
	DP	Three tied at	3
	E	Araujo, Yoel, Princeton	10

MINOR LEAGUES

BY JIM SHONERD

Idaho Falls stumbled to a 4-12 start in 2013, but the Chukars rallied to win a second-half division title and claim the franchise's first Pioneer League championship since 2000. The Chukars were led for most of the season by third baseman Hunter Dozier, the Royals' first-round pick in June, who hit .303/.403/.509 in the regular season before being promoted, then returned in the post-season to hit .375.

Both of Idaho Falls' playoff series were extended to the full three games. The Chukars outlasted Grand Junction in the first round, winning the decisive third game on the road behind seven strong innings from righthander Yender Caramo, moving on to face Helena in the finals.

The Brewers took down Great Falls, which posted the league's best regular-season record, in the first round. The finals also lasted three games, and again Idaho Falls won a winner-takes-all third game on the road, 6-0, in Helena to take the title.

Dozier not only led his team to a championship but was also the PL's best prospect, as the league again lived up to its reputation as an offense-oriented circuit. Most of the league's high-profile prospects were hitters, other than a stopover from the Rockies' Jonathan Gray, the righthander who was the third pick in the draft. Dozier and Reds first-rounder Phillip Ervin, an outfielder, were the best prospects to see meaningful time in the league, while Pioneer League pitching staffs averaged a 4.90 ERA as a group.

Great Falls came up short in the postseason, but the Voyagers were the exception to the all-offense, all-the-time trend in the regular season. The Voyagers boasted the league's stingiest pitching staff in the regular season by a sizeable margin, their 4.03 collective ERA more than 30 points better than their nearest competition. Righthander Jake Sanchez, the league's pitcher of the year, led the charge. Sanchez, a former independent league pitcher, came close to winning the pitching triple crown in the PL, leading the way in ERA (2.87) and strikeouts (76) and finishing one off the wins

lead with six.

Helena outfielder Michael Ratterree captured MVP honors. The Brewers' 2013 10th-round pick led the Pioneer League in slugging percentage (.585) while batting .314 with 12 homers and 58 RBIs. Ratterree also won a postseason showdown with Sanchez, homering off the Great Falls right-hander in the first inning of their first playoff game, which the Brewers went on to win 16-5 en route to sweeping the series. Ratterree would go on to hit .563 with six RBIs in five playoff games.

TOP 20 PROSPECTS

1. Hunter Dozier, 3b, Idaho Falls (Royals)
2. Phillip Ervin, of, Billings (Reds)
3. Raimel Tapia, of, Grand Junction (Rockies)
4. Ryan McMahon, 3b, Grand Junction (Rockies)
5. Emerson Jimenez, ss, Grand Junction (Rockies)
6. Ben Lively, rhp, Billings (Reds)
7. Zach Bird, rhp, Ogden (Dodgers)
8. Stryker Trahan, c, Missoula (Diamondbacks)
9. Jacob Scavuzzo, of, Ogden (Dodgers)
10. Jose Briceno, c, Grand Junction (Rockies)
11. Elier Hernandez, of, Idaho Falls (Royals)
12. Adam Engel, of, Great Falls (White Sox)
13. Zane Evans, c, Idaho Falls (Royals)
14. Cody Reed, lhp, Idaho Falls (Royals)
15. Jose Rondon, ss, Orem (Angels)
16. Michael Ratterree, of, Helena (Brewers)
17. Barrett Astin, rhp, Helena (Brewers)
18. Geordy Parra, rhp, Missoula (Diamondbacks)
19. Dustin Houle, c, Helena (Brewers)
20. Scott Barlow, rhp, Ogden (Dodgers)

STANDINGS: SPLIT SEASON

FIRST HALF					SECOND HALF				
NORTH	W	L	PCT	GB	**NORTH**	W	L	PCT	GB
Helena	23	15	.605	—	Great Falls	29	9	.763	—
Great Falls	19	19	.500	4	Helena	20	18	.526	9
Missoula	16	22	.421	7	Missoula	15	20	.429	12½
Billings	14	24	.368	9	Billings	14	22	.389	14
SOUTH	W	L	PCT	GB	**SOUTH**	W	L	PCT	GB
G. Junction	21	17	.553	—	Idaho Falls	22	16	.579	—
Ogden	20	18	.526	1	Orem	19	18	.514	2
Orem	20	18	.526	1	Ogden	16	22	.421	6
Idaho Falls	19	19	.500	2	G. Junction	14	24	.368	8

PLAYOFFS—Semifinals: Helena defeated Great Falls 2-0 and Idaho Falls defeated Grand Junction 2-1 in best-of-three series. **Finals:** Idaho Falls defeated Helena 2-1 in a best-of-three series.

OVERALL STANDINGS

Team (Organization)	W	L	PCT	GB	Manager	Attendance	Average	Last Pennant
Great Falls Voyagers (White Sox)	48	28	.632	—	Pete Rose Jr.	58,386	1,622	2011
Helena Brewers (Brewers)	43	33	.566	5	Tony Diggs	33,515	882	2010
Idaho Falls Chukars (Royals)	41	35	.539	7	Omar Ramirez	96,367	2,536	2013
Orem Owlz (Angels)	39	36	.520	8½	Bill Richardson	85,630	2,314	2009
Ogden Raptors (Dodgers)	36	40	.474	12	Damon Berryhill	124,687	3,370	Never
Grand Junction Rockies (Rockies)	35	41	.461	13	Anthony Sanders	87,436	2,363	Never
Missoula Osprey (Diamondbacks)	31	42	.425	15½	Robby Hammock	81,686	2,269	2012
Billings Mustangs (Reds)	28	46	.378	19	Pat Kelly	105,417	2,928	2001

CLUB BATTING

	AVG	G	AB	R	H	2B	3B	HR	RBI	BB	SO	SB	OBP	SLG
Idaho Falls	.298	76	2745	508	819	177	32	57	455	242	473	69	.362	.448
Ogden	.291	76	2639	470	768	159	28	66	410	267	557	73	.362	.448
Great Falls	.280	76	2660	457	745	151	27	49	411	299	575	73	.360	.412
Helena	.279	76	2603	472	726	133	21	54	397	280	545	88	.359	.408
Orem	.279	75	2601	482	726	172	26	61	420	287	576	94	.361	.436
Grand Junction	.277	76	2575	431	712	154	25	69	365	208	583	95	.339	.436
Missoula	.267	73	2516	406	671	150	21	47	360	270	603	56	.342	.399
Billings	.241	74	2484	328	598	112	20	50	277	236	552	94	.313	.362

CLUB PITCHING

	ERA	G	CG	SHO	SV	IP	H	R	ER	HR	BB	SO	AVG
Great Falls	4.03	76	1	4	27	676	669	377	303	38	284	573	.260
Billings	4.36	74	0	1	20	649	683	382	314	58	216	573	.268
Helena	4.62	76	0	2	22	665	686	429	341	57	311	521	.264
Missoula	4.86	73	2	3	16	638	706	449	345	51	246	536	.279
Idaho Falls	5.10	76	0	3	13	671	735	476	380	48	267	590	.278
Orem	5.23	75	0	3	20	661	777	464	384	63	241	532	.295
Grand Junction	5.47	76	1	0	17	666	747	493	405	67	277	529	.283
Ogden	5.51	76	0	1	16	663	762	484	406	71	247	610	.287

CLUB FIELDING

	PCT	PO	A	E	DP		PCT	PO	A	E	DP
Great Falls	.968	2028	863	96	62	Billings	.961	1946	728	109	53
Ogden	.963	1988	778	106	71	Orem	.959	1982	868	122	78
Helena	.962	1994	871	114	59	Missoula	.955	1915	826	129	65
Idaho Falls	.962	2013	862	114	74	Grand Junction	.950	1999	840	150	72

INDIVIDUAL BATTING LEADERS (Minimum 2.7 PA/Team Game)

Batter, Club	AVG	G	AB	R	H	HR	RBI
* Tapia, Raimel, Grand Junction	.357	66	258	53	92	7	47
Garcia, Carlos, Idaho Falls	.329	64	228	52	75	5	42
Curletta, Joey, Ogden	.326	62	230	41	75	5	42
Santana, Alex, Ogden	.322	55	205	39	66	2	27
Taylor, Dominique, Idaho Falls	.322	62	233	50	75	8	37
* McMahon, Ryan, Grand Junction	.321	59	218	42	70	11	52
* Towey, Cal, Orem	.317	70	230	69	73	8	53
Voight, Zach, Great Falls	.316	60	225	42	71	6	41
Ratterree, Michael, Helena	.310	65	258	63	80	12	56
Thompson, Corey, Great Falls	.310	56	226	31	70	4	40

INDIVIDUAL PITCHING LEADERS (Minimum 0.8 IP/team game)

Pitcher, Club	W	L	ERA	IP	H	BB	SO
Sanchez, Jake, Great Falls	6	3	2.87	82	71	14	76
* Conroy, Patrick, Idaho Falls	6	2	3.30	71	65	33	64
Caramo, Yender, Idaho Falls	6	3	3.84	61	72	8	37
Haselden, David, Great Falls	6	5	4.03	83	90	13	50
Villa, Francisco, Ogden	3	5	4.35	62	68	26	48
Perez, Felipe, Missoula	7	5	4.55	89	100	19	50
Moran, Luke, Billings	4	6	4.74	74	89	16	71
Fernandez, Arjenis, Orem	4	3	4.89	77	97	16	39
Hernandez, Carlos, Missoula	4	5	5.06	69	66	40	63
Diaz, Pedro, Billings	2	8	5.14	61	77	17	34

ALL-STAR TEAM

C: Zane Evans, Idaho Falls. **1B:** Daniel Palka, Missoula. **2B:** Carlos Garcia, Idaho Falls. **3B:** Cal Towey, Orem. **SS:** Jose Rondon, Orem. **OF:** Michael Ratterree, Helena; Jacob Scavuzzo, Ogden; Raimel Tapia, Grand Junction. **DH:** Jacob Morris, Great Falls. **P:** Devin Burke, Grand Junction; Patrick Conroy, Idaho Falls; Ben Lively, Billings; Jake Sanchez, Idaho Falls; Jonathan Van Eaton, Orem.
Most Valuable Player: Michael Ratterree, Helena. **Pitcher of the Year:** Jake Sanchez, Great Falls.
Manager of the Year: Tony Diggs, Helena.

DEPARTMENT LEADERS

BATTING

OBP	Towey, Cal, Orem	.492
SLG	Ratterree, Michael, Helena	.585
OPS	Towey, Cal, Orem	1.036
R	Towey, Cal, Orem	69
H	Tapia, Raimel, Grand Junction	92
TB	Ratterree, Michael, Helena	151
XBH	Ratterree, Michael, Helena	40
2B	Dozier, Hunter, Idaho Falls	24
3B	Hernandez, Elier, Idaho Falls	8
HR	Scavuzzo, Jacob, Ogden	14
RBI	Arteaga, Humberto, Idaho Falls	58
	Ratterree, Michael, Helena	58
SAC	Arteaga, Humberto, Idaho Falls	10
BB	Towey, Cal, Orem	67
HBP	Patterson, Jordan, Grand Junction	16
SO	Morris, Jacob, Great Falls	97
SB	Engel, Adam, Great Falls	31
CS	Bray, Colin, Missoula	9
	Tapia, Raimel, Grand Junction	9
AB/SO	Jirschele, Justin, Great Falls	11.43

PITCHING

G	Yan, Carlos, Grand Junction	26
GS	Seven tied at	15
GF	Bracho, Silvino, Missoula	23
SV	Bracho, Silvino, Missoula	11
W	Kibby, Todd, Great Falls	7
	Perez, Felipe, Missoula	7
L	Diaz, Pedro, Billings	8
IP	Perez, Felipe, Missoula	89
H	Perez, Felipe, Missoula	100
R	Perez, Felipe, Missoula	67
ER	Araujo, Victor, Ogden	55
HB	Two tied at	10
BB	Hernandez, Carlos, Missoula	40
SO	Sanchez, Jake, Great Falls	76
SO/9	Araujo, Victor, Ogden	8.84
SO/9(RP)	Sparkman, Glenn, Idaho Falls	11.5
BB/9	Caramo, Yender, Idaho Falls	1.18
WP	Tago, Peter, Grand Junction	16
BK	Two tied at	3
HR	Barlow, Scott, Ogden	13
	Junis, Jake, Idaho Falls	13
AVG	Sanchez, Jake, Great Falls	.230

FIELDING

C	PCT	Ortiz, Jose, Billings	.985
	PO	Ortiz, Jose, Billings	301
	A	Trahan, Stryker, Missoula	51
	DP	Rosario, Jairo, Grand Junction	5
	E	Trahan, Stryker, Missoula	11
	PB	Trahan, Stryker, Missoula	17
1B	PCT	Sanchez, Carlos, Orem	.996
	PO	Stubbs, Cody, Idaho Falls	534
	A	Hayes, Danny, Great Falls	44
		Stubbs, Cody, Idaho Falls	44
	DP	Stubbs, Cody, Idaho Falls	57
	E	Aguilera, Eric, Orem	10
		Prime, Correlle, Grand Junction	10
2B	PCT	Eaves, Kody, Orem	.960
	PO	Eaves, Kody, Orem	141
	A	Eaves, Kody, Orem	193
	DP	Eaves, Kody, Orem	51
	E	Garcia, Carlos, Idaho Falls	18
3B	PCT	Voight, Zach, Great Falls	.933
	PO	McMahon, Ryan, Grand Junction	49
	A	Brennan, Taylor, Helena	121
	DP	McMahon, Ryan, Grand Junction	12
		Voight, Zach, Great Falls	12
	E	Santana, Alex, Ogden	19
SS	PCT	Rondon, Jose, Orem	.955
	PO	Ortega, Angel, Helena	120
	A	Ortega, Angel, Helena	223
	DP	Rondon, Jose, Orem	49
	E	Jimenez, Emerson, G. Junction	21
		Munoz, Joe, Missoula	21
OF	PCT	Engel, Adam, Great Falls	.986
	PO	Bray, Colin, Missoula	144
	A	Engel, Adam, Great Falls	9
		Garvey, Ryan, Grand Junction	9
	DP	Rockett, Daniel, Idaho Falls	3
	E	Tapia, Raimel, Grand Junction	11

MINOR LEAGUES

BY VINCENT LARA-CINISOMO

Led by top pick Christian Arroyo, the Giants dominated the Arizona League in 2013 and beat the Dodgers 4-0 to win the league championship.

The Giants won 23 of their first 28 games and stormed to the Eastern Division crown with a 41-14 record. Arroyo was the catalyst. After being picked 25th overall in the 2013 draft, the shortstop hit .326/.388/.511 and tied for first in the league in slugging despite hitting just two home runs—his league-leading 18 doubles certainly helped make up the difference.

Arroyo, 18, also topped the AZL in RBIs (39) and runs (47) was chosen as MVP. Overall, the Giants had four players on the Arizona League's all-star team: Arroyo, third baseman Ryder Jones—a 2013 second-round pick who hit .317—catcher Fernando Puijadas and lefthander Luis Ysla.

Another 2013 first-rounder, outfielder Clint Frazier, who was picked fifth overall by the Indians, was the league's top prospect. Frazier hit .297/.362/.506 with five home runs and 28 RBIs.

One of the teams the Giants beat on their way to the Arizona League crown was the Padres, who also had four all-stars, including 18-year-old short-stop Franchy Cordero, who had an OPS of .891, and righty Pete Kelich, who at 22 was old for the league but dominated. A 38th-round pick in June out of Bryant College, Kelich went 7-1, 1.40 with one walk and 69 strikeouts in 58 innings. The Padres also had 19-year-old DH Jose Urena, who hit nine homers in 191 at-bats, while lefty reliever Payton Baskette had a 1.37 ERA.

Other standouts included Angels second baseman Ismael Dionicio, who hit .354, and Dodgers third baseman Adam Law, who batted .357 in just 33 games.

Although the league had standout performances, it largely missed out on heralded Cubs pick Kris Bryant. Drafted second overall, Bryant got only six AZL at-bats before moving up—and tearing up—the Northwest and Florida State leagues.

TOP 20 PROSPECTS

1. Clint Frazier, of, Indians
2. Christian Arroyo, ss, Giants
3. Franchy Cordero, ss, Padres
4. Sergio Alcantara, ss, Diamondbacks
5. Jose Urena, of, Padres
6. Akeem Bostick, rhp, Rangers
7. Francisco Mejia, c, Indians
8. Billy McKinney, of, Athletics
9. Travis Demeritte, ss/3b, Rangers
10. Jairo Beras, of, Rangers
11. Justin Williams, of, Diamondbacks
12. Devin Williams, rhp, Brewers
13. Natanael Delgado, of, Angels
14. Keury Mella, rhp, Giants
15. Dustin Peterson, 3b, Padres
16. Samir Duenez, 1b, Royals
17. Adrian De Horta, rhp, Padres
18. Ryder Jones, 3b, Giants
19. Brad Keller, rhp, Diamondbacks
20. Cole Wiper, rhp, Rangers

STANDINGS: SPLIT SEASON

FIRST HALF				
EAST				
Giants	23	5	.821	—
Angels	15	13	.536	8
D-backs	15	13	.536	8
Cubs	13	15	.464	10
Athletics	12	16	.429	11
CENTRAL				
Dodgers	17	11	.607	—
Indians	13	15	.464	4
Reds	10	18	.357	7
Brewers	9	19	.321	8
SOUTH				
Rangers	17	11	.607	—
Mariners	15	13	.536	2
Padres	13	15	.464	4
Royals	10	18	.357	7

SECOND HALF				
EAST				
Giants	18	9	.667	—
Angels	15	13	.536	3 ½
Cubs	14	13	.519	4
D-backs	14	14	.500	4 ½
Athletics	13	14	.481	5
CENTRAL				
Dodgers	17	11	.607	—
Indians	15	13	.536	2
Brewers	14	14	.500	3
Reds	8	19	.296	8 ½
WEST				
Padres	15	11	.577	—
Rangers	15	12	.556	½
Royals	12	15	.444	3 ½
Mariners	7	19	.269	8

OVERALL STANDINGS

Team (Organization)	W	L	PCT	GB	Manager(s)	Last Pennant
Giants	41	14	.745	—	Derin McMains/Nestor Rojas	2013
Dodgers	34	22	.607	7 ½	P.J. Forbes	2011
Rangers	32	23	.582	9	Kenny Holmberg	2012
Angels	30	26	.536	11 ½	Denny Hocking	Never
Padres	28	26	.519	12 ½	Michael Collins	2006
Diamondbacks	29	27	.518	12 ½	Luis Urueta	Never
Indians	28	28	.500	13 ½	Anthony Medrano	Never
Cubs	27	28	.491	14	Bobby Mitchell	2002
Athletics	25	30	.455	16	Marcus Jensen	2001
Brewers	23	33	.411	18 ½	Nestor Corredor	2010
Mariners	22	32	.407	18 ½	Darrin Garner	2009
Royals	22	33	.400	19	Darryl Kennedy	2003
Reds	18	37	.327	23	Eli Marrero	Never

PLAYOFFS—Quarterfinals: Rangers defeated Indians and Padres defeated Angels in one-game playoffs; **Semifinals:** Giants defeated Padres and Dodgers defeated Rangers in one-game playoffs; **Finals:** Giants defeated Dodgers in a one-game playoff.

CLUB BATTING

	AVG	G	AB	R	H	2B	3B	HR	RBI	BB	SO	SB	OBP	SLG
Giants	.279	55	1978	368	552	129	31	26	320	217	481	44	.360	.415
Angels	.270	56	1955	308	527	107	21	20	243	180	486	103	.338	.376
Padres	.268	54	1890	286	506	95	27	22	243	168	460	60	.336	.381
Rangers	.260	55	1906	282	495	89	22	29	231	201	453	59	.338	.375
Brewers	.259	56	1880	270	486	85	22	19	223	204	446	103	.336	.357
Mariners	.258	54	1883	246	486	86	24	14	207	201	509	42	.337	.352
Royals	.256	55	1907	270	489	83	21	11	223	178	460	77	.343	.339
Indians	.255	56	1928	296	492	103	24	24	243	222	483	66	.338	.371
Athletics	.249	55	1873	267	466	84	20	30	218	195	475	36	.328	.363
Reds	.248	55	1904	260	472	98	21	21	212	169	427	50	.322	.355
Dodgers	.244	56	1889	317	460	87	23	38	261	241	524	76	.337	.374
Diamondbacks	.242	56	1895	262	458	77	30	11	212	228	511	45	.328	.331
Cubs	.238	55	1820	265	433	82	25	7	221	207	449	67	.323	.322

CLUB PITCHING

	ERA	G	CG	SHO	SV	IP	H	R	ER	HR	BB	SO	AVG
Giants	3.19	55	0	3	20	493	427	218	175	9	220	560	.232
Rangers	3.42	55	0	3	14	489	444	218	186	15	191	475	.241
Dodgers	3.63	56	0	2	19	501	454	276	202	26	202	463	.238
Cubs	3.83	55	0	2	12	484	488	265	206	18	175	490	.257
Diamondbacks	3.91	56	0	2	13	500	493	280	217	21	213	527	.255
Royals	3.93	55	0	1	11	497	521	300	217	23	185	458	.266
Angels	3.99	56	0	3	15	505	520	294	224	22	192	429	.264
Brewers	4.14	56	0	2	12	494	508	305	227	23	178	478	.262
Athletics	4.28	55	0	0	8	479	487	283	228	27	177	431	.263
Reds	4.31	55	0	2	5	488	506	313	234	27	202	440	.265
Mariners	4.40	54	0	2	15	485	502	299	237	23	220	455	.268
Indians	4.82	56	0	3	11	499	481	308	267	25	254	481	.252
Padres	5.09	54	1	2	15	479	491	338	271	13	242	477	.262

CLUB FIELDING

	PCT	PO	A	E	DP		PCT	PO	A	E	DP
Giants	.966	1479	588	72	39	Dodgers	.956	1502	603	96	50
Rangers	.965	1468	608	75	55	Padres	.956	1437	589	94	35
Athletics	.963	1438	565	76	45	Cubs	.955	1453	584	97	44
Angels	.960	1514	693	93	63	Diamondbacks	.951	1500	617	108	44
Indians	.959	1496	604	90	45	Royals	.951	1492	586	106	49
Mariners	.958	1454	596	89	49	Reds	.948	1465	585	113	48
Brewers	.956	1482	589	95	40						

INDIVIDUAL BATTING LEADERS (Minimum 2.7 PA/Team Game)

Batter, Club	AVG	G	AB	R	H	HR	RBI
# Dionicio, Ismael, Angels	.360	47	164	24	59	0	20
* Williams, Justin, Diamondbacks	.354	36	144	16	51	1	32
Garcia, Kevin W, Reds	.328	50	195	38	64	3	22
* Cordero, Franchy, Padres	.326	35	141	23	46	3	17
Arroyo, Christian, Giants	.326	45	184	47	60	2	42
Kiner-Falefa, Isiah, Rangers	.322	41	149	36	48	0	11
* McKinney, Billy, Athletics	.320	46	181	31	58	2	20
* Jones, Ryder, Giants	.317	37	145	29	46	1	18
Reyes, Franmil, Padres	.315	45	165	24	52	3	30
Rubio, Elvis, Brewers	.314	42	137	18	43	4	26

INDIVIDUAL PITCHING LEADERS (Minimum 0.8 IP/team game)

Pitcher, Club	W	L	ERA	IP	H	BB	SO
Kelich, Pete, Padres	6	1	1.40	58	43	1	70
* Baskette, Payton, Padres	2	2	1.57	46	36	11	43
* Terry, Clint, Brewers	3	1	1.58	46	36	10	55
Keller, Brad, Diamondbacks	7	3	2.22	57	53	26	61
Furney, Sean, Diamondbacks	1	4	2.25	52	48	13	64
Medina, Jefferson, Mariners	4	3	2.58	52	44	14	34
* Ysla, Luis, Giants	4	0	2.65	51	38	13	52
Leal, Erick, Cubs	3	2	2.77	49	50	8	52
Tobik, Dan, Angels	4	1	2.89	47	37	16	39
Torrez, Daury, Cubs	4	2	3.12	49	49	5	49

ALL-STAR TEAM

C: Fernando Pujadas, Giants. **1B:** Logan Uxa, Reds. **2B:** Ismael Dionicio, Angels. **3B:** Ryder Jones, Giants. **SS:** Christian Arroyo, Giants; Franchy Cordero, Padres. **OF:** Kevin Garcia, Reds; Clint Frazier, Indians; Justin Williams, Diamondbacks. **DH:** Samir, Duenez, Royals; Jose Urena, Padres. **RHSP:** Pete Kelich, Padres. **LHSP:** Luis Ysla, Giants. **RHRP:** Ben Carlson, Angels. **LHRP:** Payton Baskette, Padres. **Most Valuable Player:** Christian Arroyo, Giants. **Manager of the Year:** Nestor Rojas, Giants.

DEPARTMENT LEADERS

BATTING

OBP	Law, Adam, Dodgers	.430
SLG	Arroyo, Christian, Giants	.511
OPS	Arroyo, Christian, Giants	.898
R	Arroyo, Christian, Giants	47
H	Garcia, Kevin, Reds	64
TB	Urena, Jose, Padres	97
XBH	Three tied at	25
2B	Arroyo, Christian, Giants	18
3B	Westbrook, Jamie, D-backs	8
HR	Urena, Jose, Padres	9
RBI	Arroyo, Christian, Giants	39
SAC	Harris, Jaylen, Dodgers	7
BB	Alcantara, Sergio, D-backs	44
HBP	Thompson, Cory, Reds	12
SO	McFarland, Dane, D-backs	68
SB	Baez, Jeffrey, Cubs	25
CS	Diaz, Brandon, Brewers	9
AB/SO	Garcia, Kevin, Reds	8.48

PITCHING

G	Holland, Samuel, Padres	27
GS	Stewart, Cam, Brewers	13
GF	Holland, Samuel, Padres	23
SV	Carlson, Ben, Angels	10
W	Kelich, Pete, Padres	7
	Keller, Brad, D-backs	7
L	Lovegrove, Kieran, Indians	7
IP	Herrera, Ronald, Athletics	70.2
H	Herrera, Ronald, Athletics	76
R	Newton, Dallas, D-backs	46
ER	Lovegrove, Kieran, Indians	34
	Marcano, Ivan, Padres	34
HB	Three tied at	9
BB	Hernandez, Luis, D-backs	39
SO	Samayoa, Jose, Rangers	75
SO/9	Samayoa, Jose, Rangers	12.05
SO/9(RP)	McCoy, Kevin, Mariners	13.3
BB/9	Kelich, Pete, Padres	0.16
WP	Diaz, Malcom, Padres	28
BK	Perez, Kevin, Royals	4
HR	Four tied at	5
AVG	Gardewine, Nick, Rangers	.193

FIELDING

C	PCT	Paz, Andy, Athletics	1.000
	PO	Ruiz, Jose, Padres	264
	A	Lopez, B.J., D-backs	44
	DP	Petit, Wilfredo, Cubs	5
	E	Ruiz, Jose, Padres	11
	PB	Gonzalez, Cesar, Royals	22
1B	PCT	Fink, Grant, Indians	.990
	PO	Johnson, Taylor, Angels	461
	A	Johnson, Taylor, Angels	36
	DP	Johnson, Taylor, Angels	47
1B-E		Three tied at	8
2B	PCT	Valdez, Ordomar, Indians	.945
	PO	Valdez, Ordomar, Indians	71
	A	Castillo, Francisco, Brewers	111
		Pellant, Kirby, Angels	111
	DP	Patino, Alfredo, Royals	28
	E	Berroa, Noe, Mariners	16
3B	PCT	Ahmed, Michael, Dodgers	.961
	PO	Ahmed, Michael, Dodgers	33
		Franklin, Kevin, Reds	33
	A	Ahmed, Michael, Dodgers	89
	DP	Dionicio, Ismael, Angels	34
	E	Franklin, Kevin, Reds	20
SS	PCT	Arroyo, Christian, Giants	.958
	PO	Thompson, Cory, Reds	77
	A	Salcedo, Erick, Angels	167
	DP	Salcedo, Erick, Angels	34
	E	Gomez, Cristian, Dodgers	24
		Thompson, Cory, Reds	24
OF	PCT	Baez, Jeffrey, Cubs	.989
	PO	Aquino, Aristides, Reds	83
		Gomez, Brawlun, Royals	83
	A	Aquino, Aristides, Reds	10
		Baez, Jeffrey, Cubs	10
	DP	Gomez, Brawlun, Royals	3
		Law, Adam, Dodgers	3
	E	Delgado, Natanael, Angels	9

MINOR LEAGUES

BY BEN BADLER

No team dominated its league like the Gulf Coast League Nationals did.

Including the playoffs, the Nationals ended the year with only single-digit losses, rolling through the regular season with a 49-9 record before beating the Pirates in the semifinals and sweeping the Red Sox in two games in the finals to win the league title.

The Nationals had a dominant offense and outstanding pitching, ranking first in the league in runs scored while allowing the fewest runs in the league by a wide margin.

Righthander Lucas Giolito, Washington's first-round pick in the 2012 draft, pitched in the league after recovering from Tommy John surgery that limited him to just two innings in 2012. The 19-year-old ranked as the league's best pitching prospect, flashing a fastball that hit 100 mph with a wipeout breaking ball. Righthander Wander Suero (1.65) and lefthander Hector Silvestre (1.82) carried the pitching staff and finished with the two lowest ERAs in the league.

Drew Ward, a third-round pick in the 2013 draft, was one of the keys to the Nationals' offense, hitting .292/.402/.387 in 49 games to finish fifth in the league in OBP. Speedy center fielder Rafael Bautista was a weapon on both sides of the ball, batting .322/.400/.391 with 26 stolen bases in 52 games while playing excellent defense.

The GCL was loaded with 2013 first-round picks out of high school, most of whom showed performance to match the pedigree in their pro debuts. Pirates center fielder Austin Meadows, the No. 9 overall pick, hit .294/.399/.519 in 43 games to rank as the league's top prospect. Catcher Reese McGuire, whom the Pirates popped six picks later,

also made a strong impression with his hitting—he ranked third in the GCL with a .330 average—and advanced defensive skills. Phillies shortstop J.P. Crawford, the No. 16 overall pick, won the batting title (.345) and led the league in on-base percentage (.443) while ranking fifth in slugging (.465). Mets first baseman Dominic Smith, who went 11th overall, showed a smooth swing, a keen batting eye and Gold Glove potential.

It was a deep year in the GCL for prospects thanks also to an assortment of international talent. Blue Jays shortstop Franklin Barreto, regarded by many teams as the top international prospect last year when he signed out of Venezuela, batted .299/.368/.529 to lead the league in slugging as a 17-year-old. Twins lefthander Lewis Thorpe, a $500,000 signing in 2012 out of Australia, posted a superlative 64-6 K-BB mark while maintaining a 2.05 ERA over 44 innings at age 17.

TOP 20 PROSPECTS

1. Austin Meadows, of, Pirates
2. Lucas Giolito, rhp, Nationals
3. Reese McGuire, c, Pirates
4. Dominic Smith, 1b, Mets
5. Franklin Barreto, ss, Blue Jays
6. J.P. Crawford, ss, Phillies
7. Lewis Thorpe, lhp, Twins
8. Rob Kaminsky, lhp, Cardinals
9. Wendell Rijo, 2b, Red Sox
10. Luis Torrens, c, Yankees
11. Miguel Andujar, 3b, Yankees
12. Nick Ciuffo, c, Rays
13. Abiatal Avelino, ss, Yankees
14. Victor Reyes, of, Braves
15. Gosuke Katoh, 2b, Yankees
16. Jose Mujica, rhp, Rays
17. Luis Severino, rhp, Yankees
18. Javier Betancourt, ss, Tigers
19. Jose Castillo, lhp, Rays
20. Thairo Estrada, ss, Yankees

OVERALL STANDINGS

Team (Organization)	W	L	PCT	GB	Manager(s)	Last Pennant
Nationals	49	9	.845	—	Patrick Anderson	2009
Yankees2	36	24	.600	14	Mario Garza	Never
Red Sox	35	25	.583	15	Darren Fenster	2006
Pirates	33	27	.550	17	Milver Reyes	2012
Tigers	32	28	.533	18	Basillo Cabrera	Never
Orioles	30	30	.500	20	Orlando Gomez	Never
Phillies	30	30	.500	20	Roly De Armas	2010
Blue Jays	28	32	.467	22	John Schneider	Never
Twins	28	32	.467	22	Ramon Borrego	Never
Yankees1	28	32	.467	22	Tom Nieto	2011
Astros	27	33	.450	23	Ed Alfonzo	Never
Rays	27	33	.450	23	Jim Morrison	Never
Braves	26	34	.433	24	Rocket Wheeler	2003
Marlins	25	34	.424	24 ½	Julio Garcia	Never
Cardinals	24	35	.407	25 ½	Steve Turco	Never
Mets	20	40	.333	30	Jose Carreno	Never

Semifinals: Nationals defeated Pirates and Red Sox defeated Yankees 2 in one-game playoffs. **Finals:** Nationals defeated Red Sox 2-0 in a best-of-three series.

CLUB BATTING

	AVG	G	AB	R	H	2B	3B	HR	RBI	BB	SO	SB	OBP	SLG
Nationals	.281	58	1881	319	528	98	16	15	259	184	392	110	.359	.374
Tigers	.257	60	1900	278	488	87	18	30	244	193	426	45	.338	.369
Pirates	.256	60	1969	274	505	98	27	13	240	180	418	50	.331	.353
Phillies	.255	60	1964	267	500	91	17	35	224	198	434	46	.332	.372
Yankees2	.254	60	1966	286	500	118	19	24	242	218	436	88	.337	.370
Astros	.246	60	1948	272	480	95	24	23	237	177	429	69	.321	.355
Cardinals	.243	59	1938	234	471	83	20	19	194	167	439	48	.311	.336
Rays	.241	60	1907	220	460	69	28	5	175	176	482	78	.314	.315
Orioles	.240	60	1901	225	456	93	15	16	195	210	419	68	.323	.330
Braves	.236	60	1933	248	456	75	14	7	212	198	483	81	.316	.300
Mets	.236	60	1906	236	449	69	16	15	203	224	496	61	.323	.312
Blue Jays	.235	60	1937	265	455	92	22	20	230	214	466	40	.322	.336
Red Sox	.235	60	1836	216	431	112	15	5	186	206	475	85	.323	.320
Yankees1	.233	60	2011	252	468	104	17	20	219	198	513	53	.309	.331
Twins	.227	60	1915	238	435	85	25	25	202	184	397	72	.304	.337
Marlins	.213	59	1817	182	387	74	12	20	157	179	447	16	.301	.300

CLUB PITCHING

	ERA	G	CG	SHO	SV	IP	H	R	ER	HR	BB	SO	AVG
Nationals	2.45	58	0	11	22	496	392	161	135	18	158	435	.217
Yankees2	2.92	60	0	3	15	524	430	231	170	10	200	498	.220
Twins	2.94	60	0	3	16	514	463	228	168	9	176	520	.238
Red Sox	3.04	60	0	6	19	500	409	209	169	11	210	397	.224
Orioles	3.24	60	0	3	17	513	434	225	185	11	211	465	.229
Marlins	3.41	59	0	4	14	488	470	247	185	11	161	448	.249
Rays	3.49	60	0	4	18	503	476	237	195	20	179	391	.251
Tigers	3.61	60	0	4	17	502	473	245	201	28	183	438	.251
Cardinals	3.73	59	0	2	8	507	465	269	210	20	214	499	.244
Phillies	3.76	60	0	2	12	517	507	269	216	16	184	369	.257
Yankees1	3.82	60	0	5	17	526	516	266	223	18	181	550	.256
Pirates	3.86	60	0	5	16	518	459	265	222	33	195	424	.236
Astros	3.91	60	0	2	8	511	487	289	222	20	219	473	.247
Braves	3.98	60	0	3	14	509	469	287	225	34	202	407	.242
Blue Jays	4.23	60	0	5	12	506	511	290	238	13	212	446	.262
Mets	4.28	60	1	4	10	509	508	294	242	20	221	392	.261

CLUB FIELDING

	PCT	PO	A	E	DP		PCT	PO	A	E	DP
Nationals	.977	1488	568	49	48	Yankees1	.962	1577	598	86	44
Red Sox	.975	1501	637	54	51	Astros	.961	1532	602	86	54
Tigers	.971	1505	631	63	52	Braves	.960	1528	602	89	46
Orioles	.969	1540	606	68	38	Twins	.960	1541	588	89	52
Phillies	.967	1550	620	74	49	Yankees2	.959	1572	598	93	45
Rays	.967	1508	603	72	46	Cardinals	.958	1522	526	89	44
Blue Jays	.962	1518	629	84	46	Marlins	.956	1463	596	95	56
Pirates	.962	1553	668	88	54	Mets	.956	1528	644	99	52

INDIVIDUAL BATTING LEADERS (Minimum 2.7 PA/Team Game)

Batter, Club	AVG	G	AB	R	H	HR	RBI
* Crawford, J.P., Phillies	.345	39	142	24	49	1	19
Betancourt, Javier, Tigers	.333	50	177	28	59	2	22
* McGuire, Reese, Pirates	.330	46	176	30	58	0	21
* Wong, Kean, Rays	.328	46	177	27	58	0	22
# Mejia, Yonathan, Astros	.327	59	223	27	73	2	32
Bautista, Rafael, Nationals	.322	52	202	44	65	1	27
* Oberto, Wilmer, Phillies	.316	51	187	31	59	6	45
* Brown, Rashad, Tigers	.313	42	144	16	45	0	13
* Katoh, Gosuke, Yankees1	.310	50	184	28	57	6	25
* Wade, Tyler, Yankees1	.309	46	162	37	50	0	12

INDIVIDUAL PITCHING LEADERS (Minimum 0.8 IP/team game)

Pitcher, Club	W	L	ERA	IP	H	BB	SO
Suero, Wander, Nationals	8	1	1.65	49	27	13	46
* Silvestre, Hector, Nationals	7	0	1.82	49	33	8	40
Maher, Joey, Yankees2	5	3	1.91	57	37	17	28
* Caicedo, Oriel, Braves	1	1	2.06	52	48	16	27
Alonzo, Jose, Rays	7	2	2.22	57	47	14	35
Gonzalez, Felipe, Yankees2	4	1	2.23	48	40	17	45
Lail, Brady, Yankees1	4	1	2.33	54	39	5	51
* Perez, Randy, Red Sox	3	2	2.39	49	32	18	38
Rodriguez, Jefry, Nationals	3	0	2.45	48	40	20	43
Perez, Fernando, Tigers	5	2	3.23	56	47	26	38

ALL-STAR TEAM

C: Reese McGuire, Pirates. **1B:** Wilmer Oberto, Phillies. **2B:** Gosuke Katoh, Yankees1. **3B:** Drew Ward, Nationals. **SS:** J.P. Crawford, Phillies. **OF:** Rafael Bautista, Nationals; Boomer Collins, Blue Jays; Austin Meadows, Pirates. **DH:** Yonathan Mejia, Astros. **UT:** Javier Betancourt, Tigers. **RHP:** Wander Suero, Nationals. **LHP:** Hector Silvestre, Nationals. **RP:** Victor Beriguete, Yankees1. **Most Valuable Player:** Wilmer Oberto, Phillies. **Manager of the Year:** Patrick Anderson, Nationals.

DEPARTMENT LEADERS

BATTING

OBP	Crawford, J.P., Phillies		.443
SLG	Barreto, Franklin, Blue Jays		.529
OPS	Katoh, Gosuke, Yankees1		.924
R	Bautista, Rafael, Nationals		44
H	Mejia, Yonathan, Astros		72
TB	Mejia, Yonathan, Astros		97
XBH	Barreto, Franklin, Blue Jays		26
2B	Mejia, Yonathan, Astros		19
3B	Mejia, Bryan, Nationals		7
HR	Five tied at		6
RBI	Oberto, Wilmer, Phillies		45
SAC	Four tied at		7
BB	Unroe, Riley, Rays		33
HBP	Williams, Miles, Marlins		11
SO	Sanchez, Fernelys, Braves		73
SB	Avelino, Abiatal, Yankees1, Yankees2		26
	Bautista, Rafael, Nationals		26
CS	Simon, Hector, Rays		8
AB/SO	Zambrano, Jose, Tigers		15.4

PITCHING

G	Villegas, Kinder, Cardinals		22
GS	Three tied at		12
GF	Ciriaco, Ricardo, Tigers		20
	Pena, Jose, Yankees2		20
SV	Ciriaco, Ricardo, Tigers		15
W	Suero, Wander, Nationals		8
L	Barrios, Agapito, Astros		7
IP	Alonzo, Jose, Rays		56.2
	Maher, Joseph, Yankees2		56.2
H	Casimiro, Ranfi, Phillies		66
R	Gonzalez, Francisco, Braves		38
ER	Gonzalez, Francisco, Braves		36
HB	Smoral, Matthew, Blue Jays		10
BB	Perez, Juan, Cardinals		37
SO	Thorpe, Lewis, Twins		64
SO/9	Lail, Brady, Yankees1		8.5
SO/9(RP)	Ruth, Eric, Yankees1		15
BB/9	Lail, Brady, Yankees1		0.83
WP	Salazar, Hector, Cardinals		13
BK	Lara, Confesor, Tigers		4
	Meisner, Casey, Mets		4
HR	Chavez, Emanuel, Tigers		6
AVG	Suero, Wander, Nationals		.156

FIELDING

C	PCT	Three tied at	1.000
	PO	de Oleo, Eduardo, Yankees1	256
	A	Torrens, Luis, Yankees2	41
	DP	Seven tied at	3
	E	Hawkins, Taylor, Rays	12
	PB	Rodriguez, Eric, Cardinals	16
1B	PCT	Simon, Alexander, Rays	.994
	PO	Simon, Alexander, Rays	475
	A	Simon, Alexander, Rays	34
	DP	Mejia, Yonathan, Astros	45
	E	Mejia, Yonathan, Astros	10
2B	PCT	Katoh, Gosuke, Yankees1	.977
	PO	Katoh, Gosuke, Yankees1	82
	A	Rijo, Wendell, Red Sox	126
	DP	Wong, Kean, Rays	29
	E	Olivencia, Iramis, Marlins	11
3B	PCT	Fuentes, Edwin, Blue Jays	.968
	PO	Medina, Rafael, Cardinals	45
	A	Fuentes, Steven, Tigers	101
	DP	Fuentes, Steven, Tigers	12
	E	Urena, Jhoan, Mets	17
SS	PCT	Flores, Raymel, Red Sox	.967
	PO	Viele, Justin, Orioles	81
	A	Blanton, Aaron, Marlins	140
	DP	Blanton, Aaron, Marlins	31
	E	Arbet, Trae, Pirates	21
OF	PCT	Seven tied at	1.000
	PO	Wilson, Ivan, Mets	106
	A	Kanzler, Jason, Twins	9
	DP	Kanzler, Jason, Twins	3
	E	Sanchez, Fernelys, Braves	8
		Woods, K.J., Marlins	8

MINOR LEAGUES

DOMINICAN SUMMER LEAGUE

After finishing with the best record during the Dominican Summer League regular season, the Rangers dropped the first game of the finals, but they rebounded to beat the Tigers in three straight games to capture the championship.

The Rangers allowed the fewest runs in the league and also outscored every team in the league, with an offensive that accomplished the rare team feat of having more walks (336) than strikeouts (314).

In his first pro season, 17-year-old Domingo Leyba hit .348/.446/.577 in 247 plate appearances to lead the DSL in OPS while splitting time between shortstop and second base. Pirates center fielder Michael de la Cruz also stood out in his pro debut while playing most of the season at age 16, hitting .292/.436/.367 in 62 games to rank eighth in OBP.

STANDINGS

BOCA CHICA NORTH

TEAM	W	L	PCT	GB
Rangers	53	18	.746	–
Mets2	45	26	.634	8
Pirates1	40	31	.563	13
Phillies	37	34	.521	16
Angels	36	35	.507	17
Rockies	32	39	.451	21
Marlins	26	45	.366	27
Yankees2	15	56	.211	38

BOCA CHICA SOUTH

TEAM	W	L	PCT	GB
Cubs	50	21	.704	–
Pirates2	46	26	.639	4 ½
Yankees1	40	30	.571	9 ½
Nationals	38	31	.551	11
Cardinals	35	36	.493	15
Orioles2	33	38	.465	17
Mets1	21	50	.296	29
Rojos	18	53	.254	32

BOCA CHICA NORTHWEST

TEAM	W	L	PCT	GB
Red Sox	46	24	.657	–
Royals	41	29	.586	5
Astros	39	31	.557	7
Mariners	37	33	.529	9

TEAM	W	L	PCT	GB
Rays	36	35	.507	10 ½
Athletics	31	41	.431	16
Dodgers	27	43	.386	19
Indians	25	46	.352	21 ½

BOCA CHICA BASEBALL CITY

TEAM	W	L	PCT	GB
Giants	45	22	.672	–
Reds	37	31	.544	8 ½
Orioles1	37	33	.529	9 ½
Twins	36	33	.522	10
White Sox	30	39	.435	16
D-backs	29	39	.426	16 ½
Padres	26	43	.377	20

SAN PEDRO DE MACORIS

TEAM	W	L	PCT	GB
Tigers	49	23	.681	–
Blue Jays	41	29	.586	7
Braves	27	42	.391	20 ½
Brewers	26	45	.366	22 ½

PLAYOFFS—Division Series: Red Sox defeated Giants 2-0 and Tigers defeated Pirates 2-1 in best-of-three series; **Semifinals:** Rangers defeated Red Sox 2-0 and Tigers defeated Cubs 2-1 in best-of-three series; **Finals:** Rangers defeated Tigers 3-1 in a best-of-three series.

INDIVIDUAL BATTING LEADERS

PLAYER, TEAM	AVG	G	AB	R	H	2B	3B	HR	RBI	BB	SO	SB
Leyba, Domingo, Tigers	.348	57	201	51	70	15	8	5	36	34	26	16
Ortiz, Dalfis, Cubs	.343	47	172	39	59	7	9	1	26	25	23	14
Sanchez, Richi, Dbacks	.338	58	198	43	67	13	4	3	27	49	29	10
Marte, Olvy, Phillies	.338	63	213	41	72	12	6	1	29	25	33	21
Joseph, Manuel, Tigers	.338	61	222	37	75	15	2	3	48	20	32	24
Mercedes, Alex, Orioles1	.336	67	250	47	84	15	10	1	28	31	20	19
Baez, Dubal, Twins	.335	57	164	43	55	8	1	0	14	29	37	27
Mendez, Miguel, Reds	.333	63	234	45	78	20	2	0	28	28	23	32
Lacrus, Sherman, Rangers	.330	54	179	36	59	4	1	3	21	21	18	8
Vargas, Hector, Reds	.327	61	226	41	74	11	0	33	24	18	21

INDIVIDUAL PITCHING LEADERS

PLAYER, TEAM	W	L	ERA	G	GS	CG	SV	IP	H	R	BB	SO
Morel, Jose, Giants	6	0	1.22	22	1	0	6	59	48	13	6	55
Moreno, Rafael, Orioles1	7	2	1.23	14	14	1	0	80.7	74	19	16	63
Veliz, Victor, Athletics	5	3	1.39	14	14	0	0	71	53	17	18	46
Reyes, Scarlyn, Mets	5	3	1.41	12	11	1	0	64	51	19	18	56
Santos, Gregorio, Phillies	9	1	1.47	14	14	1	0	86	58	15	57
Gracia, Ariel, Rays	3	1	1.48	14	14	0	0	66.7	60	20	12	59
Jimenez, Dedgar, Red Sox	4	3	1.5	13	13	0	0	60	45	18	9	55
Floranus, Wendell, Orioles1	3	3	1.51	15	15	1	0	77.7	66	15	18	43
Jimenez, Francisco, Orioles2	4	4	1.6	14	13	0	0	67.7	52	24	19	63
Gonzalez, Yeuri, Mariners	8	3	1.63	14	14	1	0	83	75	33	14	55

VENEZUELAN SUMMER LEAGUE

The Cubs reached the finals in their first season back in the five-team Venezuelan Summer League, but the Mariners finished with the best regular season record before sweeping the Cubs in two games in the finals to win the VSL championship.

The Mariners scored the most runs and allowed the fewest in the league. Yordi Calderon, a 19-year-old who split time between third base, first base and left field, hit .343/.448/.590 in 68 games to lead the league in on-base percentage and rank second with 11 home runs.

Rays catcher David Rodriguez, a top prospect signed out of Venezuela in 2012, led the league with 12 home runs and ranked third in OBP, batting .329/.409/.540 over 64 games as a 17-year-old in his pro debut.

PLAYOFFS— Finals: Mariners defeated Cubs 2-0 in a best-of-three series.

STANDINGS

TEAM	W	L	PCT	GB
Mariners	48	20	.706	–
Cubs	36	32	.529	12
Phillies	36	32	.529	12

TEAM	W	L	PCT	GB
Tigers	32	36	.471	16
Rays	18	50	.265	30

INDIVIDUAL BATTING LEADERS

PLAYER, TEAM	AVG	G	AB	R	H	2B	3B	HR	RBI	BB	SO	SB
Alcala, Roney, Cubs	.353	64	241	43	85	15	2	9	49	13	34	5
Calderon, Yordi, Mariners	.343	68	239	68	82	20	3	11	42	39	48	16
Padron, Victor, Tigers	.341	60	214	38	73	6	0	11	24	28	23
Rodriguez, David, Rays	.329	64	237	44	78	14	0	12	29	24	62	5
Wawoe, Gianfranco, Mariners	.328	68	244	63	80	19	4	6	30	33	25	21
Arcila, Delbis, Cubs	.321	64	240	48	77	21	0	10	42	32	62	3
Morales, Jhonbaker, Mariners	.314	51	172	30	54	10	0	1	24	11	20	1
Duran, Carlos, Phillies	.305	58	203	32	62	14	2	3	19	29	33	20
Garcia, Wilson, Phillies	.304	57	191	19	58	14	2	1	31	13	16	3
Zorrilla, Freddy, Phillies	.299	58	197	29	59	11	1	4	26	15	61	2

INDIVIDUAL PITCHING LEADERS

PLAYER, TEAM	W	L	ERA	G	GS	CG	SV	IP	H	R	BB	SO
Alzolay, Adbert, Cubs	5	3	1.07	15	12	0	0	67	49	16	10	61
Rivero, Alexis, Phillies	5	2	2.03	14	13	0	0	71	57	22	15	43
Chavez, Jesus, Phillies	9	0	2.18	14	14	0	0	74.3	67	21	9	72
Lopez, Pablo, Mariners	7	1	2.56	12	12	0	0	66.7	51	25	11	38
Gadea, Kevin, Mariners	9	1	2.65	14	14	0	0	71.3	71	28	23	48
Castro, Anthony, Tigers	2	2	2.73	13	11	0	0	56	45	24	17	55
Pinto, Ricardo, Phillies	3	5	2.86	14	14	0	0	63	55	29	12	51
Jimenez, Eduardo, Tigers	4	2	3.21	14	13	0	0	61.7	52	26	25	55
Chirinos, Yonny, Rays	3	3	3.27	13	12	0	0	55	59	21	11	42
Breto, Liarvis, Mariners	5	3	3.57	13	11	0	0	58	48	28	26	50

BY JOHN MANUEL

The bases were loaded, thanks in part to his own error. His team, the Surprise Saguaros, had a 1-0 sixth-inning lead, but lefthander Tim Berry would have to retire the Arizona Fall League's MVP and the Mesa Solar Sox's cleanup hitter and league batting champion to preserve the lead.

"The whole inning was moving really fast," the Orioles farmhand said. "It's rare when you have all your pitches working, and it's rare when you have none of your pitches working. That's how it was for me; nothing was working, and next thing you know, there's first and second, and then I make the error."

With the sacks jacked, Berry faced Kris Bryant (Cubs), whose six homers led the AFL, and C.J. Cron, who hit .413 this fall. But he was able to retire both, Bryant on a foul popup to first base, and Cron on a swinging strikeout, to escape the threat.

Three innings later, Berry and his fellow Saguaros celebrated their championship as they defeated the Solar Sox 2-0 for the first title in the nickname's history since 1995.

The Saguaros have shifted from Mesa to Maryvale and now to Surprise, and the affiliated major league clubs have changed over the years, so the significance of the title in Saguaros' lore is certainly debatable. But the victory did mean something to players such as Berry, who pitched only the scoreless sixth, one of six Surprise pitchers who combined to hold the Solar Sox to five hits. The Saguaros rushed out from the dugout and bullpen to celebrate around the pitcher's mound after David Goforth (Brewers) struck out Steven Souza (Nationals) to end the game.

"I've never played on a winning team, really," said Berry, a 50th-round pick in 2009 out of San Marcos (Calif.) High. "I've seen other teams celebrate like that but I've never been in one. It's actually pretty fun once you're in the middle of one."

Fellow Orioles farmhand Henry Urrutia had two doubles to pace Surprise's offense and scored the game's first run. He doubled to right-center field in the bottom of the second with two outs off Dallas Beeler (Cubs), then came home to score on a single to center by Jorge Alfaro (Rangers).

"I hit two fastballs," Urrutia said through translator Jonathan Schoop (Orioles). "When I got up this morning, I told myself I was going to be aggressive if I had pitches to hit, and I was able to get some pitches and do that today, and I hit it

hard twice and got two doubles.

Alfaro also shined defensively from behind the plate. Well-regarded for his throwing arm, which earns 70 grades from scouts, he threw a laser to second to catch Souza trying to steal. He also nabbed Devon Travis in the top of the fourth inning.

"It's huge to have a catcher who's with you like that, because as a pitcher, you're not alone," Berry said. "When the bases were loaded, he came out and talked to me and took me through how to go after Bryant, and we were able to execute that pitch, and it got me back on track. The at-bat against Cron was a tough at-bat, but he's just a great catcher to throw to and helped get me through that inning."

Surprise got an insurance run in the eighth on a single by Schoop, who ultimately scored on Mookie Betts' single. Goforth followed with his scoreless inning, completing the work started by lefthander Eduardo Rodriguez (Orioles), who threw three scoreless frames and was followed by Tyler Cravy (Brewers), Berry, Noe Ramirez (Red Sox) and Keone Kela (Rangers).

Beeler tossed five fine innings in the losing effort, giving up just the two hits and one walk while striking out five.

Bryant, the No. 2 pick in the draft who led the league with six homers and a .727 slugging percentage while batting .364, was named the AFL's Joe Black Award winner as MVP. It was a strong finish to a long season for Bryant, who was Baseball America's College Player of the Year and the Golden Spikes Award winner after his spring season at San Diego.

Red Sox farmhand Gerin Cecchini won the Dernell Stenson Sportsmanship award. The award, instituted in 2004 in memory of former Red Sox farmhand Dernell Stenson, is presented annually to the AFL player who best exemplifies unselfishness, hard work and leadership. Stenson was killed in Arizona while playing in the AFL in 2003.

TOP 10 PROSPECTS

1. Byron Buxton, of, Desert Dogs (Twins)
2. Addison Russell, ss, Solar Sox (Athletics)
3. Kris Bryant, 3b, Solar Sox (Cubs)
4. Alex Meyer, rhp, Desert Dogs (Twins)
5. Austin Hedges, c, Javelinas (Padres)
6. Jorge Alfaro, c, Saguaros (Rangers)
7. Aaron Sanchez, rhp, Rafters (Blue Jays)
8. Andrew Heaney, lhp, Desert Dogs
9. Marcus Stroman, rhp, Rafters
10. Kyle Crick, rhp, Scorpions (Giants)

MINOR LEAGUES

MINOR LEAGUES

STANDINGS

EAST	W	L	PCT	GB		WEST	W	L	PCT	GB
Mesa Solar Sox	19	11	.630	—		Surprise Saguaros	18	12	.600	—
Salt River Rafters	19	12	.610			Glendale Desert Dogs	13	16	.450	5
Scottsdale Scorpions	10	21	.320	10		Peoria Javelinas	12	19	.390	7

INDIVIDUAL BATTING LEADERS
(Minimum 2 Plate Appearances/League Games)

Player, Team	AVG	G	AB	R	H	HR	RBI
Cron, C.J., Mesa	.413	20	80	17	33	5	20
Alfaro, Jorge, Surprise	.386	19	70	18	27	0	11
Urrutia, Henry, Surprise	.377	18	69	8	26	3	15
Piscotty, Stephen, Salt River	.371	23	89	20	33	1	18
Bryant, Kris, Salt River	.364	20	77	22	28	6	17
Shaw, Travis, Surprise	.361	17	61	18	22	5	19
Susac, Andrew, Scottsdale	.360	17	50	7	18	2	7
Naquin, Tyler, Surprise	.339	27	115	22	39	1	18
Keys, Brent, Glendale	.319	17	69	11	22	1	5

INDIVIDUAL PITCHING LEADERS
(Minimum .4 Innings Pitched/League Games)

Player, Team	W	L	ERA	IP	H	BB	SO
Law, Derek, Scottsdale	1	0	0.00	12	8	6	16
Collier, Tommy, Mesa	0	0	0.64	14	11	2	10
Rogers, Chad, Glendale	1	0	0.66	13	10	4	12
Wittgren, Nick, Glendale	0	0	0.66	13	6	2	19
Sanchez, Aaron, Salt River	2	1	1.16	23	11	11	21
Frankoff, Seth, Mesa	0	0	1.46	12	8	3	15
Berry, Tim, Surprise	2	0	1.84	14	11	3	11
Ramirez, Noe, Surprise	1	0	1.93	14	9	3	11
Heaney, Andrew, Glendale	2	1	1.95	27	19	9	24
Morin, Mike, Mesa	0	1	2.03	13	7	4	12

MESA SOLAR SOX

BATTERS	AVG	AB	R	H	2B	3B	HR	RBI	BB	SO	SB
Almora, Albert	.307	75	8	23	6	2	1	12	4	9	0
Bandy, Jett	.258	31	3	8	2	0	1	6	0	7	0
Borenstein, Zach	.136	44	6	6	1	0	1	3	11	9	0
Bryant, Kris	.364	77	22	28	8	1	6	17	14	23	3
Collins, Tyler	.260	73	16	19	1	0	2	9	15	18	2
Cron, C.J.	.413	80	17	33	6	1	5	20	8	11	0
Darvill, Wes	.171	35	4	6	1	0	1	5	3	5	0
Freitas, David	.222	27	8	6	0	0	1	4	4	6	1
Goodwin, Brian	.296	81	9	24	4	1	2	12	4	22	3
Lindsey, Taylor	.225	80	10	18	3	1	2	10	6	17	0
Machado, Dixon	.158	38	5	6	0	0	0	4	7	12	1
Maxwell, Bruce	.000	4	0	0	0	0	0	0	0	1	0
Muncy, Max	.224	49	4	11	0	1	0	3	10	10	0
Nieto, Adrian	.271	48	6	13	1	1	0	6	6	10	0
Russell, Addison	.282	85	15	24	8	1	1	5	10	15	5
Skole, Matt	.184	49	8	9	1		3	7	15	18	0
Soler, Jorge	.271	85	11	23	6	0	1	14	5	21	0
Souza, Steven	.357	42	8	15	2	0	1	8	5	11	10
Travis, Devon	.236	72	12	17	3	0	2	12	7	14	3

PITCHERS	W	L	ERA	G	GS	SV	IP	H	BB	SO	AVG
Alvarez, R.J.	0	1	5.40	10	0	0	10	12	2	12	.279
Bedrosian, Cam	0	0	2.89	9	0	0	9	5	2	13	.156
Beeler, Dallas	4	1	2.49	6	6	0	22	24	5	9	.300
Benincasa, Robert	0	0	4.00	9	0	0	9	11	4	7	.306
Castillo, Lendy	0	0	1.74	11	0	1	10	9	12	7	.257
Collier, Tommy	0	0	0.64	4	3	0	14	11	2	10	.216
Dull, Ryan	0	1	4.91	10	0	2	11	11	4	9	.262
Duran, Omar	0	1	5.59	8	0	0	10	9	7	6	.265
Faulk, Kenny	1	1	6.97	10	0	0	10	7	11	11	.206
Frankoff, Seth	0	0	1.46	12	0	0	12	8	3	15	.170
Hardy, Blaine	2	0	3.38	8	2	0	16	19	5	16	.292
Knebel, Corey	0	0	4.15	9	0	2	9	7	3	11	.219
Loosen, Matt	2	1	3.29	8	1	0	14	15	6	14	.288
Mirowski, Richie	0	0	2.25	9	0	1	12	8	2	10	.182
Morin, Mike	0	1	2.03	11	0	1	13	7	4	12	.149
Purke, Matt	3	1	3.91	6	6	0	23	20	9	17	.238
Rivero, Armando	0	1	4.91	11	0	0	11	14	5	9	.326
Roth, Michael	1	0	3.43	6	6	0	21	18	10	10	.237
Solis, Sammy	5	2	2.17	7	7	0	29	32	7	29	.278
Urlaub, Jeff	1	0	2.77	11	0	0	13	14	3	16	.292
Wright, Mike	0	5	6.43	7	7	0	21	37	7	15	.389
Zych, Tony	1	0	3.86	13	0	1	14	18	2	4	.327

PEORIA JAVELINAS

BATTERS	AVG	AB	R	H	2B	3B	HR	RBI	BB	SO	SB
Adams, Lane	.146	48	3	7	1	0	0	1	7	20	1
Altherr, Aaron	.200	45	6	9	3	0	0	3	2	8	2
Amador, Japhet	.284	67	7	19	3	0	4	12	1	17	0
Bonifacio, Jorge	.213	61	6	13	5	0	0	4	6	14	0
Calixte, Orlando	.182	55	6	10	2	1	1	6	1	15	1
Cuthbert, Cheslor	.182	44	5	8	2	0	1	5	4	8	0
DeShields, Delino	.275	69	7	19	4	1	0	6	12	21	8
Fontana, Nolan	.111	54	8	6	2	0	0	1	13	16	0
Hedges, Austin	.273	55	2	15	5	1	0	6	5	14	0
Kivlehan, Patrick	.164	61	1	10	0	0	1	5	3	17	1
Lowery, Jake	.240	25	0	6	0	1	0	5	3	4	0
Medica, Tommy	.121	66	2	8	2	0	0		7	22	0
Meyer, Jonathan	.286	49	8	14	3	0	1	7	4	12	0
Perkins, Cameron	.216	51	8	11	4	2	0	3	5	7	1
Romero, Stefen	.212	66	9	14	2	0	2	6	4	19	1
Rupp, Cameron	.278	54	7	15	4	1	1	6	5	19	1
Spangenberg, Cory	.308	65	12	20	4	1	2	7	5	17	7
Taylor, Chris	.294	68	8	20	4	1	1	5	6	15	5

PITCHERS	W	L	ERA	G	GS	SV	IP	H	BB	SO	AVG
Adam, Jason	2	2	4.03	7	7	0	29	25	7	24	.225
Arguelles, Noel	0	1	8.76	9	0	0	12	12	15	7	.293
Baez, Angel	2	0	7.82	9	0	0	13	14	9	19	.269
Barbato, Johnny	0	3	5.79	5	5	0	14	19	6	11	.339
Culver, Malcom	0	1	4.26	10	0	0	13	9	3	7	.205
Dufek, Jonas	0	1	2.89	7	0	0	9	8	2	12	.216
Giles, Ken	0	0	5.23	10	0	3	10	8	8	16	.211
Heidenreich, Matt	2	1	2.14	6	6	0	21	14	9	18	.194
Hunter, Kyle	0	3	8.10	8	5	0	17	29	7	12	.403
Leone, Dominic	0	1	3.00	11	0	6	12	14	1	15	.286
Maurer, Brandon	1	2	5.95	6	6	0	20	21	12	17	.288
Nesseth, Mike	0	2	9.20	9	0	0	15	21	8	9	.344
O'Grady, Dennis	1	0	0.00	8	0	0	9	9	3	8	.250
Portillo, Adys	1	1	8.74	9	0	0	11	10	13	9	.244
Robinson, Andrew	1	0	3.97	10	0	1	11	15	7	9	.300
Sampson, Keyvius	0	0	0.79	7	1	0	11	8	5	10	.200
Simon, Kyle	0	0	3.14	9	0	1	14	12	6	11	.231
Smith, Carson	0	0	12.60	5	0	1	5	7	4	4	.318
Sogard, Alex	2	1	3.65	10	1	0	12	11	8	10	.234
Wieland, Joe	0	0	4.50	2	0	0	2	3	0	1	.375
Wright, Austin	0	0	5.91	10	0	0	11	16	6	11	.333

GLENDALE DESERT DOGS

BATTERS	AVG	AB	R	H	2B	3B	HR	RBI	BB	SO	SB
Barnhart, Tucker	.245	49	5	12	3	0	0	2	9	7	0
Black, Danny	.267	60	5	16	1	0	0	5	5	17	2
Buxton, Byron	.212	52	10	11	1	0	3	8	5	15	2
Cavazos-Galvez, Brian	.269	67	7	18	6	0	2	7	7	14	1
Jacobs, Brandon	.256	43	12	11	5	0	2	5	5	16	0
Johnson, Micah	.320	25	6	8	3	1	0	6	3	5	3
Kepler, Max	.234	64	8	15	5	0	0	4	7	13	0
Keys, Brent	.319	69	11	22	2	0	1	5	7	8	3
LaMarre, Ryan	.400	5	0	2	0	0	0	1	1	1	
Mattair, Travis	.236	72	7	17	3	0	2	7	9	16	0
Maynard, Pratt	.115	26	2	3	0	0	1	3	6	8	0
Mitchell, Jared	.304	69	12	21	2	1	5	11	14	17	6
Moran, Colin	.230	87	7	20	3	0	0	10	12	18	0
O'Brien, Chris	.213	47	3	10	4	0	1	8	10	11	1
Rodriguez, Yorman	.271	85	14	23	2	0	4	13	7	27	3
Rosario, Eddie	.238	80	3	19	1	1	0	7	3	13	2
Seager, Corey	.181	72	9	13	3	0	2	10	7	25	0
Semien, Marcus	.156	77	9	12	3	0	2	8	10	23	0

PITCHERS	W	L	ERA	G	GS	SV	IP	H	BB	SO	AVG
Achter, A.J.	1	1	5.25	11	0	0	12	11	4	10	.229
Baez, Pedro	0	0	0.00	4	0	0	4	3	3	6	.188
Bassitt, Chris	1	0	0.90	10	0	0	10	8	8	9	.216
Garcia, Onelki	0	0	0.00	1	0	0	1	0	1	1	.000
Garcia, Yimi	0	1	2.84	10	0	1	12	10	3	8	.227
Hayes, Drew	2	0	0.82	11	0	0	11	7	7	11	.184
Heaney, Andrew	2	1	1.95	7	7	0	27	19	9	24	.192
Jones, Zack	0	1	18.00	7	0	0	6	10	9	9	.400
Leesman, Charlie	0	1	1.74	7	1	0	10	8	3	6	.242
Lorenzen, Michael	0	3	11.42	6	6	0	17	29	12	5	.382
Martin, Jarret	0	1	5.40	13	0	0	15	13	16	15	.245
May, Trevor	0	2	3.21	9	1	0	14	13	4	12	.265
McCray, Stephen	2	2	2.57	6	6	0	21	19	10	9	.244
Meyer, Alex	2	1	3.12	7	7	0	26	20	7	28	.213
Olmos, Edgar	0	1	8.03	12	0	0	12	15	10	10	.294
Rogers, Chad	1	0	0.66	9	0	0	13	10	4	12	.200
Stem, Craig	0	0	9.00	4	0	0	4	4	0	0	.267
Suggs, Colby	0	0	5.40	12	0	0	11	7	8	8	.175
Thomas, Mike	0	1	4.76	5	0	0	5	7	3	7	.318
Vance, Kevin	0	0	2.13	10	0	0	12	9	6	13	.200
Walczak, Jamie	2	0	4.11	8	3	0	15	9	10	16	.180
Wittgren, Nick	0	0	0.66	13	0	3	13	6	2	19	.130

SALT RIVER RAFTERS

BATTERS	AVG	AB	R	H	2B	3B	HR	RBI	BB	SO	SB
Adames, Cristhian	.293	58	9	17	3	2	1	16	4	7	1
Ahmed, Nick	.219	64	12	14	1	0	1	6	11	13	1
Brett, Ryan	.154	52	9	8	2	2	0	1	11	9	7
Burns, Andy	.312	77	16	24	5	.1	0	13	12	13	6
Casali, Curt	.250	4	1	1	0	0	0	0	2	0	0
Chung, Derrick	.390	41	4	16	2	0	0	2	4	7	0
Freeman, Mike	.268	56	5	15	4	0	0	10	7	12	5
Garneau, Dustin	.167	48	7	8	2	0	4	8	7	9	0
Glaesmann, Todd	.105	19	0	2	1	0	0	1	1	4	0
Lamb, Jake	.299	77	14	23	6	0	1	7	11	25	0

PITCHERS	W	L	ERA	G	GS	SV	IP	H	BB	SO	AVG
Anderson, Chase	3	1	3.47	6	6	0	23	19	9	26	.218
Barrett, Aaron	0	0	3.27	10	0	0	11	15	2	10	.333
Chatwood, Tyler	1	1	4.60	4	4	0	16	15	10	15	.273
Demny, Paul	0	0	3.94	10	1	0	16	18	8	12	.310
Dyson, Sam	0	0	7.04	7	0	0	8	12	1	8	.353
Froneberger, Isaiah	1	1	8.25	11	0	0	12	16	5	10	.314
Kadish, Ian	0	1	7.00	10	0	0	9	14	4	6	.350
Kimball, Cole	0	0	4.80	11	0	0	15	18	9	10	.290
Marbry, Mike	0	0	2.70	3	0	0	3	3	0	3	.250
Marshall, Evan	0	1	2.19	11	0	2	12	15	0	6	.294
McGuire, Deck	2	1	3.95	11	1	0	14	9	7	11	.191
Munson, Kevin	0	0	6.75	11	0	1	9	13	6	12	.310
Perry, Ryan	2	0	4.98	6	6	0	22	17	8	16	.213
Rienzo, Andre	1	1	4.74	6	6	0	25	21	15	24	.241
Riordan, Cory	3	1	5.65	11	2	0	14	21	3	11	.344
Rodriguez, Santos	0	1	4.76	11	0	0	11	11	10	13	.262
Sanchez, Salvador	0	1	2.31	11	0	0	12	9	3	9	.220
Smith, Eric	1	1	3.46	11	0	1	13	16	7	4	.302
Tepera, Ryan	1	2	6.75	6	6	0	17	29	8	20	.367
Thompson, Taylor	1	0	3.38	10	0	0	13	16	4	10	.314
Woods, Coty	1	0	3.18	10	0	2	11	7	4	9	.171

SCOTTSDALE SCORPIONS

BATTERS	AVG	AB	R	H	2B	3B	HR	RBI	BB	SO	SB
Austin, Tyler	.333	12	2	4	0	1	0	3	2	1	0
Dickerson, Alex	.290	69	5	20	4	0	0	3	5	20	1
Hanson, Alen	.253	79	11	20	1	1	1	10	4	17	6
Hefflinger, Robby	.189	74	8	14	2	1	1	7	4	30	0
Kubitza, Kyle	.305	59	11	18	2	2	1	5	13	22	1
La Stella, Tommy	.290	62	6	18	6	1	1	10	16	4	1
Maron, Cam	.216	51	5	11	2	0	0	1	12	12	0
Maruszak, Addison	.281	32	8	9	2	0	0	2	10	5	1
Ngoepe, Gift	.078	51	5	4	1	0	0	3	6	19	2
O'Brien, Peter	.190	63	5	12	2	0	4	13	2	26	0
Parker, Jarrett	.300	60	6	18	0	1	0	6	8	19	1
Reyes, Elmer	.256	43	6	11	4	0	0	3	5	8	0
Rodriguez, Aderlin	.194	72	2	14	2	0	0	3	0	18	0
Susac, Andrew	.360	50	7	18	0	0	2	7	16	11	0
Vaughn, Cory	.250	88	8	22	2	3	1	9	8	25	8
Villalona, Angel	.200	65	2	13	3	0	0	7	3	19	0
Williams, Mason	.267	86	11	23	6	0	0	4	8	18	4

PITCHERS	W	L	ERA	G	GS	SV	IP	H	BB	SO	AVG
Benedict, Matt	0	0	2.81	11	0	0	16	14	5	11	.233
Bradford, Chasen	2	0	0.00	10	0	1	11	6	1	10	.146
Cornely, John	1	0	4.63	11	0	1	11	10	13	16	.213
Crick, Kyle	0	1	2.87	7	5	0	15	9	11	24	.161
Familia, Jeurys	0	2	6.48	8	0	0	8	8	4	11	.229
Gerritse, Brett	0	2	9.26	9	0	0	11	12	11	12	.286
Hall, Cody	0	0	3.00	9	0	0	9	13	4	7	.317
Irwin, Phil	1	2	8.62	5	5	0	15	21	6	14	.318
Jaime, Juan	0	0	6.10	10	0	0	10	11	7	15	.268
Law, Derek	1	0	0.00	11	0	0	12	8	6	16	.186
Lewis, Fred	0	0	0.00	11	0	0	11	8	5	10	.205
Mejia, Adalberto	1	3	8.47	7	3	0	17	18	8	14	.281
Northcraft, Aaron	1	5	8.00	7	7	0	18	23	15	19	.307
Nuno, Vidal	0	1	3.20	5	4	0	19	20	3	18	.250
Pazos, James	1	0	1.74	10	0	0	10	13	7	9	.310
Robles, Hansel	0	2	4.00	6	6	0	18	17	5	19	.246
Satterwhite, Cody	1	1	2.77	11	0	1	13	12	4	13	.240
Simmons, Shae	0	0	0.90	9	0	0	10	6	7	13	.182
Taillon, Jameson	0	0	0.00	1	1	0	2	1	1	3	.143
Thornton, Zack	0	0	3.07	11	0	1	14	8	3	14	.157
Waldron, Tyler	1	2	6.43	9	0	0	14	17	6	10	.293

SURPRISE SAGUAROS

BATTERS	AVG	AB	R	H	2B	3B	HR	RBI	BB	SO	SB
Alfaro, Jorge	.386	70	18	27	6	1	0	11	5	17	2
Alvarez, Dariel	.239	67	8	16	3	1	0	9	3	7	0
Betts, Mookie	.271	59	11	16	3	0	1	5	9	10	8
Cecchini, Garin	.277	65	9	18	4	0	0	9	17	14	3
Gibson, Derrik	.125	40	7	5	1	0	1	2	9	10	0
Haniger, Mitch	.280	100	19	28	8	0	4	24	11	18	1
Naquin, Tyler	.339	115	22	39	4	1	1	18	11	18	4
Nicholas, Brett	.230	61	7	14	7	0	1	6	3	11	0
Ohlman, Michael	.290	31	11	9	3	0	4	9	11	6	0
Rogers, Jason	.311	61	8	19	3	0	2	8	12	21	2
Rua, Ryan	.175	63	13	11	0	0	4	15	7	24	0
Schoop, Jonathan	.177	62	11	11	0	0	3	6	8	17	0
Shaw, Travis	.361	61	18	22	6	0	5	19	10	14	0
Urrutia, Henry	.377	69	8	26	3	0	3	15	7	8	1
Weisenburger, Adam	.200	35	2	7	1	0	0	4	3	12	0
Wendle, Joe	.311	61	8	19	4	2	1	12	6	11	0
Wolters, Tony	.178	45	6	8	1	0	0	3	10	11	1

PITCHERS	W	L	ERA	G	GS	SV	IP	H	BB	SO	AVG
Armstrong, Shawn	1	0	1.59	10	0	0	11	6	10	16	.158
Berry, Tim	2	0	1.84	7	2	0	14	11	3	11	.212
Bonilla, Lisalverto	1	0	0.00	3	0	0	5	3	2	8	.167
Couch, Keith	0	0	4.05	11	0	1	13	15	5	12	.278
Cravy, Tyler	0	1	2.76	10	1	0	16	12	9	16	.214
Goforth, David	1	1	3.75	12	0	4	12	11	4	15	.234
Gurka, Jason	2	0	3.38	11	0	0	13	19	3	8	.339
Haley, Trey	0	0	0.00	2	0	1	1	2	2	2	.286
Harvey, Ryan	0	1	5.40	3	0	1	3	3	2	6	.273
Johnson, Jeff	1	0	9.00	4	0	0	4	5	4	5	.333
Jungmann, Taylor	0	0	9.82	3	3	0	7	9	7	7	.300
Kela, Keone	0	0	0.00	7	0	2	8	5	5	10	.172
Kline, Branden	1	1	10.54	10	0	0	13	23	5	14	.390
Lamb, Will	1	1	8.69	6	6	0	19	29	19	10	.349
McBride, Nick	0	0	6.43	10	0	0	14	21	8	9	.339
Pena, Miguel	3	2	4.55	7	7	0	27	28	10	19	.255
Ramirez, Noe	1	0	1.93	10	0	2	14	9	3	11	.196
Roberts, Will	0	3	6.67	7	7	0	28	40	8	21	.342
Rodriguez, Eduardo	0	1	5.52	5	5	0	14	16	6	16	.267
Ruiz, Pete	1	0	4.76	5	0	0	5	6	5	7	.273
Shackelford, Kevin	1	1	3.09	11	0	0	11	11	4	13	.239
Sturdevant, Tyler	0	0	0.00	4	0	0	4	3	0	3	.200
West, Matt	1	0	3.72	10	0	0	9	12	7	10	.293

MINOR LEAGUES

INDEPENDENT LEAGUES

Smaller indy leagues struggle to keep up

BY J.J. COOPER

When the idea of independent baseball started to gain currency in the early 1990s, it was a chance for the have-nots to try to emulate their richer affiliated league cousins. Cities that had ballparks that didn't meet standards required by the new Professional Baseball Agreement could have a team in the new independent leagues, as could cities shut out of affiliated baseball because of territorial restrictions.

Now, independent baseball has its own haves and have-nots. Teams in the Atlantic, American Association and Frontier Leagues are the haves. The Can-Am League exists in a purgatory and everyone else is trying to scrape out an existence.

At the top of the ladder, the Atlantic League and American Association each had five of the top 10 franchises in indy ball in terms of average attendance in 2013. Every Atlantic League club and all but one American Association club drew an announced average attendance of at least 2,000 fans per game. All but one Frontier League team drew at least 1,700 fans in announced attendance per game.

With those kind of numbers of fans buying hot dogs and beers, all three leagues have been on solid footings for years. Every now and then there are individual teams in each league that may run into trouble but with strength in numbers, each league can survive a troubled team or two with no significant issues.

That's not true elsewhere in indy ball. The Can-Am League has struggled to keep five viable franchises running to stay at six teams (with a travel club). The United League has had teams fail to make it to the end of the season in each of the past two years, both times leading the league to finish the year with four viable clubs. The Pacific Association has worked hard to field four teams.

Overall, the number of fans attending independent league games has declined significantly. In 2010, independent league teams announced attendance of more than 8 million. This year, that number dipped to 6.6 million fans for announced attendance.

Every year, new leagues announce plans for upcoming years. But in reality, they face a very difficult proposition—the haves have been around in one form or another for anywhere from 14 to 20 years. And the haves have locked up most of the viable markets. The rise of summer college leagues has largely taken the bottom out of the independent league market as well.

On the field, the independent league product may be better than ever. Where it used to be shocking to see an independent league pitcher with an average fastball, teams now often fill bullpens with numerous pitchers whose fastballs sit at 90-plus mph.

C.J. Ziegler set an American Association record with 30 home runs. Bridger Hunt topped .400 (.402) in the Can-Am League. The Sugar Land Skeeters set an Atlantic League record with 95 regular season wins.

And owner Pat Salvi pulled off a very rare two-fer as Salvi's American Association club, the Gary Southshore Railcats, won the American Association crown while his other team, the Schaumburg Boomers, were Frontier League champs.

It was Salvi's first, and quickly his second, championship in six years as an owner.

Wichita's C.J. Ziegler set an American Association home run record with 30

Ziegler smashes home run record

There wasn't a specific moment during the season when it became clear to C.J. Ziegler that he could break records. Nor was his performance particularly surprising.

That's not to say it wasn't impressive. Ziegler hit 30 home runs, which broke the American Association record. He had 99 RBIs, 13 more than his closest competitor, and also hit for a .318 average and a 1.053 OPS.

That mammoth offensive campaign has earned him the honor of Baseball America Independent League Player of the Year.

But look back to last year: In 2012, Ziegler's first with the Wichita Wingnuts, he had 18 home runs and 61 RBIs—in just 58 games. If he hadn't spent part of the season with Tabasco of the Mexican League, Ziegler likely could have put up similar or better numbers than 2013. He came into this year with a plan, though, and everything fell into place.

Ziegler entered the season with a sense of relaxation thanks to returning to the same team and league, as well as a particular focus on mental preparation. He homered in each of the Wingnuts' first three games of the season and never slowed down. He had 10 homers and 30 RBIs just over a month into the season.

He hit his 28th homer, breaking the record of 27 held by Brandon Sing of the Sioux Falls Canaries, in a home game against Grand Prairie on Aug. 24. Ziegler's 30th came against the Lincoln Saltdogs two days later.

His production was also aided by an extremely potent lineup that reduced pitchers' chances to throw around him. Ziegler hit in the middle of the order for a Wichita squad that led the league in hitting and OPS and included former major leaguers Brent Clevlen and John Rodriguez, and league batting champion Abel Nieves.

PLAYER OF THE YEAR

"That's what we tried to preach to him," Hooper said, referring to the team's insistence that Ziegler be patient at the plate. "Just know who's hitting behind you, know who's in front of you, know what's going to be going on at that time in the game. With an open base, know that you're probably not going to see something to hit right here."

And if he needed another boost, Ziegler could just call on the fact that somebody else was chasing the home run record along with him. Sioux Falls designated hitter Tim Pahuta didn't get off to as hot of a start, but he had 11 homers in June and 11 in August. The day after Ziegler tied the previous record, Pahuta hit two homers to break it and take the lead in the race.

"I wasn't battling with the record, I was battling with somebody that was actually playing," Ziegler said. "Him and I kept going back and forth. You saw that with Chris Davis and Miguel Cabrera, those guys kept going back and forth with the home runs this year. When you're putting pressure on each other, I think that's the best thing in baseball."

Though he fell just short of the 100-RBI goal he set before the season, Ziegler broke a record, won the league player of the year award and led the Wingnuts to the league championship series.

The last impression that he wants people to get, though, is that he's satisfied with what he has accomplished in baseball.

"Whether that be affiliated (baseball), Mexico, Japan, that's the big thing," he said. "I want people to know that I don't want to just be in independent ball for the rest of my life."

Hooper said that Ziegler easily has the most power of any player he's managed during his five-year stint with the club.

PREVIOUS WINNERS

1996: Darryl Motley, of, Fargo-Moorhead (Northern)
1997: Mike Meggers, of, Winnipeg/Duluth (Northern)
1998: Morgan Burkhart, 1b, Richmond (Frontier)
1999: Carmine Cappucio, of, New Jersey (Northeast)
2000: Anthony Lewis, 1b, Duluth-Superior (Northern)
2001: Mike Warner, of, Somerset (Atlantic)
2002: Bobby Madritsch, lhp, Winnipeg (Northern)
2003: Jason Shelley, rhp, Rockford (Frontier)
2004: Victor Rodriguez, ss, Somerset (Atlantic)
2005: Eddie Lantigua, 3b, Quebec (Can-Am)
2006: Ian Church, of, Kalamazoo (Frontier)
2007: Darryl Brinkley, of, Calgary (Northern)
2008: Patrick Breen, of, Orange County (Golden)
2009: Greg Porter, of, Wichita (American Association)
2010: Beau Torbert, of, Sioux Falls (American Association)
2011: Chris Collabello, 1b, Worcester (Can-Am League)
2012: Blake Gailen, of, Lancaster (Atlantic)

AMERICAN ASSOCIATION

This was supposed to be a rebuilding year for the Gary Southshore Railcats.

Gary had won two titles and finished as league runners-up three more times in a five-year stretch from 2005-2009, but the Railcats had failed to make the playoffs in both 2011 and 2012, leading manager Greg Tagert to put together a large group of rookies to go with a few long-time veterans to build a team that looked set to contend in 2014.

The Railcats sped up that timetable. After finishing second in their division to the Wichita Wingnuts, Gary made it into the playoffs with a wild-card spot. Gary then knocked off favored Fargo-Moorhead and topped the Wingnuts in the championship series to earn the club its first American Association title and third championship overall (the first two titles came as part of the Northern League).

The finish was a disheartening end to an outstanding season for Wichita. The Wingnuts set a league record with a .680 regular season winning percentage. Wichita's 3.38 team ERA also set a league record. First baseman C.J. Ziegler broke the American Association home run record with 30 homers.

NORTH DIVISION

	W	L	PCT	GB
Fargo-Moorhead RedHawks	62	38	.620	—
Winnipeg Goldeyes	56	44	.560	6
St Paul Saints	47	53	.470	15
Sioux Falls Canaries	42	58	.420	20

CENTRAL DIVISION

	W	L	PCT	GB
Wichita Wingnuts	68	32	.680	—
*Gary SouthShore RailCats	58	41	.586	9.5
Lincoln Saltdogs	49	51	.490	19
Kansas City T-Bones	40	60	.400	28
Sioux City Explorers	38	62	.380	30

SOUTH DIVISION

	W	L	PCT	GB
Grand Prairie AirHogs	54	46	.540	—
Laredo Lemurs	52	47	.525	1.5
Amarillo Sox	52	48	.520	2
El Paso Diablos	39	61	.390	15
*Wild Card				

PLAYOFFS: Semifinals—Gary defeated Fargo-Moorhead 3-1 and Wichita defeated Grand Prairie 3-0 in best-of-5 series. **Finals**—Gary defeated Wichita 3-1 in best-of-5 series.

ATTENDANCE: Winnipeg Goldeyes 276,359, Kansas City T-Bones 265,596, St Paul Saints 239,399, Fargo-Moorhead RedHawks 186,091, Lincoln Saltdogs 177,982, Gary SouthShore RailCats 165,024, Sioux Falls Canaries 161,131, Laredo Lemurs 151,055, Wichita Wingnuts 147,119, Grand Prairie AirHogs 111,195, El Paso Diablos 111,230, Amarillo Sox 105,798, Sioux City Explorers 52,052.

MANAGERS: Amarillo—Bobby Brown. **El Paso**—Tim Johnson. **Fargo-Moorhead**—Doug Simunic. **Gary SouthShore**—Greg Tagert. **Grand Prairie**—Ricky VanAsselberg. **Kansas City**—Kenny Hook. **Laredo**—Pete Incaviglia. **Lincoln**—Ken Oberkfell. **Sioux City**—Stan Cliburn. **Sioux Falls**—Steve Shirley. **St. Paul**—George Tsamis. **Wichita**—Kevin Hooper. **Winnipeg**—Rick Forney.

ALL-STAR TEAM: C—Brian Peterson (Laredo). **1B**—C.J. Ziegler (Wichita). **2B**—Jake Kahaulelio (Wichita). **3B**—Abel Nieves (Wichita). **SS**—Maikol Gonzalez (El Paso). **OF**—Nick Van Stratten (Sioux Falls); Brent Clevlen (Wichita); Chris Valencia (Amarillo). **DH**—John Rodriguez (Wichita). **SP**—Taylor Stanton (Fargo-Moorhead). **RP**—Patrick Mincey

(Grand Prairie).

PLAYER OF THE YEAR: C.J. Ziegler, Wichita. **MANAGER OF THE YEAR:** Kevin Hooper, Wichita.

BATTING LEADERS

PLAYER	TEAM	AVG	G	AB	R	H	HR	RBI
Nieves, Abel	WI	.357	99	359	59	128	5	51
Van Stratten, Nick	SF	.352	96	406	75	143	6	54
Scoma, Ryan	WP	.341	81	293	63	100	4	46
Boyer, Brad	SP	.337	78	303	64	102	7	50
Rodriguez, John	WI	.337	100	409	85	138	19	86
Padgett, Matt	KC	.337	82	300	56	101	19	66
Gonzalez, Maikol	LN	.337	99	386	85	130	1	43
Kain, Harrison	LL	.330	70	261	55	86	4	35
Valencia, Chris	AM	.328	98	406	68	133	1	54
Weik, Joe	AM	.327	97	392	69	128	7	81

PITCHING LEADERS

PLAYER	TEAM	W	L	ERA	IP	H	BB	SO
Stanton, Taylor	FM	9	4	2.43	126	115	29	108
Irvine, Lucas	KC	6	5	2.96	121.2	118	21	94
Claggett, Anthony	SP	9	6	3.11	142	143	43	83
Hamburger, Mark	SP	6	8	3.26	149	162	47	120
Guerra, Javy	WI	9	4	3.3	122.2	118	58	126
Spottiswood, Billy	SP	6	4	3.42	94.2	104	31	48
Parise, Pete	LN	10	7	3.43	118	119	25	63
Hardy, Mark	WP	7	3	3.48	82.2	78	30	62
Smith, Carson	WI	8	4	3.55	132	119	35	112
Newby, Joe	AM	7	5	3.63	124	113	51	109

AMARILLO SOX

PLAYER	POS	AVG	OBP	SLG	AB	R	H	HR	RBI	SB
Joe Anthonsen	IF	.244	.389	.268	41	9	10	0	7	0
Adam De La Garza	IF	.266	.352	.317	139	29	37	1	14	2
Jorge Delgado	1B	.354	.462	.445	164	21	58	2	27	1
Dan Evatt	OF	.000	.071	.000	12	1	0	0	1	0
Trey Ford	C	.233	.362	.387	300	56	70	9	51	7
Chris Grossman	C	.291	.384	.388	327	51	95	4	49	3
Brandon Jones	3B	.277	.314	.449	336	53	93	13	49	2
Jermel Lomack	IF	.261	.342	.290	69	8	18	0	8	7
Jason Martin	OF	.265	.334	.338	302	49	80	2	30	14
Kyle Nichols	1B	.319	.398	.639	72	17	23	6	16	1
Cory Patton	OF	.305	.362	.499	387	68	118	11	71	2
David Peralta	OF	.352	.381	.604	182	42	64	8	38	4
Steve Rinaudo	IF	.083	.214	.083	12	0	1	0	1	0
KC Serna	IF	.304	.362	.424	375	68	114	1	45	17
Chris Valencia	OF	.328	.380	.426	406	68	133	1	54	12
Joe Weik	OF	.327	.371	.477	392	69	128	7	81	3

PLAYER	W	L	ERA	G	GS	IP	H	BB	SO
Chandler Barnard	0	2	8.42	27	0	26	34	11	28
Erik Draxton	1	6	3.08	46	0	50	39	20	61
Josh Giles	2	4	3.05	43	0	38	33	21	36
Chris Grossman	0	0	0.00	1	0	2	0	0	3
Jason Hirsh	1	0	6.75	1	1	4	4	0	3
Chris Holguin	0	0	3.38	5	0	5	6	6	6
Cephas Howard	0	0	1.80	5	0	5	5	1	5
Jason Johnson	5	6	5.40	19	18	108	135	31	50
Matt Larkins	5	2	5.67	27	7	73	92	22	50
Kristhiam Linares	4	2	4.48	30	7	60	48	27	47
Jeff Lyman	0	1	6.23	4	0	4	5	4	2
Corey Madden	0	0	11.12	7	0	6	13	2	4
Greg Miller	0	0	13.50	4	0	2	5	1	5
Jason Mitchell	8	6	4.72	23	18	111	132	24	86
Ryan Mitchell	9	5	4.07	21	19	113	103	41	105
Joe Newby	7	5	3.63	20	20	124	113	51	109
Cory Patton	2	2	5.31	18	0	20	30	11	20
Andrew Romo	1	1	8.71	14	0	21	36	7	26
Joe Testa	0	1	8.16	17	0	14	21	12	16
Brad Wilson	4	3	3.04	9	8	47	46	27	17

EL PASO DIABLOS

PLAYER	POS	AVG	OBP	SLG	AB	R	H	HR	RBI	SB
Rodrigo Aguirre	2B	.288	.317	.356	59	8	17	0	10	0
Juan Apodaca	C	.300	.370	.400	120	13	36	0	22	1
Chris Canedo	IF	.154	.154	.154	13	0	2	0	0	0
Miguel Chacoa	IF	.210	.272	.232	138	19	29	0	12	6
Edgar Corcino	OF	.232	.313	.384	112	12	26	2	15	0
Mitch Einertson	OF	.252	.317	.323	322	42	81	1	28	6
Shelby Ford	IF	.385	.467	.615	13	1	5	0	1	0
Reid Fronk	OF	.294	.407	.441	68	13	20	1	10	6
Jose G. Garcia	2B	.320	.371	.399	338	58	108	1	45	25
Brian Joynt	OF	.300	.353	.456	377	59	113	6	51	8
Omar Luna	IF	.360	.407	.440	50	6	18	0	6	2
Thomas McAlpine	C	.350	.420	.517	60	8	21	1	9	0
Moises Montero	C	.240	.316	.380	121	17	29	2	13	0
JJ Muse	OF	.238	.275	.286	63	8	15	0	3	1
Rogelio Noris	OF	.226	.244	.369	84	8	19	3	12	0
Rolando Petit	IF	.038	.138	.038	26	2	1	0	2	0
Roberto Ramirez	IF	.304	.329	.329	79	6	24	0	7	2
Gabe Suarez	OF	.261	.318	.322	264	34	69	0	21	10
Devin Thaut	IF	.231	.302	.313	147	23	34	0	12	3
Murray Watts	1B	.242	.367	.404	99	16	24	2	17	5
Bubby Williams	C	.158	.238	.211	19	2	3	0	1	0

PLAYER	W	L	ERA	G	GS	IP	H	BB	SO
Chandler Barnard	0	2	8.42	27	0	26	34	11	28
Ryan Bean	0	3	7.71	5	5	23	28	25	10
Austin Carden	3	1	4.55	6	5	30	29	13	14
David Casillas	1	5	5.44	9	7	43	44	23	47
Miguel Chacoa	0	0	4.09	9	0	11	14	5	3
Drew Coffey	0	1	5.14	2	1	7	5	6	3
Hector Contin	0	0	7.20	4	0	5	9	7	5
Kevin Cooper	3	5	5.80	18	11	76	95	32	41
Jesse Estrada	2	2	5.40	7	7	40	54	11	19
Victor Ferrante	1	0	6.14	7	0	7	9	4	5
Derek Forbes	0	1	8.76	13	1	25	43	14	17
Charlie Hejny	0	1	5.14	6	0	7	4	6	7
Santo Hernandez	3	0	5.11	11	1	25	27	10	25
Jason Hirsh	1	0	6.75	1	1	4	4	0	3
Jon Jones	0	3	6.04	11	4	28	23	28	23
Mike Koons	1	2	5.06	10	0	11	14	3	12
Seth Lintz	0	3	8.87	8	4	23	43	10	20
Jorge Lugo	3	2	6.67	6	6	28	32	13	17
Greg Miller	0	1	2.70	4	0	7	5	7	4
Carlos Monasterios	1	7	8.65	23	8	52	79	23	33
Alberto Montes	0	2	10.22	5	1	12	23	2	1
Jacob Reding	0	1	7.50	1	1	6	10	3	3
Matt Schimpf	0	1	10.13	1	1	3	6	4	0
Anthony Smith	0	1	4.50	1	1	8	8	2	6
Carlos Teller	3	0	4.15	12	4	30	36	10	22
Adam Tollefson	1	1	3.38	14	0	19	19	5	16
Jake Wortham	0	0	18.00	1	0	2	6	1	2

FARGO-MOORHEAD REDHAWKS

PLAYER	POS	AVG	OBP	SLG	AB	R	H	HR	RBI	SB
Nick Akins	RF	.273	.360	.455	22	0	6	0	3	1
Tim Alberts	OF	.293	.326	.523	396	65	116	16	60	5
Ronnie Bourquin	3B	.296	.411	.523	331	77	98	18	65	2
Keith Brachold	1B	.285	.353	.445	362	49	103	11	62	8
Dionys Cesar	2B	.189	.189	.243	37	4	7	0	1	1
Mitch Einertson	OF	.252	.317	.323	322	42	81	1	28	6
Jose G. Garcia	2B	.320	.371	.399	338	58	108	1	45	25
Jose Hernandez	OF	.265	.332	.383	347	45	92	7	37	9
Nic Jackson	CF	.297	.381	.453	384	64	114	11	69	6
Todd Jennings	C	.219	.297	.252	302	29	66	0	23	0
Clint Ourso	C	.164	.246	.255	55	5	9	1	3	0
Zach Penprase	SS	.257	.330	.314	404	81	104	3	36	40
Jeremiah Piepkorn	IF	.259	.271	.414	58	7	15	3	13	1
Ryan Pineda	IF	.351	.467	.405	37	5	13	0	4	2
C.J. Retherford	2B	.270	.309	.433	326	47	88	8	65	13

PLAYER	W	L	ERA	G	GS	IP	H	BB	SO
Alex Caldera	8	6	4.32	19	19	115	106	55	97
Joe Cruz	0	1	4.66	2	2	10	9	4	9
Brian Ernst	7	2	4.34	13	13	77	77	34	45
Danny Gutierrez	0	3	4.26	17	5	44	43	21	39

Joe Harris	10	3	1.55	53	0	70	47	18	59
Tyler Hess	1	0	9.00	10	0	10	13	7	8
Nathan Kilcrease	4	2	1.67	43	0	54	40	19	54
Kyle Kingsley	0	0	0.00	1	0	2	1	1	0
Jake Laber	10	5	3.82	20	20	118	137	37	73
Pete Levitt	0	0	4.12	12	0	20	18	12	12
Derrick Miramontes	2	2	3.88	41	2	58	48	18	48
Ethan Opsahl	1	2	3.73	26	7	51	57	17	33
Taylor Stanton	9	4	2.43	19	19	126	115	29	108
Alex Sunderland	0	0	0.00	2	0	4	4	2	2

GARY SOUTHSHORE RAILCATS

PLAYER	POS	AVG	OBP	SLG	AB	R	H	HR	RBI	SB
Ryan Babineau	C	.251	.320	.337	199	27	50	3	24	8
Ryan Brockett	IF	.364	.417	.418	55	12	20	0	6	0
Reid Fronk	OF	.294	.407	.441	68	13	20	1	10	6
Cristian Guerrero	OF	.233	.294	.343	382	33	89	5	55	3
Adam Klein	OF	.288	.416	.386	365	62	105	0	40	21
Brian Kolb	IF	.311	.373	.371	318	51	99	0	36	12
Steven Liddle	OF	.226	.321	.290	93	12	21	0	8	1
Nick Liles	OF	.255	.301	.288	274	27	70	0	23	9
Craig Maddox	C	.261	.358	.397	234	42	61	5	29	1
Drew Martinez	OF	.294	.349	.356	323	45	95	1	42	17
Mike Massaro	OF	.303	.375	.455	396	60	120	2	60	11
Zac Mitchell	IF	.237	.312	.297	283	35	67	2	40	5
Daniel Pulfer	IF	.284	.360	.335	197	30	56	1	33	9
Chase Tucker	IF	.206	.297	.243	136	20	28	0	13	5
Christian Vitters	IF	.306	.365	.410	183	27	56	0	20	5

PLAYER	W	L	ERA	G	GS	IP	H	BB	SO
James Adkins	1	3	4.54	15	6	36	47	14	13
Josh Biggs	0	0	40.50	2	0	2	7	3	1
Kevin Brahney	0	5	4.70	27	9	69	72	54	60
Morgan Coombs	6	3	4.95	21	16	93	100	32	69
Ian Durham	2	2	3.20	43	0	45	41	14	38
Chuck Fontana	2	0	5.27	8	0	14	14	5	12
Marco Gonzalez	0	3	1.89	32	0	33	31	10	25
Mike Hanley	0	0	0.00	5	0	6	7	2	1
Stephen Hiscock	4	2	3.26	11	11	69	68	16	50
Matt Jernstad	0	0	3.97	8	1	11	14	7	7
Will Krout	3	5	5.57	17	13	84	114	14	49
Kyle Lindquist	2	2	2.17	32	0	50	35	13	18
Alain Quijano	12	7	4.05	21	21	133	141	32	82
Osvaldo Rodriguez	1	1	4.77	5	2	17	18	7	7
Ari Ronick	6	5	4.18	13	13	75	79	22	57
Marshall Schuler	1	0	5.93	9	0	14	14	6	13
Billy Spottiswood	6	4	3.42	22	14	95	104	31	48
Estevan Uriegas	2	1	2.65	21	0	17	15	5	21
Tim Verthein	0	0	1.69	1	1	5	2	3	1
Clay Zavada	6	1	1.65	15	0	16	10	6	18

GRAND PRAIRE AIRHOGS

PLAYER	POS	AVG	OBP	SLG	AB	R	H	HR	RBI	SB
John Alonso	IF	.215	.305	.364	121	19	26	5	11	0
Bubba Dotson	OF	.204	.338	.296	54	11	11	1	10	5
Angel Flores	C	.263	.347	.395	319	33	84	6	38	0
Micah Gibbs	C	.196	.315	.283	46	3	9	0	3	0
Frazier Hall	IF	.268	.299	.491	112	15	30	2	18	1
Kenny Held	OF	.225	.294	.304	289	31	65	3	33	4
Jorge Jimenez	IF	.231	.318	.231	39	3	9	0	2	1
Palmer Karr	OF	.239	.317	.417	180	25	43	10	32	2
Aaron King	OF	.389	.421	.694	36	8	14	2	5	0
Rian Kiniry	OF	.263	.380	.354	175	22	46	0	15	15
Chad Mozingo	OF	.255	.355	.363	102	16	26	0	15	6
Brian Myrow	IF	.274	.403	.395	248	38	68	4	34	1
Austin Newell	OF	.301	.430	.369	103	12	31	0	16	3
Yasutsugu Nishimoto	IF	.238	.361	.298	181	27	43	0	19	7
Brandon Pearl	C	.182	.182	.182	11	1	2	0	1	0
Brandon Pinckney	IF	.296	.367	.378	402	57	119	4	45	2
Juan M. Richardson	IF	.290	.399	.402	169	32	49	4	22	0
Andres Rodriguez	IF	.285	.360	.481	362	58	103	15	66	0
Keanon Simon	CF	.264	.327	.382	144	23	38	2	10	8
Joe Staley	C	.160	.160	.280	25	3	4	1	5	0

PLAYER	W	L	ERA	G	GS	IP	H	BB	SO
James Adkins	1	1	6.43	3	3	14	26	6	5

	W	L	ERA	G	GS	IP	H	BB	SO
Wes Alsup	0	1	19.80	5	0	5	7	8	8
Brandon Bargas	3	6	5.33	13	13	73	87	29	43
Derek Blacksher	10	7	4.19	20	20	135	148	26	84
Curtis Camilli	0	2	5.68	4	3	19	23	2	5
Jake Cowan	0	0	5.40	5	5	25	38	8	10
Jakob Cunningham	2	0	3.35	37	0	38	36	10	19
Justin Dowdy	2	4	3.58	31	0	28	31	14	25
Drew Gagnier	0	0	7.94	4	0	6	9	1	4
Gabriel Garcia	2	3	4.99	9	8	43	50	16	27
Cole Green	0	1	15.00	1	1	3	6	3	1
Chase Johnson	1	1	3.64	34	0	30	29	20	28
Jorge Lugo	3	2	6.67	6	6	28	32	13	17
Chuck Lukanen	0	0	4.50	1	1	4	7	1	1
Patrick Mincey	5	1	1.01	50	0	53	33	14	55
Jared Mortensen	4	6	3.77	17	15	100	102	25	94
Stephen Nikonchik	2	0	1.02	11	0	18	12	8	11
Boomer Potts	6	1	2.51	33	0	32	29	15	32
David Quinowski	4	4	4.05	43	0	40	37	15	37
Josh Renfro	0	0	7.71	2	0	2	7	3	4
Marshall Schuler	1	0	5.93	9	0	14	14	6	13
Josh Strawn	9	7	4.09	21	21	139	162	27	67
Aaron Wilkerson	1	1	1.84	3	3	15	6	5	8

KANSAS CITY T-BONES

PLAYER	POS	AVG	OBP	SLG	AB	R	H	HR	RBI	SB
Justin C. Bass	OF	.273	.345	.419	198	27	54	4	21	10
Jonathan Cisneros	IF	.249	.343	.316	269	34	67	1	46	0
Trevor Coleman	C	.276	.364	.381	181	17	50	4	20	0
Anthony Davis	IF	.235	.288	.235	68	8	16	0	3	2
David Espinosa	IF	.297	.402	.443	370	72	110	12	50	13
Joey Gathright	OF	.301	.389	.322	183	26	55	0	20	10
Devin Goodwin	3B	.293	.340	.502	273	48	80	12	38	15
Kody Hightower	IF	.179	.304	.205	39	6	7	0	2	1
Brandon Jones	3B	.277	.314	.449	336	53	93	13	49	2
Kennard Jones	OF	.292	.354	.390	415	65	121	3	34	28
KJ Miramontes	IF	.143	.143	.143	14	1	2	0	0	1
Felix Molina	IF	.263	.324	.318	358	42	94	2	43	24
Kyle Nichols	1B	.224	.361	.432	125	17	28	8	34	0
Matt Padgett	IF	.337	.442	.650	300	56	101	19	66	1
Petey Paramore	C	.264	.403	.431	144	25	38	4	21	1
Brandon Pearl	C	.182	.182	.182	11	1	2	0	1	0
Jairo Perez	IF	.309	.359	.539	375	58	116	19	72	7
Nathan Ramler	OF	.222	.275	.250	36	3	8	0	3	0
Luis Rivera	RF	.276	.340	.418	170	24	47	5	24	4
Norberto Susini	C	.290	.450	.323	31	4	9	0	2	0
Stephen Yoo	C	.192	.222	.308	26	5	5	0	4	0
Steve Yoo	C	.183	.226	.248	109	16	20	1	8	0

PLAYER	W	L	ERA	G	GS	IP	H	BB	SO
Justin Albert	0	0	6.75	8	0	7	12	4	5
Devin Anderson	1	1	10.57	3	1	8	12	4	5
Ethan Cole	0	8	6.30	39	10	80	120	19	50
Ryan Fennell	0	0	0.93	7	0	10	7	6	9
Shaun Garceau	6	9	4.31	23	20	134	154	33	93
Eric Gonzalez	1	4	7.43	7	7	40	54	17	20
Connor Graham	0	2	11.76	4	4	21	36	9	10
Josh Hildebrand	2	3	5.65	27	0	37	37	13	14
Lucas Irvine	6	5	2.96	17	17	122	118	21	94
Jose Jimenez	1	1	3.59	47	0	43	42	19	46
Michael Joyce	1	1	5.34	35	5	59	76	31	37
Dustin Loggins	7	6	4.13	30	13	105	117	38	101
Aaron Meade	3	5	5.10	10	10	55	48	36	39
Jhonny Montoya	1	1	12.96	10	0	8	11	10	7
Brian Murphy	1	2	9.00	3	3	15	26	10	8
Devon Pearson	0	1	16.88	3	0	3	7	3	4
Keith Picht	0	1	4.59	9	1	18	17	10	9
Josh Rainwater	1	6	9.73	8	6	37	58	16	16
Chad Robinson	3	3	4.07	24	0	24	20	13	27
Alex Thieroff	1	0	7.36	11	0	11	12	10	7
Sean Toler	2	4	5.27	41	0	41	52	11	23
Aaron Tullo	4	0	6.81	7	6	36	39	27	30
Rick Zagone	1	4	4.47	7	7	44	54	15	18

LAREDO LEMURS

PLAYER	POS	AVG	OBP	SLG	AB	R	H	HR	RBI	SB
John Allen	OF	.308	.382	.494	344	56	106	13	56	2

	POS	AVG	OBP	SLG	AB	R	H	HR	RBI	SB
John Alonso	IF	.305	.372	.462	236	33	72	8	55	0
Garrett Buechele	C	.304	.358	.421	171	22	52	3	27	1
Sawyer Carroll	OF	.311	.416	.479	219	43	68	4	41	7
Stephen Douglas	OF	.274	.331	.397	325	38	89	8	44	4
Balbino Fuenmayor	C	.262	.300	.431	65	8	17	2	13	0
Philip Incaviglia	C	.080	.115	.080	25	1	2	0	1	0
Harrison Kain	IF	.330	.394	.475	261	55	86	4	35	19
Palmer Karr	OF	.259	.315	.459	185	25	48	8	30	1
Jimmy Mojica	SS	.312	.373	.452	372	65	116	10	61	10
Jake Opitz	2B	.212	.295	.318	85	8	18	0	4	1
Brian Peterson	C	.289	.383	.398	339	49	98	5	47	4
Daniel Poma	CF	.319	.388	.378	135	20	43	1	15	19
Mike Provencher	IF	.268	.335	.412	347	47	93	4	38	9
Garrett Rau	IF	.276	.331	.346	228	38	63	1	21	9
Mike Sheridan	1B	.258	.334	.330	267	32	69	1	23	3

PLAYER	W	L	ERA	G	GS	IP	H	BB	SO
Mike Benacka	0	1	4.50	19	0	18	17	10	30
Bradley Blanks	5	1	1.38	27	0	33	26	8	21
Jake Cowan	2	3	4.30	10	7	44	51	13	31
Jacob Douglas	0	0	2.25	3	0	4	2	8	2
Justin Garcia	7	7	5.35	21	19	116	128	34	83
Leonard Giammanco	1	3	6.67	6	6	27	35	12	12
Mark Haynes	4	2	2.35	51	0	54	42	24	61
Fernando Hernandez	0	1	9.00	2	2	11	15	8	6
Jon Jones	0	3	6.04	11	4	28	23	28	23
Jonathan Kountis	0	1	12.27	4	0	4	9	2	3
Seth Lintz	2	1	7.31	14	2	28	38	14	24
Jameson Maj	3	2	2.68	42	0	47	50	13	41
James Mannara	0	0	3.86	4	0	5	5	1	1
Manolo Mendoza	0	0	9.00	3	0	4	6	0	3
David Newmann	4	4	4.06	14	13	64	81	25	49
Tyler Pearson	1	3	6.04	6	6	25	33	17	30
Chad Povich	3	2	2.77	49	0	52	45	20	67
Garrett Rau	2	5	6.84	15	2	26	36	10	10
Ryan Sasaki	2	4	5.36	8	8	40	54	18	24
Mark Serrano	4	1	2.41	6	5	37	31	6	27
Michael Suk	2	2	5.60	12	7	45	62	15	20
Adam Tollefson	1	1	3.38	14	0	19	19	5	16
Sean Tracey	2	1	4.94	5	4	24	35	5	15
Edwin Walker	1	2	7.55	12	1	31	35	23	24
Greg Wilborn	6	2	4.81	16	15	82	101	35	64
Fabian Williamson	6	2	3.42	18	12	74	67	33	75
Kyle Wilson	0	2	7.12	8	5	37	47	16	21

LINCOLN SALTDOGS

PLAYER	POS	AVG	OBP	SLG	AB	R	H	HR	RBI	SB
Sergio Burruel	C	.287	.352	.361	108	12	31	0	14	0
Dan Carroll	OF	.303	.383	.483	201	41	61	7	30	22
Michael Coles	OF	.232	.329	.305	259	47	60	2	15	24
Anthony DAlfonso	OF	.346	.368	.469	130	14	45	0	22	0
Welington Dotel	OF	.297	.340	.464	138	24	41	4	27	8
Brian Embery	IF	.203	.261	.285	158	15	32	2	9	3
Matt Forgatch	IF	.245	.305	.361	380	39	93	6	56	34
Ian Gac	1B	.319	.368	.613	238	44	76	18	63	0
Jon Gaston	OF	.260	.332	.390	223	30	58	3	30	8
Jose Gil	C	.160	.222	.280	25	2	4	1	1	0
Yasel Gomez	IF	.244	.305	.330	291	35	71	4	17	4
Maikol Gonzalez	IF	.337	.423	.446	386	85	130	1	43	47
Tyler Goodro	IF	.239	.313	.340	188	13	45	3	25	0
Brian Joynt	OF	.300	.353	.456	377	59	113	6	51	8
Jeremy Mayo	C	.136	.313	.258	66	11	9	2	4	1
Oscar Mesa	OF	.293	.397	.399	263	47	77	1	32	17
Sean OConnell	C	.174	.233	.242	161	12	28	1	13	1
Brad Payne	IF	.163	.258	.225	80	17	13	0	7	4
Bryan Pounds	IF	.267	.334	.432	352	38	94	8	50	0
Dennis Raben	1B	.409	.455	.818	88	17	36	10	25	3
Curt Smith	IF	.316	.383	.469	196	27	62	5	27	2
Brian Wuest	OF	.200	.259	.280	50	6	10	0	5	1

PLAYER	W	L	ERA	G	GS	IP	H	BB	SO
Joe Bisenius	3	2	3.89	6	6	37	25	9	43
Stephen Bougher	3	8	3.90	14	13	83	87	35	49
Mike Burns	7	5	4.15	16	16	108	123	18	72
Matt Bywater	2	3	4.46	8	8	40	34	13	39
Luis Chirinos	3	4	4.96	23	16	94	127	33	57

INDEPENDENT LEAGUES

	W	L	ERA	G	GS	IP	H	BB	SO
Reyes Dorado	4	2	3.88	10	9	51	58	20	34
Trevor Harden	0	1	6.00	8	0	9	11	5	8
Ben Henry	0	3	6.84	6	5	25	29	17	12
Justin Kuks	3	2	3.03	14	5	39	45	18	18
Eddie McKiernan	6	1	2.34	13	2	35	27	13	29
Jake Meiers	2	2	3.41	25	0	32	31	12	21
Moises Melendez	3	6	5.02	22	18	104	116	55	68
Danny Meszaros	4	2	5.52	22	0	29	32	8	29
Nathan Moreau	0	2	7.41	4	4	17	26	14	13
Pete Parise	10	7	3.43	18	18	118	119	25	63
Travis Parker	2	2	5.78	25	3	62	76	27	54
RJ Rodriguez	0	2	4.28	36	0	34	31	10	27
Marshall Schuler	7	2	1.48	32	0	43	31	19	45
Conor Spink	1	1	3.35	34	0	43	45	18	33
Stayton Thomas	2	4	4.94	30	1	51	73	17	30
PJ Zocchi	6	1	1.61	44	0	45	36	14	56

SIOUX CITY EXPLORERS

PLAYER	POS	AVG	OBP	SLG	AB	R	H	HR	RBI	SB
Wally Backman	IF	.192	.270	.231	104	11	20	0	7	1
Leugim Barroso	IF	.260	.288	.307	362	33	94	2	32	24
Peter Barrows	OF	.279	.347	.463	348	54	97	13	55	6
Brian Bistagne	IF	.221	.295	.279	86	9	19	0	7	4
Gilbert Briones	IF	.150	.227	.200	20	2	3	0	1	1
Alberto Espinosa	C	.240	.262	.302	258	19	62	2	23	0
Austin Gallagher	IF	.293	.352	.359	198	18	58	0	26	2
Tyler Graham	OF	.296	.342	.339	274	43	81	1	15	31
Yusuke Inoguchi	OF	.281	.351	.364	327	43	92	0	31	11
Sam Judah	OF	.284	.310	.391	289	34	82	5	38	1
Palmer Karr	OF	.259	.315	.459	185	25	48	8	30	1
Anthony Kaskadden	IF	.245	.300	.304	257	31	63	2	18	9
Adrian Martinez	C	.262	.319	.369	168	20	44	4	17	0
Eliezer Mesa	OF	.293	.322	.332	386	49	113	0	24	26
Kevin Moesquit	IF	.245	.312	.338	139	26	34	2	18	4
Luke Murton	IF	.255	.328	.363	278	37	71	6	34	4
Clint Ourso	C	.164	.246	.255	55	5	9	1	3	0
Ryan Pineda	IF	.280	.356	.409	328	52	92	6	45	6
Bryan Pounds	IF	.267	.334	.432	352	38	94	8	50	0
Jeff Squier	IF	.117	.218	.184	103	16	12	1	7	4
Eddie Young	IF	.174	.259	.261	23	4	4	0	4	0

PLAYER	W	L	ERA	G	GS	IP	H	BB	SO
Chris Bodishbaugh	3	2	3.99	39	0	50	49	23	51
Yunier Colon	0	0	7.71	3	0	5	7	4	1
Cody Hall	1	1	2.53	4	3	21	20	11	6
Mike Hepple	0	0	4.91	6	0	11	17	2	4
John Holdzkom	3	4	2.89	42	0	44	36	36	52
Mike Jefferson	1	2	6.06	8	1	16	13	6	16
Dan Jurik	1	8	4.59	14	14	80	80	32	64
Jimmer Kennedy	4	5	2.89	43	0	62	49	21	50
Kyle Kingsley	0	0	3.38	8	0	16	16	6	8
Ryan Lucero	3	4	4.30	11	8	59	70	18	25
Andy Noga	4	12	5.73	20	19	116	139	39	64
Preston Olson	1	6	6.28	16	12	62	84	26	45
Edgar Osuna	3	2	3.19	6	6	37	25	16	33
Jon Plefka	1	0	3.50	23	0	36	27	16	28
Josh Poytress	0	0	10.13	9	0	8	9	13	8
Josh Rainwater	1	6	9.73	8	6	37	58	16	16
Jonathan Rodriguez	0	0	4.70	11	0	15	14	14	12
Richard Salazar	10	3	3.86	19	19	114	112	39	89
Cody Satterwhite	2	1	0.65	19	0	28	14	7	31
Nathan Stewart	0	2	8.25	8	0	12	20	7	6
Ryan Wilkins	0	0	13.50	3	0	5	9	1	3
Joe Zeller	0	1	6.48	4	1	8	10	3	6

SIOUX FALLS CANARIES

PLAYER	POS	AVG	OBP	SLG	AB	R	H	HR	RBI	SB
Reggie Abercrombie	OF	.298	.315	.524	124	18	37	7	26	4
John Alonso	IF	.215	.305	.364	121	19	26	5	11	0
Joe Anthonsen	IF	.244	.389	.268	41	9	10	0	7	0
Nate Baumann	OF	.240	.275	.429	196	26	47	8	19	8
Jared Clark	1B	.236	.358	.463	348	56	82	20	59	2
Steve Domecus	C	.242	.297	.439	66	7	16	4	12	0
Kevin Dultz	C	.256	.349	.346	211	34	54	2	14	6
Stephen King	IF	.234	.306	.360	197	21	46	3	26	7

PLAYER	POS	AVG	OBP	SLG	AB	R	H	HR	RBI	SB
Chandler Laurent	OF	.000	.154	.000	11	0	0	0	0	1
Cory Morales	IF	.238	.291	.303	403	50	96	3	43	17
Tim Pahuta	IF	.264	.325	.554	363	65	96	29	79	1
JP Ramirez	OF	.300	.341	.441	363	44	109	9	54	2
Marcos Rodriguez	OF	.320	.368	.434	334	48	107	5	45	4
Anthony Trajano	IF	.263	.336	.336	137	20	36	0	12	0
Nick Van Stratten	OF	.352	.404	.527	406	75	143	6	54	25

PLAYER	W	L	ERA	G	GS	IP	H	BB	SO
Chris Allen	2	0	4.88	25	0	24	23	8	27
Austin Brough	0	5	9.70	9	4	34	57	18	18
Adam Champion	6	11	6.29	24	24	133	159	58	74
Kirk Clark	1	4	3.86	36	0	37	47	14	38
Mitchell Clegg	4	5	5.79	16	16	79	106	30	39
Matt Daly	3	2	3.18	42	0	57	47	25	57
Alan DeRatt	0	3	3.20	41	0	39	35	6	39
Peter Gehle	4	8	5.25	20	17	96	120	42	49
Ben Moore	10	8	4.11	23	23	155	163	23	131
Kyle Ruwe	11	7	3.71	22	22	155	184	32	58
Jack Van Leur	2	2	7.36	36	0	22	28	16	16
Kyle Vazquez	3	5	5.35	33	6	72	84	31	58
Jordan Whatcott	2	6	5.78	34	5	67	76	34	58

ST. PAUL SAINTS

PLAYER	POS	AVG	OBP	SLG	AB	R	H	HR	RBI	SB
Nick Ammirati	C	.083	.267	.167	12	1	1	0	0	0
Joey Becker	IF	.259	.308	.335	379	50	98	4	40	4
Donald Blunt	IF	.253	.356	.402	87	12	22	3	14	0
Brad Boyer	IF	.337	.395	.512	303	64	102	7	50	6
Craig Brazell	IF	.347	.389	.564	101	13	35	4	21	0
Brian Burgamy	IF	.295	.387	.600	95	16	28	8	25	0
Willie Cabrera	OF	.317	.382	.517	315	50	100	13	63	0
Dwight Childs	C	.241	.273	.398	261	33	63	7	36	2
Adam Frost	SS	.276	.325	.414	377	66	104	10	43	38
Trevor Hairgrove	IF	.152	.212	.190	79	6	12	0	5	1
Andy Henkemeyer	OF	.267	.327	.267	45	6	12	0	0	0
Dan Kaczrowski	IF	.276	.358	.350	337	49	93	4	29	7
Chris Manning	C	.171	.194	.171	35	3	6	0	2	0
Jeremy Mayo	IF	.278	.350	.306	36	3	10	0	3	0
Mark Radmacher	C	.111	.158	.167	18	2	2	0	0	0
Ole Sheldon	IF	.299	.370	.462	184	27	55	7	28	1
Buddy Sosnoskie	OF	.246	.289	.368	329	36	81	8	37	12
Jake Taylor	C	.286	.339	.406	266	36	76	5	28	9
Brandon Tripp	OF	.287	.357	.524	328	58	94	19	75	5
Jordan Tripp	OF	.238	.282	.425	80	9	19	3	7	2

PLAYER	W	L	ERA	G	GS	IP	H	BB	SO
Hugh Adams	0	0	9.72	7	0	8	12	6	6
Luke Anderson	2	2	6.15	9	9	41	51	18	29
Paul Burnside	6	5	5.65	17	15	73	88	42	55
Anthony Claggett	9	6	3.11	21	21	142	143	43	83
Aaron Correa	0	1	11.81	5	1	5	17	3	1
Drew Gay	1	2	7.27	5	4	17	16	17	7
Danny Gutierrez	0	3	4.26	17	5	44	43	21	39
Mark Hamburger	6	8	3.26	21	21	149	162	47	120
Bryan Henry	0	1	2.16	7	0	8	6	0	4
T.J. Hose	0	1	3.38	6	0	11	11	2	8
George Jensen	0	3	11.17	7	2	19	28	8	12
Mackenzie Ivers	3	3	4.06	37	0	69	67	25	34
Dustin Klabunde	2	0	4.72	30	0	48	46	24	29
Mike Koons	2	2	4.61	14	8	53	66	20	22
Mikey Mehlich	4	3	2.92	34	0	49	37	28	40
Matt Meyer	6	5	4.12	39	0	39	31	27	43
Kyle Morrison	0	1	5.71	10	0	17	20	12	16
Cole Nelson	5	3	3.64	13	11	64	55	35	42
Jon Plefka	1	0	0.79	16	0	23	14	5	18
Wes Roemer	4	5	6.88	9	9	51	67	14	37
Billy Soule	3	2	7.58	18	9	65	77	33	30
Billy Spottiswood	6	4	3.42	22	14	95	104	31	48
Dylan Thomas	1	6	10.63	13	5	31	50	22	19
Connor Whalen	1	0	6.75	14	0	8	11	8	7

WICHITA WINGNUTS

PLAYER	POS	AVG	OBP	SLG	AB	R	H	HR	RBI	SB
David Amberson	OF	.280	.335	.360	214	38	60	2	29	15
Cole Armstrong	C	.241	.314	.356	278	31	67	8	47	1

Player	POS	AVG	OBP	SLG	AB	R	H	HR	RBI	SB
Madison Beaird	OF	.304	.396	.430	79	14	24	0	6	8
Johnny Bowden	C	.220	.319	.390	41	4	9	1	6	0
Brent Clevlen	CF	.322	.413	.582	261	57	84	14	51	14
Scott Dalrymple	C	.061	.114	.061	33	1	2	0	0	
0 Jonathan Davis	RF	.100	.357	.250	20	2	2	1	3	1
Jake Kahaulelio	2B	.322	.408	.544	373	91	120	17	68	16
Ryan Khoury	IF	.244	.354	.312	398	71	97	3	46	26
Colt Loehrs	OF	.279	.326	.402	122	13	34	2	14	7
Jared McDonald	IF	.301	.367	.433	326	42	98	5	54	22
Mike Mobbs	OF	.333	.556	.583	12	6	4	0	0	0
Abel Nieves	IF	.357	.446	.479	359	59	128	5	51	17
Derek Perren	OF	.243	.317	.270	37	4	9	0	5	1
John Rodriguez	OF	.337	.396	.560	409	85	138	19	86	14
Tim Rotola	OF	.286	.348	.333	21	4	6	0	2	1
Waylen Sing Chow	OF	.100	.100	.100	10	1	1	0	0	0
Stephen Yoo	C	.192	.222	.308	26	5	5	0	4	0
CJ Ziegler	IF	.318	.408	.645	380	81	121	30	99	3

PLAYER	W	L	ERA	G	GS	IP	H	BB	SO
Andrew Aizenstadt	1	1	2.67	31	0	30	21	17	23
Daniel Bennett	1	3	2.79	48	0	52	43	27	56
Anthony Capra	7	2	3.96	22	17	100	85	59	122
Josh Dew	3	2	1.56	41	0	40	21	19	44
James Giulietti	4	0	3.18	4	4	23	16	13	19
Junior Guerra	9	4	3.30	21	19	123	118	58	126
Ryan Hinson	7	2	1.53	10	10	71	49	13	57
Lincoln Holdzkom	2	4	3.72	40	0	39	34	20	30
Justin Klipp	8	3	3.89	17	15	93	103	21	56
Erik Lambe	1	0	4.50	3	0	4	4	1	3
Kristhiam Linares	0	2	8.00	2	2	9	12	8	6
Jon Link	6	1	1.74	7	7	52	39	11	38
Ryan Scoles	2	2	5.25	6	4	24	26	17	11
Christopher M. Smith	8	4	3.55	20	20	132	119	35	112
Joshua Stone	3	0	4.78	21	2	32	32	24	20
Joe Testa	0	1	8.16	17	0	14	21	12	16
Nick Walters	6	1	3.52	50	0	38	33	22	47
Tyler White	0	0	7.04	8	0	8	10	6	10

WINNIPEG GOLDEYES

PLAYER	POS	AVG	OBP	SLG	AB	R	H	HR	RBI	SB
Luis Alen	C	.315	.376	.408	346	40	109	5	54	9
Michael Coles	OF	.232	.329	.305	259	47	60	2	15	24
Leonard Davis	IF	.269	.321	.438	130	18	35	5	18	4
Yurendell de Caster	IF	.233	.297	.356	90	8	21	3	12	1
Jordan Guida	C	.184	.279	.211	38	7	7	0	1	0
Casey Haerther	IF	.307	.340	.445	384	52	118	10	66	2
Fehlandt Lentini	OF	.271	.307	.398	384	51	104	7	45	20
Josh Mazzola	IF	.293	.365	.496	379	64	111	16	64	7
Amos Ramon	IF	.268	.351	.395	339	44	91	8	52	6
Ray Sadler	RF	.276	.343	.525	377	73	104	21	72	12
Nate Samson	IF	.216	.264	.297	148	11	32	1	15	1
Ryan Scoma	OF	.341	.443	.454	293	63	100	4	46	8
Tim Smith	OF	.254	.315	.328	67	8	17	1	6	1

PLAYER	W	L	ERA	G	GS	IP	H	BB	SO
Gabe Aguilar	1	0	5.05	24	0	41	59	9	23
Wes Alsup	0	1	19.80	5	0	5	7	8	8
Allen Caldwell	1	0	1.80	13	0	15	13	13	18
Alex Capaul	1	4	10.64	6	5	22	44	7	8
Aaron Correa	0	0	5.00	9	1	18	18	10	10
Kaohi Downing	4	4	3.40	42	0	45	39	23	33
Peter Gehle	4	8	5.25	20	17	96	120	42	49
Mark Hardy	7	3	3.48	15	13	83	78	30	62
Matthew Jackson	3	0	3.70	7	6	41	48	5	37
Jason Jarvis	7	11	3.92	22	22	147	158	43	60
Patrick Keating	4	3	3.76	36	0	41	47	5	32
Chris Kissock	2	4	2.70	50	0	53	47	9	56
Brendan Lafferty	5	2	3.49	53	0	49	38	20	50
Matthew Rusch	7	4	4.11	23	23	145	149	34	111
Chris Salamida	7	1	2.23	9	9	61	51	13	44
Ryan Sasaki	2	4	5.36	8	8	40	54	18	24
Taylor Sewitt	4	1	4.71	40	0	57	73	15	26

ATLANTIC LEAGUE

There was no debate over who was the Atlantic League's dominant team during the 2013 season. In only their second season, the Sugar Land Skeeters set a league record by winning 95 games, topping Lancaster's previous record of 88 wins, set in 2012.

But come playoff time, the Skeeters regular season dominance meant nothing. Long Island, only 63-77 during the regular season, won its second straight Atlantic League crown while Sugar Land was quickly eliminated after being swept in three games by Somerset in the first round of the playoffs.

Long Island also swept its way through the first round, and the Ducks managed to edge Somerset with a 6-4 win in the deciding Game 5 of the championship series.

Somerset had forced a winner-takes-all Game 5 with a 16-inning win in Game 4. But a Ray Navarette three-run home run provided the big blow for Long Island in the deciding game. Navarette, the 2009 Atlantic League MVP, announced his retirement after the game.

Former big leaguer Jake Fox was named the league MVP. Fox, who was signed by the Diamondbacks during the season, had an amazing stretch where he hit walk-off hits in three consecutive games.

FREEDOM DIVISION	W	L	PCT	GB
Sugar Land Skeeters	95	45	.679	—
Somerset Patriots	90	49	.647	4.5
Lancaster Barnstormers	72	67	.518	22.5
York Revolution	65	75	.464	30

LIBERTY DIVISION	W	L	PCT	GB
Southern Maryland Blue Crabs	65	74	.468	—
Long Island Ducks	63	77	.450	2.5
Bridgeport Bluefish	54	85	.388	11
Camden Riversharks	54	86	.386	11.5

PLAYOFFS: Semifinals—Somerset defeated Sugar Land 3-0 and Long Island defeated Southern Maryland 3-0 in best-of-5 series. **Finals**—Long Island defeated Somerset 3-2 in best-of-5 series.

ATTENDANCE: Sugar Land 382,059; Long Island 371,186; Somerset 339,468; Lancaster 290,165; York 254,370; Southern Maryland 242,894; Camden 217,145; Bridgeport 157,267.

MANAGERS: Sugar Land—Gary Gaetti; Bridgeport—Willie Upshaw; Lancaster—Butch Hobson; Southern Maryland—Pat Osborn; Somerset—Brett Jodie; York—Andy Etchebarren; Long Island—Kevin Baez; Camden—Ron Karkovice.

ALL-STAR TEAM: Cs—Salvador Paniagua, York; Travis Scott, Sugar Land. **1B**—Aaron Bates, Sugar Land. **2B**—Andres Perez, York. **3B**—Corey Smith, Somerset. **SS**—Wilson Valdez, Camden. **Util.**—Renny Osuna, Southern Maryland. **OF**—Jerry Owens, Lancaster; Cyle Hankerd, Southern Maryland; Ryan Harvey, Lancaster; Adam Godwin, Sugar Land. **DH**—Jake Fox, Somerset. **RHP**—Dwayne Pollok, Lancaster. **LHP**—Chris Cody, York. **RP**—Jon Hunton, Somerset. **CL**—Jim Ed Warden, Southern Maryland.

PLAYER OF THE YEAR: Jake Fox, Somerset. **PITCHER OF THE YEAR:** Dwayne Pollok, Lancaster. **MANAGER OF THE YEAR:** Gary Gaetti, Sugar Land.

BATTING LEADERS

PLAYER	TEAM	AVG	G	AB	R	H	HR	RBI
Owens, Jerry	LAN	.341	117	478	76	163	2	48
Valdez, Wilson	CMD	.310	90	342	45	106	0	27
Fox, Jake	SOM	.310	96	374	62	116	25	82
Brodin, Joash	LI	.307	106	417	79	128	11	49
Mayora, Daniel	BPT	.306	108	434	61	133	7	44
Bates, Aaron	SL	.306	126	448	71	137	7	57
Gomez, Alexis	BPT	.305	125	472	55	144	11	71

Batista, Wilson	YRK	.304	122	473	55	144	6	67		
Marte, Andy	YRK	.301	96	369	61	111	19	74		
Nelson, Bry	LI	.298	124	483	72	144	11	71		

PITCHING LEADERS

PLAYER	TEAM	W	L	ERA	IP	H	BB	SO
Lowey, Josh	SOM	14	8	2.89	156	125	48	124
Pollok, Dwayne	LAN	18	3	2.92	173	163	37	124
Cody, Chris	YRK	15	9	3.12	176	189	45	139
Thompson, Daryl	SMD	10	5	3.18	125	114	39	73
Arnesen, Erik	SOM	13	4	3.19	150	161	16	103
Martinez, Miguel	CMD	5	6	3.29	115	104	29	68
Taylor, Graham	SOM	10	6	3.40	159	171	36	106
Grening, Brian	LAN	6	7	3.74	113	116	32	79
Brownell, John	LI	9	10	3.90	166	172	48	133
Marshall, Ian	SMD	12	8	4.00	158	180	40	98

BRIDGEPORT BLUEFISH

PLAYER	POS	AVG	OBP	SLG	AB	R	H	HR	RBI	SB
Daniel Barbero	IF	.200	.310	.240	25	4	5	0	0	0
Yusuf Carter	C	.265	.301	.522	253	36	67	16	54	1
Brandon Chaves	IF	.273	.356	.314	245	31	67	0	20	6
Collin DeLome	OF	.214	.241	.429	28	4	6	1	3	0
Karl Derbacher	OF	.125	.176	.125	16	2	2	0	1	0
Victor Diaz	IF	.172	.242	.259	116	10	20	2	12	0
Alexis Gomez	OF	.305	.366	.449	472	55	144	11	71	26
Adam Greenberg	OF	.220	.351	.303	109	19	24	0	7	7
Austin Krum	OF	.274	.330	.349	493	67	135	2	37	10
Luis Lopez	IF	.260	.304	.338	527	53	137	6	63	0
Juan Martinez	IF	.325	.374	.467	120	16	39	4	15	4
Daniel Mayora	IF	.306	.356	.419	434	61	133	7	44	12
Prentice Redman	OF	.259	.326	.399	464	56	120	10	70	3
Luis Rodriguez	IF	.241	.277	.294	323	27	78	2	32	0
Eddie Rogers	IF	.318	.356	.412	85	9	27	1	9	4
James Simmons	OF	.263	.330	.387	315	49	83	6	35	11
Stantrel Smith	OF	.244	.247	.311	164	14	40	1	11	4
Iggy Suarez	IF	.233	.309	.316	288	36	67	4	27	1

PLAYER	W	L	ERA	G	GS	IP	H	BB	SO
Winston Abreu	2	0	1.47	54	0	55	34	21	49
Joe Bateman	3	1	2.38	28	1	42	27	7	37
Keith Bilodeau	1	4	4.42	16	12	77	77	41	59
Josh Butler	3	11	5.64	18	18	89	111	47	45
Adam Carr	2	2	9.64	9	0	9	13	8	6
Michael Colla	2	4	3.83	9	9	52	54	17	47
Jesse English	0	2	2.66	23	0	20	18	13	24
Emiliano Fruto	1	3	3.58	33	0	38	33	14	46
Jeff Fulchino	1	1	1.29	34	0	35	23	8	36
TyRelle Harris	2	3	2.76	10	3	29	31	11	38
Alex Hinshaw	0	1	9.82	13	0	11	6	16	17
Mickey Jannis	0	1	7.56	10	0	17	30	6	6
Hunter Jones	8	13	4.19	26	26	157	167	52	105
Ruddy Lugo	5	2	3.82	25	0	33	31	10	16
Cole McCurry	0	2	6.03	7	4	31	40	12	18
Travis Minix	0	0	6.41	11	1	20	29	9	10
Mike Parisi	8	16	4.71	28	27	162	181	67	111
Hayden Penn	0	0	7.45	8	0	10	10	5	9
Trevor Reckling	4	4	4.95	12	12	56	57	29	21
Jordan Roberts	0	0	5.79	5	0	5	7	3	2
Edward Rodriguez	0	2	12.15	5	0	7	10	10	6
Josh Schmidt	0	0	14.40	4	0	5	9	5	2
Matt Sommo	2	1	3.67	31	0	42	40	21	35
Wardell Starling	0	1	13.50	2	2	4	7	6	3
Kanekoa Texeira	3	2	3.18	28	0	34	32	13	16
Kelvin Villa	3	2	5.88	5	5	34	44	13	31

CAMDEN RIVERSHARKS

PLAYER	POS	AVG	OBP	SLG	AB	R	H	HR	RBI	SB
Michael Albaladejo	C	.194	.257	.204	93	8	18	0	5	0
Rob Benedict	IF	.200	.259	.200	25	1	5	0	2	1
Danny Bomback	IF	.213	.288	.340	47	2	10	0	8	1
Dionys Cesar	IF	.262	.301	.362	301	29	79	6	46	11
Johnny Drennen	OF	.212	.288	.311	222	26	47	5	35	0
Yasser Gomez	OF	.278	.335	.309	443	48	123	0	30	16
Michael Grieco	C	.158	.200	.158	19	0	3	0	2	0

PLAYER	POS	AVG	OBP	SLG	AB	R	H	HR	RBI	SB
DAngelo Jimenez	IF	.218	.353	.277	285	37	62	3	27	7
Erik Lis	IF	.176	.317	.235	34	5	6	0	3	0
Salomon Manriquez	C	.247	.294	.373	158	20	39	2	16	0
Juan Martinez	IF	.223	.284	.336	283	31	63	4	35	6
Paddy Matera	IF	.304	.365	.525	158	31	48	6	18	0
Manuel Mayorson	IF	.197	.228	.211	76	5	15	0	4	0
Tommy Mendonca	3B	.292	.419	.292	24	2	7	0	2	0
Raul Padron	C	.274	.347	.391	481	64	132	9	59	4
Valentino Pascucci	IF	.240	.394	.452	250	48	60	15	45	1
Eduardo Perez	IF	.227	.298	.339	304	37	69	8	37	2
Burt Reynolds	OF	.247	.296	.411	190	20	47	6	14	7
Billy Rice	OF	.269	.327	.329	283	34	76	2	21	7
Kalian Sams	OF	.667	.750	1.533	15	3	10	3	9	2
Stantrel Smith	OF	.276	.323	.310	29	1	8	0	1	1
Wilson Valdez	IF	.310	.384	.371	342	45	106	0	27	37
Chris Walker	OF	.255	.312	.378	278	36	71	4	29	21
Delwyn Young	IF	.269	.342	.409	443	57	119	13	67	1

PLAYER	W	L	ERA	G	GS	IP	H	BB	SO
Chris Andujar	0	1	4.66	6	1	10	14	7	7
Mike Antonini	0	1	7.84	13	1	21	29	6	15
Brian Bass	2	10	5.88	14	14	75	87	44	58
Andrew Battisto	3	1	3.13	5	4	32	32	8	21
Pat Butler	1	1	27.00	3	1	3	6	5	0
Jordan Ellis	1	1	4.50	38	0	40	45	16	39
Jeff Farnsworth	3	0	6.67	19	7	53	71	25	30
Armando Gabino	4	8	4.93	41	6	91	97	43	85
Eric Gonzalez	0	0	9.72	5	0	8	10	8	6
Scott Gorgen	0	8	6.34	14	11	55	64	31	30
Jake Hale	3	7	5.43	27	14	106	127	33	65
Zach Hammes	2	0	1.93	13	0	14	9	5	8
Andrew Johnston	3	1	4.93	36	1	53	69	11	32
Rusty Jones	0	3	2.08	36	0	35	25	21	34
Ryan Kulik	2	11	5.83	24	20	108	131	41	83
Adrian Martin	5	5	2.14	57	0	59	66	3	37
Miguel Martinez	5	6	3.29	18	18	115	104	29	68
Mike McGuire	2	4	6.16	10	10	50	56	23	24
Valentino Pascucci	0	0	0.00	3	0	3	4	1	0
Ryan Quigley	2	3	1.36	29	0	33	23	10	44
Chris Rollins	0	1	19.29	4	0	5	9	6	3
Aaron Tullo	3	1	3.99	8	8	47	40	29	39
Jon Velasquez	6	2	1.96	61	0	74	58	26	82
Josh Walter	5	9	6.48	20	19	99	112	46	44
Keith Weiser	1	4	8.08	7	7	36	53	8	23
Joey Williamson	3	2	3.98	11	11	61	50	24	56
Eric Wordekemper	0	0	3.65	10	0	12	13	17	5
Corey Young	0	1	6.43	10	0	7	6	5	2

LANCASTER BARNSTORMERS

PLAYER	POS	AVG	OBP	SLG	AB	R	H	HR	RBI	SB
Dayton Buller	C	.310	.385	.405	84	12	26	1	10	1
Anthony Contreras	IF	.247	.284	.364	77	15	19	2	8	2
Travis Denker	2B	.275	.339	.461	510	77	140	22	79	3
Blake Gailen	OF	.288	.385	.454	434	72	125	11	52	20
Austin Gallagher	IF	.237	.336	.301	93	15	22	1	6	0
Kyle Haines	IF	.243	.307	.272	136	14	33	0	9	1
Ryan Harvey	OF	.250	.288	.500	448	52	112	29	92	2
Stephen Holdren	OF	.130	.259	.130	23	1	3	0	0	1
Kevin Howard	SS	.237	.277	.334	299	27	71	5	27	3
Kody Kirkland	IF	.237	.306	.396	169	22	40	4	15	2
Joe Mather	OF	.271	.280	.458	48	4	13	2	4	1
Gustavo Molina	C	.221	.274	.335	281	29	62	6	30	0
Jerry Owens	CF	.341	.396	.402	478	76	163	2	48	32
Preston Paramore	C	.158	.246	.208	101	11	16	0	7	0
Fernando Perez	OF	.136	.208	.273	22	2	3	0	1	1
Kyle Russell	OF	.191	.275	.323	220	22	42	5	21	3
Matt Spencer	OF	.260	.313	.379	177	18	46	0	16	0
Tsuyoshi Takashima	IF	.146	.222	.244	41	4	6	1	4	1
Jason Taylor	IF	.292	.374	.410	144	28	42	2	16	8
Joe Thurston	IF	.329	.404	.447	76	11	25	1	18	0
Daryle Ward	1B	.280	.348	.490	306	39	89	17	54	0
Jeremy Williams	OF	.238	.256	.286	42	5	10	0	2	0

PLAYER	W	L	ERA	G	GS	IP	H	BB	SO
Jeff Bennett	1	1	3.12	6	3	26	23	3	14
Zach Braddock	0	1	12.71	10	0	6	6	8	8

	W	L	ERA	G	GS	IP	H	BB	SO
Jay Buente	1	3	6.20	6	5	20	18	12	9
Tim Dillard	0	0	0.00	6	0	7	3	0	5
Lenny DiNardo	5	9	5.25	20	19	105	140	35	70
Justin Dowdy	1	0	2.13	17	0	13	9	4	6
Brodie Downs	1	4	1.44	48	0	56	49	15	36
Cody Eppley	0	1	2.08	6	0	4	3	4	4
Brian Grening	6	7	3.74	30	15	113	116	32	79
Yoslan Herrera	2	1	3.74	59	0	53	46	17	54
Robert Hinton	0	0	8.31	8	0	9	15	4	6
Alan Johnson	1	3	8.02	10	7	34	52	21	20
Derrick Loop	5	7	4.26	39	14	106	82	62	107
John Parrish	0	0	6.75	6	0	4	5	3	5
Ross Peeples	2	1	4.60	47	3	63	75	15	39
Dwayne Pollok	18	3	2.92	27	27	173	163	37	124
Horacio Ramirez	5	1	3.51	9	8	49	50	8	35
Nate Reed	6	5	2.87	45	5	75	68	32	71
Kris Regas	0	0	1.23	13	0	15	8	2	7
Jason Richardson	3	3	3.72	43	0	39	38	8	38
Rich Rundles	3	5	5.83	13	13	63	78	28	48
Brian Tallet	0	1	4.57	18	0	22	18	7	18
Jason Urquidez	3	1	0.25	39	0	36	19	7	48
Esmerling Vasquez	0	0	17.18	5	0	4	5	5	2

LONG ISLAND DUCKS

PLAYER	POS	AVG	OBP	SLG	AB	R	H	HR	RBI	SB
Adam Bailey	OF	.254	.292	.409	511	54	130	15	57	2
Josh Barfield	IF	.295	.334	.429	352	46	104	7	36	4
Kraig Binick	OF	.265	.332	.342	234	24	62	2	19	4
Joash Brodin	OF	.307	.376	.441	417	79	128	11	49	14
Ben Broussard	IF	.302	.344	.509	169	24	51	8	20	0
Ramon Castro	C	.260	.295	.378	296	21	77	8	31	0
Lew Ford	OF	.377	.413	.435	69	11	26	0	7	0
Bill Hall	OF	.239	.330	.447	318	46	76	16	63	2
Ralph Henriquez	C	.242	.301	.381	260	29	63	7	28	0
Rian Kiniry	OF	.233	.346	.310	116	12	27	0	6	5
Dan Lyons	IF	.217	.274	.260	346	45	75	0	27	4
Ray Navarrete	IF	.231	.290	.346	364	38	84	7	38	0
Bryant Nelson	IF	.298	.344	.429	483	72	144	11	71	11
Willis Otanez	IF	.150	.235	.283	60	3	9	2	8	0
Danny Perales	OF	.288	.323	.517	205	28	59	11	41	2
P.J. Phillips	IF	.222	.266	.335	221	33	49	4	19	13
Ryan Strieby	IF	.251	.330	.369	195	23	49	4	24	0
Gabe Suarez	IF	.221	.287	.337	86	13	19	2	6	3
Murray Watts	IF	.254	.273	.317	63	5	16	0	3	0

PLAYER	W	L	ERA	G	GS	IP	H	BB	SO
Derek Blacksher	0	1	15.75	1	1	4	10	2	2
Bobby Blevins	1	1	4.85	2	2	13	14	4	10
John Brownell	9	10	3.90	26	26	166	172	48	133
Pete Budkevics	2	5	5.80	22	4	45	55	27	31
Nick DeBarr	5	10	6.71	35	16	109	122	49	70
Shaun Garceau	2	1	1.17	3	3	23	15	4	17
Connor Graham	3	4	5.90	16	7	50	56	22	31
Daniel Herrera	2	1	5.03	23	0	20	29	6	14
Alex Hinshaw	0	1	9.82	13	0	11	6	16	17
T.J. Hose	2	2	5.31	38	0	39	39	21	30
James Houser	8	3	3.30	31	14	90	72	28	95
Rusty Jones	0	3	2.08	36	0	35	25	21	34
Jared Lansford	1	1	4.29	47	0	50	54	21	48
Josh Lansford	1	3	3.22	43	0	45	55	7	30
Chris McCoy	0	2	11.57	3	2	12	25	3	4
Bill Murphy	4	14	5.50	28	24	128	148	61	79
Eric Niesen	4	0	3.23	35	0	39	34	12	39
Eddy Ramos	0	0	0.93	10	0	10	7	1	3
Royce Ring	0	1	8.10	4	0	3	9	1	2
Leo Rosales	2	2	2.35	39	0	38	38	16	45
Ian Snell	2	3	4.56	50	0	51	48	12	58
Josh Strawn	0	0	6.75	2	0	3	6	0	1
Erick Threets	0	3	7.04	27	0	23	21	19	15
Matt Way	4	5	4.04	16	16	76	69	31	73
Dontrelle Willis	5	4	2.57	14	14	88	78	43	52
Bob Zimmermann	4	4	4.47	28	11	95	97	39	62

SOMERSET PATRIOTS

PLAYER	POS	AVG	OBP	SLG	AB	R	H	HR	RBI	SB
Cory Aldridge	OF	.284	.368	.462	331	44	94	12	53	5
Jeff Baisley	IF	.234	.299	.399	303	41	71	10	51	5
Jorge Cortes	OF	.283	.373	.417	187	23	53	4	25	2
Adam Donachie	C	.235	.298	.352	264	29	62	6	40	1
Aharon Eggleston	OF	.294	.380	.410	429	93	126	8	56	12
Jake Fox	IF	.310	.387	.572	374	62	116	25	82	0
Dan Hennigan	IF	.213	.351	.236	127	34	27	0	7	6
Joe Holden	OF	.305	.374	.344	154	25	47	0	11	15
Josh Kroeger	OF	.254	.299	.286	126	15	32	0	14	1
Eddy Martinez-Esteve	IF	.355	.429	.462	262	29	93	5	48	1
Luis Montanez	OF	.313	.359	.478	201	39	63	6	41	1
Angel Sanchez	IF	.228	.365	.327	101	18	23	1	11	1
Yunesky Sanchez	IF	.312	.323	.519	154	21	48	8	34	0
James Skelton	C	.268	.397	.417	235	46	63	4	28	20
Corey Smith	IF	.269	.330	.442	513	82	138	20	84	11
Bobby Stevens	IF	.254	.323	.362	307	45	78	7	36	17
Jonny Tucker	OF	.262	.348	.340	523	85	137	3	56	25
Mike Wilson	OF	.325	.406	.518	83	14	27	3	18	4

PLAYER	W	L	ERA	G	GS	IP	H	BB	SO
Erik Arnesen	13	4	3.19	22	22	150	161	16	103
Mitch Atkins	3	2	3.98	7	7	43	42	13	39
Cedrick Bowers	2	0	1.69	14	0	16	5	12	19
Brandon Braboy	1	1	5.74	27	0	27	28	11	16
David Harden	10	2	3.39	20	14	101	110	21	63
Fernando Hernandez	1	0	0.00	7	0	9	8	3	3
Alex Hinshaw	0	1	9.82	13	0	11	6	16	17
Jim Hoey	1	2	2.51	46	0	43	38	10	41
Jon Hunton	3	6	3.00	57	0	54	59	12	37
Ben Kozlowski	0	0	12.60	12	0	10	16	6	9
Jason Lowey	7	4	1.77	55	0	51	31	24	56
Josh Lowey	14	8	2.89	26	25	156	125	48	124
Derell McCall	8	0	3.46	29	8	81	77	23	35
Roy Merritt	4	2	1.96	38	7	64	39	31	71
Paul Phillips	4	5	6.72	28	10	72	90	26	66
Josh Schmidt	0	0	4.50	2	0	2	1	4	4
Carlton Smith	2	1	4.74	32	0	38	49	6	33
Graham Taylor	10	6	3.40	27	27	159	171	36	106
Brad Thompson	6	6	5.00	19	19	124	143	27	61
Joe Torres	1	0	2.38	11	0	11	11	7	9
Ryan Zamorsky	0	0	0.00	2	0	2	3	0	1

SOUTHERN MARYLAND BLUE CRABS

PLAYER	POS	AVG	OBP	SLG	AB	R	H	HR	RBI	SB
Brian Barton	OF	.262	.315	.378	370	46	97	4	37	12
George Carroll	C	.105	.105	.105	19	1	2	0	0	0
Alvin Colina	C	.231	.278	.404	329	37	76	13	40	3
Ian Gac	IF	.276	.333	.655	29	5	8	3	9	0
Cole Garner	OF	.147	.205	.250	68	4	10	2	6	1
Cyle Hankerd	OF	.322	.396	.641	301	56	97	22	61	1
Kody Hightower	IF	.241	.267	.276	29	2	7	0	1	1
Brandon Jones	IF	.229	.282	.365	96	14	22	3	13	0
Jose Julio-Ruiz	1B	.272	.324	.357	471	47	128	5	53	15
Ryan Mulhern	IF	.308	.374	.503	195	31	60	9	31	0
Cesar Nicolas	3B	.234	.311	.337	410	46	96	8	34	0
Jake Opitz	IF	.281	.356	.454	185	31	52	5	23	4
Renny Osuna	IF	.296	.360	.393	450	70	133	6	53	33
Jeremy Owens	OF	.220	.317	.358	341	49	75	8	34	20
Mike Richard	IF	.273	.349	.356	132	22	36	0	16	6
Jose Salas	C	.273	.322	.349	395	36	108	3	52	5
Nick Schwaner	IF	.286	.354	.405	42	6	12	1	9	0
Sean Smith	OF	.253	.316	.397	443	73	112	13	50	36
Troy Snitker	C	.353	.450	.588	17	4	6	1	2	0
Wladimir Sutil	IF	.240	.324	.309	362	38	87	5	43	11
Donnie Webb	OF	.250	.313	.432	44	8	11	0	8	2

PLAYER	W	L	ERA	G	GS	IP	H	BB	SO
Michael Ballard	7	7	4.89	17	17	92	106	26	60
Jordan Conley	1	0	1.42	12	0	13	10	6	8
Joe Gannon	1	2	5.82	12	4	34	40	15	29
Gabriel Hernandez	7	12	4.29	28	24	145	137	45	111
Wade Korpi	3	7	4.81	24	19	97	113	45	55
Charlie Manning	2	4	2.26	74	0	60	46	26	55
Ian Marshall	12	8	4.00	27	27	158	180	40	98
Tommy Mendoza	0	2	24.75	2	1	4	14	4	2
Kyle Mertins	1	2	4.19	73	0	67	61	28	58
Eduardo Morlan	1	4	3.33	56	0	51	43	16	40

	W	L	ERA	G	GS	IP	H	BB	SO
Mike OConnor	1	1	3.60	5	5	20	28	2	16
Tim Redding	1	2	5.94	19	0	17	20	5	13
Nick Sarianides	0	1	6.75	6	0	7	9	3	1
Peter Sikaras	0	1	7.27	9	0	9	17	5	4
Jeremy Sowers	1	3	4.30	8	8	44	41	16	25
Jeff Stevens	4	3	3.98	47	0	61	55	32	43
Deinys Suarez	0	0	17.18	2	0	4	6	2	4
Daryl Thompson	10	5	3.18	22	22	125	114	39	73
Jim Ed Warden	3	4	1.50	61	0	60	51	19	49
Logan Williamson	5	3	3.66	31	12	76	83	30	47
Kyle Zaleski	4	2	6.40	49	0	51	65	19	46

SUGAR LAND SKEETERS

PLAYER	POS	AVG	OBP	SLG	AB	R	H	HR	RBI	SB
Aaron Bates	IF	.306	.397	.411	448	71	137	7	57	0
Brian Burgamy	IF	.323	.430	.542	192	40	62	9	41	3
Koby Clemens	C	.219	.336	.461	319	57	70	21	60	4
Jeff Dominguez	IF	.277	.332	.424	347	55	96	8	48	15
Adam Godwin	OF	.282	.325	.338	556	86	157	3	36	50
Reid Gorecki	OF	.228	.320	.388	237	38	54	9	35	20
Anthony Granato	IF	.293	.393	.350	123	19	36	0	17	5
Chase Lambin	IF	.305	.347	.474	95	18	29	5	13	1
Ryan Langerhans	OF	.287	.420	.500	150	33	43	5	28	4
Dustin Martin	OF	.245	.331	.455	110	22	27	4	16	11
Russ Mitchell	IF	.211	.344	.333	261	35	55	7	24	1
Steve Moss	OF	.318	.380	.521	236	35	75	9	43	13
Eduardo Perez	IF	.227	.298	.339	304	37	69	8	37	2
Fernando Perez	OF	.278	.316	.407	54	7	15	1	5	3
Josh Pressley	IF	.271	.360	.452	314	35	85	12	52	2
Dominic Ramos	IF	.230	.267	.332	452	48	104	10	58	16
Kevin Rios	IF	.251	.324	.377	183	27	46	3	25	2
Michael Rockett	OF	.221	.267	.329	258	33	57	6	27	3
Travis Scott	C	.276	.353	.447	387	59	107	11	59	6

PLAYER	W	L	ERA	G	GS	IP	H	BB	SO
Greg Aquino	7	4	4.20	30	15	99	89	28	65
Doug Arguello	2	0	3.68	7	6	29	31	17	22
Jason Bergmann	2	0	0.30	30	0	30	15	2	33
Cesar Carrillo	2	2	4.02	9	9	47	42	31	22
Roy Corcoran	6	4	2.73	49	1	56	57	21	36
Gilbert De La Vara	4	1	3.49	12	9	57	50	24	32
Scott Elarton	6	6	5.03	19	18	102	130	31	42
Clint Everts	5	2	2.71	23	7	63	49	27	40
Sean Gallagher	2	0	2.05	4	4	22	13	4	16
Roberto Giron	4	4	2.19	55	0	58	46	21	65
Clay Hensley	2	0	0.63	14	0	14	4	7	16
Ben Kozlowski	1	1	1.86	19	3	39	32	8	26
Jason Lane	8	4	2.98	17	17	106	85	13	53
Bobby Livingston	3	3	7.11	7	6	32	41	16	14
Gary Majewski	5	2	1.79	62	0	70	70	8	35
Jay Marshall	3	0	2.50	56	0	50	46	24	6
Adam Miller	4	4	4.79	36	5	62	67	26	36
Michael Nix	9	2	1.88	14	12	77	50	30	63
David Pauley	5	3	3.44	12	12	68	72	23	52
Dustin Richardson	0	0	1.04	6	1	9	8	2	5
Travis Schlichting	1	1	4.15	14	0	13	12	3	9
Jared Wells	2	1	4.13	40	0	48	35	37	60
Matt Wright	10	1	2.63	15	15	92	65	28	68

YORK REVOLUTION

PLAYER	POS	AVG	OBP	SLG	AB	R	H	HR	RBI	SB
Patrick Arlis	C	.211	.301	.211	71	9	15	0	7	0
Wilson Batista	SS	.304	.346	.397	473	55	144	6	67	10
Ofilio Castro	IF	.290	.372	.321	162	23	47	0	11	0
Mike Coles	OF	.083	.267	.083	12	2	1	0	0	0
Jeff Fiorentino	OF	.328	.392	.453	137	21	45	3	21	1
Andy Gonzalez	IF	.273	.337	.312	77	8	21	0	7	1
Tyler Graham	OF	.245	.290	.298	94	10	23	0	9	2
Michael Hernandez	OF	.238	.305	.344	160	16	38	3	11	0
Cody Johnson	OF	.268	.358	.506	168	31	45	10	29	1
Kody Kirkland	IF	.237	.293	.377	236	33	56	3	16	5
Johan Limonta	1B	.295	.368	.459	61	8	18	2	12	1
Val Majewski	OF	.091	.091	.091	11	1	1	0	0	1
Andy Marte	3B	.301	.367	.526	369	61	111	19	74	0
Manny Mayorson	IF	.281	.311	.351	114	14	32	0	8	1

	POS	AVG	OBP	SLG	AB	R	H	HR	RBI	SB
Dallas McPherson	IF	.286	.333	.357	14	1	4	0	1	0
Charlie Neil	C	.227	.301	.253	75	8	17	0	3	0
Salvador Paniagua	C	.279	.292	.427	426	44	119	14	54	0
Eric Patterson	IF	.275	.342	.527	262	54	72	13	38	5
Andres Perez	2B	.290	.355	.442	520	77	151	13	71	4
Jason Repko	OF	.253	.330	.368	95	18	24	1	11	5
James Shanks	OF	.172	.228	.237	93	12	16	1	11	0
Matt Spencer	OF	.267	.341	.436	202	27	54	8	31	0
Mark Teahen	OF	.270	.355	.406	281	40	76	6	30	1
Chad Tracy	IF	.289	.369	.488	211	29	61	9	37	0
Ruddy Yan	OF	.238	.290	.287	425	46	101	0	44	8

PLAYER	W	L	ERA	G	GS	IP	H	BB	SO
Anthony Claggett	0	1	1.54	2	2	12	13	7	6
Chris Cody	15	9	3.12	28	28	176	189	45	139
Julio DePaula	2	2	2.89	50	0	56	48	22	36
Matt Fox	1	0	1.59	5	4	17	15	3	18
Nick Green	4	5	5.42	19	17	101	120	26	66
Josh Judy	1	0	2.25	4	0	4	3	1	5
Rommie Lewis	0	1	1.51	47	0	42	30	12	35
Pedro Liriano	7	4	4.87	27	16	94	105	41	63
Yunior Novoa	5	2	3.79	43	0	55	52	15	60
Edward Paredes	2	2	2.96	33	0	27	31	15	22
Dustin Pease	0	0	7.50	6	0	6	6	2	2
Stephen Penney	5	2	3.35	57	0	54	64	9	52
Kris Regas	1	2	8.22	10	4	23	32	12	10
Juan Rincon	1	8	3.26	47	0	47	46	19	43
Will Savage	9	11	4.41	25	23	127	161	30	87
Zack Segovia	3	5	5.30	10	8	53	66	16	27
Anthony Slama	1	1	3.71	13	0	17	12	12	10
Corey Thurman	4	14	6.49	28	28	146	196	55	107
Brett Tomko	4	8	4.98	19	19	125	137	30	90
Joe Torres	2	2	4.43	38	0	41	47	17	38
Beau Vaughan	2	2	3.69	45	3	61	55	17	39
Michael Wuertz	4	2	2.86	53	0	50	35	23	62
Rick Zagone	2	3	5.93	9	8	41	49	20	23

CAN-AM LEAGUE

The New Jersey Jackals came as close as anyone has in the past five years to ending Quebec's stranglehold over the Can-Am League, but in the end, the dynasty continued.

The Capitales fell behind by four runs early in the deciding Game 7 of the Can-Am League championship series, but Quebec rallied for a 12-7 win to clinch its fifth straight Can-Am League title. It's Quebec's sixth title in the nine-year history of the league.

Quebec's dominance stretches beyond some excellent work in the playoffs--Quebec has finished the regular season with the league's best record in each of the past four years.

Quebec third baseman Jonathan Malo was named the league's player of the year for a season that saw him finish in the top 10 in batting average (.305) and home runs (11). Newark's Bridger Hunt managed to become one of the few independent league players to top .400 for a season with a .402 average. Hunt signed with the Padres during the season, but he had enough at-bats to qualify as the league leader.

STANDINGS	W	L	PCT	GB
Quebec Capitales	56	42	.571	——
New Jersey Jackals	55	44	.556	1.5
Newark Bears	37	63	.370	20
Rockland Boulders	49	51	.490	8
Trois-Rivieres Aigles	43	56	.434	13.5

PLAYOFFS: Finals—Quebec defeated New Jersey 4-3 in best-of-7 series.

ATTENDANCE: Rockland 143,231; Quebec 141,396; New Jersey 76,883; Trois-Rivieres 71,568; Newark 21,288.
ALL-STAR TEAM: C—Josue Peley (Quebec). 1B—Chris Duffy (New Jersey). 2B—Jose Cuevas (New Jersey). 3B—Jonathan Malo (Quebec). SS—Jeremy Barnes (New Jersey). OFs—Jerod Edmondson (Rockland); Donnie Webb (Rockland); Steve Brown (Trois-Rivieres). DH—Rene Leveret (Quebec).
SP—Alex Burkard (Trois-Rivieres); RP—Tim Adleman (New Jersey).
PLAYER OF THE YEAR: Jonathan Malo, Quebec. ROOKIE OF THE YEAR: Can Kneeland, Trois-Rivieres.

BATTING LEADERS

PLAYER	TEAM	AVG	G	AB	R	H	HR	RBI
Hunt, Bridger	NEW	.402	69	266	54	107	4	36
Barnes, Jeremy	NJ	.319	90	335	64	107	16	57
Shah, Asif	QC	.319	87	288	45	92	9	57
Kneeland, Cam	QC	.306	99	372	54	114	9	62
Malo, Jonathan	QC	.305	95	374	76	114	11	57
Cuevas, Jose	NJ	.304	96	358	55	109	3	40
Peley, Josue	QC	.303	98	390	46	118	9	59
Boucher, Sebastien	QC	.302	88	328	64	99	6	45
Alvino, Billy	ROC	.300	76	260	36	78	2	30
Walton, Jamar	NEW	.299	78	294	36	88	9	48

PITCHING LEADERS

PLAYER	TEAM	W	L	ERA	IP	H	BB	SO
Shields, Jeff	TRV	9	9	2.44	137	114	44	68
Burkard, Alex	TRV	9	6	2.88	100	93	47	49
Gelinas, Karl	QC	10	4	2.98	100	95	17	80
Duda, Jeff	QC	7	2	3.23	114	116	26	67
Bennigson, Craig	NJ	8	4	3.61	120	125	27	46
Moran, Pat	ROC	6	7	3.87	140	138	41	100
Perez, Leondy	NEW	7	8	4.04	111	127	36	89
Lucas, Jonathan	NJ	9	5	4.12	94	110	30	52
Ness, Mike	NEW	5	7	4.15	80	89	23	50
Blevins, Bobby	ROC	9	10	4.24	144	143	32	82

NEW JERSEY JACKALS

PLAYER	POS	AVG	OBP	SLG	AB	R	H	HR	RBI	SB
Yasanberty Arbelo	IF	.208	.263	.321	106	12	22	3	14	0
Jeremy Barnes	IF	.319	.378	.528	335	64	107	16	57	2
Rob Benedict	IF	.263	.375	.316	38	8	10	0	6	7
Ryan Breen	C	.080	.207	.120	25	3	2	0	2	0
Jose Cuevas	IF	.304	.350	.416	358	55	109	3	40	16
Chris Curran	CF	.287	.362	.337	359	61	103	0	18	45
Chris Duffy	1B	.293	.387	.487	335	50	98	13	62	1
Nick Giarraputo	IF	.281	.331	.377	324	50	91	5	45	1
Gaetano Giunta	IF	.228	.305	.281	167	21	38	1	11	9
Benji Johnson	C	.217	.245	.302	106	6	23	1	10	0
Cody Johnson	OF	.191	.208	.362	47	4	9	2	5	0
Brandon Jones	OF	.263	.335	.343	175	25	46	2	27	1
John Lindsey	1B	.250	.328	.500	56	8	14	3	16	0
Matt Nandin	IF	.273	.342	.302	172	23	47	0	26	5
Matt Padgett	IF	.324	.415	.620	71	16	23	5	19	2
Danny Rams	C	.260	.330	.389	285	32	74	6	41	0
Bryan Sabatella	OF	.291	.355	.435	361	63	105	10	47	33

PLAYER	W	L	ERA	G	GS	IP	H	BB	SO
Tim Adleman	0	0	1.46	40	0	49	32	13	62
Craig Bennigson	8	4	3.61	19	19	120	125	27	46
Keith Cantwell	7	5	3.72	42	3	58	59	16	57
Ryan Fennell	1	3	5.98	23	3	47	61	32	38
David Filak	2	1	8.15	4	4	18	18	15	6
Mike Francisco	0	0	6.48	19	0	25	30	11	23
Marcos Frias	0	0	4.50	3	0	4	3	0	9
Jeremy Gigliotti	0	0	5.79	4	0	5	12	1	5
Kyle Greenwalt	1	5	7.16	6	6	28	38	11	23
Craig Heyer	6	5	6.00	11	11	60	88	24	30
Lucas Irvine	2	1	2.35	4	4	23	17	10	17
George Isabel	0	0	3.38	2	0	3	3	2	3
Pete Levitt	0	1	7.84	7	0	10	10	7	6
Bobby Lucas	0	0	6.91	13	0	14	17	11	12
Jon Lucas	9	5	4.12	28	14	94	110	30	52
Mike McGuire	1	4	7.62	6	6	28	50	10	21

PLAYER	W	L	ERA	G	GS	IP	H	BB	SO
Brandon Moore	5	3	3.66	13	13	76	80	21	65
Bryan Morgado	0	1	9.00	12	0	11	12	18	9
Nick Mutz	1	1	0.90	8	0	10	3	6	11
Isaac Pavlik	4	4	3.38	10	10	61	60	17	46
Wes Roemer	3	3	4.63	9	9	56	53	19	33
Chad Rose	6	1	2.24	46	0	56	48	16	53
Corey Vogt	0	0	4.50	11	0	14	12	8	14

NEWARK BEARS

PLAYER	POS	AVG	OBP	SLG	AB	R	H	HR	RBI	SB
Richard Arias	IF	.284	.324	.379	169	24	48	2	22	4
Ernie Banks Jr.	1B	.278	.319	.429	345	42	96	13	59	1
Sandy DeLeon	C	.182	.182	.182	22	0	4	0	3	0
Ryan DiMascio	3B	.138	.167	.138	29	1	4	0	1	0
Mike Gedman	1B	.219	.298	.325	237	36	52	5	32	18
Antoin Gray	IF	.269	.296	.308	26	1	7	0	0	0
Matt Huggins	1B	.182	.280	.227	22	2	4	0	2	0
Bridger Hunt	IF	.402	.438	.541	266	54	107	4	36	14
DAngelo Jimenez	3B	.281	.349	.439	57	6	16	1	10	2
Jonny Kaplan	IF	.310	.379	.429	126	22	39	2	13	8
Danny Lackner	OF	.143	.280	.190	21	0	3	0	3	0
Kyle Lafrenz	C	.288	.319	.401	299	35	86	4	32	1
Stephen Malcolm	CF	.234	.253	.286	154	20	36	0	7	8
Manny Mayorson	IF	.258	.324	.290	62	9	16	0	5	3
Elvin Millan Jr.	C	.211	.259	.294	109	8	23	3	16	1
Jereme Milons	OF	.243	.263	.243	37	2	9	0	1	1
Brandon Mims	SS	.316	.381	.474	19	3	6	1	2	1
Brandon Newton	IF	.263	.315	.316	133	21	35	0	4	8
Wander Nunez	IF	.302	.308	.411	129	15	39	1	19	3
Sean OHare	IF	.235	.333	.382	102	17	24	3	10	3
Derek Perren	OF	.238	.273	.238	21	1	5	0	1	0
Joseph Poletsky	IF	.255	.323	.336	149	14	38	0	15	0
Derrick Pyles	OF	.325	.357	.375	40	7	13	0	5	0
Manny Reyes	C	.091	.167	.091	11	0	1	0	1	0
JJ Sherrill	IF	.188	.235	.271	48	6	9	1	4	4
Charlie Stewart	OF	.143	.200	.143	14	0	2	0	0	0
Nathan Tomaszewski	IF	.114	.133	.205	44	6	5	1	2	0
Victor Torres	OF	.176	.263	.176	17	2	3	0	0	0
Jamar Walton	OF	.299	.319	.480	294	36	88	9	48	2
Travis Weaver	IF	.253	.291	.294	269	31	68	1	14	7
Johnny Welch	IF	.226	.303	.350	177	21	40	5	26	0
Trent Wilkins	OF	.217	.379	.261	23	6	5	0	3	0

PLAYER	W	L	ERA	G	GS	IP	H	BB	SO
Wander Alvino	0	0	6.23	8	0	13	16	6	20
Bryan Banes	0	2	3.38	3	3	16	11	7	10
Cameron Bayne	0	1	4.00	6	0	9	9	2	6
Ryan Carr	1	2	8.81	18	0	32	48	19	14
Brian Chandler	0	0	2.25	2	0	4	4	1	0
David Dinelli	5	5	5.65	24	8	72	74	48	71
Sergio Espinosa	0	0	2.65	36	1	51	57	12	42
Adam Gabel	3	6	5.23	14	14	74	92	43	35
Leonard Giammanco	0	4	6.75	4	4	21	35	12	7
Omar Javier	1	0	3.38	4	3	11	15	6	4
Leandro Mella	1	0	27.00	2	0	3	5	9	3
Steve Merslich	1	0	11.42	5	0	9	9	13	6
Kyle Morrison	1	0	2.37	21	0	30	20	22	34
Mike Ness	5	7	4.15	12	12	80	89	23	50
Brian Parker	5	6	5.91	25	8	81	101	30	46
Leondy Perez	7	8	4.04	19	19	111	127	36	89
Kevin Reese	1	0	6.64	6	1	20	28	4	12
Jim Schult	1	4	6.81	8	7	36	44	26	26
Joe Testa	1	5	6.09	9	4	44	52	27	37
Jorge Vasquez	2	2	3.12	40	0	43	35	20	59

QUEBEC CAPITALES

PLAYER	POS	AVG	OBP	SLG	AB	R	H	HR	RBI	SB
Jean-Luc Blaquiere	C	.275	.351	.380	171	27	47	3	18	5
Sebastien Boucher	CF	.302	.410	.418	328	64	99	6	45	18
Marc Bourgeois	CF	.333	.333	.524	21	2	7	1	3	0
Royce Consigli	OF	.254	.327	.404	354	52	90	11	46	15
Patrick DAoust	C	.144	.231	.202	104	12	15	1	9	1
Dany Deschamps	OF	.192	.299	.232	125	16	24	0	9	1
Josh Garton	OF	.107	.138	.214	28	2	3	1	5	0
Mike Grieco	C	.115	.281	.115	26	2	3	0	0	0

		AVG	OBP	SLG	AB	R	H	HR	RBI	SB
Jeff Helps	IF	.261	.368	.314	299	43	78	1	25	13
Cam Kneeland	IF	.306	.364	.468	372	54	114	9	62	10
Chase Larsson	OF	.083	.313	.083	24	1	2	0	0	1
Maxime Lefevre	IF	.224	.348	.302	205	45	46	2	24	20
Rene Leveret	1B	.292	.376	.432	329	47	96	11	71	0
Jonathan Malo	3B	.305	.399	.455	374	76	114	11	57	27
Josue Peley	C	.303	.336	.433	390	46	118	9	59	14
Asif Shah	OF	.319	.419	.462	288	45	92	9	57	3
Blair Springfield	2B	.190	.312	.270	63	7	12	1	5	3
Carlos Willoughby	IF	.200	.280	.234	145	21	29	1	11	6

PLAYER	W	L	ERA	G	GS	IP	H	BB	SO
Chris Cox	0	3	2.81	41	0	42	36	14	41
Dustin Crenshaw	9	7	4.35	22	15	110	138	13	48
Jeff Duda	7	2	3.23	19	19	114	116	26	67
Guillaume Duguay	0	0	8.10	1	1	3	6	0	1
Karl Gelinas	10	4	2.98	15	15	100	95	17	80
Casey Harman	3	2	2.77	42	0	52	51	13	43
Chad Jones	6	4	4.94	29	5	62	63	18	47
Jeff Kaplan	4	3	5.65	12	12	65	79	24	34
Eduardo Nunez	0	2	7.90	9	0	14	14	20	13
Kyle Regnault	4	2	3.82	30	4	61	55	27	60
Bryan Rembisz	6	6	4.65	19	19	108	123	40	53
Ryan Rogers	0	0	9.00	2	0	3	4	4	3
Charle Rosario	0	2	3.78	17	2	33	27	12	22
Dan Sausville	0	1	6.75	3	1	8	15	4	4
Shawn Smith	3	1	3.59	7	6	43	34	25	32
Stosh Wawrzasek	0	0	0.00	2	0	4	2	0	5

ROCKLAND BOULDERS

PLAYER	POS	AVG	OBP	SLG	AB	R	H	HR	RBI	SB
Billy Alvino	C	.300	.375	.362	260	36	78	2	30	3
Danny Bomback	IF	.283	.359	.429	357	53	101	6	48	18
Stephen Cardullo	IF	.267	.349	.417	360	51	96	6	56	19
Nick DelGuidice	SS	.218	.250	.352	142	14	31	4	19	0
Chris Edmondson	OF	.413	.513	.738	126	40	52	8	35	19
Jerod Edmondson	OF	.299	.361	.475	394	73	118	12	71	21
Mike Gedman	1B	.219	.298	.325	237	36	52	5	32	18
Robert Kelly	1B	.240	.286	.440	25	2	6	1	4	0
Scott Knazek	C	.181	.286	.305	177	19	32	4	19	0
Jaren Matthews	OF	.249	.307	.333	237	42	59	2	21	9
Angel Molina	OF	.214	.299	.259	112	7	24	0	7	0
Steve Nyisztor	IF	.257	.293	.352	210	28	54	3	21	10
Carlos Rivera	IF	.240	.293	.333	75	2	18	2	10	0
Donnie Webb	OF	.297	.382	.445	380	73	113	10	46	30
Johnny Welch	IF	.226	.303	.350	177	21	40	5	26	0

PLAYER	W	L	ERA	G	GS	IP	H	BB	SO
Cameron Bayne	4	4	5.43	18	10	60	86	23	40
Bobby Blevins	9	10	4.24	20	20	144	143	32	82
Adam Brown	0	0	1.80	2	1	5	4	4	2
Bo Budkevics	2	4	4.48	16	9	68	73	26	53
Marcos Frias	0	1	12.27	8	0	11	19	8	9
Kevin Fuqua	3	2	1.71	42	0	42	31	17	36
Min Hur	0	1	15.00	1	1	3	5	4	0
Garrett Johnson	5	3	3.12	35	0	43	35	23	36
Bobby Jones	0	1	6.23	1	1	4	4	3	2
Alex Kreis	2	0	3.10	38	0	41	34	25	48
Charlie Law	4	3	3.20	7	7	39	39	28	21
Fray Martinez	4	7	5.95	25	7	56	63	36	43
Pat Moran	6	7	3.87	22	21	140	138	41	100
Kilby Pena	0	0	36.00	1	2	2	3	9	7 2
Marty Popham	4	5	4.50	13	12	80	81	23	63
Nathaniel Roe	0	3	5.79	8	3	19	31	10	9
Dan Sausville	3	4	4.97	18	10	71	96	27	42
Jim Schult	1	4	6.81	8	7	36	44	26	26
Nick Serino	6	2	2.25	39	2	52	40	29	45
Evan Stermer	0	0	5.40	8	0	7	12	4	4

TROIS RIVIERES AIGLES

PLAYER	POS	AVG	OBP	SLG	AB	R	H	HR	RBI	SB
John Bobillo	C	.286	.318	.333	21	4	6	0	1	1
Steve Brown	OF	.288	.351	.516	364	73	105	19	58	23
Josh Colafemina	2B	.236	.313	.281	178	21	42	0	15	18

		AVG	OBP	SLG	AB	R	H	HR	RBI	SB
David JL Cooper	2B	.239	.379	.281	306	51	73	2	28	30
Phil DeLisle	IF	.200	.200	.200	10	0	2	0	1	0
Jonathan Dziomba	IF	.152	.152	.217	46	4	7	0	3	0
Brett Flowers	1B	.283	.363	.324	293	38	83	0	37	2
Emerson Frostad	C	.274	.348	.365	285	37	78	5	43	6
Carlos Guzman	OF	.281	.359	.373	359	44	101	5	56	9
Cam Kneeland	OF	.306	.364	.468	372	54	118	9	62	10
Drew Miller	OF	.292	.428	.453	342	59	100	11	45	0
Charles Neil	C	.125	.243	.156	32	2	4	0	1	0
Kyle Nisson	C	.204	.258	.252	147	6	30	0	14	0
Jeremy Nowak	OF	.241	.304	.361	316	42	76	4	38	3
Luis Piterson	IF	.157	.221	.157	70	7	11	0	8	3
Dominique Samyn	3B	.111	.200	.111	18	1	2	0	1	0
Jon Smith	OF	.249	.355	.455	334	53	83	16	55	18
Bubby Williams	C	.080	.143	.080	25	1	2	0	1	0

PLAYER	W	L	ERA	G	GS	IP	H	BB	SO
Dan Britton-Foster	3	3	5.06	19	8	64	77	14	46
Garrett Bullock	5	5	3.72	16	13	77	83	33	47
Alexander Burkard	9	6	2.88	16	16	100	93	47	49
Rob Cooper	0	2	6.92	30	0	26	26	16	31
Guillaume Duguay	0	0	8.10	1	1	3	6	0	1
Brian Gump	0	2	14.18	3	3	13	25	6	6
Sean Keeler	0	4	5.16	28	0	30	29	25	26
David Leblanc	1	2	4.99	27	0	40	46	17	25
Matt McDonald	3	2	4.78	24	2	43	47	16	37
Luis Munoz	4	4	3.95	11	11	73	90	16	55
Nick Purdy	1	3	2.31	33	0	39	27	19	45
Nick Sarianides	1	5	4.78	40	0	38	37	20	35
Jeff Shields	9	9	2.44	20	20	137	114	44	68
Oliver Vanzant	0	0	7.94	2	1	6	3	6	6
Charlie Weatherby	1	2	7.50	5	5	24	32	13	15
Tyler Wilson	6	7	4.61	19	19	121	125	42	88

FRONTIER LEAGUE

When the playoffs began, the Schaumburg Boomers were considered the favorites to claim the crown. Two weeks later, they had lived up to every expectation.

The Boomers cruised through the playoffs, winning all six games in a seemingly easy trip to their first Frontier League title in only their second year in the league.

While the 6-0 record meant the Boomers never faced a do-or-die game, they had few blowouts in the playoffs. Five of the six playoff wins came in games decided by two runs or less.

EAST DIVISION	W	L	PCT	GB
Lake Erie Crushers	56	40	.583	—
Traverse City Beach Bums	55	41	.573	1
Florence Freedom	53	43	.552	3
Evansville Otters	51	45	.531	5
Southern Illinois Miners	50	46	.521	6
Washington Wild Things	41	55	.427	15
Frontier Greys	33	62	.347	22.5

WEST DIVISION	W	L	PCT	GB
Schaumburg Boomers	59	37	.615	—
Gateway Grizzlies	53	43	.552	6
Windy City ThunderBolts	50	46	.521	9
River City Rascals	50	46	.521	9
Normal CornBelters	46	50	.479	13
Joliet Slammers	38	57	.400	20.5
Rockford Aviators	36	60	.375	23

PLAYOFFS: Semifinals—Schaumburg defeated Florence 3-0 and Lake Erie defeated Traverse City 3-2 in best-of-5 series. **Finals**—Schaumburg defeated Lake Erie 3-0 in best-of-5 series.

ATTENDANCE: Traverse City 164,915; Gateway 162,572; Schaumburg 150,254; Evansville 140,786; Normal 126,367; Southern Illinois 126,084; Lake Erie 122,097; Florence 112,270; Joliet 93,875; River City 92,652; Rockford 87,612; Washington 87,076; Windy City 74,609.

MANAGERS: Evansville—Andy McCauley; **Florence**—Fran Riordan; **Frontier**—Brent Metheny; **Gateway**—Phil Warren; **Joliet**—Mike Breyman; **Lake Erie**—Jeff Isom; **Normal**—Brooks Carey; **River City**—Steve Brook; **Rockford**—Richard Austin; **Schaumburg**—Jamie Bennett; **Southern Illinois**—Mike Pinto; **Traverse City**—Gregg Langbehn; **Washington**—Bart Zeller; **Windy City**—Ron Biga.

ALL-STARS: C—Landon Hernandez, Gateway. **1B**—Russell Moldenhauer, Lake Erie. **2B**—C.J. Beatty, Washington. **3B**—Jacob Tanis, Florence. **SS**—Patrick McKenna, Normal. **OF**—Jon Myers, Gateway; Nick Akins, Joliet; Daniel Bowman, Lake Erie. **DH**—Steve McQuail, Schaumburg.

SP—Scott Dunn, Traverse City. **RP**—Eric Massingham, Evansville.

MOST VALUABLE PLAYER: Jacob Tanis, Florence. **PITCHER OF THE YEAR:** Scott Dunn, Traverse City. **ROOKIE OF THE YEAR:** Danny Canela, River City. **MANAGER OF THE YEAR:** Jamie Bennett, Schaumburg.

BATTING LEADERS

PLAYER	TEAM	AVG	G	AB	R	H	HR	RBI
Canela, Danny	RIV	.360	67	225	38	81	12	53
Kremer, Jeff	RCK	.357	69	266	36	95	3	41
Mendez, Carlos	SOU	.337	93	380	57	128	4	50
Harrilchak, Cory	SOU	.332	61	211	45	70	5	33
McClendon, Chris	GAT	.327	82	309	66	101	7	49
Rhoney, Cory	SOU	.321	66	240	40	77	7	40
Mahley, Sean	SCH	.312	78	266	39	83	0	44
Bowman, Daniel	LER	.309	93	366	73	113	9	53
Beatty, C.J.	WSH	.305	96	351	65	107	18	66
Greener, Matt	RCK	.305	91	347	53	106	7	47

PITCHING LEADERS

PLAYER	TEAM	W	L	ERA	IP	H	BB	SO
Oros, Michael	FLO	7	5	2.16	87	73	39	80
Demmin, Ryan	NOR	6	5	2.20	98	77	23	90
Phelan, Chris	SCH	7	2	2.21	106	87	29	62
Rein, Matt	LER	8	6	2.37	121	99	34	89
Middendorf, Dave	LER	12	7	2.60	138	102	32	94
Dunn, Scott	TRA	15	1	2.61	124	120	29	73
Nation, Blake	SOU	11	2	2.61	117	84	66	78
Kuna, Matt	SCH	6	3	2.81	77	77	22	49
Rucinski, Drew	RCK	4	6	2.88	100	86	27	101
DeSimone, Daniel	FLO	8	4	2.92	86	83	21	57

EVANSVILLE OTTERS

PLAYER	POS	AVG	OBP	SLG	AB	R	H	HR	RBI	SB
Taylor Black	IF	.176	.298	.207	193	21	34	1	12	14
Andrew Clark	1B	.425	.535	.800	80	14	34	7	24	0
Chris Elder	OF	.311	.365	.466	103	13	32	2	17	6
Brian Erie	C	.294	.325	.349	109	9	32	0	7	0
C.J. Henry	OF	.332	.410	.523	214	38	71	4	29	9
J.R. Higley	OF	.228	.333	.377	114	13	26	3	14	1
Ryan Kresky	IF	.268	.357	.397	295	53	79	7	43	9
Ricardo Lizcano	OF	.243	.309	.336	214	22	52	2	15	1
Sam Mahoney	C	.185	.290	.185	27	3	5	0	2	0
James Mallard	1B	.196	.275	.261	46	2	9	1	8	0
Steve Marino	IF	.246	.288	.363	350	38	86	9	37	0
Frank Martinez	IF	.275	.327	.397	363	40	100	6	48	9
Jimmy Maxwell	1B	.194	.237	.250	36	3	7	0	1	0
Chris Munoz	IF	.182	.341	.212	33	3	6	0	3	1
John Nester	C	.287	.360	.490	286	40	82	5	28	2
John Schultz	OF	.289	.377	.438	336	63	97	4	30	4
Nick Schwaner	1B	.301	.373	.469	352	49	106	13	61	15
Jordan Tripp	OF	.200	.214	.309	55	2	11	0	2	0
Luis Uribe	OF	.233	.324	.233	30	5	7	0	2	0
Deaun Williams	OF	.107	.265	.107	28	0	3	0	2	3

PLAYER	W	L	ERA	G	GS	IP	H	BB	SO
Ricky Bowen	0	0	9.00	4	1	4	2	9	2
Anthony Collazo	3	2	3.33	28	4	49	44	23	55
Caleb Cuevas	0	4	6.91	15	0	14	16	9	9
Ryan Gibson	1	5	3.28	12	12	58	46	49	53
Pat Goelz	1	0	18.47	6	0	6	21	4	7
Mike Hanley	4	0	2.31	29	0	35	27	19	24
Rich Hawkins	1	5	6.15	13	7	41	67	13	19

	0	1	5.92	14	3	24	24	16	17
Michael Hepple	0	1	5.92	14	3	24	24	16	17
Josh Joseph	0	1	6.19	11	0	16	16	10	8
Christian Kowalchuk	0	1	30.86	4	0	2	7	2	2
Eric Massingham	3	1	1.25	35	0	36	34	10	37
Blake Monar	0	1	3.86	2	2	7	8	4	6
Bryce Morrow	6	2	3.30	11	11	71	64	13	59
Evan Mott	2	1	2.95	20	2	40	31	15	26
John Nester	0	0	4.50	2	0	2	1	2	2
Robert Ramer	3	1	3.93	6	6	34	30	8	11
Jason Ridenhour	0	1	3.32	14	3	22	20	18	18
Orlando Santos	2	1	2.48	34	0	40	34	24	33
Coty Saranthus	1	0	4.58	20	0	20	23	12	17
Alex Sunderland	0	0	8.68	11	0	9	8	16	12
Jose Velez	0	1	1.00	4	2	9	6	6	8
Trevor Walch	3	3	3.36	17	7	56	63	17	35
Scott Weismann	5	2	3.23	42	0	64	60	15	73
Kyle Wormington	0	0	7.94	3	0	6	7	2	2
Ryan Zamorsky	5	7	4.31	20	15	94	89	31	63
Matt Zielinski	9	7	3.40	20	20	124	117	39	114

FLORENCE FREEDOM

PLAYER	POS	AVG	OBP	SLG	AB	R	H	HR	RBI	SB
Junior Arrojo	IF	.262	.401	.364	343	71	90	4	34	39
Pablo Bermudez	OF	.266	.398	.339	218	36	58	2	25	7
Kyle Bluestein	OF	.164	.252	.261	134	16	22	3	17	5
David Carrillo	C	.091	.333	.091	11	1	1	0	3	0
Aljay Davis	IF	.250	.361	.330	112	17	28	1	17	6
J.C. Figueroa	IF	.200	.308	.222	90	9	18	0	4	1
Bo Folkinga	IF	.167	.250	.167	18	1	3	0	2	1
Eric Groff	IF	.282	.342	.451	71	15	20	2	18	6
Jeremy Hamilton	IF	.286	.385	.435	301	43	86	8	42	2
David Harris	OF	.272	.383	.467	345	55	94	14	51	13
Jim Jacquot	C	.246	.327	.392	309	46	76	8	42	3
Collin Janssen	C	.040	.111	.040	50	2	2	0	2	0
Wes Meadows	C	.222	.217	.190	21	2	4	0	3	0
Esteban Meletiche	IF	.205	.289	.281	171	27	35	1	15	8
Cole Miles	OF	.205	.244	.231	39	6	8	0	6	1
Gary Owens	OF	.294	.415	.382	34	4	10	0	5	4
Edwin Padua	IF	.286	.341	.314	35	3	10	0	4	0
Josh Richmond	OF	.267	.389	.467	15	2	4	0	0	0
Brian Sheehan	C	.250	.294	.313	16	2	4	0	0	1
Ryan Skellie	OF	.179	.246	.304	56	6	10	2	8	0
Nick Stein	OF	.291	.361	.455	55	4	16	2	7	4
Jacob Tanis	IF	.264	.326	.488	371	61	98	17	72	6
Bobby Joe Tannehill	IF	.210	.313	.310	100	9	21	1	9	1
Byron Wiley	OF	.290	.425	.490	314	66	91	15	53	11

PLAYER	W	L	ERA	G	GS	IP	H	BB	SO
Andres Caceres	0	0	16.88	4	2	5	7	13	3
Kit Carter	0	1	6.33	20	0	21	25	8	11
Brent Choban	4	6	4.95	26	7	56	68	39	39
Andy Clark	3	0	2.66	4	4	24	24	9	16
Jordan Conley	1	0	3.68	7	0	7	15	2	9
Corey Deighan	1	0	3.55	11	0	13	11	7	7
Daniel DeSimone	8	4	2.92	47	3	86	83	21	57
Justice French	0	2	5.61	6	6	26	28	10	14
Casey Henn	5	0	3.67	9	8	49	39	20	38
Dan Jensen	6	3	4.31	15	15	86	109	24	38
Jorge Marban	2	4	2.05	42	0	44	26	23	61
Brandon Mathes	5	7	4.78	39	5	70	65	35	67
Steve Matre	2	0	2.53	29	0	43	44	19	32
Michael Oros	7	5	2.16	21	13	87	73	39	80
Dan Osterbrock	1	3	4.81	4	4	24	29	4	21
Patrick Robinson	0	1	9.82	2	1	7	6	7	5
Andrew Strenge	0	0	0.00	2	0	5	5	1	3
Jose Velazquez	0	0	7.04	6	0	8	9	6	8
Chuck Weaver	4	2	3.70	14	12	73	81	23	41
Aaron Wilkerson	0	0	5.54	3	3	13	8	7	11

FRONTIER GREYS

PLAYER	POS	AVG	OBP	SLG	AB	R	H	HR	RBI	SB
Alex Williams	1B	.262	.324	.393	61	4	16	1	10	0
Michael Allen	C	.246	.329	.323	65	3	16	0	9	1
Calvin Anderson	IF	.297	.350	.378	37	2	11	0	0	0

INDEPENDENT LEAGUES

PLAYER	POS	AVG	OBP	SLG	AB	R	H	HR	RBI	SB
Eric Avila	IF	.243	.273	.357	185	24	45	2	24	1
Blake Bergeron	IF	.269	.316	.426	324	45	87	7	42	11
Mike Bolling	OF	.120	.241	.120	25	3	3	0	2	2
Nick DelGuidice	IF	.283	.317	.367	60	3	17	0	4	1
Bubba Dotson	OF	.229	.304	.313	48	9	11	1	5	2
Balbino Fuenmayor	IF	.322	.370	.554	177	26	57	11	32	5
Mike Gallic	OF	.202	.265	.348	89	11	18	2	11	5
Kenny Gilbert	OF	.103	.188	.138	29	1	3	0	1	0
Chris Kay	C	.149	.234	.223	94	6	14	1	10	1
Ryan Kiesel	IF	.222	.294	.244	45	7	10	0	2	0
Tyler Kolodny	IF	.219	.261	.500	64	12	14	5	10	1
Brock McCallister	IF	.242	.304	.309	285	37	69	1	25	3
Justin McDavid	C	.211	.237	.273	161	14	34	2	16	3
Esteban Meletiche	IF	.205	.289	.281	171	27	35	1	15	8
Mark Micowski	IF	.284	.357	.464	306	35	87	9	46	11
JJ Muse	OF	.234	.262	.342	269	29	63	7	31	2
Tillman Pugh	IF	.154	.211	.288	52	6	8	1	4	3
Alvaro Ramirez	OF	.239	.283	.313	310	42	74	2	20	17
Jonathan Sigado	IF	.265	.345	.286	49	6	13	0	4	1

PLAYER	W	L	ERA	G	GS	IP	H	BB	SO
Ryan Berry	1	2	11.48	13	0	13	23	12	4
Kyle Brady	3	2	3.77	40	0	60	55	37	72
Alfonso Cardenas	2	0	6.17	37	0	23	26	14	21
Matt Costello	2	9	4.45	22	14	91	105	28	74
Casey Delgado	2	6	3.51	15	13	67	56	29	57
Sean Hille	0	1	12.91	4	1	8	17	5	2
Graham Johnson	2	6	4.46	15	15	71	64	41	40
Jonathan Kountis	1	5	7.08	9	7	34	35	27	36
Devon Pearson	3	3	3.55	25	1	25	19	18	24
Mark Pope	3	2	3.14	11	10	52	49	11	32
Coty Saranthus	1	0	4.58	20	0	20	23	12	17
Bryce Shafer	0	5	4.54	38	0	40	41	20	39
Jon Shepard	1	4	3.02	47	0	54	48	19	40
Cole Stephens	1	1	4.60	3	3	16	19	5	12
Tyler Vaske	1	4	6.96	10	6	32	39	24	20
Dillon Wilson	0	4	5.49	26	3	41	47	25	30
Ryan Woolley	2	2	2.67	25	0	27	25	13	20
Eric Wooten	4	1	2.50	6	6	40	32	3	37
Justin Yackee	0	0	10.80	7	0	10	17	3	4
Joe Zeller	8	7	3.23	18	16	106	93	40	72

GATEWAY GRIZZLIES

PLAYER	POS	AVG	OBP	SLG	AB	R	H	HR	RBI	SB
Max Ayarza	IF	.186	.214	.221	113	8	21	0	9	1
Scott Dalrymple	C	.225	.267	.338	71	8	16	1	4	1
Antone Ramirez	OF	.330	.406	.470	215	41	71	5	27	12
Nick DeLorenzo	OF	.186	.222	.209	43	4	8	0	2	1
Vladimir Frias	IF	.275	.342	.456	204	28	56	7	33	11
Alex Guthrie	IF	.247	.346	.408	223	32	55	8	25	5
Landon Hernandez	C	.290	.366	.489	321	51	93	16	65	1
Jonathan Johnson	IF	.239	.384	.323	356	74	85	5	34	22
Sam Mahoney	C	.185	.290	.185	27	3	5	0	2	0
Chris McClendon	IF	.327	.415	.469	309	66	101	7	49	14
Jon Myers	OF	.283	.332	.560	361	56	102	25	64	2
Michael Pair	C	.211	.321	.361	180	18	38	6	28	3
Michael Wing	IF	.249	.292	.401	337	40	84	7	49	6

PLAYER	W	L	ERA	G	GS	IP	H	BB	SO
Edison Alvarez	0	2	8.68	2	2	9	13	5	4
Aaron Baker	1	4	7.04	12	4	31	46	7	19
Richard Barrett	2	2	3.15	35	0	34	25	16	33
Tim Brown	13	3	2.97	19	19	136	133	24	72
Rey Cotilla	0	0	7.16	15	0	16	20	10	14
Gregg Downing	2	3	6.26	8	8	42	44	37	41
Chris Enourato	2	2	7.54	12	3	29	32	21	20
Justin Erasmus	4	2	1.57	33	0	34	20	13	26
Jonathan Gonzalez	1	1	4.75	21	0	30	27	17	21
Clayton Hicks	0	1	12.15	3	1	7	8	6	9
Brett Higginbotham	2	3	2.63	30	3	51	38	10	24
Tucker Jensen	7	7	3.98	20	18	118	121	46	70
Logan Mahon	0	0	3.96	26	0	25	32	9	12
Ethan McKinzie	0	1	13.50	2	2	5	7	1	6
Matt Sergey	2	4	5.19	10	10	50	54	25	47
Jake Stephens	5	3	4.17	9	9	54	49	14	25
Zac Treece	5	3	2.13	41	0	51	38	26	57

JaVaun West	8	3	3.02	17	17	104	93	42	71
Luke Westphal	0	0	1.59	13	0	17	13	11	21

JOLIET SLAMMERS

PLAYER	POS	AVG	OBP	SLG	AB	R	H	HR	RBI	SB
Nick Akins	OF	.302	.403	.609	248	41	75	21	62	1
David Christensen	OF	.159	.263	.250	132	13	21	3	12	9
Zak Colby	C	.319	.397	.391	69	10	22	0	4	1
Kolin Conner	C	.203	.311	.283	138	13	28	2	8	0
Grant DeBruin	IF	.231	.310	.303	264	26	61	1	31	1
Erick Gaylord	OF	.150	.261	.200	20	2	3	0	0	3
Tyler Goodro	C	.182	.357	.182	22	4	4	0	2	0
Ben Hewett	C	.220	.301	.231	91	11	20	0	9	0
Goose Kallunki	IF	.275	.283	.333	51	1	14	0	8	0
Robby Kuzdale	OF	.125	.276	.125	24	1	3	0	2	1
Kyle Maunus	IF	.219	.354	.335	251	36	55	5	27	5
Joe Meggs	OF	.289	.353	.364	121	15	35	0	12	0
Marquis Riley	IF	.301	.343	.407	332	53	100	5	50	11
Darian Sandford	IF	.245	.321	.297	323	51	79	1	20	65
S. Schwindenhammer	OF	.208	.294	.335	173	23	36	5	19	0
Matthew Scruggs	OF	.161	.235	.226	31	4	5	0	3	0
Niko Vasquez	IF	.245	.317	.407	241	38	59	8	29	2
Nate Wilder	IF	.159	.270	.239	138	14	22	1	10	0
Javan Williams	OF	.250	.325	.292	72	9	18	1	7	5
Jerod Yakubik	OF	.244	.360	.321	271	38	66	3	25	2

PLAYER	W	L	ERA	G	GS	IP	H	BB	SO
Jairo Acevedo	0	0	0.00	4	0	4	5	2	5
Evan Anundsen	4	6	6.10	10	10	52	72	21	46
Mike Barsotti	2	3	3.16	24	5	63	49	25	48
Andrew Busby	0	6	3.08	10	8	53	45	24	44
Rey Cotilla	0	0	7.16	15	0	16	20	10	14
Chris DeBoo	0	0	5.52	7	0	15	22	3	7
Amalio Diaz	0	2	2.00	25	0	27	14	10	28
Matt Dillon	1	3	5.97	11	5	32	34	14	40
Chase Doremus	4	4	2.67	42	2	64	46	23	76
Anthony Figliolia	0	0	9.00	3	0	4	9	0	2
Jonathan Gonzalez	1	1	4.75	21	0	30	27	17	21
Lucas Goodgion	1	2	3.82	36	0	35	38	24	37
Ian Haley	0	1	14.90	3	2	10	13	7	9
Ryan Hartman	0	1	3.52	27	0	31	23	25	28
Shawn Kale	5	5	3.81	24	15	102	95	41	95
Corey Kimes	4	7	5.56	23	15	89	101	41	57
Seth Lintz	0	0	10.13	2	0	3	6	4	1
Chuck Lofgren	7	7	4.27	19	18	99	89	57	72
Hart Mizell	0	0	5.19	6	0	9	12	8	6
Jacob Sanchez	2	2	2.36	5	4	27	18	6	29
Jason Sullivan	3	1	4.19	32	0	39	38	19	27
Brian Valente	0	0	18.00	2	0	2	5	4	0
Brett Zawacki	6	7	4.56	30	11	81	89	29	85

LAKE ERIE CRUSHERS

PLAYER	POS	AVG	OBP	SLG	AB	R	H	HR	RBI	SB
Kevin Berard	IF	.242	.316	.329	231	24	56	2	19	18
Daniel Bowman	OF	.309	.360	.495	366	73	113	9	53	21
Max Casper	IF	.231	.311	.252	234	31	54	0	14	4
Andrew Davis	IF	.252	.316	.463	365	53	92	17	66	3
Gauntlett Eldemire	OF	.253	.309	.333	87	8	22	0	5	2
J.C. Figueroa	IF	.200	.308	.222	90	9	18	0	4	1
Seth Granger	OF	.261	.333	.375	283	32	74	4	39	11
Craig Hertler	OF	.296	.416	.389	321	60	95	1	35	18
Anderson Hidalgo	IF	.281	.354	.371	310	24	87	3	37	3
Vincent Mejia	IF	.167	.219	.200	30	1	5	0	3	0
Russell Moldenhauer	IF	.275	.355	.474	346	55	95	14	54	3
Emmanuel Quiles	C	.237	.272	.324	241	30	57	2	23	2
David Roney	C	.121	.304	.143	91	9	11	0	3	2
Juan Sanchez	IF	.231	.306	.283	321	30	74	1	29	11

PLAYER	W	L	ERA	G	GS	IP	H	BB	SO
Adam Beach	3	1	4.08	8	6	29	33	14	14
Ricky Bowen	0	0	9.00	4	1	4	2	9	2
Spencer Clifft	0	0	4.22	3	1	11	11	5	8
Dale Dickerson	1	2	4.50	41	0	40	34	23	33
Brad Duffy	2	2	2.88	31	1	41	35	13	38
Michael Jahns	1	1	8.31	11	0	13	9	13	9
Mickey Jannis	7	2	2.42	24	4	74	58	26	56

Alex Kaminsky	7	5	3.28	19	19	110	100	40	79
Ben Klafczynski	0	1	8.44	9	0	11	10	7	8
Trevor Longfellow	2	2	6.96	5	4	22	18	12	15
Dave Middendorf	12	7	2.60	21	19	138	102	32	94
Matt Rein	8	6	2.37	20	18	121	99	34	89
Devyn Rivera	0	1	5.59	3	2	10	11	9	8
Kyle Shaw	0	1	11.57	1	1	5	9	1	4
Doug Shields	0	0	3.57	13	0	18	16	6	8
Brandon Smith	2	1	1.35	13	0	20	13	2	19
Matt Smith	5	6	4.36	22	17	99	100	45	70
Jordan Wellander	4	2	2.31	35	0	51	32	19	52
Connor Whalen	2	0	1.80	19	0	25	23	12	25
Jason Wilson	4	5	5.20	19	17	97	109	21	59

NORMAL CORNBELTERS

PLAYER	POS	AVG	OBP	SLG	AB	R	H	HR	RBI	SB
Eric Arce	OF	.176	.364	.294	34	3	6	1	4	1
Santiago Chirino	IF	.254	.303	.316	323	36	82	3	27	17
Luis De La Cruz	C	.154	.233	.205	39	0	6	0	3	1
Adam Derner	IF	.158	.238	.158	19	2	3	0	1	0
Aaron Dudley	OF	.289	.400	.495	97	12	28	4	12	0
Steven Felix	OF	.209	.281	.349	86	15	18	3	19	3
Oscar Garcia	OF	.267	.330	.362	210	21	56	3	23	18
T.J. Gavlik	IF	.224	.277	.347	219	26	49	4	28	5
Ryan Lashley	IF	.241	.293	.312	170	20	41	2	15	6
Keoni Manago	OF	.291	.331	.355	327	40	95	1	25	12
Jason Matusik	OF	.229	.325	.329	70	10	16	1	11	2
Patrick McKenna	IF	.281	.393	.572	285	57	80	18	60	8
David Medina	OF	.281	.363	.427	89	11	25	4	13	2
Mike Mobbs	OF	.169	.303	.225	89	9	15	1	11	4
Rogelio Noris	OF	.211	.287	.278	90	9	19	1	5	1
Luis Parache	IF	.220	.308	.353	255	33	56	6	28	7
David Remedios	C	.143	.143	.250	28	1	4	0	2	0
Romulo Ruiz	IF	.245	.295	.431	102	13	25	5	25	0
Alex San Juan	C	.343	.361	.400	35	5	12	0	4	0
Mike Schwartz	IF	.264	.373	.425	360	67	95	12	42	10
Tyler Shover	C	.283	.360	.361	180	17	51	1	24	11
Devin Thaut	IF	.212	.317	.250	52	5	11	0	1	0
Jenzen Torres	C	.120	.267	.213	75	8	9	1	3	0
Chris Wilson	C	.133	.188	.167	30	3	4	0	1	1
Matt Wright	OF	.167	.227	.322	90	12	15	2	7	1

PLAYER	W	L	ERA	G	GS	IP	H	BB	SO
Jason Boyer	0	0	3.06	17	0	18	16	12	21
Ross Davis	3	5	4.67	19	3	44	48	27	48
Ryan Demmin	6	5	2.20	14	14	98	77	23	90
Sean Gregory	0	0	5.40	7	0	8	10	3	2
Kyle Hassna	1	0	2.28	5	5	28	27	10	20
Josh Joseph	0	1	6.19	11	0	16	16	10	8
Tyler Lavigne	4	8	3.89	18	18	104	98	50	60
Jacob Liedka	2	1	3.80	24	4	47	55	22	50
Mitch Mormann	4	6	3.63	34	0	57	48	26	39
Luis Noel	6	5	4.52	14	14	84	73	35	71
Alan Oaks	2	4	1.99	37	0	50	31	19	59
Drew Provence	6	6	3.06	18	18	112	100	42	81
Michael Schweiss	5	4	3.79	19	12	95	101	17	58
Matt Suschak	0	0	11.57	3	0	2	6	2	2
Jose Trinidad	6	6	4.55	22	8	65	59	48	62
Casey Upperman	1	0	3.97	8	0	11	7	8	17
Benjamin Weil	0	0	3.78	9	0	17	13	9	16

RIVER CITY RASCALS

PLAYER	POS	AVG	OBP	SLG	AB	R	H	HR	RBI	SB
Bryan Aanderud	IF	.286	.318	.286	21	0	6	0	2	0
Jake Atwell	OF	.257	.319	.339	280	24	72	3	34	9
Will Block	2B	.241	.354	.447	311	51	75	13	45	12
Sean Borman	IF	.268	.393	.358	123	13	33	1	13	2
Danny Canela	C	.360	.455	.582	225	38	81	12	53	0
Steve Carrillo	IF	.222	.288	.331	266	32	59	4	35	7
Evan Crawford	OF	.301	.381	.382	259	41	78	1	26	30
Bo Cuthbertson	IF	.184	.311	.184	38	3	7	0	1	3
Scott Dalrymple	C	.225	.267	.338	71	8	16	1	4	1
Andrew Edge	C	.150	.292	.200	20	3	3	0	0	0
Anthony Foulk	C	.200	.288	.231	65	8	13	0	2	2
Ben Hewett	C	.220	.301	.231	91	11	20	0	9	0

Johnny Morales	IF	.238	.317	.297	286	43	68	1	24	9
Curran Redal	OF	.291	.345	.350	374	43	109	2	48	25
Andy Scott	IF	.282	.378	.359	39	6	11	0	5	2
Jason Taylor	IF	.169	.355	.337	83	18	14	3	11	4
Eric Williams	OF	.253	.424	.299	304	63	77	1	19	14
Phil Wunderlich	IF	.264	.321	.413	375	46	99	14	64	3

PLAYER	W	L	ERA	G	GS	IP	H	BB	SO
Casey Barnes	7	3	3.68	20	20	120	140	29	66
Cameron Bayne	0	1	19.80	2	1	5	12	1	2
Drew Benes	2	2	6.46	7	7	31	35	11	21
Cory Caruso	5	2	4.02	13	10	63	64	23	42
Patrick Crider	3	1	2.97	49	0	36	40	6	38
Brandon Cunniff	0	0	0.00	12	0	12	4	3	23
Kaleb Engelke	0	0	0.00	10	0	3	1	5	4
Craig Goodman	7	3	3.81	17	17	102	98	26	77
Ray Hanson	4	1	4.85	8	4	30	19	12	32
Brett Harman	0	5	3.27	6	6	33	35	5	30
Chandler Jagodzinski	2	3	2.20	37	0	57	39	11	49
Nick Kennedy	3	3	2.44	51	0	59	50	16	64
Dan Lazzaroni	1	1	7.20	12	0	15	20	15	8
Jon Levin	1	1	2.74	27	0	23	22	8	11
Tommy Mendoza	4	8	6.51	18	18	86	106	32	62
Kyle Owings	6	3	3.48	29	1	52	41	16	40
Justin Sarratt	2	5	5.55	10	10	49	57	19	38
Gabriel Shaw	2	3	2.54	45	0	50	50	8	49
Doug Shields	0	0	3.57	13	0	18	16	6	8
Alex Sunderland	0	0	8.68	11	0	9	8	16	12
Andy Urban	4	0	5.27	18	1	27	30	8	20
Andrew Virgili	0	1	10.50	3	1	6	6	6	5
Ryan Wilkins	0	0	9.39	4	0	8	16	2	9
Kelii Zablan	0	1	15.88	7	0	6	14	8	4

ROCKFORD AVIATORS

PLAYER	POS	AVG	OBP	SLG	AB	R	H	HR	RBI	SB
Eric Bainer	C	.270	.356	.381	63	10	17	0	5	0
Brian Bistagne	IF	.280	.356	.364	143	25	40	1	16	2
Jeremy Boyd	OF	.103	.188	.103	29	1	3	0	0	0
Kenny Bryant	IF	.261	.332	.372	352	38	92	6	45	14
Edgar Corcino	OF	.312	.384	.482	218	34	68	6	28	9
Ray Delvalle	IF	.232	.328	.321	56	6	13	0	2	2
Gabe DeMarco	C	.269	.360	.352	108	8	29	0	13	1
Aritz Garcia	SS	.165	.258	.200	85	10	14	0	6	1
Matt Greener	IF	.305	.350	.432	347	53	106	7	47	2
Ray Hernandez	IF	.228	.353	.263	57	9	13	0	2	2
Will Howard	OF	.161	.212	.161	31	4	5	0	1	0
Michael Hur	OF	.273	.323	.379	330	49	90	3	40	9
Nash Hutter	IF	.182	.182	.182	11	0	2	0	2	0
Jeff Kremer	OF	.357	.436	.444	266	36	95	3	41	5
Chase Larsson	OF	.185	.333	.407	54	6	10	3	10	0
Jake Luce	LF	.000	.063	.000	15	0	0	0	1	0
Jeremy Mayo	IF	.000	.059	.000	16	0	0	0	0	0
Mike Mergenthaler	OF	.122	.163	.146	41	2	5	0	0	0
Brandon Newton	IF	.276	.352	.356	239	39	66	1	22	7
Ted Obregon	SS	.197	.287	.260	127	17	25	1	9	5
Elvin Rodriguez	SS	.175	.293	.254	114	16	20	1	6	2
Tyler Smith	C	.229	.292	.264	140	11	32	0	14	0
Joseph Taylor	IF	.000	.167	.000	10	0	0	0	0	0
Greg Van Horn	C	.173	.311	.204	98	9	17	0	8	3
Cohl Walla	OF	.222	.333	.370	27	4	6	1	4	2

PLAYER	W	L	ERA	G	GS	IP	H	BB	SO
Nick Anderson	5	10	6.42	16	16	81	94	38	69
Kyle Brueggemann	0	0	1.29	10	0	14	5	5	19
Nick Cicio	4	6	4.10	29	8	75	69	23	86
Jordan Cudney	0	1	8.31	4	1	4	8	3	1
Jesus Del Rosario	1	1	4.56	16	1	26	28	15	26
Matt Frahm	6	1	3.05	37	0	41	37	12	20
Garrett Granitz	0	2	12.27	5	0	4	11	2	0
Nick Grim	2	4	5.01	17	7	50	51	31	26
Jon Gulbransen	1	6	4.72	11	11	61	66	19	48
Trevor Harden	2	4	3.28	22	11	82	84	23	77
Seafth Howe	4	5	5.75	23	13	81	94	27	75
Connor Little	0	1	9.53	8	0	11	18	3	13
Dan Meyer	2	1	3.55	5	4	25	25	12	20
Jake Nicholson	0	3	4.25	22	0	30	31	16	19

INDEPENDENT LEAGUES

PLAYER	W	L	ERA	G	GS	IP	H	BB	SO
Nathan OBryan	1	1	6.44	35	0	36	45	14	23
Drew Rucinski	4	6	2.88	15	15	100	86	27	101
Josh Schneider	0	0	3.54	9	1	20	20	13	21
Hayden Shirley	0	0	9.00	7	0	8	6	14	11
Andrew Snowdon	3	2	0.94	22	0	29	21	7	28
Derrick Stultz	1	4	7.08	10	8	41	50	20	22
Alex Sunderland	0	0	8.68	11	0	9	8	16	12
Kelley Wagner	0	2	10.57	6	0	8	12	5	4

SCHAUMBURG BOOMERS

PLAYER	POS	AVG	OBP	SLG	AB	R	H	HR	RBI	SB
Ryan Brockett	IF	.333	.368	.333	18	1	6	0	0	0
Alexi Colon	OF	.255	.332	.417	247	35	63	5	31	5
Jordan Dean	IF	.275	.344	.325	200	28	55	0	18	8
Mike Demperio	IF	.179	.247	.239	67	9	12	0	3	1
Bubba Dotson	OF	.229	.304	.313	48	9	11	1	5	2
Gerard Hall	SS	.273	.331	.441	363	50	99	10	51	3
Sean Mahley	OF	.312	.397	.406	266	39	83	0	44	17
Bobby Martin	OF	.177	.336	.250	96	27	17	1	13	5
Brian McConkey	IF	.246	.323	.380	329	45	81	6	44	9
Steve McQuail	IF	.296	.390	.548	345	62	102	20	58	5
Chad Mozingo	OF	.295	.352	.406	244	36	72	5	31	10
Ty Nelson	C	.231	.325	.315	143	18	33	0	12	1
Frank Pfister	3B	.234	.272	.326	350	36	82	3	43	13
Michael Valadez	C	.286	.333	.329	213	25	61	0	25	2
Justin Vasquez	OF	.268	.359	.412	325	60	87	7	40	7
Keith Werman	IF	.197	.265	.224	76	10	15	0	3	3

PLAYER	W	L	ERA	G	GS	IP	H	BB	SO
Chris Armstrong	0	0	6.00	8	0	15	20	8	10
James Bierlein	2	1	3.77	35	0	45	36	18	47
Edwin Carl	0	0	0.00	2	1	6	3	2	5
Tony Delmonico	1	1	5.35	17	5	37	40	18	31
Kaleb Engelke	0	0	0.00	10	0	3	1	5	4
Mike Giovenco	9	7	3.85	24	19	115	112	57	95
Cody Griebling	5	5	4.97	15	15	83	89	29	43
Preston Hatcher	2	3	4.30	23	0	23	22	18	22
Danny Jimenez	2	4	3.90	10	10	55	58	19	48
James Jones	0	0	6.75	3	0	3	3	2	3
Matt Kuna	6	3	2.81	26	11	77	77	22	49
Clark Labitan	2	1	1.29	22	0	28	18	8	25
Matt LaMothe	1	0	5.14	6	1	14	21	7	8
Dan Lazzaroni	1	1	7.20	12	0	15	20	15	8
Sean Mahley	1	0	2.76	18	0	16	14	8	15
Joe Parsons	1	2	11.64	4	4	19	34	7	18
Delvin Perez	0	0	2.35	8	0	8	3	11	7
Chris Phelan	7	2	2.21	19	16	106	87	29	62
Dexter Price	6	1	2.16	37	0	42	37	7	36
Josh Renfro	0	0	13.50	5	0	7	11	4	4
Jose Rodriguez	1	0	3.38	3	0	3	3	2	2
Shawn Sanford	10	6	2.97	21	19	130	116	39	100
Adam Tollefson	3	1	3.68	16	0	15	13	5	12
Seth Webster	6	1	2.40	11	11	75	63	13	52

SOUTHERN ILLINOIS MINERS

PLAYER	POS	AVG	OBP	SLG	AB	R	H	HR	RBI	SB
Logan Brumley	IF	.053	.122	.053	38	2	2	0	2	1
Phil Butler	C	.212	.259	.282	273	28	58	3	29	2
Andrew Cohn	IF	.269	.338	.363	182	31	49	2	18	3
Carlos Colmenares	OF	.258	.296	.320	178	25	46	3	17	2
Ryan Curl	OF	.161	.212	.161	31	4	5	0	1	1
Scott Dalrymple	C	.225	.267	.338	71	8	16	1	4	1
Jon Eisen	IF	.252	.361	.285	123	19	31	0	10	7
Jason Ganek	IF	.232	.365	.343	181	25	42	3	26	4
Ken Gregory	OF	.263	.318	.389	262	24	69	4	43	1
Tyler Hall	OF	.243	.330	.335	173	33	42	1	9	6
Cory Harrilchak	OF	.332	.453	.450	211	45	70	5	33	20
Danny Hernandez	IF	.204	.250	.278	54	8	11	1	13	1
Cannon Lester	IF	.283	.368	.432	329	43	93	3	43	7
Steven Liddle	OF	.265	.352	.404	223	31	59	6	24	6
Carlos Mendez	IF	.337	.375	.437	380	57	128	4	50	3
Jereme Milons	OF	.280	.376	.369	268	40	75	2	32	11
Austin Montgomery	OF	.083	.083	.083	12	1	1	0	1	0

PLAYER	POS	AVG	OBP	SLG	AB	R	H	HR	RBI	SB
Corey Rhoney	IF	.321	.383	.471	240	40	77	7	40	4
Shane Street	C	.206	.229	.206	34	1	7	0	1	0
Tyler Stubblefield	IF	.305	.376	.486	105	16	32	2	12	3
Trevor Whyte	IF	.250	.382	.429	28	4	7	1	1	0

PLAYER	W	L	ERA	G	GS	IP	H	BB	SO
Jon Mark Abbey	0	2	5.06	14	0	16	23	8	9
Wes Alsup	0	0	3.50	18	0	18	11	17	30
Drew Bailey	0	2	11.37	4	1	6	7	5	8
Travis Bradshaw	3	0	2.84	13	12	70	61	22	47
Michael Carden	0	5	4.76	24	3	53	55	26	35
John Colella	2	0	2.05	22	0	26	19	23	22
Matt Crim	2	6	6.57	21	11	62	88	24	47
Brandon Cunniff	0	0	0.00	12	0	12	4	3	21
Nelson Curry	0	1	13.50	5	0	5	7	6	2
Jason Ganek	0	0	4.50	2	0	2	4	1	1
Bryant George	0	0	2.46	4	0	4	4	3	3
Cody Hall	4	5	4.81	16	10	67	78	26	21
Trevor Harden	2	4	3.28	22	11	82	84	23	77
Michael Hepple	0	1	5.92	14	3	24	24	16	17
Bobby Hurst	0	0	4.50	4	0	4	2	4	5
Brett Kennedy	1	1	9.39	6	4	23	35	12	7
Cannon Lester	0	0	9.00	4	0	4	4	1	2
Blake Nation	11	2	2.61	19	19	117	84	66	78
Race Parmenter	3	1	0.57	20	0	32	16	11	27
Pete Perez	4	3	3.03	27	1	39	34	18	41
Dayne Quist	8	4	3.16	27	11	88	81	33	59
Matt Royal	0	0	9.00	3	0	4	7	1	2
Matthew Sergey	0	1	4.32	16	0	17	14	8	24
Hayden Simpson	0	1	15.96	3	2	7	17	5	4
Richard Sullivan	2	4	5.40	9	8	47	55	13	33
Ronald Uviedo	1	0	2.79	17	0	19	19	5	23
Preston Vancil	9	6	3.97	18	18	107	97	49	63
Kyle Wahl	1	1	3.24	9	0	8	6	5	8

TRAVERSE CITY BEACH BUMS

PLAYER	POS	AVG	OBP	SLG	AB	R	H	HR	RBI	SB
Jeremy Banks	IF	.263	.328	.342	114	9	30	1	13	2
Chase Burch	1B	.264	.387	.481	318	61	84	15	66	3
Chris Cowell	C	.198	.325	.310	126	12	25	3	11	0
Sean Gusrang	IF	.229	.308	.348	328	35	75	8	40	1
Andrew Heck	SS	.200	.227	.250	40	2	8	0	5	2
Matt Howard	OF	.270	.348	.389	185	23	50	4	16	14
D'Marcus Ingram	OF	.144	.304	.222	90	10	13	1	6	3
Zach Kometani	C	.270	.317	.436	344	42	93	8	58	2
Marcus Nidiffer	C	.220	.325	.371	232	37	51	6	26	1
Ryan Still	IF	.187	.411	.260	289	56	54	0	20	2
Carlo Testa	OF	.271	.325	.436	280	47	76	7	42	31
Jose Vargas	3B	.262	.315	.464	321	49	84	12	57	9
Scott Woodward	OF	.224	.332	.350	183	30	41	2	16	10
Taylor Wrenn	IF	.288	.312	.473	243	44	70	8	43	3

PLAYER	W	L	ERA	G	GS	IP	H	BB	SO
Vladimir Camacho	0	0	3.86	2	0	2	1	4	5
Nick Capito	3	0	0.71	40	0	63	32	22	65
Jacob Clem	6	7	5.35	18	12	79	97	17	31
Michael Devine	6	2	3.95	19	15	87	80	34	65
Scott Dunn	15	1	2.61	20	20	124	120	29	73
Jason Mattila	0	0	5.00	7	0	9	13	4	2
Matt Miller	2	4	2.18	35	0	54	40	14	38
Burny Mitchem	0	4	3.67	26	1	42	34	24	40
Andrew Morris	0	1	6.75	2	1	5	7	5	2
Scott Mueller	0	1	7.56	7	0	8	12	3	6
Johnny Omahen	8	9	3.37	21	19	115	103	41	78
Ben Rawding	2	0	1.64	11	5	38	29	16	37
Jake Sabol	10	6	3.19	21	21	127	131	29	65
Chris Squires	1	2	2.60	33	0	55	37	18	61
Kyle Teague	2	4	5.06	15	2	32	34	20	33

WASHINGTON WILD THINGS

PLAYER	POS	AVG	OBP	SLG	AB	R	H	HR	RBI	SB
C.J. Beatty	IF	.305	.378	.550	351	65	107	18	66	7
Gus Benusa	OF	.231	.294	.333	108	17	25	2	14	8
Nick Boggan	IF	.228	.237	.298	57	10	13	1	2	0

Chris Costantino	IF	.125	.125	.125	16	2	2	0	0	1
Calvin Culver	OF	.133	.176	.133	15	0	2	0	4	0
Rick Devereaux	C	.139	.162	.167	36	0	5	0	4	0
Matt Fleishman	OF	.118	.167	.118	17	1	2	0	0	2
Maxx Garrett	C	.154	.250	.333	39	3	6	1	6	1
Andrew Heck	OF	.182	.270	.182	33	2	6	0	3	1
Stewart Ijames	OF	.297	.359	.560	316	50	94	16	45	2
Scott Kalamar	OF	.185	.256	.229	157	13	29	0	9	2
Quincy Latimore	OF	.232	.308	.371	151	20	35	6	22	5
Mario Mercedes	C	.242	.280	.261	207	9	50	1	18	0
Matt Mirabal	C	.219	.296	.274	73	9	16	1	6	2
AJ Nunziato	SS	.269	.338	.444	297	38	80	6	37	5
Jovan Rosa	IF	.284	.332	.432	303	35	86	7	37	0
Mark Samuelson	IF	.247	.332	.429	296	37	73	12	39	4
Shain Stoner	IF	.231	.341	.378	294	43	68	9	35	9
Jim Vahalik	C	.260	.329	.389	131	21	34	3	12	2
Tim Williams	OF	.370	.433	.370	27	2	10	0	1	1

PLAYER	W	L	ERA	G	GS	IP	H	BB	SO
Shawn Blackwell	4	10	5.36	19	18	101	99	59	54
Pat Butler	1	2	4.15	7	0	9	14	3	8
Amalio Diaz	0	2	2.00	25	0	27	14	10	28
Tyler Elrod	2	0	4.43	5	3	22	18	12	24
Zach Fleshman	1	2	3.00	26	1	33	36	15	22
Dan Goldstein	1	2	5.33	8	4	27	27	21	23
Justin Hall	2	0	0.53	2	2	17	8	3	9
Michael Hepple	0	1	5.92	14	3	24	24	16	17
Zach LeBarron	3	2	3.91	5	5	23	24	11	14
Gary Lee	5	9	4.20	21	20	135	144	21	91
Steve Messner	0	1	4.70	8	0	8	10	6	5
Jhonny Montoya	3	3	4.41	25	2	35	23	28	24
Matt Phillips	3	3	2.96	40	0	46	29	23	44
Dayne Quist	8	4	3.16	27	11	88	81	33	59
William Scott	1	2	5.28	11	0	15	15	7	13
Shawn Smith	3	5	5.43	13	13	66	68	37	61
Andy Smithmyer	0	1	5.87	13	1	15	10	12	10
Alfonso Yevoli	1	1	6.65	12	0	22	27	4	25

WINDY CITY THUNDERBOLTS

PLAYER	POS	AVG	OBP	SLG	AB	R	H	HR	RBI	SB
Zach Aakhus	C	.301	.405	.410	322	47	97	6	38	0
Andrew Brauer	OF	.271	.338	.375	317	47	86	3	37	15
Evan Button	IF	.272	.323	.427	302	42	82	8	43	14
John Clark	IF	.091	.167	.091	11	0	1	0	1	0
Chad Cregar	1B	.218	.306	.387	266	36	58	11	39	3
Adam Davis	C	.248	.321	.317	101	8	25	0	5	2
Lyndon Estill	OF	.237	.275	.289	38	2	9	0	2	2
C.J. Gillman	IF	.230	.284	.264	87	11	20	0	6	4
Jeff Harkensee	OF	.279	.413	.377	61	12	17	1	9	2
Doug Joyce	C	.228	.330	.358	232	28	53	6	38	3
Nathan Pittman	OF	.160	.282	.200	100	14	16	1	5	4
Jayce Ray	OF	.286	.393	.321	112	16	32	0	13	5
Anthony Renteria	OF	.091	.167	.091	11	0	1	0	0	0
Kyle Robinson	OF	.307	.337	.429	163	21	50	3	22	6
Ryan Soares	IF	.290	.323	.369	379	41	110	3	49	7
Louie Templeton	IF	.250	.321	.282	124	13	31	0	9	2
Nathan Tomaszewski	IF	.179	.273	.231	39	8	7	0	2	2
Mike Torres	IF	.262	.345	.325	363	50	95	3	43	26
Chase Tucker	IF	.224	.313	.296	98	17	22	0	10	6
Miles Walding	IF	.156	.265	.195	128	13	20	0	8	9

PLAYER	W	L	ERA	G	GS	IP	H	BB	SO
Jared Christensen	0	0	9.82	4	0	4	7	3	2
Tyler Claburn	2	1	5.34	30	0	30	45	15	26
Michael Click	3	0	0.90	46	0	50	34	19	71
Rey Cotilla	0	0	7.16	15	0	16	20	10	14
Daniel Cropper	8	5	4.33	19	18	116	117	24	61
Evan DeLuca	0	1	20.77	4	0	4	10	4	2
Rich Hawkins	1	5	6.15	13	7	41	67	13	19
Mark Kuzma	0	0	4.15	6	0	4	2	5	4
Reese McGraw	2	3	2.83	33	0	35	26	14	44
Andy Mee	0	2	3.18	14	0	17	14	9	25
Dyllon Nuernberg	6	1	2.68	15	10	74	61	32	72
Colin OConnell	3	0	1.39	19	0	39	33	10	25
Brian Oliver	5	9	4.58	19	19	108	120	42	65
Mike Recchia	1	3	3.70	5	5	32	26	14	47

Jake Roberts	1	1	1.66	17	0	22	15	13	11
Jessie Snodgrass	3	0	1.93	26	0	33	20	12	25
Markus Solbach	5	1	3.27	10	5	41	39	11	35
Travis Strong	1	5	6.23	8	8	39	49	16	42
Travis Tingle	5	6	4.18	21	17	97	118	26	64
Wes Torrez	0	0	2.25	4	0	8	5	2	8
Blayne Weller	0	1	0.79	2	2	11	7	6	18
Matt Wickswat	7	11	4.82	20	20	116	113	54	99
Kyle Zegarac	0	0	7.94	4	0	6	10	3	3

PACIFIC ASSOCIATION

The San Rafael Pacifics dominated the Pacific Association regular season, but that meant very little in a one-game, winner-takes-all championship. With the title on the line, Na Koa Ikaika Maui knocked off San Rafael 6-1.

Maui starter Jesse Smith held San Rafael to two hits in seven innings. Tucker Cordova picked up the save with two scoreless innings of work.

STANDINGS	W	L	PCT	GB
San Rafael	54	21	.720	—
Maui	46	29	.613	8
Vallejo	26	32	.448	19.5
Hawaii	27	39	.410	22.5
East Bay	7	29	.194	27.5

PLAYOFFS: SEMIFINALS—Maui defeated Vallejo in one-game playoff.
FINALS—Maui defeated San Rafael in one-game playoff.

UNITED LEAGUE

The United League continues to survive, it's still working on figuring out how to thrive.

Edinburg beat Fort Worth three games to two in the championship series for its first United League title after two previous trips to the United League championship series.

But that was a happy ending to what was a rough summer for the league. The league's website has been inactive for more than a year. The Alexandria Aces club was shut down 48 games into the season thanks to low attendance in a ballpark where some sections of the stands were closed because of concerns about their structural integrity. The league shut down the McAllen Thunder, a travel team, at the same time so the league played the rest of the season with four teams.

STANDINGS	W	L	PCT	GB
Fort Worth Cats	49	30	.620	—
*Alexandria Aces	24	20	.545	7.5
Edinburg Roadrunners	40	39	.506	9
San Angelo Colts	39	40	.494	10
Rio Grande Valley WhiteWings	32	43	.427	15
*McAllen Thunder	18	29	.383	15

*Did not complete season

PLAYOFFS: Finals—Edinburg defeated Fort Worth 3-2 in best-of-5 series.

ATTENDANCE: Fort Worth 90,058; Edinburg 48,871; San Angelo 45,478; Rio Grande Valley 38,202; Alexandria 7,660.

BATTING LEADERS

PLAYER	TEAM	AVG	G	AB	R	H	HR	RBI
Dziomba, Jon	SAN	.354	79	328	59	116	2	39
Newell, Austin	ALX	.340	41	141	38	48	4	36
Davis, Aljay	FTW	.337	54	196	52	66	1	24
Whyte, Trevor	EDB	.327	57	223	32	73	1	23
Ellison, Chris	FTW	.322	72	273	43	88	2	51
Carpen, Albert	RGV	.319	75	273	52	87	0	46
Monger, Cam	FTW	.318	71	255	46	81	3	40

Player	Team	AVG	G	AB	R	H	HR	RBI
Mahin, Nick	ALX	.313	42	150	40	47	3	31
Bergin, David	FTW	.310	73	274	53	85	19	66
Hicks, Joe	SAN	.309	75	285	51	88	4	50

PITCHING LEADERS

PLAYER	TEAM	W	L	ERA	IP	H	BB	SO
Kennedy, Brett	RGV	6	3	2.67	84	70	22	58
Wilkerson, Aaron	FTW	9	1	2.74	76	58	37	97
Camilli, Curtis	EDB	7	5	2.9	96	87	35	82
Jones, Jon	ALX	4	1	3.18	51	36	26	51
Banks, Demetrius	SAN	4	3	3.49	90	93	31	72
Loseke, Mike	EDB	6	2	3.68	81	90	30	43
Sheridan, Eric	SAN	8	3	3.71	90	88	38	68
Stephens, Cole	FTW	7	2	3.95	100	105	27	55
Smouse, A.J.	RGV	4	7	4.36	85	105	29	45
Frerichs, Corey	SAN	5	6	4.5	88	90	29	58

ALEXANDRIA ACES

PLAYER	POS	AVG	OBP	SLG	AB	R	H	HR	RBI	SB
Josh Band	2B	.310	.444	.379	87	18	27	0	6	7
Eldred Barnett	CF	.161	.235	.258	31	5	5	1	1	3
Chad Bunting	OF	.242	.348	.311	132	20	32	1	18	10
Zack Cadet	RF	.227	.345	.362	141	27	32	3	21	10
Alex Foltz	OF	.247	.344	.299	77	13	19	0	7	3
Doug Freeman	C	.186	.288	.243	140	16	26	2	12	1
Ryan Gasporra	C	.254	.438	.352	71	10	18	1	11	1
Daiki Komori	OF	.286	.394	.393	28	4	8	1	3	1
Craig Littleman	IF	.175	.250	.300	40	2	7	0	3	0
Nick Mahin	1B	.313	.446	.447	150	40	47	3	31	2
Trevor McDonald	2B	.167	.244	.179	78	9	13	0	6	1
Eddie Murray	SS	.283	.457	.363	113	35	32	1	15	13
Austin Newell	LF	.340	.487	.532	141	38	48	4	36	1
Brandon Spencer	C	.208	.269	.292	24	3	5	0	3	1
Jason Thomas	2B	.217	.357	.391	23	4	5	1	2	0

PLAYER	W	L	ERA	G	GS	IP	H	BB	SO
Michael Calderon	2	0	4.50	7	0	8	7	1	8
Brandon Creath	0	0	3.00	5	0	6	6	7	12
Aryo Fleming	0	1	12.00	4	2	12	22	11	10
Gabe Grammer	1	4	5.79	18	0	19	18	13	31
Jon Jones	4	1	3.18	11	9	51	36	26	51
James LoPresti	0	0	2.70	3	0	3	5	5	4
Andrew Loynaz	0	1	23.14	3	0	2	4	7	4
Leo Madrid	3	3	3.93	21	1	37	39	19	22
Trey Mayeux	0	0	9.00	2	2	5	7	6	1
Alex Schmarzo	2	3	2.73	32	0	36	32	22	46
Jadd Schmeltzer	1	0	4.85	13	3	39	44	17	34
Nathan Stewart	2	2	2.46	20	0	22	18	22	23
Clay Vanderlaan	0	3	7.27	9	6	26	43	20	12
Ryan Waters	0	1	4.96	6	1	16	18	7	21

EDINBURG ROADRUNNERS

PLAYER	POS	AVG	OBP	SLG	AB	R	H	HR	RBI	SB
Jeff Allen	C	.231	.286	.231	26	1	6	0	1	2
Todd Alls	IF	.143	.200	.143	14	0	2	0	0	0
Tim Battle	OF	.284	.348	.411	292	50	83	6	32	31
Juan Cabrera	OF	.273	.333	.273	22	1	6	0	1	0
Chris Christopoulos	C	.260	.394	.403	77	12	20	2	12	4
Travis Clark	IF	.278	.333	.344	180	28	50	2	31	11
Dan Coury	C	.250	.297	.417	204	27	51	7	31	1
Fernando De los Santos	IF	.264	.343	.385	174	23	46	3	20	3
Tyler Diaz	IF	.000	.158	.000	16	1	0	0	0	0
Jordan Etier	IF	.257	.359	.330	109	16	28	1	12	4
James Frederick	IF	.160	.222	.160	25	1	4	0	0	0
Eric Gonzalez	IF	.071	.133	.143	14	3	1	0	1	2
Michael Haynes	IF	.283	.356	.343	265	51	75	2	30	22
Nicholas Lancisi	C	.000	.069	.000	27	0	0	0	1	0
Bunyu Maeda	IF	.180	.272	.280	100	10	18	2	10	0
Tim Maitland	OF	.286	.399	.344	224	51	64	0	29	13
Trevor McDonald	IF	.167	.244	.179	78	9	13	0	6	1
Wes Patterson	IF	.256	.333	.359	39	4	10	1	8	0
Tylor Prudhomme	IF	.233	.314	.233	30	4	7	0	1	0
Derrick Pyles	OF	.307	.381	.428	257	44	79	6	55	3
Bobby Rinard	OF	.269	.367	.375	104	21	28	2	13	4
Ryde Rodriguez	OF	.250	.289	.348	184	18	46	4	24	7

Player	Team	AVG	G	AB	R	H	HR	RBI
Carlton Salters	OF	.277	.353	.451	213	28	59	7	32	17
Agustin Septimo	IF	.277	.339	.416	202	34	56	5	26	10
Kaz Smith	C	.105	.150	.158	19	0	2	0	1	0
Tomochika Tsuboi	OF	.256	.383	.385	39	7	10	0	5	1
Trevor Whyte	IF	.327	.390	.439	223	32	73	1	23	9

PLAYER	W	L	ERA	G	GS	IP	H	BB	SO
Cullen Babin	6	1	3.53	15	2	36	39	9	25
Guadalupe Barrera	1	2	6.23	6	3	26	33	15	17
Ryan Bean	0	1	4.50	5	2	14	13	14	10
Antony Bello	3	8	7.97	16	12	67	84	36	42
Curtis Camilli	7	5	2.90	15	14	96	87	35	82
Julio Castro	1	1	3.00	6	0	6	3	1	4
Drew Coffey	2	3	4.31	7	7	31	35	14	33
Yunier Colon	0	1	4.09	8	0	22	22	8	20
Maximino De la Cruz	5	1	3.39	12	11	64	62	18	43
Frank DeJuilio	3	3	4.88	14	3	28	20	25	31
Cameron Dullnig	0	0	1.23	15	0	22	18	9	18
Jordan Etier	0	0	1.80	3	0	5	6	2	8
Austin Fraker	1	2	7.06	11	5	29	29	24	16
Charlie Hajny	0	0	0.00	1	0	3	3	0	6
Kasuma Isabachi	0	1	4.79	8	2	26	33	8	28
Justin Klipp	2	1	1.25	3	3	22	18	5	36
Bryan Kloppe	0	0	5.65	7	0	14	15	7	2
Mike Loseke	6	2	3.68	16	13	81	90	30	43
Makoto Ozone	0	2	6.75	9	2	20	23	14	16
Taylor Reid	0	2	5.06	10	2	27	30	22	32
Alex Schmarzo	2	3	2.73	32	0	36	32	22	46
Dan Schmidt	5	2	3.03	13	9	59	66	15	30
Damian Seguen	3	1	1.50	17	0	24	13	14	25
Ryan Turner	0	0	1.08	5	0	8	5	1	7
Elroy Urbina	0	2	7.62	16	2	28	33	30	20
Kyle Wilson	4	2	2.77	9	8	52	43	18	49
Ryan Zimmerman	5	3	4.14	11	11	63	58	38	49

FORT WORTH CATS

PLAYER	POS	AVG	OBP	SLG	AB	R	H	HR	RBI	SB
Greg Bachman	3B	.273	.374	.336	238	33	65	1	37	5
Josh Band	2B	.310	.444	.379	87	18	27	0	6	7
David Bergin	1B	.310	.395	.551	274	53	85	19	66	2
Cody Bishop	CF	.261	.326	.338	284	35	74	2	36	4
Cody Brooks	C	.105	.261	.105	19	0	2	0	2	0
Logan Brumley	SS	.296	.367	.333	54	9	16	0	7	1
Jose Canseco	1B	.238	.360	.429	21	2	5	1	7	0
Chris Christopoulos	C	.143	.244	.190	105	11	15	1	10	1
Aljay Davis	IF	.337	.464	.444	196	52	66	1	24	12
Chris Ellison	RF	.322	.399	.410	273	43	88	2	51	8
Shelby Ford	SS	.315	.369	.476	143	23	45	2	34	0
Nick Kuroczko	IF	.133	.235	.200	45	4	6	0	1	0
Daniel Meeley	LF	.278	.359	.353	241	34	67	1	36	1
Kori Melo	IF	.220	.363	.236	182	35	40	0	12	5
Ryan Miller	IF	.323	.446	.374	155	31	50	0	21	13
Cameron Monger	OF	.318	.411	.427	255	46	81	3	40	10
Kyle Pearson	IF	.120	.258	.240	25	3	3	1	5	0
Luany Sanchez	C	.147	.275	.176	34	3	5	0	3	0
Mark Sobolewski	IF	.224	.316	.327	49	6	11	0	4	0
Brian White	C	.163	.308	.163	43	7	7	0	0	0

PLAYER	W	L	ERA	G	GS	IP	H	BB	SO
Wes Alsup	0	0	0.00	11	0	12	6	7	20
T.J. Bozeman	4	0	3.78	17	6	48	39	26	55
Hector Contin	2	1	4.05	11	0	13	7	14	14
Matt Eshleman	2	1	3.05	18	0	21	21	8	22
James Giulietti	4	3	1.56	25	6	58	45	23	52
Roman Gomez	3	5	4.59	12	12	71	88	22	52
Nick Huff	0	1	3.38	4	2	16	15	5	12
Will Krout	1	1	3.33	4	4	27	23	3	13
Trevor Longfellow	1	2	3.20	21	0	25	18	16	34
Stephen Nikonchik	3	6	3.45	18	4	60	52	28	61
Boomer Potts	0	2	5.54	12	0	13	13	6	16
Matt Redding	1	0	0.57	10	0	16	8	6	15
Chad Robinson	2	0	1.32	9	0	14	6	4	15
Jorge Rodriguez	0	0	8.44	5	0	5	4	4	8
Osvaldo Rodriguez	1	1	3.60	2	2	10	9	8	8
Jeff Sakowski	2	0	4.24	8	3	17	18	8	15
Hayden Shirley	0	1	1.50	6	0	6	4	8	7

Cole Stephens	7	2	3.95	17	15	100	105	27	55
Aaron Wilkerson	9	1	2.74	13	13	76	58	37	97
Kyle Wilson	4	2	2.77	9	8	52	43	18	49

MCALLEN THUNDER

PLAYER	POS	AVG	OBP	SLG	AB	R	H	HR	RBI	SB
Jorge Bishop	SS	.227	.272	.383	128	26	29	4	16	3
Jacinto Cipriota	IF	.274	.367	.323	164	20	45	0	21	5
Vince Coleman Jr.	OF	.233	.283	.356	90	14	21	2	14	1
Jacob Douglas	IF	.235	.278	.319	119	15	28	1	9	2
Ramon Geronimo	1B	.103	.206	.103	29	2	3	0	1	0
Temar Hudson	IF	.192	.400	.308	26	4	5	0	1	2
Adam Humes	IF	.214	.241	.286	28	2	6	0	3	0
Bunyu Maeda	IF	.180	.272	.280	100	10	18	2	10	0
Joe Manboud	IF	.154	.313	.154	13	0	2	0	1	1
Mario Mercedes	C	.286	.370	.333	21	3	6	0	5	2
Wes Moody	C	.059	.158	.059	17	2	1	0	0	0
Mauricio Nagahashi	IF	.205	.295	.231	78	10	16	0	4	2
Lucas Nakandakare	C	.213	.300	.225	80	6	17	0	8	0
Jonathan Perea	C	.077	.143	.077	13	1	1	0	0	0
Mario Perez	IF	.297	.348	.344	64	8	19	0	8	6
Jose Soledad	3B	.109	.138	.109	55	1	6	0	6	2
Andy White	IF	.212	.296	.280	118	17	25	2	10	0

PLAYER	W	L	ERA	G	GS	IP	H	BB	SO
Yunier Colon	0	1	4.09	8	0	22	22	8	20
Rick Croshaw	0	0	3.86	2	0	2	3	3	0
Eddie Dennis Jr.	0	1	9.39	4	2	8	7	12	7
Jacob Douglas	3	3	6.80	13	6	42	47	24	24
Patrick Durland	1	0	15.88	3	0	6	5	12	1
Trent Evins	7	5	4.61	14	14	98	116	18	47
Alex Fernandez	0	2	5.85	14	1	20	28	16	9
Gabriel Garcia	1	2	3.78	4	1	17	18	7	13
Ramon Geronimo	0	0	3.86	1	0	2	2	1	0
Jose Hernandez	1	0	4.08	12	0	29	31	17	13
Leo Madrid	0	0	1.80	1	0	5	11	0	2
Steven Romero	4	4	5.40	10	10	60	54	32	35
Chris Treibt	0	2	4.44	13	0	26	21	11	19
Ernesto Verrier	2	4	8.33	9	7	27	28	21	12
Jackson Yedi	0	3	36.00	4	3	3	8	7	3

RIO GRANDE VALLEY WHITEWINGS

PLAYER	POS	AVG	OBP	SLG	AB	R	H	HR	RBI	SB
Brycen Bell	SS	.091	.167	.182	11	0	1	0	0	0
Johnny Bowden	C	.318	.490	.383	107	22	34	0	9	0
Kieran Bradford	C	.238	.328	.295	105	13	25	1	12	1
Cody Brooks	C	.105	.261	.105	19	0	2	0	2	0
Chad Bunting	OF	.242	.348	.311	132	20	32	1	18	10
Albert Carpen	OF	.319	.423	.407	273	52	87	0	46	13
Cody Collins	IF	.260	.317	.301	73	7	19	0	8	1
Andrew Deeds	OF	.281	.361	.344	32	7	9	0	6	0
Buddy Elmore	1B	.115	.303	.115	26	3	3	0	0	1
Dan Evatt	OF	.191	.319	.383	94	17	18	4	16	3
Hector Garcia	SS	.320	.340	.420	50	4	16	1	5	0
Michael Garcia	CF	.247	.360	.349	166	28	41	1	13	6
Aaron Gates	LF	.379	.453	.592	103	17	39	4	21	3
Fidel Hernandez	OF	.296	.296	.296	27	2	8	0	4	2
Hiroki Itakura	CF	.212	.247	.224	85	9	18	0	6	2
Justin Juneau	RF	.191	.240	.213	47	4	9	0	2	0
Goose Kallunki	IF	.240	.316	.327	104	10	25	2	16	0
Scott Lacey	OF	.143	.235	.143	14	3	2	0	1	0
Logan Lotti	RF	.200	.250	.267	15	1	3	0	2	0
Kevin Lusson	3B	.203	.329	.210	143	24	29	0	12	0
Tyler McIntyre	1B	.125	.176	.125	16	1	2	0	1	0
Kiego Miyagi	IF	.118	.281	.118	51	9	6	0	0	4
Wes Moody	C	.059	.158	.059	17	2	1	0	0	0
Kenta Nishii	3B	.188	.188	.188	16	1	3	0	3	0
Dan Pembroke	1B	.190	.217	.228	79	5	15	0	6	0
Rolando Petit	C	.231	.375	.256	39	1	9	0	5	0
Roberto Ramirez	IF	.380	.422	.465	187	26	71	0	26	17
Ryde Rodriguez	OF	.250	.289	.348	184	18	46	4	24	7

Thomas Shull	IF	.241	.338	.297	232	32	56	1	32	11
James Simpson	SS	.200	.333	.200	10	2	2	0	0	0
Eduardo Sosa	OF	.190	.266	.207	58	5	11	0	3	1
Cohl Walla	RF	.133	.235	.200	15	2	2	0	2	0
Troy Zawadzki	SS	.219	.329	.234	128	22	28	0	14	2

PLAYER	W	L	ERA	G	GS	IP	H	BB	SO
J.R. Bromberg	0	1	5.19	4	4	17	18	13	11
Drew Coffey	2	3	4.31	7	7	31	35	14	33
Nelson Curry	3	3	1.67	23	0	27	21	8	34
Danny Gidora	0	1	5.87	2	1	8	9	5	8
Jordan Goldschmidt	0	0	5.96	25	0	26	30	15	19
Ray Hanson	5	3	3.00	9	9	60	50	18	60
Tyler Herr	1	2	5.67	14	2	27	21	21	36
Brett Kennedy	6	3	2.67	13	12	84	70	22	58
Brett Miller	4	6	4.74	13	12	82	89	23	53
Paul Montalbano II	2	1	2.18	26	0	33	31	11	41
Bobby ONeill	2	6	6.87	10	10	55	76	15	30
Brad Orsey	0	1	3.38	1	1	8	7	2	4
Kyle Roliard	0	0	6.20	21	0	25	33	19	16
Brian Smith	1	2	3.20	3	3	20	23	10	23
AJ Smouse	4	7	4.36	15	13	85	105	29	45
Kyle Wahl	0	0	2.65	17	0	17	10	8	28
Mike Wolford	1	3	3.44	27	0	34	27	17	28

SAN ANGELO COLTS

PLAYER	POS	AVG	OBP	SLG	AB	R	H	HR	RBI	SB
Miguel Alfonzo	IF	.250	.333	.333	60	5	15	0	7	2
Jorge Bishop	SS	.227	.272	.383	128	26	29	4	16	3
Chris Caves	C	.225	.293	.393	89	7	20	3	17	0
Jon Dziomba	IF	.354	.397	.482	328	59	116	2	39	13
Braden Embry	OF	.232	.333	.374	211	25	49	4	28	1
Dan Evatt	OF	.191	.319	.383	94	17	18	4	16	3
Oscar Garcia	OF	.331	.395	.398	133	18	44	0	11	12
Danny Hernandez	IF	.266	.339	.361	158	30	42	2	19	5
Joseph Hicks	LF	.309	.375	.442	285	51	88	4	50	30
Cody Hudson	OF	.314	.368	.390	105	18	33	2	14	13
Ryan Hutson	IF	.289	.416	.413	121	14	35	4	22	0
Preston Lyon	IF	.231	.412	.231	13	4	3	0	1	0
Jordan Marks	IF	.214	.313	.347	196	29	42	6	28	5
Mike Mobbs	OF	.388	.473	.550	80	18	31	2	12	8
Kyle Nichols	1B	.260	.378	.527	150	29	39	10	43	0
Nathan Ramler	1B	.087	.087	.087	23	0	2	0	1	0
Justin Reed	OF	.232	.376	.275	69	5	16	0	9	1
Steve Rinaudo	IF	.279	.341	.469	326	64	91	10	45	12
Tyler Wagner	C	.216	.301	.297	74	9	16	1	10	0
Bubby Williams	C	.254	.283	.324	213	33	54	1	14	2
Matt Wright	OF	.227	.227	.273	22	2	5	0	4	0

PLAYER	W	L	ERA	G	GS	IP	H	BB	SO
Demetrius Banks	4	3	3.49	14	14	90	93	31	72
Chandler Barnard	2	1	3.27	3	3	22	20	5	17
Alex Bates	4	7	5.72	19	11	72	82	31	54
Kristian Bueno	0	1	3.52	2	2	8	6	10	4
Alfredo Caballero	2	4	3.45	27	0	29	21	15	30
Derek Christensen	5	4	5.33	14	12	74	81	27	40
Corey Frerichs	5	6	4.50	18	13	88	90	29	58
Scott Hartling	1	1	4.50	2	0	2	3	1	1
Cephas Howard	4	3	1.53	33	0	35	33	8	34
B.J. Hyatt	3	1	4.37	13	5	35	39	21	22
Frank James	0	1	4.73	5	2	13	15	4	6
Andrew Jessup	0	0	6.14	9	0	15	13	10	15
Russell Johns	0	1	14.36	11	1	16	29	12	14
Jeff Lyman	0	0	13.50	3	0	2	3	2	3
Preston Lyon	0	0	12.00	1	0	3	6	0	2
Leandro Mella	0	0	5.79	3	1	5	4	9	4
Steve Merslich	1	1	5.74	12	1	27	31	22	23
Brian Murphy	0	0	4.70	1	1	8	5	3	3
Jake Negrete	0	2	6.00	2	2	9	10	0	5
Adam Rowe	2	0	3.86	4	4	28	29	7	17
Eric Sheridan	8	3	3.71	15	14	90	88	38	68
Jeremy Tietze	2	2	6.12	24	0	32	44	12	33
Derek Vaughn	0	2	4.66	8	2	19	24	5	19

INDEPENDENT LEAGUES

INTERNATIONAL

Dominican Republic claims first WBC title

BY JOHN MANUEL

SAN FRANCISCO

I n the 2013 World Baseball Classic, Puerto Rico took out one baseball giant after another.

It beat Venezuela in the first round, the United States in the second and Japan in a semifinal game at AT&T Park.

But Puerto Rico got three shots at "The Republic of Baseball," as manager Tony Pena likes to call his homeland, the Dominican Republic. And it came up empty all three times.

Puerto Rico came up empty all night in the WBC finale against Dominican starter Sam Deduno and four relievers—Octavio Dotel, Pedro Strop, Santiago Casilla and finally Fernando Rodney—who combined to throw a three-hit shutout. Deduno tossed five scoreless, every reliever pitched a scoreless frame and Rodney got his seventh save in eight games as the Dominican Republic beat Puerto Rico 3-0 and won the World Baseball Classic for the first time.

"Samuel Deduno did a great job, not only tonight but throughout the WBC," Pena said. "He pitched three times for us, and all were successful games . . . He could have thrown 95 pitches easy tonight, but we have the horses (in our bullpen).

"As I said from the start, our bullpen is the root of our team. We only need five innings from our starters. After that, I turn it over to them."

It worked eight times in a row as the DR became the first nation other than Japan to win the WBC and redeemed itself from an embarrassing first-round exit in 2009. Moreover, the Dominicans became the first undefeated WBC champ, winning all eight of their games.

On a rainy night with 35,703 on hand at AT&T, the Dominicans seized control early and survived as Puerto Rico couldn't plate a run despite getting the leadoff man on in five of the last six innings. Meanwhile, the DR scored two in the first as Jose Reyes doubled to lead off, and he and Robinson Cano (who was intentionally walked) scored on Edwin Encarnacion's double to right-center field. Erick Aybar doubled home an insurance run in the fifth, which was more than enough for Deduno and the Dominican bullpen.

"When I did that, the first thing that come through my mind when I hit that double is that

Fernando Rodney and the Dominican Republic were a perfect 8-0 in the WBC

CLIFF WELCH

was going to pull not just my team, but the whole Dominican Republic in front of me, because we have a very good opportunity to score a run, and we did it," Reyes said through a translator. "We scored two runs right then in the first inning. That was huge.

"I can't describe this feeling right now because like I said before, right now in the Dominican Republic, they were waiting for this moment so bad, and we did it for the whole Dominican Republic."

Deduno showed plenty of emotion, particularly when he ended the fifth by striking out Angel Pagan to end a two-on, two-out threat. Pagan didn't take kindly to the outsized reaction, but passion and pride played huge roles in the Dominicans' WBC unbeaten streak.

"The DR has huge talent," Puerto Rico manager Edwin Rodriguez said via a translator. "Other teams also had great talent and stars from the major leagues. But the DR has a passion, desire, the drive to really show this kind of amazing performance, and they did accomplish it."

Deduno, who went on to earn a spot in the Twins' big league rotation, went five scoreless for the victory, giving up two of Puerto Rico's three hits. He walked three but also struck out five. The four Dominican relievers got five more strikeouts and extended the bullpen's streak of scoreless innings in WBC play to 25⅔ innings.

"They based that team on that (bullpen)" Netherlands manager Hensley Meulens said after his team lost 4-1 to the Dominicans in the semifinal. "I think they only have a couple starters, and then most of the guys on the roster were bullpen guys. It showed tonight."

Robinson Cano was named MVP despite an 0-for-3 showing in the finale that included a walk and run scored. He went 15-for-32 with two homers and six RBIs and a .469/.514/.781 slash line, and the Yankees second baseman was emotional in the postgame celebration.

"As Tony said, you always remember the first time for everything: your first hit, playoffs, everything," Cano said. "This is always going to be in our hearts for the rest of our lives. Everyone of us who played in this game will always remember the World Classic. This is such a thrill."

Disappointments For Japan, U.S.

The Classic showed that international baseball has plenty of parity, a hallmark of increased competition. Japan had won the first two Classics and reached the semifinals but was upset by Puerto Rico, losing 3-1 in a game marked by sloppy fielding, terrible decision-making and panicked plate approaches.

Catcher Yadier Molina steadied Puerto Rico's young pitching staff, and Japan manager Koji Yamamoto made two questionable choices that backfired. He left lefthander Atsushi Nohmi in to face righthanded-hitting Mike Aviles and Alex Rios in the sixth inning, and Aviles singled and scored on Rios' homer, the game's key blow.

In the eighth, Japan rallied with runners at first and second in one out. With Randy Fontanez, a Mets farmhand who hadn't pitched above low Class A, on the mound Yamamoto called for his runners to double steal if they could get a good jump, even with Molina behind the plate and Japan's top hitter, Shinnosuke Abe, batting.

Fontanez had allowed three straight singles to plate a run, but lead runner Horikazu Ibata dutifully tried to steal third while Seiichi Uchikawa took off from first. Ibata stumbled in his jump and opted to stay put while Uchikawa kept going, getting in a rundown as Molina ran at him. Molina wound up tagging out Uchikawa, and ex-big

WORLD BASEBALL CLASSIC

RESULTS: FIRST ROUND (ROUND ROBIN)

POOL A: March 2-6, Fukuoka, Japan
Japan 5, Brazil 3
Cuba 5, Brazil 2
Japan 5, China 2
Cuba 12, China 0
China 5, Brazil 2
Cuba 6, Japan 3
Cuba, Japan Advance

POOL C: March 7-10, San Juan, P.R.
D.R. 9, Venezuela 3
P.R. 3, Spain 0
D.R. 6, Spain 3
P.R. 6, Venezuela 3
Venezuela 11, Spain 6
D.R. 4, P.R. 2
D.R., P.R. Advance

POOL B: March 2-5, Taichung, Taiwan
Taiwan 4, Australia 1
Netherlands 5, South Korea 0
Taiwan 8, Netherlands 3
South Korea 6, Australia 0
Netherlands 4, Australia 1
South Korea 3, Taiwan 2
Taiwan, Netherlands Advance

POOL D: March 7-10, Phoenix
Italy 6, Mexico 5
Italy 14, Canada 4
Mexico 5, USA 2
Canada 10, Mexico 3
USA 6, Italy 1
USA 9, Canada 4
USA, Italy Advance

SECOND ROUND (DOUBLE-ELIMINATION)

POOL 1: March 8-12, Tokyo
Netherlands 6, Cuba 2
Japan 4, Taiwan 3
Cuba 14, Taiwan 0
Japan 16, Netherlands 4
Netherlands 7, Cuba 6
Japan 10, Netherlands 6
Japan, Netherlands Advance

POOL 2: March 12-16, Miami
D.R. 5, Italy 4
USA 7, P.R. 1
P.R. 4, Italy 3
D.R. 3, USA 1
P.R. 4, USA 3
D.R. 2, P.R. 0
DR, PR Advance

CHAMPIONSHIP ROUND

March 17-19, San Francisco: Semifinals
P.R. 3, Japan 1; D.R. 4, Netherlands 1

Championship
D.R. 3, P.R. 0

BATTING LEADERS

Player	Team	AVG	AB	R	H	2B	3B	HR	RBI	BB	SO	SB
Michael Saunders	CAN	.727	11	4	8	3	0	1	7	2	1	1
Justin Morneau	CAN	.636	11	4	7	3	0	0	3	1	1	0
Yunesky Sanchez	ESP	.636	11	2	7	1	0	0	1	0	1	0
Hirokazu Ibata	JPN	.556	18	6	10	1	0	0	4	5	3	0
Chris Robinson	CAN	.556	9	1	5	0	0	0	1	0	1	0
Eduardo Arredondo	MEX	.545	11	6	6	1	0	0	1	1	0	0
Jose Fernandez	CUB	.524	21	7	11	3	0	0	6	1	0	0
Frederich Cepeda	CUB	.474	19	7	9	3	1	1	5	7	3	0
Robinson Cano	DOM	.469	32	6	15	4	0	2	6	3	7	0
Dae Ho Lee	KOR	.455	11	2	5	0	0	0	2	2	0	0
Martin Prado	VEN	.455	11	2	5	3	0	0	2	2	0	0
Mike Walker	AUS	.455	11	0	5	0	0	0	0	0	3	0
Omar Infante	VEN	.444	9	2	4	2	0	0	1	0	0	1
David Wright	USA	.438	16	4	7	2	0	1	10	3	0	0
Adrian Gonzalez	MEX	.429	7	2	3	0	0	1	3	6	1	0
Anthony Granato	ITA	.429	14	2	6	1	0	0	1	1	1	1
Salomon Manriquez	ESP	.429	7	1	3	0	0	0	2	1	2	0
Joe Mauer	USA	.429	21	4	9	2	1	0	2	5	4	0
Nick Punto	ITA	.421	19	5	8	2	0	0	2	4	0	—
Seung Yuop Lee	KOR	.400	10	3	4	3	0	0	1	0	2	0

PITCHING LEADERS

Player	Team	W	LERA	G	GS	SV	IP	H	BB	SO	WHIP
Danny Betancourt	CUB	2	0	2	2	0	11	4	3	11	0.66
Richard Castillo	ESP	0	0	1	1	0	3	4	0	2	1.33
Gio Gonzalez	USA	1	0	1	1	0	5	3	0	5	0.6
Chris Leroux	CAN	1	0	1	1	0	3	2	1	4	1
Jiangang Lu	CHN	0	0	2	0	0	4	1	1	3	0.55
Dustin Molleken	CAN	0	0	2	0	0	4	2	2	0	1
Seunghwan Oh	KOR	0	0	3	0	1	3	0	0	6	0
Wei-Lun Pan	TPE	1	0	2	0	0	5	2	1	0	0.56
Hee-soo Park	KOR	0	0	2	0	0	3	1	0	3	0.33
Fernando Rodney	DOM	0	0	8	0	7	7	1	3	8	0.55
Richard Salazar	ESP	0	0	1	0	0	5	2	1	2	0.6
Seung Song	KOR	1	0	1	1	0	4	2	2	5	1
Pedro Strop	DOM	3	0	6	0	0	7	3	0	7	0.45
Chien-Ming Wang	TPE	1	0	2	2	0	12	10	1	3	0.92
Carlos Yoshimura	BRA	0	0	1	0	0	2	2	0	2	0.86

leaguer J.C. Romero retired Abe on a grounder to end the threat, and Japan's chances at a three-peat.

While the DR and Japan were WBC favorites, Puerto Rico and the Netherlands had worn Cinderella's slipper. The Dutch continued their international mastery of Cuba by eliminating the Cubans in a thriller in second-round pool play in Tokyo, its sixth straight win over Cuba in top-level tournaments. Five double plays helped, as did a game-tying eighth-inning home run by Andrelton Simmons, and the Dutch won in walk-off fashion in the ninth after an error by Yulieski Gourriel and a sacrifice fly by Kalian Sams. The Netherlands had advanced out of the first round in Taiwan along with the host country, eliminating Korea, which had posted the best record in the first two Classics overall.

"Back when I started, say 15 years ago, when we played Cuba, we didn't put our ace in the game. We knew we were going to lose," 38-year-old Dutch righthander Rob Cordemans said. "There was no chance we were going to win. Now we've won I think six consecutive games against Cuba. I mean, that's what it's all about. If you beat those guys six times in a row, that's a real, real good team."

Puerto Rico and the Dominican had started in the same first-round pool, and the Puerto Ricans eliminated favored Venezuela in the first round. They advanced to the second round in Miami with the United States, underdog Italy and the D.R., losing its first game to the U.S., then rallying to beat Italy and the U.S. by identical 4-3 scores to advance to the semifinals.

The loss was a disappointment for the U.S., which has an all-time record of 10-10 in Classic play. The American team, managed by former Yankees skipper Joe Torre, was shut out over six, two-hit innings by 38-year-old journeyman Nelson Figueroa and couldn't complete a comeback.

The Americans' struggles on the field, and attendance that was down 2 percent from March 2009 to March 2013, did not dim Major League Baseball's enthusiasm for the Classic.

"This has been a great success—over the top, unqualified," MLB executive vice president of business operations Tim Brosnan said after the title game. "It's a worldwide event, and it's about growing the game. For any negative you can bring up, I can give you a thousand successes."

Brosnan and Paul Archey, senior VP of MLB's International operations, cited strong television viewership around the world; for example, the championship game was the most-watched sporting event in the DR in the last decade.

"You have to start on the field with the competi-

tive games we have had," Archey said. "From '06 to '09 to now, each year the gap has narrowed, and this year the games were unbelievable.

"This tournament is accomplishing what we wanted it to accomplish . . . In Taiwan, we had the No. 1 and No. 2 highest-rated cable shows of all time. We had a 75 share in Puerto Rico for the semifinal . . . and we had attendance that was higher in Puerto Rico than last time, set a record in Japan, did better than last time in Phoenix, did better than last time in Miami. So this event is getting better and better."

Olympic Dream Dashed?

The WBC will remain the ultimate international baseball competition for some time. Meeting in Buenos Aires, Argentina, in September the International Olympic Committee put wrestling back into the Olympics, choosing it over the combined baseball/softball bid for the 2020 and 2024 Games.

Baseball and softball had made the cut in May to the final three sports along with wrestling and squash being considered by the IOC's executive board. Wrestling won the final vote in a simple majority, according to a press release by the IOC. A USA Today report said the vote was 49 for wrestling, 24 for baseball/softball and 22 for squash.

Baseball was added to the Olympics in 1984 in Los Angeles as a demonstration sport, with the first medals awarded in 1992 in Barcelona. Cuba won the gold in 1992, 1996 and 2004, while the U.S. won gold in 2000 and South Korea won the final event in 2008 in Beijing.

Baseball and softball were voted out in 2005 as the IOC moved to streamline the Games program. The vote also was seen as an anti-American move in the wake of the U.S. invasion of Iraq, and also as a political maneuver by IOC president Jacques Rogge, who later steered rugby sevens and golf onto the Olympic program, sports he and his wife long have championed.

With Tokyo chosen as the host of the 2020 Games, baseball and softball could have rejoined the Olympics in style, in one of the countries most familiar with the sports. It would have been more difficult to imagine baseball and softball returning in Istanbul or Madrid, the other finalists for 2020.

While MLB has moved on from the Olympics with the creation of the World Baseball Classic, USA Baseball and other governing bodies around the world crave the government funding that comes with being on the Olympic program. So the IOC's decision, while not surprising considering wrestling's historic place in the Olympics dating back to ancient Greece, was a blow.

Cubans make mark with Quintana Roo

Former major leaguer Matias Carrillo managed Quintana Roo to its second Mexican League championship in three seasons. The Tigers had the league's third-best regular-season record but won 11 of 14 playoff contests to win its 10th championship since the team's inception in 1955.

Two Cubans played major roles in the Tigers' run. Reliever Hassan Pena proved to be a workhorse in the playoffs, recording seven saves in 11 apperances after picking up 24 regular-season saves. Pena was in his first Mexican League season after seven years in the Nationals organization. Fellow righthander Amaury Sanit, in his second season in Mexico, was Quintana Roo's ace, as the 34-year-old finished tied for the league lead with 12 wins, ranked second in ERA (3.27) and third in strikeouts (103). Sanit won three of his five playoff starts as well, including the clincher in Game Five.

Not all of Quintana Roo's stars were Cuban. Righy reliever Luis Ramirez, a Venezuelan who was previously in the Orioles and Athletics organizations, proved a crucial setup man, tossing 11 innings without giving up an earned run. Meanwhile, veteran Mexicans such as outfielders Albino Contreras (.346, five home runs in playoffs) and Karim Garcia (.377 in playoffs) and first baseman Jorge Vazquez (five homers in playoffs) made up for the loss of veteran Jorge Cantu, who ranked third in the league in home runs despite being sidelined in early July with a left leg injury.

The biggest-name import in the league in 2013, though, was a Cuban. Campeche secured the services of outfielder Alfredo Despaigne, the reigning home run champion of Cuba's Serie Nacional, and the 5-foot-9 slugger hit .338/.364/.564 with eight home runs over 33 games before his season ended in early August. Fellow Cuban national team veteran Michel Enriquez (.240 in seven games) and outfielder Yordanis Samon (2-for-18 in seven games) also had brief trials with Campeche, as Cuba tests out allowing its players to play for money outside the island. Several other Cubans who had left the island for the U.S. minor leagues, only to fail to stick in the majors, have relocated to the Mexican League. That list includes Laguna first baseman Juan Miranda (.367/.498/.633, 26 home

runs), the former Yankee and Diamondback who led the league in walks and on-base percentage; as well as sevearl members of Spain's 2013 World Baseball Classic team such as Oaxaca's Yunesky Sanchez (.346) and Barbaro Canizares (.374).

With no club managing a .600 winning percentage, veteran Ruben Mateo led third-year club Ciudad del Carmen to the league's best record. The former Rangers prospect led the Mexican League with 37 homers, but the Dolphins lost their first-round playoff series to Veracruz in four games.

STANDINGS & LEADERS

NORTH	W	L	PCT	GB
Saraperos de Saltillo	63	50	.558	—
Sultanes de Monterrey	62	50	.554	½
Pericos de Puebla	58	48	.547	1 ½
Diablos Rojos del Mexico	58	51	.532	3
Acereros del Norte	53	57	.482	8 ½
Rieleros de Aguascalientes	53	58	.477	9
Broncos de Reynosa	53	60	.469	10
Vaqueros de la Laguna	51	60	.459	11

SOUTH	W	L	PCT	GB
Delfines de Ciudad del Carmen	63	46	.578	—
Guerreros de Oaxaca	64	48	.571	½
Tigres de Quintana Roo	62	48	.564	1 ½
Rojos del Aguila de Veracruz	56	57	.496	9
Olmecas de Tabasco	54	56	.491	9 ½
Leones de Yucatan	50	61	.450	14
Piratas de Campeche	47	63	.427	16 ½
Petroleros de Minatitlan	37	71	.343	25 ½

INDIVIDUAL BATTING LEADERS

PLAYER, TEAM	AVG	AB	R	H	2B	3B	HR	RBI	BB	SO	SB
Suarez, Luis, PUE	.413	351	85	145	27	2	6	57	52	46	5
Madera, Sandy, PUE	.390	426	85	166	28	3	19	92	36	60	1
Terrero, Luis, MEX	.388	273	72	106	14	1	27	72	30	60	14
Morejon, Oswaldo, LAG	.383	473	83	181	36	1	9	66	14	25	8
Fonseca, Luis, MIN	.376	386	72	145	21	9	20	73	42	77	8
Canizares, Barbaro, OAX	.374	431	93	161	32	0	29	112	60	51	4
Robles, Oscar, MEX	.373	407	73	152	25	2	4	70	40	41	10
Castillo, Jose, PUE	.369	420	87	155	29	4	25	108	27	41	6
Amador, Japhet, MEX	.368	400	76	147	22	0	36	121	38	59	0
Miranda, Juan, LAG	.367	357	88	131	15	1	26	86	86	76	2
Diaz, Frank, REY	.360	442	75	159	29	2	21	83	35	66	3
Otanez, Willis, AGS	.356	354	73	126	22	0	26	93	46	57	0
Brena, Jaime, OAX	.351	373	72	131	22	1	5	49	61	38	3
Valenzuela, Fernando, YUC	.346	379	53	131	26	2	5	56	33	40	1
Tapia, Cesar, PUE	.345	357	63	123	25	3	11	80	27	37	5

INDIVIDUAL PITCHING LEADERS

PITCHER, TEAM	W	L	ERA	G	GS	CG	SV	IP	H	HR	BB	SO
*Oseguera, Paul, REY	8	7	3.00	19	19	4	0	123	120	10	37	124
Sanit, Amauri, TIG	12	4	3.27	22	22	1	0	135	122	12	32	103
Valenzuela, Vanny, CDC	7	4	3.38	18	17	0	0	96	75	11	47	75
Marti, Yadel, YUC	7	5	3.45	21	21	0	0	125	118	10	39	87
Meza, Andres, PUE	9	5	3.48	18	18	0	0	98	123	9	13	70
Medrano, Leo, TAB	6	6	3.55	29	15	0	1	104	106	11	28	93
Pina, Jose, TAB	11	3	3.69	22	19	0	0	124	113	10	40	85
Gonzalez, Mario, CDC	9	6	3.70	21	21	4	0	124	109	13	24	100
Carrillo, Marco, MTY	7	3	3.76	22	16	1	0	96	104	12	20	84
Valdez, Salvador, LAG	5	5	3.76	31	13	1	1	96	97	8	34	69
*Garate, Victor, SAL	9	4	3.78	19	18	0	0	100	106	9	40	112
Flores, Manuel, VER	8	6	3.81	20	19	0	0	104	117	11	23	79
Oyervidez, Jose, MVA	8	4	3.91	20	19	0	0	101	119	13	26	100
Montes, Aldo, CAM	7	5	3.96	23	22	0	0	109	113	15	47	64
*Solis, Tomas, VER	6	8	4.00	21	21	1	0	117	132	17	28	71

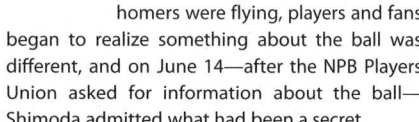
Offenses surge in NPB

BY WAYNE GRACZYK

The Tohoku Rakuten Golden Eagles, playing their ninth season after joining Japan pro baseball as an expansion team in 2005, ousted the Tokyo Yomiuri Giants four games to three and claimed their first Japan Series championship. The 2013 Eagles rode the emotions of the fans in the Tohoku area devastated by the Great East Japan Earthquake and subsequent tsunami of March 11, 2011, that left more than 19,000 people dead or missing.

Led by veteran hard-nosed manager Senichi Hoshino, the Eagles also rode the arm of right-hander Masahiro Tanaka, who turned in a perfect 24-0 regular season record with an ERA of 1.27. Rakuten won the Pacific League pennant and defeated the Chiba Lotte Marines in the Climax Series of playoffs to earn the Japan Series berth.

Wladimir Balentien

Yomiuri, led by manager Tatsunori Hara, was trying to win back-to-back Japan Series titles for the first time since 1973 but fell short. The Giants made it to the finals by winning their 35th Central League pennant and advanced after beating the Hiroshima Carp in the Central's Climax Series.

Tanaka also won a playoff game and Game Two of the Japan Series but finally lost to the Giants in Game Six despite throwing 160 pitches in a complete-game defeat. However, he bounced back to pitch the ninth inning and pick up a save as the Eagles won 3-0 in Game Seven. He was on the mound when the Series ended.

Playing their first season in Japan, former big leaguers Andruw Jones and Casey McGehee also made significant contributions to the Eagles' championship run. Jones batted .243 with 26 homers and 94 RBIs, while McGehee hit .292 with 28 home runs and 93 RBIs.

Yakult Swallos slugger Wladimir Balentien provided another big story in Japan in 2013 by hitting a record-setting 60 home runs. The Curacao native broke the single-season Japanese homer mark of 55 held jointly by all-time home run king Sadaharu Oh and former foreign stars Tuffy Rhodes and Alex Cabrera. Despite missing the first 12 games of the season because of a groin injury sustained during the World Baseball Classic, Balentien hit his 56th and 57th home runs of the year on Sept. 15, setting the new record.

Balentien flirted with a Triple Crown title until late in the season but saw fellow foreign slugger Tony Blanco of the Yokohama Baystars take the Central League batting (.333) and RBI (136) titles. Balentien finished second in batting (.330) and RBIs (131), while Blanco finished second in home runs (41).

The performances of the pair call to mind another big story in Japanese baseball in 2013; the altering of the ball used, without an announcement from the Nippon Professional Baseball Commissioner's Office. In order to provide more offense after two years of playing with a "deadened" baseball, the NPB office decided to change to a more "lively" ball. Without any mention, NPB secretary general Kunio Shimoda decided prior to the start of the 2013 season to change the ball. Two weeks into the season in mid-April, as the homers were flying, players and fans began to realize something about the ball was different, and on June 14—after the NPB Players Union asked for information about the ball—Shimoda admitted what had been a secret.

Commissioner Ryozo Kato claimed even he did not know about the change, although his name is stamped on every game ball. A subsequent investigation by an independent panel followed. In the end, Kato resigned on Oct. 25, and Shimoda was suspended for three months and demoted. A new commissioner was to be named during the 2013-2014 offseason.

Two teams have changed managers. In the Central, Chunichi Dragons skipper Morimichi Takagi stepped down and was replaced by Motonobu Tanishige, a still-active catcher who will serve as a player-manager. In the Pacific League, Seibu Lions manager Hisanobu Watanabe also resigned and will be succeeded by Haruki Ihara, a former Lions and Orix BlueWave manager.

Other news in 2013 included Yokohama Baystars outfielder Alex Ramirez becoming the first foreign-born player to reach 2,000 career hits in Japan. The Venezuelan native and 13-year Central League veteran got the milestone hit on April 6 with a home run at Tokyo's Jingu Stadium.

CENTRAL LEAGUE

	W	L	T	PCT.	GB
Yomiuri Giants	84	53	7	.613	—
Hanshin Tigers	73	67	4	.521	12 ½
Hiroshima Carp	69	72	3	.489	17
Chunichi Dragons	64	77	3	.454	22
Yokohama DeNA Baystars	64	79	1	.448	23
Tokyo Yakult Swallows	57	83	4	.407	28 ½

CLIMAX SERIES PLAYOFFS—First Stage: Hiroshima defeated Hanshin 2-0 in best-of-three series. **Final Stage:** Yomiuri defeated Hiroshima 4-0 in best-of-seven series.

INDIVIDUAL BATTING LEADERS
(MINIMUM 446 PLATE APPEARANCES)

	AVG	AB	R	H	2B	3B	HR	RBI	SB
Blanco, Tony, Baystars	.333	483	74	161	22	0	41	136	1
Balentien, Wladimir, Swallows	.330	439	94	145	17	0	60	131	0
Murata, Shuichi, Giants	.316	519	76	164	26	0	25	87	1
Murton, Matt, Tigers	.314	566	55	178	37	1	19	85	6
Lopez, Jose, Giants	.303	429	45	130	26	0	18	55	1
Abe, Shinnosuke, Giants	.296	422	81	125	17	0	32	91	0
Nishioka, Tsuyoshi, Tigers	.290	497	57	144	28	3	4	44	11
Morino, Masahiko, Dragons	.286	399	53	114	20	1	16	51	1
Toritani, Takashi, Tigers	.282	532	74	150	30	4	10	65	15
Chono, Hisayoshi, Giants	.281	590	82	166	21	3	19	65	14
Nakamura, Norihiro, Baystars	.281	431	37	121	19	1	14	61	1
Wada, Kazuhiro, Dragons	.275	449	53	136	21	2	18	76	2
Ishikawa, Takehiro, Baystars	.275	459	75	126	12	4	5	41	5
Maeda, Yamato, Tigers	.273	384	51	105	12	8	0	21	19
Maru, Yoshihiro, Carp	.273	506	82	138	25	5	14	58	29

REMAINING NORTH AMERICAN AND LATIN PLAYERS

	AVG	AB	R	H	2B	3B	HR	RBI	SB
Luna, Hector, Dragons	.350	329	46	115	23	3	9	51	4
Morgan, Nyjer, Baystars	.294	371	57	109	15	2	11	50	3
Lewis, Fred, Carp	.268	265	36	71	19	0	4	20	12
Bowker, John, Giants	.262	271	27	71	17	3	14	46	0
Ka'aihue, Kila, Carp	.259	224	31	58	7	0	14	45	0
Milledge, Lastings, Swallows	.251	374	56	94	21	0	16	49	7
Eldred, Brad, Carp	.247	235	24	58	11	0	13	32	3
Ramirez, Alex, Baystars	.185	130	6	24	0	0	2	14	0
Conrad, Brooks, Tigers	.175	57	1	10	6	0	0	0	0
Stavinoha, Nick, Carp	.154	39	2	6	0	0	1	3	0

INDIVIDUAL PITCHING LEADERS
(MINIMUM 144 INNINGS)

	W	L	ERA	G	SV	IP	H	BB	SO
Maeda, Kenta, Carp	15	7	2.10	26	0	176	129	40	158
Nomi, Atsushi, Tigers	11	7	2.69	25	0	181	155	41	127
Standridge, Jason, Tigers	8	12	2.74	26	0	161	161	47	124
Messenger, Randy, Tigers	12	8	2.89	30	0	196	174	56	183
Ogawa, Yasuhiro, Swallows	16	4	2.93	26	0	178	155	45	135
Sugano, Tomoyuki, Giants	13	6	3.12	27	0	176	166	37	155
Sawamura, Hirokazu, Giants	5	10	3.13	34	0	158	138	43	148
Bullington, Bryan, Carp	11	9	3.23	28	0	173	154	41	117
Utsumi, Tetsuya, Giants	13	6	3.31	25	0	160	157	47	107
Sugiuchi, Toshiya, Giants	11	6	3.35	24	0	153	122	49	149

REMAINING NORTH AMERICAN AND LATIN PLAYERS

	W	L	ERA	G	SV	IP	H	BB	SO
Socolovich, Miguel, Carp	0	0	0.79	11	0	11	6	4	6
Mathieson, Scott, Giants	2	2	1.03	63	0	61	36	18	77
Sosa, Jorge, Baystars	3	4	1.79	55	19	60	51	21	54
Mickolio, Kam, Carp	2	4	2.04	57	27	57	48	22	39
Boyer, Blaine, Tigers	3	1	2.67	22	0	27	20	4	21
Cabrera, Daniel, Dragons	6	5	3.09	20	0	117	109	36	98
Bergesen, Brad, Dragons	2	2	3.71	14	0	53	61	16	22
Houlton, D.J., Giants	9	4	3.73	18	0	103	85	32	67
Roman, Orlando, Swallows	3	6	4.24	30	1	64	166	27	44
Zarate, Robert, Tigers	0	0	5.40	2	0	12	2	2	1
Acosta, Manny, Giants	1	0	5.54	14	0	13	15	4	12
Corcoran, Tim, Baystars	1	3	5.65	7	0	34	43	18	14
Barnette, Tony, Swallows	1	8	6.02	47	7	40	36	19	62
LeRoux, Chris, Swallows	0	2	9.00	5	0	22	37	11	14

PACIFIC LEAGUE

	W	L	T	PCT.	GB
Tohoku Rakuten Golden Eagles	82	59	3	.582	—
Saitama Seibu Lions	74	66	4	.529	7 ½
Chiba Lotte Marines	74	68	2	.521	8 ½
Fukuoka SoftBank Hawks	73	69	2	.514	9 ½
Orix Buffaloes	66	73	5	.475	15
Hokkaido Nippon Ham Fighters	64	78	2	.451	18 ½

CLIMAX SERIES PLAYOFFS—First Stage: Chiba Lotte defeated Saitama Seibu 2-1 in best-of-three series. **Final Stage:** Tohoku Rakuten defeated Chiba Lotte 4-1 in best-of-seven series.

INDIVIDUAL BATTING LEADERS
(MINIMUM 446 PLATE APPEARANCES)

	AVG	AB	R	H	2B	3B	HR	RBI	SB
Hasegawa, Yuya, Hawks	.341	580	92	198	29	6	19	83	12
Imae, Toshiaki, Marines	.325	508	44	165	26	0	10	74	5
German, Esteban, Lions	.319	518	74	165	22	3	4	55	40
Akaminai, Ginji, Eagles	.317	482	63	153	24	3	4	54	3
Asamura, Hideto, Lions	.317	543	85	172	38	5	27	110	14
Uchikawa, Seiichi, Hawks	.316	570	76	180	33	1	19	92	1
Nakamura, Akira, Hawks	.307	427	77	131	22	2	5	44	7
Nakata, Sho, Fighters	.305	407	67	124	13	1	28	73	1
Lee, Dae Ho, Buffaloes	.303	521	60	156	27	0	24	91	0
Itoi, Yoshio, Buffaloes	.300	524	75	157	33	2	17	61	33
Iguchi, Tadahito, Marines	.297	485	68	144	31	2	23	83	4
McGehee, Casey, Eagles	.292	513	78	150	30	0	28	93	2
Baldiris, Aarom, Buffaloes	.289	512	60	148	25	1	17	91	1
Kakunaka, Katsuya, Marines	.288	462	65	133	26	6	5	43	10
Ito, Hikaru, Buffaloes	.285	410	36	117	20	2	3	40	4

REMAINING NORTH AMERICAN AND LATIN PLAYERS

	AVG.	AB	R	H	2B	3B	HR	RBI	SB
Brazell, Craig, Marines	.265	185	20	49	6	0	11	33	0
Spilborghs, Ryan, Lions	.234	214	20	50	5	1	3	25	1
Pena, Wily Mo, Hawks	.233	150	8	35	6	1	1	16	0
LaHair, Bryan, Hawks	.230	348	38	80	19	1	16	57	2
Ortiz, Jose, Lions	.210	100	6	21	5	0	0	9	0
Rottino, Vinny, Buffaloes	.206	97	7	20	5	0	4	8	1
Whitesell, Josh, Marines	.200	70	8	14	4	0	4	14	0
Fernandez, Jose, Buffaloes	.188	80	4	15	2	0	1	4	0
Hoffpauir, Micah, Fighters	.186	145	13	27	3	0	5	15	0
Carter, Chris, Lions	.133	30	0	4	0	0	0	3	0

INDIVIDUAL PITCHING LEADERS
(MINIMUM 144 INNINGS)

	W	L	ERA	G	SV	IP	H	BB	SO
Tanaka, Masahiro, Eagles	24	0	1.27	28	1	212	168	32	183
Kaneko, Chihiro, Buffaloes	15	8	2.01	29	0	223	166	58	200
Makita, Kazuhisa, Lions	8	9	2.60	26	0	166	169	39	87
Settsu, Tadashi, Hawks	15	8	3.05	25	0	162	138	42	146
Kishi, Takayuki, Lions	11	5	3.08	26	0	178	155	31	138
Yoshikawa, Mitsuo, Fighters	7	15	3.31	26	0	160	150	57	125
Norimoto, Takahiro, Eagles	15	8	3.34	27	0	170	142	51	134
Togame, Ken, Lions	8	8	3.45	28	0	164	158	44	122
Nishi, Yuuki, Buffaloes	9	8	3.63	28	0	166	178	42	137
Kisanuki, Hiroshi, Fighters	9	8	3.66	24	0	145	141	50	95

REMAINING NORTH AMERICAN AND LATIN PLAYERS

	W	L	ERA	G	SV	IP	H	BB	SO
Schultz, Mike, Buffaloes	0	0	0.00	1	0	1	0	0	1
Sarfate, Dennis, Lions	9	1	1.87	58	10	58	29	24	66
Williams, Randy, Lions	1	2	1.89	47	3	38	20	23	45
Oseguera, Paul, Hawks	3	1	2.00	6	0	36	29	15	23
Falkenborg, Brian, Hawks	0	4	2.04	41	10	40	17	16	49
Rosa, Carlos, Marines	0	1	2.08	52	0	48	46	11	48
Dickson, Brandon, Buffaloes	8	8	2.77	23	0	130	128	47	88
Wolfe, Brian, Fighters	9	6	3.05	22	0	130	134	32	60
Ledezma, Wil, Marines	3	3	3.23	26	0	31	31	13	22
Ray, Kenny, Eagles	0	1	3.26	5	0	19	13	10	10
Rasner, Darrell, Eagles	1	2	3.35	37	17	38	31	11	40
Mollekin, Dustin, Fighters	0	0	3.68	5	0	7	9	2	5
Padilla, Vincente, Hawks	3	6	3.84	16	0	59	50	17	40
Duckworth, Brandon, Eagles	5	5	4.31	18	0	88	91	37	64

Lions Make It 3

The Samsung Lions completed an epic Koeran Series comeback and thrilled their home crowd at Daegu Stadium by ralling for five runs in the sixth inning of Game Seven, pulling off a 7-3 victory and winning the championship series for the third straight series.

The Lions trailed the series three games to one to the Doosan Bears before winning a see-saw Game Five, 7-5. Then the Bears' bats went silent as they lost Game Six 6-2 while stranding 14 runners. Doosan led Game Seven 3-2 in the sixth inning and installed American import Derek Hankins on the mound..

However, Samsung rallied with five runs, with two coming on a bases loaded fielder's choice and error at the plate. Park Seok-min and Kim Tae-wan then hit consecutive singles to drive home three more runs and chase Hankins.

Nexen Heroes first baseman Park Byung Ho was named league MVP after improving on his 2012 season, leading the league in home runs (37) and RBIs (117) while batting .318/.437/.602 overall.

STANDINGS & LEADERS

Team	W	L	T	PCT	GB
Samsung Lions	75	51	2	.595	—
LG Twins	74	54	0	.578	2
Nexen Heroes	72	54	2	.571	3
Doosan Bears	71	54	3	.568	3 ½
Lotte Giants	66	58	4	.532	8
SK Wyverns	62	63	3	.496	12 ½
NC Dinos	52	72	4	.419	22
KIA Tigers	51	74	3	.408	23 ½
Hanwha Eagles	42	85	1	.331	33 ½

BATTING LEADERS

Player, Team	AVG	AB	R	H	2B	3B	HR	RBI	SB	BB	SO
Lee, Byeong Kyu, LG	.348	374	39	130	19	3	5	74	2	22	40
Son, Ah Seop, Lotte	.345	498	83	172	23	4	11	69	36	64	88
Lee, Jin Young, LG	.329	368	41	121	26	1	3	62	6	37	42
Park, Yong Taik, LG	.328	476	79	156	22	4	7	67	13	52	71
Min, Byeong, Doosan	.319	383	71	122	21	7	9	65	27	40	62
Kim, Tae Kyun, Han	.319	345	41	110	24	0	10	52	0	73	67
Park, Seok Min, Sam	.318	396	61	126	24	0	18	76	4	54	73
Park, Byung Ho, Nexen	.318	450	91	143	17	0	37	117	10	92	96
Choi, Jeong, SK	.316	434	75	137	18	0	28	83	24	64	109
Jeong, Seong Hoon, LG	.312	407	64	127	22	1	9	62	13	59	58

PITCHING LEADERS

Player, Team	W	L	ERA	G	SV	IP	H	BB	SO
Shirek, Charlie, NC	11	7	2.48	29	0	189	175	60	116
Lee, Jae Hak, NC	10	5	2.88	27	1	156	123	59	144
Seddon, Chris, SK	14	6	2.98	30	0	187	169	73	160
Liz, Radhames, LG	10	13	3.06	32	0	203	153	88	188
Cha, Woo Chan, Samsung	10	7	3.25	43	0	122	100	67	111
Yun, Sung Hwan, Samsung	13	8	3.27	22	0	171	167	37	122
Oxspring, Chris, Lotte	13	7	3.29	30	0	183	164	69	144
Youman, Shane, Lotte	13	4	3.54	31	0	193	186	78	141
Nippert, Dustin, Doosan	12	4	3.58	19	0	118	108	34	104
Vandenhurk, Rick, Samsung	7	9	3.95	24	0	144	127	48	137

Uni-President takes CPBL title

The Eda Rhinos, formerly known as the Sinon Bulls, made quite a splash in their first season with their new name.

First, the Rhinos brought Manny Ramirez to Taiwan. The former big leaguer, owner of 555 career major league home runs, a .312 average and a PED suspension in 2011, played 49 games for the Rhinos, hitting eight home runs in 206 plate appearances while posting a .352/.422/.555 line.

Ramirez, whose first home run in Taiwan in early April was also reportedly the 7,000th in CPBL history, helped Eda win the first half of the regular season, while the Uni-President 7-Eleven Lions won the second half.

Ramirez was long gone, having signed with the Texas Rangers, when the two teams matched up in the Chinese Professional Baseball League finals, which the Lions won with a four-game sweep.

First baseman Kao Kuo-ching earned the finals MVP, with seven hits, a .467 average and four RBIs in the series. Uni-President won its ninth CPBL championship, most of any franchise in league history, behind manager Terushi Nakajima, a Japanese national.

Former major leaguers Nelson Figueroa, Boof Bonser and Luis Vizcaino were all late-season signees who helped the Lions' pitching staff down the stretch of the season.

STANDINGS & LEADERS

Team	W	L	T	Pct	GB
Uni-President 7-Eleven Lions	62	54	3	.534	—
Eda Rhinos	62	57	1	.521	1 ½
Lamigo Monkeys	57	60	2	.487	5 ½
Brother Elephants	55	65	0	.458	9

INDIVIDUAL BATTING LEADERS

PLAYER, TEAM	AVG	AB	R	H	2B	3B	HR	RBI	BB	SO	SB
Lin Yi-chuan, Eda	.357	417	66	149	26	0	18	45	38	42	4
Gao Guo-hui, Eda	.350	357	60	125	31	2	14	38	34	45	5
Hu Jin-long, Eda	.344	393	71	135	27	3	5	17	15	24	12
Lin Wang-yu, Lamigo	.342	398	66	136	22	2	11	52	34	79	2
Peng Cheng-min, Brother	.318	403	60	128	25	0	10	74	60	63	15

INDIVIDUAL PITCHING LEADERS

PITCHER, TEAM	W	L	ERA	G	GS	SV	IP	H	BB	SO
Andy Sisco, Brother	8	6	2.70	21	21	0	133	120	38	91
Mike Loree, Lamigo	10	12	3.40	33	33	0	212	229	39	150
Lin Yu Qing, Brother	10	10	3.42	26	26	0	158	178	57	125
Brian Burres, Lamigo	9	5	3.49	20	20	0	121	121	28	93
Lin Chen-hua, Eda	15	8	3.71	25	25	0	136	144	23	74

INTERNATIONAL

Magrane's arm leads Rimini to Italy Three-peat

BY HARVEY SAHKER

San Marino defeated Rimini three games to two in the Italy Series, its third straight title. The last team to win three consecutive Italian national championships was Europhon Milan, from 1966 to 1968.

The visiting team won all five games of the Italy Series. Rimini—which had swept Nettuno in the semifinals—won the first two games in San Marino, then wasn't able to close out the series as it lost three straight at home.

Righthander Jim Magrane of San Marino was voted Italy Series MVP. A journeyman whose last season in affiliated ball was 2007, Magrane has since pitched in independent leagues as well as Venezuela, Taiwan, Puerto Rico and Mexico. He shined

KEVIN PATAKY
Alex Romero

in Italy, leading the league in wins and games started. He pitched three of the five Italy Series games, allowing two runs in 21 innings while winning Games Three and Five, the final with seven shutout frames.

In addition to having the two best records, Rimini and Bologna each boasted the top two batting averages and ERAs in the league during the regular season. Three teams were tied for third place in the IBL going into the last day of the regular season: Nettuno, San Marino and Parma. Only two of those teams could make the playoffs. Nettuno and San Marino each won their final game, while Parma lost to drop out of the postseason picture. San Marino finished fourth, leaving it with the toughest possible route to the title. It defeated Bologna in the semifinals, winning a best-of-five series in four games, before going on to the finals against Rimini.

Wuillians Vasquez won his second IBL home run title in three years. The 2013 season was the Venezuelan outfielder's third stint with San Marino. Vasquez also played for the club in 2008, 2009 and 2011.

Former Diamondbacks outfielder Alex Romero won the IBL batting title in his first Italian season. The 30-year old Venezuelan hit .444, the second-highest league leading average in IBL history except for a period in which metal bats were used. Romero is the first IBL player to hit at least .400 since 2004.

Reggio Emilia and Grosseto played a triple-header on August 17. Two of the three contests were make-up games. Grosseto was shut out in all three.

Bologna successfully defended its 2012 European Cup title by defeating Rimini in the annual continental club championship. The format of the competition was modified in 2013, with the winners of two separate tournaments playing a best-of-three series.

STANDINGS & LEADERS

REGULAR SEASON	W	L	PCT	GB
Bologna	28	8	.778	—
Rimini	27	9	.750	1
Nettuno	25	11	.694	3
San Marino	25	11	.694	3
Parma	24	12	.667	4
Reggio Emilia	18	18	.500	10
Ronchi	12	24	.333	16
Godo	9	27	.250	19
Novara	9	27	.250	19
Grosseto	3	33	.083	25

INDIVIDUAL BATTING LEADERS

PLAYER, TEAM	AVG	AB	R	H	2B	3B	HR	RBI	BB
Romero, Alex, RIM	.444	142	27	63	12	0	5	41	17
Duran, Carlos, RSM	.421	126	26	53	8	3	5	37	18
Vaglio, Alessandro, BOL	.410	144	36	59	12	0	4	42	15
Marval, Osman, PAR	.404	114	21	46	9	1	1	24	24
Santora, Jack, RIM	.384	138	38	53	8	0	0	23	20
Infante, Juan Carlos, BOL	.370	119	38	44	7	1	2	16	35
Desimoni, Stefano, PAR	.356	132	33	47	7	3	0	25	20
Fondin, Onelio, NET	.352	122	24	43	4	0	0	13	7
Molina, Rolexis, NOV	.348	132	15	46	10	0	2	22	12
Mazzanti, Giuseppe, NET	.342	120	21	41	11	0	3	20	16
Sanchez, Danilo, GOD	.333	114	21	38	4	0	5	26	39
Vasquez, Wuillians, RSM	.328	134	36	44	12	0	7	27	25
Harrison, Ben, NET	.325	120	28	39	7	0	6	26	22
Chiarini, Mario, RIM	.324	142	43	46	13	1	2	39	18
Silva, Conrado, NOV	.322	121	11	39	12	0	0	16	5

INDIVIDUAL PITCHING

PITCHER, TEAM	W	L	ERA	SV	IP	H	R	ER	BB	SO
Rivero, Raul, BOL	9	1	1.12	2	80	46	12	10	27	105
Acosta, Nibaldo E., REG	4	1	1.26	0	57	40	12	8	13	49
Marquez, Enorbel, RIM	7	1	1.33	6	74	50	17	11	27	86
Sanchez, Jose, PAR	12	2	1.37	0	119	77	26	18	24	143
Cubillan, Darwin, RSM	1	0	1.48	4	30	21	8	5	11	51
Corradini, Roberto, RIM	11	3	1.79	0	96	73	21	19	16	70
D'Angelo, Matteo, BOL	7	2	1.92	0	70	60	24	15	20	58
Crepaldi, Filippo, REG	4	2	1.94	2	70	55	16	15	20	55
Da Silva, Tiago, RSM	12	1	2.07	1	118	80	34	27	24	126
Calero, Angel, NOV	6	4	2.43	0	93	83	36	25	46	122

Markwell Leads Neptunus

Neptunus won the Dutch Major League pennant and beat the Hoofddorp Pioniers four games to none in the Holland Series to claim its 14th national championship.

Belgian second baseman Benjamin Dille won the Holland Series MVP award. The 27-year old Antwerp native was 7-for-17 in the series, hitting second in the Neptunus batting order. Dille also won the award in 2009.

World Baseball Classic veteran and former Blue Jays farmhand Diegomar Markwell, 33, was outstanding in the Holland Series. The southpaw won Games One and Three, allowing just one run in 15 innings. Australian reliever Brendan Wise was the victor in Games Two and Four. Wise, who pitched as high as Triple-A in the Tigers and Twins organizations and was a member of the Aussie World Baseball Classic team, was a combined 5-0, 0.68

Diegomar Markwell

with two saves in 18 regular and postseason appearances.

Kinheim set a DML record by scoring 20 runs in the first inning of an August game against cellar-dweller ADO at Pim Mulier Stadium in Haarlem. Six-time DML home run king Bryan Engelhardt had three hits, including a homer, and six RBIs in the inning and went 6 for 6 in the game with a double, two homers, nine RBIs and five runs scored. The final score was 26-0.

ADO struggled all season long, winning just two games and finishing last in the league with a .185 batting average and an 8.67 ERA. The Hague-based club narrowly avoided relegation to Holland's second tier league by defeating the Oosterhout Twins three games to two in the promotion-relegation playoff finals. ADO won the series despite being outscored 25-11.

In June, Hoofddorp first baseman De Flanegin became only the seventh player to appear in 700 DML games. The 41-year old Aruba native is the first to reach that milestone with only one club.

Rob Cordemans of the Amsterdam Pirates had another outstanding season (10-1, 1.11). The best pitcher in DML history led the league in wins and finished in the top five in ERA, strikeouts, opposing batting average and WHIP.

AROUND EUROPE

■ The Rouen Huskies won their tenth French title. Rouen defeated the Senart Templars three games to two in the best-of-five finals.

■ Buchbinder Legionäre of Regensburg defeated the Solingen Alligators three games to two in the German Bundesliga finals. Regensburg has won four consecutive German championships. Buchbinder won Game Five 9-7, coming back from a 5-1 deficit in the sixth inning before a sellout crowd of 3,000.

■ There were five no-hitters during the Bundesliga regular season. Two occurred on June 8: Brian Fields of Haar threw one against Mannheim and Nick Renault of Solingen threw the other, a seven-inning perfect game, against Berlin.

■ Draci Brno won its 18th Czech national championship, defeating Kotlaka Prague three games to one in the finals.

STANDINGS & LEADERS

Team	W	L	T	GB
Neptunus	34	8	0	—
Kinheim	31	11	0	3
Hoofddorp	29	12	1	4 ½
Amsterdam	28	13	1	5 ½
UVV	17	25	0	17
HCAW	14	27	1	19 ½
Dordrecht	11	30	1	22 ½
ADO	2	40	0	32

BATTING LEADERS

PLAYER, TEAM	AVG	AB	R	H	2B	3B	HR	RBI	BB	SO	SB
De Jong, Bas, AMS	.369	168	35	62	12	4	2	34	10	12	12
Isenia, Percy, AMS	.368	136	24	50	7	0	2	26	18	10	1
Draijer, Remco, KIN	.362	130	32	47	5	3	1	21	33	9	4
Ortez, Philip, PIO	.361	169	41	61	11	3	1	27	19	19	3
Berkenbosch, Kenny, AMS	.359	128	34	46	7	0	2	17	25	6	8
Rooi, Vince, PIO	.357	154	37	55	10	2	3	32	31	8	1
Hato, Bjorn, AMS	.346	104	23	36	1	2	1	20	10	11	8
Legito, Raily, NEP	.346	133	23	46	13	0	2	25	21	10	11
Duursma, Mark, PIO	.336	131	29	44	9	0	0	23	17	11	3
Dille, Benjamin, NEP	.327	162	36	53	19	2	0	28	16	6	1
Rombley, Danny, PIO	.325	163	42	53	11	1	3	28	24	24	12
Balentina, Ramiro, KIN	.320	147	32	47	17	2	1	35	6	20	3
Daantji, Shaldimar, NEP	.319	144	43	46	11	6	1	27	15	22	11
Cremer, Rene, KIN	.318	157	44	50	8	2	1	30	16	26	12
Kemp, Urving, HWK	.317	145	20	46	14	2	0	14	24	19	3

PITCHING LEADERS

PITCHER, TEAM	W	L	ERA	SV	IP	H	R	ER	BB	SO
Heijstek, Kevin, AMS	6	2	1.03	0	78	54	14	9	10	55
Cordemans, Rob, AMS	10	1	1.11	1	81	58	14	10	12	88
Bergman, David, KIN	9	2	1.13	0	96	68	17	12	17	101
Veltkamp, Nick, KIN	9	0	1.76	0	82	57	19	16	22	78
Markwell, Diegomar, NEP	9	3	1.77	0	102	70	32	20	22	92
Rickards, Josh, PIO	9	2	2.11	0	90	59	22	21	32	92
Mezger, Chris, UVV	3	5	2.36	0	46	38	17	12	8	45
Buring, Dennis, PIO	2	2	2.43	0	37	33	16	10	17	16
Granados, Ivan, HCA	6	5	2.50	0	90	74	30	25	21	77
Yntema, Orlando, NEP	7	2	2.90	0	81	66	31	26	37	58

Pestano leads Villa Clara back

Cuba's 52nd Serie Nacional, held in the 2012-2013 winter, brought more changes to an island nation where change has come slowly since the 1959 revolution.

The league dropped back to 16 teams after adding a 17th team in 2011-2012. It also adopted a shorter, 45-game season to accommodate the World Baseball Classic. The shorter season meant a one-division setup, with the top eight teams reaching a modified playoff round. The top four teams in the second round faced each other in best-of-seven semifinals to set up the champoinship round.

Villa Clara won its first championship since winning three in a row from 1993-1995, claiming a best-of-seven series against Matanzas in five games. Vetearn catcher Ariel Pestano, a 39-year-old who played for those mid-90s title teams, proved to be the hero again with a game-winning grand slam in the fifth game. The pitching hero was righthander Freddy Asiel Alvarez, who won two games in the finals and broke Pedro Luis Lazo's record for consecutive scoreless innings in the playoffs. Alvarez ran his streak to 40 2/3 before giving up a run in a 4-1 Game Four victory.

Jose Dariel Abreu of Cienfuegos, in what proved to be his final season in Cuba's top league, again proved too much for Cuban pitchers to handle. The massive first baseman ranked second in the league in batting while leading the league in home runs. After playing for Cuba in the World Baseball Classic, Abreu found his way off the island and signed in the fall with the Chicago White Sox.

Another star passed from the scene shortly after the WBC in tragic fashion. Righthander Yadier Pedroso, a veteran of Olympic and WBC rosters, died in a car crash at age 26. He was a member of the silver-medal '08 Olympic team and had starred for both La Habana and Artemisa in Serie Nacional.

LARRY GOREN

Ariel Pestano

Younger stars such as second baseman Jose Fernandez, who beat out Abreu for the batting title, began to emerge. But Cuba also began testing a policy of allowing younger players to leave the island to play in professional leagues, as Alfredo Despaigne played for Campeche in the Mexican League for the final 33 games of that league's season.

STANDINGS & LEADERS

Team	Round 1	Round 2
Cienfuegos	30-15	26-16
Sancti Spiritus	31-14	22-19
Matanzas	27-18	25-16
Villa Clara	24-21	26-16
Ciego de Avila	24-21	21-21
Industriales	27-18	18-24
Isla de la Juventud	26-19	17-24
Pinar del Rio	24-21	12-30
Las Tunas	23-22	N/A
Granma	19-26	N/A
Guantanamo	19-26	N/A
Holguin	18-27	N/A
Santiago de Cuba	18-27	N/A
Mayabeque	18-27	N/A
Camaguey	17-28	N/A
Artemisa	15-30	N/A

Semifinals
Villa Clara defeated Cienfuegos, 4 games to 2
Matanzas defeated Sancti Spiritus, 4 games to 3
Finals
Villa Clara defeated Matanzas, 4 games to 1

INDIVIDUAL BATTING LEADERS

PLAYER, TEAM	AVE	AB	R	H	2B	3B	HR	RBI	BB	SO	SB
Jose Fernandez, MTZ	.393	150	28	59	9	0	7	35	27	5	0
Jose Dariel Abreu, CFG	.382	136	37	52	9	0	13	36	37	21	1
A. Dairon Varona, CMG	.373	150	19	56	8	2	4	22	12	17	1
Frederich Cepeda, SSP	.362	152	30	55	9	4	7	32	46	22	0
Ariel Sanchez, MTZ	.347	170	32	59	13	1	0	10	22	16	2
Yasmani Tomas, MTZ	.346	127	24	44	9	2	8	25	12	19	1
Alf. Despaigne, GRA	.345	139	30	48	12	0	11	33	43	25	0
Yosvany Peraza , PRI	.345	168	21	58	10	0	9	42	25	24	0
Lorenzo Quintana, PRI	.343	175	23	60	10	2	2	33	7	16	4
Danger Guerrero, MAY	.342	120	12	41	9	0	3	25	21	6	0
Adir Ferran, CFG	.333	165	24	55	10	2	6	29	9	15	2
Andres Reyna, SCU	.327	113	17	37	3	2	0	9	13	16	2
Marino Luis, CMG	.327	168	18	55	5	0	0	14	10	14	10
Yulieski Gourriel, SSP	.325	154	31	50	11	2	4	29	25	14	4
Pavel Quesada, CFG	.324	145	24	47	14	0	4	18	26	18	0

INDIVIDUAL PITCHING LEADERS

PITCHER, TEAM	W	L	ERA	G	IP	R	ER	BB	SO
Ismel Jimenez, SSP	9	0	1.06	11	0	76	56	7	60
Diosdani Castle, VCL	1	1	1.17	24	8	46	27	10	33
Yander Guevara, CAV	8	2	1.42	13	0	83	63	29	31
Wilber Perez, IJV	9	2	1.60	11	0	67	57	29	44
Juan Carlos Viera, LTU	4	3	1.65	20	12	49	32	15	33
Raicel Iglesias, IJV	4	2	1.68	15	6	54	35	20	50
Maykel Martinez, MTZ	4	2	1.83	16	2	69	47	14	16
Misael Siverio, VCL	5	5	1.87	10	0	63	55	13	42
Vladimir Garcia, CAV	4	3	2.02	13	0	85	62	18	57
Olexis Carlos Gonzalez, HOL	3	5	2.10	10	0	56	44	23	29
Yoanys Quiala, HOL	3	2	2.22	16	0	53	49	14	33
Joel Suarez, MTZ	6	1	2.26	10	0	64	50	19	36
Norberto Gonzalez, CFG	4	2	2.30	10	0	63	67	13	34
Alberto Bicet, SCU	5	4	2.31	11	0	62	54	11	35
Yasmani Hernandez, VCL	6	1	2.32	10	0	54	47	22	39

Mexico's Luis Mendoza authored 13⅓ scoreless innings over two Caribbean Series starts

BILL MITCHELL

Mexico outlasts D.R., claims Caribbean title

Host Mexico showed off a new state-of-the-art stadium in Hermosillo, then made history by winning the longest game in Caribbean Series history for its seventh title.

Mexico's Yaquis de Ciudad Obregon won their second Caribbean Series in three seasons, beating the Dominican Republic's Leones del Escogido 4-3 in a game that took 7 hours, 28 minutes to play. The 18-inning game finally ended when Mexico's Doug Clark broke a 3-3 tie with a solo homer in the top of the inning. Reliever Marco Carillo got the final three outs to seal the victory.

"It was a crazy game," said Clark, who reached the majors briefly in 2005 and 2006 with the Giants and Athletics and has played year-round in Mexico since 2011. "I wasn't looking for a home run, but now it's time to celebrate."

The two teams made 19 pitching changes and threw more than 500 pitches in the finale.

The Dominican had dominated the Series to that point, winning five of its first six games behind strong pitching, including four scoreless outings by Fernando Rodney, and Miguel Tejada, the team's captain and steadiest player. Tejada hit a pair of home runs and had tied the finale with an RBI single in the 14th inning, answering a potential game-winning homer by Karim Garcia.

AUSTRALIAN BASEBALL LEAGUE

	W	L	PCT	GB
Canberra Cavalry	27	19	.587	—
Sydney Blue Sox	26	19	.578	½
Perth Heat	25	21	.543	2
Brisbane Bandits	23	22	.511	3½
Adelaide Bite	21	25	.457	6
Melbourne Aces	15	31	.326	12

SEMIFINALS: Perth def. Sydney, 2-0. **FINALS:** Canberra def. Perth, 2-0.

BATTING LEADERS

PLAYER	TEAM	AVG	AB	R	H	2B	3B	HR	RBI	BB	SO	SB
Buschini, Adam	CAN	.363	168	37	61	10	0	15	50	17	27	7
Dening, Mitch	SYD	.347	173	29	60	13	2	5	32	17	15	6
Barnes, Jeremy	CAN	.343	166	21	57	16	0	7	32	22	22	1
Hightower, Kody	CAN	.325	169	37	55	12	0	5	22	25	21	3
Adamson, Corey	PER	.321	134	24	43	10	2	1	18	17	18	10
Stovall, Ryan	CAN	.320	153	32	49	11	4	7	24	9	34	8
Ohlman, Michael	PER	.317	167	30	53	15	1	6	27	14	30	5
Choi, Ji-Man	ADE	.309	139	26	43	6	1	8	31	26	27	1
Onaka, Hirotoshi	BRI	.308	107	16	33	6	0	0	5	20	31	7
D'Antonio, Trent	SYD	.304	115	25	35	8	1	6	27	18	17	4

PITCHING LEADERS

PITCHER	TEAM	W	L	ERA	G	SV	IP	H	BB	SO	AVG
Anderson, Craig	SYD	8	2	2.10	12	0	81	81	5	39	.255
Smith, Chris	BRI	3	3	2.31	9	0	51	36	7	65	.199
Atherton, Tim	SYD	2	1	2.44	9	0	44	34	10	39	.209
Schult, James	BRI	4	2	2.47	8	0	44	33	16	41	.210
Oxspring, Chris	SYD	4	2	2.71	12	0	80	80	17	86	.251
Hussey, John	MEL	3	2	2.77	16	3	39	32	16	28	.222
Vasquez, Virgil	PER	4	3	2.77	9	0	62	56	14	55	.235
Grening, Brian	CAN	4	2	2.87	12	0	75	76	11	64	.260
Lofgren, Chuck	BRI	4	3	3.05	11	0	62	56	24	59	.239
Ruzic, Dushan	ADE	5	2	3.18	16	0	74	59	42	70	.223

INTERNATIONAL

DOMINICAN LEAGUE

	W	L	PCT	GB
Aguilas Cibaenas	32	18	.640	—
Estrellas de Oriente	30	20	.600	2
Toros del Este	23	27	.460	9
Leones del Escogido	23	28	.451	9 ½
Gigantes del Cibao	22	29	.431	10 ½
Tigres del Licey	21	29	.420	11

LIDOM CHAMPIONSHIP: Escogido defeated Aguilas, 4-0

BATTING LEADERS

PLAYER	TEAM	AVG	AB	R	H	2B	3B	HR	RBI	BB	SO	SB
Segura, Jean	GIG	.324	148	26	48	5	2	2	21	10	16	11
Taveras, Oscar	AGU	.316	152	27	48	12	1	5	17	14	21	3
Ramirez, Jose	TOR	.312	141	22	44	5	1	0	22	18	23	10
Lake, Junior	EST	.312	154	23	48	8	1	5	24	15	46	11
Nanita, Ricardo	TOR	.308	117	12	36	7	0	1	12	18	11	5
Francisco, Juan	LIC	.307	127	15	39	7	0	9	29	12	38	0
Luna, Hector	AGU	.303	175	29	53	12	2	7	25	29	30	2
Hernandez, Anderson	LIC	.295	190	25	56	13	2	1	22	19	28	4
Casilla, Alexi	GIG	.289	152	24	44	9	3	2	11	12	17	7
Garcia, Leury	GIG	.285	144	16	41	5	1	2	10	8	34	9

PITCHING LEADERS

PITCHER	TEAM	W	L	ERA	G	SV	IP	H	BB	SO	AVG
Cabrera, Daniel	ESC	5	0	2.16	11	0	58	52	16	32	.244
Baez, Manauris	EST	1	0	2.23	9	0	40	34	15	18	.231
Castro, Fabio	GIG	0	1	2.38	12	0	42	43	15	42	.259
Barcelo, Lorenzo	AGU	4	2	2.63	12	1	65	67	8	40	.264
Castro, Angel	AGU	4	4	2.90	19	0	40	32	9	19	.225
Corcoran, Tim	AGU	1	1	3.73	8	0	41	38	8	30	.242
Valdez, Edward	ESC	0	3	3.99	14	1	47	48	17	32	.262
De Paula, Jose	GIG	0	3	4.05	14	0	40	38	11	42	.244

MEXICAN PACIFIC LEAGUE

	W	L	PCT	GB
Tomateros de Culiacan	43	23	.652	—
Algodoneros de Guasave	37	30	.552	6 ½
Yaquis de Obregon	37	30	.552	6 ½
Aguilas de Mexicali	36	31	.537	7 ½
Naranjeros de Hermosillo	33	35	.485	11
Mayos de Navojoa	30	38	.441	14
Venados de Mazatlan	27	40	.403	16 ½
Caneros de los Mochis	25	41	.379	18

CHAMPIONSHIP: Obregon defeated Mexicali, 4-0

BATTING LEADERS

PLAYER	TEAM	AVG	AB	R	H	2B	3B	HR	RBI	BB	SO	SB
Amezaga, Alfredo	OBR	.344	227	40	78	12	2	5	26	15	39	5
Botts, Jason	MOC	.342	228	36	78	17	0	17	47	30	57	0
Colabello, Chris	GSV	.332	205	38	68	13	0	17	44	23	47	0
Binick, Kraig	GSV	.328	265	45	87	14	0	1	25	31	26	19
Wheeler, Zelous	GSV	.328	244	52	80	21	0	10	42	34	39	11
Weber, Jon	MXC	.325	231	43	75	19	1	5	35	39	47	2
Canizares, Barbaro	OBR	.324	244	45	79	17	0	17	66	42	35	4
Byrd, Marlon	CUL	.318	220	44	70	13	0	16	46	26	57	3
Gomez, Heber	MAZ	.314	242	44	76	11	2	2	22	18	25	2
Acosta, Rolando	NAV	.312	215	28	67	13	1	8	30	20	40	3

PITCHING LEADERS

PITCHER	TEAM	W	L	ERA	G	SV	IP	H	BB	SO	AVG
Armenta, Alejandro	CUL	6	1	2.52	12	0	75	63	14	45	.231
Carrillo, Marco	OBR	6	5	3.13	14	0	86	83	36	54	.263
Campos, Francisco	CUL	6	1	3.18	12	0	68	62	12	44	.241
Sisco, Andrew	GSV	4	3	3.66	14	0	84	65	35	64	.217
Martinez, Javier	NAV	3	4	4.15	14	0	78	77	32	70	.271
Delgadillo, Juan	GSV	5	3	4.26	13	0	80	75	24	60	.252
Lopez, Arturo	OBR	4	3	4.79	13	0	71	77	31	58	.280
Silva, Walter	MAZ	4	7	4.90	15	0	79	86	30	43	.276
Valdez, Rolando	OBR	6	5	5.25	14	0	70	86	23	58	.298
Solis, Tomas	MOC	5	6	5.29	14	0	68	84	24	40	.304

PUERTO RICAN LEAGUE

	W	L	PCT	GB
Criollos de Caguas	24	16	.600	—
Indios de Mayaguez	23	17	.575	1
Cangrejeros de Santurce	21	18	.538	2 ½
Gigantes de Carolina	19	21	.475	5
Leones de Ponce	17	23	.425	7
Atenienses de Manati	15	24	.385	8 ½

PLAYOFFS: Caguas defeated Mayaguez, 4-2.

BATTING LEADERS

PLAYER	TEAM	AVG	AB	R	H	2B	3B	HR	RBI	BB	SO	SB
De Jesus, Ivan	MAN	.364	143	27	52	11	0	3	24	13	23	2
Rosario, Eddie	MAY	.338	133	18	45	9	0	4	20	11	27	2
Navarro, Rey	CAG	.333	114	17	38	8	2	0	18	6	13	4
Ortiz, Daniel	MAY	.331	133	18	44	9	0	1	19	10	19	0
Falu, Irving	MAY	.324	142	30	46	8	4	1	16	14	11	4
Hernandez, Enrique	CAR	.320	147	24	47	12	2	2	17	11	17	4
Mateo, Luis	CAG	.313	134	19	42	7	1	1	15	8	28	7
Gonzalez, Andy	CAG	.311	135	24	42	9	0	5	27	26	30	2
Padilla, Jorge	CAG	.310	113	23	35	9	0	1	12	11	20	3
Gonzalez, Danny	MAY	.308	107	16	33	4	0	0	10	14	26	0

PITCHING LEADERS

PITCHER	TEAM	W	L	ERA	G	SV	IP	H	BB	SO	AVG	AB
Santiago, Tomas	PON	2	1	1.85	10	0	44	32	18	40	.200	160
Durbin, J.D.	SAN	2	1	1.88	7	0	38	29	11	17	.209	139
Romanski, Josh	MAN	3	3	2.83	7	0	35	31	8	29	.237	131
Villa, Kelvin	CAG	3	2	2.93	9	0	43	48	12	41	.284	169
Kehrt, Jeremy	MAY	4	2	3.00	9	0	42	43	12	21	.272	158
Alvarado, Giancarlo	PON	3	2	3.04	8	0	47	39	19	36	.227	172
Lowey, Josh	SAN	3	2	3.14	10	0	52	52	17	41	.259	201
Segovia, Zack	PON	2	5	3.30	11	2	44	42	13	28	.253	166
Collazo, Willie	CAR	3	3	3.46	9	0	42	49	11	14	.308	159
Colon, Joseph	SAN	2	4	3.46	9	0	39	32	17	31	.229	140

VENEZUELAN LEAGUE

	W	L	PCT	GB
Navegantes del Magallanes	36	27	.571	—
Aguilas del Zulia	35	28	.556	1
Caribes de Anzoategui	35	28	.556	1
Leones del Caracas	35	28	.556	1
Cardenales de Lara	34	29	.540	2
Tiburones de La Guaira	29	33	.468	6 ½
Bravos de Margarita	23	38	.377	12
Tigres de Aragua	23	39	.371	12 ½

CHAMPIONSHIP: Magallanes defeated Lara, 4-3.

BATTING LEADERS

PLAYER	TEAM	AVG	AB	R	H	2B	3B	HR	RBI	BB	SO	SB
Hernandez, Gorkys	ORI	.367	226	48	83	13	2	2	23	28	42	15
Castillo, Jose	ORI	.330	233	19	77	9	1	4	45	18	22	4
Jimenez, Luis	LAR	.324	170	33	55	9	1	9	40	39	29	1
Suarez, Cesar	LAG	.320	250	37	80	18	1	6	30	17	26	3
Lopez, Jose	LAR	.311	164	25	51	12	1	3	33	24	23	0
Romero, Alex	ARA	.308	221	30	68	12	2	2	22	31	20	0
Flores, Jose	ZUL	.307	166	20	51	8	0	1	18	18	25	3
Valbuena, Luis	LAR	.306	183	32	56	15	1	6	39	34	33	3
Diaz, Frank	MAR	.303	201	27	61	15	2	2	25	20	37	2
Gattis, Evan	ZUL	.303	195	32	59	9	0	16	44	16	30	1

PITCHING LEADERS

PITCHER	TEAM	W	L	ERA	G	SV	IP	H	BB	SO	AVG
Boscan, Wilfredo	ZUL	3	1	1.80	12	0	55	45	20	40	.228
Bibens-Dirkx, Austin	ZUL	2	2	2.35	12	1	54	51	15	57	.263
Pollok, Dwayne	ZUL	7	2	2.36	13	0	72	79	10	46	.284
Negrin, Yoanner	CAR	4	1	2.61	12	0	59	64	18	38	.281
Schmidt, Josh	ZUL	2	3	3.17	11	0	60	50	21	57	.234
Perez, Sergio	MAG	9	4	3.50	14	0	72	65	21	59	.243
Brummett, Tyson	LAG	4	1	3.79	11	0	57	50	19	27	.238
Chacin, Gustavo	MAG	4	4	3.80	14	0	69	70	18	39	.266
Chirinos, Luis	MAR	3	3	4.13	14	0	61	72	28	43	.306

COLLEGE

ANDREW WOOLLEY

UCLA won its first national championship behind historically good pitching and timely hitting

Blue-collar Bruins win title their own way

BY AARON FITT

OMAHA

UCLA head coach John Savage stood off to the side of the makeshift stage that had been erected around home plate, cradling the national championship trophy in both hands, a huge grin plastered across his face.

"Can you believe we did it?" he said, as his grin turned sly. "And the *way* we did it!"

UCLA won its first national championship with an 8-0 victory against Mississippi State in the second game of the College World Series Finals. The *way* the Bruins marched unbeaten through the postseason wasn't quite like any champion that came before them.

UCLA scored just 19 runs in its five games in the College World Series—the fewest ever for a national champion. The Bruins slugged .193 in Omaha—the lowest ever for a national champion by a wide margin (the next closest was the 1970 Southern California team at .274). UCLA hit .227 in Omaha, the lowest of any champion in the metal-bat era. The Bruins did not hit a home run in Omaha—they didn't even come close—making them the first homerless champion since 1966.

But in becoming the seventh member of the Pacific-12 Conference to win the CWS, UCLA also became the first team to allow one run or fewer in every Series game en route to the national championship. The Bruins, who allowed just 14 runs total during their 10-0 run through the NCAA tournament, pitched historically well in the postseason.

The title-clinching victory featured yet another dominating performance by a UCLA starter, as righthander Nick Vander Tuig allowed just five hits over eight shutout innings, striking out six. In two CWS starts, Vander Tuig gave up one run in 15 innings.

Back on March 16, after Vander Tuig threw his first career shutout against Washington, Savage sat in his office at UCLA's Jackie Robinson Stadium, leaned back in his chair and tried to assess his team, which was off to a 14-3 start.

"We're still trying to find out what we've got," Savage said then. "We haven't swung the bats very well—it's no secret—but we think we have some good, young, capable players. We feel like we are deep. We don't have that star power right now, certainly on offense. We have a bunch of

COACHING CAROUSEL

SCHOOL	IN (PREVIOUS JOB)	OUT (REASON/NEW JOB)
Army	* Matt Reid (Army associate head coach)	Joe Sottolano (fired)
Auburn	Sunny Golloway (Oklahoma head coach)	John Pawlowski (fired)
Cal State Northridge	Greg Moore (San Francisco associate head coach)	Matt Curtis (fired)
Cincinnati	Ty Neal (Indiana assistant)	Brian Cleary (fired)
Georgia	Scott Stricklin (Kent State head coach)	David Perno (resigned)
Indiana State	Mitch Hannahs (Lincoln Trail, Ill., CC head coach)	Rick Heller (Iowa head coach)
Iowa	Rick Heller (Indiana State head coach)	Jack Dahm (fired)
Kent State	Jeff Duncan (Purdue associate head coach)	Scott Stricklin (Georgia head coach)
Longwood	Brian McCullough (Longwood assistant)	Buddy Bolding (retired)
McNeese State	Justin Hill (La.-Monroe associate head coach)	Terry Burrows (resigned)
Miami (Ohio)	Danny Hayden (Xavier assistant)	Dan Simonds (Indiana associate head coach)
Nevada	Jay Johnson (San Diego associate head coach)	Gary Powers (retired)
New Orleans	Ron Maestri (former UNO head coach)	Bruce Peddie (fired)
Oklahoma	Pete Hughes (Virginia Tech head coach)	Sunny Golloway (Auburn head coach)
Pennsylvania	John Yurkow (Penn assistant)	John Cole (fired)
Penn State	Rob Cooper (Wright State head coach)	Robbie Wine (resigned)
Richmond	Tracy Woodson (Valparaiso head coach)	Mark McQueen (resigned)
St. Mary's	Eric Valenzuela (San Diego State assistant)	Jedd Soto (resigned)
Southeastern Louisiana	* Matt Riser (SELU Assistant)	Jay Artigues (SELU Athletic director)
Tennessee-Martin	* Brad Goss (UT Martin assistant)	Bubba Cates (reassigned)
Valparaiso	Brian Schmack (Valparaiso assistant)	Tracy Woodson (Richmond head coach)
Virginia Tech	Pat Mason (Virginia Tech associate head coach)	Pete Hughes (Oklahoma head coach)
Wichita State	Todd Butler (Arkansas associate head coach)	Gene Stephenson (fired)
Wright State	Greg Lovelady (Wright State associate head coach)	Rob Cooper (Penn State head coach)

*Acting/interim head coach

guys that are blue-collar guys on the mound, with good stuff. It's not crazy stuff, but it's guys that are pounding the zone with multiple pitches. They're good enough."

As it turned out, Savage knew exactly what he had, because his assessment in mid-March rang truer than ever in late June. UCLA might have lacked star power on offense, but its pitching was most definitely good enough. Vander Tuig and fellow junior righthander Adam Plutko will go down as one of the great pitching tandems in College World Series history. Each of them started twice in Omaha, and each of them won twice; they allowed a combined three runs in 28 innings (0.96 ERA). Plutko, who won UCLA's CWS opener against Louisiana State and its Finals opener against Mississippi State, was named CWS Most Outstanding Player.

Afterward, Plutko recalled a meeting he had with Savage when he returned to campus last summer, shortly after having knee surgery.

"He told this story one time about how he had Mark Prior and Barry Zito at USC, and they could never win a national championship for him," Plutko said, referencing Savage's days as Southern California's pitching coach. "And a guy named Seth Etherton, a guy most people have never heard of, did. I sat down in that chair, and I looked him

right in the eye, and I said, 'I'm going to be that Seth Etherton for us. I'm going to take it home.'"

He did just that, and so did sophomore lefty Grant Watson (who shut down North Carolina in a 4-1 Series victory) and Vander Tuig, who had Tommy John surgery before he ever showed up at UCLA and started his collegiate career in the bullpen. He joined Plutko in the rotation as a sophomore and helped lead the Bruins to Omaha, and he said that experience helped prepare him to take home the big prize this year.

Before the season started, Vander Tuig said, the Bruins visited the school's Hall of Champions on the day of their first weight-lifting session.

"(Savage) took us to the national championships, and there were so many," Vander Tuig said, referencing the school's 108 trophies for NCAA team championships. "Then we went to baseball, and there were none. And I remember Coach was saying, 'We've got to get our name on that board.' So I think we worked hard from Day One."

Sophomore closer David Berg, who broke the NCAA single-season saves record in the Finals opener and tied the single-season appearances record with his 51st of the year a day later, harkened back to another team meeting, in early April after the Bruins had dropped a home series against Oregon State—their second straight series loss.

"We all sat in the locker room and looked at each other . . . we had gone through a little bit of a rough patch," Berg said. "The bats weren't goin' and it felt like, 'Hey, we're not achieving what we could,' and we weren't sure we were putting our all into everything we did. So we sat in that meeting and looked each other in the eyes and made that commitment to each other that, hey, we have a chance to do something special here."

After that meeting, Berg said, "you could really just see a spark where every single detail, we really put 100 percent into everything we did." From weight lifting to practice to cleaning the bus, the Bruins became wholly dedicated to getting every little detail right.

That unwavering focus was critical in Omaha, where UCLA played superb defense and consistently took advantage when its opponents made mistakes. The Bruins cobbled together just enough offense to win for most of the CWS, moving runners over when they reached via walks, errors, wild pitches or even hits. In fact, UCLA tied the CWS record with 12 sacrifice bunts, matching the 1962 Santa Clara team. And when the Bruins needed

a timely hit in the postseason, they generally got one.

They got a whole bunch in the final game, from the first inning on. The game started in typical UCLA fashion, with leadoff man Brian Carroll getting hit by a pitch, reaching third when MSU committed two errors on Kevin Kramer's sacrifice bunt attempt, and scoring on Eric Filia's sacrifice fly. It was the kind of opportunism UCLA had illustrated throughout the postseason.

In the third, UCLA's bats started to heat up in a way they hadn't previously in Omaha. The Bruins added two more runs in that frame on a pair of singles and a perfect safety squeeze by Filia. They added two more in the fourth on two hits, a sacrifice bunt and a sacrifice fly. And they strung together four straight hits in the eighth to break the game wide open with two more runs. Filia led UCLA's 12-hit barrage, going 2-for-3 with five RBIs, capped by a two-run single in the eighth. In the postseason, he hit a team-best .444 with 11 RBIs.

In the end, it was a team effort. Sure, UCLA's pitching and defense were its biggest strengths, but

COLLEGE WORLD SERIES CHAMPIONS

YEAR	CHAMPION	COACH	RECORD	RUNNER-UP	MOST OUTSTANDING PLAYER
1948	Southern California	Sam Barry	40-12	Yale	None selected
1949	Texas*	Bibb Falk	23-7	Wake Forest	Charles Teague, 2b, Wake Forest
1950	Texas	Bibb Falk	27-6	Washington State	Ray VanCleef, of, Rutgers
1951	Oklahoma*	Jack Baer	19-9	Tennessee	Sid Hatfield, 1b-p, Tennessee
1952	Holy Cross	Jack Barry	21-3	Missouri	Jim O'Neill, p, Holy Cross
1953	Michigan	Ray Fisher	21-9	Texas	J.L. Smith, p, Texas
1954	Missouri	Hi Simmons	22-4	Rollins	Tom Yewcic, c, Michigan State
1955	Wake Forest	Taylor Sanford	29-7	Western Michigan	Tom Borland, p, Oklahoma State
1956	Minnesota	Dick Siebert	33-9	Arizona	Jerry Thomas, p, Minnesota
1957	California*	George Wolfman	35-10	Penn State	Cal Emery, 1b-p, Penn State
1958	Southern California	Rod Dedeaux	35-7	Missouri	Bill Thom, p, Southern California
1959	Oklahoma State	Toby Greene	27-5	Arizona	Jim Dobson, 3b, Oklahoma State
1960	Minnesota	Dick Siebert	34-7	Southern California	John Erickson, 2b, Minnesota
1961	Southern California*	Rod Dedeaux	43-9	Oklahoma State	Littleton Fowler, p, Oklahoma State
1962	Michigan	Don Lund	31-13	Santa Clara	Bob Garibaldi, p, Santa Clara
1963	Southern California	Rod Dedeaux	37-16	Arizona	Bud Hollowell, c, Southern California
1964	Minnesota	Dick Siebert	31-12	Missouri	Joe Ferris, p, Maine
1965	Arizona State	Bobby Winkles	54-8	Ohio State	Sal Bando, 3b, Arizona State
1966	Ohio State	Marty Karow	27-6	Oklahoma State	Steve Arlin, p, Ohio State
1967	Arizona State	Bobby Winkles	53-12	Houston	Ron Davini, c, Arizona State
1968	Southern California*	Rod Dedeaux	45-14	Southern Illinois	Bill Seinsoth, 1b, Southern California
1969	Arizona State	Bobby Winkles	56-11	Tulsa	John Dolinsek, of, Arizona State
1970	Southern California	Rod Dedeaux	51-13	Florida State	Gene Ammann, p, Florida State
1971	Southern California	Rod Dedeaux	53-13	Southern Illinois	Jerry Tabb, 1b, Tulsa
1972	Southern California	Rod Dedeaux	50-13	Arizona State	Russ McQueen, p, Southern California
1973	Southern California*	Rod Dedeaux	51-11	Arizona State	Dave Winfield, of-p, Minnesota
1974	Southern California	Rod Dedeaux	50-20	Miami	George Milke, p, Southern California
1975	Texas	Cliff Gustafson	56-6	South Carolina	Mickey Reichenbach, 1b, Texas
1976	Arizona	Jerry Kindall	56-17	Eastern Michigan	Steve Powers, dh-p, Arizona
1977	Arizona State	Jim Brock	57-12	South Carolina	Bob Horner, 3b, Arizona State
1978	Southern California*	Rod Dedeaux	54-9	Arizona State	Rod Boxberger, p, Southern California
1979	Cal State Fullerton	Augie Garrido	60-14	Arkansas	Tony Hudson, p, Cal State Fullerton
1980	Arizona	Jerry Kindall	45-21	Hawaii	Terry Francona, of, Arizona

the Bruins were simply sharper, more focused and more cohesive than every other team they played in the postseason. That is how they vanquished one juggernaut after another, from Cal State Fullerton in super regionals to Louisiana State, N.C. State, North Carolina and Mississippi State in Omaha. All five were No. 1 regional seeds and hosts, while North Carolina (No. 1), LSU (No. 4) and Cal State Fullerton (No. 5) were national seeds.

Now, with three CWS trips in four years capped by an undefeated postseason run to a national championship, UCLA can count itself among college baseball's truly elite programs.

"I'm so proud of our program, players, coaches," Savage said. "This is for the UCLA baseball family: Coach (Gary) Adams, coach (Art) Reichle, (athletics director) Dan Guerrero, all the people that have been meaningful to this program for many, many years, certainly before I got there, and it's an honor and a privilege to be the coach at UCLA.

"I'm just so proud of these guys. They did it on the field. I don't think any of the experts thought we would be here at this stage, and we did it the right way. We played baseball. We played good baseball. We pitched, we defended. We had quality offense, opportunistic offense for sure, and at the end of the day, I think we outlasted everybody."

It wasn't the same way Arizona dominated during its unbeaten run to the 2012 national title. It was different from South Carolina's 10-0 run to the 2011 championship.

It was UCLA's way, all the way.

Bulldogs Reach New Heights

Before the season began, Mississippi State's coaches asked every one of their players to give a three- to five-minute presentation to the rest of the team on any topic they wanted. Junior shortstop Adam Frazier opted to make his own PowerPoint presentation.

"He had slides, pictures of this stadium," Mississippi State coach John Cohen recalled, gesturing around him at TD Ameritrade Park. "And he said, 'When we get there, I don't want it to be new to us. We will have already seen the dugouts. We will have already seen the locker rooms. We will have already seen the playing surfaces, the stands.' How can you not be moved by that?

*Undefeated

YEAR	CHAMPION	COACH	RECORD	RUNNER-UP	MOST OUTSTANDING PLAYER
1981	Arizona State	Jim Brock	55-13	Oklahoma State	Stan Holmes, of, Arizona State
1982	Miami	Ron Fraser	57-18	Wichita State	Dan Smith, p, Miami
1983	Texas	Cliff Gustafson	66-14	Alabama	Calvin Schiraldi, p, Texas
1984	Cal State Fullerton	Augie Garrido	66-20	Texas	John Fishel, of, Cal State Fullerton
1985	Miami*	Ron Fraser	64-16	Texas	Greg Ellena, dh, Miami
1986	Arizona	Jerry Kindall	49-19	Florida State	Mike Senne, of, Arizona
1987	Stanford	Mark Marquess	53-17	Oklahoma State	Paul Carey, of, Stanford
1988	Stanford	Mark Marquess	46-23	Arizona State	Lee Plemel, p, Stanford
1989	Wichita State	Gene Stephenson	68-16	Texas	Greg Brummett, p, Wichita State
1990	Georgia	Steve Webber	52-19	Oklahoma State	Mike Rebhan, p, Georgia
1991	Louisiana State*	Skip Bertman	55-18	Wichita State	Gary Hymel, c, Louisiana State
1992	Pepperdine*	Andy Lopez	48-11	Cal State Fullerton	Phil Nevin, 3b, Cal State Fullerton
1993	Louisiana State	Skip Bertman	53-17	Wichita State	Todd Walker, 2b, Louisiana State
1994	Oklahoma*	Larry Cochell	50-17	Georgia Tech	Chip Glass, of, Oklahoma
1995	Cal State Fullerton*	Augie Garrido	57-9	Southern California	Mark Kotsay, of-p, Cal State Fullerton
1996	Louisiana State*	Skip Bertman	52-15	Miami	Pat Burrell, 3b, Miami
1997	Louisiana State*	Skip Bertman	57-13	Alabama	Brandon Larson, ss, Louisiana State
1998	Southern California	Mike Gillespie	49-17	Arizona State	Wes Rachels, 2b, Southern California
1999	Miami*	Jim Morris	50-13	Florida State	Marshall McDougall, 2b, Florida State
2000	Louisiana State*	Skip Bertman	52-17	Stanford	Trey Hodges, rhp, Louisiana State
2001	Miami*	Jim Morris	53-12	Stanford	Charlton Jimerson, of, Miami
2002	Texas*	Augie Garrido	57-15	South Carolina	Huston Street, rhp, Texas
2003	Rice	Wayne Graham	58-12	Stanford	John Hudgins, rhp, Stanford
2004	Cal State Fullerton	George Horton	47-22	Texas	Jason Windsor, rhp, Cal State Fullerton
2005	Texas*	Augie Garrido	56-16	Florida	David Maroul, 3b, Texas
2006	Oregon State	Pat Casey	50-16	North Carolina	Jonah Nickerson, rhp, Oregon State
2007	Oregon State*	Pat Casey	49-18	North Carolina	Jorge Reyes, rhp, Oregon State
2008	Fresno State	Mike Batesole	47-31	Georgia	Tommy Mendonca, 3b, Fresno State
2009	Louisiana State	Paul Mainieri	56-17	Texas	Jared Mitchell, of, Louisiana State
2010	South Carolina	Ray Tanner	54-16	UCLA	Jackie Bradley Jr., of, South Carolina
2011	South Carolina*	Ray Tanner	55-14	Florida	Scott Wingo, 2b, South Carolina
2012	Arizona*	Andy Lopez	48-17	South Carolina	Robert Refsnyder, of, Arizona
2013	UCLA*	John Savage	49-17	Mississippi State	Adam Plutko, rhp, UCLA

COLLEGE

"Everything he did in that PowerPoint and all the things did in the presentations really came to fruition. It's pretty remarkable when you get 18-22-year-olds—35 of them—and everything they talk about is within an eyelash of coming true."

The Bulldogs handled Omaha like seasoned veterans, not like a program making its first College World Series appearance in six years. They acted as if they felt right at home in TD Ameritrade Park, and they played at a very high level for three games to reach the CWS Finals for the first time ever. But they fell just short of their ultimate goal.

After toppling No. 6 national seed Virginia in the Charlottesville Super Regional, the Bulldogs dispatched another power in Omaha, twice beating No. 3 national seed Oregon State. They also showed plenty of heart in a come-from-behind Series win against a quality Indiana club. But MSU could not sustain its high level of play in the Finals, as UCLA played cleaner defense, executed better on offense, and pitched better than the Bulldogs did.

"It bothers me that we didn't play well the last two days, but I think we played 15 postseason games, and I feel like we didn't play well in two of them," Cohen said. "That is disappointing, but I will always have a special spot in my heart for this group of kids, because everything they were doing was new to them."

Cohen inherited a program five years ago that was coming off a 23-win season. By 2011, Cohen and his fine coaching staff saw their rebuilding effort accelerate, as they took the Bulldogs to the Gainesville Super Regional, where they pushed mighty Florida to the brink. In 2012, they caught fire down the stretch and won the SEC tournament, though they ran out of gas in regionals.

Mississippi State entered 2013 ranked No. 5 in the BA Top 25, and the Bulldogs justified those lofty preseason expectations by getting back to Omaha, and making it deeper into the tournament than any MSU team before them. The Bulldogs won over college baseball fans around the country with their dugout antics, their shaggy looks and their cohesiveness. Baseball is supposed to be fun, and this team made it fun.

UCLA's domination of the final game sucked much of the life out of TD Ameritrade Park, which was overrun with maroon shirts. Mississippi State reinforced that its fans are among the most dedicated and passionate in college baseball, and the folks in maroon were justifiably proud of MSU's season. Longtime CWS observers couldn't remember a fan base turning out in such numbers

RPI RANKINGS

The Ratings Percentage Index is an important tool used by the NCAA in selecting at-large teams for the 64-team Division I regional tournament. The NCAA now releases its RPI rankings during the season. These were the top 100 finishers for 2013. A team's rank in the final Baseball America Top 25 is indicated in parentheses, and College World Series teams are in bold.

1. **North Carolina** (3)	59-12	51. San Francisco	35-24
2. Vanderbilt (9)	54-12	52. Oklahoma State (24)	41-19
3. **Louisiana State** (5)	57-11	53. Coastal Carolina	37-23
3. **Oregon State** (4)	52-13	54. Brigham Young	32-21
5. Virginia (11)	50-12	55. Western Carolina	39-20
6. Cal State Fullerton (10)	51-10	56. Elon	34-30
7. **N.C. State** (6)	50-16	57. UC Santa Barbara	35-25
8. **Mississippi State** (2)	51-20	58. Southeastern La.	36-24
9. **UCLA** (1)	49-17	59. Arizona	34-21
10. Florida State (12)	47-17	60. New Mexico	37-22
11. Oregon (17)	48-16	61. Wake Forest	28-27
12. **Indiana** (7)	49-16	62. Pittsburgh	42-17
13. South Carolina (14)	43-20	63. Stanford	32-22
14. **Louisville** (8)	51-14	64. Creighton	30-18
15. Virginia Tech (19)	40-22	65. Ohio State	35-23
16. Kansas State (13)	45-19	66. Rutgers	28-30
17. Clemson	40-22	67. Houston	36-22
18. South Alabama	43-20	68. Illinois State	39-19
19. Miami	37-25	69. Kansas	34-25
20. Arizona State (22)	37-22	70. North Florida	40-19
21. Georgia Tech	37-27	71. Connecticut	35-28
22. Mississippi	38-24	72. The Citadel	35-25
23. Louisiana-Lafayette	43-20	72. South Florida	36-22
24. Florida Atlantic (20)	42-22	74. Texas	27-24
25. Rice (16)	44-20	75. Long Beach State	29-27
26. Austin Peay State (21)	47-15	76. Baylor	27-28
27. Oklahoma (15)	43-21	77. Saint Louis	41-21
28. Cal Poly	40-19	78. Lamar	39-20
29. Alabama	35-28	79. Duke	26-29
30. Arkansas (18)	39-22	80. UC Irvine	33-22
31. Nebraska	29-30	81. West Virginia	33-26
32. Texas A&M	34-29	82. Towson	30-30
33. Notre Dame	34-24	83. East Carolina	31-26
34. William & Mary	39-24	84. Nevada-Las Vegas	37-20
35. Troy (25)	42-20	85. Florida Gulf Coast	37-20
36. Illinois	35-20	86. Belmont	38-20
37. Mercer	43-18	87. Kent State	36-23
38. Sam Houston State	38-22	88. East Tennessee State	36-24
39. San Diego (23)	37-25	89. Canisius	42-17
40. UNC Wilmington	38-23	90. Washington	24-32
41. Michigan State	33-17	91. Appalachian State	30-24
42. Campbell	49-10	92. Columbia	28-21
43. Bryant	45-18	93. Middle Tenn. State	28-28
44. Seton Hall	37-19	94. TAMU-Corpus Christi	33-24
45. Central Arkansas	42-22	95. Tennessee Tech	40-17
46. Maryland	30-25	96. Memphis	35-24
47. Auburn	33-23	97. San Diego State	31-31
48. Florida	29-30	98. Cal State Northridge	31-26
49. Liberty	36-29	99. College of Charleston	31-26
50. Kentucky	30-25	100. Delaware	33-22

as Bulldogs fans did for the Finals.

"I really appreciate the comments about this team going further than any other (in school history), but what they have done is laid the foundation for some future teams," Cohen said. "Because we're going to come back here, and we're going to win this thing. That's what we're here to do—that's why I came to Mississippi State, and we're going to

COLLEGE ALL-AMERICA TEAM

FIRST TEAM

POS.	NAME	YEAR	AVG	OBP	SLG	AB	R	H	HR	RBI	BB	SO	SB
C	Stuart Turner, Mississippi	Jr.	.374	.444	.518	222	44	83	5	51	28	37	2
1B	D.J. Peterson, New Mexico	Jr.	.408	.520	.807	218	68	89	18	72	46	35	5
2B	Tony Kemp, Vanderbilt	Jr.	.391	.471	.485	266	64	104	0	33	35	32	34
3B	Kris Bryant, San Diego	Jr.	.329	.493	.820	228	80	75	31	62	66	44	7
SS	Alex Bregman, Louisiana State	Fr.	.369	.417	.546	282	59	104	6	52	24	25	16
OF	Daniel Palka, Georgia Tech	Jr.	.342	.436	.637	237	55	81	17	66	31	60	6
OF	Mike Papi, Virginia	So.	.381	.517	.619	176	57	67	7	57	45	25	6
OF	Hunter Renfroe, Mississippi State	Jr.	.345	.431	.620	255	56	88	16	65	35	43	9
DH	Colin Moran, North Carolina	Jr.	.357	.485	.579	235	69	84	13	84	55	20	1
UT	Michael Lorenzen, Cal State Fullerton	Jr.	.335	.412	.515	227	40	76	7	54	19	39	12

POS.	NAME	YEAR	W	L	ERA	G	CG	SV	IP	H	BB	SO	AVG
SP	Thomas Eshelman, Cal State Fullerton	Fr.	12	3	1.48	17	2	0	116	86	3	83	.204
SP	Jonathan Gray, Oklahoma	Jr.	10	3	1.64	17	4	0	126	83	24	147	.189
SP	Andrew Moore, Oregon State	Fr.	14	2	1.79	19	3	1	131	93	28	72	.207
SP	Aaron Nola, Louisiana State	So.	12	1	1.57	17	5	0	126	83	18	122	.188
RP	David Berg, UCLA	So.	7	0	0.92	51	0	24	78	55	11	78	.198
UT	Michael Lorenzen, Cal State Fullerton	Jr.	3	0	1.99	22	0	19	23	17	4	20	.205

SECOND TEAM

POS.	NAME	YEAR	AVG	OBP	SLG	AB	R	H	HR	RBI	BB	SO	SB
C	Kyle Schwarber, Indiana	So.	.366	.456	.647	235	65	86	18	54	42	37	4
1B	Ryan Kinsella, Elon	Jr.	.313	.409	.656	256	56	80	21	78	38	59	7
2B	Michael Bass, UNC Wilmington	Sr.	.380	.479	.560	216	62	82	4	36	33	28	26
3B	Eric Jagielo, Notre Dame	Jr.	.388	.500	.633	196	47	76	9	53	35	33	3
SS	Hunter Dozier, Stephen F. Austin State	Jr.	.396	.482	.755	212	47	84	17	52	34	35	12
OF	Philip Ervin, Samford	Jr.	.337	.459	.597	196	58	66	11	40	39	25	21
OF	Justin Parr, Illinois	Sr.	.398	.453	.576	231	43	92	6	53	22	26	16
OF	Mike Tauchman, Bradley	Sr.	.425	.513	.597	186	52	79	2	41	27	24	28
DH	Matt Oberste, Oklahoma	Jr.	.373	.458	.622	241	53	90	11	60	26	33	13
UT	Marco Gonzales, Gonzaga	Jr.	.311	.375	.389	167	16	52	2	26	19	34	3

POS.	NAME	YEAR	W	L	ERA	G	CG	SV	IP	H	BB	SO	AVG
SP	Mark Appel, Stanford	Sr.	10	4	2.12	14	4	0	106	80	23	130	.203
SP	Tyler Beede, Vanderbilt	So.	14	1	2.32	17	0	0	101	64	63	103	.187
SP	Justin Garza, Cal State Fullerton	Fr.	12	0	2.03	17	0	0	115	84	17	95	.205
SP	Ryne Stanek, Arkansas	Jr.	10	2	1.39	16	1	0	97	72	41	79	.207
RP	Jonathan Holder, Mississippi State	So.	2	0	1.65	34	0	21	55	33	17	90	.175
UT	Marco Gonzales, Gonzaga	Jr.	7	3	2.80	17	2	1	106	102	25	96	.256

THIRD TEAM

POS.	NAME	YEAR	AVG	OBP	SLG	AB	R	H	HR	RBI	BB	SO	SB
C	Zane Evans, Georgia Tech	Jr.	.361	.430	.590	244	47	88	14	66	33	40	0
1B	Jimmy Yezzo, Delaware	Jr.	.410	.453	.714	234	52	96	13	64	20	30	1
2B	Ross Kivett, Kansas State	Jr.	.360	.440	.483	261	57	94	3	39	29	27	26
3B	Dustin DeMuth, Indiana	Jr.	.377	.433	.545	244	46	92	5	41	19	40	11
SS	Trea Turner, North Carolina State	So.	.368	.455	.553	228	66	84	7	42	38	31	30
OF	Forrestt Allday, Central Arkansas	Sr.	.365	.503	.472	233	59	85	3	36	53	23	15
OF	Danny Collins, Troy	Jr.	.360	.452	.631	236	62	85	11	68	32	33	1
OF	Ben McQuown, Campbell	Jr.	.329	.443	.468	222	65	73	4	30	37	29	54
DH	L.B. Dantzler, South Carolina	Sr.	.322	.444	.617	214	46	69	15	53	42	50	2
UT	C.K. Irby, Samford	Jr.	.383	.450	.599	222	49	85	8	59	28	32	6

POS.	NAME	YEAR	W	L	ERA	G	CG	SV	IP	H	BB	SO	AVG
SP	Matt Boyd, Oregon State	Sr.	11	4	2.04	18	4	1	133	92	33	122	.197
SP	Nick Petree, Missouri State	Jr.	8	1	1.61	14	2	0	100	79	19	111	.217
SP	Carlos Rodon, North Carolina State	So.	10	3	2.99	19	3	0	132	94	45	184	.200
SP	Kevin Ziomek, Vanderbilt	Jr.	11	3	2.12	17	3	0	119	79	40	115	.188
RP	Zech Lemond, Rice	So.	6	1	1.12	29	0	14	64	42	18	61	.186
UT	C.K. Irby, Samford	Jr.	7	6	4.14	15	3	0	91	80	33	90	.241

keep knocking that door down."

CWS NOTES

■ The lack of offense at TD Ameritrade Park dominated discussion during most of the College World Series. In the third year of the new park and the BBCOR bats, offense tumbled to historically low levels. There were just 86 runs scored in the 14 CWS games, the fewest in CWS history dating back to 1950. The previous low was 98 in 1973—the last year before metal bats and the DH were implemented. The wind blew in throughout

COLLEGE

most of the tournament, often causing line drives that looked like extra-base hits to hang up in the gaps long enough for defenders to get underneath them. And of course, the wind repeatedly killed shots that looked like surefire home runs off the bat. Just three home runs were hit in 14 games in Omaha, the fewest at a CWS since 1966. In the metal-bat era, the previous low for home runs in the CWS was nine in 2011.

Obviously, BBCOR bats have suppressed offense nationwide, but the home run is still part of the game in other parks—just not at TDAP, which has never seen a home run hit between the 375-foot power alleys in three seasons.

■ Plenty of fans and reporters lamented the fact that most of the CWS games had a similar feel. With the exception of an 11-4 Oregon State win against Louisville, the games were all low-scoring affairs loaded with sacrifice bunts, and three-run leads felt insurmountable. In fact, teams that lead after eight innings at TDAP are 38-0 in the CWS play over the last three years. But fans keep showing up. The 2013 CWS drew 341,483 fans, an all-time record. The session-by-session average was 24,392, which beats the previous record set in 2005 (23,952). And the attendance in the final game was 27,127, a new TD Ameritrade Park record.

■ Since 2000, teams from the Pac-12 and SEC have won eight of 14 championships. Seven of the last eight champions have come from those two leagues, with the only exception being Fresno State in 2008. The Pac-12 has claimed four of the last eight titles, while the SEC has had a CWS finalist in six straight seasons.

■ Just three national seeds reached Omaha—No. 1 North Carolina, No. 3 Oregon State, and No. 4 LSU. That is tied for the fewest national seeds to reach the CWS since the 64-team era began in 1999. But it was still a CWS field jammed with powerhouses. For the first time in the 64-team era, all eight CWS participants were No. 1 seeds in regionals.

■ A year after Kent State and Stony Brook crashed the College World Series, Indiana became the first Big Ten team to reach Omaha since Barry Larkin's Michigan Wolverines in 1984. The Hoosiers opened their sparkling new Bart Kaufman Field with a bang, winning the Big Ten regular-season title outright for the first time since 1932, then winning the conference tournament and earning a trip to regionals for the third time ever. The Hoosiers broke into the BA Top 25 for the first time ever after taking two of three at Florida in Week Four, and they stayed in the rankings from that point on. After winning their home regional in three games, the Hoosiers went to Tallahassee and outslugged Florida State in two games, propelling them to Omaha for the first time ever. IU went 1-2 in Omaha, and it was was shut out for the first time all season in its final game against MSU.

■ Indiana was the only first-timer in the CWS field. Half of the field also participated in the 2007 CWS (UNC, Louisville, Mississippi State and Oregon State). N.C. State made its first appearance since 1968 (and its second in school history). The Wolfpack faced rival North Carolina twice in Omaha, winning the opener behind ace Carlos Rodon but losing the rematch with

COLLEGE WORLD SERIES

STANDINGS

BRACKET ONE	W	L
Mississippi State	3	0
Oregon State	2	2
Indiana	1	2
Louisville	0	2

BRACKET TWO	W	L
UCLA	3	0
North Carolina	2	2
N.C. State	1	2
Louisiana State	0	2

CWS FINALS (BEST OF THREE)
June 24: UCLA 3, Mississippi State 1
June 25: UCLA 4, Mississippi State 0

ALL-TOURNAMENT TEAM
C: Brian Holberton, North Carolina. **1B:** Wes Rea, Mississippi State. **2B:** Brett Pirtle, Mississippi State. **3B:** Colin Moran, North Carolina. **SS:** Pat Valaika, UCLA. **OF:** Michael Conforto, Oregon State; Eric Filia, UCLA; Hunter Renfroe, Mississippi State. **DH:** Trey Porter, Mississippi State. **P:** *Adam Plutko, UCLA; Nick Vander Tuig, UCLA.
*Named Most Outstanding Player.

BATTING
(Minimum 8 PA)

PLAYER	AVG	AB	R	H	2B	3B	HR	RBI	SB
Cole Sturgeon, UofL	.714	7	0	5	0	0	0	0	0
Mason Katz, LSU	.600	5	1	3	0	0	1	2	0
Mark Laird, LSU	.556	9	0	5	1	0	0	0	0
Michael Conforto, OSU	.438	16	2	7	4	0	0	2	0
Andy Peterson, OSU	.400	15	4	6	0	0	0	1	1
Bryan Adametz, NCSU	.400	10	2	4	0	0	0	1	0
Colin Moran, UNC	.375	16	3	6	0	0	0	3	0
Sam Frost, MSU	.375	8	0	3	0	0	0	1	0
Grant Clyde, NCSU	.375	8	2	3	0	0	0	1	0
Cody Stubbs, UNC	.364	11	2	4	0	0	0	0	0

PITCHING
(Minimum 6 IP)

PITCHER	W-L	ERA	G	SV	IP	H	BB	SO
Joey DeNato, IU	1-0	0.00	1	0	9	4	3	8
Hobbs Johnson, UNC	1-0	0.00	1	0	8	5	2	6
Aaron Nola, LSU	0-1	0.00	1	0	8	5	1	5
Grant Watson, UCLA	1-0	0.00	1	0	6	4	1	3
Nick Vander Tuig, UCLA	2-0	0.60	2	0	15	9	1	12
Matt Boyd, OSU	1-1	0.90	2	0	10	6	3	12
Aaron Slegers, IU	0-1	1.00	1	0	9	7	2	5
Chad Girodo, MSU	1-0	1.29	2	0	14	10	3	19
Carlos Rodon, NCSU	1-1	1.29	2	0	14	9	3	14
David Berg, UCLA	0-0	1.35	5	3	7	6	3	5

Rodon on the mound on short rest, ending N.C. State's season. A few weeks earlier in the ACC tournament, Rodon struck out 14 over 10 innings of one-hit ball in a no-decision against the Tar Heels, who eventually won the epic battle 2-1 in 18 innings. That game drew 11,392 fans at Durham Bulls Athletic Park, the largest attendance ever for a college baseball game in the state of North Carolina. The Wolfpack and Tar Heels, who shared the cover of BA's College Preview issue, each entered the season with their highest-ever preseason rankings (No. 8 and No. 1, respectively), and they lived up to expectations to deliver the most memorable college baseball season in the state's history.

REGIONALS

MAY 31-JUNE 1
64 teams, 16 four-team, double-elimination tournaments. Winners advance to super regionals.

CHAPEL HILL, N.C.
Host: North Carolina (No. 1 national seed).
Participants: No. 1 North Carolina (52-8), No. 2 Florida Atlantic (39-20), No. 3 Towson (29-28), No. 4 Canisius (42-15).
Champion: North Carolina (3-1).
Runner-up: Florida Atlantic (3-2).
Outstanding player: Cody Stubbs, 1b, North Carolina.

COLUMBIA, S.C.
Host: South Carolina.
Participants: No. 1 South Carolina (39-18), No. 2 Clemson (39-20), No. 3 Liberty (34-27), No. 4 Saint Louis (41-19).
Champion: South Carolina (3-0).
Runner-up: Liberty (2-2).
Outstanding player: Kyle Martin, 1b, South Carolina.

RALEIGH
Host: North Carolina State.
Participants: No. 1 North Carolina State (44-14), No. 2 Mississippi (37-22), No. 3 William & Mary (37-22), No. 4 Binghamton (30-23).
Champion: North Carolina State (3-0).
Runner-up: William & Mary (2-2).
Outstanding player: Tarran Senay, 1b, North Carolina State.

EUGENE, ORE.
Host: Oregon (No. 8 national seed).
Participants: No. 1 Oregon (45-14), No. 2 Rice (41-17), No. 3 San Francisco (34-22), No. 4 South Dakota State (35-22).
Champion: Rice (3-1).
Runner-up: Oregon (3-2).
Outstanding player: Jordan Stephens, rhp, Rice.

FULLERTON, CALIF.
Host: Cal State Fullerton (No. 5 national seed).
Participants: No. 1 Cal State Fullerton (48-8), No. 2 Arizona State (35-20), No. 3 New Mexico (37-20), No. 4 Columbia (27-19).
Champion: Cal State Fullerton (3-0).
Runner-up: Arizona State (2-2).
Outstanding player: Justin Garza, rhp, Cal State Fullerton.

LOS ANGELES
Host: UCLA.
Participants: No. 1 UCLA (39-17), No. 2 Cal Poly (39-17), No. 3 San Diego (35-23), No. 4 San Diego State (31-29).
Champion: UCLA (3-0).
Runner-up: San Diego (2-2).
Outstanding player: Pat Gallagher, 1b, UCLA.

BLACKSBURG, VA.
Host: Virginia Tech.
Participants: No. 1 Virginia Tech (38-20), No. 2 Oklahoma (40-19), No. 3 Coastal Carolina (37-21), No. 4 Connecticut (34-26).
Champion: Oklahoma (3-0).
Runner-up: Virginia Tech (2-2).
Outstanding player: Max White, of, Oklahoma.

BATON ROUGE, LA.
Host: Louisiana State (No. 4 national seed).
Participants: No. 1 Louisiana State (52-9), No. 2 Louisiana-Lafayette (41-18), No. 3 Sam Houston State (37-20), No. 4 Jackson State (34-20).
Champion: Louisiana State (3-0).
Runner-up: Louisiana-Lafayette (2-2).
Outstanding player: Alex Bregman, ss, LSU.

NASHVILLE
Host: Vanderbilt (No. 2 national seed).
Participants: No. 1 Vanderbilt (51-9), No. 2 Georgia Tech (34-25), No. 3 Illinois (34-18), No. 4 East Tennessee State (36-22).
Champion: Vanderbilt (3-1).
Runner-up: Georgia Tech (3-2).
Outstanding player: Mike Yastrzemski, of, Vanderbilt.

LOUISVILLE
Host: Louisville.
Participants: No. 1 Louisville (46-12), No. 2 Miami (36-23), No. 3 Oklahoma State (39-17), No. 4 Bowling Green State (24-29).
Champion: Louisville (3-0).
Runner-up: Oklahoma State (2-2).
Outstanding player: Coco Johnson, of, Louisville.

BLOOMINGTON, IND.
Host: Indiana.
Participants: No. 1 Indiana (43-14), No. 2 Austin Peay State (45-13), No. 3 Florida (29-28), No. 4 Valparaiso (31-26).
Champion: Indiana (3-0).
Runner-up: Austin Peay State (2-2).
Outstanding player: Sam Travis, 1b, Indiana.

TALLAHASSEE, FLA.
Host: Florida State (No. 7 national seed).
Participants: No. 1 Florida State (44-15), No. 2 Alabama (34-26), No. 3 Troy (40-18), No. 4 Savannah State (33-21).
Champion: Florida State (3-0).
Runner-up: Troy (2-2).
Outstanding player: Luke Weaver, rhp, Florida State.

CHARLOTTESVILLE, VA.
Host: Virginia (No. 6 national seed).
Participants: No. 1 Virginia (47-10), No. 2 UNC Wilmington (37-21), No. 3 Elon (32-28), No. 4 Army (29-21).
Champion: Virginia (3-0).
Runner-up: Elon (2-2).
Outstanding player: Kyle Crockett, lhp, Virginia.

STARKVILLE, MISS.
Host: Mississippi State.
Participants: No. 1 Mississippi State (43-17), No. 2 South Alabama (42-18), No. 3 Mercer (43-16), No. 4 Central Arkansas (39-20).
Champion: Mississippi State (3-1).
Runner-up: Central Arkansas (3-2).
Outstanding player: Alex Detz, 3b, Mississippi State.

MANHATTAN, KAN.
Host: Kansas State.
Participants: No. 1 Kansas State (41-17), No. 2 Arkansas (37-20), No. 3 Bryant (44-16), No. 4 Wichita State (39-26).
Champion: Kansas State (3-0).
Runner-up: Arkansas (2-2).
Outstanding player: Ross Kivett, 2b, Kansas State.

CORVALLIS, ORE.
Host: Oregon State (No. 3 national seed).
Participants: No. 1 Oregon State (45-10), No. 2 Texas A&M (32-27), No. 3 UC Santa Barbara (34-23), No. 4 Texas-San Antonio (35-23).
Champion: Oregon State (3-0).
Runner-up: Texas A&M (2-2).
Outstanding player: Dylan Davis, of, Oregon State.

SUPER REGIONALS

JUNE 7-10
16 teams, best-of-three series. Winners advance to College World Series.

SOUTH CAROLINA AT NORTH CAROLINA
Site: Chapel Hill, N.C.
North Carolina wins 2-1, advances to CWS.

RICE AT NORTH CAROLINA STATE
Site: Raleigh.
N.C. State wins 2-0, advances to CWS.

UCLA AT CAL STATE FULLERTON
Site: Fullerton, Calif.
UCLA wins 2-0, advances to CWS.

OKLAHOMA AT LOUISIANA STATE
Site: Baton Rouge, La.
LSU wins 2-0, advances to CWS.

LOUISVILLE AT VANDERBILT
Site: Nashville.
Louisville wins 2-0, advances to CWS.

INDIANA AT FLORIDA STATE
Site: Tallahassee, Fla.
Indiana wins 2-0, advances to CWS.

MISSISSIPPI STATE AT VIRGINIA
Site: Charlottesville, Va.
Mississippi State wins 2-0, advances to CWS.

KANSAS STATE AT OREGON STATE
Site: Corvallis, Ore.
Oregon State wins 2-1, advances to CWS.

Bryant dazzles with huge power

BY AARON FITT

Everyone has a favorite Kris Bryant story. Baseball America's 2013 College Player of the Year left a trail of gaping mouths and shaking heads in his wake this spring, on his way to 31 home runs—the most by a college player since 2003, and 10 more than any other player in 2013. So naturally, the most common story about San Diego's junior third baseman involves a massive display of power.

Longtime USD radio play-by-play man Jack Murray can't stop talking about the ball Bryant hit over the light tower against Saint Louis on a cool night in March. Murray swears the ball traveled 600 feet—or more.

Bryant's father, Mike Bryant, won't argue with that estimate.

"It was 20 feet above the light tower, and it was going up," Mike Bryant said. "Look—I get goose bumps talking about it."

Mike Bryant has plenty of favorite stories, of course. A ninth-round pick out of Massachusetts-Lowell in 1980 who played two minor league seasons in the Red Sox system, Mike introduced his sons to baseball at an early age. He still clearly remembers the day he realized Kris was special.

"We were on an elementary school playground, he was 5 years old, at his older brother's practice," Mike Bryant recalled. "At the end of the practice, the coach let the younger siblings take a couple hacks. So I went up there, I

Kris Bryant

LARRY GOREN

was throwing some overhand tosses. The other other kids took a couple swings. The first ball I threw to Kris, he launched it into the air—it had to go 30 feet into the outfield. He had this huge bat, like a 31-inch bat, and he was tiny. The ball just—it jumped, it soared."

San Diego recruiting coordinator Jay Johnson remembers the first time he ever saw Bryant.

"It was a game his sophomore year at Bonanza High School," Johnson said. "I think he hit two triples to right field, a couple walks, played unbelievable defense. And all that's great, but what really separated him was his character and makeup."

Bryant's total package—not just his 80 power—makes him the kind of player that San Diego coach Rich Hill said "comes along once in a coach's career." So it's fitting that Hill's favorite Bryant story wasn't some monstrous home run. It came in a game a couple of weeks before San Diego's season ended at the Los Angeles regional.

"He made a play on a bunt that was absolutely spectacular," Hill said. "The next inning, he went first to third, and basically ran in the center fielder's face, head-first slide into third base. Then you think to yourself, 'This guy's got 25 home runs, he just made that play, and he just went first to third like that?' I mean, that's crazy. So that really is my Kris Bryant moment. It's not the longest home run in the world, and it's not going 5-for-7 (in his final home game)—it's that spectacular play on the bunt, and going first to third. That's what separates him."

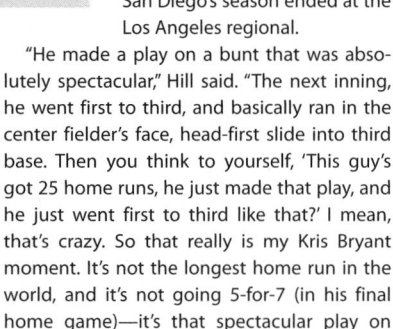

PREVIOUS WINNERS

1982: Jeff Ledbetter, of/lhp, Florida State	**1993:** Brooks Kieschnick, dh/rhp, Texas	**2004:** Jered Weaver, rhp, Long Beach State
1983: Dave Magadan, 1b, Alabama	**1994:** Jason Varitek, c, Georgia Tech	**2005:** Alex Gordon, 3b, Nebraska
1984: Oddibe McDowell, of, Arizona State	**1995:** Todd Helton, 1b/lhp, Tennessee	**2006:** Andrew Miller, lhp, North Carolina
1985: Pete Incaviglia, of, Oklahoma State	**1996:** Kris Benson, rhp, Clemson	**2007:** David Price, lhp, Vanderbilt
1986: Casey Close, of, Michigan	**1997:** J.D. Drew, of, Florida State	**2008:** Buster Posey, c/rhp, Florida State
1987: Robin Ventura, 3b, Oklahoma State	**1998:** Jeff Austin, rhp, Stanford	**2009:** Stephen Strasburg, rhp, San Diego St.
1988: John Olerud, 1b/lhp, Washington St.	**1999:** Jason Jennings, rhp, Baylor	**2010:** Anthony Rendon, 3b, Rice
1989: Ben McDonald, rhp, Louisiana State	**2000:** Mark Teixeira, 3b, Georgia Tech	**2011:** Trevor Bauer, rhp, UCLA
1990: Mike Kelly, of, Arizona State	**2001:** Mark Prior, rhp, Southern California	**2012:** Mike Zunino, c, Florida
1991: David McCarthy, 1b, Stanford	**2002:** Khalil Greene, ss, Clemson	
1992: Phil Nevin, 3b, Cal State Fullerton	**2003:** Rickie Weeks, 2b, Southern	

Savage turns UCLA into force

OMAHA

When John Savage finally held the national championship trophy above his head in triumph on the field at TD Ameritrade Park, it felt like destiny realized—for Savage, and for UCLA.

For decades, coaches and scouts considered the Bruins a sleeping giant on the West Coast. They produced major league talent on a consistent basis, but they made just two College World Series appearances in their history before Savage was hired to wake the giant in the summer of 2004.

In the last four years, Savage has led the Bruins to Omaha three times, capped by their first national title in 2013. He has built UCLA into a model program, and into the premier program on the West Coast— even surpassing old nemesis Cal State Fullerton, for the time being, at least. Savage has been a great coach for a long time, but he turned in his best coaching job this season, shepherding a team that hit just .250 to an undefeated postseason run. For building the Bruins into a juggernaut, Savage is Baseball America's 2013 College Coach of the Year.

This bunch of Bruins succeeded through focus and discipline as much as through talent. They committed themselves to getting every small detail right—an approach they learned from Savage. And that approach allowed the Bruins to execute defensively, on the mound and even at the plate, despite their lack of punch.

"We call ours a good practice team," Savage

John Savage

ANDREW WOOLLEY

said. "For us to play good in the games, you have to do it in practice, and you have to do it in front of the coaches. We work hard, conditioning, weights, practice. We got better; we got better in this tournament. That was one of our goals was to get better with our time off."

Other coaches and scouts rave about Savage's work ethic, on the recruiting trail as well as the practice field. He takes a very active role in recruiting, and he has an uncanny ability to break down the strengths and weaknesses of countless players off the top of his head. Evaluating talent comes naturally to him, which combines with his work ethic to make him a recruiting master.

"No one works harder than Coach Savage," ace righty and CWS Most Outstanding Player Adam Plutko said. "I guarantee he got about five hours of sleep in two weeks out here."

Plutko and Nick Vander Tuig are ideal Savage pitchers because they thrive off fastball command. Rare in the college ranks, Savage prefers to pound away with fastballs—he calls fastball command the foundation of his philosophy. That's one reason Savage has earned the admiration of professional scouts. Another reason is his personality.

"John treats everyone with respect," a West Coast crosschecker said. "He doesn't big league anyone."

Everyone who knows Savage can attest to that.

"He's the most genuine human I've ever met," Plutko said. "I couldn't be happier for Coach, what this means for his career."

PREVIOUS WINNERS

1982: Gene Stephenson, Wichita State
1983: Barry Shollenberger, Alabama
1984: Augie Garrido, Cal State Fullerton
1985: Ron Polk, Mississippi State
1986: Skip Bertman, LSU/Dave Snow, LMU
1987: Mark Marquess, Stanford
1988: Jim Brock, Arizona State
1989: Dave Snow, Long Beach State
1990: Steve Webber, Georgia
1991: Jim Hendry, Creighton
1992: Andy Lopez, Pepperdine

1993: Gene Stephenson, Wichita State
1994: Jim Morris, Miami
1995: Pat Murphy, Arizona State
1996: Skip Bertman, Louisiana State
1997: Jim Wells, Alabama
1998: Pat Murphy, Arizona State
1999: Wayne Graham, Rice
2000: Ray Tanner, South Carolina
2001: Dave Van Horn, Nebraska
2002: Augie Garrido, Texas
2003: George Horton, Cal State Fullerton

2004: David Perno, Georgia
2005: Rick Jones, Tulane
2006: Pat Casey, Oregon State
2007: Dave Serrano, UC Irvine
2008: Mike Fox, North Carolina
2009: Paul Mainieri, Louisiana State
2010: Ray Tanner, South Carolina
2011: Kevin O'Sullivan, Florida
2012: Mike Martin, Florida State

Hungry Bregman does it all for LSU

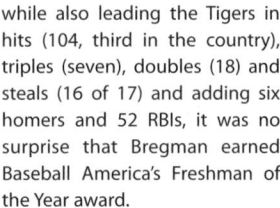

The precocious nature of Alex Bregman's passion displayed itself well before he reached the Louisiana State campus.

As a slight high school freshman, Bregman drilled a ball well out of Albuquerque's Isotopes Park during the 2009 high school state championship game. It was a thunderclap of a statement from Bregman that while young, he could play with the big boys.

So when it came time for Tigers head coach Paul Mainieri to fill out the first lineup card this spring, it was no surprise to Bregman that his name was written as the starting shortstop and batting third for the veteran-laden Tigers.

"I had confidence that I could do it," Bregman explained. "I set my goals high but I'm not satisfied with my year. I can't wait to prove that I can do more."

Mainieri also had confidence the youngster

ANDREW WOOLLEY

Alex Bregman

could do it, even if he was coming off a finger injury that robbed him of much of his high school senior season.

"Probably from the day we first started recruiting him, we knew he could do it," Mainieri said. "He was a special player."

So after a season in which Bregman hit .369 while also leading the Tigers in hits (104, third in the country), triples (seven), doubles (18) and steals (16 of 17) and adding six homers and 52 RBIs, it was no surprise that Bregman earned Baseball America's Freshman of the Year award.

"If he isn't Freshman of the Year, then they ought to quit giving out the award," Mainieri said.

But 2013 is just a season to build on for Bregman, whose work ethic also draws rave reviews.

"I feel I could have hit the ball a lot better," he said. "I know I could have played better. I just want to keep improving on every aspect of the game."

PREVIOUS WINNERS

1982: Cory Snyder, 3b, Brigham Young
1983: Rafael Palmeiro, of, Mississippi State
1984: Greg Swindell, lhp, Texas
1985: Jack McDowell, rhp, Stanford
1986: Robin Ventura, 3b, Oklahoma State
1987: Paul Carey, of, Stanford
1988: Kirk Dressendorfer, rhp, Texas
1989: Alex Fernandez, rhp, Miami
1990: Jeffrey Hammonds, of, Stanford
1991: Brooks Kieschnick, rhp-dh, Texas
1992: Todd Walker, 2b, Louisiana State
1993: Brett Laxton, rhp, Louisiana State
1994: R.A. Dickey, rhp, Tennessee
1995: Kyle Peterson, rhp, Stanford
1996: Pat Burrell, 3b, Miami
1997: Brian Roberts, ss, North Carolina
1998: Xavier Nady, 2b, California
1999: James Jurries, 2b, Tulane
2000: Kevin Howard, 3b, Miami
2001: Michael Aubrey, of/lhp, Texas
2002: Stephen Drew, ss, Florida State
2003: Ryan Braun, ss, Miami
2004: Wade LeBlanc, lhp, Alabama
2005: Joe Savery, lhp, Rice
2006: Pedro Alvarez, 3b, Vanderbilt
2007: Dustin Ackley, 1b, North Carolina
2008: Chris Hernandez, lhp, Miami
2009: Anthony Rendon, 3b, Rice
2010: Matt Purke, lhp, Texas Christian
2011: Colin Moran, 3b, North Carolina
2012: Carlos Rodon, lhp, N.C. State

FRESHMAN ALL-AMERICA TEAMS

FIRST TEAM

POS.		AVG	OBP	SLG	AB	R	H	HR	RBI	SB
C	Mitch Ghelfi, UW-Milwaukee	.322	.380	.473	146	18	47	3	19	6
1B	Patrick Mazeika, Stetson	.382	.488	.495	212	38	81	3	33	1
2B	Ian Happ, Cincinnati	.322	.451	.483	205	41	66	6	36	25
3B	Xavier Turner, Vanderbilt	.324	.387	.370	219	40	71	0	36	22
SS	Alex Bregman, Louisiana State	.369	.417	.546	282	59	104	6	52	16
OF	Skye Bolt, North Carolina	.349	.499	.550	169	42	59	6	47	10
OF	Joe McCarthy, Virginia	.336	.469	.453	223	48	75	4	51	11
OF	D.J. Stewart, Florida State	.364	.469	.560	225	50	82	5	59	8
DH	Landon Lassiter, North Carolina	.348	.498	.449	207	67	72	1	26	8
UT	Jacob Cronenworth, Michigan	.320	.386	.429	203	33	65	2	41	12

		W	L	ERA	G	SV	IP	H	BB	SO	BAA
SP	Thomas Eshelman, CS Fullerton	12	3	1.48	17	0	116	86	3	83	.204
SP	Justin Garza, Cal State Fullerton	12	0	2.03	17	0	115	84	17	95	.205
SP	Cole Irvin, Oregon	12	3	2.48	16	0	116	105	22	60	.248
SP	Andrew Moore, Oregon State	14	1	1.57	18	1	126	84	28	72	.196
RP	Trent Thornton, North Carolina	9	1	1.29	23	6	70	47	12	60	.185
UT	Jacob Cronenworth, Michigan	0	3	1.93	15	7	23	23	5	24	.261

SECOND TEAM

C–Ryan Hissey, William & Mary (.281-1-36). **1B**–Carl Wise, College of Charleston (.321-10-30). **2B**–Max Schrock, South Carolina (.282-6-39). **3B**–Tyler France, San Diego State (.317-5-36). **SS**–Edwin Rios, Florida International (.332-9-52). **OF**–Jacob Hanneman, Brigham Young (.344-5-29); Austin Listi, Dallas Baptist (.285-9-46); Tate Matheny, Missouri State (.336-4-26). **DH**–Robby Nesovic, UC Santa Barbara (.326-4-33). **UT**–Corbin Olmstead, North Florida (.307-0-19; 4-1, 2.81, 6 SV, 42 IP/44 SO). **SP**–Matthew Crownover, Clemson (7-3, 2.19, 70 IP/45 SO); Kevin Duchene, Illinois (9-1, 2.79, 81 IP/68 SO); Jimmy Herget, South Florida (6-2, 1.72, 94 IP/60 SO); Ryan Kellogg, Arizona State (11-1, 3.15, 103 IP/54 SO). **RP**–Jake Matthys, Kansas State (9-2, 2.05, 9 SV, 61 IP/44 SO).

COLLEGE

HITTING Minimum 120 plate appearances, 3.0 plate appearances per team game

BATTING AVERAGE

RANK NAME, TEAM	YEAR	G	AB	H	AVG
1. Mike Tauchman, Bradley	Sr.	49	186	79	.425
2. Christian Wolfe, UNC Greensboro	Sr.	48	209	88	.421
3. Jimmy Yezzo, Delaware	Jr.	55	234	96	.410
4. D.J. Peterson, New Mexico	Jr.	55	218	89	.408
5. Jason Radwan, St. Bonaventure	Sr.	48	185	75	.405
6. Chesny Young, Mercer	So.	61	262	105	.401
7. Rob Dickinson, VMI	Sr.	52	198	79	.399
8. Justin Parr, Illinois	Jr.	55	231	92	.398
9. Jensen Park, Northern Colo.	So.	53	209	83	.397
10. Hunter Dozier, Stephen F. Austin	Jr.	55	212	84	.396
11. Chad Prain, Georgia State	Jr.	55	226	89	.394
12. Mark Payton, Texas	Jr.	50	178	70	.393
13. Tony Kemp, Vanderbilt	Jr.	66	266	104	.391
14. Mitch Garver, New Mexico	Sr.	59	246	96	.390
15. Trey Mancini, Notre Dame	Jr.	57	229	89	.389
16. Chad Carroll, James Madison	So.	51	193	75	.389
17. Dex Kjerstad, La.-Lafayette	Jr.	61	255	99	.388
18. Eric Jagielo, Notre Dame	Jr.	56	196	76	.388
19. Colby Roberts, James Madison	Sr.	44	132	51	.386
20. Joe Jackson, Citadel	Jr.	60	228	88	.386
21. Luke Campbell, New Mexico	Sr.	51	200	77	.385
22. Craig Massoni, Austin Peay	Jr.	62	239	92	.385
23. Patrick Mazeika, Stetson	Fr.	57	212	81	.382
24. Ryan Deitrich, Penn	Sr.	43	144	55	.382
25. Chase Raffield, Georgia State	Jr.	52	186	71	.382
26. Brenden Kalfus, St. Mary's	Sr.	52	194	74	.381
27. Mike Papi, Virginia	So.	55	176	67	.381
28. Tom Healy, Mount St. Mary's	Sr.	44	158	60	.380
29. Michael Bass, UNC Wilmington	Sr.	55	216	82	.380
30. Hughston Armstrong, Citadel	Jr.	59	224	85	.379
31. Garrett Bayliff, Wichita State	Jr.	63	240	91	.379
32. C.K. Irby, Samford	Jr.	57	222	84	.378
33. Alec Keller, Princeton	Jr.	40	143	54	.378
34. Dustin DeMuth, Indiana	Jr.	65	244	92	.377
35. Julian Ridings, Western Carolina	Jr.	48	199	75	.377
36. Nathan Orf, Baylor	Sr.	55	215	81	.377
37. Curt Powell, Georgia	Sr.	53	218	82	.376
38. Kane Sweeney, Morehead State	So.	53	197	74	.376
39. Nick Miller, Northern Colo.	Jr.	56	200	75	.375
Tanner Rust, New Mexico State	Jr.	57	216	81	.375
41. Owen Stewart, Monmouth	Sr.	55	195	73	.374
42. Stuart Turner, Mississippi	Jr.	62	222	83	.374
43. Brent Graham, Campbell	Sr.	57	190	71	.374
44. Matt Oberste, Oklahoma	Jr.	64	241	90	.373
45. Patrick Armstrong, UNLV	Jr.	49	161	60	.373
46. Connor Spencer, UC Irvine	So.	55	212	79	.373
47. Darian Johnson, Lamar	Sr.	59	240	89	.371
48. Jake Thomas, Binghamton	So.	55	178	66	.371
49. Michael Felton, Campbell	Sr.	59	224	83	.371
50. Mason Katz, LSU	Sr.	68	243	90	.370
51. Ryan Lagrange, UNC Wilmington	Jr.	57	211	78	.370
Zach Shank, Marist	Sr.	52	211	78	.370
53. Luke Tendler, N.C. A&T	Jr.	52	195	72	.369
54. Brandon Dixon, Arizona	Jr.	55	214	79	.369
55. Aaron Judge, Fresno State	Jr.	56	206	76	.369
56. Alex Bregman, LSU	Fr.	67	282	104	.369
Jeff Keller, Dartmouth	Jr.	40	141	52	.369
58. Trea Turner, North Carolina State	So.	56	228	84	.368
59. Ryan Huck, Western Ky.	Sr.	53	196	72	.367
Ben Verlander, Old Dominion	Jr.	53	196	72	.367
61. John Murphy, Sacred Heart	Sr.	58	207	76	.367
62. Mike Alexander, Delaware State	Jr.	48	169	62	.367
63. Bobby Ison, Charleston So.	So.	56	229	84	.367
64. Kevin Brown, Bryant	Sr.	64	221	81	.367
65. Justin Pacchioli, Lehigh	So.	39	142	52	.366
66. Kyle Schwarber, Indiana	So.	61	235	86	.366
67. Hassan Evans, Delaware State	Jr.	40	134	49	.366
68. Adam Law, BYU	Jr.	53	208	76	.365
69. Kyle Ruchim, Northwestern	Jr.	43	167	61	.365
70. Forrestt Allday, Central Arkansas	Sr.	64	233	85	.365
Giuseppe Papaccio, Seton Hall	Sr.	56	233	85	.365
72. Colby Harrison, Northern Colo.	Jr.	52	181	66	.365
73. Cody Stubbs, North Carolina	Sr.	71	277	101	.365
74. Chad Christensen, Nebraska	Jr.	59	225	82	.364
D.J. Stewart, Florida State	Fr.	60	225	82	.364
76. Mike Fish, Siena	Sr.	57	231	84	.364
Logan Pierce, Troy	Sr.	62	242	88	.364
Michael Porcaro, Milwaukee	So.	49	187	68	.364
79. Aaron Attaway, Western Carolina	Jr.	59	267	97	.363
80. Cody Hudson, Austin Peay	Sr.	62	245	89	.363
81. Cole McInturff, James Madison	Sr.	52	179	65	.363
82. Troy Black, Maine	Jr.	54	182	66	.363
83. Tyler White, Western Carolina	Sr.	59	251	91	.363
84. Steve Laurino, Marist	So.	39	127	46	.362
85. Matt Shortall, Texas-Arlington	Jr.	55	232	84	.362
86. Nick Ferdinand, Delaware	Sr.	54	210	76	.362
87. Oscar Sanay, Bakersfield	Jr.	59	224	81	.362
88. Caleb Howell, Eastern Illinois	So.	46	177	64	.362
89. Christiaan Durdaller, Samford	Sr.	54	194	70	.361
90. Zane Evans, Georgia Tech	Jr.	64	244	88	.361
Scott Price, Tennessee	Jr.	45	183	66	.361
92. Austin Fisher, Kansas State	So.	60	208	75	.361
93. Taylor Sparks, UC Irvine	So.	55	222	80	.360
94. Kyle Wren, Georgia Tech	Jr.	64	272	98	.360
95. Danny Collins, Troy	Jr.	62	236	85	.360
96. Ross Kivett, Kansas State	Jr.	64	261	94	.360
97. Jimmy Luppens, Canisius	Jr.	54	200	72	.360
98. Tyler Girouard, La.-Lafayette	So.	55	178	64	.360
99. Marlon Gibbs, Florida A&M	So.	49	153	55	.359
100. Tom Bouck, NJIT	Sr.	42	128	46	.359

ON-BASE PERCENTAGE

RANK NAME, TEAM	OBP
1. D.J. Peterson, New Mexico	.520
2. Mike Papi, Virginia	.517
3. Jake Thomas, Binghamton	.517
4. Mike Tauchman, Bradley	.513
5. Forrestt Allday, Central Arkansas	.503
6. Ryan Deitrich, Penn	.500
Eric Jagielo, Notre Dame	.500
8. Kevin Brown, Bryant	.498
9. Joe Jackson, Citadel	.495
10. Evan Stephens, Wake Forest	.494
11. Kris Bryant, San Diego	.493
12. Landon Lassiter, North Carolina	.491
13. Patrick Mazeika, Stetson	.488
14. Johnny Bladel, James Madison	.487
15. Jordan Patterson, South Alabama	.485
16. Mark Payton, Texas	.483
17. Hunter Dozier, Stephen F. Austin	.482
18. Jason Radwan, St. Bonaventure	.481
19. Garrett Cooper, Auburn	.481
20. Steven Shelinsky, Pittsburgh	.480
21. Michael Bass, UNC Wilmington	.479
22. Tom Bouck, NJIT	.478
23. Zack Weigel, Seton Hall	.477
24. Craig Massoni, Austin Peay	.475
25. Charles Tillery, Jackson State	.475
26. Kane Sweeney, Morehead State	.475
27. Cameron Cecil, Delaware State	.473
28. Brent Graham, Campbell	.472
29. Patrick Armstrong, UNLV	.472
30. Bo Thompson, Citadel	.472
31. Richard Gonzalez, Alabama State	.472
32. George Roberts, Kent State	.471
33. Tony Kemp, Vanderbilt	.471
34. Colin Moran, North Carolina	.470
35. Nathan Orf, Baylor	.470
36. D.J. Stewart, Florida State	.469
37. Joe McCarthy, Virginia	.469
Tanner Rust, New Mexico State	.469
39. Ryan Huck, Western Ky.	.469
40. Jordan McCoy, Houston Baptist	.468
41. Logan Pierce, Troy	.467
42. David Olson, Campbell	.467
43. Brenden Kalfus, St. Mary's	.466
44. Jimmy Luppens, Canisius	.465
45. Connor Brown, James Madison	.465
46. Branden Cogswell, Virginia	.464

RANK NAME, TEAM	
47. Mason Katz, LSU	.464
48. Cole McInturff, James Madison	.464
49. Christian Wolfe, UNC Greensboro	.463
50. Aaron Nardone, Delaware State	.463

SLUGGING PERCENTAGE

RANK NAME, TEAM	SLG
1. Kris Bryant, San Diego	.820
2. D.J. Peterson, New Mexico	.807
3. Hunter Dozier, Stephen F. Austin	.755
4. Jimmy Yezzo, Delaware	.714
5. Jeff Keller, Dartmouth	.702
6. Ryan Huck, Western Ky.	.694
7. Nick Ferdinand, Delaware	.690
8. Julian Ridings, Western Carolina	.663
9. Kelvin Freeman, N.C. A&T	.663
10. Duncan McAlpine, Dallas Baptist	.662
11. Tyler White, Western Carolina	.661
12. Craig Massoni, Austin Peay	.661
13. Joe Jackson, Citadel	.658
14. Ryan Kinsella, Elon	.656
15. Aaron Judge, Fresno State	.655
16. Caleb Adams, La.-Lafayette	.651
17. Christiaan Durdaller, Samford	.649
18. Robert Lecount, New Mexico State	.647
19. Kyle Schwarber, Indiana	.647
20. Chase Raffield, Georgia State	.645
21. Mason Katz, LSU	.642
22. Kurt Wertz, Towson	.640
23. Ben Verlander, Old Dominion	.638
24. Daniel Palka, Georgia Tech	.637
25. Eric Jagielo, Notre Dame	.633
26. Jeff Gardner, Louisville	.632
27. Danny Collins, Troy	.631
28. Colby Roberts, James Madison	.629
29. Matt Oberste, Oklahoma	.622
30. Hunter Renfroe, Mississippi State	.620
31. Mike Papi, Virginia	.619
32. LB Dantzler, South Carolina	.617
33. Zach Stephens, Tennessee Tech	.616
34. Luke Tendler, N.C. A&T	.615
35. Trae Santos, Troy	.612
36. Jaycob Brugman, BYU	.609
37. Dex Kjerstad, La.-Lafayette	.608
38. Tom Healy, Mount St. Mary's	.608
39. Wise Carl, Col. of Charleston	.606
40. Nick Miller, Northern Colo.	.605
41. Jason Kanzler, Buffalo	.604
42. Tyler Horan, Virginia Tech	.603
43. Daniel Miles, Tennessee Tech	.603
44. Trey Mancini, Notre Dame	.603
45. Mike Fish, Siena	.602
46. Phillip Ervin, Samford	.597
47. Patrick Armstrong, UNLV	.596
48. Rob Dickinson, VMI	.596
49. Luke Campbell, New Mexico	.595
50. Joe Purritano, Dartmouth	.593

HOME RUNS

RANK NAME, TEAM	HR
1. Kris Bryant, San Diego	31
2. Ryan Kinsella, Elon	21
3. D.J. Peterson, New Mexico	18
Trae Santos, Troy	18
Kyle Schwarber, Indiana	18
6. Hunter Dozier, Stephen F. Austin	17
Duncan McAlpine, Dallas Baptist	17
Daniel Palka, Georgia Tech	17
9. Caleb Adams, La.-Lafayette	16
Kelvin Freeman, N.C. A&T	16
Ryan Huck, Western Ky.	16
Mason Katz, LSU	16
Craig Massoni, Austin Peay	16
Hunter Renfroe, Mississippi State	16

RANK NAME, TEAM	
Tyler White, Western Carolina	16
16. LB Dantzler, South Carolina	15
Nick Ferdinand, Delaware	15
Robert Lecount, New Mexico State	15
Zach Stephens, Tennessee Tech	15
20. Christiaan Durdaller, Samford	14
Zane Evans, Georgia Tech	14
Chris Ohmstede, Furman	14
Bo Thompson, Citadel	14
24. Nick Backlund, Mercer	13
T.D. Davis, Ga. Southern	13
Trevor Edwards, UNC Greensboro	13
Joe Jackson, Citadel	13
Colin Moran, North Carolina	13
A.J. Reed, Kentucky	13
Kurt Wertz, Towson	13
Jimmy Yezzo, Delaware	13
32. Aaron Attaway, Western Carolina	12
Andrew Barna, Davidson	12
Mike Fish, Siena	12
Tyler Griffin, Citadel	12
Connor Harrell, Vanderbilt	12
Brian Holberton, North Carolina	12
Aaron Judge, Fresno State	12
Jason Kanzler, Buffalo	12
Alex Kelly, Saint Louis	12
Dex Kjerstad, La.-Lafayette	12
Ryan McBroom, West Virginia	12
Daniel Miles, Tennessee Tech	12
Rj Perucki, UTSA	12
Steven Shelinsky, Pittsburgh	12
Brandon Thomasson, Tennessee Tech	12

RUNS BATTED IN

RANK NAME, TEAM	RBI
1. Colin Moran, North Carolina	91
2. Ryan Kinsella, Elon	78
3. Cody Stubbs, North Carolina	76
4. D.J. Peterson, New Mexico	72
5. Zach Stephens, Tennessee Tech	71
6. Mason Katz, LSU	70
Trae Santos, Troy	70
8. Robert Lecount, New Mexico State	69
9. Nick Backlund, Mercer	68
Danny Collins, Troy	68
Mitch Garver, New Mexico	68
Craig Massoni, Austin Peay	68
13. Connor Harrell, Vanderbilt	67
Joe Jackson, Citadel	67
15. Zane Evans, Georgia Tech	66
Daniel Palka, Georgia Tech	66
Tyler White, Western Carolina	66
18. Hunter Renfroe, Mississippi State	65
Casey Roche, Pittsburgh	65
Kurt Wertz, Towson	65
Chesny Young, Mercer	65
22. Jimmy Yezzo, Delaware	64
23. Logan Pierce, Troy	63
24. Kris Bryant, San Diego	62
Marcus Davis, Florida State	62
Andrew Rash, Virginia Tech	62
Zachary Turner, San Francisco	62
28. Scott Donley, Indiana	61
Nick Ferdinand, Delaware	61
Alex Kelly, Saint Louis	61
Nick Miller, Northern Colo.	61
32. Dylan Davis, Oregon State	60
Matt Oberste, Oklahoma	60
34. Brandon Downes, Virginia	59
Nolan Earley, South Alabama	59
Kelvin Freeman, N.C. A&T	59
Reed Harper, Austin Peay	59
Michael Marietta, Central Arkansas	59
Tarran Senay, North Carolina State	59

RANK NAME, TEAM	
D.J. Stewart, Florida State	59
41. Eric Aguilera, Illinois State	58
C.K. Irby, Samford	58
Duncan McAlpine, Dallas Baptist	58
Ty Young, Louisville	58
45. Clinton Freeman, East Tenn. State	57
Brian Holberton, North Carolina	57
Mike Papi, Virginia	57
Sam Travis, Indiana	57

DOUBLES

RANK NAME, TEAM	2B
1. Jimmy Yezzo, Delaware	28
2. Brad Collins, Gardner-Webb	27
Tyler White, Western Carolina	27
4. Tyler Horan, Virginia Tech	26
Cody Stubbs, North Carolina	26
6. Danny Collins, Troy	25
Hunter Dozier, Stephen F. Austin	25
Jordan Patterson, South Alabama	25
D.J. Peterson, New Mexico	25
D.J. Stewart, Florida State	25
Luke Tendler, N.C. A&T	25
12. Dustin DeMuth, Indiana	24
Giuseppe Papaccio, Seton Hall	24
Logan Pierce, Troy	24
15. Michael Katz, William & Mary	23
Tyler Mautner, Buffalo	23
Michael Strentz, La.-Lafayette	23
18. Josh Anderson, FIU	22
Nick Backlund, Mercer	22
Garrett Custons, Air Force	22
Dylan Davis, Oregon State	22
Jimmy Falla, South Florida	22
Andrew Rash, Virginia Tech	22
Justin Seager, Charlotte	22
Sam Travis, Indiana	22
26. Brett Austin, North Carolina State	21
Anthony Azar, Sam Houston State	21
Michael Bass, UNC Wilmington	21
Michael Bishop, Jacksonville State	21
Jason Blum, Southeast Mo. State	21
Mitch Garver, New Mexico	21
Cody Hudson, Austin Peay	21
Eric Kalbfleisch, UNC Greensboro	21
Jeff Keller, Dartmouth	21
Zach Lauricella, St. John's	21
Randy McCurry, Oklahoma State	21
Frank Schwindel, St. John's	21
38. Michael Benjamin, Arizona State	20
Dylan Bosheers, Tennessee Tech	20
Alex Calbick, Maine	20
Marcus Davis, Florida State	20
Brandon Downes, Virginia	20
Austin Fisher, Kansas State	20
Adam Frazier, Mississippi State	20
Ryon Healy, Oregon	20
Trent Miller, Middle Tenn.	20
Edwin Rios, FIU	20
Tyler Rocklein, Florida Atlantic	20
Tyler Vaughn, Troy	20
Treysen Vavra, Eastern Illinois	20

TRIPLES

RANK NAME, TEAM	3B
1. Jeff DeBlieux, South Alabama	10
2. Chad Carroll, James Madison	8
John Murphy, Sacred Heart	8
Mark Payton, Texas	8
Frankie Ratcliff, Houston	8
6. Alex Bregman, LSU	7
Brandon Downes, Virginia	7
Johnny Field, Arizona	7
Adam Frazier, Mississippi State	7

Name, Team	
Jacob Hannemann, BYU	7
Gunnar Heidt, Col. of Charleston	7
Matt Lowenstein, Loyola Marymount	7
Trey Mancini, Notre Dame	7
Tyler Marincov, North Florida	7
Aaron Nardone, Delaware State	7
Logan Regnier, Central Mich.	7
Daniel Russell, Eastern Mich.	7
Kurt Wertz, Towson	7
Ty Young, Louisville	7
20. Trever Allen, Arizona State	6
Joe Chavez, UC Riverside	6
Dan Dispensa, Western Illinois	6
Jordan Ellis, Cal Poly	6
Nolan Gaige, Albany	6
Mike Gerber, Creighton	6
Riley Good, UTSA	6
Zack Granite, Seton Hall	6
Mitchell Gunsolus, Gonzaga	6
C.J. Jarvis, Houston Baptist	6
Scott Kalamar, Seton Hall	6
Jason Kanzler, Buffalo	6
Tony Kemp, Vanderbilt	6
Robby Ort, Indiana State	6
Oscar Sanay, Bakersfield	6
Elvin Soto, Pittsburgh	6
Alex Swim, Elon	6
Caleb Whalen, Portland	6
Kyle Wren, Georgia Tech	6
John Ziznewski, LIU Brooklyn	6

STOLEN BASES

RANK NAME, TEAM	SB	CS
1. Ben McQuown, Campbell	54	7
2. Ian Miller, Wagner	46	8
3. Adam Engel, Louisville	41	12
4. Edmund Cheatham, Miss. Valley	39	15
Charlie White, Maryland	39	7
6. Mike Alexander, Delaware State	36	2
Tyler Grogg, Toledo	36	4
8. Zack Granite, Seton Hall	35	8
9. Richard Amion, Alabama State	34	7
Chris Kashangaki, Coppin State	34	8
Tony Kemp, Vanderbilt	34	14
12. Chad Hinshaw, Illinois State	33	4
13. Brian Carroll, UCLA	32	8
Cody Hudson, Austin Peay	32	8
Jay Knight, Mount St. Mary's	32	11
16. Brett Bell, Texas Tech	31	8
Blake Marchal, Central Arkansas	31	4
18. Brandon Dixon, Arizona	30	7
Jeff Roy, Rhode Island	30	0
Trea Turner, North Carolina State	30	6
21. Justin Albright, George Washington	29	8
L.J. Mazzilli, Connecticut	29	4
John Murphy, Sacred Heart	29	8
Tyler Shepherd, IPFW	29	5
Derek Toadvine, Kent State	29	3
26. Ryan Cordell, Liberty	28	4
Ryan Cusick, Massachusetts	28	2
Mike Tauchman, Bradley	28	2
Kyle Wren, Georgia Tech	28	13
30. Billy Ferriter, Connecticut	27	10
J.P. Frey, Delaware State	27	6
William Head, Appalachian State	27	4
Ben Morgan, Ga. Southern	27	8
Jordan Serena, Columbia	27	3
Brandon Turner, Bethune-Cookman	27	0
36. Aaron Barbosa, Northeastern	26	2
Michael Bass, UNC Wilmington	26	1
Michael Green, Charlotte	26	4
Josh Hyman, Wofford	26	5
Ross Kivett, Kansas State	26	10

Name, Team		
Aneko Knowles, Jackson State	26	7
Kevin Sah, Texas State	26	9
Charles Tillery, Jackson State	26	5
Joe Torres, Iona	26	3
Ty Young, Louisville	26	5

RUNS

RANK NAME, TEAM	R
1. Kris Bryant, San Diego	80
2. Colin Moran, North Carolina	76
3. Landon Lassiter, North Carolina	75
4. Tyler Vaughn, Troy	72
5. Jordan Hankins, Austin Peay	71
6. Jordan Patterson, South Alabama	69
7. Aaron Attaway, Western Carolina	68
Sasha LaGarde, Mercer	68
D.J. Peterson, New Mexico	68
10. Brandon Downes, Virginia	67
11. Joe Jackson, Citadel	66
Trea Turner, North Carolina State	66
13. Tyler McFarland, James Madison	65
Ben McQuown, Campbell	65
Logan Pierce, Troy	65
Kyle Schwarber, Indiana	65
Stephen Vranka, Pittsburgh	65
18. Tony Kemp, Vanderbilt	64
Tyler Marincov, North Florida	64
Cody Stubbs, North Carolina	64
21. Ryan Brown, William & Mary	63
Dex Kjerstad, La.-Lafayette	63
23. Michael Bass, UNC Wilmington	62
Danny Collins, Troy	62
Mason Davis, Citadel	62
Adam Frazier, Mississippi State	62
Tyler Grogg, Toledo	62
Mark Zagunis, Virginia Tech	62
29. Ryan Lindemuth, William & Mary	61
30. Johnny Bladel, James Madison	60
Connor Harrell, Vanderbilt	60
32. Forrestt Allday, Central Arkansas	59
Alex Bregman, LSU	59
Justin Cureton, Indiana	59
Chaz Frank, North Carolina	59
Zack Granite, Seton Hall	59
Craig Massoni, Austin Peay	59
Zach Stephens, Tennessee Tech	59
39. Antonio Alvarez, Elon	58
Phillip Ervin, Samford	58
Johnny Field, Arizona	58
Sam Haggerty, New Mexico	58
Seth Harrison, La.-Lafayette	58
Tyler Horan, Virginia Tech	58
Ronnie Mitchell, Dallas Baptist	58
Derek Toadvine, Kent State	58

HITS

RANK NAME, TEAM	H
1. Adam Frazier, Mississippi State	107
2. Chesny Young, Mercer	105
3. Alex Bregman, LSU	104
Tony Kemp, Vanderbilt	104
5. Cody Stubbs, North Carolina	101
6. Dex Kjerstad, La.-Lafayette	99
7. Kyle Wren, Georgia Tech	98
8. Aaron Attaway, Western Carolina	97
Colin Moran, North Carolina	97
10. Mitch Garver, New Mexico	96
Jimmy Yezzo, Delaware	96
12. Ross Kivett, Kansas State	94
13. Dustin DeMuth, Indiana	92
Landon Lassiter, North Carolina	92
Craig Massoni, Austin Peay	92
L.J. Mazzilli, Connecticut	92
Justin Parr, Illinois	92

Name, Team	
18. Garrett Bayliff, Wichita State	91
Tyler White, Western Carolina	91
20. Mason Katz, LSU	90
Matt Oberste, Oklahoma	90
22. Cody Hudson, Austin Peay	89
Darian Johnson, Lamar	89
Trey Mancini, Notre Dame	89
D.J. Peterson, New Mexico	89
Chad Prain, Georgia State	89
Tyler Shryock, Bakersfield	89
28. Zane Evans, Georgia Tech	88
Tyler Horan, Virginia Tech	88
Joe Jackson, Citadel	88
Ryan Lindemuth, William & Mary	88
Logan Pierce, Troy	88
Hunter Renfroe, Mississippi State	88
Tanner Witt, Kansas State	88
Christian Wolfe, UNC Greensboro	88
36. Denver Chavez, Cal Poly	87
Mike Vigliarolo, Saint Louis	87
38. Gaither Bumgardner, USC Upstate	86
Scott Donley, Indiana	86
Jordan Hankins, Austin Peay	86
Kyle Schwarber, Indiana	86
Tim Zier, San Diego State	86
43. Forrestt Allday, Central Arkansas	85
Hughston Armstrong, Citadel	85
Danny Collins, Troy	85
Shane Conlon, Kansas State	85
Pat Kelly, Nebraska	85
Michael O'Neill, Michigan	85
Giuseppe Papaccio, Seton Hall	85

TOTAL BASES

RANK NAME, TEAM	TB
1. Kris Bryant, San Diego	187
2. D.J. Peterson, New Mexico	176
3. Ryan Kinsella, Elon	168
4. Jimmy Yezzo, Delaware	167
5. Tyler White, Western Carolina	166
6. Hunter Dozier, Stephen F. Austin	160
7. Cody Stubbs, North Carolina	159
8. Aaron Attaway, Western Carolina	158
Craig Massoni, Austin Peay	158
Hunter Renfroe, Mississippi State	158
11. Mason Katz, LSU	156
12. Tyler Horan, Virginia Tech	155
Dex Kjerstad, La.-Lafayette	155
14. Alex Bregman, LSU	154
15. Colin Moran, North Carolina	153
16. Kyle Schwarber, Indiana	152
17. Daniel Palka, Georgia Tech	151
18. Joe Jackson, Citadel	150
Matt Oberste, Oklahoma	150
20. Danny Collins, Troy	149
21. Nick Ferdinand, Delaware	145
Mitch Garver, New Mexico	145
Trae Santos, Troy	145
24. Brandon Downes, Virginia	144
Zane Evans, Georgia Tech	144
26. Duncan McAlpine, Dallas Baptist	143
27. Kurt Wertz, Towson	142
28. Adam Frazier, Mississippi State	141
Zach Stephens, Tennessee Tech	141
Chesny Young, Mercer	141
31. Nick Backlund, Mercer	140
32. Mike Fish, Siena	139
33. Trey Mancini, Notre Dame	138
Tyler Marincov, North Florida	138
Logan Pierce, Troy	138
36. Jason Kanzler, Buffalo	137
Alex Kelly, Saint Louis	137
38. Clinton Freeman, East Tenn. State	136
Ryan Huck, Western Ky.	136

40.	Michael Benjamin, Arizona State	135
	Aaron Judge, Fresno State	135
42.	L.J. Mazzilli, Connecticut	134
	Andrew Rash, Virginia Tech	134
	Mike Vigliarolo, Saint Louis	134
45.	Dustin DeMuth, Indiana	133
	Jordan Hankins, Austin Peay	133
	Justin Parr, Illinois	133
	Sam Travis, Indiana	133

WALKS

RANK NAME, TEAM	BB
1. Kris Bryant, San Diego	66
2. Colin Moran, North Carolina	63
3. Casey Gillaspie, Wichita State	62
4. Pat Blair, Wake Forest	57
5. Stephen McGee, Florida State	55
6. Conrad Gregor, Vanderbilt	54
Joe McCarthy, Virginia	54
Bo Thompson, Citadel	54
9. Forrestt Allday, Central Arkansas	53
Alex Detz, Mississippi State	53
Landon Lassiter, North Carolina	53
12. Johnny Bladel, James Madison	52
13. Steven Shelinsky, Pittsburgh	51
14. Josh Vidales, Houston	49
15. Antonio Alvarez, Elon	48
Nathan Pittman, Florida Atlantic	48
Jordan Tarsovich, VMI	48
18. Kevin Brown, Bryant	47
Sam Haggerty, New Mexico	47
Ian Happ, Cincinnati	47
21. D.J. Peterson, New Mexico	46
Logan Pierce, Troy	46
23. Luis Diaz, N.C. Central	45
Ryan Emery, Arkansas State	45
Tyler McFarland, James Madison	45
Michael Medina, New Mexico State	45
Mike Papi, Virginia	45
Richy Pedroza, Cal State Fullerton	45
Jake Thomas, Binghamton	45
30. Leon Byrd, Rice	44
Michael Ratterree, Rice	44
Christian Stringer, Rice	44
Jude Vidrine, Lamar	44
34. Brian Holberton, North Carolina	43
Joe Jackson, Citadel	43
36. Ted Blackman, Coastal Carolina	42
LB Dantzler, South Carolina	42
Drew Ferguson, Belmont	42
Chris McGowan, Kennesaw State	42
Brandon Murray, Col. of Charleston	42
Alex Perez, Virginia Tech	42
Willie Pratt, Utah Valley	42
Kyle Schwarber, Indiana	42
Evan Stephens, Wake Forest	42

TOUGHEST TO STRIKE OUT

RANK PLAYER	AB/SO
1. Nick Ratajczak, Louisville	26.7
2. Tyler Vaughn, Troy	25.7
3. Brad Elwood, Charlotte	23.3

4.	Reed Gragnani, Virginia	21.7
5.	Mike Alexander, Delaware State	21.1
6.	Bobby Ison, Charleston So.	20.8
7.	Steven Patterson, UC Davis	20.4
8.	Billy Urban, St. Bonaventure	20.2
9.	Jeff McNeil, Long Beach State	20.1
10.	Devyn Bolasky, UC Riverside	19.3
11.	Darian Johnson, Lamar	18.5
12.	Griff Gordon, Jacksonville State	18.3
13.	Kyle Farmer, Georgia	17.5
14.	Bennie Robinson, Florida A&M	17.1
15.	Jacob Valdez, San Jose State	17.1
16.	Anthony Hajjar, Fairfield	16.7
17.	Kai Hatch, Utah Valley	16.7
	Kevin Newman, Arizona	16.7
19.	Joey Cujas, VCU	16.6
20.	Alex Lipson, UC Davis	16.5
21.	Austin Anderson, Mississippi	16.4
22.	Zach Shank, Marist	16.2
23.	Whitt Dorsey, South Alabama	16.1
24.	Michael Felton, Campbell	16
25.	Cody Dolan, Winthrop	15.8

HIT BY PITCH

RANK NAME, TEAM	HBP
1. Troy Marrow, N.C. Central	28
Bryce Taylor, Jackson State	28
Tom Verdi, Connecticut	28
4. Jonathan Davis, Central Arkansas	25
5. Richard Gonzalez, Alabama State	24
David Olson, Campbell	24
7. Jason Blum, Southeast Mo. State	23
Coco Johnson, Louisville	23
Ryan Lindemuth, William & Mary	23
Mike Warren, UTSA	23
11. Keith Brand, Iowa	22
Ryan Haas, Delaware State	22
13. Kyle Convissar, Maryland	21
Austin Cousino, Kentucky	21
Jon Davis, Kansas State	21
Charles Galiano, Fordham	21
Kash Kalkowski, Nebraska	21
Nick Lynch, UC Davis	21
Spencer Navin, Vanderbilt	21
Jordan Patterson, South Alabama	21
Michael Strentz, La.-Lafayette	21
22. Jake Armstrong, North Carolina State	20
Ryan Brown, William & Mary	20
Adam Engel, Louisville	20
Eric Gutierrez, Texas Tech	20
C.J. Jarvis, Houston Baptist	20
Alex Jensen, Army	20
Brett Pirtle, Mississippi State	20
Paul Rambaud, Villanova	20

SACRIFICE BUNTS

RANK NAME, TEAM	SH
1. Kevin Kuntz, Kansas	30
2. Aaron Payne, Oregon	23
3. Andrew Ely, Washington	22
4. Andy Peterson, Oregon State	21
Alex Potts, Arkansas State	21

6.	Jack Lupo, Vanderbilt	20
7.	Craig Aikin, Oklahoma	19
	Krey Bratsen, Texas A&M	19
	Federico Castagnini, Creighton	19
	Mike Reeves, Florida Gulf Coast	19
	Mike Small, Richmond	19
	Tanner Vavra, Valparaiso	19
13.	Alec Paradowski, Wofford	18
	Donnie Walton, Oklahoma State	18
15.	Michael Green, Charlotte	17
	Matt Roberts, North Carolina	17
17.	Alex Diaz, Florida Gulf Coast	16
	Brian Estevez, Hartford	16
	Sam Haggerty, New Mexico	16
	Tyler Oertle, Ark.-Pine Bluff	16
	Jaren Sustar, Charleston So.	16
22.	Jonathan Davis, Central Arkansas	15
	Jacob May, Coastal Carolina	15
	Chris Riopedre, East Tenn. State	15
	Joe Serrano, Arkansas	15
	Kyle Teaf, South Florida	15
	Justin Treece, Central Arkansas	15

SACRIFICE FLIES

RANK NAME, TEAM	SF
1. Kyle Farmer, Georgia	12
2. Sean Dwyer, Florida Gulf Coast	11
Zachary Turner, San Francisco	11
4. Jacob Cronenworth, Michigan	10
Michael Felton, Campbell	10
Conrad Gregor, Vanderbilt	10
Jake Rodriguez, Oregon State	10
Elijah Trail, Campbell	10
Ty Young, Louisville	10
10. Cael Brockmeyer, Bakersfield	9
Will Callaway, Appalachian State	9
Jose Cruz, Jackson State	9
Darren Farmer, Grambling	9
L.J. Mazzilli, Connecticut	9
J.P. Sportman, Central Conn. State	9
Nick Torres, Cal Poly	9
Stuart Turner, Mississippi	9
18. Alex Albritton, New Mexico	8
Bradley Brown, Houston Baptist	8
Trevor Edwards, UNC Greensboro	8
Kelvin Freeman, N.C. A&T	8
Zac Johnson, Illinois State	8
Alex Johnson, Miami (Ohio)	8
Robert Lecount, New Mexico State	8
Trey Mancini, Notre Dame	8
Michael Marietta, Central Arkansas	8
Sean McMullen, LSU	8
Jeff Melillo, Rutgers	8
Patrick Mescher, Army	8
Tommy Monnot, Kent State	8
Michael Porcaro, Milwaukee	8
Graham Saiko, South Carolina	8
Vinny Siena, Connecticut	8
Sam Travis, Indiana	8
Chase Vergason, South Carolina	8

PITCHING Minimum 50 IP, 1 IP per team game

EARNED RUN AVERAGE

RANK NAME, TEAM	YEAR	G	IP	R	ER	ERA
1. Ryan Thompson, Campbell	Jr.	31	72	9	7	0.88
2. David Berg, UCLA	So.	51	78	8	8	0.92
3. Mike Ford, Princeton	Jr.	9	64	15	7	0.98
4. Steve Janas, Kennesaw State	Jr.	13	79	15	10	1.14
5. Dan Slania, Notre Dame	Jr.	24	59	12	8	1.21
6. Aaron Michel, Western Illinois	Fr.	21	66	17	9	1.23
7. Trent Thornton, North Carolina	Fr.	29	92	22	14	1.37
8. Ryne Stanek, Arkansas	Jr.	16	97	23	15	1.39
9. Sean Manaea, Indiana State	Jr.	13	73	17	12	1.47
10. Thomas Eshelman, Cal State Fullerton	Fr.	17	116	26	19	1.48
11. Jordan Montgomery, South Carolina	So.	13	79	19	13	1.48
12. Preston Morrison, TCU	So.	15	107	27	18	1.51
13. Ross Mitchell, Mississippi State	So.	34	94	22	16	1.53
14. Aaron Nola, LSU	So.	17	126	30	22	1.57
15. Nick Petree, Missouri State	Jr.	14	100	23	18	1.61
16. Jonathan Gray, Oklahoma	Jr.	17	126	27	23	1.64

17. Chris Diaz, Miami	So.	16	110	29	20	1.64
18. John Straka, North Dakota State	Sr.	15	108	25	20	1.67
19. Jordan Piche', Kansas	Jr.	32	64	12	12	1.68
20. Heath Bowers, Campbell	So.	15	90	27	17	1.69
21. Zach McCulley, Cornell	Jr.	11	42	12	8	1.70
22. Chris Razo, Illinois State	Sr.	20	89	22	17	1.71
23. Jimmy Herget, South Florida	Fr.	15	94	25	18	1.72
24. Parker Ray, Texas A&M	Sr.	23	68	14	13	1.73
25. Jake Long, Milwaukee	Sr.	13	83	22	16	1.73
26. Steve Moyers, Rhode Island	Fr.	14	61	17	12	1.78
Bryan Radziewski, Miami	Jr.	15	91	24	18	1.78
28. Andrew Moore, Oregon State	Fr.	19	131	33	26	1.79
29. Barrett Astin, Arkansas	Jr.	18	91	26	18	1.79
30. Dan Savas, Illinois State	Jr.	15	100	29	20	1.79
31. Michael Renner, North Florida	Sr.	16	95	31	19	1.81
32. Michael Johnson, Dartmouth	Sr.	9	59	14	12	1.82
33. Trey Masek, Texas Tech	Jr.	11	79	18	16	1.82
34. Alex Gonzalez, Oral Roberts	Jr.	15	113	33	23	1.83
35. Kyle Hunter, Dartmouth	Sr.	9	54	14	11	1.83
36. Layne Somsen, South Dakota State	Sr.	15	92	26	19	1.87
37. Jeff McKenzie, Bakersfield	Sr.	15	115	27	24	1.88
38. Andrew Morales, UC Irvine	Jr.	17	95	20	20	1.89
39. Tyler Nurdin, Oklahoma State	So.	14	86	22	18	1.89
40. Haden Hinkle, San Francisco	Sr.	19	80	18	17	1.90
41. Will Coursen-Carr, Indiana	Fr.	17	65	18	14	1.93
Sean Furney, Rhode Island	Sr.	15	98	29	21	1.93
43. Ryan Mattes, Campbell	Sr.	16	107	31	23	1.94
44. Vince Wheeland, Oklahoma State	Jr.	30	73	20	16	1.97
45. Dillon Peters, Texas	So.	14	87	23	19	1.97
46. Kyle McGowin, Savannah State	Jr.	17	120	37	27	2.02
47. Zech Lemond, Rice	So.	32	76	19	17	2.02
48. Randall Fant, Arkansas	Sr.	14	67	17	15	2.03
49. Bobby Wahl, Mississippi	Jr.	16	98	25	22	2.03
50. Justin Garza, Cal State Fullerton	Fr.	17	115	27	26	2.03
51. Matt Boyd, Oregon State	Sr.	20	133	33	30	2.04
52. Ben Lively, UCF	Jr.	15	106	31	24	2.04
Aaron Slegers, Indiana	So.	18	106	35	24	2.04
54. Austin Kubitza, Rice	Jr.	18	109	35	25	2.06
55. Scott Sitz, Florida State	Sr.	16	95	40	22	2.09
56. Jacob Mayers, Richmond	Sr.	10	56	18	13	2.10
57. Ricky Knapp, Florida Gulf Coast	Jr.	14	103	30	24	2.10
58. Ryan Connolly, Coastal Carolina	Sr.	32	81	23	19	2.11

59. Mike Connolly, Maine	Jr.	14	77	22	18	2.11
60. Daniel Mengden, Texas A&M	So.	16	111	34	26	2.11
61. Mark Appel, Stanford	Sr.	14	106	37	25	2.12
62. Kevin Ziomek, Vanderbilt	Jr.	17	119	33	28	2.12
63. Andrew McGee, Monmouth	Jr.	13	110	28	26	2.12
64. Conner Kendrick, Auburn	Jr.	19	80	34	19	2.13
65. Luke Farrell, Northwestern	Sr.	12	84	29	20	2.13
66. Tom Windle, Minnesota	Jr.	14	93	27	22	2.14
67. Kerry Doane, East Tenn. State	Sr.	20	147	43	35	2.14
68. D.J. Snelten, Minnesota	Jr.	10	59	18	14	2.15
69. Thomas Thorpe, Oregon	So.	16	104	28	25	2.16
70. Trevor Dunlap, Washington	Jr.	29	67	19	16	2.16
Bobby Zarubin, Stanford	Fr.	15	58	23	14	2.16
72. Nick Vander Tuig, UCLA	Jr.	19	129	34	31	2.16
73. PJ Conlon, San Diego	Fr.	25	87	32	21	2.16
74. Harrison Musgrave, West Virginia	So.	14	95	24	23	2.17
75. Dan Gautieri, Penn	So.	9	58	21	14	2.17
76. Scott Baker, Ball State	So.	17	112	38	27	2.18
77. Eli Anderson, Northern Illinois	Jr.	15	115	32	28	2.18
78. Matthew Crownover, Clemson	Fr.	15	70	19	17	2.19
79. T.J. Renda, Alabama State	So.	14	95	28	23	2.19
80. Jeff Thompson, Louisville	Jr.	17	107	31	26	2.19
81. Mitch Horacek, Dartmouth	Jr.	8	45	13	11	2.20
82. Mark Lukowski, Creighton	So.	25	49	14	12	2.22
83. Tony Rizzotti, Tulane	So.	12	81	28	20	2.22
84. A.J. Helms, Prairie View	Jr.	18	57	26	14	2.22
85. Jessie Snodgrass, Belmont	Sr.	44	73	19	18	2.23
86. Ben Smith, Coastal Carolina	So.	16	93	30	23	2.23
87. Adam Plutko, UCLA	Jr.	19	124	35	31	2.25
88. Travis Felax, SIU Edwardsville	Jr.	11	76	25	19	2.26
89. Lee Ridenhour, Austin Peay	Jr.	13	79	24	20	2.27
90. Brian McAfee, Cornell	So.	9	55	17	14	2.28
91. Chase Brookshire, Belmont	Sr.	11	71	20	18	2.28
92. Reed Reilly, Cal Poly	So.	32	59	19	15	2.29
Luke Weaver, Florida State	So.	17	98	26	25	2.29
94. Sam Moll, Memphis	Jr.	15	94	34	24	2.30
Colin Welmon, Loyola Marymount	So.	12	78	25	20	2.30
96. Steven Spann, Northwestern State	Jr.	27	59	25	15	2.30
97. Jon Richard, Xavier	Sr.	15	105	38	27	2.31
98. Tyler Beede, Vanderbilt	So.	17	101	32	26	2.32
99. Adam Westmoreland, South Carolina	Sr.	29	66	22	17	2.32
100. Tommy Lawrence, Maine	Jr.	16	105	31	27	2.32

WINS

RANK NAME, TEAM	W	L
1. Tyler Beede, Vanderbilt	14	1
Andrew Moore, Oregon State	14	2
Nick Vander Tuig, UCLA	14	4
4. Ross Mitchell, Mississippi State	13	0
Kerry Doane, East Tenn. State	13	2
Jeff McKenzie, Bakersfield	13	2
Joey Wagman, Cal Poly	13	3
8. Justin Garza, Cal State Fullerton	12	0
Aaron Nola, LSU	12	1
Trent Thornton, North Carolina	12	1
Scott Baker, Ball State	12	2
Kyle McGowin, Savannah State	12	2
Thomas Eshelman, CS Fullerton	12	3
Cole Irvin, Oregon	12	3
15. Ryan Kellogg, Arizona State	11	1
Kurt Sowa, Rider	11	1
Josh Walker, New Mexico	11	1
Dan Ludwig, Belmont	11	2
Jeff Thompson, Louisville	11	2
Devin Burke, Virginia Tech	11	3
John Farrell, William & Mary	11	3
Tommy Lawrence, Maine	11	3
Kevin Ziomek, Vanderbilt	11	3
Matt Boyd, Oregon State	11	4
Garrett Cortright, Canisius	11	4
Kent Emanuel, North Carolina	11	5
27. Andrew Morales, UC Irvine	10	0
Dan Savas, Illinois State	10	0

Bobby Wahl, Mississippi	10	0
Chad Girodo, Mississippi State	10	1
Ben Wetzler, Oregon State	10	1
Taylor Williams, Kent State	10	1
Joey DeNato, Indiana	10	2
Chad Kuhl, Delaware	10	2
Scott Silverstein, Virginia	10	2
Scott Sitz, Florida State	10	2
Ryne Stanek, Arkansas	10	2
Jonathan Gray, Oklahoma	10	3
Ethan Mildren, Pittsburgh	10	3
Austin Pettibone, UC Santa Barbara	10	3
Adam Plutko, UCLA	10	3
Carlos Rodon, N.C. State	10	3
Sam Street, Texas-Pan American	10	3
Mike Volpe, Towson	10	3
Mark Appel, Stanford	10	4
Daniel Gossett, Clemson	10	4
Chad Green, Louisville	10	4
Brandon Leibrandt, Florida State	10	4
Craig Schlitter, Bryant	10	4
Adam Norton, Notre Dame	10	5

SAVES

RANK NAME, TEAM	SV
1. David Berg, UCLA	24
2. Tyler Rogers, Austin Peay	23
3. Jonathan Holder, Mississippi State	21
Jimmie Sherfy, Oregon	21
5. Michael Lorenzen, Cal State Fullerton	19
6. Hugh Adams, Florida Atlantic	18

7. Sutter McLoughlin, Sacramento State	17
Trace Dempsey, Ohio State	17
Travis Stout, Jacksonville State	17
Tyler Webb, South Carolina	17
11. Nick Burdi, Louisville	16
Brian Miller, Vanderbilt	16
Chris Cotton, LSU	16
14. Michael Swanner, Pepperdine	14
Drew Reynolds, East Carolina	14
Preston Hatcher, Western Carolina	14
Zech Lemond, Rice	14
Reed Reilly, Cal Poly	14
Jason Jester, Texas A&M	14
20. Colby Suggs, Arkansas	13
Dan Slania, Notre Dame	13
Eric Nedeljkovic, Miami	13
J.D. Moore, South Dakota State	13
Jonathan Van Eaton, Memphis	13
Jacob Dorris, TAMU-Corpus Christi	13
Skylar Hunter, Citadel	13
27. Brett Huber, Mississippi	12
Kyle Bartsch, South Alabama	12
Trevor Gott, Kentucky	12
Karch Kowalczyk, Valparaiso	12
Ray Castillo, Alabama	12
Ian Gibaut, Tulane	12
River McWilliams, Buffalo	12
Kyle Crockett, Virginia	12
Josh Davis, Belmont	12
Johnny Magliozzi, Florida	12

Seth Lucio, Tennessee Tech	12
Ryan Burr, Arizona State	12
Jordan Piche', Kansas	12
40. Pat Christensen, La Salle	11
Chase Wellbrock, Houston	11
Eric Yardley, Seattle	11
Mason Klotz, Southeastern La.	11
Ryan Halstead, Indiana	11
Matt Hicks, La.-Lafayette	11
Clark Labitan, Virginia Tech	11
Ryan Connolly, Coastal Carolina	11
Jordan Dailey, Bethune-Cookman	11

STRIKEOUTS

RANK NAME, TEAM	SO
1. Carlos Rodon, North Carolina State	184
2. Jonathan Gray, Oklahoma	147
3. Austin Kubitza, Rice	134
Kyle McGowin, Savannah State	134
5. Mark Appel, Stanford	130
6. Alex Gonzalez, Oral Roberts	126
7. Matt Boyd, Oregon State	122
Buck Farmer, Georgia Tech	122
Aaron Nola, LSU	122
10. Justin Hess, Ga. Southern	120
11. Luke Weaver, Florida State	119
12. Kevin Ziomek, Vanderbilt	115
13. Mat Batts, UNC Wilmington	114
14. Jeff Thompson, Louisville	113
15. Nick Petree, Missouri State	111
16. Taylor Williams, Kent State	110
17. Michael Cederoth, San Diego State	109
Jeremy Null, Western Carolina	109
Bryan Radziewski, Miami	109
20. Jonathan Dziedzic, Lamar	106
Mark Leiter, NJIT	106
Sam Moll, Memphis	106
23. Casey Delgado, Austin Peay	105
Shane McCain, Troy	105
25. Sam Street, Texas-Pan American	104
26. Tyler Beede, Vanderbilt	103
Trevor Foss, TAMU-Corpus Christi	103
Austin Gomber, Florida Atlantic	103
Joey Wagman, Cal Poly	103
30. Jesse Morris, Wofford	102
Braden Shipley, Nevada	102
Tyler Skulina, Kent State	102
33. Tyler Alexander, FIU	101
Chris Anderson, Jacksonville	101
Ben Lively, UCF	101
36. Jordan Stephens, Rice	100
37. Jason Inghram, William & Mary	99
Kyle Lloyd, Evansville	99
39. Kent Emanuel, North Carolina	98
Zack Godley, Tennessee	98
Andrew Pierce, Southern Miss.	98
Dan Savas, Illinois State	98
John Simms, Rice	98
Nate Smith, Furman	98

Austin Voth, Washington	98
46. Tristan Archer, Tennessee Tech	97
Kyle Webb, Elon	97
48. Matt Fraudin, Gardner-Webb	96
Marco Gonzales, Gonzaga	96
Dusten Knight, Texas-Pan American	96
Daniel Wright, Arkansas State	96

STRIKEOUTS PER NINE INNINGS

RANK NAME, TEAM	SO/9
1. Carlos Rodon, North Carolina State	12.51
2. Sean Newcomb, Hartford	11.5
3. Sean Manaea, Indiana State	11.41
4. Justin Hess, Ga. Southern	11.37
5. Nathan Hill, Troy	11.14
6. Dusten Knight, Texas-Pan American	11.08
7. Austin Kubitza, Rice	11.03
8. Mark Appel, Stanford	11
9. Jesse Morris, Wofford	10.97
10. Joey Donino, Columbia	10.96
11. Luke Weaver, Florida State	10.89
12. Jeremy Null, Western Carolina	10.78
Bryan Radziewski, Miami	10.78
14. Dace Kime, Louisville	10.77
15. David Hess, Tennessee Tech	10.55
16. Reed Reilly, Cal Poly	10.53
17. Jonathan Gray, Oklahoma	10.47
18. Chase Brookshire, Belmont	10.39
19. Dan Tobik, UT Martin	10.31
20. Michael Cederoth, San Diego State	10.29
21. Kyle Westwood, North Florida	10.25
22. David Lucroy, East Carolina	10.2
23. Sam Moll, Memphis	10.15
24. Mark Leiter, NJIT	10.08
25. Tyler Alexander, FIU	10.06
26. Kyle McGowin, Savannah State	10.02
27. Alex Gonzalez, Oral Roberts	10.01
28. Nick Petree, Missouri State	9.96
29. Bradley Wallace, Arkansas State	9.93
30. Casey Delgado, Austin Peay	9.81
31. Jordan Brink, Fresno State	9.8
32. Tyler Skulina, Kent State	9.8
33. Matt Soren, Delaware	9.76
Brandon Finnegan, TCU	9.76
35. Troy Scribner, Sacred Heart	9.72
36. Buck Farmer, Georgia Tech	9.69
37. Matt Marksberry, Campbell	9.66
38. Shane McCain, Troy	9.61
39. Ryan Beck, New Mexico State	9.56
40. Jessie Snodgrass, Belmont	9.54
41. Jeff Thompson, Louisville	9.5
42. Kyle Lloyd, Evansville	9.48
43. Ryan West, Col. of Charleston	9.44
44. Cole Sulser, Dartmouth	9.39
45. Max Povse, UNC Greensboro	9.39
46. Benton Moss, North Carolina	9.37
47. Taylor Williams, Kent State	9.37
48. Sam Howard, Ga. Southern	9.28
49. Tyler Willman, Western Illinois	9.24

50. Aaron Blair, Marshall	9.22

FEWEST HITS PER NINE INNINGS

RANK NAME, TEAM	H/9
1. Bryan Radziewski, Miami	5.24
2. David Napoli, Tulane	5.32
3. Aaron Michel, Western Illinois	5.48
4. Steve Moyers, Rhode Island	5.49
5. Jeff Thompson, Louisville	5.64
6. Brian Hunter, Hartford	5.69
7. Tyler Beede, Vanderbilt	5.7
8. Chase Brookshire, Belmont	5.7
9. Cody Dickson, Sam Houston State	5.78
10. Kurt Sowa, Rider	5.79
11. Dan Savas, Illinois State	5.83
12. Austin Kubitza, Rice	5.84
13. Jonathan Gray, Oklahoma	5.91
14. Aaron Nola, LSU	5.93
15. Jimmy Herget, South Florida	5.94
16. Kevin Ziomek, Vanderbilt	5.97
17. Sean Manaea, Indiana State	6.01
18. David Lucroy, East Carolina	6.1
19. Harrison Musgrave, West Virginia	6.14
20. Haden Hinkle, San Francisco	6.16
21. Matt Hall, Missouri State	6.17
22. Mike Ford, Princeton	6.19
23. A.J. Helms, Prairie View	6.19
24. Layne Somsen, South Dakota State	6.21
25. Jaime Schultz, High Point	6.23

FEWEST WALKS PER NINE INNINGS

RANK NAME, TEAM	BB/9
1. Thomas Eshelman, Cal St. Fullerton	0.23
2. Sam Kmiec, Winthrop	0.57
3. Dillon Newman, Baylor	0.58
4. Travis Felax, SIU Edwardsville	0.71
5. Cameron White, Air Force	0.76
6. Caleb McClanahan, Central Ark.	0.89
7. John Straka, North Dakota State	0.92
8. Matt McClain, Delaware State	0.97
9. Brett Koehler, William & Mary	0.98
10. Seth Greene, VCU	1.05
11. Brian King, Ohio State	1.07
12. Jon Prosinski, Seton Hall	1.08
13. Grahamm Wiest, Cal State Fullerton	1.12
14. Brandon Lee, South Carolina-Upstate	1.12
15. Ryan Wilkinson, Toledo	1.13
16. Jacob Mayers, Richmond	1.13
Taylor Thurber, Appalachian State	1.13
18. Adam Norton, Notre Dame	1.16
19. Andrew McGee, Monmouth	1.22
20. Kurt Yinger, Portland	1.23
21. Nolan Belcher, South Carolina	1.23
22. John Farrell, William & Mary	1.23
23. Nick Vander Tuig, UCLA	1.26
24. Bryan Goossens, Siena	1.26
25. David Berg, UCLA	1.27

TEAM LEADERS
BATTING

SCORING

RANK TEAM	G	R	R/G
1. New Mexico	59	487	8.3
2. James Madison	55	436	7.9
3. Virginia	62	489	7.9
4. Georgia State	56	432	7.7
5. North Carolina	71	542	7.6
6. La.-Lafayette	63	478	7.6
7. Pittsburgh	59	444	7.5
8. Mercer	61	446	7.3
9. Western Carolina	59	430	7.3
10. Tennessee Tech	57	415	7.3
11. Citadel	60	434	7.2
12. Delaware State	48	342	7.1
13. Troy	62	441	7.1
14. Samford	57	405	7.1
15. Campbell	59	419	7.1
16. UNLV	57	403	7.1
17. Towson	60	423	7.1
18. Canisius	59	414	7
19. Vanderbilt	66	459	7
20. New Mexico State	57	394	6.9
21. North Florida	59	403	6.8
22. Florida State	64	435	6.8
23. South Alabama	63	426	6.8
24. Delaware	55	371	6.7
25. Austin Peay	62	418	6.7
26. Arizona	55	368	6.7
27. Indiana	65	434	6.7
28. Seton Hall	56	372	6.6

29. Central Arkansas	64	425	6.6
30. Jackson State	56	370	6.6
31. Eastern Kentucky	57	374	6.6
32. UNC Greensboro	55	359	6.5
33. Elon	64	417	6.5
34. Dartmouth	41	267	6.5
35. San Diego	62	402	6.5
36. Georgia Tech	64	414	6.5
37. Lamar	59	381	6.5
38. LSU	68	439	6.5
39. Kansas State	64	412	6.4
40. Virginia Tech	62	398	6.4
41. UNC Wilmington	61	387	6.3
42. Eastern Michigan	54	342	6.3
43. Alabama State	57	359	6.3
Florida Gulf Coast	57	359	6.3
45. Dallas Baptist	60	377	6.3
46. Arizona State	60	375	6.3
47. Furman	57	356	6.2
48. Milwaukee	50	312	6.2
49. Louisville	65	404	6.2
50. Illinois State	58	359	6.2

BATTING AVERAGE

RANK TEAM	AVG
1. New Mexico	.334
2. Kansas State	.322
3. Georgia State	.321
4. James Madison	.318
5. Delaware State	.317
6. Louisiana-Lafayette	.317
7. North Florida	.316
8. Campbell	.314
9. Vanderbilt	.313
10. Austin Peay	.312

HOME RUNS

RANK TEAM	HR
1. Louisiana-Lafayette	74
2. Western Carolina	71
3. Citadel	66
4. San Diego	64
5. Dallas Baptist	61
6. Georgia Tech	58
7. Mercer	56
8. Virginia Tech	55
Arkansas-Little Rock	55

10. Austin Peay	54
Troy	54
Towson	54
Tennessee Tech	54

DOUBLES

RANK TEAM	2B
1. Troy	151
2. New Mexico	149
3. Florida State	146
4. Western Carolina	145
5. Louisiana-Lafayette	142
6. Indiana	134
Georgia State	134
Virginia	134
9. Towson	133
10. Virginia Tech	129

TRIPLES

RANK TEAM	3B
1. Arizona	35
2. Seton Hall	32
3. Virginia	31
New Mexico	31

5. Kansas State	28
6. Arizona State	26
Louisville	26
Canisius	26
9. James Madison	25
Houston	25

SLUGGING PERCENTAGE

RANK TEAM	SLG
1. New Mexico	.504
2. Louisiana-Lafayette	.503
3. Western Carolina	.493
4. Citadel	.476
5. Georgia State	.468
6. James Madison	.467
7. Tennessee Tech	.464
8. Virginia	.462
9. Troy	.457
10. Georgia Tech	.455

STOLEN BASES

RANK TEAM	SB	CS
1. Wofford	163	46
2. Louisville	150	45

3. Delaware State	145	20
4. Vanderbilt	139	36
5. Seton Hall	132	24
6. Campbell	130	35
7. Jackson State	127	32
Hofstra	127	45
Savannah State	127	31
10. Alcorn	124	33

WALKS

RANK TEAM	BB
1. North Carolina	369
2. Central Arkansas	363
3. Florida State	359
4. New Mexico State	316
5. Virginia	312
6. Mercer	309
7. Vanderbilt	295
8. Towson	294
9. LSU	293
10. Pittsburgh	292

PITCHING

EARNED RUN AVERAGE

RANK TEAM	ERA
1. Arkansas	1.89
2. Oregon State	2.33
3. LSU	2.40
4. Cal State Fullerton	2.47
5. Louisville	2.52
6. UCLA	2.55
7. Texas	2.61
8. Campbell	2.63
9. Indiana	2.64
10. Bryant	2.73
11. Dartmouth	2.75
12. Vanderbilt	2.76
13. Texas Christian	2.78
14. Oregon	2.78
15. Mississippi State	2.79
16. North Carolina	2.81
17. Central Arkansas	2.82
18. Rice	2.84
19. Minnesota	2.90
20. Florida State	2.92
21. Oklahoma	2.95
22. Rhode Island	3.01
23. South Carolina	3.02
24. Oklahoma State	3.04
25. Memphis	3.05
26. Mississippi	3.07
27. North Carolina State	3.08
28. Seton Hall	3.11
29. Virginia	3.12
30. Cornell	3.13
31. Missouri State	3.14
32. North Florida	3.16
33. Charlotte	3.16
34. Loyola Marymount	3.17
35. Clemson	3.21
36. Michigan State	3.22
37. Coastal Carolina	3.24
38. Ohio State	3.24
39. Gardner-Webb	3.35
40. San Francisco	3.36
41. Miami	3.38
42. Florida Gulf Coast	3.38
43. Stanford	3.38
44. Auburn	3.40
45. Connecticut	3.40
46. South Dakota State	3.41
47. Northwestern	3.41
48. Bakersfield	3.42
49. Cal Poly	3.42
50. Texas A&M	3.43

STRIKEOUTS PER NINE INNINGS

RANK TEAM	SO/9
1. Louisville	9.6
2. Tennessee Tech	9
3. North Carolina State	8.8
4. New Mexico State	8.7
5. Troy	8.6
6. Florida International	8.5
7. Western Kentucky	8.4
8. Wofford	8.4
9. Western Carolina	8.3
10. Mississippi State	8.2

FEWEST WALKS PER NINE INNINGS

RANK TEAM	BB/9
1. Cal State Fullerton	1.41
2. Central Arkansas	2.05
3. North Florida	2.22
4. William & Mary	2.26
5. South Carolina	2.36
6. Virginia	2.36
7. UC Irvine	2.4
8. UCLA	2.44
9. Ohio State	2.45
10. Valparaiso	2.47

FIELDING

FIELDING PERCENTAGE

RANK TEAM	PCT
1. Mercer	.982
2. Nebraska	.981
3. Oregon	.981
4. UC Irvine	.981
5. UCLA	.980
6. LSU	.980
7. VCU	.980
8. Troy	.979
9. Creighton	.979
10. Sacramento State	.979
11. Hawaii	.979
12. Dartmouth	.979
13. Tennessee Tech	.979
14. Seton Hall	.978
15. San Diego State	.978
16. Maryland	.977
17. Lamar	.977
18. Vanderbilt	.977
19. Wichita State	.977
20. Alabama	.976
21. Washington	.976
22. Ohio State	.976
23. North Carolina	.976
24. Binghamton	.976
25. Southeastern Louisiana	.976

DOUBLE PLAYS PER NINE INNINGS

RANK TEAM	DP
1. Towson	81
2. Mississippi State	80
Alabama	80
4. Southern Mississippi	78
5. Indiana	71
6. Rice	69
7. Texas Tech	68
8. Louisiana-Lafayette	66
9. Oregon State	65
10. Virginia Tech	62

Batters: 10 or more at-bats. **Pitchers:** 5 or more innings.

1. UCLA

Coach: John Savage. **Record:** 49-17.

PLAYER, POS., YEAR	AVG	AB	R	H	2B	3B	HR	RBI	SB
Eric Filia, rf, So.	.281	242	42	68	14	1	1	33	9
Kevin Kramer, 3b, So.	.278	245	41	68	11	2	3	42	9
Pat Gallagher, 1b, Jr.	.274	175	20	48	7	0	1	20	0
Brian Carroll, cf, Jr.	.258	244	50	63	3	2	0	20	32
Trent Chatterton, inf, Fr.	.257	105	18	27	4	0	0	10	2
Pat Valaika, ss, Jr.	.253	249	32	63	14	3	5	48	8
Brenton Allen, lf, Jr.	.250	108	16	27	3	1	2	13	1
Cody Regis, 2b, Sr.	.234	171	19	40	8	0	0	20	1
Kevin Williams, dh, Jr.	.227	128	15	29	4	1	1	12	4
Shane Zeile, c, So.	.226	199	22	45	9	0	2	20	2
Justin Hazard, inf/c, R-Fr.	.333	21	2	7	1	0	0	1	0
Ty Moore, of, Fr.	.219	73	10	16	4	1	0	10	0
Christoph Bono, of, R-Fr.	.216	74	10	16	2	0	2	10	2
Chris Keck, inf, So.	.186	70	9	13	3	1	1	10	0
Darrell Miller Jr., c, Fr.	.143	14	1	2	1	0	0	3	0
Brett Urabe, inf, Fr.	.083	12	4	1	0	0	0	4	1

PLAYER, POS., YEAR	W	L	ERA	G	SV	IP	H	BB	SO
David Berg, rhp, So.	7	0	0.92	51	24	78	55	11	78
James Kaprielian, rhp, Fr.	0	0	1.55	34	2	41	19	24	53
Nick Vander Tuig rhp, Jr.	14	4	2.16	19	0	129	108	18	93
Adam Plutko, rhp, Jr.	10	3	2.25	19	0	124	92	30	81
Zack Weiss, rhp, Jr.	2	1	2.25	43	0	40	36	12	27
Grant Watson, lhp, So.	9	3	3.01	18	0	93	93	16	55
Cody Poteet, rhp, Fr.	4	6	4.84	29	0	71	57	31	56
Ryan Deeter, rhp, Jr.	2	0	4.24	21	0	17	12	12	10

2. MISSISSIPPI STATE

Coach: John Cohen. **Record:** 51-20.

PLAYER, POS., YEAR	AVG	AB	R	H	2B	3B	HR	RBI	SB
Adam Frazier, ss, Jr.	.352	304	62	107	20	7	0	38	9
Hunter Renfroe, rf, Jr.	.345	255	56	88	16	3	16	65	9
Alex Detz, dh, Jr.	.318	239	43	76	14	1	1	31	1
Brett Pirtle, 2b, Jr.	.310	229	40	71	9	2	2	33	9
Sam Frost, 3b, Sr.	.302	96	20	29	3	1	0	10	7
Wes Rea, 1b, So.	.291	196	30	57	12	0	7	40	0
C.T. Bradford, cf, Jr.	.281	260	44	73	4	0	1	27	8
Demarcus Henderson, lf, Jr.	.274	175	23	48	3	0	0	23	3
Derrick Armstrong, cf, Jr.	.266	64	14	17	1	0	0	8	4
Tyler Fullerton, of, So.	.263	19	6	5	0	0	0	4	1
Trey Porter, 1b, Sr.	.257	105	8	27	6	0	1	22	0
Matthew Britton, inf, So.	.250	20	6	5	1	0	0	1	1
Nick Ammirati, c, Sr.	.246	167	23	41	3	0	1	23	2
Mitch Slauter, c, Sr.	.242	99	11	24	6	1	1	15	2
Daryl Norris, inf, Jr.	.219	64	9	14	3	0	0	8	0
Kyle Hann, 2b, Fr.	.219	32	7	7	0	0	0	1	0
Jacob Robson, lf, Fr.	.206	97	10	20	2	0	0	16	3

PLAYER, POS., YEAR	W	L	ERA	G	SV	IP	H	BB	SO
John Marc Shelly, rhp, Fr.	0	0	0.00	6	0	7	5	2	5
Chad Girodo lhp, Sr.	9	1	1.36	36	0	60	47	19	82
Ross Mitchell, lhp, Sr.	13	0	1.53	34	2	94	72	29	44
Johnathan Holder, rhp, So.	2	0	1.65	34	21	55	33	17	90
Ben Bracewell, rhp, Jr.	1	1	1.76	21	1	31	19	12	28
C.T. Bradford, lhp, Jr.	0	1	1.80	9	0	5	3	3	4
Will Cox, rhp, So.	3	1	2.45	18	0	29	12	10	30
Trevor Fitts, rhp, So.	0	1	3.03	18	0	30	27	9	26
Kendall Graveman rhp, Sr.	8	5	3.09	19	0	114	115	29	69
Preston Brown, rhp, Fr.	0	0	3.38	8	0	8	6	3	5
Myles Gentry, rhp, Fr.	4	1	3.69	23	0	32	22	11	30
Evan Mitchell, rhp, Jr.	0	1	3.74	9	0	22	8	18	65
Jacob Lindgren, lhp, Jr.	4	3	4.18	14	0	56	52	18	65
Louis Pollorena, lhp, So.	6	4	4.27	20	0	78	76	35	59
Brandon Woodruff, rhp, So.	1	1	4.34	7	0	19	17	9	15

3. NORTH CAROLINA

Coach: Mike Fox. **Record:** 59-12.

PLAYER, POS., YEAR	AVG	AB	R	H	2B	3B	HR	RBI	SB
Cody Stubbs, 1b, Sr.	.366	276	64	101	26	4	8	76	5
Landon Lassiter, dh, Fr.	.358	257	75	92	14	3	1	28	8
Colin Moran, 3b, Jr.	.345	281	76	97	11	3	13	91	1
Skye Bolt, rf, Fr.	.321	212	48	68	14	2	6	51	10
Brian Holberton, c, Jr.	.308	250	54	77	13	0	12	58	8
Michael Russell, ss, So.	.298	265	56	79	10	3	2	39	18
Chaz Frank, cf, Sr.	.292	274	59	80	15	5	1	35	24
Mike Zolk, 2b, So.	.269	242	32	65	9	1	2	40	6
Parks Jordan, lf, Jr.	.252	159	25	40	2	0	1	27	3
Tom Zengel, of, Jr.	.357	14	1	5	1	0	0	4	0
Zach Daily, of, Fr.	.300	10	4	3	0	0	0	0	0
Matt Campbell, ss, Fr.	.231	13	5	3	0	1	0	2	0
Grayson Attwood, 1b, So.	.217	23	5	5	0	0	1	6	0
Matt Rubino, c, So.	.200	10	3	2	0	0	0	2	0
Matt Roberts, c, Jr.	.195	118	18	23	6	2	2	16	2
Alex Raburn, util, Fr.	.191	48	8	9	2	0	0	5	1
Korey Dunbar, c, Fr.	.159	44	5	7	2	0	0	3	1

PLAYER, POS., YEAR	W	L	ERA	G	SV	IP	H	BB	SO
Trent Thornton, rhp, Fr.	12	1	1.37	29	8	92	69	19	81
Hobbs Johnson, lhp, Jr.	5	1	2.37	18	0	87	62	51	78
Kent Emanuel, lhp, Jr.	11	5	3.14	21	1	132	121	32	98
Benton Moss, rhp, So.	8	1	3.77	19	0	88	79	34	92
Mason McCullough rhp, So.	0	1	0.73	17	0	12	4	7	14
Tate Parrish, lhp, Jr.	1	0	1.35	20	2	7	4	4	10
Reilly Hovis, rhp, Fr.	4	0	2.36	18	0	34	20	24	26
Chris Munnelly, rhp, Sr.	6	0	2.39	22	1	60	36	27	63
Shane Taylor, rhp, Jr.	2	0	3.00	11	0	12	14	10	7
Trevor Kelley, rhp, So.	2	1	3.63	32	2	45	33	19	36
Taylore Cherry, rhp, Fr.	1	0	8.10	8	0	10	16	5	4
Luis Paula, rhp, So.	0	0	8.59	8	0	7	5	10	6

4. OREGON STATE

Coach: Pat Casey. **Record:** 52-13.

PLAYER, POS., YEAR	AVG	AB	R	H	2B	3B	HR	RBI	SB
Dylan Davis, rf, So.	.335	257	45	86	22	3	5	61	9
Andy Peterson, 2b, Jr.	.333	246	49	82	5	0	0	28	14
Michael Conforto, lf, So.	.328	247	48	81	14	1	11	47	6
Kavin Keyes, 3b, Jr.	.316	212	35	67	12	2	2	34	3
Beau Day, c, Jr.	.313	32	3	10	1	1	0	5	0
Tyler Smith, ss, Jr.	.308	224	48	69	10	2	2	28	9
Ryan Barnes, dh, Sr.	.286	189	27	54	9	1	2	24	2
Joey Jansen, of, Jr.	.279	43	3	12	2	0	0	6	1
Danny Hayes, 1b, Sr.	.269	216	38	58	14	0	6	41	2
Jake Rodriguez, c, Jr.	.366	192	24	51	11	0	2	36	2
Jeff Hendrix, of, Fr.	.259	27	4	7	0	0	0	3	4
Max Gorgon, of, Jr.	.236	123	22	29	1	0	0	7	3
Joey Matthews, cf, Sr.	.194	36	6	7	3	0	0	6	0
Jerad Casper, if, Jr.	.167	66	9	11	4	0	0	11	0
Gabe Clark, if, Fr.	.161	31	3	5	1	1	0	4	0
Nate Esposito, c, So.	.135	37	4	5	0	0	0	3	0

PLAYER, POS., YEAR	W	L	ERA	G	SV	IP	H	BB	SO
Max Engelbrekt, lhp, Fr.	5	1	1.30	22	5	28	21	10	20
Tony Bryant, rhp, Sr.	1	0	1.76	21	1	31	15	14	28
Andrew Moore, rhp, Fr.	14	2	1.79	19	1	131	93	28	72
Matt Boyd, lhp, Sr.	11	4	2.04	20	1	133	92	33	122
Scott Shultz, rhp, Jr.	2	1	2.08	27	10	43	31	8	34
Ben Wetzler, lhp, Sr.	10	1	2.26	16	0	96	83	32	83
Tyler Painton, lhp, So.	0	0	2.40	11	0	15	7	6	10
Brandon Jackson, rhp, Jr.	4	1	2.48	19	1	29	27	9	21
Dan Child, rhp, Jr.	4	1	3.29	12	0	38	36	16	28
Cole Brocker, rhp, Sr.	1	0	3.86	14	0	12	15	1	11
Taylor Starr, rhp, Sr.	0	1	3.94	10	0	16	19	5	10
Jace Fry, lhp, So.	0	1	4.70	6	0	8	6	2	2

5. LOUISIANA STATE

Coach: Paul Mainieri. **Record:** 57-11.

PLAYER, POS., YEAR	AVG	AB	R	H	2B	3B	HR	RBI	SB
Mason Katz, 1b, Sr.	.370	243	53	90	14	2	16	70	5
Alex Bregman, ss, Fr.	.369	282	59	104	18	7	6	52	16
Raph Rhymes, lf, Sr.	.331	254	53	84	15	1	4	46	3
Sean McMullen, dh, Jr.	.314	175	26	55	18	1	2	30	1
Mark Laird, rf, Fr.	.307	241	48	74	7	1	0	18	6
Christian Ibarra 3b, Jr.	.305	223	34	68	17	0	6	39	0
JaCoby Jones, 2b, Jr.	.294	201	42	59	11	1	6	31	12
Ty Ross, c, Jr.	.217	207	26	45	3	0	3	32	1
Jared Foster, rf, So.	.359	64	19	23	2	0	2	12	3
Tyler Moore, c, So.	.281	96	12	27	9	1	0	12	0
Chris Chinea, c, Fr.	.277	47	5	13	4	0	0	11	0
Casey Yocum, inf, Sr.	.273	33	4	9	0	0	0	5	0
Michael Barash, c, Fr.	.269	26	8	7	1	0	1	4	0
Chris Sciambra, of, So.	.265	98	22	26	5	1	0	9	2
Alex Edward, of, Jr.	.245	53	6	13	3	1	0	9	0
Andrew Stevenson, of, Fr.	.193	119	22	23	0	0	1	14	5

PLAYER, POS., YEAR	W	L	ERA	G	SV	IP	H	BB	SO
Aaron Nola, rhp, So.	12	1	1.57	17	0	126	83	18	122
Cody Glenn, lhp, So.	7	3	2.68	15	0	84	75	17	38
Ryan Eades, rhp, Jr.	8	1	2.79	17	0	100	101	32	78
Chris Cotton, lhp, Sr.	4	1	1.16	37	16	47	25	3	47
Russell Reynolds, rhp, Fr.	1	0	1.89	7	0	19	12	3	8
Joey Bourgeois, rhp, Sr.	3	2	2.25	34	0	32	26	10	32
Hunter Newman, rhp, Jr.	2	0	2.55	13	0	25	13	11	16
Hunter Devall, lhp, Fr.	3	0	2.65	16	0	17	15	5	15
Kurt McCune, rhp, Jr.	4	1	2.66	11	0	24	23	6	18
Brent Bonvillain, lhp, Jr.	3	0	2.70	21	0	50	35	25	37
Nate Fury, rhp, Jr.	2	1	2.95	20	0	18	14	4	16
Nick Rumbelow, rhp, Jr.	1	0	3.31	31	0	33	24	15	36
Will LaMarche, rhp, Jr.	3	0	3.42	24	0	26	20	13	25
Kevin Berry, rhp, Sr.	4	1	3.78	20	0	17	17	10	15

6. NORTH CAROLINA STATE

Coach: Elliott Avent. **Record:** 50-16.

PLAYER, POS., YEAR	AVG	AB	R	H	2B	3B	HR	RBI	SB
Trea Turner, ss, So.	.368	228	66	84	13	4	7	42	30
Jake Fincher, rf, So.	.313	265	50	83	9	1	0	29	14
Bryan Adametz, lf, Sr.	.303	228	32	69	13	1	0	32	3
Tarran Senay, 1b, Sr.	.288	257	33	74	16	2	8	59	3
Grant Clyde, 3b, Sr.	.282	195	40	55	16	0	4	26	4
Jake Armstrong, dh, So.	.266	154	31	41	9	2	1	30	7
Brett Williams, cf, Sr.	.251	235	36	59	12	1	3	32	19
Brett Austin, c, So.	.251	263	38	66	21	1	2	37	13
Logan Ratledge, 2b , So.	.250	176	28	44	6	2	0	17	11
Sam Morgan, of, Jr.	.254	122	18	31	6	0	3	18	2
Carlos Rodon, dh, Jr.	.217	23	0	5	0	0	0	4	0
Will Nance, of, Fr.	.205	73	10	15	2	0	1	8	1
Matt Berrquist, 2b, Sr.	.169	59	9	10	2	0	0	7	1
John Mangum, c, Fr.	.154	13	1	2	0	0	0	3	1
Bryan Taylor, of, R-Fr.	.130	23	8	3	2	0	0	2	1

PLAYER, POS., YEAR	W	L	ERA	G	SV	IP	H	BB	SO
Ethan Ogburn, rhp, Sr.	5	3	2.70	15	0	60	46	14	38
Carlos Rodon, lhp, So.	10	3	2.99	19	0	132	94	45	184
Brad Stone, rhp, Jr.	3	2	5.49	17	1	61	54	24	60
Chris Overman, rhp, Sr.	1	1	0.33	21	6	27	10	9	26
Grant Sasser, lhp, Sr.	3	0	1.03	33	8	44	29	13	44
Josh Easley, rhp, Sr.	7	2	1.38	25	1	46	37	13	42
Travis Orwig, lhp, So.	3	0	1.50	15	1	18	13	5	16
Logan Jernigan, rhp, So.	1	1	1.56	11	0	35	23	28	30
Will Gilbert, lhp, Fr.	0	0	2.70	11	0	7	8	7	6
D.J. Thomas, lhp, Jr.	2	0	2.89	14	0	28	29	10	17
Andrew Woeck, rhp, Jr.	6	1	3.09	26	0	47	38	10	45
Karl Keglovits, rhp, Jr.	1	0	4.05	7	0	13	13	6	6
Ryan Wilkins, rhp, Sr.	6	2	4.21	24	0	47	41	12	47
Anthony Tzamtzis, rhp, Jr.	2	1	5.40	11	0	28	24	30	25
Jon Olezak, rhp, Fr.	0	0	7.00	5	0	9	8	3	5
Dillon Frye, rhp, So.	0	0	8.53	8	0	6	9	2	4

7. INDIANA

Coach: Tracy Smith. **Record:** 49-16.

PLAYER, POS., YEAR	AVG	AB	R	H	2B	3B	HR	RBI	SB
Dustin DeMuth, 3b, Jr.	.377	244	46	92	24	1	5	41	11
Kyle Schwarber, c, So.	.366	235	65	86	10	1	18	54	4
Scott Donely, dh, So.	.358	240	40	86	16	2	5	61	2
Sam Travis, 1b, So.	.316	244	53	77	22	2	10	57	4
Michael Basil, ss, Sr.	.313	243	44	76	15	2	3	49	7
Casey Smith, rf, Jr.	.309	175	25	54	9	0	5	34	2
Will Nolden, rf, So.	.303	142	31	43	5	2	0	12	5
Brian Wilhite, if, Fr.	.292	24	3	7	0	0	0	0	1
Chris Sujka, lf, So.	.286	77	18	22	4	0	0	8	9
Ricky Alfonso, of, So.	.237	38	4	9	2	1	0	10	0
Chad Clark, 2b, So.	.232	198	19	46	8	0	1	32	1
Nick Ramos, if, Fr.	.228	92	13	21	5	0	5	23	0
Justin Cureton, cf, Sr.	.216	231	59	50	11	1	1	17	22
Tim O'Connor, of, So.	.150	20	3	3	0	1	0	6	3
Trace Knoblauch, if, So.	.069	29	4	2	1	0	0	2	1

PLAYER, POS., YEAR	W	L	ERA	G	SV	IP	H	BB	SO
Brian Korte, lhp, Jr.	1	0	1.65	17	1	16	14	8	7
Wil Coursen-Carr, lhp, Fr.	5	0	1.93	17	1	65	54	27	37
Aaron Slegers, rhp, So.	9	2	2.04	18	0	106	108	17	59
Scott Effross, rhp, Jr.	6	1	2.44	28	5	63	53	13	34
Joey DeNato, lhp, Jr..	10	2	2.52	19	0	104	97	43	87
Luke Harrison, rhp, So.	4	2	2.82	22	0	38	36	9	32
Ryan Halstead, rhp, Jr.	4	5	2.89	28	11	44	30	12	48
Kyle Hart, lhp, So.	8	2	3.01	15	0	84	83	27	50
Evan Bell, rhp, Fr.	1	0	3.41	14	0	29	29	5	17
Christian Morris, rhp, Fr.	1	1	4.68	13	0	25	35	7	12
Walker Stadler, rhp, Jr.	0	0	4.82	6	0	9	3	11	6
Matt Dearden, lhp, So.	0	1	4.50	5	0	6	5	4	4

8. LOUISVILLE

Coach: Dan McDonnell. **Record:** 51-14.

PLAYER, POS., YEAR	AVG	AB	R	H	2B	3B	HR	RBI	SB
Cole Sturgeon, rf, Jr.	.339	221	38	75	9	2	1	33	13
Jeff Gardner, dh, Jr.	.337	163	28	55	15	3	9	43	1
Ty Young, 3b, Jr.	.335	236	54	79	13	7	4	58	26
Coco Johnson, lf, Jr.	.324	204	41	66	11	2	8	50	22
Sutton Whiting, ss, So.	.308	201	41	62	6	4	1	30	24
Nick Ratajczak, 2b, Sr.	.283	240	52	68	6	3	2	34	9
Adam Engel, cf, Sr.	.236	246	51	58	9	2	1	28	41
Zak Wasserman, 1b, Sr.	.230	174	18	40	9	0	0	25	1
Kyle Gibson, c, Jr.	.305	105	24	32	5	0	0	13	3
Matt Helms, rf, Sr.	.286	42	4	12	1	1	0	5	2
Zach Lucas, 2b, So.	.283	53	3	15	2	0	0	5	1
Danny Rosenbaum, 3b, Fr.	.258	93	15	24	3	1	1	13	1
Shane Crain, c, Jr.	.228	123	15	28	5	0	1	16	1
Mike White, cf, So.	.214	28	12	6	1	1	1	5	5
Alex Chittenden, ss, Jr.	.194	36	8	7	3	0	0	3	0

PLAYER, POS., YEAR	W	L	ERA	G	SV	IP	H	BB	SO
Jeff Thompson, rhp, Jr.	11	2	2.19	17	0	107	67	34	113
Chad Green, rhp, Jr.	10	4	2.42	18	0	104	97	27	74
Dace Kime, rhp, Jr.	6	1	2.99	27	1	69	64	20	83
Nick Burdi, rhp, So.	3	3	0.76	29	16	36	25	13	62
Cody Ege, lhp, Jr.	4	1	1.04	38	1	35	13	12	52
Anthony Kidston, rhp, Fr.	5	0	1.31	13	1	48	25	22	58
Cole Sturgeon, lhp, Jr.	0	0	2.08	14	1	13	11	4	16
Kyle Funkhouser, rhp, Fr.	5	1	2.14	22	1	55	43	25	55
Kyle McGrath, lhp, So.	6	1	2.27	25	2	48	33	16	48
Jonah Philley, rhp, Fr.	0	0	3.38	14	0	8	7	9	6
Joe Filomeno, lhp, Jr.	1	0	5.30	14	0	19	12	14	22
Jared Ruxer, rhp, So.	0	1	5.63	19	0	38	43	21	35
Jordan Simons, rhp, Fr.	0	0	10.80	6	0	7	11	3	3

9. VANDERBILT

Coach: Tim Corbin. **Record:** 54-12.

PLAYER, POS., YEAR	AVG	AB	R	H	2B	3B	HR	RBI	SB
Tony Kemp, 2b, Jr.	.391	266	64	104	13	6	0	33	34
Xavier Turner, 3b, Fr.	.324	219	40	71	10	0	0	36	22
Mike Yastrzemski, rf, Sr.	.312	247	52	77	19	3	3	43	20

PLAYER, POS., YEAR	AVG	AB	R	H	2B	3B	HR	RBI	SB
Connor Harrell, cf, Sr.	.312	247	60	77	12	3	12	67	9
Conrad Gregor, 1b, Jr.	.308	227	47	70	14	0	3	48	21
Vince Conde, ss, So.	.307	238	43	73	18	0	6	44	3
Spencer Navin, c, Jr.	.302	182	38	55	5	0	4	34	7
Jack Lupo, lf, Sr.	.297	175	25	52	10	0	0	24	15
John Norwood, lf, So.	.328	58	14	19	4	0	1	10	0
Tyler Campbell, if, Fr.	.313	16	3	5	1	0	0	6	0
Zander Wiel, if, R-Fr.	.305	82	13	25	5	0	5	27	0
Rhett Wiseman, of, Fr.	.289	121	21	35	7	1	3	17	6
Chris Harvey, c, So.	.250	52	12	13	4	3	0	9	0
Kyle Smith, if, Fr.	.250	40	16	10	2	1	4	16	1
Joel McKeithan, if, Jr.	.220	41	6	9	0	0	0	6	0
Dansby Swanson, if, Fr.	.188	16	4	3	1	0	0	1	1

PLAYER, POS., YEAR	W	L	ERA	G	SV	IP	H	BB	SO
Kevin Ziomek, lhp, Jr.	11	3	2.12	17	0	119	79	40	115
Tyler Beede, rhp, So.	14	1	2.32	17	0	101	64	63	103
Brian Miller, rhp, So.	5	2	1.58	32	16	57	37	11	48
Jared Miller, lhp, So.	2	1	2.31	22	2	23	22	15	24
Carson Fulmer, rhp, Fr.	3	0	2.39	26	4	53	37	25	51
Steven Rice, lhp, Jr.	4	0	2.57	21	0	35	28	12	28
Walker Buehler, rhp, Fr.	4	3	3.14	16	1	63	64	25	57
Adam Ravenelle, rhp, So.	0	0	3.18	11	0	17	13	8	9
Philip Pfeifer, lhp, So.	4	0	3.68	15	0	64	62	30	47
Tyler Ferguson, rhp, Fr.	3	1	4.21	8	0	26	24	11	21
TJ Pecoraro, rhp, Jr.	4	1	5.97	10	1	35	38	14	15

10. CAL STATE FULLERTON

Coach: Rick Vanderhook. **Record:** 51-10.

PLAYER, POS., YEAR	AVG	AB	R	H	2B	3B	HR	RBI	SB
Carlos Lopez, 1b, Sr.	.339	236	52	80	11	3	4	34	15
Michael Lorenzen, cf, Jr.	.335	227	40	76	12	4	7	54	12
J.D. Davis, if, So.	.318	211	40	67	11	1	4	50	1
Chad Wallach, c, Jr.	.309	162	24	50	14	1	2	32	2
Matt Chapman, 3b, So.	.285	186	41	53	11	3	5	37	6
Richy Pedroza, ss, Sr.	.274	223	48	61	8	4	1	24	10
A.J. Kennedy, c, Fr.	.429	14	4	6	2	0	0	4	8
Austin Diemer, rf, So.	.311	122	21	38	5	2	0	12	8
Jared Deacon, c, Jr.	.300	50	8	15	0	0	0	8	0
Greg Velazquez, of, Jr.	.273	66	10	18	4	0	3	11	1
Jake Jefferies, 2b, Fr.	.260	150	18	39	7	1	2	24	4
Anthony Hutting, lf, Sr.	.256	121	16	31	3	0	5	27	1
Nico Darras, 1b, Fr.	.250	12	2	3	0	0	0	2	0
Austin Kingsolver, of, Sr.	.204	103	14	21	0	2	2	7	8
Keegan Dale, if, Jr.	.192	73	19	14	0	1	0	7	4
Clay Williamson, rf, So.	.143	49	9	7	0	2	0	3	1
Matt Orloff, if, Sr.	.121	33	2	4	0	0	0	2	0

PLAYER, POS., YEAR	W	L	ERA	G	SV	IP	H	BB	SO
Thomas Eshelman, rhp, Fr.	12	3	1.48	17	0	116	86	3	83
Justin Garza, rhp, Fr.	12	0	2.03	17	0	115	84	17	95
Grahamm Wiest, rhp, Jr.	9	3	3.27	16	0	105	94	13	76
Tyler Peitzmeier, lhp, So.	3	0	0.57	28	1	32	22	4	24
David Birosak, lhp, Sr.	1	0	1.80	5	0	5	6	1	0
Michael Lorenzen, rhp, Jr.	3	0	1.99	22	19	23	17	4	20
Koby Gauna, rhp, So.	4	1	2.60	22	2	55	49	7	33
J.D. Davis, rhp, So.	1	2	2.74	16	4	23	19	7	17
Willie Kuhl, rhp, So.	1	0	3.38	24	1	29	26	13	39
Jose Cardona, rhp, So.	2	1	3.38	11	0	11	15	4	10
Michael Lopez, rhp, So.	1	0	3.38	8	0	11	10	1	1
Bryan Conant, lhp, Fr.	1	0	5.40	7	0	8	6	3	10
Kyle Murray, rhp, Fr.	1	0	6.35	5	0	6	13	2	5

11. VIRGINIA

Coach: Brian O'Connor. **Record:** 50-12.

PLAYER, POS., YEAR	AVG	AB	R	H	2B	3B	HR	RBI	SB
Mike Papi, lf, So.	.381	176	57	67	15	3	7	57	6
Branden Cogswell, ss, Jr.	.346	182	55	63	11	4	0	22	12
Joe McCarthy, rf, Fr.	.336	223	48	75	10	2	4	51	11
Nick Howard, ss, So.	.323	198	37	64	12	2	3	38	2
Brandon Downes, cf ,So.	.316	253	67	80	20	7	10	59	6
Reed Gragnani, 2b, Sr.	.304	217	44	66	11	3	3	49	4
Derek Fisher, dh, So.	.293	205	43	60	12	3	7	48	8
Kenny Towns, 3b, So.	.290	186	38	54	11	5	7	44	5

PLAYER, POS., YEAR	AVG	AB	R	H	2B	3B	HR	RBI	SB
Jared King, 1b, Sr.	.288	240	41	69	17	1	1	38	8
Nate Irving, c, So.	.284	183	39	52	11	0	0	33	2
Colin Harrington, of, Jr.	.583	12	3	7	1	0	1	5	0
George Ragsdale, if, Fr.	.333	6	2	2	0	0	0	2	0
Rob Bennie, of, Fr.	.200	15	4	3	0	0	0	2	0
Robbie Coman, c, Fr.	.190	21	2	4	3	0	0	3	0
John LaPrise, if, Fr.	.171	35	7	6	0	1	0	6	0

PLAYER, POS., YEAR	W	L	ERA	G	SV	IP	H	BB	SO
Scott Silverstein, lhp, Sr.	10	2	3.15	16	0	91	93	28	70
Brandon Waddell, lhp, Fr.	6	3	3.96	16	0	89	100	23	84
David Rosenberger, lhp, Fr.	3	0	1.38	20	0	33	31	3	23
Kyle Crockett, lhp, Jr.	4	1	1.70	29	12	58	42	7	71
Josh Sborz, rhp, Fr.	3	0	1.98	30	2	50	37	12	47
Austin Young, rhp, Jr.	5	0	2.25	28	0	32	22	12	32
Whit Mayberry, rhp, Fr.	4	0	2.45	22	2	51	44	9	34
Nick Howard, rhp, So.	6	4	3.38	13	0	61	67	15	52
Trey Oest, rhp, Fr.	5	0	4.28	12	0	40	36	12	30
Nathan Kirby, lhp, Fr.	4	1	6.06	24	0	33	43	13	37
Nathaniel Abel, lhp, So.	0	0	6.43	6	0	7	6	6	6

12. FLORIDA STATE

Coach: Mike Martin. **Record:** 47-17.

PLAYER, POS., YEAR	AVG	AB	R	H	2B	3B	HR	RBI	SB
DJ Stewart, of, Fr.	.364	225	50	82	25	2	5	59	8
Jose Brizuela, if, So.	.324	216	40	70	14	3	4	44	7
Marcus Davis, of, Jr.	.301	239	56	72	20	0	9	62	6
Stephen McGee, c, Jr.	.286	206	50	59	16	1	9	52	4
John Nogowski, 1b, So.	.277	159	36	44	11	2	2	33	2
Seth Miller, of, Sr.	.276	170	38	47	15	4	0	19	4
Josh Delph, of, So.	.270	111	32	30	6	0	1	21	5
Giovanny Alfonzo, if, So.	.263	205	31	54	6	0	0	26	2
Jameis Winston, of, Fr.	.235	119	21	28	7	3	0	9	2
John Sansone, if, Fr.	.233	193	36	45	11	0	2	32	2
Brett Knief, of, Jr.	.333	87	16	29	5	2	1	14	1
Casey Smit, if, Jr.	.299	97	18	29	9	0	0	13	1
Justin Gonzalez, if, Sr.	.278	18	5	5	0	1	2	5	0
Ladson Montgomery, c, Jr.	.267	30	1	8	1	0	0	3	0

PLAYER, POS., YEAR	W	L	ERA	G	SV	IP	H	BB	SO
Scott Sitz, rhp, Sr.	10	2	2.09	16	0	95	92	22	80
Luke Weaver, rhp, So.	7	2	2.29	17	0	98	78	19	119
Brandon Leibrandt, lhp, So.	10	4	3.44	16	0	89	89	30	77
Peter Miller, rhp, Jr.	6	2	3.55	14	0	58	60	21	47
Dylan Silva, lhp, Fr.	0	0	0.82	7	0	11	4	10	7
Robby Coles, rhp, Jr.	4	2	2.25	30	9	36	30	16	35
Gage Smith, rhp, Jr.	4	2	2.41	35	1	41	35	8	32
Billy Strode, lhp, So.	1	0	2.43	20	1	37	30	8	33
Jameis Winston, rhp, Fr.	1	2	3.00	17	2	27	18	12	21
Brandon Johnson, lhp, Jr.	1	1	3.98	15	0	20	23	8	13
Bryant Holtmann, lhp, So.	3	0	4.00	22	0	36	31	19	23
Kyle Bird, lhp, So.	0	0	6.10	12	0	10	16	10	10
Kenny Burkhead, rhp, Fr.	0	0	7.04	7	0	7	9	6	3

13. KANSAS STATE

Coach: Brad Hill. **Record:** 45-19.

PLAYER, POS., YEAR	AVG	AB	R	H	2B	3B	HR	RBI	SB
Austin Fisher, ss, So.	.361	208	43	75	20	3	2	38	3
Ross Kivett, 2b, Jr.	.360	261	57	94	15	4	3	39	26
Shane Conlon, 1b, So.	.341	249	56	85	13	3	7	28	17
Tanner Witt, lf, Sr.	.337	261	49	88	8	3	1	35	7
Jared King, cf, Jr.	.335	218	52	73	16	2	7	53	14
Blair DeBord, c, Jr.	.327	199	33	65	11	1	0	37	6
RJ Santigate, 3b, Jr.	.324	222	32	72	4	2	0	29	11
John Davis, rf, So.	.302	212	49	64	14	4	5	42	10
Mitch Meyer, of, So.	.281	128	16	36	5	5	4	34	2
Clayton Dairymple, of, Fr.	.343	35	6	12	2	0	0	6	2
Joe Goodwin, if, Jr.	.267	45	7	12	3	1	0	5	0
Damion Lovato, of, Jr.	.262	42	3	11	2	0	0	7	0
Lance Miles, dh, Fr.	.241	58	5	14	0	0	0	9	1
Kyle Speer, of, So.	.143	35	4	5	2	0	0	4	0
Alex Bee, c, Fr.	.105	19	0	2	0	0	0	0	0

PLAYER, POS., YEAR	W	L	ERA	G	SV	IP	H	BB	SO
Nate Williams, rhp, So.	4	3	2.81	24	0	67	55	33	54
Joe Flattery, lhp, Sr.	5	4	3.86	19	0	79	85	20	52
Matt Wivinis, rhp, So.	6	2	4.72	21	0	76	77	22	50
Jake Matthys, rhp, Fr.	9	2	2.05	34	9	61	46	9	44
Tanner Witt, rhp, Sr.	0	0	3.18	17	7	17	15	5	18
Jake Doller, rhp, Sr.	2	3	3.54	13	0	41	33	22	29
Jordan Witcig, rhp, Fr.	0	0	3.68	9	0	15	10	7	9
Jared Moore, lhp, Jr.	4	0	3.73	21	0	31	37	9	23
Gerardo Esquivel, rhp, Jr.	2	2	3.99	20	1	29	31	7	17
Landon Busch, rhp, Fr.	0	0	4.58	15	1	18	13	11	11
Levi MaVorhis, rhp, Fr.	5	0	4.77	23	0	55	76	13	30
Blake McFadden, rhp, Fr.	6	3	4.97	17	0	58	63	17	35
Hayden Nixon, lhp, Fr.	2	0	5.89	14	1	18	22	12	8

14. SOUTH CAROLINA
Coach: Chad Holbrook. Record: 43-20.

PLAYER, POS., YEAR	AVG	AB	R	H	2B	3B	HR	RBI	SB
LB Dantzler, dh, Sr.	.322	214	46	69	16	1	15	53	2
Joey Pankake, ss, So.	.311	238	40	74	9	1	11	42	7
Grayson Greiner, c, So.	.298	205	32	61	10	2	4	38	5
Connor Bright, rf, So.	.288	177	27	51	11	1	4	22	2
Tanner English, cf, Jr.	.283	166	30	47	11	3	1	25	9
Max Schrock 2b, Fr.	.282	227	40	64	9	2	6	39	14
Graham Saiko, lf, Jr.	.263	198	38	52	7	0	2	29	12
Chase Vergason, 3b, Sr.	.262	229	40	60	9	2	4	27	1
Dante Rosenberg, c, Sr.	.339	56	10	19	4	0	1	13	0
Sean Sullivan, of, Sr.	.313	32	8	10	2	0	0	6	3
Brison Celek, 1b, Jr.	.307	88	12	27	4	0	1	18	0
Kyle Martin, 1b, So.	.288	80	15	23	2	0	2	10	1
TJ Costen, of, So.	.250	80	19	20	5	1	1	8	3
George Iskenderian, if, Fr.	.250	36	6	9	1	0	0	6	1
Shon Carson of, Fr.	.194	31	7	6	1	0	0	2	2
Erik Payne, if, Jr.	.185	27	2	5	1	0	0	4	0
DC Arendas, if, Fr.	.071	14	2	1	1	0	0	0	0

PLAYER, POS., YEAR	W	L	ERA	G	SV	IP	H	BB	SO
Jordan Montgmery, lhp, So.	6	1	1.48	13	0	79	64	18	60
Adam Westmoreland, lhp, Sr.	7	4	2.32	29	3	66	52	15	62
Nolan Belcher, lhp, Sr.	7	5	2.38	17	0	117	108	16	95
Tyler Webb, lhp, Sr.	3	3	1.47	32	17	43	33	14	60
Patrick Sullivan, rhp, Sr.	2	0	2.84	19	1	25	31	11	23
Jack Wynkoop, lhp, Fr.	7	3	3.09	17	0	64	70	11	36
Colby Holmes, rhp, Sr.	5	2	3.76	19	0	55	52	15	42
Vince Fiori, lhp, Fr.	1	0	3.92	14	0	21	22	4	21
Joel Seddon, rhp, So.	1	1	4.50	11	0	18	25	9	20
Evan Beal, rhp, So.	2	1	4.78	13	0	32	31	16	36
Curt Britt, rhp, Fr.	2	0	5.12	11	1	19	24	3	10
Forrest Koumas, rhp, Jr.	0	0	8.35	10	0	18	21	13	16

15. OKLAHOMA
Coach: Sunny Galloway. Record: 43-21.

PLAYER, POS., YEAR	AVG	AB	R	H	2B	3B	HR	RBI	SB
Matt Oberste, 1b, Jr.	.373	241	53	90	19	4	11	60	13
Max White, cf, Sr.	.310	255	53	79	12	2	3	33	9
Craig Aikin, lf, Fr.	.286	252	42	72	5	3	0	23	16
Anthony Hermelyn, c, Fr.	.275	178	18	49	6	0	0	26	2
Hector Lorenzana, 2b, Jr.	.274	237	33	65	12	1	2	42	1
Garrett Carey, 3b, Sr.	.273	209	32	57	11	2	3	23	0
Kolbey Carpenter, if, Fr.	.264	197	18	52	10	2	2	24	1
Hunter Haley rf, Fr.	.264	144	22	38	4	4	2	20	8
Jack Mayfield, ss, Sr.	.254	268	55	68	14	1	7	35	7
Colt Bickerstaff, dh, So.	.238	84	8	20	6	0	2	13	1
Justin Burba, of, Fr.	.214	14	7	3	1	0	0	3	4
Taylor Alspaugh, rf, So.	.189	37	6	7	1	0	0	1	0
Dylan Neal, c, Jr.	.158	38	2	6	2	0	0	8	0

PLAYER, POS., YEAR	W	L	ERA	G	SV	IP	H	BB	SO
Jonathan Gray, rhp, Jr.	10	3	1.64	17	0	126	83	24	147
Dillon Overton, lhp, Jr.	9	3	3.02	16	0	92	91	23	79
Drew Krittenbrink, rhp, Jr.	0	0	0.00	3	0	7	3	6	7
Jacob Evans, lhp, Fr.	7	2	2.06	30	9	52	37	10	41
Jake Fisher, lhp, Sr.	3	2	2.50	21	0	54	59	14	51
Ralph Garza Jr., rhp, Jr.	5	1	2.76	24	0	59	53	23	38
Kyle Hayes, rhp, Jr.	1	0	3.23	17	2	31	31	12	23

PLAYER, POS., YEAR	W	L	ERA	G	SV	IP	H	BB	SO
Robert Tasin, rhp, So.	1	0	3.29	15	2	14	14	8	11
Kindle Ladd, rhp, Jr.	0	0	3.65	13	0	25	31	6	17
Ethan Carnes, lhp, Jr.	2	3	4.42	14	0	37	42	7	26
Billy Waltrip, rhp, Jr.	2	3	5.15	20	0	37	39	30	45
Adam Choplick, lhp, R-Fr.	3	3	5.56	12	0	34	32	17	36
Corey Chopping, rhp, Fr.	0	1	5.74	5	0	16	16	4	12

16. RICE
Coach: Wayne Graham. Record: 44-20.

PLAYER, POS., YEAR	AVG	AB	R	H	2B	3B	HR	RBI	SB
Shane Hoelscher, 3b, Jr.	.320	150	21	48	7	1	0	25	3
Michael Aquino, dh, Jr.	.315	248	45	78	13	4	9	43	2
Christian Stringer, 2b, Sr.	.308	247	50	76	15	4	4	31	3
Ford Stainback, ss, So.	.295	275	37	81	9	0	0	25	6
Keenan Cook, lf, Jr.	.292	233	38	68	9	3	0	32	5
Leon Byrd, cf, Fr.	.275	233	36	64	9	1	1	21	9
Geoff Perrott, c, Sr.	.271	181	22	49	9	1	1	26	2
Michael Ratterree, rf, Sr.	.261	226	48	59	10	0	9	41	13
Skyler Ewing, 1b, So.	.226	146	16	33	5	0	4	23	1
Hunter Kopycinski, c, Fr.	.300	40	3	12	0	1	1	11	0
Blake Fox, if, Fr.	.241	54	0	13	0	0	0	7	0
Connor Teykl, if, Fr.	.239	109	7	26	2	0	0	14	0
Kirby Taylor, if, So.	.154	26	3	4	1	0	0	0	0
John Williamson, of, So.	.100	20	6	2	0	0	0	0	0

PLAYER, POS., YEAR	W	L	ERA	G	SV	IP	H	BB	SO
Zach Lemond, rhp, So.	7	2	2.02	32	14	76	56	21	71
Austin Kubitza, rhp, Jr.	8	4	2.06	18	0	109	71	48	134
Jordan Stephnes, rhp, So.	8	4	2.43	21	1	119	91	31	100
John Simms, rhp, Jr.	8	5	2.51	24	1	111	85	37	98
Tyler Spurlin, rhp, Sr.	0	0	2.61	9	0	10	11	5	6
Connor Mason, rhp, So.	0	1	3.00	3	0	6	5	1	4
Blake Fox, lhp, Fr.	6	0	3.41	20	1	37	40	13	23
Evan Rutter, rhp, So.	0	0	3.86	11	0	14	16	6	6
Chase McDowell, rhp, Jr.	4	2	4.25	17	0	53	49	20	26
Kevin McCanna, rhp, So.	3	1	4.50	16	0	40	30	17	18
Matt Ditman, rhp, So.	0	1	5.50	16	0	18	20	3	17

17. OREGON
Coach: George Horton. Record: 48-16.

PLAYER, POS., YEAR	AVG	AB	R	H	2B	3B	HR	RBI	SB
Ryon Healy, 1b, Jr.	.333	228	44	76	20	0	11	56	5
Brett Thomas, lf, Jr.	.317	208	45	66	15	0	2	28	12
Mitchell Tolman, dh, Fr.	.315	165	16	52	9	1	1	37	2
Scott Heineman, lf, So.	.278	230	28	64	14	1	4	38	12
J.J. Altobelli, ss, Sr.	.276	199	38	55	6	1	0	24	8
Aaron Payne, 2b, Jr.	.241	203	39	49	3	3	0	19	16
Craig Meredith, if, Jr.	.273	11	0	3	1	0	0	1	0
Tyler Baumgartner, lf, Jr.	.272	162	23	44	10	4	2	22	7
Kevin Minjares, if, Jr.	.267	15	4	4	0	0	0	2	1
Nick Catalano, of, Fr.	.237	38	8	9	3	0	0	1	0
Steven Packard, of, So.	.232	95	10	22	3	1	0	7	4
Shaun Chase, c, So.	.207	87	11	18	3	0	3	17	0
Connor Hofmann, cf, Fr.	.194	134	14	26	6	1	0	10	9
Ryan Hambright, 3b, Jr.	.182	143	10	26	5	1	0	11	3
Josh Graham, c, Fr.	.147	102	13	15	5	0	1	11	0
Kyle Garlick, of, Jr.	.097	31	4	3	1	2	0	4	1
Desmond Santos, if, Jr.	.063	16	6	1	1	0	0	1	1

PLAYER, POS., YEAR	W	L	ERA	G	SV	IP	H	BB	SO
Tommy Thorpe, lhp, So.	7	5	2.16	16	0	104	82	39	87
Cole Irvin, lhp, Fr.	12	3	2.48	16	0	116	105	22	60
Jake Reed, rhp, So.	6	6	3.50	17	0	100	93	30	65
Derek Smith, rhp, R-Fr.	0	0	0.00	4	1	5	5	2	3
Garrett Cleavinger, lhp, Fr.	9	0	1.24	37	2	44	20	24	57
Jeff Gold, rhp, Jr.	4	0	2.20	13	0	41	37	8	35
Jimmie Sherfy, rhp, Jr.	2	0	2.25	38	21	40	33	14	55
Brando Tessar, rhp, Jr.	1	0	2.70	4	0	7	5	3	2
Darrell Hunter, rhp, Sr.	2	0	3.40	28	1	40	34	15	29
Christian Jones, lhp, Jr.	1	1	3.42	21	1	24	18	10	20
Jordan Spencer, lhp, So.	2	0	4.00	12	0	18	19	11	10
Jared Priestley, rhp, Jr.	0	0	4.15	7	0	9	8	1	6
Clayton Crum rhp, Jr.	0	0	5.27	8	0	14	14	5	7
Cole Wiper, rhp, R-Fr.	2	1	7.11	7	0	13	19	10	4

18. ARKANSAS

Coach: Dave Van Horn. **Record:** 39-22.

PLAYER, POS., YEAR	AVG	AB	R	H	2B	3B	HR	RBI	SB
Brian Anderson, cf, So.	.325	209	47	68	12	5	4	36	6
Joe Serrano, lf, So.	.295	193	34	57	9	0	1	18	3
Tyler Spoon, rf, R-Fr.	.288	236	28	68	7	0	4	49	7
Matt Vinson, of, Sr.	.286	213	37	61	8	3	2	24	8
Jacob Mahan, 3b, Sr.	.281	185	28	52	7	0	2	23	1
Brett McAfee, ss, So.	.263	156	14	41	6	2	1	18	6
Dominic Ficociell, 2b, Jr.	.247	166	21	41	7	0	3	17	2
Jake Wise, c, Jr.	.212	179	19	38	3	1	3	23	3
Eric Fisher, 1b, So.	.238	122	18	29	3	0	2	13	2
Jordan Farris, 2b, Fr.	.222	99	14	22	6	0	3	20	3
Willie Schwanke, 3b, Fr.	.214	70	9	15	0	0	1	5	0
Isaac Hellbusch, if, Fr.	.190	21	1	4	1	0	1	6	0
Michael Gunn, dh, So.	.189	37	2	7	2	0	0	3	0
Jean Ramirez, c, R-Fr.	.172	29	7	5	1	0	0	1	0
Jacob Morris, cf, Jr.	.160	100	19	16	3	1	0	14	8

PLAYER, POS., YEAR	W	L	ERA	G	SV	IP	H	BB	SO
Ryne Stanek, rhp, Jr.	10	2	1.39	16	0	97	72	41	79
Barrett Astin, rhp, Jr.	4	4	1.79	18	1	91	85	20	74
Randall Fant, lhp, Jr.	6	1	2.03	14	0	67	50	19	52
Tyler Wright, lhp, Sr.	1	1	0.00	11	0	20	9	11	19
Michael Gunn, lhp, So.	1	1	1.21	18	1	30	13	8	35
Colin Poche, lhp, Fr.	3	0	1.37	8	0	20	12	11	23
Thomas Altimont, rhp, Jr.	1	0	1.59	6	0	6	5	4	4
Colby Suggs, rhp, Jr.	0	0	1.74	23	13	21	10	17	29
Landon Simpson, rhp, R-Fr.	1	1	1.88	14	1	24	23	6	20
Jalen Beeks, lhp, So.	6	2	2.20	29	2	41	33	7	28
Chris Oliver, rhp, So.	2	2	2.25	14	0	20	14	8	21
Trent Daniel, lhp, Sr.	0	1	2.55	22	1	25	28	11	24
Brandon Moore, rhp, Jr.	1	4	2.68	25	0	47	35	19	30
Trey Killian, rhp, Fr.	3	3	3.19	16	0	37	21	12	34

19. VIRGINIA TECH

Coach: Pete Hughes. **Record:** 40-22.

PLAYER, POS., YEAR	AVG	AB	R	H	2B	3B	HR	RBI	SB
Tyler Horan, lf, Jr.	.342	257	58	88	26	4	11	50	5
Mark Zagunis, rf, So.	.341	232	62	79	14	3	9	51	19
Chad Pinder, ss, Jr.	.321	240	49	77	13	1	8	50	5
Andrew Rash, 3b, Sr.	.315	234	37	75	22	2	11	62	5
Sean Keselica, 1b, So.	.307	218	40	67	11	1	5	31	2
Chad Morgan, c, Jr.	.250	176	19	44	10	1	2	25	4
Alex Perez, 2b, So.	.225	231	37	52	8	1	1	24	3
Brendon Hayden, if, So.	.208	197	24	41	9	0	4	29	2
Ryan Burns, dh, R-Fr.	.360	50	8	18	4	0	0	7	0
Gary Schneider, if, Jr.	.329	140	29	46	7	1	2	11	8
Kyle Wernicki, c, Jr.	.250	120	22	30	2	2	2	13	2
Matt Dauby, if, Fr.	.247	81	9	20	2	0	0	6	1

PLAYER, POS., YEAR	W	L	ERA	G	SV	IP	H	BB	SO
Clark Labitan, rhp, Sr.	2	5	2.58	30	11	45	38	19	37
Joe Mantiply, lhp, Sr.	6	1	2.85	15	0	76	84	25	50
Brendon Hayden, rhp, So.	2	0	3.00	10	1	21	16	11	12
Devin Burke, rhp, Jr.	11	3	3.11	16	0	104	98	34	50
Tanner McIntyre, rhp, Sr.	3	0	3.81	9	0	26	21	14	18
Jake Joyce, rhp, Sr.	7	1	4.16	30	3	63	67	30	56
Sean Keselica, lhp, So.	2	1	4.55	11	0	32	40	12	22
Ricky Hodges, lhp, So.	0	0	4.66	9	0	10	12	4	6
Brad Markey, rhp, Jr.	5	4	4.93	17	0	100	121	21	77
Eddie Campbell, lhp, Jr.	2	5	5.40	16	0	47	42	23	38
Luis Collazo, lhp, Fr.	0	0	5.82	9	0	17	22	9	10
Sean Kennedy, lhp, Fr.	0	0	7.71	8	0	12	18	4	6
Colin O'Keefe, lhp, Jr.	0	2	15.88	5	0	6	10	7	6

20. FLORIDA ATLANTIC

Coach: John McCormack. **Record:** 42-22.

PLAYER, POS., YEAR	AVG	AB	R	H	2B	3B	HR	RBI	SB
Brendon Sanger, 2b, Fr.	.347	173	49	60	6	4	3	28	5
Nathan Pittman, cf, Sr.	.330	221	50	73	14	4	5	40	14
Mitch Morales, ss, So.	.301	226	39	68	8	1	0	30	3
Levi Meyer, c, Jr.	.299	214	22	64	9	0	5	35	0

PLAYER, POS., YEAR	AVG	AB	R	H	2B	3B	HR	RBI	SB
Ricky Santiago, 3b, So.	.298	242	34	72	14	1	5	29	3
Mark Nelson, 1b, Sr.	.286	210	32	60	11	1	6	41	0
Tyler Rocklein, dh, Jr.	.281	242	40	68	20	2	10	49	7
Corey Keller, rf, Sr.	.277	188	40	52	13	1	10	31	1
Geoff Jimenez, lf, Jr.	.235	132	25	31	5	2	1	10	9
Mike Spano, c, Sr.	.211	133	9	28	3	0	0	18	0
Billy Endris, of, Fr.	.242	33	11	8	0	0	1	5	2
Robert Buckley, if, Jr.	.237	59	9	14	2	1	1	6	0
Sean Murrell, if, Jr.	.220	82	8	18	5	1	0	13	0
Nicholas Worrall, if, Jr.	.133	15	1	2	0	0	0	2	0

PLAYER, POS., YEAR	W	L	ERA	G	SV	IP	H	BB	SO
Austin Gomber, lhp, So.	8	4	2.97	18	0	106	95	28	103
Jeremy Strawn, rhp, Jr.	5	3	3.46	17	0	94	96	26	64
Jake Meiers, rhp, Sr.	6	3	4.87	19	0	68	88	18	51
Alex Koji, lhp, Jr.	0	0	1.46	12	0	12	7	9	13
Bo Logan, rhp, So.	5	1	2.68	27	1	44	39	15	41
Seth McGarry, rhp, Fr.	2	0	2.79	3	0	10	8	3	11
Kevin Alexander, rhp, Jr.	3	3	2.89	26	1	53	49	19	44
Hugh Adams, rhp, Sr.	3	0	3.49	29	18	39	38	13	38
Michael Sylvestri, rhp, Sr.	4	3	3.86	23	0	44	42	23	39
Brandon Rhodes, lhp, Fr.	3	2	4.19	13	0	39	42	10	22
Kyle Miller, rhp, Jr.	3	1	4.85	15	0	30	28	19	32
Jimmy Tornabene, rhp, Jr.	0	1	6.97	7	0	10	13	7	6
Gregg Bennis, rhp, Sr.	0	0	8.31	11	0	9	12	8	9
Andrew Archer, rhp, Jr.	0	1	8.44	11	0	11	20	5	13

21. AUSTIN PEAY STATE

Coach: Gary McClure. **Record:** 47-15.

PLAYER, POS., YEAR	AVG	AB	R	H	2B	3B	HR	RBI	SB
Craig Massoni, 1b, Jr.	.385	239	59	92	18	0	16	68	6
Cody Hudson, lf, Sr.	.363	245	45	89	21	2	3	40	32
Jordan Hankins, 3b, Jr.	.352	244	71	86	14	0	11	54	8
Reed Harper, ss, Sr.	.346	237	35	82	12	2	7	59	14
Rolando Gautier, of, Jr.	.329	210	56	69	16	2	3	30	3
Dylan Riner, cf, So.	.307	215	37	66	13	0	0	24	7
P.J. Torres, c, Jr.	.273	183	28	50	11	1	7	35	1
Britte Underwood, c, So.	.333	12	2	4	0	1	0	0	0
Tommy Hager, rf, Jr.	.278	79	12	22	5	0	0	6	5
Michael Davis, dh, Jr.	.262	130	22	34	8	0	6	19	5
Mason Dillon, if, Jr.	.250	12	0	3	1	0	0	0	0
Brett Carlson, 2b, So.	.235	85	18	20	3	0	0	11	4
Kevin Corey, if, Jr.	.220	150	24	33	0	0	1	17	5
Kyle Schlatter, 1b, Fr.	.211	57	6	12	1	0	0	8	1
Matt Wollenzin, c, Jr.	.191	47	3	9	0	1	0	3	0

PLAYER, POS., YEAR	W	L	ERA	G	SV	IP	H	BB	SO
Lee Ridenhour, rhp, Jr.	8	1	2.27	13	0	79	62	20	67
Zach Hall, lhp, Jr.	8	2	4.53	19	0	89	92	42	66
Casey Delgado, rhp, Sr.	9	3	5.14	20	0	96	107	35	105
Tyler Rogers, rhp, Sr.	7	2	1.63	41	23	50	29	27	41
Alex Belew, lhp, Jr.	0	1	2.65	13	0	17	9	11	13
A.J. Gaura, rhp, Jr.	1	1	3.21	3	0	14	20	1	15
Kacy Kemmer, rhp, Jr.	6	0	3.31	34	1	54	60	18	33
Hunter Lindely, rhp, Fr.	0	1	3.65	15	0	12	12	14	5
Ryan Quick, rhp, Jr.	5	2	5.76	22	0	59	72	41	56
Tommy Hager, lhp, Jr.	0	0	6.16	14	0	19	14	12	17
Jared Carkuff, rhp, Fr.	0	0	6.89	19	0	33	47	17	27
Kevin Corey, rhp, Jr.	2	2	6.92	10	0	13	19	11	9
Don Whiston, rhp, Jr.	1	0	10.38	17	0	17	25	12	12

22. ARIZONA STATE

Coach: Tim Esmay. **Record:** 37-22.

PLAYER, POS., YEAR	AVG	AB	R	H	2B	3B	HR	RBI	SB
Michael Benjamin, 3b, Jr.	.335	248	53	83	20	4	8	47	4
Kasey Coffman, cf, Jr.	.332	232	57	77	13	5	8	44	9
R.J. Ybarra, c, Fr.	.313	112	20	35	7	0	5	22	0
Dalton DiNatale, 1b, Fr.	.302	126	26	38	7	0	2	25	3
Trever Allen, rf, So.	.297	219	41	65	6	6	9	49	7
Drew Stankiewicz, ss, Fr.	.295	217	34	64	10	3	2	25	7
Nathaniel Causey, c, So.	.274	135	20	37	6	1	5	26	1
Max Rossiter, c, Sr.	.272	195	31	53	12	1	1	26	2
David Graybill, of, Fr.	.268	56	8	15	5	0	0	7	0
James McDonald, 2b, Jr.	.257	230	32	59	14	1	6	41	7

PLAYER, POS., YEAR	AVG	AB	R	H	2B	3B	HR	RBI	SB
Jake Peevyhouse, lf, So.	.251	187	37	47	12	5	2	26	3
Johnny Sewald, cf, Fr.	.239	46	3	11	3	0	0	4	1
Rouric Bridgewater, if, So.	.222	36	5	8	2	0	0	4	0
Jordan Aboites, if, Fr.	.154	13	0	2	0	0	0	0	0
Tucker Esmay, if, So.	.000	12	4	0	0	0	0	0	0

PLAYER, POS., YEAR	W	L	ERA	G	SV	IP	H	BB	SO
Josh McAlister, rhp, Jr.	0	1	0.89	13	0	20	15	10	12
Matt Dunbar, lhp, Sr.	1	1	1.96	36	1	41	36	25	30
Ryan Burr, rhp, Fr.	4	2	2.20	31	12	45	21	23	60
Ryan Kellogg, lhp, Fr.	11	1	3.15	16	0	103	96	17	54
Brett Lilek, lhp, Fr.	2	1	4.05	11	0	20	18	8	17
Trevor Williams, rhp, Jr.	6	6	4.12	16	0	111	124	26	81
Darin Gillies, So.	2	2	4.67	28	1	35	28	17	28
Zak Miller, rhp, Jr.	4	0	4.85	13	0	52	65	27	24
Alex Blackford, rhp, Sr.	5	1	4.93	24	1	35	29	24	36
Billy Young, rhp, Jr.	0	2	6.75	10	0	23	32	10	10
Adam McCreery, lhp, So.	2	4	6.93	15	0	38	38	40	31
Mark Lambson, rhp, So.	0	0	7.94	7	0	11	15	5	4
Eric Melbostad, rhp, Fr.	0	1	17.18	7	0	7	19	4	0

23. SAN DIEGO

Coach: Rich Hill. **Record:** 37-25.

PLAYER, POS., YEAR	AVG	AB	R	H	2B	3B	HR	RBI	SB
Kris Bryant, 3b, Jr.	.329	228	80	75	13	3	31	62	7
Connor Joe, 1b, So.	.319	232	43	74	14	0	7	43	3
AJ Robinson, rf, Sr.	.307	192	38	59	8	5	1	30	9
Austin Green, c, Sr.	.301	176	28	53	13	0	5	39	1
Dillon Haupt, c, Sr.	.277	206	30	57	17	1	11	49	2
Andrew Daniel, ss, So.	.265	211	37	56	8	0	4	24	8
Louie Lechich, cf, Jr.	.265	189	31	50	10	4	1	25	1
Logan Davis, ss, Jr.	.319	113	16	36	3	1	0	10	3
Austin Bailey, 2b, So.	.301	103	20	31	5	0	2	28	2
Jerod Smith, if, R-Fr.	.286	56	6	16	2	0	0	11	1
Chris Woolley, util, Jr.	.274	124	20	34	2	0	1	18	2
Troy Conyers, dh, Fr.	.273	22	4	6	2	0	0	5	0
Dillon Checkal, lf, Sr.	.241	112	23	27	1	0	0	7	3
Lucas Hasberg, lf, Sr.	.196	143	20	28	9	0	1	17	4

PLAYER, POS., YEAR	W	L	ERA	G	SV	IP	H	BB	SO
P.J. Conlon, lhp, Fr.	9	1	2.16	25	0	87	81	28	71
Max Homick, lhp, So.	5	2	3.34	27	6	70	70	25	57
Michael Wagner, rhp, Jr.	2	5	4.55	23	2	89	94	32	84
Trevor Bayless, rhp, Sr.	3	3	2.10	28	3	34	32	16	40
Louie Lechich, lhp, Jr.	3	3	3.24	16	0	50	53	17	35
Sheldon Ekstrand, rhp, Jr.	2	0	4.21	19	0	26	35	10	20
Wes Judish, rhp, R-Fr.	1	1	4.94	20	0	24	15	19	11
Dylan Covey, rhp, Jr.	5	4	5.05	18	1	77	90	43	65
Jack Shannon, lhp, Sr.	1	0	5.56	19	0	11	15	9	11
Troy Conyers, lhp, Fr.	3	2	5.70	17	1	24	27	15	27
Ryan Keller, rhp, So.	0	0	5.79	11	0	9	13	11	6
Daniel Reitzler, rhp, Fr.	0	0	5.79	12	0	9	11	2	6
Max MacNabb, lhp, Jr.	4	4	6.19	25	3	48	51	28	44

24. OKLAHOMA STATE

Coach: Josh Holliday. **Record:** 41-19.

PLAYER, POS., YEAR	AVG	AB	R	H	2B	3B	HR	RBI	SB
Tanner Krietemeier, 1b, Jr.	.314	229	42	72	14	2	4	45	7
Randy McCurry, ss, Sr.	.314	223	32	70	21	0	3	41	5
Saulyer Saxon, cf, Sr.	.301	166	30	50	8	1	0	18	6
Victor Romero, c, Sr.	.300	170	26	51	12	0	4	29	4
Donnie Walton, 2b, Fr.	.287	188	27	54	8	1	1	27	7

PLAYER, POS., YEAR	AVG	AB	R	H	2B	3B	HR	RBI	SB
Gage Green, lf, So.	.287	178	33	51	9	3	2	21	13
Zach Fish, rf, So.	.283	237	35	67	17	1	7	41	10
Robbie Rea, 3b, Sr.	.259	212	34	55	12	2	5	26	3
Craig McConaughy, ss, Jr.	.364	22	4	8	1	0	0	4	0
Aaron Cornell, of, Jr.	.280	132	29	37	7	0	2	17	12
Rick Stover, c, Jr.	.275	40	4	11	4	0	1	6	0
Corey Hassel, of, Fr.	.263	19	6	5	0	0	0	3	1
Trey Whaley, of, Sr.	.238	63	13	15	5	0	1	7	1
Jarrett Higgins, dh, Sr.	.183	93	18	17	3	2	0	12	10
Brendan McCurry, if, Jr.	.167	36	4	6	0	0	1	3	1

PLAYER, POS., YEAR	W	L	ERA	G	SV	IP	H	BB	SO
Tyler Nurdin, lhp, So.	5	3	1.89	14	0	86	74	24	69
Vince Wheeland, rhp, Jr.	8	2	1.97	30	2	73	58	13	64
Jason Hursh, rhp, So.	6	5	2.79	16	0	106	105	28	86
Mark Robinette, rhp, Jr.	6	1	3.58	17	0	70	60	22	54
Kyle Gehrs, rhp, Jr.	0	0	1.26	16	0	14	15	6	14
Alex Hackerott, lhp, Fr.	1	0	1.64	16	0	22	13	6	24
Reid Barnett, rhp, Jr.	0	0	2.16	7	0	8	6	3	6
Brendan McCurry, rhp, Jr.	6	3	2.72	29	8	46	40	11	35
Jon Perrin, rhp, So.	4	0	3.23	23	0	47	51	11	41
Randy McCurry, rhp, Sr.	2	1	3.63	10	1	17	14	7	14
Kenton Bevacqua, lhp, Sr.	2	3	6.45	13	0	38	53	4	32
Phillip Wilson, rhp, Jr.	1	1	9.95	5	0	6	12	7	7

25. TROY

Coach: Bobby Pierce. **Record:** 42-20.

PLAYER, POS., YEAR	AVG	AB	R	H	2B	3B	HR	RBI	SB
Logan Pierce, 3b, Sr.	.364	242	65	88	24	1	8	63	2
Danny Collins, rf, Jr.	.360	236	62	85	25	3	11	68	1
Tyler Vaughn, ss, Jr.	.327	257	72	84	20	1	0	26	9
Josh McDorman, lf, Sr.	.322	199	42	64	12	0	6	38	17
Trae Santos, 1b, Jr.	.300	237	51	71	12	4	18	70	2
Matthew Howard, dh, Jr.	.273	132	24	36	11	1	2	23	3
Brandon Brown, c, Sr.	.252	139	24	35	6	1	1	13	4
Garrett Pitts, 2b, Jr.	.241	158	20	38	10	0	2	21	2
Justin Hancock, c, Jr.	.300	50	9	15	5	0	1	10	0
Kyle Brown, 1b, So.	.286	35	2	10	3	0	0	6	0
Peyton Fuller, if, R-Fr.	.243	37	4	9	2	0	1	5	1
Ali Knowles, of, Jr.	.230	113	21	26	7	1	1	20	8
Jacob Nixon, if, Jr.	.218	55	9	12	2	1	1	6	1
Clay Holcomb, cf, So.	.200	55	17	11	4	0	0	10	9
David Hall, of, Jr.	.200	25	5	5	2	0	0	7	0
Jo-El Bennett, of, So.	.190	42	5	8	2	2	1	6	1
Jake Harrell, c, So.	.184	49	5	9	4	0	1	5	0
Chase Mathis, of, Sr.	.091	22	2	2	0	0	0	1	1

PLAYER, POS., YEAR	W	L	ERA	G	SV	IP	H	BB	SO
Shane McCain, lhp, Jr.	9	1	3.48	16	0	98	84	18	105
Tanner Hicks, rhp, Jr.	8	4	3.61	18	2	100	87	32	94
Nate Hill, lhp, Sr.	4	2	3.75	37	5	74	66	30	92
Ryan Sorce, lhp, Jr.	6	3	4.81	17	0	58	76	12	45
Levi Tate, lhp, Fr.	1	0	1.32	6	0	14	11	10	12
Jeremy McGowan, rhp, So.	2	1	3.44	10	0	18	20	10	19
Joe Hernandez, rhp, Jr.	1	0	4.34	7	0	19	16	18	16
Thomas Austin, rhp, Sr.	3	1	4.65	26	1	41	47	15	23
Austin Sullivan, rhp, Jr.	0	0	4.70	8	0	8	6	7	8
Robert Price, lhp, Jr.	0	0	4.76	8	0	11	13	7	8
William Teal, rhp, Sr.	1	1	5.12	15	0	19	16	8	13
Matthew Howard, rhp, Jr.	2	2	5.20	22	5	28	24	12	26
Will Starling, rhp, Jr.	4	3	6.31	10	0	41	50	19	46
Ryan Brady, rhp, Sr.	1	2	8.59	5	0	7	12	7	7

CONFERENCE STANDINGS & LEADERS

NCAA regional teams in bold. Conference category leaders in bold.
*Team won conference's automatic regional bid. #Category leader who did not qualify for batting or pitching title.

AMERICA EAST CONFERENCE

Team	Conference		Overall	
	W	L	W	L
Maine	21	3	52	15
*Binghamton	16	8	22	32
Albany	13	9	23	26
Stony Brook	11	11	28	28
Hartford	7	17	16	40
Maryland-Baltimore County	2	22	10	42

ALL-CONFERENCE TEAM: C—Mike Connolly, Jr., Maine. **1B**—Kevin Courtney, Jr., Stony Brook. **2B**—Daniel Nevares, Jr., Binghamton. **SS**—Michael Fransoso, Sr., Maine. **3B**—Eric White, Jr., Maine. **OF**—Josh Nethaway, Jr., Albany; Jack Parenty, Fr., Stony Brook; Jake Thomas, So., Binghamton. **DH**—Shaun McGraw, Jr., Binghamton. **SP**—Tommy Lawrence, Jr., Maine; Jay Lynch, Sr., Binghamton; Sean Newcomb, So., Hartford; Frankie Vanderka, Jr., Stony Brook. **RP**—Jon Cohn, Jr., Maryland-Baltimore County. **Player of the Year:** Michael Fransoso, Maine. **Pitcher of the Year:** Tommy Lawrence, Maine. **Coach of the Year:** Steve Trimper, Maine. **Rookie of the Year:** Jack Parenty, Stony Brook.

INDIVIDUAL BATTING LEADERS
(Minimum 2.5 at-bats per team game)

	AVG	AB	R	H	2B	3B	HR	RBI	SB
Thomas, Jake, Binghamton	.371	178	42	66	10	1	5	37	6
Black, Troy, Maine	.363	182	31	66	5	2	1	24	13
Fransoso, Michael, Maine	.352	210	45	74	17	2	4	49	20
White, Eric, Maine	.347	193	38	67	10	1	6	37	6
Parenty, Jack, Stony Brook	.333	210	30	70	6	1	0	17	6
Doran, Brian, Maine	.312	173	32	54	11	1	1	23	3
Nevares, Daniel, Binghamton	.311	196	25	61	19	0	2	34	0
Nethaway, Josh, Albany	.310	184	26	57	17	0	3	35	1
Gaige, Nolan, Albany	.308	185	33	57	9	6	1	30	9
Muller, Greg, Albany	.306	173	28	53	10	2	1	39	5
LaChance, Kevin, UMBC	.303	175	21	53	12	2	1	19	13
Balzano, Sam, Maine	.299	204	42	61	5	0	0	21	21
Bullard, Brian, Albany	.296	125	23	37	5	1	3	14	2
Lukach, Ryan, Hartford	.292	171	28	50	14	1	4	27	4
Blanden, Zach, Binghamton	.289	218	38	63	12	4	2	29	11
Peragine, Cole, Stony Brook	.289	201	28	58	5	2	1	19	6
Madej, Gordon, Albany	.285	179	30	51	5	0	0	22	5
Calbick, Alex, Maine	.280	207	30	58	20	1	2	33	1
McCabe, Rob, UMBC	.280	161	25	45	4	0	0	10	10
DelDebbio, Chris, Hartford	.279	190	23	53	10	4	0	28	4
Sheetz, Brady, Hartford	.274	197	31	54	12	1	1	20	6
Caputo, Johnny, Stony Brook	.271	225	22	61	10	5	0	20	5
Stover, Trey, Hartford	.271	181	25	49	7	1	0	14	6
Gay, Colin, Maine	.259	220	39	57	8	2	2	26	18
Coluccio, Brandon, UMBC	.246	122	9	30	2	0	0	16	0
Barnes, Jake, UMBC	.239	159	19	38	12	0	2	17	4
Ruby, Brian, Binghamton	.239	180	37	43	5	0	0	24	3
Nivins, Tanner, Stony Brook	.238	181	18	43	5	3	1	27	10
Courtney, Kevin, Stony Brook	.237	169	29	40	13	1	6	28	2
Alfonso, James, Hartford	.231	160	14	37	10	0	2	22	2

INDIVIDUAL PITCHING LEADERS
(Minimum 1 IP per team game)

	W	L	ERA	G	SV	IP	H	BB	SO
Connolly, Mike, Maine	6	4	2.11	14	1	77	60	26	46
Lawrence, Tommy, Maine	11	3	2.32	16	0	105	95	25	78
Ladner, Kevin, UMBC	4	2	2.78	22	1	45	40	23	17
Vanderka, Frankie, Stony Brook	8	4	2.80	15	0	100	84	24	59
Cohn, Jon, UMBC	4	4	2.92	19	0	52	51	9	14
Gomez, Mike, UMBC	2	4	3.00	18	4	60	56	16	41
Rogiala, Jack, Binghamton	5	5	3.01	15	0	90	87	13	55
Lynch, Jay, Binghamton	6	5	3.09	15	0	84	83	18	54
Lambert, Jake, Binghamton	7	3	3.12	16	0	101	104	16	84
McNitt, Brandon, Stony Brook	4	6	3.36	15	0	102	91	30	63
Bazdanes, A.J., Maine	6	6	3.47	15	0	96	88	25	70
Chase, Austin, Albany	6	5	3.60	14	1	75	62	21	57
Hunter, Brian, Hartford	2	5	3.71	13	0	68	43	52	58
Newcomb, Sean, Hartford	5	4	3.75	13	0	72	53	37	92
Graham, Kasceim, Albany	7	5	3.82	13	0	73	70	22	52
Charles, Jeremy, Hartford	1	3	4.03	17	6	22	27	10	17
Gill, Mac, UMBC	3	5	4.03	12	0	74	88	20	24
Sorgie, Cameron, Albany	2	5	4.94	13	1	51	53	31	51
Zamora, Daniel, Stony Brook	2	8	4.95	15	0	84	80	31	77
Stephenson, Riley, UMBC	2	7	6.20	11	0	49	71	20	22
Gauthier, Kyle, Hartford	1	7	6.60	14	0	60	78	16	30

ATLANTIC COAST CONFERENCE

	Conference		Overall	
ATLANTIC	W	L	W	L
Florida State	20	10	47	17
North Carolina State	19	10	50	16
Clemson	18	12	40	22
Maryland	11	19	30	25
Wake Forest	9	20	28	27
Boston College	4	25	12	40
COASTAL	**W**	**L**	**W**	**L**
*North Carolina	21	7	59	12
Virginia	22	8	50	12
Virginia Tech	15	14	40	22
Georgia Tech	15	15	37	27
Miami	14	16	37	25
Duke	9	21	26	29

ALL-CONFERENCE TEAM: C—Zane Evans, Jr., Georgia Tech. **1B**—Cody Stubbs, Sr., North Carolina. **2B**—Reed Gragnani, Sr. Virginia. **SS**—Trea Turner, So., N.C. State. **3B**—Colin Moran, Jr. North Carolina; Chad Pinder, Jr., Virginia Tech. **OF**—Tyler Horan, Jr. Virginia Tech; Daniel Palka, Jr., Georgia Tech; Mike Papi, So., Virginia. **DH**—Nick Howard, So., Virginia. **SP**—Kent Emanuel, Jr., North Carolina; Buck Farmer, Sr., Georgia Tech; Bryan Radziewski, Jr., Miami; Carlos Rodon, So., N.C. State; Scott Sitz, Sr., Florida State. **RP**—Kyle Crockett, Jr., Virginia. **Player of the Year:** Colin Moran, North Carolina. **Pitcher of the Year:** Kent Emanuel, North Carolina. **Freshman of the Year:** Joe McCarthy, Virginia. **Coach of the Year:** Brian O'Connor, Virginia.

INDIVIDUAL BATTING LEADERS
(Minimum 2.5 at-bats per team game)

	AVG	AB	R	H	2B	3B	HR	RBI	SB
Papi, Mike, Virginia	.381	176	57	67	15	3	7	57	6
Turner, Trea, N.C. State	.368	228	66	84	13	4	7	42	30
Stubbs, Cody, UNC	.366	276	64	101	27	4	8	76	5
Stewart, D.J., FSU	.364	225	50	82	25	2	5	59	8
Evans, Zane, Georgia Tech	.361	244	47	88	12	1	14	66	0
Wren, Kyle, Georgia Tech	.360	272	50	98	11	6	2	28	28
Lassiter, Landon, UNC	.358	257	75	92	14	3	1	28	8
Stephens, Evan, Wake Forest	.358	190	43	68	5	2	0	22	15
White, Charlie, Maryland	.350	214	44	75	3	6	0	29	39
Cogswell, Brandon, Virginia	.346	182	55	63	11	4	0	22	12
Moran, Colin, UNC	.345	281	76	97	11	3	13	91	1
Horan, Tyler, Virginia Tech	.342	257	58	88	26	4	11	50	5
Palka, Daniel, Georgia Tech	.342	237	55	81	13	3	17	66	6
Zagunis, Mark, Virginia Tech	.341	232	62	79	14	3	9	51	19
McCarthy, Joe, Virginia	.336	223	48	75	10	2	4	51	11
Conway, Matt, Wake Forest	.335	188	27	63	18	0	3	36	4
Convissar, Kyle, Maryland	.325	157	27	51	11	1	1	37	7
Hagel, Jordan, Maryland	.324	148	34	48	15	2	4	24	13
Brizuela, Jose, FSU	.324	216	40	70	14	3	4	44	7
Howard, Nick, Virginia	.323	198	37	64	12	1	3	38	2
Pinder, Chad, Virginia Tech	.321	240	49	77	13	1	8	50	5
Bolt, Skye, UNC	.321	212	48	68	14	2	6	51	10

	AVG	AB	R	H	2B	3B	HR	RBI	SB
Thomas, Brandon, Ga. Tech	.321	209	49	67	15	4	1	30	9
Kennedy, Shane, Clemson	.317	218	47	69	5	4	5	35	22
Downes, Brandon, Virginia	.316	253	67	80	20		10	59	6
Perez, Andy, Duke	.316	212	40	67	8	5	4	25	18
Rash, Andrew, Virginia Tech	.315	238	37	75	22	2	11	62	5
Fincher, Jake, N.C. State	.313	265	50	83	9	1	0	29	14
Kremer, Jeff, Duke	.311	206	42	64	12	0	0	26	4
Boulware, Garrett, Clemson	.308	227	43	70	12	1	8	45	2
Holberton, Brian, UNC	.308	250	54	77	13	0	12	58	8
Keselica, Shane, Virginia Tech	.307	218	40	67	11	1	5	31	2

INDIVIDUAL PITCHING LEADERS
(Minimum 1 IP per team game)

	W	L	ERA	G	SV	IP	H	BB	SO
Trent Thornton, UNC	12	1	1.37	29	8	92	69	19	81
#Nedeljkovic, Eric, Miami	2	2	1.37	25	13	26	18	4	30
Diaz, Chris, Miami	7	5	1.64	16	0	110	101	27	78
Radziewski, Brian, Miami	9	3	1.78	15	0	91	53	30	109
Sitz, Scott, FSU	10	2	2.09	16	0	95	92	22	80
Crownover, Matthew, Clemson	7	3	2.19	15	0	70	64	17	45
Weaver, Luke, FSU	7	3	2.29	17	0	98	78	19	119
Reed, Jimmy, Maryland	6	4	2.33	13	0	89	80	32	74
Johnson, Hobbs, UNC	5	1	2.37	18	0	87	62	51	78
#Smith, Gage, FSU	4	2	2.41	35	1	41	35	8	32
Gossett, Daniel, Clemson	10	4	2.56	16	0	98	78	38	91
Gordon, Hunter, BC	2	4	2.67	13	0	57	47	19	33
Swart, Trent, Duke	4	4	2.75	13	0	85	76	26	71
Farmer, Buck, Georgia Tech	9	5	2.78	17	0	113	100	35	122
Stinnett, Jake, Maryland	6	5	2.83	16	2	64	46	24	48
Mantiply, Joe, Virginia Tech	6	1	2.85	15	0	76	84	25	50
Rodon, Carlos, N.C. State	10	3	2.99	19	0	132	94	45	
Burke, Devin, Virginia Tech	11	3	3.11	16	0	104	98	34	50
Emanuel, Kent, UNC	11	5	3.14	21	1	132	121	32	98
Silverstein, Scott, Virginia	10	2	3.15	16	0	91	93	28	70
Salas, Javi, Miami	5	5	3.18	17	0	71	68	19	44
Leibrandt, Brandon, FSU	10	4	3.44	16	0	89	89	30	77
Stadler, Austin, Wake Forest	5	3	3.50	13	0	69	79	28	60

ATLANTIC SUN CONFERENCE

	Conference		Overall	
	W	L	W	L
Mercer	20	7	43	18
Florida Gulf Coast	19	8	37	20
North Florida	18	9	40	19
* East Tennessee State	17	10	36	24
Stetson	15	12	26	31
Kennesaw State	13	14	30	30
Lipscomb	13	14	25	34
South Carolina-Upstate	9	18	28	30
Jacksonville	8	19	17	38
Northern Kentucky	3	24	8	47

ALL-CONFERENCE TEAM: C—Corey Bass, Sr., North Florida. 1B—Patrick Mazeika, Fr., Stetson. 2B—Brandon Bednar, Jr., Florida Gulf Coast. SS—Kal Simmons, Fr., Kennesaw State. 3B—Chesny Young, So., Mercer. OF—Gaither Bumgardner, Sr., S. Carolina-Upstate; Sean Dwyer, Jr., Florida Gulf Coast; Tyler Marincov, Jr. North Florida; Derrick Workman, Jr., Mercer. DH—Nick Backlund, Jr., Mercer. SP—Kerry Doane, Sr., East Tennessee; Steve Janas, Jr., Kennesaw State; Ricky Knapp, Jr., Florida Gulf Coast. RP—Dimitri Kourtis, So., Mercer. Player of the Year: Chesny Young, Mercer. Pitcher of the Year: Kerry Doane, East Tennessee State. Freshman of the Year: Patrick Mazeika, Stetson. Coach of the Year: Craig Gibson, Mercer.

INDIVIDUAL BATTING LEADERS
(Minimum 2 at-bats per team game)

	AVG	AB	R	H	2B	3B	HR	RBI	SB
Young, Chesny, Mercer	.401	262	56	105	18	3	4	65	9
Mazeika, Patrick, Stetson	.382	212	38	81	11	2	3	33	1
Bumgardner, Gaither, S.C.-Upstate	.354	243	44	86	6	1	0	34	6
Dewees, Donnie, N. Florida	.347	213	47	74	19	3	5	47	3
Roberson, Ryan, N. Florida	.342	187	28	64	11	0	6	40	0
Wielbruda, Joe, N. Florida	.339	236	48	80	7	0	0	25	8
Workman, Derrick, Mercer	.338	216	45	73	17	2	9	48	3

	AVG	AB	R	H	2B	3B	HR	RBI	SB
Bednar, Brandon, Fla. Gulf Coast	.336	247	52	83	16	3	1	46	7
Freeman, Clinton, ETSU	.335	239	39	80	18	4	10	57	2
Weber, Luke, S.C.-Upstate	.332	217	35	72	16	1	5	42	0
Dwyer, Sean, Fla. Gulf Coast	.332	217	44	72	11	5	4	25	18
Marincov, Tyler, N. Florida	.331	245	64	81	19	7	8	54	21
Reeves, Mike, Fla. Gulf Coast	.327	223	47	73	8	1	1	27	0
Backlund, Nick, Mercer	.326	242	45	79	22	0	13	68	0
Tritsch, Dylan, ETSU	.324	222	37	72	11	2	2	19	21
Green, Andrew, ETSU	.324	238	56	77	15	3	5	32	24
Beisner, Brooks, Fla. Gulf Coast	.323	223	38	72	9	1	6	43	1
Greer, Brody, S.C.-Upstate	.318	223	40	71	15	1	1	34	5
Richardson, Trey, S.C.-Upstate	.316	212	34	67	17	0	8	49	0
Bruce, Jacob, Kennesaw	.316	228	31	72	12	3	1	25	6
Sucy, Michael, Fla. Gulf Coast	.314	226	37	71	7	1	9	46	7
Way, Bo, Kennesaw	.313	240	41	75	12	4	2	27	8
Karmeris, Paul, N. Florida	.311	228	37	71	10	0	4	31	7
Patterson, Brandon, S.C.-Upstate	.311	206	30	64	11	1	1	46	3
Barrett, Austin, Mercer	.309	217	33	67	11	0	6	45	2
LaGarde, Sasha, Mercer	.308	237	68	73	9	1	7	34	15
Brooks, Kyle, N. Florida	.307	192	34	59	7	2	2	20	6
Olmstead, Corbin, N. Florida	.307	150	20	46	4	3	0	19	1
Niesman, Derek, ETSU	.307	199	32	61	7	0	3	32	4
Huxtable, Jake, Jacksonville	.304	171	21	52	4	0	4	14	0

INDIVIDUAL PITCHING LEADERS
(Minimum 1 IP per team game)

	W	L	ERA	G	SV	IP	H	BB	SO
Janas, Steve, Kennesaw	9	1	1.14	13	0	79	74	14	55
Renner, Michael, N. Florida	9	2	1.81	16	0	95	90	16	54
Knapp, Ricky, Fla. Gulf Coast	9	3	2.10	14	0	103	89	15	74
Doane, Kerry, ETSU	13	2	2.14	20	0	147	129	24	77
Anderson, Chris, Jacksonville	7	5	2.49	14	0	105	90	27	101
Barker, Brandon, Mercer	7	2	2.66	17	0	85	85	27	79
Perez, Austin, Stetson	7	2	2.81	15	0	90	89	26	66
Murray, Michael, Fla. Gulf Coast	5	1	2.93	15	0	86	79	19	55
Kourtis, Dimitri, Mercer	5	3	2.94	34	9	67	63	15	60
Johnson, D.J., Mercer	7	2	3.06	19	0	85	79	18	67
Rice, Logan, ETSU	6	3	3.23	19	0	64	68	24	27
Cooney, Harrison, Fla. Gulf Coast	6	2	3.24	21	5	67	57	30	59
Powers, Josh, Stetson	1	8	3.41	15	0	106	125	15	54
Bumgardner, Gaither, S.C.-Upstate	5	2	3.57	17	1	68	72	24	52
Lee, Brandon, S.C.-Upstate	7	6	3.62	14	0	104	112	13	80
Westwood, Kyle, N. Florida	4	1	3.75	15	0	62	68	12	71
Allbritton, Nick, N. Florida	5	7	3.80	17	0	92	109	21	49
Organ, Tommy, N. Florida	5	2	4.11	17	0	85	100	25	54
Roseboom, David, S.C.-Upstate	5	4	4.35	16	0	83	80	31	53
Jefferson, Matt, N. Kentucky	1	8	4.76	14	0	87	124	27	51
#Teasley, David, Mercer	8	2	5.57	46	4	53	49	34	60

ATLANTIC 10 CONFERENCE

	Conference		Overall	
	W	L	W	L
* Saint Louis	17	7	41	21
Charlotte	17	7	37	23
Rhode Island	17	7	35	24
Xavier	16	8	32	26
La Salle	15	9	24	29
George Washington	15	9	26	32
Richmond	13	11	31	24
Virginia Commonwealth	12	12	28	26
St. Joseph's	12	12	26	26
Butler	12	12	25	27
St. Bonaventure	9	15	20	28
Fordham	8	16	22	33
Temple	7	17	18	28
Massachusetts	7	17	14	31
Dayton	3	21	11	39

ALL-CONFERENCE TEAM: C—Grant Nelson, Sr., Saint Louis. 1B—Mike Vigliariolo, So., Saint Louis. 2B—Jason Radwan, Sr., St. Bonaventure. SS—Alec Solé, So., Saint Louis. 3B—Billy Urban, Sr., St. Bonaventure. OF—Alex Kelly, Sr., Saint Louis; Justin Seager, Sr., Charlotte; Tanner Stanley, Fr., Richmond. DH—Jacob Mayers, Sr., Richmond. SP—Sean

Furney, Sr., Rhode Island; Brock Hudgens, Jr., Charlotte. **RP**—Pat Christensen, Sr., La Salle. **Player of the Year:** Justin Seager, Charlotte; Mike Vigliariolo, Saint Louis. **Pitcher of the Year:** Sean Furney, Rhode Island. **Rookie of the Year:** Tanner Stanley, Richmond. **Coach of the Year:** Gregg Ritchie, George Washington.

INDIVIDUAL BATTING LEADERS
(Minimum 2.5 at-bats per team game)

	AVG	AB	R	H	2B	3B	HR	RBI	SB
Radwan, Jason, St. Bonaventure	.405	185	37	75	10	3	0	21	2
Mayers, Jacob, Richmond	.359	209	43	75	11	2	7	37	0
Seager, Justin, Charlotte	.351	225	46	79	22	1	2	40	5
Risi, Jimmy, Butler	.347	170	26	59	19	1	7	41	3
Knabe, Henry, Temple	.345	174	23	60	12	2	1	32	21
Elwood, Brad, Charlotte	.343	233	37	80	14	2	3	41	5
Vigliariolo, Mike, SLU	.341	255	36	87	19	2	8	42	9
Urban, Billy, St. Bonaventure	.341	182	29	62	11	0	2	35	3
Nelson, Grant, SLU	.338	228	45	77	8	3	5	32	4
Kelly, Alex, SLU	.337	246	45	83	17	0	12	62	9
Cujas, Joey, VCU	.333	216	31	72	16	0	1	40	1
Elwell, Mark, Xavier	.332	211	38	70	11	0	1	26	15
Williams, Bret, Richmond	.326	178	23	58	14	0	1	37	1
Sole, Alec, SLU	.326	218	36	71	6	2	0	34	10
Cirillo, Anthony, St. Joseph's	.325	169	35	55	10	0	0	26	10
Zink, Matt, Richmond	.318	157	34	50	7	2	2	23	16
Martinez, Braxton, SLU	.314	242	32	76	12	0	7	29	1
Levine, Mike, SLU	.314	223	36	70	11	3	0	31	3
Peterson, Derek, Temple	.314	188	27	59	13	2	2	31	6
Forney, Joe, Xavier	.313	182	31	57	4	0	1	22	6
Klem, Dan, LaSalle	.313	198	24	62	13	0	0	20	9
Hueth, Chris, St. Joseph's	.312	189	39	59	15	4	3	29	12
McLam, Rob, Massachusetts	.311	177	29	55	11	1	0	27	11
Chidemo, Selby, Xavier	.311	161	22	50	4	1	1	24	8
Poulos, Nick, Richmond	.310	187	26	58	2	2	1	15	8
Ravert, Joey, LaSalle	.310	142	16	44	10	1	0	19	0
Stanley, Tanner, Richmond	.308	221	44	68	17	3	1	38	9
Williams, Mark, LaSalle	.308	156	26	48	13	3	2	29	2
Basen, Shane, Charlotte	.307	244	45	75	9	2	4	49	16
Rosencrance, Joel, St. Bonaventure	.305	131	20	40	14	0	4	26	0
#Albright, Justin, GWU	.300	210	29	63	11	0	0	19	29
#Korenblatt, Justin, La Salle	.297	192	25	57	9	5	1	26	4
#Caputo, Tim, Rhode Island	.295	227	49	67	13	2	0	30	13

INDIVIDUAL PITCHING LEADERS
(Minimum 1 inning pitched per team game)

	W	L	ERA	G	SV	IP	H	BB	SO
#Levin, John, SLU	3	0	1.21	30	2	22	14	6	17
#Lees, Matt, VCU	2	6	1.22	30	11	52	51	13	39
Moyers, Steve, Rhode Island	4	1	1.78	14	1	61	37	25	52
Furney, Sean, Rhode Island	7	4	1.93	15	0	98	85	22	75
Mayers, Jacob, Richmond	3	2	2.10	10	2	56	42	7	41
Richard, Jon, Xavier	9	4	2.31	15	0	105	87	27	65
#Christensen, Pat, La Salle	6	1	2.52	24	11	50	45	10	58
Bradstreet, Mike, Rhode Island	8	5	2.64	14	0	102	87	15	76
Hamilton, John, Charlotte	6	3	2.76	15	0	98	90	22	67
Hudgens, Brock, Charlotte	7	1	2.77	16	0	84	62	35	77
Dwyer, Heath, VCU	7	6	2.78	14	0	107	104	20	74
Westrick, Alex, Xavier	3	3	2.79	12	0	61	56	25	29
Greene, Seth, VCU	5	1	2.90	19	2	68	67	8	38
Peterson, Eric, Temple	6	3	3.03	13	0	74	64	15	69
Mullen, Kyle, St. Joseph's	8	4	3.16	14	0	91	88	31	77
Weisberg, Aaron, GWU	6	4	3.32	17	0	81	84	22	53
Alemann, Alex, SLU	6	6	3.36	15	0	94	102	33	70
Staub, Luke, GWU	4	6	3.44	17	0	92	93	23	55

BIG EAST CONFERENCE

	Conference		Overall	
	W	L	W	L
Louisville	20	4	51	14
Pittsburgh	18	6	42	17
Seton Hall	18	6	37	19
South Florida	17	7	36	22
Rutgers	14	10	28	30

Notre Dame	10	14	34	24
St. John's	10	14	23	35
* **Connecticut**	9	15	35	28
Cincinnati	6	18	24	32
Georgetown	5	19	25	28
Villanova	5	19	14	40

ALL-CONFERENCE TEAM: C—Elvin Soto, So., Pittsburgh. **1B**—Trey Mancini, Jr., Notre Dame. **2B**—L.J. Mazzilli, Sr., Connecticut. **SS**—Giuseppe Papaccio, Sr., Seton Hall. **3B**—Eric Jagielo, Jr., Notre Dame. **OF**—Zack Granite, Jr., Seton Hall; James Ransay, Jr., South Florida; Casey Roche, Jr., Pittsburgh. **DH**—Jeff Gardner, Jr., Louisville. **SP**—Adam Norton, Sr., Notre Dame; Ethan Mildren, Jr., Pitts.; Jon Prosinski, Jr., Seton Hall; Jeff Thompson, Jr., Louisville. **RP**—Nick Burdi, So., Louisville. **Player of the Year:** Eric Jagielo, Notre Dame. **Pitcher of the Year:** Jeff Thompson, Louisville. **Rookie of the Year:** Jimmy Herget, South Florida. **Coach of the Year:** Joe Jordano, Pittsburgh.

INDIVIDUAL BATTING LEADERS
(Minimum 2.5 at-bats per team game)

	AVG	AB	R	H	2B	3B	HR	RBI	SB
Mancini, Trey, Notre Dame	.389	229	29	89	14	7	7	54	3
Jagielo, Eric, Notre Dame	.388	196	47	76	19	1	9	53	3
Papaccio, Giuseppe, Seton Hall	.365	233	43	85	24	4	4	53	9
Mazzilli, L.J., UConn	.354	260	50	92	16	4	6	51	29
Schwindel, Frank, St. John's	.349	235	39	82	21	0	5	53	1
Sturgeon, Cole, Louisville	.339	221	38	75	9	2	1	33	13
Roche, Casey, Pitt	.339	233	53	79	12	2	9	65	10
Ramsay, James, S. Florida	.337	243	37	82	14	2	3	43	12
Vazquez, Boo, Pitt	.337	199	31	67	13	1	2	30	1
Young, Ty, Louisville	.335	236	54	79	13	7	4	58	26
Alonso, Nik, S. Florida	.331	181	23	60	6	0	0	23	1
Zarrillo, Vinny, Rutgers	.330	221	35	73	13	5	0	24	12
Zavala, Steve, Rutgers	.330	188	35	62	11	0	4	30	5
Parente, Sam, Pitt	.329	216	38	71	14	4	6	51	3
Collins, Nick, Georgetown	.328	180	20	59	6	2	3	30	0
Johnson, Coco, Louisville	.324	204	41	66	11	2	8	50	22
Glass, Justin, Cincinnati	.322	239	41	77	12	0	5	39	11
Happ, Ian, Cincinnati	.322	205	41	66	13	1	6	36	25
Leeson, Justin, Georgetown	.321	218	35	70	9	2	1	23	13
Soto, Elvin, Pitt	.320	222	50	71	13	6	6	43	3
Lauricella, Zach, St. John's	.320	197	31	63	21	1	4	40	3
Selden, Chris, Seton Hall	.320	169	31	54	8	0	2	33	17
Bull, Ryan, Louisville	.319	216	24	69	9	5	2	38	2
Annunziata, Sal, Seton Hall	.319	213	36	68	14	1	6	38	7
Vranka, Stephen, Pitt	.318	236	65	75	18	5	7	47	16
Williams, Matt, Cincinnati	.317	167	26	53	9	1	2	24	12
Favatella, Nick, Rutgers	.316	234	41	74	12	5	3	29	12
Falla, Jimmy, S. Florida	.315	232	40	73	22	0	2	50	8
Law, Charlie, Rutgers	.312	199	24	62	13	0	4	47	1
Shelinsky, Steven, Pitt	.311	183	50	57	8	1	12	54	6
#Engel, Adam, Louisville	.236	246	51	58	9	2	1	28	41
#Ferriter, Billy, UConn	.286	262	63	75	15	0	1	19	27

INDIVIDUAL PITCHING LEADERS
(Minimum 1 IP per team game)

	W	L	ERA	G	SV	IP	H	BB	SO
#Burdi, Nick, Louisville	3	3	0.76	29	16	36	25	13	62
#Ege, Cody, Louisville	4	1	1.04	38	1	35	13	12	52
Slania, Dan, Notre Dame	3	1	1.21	24	13	59	47	11	43
Herget, Jimmy, S. Florida	6	2	1.72	15	0	94	62	27	60
Thompson, Jeff, Louisville	11	2	2.19	17	0	107	67	34	113
Horstman, Ryan, St. John's	6	6	2.33	16	0	66	59	30	56
Terhune, Greg, Seton Hall	7	3	2.33	18	0	81	64	27	58
Mildren, Ethan, Pitt	10	3	2.35	16	0	115	88	25	76
Norton, Adam, Notre Dame	10	5	2.40	16	0	116	125	15	70
Green, Chad, Louisville	10	4	2.42	18	0	104	97	27	74
Cross, Carson, UConn	9	4	2.44	16	0	111	104	24	86
Tabakman, Jordan, UConn	6	2	2.57	22	5	67	65	21	40
Prosinski, Jon, Seton Hall	7	4	2.58	15	0	108	91	13	82
Aldenhoven, Rhys, Pitt	8	1	2.76	15	0	88	81	27	54
Kime, Dace, Louisville	6	1	2.99	27	1	69	64	20	83
Prevost, Josh, Seton Hall	5	2	3.24	15	0	58	58	21	31
Smorol, Rob, Rutgers	5	7	3.63	15	0	89	89	33	62

Gonzalez, Nick, S. Florida	3	4	3.63	15	0	87	76	37	77
Wotherspoon, Matt, Pitt	9	3	3.70	16	0	107	103	33	85
Gebler, Tyler, Rutgers	4	6	3.71	17	3	85	99	14	39
Marzi, Anthony, UConn	5	7	3.75	17	0	98	93	31	78
Harris, Josh, Villanova	5	7	3.75	13	0	86	94	20	56

BIG SOUTH CONFERENCE

	Conference		Overall	
NORTH	W	L	W	L
Campbell	19	5	49	10
High Point	15	9	29	29
Radford	14	10	30	26
*Liberty	13	11	36	29
Longwood	12	12	26	28
Virginia Military Institute	6	18	20	35
SOUTH	W	L	W	L
Coastal Carolina	18	6	37	23
Gardner-Webb	12	11	29	27
Charleston Southern	11	13	22	34
Presbyterian	10	14	24	32
Winthrop	8	15	21	33
UNC Asheville	4	18	16	35

ALL-CONFERENCE TEAM: C—Trey Wimmer, Sr., Liberty. **1B**—Spencer Angelis, So., High Point. **2B**—Michael Felton, Sr., Campbell. **SS**—Jeff Kemp, Sr., Radford. **3B**—Alex Owens, Jr., Longwood; Elijah Trail, Jr., Campbell. **OF**—Rob Dickinson, Sr., VMI; Bobby Ison, So., Charleston Southern; Ben McQuown, Jr., Campbell. **DH**—Zack Hagaman, Jr., Charleston Southern. **SP**—Matt Fraudlin, So., Gardner-Webb; Ryan Mattes, Sr., Campbell; Ben Smith, Coastal Carolina. **RP**—Ryan Thompson, Jr., Campbell. **Player of the Year:** Rob Dickinson, VMI. **Pitcher of the Year:** Ryan Thompson, Campbell. **Freshman of the Year:** Seth Lamando, Coastal Carolina. **Coach of the Year:** Greg Goff, Campbell.

INDIVIDUAL BATTING LEADERS
(Minimum 2.5 at-bats per team game)

	AVG	AB	R	H	2B	3B	HR	RBI	SB
Dickinson, Rob, VMI	.399	198	34	79	12	3	7	46	15
Graham, Brent, Campbell	.374	190	57	71	11	3	2	37	15
Felton, Michael, Campbell	.371	224	49	83	15	1	2	53	13
Ison, Bobby, Charleston So.	.367	229	39	84	14	2	3	27	9
Olson, David, Campbell	.347	196	45	68	10	0	3	37	2
Retz, Ryan, High Point	.347	222	42	77	18	0	6	39	0
Tomasovich, Alex, Charleston So.	.343	207	41	71	13	0	2	20	8
Winn, Matt, VMI	.333	153	16	51	11	1	2	18	0
Dickason, Matt, Liberty	.331	181	26	60	13	1	0	18	2
Aanderud, Bryan, Liberty	.329	252	31	83	8	0	1	39	4
McQuown, Ben, Campbell	.329	222	65	73	11	4	4	30	54
May, Jacob, Coastal Carolina	.324	216	42	70	12	2	7	31	16
Houmard, Tommy, UNCA	.321	184	27	59	10	3	2	31	1
Angelis, Spencer, High Point	.319	188	29	60	14	1	1	26	0
Reavis, Josh, Radford	.319	182	30	58	5	0	0	25	4
Shelton, Chase, Charleston So.	.318	195	28	62	12	0	2	32	2
Delucia, Michael, Campbell	.316	152	21	48	5	4	2	30	8
Spano, Josh, High Point	.316	225	34	71	11	0	2	31	1
Joyner, Todd, UNCA	.315	203	22	64	9	2	2	28	1
Graham, Ian, UNCA	.314	172	32	54	12	0	4	28	0
Paul, Brandon, Presbyterian	.313	211	23	66	10	2	0	24	8
McIntosh, Robert, UNCA	.309	165	22	51	11	1	2	24	1
Gardiner, Josh, Radford	.308	224	47	69	11	2	1	24	20
Jackson, Benji, Gardner-Webb	.305	187	34	57	19	0	3	26	5
Burkett, Scott, Longwood	.304	204	29	62	11	0	4	30	0
Blackman, Ted, Coastal Caro.	.303	195	45	59	10	1	5	24	7
Dolan, Cody, Winthrop	.300	190	30	57	13	0	3	19	4
Woolcock, Zach, Radford	.299	187	28	56	9	3	2	29	5
Tarsovich, Jordan, UNCA	.299	204	45	61	16	3	2	28	18
Hering, Colin, Coastal Carolina	.297	192	26	57	6	0	3	26	9
Wimmer, Trey, Liberty	.296	243	43	72	17	3	5	44	2
#Kemp, Jeff, Radford	.284	148	38	42	11	2	10	34	8
#Collins, Brad, Gardner-Webb	.296	216	29	64	27	0	5	41	2
#Coleman, Scott, Gardner-Webb	.294	194	35	55	10	4	2	28	6
#Cordell, Ryan, Liberty	.261	261	42	68	12	2	6	40	28

INDIVIDUAL PITCHING LEADERS
(Minimum 1 IP per team game)

	W	L	ERA	G	SV	IP	H	BB	SO
Thompson, Ryan, Campbell	9	1	0.88	31	10	72	51	15	57
Bowers, Heath, Campbell	9	0	1.69	15	0	90	75	22	80
Mattes, Ryan, Campbell	8	3	1.94	16	0	107	101	18	76
Connolly, Ryan, Coastal Caro.	6	4	2.11	32	11	81	61	20	69
Smith, Ben, Coastal Carolina	5	4	2.23	16	0	93	73	53	83
Richardson, Josh, Liberty	4	4	2.40	23	2	71	66	18	48
Scarborough, Conner	1	6	2.45	27	1	59	67	9	41
Bach, Connor, VMI	2	4	2.81	13	0	83	62	35	45
Fraudin, Matt, Gardner-Webb	8	5	2.88	16	0	106	76	40	96
Jeter, Bud, Presbyterian	5	7	2.89	14	0	106	99	34	84
Dees, Beau, Presbyterian	5	7	3.05	14	0	91	79	29	56
Newberry, Jacob, High Point	4	3	3.07	14	0	88	93	24	78
Barnett, Andrew, Gardner-Webb	5	3	3.14	15	0	92	99	17	93
Myers, Aaron, Longwood	4	2	3.30	23	10	79	78	24	67
Maxwell, Jeff, Radford	0	3	3.32	30	4	57	67	9	31
Roy, Brooks, Liberty	7	6	3.36	16	0	88	79	32	51
Pierpont, Matt, Winthrop	4	5	3.38	13	0	91	94	19	80
Cedano, Hector	8	2	3.50	16	0	72	78	29	57
Schroff, Tory, Charleston So.	6	5	3.52	15	0	79	72	29	73
Lambert, Trey, Liberty	8	3	3.54	15	0	89	76	23	48

BIG TEN CONFERENCE

	Conference		Overall	
	W	L	W	L
*Indiana	17	7	49	16
Ohio State	15	9	35	23
Nebraska	15	9	29	30
Minnesota	13	8	32	22
Illinois	14	10	35	20
Michigan	14	10	29	27
Michigan State	12	9	33	17
Iowa	10	14	22	27
Northwestern	9	15	22	26
Purdue	6	18	17	34
Penn State	4	20	14	36

ALL-CONFERENCE TEAM: C—Kyle Schwarber, So., Indiana. **1B**—David Kerian, So., Illinois. **2B**—Pat Kelly, So., Nebraska. **SS**—Thomas Lindauer, Jr., Illinois; Kirby Pellant, Sr., Ohio State. **3B**—Dustin DeMuth, Jr., Indiana. **OF**—Michael O'Neill, Jr., Michigan; Chad Christensen, Sr., Nebraska; Justin Parr, Sr., Illinois. **DH**—Scott Donley, So., Indiana. **SP**—Aaron Slegers, So., Indiana; D.J. Snelten, Jr., Minnesota; Tom Windle, Jr., Minnesota. **RP**—Trace Dempsey, So., Ohio State. **Player of the Year:** Justin Parr, Illinois. **Pitcher of the Year:** Aaron Slegers, Indiana. **Freshman of the Year:** Kevin Duchene, Illinois. **Coach of the Year:** Tracy Smith, Indiana.

INDIVIDUAL BATTING LEADERS
(Minimum 2.5 at-bats per team game)

	AVG	AB	R	H	2B	3B	HR	RBI	SB
Parr, Justin, Illinois	.398	231	43	92	15	4	6	53	16
DeMuth, Dustin, Indiana	.377	244	46	92	24	1	5	41	11
Schwarber, Kyle, Indiana	.366	235	65	86	10	1	18	54	4
Ruchim, Kyle, Northwestern	.365	167	32	61	16	3	2	26	10
Christensen, Chad, Nebraska	.364	225	45	82	8	3	2	39	8
Donley, Scott, Indiana	.358	240	40	86	16	2	5	61	2
O'Neill, Michael, Michigan	.356	239	46	85	11	1	5	37	23
Salter, Blaise, MSU	.343	181	28	62	14	0	5	35	1
Toole, Eric, Iowa	.337	175	32	59	6	1	0	11	22
Pritchard, Michael, Nebraska	.333	198	34	66	13	1	0	18	4
Kelly, Pat, Nebraska	.331	257	33	85	12	1	2	33	5
Gibson, Cam, MSU	.325	163	34	53	5	3	0	17	12
Cronenworth, Jacob, Michigan	.320	203	33	65	12	2	2	41	12
Travis, Sam, Indiana	.316	244	53	77	22	2	10	57	4
Maezes, Travis, Michigan	.313	217	35	68	10	3	3	44	16
Kerian, David, Illinois	.313	195	30	61	11	1	1	39	23
Basil, Michael, Indiana	.311	244	44	76	15	2	3	49	7
Lindauer, Thomas, Illinois	.309	223	45	69	12	1	9	38	15
Biondi, Patrick, Michigan	.309	165	40	51	9	0	1	16	15
Smith, Casey, Indiana	.309	175	25	54	9	0	5	34	2

	AVG	AB	R	H	2B	3B	HR	RBI	SB
Henkemeyer, Andy, Minnesota	.308	201	24	62	13	3	1	28	5
Havey, Jack, Northwestern	.307	166	19	51	9	0	2	28	2
Parr, Jordan, Illinois	.305	213	50	65	6	1	9	47	**23**
Kalkowski, Kash, Nebraska	.304	214	40	65	13	3	3	44	7
Larson, Troy, Minnesota	.304	168	24	51	6	2	0	14	8
Sanguinetti, Rich, Nebraska	.303	221	41	67	8	1	1	16	8
Pickens, Jimmy, MSU	.303	195	39	59	13	2	9	42	6
Pellant, Kirby, Ohio State	.301	186	20	56	5	3	2	15	12
McHugh, Sean, Purdue	.298	198	28	59	9	3	4	31	5
Porter, Patrick, Ohio State	.296	199	42	59	13	**5**	4	33	11
#Cheky, Anthony, MSU	.278	176	34	49	7	0	1	12	**23**

INDIVIDUAL PITCHING LEADERS
(Minimum 1 IP per team game)

	W	L	ERA	G	SV	IP	H	BB	SO
#Dempsey, Trace, Ohio State	3	0	1.02	**31**	**17**	35	22	11	28
Coursen-Carr, Will, Indiana	5	0	**1.93**	17	1	65	54	27	37
Slegers, Aaron, Indiana	9	2	2.04	18	0	**106**	108	17	59
Farrell, Luke, Northwestern	3	4	2.13	12	0	84	68	26	80
Windle, Tom, Minnesota	6	4	2.14	14	0	93	70	33	86
Snelten, D.J., Minnesota	5	2	2.15	10	0	59	50	19	42
Waszak, Andrew, MSU	6	3	2.36	13	0	92	79	18	57
DeNato, Joey, Indiana	**10**	2	2.52	19	0	104	97	43	**87**
King, Brian, Ohio State	7	6	2.68	15	0	101	91	12	56
Duchene, Kevin, Illinois	9	1	2.79	18	0	81	78	34	68
Meyer, Ben, Minnesota	5	4	2.80	15	0	64	68	11	49
Morton, Zach, Northwestern	3	5	2.86	14	0	85	91	22	46
VanVossen, Mick, MSU	5	2	2.97	11	0	76	58	20	32
Goldberg, Brad, Ohio State	6	1	2.99	15	0	81	71	46	68
Hart, Kyle, Indiana	8	2	3.01	15	0	84	83	27	50
DeLeon, Christian, Nebraska	7	4	3.21	14	0	93	101	15	46
Johnson, Kevin, Illinois	6	3	3.22	11	0	67	69	18	44
Magallones, Brandon, Northwestern	5	6	3.30	13	0	85	84	24	48
Hill, Steven, Penn State	1	7	3.39	11	0	74	81	27	45
McAnallen, Logan, Michigan	3	3	3.50	19	0	72	80	20	50
Hill, Evan, Michigan	7	3	3.51	14	0	82	66	41	47

BIG 12 CONFERENCE

	Conference		Overall	
	W	L	W	L
Kansas State	16	8	45	19
Oklahoma State	13	10	41	19
*Oklahoma	13	11	43	21
West Virginia	13	11	33	26
Baylor	12	11	27	28
Kansas	12	12	34	25
Texas Christian	12	12	29	28
Texas Tech	9	15	26	30
Texas	7	17	27	24

ALL-CONFERENCE TEAM: C—Blair DeBord, Jr., Kansas State. **IF**—Shane Conlon, So., Kansas State; Austin Fisher, So., Kansas State; Ross Kivett, Jr., Kansas State; Matt Oberste, Jr., Oklahoma; Cal Towey, Sr., Baylor. **OF**—Zach Fish, So., Oklahoma State; Jared King, Jr., Kansas State; Mark Payton, Jr., Texas. **DH**—Nathan Orf, Sr., Baylor. **SP**—Jonathan Gray, Jr., Oklahoma; Preston Morrison, So., Texas Christian; Harrison Musgrave, So., West Virginia. **RP**—Jordan Piché, Jr., Kansas; Jake Matthys, Fr., Kansas State; Vince Wheeland, Jr., Oklahoma State. **Player of the Year:** Ross Kivett, Kansas State. **Pitcher of the Year:** Harrison Musgrave, West Virginia. **Freshman of the Year:** Jake Matthys, Kansas State. **Newcomer of the Year:** Jordan Piché, Kansas. **Coach of the Year:** Brad Hill, Kansas State.

INDIVIDUAL BATTING LEADERS
(Minimum 2.5 at-bats per team game)

	AVG	AB	R	H	2B	3B	HR	RBI	SB
Payton, Mark, Texas	**.393**	178	27	70	11	**8**	0	29	3
Orf, Nathan, Baylor	.377	215	36	81	15	1	1	34	4
Oberste, Matt, Oklahoma	.373	241	53	90	19	4	11	**60**	13
Fisher, Austin, Kansas State	.361	208	43	75	20	3	2	38	3
Kivett, Ross, Kansas State	.360	261	**57**	**94**	15	4	3	39	26
Conlon, Shane, Kansas State	.341	249	56	85	13	3	7	28	17
Witt, Tanner, Kansas State	.337	261	49	88	8	3	1	36	7
King, Jared, Kansas State	.335	218	52	73	16	2	7	53	14

	AVG	AB	R	H	2B	3B	HR	RBI	SB
Rice, Jacob, W. Virginia	.333	219	34	73	13	0	2	30	12
DeBord, Blair, Kansas State	.327	199	33	65	11	1	0	37	6
Tuntland, Ryan, W. Virginia	.325	200	32	65	9	1	3	36	7
Santigate, R.J., Kansas State	.324	222	32	72	4	2	0	29	11
Alex DeLeon, Kansas	.319	204	35	65	19	0	10	46	4
Krietemeier, Tanner, OSU	.314	229	42	72	14	2	4	45	7
Boyd, Bobby	.314	210	33	66	7	3	0	24	17
McCurry, Randy, OSU	.314	223	32	70	**21**	0	3	41	5
White, Boomer, TCU	.314	188	18	59	13	1	1	27	2
Hinojosa, C.J., Texas	.311	190	19	59	10	2	2	29	3
White, Max, Oklahoma	.310	255	53	79	12	2	3	33	9
Kuntz, Kevin, Kansas	.310	168	24	52	6	0	0	22	12
Suiter, Michael, Kansas	.309	223	40	69	10	1	1	29	17
Davis, Jon, Kansas State	.302	212	49	64	14	4	5	42	10
Saxon, Saulyer, OSU	.301	166	30	50	8	1	0	18	6
Romero, Victor, OSU	.300	170	26	51	12	0	4	29	4
Barrios, Jake, Texas Tech	.297	185	27	55	8	4	3	48	2
Fleming, Billy, W. Virginia	.294	197	27	58	11	1	0	23	2
Erich Weiss, Texas	.294	177	28	52	7	3	1	24	7
Witte, Jantzen, TCU	.293	208	28	61	15	2	3	34	3
Towey, Cal, Baylor	.291	199	34	58	11	5	4	45	10
Wilson, Brady, W. Virginia	.290	217	31	63	4	2	3	19	20
#Bell, Brett, Texas Tech	.278	187	38	52	2	0	0	15	**31**
#McBroom, Ryan, W. Virginia	.268	220	39	59	19	0	**12**	48	5
#Mayfield, Jack, Oklahoma	.254	**268**	55	68	14	1	7	35	7

INDIVIDUAL PITCHING LEADERS
(Minimum 1 IP per team game)

	W	L	ERA	G	SV	IP	H	BB	SO
Morrison, Preston, TCU	7	3	**1.51**	15	0	107	85	18	64
Gray, Jonathan, Oklahoma	**10**	3	1.64	17	0	**126**	83	24	**147**
Piche', Jordan, Kansas	6	4	1.68	17	**12**	64	53	10	49
Masek, Trey, Texas Tech	5	2	1.82	11	0	79	56	22	69
Nurdin, Tyler, OSU	5	3	1.89	14	0	86	74	24	69
Wheeland, Vince, OSU	8	2	1.97	30	2	73	58	13	64
Peters, Dillon, Texas	6	3	1.97	14	0	87	71	24	57
#Matthys, Jake, Kansas State	9	2	2.05	**34**	9	61	46	9	44
Musgrave, Harrison, W. Virginia	9	1	2.17	14	0	95	65	29	81
Taylor, Thomas, Kansas	6	2	2.33	14	0	97	84	28	66
Thornhill, Nathan, Texas	3	6	2.64	14	0	85	75	15	60
Williams, Nate, Kansas State	4	3	2.67	24	0	67	55	33	54
French, Parker, Texas	4	5	2.68	13	0	77	69	24	46
Hursh, Jason, OSU	6	5	2.79	16	0	106	105	28	86
Newman, Dillon, Baylor	3	4	2.91	12	0	77	63	5	52
Overton, Dillon, Oklahoma	9	3	3.02	16	0	92	91	23	79
Finnegan, Brandon, TCU	0	8	3.18	16	0	79	74	35	86
John Means, W. Virginia	4	4	3.34	13	0	73	72	22	54
Drozd, Jonny, TCU	4	5	3.48	15	1	67	74	13	43
Robinette, Mark, OSU	6	1	3.58	17	0	70	60	22	54
Walter, Corey, W. Virginia	5	5	3.65	15	1	67	74	28	38

BIG WEST CONFERENCE

	Conference		Overall	
	W	L	W	L
*Cal State Fullerton	23	4	51	10
Cal Poly	17	10	40	19
UC Santa Barbara	17	10	35	25
UC Irvine	15	12	33	22
Cal State Northridge	15	12	31	26
Long Beach State	15	12	29	27
Hawaii	11	16	16	35
UC Riverside	10	17	22	32
Pacific	7	20	15	39
UC Davis	5	22	19	37

ALL-CONFERENCE TEAM: C—Ronnie Shaeffer, Sr., UC Irvine. **1B**—Carlos Lopez, Sr., CS Fullerton. **2B**—Denver Chavez, Sr., Cal Poly. **SS**—Richy Pedroza, Jr., CS Fullerton. **3B**—Taylor Sparks, Jr., UC Irvine. **OF**—Michael Lorenzen, Jr., CS Fullerton; Dominique Taylor, Jr., UC Irvine; Nick Torres, So., Cal Poly. **DH**—J.D. Davis, So., CS Fullerton. **UT**—Jeff McNeil, Jr., Long Beach State. **SP**—Thomas Eshelman, Fr., CS Fullerton; Justin Garza, Fr., CS Fullerton; Andrew Morales, Jr., UC Irvine; Joey Wagman, Sr., Cal Poly. **RP**—Reed Reilly, So., Cal Poly. **CP**—Michael Lorenzen, Jr., CS

Fullerton. **Players of the Year:** Carlos Lopez, CS Fullerton; Taylor Sparks, UC Irvine. **Pitcher of the Year:** Justin Garza, CS Fullerton. **Defensive Player of the Year:** Richy Pedroza, CS Fullerton. **Freshman Pitcher of the Year:** Thomas Eshelman, CS Fullerton. **Freshman Player of the Year:** Robby Nesovic, UC Santa Barbara. **Coach of the Year:** Rick Vanderhook, CS Fullerton.

INDIVIDUAL BATTING LEADERS
(Minimum 2.5 at-bats per team game)

	AVG	AB	R	H	2B	3B	HR	RBI	SB
Spencer, Connor, UC Irvine	.373	212	42	79	19	3	0	35	3
Sparks, Taylor, UC Irvine	.360	222	38	80	11	4	10	50	7
Lynch, Nick, UC Davis	.359	170	24	61	6	1	2	28	2
Chavez, Denver, Cal Poly	.357	244	56	87	14	3	1	23	17
Prestridge, Clayton, UC Riverside	.355	197	34	70	12	0	1	30	14
McNeil, Jeff, LBSU	.348	221	35	77	16	2	0	23	13
Lipson, Tino, UC Davis	.339	165	31	56	2	3	0	18	10
Lopez, Carlos, CS Fullerton	.339	236	52	80	11	3	4	34	15
Andriese, David, UC Riverside	.335	209	21	70	10	3	1	43	3
Lorenzen, Michael, CS Fullerton	.335	227	40	76	12	4	7	54	12
Torres, Nick, Cal Poly	.333	225	39	75	19	1	7	49	6
Bolasky, Devyn, UC Riverside	.333	174	38	58	3	0	0	13	5
Woodward, Woody, UCSB	.330	188	34	62	10	2	1	34	7
Nesovic, Robby, UCSB	.326	187	28	61	9	0	4	33	1
Patterson, Steven, UC Davis	.324	204	31	66	12	0	2	33	1
Ellis, Jordan, Cal Poly	.323	161	20	52	7	6	0	18	3
Davis, J.D., CS Fullerton	.318	211	40	67	11	1	4	50	1
Chavez, Joe, UC Riverside	.313	198	43	62	17	6	2	30	17
Newell, Cameron, UCSB	.309	223	37	69	6	1	0	26	12
Taylor, Dominique, UC Irvine	.309	230	42	71	14	4	3	34	10
Wallach, Chad, CS Fullerton	.309	162	24	50	14	1	2	32	2
Lockwood, Erik, Pacific	.304	194	23	59	12	0	1	19	0
Prigatano, Richard, LBSU	.302	159	22	48	11	2	1	23	7
Patron, Ino, LBSU	.301	209	26	63	15	5	1	30	1
Shaeffer, Ronnie, UC Irvine	.300	220	31	66	11	0	3	35	2
Allen, Jimmy, Cal Poly	.299	241	29	72	12	2	1	39	6
Kuresa, Tyler, UCSB	.296	233	36	69	16	3	5	46	3
Swenson, Luke, UCSB	.295	183	35	54	8	1	9	23	11
Avila, Juan, LBSU	.292	168	29	49	9	0	2	28	0
Sullivan, Tyler, Pacific	.291	199	38	58	12	2	1	16	10
#Mundell, Brian, Cal Poly	.265	204	38	54	6	2	11	42	2

INDIVIDUAL PITCHING LEADERS
(Minimum 1 IP per team game)

	W	L	ERA	G	SV	IP	H	BB	SO
Eshelman, Thomas, CS Fullerton	12	3	1.48	17	0	116	86	3	83
Morales, Andrew, UC Irvine	10	0	1.89	17	0	95	78	21	85
#Lorenzen, Michael, CS Fullerton	3	0	1.99	22	19	23	17	4	20
Garza, Justin, CS Fullerton	12	0	2.03	17	0	115	84	17	95
Reilly, Reed, Cal Poly	2	4	2.29	32	14	59	55	20	69
Keel, Jerry, CS Northridge	7	3	2.59	17	0	94	90	21	69
Imhof, Matt, Cal Poly	7	3	2.74	16	0	102	95	30	95
Wagman, Joey, Cal Poly	13	3	2.96	16	0	112	106	29	103
Pettibone, Austin, UCSB	10	3	2.98	16	0	118	120	20	61
Cooper, Matt, Hawaii	3	8	3.14	16	0	86	83	19	69
Thurman, Andrew, UC Irvine	6	4	3.23	14	0	100	85	19	91
Wiest, Grahamm, CS Fullerton	9	3	3.27	16	0	105	94	13	76
Whitehouse, Matt, UC Irvine	5	6	3.29	16	0	93	86	18	84
Stassi, Jake, LBSU	4	4	3.32	16	0	81	77	21	38
Salas, John, CS Northridge	4	6	3.49	21	0	80	76	12	52
Carle, Shane, LBSU	4	9	3.57	15	0	93	94	30	75
Jacome, Justin, UCSB	5	4	3.89	14	0	83	85	15	53
Copping, Calvin, CS Northridge	5	5	3.90	15	0	83	88	21	51
Hill, David, LBSU	4	2	4.05	17	1	67	69	31	31
MacDonald, Corey, Hawaii	7	6	4.08	14	0	99	102	25	57
Little, Connor, Hawaii	3	6	4.12	14	0	96	106	18	52
#Mahle, Greg, UCSB	7	5	4.28	32	2	61	71	19	47

COLONIAL ATHLETIC ASSOCIATION

	Conference		Overall	
	W	L	W	L
UNC Wilmington	18	8	38	23
William & Mary	17	10	39	24
Delaware	15	12	33	22
Old Dominion	15	12	30	24
Georgia State	14	13	35	21
*Towson	14	13	30	30
Northeastern	12	15	31	26
James Madison	11	15	25	30
Hofstra	11	16	26	27
George Mason	7	20	18	35

ALL-CONFERENCE TEAM: C—Matt Reistetter, Jr., Hofstra. **1B**—Jimmy Yezzo, Jr., Delaware. **2B**—Michael Bass, Sr., UNC Wilmington. **SS**—Chad Prain, Jr., Georgia State. **3B**—Ryan LaGrange, Jr., UNC Wilmington. **OF**—Chad Carroll, So., James Madison; Nick Ferdinand, Sr., Delaware; Ben Verlander, Jr., Old Dominion. **DH**—Kurt Wertz, Jr., Towson. **UT**—Anthony Montefusco, Jr., George Mason. **SP**—Mat Batts, Jr., UNC Wilmington; John Farrell, Sr., William & Mary. **RP**—Kelly Secrest, Jr., UNC Wilmington. **Player of the Year:** Jimmy Yezzo, Delaware. **Pitcher of the Year:** Mat Batts, UNC Wilmington. **Defensive Player of the Year:** Andrew Parker, Towson. **Rookie of the Year:** Josh Merrigan, George Mason. **Coaches of the Year:** Jamie Pinzino, William & Mary; Mark Scalf, UNC Wilmington.

INDIVIDUAL BATTING LEADERS
(Minimum 125 at-bats)

	AVG	AB	R	H	2B	3B	HR	RBI	SB
Yezzo, Jimmy, Delaware	.410	234	52	96	28	2	13	64	1
Prain, Chad, Georgia State	.394	226	40	89	16	1	4	48	15
Carroll, Chad, JMU	.389	193	50	75	14	8	3	55	21
Roberts, Colby, JMU	.386	132	33	51	11	3	5	37	5
Raffield, Chase, Georgia State	.382	186	42	71	19	0	10	51	4
Bass, Michael, UNCW	.380	216	62	82	21	3	4	36	26
LaGrange, Ryan, UNCW	.370	211	41	78	14	1	5	38	3
Verlander, Ben, ODU	.367	196	46	72	12	4	11	37	13
McInturff, Cole, JMU	.363	179	36	65	7	3	1	41	11
Ferdinand, Nick, Delaware	.362	210	48	76	16	4	15	61	2
Katz, Michael, William & Mary	.358	212	49	76	23	1	5	47	3
Merrigan, Josh, Georgia State	.353	238	52	84	15	5	4	36	12
Bailey, Caden, Georgia State	.353	204	40	72	9	2	1	33	8
Lindemuth, Ryan, William & Mary	.351	251	61	88	13	2	4	49	3
Fratantuono, Dominic, Towson	.342	231	48	79	17	5	8	53	15
Brown, Conner, JMU	.341	179	44	61	12	3	9	47	3
Goss, Casey, JMU	.340	188	36	64	9	1	2	43	4
McFarland, Ty, JMU	.339	218	65	74	12	1	4	42	2
Dunlap, Luke, UNCW	.338	219	51	74	15	1	6	46	0
Wertz, Kurt, Towson	.338	222	43	75	14	7	13	65	8
Tobin, Tucker, GMU	.335	188	32	63	15	2	8	37	6
Bowles, Peter, Towson	.335	194	39	65	16	1	8	50	4
Fernandez, Blaise, GMU	.330	209	27	69	18	2	2	26	3
Reistetter, Matt, Hofstra	.326	178	25	58	10	1	2	34	6
Brown, Ryan, William & Mary	.322	236	63	76	12	1	2	30	21
Bladel, Johnny, JMU	.319	207	60	66	13	1	2	26	10
Fisher, Sam, JMU	.318	242	48	77	11	1	3	40	15
Triplett, Chris, Georgia State	.313	182	41	57	12	1	6	29	2
Slaton, Ben, ODU	.312	138	20	43	14	1	3	35	0
Hogan, Mark, Georgia State	.309	152	36	47	10	1	2	26	3
#Barbosa, Aaron, Northeastern	.307	231	47	71	7	4	0	17	26

INDIVIDUAL PITCHING LEADERS
(Minimum 50 IP)

	W	L	ERA	G	SV	IP	H	BB	SO
Ramsey, Jordan, UNCW	6	6	2.34	17	0	104	91	30	83
Schreiber, Brett, Hofstra	3	3	2.48	28	6	54	49	12	47
Ferguson, Kevin, Northeastern	7	4	2.59	14	0	104	90	28	93
Farrell, John, William & Mary	11	3	2.70	17	0	117	118	16	92
Roberts, Andy, ODU	5	3	2.92	14	0	74	59	22	37
Ali, Dean, ODU	4	3	3.02	16	0	80	72	30	65
Fessler, Andrew, Georgia State	6	2	3.04	13	0	77	61	33	51
Yarbrough, Ryan, ODU	4	4	3.27	17	1	83	78	25	60

COLLEGE

	W	L	ERA	G	SV	IP	H	BB	SO
Gatto, Dan, Delaware	4	3	3.36	18	0	67	66	20	47
Inghram, Jason, William & Mary	9	6	3.36	16	0	104	96	24	99
Batts, Mat, UNCW	9	4	3.47	16	0	112	100	27	**114**
Berger, Nick, Northeastern	6	6	3.56	14	0	94	93	29	53
Secrest, Kelly, UNCW	3	1	3.57	31	8	53	49	16	53
Volpe, Mike, Towson	10	3	3.59	16	0	103	108	35	78
Soren, Matt, Delaware	4	5	3.62	15	1	75	65	34	81
Kuhl, Chad, Delaware	10	2	3.75	15	0	106	107	31	76
Cook, Matt, Northeastern	4	5	3.83	20	0	52	43	30	35
MacDonald, Christian, UNCW	5	1	3.86	22	0	70	67	24	29
Davis, Adam, Delaware	5	7	3.99	15	0	97	114	15	74
Koehler, Brett, William & Mary	7	5	4.08	17	0	110	142	12	70
#Wainman, Matt, William & Mary	4	4	4.21	26	9	66	65	26	61
#Lane, Jack, UNCW	2	2	6.65	31	0	22	20	9	16

CONFERENCE USA

	Conference		Overall	
	W	L	W	L
*Rice	15	9	44	20
Southern Mississippi	15	9	30	27
Memphis	14	10	35	24
East Carolina	14	10	31	26
Houston	13	11	36	22
Central Florida	13	11	29	30
Tulane	11	13	30	28
Alabama-Birmingham	7	17	23	36
Marshall	6	18	20	34

ALL-CONFERENCE TEAM: C—Chase Fowler, Sr., Southern Miss. **IF**—John Frost, Sr., UAB; Chase McDonald, Jr., East Carolina; Isaac Rodriguez, Sr., Southern Miss.; Chris Taladay, Sr., Central Florida. **OF**—Isaac Ballou, Sr., Marshall; Erik Hempe, Sr., Central Florida; Michael Ratterree, Sr., Rice. **DH/UT**—Drew Reynolds, Jr., East Carolina. **P**—Aaron Blair, Jr., Marshall; Sam Moll, Jr., Memphis; Andrew Pierce, Sr., Southern Miss.; Erik Schoenrock, Jr., Memphis. **RP**—Zech Lemond, So., Rice. **Player of the Year:** Chris Taladay, Central Florida. **Pitcher of the Year:** Erik Schoenrock, Memphis. **Freshman of the Year:** Justin Montemayor, Houston. **Newcomer of the Year:** Frankie Ratcliff, Houston. **Coach of the Year:** Daron Schoenrock, Memphis.

INDIVIDUAL BATTING LEADERS
(Minimum 150 at-bats)

	AVG	AB	R	H	2B	3B	HR	RBI	SB
Rodriguez, Isaac, S. Miss.	.348	201	37	70	15	0	2	30	3
Taladay, Chris, UCF	.342	228	38	78	14	1	3	43	6
Prinzing, Ryan, UAB	.335	203	38	68	11	2	3	32	1
Frost, John, UAB	.329	225	27	74	**19**	2	2	39	11
Montemayor, Justin, Houston	.329	222	42	73	10	2	3	27	3
Ballou, Isaac, Marshall	.328	201	40	66	17	2	0	18	13
Tubbs, Tucker, Memphis	.327	214	34	70	7	1	4	32	2
White, Carter, Memphis	.325	166	27	54	6	0	0	15	2
Day, Dillon, S. Miss.	.324	176	29	57	12	0	1	18	12
Fowler, Chase, S. Miss.	.323	186	27	60	9	3	1	30	4
Reynolds, Drew, E. Carolina	.322	211	30	68	13	0	0	22	5
Hempe, Erik, UCF	.320	222	41	71	17	1	8	38	6
Houchins, Zach, E. Carolina	.317	189	34	60	18	2	5	42	3
Robbins, Mason, S. Miss.	.317	224	31	71	10	2	2	40	2
Aquino, Michael, Rice	.315	248	45	78	13	4	9	43	2
Stringer, Christian, Rice	.308	247	**50**	76	15	4	4	31	3
Willis, Michael, Memphis	.305	223	36	68	11	1	1	24	8
Griffin, Drew, Memphis	.304	207	29	63	13	0	2	36	11
Bass, Bryan, E. Carolina	.302	235	36	71	4	0	1	15	7
Ratcliff, Frankie, Houston	.300	210	38	63	13	**8**	2	44	11
McDonald, Chase, E. Carolina	.299	187	24	56	8	0	**11**	**46**	0
Survance, Kyle, Houston	.299	167	36	50	4	2	0	20	**20**
Dundon, Andrew, Marshall	.298	198	19	59	7	0	0	16	11
Middleton, Brennan, Tulane	.295	220	35	65	8	1	0	13	9
Stainback, Ford, Rice	.295	275	37	**81**	9	0	0	25	6
Cook, Keenan, Rice	.292	233	38	68	9	3	0	32	5
Bryant, Tanner, UAB	.283	173	19	49	7	1	0	19	2
Garner, Andrew, Tulane	.283	205	27	58	17	1	2	35	4
Byrd, Leon, Rice	.275	233	36	64	9	1	1	21	9
Gomez, Nathan, Marshall	.275	193	18	53	8	1	2	24	0

INDIVIDUAL PITCHING LEADERS
(Minimum 1 IP per team game)

	W	L	ERA	G	SV	IP	H	BB	SO
Lemond, Zech, Rice	7	2	**2.02**	32	**14**	76	56	21	71
Lively, Ben, UCF	7	5	2.04	15	0	106	88	28	101
Kubitza, Austin, Rice	8	4	2.06	18	0	109	71	48	**134**
Rizzotti, Tony, Tulane	5	4	2.22	12	0	81	71	23	57
Moll, Sam, Memphis	9	3	2.30	15	0	94	66	32	106
Stephens, Jordan, Rice	8	4	2.43	21	1	**119**	91	31	100
Lucroy, David, E. Carolina	4	2	2.49	15	0	72	49	42	82
Simms, Brian, Rice	8	5	2.51	24	1	111	85	37	98
Pierce, Andrew, S. Miss.	9	2	2.57	16	0	112	93	26	98
Pruitt, Austin, Houston	**10**	5	2.85	15	0	114	105	24	92
Blair, Aaron, Marshall	5	5	2.85	13	0	82	59	36	84
Byo, Alex, Tulane	6	4	2.91	14	0	99	102	27	49
#Reynolds, Drew, E. Carolina	3	2	2.92	28	1	41	40	35	19
Napoli, David, Tulane	5	3	3.00	15	0	66	39	33	51
Schoenrock, Eric, Memphis	7	4	3.02	15	0	98	82	28	86
Gunn, Alex, Memphis	3	4	3.11	15	0	64	62	17	42
Hoffman, Jeff, E. Carolina	6	7	3.20	15	0	110	99	39	84
Fisk, Conor, S. Miss.	4	3	3.23	12	0	70	67	26	50
Lemoine, Jake, Houston	7	4	3.49	18	0	70	71	33	45
Drehoff, Jake, S. Miss.	5	5	3.54	15	0	81	86	30	69
Garza, Aaron, Houston	5	5	3.88	13	0	67	77	18	43

GREAT WEST CONFERENCE

	Conference		Overall	
	W	L	W	L
Northern Colorado	20	7	33	24
Houston Baptist	17	10	34	24
Texas-Pan American	17	10	28	30
Utah Valley	15	9	24	30
North Dakota	13	11	25	22
New Jersey Tech	11	16	20	34
New York Tech	8	20	10	47
Chicago State	5	23	10	45

ALL-CONFERENCE TEAM: C—Taylor Petersen, Jr., North Dakota. **1B**—Colby Harrison, Jr., N. Colorado. **2B**—Ali Rodriguez, Sr., New York Tech. **SS**—Kai Hatch, Sr., Utah Valley. **3B**—Mattingly Romanin, So., Chicago State. **OF**—Luke Clements, Sr., Houston Baptist; Jake Gonzalez, Sr., Houston Baptist; Jensen Park, So., N. Colorado. **DH**—Stephan Halibej, Fr., New Jersey Tech. **UT**—Alberto Morales, Jr., Texas-Pan American. **SP**—Mark Leiter, Jr., Sr., New Jersey Tech; Ryan Lower, Jr., Houston Baptist; Sam Street, Jr., Texas-Pan American. **RP**—Kevin Willman, Sr., N. Colorado. **Player of the Year:** Jensen Park, N. Colorado. **Pitcher of the Year:** Sam Street, Texas-Pan American. **Newcomer of the Year:** Sam Street, Texas-Pan American. **Coach of the Year:** Carl Iwasaki, N. Colorado.

INDIVIDUAL BATTING LEADERS
(Minimum 125 at-bats)

	AVG	AB	R	H	2B	3B	HR	RBI	SB
Park, Jensen, N. Colorado	**.397**	209	44	**83**	13	2	4	34	7
Miller, Nick, N. Colorado	.375	200	47	75	**18**	5	6	**61**	2
Harrison, Colby, N. Colorado	.365	181	32	66	9	3	1	31	5
Bouck, Tom, NJIT	.359	128	23	46	10	1	2	24	0
Ammon, Shane, UTPA	.353	136	32	48	9	1	0	24	9
Clements, Luke, HBU	.341	214	**55**	73	11	4	6	35	10
McCoy, Jordan, HBU	.330	206	46	68	13	1	0	26	4
Vandoorne, Patrick, N. Dakota	.328	131	22	43	6	0	0	12	8
Rodriguez, Ali, NYIT	.328	180	34	59	12	3	1	23	**24**
Krueger, Mark, Utah Valley	.323	192	31	62	17	1	2	26	4
Hatch, Kai, Utah Valley	.323	**217**	28	70	18	1	0	35	6
Gonzalez, Jake, HBU	.316	209	40	66	15	1	3	33	9
Howe, Alex, UTPA	.315	165	31	52	9	3	0	38	10
Chamberlain, Mike, HBU	.311	135	27	42	4	1	0	17	4
Trygstad, Zack, N. Dakota	.309	152	28	47	7	5	1	27	2
Ramsey, Stone, Utah Valley	.307	140	33	43	11	5	0	27	6
Threlkeld, Jacob, N. Dakota	.306	170	24	52	7	4	0	25	17
White, Riley, Utah Valley	.305	210	35	64	11	2	1	34	5
Goulding, Riley, UTPA	.304	204	37	62	9	1	2	29	4
Follis, Tyler, N. Dakota	.303	155	31	47	5	0	0	16	2
Yamane, Ryan, N. Colorado	.301	206	38	62	10	1	0	27	7

	AVG	AB	R	H	2B	3B	HR	RBI	SB
Klausing, Will, UTPA	.299	157	28	47	8	0	1	20	2
Klemcke, Shane, UTPA	.297	182	34	54	6	4	0	25	5
Petersen, Taylor, N. Dakota	.295	149	38	44	11	0	4	31	4
Charlton, Ed, NJIT	.294	180	28	53	8	4	3	24	16
Hagy, Derek, UTPA	.291	196	29	57	5	0	1	30	5
Kwak, Kris, N. Dakota	.285	137	25	39	6	0	1	23	9
Moraies, Alberto, UTPA	.284	162	30	46	13	1	8	33	2
Romain, Mattingly, Chicago State	.284	162	21	46	9	2	1	32	12
Canabal, Joshua, NYIT	.282	170	15	48	6	2	0	21	9
#Jarvis, C.J., HBU	.259	212	34	55	9	6	1	34	11

INDIVIDUAL PITCHING LEADERS
(Minimum 50 IP)

	W	L	ERA	G	SV	IP	H	BB	SO
#Willman, Kevin, N. Colorado	4	3	2.27	24	10	44	39	18	24
Twenge, Alex, N. Dakota	7	1	2.52	11	0	64	54	16	37
Lower, Ryan, HBU	8	4	2.69	14	9	87	77	35	57
Street, Sam, UTPA	10	3	2.73	17	0	115	91	28	104
Badura, Dylan, UTPA	3	7	3.52	15	0	79	84	21	48
Nelson, Devin, Utah Valley	4	5	3.55	17	0	79	79	17	61
Tinnon, Josh, North Colorado	6	3	3.55	16	1	79	78	26	48
Knight, Dusten, UTPA	5	4	3.58	15	0	78	68	39	96
Kennell, Ross, HBU	7	4	3.73	15	0	82	86	20	43
Hoeschler, Tyler, HBU	8	5	3.89	14	0	90	97	34	41
Thome, Andrew, N. Dakota	5	5	4.14	12	0	78	76	26	57
Wellwerts, Andrew, Chicago State	4	10	4.28	17	0	90	97	38	65
Coughlin, Matt, NJIT	4	6	4.33	15	0	71	95	32	35
Miller, Nick, N. Colorado	6	4	4.58	13	0	71	83	26	50
Davis, Tripp, NJIT	5	7	4.72	15	0	97	113	28	87
Hammerly, Brandon, HBU	2	5	4.74	12	0	63	57	37	40
Tucker, James, Chicago State	3	6	4.89	20	0	81	91	40	19
Gunn, Adam, Utah Valley	5	4	4.92	15	0	82	82	29	58
Leiter, Mark, NJIT	5	9	4.94	15	0	95	92	42	106
Bulva, James, NYIT	1	8	4.98	11	0	60	57	41	44
Sterett, Dylan, Chicago State	1	11	5.12	14	0	90	101	46	49
#Silva, Jerry, Chicago State	0	3	6.03	27	1	60	75	18	27

HORIZON LEAGUE

	Conference		Overall	
	W	L	W	L
Wisconsin-Milwaukee	14	7	29	21
* Valparaiso	13	11	32	28
Illinois-Chicago	13	11	27	28
Wright State	9	12	25	30
Youngstown State	8	16	14	43

ALL-CONFERENCE TEAM: C—Garret Gray, Sr., Wright State. 1B—Alex Grunenwald, Sr., Illinois-Chicago. 2B—Michael Porcaro, So., Wisconsin-Milwaukee. SS—Spencer Mahoney, So., Valparaiso. 3B—Drew Dosch, Jr., Youngstown State. OF—Kieston Greene, Jr., Wright State; Chris Manning, Jr., Valparaiso; Derek Peake, So., Wisconsin-Milwaukee. DH—Will Fadness, Sr., Wisconsin-Milwaukee. UT—Andrew Bain, Sr., Valparaiso. P—Jake Long, Sr., Wisconsin-Milwaukee; Tomas Michelson, So., Illinois-Chicago. Player of the Year: Michael Porcaro, Wisconsin-Milwaukee. Pitcher of the Year: Jake Long, Wisconsin-Milwaukee. Relief Pitcher of the Year: Karch Kowalczyk, Valparaiso. Newcomer of the Year: Mitch Ghelfi, Wisconsin-Milwaukee. Coach of the Year: Scott Doffek, Wisconsin-Milwaukee.

INDIVIDUAL BATTING LEADERS
(Minimum 125 at-bats)

	AVG	AB	R	H	2B	3B	HR	RBI	SB
Porcaro, Michael, Milwaukee	.364	187	41	68	14	4	1	43	8
Dosch, Drew, YSU	.338	201	40	68	15	3	3	30	3
Greene, Kieston, Wright State	.335	185	36	62	11	3	4	23	6
Vavra, Tanner, Valparaiso	.333	210	42	70	10	1	0	17	11
Gray, Garrett, Wright State	.328	204	34	67	13	3	4	30	12
Peake, Derek, Milwaukee	.327	165	35	54	2	3	0	17	16
Ghelfi, Mitch, Milwaukee	.322	146	18	47	11	1	3	18	6
Manning, Chris, Valparaiso	.320	203	38	65	10	2	3	32	12
Capasso, Jonathan, Milwaukee	.320	169	24	54	7	2	0	23	2
Dinello, Nick, YSU	.311	132	20	41	4	0	2	23	6
Fadness, Will, Milwaukee	.310	158	26	49	8	0	4	33	3
Boss, Ryan, UIC	.308	201	32	62	12	5	6	40	4

	AVG	AB	R	H	2B	3B	HR	RBI	SB
Fowler, Mark, Wright State	.308	182	31	56	8	2	1	32	11
Bain, Andrew, Valparaiso	.306	222	31	68	10	0	0	23	7
White, Josh, YSU	.303	165	18	50	8	0	0	26	3
Detmer, Tyler, UIC	.295	200	26	59	16	1	0	28	3
Loeffler, John, Valparaiso	.288	184	25	53	5	1	2	38	2
Solberg, Ryan, Milwaukee	.288	153	29	44	8	0	4	24	5
Picchiotti, Sam, Wright State	.287	136	18	39	8	1	2	19	2
Koenig, Sam, Milwaukee	.286	133	28	38	11	1	2	24	5
Meeteer, Luke, Milwaukee	.285	179	37	51	5	1	2	27	18
Kopale, Justin, Wright State	.280	168	22	47	5	2	1	28	3
Schroth, Neil, YSU	.278	133	30	37	9	1	1	13	4
Cribbs, Billy, Valparaiso	.276	152	12	42	5	0	0	20	0
Coen, John, UIC	.271	181	40	49	5	2	1	26	14
De LaRosa, Alex, UIC	.270	174	18	47	6	1	0	17	5
Lipari, Phil, YSU	.263	194	23	51	12	1	0	27	9
Mahoney, Spencer, Valparaiso	.261	180	34	47	6	3	0	18	7
Jurich, Alex, UIC	.256	133	22	34	5	3	0	9	5
Betcher, Joe, UIC	.255	196	32	50	7	3	2	22	7
#Grunenwald, Alex, UIC	.243	202	31	49	12	2	8	44	1
#Shober, Ryan, UIC	.236	174	21	41	10	0	1	18	19

INDIVIDUAL PITCHING LEADERS
(Mimimum 50 IP)

	W	L	ERA	G	SV	IP	H	BB	SO
#Kowalczyk, Karch, Valparaiso	1	0	0.36	22	12	25	12	7	17
Long, Jake, Milwaukee	8	3	1.73	13	0	83	72	27	46
McKinley, Mike, UIC	3	3	2.89	16	1	53	38	21	30
Michelson, Tomas, UIC	6	6	3.08	15	0	102	102	26	65
Lewandowski, Ian, UIC	5	3	3.26	21	2	77	76	35	39
Henn, Casey, Wright State	4	8	3.57	15	0	91	88	23	81
Webb, Cole, Valparaiso	5	7	3.59	14	0	90	95	25	54
Schneider, Mike, Milwaukee	8	3	3.64	16	0	72	64	50	55
Lundeen, Dalton, Valparaiso	5	1	3.90	12	0	65	68	17	45
Wormington, Kyle, Valparaiso	5	7	4.00	17	1	72	97	14	47
Tassi, Cale, Milwaukee	5	6	4.11	14	0	70	71	41	53
Begel, Joey, UIC	2	7	4.46	17	2	75	81	20	40
DeBoo, Chris, Valparaiso	5	7	4.52	15	0	94	108	16	38
Hoelzel, Joey, Milwaukee	5	5	4.62	17	1	74	65	45	54
#Kopilchack, Cody, Wright State	2	1	4.82	31	0	47	30	37	65
O'Brien, Patrick, YSU	3	8	4.85	15	0	91	108	18	51
Andersen, Jack, UIC	4	5	5.09	20	3	53	68	16	25
Aquadro, Blake, YSU	3	10	5.42	15	0	81	103	29	27
Braun, Taylor, Wright State	0	5	6.63	16	1	54	76	23	31

IVY LEAGUE

	Conference		Overall	
GEHRIG	W	L	W	L
Dartmouth	15	5	32	9
Yale	10	10	13	25
Harvard	7	13	10	31
Brown	3	17	7	33

ROLFE	W	L	W	L
* Columbia	16	4	28	21
Cornell	11	9	23	17
Princeton	11	9	14	28
Pennsylvania	7	13	22	21

ALL-CONFERENCE TEAM: C—Matt MacDowell, So., Dartmouth; Chris Piwinski, Sr., Yale. 1B—Mike Ford, Jr., Princeton. 2B—Matt Parisi, So., Dartmouth. SS—Aaron Silbar, Jr., Columbia. 3B—Nick Lombardi, So., Dartmouth. OF—Ennis Coble, Sr., Dartmouth; Ryan Deitrich, Sr., Penn.; Jeff Keller, Jr., Dartmouth; Alec Keller, Jr., Princeton; Jordan Serena, So., Columbia. DH—Joe Purritano, Fr., Dartmouth. UT—Rick Brebner, Jr., Penn. P—Mike Ford, Jr., Princeton; Michael Johnson, Sr., Dartmouth; David Speer, Jr., Columbia. RP—Thomas Olson, So., Dartmouth. Player/Pitcher of the Year: Mike Ford, Princeton. Rookie of the Year: Joe Purritano, Fr., Dartmouth.

INDIVIDUAL BATTING LEADERS
(Minimum 2.5 at-bats per team game)

	AVG	AB	R	H	2B	3B	HR	RBI	SB
Deitrich, Ryan, Penn.	.382	144	31	55	8	3	4	23	11
Keller, Alec, Princeton	.378	143	32	54	9	1	4	17	6

COLLEGE

	AVG	AB	R	H	2B	3B	HR	RBI	SB
Keller, Jeff, Dartmouth	.369	141	**39**	52	**21**	4	6	**41**	8
Black, Alex, Columbia	.331	166	32	**55**	8	0	**8**	31	4
Parisi, Matt, Dartmouth	.329	167	31	**55**	12	1	1	15	3
Coble, Ennis, Dartmouth	.325	151	33	49	12	1	2	22	11
Marcal, Will, Brown	.324	145	20	47	9	2	3	22	3
Vilardo, Michael, Penn.	.320	172	25	**55**	19	1	2	31	7
Ford, Mike, Princeton	.320	147	25	47	9	0	6	38	4
Branigan, Spencer, Penn.	.308	143	21	44	14	0	0	19	0
Hoy, Danny, Princeton	.307	150	26	46	14	1	2	21	12
Silbar, Aaron, Columbia	.309	170	22	52	11	0	0	22	8
Massey, Daniel, Brown	.303	119	10	36	4	0	4	15	1
MacDowell, Matt, Dartmouth	.301	113	13	34	6	2	2	26	0
Whetsel, J.D., Cornell	.300	140	27	42	11	0	1	12	19
Kregel, Brandon, Harvard	.294	153	23	45	13	2	2	20	1
Lombardi, Nick, Dartmouth	.294	143	26	42	12	1	4	39	0
Lawson, Brent, Yale	.290	124	17	36	7	0	0	13	1
Hsieh, Eric, Yale	.289	121	17	35	2	0	0	5	3
Selzer, Dustin, Dartmouth	.283	138	26	39	10	0	3	25	0
Martin, Mike, Harvard	.279	111	21	31	9	3	0	6	7
Serena, Jordan, Columbia	.278	**176**	39	49	16	1	1	13	**27**
Ferraresi, Nick, Columbia	.278	**176**	23	49	9	0	3	26	10
Bossart, Austin, Penn.	.278	144	25	40	8	**4**	3	25	9
Anderson, Tanner, Harvard	.274	113	10	31	7	0	1	17	1
Hall, Matt, Cornell	.271	118	12	32	8	0	0	16	1
Piwinski, Chris, Yale	.267	101	8	27	2	0	0	9	4
Peters, Breton, Cornell	.267	120	14	32	6	2	0	6	5
Crucet, Nick, Columbia	.265	155	21	41	5	0	0	25	20
Bailey, Carlton, Harvard	.264	125	13	33	2	0	0	12	2
#Vandercook, David, Columbia	.199	146	23	29	5	**4**	2	17	4

INDIVIDUAL PITCHING LEADERS
(Minimum 1 IP per team game)

	W	L	ERA	G	SV	IP	H	BB	SO
Ford, Mike, Princeton	6	0	**0.98**	9	0	64	44	13	32
McCulley, Zach, Cornell	4	2	1.70	11	1	42	38	8	30
Johnson, Michael, Dartmouth	**7**	0	1.82	9	0	59	43	13	47
#Beasley, John, Penn.	1	2	1.99	**17**	1	32	25	12	26
Hunter, Kyle, Dartmouth	4	1	1.83	9	0	54	45	17	52
Hickey, David, Yale	4	2	2.15	10	1	38	38	9	35
Gauteri, Dan, Penn.	5	3	2.17	9	0	58	55	12	42
Horacek, Mitch, Dartmouth	6	2	2.20	8	0	45	40	10	42
McAfee, Brian, Cornell	3	2	2.28	9	0	55	46	8	32
Speer, David, Columbia	6	3	2.34	11	0	73	60	16	**66**
Hermans, Zak, Princeton	3	4	2.40	9	0	56	44	12	55
Sulser, Cole, Dartmouth	3	3	2.52	9	0	54	46	14	56
Donino, Joey, Columbia	**7**	0	2.86	13	1	57	47	19	69
Mingo, Cameron, Princeton	1	4	2.92	10	0	49	56	15	33
Moates, Chris, Yale	1	4	2.98	13	1	42	46	7	29
Coleman, Michael, Yale	3	4	3.13	10	0	55	56	13	18
Giel, Tim, Columbia	3	3	3.20	11	0	65	68	13	51
Cerfolio, Rob, Yale	1	5	3.31	10	0	49	54	8	29
Busto, Nick, Cornell	5	2	3.34	9	0	57	53	19	34
Carlow, Kevin, Brown	0	7	4.02	10	0	56	46	27	55
Cuff, Connor, Penn.	5	3	4.38	9	0	51	62	17	43
#Glenn, Ronnie, Penn.	1	1	4.42	15	**8**	18	18	9	24

METRO ATLANTIC ATHLETIC CONFERENCE

	Conference		Overall	
	W	L	W	L
Rider	18	6	35	22
Marist	17	7	27	24
*Canisius	15	9	42	17
Siena	15	9	27	30
Manhattan	11	13	24	28
Fairfield	11	13	20	29
St. Peter's	9	15	17	34
Niagara	9	15	16	38
Iona	3	21	8	43

ALL-CONFERENCE TEAM: C—Ramon Ortega, Sr., Manhattan. **1B**—Jimmy Luppens, Jr., Canisius. **2B**—Nick Camastro, Sr., Manhattan. **SS**—Zach Shank, Sr., Marist. **3B**—Adam Wayman, Sr., Rider. **OF**—Mike Fish, Sr., Siena; Jesse Kelso, Jr., Canisius; Ryan Plourde, Jr., Fairfield. **DH**—

Jerry Mulderig, Jr., Rider. **UT**—Matt Kriss, Sr., Iona. **P**—Garrett Cortright, Jr., Canisius; Matt Gage, So., Siena; Kurt Sowa, So., Rider. **Player of the Year:** Mike Fish, Siena. **Pitcher of the Year:** Kurt Sowa, Rider. **Relief Pitcher of the Year:** Jon Fitzsimmons, Canisius; Kevin McCarthy, Marist. **Rookie of the Year:** Alex Godzak, Canisius. **Coach of the Year:** Barry Davis, Rider.

INDIVIDUAL BATTING LEADERS
(Minimum 125 at-bats)

	AVG	AB	R	H	2B	3B	HR	RBI	SB
Shank, Zach, Marist	**.370**	211	50	78	14	4	3	37	6
Luppens, Jimmy, Canisius	.368	193	40	71	10	1	5	47	4
Fish, Mike, Siena	.364	**231**	55	**84**	17	1	**12**	51	14
Plourde, Ryan, Fairfield	.354	175	37	62	8	4	3	36	15
Orefice, Mike, Marist	.338	195	32	66	**18**	0	2	**52**	1
Pagano, Matt, Marist	.337	172	40	58	7	**5**	1	26	5
Mulderig, Jerry, Rider	.328	192	26	63	9	1	2	31	16
McCauley, Ryan, Niagara	.328	180	37	59	15	1	5	31	3
Panas, Connor, Canisius	.321	162	39	52	6	3	1	18	6
Ortega, Ramon, Manhattan	.320	169	27	54	10	2	4	33	2
McQuail, Nick, Marist	.319	182	34	58	8	0	1	32	4
Giannini, Jack, Fairfield	.317	186	25	59	5	1	0	27	10
Wayman, Adam, Rider	.313	217	37	68	12	0	2	34	9
Hajjar, Anthony, Fairfield	.304	184	37	56	15	0	2	37	5
Kelso, Jesse, Canisius	.299	177	44	52	9	4	4	38	12
Mancini, Matt, St. Peter's	.298	181	28	54	3	0	0	9	13
LoPinto, Rob, Fairfield	.292	192	34	56	7	2	1	21	5
Allen, Mike, Siena	.290	193	28	56	14	2	3	39	6
Crecenzo, Nick, Rider	.290	200	35	58	8	4	1	36	20
Fay, Brian, Siena	.289	197	27	57	13	1	3	37	0
Kriss, Matthew, Iona	.287	188	15	54	7	1	0	20	6
Smith, James, St. Peter's	.285	130	21	37	10	0	1	25	1
Rooney, John, Siena	.284	208	39	59	9	0	0	24	11
Citro, Vincent, Siena	.282	209	43	59	9	1	1	17	14
Henriquez, Nicholas, St. Peter's	.282	163	22	46	4	0	0	19	4
Parsons, Mike, Rider	.282	195	40	55	12	0	0	25	14
Rodrigues, Thomas, Niagara	.282	181	31	51	7	0	0	18	5
Speckmann, Matt, St. Peter's	.279	194	34	50	7	2	1	32	11
Camastro, Nick, Manhattan	.279	190	29	53	11	0	1	13	15
Thomas, Eric, Rider	.276	210	35	58	12	0	1	24	4
#Torres, Joe, Iona	.263	190	30	50	3	0	2	11	**26**

INDIVIDUAL PITCHING LEADERS
(Minimum 50 IP)

	W	L	ERA	G	SV	IP	H	BB	SO
#Fitzsimmons, Jon, Canisius	4	0	1.19	20	**10**	30	15	18	36
Cortright, Garrett, Canisius	**11**	3	2.24	15	0	**109**	83	25	72
Vrana, Rich, Marist	5	1	2.87	14	0	60	51	24	40
Smith, Tyler, Rider	7	5	3.10	14	0	93	91	24	82
Godzak, Alex, Canisius	8	3	3.22	15	0	78	65	26	66
Ashworth, E.J., Fairfield	3	4	3.33	12	0	76	79	13	32
Wallace, Mike, Fairfield	6	4	3.39	12	0	66	70	19	37
Sowa, Kurt, Rider	**11**	1	3.40	14	0	79	51	37	54
Gage, Matt, Siena	6	6	3.42	15	0	97	96	30	**88**
#Kuberiet, Sean, Rider	3	1	3.53	**27**	1	36	31	12	19
Bielak, Chris, Marist	7	3	3.59	13	0	83	78	33	64
Goossens, Bryan, Siena	1	5	3.64	15	0	64	82	9	18
Soldinger, John, Manhattan	4	3	3.69	15	1	85	71	39	53
Hopf, Zach, St. Peter's	2	10	3.70	13	0	90	94	23	64
Howell, Aaron, Fairfield	4	2	3.71	11	0	53	56	20	32
Lewicki, Ed, Siena	4	3	3.92	17	0	64	86	32	33
Murphy, Mike, Rider	4	4	4.06	14	1	78	84	22	45
McCarthy, Kevin, Marist	4	3	4.24	22	8	68	76	19	62
Houseal, Brett, Marist	7	7	4.36	15	0	95	108	24	49
Macaluso, Eddie, Iona	1	9	4.94	14	0	75	82	38	43
Stewart, Devon, Canisius	5	5	4.98	14	0	78	87	24	47
Pierce, Rohn, Canisius	3	1	5.12	15	0	58	67	19	45

464 · Baseball America 2014 Almanac   **BaseballAmerica**.com

MID-AMERICAN CONFERENCE

EAST	Conference		Overall	
	W	L	W	L
Kent State	20	7	36	23
Buffalo	19	7	33	24
Miami (Ohio)	14	13	26	30
* Bowling Green State	13	14	24	31
Akron	10	16	15	37
Ohio	9	18	14	39

WEST	W	L	W	L
Northern Illinois	16	11	22	34
Ball State	15	12	31	24
Toledo	13	14	25	33
Eastern Michigan	12	15	26	28
Central Michigan	12	15	25	32
Western Michigan	8	19	16	38

ALL-CONFERENCE TEAM: C—T.J. Losby, Jr., Bowling Green. **1B**—George Roberts, Sr., Kent State. **2B**—Alex Klonowski, Jr., N. Illinois. **SS**—Andrew Sohn, Jr., W. Michigan. **3B**—Billy Wellman, Sr., Ball State. **OF**—Ben Hammer, Sr., Toledo; Matt Honchel, So., Miami; Jason Kanzler, Sr., Buffalo. **SP**—Eli Anderson, Jr., N. Illinois; Scott Baker, So., Ball State; Ryan Wilkinson, Jr., Toledo; Taylor Williams, Jr., Kent State. **RP**—Brian Clark, So., Kent State. **DH**—Lee Longo, Jr., E. Michigan. **UT**—Mike Burke, Jr., Buffalo. **Player of the Year:** Jason Kanzler, Buffalo. **Pitcher of the Year:** Scott Baker, Ball State. **Freshman of the Year:** Jake Romano, Miami. **Coach of the Year:** Ron Torgalski, Buffalo.

INDIVIDUAL BATTING LEADERS
(Minimum 125 at-bats)

	AVG	AB	R	H	2B	3B	HR	RBI	SB
Roberts, George, Kent State	.358	165	33	59	14	2	2	41	10
Grogg, Tyler, Toledo	.357	207	62	74	7	1	1	20	36
Leichman, Cody, C. Michigan	.341	176	21	60	9	0	3	30	6
Honchel, Matt, Miami	.340	235	51	80	13	2	0	18	18
Sohn, Andrew, W. Michigan	.337	208	29	70	9	2	2	36	17
Hammer, Ben, Toledo	.333	195	28	65	12	1	4	48	6
Kanzler, Jason, Buffalo	.330	227	46	75	14	6	12	53	21
Shay, Jeremy, BGSU	.330	191	35	63	15	2	6	38	2
Godfrey, Sean, Ball State	.329	222	45	73	15	2	5	30	18
Losby, T.J., BGSU	.327	211	31	69	5	1	6	39	3
Ott, Sam, E. Michigan	.327	211	47	69	18	3	2	44	5
Madsen, Jake, Ohio	.326	221	26	72	18	0	2	37	6
Sonabend, Adam, E. Michigan	.325	200	35	65	12	0	2	38	3
Delewski, Matt, Toledo	.324	244	31	79	9	1	0	45	4
Buglione, Steve, W. Michigan	.323	161	17	52	3	0	0	17	4
Piccirilli, Theo, W. Michigan	.322	211	31	68	4	0	0	18	7
Regnier, Nick, C. Michigan	.321	221	44	71	12	2	5	38	21
Zimmerman, Jeff, N. Illinois	.321	218	24	70	17	3	0	30	5
Sedio, Chad, Miami	.318	148	30	47	7	3	0	22	6
Crummy, John, Miami	.317	180	30	57	11	1	2	31	0
Topps, Jim, Buffalo	.314	175	36	55	7	2	0	21	11
Polen, Sawyer, Kent State	.312	234	42	73	11	2	0	24	6
Wellman, Billy, Ball State	.310	197	25	61	12	0	4	36	3
Campbell, Evan, Kent State	.308	221	43	68	9	5	2	47	16
Smith, Anthony, Toledo	.304	171	25	52	10	1	0	22	1
Tansel, Deion, Toledo	.301	173	30	52	5	1	0	15	10
Bower, Kevin, Miami	.299	201	34	60	16	0	2	31	2
Hook, Tommy, N. Illinois	.298	171	28	51	8	2	0	22	3
Sutton, T.J., Kent State	.297	212	28	63	10	1	1	36	2
Toadvine, Derek, Kent State	.297	239	58	71	5	1	1	21	29
#Mautner, Tyler, Buffalo	.295	200	35	59	23	0	2	35	2
#Regnier, Logan, C. Michigan	.288	215	37	62	7	7	1	27	25
#Russell, Daniel, E. Michigan	.245	200	45	49	8	7	2	22	10

INDIVIDUAL PITCHING LEADERS
(Minimum 50 IP)

	W	L	ERA	G	SV	IP	H	BB	SO
McKenney, Ethan, BGSU	3	1	1.99	21	2	50	49	16	28
Hartz, Ben, Buffalo	6	1	2.01	18	1	40	35	11	19
Baker, Scott, Ball State	12	2	2.18	17	1	112	94	35	88
Anderson, Eli, N. Illinois	9	4	2.18	15	0	115	101	26	76
Williams, Taylor, Kent State	10	1	2.47	15	0	106	83	18	110

Bruns, Nick, BGSU	6	2	2.52	29	6	53	46	18	46
Burke, Mike, Buffalo	8	2	2.66	14	0	102	84	21	75
Wilkinson, Ryan, Toledo	7	3	2.82	16	0	112	109	14	53
Doodridge, Rick, C. Michigan	4	4	2.99	13	0	69	75	41	46
Cisna, Jon, Ball State	3	3	3.04	17	1	53	50	25	25
Foley, Jordan, C. Michigan	6	6	3.08	15	0	90	70	44	90
Beaver, Zach, Akron	3	2	3.09	25	0	44	48	10	20
Shaw, Kyle, Toledo	5	8	3.12	15	0	104	96	18	66
McWilliams, River, Buffalo	3	5	3.30	29	12	57	58	17	41
Skulina, Tyler, Kent State	6	4	3.36	15	0	94	74	34	102
Laudicina, Steve, W. Michigan	3	9	3.44	14	0	89	97	35	62
Jordan, Tyler, Ball State	2	7	3.54	32	3	48	49	20	31
Wilson, Casey, Kent State	8	5	3.61	15	0	95	95	26	50
McNamara, Jimmy, C. Michigan	1	3	3.67	18	1	56	69	17	39
Fiala, Brooks, Miami	6	6	3.71	15	0	102	108	22	93
#Cozart, Logan, Ohio	1	4	6.21	33	1	42	52	17	34

MID-EASTERN ATHLETIC CONFERENCE

NORTH	Conference		Overall	
	W	L	W	L
Delaware State	21	3	33	15
Norfolk State	12	12	19	29
Coppin State	11	13	18	33
Maryland-Eastern Shore	4	20	8	45

SOUTH	W	L	W	L
* Savannah State	17	7	33	23
Bethune-Cookman	17	7	34	25
North Carolina Central	12	12	27	29
North Carolina A&T	8	16	16	38
Florida A&M	6	18	7	47

ALL-CONFERENCE TEAM: C—Eddie Sorondo, Jr., Delaware State. **1B**—Kelvin Freeman, Sr., N.C. A&T. **2B**—J.P. Frey, Sr., Delaware State. **SS**—Luke Tendler, Jr., N.C. A&T. **3B**—Cameron Cecil, Jr., Delaware State. **OF**—Luis Diaz, Sr., N.C. Central; Josh Johnson, Jr., Bethune-Cookman; Aaron Nardone, Jr., Delaware State. **DH**—Mike Alexander, Jr., Delaware State. **P**—Montana Durupau, Jr., Bethune-Cookman; Kyle McGowin, Jr., Savannah State. **RP**—Jordan Dailey, Sr., Bethune-Cookman. **Player of the Year:** Kelvin Freeman, N.C. A&T. **Pitcher of the Year:** Kyle McGowin, Savannah State. **Rookie of the Year:** Mendez Elder, Savannah State. **Coach of the Year:** Carlton Hardy, Savannah State.

INDIVIDUAL BATTING LEADERS
(Minimum 2 at-bats per team game)

	AVG	AB	R	H	2B	3B	HR	RBI	SB
Gibbs, Marlon, Fla. A&M	.374	147	20	55	2	3	0	13	9
Tendler, Luke, N.C. A&T	.369	195	41	72	25	5	3	34	17
Alexander, Mike, Del. State	.367	169	43	62	6	1	0	43	36
Evans, Hassan, Del. State	.366	134	20	49	8	3	0	29	15
Frey, J.P., Del. State	.360	200	47	72	6	2	0	22	27
Cecil, Cameron, Del. State	.356	160	49	57	11	3	0	25	17
Nardone, Aaron, Del. State	.351	168	42	59	11	7	3	44	23
Freeman, Kelvin, N.C. A&T	.342	193	43	66	12	1	16	59	14
Robinson, Bennie, Fla. A&M	.328	180	17	59	6	0	1	29	2
Johnson, Josh, B-CU	.327	223	32	73	14	2	0	19	15
Hamlett, David, Coppin State	.321	137	17	44	8	4	1	35	10
Hagen, Todd, Savannah State	.321	209	40	67	13	1	0	26	16
Markel, Zach, Norfolk State	.320	175	25	56	11	0	2	35	2
Diaz, Luis, N.C. Central	.320	194	44	62	14	4	2	35	19
Day, Cameron, Norfolk State	.318	176	26	56	11	3	2	30	6
Kashangaki, Chris, Coppin State	.312	170	32	53	8	0	0	14	33
Bull, Stephen, UMES	.309	165	30	41	8	2	1	13	4
Kraft, Jack, Coppin State	.308	159	13	49	9	1	0	14	4
Richards, David, Savannah State	.308	117	22	36	7	5	2	18	3
Elder, Mendez, Savannah State	.306	144	23	44	7	2	1	23	10
Haas, Ryan, Del. State	.304	148	30	45	8	0	2	39	7
Onderko, Cameron, Del. St.	.298	131	29	39	6	1	0	21	5
Lee, Zack, N.C. Central	.295	176	31	52	5	3	0	14	11
McCrary, Joseph, Savannah State	.294	211	37	62	12	4	0	32	13
Jergens, Cameron, N.C. A&T	.294	194	15	57	10	0	2	35	4
Stokes, Anthony, B-CU	.293	164	23	48	12	1	5	34	0
Campbell, Byron, UMES	.291	179	31	52	15	2	1	21	13
Wilkerson, Brandon, N.C. A&T	.288	153	22	44	7	2	0	21	14

	AVG	AB	R	H	2B	3B	HR	RBI	SB
Nix, Parker, Savannah State	.284	201	35	57	13	1	0	29	18
Ellis, Cody, Norfolk State	.276	105	13	29	2	1	0	10	2

INDIVIDUAL PITCHING LEADERS
(Minimum 1 IP per team game)

	W	L	ERA	G	SV	IP	H	BB	SO
#Dailey, Jordan, B-CU	5	1	1.14	**34**	**11**	55	36	12	55
McGowin, Kyle, Savannah State	12	2	**2.02**	17	2	**120**	101	31	**134**
Gardner, Elliott, Del. State	5	1	2.47	14	1	58	56	28	46
Elliott, Jordan, Del. State	9	2	2.77	13	0	91	73	30	73
Durapau, Montana, B-CU	9	3	2.89	16	0	109	93	22	78
Michaels, George, Del. State	6	1	3.04	17	4	50	38	18	30
McClain, Matt, Del. State	6	2	3.06	12	0	65	66	7	50
Horne, Chris, Norfolk State	5	5	3.24	18	1	100	98	21	57
Quinn, Jordan, N.C. Central	5	3	3.56	12	0	73	81	24	37
Bhatti, Justin, Norfolk State	2	7	3.59	20	1	78	79	41	64
Moore, Brent, N.C. A&T	4	7	3.69	14	0	90	107	27	53
Frye, Glenn, N.C. Central	4	4	3.75	12	0	82	85	14	58
Taylor, Myles, Coppin State	2	8	3.77	11	0	57	45	44	29
Boone, Tyler, N.C. A&T	4	5	3.78	15	1	81	96	21	43
Ganus, Josh, N.C. A&T	3	8	3.81	14	0	85	102	25	41
Davies, Shane, Coppin State	5	6	4.15	13	0	65	71	20	25
May, Jackson, Savannah State	5	4	4.32	18	0	77	83	23	40
Grebenstein, Will, Coppin State	3	0	4.36	18	1	54	55	23	23
McNabb, Terry, N.C. Central	5	6	4.43	13	0	81	82	18	50
Garner, Scott, B-CU	6	5	4.62	14	0	76	72	32	51
Turley, Will, UMES	1	4	5.13	11	0	54	66	16	13

MISSOURI VALLEY CONFERENCE

	Conference		Overall	
	W	L	W	L
Illinois State	16	5	39	19
* Wichita State	15	6	39	28
Creighton	13	8	30	18
Missouri State	12	9	31	23
Evansville	10	10	24	34
Indiana State	9	11	26	25
Southern Illinois	6	15	25	33
Bradley	2	19	17	32

ALL-CONFERENCE TEAM: C—Mike Hollenbeck, Jr., Illinois State. **1B**—Kyle Stanton, Sr., Illinois State. **2B**—Eric Cheray, So., Missouri State. **SS**—Brett Kay, Sr., Illinois State. **3B**—Zac Johnson, Sr., Illinois State. **OF**—Eric Aguilera, Sr., Illinois State; Kevin Kaczmarski, So., Evansville; Mike Tauchman, Sr., Bradley. **DH**—Greg Partyka, Jr., Bradley. **UT**—Tyler Baker, So., Wichita State. **SP**—Nick Petree, Jr., Missouri State; Chris Razo, Sr., Illinois State; Dan Savas, So., Illinois State. **RP**—Brandon Peterson, Jr., Wichita State; Jeremy Rhoades, So., Illinois State. **Player of the Year:** Mike Tauchman, Bradley. **Pitcher of the Year:** Chris Razo, Illinois State. **Newcomer of the Year:** Brandon Peterson, Wichita State. **Freshman of the Year:** Tate Matheny, Missouri State. **Defensive Player of the Year:** Brett Kay, Illinois State. **Coach of the Year:** Mark Kingston, Illinois State.

INDIVIDUAL BATTING LEADERS
(Minimum 2.5 at-bats per team game)

	AVG	AB	R	H	2B	3B	HR	RBI	SB
Tauchman, Mike, Bradley	**.425**	186	52	79	16	5	2	41	28
Bayliff, Garrett, Wichita State	.379	240	44	**91**	9	1	0	38	11
Peter, Jake, Creighton	.350	203	33	71	10	5	1	35	8
Montgomery, Austin, SIU	.350	226	35	79	17	2	7	46	0
Aguilera, Eric, Illinois State	.346	231	38	80	14	3	7	**58**	4
Stanton, Kyle, Illinois State	.344	212	33	73	19	0	3	41	4
Kaczmarski, Kevin, Evansville	.339	236	48	80	15	3	6	31	15
Matheny, Tate, Missouri State	.336	229	40	77	14	1	4	26	4
Lamb, Kevin, Creighton	.331	121	16	40	4	1	1	25	1
Gerber, Mike, Creighton	.328	134	20	44	5	**6**	5	31	2
Baker, Tyler, Wichita State	.328	238	41	78	15	3	4	47	1
Castagnini, Federico, Creighton	.320	169	33	54	8	0	1	27	2
Welch, Jake, SIU	.317	**249**	51	79	10	1	1	22	20
Leffler, Tyler, Bradley	.311	151	31	47	12	0	0	24	4
Johnson, Dylan, Illinois State	.311	222	50	69	14	1	7	47	2
Jones, Matt, SIU	.310	232	35	72	15	1	4	42	1
Partyka, Greg, Bradley	.309	178	26	55	16	1	3	33	0
Ort, Robby, Indiana State	.308	208	35	64	9	**6**	5	44	10

	AVG	AB	R	H	2B	3B	HR	RBI	SB
McKewon, Brad, Creighton	.308	195	42	60	8	2	0	21	8
Hockemeyer, Jason, Evansville	.306	206	44	63	8	3	1	31	11
Dearman, Tanner, Wichita State	.301	176	30	53	4	1	0	23	12
Kay, Brett, Illinois State	.301	216	48	65	9	3	3	35	10
Gillaspie, Casey, Wichita State	.299	234	49	70	16	1	**11**	46	5
Voit, Luke, Missouri State	.299	211	28	63	14	0	2	30	8
Pearson, Chris, Evansville	.299	211	28	63	7	0	4	32	2
Hinshaw, Chad, Illinois State	.298	228	**54**	68	11	4	4	35	**33**
Hollenbeck, Miek, Illinois State	.296	186	32	55	6	0	1	26	1
Maddox, Keenen, Mo. State	.292	216	29	63	16	0	1	28	3
Casillas, Ryan, SIU	.291	199	25	58	8	0	2	30	1
Kraemer, Koby, Indiana State	.287	188	31	54	15	2	3	29	6

INDIVIDUAL PITCHING LEADERS
(Minimum 1 IP per team game)

	W	L	ERA	G	SV	IP	H	BB	SO
#Peterson, Brandon, Wichita State	3	1	1.12	26	**10**	40	27	15	42
Manaea, Sean, Indiana State	5	4	**1.47**	13	0	73	49	27	93
Petree, Nick, Missouri State	8	1	1.61	14	0	100	79	19	**111**
Savas, Dan, Illinois State	**10**	0	1.79	15	0	100	65	41	98
Razo, Chris, Illinois State	8	2	1.81	20	4	89	67	32	79
Lukowski, Mark, Creighton	4	2	2.22	25	1	49	38	13	18
Hall, Matt, Missouri State	5	3	2.50	19	0	54	37	23	53
Lloyd, Kyle, Evansville	7	4	2.68	14	0	94	76	34	99
Moore, Devin, Indiana State	5	4	2.90	14	0	81	69	28	63
Forsythe, Cody, SIU	4	5	3.03	15	0	**101**	85	22	67
Cheray, Eric, Missouri State	1	5	3.14	12	0	57	47	20	34
Elam, Cale, Wichita State	7	5	3.17	17	0	94	90	30	75
Stong, Brent, Bradley	4	3	3.60	15	1	50	46	25	42
Sorkin, Brad, Illinois State	8	4	3.77	15	0	91	95	34	44
Harris, Tyler, Missouri State	8	2	3.87	13	0	77	74	31	61
Strunc, Tommy, Creighton	7	3	4.14	14	0	72	50	44	55
Coonrod, Sam, SIU	3	6	4.29	15	0	80	79	49	68
Freeland, Kyle, Evansville	4	8	4.34	14	0	94	107	26	84
Ladwig, A.J., Wichita State	5	6	4.54	16	0	85	106	15	68
Isom, Cole, Evansville	4	6	4.57	14	0	69	79	25	48
Peterson, Daniel, Indiana State	1	5	4.61	15	0	53	68	10	43
#Winkleman, Mark, Creighton	6	0	4.70	**31**	1	54	61	19	31

MOUNTAIN WEST CONFERENCE

	Conference		Overall	
	W	L	W	L
New Mexico	25	5	37	22
Nevada-Las Vegas	18	12	37	20
* San Diego State	15	15	31	31
Fresno State	14	16	23	33
Nevada	11	19	25	32
Air Force	7	23	15	39

ALL-CONFERENCE TEAM: C—Mitch Garver, Sr., New Mexico. **1B**—Seth Kline, Jr., Air Force. **2B**—Tim Zier, Jr., San Diego State. **SS**—Alex Allbritton, Jr., New Mexico. **3B**—D.J. Peterson, Jr., New Mexico. **OF**—Brandon Bayard, Sr., UNLV; Aaron Judge, Jr., Fresno State; Josh Melendez, Sr., New Mexico. **DH/UT**—Buddy Borden, Jr., UNLV; Garrett Custons, Sr., Air Force. **P**—Braden Shipley, Jr., Nevada; Ryan Doran, Sr., San Diego State; Sam Wolff, Sr., New Mexico. **RP**—Gabe Auilar, Sr., New Mexico. **Players of the Year:** Mitch Garver, New Mexico; D.J. Peterson, New Mexico. **Pitchers of the Year:** Buddy Borden, UNLV; Braden Shipley, Nevada. **Freshmen of the Year:** Sam Haggerty, New Mexico; Blake Quinn, Fresno State. **Coach of the Year:** Ray Birmingham, New Mexico.

INDIVIDUAL BATTING LEADERS
(Minimum 125 at-bats)

	AVG	AB	R	H	2B	3B	HR	RBI	SB
Peterson, D.J., New Mexico	**.408**	218	68	89	25	4	**18**	**72**	5
Garver, Mitch, New Mexico	.390	246	55	**96**	21	5	6	68	12
Campbell, Luke, New Mexico	.385	200	49	77	15	3	7	49	8
Armstrong, Patrick, UNLV	.373	161	29	60	15	0	7	40	2
Judge, Aaron, Fresno State	.369	206	45	76	15	4	12	36	12
Kline, Seth, Air Force	.356	194	34	69	16	1	2	40	6
Custons, Garrett, Air Force	.353	215	48	76	22	3	1	25	14
Byler, Austin, Nevada	.346	182	35	63	10	3	8	40	3
Klein, Brooks, Nevada	.346	217	36	75	14	4	7	42	3
Zier, Tim, SDSU	.341	252	43	86	14	2	1	41	18

	AVG	AB	R	H	2B	3B	HR	RBI	SB
Bayardi, Brandon, UNLV	.341	232	45	79	13	3	11	50	8
White, T.J., UNLV	.335	212	55	71	11	2	1	36	12
Melendez, Josh, New Mexico	.329	225	47	74	15	5	3	41	13
Armstrong, Joey, UNLV	.324	219	42	71	8	3	0	33	10
Harris, Chase, New Mexico	.321	262	57	84	15	3	5	48	19
Real, Alex, New Mexico	.317	208	41	66	18	0	8	36	2
France, Tyler, SDSU	.317	218	28	69	14	0	5	36	1
Johnson, Peter, Air Force	.313	179	17	56	8	1	1	31	1
Allbritton, Alex, New Mexico	.312	205	27	64	10	2	2	39	3
Shannon, Mark, UNLV	.309	230	48	71	17	1	3	39	11
Baska, David, Air Force	.304	181	40	55	13	1	6	21	6
Romanski, Jake, SDSU	.303	228	38	69	9	1	3	33	6
Meyer, Kewby, Nevada	.302	182	28	55	11	1	2	18	2
VanMeetren, Erik, UNLV	.299	187	38	56	11	0	0	32	4
Allen, Greg, SDSU	.299	254	51	76	11	1	0	28	25
Swanner, Joey, UNLV	.299	221	42	66	17	2	0	33	5
Mariscal, Chris, Fresno State	.298	218	32	65	13	0	2	21	3
Munoz, Matt, SDSU	.298	161	24	48	9	0	2	23	6
Holley, Jared, New Mexico	.293	157	34	46	6	0	0	23	3
Thorne, Matt, Air Force	.290	145	18	42	13	0	1	17	6
#Haggerty, Sam, New Mexico	.280	225	58	63	9	5	1	32	4
#Brink, Jordan, Fresno State	.226	164	20	37	4	5	2	21	1

INDIVIDUAL PITCHING LEADERS
(Minimum 50 IP)

	W	L	ERA	G	SV	IP	H	BB	SO
Borden, Buddy, UNLV	8	2	2.59	15	0	101	88	35	77
Shipley, Braden, Nevada	7	3	2.77	15	0	107	84	34	102
Doran, Ryan, SDSU	8	4	2.82	17	0	112	117	27	86
Wolff, Sam, New Mexico	7	3	2.90	16	0	93	84	39	75
Quinn, Blake, Fresno State	3	3	3.02	14	0	51	42	18	34
Oakley, Kenny, UNLV	4	2	3.21	16	1	53	55	17	48
Robards, Mike, SDSU	4	1	3.58	19	0	55	56	22	37
Walker, Josh, New Mexico	11	1	3.66	29	7	79	76	22	55
#Derby, Bubba, SDSU	4	3	3.79	24	10	36	33	14	44
Walby, Philip, SDSU	5	3	3.82	17	0	94	87	51	57
Brink, Jordan, Fresno State	4	4	3.92	17	0	60	50	25	65
Fedde, Erick, UNLV	7	3	3.92	15	0	96	98	28	83
Borst, Tim, Fresno State	3	2	4.12	22	4	63	83	21	32
Cederoth, Michael, SDSU	3	9	4.25	15	0	95	72	48	109
Richy, John, UNLV	7	5	4.33	19	1	89	87	20	61
Wells, Tyler, Nevada	4	6	4.39	15	0	82	93	39	68
Velazquez, Derick, Fresno State	4	2	4.40	17	0	76	94	36	52
White, Cameron, Air Force	3	11	5.21	15	0	107	149	9	70
Munro, William, Fresno State	2	4	5.23	17	0	53	59	34	28
Baker, Alex, Air Force	4	3	5.44	15	0	51	69	16	46
Linehan, Tyler, Fresno State	3	7	5.90	19	1	50	72	28	47
#Hourin, Jack, Air Force	0	4	8.23	31	1	43	61	19	25
#McClain, Hobie, New Mexico	3	1	4.98	31	1	47	50	21	33

NORTHEAST CONFERENCE

	Conference		Overall	
	W	L	W	L
* Bryant	27	5	45	18
Sacred Heart	23	9	34	24
Monmouth	19	11	30	24
Long Island-Brooklyn	16	14	21	33
Central Connecticut State	16	16	28	25
Wagner	16	16	24	31
Quinnipiac	12	20	17	36
Fairleigh Dickinson	7	25	12	36
Mount St. Mary's	6	26	11	37

ALL-CONFERENCE TEAM: C—Nick Dini, So., Wagner. 1B—Dave Boisture, Sr., Sacred Heart. 2B—Jake Gronsky, Jr., Monmouth. SS—John Murphy, Sr., Sacred Heart. 3B—Kevin Brown, Sr., Bryant. OF—Carl Anderson, So., Bryant; Dylan DelaCruz, Jr., Central Conn.; Ian Miller, Jr., Wagner. DH—Dan Perez, Jr., Sacred Heart. UT—Mark Quaranta, Sr., Mount St. Mary's. SP—Peter Kelich, Sr., Bryant; Andy McGee, Jr., Monmouth. RP—Sal Lisanti, Sr. Bryant. Player of the Year: Kevin Brown, Bryant. Pitcher of the Year: Andy McGee, Monmouth. Rookie of the Year: A.J. Zarozny, Bryant. Coach of the Year: Steve Owens, Bryant.

INDIVIDUAL BATTING LEADERS
(Minimum 125 at-bats)

	AVG	AB	R	H	2B	3B	HR	RBI	SB
Healy, Tom, Mount St. Mary's	.380	158	30	60	12	3	6	25	10
Stewart, Owen, Monmouth	.374	195	31	73	4	0	0	30	3
Murphy, John, Sacred Heart	.367	207	35	76	13	8	4	47	29
Brown, Kevin, Bryant	.367	221	49	81	16	2	7	48	22
Ziznewski, John, LIU-Brooklyn	.361	205	43	74	11	6	5	31	17
DelaCruz, Dylan, CCSU	.352	210	42	74	17	5	6	34	5
Knight, Jay, Mount St. Mary's	.345	177	44	61	9	2	2	14	32
Anderson, Carl, Bryant	.341	214	42	73	9	0	2	49	20
Boisture, Dave, Sacred Heart	.331	172	32	57	12	1	3	33	3
Miller, Ian, Wagner	.329	234	46	77	4	1	0	30	46
Leonello, Pete, LIU-Brooklyn	.329	207	39	68	9	4	4	26	10
Sportman, J.P., CCSU	.327	202	31	66	18	3	1	33	13
McIntyre, Tyler, CCSU	.324	185	31	60	16	1	5	40	0
Mountford, Jordan, Bryant	.317	189	50	60	17	3	3	22	17
Weeks, , Fairleigh Dickinson	.316	171	23	54	13	0	0	24	3
Perez, Dan, Sacred Heart	.313	179	23	56	11	1	3	28	2
Dini, Nick, Wagner	.312	215	39	67	14	2	4	46	13
Needham, Kevin, LIU-Brooklyn	.310	187	30	58	7	0	4	36	0
Zarozny, A.J., Bryant	.310	184	43	57	14	1	2	28	10
Bamford, Joe, Monmouth	.307	179	24	55	7	1	1	27	4
Gronsky, Jake, Monmouth	.302	212	35	64	13	4	3	27	3
Smith, Chris, Wagner	.299	177	38	53	11	3	4	32	17
Untereiner, Chris, LIU-Brooklyn	.297	202	23	60	13	0	1	24	2
Wilgus, Steve, Monmouth	.297	209	35	62	10	2	2	28	6
Perret, Chris, Monmouth	.297	172	44	51	13	1	4	30	2
Moonan, Riley, FDU	.293	184	29	54	14	5	0	19	6
Rinn, Robby, Bryant	.292	185	23	54	7	1	0	26	1
St. George, Daniel, Bryant	.290	155	26	45	9	1	1	31	4
Lamboy, Brian, Sacred Heart	.290	176	33	51	9	1	0	23	8
Perry, Kyle, Monmouth	.288	177	23	51	7	0	0	15	7
Nott, Sam, Mount St. Mary's	.232	168	25	39	6	0	9	44	3

INDIVIDUAL PITCHING LEADERS
(Minimum 50 IP)

	W	L	ERA	G	SV	IP	H	BB	SO
#Lisanti, Salvatore, Bryant	2	2	1.11	23	10	32	20	12	30
Morris, Matt, Wagner	4	4	1.98	12	0	50	44	18	42
McGee, Andrew, Monmouth	8	2	2.12	13	0	110	89	15	69
LaMacchia, Derek, Quinnipiac	3	7	2.39	10	0	75	64	22	56
Healy, John, Bryant	9	1	2.45	16	1	81	62	24	69
Kelich, Peter, Bryant	7	4	2.49	15	0	98	79	19	89
Kerski, Kerski, Sacred Heart	7	2	2.57	11	0	74	61	25	63
Schlitter, Craig, Bryant	10	4	2.58	14	0	84	61	16	80
Scribner, Troy, Sacred Heart	5	2	2.59	13	1	83	66	17	90
Stoddard, Jeff, Sacred Heart	8	3	2.64	13	0	78	69	16	48
Michaud, Joseph, Bryant	5	3	3.00	14	2	63	52	28	61
Trimarco, Frank, Monmouth	5	2	3.08	12	0	53	55	11	30
Brown, Cody, CCSU	5	5	3.47	13	0	86	95	19	45
Mammino, Paul, Wagner	6	2	3.53	14	0	71	70	27	41
Zerff, Evan, LIU-Brooklyn	2	1	3.61	27	2	52	51	19	49
Kane, Spencer, Quinnipiac	4	5	3.82	12	0	73	79	24	47
McAvoy, Kevin, Bryant	7	3	3.83	15	0	85	78	29	57
Neumann, Nick, CCSU	5	5	3.97	12	0	70	74	15	44
Topa, Justin, Long Island	8	6	4.05	14	0	100	94	29	81
Casey, Ryan, Wagner	5	5	4.33	13	0	89	100	20	35
Thomas, Justin, Quinnipiac	4	1	4.50	11	0	52	58	29	30
#Calise, Anthony, FDU	0	2	7.18	31	0	31	34	20	18

OHIO VALLEY CONFERENCE

Team	Conference		Overall	
	W	L	W	L
Tennessee Tech	24	6	40	17
* Austin Peay State	22	7	47	15
Belmont	22	8	38	20
Jacksonville State	22	8	32	26
Eastern Kentucky	16	13	23	34
Southeast Missouri State	13	17	26	33
Eastern Illinois	11	17	22	27
Southern Illinois-Edwardsville	10	20	16	35
Morehead State	10	20	16	35

Murray State	9	21	21	33
Tennessee-Martin	4	26	11	40

ALL-CONFERENCE TEAM: C—Sean Hagen, Jr., E. Kentucky. **1B**—Craig Massone, Jr., Austin Peay. **2B**—Jordan Hankins, Jr., Austin Peay. **SS**—Reed Harper, Sr., Austin Peay. **3B**—Daniel Miles, Jr., Tenn. Tech. **OF**—Shaun Ball, Sr., E. Kentucky; Michael Bishop, Jr., Jacksonville State; Cody Hudson, Sr., Austin Peay. **DH**—Brandon Thomasson, Jr., Tenn. Tech. **UT**—Josh Davis, Sr., Belmont. **SP**—Tristan Archer, Sr., Tenn. Tech; Dan Ludwig, So., Belmont; Lee Ridenhour, Jr., Austin Peay; Tyler Rogers, Sr., Austin Peay. **Player of the Year:** Craig Massoni, Austin Peay. **Pitcher of the Year:** Tyler Rogers, Austin Peay. **Rookie of the Year:** Kyle Nowlin, E. Kentucky. **Coach of the Year:** Matt Bragga, Tenn. Tech.

INDIVIDUAL BATTING LEADERS
(Minimum 2.5 at-bats per team game)

	AVG	AB	R	H	2B	3B	HR	RBI	SB
Massoni, Craig, Austin Peay	.385	239	59	92	18	0	16	68	6
Sweeney, Kane, Morehead State	.376	197	31	74	13	1	4	28	3
Hudson, Cody, Austin Peay	.363	245	45	89	21	2	3	40	32
Howell, Caleb, E. Illinois	.362	177	29	64	7	1	2	20	4
Hankins, Jordan, Austin Peay	.354	243	71	86	14	0	11	54	8
Hagen, Sean, E. Kentucky	.353	204	34	72	14	0	4	41	10
Diamond, Alec, Belmont	.351	154	19	54	3	1	0	26	5
Abraham, James, Tenn. Tech	.347	199	40	69	8	2	1	31	14
Harper, Reed, Austin Peay	.346	237	35	82	12	2	7	59	14
Hewitt, Dalton, Southeast Mo.	.345	177	29	61	10	0	0	26	8
Gordon, Griff, JSU	.341	220	47	75	8	4	2	40	4
Bishop, Michael, JSU	.340	206	53	70	21	4	4	26	17
Eggenschwiler, Brand, Murray State	.340	212	34	72	13	0	1	40	2
Greenwell, Chase, Morehead State	.339	227	29	77	13	0	1	34	4
Miles, Daniel, Tenn. Tech	.337	199	43	67	11	3	12	53	2
Stetson, Ty, Murray State	.336	217	46	73	9	3	0	27	5
Stephens, Zach, Tenn. Tech	.336	229	59	77	17	1	15	71	0
Gibson, Derek, Southeast Mo.	.332	211	37	70	10	0	3	31	6
Valach, Brant, E. Illinois	.332	193	34	64	19	0	4	35	0
Bosheers, Dylan, Tenn. Tech	.329	216	39	71	20	2	6	46	6
Gautier, Rolando, Austin Peay	.329	210	56	69	16	2	3	30	3
Greatting, Joel, SIU-Edwardsville	.326	181	32	59	8	0	7	34	1
Evans, Clayton, Southeast Mo.	.325	160	27	52	8	2	2	24	8
Blum, Jason, Southeast Mo.	.323	226	53	73	21	3	4	33	9
Vavra, Treysen, E. Illinois	.318	192	37	61	20	2	8	47	5
Turner, Drew, Belmont	.318	211	40	67	15	1	3	29	12
Hughes, Alex, E. Kentucky	.317	183	39	58	16	2	3	26	4
Priessman, Nick, E. Illinois	.311	177	35	55	12	0	1	24	7
Tellor, Matt, Southeast Mo.	.311	235	38	73	15	1	8	46	3
Riner, Dylan, Austin Peay	.307	215	37	66	13	0	0	24	7
#Blanchard, Coty, JSU	.305	220	54	67	19	4	4	37	15
#Lennington, Andy, Southeast Mo.	.282	181	31	51	14	4	2	32	7
#Elmore, Duran, Morehead State	.273	132	22	36	7	4	1	11	7

INDIVIDUAL PITCHING LEADERS
(Minimum 1 IP per team game)

	W	L	ERA	G	SV	IP	H	BB	SO
#Rogers, Tyler, Austin Peay	7	2	1.63	41	23	50	29	27	41
Snodgrass, Jessie, Belmont	5	2	2.23	44	2	73	65	20	77
Felax, Travis, SI-Edwardsville	3	6	2.26	11	0	76	74	6	58
Ridenhour, Lee, Austin Peay	8	1	2.27	13	0	79	62	20	67
Brookshire, Chase, Belmont	5	2	2.28	11	0	71	45	12	82
Archer, Tristan, Tenn. Tech	9	4	3.34	9	0	97	102	23	97
Greenfield, Joe, E. Illinois	3	6	3.66	18	2	93	106	31	63
Cobb, Brent, E. Kentucky	7	6	3.69	15	0	95	93	28	50
Ludwig, Dan, Belmont	11	2	3.83	20	0	94	102	26	72
Hess, David, Tenn. Tech	7	2	3.84	22	0	66	73	21	77
Shields, Taylor, JSU	8	3	4.15	18	0	85	99	21	42
Borens, Matt, E. Illinois	4	4	4.30	16	0	88	96	25	65
Finch, Cameron, Murray State	5	4	4.32	14	0	81	82	28	48
Smith, Blake, Morehead State	4	4	4.46	16	0	79	86	50	51
Hall, Zach, Austin Peay	8	2	4.53	19	0	89	92	42	66
Schaeffer, Tony, SIU-Edwardsville	2	5	4.94	18	4	51	66	12	37
Antley, Casey, JSU	6	5	5.02	16	0	86	99	25	65
Delgado, Casey, Austin Peay	9	3	5.14	20	0	96	107	35	105
DeLeeuw, Cashtyn, Murray State	3	5	5.32	12	0	71	89	24	38
Smith, Zack, Southeastern Mo.	2	6	5.43	14	0	71	89	25	49
Smallwood, Noah, Morehead State	1	7	5.51	16	0	85	114	26	54

PACIFIC-12 CONFERENCE

	Conference		Overall	
	W	L	W	L
* Oregon State	24	6	52	13
Oregon	22	8	48	16
UCLA	21	9	49	17
Arizona State	16	14	37	22
Stanford	16	14	32	22
Arizona	15	15	34	21
Washington	15	15	24	32
California	10	20	23	31
Southern California	10	20	20	36
Washington State	9	21	23	32
Utah	7	23	21	31

ALL-CONFERENCE TEAM: C—Andrew Knapp, Jr., California; Jake Rodriguez, Jr., Oregon State. **1B**—Ryon Healy, Jr., Oregon; Brian Ragira, Jr., Stanford. **SS**—J.J. Altobelli, Sr., Oregon; Kevin Newman, Fr., Arizona; Tyler Smith, Sr., Oregon State; Pat Valaika, Jr., UCLA. **3B**—Michael Benjamin, Jr., Arizona State; Brandon Dixon, Jr., Arizona. **OF**—Kasey Coffman, Jr., Oregon State; Michael Conforto, So., Oregon State; Dylan Davis, So., Oregon State; Johnny Field, Jr., Arizona. **DH**—Justin Ringo, Sr., Stanford. **P**—Mark Appel, Sr., Stanford; David Berg, So., UCLA; Matt Boyd, Sr., Oregon State; Ryan Kellogg, Fr., Arizona State; Andrew Moore, Fr., Oregon State; Adam Plutko, Jr., UCLA; Jimmie Sherfy, Jr., Oregon; Tommy Thorpe, So., Oregon; Nick Vander Tuig, Jr., UCLA; Ben Wetzler, Jr., Oregon State. **Player of the Year:** Michael Conforto, Oregon State. **Pitcher of the Year:** David Berg, UCLA. **Defensive Player of the Year:** Pat Valaika, UCLA. **Freshman of the Year:** Andrew Moore, Oregon State. **Coach of the Year:** Pat Casey, Oregon State.

INDIVIDUAL BATTING LEADERS
(Minimum 2.5 at-bats per team game)

	AVG	AB	R	H	2B	3B	HR	RBI	SB
Dixon, Brandon, Arizona	.369	214	57	79	13	5	6	51	30
Landecker, Adam, USC	.351	202	31	71	18	1	2	25	6
Knapp, Andrew, California	.350	206	34	72	16	0	8	41	4
Field, Johnny, Arizona	.347	222	58	77	11	7	5	39	16
Gilbert, Trent, Arizona	.344	221	45	76	13	5	0	49	5
Zebrack, Greg, USC	.340	200	35	68	15	3	3	23	5
Ely, Andrew, Washington	.338	201	29	68	4	1	0	14	1
Newman, Kevin, Arizona	.336	217	40	73	6	3	0	42	11
Benjamin, Michael, Ariz. State	.335	248	53	83	20	4	8	47	4
Conforto, Michael, Ore. State	.333	243	48	81	14	1	11	47	6
Healy, Ryon, Oregon	.333	228	44	76	20	0	11	56	5
Davis, Dylan, Oregon State	.332	253	45	84	22	3	5	61	8
Coffman, Kasey, Oregon State	.332	232	57	77	13	5	8	44	9
Stemp, Trek, Wash. State	.331	145	27	48	6	2	1	15	3
Peterson, Andy, Oregon State	.331	242	49	80	5	0	0	27	13
Ringo, Justin, Stanford	.325	194	38	63	10	2	6	33	9
Ragira, Brian, Stanford	.323	217	34	70	9	1	8	40	4
Gibbons, Zach, Arizona	.320	178	33	57	5	4	0	27	11
Roberts, James, USC	.320	203	19	65	10	0	4	28	0
Maggi, Joseph, Arizona	.320	150	31	48	6	1	0	27	3
Slaybaugh, Collin, Wash. State	.317	189	32	60	7	1	0	16	12
Thomas, Brett, Oregon	.317	208	45	66	15	0	2	29	12
Keyes, Kavin, Oregon State	.317	208	35	66	12	2	2	34	3
Tolman, Mitchell, Oregon	.315	165	16	52	9	1	1	37	2
Rosen, Yale, Washington State	.314	210	26	66	12	2	7	35	0
Smith, Tyler, Oregon State	.314	220	48	69	10	2	2	28	8
Ray, Jayce, Washington	.309	220	35	68	11	4	0	36	3
Swick, Kevin, USC	.305	167	25	51	12	1	2	16	5
Pearson, Devin, California	.302	179	26	54	8	0	2	17	7
Diekroeger, Danny, Stanford	.300	217	29	65	10	2	2	28	6
#Carroll, Brian, UCLA	.261	238	45	62	3	2	0	20	30

INDIVIDUAL PITCHING LEADERS
(Minimum 1 IP per team game)

	W	L	ERA	G	SV	IP	H	BB	SO
Berg, David, UCLA	7	0	0.85	48	23	74	51	9	76
Moore, Andrew, Oregon State	14	1	1.57	18	1	126	84	28	72
Boyd, Matt, Oregon State	11	4	2.04	20	1	133	92	33	122
Appel, Mark, Stanford	10	4	2.12	14	0	106	80	23	130
Thorpe, Tommy, Oregon	7	5	2.16	16	0	104	82	39	87

	W	L	ERA	G	SV	IP	H	BB	SO
Dunlap, Trevor, Washington	4	3	2.16	29	6	67	56	20	52
Wetzler, Ben, Oregon State	10	1	2.25	16	0	96	83	32	83
Plutko, Adam, UCLA	9	3	2.29	18	0	118	88	29	79
Vander Tuig, Nick, UCLA	13	4	2.31	18	0	121	103	17	87
Zarubin, Bobby, Stanford	3	3	2.32	14	0	54	46	27	34
Strahan, Wyatt, USC	4	3	2.45	13	0	81	72	41	45
Irvin, Cole, Oregon	12	3	2.48	16	0	116	105	22	60
Pistorese, Joe, Wash. State	5	5	2.78	15	0	100	100	26	61
Wheatley, Bo, USC	3	4	2.78	13	0	78	94	19	38
Watrous, Mitch, Utah	4	4	2.81	17	1	93	92	31	64
Voth, Austin, Washington	7	6	2.99	17	1	105	99	38	98
Kellogg, Ryan, Arizona State	11	1	3.15	16	0	103	96	17	54
Wright, Zach, Washington	4	5	3.20	33	0	70	61	43	27
Fisher, Jared, Washington	2	2	3.20	11	0	59	56	19	25
Watson, Grant, UCLA	8	3	3.22	17	0	87	89	15	52
Reed, Jake, Oregon	6	6	3.41	17	0	100	93	30	65

PATRIOT LEAGUE

	Conference		Overall	
	W	L	W	L
Holy Cross	15	5	28	25
Navy	13	7	28	23
* Army	11	9	29	23
Bucknell	10	10	16	33
Lafayette	6	14	10	40
Lehigh	5	15	18	29

ALL-CONFERENCE TEAM: C—Dave Milanes, Sr., Navy. **1B**—Jordan Enos, Sr., Holy Cross. **2B**—Kevin Casey, Sr., Lafayette. **SS**—Alex Jensen, So., Army. **3B**—Mike Ahmed, Jr., Holy Cross. **OF**—Evan Ocello, So., Holy Cross; Patrick Puentes, Sr., Holy Cross; Greg Dupell, Sr., Navy. **DH**—Corey Furman, Jr., Bucknell. **Player of the Year:** Jordan Enos, Sr., Holy Cross. **Pitcher of the Year:** John Colella, Sr., Holy Cross. **Rookie of the Year:** Andrew Andreychik, Fr., Bucknell. **Coach of the Year:** Greg DiCenzo, Holy Cross.

INDIVIDUAL BATTING LEADERS
(Minimum 2.5 at-bats per team game)

	AVG	AB	R	H	2B	3B	HR	RBI	SB
Pacchioli, Justin, Lehigh	.366	142	31	52	10	5	0	14	11
Mescher, Patrick, Army	.341	173	35	59	4	0	2	40	10
Ocello, Evan, Holy Cross	.338	198	46	67	14	3	3	25	15
Turner, Casey, Lehigh	.337	172	40	58	14	2	1	28	16
Manzelli, Kash, Navy	.335	191	35	64	9	1	2	30	1
Cipolla, Brandon, Holy Cross	.333	186	37	62	15	3	2	30	7
Enos, Jordan, Holy Cross	.332	184	33	61	18	0	2	37	4
Dupell, Greg, Navy	.320	200	35	64	18	4	3	39	6
Puentes, Patrick, Holy Cross	.320	169	31	54	9	2	7	34	6
Ruck, Andrew, Lafayette	.318	176	15	56	7	1	3	18	9
Casey, Kevin, Lafayette	.317	164	35	52	10	1	2	16	9
McCants, Mark, Army	.314	137	25	43	6	2	0	24	10
Abeln, Joe, Lehigh	.311	164	29	51	8	1	0	28	7
Milanes, Dave, Navy	.311	193	33	60	13	0	1	32	1
Page, Jacob, Army	.307	179	29	55	8	4	3	35	11
Jensen, Alex, Army	.292	192	42	56	9	1	3	38	10
Beans, Brandon, Navy	.291	179	33	52	12	2	1	21	13
Furman, Corey, Bucknell	.291	179	31	52	6	2	1	21	1
Barry, Andrew, Holy Cross	.286	196	29	56	8	0	0	27	4
Elson, Brandon, Lehigh	.284	183	23	52	8	2	2	29	12
Wadsworth, Stephen, Holy Cross	.284	148	21	42	8	1	2	26	6
Ahmed, Mike, Holy Cross	.279	140	33	39	6	0	4	28	14
Clark, Travis, Bucknell	.278	194	29	54	16	1	2	19	11
Brong, Tyler, Lehigh	.278	162	31	45	9	0	2	23	5
Bumgardner, Carter, Bucknell	.277	159	17	44	7	0	1	30	2
Currie, Robert, Navy	.273	150	24	41	5	1	0	19	8
Garzillo, Mike, Lehigh	.273	154	23	42	15	1	0	16	15
Ogren, Joe, Bucknell	.263	137	21	36	11	0	2	19	1
Crucitti, Jon, Army	.260	173	43	45	1	2	0	6	16
Santomauro, Andrew, Lafayette	.258	182	28	47	11	5	0	16	15
#Borosak, Brad, Navy	.245	139	21	34	2	2	0	18	16

INDIVIDUAL PITCHING LEADERS
(Minimum 1 IP per team game)

	W	L	ERA	G	SV	IP	H	BB	SO
Rowley, Chris, Army	9	4	2.67	14	0	98	99	21	75
Gillingham, Luke, Navy	4	3	3.23	14	0	53	60	9	45
Moore, Stephen, Navy	4	3	3.24	12	0	58	56	10	46
Massa, Michael, Lafayette	3	6	3.41	11	0	66	51	38	37
Robinett, Alex, Army	7	4	3.43	15	0	87	83	25	62
#Colella, John, Holy Cross	2	4	3.47	25	8	49	51	31	56
Gotzon, Colin, Lehigh	5	5	3.56	11	0	56	53	22	52
Goldstien, Dan, Bucknell	4	5	3.60	12	0	70	61	34	59
Andreychik, Andrew, Bucknell	4	3	3.73	12	0	51	49	18	32
Hough, Bryson, Bucknell	3	6	4.28	12	0	74	78	24	39
Weigel, Dan, Bucknell	2	8	4.33	11	0	81	88	17	59
Murray, Donny, Holy Cross	7	3	4.33	14	0	73	76	24	61
Parenti, Anthony, Navy	3	4	4.38	12	0	64	67	22	65
Davidson, Brock, Army	2	3	4.45	11	0	59	62	12	26
Schwartz, Toby, Lafayette	4	4	4.96	13	0	53	71	26	25
Marra, Tom, Holy Cross	4	5	5.28	13	0	61	68	30	44
Ortolf, Connor, Lafayette	1	5	5.73	10	0	55	75	28	25
Schoberl, Johnny, Navy	4	5	6.02	12	0	52	55	33	35
#Boyce, Andrew, Holy Cross	5	4	6.94	28	3	47	59	21	41

SOUTHEASTERN CONFERENCE

EAST	Conference		Overall	
	W	L	W	L
Vanderbilt	26	3	54	12
South Carolina	17	12	43	20
Florida	14	16	29	30
Kentucky	11	19	30	25
Missouri	10	20	18	32
Tennessee	8	20	22	30
Georgia	7	20	21	32
WEST	W	L	W	L
* Louisiana State	23	7	57	11
Arkansas	18	11	39	22
Mississippi State	16	14	51	20
Mississippi	15	15	38	24
Alabama	14	15	35	28
Texas A&M	13	16	34	29
Auburn	13	17	33	23

ALL-CONFERENCE TEAM: C—Stuart Turner, Jr., Mississippi. **1B**—Mason Katz, Sr., Louisiana State. **2B**—Tony Kemp, Jr., Vanderbilt. **SS**—Alex Bregman, Fr., Louisiana State. **3B**—Christian Ibarra, Jr., Louisiana State. **OF**—Hunter Renfroe, Jr., Mississippi State; Raph Rhymes, Sr., Louisiana State; Mike Yastrzemski, Sr., Vanderbilt. **DH/UTIL**—A.J. Reed, So., Kentucky; Keaton Steele, Jr., Missouri. **SP**—Aaron Nola, So., Louisiana State; Ryne Stanek, Jr., Arkansas. **RP**—Jonathan Holder, So., Mississippi State. **Player of the Year:** Tony Kemp, Vanderbilt. **Pitcher of the Year:** Aaron Nola, Louisiana State. **Freshman of the Year:** Alex Bregman, Louisiana State. **Coach of the Year:** Tim Corbin, Vanderbilt.

INDIVIDUAL BATTING LEADERS
(Minimum 3 plate appearances per team game)

	AVG	AB	R	H	2B	3B	HR	RBI	SB
Kemp, Tony, Vanderbilt	.391	266	64	104	13	6	0	33	34
Powell, Curt, Georgia	.376	218	32	82	8	1	0	21	6
Turner, Stuart, Mississippi	.374	222	44	83	15	1	5	51	2
Katz, Mason, LSU	.370	243	53	90	14	2	16	70	5
Bregman, Alex, LSU	.369	282	59	104	18	7	6	52	16
Price, Scott, Tennessee	.359	184	25	66	10	1	2	25	4
Cooper, Garrett, Auburn	.354	189	31	67	12	1	7	37	1
Frazier, Adam, Miss. State	.352	304	62	107	20	7	0	38	9
Lankford, Cole, Texas A&M	.352	216	26	76	18	4	3	40	4
Renfroe, Hunter, Miss. State	.345	255	56	88	16	3	16	65	9
Reynolds, Mikey, Texas A&M	.342	225	43	77	15	1	1	25	19
Maddox, Will, Tennessee	.333	207	42	69	8	2	0	20	22
Rhymes, Raph, LSU	.331	254	53	84	15	1	4	46	3
Anderson, Brian, Arkansas	.325	209	47	68	12	5	4	36	6
Turner, Xavier, Vanderbilt	.324	219	40	71	10	0	0	36	22
Danztler, L.B., S. Carolina	.322	214	46	69	16	1	15	53	2
Wacker, Cullen, Auburn	.320	200	24	64	12	1	2	34	0

	AVG	AB	R	H	2B	3B	HR	RBI	SB
Detz, Alex, Miss. State	.318	239	43	76	14	1	1	31	1
Mistone, Andrew, Mississippi	.317	227	35	72	12	1	0	25	1
McMullen, Sean, LSU	.314	175	26	55	18	1	2	30	1
Bader, Harrison, Florida	.312	221	37	69	7	2	1	22	15
Harrell, Connor, Vanderbilt	.312	247	60	77	12	3	12	67	9
Yastrzemski, Mike, Vanderbilt	.312	247	52	77	19	3	3	43	20
Pankake, Joey, S. Carolina	.311	238	40	74	9	1	11	42	7
Pirtle, Brett, Miss. State	.310	229	40	71	9	2	2	33	8
Laird, Mark, LSU	.310	242	48	75	7	1	0	18	6
Anderson, Austin, Mississippi	.310	213	41	66	12	1	3	39	4
Gregor, Conrad, Vanderbilt	.308	227	47	70	14	0	3	48	21
Conde, Vince, Vanderbilt	.307	238	43	73	18	0	6	44	3
Ward, Nelson, Georgia	.306	186	36	57	7	3	2	19	8

INDIVIDUAL PITCHING LEADERS
(Minimum 1 IP per team game)

	W	L	ERA	G	SV	IP	H	BB	SO
#Cotton, Chris, LSU	4	1	1.16	37	16	47	25	3	47
Stanek, Ryne, Arkansas	10	2	1.39	16	0	97	72	41	79
Montgomery, Jordan, S. Carolina	6	1	1.48	13	0	79	64	18	60
Mitchell, Ross, Miss. State	13	0	1.53	34	2	94	72	29	44
Nola, Aaron, LSU	12	1	1.57	17	0	126	83	18	122
#Holder, Jonathan, Miss. State	2	0	1.65	34	21	55	33	17	90
Ray, Parker, Texas A&M	2	1	1.73	23	0	68	51	19	44
Astin, Barrett, Arkansas	4	4	1.79	18	1	91	85	20	74
Fant, Randall, Arkansas	6	1	2.03	14	0	67	50	19	52
Wahl, Bobby, Mississippi	10	0	2.03	16	0	98	69	44	78
Mengden, Daniel, Texas A&M	8	4	2.11	16	0	111	78	24	94
Ziomek, Kevin, Vanderbilt	11	3	2.12	17	0	119	79	40	115
Kendrick, Conner, Auburn	5	3	2.13	19	2	80	78	29	75
Beede, Tyler, Vanderbilt	14	1	2.32	17	0	101	64	63	103
Westmoreland, Adam, S. Carolina	7	4	2.32	29	3	66	52	15	62
Belcher, Nolan, S. Carolina	7	5	2.38	17	0	117	108	16	51
Magliozzi, Johnny, Florida	4	2	2.67	29	12	67	53	16	57
Glenn, Cody, LSU	7	3	2.68	15	0	84	75	17	38
O'Neal, Michael, Auburn	8	4	2.73	14	0	89	73	21	36
Shepherd, Chandler, Kentucky	5	0	2.77	26	0	55	50	17	39
Eades, Ryan, LSU	8	1	2.79	17	0	100	101	32	78
Mayers, Mike, Mississippi	5	6	2.83	16	0	92	77	37	73
Harris, Ryan, Florida	5	4	3.07	37	0	59	53	15	51

SOUTHERN CONFERENCE

	Conference		Overall	
	W	L	W	L
Western Carolina	23	7	39	20
College of Charleston	18	11	31	26
*Elon	18	11	34	30
The Citadel	18	12	35	25
Appalachian State	13	14	30	24
Furman	14	16	32	35
Georgia Southern	13	17	27	32
Samford	12	17	27	30
Davidson	12	18	18	31
UNC Greensboro	11	19	24	31
Wofford	10	20	20	36

ALL-CONFERENCE TEAM: C—Joe Jackson, Jr., The Citadel. **1B**—Ryan Kinsella, Jr., Elon. **2B**—Hector Crespo, Sr., Appalachian State. **SS**—Aaron Attaway, Jr., W. Carolina. **3B**—Tyler White, Sr., W. Carolina. **OF**—Phillip Ervin, Jr., Samford; Julian Ridings, Jr., W. Carolina; Christian Wolfe, Sr., UNC Greensboro. **DH**—C.K. Irby, Jr., Samford. **SP**—Jamie Nunn, So., Appalachian State; Austin Pritcher, Sr., The Citadel. **RP**—Preston Hatcher, Sr., W. Carolina. **Player of the Year:** Ryan Kinsella, Elon. **Pitcher of the Year:** Austin Pritcher, The Citadel. **Freshman of the Year:** Jaylin Davis, Appalachian State. **Coach of the Year:** Bobby Moranda, W. Carolina.

INDIVIDUAL BATTING LEADERS
(Minimum 2.5 at-bats per team game)

	AVG	AB	R	H	2B	3B	HR	RBI	SB
Wolfe, Christian, UNCG	.421	209	47	88	17	2	4	39	5
Jackson, Joe, The Citadel	.386	228	66	88	19	2	13	67	3
Irby, C.K., Samford	.383	222	49	85	16	4	8	59	6
Armstrong, Hughston, Citadel	.379	224	57	85	11	2	1	23	18
Ridings, Julian, W. Carolina	.377	199	49	75	16	4	11	49	14

	AVG	AB	R	H	2B	3B	HR	RBI	SB
Attaway, Aaron, W. Carolina	.363	267	68	97	15	5	12	54	12
White, Tyler, W. Carolina	.363	251	52	91	27	0	16	66	3
Durdaller, Christiaan, Samford	.361	194	53	70	14	0	14	53	6
Marrero, Benigno, UNCG	.352	199	36	70	10	0	3	28	5
Heidt, Gunnar, CofC	.349	232	49	81	17	7	4	54	13
Callaway, Will, App. State	.344	215	42	74	12	0	4	40	14
Hyman, Josh, Wofford	.338	210	43	71	14	3	6	36	26
Ervin, Phillip, Samford	.337	196	58	66	14	2	11	40	21
Crespo, Hector, App. State	.336	235	48	79	14	3	4	40	22
Abrams, Alex, Furman	.335	185	39	62	11	1	6	35	1
Johnson, Taylor, Furman	.332	247	47	82	17	0	10	56	5
Gomez, Sebastian, Elon	.323	232	39	75	16	1	3	42	11
Butler, Blake, CofC	.321	209	52	67	7	2	1	21	9
Neely, Seth, Wofford	.319	216	24	69	7	1	0	38	17
Spina, T.J., UNCG	.319	204	46	65	10	4	2	26	10
Simpson, Jordan, Furman	.317	202	28	64	9	1	2	29	9
Orth, Calvin, Citadel	.316	215	32	68	10	2	7	33	0
Griffin, Tyler, Citadel	.314	159	39	50	7	2	12	52	0
Kinsella, Ryan, Elon	.313	256	56	80	19	3	21	78	7
Hoyle, Jacob, W. Carolina	.310	213	40	66	16	2	11	52	1
Kalbfleisch, Eric, UNCG	.310	197	30	61	21	2	4	31	4
Stokes, Johnathan, Citadel	.309	236	33	73	13	0	5	52	3
Leach, Zach, UNCG	.308	143	23	44	10	1	2	17	9
Morgan, Ben, Georgia So.	.307	241	48	74	16	2	6	36	27
Dodds, Robbie, Georgia So.	.305	213	29	65	11	2	3	33	2
#Davis, Mason, Citadel	.305	272	62	83	11	4	5	25	22
#Head, William, App. State	.288	163	34	47	5	2	1	25	27

INDIVIDUAL PITCHING LEADERS
(Miminum 1 IP per team game)

	W	L	ERA	G	SV	IP	H	BB	SO
Abrams, Alex, Furman	5	1	2.43	17	0	63	54	17	48
Zokan, Jake, CofC	4	3	2.85	17	0	79	81	15	80
Thurber, Taylor, App. State	3	2	2.91	26	2	56	61	7	36
Pritcher, Austin, The Citadel	8	3	2.99	16	0	99	93	38	80
Null, Jeremy, W. Carolina	9	2	3.46	14	0	91	82	27	109
Smith, Nate, Furman	7	4	3.59	17	0	100	104	34	98
Cribb, Logan, Citadel	4	3	3.60	20	0	75	74	25	64
Pegier, Matt, CofC	4	2	3.62	16	0	87	79	13	70
Gilliam, Lee, UNCG	2	4	3.69	12	0	68	63	33	58
Hess, Justin, Georgia So.	5	6	3.69	23	4	95	50	34	120
Smith, Jordan, W. Carolina	7	3	3.73	15	0	94	87	33	70
Webb, Kyle, Elon	7	3	3.89	18	1	104	117	21	97
Clark, Dylan, Elon	6	4	3.95	13	0	80	86	16	54
Nunn, Jamie, App. State	9	5	3.96	15	0	98	94	37	77
Irby, C.K., Samford	7	6	4.14	15	0	91	80	33	90
Yarusi, Brandon, Wofford	2	3	4.14	12	0	63	72	17	54
#Sherrill, Zach, Citadel	3	1	4.14	48	0	46	39	17	38
McKinney, Morgan, W. Carolina	4	3	4.25	12	0	66	76	34	52
#Hatcher, Preston, W. Carolina	6	3	4.35	32	14	41	43	25	45
Milazzo, Alex, Samford	6	2	4.40	12	0	61	65	31	50
West, Ryan, Col. of Charleston	4	3	4.66	20	0	68	71	21	71
Mooney, Danny, Davidson	6	4	4.71	14	0	78	94	29	70

SOUTHLAND CONFERENCE

	Conference		Overall	
	W	L	W	L
Sam Houston State	20	7	38	22
Texas A&M-Corpus Christi	17	10	33	24
Southeastern Louisiana	16	11	36	24
Oral Roberts	16	11	25	32
Lamar	15	12	39	20
Stephen F. Austin State	15	12	28	29
*Central Arkansas	12	15	42	22
NcNeese State	10	17	23	31
Nicholls State	9	18	26	29
Northwestern State	5	22	16	40

ALL-CONFERENCE TEAM: C—Anthonay Azar, Jr., Sam Houston State. **1B**—Brad Porras, Sr., Texas A&M-Corpus Christi. **2B**—V.J. Bunner, Sr., Lamar. **SS**—Hunter Dozier, Jr., Stephen F. Austin. **3B**—Kevin Miller, Sr. Sam Houston State. **OF**—Forrestt Allday, Sr., Central Arkansas; Darian Johnson, Sr., Lamar; Eric Weiss, Sr., Texas A&M-Corpus Christi. **DH**—

Jonathan Gonzales, Sr., Texas A&M-Corpus Christi. **P**—Alex Gonzalez, Jr., Oral Roberts; Eric Harrington, Sr., Lamar; Caleb McClanahan, Sr., Central Arkansas. **Player of the Year:** Hunter Dozier, Stephen F. Austin. **Hitter of the Year:** Hunter Dozier, Stephen F. Austin. **Pitcher of the Year:** Alex Gonzalez, Oral Roberts. **Relief Pitcher of the Year:** Brett Higginbotham, Stephen F. Austin. **Freshman of the Year:** Bryce Kingsley, McNeese State. **Newcomer of the Year:** Sam Bumpers, Lamar. **Coach of the Year:** Davie Pierce, Sam Houston State.

INDIVIDUAL BATTING LEADERS
(Minimum 125 At-bats)

	AVG	AB	R	H	2B	3B	HR	RBI	SB
Dozier, Hunter, SFA	.396	212	47	84	25	0	17	52	12
Johnson, Darian, Lamar	.371	240	44	89	12	3	1	47	9
Allday, Forestt, Central Ark.	.365	233	59	85	14	1	3	36	15
Sanchez, Ricardo, SFA	.358	176	24	63	6	1	3	20	7
Bunner, V.J., Lamar	.341	179	49	61	14	0	6	33	5
Bumpers, Sam, Lamar	.339	236	48	80	19	2	4	40	2
Miller, Kevin, SHSU	.333	225	37	75	8	1	2	37	1
Duplantis, Tyler, Nicholls State	.330	188	33	62	7	3	0	13	5
Weiss, Eric, TAMU-CC	.327	211	42	69	10	4	4	42	8
Gonzalez, Jonathan, TAMU-CC	.323	223	35	72	16	0	5	43	1
Burgess, Carter, SHSU	.321	234	41	75	12	4	0	29	0
Fisher, Jameson, SELA	.315	219	38	69	11	2	3	27	8
Marietta, Michael, Central Ark.	.315	235	45	74	16	3	4	59	6
Porras, Brad, TAMU-CC	.314	229	34	72	17	0	3	31	3
Stephens, Cody, TAMU-CC	.313	224	48	70	4	2	2	28	19
Slade, Harry, SELA	.310	216	30	67	7	2	1	37	14
Dornak, Seth, Lamar	.309	207	36	64	16	0	2	40	1
Watson, Will, NW State	.308	198	18	61	8	1	1	23	8
Hernandez, Ben, SELA	.307	215	32	66	5	0	0	27	6
Lee, Jordan, TAMU-CC	.307	215	36	66	7	1	1	23	9
Atwood, Colt, SHSU	.303	241	40	73	6	0	0	25	9
Azar, Anthony, SHSU	.303	218	38	66	21	1	6	47	4
Gooch, Jackson, McNeese State	.301	216	40	65	15	1	5	34	0
Olivas, Aaron, Lamar	.300	213	39	64	9	0	0	40	2
Taylor, Zach, TAMU-CC	.299	187	29	56	9	2	0	27	5
Plucheck, Luke, SHSU	.298	215	42	64	11	4	9	43	11
Cho, Kevin, Oral Roberts	.296	199	30	59	3	2	0	15	6
Boss, Tyler, Oral Roberts	.295	190	29	56	10	2	7	32	9
Farney, Ryan, SHSU	.293	150	25	55	9	1	0	14	4
Vidrine, Jude, Lamar	.293	205	53	60	15	0	3	26	4
#Davis, Jonathan, Central Ark.	.268	235	48	63	11	5	3	49	25
#Marchal, Blake, Central Ark.	.263	240	44	63	7	1	3	50	31

INDIVIDUAL PITCHING LEADERS
(Minimum 50 IP)

	W	L	ERA	G	SV	IP	H	BB	SO
Gonzalez, Alex, Oral Roberts	9	5	1.83	15	0	113	83	27	126
McKinzie, Ethan, Central Ark.	4	2	2.09	21	5	52	47	14	22
Spann, Steven, NW State	2	4	2.30	27	0	59	52	23	39
#Dorris, Jacob, TAMU-CC	1	2	2.36	30	13	27	28	10	33
Harrington, Eric, Lamar	7	1	2.38	14	0	76	69	14	54
McClanahan, Caleb, Central Ark.	10	6	2.43	17	0	122	105	12	80
Greening, Chase, SFA	4	6	2.80	15	0	90	86	25	78
Dziedzic, Jonathan, Lamar	7	4	3.01	16	0	108	86	35	106
Biggerstaff, Bryce, Central Ark.	6	5	3.01	18	0	108	109	19	60
Foss, Trevor, TAMU-CC	8	6	3.09	16	0	102	77	31	103
Godail, Andrew, SHSU	5	4	3.10	16	0	81	68	49	71
Kingsley, Bryce, McNeese State	8	6	3.11	15	0	98	85	42	64
Belicek, Trevor, TAMU-CC	9	2	3.12	16	0	81	88	21	58
Byrd, Taylor, Nicholls State	5	6	3.18	15	0	74	65	43	72
Zufall, Tim, Oral Roberts	5	2	3.27	15	0	72	68	32	36
Ware, Blake, McNeese State	5	7	3.27	15	0	107	98	36	55
Eppler, Tyler, SHSU	5	2	3.41	17	0	69	65	30	44
Enloe, Jeffrey, Central Ark.	7	5	3.43	16	0	110	128	25	86
Smith, Caleb, SHSU	7	5	3.44	18	0	89	66	60	68
Bowen, Drew, Oral Roberts	4	3	3.48	13	0	67	52	19	42
Kennel, Sean, SELA	6	3	3.49	14	0	70	79	13	36
#McCoy, Jordan, Nicholls State	2	2	3.93	30	8	34	32	13	33

SOUTHWESTERN ATHLETIC CONFERENCE

	Conference		Overall	
EAST	**W**	**L**	**W**	**L**
* Jackson State	19	5	34	22
Alabama State	18	6	32	25
Alcorn State	13	10	15	41
Alabama A&M	6	15	8	40
Mississippi Valley State	1	21	5	44
WEST	**W**	**L**	**W**	**L**
Southern	14	10	21	23
Arkansas-Pine Bluff	13	11	21	32
Prairie View A&M	12	12	27	27
Texas Southern	12	12	22	29
Grambling State	9	15	18	30

ALL-CONFERENCE TEAM: C—Jose Cruz, Jr., Jackson State. **1B**—Dominiq Harris, Jr., Prairie View A&M. **2B**—Edmund Cheatham, Sr., Miss. Valley State. **SS**—Isias Alcantar, Sr., Arkansas-Pine Bluff. **3B**—Austin Hulsey, Fr., Alabama A&M. **OF**—Darren Farmer, Sr., Grambling State; Tyler Kirksey, So., Southern; Ellis Stephney, Jr., Texas Southern. **DH**—Malcolm Tate, Sr., Jackson State. **SP**—Jose DeLeon, Jr., Southern; T.J. Renda, So., Alabama State. **RP**—Andre Rodriguez, Jr., Jackson State. **Player of the Year:** Isias Alcantar, Arkansas-Pine Bluff. **Pitcher of the Year:** T.J. Renda, Alabama State. **Hitter of the Year:** Darren Farmer, Grambling State. **Newcomer of the Year:** Charles Tillery, Jackson State. **Freshman of the Year:** Dillon Cooper, Alabama State. **Coach of the Year:** Carlos James, Arkansas-Pine Bluff.

INDIVIDUAL BATTING LEADERS
(Minimum 100 at-bats)

	AVG	AB	R	H	2B	3B	HR	RBI	SB
Farmer, Darren, Grambling	.361	166	33	60	5	3	3	36	9
Tillery, Charles, Jackson State	.352	193	50	68	10	2	1	35	26
Gonzalez, Richard, Ala. State	.348	181	29	63	10	3	1	35	11
Alcantar, Isias, UAPB	.345	206	32	71	11	1	6	44	7
Estrada, Waldyvan, Ala. State	.333	204	28	68	6	0	7	51	5
Dodson, Patrick, Ala. A&M	.333	192	35	64	10	1	0	31	11
Ford II, Jerry, Texas So.	.324	139	27	45	6	0	1	15	20
Stephney, Ellis, Texas So.	.321	184	36	59	13	4	3	30	10
Rojas, Leo, Alabama State	.314	172	45	54	11	5	1	30	14
Hulsey, Austin, Ala. A&M	.313	182	27	57	10	2	1	36	13
Hays, German, Miss. Valley	.310	145	17	45	6	0	1	21	6
Bueno, Juan, Grambling	.307	189	33	58	10	5	4	32	7
Curtis, Stephen, Jackson State	.305	164	26	50	13	1	1	38	12
Taylor, Bryce, Jackson State	.304	181	38	55	13	1	1	26	13
Cooper, Dillon, Alabama State	.301	196	34	59	12	1	3	26	5
Harris, Dominiq, Prairie View	.301	193	31	58	11	1	8	40	3
Salcido, Greg, Prairie View	.300	180	26	54	13	1	2	40	5
Rosa, Angel, Alcorn State	.294	160	27	47	7	2	2	28	17
Cheatham, Edmund, MVSU	.292	154	30	45	5	0	2	21	39
Curry, Marquis, Texas So.	.292	144	20	42	7	3	2	32	12
Campbell, Kirby, UAPB	.288	163	26	47	6	0	0	19	3
Thomas, Gary, Jackson State	.288	170	34	49	9	1	0	13	12
Jackson, Alvin, Alcorn State	.288	191	26	55	11	4	1	26	17
Bright, Evan, Jackson State	.286	210	32	60	16	1	4	36	1
Todman, Elias, Grambling	.286	189	23	54	10	3	4	34	3
Black, Bradley, Ala. A&M	.285	179	27	51	12	1	4	26	10
Hall, Korey, Grambling	.283	152	35	43	9	2	1	21	2
Marrero, Emmanuel, Ala. State	.282	163	33	46	8	0	1	17	11
De Mera, Cody, UAPB	.281	192	32	54	9	0	1	28	9
Knowles, Aneko, Jackson State	.281	178	37	50	3	4	1	20	26
#Washington, Sean, Southern	.275	131	26	36	9	5	2	14	2
#Amion, Richard, Ala. State	.269	201	56	54	9	1	2	37	34
#Hines, Colby, Prairie View	.237	194	31	46	7	5	1	19	5
#Price, Dexter, Alabama State	.236	195	35	46	11	1	8	27	9

INDIVIDUAL PITCHING LEADERS
(Minimum 50 IP)

	W	L	ERA	G	SV	IP	H	BB	SO
Helms, A.J., Prairie View	3	2	2.22	18	3	57	39	17	47
Renda, T.J., Alabama State	9	1	2.38	14	0	95	73	14	85
Baker, Brock, Grambling	3	5	2.82	13	0	61	52	17	21
Holliday, Jesse, Southern	7	3	2.87	12	0	82	69	15	72

	W	L	ERA	G	SV	IP	H	BB	SO
Lara, Marcos, Texas So.	4	2	2.91	17	0	59	54	16	47
Alvira, Joel, Alabama State	6	0	3.15	12	0	66	51	38	51
DeLeon, Jose, Southern	4	3	3.28	12	0	82	63	31	73
Jones, Stanten, UAPB	5	5	3.44	31	0	55	46	21	53
Juday, Alexander, Jackson State	7	5	3.67	22	1	115	118	37	60
Schwartz, Kyle, UAPB	4	6	3.74	13	0	79	80	21	55
Hernandez, Stef, Prairie View	4	4	3.90	12	0	67	60	30	39
#Moreau, Zach, Grambling	0	4	3.90	18	5	32	25	11	31
Ricciardi, Anthony, Ala. State	3	6	3.92	11	0	57	55	21	50
Gomez, Felix, Texas So.	1	7	3.93	14	0	71	71	24	43
Ploeger, Jim, UAPB	5	4	4.11	13	0	72	73	23	65
Ramirez, Mikey, UAPB	3	3	4.22	14	1	70	79	15	48
Bautista, Richard, Grambling	6	5	4.26	11	0	70	71	24	41
#Powell, Josh, Southern	3	1	4.31	24	5	31	37	9	21
Garcia, Daniel, Southern	4	5	4.32	12	0	58	60	22	29
Pearson, Robert, Texas So.	5	5	4.37	15	0	68	62	27	51
Gary, Harrison, Alcorn State	5	3	4.61	15	0	70	76	38	46
Mata, Jonathan, Prairie View	5	5	4.79	13	0	71	88	23	53

SUMMIT LEAGUE

	Conference		Overall	
	W	L	W	L
Nebraska-Omaha	20	6	27	22
* South Dakota State	16	10	35	24
Oakland	15	13	20	35
North Dakota State	11	13	26	27
Western Illinois	9	17	19	37
IPFW	9	21	22	32

ALL-CONFERENCE TEAM: C—Alex Mortensen, So., Nebraska-Omaha. **1B**—Cory Buckley, Sr., Nebraska-Omaha. **2B**—Wes Satzinger, Jr., North Dakota State. **SS**—Jameson Henning, Fr., Western Illinois. **3B**—Tyler Splichal, Jr., Nebraska-Omaha. **OF**—Tim Colwell, Jr., North Dakota State; Ryan Keele, Sr., Nebraska-Omaha; Kyle Kleinendorst, Jr., North Dakota State. **DH**—Daniel Telford, Sr., South Dakota State. **UTIL**—Jon Hechtner, Fr., North Dakota State. **SP**—Stephen Bougher, Sr., South Dakota State; Jason Hager, Jr., Oakland; Layne Somsen, Sr., South Dakota State. **RP**—Russell Luxton Jr., Sr., Oakland. **Player of the Year:** Ryan Keele, Nebraska-Omaha. **Pitcher of the Year:** Layne Somsen, South Dakota State. **Newcomer of the Year:** Ryan Keele, Nebraska-Omaha. **Coach of the Year:** Bob Herold, Nebraska-Omaha.

INDIVIDUAL BATTING LEADERS
(Minimum 2.5 plate appearances per team game)

	AVG	AB	R	H	2B	3B	HR	RBI	SB
#Telford, Daniel, SDSU	.410	122	25	50	9	3	6	36	0
Buckley, Cory, UNO	.391	128	26	50	6	2	1	13	2
Keele, Ryan, UNO	.385	156	30	60	9	1	6	33	5
Taylor, Clayton, UNO	.352	122	20	43	8	0	1	18	8
Kleinendorst, Kyle, NDSU	.333	153	23	51	11	3	2	30	7
Mortensen, Alex, UNO	.318	179	32	57	15	0	1	27	2
Schultz, Alex, UNO	.311	151	28	47	10	1	0	21	3
Satzinger, Wes, NDSU	.307	150	28	46	10	1	5	32	3
Burling, Zack, W. Illinois	.306	186	33	57	8	0	1	17	19
Colwell, Tim, UNO	.304	217	40	66	12	4	1	28	11
Bass, Brett, UNO	.301	196	26	59	5	1	0	22	11
DeCook, Neil, W. Illinois	.300	150	21	45	4	2	0	16	11
Gruber, Cole, UNO	.299	134	19	40	7	1	0	26	6
Henning, Jameson, W. Illinois	.297	182	23	54	7	1	1	26	8
Shepherd, Tyler, IPFW	.296	179	22	53	6	0	1	18	29
Jacobson, Paul, SDSU	.293	164	37	48	15	1	1	20	10
Hathaway, Clay, IPFW	.289	190	30	55	9	3	5	18	13
Soat, Brandon, IPFW	.288	125	19	36	7	2	1	20	3
Splett, Scott, SDSU	.288	205	39	59	9	2	2	32	5
Turbak, Blake, NDSU	.286	189	27	54	12	3	2	29	2
Kedroski, Steve, W. Illinois	.284	197	21	56	12	1	3	28	1
Danforth, Eric, SDSU	.278	133	24	37	5	1	1	17	5
Marra, Daniel, SDSU	.274	164	24	45	7	0	0	24	1
Splichal, Tyler, NDSU	.274	168	25	46	5	1	0	19	1
Kalber, Jason, IPFW	.271	170	17	46	16	0	2	16	0
Machbitz, Aaron, SDSU	.270	189	20	51	12	0	2	36	0
Palensky, Caleb, UNO	.266	143	21	38	7	1	1	29	2
Lowden, Steve, IPFW	.266	177	17	47	8	0	1	15	2
Dispensa, Dan, W. Illinois	.265	196	30	52	4	6	3	19	8

	AVG	AB	R	H	2B	3B	HR	RBI	SB
Brosseau, Mike, Oakland	.265	151	19	40	4	1	0	17	1
Enslen, Robby, Oakland	.264	193	30	51	13	0	3	30	2

INDIVIDUAL PITCHING LEADERS
(Minimum 1 IP per team game)

	W	L	ERA	G	SV	IP	H	BB	SO
Michel, Aaron, W. Illinois	4	2	1.23	21	0	66	40	29	44
Straka, John, NDSU	8	2	1.67	15	1	108	91	11	90
Somsen, Layne, SDSU	4	5	1.87	15	1	91	63	30	91
#Moore, J.D., SDSU	0	2	1.99	26	13	32	18	14	38
Bougher, Stephen, SDSU	8	2	2.86	15	0	88	84	23	62
Kalber, Jason, IPFW	2	7	3.16	14	0	83	85	20	60
Bray, Adam, SDSU	7	2	3.19	14	0	68	72	15	41
Hager, Jason, Oakland	3	7	3.30	16	0	95	94	21	73
Constand, Tom, W. Illinois	4	5	3.32	18	0	79	70	30	56
Williamsen, Zach, UNO	4	1	3.38	11	0	56	45	20	42
Ernst, David, NDSU	5	5	3.43	15	0	81	87	21	54
Koons, Tim, Oakland	4	5	3.44	15	0	92	79	31	72
Weaver, Chuck, IPFW	2	5	3.57	14	1	71	66	32	69
White, John, W. Illinois	3	6	3.74	16	0	77	83	24	46
Fox, Tyler, UNO	6	2	3.99	12	0	56	56	19	39
Danielak, Steve, IPFW	5	4	4.25	14	0	66	67	23	39
Emery, Kolton, SDSU	4	5	4.45	11	0	57	64	13	32
Pease, Brandon, IPFW	1	4	4.48	13	0	64	77	20	40
Tew, Matt, UNO	3	5	4.86	14	1	54	57	22	54
Paulson, Jake, Oakland	2	8	5.33	13	0	74	85	21	47
Jaunich, Trevor, NDSU	2	7	5.33	12	0	53	76	18	40

SUN BELT CONFERENCE

	Conference		Overall	
	W	L	W	L
South Alabama	20	10	43	20
Troy	20	10	42	20
Louisiana-Lafayette	19	11	43	20
* **Florida Atlantic**	19	11	42	22
Western Kentucky	16	14	28	29
Arkansas-Little Rock	13	17	28	28
Florida International	13	17	26	32
Arkansas State	12	18	28	31
Middle Tennessee State	11	19	28	28
Louisiana-Monroe	7	23	18	36

ALL-CONFERENCE TEAM: C—Aramis Garcia, So., Florida International. **1B**—Ryan Huck, Sr., Western Kentucky. **2B**—Robby Campbell, Sr., South Alabama. **SS**—Tyler Vaughn, Jr., Troy. **3B**—Logan Pierce, Sr., Troy. **OF**—Danny Collins, Jr., Troy; Seth Harrison, Jr., La.-Lafayette; Dex Kjerstad, Jr., La.-Lafayette. **DH**—Dustin Dalken, Sr., South Alabama. **UTIL**—Jordan Patterson, Jr., South Alabama. **SP**—Austin Gomber, So., Fla. Atlantic; Shane McCain, Jr., Troy; Austin Robichaux, So., La.-Lafayette; Daniel Wright, Sr., Arkansas State. **RP**—Hugh Adams, Sr., Florida Atlantic. **Player of the Year:** Jordan Patterson, South Alabama. **Pitcher of the Year:** Shane McCain, Troy. **Freshman of the Year:** Blake Trahan, La.-Lafayette. **Coach of the Year:** Mark Calvi, South Alabama.

INDIVIDUAL BATTING LEADERS
(Minimum 2.5 at-bats per team game)

	AVG	AB	R	H	2B	3B	HR	RBI	SB
Kjerstad, Dex, La.-Lafayette	.388	255	63	99	14	3	12	44	10
Huck, Ryan, W. Kentucky	.367	196	43	72	16	0	16	56	3
Pierce, Logan, Troy	.364	242	65	88	24	1	8	63	2
Collins, Danny, Troy	.360	236	62	85	25	3	11	68	1
Girouard, Tyler, La.-Lafayette	.360	178	37	64	14	3	7	41	4
Patterson, Jordan, S. Alabama	.352	233	69	82	25	1	4	49	4
Sanger, Brendon, Fla. Atlantic	.347	173	49	60	6	4	3	28	5
Burk, Chris, UALR	.340	200	39	68	15	2	5	35	6
Adams, Caleb, La.-Lafayette	.339	189	49	64	9	1	16	66	3
Harrison, Seth, La.-Lafayette	.338	210	58	71	17	2	9	45	10
Rios, Edwin, FIU	.332	217	42	72	20	0	9	52	2
Pittman, Nathan, Fla. Atlantic	.330	221	50	73	14	4	5	41	13
Dalken, Dustin, S. Alabama	.330	185	29	61	11	3	8	43	2
Stephens, Ryan, MTSU	.329	213	29	70	11	4	4	33	7
Leonards, Ryan, La.-Lafayette	.328	195	34	64	13	0	1	30	7
Vaughn, Tyler, Troy	.327	257	72	84	20	1	0	26	9
Wilcox, Scott, W. Kentucky	.326	236	40	77	16	2	0	26	2

	AVG	AB	R	H	2B	3B	HR	RBI	SB
Earley, Nolan, S. Alabama	.323	235	50	76	19	1	3	59	1
DeBlieux, Jeff, S. Alabama	.323	229	49	74	14	**10**	3	37	6
McDorman, Josh, Troy	.322	199	42	64	12	0	6	38	17
Garcia, Aramis, FIU	.321	224	37	72	12	0	11	51	0
Trahan, Blake, La.-Lafayette	.319	213	46	68	10	0	4	38	13
Ford, Ryan, MTSU	.316	234	48	74	14	2	5	30	7
Roberts, Ryan, Arkansas State	.313	150	21	47	7	0	4	25	0
Strentz, Michael, La.-Lafayette	.311	206	50	64	23	2	7	45	5
Sweety, Zach, FIU	.308	195	43	60	12	1	3	20	1
Johnson, Blake, UALR	.304	204	30	62	16	0	8	38	8
Billingsley, Cole, S. Alabama	.302	169	30	51	5	2	0	22	3
Morales, Mitch, Fla. Atlantic	.301	226	39	68	8	1	0	30	3
Santos, Trae, Troy	.300	237	51	71	12	4	**18**	**70**	2
#Crumpton, Ben, UALR	.281	224	52	63	19	2	4	27	**23**

INDIVIDUAL PITCHING LEADERS
(Minimum 1 IP per team game)

	W	L	ERA	G	SV	IP	H	BB	SO
Gomber, Austin, Fla. Atlantic	8	4	**2.97**	18	0	106	95	28	103
Robichaux, Austin, La.-Lafayette	**9**	2	3.05	16	0	109	96	22	88
Wright, Daniel, Alabama State	6	5	3.18	17	1	**110**	92	26	96
Wilson, Ryan, La.-Lafayette	6	4	3.25	22	1	83	83	27	61
Strawn, Jeremy, Fla. Atlantic	5	3	3.46	17	0	94	96	26	64
McCain, Shane, Troy	**9**	1	3.48	16	0	98	84	18	**105**
#Adams, Hugh, Fla. Atlantic	3	0	3.49	29	**18**	39	18	13	38
Cleveland, Chance, UALR	5	10	3.59	15	0	100	92	29	90
Hicks, Tanner, Troy	8	4	3.61	18	2	100	87	32	94
Noble, Jacob, S. Alabama	5	3	3.70	14	0	66	69	23	53
Bell, Matt, S. Alabama	6	2	3.70	15	0	75	68	23	54
Hill, Nate, Troy	4	2	3.75	**37**	5	74	66	30	92
Koch, John, Arkansas State	4	6	3.95	25	5	68	72	31	62
Huffman, Blake, UALR	6	5	3.99	15	0	88	88	35	69
Wine, Cale, Louisiana-Monroe	6	8	4.05	15	0	91	110	27	59
Clay, Austin, W. Kentucky	3	4	4.28	24	2	74	80	18	56
Tyler, Alexander, FIU	4	6	4.28	15	0	90	85	62	101
Adkins, Hunter, MTSU	5	5	4.31	14	0	88	87	26	65
Wallace, Bradley, Ark. State	5	2	4.33	14	0	71	65	25	78
Edwards, Andrew, W. Kentucky	6	4	4.69	15	0	81	81	38	75
Seibold, Alex, FIU	3	6	4.69	19	0	63	78	24	56

WEST COAST CONFERENCE

	Conference		Overall	
	W	L	W	L
Gonzaga	18	6	32	21
Brigham Young	15	9	32	21
*San Diego	15	9	37	25
San Francisco	15	9	35	24
Pepperdine	13	11	27	24
Loyola Marymount	12	12	24	27
St. Mary's	11	13	21	34
Portland	8	16	18	36
Santa Clara	1	23	14	39

ALL-CONFERENCE TEAM: C—Colton Plaia, Sr., Loyola Marymount. **1B**—Collin Ferguson, So., St. Mary's; Brian Frattali, Sr., Portland; Marco Gonzales, Jr., Gonzaga; Zachary Turner, Jr., San Francisco; Brock Whitney, Jr., BYU. **IF**—Connor Joe, So., San Diego. **3B**—Kris Bryant, Jr., San Diego; Austin Davidson, So., Pepperdine; Adam Law, Jr., BYU; Jeff Melby, Sr., Portland. **OF**—Jaycob Brugman, Jr., BYU; Jacob Hannemann, Fr., BYU; Cory Lebrun, So., Gonzaga; A.J. Robinson, Jr., San Diego; Bradley Zimmer, So., San Francisco. **P**—Abe Bobb, Jr., San Francisco; P.J. Conlon, Fr., San Diego; Marco Gonzales, Jr., Gonzaga; Aaron Griffin, Sr., Loyola Marymount; Haden Hinkle, Sr., San Francisco; Jordan Mills, Jr., St. Mary's; Tyler Olson, Sr., Gonzaga; Colin Welmon, So., Loyola Marymount. **Player of the Year:** Kris Bryant, San Diego; Marco Gonzales, Gonzaga. **Pitcher of the Year:** Tyler Olson, Gonzaga. **Defensive Player of the Year:** Colton Plaia, Loyola Marymount. **Freshman of the Year:** Jacob Hannemann, BYU. **Coach of the Year:** Mack Machtolf, Gonzaga.

INDIVIDUAL BATTING LEADERS
(Minimum 3 plate appearances per team game)

	AVG	AB	R	H	2B	3B	HR	RBI	SB
Kalfus, Brenden, St. Mary's	**.381**	194	31	74	12	0	1	45	11
Law, Adam, BYU	.365	208	46	**76**	10	4	4	46	14

	AVG	AB	R	H	2B	3B	HR	RBI	SB
Hannemann, Jacob, BYU	.344	215	53	74	16	**7**	5	29	14
Melby, Jeff, Portland	.339	171	18	58	11	0	1	22	3
Turner, Zachary, USF	.333	228	32	**76**	15	0	8	**62**	1
Bryant, Kris, San Diego	.329	228	**80**	75	13	3	**31**	**62**	7
Melgosa, Markus, St. Mary's	.326	144	33	47	10	0	0	17	8
Zimmer, Bradley, USF	.320	203	48	65	12	3	7	37	19
Joe, Connor, San Diego	.319	232	43	74	14	0	7	43	3
Brugman, Jaycob, BYU	.317	202	39	64	16	5	11	52	8
Gonzales, Marco, Conzaga	.311	167	16	52	7	0	2	26	3
Plaia, Colton, LMU	.311	193	24	60	16	0	3	25	4
LeBrun, Cory, Gonzaga	.308	185	27	57	11	2	2	34	8
Munoz, Casey, Santa Clara	.308	208	21	64	10	1	1	31	2
Robinson, A.J., San Diego	.307	192	38	59	8	5	1	30	9
Cheek, Tommy, LMU	.305	141	11	43	8	1	0	18	0
Lowe, Ranny, Pepperdine	.304	171	19	52	6	0	0	26	7
Green, Austin, San Diego	.301	176	28	53	13	0	5	39	1
Lenahan, Cody, Portland	.300	190	20	57	9	0	0	18	4
Harisis, Greg, Santa Clara	.293	167	27	49	9	1	2	25	13
Whitney, Brock, BYU	.293	208	38	61	12	1	3	35	1
Ferguson,Collin, St. Mary's	.293	205	25	60	17	1	4	31	2
Maffei, Justin, USF	.292	**253**	43	74	12	0	5	22	15
Mahoney, Cullen, LMU	.291	203	29	59	11	4	0	20	7
Davidson, Austin, Pepperdine	.288	198	30	57	14	0	6	24	2
Gunsolus, Mitchell, Gonzaga	.288	212	38	61	7	6	0	21	5
Lowenstein, Matt, LMU	.287	195	31	56	4	7	0	17	5
Cruikshank, Bob, USF	.286	210	14	60	**19**	0	1	32	0
Villa, Anthony, St. Mary's	.286	196	25	56	14	0	0	32	2
Fujimoto, Zac, LMU	.282	156	22	44	8	1	0	19	14
#Clark, DonAndre, St. Mary's	.245	147	35	36	0	2	0	9	**21**

INDIVIDUAL PITCHING LEADERS
(Minimum 1 IP per team game)

	W	L	ERA	G	SV	IP	H	BB	SO
#Swanner, Michael, Pepperdine	1	1	1.50	23	**14**	24	14	9	26
Hinkle, Haden, USF	**9**	1	**1.90**	19	2	80	55	18	61
Conlon, P.J., San Diego	**9**	1	2.16	25	0	87	81	28	71
Welmon, Colin, LMU	5	4	2.30	12	0	78	65	25	64
McGrath, Patrick, LMU	5	2	2.43	14	0	74	63	16	55
Mills, Jordan, St. Mary's	4	4	2.47	14	0	84	86	21	78
Olson, Tyler, Gonzaga	**9**	4	2.48	16	1	102	94	31	91
Miller, Corey, Pepperdine	5	5	2.71	13	0	90	83	26	67
Gonzales, Marco, Gonzaga	7	3	2.80	17	1	**106**	102	25	**96**
Griffin, Aaron, LMU	4	5	3.07	13	0	88	78	19	72
Poulson, Desmond, BYU	7	2	2.24	15	0	100	90	25	70
Homick, Max, San Diego	5	2	3.34	27	6	70	70	25	57
Griset, Ben, St. Mary's	4	4	3.62	13	0	82	88	23	78
Balog, Alex, USF	3	4	3.63	14	0	92	94	33	67
Barker, Jeff, BYU	6	3	3.67	14	0	69	71	31	41
Brockett, Ryan, St. Mary's	5	5	3.70	15	0	83	72	30	67
Bobb, Abe, USF	5	6	3.70	19	2	75	85	20	49
Reyes, Arturo, Gonzaga	6	3	3.79	20	3	59	58	16	52
Mendoza, Chris, Santa Clara	3	2	3.86	26	1	58	66	25	41
Cecilio, Christian, USF	3	3	3.96	18	0	75	74	19	49
Frazier, Scott, Pepperdine	5	5	4.06	13	0	89	75	40	83
#Cimber, Adam, USF	6	3	3.74	34	9	53	57	11	59

WESTERN ATHLETIC CONFERENCE

	Conference		Overall	
	W	L	W	L
Cal State Bakersfield	18	9	37	22
Texas-Arlington	18	9	31	27
Texas State	16	11	29	29
*Texas-San Antonio	15	11	35	25
Sacramento State	14	13	34	25
New Mexico State	13	14	29	28
Dallas Baptist	13	14	30	30
San Jose State	11	16	17	41
Seattle	10	16	21	33
Louisiana Tech	6	21	19	37

ALL-CONFERENCE TEAM: C—Cael Brockmeyer, Jr., Cal State Bakersfield; Michael Miller, Jr., Dallas Baptist. **IF**—Robert Lecount, Sr., New Mexico State; Duncan McAlpine, Sr., Dallas Baptist; R.J. Perucki, Jr., UTSA; Nate

Roberts, Sr., Seattle; Tanner Rust, Jr., New Mexico State; Oscar Sanay, Jr., Cal State Bakersfield; Tyler Shryock, Jr., Cal State Bakersfield. **OF**—Cody Lovejoy, So., Texas State. **DH**—Chris Lewis, Fr., Sacramento State; Matt Shortall, Jr., Texas-Arlington. **P**—Scott Brattvet, Sr., Cal State Bakersfield; Brennan Leitao, So., Sacramento State; Phil Maton, So., Louisiana Tech; Jeff McKenzie, Sr., Cal State Bakersfield; Sutter McLoughlin, Fr., Sacramento State; Michael Smith, Sr., Dallas Baptist. **Player of the Year:** Tyler Shryock, Cal State Bakersfield. **Pitcher of the Year:** Jeff McKenzie, Cal State Bakersfield. **Freshman of the Year:** Chris Lewis, Sacramento State. **Coach of the Year:** Bill Kernen, Cal State Bakersfield.

INDIVIDUAL BATTING LEADERS
(Minimum 2.5 at-bats per team game)

	AVG	AB	R	H	2B	3B	HR	RBI	SB
Rust, Tanner, NMSU	**.375**	216	54	81	15	2	7	54	8
Shortall, Matt, UT Arlington	.362	232	33	84	**18**	2	8	54	0
Sanay, Oscar, Bakersfield	.362	224	48	81	13	**6**	1	45	4
Shyrock, Tyler, Bakersfield	.357	249	46	**89**	11	3	0	28	4
Perucki, R.J., UTSA	.350	240	49	84	12	0	12	48	1
Lewis, Chris, Sacramento State	.349	215	33	75	15	1	4	46	4
Carroll, Matt, San Jose State	.340	212	27	72	15	0	2	39	5
Lovejoy, Cody, Texas State	.337	187	32	63	12	0	1	22	8
Good, Riley, UTSA	.335	251	50	84	11	**6**	2	33	11
Miller, Michael, Dallas Baptist	.333	243	37	81	**18**	1	9	51	0
Jones, Mylz, Bakersfield	.333	225	32	75	11	0	0	37	1
McAlpine, Duncan, DBU	.333	216	44	72	**18**	1	**17**	58	3
Brockmeyer, Cael, Bakersfield	.330	221	48	73	13	4	4	51	6
Rockett, Daniel, UTSA	.328	201	39	66	13	2	10	48	6
Lecount, Robert, NMSU	.326	187	39	61	13	1	15	**69**	0
Medina, Michael, NMSU	.324	207	54	67	7	2	0	31	11
Targun, Colby, Texas State	.321	159	30	51	9	2	3	20	3
Mattlage, Garrett, Texas State	.320	231	43	74	13	4	3	44	5
Warren, Mike, UTSA	.318	217	43	69	11	1	3	29	5
Valdez, Jacob, San Jose State	.317	205	43	65	12	2	0	28	8
Mercurio, Andre, San Jose State	.315	235	38	74	5	4	0	22	7
Lukes, Nathan, Sac. State	.315	232	40	73	13	4	2	32	4
Cray, Landon, Seattle	.313	163	29	51	4	3	3	24	3
Quiery, Tim, San Jose State	.305	187	22	57	2	0	0	19	7
Copeland, Justin, UT Arlington	.305	187	29	57	6	2	0	23	5
Fields, Chase, Seattle	.305	174	37	53	7	0	1	12	14
Correa, Horacio, UTSA	.304	230	31	70	9	0	1	37	1
Walker, Ryan, UT Arlington	.304	247	43	75	2	2	1	28	6
Phillips, Kyle, NMSU	.301	209	36	63	14	2	6	31	3
Hipp, Parker, NMSU	.300	190	45	57	7	0	9	50	7
#Sah, Kevin, Texas State	.293	205	45	60	12	2	2	28	**26**
#Mitchell, Ronnie, DBU	.283	237	58	67	15	3	4	31	12
#Collins, Boomer, DBU	.271	**258**	48	70	16	2	7	42	5

INDIVIDUAL PITCHING LEADERS
(Minimum 1 IP per team game)

	W	L	ERA	G	SV	IP	H	BB	SO
McKenzie, Jeff, Bakersfield	**13**	2	**1.88**	15	0	**115**	103	24	88
#McLoughlin, Sutter, Sac. State	1	3	2.11	28	**17**	38	27	9	26
#Hart, Donnie, Texas State	1	1	2.13	**41**	0	42	32	13	34
Brattvet, Scott, Bakersfield	9	1	2.65	15	0	99	95	42	70
Maton, Phil, La. Tech	6	6	2.70	15	0	97	75	30	**89**
Leitao, Brennan, Sac. State	8	3	2.77	17	1	101	79	20	47
Vachon, Brad, UT Arlington	7	4	3.18	16	0	96	77	42	75
Aikenhead, Taylor, Bakersfield	5	2	3.24	26	5	67	57	30	36
Hassna, Kyle, San Jose State	3	6	3.26	25	2	58	57	16	49
Humpal, Lucas, Texas State	5	2	3.30	25	0	63	67	16	41
Hartson, Brock, UTSA	9	5	3.40	17	0	106	108	27	50
Morgan, Zach, Sac. State	7	1	3.45	16	0	76	74	22	33
Weaver, Chase, UT Arlington	4	1	3.92	20	1	62	59	27	38
Montoya, Jonathan, Bakersfield	4	3	3.94	15	0	78	70	31	32
Petersen, Trevor, La. Tech	3	6	3.95	15	0	80	84	34	27
Nichols, Ty, Sacramento State	4	6	4.01	16	0	74	68	19	43
Slaton, D.J., San Jose State	4	8	4.04	15	0	91	98	37	49
Kraft, Michael, UTSA	4	5	4.10	17	0	68	70	40	62
Olson, Andrew, Seattle	7	5	4.18	15	0	67	84	12	37
Pacheco, Jordan, UTSA	7	2	4.25	25	1	72	76	18	40
Trabanino, Nolan, UTSA	4	3	4.38	20	0	74	90	15	33
Black, Taylor, Texas State	3	7	4.43	15	0	85	91	40	68

NCAA DIVISION II

Tampa brought a high-powered offense. Minnesota State-Mankato brought a top-notch pitching staff. In the end, Tampa's bats prevailed, earning the Spartans an NCAA Division II championship with an 8-2 victory at the USA Baseball Training Complex in Cary, N.C. It was Tampa's sixth championship, and its third under coach Joe Urso, who led the Spartans to titles in 2006 and '07.

"My fear coming into this year was that I knew I had a special group of guys," Urso told NCAA. com. "I just wanted this to end well for them. This will go down as my favorite team ever. I didn't think anyone would ever beat that 2006 team. That's how proud I am of these young men."

The Spartans jumped on MSU ace righthander Harvey Martin (9-1, 2.06)—who came in with a handful of pitcher of the year awards—for five runs in the second inning, knocking him out of the game and building a cushion that the Mavericks would never threaten.

"We had seen (Martin) in the tournament," Urso said. "We knew his strengths were away, and we told our guys not to worry about any strikeouts inside. Those would be on the coaching staff. We needed to take that outside part of the plate away from him, because he can point that ball right where he wants it on the corner. That's why he's so good."

Tampa third baseman Jake Schrader knocked in the first Spartan run on an RBI double, and he went on to win the tournament's most outstanding player award after going 8-for-18 with two home runs and six RBIs. Meanwhile, former Nebraska pitcher Jon Keller (6-3, 3.58) tossed seven scoreless innings to earn his second win of the tournament.

Keller wasn't the only notable Division I bounceback to help lead the Spartans to the title. Cleanup man Sean O'Brien (.341/.450/.436) was a transfer from Florida State, and other players on the roster transferred from Miami, Auburn, Tulane and Troy. The Spartans opened the year ranked No. 3 in Division II in Baseball America's College Preview, and they stayed in the top 10 in D-II polls all year long.

UT hit a speedbump in the semifinals in Cary, getting shut out by Grand Valley State 4-0, forcing a rematch the next day with a trip to the championship game on the line. Tampa's top pitcher, Mike Adams, spent most of the season anchoring the back of the bullpen, but he made his second start of the season in the rematch against Grand Valley, and he delivered six innings of shutout ball in a 10-1 win.

"I felt like we came out of that game just hoping to get through it to get to the finals," Urso said. "We talked about that. You've got to come out and fight to get to the finals. But these guys were resilient all year. That shows you what the personality of this team was all about. They were not going to give up. They came out and fought for us the next day."

Adams finished 8-0, 2.10 with six saves and a 77-8 strikeout-walk in 64 innings. The lefthander was drafted in the seventh round by the Red Sox.

The Mavericks had been undefeated in Cary going into the championship game, relying on strong starting pitching from Martin and rotationmate Jason Hoppe (8-1, 1.26), who capped a streak of 55⅓ scoreless innings in a semifinal win against St. Edward's. The streak broke the D-II record of 54 consecutive scoreless innings set by Southern Illinois-Edwardsville's Kyle Jones in 2006.

DIVISION II WORLD SERIES

Site: Cary, N.C.
Participants: Coker, S.C. (38-14); Franklin Pierce, N.H. (36-17); Grand Canyon, Ariz. (39-17); Grand Valley State, Mich. (35-17); Minnesota State-Mankato (39-8); St. Edward's, Texas (42-16); Shippensburg, Pa. (32-21); Tampa (43-11).
Champion: Tampa.
Runner-up: Minnesota State-Mankato.
Outstanding player: Jake Schrader, 3b, Tampa.
PRELIMINARIES
Franklin Pierce 1, Shippensburg 0
Minnesota State-Mankato 2, Grand Valley State 0
Tampa 12, Coker 4
St. Edwards 1, Grand Canyon 0
Grand Valley State 8, Shippensburg 4 (Shippensburg eliminated)
Minnesota State-Mankato 10, Franklin Pierce 5
Grand Canyon 10, Coker 2 (Coker eliminated)
Tampa 10, St. Edward's 3
Grand Valley State 10, Franklin Pierce 3 (Franklin Pierce eliminated)
St. Edward's 8, Grand Canyon 5 (Grand Canyon eliminated)
SEMINIFINALS
Grand Valley State 4, Tampa 0
Minnesota State-Mankato 6, St. Edwards 5 (St. Edwards eliminated)
Tampa 10, Grand Valley State 1 (Grand Valley State eliminated)
FINALS
Tampa 8, Minnesota State-Mankato 2
(Minnesota State-Mankato eliminated)

NCAA DIVISION III

Linfield (Ore.) rode a complete-game performance from sophomore righthander Chris Haddeland to beat Southern Maine, 4-1, and win its first NCAA title. The Wildcats had won NAIA titles in 1966 and 1971.

Linfield, coached by former New York Yankee Scott Brosius, was the top-ranked team in the country heading into regional play and went 8-2 on its way to the title. The Wildcats beat Southern Maine 10-1 in the second round of the CWS, forcing the Huskies to run through the losers' bracket. Linfield started the CWS 3-0 before losing to Ithaca, which then lost to Southern Maine, setting up the winner-take-all final.

In the championship game, Southern Maine took an early one-run lead and ended up outhitting Linfield, but a four-run fourth put the Wildcats on top. Haddeland, one of four Linfield players who earned a spot on the all-tournament team, cruised the rest of the way to get his 15th win of the season. He was named the Most Outstanding Player of the CWS and finished 15-1, 1.07 on the season.

"We came close to getting them in the first inning, and then they had the big fourth inning," Southern Maine coach Ed Flaherty said. "And the kid Haddeland, he's a first-team All-American, and there's a reason for it. He kept us off balance, got some big double plays when it counted. The kid's good."

Brosius, a Linfield alumnus who won three World Series titles with the Yankees, said leading his alma mater to the title was special.

"This ranks up there, believe me," Brosius said. "You win as a professional and certainly there is a part of that that you carry with you. But this is a special deal. This is about more than just me, about more than us. This is a college campus, a community. This is a big deal."

DIVISION III WORLD SERIES

Site: Appleton, Wis.
Participants: Ithaca, N.Y. (38-5); Kean, N.J. (37-11); Linfield, Ore. (37-7); Manchester, Ind. (39-4-1); Millsaps, Miss. (38-11); Southern Maine (41-8); Webster, Mo. (36-9); Wisconsin-Stevens Point (38-9).
Champion: Linfield.
Runner-up: Southern Maine.
Outstanding player: Chris Haddeland, rhp, Linfield.
RESULTS
Southern Maine 2, Millsaps 1
Linfield 8, Ithaca 6
UW-Stevens Point 6, Manchester 5
Kean 14, Webster 8
Ithaca 5, Millsaps 2 (Millsaps eliminated)
Webster 5, Manchester 3 (Manchester eliminated)
Linfield 10, Southern Maine 1
UW-Stevens Point 4, Kean 3

Southern Maine 7, Webster 2 (Webster eliminated)
Ithaca 3, Kean 1 (Kean eliminated)
Linfield 5, UW-Stevens Point 3
Southern Maine 8, UW-Stevens Point 1
(UW-Stevens Point eliminated)
Ithaca 6, Linfield 4
Southern Maine 5, Ithaca 4 (Ithaca eliminated)
Linfield 4, Southern Maine 1 (Southern Maine eliminated)

NAIA

In the Avisa-NAIA Baseball World Series title game, Faulkner (Ala.) lived up to its No. 1 seed and soundly beat host and perennial power Lewis-Clark State (Idaho) 11-4 for its first title.

The championship game drubbing, which was spurred by a six-run second inning, capped a perfect championship series for the Eagles. They shut out Missouri Baptist 2-0 in the opening game, then scored 25 runs over the next three games to reach the championship, where they pounded out 16 hits.

Most Outstanding Player Johnny Shuttlesworth earned the win in two of Faulkner's five World Series games, including the clincher. He posted a 2.51 ERA over 14 innings in Lewiston. His final 122-pitch outing was gritty, as he allowed 14 hits over 7⅓ innings but yielded just four runs.

"Just because a pitcher is allowing a lot of hits doesn't mean the other team is squaring balls up," said Faulker coach Patrick McCarthy, who led the Eagles to a national title in his fourth season at the helm. "Johnny has totally bought into pitching to contact and has a great mindset on the mound."

Lewis-Clark State entered the World Series as the No. 7 seed but still reached the title game for the 22nd time, finishing as runner-up for the sixth time.

Site: Lewiston, Idaho
Participants: Embry-Riddle, Fla. (49-13); Faulkner, Ala. (52-11); Lee, Tenn. (50-10); Lewis-Clark State, Idaho (42-13); Missouri Baptist (36-12); Northwood, Texas (43-12); Rogers State, Okla. (35-23); Sterling, Kan. (48-13); The Master's, Calif. (44-15); York, Neb. (44-11).
Champion: Faulkner.
Runner-up: Lewis-Clark State.
Outstanding player: Johnny Shuttlesworth, rhp, Faulkner.

NJCAA DIVISION I

Central Alabama captured its first Junior College World Series title by beating Palm Beach State (Fla.) 7-3 in the championship.

Freshman righthander Paul Young allowed three runs (one earned) on seven hits in a complete game to pick up his second victory of the World Series. He made just five previous starts all season.

Sophomore catcher Blaine Miller led the Central Alabama offense, going 3-for-4 with two RBIs and three runs. Center fielder Darius Reese went 3-for-5 with an RBI and a run scored in the final; he finished the tournament 16-for-29 (.552) with two doubles and two triples to capture Most Outstanding Player honors.

Site: Grand Junction, Colo.
Participants: Central Alabama (38-13); Cochise, Ariz. (49-17); Connors State, Okla. (52-9); Kaskaskia, Ill. (39-10); Midland, Texas (47-13); Navarro, Texas (43-15); Neosho County, Kan. (35-25); Palm Beach State, Fla. (38-19); Spartanburg Methodist, S.C. (45-13); Walters State, Tenn. (37-16).
Champion: Central Alabama.
Runner-up: Palm Beach State.
Outstanding player: Darius Reese, of, Central Alabama.

NJCAA DIVISION II

It its first appearance in the NJCAA Division II Baseball World Series, Murray State (Okla.) took home the championship, dethroning defending champion Louisiana State-Eunice 4-3 in the final. That clinched Murray State's first national championship in any sport.

Bradley Horn allowed three runs on seven hits while striking out six in a complete-game victory for the Aggies. Tournament MVP Noel Nevarez made several key plays in center field during the World Series and led Murray State's offense by hitting .400 with six RBIs, a home run and three doubles.

Site: Enid, Okla.
Participants: Brunswick, N.C. (38-13); Connecticut-Avery Point (38-8); Grand Rapids, Mich. (27-26); Heartland, Ill. (48-9); Lackawanna, Pa. (41-18); Louisiana State-Eunice (48-8); Madison, Wis. (39-11); Murray State, Okla. (41-21); North Iowa Area (29-16); Scottsdale, Ariz. (38-19).
Champion: Murray State.
Runner-up: LSU-Eunice.
Most Valuable Player: Noel Nevarez, of, Murray State.

NJCAA DIVISION III

Gloucester County (N.J.) crushed Century (Minn.) 16-4 in the title game to clinch its seventh NJCAA Division III national championship. The Roadrunners broke the game open with 10 runs in the fifth inning. Most Outstanding Player Narcisco Crook, a 23rd-round pick by the Reds, led the way, going 3-for-5 with a home run and

seven RBIs.

Site: Tyler, Texas
Participants: Brookhaven, Texas (30-18); Century, Minn. (38-11); Gloucester County, N.J. (45-3); Montgomery, Md. (40-15); Nassau, N.Y. (19-16); Niagara County, N.Y. (37-16); Northern Essex, Mass. (18-14); Waubonsee, Ill. (36-22).
Champion: Gloucester County
Runner-up: Century
Outstanding player: Narciso Crook, of, Gloucester County.

CALIFORNIA CC ATHLETIC ASSOCIATION

Cypress JC won the California Community College Athletic Association title for the fifth time, defeating Orange Empire Conference foe Fullerton JC 10-3 in the final. Coach Scott Pickler, who has 904 career victories, led the Chargers to all five of their titles.

Fullerton had won the conference in the regular season, while Cypress finished in fourth place. But Cypress allowed just six runs in its unbeaten three-game run through the state tournament. Bryson Kauhaahaa threw a complete game in the final, and the Chargers supported him with 18 hits. Cypress catcher Tyler Schultz hit .538 in three games to win Most Outstanding Player honors.

Site: Fresno, Calif.
Participants: Cypress (29-14); Feather River (29-12); Fullerton (30-13); Santa Rosa (33-7-1).
Champion: Cypress.
Runner-up: Fullerton.
Outstanding player: Tyler Schultz, c, Cypress.

NORTHWEST ATHLETIC ASSOCIATION OF CCS

Everett topped defending champion Pierce 4-1 to capture the NWAACC title. Everett's Gunnar Swanson allowed just one run on four hits and no walks while striking out nine in a complete-game gem in the final. Everett took control of the game with three runs in the fourth, and Swanson took it from there.

Site: Longview, Wash.
Participants: Bellevue, Wash. (32-20); Everett, Wash. (39-9); Linn-Benton, Ore. (28-16); Mt. Hood, Ore. (31-14); Pierce, Wash. (30-15); Tacoma, Wash. (35-16); Treasure Valley, Ore. (37-12); Yakima Valley, Wash. (33-19).
Champion: Everett.
Runner-up: Pierce.
Outstanding player: Gunnar Swanson, Everett.

DURHAM, N.C.

Carlos Rodon admitted he has developed a special affinity for Durham Bulls Athletic Park. It's where the North Carolina State lefthander pitched 10 dominating innings against North Carolina in an Atlantic Coast Conference tournament game, striking out 14. It's also where he posed with Wolfpack teammate and roommate Trea Turner and North Carolina's Kent Emanuel and Colin Moran in January of 2013 for the cover of BA's College Preview issue.

It's where his 2013 season ended, in a start against Cuba at the end of the summer schedule for USA Baseball's Collegiate National Team. And once again, it was the scene of a Rodon masterpiece.

"I love this ballpark," Rodon said with a smile after his performance, during which he tossed 6⅔ scoreless innings, giving up just two hits and striking out 11 in a dominating shutdown of Cuba. The Collegiate National Team had its biggest offensive outburst to back him and won the fifth and final game of the series with Cuba 5-3, sweeping the series. It's the first five-game sweep for a USA Collegiate National Team against Cuba.

The CNT finished with a 20-3 record for the summer, with the only three losses coming in a five-game series in Japan. Team USA won all five games against Cuba, but all the games were close, with one-run wins in the opener in Des Moines, Iowa, as well as two games in Omaha. The Americans won by a single run in Game Four, 3-2 at USA Baseball's National Training Complex in Cary, N.C., before ending the summer with Rodon's firepower, five runs and fireworks.

"It was an awesome way to end the summer," said closer Ryan Burr (Arizona State), a freshman who struck out two of the game's last three batters to notch the save, his sixth of the summer. "This was a snapshot of our entire summer—great pitching, timely hitting, just playing USA Baseball. It was awesome to be able to do it with a nice crowd in this great ballpark, against a great team like Cuba."

COLLEGIATE NATIONAL TEAM STATS
Year indicates 2013-14 class standing

PLAYER, POS.	YEAR	SCHOOL	AVG	OBP	SLG	G	AB	R	H	2B	3B	HR	RBI	BB	SO	SB
Taylor Sparks, 3b/1b	Jr.	UC Irvine	.396	.475	.434	19	53	11	21	0	1	0	10	4	13	7
Will Maddox, if/of	Jr.	Tennessee	.389	.450	.444	6	18	2	7	1	0	0	2	2	5	2
C.J. Hinojosa, ss	So.	Texas	.375	.444	.583	10	24	5	9	5	0	0	6	2	1	0
A.J. Reed, 1b	Jr.	Kentucky	.364	.462	.455	5	11	1	4	1	0	0	3	2	4	0
Alex Bregman, ss/2b	So.	Louisiana State	.361	.410	.486	18	72	16	26	7	1	0	12	7	11	7
Kyle Schwarber, c/of	Jr.	Indiana	.308	.396	.436	21	78	17	24	7	0	1	16	11	17	3
Michael Conforto, of	Jr.	Oregon State	.302	.423	.524	18	63	13	19	5	0	3	10	7	23	1
Bradley Zimmer, of	Jr.	San Francisco	.300	.383	.371	21	70	19	21	2	0	1	11	9	20	11
Mike Papi, of	Jr.	Virginia	.300	.364	.300	3	10	1	3	0	0	0	0	1	2	1
Nate Irving, c	Jr.	Virginia	.300	.462	.300	5	10	1	3	0	0	0	2	3	2	0
Matt Chapman, 3b	Jr.	Cal State Fullerton	.278	.396	.361	23	72	17	20	6	0	0	20	14	17	7
Austin Cousino, of	Jr.	Kentucky	.273	.347	.439	22	66	11	18	2	3	1	7	3	5	0
Grayson Greiner, c	Jr.	South Carolina	.255	.367	.353	16	51	4	13	2	0	1	8	8	15	0
Sam Travis, 1b	Jr.	Indiana	.222	.306	.315	19	54	9	12	2	0	1	7	5	15	3
Trea Turner, ss/2b	Jr.	N.C. State	.211	.347	.263	20	76	13	16	2	1	0	5	17	15	9
Skye Bolt, of	So.	North Carolina	.120	.214	.280	13	25	4	3	1	0	1	5	3	11	3

PITCHER, POS.	YEAR	SCHOOL	W	L	ERA	G	SV	IP	H	R	ER	BB	SO	AVG
Carlos Rodon, lhp	Jr.	N.C. State	3	0	0.00	4	0	17	5	0	0	4	21	.094
Riley Ferrell, rhp	So.	Texas Christian	0	0	0.00	9	2	9	1	0	0	4	15	.037
Trent Thornton, rhp	So.	North Carolina	1	0	0.00	3	0	6	3	0	0	2	7	.150
Cole Irvin, lhp	So.	Oregon	1	0	0.00	3	0	6	2	1	0	2	9	.105
A.J. Reed, lhp	Jr.	Kentucky	1	0	0.00	1	0	5	1	0	0	1	4	.059
Matt Chapman, rhp	Jr.	Cal State Fullerton	0	0	0.00	2	0	2	1	0	0	1	3	.125
Nick Burdi, rhp	Jr.	Louisville	0	0	0.00	2	0	2	2	0	0	0	4	.250
Matt Imhof, lhp	Jr.	Cal Poly	3	0	0.53	6	0	17	10	1	1	5	18	.175
Ryan Burr, rhp	So.	Arizona State	0	0	0.93	9	6	10	2	1	1	5	20	.067
Chris Diaz, lhp	Jr.	Miami	1	0	0.96	10	0	9	4	1	1	4	11	.138
Brandon Finnegan, lhp	Jr.	Texas Christian	3	1	1.14	6	0	24	11	4	3	10	23	.145
Daniel Mengden, rhp	Jr.	Texas A&M	1	0	1.35	6	0	13	11	3	2	1	11	.220
Luke Weaver, rhp	Jr.	Florida State	0	0	2.14	5	0	21	20	7	5	5	17	.247
David Berg, rhp	Jr.	UCLA	3	0	2.89	7	0	9	5	3	3	1	9	.147
Erick Fedde, rhp	Jr.	Nevada-Las Vegas	1	0	3.18	2	0	6	3	2	2	1	8	.150
Colin Welmon, rhp	Jr.	Loyola Marymount	0	0	3.60	2	1	5	7	3	2	0	4	.333
Preston Morrison, rhp	Jr.	Texas Christian	0	1	4.05	8	1	13	9	7	6	1	17	.173
Tommy Thorpe, lhp	Jr.	Oregon	1	0	4.50	5	0	10	12	5	5	4	11	.286
Tyler Beede, rhp	Jr.	Vanderbilt	1	1	6.59	5	0	14	9	10	10	13	10	.191

Coach Jim Schlossnagle (Texas Christian) addressed his team on its last day off, when it was coming to North Carolina after winning the first three games of the series in the Midwest. He was pleased the Americans had won the series but challenged to see if his team could do something no other U.S. club had done—sweep a five-game set. They came through for him with defensive execution, making only one error in the five-game series and none in the final two games.

"We knew the goals at the start of the year were to win the Japan series (in Japan), which hasn't been done in 40 years, and to win this Cuba series," Schlossnagle said. "When we didn't win the series in Japan, the guys were disappointed—really disappointed. We talked about it every day. We said, 'Hey, the only way to make up for it is to win this Cuba series.'"

Rodon finished the season 3-0 in four outings for the CNT, tossing 17 scoreless innings and allowing just five hits and four walks while striking out 21. He led the way as the U.S. pitching staff posted a 1.87 ERA over 23 games, with 222 strikeouts and 64 walks in 197 innings.

The American offense had its best game of the series, getting a pair of doubles from Michael Conforto (Oregon State), one of five players with an RBI. Turner scored two runs and had a stolen base out of the leadoff spot, and corner infielder Taylor Sparks (UC Irvine), who played first base in the finale after playing third a day earlier, had an infield hit and finished the summer batting a team-best .396 in 53 at-bats.

The strong finish eased the sting of losing the 39th friendly series against a team of Japanese collegiate all-stars. The bi-annual five-game series, which was played in Japan in 2013, came down to the final game after the two teams split the first four contests. Japan won the rubber game 7-4.

Cotuit Wins Cape Title

Chatham and Falmouth each won 26 games in the regular season to win their respective Cape Cod League divisions, but Orleans and Cotuit were hotter in the playoffs. The Firebirds overcame a sluggish start to win 16 of their final 20 games (counting the postseason) before getting swept by the Kettleers in the best-of-three finals. Lefthander Christian Cecilio (San Francisco) threw six scoreless innings to earn the win in the championship game, and Dons teammate Bradley Zimmer won postseason MVP honors, largely on the strength of his three-hit, two-RBI first game against Orleans. Cotuit, the most decorated team in Cape League annals, won its 14th title, and its first since 2010.

Zimmer highlighted a solid group of position-player prospects in the Cape League. The circuit featured a fairly deep supply of power hitters, athletes and skilled middle infielders, but it lacked surefire stars, and the pitching crop was thin. Scouts agreed that top prospect Jeff Hoffman (East Carolina) of Hyannis was the only likely top-five overall pick candidate in the league.

"I thought you had a lot of guys that were fourth- to 10th-round guys there," a National League crosschecker said. "And a handful of guys that were top three rounds."

Pitching dominated the Cape League in 2013, a year after juiced baseballs resulted in offensive explosions in the Cape and many other summer leagues. A return to the old baseballs resulted in a return to statistical normalcy.

SUMMER LEAGUE ROUNDUP

■ The Madison Mallards topped the Duluth Huskies 12-3 in championship game to win their second Northwoods League title and first since 2004. At 41-29, Madison had the worst regular-season record of the four playoff teams. The Waterloo Bucks, who lost in the first round of the playoffs, finished with an NWL-record 51 wins (.729 winning percentage).

■ The Newport Gulls were denied a second straight New England Collegiate Baseball League title by the Keene Swamp Bats, who took two out of three against the Gulls in the championship series. Four Keene pitchers combined to shut down Newport in the decisive third game with infielder Matt Ford (Hofstra) and outfielder J.P. Sportman (Central Connecticut State) combining to drive in five runs in Keene's 7-1 win.

■ The Peninsula Pilots went just 14-13 in the first half of the Coastal Plain League season, but they got hot when it mattered most. The Pilots went 19-9 in the second half to finish with a team-record 39 regular-season victories, then vanquished Wilmington, Edenton and Columbia in best-of-three postseason series to capture their first-ever Petitt Cup Championship. Peninsula dethroned defending champion Columbia with a pair of one-run victories in the finals.

■ The Alaska Goldpanners went 22-13 to win the Alaska League's regular-season title, then swept the defending champion Anchorage Glacier Pilots in the best-of-three ABL tournament championship series. For the first time, the ABL elected to hold a postseason round-robin tournament with every team included, save for the Peninsula Oilers, who elected not to participate. For the second consecutive summer, the ABL did not send a team to the National Baseball Congress World Series.

■ The Los Angeles Brewers toppled the 10-time defending champion Santa Barbara Foresters with a two-game sweep in the Cal Collegiate League championship series. The Foresters went on to the NBC World Series, where they saw their two-year reign end in the semifinals. The Seattle Studs, who finished as runners-up in 2008, 2010 and 2012, took home their first NBC World Series title.

COLLEGE *SUMMER LEAGUES*

CAPE COD LEAGUE

EASTERN	W	L	T	PCT	PTS
Chatham Anglers	26	17	1	.591	53
Orleans Firebirds	24	19	1	.545	49
Harwich Mariners	23	19	2	.523	48
Yarmouth-Dennis Red Sox	20	22	2	.455	42
Brewster Whitecaps	14	29	1	.318	29
WESTERN	W	L	T	PCT	PTS
Falmouth Commodores	26	18	0	.591	52
Hyannis Harbor Hawks	25	17	2	.568	52
Cotuit Kettleers	25	18	1	.568	51
Bourne Braves	21	21	1	.488	43
Wareham Gatemen	9	33	1	.209	19

CHAMPIONSHIP: Cotuit defeated Orleans 2-0 in best-of-three series.
TOP 30 PROSPECTS: 1. Jeff Hoffman, rhp, Hyannis (Jr., East Carolina). **2.** Ian Happ, 2b/3b/of, Harwich (So., Cincinnati). **3.** James Kaprielian, rhp, Yarmouth-Dennis (So., UCLA). **4.** Bradley Zimmer, of, Cotuit (Jr., San Francisco). **5.** Derek Fisher, of, Harwich (Jr., Virginia). **6.** Erick Fedde, rhp, Yarmouth-Dennis (Jr., Nevada-Las Vegas). **7.** Kyle Freeland, lhp, Hyannis (Jr., Evansville). **8.** Max Pentecost, c, Bourne (Jr., Kennesaw State). **9.** Sean Newcomb, lhp, Wareham (Jr., Hartford). **10.** Kyle Funkhouser, rhp, Chatham (So., Louisville). **11.** Kyle Twomey, lhp, Orleans (So., Southern California). **12.** J.D. Davis, 1b/3b/rhp, Chatham (Jr., Cal State Fullerton). **13.** Dylan Davis, of/rhp, Falmouth (Jr., Oregon State). **14.** Alex Blandino, 3b, Yarmouth-Dennis (Jr., Stanford). **15.** Drew Jackson, ss, Cotuit (So., Stanford). **16.** Lukas Schiraldi, rhp, Chatham (Jr., Texas). **17.** Brian Anderson, of/3b, Hyannis (Jr., Arkansas). **18.** D.J. Stewart, of, Yarmouth-Dennis (So., Florida State). **19.** Scott Heineman, of, Brewster (Jr., Oregon). **20.** Rhett Wiseman, of, Cotuit (So., Vanderbilt). **21.** Kevin Newman, ss, Falmouth (So., Arizona). **22.** Hunter Cole, of, Cotuit (Jr., Georgia). **23.** Casey Gillaspie, 1b, Falmouth (Jr., Wichita State). **24.** Ben Smith, lhp, Cotuit (Jr., Coastal Carolina). **25.** Jordan Foley, rhp, Hyannis (Jr., Central Michigan). **26.** Dillon Peters, lhp, Harwich (Jr., Texas). **27.** Branden Cogswell, ss, Harwich (Jr., Virginia). **28.** Ross Kivett, 2b, Orleans (Sr., Kansas State). **29.** Matt Troupe, rhp, Orleans (Jr., Arizona). **30.** Sam Coonrod, rhp, Yarmouth-Dennis (Jr., Southern Illinois).

INDIVIDUAL BATTING LEADERS
(MINIMUM 2.7 PLATE APPEARANCES PER TEAM GAME)

	AVG	G	AB	R	H	HR	RBI
Kevin Newman, Falmouth	.375	40	160	36	60	0	18
Kevin Cron, Falmouth	.350	42	157	28	55	4	32
Max Pentecost, Bourne	.346	35	130	20	45	6	29
Ross Kivett, Orleans	.336	34	140	20	47	3	17
Derek Fisher, Harwich	.333	36	120	14	40	0	21
Rhys Hoskins, Falmouth	.326	44	178	44	58	7	37
Jordan Luplow, Falmouth	.325	41	151	18	49	4	28
Clinton Freeman, Bourne	.322	37	143	18	46	0	17
Casey Gillaspie, Falmouth	.321	43	165	31	53	8	27
Dylan Davis, Falmouth	.317	29	104	20	33	6	34

INDIVIDUAL PITCHING LEADERS
(MINIMUM 0.8 INNINGS PITCHED PER TEAM GAME)

	W	L	ERA	IP	H	BB	SO
Lukas Schiraldi, Chatham	4	1	1.20	38	28	10	27
Aaron Bummer, Harwich	5	2	1.41	45	39	14	18
Justin Kamplain, Brewster	3	2	1.66	38	28	18	41
Bobby Poyner, Orleans	2	3	1.72	37	30	5	24
Trent Szkutnik, Orleans	3	1	1.72	37	26	9	30
John Means, Falmouth	3	3	1.99	41	25	8	35
Kyle Freeland, Hyannis	3	2	2.25	40	39	4	48
Chris Ellis, Cotuit	2	3	2.39	38	32	10	23
Tucker Simpson, Wareham	1	3	2.75	36	33	14	22
Chandler Shepherd, Harwich	2	3	2.78	36	27	9	28

BOURNE

BATTING	AVG	AB	R	H	2B	3B	HR	RBI	SB
Max Pentecost	.346	130	20	45	7	0	6	29	5
Clinton Freeman	.322	143	18	46	9	0	0	17	1
Tim Caputo	.315	143	25	45	5	0	0	15	11
Bobby Boyd	.306	98	21	30	1	1	0	4	5
Mark Laird	.292	65	9	19	2	0	0	8	2
Mason Robbins	.287	115	15	33	6	0	0	13	3

	AVG	AB	R	H	2B	3B	HR	RBI	SB
Eric Fisher	.286	98	10	28	5	2	0	14	3
Jeff Gardner	.272	92	10	25	5	1	0	8	1
Michael Martin	.250	8	0	2	0	0	0	1	0
Pat Kelly	.242	99	6	24	2	1	0	2	3
Trent Gilbert	.232	112	12	26	3	1	0	9	2
Matt Gonzalez	.224	85	4	19	5	0	0	6	1
Tyler Kuresa	.202	84	5	17	3	0	1	8	2
Richard Gonzalez	.164	73	7	12	3	0	0	1	0
Vinny Siena	.152	99	5	15	1	0	0	9	0
Joey Cujas	.143	7	0	1	0	0	0	0	1
Chad Carroll	.053	19	1	1	0	0	0	2	1

PITCHING	W	L	ERA	G	SV	IP	H	BB	SO
Christian Colletti	1	0	0.00	1	0	5	4	0	3
Michael Costello	0	0	0.00	8	0	18	16	3	9
Patrick Peterson	0	0	0.00	1	0	1	0	1	2
Jaron Long	5	1	0.30	6	0	30	19	6	25
Justin McCalvin	1	0	1.04	6	1	9	7	3	13
Ryan Kellogg	3	0	1.36	6	0	33	27	5	26
Trace Dempsey	1	1	1.39	12	4	13	13	4	17
David Speer	0	3	1.98	4	0	14	20	7	14
Nigel Nootbaar	0	1	2.31	7	0	12	6	4	10
Kody Kerski	0	0	2.35	3	0	8	5	1	5
Ryan Harris	0	0	2.57	4	0	7	4	4	5
Jacob Lindgren	2	0	2.57	6	0	14	14	1	18
Josh Laxer	1	1	2.88	12	1	25	25	9	22
Jack English	1	2	3.00	12	1	21	25	8	33
Kyle Kubat	2	4	3.13	8	0	46	48	8	21
Kris Gardner	0	4	3.41	7	0	29	36	8	12
Cody Livingston	1	0	4.24	10	0	23	20	14	24
Austin Gomber	2	2	4.35	7	0	29	22	10	14
Clinton Freeman	0	0	4.50	4	1	4	6	0	5
Michael Kraft	0	0	4.50	1	0	4	6	2	1
Hawtin Buchanan	1	0	5.40	10	0	13	15	9	16
Will Cox	0	1	6.75	9	1	12	11	4	14
Eric Skoglund	0	0	9.00	2	0	3	6	1	1
Joshua Harris	0	1	12.00	1	0	3	6	2	2
Henry Van Zant	0	0	18.00	1	0	1	3	0	2

BREWSTER

BATTING	AVG	AB	R	H	2B	3B	HR	RBI	SB
Jordan Ebert	.333	9	0	3	1	0	0	1	0
Jose Brizuela	.328	61	10	20	1	2	0	10	0
Boo Vazquez	.313	112	16	35	7	0	0	8	0
Scott Heineman	.304	148	21	45	8	3	2	8	24
Trevor Mitsui	.282	131	15	37	7	0	1	14	1
David Armendariz	.269	104	12	28	5	1	1	10	3
Trent Woodward	.255	94	7	24	2	0	0	11	0
Nick Lynch	.246	69	5	17	4	0	1	14	2
Cole Lankford	.245	110	13	27	7	0	0	17	1
Ford Stainbeck	.235	81	11	19	2	0	0	5	0
Kyle Overstreet	.232	99	9	23	3	0	1	8	7
Austin Bailey	.222	54	6	12	3	1	0	5	0
Hayden Simerly	.222	9	2	2	0	0	0	0	1
Joe Chavez	.200	10	0	2	0	0	0	1	0
Connor Schaefbauer	.196	51	9	10	1	0	0	3	3
Tucker Tubbs	.194	72	8	14	4	0	0	1	0
Keaton Aldridge	.161	56	2	9	1	1	0	4	0
Aaron Brown	.106	47	2	5	1	0	0	3	0
Chris Mariscal	.103	68	2	7	1	0	0	3	2
Timothy Costen	.077	13	1	1	0	0	0	1	1
Derek Campbell	.000	8	0	0	0	0	0	0	0
Brandon Leibrandt	.000	1	0	0	0	0	0	0	0
Evan Rutter	.000	1	0	0	0	0	0	0	0
Brad Schreiber	.000	1	0	0	0	0	0	0	0
Corey Taylor	.000	1	0	0	0	0	0	0	0

PITCHING	W	L	ERA	G	SV	IP	H	BB	SO
Scott Heineman	0	0	0.00	1	0	1	0	0	1
Eric Stevens	0	0	0.00	2	0	2	1	1	2
David Gibson	0	0	1.50	4	0	6	5	2	8
Justin Kamplain	3	2	1.66	8	0	38	28	18	41
Evan Rutter	1	1	2.33	12	0	19	17	2	17
Brandon Leibrandt	2	1	3.00	6	0	27	30	5	15

	W	L	ERA	G	SV	IP	H	BB	SO
Brad Schreiber	0	1	3.21	14	5	14	7	11	12
Corey Taylor	3	1	3.82	14	1	35	43	10	25
Trey Cochran-Gill	1	1	4.44	13	0	26	24	15	20
Dylan Toscano	1	5	4.50	8	0	32	35	15	27
Aaron Brown	1	3	5.16	7	0	30	34	7	25
Jake Stinnett	2	2	5.36	9	0	40	50	16	37
Frankie Vanderka	0	3	5.63	7	0	32	41	10	13
Matt Pirro	0	6	6.34	7	0	33	39	19	31
Matt Withrow	0	2	6.43	6	0	14	11	17	17
Jonathan Keller	0	1	7.16	10	0	16	23	10	19
Ben Meyer	0	0	9.00	3	0	4	7	2	2
John Van Eaton	0	0	21.60	2	0	2	4	5	1

CHATHAM

BATTING	AVG	AB	R	H	2B	3B	HR	RBI	SB
Ryan Plourde	.429	7	0	3	0	0	0	0	0
Dante Flores	.317	139	25	44	13	2	1	19	3
J.D. Davis	.311	103	18	32	5	0	3	19	4
Connor Joe	.308	146	19	45	9	1	3	22	6
Jimmy Pickens	.307	127	20	39	8	1	7	23	11
Kenny Koplove	.296	27	5	8	1	0	0	1	0
Mitchell Gunsolus	.293	123	18	36	3	0	0	11	8
Hunter Redman	.258	31	2	8	0	0	0	1	1
Landon Lassiter	.250	68	8	17	2	0	0	7	2
Erich Weiss	.250	40	9	10	1	1	0	3	0
Joshua Eldridge	.236	72	10	17	1	0	1	12	4
Brett Bell	.226	31	6	7	0	0	0	4	3
Michael Russell	.216	88	12	19	2	0	1	11	11
Brandon Sedell	.214	84	6	18	3	0	0	12	1
Richard Prigatano	.204	54	11	11	4	0	0	7	5
Blake Butera	.196	112	17	22	5	0	0	8	6
Ryan Phelan	.182	22	4	4	0	0	0	2	0
Sheehan Planas-Arteaga	.171	105	14	18	1	0	0	9	8
AJ Murray	.130	23	3	3	2	0	0	2	0
William Head	.059	17	1	1	0	0	0	2	1
Scott Heath	.000	3	0	0	0	0	0	1	0

PITCHING	W	L	ERA	G	SV	IP	H	BB	SO
J.D. Davis	0	1	0.00	5	2	4.2	3	2	7
Liam Rafferty	0	0	0.00	2	0	2	0	0	2
Mitch Merten	2	0	0.52	12	1	17	11	6	20
David Speer	0	0	0.79	8	1	11	10	1	11
Lukas Schiraldi	4	1	1.20	7	0	38	28	10	27
Tommy Lawrence	3	0	1.59	7	0	28	18	1	23
Ryan Leach	1	0	1.77	13	0	20	10	14	27
Stephen Marino	0	1	1.93	4	0	5	2	3	1
Chad Sobotka	2	1	2.25	15	1	24	17	16	24
Jacob Dorris	2	1	2.55	15	3	25	21	9	26
Dominic Moreno	3	1	2.89	9	0	19	15	3	19
Aaron Garza	0	4	3.57	7	0	35	41	8	21
Matthew Gage	4	2	3.89	7	0	35	40	7	25
Kyle Funkhouser	0	0	4.15	10	4	13	11	6	21
Andrew McGee	2	2	4.73	8	0	40	46	7	36
Andrew Chin	2	2	6.46	9	0	31	41	15	24
Kenny Koplove	0	0	6.75	3	0	4	5	3	2
Jimmy Litchfield	0	1	6.75	14	0	21	32	5	12
Joseph Goodman	1	0	7.36	7	1	7	8	3	3
Scott Heath	0	0	9.00	2	0	2	4	2	1

COTUIT

BATTING	AVG	AB	R	H	2B	3B	HR	RBI	SB
Jared Walsh	.455	11	0	5	1	0	0	0	0
Mike Ford	.407	86	22	35	7	0	5	18	0
Garrett Stubbs	.400	5	0	2	0	0	0	1	0
Max Schrock	.381	21	2	8	0	0	0	2	1
Danny Diekroeger	.324	102	19	33	6	0	2	7	2
Caleb Bryson	.308	13	4	4	0	0	4	5	0
Connor Castellano	.300	20	5	6	0	0	1	6	4
Will Remillard	.297	37	3	11	0	0	1	9	2
Jake Fincher	.295	112	15	33	3	0	0	12	18
Rhett Wiseman	.294	136	24	40	14	2	4	25	12
Bradley Zimmer	.281	64	10	18	3	1	1	7	6
Drew Jackson	.263	80	9	21	4	0	1	7	2
Mark Payton	.250	32	6	8	2	0	1	5	1
Hunter Cole	.241	116	14	28	5	0	2	16	6
Yale Rosen	.237	93	12	22	6	0	3	17	6
Logan Ratledge	.234	94	9	22	7	0	2	6	3

	AVG	AB	R	H	2B	3B	HR	RBI	SB
Galli Cribbs Jr.	.228	57	6	13	1	0	0	1	5
Austin Byler	.216	37	2	8	3	1	0	4	2
Steven Duggar	.209	43	1	9	0	0	0	1	3
Nolan Clark	.169	77	4	13	1	1	0	5	0
Elliott Caldwell	.167	6	2	1	0	0	1	1	0
Tim Kiene	.145	55	12	8	1	0	2	3	3
Kevin Bradley	.141	71	6	10	4	0	0	8	1
Edwin Rios	.095	21	1	2	0	0	0	0	0
Patrick Mazeika	.077	13	3	1	0	0	0	1	0
Aramis Garcia	.000	1	2	0	0	0	0	0	1

PITCHING	W	L	ERA	G	SV	IP	H	BB	SO
Derrick Capiak	0	0	0.00	1	1	1	0	0	1
James Connell	0	0	0.00	2	0	2	3	2	2
Wesley Cox	0	0	0.00	3	0	4	3	3	3
Galli Cribbs Jr.	0	0	0.00	1	0	1	0	0	0
Ryan Grant	0	0	0.00	1	0	1	0	0	0
Vaughn Hayward	1	0	0.00	1	0	5	5	3	2
Alec Palioca	0	0	0.00	1	0	1	0	0	
Liam Rafferty	0	0	0.00	2	0	1	0	3	0
Patrick Corbett	3	0	0.92	7	1	20	15	8	17
Jared Walsh	1	0	1.06	9	0	34	28	18	22
Tommy Kister	1	0	1.59	1	0	6	3	3	8
Joel Seddon	3	2	2.17	14	3	29	23	11	22
Chris Ellis	2	3	2.39	7	0	38	32	10	23
Trevor Seidenberger	0	0	2.46	4	0	7	3	1	5
Evan Beal	2	3	2.73	8	0	33	24	16	32
Alex Haines	0	1	2.79	7	0	19	18	8	26
Ben Smith	2	0	2.83	7	0	29	25	11	35
Brian Miller	1	2	3.00	19	5	27	27	7	26
Adam Ravenelle	0	1	3.12	11	1	17	14	12	16
Christian Cecilio	3	3	3.13	8	0	37	31	5	25
Dalton Potts	0	1	3.60	1	0	5	6	1	5
Eric Karch	3	0	3.90	10	2	28	25	5	19
John Hochstatter	1	1	5.87	8	0	15	16	13	10
Chris Murphy	0	1	6.75	1	0	1	1	1	1
Mike Ford	1	0	8.22	3	0	8	9	2	9
Dusty Isaacs	1	0	9.00	1	0	1	2	1	0
Michael Roberts	0	0	9.82	5	0	4	5	3	4
David Schmidt	0	0	12.19	9	0	10	19	10	10

FALMOUTH

BATTING	AVG	AB	R	H	2B	3B	HR	RBI	SB
Todd Ezold	1.000	1	0	1	0	0	0	0	0
Kevin Newman	.375	160	36	60	3	0	0	18	16
Kevin Cron	.350	157	28	55	10	1	4	32	7
Rhys Hoskins	.326	178	44	58	9	0	7	37	3
Casey Gillaspie	.321	165	31	53	9	0	8	27	4
Dylan Davis	.317	104	20	33	8	0	6	34	2
Troy Stein	.277	112	12	31	6	2	2	19	6
Sam Gillikin	.256	90	11	23	5	1	0	8	2
Conner Hale	.254	114	9	29	1	0	1	14	2
Leon Byrd Jr.	.252	139	22	35	6	1	1	6	8
Cameron OBrien	.250	60	7	15	1	1	2	7	0
Kyle Ruchim	.200	5	0	1	0	0	0	1	1
Richard Martin Jr.	.193	109	19	21	3	1	1	10	11
Joseph Maggi	.165	115	14	19	1	0	0	4	3
Max Murphy	.143	21	0	3	1	0	0	2	0
Isias Alcantar	.000	2	1	0	0	0	0	0	0
Brandon Cipolla	.000	1	0	0	0	0	0	0	0

PITCHING	W	L	ERA	G	SV	IP	H	BB	SO
Nick Friar	0	0	0.00	1	0	1	0	0	1
Preston Johnson	0	0	0.00	1	0	1	1	1	1
Jimmy ONeill	0	0	0.00	1	0	1	1	0	1
Jim Ploeger	0	0	0.00	1	0	1	1	1	1
Zechariah Lemond	0	1	1.29	6	2	7	4	4	3
Preston Morrison	1	0	1.42	2	0	6	5	0	4
John Means	3	3	1.99	7	0	41	25	8	35
Dylan Davis	0	0	2.25	4	0	4	3	0	5
Donny Murray	1	0	2.46	14	1	22	17	4	19
Alex Robinson	0	0	2.46	3	0	3.2	3	3	5
Nicolas Manuppelli	0	1	2.76	11	1	16	14	10	16
Hunter Brothers	2	0	2.81	14	2	16	8	10	27
Trey Teakell	5	1	2.85	8	0	47	47	5	21
Brandon Magallones	1	2	3.45	8	0	29	31	10	21
Daniel Koger	2	2	3.48	6	0	31	32	6	19

	W	L	ERA	G	SV	IP	H	BB	SO
Kevin Mooney	2	1	3.51	14	0	26	27	6	17
Craig Schlitter	4	2	3.63	8	0	40	40	11	33
Brandon Finnegan	1	0	3.68	2	0	7	6	2	10
Brent Stong	0	0	4.42	13	0	18	17	7	16
Jared Price	2	0	4.91	13	0	15	13	14	11
Garrett Cleavinger	0	2	6.57	12	0	12	11	9	22
Kevin McCanna	2	2	6.59	8	0	29	33	14	17
Clate Schmidt	0	1	7.27	3	0	9	15	5	4
Garrett Hayward	0	0	7.71	2	0	2	1	3	2
Daniel Brown	0	0	9.00	1	0	1	1	1	1
Jeff Dally	0	0	27.00	1	0	1	1	0	0

HARWICH

BATTING	AVG	AB	R	H	2B	3B	HR	RBI	SB
Aaron Barbosa	.344	93	18	32	2	0	0	9	19
Derek Fisher	.333	120	14	40	6	0	0	21	13
CJ Hinojosa	.316	19	1	6	1	0	0	3	3
Ian Happ	.293	147	22	43	7	2	5	22	13
Nick Howard	.276	76	9	21	5	1	0	4	2
Mark Zagunis	.273	44	5	12	4	0	0	4	4
Brendon Hayden	.271	85	11	23	3	0	0	6	2
Tanner English	.269	108	21	29	2	1	1	10	10
Blair DeBord	.239	46	7	11	1	0	0	6	2
Branden Cogswell	.231	121	16	28	1	0	0	8	6
Kevin Krause	.226	31	0	7	1	0	0	2	2
Ryan Lindemuth	.223	103	16	23	5	0	1	7	5
Ben Moore	.222	126	15	28	4	0	1	17	2
Mitch Morales	.220	50	7	11	0	0	0	5	0
AJ Reed	.218	55	3	12	4	1	1	11	0
Gunnar Heidt	.210	138	16	29	6	2	2	17	7
Brett Austin	.200	65	6	13	1	1	0	6	0
Andrew Santomauro	.167	6	0	1	0	0	0	1	0
Josh Anderson	.158	19	0	3	2	0	0	2	0
Anthony Italiano	.150	20	1	3	1	0	0	0	0
Chad Prain	.000	4	0	0	0	0	0	0	0

PITCHING	W	L	ERA	G	SV	IP	H	BB	SO
Tanner English	0	0	0.00	1	0	1	0	0	2
Alex Farina	0	0	0.00	1	1	2	0	0	2
Jake Drossner	1	1	0.82	10	0	11	8	3	6
Mason McCullough	0	0	0.90	8	1	10	9	3	15
Patrick Connaughton	1	1	1.00	2	0	9	9	5	10
Dillon Peters	2	1	1.23	5	0	22	10	3	21
Aaron Bummer	5	2	1.41	7	0	45	39	14	18
Sean Fitzgerald	1	0	2.29	9	1	20	14	4	14
Gunner Carroll	0	0	2.46	5	0	7	9	3	2
Ian Tompkins	1	1	2.55	10	0	18	14	11	27
Johnathan Frebis	1	0	2.57	11	0	28	12	14	30
Chris Oliver	1	0	2.57	10	3	14	13	3	16
Tyler Burgess	1	0	2.70	8	0	14	13	6	11
Chandler Shepherd	2	3	2.78	7	0	36	27	9	28
Jalen Beeks	3	2	3.22	7	0	36	35	9	19
AJ Reed	1	2	3.60	5	0	25	22	7	21
Logan Jernigan	0	0	3.63	8	0	22	25	12	22
Michael Costello	1	0	3.86	3	0	5	2	4	4
Keaton Haack	0	2	4.26	3	0	13	17	10	8
Nick Howard	1	2	4.38	5	0	25	29	4	25
Sam Howard	1	2	5.14	9	0	21	23	8	14
Ian Happ	0	0	9.00	1	0	1	3	0	2
Vaughn Hayward	0	0	9.00	1	0	1	3	1	1
Brendon Hayden	0	0	40.50	1	0	1	4	1	0

HYANNIS

BATTING	AVG	AB	R	H	2B	3B	HR	RBI	SB
J.C. Coban	1.000	1	0	1	0	0	0	1	0
Skyler Ewing	.287	115	18	33	8	2	4	20	3
Ryan Padilla	.282	78	6	22	5	0	1	9	3
Austin Slater	.277	141	21	39	7	1	1	8	8
Tyler Spoon	.261	165	14	43	1	1	4	15	8
Jay Baum	.259	116	12	30	5	0	0	9	10
Jake Hernandez	.246	61	4	15	4	0	0	10	1
Steve Wilkerson	.244	123	17	30	7	0	1	9	8
Landon Curry	.242	91	10	22	1	0	0	4	10
Brian Anderson	.227	132	16	30	6	0	1	9	4
Jeff Schalk	.221	86	9	19	2	0	4	12	3
Chase Griffin	.212	85	6	18	1	0	2	11	4
Levi Borders	.188	48	4	9	2	0	0	1	0

	AVG	AB	R	H	2B	3B	HR	RBI	SB
Drew Stankewicz	.179	84	5	15	3	0	0	2	0
Dominic Jose	.170	100	10	17	2	1	0	9	6
Will Maddox	.063	16	3	1	0	0	0	0	1
Mike Gunn	.000	5	0	0	0	0	0	1	0
Bobby Melley	.000	3	0	0	0	0	0	1	0

PITCHING	W	L	ERA	G	SV	IP	H	BB	SO
Jordan DeLorenzo	0	0	0.00	2	1	6	2	2	6
Colton Kibler	0	0	0.00	1	0	3	2	2	3
Sarkis Ohanian	0	0	0.00	10	3	14	6	7	13
Jeff Schalk	0	0	0.00	2	0	3	4	1	2
Ryan Thompson	0	0	0.00	2	0	3	2	1	2
Joe Harvey	0	0	1.50	3	0	6	5	2	7
Kyle Freeland	3	2	2.25	9	0	40	39	4	48
Andrew Istler	2	1	2.35	13	2	23	9		13
Rocky McCord	1	2	2.60	8	0	35	32	11	21
Cy Sneed	3	2	2.80	8	0	45	31	14	35
Mike Gunn	0	1	2.81	12	0	16	13	9	19
Kevin Doherty	0	0	3.00	2	0	3	4	0	3
Jordan Foley	1	1	3.00	10	2	27	21	10	34
Peter Fairbanks	1	0	3.12	2	0	9	8	1	2
Eric Eck	2	1	3.26	16	10	20	15	7	21
Austin Pettibone	4	1	3.34	6	0	30	41	3	15
Jeffrey Hoffman	2	0	3.70	4	0	24	20	5	33
Patrick Andrews	2	1	3.80	5	0	24	27	4	19
James Barragan	0	0	4.50	1	0	6	7	2	5
Andrew Thome	3	2	4.77	6	0	28	36	9	13
Jay Shaw	1	0	5.40	5	1	7	6	4	7
Bryant Holtmann	0	2	8.64	9	0	17	28	6	11
Joseph Shaw	0	0	11.25	1	0	4	8	2	3
Logan Carman	0	1	15.00	1	0	3	6	2	1
Brian Anderson	0	0	27.00	1	0	1	1	4	0

ORLEANS

BATTING	AVG	AB	R	H	2B	3B	HR	RBI	SB
Ross Kivett	.336	140	20	47	10	0	3	17	7
Jordan Luplow	.325	151	18	49	12	0	4	28	2
Chris Marconcini	.289	152	18	44	11	1	3	23	0
Austin Davidson	.288	153	14	44	14	0	0	24	0
Will Fulmer	.278	72	16	20	4	1	2	8	3
Collin Slaybaugh	.258	132	11	34	5	0	0	11	3
Zach Fish	.250	112	12	28	3	0	2	12	6
Jordan Betts	.248	125	18	31	7	0	3	11	0
Vince Conde	.222	99	10	22	8	0	1	8	2
Greg Allen	.221	68	11	15	1	0	0	3	11
Riley Moore	.217	106	14	23	3	0	1	8	2
Geoff DeGroot	.212	52	9	11	1	0	0	4	2
Shane Conlon	.200	35	1	7	0	0	0	1	0
Angelo La Bruna	.196	56	9	11	0	0	0	3	1
Kevin Kramer	.192	26	4	5	2	0	0	2	2

PITCHING	W	L	ERA	G	SV	IP	H	BB	SO
Conor Harber	0	0	0.00	4	0	5	1	3	4
Trent Swart	0	1	0.00	2	0	6	6	0	4
Matt Troupe	1	1	1.35	17	11	20	11	7	32
Trevor Kelley	0	0	1.53	13	1	18	12	6	17
Bobby Poyner	2	3	1.72	7	0	37	30	5	24
Trent Szkutnik	3	1	1.72	9	0	37	26	9	30
Brandon McNitt	0	0	1.74	8	0	10	16	3	12
Colin Welmon	1	1	2.16	2	0	8	10	1	4
Jared Miller	2	2	2.30	8	1	31	17	13	24
Corey Miller	5	1	3.20	8	0	39	49	5	18
Shawn ONeill	1	1	3.28	11	1	36	37	5	19
Brian Clark	1	1	4.05	19	0	20	18	5	26
Jeremy Rhoades	1	2	4.22	18	0	21	27	8	19
Garrett Cole	1	0	4.50	2	0	2	3	0	1
Kyle Twomey	2	1	4.63	12	0	23	22	15	31
Luis Paula	2	1	4.94	15	0	27	25	16	15
Josh Sborz	1	2	5.72	8	0	28	38	10	27
Lucas Long	1	0	6.23	2	0	4	7	3	4
Daniel Zamora	0	1	10.39	10	0	13	17	14	8

WAREHAM

BATTING	AVG	AB	R	H	2B	3B	HR	RBI	SB
Kyle Schwarber	.432	37	3	16	1	0	1	3	2
Tino Lipson	.278	97	11	27	4	0	0	5	4
Cole Stancil	.270	74	3	20	3	2	0	6	2

	AVG	AB	R	H	2B	3B	HR	RBI	SB
Ethan Gross	.265	151	11	40	2	2	0	15	5
Sean McMullen	.250	100	10	25	2	0	0	2	1
Mikey White	.250	32	2	8	2	0	0	3	0
Adam Toth	.248	101	13	25	7	0	0	6	4
Daniel Rosenbaum	.246	69	7	17	2	0	1	9	0
Brett Pirtle	.242	99	8	24	1	0	1	7	5
Trevor Podratz	.241	137	12	33	4	1	2	12	0
Matthew Walsh	.235	98	9	23	2	0	0	6	0
Christopher Chinea	.234	77	9	18	0	0	0	5	1
Cole Sturgeon	.215	135	11	29	6	1	1	12	5
Brock Stewart	.194	36	2	7	0	0	0	1	0
Will Schwanke	.182	99	6	18	0	0	0	6	1
Bradley Roney	.140	43	2	6	1	0	0	3	2
CJ Saylor	.097	31	2	3	0	0	0	1	0
Fred Shepard	.000	1	0	0	0	0	0	0	0

PITCHING	W	L	ERA	G	SV	IP	H	BB	SO
Cole Sturgeon	0	0	0.00	6	0	7	5	3	11
Bradley Roney	0	1	1.59	13	0	17	9	10	21
Ryan Riga	1	2	2.49	16	0	25	26	11	18
Tucker Simpson	1	3	2.75	8	0	36	33	14	22
Jared Ruxer	0	1	3.18	9	0	17	23	4	14
Spencer Turnbull	0	2	3.86	6	0	16	25	12	9
Andro Cutura	2	3	3.92	9	1	44	42	10	29
Trey Killian	0	3	4.06	7	1	38	43	9	36
Sean Newcomb	1	2	4.43	6	0	22	23	13	28
Dillon Ortman	0	2	4.50	15	0	26	22	10	31
Kyle Cody	1	1	5.00	2	0	9	7	4	9
Christopher Huffman	0	0	5.06	6	1	5	8	2	7
Fred Shepard	1	6	5.58	9	0	40	50	15	36
Jonathan Holder	0	1	5.59	7	1	10	14	3	12
Kurt McCune	2	1	5.89	6	0	26	34	7	18
Dalton Brown	0	1	7.36	3	1	7	7	6	9
Will Coursen-Carr	0	3	7.71	6	0	19	26	9	10
Michael Howerton	0	1	9.00	3	0	4	7	2	3

YARMOUTH-DENNIS

BATTING	AVG	AB	R	H	2B	3B	HR	RBI	SB
Salvatore Annunziata	.353	17	3	6	1	0	0	2	0
Terence Connelly	.333	9	2	3	1	0	0	0	1
Kyle Wood	.333	39	6	13	4	0	0	3	0
Matthew Honchel	.329	70	16	23	4	0	0	7	4
Cole Peragine	.313	80	9	25	5	0	0	8	2
Alex Blandino	.308	130	19	40	11	1	2	17	2
Andrew Daniel	.279	86	15	24	1	0	0	14	4
Auston Bousfield	.270	115	18	31	9	0	1	12	9
Demetrius Stewart	.270	115	17	31	9	1	3	24	8
Wayne Taylor	.259	81	5	21	5	1	2	5	1
Carl Anderson	.250	4	1	0	0	0	0	0	0
Brandon Downes	.246	118	14	29	6	0	4	15	2
Robert Pehl	.245	139	13	34	7	0	1	7	2
Jose Trevino	.229	105	10	24	5	0	4	21	1
Taylor Gushue	.224	76	9	17	5	1	2	9	1
Taylor White	.203	148	18	30	7	2	0	10	8
Jeffrey Keller	.190	21	3	4	2	0	0	1	2
Taylor Smart	.181	83	10	15	4	0	1	8	6
Justin Shafer	.125	8	1	1	0	0	0	0	0
Bradley Strong	.111	9	2	1	0	0	0	1	2
Eric Filia	.067	15	0	1	0	0	0	0	0
Elvin Soto	.000	8	0	0	0	0	0	0	0
Christopher Travers	.000	1	0	0	0	0	0	0	0

PITCHING	W	L	ERA	G	SV	IP	H	BB	SO
Robert Pehl	0	0	0.00	1	0	1	0	0	2
Cody Petre	0	0	0.00	1	0	0	0	0	0
Justin Shafer	0	0	0.00	1	0	1	0	0	0
Travis Stout	0	0	0.00	1	0	1	0	0	0
Graham Tebbit	1	0	0.00	1	0	3	2	1	4
Jose Trevino	0	0	0.00	2	0	2	0	0	0
Taylor White	0	0	0.00	1	0	1	1	0	1
James Kaprielian	0	0	1.80	5	0	20	13	4	28
Sam Lindquist	1	0	1.80	6	0	20	18	9	13
Kody Kerski	3	3	2.08	13	1	22	18	6	18
Erick Fedde	3	1	2.35	5	0	31	21	8	26
Daniel Savas	3	0	3.00	8	0	36	31	12	34
Daniel Altavilla	2	0	3.10	12	2	20	15	13	22
Alexander Katz	0	0	3.38	2	0	3	2	3	2

	W	L	ERA	G	SV	IP	H	BB	SO
Nick Kozlowski	0	0	3.60	5	0	5	2	7	5
Clayton Smith	2	2	3.89	9	0	44	47	8	16
Jordan Minch	0	2	4.42	10	0	37	44	12	22
Kevin McAvoy	2	3	4.65	9	0	31	36	7	28
Samuel Coonrod	1	1	4.86	8	0	17	15	13	14
Jose Lopez	0	4	4.88	9	0	24	26	7	24
Darrell Hunter	1	2	5.00	13	7	18	19	8	21
Jonathan Danielczyk	0	0	5.09	12	0	18	22	7	9
Jeremy Null	0	1	6.00	5	1	12	15	4	15
Kyle Wood	1	3	10.05	6	0	14	24	5	4
Kellen Urbon	0	0	12.00	3	0	3	6	1	0
Michael Matuella	0	0	13.50	4	0	5	9	4	5

ALASKA LEAGUE

	W	L	PCT	GB
Alaska Goldpanners	22	13	.629	—
Anchorage Bucs	20	15	.571	2
Matsu Miners	20	15	.571	2
Peninsula Oilers	18	17	.514	4
Anchorage Glacier Pilots	17	18	.486	5
Chugiak Chinooks	8	27	.229	14

CHAMPIONSHIP: Alaska Goldpanners defeated the Anchorage Glacier Pilots 2-0 in best-of-three series.
TOP 10 PROSPECTS: 1. A.J. Simcox, ss, Mat-Su (So., Tennessee). 2. Christin Stewart, of, Mat-Su (So., Tennessee). 3. Garrett Mundell, rhp, Anchorage Bucs (Jr., Fresno State). 4. Gio Brusa, of, Mat-Su (So., Pacific). 5. Drew Smith, rhp, Mat-Su (So., Dallas Baptist). 6. David Fletcher, ss, Alaska (Fr., Loyola Marymount). 7. Andrew Sopko, rhp, Anchorage Bucs (So., Gonzaga). 8. Brody Russell, of/2b, Anchorage Glacier Pilots (So., Fresno State). 9. Austin Stone, rhp, Anchorage Bucs (Jr., Baylor). 10. Cody Moffett, lhp, Alaska (So., Arizona).

INDIVIDUAL BATTING LEADERS
(MINIMUM 2.7 PLATE APPEARANCES PER TEAM GAME)

	AVG	AB	R	H	2B	3B	HR	RBI	SB
A.J. Simcox, Matsu	.356	135	27	48	4	1	1	20	10
Christin Stewart, Matsu	.336	125	26	42	14	2	5	31	4
Andre Mercurio, Peninsula	.319	113	10	36	4	1	0	13	6
Casey Munoz, Alaska	.315	89	12	28	2	0	2	15	5
Collin Radack, Chugiak	.310	113	13	35	6	3	1	13	6
Spencer Mahoney, Matsu	.302	106	16	32	5	0	0	6	1
Jake Alvarez, Peninsula	.301	123	11	37	6	0	0	6	1
Andy Crowley, Bucs	.292	120	13	35	8	0	0	11	1
Rick Reigner, Alaska	.287	94	14	27	1	0	0	5	6
A.J. Ramirez, Peninsula	.282	110	6	31	6	2	1	11	1

INDIVIDUAL PITCHING LEADERS
(MINIMUM 0.8 INNINGS PITCHED PER TEAM GAME)

	W	L	ERA	G	SV	IP	H	BB	SO
Garrett Mundell, Bucs	4	1	0.63	7	0	43	26	13	30
Cody Moffett, Alaska	2	0	0.76	11	4	35	23	5	34
Sean Buckle, Glacier Pilots	3	2	1.00	7	0	36	23	16	22
Logan McAnallen, Peninsula	1	3	1.14	9	0	39	24	13	37
A.J. Quintero, Peninsula	1	1	1.54	7	0	41	29	8	26
GJ Strauss, Peninsula	4	1	1.64	6	0	33	18	14	26
Philip Orr, Matsu	1	0	2.01	6	0	31	20	19	19
Carlos Fuentes, Glacier Pilots	1	2	2.20	7	0	41	41	13	35
Nathan Bannister, Alaska	6	0	2.25	8	0	44	40	3	32
Mikey Ramirez, Alaska	4	1	2.36	9	1	42	32	11	28

ATLANTIC COLLEGIATE LEAGUE

	W	L	T	PCT	GB
Allentown Railers	27	13	0	.675	—
Trenton Generals	27	13	0	.675	—
Staten Island Tide	25	14	1	.625	1 ½
North Jersey Eagles	21	18	1	.525	5 ½
Quakertown Blazers	20	20	0	.500	7
Jersey Pilots	10	30	0	.250	17
Lehigh Valley Catz	9	31	0	.225	18

CHAMPIONSHIP: North Jersey defeated Allentown in tournament final.
TOP 10 PROSPECTS: 1. Matt Alvarez, rhp, Staten Island (SIGNED: Royals). 2. Narcisco Crook, of, Trenton (SIGNED: Reds). 3. Karl Kglovits, rhp, Allentown (So., North Carolina State). 4. Heath Fillmyer, rhp, Trenton (So., Mercer County CC, N.J.). 5. Brandon Martinez, of, Quakertown (Jr., Kutztown, Pa.). 6. P.J. Higgins, 3b, Lehigh Valley

(So., Old Dominion). **7.** Vincenzo Aiello, rhp, Trenton (So., Rider). **8.** Chris Smith, of, North Jersey (Sr., Wagner). **9.** Mike Weinhold, lhp, Quakertown (Sr., Alvernia, Pa.). **10.** Anthony Ciavarella, lhp, Lehigh Valley (So., Monmouth).

INDIVIDUAL BATTING LEADERS
(MINIMUM 2.7 PLATE APPEARANCES PER TEAM GAME)

	AVG	AB	R	H	2B	3B	HR	RBI	SB
Rich Ricciardi, Trenton	.395	114	24	45	6	0	1	24	5
Brandon Martinez, Quakertown	.371	140	30	52	9	0	1	8	19
Jeff Birkofer, Allentown	.367	109	29	40	8	0	2	18	4
Kenneth Kirshner, North Jersey	.356	118	33	42	8	2	0	20	17
Drew Hercik, Allentown	.338	133	27	45	5	4	1	23	3
Jeremy Musser, Quakertown	.336	107	16	36	5	1	1	23	11
Juan Bueno, Staten Island	.336	128	22	43	7	0	1	26	1
Joseph Forcellini, Allentown	.333	138	28	46	10	1	4	31	3
Cliff Brantley Jr., Staten Island	.333	108	18	36	8	1	0	14	7
Richard Mejia, Staten Island	.331	130	31	43	7	0	4	19	1
Matt Patterson, Trenton	.331	121	22	40	5	1	2	21	3

INDIVIDUAL PITCHING LEADERS
(MINIMUM 0.8 INNINGS PITCHED PER TEAM GAME)

	W	L	ERA	G	SV	IP	H	BB	SO
Brandon Shimo, Allentown	4	2	1.23	7	0	44	35	4	39
Adam Davis, Allentown	6	1	1.33	8	0	47	34	9	37
Jeffrey Courter, Quakertown	2	1	1.54	9	0	35	41	7	24
J.B. Kole, Trenton	3	2	1.77	8	1	36	16	15	34
Jonathan Reich, North Jersey	4	3	2.17	10	0	50	49	5	25
Nick Zucchero, Trenton	2	2	2.23	6	0	32	23	7	17
Marty Martens, Quakertown	5	2	2.23	8	0	36	29	13	34
Cory Spera, Lehigh Valley	2	2	2.31	12	0	39	39	10	34
Matthew Kostalos, Staten Island	3	1	2.67	11	3	34	19	14	36
James Harrity, Trenton	1	1	2.76	10	1	33	32	15	25

CAL RIPKEN COLLEGIATE LEAGUE

	W	L	PCT	GB
Bethesda Big Train	30	14	.682	—
Alexandria Aces	27	17	.614	3
Gaithersburg Giants	26	18	.591	4
Rockville Express	25	19	.568	5
Youse's Orioles	25	19	.568	5
Baltimore Redbirds	25	19	.568	5
Vienna River Dogs	23	21	.523	7
Southern Maryland Nationals	23	21	.523	7
D.C. Grays	23	21	.523	7
Presstman Cardinals	14	30	.318	16
Silver Spring Takoma T Bolts	13	31	.295	17
Herndon Braves	10	34	.227	20

CHAMPIONSHIP: Baltimore Redbirds defeated Bethesda Big Train in final.
TOP 10 PROSPECTS: 1. Nik Nowottnick, rhp, Rockville (SIGNED: Orioles). **2.** Jack Fischer, rhp, Baltimore (Sr., Wake Forest). **3.** Bubba Derby, rhp, Bethesda (So., San Diego State). **4.** Mitch Aker, rhp, Alexandria (So., William & Mary) . **5.** K.J. Hockaday, 3b, Youse's Orioles (Jr., Harford CC, Md.). **6.** Ian Rice, c, Baltimore (So., Chipola State JC, Fla.). **7.** Mike Boyle, lhp, Bethesda (So., Radford). **8.** Brendan Butler, if/of, Youse's Orioles (Jr., Towson). **9.** Ryan Ripken, 1b, Youse's Orioles (So., Indian River State JC, Fla.). **10.** Errol Robinson, ss/2b, Silver Spring-Takoma (Fr., Mississippi).

INDIVIDUAL BATTING LEADERS
(MINIMUM 2.7 PLATE APPEARANCES PER TEAM GAME)

	AVG	AB	R	H	2B	3B	HR	RBI	SB
K.J. Hockaday, Youse's	.362	149	34	54	8	1	0	22	12
Will Kengor, Rockville	.354	147	36	52	11	3	1	13	7
Josh Ingham, Gaithersburg	.339	127	18	43	8	1	2	19	8
Ty France, Bethesda	.331	118	19	39	4	0	2	22	4
Jordon Glover, Presstman	.331	124	17	41	10	0	0	13	7
Ian Rice, Baltimore	.317	145	25	46	12	1	7	34	2
Ryan Mincher, Alexandria	.315	143	27	45	7	0	2	20	4
Nicholas Collins, Alexandria	.313	150	16	47	14	1	0	30	0
Ryan Metzler, S. Maryland	.310	116	20	36	8	1	0	4	10
R.J. Dennard, Baltimore	.310	100	17	31	9	0	3	20	2

INDIVIDUAL PITCHING LEADERS
(MINIMUM 0.8 INNINGS PITCHED PER TEAM GAME)

	W	L	ERA	G	SV	IP	H	BB	SO
Bubba Derby, Bethesda	6	2	0.76	9	0	47	24	14	56
Michael Taylor, Youse's	1	1	0.87	8	0	41	31	12	43
Robin Mowatt, Gaithersburg	5	1	1.00	11	0	45	44	5	22
Danny Mooney, Bethesda	2	1	1.57	9	0	46	38	9	34
Bryan McHale, S. Maryland	3	3	1.96	6	0	37	26	9	25
Jordan Santak, Rockville	3	1	2.02	6	0	36	29	7	12
Jesse Frawley, Gaithersburg	4	0	2.14	8	0	42	36	10	29
Bryson Hough, Vienna	3	2	2.15	7	0	38	30	10	28
Colin Milon, Alexandria	5	1	2.20	7	0	41	26	14	35

CALIFORNIA COLLEGIATE LEAGUE

	W	L	PCT	GB
Los Angeles Brewers	25	13	.658	—
Santa Barbara Foresters	22	16	.579	3
San Luis Obispo	22	17	.564	3 ½
Conejo Oaks	20	18	.526	5
Santa Paula Halos	20	19	.513	5 ½
Academy Barons	19	20	.487	6 ½
Southern California Catch	18	20	.474	7
Bakersfield Sound	8	31	.205	17 ½

CHAMPIONSHIP: Los Angeles Brewers defeated Santa Barbara Foresters 2-0 in best-of-three final.
TOP 10 PROSPECTS: 1. Caleb Whalen, 2b/3b/of, Los Angeles Brewers (Jr., Portland). **2.** Parker French, rhp, Santa Barbara (Jr., Texas). **3.** Drake Owenby, lhp, San Luis Obispo (So., Tennessee). **4.** Grayson Long, rhp, San Luis Obispo (So., Texas A&M). **5.** Patrick Weigel, rhp, Santa Barbara (So., Pacific). **6.** Drew Van Orden, rhp, Santa Barbara (Sr., Duke). **7.** Corey Ray, rhp, San Luis Obispo (Jr., Texas A&M). **8.** Ben Johnson, of, Santa Barbara (So., Texas). **9.** Jordan Brower, 1b, Santa Paula (Jr., Azusa Pacific, Calif.). **10.** Kyle Johnson, of/rhp, San Luis Obispo (So., Purdue).

INDIVIDUAL HITTING LEADERS
(MINIMUM 100 AT-BATS)

	AVG	AB	R	H	2B	3B	HR	RBI	SB
Michael Pritchard, SLO	.386	171	38	66	12	4	1	34	18
Rob Fonseca, Los Angeles	.383	141	31	54	8	2	8	35	1
Caleb Whalen, Los Angeles	.361	158	33	57	15	4	1	22	9
Tim Ginther, Conejo	.358	165	35	59	8	2	2	25	4
Matt Tietz, Los Angeles	.357	171	36	61	11	3	9	32	12
Conor Smith, SoCal	.354	175	31	62	15	3	6	41	4
Aaron Attaway, SLO	.347	150	30	52	13	1	2	28	12
Jordan Brower, Santa Paula	.346	136	23	47	13	1	2	23	7
Jordan Hinshaw, Academy	.343	143	27	49	14	3	2	34	8
Kyle Johnson, SLO	.336	107	26	36	7	0	2	16	7

INDIVIDUAL PITCHING LEADERS
(MINIMUM 20 INNINGS PITCHED)

	W	L	ERA	G	SV	IP	H	BB	SO
Billy Kirkpatrick, SoCal	1	2	0.52	17	5	34	21	8	18
Drake Owenby, SLO	1	1	1.01	20	8	27	18	9	50
Jordan Smith, SLO	3	2	1.27	7	0	28	20	8	24
Drew Van Orden, Santa Barbara	5	2	1.29	9	0	49	35	13	65
Jeff Paschke, Santa Paula	2	1	1.54	9	1	23	8	13	14
Tejay Antone, Santa Barbara	4	0	1.80	19	1	35	26	13	36
Anthony Shew, Los Angeles	4	0	1.87	11	3	43	34	13	38
Grayson Long, SLO	2	3	1.88	11	0	38	32	7	32
Travis Evans, SLO	4	0	1.99	7	0	32	26	14	28
Tre Haliburton-Goeas, Santa Paula	4	1	2.01	12	0	40	21	25	32

COASTAL PLAIN LEAGUE

EAST	W	L	PCT	GB
Edenton Steamers	40	11	.784	—
Peninsula Pilots	33	22	.600	9
Wilmington Sharks	31	23	.574	10 ½
Fayetteville SwampDogs	29	23	.558	11 ½
Wilson Tobs	29	24	.547	12
Morehead City Marlins	24	32	.429	18 ½
Petersburg Generals	9	43	.173	31 ½

WEST	W	L	PCT	GB
Asheboro Copperheads	35	18	.660	—
Columbia Blowfish	31	20	.608	3
High Point—Thomasville HiToms	26	28	.481	9 ½

Martinsville Mustangs	22	31	.415	13
Florence RedWolves	20	31	.392	14
Forest City Owls	17	32	.347	16

CHAMPIONSHIP: Peninsula Pilots defeated Columbia Blowfish in best-of-three finals.

TOP 10 PROSPECTS: 1. John Tuttle, rhp, Asheboro (Sr., Catawba). **2.** Tyler Bolton, rhp, Wilmington (Jr., East Carolina). **3.** Luke Tendler, of, Asheboro (Sr., North Carolina A&T). **4.** Matt Reistetter, c, Asheboro (SIGNED: Nationals). **5.** Jordan Negrini, 3b, Peninsula (Sr., Old Dominion). **6.** Evan Stephens, of, High Point-Thomasville (Sr., Wake Forest). **7.** Nick Thompson, 2b, Edenton (Jr., William & Mary). **8.** Derrick Smith, rhp, Columbia (R-Sr., College of Charleston). **9.** Ryan Cranmer, 1b, Morehead City (Sr., Newberry College, S.C.). **10.** Cord Cockrell, rhp, Columbia (Jr., Louisiana-Lafayette).

INDIVIDUAL HITTING LEADERS
(MINIMUM 143 PLATE APPEARANCES)

	AVG	AB	R	H	2B	3B	HR	RBI	SB
Luke Tendler, Asheboro	.351	174	29	61	8	2	8	40	13
Trent Miller, Edenton	.347	150	31	52	8	0	7	32	10
Evan Stephens, High Point	.338	139	21	47	7	2	4	20	15
Jordan Negrini, Peninsula	.329	140	26	46	11	3	2	27	10
Oscar Sanay, Asheboro	.327	113	29	37	3	1	2	16	5
Brad Elwood, Florence	.318	129	24	41	8	1	0	10	5
Ransom LaLonde, Fayetteville	.316	117	18	37	9	0	0	12	9
Keelin Rasch, Martinsville	.316	190	25	60	16	0	0	19	3
John Rooney, Fayetteville	.315	127	26	40	5	0	0	15	8
Daniel Fraga, Gastonia	.315	143	21	45	2	1	0	21	11

INDIVIDUAL PITCHING LEADERS
(MINIMUM 42 INNINGS PITCHED)

	W	L	ERA	G	SV	IP	H	BB	SO
John Tuttle, Asheboro	9	1	0.78	12	0	58	36	12	50
Tyler Bolton, Wilmington	5	0	0.87	8	0	52	24	15	49
Nick Miller, Edenton	5	1	1.02	8	0	53	45	14	25
Brandon Vick, Peninsula	3	0	1.17	11	1	46	34	13	27
John Williams, Edenton	5	0	1.41	10	2	45	32	8	36
David Duncan, Columbia	3	3	1.45	10	0	56	35	14	43
Shawn Talkington, Fayetteville	2	1	1.50	7	0	42	26	10	33
Cord Cockrell, Columbia	5	1	1.66	9	0	43	35	9	39
Jared Lyons, Peninsula	5	1	1.71	9	0	42	29	10	39
Beau Dees, Wilmington	2	1	1.84	9	0	44	36	7	25

FAR WEST LEAGUE

	W	L	PCT	GB
Humboldt Crabs	25	8	.758	—
Top Speed Baseball	23	9	.719	1 ½
California Warriors	14	16	.467	9 ½
Menlo Park Legends	14	16	.467	9 ½
Neptune Beach Pearl	13	15	.464	9 ½
Walnut Creek Crawdads	13	16	.448	10
Seals Baseball Club	9	17	.346	12 ½
Redding Colt .45s	7	21	.250	15 ½

CHAMPIONSHIP: Humboldt Crabs defeated Top Speed Baseball in tournament finals.

TOP 10 PROSPECTS: 1. Francis Christy, c, California (Fr., Oregon). **2.** David Hearne, rhp, Redding (So., Notre Dame). **3.** Trevin Haseltine, rhp, California (Fr., California). **4.** Jordan Desguin, rhp/if, Redding (So., Feather River CC, Calif.). **5.** Greg Kuhlman, lhp, Top Speed (R-Jr., Indiana State). **6.** Tyler Mautner, 3b, Top Speed (R-So., Buffalo). **7.** Cameron Olson, c, Humboldt Crabs (So., UC Davis). **8.** Manny Ramirez Jr., 1b, California (Fr., Central Arizona CC). **9.** Tyler Cyr, rhp, Top Speed (Jr., Embry Riddle, Fla.). **10.** Justin Hovis, 3b/ss, Redding (So., Michigan State).

INDIVIDUAL BATTING LEADERS
(MINIMUM 2.7 PLATE APPEARANCES PER TEAM GAME)

	AVG	AB	R	H	2B	3B	HR	RBI	SB
Tyler Mautner, Top Speed	.390	231	58	90	26	1	13	57	1
Kyle Moses, Humboldt	.349	189	53	66	17	3	2	27	19
Alex Sortwell, Top Speed	.344	180	38	62	18	3	7	46	3
Danny Miller, Menlo Park	.340	159	30	54	12	2	9	41	2
Matt Owen, Top Speed	.338	148	30	50	9	0	4	29	6
Allen Smoot, Walnut Creek	.336	137	24	46	7	0	0	30	4
Ariel Aracena-Sanchez, Redding	.336	146	31	49	11	1	7	22	8
Michael Brdar, Walnut Creek	.333	147	24	49	7	0	3	21	9
Cole Gleason, Top Speed	.323	155	38	50	8	2	11	32	4
Cameron Olson, Humboldt	.322	143	32	46	11	1	8	47	3

INDIVIDUAL PITCHING LEADERS
(MINIMUM 0.8 INNINGS PITCHED PER TEAM GAME)

	W	L	ERA	G	SV	IP	H	BB	SO
Chad Hodges, Humboldt	7	0	2.47	9	0	62	57	18	55
Drew Bradshaw, Humboldt	3	5	2.49	10	0	69	59	17	48
Adam Cline, Top Speed	6	4	2.57	16	1	63	52	11	56
Andrew Herrera, Menlo Park	5	3	2.59	13	0	66	65	15	46
Tyler Rios, Menlo Park	2	1	2.68	18	0	37	28	20	36
Mike Dodakian, Menlo Park	3	3	2.84	14	6	38	31	5	34
Johnny Melero, Humboldt	5	1	2.86	10	0	66	77	14	34
Austin Lee, Walnut Creek	1	2	3.48	8	2	44	37	22	37
DJ Zapata, Menlo Park	1	3	3.53	12	1	43	47	18	43
Chris Muse-Fisher, Walnut Creek	1	5	3.77	9	0	43	43	15	40

FLORIDA COLLEGIATE SUMMER LEAGUE

	W	L	PCT	GB
Winter Park Diamond Dawgs	27	13	.675	—
Leesburg Lightning	25	14	.641	1 ½
Sanford River Rats	21	19	.525	6
Orlando Monarchs	17	19	.472	8
DeLand Suns	16	21	.432	9 ½
College Park Freedom	10	30	.250	17

CHAMPIONSHIP: Winter Park Diamond Dawgs defeated Leesburg Lightning in finals.

TOP 10 PROSPECTS: 1. Tyler Palmer, mif/of, Sanford (So., Seminole State JC, Fla.). **2.** Erik Skoglund, lhp, Orlando (Jr., Central Florida). **3.** Rock Rucker, of/lhp, Sanford (So., Auburn). **4.** John Sever, lhp, Sanford (Jr., Embry-Riddle, Fla.). **5.** Cory Taylor, rhp, Leesburg (So., Dallas Baptist). **6.** Daniel Sweet, of, Winter Park (So., Polk State JC, Fla.). **7.** Arturo Martoral, rhp, Sanford (So., Cisco JC, Texas). **8.** Emilio Ogando, lhp, Winter Park (Jr., St. Thomas, Fla.). **9.** Tanner Stanley, of, Winter Park (So., Richmond). **10.** Michael Gouge, 3b, Winter Park (So., Valdosta State, Ga.).

INDIVIDUAL BATTING LEADERS
(MINIMUM 2.7 PLATE APPEARANCES PER TEAM GAME)

	AVG	AB	R	H	2B	3B	HR	RBI	SB
AC Carter, Winter Park	.354	96	16	34	6	0	0	22	3
Tyler Palmer, Sanford	.350	140	35	49	10	2	9	32	24
Tyler Neslony, Leesburg	.346	130	17	45	4	0	0	19	0
Jared Watson, College Park	.340	100	16	34	8	0	0	6	10
Brett Jones, Leesburg	.338	133	25	45	6	3	2	18	10
Tyler Kellmann, Leesburg	.314	86	10	27	9	0	0	9	1
Joshua Johnson, Orlando	.303	119	20	36	2	1	0	12	18
Tanner Stanley, Winter Park	.300	110	21	33	8	0	0	15	12
Kevin Lindheim, Winter Park	.297	91	11	27	5	0	1	7	4
Daniel Sweet, Winter Park	.295	95	25	28	6	0	1	17	20

INDIVIDUAL PITCHING LEADERS
(MINIMUM 0.8 INNINGS PITCHED PER TEAM GAME)

	W	L	ERA	G	SV	IP	H	BB	SO
Emilio Ogando, Winter Park	7	1	0.63	8	0	43	21	7	46
Cory Taylor, Leesburg	3	1	1.44	9	0	44	28	27	42
Josh Strong, DeLand	1	3	1.56	8	0	40	28	15	21
Dylan Hathcock, Leesburg	3	1	1.58	7	0	40	32	10	25
Connor OBrien, Sanford	2	1	2.08	9	0	48	33	14	37
Ben Anchetf, Winter Park	5	2	2.18	7	0	41	38	11	31
Evan Incinelli, Winter Park	4	1	2.60	9	0	55	52	19	36
Byron Ferguson, Orlando	1	0	2.97	11	1	36	29	25	37
David Lidyard, DeLand	3	3	2.98	9	0	39	45	7	29
Arturo Martoral, Sanford	5	2	3.04	17	5	47	40	15	41

FUTURES COLLEGIATE LEAGUE

	W	L	PCT	GB
Martha's Vineyard Sharks	35	18	.660	—
Nashua Silver Knights	34	19	.642	1
North Shore Navigators	26	25	.510	8
Old Orchard Beach Raging Tide	26	27	.491	9
Pittsfield Suns	25	27	.481	9 ½
Brockton Rox	24	26	.480	9 ½
Torrington Titans	22	28	.440	11 ½
Seacoast Mavericks	21	32	.396	14
Wachusett Dirt Dawgs	20	31	.392	14

CHAMPIONSHIP: Martha's Vineyard Sharks defeated Nashua Silver Knights 2-0 in best-of-three finals.

TOP 10 PROSPECTS: 1. Jamill Moquette, of, Wachusett (Jr., Massachusetts-Boston). **2.** John Sheehan, rhp, Brockton (Sr., William & Mary). **3.** Tim Holmes, rhp, Seacoast, (So., San Jacinto JC, Texas). **4.** Mitch Elliot, of, Brockton (Sr., Xavier). **5.** Michael Odenwaelder, of, Torrington (So., Amherst, Mass.). **6.** Johnny Adams, ss/3b, Nashua (Fr., Boston College). **7.** Dylan Tice, ss/2b, Martha's Vineyard (Jr., Indiana U., Pa.). **8.** Ryan Siegel, of, Martha's Vineyard (Jr., Mercyhurst, Pa.). **9.** Matt Tulley, rhp, Nashua (So., Virginia Tech). **10.** Bob Carbaugh, rhp, Martha's Vineyard (Sr., Seton Hill, Pa.).

INDIVIDUAL BATTING LEADERS
(MINIMUM 2.7 PLATE APPEARANCES PER TEAM GAME)

	AVG	AB	R	H	2B	3B	HR	RBI	SB
Ryan Siegel, Martha's Vineyard	.373	169	40	63	7	1	1	23	6
Mitch Elliott, Brockton	.358	151	25	54	7	3	3	33	8
T.J. Lynch, Seacoast	.357	154	29	55	10	1	0	28	0
Tim Hendricks, North Shore	.354	192	23	68	6	1	1	28	15
Jamill Moquette, Wachusetts	.350	140	34	49	10	0	7	29	4
Dylan Tice, Martha's Vineyard	.338	207	39	70	9	1	6	39	7
Ryan Coppinger, Seacoast	.326	138	24	45	5	2	5	24	7
John Kinne, Pittsfield	.323	164	27	53	5	0	0	28	4
Josh Raymond, Wachusetts	.309	165	30	51	14	0	7	35	3
Kyle Singleton, Pittsfield	.306	160	26	49	7	1	6	34	0

INDIVIDUAL PITCHING LEADERS
(MINIMUM 0.8 INNINGS PITCHED PER TEAM GAME)

	W	L	ERA	G	SV	IP	H	BB	SO
Tom Hudon, Nashua	4	1	1.49	0	0	48	36	19	33
Trevor Breton, Martha's Vineyard	4	0	1.55	10	0	58	37	22	55
Derek Dubois, North Shore	4	2	1.69	9	0	43	37	15	43
Bob Carbaugh, Martha's Vineyard	8	0	1.85	10	0	63	42	17	50
Dylan Driscoll, Brockton	4	3	2.00	9	0	54	59	11	27
Jake Mellin, Nashua	4	0	2.02	8	0	45	33	16	32
Tim Cashman, Nashua	2	4	2.02	8	0	45	42	16	26
Nick Fuller, Torrington	5	1	2.17	9	0	50	29	22	41
Matt Tulley, Nashua	2	1	2.33	9	0	46	36	23	24
Brendan Doonan, Brockton	2	3	2.68	9	0	47	38	12	39

GREAT LAKES LEAGUE

	W	L	PCT	GB
Southern Ohio Copperheads	25	15	.625	—
Cincinnati Steam	24	16	.600	1
Licking County Settlers	24	16	.600	1
Lima Locos	22	16	.579	2
Dayton Docs	20	19	.513	4 ½
Grand Lake Mariners	20	20	.500	5
Xenia Scouts	17	23	.425	8
Hamilton Joes	17	23	.425	8
Lexington Hustlers	14	24	.368	10
Lake Erie Monarchs	14	25	.359	10 ½

CHAMPIONSHIP: Licking County Settlers defeated Lima Locos 2-0 in best-of-three finals.
TOP 10 PROSPECTS: 1. Ashton Perritt, rhp/of, Licking County (Jr., Liberty). **2.** Anthony Misiewicz, lhp, Southern Ohio (So., Michigan State). **3.** Scott Effross, rhp, Licking County (So., Indiana). **4.** Cameron Vieaux, lhp, Southern Ohio (So., Michigan State). **5.** Will Solomon, lhp, Lima (Jr., Kennesaw State). **6.** Justin McCalvin, rhp, Lima (R-Jr., Kennesaw State). **7.** Jared Kujawa, of, Lake Erie (Jr., Western Michigan). **8.** Will Drake, of, Cincinnati (R-So., Cincinnati). **9.** Austin Crutcher, of, Dayton (Jr., Bellarmine, Ky.). **10.** Adam Hall, rhp, Cincinnati (R-So., Xavier).

INDIVIDUAL BATTING LEADERS
(MINIMUM 2.7 PLATE APPEARANCES PER TEAM GAME)

	AVG	AB	R	H	2B	3B	HR	RBI	SB
Ashton Perritt, Licking County	.356	104	23	37	3	1	0	14	12
Robby Sunderman, Cincinnati	.355	141	14	50	9	1	1	24	20
Jared Kujawa, Lake Erie	.346	107	15	37	8	0	1	8	5
Austin Crutcher, Dayton	.336	134	16	45	8	0	2	24	13
Mike Accardi, So. Ohio	.324	142	41	46	5	2	0	15	9
Jesse Puscheck, So. Ohio	.321	156	26	50	6	0	3	44	4
Tyler Grogg, Lima	.320	128	29	41	5	0	0	14	41
Tyler Gray, Grand Lake	.317	126	24	40	8	0	2	26	3
Matthew Paculan, Grand Lake	.314	137	23	43	2	0	0	15	4
Ryan Huber, Licking County	.309	123	24	38	6	0	0	8	6

INDIVIDUAL PITCHING LEADERS
(MINIMUM 0.8 INNINGS PITCHED PER TEAM GAME)

	W	L	ERA	G	SV	IP	H	BB	SO
Matt Jefferson, Cincinnati	3	1	0.65	7	0	41	33	7	40
Michael Danielak, Licking County	4	0	0.77	6	0	35	19	8	28
Connor Murphy, Licking County	4	2	1.26	12	0	43	36	7	25
Tommy Kister, Xenia	6	0	1.29	10	0	49	21	7	36
Will Solomon, Lima	2	0	1.45	7	0	31	23	8	24
Eric Martin, Cincinnati	4	0	1.64	9	0	49	37	11	36
Ryan Wells, Dayton	3	1	1.71	7	0	32	25	13	23
Charles Cooper, Licking County	3	0	1.75	8	0	36	26	13	17
Austin Clay, Lexington	3	1	1.92	8	0	47	40	3	33
Logan Sendelbach, Dayton	4	0	1.98	8	0	41	28	18	32

HAMPTONS COLLEGIATE LEAGUE

	W	L	PCT	GB
Sag Harbor	24	16	.600	—
Westhampton	24	16	.600	—
North Fork	22	18	.550	2
Center Moriches	21	19	.525	3
Riverhead	18	22	.450	6
Shelter Island	17	23	.425	7
Southampton	14	26	.350	10

CHAMPIONSHIP: North Fork Ospreys defeated Center Moriches Battlecats 2-1 in best-of-three finals.
TOP 10 PROSPECTS: 1. Nick Heath, of, North Fork (R-Fr., Northwestern State). **2.** Alex Katz, lhp, Shelter Island (So., St. John's). **3.** Justin Montemayor, if, Sag Harbor (So., Houston). **4.** T.J. Pecoraro, rhp, Southampton (Sr., Vanderbilt). **5.** Max Watt, rhp, Center Moriches (So., Hillsborough, Fla., CC). **6.** Jacob Bodner, rhp, Sag Harbor (Jr., Xavier). **7.** Brandon Thomas, lhp, Center Moriches (Jr., San Diego State). **8.** Charles Galiano, c, Center Moriches (So., Fordham). **9.** Andre Jernigan, if, Riverhead (R-Fr., Xavier). **10.** Jack Sundberg, of, Riverhead (So., Connecticut).

INDIVIDUAL BATTING LEADERS
(MINIMUM 2.7 PLATE APPEARANCES PER TEAM GAME)

	AVG	AB	R	H	2B	3B	HR	RBI	SB
J.C. Brandmaier, Westhampton	.375	144	26	54	8	1	6	28	2
Kyle Zech, Southampton	.343	102	21	35	2	1	1	13	12
Ben Ruta, Southampton	.329	149	20	49	9	1	0	19	10
Nick Heath, North Fork	.326	138	35	45	7	4	2	18	34
Jack Sundberg, Riverhead	.316	133	31	42	5	1	0	11	35
Dan Rizzie, Sag Harbor	.315	89	15	28	5	1	1	12	1
Mac James, Shelter Island	.311	106	15	33	5	0	1	12	8
Dan Shea, Sag Harbor	.311	106	20	33	8	1	2	19	6
Joe Burns, Shelter Island	.311	132	15	41	11	0	0	17	11
Michael Brosseau, Riverhead	.310	116	21	36	1	0	1	11	16

INDIVIDUAL PITCHING LEADERS
(MINIMUM 0.8 INNINGS PITCHED PER TEAM GAME)

	W	L	ERA	G	SV	IP	H	BB	SO
Brendan Mulligan, Riverhead	3	1	1.49	11	1	36	20	21	27
Jonathan Mulford, Sag Harbor	6	0	1.69	9	0	53	47	6	26
Max Watt, Center Moriches	2	1	1.70	8	0	37	28	9	29
Max Almonte, Southampton	3	3	1.76	7	0	46	39	17	45
Joe Salanitri, North Fork	3	2	1.84	9	2	34	26	12	22
Reed Bastie, Sag Harbor	3	2	1.92	8	0	47	31	14	29
Mike Wallace, Shelter Island	4	2	2.25	9	0	52	57	7	40
David Jesch, North Fork	5	0	2.38	8	0	53	38	20	52
Mike OReilly, Center Moriches	2	2	2.42	8	0	41	42	6	44
Mike Dolce, Riverhead	3	2	2.62	9	0	45	32	26	42

JAYHAWK LEAGUE

	W	L	PCT	GB
Hays Larks	23	10	.697	—
Wellington Heat	20	14	.588	3 ½
El Dorado Broncos	19	14	.576	4
Liberal BeeJays	17	17	.500	6 ½
Derby Twins	14	20	.412	9 ½
Dodge City A's	8	26	.235	15 ½

CHAMPIONSHIP: None.
TOP 10 PROSPECTS: 1. Dalton Viner, rhp, Hays (So., San Jacinto, Texas, JC). **2.** Darien McLemore, 2b, Liberal (So., Texas-Arlington). **3.** Dylan

Boston, 1b, Derby (Jr., North Alabama). **4.** Aaron Cornell, of, Hays (Sr., Oklahoma State). **5.** Graylon Brown, rhp, Derby (R-So., Angelo State, Texas). **6.** Joe Williams, ss, Wellington (Graduated, Sterling, Kan.). **7.** David Owen, rhp, Hays (So., Arkansas State). **8.** Cody Robinson, of, Derby (Sr., Northeastern State, Okla.). **9.** Aaron Siple, of, Wellington (So., New Mexico). **10.** Chad Nack, rhp, Liberal (Jr., Texas-Arlington).

INDIVIDUAL BATTING LEADERS
(MINIMUM 2.7 PLATE APPEARANCES PER TEAM GAME)

	AVG	AB	R	H	2B	3B	HR	RBI	SB
Joe Williams, Wellington	.406	96	22	39	4	2	5	16	5
Clayton Garland, Hays	.370	119	18	44	3	0	4	29	7
Aaron Cornell, Hays	.357	98	26	35	9	2	5	28	4
Nick Billinger, Wellington	.350	137	26	48	10	0	0	18	8
Casey Scott, Derby	.346	113	22	39	8	0	0	19	3
Ty Gilmore, Hays	.345	113	22	39	8	0	1	18	4
Jake Placzek, Hays	.330	109	33	36	11	0	1	18	19
Kirk Rocha, Wellington	.325	117	27	38	5	1	1	18	19
T.C. Mark, Wellington	.319	116	11	37	5	0	2	26	0
Dylan Boston, Derby	.317	139	21	44	5	0	9	24	0

INDIVIDUAL PITCHING LEADERS
(MINIMUM 0.8 INNINGS PITCHED PER TEAM GAME)

	W	L	ERA	G	SV	IP	H	BB	SO
David Owen, Hays	2	1	0.36	17	5	25	19	6	25
Justin Bethard, Liberal	2	1	1.66	7	0	44	42	11	40
Jacob Westerhouse, Derby	1	2	2.00	17	2	26	25	5	15
Eric Shuermann, Derby	2	2	2.30	5	0	27	22	8	19
Ian Bentley, Hays	4	1	2.31	13	0	23	27	8	27
Chad Nack, Liberal	2	4	2.51	8	1	32	30	5	12
Nick Gora, Hays	5	1	2.55	8	0	53	40	14	25
Derek Fischer, Wellington	5	2	2.61	8	4	48	45	9	46
Graylon Brown, Derby	1	1	2.63	14	5	24	17	9	30
Vince Lujan, Wellington	1	1	2.63	8	0	27	23	11	18

MINK LEAGUE

NORTH	W	L	PCT	GB
Clarinda A's	28	14	.667	—
St. Joseph Mustangs	21	21	.500	7
Chillicothe Mudcats	20	20	.500	7
Omaha Diamond Spirit	15	25	.375	12
SOUTH	W	L	PCT	GB
Nevada Griffons	25	17	.595	—
Sedalia Bombers	24	18	.571	1
Ozark Generals	22	21	.512	3 ½
Joplin Outlaws	12	30	.286	13

CHAMPIONSHIP: Clarinda A's defeated Nevada Griffons 2-0 in best-of-three finals.

TOP 10 PROSPECTS: 1. Blake Trahan, ss, Clarinda (So., Louisiana-Lafayette). **2.** Brandon Dulin, 1b/of, Chillicothe (SIGNED: Royals). **3.** Michael Schulze, ss, St. Joseph's (SIGNED: Cardinals). **4.** Cory Raley, ss/2b, Clarinda (R-Fr., Temple JC, Texas). **5.** Robert Greco, rhp, Sedalia (Sr., Nebraska). **6.** Jake Meloche, lhp, Clarinda (R-Fr., San Bernardino Valley JC, Calif.). **7.** Tyler House, lhp, Omaha (R-Fr., Missouri). **8.** Mylz Jones, 3b/ss, Sedalia (So., Cal State Bakersfield). **9.** Nathan Lukes, of, Chillicothe (So., Sacramento State). **10.** Robert Prieto, 2b, Ozark (Sr., Freed-Hardeman, Tenn.).

INDIVIDUAL BATTING LEADERS
(MINIMUM 2.7 PLATE APPEARANCES PER TEAM GAME)

	AVG	AB	R	H	2B	3B	HR	RBI	SB
Paul Trenhaile, Chillicothe	.434	122	31	53	8	2	2	22	6
Robert Prieto, Ozark	.387	150	26	58	8	0	3	19	7
Trevor Jones, Chillicothe	.386	114	32	44	3	3	0	24	21
Nathan Lukes, Chillicothe	.362	130	31	47	4	1	1	24	7
Payton Reed, Ozark	.359	142	25	51	11	1	2	20	1
Paul Richmond, Ozark	.353	116	23	41	5	0	0	16	7
Dean Long, Clarinda	.352	145	38	51	10	2	1	34	13
Zac Stewart, Joplin	.350	143	21	50	6	5	0	20	9
Michael Douglas, Nevada	.350	117	26	41	5	0	7	30	9
Kevin Connolly, Omaha	.347	121	14	42	7	1	1	16	15

INDIVIDUAL PITCHING LEADERS
(MINIMUM 0.8 INNINGS PITCHED PER TEAM GAME)

	W	L	ERA	G	SV	IP	H	BB	SO
Aaron Baker, St. Joseph	5	1	1.10	9	0	49	36	7	34
Mitch Weis, Nevada	3	2	1.10	14	4	33	18	13	27
Jake Meloche, Clarinda	6	0	1.41	8	0	51	29	14	49
Trevor Richards, Sedalia	2	4	1.52	7	0	41	33	8	36
Logan Thune, Omaha	2	0	1.54	6	1	23	14	13	19
Marc Picciola, Omaha	1	3	1.59	12	3	23	28	3	17
Chris Bradley, Omaha	1	0	1.64	4	0	22	16	7	23
Robert Greco, Sedalia	3	2	1.98	8	0	59	44	24	62
Tei Vanderford, Clarinda	1	1	2.18	7	0	33	25	11	20
Derek Birginske, Chillicothe	3	1	2.56	9	1	32	24	14	22

NEW ENGLAND COLLEGIATE LEAGUE

EASTERN	W	L	PCT	GB
Newport Gulls	30	14	.682	—
Ocean State Waves	24	20	.545	6
Mystic Schooners	22	22	.500	8
Sanford Mainers	22	23	.489	8 ½
Laconia Muskrats	21	24	.467	9 ½
New Bedford Bay Sox	20	24	.455	10
Plymouth Pilgrims	15	28	.349	14½
WESTERN	W	L	PCT	GB
Keene Swamp Bats	27	17	.614	—
Vermont Mountaineers	24	20	.545	3
North Adams SteepleCats	22	22	.500	5
Holyoke Blue Sox	22	23	.489	5 ½
Saratoga Brigade	21	24	.467	6 ½
Danbury Westerners	17	26	.395	9 ½

CHAMPIONSHIP: Keene Swamp Bats defeated Newport Gulls 2-1 in best-of-three finals.

TOP 10 PROSPECTS: 1. Nathan Kirby, lhp, Keene (So., Virginia). **2.** Scott Squier, lhp, North Adams (Jr., Hawaii). **3.** Kyle Wilcox, rhp, Newport (So., Bryant). **4.** Ben Roberts, of, Newport (R-So., Washington State). **5.** Brett Lilek, lhp, Newport (So., Arizona State). **6.** Chris Shaw, 1b, New Bedford (So., Boston College). **7.** Brett Graves, rhp, Newport (Jr., Missouri). **8.** Trace Tam Sing, ss, Newport (R-Jr., Washington State). **9.** Steven Rice, lhp, Sanford (Sr., Vanderbilt). **10.** Cole Martin, c, Sanford (Sr., Michigan).

INDIVIDUAL BATTING LEADERS
(MINIMUM 2.7 PLATE APPEARANCES PER TEAM GAME)

	AVG	AB	R	H	2B	3B	HR	RBI	SB
Joe Landi, North Adams	.348	138	27	48	8	0	0	6	22
Brendan Hendriks, Holyoke	.342	152	15	52	10	1	1	26	3
Mike Gerber, Ocean State	.340	147	25	50	10	1	7	30	0
Nico Darras, Mystic	.340	100	15	34	6	0	2	12	6
JP Sportman, Keen	.340	147	24	50	13	1	4	31	12
Chandler Brock, Vermont	.339	124	22	42	6	1	0	12	12
Christopher Shaw, New Bedford	.335	155	24	52	11	0	5	39	1
Zach Lucas, Keen	.331	130	22	43	5	0	5	17	6
Evan Ocello, Ocean State	.331	133	30	44	10	0	4	15	16
Daniel Spingola, Danbury	.325	157	21	51	9	2	2	13	4

INDIVIDUAL PITCHING LEADERS
(MINIMUM 0.8 INNINGS PITCHED PER TEAM GAME)

	W	L	ERA	G	SV	IP	H	BB	SO
Michael Burke, Holyoke	3	1	0.55	9	0	65	58	9	56
Brett Graves, Newport	4	0	1.01	6	0	36	20	15	30
John Miles, Vermont	3	1	1.20	8	2	38	18	11	32
Zachary Tax, Danbury	3	1	1.26	14	2	36	27	7	18
Nathan Kirby, Keene	3	0	1.67	8	0	43	28	18	60
Jordan Kutzer, Holyoke	1	1	1.73	8	0	42	31	12	20
Brian Hunter, Keene	3	2	1.88	8	0	38	27	17	52
James Mulry, Newport	4	1	1.93	8	0	37	26	13	30
Tyler Bowditch, Ocean State	3	0	2.25	9	0	40	37	12	27
James Bessell, Ocean State	4	0	2.40	8	0	41	29	16	31

NEW YORK COLLEGIATE LEAGUE

	W	L	PCT	GB
Oneonta Outlaws	25	15	.625	—
Hornell Dodgers	23	17	.575	2
Olean Oilers	22	18	.550	3
Wellsville Nitros	22	18	.550	3
Syracuse JR Chiefs	22	18	.550	3

	W	L	PCT	GB
Syracuse Salt Cats	21	19	.525	4
Geneva Twins	20	20	.500	5
Geneva Red Wings	20	20	.500	5
Sherrill Silversmiths	16	24	.400	9
Rochester Ridgemen	16	24	.400	9
Niagara Power	13	27	.325	12

CHAMPIONSHIP: Oneonta Outlaws defeated Hornell Dodgers in finals.
TOP 10 PROSPECTS: 1. Robert Winemiller, rhp, Geneva Red Wings (Jr., Case Western Reserve, Ohio). **2.** Ryan Clark, rhp, Syracuse Jr. Chiefs (So., UNC Greensboro). **3.** Thomas Bergjans, rhp, Geneva Red Wings (Jr., Haverford College, Pa.). **4.** Luke Crumley, rhp, Oneonta (Jr. Georgia). **5.** Zac Fowler, rhp, Geneva Twins (Jr., Jacksonville State).

INDIVIDUAL BATTING LEADERS
(MINIMUM 2.7 PLATE APPEARANCES PER TEAM GAME)

	AVG	AB	R	H	2B	3B	HR	RBI	SB
Carlos Guzman, Salt Cats	.388	139	34	54	9	5	0	15	10
Aaron Pigna, JR Chiefs	.377	130	29	49	5	0	1	28	23
Kirby Campbell, Twins	.373	102	12	38	7	1	0	18	2
Alec Bahnick, Wellsville	.364	107	28	39	4	0	0	17	16
Cristian Fiorito, Salt Cats	.362	127	23	46	13	3	5	38	0
Alex Caruso, JR Chiefs	.350	103	27	36	4	0	0	16	7
Stanley Susana, JR Chiefs	.344	122	26	42	8	0	1	27	5
Shane Barley, Wellsville	.343	137	29	47	9	0	8	36	4
Nicholas Sinay, JR Chiefs	.342	111	28	38	4	4	2	14	12
Connor Mathis, JR Chiefs	.341	123	22	42	7	0	2	16	4

INDIVIDUAL PITCHING LEADERS
(MINIMUM 0.8 INNINGS PITCHED PER TEAM GAME)

	W	L	ERA	G	SV	IP	H	BB	SO
Thomas Bergjans, Red Wings	2	2	0.82	7	0	44	22	18	50
Luke Crumley, Oneonta	3	0	1.29	6	0	42	22	18	38
Dwayne Snider, Rochester	2	2	1.63	9	0	55	38	13	56
Brandon Valentin, Olean	3	1	1.67	7	0	43	35	16	26
Chris Jansen, Hornell	6	0	1.82	9	0	40	34	10	24
Jeff Beall, Hornell	4	1	2.05	18	1	44	32	12	34
Matthew Milburn, Oneonta	5	1	2.12	8	0	51	39	12	30
Karney Boff, Twins	3	0	2.13	14	1	38	41	9	29
Michael Bittel, JR Chiefs	4	1	2.21	8	0	41	31	16	32
Josh Webb, Sherrill	3	3	2.47	10	0	44	29	14	34

NORTHWOODS LEAGUE

NORTH

	W	L	PCT	GB
Waterloo Bucks	51	19	.729	—
Duluth Huskies	43	27	.614	8
Willmar Stingers	41	29	.586	10
Mankato MoonDogs	38	32	.543	13
St. Cloud Rox	36	34	.514	15
Rochester Honkers	28	42	.400	23
Alexandria Blue Anchors	24	46	.343	27
Thunder Bay Border Cats	21	49	.300	30

SOUTH

	W	L	PCT	GB
Lakeshore Chinooks	44	26	.629	—
La Crosse Loggers	43	27	.614	1
Madison Mallards	41	29	.586	3
Eau Claire Express	33	37	.471	11
Wisconsin Rapids Rafters	31	39	.443	13
Wisconsin Woodchucks	29	41	.414	15
Battle Creek Bombers	29	41	.414	15
Green Bay Bullfrogs	28	42	.400	16

CHAMPIONSHIP: Madison Mallards defeated Duluth Huskies in finals.
TOP 25 PROSPECTS: 1. Colin Poche, lhp, Willmar (So., Arkansas). **2.** Eric Hanhold, rhp, Lakeshore (So., Florida). **3.** Mike Papi, of/1b, Lakeshore (Jr., Virginia). **4.** Paul Voelker, rhp, Eau Claire (Jr., Dallas Baptist). **5.** Blake Hickman, rhp/c, Waterloo (So., Iowa). **6.** Alex Young, lhp, Lakeshore (So., Texas Christian). **7.** Taylore Cherry, rhp, Madison Mallards (So., North Carolina) . **8.** J.P. Feyereisen, rhp, Wisconsin Rapid Rafters (Jr., Wisconsin-Stevens Point). **9.** John LaPrise, 3b/2b, Madison (So., Virginia). **10.** Chesny Young, 3b/2b, Waterloo (Jr., Mercer). **11.** Michael Suchy, of, Willmar (Jr., Florida Gulf Coast). **12.** Tyler Eppler, rhp, Rochester (Jr., Sam Houston State). **13.** Adam Dian, rhp, Waterloo (Jr., Temple). **14.** Georgie Salem, of, Alexandria (So., Alabama). **15.** Cam Gibson, of, Battle Creek (So., Michigan State). **16.** Garrett Harrison, lhp, Green Bay (R-So., St. Cloud State, Minn.). **17.** Jake Jefferies, 2b/ss, Wisconsin Woodchucks (So., Cal State Fullerton). **18.** Mitch Sewald, rhp, Lakeshore (So., Louisiana State).

19. Tate Matheny, of, Madison (So., Missouri State). **20.** Matt Trowbridge, lhp, Eau Claire (Jr., Central Michigan). **21.** Aaron Rhodes, rhp, Waterloo (R-So., Florida). **22.** Donnie Hissa, rhp, Lakeshore (Sr., Notre Dame). **23.** Marc Flores, 1b/of, Willmar (Sr., Hawaii) . **24.** Keith Curcio, of/if, Duluth (Jr., Florida Southern). **25.** Nate Carter, rhp, Duluth (Sr., Florida Southern).

INDIVIDUAL BATTING LEADERS
(MINIMUM 2.7 PLATE APPEARANCES PER TEAM GAME)

	AVG	AB	R	H	2B	3B	HR	RBI	SB
John LaPrise, Madison	.407	189	45	77	6	3	0	29	14
Keith Curcio, Duluth	.367	278	48	102	18	1	3	53	28
Zack Tillery, Willmar	.358	165	33	59	9	0	4	40	1
Marc Flores, Willmar	.352	270	58	95	26	0	13	64	8
Andrew Sohn, Alexandria	.349	229	40	80	14	0	5	30	24
Timothy Arakawa, Mankato	.346	254	56	88	16	1	1	30	30
Cam Gibson, Battle Creek	.345	220	43	76	11	3	1	26	23
John Ziznewski, Waterloo	.343	204	43	70	10	2	4	40	9
Georgie Salem, Alexandria	.337	190	35	64	11	0	5	27	14
Micael Suiter, Duluth	.335	251	40	84	16	1	0	37	9

INDIVIDUAL PITCHING LEADERS
(MINIMUM 0.8 INNINGS PITCHED PER TEAM GAME)

	W	L	ERA	G	SV	IP	H	BB	SO
Clay Chapman, Duluth	4	4	1.99	12	0	72	46	26	66
Matt Kent, Rochester	5	3	2.50	12	0	72	67	19	66
Joe Greenfield, Lakeshore	3	3	2.84	11	0	63	56	21	58
Brad Stroik, Wisconsin	4	4	2.99	15	0	84	77	31	74
Aaron Rhodes, Waterloo	5	4	3.19	11	0	59	52	18	74
Eric Nyquist, St. Cloud	5	3	3.26	10	0	58	73	13	47
John Kravetz, Wisconsin	4	3	3.26	10	0	61	60	12	54
Josh Frye, La Crosse	6	3	3.32	12	0	76	70	32	79
Taylor Lehnert, Eau Claire	7	3	3.39	11	0	61	64	25	34
Cam Verbeke, Madison	5	4	3.47	15	0	57	48	20	57

PERFECT GAME COLLEGIATE LEAGUE

EAST

	W	L	PCT	GB
Amsterdam Mohawks	31	16	.660	—
Mohawk Valley DiamondDawgs	26	19	.578	4
Albany Dutchmen	26	22	.542	5 ½
Glens Falls Golden Eagles	26	22	.542	5 ½
Cooperstown Hawkeyes	18	25	.419	11

WEST

	W	L	PCT	GB
Watertown Rams	29	19	.604	—
Newark Pilots	22	25	.469	6 ½
Elmira Pioneers	21	26	.447	7 ½
Utica Brewers	16	28	.364	11
Adirondack Trail Blazers	17	30	.362	11 ½

CHAMPIONSHIP: Amsterdam Mohawks defeated Elmira Pioneers 2-1 in best-of-three finals.
TOP 10 PROSPECTS: 1. Trey Wingenter, rhp, Amsterdam (So., Auburn). **2.** Mike Urbanski, rhp, Amsterdam (Jr., Binghamton). **3.** Kyle Barrett, of, Amsterdam (So., Kentucky). **4.** Zach Remillard, 3b, Albany (So., Coastal Carolina). **5.** Matt Thaiss, c, Watertown (Fr., Virginia). **6.** Jordan Ebert, 2b/of, Amsterdam (So., Auburn). **7.** Matt Snyder, lhp, Amsterdam (So., Fulton-Montgomery C.C., N.Y.). **8.** Matt Dacey, 1b, Albany (R-Fr., Richmond). **9.** Joe Purritano, 1b, Albany (So., Dartmouth). **10.** Jay Gonzalez, of, Utica (Sr., Auburn).

INDIVIDUAL BATTING LEADERS
(MINIMUM 3 AT-BATS PER TEAM GAME)

	AVG	AB	R	H	2B	3B	HR	RBI	SB
Michael Pierson, Utica	.404	156	34	63	10	1	2	30	10
Chris Kalousdian, Elmira	.376	170	38	64	19	1	2	32	12
John Nogowski, Amsterdam	.365	148	33	54	14	1	3	24	4
Jay Gonzalez, Utica	.362	149	36	54	10	1	1	21	17
Dalton Herrington, MV	.359	156	36	56	11	2	1	33	34
Nate Lotze, Cooperstown	.350	157	26	55	7	1	1	16	1
Max Rosing, Newark	.345	168	30	58	14	0	2	20	1
Anthony Marks, Albany	.342	161	31	55	4	0	0	12	18
Cameron Day, Cooperstown	.338	136	21	46	5	0	0	21	1
Josh Gardiner, Amsterdam	.327	150	40	49	15	1	4	33	15

INDIVIDUAL PITCHING LEADERS
(MINIMUM 1 INNING PITCHED PER TEAM GAME)

	W	L	ERA	G	SV	IP	H	BB	SO
Dylan Collett, Albany	3	1	1.71	15	2	53	40	14	47
Eann Cox, Cooperstown	6	0	2.11	9	0	55	42	19	64

	W	L	ERA	G	SV	IP	H	BB	SO
Zach Hopf, Glens Falls	6	1	2.63	8	0	51	52	8	42
Keegan Long, Mohawk Valley	4	1	2.78	10	0	45	40	11	51
Bryan Carr, Albany	3	3	2.79	10	0	48	52	15	25
Gavin Culpepper, MV	3	3	2.91	9	0	53	39	21	39
Sean Spicer, Albany	3	2	3.42	10	0	55	50	26	38
Matt Gallup, Albany	3	1	3.56	10	0	48	54	16	22
Will Spitzfaden, Newark	2	5	3.83	8	0	56	56	5	17
Chas Parsons, Adirondack	0	4	3.99	11	0	50	54	17	33

PROSPECT LEAGUE

EAST	W	L	PCT	GB
West Virginia Miners	38	22	.633	—
Chillicothe Paints	34	26	.567	4
Butler Blue Sox	33	26	.559	4 ½
Slippery Rock Sliders	28	32	.467	10
Richmond RiverRats	24	36	.400	14
Lorain County Ironmen	22	37	.373	15 ½

WEST	W	L	PCT	GB
Danville Dans	41	19	.683	—
Quincy Gems	34	25	.576	6 ½
Terre Haute Rex	32	28	.533	9
Hannibal Cavemen	29	28	.509	10 ½
Springfield Sliders	11	47	.190	29

CHAMPIONSHIP: West Virginia Miners defeated Quincy Gems 2-0 in best-of-three finals.

TOP 10 PROSPECTS: 1. Troy Conyers, lhp, Danville (So., San Diego). **2.** Steve Pallares, ss, Quincy (Jr., San Diego State). **3.** Spencer Herrmann, 1b/lhp, Danville (Jr., North Florida). **4.** David Hess, rhp, West Virginia (Jr., Tennessee Tech). **5.** Brandon Koch, rhp, West Virginia (So., Dallas Baptist). **6.** Jacob Bosiokovic, 3b, Richmond (So., Ohio State). **7.** Jaesung Hwang, rhp, West Virginia (Sr., Lipscomb). **8.** Dan Zuchowski, inf/of, Chillicothe (R-so., Toledo). **9.** Matt Peters, 2b, Butler (Sr., California University of Pennsylvania). **10.** Giancarlo Brugnoni, 1b, Chillicothe (Sr., Grand Valley State).

INDIVIDUAL BATTING LEADERS
(MINIMUM 2.7 PLATE APPEARANCES PER TEAM GAME)

	AVG	AB	R	H	2B	3B	HR	RBI	SB
Kaeo Aliviado, West Virginia	.370	154	34	57	10	0	0	15	11
Matthew Calhoun, Slippery Rock	.358	173	28	62	10	1	7	26	7
Thomas Richards, Quincy	.347	176	31	61	7	3	8	33	1
Tyler Wampler, Terre Haute	.341	185	32	63	11	2	0	23	9
Kyle Kempf, Terre Haute	.336	217	31	73	17	5	2	25	19
Matthew Peters, Butler	.330	212	23	70	11	7	0	22	13
Steven Pallares, Quincy	.318	184	26	54	12	2	2	22	22
Caleb Howell, Quincy	.310	197	29	61	8	2	0	19	9
Zach Woolcock, West Virginia	.310	171	26	53	11	1	3	27	6
Robbie Stein, Richmond	.303	231	32	70	8	2	1	24	5

INDIVIDUAL PITCHING LEADERS
(MINIMUM 0.8 INNINGS PITCHED PER TEAM GAME)

	W	L	ERA	G	SV	IP	H	BB	SO
Jaesung Hwang, West Virginia	5	1	0.36	7	0	51	28	5	44
Adam Aldred, Butler	2	0	1.59	8	0	51	39	18	41
Spencer Herrmann, Danville	2	2	1.69	9	0	48	34	20	48
Rolando Celis, West Virginia	2	3	1.77	12	1	51	40	13	41
Travis McDonald, Hannibal	4	4	1.77	10	1	61	39	20	57
Steve Laudicina, Chillicothe	7	3	1.98	10	0	59	42	13	41
Cam Knott, Lorain County	6	2	2.13	12	0	63	50	17	60
Mike Deitsch, Chillicothe	2	3	2.13	12	0	51	47	16	44
Jon Anderson, Butler	5	2	2.17	10	0	58	39	25	44
Jake Powers, Quincy	6	0	2.23	13	0	65	41	25	52

TEXAS COLLEGIATE LEAGUE

	W	L	PCT	GB
Brazos Valley Bombers	46	14	.767	—
Acadiana Cane Cutters	32	28	.533	14
East Texas Pump Jacks	30	28	.517	15
Victoria Generals	30	29	.508	15 ½
Woodlands Strykers	21	39	.350	25
Texas Marshals	19	40	.325	26 ½

CHAMPIONSHIP: Brazos Valley Bombers defeated Victoria Generals 2-1 in best-of-three finals.

TOP 10 PROSPECTS: 1. Logan Taylor, ss, Acadiana (So., Texas A&M). **2.** Parker Ray, rhp, Brazos Valley (Sr., Texas A&M). **3.** Connor Barron, ss/of,

Acadiana (Jr., Southern Mississippi). **4.** Zac Curtis, lhp, Brazos Valley (Sr., Middle Tennessee State). **5.** Mitchell Nau, c, Acadiana (Jr., Texas A&M). **6.** Ty Marlow, rhp, East Texas (Sr., Texas). **7.** Blake Kopetsky, of, Brazos Valley (So., Temple JC, Texas). **8.** Guillermo Trujillo, rhp, Brazos Valley (So., Oral Roberts). **9.** Kyle Keller, rhp, Victoria (Jr., Southeastern Louisiana). **10.** Shay Maltese, rhp, Brazos Valley (Sr., Cal State Northridge).

INDIVIDUAL BATTING LEADERS
(MINIMUM 2.7 PLATE APPEARANCES PER TEAM GAME)

	AVG	AB	R	H	2B	3B	HR	RBI	SB
Mitchell Nau, Acadiana	.350	180	33	63	18	0	6	39	9
Logan Taylor, Acadiana	.339	177	38	60	11	1	3	29	17
Dirk Masters, Woodlands	.330	182	34	60	10	2	7	37	1
Matthew Dickey, East Texas	.322	171	32	55	6	0	0	18	40
Horacio Correa III, Brazos Valley	.314	159	35	50	8	1	1	28	6
Brett Kauten, Brazos Valley	.312	186	42	58	7	0	3	37	20
Blake Kopetsky, Brazos Valley	.309	162	34	50	6	1	5	30	11
G.R. Hinsley, Brazos Valley	.309	217	42	67	14	0	6	55	11
Ricardo Sanchez, Woodlands	.306	170	26	52	10	1	2	17	12
Kyle Cedotal, Acadiana	.305	141	26	43	7	2	0	15	11

INDIVIDUAL PITCHING LEADERS
(MINIMUM 0.8 INNINGS PITCHED PER TEAM GAME)

	W	L	ERA	G	SV	IP	H	BB	SO
Nick Rossetta, East Texas	6	2	1.23	10	0	58	49	18	41
Parker Ray, Brazos Valley	4	0	1.69	6	0	48	32	14	49
Jake Winston, Acadiana	7	2	2.12	11	0	68	54	20	53
Justin Sinibaldi, Acadiana	5	0	2.25	11	0	68	50	24	58
Robert Parucha, East Texas	5	0	2.63	7	0	51	50	5	33
Bryce Rutherford, Brazos Valley	6	1	2.89	9	0	56	48	19	58
Matt Danton, Woodlands	5	2	3.06	11	0	68	78	8	51
Kyle Cedotal, Acadiana	3	4	3.39	10	0	61	62	16	41
Nick Zaunbrecher, Acadiana	1	4	3.42	10	1	50	43	18	31
Keaton Brewer, Texas	4	4	3.84	14	0	63	74	24	30

VALLEY LEAGUE

NORTH	W	L	PCT	GB
Woodstock River Bandits	26	17	.605	—
Charles Town Cannons	23	21	.523	3 ½
Strasburg Express	22	21	.512	4
Aldie Senators	22	22	.500	4 ½
Front Royal Cardinals	19	25	.432	7 ½
Winchester Royals	13	30	.302	13

SOUTH	W	L	PCT	GB
Harrisonburg Turks	32	12	.727	—
New Market Rebels	28	15	.651	3 ½
Staunton Braves	24	20	.545	8
Waynesboro Generals	22	22	.500	10
Covington Lumberjacks	17	27	.386	15
Rockbridge Rapids	14	30	.318	18

CHAMPIONSHIP: Waynesboro Generals defeated Strasburg Express 2-1 in best-of-three finals.

TOP 10 PROSPECTS: 1. Max Povse, rhp, Strasburg (Jr., UNC Greensboro). **2.** Connor Kaden, rhp, Harrisonburg (Jr., Wake Forest). **3.** Luke Leftwich, rhp, Aldie (So., Wofford). **4.** Jordan DeLorenzo, lhp, Front Royal (Jr., West Florida). **5.** Aaron Cressley, rhp, New Market (Jr., Pittsburgh-Bradford). **6.** Brandon Gum, ss, New Market (So., George Mason). **7.** Aaron Weisberg, rhp, Staunton (Sr., George Washington). **8.** Jordan Tarsovich, of, Strasburg (Sr., Virginia Military Institute). **9.** James Vasquez, 1b/dh, Staunton, (Sr., Central Florida). **10.** Adam Emerson, rhp, Strasburg (Jr., Christopher Newport, Va.).

INDIVIDUAL BATTING LEADERS
(MINIMUM 2.7 PLATE APPEARANCES PER TEAM GAME)

	AVG	AB	R	H	2B	3B	HR	RBI	SB
Jordan Tarsovich, Strasburg	.414	157	34	65	10	1	2	10	13
Brandon Gum, New Market	.366	145	21	53	11	2	0	15	17
Eric Kalbfleisch, Harrisonburg	.354	158	23	56	8	2	1	18	1
Thomas Smith, Harrisonburg	.341	132	23	45	10	2	2	23	4
Tyler Hibbert, Charles Town	.333	114	26	38	5	0	0	13	16
Jimmy Dowdell, Aldie	.333	156	18	52	7	1	1	14	4
Waldyvan Estrada, Charles Town	.331	166	23	55	11	1	3	32	9
Phil Lipari, Staunton	.321	162	28	52	7	0	1	22	24
Tyler Bocock, Waynesboro	.311	177	28	55	10	1	1	23	9
Matt Durst, Charles Town	.310	158	17	49	6	2	4	29	2

INDIVIDUAL PITCHING LEADERS
(MINIMUM 0.8 INNINGS PITCHED PER TEAM GAME)

	W	L	ERA	G	SV	IP	H	BB	SO
Richard Winters, Winchester	5	0	0.44	11	0	41	22	7	43
Aaron Cressley, New Market	4	0	0.63	7	0	43	32	17	37
Daniel Thorpe, Aldie	3	2	1.07	8	0	42	26	12	31
Justin Cooper, New Market	6	0	1.12	9	0	56	40	33	32
Justin Camp, Harrisonburg	6	1	1.37	9	0	59	33	16	45
Parks Smithey, Covington	4	1	1.62	10	2	39	36	14	27
Abdel Rivera, Covington	0	4	1.62	7	0	50	46	10	23
Jordan DeLorenzo, Front Royal	4	3	1.69	8	0	59	39	9	64
Matt Hockenberry, Woodstock	2	1	1.77	8	0	46	39	10	32
Graham Tebbit, Aldie	1	3	1.81	10	0	50	38	6	44

WEST COAST LEAGUE

NORTH

	W	L	PCT	GB
Walla Walla Sweets	31	22	.585	—
Wenatchee AppleSox	29	24	.547	2
Bellingham Bells	27	27	.500	4 ½
Victoria HarbourCats	22	32	.407	9 ½
Kelowna Falcons	19	35	.352	12 ½

SOUTH

	W	L	PCT	GB
Corvallis Knights	37	17	.685	—
Medford Rogues	30	24	.556	7
Bend Elks	30	24	.556	7
Cowlitz Black Bears	28	26	.519	9
Klamath Falls Gems	25	29	.463	12
Kitsap BlueJackets	18	36	.333	19

CHAMPIONSHIP: Corvallis defeated Wenatchee 2-0 in best-of-three final.
TOP 10 PROSPECTS: 1. Cody Poteet, rhp, Walla Walla (So., UCLA) . **2.** Jorge Perez, rhp, Corvallis (Jr., Grand Canyon, Ariz.). **3.** Blake Drake, of, Corvallis (Jr., Concordia, Ore.). **4.** Dylan Hecht, rhp, Corvallis (So., UC Santa Barbara). **5.** Alex Real, c, Victoria (Jr., New Mexico). **6.** Nick Sabo, lhp, Klamath Gems (Jr., Long Beach State). **7.** Marc Huberman, lhp, Bellingham (So., Southern California). **8.** Connor Spencer, 1b/of/3b, Wenatchee (Jr., UC Irvine). **9.** Joe Mello, ss, Wenatchee (Jr., Lewis-Clark State, Idaho). **10.** Alex Calbick, 3b/1b, Bellingham (Sr., Maine).

INDIVIDUAL BATTING LEADERS
(MINIMUM 2.7 PLATE APPEARANCES PER TEAM GAME)

	AVG	AB	R	H	2B	3B	HR	RBI	SB
Alex Calbick, Bellingham	.384	185	31	71	13	0	5	26	2
Connor Spencer, Wenatchee	.380	166	28	63	14	0	3	36	2
Kyle Knigge, Cowlitz	.373	118	20	44	6	0	1	25	5
Kevin Davidson, Medford	.361	147	22	53	7	0	5	33	2
Jarryd Klemm, Kelowna	.353	133	23	47	13	0	3	29	1
Dane Lund, Corvallis	.343	140	26	48	7	0	0	16	25
Alex Real, Victoria	.339	168	26	57	10	1	6	27	4
Devyn Bolasky, Cowlitz	.337	172	22	58	8	2	1	23	5
Ryan Aguilar, Cowlitz	.329	161	41	53	8	1	0	20	10
Darren Kolk, Kelowna	.327	171	31	56	14	0	0	11	25

INDIVIDUAL PITCHING LEADERS
(MINIMUM 0.8 INNINGS PITCHED PER TEAM GAME)

	W	L	ERA	G	SV	IP	H	BB	SO
Elliot Surrey, Corvallis	5	1	1.27	10	1	50	49	12	33
Nick Baker, Bellingham	1	3	1.63	11	0	55	46	9	32
Brandon Horth, Klamath Falls	4	1	1.64	10	0	55	51	18	49
Nate Cole, Bellingham	4	2	1.71	11	0	58	53	16	41
Bryan Conant, Victoria	4	1	1.81	8	0	55	40	11	45
Andrew Olson, Bellingham	3	2	1.84	9	0	44	32	6	43
Brandon Williams, Medford	4	3	2.23	16	2	48	32	9	45
Matt Hall, Walla Walla	5	2	2.25	11	0	52	39	23	45
Nick Sabo, Klamath Falls	6	3	2.63	12	0	75	69	16	57
Sean Silva, Walla Walla	4	0	2.64	12	0	44	47	22	29

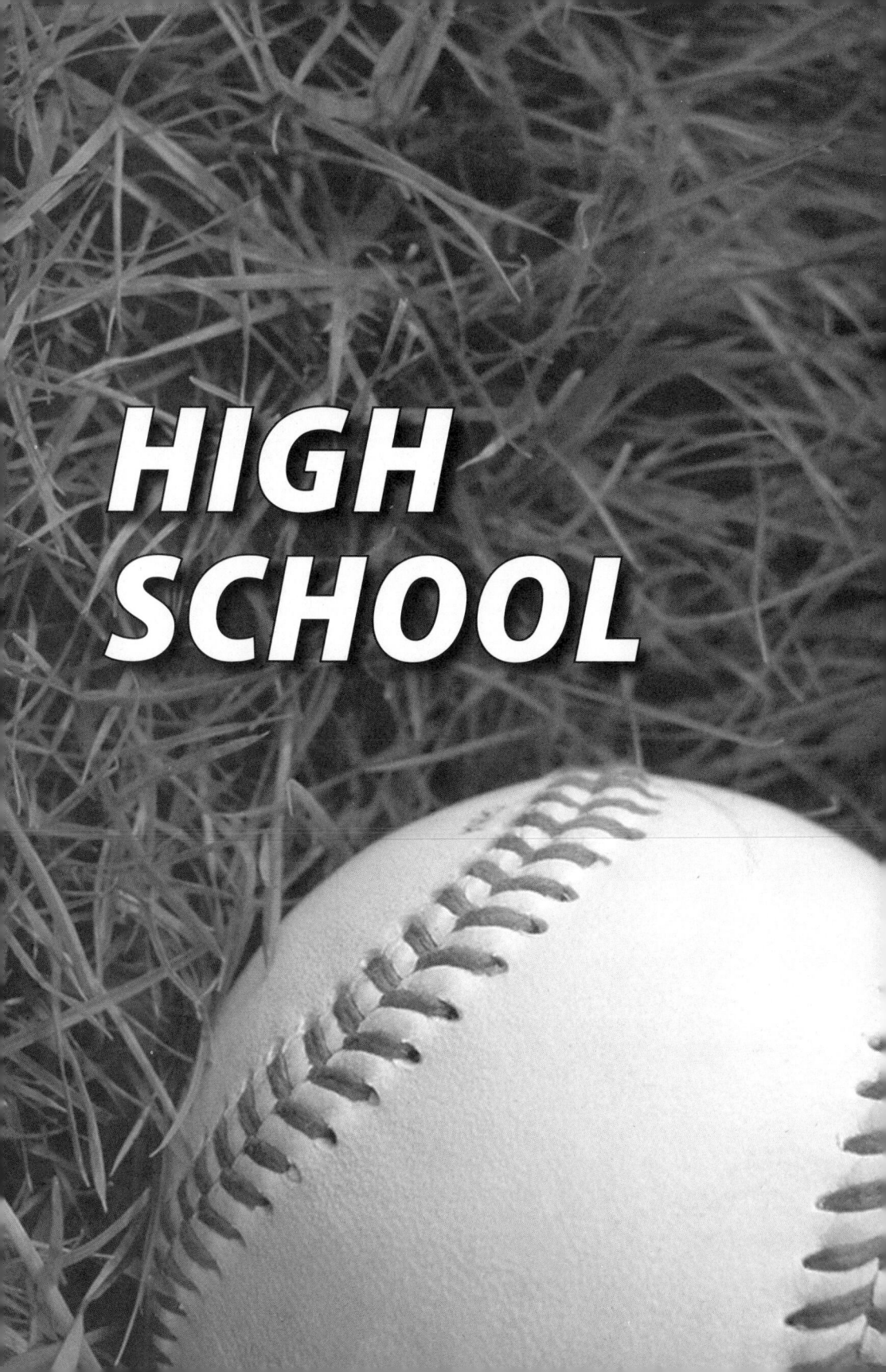

HIGH SCHOOL

ALYSON BOYER RODE

Conor Cuse followed in the footsteps of first-round picks and lifted Harvard-Westlake to a title

Harvard-Westlake gets its title

BY NATHAN RODE

The game of baseball works in funny ways, especially at the high school level. Just ask Harvard-Westlake High, whose run to national glory came one year later than expected.

The script for the private school in Studio City, Calif.—where it is sandwiched between Hollywood lots and million-dollar Beverly Hills homes—was written for 2012, with two first-round picks on one pitching staff and plenty of national hype. But the storybook run never came. The staff ace was lost to injury and the Wolverines were upset in the postseason.

A year later, the pitching superstars—righthander Lucas Giolito and lefthander Max Fried—were gone and their younger protégé, righthander/third baseman Jack Flaherty, was left to lead a staff with modest experience and less punch. Add in nearly an entire offensive lineup returning, a young coach with a bright future, his own all-star staff, and a desire for redemption and the real story was writing itself as Harvard-Westlake High marched to a wild win in California's Southern Section championship and was ultimately named Baseball America's Team of the Year.

Most would write off a team that lost two first-round arms to graduation and not expect the team to compete at the same level, but Harvard-Westlake head coach Matt LaCour knew his team would be a threat offensively with most of his everyday players back, and he was confident that the hard work everyone put in would pay off.

"I felt like this was a culmination of the past seven years of really hard work by our staff and our players—daily putting in the grind and trying to do things the right way with the hope that it would all pay off," he said. "This group of seniors, there's no transfers, there's no kid that just came in and made us better. It was just a culmination guys that worked hard together, that got better on a daily basis and at the end just became an unbelievable team in terms of trusting each other and quite honestly, teaching me as a coach how to trust players a little bit more."

The Wolverines hit .323 as a team, living up to expectations at the plate and on defense, consistently making the routine plays and executing on fundamentals. Junior Brian Ginsberg solidified the infield with his play at shortstop and on days he wasn't pitching, Flaherty strengthened the left side by holding down the hot corner. LaCour and his staff knew hitting and defense would be their

HIGH SCHOOL TOP 25

Rank	School	Record	Season conclusion
1	Harvard-Westlake HS, Studio City, Calif.	28-4	CIF Southern Section D-I Champion
2	Venice (Fla.) HS	28-3	7A State Champ
3	The Woodlands (Texas) HS	38-4	5A State Champ
4	Owasso (Okla.) HS	36-0	6A State Champ
5	Pensacola (Fla.) Catholic HS	30-0	4A State Champ
6	St. Francis HS, Mountain View, Calif.	30-4	CIF Central Coast Section Champion
7	Lexington (S.C.) HS	28-3	4A State Champ
8	Rancho Bernardo HS, San Diego	30-5	CIF San Diego Section Champion
9	Tomball (Texas) HS	35-5	4A State Champ
10	Coronado HS, Las Vegas	36-4	Division I State
11	Desert Mountain HS, Scottsdale, Ariz.	31-4	Division I State
12	Lake Brantley HS, Altamonte Springs, Fla.	27-5	8A State Champ
13	Oaks Christian HS, Westlake Village, Calif.	29-3	CIF Southern Section D-IV Champion
14	Archbishop McCarthy HS, Southwest Ranches, Fla.	27-3	6A State Champ
15	Cypress (Calif.) HS	26-8	CIF Southern Section D-II Champion
16	Dulles HS, Sugar Land, Texas	32-8	6A State Runner Up
17	Mater Dei HS, Santa Ana, Calif.	24-3	CIF Southern Section D-I First Round
18	Martin HS, Arlington, Texas	36-8	5A State Semi-finalist
19	Carroll HS, Southlake, Texas	34-6	5A Region Finalist
20	Milton (Ga.) HS	29-9	6A State Champ
21	Pope HS, Marietta, Ga.	28-11	5A State Champ
22	Thunder Ridge HS, Highlands Ranch, Colo.	21-5	5A State Champ
23	Christian Brothers HS, Memphis	36-8	Division II Class AA State Champion
24	Howell HS, St. Charles, Mo.	35-5	5A State Champ
25	Archbishop Moeller HS, Cincinnati	32-2	Division I State Champ

strengths and keep them in games, but pitching is what would help the Wolverines get over the hurdle they failed to clear in 2012.

"Going into the year, we had two pitchers that we felt really comfortable with in Jack and Hans (Hansen)," LaCour said. "We knew what we were going to have in those two guys. But in order to get through our playoffs here and the grind of season, you need to have a solidified No. 3 guy, a third guy you can throw out there that can do a really good job. That was (righthander) Conor Cuse for us. The strides he has made in the last 12 months, we haven't really seen as a staff in an individual player in our career."

Bouts of wildness and strong alternatives to him kept Cuse buried in the rotation through his junior season. He had the size, strength and arm to attract college recruiters, but no one was biting. But Cuse didn't let the lack of a college scholarship or the pressure of stepping up deter him. He made great advancements on the mound and after a strong outing in the National High School Invitational, Cuse was offered a scholarship to pitch at Stanford.

"That's what I've been working toward my high school career, but things didn't always work out in the beginning," Cuse said. "I had command issues and that's what has held me back. After I got enough repetitions and confidence, it kind of clicked for me. I built up a lot of confidence over the winter and continued through the spring."

Cuse had good examples to draw from, seeing the work ethic and competitive edge of Giolito and Fried firsthand, and didn't hesitate to put the time in off the field to get better.

"I always knew Conor was going to be good because he's one of the hardest working kids I've ever seen," catcher Arden Pabst said. "He's always there before doing his exercises. He gets there before practice and stays after. I always knew that was going to pay off."

The work of Cuse and Hansen on the mound was a huge piece of Harvard-Westlake's success, but Flaherty took his own step forward with his work as the team ace and No. 3 hitter. Thrust into the No. 2 role as a sophomore in 2012 when Giolito went down with an elbow injury, Flaherty polished his raw tools and athleticism in the months after the Wolverines' disappointing finish.

"The thing about Jack is that he learns from things that are going on around him and he can apply it to his game," LaCour said. "He learned from the preparation that he saw from Max Fried and Lucas Giolito. My biggest problem with Jack for the first two and a half years of his high school career were offensively he did not have the same aggressiveness that he had on the mound."

That all changed after Harvard-Westlake returned to Cary, N.C., for the second edition of the NHSI. In 2012, the Wolverines lost to Southern California power Mater Dei High (Santa Ana, Calif.) and a rematch came to fruition. The Monarchs prevailed for a second straight season, leaving the Wolverines with a bitter taste in their mouths, a taste that would fuel the rest of their season.

"Getting out there, for this team building a new

identity, was a big deal," LaCour said. "I'll be honest, losing that championship game, that lit a fire. We were ready to play, but that really just pissed us off. We played with a chip on our shoulder from that point on that was really fun to watch."

Flaherty took a turn at the plate, going from a passive approach to one that had him smoking balls to his pull side. His emergence with the bat set the stage for others around him like Ginsberg, Pabst, Joe Corrigan and Alex Horowitz to make noise offensively.

Harvard-Westlake won nine straight following the loss in the NHSI championship, stumbling just once more in the regular season. The Wolverines dropped a game to Notre Dame High (Sherman Oaks, Calif.), but LaCour encouraged his team to make the loss a positive development. They got one last look at what else they needed to do to win—before a loss would bring the season to an end—and focused on going on a seven-game win streak, which would end with a dogpile at Dodger Stadium in the Southern Section Division I final.

The Wolverines powered through the next six games, again getting big starts from Cuse, and found themselves warming up on a major league field, ranked No. 1 in the country and one win away from a national championship.

Like so many other games on their schedule, the championship against Marina High (Huntington Beach, Calif.) was a dramatic battle with Flaherty fittingly on the mound, stifling opposing hitters and driving in the game's lone run. The story that is Harvard-Westlake's run to a championship climaxed not with the final out of the seventh inning, but the one just prior.

Marina started the top of the seventh with a single and sacrificed the runner to second. The next hitter then roped a single through the left side and the runner on second made the turn for home. Approaching the ball in left field was Jackson Grayson, a sophomore who had been used as a defensive replacement for most of the season. The day before the championship tilt, LaCour protested Grayson's tendency to air out his throws from the outfield.

"I expressed my displeasure in Jackson Grayson throwing the ball air to air to every single base and how much I wanted to see him get on top of the ball and use one hop," LaCour said.

So as the Marina runner made his turn and Grayson lined himself up for the throw, LaCour and the rest of his team could only watch as he uncorked a strike to home plate where Pabst threw up a brick wall and the runner was cut down, two feet from tying the game.

"It was a perfect throw and it was bang-bang," Pabst said. "I was holding onto that ball for my life."

"That was one of the best things I ever watched," Flaherty said. "With where I was positioned—I gave up the hit and went to go back up home—and I see Jackson come up and throw the ball. I looked and saw the runner coming. He was about halfway down the line and the ball was almost in Arden's glove. I thought, 'He's out and we're going to win this thing.' "

After a routine groundout to Ginsberg, the Wolverines stormed the pitcher's mound, celebrating the school's first-ever section title, securing the No. 1 spot atop the High School Top 25 with a 28-4 record and wrapping a story of hard work and perseverance that would satisfy any baseball fan.

Mater Dei Wins NHSI, Again

Southern California is a baseball kingdom and the Monarchs continued their reign. Mater Dei High of Santa Ana, Calif., returned to defend its 2012 National High School Invitational and faced a familiar foe on the final day. It was deja vu all over again with Mater Dei and Havard-Westlake matching up in the NHSI championship for the second straight year.

Mater Dei maintained its hold on the trophy, getting a complete-game performance from lefthander Jacob Erickson and beating the Wolverines 4-0. Erickson allowed just four hits and a walk while striking out eight.

"It's unbelievable, coming from a guy who is just a reliever to get the start in the biggest game in the country," Erickson said. "I had confidence in my team, confidence that they were going to score runs and I also had confidence they were going to play good defense out there. I just knew I had to go in there, pound the zone and throw strikes."

Erickson found himself in a serious jam early when he had the bases loaded, one out and third baseman Jack Flaherty up to bat. With a 3-1 count, Erickson got Flaherty to look at two straight strikes, ringing him up on a fastball.

"Everyone in the country knows who Jack Flaherty is," Erickson said. "Everyone knows he can easily put a ball in the gap and score three runs right there. I knew I just had to settle down and make pitches."

Harvard-Westlake shortstop Brian Ginsberg came up with a chance to pick up Flaherty, but grounded out to third baseman Ryan McMahon and Erickson escaped the jam—a huge blow to Harvard-Westlake's momentum.

"Their guy, who we had not seen pitch before and we've seen them a couple times already, made some pitches," Harvard-Westlake head coach Matt LaCour said. "Jack got caught leaning on a different pitch. He thought he was going to get an offspeed pitch and the guy snuck a fastball by him. Brian put a swing on a pitch that was there to hit. He just didn't get good contact on it. That was a definite blow to us. We could've seized some momentum in the game by putting a number on the board right there. That's a tough one to give away."

Mater Dei opened scoring in the third inning when freshman outfielder Josh Stephen drew a leadoff walk and advanced on a sacrifice bunt. Outfielder Austin Grebeck, an Oregon signee, then singled to left field to bring Stephen home.

Both sides traded zeros until the sixth when Mater Dei put two more runs on the board to go up 3-0. McMahon, a Southern California recruit and top draft prospect, smoked a single to right-center field. Sophomore shortstop Brandon Perez moved him over with a sacrifice bunt and McMahon moved up on a wild pitch before Brian Soper walked. With runners at first and third, Wolverines sophomore righthander Michael Vokulich attempted the typical fake to third, throw to first play, but it backfired and he was called for a balk, which made it 2-0. Stephen then came through with a hard single to right that brought Soper home.

Perez singled again in the seventh to bring Grebeck home and pad Mater Dei's lead. Grebeck went 2-for-3 with a run and RBI. He also chased down a fly ball in the left-center field gap that took some wind out of Harvard-Westlake's sails.

"I knew I had a bead on it, but I didn't know if I had to dive or not," He said. "Tyler (Adkison) and me communicated really well and he said I had it. It turned out good."

In the 2012 NHSI, the Monarchs' bats rolled the competition in the first three games before a tightly contest tilt with Harvard-Westlake. This year, it was all about pitching as Mater Dei got three complete games out of its starters and surrendered just six runs in 28 innings.

Losing in the championship for the second straight year was tough for Harvard-Westlake to swallow, but the Wolverines used the loss as motivation in their drive to a national title.

"If you had told me when I woke up this morning that we would've given up four runs, seven hits to that team on Day Four of a tournament, I probably would've taken that," LaCour said. "I count it out as a great experience and a great tournament for us overall. Going 3-1 against the teams we faced out here, I'm pleased with our effort. I'm pleased with the conduct of our guys. I'm pleased

with how the tournament was run. I don't have enough good things to say, but you leave here for the second year in a row without that trophy in your luggage, we want to win. We're not real happy when we don't win.

"But I think we'll look back a couple weeks from now and say it was a great experience and got us ready for what we're going to face down the road."

Two years into the NHSI and only Southern California teams have appeared in the finals, reinforcing the argument that the region has the best high school competition in the country. They believe it and so will fans until another state finds a way to beat them.

"I think Southern California baseball is extremely strong," Mater Dei head coach Burt Call said. "There's a lot of great teams. It seems like every game we're in a fight and I think that competitiveness helps us down the stretch build mental toughness. Anytime you're put in a situation you're competing every day and have that experience, you're just going to get better and better. By playing quality teams and good competition, you're just going to keep getting better and better. That's always been my philosophy in scheduling games, to always play the top teams out there so when we get to the playoffs or in a national tournament, so that we have that mental toughness to compete and win it."

U.S. Claims 18U World Cup

USA Baseball's 18-and-under national team defeated Japan 3-2 in the gold-medal game in Taichung, Taiwan, to win the 18-and-under World Cup. The gold medal in 2012 was the first for the U.S. at the 18U level since 1999, and now the Americans have won back-to-back 18U world championships for the first time since 1988-89.

Lefthander Brady Aiken (Cathedral Catholic High, San Diego), one of the top pitchers in the class, turned in his second straight strong start in the championship victory. He allowed five hits and one run in seven innings, walking just two while striking out 10. He'd beaten Korea in his first start.

"To have the coaches and my teammates have the faith in me to go out and start this game means everything," Aiken said. "It was such an honor. Winning this championship means everything."

Japan had scored the most runs and allowed the fewest runs in the tournament and entered the final rounds of competition undefeated in the tournament. The Americans beat Japan on consecutive days though, winning 10-4 to end the second round, then winning the title game.

The U.S. overcame a 1-0 deficit, tying the game

USA BASEBALL

Event	Site	Champion	Runner-up
Tournament of Stars (18U)	Cary, N.C.	Babe Ruth	Dixie
USA Baseball 17U—East	Palm Beach Co., Fla.	Ostingers Baseball Academy	Boca Thunder
USA Baseball 17U—West	Goodyear, Ariz.	Placentia Mustangs	Team Northwest
USA Baseball 15U—East	Fort Myers, Fla.	Team Elite	SW Florida Baseball
USA Baseball 15U—West	Goodyear, Ariz.	GBG Marucci	Pacific Baseball Academy
USA Baseball 14U—East	Cary, N.C.	Miami Suns	CFBL Mizuno Elite
USA Baseball 14U—West	Goodyear, Ariz.	Rawlings Elite	San Diego Show

ALL-AMERICAN AMATEUR BASEBALL ASSOCIATION (AAABA) · Headquarters: Zanesville, Ohio

Event	Site	Champion	Runner-up
World Series (21-and-Under)	Johnstown, Pa.	Baltimore	Johnstown

AMATEUR ATHLETIC UNION (AAU) · Headquarters: Lake Buena Vista, Fla.

Event	Site	Champion	Runner-up
10-and-Under Diamond (60-foot)	Orlando	Central Florida Wolverines	Central Florida Redhawks Elite
10-and-Under Gold (60-foot)	Orlando	Wesley Chapel Storm	Young Guns Baseball Elite
11-and-Under Diamond (70-foot)	Orlando	Central Florida Wolverines	Team Florida
11-and-Under Gold (70-foot)	Orlando	Central Florida Thunder	Fca Blueclaws
12-and-Under Diamond (70-foot)	Orlando	Diamond Sports Stealth USA	Stingrays
12-and-Under Gold (70-foot)	Orlando	South Texas Show	Titans Baseball
13-and-Under Diamond (90-foot)	Orlando	Connecticut Wolfpack	Taylormade Mizuno
13-and-Under Gold (90-foot)	Orlando	Clermont Bonecrushers	West Florida Gators
14-and-Under Super Showcase	Orlando	Rawlings Arkansas Prospects	Carrollwood Gators
Upperclassmen Super Showcase	Orlando	Jacksonville Dynasty	Carrollwood Gators

AMERICAN AMATEUR BASEBALL CONGRESS (AABC) · Headquarters: Farmington, N.M.

Event	Site	Champion	Runner-up
Gil Hodges	Brooklyn, N.Y.	CT Yard Dogs	UPS NY Stars
Pee Wee Reese (12 & U)	Toa Baja, P.R.	Team-MVP	Lamorinda Spartans
Sandy Koufax (14 & U)	Bartlesville, Okla.	Woodinville Rijo Athletics	Aquilas de Carolina
Ken Griffey, Jr. (15 & U)	Surprise, Ariz.	All Star Baseball Cafarelli	520 Elite
Mickey Mantle (16 & U)	McKinney, Texas	Ontario Blue Jays	SGV Arsenal
Don Mattingly (17 & U)	Surprise, Ariz.	Trombly Braves	South Troy
Connie Mack (18 & U)	Farmington, N.M.	East Cobb Yankees	So Cal Renegades
Stan Musial (open)	Farmingdale, N.Y.	Bellows Storm	Northwest Texas Wildcats

AMERICAN LEGION BASEBALL · Headquarters: Indianapolis

Event	Site	Champion	Runner-up
World Series (19 & U)	Shelby, N.C.	New Orleans	Brooklawn, N.J.

BABE RUTH BASEBALL · Headquarters: Trenton, N.J.

Event	Site	Champion	Runner-up
Cal Ripken (10 & U)	Ocala, Fla.	Visalia, Calif.	South Lexington, Ky.
Cal Ripken 12-year-old (60 feet)	Hammond, Ind.	Crown Point, Ind.	Kingsbridge, N.Y.
Cal Ripken 13-year-old (70 feet)	Aberdeen, Md.	Japan	West Raleigh, N.C.
13-year-old	Williston, N.D.	El Segundo, Calif.	Lawrenceburg, Tenn.
14-year-old	Moses Lake, Wash.	Westchester, Calif.	Tualatin Hills, Ore.
13-15-year-olds	Loudoun County, Va.	Greater Vienna, Va.	Westchester, Calif.
16-18-year-old	Covington County, Ala.	Gulf Coast, Ala.	Mid County, Texas

CONTINENTAL AMATEUR BASEBALL ASSOCIATION (CABA) · Headquarters: Westerville, Ohio

Event	Site	Champion	Runner-up
10-and-Under	Westfield, Ind.	Butler County Bombers	Indiana Mustangs Blue
11-and-Under	Marietta, Ga.	Georgia Pirates	Elite Gamers
12-and-Under	Mason, Ohio	Indiana Prospects Blue	At The Yard Baseball Club
13-and-Under	Westfield, Ind.	East Cobb Astros	GRB Rays
14-and-Under (60x90)	Lebanon, Tenn.	Showtime Sports Academy	Sandy Plains Wildcats

in the bottom of the fifth, then taking the lead on a two-out, RBI single by Bryson Brigman (Valley Christian HS, San Jose). The lead expanded to 3-1 in the seventh on an RBI single by first baseman Keaton McKinney (Ankeny, Iowa, HS).

Sanger (Calif.) High righthander Luis Ortiz, who struck out eight without allowing a walk in four previous outings, entered in the eighth inning. Japan scored a run to shave the U.S. lead to one, but Ortiz struck out the side in the ninth to secure the victory. Ortiz was named the World Cup MVP for saving three games with 11 strikeouts against one walk in 8⅓ innings. He appeared in five games and allowed three runs.

"I'm not sure I can totally describe this feeling," 18U national team manager Rob Cooper (Penn State) said. "What I do want to say is how proud I am to be associated with these 20 young

15-and-Under (Aluminum)	Jacksonville, Ill.	Georgia Roadrunners	Bergen Beach
15-and-Under (Wood)	Charleston, S.C.	Team DiMarini Cyclones	Aiken Baseball Academy
16-and-Under	Marietta, Ga.	East Cobb Astros	Homeplate Chilidogs
17-and-Under/HS (Aluminum)	Euclid, Ohio	Northern Ohio Pastors	Northwest Pelicans
17-and-Under/HS (Wood)	Charleston, S.C.	Baseball Scoutz	West End Baseball Academy
18-and-Under (Aluminum)	Struthers, Ohio	Creeksite Fitness	Kuboff & Associates
18-and-Under (Wood)	Charleston, S.C.	East Cobb Yankees	East Cobb Astros

LITTLE LEAGUE BASEBALL · Headquarters: Williamsport, Pa.

Event	Site	Champion	Runner-up
Little League (11-12)	Williamsport, Pa.	Japan	Chula Vista, Calif.
Junior League (13-14)	Taylor, Mich.	Chinese Taipei	Rio Rico, Ariz.
Senior League (15-16)	Bangor, Maine	Panama	Kennett Square, Pa.
Big League (17-18)	Easley, S.C	Greenville District 7	Venezuela

NATIONAL AMATEUR BASEBALL FEDERATION (NABF) · Headquarters: Bowie, Md.

Event	Site	Champion	Runner-up
Sophomore (14 & U)	Altavista,Va.	Saratoga Stampede	Suffolk's PAL Rangers
Junior (16 & U)	Northville, Mich.	Team Cincinnati	SAYO Grays
High School (17 & U)	Knoxville, Tenn.	Marucci Titans	Maryland Monarchs
Senior (18 & U)	Struthers, Ohio	Maryland Monarchs	Creekside Fitness

PERFECT GAME/BCS FINALS · Headquarters: Cedar Rapids, Iowa

Event	Site	Champion	Runner-up
14-and-Under	Fort Myers, Fla.	Arena Starz	Houston Banditos Black
15-and-Under	Fort Myers, Fla.	Texas Drillers	Indiana Prospects Blue
16-and-Under	Fort Myers, Fla.	SWFL	Boca Thunder
17-and-Under	Fort Myers, Fla.	East Cobb Astros	Midwest Elite Baseball
18-and-Under	Fort Myers, Fla.	FTB Mizuno-Chandler	Team IMPACT

PERFECT GAME/WORLD WOOD BAT ASSOCIATION SUMMER CHAMPIONSHIPS · Headquarters: Cedar Rapids, Iowa

Event	Site	Champion	Runner-up
14-and-Under	Fort Myers, Fla.	Kentucky Baseball Club-Boggs	Louisiana Tigers
15-and-Under	Marietta, Ga.	Dulin Dodgers	Lids Indiana Bulls
16-and-Under	Marietta, Ga.	EvoShield Canes 16U	EvoShield Canes North 16U
17-and-Under	Marietta, Ga.	Orlando Scorpions Prime	FTB Chandler
18-and-Under	Marietta, Ga.	Dulin Dodgers	NBS

PONY BASEBALL · Headquarters: Washington, Pa.

Event	Site	Champion	Runner-up
Mustang (9-10)	Burleson, Texas	Keller (Texas) Knights	Tijuana, Mex.
Bronco (11-12)	Chesterfield, Va.	Chesterfield (CBC), Va.	Torrance, Calif.
Pony (13)	Jurupa, Calif.	Jurupa, Calif.	McCuthcheon, Ind.
Pony (13-14)	Washington, Pa.	Okinawa, Japan	Sinaloa, Mex.
Colt (15-16)	Lafayette, Ind.	Los Gatos, Calif.	Caguas, P.R.
Palomino (17-18)	Compton, Calif.	Urban Youth Academy, Calif.	Bayamon, P.R.

REVIVING BASEBALL IN INNER CITIES (RBI) · Headquarters: New York

Event	Site	Champion	Runner-up
Junior (13-15)	Minneapolis	Venice, Fla.	Dominican RBI
Senior (16-18)	Minneapolis	Harrisburg, Pa.	Tampa, Fla.

U.S. SPECIALTY SPORTS ASSOCIATION (USSSA) · Headquarters: Petersburg, Va.

Event	Site	Champion	Runner-up
10-and-Under/Majors Elite	Orlando	Diamond MVP	East Cobb Astros
11-and-Under/Majors Elite	Orlando	Team MVP	Florida Battalion
12-and-Under/Majors Elite	Orlando	EM Majors	Diamond MVP
13-and-Under/Majors Elite	Orlando	Dig In Baseball Duffy	Gulf Coast Elite
14-and-Under/Majors Elite	Orlando	East Cobb Astros	Louisiana Tigers

men: what they've gone through, how they came together and how they stayed together. In this tournament you saw 20 guys come together for something far more important than themselves and play for the letter on their chest."

Left fielder Adam Haseley (The First Academy, Windermere, Fla.). Haseley was the leading hitter of the event with a .484 average (.484/.515/.800) and hit three doubles, two triples and an inside-

the-park home run to go with two steals.

In total, Aiken threw 12 2/3 innings and allowed just two runs (1.42 ERA). He walked three against 17 strikeouts, the fourth most of any pitcher. Aiken held the Japanese, who entered the championship game averaging nearly nine runs scored a game, to one run in seven innings, registering 10 strikeouts, the most recorded against the contact-oriented Japanese team.

Frazier personifies power, passion

Clint Frazier has never been one to shy away from the spotlight. He stepped right into it early in the 2013 season by delivering a memorable performance in the most-hyped high school game of the year, as his Loganville (Ga.) High team played crosstown rival Grayson High.

Facing a ranked opponent and another highly rated prospect (outfielder Austin Meadows) in front of 1,300 people—including dozens of scouts, crosscheckers, scouting directors and even a couple of general managers—Frazier blasted two home runs that sent the amateur baseball world into a frenzy.

He might as well have clinched it that night, but Frazier's energetic play and electric performance—he hit .485 with 17 home runs, 45 RBIs and 22 stolen bases before becoming the fifth overall pick in the draft—is what makes him Baseball America's 2013 High School Player of the Year. Frazier went on to be the fifth overall pick in the 2013 draft, by the Indians.

Loganville (Ga.) High head coach Jeff Segars has known Frazier since he became the team manager as a seventh-grader; he made the ninth-grade team as an eighth-grader.

"He's always had good tools as a player, always had that power," Segars said. "He's definitely made a lot of strides getting more fundamental and getting his mechanics better hitting wise. He's really worked hard to improve."

It would be easy for anyone to get caught up in hype, but Segars quickly learned that any concerns he had about Frazier's ego were unwarranted.

"Clint has always been a great teammate. People knew him around Gwinnett County, but when he blew up like he did, I was concerned that he would lose focus on the high school season," Segars said. "But he did a really good job this year of enjoying the process of it being his last year, being a senior. He handled all the scouts, the GMs, the media. Everything that came in, he handled it really well coming out to practice and just being one of the guys. He's not a rah-rah guy anyway. He's just going to work hard."

Brad Bouras, the founder and head coach of the Team Elite travel ball club, was a coach at Loganville when Frazier was in middle school and says he immediately knew he was some-

PLAYER OF THE YEAR

PREVIOUS WINNERS

1992: Preston Wilson, of/rhp, Bamberg-Ehrhardt (S.C.) HS
1993: Trot Nixon, of/lhp, New Hanover HS, Wilmington, N.C.
1994: Doug Million, lhp, Sarasota (Fla.) HS
1995: Ben Davis, c, Malvern (Pa.) Prep
1996: Matt White, rhp, Waynesboro Area (Pa.) HS
1997: Darnell McDonald, of, Cherry Creek HS, Englewood, Colo.
1998: Drew Henson, 3b/rhp, Brighton (Mich.) HS
1999: Josh Hamilton, of/lhp, Athens Drive HS, Raleigh, N.C.
2000: Matt Harrington, rhp, Palmdale (Calif.) HS
2001: Joe Mauer, c, Cretin-Derham Hall HS, St. Paul, Minn.
2002: Scott Kazmir, lhp, Cypress Falls HS, Houston
2003: Jeff Allison, rhp, Veterans Memorial HS, Peabody, Mass.
2004: Homer Bailey, rhp, LaGrange (Texas) HS
2005: Justin Upton, ss, Great Bridge HS, Chesapeake, Va.
2006: Adrian Cardenas, ss/2b, Mons. Pace HS, Opa Locka, Fla.
2007: Mike Moustakas, ss, Chatsworth (Calif.) HS
2008: Ethan Martin, rhp/3b, Stephens County HS, Toccoa, Ga.
2009: Bryce Harper, c, Las Vegas HS
2010: Kaleb Cowart, rhp/3b, Cook HS, Adel, Ga.
2011: Dylan Bundy, rhp, Owasso (Okla.) HS
2012: Byron Buxton, of, Appling County HS, Baxley, Ga.

thing special.

"We saw how strong he was back when he was 12, 13 years old," Bouras said. "I think he set some pushup record when he was in eighth or ninth grade here—beat a senior in pushups. There was always some story going around about his freakish strength.

"The question was what type of baseball player he was going to be, but he kept getting better and better through the coaching at Loganville. We all see the tools—great arm strength, the running speed, the bat speed, we all see that—but the best part of his game is he knows how to play the game hard every day. Over a pro season, 150, 162 games, I think he's a guy who's going to be successful in pro ball because he's going to play hard every day."

The quote that perhaps best sums up Frazier's game came from a scout as he broke down the differences between Frazier and Meadows, who was a Pirates first-round pick.

"The bigger the stage, the bigger the game, he's just an animal," an American League area scout said. "You could take the top 40 kids in the country and put them in a steel cage and say, 'Who comes out with the baseball will go first,' and I'd bet you that kid (Frazier) would go first. That's just his mentality."

Clint Frazier

ALYSON BOYER RODE

Tyler Danish

TONY FARLOW

FIRST TEAM

Pos.	Name	School	Yr.	AVG	AB	R	H	2B	3B	HR	RBI	SB	DRAFTED
C	Jacob Nottingham	Redlands (Calif.) HS	Sr.	.545	66	29	36	5	2	7	31	15	Astros (6)
IF	Christian Arroyo	Hernando HS, Brooksville, Fla.	Sr.	.524	105	42	55	13	3	11	35	9	Giants (1)
IF	Dominic Smith	Serra HS, Gardena, Calif.	Sr.	.493	67	33	33	6	4	7	37	4	Mets (1)
IF	Rowdy Tellez	Elk Grove (Calif.) HS	Sr.	.500	94	41	47	16	1	9	46	10	Blue Jays (30)
IF	Riley Unroe	Desert Ridge HS, Mesa, Ariz.	Sr.	.553	94	54	52	14	5	10	25	25	Rays (2)
OF	Jake Bauers	Marina HS, Huntington Beach, Calif.	Sr.	.571	84	37	48	7	1	10	26	8	Padres (7)
OF	Clint Frazier	Loganville (Ga.) HS	Sr.	.485	97	56	47	4	4	17	45	22	Indians (1)
OF	Cody Thomas	Colleyville (Texas) Heritage HS	Sr.	.470	117	48	55	15	3	15	54	16	Yankees (1)
DH	Cameron Miller	Bellaire (Texas) HS	Sr.	.568	76	27	43	10	0	12	52	2	Not eligible
UT	Jack Flaherty	Harvard-Westlake HS, Studio City, Calif.	Jr.	.360	86	31	31	4	1	2	13	13	Not eligible

Pos.	Name	School	Yr.	W	L	ERA	G	SV	IP	H	BB	K	DRAFTED
RHP	Phil Bickford	Oaks Christian HS, Westlake Village, Calif.	Sr.	10	0	0.69	14	0	71	31	11	118	Blue Jays (1)
LHP	Ryan Burnett	The Woodlands (Texas) HS	Sr.	14	1	0.98	16	0	100	40	16	142	Undrafted
RHP	Tyler Danish	Durant HS, Plant City, Fla.	Sr.	15	1	0.00	17	0	94	32	16	156	White Sox (2)
RHP	Wil Crowe	Pigeon Forge (Tenn.) HS	Sr.	16	1	0.64	20	0	98	37	14	187	Indians (31)
RHP	Carlos Salazar	Kerman (Calif.) HS	Sr.	9	2	0.09	13	0	74	22	26	147	Braves (3)
UT	Jack Flaherty	Harvard-Westlake HS, Studio City, Calif.	Sr.	13	0	0.63	16	1	89	40	10	112	Not eligible

SECOND TEAM

Pos.	Name	School	Yr.	AVG	AB	R	H	2B	3B	HR	RBI	SB	DRAFTED
C	Mike Rivera	Venice (Fla.) HS	Jr.	.528	89	11	47	21	1	1	28	3	Not eligible
IF	Gosuke Katoh	Rancho Bernardo HS, San Diego	Sr.	.429	105	46	45	13	3	10	32	9	Yankees (2)
IF	Gavin LaValley	Albert HS, Midwest City, Okla.	Jr.	.477	128	61	53	19	1	20	76	0	Not eligible
IF	Dustin Peterson	Gilbert (Ariz.) HS	Sr.	.540	87	43	47	11	6	10	39	8	Padres (2)
IF	Silento Sayles	Port Gibson (Miss.) HS	Sr.	.541	85	38	46	16	3	2	27	103	Indians (14)
OF	Andrew Benintendi	Madeira HS, Cincinnati	Sr.	.564	101	63	57	15	6	12	57	38	Reds (31)
OF	Kenny Meimerstorf	Bishop Gorman HS, Las Vegas	Sr.	.437	119	42	52	15	0	15	56	7	Brewers (40)
OF	J.B. Woodman	Edgewater HS, Orlando	Sr.	.575	87	46	50	10	3	3	33	22	Mets (40)
DH	Alex Jackson	Rancho Bernardo HS, San Diego	Jr.	.343	108	50	37	8	0	14	33	8	Not eligible
UT	Keegan Thompson	Cullman (Ala.) HS	Sr.	.420	150	35	63	19	1	9	45	4	Undrafted

Pos.	Name	School	Yr.	W	L	ERA	G	SV	IP	H	BB	K	DRAFTED
LHP	Ian Clarkin	Madison HS, San Diego	Sr.	9	2	0.95	14	1	73	41	24	133	Yankees (1)
LHP	Eric Lauer	Midview HS, Grafton, Ohio	Sr.	6	0	0.00	7	0	42	8	4	82	Blue Jays (17)
RHP	Zach Jackson	Berryhill (Okla.) HS	Sr.	13	1	0.38	15	1	72	20	24	147	Undrafted
LHP	Rob Kaminsky	St. Joseph Regional HS, Montvale, N.J.	Sr.	10	0	0.10	10	0	64	27	14	126	Cardinals (1)
RHP	Brett Morales	King HS, Tampa	Sr.	10	1	0.39	12	0	71	35	20	100	Reds (24)
UT	Keegan Thompson	Cullman (Ala.) HS	Sr.	9	2	1.25	15	2	73	48	8	124	Undrafted

DRAFT

New draft rules limit signing drama

For 29 of baseball's 30 teams, there was no drama at the July 12 draft signing deadline. For the Blue Jays, there was plenty.

Toronto became the only club not to sign its 2013 first-round pick when No. 10 overall choice Phil Bickford didn't come to terms. But the Blue Jays did make two big splashes by signing 30th-rounder Rowdy Tellez for $850,000 and 11th-rounder Jake Brentz for $700,000, less than 15 minutes before the 5 p.m. deadline on July 12.

The day before the deadline, Toronto general manager Alex Anthopoulos announced that he didn't expect to land Bickford. He didn't elaborate much, beyond saying that the impasse wasn't financial. There has been speculation that the Jays might have detected a physical issue or that Bickford had his heart set on attending Cal State Fullerton, but no one on either side of the negotiations has been willing to discuss exactly what happened.

"We would have liked to have gotten him done," but it didn't work out," Blue Jays scouting director Brian Parker said. "We wish Phil and his family good luck going forward."

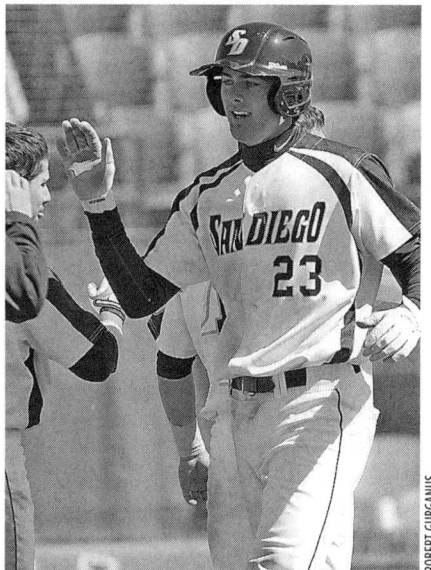

Kris Bryant went No. 2 overall to the Cubs but received the largest bonus in the class

FIRST-ROUND BONUS PROGRESSION

Current draft rules have been effective in slowing overall draft spending, but teams continue to pay for premium talent, spending an average of $2,641,538 on first-round picks in 2013, the second-highest ever and a nearly 7 percent increase over 2012. The highest ever was the $2,653,375 average from 2011, the last year of the old draft rules.

After the first draft in 1965, first-round bonuses rose by an average of just 0.6 percent annually for the rest of the 1960s and 5.2 percent per year in the 1970s. Bonus inflation picked up in the 1980s, averaging 10.2 percent annually, and soared to 26.9 percent per year in the 1990s. When MLB instituted an informal slotting system from 2000-11, first-round bonuses rose by an average of 3.8 percent.

Below are the annual averages for first-round bonuses since the draft started in 1965. The 1996 total does not include four players who became free agents through a draft loophole and signed lucrative contracts.

YEAR	AVERAGE	CHANGE	YEAR	AVERAGE	CHANGE	YEAR	AVERAGE	CHANGE
1965	$42,516	—	1982	$82,615	+5.1%	1999	$1,809,767	+10.5%
1966	$44,430	+4.5%	1983	$87,236	+5.6%	2000	$1,872,586	+3.5%
1967	$42,898	-3.4%	1984	$105,391	+20.8%	2001	$2,154,280	+15.0%
1968	$43,850	+2.2%	1985	$118,115	+12.1%	2002	$2,106,793	-2.2%
1969	$43,504	-0.8%	1986	$116,300	-1.6%	2003	$1,765,667	-16.2%
1970	$45,230	+3.9%	1987	$128,480	+10.5%	2004	$1,958,448	+10.9%
1971	$45,197	-0.1%	1988	$142,540	+10.9%	2005	$2,018,000	+3.0%
1972	$44,952	-0.5%	1989	$176,008	+23.5%	2006	$1,933,333	-4.2%
1973	$48,832	+8.6%	1990	$252,577	+43.5%	2007	$2,098,083	+8.5%
1974	$53,333	+9.2%	1991	$365,396	+44.7%	2008	$2,458,714	+17.2%
1975	$49.333	-7.5%	1992	$481,893	+31.9%	2009	$2,434,800	-1.0%
1976	$49,631	+0.6%	1993	$613,037	+27.2%	2010	$2,220,966	-8.8%
1977	$48,813	-1.6%	1994	$790,357	+28.9%	2011	$2,653,375	+19.5%
1978	$67,892	+39.1%	1995	$918,019	+16.1%	2012	$2,475,167	-6.7%
1979	$68,094	+0.2%	1996*	$944,404	+2.9%	2013	$2,641,538	+6.7%
1980	$74,025	+8.7%	1997	$1,325,536	+40.4%			
1981	$78,573	+6.1%	1998	$1,637,667	+23.1%			

A righthander from Oaks Christian High in Westlake Village, Calif., Bickford's stock rose along with the quality of his fastball this spring. After throwing 88-92 mph last summer, he worked from 90-96 mph as a senior with tremendous life and the ability to command it to both sides of the plate. He wowed scouts in his final start of the season, striking out 18 in seven innings (including the final 11 hitters he faced) five days before the draft.

Bickford reportedly communicated a $4.25 million price tag, significantly more than the $2,921,400 assigned value for the No. 10 selection. The Blue Jays did wind up saving $423,520 against their bonus pool for the first 10 rounds and could have paid him $3,664,830 without forfeiting a future first-round pick. Sources said the team didn't make any further attempts to sign Bickford on deadline day.

Toronto will get the 11th overall pick in 2014 as compensation for failing to land Bickford. The Blue Jays softened the blow of missing out on Bickford by getting Tellez and Brentz, who were 59th and 80th on Baseball America's predraft rankings. Tellez's bonus set a new record for a post-10th-round pick since the new draft rules came into play last year, eclipsing the $750,000 that the Cardinals paid 11th-rounder Steven Farinaro in June, while Brentz's was the third-highest.

"Brentz and Tellez weren't connected to Bickford," Parker said. "There were five or six guys we wanted to make a run at after the 10th round. We knew all along we were going to try to do that. We were trying to get more than them. The signing bonuses they got reflected how much we liked Brentz and Tellez. We added two higher-level talents to our system."

Tellez, a first baseman from Elk Grove (Calif.) High, had the best lefthanded power in the 2013 draft. A lefthander from Parkway South High (Manchester, Mo.), Brentz has pitched regularly for less than a year but throws strikes and runs his fastball up to 96 mph.

Bryant Takes Cubs Past $11 Million

Toronto's signings and non-signing dominated deadline news. Just 19 players officially finalized contracts on July 12, receiving bonuses totaling $12,515,900. The vast majority of that went to first-rounders Kris Bryant ($6,708,400 at No. 2 from the Cubs) and Aaron Judge ($1.8 million at No. 32 from the Yankees), and both deals had been agreed to and reported by Baseball America in the previous two days.

BA's College Player of the Year, Bryant led NCAA Division I with 31 homers, more than 223

BONUS SPENDING BY TEAM

Teams combined to spend $219.3 million on draft bonuses in 2013, the second-highest total ever. The record was set in 2011, the final year of the previous Collective Bargaining Agreement, when clubs spent $228 million on bonuses and another $8.1 million on guaranteed salaries that were part of major league contracts.

The current labor agreement took effect in 2012 and drastically changed the draft rules. Rather than having the freedom to spend whatever they wanted on the draft, clubs now are assigned a bonus pool for the first 10 rounds and lose draft picks if they exceed it by more than 5 percent. Also, major league contracts are no longer permitted. In the first year under the new rules, teams spent $207.9 million on bonuses.

Teams at the top of the draft get more money in their pools, so it's no surprise that the clubs selecting second (Cubs, $11,724,900), first (Astros, $11,441,000) and third (Rockies, $10,368,200) led the industry in spending. The Angels ($3,168,200) and Nationals ($3,176,200) brought up the rear after forfeiting their first-round picks to sign free agents.

TEAM	2013	2012	2011
Cubs	$11,724,900	$9,164,700	$11,994,550
Astros	$11,441,000	$12,074,200	$5,545,800
Rockies	$10,368,200	$6,978,700	$3,967,900
Pirates	$9,887,400	$3,830,700	$17,005,700
Royals	$9,581,900	$7,573,000	$14,066,000
Yankees	$9,197,400	$4,898,400	$6,324,500
Twins	$8,776,400	$12,602,400	$5,902,300
Cardinals	$8,526,400	$9,909,490	$4,554,000
Diamondbacks	$8,049,100	$4,594,800	$11,930,000
Marlins	$7,951,000	$5,755,700	$4,135,000
Padres	$7,895,000	$10,993,000	$11,020,600
Mets	$7,854,400	$7,007,400	$6,782,500
Rangers	$7,696,500	$7,394,400	$4,193,000
Mariners	$7,376,700	$9,325,200	$11,330,500
Orioles	$7,235,000	$7,433,200	$8,432,100
Red Sox	$7,210,900	$7,908,000	$10,978,700
Rays	$7,147,000	$4,427,300	$11,482,900
Tigers	$6,839,100	$3,172,300	$2,878,700
Reds	$6,757,800	$7,450,400	$6,378,900
Indians	$6,713,600	$5,330,000	$8,225,000
Athletics	$6,506,100	$8,301,600	$3,067,300
Dodgers	$6,366,100	$6,277,300	$3,509,300
Phillies	$6,186,900	$4,787,800	$4,689,800
Giants	$6,063,800	$4,630,500	$6,266,000
White Sox	$5,810,800	$6,452,100	$2,786,300
Braves	$5,410,500	$4,758,000	$3,735,700
Brewers	$4,637,300	$7,200,100	$7,509,300
Blue Jays	$3,747,280	$10,486,000	$10,996,500
Nationals	$3,176,200	$4,880,500	$15,002,100
Angels	$3,168,200	$2,289,800	$3,318,100
Total	**$219,302,880**	**$207,886,990**	**$228,009,050**
Average	**$7,310,096**	**$6,929,566**	**$7,600,302**

of the 296 teams at that level and more than any player has hit since college bats were toned down three years ago. His bonus eclipsed draft records under the revamped rules (No. 1 pick Mark Appel got $6.35 million from the Astros), for a college position player in the draft (Buster Posey, $6.2 million from the Giants in 2008) and for the Cubs (Jorge Soler, $6 million in 2012).

Bryant's bonus pushed the Cubs' total for the 2013 draft to $11,724,900, more than any other team. The Astros ($11,441,000) and Rockies ($10,368,200) also topped $10 million, and all 30 clubs combined to spend $219,302,880. That's the second-highest total ever, behind $228 million in 2011, and up from $207.9 million last year.

No team overspent its bonus pool by more than 5 percent, which would have triggered the loss of a first-round pick. The Dodgers pushed the envelope the most, coming within $7,186 of losing a first-rounder. The Braves, Cardinals, Cubs, Giants, Mariners, Phillies, Pirates, Rangers, Royals and Yankees also exceeded their pools by less than 5 percent, which carries a penalty of a 75 percent tax on their overage. The total tax bill for those 11 clubs comes to $1,807,725, which will be divided among 10 revenue-sharing recipients who didn't exceed their pools: the Athletics, Brewers, Diamondbacks, Indians, Marlins, Orioles, Padres, Rays, Reds and Rockies.

Because they didn't sign Bickford, the Blue Jays spent a lower percentage (47.7) of their original pool than any club. Despite outspending everyone but the Cubs, the Astros saved more money ($877,300) relative to their pool than any team.

The new draft rules have taken most of the drama out of the signing process. Before the latest Collective Bargaining Agreement took effect for the 2012 season, bringing with it sweeping new draft regulations, top draft prospects often held

Lefthander Sean Manaea fell out of the first round but still got a significant bonus

HIGHEST BONUSES EVER

The 2013 saw just two players, Kris Bryant and Mark Appel, join the list of top bonuses. Three of the top five bonuses in draft history, including the record, came in the 2011 draft.

PLAYER, POS.	TEAM, YEAR (PICK)	BONUS
Gerrit Cole, rhp	Pirates, 2011 (No. 1)	$8,000,000
Stephen Strasburg, rhp	Nationals, 2009 (No. 1)	*$7,500,000
Bubba Starling, of	Royals, 2011 (No. 5)	+$7,500,000
Kris Bryant, 3b	Cubs, 2013 (No. 2)	$6,708,400
Jameson Taillon, rhp	Pirates, 2010 (No. 2)	$6,500,000
Danny Hultzen, lhp	Mariners, 2011 (No. 2)	*$6,350,000
Mark Appel, rhp	Astros, 2013 (No. 1)	$6,350,000
Donavan Tate, of	Padres, 2009 (No. 3)	+$6,250,000
Bryce Harper, of	Nationals, 2010 (No. 1)	*$6,250,000
Buster Posey, c	Giants, 2008 (No. 5)	$6,200,000
Tim Beckham, ss	Rays, 2008 (No. 1)	+$6,150,000
Justin Upton, ss	D'backs, 2005 (No. 1)	+$6,100,000
Matt Wieters, c	Orioles, 2007 (No. 5)	$6,000,000
Pedro Alvarez, 3b	Pirates, 2008 (No. 2)	*$6,000,000
Eric Hosmer, 1b	Royals, 2008 (No. 3)	$6,000,000
Dustin Ackley, of	Mariners, 2009 (No. 2)	*$6,000,000
Anthony Rendon, 3b	Nationals, 2011 (No. 6)	*$6,000,000
Byron Buxton, of	Twins, 2012 (No. 2)	$6,000,000
David Price, lhp	Devil Rays, 2007 (No. 1)	*$5,600,000
Joe Borchard, of	White Sox, 2000 (No. 12)	+$5,300,000
Manny Machado, ss	Orioles, 2010 (No. 3)	$5,250,000
Zach Lee, rhp	Dodgers, 2010 (No. 28)	+$5,250,000
Joe Mauer, c	Twins, 2001 (No. 1)	+$5,150,000
Archie Bradley, rhp	Diamondbacks, 2011 (No. 7)	+$5,000,000
Josh Bell, of	Pirates, 2011 (No. 61)	$5,000,000

*Part of major league contract.
+Bonus spread over multiple years under MLB provisions for two-sport athletes.

out until the old mid-August signing deadline. In 2011, 22 of the 33 first-round picks signed on Aug. 15, and teams combined to spend $139.1 million on draftees that day.

But with a formal slotting process and strict penalties now in place for clubs that surpass their allocated bonus pools for the first 10 rounds by more than 5 percent, Major League Baseball no longer has to police every individual signing. The process also has accelerated because the signing deadline is in mid-July now.

One of the most notable bonuses from the 2013 proceedings went to a player who slid out of the first round. Indiana State lefthander Sean Manaea put himself in position to go at the top of the 2013 draft by starring in the Cape Cod League, but he was the 34th overall pick after battling a hip injury in the spring. Nevertheless, the Royals signed him for $3.55 million on June 21, breaking the supplemental first-round record held by Nick Castellanos, who got $3.45 million from the Tigers in 2010. Manaea's bonus was more than double the assigned value for his slot ($1,623,000) and slightly more than the value of the No. 6 pick ($3,516,000).

His physical problems began March 15, when he rolled his right ankle while celebrating a dramatic win over Minnesota ace Tom Windle. Manaea's hip began to bother him shortly afterward, and teams found out he had a labrum tear in his hip that will require surgery but isn't expected to hinder him in the long term. One Royals executive said the team strongly considered taking Manaea with its No. 8 overall pick after reviewing his medical records. Instead, they took third baseman Hunter Dozier at No. 8 and signed him to a below-slot deal, saving the money needed to sign Manaea.

Appel Finally Goes No. 1

It's likely no other player chosen No. 1 overall has been as dissected and thoroughly vetted as Mark Appel.

The Stanford righthander was a 15th-round pick out of high school in Houston in 2009. After his freshman year in 2010, he ranked as the No. 2 prospect in the New England Collegiate League, and the next summer he ranked No. 1 among the players on USA Baseball's Collegiate National Team. He entered the 2012 draft ranked fourth on the BA 500 and was in the mix until the end as the hometown Astros selected with the first overall pick. When the Astros decided to take Puerto Rican shortstop Carlos Correa instead, Appel fell to the eighth overall selection, where the Pirates took a shot at him.

Appel spurned the Pirates' $3.8 million offer and went back to Stanford, and went through the process again. Along the way, he became the Cardinal's career strikeouts leader and kept getting better. His continued improvement, to go with his consistency and polish, landed the 6-foot-5, 215-pound Appel atop Houston's draft board again. And this time, the Astros made him their man, selecting him No. 1 overall in the 2013 draft. Appel signed well before the deadline this time, agreeing to terms with the Astros on June 19 for $6.35 million. The Stanford righthander set a new record for a college senior, surpassing the $2 million Matt LaPorta got from the Brewers as the No. 7 choice in 2007.

"This guy was under the microscope for two years," scouting director Mike Elias said. "He took every turn. You could set your watch to him, he was so consistent in how he gave Stanford quality start after quality start. The enormity of his consistency really stood out.

"Plus he got better. As has been documented, he raised the angle of his arm a little bit, and that helped his fastball have more life when it was down, more angle, gave it a little run. His secondary stuff also took a step forward."

Appel became the first Cardinal player to go No. 1 over-

NO. 1 OVERALL PICKS

YEAR	TEAM: PLAYER, POS., SCHOOL	BONUS
1965	Athletics: Rick Monday, of, Arizona State	$100,000
1966	Mets: Steve Chilcott, c, Antelope Valley HS, Lancaster, Calif.	$75,000
1967	Yankees: Ron Blomberg, 1b, Druid Hills HS, Atlanta	$65,000
1968	Mets: Tim Foli, ss, Notre Dame HS, Sherman Oaks, Calif.	$74,000
1969	Senators: Jeff Burroughs, of, Centennial HS, Long Beach	$88,000
1970	Padres: Mike Ivie, c, Walker HS, Atlanta	$75,000
1971	White Sox: Danny Goodwin, c, Peoria (Ill.) HS	Did Not Sign
1972	Padres: Dave Roberts, 3b, Oregon	$70,000
1973	Rangers: David Clyde, lhp, Westchester HS, Texas	*$65,000
1974	Padres: Bill Almon, ss, Brown	*$90,000
1975	Angels: Danny Goodwin, c, Southern	*$125,000
1976	Astros: Floyd Bannister, lhp, Arizona State	$100,000
1977	White Sox: Harold Baines, of, St. Michaels (Md.) HS	$32,000
1978	Braves: Bob Horner, 3b, Arizona State	*$162,000
1979	Mariners: Al Chambers, 1b, Harris HS, Harrisburg, Pa.	$60,000
1980	Mets: Darryl Strawberry, of, Crenshaw HS, Los Angeles	$152,500
1981	Mariners: Mike Moore, rhp, Oral Roberts	$100,000
1982	Cubs: Shawon Dunston, ss, Jefferson HS, New York	$135,000
1983	Twins: Tim Belcher, rhp, Mount Vernon Nazarene (Ohio)	Did Not Sign
1984	Mets: Shawn Abner, of, Mechanicsburg (Pa.) HS	$150,500
1985	Brewers: B.J. Surhoff, c, North Carolina	$150,000
1986	Pirates: Jeff King, 3b, Arkansas	$180,000
1987	Mariners: Ken Griffey Jr., of, Moeller HS, Cincinnati	$160,000
1988	Padres: Andy Benes, rhp, Evansville	$235,000
1989	Orioles: Ben McDonald, rhp, Louisiana State	*$350,000
1990	Braves: Chipper Jones, ss, The Bolles School, Jacksonville	$275,000
1991	Yankees: Brien Taylor, lhp, East Carteret HS, Beaufort, N.C.	$1,550,000
1992	Astros: Phil Nevin, 3b, Cal State Fullerton	$700,000
1993	Mariners: Alex Rodriguez, ss, Westminster Christian HS, Miami	*$1,000,000
1994	Mets: Paul Wilson, rhp, Florida State	$1,550,000
1995	Angels: Darin Erstad, of, Nebraska	$1,575,000
1996	Pirates: Kris Benson, rhp, Clemson	$2,000,000
1997	Tigers: Matt Anderson, rhp, Tigers	$2,505,000
1998	Phillies: Pat Burrell, 3b, Miami	*$3,150,000
1999	Devil Rays: Josh Hamilton, of, Athens Drive HS, Raleigh	$3,960,000
2000	Marlins: Adrian Gonzalez, 1b, Eastlake HS, Chula Vista, Calif.	$3,000,000
2001	Twins: Joe Mauer, c, Cretin-Derham Hall, St. Paul	$5,150,000
2002	Pirates: Bryan Bullington, rhp, Ball State	$4,000,000
2003	Devil Rays: Delmon Young, of, Camarillo (Calif.) HS	*$3,700,000
2004	Padres: Matt Bush, ss, Mission Bay HS, San Diego	$3,150,000
2005	Diamondbacks: Justin Upton, ss, Great Bridge HS, Chesapeake, Va.	$6,100,000
2006	Royals: Luke Hochevar, rhp, Fort Worth (American Association)	*$3,500,000
2007	Devil Rays: David Price, lhp, Vanderbilt	*$5,600,000
2008	Rays: Tim Beckham, ss, Griffin (Ga.) HS	$6,150,000
2009	Nationals: Stephen Strasburg, rhp, San Diego State	*$7,500,000
2010	Nationals: Bryce Harper, of, JC of Southern Nevada	*$6,250,000
2011	Pirates: Gerrit Cole, rhp, UCLA	$8,000,000
2012	Astros: Carlos Correa, ss, Puerto Rico Baseball Academy, Gurabo, P.R.	$4,800,000
2013	Astros: Mark Appel, rhp, Stanford	$6,350,000

*Part of major league contract.

all in the draft. He already has his degree in management, science and engineering, but now he finally can move into his chosen profession—baseball—and do so in his hometown. As he tweeted after being selected, echoing the Skylar Grey song, "I'm coming home, I'm coming home! Tell the world, I'm coming home!"

Getting Appel off the board helped the first round go in a fairly straightforward manner, with few surprises. The top three players on the board for most clubs went in the first three picks, with the Cubs surprising many by taking Bryant instead of a pitcher. That left Oklahoma's flamethrowing ace, righthander Jonathan Gray, for the Rockies at No. 3. His positive test for the banned stimulant Adderall didn't hurt his draft stock.

Draft Dots

■ The Peterson brothers missed becoming the first brother tandem drafted in the same first round since J.D. and Tim Drew in 1997, but not by much. New Mexico corner bat D.J. Peterson went 12th overall to the Mariners, while younger brother Dustin was the 50th overall pick to the Padres. They should see plenty of each other in pro ball, because the Padres and Mariners share a spring training complex in Peoria, Ariz.

■ Several high-profile picks had big league bloodlines, starting with Marlins first-rounder Colin Moran, the nephew of B.J. Surhoff, who was the No. 1 overall pick back in 1985. Hunter Harvey (No. 22 overall, Orioles) was the highest-drafted big league progeny. His father Bryan was a former all-star relief pitcher. Other selections with prominent bloodlines include Rays second-rounder Riley Unroe (son of Tim Unroe), Dodgers fourth-rounder Cody Bellinger (son of Clay Bellinger) and Marlins fifth-rounder Chad Wallach (son of Tim Wallach). Two sons of Hall of Fame-caliber players went later, though, as Craig Biggio's son Cavan went to the Phillies in the 29th round, while Roger Clemens' son Kacy was the Astros' 35th-round pick.

■ Several clubs had extra selections, none more than the Yankees with three picks at the back of the first round. At No. 26, New York got one of its rumored targets in Notre Dame third baseman Eric Jagielo, a lefthanded hitter with power who fits the third-base profile. Then the Yankees drafted Fresno State outfielder Aaron Judge, the 6-foot-7 physical specimen, and prep lefthander Ian Clarkin from the San Diego area. New York went off the board a bit in the second round with California prep second baseman Gosuke Katoh, a UCLA signee who had late helium despite his

tough profile. New York also snagged Michigan outfielder Michael O'Neill, the nephew of former Yankees outfielder and current YES Network analyst Paul O'Neill, in the third round.

■ Arkansas, ranked No. 3 in the preseason but knocked out in regional play after a disappointing regular season, led all schools with 11 players drafted. Righthander Ryne Stanek led the way as the Rays' first-rounder. Louisiana State, which advanced to the College World Series, ranked second with nine, while Bryant was the first of eight San Diego players selected.

■ Eight first-round picks were on hand at MLB Network's Studio 42 for the draft, as was Oklahoma prep catcher Jonathan Denney, who went in the third round to the Red Sox. And though there was no memorable moment to rival Courtney Hawkins' backflip when the White Sox drafted him in 2012, the show went off without a hitch. The baseball draft as a TV product continues to mature and grow, with a ways to go but improvements year after year.

■ The Astros secured the first overall pick in the 2014 draft for an unprecedented third straight year, but the Rockies secured a top selection of their own by winning Major League Baseball's competitive-balance lottery. The Rockies secured the first of six selections that will follow the final pick of the first round in the second competitive-balance lottery, a provision of the new draft rules that took effect last year. The next five slots will go to the Orioles, Indians, Marlins, Royals and Brewers.

Competitive-balance picks are the only draft picks that can be traded, as they were in 2012 when the Pirates traded their competitive-balance pick to the Marlins as part of the Gaby Sanchez deal. Miami used that pick to select Arkansas righthander Colby Suggs in June.

Extra draft picks have also become more valuable under the more stringent free agent compensation rules. With spending limits restricting teams' total expenditures, the importance of the selection comes not just from the potential player, but also the pick value. In 2013, the assigned pick values for the competitive balance slots were around $1.5 million.

The Royals provided a blueprint for how the extra pick can be used, taking Manaea with the first pick of the supplemental round before the Astros—who also had their eye on Manaea—could take him with the first pick of the second round. The Royals gave Manaea $3.55 million, the fifth-largest bonus in the draft.

Teams eligible for the lottery either play in one of the 10 smallest markets, rank in the bottom 10 in revenue, or receive revenue sharing. With overlap, 14 teams were eligible. Team odds were in inverse order of 2012 winning percentage, which gave Colorado the highest odds at 17 percent.

Six additional competitive-balance selections

BONUSES VS. PICK VALUES

Just as they did in 2012 in the first draft under the revamped rules, the signing bonuses and the assigned pick values for 2013 tracked each other nicely. To give the worst teams extra spending power, the values for the selections at the top of the draft have been set higher than the perceived market value. As a result, just four of the top 11 choices received their full pick value, and three of the 33 first-rounders exceeded theirs.

But all told, the top 50 bonuses added up to $110.5 million, while the first 50 pick values totaled $114.5 million. By comparison, when MLB unilaterally determined slot recommendations in the last year of the previous Collective Bargaining Agreement (2011) but had no enforcement mechanism, the total of the first 50 bonuses ($120.5 million) dwarfed that of the top 50 slots ($70 million).

PLAYER, POS., TEAM (ROUND/OVERALL PICK)	BONUS	PICK VALUE
1. Kris Bryant, 3b, Cubs (1st round/No. 2)	$6,708,400	$7,790,400
2. Mark Appel, rhp, Astros (1st round/No. 1)	$6,350,000	$6,708,400
3. Jonathan Gray, rhp, Rockies (1st round/No. 3)	$4,800,000	$5,626,400
4. Kohl Stewart, rhp, Twins (1st round/No. 4)	$4,544,400	$4,544,400
5. Sean Manaea, lhp, Royals (supp. 1st round/No. 34)	$3,550,000	$3,787,000
6. Colin Moran, 3b, Marlins (1st round/No. 6)	$3,516,500	$3,516,500
7. Clint Frazier, of, Indians (1st round/No. 5)	$3,500,000	$3,246,000
8. Austin Meadows, of, Pirates (1st round/No. 9)	$3,029,600	$3,137,800
9. D.J. Peterson, 3b, Mariners (1st round/No. 12)	$2,759,100	$3,029,600
10. Trey Ball, lhp, Red Sox (1st round/No. 7)	$2,750,000	$2,921,400
11. Hunter Renfroe, of, Padres (1st round/No. 13)	$2,678,000	$2,840,300
12. Dominic Smith, 1b, Mets (1st round/No. 11)	$2,600,000	$2,759,100
13. Reese McGuire, c, Pirates (1st round/No. 14)	$2,369,800	$2,678,000
14. J.P. Crawford, ss, Phillies (1st round/No. 16)	$2,299,300	$2,569,800
15. Braden Shipley, rhp, D-backs (1st round/No. 15)	$2,250,000	$2,434,500
16. Alex Gonzalez, rhp, Rangers (1st round/No. 23)	$2,215,000	$2,299,300
17. Hunter Dozier, 3b, Royals (1st round/No. 8)	$2,200,000	$2,164,000
18. Tim Anderson, ss, White Sox (1st round/No. 17)	$2,164,000	$2,109,900
19. Chris Anderson, rhp, Dodgers (1st round/No. 18)	$2,109,900	$2,055,800
20. Jonathon Crawford, rhp, Tigers (1st round/No. 20)	$2,001,700	$2,001,700
21. Nick Ciuffo, c, Rays (1st round/No. 21)	$1,972,200	$1,974,700
22. Hunter Harvey, rhp, Orioles (1st round/No. 22)	$1,947,600	$1,947,600
23. Travis Demeritte, ss, Rangers (1st round/No. 30)	$1,900,000	$1,920,600
24. Christian Arroyo, ss, Giants (1st round/No. 25)	$1,866,500	$1,893,500
25. Marco Gonzales, lhp, Cardinals (1st round/No. 19)	$1,850,000	$1,866,500
26. Eric Jagielo, 3b, Yankees (1st round/No. 26)	$1,839,400	$1,839,400
27. Phillip Ervin, of, Reds (1st round/No. 27)	$1,812,400	$1,812,400
28. Billy McKinney, of, Athletics (1st round/No. 24)	$1,800,000	$1,785,300
Aaron Judge, of, Yankees (1st round/No. 32)	$1,800,000	$1,758,300
30. Rob Kaminsky, lhp, Cardinals (1st round/No. 28)	$1,785,300	$1,731,200
31. Ryne Stanek, rhp, Rays (1st round/No. 29)	$1,755,800	$1,704,200
32. Jason Hursh, rhp, Braves (1st round/No. 31)	$1,704,200	$1,677,100
33. Austin Wilson, of, Mariners (2nd round/No. 49)	$1,700,000	$1,650,100
34. Ian Clarkin, lhp, Yankees (1st round/No. 33)	$1,650,100	$1,623,000
35. Michael Lorenzen, rhp, Reds (supp. 1st/No. 38)	$1,500,000	$1,587,700
Oscar Mercado, ss, Cardinals (2nd round/No. 57)	$1,500,000	$1,547,700
37. Josh Hart, of, Orioles (supp. 1st round/No. 37)	$1,450,000	$1,508,600
38. Aaron Blair, rhp, D-backs (supp. 1st round/No. 36)	$1,435,000	$1,470,500
39. Corey Knebel, rhp, Tigers (supp. 1st round/No. 39)	$1,433,400	$1,433,400
40. Dustin Peterson, ss, Padres (2nd round/No. 50)	$1,400,000	$1,397,200
41. Andrew Thurman, rhp, Astros (2nd round/No. 40)	$1,397,200	$1,361,900
42. Devin Williams, rhp, Brewers (2nd round/No. 54)	$1,350,000	$1,327,600
43. Ryan McMahon, 3b, Rockies (2nd round/No. 42)	$1,327,600	$1,294,100
44. Ryan Eades, rhp, Twins (2nd round/No. 43)	$1,294,100	$1,261,400
45. Trevor Williams, rhp, Marlins (2nd round/No. 44)	$1,261,400	$1,229,600
46. Cody Reed, lhp, Royals (2nd round/No. 46)	$1,198,500	$1,198,500
47. Rob Zastryzny, lhp, Cubs (2nd round/No. 41)	$1,100,000	$1,168,200
48. Justin Williams, of, D-backs (2nd round/No. 52)	$1,050,000	$1,138,800
49. Andrew Knapp, c, Phillies (2nd round/No. 53)	$1,033,100	$1,110,000
50. Tyler Danish, rhp, White Sox (2nd round/No. 55)	$1,001,800	$1,082,000
Total	$110,511,300	$114,521,400

were awarded after the second round. Those went to the Padres, Diamondbacks, Cardinals, Rays, Pirates and Mariners. The Reds and Athletics, who had the two lowest odds, were the only eligible teams that did not receive a selection.

TOP 100 PICKS

ANDREW WOOLLEY

DRAFT

Jonathan Gray made a strong first impression on the Rockies after they took him third overall

TEAM. PLAYER, POS., SCHOOL	BONUS	TEAM. PLAYER, POS., SCHOOL	BONUS
1. Astros. Mark Appel, rhp, Stanford	$6,350,000	51. Pirates. Blake Taylor, lhp, HS—Dana Point, Calif.	$750,000
2. Cubs. Kris Bryant, 3b, San Diego	$6,708,400	52. Diamondbacks. Justin Williams, ss, HS—Houma, La.	$1,050,000
3. Rockies. Jonathan Gray, rhp, Oklahoma	$4,800,000	53. Phillies. Andrew Knapp, c, California	$1,033,100
4. Twins. Kohl Stewart, rhp, HS—Houston	$4,544,400	54. Brewers. Devin Williams, rhp, HS—Hazelwood, Mo.	$1,350,000
5. Indians. Clint Frazier, of, HS—Loganville, Ga.	$3,500,000	55. White Sox. Tyler Danish, rhp, HS—Plant City, Fla.	$1,001,800
6. Marlins. Colin Moran, 3b, North Carolina	$3,516,500	56. Dodgers. Tom Windle, lhp, Minnesota	$986,500
7. Red Sox. Trey Ball, lhp, HS—New Castle, Ind.	$2,750,000	57. Cardinals. Oscar Mercado, ss, HS—Tampa	$1,500,000
8. Royals. Hunter Dozier, ss, Stephen F. Austin State	$2,200,000	58. Tigers. Kevin Ziomek, lhp, Vanderbilt	$956,600
9. Pirates. Austin Meadows, of, HS—Loganville, Ga.	$3,029,600	59. Angels. Hunter Green, lhp, HS—Bowling Green, Ky.	$942,000
10. Blue Jays. Phil Bickford, rhp, HS—Westlake Village, Calif.	Did not sign	60. Rays. Riley Unroe, ss, HS—Mesa, Ariz.	$997,500
11. Mets. Dominic Smith, 1b, HS—Gardena, Calif.	$2,600,000	61. Orioles. Chance Sisco, c, HS—Lake Elsinore, Calif.	$785,000
12. Mariners. D.J. Peterson, 3b, New Mexico	$2,759,100	62. Rangers. Akeem Bostick, rhp, HS—West Florence, S.C.	$520,600
13. Padres. Hunter Renfroe, of, Mississippi State	$2,678,000	63. Athletics. Dillon Overton, lhp, Oklahoma	$400,000
14. Pirates. Reese McGuire, c, HS—Covington, Wash.	$2,369,800	64. Giants. Ryder Jones, 3b, HS—Boone, N.C.	$880,000
15. Diamondbacks. Braden Shipley, rhp, Nevada	$2,250,000	65. Braves. Victor Caratini, c, Dade JC	$800,000
16. Phillies. J.P. Crawford, ss, HS—Lakewood, Calif.	$2,299,300	66. Yankees. Gosuke Katoh, 2b, HS—San Diego	$845,700
17. White Sox. Tim Anderson, ss, East Central (Miss.) CC	$2,164,000	67. Reds. K.J. Franklin, 3b, HS—Cerritos, Calif.	$675,000
18. Dodgers. Chris Anderson, rhp, Jacksonville	$2,109,900	68. Nationals. Jake Johansen, rhp, Dallas Baptist	$820,000
19. Cardinals. Marco Gonzales, lhp, Gonzaga	$1,850,000	69. Padres. Jordan Paroubeck, of, HS—San Mateo, Calif.	$650,000
20. Tigers. Jonathon Crawford, rhp, Florida	$2,001,700	70. Rockies. Alex Balog, rhp, San Francisco	$795,200
21. Rays. Nick Ciuffo, c, HS—Lexington, S.C.	$1,972,200	71. Athletics. Chad Pinder, ss, Virginia Tech	$750,000
22. Orioles. Hunter Harvey, rhp, HS—Catawba, N.C.	$1,947,600	72. Brewers. Tucker Neuhaus, ss, HS—Tampa	$771,000
23. Rangers. Alex Gonzalez, rhp, Oral Roberts	$2,215,000	73. Marlins. Colby Suggs, rhp, Arkansas	$600,000
24. Athletics. Billy McKinney, of, HS—Plano, Texas	$1,800,000	74. Astros. Kent Emanuel, lhp, North Carolina	$747,700
25. Giants. Christian Arroyo, ss, HS—Brooksville, Fla.	$1,866,500	75. Cubs. Jacob Hannemann, of, Brigham Young	$1,000,000
26. Yankees. Eric Jagielo, 3b, Notre Dame	$1,839,400	76. Mets. Ivan Wilson, of, HS—Ruston, La.	$624,900
27. Reds. Phillip Ervin, of, Samford	$1,812,400	77. Rockies. Sam Moll, lhp, Memphis	$600,000
28. Cardinals. Rob Kaminsky, lhp, HS—Montvale, N.J.	$1,785,300	78. Twins. Stuart Turner, c, Mississippi	$550,000
29. Rays. Ryne Stanek, rhp, Arkansas	$1,755,800	79. Indians. Dace Kime, rhp, Louisville	$525,000
30. Rangers. Travis Demeritte, ss, HS—Winder, Ga.	$1,900,000	80. Marlins. Ben DeLuzio, ss, HS—Orlando	Did not sign
31. Braves. Jason Hursh, rhp, Oklahoma State	$1,704,200	81. Red Sox. Jonathan Denney, c, HS—Yukon, Okla.	$875,000
32. Yankees. Aaron Judge, of, Fresno State	$1,800,000	82. Royals. Carter Hope, rhp, HS—The Woodlands, Texas	$560,900
33. Yankees. Ian Clarkin, lhp, HS—San Diego	$1,650,100	83. Blue Jays. Patrick Murphy, rhp, HS—Chandler, Ariz.	$500,000
34. Royals. Sean Manaea, lhp, Indiana State	$3,550,000	84. Mets. Casey Meisner, rhp, HS—Cypress, Texas	$500,000
35. Marlins. Matt Krook, lhp, HS—San Francisco	Did not sign	85. Mariners. Tyler O'Neill, of, HS—Maple Ridge, B.C.	$650,000
36. Diamondbacks. Aaron Blair, rhp, Marshall	$1,435,000	86. Padres. Bryan Verbitsky, rhp, Hofstra	$400,000
37. Orioles. Josh Hart, of, Parkview HS, Lilburn, Ga.	$1,450,000	87. Pirates. JaCoby Jones, of, Louisiana State	$612,000
38. Reds. Michael Lorenzen, rhp, Cal State Fullerton	$1,500,000	88. Diamondbacks. Daniel Palka, 1b, Georgia Tech	$550,000
39. Tigers. Corey Knebel, rhp, Texas	$1,433,400	89. Phillies. Cord Sandberg, of, HS—Bradenton, Fla.	$775,000
40. Astros. Andrew Thurman, rhp, UC Irvine	$1,397,200	90. Brewers. Barrett Astin, rhp, Arkansas	$584,300
41. Cubs. Rob Zastryzny, lhp, Missouri	$1,100,000	91. White Sox. Jacob May, of, Coastal Carolina	$525,000
42. Rockies. Ryan McMahon, 3b, HS—Santa Ana, Calif.	$1,327,600	92. Dodgers. Brandon Dixon, 3b, Arizona	$566,500
43. Twins. Ryan Eades, rhp, Louisiana State	$1,294,100	93. Cardinals. Mike Mayers, rhp, Mississippi	$510,000
44. Marlins. Trevor Williams, rhp, Arizona State	$1,261,400	94. Tigers. Jeff Thompson, rhp, Louisville	$549,400
45. Red Sox. Ted Stankiewicz, rhp, Seminole State (Okla.) JC	$915,000	95. Angels. Keynan Middleton, rhp, Lane (Ore.) CC	$450,000
46. Royals. Cody Reed, lhp, Northwest Mississippi CC	$1,198,500	96. Phillies. Jan Hernandez, ss, HS—Florida, P.R.	$550,000
47. Blue Jays. Clint Hollon, rhp, HS—Versailles, Ky.	$467,280	97. Rays. Thomas Milone, of, HS—Monroe, Conn.	$528,100
48. Mets. Andrew Church, rhp, HS—Henderson, Nev.	$850,000	98. Orioles. Stephen Tarpley, lhp, Scottsdale (Ariz.) CC	$525,500
49. Mariners. Austin Wilson, of, Stanford	$1,700,000	99. Rangers. David Ledbetter, rhp, Cedarville (Ohio)	$350,000
50. Padres. Dustin Peterson, ss, HS—Gilbert, Ariz.	$1,400,000	100. Athletics. Ryon Healy, 1b, Oregon	$500,000

ORDER OF SELECTION IN PARENTHESES   PLAYERS SIGNED IN BOLD

ARIZONA DIAMONDBACKS (14)

1. **Braden Shipley, rhp, Nevada**
1s. **Aaron Blair, rhp, Marshall** (Competitive balance selection)
2. **Justin Williams, ss, Terrebonne HS, Houma, La.**
3. **Daniel Palka, 1b, Georgia Tech**
4. **Matt McPhearson, of, Riverdale Baptist HS, Upper Marlboro, Md.**
5. **Jamie Westbrook, ss, Basha HS, Chandler, Ariz.**
6. **Colin Bray, of, Faulkner State (Ala.) CC**
7. **Daniel Gibson, lhp, Florida**
8. **Brad Keller, rhp, Flowery Branch (Ga.) HS**
9. **Grant Nelson, c, Saint Louis**
10. **Jimmie Sherfy, rhp, Oregon**
11. **Jacob Cordero, ss, Puerto Rico Baseball Academy, Gurabo, P.R.**
12. **Dane McFarland, of, JSerra Catholic HS, San Juan Capistrano, Calif.**
13. **Taylor Ratliff, of, Florida**
14. **Steven Hathaway, lhp, Franklin Pierce (N.H.)**
15. **Jordan Parr, 3b, Illinois**
16. **Elvin Soto, c, Pittsburgh**
17. **Ryan Gebhardt, ss, Louisiana Tech**
18. **Ryan Kinsella, 1b, Elon**
19. **Jacob Mayers, 3b, Richmond**
20. **Adam Miller, rhp, Brigham Young**
21. Andy Ravel, rhp, Wilson HS, Reading, Pa.
22. **Antonio Alvarez, ss, Elon**
23. **Randy McCurry, ss, Oklahoma State**
24. **Zach Esquerra, of, California Baptist**
25. **Bud Jeter, rhp, Presbyterian**
26. **George Roberts, 1b, Kent State**
27. **Jake Miller, ss, Baylor**
28. **Johnny Shuttlesworth, rhp, Faulkner (Ala.)**
29. Matt Foster, rhp, Valley (Ala.) HS
30. **Denver Chavez, 2b, Cal Poly**
31. **Joel Thys, c, Arizona Christian**
32. **Dallas Newton, rhp, Pitt (N.C.) CC**
33. **Alex Byo, rhp, Tulane**
34. Cory Hahn, of, Arizona State
35. **Tyler Toyfair, rhp, Massachusetts-Lowell**
36. Matt Vogel, rhp, Patchogue-Medford HS, Medford, N.Y.
37. **Matt Vinson, of, Arkansas**
38. **Kurtis Kostuk, rhp, Yale SS, Abbotsford, B.C.**
39. Mark Karaviotis, ss, Maui HS, Kahului, Hawaii
40. Frankie Ratcliff, ss, Houston

ATLANTA BRAVES (27)

1. (Pick forfeited for signing of free agent B.J. Upton)
1. **Jason Hursh, rhp, Oklahoma State** (Compensation pick for loss of free agent Michael Bourn)
2. **Victor Caratini, c, Miami Dade JC**
3. **Carlos Salazar, rhp, Kerman (Calif.) HS**
4. **Tanner Murphy, c, Malden (Mo.) HS**
5. **Mikey Reynolds, ss, Texas A&M**
6. **Stephen Janas, rhp, Kennesaw State**
7. **Ian Stiffler, rhp, Somerset (Pa.) HS**
8. **Kyle Wren, of, Georgia Tech**
9. **Dylan Manwaring, 3b, Horseheads (N.Y.) HS**
10. **Ian Hagenmiller, 3b, Palm Beach Central HS, Wellington, Fla.**
11. **Alec Grosser, rhp, Williams HS, Alexandria, Va.**
12. **Ryan Gunther, rhp, Charleston Southern**
13. **Joseph Odom, c, Huntingdon (Ala.)**
14. Tyler Kuresa, 1b, UC Santa Barbara
15. **Matt Marksberry, lhp, Campbell**
16. **Michael Swanner, rhp, Pepperdine**
17. **Jared Dettmann, lhp, Century (Minn.) CC**
18. **Chuck Buchanan, lhp, Cal State Bakersfield**

19. **Jordan Sechler, lhp, Cal State Los Angeles**
20. **Tyler Vail, rhp, Temple (Texas) JC**
21. **Tyler Brosius, rhp, Walters State (Tenn.) CC**
22. **Andrew Waszak, rhp, Michigan State**
23. **Connor Oliver, of, Manatee (Fla.) JC**
24. **Orrin Sears, c, Arizona Christian**
25. **Reed Harper, ss, Austin Peay State**
26. **Dakota Dill, rhp, Sul Ross State (Texas)**
27. **Jake Schrader, 1b, Tampa**
28. Stephen Wrenn, of, Walton HS, Marietta, Ga.
29. Tim Hergert, ss, Heritage HS, Vancouver, Wash.
30. Sterling Sharp, rhp, North Farmington HS, Farmington Hills, Mich.
31. Johnny Slater, of, Southfield-Lathrup HS, Southfield, Mich.
32. Jack Klein, of, St. Ignatius HS, San Francisco
33. Trevor Sprowl, 2b, Shelton State (Ala.) CC
34. Mac Seibert, 2b, Meridian (Miss.) CC
35. Angel Perez, ss, Collegio San Felipe, Arecibo, P.R.
36. Tyler Stubblefield, lhp, Lufkin (Texas) HS
37. Geoffrey Bramblett, rhp, Hoover (Ala.) HS
38. Jacob Heyward, of, Eagle's Landing Acad., McDonough, Ga.
39. Francisco Cruz, of, Puerto Rico Baseball Acad., Gurabo, P.R.
40. Connor Brogdon, rhp, Brentwood HS, Los Angeles

BALTIMORE ORIOLES (23)

1. **Hunter Harvey, rhp, Bandys HS, Catawba, N.C.**
1s. **Josh Hart, of, Parkview HS, Lilburn, Ga.** (Competitive balance selection)
2. **Chance Sisco, c, Temescal Canyon HS, Lake Elsinore, Calif.**
3. **Stephen Tarpley, lhp, Scottsdale (Ariz.) CC**
4. **Jonah Heim, c, Amherst (N.Y.) Central HS**
5. **Travis Seabrooke, lhp, Crestwood SS, North Monaghan, Ont.**
6. **Alex Murphy, c, Calvert Hall College HS, Towson, Md.**
7. **Drew Dosch, 3b, Youngstown State**
8. **Trey Mancini, 1b, Notre Dame**
9. **Mitch Horacek, lhp, Dartmouth**
10. **Austin Wynns, c, Fresno State**
11. **Steven Brault, lhp, Regis (Colo.)**
12. **Jake Bray, rhp, Feather River (Calif.) JC**
13. **Jimmy Yacabonis, rhp, St. Joseph's**
14. **Mike Yastrzemski, of, Vanderbilt**
15. Tyler Walsh, ss, Mater Dei HS, Evansville, Ind.
16. **Randolph Gassaway, 1b, Riverwood International HS, Sandy Springs, Ga.**
17. **Caleb Kellogg, rhp, Tampa**
18. Reed Reilly, rhp, Cal Poly
19. **Dylan Rheault, rhp, Central Michigan**
20. **Nick Cunningham, rhp, Arizona**
21. Levi Scott, 1b, Howard (Texas) JC
22. **Jon Keller, rhp, Tampa**
23. **Stefan Crichton, rhp, Texas Christian**
24. **Jared Breen, ss, Belmont**
25. **Danny Ayers, lhp, Columbus (Ind.) North HS**
26. Layne Bruner, lhp, Montesano (Wash.) HS
27. **Donnie Hart, lhp, Texas State**
28. Robert Tyler, rhp, Crisp County HS, Cordele, Ga.
29. **Conor Bierfeldt, of, Western Connecticut State**
30. **Federico Castagnini, ss, Creighton**
31. Dustin Hagy, rhp, Trinity Christian Academy, Deltona, Fla.
32. **Max Homick, lhp, San Diego**
33. **Jeff Kemp, ss, Radford**
34. Parker Bugg, rhp, Rancho Bernardo HS, San Diego
35. D.J. McKnight, of, Madison County HS, Madison, Fla.
36. **Eric Green, lhp, Embry-Riddle (Fla.)**
37. **Justin Viele, ss, Santa Clara**
38. Conor Harber, of, Western Nevada JC
39. **Augey Bill, lhp, Arizona**
40. **Garrett Cortright, rhp, Canisius**

BOSTON RED SOX (7)

1. **Trey Ball, lhp, New Castle (Ind.) HS**
2. **Teddy Stankiewicz, rhp, Seminole State (Okla.) JC**
3. **Jonathan Denney, c, Yukon (Okla.) HS**
4. **Myles Smith, rhp, Lee (Tenn.)**
5. **Corey Littrell, lhp, Kentucky**
6. **Jordon Austin, of, Forest HS, Ocala, Fla.**
7. **Mike Adams, lhp, Tampa**
8. **Forrestt Allday, of, Central Arkansas**
9. **Kyle Martin, rhp, Texas A&M**
10. **Taylor Grover, rhp, South Carolina-Aiken**
11. **Carlos Asuaje, ss, Nova Southeastern (Fla.)**
12. **Jake Drehoff, lhp, Southern Mississippi**
13. Jordan Sheffield, rhp, Tullahoma (Tenn.) HS
14. **Jake Romanski, c, San Diego State**
15. **Bryan Hudson, of, Mill Creek HS, Hoschton, Ga.**
16. **Jalen Williams, rhp, Westminster Christian Academy, Opelousas, La.**
17. **Joseph Monge, of, Beltran Academy, Florida, P.R.**
18. **Joe Gunkel, rhp, West Chester (Pa.)**
19. **Gabe Speier, lhp, Dos Pueblos HS, Goleta, Calif.**
20. Derek Burkamper, rhp, Muscatine (Iowa) HS
21. **Reed Gragnani, 2b, Virginia**
22. Ryan Boldt, of, Red Wing (Minn.) HS
23. Jimmy Allen, 2b, Cal Poly
24. **Jantzen Witte, 3b, Texas Christian**
25. Derik Beauprez, rhp, Cherry Creek HS, Greenwood Vill., Colo.
26. **Mauricio Dubon, ss, Capital Christian HS, Sacramento**
27. Mark Nowaczewski, rhp, Reed HS, Sparks, Nev.
28. Nick Zammarelli, 3b, Lincoln (R.I.) HS
29. **Jeff Driskel, of, Florida**
30. **Nick Longhi, of, Venice (Fla.) HS**
31. Ryan Rippee, 1b, Jefferson (Mo.) CC
32. Matt Thaiss, c, Jackson (N.J.) Memorial HS
33. Andrew Rosa, ss, Owasso (Okla.) HS
34. **Danny Bethea, c, St. John's**
35. **Rafael Oliveras, 3b, Loaiza Cordero Del Rosario HS, Yauco, P.R.**
36. **Pat Goetze, rhp, Wake County Home Schools, Raleigh, N.C.**
37. Max Watt, rhp, Hillsborough (Fla.) CC
38. Trever Morrison, ss, Archbishop Murphy HS, Everett, Wash.
39. **K.J. Trader, rhp, Delmar (Del.) HS**
40. Ryan Lidge, c, Barrington (Ill.) HS

CHICAGO CUBS (2)

1. **Kris Bryant, 3b, San Diego**
2. **Rob Zastryzny, lhp, Missouri**
3. **Jacob Hannemann, of, Brigham Young**
4. **Tyler Skulina, rhp, Kent State**
5. **Trey Masek, rhp, Texas Tech**
6. **Scott Frazier, rhp, Pepperdine**
7. **David Garner, rhp, Michigan State**
8. **Sam Wilson, lhp, Lamar (Colo.) CC**
9. **Charcer Burks, of, Travis HS, Richmond, Texas**
10. **Zack Godley, rhp, Tennessee**
11. **Jordan Hankins, c, Austin Peay State**
12. **Trevor Clifton, rhp, Heritage HS, Maryville, Tenn.**
13. **Trevor Graham, rhp, Franklin Pierce (N.H.)**
14. Daniel Poncedeleon, rhp, Houston
15. **Michael Wagner, rhp, San Diego**
16. **Cael Brockmeyer, c, Cal State Bakersfield**
17. **Kelvin Freeman, 1b, North Carolina A&T**
18. **Giuseppe Papaccio, ss, Seton Hall**
19. **Will Remillard, c, Coastal Carolina**
20. **Zak Blair, 2b, Mercyhurst**
21. Josh McCauley, rhp, Shepherd (W.Va.)
22. **Kevin Brown, of, Bryant**
23. **Tyler Ihrig, lhp, Marin (Calif.) CC**
24. **Tyler Alamo, c, Cypress (Calif.) HS**
25. Marcus Doi, of, Mid-Pacific Institute, Honolulu

26. **Carlos Pena, c, Southwest HS, Miami**
27. Tyler Sciacca, 2b, Villanova
28. **Brad Renner, rhp, Florida State JC**
29. John Garcia, of, Denbigh HS, Newport News, Va.
30. **Zak Hermans, rhp, Princeton**
31. Sean Johnson, rhp, Iowa Western CC
32. Keaton Leach, rhp, Glendale (Calif.) CC
33. Chris Madera, of, Northwest Florida State JC
34. Jake Thompson, rhp, Central HS, Independence, Ore.
35. Ramsey Romano, ss, Valhalla HS, El Cajon, Calif.
36. Derek Campbell, ss, California
37. Jeremy Martinez, c, Mater Dei HS, Santa Ana, Calif.
38. Zack Brown, rhp, Seymour (Ind.) HS
39. Josh Greene, of, Forest HS, Ocala, Fla.
40. Bubby Riley, of, Delgado (La.) CC

CHICAGO WHITE SOX (17)

1. **Tim Anderson, ss, East Central (Miss.) CC**
2. **Tyler Danish, rhp, Durant HS, Plant City, Fla.**
3. **Jacob May, of, Coastal Carolina**
4. **Andrew Mitchell, rhp, Texas Christian**
5. **Thaddius Lowry, rhp, Spring (Texas) HS**
6. **James Dykstra, rhp, Cal State San Marcos**
7. **Trey Michalczewski, 3b, Jenks (Okla.) HS**
8. **Chris Freudenberg, lhp, South Mountain (Ariz.) CC**
9. **Nick Blount, rhp, Southern Polytechnic State (Ga.)**
10. **Brad Goldberg, rhp, Ohio State**
11. **Matt Ball, rhp, Bonita Vista HS, Chula Vista, Calif.**
12. **Tyler Shryock, ss, Cal State Bakersfield**
13. **Danny Hayes, 1b, Oregon State**
14. **Tyler Barnette, rhp, Charlotte**
15. **Andre Wheeler, lhp, Texas Tech**
16. **John Stringer, ss, Rice**
17. **Joey Wagman, rhp, Cal Poly**
18. **Michael Carballo, of, Tennessee Wesleyan**
19. **Adam Engel, of, Louisville**
20. **Dillon Haupt, c, San Diego**
21. **Toby Thomas, ss, Pensacola State (Fla.) JC**
22. **Nolan Earley, of, South Alabama**
23. **Trey Wimmer, c, Liberty**
24. **Jacob Morris, of, Arkansas**
25. **Alex Powers, rhp, Southern New Hampshire**
26. **Charlie Sharrer, rhp, Cal State East Bay**
27. **Devin Moore, rhp, Indiana State**
28. **Jeff McKenzie, lhp, Cal State Bakersfield**
29. **Matt Abramson, rhp, Tampa**
30. **Jon Bengard, rhp, California Baptist**
31. **Sean Hagan, lhp, St. John's**
32. **Darian Johnson, of, Lamar**
33. Tavo Rodriguez, lhp, Franklin HS, El Paso
34. Tyrell King, lhp, Yavapai (Ariz.) JC
35. **Sam Macias, of, San Diego**
36. **Nick Parent, 1b, Cal State Monterey Bay**
37. **Cody Yount, 1b, Virginia Commonwealth**
38. **Audry Santana, ss, Eckerd (Fla.)**
39. Wolfie Tash, 3b, Venice HS, Los Angeles
40. Ro Coleman, 2b, Simeon HS, Chicago

CINCINNATI REDS (29)

1. **Phillip Ervin, of, Samford**
1s. **Michael Lorenzen, rhp, Cal State Fullerton** (Competitive balance selection)
2. **K.J. Franklin, 3b, Gahr HS, Cerritos, Calif.**
3. **Mark Armstrong, rhp, Clarence (N.Y.) HS**
4. **Ben Lively, rhp, Central Florida**
5. **Cory Thompson, ss, Mauldin (S.C.) HS**
6. **Zack Weiss, rhp, UCLA**
7. **Tyler Mahle, rhp, Westminster (Calif.) HS**
8. **Scott Brattvet, rhp, Cal State Bakersfield**
9. **Chad Jones, lhp, New Orleans (no school)**

10. **Daniel Wright, rhp, Arkansas State**
11. **Ty Boyles, lhp, Quartz Hill (Calif.) HS**
12. **Shedric Long, c, Jacksonville (Ala.) HS**
13. **Evan Mitchell, rhp, Mississippi State**
14. Willie Abreu, of, Mater Academy, Hialeah Gardens, Fla.
15. **Jarrett Freeland, c, Parkview HS, Lilburn, Ga.**
16. **Fabian Roman, rhp, Lubbock Christian (Texas)**
17. **Dalton Carter, of, Winder-Barrow HS, Winder, Ga.**
18. **Joe Mantoni, rhp, Merrimack (Mass.)**
19. Alex Krupa, of, Greenwood (Ind.) Community HS
20. **Morgan Lofstrom, c, Mt. Boucherie SS, Kelowna, B.C.**
21. Eric Dorsch, rhp, Kent State
22. **Layne Somsen, rhp, South Dakota State**
23. **Narciso Crook, of, Gloucester County (N.J.) JC**
24. Brett Morales, rhp, King HS, Tampa
25. Eduardo Garcia, rhp, Alexander HS, Laredo, Texas
26. Eli White, ss, Wren HS, Anderson, S.C.
27. Zack Collins, c, American Heritage HS, Plantation, Fla.
28. Carter Austin, 1b, Maine-Endwell HS, Endwell, N.Y.
29. **Alex Greer, of, Iowa Western CC**
30. **Taylor Terrasas, 3b, Louisiana Tech**
31. Andrew Benintendi, of, Madeira HS, Cincinnati
32. **Logan Uxa, 1b, Arkansas State**
33. Matt Blandino, rhp, Bristol (Conn.) Central HS
34. Luke Bolka, rhp, Atlee HS, Mechanicsville, Va.
35. Conner Simonetti, of, Fairport (N.Y.) HS
36. Taylor Hearn, lhp, San Jacinto (Texas) JC
37. Alec Byrd, lhp, St. Thomas Aquinas HS, Fort Lauderdale
38. Dan Grauer, rhp, Liberty
39. Manny Cruz, ss, Wolcott (Conn.) HS
40. **P.J. Cerreto, rhp, Ramapo (N.J.)**

CLEVELAND INDIANS (5)

1. **Clint Frazier, of, Loganville (Ga.) HS**
2. (Pick forfeited for signing of free agent Nick Swisher)
2s. (Competitive balance selection; forfeited for signing of free agent Michael Bourn)
3. **Dace Kime, rhp, Louisville**
4. **Kyle Crockett, lhp, Virginia**
5. **Sean Brady, lhp, Baker HS, Cape Coral, Fla.**
6. **Casey Shane, rhp, Centennial HS, Burleson, Texas**
7. **Kenny Mathews, lhp, Riverside (Calif.) CC**
8. **Trevor Frank, rhp, UC Riverside**
9. **Thomas Pannone, lhp, JC of Southern Nevada**
10. Ross Kivett, 2b, Kansas State
11. **Adam Plutko, rhp, UCLA**
12. Heath Quinn, of, Oak Mountain HS, Birmingham
13. **Sicnarf Loopstok, c, Western Oklahoma State JC**
14. **Silento Sayles, of, Port Gibson (Miss.) HS**
15. James Roberts, ss, Southern California
16. Mark Payton, of, Texas
17. Ryan Hendrix, rhp, Cypress Woods HS, Cypress, Texas
18. **Paul Hendrix, ss, Texas Christian**
19. **Matt Whitehouse, lhp, UC Irvine**
20. **Shane Rowland, c, Tampa**
21. Paul Young, rhp, Central Alabama CC
22. **Ben Heller, rhp, Olivet Nazarene (Ill.)**
23. **Grant Fink, 3b, Missouri Western State**
24. **Kerry Doane, rhp, East Tennessee State**
25. **Cole Sulser, rhp, Dartmouth**
26. Danny Cogan, rhp, Rocklin (Ca.) HS
27. **Juan Gonzalez, c, Puerto Rico Baseball Acad., Gurabo, P.R.**
28. Stephen Kane, rhp, Cypress (Calif.) JC
29. Ridge Smith, 3b, Germantown (Tenn.) HS
30. Aaron Brown, lhp, Pepperdine
31. Wil Crowe, rhp, Pigeon Forge (Tenn.) HS
32. **Cortland Cox, rhp, Riverside (Calif.) CC**
33. Joey Wise, lhp, Cactus Shadows HS, Cave Creek, Ariz.
34. Dustin Cook, rhp, San Jacinto (Texas) JC
35. **Jordan Milbrath, rhp, Augustana (S.D.)**

36. **Mike Giuffre, 2b, Tottenville HS, Staten Island, N.Y.**
37. **Garrett Smith, 2b, California Lutheran**
38. **Justin Garcia, rhp, Weatherford (Texas) JC**
39. Frank Duncan, rhp, Kansas
40. Dan Pellinen, 3b, North Woods HS, Cook, Minn.

COLORADO ROCKIES (3)

1. **Jonathan Gray, rhp, Oklahoma**
2. **Ryan McMahon, 3b, Mater Dei HS, Santa Ana, Calif.**
2s. **Alex Balog, rhp, San Francisco** (Competitive balance selection)
3. **Sam Moll, lhp, Memphis**
4. **Jordan Patterson, of, South Alabama**
5. **Blake Shouse, rhp, Middle Georgia JC**
6. **Dom Nunez, 3b, Elk Grove (Calif.) HS**
7. **Konner Wade, rhp, Arizona**
8. **Terry McClure, of, Riverwood International HS, Sandy Springs, Ga.**
9. **Pat Valaika, ss, UCLA**
10. **Mike Tauchman, of, Bradley**
11. **Sean Dwyer, of, Florida Gulf Coast**
12. **Billy Waltrip, rhp, Oklahoma**
13. **Mike Benjamin Jr., 3b, Arizona State**
14. **Dylan Stamey, rhp, South Alabama**
15. **John Beck, rhp, Texas-Arlington**
16. **Alex Rodriguez, lhp, Indian River (Fla.) JC**
17. **Trent Daniel, lhp, Arkansas**
18. **Jacob Newberry, rhp, High Point**
19. **Scott Firth, rhp, Clemson**
20. M.T. Minacci, rhp, North Fla. Christian HS, Tallahassee, Fla.
21. **Eric Nedeljkovic, rhp, Miami**
22. Brody Weiss, ss, Regis Jesuit HS, Aurora, Colo.
23. **Jerad McCrummen, rhp, Texas Tech**
24. Hunter Brothers, rhp, Lipscomb
25. Alec Hansen, rhp, Loveland (Colo.) HS
26. **Matt Pierpont, rhp, Winthrop**
27. **Daniel Palo, rhp, Middle Tennessee State**
28. Heath Fillmyer, rhp, Mercer County (N.J.) JC
29. Kyle Serrano, rhp, Farragut (Tenn.) HS
30. Jacob Stone, rhp, Weatherford (Texas) JC
31. **Wesley Jones, ss, Redan HS, Stone Mountain, Ga.**
32. Thomas Hatch, rhp, Jenks (Okla.) HS
33. Alex Haines, lhp, Seton Hill (Pa.)
34. Kyle Thornell, 3b, McLennan (Texas) CC
35. Ronnie Gideon, 3b, Hallsville (Texas) HS 36.Andy McGuire, ss, Madison HS, Vienna, Va.
37. Luke Persico, of, Great Oak HS, Temecula, Calif.
38. Scott Moss, lhp, Deland (Fla.) HS
39. **Cole Norton, of, St. Mary's**
40. Tyler Stover, 1b, Vacaville (Calif.) HS

DETROIT TIGERS (20)

1. **Jonathon Crawford, rhp, Florida**
1s. **Corey Knebel, rhp, Texas** (Competitive balance selection, obtained in trade from Marlins)
2. **Kevin Ziomek, lhp, Vanderbilt**
3. **Jeff Thompson, rhp, Louisville**
4. **Austin Kubitza, rhp, Rice**
5. **Buck Farmer, rhp, Georgia Tech**
6. **Calvin Drummond, rhp, Arizona Christian**
7. **Connor Harrell, of, Vanderbilt**
8. **Zach Reininger, rhp, Hill (Texas) JC**
9. **Will LaMarche, rhp, Louisiana State**
10. **Kasey Coffman, of, Arizona State**
11. **Chad Green, rhp, Louisville**
12. **Dominic Ficociello, 3b, Arkansas**
13. **Austin Green, c, San Diego**
14. **Ben Verlander, of, Old Dominion**
15. **Raph Rhymes, of, Louisiana State**
16. **Duncan McAlpine, c, Dallas Baptist**
17. **Steven Negron, ss, Miami Dade JC**

18. Jon Maciel, rhp, Long Beach State
19. Austin Pritcher, rhp, Citadel
20. Matt Wotherspoon, rhp, Pittsburgh
21. Curt Powell, ss, Georgia
22. Daryl Norris, rhp, Mississippi State
23. Tyler Alexander, lhp, Carroll HS, Southlake, Texas
24. Chase Edwards, rhp, Hill (Texas) JC
25. Johnnie Kirkland, rhp, Southeastern (Fla.)
26. Adrian Castano, of, Cardozo HS, New York
27. Joe Mantiply, lhp, Virginia Tech
28. Scott Sitz, rhp, Florida State
29. Charley Sullivan, rhp, Alabama
30. Ryan Beck, lhp, New Mexico State
31. Brett Huber, rhp, Mississippi
32. Tanner Bailey, rhp, Mississippi
33. John Armstrong, 2b, Bishop Carroll HS, Wichita, Kan.
34. Brad Holland, 2b, Mesquite HS, Gilbert, Ariz.
35. A.J. Puk, lhp, Washington HS, Cedar Rapids, Iowa
36. Torii Hunter Jr., of, Prosper (Texas) HS
37. Nick Deeg, lhp, Lake Orion (Mich.) HS
38. Harrison Wenson, c, University of Detroit Jesuit HS
39. Anfernee Grier, of, Russell County HS, Seale, Ala.
40. Taylor Johnson, 2b, St. Edward's (Texas)

HOUSTON ASTROS (1)

1. Mark Appel, rhp, Stanford
2. Andrew Thurman, rhp, UC Irvine
3. Kent Emanuel, lhp, North Carolina
4. Conrad Gregor, 1b, Vanderbilt
5. Tony Kemp, 2b, Vanderbilt
6. Jacob Nottingham, c, Redlands (Calif.) HS
7. James Ramsay, of, South Florida
8. Jason Martin, of, Orange (Calif.) Lutheran HS
9. Brian Holberton, c, North Carolina
10. Austin Nicely, lhp, Spotswood HS, Penn Laird, Va.
11. Devonte German, rhp, Bishop Manogue HS, Reno, Nev.
12. Chase McDonald, 1b, East Carolina
13. Kyle Westwood, rhp, North Florida
14. Chris Cotton, lhp, Louisiana State
15. James Farris, rhp, Arizona
16. Dillon Newman, rhp, Baylor
17. Alex Schick, rhp, Cathedral Catholic HS, San Diego
18. Adam Nelubowich, 3b, Washington State
19. Jake Rodriguez, c, Oregon State
20. Daniel Pinero, ss, Humberside Collegiate Institute, Toronto
21. Jon Kemmer, of, Brewton-Parker (Ga.)
22. Sebastian Kessay, lhp, Scottsdale (Ariz.) CC
23. Thomas Lindauer, ss, Illinois
24. Nathan Thornhill, rhp, Texas
25. Albert Minnis, lhp, Wichita State
26. Austin Chrismon, rhp, Christopher Newport (Va.)
27. Pat Christensen, rhp, La Salle
28. Jordan Mills, lhp, St. Mary's
29. Randall Fant, lhp, Arkansas
30. Jorge Perez, rhp, Seminole State (Okla.) JC
31. Scott Burke, rhp, Glendora (Calif.) HS
32. Zach Morton, rhp, Northwestern
33. Tyler White, 3b, Western Carolina
34. Brett Booth, c, Alabama
35. Kacy Clemens, rhp, Memorial HS, Houston
36. J.D. Osborne, lhp, Wofford
37. Josh Melendez, of, New Mexico
38. Ronnie Mitchell, of, Dallas Baptist
39. Juan Santos, rhp, Arlington Country Day School, Jacksonville
40. Tyler Brunnemann, rhp, Hardin-Simmons (Texas)

KANSAS CITY ROYALS (8)

1. Hunter Dozier, ss, Stephen F. Austin State
1s. Sean Manaea, lhp, Indiana State (Competitive balance selection)

2. Cody Reed, lhp, Northwest Mississippi CC
3. Carter Hope, rhp, The Woodlands (Texas) HS
4. Zane Evans, c, Georgia Tech
5. Amalani Fukofuka, of, Logan HS, Union City, Calif.
6. Luke Farrell, rhp, Northwestern
7. Kyle Bartsch, lhp, South Alabama
8. Cody Stubbs, 1b, North Carolina
9. Daniel Rockett, of, Texas-San Antonio
10. Alex Newman, of, Cypress (Calif.) JC
11. Xavier Fernandez, c, Puerto Rico Baseball Academy, Gurabo, P.R.
12. Brandon Dulin, 1b, Metropolitan CC-Longview (Mo.)
13. Jonathan Dziedzic, lhp, Lamar
14. Chase Darhower, rhp, Northwest Florida State JC
15. Dominique Taylor, of, UC Irvine
16. Kevin McCarthy, rhp, Marist
17. Kevin Perez, rhp, Miami Dade JC
18. Frank Schwindel, c, St. John's
19. Andrew Edwards, rhp, Western Kentucky
20. Glenn Sparkman, rhp, Wharton (Texas) JC
21. Shane Conlon, 1b, Kansas State
22. Andrew Brockett, rhp, Richmond
23. Javier Reynoso, lhp, Middle Georgia JC
24. Riley King, of, Carroll (Mont.)
25. Logan Gray, ss, Rockhurst HS, Kansas City, Mo.
26. Trace Tam Sing, ss, Washington State
27. Christian Flecha, lhp, Caguas (P.R.) Military Academy
28. Kevin Kuntz, ss, Kansas
29. Alex Black, rhp, Columbia
30. Andrew Ayers, 2b, Sacramento State
31. T.J. Zeuch, rhp, Mason (Ohio) HS
32. Mike Shawaryn, rhp, Gloucester Catholic HS, Gloucester City, N.J.
33. Dalton Moats, lhp, Park Hill HS, Kansas City, Mo.
34. Isaac Anderson, rhp, JC of Southern Idaho
35. Clay Miller, lhp, Bayfield (Colo.) HS
36. Ryan McBroom, 1b, West Virginia
37. Will Craig, 3b, Science HIII HS, Johnson City, Tenn.
38. Jake Matthews, of, Ironwood Ridge HS, Oro Valley, Ariz.
39. John Sternagel, ss, Rockledge (Fla.) HS
40. Keaton Steele, rhp, Missouri

LOS ANGELES ANGELS (21)

1. (Pick forfeited for signing of free agent Josh Hamilton)
2. Hunter Green, lhp, Warren East HS, Bowling Green, Ky.
3. Keynan Middleton, rhp, Lane (Ore.) CC
4. Elliot Morris, rhp, Pierce (Wash.) JC
5. Kyle McGowin, rhp, Savannah State
6. Harrison Cooney, rhp, Florida Gulf Coast
7. Garrett Nuss, rhp, Seminole State (Fla.) JC
8. Nate Smith, lhp, Furman
9. Stephen McGee, c, Florida State
10. Grant Gordon, rhp, Missouri State
11. Jonah Wesely, lhp, Tracy (Calif.) HS
12. Blake Goins, rhp, Pearland (Texas) HS
13. Angel Rosa, ss, Alcorn State
14. Riley Good, of, Texas-San Antonio
15. Chad Hinshaw, of, Illinois State
16. Ryan Etsell, rhp, Hillsborough (Fla.) JC
17. Cal Towey, 3b, Baylor
18. Garrett Cannizaro, 3b, Tulane
19. Cole Swanson, lhp, Concordia (Calif.)
20. Brian Loconsole, rhp, Western Illinois
21. Alex Allbritton, ss, New Mexico
22. Trevor Foss, rhp, Texas A&M-Corpus Christi
23. Matt Hernandez, lhp, Houston
24. Mark Shannon, of, Nevada-Las Vegas
25. Alan Busenitz, rhp, Kennesaw State
26. Kirby Pellant, ss, Ohio State
27. Nate Goro, ss, Oral Roberts
28. Michael Hermosillo, of, Ottawa (Ill.) HS
29. Michael Smith, rhp, Dallas Baptist

30. Cambric Moye, c, UNC Greensboro
31. Taylor Johnson, of, Furman
32. Michael Fish, of, Siena
33. Colin O'Keefe, lhp, Virginia Tech
34. Eric Aguilera, of, Illinois State
35. Eric Weiss, c, Texas A&M-Corpus Christi
36. Brandon Bayardi, of, Nevada-Las Vegas
37. Alex Blackford, rhp, Arizona State
38. Clint Sharp, rhp, Texas-San Antonio
39. Dan Tobik, rhp, Tennessee-Martin
40. Ben Carlson, rhp, Furman

LOS ANGELES DODGERS (18)

1. Chris Anderson, rhp, Jacksonville
2. Tom Windle, lhp, Minnesota
3. Brandon Dixon, 3b, Arizona
4. Cody Bellinger, 1b, Hamilton HS, Chandler, Ariz.
5. J.D. Underwood, rhp, Palm Beach State (Fla.) JC
6. Jacob Rhame, rhp, Grayson County (Texas) CC
7. Brandon Trinkwon, ss, UC Santa Barbara
8. Kyle Farmer, c, Georgia
9. Henry Yates, of, Texas Wesleyan
10. Nick Keener, rhp, Mansfield (Pa.)
11. Spencer Navin, c, Vanderbilt
12. Adam Law, 3b, Brigham Young
13. Ty Damron, lhp, Krum (Texas) HS
14. Michael Johnson, lhp, Dartmouth
15. Billy Flamion, lhp, Grossmont (Calif.) JC
16. Peter Miller, rhp, Florida State
17. Greg Harris, rhp, Los Alamitos (Calif.) HS
18. James McDonald, 2b, Arizona State
19. Blake Hennessey, ss, Arlington Country Day HS, Jacksonville
20. Mike Ahmed, of, Holy Cross
21. Jamie Baune, rhp, Southern Arkansas
22. Jake Fisher, lhp, Oklahoma
23. M.J. Villegas, rhp, Seton Catholic HS, Chandler, Ariz.
24. Jose DeLeon, rhp, Southern
25. Kyle Hooper, rhp, UC Irvine
26. Thomas Taylor, rhp, Kansas
27. Tanner Kiest, rhp, Riverside (Calif.) CC
28. Crayton Bare, lhp, Baylor
29. Sam Finfer, c, Interlake HS, Bellevue, Wash.
30. Ryan Scott, c, Notre Dame HS, Scottsdale, Ariz.
31. Andrew McWilliam, 3b, Westview HS, San Diego
32. Rob Rogers, rhp, Keystone (Pa.)
33. Tyger Pederson, 2b, Pacific
34. Rob Cerfolio, lhp, Yale
35. Kaleb Holbrook, c, South Georgia JC
36. James Lynch, of, Glendale (Ariz.) CC
37. Justin Dunn, rhp, The Gunnery School, Washington, Conn.
38. Dillon Moyer, ss, UC San Diego
39. Jake Sidwell, c, Olympia HS, Orlando
40. Matt Haggerty, of, Seton Catholic HS, Chandler, Ariz.

MIAMI MARLINS (6)

1. Colin Moran, 3b, North Carolina
1s. Matt Krook, lhp, St. Ignatius HS, San Francisco (Competitive balance selection; obtained in trade from Pirates)
2. Trevor Williams, rhp, Arizona State
2s. Colby Suggs, rhp, Arkansas (Competitive balance selection; obtained in trade from Tigers)
3. Ben DeLuzio, ss, The First Academy, Orlando
4. K.J. Woods, of, Fort Mill (S.C.) HS
5. Chad Wallach, c, Cal State Fullerton
6. Ryan Aper, of, Lincoln Land (Ill.) CC
7. Justin Bohn, ss, Feather River (Calif.) JC
8. Iramis Olivencia, 2b, Arlington Country Day HS, Jacksonville
9. Aaron Blanton, ss, Richland (Texas) JC
10. Carlos Lopez, 1b, Cal State Fullerton
11. Coco Johnson, of, Louisville

12. C.J. Robinson, rhp, St. John's River (Fla.) JC
13. J.T. Riddle, 2b, Kentucky
14. Scott Carcaise, 1b, Florida Tech
15. Miles Williams, of, Cal State Northridge
16. Tyler Kinley, rhp, Barry (Fla.)
17. Scott Schultz, rhp, Oregon State
18. Max Garner, rhp, Baylor
19. Will White, lhp, Marin (Calif.) CC
20. Juan Avila, 3b, Long Beach State
21. Sam Alvis, lhp, Louisiana Tech
22. Nelson Zulueta, rhp, Faith Baptist Christian HS, Brandon, Fla.
23. Josh Easley, rhp, North Carolina State
24. Cody Harris, rhp, The Masters (Calif.)
25. Sean Townsley, lhp, High Point
26. Adam Westmoreland, lhp, South Carolina
27. Matt Young, rhp, Glendora (Calif.) HS
28. Joel Effertz, rhp, Wisconsin-LaCrosse
29. Kevin Williams, ss, UCLA
30. Eric Fisher, 1b, Arkansas
31. Dalton Viner, rhp, Eastern Oklahoma State JC
32. Cody Crabaugh, rhp, Oklahoma City
33. Blake Douglas, rhp, Weatherford (Texas) JC
34. Edward Cruz, rhp, Western Oklahoma State JC
35. Cole Stapler, rhp, Dutchtown HS, Geismar, La.
36. Chandler Eden, rhp, Yuba City (Calif.) HS
37. Michael Bell, ss, Hughes HS, Fairburn, Ga.
38. Tyler Kane, rhp, Washington
39. Daulton Jefferies, rhp, Buhach Colony HS, Atwater, Calif.
40. Timmy Richards, ss, Wilson HS, Long Beach

MILWAUKEE BREWERS (16)

1. (Pick forfeited for signing of free agent Kyle Lohse)
2. Devin Williams, rhp, Hazelwood (Mo.) West HS
2s. Tucker Neuhaus, ss, Wharton HS, Tampa (Competitive balance selection)
3. Barrett Astin, rhp, Arkansas
4. Taylor Williams, rhp, Kent State
5. Josh Uhen, rhp, Wisconsin-Milwaukee
6. Garrett Cooper, 1b, Auburn
7. Omar Garcia, of, Miami Dade JC
8. Brandon Diaz, of, American Heritage HS, Plantation, Fla.
9. Tyler Linehan, lhp, Fresno State
10. Michael Ratterree, of, Rice
11. Andy Hillis, rhp, Lee (Tenn.)
12. Trevor Seidenberger, lhp, Texas Christian
13. Tanner Norton, c, Bishop Brossart HS, Alexandria, Ky.
14. Hobbs Johnson, lhp, North Carolina
15. David Denson, 1b, South Hills HS, West Covina, Calif.
16. Corey Miller, rhp, Pepperdine
17. Brandon Moore, rhp, Arkansas
18. Clint Terry, lhp, Lee (Tenn.)
19. Josh Matheson, rhp, Minnesota State-Mankato
20. Ryan Yarbrough, lhp, Brigham Young
21. Tristan Archer, rhp, Tennessee Tech
22. Johnny Davis, of, West Los Angeles JC
23. Eric Williams, of, Sachse (Texas) HS
24. Chris Razo, rhp, Illinois State
25. Drew Ghelfi, rhp, Minnesota
26. Ky Parrott, of, Herndon (Va.) HS
27. Tyler Alexander, lhp, Florida International
28. Alex Moore, rhp, Lee (Tenn.)
29. Nick Eicholtz, rhp, Cambridge Christian HS, Tampa
30. Luis Aviles, ss, Southwest HS, Miami
31. Tanner Poppe, rhp, Kansas
32. Ryan Deeter, rhp, UCLA
33. Charles LeBlanc, ss, Vanier SS, Toronto
34. Dylan Brock, rhp, Glendale (Ariz.) CC
35. Jesse Travis, rhp, Southwest Mississippi CC
36. Jesse Weiss, 1b, Kenyon (Ohio)
37. JaVon Shelby, ss, Tates Creek HS, Lexington, Ky.

38. Charlie Markson, of, Notre Dame
39. John Cleary, c, Maryland
40. Kenny Meimerstorf, of, Bishop Gorman HS, Las Vegas

MINNESOTA TWINS (4)

1. Kohl Stewart, rhp, St. Pius X HS, Houston
2. Ryan Eades, rhp, Louisiana State
3. Stuart Turner, c, Mississippi
4. Stephen Gonsalves, lhp, Cathedral HS, San Diego
5. Aaron Slegers, rhp, Indiana
6. Brian Navarreto, c, Arlington Country Day HS, Jacksonville
7. Brian Gilbert, rhp, Seton Hall
8. Dustin DeMuth, 3b, Indiana
9. Mitchell Garver, c, New Mexico
10. C.K. Irby, rhp, Samford
11. Nelson Molina, ss, Luchetti HS, Arecibo, P.R.
12. Ethan Mildren, rhp, Pittsburgh
13. Brandon Peterson, rhp, Wichita State
14. Zack Granite, of, Seton Hall
15. Derrick Penilla, lhp, Mount San Antonio (Calif.) JC
16. Brandon Bixler, lhp, Florida Gulf Coast
17. Tanner Mendonca, rhp, Sacramento State
18. Ryan Walker, ss, Texas-Arlington
19. Jared Wilson, rhp, UC Santa Barbara
20. Jason Kanzler, of, Buffalo
21. Tyler Stirewalt, rhp, Fresno State
22. Alex Swim, c, Elon
23. Zach Hayden, rhp, South Carolina-Aiken
24. Brandon Easton, lhp, Lakeland (Ohio) CC
25. Chad Christensen, of, Nebraska
26. Ryan Halstead, rhp, Indiana
27. Taylor Blatch, rhp, Jensen Beach (Fla.) HS
28. Chris Erwin, lhp, Grayson HS, Loganville, Ga.
29. Logan Shore, rhp, Coon Rapids (Minn.) HS
30. Tanner Vavra, 2b, Valparaiso
31. A.J. Bogucki, rhp, Boyertown (Pa.) Area HS
32. Carlos Avila, ss, Cal State Dominguez Hills
33. Steven Sensley, of, University HS, Baton Rouge
34. Ivory Thomas, of, Cal State Dominguez Hills
35. Nick Lemoncelli, lhp, Lower Columbia (Wash.) JC
36. Joe Greenfield, rhp, Eastern Illinois
37. Julian Service, of, Northeast Texas CC
38. Javier Salas, rhp, Miami
39. Seth Wagner, lhp, Mifflin County HS, Lewistown, Pa.
40. Kelly Starnes, of, Los Medanos (Calif.) JC

NEW YORK METS (10)

1. Dominic Smith, 1b, JSerra HS, Gardena, Calif.
2. Andrew Church, rhp, Basic HS, Henderson, Nev.
3. Ivan Wilson, of, Ruston (La.) HS (Compensation pick for failure to sign 2012 second-round pick Teddy Stankiewicz)
3. Casey Meisner, rhp, Cypress Woods HS, Cypress, Texas
4. L.J. Mazzilli, 2b, Connecticut
5. Jared King, of, Kansas State
6. Champ Stuart, of, Brevard (N.C.)
7. Matt Oberste, 1b, Oklahoma
8. Ricky Knapp, rhp, Florida Gulf Coast
9. Patrick Biondi, of, Michigan
10. Luis Guillorme, ss, Coral Springs (Fla.) HS
11. Ty Bashlor, rhp, South Georgia JC
12. Jeff McNeil, ss, Long Beach State
13. Kevin McGowan, rhp, Franklin Pierce (N.H.)
14. J.D. Leckenby, rhp, Washington State
15. Colton Plaia, c, Loyola Marymount
16. Zach Mathieu, 1b, Franklin Pierce (N.H.)
17. John Magliozzi, rhp, Florida
18. Brent McMinn, rhp, Nevada
19. Cody Crouse, rhp, Bloomingdale HS, Valrico, Fla.
20. Dan Herrmann, rhp, Christian Brothers HS, St. Louis
21. Morgan Earman, rhp, Desert Acad., Bermuda Dunes, Calif.

22. Daniel Procopio, rhp, Central Technical School, Toronto
23. Gaither Bumgardner, rhp, South Carolina-Upstate
24. Matt Brill, rhp, Moline (Ill.) HS
25. Ricky Jacquez, rhp, Central Arizona JC
26. Owen Spiwak, c, Cawthra Park SS, Mississauga, Ont.
27. Austin Coley, rhp, Belmont
28. Robby Coles, rhp, Florida State
29. Anthony Kay, lhp, Melville HS, East Setauket, N.Y.
30. David McKay, rhp, Viera (Fla.) HS
31. Ben Hecht, rhp, St. Anthony HS, Effingham, Ill.
32. Juan Escarra, c, Mater Academy, Hialeah Gardens, Fla.
33. Ryan Chapman, rhp, Santa Ana (Calif.) JC
34. Cameron Griffin, rhp, Columbus State (Ga.)
35. Ty Williams, rhp, Seminole State (Okla.) JC
36. Brandon Brosher, 1b, Springstead HS, Spring Hill, Fla.
37. Juan Avena, 1b, Compton (Calif.) JC
38. Paul Paez, lhp, Rio Hondo (Calif.) JC
39. Logan Quimuyog, 1b, Mosley HS, Lynn Haven, Fla.
40. J.B. Woodman, of, Edgewater HS, Orlando

NEW YORK YANKEES (28)

1. Eric Jagielo, 3b, Notre Dame
1. Aaron Judge, of, Fresno State (Compensation pick for loss of free agent Nick Swisher)
1. Ian Clarkin, lhp, Madison HS, San Diego (Compensation pick for loss of free agent Rafael Soriano)
2. Gosuke Katoh, 2b, Rancho Bernardo HS, San Diego
3. Michael O'Neill, of, Michigan
4. Tyler Wade, ss, Murrieta Valley HS, Murrieta, Calif.
5. David Palladino, rhp, Howard (Texas) JC
6. John Murphy, ss, Sacred Heart
7. Nick Rumbelow, rhp, Louisiana State
8. Brandon Thomas, of, Georgia Tech
9. Conner Kendrick, lhp, Auburn
10. Tyler Webb, lhp, South Carolina
11. Kendall Coleman, of, Rockwall (Texas) HS
12. Philip Walby, rhp, San Diego State
13. Cale Coshow, rhp, Oklahoma Christian
14. Caleb Smith, lhp, Sam Houston State
15. Jordan Barnes, of, Northwest Mississippi CC
16. Ryan Butler, rhp, Central Piedmont (N.C.) CC
17. Hever Bueno, rhp, Westwood HS, Mesa, Ariz.
18. Dustin Fowler, of, West Laurens HS, Dexter, Ga.
19. Andy Beresford, rhp, Nevada-Las Vegas
20. Drew Bridges, 3b, Carthage (Mo.) HS
21. Ethan Carnes, lhp, Oklahoma
22. Derek Toadvine, 2b, Kent State
23. Alex Polanco, rhp, Western Oklahoma State JC
24. Sam Agnew-Wieland, rhp, Appalachian State
25. Jordan Floyd, lhp, Shawnee Heights HS, Tecumseh, Kan.
26. Cal Quantrill, rhp, Trinity College School, Port Hope, Ont.
27. Dillon McNamara, rhp, Adelphi (N.Y.)
28. Trent Garrison, c, Fresno State
29. Charlie White, of, Maryland
30. Cody Thomas, of, Colleyville (Texas) Heritage HS
31. Kevin Cornelius, ss, Grayson County (Texas) CC
32. Chaunsey Sumner, 3b, Hawaii Pacific
33. Shane McCarley, rhp, Manvel (Texas) HS
34. Hector Crespo, 2b, Appalachian State
35. Nick Green, rhp, Fountain-Fort Carson HS, Fountain, Colo.
36. Nestor Cortes, lhp, Hialeah (Fla.) HS
37. Josh Pettitte, rhp, Deer Park (Texas) HS
38. Andrew Schmidt, of, Regis Jesuit HS, Aurora, Colo.
39. Ty Afenir, ss, Washington
40. Kyle Buchanan, of, Florida Gulf Coast

OAKLAND ATHLETICS (25)

1. Billy McKinney, of, Plano (Texas) West HS
2. Dillon Overton, lhp, Oklahoma
2s. Chad Pinder, ss, Virginia Tech (Competitive balance selection)

3. **Ryon Healy, 1b, Oregon**
3s. **Chris Kohler, lhp, Los Osos HS, Rancho Cuca., Calif.**
(Compensation pick for failure to sign 2012 third-round pick Kyle Twomey)
4. **Dylan Covey, rhp, San Diego**
5. **Bobby Wahl, rhp, Mississippi**
6. **Kyle Finnegan, rhp, Texas State**
7. **Dustin Driver, rhp, Wenatchee (Wash.) HS**
8. **Tyler Marincov, of, North Florida**
9. **Matt Stalcup, lhp, Pittsburg State (Kan.)**
10. **Jerad Grundy, lhp, Kentucky**
11. **Lou Trivino, rhp, Slippery Rock (Pa.)**
12. **Dakota Freese, rhp, Des Moines Area CC**
13. **Justin Higley, of, Sacramento State**
14. James Lomangino, rhp, St. John's
15. **Edwin Diaz, ss, Martine HS, Vega Alta, P.R.**
16. **Junior Mendez, rhp, Southern New Hampshire**
17. **Jaycob Brugman, of, Brigham Young**
18. **Sam Bragg, rhp, Georgia Perimeter JC**
19. A.J. Vanegas, rhp, Stanford
20. **Iolana Akau, c, St. Louis HS, Honolulu**
21. **Scott Masik, of, Cal State Los Angeles**
22. **Trevor Bayless, rhp, San Diego**
23. **Josh Miller, c, South Carolina-Aiken**
24. **Kevin Johnson, rhp, Illinois**
25. **Jon Massad, rhp, Southern New Hampshire**
26. **Kyle Wheeler, c, Belhaven (Miss.)**
27. **Ryan Huck, 1b, Western Kentucky**
28. **Joe Bennie, 2b, East Stroudsburg (Pa.)**
29. **Blake McMullen, rhp, Science and Arts of Oklahoma**
30. **Ben McQuown, of, Campbell**
31. **A.J. Burke, rhp, Western Oregon**
32. **Dominique Vattuone, rhp, UNC Greensboro**
33. **Joe Michaud, rhp, Bryant**
34. **A.J. Kubala, 1b, Arlington Country Day HS, Jacksonville**
35. A.J. Puckett, rhp, De La Salle HS, Concord, Calif.
36. **Cooper Goldby, c, Yuba City (Calif.) HS**
37. Francis Christy, c, Casa Grande HS, Petaluma, Calif.
38. Hunter Mercado-Hood, of, De La Salle HS, Concord, Calif.
39. Hayden Howard, lhp, Seward County (Kan.) CC
40. Dominic Miroglio, c, Bishop O'Dowd HS, Oakland

PHILADELPHIA PHILLIES (15)

1. **J.P. Crawford, ss, Lakewood (Calif.) HS**
2. **Andrew Knapp, c, California**
3. **Cord Sandberg, of, Manatee HS, Bradenton, Fla.**
(Compensation pick for failure to sign 2012 second-round pick Alec Rash)
3. **Jan Hernandez, ss, Beltran Academy, Florida, P.R.**
4. **Jake Sweaney, c, Garces HS, Bakersfield, Calif.**
5. Ben Wetzler, lhp, Oregon State
6. Jason Monda, of, Washington State
7. **Trey Williams, 3b, JC of the Canyons (Calif.)**
8. **Justin Parr, of, Illinois**
9. **Shane Martin, rhp, Southwestern Oklahoma State**
10. **Jon Prosinski, rhp, Seton Hall**
11. **Denton Keys, lhp, Rye (Colo.) HS**
12. Griffin Jax, rhp, Cherry Creek HS, Greenwood Village, Colo.
13. Joey Martarano, 3b, Fruitland (Idaho) HS
14. **Sam Dove, 2b, Georgia Tech**
15. **Logan Pierce, 3b, Troy**
16. **Lee Ridenhour, rhp, Austin Peay State**
17. **Rob Marcello, lhp, Appalachian State**
18. **Dan Child, rhp, Oregon State**
19. **Matt Soren, rhp, Delaware**
20. **Corey Bass, c, North Florida**
21. **Mark Meadors, rhp, Cowley County (Kan.) CC**
22. **Mark Leiter Jr., rhp, New Jersey Tech**
23. **Chris O'Hare, lhp, Fisher (Mass.)**
24. **Will Morris, rhp, JC of Southern Nevada**
25. **Cody Forsythe, lhp, Southern Illinois**

26. **Chris Burgess, rhp, Oklahoma Christian**
27. **Tyler Buckley, rhp, Arkansas-Little Rock**
28. **Matt Southard, rhp, Yavapai (Ariz.) JC**
29. Cavan Biggio, 2b, St. Thomas HS, Houston
30. **Venn Biter, of, Rossview HS, Clarksville, Tenn.**
31. Matt Grimes, rhp, Georgia Tech
32. **Tyler Viza, rhp, Desert Vista HS, Phoenix**
33. Harrison Musgrave, lhp, West Virginia
34. **David Whitehead, rhp, Elon**
35. **Nick Ferdinand, of, Delaware**
36. Dalton Dulin, 2b, Memphis University HS
37. Ryley MacEachern, rhp, Salisbury (Conn.) School
38. Dimitri Casas, rhp, Cherry Creek HS, Greenwood Village, Colo.
39. Brandon Wagner, 3b, Immaculata HS, Somerville, N.J.
40. Jose Haros, ss, San Fernando (Calif.) HS

PITTSBURGH PIRATES (13)

1. **Austin Meadows, of, Grayson HS, Loganville, Ga.**
(Compensation pick for failure to sign 2012 first-round pick Mark Appel)
1. **Reese McGuire, c, Kentwood HS, Covington, Wash.**
2. **Blake Taylor, lhp, Dana Hills HS, Dana Point, Calif.**
3. **JaCoby Jones, of, Louisiana State**
4. **Cody Dickson, lhp, Sam Houston State**
5. **Trae Arbet, ss, Great Oak HS, Temecula, Calif.**
6. **Adam Frazier, ss, Mississippi State**
7. **Buddy Borden, rhp, Nevada-Las Vegas**
8. **Neil Kozikowski, rhp, Avon (Conn.) Old Farms School**
9. **Chad Kuhl, rhp, Delaware**
10. **Shane Carle, rhp, Long Beach State**
11. **Erich Weiss, 3b, Texas**
12. **Beau Wallace, 3b, Hinds (Miss.) CC**
13. **Danny Collins, 1b, Troy**
14. **Nick Buckner, of, North Shore HS, Houston**
15. **Max Rossiter, c, Arizona State**
16. **Billy Roth, rhp, Vista (Calif.) HS**
17. **Justin Topa, rhp, Long Island-Brooklyn**
18. **Jeff Roy, of, Rhode Island**
19. **Brett McKinney, rhp, Ohio State**
20. Ryan Lindemuth, 2b, William & Mary
21. **Adam Landecker, 2b, Southern California**
22. **Henry Hirsch, rhp, New Haven (Conn.)**
23. **Cameron Griffin, lhp, Stetson**
24. Carson Cross, rhp, Connecticut
25. **Justin Maffei, of, San Francisco**
26. Grant Tyndall, of, South Lenoir HS, Deep Run, N.C.
27. **Mike Fransoso, ss, Maine**
28. **Jerry Mulderig, rhp, Rider**
29. Jake Stinnett, rhp, Maryland
30. **Will Kendall, lhp, Auburn**
31. Tevin Johnson, of, Gulf Coast (Fla.) CC
32. Christian Ibarra, 3b, Louisiana State
33. Reagan Bazar, rhp, Salado HS, South Bell, Texas
34. Connor Goedert, 3b, Neosho County (Kan.) CC
35. Cody Beam, rhp, Dallas Baptist
36. Scot Hoffman, rhp, South Mountain (Ariz.) CC
37. **Andrew Dennis, c, Wallace State (Ala.) CC**
38. Luke Voiron, c, Delgado (La.) CC
39. Jacob Smigelski, rhp, UC Riverside
40. Bryan Baker, rhp, Choctawhatchee HS, Fort Walton Beach, Fla.

ST. LOUIS CARDINALS (19)

1. **Marco Gonzales, lhp, Gonzaga**
1. **Rob Kaminsky, lhp, Saint Joseph Regional HS, Montvale, N.J.**
(Compensation pick for loss of free agent Kyle Lohse)
2. **Oscar Mercado, ss, Gaither HS, Tampa**
3. **Mike Mayers, rhp, Mississippi**
4. **Mason Katz, 2b, Louisiana State**
5. **Ian McKinney, lhp, Boone HS, Orlando**
6. **Jimmy Reed, lhp, Maryland**

DRAFT

7. Chris Rivera, ss, El Dorado HS, Placentia, Calif.
8. Andrew Pierce, rhp, Southern Mississippi
9. Nick Petree, rhp, Missouri State
10. Malik Collymore, ss, Port Credit SS, Mississauga, Ont.
11. Steven Farinaro, rhp, Head Royce HS, Oakland
12. Ricardo Bautista, of, Martinez HS, Vega Alta, P.R.
13. Jimmy Bosco, of, Menlo (Calif.)
14. Elier Rodriguez, c, Immaculata-LaSalle HS, Miami
15. De'Andre Asbury, of, Brookland-Cayce HS, Cayce, S.C.
16. Blake Higgins, rhp, Jackson (Mich.) CC
17. Richy Pedroza, ss, Cal State Fullerton
18. J.J. Altobelli, ss, Oregon
19. Michael Schulze, ss, Missouri Western State
20. Chase Brookshire, lhp, Belmont
21. Zach Loraine, rhp, Coker (S.C.)
22. Luke Voit, c, Missouri State
23. Alex DeLeon, c, Kansas
24. Devante Lacy, of, Cedar Valley (Texas) JC
25. Michael Holback, rhp, Cal Poly
26. Will Anderson, rhp, Fresno State
27. Jake Stone, 1b, Tennessee Wesleyan
28. Justin Ringo, 1b, Stanford
29. Bryan Radziewski, lhp, Miami
30. Trey Nielsen, rhp, Utah
31. Calvin Munson, rhp, Howell HS, St. Charles, Mo.
32. Kyle Webb, rhp, Elon
33. Nick Frey, rhp, Texas Christian
34. Nick Lomascolo, lhp, Catawba (N.C.)
35. Vaughn Bryan, of, Broward (Fla.) CC
36. Anthony Ray, of, St. Rita HS, Chicago
37. Alan Kruzel, 2b, Sinclair (Ohio) CC
38. Blake McKnight, rhp, Evangel (Mo.)
39. Kevin Herget, rhp, Kean (N.J.)
40. Artie Reyes, rhp, Gonzaga

SAN DIEGO PADRES (12)

1. Hunter Renfroe, of, Mississippi State
2. Dustin Peterson, ss, Gilbert (Ariz.) HS
2s. Jordan Paroubeck, of, Serra HS, San Mateo, Calif. (Competitive balance selection)
3. Bryan Verbitsky, rhp, Hofstra
4. Mason Smith, of, Rocky Mtn. HS, Meridian, Idaho
5. Josh VanMeter, of, Norwell HS, Ossian, Ind.
6. Trevor Gott, rhp, Kentucky
7. Jake Bauers, 1b, Marina HS, Huntington Beach, Calif.
8. Adrian De Horta, rhp, South Hills HS, West Covina, Calif.
9. Adam Cimber, rhp, San Francisco
10. Justin Livengood, rhp, UNC Wilmington
11. Erik Schoenrock, lhp, Memphis
12. Rod Boykin, of, Edgewood Academy, Elmore, Ala.
13. Travis Remillard, rhp, NE Oklahoma A&M JC
14. Ryan Miller, c, San Bernardino Valley (Calif.) JC
15. Tyler Dial, c, Gulf Coast State (Fla.) JC
16. Payton Baskette, lhp, Grayson County (Texas) CC
17. Trae Santos, 1b, Troy
18. Brandon Fry, lhp, Pearl River (Miss.) CC
19. Christian Summers, ss, Angelo State (Texas)
20. Michael Miller, c, Dallas Baptist
21. Connor Jones, rhp, Great Bridge HS, Chesapeake, Va.
22. Chase Jensen, ss, Oklahoma City
23. Chris Long, rhp, Darton State (Ga.) JC
24. Marcus Davis, of, Florida State
25. Tony Rizzotti, rhp, Tulane
26. Josh Richardson, rhp, Liberty
27. Michael Bass, 2b, UNC Wilmington
28. Jace Chancellor, rhp, Lubbock Christian (Texas)
29. Kyle Lloyd, rhp, Evansville
30. Jason Jester, rhp, Texas A&M
31. Chris Okey, c, Eustis (Fla.) HS
32. Max Beatty, rhp, Pacific Lutheran (Wash.)
33. Garrett Williams, lhp, Calvary Academy, Shreveport, La.

34. Sean Carley, rhp, West Virginia
35. Taylor Blair, rhp, Lexington (Ky.) Christian HS
36. Cornelius Copeland, ss, Lakewood HS, St. Petersburg, Fla.
37. Jeffery Enloe, lhp, Central Arkansas
38. Peter Kelich, rhp, Bryant
39. Brock Carpenter, ss, Fife (Wash.) HS
40. Chris Thibideau, ss, Vauxhall HS, Alberta, Canada

SAN FRANCISCO GIANTS (26)

1. Christian Arroyo, ss, Hernando HS, Brooksville, Fla.
2. Ryder Jones, 3b, Watauga HS, Boone, N.C.
3. Chase Johnson, rhp, Cal Poly
4. Brian Ragira, 1b, Stanford
5. Dan Slania, rhp, Notre Dame
6. Nick Vander Tuig, rhp, UCLA
7. Brandon Bednar, ss, Florida Gulf Coast
8. Tyler Horan, of, Virginia Tech
9. D.J. Snelten, lhp, Minnesota
10. Tyler Rogers, rhp, Austin Peay State
11. Johneshwy Fargas, of, Puerto Rico Baseball Academy, Gurabo, P.R.
12. Ty Ross, c, Louisiana State
13. Pat Young, rhp, Villanova
14. Nick Jones, lhp, Chattahoochee Valley (Ala.) CC
15. Geno Escalante, c, Mount Olive (N.C.)
16. Jonah Arenado, 3b, El Toro HS, Lake Forest, Calif.
17. Rene Melendez, c, Caguas (P.R.) Military Academy
18. Christian Jones, lhp, Oregon
19. Garrett Hughes, lhp, Stanford
20. Brett Kay, ss, Illinois State
21. Caleb Simpson, rhp, Seminole State (Okla.) JC
22. Ethan Miller, rhp, San Diego State
23. Brandon Zajac, lhp, Cleveland State (Tenn.) CC
24. Nick Gonzalez, lhp, South Florida
25. Blake Miller, ss, Western Oregon
26. Jake McCasland, rhp, New Mexico
27. Mike Connolly, rhp, Maine
28. Dusten Knight, rhp, Texas-Pan American
29. Ryan Tuntland, 3b, West Virginia
30. Dylan Brooks, rhp, Lord Dorchester SS, North Dorchester, Ont.
31. John Riley, c, Willow Glen HS, San Jose
32. Nick Cieri, c, Rancocas Valley Regional HS, Mount Holly, N.J.
33. Craig Massoni, 1b, Austin Peay State
34. Rayan Hernandez, rhp, Puerto Rico Baseball Academy, Gurabo, P.R.
35. Aubrey McCarty, 1b, Colquitt County HS, Moultrie, Ga.
36. Grant Goodman, rhp, Burlingame (Calif.) HS
37. Will Callaway, 2b, Appalachian State
38. Osvaldo Garcia, rhp, Miami Southridge HS
39. Chris Viall, rhp, Soquel (Calif.) HS
40. Ryan Kirby, of, Granada HS, Livermore, Calif.

SEATTLE MARINERS (11)

1. D.J. Peterson, 3b, New Mexico
2. Austin Wilson, of, Stanford
3. Tyler O'Neill, of, Garibaldi SS, Maple Ridge, B.C.
4. Ryan Horstman, lhp, St. John's
5. Jack Reinheimer, ss, East Carolina
6. Corey Simpson, of, Sweeny (Texas) HS
7. Tyler Olson, lhp, Gonzaga
8. Tyler Smith, ss, Oregon State
9. Jake Zokan, lhp, College of Charleston
10. Emilio Pagan, rhp, Belmont Abbey (N.C.)
11. Zack Littell, rhp, Eastern Alamance HS, Mebane, N.C.
12. Justin Seager, 1b, Charlotte
13. Lachlan Fontaine, 3b, Sutherland SS, North Vancouver, B.C.
14. Ian Miller, of, Wagner
15. Eddie Campbell, lhp, Virginia Tech
16. Lonnie Kauppila, ss, Stanford
17. Paul Fry, lhp, St. Clair County (Mich.) CC

18. Troy Scott, rhp, Riverside (Calif.) CC
19. Jeff Zimmerman, 1b, Northern Illinois
20. Dan Torres, c, St. Leo (Fla.)
21. Brett Thomas, of, Oregon
22. Tommy Burns, rhp, Howard (Texas) JC
23. Kyle Petty, 1b, California (Pa.)
24. Kevin McCoy, rhp, Kennesaw State
25. Will Mathis, lhp, New Mexico
26. Tyler Wright, lhp, Arkansas
27. Ricky Claudio, rhp, St. Thomas (Fla.)
28. Zach Shank, ss, Marist
29. Chantz Mack, of, Miami
30. Rafael Pineda, rhp, Texas A&M
31. Michael Guzman, lhp, La Selva, Calif. (No school)
32. Nate Maggio, 1b, Blessed Trinity HS, Roswell, Ga.
33. Corey Ray, of, Simeon HS, Chicago
34. Taylor Snyder, 2b, Salem Hills HS, Salem, Utah
35. Marshawn Taylor, ss, Simeon HS, Chicago
36. JC Snyder, 3b, Salt Lake (Utah) CC
37. Jordan Cowan, ss, Kentlake HS, Kent, Wash.
38. Michael Sexton, 3b, Rogers HS, Puyallup, Wash.
39. Sam Hellinger, rhp, West Seattle HS
40. Mike McCann, c, Columbia River HS, Vancouver, Wash.

TAMPA BAY RAYS (22)

1. Nick Ciuffo, c, Lexington (S.C.) HS
1. Ryne Stanek, rhp, Arkansas (Compensation pick for loss of free agent B.J. Upton)
2. Riley Unroe, ss, Desert Ridge HS, Mesa, Ariz.
3. Thomas Milone, of, Masuk HS, Monroe, Conn.
4. Kean Wong, 2b, Waiakea HS, Hilo, Hawaii
5. Johnny Field, 2b, Arizona
6. Stephen Woods, rhp, Half Hollow Hills East HS, Dix Hills, N.Y.
7. Ty Young, 3b, Louisville
8. Roel Ramirez, rhp, United South HS, Laredo, Texas
9. Austin Pruitt, rhp, Houston
10. Aaron Griffin, rhp, Loyola Marymount
11. Hunter Lockwood, of, Weatherford (Texas) JC
12. Pat Blair, ss, Wake Forest
13. Ben Griset, lhp, St. Mary's
14. Jaime Schultz, rhp, High Point
15. Coty Blanchard, 2b, Jacksonville State
16. Darren Fischer, lhp, Central Florida CC
17. Willie Calhoun, 2b, Benicia (Calif.) HS
18. Julian Ridings, of, Western Carolina
19. Josh Kimborowicz, rhp, Everett (Wash.) CC
20. Harmen Sidhu, rhp, Sonoma State (Calif.)
21. John Farrell, rhp, William & Mary
22. Andrew Hanse, rhp, Iowa
23. Rick Teasley, lhp, St. Leo (Fla.)
24. Jeremy Hadley, of, Sachse (Texas) HS
25. Stone Speer, lhp, New Orleans
26. Christian Talley, rhp, Pearl River (Miss.) CC
27. Hyrum Formo, rhp, Pima (Ariz.) CC
28. Derek Loera, lhp, Lubbock Christian (Texas)
29. Hunter Wood, rhp, Howard (Texas) JC
30. Colton Reavis, rhp, Northwood (Texas)
31. Dalton Martinez, of, Dunedin (Fla.) HS
32. Anthony Tzamtzis, rhp, North Carolina State
33. Hector Montes, 3b, Southwestern (Calif.) JC
34. Devin Ceciliani, of, Madras (Ore.) HS
35. Cory Jordan, rhp, Grambling State
36. Ryan Moseley, rhp, Lubbock-Cooper HS, Lubbock, Texas
37. D.J. Slaton, rhp, San Jose State
38. David Sheaffer, c, North Surry HS, Mount Airy, N.C.
39. Johnny Meszaros, rhp, Service HS, Anchorage
40. Ryan Henley, 2b, Azusa Pacific (Calif.)

TEXAS RANGERS (24)

1. Alex Gonzalez, rhp, Oral Roberts
1. Travis Demeritte, ss, Winder-Barrow HS, Winder, Ga. (Compensation pick for loss of free agent Josh Hamilton)
2. Akeem Bostick, rhp, West Florence (S.C.) HS
3. David Ledbetter, rhp, Cedarville (Ohio)
4. Isiah Kiner-Falefa, ss, Mid-Pacific Institute, Honolulu
5. Joe Jackson, c, The Citadel
6. Sam Wolff, rhp, New Mexico
7. Nick Gardewine, rhp, Kaskaskia (Ill.) CC
8. Evan Van Hoosier, 2b, JC of Southern Nevada
9. Jose Samayoa, rhp, Lee (Tenn.)
10. Cole Wiper, rhp, Oregon
11. Ryan Cordell, of, Liberty
12. Derek Thompson, lhp, John A. Logan (Ill.) CC
13. Taylor Olmstead, of, Greenwich (Conn.) HS
14. Jarred Smith, rhp, Manatee (Fla.) JC
15. Cody Ege, lhp, Louisville
16. Marcus Greene, c, New Mexico JC
17. Sean Labsan, lhp, Riverview HS, Sarasota, Fla.
18. David Gates, rhp, Howard (Texas) JC
19. Ryan Ledbetter, rhp, Cedarville (Ohio)
20. Jackson Lamb, rhp, Bedford HS, Temperance, Mich.
21. Luke Lanphere, rhp, Citrus Valley HS, Redlands, Calif.
22. Zach Winn, rhp, Show Low (Ariz.) HS
23. Luis Pollorena, lhp, Mississippi State
24. Darryn Sheppard, of, Dulles HS, Sugar Land, Texas
25. Chris Dula, rhp, Catawba (N.C.)
26. Travis Dean, rhp, Kennesaw State
27. Sherman Lacrus, c, Western Oklahoma State JC
28. Ryan Williamson, lhp, Cranford (N.J.) HS
29. Justin Sprenger, rhp, Tennessee Wesleyan
30. Joe Palumbo, lhp, St. John the Baptist HS, West Islip, N.Y.
31. Michael Peterson, rhp, West Valley (Calif.) JC
32. John Straka, rhp, North Dakota State
33. Danny de la Calle, c, Miami Dade JC
34. Easton Napiontek, rhp, Lower Columbia (Wash.) JC
35. Buddy Reed, of, St. George's HS, Middletown, R.I.
36. Dakota Hudson, rhp, Sequatchie County HS, Dunlap, Tenn.
37. Cody Lavalli, of, Lewis-Clark State (Idaho)
38. Sheldon Neuse, ss, Fossil Ridge HS, Fort Worth
39. Jay Gonzalez, of, Auburn
40. Sal Mendez, lhp, Weehawken (N.J.) HS

TORONTO BLUE JAYS (9)

1. Phil Bickford, rhp, Oaks Christian HS, Westlake Village, Calif.
2. Clinton Hollon, rhp, Woodford Co. HS, Versailles, Ky.
3. Patrick Murphy, rhp, Hamilton HS, Chandler, Ariz.
4. Evan Smith, lhp, Montgomery HS, Semmes, Ala.
5. Daniel Lietz, lhp, Heartland (Ill.) CC
6. Matt Boyd, lhp, Oregon State
7. Conner Greene, rhp, Santa Monica (Calif.) HS
8. Kendall Graveman, rhp, Mississippi State
9. Chad Girodo, lhp, Mississippi State
10. Garrett Custons, c, Air Force
11. Jake Brentz, lhp, Parkway South HS, Manchester, Mo.
12. Tim Mayza, lhp, Millersville (Pa.)
13. Tim Locastro, ss, Ithaca (N.Y.)
14. L.B. Dantzler, 1b, South Carolina
15. Jonathan Davis, of, Central Arkansas
16. Danny Jansen, c, Appleton (Wis.) West HS
17. Eric Lauer, lhp, Midview HS, Grafton, Ohio
18. Sean Ratcliffe, rhp, Pickering HS, Ajax, Ont.
19. Christian Vazquez, ss, Lubbock Christian (Texas)
20. Chaz Frank, of, North Carolina
21. Mike Reeves, c, Florida Gulf Coast
22. Sam Tewes, rhp, Waverly (Neb.) HS
23. Brenden Kalfus, of, St. Mary's
24. Sean Hurley, of, Central Arizona JC
25. Scott Silverstein, lhp, Virginia

26. Tanner Cable, rhp, Northwest Mississippi CC
27. **Andrew Florides, ss, Holy Cross HS, Flushing, N.Y.**
28. **Matt Dermody, lhp, Iowa**
29. **Garrett Pickens, rhp, Delta State (Miss.)**
30. **Rowdy Tellez, 1b, Elk Grove (Calif.) HS**
31. Brison Celek, 1b, South Carolina
32. Josh Sawyer, lhp, Central HS, San Angelo, Texas
33. Edgar Cabral, c, Knight HS, Palmdale, Calif.
34. Dane Dunning, rhp, Clay HS, Green Cove Springs, Fla.
35. Akoni Arriaga, rhp, Baldwin HS, Wailuku, Hawaii
36. **David Harris, ss, Southern Arkansas**
37. **Brett Barber, rhp, Ohio**
38. Jon Nunnally, of, Horizon HS, Scottsdale, Ariz.
39. Zach Levinson, ss, Wagner HS, New York
40. Antonio Ruiz, 1b, San Gabriel (Calif.) HS

WASHINGTON NATIONALS (30)

1. (Pick forfeited for signing of free agent Rafael Soriano)
2. **Jake Johansen, rhp, Dallas Baptist**
3. **Drew Ward, 3b, Leedey (Okla.) HS**
4. **Nic Pivetta, rhp, New Mexico JC**
5. **Austin Voth, rhp, Washington**
6. **Cody Gunter, 3b, Grayson County (Texas) CC**
7. **Jimmy Yezzo, 1b, Delaware**
8. **David Napoli, lhp, Tulane**
9. **Jake Joyce, rhp, Virginia Tech**
10. **Brennan Middleton, ss, Tulane**
11. **John Simms, rhp, Rice**

12. **Andrew Cooper, rhp, Sierra (Calif.) JC**
13. **John Costa, rhp, Palm Beach State (Fla.) JC**
14. **David Masters, ss, Central Arizona JC**
15. **Isaac Ballou, of, Marshall**
16. Willie Allen, of, Western Oklahoma State JC
17. Geoff Perrott, c, Rice
18. **Cory Bafidis, lhp, Texas Wesleyan**
19. **Niko Spezial, lhp, Wake Forest**
20. **Brenton Allen, of, UCLA**
21. **Justin Thomas, lhp, Southern Arkansas**
22. **Cody Dent, ss, Florida**
23. **Garrett Gordon, of, Wabash Valley (Ill.) CC**
24. **Matt Derosier, rhp, Southwestern (Calif.) JC**
25. **Travis Ott, lhp, Shippensburg (Pa.)**
26. Garrett Hampson, ss, Reno (Nev.) HS
27. Bryce Harman, of, Bird HS, Richmond
28. **Joey Webb, lhp, Menlo (Calif.)**
29. **Mike Sylvestri, rhp, Florida Atlantic**
30. **Ryan Ullmann, rhp, Concordia (Texas)**
31. **Willie Medina, ss, High Point**
32. Pat Boling, lhp, Georgia
33. Andrew Dunlap, rhp, Houston (no school)
34. **Jake Walsh, lhp, Missouri**
35. Lukas Schiraldi, rhp, Navarro (Texas) JC
36. Reid Humphreys, ss, Northwest Rankin HS, Flowood, Miss.
37. Karsten Whitson, rhp, Florida
38. Caleb Hamilton, ss, Woodinville (Wash.) HS
39. Robbie Tenerowicz, 2b, Campolindo HS, Moraga, Calif.
40. Shaun Anderson, rhp, Amer. Heritage HS, Plantation, Fla.

APPENDIX

■ **Rogelio Alvarez,** a first baseman who played in parts of two seasons for the Reds, died Nov. 30, 2012, in Hialeah, Fla. He was 74.

Alvarez, a native of Cuba, started his pro career in 1956 in the Reds organization and reached the big leagues in 1960. Alvarez's only other big league experience came in September 1962, when he got into 14 games for the Reds and hit .214.

■ **Joe Astroth,** a catcher who played 10 seasons with the Philadelphia and Kansas City Athletics, died May 3 in Boca Raton, Fla. He was 90.

Astroth spent the first half of his career as a reserve but did surpass 80 games three times from 1952 to '55. He was a .254 lifetime hitter, the high point of his career coming in 1950, when he hit .327 with one homer in 110 at-bats. Astroth moved with the A's from Philadelphia to Kansas City in 1955, last playing in the majors in 1956.

■ **Boyd Bartley,** a shortstop who played in one major league season, died Dec. 21, 2012, in Fort Worth. He was 92.

Bartley signed with the Brooklyn Dodgers out of the University of Illinois in 1943 and went straight to the majors. He played in nine games for the Dodgers and had one hit and one RBI. He went on to work as a scout for the Dodgers, with Orel Hershiser his most notable signing.

■ **Matt Batts,** a catcher who played 10 seasons in the majors from 1947-56, died July 14 in Baton Rouge. He was 90.

Batts logged 546 games for five teams in a career spent primarily as a backup catcher. He played the first half of his career with the Red Sox after debuting in September 1947. The Red Sox traded him to the St. Louis Browns in May 1951, and he went on to play for the Tigers, White Sox and Reds through 1956. He topped 100 games played in a season only once, when he played 116 games for the Tigers in 1953, hitting .278 with six homers.

■ **Tom Borland,** a lefthander who pitched in two seasons with the Red Sox, died March 2 in Stillwater, Okla. He was 80.

Borland made 26 appearances, including four starts, for the 1960 Red Sox, going 0-4, 6.53 in 51 innings. He made only one appearance for Boston in 1961.

■ **Ed Bouchee,** a first baseman who played seven seasons in the major leagues form 1956-62, died Jan. 23 in Phoenix. He was 79.

Bouchee got off to a flying start in the majors, hitting .293 with 17 homers and 76 RBIs for the Phillies in 1957, his first full year in the big leagues. He finished second to teammate Jack

Sanford in the National League rookie of the year voting, but '57 would prove to be Bouchee's career year. The Phillies traded him to the Cubs in May 1960, and he played his final big league season in 1962 for the expansion Mets.

■ **Gates Brown,** an outfielder who played 13 seasons for the Tigers from 1963-75, died Sept. 27 in Detroit. He was 74.

Brown hit a pinch-hit home run in his first big league at-bat on June 19, 1963, and he went on to carve out a lengthy big league career largely on the strength of his pinch-hitting exploits. Brown slugged 16 career pinch-hit home runs, a figure that trails only Matt Stairs, Cliff Johnson, Jerry Lynch and John Vander Wal on the all-time list. His 107 career pinch-hits ranked in the top 10 all-time at the time of his retirement in 1975..

■ **Ellis Burton,** an outfielder who played in five major league seasons between 1958 and 1965, died Oct. 1 in Fontana, Calif. He was 77.

Burton worked as a reserve outfielder for the Cardinals, Indians and Cubs, getting most of his time with Chicago from 1963-65. He hit 13 homers for the Indians and Cubs in '63, his only season getting regular action.

■ **Rick Camp,** a righthander who pitched nine seasons with the Braves, died April 25 in Rydal, Ga. He was 59.

Camp pitched over 900 innings in the majors but was best known for something he did at the plate. On July 4, 1985, Camp, a career .074 hitter, came to bat in the bottom 18th inning against the Mets and hit a two-out, game-tying home run. It was the only home run of his career.

■ **Frank Castillo,** a righthander who pitched 13 seasons in the majors between 1991 and 2005, died July 28 in Bartlett Lake, Ariz. He was 44.

Castillo came up through the Cubs system after being their sixth-round pick in 1987 and debuted in the majors in 1991. He logged parts of seven seasons in Chicago's rotation from 1991-97. The Cubs traded him to the Rockies in July 1997, and he went on to pitch for the Tigers, Blue Jays, Red Sox and Marlins between 1998 and 2005.

■ **Bob Chance,** a first baseman who played in six big league seasons in the 1960s, died Oct. 2 in Charleston, W.Va. He was 73.

Chance was a reserve for most of his big league career, which began in 1963. He saw regular action only once, hitting .279 with 14 homers as the Indians' everyday first baseman in 1964.

■ **Neil Chrisley,** an outfielder who played five years in the majors from 1957-61, died May 18 in Conway, S.C. He was 81.

Used mostly as a utility outfielder, Chrisley surpassed 100 games played in a season only once in the majors, when he hit .215 with five homers in 105 games for the Washington Senators in 1958. He went on to play for the Tigers (1959-60) and Milwaukee Braves (1961).

■ **Jim Cosman,** a righthander who pitched in three big league seasons, died Jan. 7 in Sewickley, Pa. He was 69.

Cosman came up through the Cardinals system and made a splash in his big league debut on the final day of the 1966 season, pitching a two-hit shutout against the Cubs. He made 10 appearances, including five starts, for the Cardinals in 1967, going 1-0, 3.16 in 31 innings while spending most of the year back in the minors. He made only one more appearance in the big leagues, pitching one inning for the Cubs on April 30, 1970.

■ **Rocky Craig,** an outfielder who played in parts of four big league seasons between 1979 and 1986, died Aug. 17 in Los Angeles. He was 55.

Craig spent parts of two seasons with the Mariners from 1979-80 and later saw limited action with the 1982 Indians and 1986 White Sox.

■ **Jack Daniels,** an outfielder who played one season for the Boston Braves, died April 16 in Shreveport, La. He was 85.

Daniels played 13 years of pro ball, but his only experience in the majors came in 1952. He appeared in 106 games but hit just .187 with two homers in 219 at-bats.

■ **Mike Davison,** a lefthander who pitched in parts of two seasons for the Giants, died May 11 in Glencoe, Minn. He was 67.

Davison reached the majors at the tail end of the 1969 season, making his big league debut for the Giants on Oct. 1. He was a regular piece of the Giants' middle-relief corps in 1970, making 31 appearances and going 3-5, 6.50 in 36 innings.

■ **Ellis "Cot" Deal,** a righthander who pitched in parts of four major league seasons, died May 21 in Oklahoma City. He was 90.

Deal made a handful of appearances for the Red Sox in 1947 and '48, then was traded to the Cardinals in 1949. He got back to the majors to make three appearances for St. Louis in 1950. He didn't pitch in the majors again until 1954, when he spent the entire season with the Cardinals and made 33 appearances, all in relief, going 2-3, 6.28 in 72 innings.

■ **Robert "Ducky" Detweiler,** a third baseman who played in parts of two big league seasons, died March 17 in Easton, Md. He was 94.

Detweiler worked his way up to the majors

with the Boston Braves in 1942, when he was a late-season callup. He also made one appearance for the '46 Braves.

■ **Harry Elliott,** an outfielder who played in parts of two seasons with the Cardinals, died Aug. 9 in Little Falls, Kan. He was 89.

Elliott was 29 years old when he reached the majors for the first time with St. Louis in August 1953. He appeared in 24 games over the remainder of the season and hit .254 with one homer. Elliott didn't get back to the majors until 1955 when the Cardinals played him in 68 games and he hit .256 with 12 RBIs.

■ **Eddie Erautt,** a righthander who pitched in six major league seasons between 1947 and 1953, died Oct. 27 in La Mesa, Calif. He was 89.

Erautt made all but 20 of his 164 big league appearances with the Reds, seeing regular action out of their bullpen from 1947-51. He had his best year in 1949, posting a 3.36 RA over 113 innings and 39 appearances, including nine starts.

■ **Ron Fraser,** the legendary former head coach at the University of Miami, died Jan. 20 in Weston, Fla. He was 79.

Fraser is one of the most significant figures in the history of college baseball for his efforts to raise the sport's profile, in addition to establishing the Hurricanes as a college baseball power. Fraser led Miami to 12 College World Series appearances and two national titles, in 1982 and '85. He retired as the third winningest coach in NCAA history with a 1271-438-9 record.

■ **Ryan Freel,** an outfielder who played eight seasons in the majors through 2009, died Dec. 22, 2012, in Jacksonville in an apparent suicide. He was 36.

A 10th-round pick of the Blue Jays in 1995, Freel made his big league debut with Toronto in 2001, but he was best known for his time with the Reds from 2003-08. Freel stood out for his versatility—playing second base, third base and all three outfield spots during his career—and his all-out style, though it contributed to his career being plagued by injuries. Freel stole 36 and 37 bases in 2005 and '06, respectively, but injuries began taking their toll afterward. He left the big leagues with a .268 career average, 22 homers and 143 stolen bases.

■ **Gene Freese,** a third baseman who played in the majors from 1955-66, died June 19 in New Orleans. He was 79.

Freese had a well-travelled career, playing for six major league teams in 12 seasons. A .254 career hitter, he did have a couple big seasons, hitting 23 homers for the Phillies in 1959 and a career-best 26 for the Reds in 1961. Unfortunately, he wasn't able to build on that season, as he missed most of the '62 season after breaking his ankle during spring training. He hit just 19 home runs from 1962-66 combined, finishing his career with the Astros in 1966.

■ **Joe Ginsberg,** a catcher who played 13 seasons in the major leagues between 1948 and '62, died Nov. 2, 2012, in West Bloomfield, Mich. He was 86.

Ginsberg was a reserve for most of his big league career, which saw him play for seven different teams in 13 seasons. He originally got to the majors with the Tigers in 1948 was Detroit's regular catcher for two seasons in 1951 and '52. He hit .260 with eight homers in 304 at-bats in '51, but his average dipped to .221 over 307 at-bats in '52, and those would be his only big league seasons with more than 300 plate appearances.

After stints with the Indians and Kansas City Athletics from 1953-56, Ginsberg played five seasons for the Orioles from 1956-60, during which he posted a cumulative .219 average. He finished out his career with stops with the White Sox, Red Sox and Mets.

■ **Bill Glynn,** a first baseman who played in parts of four major league seasons between 1949 and '54, died Jan. 15 in San Diego. He was 87.

Glynn first made it to the majors with the Phillies in 1949, appearing in eight games, but he didn't see his first meaningful action until 1952 at age 26, when he hit .272 with two homers in 92 at-bats for the Indians. He saw regular action in 1953, hitting .243 with three homers, and in '54, when he hit .251 with five homers. Glynn's final big league action occurred in the 1954 World Series, during which he appeared in two games, both as a pinch-hitter, and went 2-for-2 at the plate as the Indians were swept by the New York Giants. He continued playing Triple-A ball through 1958.

■ **Lonnie Goldstein,** a first baseman who played in parts of two big league seasons, died Jan. 28 in Fort Worth. He was 92.

Goldstein played 15 seasons of pro ball but only appeared briefly in the big leagues. He got into five games as a late-season callup for the Reds in 1943, then he went into the military and missed most of the next two seasons. He got back to the Reds in 1946, appearing in six games, but that was his last big league experience. He continued playing in the minors through 1955.

■ **Dick Gray,** a third baseman who played in

parts of three big league seasons from 1958-60, died July 8 in Anaheim. He was 81.

Gray's greatest claim to fame is that he hit the newly relocated Los Angeles Dodgers' first-ever home run on April 16, 1958, against the Giants. Gray made his big league debut that season as the Dodgers' Opening Day third baseman and hit .249 with nine homers before being sent back to the minors in July. He returned to Los Angeles in 1959 but was dealt to the Cardinals that June, hitting a combined .233, and he played just nine games for St. Louis in 1960. Gray finished out his career in the minors in 1962.

■ **Charles "Bubba" Harris,** a righthander who pitched in three major league seasons, died Jan. 12 in Nobleton, Fla. He was 86.

Harris got to the majors for the first time with the Philadelphia Athletics in 1948. He worked as a starter at times in the minors but was exclusively a reliever in the big leagues, beginning with his 5-2, 4.13 line over 45 appearances in '48. He went 1-1, 5.44 in 84 relief innings for the A's in 1949, which would be his last full year in the majors. His only other big league time came in 1951, when he made five combined appearances with the A's and Indians.

■ **Jack Harshman,** a lefthander and first baseman who played in 10 big league seasons, died Aug. 17 in Georgetown, Texas. He was 86.

Harshman originally reached the majors as a power-hitting first baseman for the New York Giants in 1948. He won three minor league home run titles in his career, twice hitting over 40, but he went just 6-for-42 (.143) in big league action between 1948 and '52. He began seeing increasing time on the mound while with Minneapolis (American Association) in 1952 and then went 23-7, 3.27 for Nashville (Southern Association) in '53. The White Sox purchased him from the Giants in September 1953 and he returned to the majors as a full-time pitcher in '54.

Harshman spent four years in the White Sox rotation from 1954-57, his best year coming in '54 when he went 14-8, 2.95 in 177 innings. He finished in the top 10 in the American League in ERA three times, including a third-place finish in 1958 with the Orioles after going 12-15, 2.89.

■ **Grady Hatton,** a third baseman who played 12 seasons in the majors and was a big-league manager for three, died April 11 in Warren, Texas. He was 90.

The Reds signed Hatton out of the military after World War II and he went straight to the big leagues with no prior professional experience. The

Reds installed him as their regular third baseman in 1946 and he hit a solid .271 with 14 homers as a rookie. He had his best offensive season in 1947 when he hit a career-high 16 homers to go with a .281 average. His numbers never got back to those levels, though he remained a regular spot in the Reds' lineup through 1953, shifting from third base to second in 1952.

After eight seasons in Cincinnati, Hatton was traded twice in just over a month in 1954, first going from the Reds to the White Sox and then to the Red Sox. His big league career effectively ended with the Orioles in 1956, and he subsequently got into managing in the Cubs organization, though they briefly brought him back as a player in 1960 and he appeared in 28 games. He did make it to the majors as a manager with the Astros from 1966-68 but went 164-221.

■ **Enzo Hernandez,** a shortstop who played eight seasons in the majors from 1971-78, died Jan. 13 in El Tigre, Venezuela. He was 63.

Hernandez was the Padres' everyday shortstop for most of the early 1970s. He began his pro career in the Astros organization but was traded twice while in the minors, getting his first big league chance with San Diego in 1971. He was best known for his defensive prowess, and he was just a .224 career hitter and had only one season in which he hit more than .240, when he hit .256 in 1976. He did finish in the top 10 in the National League in stolen bases three times, peaking at 37 in 1974. He was limited to just seven games in 1977 and the Padres released him during '78 spring training. He latched on with the Dodgers but appeared in just four games in the 1978 season.

■ **Chuck Hinton,** an outfielder who played 11 years in the majors from 1961-71, died Jan. 27 in Washington. He was 78.

Hinton was coming up through the Orioles system when the Washington Senators selected him in the 1960 expansion draft, and he made his big league debut the following year. Hinton's second season was his best, when he hit .310 with 17 homers in 1962, but he continued putting up solid numbers in what was pitching-dominated era. He hit .275/.343/.434 collectively from 1962-66 and made the AL all-star team in 1964. However, Hinton didn't make the majors until he was 27 years old, having served two years in the military while he was in the minors, and his production began tailing off after 1966, when he was 32. He had been traded from the Senators to the Indians after his all-star season in 1964 and spent the rest of his career in Cleveland, save for one season with

the California Angels in 1968. Hinton hit 113 home runs for his career and also registered 130 stolen bases.

■ **Glen Hobbie,** a righthander who pitched eight years in the big leagues from 1957-64, died Aug. 9 in Springfield, Ill. He was 77.

Hobbie was just 21 when he made his big league debut for the Cubs at the tail end of the 1957 season, and he stayed with Chicago full-time starting in 1958. He began pitching primarily in the Cubs' rotation in 1959 and finished 10th in the National League in strikeouts that year with 138 while going 16-13, 3.69. Hobbie won 16 games again in 1960, but he also lost a league-worst 20. Hobbie, who threw 259 innings in 1960, never won more than seven games in a season again and his career was ultimately derailed by shoulder problems.

■ **Larry Johnson,** a catcher who played in parts of five big league seasons in the 1970s, died May 26 in Tampa. He was 62.

Johnson had a long pro career, playing in the minors from 1968-81, then briefly coming back in the Mexican League in 1992. His big league experience consisted of 12 appearances between 1972 and 1978, in which he went 5-for-26 at the plate. He got his longest big league exposure in 1976, playing in six games for the Montreal Expos. Johnson also appeared in single games for the Indians in 1972 and '74, one game for the Expos in 1975 and three games for the 1978 White Sox.

■ **Paul Keyes,** the head baseball coach at Virginia Commonwealth, died Nov. 3, 2012, after a battle with cancer. He was 50.

Keyes was VCU's head coach for the past 18 seasons, making eight trips to the NCAA tournament and capturing five Colonial Athletic Association titles. He compiled a 603-428-1 record, including 12 consecutive winning seasons from 1996-2007, and won four CAA coach of the year awards. VCU produced six major leaguers under Keyes, most notably Brandon Inge and Sean Marshall, and a total of 36 of his players went on to pro ball.

■ **Dan Kravitz,** a catcher who played five years in the big leagues from 1956-60, died June 19 in Danville, Pa. He was 82.

Kravitz didn't reach the majors until he was 25 in part because he missed two years in the minors to serve in the military. He logged four years as a reserve catcher for the Pirates from 1956-59, putting up a cumulative .240 average with six homers in 371 at-bats over that time. The Pirates traded him to the Kansas City Athletics in June 1960, and he got the most playing time of his big league career over the remainder of that season, appearing in 59 games for the A's and hitting .234 with four homers. The A's dealt him to the Reds after the '60 season, but he played out the rest of his career in the minors.

■ **Brad "Animal" Lesley,** a righthander who pitched four seasons in the majors, died April 27 in Marina del Rey, Calif. He was 54.

Lesley burst onto the scene in 1982, when he had a 2.58 ERA and four saves as a 23-year-old rookie with the Reds. That was the peak of his big league career, though, as he only pitched in 26 more big league games over the next three years before going over to Japan and playing two seasons there. Lesley became much better known for his unusual antics more so than his pitching, ranging from his demonstrative behavior on the mound to his appearing on a comedy television show in Japan. His baseball career ended in 1987 but he continued to pursue acting, including appearing as a pitcher in the 1994 movie "Little Big League."

■ **Johnny Logan,** a shortstop who was a four-time all-star for the Milwaukee Braves, died Aug. 9 in Milwaukee. He was 86.

Hank Aaron and Eddie Mathews were bigger stars for the 1950s Braves, but Logan was one of the team's emotional leaders. He didn't reach the majors until he was 25 in 1951, but he took over as the Braves' everyday shortstop in 1952, their last season in Boston, and led NL shortstops in fielding percentage in each of his first three full years from 1952-54. He had his best offensive season in 1955 and made his first all-star team, batting .297 with 13 homers and an NL-best 37 doubles. Logan cracked double digits in homers for five straight years from 1955-59, peaking with 15 in 1956.

■ **Stan Lopata,** a catcher who was a two-time all-star for the Phillies, died June 15 in Philadelphia. He was 87.

Lopata reached the majors as a 22-year-old in 1948 but spent most of the first half of this career splitting time with Andy Seminick and then Smoky Burgess, never playing in more than 86 games in a season until 1955, his eighth year in the majors. Lopata made the most of his chances in 1954, batting .290 with 14 homers in 259 at-bats, and he broke through to his first All-Star Game when given the bulk of the catching duties in 1955, belting 22 homers to go with a .271 average in 303 at-bats. He continued putting up big power numbers in 1945, finishing eighth in the National League with 32 homers and making another all-star trip. His production began dropping off after 1956.

■ **Boris "Babe" Martin,** a catcher who played in parts of six big league seasons, died Aug. 1 in Tucson. He was 93.

Martin's pro career spanned 1940 to 1954, missing one season due to military service. He appeared in 69 big league games between 1944 and 1953, his only extensive big league time coming in 1945. Martin got into 54 games for the St. Louis Browns in '45 and batted .200 with two homers in 185 at-bats.

■ **Ray Martin,** a righthander who pitched in three big league seasons, died March 7 in Norwood, Mass. He was 87.

Martin debuted with the Boston Braves in 1943 shortly after signing with them as an 18-year-old, pitching in two games. He then went into the military and didn't get back to the majors until 1947. He got into one game for the Braves in '47 and two in '48 while spending the rest of his time in the minors.

■ **Justin Miller,** a righthander who pitched in seven major league seasons, died June 26 in Palm Harbor, Fla. He was 35.

Miller made 25 appearances, including 18 starts for the Blue Jays in 2002, going 9-5, 5.54. Miller missed most of the 2003 season with a shoulder injury before returning to go 3-4, 6.06 for the Blue Jays in 2004. The Blue Jays released Miller in July 2005, and he didn't resurface in the majors again until 2007 with the Marlins. Now a full-time reliever, Miller logged 62 innings with a 3.65 ERA for the Marlins in 2007. He continued to pitch well out of the bullpen over the next three years for the Marlins, Giants and Dodgers, posting a cumulative 3.81 ERA from 2008-10.

■ **Rudy Minarcin,** a righthander who pitched in parts of three big league seasons from 1955-57, died Oct. 15 in Cabot, Pa. He was 83.

Minarcin logged 115 innings for the Reds in 1955, going 5-9, 4.90 while splitting time as a starter and reliever. He was sold to the Red Sox in 1956 and pitched just 54 innings over his final two seasons in the majors from 1956-57.

■ **Stan Musial,** a Hall of Fame outfielder and one of the greatest hitters of all time, died Jan. 19 in Ladue, Mo. He was 92.

Musial made his big league debut with the Cardinals as a 20-year-old in September 1941. He took off almost immediately, hitting .315/.397/.490 in his first full season in 1942 as St. Louis won the World Series. He led the National League in all three slash categories in 1943, batting .357/.425/.562, on his way to capturing his first of three NL MVP awards. After Musial's Cardinals won another title in 1944, he missed the '45 season while serving in the U.S. Navy. He didn't skip a beat after returning the Cardinals in 1946, winning his second batting title with a .365 average and helping St. Louis win their third World Series during his career. Musial rarely let up in the postwar years. He won five NL batting titles in seven seasons from 1946-52, with the '48 season standing out as his most dominant. That year, Musial hit .376 to win the batting title by 43 points while also leading the NL in, among other categories, RBIs (131), doubles (46), on-base (.450) and slugging (.702) percentage.

When Musial retired in 1963, he was the NL's all-time hits leader (3,630) and ranked second behind Ty Cobb in the majors. He now ranks fourth all time behind Pete Rose, Cobb and Hank Aaron. He retired with a .331 career average and 475 home runs, and he was the first player with both 3,000 hits and 400 homers. He was named to 20 All-Star Games and elected to the Hall of Fame in 1969. Musial was then general manager for the 1967 Cardinals team that won the World Series and worked in their front office until 1980.

■ **George O'Donnell,** a righthander who pitched one season in the majors, died Dec. 19, 2012, in Springfield, Ill. He was 83.

O'Donnell pitched 13 seasons in pro ball, but his only big league experience came with the 1954 Pirates. He made 21 appearances for Pittsburgh that season, including 10 starts, going 3-9, 4.53 in 87 innings.

■ **Dan Osinski,** a righthander who pitched in eight big league seasons between 1962 and 1970, died Sept. 13 in Sun City, Ariz. He was 79.

Osinski pitched for six big league teams. He made 16 starts for the Angels in 1963 but spent the rest of his big league career in the bullpen. His best year came in 1965, when he made 61 appearances with a 2.82 ERA for the Milwaukee Braves. He made 324 appearances for his career, all but 21 of them in relief.

■ **Andy Pafko,** an outfielder who was a five-time all-star with the Cubs, died Oct. 8 in Bridgman, Mich. He was 92.

Pafko played 17 years in the majors from 1943-59 but was best remembered for his years with the Cubs from 1943-51. Pafko broke out in 1945, his second full year in the majors, when he batted .298 with 12 home runs for the Cubs' last World Series team. His power really came into its own in 1948, when he belted 26 homers and batted .312 in 548 at-bats. In 1950, Pafko accomplished the rare feat of hitting more home runs (36) than he recorded strike outs (32). He finished second in

the National League home run race that year and did it while batting .304. He hit 30 homers again in 1951, but the Cubs traded him to the pennant-contending Brooklyn Dodgers in June of that year. He hit 18 home runs during his time in Brooklyn, but the Dodgers famously lost a 13-game lead to the New York Giants.

■ **Frank Pastore,** a righthander who pitched eight seasons in the majors, died Dec. 17, 2012, in Upland, Calif. He was 55.

The Reds' second-round pick in 1975 out of a California high school, Pastore reached the majors in 1979. He went 6-7, 4.25 as a 21-year-old rookie in '79, splitting his time between the rotation and bullpen. He moved into the Reds' rotation full-time in 1980 and had his best year, going 13-7, 3.27 in 185 innings. Pastore continued to be a serviceable starter for the next two seasons, posting a cumulative 3.99 ERA in 1981 and '82. His numbers began falling off in subsequent seasons, though, and he lost his place in Cincinnati's rotation in 1984.

■ **Pascual Perez,** a righthander who pitched 11 seasons in the major leagues, died Nov. 1, 2012, in San Gregonio de Nigua, Dominican Republic. He was 55.

Perez made his big league debut with the Pirates in 1980 but didn't establish himself until after a trade to the Braves in June 1982. He went 4-4, 3.06 in 79 innings for Atlanta over the remainder of the season, then had a breakout year in 1983. Perez made the All-Star Game and won 15 games to go with a 3.43 ERA over 215 innings.

He had another solid year in 1984 but then plummeted to a 1-13, 6.14 season in 1985. The Braves released him at the end of spring training in 1986 and he didn't pitch that season. Perez's career got a second wind with the Montreal Expos in 1987, going 7-0, 2.30 in 70 innings. He won 21 games with a 2.89 ERA over the next two seasons for Montreal, then finished his career with two seasons with the Yankees in 1990 and '91.

■ **Tony Pierce,** a lefthander who pitched in the majors in 1967 and '68, died Jan. 31 in Columbus, Ga. He was 67.

Pierce was just 21 years old when he made the Kansas City Athletics' Opening Day roster in 1967, and he went on to go 3-4, 3.04 in 49 appearances, including six starts, for the A's that year. He had another promising season in 1968, going 1-2, 3.86 through 33 innings, before an elbow injury ended his career.

■ **Bob Savage,** a righthander who pitched in five big league seasons in the 1940s, died July 26 in Berlin, N.H. He was 91.

Savage pitched in eight games for the Philadelphia Athletics in 1942 at age 20 before joining the U.S. Army. He returned to the mound in 1946 and appeared in 40 games (19 starts) for the A's. Savage primarily worked in relief in 1947 and went 8-10, 3.76. His ERA jumped to 6.21 in 1948, though, after which he was waived and picked up by the St. Louis Browns. Savage made just four appearances for the Browns in 1949 and spent the rest of his career in the minors.

■ **George Scott,** a first baseman who played 14 seasons in the majors and was a three-time all-star, died July 28 in Greenville, Miss. He was 69.

Scott was one of the majors' best power hitters in the 1960s and '70s. He hit 271 homers in a career spanning 1966-79, which ranked 14th among all big leaguers during those years. He arrived in the majors fresh off winning the Eastern League triple crown in 1965 and slugged 27 homers as a 22-year-old rookie with the Red Sox in 1966. He made the All-Star Game but lost out to Tommy Agee for American League Rookie of the Year honors.

The Red Sox traded Scott to the Brewers after the 1971 season, just as he was beginning a stretch of three straight 20-homer and six straight Gold Glove seasons. Scott won the AL home run (36) and RBI (109) titles in 1975 for the Brewers. He was traded back to Boston after the 1976 season in a deal for Cecil Cooper and hit 33 homers in his first year back with the Red Sox in 1977. However, his production dropped off quickly, and he was out of the major leagues two years later. In addition to his six 20-homer seasons, Scott finished his career with a .268 lifetime average and eight Gold Gloves.

■ **Lou Sleater,** a lefthander who pitched seven seasons in the major leagues, died March 25 in Timonium, Md. He was 85.

Sleater logged 300 major league innings in a well-traveled career, during which he played for five different big league teams. Primarily a reliever throughout his career, Sleater's best season came with the Milwaukee Braves in 1956, when he went 2-2, 3.15 in 46 innings. He left pro ball in 1958 with a 12-18, 4.70 career record in the majors.

■ **Jose Sosa,** a righthander who pitched in the big leagues in 1975 and '76, died June 8 in Santo Domingo, Dominican Republic. He was 60.

A cousin on Felipe, Jesus and Matty Alou, Sosa began his pro career in the Astros system at age 17 in 1970 and reached the big leagues with Houston in 1975. He got into 25 games, including two starts, and went 1-3, 4.02 in 47 innings. He spent most of the '76 season back in the minors but did log nine appearances (all in relief) for the Astros, recording a 6.94 ERA without figuring in any decisions.

■ **Jake Striker,** a lefthander who pitched in parts of two seasons in the majors in 1959 and '60, died March 7 in Dallas, Ore. He was 79.

Striker made his big league debut in fine fashion, coming up with the Indians on Sept. 25, 1959. He tossed 62/3 innings and allowed just two runs to beat the Kansas City Athletics. However, Striker made just two more relief appearances in the majors following a trade to the White Sox in December 1959. He continued pitching in the minors through 1962.

■ **Harry Taylor,** a righthander who pitched briefly in the majors in 1957, died Jan. 24 in Fort Worth. He was 77.

Taylor reached the majors in his first season as a pro in 1957, making two relief appearances for the Kansas City Athletics that September.

■ **Gus Triandos,** a catcher who was a three-time all-star with the Orioles, died March 28 in San Jose. He was 82.

Triandos originally came up with the Yankees in 1953, but with Yogi Berra entrenched behind the plate in New York, Triandos was traded to the Orioles after the 1954 season. He quickly established himself in Baltimore, hitting 21 homers in 1956 and making his first All-Star Game in '57, the first of three straight all-star seasons for him. He belted a career-high 30 homers in 1958, followed by another 25 in '59. Triandos had a strong arm behind the plate as well. He led the American League in caught-stealing percentage in 1957 and finished in the top five in each of the next five years.

■ **Virgil "Fire" Trucks,** a righthander who pitched 17 seasons in the majors and was a two-time all-star, died March 23 in Calera, Ala. He was 95.

Trucks pitched the first half of his career with the Tigers, winning 108 games in a Detroit uniform from 1941-52. He first to got the majors in 1941 and posted sub-3.00 ERAs in each of his first two full big league seasons in 1942 and '43, but he went into the U.S. Navy and missed the 1944 and most of the '45 seasons. Trucks made his first All-Star Game in 1949, when he went 19-11, 2.81, won the majors' strikeout crown and also led the league in shutouts (six). His other biggest highlights as a Tiger came in 1952, when Trucks threw two no-hitters in the same season, first against the

Washington Senators on May 15 and then against the Yankees on Aug. 25.

The Tigers traded Trucks to the St. Louis Browns after the 1952 season, and he was more of a journeyman during the latter stages of his career, pitching for five different teams from 1953-58. He did have his lone 20-win season in 1953, which he split between the Browns and White Sox.

■ **Bob Turley,** a righthander who won the 1958 Cy Young Award and pitched 12 years in the majors, died March 30 in Atlanta. He was 82.

Turley came up with the St. Louis Browns in 1951 and went to the Yankees after the '54 season in the largest trade in major league history, a massive 17-player swap. Turley had made his first all-star appearance in 1954 and kept rolling with New York. He went 17-13, 3.06 in his first season with the Yankees and made another All-Star Game. He had his finest season in 1958, when he went 21-7, 2.97 and won the Cy Young Award (there was only one given out in those days).

A power pitcher, Turley led the American League in strikeouts in 1954 and finished in the top five three other times, but he also allowed the most walks three times. Turley won four World Series (1956, '58, '60 and '61) during his time with the Yankees and went 4-3, 3.19 overall in 15 career postseason appearances.

■ **Preston Ward,** a first baseman who played in parts of nine big league seasons, died June 2 in Las Vegas. He was 85.

Ward played for five teams in a career that spanned 1948 to 1959, also missing two seasons due to military service. He saw his most extensive time with the Pirates from 1953-56, hitting a career-high 12 homers in 1953 and getting regular time at first base. He reached double-digits in homers twice and hit 50 for his career, playing in 744 big league games.

■ **Earl Weaver,** a Hall of Fame manager with the Orioles, died Jan. 19. He was 82.

Weaver played 14 seasons in the minor leagues as a second baseman and began his managing career as a player-manager in the minors in 1956. He took over as the Orioles' manager in July 1968 and promptly reeled off a series of dominant seasons. Led by stars like Brooks Robinson, Frank Robinson, Jim Palmer and Boog Powell, Weaver's Orioles won three straight American League pennants from 1969-71, winning more than 100 games each season. Baltimore captured the 1970 World Series title, beating the Reds in five games.

They won two more division titles in 1973 and '74, and another pennant in '79. During his first tenure as manager from 1968-82, Weaver's teams never had a losing season. Weaver retired after the '82 season but returned to the Orioles dugout in mid-1985 and stayed on through 1986, his only losing season. He retired for good with a 1480-1060 record, one World Series title and four AL pennants.

Of course, Weaver was known as much for his style as for his winning. His highly animated, profanity-laced arguments with umpires were legendary. Weaver was also an advocate of the four-man rotation, sticking with it after the five-man rotation had come into vogue. He famously believed in the three-run homer more than playing small ball, and he had a knack for getting the most out of platoon players.

■ **Fred Whitfield,** a first baseman who played nine seasons in the major leagues from 1962-70, died Jan. 31 in Gadsden, Ala. He was 75.

Whitfield debuted with the Cardinals in 1962, batting .266 with eight homers, but he established himself following a trade to the Indians in December 1962. Whitfield hit 21 homers in 1963, his first full year in the majors, while batting .251. He continued putting up strong power numbers over the next few seasons, finishing in the top 10 in the American League for home runs in both 1965 (26) and '66 (27). He also hit a career-best .293 in 468 at-bats in '65, but his production began falling off in the late '60s, and he was traded to the Reds after the 1967 season. He last played in the majors with the Montreal Expos in 1970, ending his career with 108 homers and a .253 lifetime average.

■ **Earl Williams,** a catcher/first baseman who won the 1971 National League Rookie of the Year Award, died Jan. 28 in Somerset, N.J. He was 64.

Williams was a sensation in his rookie season with the Braves, belting 33 homers to go with a .260 average as a 22-year-old catcher. He finished fifth in the NL in homers and won ROY honors over Willie Montanez. His '71 season proved to be a career year. Williams had another solid season in 1972, hitting 28 homers, but he never matched his rookie figures for average or homers.

Enamored of Williams' power, the Orioles traded for him as part of a six-player deal after the '72 season. Williams lasted just two seasons in Baltimore though, hitting 22 and 14 homers in 1973 and '74, respectively, before being traded back to the Braves. He spent the latter years of his big league career moving between the Braves, Montreal Expos and Athletics. He last played in the majors in 1977.

STATISTICS INDEX

APPENDIX